HANDBOOK OF
CHILD PSYCHOLOGY

HANDBOOK OF CHILD PSYCHOLOGY

SIXTH EDITION

Volume Four: Child Psychology in Practice

Volume Editors

K. ANN RENNINGER and IRVING E. SIGEL

Editors-in-Chief

WILLIAM DAMON and RICHARD M. LERNER

WILEY

John Wiley & Sons, Inc.

Library of Congress Cataloging-in-Publication Data:

Handbook of child psychology / editors-in-chief, William Damon & Richard M. Lerner.—
  6th ed.
      p.   cm.
    Includes bibliographical references and indexes.
    Contents: v. 1. Theoretical models of human development / volume editor,
Richard M. Lerner — v. 2. Cognition, perception, and language / volume editors,
Deanna Kuhn, Robert Siegler — v. 3. Social, emotional, and personality development /
volume editor, Nancy Eisenberg — v 4. Child psychology in practice / volume editors, K.
Ann Renninger, Irving E. Sigel.
    ISBN 0-471-27287-6 (set : cloth)
    — ISBN 0-471-27288-4 (v. 1 : cloth) — ISBN 0-471-27289-2 (v. 2 : cloth)
    — ISBN 0-471-27290-6 (v. 3 : cloth) — ISBN 0-471-27291-4 (v. 4 : cloth)
    1. Child psychology.   I. Damon, William, 1944–   II. Lerner, Richard M.
  BF721.H242   2006
  155.4—dc22
                                                                2005043951

Printed in the United States of America.
10 9 8 7 6 5 4 3 2 1

In memory of Paul Mussen, whose generosity of spirit
touched our lives and helped build a field.

Contributors

Lieselotte Ahnert
Free University of Berlin
Berlin, Germany

Nikki L. Aikens
University of North Carolina at Chapel Hill
Chapel Hill, North Carolina

Virginia W. Berninger
Area of Educational Psychology
College of Education
University of Washington
Seattle, Washington

Phyllis C. Blumenfeld
School of Education
University of Michigan
Ann Arbor, Michigan

Monique Boekaerts
Center for the Study of Education
    and Instruction
Leiden University
Leiden, The Netherlands

Marc H. Bornstein
Child and Family Research
National Institute of Child Health and
    Human Development
National Institutes of Health
Bethesda, Maryland

Maggie Bruck
Department of Psychiatry
School of Medicine
Johns Hopkins University
Baltimore, Maryland

Linda M. Burton
The Center for Human Development and Family
    Research in Diverse Contexts
College of Health and Human Development
The Pennsylvania State University
University Park, Pennsylvania

Stephen J. Ceci
Human Development
Cornell University
Ithaca, New York

Dante Cicchetti
Institute of Child Development
University of Minnesota
Minneapolis, Minnesota

George Comstock
The Newhouse School
Syracuse University
Syracuse, New York

Carol Copple
National Association for the Education of
    Young Children
Washington, District of Columbia

Erik De Corte
Department of Educational Sciences
Center for Instructional Psychology and Technology
University of Leuven
Leuven, Belgium

Amy J. Dray
Human Development and Psychology
Graduate School of Education
Harvard University
Cambridge, Massachusetts

Elisabeth M. Dykens
Psychology and Human Development and
John F. Kennedy Center for Research on
    Human Development
Vanderbilt University
Nashville, Tennessee

Maurice J. Elias
Department of Psychology
Rutgers University
Piscataway, New Jersey

Patricia M. Greenfield
Department of Psychology
University of California, Los Angeles
Los Angeles, California

Christopher J. Harris
College of Education
University of Arizona
Tucson, Arizona

Robert M. Hodapp
Special Education and
John F. Kennedy Center for Research on
    Human Development
Vanderbilt University
Nashville, Tennessee

Marilou Hyson
National Association for the Education of
    Young Children
Washington, District of Columbia

Jacqueline Jones
Educational Testing Service
Princeton, New Jersey

Jennifer Yusun Kang
Graduate School of Education
Harvard University
Cambridge, Massachusetts

Avigdor Klingman
Faculty of Education
University of Haifa
Haifa, Israel

Jeffrey S. Kress
William Davidson Graduate School of
    Jewish Education
Jewish Theological Seminary
New York, New York

Michael E. Lamb
Social and Political Sciences
Cambridge University
Cambridge, United Kingdom

Robin G. Lanzi
The Georgetown Center on Health
    and Education
Georgetown University
Washington, District of Columbia

Daniel K. Lapsley
Teachers College
Ball State University
Muncie, Indiana

Richard Lehrer
Department of Teaching and Learning
Peabody College of Vanderbilt University
Nashville, Tennessee

Lynn S. Liben
Department of Psychology
The Pennsylvania State University
University Park, Pennsylvania

Ronald W. Marx
School of Education
University of Arizona
Tucson, Arizona

Vonnie C. McLoyd
Department of Psychology
University of North Carolina at
    Chapel Hill
Chapel Hill, North Carolina

Darcia Narvaez
Department of Psychology
University of Notre Dame
Notre Dame, Indiana

Alison H. Paris
Department of Psychology
Claremont McKenna College
Claremont, California

Scott G. Paris
Department of Psychology
University of Michigan
Ann Arbor, Michigan

Douglas R. Powell
Child Development and Family Studies
Purdue University
West Lafayette, Indiana

Gabrielle F. Principe
Department of Psychology
Ursinus College
Collegeville, Pennsylvania

Craig T. Ramey
Health Studies
Georgetown Center on Health and Education
Georgetown University
Washington, District of Columbia

Sharon Landesman Ramey
Child and Family Studies
Georgetown Center on Health and Education
Georgetown University
Washington, District of Columbia

K. Ann Renninger
Department of Educational Studies
Swarthmore College
Swarthmore, Pennsylvania

Carrie Rothstein-Fisch
Department of Educational Psychology
    and Counseling
California State University, Northridge
Northridge, California

Erica Scharrer
Department of Communication
University of Massachusetts
Amherst, Massachusetts

Leona Schauble
Department of Teaching and Learning
Peabody College of Vanderbilt University
Nashville, Tennessee

Robert L. Selman
Human Development and Psychology
Graduate School of Education
Harvard University
Cambridge, Massachusetts

Irving E. Sigel
Educational Testing Service
Center for Education Policy and Research
Princeton, New Jersey

Catherine E. Snow
Graduate School of Education
Harvard University
Cambridge, Massachusetts

Lalita K. Suzuki
HopeLab
Palo Alto, California

Sheree L. Toth
Mount Hope Family Center
University of Rochester
Rochester, New York

Lieven Verschaffel
Department of Educational Sciences
Center for Instructional Psychology and Technology
University of Leuven
Leuven, Belgium

Reviewers

Jay Belsky
Institute for the Study of Children,
   Families and Social Issues
Birkbeck University of London
London, United Kingdom

Carolyn Pape Cowan
Institute of Human Development
University of California, Berkeley
Berkeley, California

Philip A. Cowan
Department of Psychology
University of California, Berkeley
Berkeley, California

Keith A. Crnic
Clinical Psychology
Arizona State University
Tempe, Arizona

Roger Downs
Department of Geography
Penn State University
University Park, Pennsylvania

Byron Egeland
Child Development
Institute of Child Development
University of Minnesota
Minneapolis, Minnesota

Linda M. Espinosa
Learning Teaching and Curriculum
University of Missouri, Columbia
Columbia, Missouri

Douglas A. Gentile
Department of Psychology
Iowa State University
Ames, Iowa

Herbert P. Ginsburg
Department of Human Development
Teachers College
Columbia University
New York, New York

Joan E. Grusec
Department of Psychology
University of Toronto
Toronto, Ontario, Canada

Rogers Hall
Vanderbilt University
Nashville, Tennessee

James E. Johnson
Curriculum and Instruction
The Pennsylvania State University
University Park, Pennsylvania

Melanie Killen
Department of Human Development
Center for Children, Relationships, and Culture
University of Maryland
College Park, Maryland

Cynthia Lanius
The Math Forum
Drexel University
Philadelphia, Pennsylvania

Alicia Lieberman
Psychology, Academic Affairs, and Child Trauma
    Research Project
University of California, San Francisco
San Francisco General Hospital
San Francisco, California

James Marcia
Department of Psychology
Simon Fraser University
Vancouver, British Columbia, Canada

Steven McGee
Learning Technologies and Assessment
Academic Affairs
Lake Shore Campus
Loyola University Chicago
Chicago, Ilinois

Katheen E. Metz
Cognition and Development
Graduate School of Education
University of California, Berkeley
Berkeley, California

Carolyn B. Morgan
Department of Psychology
University of Wisconsin, Whitewater
Whitewater, Wisconsin

Ageliki Nicolopoulou
Department of Psychology
Lehigh University
Bethlehem, Pennsylvania

Catherine Tamis-Lemonda
Department of Applied Psychology
The Steinhardt School of Education
New York University
New York, New York

Daniel A. Wagner
Department of Education
National Center on Adult Literacy/International
    Literacy Institute
University of Pennsylvania
Philadelphia, Pennsylvania

Aida Walqui
Teacher Professional Development Program
WestEd
San Francisco, California

Roger P. Weissberg
Department of Psychology
The Collaborative for Academic, Social, and Emotional
    Learning
University of Illinois at Chicago
Chicago, Illinois

Dylan Wiliam
Learning and Teaching Research Center
Educational Testing Service
Princeton, New Jersey

Preface to Handbook of Child Psychology, *Sixth Edition*

WILLIAM DAMON

Scholarly handbooks play several key roles in their disciplines. First and foremost, they reflect recent changes in the field as well as classic works that have survived those changes. In this sense, all handbooks present their editors' and authors' best judgments about what is most important to know in the field at the time of publication. But many handbooks also influence the fields that they report on. Scholars—especially younger ones—look to them for sources of information and inspiration to guide their own work. While taking stock of the shape of its field, a handbook also shapes the stock of ideas that will define the field's future. It serves both as an indicator and as a generator, a pool of received knowledge and a pool for spawning new insight.

THE *HANDBOOK'S* LIVING TRADITION

Within the field of human development, the *Handbook of Child Psychology* has served these key roles to a degree that has been exceptional even among the impressive panoply of the world's many distinguished scholarly handbooks. The *Handbook of Child Psychology* has had a widely heralded tradition as a beacon, organizer, and encyclopedia of developmental study for almost 75 years— a period that covers the vast majority of scientific work in this field.

It is impossible to imagine what the field would look like if it had not occurred to Carl Murchison in 1931 to assemble an eclectic assortment of contributions into the first *Handbook of Child Psychology.* Whether or not Murchison realized this potential (an interesting speculation in itself, given his visionary and ambitious nature), he gave birth to a seminal publishing project that

not only has endured over time but has evolved into a thriving tradition across a number of related academic disciplines.

All through its history, the *Handbook* has drawn on, and played a formative role in, the worldwide study of human development. What does the *Handbook*'s history tell us about where we, as developmentalists, have been, what we have learned, and where we are going? What does it tell us about what has changed and what has remained the same in the questions that we ask, in the methods that we use, and in the theoretical ideas that we draw on in our quest to understand human development? By asking these questions, we follow the spirit of the science itself, for developmental questions may be asked about any endeavor, including the enterprise of studying human development. To best understand what this field has to tell us about human development, we must ask how the field itself has developed. In a field that examines continuities and changes, we must ask, for the field itself, what are the continuities and what are the changes?

The history of the *Handbook* is by no means the whole story of why the field is where it is today, but it is a fundamental part of the story. It has defined the choices that have determined the field's direction and has influenced the making of those choices. In this regard, the *Handbook*'s history reveals much about the judgments and other human factors that shape a science.

THE CAST OF CHARACTERS

Carl Murchison was a scholar/impresario who edited *The Psychological Register;* founded and edited key psychological journals; wrote books on social psychology, politics, and the criminal mind; and compiled an assortment of handbooks, psychology texts, autobiographies of renowned psychologists, and even a book on psychic beliefs (Sir Arthur Conan Doyle and Harry Houdini were among the contributors). Murchison's initial *Handbook of Child Psychology* was published by a small university press (Clark University) in 1931, when the field itself was still in its infancy. Murchison wrote:

> Experimental psychology has had a much older scientific and academic status [than child psychology], but at the present time it is probable that much less money is being spent for pure research in the field of experimental psychology than is being spent in the field of child psychology. In spite of this obvious fact, many experimental psychologists continue to look upon the field of child psychology as a proper field of research for women and for men whose experimental masculinity is not of the maximum. This attitude of patronage is based almost entirely upon a blissful ignorance of what is going on in the tremendously virile field of child behavior. (Murchison, 1931, p. ix)

Murchison's masculine allusion, of course, is from another era; it could furnish some good material for a social history of gender stereotyping. That aside, Murchison was prescient in the task that he undertook and the way that he went about it. At the time Murchison wrote the preface to his *Handbook,* developmental psychology was known only in Europe and in a few forward-looking American labs and universities. Nevertheless, Murchison predicted the field's impending ascent: "The time is not far distant, if it is not already here, when nearly all competent psychologists will recognize that one-half of the whole field of psychology is involved in the problem of how the infant becomes an adult psychologically" (Murchison, 1931, p. x).

For his original 1931 *Handbook,* Murchison looked to Europe and to a handful of American centers (or "field stations") for child research (Iowa, Minnesota, the University of California at Berkeley, Columbia, Stanford, Yale, Clark). Murchison's Europeans included a young "genetic epistemologist" named Jean Piaget, who, in an essay on "Children's Philosophies," quoted extensively from interviews with 60 Genevan children between the ages of 4 and 12 years. Piaget's chapter would provide American readers with an introduction to his seminal research program on children's conceptions of the world. Another European, Charlotte Bühler, wrote a chapter on children's social behavior. In this chapter,

which still is fresh today, Bühler described intricate play and communication patterns among toddlers, patterns that developmental psychology would not rediscover until the late 1970s. Bühler also anticipated the critiques of Piaget that would appear during the socio-linguistics heyday of the 1970s:

> Piaget, in his studies on children's talk and reasoning, emphasizes that their talk is much more egocentric than social . . . that children from 3 to 7 years accompany all their manipulations with talk which actually is not so much intercourse as monologue . . . [but] the special relationship of the child to each of the different members of the household is distinctly reflected in the respective conversations. (Buhler, 1931, p. 138)

Other Europeans included Anna Freud, who wrote on "The Psychoanalysis of the Child," and Kurt Lewin, who wrote on "Environmental Forces in Child Behavior and Development."

The Americans whom Murchison chose were equally notable. Arnold Gesell wrote a nativistic account of his twin studies, an enterprise that remains familiar to us today, and Stanford's Louis Terman wrote a comprehensive account of everything known about the "gifted child." Harold Jones described the developmental effects of birth order, Mary Cover Jones wrote about children's emotions, Florence Goodenough wrote about children's drawings, and Dorothea McCarthy wrote about language development. Vernon Jones's chapter on "children's morals" focused on the growth of *character,* a notion that was to become lost to the field during the cognitive-developmental revolution, but that reemerged in the 1990s as the primary concern in the study of moral development.

Murchison's vision of child psychology included an examination of cultural differences as well. His *Handbook* presented to the scholarly world a young anthropologist named Margaret Mead, just back from her tours of Samoa and New Guinea. In this early essay, Mead wrote that her motivation in traveling to the South Seas was to discredit the views that Piaget, Levy-Bruhl, and other nascent "structuralists" had put forth concerning "animism" in young children's thinking. (Interestingly, about a third of Piaget's chapter in the same volume was dedicated to showing how Genevan children took years to outgrow animism.) Mead reported some data that she called "amazing": "In not one of the 32,000 drawings (by young 'primitive' children) was there a single case of personalization of animals, material phenomena, or inanimate objects" (Mead, 1931, p. 400). Mead parlayed these data into a tough-minded critique of Western psychology's ethnocentrism, making the point that animism and other beliefs are more likely to be culturally induced than intrinsic to early cognitive development. This is hardly an unfamiliar theme in contemporary psychology. Mead also offered a research guide for developmental fieldworkers in strange cultures, complete with methodological and practical advice, such as the following: Translate questions into native linguistic categories; don't do controlled experiments; don't do studies that require knowing ages of subjects, which are usually unknowable; and live next door to the children whom you are studying.

Despite the imposing roster of authors that Murchison assembled for the 1931 *Handbook of Child Psychology*, his achievement did not satisfy him for long. Barely 2 years later, Murchison put out a second edition, of which he wrote: "Within a period of slightly more than 2 years, this first revision bears scarcely any resemblance to the original *Handbook of Child Psychology*. This is due chiefly to the great expansion in the field during the past 3 years and partly to the improved insight of the editor" (Murchison, 1933, p. vii). The tradition that Murchison had brought to life was already evolving.

Murchison saw fit to provide the following warning in his second edition: "There has been no attempt to simplify, condense, or to appeal to the immature mind. This volume is prepared specifically for the scholar, and its form is for his maximum convenience" (Murchison, 1933, p. vii). It is likely that sales of Murchison's first volume did not approach textbook levels; perhaps he received negative comments regarding its accessibility.

Murchison exaggerated when he wrote that his second edition bore little resemblance to the first. Almost half of the chapters were virtually the same, with minor additions and updating. (For the record, though, despite Murchison's continued use of masculine phraseology, 10 of the 24 authors in the second edition were women.) Some of the authors whose original chapters were dropped were asked to write about new topics. So, for example, Goodenough wrote about mental testing rather than about children's drawings, and Gesell wrote a general statement of his maturational theory that went well beyond the twin studies.

But Murchison also made some abrupt changes. He dropped Anna Freud entirely, auguring the marginalization of psychoanalysis within academic psychology. Leonard Carmichael, who was later to play a pivotal role

in the *Handbook* tradition, made an appearance as author of a major chapter (by far the longest in the book) on prenatal and perinatal growth. Three other physiologically oriented chapters were added as well: one on neonatal motor behavior, one on visual-manual functions during the first 2 years of life, and one on physiological "appetites" such as hunger, rest, and sex. Combined with the Goodenough and Gesell shifts in focus, these additions gave the 1933 *Handbook* more of a biological thrust, in keeping with Murchison's longstanding desire to display the hard science backbone of the emerging field.

Leonard Carmichael was president of Tufts University when he organized Wiley's first edition of the *Handbook*. The switch from a university press to the long-established commercial firm of John Wiley & Sons was commensurate with Carmichael's well-known ambition; indeed, Carmichael's effort was to become influential beyond anything that Murchison might have anticipated. The book (one volume at that time) was called the *Manual of Child Psychology*, in keeping with Carmichael's intention of producing an "advanced scientific manual to bridge the gap between the excellent and varied elementary textbooks in this field and the scientific periodical literature" (Carmichael, 1946, p. viii).

The publication date was 1946, and Carmichael complained that "this book has been a difficult and expensive one to produce, especially under wartime conditions" (Carmichael, 1946, p. viii). Nevertheless, the project was worth the effort. The *Manual* quickly became the bible of graduate training and scholarly work in the field, available virtually everywhere that human development was studied. Eight years later, now head of the Smithsonian Institution, Carmichael wrote, in the preface to the 1954 second edition, "The favorable reception that the first edition received not only in America but all over the world is indicative of the growing importance of the study of the phenomena of the growth and development of the child" (Carmichael, 1954, p. vii).

Carmichael's second edition had a long life: Not until 1970 did Wiley bring out a third edition. Carmichael was retired by then, but he still had a keen interest in the book. At his insistence, his own name became part of the title of the third edition; it was called, improbably, *Carmichael's Manual of Child Psychology*, even though it had a new editor and an entirely different cast of authors and advisors. Paul Mussen took over as the editor, and once again the project flourished. Now a two-volume set, the third edition swept across the social sciences, generating widespread interest in developmental psychology and its related disciplines. Rarely had a scholarly compendium become both so dominant in its own field and so familiar in related disciplines. The set became an essential source for graduate students and advanced scholars alike. Publishers referred to *Carmichael's Manual* as the standard against which other scientific handbooks were compared.

The fourth edition, published in 1983, was now redesignated by John Wiley & Sons to become once again the *Handbook of Child Psychology.* By then, Carmichael had passed away. The set of books, now expanded to four volumes, became widely referred to in the field as "the Mussen handbook."

WHAT CARMICHAEL CHOSE FOR THE NOW EMERGENT FIELD

Leonard Carmichael, who became Wiley's editor for the project in its now commercially funded and expanded versions (the 1946 and 1954 *Manuals*), made the following comments about where he looked for his all-important choices of content:

> Both as editor of the *Manual* and as the author of a special chapter, the writer is indebted . . . [for] extensive excerpts and the use of other materials previously published in the *Handbook of Child Psychology, Revised Edition.* (1946, p. viii)

> Both the *Handbook of Child Psychology* and the *Handbook of Child Psychology, Revised Edition,* were edited by Dr. Carl Murchison. I wish to express here my profound appreciation for the pioneer work done by Dr. Murchison in producing these handbooks and other advanced books in psychology. The *Manual* owes much in spirit and content to the foresight and editorial skill of Dr. Murchison. (1954, p. viii)

The first quote comes from Carmichael's preface to the 1946 edition, the second from his preface to the 1954 edition. We shall never know why Carmichael waited until the 1954 edition to add the personal tribute to Carl Murchison. Perhaps a careless typist dropped the laudatory passage from a handwritten version of the 1946 preface and its omission escaped Carmichael's notice. Or perhaps 8 years of further adult development increased Carmichael's generosity of spirit. (It also may be possible that Murchison or his family com-

plained.) In any case, Carmichael acknowledged the roots of his *Manuals,* if not always their original editor. His choice to start with those roots is a revealing part of the *Handbook*'s history, and it established a strong intellectual legacy for our present-day descendants of the early pioneers who wrote for the Murchison and Carmichael editions.

Although Leonard Carmichael took the 1946 *Manual* in much the same direction established by Murchison back in 1931 and 1933, he did bring it several steps further in that direction, added a few twists of his own, and dropped a couple of Murchison's bolder selections. Carmichael first appropriated five Murchison chapters on biological or experimental topics, such as physiological growth, scientific methods, and mental testing. He added three new biologically oriented chapters on animal infancy, physical growth, and motor and behavioral maturation (a tour de force by Myrtal McGraw that instantly made Gesell's chapter in the same volume obsolete). Then he commissioned Wayne Dennis to write an adolescence chapter that focused exclusively on physiological changes associated with puberty.

On the subject of social and cultural influences in development, Carmichael retained five of the Murchison chapters: two chapters on environmental forces on the child by Kurt Lewin and by Harold Jones, Dorothea McCarthy's chapter on children's language, Vernon Jones's chapter on children's morality (now entitled "Character Development—An Objective Approach"), and Margaret Mead's chapter on "primitive" children (now enhanced by several spectacular photos of mothers and children from exotic cultures around the world). Carmichael also stayed with three other Murchison topics (emotional development, gifted children, and sex differences), but he selected new authors to cover them. But Carmichael dropped Piaget and Bühler.

Carmichael's 1954 revision, his second and final edition, was very close in structure and content to the 1946 *Manual.* Carmichael again retained the heart of Murchison's original vision, many of Murchison's original authors and chapter topics, and some of the same material that dated all the way back to the 1931 *Handbook.* Not surprisingly, the chapters that were closest to Carmichael's own interests got the most significant updating. Carmichael leaned toward the biological and physiological whenever possible. He clearly favored experimental treatments of psychological processes. Yet he still kept the social, cultural, and psychological analyses by Lewin, Mead, McCarthy, Terman, Harold Jones, and

Vernon Jones, and he even went so far as to add one new chapter on social development by Harold and Gladys Anderson and one new chapter on emotional development by Arthur Jersild.

The Murchison and Carmichael volumes make for fascinating reading, even today. The perennial themes of the field were there from the start: the nature-nurture debate; the generalizations of universalists opposed by the particularizations of contextualists; the alternating emphases on continuities and discontinuities during ontogenesis; and the standard categories of maturation, learning, locomotor activity, perception, cognition, language, emotion, conduct, morality, and culture—all separated for the sake of analysis, yet, as authors throughout each of the volumes acknowledged, all somehow inextricably joined in the dynamic mix of human development.

These things have not changed. Yet, much in the early editions is now irrevocably dated. Long lists of children's dietary preferences, sleeping patterns, elimination habits, toys, and somatic types look quaint and pointless through today's lenses. The chapters on children's thought and language were written prior to the great contemporary breakthroughs in neurology and brain/behavior research, and they show it. The chapters on social and emotional development were ignorant of the processes of social influence and self-regulation that soon would be revealed through attribution research and other studies in social psychology. Terms such as *cognitive neuroscience, neuronal networks, behavior genetics, social cognition, dynamic systems,* and *positive youth development* were of course unknown. Even Mead's rendition of the "primitive child" stands as a weak straw in comparison to the wealth of cross-cultural knowledge available in today's *cultural psychology.*

Most telling, the assortments of odd facts and normative trends were tied together by very little theory throughout the Carmichael chapters. It was as if, in the exhilaration of discovery at the frontiers of a new field, all the facts looked interesting in and of themselves. That, of course, is what makes so much of the material seem odd and arbitrary. It is hard to know what to make of the lists of facts, where to place them, which ones were worth keeping track of and which ones are expendable. Not surprisingly, the bulk of the data presented in the Carmichael manuals seems not only outdated by today's standards but, worse, irrelevant.

By 1970, the importance of theory for understanding human development had become apparent. Looking back

on Carmichael's last *Manual,* Paul Mussen wrote, "The 1954 edition of this *Manual* had only one theoretical chapter, and that was concerned with Lewinian theory which, so far as we can see, has not had a significant lasting impact on developmental psychology" (Mussen, 1970, p. x). The intervening years had seen a turning away from the norm of psychological research once fondly referred to as "dust-bowl empiricism."

The Mussen 1970 edition—or *Carmichael's Manual,* as it was still called—had a new look and an almost entirely new set of contents. The two-volume edition carried only one chapter from the earlier books, Carmichael's updated version of his own long chapter on the "Onset and Early Development of Behavior," which had made its appearance under a different title in Murchison's 1933 edition. Otherwise, as Mussen wrote in his preface, "It should be clear from the outset . . . that the present volumes are not, in any sense, a *revision* of the earlier editions; this is a completely new *Manual*" (Mussen, 1970, p. x).

And it was. In comparison to Carmichael's last edition 16 years earlier, the scope, variety, and theoretical depth of the Mussen volumes were astonishing. The field had blossomed, and the new *Manual* showcased many of the new bouquets that were being produced. The biological perspective was still strong, grounded by chapters on physical growth (by J. M. Tanner) and physiological development (by Dorothy Eichorn) and by Carmichael's revised chapter (now made more elegant by some excerpts from Greek philosophy and modern poetry). But two other cousins of biology also were represented, in an ethological chapter by Eckhard Hess and a behavior genetics chapter by Gerald McClearn. These chapters were to define the major directions of biological research in the field for at least the next 3 decades.

As for theory, Mussen's *Handbook* was thoroughly permeated with it. Much of the theorizing was organized around the approaches that, in 1970, were known as the "three grand systems": (1) Piaget's cognitive-developmentalism, (2) psychoanalysis, and (3) learning theory. Piaget was given the most extensive treatment. He reappeared in the *Manual,* this time authoring a comprehensive (and, some say, definitive) statement of his entire theory, which now bore little resemblance to his 1931/1933 sortings of children's intriguing verbal expressions. In addition, chapters by John Flavell, by David Berlyne, by Martin Hoffman, and by William Kessen, Marshall Haith, and Philip Salapatek all gave major treatments to one or another aspect of Piaget's body of work. Other approaches were represented as well. Herbert and Ann Pick explicated Gibsonian theory in a chapter on sensation and perception, Jonas Langer wrote a chapter on Werner's organismic theory, David McNeill wrote a Chomskian account of language development, and Robert LeVine wrote an early version of what was soon to become "culture theory."

With its increased emphasis on theory, the 1970 *Manual* explored in depth a matter that had been all but neglected in the book's previous versions: the mechanisms of change that could account for, to use Murchison's old phrase, "the problem of how the infant becomes an adult psychologically." In the process, old questions such as the relative importance of nature versus nurture were revisited, but with far more sophisticated conceptual and methodological tools.

Beyond theory building, the 1970 *Manual* addressed an array of new topics and featured new contributors: peer interaction (Willard Hartup), attachment (Eleanor Maccoby and John Masters), aggression (Seymour Feshbach), individual differences (Jerome Kagan and Nathan Kogan), and creativity (Michael Wallach). All of these areas of interest are still very much with us in the new millennium.

If the 1970 *Manual* reflected a blossoming of the field's plantings, the 1983 *Handbook* reflected a field whose ground cover had spread beyond any boundaries that could have been previously anticipated. New growth had sprouted in literally dozens of separate locations. A French garden, with its overarching designs and tidy compartments, had turned into an English garden, a bit unruly but glorious in its profusion. Mussen's two-volume *Carmichael's Manual* had now become the four-volume Mussen *Handbook*, with a page-count increase that came close to tripling the 1970 edition.

The grand old theories were breaking down. Piaget was still represented by his 1970 piece, but his influence was on the wane throughout the other chapters. Learning theory and psychoanalysis were scarcely mentioned. Yet the early theorizing had left its mark, in vestiges that were apparent in new approaches, and in the evident conceptual sophistication with which authors treated their material. No return to dust bowl empiricism could be found anywhere in the set. Instead, a variety of classical and innovative ideas were coexisting: Ethology, neurobiology, information processing, attribution theory, cultural approaches, communications theory, behavioral genetics, sensory-perception models, psycholinguistics, sociolinguistics, discontinuous stage theories, and continuous memory theories all took their places, with none

quite on center stage. Research topics now ranged from children's play to brain lateralization, from children's family life to the influences of school, day care, and disadvantageous risk factors. There also was coverage of the burgeoning attempts to use developmental theory as a basis for clinical and educational interventions. The interventions usually were described at the end of chapters that had discussed the research relevant to the particular intervention efforts, rather than in whole chapters dedicated specifically to issues of practice.

This brings us to the efforts under the present editorial team: the *Handbook*'s fifth and sixth editions (but really the seventh and eighth editions, if the germinal two pre-Wiley Murchison editions are counted). I must leave it to future commentators to provide a critical summation of what we have done. The volume editors have offered introductory and/or concluding renditions of their own volumes. I will add to their efforts here only by stating the overall intent of our design and by commenting on some directions that our field has taken in the years from 1931 to 2006.

We approached our editions with the same purpose that Murchison, Carmichael, and Mussen before us had shared: "to provide," as Mussen wrote, "a comprehensive and accurate picture of the current state of knowledge—the major systematic thinking and research—in the most important research areas of the psychology of human development" (Mussen, 1983, p. vii). We assumed that the *Handbook* should be aimed "specifically for the scholar," as Murchison declared, and that it should have the character of an "advanced text," as Carmichael defined it. We expected, though, that our audiences may be more interdisciplinary than the readerships of previous editions, given the greater tendency of today's scholars to cross back and forth among fields such as psychology, cognitive science, neurobiology, history, linguistics, sociology, anthropology, education, and psychiatry. We also believed that research-oriented practitioners should be included under the rubric of the "scholars" for whom this *Handbook* was intended. To that end, for the first time in 1998 and again in the present edition, we devoted an entire volume to child psychology in practice.

Beyond these very general intentions, we have let chapters in the *Handbook*'s fifth and sixth editions take their own shape. We solicited the chapters from authors who were widely acknowledged to be among the leading experts in their areas of the field, although we know that, given an entirely open-ended selection process and no limits of budget, we would have invited a large number of other leading researchers whom we did not have the space—and thus the privilege—to include. With very few exceptions, every author whom we invited agreed to accept the challenge. Our only real, and great, sadness was to hear of the passing of several authors from the 1998 edition prior to our assembly of the present edition. Where possible, we arranged to have their collaborators revise and update their chapters.

Our directive to authors was simple: Convey your area of the field as you see it. From then on, the authors took center stage—with, of course, much constructive feedback from reviewers and volume editors. No one tried to impose a perspective, a preferred method of inquiry, or domain boundaries on any of the chapters. The authors expressed their views on what researchers in their areas attempt to accomplish, why they do so, how they go about it, what intellectual sources they draw on, what progress they have made, and what conclusions they have reached.

The result, in my opinion, is still more glorious profusion of the English garden genre, but perhaps contained a bit by some broad patterns that have emerged over the past decade. Powerful theoretical models and approaches—not quite unified theories, such as the three grand systems—have begun once again to organize much of the field's research and practice. There is great variety in these models and approaches, and each is drawing together significant clusters of work. Some have been only recently formulated, and some are combinations or modifications of classic theories that still have staying power.

Among the formidable models and approaches that the reader will find in this *Handbook* are the dynamic system theories, the life span and life course approaches, cognitive science and neuronal models, the behavior genetics approach, person-context interaction theories, action theories, cultural psychology, and a wide assortment of neo-Piagetian and neo-Vygotskian models. Although some of these models and approaches have been in the making for some time, they have now come into their own. Researchers are drawing on them directly, taking their implied assumptions and hypotheses seriously, using them with specificity and control, and exploiting their implications for practice.

Another pattern that emerges is a rediscovery and exploration of core processes in human development that had been underexamined by the generation of researchers just prior to the present one. Scientific interest

has a way of moving in alternating cycles (or spirals, for those who wish to capture the progressive nature of scientific development). In our time, developmental study has cycled away from classic topics such as motivation and learning—not in the sense that they were entirely forgotten, or that good work ceased to be done in such areas, but in the sense that they no longer were the most prominent subjects of theoretical reflection and debate. Some of the relative neglect was intentional, as scholars got caught up in controversies about whether psychological motivation was a "real" phenomenon worthy of study or whether learning could or should be distinguished from development in the first place. All this has changed. As the contents of our current edition attest, developmental science always returns, sooner or later, to concepts that are necessary for explaining the heart of its concerns, progressive change in individuals and social groups over time, and concepts such as learning and motivation are indispensable for this task. Among the exciting features of this *Handbook* edition are the advances it presents in theoretical and empirical work on these classic concepts.

The other concept that has met some resistance in recent years is the notion of development itself. For some social critics, the idea of progress, implicit in the notion of development, has seemed out of step with principles such as equality and cultural diversity. Some genuine benefits have accrued from that critique; for example, the field has worked to better appreciate diverse developmental pathways. But, like many critique positions, it led to excesses. For some, it became questionable to explore issues that lie at the heart of human development. Growth, advancement, positive change, achievement, and standards for improved performance and conduct, all were questioned as legitimate subjects of investigation.

Just as in the cases of learning and motivation, no doubt it was inevitable that the field's center of gravity sooner or later would return to broad concerns of development. The story of growth from infancy to adulthood is a developmental story of multifaceted learning, acquisitions of skills and knowledge, waxing powers of attention and memory, growing neuronal and other biological capacities, formations and transformations of character and personality, increases and reorganizations in the understanding of self and others, advances in emotional and behavioral regulation, progress in communicating and collaborating with others, and a host of other achievements documented in this edition. Parents, teachers, and other adults in all parts of the world recognize and value such developmental achievements in children, although they do not always know how to understand them, let alone how to foster them.

The sorts of scientific findings that the *Handbook*'s authors explicate in their chapters are needed to provide such understanding. The importance of sound scientific understanding has become especially clear in recent years, when news media broadcast story after story based on simplistic and biased popular speculations about the causes of human development. The careful and responsible discourse found in these chapters contrasts sharply with the typical news story about the role of parents, genes, or schools in children's growth and behavior. There is not much contest as to which source the public looks to for its information and stimulation. But the good news is that scientific truth usually works its way into the public mind over the long run. The way this works would make a good subject for developmental study some day, especially if such a study could find a way to speed up the process. In the meantime, readers of this edition of the *Handbook of Child Psychology* will find the most solid, insightful and current set of scientific theories and findings available in the field today.

February 2006
Palo Alto, California

REFERENCES

Bühler, C. (1931). The social participation of infants and toddlers. In C. Murchison (Ed.), *A handbook of child psychology.* Worcester, MA: Clark University Press.

Carmichael, L. (Ed.). (1946). *Manual of child psychology.* New York: Wiley.

Carmichael, L. (Ed.). (1954). *Manual of child psychology* (2nd ed.). New York: Wiley.

Mead, M. (1931). The primitive child. In C. Murchison (Ed.), *A handbook of child psychology.* Worcester, MA: Clark University Press.

Murchison, C. (Ed.). (1931). *A handbook of child psychology.* Worcester, MA: Clark University Press.

Murchison, C. (Ed.). (1933). *A handbook of child psychology* (2nd ed.). Worcester, MA: Clark University Press.

Mussen, P. (Ed.). (1970). *Carmichael's manual of child psychology.* New York: Wiley.

Mussen, P. (Ed.). (1983). *Handbook of child psychology.* New York: Wiley.

Acknowledgments

A work as significant as the *Handbook of Child Psychology* is always produced by the contributions of numerous people, individuals whose names do not necessarily appear on the covers or spines of the volumes. Most important, we are grateful to the more than 150 colleagues whose scholarship gave life to the Sixth Edition. Their enormous knowledge, expertise, and hard work make this edition of the *Handbook* the most important reference work in developmental science.

In addition to the authors of the chapters of the four volumes of this edition, we were fortunate to have been able to work with two incredibly skilled and dedicated editors within the Institute for Applied Research in Youth Development at Tufts University, Jennifer Davison and Katherine Connery. Their "can-do" spirit and their impressive ability to attend to every detail of every volume were invaluable resources enabling this project to be completed in a timely and high quality manner.

It may be obvious, but we want to stress also that without the talent, commitment to quality, and professionalism of our editors at John Wiley & Sons, this edition of the *Handbook* would not be a reality and would not be the cutting-edge work we believe it to be. The breadth of the contributions of the Wiley staff to the *Handbook* is truly enormous. Although we thank all these colleagues for their wonderful contributions, we wish to make special note of four people in particular: Patricia Rossi, Senior Editor, Psychology, Linda Witzling, Senior Production Editor, Isabel Pratt, Associate Editor, and Peggy Alexander, Vice President and Publisher. Their creativity, professionalism, sense of balance and perspective, and unflagging commitment to the tradition of quality of the *Handbook* were vital ingredients for any success we may have with this edition. We are also deeply grateful to Pam Blackmon and her colleagues at Publications Development Company for undertaking the enormous task of copy editing and producing the thousands of pages of the Sixth Edition. Their professionalism and commitment to excellence were invaluable resources and provided a foundation upon which the editors' work was able to move forward productively.

Child development typically happens in families. So too, the work of editors on the *Handbook* moved along productively because of the support and forbearance of spouses, partners, and children. We thank all of our loved ones for being there for us throughout the several years on which we have worked on the Sixth Edition.

Numerous colleagues critiqued the chapters in manuscript form and provided valuable insights and suggestions that enhanced the quality of the final products. We thank all of these scholars for their enormous contributions.

William Damon and Richard M. Lerner thank the John Templeton Foundation for its support of their respective scholarly endeavors. In addition, Richard M. Lerner thanks the National 4-H Council for its support of his work. Nancy Eisenberg thanks the National Institute of Mental Health, the Fetzer Institute, and The Institute for Research on Unlimited Love—Altruism, Compassion, Service (located at the School of Medicine, Case Western Reserve University) for their support. K. Ann Renninger and Irving E. Sigel thank Vanessa Ann Gorman for her editorial support for Volume 4. Support from the Swarthmore College Provost's Office to K. Ann Renninger for editorial assistance on this project is also gratefully acknowledged.

Finally, in an earlier form, with Barbara Rogoff's encouragement, sections of the preface were published in *Human Development* (April 1997). We thank Barbara for her editorial help in arranging this publication.

Contents

Section One: Research Advances and Implications for Practice in Education

Section Two: Research Advances and Implications for Clinical Applications

Section Three: Research Advances and Implications for Social Policy and Social Action

Introduction: Child Psychology Research in Practice

K. ANN RENNINGER and IRVING E. SIGEL

APPLIED DEVELOPMENTAL RESEARCH

We undertook the job of editing this volume of the *Handbook of Child Psychology* with a sincere interest in and concern for supporting research that is use-inspired and will impact practice. The applied developmental researcher is a conduit between basic research and real people and activity. By studying questions about a person or a group in context, rather than focusing on some aspect of a person's cognitive and affective functioning in isolation, the applied developmental researcher is positioned to contribute to the ways in which professional activity, including educational or clinical intervention, is carried out and/or text, software, curriculum, and media are designed. This form of developmental research draws on both theory and basic research to address the potential for change and development (age-related and/or content-related). It also can validate basic methods and developmental theory.

The basic methods of the applied developmental researcher may include rich description (participant observation, in-depth interviews, discourse analysis, micro-analysis) that supports hypothesis generation and, in later phases of the research process, serves to illustrate and explain quantitative findings. Basic methods may also include controlled hypothesis testing and use of control groups, randomized sampling, and existing questionnaires and tests. The choice of methods reflects the requirements of the research question.

Identifying relevant indicators for study and tracking change and development is critical to establishing and meeting curricular, therapeutic, and/or social policy goals, as is care in their measurement. A developmental focus assumes that (a) change is dynamic and requires time, (b) the process of effecting change may involve what can look like forward and backward movement, and (c) change needs to be studied in terms of the individual or group as well as the context.

Although no form of research is a prescription for practice, research can inform practice if it is undertaken as a collaboration. Research collaborations in educational, clinical, and social policy contexts typically involve at least one party who is trained in and/or reads research and other(s) who may lack an understanding of, a real interest in, or a readiness to think about either the research literature or its process. These are most successful when all participants hold a jointly articulated vision of purpose and a readiness to build on serendipity, to build on new information, and to delve into and work through problems and/or differences of abilities, interests, prior experiences, and beliefs.

USE-INSPIRED BASIC RESEARCH

Although psychologists such as Binet (1901) and Murchison (1933) used research to inform practice, it is only in recent years that basic research and practice have not been considered distinct efforts. In fact, there has been increasing interest in using developmental research to address problems of practice, or what Stokes (1996) calls "use-inspired basic research." This increased interest can be attributed, in part, to Stokes's articulation of the importance of grounding research in practice in order to meet societal needs. Stokes argues that neither basic nor applied research needs to be exclusive or linear. Rather, he suggests that the study of practice is enhanced by the rigor that characterizes basic research methods and that government would effect change if it supported research that was use-inspired. In *Pasteur's Quadrant* (Stokes, 1997), he describes Louis Pasteur's work on vaccination and pasteurization as emblematic. Pasteur was a scientist and a humanitarian who was as interested in understanding microbiological processes as he was in how he might control the influences of these processes. Pasteur's interest in finding the source of germs inspired his work on a basic research problem. Stokes notes that information from basic research and the field informed Pasteur's work, and that Pasteur's work, in turn, made contributions to basic research as well as to practice.

Child development research that focuses on change and development in contexts of practice is use-inspired research. The first edition of this volume of the *Handbook of Child Psychology, Child Psychology and Practice,* was in press as Stokes's volume was being published. A newsletter (*Quarterly Newsletter of the Laboratory of Comparative Human Cognition*) and three journals (*Applied Developmental Science, Cognition and Instruction, and Journal of Applied Developmental Psychology*) focused on the application of child psychology to practice had preceded this effort, and a number of significant volumes have followed (e.g., Bransford, Brown, & Cocking's, 1999, *How people learn: Brain, mind, experience, and school*; Lerner, Jacobs, & Wertlieb's, 2002, *Handbook of applied developmental science: Promoting positive child, adolescent, and family development through research, policies, and programs*). Each of these publications highlights the importance of research to addressing problems related to education, clinical practice, and social policy. They also reflect a belief that research can provide needed data that make a case for changed and improved practice and evaluate its effectiveness.

Consistent with the model of use-inspired basic research, government and private foundations have begun championing research specific to practice in contexts that are sorely challenged (e.g., schools, out-of-school care, health care). Such initiatives highlight the importance of evaluating change, or impact. It is expected that studies will: include an evaluation component; demonstrate clear impact; document change; and use the information gathered as a basis for developing models that can be used to scale impact.

In this funding climate, the researcher trained in developmental methods with some experience in practical settings (and/or the possibility of partnering with others who have experience) is positioned to: (a) identify relevant indicators of change, (b) select methods that will provide information about these indicators, and (c) develop partnerships that support and effect change even when the researcher is no longer present. This is a creative endeavor, one that involves building on existing theoretical models, research methods and findings—but not directly. Rather, theory, method, and prior research provide a basis for collaborating on the identification and prioritizing of questions to be investigated and methods to be used in the practice setting, so that change can be both assessed and effected.

Importantly, what counts as theory, method, and prior research is not necessarily all "developmental" in its origin. While developmental approaches that enable attention to change and human development have particular relevance to questions of practice, use-inspired basic research does not draw on a single theoretical or research tradition. Of necessity, developmental research that applies to practice builds on research specific to the context of inquiry, research focused on the general nature of context, and identifiable principles for practice. Depending on their questions, researchers studying human development may draw on other fields of psychology (clinical, cognitive, educational, neuropsychology, social) and/or disciplines as wide-ranging as anthropology, biology, communications, economics, learning sciences, linguistics, mathematics, and political science.

THE CONTENTS OF THE PRESENT HANDBOOK

In planning the contents of this volume, we selected three fields that are exemplars of how research is informing practice in contexts that are challenged and of social significance: education, clinical practice, and social policy. Within each of these areas we sought authors who, because of their involvement with practice over time, could speak to their decision-making as researchers using basic research to address issues of practice.

For this volume, we specifically invited authors working in a wide variety of practice contexts to write a chapter that included a selective review of the literature and a description of their own research program as an exemplar. Summaries of prior research were considered to be informative, but not sufficient since the aim of this volume of the *Handbook* is to support use-inspired basic research. Similarly, while theoretical models can provide a language with which to think about practice, they typically do not map the particulars of use and how its study might be undertaken.

We encouraged the authors to include case material in order to provide (a) readers with a context for thinking about the study of change and development and (b) a basis for discussing points raised in the empirical literature and the ways in which these do (or do not) inform practice. We also asked authors to consider a number of questions:

- What are the working assumptions in the research questions being asked? What are the competing hypotheses?

- What are the methods or interventions? On what are they based? What types of adjustments or iterations have they required?

- What principles for practice are suggested by the findings; and what are the caveats about their generalizability? Are there considerations of culture, individual and group needs, gender, and so forth that need to be acknowledged? Was the implementation mandated? What are the ethical issues that need to be addressed?

- What types of decisions get made all of the time in practice even when there is no research to inform practice? What kind of formative assessments can be used in these instances?

- What are the questions with which you and/or the field are still wrestling or still need to wrestle? What are the open questions that are suggested by practice that researchers need to address?

The inclusion of case material, a selected review of the literature, and discussions of decision making were intended to enhance the readability and the utility of chapter contents. These features should also distinguish this volume from others.

Importantly, a volume such as this is expected to hold different meanings for each reader. In fact, each reader is expected to find his or her own favorite or most useful chapters, and these can be expected to differ from those of the next reader. Together, these chapters showcase the thinking that informs use-inspired research on change and development. The chapters provide a basis for thinking about both the ways in which theory and methods inform child psychology research in practice. This volume also addresses the way in which research can inform those working together in practice and mediate decision-making that influences children, their families and/or caretakers, and the professionals who work with them.

REFERENCES

Binet, A. (1901). *The psychology of reasoning: Based on experimental researches in hypnotism* (A. G. Whyte, Trans.). Chicago: Open Court.

Bransford, J. D., Brown, A. L., & Cocking, R. R. (Eds.). (1999). *How people learn: Brain, mind, experience, and school.* Washington, DC: National Academy Press.

Lerner, R. M., Jacobs, F., & Wertlieb, D. (Eds.). (2002). *Handbook of applied developmental science: Promoting positive child, adolescent, and family development through research, policies, and programs.* Thousand Oaks, CA: Sage.

Murchison, C. (Ed.). (1931). *A handbook of child psychology.* Worcester, MA: Clark University Press.

Stokes, D. S. (1997). *Pasteur's quadrant: Basic science and technological innovation.* Washington, DC: Brookings Institution Press.

Research Advances and Implications for Practice in Education

CHAPTER 1

Early Childhood Development and Education

MARILOU HYSON, CAROL COPPLE, and JACQUELINE JONES

The children in Linda Sims's class have gathered on the rug first thing in the morning. All of the children in this Head Start class live in poverty. Four of the children are living in homeless shelters and several others have par-

ents who are in substance abuse treatment programs. Two children have Autism and three have speech and language disabilities. Four of the children speak a language other than English at home.

The authors of this chapter express sincere appreciation to Elena Bodrova and Deborah Leong for their frank and generous discussions of the Tools of the Mind curriculum; to the Tools of the Mind teachers in Maryland and New Jersey, who allowed us to visit their classrooms; to reviewers Linda Espinosa and James

Johnson, and to Martha Bronson and Susanne Denham, for their helpful comments on an earlier draft of this chapter; and to supportive staff and colleagues at the National Association for the Education of Young Children and the Educational Testing Service.

The teacher begins to lead the children through a series of beginning-the-day activities that, on the surface, might look familiar to anyone who has been around preschools. However, significant and purposeful differences—driven by specific developmental theory and related research—influence the curriculum and teaching strategies in this classroom. For example, because it is Monday the children are planning their "jobs" for the week. Rather than assigning jobs, however, the teacher guides the children to look at the labels and pictorial representations on the wall and match their names to their preferred job, placing their names in the slots beside the job listing. Those who do not get jobs are reminded that next week there will be another chance to have a special job.

Although the jobs choices and other seated activities have taken no more than 15 minutes, the teacher spontaneously decides to lead the children in a familiar physical activity, the Freeze Game, before moving on. Putting on a tape, she gets the children on their feet, moving in time to lively music. While they are still dancing, she holds up a stick figure in a pose. Knowing the game, the children continue dancing as usual but remember the stick figure's position. When the music stops, they "freeze" in an approximation of the pose they had seen—this time, with their arms raised. The music starts again, and they dance with vigor, once again ignoring the stick figure's new pose until the music signals them to stop dancing and they freeze in the pose. At one point, Ms. Sims holds up a particularly complex drawing (two figures, each with one foot up and holding hands) and says "Wow! I know this is hard!" The children grin, dance, and then pair up and respond with extra efforts.

Afterward, the children settle onto the rug again for the final activity of the day's opening meeting: Share the News. Many preschool classrooms have something like a show-and-tell or other time for each child to tell something to the rest of the class. Share the News is organized differently: Each child is paired with another and invited to share the news on a topic suggested by the teacher, this time, "Tell your friend what your favorite snack is." The children are accustomed to this ritual and take turns talking and listening with minimal prompting from Ms. Sims. Many children are talking at once as they share their news in partner fashion, but Ms. Sims leans over and listens with interest to each pair, sometimes suggesting a question or reminding a pair of the turn-taking procedures.

This vignette, and others from the same program, provides a real-world context for this chapter's discussion of developmental theory and research in relation to early childhood programs. The *Handbook of Child Psychology* has not previously included a chapter specifically focused on early childhood education, although early childhood issues have formed an important part of chapters on child care, prevention and intervention, and other related topics. The presence of this chapter in Volume 4 attests to the increased recognition that early childhood education is a powerful tool to promote positive development and learning. Clearly, the scope of early childhood education is far too broad and complex to be comprehensively addressed in a chapter of this length. Rather than attempting to review many aspects of the education of young children, the authors have chosen a different approach, one that is consistent with the overall focus of Volume 4 of this *Handbook*.

THE CHAPTER'S FOCUS AND AIMS

Along with other influences and aims, to a notable extent early childhood education programs have grown out of, and aim to promote, child development. Chapters in the first three volumes of this *Handbook* and other chapters in Volume 4 provide extensive summaries and analyses of research in critical domains of early development and learning.

Despite this abundance of data, a continuing challenge is to make effective connections between developmental theory and research on the one hand, and early childhood programmatic and pedagogical decisions, on the other. As this chapter suggests, that relationship is both critically important and more complex than it may appear at first glance. In this chapter, we illustrate and examine these complex relationships by focusing on two foundations of early development and education: the development of cognitive essentials, specifically children's representational thinking, self-regulation, and planning; and the development of children's emotional competence, taking as examples the key areas of emotional security and emotion regulation (ER). Although other developmental domains play a central role, these areas have been identified as critical underpinnings of literacy and other academic skills and of longer-term life success. Both of these foundational areas are also supported by extensive developmental research. Yet at times, each has been inadequately represented in early childhood education policies and practices. Connecting and strengthening the two foundational areas is a third focus: the implementation of developmentally appropriate, classroom-embedded assessment practices that can document children's progress and guide teachers' decision making. Here again, research has great potential to inform the selection and use of assessment tools, and yet developmental perspectives have been insufficiently emphasized in early childhood assessment practices.

We focus our discussion on research and programs for children ages 3 to 6, where much public policy attention is currently directed and where a wealth of developmental and educational research is available, although we describe earlier developmental manifestations and, where available, trajectories in each of the areas highlighted in the chapter. Although the chapter has a preschool emphasis, many of our conclusions can be applied to curriculum and educational practices for both younger and older children.

Rather than confining the analysis of these research and practice relationships to an abstract level, we link this discussion to a specific case example: the Tools of the Mind curriculum developed by Elena Bodrova and Deborah Leong (Bodrova & Leong, 1996; Leong, 2005). The selection of this curriculum is not intended as an endorsement of one approach over all others. Rather, we have chosen the Tools of the Mind curriculum as a case example for other reasons. First, in line with this chapter's focus, the Tools curriculum is strongly influenced by developmental theory and research, specifically, by Vygotskian theory and a related body of social constructivist research. Second, unlike some other, more widely adopted curricula such as High/Scope (Hohmann & Weikart, 2002; Schweinhart, Barnes, & Weikart, 1993) and the Creative Curriculum (Dodge, Colker, & Heroman, 2002), the Tools of the Mind curriculum is still in the relatively early stages of implementation and evaluation. Third, as the curriculum becomes better known in the early childhood community, it is facing the challenges of going to scale. Finally, the nature of this curriculum is such that teachers need to assimilate and be committed to a relatively complex set of guidelines. As the curriculum becomes more widely implemented, it is likely that not all of these teachers will have participated in the curriculum's development; indeed, some may disagree with aspects of its approach. For these reasons, Tools of the Mind seems to be a fruitful example to illustrate the important and complicated connections between theory and research on the one hand, and the world of early childhood practice on the other.

Specifically, we hope this chapter will provide a wide audience of readers with:

- A sense of the contexts within which developmental theory and research have exerted, and continue to exert, influence on early childhood education programs.
- An overview of developmental research in several domains that are essential priorities in early childhood education programs.
- A sense of the opportunities and obstacles facing efforts to use developmental research in designing early education programs.
- Consideration of the implications of these complex relationships for developing, implementing, and evaluating early childhood education programs.

CHAPTER OVERVIEW

The chapter begins by placing the preceding classroom vignette in contemporary contexts for and trends in early education in the United States. Next we discuss the functions and limitations of developmental theory and research in informing the content and implementation of early childhood education programs, previewing some of the challenges that will become apparent in later parts of this chapter.

This background is followed by discussion and analysis of several essential foundations for young children's learning and development (children's cognitive competence, with a focus on representational thought, self-regulation, and planning; and children's emotional competence, with a focus on security and emotion regulation), with effective assessment practices serving to connect, document, and support these two domains. Again we emphasize that these topics do not tell the whole story of what needs to be considered in early childhood education, but they were selected for their centrality, and they will provide key points for analysis. Throughout this discussion, we place special emphasis on the role of the teacher and other significant adults in actively promoting early development and learning. We also examine what research has not yet told us, or may not be able to tell us, about how these essential foundations may best contribute to children's competence in early childhood education programs.

We then turn to a more extended analysis of our case example, the Tools curriculum. We describe the theoretical foundations, key features, and current status of this educational approach. The primary task is to examine how the developmental examples that this chapter has presented (representational thinking, self-regulation, and planning; security and emotion regulation; and developmentally appropriate early childhood assessment) are or might be embodied in this still-evolving curriculum approach.

The broader practical, systemic, and policy challenges of linking developmental theory and research with early childhood curriculum, teaching practices, and assessment are the focus of the final section of the chapter. In this discussion, we again build on the examples from Tools of the Mind, identifying the challenges involved in taking a demonstration program to scale; issues of variability and quality in the system of U.S. early care and education; issues in delivering professional development; challenges of maintaining integrity and coherence; expectations for evidence and accountability; and the continuing, critical gaps in the field's knowledge base. The chapter concludes with a summary and recommendations for linking research with practice.

CONTEXTS FOR EARLY CHILDHOOD EDUCATION TODAY: THROUGH THE LENS OF ONE CLASSROOM

The Tools of the Mind classroom just introduced, and revisited in vignettes throughout the chapter, operates in a context that mirrors larger trends in early childhood education. This context provides a framework for our later discussion of relevant developmental theories and research.

The local program of which Linda Sims's classroom is a part would not have existed 5 years ago. Not only is the curriculum itself new, but the program is in session for more hours per day than Head Start programs typically operated in the past: The children attend for 6 hours per day rather than 3 or 4 hours. This shift is consistent with national trends in Head Start and with evidence that the "dosage" of interventions must be adequate to produce results (McCall, Larsen, & Ingram, 2003; S. L. Ramey & Ramey, 1992). Down the hall from Linda Sims's Head Start class is another classroom for 4-year-olds, also using the Tools of the Mind model. This classroom is part of the state prekindergarten sys-

tem. Maryland, where this school is located, is one of at least 38 states investing some resources in this form of early intervention (Barnett, Hustedt, Robin, & Schulman, 2004).

As part of Head Start, Linda Sims's classroom serves children living in poverty; her students are among the millions of young children who are statistically at risk for negative educational and developmental outcomes because of poverty and other forms of adversity (Lee & Burkham, 2002). Furthermore, the many cultural, ethnic, and language groups represented by the children in Linda Sims's class are typical of today's increasingly diverse preschool population (U.S. Census Bureau, 2003). Because she also has in her class a number of children with disabilities and individualized education programs (IEPs), Linda Sims must continually adapt her curriculum and teaching practices to multiple developmental and educational needs.

Despite the children's many challenges, Linda Sims's hopes for her class are high, but they are not unrealistic. The goals and desired outcomes of the Tools of the Mind program are consistent with the research base, synthesized in several major reports (Bowman, Donovan, & Burns, 2001; Shonkoff & Phillips, 2000; Snow, Burns, & Griffin, 1998), that documents the rapid development and great learning potential of the early years. Linda Sims's classroom functions within an educational and policy environment that reflects an ever greater concern with school readiness and a growing discussion of the potential return on investments in early education (Lynch, 2004). The stage was set in 1993 by the National Education Goals Panel's definition of "Goal One": that all children, including children living in poverty, would enter school "ready to learn."

Since that time, policymakers at the federal and state levels have continued to view early childhood education as a strategy, urging even greater attention to cognitive and academic skill development, especially in early literacy. The 1994 reauthorization of Head Start required programs to ensure that all children acquire specific skills and knowledge, including knowing 10 letters of the alphabet. Although Head Start has broader goals than alphabet knowledge (Zigler & Styfco, 2003), and school readiness is often defined more broadly than in some of these policy initiatives (Child Trends, 2001; Kagan, Moore, & Bredekamp, 1995; National Association for the Education of Young Children, 1995; Shore, 1998), a policy climate that prioritizes an academic and literacy-driven definition of school readiness forms part of the context in which Tools of the Mind is being implemented and evaluated.

This context underscores the potentially significant role of developmental theory and research, both for the new Tools of the Mind curriculum and for many other efforts to create better outcomes for young children. The following section examines the functions and past uses of child development knowledge, as well as trends, challenges, and critical perspectives in bringing child development knowledge to bear on early childhood education.

DEVELOPMENTAL THEORY, RESEARCH, AND EARLY CHILDHOOD EDUCATION

Child development theory and research have a long relationship with early childhood education. Ideas about the potential of early childhood education and early intervention, as well as critical decisions about curriculum, teaching practices, and assessment and evaluation approaches, have frequently been grounded in developmental perspectives.

Major Functions

Over the years, developmental theory and research have served several critical functions with respect to early childhood education:

- *Providing developmental rationales for why early childhood education and early intervention may support positive child outcomes.* Examples include rationales stemming from evidence of the importance of early experiences for the development of critical language and literacy skills (Hart & Risley, 1995) and rationales from cognitive developmental theory and research (e.g., the High/Scope Piagetian-influenced curriculum; Schweinhart & Weikart, 1997).
- *Helping to identify specific desired outcomes of early education programs and curricula.* Research on the developmental course of social competence, for example, identifies specific social and emotional outcomes as of particular significance in early childhood (*Handbook,* Vol. 3); studies of literacy development highlight developmental precursors of later reading and writing, such as vocabulary and phonemic awareness (Snow et al., 1998).
- *Helping to specify interventions, curriculum models, experiences, and practices that would be likely to produce positive developmental outcomes.* For example,

Bronfenbrenner's (Bronfenbrenner & Morris, 1998) ecological theory suggests that interventions emphasizing family and community contexts would be likely to produce better outcomes. Social constructivist theory and research (Rogoff, 1998; Tharp & Gallimore, 1988; Wertsch, 1991) suggest that interventions should emphasize peer interactions and scaffolded interactions with more skilled children and adults.

- *Helping to identify what kinds of developmental indicators should be assessed and tracked so as to document children's individual progress in early education programs and to provide evidence of program effectiveness.* What are the connections between earlier and later development, and between earlier and later forms of a behavior? The sequence of early motor development is clearly mapped out, but developmental sequences or trajectories can be difficult to describe in many areas of early development and learning, such as the growth of mathematical understanding. Although more work is needed (Love, 2003), developmental theory and research can help identify the precursors of later competence and can help identify a variety of possible typical and atypical developmental pathways or trajectories.

Developmental theory and research, then, have been sources for goals and practices in early childhood education in general, and early childhood curriculum in particular. A few examples will underscore this point.

Historical Examples

A full history and a critical analysis of the child development-early education connection are beyond the scope of this chapter but are addressed in several other accounts (Chafel & Reifel, 1996; Goffin & Wilson, 2001; Mallory & New, 1994; Stott & Bowman, 1996). However, even a quick overview of this history illustrates the ways that different conceptualizations of children's development have helped shape not only the content but also the specification of outcomes in programs for young children. This history also illustrates the complexity of, and challenges to, the use of developmental theory and research as a basis for early childhood curriculum.

For developmentalists, but also for those in the public policy and advocacy community, interest in U.S. early childhood education has resided in its potential to positively influence the trajectory of children's development and learning, for example, in Head Start (Zigler & Valentine, 1997). Early optimism about the developmental efficacy of early childhood education was replaced by caution as research appeared to show what were called "fade-out" effects (Cicirelli, 1969), with many short-term gains disappearing in the early years of school.

Yet this perspective on the developmental power of Head Start began, in more recent years, to be replaced with or at least accompanied by another perspective. Longitudinal studies of children enrolled in Head Start and other programs began to show longer-term developmental benefits (Barnett, 1995). Together, these studies provide converging, though still debated, evidence of a set of benefits that go beyond short-term academic outcomes. Indeed, this research suggests that these effects are more likely to be found in other developmental domains and in a different time frame. Over time, children who attended the programs evaluated in these studies were less likely to be retained in grade, less likely to be assigned to special education, more likely to graduate from high school and hold a job, and less likely to engage in a variety of forms of antisocial behavior (Nelson, Westhues, & MacLeod, 2003; C. T. Ramey et al., 2000; Reynolds, 2000; Reynolds, Ou, & Topitzes, 2004; Schweinhart et al., 2005).

Curriculum Models in Early Childhood Education

Research on the outcomes of early childhood education has also examined the relative effectiveness of various curriculum models. As outlined by Goffin and Wilson (2001), theories of child development have served as the principal foundation, though not the only foundation, for curriculum model development, varying according to values about children's learning and according to beliefs about the processes by which children develop and learn. Interpretations of the results of some past curriculum comparison studies have been mixed. Some have concluded that, although differences in child outcomes tend to reflect the curriculum's intent, early childhood curriculum models do affect child outcomes, with potential negative consequences associated with highly structured, academic preschool programs (Goffin & Wilson, 2001; Marcon, 1999, 2002; Schweinhart & Weikart, 1997). Yet the National Research Council's report *Eager to Learn: Educating Our Preschoolers* (Bowman et al., 2001) came to a different conclusion, questioning whether evidence existed to

show that any one curriculum had a clear developmental and educational advantage.

The Questions Reframed: Current Research Initiatives in Early Intervention and Curriculum Comparison Studies

Many writers agree that the debate over questions such as Is early intervention effective? or Does quality in early childhood education matter? or Which curriculum is the best? is over (Guralnick, 1997), or at least has been significantly recast. Now the questions are more complicated, and more interesting: How does early childhood education in general, or a particular curriculum, make a difference? In what domains does early childhood education, or a particular curriculum model, make a difference? A difference in what and for whom and under what conditions (conditions both within the child and within the program, curriculum, and teacher characteristics)? What are the environmental factors that promote or hinder children's movement toward important developmental and educational goals? Recent conceptual frameworks for thinking about early educational interventions reflect this complexity (e.g., C. T. Ramey & Ramey, 1998).

It has not been easy to disentangle what it is about early childhood education programs that produces positive effects, or what types of curriculum and teaching practices, combined with what other family and child supports, may yield the greatest benefits in critical areas of development and learning. These kinds of questions have become the focus of several recent federal initiatives funding large-scale research projects, using carefully designed studies to investigate complex issues around approaches to early childhood curriculum and intervention.

For example, a group of eight research centers, funded in 2003 as part of the Interagency Early Childhood Research Initiative, aims to answer an overarching question: Which early childhood programs, and combination of program components and interactions with adults and peers, are effective or ineffective in promoting early learning and development, for which children, and under which conditions? Projects include an evaluation of an enhanced Head Start curriculum that places emphasis on both evidence-based literacy practices and social and emotional competence, and a study comparing different versions of an intervention to decrease behavior problems and thereby promote school readiness, using teacher professional development, the presence of teachers' aides, and access to mental health professionals. The Head Start Quality Research Center Consortium is supporting the development, testing, and refinement of eight interventions to enhance literacy, social-emotional development, and other domains of school readiness. Finally, another program of research is supported by the U.S. Department of Education's Institute of Education Sciences, with grantees evaluating existing curricula with a focus on the conditions under which curricula may be more or less effective in promoting positive cognitive, academic, and social outcomes.

Complexities and Cautions

These examples from the history of early childhood education, as well as from more recent initiatives, show how extensively a developmental focus has informed the shape, direction, and evaluation of early childhood education programs. However, numerous concerns and cautions have been expressed about the use of child development knowledge in early childhood education.

First, child development knowledge is not the only source of influence on early childhood education. Educators have frequently emphasized that curriculum and program development are shaped by sources other than child development theory and research (Goffin & Wilson, 2001; Stott & Bowman, 1996; Zimiles, 2000). For example, developmental research does not always provide clear guidance about what pedagogical approaches may best produce positive outcomes, and attention to developmental competence has not always been connected to a "knowledge-centered environment" (Bransford, Brown, & Cocking, 2000) needed to promote school success for young children living in poverty (Bowman, 2004). Further, the reconceptualist movement in early childhood education, like other critical perspectives in the broader field of education, has articulated strong challenges to the field's reliance on a child development knowledge base, asserting that generalizations from past developmental research do not hold up across cultures, genders, and other sources of variation, and that the imposition of narrow theoretical perspectives perpetuates imbalances of power and control (Bloch, 1992; Kessler & Swadener, 1992; Mallory & New, 1994). Others have noted that practitioners' insights and "bottom-up" theories of practice are frequently ignored in an emphasis on "top-down" application of formal theory and research (Williams, 1996).

These critical perspectives are important to keep in mind, providing a context in which this chapter's discussion of developmental perspectives should be placed.

Another caution comes from past experiences in which child development research and developmental theory have been misunderstood or misapplied. The 1960s' early optimism about the potential effects of a brief summer dose of Head Start stemmed in part from what Zigler has characterized as the naive environmentalism of that period (Zigler & Styfco, 2004). As developmental knowledge has accumulated, these views have yielded to a more complex and nuanced version of development, but the misuses of the so-called new brain research sounds another cautionary note (Bailey, Bruer, Symons, & Lichtman, 2001). Still another example is the persistent influence of maturationist theory (Gesell & Ilg, 1943) regarding school readiness and school entry age, despite assertions that the theory lacks research support (Graue &DePerna, 2000).

SOME DEVELOPMENTAL ESSENTIALS FOR HIGH-QUALITY EARLY CHILDHOOD EDUCATION

The preceding overview of the history, functions, and limitations of developmental theory and research in relation to early childhood education will serve to frame the discussion that follows. As we will see, research makes a strong case for attention to two significant developmental areas that are the focus of a number of early childhood education curricula, including this chapter's case example, Tools of the Mind: (1) *cognitive competence,* of which *representational thinking, self-regulation,* and *planning* are examples, and (2) *emotional competence,* focusing on the examples of *security* and *emotion regulation.* This analysis is followed by a discussion of the need for high-quality early childhood assessment practices to ensure effective teaching and appropriate accountability.

As the next section of this chapter shows, these essentials have a number of points in common. Both cognitive and emotional competence have long been priorities, although, as noted earlier, they are far from the only priorities in early childhood education. Both have been enriched by recent theoretical and research advances in developmental psychology and in some promising applications in early childhood education settings. Yet both have suffered from periods of neglect. At various times, public policies, competing priorities, and other factors have served to limit the field's ability to implement evidence-based practices in these critically important areas. Although other developmental domains are also significant—such as language, social, and physical development—the breadth and power of both dimensions have great potential to positively influence the direction of early childhood education in ways that benefit not just these specific areas, but other aspects of development and learning as well.

We should also emphasize that, although separated for purposes of review and discussion, cognitive and emotional competence are far from disconnected either at the conceptual or the neurobiological level (Blair, 2002). In the following pages, repeated examples underscore how cognitive and emotional dimensions mutually influence and connect with one another in the early years: how, for example, children's emotional security allows access to cognitive representations, how the emergence of planning skills may be used in the service of emotion regulation, and how adult interactions that support emotional competence also lead to cognitive competence.

If the knowledge base for these essential foundations of early learning is to have a positive influence on curriculum and teaching practices, and therefore on outcomes for the children enrolled in early childhood programs, *assessment* must be another essential and unifying tool. We therefore discuss the multiple challenges of effective early childhood assessments, for example, to inform curriculum implementation and teaching practices and to help evaluate curriculum effectiveness.

An important theme throughout this part of the chapter is the central role of early childhood teachers as potential catalysts for children's cognitive and emotional growth and for gathering, interpreting, and using assessment information about that growth. The field of early childhood education has held, and continues to hold, divergent views about how active teachers should be in direct instruction, coaching, modeling, or otherwise promoting children's development and learning, rather than providing more indirect support and facilitation by setting up the environment and creating conditions for exploration and play. The authors of this chapter are persuaded by research and promising practices that identify teachers' intentional involvement, scaffolding, and collaboration as key supports for early development and learning (e.g., Bowman et al., 2001; Bransford et al., 2000; Edwards, Gandini, & Forman, 1998; Rogoff, Goodman, Turkanis, & Bartlett, 2001).

FOSTERING COGNITIVE ESSENTIALS IN THE EARLY CHILDHOOD YEARS

As an observer watches, 4-year-old Monique asks the teacher in her Tools of the Mind classroom for paper to draw the house she and her friend Ashid had made with the blocks. "I need paper so we can remember what we did," she says to the teacher. Monique and Ashid take the paper and begin to draw. "Should I draw this?" Monique asks as she points to a part of their block structure. "Yeah, well, I'll do this part," Ashid responds. Together they draw what represents the structure. The next day, they get the paper and huddle together to confer on how to rebuild their block house.

Many experts and policymakers today contend that early childhood programs should stress the literacy and mathematical skills that children need to succeed in school and beyond. Important as these skills are, they could be said to be the tip of the iceberg in early education: critical, but dependent on other vital capacities that should be fostered during the years from 3 to 6. A number of researchers and educators have pointed to fundamental abilities that not only underlie reading, mathematics, and other discipline learning but also make possible children's development of focused attention, problem solving, and metacognition, all key in school success. Of these fundamental cognitive abilities, we focus here on three: representational thought, self-regulation, and planning.

Theory and research in these areas are briefly summarized in the following sections. Also described are a number of educational approaches in which representational abilities, self-regulation, and planning are major themes. These include Montessori (1949/1967), High/Scope (Hohmann & Weikart, 2002), Reggio Emilia (Edwards et al., 1998), the Brookline Early Education Project (M. B. Bronson, Pierson, & Tivnan, 1985), Educating the Young Thinker (Copple, Sigel, & Saunders, 1984), and, most recently, Tools of the Mind (Bodrova & Leong, 2003a, 2003b).

Representational Thought

At approximately the same time in their development, children begin to engage in pretend play, develop receptive and expressive language, and show signs of representing objects and events that are not present. Developmental psychologists thus hypothesize strong relationships among these processes. For Piaget, the common factor among these new achievements of the child was what he called the *semiotic* (or symbolic) function, which he saw as developing through the individual child's interaction with the physical and social world. Vygotsky strongly emphasized the social context as the means through which an object, word, or gesture becomes symbolic for the child. For instance, Vygotsky (1981, pp. 160–161) wrote:

> At first the indicatory gesture [pointing] is simply an unsuccessful grasping movement directed at an object and designating a forthcoming action. The child tries to grasp an object that is too far away. The child's hands, reaching toward the object, stop and hover in midair. . . . When the mother comes to the aid of the child and comprehends the movement as an indicator, the situation changes in an essential way. The indicatory gesture becomes a gesture for others.

In other words, the gesture takes on a representational meaning.

Whatever view one takes from these and other perspectives on the dawn of representation, it is clear that a major transition takes place in the 2nd year of life. The ability to form mental images allows children to anticipate and remember objects, people, and events that are not present, that is, to mentally represent (Bruner, 1966, 1983; Piaget, 1926/1955, 1952; Vygotsky, 1962, 1930–1935/1978). It is during this period that children begin to reflect on their actions and perceptions and form symbolic relations among things.

The Burgeoning of Representational Thought

Near the end of the 2nd year, mental representation can be seen in the child's reproducing an event seen earlier, called *deferred imitation* (Piaget, 1962). Also emerging at this time are the more advanced levels of object permanence. Children now systematically search for an object hidden with invisible displacements (Piaget, 1952; Uzgiris & Hunt, 1975). Besides being documented in

systematic research, object permanence can also be seen in children's daily activities. For instance, children late in the 2nd year of life find it necessary to make only occasional visual checks for their mother, far fewer than they did at a younger age (W. C. Bronson, 1973). In all these ways, children manifest the transition to representational thinking at around 18 to 24 months. This advance in thinking is also apparent in children's symbolic or pretend play.

Representation in Pretend Play

The early childhood field has long recognized the many ways pretend play nourishes children's well-being and promotes emotional, social, cognitive, and imaginative development (Bergen, 1988; Johnson, Christie, & Wardle, 2005; Russ, 1994; D. G. Singer & Singer, 1990; Smilansky & Shefatya, 1990). Volumes are written about each of these functions; in this chapter, the major focus is play's cognitive aspects. In considering cognition and play, Vygotsky's work has been a major force.

For Vygotskians, the importance of play lies partly in the fact that children learn to use objects and actions in their symbolic function and thus become more able to think symbolically. Additionally, Vygotsky (1966/1977) saw the dramatic play context, with its system of roles and rules—who does what and what is allowed in the play scenario—as uniquely supportive of self-regulation. Children's eagerness to stay in the play motivates them to attend to and operate within the structure, conforming to what is required by the other players and by the play scenario. Motivation is the first of the four principal ways children's dramatic play influences their development, as identified by Vygotsky's colleague Daniel Elkonin (1977, 1978). In the intensely engrossing play context, children for the first time harness their immediate wants and impulses.

Second, from a Vygotskian perspective, dramatic play facilitates cognitive decentering or perspective taking (Elkonin, 1977, 1978; Vygotsky, 1966/1977). The argument is that taking on a pretend role—being another person for a while—helps the child to move to another perspective and then back to his or her own. In addition, attention to the perspectives of other players is critical for coordinating multiple roles and negotiating play scenarios. Vygotsky and Elkonin also saw cognitive decentering as involved in the assigning of different pretend functions to the same object. Later, children will use this ability in school to recognize another's perspective, coordinating their cognitive perspectives with those of their teachers and learning partners. In time, the ability to coordinate multiple perspectives becomes less outward and more mental, leading to the development of reflective thinking and metacognition (Elkonin, 1977, 1978). The gradual development of this reflectivity and metacognition, including children's notions about their own mental activities and those of others, has also been evident in "theory of mind" research (Bialystok & Senman, 2004; Chandler, 1988; Dunn, 1988).

A third developmental function of play noted in the literature is promoting mental representations, crucial for higher-level thinking. In pretend play, the child begins to separate the meaning of objects from their physical form. At first, children are able only to use replicas of real objects in their pretend play. If this type of play is supported, children then begin to substitute objects that do not closely resemble the object but can perform its function, such as a pencil to serve as a spoon for stirring make-believe soup (Copple, Cocking, & Matthews, 1984; Pulaski, 1973). Finally, experienced players are able to dispense with the object when they choose to do so, often using gestures or speech to bridge the gap, as in "Now I'm carrying a heavy box" (Bornstein, Haynes, Legler, O'Reilly, & Painter, 1997; Corrigan, 1987; Fenson, 1984). Experience in using object substitutes in play appears to help children move from thought that is entirely bound to actions (sensorimotor intelligence) to operational thought, Vygotskian theorists argue. As thought becomes uncoupled from specific actions and objects, children begin to be able to use words and eventually other symbols and signs to represent concepts and abstractions (Piaget, 1962; Vygotsky, 1962).

The final function of play in Elkonin's framework is the development of "deliberateness," or self-regulation, in children's behavior. To stay in the play, the child needs to follow the rules of the play, and play partners monitor each other continually to make sure that everyone is doing so (Bodrova & Leong, 2003a). In early play, this self-regulation is evident in children's physical actions and modification of speech, as in walking heavily to play an elephant, staying still when playing a guard, or talking in a high, babyish voice to portray an infant. Although these are not the only reasons symbolic play occupies a central place in early childhood education, they are the rationales that are most pertinent to our discussion here. For Vygotskians and other constructivists, play is therefore key in preparing children for the learning demands, social interactions, and behavioral expectations they will experience in and out of school.

Influences on Representational Thinking

The influence of children's experiences on the quantity and representational levels of make-believe play can be seen in the variation found in children of different socioeconomic and family backgrounds (Freyberg, 1973; Fromberg, 1992; Sigel & McBane, 1967; Smilansky, 1968; Smilansky & Shefatya, 1990). Evidence also suggests that training and forms of direct support from adults can increase children's ability to use representation and pretense in their dramatic play (Freyberg, 1973; E. Saltz & Brodie, 1982; Smilansky, 1968). Although differences in mental representation are harder to observe, children who have certain kinds of early education experiences may increase their skills or dispositions with respect to use of mental representations, as the work reported next suggests.

Developing Representational Abilities in Early Childhood Programs

Two programs, one early program and one that is ongoing, are particularly known for their emphasis on children's representations and representational thinking: Irving Sigel's Educating the Young Thinker program (Copple, Sigel, et al., 1984; Sigel, 2000), and the Reggio Emilia approach (Edwards et al., 1998; Malaguzzi, 1998).

In 1975, Irving Sigel, along with colleagues Ruth Saunders and Carol Copple, began the Educating the Young Thinker program in Princeton, New Jersey. It was based on Sigel's work on representational competence and the importance of what he calls "distancing" experiences: those that place on the child the cognitive demand of considering objects, actions, or events that are separate in time and/or space from the immediate present (Copple, Sigel, et al., 1984). Based on the idea that actively engaging in mental construction and representation promotes children's representational abilities and dispositions, teachers in the program frequently engaged preschoolers in anticipating, predicting, recalling, or reconstructing experiences. For example, children planned in considerable detail how to make changes in their playground, prepare for a family night at the preschool, or investigate a science problem. Teachers actively encouraged metacognitive thinking with questions such as, "How can we make sure to remember our plan?"

Children randomly assigned to classrooms using such strategies were found to differ on a number of measures from children in control classrooms that were comparable in materials, teacher training, parent involvement, and other aspects that might be expected to affect child outcomes (Sigel, 2000). Additional evidence for the effects of such inputs on children's representational competence comes from laboratory studies in which parents were instructed to teach their children a task (e.g., McGillicuddy-DeLisi, Sigel, & Johnson, 1979). In such teaching situations, parents' use of distancing strategies was significantly associated with children's representational competence.

For more than 30 years, educators, together with parents and community members, worked together to develop an acclaimed public system of early care and education in the city of Reggio Emilia, Italy. Numerous early childhood specialists have explored the implications of the Reggio Emilia programs for the theory, practice, and improvement of U.S. early childhood education (e.g., Edwards et al., 1998). Although Reggio programs highly value the role of play in children's development, they are especially well-known for the complex, long-term projects in which children and teachers become engaged over weeks and months. At the start of a project, teachers engage children in bringing to mind what they know and think about the topic or problem of their investigation and about what they want to learn and accomplish in the project. Malaguzzi (1998) sees these predictions and hypotheses at the outset as key in organizing and galvanizing the project work.

For the duration of the project, teachers make observations, tape and make transcriptions of children's discussions, take photographs showing work in progress, and otherwise document the ongoing work. The documentation of the children's thoughts and ideas, which the group comes back to repeatedly, helps them remember significant points and get new ideas. Participating in and making use of the documentation also expands children's understanding of representational modes, including language and visual representation in various media—the "hundred languages of children" of which Reggio Emilians speak (Edwards et al., 1998). In Reggio Emilia, graphic representation is viewed as a communication tool much simpler and clearer than words, and thus as an invaluable way to help children clarify and extend their thinking. Children make extensive use of drawing, as well as models and other concrete forms of representation, as they work together on a project (Malaguzzi, 1998). Because children are trying to communicate with others in these graphic efforts, they often

pause to clarify their ideas before putting them down on paper and making them visible to other people.

Although systematic research, such as comparisons with control and experimental groups, has not been part of the Reggio Emilia tradition or emphasis, some of the program's effects are quite visible. Those who see the products children produce and documentation of the conversations and procedures they engage in along the way are struck by the sophistication and thoughtfulness of the work (Edwards et al., 1998; Katz & Cesarone, 1994; New, 1998).

Several other programs and interventions relating to mental representation are discussed in "Developing Planning Skills in Early Childhood Programs" later in the chapter.

Self-Regulation

Related to but not identical with the domain of emotion regulation discussed later in this chapter, self-regulation is a significant dimension of cognitive competence, with implications for a wide array of developmental and learning outcomes. Self-regulation is by no means a simple or singular construct. It has been defined and studied in various ways, including self-direction, self-regulated learning, self-control, and impulse control (M. B. Bronson, 2000). Although it is beyond the scope of this chapter to detail the distinctions among these various terms and the paradigms used to study them, these differences clearly need to be considered when interpreting implications for developmental expectations and for what supports and educational practices are useful at various ages and in different situations (Blair, 2002; M. B. Bronson, 2000).

Early childhood educators (e.g., Bredekamp, 1987; Hymes, 1955; Montessori, 1949/1967) have long viewed children's development of self-regulation as a primary goal for the preschool years. Research evidence links self-regulation to focusing of attention (Barkley, 1997; Holtz & Lehman, 1995), self-directed thinking and problem solving (Brown & DeLoache, 1978; DeLoache & Brown, 1987), planning, and metacognition (Flavell, 1987; Wellman, Fabricius, & Sophian, 1985). Presumably through this association with behaviors and skills needed in school, self-regulation in school-age children is predictive of academic success (Blair, 2002; Ladd, Birch, & Buhs, 1999; Normandeau & Guay, 1998; Zimmerman, Bonner, & Kovach, 1996; Zimmerman & Schunk, 1989).

Over the early childhood years, children become less reactive and more self-regulated and deliberate. With development, they are better able to control their behavior and attention (Barkley, 1997; Holtz & Lehman, 1995; Mischel & Mischel, 1983). They become increasingly capable of self-directed thinking, planning, and problem solving (Berg, Strough, Calderone, Meegan, & Sansone, 1997; Brown & DeLoache, 1978; DeLoache & Brown, 1987; Rogoff, Gauvain, & Gardner, 1987).

In the preschool years, a major force in increasing self-regulation appears to be children's engagement in pretend play. Erik Erikson (1950) describes how children gain control of their emotions and social behavior through their play. In play, they express the world inside them and impose order on the world outside. Thus, in Erikson's view, if children lack sufficient play opportunities or are pushed prematurely out of this stage by external demands, they may not become as self-regulated as other children are.

Elias and Berk (2002) investigated the relationship between play and self-regulation that Erikson, Vygotsky, and others have posited. Observing the complexity of children's dramatic play and recording self-regulation during cleanup and circle time, they found a positive relationship between the time spent in mature dramatic play and the child's self-regulation during cleanup.

The role of language in developing internal control of action and thought has also been emphasized by theorists. Vygotsky (1962, 1930–1935/1978) considered language to be the primary means for developing both understanding and self-regulation, and a substantial body of research supports this idea (Berk, 1992; Fuson, 1979, Luria, 1961). Children repeat the kinds of instruction and guidance that others have given them and begin to give themselves audible directions (e.g., "Put the red ones there"; "That piece doesn't fit"). According to Vygotsky (1962, 1930–1935/1978), in time this private speech becomes internalized as thought.

The ability to store and retrieve mental images, greatly expanded by use of language, enables children to apply past experience in a variety of situations. Moreover, the growing capacity for mental representation allows children to make plans before taking action; their activities take on a more purposeful, goal-directed character (Friedman & Scholnick, 1997; Friedman, Scholnick, & Cocking, 1987; Wellman et al., 1985).

Influences on Self-Regulation

Zimmerman and his colleagues (e.g., Schunk & Zimmerman, 1997; Zimmerman, 1989; Zimmerman, Bandura, & Martinez-Pons, 1992), working from a social-cognitive perspective, conjecture that parents function as implicit and explicit role models in their children's acquisition of self-regulatory skills. With path analysis (Martinez-Pons, 1996) and training-study methods (Zimmerman & Kitsantas, 1999, 2001), they have demonstrated the causal influence of self-regulatory models, such as parents, on children ranging from elementary through high school. The researchers posit that modeling and encouragement of self-regulation are part of the "hidden curriculum" that some children experience and others do not. They offer school-based interventions, such as one at the middle school level (Zimmerman et al., 1996).

Developing Self-Regulation in Early Childhood Programs

Early childhood educators would argue that this focus on self-regulation should take place much earlier than in middle school. Besides the emphasis on promoting children's self-control and self-regulation that runs through much of early childhood education literature (see section on "Fostering Emotional Essentials in the Early Childhood Years"), two early childhood education approaches stand out as particularly concerned with this area.

The Montessori (1949/1967) method values children's becoming independent learners. Developmental milestones such as weaning, walking, and talking are seen as events that enable the child to achieve increased autonomy and self-regulation. A wide range of activities are available to children at all age and maturity levels to reinforce Montessori goals of individualized work, progress, and independence. By encouraging children to make decisions from an early age, Montessori programs seek to develop self-regulated problem solvers who can make choices and manage their time well. Some evidence of these associations comes from research by Kendall (1992), who examined the autonomous behavior among groups of Montessori schools and traditional public schools, finding that Montessori students demonstrated higher levels of self-regulation, independence, and initiative than those from traditional schools.

Similarly, self-regulation is a central goal in the Vygotsky-based Tools approach, the case example examined later in this chapter. The methods used in Tools of the Mind programs to help children become more self-regulated are described there.

Planning

Planning may be defined as the deliberate organization of actions oriented toward a goal (Prevost, Bronson, & Casey, 1995). Both adults and children plan in their daily lives, although young children's planning is far less complex and frequent than it later becomes (e.g., Benson, 1994, 1997; Hudson, Shapiro, & Sosa, 1995). Because planning is a factor in how children approach school tasks, manage their time, and create and modify strategies to reach goals, it is not surprising that planning ability has been found to be associated with school achievement (Naglieri & Das, 1987).

Development of Planning and Related Processes

Early precursors of planning appear in the sensorimotor period when infants and young toddlers begin to vary their actions to get interesting effects (Lewis, 1983; Piaget, 1952). For example, when an infant clutching a rattle in his hand moves his arms and hears the sound, he begins to move his arms more vigorously to create more sound.

Behavior becomes increasingly intentional in the 2nd year of life. Part of what allows embryonic planning to occur at this point is the child's development of mental representation. As Haith (1997) notes, planning seems to depend on the individual's ability both to mentally represent and to have control over action alternatives. Because representation of events is necessary for planning, research on recall and representation of events is relevant here. Research by Bauer and colleagues (Bauer & Hertsgaard, 1993; Bauer & Mandler, 1989, 1990, 1992) demonstrates that preschool children can reproduce a modeled series of actions, thus showing their ability to represent the sequence of events mentally.

Further evidence suggests that young children's knowledge about familiar events is both organized and general (Hudson & Shapiro, 1991; Nelson, 1986; Slackman, Hudson, & Fivush, 1986). Asked about a familiar activity such as going to the grocery store, children give generalized accounts derived from knowledge of what usually happens across many instances. For example, Hudson, Sosa, and Shapiro (1997, p. 77) quote a 3-year-old who was asked to tell what happens when he goes to the store: "I just buy things to eat. We get a cart or box to hold it. When we're done, we just get in the car and go home." What is noteworthy here is that the child gives a general rather than a specific account: He knows that various things may be purchased, that either a cart or a box may be used to carry the groceries, and that one buys the items before leaving. Having found that young children have considerable event knowledge of this kind, Nelson sees these "generalized event representations" as a significant resource that children bring to the task of planning. Even preschoolers apparently have considerable knowledge about the sequence and steps in familiar events, which they can put to use in planning (Hudson, Shapiro, et al., 1995).

Influences on Planning

Whether it is possible to increase such knowledge and children's access to it by purposeful intervention has not been determined, at least not in controlled studies. Some early childhood approaches (including High/Scope and the Tools of the Mind model) have emphasized planning and reflection experiences and engaged children regularly in both representing past experiences and planning future actions. We look at several of these in the later section on "Developing Planning Skills in Early Childhood Programs."

Language comes into play in children's developing ability to plan. Vygotsky (1966/1977, 1930–1935/1978) viewed the child's private speech, also called egocentric speech or self-speech, as important in the development of thought. Children use private speech to regulate their own behavior in problem-solving situations and as a tool in planning solutions before trying them out (Berk & Winsler, 1995). Moreover, when children employ words to plan and reflect, their language use is decontextualized, that is, focused on nonimmediate events (Dickinson & Smith, 1994), and decontextualized language use is important in reading and other learning tasks in school. In other words, incorporating experiences with planning and reflecting in early childhood settings appears to be a promising way to nurture the kind of language development particularly useful for school learning.

Preschool children vary widely in how planful they are. Casey and her colleagues (Casey, Bronson, Tivnan, Riley, & Spenciner, 1991) found that some 4- and 5-year-olds were very organized and systematic across a variety of tasks, whereas other children of equivalent intelligence showed little evidence of thinking ahead.

Numerous researchers have shown external influences on children's planning processes and their use of planning. Variations in children's experiences with respect to planning or future orientation at home have been documented (e.g., Benson, 1997; Hudson, Sosa, et al., 1997; Rogoff, 1990). Jacqueline Goodnow (1987) investigated how planning varies in differing social contexts. Studying children's conversations while they planned and executed drawings, Cocking and Copple (1987) observed that children react to their peers' plans and comments, at times by rethinking their own plans. Ellis and Siegler (1997) examined the conditions under which children plan and fail to plan, summarizing the results of numerous studies. The studies included a variety of tasks such as 20 Questions, the Tower of Hanoi (in which the subject faces the problem of transferring rings stacked on a pole in increasing size order to another pole without violating the size order), and other problems that involve multiple moves or choices and may be approached in numerous ways.

Developing Planning Skills in Early Childhood Programs

Children's experiences with planning in education and care settings vary. Generally, the development of planning skills is not an explicit program goal, but some common teacher practices are likely to support a degree of thinking ahead and awareness of temporal sequence. For example, most early childhood teachers usually follow a regular daily schedule of activities and often draw children's attention to the event sequences by saying things like "We will have time for you to finish your building right after we come in from the playground." Beyond such commonplace preschool experiences, one can point to a number of educational approaches in which enhancing children's planning and reflection has been a major objective. Several of these are briefly described here.

The Brookline Early Education Project (BEEP), the first comprehensive school-based early intervention program in the United States, began in 1972. The program involved preschoolers in daily planning in a variety of ways. At the beginning of the day, children discussed with the teacher and decided what they would do during the session. They used planning boards to represent the structure and sequence of their activities. At the end of the day, they gathered with the teacher to review and evaluate their follow-through on their plans: what they actually did and how it turned out. At times, they put together visual examples of what they had done during the day, and sometimes were even able to show the sequence of their activities. Program evaluation indicated that children in the BEEP program outperformed controls on observational measures of mastery skills, social skills, and use of time (M. B. Bronson et al., 1985; Tivnan,

1988). A follow-up study when the BEEP children were young adults suggests long-term differences for program participants as compared to their urban peers. BEEP graduates, especially those living in urban settings, had significantly higher incomes, more years of education, higher rates of employment and college attendance, higher health ratings, and fewer risky health behaviors than those in the comparison group (Palfrey, Bronson, Erickson-Warfield, Hauser-Cram, & Sirin, 2002).

The High/Scope preschool curriculum, initially developed in 1962 by David Weikart and colleagues (Weikart, Rogers, Adcock, & McClelland, 1971), is widely used in the United States and other countries. The curriculum approach is based on constructivist theories of development and learning, particularly that of Piaget (Hohmann & Weikart, 2002). The Piagetian influence is apparent in the curriculum goals, which give priority to the cognitive skills of language, experiencing, and representing, along with classification, number, and other conceptual areas prominent in Piaget's work. A substantial body of research, including longitudinal data more than 35 years after participants attended High/Scope's Perry Preschool Program (Schweinhart & Weikart, 1997; Schweinhart et al., 2005), confirms the positive effects of the program in terms of cognitive, social, and real-world outcomes, such as lower crime rates and unemployment decades after participating in the program.

The plan-do-review sequence is a hallmark of the High/Scope approach (Hohmann & Weikart, 2002). It includes a small-group time of 5 to 10 minutes during which children plan what they want to do during work time: the area they plan to visit, the materials they will use, and the peers they will play with. The children then have a work time of 45 minutes to an hour for carrying out their plans, followed by another small-group time for reviewing and recalling with the teacher and the other children what they have done and learned. Both the planning and review periods become longer and more detailed when children are older and more experienced in the processes of planning and reflecting. Although specific assessment of planning has not been included in evaluations of High/Scope, findings (Epstein, 2003) suggest that High/Scope children score higher than do controls on measures of language, literacy, social skills, and overall development.

Tools of the Mind, described at length later in the chapter, also engages children in a range of planning and reflection experiences, particularly daily planning of their play and then revisiting and reflecting on their play experiences on the following day.

Summary

This review of the development and educational relevance of three cognitive essentials—representation, self-regulation, and planning—is far from exhaustive. Many other dimensions of cognitive competence are related to those discussed and are also educationally important, such as children's social-cognitive development, theories of mind, and linguistic abilities. Considerable research, too extensive to be discussed in this chapter, is available in each of these and other areas of developmental and educational significance.

Similarly, the next section of this chapter highlights two specific aspects of emotional competence out of a much broader set of dimensions. First, we make a case for *emotional security,* grounded in positive adult-child relationships, as an essential underpinning of young children's ability to benefit from educational experiences. Related to but also distinct from the self-regulation just discussed, *emotion regulation* is highlighted as an area that makes substantial contributions to positive development and learning.

FOSTERING EMOTIONAL ESSENTIALS IN THE EARLY CHILDHOOD YEARS

An observer visits a Tools of the Mind classroom in September. During group time, one child, Shana, wanders around the classroom looking at the objects on the shelf. As the children begin their play time, Shana continues to wander, unable to engage in any activity. Going to the sand table where children are playing together, she takes the shovel out of another child's hand as she looks at the teacher. A pushing match ensues, and the other child raises her fist, threatening to hit Shana. As the teacher approaches, Shana turns her head, struggling to get away, kicking and pushing the furniture over. Picking Shana up, the teacher begins to talk softly to her. When the observer returns in April, she notices a girl and a boy playing with blocks. "Be careful," the boy says. "I don't want you to knock this over. But go and get your things and we'll go on vacation." The little girl gets up and carefully steps around the structure. For about 40 minutes they play out an elaborate scenario about going on vacation together. The little girl is Shana, the same

child who had shown such disorganized, disruptive, and distressed behavior in September.

Emotional development has been a recurring emphasis in early childhood education, forming part of the field's core tradition (Bredekamp & Copple, 1997; M. C. Hyson, 2003). In the past few decades, developmental researchers have generated extensive knowledge of young children's emotions, as reviewed in the chapter by Saarni, Camras, and Campos (Chapter 5, this *Handbook,* Volume 3). Despite this shared attention, research on emotions has not had a significant impact on program developers, practitioners, and policymakers in early childhood education settings. Several factors account for this state of affairs. Until recently, theory and research on emotional development was disseminated primarily through academic journals and conferences in psychology. Although the gap has narrowed with a series of publications that have been disseminated to policymakers and practitioners (e.g., Denham, 1998; Hyson, 2003a; Kauffman Early Education Exchange, 2002; Peth-Pierce, 2000; Raver, 2002), other trends have worked in the opposite direction. In a climate of strong focus on academic content standards and high-stakes skills testing, observers find numerous early childhood programs diminishing rather than heightening their emphasis on emotions.

Reflecting and foreshadowing these trends, the National Research Council's report *Neurons to Neighborhoods: The Science of Early Childhood Development* (Shonkoff & Phillips, 2000, pp. 387–388) urged the following:

> Resources on a par with those focused on literacy and numerical skills should be devoted to translating the knowledge base on young children's emotional, regulatory, and social development into effective strategies for fostering (1) the development of curiosity, self-direction, and persistence in learning situations; (2) the ability to cooperate, demonstrate caring, and resolve conflict with peers; and (3) the capacity to experience the enhanced motivation associated with feeling competent and loved.

The next section of this chapter begins by defining the domain and components of emotional development, and then describes two specific dimensions of emotional competence.

The Domain and Components of Emotional Development

Rather than being subsumed under the "socioemotional" umbrella, emotional development is now viewed as a distinct domain, with a rich theoretical and research base deserving of attention in its own right, yet conceptually and empirically linked both to social development and to every other domain of early development and learning.

Emotional development has many components. The construct of *emotional security,* whether indexed by attachment status or in other ways, is generally regarded as an essential developmental foundation. In addition to this dimension, Denham (1998) groups the components of early emotional competence into three areas: *emotion expression* (including using gestures to convey emotional messages, demonstrating empathic involvement, displaying complex emotions appropriately, realizing one may feel one way and outwardly express a different feeling); *emotional understanding* (discerning one's own feelings, discerning others' emotional states, and using emotion vocabulary); and *emotion regulation* (coping with unpleasant feelings or emotion-eliciting situations, coping with strong positive feelings such as excitement, and strategically exaggerating the expression of some feelings to get a desired result).

For the purposes of this chapter, just two components will receive in-depth attention: emotional security and emotion regulation. Closely related to each other and to the previously discussed cognitive constructs of representational thinking, self-regulation, and planning, they appear foundational to young children's successful development and learning in early childhood education programs.

Emotional Security

No single definition of emotional security has dominated the field of child development, and yet the construct has been a consistent emphasis. Erikson (1950, 1959) believed the achievement of "basic trust" to be the first accomplishment of infancy, revisited in different ways at each stage of the life course. Bowlby (1969/1982) and, later, Ainsworth (Ainsworth, Blehar, Waters, & Wall, 1978) posited a universal human need for attachments between children and adults. Building on attachment theory, the "emotional security hypothesis" (Davies & Cummings, 1998; Davies, Harold, Goeke-Morey, & Cummings, 2002) holds that children's adaptive behavior is strongly influenced by the underlying goal of maintaining emotional security within and beyond the family.

Why Is Emotional Security Significant for Children's Development and Learning?

Essentially, "relationships shape the development of self-regulation, social competence, conscience, emotional growth and emotion regulation, learning and cognitive growth, and a variety of other foundational developmental accomplishments" (Shonkoff & Phillips, 2000, p. 265). Consistent, warm, responsive and nurturing relationships with mothers, fathers, family child care providers, preschool teachers, and others are thought to build a sense of emotional security in young children, with specific cultural practices and traditions influencing how that security is experienced and expressed (e.g., Miller & Goodnow, 1995).

Much evidence for the importance of emotionally secure relationships comes from mother-child attachment research (Ainsworth et al., 1978; Cassidy & Shaver, 1999; Thompson, 1999). Secure attachments or, more broadly, emotionally positive relationships have a number of short- and long-term benefits. For example, secure attachment relationships appear to buffer the presence of stress hormones (Gunnar, Brodersen, Nachmias, Buss, & Rigatuso, 1996), serving as a protective factor for children at risk. Research syntheses suggest that secure attachments may make children more receptive to adults' socialization efforts and instruction, and that securely attached children are also less likely to have behavior problems (Shonkoff & Phillips, 2000).

Emotional security tends to generalize: Even at a young age, children develop representations or "internal working models" (Main, Kaplan, & Cassidy, 1985) of how future partners in the child's social world may respond. Thus, the child's ability to build secure relationships with others, or to use relationships as a base for future exploration and learning, is powerfully affected by experiences with these early relationships (Thompson, 1999).

The Development of Emotional Security in Infants, Toddlers, and Preschoolers

From the perspective of attachment theory, the development of children's close relationships with important adults follows a predictable course (Ainsworth, 1973; Bowlby, 1969/1982), although with important cultural variations (Shonkoff & Phillips, 2000). In the first 3 or 4 months of life, infants orient themselves to the adults in their environment and begin to signal to them, but do not yet discriminate particular adults as "attachment figures." Over the next months, infants begin to show these kinds of preferences, usually for their mother but also for others, depending on who participates in caregiving. After about 8 months of age, most children develop clear signs of attachment relationships, becoming distressed when mother or another preferred person leaves, and following or seeking physical proximity to that adult, especially when the child is distressed or fearful. Over time, and generally by the 3rd or 4th year of life, this relationship is thought to develop into what Bowlby called a "goal corrected partnership," in which the child is able to tolerate separations and use attachment figures as secure bases for exploration and risk taking. The long-term goal and organizing principle of the attachment relationship is not to maintain physical closeness but for the child to experience "felt security" (Sroufe & Waters, 1977)—an important consideration as we turn to secure relationships in out-of-home settings.

Emotional Security in Early Childhood Education Programs: Characteristics, Influences, and Outcomes

Children of the ages emphasized in this chapter (3 to 6) have typically formed attachments to one or more primary caregivers and are able to hold representations of those figures in mind even in their absence. Building from this body of theory and research, several investigators have recently examined the characteristics of, influences on, and consequences of positive, secure teacher-child relationships in the early years. The premise of much of this research is that adults who are not parents can serve as attachment figures in young children's lives (Howes, 1999, 2000). These relationships do not entirely replicate the bonds between parents and children, and their developmental course may differ depending on when the relationships are established, but they nevertheless have similar features and functions in early development and learning (Howes, 1999; Howes & Hamilton, 1992). Many children develop a clear desire to stay physically close to their favorite teachers, appear to use them as a base from which to explore the environment, and seek physical proximity when hurt or distressed. Further, these relationships can be classified as secure or insecure using criteria similar to those that have been used in studies of parent-child attachment— again, with attention to cultural differences in how adult-child relationships may be manifested.

Prevalence of Emotionally Supportive Relationships and Environments in Early Childhood Programs. How likely is it that young children will have supportive, emotionally secure relationships with their teachers? According to Howes (1999; Howes & Ritchie, 2002), as many as 70% of young children may fail to develop secure attachments to their teachers, as indexed by, for example, scores on the Attachment Styles Questionnaire (Howes & Ritchie, 2002). Many teachers' interactions with young children lack the warmth and responsiveness that appear to be essential underpinnings of growth-promoting relationships. For example, in a study of 90 middle-class children and their families, Hyson, Hirsh-Pasek, and Rescorla (1990) found that only about one-third of preschool teachers were observed to spend time talking about feelings. Large-scale child care studies (e.g., Cost, Quality, and Child Outcomes Study Team, 1995; National Institute of Child Health and Human Development Early Child Care Research Network, 2000) have found frequent evidence of emotional insensitivity, detachment, and even harshness among teachers of young children.

Relationships between Teacher-Child Relationships and Outcomes for Children. This lack of consistently secure, emotionally supportive teacher-child relationships is of particular concern in light of recent evidence that positive relationships with teachers have short- and longer-term benefits both in the behavioral or social domains and in cognitive and academic development.

Evidence is accumulating that when young children are able to feel emotionally secure with their teacher, they are more active in exploring the environment and, therefore, have more opportunities to learn (Birch & Ladd, 1997; Howes & Smith, 1995; Pianta, 1999). One of the consistent findings in early education, summarized in the National Research Council's report *Eager to Learn: Educating Our Preschoolers,* is that an emotionally warm and positive approach in learning situations leads to more constructive behavior in children (Bowman et al., 2001). For example, Howes and colleagues (Howes, 2000; Howes & Smith, 1995) have found that children with more secure attachments to their child care teachers have more competent interactions with adults, play more maturely with other children, and engage in more cognitively complex activities.

Other researchers have investigated the importance of teacher-child relationships for school adjustment and academic success (Birch & Ladd, 1997; Hamre & Pianta, 2001; Pianta, 1999; Pianta, La Paro, Payne, Cox, & Bradley, 2002; Pianta, Nimetz, & Bennett, 1997). For example, children who have emotionally close relationships with kindergarten teachers are more likely to adjust well to school than those whose relationships are less close. Kindergarten children who were predicted to be retained in grade or referred to special education—but who did not experience those outcomes—were found to have had especially positive relationships with their kindergarten teachers (Pianta, Steinberg, & Rollins, 1995).

Two longitudinal studies support the predictive power of early, positive teacher-child relationships. In a study of children from kindergarten through eighth grade, children who had negative relationships with their kindergarten teachers (either conflicted or overly dependent) were more likely to experience social and academic difficulties in later years (Hamre & Pianta, 2001). Another longitudinal study (Stipek & Greene, 2001) shows that kindergarten and first-grade teachers' ratings of their affectionate and warm versus "conflicted" relationships with individual students in the class predicted those children's feelings about school as well as the children's ratings of their own academic performance.

In addition to their social and academic benefits, children's relationships with teachers can compensate to some extent for troubled family relationships. Several studies (Howes & Smith, 1995; Mitchell-Copeland, Denham, & DeMulder, 1997) indicate that secure attachments to child care teachers can support positive development even if children's attachments to their parents are insecure. For example, Howes and Ritchie (2002) found that children who had insecure attachments to their parents were able to compensate to some extent, both socially and academically, if they had a secure relationship with their teacher.

Emotional Security's Associations with Teacher Characteristics, Curriculum, and Teaching Practices.   What conditions promote or diminish the likelihood that teachers will indeed develop these kinds of secure relationships with young children? A number of studies have looked at the effects of teachers' levels of education and training on the provision of emotionally responsive, supportive classroom environments and relationships. In general, higher levels of formal education and specialized training seem to be associated with warmer relationships and interactions with children

(Arnett, 1989; Howes, 1997), although researchers have found it difficult to identify underlying reasons for these associations.

Furthermore, several programs of research have examined relationships between the emphasis of a specific early childhood curriculum or set of teaching practices and the likelihood that the teacher has warm and emotionally positive relationships with children. For example, a study by Hyson et al. (1990) included preschool classroom observations in which the emotional climate of the classroom was rated, along with other features of the curriculum and teaching practices. The results indicated that classrooms with higher levels of adult direction and more didactic approaches to teaching were significantly less likely to be characterized by teacher-child affection and warmth.

In a related set of studies, Stipek and colleagues (Stipek, Daniels, Galluzzo, & Milburn, 1992; Stipek et al., 1998; Stipek, Feiler, Daniels, & Milburn, 1995) examined classrooms that varied in their emphasis on structured, teacher-directed instruction in basic skills, rather than on child choice and autonomy. These studies included systematic observations of teachers' acceptance/warmth and of the classroom's emotional climate. Again, Stipek and colleagues found that highly didactic, basic skills-oriented approaches that emphasized individual success and failure were associated with less teacher warmth and nurturance and less attention to children's individual needs than in the more child-focused classrooms.

Despite these findings, it is impossible to conclude that the only pedagogical approach that supports emotionally secure teacher-child relationships is a strongly child-centered one. A number of recent trends have blurred the distinction between teacher-directed and child-centered early childhood curricula and teaching practices. Influenced by Vygotskian and other social constructivist perspectives, as well as by research on early language, literacy, and mathematical development, by the growing presence of content standards in kindergarten and prekindergarten education, by new position statements from national organizations (Bredekamp & Copple, 1997; Neuman, Copple, & Bredekamp, 2000), and by greater knowledge of the wide cultural variations in approaches to early childhood education (Mallory & New, 1994), there are now a greater number of early childhood curricula that cannot neatly be categorized as child-centered versus didactic. These approaches, like the Tools of the Mind curriculum described in this chapter, place greater emphasis on teachers' active promotion of cognitive and academic competencies (Mayer, 2004) through scaffolding, reflection, and representation, while still embedding these in firsthand experiences linked to young children's interests and within the context of close relationships, rich social interactions, and play.

However, the emotional climate and motivational impact of these curricula have not yet been systematically studied. The previously described federally funded programs of early childhood education research, including curriculum comparisons and effectiveness studies, have potential to answer some of these questions.

Emotion Regulation

In addition to emotional security, a second critical component of early emotional competence is the development of emotion regulation. As suggested earlier in this chapter, emotion regulation is related to but distinct from the more cognitively focused self-regulation, an ability strongly emphasized in the Tools of the Mind curriculum. Kopp (1989, 2002) views ER as "modulating the intensity of emotion responses such as anger, fear, pleasure, sadness, and other emotions. Effective ER means a response is appropriate to context, enhances rather than jeopardizes bio-behavioral well-being, and guides subsequent social and cognitive activities" (2002, p. 11).

Emotion regulation involves a number of crucial skills and dispositions (Denham, 1998; Dunn & Brown, 1991; Saarni, 1999). Children who are acquiring these skills are increasingly able to:

- Keep in touch with their own emotional responses.
- Stop themselves from displaying inappropriate behavior motivated by strong positive or negative feelings.
- Calm, distract, or soothe themselves when strong feelings threaten to overwhelm them.
- Use varied and flexible coping strategies to change the intensity of their emotions.
- Coordinate feelings, thoughts, and actions to reach goals that are important to them.
- Use emotions to help focus and sustain attention.
- Influence others by the use of emotions.
- Follow the standards of their culture about when and how to show emotions.

Why Is Emotion Regulation Significant for Children's Development and Learning?

Like emotional security, emotion regulation has increasingly been viewed as a critical outcome in the preschool years, for all children but especially for those at risk of negative developmental and educational outcomes. Head Start children who begin the year with emotion regulation difficulties are likely to make a poor adjustment to school, including problems adapting to routines, complying with limits, getting along with other children, acquiring academic skills, and developing positive attitudes toward learning (Eisenberg et al., 2001; Shields et al., 2001). Early problems with emotion regulation, especially with the regulation of negative emotions, are consistently found to predict both social-emotional and academic difficulties in later years of school (Raver, 2002). Three- and 4-year-olds who are prone to venting anger and other negative emotions are likely to be lower in social competence when they reach kindergarten (Denham et al., 2003); similarly, children who are unable to maintain "effortful control" are at risk for later difficulties in maintaining good relationships with peers (Kochanska, Murray, & Harlan, 2000). Children with serious regulatory difficulties are on a trajectory that tends to alienate them from other children, from teachers, and from access to learning opportunities. Thus, widespread agreement exists that attention to emotion regulation is an essential priority and goal of early childhood education and early intervention programs.

The Development of Emotion Regulation in Infants, Toddlers, and Preschoolers

At whatever age children enter early childhood education programs, they have begun to develop important emotion regulation abilities. The following brief description is influenced by Kopp's (1989) analysis, focused on the developmental course of children's regulation of distress. It also draws on other reviews, for example, Denham (1998); Fox (1994); Saarni, Camras, Campos, and Witherington (Chapter 5, this *Handbook*, Volume 3); Shonkoff and Phillips (2000); and Thompson (1994).

As Kopp (1989) outlines, the earliest emotion regulation begins in the first days of life, as infants' reflexive reactions help them avoid unpleasant stimuli. Crying babies learn to suck their thumbs and use other strategies to manage their distress, while still relying on adults to scaffold and support their emotion modulation. In the 2nd year of life and beyond, toddlers' expanding cognitive abilities (e.g., anticipation and planfulness) are used in the service of emotion regulation, and they communicate their needs more clearly. The expansion of language competence provides additional tools to communicate, represent, and regulate emotions. Of course, toddlers and young preschoolers still require a good deal of adult support, as they continue to have difficulty independently managing strong negative or positive emotions.

As children move into the later preschool years, most are increasingly self-reflective about their regulation of their own and others' emotions. Children are able to use a wider repertoire of cognitively oriented coping strategies when faced with distressing situations (Denham, 1998). Preschoolers are increasingly able to distract themselves and use symbolic thought to reframe the meaning of a situation, and they can look at an emotionally arousing situation from multiple perspectives (Saarni, 1999).

Several observations should be made about this description of the early developmental course of emotion regulation. First, it underscores the close relationships between cognitive and emotional development, relationships that recur throughout this chapter. Second, it focuses primarily on the development of regulation of negative emotions, in particular, distress. The regulation of positive emotions is also important, yet has been studied less frequently. In educational settings, children's ability to regulate their excitement or to direct their interest into specific channels is a significant task. Finally, most of the research on which these developmental trajectories are based has not included culturally and linguistically diverse groups of children, and few studies have examined the development of emotion regulation outside of the family.

Emotion Regulation in Early Childhood Programs: Characteristics, Influences, and Outcomes

Much of the research on emotion regulation has focused on the predictors of, or influences on, its development. However, few of these studies have been done in early childhood education programs. As outlined here, research in family contexts suggests some factors that may be relevant for curriculum and teaching practices in early childhood education settings.

Emotion Regulation and Security of Attachment. A number of studies have found that secure mother–child attachments predict greater ability to manage distress and regulate negative emotions. Saarni (1999) speculates about the mechanisms that may underlie this relationship: Perhaps securely attached children are able to explore a wider array of feelings with the support and emotion sharing provided by the adult.

Might secure attachments to teachers, or other non-family caregivers, have a similar benefit for children's emotion regulation? There is growing evidence of this link. Preschool children who have secure attachments to their teachers are less likely to have emotion-regulation problems such as unregulated anger displays (DeMulder, Denham, Schmidt, & Mitchell, 2000). And children whose Head Start teachers reported less conflicted, warmer relationships with those children early in the year were seen by their teachers as more emotionally regulated and less angry later in the year (Shields et al., 2001).

Language and Cognitive Skills as Influences on Emotion Regulation. As Vygotsky (1930–1935/1978) and others (Kopp, 1989) have emphasized, children's competence in language supports their ability to regulate their emotions and behavior, as well as to engage in positive relationships with others. Children whose language skills are limited relative to their peers' are also at risk for regulatory difficulties (Greenberg, Kusché, & Speltz, 1991).

Caregivers' Assistance and Modeling to Support Emotion Regulation. Thompson (1994) emphasizes how important caregivers are in helping very young children to modulate their emotional arousal, directly soothing babies and then helping them learn to soothe themselves. Adult modeling is also a significant influence, as studies by Eisenberg and Fabes (1992) and others have shown. In those studies, taking anger expressions seriously and working on anger issues constructively with children led to better, more regulated responses to peer aggression.

Adults also support emotion regulation by talking with young children about emotions (Dunn & Brown, 1991; Kopp, 1989), giving children language and labels for emotional experiences; these labels then begin to be internalized and used by children as they regulate their own emotional expression. In addition, adults respond in different ways to children's negative emotion expressions, and these differences seem to be related to how the children themselves express and regulate emotion.

For example, mothers who said they were likely to punish children's negative emotion expressions had children who were unlikely to seek help from their parents when distressed (Eisenberg & Fabes, 1998).

It is likely that this kind of socialization goes on in early childhood education programs as well, although it has not been studied systematically, widely, and longitudinally. As Shields and colleagues (2001) point out, we still know little about teachers' everyday influences on children's emotional competence, including their emotion regulation.

Provision of Opportunities for Pretend Play. Significant in the development of self-regulation, pretend play may benefit emotion regulation as well. In one of a small number of studies relating pretend play to emotion regulation, Galyer and Evans (2001) found that children whose parents had reported greater prior involvement in pretend play, especially play with adults, showed greater emotion regulation in a distressing experimental situation, and were also rated by their parents as having better emotion regulation skills. If replicated in other studies, this finding may have implications for early childhood programs.

Other Features of Early Childhood Program Quality, Curriculum, and Teaching Practices. It is now understood that many of the challenging behaviors, aggression, and other behavioral difficulties in early childhood and beyond are fundamentally problems with emotion regulation (Raver, 2002). On the positive side, a long-term outcome of several high-quality early intervention programs has been a reduction in antisocial behaviors that are thought to stem from emotion regulation difficulties (Campbell, Ramey, Pungello, Sparling, & Miller-Johnson, 2002; Reynolds, Temple, Robertson, & Mann, 2001; Schweinhart & Weikart, 1997). It is not clear what aspects of these programs contributed to this long-term effect, but McCall and colleagues (2003, p. 269) observe that "the establishment of close, meaningful, warm, caring, stable parent-child, caretaker-child, and child-child relationships is a plausible working hypothesis." Thus, it may be said that high-quality early childhood programs have the potential to serve as a protective factor in supporting emotion regulation, especially for children living in poverty or other adverse conditions.

Looking specifically at curriculum and teaching practices, there is limited evidence that some forms of highly didactic, adult-dominated curricula in preschool and kindergarten may be associated with child behaviors indicative of stress, or, in other words, of difficulty regulating anxiety or frustration. Higher levels of stress behaviors—nail biting, stuttering, and so on (Burts, Durland, Charlesworth, DeWolf, & Fleege, 1998)—and higher levels of test anxiety (Hirsh-Pasek, Hyson, & Rescorla, 1990) have been observed in classrooms that were more "developmentally inappropriate" or teacher-dominated than in more child-focused classroom environments. But as noted in this chapter's discussion of emotional security and early childhood curricula, an increasing number of curricula combine child choice and playful activities with a high degree of intentional teacher scaffolding and "structure," making the classification of curriculum approaches more complex than in the past.

School-Based Interventions to Support Emotional Competence

The research presented in this part of the chapter makes a compelling case for the importance of children's emotional competence, including their emotional security and emotion regulation abilities. High-quality early childhood education that includes an "emotion-focused" approach to the curriculum provides a foundation for this competence (M. C. Hyson, 2003). Several practitioner-oriented publications (Howes & Ritchie, 2002; M. C. Hyson, 2003) also provide teachers with suggestions about how to create conditions that promote secure and supportive relationships. In addition, as discussed by Denham and Burton (2003), Raver (2002), and Raver and Knitzer (2002), a number of specific interventions have been designed to address various components of emotional competence. These interventions may be targeted either at all children in a class or, in some cases, at those children who are at special risk.

The theme of emotional security is prominent in some interventions. For example, Pianta (1999; Hamre & Pianta, 2001) and others (Greenspan & Weider, 1998) have recommended specific interventions to help teachers build positive relationships with children, especially children who are at risk for developmental and educational difficulties. Other interventions focus more intensely on building children's understanding and regulation of emotions (e.g., Denham & Burton, 1996; Kusche & Greenberg, 2001; Webster-Stratton, Reid, & Hammond, 2001).

Whether these interventions are universal or targeted, whether they are focused on building security or strengthening regulatory competence, reviews of the effectiveness of emotion-related interventions draw some clear conclusions (Raver, 2002; Raver & Knitzer, 2002). To be effective, interventions designed to promote emotional competence must be implemented with a high degree of fidelity. And for children at the highest risk of serious emotional difficulties, dosage and intensity matter a great deal. For those children, a promising approach is to combine a universal intervention (intended for all children in a class) with more focused and intense individual interventions, together with family involvement.

Summary

A persuasive body of research has identified emotional competence as essential to young children's positive development and learning. The dimensions of *emotional security* and *emotion regulation* are related to each other in mutually influencing ways, and they are also connected to the cognitive essentials discussed in the preceding section of this chapter. Although primarily relying on studies within families, the research is beginning to identify teaching practices and features of educational programs that may promote children's emotional development and prevent later difficulties.

To reap the benefits of this research and of research related to representational abilities, self-regulation, and planning, practitioners also require a developmental and evidence-based approach to assessing children's progress and needs in these and other areas. The next section of the chapter addresses this requirement.

IMPLEMENTING EFFECTIVE ASSESSMENT PRACTICES

Two boys are playing in the literacy center in a Tools of the Mind classroom. Four-year-old Josh is decorating the pieces of paper with a rubber stamp after his friend Chris copies the names of other children on each piece. Chris is writing carefully and slowly. Having finished stamping the last piece of paper Chris gave him, Josh has nothing to do. He starts stamping the paper that Chris is writing on, and then he stamps Chris's hand. Upset, Chris looks up as Josh holds the stamp in the air, ready to descend on the arm that was under it. "Was that your plan?" he asks Josh, referring to the play plans the children develop each

morning. Josh stops, with the stamp hovering over the piece of paper. "Well, I'm supposed to stamp. That's my plan." "But I'm not done," Chris protests. Josh responds with "Okay, I'll . . . hmmm" (pondering the options). Encouraged, Chris offers a suggestion: "Why don't you fold them and put them in there?" (he points to the envelopes next to the paper). "Okay!" Josh says. "Then I'll stamp them again." He starts folding the paper and looks at the other side. "Oh look, I didn't stamp here," he says, as he stamps the other side of the paper. They smile at each other and continue working together.

The preceding sections of this chapter have reviewed and discussed what we know about some cognitive and emotional essentials for young children's development and learning: representation, planning, self-regulation, emotional security, and emotion regulation. Although the chapter has emphasized the relevance, as well as the limitations, of this research for early childhood programs and practices, we have not yet addressed a different and important question: How might one assess young children's progress in these and other areas? The way this question is framed and answered is different in the cases of classroom teachers, policymakers, and developmental researchers. This section focuses primarily on classroom-based assessment, but places it in a wider context.

The heightened interest in early learning and the increased calls for accountability and scrutiny of instructional programs have placed assessment and testing of young children at center stage. Classroom teachers, school administrators, parents, and policymakers have legitimate concerns about young children's development and the effectiveness of educational programs. With the Tools of the Mind case example in mind, this section culls from the literature some of the major issues in the implementation of appropriate assessment practices designed to support children's learning in the classroom. The central role of the teacher and the inherent challenges in this type of assessment are discussed.

Defining Assessment

In the *Standards for Educational and Psychological Testing* (American Educational Research Association [AERA], American Psychological Association, & National Council on Measurement in Education, 1999, p. 172), assessment is defined as "any systematic method of obtaining information from tests and other sources, used to draw inferences about characteristics of people, objects, or programs." This definition consists of three critical components: (1) engaging in systematic (intentional) procedures, (2) collecting information on (evidence of) learning, and (3) making inferences (generalizations) in response to the assessment results.

The intentional ongoing process of identifying, collecting, and evaluating evidence to make informed decisions about young children's learning is an integral component of any effective instructional intervention, including interventions such as those discussed in this chapter. These three components of assessment frame this discussion.

Intentionality: Purpose Matters

As part of the systematic nature of the assessment process, the major purposes for the assessment of young children, as defined by Shepard, Kagan, and Wurtz (1998) in their report to the National Education Goals Panel, have been widely accepted:

- To support learning.
- For identification of special needs.
- For program evaluation and monitoring trends.
- For high-stakes accountability.

Clarifying the purpose of an assessment process is analogous to crafting a clear research question at the beginning of a study. Defining why the assessment process should take place shapes the content, form, and amount of the evidence that will be needed. The purpose can also have an impact on the format of the results (AERA et al., 1999; Bowman et al., 2001; J. Jones, 2004; Millman & Greene, 1989). For example, assessments intended to provide parents with information on the progress of their 4-year-old's ability to play with others may look very different from a research report on national trends in the social pretend play of subgroups of children. Both are important, but the tasks, sample size, reporting format, and implications may be quite different. The Tools of the Mind vignettes presented throughout this chapter have provided a glimpse into classrooms in which the primary assessment goal is to support children's learning. Implicit in these vignettes is that the overarching goal of the teacher's observations, questions, and conversations with the children is to gather an array of "up close and personal" information on the

learning of a specific child or a group of children and to determine what strategies will advance their learning.

Challenges to the Assessment of Young Children

Researchers have acknowledged that young children present a unique set of assessment challenges (Bowman et al., 2001; Dyer, 1973; Kagan, Scott-Little, & Clifford, 2003; Love, 2003; Shepard, 1994). As described in earlier sections of this chapter and in other parts of the *Handbook,* children's cognitive and emotional capacities, astonishing in many respects, can constrain the ways those capacities may be assessed validly. The nature of early childhood, with its periods of rapid and episodic growth, can pose significant measurement challenges. Young children's development may be highly variable, both within and across individuals, posing a potentially negative impact on the reliability of any test and the validity of score interpretation (Messick, 1987, 1989; Powell & Sigel, 1991; Salvia & Ysseldyke, 2004; Shepard et al., 1998). The child's level of cognitive, linguistic, and physical development will also play a role in how he or she can represent knowledge in ways that educators can interpret. For example, with children from birth to 3 years, teachers and parents are primarily observing and recording children's linguistic and physical development. From age 3 to 4 years, when linguistic and physical skills have developed to a point where conversation and some drawing is possible, records of language and samples of drawings and constructions may be collected. By age 5, children may be able to respond to developmentally appropriate formal and informal measures (Shepard et al., 1998). Therefore, many of the assessment approaches that work well with older children are ineffective in early childhood education. As Salvia and Ysseldyke state, "Infants and young children are not miniature adults possessed of adult abilities and behavior" (p. 663).

Furthermore, deciding what aspect of young children's learning should be measured, and by what metric, is a nontrivial matter. The National Research Council's synthesis of early childhood research (National Research Council and Institute of Medicine, 2000, pp. 82–83) reported:

> Measuring growth in psychological domains (e.g., vocabulary, quantitative reasoning, verbal memory, hand-eye coordination, self-regulation) is more problematic. Disagreement is more likely to arise about the definition of the construct to be assessed. This occurs, in part, because there are often no natural units of measurement

(i.e., nothing comparable to the use of inches when measuring height). As a result, units of measurement must be created and defended, and errors of measurement are likely to be quite large.

Regardless of the methodological complexities that are involved in the assessment of young children, to promote children's positive development and learning, early childhood teachers must be engaged in the assessment process in some form in the context of their classrooms.

Classroom-Based Assessment

Early childhood assessment specialists argue that the central purpose of early childhood assessment is to improve instruction for young children (Bowman et al., 2001; Shepard et al., 1998). Specifically, in the context of this chapter, the goal is to better understand children's cognitive and emotional development so as to devise more effective curriculum and teaching strategies. The educational research literature on K–12 classroom-based assessment practices, also termed authentic or formative assessments, can support this goal (Black & Wiliam, 1988; Phye, 1997; Stiggins, 2001, 2002). These assessment practices are linked directly to the instructional program and use teacher observational notes, records of children's language, and work samples as part of a collection of evidence of learning that will guide instruction. Research suggests that assessment procedures that inform teachers' instructional practice can also increase student performance (Black, Harrison, Lee, Marshall, & Wiliam, 2003; Black & Wiliam, 1988). However, using appropriate classroom-based assessment strategies places a greater responsibility on the teacher to take a stance or attitude of inquiry into children's learning and to acquire a considerable understanding of assessment design, use, and interpretation (Calfee & Masuda, 1997; Chittenden, Salinger, & Bussis, 2001; Stiggins, 1999).

Evidence

The second component of the preceding definition of assessment (AERA et al., 1999) is collecting evidence of children's learning. On a daily basis, teachers of young children must provide environments that support and promote the development of each child in their classroom. When asked, many teachers might readily answer such questions as "Is Johnny increasing his ability to follow a plan?" or "Is Maria developing better strategies to cope with her frustration?" Yet, without sufficient, high-quality evidence of young children's learning, teachers may reach qualitatively different and perhaps erroneous conclusions about what children know and are able to do in these and other areas.

The early childhood literature has embraced the use of classroom-based evidence of children's learning. Many early childhood assessment specialists argue that this type of evidence is closer to the child's classroom experiences, more aligned with the child's level of development, has a direct bearing on classroom practices, and can be part of the teaching/learning process (McAfee & Leong, 1997; Meisels, Liaw, Dorfman, & Nelson, 1995; Mindes, 2003; Puckett & Black, 2000).

Rather than a passive recipient of test results, in this approach to early childhood assessment the teacher must become actively involved in setting appropriate developmental and learning goals; creating the opportunities for children to demonstrate what they know; collecting, describing, and analyzing samples of work; evaluating the work against standards; and applying evidence that children are learning (Blythe, Allen, & Powell, 1999; Calfee & Masuda, 1997; Carini, 2000; J. Jones & Courtney, 2003; Martin, 1999).

Observation

The early childhood literature has made a consistent case that teachers' powers of observation, documentation, and deep understanding of child development are critical to achieving high-quality early childhood programs (Dyer, 1973; Genishi, 1992, 1993, 1997; Jablon, Dombro, & Dichtelmiller, 1999). Ongoing careful observation allows teachers to see children's behaviors and work samples and listen to their language. These are the central sources of evidence that will lead to informed inferences about how children are developing and what instructional strategies will be most supportive. Yet, observation alone is not sufficient. The literature describes a rich history of careful description of children's development that includes in-depth case studies, which describe a child's learning styles, interests, and methods of representing knowledge (Avidon, Hebron, & Kahn, 2000; Chittenden et al., 2001; Gruber & Voneche, 1977; Piaget, 1926/1955). The competencies emphasized in this chapter, such as representation, planning, and emotion regulation, appear to be more effectively assessed through this kind of systematic observation than through one-time tests.

It is also clear from the literature that developing the strategies to conduct careful observation and documentation requires some effort and practice (Allen, 1998; Garbarino & Stott, 1989; Genishi, 1997; Helm, Beneke, & Steinheimer, 1998; J. Jones, 2003). Systematic observation is a highly structured process, grounded in classroom practice that reflects the learning goals that have been set for the children. It is the teacher's role to provide the opportunities and classroom settings in which the child can make learning visible—that is, demonstrate what he or she knows and is able to do.

Tests as Evidence

Thus far, the discussion has focused on the use of classroom-based evidence. A more formal form of evidence of children's learning is a test, which is defined in the *Standards for Educational and Psychological Testing* (AERA et al., 1999, p. 183) as "an evaluative device or procedure in which a sample of an examinee's behavior in a specified domain is obtained and subsequently evaluated and scored using a standardized process." This is a specific form of evidence, gathered at a single session or during multiple time periods, as part of the overall assessment process. When all or a sample of children are asked to perform the same task under the same conditions with a common scoring rubric, a standardized test has been administered. The controversy appears to arise when tests are not linked directly to the teacher's curriculum, may not be aligned with children's developmental levels, and may not be sensitive to the range of cultural and linguistic differences. However, when the purpose of the child assessment is part of an overall evaluation of program effectiveness, a well-constructed test that is administered to an appropriate sample of children can provide important information about a group, rather than about a specific child. As emphasized earlier in this section, a challenge is that very young children may lack thecognitive, linguistic, social-emotional, and physical resources to respond validly to formal tests. These assessment difficulties are multiplied when children are living in difficult circumstances, have disabilities, or speak a language other than the one in which assessments are conducted.

Technically Sound Assessment Evidence

Classroom-based evidence can provide a particularly rich picture of a young child's development and learning. This picture may provide teachers with information that is directly tied to decisions about curriculum and teaching practices. However, this type of assessment has not been the standard by which programs are held accountable to policymakers (Stiggins, 2001). The tension between standardized, norm-referenced assessments and classroom-based assessments may have roots in the fundamentally different perspectives taken by educational researchers and early childhood educators on what constitutes the evidence of young children's learning. Some major theories of child development have emerged from careful observational studies of just a few children (Gruber & Voneche, 1977; Piaget, 1926/1955; Wertsch, 1985), whereas the educational measurement literature has often looked to the large-scale random assignment experimental design as the gold standard. In addition, many measurement experts have expressed limited confidence in the objectivity of teachers' judgments and in their overall understanding of assessment design and use (Plake & Impara, 1997; Stiggins, 1999, 2001).

There appears to be some progress in bridging the essential differences between traditional large-scale assessment procedures and classroom-based assessment. Educational researchers are examining a reconceptualization of the measurement framework that would acknowledge the complex and dynamic nature of classrooms (Brookhart, 2003; Moss, 2003; Smith, 2003). Articulating three aspects of classroom assessment that strain traditional measurement theory—the context-dependence of classroom assessment, its inextricable relationship with instruction, and its simultaneous formative and summative functions—Brookhart states:

> Both classical and modern test theory for large-scale assessment consider context a source of irrelevant variance; the aim is to generalize across contexts. In contrast, for classroom assessment, items or tasks are dependent on, and nested within, the instructional environment. For another example, in large-scale assessment, items or tasks are usually assumed to be independent, whereas in classroom assessment they are linked together in students' classroom experiences. For yet another example, large-scale assessment theories usually make assumptions that require large sample sizes. Class sizes are small in comparison, and sometimes classroom assessments are given to even smaller subgroups or to individuals within classes. (p. 5)

Creating this new paradigm will be a challenge to the fields of child development and educational measurement, requiring much greater collaboration. Professionals in both fields can profit from the realization that both types of assessments have value, depending on the purpose of the assessment. Constructing assessment systems that are based on credible and useful evidence can enhance our understanding of children's learning and development and broaden our perspectives on program effectiveness.

Inferences

The third component in the definition of assessment (AERA et al., 1999) refers to the conclusions, generalizations, and inferences that are made in response to assessment results. The purpose of the assessment and the types of inferences to be made should be clearly articulated and should guide the assessment design process (AERA et al., 1999; Millman & Greene, 1989). However, interpreting assessment results is not always a simple task. The literature suggests that classroom teachers are alarmingly underprepared to design sound classroom assessments and to interpret assessment results appropriately (Plake & Impara, 1997; Stiggins, 1999).

A Documentation Assessment Model

A five-stage model outlines the documentation/assessment process for classroom-based assessment, from identifying learning goals to collecting and evaluating evidence (Figure 1.1). This model places inferences within a cycle in which teachers, including early childhood teachers, identify learning goals, collect evidence, describe and analyze the evidence, interpret results in light of learning goals, and apply this information to future planning.

Identifying

The first stage in designing assessments to support children's learning is the identification of learning goals. Although debates may develop about what constitutes appropriate learning goals, meaningful assessment systems will require some consensus on the major goals for children and the classroom settings in which evidence of learning may be apparent. For example, is the goal to increase children's sense of security and close relationships with their teachers?

Collecting

The evidence of young children's development and learning, their drawings, constructions, and records of their language and behaviors, is apparent in the everyday life of high-quality early childhood classrooms. Teachers

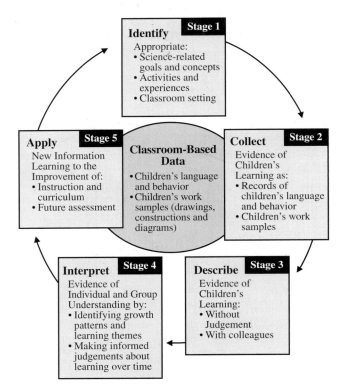

Figure 1.1 A five-stage documentation/assessment cycle.

need to collect this evidence in a purposeful manner, not simply to amass artifacts but to document the learning that occurs. In the case of developing secure relationships, might children's drawings be informative? Would it be useful to collect information from systematic observations of distressed children's behavior with teachers?

Describing

Merely collecting the evidence of learning does not translate it into instructional information. Careful analysis of children's work using strategies such as those outlined in Carini's (1993) descriptive review provide a window into children's thinking, as well as into their emotional responses. The accuracy of a child's response to a specific question provides a background for the teacher's active inquiry into how the child is coming to understand a phenomenon. In the context of this chapter, for example, how might teachers analyze young children's pictorial or written plans for their play activities?

Interpreting/Evaluating

After a careful study and description of children's work, teachers return to their learning goals to evaluate what the classroom-based data reveal about children's progress toward these goals. Again, what if only a few children are able, at this point in the year, to use teachers as a secure base? Do goals related to emotional security need greater attention?

Applying

This information about how children are learning can inform future instructional planning. What additional teaching strategies can support the child's development? In turn, new questions will inevitably be raised, questions that will require teachers to move once again and continuously through the cycle. This focus on application can inform teachers' decisions as they focus on representation, planning, self-regulation, emotional security, emotion regulation, and other key components of young children's growing competence throughout the year.

Beyond Yet Connected with the Classroom: Guidelines for Researchers

Although the primary focus of this section of the chapter has been classroom-based assessment by teachers of young children, the domains discussed here are also of great interest to developmental and educational researchers. Their studies can also assist in creating more effective learning opportunities. A synthesis of early childhood research (National Research Council and Institute of Medicine, 2000, p. 84) defined the following key components to guide the design of quantitative developmental research:

- A clear definition of the outcome variable or the construct on which the children are believed to be growing.
- A measurement unit or scale that has constant meaning over the age range of interest (e.g., height in inches or the number of words in a child's expressive vocabulary).
- An outcome that can be measured on a common scale across ages, such that the alternative, age-appropriate forms of the assessment can be equated, that is, put onto the same meaningful scale.
- A statistical model for individual change over time. . . .
- A longitudinal study that is optimally designed to ensure a given level of statistical precision for the question at hand. Trade-offs among the length of the study, the frequency of observation, and the sample size are invariably involved.

Whatever their experience with young children, those who intend to conduct research in early childhood programs need to become familiar with the goals and climate of the program within which children are functioning. Program goals, curriculum and teaching practices, interactions between teachers and children, other assessments being conducted as part of an ongoing system, as well as knowledge of the children's cultures and languages provide an essential context. Understanding this context allows researchers to conduct more effective research and may suggest important variables to include in their analyses.

Establishing mutually respectful and beneficial relationships between the program administrator and staff on the one hand, and the research team on the other, is also essential (Frede & Barnett, 2001). Ethically and practically, benefits should accrue to the early childhood program as a result of being involved in research. To the greatest extent possible, researchers should attempt to incorporate their assessments into the ongoing fabric of the program. When research instruments must be administered through individual, direct assessment procedures, it is important to work with the teacher to minimize disruption and to ensure that the researcher is obtaining the child's best performance. Recommendations about the use of assisted or dynamic assessment procedures (Campione & Brown, 1987; Tzuriel, 2001), such as are emphasized in Tools of the Mind, are worth considering in this regard.

Summary

It is rarely the case that a single assessment question is being asked. Simultaneously, teachers are trying to plan better instruction, administrators are weighing the efficacy of specific curriculum models for various subgroups of children, and policymakers are identifying effective and struggling programs. Thus, the challenge of early childhood assessment is to construct a system of assessment strategies that are methodologically sound, developmentally appropriate, and responsive to the specific questions that are raised by multiple audiences (J. Jones, 2003; Kagan et al., 2003). The dimensions of early development and learning identified in this chapter can indeed be assessed in ways that answer to these multiple constituencies, while keeping young children's characteristics and needs at the forefront of educational decision making.

CASE EXAMPLE: TOOLS OF THE MIND

During play time, Roy walks into the dramatic play or house area dressed up in a man's jacket, accompanied by his friend Vanessa, who is decked out in a too-big fancy dress, high heels, and a purse. For several minutes they walk silently around the dramatic play area, opening and closing cupboards. Observing this, the teacher thinks this may be immature play; she sees no play scenario and hears no language. She moves in closer to listen. "Look here," Roy says, as he opens a cupboard. Vanessa leans over, looks in, and nods. Finally, they sit down with a piece of paper and a pencil. Curious, the teacher finally asks, "What are you two doing?" Roy answers, "She's looking at the place. She's signing."

As the teacher thought back, she knew that Roy's family had been homeless, and his parents had found a new place to live the previous weekend. In the dramatic play area, Roy was playing the role of the apartment manager showing the apartment, and his friend Vanessa was signing a lease.

In this section, we return, in more detail, to our case example: the Tools of the Mind curriculum that has been previewed in earlier sections of this chapter. After providing some background on its history and main features, we examine relationships between this curriculum approach and the cognitive, emotional, and assessment research that has been outlined in the chapter.

Background

Based on Vygotskian theory, the Tools of the Mind approach emphasizes children's development of self-regulation and the cognitive and metacognitive foundations of literacy. Founders and directors Elena Bodrova and Deborah Leong began their collaboration in 1992 (Bodrova & Leong, 2001), when Bodrova came to the United States from the Russian Federation, so Tools of the Mind is a relatively new program. Since the program's inception, roughly 4,000 children have participated in the several hundred Tools of the Mind classrooms. As was typical of the children in Linda Sims's class, profiled in the chapter's introduction, virtually all the children have been classified as at risk in terms of living in difficult circumstances. Some are homeless, some have substance abuse in their families, and nearly all live in poverty. Some of the children also have developmental disabilities and other special needs. In recent years, over half the participating children have been English-language learners.

As in any well-rounded preschool program, Tools classrooms include many activities, routines, interactions, and environmental features that are designed to foster children's learning and development in all areas. In addition, Tools of the Mind has its own distinctive features, some of which we do not examine here. For the purposes of this chapter, we are focusing on a few program features that link most directly to our chapter emphases: the program's deliberate attention to pretend play and play planning, as well as other activities designed to support self-regulation and emotion regulation. We also look at the program's approach to developing children's emotional security. Finally, we make some observations about the Tools approach to assessment. Throughout, a theme is how the developmental research summarized earlier has relevance for, informs, and may create challenges for the curriculum and teaching practices of this specific educational model.

Play and Play Planning

Vygotsky (1930–1935/1978) saw pretend play as the leading activity in young children's development, that is, the activity that promotes development to the highest degree. It is not surprising that pretend or dramatic play occupies a key place in a Vygotsky-based program such as Tools of the Mind. Dramatic play elements are woven through many of the day's activities. During the 40- to 50-minute choice time, children can opt to play in the designated dramatic play area or in other centers, such as the block area, where pretend play themes abound. Although teachers in other early childhood programs may give children time and opportunity to engage in pretend play, relatively few work to actively promote mature dramatic play and have explicit strategies to do so. A notable exception is the High/Scope curriculum (Epstein, 2003). A number of other programs around the country (e.g., Davidson, 1996) have built on the play-training research in developing strategies for enhancing the complexity and symbolic levels of children's play (R. Saltz & Saltz, 1986; Smilansky, 1968; Smilansky & Shefatya, 1990).

Many children are able to sustain rich, interactive dramatic play as soon as they enter a preschool program. However, in some settings, particularly those serving children from difficult circumstances, children may enter with more limited dramatic play experience and skills (Smilansky, 1968; Smilansky & Shefatya, 1990). For this reason, Tools teachers regularly use a variety of strategies consistent with Vygotsky's work and the research literature to set the stage and actively promote the high-level play that is viewed as essential for young children's development and learning.

Setting the Stage

To help children initiate and sustain an imaginary situation, the Tools teacher works to ensure that the children have a repertoire of themes—hospital, grocery store, restaurant, and library, to name a few—to inspire their pretend play and have sufficient knowledge of the roles and activities involved in each. The teachers also use field trips, visitors' presentations, videos, and books. Providing such experiences to nourish children's dramatic play and project work is relatively common (Bredekamp & Copple, 1997; Davidson, 1996; Katz & Chard, 2000). What Tools teachers do reflects their specific, theoretically influenced goals for children's play. For example, when a class visits the fire station, the teachers invite the firefighters to tell the children who they are and what they do and say in their work. On one such trip, one man showed the children how the firefighters relax and live, and another showed how he uses a hose to fight the fire. When the children came back to the classroom, they created their own props for play. They used cardboard tubes for the hoses, and they pretended to cook firefighter stew, which they had learned about on the visit. As the teachers had hoped, the trip inspired the children to engage in firehouse play for many days.

Teachers in Tools of the Mind classrooms also make strategic use of props to stimulate children's interest and help sustain their play in an imaginary situation. Some early childhood programs stock the dramatic play area with lots of realistic props. In contrast, Tools of the Mind uses a mix of realistic and open-ended props, like the cardboard tubes the children used to make hoses after the firehouse visit. In the early weeks of the school year, teachers find that many children in Tools classrooms do not seem to be able to play without the realistic props, and they do not stray far from each item's designated use. Teachers work to reduce children's dependence on realistic props and help them progress to more symbolic object use. Strategies include games in which children come up with different ways to play with ordinary objects: A wooden block can be used as a baby, a ship, or a chair for a doll. With such practice, along with on-the-spot teacher modeling and encouragement, children begin to make use of simple objects to represent things they need in their play.

Again, the play-promoting practices described here are not unique to Tools of the Mind. Early childhood experts typically call for a mix of open-ended and realistic props (e.g., Bredekamp & Copple, 1997; Davidson, 1996; Dodge, Colker, & Heroman, 2002), and a variety of education programs and interventions have actively promoted mature dramatic play (Hohmann & Weikart, 2002; Nevile & Bachor, 2002; Smilansky & Shafatya, 1990). Teacher-initiated experiences designed to build children's symbolic abilities outside the play context are less frequently used in other early childhood programs, but they can be found here and there. The most distinctive element of Tools of the Mind with respect to play is the approach to play planning.

Play Planning in Tools of the Mind

Every day, teachers involve children in planning for their center-time activities, asking each child what he or she will do that day. Over the course of the year, the discussion becomes more detailed, going well beyond the "Where will you play today?" question that many teachers ask to give preschoolers a degree of choice. For dramatic play, teachers encourage children to discuss the roles in the play (who they are going to be), the play scenario (what they are going to play, such as grocery shopping or having a picnic), and how the play will unfold.

Early in the year, teachers need to do quite a bit of prompting. Many of the children initially respond by simply naming the center where they intend to play. The eventual goals are more elaborated planning and children's discussing their plans together without teacher prompting. After some months, teachers see children discussing play on their own more often and more fully, both before and during the actual play.

Another key aspect of the program's approach to planning is having children put their plans on paper. When teachers initially tried purely oral planning, the children and the teachers often forgot the plan. The plan on paper is a tangible record of what the child wants to do, and it can be consulted by the child, the teacher, and even other children. Initially, teachers may take dictation and write what the child says about the plan, which is a useful step in literacy learning as well as planning.

In the Vygotskian framework that Tools is based on, planning on paper would be viewed as a "mediator," strengthening play's self-regulation function. In creating, discussing, and revising their plans, children learn to control their behaviors in play, and teachers report that this tendency carries over to situations outside the play context. Further, the creation of play plans allows teachers to influence play without intervening and disrupting it as it occurs, which those who study children's play see as important (E. Jones & Reynolds, 1992; Rogers & Sawyers, 1988). Instead, the teacher may suggest to children ahead of time how they can try out new roles, add new twists to the play scenario, or devise substitutes for missing props.

Tools teachers engage children in thinking back to and reflecting on their play as well as planning it. This is not the only approach that emphasizes reflection; as part of their curriculum's plan-do-review sequence, High/Scope teachers also make a point of involving children in reflection on what they have done in the centers. A difference is that Tools teachers wait until the following day to elicit children's reconstructions and comments on a play episode. In the early stages of the program, the teachers observed that being asked about changes in plans immediately after play ("Did you do what you said you had planned?") tended to make children feel they shouldn't change their plan or admit to doing so. A day later, the teachers have found, children are able to discuss more freely what happened in a previous play session. Each approach—same-day or next-day reflection—may have its own advantages; this difference has not been investigated to date.

Giving advance thought to their play and reflecting on it later appears to enable children to develop more mature, interactive play (Bodrova & Leong, 2003b). The literature suggests that play of this kind contributes to language skills, problem solving, self-regulation, and appreciation of others' play efforts (E. Saltz & Brodie, 1982; Smilansky & Shefatya, 1990). Over the course of the year, children in Tools classrooms move from engaging in very limited dramatic play to more frequent and substantially more complex, mature levels of play. Some of this progress may be a function of children's development over 8 or 9 months, but research suggests that without interventions, children with low initial levels of play rarely make significant progress (Smilansky & Shefatya, 1990).

Equally striking to observers is each year's marked decrease in peer conflicts from fall to winter to spring. After plans have been used for several months, teachers find that there are far fewer conflicts because potential problems are defused before play begins. Because peer conflicts appear to reflect difficulties in emotion regulation as well as in other capacities such as social perspective taking, these changes, if confirmed, will be theoretically interesting as well as beneficial to children themselves and to the overall classroom environment.

Other Experiences That Foster Self-Regulation and Emotion Regulation

The play planning process in Tools of the Mind appears to prompt the development of planning and representational skills (writing and drawing about the intended activities). Other aspects of the curriculum support the closely related goals of self-regulation and emotion regulation.

In the Vygotskian tradition, Tools of the Mind sees as an overarching goal the development of self-regulation. As Kopp (1982, 1989, 2002) and others have clarified, self-regulation is focused on children's regulation of their behavior in accordance with societal and cultural norms, including compliance and effortful control (Kochanska et al., 2000). On the other hand, emotion regulation emphasizes children's ability to modulate and direct the experience and expression of feelings, including but not limited to negative emotions, in the service of important goals. Obviously, the two are closely related, both conceptually and in how they are addressed in the Tools curriculum approach.

Children who experience multiple forms of adversity often arrive at preschool with limited capacity for self-regulation and emotion regulation (Raver, 2002). Teachers in Tools of the Mind classrooms confirm that this is the case for many of their children. Accordingly, the curriculum's developers (Bodrova & Leong, 1996) have made regulatory issues an extremely high priority, especially early in the year. Consistent with the program's theoretical perspective, Bodrova and Leong usually frame their discussion in terms of self-regulation rather than emotion regulation, believing that until children have begun to exhibit some degree of physical and self-regulation (and stemming from that, emotion regulation and the integration of emotions and thinking) they will be unable to take advantage of the classroom's learning opportunities. Although informed most directly by Vygotskian theory, this view is generally consistent with research on self- and emotion regulation discussed earlier in this chapter.

A number of specific features of the Tools program are intended to promote self-regulation and emotion regulation. The Freeze Game described in the first vignette of this chapter is an example. The game is designed to help children practice physical self-regulation;

in this case, as children dance, they see a posed stick figure that the teacher holds up, but they keep dancing until the music stops, and they then reproduce the pose they had previously seen. Another example is what the curriculum's developers call Buddy Reading. Sitting in a group, pairs of children select books to "read" together. To help mediate the turn-taking task, each pair of children is given a set of cardboard lips and ears. Whichever child is holding the ears is the listener, and the child holding the lips is the talker. When they exchange props, the roles are reversed.

Many children in Tools classrooms come into preschool with limited language skills or are English-language learners. As in many other early intervention programs, promoting language development is a priority. The curriculum's focus on language, including encouraging children's private speech to guide behavior, may provide at-risk children with resources to help them regulate their emotional responses and behaviors in frustrating or conflict-ridden situations.

Contributions to Secure Relationships

Vygotskian theory is typically viewed as strongly cognitive. Thus, one might expect less emphasis in Tools of the Mind on emotions and on promoting children's emotional development than in programs influenced by, for example, Eriksonian theory. Bodrova and Leong (2003b) point out that Vygotsky did address emotional development, although in a less elaborated way than in the cognitive domain, and several neo-Vygotskians further developed these ideas about emotions. Their formulations have influenced the perspective on emotional development that is evident in Tools of the Mind.

Besides their Vygotskian focus, the developers of the Tools of the Mind curriculum appear to be incorporating other perspectives on the importance of teacher-child relationships (e.g., Hamre & Pianta, 2001). As the curriculum has become more widely implemented, the developers report that many teachers do not easily or intentionally build nurturing relationships with children, especially children whose behavior is challenging. For this reason, the curriculum's developers have worked on two fronts. First, the developers have tried to build teachers' understanding of the importance of and techniques for creating secure relationships. Second, they work to help children become more self-regulated, thereby making it easier for inexperienced teachers to

have positive feelings about the children in their class. The training manual (Leong, 2005) includes suggestions for how teachers may take advantage of everyday opportunities to establish emotional communication and create secure relationships with children, especially at the beginning of the year.

As reviewed earlier in this chapter, some prior research appears to favor child-centered curriculum models in building emotional security and warm teacher-child interactions. Consistent with broader trends and recommendations (e.g., Bowman, Donovan, & Burns, 2001; Bredekamp & Copple, 1997), Tools of the Mind is one of a number of curriculum approaches that do not fit neatly into these categories, emphasizing both a so-called academic emphasis in its focus on literacy and cognitive development, and a strong emphasis on pretend play and social activity. Although the teacher-child relationships in Tools programs have not yet been studied systematically, observations and discussions with teachers and curriculum developers suggest that close relationships may be prevalent. With few exceptions, once the year is well under way, children—including those at risk for relationship difficulties—function calmly and independently in the classroom, checking in with the teacher and appearing to use him or her as a secure base for their exploration and problem-solving activities.

A contribution to the formation of these bonds may be the sequential nature of the year-long curriculum and the changing priorities over the course of the year. As in a number of other early childhood programs, time is deliberately set aside early in the year for a number of foundational priorities, including the development of nurturing teacher-child relationships (Leong, 2005). The daily schedule is also weighted heavily toward peer collaboration and interaction during pretend play and in activities such as shared book reading. Teachers rarely need to put their energy into being in charge of an entire group and need to impose few sanctions on the class. Freed of these constraints, the teacher is better able to spend time getting to know children on a personal level and responding in contingent, nurturing ways. Further, the frequent "scaffolding" interactions, a key component of the Vygotskian curriculum, also create the conditions for relationship building. In an emotional as well as a cognitive sense, the teacher's supportive assistance allows the child to reach desired ends, further cementing the relationship.

Assessment Perspectives on Tools of the Mind

Assessment has an important role in the Tools of the Mind curriculum. Consistent with recommendations for early childhood assessment (National Association for the Education of Young Children & National Association of Early Childhood Specialists in State Departments of Education, 2003; Shepard et al., 1998), in these programs the primary purpose of assessment is to help teachers make the daily classroom decisions that support children's learning. Specifically, in Tools of the Mind classes, the ongoing assessment is intended not just to let the teacher know where the child is functioning, but to give the teacher insight into how to move each child forward to the next level of learning.

In general, there appears to be alignment between the goals of the program and the curriculum-related assessments used by the teachers. For example, teachers use checklists to track children's growth in play planning and in the maturity of their pretend play—significant emphases in the developmental framework of Tools of the Mind. The Tools of the Mind curriculum focuses on explicit development of self-regulation in the context of intentional play (Bodrova & Leong, 1996). Teachers in Tools of the Mind classes must be deliberate in setting up the conditions in which children will interact with one another and must be careful observers of children's interactions. They must constantly observe and listen as children talk, draw, construct, and carry out their activities.

The day-to-day implementation of the curriculum is continually informed by teachers' assessments as they become involved with and observe children's performance. Only through focused observation will the teacher recognize those moments when children need assistance (scaffolding) to move to the next level. Based on those assessments, for example, teachers provide supports in the form of certain external mediators, such as more concrete props for pretend play, gradually withdrawing these supports as children become more cognitively and behaviorally independent. Valuable as this scaffolding may be, some have observed that it may create tension for more traditional approaches to assessment:

> Help and coaching that students receive for assessments conducted during and as part of instruction would be seen as contributing to lack of independence of observations or "cheating" and thus a threat to reliability and validity. However, one of the basics in constructivism is that

this is precisely where the learning occurs—in the zone of proximal development (Vygotsky, 1978), that space between what the individual can accomplish independently and what he or she can do with assistance. (Brookhart, 2003, p. 7)

More specifically, the Vygotskian theoretical framework that has shaped the Tools of the Mind curriculum has implications for how assessment is conceptualized and conducted. In Tools of the Mind and other Vygotsky-influenced programs, the assessment approach has been termed "dynamic assessment" (Tzuriel, 2001). Rather than gathering summative information at the end of each unit, from a dynamic assessment perspective teachers are always facilitators of children's learning (Feuerstein, 1979). The teacher's role is to begin by identifying the child's level of independent performance: What can the child do alone? The supports the child needs to learn the target skill or knowledge must also be identified and provided. For example, if the teacher observes that a child needs help in planning for play, several scaffolding strategies are available:

- *Oral language:* The teacher asks the child to put the plan into words.
- *Social interactions:* The teacher anticipates potential trouble spots that might influence the first interactions in the play.
- *Representational drawing/symbolic thinking:* The teacher asks the child to represent the idea on paper.
- *Memory:* The teacher asks the child to repeat the plan after drawing.
- *Literacy:* The teacher models how to put an oral message into print.

The professional development implications of these assessment approaches are substantial. Teachers implementing the Tools curriculum must develop an understanding of human development in general and of the specific ways their children learn and develop. Teachers also need an array of scaffolding procedures and the ability to select the most appropriate strategy for a specific child and a specific point in his or her learning. Clearly, this type of assessment requires a skilled teacher, and therefore teacher professional development is a critical component of the Tools of the Mind approach to early childhood education.

This description of the assessments used in Tools programs reflects the difficulty of implementing comprehensive and ongoing assessment. It also underscores the complex relationships between assessment within a specific curriculum and the larger context of assessments that may be (as the next section details) driven by larger federal or state imperatives around assessment and accountability. With its emphasis on self-regulation, the Tools of the Mind curriculum raises interesting questions regarding the use of direct standardized assessment of self-regulation skills in any evaluation of this curriculum. Although some measures currently exist (McCabe, Hernandez, Lara, & Brooks-Gunn, 2000; McCabe, Rebello-Britto, Hernandez, & Brooks-Gunn, 2004), significant work is needed to develop technically sound, culturally and linguistically sensitive direct measures of self-regulation from which generalizations about programs can be made.

THE CHALLENGES OF IMPLEMENTATION

So far, this chapter has illustrated the general relationships between child development research and early childhood education programs, using selected examples. It has described evidence that supports an emphasis on some specific aspects of cognitive and emotional competence in early childhood education and a systematic, developmentally appropriate approach to assessing children's progress in these and other areas. We have just analyzed the components of the Tools of the Mind preschool curriculum in light of these developmental essentials.

However, the process of actually implementing a complex, developmentally based curriculum such as Tools of the Mind is more challenging than this story may have conveyed. This part of the chapter returns to the larger context of early childhood education in the United States, highlighting ways in which difficult societal, policy, and practical issues must be taken into account, not only by this curriculum but also by any effort to implement high-quality early childhood education.

The Challenges of Going to Scale

At present, the Tools of the Mind curriculum has been implemented in a relatively small number of settings, and oversight of implementation and training has remained primarily in the hands of the curriculum's original developers (Bodrova & Leong, 1996). Clearly, the developers would like to see their approach to early childhood programming used more widely, yet obstacles face any such efforts.

Over the years, early intervention research has raised cautions about the difficulty of taking promising demonstration programs to a larger scale. A point made repeatedly is that the most positive long-term effects of early intervention have been found in programs that were essentially demonstrations, often linked with a major research center, such as the Perry Preschool Project (Schweinhart et al., 1993) and the Abecedarian Project (Campbell et al., 2002). These and other demonstration programs were typically implemented in one setting, with close involvement of the curriculum developers and with highly trained and committed teaching staff and ongoing evaluation. With a few exceptions, such as the Chicago Parent-Child Project (Reynolds, 2000), larger-scale program implementations such as in Head Start—although having clear benefits—have had less dramatic impact. Some specific curriculum models have been scaled up with positive results (the High/Scope curriculum, the Creative Curriculum), but this has taken extensive development and revision of print resources, teacher training materials and training of trainers, assessment tools, and other supports for implementation.

Tools of the Mind is just beginning to face these kinds of challenges. Its training manual is still under development, and training is conducted only by the developers and several other individuals who have worked closely with the developers. Although the curriculum provides many scaffolds for teachers as well as for children, it is not tightly scripted and requires a fairly high level of theoretical and pedagogical insight, as teachers use careful observation and assessment to tailor their interactions to children's individual zones of proximal development. It also assumes a high degree of buy-in or commitment on the part of teachers, which is less likely as any curriculum approach is taken to scale or mandated for adoption (Ryan, 2004).

Ironically, the very features that promise the greatest benefits for children, such as Tools of the Mind's flexible, individualized interactions, make it difficult to quickly and simply communicate the essentials to a wide range of teachers and administrators. In the current climate of limited time and resources, school districts and agencies are often inclined to adopt a curriculum that seems easier to implement on a large scale without a great deal of effort, despite the potential developmental advantages of approaches like Tools of the Mind.

Quality Issues in Early Care and Education

Furthermore, taking any curriculum to scale in the complex and highly variable environment of U.S. early child care and education is far more daunting than in the relatively more homogeneous system of K–12 public education. Ideally, one would want a promising curriculum model to be implemented in a wide range of settings, including Head Start classrooms, state prekindergarten programs, and community-based child care programs that are not part of Head Start or state prekindergarten. However, wide variations exist across these settings in who sets the standards and in what standards apply in areas such as teacher qualifications, adult-child ratios, and group size. For example, child care programs are regulated by state licensing standards, which vary widely from one state to another but that typically emphasize health and safety requirements. State-funded prekindergarten programs operate under the aegis of public schools and typically have higher requirements for teacher qualifications than other child care programs in the same community. Head Start programs operate under a set of performance standards (U.S. Department of Health and Human Services, 1997), higher teacher qualifications than most child care centers, and a well-defined monitoring system, with grantee agencies varying from public schools to community agencies to universities.

Not only does this variation create administrative challenges to implementation, but it also underscores the need for a consistent floor of quality. It is much easier to layer a curriculum such as Tools of the Mind onto a program that already has a relatively high level of quality. The reality is that in this diverse and underfunded collection of early child care and education settings, quality varies widely (Lombardi, 2003) and is generally rated mediocre if not actually harmful to children's development (Cost, Quality, and Child Outcomes Study Team, 1995).

Professional Development Challenges

Related to these concerns, an inconsistent and underfunded system has great difficulty sustaining a well-educated and motivated workforce adequate to implement a developmentally based, cognitively challenging curriculum. Research has consistently identified early childhood teachers' education and training as important to program quality, often predicting the kinds of teacher-child interactions that are associated with better child outcomes (Barnett, 2003; Tout, Zaslow, & Berry, in press). Tools of the Mind is primarily implemented in classrooms staffed by experienced, committed lead teachers like Linda Sims, who have the bachelor's degrees and early childhood competencies recommended in national reports and professional standards (Bowman et al., 2001; M. Hyson, 2003). As the curriculum is taken to scale, the trainers are likely to be faced with a far less educated and motivated workforce.

Even with highly qualified teachers, an ongoing challenge is to design and deliver effective professional development. The developers of Tools of the Mind have found, and research suggests, that something considerably beyond the usual one-shot workshop is needed (Bransford et al., 2000; National Staff Development Council, 2001). At present, the developers rely on a mix of intensive workshops early in the year, along with regular observation, feedback, and coaching from trainers. Working with teachers who have often spent years implementing quite different approaches can be challenging. Again, as the program attempts to reach a larger audience, the intensive and personalized training approach currently used may come under closer scrutiny, or it may need adaptation and implementation by a much larger group of trainers, running the risk that the curriculum's key emphases may be diluted or distorted.

Selection of important content for professional development is a challenge for the field. With limited time and resources, what is most worth knowing and emphasizing? The Tools training manual clearly emphasizes Vygotskian theory and related research, as well as rationales and techniques for implementing a variety of specific activities and assessment systems in the classroom. Training does not address all aspects of delivering an early education program in comprehensive fashion; to some extent, the Tools programs may be relying on other professional development systems (e.g., Head Start programs have other training in place) to deliver some important content. A concern is that some content may fall through the cracks; for example, a recurring theme in the literature (Raver, 2002; Shonkoff & Phillips, 2000) is the lack of high-quality professional development for teachers who are addressing emotional issues in their classrooms and who are trying to deal with children's challenging behaviors.

The Challenges of Maintaining Integrity and Coherence

Although research has not yet provided evidence for the superiority of any single curriculum model (Bowman et al., 2001; Goffin & Wilson, 2001), it does seem that a planned, coherent curriculum, implemented with fidelity by qualified teachers, indeed makes a difference for children. A difficult question is how coherent or theoretically consistent a curriculum should optimally be. Tools of the Mind is one of the most theory-driven curricula currently being implemented in early childhood education.

Maintaining this coherence is a challenge, and there may be trade-offs. On a conceptual level, it is not clear that all the answers can be found in Vygotsky and the neo-Vygotskians. For example, the developers make an effort to draw on neo-Vygotskians to inform their approach to emotional development, yet this insistence on Vygotskian underpinnings may result in too little attention to other current work in early emotional development. Similarly, recent work by developmental psychologists on planning, representation, and self-regulation might further strengthen these curriculum emphases.

In addition, as discussed earlier in this chapter, there are many critics of the use of child development theory and research as the primary basis for early childhood curriculum and teaching practices (e.g., Stott & Bowman, 1996; Zimiles, 2000). Early childhood reconceptualists and others note that multiple sources provide knowledge and insight about early childhood education, including the insights of teachers (Ryan, 2004; Williams, 1996).

These suggestions should be tempered with caution. Might a too enthusiastic search for evidence from multiple perspectives and multiple theories, researchers, and practitioners drive the curriculum in the direction of a scattered eclecticism? Maintaining a more "pure" Vygotskian emphasis may run the risk of losing the benefit of key evidence and insights in areas important to the curriculum's goals; on the other hand, incorporating widely divergent viewpoints and related research evidence runs the risk of diluting the curriculum's integrity and focus.

Expectations for Evidence and Accountability

The public, policymakers, program developers, and others want clear and credible evidence of the impact of public investments in programs for young children. National reports and government mandates have raised expectations for early childhood teachers. Teachers today are expected to implement more effective and challenging curricula in language, literacy, mathematics, and other content areas and to use more complex assess-

ments of children's progress (Bowman et al., 2001). Doing this in a developmentally appropriate way is a continuing challenge.

Today, every state has K–12 standards, specifying what children are expected to know and be able to do in various content areas (Align to Achieve, 2004), and a recent survey (Scott-Little, Kagan, & Frelow, 2005) found that more than forty states had or were developing "early learning standards" for children below kindergarten age. As the Tools of the Mind curriculum or other curricula are developed and implemented, they do not exist in a vacuum. These standards and other expectations—which may or may not be theoretically and practically consistent with the curriculum's emphasis—must be taken into account. In some cases, this integration may be smooth, but in other cases, the expectations of various "masters" may be contradictory and challenging to reconcile.

Tools teacher Linda Sims and other teachers also function within the larger context of evidence expectations: in this case, the expectations of the curriculum's developers and evaluators (evaluation is ongoing and has not yet been published); the expectations of the state's early learning standards and assessment system; and, because Linda Sims's classroom is part of Head Start, regular screening and assessment guided by Head Start's Program Performance Standards and Child Outcomes Framework. Linda Sims also needs to take into account a newly implemented and controversial Head Start National Reporting System, which was designed to administer standardized tests to every child twice a year on language, literacy, and mathematical knowledge (Administration for Children and Families, 2003; Raver & Zigler, 2004). All of these expectations must be taken into consideration, along with other goals and priorities. The developers of Tools of the Mind comment on these challenges, noting that many of the mandated assessments linked to Head Start, state, or other accountability systems are not well aligned with their curriculum's developmental assumptions and goals.

The Challenge of Gaps in the Research

Despite the significant body of work discussed in this chapter, a challenge in implementing early childhood curricula such as Tools of the Mind is the continuing lack of developmental and educational research in a number of critical areas. The need for additional research has been noted throughout the chapter, but examples can be summarized here.

Research priorities include:

- Studies of the development of specific cognitive and emotional competencies in child care and other out-of-home settings.
- Further study of the importance of culture and language in children's cognitive and emotional development and in the early educational approaches that are most effective in promoting the development of linguistically and culturally diverse young children.
- Further specification of what aspects of early childhood curricula, implemented under what conditions and with what resources, lead to more favorable child outcomes.
- Further investigation of what curriculum features, and what teaching practices, are most likely to support the development of warm, secure relationships between teachers and children.
- Closer examination of the characteristics and effects of curriculum approaches that combine intentional, focused teaching with promotion of children's play, social interaction, and exploration.
- Investigation of the conditions that promote teachers' commitment to and involvement in developing and implementing early childhood curriculum and teaching practices.
- Additional studies of the role of pretend play in the development of self- and emotion regulation.
- More precise definition of the critical components of effective classroom-based or formative assessments.
- Design and validation of direct child assessments of social-emotional and vocabulary development that are sensitive to linguistic and cultural differences.
- Studies that lead to a reconceptualization of the constructs of validity and reliability in the context of classroom-based assessment.

To refine and move this research agenda forward, greater communication and collaboration are essential—between researchers with differing specializations (such as cognitive and emotional development) and between researchers, early childhood program and policy specialists, and teachers, who know best what kinds of research questions are most in need of answers.

Certainly, the new directions in curriculum research and in other early intervention research are promising, going beyond winners or losers in the curriculum race to seek more nuanced understandings of complex patterns and effects. As this work goes forward, several additional features will enhance its value. First, as the ecological perspective on development emphasizes, young children participate in many settings beyond the hours they spend in any preschool program. The potential of early childhood education needs to be studied in contexts, including the kind and quality of interactions experienced by children in families and neighborhoods and in informal as well as formal child care. Those experiences may influence and be influenced by the more formal educational program. Second, in-depth studies of the process of developing and implementing new approaches to early childhood education, such as the Tools of the Mind curriculum, will help with the task of bringing developmental knowledge into classrooms and communities, anticipating what some of the barriers and promising pathways may be. Finally, young children will be well served if developmental researchers' own professional development includes attention to skills in identifying program- and policy-relevant research and communicating the results of that research to policymakers in clear, objective ways.

SUMMARY AND CONCLUSIONS

In this chapter, we have examined the complex relationships between early childhood education programs and child development research, using as a case example the relatively new and still evolving Tools of the Mind curriculum. After an overview of the functions and limitations of developmental theory and research in relation to early childhood education, the chapter focused on two educationally relevant areas: the development of cognitive essentials, specifically children's representational thinking, self-regulation, and planning, and the development of emotional competence, specifically emotional security and emotion regulation. We reviewed principles and research on the assessment of young children's development and learning, emphasizing classroom-based assessment intended to support teachers' ongoing decision making. The practical, systemic, and policy challenges of linking developmental theory and research with early childhood curriculum and teaching practices were the focus of the final section of the chapter, including the challenges of taking a demonstration program to scale; issues of variability and quality in the system of U.S. early care and education; issues in delivering professional development; challenges of maintaining integrity and coherence; expectations for evidence and accountability; and gaps in the field's current knowledge base.

Despite these challenges and research gaps, the work discussed in this chapter does have some clear implications for practice. Among other emphases, it guides programs toward the following:

- Greater intentionality on the part of teachers, as they plan and implement curriculum.
- A focus on the big picture in development, giving priority to competencies that have the greatest likelihood of influencing later development and learning in far-reaching and positive ways.
- Attention to the modes of learning found to be especially powerful in early childhood, such as pretend play and other forms of representation.
- Giving high priority to teacher-child relationships.
- A view of assessment as an ongoing process, conducted by knowledgeable and interested teachers, to help them promote the development and learning of every child in their class.
- Creating the kinds of professional development and other resources that can support teachers' ability to implement curriculum and teaching practices and to assess children's progress.

The consequences of not moving in these directions, and others articulated in this chapter, are serious, especially for children most at risk for developmental and academic difficulties. As the research has suggested, lack of planning skills, inadequate development of self- and emotion regulation, lack of enthusiasm and persistence in the face of learning challenges, and an absence of secure and nurturing relationships with teachers will multiply the difficulties young children face as they enter kindergarten and the primary grades.

The challenges described here should be understood in light of the high stakes involved. Growing research that shows the potential to foster positive development through early childhood education is paralleled by the growing number of developmentally vulnerable young children in child care, Head Start, prekindergarten, and other programs. Working together, early childhood educators and researchers have the potential to identify the most promising curriculum and assessment practices to serve all young children and to devise effective ways to integrate those practices into programs staffed by committed and well-compensated professionals.

REFERENCES

Administration for Children and Families. (2003). *Implementation of the Head Start national reporting system on child outcomes.* Available from http://www.headstartinfo.org/publications/im03/im03_07.htm.

Ainsworth, M. D. S. (1973). The development of infant-mother attachment. In B. M. Caldwell & H. N. Ricciuti (Eds.), *Review of child development research* (Vol. 3, pp. 1–94). Chicago: University of Chicago Press.

Ainsworth, M. D. S., Blehar, M. C., Waters, E., & Wall, S. (1978). *Patterns of attachment.* Hillsdale, NJ: Erlbaum.

Align to Achieve. (2004). *The standards database.* Watertown, MA: Author. Available from www.aligntoachieve.org/AchievePhaseII/basic-search.cfm.

Allen, D. (Ed.). (1998). *Assessing student learning: From grading to understanding—The series on school reform.* New York: Teachers College Press.

American Educational Research Association, American Psychological Association, & National Council on Measurement in Education. (1999). *Standards for educational and psychological testing.* Washington, DC: American Educational Research Association.

Arnett, J. (1989). Caregivers in day-care centers: Does training matter? *Journal of Applied Developmental Psychology, 10*(4), 541–552.

Avidon, E., Hebron, M., & Kahn, K. (2000). Gabriel. In M. Himley & P. F. Carini (Eds.), *From another angle: Children's strengths and school standards* (pp. 23–55). New York: Teachers College Press.

Bailey, D. B., Bruer, J. T., Symons, F. J., & Lichtman, J. W. (Eds.). (2001). *Critical thinking about critical periods.* Baltimore: Paul H. Brookes.

Barkley, R. A. (1997). Behavioral inhibition, sustained attention, and executive functions: Constructing a unifying theory of ADHD. *Psychological Bulletin, 121,* 65–94.

Barnett, W. S. (1995). Long-term effects of early childhood programs on cognitive and school outcomes. *Future of Children, 5*(3), 25–50.

Barnett, W. S. (2003). *Preschool policy matters: Vol. 2. Better teachers, better preschools—Student achievement linked to teacher qualifications.* New Brunswick, NJ: National Institute for Early Education Research.

Barnett, W. S., Hustedt, J. T., Robin, K. B., & Schulman, K. L. (2004). *The state of preschool: 2004 state preschool yearbook.* New Brunswick, NJ: National Institute for Early Education Research.

Bauer, P., & Mandler, J. M. (1989). One thing follows another: Effects of temporal structure on 1- to 2-year-olds' recall of events. *Developmental Psychology, 25*(2), 197–206.

Bauer, P. J., & Hertsgaard, L. A. (1993). Increasing steps in recall of events: Factors facilitating immediate and long-term memory in 13.5- and 16.5-month-old children. *Child Development, 64,* 1204–1223.

Bauer, P. J., & Mandler, J. M. (1990). Remembering what happened next: Very young children's recall of event sequences. In R. Fivush & J. Hudson (Eds.), *Knowing and remembering in young children* (pp. 9–29). New York: Cambridge University Press.

Bauer, P. J., & Mandler, J. (1992). Putting the horse before the cart: The use of temporal order in recall of events by 1-year-old children. *Developmental Psychology, 28*(3), 441–452.

Benson, J. B. (1994). The origins of future orientation in the everyday lives of infants and toddlers. In M. M. Haith, J. B. Benson, R. R. Roberts, & B. Pennington (Eds.), *The development of future-oriented processes* (pp. 375–407). Chicago: University of Chicago Press.

Benson, J. B. (1997). The development of planning: It's about time. In S. Friedman & E. Skolnick (Eds.), *The developmental psychology of planning* (pp. 43–75). Hillsdale, NJ: Erlbaum.

Berg, C. A., Strough, J., Calderone, K. S., Meegan, S., & Sansone, C. (1997). Planning to prevent problems from occurring. In S. L. Friedman & E. K. Scholnick (Eds.), *Why, how, and when do we plan? The developmental psychology of planning* (pp. 209–236). Hillsdale, NJ: Erlbaum.

Bergen, D. (1988). *Play as a medium for learning and development.* Portsmouth, NH: Heinemann.

Berk, L. E. (1992). Children's private speech: An overview of theory and the status of research. In R. M. Diaz & L. E. Berk (Eds.), *Private speech: From social interaction to self-regulation* (pp. 17–53). Hillsdale, NJ: Erlbaum.

Berk, L. E., & Winsler, A. (1995). *Scaffolding children's learning: Vygotsky and early childhood education.* Washington, DC: National Association for the Education of Young Children.

Bialystok, E., & Senman, L. (2004). Executive processes in appearance-reality tasks: The role of inhibition of attention and symbolic representation. *Child Development, 75*(2), 562–579.

Birch, S. H., & Ladd, G. W. (1997). The teacher-child relationship and children's early school adjustment. *Journal of School Psychology, 35*, 61–79.

Black, P., Harrison, C., Lee, C., Marshall, B., & Wiliam, D. (2003). *Assessment for learning: Putting it into practice.* London: Open University Press.

Black, P., & Wiliam, D. (1988). Inside the black box: Raising standards through classroom assessment. *Phi Delta Kappan, 80*(2), 139–148.

Blair, C. (2002). School readiness: Integrating cognition and emotion in a neurobiological conceptualization of children's functioning at school entry. *American Psychologist, 57*(2), 111–127.

Bloch, M. (1992). Critical perspectives on the historical relationship between child development and early childhood education research. In S. A. Kessler & B. B. Swadener (Eds.), *Reconceptualizing the early childhood curriculum: Beginning the dialogue* (pp. 3–20). New York: Teachers College Press.

Blythe, T., Allen, D., & Powell, B. S. (1999). Critical considerations: Description, interpretation, evaluation, and context. In T. Blythe, D. Allen, & B. S. Powell (Eds.), *Looking together at student work: A companion guide to assessing student work* (pp. 21–25). New York: Teachers College Press.

Bodrova, E., & Leong, D. (1996). *Tools of the Mind: The Vygotskian approach to early childhood education.* Englewood Cliffs, NJ: Merrill/Prentice-Hall.

Bodrova, E., & Leong, D. J. (2001) "About the authors," in *Tools of the mind: A Case Study of Implementing the Vygotskian Approach in American Early Childhood and Primary Classrooms* [Monograph]. Switzerland: International Bureau of Education, UNESCO. Available from http://www.ibe.unesco.org/International/Publications/INNODATAMonograph/inno07.pdf.

Bodrova, E., & Leong, D. J. (2003a). Chopsticks and counting chips: Do play and foundational skills need to compete for the teacher's attention in an early childhood classroom? *Young Children, 58*(3), 10–17.

Bodrova, E., & Leong, D. J. (2003b). Learning and development of preschool children: The Vygotskian perspective. In A. Kozulin, V. Ageyev, S. Miller, & B. Gindis (Eds.), *Vygotsky's theory of education in cultural context* (pp. 156–176). New York: Cambridge University Press.

Bornstein, M. H., Haynes, O. M., Legler, J. M., O'Reilly, A. W., & Painter, K. M. (1997). Symbolic play in childhood: Interpersonal and environmental context and stability. *Infant Behavior and Development, 20*, 197–207.

Bowlby, J. (1982). *Attachment and loss: Vol. 1. Attachment.* New York: Basic Books. (Original work published 1969)

Bowman, B. T. (2004). The future of Head Start. In E. Zigler & S. J. Styfco (Eds.), *The Head Start debates* (pp. 533–544). Baltimore: Paul H. Brookes.

Bowman, B. T., Donovan, M. S., & Burns, M. S. (Eds.). (2001). *Eager to learn: Educating our preschoolers.* Washington, DC: National Academy Press.

Bransford, J., Brown, A. L., & Cocking, R. R. (Eds.). (2000). *How people learn: Brain, mind, experience, and school* (Expanded ed.). Washington, DC: National Academy Press.

Bredekamp, S. (Ed.). (1987). *Developmentally appropriate practice in early childhood programs serving children from birth through age 8* (Expanded ed.). Washington, DC: National Association for the Education of Young Children.

Bredekamp, S., & Copple, C. (1997). *Developmentally appropriate practice in early childhood programs* (Rev. ed.). Washington, DC: National Association for the Education of Young Children.

Bronfenbrenner, U., & Morris, P. A. (1998). The ecology of developmental processes. In W. Damon (Editor-in-Chief) & Richard M. Lerner (Vol. Ed.), *Handbook of child psychology: Vol. 1. Theoretical issues* (5th ed., pp. 993–1028). New York: Wiley.

Bronson, M. B. (2000). Recognizing and supporting the development of self-regulation in young children. *Young Children, 55*(2), 32–37.

Bronson, M. B., Pierson, D. E., & Tivnan, T. (1985). The effects of early education on children's competence in elementary school. In L. H. Aiken & B. H. Kehrer (Eds.), *Evaluation studies review annual* (Vol. 10, pp. 243–256). Beverly Hills, CA: Sage.

Bronson, W. C. (1974). Mother-toddler interaction: A perspective on studying the development of competence. *Merrill-Palmer Quarterly, 20*(4), 275–301.

Brookhart, S. M. (2003). Developing measurement theory for classroom assessment purposes and uses. *Educational Measurement: Issues and Practice, 22*(4), 5–12.

Brown, A. L., & DeLoache, J. S. (1978). Skills, plans and self-regulation. In R. Siegler (Ed.), *Children's thinking: What develops?* (pp. 3–35). Hillsdale, NJ: Erlbaum.

Bruner, J. S. (1966). *Toward a theory of instruction.* Cambridge, MA: Belknap Press of Harvard University.

Bruner, J. S. (1983). *Child's talk: Learning to use language.* New York: Norton.

Burts, D. C., Durland, M. A., Charlesworth, R., DeWolf, M., & Fleege, P. O. (1998). Stress behaviors and activity type participation of preschoolers in more and less developmentally appropriate classrooms: SES and gender differences. *Journal of Research in Childhood Education, 12*(2), 176–196.

Calfee, R. C., & Masuda, W. V. (1997). Classroom assessment as inquiry. In G. D. Phye (Ed.), *Handbook of classroom assessment: Learning, adjustment, and achievement* (pp. 69–102). San Diego: Academic Press.

Campbell, F. A., Ramey, C. T., Pungello, E. P., Sparling, J., & Miller-Johnson, S. (2002). Early childhood education: Young adult outcomes from the Abecedarian Project. *Applied Developmental Science, 6,* 42–57.

Campione, J. C., & Brown, A. L. (1987). Linking dynamic assessment with school achievement. In C. S. Lidz (Ed.), *Dynamic assessment: An interactional approach to evaluating learning potential* (pp. 82–115). New York: Guilford Press.

Carini, P. F. (1993). *The descriptive review of the child: A revision.* Prospect Center, North Bennington, VT.

Carini, P. F. (2000). Prospect's descriptive process. In M. Himley & P. F. Carini (Eds.), *From another angle: Children's strengths and school standards* (pp. 8–19). New York: Teachers College Press.

Casey, M. B., Bronson, M. B., Tivnan, T., Riley, E., & Spenciner, L. (1991). Differentiating preschoolers' sequential planning ability from general intelligence: A study of organization, systematic responding, and efficiency in young children. *Journal of Applied Developmental Psychology, 12,* 19–32.

Cassidy, J., & Shaver, P. R. (Eds.). (1999). *Handbook of attachment theory and research.* New York: Guilford Press.

Chafel, J. A., & Reifel, S. (Eds.). (1996). *Advances in early education and day care: Vol. 8. Theory and practice in early childhood teaching.* Greenwich, CT: JAI Press.

Chandler, M. (1988). Doubt and developing theories of mind. In J. W. Astington, P. L. Harris, & D. R. Olson (Eds.), *Developing theories of mind* (pp. 387–413). Cambridge, England: Cambridge University Press.

Child Trends. (2001). *Research brief—School readiness: Helping communities get children ready for school and schools ready for children.* Washington, DC: Author.

Chittenden, E., Salinger, T., & Bussis, W. A. (2001). *Inquiry into meaning: An investigation of learning to read* (Rev. ed.). New York: Teachers College Press.

Cicirelli, V. G. (1969). *The impact of Head Start: An evaluation of the effects of Head Start on children's cognitive and affective development.* Washington, DC: Westinghouse Learning Corporation. (Report No. PB 184 328, presented to the Office of Economic Opportunity)

Cocking, R. R., & Copple, C. (1987). Social influences on representational awareness, plans for representing and plans as representation. In S. L. Friedman, E. K. Scholnick, & R. R. Cocking (Eds.), *Blueprints for thinking: The role of planning in cognitive development* (pp. 428–465). Cambridge, England: Cambridge University Press.

Copple, C., Sigel, I. E., & Saunders, R. (1984). *Educating the young thinker: Classroom strategies for cognitive growth.* Hillsdale, NJ: Erlbaum.

Copple, C. E., Cocking, R. R., & Matthews, W. S. (1984). Objects, symbols, and substitutes: The nature of the cognitive activity during symbolic play. In T. D. Yawkey & A. D. Pellegrini (Eds.), *Child's play: Developmental and applied* (pp. 105–124). Hillsdale, NJ: Erlbaum.

Corrigan, R. (1987). A developmental sequence of actor-object pretend play in young children. *Merrill-Palmer Quarterly, 33,* 87–106.

Cost, Quality, and Child Outcomes Study Team. (1995). *Cost, quality, and child outcomes in child care centers* [Technical report]. Denver, CO: University of Colorado, Center for Research in Economics and Social Policy, Department of Economics.

Davidson, J. I. (1996). *Emergent literacy and dramatic play in early education.* Albany, NY: Delmar.

Davies, P. T., & Cummings, E. M. (1998). Exploring children's emotional security as a mediator of the link between marital relations and child adjustment. *Child Development, 69,* 124–139.

Davies, P. T., Harold, G. T., Goeke-Morey, M. C., & Cummings, E. M. (2002). Children's emotional security and interparental conflict. *Monographs of the Society for Research in Child Development, 67,* 1–129.

DeLoache, J. S., & Brown, A. L. (1987). The emergence of plans and strategies. In H. Weinreich-Haste & J. Bruner (Eds.), *Making sense: A child's construction of the world* (pp. 108–130). London: Methuen.

DeMulder, E. K., Denham, S., Schmidt, M., & Mitchell, J. (2000). Q-sort assessment of attachment security during the preschool years: Links from home to school. *Developmental Psychology, 36,* 274–282.

Denham, S. (1998). *Emotional development in young children.* New York: Guilford Press.

Denham, S., & Burton, R. (1996). A social-emotional intervention for at-risk 4-year-olds. *Journal of School Psychology, 34,* 225–246.

Denham, S. A., Blair, K. A., DeMulder, E., Levitas, J., Sawyer, K., Auerbach-Major, S., et al. (2003). Preschool emotional competence: Pathway to social competence? *Child Development, 74*(1), 238–256.

Denham, S. A., & Burton, R. (2003). *Social and emotional prevention and intervention programming for preschoolers.* New York: Kluwer/Plenum Press.

Dickinson, D. K., & Smith, M. W. (1994). Long-term effects of preschool teachers' book reading on low-income children's vocabulary and story comprehension. *Reading Research Quarterly, 29*(2), 105–122.

Dodge, D. T., Colker, L., & Heroman, C. (2002). *The creative curriculum for early childhood* (4th ed.). Washington, DC: Teaching Strategies.

Dunn, J. (1988). *The beginnings of social understanding.* Cambridge, MA: Harvard University Press.

Dunn, J., & Brown, J. (1991). Relationships, talk about feelings, and the development of affect regulation in early childhood. In J. Garber & K. A. Dodge (Eds.), *The development of emotion regulation and dysregulation* (pp. 89–108). New York: Cambridge University Press.

Dyer, H. S. (1973). Testing little children: Some old problems in new settings. *Childhood Education, 49*(7), 362–367.

Edwards, C. P., Gandini, L., & Forman, G. E. (Eds.). (1998). *The hundred languages of children: The Reggio Emilia approach—Advanced reflections* (2nd ed.). Greenwich, CT: Ablex.

Eisenberg, N., Cumberland, A., Spinrad, T. L., Fabes, R. A., Shepard, S. A., Reiser, M., et al. (2001). The relations of regulation and emotionality to children's externalizing and internalizing problem behavior. *Child Development, 72*(4), 1112–1134.

Eisenberg, N., & Fabes, R. (1992). Emotion regulation and the development of social competence. In M. S. Clark (Ed.), *Review of personality and social psychology: Vol. 14. Emotion and social behavior* (pp. 119–150). Newbury Park, CA: Sage.

Eisenberg, N., & Fabes, R. (1998). Prosocial development. In W. Damon (Editor-in-Chief) & N. Eisenberg (Ed.), *Handbook of child psychology: Vol. 3. Social, emotional, and personality development* (5th ed., pp. 701–778). New York: Wiley.

Elias, C., & Berk, L. E. (2002). Self-regulation in young children: Is there a role for sociodramatic play? *Early Childhood Research Quarterly, 17,* 216–238.

Elkonin, D. (1977). Toward the problem of stages in the mental development of the child. In M. Cole (Ed.), *Soviet developmental psychology* (pp. 538–563). Armonk, NY: M. E. Sharpe. (Original work published 1971)

Elkonin, D. (1978). *Psychologija igry* [The psychology of play]. Moscow: Pedagogika.

Ellis, S. A., & Siegler, R. S. (1997). Planning as a strategy choice: Why don't children plan when they should? In S. Friedman & E. Scholnick (Eds.), *Why, how, and when do we plan? The developmental psychology of planning* (pp. 183–208). Hillsdale, NJ: Erlbaum.

Epstein, A. S. (2003). How planning and reflection develop young children's thinking skills. *Young Children, 58*(4), 28–36.

Erikson, E. H. (1950). *Childhood and society.* New York: Norton.

Erikson, E. H. (1959). *Identity and the life cycle.* New York: Norton.

Fenson, L. (1984). Developmental trends for action and speech in pretend play. In I. Bretherton (Ed.), *Symbolic play: The development of social understanding* (pp. 249–270). Orlando, FL: Academic Press.

Feuerstein, R. (1979). *Dynamic assessment of retarded performance: The learning potential assessment device, theory, instrument, and techniques.* Baltimore: University Park Press.

Flavell, J. H. (1987). Speculations about the nature and development of metacognition. In F. E. Weinert & R. H. Kluwe (Eds.), *Metacognition, motivation, and understanding* (pp. 21–64). Hillsdale, NJ: Erlbaum.

Fox, N. (Ed.). (1994). The development of emotion regulation: Biological and behavioral considerations. *Monographs of the Society for Research in Child Development, 59*(2/3, Serial No. 240), 228–249.

Frede, E. C., & Barnett, W. S. (2001). And so we plough along: The nature and nurture of partnerships for inquiry. *Early Childhood Research Quarterly, 16*(1), 3–17.

Freyberg, J. T. (1973). Increasing the imaginative play of urban disadvantaged kindergarten children through systematic training. In J. L. Singer (Ed.), *The child's world of make-believe* (pp. 129–154). New York: Academic Press.

Friedman, S. L., Scholnick, E. K. (Eds.). (1997). *The developmental psychology of planning: Why, how, and when do we plan?* Mahwah, NJ: Erlbaum.

Friedman, S. L., Scholnick, E. K., & Cocking, R. R. (Eds.). (1987). *Blueprints for thinking: The role of planning in cognitive development.* Cambridge, England: Cambridge University Press.

Fromberg, D. P. (1992). A review of research on play. In C. Seefeldt (Ed.), *The early childhood curriculum: A review of current research* (2nd ed., pp. 42–84). New York: Teachers College Press.

Fuson, K. C. (1979). The development of self-regulating aspects of speech: A review. In G. Zivin (Ed.), *The development of self-regulation through private speech* (pp. 135–217). New York: Wiley.

Galyer, K. T., & Evans, I. M. (2001). Pretend play and the development of emotion regulation in preschool children. *Early Child Development and Care, 166,* 93–108.

Garbarino, J., & Stott, F. M. (1989). *What children can tell us: Eliciting, interpreting, and evaluating information from children.* San Francisco: Jossey-Bass.

Genishi, C. (Ed.). (1992). *Ways of assessing children and curriculum.* New York: Teachers College Press.

Genishi, C. (1993). Assessing young children's language and literacy: Tests and their alternatives. In B. Spodek & O. N. Saracho (Eds.), *Language and literacy in early childhood education* (pp. 60–81). New York: Teachers College Press.

Genishi, C. (1997). Assessing against the grain: A conceptual framework for alternative assessment. In L. Goodwin (Ed.), *Assessment for equity and inclusion* (pp. 35–50). London: Routledge.

Gesell, A., & Ilg, F. L. (1943). *Infant and child in the culture of today.* New York: Harper & Row.

Goffin, S. G., & Wilson, C. (2001). *Curriculum models and early childhood education: Appraising the relationship* (2nd ed.). Upper Saddle River, NJ: Merrill/Prentice-Hall.

Goodnow, J. J. (1987). Social aspects of planning. In S. L. Friedman, E. K. Scholnick, & R. R. Cocking (Eds.), *Blueprints for thinking: The role of planning in cognitive development* (pp. 179–201). Cambridge, England: Cambridge University Press.

Graue, M. E., & DiPerna, J. (2000). Redshirting and early retention: Who gets the "gift of time" and what are its outcomes? *American Educational Research Journal, 37*(2), 509–534.

Greenberg, M. T., Kusché, C. A., & Speltz, M. (1991). Emotional regulation, self-control, and psychopathology: The role of relationships in early childhood. In D. Cicchetti & S. Toth (Eds.), *Rochester Symposium on Developmental Psychopathology* (pp. 21–55). Hillsdale, NJ: Erlbaum.

Greenspan, S. I., & Weider, S. (1998). *The child with special needs: Encouraging intellectual and emotional growth.* Reading, MA: Addison-Wesley.

Gruber, H. E., & Voneche, J. J. (Eds.). (1977). *The essential Piaget: An interpretive reference and guide.* New York: Basic Books.

Gunnar, M., Brodersen, L., Nachmias, M., Buss, K., & Rigatuso, R. (1996). Stress reactivity and attachment security. *Developmental Psychobiology, 29,* 191–204.

Guralnick, M. J. (Ed.). (1997). *The effectiveness of early intervention.* Baltimore: Paul H. Brookes.

Haith, M. M. (1997). The development of future thinking as essential for the emergence of skill in planning. In S. Friedman & E. Scholnick (Eds.), *Why, how and when do we plan? The developmental psychology of planning* (pp. 25–42). Hillsdale, NJ: Erlbaum.

Hamre, B. K., & Pianta, R. C. (2001). Early teacher-child relationships and the trajectory of children's school outcomes through eighth grade. *Child Development, 72,* 625–638.

Hart, B., & Risley, T. R. (1995). *Meaningful differences in the everyday experience of young American children.* Baltimore: Paul H. Brookes.

Helm, J., Beneke, S., & Steinheimer, K. (1998). *Windows on learning: Documenting young children's work.* New York: Teachers College Press. (ERIC/EECE No. PS 026 639)

Hirsh-Pasek, K., Hyson, M. C., & Rescorla, L. (1990). Academic environments in early childhood: Do they pressure or challenge young children? *Early Education and Development, 1,* 401–423.

Hohmann, M., & Weikart, D. P. (2002). *Educating young children: Active learning practices for preschool and child care programs* (2nd ed.). Ypsilanti, MI: High/Scope.

Holtz, B. A., & Lehman, E. B. (1995). Development of children's knowledge and use of strategies for self-control in a resistance-to-distraction task. *Merrill-Palmer Quarterly, 41*, 361–380.

Howes C. (1997). Children's experiences in center-based child care as a function of teacher background and adult:child ratio. *Merrill-Palmer Quarterly, 43*(3), 404–425.

Howes, C. (1999). Attachment relationships in the context of multiple caregivers. In J. Cassidy & P. R. Shaver (Eds.), *Handbook of attachment theory and research* (pp. 671–687). New York: Guilford Press.

Howes, C. (2000). Social-emotional classroom climate in child care, child-teacher relationships and children's second grade peer relations. *Social Development, 9*(2), 191–204.

Howes, C., & Hamilton, C. E. (1992). Children's relationships with child care teachers: Stability and concordance with parental attachments. *Child Development, 63*(4), 867–878.

Howes, C., & Ritchie, S. (2002). *A matter of trust: Connecting teachers and learners in the early childhood classroom.* New York: Teachers College Press.

Howes, C., & Smith, E. (1995). Relations among child care quality, teacher behavior, children's play activities, emotional security, and cognitive activity in child care. *Early Childhood Research Quarterly, 10*, 381–404.

Hudson, J., & Shapiro, L. (1991). From knowing to telling: The development of children's scripts, stories, and personal narratives. In A. McCabe & C. Peterson (Eds.), *Developing narrative structure* (pp. 89–136). Hillsdale, NJ: Erlbaum.

Hudson, J. A., Sosa, B. B., & Shapiro, L. R. (1997). Scripts and plans: The development of preschool children's event knowledge and event planning. In S. L. Friedman & E. K. Scholnick (Eds.), *The developmental psychology of planning: Why, how, and when do we plan.* Mahwah, NJ: Erlbaum.

Hymes, J. L. (1955). *Behavior and misbehavior: A teacher's guide to action.* Englewood Cliffs, NJ: Prentice-Hall.

Hyson, M. C. (Ed.). (2003). *Preparing early childhood professionals: National Association for the Education of Young Children's standards for programs.* Washington, DC: National Association for the Education of Young Children.

Hyson, M. C. (2003). *The emotional development of young children: Building an emotion-centered curriculum.* New York: Teachers College Press.

Hyson, M. C., Hirsh-Pasek, K., & Rescorla, L. (1990). The Classroom Practices Inventory: An observation instrument based on National Association for the Education of Young Children's guidelines for developmentally appropriate practices for 4- and 5-year-old children. *Early Childhood Research Quarterly, 5*, 475–494.

Jablon, J. R., Dombro, A. L., & Dichtelmiller, M. L. (1999). *The power of observation.* Washington, DC: Teaching Strategies.

Johnson, J. E., Christie, J. F., & Wardle, F. (2005). *Play, development, and early education.* Boston: Pearson.

Jones, E., & Reynolds, G. (1992). *The play's the thing: Teachers' roles in children's play.* New York: Teachers College Press.

Jones, J. (2003). *Early literacy assessment systems: Essential elements.* Princeton, NJ: Educational Testing Service, Policy Information Center.

Jones, J. (2004). Framing the assessment discussion. *Young Children, 59*(1), 14–18.

Jones, J., & Courtney, R. (2003). Documenting early science learning. In D. Koralek & L. J. Colker (Eds.), *Spotlight on young children and science* (pp. 27–32). Washington, DC: National Association for the Education of Young Children.

Kagan, S. L., Moore, E., & Bredekamp, S. (Eds.). (1995). *Reconsidering children's early development and learning: Toward common views and vocabulary.* Washington, DC: National Education Goals Panel.

Kagan, S. L., Scott-Little, C., & Clifford, R. M. (2003). Assessing young children: What policymakers need to know. In C. Scott-Little, S. L. Kagan, & R. M. Clifford (Eds.), *Assessing the state of state assessments: Perspectives on assessing young children* (pp. 5–11). Greensboro, NC: SERVE.

Katz, L. G., & Cesarone, B. (Eds.). (1994). *Reflections on the Reggio Emilia approach.* Urbana, IL: ERIC Clearinghouse on Elementary and Early Childhood Education. (ERIC Document Reproduction No. ED375 986)

Katz, L. G., & Chard, S. C. (2000). *Engaging children's minds: The project approach* (2nd ed.). Norwood, NJ: Ablex.

Kauffman Early Education Exchange. (2002). *Set for success: Building a strong foundation for school readiness based on the social-emotional development of young children.* Kansas City, MO: Ewing Marion Kauffman Foundation.

Kendall, S. (1992). *The development of autonomy in children: An examination of the Montessori educational model.* Unpublished doctoral dissertation, Walden University, Minneapolis, MN.

Kessler, S., & Swadener, B. B. (1992). *Reconceptualizing the early childhood curriculum: Beginning the dialogue.* New York: Teachers College Press.

Kochanska, G., Murray, K. T., & Harlan, E. (2000). Effortful control in early childhood: Continuity and change, antecedents, and implications for social development. *Developmental Psychology, 36*, 220–232.

Kopp, C. B. (1982). The antecedents of self-regulation: A developmental perspective. *Developmental Psychology, 18*, 199–214.

Kopp, C. B. (1989). Regulation of distress and negative emotions: A developmental view. *Developmental Psychology, 25*, 343–354.

Kopp, C. B. (2002). School readiness and regulatory processes. In C. Raver (Ed.), Emotions matter: Making the case for the role of young children's emotional development for early school readiness. *SRCD Social Policy Report, 16*(3), 11. Ann Arbor, MI: Society for Research in Child Development.

Kusche, C. A., & Greenberg, M. T. (2001). PATHS in your classroom: Promoting emotional literacy and alleviating emotional distress. In J. Cohen (Ed.), *Social emotional learning and the elementary school child: A guide for educators* (pp. 140–161). New York: Teachers College Press.

Ladd, G. W., Birch, S. H., & Buhs, E. S. (1999). Children's social and scholastic lives in kindergarten: Related spheres of influence? *Child Development, 70*(6), 1373–1400.

Lee, V. E., & Burkham, D. T. (2002). *Inequality at the starting gate: Social background differences in achievement as children begin school.* Washington, DC: Economic Policy Institute.

Leong, D. J. (2005). *Tools of the Mind preschool curriculum research manual* (3rd ed.). Denver, CO: Center for Improving Early Learning, Metropolitan State College of Denver.

Lewis, M. (Ed.). (1983). *Origins of intelligence: Infancy and early childhood.* New York: Plenum Press.

Lombardi, J. (2003). *Time to care: Redesigning child care to promote education, support families, and build communities.* Philadelphia: Temple University Press.

Love, J. M. (2003). Instrumentation for state readiness assessment: Issues in measuring children's early development and learning. In C. Scott-Little, S. L. Kagan, & R. M. Clifford (Eds.), *Assessing the state of state assessments: Perspectives on assessing young children* (pp. 43–55). Greensboro, NC: SERVE.

Luria, A. R. (1961). *The role of speech in the regulation of normal and abnormal behavior.* New York: Liveright.

Lynch, R. G. (2004). *Exceptional returns: Economic, fiscal, and social benefits of investment in early childhood development.* Washington, DC: Author.

Main, M., Kaplan, N., & Cassidy, J. (1985). Security in infancy, childhood, and adulthood: A move to the level of representation. In I. Bretherton & E. Waters (Eds.), Growing points in attachment theory and research (pp. 66–104). *Monographs of the Society for Research in Child Development, 50*(1–2, Serial No. 209).

Malaguzzi, L. (1998). History, ideas, and basic philosophy. In C. Edwards, L. Gandini, & G. Forman (Eds.), *The hundred languages of children: The Reggio Emilia approach—Advanced reflections* (2nd ed., pp. 49–97). Norwood, NJ: Ablex.

Mallory, B., & New, R. (Eds.). (1994). *Diversity and developmentally appropriate practices: Challenges for early childhood education.* New York: Teachers College Press.

Marcon, R. (2002). Moving up the grades: Relationship between preschool model and later school success. *Early Childhood Research and Practice, 4*(1). Available from http://ecrp.uiuc.edu/v4n1/marcon.html.

Marcon, R. A. (1999). Differential impact of preschool models on development and early learning of inner-city children: A three-cohort study. *Developmental Psychology, 35*(2), 358–375.

Martin, S. (1999). *Take a look: Observation and portfolio assessment in early childhood* (2nd ed.). Reading, MA: Addison-Wesley.

Martinez-Pons, M. (1996). Test of a model of parental inducement of academic self-regulation. *Journal of Experimental Education, 64*, 213–227.

Mayer, R. E. (2004). Should there be a three-strikes rule against pure discovery learning? The case for guided methods of instruction. *American Psychologist, 59*(1), 14–19.

McAfee, O., & Leong, D. (1997). *Assessing and guiding young children's development and learning* (2nd ed.). Boston: Allyn & Bacon.

McCabe, L. A., Hernandez, M., Lara, S. L., & Brooks-Gunn, J. (2000). Assessing preschoolers' self-regulation in homes and classrooms: Lessons from the field. *Behavioral Disorders, 26*, 42–52.

McCabe, L. A., Rebello-Britto, P., Hernandez, M., & Brooks-Gunn, J. (2004). Games children play: Observing young children's self-regulation across laboratory, home, and school settings. In R. DelCarmen-Wiggins & A. Carter (Eds.), *Handbook of infant, toddler, and preschool mental health assessment* (pp. 491–521). New York: Oxford University Press.

McCall, R. B., Larsen, L., & Ingram, A. (2003). The science and policies of early childhood education and family services. In A. J. Reynolds, M. C. Wang, & H. J. Walberg (Eds.), *Early childhood programs for a new century* (pp. 255–298). Washington, DC: CWLA Press.

McGilliuddy-DeLisi, A. V., Sigel, I., & Johnson, J. E. (1979). The family as a system of mutual influences: Parent beliefs, distancing behaviors, and children's representational thinking. In M.

Lewis & L. Rosenblum (Eds.), *The child and its family: Genesis of behavior* (pp. 91–106). New York: Plenum Press.

Meisels, S. J., Liaw, F., Dorfman, A., & Nelson, R. F. (1995). The work sampling system: Reliability and validity of a performance assessment for young children. *Early Childhood Research Quarterly, 10*(3), 277–296.

Messick, S. (1987). *Assessment in the schools: Purposes and consequences.* Princeton, NJ: Educational Testing Service.

Messick, S. (1988). Assessment in the schools: Purposes and consequences. In P. W. Jackson (Ed.), *Contributing to educational change: Perspectives on research and practice* (pp. 107–125). Berkeley, CA: McCutchan.

Messick, S. (1989). Validity. In R. L. Linn (Ed.), *Educational measurement* (3rd ed., pp. 13–103). New York: American Council on Education/Macmillan.

Miller, P. J., & Goodnow, J. J. (1995). Cultural practices: Toward an integration of culture and development. *New Directions for Child Development, 67*, 5–16.

Millman, J., & Greene, J. (1989). The specification and development of tests of achievement and ability. In R. L. Linn (Ed.), *Educational measurement* (3rd ed., pp. 335–366). New York: American Council on Education.

Mindes, G. (2003). *Assessing young children* (2nd ed.). Pearson Education, Inc.

Mischel, H. M., & Mischel, W. (1983). The development of children's knowledge of self-control strategies. *Child Development, 54*, 603–619.

Mitchell-Copeland, J., Denham, S. A., & DeMulder, E. K. (1997). Q-sort assessment of child-teacher attachment relationships and social competence in the preschool. *Early Education and Development, 8*(1), 27–39.

Montessori, M. (1967). *The absorbent mind.* New York: Holt, Rinehart and Winston. (Original work published 1949)

Moss, P. A. (2003). Reconceptualizing validity for classroom assessment. *Educational Measurement: Issues and Practice, 22*(4), 13–25.

Naglieri, J. A., & Das, J. P. (1987). Construct and criterion related validity of planning, simultaneous and successive cognitive processing tasks. *Journal of Psychoeducational Assessment, 4*, 353–363.

National Association for the Education of Young Children. (1995). *Position statement on school readiness* (Rev. ed.). Available from http://www.naeyc.org/resources/position_statements/psredy98.htm.

National Association for the Education of Young Children and National Association of Early Childhood Specialists in State Departments of Education. (2003, November). *Joint position statement, early childhood curriculum, assessment, and program evaluation: Building an effective, accountable system in programs for children birth through age 8.* Available from http://www.naeyc.org/resources/position_statements/pscape.asp.

National Education Goals Panel. (1993). *The national education goals report: Vol. 1. The national report.* Washington, DC: U.S. Government Printing Office.

National Institute of Child Health and Human Development Early Child Care Research Network. (2000). Characteristics and quality of child care for toddlers and preschoolers. *Applied Developmental Science, 4*, 116–135.

National Research Council and Institute of Medicine. (2000). *From neurons to neighborhoods: The science of early childhood development.* Washington, DC: National Academy Press.

National Staff Development Council. (2001). *NSDC's standards for staff development* (Revised). Oxford, OH: Author.

Nelson, G., Westhues, A., & MacLeod, J. (2003). A meta-analysis of longitudinal research on preschool prevention programs for children. *Prevention and Treatment, 6*(31). Copyright 2003 by the American Psychological Association. Available from http://journals.apa.org/prevention/volume6/pre0060031a.html.

Nelson, K. (1986). *Event knowledge: Structure and function in development.* Hillsdale, NJ: Erlbaum.

Nevile, M., & Bachor, D. G. (2002). A script-based symbolic play intervention for children with developmental delay. *Developmental Disabilities Bulletin, 30*(2), 140–172.

New, R. S. (1998). Theory and praxis in Reggio Emilia: They know what they are doing, and why. In C. Edwards, L. Gandini, & G. Forman (Eds.), *The hundred languages of children: The Reggio Emilia approach—Advanced reflections* (2nd ed., pp. 261–284). Greenwich, CT: Ablex.

Normandeau, S., & Guay, F. (1998). Preschool behavior and first-grade school achievement: The mediational role of cognitive self-control. *Journal of Educational Psychology, 90*(1), 111–121.

Palfrey, J., Bronson, M. B., Erickson-Warfield, M., Hauser-Cram, P., & Sirin, S. R. (2002). *BEEPers come of age: The Brookline Early Education Project follow-up study—Final report to the Robert Wood Johnson Foundation.* Chestnut Hill, MA: Boston College.

Peth-Pierce, R. (2000). *A good beginning: Sending America's children to school with the social and emotional competence they need to succeed* [Monograph: Child Mental Health Foundations and Agencies Network]. Bethesda, MD: National Institute of Mental Health, Office of Communications and Public Liaison.

Phye, G. D. (1997). Classroom assessment: A multidimensional perspective. In G. D. Phye (Ed.), *Handbook of classroom assessment: Learning, adjustment, and achievement* (pp. 33–51). San Diego: Academic Press.

Piaget, J. (1952). *The origins of intelligence in children.* New York: International Universities Press.

Piaget, J. (1955). *The language and thought of the child.* New York: Meridian Books. (Original work published 1926)

Piaget, J. (1962). *Play, dreams and imitation in childhood.* New York: Norton. (Original work published 1945)

Pianta, R. (1999). *Enhancing relationships between children and teachers.* Washington, DC: American Psychological Association.

Pianta, R., La Paro, K., Payne, C., Cox, M. J., & Bradley, R. (2002). The relation of kindergarten classroom environment to teacher, family, and school characteristics and child outcomes. *Elementary School Journal, 102,* 225–238.

Pianta, R. C., Nimetz, S. L., & Bennett, E. (1997). Mother-child relationships, teacher-child relationships, and school outcomes in preschool and kindergarten. *Early Childhood Research Quarterly, 12,* 263–280.

Pianta, R. C., Steinberg, M., & Rollins, K. (1995). The first 2 years of school: Teacher-child relationships and reflections in children's classroom adjustment. *Development and Psychopathology, 7,* 297–312.

Plake, B. S., & Impara, J. C. (1997). Teacher assessment literacy: What do teachers know about assessment? In G. D. Phye (Ed.), *Handbook of classroom assessment: Learning, adjustment, and achievement* (pp. 53–68). San Diego: Academic Press.

Powell, D. R., & Sigel, I. E. (1991). Searches for validity in evaluating young children and early childhood programs. In B. Spodek & O. N. Saracho (Eds.), *Yearbook in early childhood education: Vol. 2. Issues in early childhood curriculm* (pp. 190–212). New York: Teachers College Press.

Prevost, R., Bronson, M. B., & Casey, M. B. (1995). Planning processes in preschool children. *Journal of Applied Developmental Psychology, 16,* 505–527.

Puckett, M. B., & Black, J. K. (2000). *Authentic assessment of the young child* (2nd ed.). Englewood Cliffs, NJ: Merrill.

Pulaski, M. A. (1973). Toys and imaginative play. In J. L. Singer (Ed.), *The child's world of make-believe* (pp. 73–103). New York: Academic Press.

Ramey, C. T., Campbell, F. A., Burchinal, M., Skinner, J. L., Gardner, D. M., & Ramey, S. L. (2000). Persistent effects on early childhood education on high-risk children and their mothers. *Applied Developmental Science, 4,* 2–14.

Ramey, C. T., & Ramey, S. L. (1998). Early intervention and early experience. *American Psychologist, 53,* 109–120.

Ramey, S. L., & Ramey, C. T. (1992). Early educational intervention with disadvantaged children: To what effect? *Applied and Preventive Psychology, 1,* 131–140.

Raver, C. (2002). *Emotions matter: Making the case for the role of young children's emotional development for early school readiness—Social policy report.* Ann Arbor, MI: Society for Research in Child Development. Available from http://www.srcd.org/spr16-3.pdf.

Raver, C., & Knitzer, J. (2002). *Ready to enter: What research tells policymakers about strategies to promote social and emotional school readiness among 3- and 4-year-old children.* New York: National Center for Children in Poverty, Columbia University Mailman School of Public Health.

Raver, C., & Zigler, E. F. (2004). Another step back? Assessing readiness in Head Start (Public policy viewpoint). *Young Children, 59*(1), 58–63.

Reynolds, A. J. (2000). *Success in early intervention: The Chicago Child-Parent Centers.* Lincoln: University of Nebraska Press.

Reynolds, A. J., Ou, S., & Topitzes, J. D. (2004). Paths of effects of early childhood intervention on educational attainment and delinquency: A confirmatory analysis of the Chicago Child-Parent Centers. *Child Development, 75*(5), 1299–1238.

Reynolds, A. J., Temple, J. A., Robertson, D. L., & Mann, E. A. (2001). Long-term effects of an early childhood intervention on educational achievement and juvenile arrest: A 15-year follow-up of low-income children in public schools. *Journal of the American Medical Association, 285*(18), 2339–2346.

Rogers, C., & Sawyers, J. (1988). *Play in the lives of children.* Washington, DC: National Association for the Education of Young Children.

Rogoff, B. (1990). *Apprenticeship in thinking: Cognitive development in social context.* New York: Oxford University Press.

Rogoff, B. (1998). Cognition as a collaborative process. In W. Damon (Editor-in-chief) & D. Kuhn & R. S. Siegler (Vol. Eds.), *Handbook of child psychology: Vol. 2. Cognition, perception and language* (5th ed., pp. 679–744). New York: Wiley.

Rogoff, B., Gauvain, M., & Gardner, W. (1987). Children's adjustment of plans to circumstances. In S. Freidman, E. Scholnick, & R. Cocking (Eds.), *Blueprints for thinking* (pp. 303–320). Cambridge, England: Cambridge University Press.

Rogoff, B., Goodman Turkanis, C., & Bartlett, L. (Eds.) (2001). *Learning together: Children and adults in a school community.* New York: Oxford University Press.

Russ, S. W. (1994). *Affect and creativity: The role of affect and play in the creative process*. Hillsdale, NJ: Erlbaum.

Ryan, S. (2004). Message in a model: Teachers' responses to a court-ordered mandate for curriculum reform. *Educational Policy, 18*(5), 661–685.

Saarni, C. (1999). *The development of emotional competence*. New York: Guilford Press.

Saltz, E., & Brodie, J. (1982). Pretend-play training in childhood: A review and critique. *Contributions to Human Development, 6,* 97–113.

Saltz, R., & Saltz, E. (1986). Pretend play training and its outcomes. In G. Fein & M. Rivkin (Eds.), *The young child at play: Vol. 4. Reviews of research* (pp. 155–173). Washington, DC: National Association for the Education of Young Children.

Salvia, J., & Ysseldyke, J. E. (2004). *Assessment in special and inclusive education*. Boston: Houghton Mifflin.

Schunk, D. H., & Zimmerman, B. J. (1997). Social origins of self-regulatory competence. *Educational Psychologist, 32,* 195–208.

Schweinhart, L. J., Montie, J., Xiang, Z., Barnett, W. S., Belfield, C. R., & Nores, M. (2005). Lifetime effects: The High/Scope Perry Preschool study through age 40. *Monographs of the High/Scope Educational Research Foundation, 14.* Ypsilanti, MI: High/Scope Press.

Schweinhart, L. J., & Weikart, D. P. (1997). The High/Scope Preschool Curriculum Comparison Study through age 23. *Early Childhood Research Quarterly, 12*(2), 117–143.

Scott-Little, C., Kagan, S. L., & Frelow, V. (2005). *Inside the content: The depth and breadth of early learning standards*. University of North Carolina at Greensboro: SERVE Center for Continuous Improvement.

Shepard, L., Kagan, S. L., & Wurtz, E. (Eds.). (1998). *Principles and recommendations for early childhood assessments*. Washington, DC: National Education Goals Panel.

Shepard, L. A. (1994). The challenges of assessing young children appropriately. *Phi Delta Kappan, 75*(6), 206–212.

Shields, A., Dickstein, S., Seifer, R., Guisti, L., Dodge-Magee, K. D., & Spritz, B. (2001). Emotional competence and early school adjustment: A study of preschoolers at risk. *Early Education and Development, 12*(1), 73–96.

Shonkoff, J. P., & Phillips, D. A. (Eds.). (2000). *From neurons to neighborhoods: The science of early childhood development*. Washington, DC: National Academy Press.

Shore, R. (1998). *Ready schools: A report of the Goal 1 Ready Schools Resource Group*. Washington, DC: National Education Goals Panel. Available from www.negp.gov/reports/readysch.pdf.

Sigel, I. E. (2000). Educating the young thinker model from research to practice: A case study of program development, or the place of theory and research in the development of educational programs. In J. L. Roopnarine & J. E. Johnson (Eds.), *Approaches to early childhood education* (3rd ed., pp. 315–340). Columbus, OH: Merrill/Macmillan.

Sigel, I. E., & McBane, B. (1967). Cognitive competence and level of symbolization among 5-year-old children. In J. Hellmuth (Ed.), *The disadvantaged child* (Vol. 1, pp. 433–453). New York: Brunner/Mazel.

Singer, D. G., & Singer, J. L. (1990). *The house of make-believe: Children's play and the developing imagination*. Cambridge, MA: Harvard University Press.

Slackman, E., Hudson, J. A., & Fivush, R. (1986). Actors, actions, links and goals: The structure of children's event representations. In K. Nelson (Ed.), *Event knowledge: Structure and function in development* (pp. 47–70). Hillsdale, NJ: Erlbaum.

Smilansky, S. (1968). *The effects of sociodramatic play on disadvantaged preschool children*. New York: Wiley.

Smilansky, S., & Shefatya, L. (1990). *Facilitating play: A medium for promoting cognitive, socio-emotional, and academic development in young children*. Gaithersburg, MD: Psychological and Educational Publications.

Smith, J. (2003). Reconsidering reliability in classroom assessment and grading. *Educational Measurement: Issues and Practice, 22*(4), 26–33.

Snow, C. E., Burns, M. S., & Griffin, P. (Eds.). (1998). *Preventing reading difficulties in young children*. Washington, DC: National Academy Press.

Sroufe, L. A., & E. Waters. (1977). Attachment as an organizational construct. *Child Development, 48,* 1184–1199.

Stiggins, R. J. (1999). Evaluating classroom assessment training in teacher education programs. *Educational Measurement: Issues and Practice, 18*(1), 23–27.

Stiggins, R. J. (2001). The unfulfilled promise of classroom assessment. *Educational Measurement: Issues and Practice, 20*(3), 5–15.

Stiggins, R. J. (2002, March 13). Assessment for learning. *Education Week, 21,* 30, 32–33.

Stipek, D., Daniels, D., Galluzzo, D., & Milburn, S. (1992). Characterizing early childhood education programs for poor and middle-class children. *Early Childhood Research Quarterly, 7,* 1–19.

Stipek, D., Feiler, R., Byler, P., Ryan, R., Milburn, S., & Salmon, J. M. (1998). Good beginnings: What difference does the program make in preparing children for school? *Journal of Applied Developmental Psychology, 19*(1), 41–66.

Stipek, D., Feiler, R., Daniels, D., & Milburn, S. (1995). Effects of different instructional approaches on young children's achievement and motivation. *Child Development, 66,* 209–233.

Stipek, D. J., & Greene, J. K. (2001). Achievement motivation in early childhood: Cause for concern or celebration? In S. L. Golbeck (Ed.), *Psychological perspectives on early childhood education* (pp. 64–91). Mahwah, NJ: Erlbaum.

Stott, F., & Bowman, B. (1996). Child development knowledge: A slippery base for practice. *Early Childhood Research Quarterly, 11*(1), 169–183.

Tharp, R. G., & Gallimore, R. (1988). *Rousing minds to life: Teaching, learning, and schooling in social context*. Cambridge: Cambridge University Press.

Thompson, R. (1994). Emotion regulation: A theme in search of a definition. *Monographs of the Society for Research in Child Development, 59*(2–3, Serial No. 240), 25–52.

Thompson, R. (1999). Early attachment and later development. In J. Cassidy & P. R. Shaver (Eds.), *Handbook of attachment theory and research* (pp. 265–286). New York: Guilford Press.

Tivnan, T. (1988). Lessons from the evaluation of the Brookline Early Education Project. In H. E. Weiss & F. H. Jacobs (Eds.), *Evaluating early childhood demonstration programs* (pp. 221–238). Hawthorne, NY: Aldine.

Tout, K., Zaslow, M., & Berry, D. (in press). What is known about the linkages between education and training and the quality of early childhood care and education environments. In M. Zaslow & I. Martinez-Beck (Eds.), *Early childhood professional development and children's successful transition to elementary school*. Baltimore: Paul H. Brookes.

Tzuriel, D. (2001). *Dynamic assessment of young children*. New York: Kluwer Academic/Plenum Press.

U.S. Census Bureau. (2003, Spring). *Child care arrangements for preschoolers by family characteristics and employment status of mother: Survey of income and program participation*. Washington, DC: Author.

U.S. Department of Health and Human Services. (1997). *Program performance standards for the operation of Head Start programs by grantee and delegate agencies* (45 CFR Part 1304, Federal Register, 61, 57186–57227). Washington, DC: U.S. Government Printing Office.

Uzgiris, I. C., & Hunt, J. M. (1975). *Assessment in infancy: Ordinal scales of psychological development*. Urbana: University of Illinois Press.

Vygotsky, L. S. (1962). *Thought and language*. Cambridge, MA: MIT Press.

Vygotsky, L. S. (1977). Play and its role in the mental development of the child. In M. Cole (Ed.), *Soviet developmental psychology* (pp. 76–99). Armonk, NY: M. E. Sharpe. (Original work published 1966)

Vygotsky, L. S. (1978). *Mind in society: The development of higher psychological processes*. Cambridge, MA: Harvard University Press. (Original work published 1930–1935)

Vygotsky, L. S. (1981). The development of higher forms of attention in childhood. In J. V. Wertsch (Ed.), *The concept of activity in Soviet psychology* (pp. 189–240). Armonk, NY: M. E. Sharpe.

Webster-Stratton, C., Reid, M. J., & Hammond, M. (2001). Preventing conduct problems, promoting social competence: A parent and teacher training partnership in Head Start. *Journal of Child Clinical Psychology, 30*, 283–302.

Weikart, D. P., Rogers, L., Adcock, C., & McClelland, D. (1971). *The cognitively oriented curriculum: A framework for preschool teachers*. Urbana: University of Illinois.

Wellman, H. M., Fabricius, W. V., & Sophian, C. (1985). The early development of planning. In H. M. Wellman (Ed.), *Children's searching: The development of search skill and spatial representation* (pp. 123–149). Hillsdale, NJ: Erlbaum.

Wertsch, J. V. (1985). *Vygotsky and the social formation of mind*. Cambridge, MA: Harvard University Press.

Wertsch, J. V. (1991). *Voices of the mind: A sociocultural approach to mediated action*. Cambridge, MA: Harvard University Press.

Williams, L. R. (1996). Does practice lead theory? Teachers' constructs about teaching—Bottom-up perspectives. In J. A. Chafel & S. Reifel (Eds.), *Advances in early education and day care: Vol. 8. Theory and practice in early childhood teaching* (pp. 153–184). Greenwich, CT: JAI Press.

Zigler, E., & Styfco, S. J. (2003). The federal commitment to preschool education: Lessons from and for Head Start. In A. J. Reynolds, M. C. Wang, & H. J. Walberg (Eds.), *Early childhood programs for a new century* (pp. 3–33). Washington, DC: Child Welfare League of America Press.

Zigler, E., & Styfco, S. (Eds.) (2004). *The Head Start debates*. Baltimore: Paul H. Brookes.

Zigler, E., & Valentine, J. (1997). *Project Head Start: A legacy of the war on poverty*. Alexandria, VA: National Head Start Association.

Zimiles, H. (2000). On reassessing the relevance of the child development knowledge base to education. *Human Development, 43*(4/5), 235–245.

Zimmerman, B. J. (1989). A social cognitive view of self-regulated academic learning. *Journal of Educational Psychology, 81*, 329–339.

Zimmerman, B. J., Bandura, A., & Martinez-Pons, M. (1992). Self-motivation for academic attainment: The role of self-efficacy beliefs and personal goal setting. *American Educational Research Journal, 29*, 663–676.

Zimmerman, B. J., Bonner, S., & Kovach, R. (1996). *Developing self-regulated learners: Beyond achievement to self-efficacy*. Washington, DC: American Psychological Association.

Zimmerman, B. J., & Kitsantas, A. (1999). Acquiring writing revision skill: Shifting from process to outcome self-regulatory goals. *Journal of Educational Psychology, 91*, 1–10.

Zimmerman, B. J., & Kitsantas, A. (2001). *Acquiring writing revision proficiency through observation and emulation*. Manuscript submitted for publication.

Zimmerman, B. J., & Schunk, D. H. (1989). *Self-regulated learning and academic achievement*. New York: Springer-Verlag.

CHAPTER 2

Assessments of Early Reading

SCOTT G. PARIS and ALISON H. PARIS

Child psychology and education share a long history of mutual interests and reciprocity in their methods of study, theories of development, and practical goals for improving the lives of children. Educational psychologists, for example, have studied learning and motivation, curriculum and instruction, and assessment and intervention in schools for more than 100 years (S. Paris & Cunningham, 1996; Renninger, 1998). The synergy between the fields has improved the knowledge of parents and caregivers as well as the professional development of teachers. Perhaps the area where the synergy is most evident is the field of reading education because developmental research has informed teachers' practices and educational policies directly. At the beginning of the twenty-first century, educators and policymakers show an increasing reliance on scientific research and evidence-based practices to substantiate what works in the classroom for reading instruction and assessment. The national and state policies concerning achievement testing and educational accountability through assessment are based on developmental research, and they have strong consequences for the ways that young children are taught to read.

This chapter examines the developmental issues that surround assessment and instruction of beginning readers. We review the prevailing view of the development and coordination of reading skills and show how assessments of different concepts and skills are important for beginning readers. We suggest that many early reading assessments are confounded by different developmental trajectories of reading skills, and we show how confounded correlations can be misinterpreted to privilege some skills over others in early reading practices. Thus, the chapter connects conceptual, methodological, and practical aspects of children's reading development to show the value of an applied psychological perspective on educational issues. We begin with an example of a typical reading assessment of a first grade student.

CASE EXAMPLE: ROBERT, A FIRST-GRADE STUDENT

Ms. Jones tries to assess the reading skills of every child in her first-grade class at the beginning of the school year, but it often takes 6 to 8 weeks to administer individual assessment tasks to each child. Now it is October and she has had many opportunities to test Robert and to observe him during small group instruction. She used the state-sponsored battery of reading assessments and recorded Robert's performance on letter knowledge, concepts of print, phonemic awareness, and oral reading, as well as his daily interactions with texts. He correctly identified 18 uppercase letters of the alphabet, but he had more difficulty with lowercase letters. When given a book, Robert knew how to hold the book and turn pages one at a time and how to track print from left to right. He was able to read some words in a preprimer text, but he did not understand punctuation so he did not know when to pause at the end of a sentence. He guessed at words that he did not know, and his intonation was flat while he read.

Ms. Jones recorded a low score for Robert on the Concepts of Print task because of his problems with punctuation and discriminating words. She noted that he read only 22 words correctly per minute in his oral reading assessment. Because Ms. Jones worried that Robert did not know the correspondence between letters and their sounds, she gave him several assessments of phonological processing skills. Although Robert could supply rhyming words for 6 of the 8 words she gave him, he had more trouble segmenting words into separate sounds (e.g., d-o-g) and blending sounds to form words (e.g., t-a-p), so Ms. Jones recorded low scores for his phonemic awareness.

Based on the assessments and her observations, Ms. Jones noted that Robert was a reluctant reader who guessed at words often. The only comprehension assessment in the state battery was a listening task, but Ms. Jones had observed that Robert seemed to have difficulty retelling stories and answering questions about text. His problems with letter-sound correspondences seemed to hinder his decoding. She identified Robert as a child who needed extra tutoring and placed him in her lowest reading group. She advised the parents to help Robert learn the letters of the alphabet and their sounds. She provided a tutor to drill Robert each day on phonological processing skills such as identifying initial consonants, discriminating long and short vowels sounds, and segmenting and blending sounds in words. She also tried to work one-on-one with Robert several times each week with repeated readings (of the same text they read in small groups) to increase his fluent oral reading.

This kind of report is representative of many first graders, perhaps half the class in schools that serve low-socioeconomic status (SES) families and students at risk for educational problems (S. Paris & Hoffman, 2004). The positive features of Ms. Jones's report include early testing by the teacher, combining formal assessments and informal observations, and making clear instructional suggestions to help Robert. However, there are some problems with the assessment, mostly in terms of omissions. Because Robert could not read much text, his comprehension and vocabulary skills were not assessed as thoroughly as other skills, and, consequently, the remedial instruction focused on basic skills rather than strategies for understanding words and text. Ms. Jones discussed text genres (e.g., the differences between narrative and informational texts) with her best readers, and she connected writing and reading for them. Robert's motivation and interest in the content of texts were not assessed, so most of his interactions with reading were focused on sounding out words correctly and quickly rather than thinking about the meaning or enjoying the content of the text. Ms. Jones gave priority to Robert's weakest skills, with the understanding that assessment and instruction on comprehension and writing would be deferred until his decoding skills improved. There simply was not enough time in the 90-minute language arts block to teach Robert listening, speaking, and writing skills while he was trying to catch up to the decoding prowess of his classmates. The end result for Robert, as for many struggling readers, is a skill-and-drill approach to reading that is qualitatively different from the curriculum provided to better readers (Allington, 1983).

Many readers will recognize the choice of instructional emphases between Robert's decoding skills and a broader variety of literacy skills as a reflection of a larger polarization between two approaches to reading instruction labeled the "great debate" between basic skills and whole language (Chall, 1967). It has also been referred to as a contrast between top-down and bottom-up processing of text, although Stanovich (1980) showed that both kinds of processes can be mutually compensatory during reading. Adams, Treiman, and Pressley (1998) provided a thoughtful review of this controversy and why it disappeared in the 1990s. They concluded:

> Repeatedly and convergingly, the heavy majority of the variance in beginning reading success has been traced to just two factors—familiarity with the letters of the alphabet and phonemic awareness—whereas the measurable contributions of even our most intuitively compelling contenders appears weak, evanescent, and remote. (p. 310)

This conclusion has been supported widely in seminal publications, including *The Prevention of Reading Difficulties* (Snow, Burns, & Griffin, 1998) and the National Reading Panel (2000) report.

The consequences of the research evidence for educational practice have been powerful and widespread, facilitated greatly by the federal legislation in the No Child Left Behind Act (2002) that raised the stakes for educational accountability. Assessment of achievement, especially reading, is required annually for grades 3 through 8, and there is increased pressure to demonstrate measures of adequate yearly progress in grades kindergarten through 3. Assessments of progress have focused on early decoding skills and precursors such as letter knowledge because research has shown that they predict later reading proficiency. At the same time that assessment of reading achievement was becoming more frequent and more important at primary grades, instruction was becoming more aligned with the same basic skills on the assessments. Thus, federal policies emphasizing assessment and instruction of basic reading skills have been implemented across the nation. It has been a remarkably swift transformation of early reading practices and policies, built mainly on research evidence about the developmental importance of basic decoding skills for beginning readers. In this chapter, we examine and reinterpret the evidence for these policies, and we suggest an alternative interpretation of the research. To understand the bases for the current practices and policies in reading education, we turn to an examination of the prevailing view of reading development and then to a critical evaluation of the research evidence that supports it.

THE COMPONENT VIEW OF READING DEVELOPMENT

Assessment of reading depends on fundamental theoretical and methodological assumptions about the skills that are measured. Most theories of reading development regard proficient reading as the assembly, coordination, and automatic use of multiple component processes (Adams, 1990; Stanovich, 2000). These processes include a variety of knowledge and skills, some specific to print and some not, that develop into a coordinated activity of skilled reading, usually during childhood. For example, Rathvon (2004) lists 10 components of reading that predict reading acquisition or diagnose reading problems: phonological processing, rapid letter naming, orthographic processing, oral language, print awareness

and concept of word, alphabet knowledge, single-word reading, oral reading in context, reading comprehension, and written language. The National Reading Panel (2000) identified a shorter list of five essential components of early reading: the alphabetic principle, phonemic awareness, oral reading fluency, vocabulary, and comprehension. The same five skills were endorsed in the Reading First part of the No Child Left Behind Act (2002) as fundamental for K–3 reading instruction and assessment. Researchers and educators generally regard the acquisition and integration of these components to be essential for reading development.

It is surprising, however, that differences among component skills have not been taken into account in research that compares skills during acquisition. There are several consequences of the developmental differences in component skills that influence assessment considerably (S. Paris, 2005). Consider some differences among skills. First, the five essential skills are not differentiated by the scope of knowledge that needs to be learned. Alphabet knowledge (in English), for example, is limited to the names and sounds of 26 letters, and it is much smaller in scope than comprehension. Skills that are smaller in scope may be learned earlier or faster than skills with larger scope. Second, the duration of acquisition differs dramatically for various skills. For example, the basic concepts of print are acquired in a few years, but vocabulary develops throughout the life span. The same is true for awareness of written language conventions compared with spelling abilities. The developmental trajectories of acquisition and automatic use can vary widely for various components. Third, some skills are mastered universally to the same level, that is, every literate person knows the same information, such as learning the alphabet, whereas other skills, such as vocabulary, vary widely among individuals in what they know and how much they know. Universally mastered skills have no variance among novices (because of floor effects) and no variance among experts (because of ceiling effects) and considerable variance during learning. In contrast, skills such as comprehension and vocabulary that develop continuously may exhibit more stable patterns of variance for both individuals and age cohorts, and the variance for unconstrained skills will be evident among beginning and proficient readers too.

Fourth, assembly models of skills regard each skill independently and ignore sequential or codependent relations between them. For example, both orthographic and phonological processing are required for word reading, and it is difficult to separate their contributions. Likewise, reading comprehension depends on multiple visual, cognitive, and linguistic skills. Some skills must meet thresholds of performance to enable other skills to operate. For example, when oral reading accuracy is less than 90% of the words in text, comprehension is seriously degraded. Why is this a problem? Because researchers often use multivariate statistics such as regression analyses and hierarchical linear modeling (HLM) to compare the predictive strength of different skills, but these methods fail to consider codependency among skills or different onsets, slopes, or durations of their developing trajectories.

The failure to differentiate reading skills conceptually is evident in the methods used to analyze developmental data. Consider cross-sectional and longitudinal studies of reading achievement (cf. Lonigan, Burgess, & Anthony, 2000; Morris, Bloodgood, Lomax, & Perney, 2003; Scarborough, 1998). It is common practice to assess a variety of reading skills and use the data to calculate correlations among skills, to conduct factor analyses to determine if skills are closely related, and to conduct regression analyses to determine which skills predict an outcome variable. Correlations are also used routinely to calculate concurrent and criterion-referenced validity for reading components. For example, Snow et al. (1998, p. 110), in a chapter entitled "Predictors of Success and Failure in Reading," include a table of correlations between reading components and difficulties at school entry that are summed over many studies. The median Pearson r correlations are .53 for letter identification, .49 for concepts of print, .42 for phonological awareness, and .33 for receptive vocabulary. Thus, these factors are implicated as predictors, correlates, and perhaps causes of reading difficulties at school entry. These conclusions, and the research methods used to establish validity of reading components, are accepted as robust and scientific evidence in federally endorsed reports on reading (e.g., Adams, 1990; Adams et al., 1998; National Reading Panel, 2000; Snow et al., 1998).

Despite a massive amount of evidence about the development of early reading skills, and the importance of letter knowledge and phonemic awareness, we think there is a different interpretation of the scientific evidence that merits consideration. Our reasoning in this chapter is inductive. We begin by focusing on skills that enable reading and note differences in their developmental courses of acquisition. Some skills, like knowledge of

the alphabet, are mastered completely by all skilled readers. The rate of learning may vary, but the asymptote, that is, the final knowledge shared among readers, is the same for everyone. The developmental curve is sigmoidal in shape, like an S curve, with gradual learning initially, followed by rapid learning, and slowing down as an expert level is approached. Most important, letter knowledge has the *same* end point or intercept for all readers, that is, knowing the names and sounds of 26 letters. We suggest that decoding skills, including basic phonemic awareness, have similar trajectories, and furthermore, these trajectories are different from other less-constrained skills, such as vocabulary knowledge, that continue to develop continuously and do not reach identical asymptotes. We attribute the fundamental differences in developmental trajectories to the nature of the skills, the course of learning, and the universality of some skill asymptotes. The implications of these different skill trajectories are profound for research, practice, and policymaking because they have been neglected for 100 years. The arguments may be extended to other skills, such as arithmetic, that are constrained by mastery and similar asymptotic growth curves. Thus, the lessons from assessments of reading skills have implications for psychoeducational assessment of other developing skills.

There are potentially many alternatives to the componential view of reading. Not all theories need to assume that skills are equal on many dimensions, nor that growth is linear. For example, Fischer and Bidell (1998) describe dynamic systems theories that can account for variability and uniformity using newer approaches than stages and traditional learning mechanisms. They suggest that many features of development are not linear, and that logistic growth, like the S curve we advocate for some constrained reading skills, is common. They propose methods of analysis to accompany dynamic and nonlinear models of development. However, their approach does not address universally mastered and constrained skills nor the implications of parametric data analyses of such skills, so we do not attempt in this chapter to integrate their approach with our own interpretation of constrained reading skills.

THE ASSESSMENT OF ALPHABET KNOWLEDGE

As children are exposed to print, they learn to identify letter names and the sounds associated with them. This is generally referred to as the alphabetic principle, letter knowledge, or graphophonic knowledge. With practice, fluency (i.e., speed) increases for identifying and producing letters and their sounds. The letter names that are easiest to learn occur early in the alphabet and may occur in the child's name. Letter sounds are easiest to learn when the sound of the letter is in the letter name and when letters usually occur in the initial position of words rather than in the final position (McBride-Chang, 1999). Learning the names of letters precedes and facilitates learning letter-sound correspondence because the latter includes identification of phonemes (Stahl & Murray, 1994). Thus, letter-naming knowledge "does not appear to have a direct causal influence on word reading skills" (Rathvon, 2004, p. 122) but does promote phonemic awareness. This may explain why teaching children the names of letters and improving their letter-naming fluency do not improve reading skills (Fugate, 1997). In contrast, letter-sound knowledge may contribute directly to phonemic awareness, decoding, and word recognition (Treiman, 2000).

Alphabet knowledge is one of the five essential components of early reading identified by Snow et al. (1998) and the National Reading Report (2000), so it is not surprising that it is included in many early reading assessments. For example, it is part of the Texas Primary Reading Inventory (TPRI, 2002), the Virginia Phonological Awareness Literacy Screening (PALS, 2002), the Michigan Literacy Progress Profile (MLPP, 2002), and the Illinois Snapshots of Early Literacy (ISEL, 2003). Rathvon (2004) lists 26 different assessments of alphabet knowledge and letter-naming fluency; it is clearly a popular and frequent part of early reading assessments. Alphabet knowledge can be assessed with a variety of tasks, including letter identification, letter naming, rapid automatic naming, spelling, and phonological awareness. The format of assessment can require recitation, recognition, identification, or production. Rathvon notes that identification or recall methods are the most common, but the format may contribute to differences in sensitivity of the assessments. Whether the letters are presented in uppercase, which is easier to decode, or lowercase or even cursive, may also affect the assessment. Few assessments include all 26 letters of the alphabet, and assessments vary widely on whether they include all single-letter sounds, digraphs, blends, and diphthongs. Usually, the assessments use prototypical sounds such as initial consonants and frequent long and short vowel patterns. Fluency of alphabet knowledge is measured in only a few assessments, usually by counting the numbers of letter names or sounds produced in 1 minute, because the speed of saying individual letter names and sounds is not correlated with reading ability (Stanovich, Cunningham, & West, 1981). Rathvon says it is surprising that no fluency norms are available for either letter-naming or letter-sound fluency, and the lack of benchmarks may contribute to the less frequent assessment of the fluency of letter-name and letter-sound production.

The reason alphabet knowledge is such a popular assessment is because of the strong correlations with subsequent reading skill. Knowing the names of letters in kindergarten is one of the best predictors of future reading achievement in first grade and beyond (Scanlon & Vellutino, 1996; Share, Jorm, Maclean, & Matthews, 1984: Stevenson & Newman, 1986). Although there is less evidence about the predictive strength of letter-sound knowledge, when it is assessed in kindergarten, it predicts word identification in first grade and reading group status in fourth grade (Badian, McAnulty, Duffy, & Als, 1990; Byrne & Fielding-Barnsley, 1993). Lonigan et al. (2000, p. 597) write, "Knowledge of the alphabet (i.e., knowing the names of letters and the sounds they represent) at entry into school is one of the strongest single predictors of short- and long-term success in learning to read." Thus, alphabet knowledge is relatively easy to assess, and there is considerable evidence that it predicts subsequent reading achievement.

The correlation between early alphabet knowledge and later reading achievement, however, has been oversimplified and misinterpreted. Although researchers do not suggest a causal relation between them, the inference is so seductive that instruction in kindergarten and remedial help for struggling readers often targets letter names and sounds. This was portrayed in the example of Robert, a struggling first-grade reader whose teacher emphasized sounding out words correctly and quickly. When this happens, three risks are likely. One is that children with few literacy experiences before kindergarten, usually children from homes with low SES or families who do not speak English as a native language, are identified for special remediation. Second, these students are given a curriculum that is focused on isolated skill instruction, such as letter identification, rather than on rich and diverse literacy experiences. The third risk is that the lack of rich and diverse literacy experiences has detrimental consequences for disadvantaged students' learning and motivation. Beginning readers who have more difficulty breaking the code than their peers are usually exposed to less text with less emphasis on meaning making, which can increase, not decrease, the disparities between children (Stanovich, 2000). Children would be in less jeopardy of these risks if the assessments of alphabet knowledge were interpreted as indicators of different developmental trajectories rather than specific skill deficits. The causes for the slower learning of the alphabet can include a range of factors, such as less exposure to books, less print in the home environment, or less adult guidance and instruction, and interventions can accommodate these factors in addition to teaching letter names and sounds.

Unstable Correlations

Although many studies have shown that alphabet knowledge at entry to kindergarten is a strong predictor of later reading, the strength of the correlation declines when alphabet knowledge is assessed in late kindergarten or first grade. Longitudinal research also reveals declining correlations as the same children acquire knowledge about letter names and sounds. For example, McBride-Chang (1999) collected data on children's letter knowledge at four time points and correlated the data longitudinally with measures of word identification and phonological awareness. At time 1, letter knowledge had a mean of 12.4 (SD = 8.8). By time point 4, the variable lost 60% of its variance and had a mean of 24.5 (SD = 3.4), near ceiling on the task. The effects of ceiling performance on the correlations with other variables were consistent and dramatic. Correlations between letter knowledge and the Word Attack test decreased from r = .54 at time 1 to r = .23 at the final time point. Similarly, correlations between letter knowledge and phoneme elision decreased from r = .51 to r = .18. The same decreasing pattern was found for correlations between letter knowledge and every other predictor.

A similar pattern of variable correlations is evident in other longitudinal studies. Hecht, Burgess, Torgesen, Wagner, and Rashotte (2000) analyzed the effects of SES on children's early reading skills from kindergarten to fourth grade with a subset of the data used in previous research by Wagner et al. (1997). Among the 20 measures were three tasks used to assess print knowledge. Print Concepts included 13 items derived from

Clay's (1979) Concepts About Print task, Letter Names required children to name all 26 uppercase letters, and Letter Sounds required children to provide sounds for letters shown on cards. These tasks were given to 197 children in the beginning of kindergarten, and the data were correlated with other variables collected in the beginning of first, second, third, and fourth grades.

The canonical correlations of the three print knowledge tasks with the other 17 variables ranged from r = .24 to r = .60, all significant at levels similar to previous research. The researchers used a measurement model based on factor analyses and created a latent factor for Print Knowledge composed of an aggregate of the three tasks. This factor was highly correlated with other latent factors across years. For example, Print Knowledge was correlated with Reading Comprehension at grades 2, 3, and 4, respectively, with rs = .74, .60, and .53. These are impressive correlations, but note the decline with age. Next, HLM procedures were used to determine the amount of variance that each factor accounted for in the longitudinal predictions. The authors found that Print Knowledge scores at kindergarten accounted for significant variance in reading comprehension scores at grade 2 (33%), grade 3 (16%), and grade 4 (9%), again a declining pattern. It should be noted that all other variables accounted for significant variance in reading comprehension across years, with a general decline with increasing grade level. However, the variance accounted for ranged only between 2% and 19%.

Reinterpreting Correlations with Alphabet Knowledge

Many researchers have described decreasing correlations between alphabet knowledge and reading achievement with increasing age (e.g., Adams, 1990; Johnston, Anderson, & Holligan, 1996; Muter & Diethelm, 2001; Muter, Hulme, Snowling, & Taylor, 1998). The developmental trajectory of alphabet knowledge may account for the decreasing correlations longitudinally. Consider several points about the shape of the curve that describes letter naming. First, the trajectory of letter naming from knowing a few letters to 100% accurate performance is relatively brief and rapid, perhaps a year or two, and this learning often occurs by 5-6 years of age. Second, the end point of the skill is the same for everyone: knowing the names of the 26 letters in the English alphabet. The universal intercept is a critical feature of mastery learning that is 100% of alphabet knowledge (or close to it). Third, the shape of the developmental trajectory is not linear but sigmoidal (for individual data) because the period of rapid learning is brief and accelerated compared to longer periods of floor and ceiling performance on the skill. Consequently, correlations between developing knowledge of letter names and other variables will vary depending on the distribution of individual mastery and the location of data on the sigmoidal curve. When floor and ceiling effects are evident in the data, the skew will attenuate correlations, and only when the data fall mostly in the middle of the acquisition curve will the variance be large and approximate a normal distribution. Thus, the degree of correlation with an emerging skill like letter naming depends on the characteristics of the sample, their degree of knowledge, and the timing of the assessment.

Three problems are evident. The first is the special selection of children who do not exhibit floor or ceiling performance on assessments of alphabet knowledge. Researchers understand the need to avoid floor and ceiling effects in the data, so they are careful to assess alphabet knowledge in 5- to 6-year-olds who know some, but not all, letter names. Although common practice, this sampling technique leads to replicable patterns of correlations but only with children who know some of the alphabet. The observed strong correlations are entirely dependent on the relative skill mastery of the sample. The correlations are transitory and special cases, not enduring stable relations, between two variables. When the sample includes a large number of children with either little or great knowledge, the data reveal floor and ceiling effects. These minimize the variance in the measures and attenuate correlations with other variables. Actually, there is zero predictive power for reading comprehension (or any other variable) when there are ceiling effects in the data. Hecht et al. (2000) minimized the problem of ceiling effects by testing children at the beginning of kindergarten. Their data indicate mean scores on Print Concepts of 11.4 (maximum = 18; SD = 4.1), Letter Names of 21.2 (maximum = 26; SD = 7.5), and Letter Sounds of 10.4 (maximum = 36; SD = 10.4). It is clear that the researchers avoided ceiling effects and there was great variability among the children, but this variability does not reflect stable individual differences. Those two features underlie the positive correlations evident in their data. In contrast, McBride-Chang (1999) encountered ceiling effects in the sample that diminished the correlations longitudinally.

The second interpretive problem is the transitory nature of the purported relation between print knowledge and reading comprehension. The predictive power of letter naming and print knowledge is restricted to a period of approximately a year or less when children know about half of the alphabet, or at least score near the midpoints on the reading assessments. These are transitory and unstable relations, statistically as well as cognitively, and they yield significant relations only during a brief period of growth. Thus, had Ms. Jones tested Robert just 1 year earlier or later than October of first grade, the state assessment of letter knowledge would likely have revealed a floor or ceiling effect that would not predict later reading comprehension.

Walsh, Price, and Gillingham (1988) described the transitory relation problem as one of diminishing returns. They examined the longitudinal relations between letter-naming accuracy and letter-naming speed at kindergarten with reading development at grade 2 on a multilevel reading inventory and the Gates-MacGinitie Reading Test. Accuracy of letter naming improved from a mean of 67% correct at kindergarten to 100% correct at second grade. The correlation with later reading achievement was zero for the kindergarten data and meaningless for the second graders because of the ceiling effect. The researchers found that letter-naming speed was a significant predictor of reading development and comprehension at kindergarten but not grade 2. This interaction with grade suggests that letter naming has transitory importance. They hypothesized that there is a speed threshold for letter naming, and once the threshold is exceeded, there is little benefit of further increases in letter-naming speed. The diminishing returns hypothesis reflects (a) mastery of a skill (b) within a narrow age range and (c) nonlinear growth that reaches asymptotic levels so that (d) there is little variance left to relate to other variables. The diminishing returns and transitory effects hypotheses appear to describe the case for print concepts, letter naming, and letter-sound correspondence variables.

What is the problem with a transitory relation? First, the transitory qualification is rarely attached to interpretations of the relation between alphabet knowledge and subsequent reading achievement, so policymakers (and others) wrongfully infer that letter-sound or alphabet knowledge is correlated with reading achievement at all ages and skill levels. It has led to policies that emphasize the importance of letter naming and letter-sound knowledge first and foremost in early reading assessment and instruction. Second, experimental evidence can be marshaled to show that intervention in the early and intermediate phases of skill learning can accelerate learning letter names and sounds, and, sometimes but not always, it increases growth among other skills such as word recognition and comprehension. For example, Foorman, Fletcher, Francis, Schatschneider, and Metha (1998) suggested that explicit teaching of phonics is more effective for helping at-risk children develop phonemic awareness and phonics skills than embedded phonics and whole-language programs. However, no significant differences in comprehension were found among the groups.

The experimental evidence that alphabet knowledge can be enhanced through direct instruction, coupled with the erroneous inferences made from the correlations between enabling skills and reading comprehension, has led to claims that alphabet skills cause/promote/facilitate reading comprehension and achievement across ages and skill levels. This causal claim is seductive but unwarranted. At best, explicit teaching of phonics leads to better alphabet knowledge and word recognition, and that is usually confined to children who have the least developed alphabet skills. Better word recognition may enable reading comprehension for these children, but it is not the sufficient or causal link. The significant transitory relation focuses too much attention and time on assessment of alphabet skills. When the goals of assessment are focused on mastery of enabling skills, instructional goals become narrowed and the public standards of accountability are reduced to a basic and uninformative level. The age or time at which children know the names and sounds of 5, 10, or 20 letters is not as important as instructing them to mastery quickly and efficiently.

The third interpretive problem is that print knowledge variables are correlated with many other features of children and their development, so they may serve only as proxies for other relations. This is the problem of multicolinearity that confounds all multivariate longitudinal studies, but it is often overlooked in the interpretations of canonical correlations in reading research. For example, Hecht et al. (2000) noted that the effects of SES were severely attenuated by 30% to 50% when print knowledge scores were controlled. They concluded that, "most of the SES related variance in growth of reading skills was accounted for by beginning kindergarten lev-

els of print knowledge" (p. 119). These results led the authors to conclude:

> A practical consequence of the present results is that measures of reading related abilities should be included in test batteries used to identify beginning kindergarten children, particularly those from lower social class backgrounds, at risk for later reading failure. . . . In addition, the results suggest that preschool and kindergarten interventions involving intensive training in print knowledge, phonological awareness, and/or rate of access skills may help reduce the incidence of later reading failure among children from lower SES families. (p. 122)

We think this is a misinterpretation of proxy variables as causal variables and that the prescription for instruction is unwarranted. In the Hecht et al. (2000) data, the researchers found that composite scores for SES and Print Knowledge were correlated at $r = .41$, and that when they controlled the effects of Print Knowledge on SES, the effects of SES were attenuated. This led them to conclude that kindergarten Print Knowledge mediated reading scores at grades 3 and 4. However, it is more plausible to interpret Print Knowledge scores at kindergarten as measures of other factors (perhaps related to SES) such as parental assistance and involvement in helping their children learn to read. Those kindergarten children who scored high on Print Concepts, Letter Names, and Letter Sounds were most likely to have had more social supports and opportunities for reading, learning, and education than those kindergarten children who scored lower on these tasks. That should be expected by the strong correlation with SES and might be evident if other data were available, such as preschool experiences, parental education levels, parental time spent with children, or quality of children's literacy materials in the home. Therefore, knowing letter names in kindergarten is probably *not* the mediator of reading comprehension at grades 3 and 4. Instead, home environment, SES, and other enduring variables associated with parent-child interactions probably account for better comprehension in later grades, especially if those same factors continued to be influential several years later. Thus, interventions with parents in the home, not teaching letter names in isolation, are the route to fostering successful readers.

Simplistic interpretations of correlations are easy to recognize, but the relations can be obscured in sophisticated statistical analyses. For example, researchers can aggregate data from different tasks to minimize floor and ceiling effects. The Hecht et al. (2000) data have highly skewed data for Letter Names that are aggregated with less skewed data on Print Concepts and Letter Sounds. When composite scores are created based on factor analyses or HLM or item response theory, the result may be an artificially normalized distribution that is more influenced by scores on one measure than another. For example, composite scores might disguise floor and ceiling effects on some skills or suggest inappropriately that all subskills are important in the composite score. This problem is exacerbated when researchers aggregate data from highly constrained and less constrained variables.

The problem is also evident when data are transformed to normalize the distributions, when the sample size is so large that it includes many subjects with floor and ceiling effects, and when the skewed data are blocked to create categorical data. For example, the Early Childhood Longitudinal Study—Kindergarten Class of 1998–99 confounds early reading measures with these practices, and the aggregated variables obscure developmental differences among the component knowledge and skills (U.S. Department of Education, 2000). These problems are rarely acknowledged in aggregated data, and alternative explanations based on developmental proxies are rarely offered. It is clear that lack of knowledge about letter names and sounds impedes reading temporarily, but learning letter names and sounds is necessary but not sufficient for successful reading. It is more likely that the enduring effects of SES and early literacy experiences are signaled by poor alphabet knowledge in kindergarten, and if they persist, they are obstacles to successful reading.

Learning the letter names and sounds, and practicing them until fluency is achieved, occurs faster for some children than others. Those who acquire the knowledge sooner are likely to be better readers a year or two later, but this relation must be interpreted cautiously. It is paradoxical that (a) the strong correlations between alphabet knowledge and later reading achievement are only evident when alphabet knowledge is measured early in kindergarten, when the differences due to preschool experiences are greatest; (b) directly teaching letter names does not improve reading skill; and (c) all children learn the names of the letters eventually, so letter-naming knowledge is not an enduring individual difference nor a stable predictor of reading achievement.

The developmental trajectory for letter naming provides a clear example of the onset, rate, and intercept of a skill that is relatively small in scope and mastered completely and universally. The trajectory for letter-sound knowledge may be parallel to letter naming, but it may have a later onset, a longer period and rate of learning, and a less identical intercept because of the greater number and complexity of letter sounds to master. The developmental trajectories are constrained, but not to the same degree. These constraints involve the set size of knowledge, the universal mastery of the set so that intercepts of learning are identical for everyone, and the consequent effects on the distributions of data. Only in samples that exhibit partial mastery does the distribution of data exhibit wide variance and approach normality. Except for these special cases, the data are never normally distributed empirically or conceptually. The same constraints apply to learning to read in languages other than English, but the number of letters or symbols in any language will determine the set to master and influence the rate of learning.

It is worth noting that some researchers have recognized the potential problems with some component reading skills like alphabet knowledge that are mastered quickly and completely (Adams, 1990; Stanovich, 2000), but no one has provided a coherent account of the connections between different developmental trajectories, statistical analyses, and interpretations of the data. Ironically, Adams et al. (1998) identified similar problems for hypotheses about the importance of variables *other than* letter knowledge and phonemic awareness. In their review of Scarborough and Dobrich's (1994) research on parenting variables, they noted that some variables were nonlinear, some may have thresholds of influence, and some are proxies for other accomplishments: "What is at issue here is not merely the precision, but the very appropriateness of the linear statistical models on which the field so strongly relies" (Adams et al., 1998, p. 211). We think the same statement applies to variables derived from assessments of letter knowledge and phonemic awareness.

ASSESSMENTS OF OTHER EARLY READING SKILLS

There are many skills that precede and accompany early reading so the sequence and relations among them are difficult to identify. We describe three types of skills that are frequently assessed, and we show how each might be constrained developmentally.

Concepts about Print

Other assessments of early reading knowledge and skills may exhibit trajectories that are similar to letter naming.

Print knowledge or concepts about print refers to a small set of knowledge that is learned by beginning readers. For example, Clay (1972) presented a little book to 5-year-olds and asked them to indicate the front of the book, the direction of reading, errors in inverted text, and the function of punctuation marks. The 24 items included a variety of concepts about both functions and conventions of print. Rathvon (2004) summarized the seven typical concepts included in assessments of print knowledge as book orientation; meaning conveyed by print versus pictures; print directionality; voice-word matching; boundaries between letters, words, and sentences; order of letters and words; and punctuation marks. Clay (1979) included concepts about print in a battery of early reading assessments called the Observation Survey, and she cautioned against the use of the assessment as a stand-alone instrument to signal reading readiness or progress. Nonetheless, it has been appropriated and abbreviated as a research tool and is an isolated skill assessment in the PALS, TPRI, MLPP, and other assessments. Assessments vary widely in the number of concepts tested from as few as 4 to 5 to as many as 24, and the concepts vary in difficulty. Most 5-year-olds can identify the front of the book and the left-right direction of reading, but punctuation marks may confuse even 7-year-olds. Thus, the relative difficulty of an assessment depends on the number of items and the difficulty of the assessed concepts.

Concepts about print, like letter naming, is a small set of knowledge that is universally mastered by children, and the same kinds of constraints operate empirically and theoretically. Data from around the world reveal that children learning English understand only a few of the basic concepts about print before age 5, but they understand most, except for punctuation marks, by age 6 (cf. Clay, 1979). The period of acquisition is rapid and reaches the same asymptote for all children, so the variance in any group is small before age 5 and after age 7. Thus, it is only during the period of rapid learning that variance is large and approaches a normal distribution, which is, not by coincidence, the age at which concepts about print are usually assessed and described as the most diagnostic. Several problems are revealed by the developmental trajectory and common asymptote.

First, concepts about print is an assessment of specific rules and conventions that are acquired with reading expertise. All skilled readers of a language learn the same concepts. They are not emergent, universal developmental concepts like conservation in the Piagetian sense; they are language-specific rules that depend on didactic experiences more than maturation. Thus, they

can be taught directly. Second, the knowledge set is small and can be learned relatively quickly given a rich literacy environment and contextualized instruction such as shared reading. Third, the calculation of norms for mastery seems inappropriate because it implies that the knowledge is normally distributed when it is not. For example, Clay (1979) presents normalized scores in stanine groups that show how many concepts are mastered by samples of children. The technical manual of the ISEL also provides age norms. Although there is value in providing norm-referenced rates of acquisition, it is important to note that nearly all children master all the concepts about print by 7 to 8 years of age, so the critical difference among children is in their rate of mastery, not their final knowledge. Norms, therefore, reveal only averages for a particular group, and those norms may vary widely by country, community, and SES.

The characteristics of children's concepts about print can shed light on empirical findings. Rathvon's (2004) review indicates that assessments of children's print awareness may be correlated with other measures of early reading, but they have little predictive power when measures of letter naming and phonemic awareness are included in the regressions. This may be due to the multicolinearity of the variables. Letter naming and phonemic awareness usually are taught at about the same age as print awareness skills, and they emerge from the same kinds of shared reading experiences, so the intercorrelations of the three variables remove their unique variance. Lonigan et al. (2000) suggested that print awareness serves as a proxy measure for print exposure and literacy experiences. This means that children who score high on assessments of concepts about print are ahead of their age-mates, but their superior print awareness is temporary and an indicator only of different previous literacy experiences and not of stable individual differences. A second reason for the lack of predictive power could be the lack of relation between simple concepts about print and more complex decoding and comprehension skills. Thus, print knowledge is easy to assess, and it leads to diagnoses of specific weaknesses, but it does not predict future reading achievement and may be unrelated to other cognitive skills required for proficient reading. Given these problems, concepts about print may have value only for guiding instruction in the first year or two of schooling.

A caveat needs to be added about children's concepts of words, however, because the ability to identify an orthographic unit as a word involves more than a simple concept. When children can point their finger to a spoken word, they understand boundaries between letters and words as well as some resemblance between letters and sounds. They can even use comprehension and rhythm to identify which word goes with what spoken sounds. Thus, the line is blurred between understanding an entity called a word and the ability to match graphemes and phonemes. Some researchers suggest that understanding the concept of a word facilitates phonemic segmentation (Morris, 1992), whereas other researchers suggest that phonemic segmentation facilitates word recognition. They are intercorrelated, so the direction of influence is difficult to specify. Indeed, both components could be influenced by some other factor.

Orthographic Processing

Children's orthographic processing includes their awareness and processing of printed literacy symbols. Understanding of orthography includes knowing upper- and lowercase letters, print and cursive writing, and the meanings of symbols, numerals, and punctuation marks. The skills are intertwined with developing concepts about print and words as well as phonological awareness. Orthographic processing allows readers to construct visual representations of written symbols and is critical for spelling development (Share & Stanovich, 1995). However, there is some controversy over the construct validity of orthographic processing. Vellutino, Scanlon, and Chen (1994) claim that many tasks assess spelling and word identification skills rather than visual representation of print. Cunningham, Perry, and Stanovich (2001) compared six measures of orthographic processing and found variable correlations among them rather than good convergence. Three points seem clear. First, the set of knowledge required for orthographic processing is finite and relatively small. Second, skilled readers all master the same kinds of knowledge, so the developmental trajectory should proceed from floor to ceiling effects like letter naming. Third, assessments of orthographic processing may reflect several different component skills that contribute differently to performance with increasing age.

Orthographic processing is not assessed routinely, perhaps because many of the assessments require individual administration via computers of the stimuli and recording of reaction times. There are also few norms available for interpreting the data, and the tasks are susceptible to guessing. For example, one common assessment method is to ask children to choose the word from two choices that sound alike, such as "nail and nale." Another method, the homophone choice task, asks children to choose one word, such as "Which is a number—ate or eight?" Despite these problems, there is evidence that orthographic processing differences may help identify different types of dyslexia (Castles & Coltheart, 1993).

Orthographic processing emerges later than alphabet knowledge and concurrently with beginning word identification, but the developmental trajectory of orthographic processing is difficult to identify because it depends on the specific method used to assess it. Orthographic processing is confounded with other variables such as spelling, phonological awareness, and print exposure, although orthographic processing appears to contribute some unique variance to reading achievement beyond these skills (Cunningham & Stanovich, 1990). It is clear, however, that orthographic processing becomes more important with age because the correlations between orthographic skills and reading achievement are stronger among older children (Badian, 1995; Juel, Griffith, & Gough, 1986).

Orthographic processing is necessary for identifying words and reading proficiently, but it is difficult to isolate and assess. First, the set of knowledge of letter patterns is large, so the relative difficulty of an assessment depends on the stimuli that are chosen. For example, distinguishing homophones based on "ai" versus long "a" sounds is easier than discriminating irregular "ough" sounds. On the one hand, there are a small number of high-frequency patterns of letters that need to be mastered by beginning readers, and as they are learned, the patterns may promote phonological awareness, spelling, and related skills (and vice versa). Performance on those patterns may be poor among 5-year-olds and very high among 7-year-olds, so the trajectories may be constrained, as in alphabet knowledge. On the other hand, more complex orthographic discriminations may be difficult for older readers, so the level of skill does not reach ceiling, the period of acquisition is protracted, and the rate of learning may be slower. Thus, the trajectories of learning depend on the particular task and stimuli. Second, measures of orthographic processing may be confounded by individual differences in response speed, print exposure, guessing, and phonological awareness that contribute variance in addition to orthographic processing skills (Swanson & Alexander, 1997). Thus, the resulting measures may be normally distributed because of these confounds rather than in the normal distribution of underlying orthographic skills.

Phonological Processing

Understanding the sounds of oral and written language includes (a) phonological awareness, (b) phonological memory, and (c) phonological naming, usually assessed as the speed of naming sounds. These important processes begin to develop before exposure to print and continue to develop concurrently with alphabet knowledge, orthographic skills, and other components of reading. Stanovich (1991, p. 78) wrote, "The specification of the role of phonological processing in the earliest stages of reading acquisition is one of the more notable scientific success stories of the last decade." Phonological processes have been hypothesized to facilitate and perhaps even to cause reading development. Children who exhibit reading disabilities and dyslexia often have deficits in phonological processing (Share & Stanovich, 1995).

The conscious perception and manipulation of the sounds of spoken words, including phonemes, rimes, and words, is referred to as phonological awareness. It has been one of the most frequently studied reading skills during the past 25 years, and it is one of the five essential components of early reading identified by the National Reading Panel (2000). Phonological awareness is usually assessed with tasks based on rhyming, segmenting, and blending distinct phonemes, and it is a core feature of the TPRI, PALS, MLPP, and ISEL. In general, children understand rhyming first, followed by segmenting and then blending phonemes. Abundant research has shown that children's phonological awareness and reading achievement are strongly related (Adams et al., 1998), but there is controversy about the causal role it might play in reading development. In an extensive review of research on phonological awareness, Castles and Coltheart (2004) found no definitive evidence, from either longitudinal studies or training studies, that phonological awareness precedes and causes reading and spelling development. Instead, they suggest that rather than one causing the other, it is possible that "once children acquire reading and spelling skills, they change *the way in which they perform phonological awareness tasks,* using their orthographic skills, either in addition to or instead of their phonological skills, to arrive at a solution" (p. 102). This interpretation suggests that the skills are highly related and that the correlation between

phonological awareness and reading development is mediated by orthographic skills.

The controversy about the causal role of phonological awareness pivots on two types of evidence: predictive validity and training studies. Consider correlations used to establish predictive validity. The landmark longitudinal study by Bradley and Bryant (1983) claimed a causal relation between phonological awareness and subsequent reading achievement. These researchers tested understanding of rhyme and alliteration among 4- and 5-year-olds (who could not read) with oddity tasks as the measure of phonological awareness. For example, children were asked to choose which word did not fit in a group (i.e., was the odd or different word) among "pin, win, sit, fin." The remarkable finding was that performance on the phonological awareness tasks predicted reading and spelling achievement 3 years later, even after controlling for the effects of memory and IQ. Many influential reports have reported similar strong correlations that imply a causal role of phonological awareness (Adams, 1990; National Reading Panel, 2000; Snow et al., 1998).

Other researchers, though, have not found strong correlations between rhyme awareness and reading achievement (Hulme et al., 2002; Stuart, 1995). Rathvon (2004) suggests that rhyming tasks administered at kindergarten are poor predictors compared to phonemic awareness measures because of ceiling effects. Castles and Coltheart (2004) suggest that rhyming tasks like the oddity tasks may be answered correctly by noticing the different ending sounds, thus confounding phonemic awareness with rhyming awareness. They also note that the reliability of oddity tasks is low, and conclude that "there is not a strong case to be made for rhyme awareness being a significant independent predictor of reading and spelling acquisition" (p. 90).

These findings can be explained by examining the developmental trajectory of rhyme awareness, and the explanation applies to other measures of phonological awareness. First, rhyme awareness refers to a potentially large set of sounds, but in practice, most assessments focus on a small set of prototypical relations that are relatively unknown by 4-year-olds but mastered by 6-year-olds. The tasks used to assess rhyme awareness are not only confounded with emerging phonemic awareness, they reveal skewed distributions in some samples and are only normally distributed as special cases of selected subjects who score in the midrange of the task. Thus, the difficulty of the task and the distribution of scores depend on the items included in the test. Second, the strength of the correlations used to establish predictive validity will depend on the relative mastery of the sample and will be diminished for children who score near the floor or ceiling on the tasks. For example, Willson and Rupley (1997) found that phonemic awareness strongly predicted comprehension in lower grades, but by third grade, background knowledge and strategy knowledge were more important. Third, reliability may be low because rhyming is learned rapidly, perhaps even in the testing situation, so children's scores should be expected to improve with retesting. Fourth, it is difficult to assess rhyme awareness in isolation because it is developing concurrently with other phonological and orthographic skills, so regression techniques that partial out variance or compare residual variance are confounded by multicolinearity.

All of these problems mean that the specific items on the assessment and the relative degree of phonological awareness among the specific children tested will determine the shape of the distributions, the degree of skew, and the strength of correlations among variables. The issue is not sampling a random and representative set of items and subjects, because all items are not equally difficult and not all children display normally distributed skills. Thus, the actual construct being assessed, rhyming or phonological awareness, is not an independent and normally distributed component of reading. It can be conceptualized better as a set of knowledge that is gradually mastered and used so the degree of mastery can be assessed and the proficiency or accuracy of use can be determined as both approach asymptotes of 100%. Norms can be calculated for both mastery and use, but it is important to recognize that the norms can vary widely depending on print exposure, joint book experiences, and direct instruction, so the norms may assess features of the literate environments more than individual abilities.

Now let us consider the evidence for the causal role of phonological awareness derived from training studies. Bus and van Ijzendoorn (1999) conducted a meta-analysis of phonological awareness studies and found that training significantly improved phonological awareness and reading (as measured by word identification and word attack skills). The overall correlations were $r = .33$ for phonological awareness and $r = .34$ for reading, so phonological training accounted for about 12% of the variance in the outcomes. Both outcome measures closely resembled the training; the average

length of training was 8 months for phonological awareness outcomes and 18 months for outcomes based on reading letters and words. Bus and van Ijzendoorn concluded, "The training studies settle the issue of the causal role of phonological awareness in learning to read: Phonological training reliably enhances phonological and reading skills" (p. 411).

This conclusion may be inflated, though, given that the set of training studies included training on letter-sound relations and more components than phonological awareness. The training was more effective for preschoolers than kindergarten or primary grade children; short-term effects were larger than long-term effects; and children with reading disabilities did not benefit more than regular children. The authors noted that ceiling effects and normal development of phonological awareness may underlie the diminished impact of training on older children. Training phonological awareness seems to benefit those who exhibit the least knowledge, and the benefits are greater if the treatment includes sustained training on multiple components of alphabet knowledge, phonological skills, and orthographic skills. Nonetheless, Bus and van Ijzendoorn (1999, p. 413) caution that phonological awareness accounted for only 12% of the variance and conclude that it is "an important but not sufficient condition for learning to read."

Castles and Coltheart (2004) examined the causal role of phonological awareness with more rigorous criteria. They reviewed studies that (a) trained only phonological awareness, (b) showed facilitation of reading-related processes beyond the target phonological skill, (c) showed positive transfer only to reading-related skills, and (d) showed improvement specifically on phonological awareness for children who had no pre-existing reading or spelling skills that may have been improved by training. Few studies met these stringent criteria. Castles and Coltheart concluded that "no single study has conclusively established that phonemic awareness training assists reading or spelling acquisition" (p. 101). Their review highlights a number of findings that can be explained by analyzing the developing trajectories of the skills. First, many different types of phonological skills have been trained, and they vary widely. Some, such as rhyming and initial consonant sounds, are learned early; other skills, such as phonemic segmentation and blending, are learned later. Training skills that are beginning to emerge leads to more gains than training skills that are nonexistent or already mostly learned. Said differently, training in the zone of proximal development leads to the largest improvements, so it is the fit of training to the level of learning that determines the effectiveness of the treatment. If training phonological awareness has only temporary benefits and only for children who have little phonological awareness, then the influence on subsequent reading achievement may be modest.

Second, multicolinearity of phonological skills makes it difficult to train one isolated phonological skill without also providing information and experience on related skills. For example, training children to recognize onset-rime patterns, such as "c—at," also provides information on letter naming, letter-sound correspondence, and orthographic features. Castles and Coltheart (2004) point out that the window of time for independent skills to develop may be small. Furthermore, emerging interdependencies among skills, such as knowing specific letter-sound relations, may predict specific spelling and reading achievements better than general phonological awareness measures. This means that the sequential facilitation of skills may be specific to letters, syllables, and phonemes, so general assessments of different phonological skills may obscure the developing relations. Third, training can provide diffuse benefits to related skills. Even though the training conditions may be described as focused, they can provide practice and feedback on related skills. Some studies did not measure transfer to other reading and nonreading skills, so the specificity of effects cannot be determined, much less the Hawthorne effects due to the training. Fourth, training may be most effective when it links different skills, such as phonological and orthographic skills (Hatcher, Hulme, Ellis, 1994), or when training includes explicit metacognitive instruction about the skills (Cunningham, 1990).

In conclusion, studies of phonological awareness have shown that children acquire a variety of related skills as they learn to read, and it is difficult to isolate, assess, or train any component skill. Indeed, phonological awareness may be mediated by, or develop concurrently with, orthographic skills. This makes it difficult to identify a direct causal relation between phonological awareness and reading development. The two findings that provide the strongest foundation for the importance of phonological awareness are evidence that struggling readers perform poorly on tasks assessing phonological awareness, and that training, even on multiple or confounded phonological skills, improves the target skill. Thus,

phonological skills may provide a necessary but not sufficient condition for subsequent reading achievement.

CONSTRAINTS ON READING SKILLS

For descriptive convenience, the constraints that influence analyses of reading development can be grouped into three categories: conceptual, developmental, and methodological. The type and degree of constraints can vary widely among reading skills. In general, letter knowledge, phonics, and concepts about print are highly constrained; phonemic awareness and oral reading fluency are less constrained; and vocabulary and comprehension are least constrained. The polarized ends of the continuum exemplify the differences between constrained and unconstrained skills most clearly, but even subtle constraints hinder analyses of reading skills.

Conceptual Constraints

Reading skills, like other psychological constructs, are defined and operationalized to establish consistent measurement and interpretation of the constructs. The validity of the construct is evaluated by reference to its definitions and measures. One fundamental constraint of a construct is the *scope*, defined by its domain, number of elements, or set size. For example, learning the names and sounds of the 26 letters in the English alphabet are two clear examples. Skills with narrow scope are learned quickly, so the trajectory of mastery is steep and the duration of acquisition is brief. The same is true of basic concepts about print (Clay, 1979); they are conceptually constrained by the relatively small number of concepts to be acquired.

The second conceptual constraint on early reading skills and concepts is *importance*, as measured by centrality or typicality of exemplars. Most assessments of children's understanding of early print concepts pertain to a small set of central and important features of text that beginning readers need to understand. Therefore, early assessments use prototypical stimuli that are mastered by all skilled readers and thus can exhibit ceiling effects. Infrequent letter sounds, for example, "x", and esoteric concepts about print, such as single quotation marks, may be in the conceptual scope of a skill, but they are rarely included in assessments of early reading because they are less important for learning to read than mastery of other skills and concepts. A third type of conceptual constraint among reading skills is the *range of influence,* both the domain and temporal range. The concomitant skills influenced by learning the alphabet and concepts about print are tied directly to decoding grapheme-phoneme relations. In contrast, vocabulary development influences (and is influenced by) linguistic, cognitive, and communicative proficiency in wide-ranging ways. Not only is the range of influence less among highly constrained skills, but the temporal range of influence is restricted in constrained skills to that period when rapid acquisition is occurring. Thus, constrained skills such as alphabet knowledge are most related to decoding in early childhood, whereas unconstrained skills such as vocabulary are related to a wide range of academic skills throughout life.

Scope, importance, and range of influence are also evident in constructs involving phonological awareness, although each is broader than alphabet knowledge and their acquisition takes longer. Most early reading assessments include tasks of phoneme identification, segmentation, blending, and rhyming, but the phonemes that are used in the tests are usually important and prototypical. They are based on phonemes and words that have a high frequency of occurrence in oral language and text, they are usually familiar, and they have a wide range of application. Thus, words such as "cat" and "sit" are frequent in early assessments of phonological awareness because the onset-rime patterns are central prototypes for young children. Because most assessments of phonological awareness are limited to a small number of rules that are assessed with central exemplars, they can be considered constrained skills (e.g., Adams & Treadway, 2000; TPRI, 2002). Although there are many distinct phonological rules, and the set size is greater than 26, it is the constrained scope, importance, and range of influence of these rules that enable 7- to 8-year-old children to learn the essential features of phonological awareness and to decode nearly all words they encounter in beginning texts.

Phonological processing is more complicated than phonological awareness because constrained and unconstrained skills may operate together. Thus, assessments of phonological processing may confound constrained and unconstrained skills. For example, the Comprehensive Test of Phonological Processing (CTOPP) by Wagner, Torgesen, and Rashotte (1999) is based on the interactions among three correlated skills: phonological awareness, phonological memory, and rapid naming that, according to the authors, become less correlated

with development. The constrained skills view provides a useful framework for understanding the CTOPP because phonological memory and rapid naming are both individual difference variables between children that endure over time, whereas phonological awareness is a constrained skill that varies within and between individuals during a period of mastery only. After mastery is achieved, phonological awareness carries little variance compared to phonological memory and rapid naming, so the correlations among the dependent skills must decrease for statistical reasons alone. What remains are individual differences in basic information-processing functions of memory and rapid naming, not skills specific to reading.

The CTOPP includes 13 subtests, 7 for children ages 5 to 6 years and 10 for people 7 to 24 years old. The older subjects actually receive all of the same subtests as the younger sample except Sound Matching, presumably because it is mastered by age 7 years, plus four more difficult subtests, blending and segmenting nonwords and rapid naming of colors and objects. The subtest scores are used to create three composite scores for Phonological Awareness, Phonological Memory, and Rapid Naming that are used to establish normative ages for performance. The composite scores are also used as correlates to establish concurrent and predictive validity. The CTOPP combines very different skills in the composite measures that confound developmental and methodological constraints; thus, the interpretations of the data may have less to do with phonological awareness than individual differences in processing speed and memory.

Examination of Table C.1 in the CTOPP manual reveals wide variation in the developmental growth rates of the performance on the subtests between ages 5 and 15. For example, Sound Matching is at 100% by 8 years 3 months; Blending Words is at 87% mastery by age 8 to 9 years; Blending Nonwords is at 80% mastery by the same age; and Phoneme Reversal is at 70% mastery by age 9 years. Floor effects are evident for Segmenting Words because all children who segment fewer than nine words receive the same low score. Growth from 0 to 9 on that scale is from ages 5-0 to 7-9 years, and increases in segmenting words only advance from a raw score of 9 to 12 between ages 7-9 and 14-9 years. Clearly, growth on the subtests is not linear or uniform; ceiling and floor effects are evident in individual subtests, so composite scores derived from the subtests reflect proficiency (or lack of it) for different skills at different ages. Consider

Memory for Digits. The scale of raw scores is from 0 to 14 between ages 5-0 and 14-9 years, but the conversions to age equivalents show that 0 to 10 scores are all expected before age 6 years, with growth during the next 9 years limited to increases of four items. Failure to consider nonlinear growth, the constraints on various skills, and different developmental trajectories of the skills undermines the construct validity of the composite scores in the CTOPP.

Details about CTOPP are presented here to provide a specific example of the differences in developmental trajectories and the asymptotes reached in assessment instruments. Similar criticisms can be directed to other early reading assessments, including the Dynamic Indicators of Basic Literacy Skills (DIBELS), the TPRI, and the PALS, because they include assessments of constrained skills such as letter knowledge, concepts about print, and phonemic awareness. It is worth noting that these early skill assessments typically report Pearson correlations to show the relations with other reading tests to establish concurrent and predictive validity. However, the psychometric data are necessarily skewed from novice to expert status, and those variable distributions influence the correlations. That is why reconsideration of the differences among skills is important.

Developmental Constraints

There are four important constraints on the developmental trajectories of reading skills. The first constraint is *unequal learning* because some letters, concepts, and phonemes are learned more quickly and thoroughly than others. They are fixed effects with heterogeneous variance that result in nonlinear learning among elements. For example, the letters x and q are learned later and more slowly than the letters m and s, and phoneme rhyming is generally easier with consonant-vowel-consonant words than more complex patterns. Unequal learning of exemplars of concepts or instances of rules becomes a problem when skills such as alphabet knowledge and phonemic awareness are treated as uniform skills, especially in assessments that presume random sampling of equivalent elements.

A second developmental constraint is *duration of learning*. Some reading skills, such as learning the alphabet, are mastered in a few years, whereas other skills, such as vocabulary, are not. Whether the learning occurs during childhood or during adulthood does not change the fact that the degree of learning is more rapid and more complete for some skills. These temporal constraints are not evident in unconstrained skills that continue to develop over the life course. Mastered skills must exhibit floor and ceiling effects in the longitudinal course of acquisition because constrained skills develop from nonexistent to fully acquired to automatic. Granted that some reading skills may not be mastered perfectly or completely, they approach an individual growth asymptote as acquisition slows or a ceiling is attained. Reading rate, for example, becomes more stable for each individual by middle school, yet reading rates vary widely between people.

The third developmental constraint is *universal mastery*. Some reading skills and concepts reveal mastery of identical information among people. All skilled readers of English know the 26 letters of the alphabet and the phonemes associated with them. Likewise, all competent readers know the identical (or nearly so) concepts about print and understand phonemic rhyming, segmentation, and blending in the same manner. On assessments of these reading skills, they would have the identical y-intercepts or asymptotes. This is a critical feature of constrained skills because it results in zero (or at least minimal) variance between individuals when the constrained skill is at asymptotic levels. Contrast a universal constraint with less constrained variables such as growth in height or vocabulary. Both may reach asymptote in adulthood, or at least exhibit slower rates of change, but the asymptotes are different across individuals and the differences in the y-intercepts are normally distributed. This is not the case for universally mastered skills that attain the identical intercepts and have no enduring individual differences. Thus, the differences during acquisition of universally mastered skills (in terms of onset, rate, or duration) are minor compared to the similarity over most of the life span. Unconstrained skills continue to develop over time and may reveal enduring differences between individuals over the life span. This is a crucial distinction that has implications for the kinds of statistical analyses and interpretations that are appropriate with each kind of skill.

The analysis of developmental trajectories is more complicated because the sigmoid growth curves of various skills can vary widely in age of onset and duration of growth. Consider the subtests in the CTOPP. The normative data reveal that Sound Matching, Blending Words, and Phoneme Reversal are acquired rapidly by 7 to 8 years of age, whereas Segmenting Nonwords and Elision are mastered more slowly. When they are combined in composite scores by statistical techniques, the fundamental differences among different growth curves are obscured. The data may have improved normality of dependent variables but at an undisclosed cost of reduced validity. Evidently, designers of the Woodcock-Johnson reading test recognized the problem with a low ceiling on letter naming, so they created composite scores of letter naming and word identification. Creating composite scores to skirt skewed data solves the normality problem but confounds what is being measured.

There are many studies that illustrate how mastery of constrained skills may confound data analyses and interpretation. For example, Morris et al. (2003) report a longitudinal study of the relations among reading skills in children during kindergarten and first grade. They used a LISREL model to test the relations among emerging skills, but they failed to consider the conceptual and methodological constraints in their data. For example, Table 2.3 in their report shows clearly that children's alphabet knowledge and beginning consonant awareness were at ceiling levels at Times 2, 3, and 4 in their study, and measures of children's word recognition and phoneme segmentation were at floor levels for Times 1, 2, and 3. Nevertheless, they used traditional statistical analyses that assume normally distributed measures. From their longitudinal analyses, they concluded that the developmental sequence of acquisition for seven reading skills is as follows: alphabet knowledge, beginning consonant awareness, concept of word in text, spelling with beginning and ending consonants, phoneme segmentation, word recognition, and contextual reading ability.

The last two skills are unconstrained and would be predicted to develop longer and slower than the other five constrained skills. It is possible to predict the order of acquisition based only on the size of successively increasing knowledge sets within each skill and greater constraints in measurement among the early emerging skills. The authors argue that concepts about words (i.e., finger pointing to words as the story is read) are important precursors to phonemic awareness and should be emphasized in instruction. This may be true only in the trivial sense that concepts about words is a smaller set of knowledge that is learned more rapidly than phonemic awareness, and it is a necessary but not sufficient condition for other skills to emerge. Although the empirical identification of patterns of emerging developmental skills is important, the interpretations would be

more accurate and complete if the conceptual distinctions among developing skills were considered.

A fourth developmental constraint on reading skills is *codependency*. Some precursors might be necessary for a skill to be acquired, so it is constrained by its relation to other skills. For example, there are many skills involved in language reception, discrimination, and production that underlie emerging literacy skills. These skills may be necessary prerequisites for literacy development. Specifically, phoneme identification of consonants precedes identification of vowels and may be a necessary precursor to segmentation and blending skills. In general, comprehension of text depends on decoding the words; decoding is a necessary but not sufficient condition for understanding text. Many constrained reading skills are dependent on cognitive and linguistic development and are acquired during childhood about the same time. The parallel and simultaneous development of language and literacy skills leads to multicolinearity of these variables in research studies and makes it especially difficult to separate the relations among the skills during periods of rapid development. The codependency also may invalidate correlational analyses.

Researchers have analyzed reading skills as if they are independent, when many are required as precursors or enabling skills for others (e.g., Fuchs, Fuchs, Hosp, & Jenkins, 2001). Thus, there is a positive correlation during acquisition between codependent skills that is logically necessary during acquisition, but the relation will disappear when both skills are fully mastered and there is minimal variance in either one. This pattern of transitory relations and later lack of relations between skills is a consequence of the developmentally codependent constraints on the skills. The constrained skills view explains the transitory correlation patterns as logical, conceptual, and empirical consequences of children's mastery of constrained skills that are developmental precursors and enablers of other skills.

It is important to note that the codependency may be asymmetrical when one skill enables another. Thus, the lack of skill A may be correlated with the lack of skill B, if B depends on A, but the proficiency of skill A does not imply that skill B is also proficient (if A is a necessary but not sufficient condition for skill B). This asymmetrical relation is evident among novice readers when the lack of oral reading fluency is correlated with the lack of comprehension, but fluency is not necessarily correlated with comprehension among skilled readers (S. Paris, Carpenter, A. Paris, & Hamilton, 2005). In more general terms, this means that emerging or novice skills may display codependent relations with other reading skills, as well as greater variance than the same subjects with highly proficient skills. Thus, positive correlations are evident only among partially developed skills and not evident at all among mastered skills. One implication of this asymmetrical relation is that positive correlations might be observed only for novice skill users, struggling readers, or readers with skill deficits because the lack of alphabet knowledge and phonemic awareness is correlated with the lack of effective word recognition, fluency, and comprehension. Consequently, models of reading skills built only on struggling readers with poor skills may overemphasize asymmetrical relations between the lack of codependent skills. The positive correlations between poor basic skills and poor reading achievement are exactly what is expected if the basic skills are necessary but not sufficient for proficient reading development. Thus, a general implication for reading theories and practices is that deficit models of unskilled reading may provide an incomplete and inaccurate characterization of the developmental relations among reading skills for older readers who have mastered basic skills.

Methodological Constraints

Some constraints result from methods used to gather data. Mundane examples of measurement constraints include rubrics with narrow ranges and unreliable interrater agreement and assessment tasks that are too easy or difficult so the data are skewed empirically but not necessarily conceptually. Codependency between skills provides a more compelling example of methodological constraints because the use of one skill may depend on a minimum or critical level of another skill. Consider two examples of reading skill "thresholds": oral reading accuracy and oral reading rate. Both are constrained skills, yet they have been treated as unconstrained variables in traditional research. Accuracy is constrained conceptually because skilled reading is not distributed around a midpoint of 50% accurate word identification. Indeed, 100% accuracy is the goal and preferred skill level, so the measure is constrained conceptually. Accuracy is also constrained as a research variable because educators and researchers consider a level of 95% accu-

rate word identification to be essential for comprehending text (Lipson & Wixson, 2003). This means that accuracy sets a threshold for comprehension and is a highly skewed skill with limited variance when compared to other reading skills.

Reading rate is constrained by speed of speech production and automatic word recognition, but in practice is less constrained than accuracy. Most children read aloud at similar rates as they learn to decode words, and few read fewer than 40 to 50 words correct per minute (wcpm). The midrange of oral reading rate for first graders in the fall is about 53 wcpm, whereas fifth graders at the 50th percentile in the fall read about 105 wcpm (Hasbrouck & Tindal, 1982). At each successive grade level, children read on average about 13 more words per minute. Thus, the range of reading rate is constrained within and between grades by a modest range of growth each year. By middle school, children's reading rate approaches adult asymptotes, about 150 to 200 wpm. Reading very slowly or very quickly may degrade comprehension, so oral reading rate is constrained by speech rate, expertise, and attempts to understand text while decoding print. Certainly, the complexity of text, the familiarity of vocabulary, the audience, and the purpose for reading also influence rate of reading. The thresholds for reading accuracy and rate increase with age and instruction, but reading accuracy, and rate to a lesser degree, are constrained skills conceptually, developmentally, and empirically.

Correlations between fluency and comprehension for highly accurate oral readers have little variance to begin with (in the data), so modest correlations are the most that can be expected. Floor effects, though, are paradoxical because of the asymmetrical codependency and because accuracy below a threshold of 90% disrupts understanding. Even though there is little variance in very low scores on fluency and comprehension, they will covary by necessity when assessed on the same text because lack of fluency ensures lack of comprehension; that is, there can be no comprehension if the words cannot be read accurately. It makes no sense to assess the relation between fluency and comprehension when oral reading accuracy is at low levels because the relation will always reveal the obvious and spurious positive correlations. It should not be surprising that children who cannot recognize many words in a passage also cannot comprehend it. The nonindependence of the variables at low levels of decoding certainly confounds and inflates the positive relation, and it may invalidate correlational analyses involving oral reading accuracy.

So, why do some studies find modest positive correlations between oral reading fluency and comprehension (Kuhn & Stahl, 2003)? Sometimes the studies include data from many readers who are reading below 90% accuracy, so the data include cases of readers who cannot decode or comprehend the text. The variance in scores below 90% accuracy is huge and yields positive correlations with comprehension because both scores are so low for poor readers. Even when the majority of subjects have accuracy scores above 90%, the correlations with comprehension are unduly influenced by the few cases with the most variance, outliers in a statistical sense, because there is little variance in fluency scores among the best readers. Readers who have less than 90% accurate oral reading may have a wide variety of reading problems, including inadequate prior knowledge, poor vocabulary, unfamiliarity with standard English, unfamiliarity with the passage genre and test format, and motivational obstacles such as low self-efficacy and self-handicapping strategies (S. Paris & A. Paris, 2001). Thus, oral reading accuracy can be influenced by many different experiences and skills, and the oral reading fluency score may be only a proxy measure for many other influences on reading development.

Some researchers have correlated fluency and comprehension scores on different tasks to avoid the codependency problem between skills. For example, oral reading fluency can be calculated on one text and comprehension can be assessed on standardized reading tests. This seems questionable because the relation between the two cognitive processes is important within texts, not between texts. Assessing the skills on independent texts treats the skills as independent abilities. Correlations between fluency scores on one reading task and comprehension scores on another task generally yield positive correlations. However, the interpretation is debatable. Advocates argue that the two skills are positively related because of the positive correlation, but the analyses of independent texts indicate that the correlation is between subjects and not cognitive processes. Subjects low in one skill tend to be low in the other skill, but fluent readers are not necessarily good comprehenders because of the asymmetry. Proxy effects also operate, though, because highly fluent readers might have better intellectual skills and more previous literacy experiences than low fluent readers. The apparently simple positive correlation is thus confounded by

the codependency between skills, the asymmetrical relation between necessary and sufficient skills, and the multicolinearity of multiple factors that affect fluency and comprehension.

IMPLICATIONS FOR RESEARCH AND POLICIES

The central point of this chapter is that fundamental conceptual and developmental differences among components of reading influence research methods, data analyses, and interpretations of relations among reading skills. The differences among skills were regarded as constraints to identify how the developing trajectories of different skills can exhibit different slopes, intercepts, durations of learning, and ranges of influence. The effects of the constraints are most evident in the data when the distributions are skewed due to floor and ceiling effects. These may be due to subject selection, task difficulty, or learning at initial or expert levels. The skewed data are not aberrations in data that are usually normally distributed, and they should not be corrected by sampling, data transformations, or data aggregations. Instead, the data are skewed as children acquire and refine the skills except for the brief time when most children in the sample exhibit partial mastery.

In any component model of reading, the skills should also be expected to become interdependent and intercorrelated as they become reciprocally beneficial. For example, as children learn to segment and blend phonemes by identifying and combining onset-rime patterns (such as d-og or b-all), they use knowledge about letter names and sounds, orthographic processes, phonemic awareness, vocabulary knowledge, and previous experience with such tasks to break and make words. Multicolinearity of component skills should be expected in developmental data on reading, and this confounds interpretations of correlations among skills, both concurrent and criterion-related correlations. For example, in the landmark evaluation of first-grade reading programs, Bond and Dykstra (1967) examined a variety of data from pupils, schools, and communities to determine how the variables are related to achievement in reading and spelling in first grade. The pupil measures included a variety of constrained (e.g., phoneme discrimination, letter naming) and unconstrained (e.g., intelligence test, word meaning) skills that were analyzed in the same ways with correlations and analyses of variance. As one example of the multicolinearity of the data, the intercorrelations among 13 pupil measures, calculated for each of 6 types of reading instruction (see Tables 2 through 7 in Bond & Dykstra, 1967) ranged from $r = .16$ to $.84$ with most correlations between .3 and .6. Similar correlations were found between all pupil measures of reading and learning and the Stanford Paragraph Meaning Test.

The Bond and Dykstra (1967) study was one of the first large-scale efforts to review reading research with the goal of identifying evidence to substantiate methods to teach reading in primary grades. Recent research reviews, such as the National Reading Panel (2000), had similar purposes with the additional goal of establishing national policies for reading assessment and instruction. Although we applaud the intentions of these efforts, we think that the methods and analyses applied to constrained reading skills should be reevaluated because the developmental differences among reading skills are numerous and important. We examine some implications for policies in the next section.

The Five Essential Components of Reading

Reviews of reading research by Adams et al. (1998), Snow et al. (1998), and the National Reading Panel (2000) provided the foundation for federal legislation based on scientific reading research and evidence-based approaches. One notable outcome of the reports was the emphasis on the five essential components of reading in both instruction and assessment. The impact on reading materials and practices in classrooms across America has been dramatic. Although many psychologists and educators were enthusiastic about the larger role of scientific research, others worried that the evidence was selective and debatable. Protests about the educational policies, however, did not challenge the scientific bases of the claims, so they were interpreted as complaints about accountability or preferences for unproven methods. The constrained skills view challenges the research methods, data analyses, and interpretations of the component view of reading on scientific grounds.

One implication of differential reading constraints is that the five essential components differ widely in developmental trajectories and scope. Alphabet knowledge and phonological awareness are undoubtedly important and necessary precursors to skilled reading, but they are learned in a few years, usually between the age of 4 and 8 years, when children are provided direct instruction and practice with the skills. During rapid acquisition, differences in relative learning are correlated with a wide variety of other developmental accomplishments (concurrent and predictive correlations) because they provide indicators of an educationally supportive environment and greater relative achievement compared to their peers. Alphabet knowledge and phonological awareness usually are mastered to a high level before other reading skills are proficient, so asymptotic performance decreases longitudinal correlations. This yields unstable and transitory correlations with subsequent reading achievement.

Oral reading fluency is a popular instructional goal and assessment target because children who can read quickly, accurately, and with expression have integrated component skills into automatic word identification. Fluent reading builds on many other component skills and is an indicator of automatic skills, but it is constrained in several ways. The developmental trajectory reveals a period of halting and disfluent word reading, usually fewer than 50 wcpm in first grade, with progressive automatic decoding in elementary grades until an asymptote of 150 to 200 wcpm is reached by adolescence. Correlations with oral reading fluency vary along the trajectory, with weaker correlations evident at both early and late phases of learning to read. Transitory effects of fluency can be explained by the longitudinal course of progressive mastery of a constrained skill.

Oral reading fluency is also constrained in the codependent relation with comprehension because readers cannot be expected to understand text when they cannot read at least 90% of the words. Past research has analyzed the relation between fluency and comprehension as if they were independent skills (Fuchs & Fuchs, 1999), but the constrained skills view suggests that there is a threshold of oral reading fluency required to enable comprehension. However, the threshold of fluency is necessary but insufficient for comprehension because many readers, especially after grades 3 to 4, can identify words fluently yet fail to comprehend the text (S. Paris et al., 2005). Correlations between oral reading fluency and comprehension are strongest when assessed in beginning readers or when assessed with different texts, and in both conditions, the variance is explained mostly by readers who have poor fluency because disfluent reading leads to comprehension failures more often than fluent reading leads to comprehension success.

The five essential components of reading, in our view, might be reinterpreted as three important foundation skills and two essential components of reading. Although we have not examined vocabulary and comprehension in detail in this chapter, both components begin to develop before print-related skills and continue to develop throughout the life span. Both have large scopes and ranges of influence, and both enable the construction of meaning during reading. Variations in vocabulary and comprehension between individuals are enduring and stable differences compared to the transient differences between children in constrained skills. Both deserve amplified instruction and assessment at all phases of learning to read because they are fundamental cognitive and language skills that transcend reading and are fundamental to education (A. Paris & S. Paris, 2003).

Reanalyses of Constrained Skill Assessments

Another implication of the constrained skills view is that traditional reading research and assessments need to be reexamined because the claims made from the data may not be valid. We summarize some of the problems mentioned throughout the chapter. One factor is subject selection. If significant relations among components and achievement measures depend on the relative degree of learning of the subjects, then the effects must be interpreted as transitory rather than enduring. This applies to cross-sectional and longitudinal data for skills that exhibit unstable and decreasing correlations with increasing mastery. A second factor is skewed data. Researchers should analyze and report the skew and kurtosis in their data. They should not apply statistical transformation to the data to normalize distributions that conceptually are not normally distributed. Third, raw scores on component skills should not be aggregated because this confounds different developmental trajectories and artificially creates normalized data. Fourth, researchers may need to use nonparametric statistics to analyze constrained skills that have nonlinear and asymptotic trajectories.

The reason for reanalyzing the data is to avoid misinterpretations of relations among component skills. Two misinterpretations persist in claims about reading components. The first is that the purported correlations between reading achievement and constrained components such as alphabet knowledge, concepts about print, and phonemic awareness are stable and enduring relations. They are not, and the claims ignore the transitory, unstable, and declining correlations with progressive mastery of constrained skills. The second problem is the seductive causal inference made from the consistent correlations between constrained skills and subsequent achievement. Although some researchers are careful to interpret the correlations between constrained components and reading achievement as an indicator, not a cause, of later achievement, the research paradigms often do not include assessments of other environmental variables that may mediate the effects, such as parental assistance and literacy experiences. The proxy effects are likely for constrained skills because early rapid learning of specific print-related knowledge and skills reflects social and environmental conditions instead of stable and enduring individual differences. For example, Scanlon and Vellutino (1996) reported a correlation between letter identification and reading achievement of $r = .56$, but they also found the correlations between number identification and reading achievement to be $r = .59$ (cited in Snow et al., 1998). Thus, early advantages in letter knowledge compared to peers may simply be a marker of generally advantageous environments that result in better learning and achievement on a variety of skills. That is precisely why it is incorrect to interpret predictive correlations as mandates for specific skill instruction.

Reliability and Validity

Traditional assessments of reading skills use correlations to establish reliability and validity, but we have shown that correlations based on nonlinear developmental trajectories, especially those with universal asymptotes, yield unstable patterns that are dependent on the specific sample tested. How can alphabet knowledge be considered a valid assessment if it yields low, strong, and no correlations with reading achievement when it is tested on the same children at three time points between 4 and 7 years of age? The assertion that it is significant and therefore "valid" for the middle time point alone does not meet the criterion of scientific validity because it is transitory. We believe that all assessments of constrained skills yield a similar pattern of unstable correlations with progressive mastery, so all claims about criterion-related validity of constrained skills are suspect. Traditional research has found significant correlations between constrained skills and later achievement, but those depend on the specific sample of children and stimulus items that yield nonskewed data. They are special cases that are not replicable across children of widely different ages and skill levels.

Another confound in the correlations is the complexity of the skill. Letter knowledge, and associated skills such as rapid letter naming, are discrete compared to answering multiple-choice questions about the meaning of text. Constrained skills are more discrete and less confounded with other skills than unconstrained skills. Discrete skills are easier to assess and quantify than more complex skills such as vocabulary and comprehension. The ease of measurement may yield higher reliability and validity estimates, too. Unconstrained skills, such as comprehension, will have lower test-retest reliability because of the learning that occurs with the first reading of text. Correlations to establish concurrent and predictive validity may also be lower than those for discrete skills because (a) there are more confounded component skills involved in comprehension, (b) the specific text and questions can vary widely in familiarity and difficulty, (c) comprehension depends on motivation and strategic reading, and (d) discrete skills have more congruence and similarity among items than complex skills (Carpenter & Paris, 2005). The last point is illustrated by the greater similarity of segmenting, blending, or rhyming different words than the similarity of reading different texts and answering questions about them. Thus, traditional psychometric criteria for measuring reliability and validity might privilege some skills over others if only the strengths of the correlations are compared.

Effects of Intervention on Different Skills

Constrained skills can be taught more readily than unconstrained skills, partly because the sets of knowledge are smaller and more discrete. For example, teaching a 5-year-old the names of 10 letters can have a dramatic effect on letter knowledge assessments, whereas teaching the same child 10 new vocabulary words is unlikely to influence a general vocabulary assessment. Of course, interventions will be most effective during a developmental window of rapid acquisition when the prerequisite knowledge and skills are available. Because the scopes of knowledge are smaller, the developmental windows more narrow, and the learning trajectories more rapid, constrained skills show larger responses to intervention than unconstrained skills.

The responses to intervention for constrained skills can be dramatic over short time intervals, but the effects often wash out over time because all children acquire the skills eventually. This is true for alphabet knowledge, concepts about print, and most aspects of phonemic awareness. Interventions on constrained skills usually have highly specific effects also with little

transfer to less related skills. In contrast, when interventions are successful on unconstrained skills, such as vocabulary and comprehension, the effects may last longer and generalize more diffusely because the skills are more complex and interrelated with other skills.

IMPLICATIONS FOR EDUCATIONAL PRACTICE

Let's return to the example of Ms. Jones, a first-grade teacher, to examine the implications of her district's assessment policies for her classroom reading instruction and assessment. Her district uses the Stanford Achievement Test, ninth edition (SAT-9) to assess reading in grades 3 to 8. They also use the state-mandated reading proficiency test in grades 4, 7, and 10. Ms. Jones, like other K–3 teachers, uses the state-sponsored battery of early reading assessments of alphabet knowledge, phonemic awareness, concepts about print, and oral reading fluency. She has attended workshops about informal reading inventories and would like to use them but does not have adequate time to assess each child individually for 20 to 30 minutes. Her district reading coordinator recognized the problem and recommended that all K–3 teachers use the DIBELS (Good & Kaminski, 2002). Part of the appeal of the DIBELS is the 1-minute samples of oral reading and other quick assessments of letter knowledge and phonemic awareness. The DIBELS allows easy scoring and data records along with prescriptions for instruction based on the results. The superintendent is impressed with the use of data to identify struggling readers, the data available to track the adequate yearly progress of each classroom and school, and the fact that the DIBELS is widely used across the country. Ms. Jones learns to administer the DIBELS assessments 3 times per year, more frequently for her poorest readers, and to use the data in reports to parents and the district. She is uncomfortable with the amount of time she spends assessing children's reading, and she wishes there were better assessments of comprehension, but she feels empowered to document students' growth and to align her assessment and instructional practices.

This scenario represents the quandaries of a typical primary grade teacher who must increase the frequency and amount of reading assessment while also increasing the amount and intensity of explicit instruction, usually within a 60- to 90-minute block of time each morning.

Inadequate time for both assessment and instruction is the main problem, but many teachers also complain about the lack of materials, resources, and professional aides needed to work with an increasingly diverse group of students. Many first-grade teachers have 25 or more students in a class, which may include children with learning difficulties, Attention-Deficit/Hyperactivity Disorder, and native languages other than English. Children with special needs often participate in special programs during and after school, so Ms. Jones tries to meet with the paraprofessionals, tutors, and parents to coordinate instruction for each child. Although Ms. Jones is an excellent teacher, she is frustrated by the lack of time to work individually with the children who most need her help to learn to read.

Prescriptive Instruction

Educational assessments should be connected to instruction so that diagnoses of difficulties lead to direct interventions. However, when the diagnoses of reading difficulties indicate incomplete mastery of constrained skills, educators run the risk of treating the symptoms rather than the underlying problems. This problem is evident in the case of Ms. Jones and can be illuminated by an analysis of the DIBELS (Good & Kaminski, 2002). The DIBELS was designed as part of a system of accountability as well as prevention by providing measures of early reading that predict reading success or difficulty (Good, Simmons, & Kame'enui, 2001). The value of the instrument is based on claims about the predictive validity of the DIBELS to assess reading development and to identify individual children who are at risk. Good et al. explain: "The premise of assessment examined in this study is that fluency as represented by accuracy and rate pervades all levels of processing involved in reading . . . and that fluency on early foundational skills can be used to predict proficiency on subsequent skills in reading" (p. 264). The DIBELS (in the original version) assesses three of the five "big ideas" in early reading: letter-sound knowledge, phonemic awareness, and fluency. All of these are constrained skills, and the evidence used to substantiate them is flawed. The same criticisms described earlier about letter-sound knowledge, phonemic awareness, and oral reading fluency undermine the validity of the DIBELS.

Reading rate, as measured by oral reading fluency, is constrained by many factors, including (a) the rate of speech production, (b) automatic decoding and word recognition, (c) developmental factors such as motor control of the vocal apparatus, and (d) social factors such as anxiety. Clearly, these variables also interact with age and situation. Children speak slower than adults, and they also read aloud more slowly because of these factors. Reading rate is constrained as a measure because beginning readers in first grade rarely read at a rate below 20 wcpm and highly skilled readers in fifth grade rarely read faster than 180 wcpm (Hasbrouck & Tindal, 1982). The average reading rate at each grade level from grades 1 to 5 increases about 10 to 20 wcpm within subjects, so there are developmental normative expectations for reading rate that are constrained within and between grade levels. This means that rate increases with age and expertise, that growth in rate within individuals is small, and that reading rate reaches different asymptotes for different individuals.

Most of the variance in young children's reading rate is accounted for by automatic decoding skills, so this may be the main factor accounting for developmental improvement in reading rate. To the extent that this is true, rate is a proxy for automatic word recognition. This explanation seems reasonable, but automaticity is only one of several factors underlying reading rate. These two factors, automatic decoding and reading rate, have been conflated in explanations of individual reading proficiency versus group differences in relative proficiency because rate generally is a correlate of better reading when compared among children.

One problem is confounding individual development over time with individual expertise at one time point. Reading rate increases within individuals over time with increasing skill, so faster reading is an indicator of better reading due to faster word recognition, automatic decoding, and so forth that improve with age. However, this does *not* imply that the same person can understand a text better if it is read quickly. In fact, there is no evidence from within-subjects research that comprehension is better if individuals are forced to read faster. On the contrary, individuals who read slowly and strategically with rereadings and comprehension checks comprehend more than when those same people read quickly. This is intuitively obvious: Readers can employ more strategies for engaging and checking their comprehension when they read slowly and silently than orally and quickly. Reading aloud prevents readers from using many strategies and places a premium on rate. Thus, reading quickly does not necessarily indicate good comprehension, and reading a text more quickly is not a within-subject measure of greater expertise when assessed at the same time.

The second problem is now evident: Reading rate is a proxy measure for developmental changes in reading because it assesses differences between subjects (or within subjects over time). Children who can read 150 wcpm are different from children who can read only 50 wcpm due to many factors, including age, automaticity, vocabulary, and reading experiences. Studies that have established the predictive validity of oral reading fluency use between-subjects data to show that reading rate correlates with other measures of reading achievement. For example, Good and Jefferson (1998) found Pearson correlations between .52 and .91 in eight different studies when fluency measures were correlated with later measures of reading achievement. These correlations indicate that children who read slowly at first testing later scored more poorly on achievement tests, and, conversely, children who read quickly at a young age scored better later. The error in method is assuming that fluency scores and achievement data are "ability estimates" of children that are independent of the text that is read (because rate and comprehension were assessed in different tasks) and independent of other concurrent experiences. The error in logic is concluding that reading faster leads to better reading that leads to better achievement test scores. Fleisher, Jenkins, and Pany (1979–1980) showed that training poor readers to decode rapidly did not improve their comprehension. The erroneous reasoning is amplified in the Good et al. (2001) prevention model that assumes that teaching children to read more quickly will make them better readers. This is spurious reasoning based on correlational evidence, and it leads to scientifically false claims about prevention of reading difficulties that are wrong and dangerous.

The errors in interpreting the data are twofold. First, researchers have examined the simple correlations between reading rate and later outcomes in isolation and interpreted them without regard for the other factors that underlie reading improvement over time. This makes the correlations about predictive validity only proxy measures or symptomatic correlations because there is no experimental evidence to support the fact that making people read faster improves their comprehension. The researchers have ignored the underlying factors that explain why reading rate varies between subjects, such as automaticity and experience, in their focus on rate alone. Second, the researchers have made within-subjects claims from between-subjects data that are not justified. Differences in reading proficiency between children may be indicated by fluency measures, but this does not mean that ameliorating the rate differences will improve reading proficiency within individuals. The prevention models advocated by special educators and school psychologists who created the DIBELS are founded on erroneous reasoning about simple correlations and misinterpretations of between-subjects data. Faster reading is an outcome of more skilled reading, but there is no evidence that it is a cause of better reading.

Does this mean that oral reading fluency is an invalid assessment? No, it can help identify children with reading difficulties, but fluency should be regarded in the same way a thermometer is used to identify illness. Children who read slowly and inaccurately may be poor readers and they may have a wide assortment of problems that contribute to their difficulties, but speedier reading is not the prescription or cure. The irony is that slow readers may benefit from instruction that helps automate decoding skills, and if the desired outcome is only speedier reading, then fluency practice and instruction may help (Rasinski & Hoffman, 2003). However, fluent, accurate oral reading does *not* lead automatically to good reading comprehension. Children may be taught to read more quickly, and some may read with better comprehension, but many will become rapid word callers with poor comprehension. This is an inappropriate educational goal. Thus, reading rate, like other constrained skills, may be a necessary but not sufficient condition for reading proficiency.

CONCLUSIONS

Assessment of children's reading has a long history in American education and remains a foundation for improving teaching and learning. The consequences for teachers and students are enormous, yet there are few analyses of the developmental parameters that underlie the assessments. Our analysis of early reading assessments reveals how developmental trajectories of different skills may contradict the prevailing component skills view of reading development. The nonlinear growth, universal mastery, and codependency of some reading skills may confound early reading assessments and lead to misinterpretations of data about early reading.

Our analyses suggest that early reading skills such as alphabet knowledge, concepts about print, orthographic processing, phonological awareness, and oral reading fluency are constrained in their development in ways that vocabulary and comprehension are not. Those constraints include conceptual, developmental, and methodological limitations that influence the developmental trajectories of the skills. Thus, some reading skills are acquired quickly, some completely, and some interdependently at different ages. Data analyses that ignore these different trajectories run the risk of overemphasizing transitory patterns of significant correlations and temporary gains due to intervention. These correlations may be misinterpreted as causal relations, and skill instruction becomes the prescribed intervention or remediation. These prescriptive errors neglect the proxy effects of the assessments and the multicolinearity of the data and result in oversimplified links between assessment and instruction. We think that consideration of the different developmental trajectories of early reading skills requires reinterpretation of data from early reading assessments as well as longitudinal studies of reading (S. Paris, 2005).

There are also implications of the constrained skills view for educational practices and policies. Teachers are frustrated with the amount and frequency of reading assessments, especially when they take time away from instruction. Repeated measures of basic skills in K–3 grades can lead to instruction that overemphasizes basic skills at the expense of comprehension, vocabulary, and other literacy skills. Just because letter knowledge, rhyming, and reading rate are easy skills to measure in beginning readers does not mean that they should become the focus of the curriculum. When oversimplified assessments are aligned with oversimplified instruction, the short-term result may be improved scores and basic skills, but the risk is that deep understanding about text, and the skills needed to discuss, analyze, and write about it, may be neglected in the K–3 curriculum. Students may exhibit frustration with boredom and lack of motivation to read. Teachers are frustrated if the assessments do not reveal the richness of their literacy instruction and the accomplishments of their students. Both risks are unnecessary, and they can be avoided with assessments of a wider variety of skills and accomplish-

ments. Vocabulary and comprehension assessments are sorely needed, but other assessments of listening, speaking, viewing, and writing are also important because they measure students' thoughtful responses to a variety of texts and genres. Educational policymakers should not be seduced by simple data and dramatic claims about assessments of basic skills among beginning readers. The developmental issues for assessment and instruction are more complex, but richer reading assessments may lead to better reading instruction.

REFERENCES

Adams, M. J. (1990). *Beginning to read: Thinking and learning about print.* Cambridge, MA: MIT Press.

Adams, M. J., & Treadway, J. (2000). *The fox in the box.* Monterey, CA: CTB/McGraw-Hill.

Adams, M. J., Treiman, R., & Pressley, M. (1998). Reading, writing, and literacy. In W. Damon (Editor-in-Chief) & I. E. Sigel & K. A. Renninger (Vol. Eds.), *Handbook of child psychology: Vol. 4. Child psychology in practice* (5th ed., pp. 275–355). New York: Wiley.

Allington, R. L. (1983). The reading instruction provided readers of differing abilities. *Elementary School Journal, 83,* 549–559.

Badian, N. A. (1995). Predicting reading ability over the long-term: The changing roles of letter naming, phonological awareness, and orthographic processing. *Annals of Dyslexia, 45,* 79–96.

Badian, N. A., McAnulty, G. B., Duffy, F. H., & Ala, H. (1990). Prediction of dyslexia in kindergarten boys. *Annals of Dyslexia, 40,* 152–169.

Bond, G., & Dykstra, R. (1967). The cooperative research program in first-grade reading instruction. *Reading Research Quarterly, 2*(4), 5–142.

Bradley, L., & Bryant, P. E. (1983). Categorizing sounds and learning to read: A causal connection. *Nature, 301*(5899), 419–421.

Bus, A. G., & van Ijzendoorn, M. H. (1999). Phonological awareness and early reading: A meta-analysis of experimental training studies. *Journal of Educational Psychology, 91*(3), 403–414.

Byrne, B., & Fielding-Barnsley, R. (1993). Evaluation of a program to teach phonemic awareness to young children: A 2- and 3-year follow-up and a new preschool trial. *Journal of Educational Psychology, 87,* 488–503.

Carpenter, R. D., & Paris, S. G. (2005). Issues of validity and reliability in early reading assessments. In S. G. Paris & S. A. Stahl (Eds.), *Children's reading comprehension and assessment* (pp. 279–304). Mahwah, NJ: Erlbaum.

Castles, A., & Coltheart, M. (1993). Varieties of developmental dyslexia. *Cognition, 47,* 149–180.

Castles, A., & Coltheart, M. (2004). Is there a causal link from phonological awareness to success in learning to read? *Cognition, 91,* 77–111.

Chall, J. S. (1967). *Learning to read: The great debate.* New York: McGraw-Hill.

Clay, M. M. (1972). *Sand: The concepts about print test.* Auckland, New Zealand: Heinemann Educational Books.

Clay, M. M. (1979). *An observation survey of early literacy achievement.* Portsmouth, NH: Heinemann.

Cunningham, A. E. (1990). Explicit versus implicit instruction in phonemic awareness. *Journal of Experimental Child Psychology, 50,* 429–444.

Cunningham, A. E., Perry, K. E., & Stanovich, K. E. (2001). Converging evidence for the concept of orthographic processing. *Reading and Writing, 14,* 549–568.

Cunningham, A. E., & Stanovich, K. E. (1990). Assessing print exposure and orthographic processing skill in children: A quick measure of reading experience. *Journal of Educational Psychology, 82,* 733–740.

Fischer, K. W., & Bidell, T. R. (1998). Dynamic development of psychological structures in action and thought. In W. Damon (Editor-in-Chief) & R. Lerner (Vol. Ed.), *Handbook of child psychology: Vol. 1. Theoretical models of human development* (5th ed., pp. 467–561). New York: Wiley.

Fleisher, L. S., Jenkins, J. R., & Pany, D. (1979–1980). Effects on poor readers' comprehension of training in rapid decoding. *Reading Research Quarterly, 15,* 30–48.

Foorman, B. R., Fletcher, J. M., Francis, D. J., Schatschneider, C., & Mehta, P. (1998). The role of instruction in learning to read: Preventing reading failure in at-risk children. *Journal of Educational Psychology, 90*(1), 37–55.

Fuchs, L. S., & Fuchs, D. (1999). Monitoring student progress toward the development of reading competence: A review of three forms of classroom-based assessment. *School Psychology Review, 28,* 659–671.

Fuchs, L. S., Fuchs, D., Hosp, M. K., & Jenkins, J. R. (2001). Oral reading fluency as an indicator of reading competence: A theoretical, empirical, and historical analysis. *Scientific Studies of Reading, 5*(3), 241–258.

Fugate, M. H. (1997). Letter training and its effect on the development of beginning reading skills. *School Psychology Quarterly, 12,* 170–192.

Good, R. H., & Jefferson, G. (1998). Contemporary perspectives on curriculum-based measurement validity. In M. R. Shinn (Ed.), *Advanced applications of curriculum-based measurement* (pp. 61–88). New York: Guilford Press.

Good, R. H., & Kaminski, R. A. (Eds.). (2002). *Dynamic indicators of basic early literacy skills* (6th ed.). Eugene, OR: Institute for the Development of Educational Achievement.

Good, R. H., Simmons, D. C., & Kame'enui, E. J. (2001). The importance and decision-making utility of a continuum of fluency-based indicators of foundational reading skills for third-grade high-stakes outcomes. *Scientific Studies of Reading, 5*(3), 257–288.

Hasbrouck, J. E., & Tindal, G. (1992). Curriculum-based oral reading fluency norms for students in grades 2 through 5. *Teaching Exceptional Children, 24*(3), 41–44.

Hatcher, J., Hulme, C., & Ellis, A. W. (1994). Ameliorating early reading failure by integrating the teaching of reading and phonological skills: The phonological linkage hypothesis. *Child Development, 65,* 41–57.

Hecht, S. A., Burgess, S. R., Torgesen, J. K., Wagner, R. K., & Rashotte, C. A. (2000). Explaining social class differences in growth of reading skills from beginning kindergarten through fourth-grade: The role of phonological awareness, rate of access, and print knowledge. *Reading and Writing: An Interdisciplinary Journal, 12,* 99–127.

Hulme, C., Hatcher, P. J., Nation, K., Brown, A., Adams, J., & Stuart, G. (2002). Phoneme awareness is a better predictor of early reading skill than onset-rime awareness. *Journal of Experimental Child Psychology, 82,* 2–28.

Illinois Snapshots of Early Literacy. (2004). Springfield, IL: State Board of Education.

Johnston, R. S., Anderson, M., & Holligan, C. (1996). Knowledge of the alphabet and explicit awareness of phonemes in pre-readers: The nature of the relation. *Reading and Writing: An Interdisciplinary Journal, 8,* 217–234.

Juel, C., Griffith, P. L., & Gough, P. B. (1986). Acquisition of literacy: A longitudinal study of children in first and second grade. *Journal of Educational Psychology, 78,* 243–255.

Kuhn, M. R., & Stahl, S. A. (2003). Fluency: A review of developmental and remedial practices. *Journal of Educational Psychology, 95*(1), 3–21.

Lipson, M. Y., & Wixson, K. K. (2003). *Assessment and instruction of reading and writing difficulty.* Boston: Allyn & Bacon.

Lonigan, C. J., Burgess, S. R., & Anthony, J. L. (2000). Development of emergent literacy and early reading skills in preschool children: Evidence from a latent-variable longitudinal study. *Developmental Psychology, 36*(5), 596–613.

McBride-Chang, C. (1999). The ABCs of the ABCs: The development of letter-name and letter-sound knowledge. *Merrill-Palmer Quarterly, 45*(2), 285–308.

Michigan Literacy Progress Profile. (2003). Lansing, MI: Department of Education.

Morris, D. (1992). Concept of word: A pivotal understanding in the learning-to-read process. In S. Templeton & D. Bear (Eds.), *Development of orthographic knowledge and the foundations of literacy: A memorial festschrift for Edmund H. Henderson* (pp. 53–77). Hillsdale, NJ: Erlbaum.

Morris, D., Bloodgood, J. W., Lomax, R. G., & Perney, J. (2003). Developmental steps in learning to read: A longitudinal study in kindergarten and first grade. *Reading Research Quarterly, 38*(3), 302–328.

Muter, V., & Diethelm, K. (2001). The contribution of phonological skills and letter knowledge to early reading development in a multilingual population. *Language Learning, 51*(2), 187–219.

Muter, V., Hulme, C., Snowling, M., & Taylor, S. (1998). Segmentation, not rhyming, predicts early progress in learning to read. *Journal of Experimental Child Psychology, 71,* 3–27.

National Reading Panel. (2000). *Teaching children to read: An evidence-based assessment of the scientific research literature on reading and its implications for reading instruction—Reports of the subgroups.* Bethesda, MD: National Institute of Child Health and Human Development.

No Child Left Behind Act of 2001, Pub. L. No. 107-110, 115 Stat. 1425 (2002).

Paris, A. H., & Paris, S. G. (2003). Assessing narrative comprehension in young children. *Reading Research Quarterly, 38*(1), 36–76.

Paris, S. G. (2005). Re-interpreting the development of reading skills. *Reading Research Quarterly, 40*(2), 184–202.

Paris, S. G., Carpenter, R. D., Paris, A. H., & Hamilton, E. E. (2005). Spurious and genuine correlates of children's reading comprehension (pp. 131–160). In S. Paris & S. Stahl (Eds.), *New directions in assessment of reading comprehension.* Mahwah, NJ: Erlbaum.

Paris, S. G., & Cunningham, A. (1996). Children becoming students. In D. Berliner & R. Calfee (Eds.) *Handbook of educational psychology* (pp. 117–147). New York: Macmillan.

Paris, S. G., & Hoffman, J. V. (2004). Early reading assessments in kindergarten through third grade: Findings from the Center for the Improvement of Early Reading Achievement. *Elementary School Journal, 105*(2), 199–217.

Paris, S. G., & Paris, A. H. (2001). Classroom applications of research on self-regulated learning. *Educational Psychologist, 36*(2), 89–101.

Phonological Awareness Literacy Screening. (2003). Richmond, VA: Department of Education.

Rasinski, T. V., & Hoffman, J. V. (2003). Theory and research into practice: Oral reading in the school literacy curriculum. *Reading Research Quarterly, 38*(4), 510–523.

Rathvon, N. (2004). *Early reading assessment: A practitioner's handbook.* New York: Guilford Press.

Renninger, K. A. (1998). Developmental psychology and instruction: Issues from and for practice. In W. Damon (Editor-in-Chief) & I. E. Sigel & K. A. Renninger (Vol. Eds.), *Handbook of child psychology: Vol. 4. Child psychology in practice* (5th ed., pp. 211–274). New York: Wiley.

Scanlon, D. M., & Vellutino, F. R. (1996). Prerequisite skills, early instruction, and success in first-grade reading: Selected results from a longitudinal study. *Mental Retardation and Developmental Disabilities Research Reviews, 2,* 54–63.

Scarborough, H. S. (1998). Predicting the future achievement of second graders with reading disabilities: Contributions of phonemic awareness, verbal memory, rapid naming, and IQ. *Annals of Dyslexia, 48,* 115–136.

Scarborough, H. S., & Dobrich, W. (1994). On the efficacy of reading to preschoolers. *Developmental Review, 14,* 245–302.

Share, D. L., Jorm, A. F., Maclean, R., & Matthews, R. (1984). Sources of individual differences in reading acquisition. *Journal of Educational Psychology, 76*(6), 1309–1324.

Share, D. L., & Stanovich, K. E. (1995). Cognitive processes in early reading development: Accommodating individual differences into a model of acquisition. *Issues in Education, 1,* 1–57.

Snow, C. E., Burns, M. S., & Griffin, P. (1998). *Preventing reading difficulties in young children.* Washington, DC: National Academy Press.

Stahl, S. A., & Murray, B. A. (1994). Defining phonological awareness and its relationship to early reading. *Journal of Educational Psychology, 86,* 221–234.

Stanovich, K. E. (1980). Toward an interactive-compensatory model of individual differences in the development of reading fluency. *Reading Research Quarterly, 16,* 32–71.

Stanovich, K. E. (1991). Changing models of reading and reading acquisition. In L. Rieben & C. Perfetti (Eds.), *Learning to read: Basic research and its implications* (pp. 19–32). Hillsdale, NJ: Erlbaum.

Stanovich, K. E. (2000). *Progress in understanding reading: Scientific foundations and new frontiers.* New York: Guilford Press.

Stanovich, K. E., Cunningham, A. E., & West, R. F. (1981). A longitudinal study of the development of automatic recognition skills in first graders. *Journal of Reading Behavior, 13,* 57–74.

Stevenson, H. W., & Newman, R. S. (1986). Long-term prediction of achievement and attitudes in mathematics and reading. *Child Development, 57,* 646–659.

Stuart, M. (1995). Prediction and qualitative assessment of 5- and 6-year old children's reading: A longitudinal study. *British Journal of Educational Psychology, 65,* 287–296.

Swanson, H., & Alexander, J. (1997). Cognitive processes as predictors of word recognition and reading comprehension in learning-disabled and skilled readers: Revisiting the specificity hypothesis. *Journal of Educational Psychology, 89*(1), 128–158.

Texas Primary Reading Inventory. (2002). Austin: Texas Education Agency.

Treiman, R. (2000). The foundations of literacy. *Current Directions in Psychological Science, 9,* 89–92.

U.S. Department of Education, National Center for Education Statistics. (2000). *Early Childhood Longitudinal Study: Kindergarten Class of 1998–1999.* Washington, DC: Author.

Vellutino, F. R., Scanlon, D. M., & Chen, R. (1994). The increasingly inextricable relationship between orthographic and phonological coding in learning to read: Some reservations about current methods of operationalizing orthographic coding. In V. W. Berninger (Ed.), *The varieties of orthographic knowledge: Pt. 2. Relationships to phonology, reading, and writing* (pp. 47–111). Dordrecht, The Netherlands: Kluwer Academic.

Wagner, R. K., Torgesen, J. K., & Rashotte, C. A. (1999). *Comprehensive test of phonological processing.* Austin, TX: ProEd.

Wagner, R. K., Torgesen, J. K., Rashotte, C. A., Hecht, S. A., Barker, T. A., Burgess, S. R., et al. (1997). Changing relations between phonological processing abilities and word-level reading as children develop from beginning to skilled readers: A 5-year longitudinal study. *Developmental Psychology, 33*(3), 468–479.

Walsh, D. J., Price, G. G., & Gillingham, M. G. (1988). The critical but transitory importance of letter naming. *Reading Research Quarterly, 23*(1), 108–122.

Willson, V. L., & Rupley, W. H. (1997). A structural equation model for reading comprehension based on background, phonemic, and strategy knowledge. *Scientific Studies of Reading, 1*(1), 45–63.

CHAPTER 3

Becoming Bilingual, Biliterate, and Bicultural

CATHERINE E. SNOW and JENNIFER YUSUN KANG

The issue of linguistic and cultural differences confronts modern societies ubiquitously. The post-World War II years have been characterized by unprecedented and increasingly massive migrations of human individuals and groups from places where they are competent in the local language and cultural rules to places where they are not (Zhou, 2001). These migrations create grave challenges, both for the migrants and for their host societies. Migrants must learn how to function in novel settings, acquiring a new language, a new set of rules for daily life, and often new work and school skills as well. The indigenous inhabitants of the places where the migrants settle must also learn to interact effectively with the newcomers—to serve them in stores, hire them, work with them, and teach them—or else suffer the economic, ethical, social, and interpersonal consequences of avoiding or failing at these interactions.

These challenges of functioning and interacting might seem, on brief reflection, to be hardest for adults. After all, adults typically have already acquired a language and a culture, so they have to suppress old knowledge while acquiring new knowledge. Adults are widely thought to be

incapable of learning a new linguistic/cultural system to a high level, and may well hold such self-defeating beliefs themselves. Indeed, though pessimism about adult capacities to acquire a second language is unfounded (see Marinova-Todd, Marshall, & Snow, 2000), opportunities for immigrants to become fluent second-language speakers are often restricted. For example, the majority of immigrants to the United States from all major sending nations except Jamaica, India, and the Philippines reported speaking "poor English" (U.S. Bureau of the Census, 1993), and political opposition to ongoing immigration in Scandinavia and the Netherlands reflects the failure of immigrant adults in those countries to acquire proficiency in the local language as much as conflicts around religion, social mores, and cultural commitments. In the Netherlands, for example, a policy of *inburgeringsplicht* (responsibility to assimilate) for immigrants tied financial compensation to participation in language courses (see Verhallen, Janssen, Jas, Snoeken, & Top, 1996, for a description). But dissatisfaction with the levels of participation and accomplishment in those courses has led to restrictions on financial support for them (http://www.inburgernet.nl/beleid/bel155.html, retrieved February 1, 2005).

We do not minimize the difficulties adult migrants face in adjusting to their new settings. Nonetheless, we focus in this chapter on the challenges confronting transplanted children and adolescents, as well as the teachers and other caregiving adults in the host cultures who are responsible for promoting their success. Future opportunities and access to educational advantages for their children are the reasons adults most frequently offer for their decision to migrate (C. Suárez-Orozco & Suárez-Orozco, 2001); evaluating the impact on children of their parents' decisions to move to a new setting, and describing the conditions under which the parental aspirations are most likely to be fulfilled, is thus of considerable practical importance.

These challenges of adaptation to a new language and culture for child migrants are reflected in data about their academic achievement. Language minority children are at demonstrably greater risk than native speakers of experiencing academic difficulty, difficulties that have been documented in the United States (Lloyd, Tienda, & Zajacova, 2002), in the Netherlands (Tesser, Merens, van Praag, Iedema, 1999; Verhoeven, 1994), in Great Britain (Runnymede Trust, 1998), and in Japan (DeVos & Wetherall, 1983; Y. Lee, 1991; Shimihara, 1991). The exact source of these academic difficulties—whether control over the target language, difficulties acquiring literacy, the more general challenges of a novel academic system, the consequences of discrimination, or the emotional and motivational challenges of functioning in a foreign culture—is not always easy to determine. Nonetheless, any society that seeks to avoid persistent socioeconomic differences associated with cultural and linguistic background must seek to understand the reasons for the poor academic achievement of immigrant and language minority children and youth.

Furthermore, the functioning of linguistic and cultural minorities in schools, and in the workplace and other institutions of the host culture, sheds light on basic questions about the language development and cultural learning, not just of immigrant or minority group members, but of all human beings. This is one of the many domains in which problems of practice—how best to assist immigrants with the social and educational challenges of adaptation—can yield insights of interest to basic scientists, by generating questions that might not otherwise have arisen, for example:

- How do children learn to function as successful members of their cultural groups?
- What is the role of parents, of peers, and of institutional and academic settings in cultural learning?
- How closely tied to one another are knowledge of language and knowledge of culture?
- Is it possible to be a "native speaker" but not a "native member"?
- Does achieving at high levels in host country schools require assimilation to the host culture?
- What are the limits, if any, on the achievement of full bilingualism, biculturalism, and biliteracy, and to whom do these limits apply?

Answers to these questions would help us understand some general principles of child development, of language acquisition, of literacy development, and of cultural learning, whether for the first time in infancy and early childhood or for the second time at a later age. In addition, answers to these questions would be of great benefit to the educators responsible for the growth and development of groups that increasingly include child immigrants and the children of immigrants, both in the United States and in other parts of the so-called developed world.

We take literacy learning as a focus in this chapter because it represents an important issue in its own right and because literacy is a litmus test—the final common pathway—for many other domains of learning. As we review here, literacy development is multiply determined; successful reading and writing in the later elementary and secondary grades is not possible without high levels of language proficiency, access to large stores of knowledge, and control over the local cultural norms for communication. Thus, through our focus on literacy, we can discuss many aspects of the challenges learners in general, and language minority learners in particular, face. We focus on the group we call L2/C2 learners: children and adolescents faced with the need to acquire a second language (L2) and/or a second culture (C2), either because they have just arrived in a new setting or because their home language (L1) and culture (C1) differ from that of the schools and the larger society. But in forefronting the specific, practice-embedded challenge of understanding and supporting L2/C2 learners, we also consider research on the general case of literacy acquisition and the challenges it presents even to monolingual children for whom home and school represent no sharp discontinuities of language and culture.

L2/C2 learners are as a group at greater than average risk of poor literacy outcomes and associated achievement problems (August & Hakuta, 1997; National Center for Education Statistics, 2003), but it is important to note that there are robust differences in academic outcomes within the language minority and immigrant population that help may shed light on some of the mechanisms by which children acquire the language, literacy, and cultural skills they need. Ogbu (1992) argued that these differences could be accounted for by factors leading to immigration—that voluntary migrants, moving to a new setting in part to promote their children's learning, were more tolerant of the stresses associated with migration, had higher aspirations for social mobility, and were more optimistic for their children's success, with the result that the children were academically more successful. Ogbu's ideas on this topic have been highly influential, but they do not entirely fit the data; Mexican immigrants, for example, are voluntary immigrants who are strongly motivated to improve their children's educational opportunities (C. Suárez-Orozco & Suárez-Orozco, 2001), but their children perform more poorly in school than nonimmigrants or other immigrant groups. It has been argued that the high regard for education Asian immigrants bring with them helps explain their children's generally good school performance, but this explanation ignores differences within the Asian population (S. Lee, 1996) and fails to clarify a mechanism by which those cultural values are transmitted to the children. Furthermore, as Ogbu has pointed out, Asian migrants perform rather poorly in settings where they are discriminated against. So, for example, if culture explains the high achievement of Korean immigrants in the United States, why does it not protect Korean children whose families have immigrated to Japan, where Korean academic achievement is relatively poor?

These disparities across and within immigrant groups suggest the importance of understanding context as well as development. If we hope to answer questions about the determinants of and limitations on academic outcomes for children in general, and for L2/C2 learners in particular, we need to expand our horizons as researchers to integrate information about processes of development with information about local and societal conditions affecting those developmental processes. In other words, these are not questions to be answered by thinking purely as developmental psychologists or educational researchers; to be addressed satisfactorily, they require insights from demography, sociology, anthropology, socio- as well as psycholinguistics, and economics.

CASE EXAMPLES: LEARNING A SECOND LANGUAGE IN CHILDHOOD

Consider the cases of two families who display some of the complexities of migration and L2 learning.

The Lopez Family

A Spanish-dominant 5-year-old girl named Rosario, whose parents have recently immigrated from Oaxaca to Austin, Texas, starts kindergarten. Her mother, trying to choose the program that will best support Rosario's learning of English, puts her in an all-English classroom. Because the adults in Rosario's family speak very little English, they of course continue to speak Spanish at home. Rosario struggles in kindergarten, partly because she doesn't understand much English, but partly because many of her classmates have had far more experience than she has being read to, playing with puzzles, learning numbers and letters, and writing. In first grade, Rosario is in the lowest reading group, which gives her access to some one-on-one tutoring from a reading specialist; as it happens the reading specialist is bilingual and reverts to Spanish occasionally in explaining particularly difficult puzzles in English spelling and word reading. Five years later, Rosario is doing well in fourth grade, reading fluently and eagerly in English and enjoying school. Her spoken English is now fluent, accent-free, and grammatically mostly correct. She still speaks Spanish at home with her parents, but increasingly uses English with her younger siblings. She has not learned to read in Spanish and now has some difficulty talking in Spanish with her parents about things that she is learning at school; she doesn't have the Spanish vocabulary to discuss math, science, or social studies. Thus, her Spanish conversations tend to focus on matters relevant to home and family; if she needs help with homework or wants an explanation about something she heard at school, she turns to her teacher rather than to her parents. By the time Rosario is in high school, she much prefers speaking English to speaking Spanish, often responds to her parents in English when they speak to her in Spanish, and finds herself occasionally unable to understand her parents' conversations, for example, when they turn to such topics as political change in Mexico or medical procedures.

The Jackson Family

Six-year-old Ashley and her 10-year-old sister, Brittany, move with their English-speaking family to Querétaro, Mexico, where their mother has taken a position at El Instituto de Neurobiología. Their mother is eager for her daughters to become bilingual and thus enrolls them in a nearby school where they are the only English speakers. Ashley has completed kindergarten in South Bend and can already read at a late second-grade level in English. Brittany is a fluent reader at an early sixth-grade level and insisted on including several dozen chapter books in the luggage the family took with them. Both Ashley and Brittany find their Spanish-speaking classroom environments intimidating to begin with; Ashley in particular often has tantrums and crying fits when it is time to go to school and seems somewhat depressed during her first months in Querétaro. Only after 4 months in school does Ashley produce any spontaneous Spanish utterances. Meanwhile, though, she is participating fairly successfully in the literacy instruction activities in her first-grade classroom; these consist mostly of filling in worksheets, copying sentences from the board, and reading aloud in chorus. Brittany is more lost at first, because the instruction she encounters involves a lot of teacher talk, which she does not understand. But within a few months, Brittany has learned enough Spanish to make some tentative friendships; she starts to rely on her desk-mate, Maricarmen, to repeat the teacher's instructions slowly or to explain how to do the assignments. Furthermore, Brittany learns to read Spanish after only a few sessions with a tutor and soon is able to understand her textbooks and the written homework instructions with little difficulty. Brittany can even help Ashley with her homework. During Christmas break, their mother insists that the girls spend some time reading books in English, to be sure they not fall behind in English reading skills. As soon as the school year is over, Ashley and Brittany are sent to spend 6 weeks with their grandparents in Maine, a pattern that will continue throughout their elementary school years. Brittany takes Spanish books with her to read on vaca-

tion, but both children are soon happily reading English books borrowed from the local public library. By the end of *primária,* both Ashley and Brittany are fully bilingual, able to talk about things they have learned in school with their parents in either Spanish or English or a mix of both languages. Their mother notes that their Spanish literacy skills are somewhat stronger than their English literacy skills and decides to enroll them in a private bilingual secondary school to ensure that they will develop the skills needed to be able to gain admittance to and to succeed at a university in the United States.

Summary of Language-Learning Cases

On the face of it, Rosario, Ashley, and Brittany all faced the same challenge: learning a new language primarily from exposure in school. Their outcomes, though, are different in important ways; Rosario ended up with greater oral proficiency in her L2 than her L1 and became literate only in the language of schooling. Ashley and Brittany ended up bilingual and biliterate, though the equilibrium between Spanish and English dominance shifted back and forth as their circumstances changed. Rosario's parents were somewhat surprised that she did not end up a fully proficient speaker of Spanish, but they did not know how to intervene to ensure full Spanish proficiency. Ashley and Brittany's parents anticipated the possibility of decline of English skills and invested heavily to ensure maintenance of English, sending the children off to an English-speaking environment every summer, buying them books in English, and choosing a bilingual secondary school.

These three child cases concretize some of the general conclusions derived from research on L2 language/literacy acquisition that:

- Acquiring an L2 in childhood can be intimidating and difficult, lead to temporary emotional problems, and take several years.
- An L1 is at some risk of loss or decline under the influence of an L2.
- A child's continued development of the L1 is more likely if the parents are bilingual and/or highly educated in the L1.
- Higher-status languages and languages associated with schooling and literacy are in general less subject to attrition than lower-status languages.
- L1 literacy skills can be a support to L2 acquisition.

- Learning to read an L2 is easier if one is already literate in an L1.
- Literacy skills contribute to higher levels of oral proficiency in both an L1 and an L2.
- Older children typically learn an L2 faster than younger children, perhaps because of their better developed literacy skills.
- Transfer of literacy skills can support L2 literacy but may not occur automatically across even closely related languages.

These case studies of individual language learners illuminate one aspect of L2/C2 learning. But understanding the full range of relevant issues requires considering a case involving policy as well.

CASE EXAMPLE: BILINGUAL EDUCATION IN THE UNITED STATES

Forty years after the establishment of the first bilingual education programs in the United States, researchers still cannot answer straightforwardly the seemingly simple question, "Does bilingual education work?" No proper experiments comparing bilingual to English-only education for English-language learners have been carried out. The debate about the effectiveness of bilingual education, reinvigorated by Ron Unz's placement of a referendum banning bilingual education on the ballot in California, Arizona, Massachusetts, and Colorado, has been minimally informed by research evidence. Supporters of bilingual education, relying on comparisons of groups that were probably not well matched to begin with, offered data that they interpreted as supporting the greater effectiveness of bilingual education (Willig, 1985). But such data were unconvincing in a political context where the opponents could identify graduates of bilingual education with clearly inadequate English and literacy skills. The slogan adopted by those who had lost faith in bilingual education, "English for the Children," was highly effective. Furthermore, researchers with integrity had to admit that good English-only instruction could also produce adequate literacy outcomes for English-language learners (e.g., Lesaux & Siegel, 2003) and that quality of instruction was more important in determining outcomes than the language in which it was delivered. The referenda greatly reducing access to bilingual education passed in California, Arizona, and

Massachusetts; the referendum failed in Colorado largely because of funding provided by a staunch and wealthy proponent of bilingual schooling. Furthermore, though some states continue to support and celebrate bilingual programs, the impact of No Child Left Behind, with its provision that all children be tested on reading and math starting in third grade and that test scores for English-language learners be reported separately, shifted attention everywhere to literacy performance in English. School districts and states have made decisions to reduce or eliminate bilingual education partly because of these political pressures and partly because its initial promise, that it would eradicate the academic deficits of language minority children, has demonstrably not been achieved. The data suggesting that bilingual education does make modest contributions to academic outcomes are insufficiently convincing to counter the political opposition raised by Unz, the accountability pressures exacerbated by No Child Left Behind, and the increasing loss of public faith in the capacities of local educators to make decisions about children's schooling.

As a National Research Council review of evaluations of bilingual education suggested long before Unz brought bilingual education to the ballot (Meyer & Fienberg, 1992), arguing for or against particular educational treatments for language minority students on the basis of evaluation studies is unlikely to be informative. For one thing, the variation within programs labeled bilingual is as great as the variation across bilingual and English-only programs. Furthermore, program quality is almost certainly more important than program type in determining outcomes. What we really want to know is under what societal circumstances, for which children, and with what educational resources certain policies are effective. Then we must analyze the mechanisms that underlie their effectiveness as a basis for designing educational treatments that will work for other groups of children, under other societal circumstances, and with access to a somewhat different set of educational resources.

In other words, we do not endorse the traditional transmission model for applied research: Work from theory (bilingual education develops and exploits a learner's "common underlying proficiency" and enables the learner to exploit transfer; see Cummins, 1991) toward application (design the program) to evaluation (compare it to some other program). Instead, we suggest reversing the arrows in Figure 3.1: Work from practice

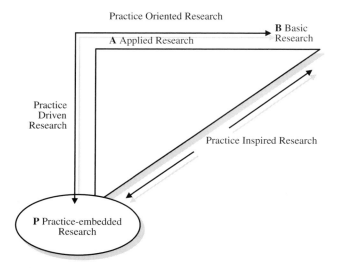

Figure 3.1 The practice-based research triangle. Adapted from Selman and Dray, Chapter 10, this *Handbook,* this volume.

(carefully describe programs that seem to have good outcomes for certain groups of children at risk) toward analysis (figure out what those programs have in common) toward theory (formulate hypotheses about how variations across programs for L2/C2 children in the practices implemented relate to the gains achieved) that can then be tested more rigorously with traditional experimental methods.

This chapter has two closely related goals: to highlight the complexity of the interplay among the various factors influencing educational advancement, in particular achievement in literacy and related academic language skills, for L2/C2 learners, and to argue for the need to substitute practice-embedded and practice-inspired research for traditional transmission-model research in this domain and in other domains similarly characterized by complexity and multidisciplinarity. The first goal relates to the argument for a multidisciplinary approach to thinking about L2/C2 learning. The second goal relates closely to the argument made by Selman and Dray (Chapter 10, this *Handbook,* this volume) about models of research in a similarly challenging domain, social development under conditions of risk.

Before turning to the specific case of language minority children, we outline the challenges of literacy development in general and the ways literacy skills form a path toward (or an obstacle to) learning across the entire range of subjects taught in middle and secondary schools. Then we review the literature on L2/C2 children's literacy development in greater depth, seeking

explanations for the overall poorer academic performance of such children. Finally, we provide an overview of the educational treatments available to L2/C2 learners and highlight a few specific programs and interventions that have been implemented for these learners in preschool and elementary school settings.

REVIEW OF EMPIRICAL LITERATURE

In this section we summarize briefly the very large body of work on literacy development from its roots in early childhood through comprehension of complex texts in the middle and secondary grades.

Literacy Development: The General Case

A large and very robust research literature is available to guide us in describing the default course of early literacy development and the factors that are related to success in learning to read during the first few years of school. A somewhat less complete, but nonetheless substantial, research literature has illuminated the processes involved in reading comprehension and the conditions likely to lead to success in reading comprehension. We summarize these bodies of work here, as a backdrop to understanding how the literacy development of the L2/C2 learner might differ from that presupposed in these descriptions.

A 1998 report of the National Research Council, *Preventing Reading Difficulties in Young Children* (Snow, Burns, & Griffin, 1998), summarized the research on the development of literacy skills, organizing it by answering three questions: What is the normal course of literacy development from birth to age 8? What group and individual factors are most associated with risk of difficulties in literacy development? What are the features of skilled reading that all learners need opportunities to acquire? Findings and conclusions from that report are summarized in the next several paragraphs.

How Early Literacy Develops

Answering the developmental question required considering literacy within the larger context of language and cognitive development. In other words, the National Research Council placed the beginnings of literacy development well before school entry. Particularly in the preschool years, before formal literacy instruction starts, children use literacy skills just as they use other emerging capacities: in play, for purposes of communication, as problems to solve, and in the context of behavioral routines. Playful, communicative, cognitively active engagement with literacy for preschoolers encompasses many sorts of activities, all of which offer opportunities to learn about letters and sounds, to learn about the functions of reading and writing, to acquire cultural rules related to literacy practices, and to develop appropriate affect.

Take as an illustrative example a typical middle-class English-speaking Euro-American child of college-educated parents. She has probably been given books to manipulate and had her attention drawn to pictures in books before her 1st birthday, is read to starting early in her 2nd year as part of a regular naptime or bedtime routine, and by age 2 may well have experienced an accumulated 500+ hours of parent-child book-reading activity (Stahl, van Kleeck, & Bauer, 2003); as a result, by the age of 3 she can recognize dozens of books by their covers, anticipate words or even whole sentences when read to from favorite books, name hundreds of pictures in books, and talk about what will happen next and why in book-based stories. This child probably plays with "refrigerator letters" while her parents are cooking dinner, scribbles with crayons or pens on pads of paper in imitation of adults writing, watches and talks about *Sesame Street* together with her mom or dad, and looks at simple or familiar books on her own; as a result, by age 3 she can write or, using magnetic letters, compose her own name, can recognize and name most upper- and lowercase letters, is starting to notice and "read" print on signs and labels, knows that her parents read the print and not the pictures in her books, and may be starting to produce initial attempts at spelling real words. This child by age 3 has probably heard dozens of different nursery rhymes and songs hundreds of times each, may have completely memorized some Dr. Seuss rhyming books, is starting to be able to respond when asked to name items in a category (fruits, animals, friends), to identify words that rhyme with *cat, dog,* or *lick,* or maybe even to select words that match on beginning sounds (*big* and *bad,* but not *moo*).

This child enters kindergarten with a vocabulary of 8,000 to 12,000 words, able to recognize and name all the letters, with sufficient phonological awareness to isolate beginning and ending phonemes in simple words, and extremely eager to learn how to read. Her kindergarten teacher uses a mildly structured phonics approach; all the kindergarteners in this middle-class

suburban school know the letter names already, so she teaches letter sounds, starting with /m/, /n/, /l/, /b/, /p/, and /d/ and four short vowels. She gives the children lots of practice with little word families in which those letter-sound combinations can be practiced, for example:

map, lap, nap

men, pen, Ben, den

lip, dip, nip

mop, lop, bop, pop

and she seeks out some books for read-aloud (e.g., Dr. Seuss's *Hop on Pop,* Nikola-Lisa's *Bein' with You This Way*) in which these words occur, so that the children can be successful in helping her read them in context.

When all the children are pretty good at these distinctions, she teaches a few more letter-sounds, and short u, so that she can expand the lists used in the word sorts (with *cap, hen, sip,* and *hop,* respectively), can add new lists (*pup, cup, sup/man, can, fan*), and can get children looking at variation at the ends of the words as well as at the beginning (*map, mad, mat, man/sip, sit, sin, sis*). Meanwhile, she also spends at least 45 minutes a day reading books to the children and leading or promoting discussions about them, teaching new vocabulary and lots of general knowledge in the process. She also has the children engage in science observation projects, during which they have to record (using a combination of drawing and writing) what they see when studying leaves, buds, and flowers, then larvae, pupae, and insects, then the behavior of ants in the class ant farm.

With this good beginning, going on to learn the various complexities of spelling and longer word reading in first and second grade is pretty easy for our well-prepared reader, and by third grade she is able to read chapter books independently, fluently, with excellent comprehension and great enthusiasm.

Of course, perfectly normal children in highly literate, middle-class households may deviate from this illustrative case in any of a number of ways. Some may have minor learning disabilities that make it harder for them to attend to individual sounds in words, remember which letter represents which sound, or focus sequentially on all the letters in words. Such children need more time to learn these things and more practice with each of them. Others may have been brought up in bilingual or non-English-speaking homes, so their English vocabularies comprise many fewer words at kindergarten entry. Such children will need to learn English words while learning to read. Others may be physically very active children, or children with short attention spans, so they have had less time being read to and have enjoyed lap-reading less. They may need more explicit instruction in the conventions of literacy because they have had fewer opportunities for incidental learning.

Risk Factors

We sketched here the development of a child who encounters no special difficulties in learning to read. She was not a member of any of the demographic groups that have a higher than average incidence of reading failure: children living in poverty, children with health or nutritional challenges, African Americans, Latinos, L2 speakers, children of parents with low literacy skills, children in homes with few literacy resources. Nor did she have any of the individual factors that are associated with a higher than average risk of reading problems: language delay, hearing loss, a dyslexic or learning-disabled parent, cognitive problems such as mental retardation.

The presence of racial, ethnic, and language minority children in the group at heightened risk of reading difficulties opens up a large set of questions: To what extent are the literacy trajectories of those different risk groups similar? Are Latino children at heightened risk primarily because of limited English skills, or because of poverty and low parental education, or because of a cultural mismatch between their home and their school? Is the risk equivalent for first-generation and later Latinos? For monolingual Spanish-speaking, bilingual, and monolingual English-speaking Latinos? Is the risk for Spanish-speaking Latinos equivalent to that of other immigrant groups of similar social composition who speak other languages, or does identification as a Latino heighten the risks associated with L2 and poverty? Although there are no definitive answers to most of these questions, there are some hints in the data we review in the section on L2/C2 learners.

Skilled Reading

What are the characteristics of skilled reading that constitute the target performance toward which literacy development is aiming? Work using techniques such as eye movement tracking has demonstrated that skilled readers are very dependent on print, looking at and processing most of the letters in almost all of the words on a page. Skilled reading feels as if it goes too fast for such detailed attention, but good readers manage to process frequently occurring sequences of letters very efficiently because they have seen them and converted them into phonological forms so often. Thus, sequences such as *-ation* and *-itude* can be processed as units. Although readers are not aware of this automatic chunking and rapid processing, it becomes obvious because of the difficulty of reading words in which unfamiliar sequences occur, for example, *Ghazi Ajil al-Yawar, Tblisi,* or *diyethyl-m-toluamide.* This aspect of skilled reading is referred to as automaticity.

Conversion of letter sequences into phonological forms is another feature of skilled reading. It seems as if beginning or poor readers are the ones who have to sound out words, whereas skilled readers can move directly from print to meaning. In fact, though, research findings make it quite clear that skilled readers access word meaning through the phonological, or sound-based, form of the word. Access to phonology is so automatic that it is largely unconscious, but failure to access the phonology of lexical items (a process we all engage in at times, for example, when we remember the names of characters in Russian novels just by their initials or first syllables) is a low-level reading strategy and one that does not work in general.

An implication of the print-dependence and phonological processing of skilled readers is that word recognition is only minimally influenced by context. Thus, for example, knowing that one is reading a report about carburetors does not make it easier to read words like *valve, displacement,* or *revolutions.* Knowing that one is reading about carburetors does, of course, help in comprehending the text in which these words occur and in realizing that *valve* refers here to a mechanical device and not a biological structure, and that *revolution* probably has to do with the turning of gears and not the uprising of the oppressed. So contextual information is very important in comprehension, but it has only very minor effects on word reading per se. Thus, good reading instruction focuses on helping children actually read the print in order to read the word, rather than guessing from context at what the word might be.

At the same time, good reading instruction also ensures that children realize that reading the words is not enough. Comprehension is an active process that can be aided by invoking various strategies while reading (e.g., read the title page or chapter headings to see what the text is about, stop and think about why you are reading it, formulate some questions you think the text might answer, stop every once in a while to summarize what you have read, be alert for words or sentences you don't understand and stop to try to figure them out). Children who have not discovered these strategies on their own can be taught them, and teachers can demonstrate how to use them by modeling comprehension work while reading aloud.

Learning to Comprehend

Comprehension is, of course, the goal of reading instruction. *Preventing Reading Difficulties in Young Children* (Snow et al., 1998) emphasized that children need opportunities to develop language skill and stores of knowledge because those capacities are crucial to success at comprehension. But because that report dealt with children only up to age 8, it did not address in detail many of the challenges of reading comprehension, which emerge for many children only in the middle school years, when the texts they are expected to read become more challenging.

The RAND Reading Study Group (RRSG) was asked in 1999 by the assistant secretary of education to formulate a research agenda for work on reading. In its report *Reading for Understanding* (2002; see also Sweet & Snow, 2003, for a more practice-focused presentation of some of the same themes), the RRSG proposed that reading comprehension should be the focus of future federal funding in the area of literacy. In the process of developing the research agenda, the RRSG summarized the topics related to reading comprehension on which research had been carried out and drew some conclusions from that literature that are relevant to understanding the challenges of achieving good comprehension outcomes for all children, and for language minority children in particular.

The RAND report analyzed variability in reading comprehension success as the product of an interaction among the reader, the text, and the reading activity being engaged in, all embedded in a sociocultural context (see Figure 3.2 for a representation of this heuristic). Reader factors that contribute to success at comprehension include skills with low-level reading processes (word recognition, fluency) and high-level reading processes (comprehension strategies), domains of knowledge (linguistic knowledge, including syntax, discourse, and vocabulary, as well as relevant content knowledge), and motivation and domains of interest. Text features include topic, linguistic complexity, and discourse organization. The category activity includes

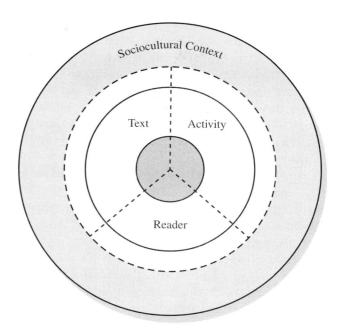

Figure 3.2 A heuristic for thinking about reading comprehension.

formulating a purpose for reading, the attentional and constructive processes involved in reading, and the impact on the reader (e.g., increment to knowledge, engagement) resulting from reading.

The most important portions of Figure 3.2 fall along the dotted lines: the interface between text features and reader capabilities, between reader capabilities and activity, and between activity and text features. Any of us can be rendered a poor comprehender by a text that is very badly written or that deals with a topic about which we lack background knowledge. Some activities—for example, reading quickly for the gist, or reading to understand and challenge the writer's argument, or reading to appreciate the writer's style—will be easier for some kinds of readers than others, and easier with some kinds of texts than others. Thus, the instructional challenge is to provide young readers with texts sufficiently accessible and motivating to keep them reading, but also sufficiently challenging to stimulate growth in their comprehension skills, vocabulary, and world knowledge.

The particular challenges of reading comprehension for the L2 reader can come in any of these domains. First, L2 readers are likely to be less advanced than monolingual or L1 readers in several of the domains that predict reading comprehension; vocabulary knowledge, knowledge of syntactic structures, and knowledge of discourse structures are all language-specific. Second, the organization of texts and world knowledge presupposed by texts are language- and culture-specific, and thus also likely to be more challenging to L2 than to L1 readers. Third, to the extent that the reading tasks being posed are specific to a particular culture and school context, they might be unfamiliar or even puzzling to the learner. For example, if a student has first learned to read in a school setting where reading for memorization is expected, then being expected to question the text or compare two texts that give different perspectives on an issue requires new learning. If a student's reading experience has been confined to narratives, then reading fact-laden science texts might be a challenge. And if a student's experiences have been limited to reading texts considered reliable and credible, for example, school-assigned history or science books, then reading the wide variety of texts of varying degrees of reliability on the Internet poses new and unfamiliar problems.

LITERACY DEVELOPMENT AMONG CHILD SECOND LANGUAGE/SECOND CULTURE LEARNERS

In this section, we turn to the evidence about the literacy development of L2/C2 learners. We briefly summarize first the evidence that such children are at heightened risk of poor academic outcomes and relate those academic risks to the other risks (health, poverty, family relations, emotional stability) they face. We then turn to a review of the literacy development of these learners, how their knowledge of an L1 (and, for some, L1 literacy) does and does not relate to their L2 literacy development, school achievement, and school adjustment. A major question we address in this section is how individual differences among L2 learners relate to outcomes. Then we consider the influence of social and instructional settings to address questions about the conditions under which language minority children do and do not thrive.

Academic Outcomes of Second Language/Second Culture Learners: A Group at Risk

Analyses of the *National Assessment of Educational Progress: Reading Assessments (NAEP)* reading data (e.g., National Center for Education Statistics [NCES], 2003) make clear that L2/C2 learners in general perform more poorly than monolingual English speakers. The *NAEP* data do not allow an easy analysis of the degree to which low proficiency in English contributes to deficits in performance, as compared to the contributions of cultural differences, as the data are disaggregated by ethnicity and not language proficiency status. However, analyses of state accountability data disaggregated by both language proficiency status and ethnicity make clear that both these factors independently are associated with poorer performance, and that when they combine, the likelihood of performing at expected levels decreases further. The *NAEP* findings can be summarized as showing that English-language learners, language minority children, and/or Latinos have on average achieved much lower levels of reading skill than English-only, monolingual, Anglo age-mates. What accounts for these effects?

The greater educational risks of this group of L2/C2 learners cannot, of course, be completely disentangled from their greater risks in other areas: poverty, poor health, experiences of family separation, emotional challenges, and so on (see papers in M. Suárez-Orozco and Páez, 2002, for an overview). Furthermore, there is considerable evidence that some immigrant groups engage in family practices that are less likely to produce 5-year-olds ready for the expectations of U.S. kindergartens. Analysis of the data from the NCES (1995) birth cohort study suggests that Latino mothers are less likely to read books to their children, to make literacy materials available, and to purchase children's books than are Anglo mothers of the same educational level. Furthermore, studies that have examined the relationship between home literacy practices (either in L1 or L2) and L2 literacy and academic achievement of language minority students have found positive effects of certain home literacy factors for immigrant and English-language learning children, and negative effects of their absence. For example, Pucci and Ulanoff (1998) reported that proficient readers were more likely to have a greater number of books in the home. On the other hand, Leseman and de Jong (1998) found that reading comprehension and word decoding skills of Turkish and Surinamese language minority children in the Netherlands at age 7 were strongly determined by age 4 vocabulary on which using Dutch (L2) as the home language had significant effects. Moreover, they reported that home literacy practice, which was found to determine school literacy achievement, was strongly determined by socioeconomic status (SES) and race.

To some extent, these effects of home literacy practices on literacy outcomes may be mediated by their contribution to children's acquisition of the L1. Walters and Gunderson (1985) showed that Chinese immigrant children who heard stories read aloud in Chinese (L1) made significant gains in English reading and experienced no negative effects on their English reading achievement. However, as there was no control group, whether exposure to Chinese storybooks had direct effects on English reading skills or whether the gain in the reading achievement was caused by other factors is unknown. At any rate, it is important to note that such L1 exposure was not detrimental to children's school achievement. Similarly, Nguyen, Shin, and Krashen (2001) reported that Vietnamese students' competence in Vietnamese had no relationship with English literacy and that competence in spoken Vietnamese and high levels of the use of Vietnamese at home were not detrimental to the development of spoken English. That is, L1 use at home had neither positive nor negative effects on English language and literacy development for this population. Likewise, Rosenthal, Baker, and Ginsburg (1983) showed that Spanish-speaking language minority children's low academic achievement was explained more by SES and race than home language. They also found that Spanish language background for Hispanic children was strongly related to deficits in reading achievement at school, but that the language effect was much stronger for preexisting achievement levels than for learning over the school year. In other words, children who used Spanish at home may have started out scoring lower on measures of English literacy, but progressed as fast as English-only speakers, thus indicating no long-term negative effect of L1 use in the home on academic achievement in L2. In fact, though, such children need to progress faster than their English-only classmates if they are to perform at expected levels in later grades.

Though the impact of home language on L2 reading is somewhat equivocal, several studies have found that the percentage of English spoken at home is highly correlated with language minority students' English reading skills (Abedi, Lord, & Plummer, 1997; Beech & Keys, 1997; Connor, 1983; Kennedy & Park, 1994; Umbel, Pearson, Fernandez, & Oller, 1992). Beech and Keys found that Asian children who preferred speaking their L1 at home were significantly behind in English vocabulary development, controlling for nonverbal intelligence, although the impact on reading development was weak. The unexpected weak effects of vocabulary on reading

development that Beech and Keys found may be explained by the monolingual control group's low SES status; low SES children, like language minority children, are considered to be at risk for poor literacy development, especially for vocabulary knowledge. Abedi et al. reported that students who always spoke their L1 at home failed to complete as many test items as students who spoke only English at home. Umbel et al. also showed that Hispanic children who spoke both English and Spanish in the home scored higher on English vocabulary tests than those who spoke only Spanish in the home. These findings contradict Rosenthal et al.'s (1983) finding about the absence of long-term detrimental effects of L1 use at home on later school achievement. This further implies that a longitudinal approach is needed to examine the true relationship between home language use and L2 literacy development. It is only natural that 7- and 8-year-old children who are exposed to and use mainly L1 before starting school need to take some time to catch up and learn the new language. Thus, we should be more concerned about these children's L2 literacy skills after they have had plenty of exposure to L2 language and literacy than about their seemingly low performance in the early grades. Beech and Keys, Umbel et al., and Abedi et al.'s studies did not control for L2 learners' length of residence or length of schooling in the L2, and thus we should not jump to the conclusion that L1 use at the home is detrimental to later academic performance.

Interestingly, Kennedy and Park (1994) found that the role of home language had differential effects on the two ethnic groups of language minority children they studied: For Mexican American students, SES was the strong predictor of academic achievement, whereas home language was not. On the other hand, home language was a strong predictor for Asian American students' reading achievement on a standardized test: Asian American students who spoke English in the home performed significantly better than those who spoke L1 in the home. Such differences may be explained by the relevant language status of the two groups' L1 in the dominant society, the potential role of structural similarities and differences between L1 and L2, length of residency, and so on. Likewise, Fernandez and Nielsen (1986) found, somewhat paradoxically, that the L1 (Spanish) proficiency of Hispanic bilingual students was associated with greater academic achievement, whereas frequency of Spanish use had a negative effect on academic achievement. Their finding may reflect the fact that the similarities in the linguistic and cultural properties of L1/C1 and L2/C2 facilitate positive influence on Spanish-speaking language minority children's L2 performance. Hence, those with high L1 proficiency may have developed an understanding about L2 linguistic properties in relation to their L1 and transferred their L1 knowledge to other relevant L2 academic settings, whereas merely speaking L1 frequently may reflect their reluctance to or inability to function well in L2.

This finding is somewhat related to what Rosowsky (2001) found with Muslim Mirpuri-Punjabi speakers in the U.K., although in that case, the children transferred their C1 literacy practice to L2 literacy skills. Although the Mirpuri-Punjabi-speaking children were not able to apply their L1 knowledge to L2 tasks, as their L1 does not share linguistic structural similarities with L2, they did as well as the English-monolingual children on English decoding tasks, possibly due to their C1, which emphasizes on accurate reading of the Qur'an. The same children, however, were lagging behind their monolingual counterparts on reading comprehension abilities, which require more C2 knowledge than decoding.

Because the literature shows considerable disagreement regarding the positive and negative effects of home language use on L2 literacy development, a firm conclusion cannot be drawn about the impact of continuity and discontinuity between home and school, which further implies that more in-depth and long-term investigation regarding the role of L1 use at home in different language minority groups' literacy and academic achievement is needed. However, these studies are quite convergent in showing that the amount and quality of home support for literacy development in either L1 or L2 relate strongly to L2 literacy achievement (Leseman & de Jong, 1998; Pucci & Ulanoff, 1998; Walters & Gunderson, 1985) and that L1 use at home does not impede L2 literacy development if it is accompanied by L2 use at home as well (Abedi et al., 1997; Beech & Keys, 1997). Thus, it is important for school literacy instruction to both provide support for and complement language minority students' home literacy experiences.

Possible Transfer Effects from First to Second Language: Evidence of Classroom Challenges Associated with Language Differences

The positive and negative effects of home language use on language minority students' literacy and school achievement imply the potential existence of both positive and negative transfer effects from L1 on their L2 literacy development. Because such transfer effects may vary for different literacy domains, it is important to examine them for each of the component skills known to contribute to literacy achievement. For the review of literature relevant to each literacy domain, only those empirical studies that involve language minority learners learning the target language in a second language setting, as opposed to foreign-language setting, were considered.

Phonological Awareness

Research with monolingual beginning readers indicates that higher levels of phonological awareness are associated with beginning reading and spelling achievement (Adams, 1990; Bradley & Bryant, 1983). But the question remains whether the same relationship holds for bilingual children who may already have some degree of phonological awareness in their L1 but not in L2. In general, bilingual children seem to be better at phonological awareness tasks than English-monolingual children (Oller, Cobo-Lewis, & Eilers, 1998). Moreover, for bilingual children whose L1 and L2 share similar orthographic and phonological characteristics, there is not only transfer of phonological awareness between the two languages, but their L1 metalinguistic and phonological awareness account for significant variance in L2 literacy skills such as spelling, word recognition, pseudoword reading, and reading comprehension (Cisero & Royer, 1995; Comeau, Cormier, Grandmaison, & Lacroix, 1999; Durgunolu, Nagy, & Hancin-Bhatt, 1993; Gottardo, Yan, Siegel, & Wade-Woolley, 2001; Oller et al., 1998; Smith & Martin, 1997). Durgunolu et al., for example, tested Spanish-speaking first graders in a transitional bilingual education program in the United States on phonological awareness tasks and word identification skills in both Spanish and English. They showed not only that phonological awareness in Spanish was closely related to Spanish word recognition, but also that children who performed well on Spanish phonological awareness tests were more likely be able to do well on English phonological awareness tests and, most important, on English word and pseudoword reading tests. That is, their L1 phonological awareness was a significant predictor of their performance on early literacy tasks both within and across languages. Similarly, Comeau et al. studied English-speaking grade 1, 3, and 5 children in French immersion classes and found cross-language transfer in phonological awareness and word decoding skills.

However, such transfer of phonological awareness, which is predictive of early literacy skills in L2, may be constrained to the cases where L1 and L2 share similar phonological and orthographic properties. In fact, unlike Oller et al. (1998), who showed that Spanish-English bilingual children are better at phonological awareness tasks than English-monolingual children, Jackson, Holm, and Dodd (1988) found no difference between English-monolingual and Cantonese-English bilingual children's phonological awareness skills and found better performance of English-monolingual children on reading and spelling tasks as well as manipulation of phonemic information tasks. They also detected bilingual children's patterns of phonological awareness to be language-specific, related to the phonemic and syllabic structure of their L1. Their findings further indicate that bilingualism itself may not be a sufficient condition to heighten phonological awareness. These conflicting findings may be related to the differences in the orthographic characteristics of the two languages (alphabetic versus morpho-syllabic). In a similar study, Liow and Poon (1998) investigated phonological awareness of three different multilingual Chinese groups and showed that phonological awareness in L2 (English) was related to L1 orthographic depth and that tonal phonological awareness of the Chinese L1 children may not be optimal for English literacy development. However, neither study tested the bilingual children in their L1, so no conclusion can be drawn regarding the possibility of negative or zero transfer of bilingual children's L1 phonological awareness. Gottardo et al. (2001), on the other hand, did measure Chinese ESL learners' L1 phonological awareness using a rhyme detection test, and in accordance with research conducted with L2 children with alphabetic L1 backgrounds, showed that children's L1 phonological awareness was related not only to their L2 phonological awareness, but also to their L2 reading skills. This is a very important finding, for it "points to an underlying process that is not specific to the child's L1 phonology but that is related to the child's ability to reflect on all phonology to which he or she has a minimum level of exposure" (p. 539). Phonological awareness requires one to reflect on and manipulate the features of oral language. Gottardo et al.'s finding implies that children's ability to reflect on and manipulate structural features of a particular language can be applied to an L2, whether it is typologically different from L1 or not.

Regardless of the language minority children's L1 backgrounds, the positive relationship between phonological awareness and other literacy skills within L2 is still apparent, as in the case of monolingual children. And for children whose L1 and L2 share similar phonological and orthographic properties, developing or building on the children's L1 phonological awareness is likely to help their L2 literacy development. Questions still remain, however, about how to help language minority children whose L1 is very different from their L2. Spanish-speaking children's acquisition of phonological awareness skills in English and Spanish was found to be in the same order across languages (Cisero & Royer, 1995), but what would it look like if the child's L1 and L2 are typologically very different? More research needs to be done with different populations of language minority children to further shed light on the development of bilingual children's phonological awareness and other language skills and classroom practices.

Word Reading and Spelling

As would be anticipated from the findings relating phonological awareness to word reading, word reading is not normally an insuperable challenge to the language minority child. Lesaux and Siegel (2003), for example, have documented that L2 learners in English-only programs can achieve native-like levels of L2 word reading by the end of grade 2, if provided with systematic instruction and appropriate interventions if they are falling behind.

Most studies of language minority students' spelling development have looked at Spanish-speaking English-language learners in the United States and identified the challenges associated with language differences between L1 and L2. For example, studies of lower-grade Spanish-speaking language minority students have shown that L1 rules for spelling dominated when they were working on new words or pseudowords in L2 and that the L1 spelling system was applied to the L2 spelling task (Ferroli & Shanahan, 1993; Nathenson-Mejía, 1989). For instance, second- and third-grade Spanish-speaking children in Ferroli and Shanahan's study produced spelling errors caused by merged voiced versus voiceless sounds in the spelling system, as Spanish does not attend to differences in voicing as systematically as English does. Thus, some spelled *drink*, as *trink*, a Spanish-influenced spelling that differs from the correct spelling in a predictable way. Likewise, studies of language minority students' spelling in higher grades also found that the influence of L1 was a predominant source of spelling errors in English (Cronnell, 1985) and that these children produced significantly more predicted L1-related errors than English-only children (Fashola, Drum, Mayer, & Kang, 1996). Moreover, L2 proficiency level was found to play an important role in spelling performance, as the less successful students produced significantly more L1-influenced errors than the more successful ones (Zutell & Allen, 1988).

Although there is not an abundance of studies with non-Spanish-speaking L1 language minority children, Wang and Geva's study (2003) with Chinese-speaking language minority students revealed similar L1 transfer effects in L2 spelling. Moreover, they were able to identify both effects of the L1 orthographic system and learning effects. The Chinese ESL students in Wang and Geva's study performed at a level similar to that of their English-monolingual counterparts in spelling real words. However, they performed significantly more poorly than English-monolingual children in pseudoword spelling. Also, the difference between real word and pseudoword spelling performance was much greater for Chinese ESL children than English-monolingual children. These results were explained by Chinese ESL children's reliance on the nonphonological route in spelling, the strategy employed and practiced for their L1 writing activities. Thus, when spelling unfamiliar words, they encountered difficulty in phoneme-grapheme mapping, which does not occur in their L1 because Chinese has a morphosyllabic orthography and is thus processed with the whole-word approach in spelling. For the same reason, the Chinese ESL children performed better than English-monolingual children in spelling visually presented orthographically legitimate/illegitimate and pronounceable/unpronounceable letter strings. That is, for the particular task that requires visual processing of letter strings, there was a positive L1-specific transfer for Chinese ESL children, who are used to processing letter strings visually as whole words.

In helping language minority children with L1 backgrounds both similar to and different from their L2, teachers need to be aware of the likely error patterns due to the L1 influence and the varying degrees of familiarity with both L1 and L2 phonological and spelling systems. To understand the differential effects of L1 spelling strategies of L2 students from diverse L1 backgrounds, however, studies need to be conducted that control for L1-specific spelling strategies, thus possibly comparing multiple ESL groups with similar L2 proficiency level but whose L1s are orthographically different from and similar to English.

Vocabulary

Although it is known that vocabulary knowledge is related to reading comprehension ability for L1 children (Freebody & Anderson, 1983; Stanovich, 1986), there have been relatively few studies looking at language minority students' L2 vocabulary development in relation to their L1 background and literacy skills. Vocabulary is a crucial domain of literacy skills for L2 learners as well as L1 students, due to the reciprocal effects of vocabulary and reading comprehension and academic achievement in general: Vocabulary knowledge helps reading comprehension, and good reading comprehension leads to a natural process of new vocabulary acquisition.

The findings from the few studies on L2 learners' vocabulary knowledge in relation to their reading comprehension ability conform with studies with L1 learners. Nagy, García, Durgunoglu, and Hancin-Bhatt (1993), for example, not only found a positive relationship between L2 vocabulary knowledge and L2 reading comprehension scores, but also showed evidence of transfer of Spanish-English bilingual upper-grade students' L1 vocabulary knowledge to L2 reading. Moreover, they showed that such transfer is dependent on students' ability to recognize L1-L2 cognates in reading L2 passages. This particular finding holds important implications for literacy and reading instruction for language minority students whose L1 shares similar morphosyntactic features with their L2. In fact, Carlo et al. (2004) showed the positive effects of cognate instructions on Spanish-speaking English learners' English reading comprehension outcomes. However, such vocabulary instruction should take into consideration the L2 learners' level of L2 proficiency, as a certain level of L2 proficiency is required for guessing meanings of unfamiliar words in L2 reading contexts (Hancin-Bhatt & Nagy, 1994; Nagy, McClure, & Mir, 1997). Specifically, it was shown that Spanish-speaking English learners' ability to recognize cognates increased with age as their knowledge of the relationships between English and Spanish derivational suffixes became more concrete. Thus, cognate instruction should take into account the English-language learners' level of understanding of L1-L2 structural relationships.

As in the case of other literacy domains, however, we must be careful about the L1 backgrounds of the language minority children in assuming the positive transfer effects of L1 vocabulary knowledge on L2 literacy skills. Verhoeven (1994), for example, found no predictive power of L1 vocabulary knowledge for L2 vocabulary development in Turkish-speaking Dutch learners in the Netherlands. Thus, more studies on the relationship between L1 vocabulary and the development of L2 literacy skills need to be carried out for language minority children whose L1 is morphosyntactically different from their L2. This, in turn, will yield useful guidelines regarding vocabulary instruction for L2 learners from diverse language backgrounds. The vocabulary (cognate) instruction for Spanish-speaking English learners was successful in Carlo et al.'s study (2004), partly because it relied on the interdependence of L1-L2. But what kind of instruction would benefit L2 learners from Vietnam, for example? What kinds of knowledge do the teachers need to know about L1-L2 relationships for those children to foster vocabulary improvement in L2? Studies addressing such questions will contribute to helping those children's academic achievement as well as reading comprehension.

Reading Comprehension

Research in the reading comprehension of language minority children has yielded evidence that L1 oral language and/or literacy skills can be both an asset and a hindrance in L2 reading comprehension, depending on age, L1 proficiency level, and L1 background.

Researchers have focused on Spanish-speaking English learners in studying the relationship between L1 literacy skills and L2 reading comprehension. Most of the studies are in agreement that those language minority children's L1 reading skills transfer to L2 reading comprehension (Calero-Breckheimer & Goetz, 1993; Langer, Bartolome, Vasquez, & Lucas, 1990; Reese, Garnier, Gallimore, & Goldenberg, 2000; Royer & Carlo, 1991). Calero-Breckheimer and Goetz, for instance, showed that third- and fourth-grade Hispanic students successfully transferred reading strategies between two languages, which contributed positively to reading comprehension in English. Likewise, Royer and Carlo found that the best predictor of English reading performance at the end of sixth grade was Spanish (L1) reading performance the previous year. In addition, Jiménez, García, and Pearson (1996) showed that successful Latina/o readers relied on various strategies, including transferring information and accessing cognate vocabulary across languages, whereas less successful readers were less effective in resolving comprehension difficulties in either language.

However, more careful investigation of the Spanish-speaking language minority children's background variables, including socioeconomic background, immigration status, and home language use, provided a more complex picture of such transfer. Buriel and Cardoza (1988) showed that Spanish oral proficiency and literacy skills predicted reading and other academic achievement variables only of the third-generation language minority children, but not the first- and second-generation children. Overall, the trend was for an increasing relationship of Spanish literacy to school achievement, including reading, across three generations. More specifically, third-generation students with greater literacy skills in L1 scored higher on the L2 reading test. Across three generations, however, L1 oral proficiency showed minimal relationship with L2 language and literacy skills, which further implies that L1 development does not hinder academic achievement in L2. The differential effect of L1 literacy skills on L2 reading across generations, however, does bring up an important issue: If a positive L1-L2 transfer of reading skills occurred only for the third-generation language minority students, those who probably had the most exposure to L2 language and literacy and spent the longest amount of time in the L2 setting, is a certain level of L2 proficiency or L2 input a prerequisite for such a positive transfer? Larger-scale studies with L2 learners from different language and cultural backgrounds within an ethnic group need to be conducted to get a more complete picture.

In addition, we need to pursue questions about L1 to L2 transfer for children from a wider array of L1 backgrounds, as most existing studies are limited to Hispanic students in the United States whose L1 rules and properties may contribute in unique ways to English reading comprehension. Connor (1983) looked at second- to 12th-grade students from 21 different L1 backgrounds and found that the percentage of English spoken at home and family SES had positive effects on reading skills in English, which, in a way, contradicts Nguyen et al.'s (2001) finding that there was no correlation between English reading performance on standardized tests and Vietnamese-speaking English learners' self-reported use of L1 at home. Nguyen et al. did not look at the relationship between the children's English use at home and English literacy outcomes to either support or argue against Connor's findings, although they did certainly show that L1 use at home is not a hindrance to L2 literacy development. On the other hand, Lasisi, Falodun, and Onyehalu (1988) reported that seventh-grade Nigerian students performed better when reading culturally familiar passages than unfamiliar passages, which implies that the presence of cultural values in texts has an important impact on language minority students' performance in English reading. However, more studies are needed to generate a portrait of challenges and benefits associated with language minority students' language background in relation to their ability to read in English.

Furthermore, one should take into account the order of literacy instruction (submersion versus immersion) and the language minority students' proficiency level in both L1 and L2 before implementing any literacy instruction. Verhoeven (1994) suggested that the transfer of L1-L2 word decoding and reading comprehension abilities could be bidirectional, depending on the order of instruction. The reading comprehension abilities of Turkish-Dutch bilingual children in the Netherlands who were in the transitional bilingual education classes were predicted from their L1 reading comprehension abilities acquired earlier; likewise, Turkish-Dutch bilingual children who underwent an L2 submersion approach showed evidence of transfer in the opposite direction. The findings from Verhoeven's study have important policy and pedagogical implications for promoting L2 learners' academic achievement.

In general, the existing literature highlights the beneficial effect of L1 literacy skills for L2 reading comprehension and the importance of knowing which strategies and knowledge to transfer from L1 to L2 reading. This, in return, points out the importance of acknowledging and promoting language minority students' L1 literacy skills and instructing them on how to effectively use their assets for L2 reading comprehension.

Writing

There has not been much attention paid to the writing (composition) development of young language minority students, although many researchers have studied it in adult language minority populations. Lanauze and Snow's (1989) study is one of the few that looked at fourth- and fifth-grade Spanish-speaking language minority students' writing skills. They showed that children who were rated good in both L1 and English and children rated poor in English but good in L1 (Spanish) scored better in English and Spanish writing than the children rated poor in both languages. The children who were rated poor in English but good in Spanish produced English writing that was equivalent to that of the children rated good in both languages in the complexity, sophistication, and semantic content of their English writing. In short, "One determinant of how early in the acquisition of the second language relevant L1 skills become available is their degree of mastery in the first language" (p. 338). Similarly, Nathenson-Mejía (1989), based on a single case study of a Spanish-speaking third-grader, suggested that the relationship between oral and written language is transactional, with benefits for language minority students. These results suggest the potentially facilitative impact of L1 literacy development on L2 literacy and academic skills. Writing is clearly an area in L2 literacy research that needs more attention and research, especially as it is a skill necessary for high academic achievement and success in upper grades and for higher education.

Possible Transfer Effects from First Culture to Second Language/Second Culture: Evidence of School/Classroom Challenges Associated with Cultural Differences

Relatively less attention has been paid to the effect of L2/C2 learners' cultural background on their literacy development in English and school achievement. The existing literature on cultural influences on literacy development falls into roughly three categories: (1) the relationship between C1/cultural familiarity with the C2 and literacy development, (2) discourse differences between home and school and their effect on L2 literacy development, and (3) the relationship between other cultural factors (e.g., SES, educational aspiration) and literacy development and school achievement.

Knowledge of the Second Culture

Research on the effect of cultural differences between home and school on L2/C2 learners' school achievement and literacy development has generated two very different findings. One set of studies found no relationship between C1 and school achievement, whereas the other set found that familiarity with C2 related to better school outcomes.

García-Vázquez (1995) found no significant relationship between measures of acculturation and reading comprehension skills of Spanish-speaking language minority students, which implies that acculturation to the dominant culture is not mandatory for high literacy achievement in English. Similarly, Abu-Rabia (1995) showed that cultural familiarity with reading material made no difference in reading comprehension outcomes among Arab students whose English proficiency was stronger than their Arabic.

A larger set of studies, though, has shown that cultural familiarity and unfamiliarity with the dominant culture does influence language minority children's performance on reading comprehension (Abu-Rabia, 1998; Droop & Verhoeven, 1998; Hannon & McNally, 1986, Jiménez, 1997; Kenner, 1999; Rosowsky, 2001). Abu-Rabia reported that Arab students performed better on comprehension of Arabic cultural content regardless of the language of the text. Droop and Verhoeven identified a facilitating effect of cultural familiarity on reading comprehension and reading efficiency for Turkish and Moroccan language minority children in the Netherlands, whereas Rosowsky showed that language minority students' comprehension was far behind due to their lack of cultural familiarity with the meaning of texts, although they were able to decode text better than monolingual English-speaking children.

From the existing studies, it seems that, although acculturation does not always have an impact on literacy performance of L2/C2 learners, especially those with a high proficiency in L2, lack of knowledge of the dominant language and culture often has detrimental effects on school performance and literacy skills. Thus, it may be necessary for school literacy instruction to support the continuity of C1 to school and explicit instruction in meaning-making strategies for culturally unfamiliar topics.

Discourse Patterns

Studies that focus on discourse patterns indicate that language minority students benefit from school interaction patterns that are similar to those in their home (Au & Mason, 1981; Ballenger, 2000; Hudicourt-Barnes, 2003; Huerta-Macias & Quintero, 1992; Wilkinson, Milosky, & Genishi, 1986). Au and Mason showed that native Hawaiian children's academic engagement, including reading activities, was facilitated when the classroom instructional interaction was compatible with that of their home. Similarly, Huerta-Macias and Quintero reported beneficial effects of code switching at school for biliteracy development of the language minority students who were used to code switching at home. Wilkinson et al. also found a positive relationship between reading achievement and displaying school-appropriate interaction patterns for Hispanic children. In short, studies are in agreement that ac-

knowledgment of and sensitivity to language minority children's C1 support their literacy development in L2.

Additional Cultural Variables

Although many researchers have examined the influence of parents, family, home culture, and community on L2 literacy and school achievement, no study has documented their exact relationships or effects. The majority of such studies failed to report significant relationships (Buriel & Cardoza, 1988; Duran & Weffer, 1992; Goldenberg, Reese, & Gallimore, 1992). Duran and Weffer, for example, found that parents' educational values were not directly related to ninth-grade reading and 12th-grade school achievement of Mexican American high school students, although they did influence student behavior at school positively; such family educational values affected students' willingness to take math/science enrichment classes, which was significantly related to increase in related academic achievement. Likewise, Goldenberg et al. showed that home literacy practice was not as strongly related to Hispanic language minority children's reading achievement as school use of literacy materials and that parent expectations changed as a result of their child's school performance but not vice versa. Monzó and Rueda (2001) indicated a positive relationship between family literacy practices and resources and children's reading motivation, but their sample size was too small ($N = 5$) to make a general claim.

Kennedy and Park (1994) reported that the significant relationship between use of English at home and reading achievement at school for Hispanic children disappeared when SES was controlled, which suggests that the SES effect on English reading achievement was stronger than the effect of L2 use for this particular language minority group. However, the same was not true for Asian students; the relationship between their home language use and achievement remained significant even with SES controlled. However, little is known about the effect of SES on literacy and school achievement of language minority students in particular, although significant influences may be assumed from other sets of research with English-speaking children (Cook, 1991; Stubbs, 1980).

Summary

Our review of the literature on L2/C2 learners' performance on the key components of literacy demonstrates the complexity of L1/C1 and L2/C2 relationships and how they vary as a function of the L1's cultural as well as linguistic characteristics, students' and parents' commitment to L1 as well as L2 language and literacy development, the social status of L1, length of residence, and immigration and socioeconomic status. In addition, the L1-L2 relationship is not always the same across different subcomponents of literacy skills, depending on the L2 learners' L1 and L2 proficiency level, degree of similarities and differences between the two languages, and home language use as well as home literacy practice. However, the literature generally agrees on the following:

- L1 and C1 knowledge and skills are not the main source of L2 learners' poor performance on L2 literacy tasks or academic failure. In most cases, they have positive effects on L2 literacy development, even when L2 is typologically different from L1.
- L1 maintenance and use does not impede L2 language and literacy development.
- L2 learners, in many cases, apply their L1 and C1 knowledge and skills to L2/C2 tasks, although sometimes they need instruction on how to transfer L1 knowledge effectively.
- L2 learners benefit from L1- and/or C1-sensitive instructions in L2 literacy development and academic achievement.
- Full acculturation may not be necessary for academic success, but knowledge of C2 does make a difference in reading comprehension and academic achievement.

In general, this survey of recent literature on transfer of L1/C1 literacy-related skills to L2 literacy development has shown both positive and negative relationships between L1 language/literacy skills and L2 literacy achievement. Except for the case of spelling, most studies show that L1 oral and literacy skills are positively correlated with equivalent skills in L2, but of course such positive correlations, though they are consistent with a transfer explanation, hardly constitute strong evidence in support of it. Perhaps learners with better skills in L1 are just smarter and thus faster in acquiring skills in L2.

Most important, we have only hints about the conditions under which transfer is most likely to occur and most likely to be positive and productive. We know, furthermore, that there are many opportunities for transfer

that are missed; for example, Spanish-speaking learners of English are unaware of the value of cognates until taught to use them (Nagy et al., 1993), and even then, students with limited literacy skills in Spanish are unable to recognize many potential cognates that give clues to word meaning. Jiménez (1997) reported on a small number of native Spanish speakers who were poor readers in English and who professed that reading in English and in Spanish were quite different, whereas his small group of better English readers said they used many of the same strategies in both languages, having evidently discovered the value of transfer on their own. Much more research needs to be done on how and when transfer functions, how it is related to differences between the L1 and the L2 and orthographic system, as well as how age, instruction, the sociolinguistics of the language community, and other factors affect the likelihood and the utility of transfer. With this enhanced knowledge base, we could offer stronger arguments about the value of encouraging language minority students' continued development of L1 language and literacy knowledge as an influence on their successful development of L2 literacy skills.

PROGRAMS DESIGNED FOR SECOND LANGUAGE/SECOND CULTURE LEARNERS

Given the long history in the United States and in northern Europe of immigration and of academic underperformance among immigrant students, it is surprising and unfortunate that we still lack incontrovertible evidence about key aspects of programs that best support the development of such children. There is, however, sufficient basis for arguing that certain instructional features contribute crucially to program effectiveness. In this section, we briefly review available evidence about the qualities of effective programs for preschoolers and elementary students, note those domains for which more evidence is needed, and provide sketches of some programs that exemplify both the features shown to be effective and the difficulties of implementing those features widely and consistently.

Preschool-Age Children

Programs designed for preschool-age L2/C2 learners should incorporate opportunities for the children to develop warm relationships with the adult caregivers/educators, rich opportunities for language interaction, varied opportunities for engagement in literacy activities, and opportunities to acquire knowledge, concepts, and theories about the physical and social world through observation, conversation, discussion, and engagement with books. These features are, of course, precisely those that characterize good preschool education for any child; considerable evidence suggests that they are of particular importance in ensuring good outcomes for children at risk of poor academic outcomes, including children who have limited control over the language and culture of the schools they will attend.

We lack direct evidence concerning language use in preschool programs serving L2/C2 learners. Some would argue that the key characteristics of good programs—warm relationships with adults, access to concepts, theories, and new knowledge, and engagement in rich language and literacy activities—are unlikely to be present in an environment where the only language children know is not used. Others would respond that young children can quickly learn enough of the L2 encountered in the preschool to establish warm relationships with responsive adults, and that the task of acquiring rich language skills in the school language is best started earlier rather than later.

A Few Illustrative Cases

U.S. Head Start programs serve a large and increasing population of English-language learners. Head Start programs are held accountable for standards set centrally but have local control over the specifics of program design. There is some disagreement within Head Start about program responsibilities for teaching children English. Some Head Start administrators and personnel interpret the responsibility to prepare children for school as dictating that they be taught English; others argue that the greater responsibility is to provide children with the social and academic skills that would ease English acquisition once they get to English-medium classrooms.

The historical shift toward all-English programs for immigrant children in elementary schools has had its influence on Head Start program design, increasing the pressure to provide English skills to preschoolers and diminishing the value associated with support for the L1 language and literacy skills. Nonetheless, one of the standards with which Head Start programs must comply is availability of adults who speak the children's native language; for English-language learners, that adult sometimes is the classroom teacher, more often is an aide, and not infrequently is someone working in the office or the kitchen rather than a part of the educational staff.

In 1996, members of the Language Diversity Project team of the New England Head Start Quality Research Center[1] started working with a large Head Start program near Boston, in a town we refer to as Witham. Witham's Head Start served a population that was approximately 40% Spanish-speaking, and that ratio was reflected in each of the classrooms in the program. Most of the classrooms had a Spanish-speaking aide or assistant teacher and an English-speaking head teacher. Because the Witham public schools had a thriving bilingual education program, it seemed to us that promoting the Head Start children's Spanish skills, and their literacy skills through Spanish-language activities, might well be an approach worth considering. Thus, we proposed to the Witham Head Start director that Spanish-medium classrooms be established to serve Spanish-speaking and bilingual children. We offered to provide professional development and other forms of support to the teachers in such classrooms and to collect data on child performance that could be used by the program.

Though initially enthusiastic about this proposal, after reflection the Witham director pointed to a number of difficulties. First, there was only one fluent Spanish speaker on his staff qualified to serve as a head teacher. Second, he felt that parents would object if 4-year-olds were not receiving opportunities to learn English in the program. Third, and most frustrating, he noted logistical difficulties because classroom assignment was determined to a large extent by bus routes; the children who were bussed together would probably be a mix of Spanish and English speakers rather than language-homogeneous.

Despite these difficulties, it did turn out to be possible to create and study a single classroom in which two Spanish-speaking teachers developed and implemented a curriculum designed for a group of 3-year-olds. The coteachers in this classroom were Ana, formerly an English-medium Head Start teacher and a native bilingual with stronger literacy skills in English than in Spanish, and Luisa, a Spanish-dominant bilingual who previously had worked as a Head Start teacher in Puerto Rico and an assistant teacher in Witham Head Start classrooms. Regular professional development with Ana and Luisa was carried out by Aceves (2003), who also systematically

[1]The Language Diversity project researchers working in Witham included Consuelo Aceves, Lilia Bartolome, Catherine Snow, and Patton Tabors; David Dickinson was the director of the New England Head Start Quality Research Center.

studied the language use and progress of the children in their class.

There are four kinds of data that cast light on the success of the language intervention in this classroom: teacher interviews conducted by Aceves and Bartolomé, observations of classroom practice conducted by Aceves, child language performance data collected by Aceves, and observations of child social and task-mastery skills collected by Bronson and Fetter (1998). In interviews, both Ana and Luisa reported that the complexity and sophistication of their curriculum was much greater in the Spanish-medium classroom than it had been in other years when they taught mixed-language groups all in English. In the observations, the sophistication of their language use, the levels of participation of their students, and the complexity of the topics they introduced into their curriculum were striking. Their classroom was characterized by curricular units (e.g., deep sea life) that one might encounter in a 4-year-old preschool classroom or even a kindergarten, and it was very different from the routine-oriented classroom, with simplified language and little formal curriculum, described by Tabors (1997) as the pedagogical response to a group composed mostly of L2/C2 learners. Language testing revealed that the children in Ana and Luisa's class made more than the expected gains in Spanish vocabulary over the year, and improved as well in English vocabulary despite the fact that their formal exposure to English was limited to 30 minutes a day of ESL. Finally, Bronson and Fetter's comparisons of these Spanish-speaking 3-year-olds to Spanish speakers in English-medium classrooms in the same Head Start program revealed them to be more socially competent and to score higher on task mastery.

In short, the experience of the adult participants and the test data strongly support the effectiveness of native-language preschool instruction in promoting children's overall development and documents the absence of negative effects on English development. Ana and Luisa taught a Spanish-language 3-year-old classroom for a 2nd year, with considerable interest from parents who had heard about the first year's experience. During the 2nd year, they became consulting teachers to their colleagues, because there was general recognition within the program that they were doing a very effective job of teaching and organizing their classroom. Given these successes, one might have expected the model to become a permanent option in the Witham Head Start program and to expand to more classrooms.

Unfortunately, neither of those things happened. The innovation was brief and limited, and both Ana and Luisa were back teaching in English-medium classrooms after 2 years. There was simply insufficient support from the administration of the Witham Head Start and insufficient data as to the value of the program to be able to keep it alive. The termination of the Language Diversity Project also meant that expectation of support and resources from Harvard associated with the intervention dwindled. Like many educational experiments, this remained a demonstration that never rose to the level of becoming standard practice.

The story of the Spanish-language classroom in Witham has been repeated dozens of times. A similar case studied by Wagenaar (1993) in the Netherlands was a preschool program delivered in Moroccan Arabic for the benefit of Moroccan children. The large numbers of Turkish and Moroccan children living in the Netherlands have very much the same achievement profile as Spanish-speaking children in U.S. schools. These children tend to live in relatively homogeneous, immigrant neighborhoods. They attend schools referred to in Holland as "black schools," emphasizing the paucity of ethnic Dutch children in them. They live in families in which the parents tend to maintain the ancestral language; many of the mothers are monolingual and have limited literacy skills in either the L1 or in Dutch.

The program Wagenaar (1993) studied started with 3-year-olds, this being the age at which public preschool normally begins in the Netherlands. It was conducted in Moroccan Arabic and welcomed mothers to spend time in the classroom and observe or take part in the activities designed to build children's classroom participation skills as well as basic numeracy, literacy, and world knowledge.

Like the Witham native language program, the Amsterdam program was judged highly successful by participating families and teachers. The children showed considerable gains in Arabic-language skills in comparison to other Moroccan children in traditional Dutch-language programs and, again like the Witham program, showed no comparative deficits in Dutch, though they continued to test below the level of monolingual Dutch-speaking children.

Again like the Witham program, the Amsterdam program (originally intended to develop into a full-fledged bilingual program as the children entered the elementary grades) lasted only 2 years. Logistical challenges that simply could not be overcome included availability of sufficient numbers of qualified teachers who were fluent in both Moroccan Arabic and Dutch, and the difficulty of either excluding from the program or serving adequately within it the minority of Berber-speaking Moroccan children, for whom the program was ill-designed. Additional contributing factors certainly included the low perceived value of Moroccan Arabic in the Netherlands, and indeed its somewhat diminished role as an academic language even in Morocco, where standard Arabic is taught as the initial language of literacy and French is the language of higher schooling.

Failure of the capacity to develop and sustain sufficient numbers of programs like the Moroccan Arabic preschool studied by Wagenaar (1993) has led Dutch educators to abandon attempts at native-language schooling and to develop instead Dutch-language enrichment preschool programs designed for nonnative speakers. Three such programs that have been studied in some detail are the Dutch adaptation of the Israeli home-based program called HIPPY and the center-based programs Kaleidoskoop (a Dutch adaptation of HighScope) and Piramide. These three programs are notable for their minimization of explicit attention to the linguistic and cultural knowledge the children bring with them. They operate on a simple target language/target culture model: There are certain skills and capacities that children who will be successful in school need to have, and because their home does not naturally provide them, the programs are designed to teach them. Parent participation in the center-based programs is encouraged, in part because it is thought to be a route toward the acquisition of Dutch linguistic and cultural knowledge for the mothers, who might otherwise be somewhat isolated from Dutch society. Evaluation studies have shown no significant effect of the HIPPY program in the Netherlands (Eldering & Vedder, 1993), but the two center-based programs, Piramide and Kaleidoskoop, have generated gains for participating children (Schonewille, Kloprogge, & van der Leij, 2000; Veen, Roeleveld, & Leseman, 2000).

Immigrants to the Netherlands share with the indigenous population a sense that Dutch norms need to be acquired, and that their own languages are somehow unsuited to schooling. Kook (1994) and Muysken, Kook, and Vedder (1996), describing parent-child interaction among Papiamento-speaking immigrants to the Netherlands from the Dutch West Indies, noted that even those

mothers whose Dutch was very limited would switch to Dutch when presenting certain "academic" content to their preschool-age children, for example, numbers, shapes, and colors. Afkir (2002), in a study of low-income Moroccan mothers interacting with their kindergarten-age children, noted a similar switch from Moroccan Arabic to French for academic content; in this case as well, the mothers themselves possessed minimal skills in French. There is indeed a general sense in multicultural and/or multilingual settings that some languages are worth more than others and are more appropriate for formal tasks, for literacy, and for academic practices; this sense, which may well be unexpressed, is shared by policymakers, the public at large (as indicated by Ron Unz's success in passing referenda limiting bilingual education), many educators, and even parents who themselves have little education and minimal control over the language of power. The specifics of these consensual valuings of language are sometimes puzzling; it may not seem strange that Creole languages like Papiamento and Haitian Kreyol, which have few native speakers and relatively brief literary traditions, easily give way before standard, national languages like Dutch and English. But why should Arabic, a language of high culture and long-standing literacy, and the fourth most widely spoken language in the world, be of less value in school than French or Dutch (a language spoken by fewer than 25 million people, almost all of whom speak another European language fairly well)? Nonetheless, Arabic has little status in Holland or in France, with severe consequences for the potential of North African immigrants in those nations to be successful students in their L2 or to maintain their L1 at high levels of proficiency or literacy.

Elementary School Programs

For elementary school programs, theory as well as the wisdom of practice would lead to the conclusion that programs that incorporate the native language have an advantage for one segment of the population: those children who are at some risk of difficulty in learning to read and who have not acquired literacy skills in their native language. The Committee on the Prevention of Reading Difficulties in Young Children (Snow et al., 1998) recommended native language literacy instruction specifically for that group; at the same time, they suggested the postponement of literacy instruction until children had acquired some oral English and strong emergent literacy skills.

The argument presented by the Committee on the Prevention of Reading Difficulties focused on literacy outcomes as the primary goal of native language instruction; in other words, it argued from the presupposition that the basics of literacy should be taught in a way that optimizes access to meaning, and that transfer of L1 literacy skills to L2 would be more efficient than teaching L2 skills directly. As noted earlier and acknowledged by the Committee, this recommendation is not strongly supported by evaluation data, though the more scholarly and politically neutral meta-analyses of English-only versus bilingual programs (e.g., Willig, 1985) generally come out showing small positive and no negative effects for bilingual education.

Transitional Bilingual Programs

The term "transitional bilingual program" is used for programs that are designed to ease the language learner's entry into schooling in the majority language. They are formally distinguished from various sorts of maintenance bilingual programs, which are designed to support development of oral and literacy skills in the native language with true bilingualism as the outcome. In fact, though, the classroom activities that go on in transitional versus maintenance programs may not be radically different. In each type of program, on the other hand, there is considerable heterogeneity of pedagogical approach and language use. The most common arrangement in bilingual programs of both types is that a single, bilingual teacher is responsible for the delivery of instruction in both the L1 and the L2, operating with some more or less formal guidelines for amounts of L1 and of L2. Very few programs separate language by teacher, pairing an English speaker with an other-language speaker in serving two classes. Some programs separate language by subject matter, teaching math, art, and music, for example, in English, and teaching reading, social studies, and science in the L1. Other programs prescribe use of both languages in all subjects, for example, presenting new material in the native language and then teaching it again in English to provide the relevant English vocabulary. Alternatively, teaching might go on primarily in English, with use of the native language to repeat and reinforce lessons that some children struggle with. Sometimes literacy is taught first in the native language and subsequently in English, but most often literacy is taught simultaneously in both languages but at different times of day. Some programs even prescribe that every teacher utterance be produced in both English and the children's L1—an approach almost certain to lead students to ignore half of what is said.

Two-Way Bilingual Programs

Some educators (e.g., Christian, 1994) have made the more millennial argument that bilingual education is of value not just as a way of reducing risk for L2/C2 learners, but as a way of promoting bilingualism. Maintenance programs, for example, are designed not only to teach English and transfer students into mainstream classrooms as quickly as possible, but to teach literacy, language arts, and content in both the native language and in English, with the goal of producing highly proficient bilinguals. A particular approach to maintenance of L1 skills for L2 learners is represented by two-way bilingual (also called two-way immersion) programs, in which L2/C2 learners and English-only students study together in classrooms where half the instruction is provided in English and half in the other language.

Evidence about the conditions under which two-way programs are successful for all their students is accumulating (Cazabon, Lambert, & Hall, 1998; Howard, Christian, & Genesee, 2004). The major challenge in such programs is not the acquisition of English by the language minority students, but the acquisition of the other language by the English speakers. Creating conditions under which English speakers devote time and energy to L2 learning is not easy (another symptom of the high status of English), and the obstacles to keeping the other language robust in such programs are many. What are these obstacles? They range from within-classroom effects to the consequences of school, district, and statewide policies. They can be overcome only by ensuring that changes are made at all four of these levels of organization simultaneously.

One study of fourth- and fifth-grade classrooms in a two-way bilingual school (Carrigo, 2000) documented the many classroom-level contexts that led to use of English, even during the part of the school day designated as Spanish time. When groups of native English speakers were working together, they were very unlikely to speak in Spanish, even if their work involved Spanish texts; teachers interacting with such groups often accommodated to their language choice. When student groups included both native English and native Spanish speakers, again there was a strong tendency for peer and teacher talk to be in English; this reflected both the fact that the Spanish speakers were more proficient in English than the English speakers were in Spanish, and that English was the high-status language among the students. Only in small groups where all the students were native Spanish speakers did group work and teacher talk reliably occur in Spanish. Although the Spanish-speaking students had access to quite sophisticated Spanish-language use during these interactions, they were not very frequent, and native English speakers had few opportunities to participate in Spanish-rich discussions.

The principal of another two-way school, which we call Clemente, recognized a similar problem in her school: The teachers deviated massively from the planned use of Spanish in the higher grades, reverting to almost 100% English. The teachers reported that many of the children in their classes simply couldn't understand Spanish, whereas everyone could understand English. How can one explain this outcome in a school that had provided systematic Spanish and English instruction from kindergarten? Several factors emerged as relevant. First, Clemente was a Success for All school, and the Success for All program, with its required daily 90-minute literacy block, was delivered entirely in English. Thus, the 50–50 split between Spanish and English started only after the most intensive teaching of the day had ended. Second, the Clemente School and the district in which it was located were under considerable pressure to show adequate improvement on the mandated statewide test. The superintendent required in-class test preparation programs be used in third and higher grades in all the schools, such as Clemente, which were in danger of showing inadequate progress. The test preparation activities absorbed at least 90 minutes a day between January and April and were, of course, all carried out in English. Third, Clemente was located in a very mixed neighborhood, not a homogeneously Latino or Spanish-speaking part of town. Every year, in every grade, new students were enrolled whose parents were not seeking a two-way program but had picked Clemente for convenience. These English-only speakers were unable, if they entered in third or fourth grade, to follow instruction offered in Spanish. All these factors led to a situation in which Clemente was offering a two-way program in name only. In kindergarten through second grade, the program was perhaps 30% Spanish, and in third and higher grades perhaps 15% Spanish. Thus, it was not surprising that many English-speaking children failed to learn much Spanish, and that Spanish speakers were soon opting as

well for the default language, English, for in- and out-of-classroom interactions.

What factors are associated with better adherence to the principles of two-way programs? First, the sociolinguistic reality that English is more highly valued than other languages has to be recognized and acknowledged in program designs; programs are more successful if they counteract that reality by making the other language unavoidable. They can do this by instituting preschool programs that are delivered entirely in the other language; such programs function as enrichment for the other-language speakers and as immersion L2 settings for English speakers. They can adopt so-called 90–10 or 80–20 designs, in which kindergarten instruction is heavily weighted to the other language, with a gradual shift to a 50–50 balance of language use by third grade. Some programs find that they still need to reinforce the other language by offering afterschool and/or summer school activities that are highly engaging and monolingual, banning the use of English in these settings.

Second, the natural tendency to accommodate to the less proficient speakers of a language has to be counteracted. Two-way programs should be able to exclude monolingual English speakers as new entrants after kindergarten or grade 1, and transfer to other programs students who are not making expected progress in the L2 within the program. Two-way programs need extra resources so they can offer L2 courses for parents, both in English for the immigrant parents and in the other language for English-only parents. How can parents help with homework, after all, if they don't speak both of the languages in which their child is studying?

Third, the value of bilingual outcomes should be acknowledged by the district and the community, for example, by reporting children's scores on tests administered in the other language as well as in English, by establishing some level of other-language proficiency as a high school graduation requirement, and by featuring the two-way programs as high-status magnet programs rather than treating them as remedial.

Supporting Second Language/Second Culture Learners in Predominantly English Instruction

We made the argument that students could transfer knowledge acquired in their L1 and C1 to be more efficient and effective L2/C2 learners. But we also presented evidence that transfer is neither automatic nor inevitable. Transfer is more or less likely, and more or less helpful, as a function of the L1-L2 and C1-C2 relationships, the specific L2/C2 learning task, the degree of metacognitive capacity of the learner, and the skill of the teacher. Many students simply fail to recognize or exploit knowledge they possess that could help them solve L2/C2 problems. Of course, this specific problem of ensuring that learners transfer knowledge from a well-established to a novel domain of functioning is ubiquitous in education. But it is particularly acute for the L2/C2 learner, who is in the position of having to learn more than the monolingual student, and to catch up with monolingual levels of functioning in less time. Helping L2/C2 learners meet or even surpass the academic achievement of their monolingual classmates requires figuring out how to help them turn their L1/C1 knowledge into an asset through transfer.

One such attempt was the Vocabulary Improvement Project (VIP), a vocabulary intervention designed to enrich fourth- and fifth-grade Spanish-speaking English-language learners' academic vocabulary in English (L2) through helping them make use of their vocabulary and linguistic knowledge in L1 and promoting L1-L2 transfer (August, Carlo, Lively, McLaughlin, & Snow, 2005; Carlo et al., 2004; Lively, August, Carlo, & Snow, 2003). The VIP was initially designed in accordance with research indicating that vocabulary knowledge was one of the key predictors of students' performance in reading comprehension; furthermore, vocabulary knowledge sufficient to ensure comprehension of moderately complex texts creates opportunities for new vocabulary learning (Fukkink & de Glopper, 1998). The VIP focused on teaching children strategies for word learning as much as new vocabulary items. Those strategies, furthermore, were directed at various aspects of lexical knowledge, including morphology (affixes, frequently occurring Latin and Greek roots), recognizing multiple meanings of words, thinking about semantic associations (e.g., superordinates, antonyms, near synonyms), and the metalinguistic knowledge required to give definitions (Lively et al., 2003). That is, the VIP not only taught *words,* but also taught *about words,* so that the children could both develop skills to infer word meanings independently and develop curiosity about words. What is more, by teaching cognate use and previewing each lesson in Spanish before introduction in English, the VIP encouraged Spanish-speaking English-language learners to use their L1 knowledge to improve their vocabulary knowledge and text comprehension.

After the 15-week intervention, introducing 10 to 12 target words each week for 30 to 45 minutes, 4 days a week, the VIP was found to improve children's performance in reading comprehension, word knowledge, and metalinguistic analysis of novel vocabulary items (Carlo et al., 2004; Dressler, 2000). Both the English-language learners and the monolingual English speakers showed improvement, but the English-language learners did not improve at a faster rate; in other words, the curriculum was effective but, in the short run at least, did not contribute to closing the gap between English-language learners and their monolingual classmates.

The VIP undertaking provides a salutary lesson about the relation of applied and basic research to practice, and vice versa (see Selman & Dray, Chapter 10, this *Handbook,* this volume). This project was conceived as one in which we collaborated with teachers to design the curriculum. Two 3-day meetings were held at which participating researchers and teachers shared insights from the research literature and from classroom practice and developed ideas about how best to promote vocabulary development. Although those meetings were energizing, they did not in fact generate a usable curriculum. Most of the participating teachers represented themselves as already paying a lot of attention to vocabulary development in their classes, but the techniques they suggested (giving children dictionaries, repeating English words with Spanish phonology so as to remember the spelling, using word walls) were neither innovative nor sufficiently effective. Thus, having failed with at least that approach to seeking inspiration from practice, the research team reverted to the traditional transmission model; we reviewed the basic and applied research about vocabulary acquisition, designed the curriculum on that basis, carefully observed its implementation and collected information from the teachers using it about its flaws, and then produced an improved design for the next year of the study.

Reverting to practice-embedded work in studying the implementation taught us a crucial lesson: This curriculum makes a very great demand on teacher knowledge. Several of the teachers would have required considerable professional development to ensure that they understood enough about linguistics and second-language acquisition to implement the curriculum faithfully (White, 2000). For example, doing a good job with the lessons devoted to promoting cognate use required some knowledge of Latin, Spanish, or another Romance language, which many of the teachers did not have. Some understanding of the morphological structure of English was presupposed in the lessons we designed. Indeed, we also presupposed (incorrectly, in a few cases) that the teachers would already know the correct pronunciation and use of the words taught in the curriculum. Knowledge about English, knowledge about linguistics, and cross-linguistic knowledge were all needed if teachers were to optimize the learning the VIP was designed for. Valuable opportunities for the teachers, especially those in diverse classrooms, to understand the exact linguistic and metalinguistic challenges their English-language learners are going through must occur in combination with supplying good teacher manuals and a well-designed curriculum.

Despite its success in promoting positive L1-L2 transfer in Spanish-speaking English-language learners as well as supporting vocabulary and reading comprehension in monolingual English speakers, the intervention has not survived as an intact instructional program in any of the classrooms where it was introduced. It has generated a published curriculum designed for fourth-, fifth-, and sixth-grade English-language learners (Lively et al., 2003); a larger-scale evaluation of the effectiveness of the curriculum is, of course, needed.

Another curriculum that aimed to promote English-language learners' academic performance by being sensitive to their linguistic and cultural background was designed by the Chèche Konnen Center for teaching science to Haitian Creole-speaking upper-elementary and middle school English-language learners. Previous studies (e.g., O. Lee & Fradd, 1996) had concluded that Haitian children were nonverbal and incompetent in science classes. Based on an understanding of the essentially oral Haitian culture and of the common Haitian practice of *Bay Odyans* ("chatting" or "science argumentation"), the research team of the Chèche Konnen Center encouraged the use of such discourse during science classes, supported the use of the students' L1, Haitian Creole, and incorporated students' existing knowledge into science teaching. Thus, the program not only supported bilingualism by encouraging the use of L1, but also showed sensitivity to the C1 by making use of their C1 discourse practice. The research team found that the Haitian students provided with a culturally familiar setting showed growth in learning behaviors and science knowledge similar to that of the mainstream students (Ballenger, 2000; Hudicourt-Barnes, 2003). More rigorous and large-scale evaluations of this approach to science instruction for Haitian immigrants are needed.

The Chèche Konnen project differed from traditional approaches to teaching Haitian children both in the contexts created for learning and in the assessment procedures used. O. Lee & Fradd's (1996) study used tradi-

tional testing, whereas the Chèche Konnen classroom used discourse-embedded assessments. Thus, curriculum design that utilizes English-language learners' L1 and C1 in academic content areas may need to be supplemented, not just by teacher professional development, but also by language- and culture-sensitive measures to assess English-language learners' growth and development in learning.

CONCLUSION

We have sketched the challenges that becoming literate poses to all learners, then elaborated evidence that learning to read is a particular challenge for the L2/C2 learner. There were two themes in our analysis. The first is the complexity of the challenges posed, both to newcomers in a society and to the locals who are responsible for teaching, working with, or interacting with the newcomers, by the need to learn each others' languages, literacies, discourse patterns, and culturally prescribed ways of operating. We have argued that, if L2/C2 learners are to catch up with monolinguals in the academic, linguistic, and literacy skills needed for success in school and in the workplace, educational procedures are needed that enhance transfer, thus exploiting the knowledge of the L1 and C1 that learners bring with them. The second theme is the need, in complex and multifaceted domains like second-language learning and education for language minorities, for practice-embedded and practice-inspired research to complement the contributions of traditional basic and applied research. The fastest route to understanding what educational treatments work best to ensure language and literacy acquisition for various subgroups of L2 learners is to study successful practice, to build on the wisdom accumulated by successful practitioners, and to systematize that wisdom to be able to test it and make it public.

REFERENCES

Abedi, J., Lord, C., & Plummer, J. (1997). *Final report of language background as a variable in NAEP mathematics performance* (CSE Technical Report No. 429). Los Angeles: University of California, National Center for Research on Evaluation, Standards and Student Testing.

Abu-Rabia, S. (1995). Attitudes and cultural background and their relationship to English in a multicultural social context: The case of male and female Arab immigrants in Canada. *Educational Psychology, 15*(3), 323–336.

Abu-Rabia, S. (1998). Attitudes and culture in second language learning among Israeli-Arab students. *Curriculum and Teaching, 13*(1), 13–30.

Aceves, C. (2003). *Dímelo en Español: The characteristics of teacher-child oral language interactions in a Spanish-language preschool classroom.* Unpublished doctoral dissertation, Harvard Graduate School of Education, Cambridge, MA.

Adams, M. J. (1990). *Beginning to read: Thinking and learning about print.* Cambridge, MA: MIT Press.

Afkir, M. (2002). *Language and literacy in Moroccan mother-child interaction.* Unpublished doctoral dissertation, Mohammed V University, Rabat, Morocco.

Au, K. H. P., & Mason, J. M. (1981). Social organizational factors in learning to read: The balance of rights hypothesis. *Reading Research Quarterly, 17*(1), 115–152.

August, D., Carlo, M., Lively, T., McLaughlin, B., & Snow, C. (2005). Promoting the vocabulary growth of English learners. In T. Young & N. Hadaway (Eds.), *Building literacy: Supporting English learners in all classrooms* (pp. 96–112). Newark, DE: International Reading Association.

August, D., & Hakuta, K. (1997). *Improving schooling for language-minority children: A research agenda.* Washington, DC: National Academies Press.

Ballenger, C. (2000). Bilingual in two senses. In Z. Beykont (Ed.), *Lifting every voice: Pedagogy and the politics of bilingualism* (pp. 95–112). Cambridge, MA: Harvard Education Publishing Group.

Beech, J. R., & Keys, A. (1997). Reading, vocabulary and language preference in 7- to 8-year-old bilingual Asian children. *British Journal of Educational Psychology, 67*(4), 405–414.

Bradley, L., & Bryant, P. E. (1983). Categorizing sounds and learning to read: A causal connection. *Nature, 301,* 419–421.

Bronson, M. B., & Fetter, A. L. (1998, July). *Fall to spring changes in the social and mastery skills of Head Start children.* Paper presented at the fourth National Head Start Research Conference, Washington, DC.

Buriel, R., & Cardoza, D. (1988). Sociocultural correlates of achievement among three generations of Mexican American high school seniors. *American Educational Research Journal, 25*(2), 177–192.

Calero-Breckheimer, A., & Goetz, E. T. (1993). Reading strategies of biliterate children for English and Spanish texts. *Reading Psychology, 14*(3), 177–204.

Carlo, M. S., August, D., McLaughlin, B., Snow, C. E., Dressler, C., Lippman, D. N., et al. (2004). Closing the gap: Addressing the vocabulary needs of English-language learners in bilingual and mainstream classrooms. *Reading Research Quarterly, 39,* 188–215.

Carrigo, D. L. (2000). *Just how much English are they using? Teacher and student language distribution patterns, between Spanish and English, in upper-grade, two-way immersion Spanish classes.* Unpublished doctoral dissertation, Harvard University, Cambridge, MA.

Cazabon, M., Lambert, W. E., & Hall, G. (1998). *Becoming bilingual in the Amigos two-way immersion program.* Santa Cruz, CA: National Center for Research on Education, Diversity and Excellence.

Christian, D. (1994). *Two-way bilingual education: Students learning through two languages* (Educational Practice Report: 12). Santa Cruz, CA: National Center for Research on Cultural Diversity and Second Language Learning.

Cisero, C. A., & Royer, J. M. (1995). The development and cross-language transfer of phonological awareness. *Contemporary Educational Psychology, 20,* 275–303.

Comeau, L., Cormier, P., Grandmaison, E., & Lacroix, D. (1999). A longitudinal study of phonological processing skills in children learning to read in a second language. *Journal of Educational Psychology, 91*(1), 29–43.

Connor, U. (1983). Predictors of second-language reading performance. *Journal of Multilingual and Multicultural Development, 4*(4), 271–288.

Cook, D. C. (1991). A developmental approach to writing. *Reading Improvement, 28,* 300–304.

Cronnell, B. (1985). Language influences in the English writing of third- and sixth-grade Mexican-American students. *Journal of Educational Research, 78*(3), 168–173.

Cummins, J. (1991). Interdependence of first and second language proficiency in bilingual children. In E. Bialystok (Ed.), *Language processing in bilingual children* (pp. 70–89). Cambridge, England: Cambridge University Press.

DeVos, G., & Wetherall, W. (1983). *Japan's minorities.* London: Minorities Rights Group.

Dressler, C. (2000). *The word-inferencing strategies of bilingual and monolingual fifth graders: A case study approach.* Unpublished qualifying paper, Harvard Graduate School of Education, Cambridge, MA.

Droop, M., & Verhoeven, L. T. (1998). Background knowledge, linguistic complexity, and second-language reading comprehension. *Journal of Literacy Research, 30*(2), 253–271.

Duran, B. J., & Weffer, R. E. (1992). Immigrants' aspirations, high school process, and academic outcomes. *American Educational Research Journal, 29*(1), 163–181.

Durgunoğlu, A. Y., Nagy, W. E., & Hancin-Bhatt, B. J. (1993). Cross-language transfer of phonological awareness. *Journal of Educational Psychology, 85*(3), 453–465.

Eldering, L., & Vedder, P. (1993). Culture sensitive home intervention: The Dutch HIPPY experiment. In L. Eldering & P. Leseman (Eds.), *Early intervention and culture* (pp. 231–252). The Netherlands: UNESCO.

Fashola, O. S., Drum, P. A., Mayer, R. E., & Kang, S. J. (1996). A cognitive theory of orthographic transitioning: Predictable errors in how Spanish-speaking children spell English words. *American Educational Research Journal, 33*(4), 825–843.

Fernandez, R. M., & Nielsen, F. (1986). Bilingualism and Hispanic scholastic achievement: Some baseline results. *Social Science Research, 15*(1), 43–70.

Ferroli, L., & Shanahan, T. (1993). Voicing in Spanish to English knowledge transfer. *Yearbook of the National Reading Conference, 42,* 413–418.

Freebody, P., & Anderson, R. (1983). Effects of vocabulary difficulty, text cohesion, and schema availability on reading comprehension. *Reading Research Quarterly, 18*(3), 277–294.

Fukkink, R. G., & de Glopper, K. (1998). Effects of instruction in deriving word meaning from context: A meta-analysis. *Review of Educational Research, 68,* 450–469.

García-Vázquez, E. (1995). Acculturation and academics: Effects of acculturation on reading achievement among Mexican-American students. *Bilingual Research Journal, 19*(2), 304–315.

Goldenberg, C., Reese, L., & Gallimore, R. (1992). Effects of literacy materials from school on Latino children's home experiences and early reading achievement. *American Journal of Education, 100*(4), 497–536.

Gottardo, A., Yan, B., Siegel, L. S., & Wade-Woolley, L. (2001). Factors related to English reading performance in children with Chinese as a first language: More evidence of cross-language transfer of phonological processing. *Journal of Educational Psychology, 93*(3), 530–542.

Hancin-Bhatt, B., & Nagy, W. E. (1994). Lexical transfer and second language morphological development. *Applied Psycholinguistics, 15*(3), 289–310.

Hannon, P., & McNally, J. (1986). Children's understanding and cultural factors in reading test performance. *Educational Review, 38*(3), 237–246.

Howard, E. R., Christian, D., & Genesee, F. (2004). *The development of bilingualism and biliteracy from grades 3 to 5: A summary of findings from the CAL/CREDE Study of two-way immersion education* (Research Report 13). Santa Cruz, CA: Center for Research on Education, Diversity and Excellence.

Hudicourt-Barnes, J. (2003). The use of argumentation in Haitian Creole science classrooms. *Harvard Education Review, 73,* 73–93.

Huerta-Macias, A., & Quintero, E. (1992). Code-switching, bilingualism, and biliteracy: A case study. *Bilingual Research Journal, 16*(3/4), 69–90.

Jackson, N., Holm, A., & Dodd, B. (1998). Phonological awareness and spelling abilities of Cantonese-English bilingual children. *Asia Pacific Journal of Speech, Language, and Hearing, 3*(2), 79–96.

Jiménez, R. T. (1997). The strategic reading abilities and potential of five low-literacy Latina/o readers in middle school. *Reading Research Quarterly, 32*(3), 224–243.

Jiménez, R. T., García, G. E., & Pearson, D. P. (1996). The reading strategies of bilingual Latina/o students who are successful English readers: Opportunities and obstacles. *Reading Research Quarterly, 31*(1), 90–112.

Kennedy, E., & Park, H. S. (1994). Home language as a predictor of academic achievement: A comparative study of Mexican- and Asian-American youth. *Journal of Research and Development in Education, 27*(3), 188–194.

Kenner, C. (1999). Children's understandings of text in a multilingual nursery. *Language and Education, 13*(1), 1–16.

Kook, H. (1994). Leren lezen en schrijven in een tweetalige context: Antilliaanse en Arubaanse kinderen in Nederland [Learning to read and write in a bilingual context: Antillean and Aruban children in the Netherlands]. Unpublished doctoral dissertation, University of Amsterdam.

Lanauze, M., & Snow, C. E. (1989). The relation between first- and second-language writing skills: Evidence from Puerto Rican elementary school children in bilingual programs. *Linguistics and Education, 4,* 323–339.

Langer, J. A., Bartolome, L., Vasquez, O., & Lucas, T. (1990). Meaning construction in school literacy tasks: A study of bilingual students. *American Educational Research Journal, 27*(3), 427–471.

Lasisi, M. J., Falodun, S., & Onyehalu, A. S. (1988). The comprehension of first and second-language prose. *Journal of Research in Reading, 11*(1), 26–35.

Lee, O., & Fradd, S. (1996). Interactional patterns of linguistically diverse students and teachers: Insights for promoting science learning. *Linguistics and Education, 8,* 269–297.

Lee, S. (1996). *Unraveling the "model minority" stereotype: Listening to Asian American youth.* New York: Teachers College Press.

Lee, Y. (1991). Koreans in Japan and the United States. In M. A. Gibson & J. U. Ogbu (Eds.), *Minority status and schooling: A comparative study of immigrants and involuntary minorities* (pp. 139–165). New York: Garland.

Lesaux, N., & Siegel, L. (2003). The development of reading in children who speak English as a second language. *Developmental Psychology, 39,* 1005–1019.

Leseman, P. P. M., & de Jong, P. F. (1998). Home literacy: Opportunity, instruction, cooperation, and social-emotional quality predicting early reading achievement. *Reading Research Quarterly, 33*(3), 294–318.

Liow, S. J. R., & Poon, K. K. L. (1998). Phonological awareness in multilingual Chinese children. *Applied Psycholinguistics, 19*(3), 339–362.

Lively, T., August, D., Carlo, M., & Snow, C. (2003). *Vocabulary improvement program for English language learners and their classmates.* Baltimore: Paul H. Brookes.

Lloyd, K. M., Tienda, M., & Zajacova, A. (2002). Trends in educational achievement of minority students since Brown v. Board of Education. In T. Ready, C. Edley Jr., & C. E. Snow (Eds.), *Achieving high educational standards for all: Conference summary* (pp. 149–182). Washington, DC: National Academy Press.

Marinova-Todd, S. H., Marshall, D. B., & Snow, C. E. (2000). Three misconceptions about age and L2 learning. *TESOL Quarterly, 34,* 9–34.

Meyer, M., & Fienberg, S. (1992). *Assessing evaluation studies: The case of bilingual education strategies.* Washington, DC: National Academy Press.

Monzó, L., & Rueda, R. (2001). *Constructing achievement orientations toward literacy: An analysis of sociocultural activity in Latino home and community contexts* (CIERA Report No. 1-011). Ann Arbor, MI: Center for the Improvement of Early Reading Achievement.

Muysken, P., Kook, H., & Vedder, P. (1996). Papiamento/Dutch code-switching in bilingual parent-child reading. *Applied Psycholinguistics, 17,* 485–505.

Nagy, W. E., García, G. E., Durgunolu, A. Y., & Hancin-Bhatt, B. (1993). Spanish-English bilingual students' use of cognates in English reading. *Journal of Reading Behavior, 25*(3), 241–259.

Nagy, W. E., McClure, E. F., & Mir, M. (1997). Linguistic transfer and the use of context by Spanish-English bilinguals. *Applied Psycholinguistics, 18*(4), 431–452.

Nathenson-Mejía, S. (1989). Writing in a second language: Negotiating meaning through invented spelling. *Language Arts, 66*(5), 516–526.

National Center for Education Statistics. (1995). *Approaching kindergarten: A look at preschoolers in the United States—Statistical analysis report.* Washington, DC: U.S. Department of Education, Office of Educational Research and Improvement.

National Center for Educaton Statistics. (2003). *National assessment of educational progress: Reading assessments.* Washington, DC: U.S. Department of Education, Institute of Education Sciences.

Nguyen, A., Shin, F., & Krashen, S. (2001). Development of the first language is not a barrier to second-language acquisition: Evidence from Vietnamese immigrants to the United States. *International Journal of Bilingual Education and Bilingualism, 4*(3), 159–164.

Ogbu, J. (1992). Understanding cultural differences and school learning. *Education Libraries, 16,* 7–11.

Oller, D. K., Cobo-Lewis, A. B., & Eilers, R. E. (1998). Phonological translation in bilingual and monolingual children. *Applied Psycholinguistics, 19*(2), 259–278.

Pucci, S. L., & Ulanoff, S. H. (1998). What predicts second language reading success? A study of home and school variables. *ITL: Review of Applied Linguistics, 121, 122,* 1–18.

RAND Reading Study Group. (2002). *Reading for understanding.* Santa Monica, CA: RAND.

Reese, L., Garnier, H., Gallimore, R., & Goldenberg, C. (2000). Longitudinal analysis of the antecedents of emergent Spanish literacy and middle-school English reading achievement of Spanish-speaking students. *American Educational Research Journal, 37*(3), 633–662.

Rosenthal, A. S., Baker, K., & Ginsburg, A. (1983). The effect of language background on achievement level and learning among elementary school students. *Sociology of Education, 56*(4), 157–169.

Rosowsky, A. (2001). Decoding as a cultural practice and its effects on the reading process of bilingual pupils. *Language and Education, 15*(1), 56–70.

Royer, J. M., & Carlo, M. S. (1991). Assessing the language acquisition progress of limited English proficient students: Problems and a new alternative. *Applied Measurement in Education, 4*(2), 85–113.

Runnymede Trust. (1998). *Race policy in education* (Briefing paper no. 1). Retrieved February 10, 2005, from http://www.runnymedetrust.org/publications/briefingPapers.html.

Schonewille, B., Kloprogge, J. J. J., & van der Leij, A. (2000). *Kaleidoskoop en piramide: Samenvattende eindrapportage* [Kaleidoskoop and piramide: Summary final report]. (Evaluatie Begeleidingscommissie projecten voor-en vroegschoolse educatie—EBC.) Utrecht, The Netherlands: Sardes.

Shimahara, A. (1991). Social mobility and education: Burakumin in Japan. In M. A. Gibson & J. U. Ogbu (Eds.), *Minority status and schooling: A comparative study of immigrants and involuntary minorities* (pp. 327–356). New York: Garland.

Smith, S. J., & Martin, D. (1997). Investigating literacy and pre-literacy skills in Panjabi/English schoolchildren. *Educational Review, 49*(2), 181–197.

Snow, C. E., Burns, S., & Griffin, P. (Eds.). (1998). *Preventing reading difficulties in young children*. Washington, DC: National Academy Press.

Stahl, S., van Kleeck, A., & Bauer, E. (2003). *On reading books to children: Parents and teachers*. Mahwah, NJ: Erlbaum.

Stanovich, K. E. (1986). Matthew effects in reading: Some consequences of individual differences in the acquisition of literacy. *Reading Research Quarterly, 21*(4), 360–407.

Stubbs, M. (1980). *Language and literacy: The sociolinguistics of reading and writing*. Boston: Routledge & Kegan Paul.

Suárez-Orozco, C., & Suárez-Orozco, M. M. (2001). *Children of immigration*. Cambridge, MA: Harvard University Press.

Suárez-Orozco, M., & Páez, M. M. (2002). *Latinos: Remaking America*. Berkeley: University of California Press.

Sweet, A. P., & Snow, C. E. (Eds.). (2003). *Rethinking reading comprehension: Solving problems in the teaching of literacy*. New York: Guilford Press.

Tabors, P. O. (1997). *One child, two languages: A guide for preschool educators of children learning English as a second language*. Baltimore: Paul H. Brookes.

Tesser, P. T. M., Merens, J. G. F., van Praag, C. S., & Iedema, J. (1999). *Rapportage minderheden: Positie in het onderwijs en op de arbeidsmarkt* [Minorities report: Position in education and the labor market]. Den Haag, The Netherlands: Sociaal Cultureel Planbureau.

Umbel, V. M., Pearson, B. Z., Fernandez, M. C., & Oller, D. K. (1992). Measuring bilingual children's receptive vocabularies. *Child Development, 63*(4), 1012–1020.

U.S. Bureau of the Census. (1993). *1990 census of the population: The foreign born population in the United States*. Washington, DC: U.S. Government Printing Office.

Veen, A., Roeleveld, J., & Leseman, P. (2000). *Evaluatie van Kaleidoskoop en Piramide, Eindrapportage* [Evaluation of Kaleidoskoop and Piramide, final report]. Amsterdam: SCO-Kohnstamm Instituut.

Verhallen, S., Janssen, K., Jas, R., Snoeken, H., & Top, W. (1996). *Taalstages op de werkvloer* [Language practica at work]. Amsterdam: Instituut voor Taalonderzoek en Taalonderwijs Anderstaligen, Universiteit van Amsterdam.

Verhoeven, L. T. (1994). Transfer in bilingual development: The linguistic interdependence hypothesis revisited. *Language Learning, 44*(3), 381–415.

Wagenaar, E. (1993). Tweetaligheid en het aanvangsonderwijs: Een onderzoek naar de effecten van tweetalig kleuteronderwijs op de schoolloopbaan van Marokkaanse kinderen [Bilingualism in preschool: A study of the effect of bilingual 3-year-old classrooms on the school trajectories of Moroccan children]. Unpublished master's thesis, University of Amsterdam.

Walters, K., & Gunderson, L. (1985). Effects of parent volunteers reading first language (L1) books to ESL students. *Reading Teacher, 39*(1), 66–69.

Wang, M., & Geva, E. (2003). Spelling performance of Chinese ESL children: Lexical and visual-orthographic processes. *Applied Psycholinguistics, 24*(1), 1–25.

White, C. E. (2000). *Implementation of a vocabulary curriculum designed for second-language-learners: Knowledge base and strategies used by monolingual and bilingual teachers*. Unpublished qualifying paper, Harvard Graduate School of Education, Cambridge, MA.

Wilkinson, L. C., Milosky, L. M., & Genishi, C. (1986). Second language learners' use of requests and responses in elementary classrooms. *Topics in Language Disorders, 6*(2), 57–70.

Willig, A. C. (1985). A meta-analysis of selected studies on the effectiveness of bilingual education. *Review of Educational Research, 55*(3), 269–318.

Zhou, M. (2001). Contemporary immigration and the dynamics of race and ethnicity. In N. Smelser, W. J. Wilson, & F. Mitchell (Eds.), *America becoming: Vol. 1. Racial trends and their consequences* (pp. 200–242). Washington, DC: National Academies Press.

Zutell, J., & Allen, V. (1988). The English spelling strategies of Spanish-speaking bilingual children. *TESOL Quarterly, 22*(2), 333–340.

CHAPTER 4

Mathematical Thinking and Learning

ERIK DE CORTE and LIEVEN VERSCHAFFEL

Mathematics education is incontestably one of the most representative examples of the subject matter orientation in instructional and developmental psychology. As shown by Kilpatrick (1992; see also Ginsburg, Klein, & Starkey, 1998), mathematics education and psychology have been intertwined throughout the past century, but for a large part of that era the approaches from both sides were complementary rather than symbiotic. On the one hand, psychologists used mathematics as a domain for studying and testing theoretical issues of cognition and learning; on the other hand, mathematics educationalists often borrowed and selectively used concepts and techniques from psychology. Sometimes the mutual attitude was critical. For instance, Freudenthal (1991) criticized psychological research for disregarding the specific nature of mathematics as a domain and of mathematics teaching; others, like Davis (1989) and Wheeler (1989), reproached psychologists for taking mathematics education as a given and uncontroversial, without questioning its current goals and practices. However, especially since the 1970s, an increasingly symbiotic and mutually fertilizing relationship between both groups has emerged, facilitated by the growing im-

pact of the cognitive movement in psychology and by the creation of interactive forums such as the International Group for the Psychology of Mathematics Education founded in 1976. Today, the domain of mathematics learning and instruction has become a fully fledged and interdisciplinary field of research and study, aiming at a better understanding of the processes underlying the acquisition and development of mathematical knowledge, skills, beliefs, and attitudes, as well as at the design—based on that better understanding—of powerful mathematics teaching-learning environments.

A parallel trend is the rapprochement in past decades between developmental and cognitive psychology. For a long time in the history of psychology, both subdisciplines adhered to different, even conflicting paradigms. Whereas developmentalists considered development as the necessary prerequisite, and sometimes even the final goal of education, learning and instructional psychologists believed that cognitive development in general is not the prerequisite but the result of education (De Corte & Weinert, 1996). In contrast to these extreme positions, there has developed, especially since the last 2 decades of the preceding century, a strong movement toward a synthesis of the concepts of development, learning, instruction, and the interactive mind. As argued by De Corte and Weinert:

> First of all, there is convincing theoretical and empirical evidence that not only the relationship between development and learning but also the relationship between instruction and learning is very complicated. Maturational precursors, implicit learning, and self-organizing processes that spontaneously integrate new information with already available knowledge all mean that cognitive development always entails more than the sum of explicit learning processes. In addition more must be learned than can be taught. These restrictions on the importance of explicit learning do not mean that school learning and deliberate practice are unimportant for cognitive development. Quite the opposite: to a considerable degree cognitive development consists in the acquisition of expertise in a variety of content domains. (p. xxvii)

As a result of these trends, the boundaries between developmental and instructional psychology, but also between those subdisciplines of psychology and research in mathematics education, have become increasingly blurred. Consequently, in this chapter, we do not attempt to make clear distinctions between or to classify investigations in those different domains.

Taking into account space restrictions, but especially the vast amount of research on mathematics learning and teaching that is now available, a comprehensive and all-inclusive coverage of the literature is beyond the scope of this chapter. Whereas school mathematics involves arithmetic, algebra, measurement, and geometry, as well as data handling and probability, we focus on arithmetic only, a focus that reflects the preponderance of current psychological and educational research on mathematics education, as well as our own research interests. In our discussion of learning and teaching arithmetic, we give special emphasis to whole number arithmetic and word problem solving, topics that have been stressed in reform documents issued over the past decade (e.g., National Council of Teachers of Mathematics [NCTM], 2000) because of their importance for the acquisition of basic competence in mathematics. Our review is also selective with regard to age range, focusing on primary school children, although some attention will be paid to lower secondary school students.

Finally, we have taken into account the excellent review on the development of children's mathematical thinking by Ginsburg, Klein, et al. (1998) in the previous edition of the *Handbook of Child Psychology*. For instance, we do not discuss the history of the field because their chapter offers a brief but very informative overview. For complementary information on issues and topics that are not reviewed here, we refer readers especially to the following sources: *The Development of Mathematical Skills*, edited by Donlan (1998); the report published by the National Research Council (NRC; 2001a), *Adding It Up: Helping Children Learn Mathematics*, edited by Kilpatrick, Swafford, and Findell; *The Development of Arithmetic Concepts and Skills: Constructing Adaptive Expertise*, edited by Baroody and Dowker (2003); *Second International Handbook of Mathematics Education*, edited by Bishop, Clements, Keitel, Kilpatrick, and Leung (2003); and the forthcoming *Second Handbook of Research on Mathematics Teaching and Learning*, edited by Lester (in press). Although our account of the domain of mathematical learning and thinking is selective in terms of mathematical content and age range, we have aimed at international representativeness of the work discussed, albeit the focus still is mostly on numerical thinking in Western societies.

As a framework for reviewing the selected literature on the development of mathematical thinking and learning, and for the presentation and discussion of research-based instructional interventions, we use a model for the design of powerful environments for learning and teaching mathematics that is structured according to four interrelated components (De Corte, Verschaffel, & Masui, 2004):

1. *Competence:* This part of the framework analyzes and describes the components of mathematical competence or proficiency; it answers the question: What has to be learned to acquire mathematical competence?

2. *Learning:* This component focuses on the characteristics of productive mathematics learning and developmental processes; it addresses the question: What kind of learning/developmental processes should be induced in students to facilitate their acquisition of competence?

3. *Intervention:* This part of the framework elaborates principles and guidelines for the design of powerful environments for mathematics learning and instruction; it should answer the question: What are appropriate instructional methods and environments to

elicit and maintain in students the required learning and developmental processes?

4. *Assessment:* This component of the model refers to forms and methods of assessment for monitoring and improving mathematics learning and teaching; the question here is: Which types of instrument are necessary to assess students' mastery of components of mathematical competence and, thus, their progress toward proficiency?

In a systematic discussion of the research literature, it is useful to distinguish among those four components of the *C*ompetence, *L*earning, *I*ntervention, *A*ssessment (CLIA) model. In the reality of curriculum development, designing learning environments, and classroom practices, the components of the framework are narrowly intertwined. For instance, stressing conceptual understanding rather than the acquisition of routine procedures as a component of competence has strong implications for the kind of learning activities in which students should get involved, as well as for the instructional interventions to induce in them those activities. Obviously, assessing conceptual understanding in mathematics requires different questions and tasks than checking to see if students can perform routine procedures. These interactive relationships among the CLIA components will become more apparent throughout this chapter.

COMPONENTS OF MATHEMATICAL COMPETENCE

Taking into account the literature of the past 15 to 20 years (see, e.g., Baroody & Dowker, 2003; De Corte, Greer, & Verschaffel, 1996; NCTM, 1989, 2000; NRC, 2001a; Schoenfeld, 1985, 1992), becoming competent in mathematics can be conceived of as acquiring a mathematical disposition:

Learning mathematics extends beyond learning concepts, procedures, and their applications. It also includes developing a disposition toward mathematics and seeing mathematics as a powerful way for looking at situations. Disposition refers not simply to attitudes but to a tendency to think and to act in positive ways. Students' mathematical dispositions are manifested in the way they approach tasks—whether with confidence, willingness to explore alternatives, perseverance, and interest—and in their tendency to reflect on their own thinking. (NCTM, 1989, p. 230)

Building up and mastering such a disposition requires the acquisition of five categories of cognitive, affective, and conative components:

1. A well-organized and flexibly accessible domain-specific knowledge base involving the facts, symbols, algorithms, concepts, and rules that constitute the contents of mathematics as a subject matter field.

2. Heuristics methods, that is, search strategies for problem solving that do not guarantee but significantly increase the probability of finding the correct solution because they induce a systematic approach to the task. Examples of heuristics are decomposing a problem into subgoals and making a graphic representation of a problem.

3. Metaknowledge, which involves knowledge about one's cognitive functioning (metacognitive knowledge, e.g., believing that one's cognitive potential can be developed and improved through learning and effort) and knowledge about one's motivation and emotions that can be used to deliberately improve volitional efficiency (e.g., becoming aware of one's fear of failure when confronted with a complex mathematical task or problem).

4. Self-regulatory skills, which embrace skills relating to the self-regulation of one's cognitive processes (metacognitive skills or cognitive self-regulation; e.g., planning and monitoring one's problem-solving processes) and skills for regulating one's volitional processes/activities (metavolitional skills or volitional self-regulation; e.g., keeping up one's attention and motivation to solve a given problem).

5. Positive beliefs about oneself in relation to mathematical learning and problem solving (self-efficacy beliefs), about the social context in which mathematical activities take place, and about mathematics and mathematical learning and problem solving.

We know from past research that knowledge and skills that students have learned are often neither accessible nor usable when necessary to solve a problem at hand (Cognition and Technology Group at Vanderbilt, 1997). Building a disposition toward skilled learning and thinking should help to overcome this phenomenon, which Whitehead already in 1929 labeled "inert knowledge." To overcome this inertia, it is necessary that these different kinds of knowledge, skills, and beliefs are acquired and mastered in an *integrated way,* resulting in the development of the intended disposition. According to Perkins (1995), two crucial aspects of such a disposition are *sensitivity* to situations in which it is relevant and appropriate to use acquired knowledge and skills and the *inclination* to do so. Perkins argues that these aspects are both determined by the beliefs a person holds. For instance, one's beliefs about what counts as a mathematical context and what one finds interesting or important have a strong impact on the situations one is sensitive to and whether or not one engages in them.

This view of mathematical competence is quite consonant with the conception of mathematical proficiency as elaborated in the report of the NRC (2001a) which defines proficiency in terms of five interwoven strands: conceptual understanding, computational fluency, strategic competence, adaptive reasoning, and productive disposition. Conceptual understanding and procedural fluency are the two most important aspects of a well-organized and flexibly accessible domain-specific knowledge base. Conceptual understanding refers to "comprehension of mathematical concepts, operations, and relations" and procedural fluency to "skill in carrying out procedures flexibly, accurately, efficiently, and appropriately" (p. 5). Strategic competence is defined as "ability to formulate, represent, and solve mathematical problems" (p. 5); this obviously implies heuristic strategies but also aspects of cognitive self-regulation. Adaptive reasoning, viewed as the "capacity for logical thought, reflection, explanation, and justification" (p. 5), involves especially skills in cognitive self-regulation (see also p. 118). Finally, a productive disposition is conceived of as a "habitual inclination to see mathematics as sensible, useful, and worthwhile, coupled with a belief in diligence and one's efficacy" (p. 5); this strand of proficiency converges with the positive beliefs mentioned earlier, but it also relates to the sensitivity and inclination aspects of a mathematical disposition.

The conceptualization of mathematical proficiency in the report of the NRC (2001a) is thus well in line with our elaboration of the competence component of the CLIA framework. Both perspectives embody also what Hatano (1982, 1988; see also Baroody, 2003) has called adaptive expertise, that is, the ability to apply meaningfully acquired knowledge and skills flexibly and creatively in a large variety of situations, familiar as well as unfamiliar. Nevertheless, some aspects of our analysis of competence are not, or at least not explicitly, included or articulated in the definition of proficiency in the NRC report, namely, metaknowledge and especially volitional self-regulation skills, which are essential to stay concentrated on a task and to sustain and persevere in achieving it (Corno et al., 2002). A major point on which both perspectives on mathematical competence do strongly agree is that the different components involved are interwoven and, therefore, need to be acquired integratively. In fact, the interdependency of the five strands outlined earlier is the leitmotif of the report: "Learning is not an all-or-none phenomenon, and as it proceeds, each strand of mathematical proficiency should be developed in synchrony with the others. That development takes time" (NRC, 2001a, p. 133).

This standpoint has very important implications from a developmental perspective. Indeed, it means that from the very beginning of mathematics education, attention has to be paid to the parallel and integrated acquisition in children of the different components of competence. In this respect, we endorse the following point of view of the NRC (2001a, p. 133) report: "One of the most challenging tasks faced by teachers in prekindergarten to grade 8 is to see that children are making progress along every strand and not just one or two."

In the next part of this section, we focus on several components of competence by reviewing a selection of the recent literature that has contributed to unravel their development in children. Thereby we will take into account the interdependency of the different strands of proficiency: number sense, single-digit computation, and multidigit arithmetic, which constitute major aspects of the domain-specific knowledge involved in the primary school mathematics curriculum; word problem solving, in which domain-specific knowledge but also heuristic strategies and self-regulation skills and even beliefs all interactively play an important role; and mathematics-related beliefs, a topic that only recently has attracted the interest of researchers. Most of these topics received relatively little attention in the chapter on the development of children's mathematical thinking in the previous edition of this *Handbook* (Ginsburg, Klein, et al., 1998), which focused more on development during infancy, toddlerhood, and the preschool years.

Number Sense

In the reform documents for mathematics education issued in different countries over the past decades, it has been stressed that the elementary mathematics curriculum should pay substantial attention to the development of number concepts and numeration skills (see, e.g., Australian Education Council, 1990; Cockcroft, 1982; NCTM, 1989). One of the most typical aspects of the reform documents in this respect is the emphasis they put—already in the early grades of primary school—on number sense (e.g., NCTM, 1989); this is not at all surprising as it typifies the current view of learning mathematics as a sense-making activity.

McIntosh, Reys, and Reys (1992, p. 3) describe number sense as follows:

> Number sense refers to a person's general understanding of number and operations. It refers to a person's general understanding of number and operations along with the ability and inclination to use this understanding in flexible ways to make mathematical judgments and to develop useful strategies for handling numbers and operations. It reflects an inclination and an ability to use numbers and quantitative methods as a means of communicating, processing and interpreting information. It results in, and reciprocally derives from, an expectation that numbers are useful and that mathematics has a certain regularity.

Further discussions and analyses have resulted in listings of the essential components of number sense (McIntosh et al., 1992; Sowder, 1992), descriptions of students displaying (lack of) number sense (Reys & Yang, 1998), and an in-depth theoretical analysis of number sense from a psychological perspective (Greeno, 1991a).

Probably the most comprehensive and most influential attempt to articulate a structure that clarifies, organizes, and interrelates some of the generally agreed upon components of basic number sense has been provided by McIntosh et al. (1992). In their model, they distinguish three areas where number sense plays a key role: number concepts, operations with number, and applications of number and operation:

1. The first component, "knowledge of and facility with numbers," involves subskills such as a sense of orderliness of number ("Indicate a number on an empty number line, given some benchmarks"), multiple representations for numbers ($\frac{3}{4} = 0.75$), a sense of rela-

tive and absolute magnitude of numbers ("Have you lived more or less than 1,000 days?"), and a system of benchmarks (recognizing that the sum of two 2-digit numbers is less than 200).

2. The second component, called "knowledge of and facility with operations," involves understanding the effect of operations (knowing that multiplication does *not* always make bigger), understanding mathematical properties (e.g., commutativity, associativity, and distributivity, and intuitively applying these properties in inventing procedures for mental computation), and understanding the relationship between operations (the inverse relationships between addition and subtraction and between multiplication and division) to solve a problem such as $11 - 9 =$ _____ by means of indirect addition, or to solve a division problem such as 480/8 by multiplying $8 \times$ _____ $= 480$.

3. The third component, "applying knowledge and facility with numbers and operations to computational settings," involves subskills such as understanding the relationship between problem contexts and the necessary computation (e.g., "If Skip spent $2.88 for apples, $2.38 for bananas, and $3.76 for oranges, could Skip pay for this fruit with $10?" can be solved quickly and confidently by adding the three *estimated* quantities rather than by *exact* calculation), awareness that multiple strategies exist for a given problem, inclination to utilize an efficient representation and/or method (not solving $(375 + 375 + 375 + 375 + 375)/5$ by first adding the five numbers and then dividing the answer by 5), and inclination to review data and results (having a natural tendency to examine one's answer in light of the original problem).

Several researchers have documented the problems children experience with the different aspects of number sense. For instance, Reys and Yang (1998) investigated the relationship between computational performance and number sense among sixth- and eight-grade students in Taiwan. Seventeen students were interviewed about their knowledge of the different aspects of number sense from the theoretical framework mentioned here. Students' overall performance on number sense was lower than their performance on similar questions requiring written computation. There was little evidence that identifiable components of number sense, such as use of benchmarks, were naturally used by Taiwanese students in their decision making.

In line with his situative view of cognition, Greeno (1991a; see also Sowder, 1992) has suggested the following metaphor for developing number sense. He characterized it as an environment, with the collection of resources needed for knowing, understanding, and reasoning all at different places within this environment: "Learning in the domain, in this view, is analogous to learning to get around in an environment and to use the resources there in conducting one's activities productively and enjoyably" (p. 45).

People who have developed number sense can move around easily within this environment because of their access to the necessary resources. Teaching becomes the act of "indicating what resources the environment has, where they can be found, what some of the easy routes are, and where interesting sites are worth visiting" (p. 48).

Given that number sense is conceptualized in such a way, it is evident that, according to Greeno (1991a), Reys and Yang (1998, p. 227), and many others, the development of number sense "is not a finite entity that a student has or does not have but rather a process that develops and matures with experience and knowledge." This development results from a whole range of mathematical activities on a day-by-day basis within each mathematics lesson, rather than from a designated set or subset of specially designed activities (Greeno, 1991a; Reys & Yang, 1998).

According to many authors, estimation is closely connected to number sense (or to numeracy). For instance, Van den Heuvel-Panhuizen (2001, p. 173) starts her didactical treatise of estimation as follows: "Estimation is one of the fundamental aspects of numeracy. It is the preeminent calculation form in which numeracy manifests itself most explicitly." Besides the fact that it is pervasively present in the daily lives of both children and adults, estimation is also important because it is related to and constitutive of other conceptual, procedural, strategic, and attitudinal aspects of mathematical ability (Siegler & Booth, in press; Sowder, 1992; Van den Heuvel-Panhuizen, 2001). In her review of the literature on estimation up to the early 1990s, Sowder differentiated three forms of estimation: computational estimation (performing some mental computation on approximations of the original numbers of a required computation), measurement estimation (estimating the length or area of a room), and numerosity estimation (estimating the number of items in a set, such as the number of people in a theater). In a more recent overview of

the literature, Siegler and Booth identify a fourth category, number line estimation (translating numbers into positions on number lines, such as a 0–100 or a 1–1,000 number line). For all these types of estimation, the older and more recent research, which is excellently reviewed in the works cited earlier, shows that both children and adults use varied estimation strategies, that the variety, efficiency, sophistication, and adaptivity of these strategies increase with age and experience, and that estimation is a domain wherein all aspects of a mathematical disposition are integratively involved.

The preceding discussion clearly shows the dispositional nature of number sense, involving not only aspects of capacity but also aspects of inclination and sensitivity; it also illustrates that number sense remains a vague notion and that its relationships with other aspects of arithmetic competence need further clarification. As stated in NCTM's (1989, p. 39) *Curriculum and Evaluation Standards for School Mathematics,* number sense is "an intuition about numbers that is drawn from all varied meanings of numbers." Nowadays, it is very common in the mathematics education community to agree that this intuition is important; however, it is hard to define and even harder to operationalize in view of the research. And recently there has been a rash of more or less related terms, such as "numeracy" and "mathematical literacy," also with little definitional precision. Indeed, in most cases where we have encountered it, number sense is defined so broadly that it includes problem solving but also most, if not all, other skills that constitute a mathematical disposition (McIntosh et al., 1992). Although we acknowledge its power in curricular reforms, we have some doubts about its usefulness for scientific research unless its specific meaning is articulated in a more clear and consistent way.

Single-Digit Computation

The domain of single-digit addition and subtraction is undoubtedly one of the most frequently investigated areas of numerical cognition and school mathematics. Much work in the domain has been done from a cognitive/rationalist, especially an information-processing perspective. Numerous older and more recent studies provide detailed descriptions of the progression in children of orally stated single-digit additions (e.g., 3 + 4 = _____): from the earliest concrete counting-all-with-materials strategy; over several types of more advanced counting strategies (such as counting-all-without-materials, counting-on-from-first, and counting-on-from-larger, and derived-fact strategies) that take advantage of certain arithmetic principles to shorten and simplify the computation; to the final state of "known facts" (for extensive reviews of this research, see Baroody & Tiilikainen, 2003; Fuson, 1992; NRC, 2001a; Thompson, 1999).

Similar levels for subtraction have been described, although this developmental sequence is somewhat less clearly defined (Thompson, 1999).

These and other studies document how, at any given time during this development, an individual child uses a variety of addition strategies, even within the same session and for the same item (for an overview, see Siegler, 1998). Even older students and adults do not always perform at the highest developmental level of "known fact use" but still demonstrate use of a range of different procedures even for simple addition problems (Siegler, 1998).

The exact organization of the store of arithmetic facts in subjects having reached the final stage of this developmental process is a special area of research in numerical cognition (for an overview, see Ashcraft, 1995; Dehaene, 1993). Most of this research has been done with adults rather than with elementary school children. Most models share the notion that in the "expert fact retriever," arithmetic facts such as $2 + 3 = 5$ are memorized in and automatically retrieved from a stored associative network or lexicon (Ashcraft, 1995). Well-known "problem size effects" (i.e., the fact that the time needed to solve single-digit addition problems increases slightly with the size of the operands) and "tie effects" (i.e., the fact that response time for ties such as $2 + 2$ remains constant or increases only moderately with operand size) are considered in this common view as reflecting the duration and difficulty of memory retrieval. According to Ashcraft (1995; Ashcraft & Christy, 1995), both effects faithfully reflect the frequency with which arithmetic facts are acquired and practiced by individuals. However, it is quite generally accepted that not all experts' knowledge of single-digit arithmetic is mentally represented in separate and independent units. Part of their knowledge about simple addition seems to be stored in rules (e.g., $N + 0 = N$) rather than as isolated facts (e.g., $1 + 0 = 1$, $2 + 0 = 2$). A related assumption is that not all problems are represented. For instance, for each commutative pair of problems (e.g., $3 + 5$ and $5 + 3$), there might be only one representational unit in the network.

It is well known that the developmental process from counting to fact retrieval does not proceed smoothly for all children. Single-digit arithmetic among children with mathematical difficulties or learning problems has also attracted a lot of research. Generally speaking, this research shows that learning-disabled children and others having difficulty with mathematics do not use procedures that differ from the progression described here. Rather, they are just slower than others in moving through it (NRC, 2001a; Torbeyns, Verschaffel, & Ghesquiere, 2005). Especially the last step of arithmetic facts mastery seems to be very difficult for them, and for some of these children, these retrieval difficulties appear to reflect a highly persistent, perhaps lifelong, deficit rather than merely a temporary developmental delay (Geary, 2003).

Several other studies have addressed the relationship between declarative and procedural knowledge by investigating which kind of knowledge develops before the other. As far as single-digit addition and subtraction is concerned, this question has focused on the relationship between children's understanding of certain mathematical principles, especially commutativity, and their progression toward more efficient counting strategies (e.g., the counting-on-from-larger strategy, otherwise known as the *min* strategy) based on these mathematical principles (for extensive reviews of this literature, see Baroody, Wilkins, & Tiilikainen, 2003; Rittle-Johnson & Siegler, 1998). This research indicates that conceptual and procedural knowledge are positively correlated, but also that most children understand the commutativity concept before they generate the procedure(s) based on it. This latter finding seems to favor, at least for the domain of single-digit addition, the "concepts first" above the "skills first" view. However, whereas in previous decades the debate about the relationship between conceptual and procedural knowledge was dominated by proponents of these two camps, most researchers now adhere to a more moderate perspective. They assume, on the one hand, that the relationship between procedural and conceptual knowledge develops more concurrently and/or iteratively than suggested by both opposite views and, on the other hand, that the nature of this relationship may differ among different mathematical (sub)domains (Baroody, 2003; Rittle-Johnson & Siegler, 1998).

Although the research concerning the development of children's strategies for multiplying and dividing single-digit numbers is less extensive than for single-digit addition and subtraction, there is a growing body of studies in this domain, too (e.g., Anghileri, 1999; Butterworth, Marschesini, & Girelli, 2003; LeFevre, Smith-Chant, Hiscock, Daley, & Morris, 2003; Lemaire & Siegler, 1995; Mulligan & Mitchelmore, 1997; Steffe & Cobb, 1998). As for single-digit addition and subtraction, this research documents how, generally speaking, children progress from concrete (material-, fingers-, or paper-based) counting-all strategies, through additive-related calculations (repeated adding and additive doubling), pattern-based (e.g., multiplying by 9 as by $10 - 1$), and derived-fact strategies (e.g., deriving 7×8 from $7 \times 7 = 49$), to a phase of learned multiplication products. However, there is less consistency between the names and the characterizations of the different categories than for addition and subtraction. As for these two operations, research on multiplication and division has shown that multiplicity and flexibility of strategy use are basic features of people doing simple number combinations, even for older children and adults (LeFevre et al., 2003). Here, too, research is unequivocal about the exact features of the organization and the functioning of the multiplication facts store and, more particularly, to what extent (part of) experts' knowledge about the multiplication table is stored in rules ($0 \times N = 0$, $1 \times N = N$, $10 \times N = N0$, etc.) rather than as strengthened associative links between particular mathematical expressions and their correct answers. Based on a recent study with third and fifth graders solving multiplication items with the larger operand either placed first ($7 \times 3 =$ _____) or second ($3 \times 7 =$ _____), Butterworth et al. (2003, p. 201) concluded:

> The child learning multiplication facts may not be passive, simply building associative connections between an expression and its answer as a result of practice. Rather, the combinations held in memory may be reorganized in a principled way that takes into account a growing understanding of the operation, including the commutativity principle, and, perhaps, other properties of multiplication.

Baroody (1993) arrived at a similar conclusion based on a study on the role of relational knowledge in the development of mastering multiplication basic fact knowledge, and especially of knowledge about the addition doubles in learning multiplication combinations involving 2 (2×6, 2×11, $2 \times 50 \ldots$).

Probably the most ambitious and most influential attempt to model this development and this variety of strategy use in single-digit arithmetic from an information-processing perspective is found in the subsequent versions of the computer model of strategy choice and strategy change in the domain of simple addition developed by Siegler and associates. We briefly describe the latest version of the Strategy Choice and Discovery Simulation (SCADS; Shrager & Siegler, 1998; see also Siegler, 2001; Torbeyns, Arnaud, Lemaire, & Verschaffel, 2004). Central in SCADS is a database with information about problems and strategies that plays a key role in the strategy choice process. The first type of information, information about problems, consists of problem-answer associations, that is, associations between individual problems and potential answers to these problems, which differ in strength. The second type of information includes global, featural, problem-specific, and novelty data about each strategy available in the database. Whenever SCADS is presented with a problem, it activates the global, featural, and problem-specific data about the speed and accuracy of each of the available strategies. The model weights these data in terms of the amount of information they reflect and how recently they were generated. Weighted efficiency and novelty data for each strategy provide the input for stepwise regression analyses, which compute the projected strength of the different strategies on the problem: The strategy with the highest projected strength has the highest probability to be chosen. In case the initially chosen strategy does not work, another strategy with less projected strength is chosen, and this process continues until a strategy is chosen that meets the model's criteria. An important advantage of SCADS (compared to its predecessors) is that it also discovers new strategies and learns about them. It does so through representing each strategy as a modular sequence of operators (rather than just a unit) and by maintaining a working memory trace of the strategy's execution (rather than just recording speed and accuracy data). A metacognitive system uses the representation of the strategies and the memory traces to formulate new strategies based on the detection of redundant sequences of behavior and the identification of more efficient orders of executing operators. SCADS evaluates these proposed strategies for consistency with a "goal sketch," which indicates the criteria that legitimate strategies in the domain of simple addition must meet. If the proposed strategy violates the conceptual constraints specified by the goal sketch filters, it is abandoned. If the proposed strategy is in accord with the conceptual constraints (approved strategies), SCADS adds it to its strategy repertoire. The newly discovered strategy thus modifies the model's database and, consequently, influences future strategy choices. According to the developers of SCADS, its performance on single-digit additions and on additions with one addend above 20 is highly consistent with the strategy choice and discovery phenomena that they observed in their studies with young children (Shrager & Siegler; 1998; Siegler & Jenkins, 1989; see also Siegler, 2001).

Siegler's strategy choice model has been tested for simple addition and also, although to a much less fine-grained extent, for multiplication. Siegler and Lemaire (1997) report a longitudinal investigation of French second graders' acquisition of single-digit multiplication skills. Speed, accuracy, and strategy data were assessed three times in the year when children learned multiplication. The data showed improvements in speed and accuracy, which reflected four different aspects of strategic changes that generally accompanied learning: origin of new strategies, more frequent use of more efficient strategies, more efficient execution of each strategy, and more adaptive choices among available strategies. According to the authors, these findings support a number of predictions of the SCADS model.

Siegler's (2001) model is considered by many as among the strongest proofs of the success of the information-processing paradigm, and it has influenced and still influences a lot of research in the domain of single-digit arithmetic. Nevertheless, this model also has its critics. First, although SCADS involves a large number of strategies, its direct application field is rather restricted. Future models will need to incorporate a wider range of strategies, such as the decomposition-to-10 strategy (e.g., $8 + 7 = (8 + 2) + (7 - 2) = 15$) or the tie strategy (e.g., $6 + 7 = (6 + 6) + 1 = 13$; Torbeyns et al., 2005), as well as the extension from single-digit to multidigit addition. The further elaboration of the model for other operations is also necessary. According to some scholars (e.g., Cowan, 2003), this may only be a matter of time; others are more skeptical about the ease with which the application range of computer models like SCADS can be meaningfully broadened to include related task domains (Baroody & Tiilikainen, 2003). More important, however, are the criticisms of the model coming from other, more recent theoretical perspectives. Starting from a constructivist and social-learning theoretical framework and from a broader data

set, Baroody and Tiilikainen performed a very critical analysis of Siegler's model of early addition performance and its underlying assumptions. These authors argue that the operation of SCADS is at odds with several key phenomena about the development and flexibility of children's addition strategies. For instance, Baroody and Tiilikainen collected evidence that even children who apparently have constructed a goal sketch sometimes used strategies that do not conform to a valid addition strategy specified in the goal sketch whereas SCADS never executes illegal strategies. Another important criticism of the model is that little or no attention is given to the social and instructional context in which the development of arithmetic skills takes place. Indeed, it seems incontrovertible to assume that the occurrence and the frequency, efficiency, and adaptivity with which certain strategies are used by children will depend heavily on the nature of instruction. And by instruction we mean more than the frequency of an arithmetic fact in an elementary school mathematics textbook (Ashcraft & Christy, 1995), the number of times a particular item has been shown, or the number of times a child has received positive or negative feedback for a particular item. For instance, several researchers (Hatano, 1982; Kuriyama & Yoshida, 1995) who examined the developmental paths of addition solution methods used by Japanese children have reported that they typically move more quickly than U.S. children do from counting-all methods to derived-fact and known-fact methods without passing through a clearly identifiable stage of more efficient counting strategies. Interestingly, many Japanese children use the number 5 as an intermediate anchor to think about numbers and to do additions and subtractions, before starting to do sums by means of retrieval or using 10 as an anchor in their derived-fact strategies. According to these authors, these developmental characteristics of Japanese children are closely related to a number of cultural and instructional supports and practices, such as the emphasis on using groups of five in the early arithmetic instruction in general and in abacus instruction in particular. Similarly, among classes of Flemish children, Torbeyns et al. (2005) found an unusually frequent, efficient, and adaptive use of a tie strategy on sums above 10, that is, solving almost-tie sums such as $7 + 8 =$ _____ by means of $(7 + 7) + 1 =$ _____, rather than by the decomposition-to-10 strategy: $(7 + 3) + 5 =$ _____. In those classes, a new textbook series was used that put great emphasis on the deliberate and flexible use of multiple solution strategies rather than on the mastery of the decomposition-to-10 strategy as the only acceptable approach to sums above 10.

Commenting on Baroody and Tiilikainen's (2003) very critical analysis of SCADS, and on the "schema-based view" they present as a more valuable alternative, Bisanz (2003) remarks that, although it is quite clear how SCADS works, this schema-based view, which speaks of a "web of conceptual, procedural, and factual knowledge," is not described in equally great detail. He concludes rightly, "When accounting for data, an unspecified model (like Baroody's) will always have an advantage over a relatively well-specified model, because the latter is constrained by its details" (p. 442). But even if Baroody and Tiilikainen's model lacks the specificity of SCADS, it certainly points to the complex mutual relationship between different kinds of knowledge (conceptual and procedural) in the development of single-digit arithmetic, as well as to the crucial role of the broader sociocultural and instructional contexts in which this development occurs.

In sum, the available research over the past decade has convincingly documented that acquiring proficiency with single-digit computations involves much more than rote memorization. This domain of whole number arithmetic demonstrates (a) how the different components of arithmetic skill (strategies, principles, and number facts) contribute to each other; (b) how children begin with understanding of the meaning of operations and how they gradually develop more efficient methods; and (c) how they choose adaptively among different strategies depending on the numbers involved (NRC, 2001a). Researchers have made considerable progress in describing these phenomena, and there are now sophisticated computer models that fit to some extent with the available empirical data. But we are nevertheless still remote from a full understanding of the development of expertise in this subdomain (Cowan, 2003). One of the most important tasks for further research relates to how these different components interact and, more precisely, exactly when and how the development of one component promotes the development of another. As argued convincingly by Siegler and others (Siegler, 2001; Torbeyns et al., 2004), further research on this issue requires the application of so-called microgenetic methods, which involve the repeated examination of children's factual, conceptual, and procedural knowledge during the whole learning process.

Another largely unresolved issue concerns the impact of cultural and instructional factors beyond the simple ones dealing with the amount of practice and reinforcement of arithmetic responses that are implemented in Siegler's computer simulation model. Remarkably, many of the available computer models seem to assume that there is a kind of universal taxonomy and/or developmental sequence of computational strategies, which is fundamentally independent of the nature of instruction or the broader cultural environment. It seems indeed plausible that some elements of this development are strongly constrained by general factors other than the instructional and cultural context wherein this development occurs, such as the inherent structure of mathematics and the unfolding of certain cognitive capacities in early childhood. However, other developmental aspects look less constrained and much more dependent on children's experiences with early mathematics at home and at school, such as the provision of cultural supports and practices as sources to move quickly beyond counting-based methods, or the immersion in a classroom climate and culture that encourages and praises flexibility.

Multidigit Arithmetic

Whereas existing theory and research offer a rather comprehensive picture of how children learn to add and subtract with small numbers, the literature about what concepts and strategies should be distinguished and how they develop over time is much more limited in the domain of multidigit arithmetic.

During the past decade, a number of studies from many different countries have documented the frequent and varied nature of children's and adults' use of informal strategies for mental addition and subtraction that depart from the formal written algorithms taught in school (Beishuizen, 1999; Carpenter, Franke, Jacobs, Fennema, & Empson, 1998; Cooper, Heirdsfield, & Irons, 1996; Jones, Thornton, & Putt, 1994; Reys, Reys, Nohda, & Emori, 1995; Thompson, 1999; Verschaffel, 1997). For instance, in the United States, Carpenter et al. (1998) did a longitudinal study investigating the development of children's multidigit addition and subtraction in relation to their understanding of multidigit concepts in grades 1 through 3. Students were individually interviewed five times on a variety of tasks involving straightforward, result-unknown addition and subtraction word problems with two-digit numbers for the first three interviews and three-digit numbers in the last two interviews. During the same interviews, children were individually administered five tasks measuring their knowledge of base-10 number concepts, together with a task wherein they had to apply a specific invented strategy to solve another problem and two unfamiliar (missing addend) problems that required some flexibility in calculation. It is important to note that all students were in classes of teachers who were participating in a 3-year intervention study designed to help them understand and build on children's mathematical thinking in line with reform-based principles. The emphasis of this intervention was on how children's intuitive mathematical ideas emerge to form the basis for the development of more formal concepts and procedures. Teachers learned about how children solve problems using base-10 materials and about the various invented strategies children often construct. The researchers identified the following categories of strategies:

- Modeling or counting by 1s.
- Modeling with 10s materials.
- Combining-units strategies (otherwise called decomposition or split strategies), wherein the 100s, 10s, and units of the different numbers are split off and handled separately (e.g., 46 + 47 is determined by taking 40 + 40 = 80 and 6 + 7 = 13, answer 80 + 13 = 93).
- Sequential strategies or jump strategies, wherein the different values of the second number are counted up or down from the first unsplit number (e.g., 46 + 47 is determined by taking 46 + 40 = 86, 86 + 7 = 93).
- Compensating strategies or varying strategies, wherein the numbers are adjusted to simplify the calculation (e.g., 46 + 47 = (45 + 45) + 1 + 2 = 93).
- Other invented mental calculation strategies.
- Algorithms (correct as well as buggy ones) wherein the answer is not found by means of mental calculation with numbers but by applying a taught algorithm on digits.

The study showed that, under favorable circumstances, children can invent mental calculation strategies for addition and subtraction problems. Also, buggy algorithms occurred more frequently among children who started out working algorithmically than among children who used invented mental strategies before or at the same time that they used standard algorithms. Students who used mental calculation strategies before using standard algorithms demonstrated better knowledge of base-10 number concepts and were more successful in extending their knowledge to new situations than students who used standard algorithms before applying mental calculation strategies. Finally, the data suggest that there is no explicit sequence in which the three basic categories of mental calculation strategies (sequential, combining units, and compensating) develop for addition; the majority of students applied all three, and the order in which they occurred was mixed. For subtraction, the sequential method was most often used, but some compensation strategies were observed, too.

Similar findings about the development of students' mental calculation strategies for multidigit addition and subtraction, in close relation to the development of their conceptual knowledge, were reported by Fuson et al. (1997) and by Hiebert and Wearne (1996). In both studies, these findings were obtained in nonconventional, reform-based classrooms. The latter authors followed children from the first to the fourth grade. They assessed conceptual understanding by asking children to identify the number of 10s in a number, to represent the value of each digit in a number with concrete materials, and to make different concrete representations of multidigit numbers. Procedural knowledge was assessed through performance on two-digit addition and subtraction story problems, which could be solved either by the standard algorithm or by an invented procedure. The size of the numbers used in the tests differed as the children grew older. Across assessment periods, children who demonstrated higher levels of conceptual understanding obtained higher scores on the procedural measures. As a second kind of support for the close relationship between procedural and conceptual knowledge, Hiebert and Wearne found that early conceptual understanding predicted not only concurrent but also future procedural skill.

Several researchers have documented that children also can invent strategies for multiplying and dividing multidigit numbers and have described some strategies they use. However, less progress has been made in characterizing such inventions than for the domain of multidigit addition and subtraction. We summarize next the main findings from an analysis by Ambrose, Baek, and Carpenter (2003) of children's invented multidigit multiplication and division procedures and the concepts and skills they depend on. We stress that these inventions did not take place in a vacuum, but in the context of a reform-based instructional environment that allowed and even stimulated children to construct, elaborate, and refine their own mental strategies rather than forcing them to follow a uniform, standardized trajectory for mental and/or written arithmetic. Very similar analyses have been reported by Anghileri (1999) and Thompson (1999) in the United Kingdom with children being taught according to the principles of the National Numeracy Strategy and by Treffers (1987) and Van Putten, Van den Brom-Snijders, and Beishuizen (2005) in the Netherlands with children being taught according to the principles of Realistic Mathematics Education.

Ambrose et al. (2003) classified children's mental calculation strategies for multiplication problems into four categories: direct modeling, complete number strategies, partitioning number strategies, and compensating strategies. A child using a *direct modeling strategy* models each of the groups using concrete manipulatives or drawings. Among these direct modeling strategies, the most elementary ones involve the use of individual counters to directly represent problems (identical to those used with single-digit numbers). As children develop knowledge of base-10 number concepts, they begin to use base-10 materials rather than individual counters to directly model and solve the problem. A second category, *complete number strategies,* describes strategies based on progressively more efficient techniques for adding and doubling. The most basic one is simply repeated addition. Others involve doubling, complex doubling, and building up by other factors. A child using the *partitioning number strategy* will split the multiplicand or multiplier into two or more numbers and create multiple subproblems that are easier to deal with. This procedure allows children to reduce the complexity of the problem and to use multiplication facts they already know. Distinction is made between strategies wherein a number is partitioned into nondecade numbers, strategies wherein a number is partitioned into decade numbers, and strategies wherein both numbers are partitioned into decade numbers. Finally, a child using a *compensating strategy* will adjust both multiplicand and multiplier or one of them based on special characteristics of the number combination to make the calculation easier. Children then make corresponding adjustments later if necessary. Ambrose et al. present a similar taxonomy for division. Many children in the study developed their mental calculation strategies for multidigit

numbers in a sequence from direct modeling to complete number, to partitioning numbers into nondecade numbers, and to partitioning numbers into decade numbers. Moreover, children's strategies for solving multidigit multiplication problems varied with their conceptual knowledge of addition, units, grouping by 10, place value, and properties of the four basic operations.

Our analysis of these studies revealed also how these researchers investigated the development of both procedural and conceptual knowledge. For the analysis of conceptual knowledge, investigators relied on a model developed by Fuson (1992; see also Fuson et al., 1997). This framework is called the UDSSI triad model, after the names of the five conceptual structures (unitary, decade, sequence, separate, integrated) distinguished in that model. Each conception involves a triad of two-way relationships among number words, written number marks, and quantities. Each of these relationships is connected to the other two. According to the model, children begin with a unitary multidigit conception, in which quantities are not differentiated into groupings, and the number word and number marks are not differentiated into parts. So, for 15 doughnuts, for example, the 1 is not related to "teen" in "fifteen" and the quantities are not meaningfully separable into 10 doughnuts and 5 doughnuts. In the most sophisticated conception, the integrated sequence-separate 10s conception, bidirectional relationships are established between the 10s and the 1s component of each of the three parts (i.e., number words, marks, quantities) of the sequence-10s and the separate-10s conceptions. This integrated conception allows children considerable flexibility in approaching and solving problems using two-digit numbers.

Fuson et al. (1997) acknowledge that this developmental model is deceptively neat in several respects. First, there are qualitative and quantitative differences depending on the language used. The European number words require some decade conception, and the written marks require some conception of separate 10s and 1s. For full understanding of the words and marks, European children need to construct all five of the UDSSI multidigit conceptions. But children speaking Chinese-based number words, for instance, that are regular and name the 10s, have a much easier task. Second, children learn the six relationships for a given number (or set of numbers) at different times and may not construct the last triad relationship for all numbers up to 99 for one kind of conception before the first triad relationships for another conception are construed. Third, not all children construct all conceptions; these constructions depend on the conceptual supports experienced by individual children in their classroom and outside of school. In this respect, it is important to note that besides these five conceptual structures, Fuson's framework also contains a sixth, inadequate conception, called the "concatenated single-digit conception," which refers to the interpretation and treatment of multidigit numbers as single-digit numbers placed adjacent to each other, rather than using multidigit meanings for the digits in different positions. According to Fuson (1992, p. 263), the use of this concatenated single-digit meaning for multidigit numbers may stem from classroom experiences "that do not sufficiently support children's construction of multiunit meanings, do require children to add and subtract multidigit numbers in a procedural, rule-directed fashion, and do set expectations that school mathematics activities do not require one to think or to access meanings."

Finally, children who have more than one multidigit conception may use different conceptions in different situations or combine parts of different triads in a single situation. For instance, even among children who already have a more meaningful conception available, the vertical instead of a horizontal presentation of an addition or subtraction problem may seduce them into using a concatenated single-digit conceptual structure. So children's multiunit conceptions do not conform to a uniform and stage-like model (Fuson et al., 1997).

We now turn to some comments on this framework. First, the empirical basis of the latest version of the model, as presented here, is somewhat unspecific. It remains unclear which aspects of this development are shaped by specific characteristics of the innovative learning environments in which it was observed, and which aspects are shaped by more general factors that are largely outside the control of instruction. Second, Fuson et al.'s (1997) model focuses on only one aspect of children's growing understanding of numbers and number relationships when they start exploring and operating on multidigit numbers (Fuson, 1992; Jones et al., 1994; Treffers, 2001), namely, their base-10 structure. Fuson (1992) herself points to the fact that besides this "collection-based" interpretation of numbers, there is also the "counting-based" interpretation. Treffers refers to these two interpretations as, respectively, the "structuring" and the "positioning"

representation of numbers. He defines "positioning" as "being able to place whole numbers on an empty number line with a fixed start and end point. . . . Positioning enables students to gain a general idea of the sizes of numbers to be placed" (p. 104). As such, Treffers's "positioning" interpretation shows some alignment with Dehaene's (Dehaene & Cohen, 1995) theory about how numbers are internally represented in the human mind (and brain), which assumes an analogue magnitude code (a kind of mental number line) as the main, if not only, semantic representation of a number. Although several mathematics educators working in the domain of multidigit arithmetic give this counting-based or positioning interpretation a prominent place in their experimental curricula, textbooks, and instructional materials (see, e.g., Beishuizen, 1999; Selter, 1998; Treffers, 2001), we are not aware of any ascertaining study that describes in a broad and systematic way the development of this latter aspect of children's growing conceptual knowledge of numbers and its relationship to the other aspect of multidigit number development.

To summarize, whereas in the 1970s and 1980s research focused on children's solutions of arithmetic problems involving relatively small whole numbers, researchers afterward paid more attention to problems that involve multidigit calculations. Significant progress has been made in identifying and characterizing the different concepts and strategies that children construct to calculate with multidigit numbers besides the regularly taught standard algorithms for written computation. Most classifications of children's procedures for operating on multidigit numbers distinguish among three basic categories of strategies of mental arithmetic:

1. Strategies where the numbers are primarily seen as objects in the counting row and for which the operations are movements along the counting row: further (+) or back (−) or repeatedly further (×) or repeatedly back (÷).

2. Strategies where the numbers are primarily seen as objects with a decimal structure and in which operations are performed by splitting and processing the numbers based on this structure.

3. Strategies based on arithmetic properties where the numbers are seen as objects that can be structured in all sorts of ways and where operations take place by choosing a suitable structure and using the appropriate arithmetic properties (see also Buys, 2001).

Each of these three basic forms can be performed at different levels of internalization, abbreviation, abstraction, and formalization. Moreover, each of these categories can be found in each of the four arithmetic operations.

The description of the past decade's research on multidigit mental arithmetic has pointed to the invented nature of some of these procedures of mental arithmetic and to the flexible or adaptive use of different strategies as a basic characteristic of expertise in multidigit arithmetic (see also Hatano, 2003). The available work has revealed the impossibility of separating the learning of the procedures for doing multidigit arithmetic from the development of base-10 number concepts as well as other, complementary conceptualizations of number. In their review of the relationship between conceptual and procedural knowledge of multidigit arithmetic, Rittle-Johnson and Siegler (1998) report several kinds of empirical evidence for this close relationship. At the same time, they refer to some research evidence (Resnick & Omanson, 1987) showing that in conventional instruction, which emphasized practicing procedures without linking this practice to conceptual understanding, the links between conceptual and procedural development are much looser. Finally, the research yielded evidence for the "dispositional nature" of multidigit arithmetic. This is convincingly documented, albeit in a negative way, by many traditionally taught children's inclination to apply their standard algorithms in a stereotyped, stubborn way, even in cases where mental arithmetic seems much more appropriate, such as for 24,000/6,000 = _____ or 4,002 − 3,998 = _____ (Buys, 2001; Treffers, 1987, 2001), and by their lack of self-confidence to have a go and take risks when leaving the safe path of standard algorithms (Thompson, 1999).

Word Problem Solving

Using the information-processing approach, research on the cognitive processes involved in solving one-step addition and subtraction as well as multiplication and division problems was flourishing during the 1980s and the early 1990s (for extensive and thorough reviews, see Fuson, 1992; Greer, 1992; see also Verschaffel & De Corte, 1997). This work has substantially advanced our understanding of the development of children's solution processes and activities for word problems. For instance, there has been considerable agreement concerning the categorization of real-world addition and subtraction situations involving three quantities in terms of their underlying semantic structure: change, combine, and compare situations. *Change* problems refer to a dynamic situation in which some event changes the value of a quantity (e.g., Joe had 3 marbles; then Tom gave him 5 more marbles; how many marbles does Joe have now?). *Combine* problems relate to static situations where there are two parts that are considered either separately or in combination as a whole (e.g., Joe and Tom have 8 marbles altogether; Joe has 3 marbles; how many marbles does Tom have?). *Compare* problems involve two amounts that are compared and the difference between them (e.g., Joe has 8 marbles; Tom has 5 marbles; how many fewer marbles does Tom have than Joe?). Within each of these three categories, further distinctions can be made depending on the identity of the unknown quantity; furthermore, change and compare problems are also subdivided depending on the direction of the transformation (increase or decrease) or the relationship (more or less), respectively.

Using a variety of techniques, such as written tests, individual interviews, computer simulation, and eye-movement registration, extensive research on these word problems has documented children's performance on the different problem types, the diversity in the solution strategies they use to solve the problems, and the nature and origin of their errors (e.g., Verschaffel & De Corte, 1993). For instance, the psychological significance of the categorization of the word problems was convincingly shown in many studies with 5- to 8-year-old children, reporting that word problems that can be solved by the same arithmetic operation but that belong to distinct semantic categories differ substantially in their level of difficulty; this demonstrates the importance of mastering knowledge of the different semantic problem structures for competent problem solving. From a developmental perspective, this research has demonstrated that most children entering primary school can solve the most simple one-step problems (e.g., change problems with the result set unknown, or combine problems with the whole unknown) using a solution strategy based on modeling the relations and actions described in them. Later on, children's proficiency gradually develops and increases in two important directions. First, informal, external, and cumbersome strategies are progressively replaced by more formalized, abbreviated and internalized, and more efficient strategies. Second, whereas initially children have a different solution method for each problem type that directly reflects the problem situation, they develop more general methods that apply to classes of problems with a similar underlying mathematical structure. Therefore, it is only in the later phases of development that children demonstrate problem-solving behavior that reflects the sequence of steps as described in models of expert problem solving: (a) representing the problem situation; (b) deciding on a solution procedure; (c) carrying out the solution procedure. Because at earlier levels of development they do not proceed through those steps, but use a solution method that directly models the situation, it is not surprising that children then solve problems correctly without first writing a corresponding number sentence (Fuson, 1992), or even without being able to write such a number sentence on request (De Corte & Verschaffel, 1985).

The research on multiplication and division word problems from the information-processing perspective during that period did not lead to a similar coherent theoretical framework as for addition and subtraction problems, but important related results were obtained (Verschaffel & De Corte, 1997). Based on a review of previous work, Greer (1992) proposed a categorization scheme representing different semantic types of multiplication and division situations. Paralleling the developmental findings for addition and subtraction, it was observed that many children can solve one-step multiplication and division problems involving small numbers before they have had any instruction about these operations. Also, here they use a large variety of informal strategies that reflect the action or relationship described in the problem situation. Likewise, the development proceeds in the direction of using more efficient, more formal, and internalized strategies. A difference from addition and subtraction that emerges from the literature, however, is that multiplicative thinking develops more slowly (Anghileri, 2001; Clark & Kamii, 1996).

Overall, the extensive body of research in the 1980s and the early 1990s relating to word problems involving the four basic operations has resulted in identifying different knowledge components of proficiency in solving such problems. This points to the significant role of domain-specific conceptual knowledge concerning semantic structures underlying additive and multiplicative problem situations, and to the diversity of strategies for solving them. Substantial progress has

been made in tracing the developmental steps that children pass through in acquiring problem-solving competence: Starting from a level that is characterized by informal, concrete, and laborious procedures, they progressively acquire more formal, abstract, and efficient strategies. Nevertheless, important issues for further inquiry remain. First, previous research that focused on the initial and middle stages of the development of additive and multiplicative concepts needs to be enlarged to more advanced developmental levels involving extension beyond the domain of positive integers (Greer, 1992; Vergnaud, 1988). Second, and as argued already in 1992 by Greer, whereas in the past the study of both conceptual fields occurred separately, future work should explicitly aim at the integration of additive and multiplicative conceptual knowledge.

A third critical comment on the research carried out in the information-processing tradition largely explains why this approach to the study of word problem solving has fallen into the background in the past decade. As argued in 1992 by Fuson, most of that research used only word problems that are restricted school versions of the real world. Indeed, researchers in this tradition have relied heavily on a narrow range of problems, namely, brief, stereotyped, contextually impoverished pieces of text that contain all the necessary numerical data and end with a clear question that can undoubtedly be answered by performing one or more arithmetic operations on these numbers. These constraints raise serious doubts about the generalizability of the theoretical assertions and the empirical outcomes (such as the importance of semantic schemata) toward solving more realistic, context-rich, and more complex problems in situations inside as well as outside the school (Verschaffel & De Corte, 1997). Therefore, researchers who stress the importance of social and cultural contexts in problem solving have engaged in investigations aimed at unraveling children's solution activities and strategies relating to more authentic and contextually embedded problems.

Well-known examples of this approach are the studies of street mathematics and school mathematics by Nunes, Schliemann, and Carraher (1993) in Recife, Brazil (see also Saxe, 1991). For example, in one study, Nunes et al. observed that young street vendors (9- to 15-year-olds) performed very well on problems in the street-vending context (such as selling coconuts), but less well on isomorphic school mathematics tasks. In addition, they found that in the street-vending situation, the children solved the problems using informal mathematical reasoning and calculation processes that differ considerably from the formal, school-prescribed procedures they tried to use with much less success on the textbook problems. These findings show in a rather dramatic way the gap that can exist in children's experience and beliefs between the world of the school and the reality of everyday life; to bridge this gap it is thus necessary in mathematics education to take into account children's informal prior knowledge.

Another line of research on mathematics problem solving goes back to the work of Polya, who in 1945 published a prescriptive model of the stages of problem solving involving the following steps: understanding the problem; devising a solution plan; carrying out the plan; and looking back or checking the solution. In each of these steps, Polya distinguishes a number of heuristics that can be applied to the problem, such as "Draw a figure" and "Do you know a related problem?" In the early days of the information-processing approach to the study of cognition, and using emerging ideas of artificial intelligence, Newell and Simon (1972) developed the well-known General Problem Solver, a computer program that solved a variety of rather artificial, puzzle-like problems (e.g., cryptograms), applying general strategies akin to Polya's heuristics, such as means-ends analysis. But research revealed over and over that children's and students' solution processes of word problems do not at all fit the stages of Polya's model. In this respect, two important phenomena observed in students' problem solving are suspension of sense making and lack of strategic approaches to problems. We next briefly review research relating to both phenomena.

A well-known and spectacular illustration of the suspension of sense making in children's problem solving was reported by French researchers in 1980 (Institut de Recherche sur l'Enseignement des Mathématiques de Grenoble, 1980; for an extensive review of this theme, see Verschaffel, Greer, & De Corte, 2000). They administered to a group of first and second graders the following absurd problem: "There are 26 sheep and 10 goats on a ship. How old is the captain?" It turned out that a large majority of the children produced a numerical answer (mostly 36) without any apparent awareness of the meaninglessness of the problem. Similar results were obtained in Germany (Radatz, 1983) and Switzerland (Reusser, 1986) with a number of related problems. The phenomenon showed also up in the United States; the

oft-cited example comes from the Third National Assessment of Educational Progress in 1983 with a sample of 13-year-olds (Carpenter, Lindquist, Matthews, & Silver, 1983): "An army bus holds 36 soldiers. If 1,128 soldiers are being bussed to their training site, how many buses are needed?" Although about 70% of the students correctly carried out the division of 1,128 by 36, obtaining the quotient 31 and remainder 12, only 23% gave 32 buses as the answer; 19% gave as answer 31 buses, and another 29% answered 31 remainder 12. In all these examples, students seem to be affected by the belief that real-world knowledge is irrelevant when solving mathematical word problems, and this results in nonrealistic mathematical modeling and problem solving.

Using the same or similar word problems under largely the same testing conditions, this phenomenon was very extensively studied and replicated independently with students in the age range of 9 to 14 years during the 1990s, initially in several European countries (Belgium, Germany, Northern Ireland, and Switzerland), but also in other parts of the world (Japan, Venezuela; for an overview of these studies, see Verschaffel et al., 2000). In the basic study (Verschaffel, De Corte, & Lasure, 1994), a paper-and-pencil test consisting of 10 pairs of problems was administered collectively to a group of 75 fifth graders (10- to 11-year-old boys and girls). Each pair of problems consisted of a standard problem, that is, a problem that can be solved by the straightforward application of one or more arithmetic operations with the given numbers (e.g., "Steve bought 5 planks of 2 meters each. How many planks of 1 meter can he saw out of these planks?"), and a parallel problem in which the mathematical modeling assumptions are problematic, at least if one seriously takes into account the realities of the context called up by the problem statement (e.g., "Steve bought 4 planks of 2.5 meters each. How many planks of 1 meter can he saw out of these planks?"). An analysis of the students' reactions to the problematic tasks yielded an alarmingly small number of realistic responses or comments based on the activation of real-world knowledge (responding to the problem about the 2.5 m planks with 8 instead of 10). Indeed, only 17% of all the reactions to the 10 problematic problems could be considered realistic, either because the realistic answer was given, or the nonrealistic answer was accompanied by a realistic comment (e.g., with respect to the planks problem, some students gave the answer 10, but added that Steve would have to glue together the four remaining pieces of .5 m two by two). The fact that these studies yielded very similar findings worldwide justifies the conclusion that children's belief that real-world knowledge is irrelevant when solving word problems in the mathematics classroom represents a very robust research result. Moreover, additional studies in our center (De Corte, Verschaffel, Lasure, Borghart, & Yoshida, 1999), but also by other European researchers (see Greer & Verschaffel, 1997), have shown that this misbelief about the role of real-world knowledge during word problem solving is very strong and resistant to change.

How is it possible that the results of some years of mathematics education could be the willingness of children to collude in negating their knowledge of reality? Gradually, researchers came to realize that this apparent "senseless behavior" should not be considered the result of a "cognitive deficit" in children, but should be construed as sense making of a different sort, namely, a strategic decision to play the "word problem game" (De Corte & Verschaffel, 1985). As expressed by Schoenfeld (1991, p. 340):

> Such behavior is sense-making of the deepest kind. In the context of schooling, such behavior represents the construction of a set of behaviors that results in praise for good performance, minimal conflict, fitting in socially and so on. What could be more sensible than that?

Students' strategies and beliefs develop from their perceptions and interpretations of the didactic contract (Brousseau, 1997) or the sociomathematical norms (Yackel & Cobb, 1996) that determine—largely implicitly—how they behave in a mathematics class, how they think, and how they communicate with the teacher. This enculturation seems to be mainly caused by two aspects of current instructional practice: the nature of the (traditional) word problems given and the way these problems are conceived and treated by teachers. Support for the latter factor comes from a study by Verschaffel, De Corte, and Borghart (1997), where preservice elementary school teachers were asked, first, to solve a set of problems themselves and, second, to evaluate realistic and unrealistic answers from imaginary students to the same set of problems. The results indicated that these future teachers shared, though in a less extreme form, students' tendency to suspend sense making.

Research has also documented convincingly the lack of strategic aspects of proficiency in students' solution activities of word problems. When confronted with a problem, they do not spontaneously use valuable heuristic strategies (such as analyzing the problem, making a drawing of the problem situation, decomposing the problem) in view of constructing a good mental representation of the problem as a lever to understanding the problem well. For instance, in a study by De Bock, Verschaffel, and Janssens (1998), 120 12- to 13-year-old seventh graders were administered a test with 12 items involving enlargements of similar plane figures, six of which were so-called proportional, and the other six nonproportional items, as illustrated by the following examples:

- *Proportional items:* Farmer Gus needs approximately 4 days to dig a ditch around a square pasture with a side of 100 m. How many days would he need to dig a ditch around a square pasture with a side of 300 m?
- *Nonproportional item:* Farmer Carl needs approximately 8 hours to manure a square piece of land with a side of 200 m. How many hours would he need to manure a piece of land with a side of 600 m?

In line with what was predicted, the proportional items were solved very well (over 90% correct), whereas performance on the nonproportional items was extremely weak (only about 2% correct). An inspection of the answer sheets revealed that only 2% of the students spontaneously made a drawing of the nonproportional items; in other words, most 12- to 13-year-olds were not at all inclined to apply to these problems the appropriate heuristic "Make a drawing of the problem." Even the encouragement to make a drawing or the presentation of a ready-made drawing when given a second test did not significantly increase performance. Continued research using individual interviews for the in-depth analysis of the thinking processes of 12- to 13- and 15- to 16-year old students has confirmed the improper use of proportional or linear reasoning, as well as its resistance to change (De Bock, Van Dooren, Janssens, & Verschaffel, 2002).

Similar outcomes revealing the lack of use of heuristic strategies, especially in weak problem solvers, have been reported by many other scholars, even with older subjects (e.g., De Corte & Somers, 1982; Hegarty, Mayer, & Monk, 1995; Van Essen, 1991). As argued in the NRC (2001a) report, weak problem solvers often rely on very superficial methods to solve problems. For example, when given the problem "At ARCO, gas sells for $1.13 per gallon. This is 5 cents less per gallon than gas at Chevron. How much does 5 gallons of gas cost at Chevron?" they focus on the numbers and on the keyword "less," which triggers the wrong arithmetic operation, in this case subtraction. In contrast, successful problem solvers build a mental representation of the problem by carefully analyzing the situation described, focusing on the known and unknown quantities and their relationships.

But not being heuristic is not the only flaw in students' (especially the weaker ones) problem-solving approach. Maybe even more important is the absence of metacognitive activities during problem solving. Indeed, research has clearly shown that the use of cognitive self-regulation skills—such as planning a solution process, monitoring that process, evaluating the outcome, and reflecting on one's solution strategy—is a major characteristic of expert mathematics problem solving (e.g., Schoenfeld, 1985, 1992). Comparative studies have convincingly documented that successful problem solvers more often apply self-regulation skills than unsuccessful ones, in the United States (see, e.g., Carr & Biddlecomb, 1998; Garofalo & Lester, 1985; Silver, Branca, & Adams, 1980) as well as in other parts of the world. For example, in the Netherlands, Nelissen (1987) found that good problem solvers among elementary school children were better at self-monitoring and reflection than poor problem solvers; Overtoom (1991) registered analogous differences between gifted and average students at the primary and secondary school levels. De Corte and Somers (1982) observed a strong lack of planning and monitoring of problem solving in a group of Flemish sixth graders, leading to poor performance on a word problem test. In his well-known studies, Krutetskii (1976) observed differences between elementary and secondary school students of different ability levels with respect to metacognitive activities during word problem solving. In summary, there is abundant evidence showing that cognitive self-regulation constitutes a major aspect of skilled mathematical learning and problem solving, but that it is often absent, especially in weak problem solvers.

The work of Krutetskii (1976) showing differences between primary and secondary school students elicits the question of whether there are developmental differences in metacognitive awareness and skills. However, based on an analysis of a number of studies, Carr and Biddlecomb (1998, p. 73) conclude that young as well as older children (up to middle and high school) fail in monitoring and evaluating their problem solving activities:

> Taken together, metacognitive research in mathematics is similar to metacognitive research in other domains: Children can benefit from both strategy-specific knowledge and from metacognitive awareness. Metacognitive research in mathematics, however, differs in showing that the use of cognitive monitoring and evaluation frequently do not appear to develop in children even in late childhood.

This raises a challenging issue for future research: Why is there, or should there be, a difference in this respect between mathematics and other domains? Indeed, the extensive literature on metacognitive development (Kuhn, 1999, 2000) suggests that metacognitive awareness emerges in children by age 3 to 4, and that starting from there, the executive control of cognitive functioning is acquired gradually through multiple developmental transitions (Zelazo & Frye, 1998). Development does not occur as a single transition, but "entails a shifting distribution in the frequencies with which more or less adequate strategies are applied, with the inhibition of inferior strategies as important an achievement as the acquisition of superior ones" (Kuhn, 2000, p. 179; see also Siegler, 1996).

Taking into account that it is plausible that the nature and development of cognitive self-regulation skills show some generality across domains (Kuhn, 2000), this current perspective on metacognitive development presents an interesting framework for future research on the development of mathematics-related self-regulation skills, especially because enhancing metacognitive awareness and skills constitutes a major component of mathematical proficiency and, thus, an important developmental and educational goal.

The preceding discussion shows that over the past 20 years substantial progress has been made in understanding the role and development of major components of a mathematical disposition in children's word problem solving. These components are domain-specific knowledge (conceptual understanding as well as computational fluency), heuristic strategies, and self-regulation skills. Although the available work points to the interwoven character of the different components, a challenge for future research consists in unraveling in greater detail the interactions among those strands in the acquisition and development of competence in mathematical problem solving.

Mathematics-Related Beliefs

Based on 2 decades of research, there is currently quite general agreement in the literature that beliefs that students hold about mathematics and about mathematics education have an important impact on their approach to mathematics learning and on their performance (Leder, Pehkonen, & Törner, 2002; Muis, 2004). In the *Curriculum and Evaluation Standards for School Mathematics* the NCTM echoed this point of view in 1989: "These beliefs exert a powerful influence on students' evaluation of their own ability, on their willingness to engage in mathematical tasks, and on their ultimate mathematical disposition" (p. 233).

To acquire the intended mathematical disposition, it is thus important that students develop positive beliefs about mathematics as a domain and about mathematics education. This converges with the component of "productive disposition," one of the five strands of mathematical proficiency proposed in the 2001 report of the NRC (2001a, p. 131): "*Productive disposition* refers to the tendency to see sense in mathematics, to perceive it as both useful and worthwhile, to believe that steady effort in learning mathematics pays off, and to see oneself as an effective learner and doer of mathematics." However, the available research shows that today the situation in mathematics classrooms is remote from this ideal. One pertinent illustration derives from studies in which students of different ages were asked to draw a mathematician at work. In one study by Picker and Berry (2000), 476 12- to 13-year-olds from several countries (United States, United Kingdom, Finland, Sweden, and Romania) were asked to make such a drawing and to comment on it in writing. A major conclusion from the study is that in all the countries involved, the gist of the images produced by the students was that of powerless little children confronted with mathematicians portrayed as authoritarian and threatening. According to the authors, the dominant picture of a mathematician that emerged from their study is in line with the images obtained in a similar investigation by Rock and Shaw (2000) with children ranging from kindergarten through the eighth grade. As it is plausible that children's drawings reflect their beliefs about mathematics, it is obvious that they do not perceive this domain as attractive and interesting.

Based on an analysis of the literature, De Corte, Op 't Eynde, and Verschaffel (2002; see also Op 't Eynde, De Corte, & Verschaffel, 2002) have made a distinction among three kinds of student beliefs: beliefs about the self in relation to mathematical learning and problem solving (e.g., self-efficacy beliefs relating to mathematics), beliefs about the social context (e.g., the social norms in the mathematics class), and beliefs about mathematics and mathematical learning and problem solving. With respect to the last type, it has been shown that, probably as a consequence of current educational practices, students of a wide range of ages and abilities acquire beliefs relating to mathematics that are naive, incorrect, or both, but that have mainly a negative or inhibitory effect on their learning activities and approaches to mathematics tasks and problems (Muis, 2004; Schoenfeld, 1992; Spangler, 1992). From a certain perspective, the research reported earlier on the suspension of sense making in solving word problems is also an illustration of these phenomena. In other words, the available data are in line with the bleak situation that emerged from the studies of Picker and Berry (2000) and Rock and Shaw (2000). According to Greeno (1991a), most students learn from their experiences in the classroom that mathematics knowledge is not something constructed by the learner, either individually or in a group, but a fixed body of received knowledge. In a similar way, Lampert (1990) characterizes the common view about mathematics as follows: Mathematics is associated with certainty and with being able to quickly give the correct answer; doing mathematics corresponds to following rules prescribed by the teacher; knowing math means being able to recall and use the correct rule when asked by the teacher; and an answer to a mathematical question or problem becomes true when it is approved by the authority of the teacher. She also argues that those beliefs are acquired through years of watching, listening, and practicing in the mathematics classroom. A case study by Boaler and Greeno (2000), this time at the secondary school level, likewise suggests that students' problematic beliefs result more or less directly from the actual curriculum and classroom practices and culture.

Convincing empirical evidence for the claim that students are afflicted by such beliefs has been reported by Schoenfeld (1988) in an article with the strange title "When Good Teaching Leads to Bad Results: The Disasters of 'Well-Taught' Mathematics Courses." Schoenfeld made a year-long intensive study of one 10th-grade geometry class with 20 students, along with periodic data collections in 11 other classes (210 students altogether) involving observations, interviews with teachers and students, and questionnaires relating to students' perceptions about the nature of mathematics. The students scored well on typical achievement measures, and the mathematics was taught in a way that would generally be considered good teaching. Nevertheless, it was found that students acquired debilitating beliefs about mathematics and about themselves as mathematics learners, such as "All mathematics problems can be solved in just a few minutes" and "Students are passive consumers of others' mathematics." It is obvious that such misbeliefs are not conducive to a mindful and persistent approach to new and challenging problems. Other strange beliefs that have been observed in students, and that are to a large extent responsible for the lack of sense making when doing word problem solving, are "Mathematics problems have one and only one right answer" and "The mathematics learned in school has little or nothing to do with the real world" (see, e.g., Schoenfeld, 1992).

With regard to beliefs about the self, it has been shown that self-efficacy beliefs are predictive of performance in mathematics problem solving in university students (Pajares & Miller, 1994). However, this seems to be the result of a developmental trend that mirrors an evolution in the nature and complexity of these beliefs. For instance, a study by Kloosterman and Cougan (1994) on a sample of 62 students in grades 1 to 6 suggests that students' confidence beliefs and liking of mathematics in the first two grades of elementary school are independent of their achievement levels, but that by the end of elementary school, these beliefs are related to performance, and that low achievers, besides having low confidence, start to dislike mathematics. Wigfield et al. (1997) also found that in the beginning of primary school, children view mathematics as important and themselves as competent to master it (see also NRC, 2001a). But later during primary school, their competence beliefs decrease. Middleton and Spanias (1999) point to the junior high school level as the crucial stage where students' beliefs about mathematics become more influential; unfortunately, a large number of students start developing more negative beliefs about the self in relation to mathematics (see also Muis, 2004; Wigfield et al., 1997).

As already stressed, several authors have argued that the negative mathematics-related beliefs of students of different ages are largely induced by current educational practices. However, although anecdotal observations and a few case studies point in that direction, this must be considered a plausible hypothesis in need of further research. Therefore, a major challenge for continued inquiry is the systematic study of the interplay between students' beliefs and instructional intervention, focusing on the design of interventions that can facilitate the acquisition of the intended productive disposition. This type of research would at the same time contribute to tracing in a more detailed way the development of mathematics-related beliefs in students. Indeed, as is the case for general epistemological beliefs (i.e., beliefs about knowing and knowledge; see Hofer & Pintrich, 2002), there is a need for better research-based knowledge about the nature and the processes of development of mathematics-related beliefs and about the internal and contextual factors that induce change in those beliefs in students (see also Muis, 2004).

Summary

The preceding selective review of research relating to components of mathematical competence shows that over the past decades, substantial progress has been made in unraveling major and educationally relevant aspects of their nature and development. The discussions have also shown the interdependency of the distinct components of proficiency in mathematics, for instance, the interconnectedness of conceptual and procedural knowledge in computation skills; the integration of domain knowledge, heuristic strategies, self-regulation skills, and beliefs in problem solving; and the complexity of number sense.

However, throughout this analysis of major components of a mathematical disposition, it has also become clear that important unanswered questions call for continued inquiry in view of the elaboration of a more encompassing and overarching theoretical framework of the development of mathematical competence. For instance, a crucial and still largely unresolved question with respect to the development of several components, such as basic conceptual and procedural knowledge structures, is to what degree they are either biologically prepared and, thus, more or less universal schemas, or are acquired in and attuned to situational contexts (see, e.g., Resnick, 1996). Whether a conceptual structure is subjected mainly to the first or to the second trend has important implications for teaching: It constrains or facilitates its sensitivity for instructional intervention. A related topic for further investigation is the more fine-grained unraveling of the interactions among the different components of mathematical competence. Future research must address more intensively the development of competence in other subdomains of mathematics, such as rational numbers, negative numbers, proportional reasoning, algebra, measurement, and geometry. Illustrative in this respect are the following quotes from the NRC (2001a) report, *Adding It Up: Helping Children Learn Mathematics:*

> Moreover, how students become proficient with rational numbers is not as well understood as with whole numbers. (p. 231)
>
> Compared with the research on whole numbers and even on noninteger rational numbers, there has been relatively little research on how students acquire an understanding of negative numbers and develop proficiency in operating with them. (p. 244)

LEARNING MATHEMATICS: ACQUIRING THE COMPONENTS OF COMPETENCE

The learning component of the CLIA model should provide us with an empirically based description and explanation of the processes of learning and development that must be elicited and kept going in students to facilitate in them the acquisition of the intended mathematical disposition and the components of competence involved in it. Research over the past decades has made progress in that direction and has resulted in the view of mathematics learning as the active and cumulative construction in a community of learners of meaning, understanding and skills based on modeling of reality (see, e.g., De Corte et al., 1996; Fennema & Romberg, 1999; Nunes & Bryant, 1997; Steffe, Nesher, Cobb, Goldin, & Greer, 1997). This conception implies that productive mathematics learning has to be a self-regulated, situated, and collaborative activity.

Learning as Cumulative Construction of Knowledge and Skills

The view that learning is a cumulative and constructive activity has nowadays become common ground among educational psychologists in general, and among mathematics educators in particular, and there is substantial empirical evidence supporting it (e.g., NRC, 2000; Simons, Van der Linden, & Duffy, 2000; Steffe & Gale, 1995). What is essential in the constructivist approach to learning is the mindful and effortful involvement of learners in the processes of knowledge and skill acquisition in interaction with the environment and building on their prior knowledge. What needs to be constructed is the process of doing mathematics rather than the mathe-

matical content (Greer, 1996). This is well illustrated in the work of Nunes et al. (1993) with Brazilian street vendors referred to earlier. In one case, the interviewer, acting as a customer, bought from a 12-year-old vendor 10 coconuts at 35 cruzeiros a piece. After the interviewer said, "I'd like 10. How much is that?" there was a pause and then the vendor reacted as follows: "Three will be 105; with three more that will be 210. [Pause] I need four more. That is . . . [pause] 315. . . . I think it is 350" (p. 19). This cumbersome but accurate calculation procedure was clearly invented by the street vendor himself. Indeed, third graders in Brazil learn to multiply any number by 10 by just putting a zero to the right of that number.

In our own work, we observed in first graders a great variety of solution strategies for one-step addition and subtraction problems (Verschaffel & De Corte, 1993). Many of these strategies were never explicitly taught in school, but they were invented by the children themselves. For example, to solve the difficult change problem "Pete had some apples; he gave 5 apples to Ann; now Pete has 7 apples; how many apples did Pete have in the beginning?" some children successfully applied a kind of trial-and-error strategy: They estimated the size of the initial amount and checked their guess by subtracting it by 5 to see if there were 7 left; if not, they made a new guess and checked again.

But the constructive nature of learning is also evidenced in a negative way in the misconceptions and defective procedures that many learners acquire in a variety of content domains, including mathematics. A well-known illustration of the latter kind of erroneous inventions are the so-called buggy algorithms, that is, systematic procedural errors made by children on multidigit arithmetic operations, such as subtracting the smaller digit from the larger one in each column regardless of position, as in the following example:

$$\begin{array}{r} 543 \\ -\,175 \\ \hline 432 \end{array}$$

Based on task analysis and using computer simulation, it has been shown that such bugs can be predicted as constructions of the child who is faced with an impasse because conditions are encountered beyond the currently mastered procedures (VanLehn, 1990).

A well-documented misconception is the idea that multiplication always makes bigger. There is, for instance, overwhelming evidence from studies with students of different ages (from 12- to 13-year-olds up to preservice teachers) supporting the most obvious manifestation of this misconception, known as the multiplier effect: When given the task to choose the operation to solve a multiplication problem with a multiplier smaller than 1, almost 50% of the preservice teachers and almost 70% of the 12- to 13-year-olds made an incorrect choice (mostly division instead of multiplication; Greer, 1988; see also De Corte, Verschaffel, & Van Coillie, 1988; Greer, 1992). Remarkable from a developmental perspective is the persistence of this multiplier effect over a broad age range. As argued by Hatano (1996, p. 201), "Procedural bugs and misconceptions are taken as the strongest pieces of evidence for the constructive nature of knowledge acquisition, because it is very unlikely that students have acquired them by being taught."

Notwithstanding the evidence showing that students construct their own knowledge, even in learning environments that are implicitly based on an information-transmission model, today we cannot pretend to have a well-elaborated constructivist learning theory. What Fischbein argued in 1990 still largely holds true, namely, "the need for a more specific definition of constructivism as a psychological model for mathematical education" (p. 12). For instance, current constructivist approaches to learning do not provide clear and detailed guidelines for the design of teaching-learning environments (Greer, 1996; see also Davis, Maher, & Noddings, 1990). This standpoint is echoed in a recent contribution by Cobb, Confrey, diSessa, Lehrer, and Schauble (2003) stating that general orientations to education, such as constructivism, often fail to offer detailed guidelines for organizing instruction. The authors present the following illustration:

> The claim that invented representations are good for mathematics and science learning probably has some merit, but it specifies neither the circumstances in which these representations might be of value nor the learning processes involved and the manner in which they are supported. (p. 11)

Indeed, it is important to stress that the view of learning as an active process does not imply that students' construction of their knowledge cannot be supported and guided by suitable interventions by teachers, peers, and educational media (see, e.g., Grouws & Cebulla, 2000). Thus, the claim that productive learning is accompanied by good teaching still holds true. Moreover, as argued in the recent volume *Beyond Constructivism* (Lesh &

Doerr, 2003), there are distinct categories of instructional objectives in mathematics education, and not all of them have to be discovered and constructed autonomously by the learners.

The present state of the art thus calls for continued theoretical and empirical research aimed at a deeper understanding and a more fine-grained analysis of the nature of constructive learning processes that are conducive to the acquisition of worthwhile knowledge, (meta)cognitive strategies, and affective components of skilled performance, and of the role and nature of instruction in eliciting and facilitating such learning processes.

Learning Is Increasingly Self-Regulated

If the process and not the product of learning is the focus of constructivism, this also implies that constructive learning has to be self-regulated. Indeed, self-regulation "refers to the degree that individuals are metacognitively, motivationally, and behaviorally active participants in their own learning process" (Zimmerman, 1994, p. 3). It is a form of action control characterized by the integrated regulation of cognition, motivation, and emotion (De Corte, Verschaffel, & Op 't Eynde, 2000; see also Boekaerts, 1997). Research has shown that self-regulated learners in school are able to manage and monitor their own processes of knowledge and skill acquisition; that is, they master and apply self-regulatory learning and problem-solving strategies on the basis of self-efficacy perceptions in view of attaining valued academic goals (Zimmerman, 1989). Skilled self-regulation enables learners to orient themselves to new learning tasks and to engage in the pursuit of adequate learning goals; it facilitates appropriate decision making during learning and problem solving, as well as the monitoring of an ongoing learning and problem-solving process by providing their own feedback and performance evaluations and by keeping themselves concentrated and motivated. It has also been established in a variety of content domains, including mathematics, that the degree of students' self-regulation correlates strongly with academic achievement (Zimmerman & Risemberg, 1997). The importance of self-regulation for mathematics learning has been stressed, especially by reflective activities, for instance, by Nelissen (1987). During learning, the student has to continuously make decisions about the next steps to be taken, for example, looking back for a formula or theorem, reconsidering a problem situation from a different perspective or restructuring it, or making an estimation of the expected outcome.

Moreover, it is necessary to monitor learning processes through intermediate evaluations of the progress made in acquiring, understanding, and applying new knowledge and skills, as well as of one's motivation and concentration on the learning task.

However, as we reported in the section on word problem solving, many students, especially the weaker ones, do not master appropriate and efficient cognitive self-regulation skills that facilitate their learning of new knowledge and skills and enhance their success in mathematical problem solving. In some ways, this is not so surprising. Indeed, observing current teaching practices in mathematics classrooms, one often has the impression that regulating students' learning and problem solving appropriately is considered to be the task of the teacher. This induces the beliefs mentioned earlier, namely, that mathematics is a fixed body of knowledge received from the teacher and that doing mathematics is following the rules prescribed by the teacher. At the same time, as shown earlier, students often develop inappropriate self-regulating learning activities that result in defective algorithmic procedures and/or misconceptions.

On a more positive note, the literature shows that the self-regulation of learning can be enhanced through appropriate guidance (see, e.g., Schunk, 1998; Zimmerman, 2000). We will come back to this in the section on intervention.

Learning Is Situated and Collaborative

The idea that learning and cognition are situated activities was strongly put forward in the late 1980s in reaction to the then dominant cognitive view of learning and thinking as highly individual and purely mental processes occurring in the brain and resulting in encapsulated mental representations (J. S. Brown, Collins, & Duguid, 1989). This cognitive view is in line with Sfard's (1998) acquisition metaphor of learning focused on individual enrichment through acquiring knowledge, skills, and so on. In contrast, the situated perspective converges with the participation metaphor: It stresses that learning is enacted essentially in interaction with social and cultural contexts and artifacts, and especially through participation in cultural activities and contexts (Greeno & the Middle School Mathematics through Applications Project Group, 1998; Lave & Wenger, 1991; see also Bruner, 1996; Greeno, Collins, & Resnick, 1996; Sfard, 1998). This situated conception of learning and cognition is nowadays quite widely shared in the

mathematics education community. The calculation procedure invented by the Brazilian street vendor in the realistic context of his business is a nice illustration of this view. It also is representative of the outcomes of a series of ethnomathematical studies of the informal calculation procedures and problem-solving strategies of particular groups of children and adults who are involved in specific everyday cultural practices of business, tailoring, weaving, carpentry, grocery, packing, cooking, and so on (Nunes, 1992; for a summary, see De Corte et al., 1996).

Although the situated nature of learning has been documented especially well in studies carried out in everyday contexts, it is obvious that situatedness applies to school learning as well. For instance, the young street vendors in the study by Nunes et al. (1993) who were so successful in using informal invented strategies and procedures when selling coconuts did not do well when solving isomorphic textbook problems in school. There they tried, without much success, to apply the formal procedures learned in the mathematics lessons. The work on the suspension of sense making when doing school word problems can be considered another line of evidence for the importance of the social and cultural situatedness of mathematical thinking and learning (Lave, 1992).

The situated perspective on learning has fueled and supported the movement toward more authentic and realistic mathematics education, although it has to be added that such an approach to mathematics teaching and learning was already introduced and developed earlier by several groups of mathematics educators; the most typical example in this respect is probably Freudenthal, who developed and implemented, together with his collaborators, Realistic Mathematics Education in the Netherlands in the 1970s (see, e.g., Streefland, 1991; Treffers, 1987).

Of special importance from an educational perspective is that the situativity view of learning and cognition has obviously also contributed to emphasis on the importance of collaboration for learning. In fact, because it emphasizes the social and participatory character of learning, the situated perspective implies the collaborative nature of learning. This means that effective learning is not a purely solo activity, but essentially a distributed one; that is, the learning efforts are distributed over the individual student, his or her partners in the learning environment, and the technological resources and tools that are available. In the past, this idea was embraced broadly by mathematics educators. For instance, Wood, Cobb, and Yackel (1991; see also Cobb & Bauersfeld, 1995) consider social interaction essential for mathematics learning, with individual knowledge construction occurring throughout processes of interaction, negotiation, and cooperation.

There is no doubt that the available literature provides substantial evidence supporting the positive effects of collaborative learning on the cognitive as well as the social and affective outcomes of learning (see, e.g., Good, Mulryan, & McCaslin, 1992; Mevarech & Light, 1992; Salomon, 1993a). In the cognitive domain, the significance of interaction, collaboration, and communication lies especially in their requiring insights, strategies, and problem-solving methods to be made explicit. This not only supports conceptual understanding, it also fosters the acquisition of heuristic strategies and metacognitive skills. Therefore, a shift toward more social interaction and participation in mathematics classrooms would represent a worthwhile move away from the traditional overemphasis on individual learning that prevails, as shown in a study by Hamm and Perry (2002). Studying the classroom discourse processes and participatory structures in six first-grade classrooms, they found that five out of the six teachers did not grant any authority to their students and did not create a classroom community in which students participated in mathematical discourse and analysis; even the one teacher who invited her students to take some responsibility as members of a mathematical community still mainly reinforced herself as the source of mathematical authority rather than the classroom community. But one should also avoid falling into the trap of the other extreme. Indeed, stressing the importance for learning of collaboration, interaction, and participation does not at all deny that students can and do develop new knowledge individually. As argued by Salomon (1993b), distributed and individual cognitions interact during productive learning (see also Salomon & Perkins, 1998; Sfard, 1998).

Summary

The preceding discussion shows that recent research provides substantial evidence supporting the view that productive mathematics learning is a constructive, progressively more self-regulated, and situated process of knowledge building and skill acquisition involving ample opportunities for interaction, negotiation, and collaboration. Therefore, it seems self-evident that we

should take these basic characteristics of this conception of learning as major guidelines for the design of curricula, textbooks, learning environments, and assessment instruments that aim at fostering in students the acquisition of a mathematical disposition as defined in the previous section of this chapter.

But, notwithstanding this positive overall result of past inquiry, numerous issues and problems have to be addressed in future research. We stressed the need to further unravel the nature of constructive learning processes and the role of instructional interventions in eliciting such processes. Continued research should also aim at tracing the development in students of self-regulatory skills, and at unpacking how and under what instructional conditions students become progressively more self-regulated learners. Similarly, it is necessary to get a better understanding of how collaborative work in small groups influences the learning and thinking of students of different ages, of the role of individual differences on group work, and of the processes that are at work during group activities.

DESIGNING POWERFUL MATHEMATICS LEARNING ENVIRONMENTS

The preceding sections elucidated the ultimate objective of mathematics education, developing a mathematical disposition, as well as major characteristics of learning processes that can facilitate the acquisition of the different components of such a disposition. All this leads us to the important and challenging question relating to the intervention component of the CLIA model: How can powerful mathematics learning environments be designed for inducing in students the intended learning activities and processes, and by so doing, fostering in them the progressive development and mastery of a mathematical disposition?

Over the past 15 years, scholars in the domain of mathematics education have been addressing this challenge mainly by using intervention studies, such as in constructional research (Becker & Selter, 1996), and design experiments (Cobb et al., 2003) or design-based research (Sandoval & Bell, 2004b). Becker and Selter define constructional research "as research that is connected with suggestions on how teaching ought to be or *could* be, to put it slightly more moderately. . . . [It is] concentrating on the development of theoretically founded and empirically tested practical *suggestions* for teaching" (p. 525). According to Cobb et al.:

> Design experiments entail both "engineering" particular forms of learning and systematically studying those forms of learning within the context defined by the means of supporting them. This designed context is subject to test and revision, and the successive iterations that result play a role similar to that of systematic variation in experiments. (p. 9)

It is important to stress that this type of research intends to advance theory building about learning from instruction, besides contributing to the innovation and improvement of classroom practices (Cobb et al., 2003; De Corte, 2000). In this respect, Sandoval and Bell (2004a, pp. 199–200) characterize design-based research as "theoretically framed, empirical research of learning and teaching based on particular designs of instruction." From a theoretical perspective, then, a major task bears on the development and validation of a coherent set of guiding principles for the design of powerful mathematics learning environments.

Due to space restrictions, we can discuss only a very small selection from the extensive number of projects that have been or still are being carried out (see, e.g., Becker & Selter, 1996), focusing on primary education and choosing examples that are in line with the constructivist perspective on learning discussed earlier. Specifically, two studies are reviewed in some detail: a learning environment for mathematical problem solving in the upper primary school (Verschaffel et al., 1999) and a program of classroom teaching experiments aiming at better understanding the development of social and sociomathematical norms in the lower grades of the primary school (Cobb, 2000; Yackel & Cobb, 1996). Besides the distinction in grade level and the geographical spread over both sides of the Atlantic, the two examples differ in two other respects. Whereas our intervention focuses on word problem solving, the work of Cobb and his coworkers relates to mental calculation with whole numbers, thus representing two distinct aspects of mathematical competence. In addition, both studies contrast and complement each other interestingly from a methodological perspective. The first one is a relatively well-controlled investigation looking for treatment effects, with some attention to differences between teachers in implementing the intervention but providing little sense of the processes that produce different outcomes; Cobb's investigations have a more longitudinal charac-

ter and pay closer attention to the ongoing processes of learning and teaching in the mathematics classroom.

A Learning Environment for Mathematical Problem Solving in Upper Primary School Children

Parallel with the rethinking of the objectives and the nature of mathematics education by researchers in the field, initiatives have been implemented in many countries to reform and innovate classroom practices (see, e.g., NCTM, 1989, 2000). This has also been the case in the Flemish part of Belgium. Since the school year 1998 to 1999, new standards for primary education became operational (Ministerie van de Vlaamse Gemeenschap, 1997). For mathematics education, these standards embody an important shift that is in line with the view of mathematical competence as defined by de-emphasizing the teaching and practicing of procedures and algorithms, and instead stressing the importance of mathematical reasoning and problem-solving skills and their application to real-life situations and problems, as well as the development of positive attitudes and beliefs toward mathematics. To implement the new standards, the Department of Education of the Flemish Ministry commissioned the present project from our center, aimed at the design and evaluation of a powerful learning environment that can elicit in upper primary school students the constructive learning processes for acquiring the intended mathematical competence (for a more detailed report, see Verschaffel et al., 1999).

Taking into account the literature discussed in the previous sections, a set of five major guidelines for designing a learning environment was derived from our present understanding of a mathematical disposition (the first component of the CLIA model) and the characteristics of constructive learning processes (the second CLIA component):

1. Learning environments should initiate and support active, constructive acquisition processes in *all* students, thus also in the more passive learners and independent of socioeconomic status and/or ethnic diversity. However, the view of learning as an active process does not imply that students' construction of their knowledge cannot be guided and mediated by appropriate interventions. Indeed, the claim that productive learning involves good teaching still holds true. In other words, a powerful learning environment

is characterized by a good balance between discovery and personal exploration, on the one hand, and systematic instruction and guidance, on the other, always taking into account individual differences in abilities, needs, and motivation among learners.

2. Learning environments should foster the development of self-regulation strategies in students. This implies that external regulation of knowledge and skill acquisition through systematic instructional interventions should be gradually removed so that students become more and more agents of their own learning.

3. Because of the importance of context and collaboration for effective learning, learning environments should embed students' constructive acquisition activities in real-life situations that have personal meaning for the learners, that offer ample opportunities for distributed learning through social interaction, and that are representative of the tasks and problems to which students will have to apply their knowledge and skills in the future.

4. Because domain-specific knowledge, heuristic methods, metaknowledge, self-regulatory skills, and beliefs play complementary roles in competent learning, thinking, and problem solving, learning environments should create opportunities to acquire general learning and thinking skills embedded in the mathematics content.

5. Powerful learning environments should create a classroom climate and culture that encourages students to explain and reflect on their learning activities and problem-solving strategies. Indeed, fostering self-regulatory skills requires that students become aware of strategies, believe that they are worthwhile and useful, and finally master and control their use (Dembo & Eaton, 1997).

Aims of the Learning Environment

The aims of our learning environment were twofold. The first aim was the acquisition of an overall cognitive self-regulatory strategy for solving mathematics application problems. This consisted of five stages and involved a set of eight heuristic strategies that are especially useful in the first two stages of that strategy (see Table 4.1). Acquiring this strategy involves (a) becoming aware of the different phases of a competent problem-solving process (awareness training); (b) being able to monitor and evaluate one's actions during the different phases of the solution process (self-regulation training); and (c) gaining mastery of the eight heuristic strategies

Table 4.1   The Competent Problem-Solving Model Underlying the Learning Environment

Step 1: Build a Mental Representation of the Problem
        Heuristics: Draw a picture.
                   Make a list, a scheme, or a table.
                   Distinguish relevant from irrelevant data.
                   Use your real-world knowledge.
Step 2: Decide How to Solve the Problem
        Heuristics: Make a flowchart.
                   Guess and check.
                   Look for a pattern.
                   Simplify the numbers.
Step 3: Execute the Necessary Calculations
Step 4: Interpret the Outcome and Formulate an Answer
Step 5: Evaluate the Solution

(heuristic strategy training). The five stages of this strategy for cognitive self-regulation parallel the models proposed by Schoenfeld (1985) and Lester, Garofalo, and Kroll (1989).

The second aim was the acquisition of a set of appropriate beliefs and positive attitudes with regard to mathematics learning and problem solving (e.g., "Mathematics problems may have more than one correct answer"; "Solving a mathematics problem may be effortful and take more than just a few minutes").

Major Characteristics and Organization of the Learning Environment

The five design principles were applied in an integrated way in the learning environment. This resulted in an intervention characterized by the following three basic features:

1. *A varied set of complex, realistic, and challenging word problems.* These problems differed substantially from the traditional textbook problems and were carefully designed to elicit the application of the intended heuristics and self-regulatory skills that constitute the model of skilled problem solving. The example that follows illustrates the type of problems used in the learning environment:

School Trip Problem*

The teacher told the children about a plan for a school trip to visit the Efteling, a well-known amusement park

---

*The problem is not presented in its original format because it takes a lot of space. Moreover, translating it from Flemish to English is somewhat cumbersome.

in the Netherlands. But if that would turn out to be too expensive, one of the other amusement parks might be an alternative.

Each group of four students received copies of folders with entrance prices for the different parks. The lists mentioned distinct prices depending on the period of the year, the age of the visitors, and the kind of party (individuals, families, groups).

In addition, each group received a copy of a fax from a local bus company addressed to the principal of the school. The fax gave information about the prices for buses of different sizes (with a driver) for a 1-day trip to the Efteling.

The first task of the groups was to determine whether it was possible to make the school trip to the Efteling given that the maximum price per child was limited to 12.50 euro.

After finding out that this was not possible, the groups received a second task: They had to find out which of the other parks could be visited for the maximum amount of 12.50 euro per child.

2. *A series of lesson plans based on a variety of activating and interactive instructional techniques.* The teacher initially modeled each new component of the metacognitive strategy; a lesson consisted of a sequence of small-group problem-solving activities or individual assignments, always followed by a whole-class discussion. During all these activities, the teacher's role was to encourage and scaffold students to engage in and to reflect on the kinds of cognitive and metacognitive activities involved in the model of competent mathematical problem solving. These encouragements and scaffolds were gradually withdrawn as the students became more competent and took more responsibility for their own learning and problem solving. In other words, external regulation was faded out as students became more self-regulated learners and problem solvers.

3. *Interventions explicitly aimed at the establishment of new social and sociomathematical norms.* A classroom climate was created that is conducive to the development in students of appropriate beliefs about mathematics and mathematics learning and teaching and to students' self-regulation of their learning. Social norms are general norms that apply to any subject matter domain and relate, for instance, to the role of the teacher and the students in the classroom (e.g., not the teacher alone, but the whole class will decide which of the different learner-generated solutions is the optimal one after an evaluation of the pros and cons of the distinct alternatives). Sociomathematical norms, on the other hand, are specific to students' activity in mathematics, such as what counts as a good mathematical problem, a good solution procedure, or a good response (e.g., sometimes a rough estimate is a better answer to a problem than an exact number; Yackel & Cobb, 1996).

The learning environment consisted of a series of 20 lessons designed by the research team in consultation and cooperation with the regular class teachers, who themselves did the teaching. With two lesson periods each week, the intervention was spread over about 3 months. Three major parts can be distinguished in the series of lessons:

1. Introduction to the content and organization of the learning environment and reflection on the difference between a routine task and a real problem (1 lesson).

2. Systematic acquisition of the five-step regulatory problem-solving strategy and the embedded heuristics (15 lessons).

3. Learning to use the competent problem-solving model in a spontaneous, integrated, and flexible way in so-called project lessons involving more complex application problems (4 lessons). The School Trip Problem is an example of such a lesson.

Teacher Support and Development

Because the class teachers taught the lessons, they were prepared for and supported in implementing the learning environment. The model of teacher development adopted reflected our views about students' learning by emphasizing the creation of a social context wherein teachers and researchers learn from each other through continuous discussion and reflection on the basic principles of the learning environment, the learning materials developed, and the teachers' practices during the lessons (De Corte, 2000). Moreover, taking into account that the mathematics teaching-learning process is too complex to be prespecified and that teaching as problem solving is mediated by teachers' thinking and decision making, the focus of teacher development and support was not on making them perform in a specific way, but on preparing and equipping them to make informed decisions (see also Carpenter & Fennema, 1992; Yackel & Cobb, 1996). Taking this into account, the teachers received the following support materials to enhance a reliable and powerful implementation of the learning environment: (a) a general teaching guide containing an extensive description of the aims, content, and structure of the learning environment; (b) a list of 10 guidelines comprising actions that they should take before, during, and after the individual or group assignments, complemented with worked-out examples of each guideline (see Table 4.2); (c) a specific teacher guide for each lesson, containing the overall lesson plan but also specific suggestions for appropriate teacher interventions and examples of anticipated correct and incorrect solutions and solution methods; and (d) all the necessary concrete materials for the students.

Procedure and Hypotheses

The effectiveness of the learning environment was evaluated in a study with a pretest-posttest-retention test design. Four experimental fifth-grade classes (11-year-olds) and seven comparable control classes from 11 different elementary schools in Flanders participated in the study. These seven classes were comparable to the experimental classes in terms of ability and socioeconomic status, and during the 4-month period they followed an equal number of lessons in word problem solving. Interviews with the teachers of these classes and analyses of the textbooks used provided us with a good overall view of what happened in those control classes. This indicated that the teaching with respect to word problem solving was representative of current instructional practice in Flemish elementary schools (see De Corte & Verschaffel, 1989).

Table 4.2   General Guidelines for the Teachers Before, During, and After the Group and Individual Assignments

Before
1. Relate the new aspect (heuristic, problem-solving step) to what has already been learned before.
2. Provide a good orientation to the new task.

During
3. Observe the group work and provide appropriate hints when needed.
4. Stimulate articulation and reflection.
5. Stimulate the active thinking and cooperation of all group members (especially the weaker ones).

After
6. Demonstrate the existence of different appropriate solutions and solution methods for the same problem.
7. Avoid imposing solutions and solution methods onto students.
8. Pay attention to the intended heuristics and metacognitive skills of the competent problem-solving model, and use this model as a basis for the discussion.
9. Stimulate as many students as possible to engage in and contribute to the whole-class discussion.
10. Address (positive as well as negative) aspects of the group dynamics.

Three pretests were collectively administered in the experimental as well as the control classes: a standardized achievement test (SAT) to assess fifth graders' general mathematical knowledge and skills, a word problem test (WPT) consisting of 10 nonroutine word problems, and a beliefs attitude questionnaire (BAQ) aimed at assessing students' beliefs about and attitudes toward (teaching and learning) word problem solving. In addition, students' WPT answer sheets for each problem were carefully scrutinized for evidence of the application of one or more of the heuristics embedded in the problem-solving strategy. Besides these collective pretests, three pairs of students of equal ability from each experimental class were asked to solve five nonroutine application problems during a structured interview. The problem-solving processes of these dyads were videotaped and analyzed by means of a self-made schema for assessing the intensity and the quality of students' cognitive self-regulation activities.

By the end of the intervention, parallel versions of all collective pretests (SAT, WPT, and BAQ) were administered in all experimental and control classes. The answer sheets of all students were again scrutinized for traces of the application of heuristics, and the same pairs of students from the experimental classes as prior to the intervention were subjected again to a structured interview involving parallel versions of the five nonroutine application problems used during the pretest. Three months later, a retention test (a parallel version of the collective WPT used as pretest and posttest) was also administered in all experimental and control classes. To assess the implementation of the learning environment by the teachers of the experimental classes, a sample of four representative lessons was videotaped in each experimental class and analyzed afterward for an "implementation profile" for each experimental teacher.

A major hypothesis was that as a result of acquiring the self-regulatory problem-solving strategy, the experimental students would significantly outperform the control children on the WPT, and that this would be accompanied by a significant increase in the use of heuristics. Furthermore, it was anticipated that the frequency and the quality of the self-regulation activities in the dyads would substantially grow.

Results

We summarize here the major results of this intervention study. Although no significant difference was found between the experimental and control groups on the WPT during the pretest, the former significantly outperformed the latter during the posttest, and this difference in favor of the experimental group was maintained in the retention test. However, it should be acknowledged that in the experimental group, students' overall performance on the posttest and retention tests was not as high as anticipated (i.e., the students of the experimental classes still produced only about 50% correct answers on these tests). In the experimental group, there was a significant improvement in students' beliefs about and attitudes toward learning and teaching mathematical problem solving, whereas in the control group there was no change in students' reactions to the BAQ from pretest to posttest. Although there was no difference in the pretest results on the SAT between the experimental and the control group, the results on the posttest revealed a significant difference in favor of the former group, indicating some transfer effect of the intervention toward mathematics as a whole. A qualitative analysis of the students' response sheets of the WPT revealed a dramatic increase from pretest to posttest and retention test in the manifest use of some of the heuristics that were specifically addressed and discussed in the learning environment; in the control classes, there was no difference in students' use of heuristics between the three testing times. In line with this result, the videotapes of the problem-solving processes of the dyads revealed substantial improvement in the intensity and quality with which the pairs from the experimental classes applied certain—but not all—(meta)cognitive skills that were specifically addressed in the learning environment. Both findings are indicative of a substantial increase in students' ability to self-regulate their problem-solving processes. Although there is some evidence that students of high and medium ability benefited more from the intervention than low-ability students, the statistical analysis revealed at the same time that all three ability groups contributed significantly to all the positive effects in the experimental group. This is a very important outcome, because it suggests that through appropriate intervention, one can also improve the cognitive self-regulatory skills of the weaker children. Finally, the positive effects of the learning environment were not observed to the same extent in all four experimental classes; actually, in one of the four classes, there was little or no improvement on most of the process and product measures. Analysis of the videotapes of the lessons in these classes indicated substantial differences in the extent to which the four

experimental teachers succeeded in implementing the major aspects of the learning environment. For three of the four experimental classes, there was a good fit between the teachers' implementation profiles and their students' learning outcomes.

Strengthening the Learning Environment with a Technology Component

The results of the previous study encouraged us to combine in a subsequent investigation the theoretical ideas and principles relating to socioconstructivist mathematics learning and to teachers' professional development with a second strand of theory and research focusing on the (meta)cognitive aspects of computer-supported collaborative knowledge construction and skill building (De Corte, Verschaffel, Lowyck, Dhert, & Vandeput, 2002). Taking into account the available empirical evidence showing that computer-supported collaborative learning (CSCL) is a promising lever for the improvement of learning and instruction (Lehtinen, Hakkarainen, Lipponen, Rahikainen, & Muukkonen, 1999), we enriched the learning environment designed in the previous study with a CSCL component. We chose Knowledge Forum (KF), a software tool for constructing and storing notes, for sharing notes and exchanging comments on them, and for scaffolding students in their acquisition of specific cognitive operations and particular concepts (Scardamalia & Bereiter, 1998). As in the preceding study, students solved the problems in small groups; afterward, they exchanged their solutions through KF and could comment on each other's solutions before a whole-class discussion was held. In the last stage of this study, the small groups generated problems themselves, which were also exchanged through KF; each group solved at least one problem posed by another group and sent its solution to that group for comments.

The learning environment was implemented in two fifth-grade and two sixth-grade classes of a Flemish primary school over a period of 17 weeks (2 hours per week). Although this study was less well-controlled than the previous one (e.g., there was no control group), the findings point in the same direction, showing that it is possible to create a high-powered computer-supported learning community for teaching and learning mathematical problem solving in the upper primary school. Of special importance is that the teachers were very enthusiastic about their participation and involvement in the investigation. Their positive appreciation related to the approach to the teaching of problem solving as well as the use of KF as a supporting tool for learning; for instance, they reported several positive developments observed in their students, such as a more mindful and reflective approach to word problems. The learning environment was also enthusiastically received by most of the students. At the end of the intervention, they expressed that they liked this way of doing word problems much more than the traditional approach. Many of the children also reported learning something new, both about information technology and about mathematical problem solving.

Summary

By combining in these intervention studies a set of carefully designed word problems, a variety of activating and interactive teaching methods (strengthened by a technology component in the second one), and the adoption of new social and sociomathematical classroom norms, a learning environment was created that aimed at the development in students of a mindful and self-regulated approach toward mathematical problem solving. In terms of the components of a mathematical disposition, the learning environment focused selectively on heuristic methods, cognitive self-regulation skills, and, albeit rather implicitly, positive beliefs about learning mathematics problem solving. As anticipated, the results show that the intervention had significant positive effects on students' performance in problem solving, their use of heuristic strategies, and their cognitive self-regulation. Moreover, in the first study, the learning environment also had a favorable influence, albeit to a lesser extent, on their beliefs about learning and teaching mathematics. Taking into account the rather short period of the intervention, this last result is not at all surprising; indeed, beliefs and attitudes do not change overnight. However, a recent study in Italy by Mason and Scrivani (2004) in which a learning environment was designed and implemented with a more explicit focus on fostering students' beliefs obtained similar good results as our study, but the outcomes were especially positive with respect to the development of students' mathematics-related beliefs.

Notwithstanding the positive outcomes of these studies, some critical comments need to be made that point at issues for continued research (for a more detailed discussion, see Verschaffel et al., 1999). First of all, due to the quasi-experimental design of the studies, the complexity of the learning environment, and the small experimental group, it is not possible to establish the rel-

ative importance of the distinct components of the intervention in producing its positive effects; in fact, it is plausible that it is the combination of the different aspects of the design, the content, and the implementation of the learning environment that is responsible for those effects. From a methodological perspective, this is often considered a weakness of teaching experiments, criticized for their lack of randomization and control (see, e.g., Levin & O'Donnell, 1999). To overcome this criticism and make a stronger contribution to theory building, one could conduct randomized classroom trial studies (Levin & O'Donnell, 1999) involving larger numbers of experimental classes, in which different versions of complex learning environments are systematically contrasted and compared in terms of identification and differentiation of the aspects that contribute especially to their power and success. However, as argued by Slavin (2002, p. 17), one should be aware of "the fact that randomized experiments of interventions applying to entire classrooms can be extremely difficult and expensive to do and are sometimes impossible."

Furthermore, some problematic aspects of the learning environment designed and implemented in these studies may explain why no stronger effects were achieved; they point to suggestions for further inquiry. First, the components of the model of competent problem solving might be reformulated in terms that are more understandable and accessible to children, and that at the same time better reflect the cyclical nature of a solution process. Second, the third basic pillar of the learning environment, the establishment of a new classroom climate through the introduction of new social and sociomathematical norms, was not implemented in this study in a sufficiently systematic and effective way. Besides the short duration of the intervention, this may also explain the rather weak impact of the intervention on students' attitudes and beliefs. Third, with respect to the instructional techniques, an issue that needs to be further addressed is how to organize and support small-group work so that all students—including the shy and low-ability ones—participate and collaborate in a task-oriented way.

Finally, although the observed outcomes are promising, we should realize that in several respects we are still far removed from the intended large-scale implementation in educational practice of the underlying conception of mathematics learning and teaching. First, the intervention was restricted to only a part of the mathematics curriculum, namely, word problem solving; for a sustained innovation, the whole mathematics curriculum, and even the entire school program, should be modeled after the socioconstructivist perspective on learning environments (see also Cognition and Technology Group at Vanderbilt, 1996). Second, the studies have shown that practicing a learning environment such as the ones designed in our project is very demanding and requires drastic changes in the role of the teacher. Instead of being the main, if not the only source of information, as is often still the case in average educational practice, the teacher becomes a "privileged" member of the knowledge-building community who creates an intellectually stimulating climate, models learning and problem-solving activities, asks thought-provoking questions, provides support to learners through coaching and guidance, and fosters students' agency in and responsibility for their own learning. Broadly scaling up this new perspective on mathematics learning and teaching into educational practice is not a minor challenge. Indeed, it is not just a matter of acquiring a set of new instructional techniques, but calls for a fundamental and profound change in teachers' beliefs, attitudes, and mentality and, therefore, requires intensive professional development and cooperation with in-service mathematics teachers (see also Cognition and Technology Group at Vanderbilt, 1997; Gearhart et al., 1999).

Developing Social and Sociomathematical Norms

In the previous subsection, we remarked that in our intervention study, one characteristic of the learning environment was not very well implemented, namely, the establishment of new social and sociomathematical norms. It is plausible that this flaw in the actualization of the learning environment accounts to a large extent for the poor effects on students' mathematics-related beliefs. The work of Cobb and his colleagues (Cobb, 2000; Cobb, Gravemeijer, Yackel, McClain, & Whitenack, 1997; Cobb, Yackel, & Wood, 1989; McClain & Cobb, 2001; Yackel & Cobb, 1996) over the past 15 years has focused on conducting design experiments in the lower grades of the primary school that explicitly aimed at developing novel social and sociomathematical norms that can enhance students' mathematics-related beliefs.

The theoretical stance of Cobb's work, called the *emergent view,* conceives of "mathematical learning as both a process of active individual construction and a process of enculturation" (Cobb et al., 1997, p. 152). By stressing the individual as well as the social aspects of

learning, this view is closely related to our socioconstructivist perspective.

The methodological approach used by Cobb (2000) is the classroom teaching experiment, an extension to the level of the classroom of the constructivist teaching experiment in which the researcher himself or herself acts as teacher interacting with students either one-on-one or in small groups. The aim of the classroom teaching experiment, or design experiment, is to study students' mathematics learning in alternative learning environments designed in collaboration with teachers. By so doing, this design can reveal "the implications of reform as they play out in interactions between teachers and students in classrooms" (p. 333).

Social and Sociomathematical Norms, and Beliefs as Their Correlates

The rather subtle distinction between social norms and sociomathematical norms, referred to in the previous subsection, can be clarified through some examples. The expectation that students explain their solution strategies and procedures is a social norm, whereas being able to recognize what counts as an acceptable mathematical explanation is a sociomathematical norm. Similarly, the rule that when discussing a problem one should come up with solutions that differ from those already presented is a social norm; knowing and understanding what constitutes mathematical difference (see later discussion) is a sociomathematical norm. Stated more generally, social norms apply to any subject matter domain of the curriculum; sociomathematical norms are domain-specific in the sense that they bear on normative aspects of students' mathematical activities and discussions (Yackel & Cobb, 1996).

Social and sociomathematical norms constitute the key constructs of the following interpretive framework put forward by Cobb (2000; see also Cobb et al., 1997) for analyzing the classroom microculture. According to Cobb and his colleagues, this framework represents both reflexive perspectives of the emergent view. The *social perspective* refers to interactive and collective classroom activities; the *psychological perspective* focuses on individual students' activities during and contributions to the collective classroom practices resulting in beliefs: beliefs about one's own role as a learner, about the role of the teacher and one's colearners, and about the general nature of the mathematical activity as correlates of the social norms; and mathematical beliefs and values as correlates of the sociomathematical norms. As Table 4.3

Table 4.3   An Interpretive Framework for Analyzing Individual and Collective Activity at the Classroom Level

Social Perspective	Psychological Perspective
Classroom social norms	Beliefs about our own role, others' roles, and the general nature of mathematical activity
Sociomathematical norms	Specifically mathematical beliefs and values
Classroom mathematical practices	Mathematical conceptions and activity

Source: From "Mathematizing and Symbolizing: The Emergence of Chains of Signification in One First-Grade Classroom" (pp. 151–233), by P. Cobb, K. Gravemeijer, E. Yackel, K. McClain, and J. Whitenack, in *Situated Cognition: Social, Semiotic, and Psychological Perspectives,* D. Kirshner and J. Whitson (Eds.), 1997, Mahwah, NJ: Erlbaum. Reprinted with permission.

shows, the social component of the framework involves a third aspect, classroom mathematical practices, which refers to taken-as-shared mathematical practices established by the classroom community. Cobb (2000, p. 324; see also Cobb et al., 1997) gives the following example:

> In the second-grade classrooms in which my colleagues and I have worked, various solution methods that involve counting by ones are established mathematical practices at the beginning of the school year. Some of the students are also able to develop solutions that involve the conceptual creation of units of 10 and 1. However, when they do so, they are obliged to explain and justify their interpretations of number words and numerals. Later in the school year, solutions based on such interpretations are taken as self-evident by the classroom community. The activity of interpreting number words and numerals in this way has become an established mathematical practice that no longer stands in need of justification. From the students' point of view, numbers simply are composed of 10s and 1s—it is a mathematical truth.

As is shown in the "Psychological Perspective" column of Table 4.3, the mathematical interpretations, conceptions, and activities of individual students are considered the psychological correlates of those classroom practices; their relationship is also conceived as reflexive.

Research Method

The interpretive framework was used over the past years in a number of teaching experiments in lower primary classrooms (first, second, and third grades) in which attempts were made to help and support teachers in radically changing their mathematics teaching practices. This implies that the researchers are present in the classroom during all the lessons of the experiment. Also, the

participating teachers become members of the research and development team. The duration of the experiments can vary from just a few weeks to an entire school year.

A variety of data are collected throughout the experiments. Video recordings of the lessons are made using two cameras, one focused mainly on the teacher, but sometimes on individual children who explain their reasoning and problem solving; the other camera tapes students while they are involved in discussions about a math task. Other data sources are copies of students' written work, field notes relating to the daily lessons, reports of the daily and weekly planning and debriefing sessions of the researchers together with the teacher, the teacher's diary, and videotapes of individual interviews with students. The method used to analyze those data is in line with the constant comparison method of B. G. Glaser and Strauss (1967) as applied in ethnographic studies. It consists of the cyclic comparison of data against conjectures derived from the preceding analysis: Issues that arise from watching the video recordings of a lesson are documented and clarified through a process of conjecture and refutation, and the trustworthiness of the final outcome can be checked against the original data tapes (McClain & Cobb, 2001; for a more detailed account, see Cobb & Whitenack, 1996).

Illustrative Results

Classroom teaching experiments were usually carried out with teachers who followed an inquiry approach to teaching and learning. The instructional tasks and problems, as well as the instructional strategies, are prepared and planned in collaboration and consultation with the teacher. The instructional strategies are very much in accordance with those applied in our own intervention study: whole-class discussions of problems led by the teacher and collaborative small-group work followed by whole-class discussions in which students explicate, argue for, and justify their strategies and solutions elaborated during the small-group activities.

The illustration of the development of social norms described later is taken from a study in a second-grade classroom. In the beginning of the school year, the teacher quickly realized that the students did not meet his expectation that they would easily explain for the whole class how they had approached and solved tasks and problems. Apparently, this expectation contradicted their belief acquired during the previous school year, in the first grade, that the only source of the right solution method and the correct answer is the teacher. To deal with these conflicting expectations, the teacher started using a procedure called the renegotiation of classroom social norms. As a result, different social norms relating to whole-class discussion were overtly considered, negotiated, and thus socially constructed through interaction in the classroom. Examples are explaining and justifying solutions, trying to understand others' explanations, expressing agreement and disagreement, and questioning alternatives when conflicting interpretations and solutions are put forward (Cobb et al., 1989). Their contributions to the social construction of the classroom social norms in the renegotiation process initiates in students developments and changes in their beliefs about their role and the role of the teacher and their fellow students in the mathematics classroom, and about the nature of mathematics. Therefore, these beliefs are considered the psychological correlates of the classroom social norms.

Whereas Cobb and his colleagues initially focused on general social norms in elaborating a social perspective on classroom activities, in the mid-1990s this was complemented by a growing attention to domain-specific norms that permeate and regulate classroom discourse, that is, norms that are specific to activities and interactions in the mathematics classroom (Yackel & Cobb, 1996; see also Voigt, 1995). Examples of such sociomathematical norms are what counts as a different mathematical solution, a sophisticated solution, an insightful solution, an elegant solution, an efficient solution, and an acceptable solution.

The mathematical difference norm and its significance was first identified in inquiry-oriented classrooms where teachers regularly solicited students to offer a different approach or solution to a task, and rejected some reactions as not being mathematically different. It was obvious that the students had no idea what a mathematically different answer could be, but became aware of it during interactions in the course of which some of their contributions were accepted and others rejected. It was thus through their reactions to the teacher's invitation to offer different solutions that students learned what mathematical difference means and also contributed to install and define the mathematical difference norm in their classroom. This shows that, as is the case for social norms, sociomathematical norms also emerge and are socially constructed through negotiation between teacher and students.

The following episode of a lesson in a second-grade classroom shows how a teacher initiates the interactive development of a mathematically different solution (Yackel & Cobb, 1996, pp. 462–463):

The number sentence $16 + 14 + 8 = $ _____ has been posed as a mental computation activity.

Lemont: I added the two 1s out of the 16 and [the 14] . . . would be 20 . . . plus 6 plus 4 would equal another 10, and that was 30 plus 8 left would be 38.

Teacher: All right. Did anyone add a little *different*? Yes?

Ella: I said 16 plus 14 would be 30 . . . and add 8 more would be 38.

Teacher: Okay! Jose? *Different?*

Jose: I took two 10s from the 14 and the 16 and that would be 20 . . . and the I added the 6 and the 4 that would be 30 . . . then I added the 8, that would be 38.

Teacher: Okay! It's almost similar to—(addressing another student) Yes? *Different?* All right.

Here, the teacher's response to Jose suggests that he is working out for himself the meaning of *different*. However, because he does not elaborate for the students how Jose's solution is similar to those already given, the students are left to develop their own interpretations. The next two solutions offered by students are more inventive and are not questioned by the teacher.

Rodney: I took one off the 6 and put it on the 14 and I had . . . 15 [and] 15 [would be] 30, and I had 8 would be 38.

Teacher: Yeah! Thirty-eight. Yes. *Different?*

Tonya: I added the 8 and the 4, that was 12. . . . So I said 12 plus 10, that would equal 22 . . . plus the other 10, that would be 32—and then I had 38.

Teacher: Okay! Dennis—*different, Dennis?*

Throughout such interactions the students progressively learned the meaning of mathematical difference as they observed that their teacher accepted solutions that consist of decomposing and recomposing numbers in a variety of ways but rejected responses that only more or less repeat solutions already presented. The episode demonstrates clearly how normative aspects of mathematical activity emerge and are constituted during classroom discourse. Correlatively with the installation of those sociomathematical norms, students develop at the individual level mathematics-related beliefs and values that enable them to become progressively more self-regulated in doing mathematics.

The initial work on sociomathematical norms from which the preceding episode is taken (Yackel & Cobb, 1996) documents through a post hoc analysis how such normative aspects of mathematical activity emerge. In a more recent classroom teaching experiment, more explicit attempts were undertaken, in collaboration between a teacher and the research team, to proactively foster the establishment of certain sociomathematical norms, thus simultaneously enhancing children's mathematics-related beliefs. In addition, this work focused on tracing the emergence of one sociomathematical norm from another throughout the classroom discourse.

Based on video data of lessons during the first 4 months of a school year, McClain and Cobb (2001) showed what first-grade teachers could do to evoke and sustain the development of sociomathematical norms at the classroom level and mathematics-related beliefs in individual children that are in line with the mathematical disposition advocated in current reform documents. One task given to the children was to figure out how many chips were shown on an overhead projector on which an arrangement of, for instance, five or seven chips was displayed. The objective was to elicit reasoning about the task and initiate a shift in students from using counting to find the answer to more sophisticated strategies based on grouping of chips. The results show how the mathematical difference norm developed in the classroom through discussions and interactions focused on the task, but later evolved into a renegotiation of the norm of a sophisticated solution. Indeed, solutions based on grouping of chips were seen not only as different from, but also as more sophisticated than counting. Similarly, from the mathematical difference norm emerged the norm of what counts as an easy, simple or efficient way to solve a problem: Some of the solutions that were accepted as being different were also considered easy or efficient, but others not. In the same way as in the previous study, students' individual beliefs about mathematics and mathematics learning were influenced in parallel with the emergence of the sociomathematical norms, and this contributed to their acquisition of a mathematical disposition.

Summary

Conducting classroom teaching experiments in collaboration with teachers as an overall research strategy, and using the interpretive framework discussed here for the in-depth qualitative analyses of video recordings of lessons (complemented with field notes and interview data), Cobb and his colleagues have shown how social and sociomathematical norms in the microculture of lower primary grades' mathematics classrooms emerge, evolve, and further develop throughout interactions between teacher and students, and also how these norms then regulate continued classroom discourse and contribute to the creation of learning opportunities for students and teacher. Besides this theoretical orientation, the work has a major pragmatic goal, namely, understanding and designing, in close collaboration with teachers, classroom learning environments that are in accordance with the basic tenets of current reform documents.

According to Cobb (2000, p. 327), the methodological issue of generalizability is of utmost importance, but the notion is not used here in the traditional sense that ignores specific features of the particular cases of the set to which a proposition generalizes: "Instead, the theoretical analysis developed when coming to understand one case is deemed to be relevant when interpreting other cases. Thus, what is generalized is a way of interpreting and acting that preserves the specific characteristics of individual cases."

Cobb (2000) concedes that the classroom teaching experiment that focuses on problems and reform issues at the classroom level is not the panacea that fits all research questions and problems. Due to the focus on the classroom as a community of learners, this type of experiment is less appropriate for investigating and documenting mathematical learning and thinking of individual students. For the same reason, the classroom teaching experiment is not well suited for studying reform issues that relate to the broader context of the school and the community, for which different approaches, such as ethnographic methods, are more strongly indicated.

Referring to the first limitation signaled by Cobb (2000), and taking into account the available publications, it seems to us that indeed this work falls short of operationalizing the psychological perspective of the interpretive framework. A major point in this respect relates to the claim that correlatively with the establishment of new social and sociomathematical norms embedded in the classroom practices, the mathematics-related beliefs of individual students develop. However, those beliefs are not at all operationalized and assessed in the reports of the experiments, although it might not be too difficult to do so.

As already remarked with regard to the previous intervention study, the second restriction of this classroom teaching experiment also raises concern about the crucial issue of upscaling promising practices that are in line with the intended reform of math education. Still, the two intervention projects support in different ways the viewpoint that it is possible to create and implement novel learning environments that induce in children learning processes that facilitate the acquisition of important components of mathematical competence as described in the beginning of this chapter.

Other projects in which innovative instructional interventions have been designed, based on similar principles, have reported converging findings. We mention here only two examples, again geographically spread over both sides of the Atlantic. In the so-called Jasper Project, learning of mathematical problem solving in the upper primary school is anchored in meaningful and challenging environments (Cognition and Technology Group at Vanderbilt, 1997, 2000). Although this project resembles our own intervention study in terms of grade level and mathematical focus, it goes far beyond it in several respects. First, anchored instruction of mathematical problem solving has been studied more intensively and over a longer period of time. Second, it involves a strong technological component, using videodisc technology to present problems. Third, efforts have been undertaken toward a more large-scale implementation of anchored instruction.

The second example, referred to earlier, is Realistic Mathematics Education (RME), which was initiated by Freudenthal and developed in the Netherlands in the 1970s. Underlying this approach to mathematics education is Freudenthal's (1983) didactic phenomenology, which involves a reaction against the traditional idea that students should first acquire the formal system of mathematics, with applications to come afterward. According to Freudenthal, this is contrary to the way mathematical knowledge has been gathered and developed, that is, starting from the study of phenomena in the real world. We refer readers to Treffers (1987), Streefland (1991), and Gravemeijer (1994) for more detailed information about the basic ideas of RME, as well as for examples of design experiments wherein these ideas have been successfully implemented and tested with respect to different aspects of the elementary school curriculum. Interesting to mention here is that in a 1-year RME-based intervention study relating to mental calculation with numbers up to 100, Menne (2001) found not

only that second graders at the end of the school year achieved one or more mastery levels higher than at the beginning of the school year, but also that this remarkable progression applied particularly to the weaker students, who mainly belonged to the group of children from non-Dutch backgrounds.

ASSESSMENT: A TOOL FOR MONITORING LEARNING AND TEACHING

The assessment component of the CLIA model is concerned with the design, construction, and use of instruments for determining how powerful learning environments are in facilitating in students the acquisition of the different aspects of a mathematical disposition. This implies that those instruments should be aligned with this view of the ultimate goal of mathematics education and with the nature of mathematics learning as discussed earlier.

Assessments of mathematics learning can either be internal or external. Internal assessments are organized by the teacher in the classroom, formally or more informally; external, usually large-scale assessments come from outside, organized at the district, state, national, or even international level using standardized tests or surveys (NRC, 2001a; Silver & Kenney, 1995). As argued by the NRC (2001b), assessments in both the classroom and a large-scale context can be set up for three broad purposes: to assist learning and teaching, to measure achievement of individual students, and to evaluate school programs. Stated somewhat differently, Webb (1992) has distinguished the following purposes of assessing mathematics: to provide evidence for teachers on what students know and can do; to convey to students what is important to know, do, and believe; to inform decision makers within educational systems; and to monitor performance of the educational system as a whole. With respect to classroom assessment, we argue that, considered within the CLIA framework, the major purpose is to use assessment *for* learning, which means that it should provide useful information for students and teachers to foster and optimize further learning (Shepard, 2000; see also Shepard, 2001). Sloane and Kelly (2003) contrast assessment *for* learning, or formative assessment, with assessment *of* learning, the goal of which is to determine what students can achieve and whether they attain a certain achievement or proficiency level. They describe this as high-stakes testing, a topic recently heavily debated in relation to the No Child Left Behind Act of 2001 (see, e.g., the special issue of *Theory into Practice* edited by Clarke & Gregory in 2003). Before focusing on classroom assessment, we address large-scale assessment, which mostly, but not necessarily, takes the form of high-stakes testing.

Large-Scale Assessment of Mathematics Learning

The massive use of standardized tests in education has always been more customary in the United States than in Europe. The 2001 No Child Left Behind Act and the related quest for accountability have even increased this practice, and also intensified the debates about the effectiveness and desirability of high-stakes testing (see, e.g., Amrein & Berliner, 2002; Clarke & Gregory, 2003). Especially since the beginning of the 1990s, the traditional tests have been criticized (see, e.g., Kulm, 1990; Lesh & Lamon, 1992; Madaus, West, Harmon, Lomax, & Viator, 1992; Romberg, 1995; Shepard, 2001). But although research has resulted in improvements in the underlying theory and the technical aspects of achievement assessment, R. Glaser and Silver (1994, p. 401) have argued, "Nevertheless, at present, much of this work is experimental, and the most common practices in the current assessment of achievement in the national educational system have changed little in the last 50 years."

Analyses of widely used standardized tests show that there is a mismatch between the new vision of mathematical competence, as described earlier, and the content covered by those tests. Due to the excessive use of the multiple-choice format, the tests focus on the assessment of memorized facts, rote knowledge, and lower-level procedural skills. They do not sufficiently yield relevant and useful information on students' abilities in problem solving, in modeling complex situations, in communicating mathematical ideas, and in other higher-order components of mathematical activity and a mathematical disposition. A related criticism points to the one-sided orientation of the tests toward the products of students' mathematics work, and the neglect of the processes underlying those products (De Corte et al., 1996; Masters & Mislevy, 1993; Silver & Kenney, 1995).

An important consequence of this state of the art is that assessment often has a negative impact on the implemented curriculum, the classroom climate, and instructional practices, dubbed the WYTIWYG (What You Test Is What You Get) principle (Bell, Burkhardt, & Swan, 1992). Indeed, the tests convey an implicit mes-sage to students and teachers that only facts, standard procedures, and lower-level skills are important and valued in mathematics education. As a result, teachers tend to "teach to the test"; that is, they adapt and narrow their instruction to give a disproportionate amount of attention to the teaching of the low-level knowledge and skills addressed by the test, at the expense of teaching for understanding, reasoning, and problem solving (Frederiksen, 1990; R. Glaser & Silver, 1994).

An additional major disadvantage of the majority of traditional evaluation instruments is that they are disconnected from learning and teaching. Indeed, also due to their static and product-oriented nature, most achievement measures do not provide feedback about students' understanding of basic concepts, or about their thinking and problem-solving processes. Hence, they fail to provide relevant information that is helpful for students and teachers in terms of guiding further learning and instruction (De Corte et al., 1996; R. Glaser & Silver, 1994; NRC, 2001b; Shepard, 2001; Snow & Mandinach, 1991). In this respect, Chudowsky and Pellegrino (2003, p. 75) question whether large-scale assessments can be developed that can both measure and support student learning, and they argue:

> We set forth the proposition that large-scale assessments can and should do a much better job of supporting learning. But for that to happen, education leaders will need to rethink some of the fundamental assumptions, values, and beliefs that currently drive large-scale assessment practices in the United States. The knowledge base to support change is available but has to be harnessed.

Indeed, apart from the previous intrinsic criticisms of traditional standardized achievement tests, a major issue of debate is their accountability use as high-stakes tests, that is, their mandatory administration for collecting data on student achievement as a basis for highly consequential decisions about students (e.g., graduation), teachers (e.g., financial rewards), and schools and school districts (e.g., accreditation). According to the No Child Left Behind Act, this accountability use should result in the progressive acquisition by all students of a proficiency level in reading and mathematics. However, a crucial question is whether current testing programs really foster and improve learning and instruction, and there are serious doubts in this regard. In a study by Amrein and Berliner (2002) involving 18 states, it was shown that there is no compelling evidence at all for increased student learning, the intended outcome of those states' high-stakes testing programs. Moreover, there are many reports of unintended unfavorable consequences, such as increased dropout rates, negative impact on minority and special education children, cheating on examinations by teachers and students, and teachers leaving the profession. In addition, students tend to focus on learning for the test at the expense of the broader scope of the standards.

For large-scale assessments to indeed foster and improve student learning, as set forth by Chudowsky and Pellegrino (2003), we will have to move away from the rationale, the constraints, and the practices of current high-stakes testing programs (Amrein & Berliner, 2002; NRC, 2001b). As one example, we briefly review an alternative approach to large-scale testing developed recently in the Flemish part of Belgium (for a more detailed discussion, see Janssen, De Corte, Verschaffel, Knoors, & Colémont, 2002).

In the preceding section of this chapter, we presented a study by our center in which we designed a learning environment for mathematical problem solving that is aligned with the new standard for primary education in Flanders that became operational in the school year 1998 to 1999. In a subsequent project, also commissioned by the Department of Education of the Flemish Ministry, we developed an instrument for the national assessment of the new standards of the entire mathematics curriculum. The instrument was used to obtain a first, large-scale baseline assessment of students' attainment of those curriculum standards at the end of primary school. The aim was thus not to evaluate individual children or schools as a basis for making high-stakes decisions, but to get an overall picture of the state of the art of achievement in mathematics across Flanders. The instrument consists of 24 measurement scales, each representing a cluster of standards and covering as a whole the entire mathematics curriculum relating to numbers, measurement, and geometry.

Item response theory was used for the construction of the scales. Using a stratified sampling design, a fairly representative sample of 5,763 sixth graders (12-year-olds) belonging to 184 schools participated in the investigation. Taking into account the aim of the assessment, it was not necessary to have individual scores of all students, and a population sampling approach could be used "whereby different students take different portions of a much larger assessment, and the results are combined to obtain an aggregate picture of student achievement" (Chudowsky & Pellegrino, 2003, p. 80). This approach

also allows for cover of the total breadth of the curriculum standards. Specifically, the instrument involved 10 booklets, each containing about 40 items belonging to two or three of the 24 measurement scales; to get booklets that were somewhat varied, the measurement scales in each booklet represented distinct mathematical contents (e.g., the items in booklet 2 related to percentages and problem solving). Each booklet was administered to a sample of more than 500 sixth graders. Four different item formats were used: short answer (67%), short answer with several subquestions (14%), multiple choice (11%), and product and process questions (8%). Especially the last type addressed higher-order skills by asking for a motivation or an explanation for the given answer. Figure 4.1 shows an example of each of the four item formats.

Estimating the proportion of students in three categories summarized performance on each of the 24 scales: insufficient, sufficient, and good mastery. Briefly stated, the results of this assessment were as follows. Scales about declarative knowledge and those involving lower-order mathematical procedures were mastered best. The scales relating to more complex procedures (e.g., calculating percentages; calculating perimeter, area, volume), and those that address higher-order thinking skills (problem solving; estimation and approximation) were not so well mastered. The latter finding is not so surprising as those scales relate to standards that are relatively new in the Flemish mathematics curriculum. It is also interesting to mention that few gender differences in performance were observed.

It is the intention of the Department of Education of the Flemish Ministry to organize such a large-scale assessment of mathematics education periodically in the future. As the present assessment was carried out recently, it is too early to see if it has an impact on mathematics learning and teaching. However, the potential is obviously there. Indeed, because this assessment covers the entire curriculum, its findings are a good starting point for continued discussion and reflection on the standards in and among all education stakeholders (policymakers, teachers, supervisors and educational counselors, parents, students). Also due to the breadth of such an assessment approach, it uncovers those (sets of) standards that are insufficiently mastered. In doing so, the assessment provides relevant feedback to practitioners (curriculum designers, teachers, counselors) by identifying those aspects of the curriculum that need special attention in learning and instruction; researchers could

a. Short-answer format
Ann buys a coat of 4.500 BF for 3.600 BF.
With how many percent is the price reduced?
_____%

b. Short-answer format with several subquestions
Put the following numbers in the table:
250   3564   816   2845   1991   1702
Note: Some numbers may not fit into the table, or may fit in several columns.

divisible through 2	divisible through 3	divisible through 5	divisible through 9	divisible through 10

c. Multiple-choice format
Three of these pictures are made of the same situation.
One picture does not belong here.
Color the round below this picture.

d. Product and process question
Chantal wants to buy a pair of Tiger sneakers and saw these ads in the local paper.

Family Shoe Center	**Van Dierens shoe shop**
Bottom prices every day	This week only
Tiger sneakers only 1200 BF	Sales: Tiger sneakers 1100 BF

The Family Shoe Center is within walking distance.
To go to Van Dierens shoe shop Chantal has to take the bus. That would cost 80 BF
for a one-way ticket.
If Chantal wants to spend <u>as little money as possible</u>, at which shop should she buy her
sneakers?
Answer: _____
Explain why.
Answer: _____

Figure 4.1   Examples of an item for each item format.

also focus intervention research of the kind discussed in the previous section on those weaknesses in students' competence. A third advantage of the alignment of the assessment and the curriculum is that the often heard complaint about teaching and learning to the test can largely be avoided, especially if appropriate counseling and follow-up care is provided after the results are published. Moreover, because the Ministry does not intend to use the results for the evaluation of individual teachers or schools, and because scores of individual children, classes, and schools are not published, the negative consequences of high-stakes testing are also avoided.

Classroom Assessment

Notwithstanding the relevance and importance of large-scale, external assessments, these necessarily need to be supplemented by internal classroom testing. Large-scale tests are a form of summative evaluation: They measure achievement after a longer period of instruction covering a more or less extensive part of the curriculum of a subject matter domain. It is obvious that assessment *for* learning, that is, to assist and support learning in the classroom, needs to be formative in nature: Teachers need to continually collect evaluative information during the instructional process about students' progress in understanding and mastering knowledge and skills as a basis for guiding and supporting further learning, and, if needed, for providing on-time corrective help and instruction for individual students or groups of students. Such formative assessments also provide students themselves with informative feedback as a basis for monitoring and regulating their own learning (see, e.g., NRC, 2001b; Shepard, 2001). Whereas external assessments are useful and important for the large-scale monitoring of trends in mathematics education, classroom assessment intends to provide information on an ongoing day-to-day basis to improve student learning, taking into account the strengths and weaknesses of the class as a group as well as of the individual students.

In view of fulfilling their expected role in supporting and fostering learning, classroom assessment instruments should be well aligned with the full breadth of the learning goals or standards, similarly to large-scale tests. And because classroom assessment is much more focused on learning of and instruction for one specific group of students (as a group but also as individual children), it should provide, even more than large-scale tests, diagnostic information about students' conceptual understanding and about their thinking processes and

solution strategies for tasks and problems. This is a conditio sine qua non for teachers to guide further learning and instruction, especially for adapting teaching appropriately to the needs of the learners (De Corte et al., 1996; R. Glaser & Silver, 1994; Shepard, 2001).

A very simple example from our own research can illustrate the importance of this diagnostic information. In a study on children's solution processes of numerical addition and subtraction problems (De Corte & Verschaffel, 1981), an item such as _____ $- 12 = 7$ elicited mainly the two wrong answers 18 and 5. Both responses are incorrect, but the underlying erroneous solution processes are totally different: The first wrong answer is due to a rather technical error in executing the arithmetic operation; the second mistake is conceptual in nature and points to a lack of understanding of the equal sign. By tracing children's solution processes and strategies, one can derive their level of understanding; this information is necessary for designing individually adapted remedial instruction.

Another striking example of the usefulness of identifying students' reasoning comes from the well-known QUASAR (Quantitative Understanding: Amplifying Student Achievement and Reasoning) project. The open-ended task shown in Figure 4.2 was given to middle school students (Silver & Kenney, 1995). The classroom teachers believed that this was a straightforward task, and expected the answer "No" accompanied by the following explanation: "Yvonne takes the bus eight times a week, which would cost $8.00. Buying the pass would

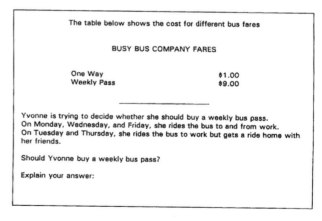

Figure 4.2 Item from the QUASAR project. *Source:* From "Sources of Assessment Information for Instructional Guidance in Mathematics" (pp. 38–86), by E. A. Silver and P. A. Kenney, in *Reform in School Mathematics and Authentic Assessment,* T. A. Romberg (Ed.), 1995, Albany, NY: State University of New York Press. Reprinted with permission.

cost $1.00 more." But surprisingly, quite a number of students came up with the answer "Yes," a response that in a traditional product-oriented test would be scored as incorrect. However, in their explanation, those children argued that the pass was a better deal because it could be used for other trips during the weekend by Yvonne, and even by other family members. This clearly illustrates that appropriately assessing students' knowledge and understanding requires that one looks not only at their answers, but also at their thinking and reasoning.

The preceding discussion shows that using assessment to assist instruction requires that the two should be integrated, as envisioned by the NRC (1989, p. 69; see also NRC, 2001b; Shepard, 2001; Snow & Mandinach, 1991): "Assessment should be an integral part of teaching. It is the mechanism whereby teachers can learn how students think about mathematics as well as what students are able to accomplish." In accordance with this perspective, Shavelson and Baxter (1992, p. 82) have rightly argued that "a good assessment makes a good teaching activity, and a good teaching activity makes a good assessment."

One can add that from the perspective of the learner, a good assessment makes a good learning activity, and a good learning activity makes a good assessment. Taking into account the conception of learning in the CLIA model, this also implies that assessment should contain assignments that are meaningful for the learners and that offer opportunities for self-regulated and collaborative—besides individual—approaches to tasks and problems (see also Shavelson & Baxter, 1992). In line with the constructivist view of learning, the increasing proficiency in self-regulating their learning should gradually lead to students acquiring the ability to self-assess their math work. Of course, from that perspective, the criteria and expectations should be made explicit to students (see also Shepard, 2001).

To gather data about students' performance and progress, teachers can use a variety of techniques: informal questions, seatwork and homework tasks, clinical interviews, portfolios, and more formal instruments such as teacher-made classroom tests, learning potential tests, and progress maps. The clinical interview initiated by Piaget (1952) is a very appropriate technique for acquiring insight into children's thinking and reasoning processes while solving mathematics tasks and problems. Due to its flexible, responsive, and open-ended nature (Ginsburg, Klein, et al., 1998) it allows

for an in-depth analysis of those processes. For an excellent and practice-oriented introduction to the use of the clinical interview as a tool for formative classroom assessment, we refer readers to the teacher's guide by Ginsburg, Jacobs, and Lopez (1998).

Another method that aims at the diagnosis of mental structures and cognitive processes is the so-called learning potential test, a concept that emerges from Vygotsky's (1978) notion of the zone of proximal development (ZPD). The purpose of a learning potential test is to diagnose the ZPD that provides an assessment of the child's learning ability (see, e.g., A. L. Brown, Campione, Webber, & McGilly, 1992; Hamers, Ruijssenaars, & Sijtsma, 1992). Such a test consists of three steps: a pretest, a learning phase, and a posttest. The pretest assesses the child's entering ability with respect to the targeted problems. In the learning phase, which often takes the format of an individual interview, the tester administers a carefully designed sequence of tasks representing a continuum of increasing difficulty/transfer levels; the amount of help needed by the child for solving the successive tasks is taken as a measure of learning efficiency. Finally, a posttest is given to measure the amount of learning that has occurred throughout the session. This learning potential test thus offers a nice example of the integration of instruction and assessment.

One type of instrument that is particularly useful for classroom assessment from a developmental perspective, especially if it is theory-based, is a progress map, which describes the typical sequence of development and acquisition of knowledge and skill in a given domain of learning. As an example, we present the Number Knowledge Test developed by Griffin and Case (1997; see also NRC, 2001b). The test was originally elaborated as an instrument for testing the authors' theory concerning the normal development in children of central conceptual structures for whole numbers. In this regard, they distinguish four stages:

1. *Initial counting and quantity schemas:* Four-year-olds can count a set of objects and have some knowledge of quantity, allowing them to answer questions about more and less when presented with arrays of objects. But they fail on such questions as "Which is more—four or five?"

2. *Mental counting line structure:* By 6 years, children are able to answer correctly the latter type of question (without objects), indicating that the two earlier structures are integrated into a mental number line,

considered by Griffin and Case as a central conceptual structure.

3. *Double counting line structure:* By 8 years, once children understand how mental counting works, they progressively form representations of multiple number lines, such as those for counting by 2s, 5s, 10s, and 100s.

4. *Understanding of full system:* By about age 10, children acquire a generalized understanding of the whole-number system and the underlying base-10 system.

Although primarily intended as a research instrument, the Number Knowledge Test has been applied in North America more and more as a diagnostic assessment tool to inform and assist arithmetic teaching. The test has already been revised to better capture 4-year-olds' understanding of number. The revised version is presented in Figure 4.3 (Griffin, 2003, 2004).

This Number Knowledge Test is administered orally and individually to children. The testing continues until a child does not answer a sufficient number of questions to proceed to the next level. It has been shown that the test yields very rich data about children's development in understanding numbers, and the instrument derives its power as an assessment tool from the underlying theory briefly outlined earlier. Although teachers often have an initial resistance to administering this individual oral test, most end up finding it very useful and worthwhile. They report that the test reveals differences in thinking among children that they were not aware of before. As a consequence, they also listen more actively to their students, and they find the results very useful for supporting and fostering children's learning.

Summary

Theoretical and empirical work over the past 15 years has resulted in important changes in the roles for assessment that are in line with a constructivist perspective on learning. The NRC (2001b, p. 4) has summarized these roles appropriately as follows:

> Assessments, especially those conducted in the context of classroom instruction, should focus on making students' thinking visible to both teachers and themselves so that instructional strategies can be selected to support an appropriate course for future learning. . . . One of the most important roles for assessment is the provision of timely and informative feedback to students during instruction

and learning so that their practice of a skill and its subsequent acquisition will be effective and efficient.

Researchers in the field of learning and instruction, as well as experts in the domain of testing and psychometrics, have started endeavors, aiming at the elaboration of new approaches and procedures for the design and construction of innovative assessment devices in line with those novel roles, as well as an explicit and research-based integration of assessment and instruction (Frederiksen, Mislevy, & Bejar, 1993; Lesh & Lamon, 1992; NRC, 2001b; Romberg, 1995; Shepard, 2001).

However, only the first steps have been taken, and so we are confronted with an extensive and long-term agenda of research and dissemination (see, e.g., Snow & Mandinach, 1991). Implementation of the new perspective on assessment requires first of all breaking out of the still prevailing traditional approach to evaluation in educational practice. Policymakers, practitioners, and the public need to be convinced of the nonproductivity of, and even the harm from, the educational perspective of current high-stakes testing and of the benefits of the assessment *for* learning. This is critical because large-scale assessments in the usual standardized testing scenarios radiate on and influence classroom assessment. As argued by Amrein and Berliner (2002), it is now time to debate high-stakes testing policies more thoroughly and seek to change them if they do not do what was intended and have some unintended negative consequences as well.

A major challenge for research in the future relates to the integration of psychometric theory with current perspectives about the nature of productive learning and effective teaching. In this regard, some progress has recently been made, as illustrated by the report of the NRC (2001b), *Knowing What Students Know: The Science and Design of Educational Assessment.* But much remains to be done to develop alternative methods for the construction of new types of assessment instruments. Another important issue for research is the development of computer-based systems for assessment. Indeed, due to its wide possibilities for varied presentation of tasks and problems, its potential for adaptive testing and feedback taking into account learners' prior knowledge and skills, and its capacities for storing and processing responses, the computer can be very helpful in achieving the challenging task of elaborating and implementing the intended forms of assessment to assist and support learning and instruction.

Number Knowledge Test

Level 0 (4-year-old level): Go to Level 1 if 3 or more correct.

1   Can you count these chips and tell me how many there are? (Place 3 counting chips in front of child in a row.)

2a (Show stacks of chips, 5 vs. 2, same color.) Which pile has more?

2b (Show stacks of chips, 3 vs. 7, same color.) Which pile has more?

3a this time I'm going to ask you which pile has less. (Show stacks of chips, 2 vs. 6, same color.) Which pile has less?

3b (Show stacks of chips, 8 vs. 3, same color.) Which pile has less?

4   I'm going to show you some counting chips. (Show a line of 3 red and 4 yellow chips in a row, as follows: R Y R Y R Y Y.) Count just the yellow chips and tell me how many there are.

5   Pick up all chips from the previous question. Then say: Here are some more counting chips. (Show mixed array [not in a row] of 7 yellow and 8 red chips.) Count just the red chips and tell me how many there are.

Level 1 (6-year-old level): Go to Level 2 if 5 or more correct.

1   If you had 4 chocolates and someone gave you 3 more, how many chocolates would you have altogether?

2   What number comes right after 7?

3   What number comes two numbers after 7?

4a Which is bigger: 5 or 4?

4b Which is bigger: 7 or 9?

5a This time, I'm going to ask you about smaller numbers. Which is smaller: 8 or 6?

5b Which is smaller: 5 or 7?

6a Which number is closer to 5: 6 or 2? (Show visual array after asking question.)

6b Which number is closer to 7: 4 or 9? Show visual array after asking question.)

7   How much is 2 + 4? (OK to use fingers for counting.)

8   How much is 8 take away 6? (OK to use fingers for counting.)

9a (Show visual array - 8 5 2 6 - and ask child to point to and name each numeral.) When you are counting, which of these numbers do you say first?

9b When you are counting, which of these numbers do you say last?

Level 2 (8-year-old level): Go to Level 3 if 5 or more correct.

1   What number comes 5 numbers after 49?

2   What number comes 4 numbers before 60?

3a Which is bigger: 69 or 71?

3b Which is bigger: 32 or 28?

4a This time I'm going to ask you about smaller numbers. Which is smaller: 27 or 32?

4b Which is smaller: 51 or 39?

5a Which number is closer to 21: 25 or 18? (Show visual array after asking the question.)

5b Which number is closer to 28: 31 or 24? (Show visual array after asking the question.)

6   How many numbers are there in between 2 and 6? (Accept either 3 or 4.)

7   How many numbers are there in between 7 and 9? (Accept either 1 or 2.)

8   (Show card 12 54) How much is 12 – 54?

9   (Show card 47 21) How much is 47 take away 21?

Level 3 (10-year-old level):

1   What number comes 10 numbers after 99?

2   What number comes 9 numbers after 999?

3a Which difference is bigger: the difference between 9 and 6 or the difference between 8 and 3?

3b Which difference is bigger: the difference between 6 and 2 or the difference between 8 and 5?

4a Which difference is smaller: the difference between 99 and 92 or the difference between 25 and 11?

4b Which difference is smaller: the difference between 48 and 36 or the difference between 84 and 73?

5   (Show card, "13, 39") How much is 13 + 39?

6   (Show card, "36, 18") How much is 36 – 18?

7   How much is 301 take away 7

Figure 4.3   Number Knowledge Test. *Source:* From "The Development of Math Competence in the Preschool and Early School Years: Cognitive Foundations and Instructional Strategies" (pp. 1–32), by S. Griffin, in *Mathematical Cognition,* J. M. Royer (Ed.), 2003, Greenwich, CT: Information Age Publishing. Reprinted with permission.

CONCLUSIONS

Using the CLIA framework as an organizing device, this chapter presents a selective review of research on development, learning, and instruction relating to mathematics that is relevant and looks promising in view of application in and innovation and improvement of mathematics classroom practices. This framework is in line with the new international perspectives on the goals and the nature of mathematics education as manifested in reform documents such as the *Principles and Standards for School Mathematics* (NCTM, 2000). The review is selective in terms of educational level (focusing on primary school) and mathematical content (whole number and word problem solving); in addition, the chapter has an emphasis on research on mathematics education in the Western world.

The review shows that with respect to each of the four interconnected components of the CLIA model, our empirically based knowledge has substantially advanced over the past decades. Progressively, a much better understanding has emerged concerning the components that constitute a mathematical disposition, concerning the nature of the learning and developmental processes that should be induced in students to facilitate the acquisition of competence, concerning the characteristics of learning environments that are powerful in initiating and evoking those processes, and concerning the kind of assessment instruments that are appropriate to help monitor and support learning and teaching.

An important question to ask is whether this expanding knowledge base (for a condensed review, see Grouws & Cebulla, 2000) is relevant and useful to bridging the long-standing gap between theory/research and practice and, thus, can contribute to improving mathematics education practices. The available intervention studies reviewed and referred to here, as well as others (e.g., Becker & Selter, 1996; Clements & Sarama, 2004; Lesh & Doerr, 2003), warrant some optimism. Indeed, the increasing number of success stories are building to a critical mass of results, showing that under certain conditions, carefully designed, research-based learning environments can yield learning outcomes in students that are in accordance with the current view of the goal of mathematics education as the acquisition of a mathematical disposition. Based on the research analyzed and reviewed here, but also taking into account the broader recent literature on innovative contexts for learning in and out of school (e.g., NRC,

2000; Schauble & Glaser, 1996), some major interconnected principles for designing powerful mathematics learning environments are the following:

- Learner-centered environments, that is, environments that help all students construct knowledge and skills, building on their prior knowledge and beliefs relating to mathematics.

- A focus on understanding of basic concepts and number sense and, where relevant, connecting conceptual with procedural knowledge.

- Learning new mathematical concepts and skills while problem solving.

- Stimulating active and progressively more self-regulated, reflective learning, starting from eliciting children's own productions and contributions.

- Use of tasks and problems that are meaningful to students, and when they have acquired a certain level of mastery, inviting them to generate their own tasks and problems.

- Use of interactive and collaborative teaching methods, especially small-group work and whole-class discussion to create a classroom learning community.

- Alignment of learning, instruction, and assessment to provide multiple opportunities for feedback that yield relevant information for improving teachers' instruction as well as students' learning.

- Attention to individual differences by assessing, acknowledging, and supporting diversity.

The optimism based on the available research is fueled by the observation that inquiry-based ideas are indeed gradually taking root in the mathematics education community, namely, in the reform documents worldwide and subsequently in curricula and textbooks, but also in the writings and practices of knowledgeable educational professionals. However, the optimism is tempered by two major challenging problems for future research and development that we cannot elaborate here due to space restrictions. The first issue, signaled in the section on intervention, relates to broadly *upscaling* the new perspective on learning and teaching mathematics, and the design principles for learning environments that derive from it. The second related and equally important problem concerns the *sustainability* of innovative learning environments. The solution to both problems has a serious price tag and is largely a matter for educational policy. Taking this into account, a major answer lies in preservice and in-service teacher professional development; an excellent example in this respect is the Cognitively Guided Instruction Project (Carpenter & Fennema, 1992; Carpenter, Fennema, & Franke, 1994; for a brief overview, see Ginsburg, Klein, et al., 1998). In terms of sustainability, a major condition is meeting teachers' need for ongoing support for feedback and reflection about their teaching practices (Cognition and Technology Group at Vanderbilt, 1997). A promising approach to such continuing professional development and support is elaborated in the Lesson Study Project, the core form of in-service training for Japanese mathematics teachers (Lewis, 2002).

REFERENCES

Ambrose, R., Baek, J.-M., & Carpenter, T. P. (2003). Children's invention of multidigit multiplication and division algorithms. In A. J. Baroody & A. Dowker (Eds.), *The development of arithmetic concepts and skills* (pp. 305–336). Mahwah, NJ: Erlbaum.

Amrein, A. L., & Berliner, D. C. (2002). High-stakes testing, uncertainty, and student learning. *Educational Policy Analysis Archives, 10*(18). Available from http://epaa.asu.edu/epaa/v10n18.

Anghileri, J. (1999). Issues in teaching multiplication and division. In I. Thompson (Ed.), *Issues in teaching numeracy in primary schools* (pp. 184–194). Buckingham, England: Open University Press.

Anghileri, J. (2001). Development of division strategies for year 5 pupils in 10 English schools. *British Educational Research Journal, 27*, 85–103.

Ashcraft, M. H. (1995). Cognitive psychology and simple arithmetic: A review and summary of new directions. *Mathematical Cognition, 1*, 3–34.

Ashcraft, M. H., & Christy, K. S. (1995). The frequency of arithmetic facts in elementary texts: Addition and multiplication in grades 1 through 6. *Journal for Research in Mathematics Education, 26*, 396–421.

Australian Education Council. (1990). *A national statement on mathematics for Australian schools.* Melbourne: Curriculum Corporation for Australian Education Council.

Baroody, A. J. (1993). Early multiplication performance and the role of relational knowledge in mastering combinations involving "two." *Learning and Instruction, 3*, 93–112.

Baroody, A. J. (2003). The development of adaptive expertise and flexibility: The integration of conceptual and procedural knowledge. In A. J. Baroody & A. Dowker (Eds.), *The development of arithmetic concepts and skills: Constructing adaptive expertise* (pp. 1–33). Mahwah, NJ: Erlbaum.

Baroody, A. J., & Dowker, A. (Eds.). (2003). *The development of arithmetic concepts and skills: Constructing adaptive expertise.* Mahwah, NJ: Erlbaum.

Baroody, A. J., & Tiilikainen, S. H. (2003). Two perspectives on addition development. In A. J. Baroody & A. Dowker (Eds.), *The development of arithmetic concepts and skills* (pp. 75–126). Mahwah, NJ: Erlbaum.

Baroody, A. J., Wilkins, J. L. M., & Tiilikainen, S. M. (2003). The development of children's understanding of additive commutativity: From protoquantitative concept to general concept. In A. J. Baroody & A. Dowker (Eds.), *The development of arithmetic concepts and skills* (pp. 127–160). Mahwah, NJ: Erlbaum.

Becker, J. P., & Selter, C. (1996). Elementary school practices. In A. Bishop, K. Clements, C. Keitel, J. Kilpatrick, & C. Laborde (Eds.), *International handbook of mathematics education* (Pt. 1, pp. 511–564). Dordrecht, the Netherlands: Kluwer Academic.

Beishuizen, M. (1999). The empty number line as a new model. In I. Thompson (Ed.), *Issues in teaching numeracy in primary schools* (pp. 157–168). Buckingham, England: Open University Press.

Bell, A., Burkhardt, H., & Swan, M. (1992). Balanced assessment of mathematical performance. In R. Lesh & S. J. Lamon (Eds.), *Assessment of authentic performance in school mathematics* (pp. 119–144). Washington, DC: American Association for the Advancement of Science.

Bisanz, J. (2003). Arithmetical development: Commentary on chapters 1 through 8 and reflections on directions. In A. J. Baroody & A. Dowker (Eds.), *The development of arithmetic concepts and skills* (pp. 435–452). Mahwah, NJ: Erlbaum.

Bishop, A. J., Clements, M. A., Keitel, C., Kilpatrick, J., & Leung, F. S. K. (Eds.). (2003). *Springer international handbooks of education: Vol. 10. Second international handbook of mathematics education.* Dordrecht, the Netherlands: Kluwer Press.

Boaler, J., & Greeno, J. G. (2000). Identity, agency, and knowing in mathematical worlds. In J. Boaler (Ed.), *Multiple perspectives on mathematics teaching and learning* (pp. 171–200). Stamford, CT: Ablex.

Boekaerts, M. (1997). Self-regulated learning: A new concept embraced by researchers, policy makers, educators, teachers, and students. *Learning and Instruction, 7*, 161–186.

Brousseau, G. (1997). *Theory of didactical situations in mathematics* (N. Balacheff, M. Cooper, R. Sutherland, & V. Warfield, Eds. & Trans.). Dordrecht, the Netherlands: Kluwer Press.

Brown, A. L., Campione, J. C., Webber, L. S., & McGilly, K. (1992). Interactive learning environments: A new look at assessment and instruction. In B. R. Gifford & M. C. O'Connor (Eds.), *Changing assessments: Alternative views of aptitude, achievement, and instruction* (pp. 121–211). Boston: Kluwer Press.

Brown, J. S., Collins, A., & Duguid, P. (1989). Situated cognition and the culture of learning. *Educational Researcher, 18*(1), 32–42.

Bruner, J. (1996). *The culture of education.* Cambridge, MA: Harvard University Press.

Butterworth, B., Marschesini, N., & Girelli, L. (2003). Basic multiplication combinations: Passive storage or dynamic reorganisation? In A. J. Baroody & A. Dowker (Eds.), *The development of arithmetic concepts and skills* (pp. 161–188). Mahwah, NJ: Erlbaum.

Buys, K. (2001). Mental arithmetic. In M. Van den heuvel (Ed.), *Children learn mathematics* (pp. 121–146). Utrecht, the Netherlands: Freudenthal Institute, University of Utrecht.

Carpenter, T. P., & Fennema, E. (1992). Cognitively guided instruction: Building on the knowledge of students and teachers. *International Journal of Educational Research, 17*, 457–470.

Carpenter, T. P., Fennema, E., & Franke, M. L. (1994). *Children thinking about whole numbers.* Madison: Wisconsin Center for Education Research.

Carpenter, T. P., Franke, M. L., Jacobs, V., Fennema, E., & Empson, S. B. (1998). A longitudinal study of intervention and understanding in children's multidigit addition and subtraction. *Journal for Research in Mathematics Education, 29,* 3–30.

Carpenter, T. P., Lindquist, M. M., Matthews, W., & Silver, E. A. (1983). Results of the third NAEP mathematics assessment: Secondary school. *Mathematics Teacher, 76,* 652–659.

Carr, M., & Biddlecomb, B. (1998). Metacognition in mathematics from a constructivist perspective. In D. J. Hacker, J. Dunlosky, & A. C. Graesser (Eds.), *Metacognition in educational theory and practice* (pp. 69–91). Mahwah, NJ: Erlbaum.

Chudowsky, N., & Pellegrino, J. W. (2003). Large-scale assessments that support learning: What will it take? *Theory into Practice, 42,* 75–83.

Clark, F. B., & Kamii, C. (1996). Identification of multiplicative thinking in children in grades 1 through 5. *Journal for Research in Mathematics Education, 27,* 41–51.

Clarke, M., & Gregory, K. (Eds.). (2003). The impact of high-stakes testing [Special issue]. *Theory into Practice, 42*(1).

Clements, D., & Sarama, J. (Eds.). (2004). Hypothetical learning trajectories [Special issue]. *Mathematical Thinking and Learning, 6,* 81–260.

Cobb, P. (2000). Conducting teaching experiments in collaboration with teachers. In A. E. Kelly & R. A. Lesh (Eds.), *Handbook of research design in mathematics and science education* (pp. 307–333). Mahwah, NJ: Erlbaum.

Cobb, P., & Bauersfeld, H. (Eds.). (1995). *The emergence of mathematical meaning: Interactions in classroom cultures.* Hillsdale, NJ: Erlbaum.

Cobb, P., Confrey, J., diSessa, A., Lehrer, R., & Schauble, L. (2003). Design experiments in educational research. *Educational Researcher, 32*(1), 9–13.

Cobb, P., Gravemeijer, K., Yackel, E., McClain, K., & Whitenack, J. (1997). Mathematizing and symbolizing: The emergence of chains of signification in one first-grade classroom. In D. Kirshner & J. Whitson (Eds.), *Situated cognition: Social, semiotic, and psychological perspectives* (pp. 151–233). Mahwah, NJ: Erlbaum.

Cobb, P., & Whitenack, J. (1996). A method for conducting longitudinal analysis of classroom videorecordings and transcripts. *Educational Studies in Mathematics, 30,* 213–228.

Cobb, P., Yackel, E., & Wood, T. (1989). Young children's emotional acts while doing mathematical problem solving. In D. B. McLeod & V. M. Adams (Eds.), *Affect and mathematical problem solving: A new perspective* (pp. 117–148). New York: Springer-Verlag.

Cockcroft, W. H. (1982). *Mathematics counts: A report of the Committee of Inquiry into the Teaching of Mathematics in Schools.* London: Her Majesty's Stationery Office.

Cognition and Technology Group at Vanderbilt. (1996). Looking at technology in context: A framework for understanding technology and education research. In D. C. Berliner & R. C. Calfee (Eds.), *Handbook of educational psychology* (pp. 807–840). New York: Macmillan.

Cognition and Technology Group at Vanderbilt. (1997). *The Jasper Project: Lessons in curriculum, instruction, assessment, and professional development.* Mahwah, NJ: Erlbaum.

Cognition and Technology Group at Vanderbilt. (2000). Adventures in anchored instruction: Lessons from beyond the ivory tower. In R. Glaser (Ed.), *Advances in instructional psychology: Vol. 5. Educational design and cognitive science* (pp. 35–99). Mahwah, NJ: Erlbaum.

Cooper, T. J., Heirdsfield, A. M., & Irons, C. J. (1996, July). *Years 2 and 3 children's mental addition and subtraction strategies for 2-*

and 3-digit word problems and algorithmic exercises. Paper presented at Topic Group 1 at ICME-8, Sevilla, Spain.

Corno, L., Cronbach, L. J., Kupermintz, H., Lohman, D. F., Mandinach, E., Porteus, A. W., et al. (2002). *Remaking the concept of aptitude: Extending the legacy of Richard E. Snow.* Mahwah, NJ: Erlbaum.

Cowan, R. (2003). Does it all add up? Changes in children's knowledge of addition combinations, strategies and principles. In A. J. Baroody & A. Dowker (Eds.), *The development of arithmetic concepts and skills* (pp. 35–74). Mahwah, NJ: Erlbaum.

Davis, R. B. (1989). Three ways of improving cognitive studies in algebra. In S. Wagner & C. Kieran (Eds.), *Research issues in the learning and teaching of algebra* (pp. 115–119). Hillsdale, NJ: Erlbaum.

Davis, R. B., Maher, C. A., & Noddings, N. (1990). Suggestions for the improvement of mathematics education. In R. B. Davis, C. A. Maher, & N. Noddings (Eds.), *Constructivist views on the teaching and learning of mathematics (Journal for Research in Mathematics Education,* Monograph No. 4, pp. 187–191). Reston, VA: National Council of Teachers of Mathematics.

De Bock, D., Van Dooren, W., Janssens, D., & Verschaffel, L. (2002). Improper use of linear reasoning: An in-depth study of the nature and the irresistibility of secondary school students' errors. *Educational Studies in Mathematics, 50,* 311–334.

De Bock, D., Verschaffel, L., & Janssens, D. (1998). The predominance of the linear model in secondary school students' solutions of word problems involving length and area of simple plane figures. *Educational Studies in Mathematics, 35,* 65–83.

De Corte, E. (2000). Marrying theory building and the improvement of school practice: A permanent challenge for instructional psychology. *Learning and Instruction, 10,* 249–266.

De Corte, E., Greer, B., & Verschaffel, L. (1996). Mathematics teaching and learning. In D. C. Berliner & R. C. Calfee (Eds.), *Handbook of educational psychology* (pp. 491–549). New York: Macmillan.

De Corte, E., Op 't Eynde, P., & Verschaffel, L. (2002). Knowing what to believe: The relevance of mathematical beliefs for mathematics education. In B. K. Hofer & P. R. Pintrich (Eds.), *Personal epistemology: The psychology of beliefs about knowledge and knowing* (pp. 297–320). Mahwah, NJ: Erlbaum.

De Corte, E., & Somers, R. (1982). Estimating the outcome of a task as a heuristic strategy in arithmetic problem solving: A teaching experiment with sixth-graders. *Human Learning, 1,* 105–121.

De Corte, E., & Verschaffel, L. (1981). Children's solution processes in elementary arithmetic problems: Analyses and improvement. *Journal of Educational Psychology, 73,* 765–779.

De Corte, E., & Verschaffel, L. (1985, October). Writing number sentences to represent addition and subtraction word problems. In S. Damarin & M. Shelton (Eds.), *Proceedings of the seventh annual meeting of the North American chapter of the International Group for the Psychology of Mathematics Education* (pp. 50–56). Columbus: Ohio State University, Department of Psychology.

De Corte, E., & Verschaffel, L. (1989). Teaching word problems in the primary school: What research has to say to the teacher. In B. Greer & G. Mulhern (Eds.), *New developments in teaching mathematics* (pp. 85–106). London: Routledge.

De Corte, E., Verschaffel, L., Lasure, S., Borghart, I., & Yoshida, H. (1999). Real-world knowledge and mathematical problem solving in upper primary school children. In J. Bliss, R. Säljö, & P. Light (Eds.), *Learning sites: Social and technological contexts for learning* (pp. 61–79). Oxford: Elsevier Science.

De Corte, E., Verschaffel, L., Lowyck, J., Dhert, S., & Vandeput, L. (2002). Collaborative learning in mathematics: Problem solving and problem posing supported by "Knowledge Forum." In D. Passey & M. Kendall (Eds.), *TelE-LEARNING: The challenge for the third millennium* (pp. 53–59). Boston: Kluwer Academic.

De Corte, E., Verschaffel, L., & Masui, C. (2004). The CLIA-model: A framework for designing powerful learning environments for thinking and problem solving. *European Journal of Psychology of Education, 19,* 365–384.

De Corte, E., Verschaffel, L., & Op 't Eynde, P. (2000). Self-regulation: A characteristic and a goal of mathematics education. In M. Boekaerts, P. R. Pintrich, & M. Zeidner (Eds.), *Handbook of self-regulation* (pp. 687–726). San Diego: Academic Press.

De Corte, E., Verschaffel, L., & Van Coillie, V. (1988). Influence of number size, problem structure, and response mode on children's solutions of multiplication word problems. *Journal of Mathematical Behavior, 7,* 197–216.

De Corte, E., & Weinert, F. E. (1996). Introduction. In E. De Corte & F. E. Weinert (Eds.), *International encyclopedia of developmental and instructional psychology* (pp. xix–xxviii). Oxford: Elsevier Science.

Dehaene, S. (1993). Varieties of numerical abilities. In S. Dehaene (Ed.), *Numerical cognition* (pp. 1–42). Cambridge, MA: Blackwell.

Dehaene, S., & Cohen, L. (1995). Towards an anatomical and functional model of number processing. *Mathematical Cognition, 1,* 83–120.

Dembo, M. H., & Eaton, M. J. (1997). School learning and motivation. In G. D. Phye (Ed.), *Handbook of academic learning: Construction of knowledge* (pp. 65–103). San Diego: Academic Press.

Donlan, C. (1998). *The development of mathematical skills.* Hove, England: Psychology Press.

Fennema, E., & Romberg, T. A. (Eds.). (1999). *Mathematics classrooms that promote thinking.* Mahwah, NJ: Erlbaum.

Fischbein, E. (1990). Introduction. In P. Nesher & J. Kilpatrick (Eds.), *Mathematics and cognition: A research synthesis by the International Group for the Psychology of Mathematics Education* (ICMI Study Series) (pp. 1–13). Cambridge, England: Cambridge University Press.

Frederiksen, N. (1990). Introduction. In N. Frederiksen, R. Glaser, A. Lesgold, & M. G. Shafto (Eds.), *Diagnostic monitoring of skill and knowledge acquisition* (pp. ix–xvii). Hillsdale, NJ: Erlbaum.

Frederiksen, N., Mislevy, R. J., & Bejar, I. I. (1993). *Test theory for a new generation of tests.* Hillsdale, NJ: Erlbaum.

Freudenthal, H. (1983). *Didactical phenomenology of mathematical structures.* Dordrecht, the Netherlands: Reidel.

Freudenthal, H. (1991). *Revisiting mathematics education.* Dordrecht, the Netherlands: Kluwer Academic.

Fuson, K. C. (1992). Research on whole number addition and subtraction. In D. A. Grouws (Ed.), *Handbook of research on mathematics teaching and learning* (pp. 243–275). New York: Macmillan.

Fuson, K. C., Wearne, D., Hiebert, J. C., Murray, H. G., Human, P. G., Olivier, A. I., et al. (1997). Children's conceptual structures for multidigit numbers and methods of multidigit addition and subtraction. *Journal for Research in Mathematics Education, 28,* 130–162.

Garofalo, J., & Lester, F. K., Jr. (1985). Metacognition, cognitive monitoring and mathematical performance. *Journal for Research in Mathematics Education, 16,* 163–176.

Gearhart, M., Saxe, G. B., Seltzer, M., Schlackman, J., Carter Ching, C., Nasir, H., et al. (1999). When can educational reforms make a difference? Opportunities to learn fractions in elementary school classrooms. *Journal for Research in Mathematics Education, 30,* 286–315.

Geary, D. C. (2003). Arithmetical development: Commentary on chapters 9 through 15 and future directions. In A. J. Baroody & A. Dowker (Eds.), *The development of arithmetic concepts and skills* (pp. 453–464). Mahwah, NJ: Erlbaum.

Ginsburg, H. P., Jacobs, S. F., & Lopez, L. S. (1998). *The teacher's guide to flexible interviewing in the classroom: Learning what children know about math.* Boston: Allyn & Bacon.

Ginsburg, H. P., Klein, A., & Starkey, P. (1998). The development of children's mathematical thinking: Connecting research with practice. In W. Damon (Editor-in-Chief) & I. E. Sigel & K. A. Renninger (Vol. Eds.), *Handbook of child psychology: Vol. 4. Child psychology in practice* (5th ed., pp. 401–476). New York: Wiley.

Glaser, B. G., & Strauss, A. L. (1967). *The discovery of grounded theory: Strategies for qualitative research.* New York: Aldine.

Glaser, R., & Silver, E. (1994). Assessment, testing, and instruction: Retrospect and prospect. In L. Darling-Hammond (Ed.), *Review of research in education* (Vol. 20, pp. 393–419). Washington, DC: American Educational Research Association.

Good, T. L., Mulryan, C., & McCaslin, M. (1992). Grouping for instruction in mathematics: A call for programmatic research on small-group processes. In D. A. Grouws (Ed.), *Handbook of research on mathematics teaching and learning* (pp. 165–196). New York: Macmillan.

Gravemeijer, K. (1994). *Developing realistic mathematics education.* Utrecht, the Netherlands: Freudenthal Institute, University of Utrecht.

Greeno, J. G. (1991a). Number sense as situated knowing in a conceptual domain. *Journal for Research in Mathematics Education, 22,* 170–218.

Greeno, J. G. (1991b). A view of mathematical problem solving in school. In M. U. Smith (Ed.), *Toward a unified theory of problem solving: Views from the content domains* (pp. 69–98). Hillsdale, NJ: Erlbaum.

Greeno, J. G., Collins, A. M., & Resnick, L. B. (1996). Cognition and learning. In D. C. Berliner & R. C. Calfee (Eds.), *Handbook of educational psychology* (pp. 15–46). New York: Macmillan.

Greeno, J. G., & the Middle School Mathematics through Applications Project Group. (1998). The situativity of knowing, learning, and research. *American Psychologist, 53,* 5–26.

Greer, B. (1988). Nonconservation of multiplication and division: Analysis of a symptom. *Journal of Mathematical Behavior, 7,* 281–298.

Greer, B. (1992). Multiplication and division as models of situations. In D. A. Grouws (Ed.), *Handbook of research on mathematics teaching and learning* (pp. 276–295). New York: Macmillan.

Greer, B. (1996). Theories of mathematics education: The role of cognitive analysis. In L. P. Steffe, P. Nesher, P. Cobb, G. A. Goldin, & B. Greer (Eds.), *Theories of mathematical learning* (pp. 179–196). Mahwah, NJ: Erlbaum.

Greer, B., & Verschaffel, L. (Eds.). (1997). Modelling reality in mathematics classrooms [Special issue]. *Learning and Instruction, 7,* 293–397.

Griffin, S. (2003). The development of math competence in the preschool and early school years: Cognitive foundations and instructional strategies. In J. M. Royer (Ed.), *Mathematical cognition* (pp. 1–32). Greenwich, CT: Information Age Publishing.

Griffin, S. (2004). Fostering the development of whole-number sense: Teaching mathematics in the primary school. In M. S. Donovan &

J. D. Bransford (National Research Council Board on Behavioral and Social Sciences and Education) (Eds.), *How students learn: History, mathematics, and science* (pp. 257–308). Washington, DC: National Academy Press.

Griffin, S., & Case, R. (1997). Re-thinking the primary school math curriculum: An approach based on cognitive science. *Issues in Education, 3*(1), 1–49.

Grouws, D. A., & Cebulla, K. J. (2000). *Improving student achievement in mathematics* (Educational Practices Series, No. 4). Geneva, Switzerland: International Academy of Education and International Bureau of Education.

Hamers, J. H. M., Ruijssenaars, A. J. J. M., & Sijtsma, K. (1992). *Learning potential assessment: Theoretical, methodological and practical issues.* Amsterdam: Swets & Zeitlinger.

Hamm, J. V., & Perry, M. (2002). Learning mathematics in first-grade classrooms: On whose authority? *Journal of Educational Psychology, 94,* 126–137.

Hatano, G. (1982). Cognitive consequences of practice in culture specific procedural skills. *Quarterly Newsletter of the Laboratory of Comparative Human Cognition, 4,* 15–18.

Hatano, G. (1988). Social and motivational bases for mathematical understanding. In G. B. Saxe & M. Gearhart (Eds.), *Children's mathematics* (pp. 55–70). San Francisco: Jossey-Bass.

Hatano, G. (1996). A conception of knowledge acquisition and its implications for mathematics education. In L. P. Steffe, P. Nesher, P. Cobb, G. A. Goldin, & B. Greer (Eds.), *Theories of mathematical learning* (pp. 197–217). Mahwah, NJ: Erlbaum.

Hatano, G. (2003). Foreword. In A. J. Baroody & A. Dowker (Eds.), *The development of arithmetic concepts and skills* (pp. xi–xiv). Mahwah, NJ: Erlbaum.

Hegarty, M., Mayer, R. E., & Monk, C. A. (1995). Comprehension of arithmetic word problems: A comparison of successful and unsuccessful problem solvers. *Journal of Educational Psychology, 87,* 18–32.

Hiebert, J., & Wearne, D. (1996). Instruction, understanding, and skill in multidigit addition and subtraction. *Cognition and Instruction, 14,* 251–284.

Hofer, B. K., & Pintrich, P. R. (Eds.). (2002). *Personal epistemology: The psychology of beliefs about knowledge and knowing.* Mahwah, NJ: Erlbaum.

Institut de Recherche sur l'Enseignement des Mathématiques de Grenoble. (1980). Quel est l' âge du capitaine? *Bulletin de l' Association des Professeurs de Mathématique de l'Enseignement Public, 323,* 235–243.

Janssen, R., De Corte, E., Verschaffel, L., Knoors, E., & Colémont, A. (2002). National assessment of new standards for mathematics in elementary education in Flanders. *Educational Research and Evaluation, 8,* 197–225.

Jones, G., Thornton, C. A., & Putt, I. J. (1994). A model for nurturing and assessing multidigit number sense among first grade children. *Educational Studies in Mathematics, 27,* 117–143.

Kilpatrick, J. (1992). A history of research in mathematics education. In P. Kloosterman & M. C. Cougan (Eds.), Students' beliefs about learning school mathematics. *Elementary School Journal, 94,* 375–388.

Kloosterman, P., & Cougan, M. C. (1994). Students' beliefs about learning school mathematics. *Elementary School Journal, 94,* 375–388.

Krutetskii, V. A. (1976). *The psychology of mathematical abilities in school children.* Chicago: University of Chicago Press.

Kuhn, D. (1999). Metacognitive development. In L. Balter & C. Tamis-LeMonda (Eds.), *Child psychology: A handbook of contemporary issues* (pp. 259–286). Philadelphia: Psychology Press.

Kuhn, D. (2000). Metacognitive development. *Current Issues in Psychological Science, 9,* 178–181.

Kulm, G. (Ed.). (1990). *Assessing higher order thinking in mathematics.* Washington, DC: American Association for the Advancement of Science.

Kuriyama, K., & Yoshida, H. (1995). Representational structure of numbers in mental addition. *Japanese Journal of Educational Psychology, 43,* 402–410.

Lampert, M. (1990). When the problem is not the question and the solution is not the answer: Mathematical knowing and teaching. *American Educational Research Journal, 27,* 29–63.

Lave, J. (1992). Word problems: A microcosm of theories of learning. In P. Light & G. Butterworth (Eds.), *Context and cognition: Ways of learning and knowing* (pp. 74–92). New York: Harvester Wheatsheaf.

Lave, J., & Wenger, E. (1991). *Situated learning: Legitimate peripheral participation.* Cambridge, England: Cambridge University Press.

Leder, G. C., Pehkonen, E., & Törner, G. (Eds.). (2002). *Beliefs: A hidden variable in mathematics education?* Dordrecht, the Netherlands: Kluwer Academic.

LeFevre, J.-A., Smith-Chant, B. L., Hiscock, K., Daley, K. E., & Morris, J. (2003). Young adults' strategic choices in simple arithmetic: Implications for the development of mathematical representations. In A. J. Baroody & A. Dowker (Eds.), *The development of arithmetic concepts and skills* (pp. 203–228). Mahwah, NJ: Erlbaum.

Lehtinen, E., Hakkarainen, K., Lipponen, L., Rahikainen, M., & Muuhkonen, H. (1999). *Computer-supported collaborative learning: A review* (The J. H. G. I. Giesbers Reports on Education, Number 10). Nijmegen, the Netherlands: University of Nijmegen, Department of Educational Sciences.

Lemaire, P., & Siegler, R. S. (1995). Four aspects of strategic change: Contributions to children's learning of multiplication. *Journal for Experimental Psychology: General, 124,* 83–97.

Lesh, R., & Doerr, H. M. (Eds.). (2003). *Beyond constructivism: Models and modeling perspectives on mathematical problem solving, learning and teaching.* Mahwah, NJ: Erlbaum.

Lesh, R., & Lamon, S. J. (Eds.). (1992). *Assessment of authentic performance in school mathematics.* Washington, DC: American Association for the Advancement of Science.

Lester, F. K., Jr. (in press). *Second handbook of research on mathematics teaching and learning* (2nd ed.). Greenwich, CT: Information Age Publishing.

Lester, F. K., Jr., Garofalo, J., & Kroll, D. L. (1989). *The role of metacognition in mathematical problem solving: A study of two grade seven classes.* (Final report to the National Science Foundation of NSF project MDR 85-50346). Bloomington: Mathematics Education Development Center, Indiana University.

Levin, J. R., & O'Donnell, A. M. (1999). What to do about educational research's credibility gap? *Issues in Education: Contributions from Educational Psychology, 5,* 177–229.

Lewis, C. C. (2002). *Lesson study: A handbook of teacher-led instructional change.* Philadelphia: Research for Better Schools.

Madaus, G. F., West, M. M., Harmon, M. C., Lomax, R. G., & Viator, K. A. (1992). *The influence of testing on teaching math and science in grades 4 through 12.* Chestnut Hill, MA: Center for the Study of Testing, Evaluation, and Educational Policy, Boston College.

Mason, L., & Scrivani, L. (2004). Developing students' mathematical beliefs: An intervention study. *Learning and Instruction, 14,* 153–176.

Masters, G. H., & Mislevy, R. J. (1993). New views of student learning: Implications for educational measurement. In N. Frederiksen, R. J. Mislevy, & I. I. Bejar (Eds.), *Test theory for a new generation of tests* (pp. 219–242). Hillsdale, NJ: Erlbaum.

McClain, K., & Cobb, P. (2001). An analysis of development of sociomathematical norms in one first-grade classroom. *Journal for Research in Mathematics Education, 32,* 236–266.

McIntosh, A., Reys, B. J., & Reys, R. E. (1992). A proposed framework for examining basic number sense. *For the Learning of Mathematics, 12*(3), 2–8.

Menne, J. J. M. (2001). *Met sprongen vooruit. Een productief oefenprogramma voor zwakke rekenaars in het getallengebied tot 100: Een onderwijsexperiment* [A productive training program for mathematically weak children in the number domain up to 100: A teaching experiment]. Utrecht, the Netherlands: CD-Beta Press.

Mevarech, Z. R., & Light, P. H. (Eds.). (1992). Cooperative learning with computers [Special issue]. *Learning and Instruction, 2,* 155–285.

Middleton, J. A., & Spanias, P. H. (1999). Motivation for achievement in mathematics: Findings, generalizations, and criticisms of the research. *Journal for Research in Mathematics Education, 30,* 65–88.

Ministerie van de Vlaamse Gemeenschap [Ministry of the Flemish Community]. (1997). *Gewoon basisonderwijs. Ontwikkelings doelen en eindtermen: Besluit van mei '97 en decreet van juli '97* [Educational standards for the elementary school]. Brussels, Belgium: Departement Onderwijs, Centrum voor Informatie en Documentatie.

Muis, K. R. (2004). Personal epistemology and mathematics: A critical review and synthesis of research. *Review of Educational Research, 74,* 317–377.

Mulligan, J., & Mitchelmore, M. (1997). Young children's intuitive models of multiplication and division. *Journal for Research in Mathematics Education, 28,* 309–330.

National Council of Teachers of Mathematics. (1989). *Curriculum and evaluation standards for school mathematics.* Reston, VA: National Council of Teachers of Mathematics.

National Council of Teachers of Mathematics. (2000). *Principles and standards for school mathematics.* Reston, VA: National Council of Teachers of Mathematics.

National Research Council. (1989). *Everybody counts.* Washington, DC: National Academy of Sciences.

National Research Council. (2000). *How people learn: Brain, mind, experience, and school* (J. D. Bransford, A. L. Brown, & R. R. Cocking, Eds., Committee on Developments in the Science of Learning and Committee on Learning Research and Educational Practice). Washington, DC: National Academy Press.

National Research Council. (2001a). *Adding it up: Helping children learn mathematics* (J. Kilpatrick, J. Swafford, & B. Findell, Eds., Mathematics Learning Study Committee, Center for Education, Division of Behavioral and Social Sciences and Education). Washington, DC: National Academy Press.

National Research Council. (2001b). *Knowing what students know: The science and design of educational assessment* (Committee on the Foundations of Assessment, J. Pellegrino, N. Chudowsky, & R. Glaser, Eds., Board on Testing and Assessment, Center for Education, Division of Behavioral and Social Sciences and Education). Washington, DC: National Academy Press.

Nelissen, J. M. C. (1987). *Kinderen leren wiskunde: Een studie over constructie en reflectie in het basisonderwijs* [Children learning mathematics: A study on construction and reflection in elementary school children]. Gorinchem, the Netherlands: Uitgeverij De Ruiter.

Newell, A., & Simon, H. (1972). *Human problem solving.* Englewood Cliffs, NJ: Prentice-Hall.

Nunes, T. (1992). Ethnomathematics and everyday cognition. In D. A. Grouws (Ed.), *Handbook of research on mathematics teaching and learning* (pp. 557–574). New York: Macmillan.

Nunes, T., & Bryant, P. (Eds.). (1997). *Learning and teaching mathematics: An international perspective.* Hove, England: Psychology Press.

Nunes, T., Schliemann, A. D., & Carraher, D. W. (1993). *Street mathematics and school mathematics.* Cambridge, England: Cambridge University Press.

Op 't Eynde, P., De Corte, E., & Verschaffel, L. (2002). Framing students' mathematics-related beliefs. In G. C. Leder, E. Pehkonen, & G. Törner (Eds.), *Beliefs: A hidden variable in mathematics education?* (pp. 13–37). Dordrecht, the Netherlands: Kluwer Academic.

Overtoom, R. (1991). *Informatieverwerking door hoogbegaafde leerlingen bij het oplossen van wiskundeproblemen* [Information processing by gifted students in solving mathematical problems]. De Lier, the Netherlands: Academisch Boeken Centrum.

Pajares, F., & Miller, M. D. (1994). Role of self-efficacy and self-concept beliefs in mathematical problem solving: A path analysis. *Journal of Educational Psychology, 86,* 193–203.

Perkins, D. N. (1995). *Outsmarting IQ: The emerging science of learnable intelligence.* New York: Free Press.

Piaget, J. (1952). *The child's conception of number.* New York: Norton.

Picker, S. H., & Berry, J. S. (2000). Investigating pupils' images of mathematicians. *Educational Studies in Mathematics, 43,* 65–94.

Polya, G. (1945). *How to solve it.* Princeton, NJ: Princeton University Press.

Radatz, H. (1983). Untersuchungen zum lösen eingekleideter aufgaben. *Zeitschrift für Mathematik-Didaktik, 4,* 205–217.

Resnick, L. B. (1996). Situated learning. In E. De Corte & F. E. Weinert (Eds.), *International encyclopedia of developmental and instructional psychology* (pp. 341–347). Oxford: Elsevier Science.

Resnick, L. B., & Omanson, S. F. (1987). Learning to understand arithmetic. In R. Glaser (Ed.), *Advances in instructional psychology* (Vol. 3, pp. 41–95). Hillsdale, NJ: Erlbaum.

Reusser, K. (1986). Problem solving beyond the logic of things: Contextual effects on understanding and solving word problems. *Instructional Science, 17,* 309–338.

Reys, R. E., Reys, B. J., Nohda, N., & Emori, H. (1995). Mental computation performance and strategy use of Japanese students in grades 2, 4, 6, and 8. *Journal for Research in Mathematics Education, 26,* 304–326.

Reys, R. E., & Yang, D.-C. (1998). Relationship between computational performance and number sense among sixth- and eighth-grade students in Taiwan. *Journal for Research in Mathematics Education, 29,* 225–237.

Rittle-Johnson, B., & Siegler, R. S. (1998). The relation between conceptual and procedural knowledge in learning mathematics: A review. In C. Donlan (Ed.), *The development of mathematical skills* (pp. 75–110). East Sussex, England: Psychology Press.

Rock, D., & Shaw, J. M. (2000). Exploring children's thinking about mathematicians and their work. *Teaching Children Mathematics, 6,* 550–555.

Romberg, T. A. (Ed.). (1995). *Reform in school mathematics and authentic assessment*. Albany: State University of New York Press.

Salomon, G. (Ed.). (1993a). *Distributed cognition: Psychological and educational considerations*. Cambridge, England: Cambridge University Press.

Salomon, G. (1993b). No distribution without individual's cognition: A dynamic interactional view. In G. Salomon (Ed.), *Distributed cognition: Psychological and educational considerations* (pp. 111–138). Cambridge, England: Cambridge University Press.

Salomon, G., & Perkins, D. N. (1998). Individual and social aspects of learning. In P. D. Pearson & A. Iran-Nejad (Eds.), *Review of research in education* (Vol. 23, pp. 1–24). Washington, DC: American Educational Research Association.

Sandoval, W. A., & Bell, P. (2004a). Design-based research methods for studying learning in context: Introduction. *Educational Psychologist, 39*, 199–201.

Sandoval, W. A., & Bell, P. (Eds.). (2004b). Design-based research methods for studying learning in context [Special issue]. *Educational Psychologist, 39*(4).

Saxe, G. B. (1991). *Culture and cognitive development: Studies in mathematics understanding*. Hillsdale, NJ: Erlbaum.

Scardamalia, M., & Bereiter, C. (1998). *Web knowledge forum: User guide*. Santa Cruz, CA: Learning in Motion.

Schauble, L., & Glaser, B. (Eds.). (1996). *Innovations in learning: New environments for education*. Mahwah, NJ: Erlbaum.

Schoenfeld, A. H. (1985). *Mathematical problem solving*. New York: Academic Press.

Schoenfeld, A. H. (1988). When good teaching leads to bad results: The disasters of "well-taught" mathematics courses. *Educational Psychologist, 23*, 145–166.

Schoenfeld, A. H. (1991). On mathematics as sense-making: An informal attack on the unfortunate divorce of formal and informal mathematics. In J. F. Voss, D. N. Perkins, & J. W. Segal (Eds.), *Informal reasoning and education* (pp. 311–343). Hillsdale, NJ: Erlbaum.

Schoenfeld, A. H. (1992). Learning to think mathematically: Problem solving, metacognition, and sense-making in mathematics. In D. A. Grouws (Ed.), *Handbook of research on mathematics teaching and learning* (pp. 334–370). New York: Macmillan.

Schunk, D. H. (1998). Teaching elementary students to self-regulate practice of mathematical skills with modeling. In D. H. Schunk & B. J. Zimmerman (Eds.), *Self-regulated learning: From teaching to self-reflective practice* (pp. 137–159). New York: Guilford Press.

Selter, C. (1998). Building on children's mathematics: A teaching experiment in grade 3. *Educational Studies in Mathematics, 36*, 1–27.

Sfard, A. (1998). On two metaphors for learning and the dangers of choosing just one. *Educational Researcher, 27*(2), 4–13.

Shavelson, R. J., & Baxter, G. P. (1992). Linking assessment with instruction. In F. K. Oser, A. Dick, & J. L. Patry (Eds.), *Effective and responsible teaching: The new synthesis* (pp. 80–90). San Francisco: Jossey-Bass.

Shepard, L. A. (2000). The role of assessment in a learning culture. *Educational Researcher, 29*(7), 4–14.

Shepard, L. A. (2001). The role of classroom assessment in teaching and learning. In V. Richardson (Ed.), *Handbook of research on teaching* (4th ed, pp. 1066–1101). Washington, DC: American Educational Research Association.

Shrager, J., & Siegler, R. S. (1998). SCADS: A model of children's strategy choices and strategy discoveries. *Psychological Sciences, 9*, 405–410.

Siegler, R. (1996). *Emerging minds: The process of change in children's thinking*. New York: Oxford University Press.

Siegler, R. S. (1998). *Children's thinking*. Upper Saddle River, NJ: Prentice-Hall.

Siegler, R. S. (2001). Children's discoveries and brain-damaged patients' rediscoveries. In J. L. McClelland & R. S. Siegler (Eds.), *Mechanisms of cognitive development: Behavioral and neural perspectives* (pp. 33–63). Mahwah, NJ: Erlbaum.

Siegler, R. S., & Booth, J. L. (in press). Development of numerical estimation: A review. In J. I. D. Campbell (Ed.), *Handbook of mathematical cognition*. New York: Psychology Press.

Siegler, R. S., & Jenkins, E. A. (1989). *How children discover new strategies*. Hillsdale, NJ: Erlbaum.

Siegler, R. S., & Lemaire, P. (1997). Older and younger adults' strategy choices in multiplication: Testing predictions of ASCM using the choice/no-choice method. *Journal of Experimental Psychology: General, 126*, 71–92.

Silver, E. A., Branca, N., & Adams, V. (1980). Metacognition: The missing link in problem solving. In R. Karplus (Ed.), *Proceedings of the fourth International Congress of Mathematical Education* (pp. 429–433). Boston: Birkhäuser.

Silver, E. A., & Kenney, P. A. (1995). Sources of assessment information for instructional guidance in mathematics. In T. A. Romberg (Ed.), *Reform in school mathematics and authentic assessment* (pp. 38–86). Albany: State University of New York Press.

Simons, R. J., Van der Linden, J., & Duffy, T. (2000). *New learning*. Dordrecht, the Netherlands: Kluwer Academic.

Slavin, R. E. (2002). Evidence-based education policies: Transforming educational practice and research. *Educational Researcher, 31*(7), 15–21.

Sloane, F. C., & Kelly, A. E. (2003). Issues in high-stakes testing programs. *Theory into Practice, 42*, 12–17.

Snow, R. E., & Mandinach, E. B. (1991). *Integrating assessment and instruction: A research and development agenda*. Princeton, NJ: Educational Testing Service.

Sowder, J. (1992). Estimation and number sense. In D. A. Grouws (Ed.), *Handbook of research on mathematics teaching and learning: A project of the National Council of Teachers of Mathematics* (pp. 371–389). New York: Macmillan.

Spangler, D. A. (1992). Assessing students' beliefs about mathematics. *Arithmetic Teacher, 40*, 148–152.

Steffe, L. P., & Cobb, P. (1998). Multiplicative and division schemes. *Focus on Learning Problems in Mathematics, 20*(1), 45–61.

Steffe, L. P., & Gale, J. (Eds.). (1995). *Constructivism in education*. Hillsdale, NJ: Erlbaum.

Steffe, L. P., Nesher, P., Cobb, P., Goldin, G. A., & Greer, B. (Eds.). (1996). *Theories of mathematical learning*. Mahwah, NJ: Erlbaum.

Streefland, L. (Ed.). (1991). *Realistic mathematics education in primary school: On the occasion of the opening of the Freudenthal Institute*. Utrecht, the Netherlands: Freudenthal Institute, University of Utrecht.

Thompson, I. (1999). Getting your head around mental calculation. In I. Thompson (Ed.), *Issues in teaching numeracy in primary schools* (pp. 145–156). Buckingham, England: Open University Press.

Torbeyns, J., Arnaud, L., Lemaire, P., & Verschaffel, L. (2004). Cognitive change as strategic change. In A. Demetriou & A. Raftopoulos (Eds.), *Emergence and transformation in the mind: Modeling and measuring cognitive change* (pp. 186–216). Cambridge, England: Cambridge University Press.

Torbeyns, J., Verschaffel, L., & Ghesquiere, P. (2005). Simple addition strategies in a first-grade class with multiple-strategy instruction. *Cognition and Instruction, 23,* 1–21.

Treffers, A. (1987). *Three dimensions: A model of goal and theory description in mathematics education—The Wiskobas Project.* Dordrecht, the Netherlands: Reidel.

Treffers, A. (2001). Numbers and number relationships. In M. Van den Heuvel-Panhuizen (Ed.), *Children learn mathematics* (pp. 101–120). Utrecht, the Netherlands: Freudenthal Institute, University of Utrecht.

Van den Heuvel-Panhuizen, M. (2001). Estimation. In M. Van den Heuvel-Panhuizen (Ed.), *Children learn mathematics* (pp. 173–202). Utrecht, the Netherlands: Freudenthal Institute, University of Utrecht.

Van Essen, G. (1991). *Heuristics and arithmetic word problems.* Unpublished doctoral dissertation, Amsterdam, the Netherlands: University of Amsterdam.

VanLehn, K. (1990). *Mind bugs: The origins of procedural misconceptions.* Cambridge, MA: MIT Press.

Van Putten, C. M., Van den Brom-Snijders, P. A., & Beishuizen, M. (2005). Progressive mathematization of long division strategies in Dutch primary schools. *Journal for Research in Mathematics Education, 36,* 44–73.

Vergnaud, G. (1988). Multiplicative structures. In J. Hiebert & M. Behr (Eds.), *Number concepts and operations in the middle grades* (Vol. 2, pp. 141–161). Hillsdale, NJ: Erlbaum.

Verschaffel, L. (1997). Young children's strategy choices for solving elementary arithmetic word problems: The role of task and context variables. In M. Beishuizen, K. Gravemeijer, & E. Van Lieshout (Eds.), *The role of contexts and models in the development of mathematical strategies and procedures* (pp. 113–126). Utrecht, the Netherlands: Center for Science and Mathematics Education, Freudenthal Institute, University of Utrecht.

Verschaffel, L., & De Corte, E. (1993). A decade of research on word problem solving in Leuven: Theoretical, methodological, and practical outcomes. *Educational Psychology Review, 5,* 239–256.

Verschaffel, L., & De Corte, E. (1997). Word problems: A vehicle for promoting authentic mathematical understanding and problem solving in the primary school. In T. Nunes & P. Bryant (Eds.), *Learning and teaching mathematics: An international perspective* (pp. 69–97). Hove, England: Psychology Press.

Verschaffel, L., De Corte, E., & Borghart, I. (1997). Pre-service teachers' conceptions and beliefs about the role of real-world knowledge in mathematical modelling of school word problems. *Learning and Instruction, 7,* 330–359.

Verschaffel, L., De Corte, E., & Lasure, S. (1994). Realistic considerations in mathematical modelling of school arithmetic word problems. *Learning and Instruction, 4,* 273–294.

Verschaffel, L., De Corte, E., Lasure, S., Van Vaerenbergh, G., Bogaerts, H., & Ratinckx, E. (1999). Learning to solve mathematical application problems: A design experiment with fifth graders. *Mathematical Thinking and Learning, 1,* 195–229.

Verschaffel, L., Greer, B., De Corte, E. (2000). *Making sense of word problems.* Lisse, the Netherlands: Swets & Zeitlinger.

Voigt, J. (1995). Thematic patterns of interaction and sociomathematical norms. In P. Cobb & H. Bauersfeld (Eds.), *The emergence of mathematical meaning: Interactions in classroom culture* (pp. 163–201). Hillsdale, NJ: Erlbaum.

Vygotsky, L. S. (1978). *Mind in society: The development of higher psychological processes.* Cambridge, MA: Harvard University Press.

Webb, N. L. (1992). Assessment of students' knowledge of mathematics: Steps toward a theory. In D. A. Grouws (Ed.), *Handbook of research on mathematics teaching and learning* (pp. 661–683). New York: Macmillan.

Wheeler, D. (1989). Contexts for research on the teaching and learning of algebra. In S. Wagner & C. Kieran (Eds.), *Research issues in the learning and teaching of algebra* (pp. 278–287). Hillsdale, NJ: Erlbaum.

Whitehead, A. N. (1929). *The aims of education.* New York: Macmillan.

Wigfield, A., Eccles, J. S., Yoon, K. S., Harold, R. D., Arbreton, A. J. A., Freedman-Doan, C., et al. (1997). Change in children's competence beliefs and subjective task values across the elementary school years: A 3-year study. *Journal of Educational Psychology, 89,* 451–469.

Wood, T., Cobb, P., & Yackel, E. (1991). Change in teaching mathematics: A case study. *American Educational Research Journal, 28,* 587–616.

Yackel, E., & Cobb, P. (1996). Sociomathematical norms, argumentation, and autonomy in mathematics. *Journal for Research in Mathematics Education, 27,* 458–477.

Zelazo, P., & Frye, D. (1998). Cognitive complexity and control: Pt. 2. The development of executive function in childhood. *Current Directions in Psychological Science, 7,* 121–125.

Zimmerman, B. J. (1989). A social cognitive view of self-regulated academic learning. *Journal of Educational Psychology, 81,* 329–339.

Zimmerman, B. J. (1994). Dimensions of academic self-regulation: A conceptual framework for education. In D. H. Schunk & B. J. Zimmerman (Eds.), *Self-regulation of learning and performance: Issues and educational implications* (pp. 3–21). Hillsdale, NJ: Erlbaum.

Zimmerman, B. J. (2000). Attaining self-regulation: A social cognitive perspective. In M. Boekaerts, P. R. Pintrich, & M. Zeidner (Eds.), *Handbook of self-regulation* (pp. 13–39). San Diego: Academic Press.

Zimmerman, B. J., & Risemberg, R. (1997). Self-regulatory dimensions of academic learning and motivation. In G. D. Phye (Ed.), *Handbook of academic learning: Construction of knowledge* (pp. 105–125). San Diego: Academic Press.

CHAPTER 5

Scientific Thinking and Science Literacy

RICHARD LEHRER and LEONA SCHAUBLE

Although there is a long tradition of research on the development of scientific reasoning, the impact of this research on science education has been limited and not always constructive. As Metz (1995) pointed out, to the extent that research has provided any guiding picture of development to inform science education, the most enduring influence has come from outmoded misinterpretations of Piagetian research. As a consequence, even now, ideas about children and science are dominated by untested conclusions about what children *cannot* do—or worse, claims about deficits that have already been refuted by evidence, but that somehow continue to hang around like unwelcome relatives, exerting their influence on education via texts, science standards, and the beliefs of educators. These assumptions about what children cannot learn show up with particular frequency in evaluations of the "developmental appropriateness" of approaches to science education or specific topics of study. Metz, for example, charts the influence of these assumptions on the national discussions about science standards and argues convincingly that the standards seriously underestimate young children's capability to learn and do science.

In the previous volume of this *Handbook,* Strauss (1998) suggested several reasons why the best of developmental psychology does not always contribute to the best of science education. He proposes, among other reasons, that developmental psychology and science education share little overlap in content, focus, underlying assumptions, and methods of inquiry. However, since his chapter was published, there has been an acceleration of activity in the intersection between these two fields. Science educators have become increasingly interested in and knowledgeable about learning and development. And some developmental scholars have begun to pursue education in a more serious and committed way. For example, there are now a number of research programs, described later in the chapter, in which investigators are deeply involved not just in studying scientific thinking, but also in changing its course in contexts of education. New programs of research emphasize the coordinated

Order of authorship is alphabetical; the contribution of both authors was equal. We gratefully acknowledge the contributions of Steven McGee and Kathleen Metz, who reviewed the manuscript and offered comments that were extremely helpful.

design and study of science learning in school class-rooms, consistent with a wider appreciation of the fact that studying interesting forms of scientific thinking cannot progress very far unless these forms of thinking are brought into being. As a result, research on the development of scientific reasoning is increasingly becoming entwined with the search for effective ways to catalyze and support it.

Typically, this approach to research entails designing and implementing instruction and then studying the resulting student learning over a relatively extended period of time (ideally, several years). These long time periods are required because the forms of thinking that are of interest do not emerge within a few months or even a year. The emphasis in this research is not on describing "naturally occurring" forms of thinking, whatever those may be, but on systematically testing effective ways to support the development of students' reasoning and knowledge over the long term. In addition, many of these projects pursue a secondary interest in the professional development of the teachers who conduct the instruction or in the institutional structures of schooling that both facilitate and constrain educational potential. Because these programs take a longitudinal perspective, they offer the opportunity for a more serious test of accounts of development than do studies that last only a few days or weeks (an opportunity, however, on which it is difficult to capitalize, as we will discuss). Moreover, they are tests of development under conditions in which development is brought into being and sustained by cultural and semiotic tools. As we will explain, the field is currently struggling to decide the extent to which mechanisms of development such as language, tasks, forms of argument, and tools, need to be incorporated into theoretical and empirical accounts.

This general approach to studying development and learning, in which intervention and investigation are conducted as part of a coordinated enterprise, has been called "design experiments" or "design studies." The merits and limitations of this approach are currently being explored and debated (Brown, 1992; Cobb, Confrey, diSessa, Lehrer, & Schauble, 2003; Shavelson & Towne, 2002; Sloane & Gorard, 2003). However, these conversations are occurring almost exclusively within the field of education research rather than the field of development. Our interest in design studies is in their potential to shed light on both origins and pathways of development, an issue that we take up in the second sec-

tion of the chapter. In that section, we survey the landscape of contemporary design studies that are informed by and, in turn, inform our knowledge about the development of scientific thinking.

In spite of the emergence of this new research in the overlap between developmental psychology and science education, we can by no means congratulate ourselves that the fields of psychology and education have achieved a comfortable and general consensus about common goals for and conclusions about children's learning. There appear to be two main reasons for this gap. First, not only between, but also within these fields, there are long-standing disagreements about what it means to learn or understand science. These disagreements are partly due to the lack of shared vision in our society about the purposes for education in general. More particular to *science* learning, there are also competing views of the nature of science, so that we lack consensus on the character of the phenomenon under investigation. Second, within the field of developmental psychology there are long-standing differences of opinion about the nature and mechanisms of development and how developmental research can best inform and be informed by the educational enterprise. These disagreements are also at play, and views of how best to study development color perspectives about how learning should be supported.

For example, some scholars emphasize mechanisms that are conceived primarily as internal qualities of the developing individual and especially emphasize those forms of development that appear to be universal to the human species and therefore relatively robust across varying contexts and cultures. Others have argued that psychology attends too much to explanations of development that are based on presumed inner mental processes, traits, or constraints operating at the level of the individual organism. These scholars argue that an adequate account of development needs to include the local and distal contexts that support and shape it. From this perspective, the focus of study should be on the structures, goals, and values associated with the activities that people are habitually immersed in; the kinds of tasks and problems they encounter in contexts of learning; the content and structure of their prior knowledge; their histories of learning; the cultural expectations, tools, and behavioral patterns that are part of an individual's world; and the social and historical contexts that shape contemporary activity. Of course, this tension between explanations based on mental qualities of individuals versus the physical and social environments is an old and ongoing story in developmental psychology, one that seems to continually reshape itself as the field evolves.

In sum, different views of science literacy and learning are at least partly the result of differences in answers to two questions: What is developing when children learn science? and What is development? Where progress is being made, it has been by reformulating and testing the implications of different answers to these enduring questions. Therefore, we begin the chapter by considering different images of the nature of science, because these images have either explicitly or tacitly guided the conduct of developmental research. The second section of the chapter revisits some familiar territory—studies of the growth of scientific reasoning—but reconsiders them in light of the images of science that they assume and also in light of longer-term studies where development is (deliberately) shaped by education. This section examines the assumptions about scientific thinking and development that inspired longer-term investigations of development and summarizes how both traditional and design approaches contribute to what we understand about learning and development.

The design studies emphasize somewhat different views of the nature of science and, taken as a group, entail a contrasting set of educational designs based on different "bets" about how to catalyze development over the long haul. This new research is important for both developmental psychologists and science educators to understand. For science educators, it is providing a beginning empirical base to inform the debates about the nature of science and resulting implications for education. For developmental psychologists, it may reframe our expectations about trajectories of cognitive development and the influences that can shape or change those trajectories.

As we will explain, classroom design studies encounter a host of challenges that laboratory research typically does not. For example, taking a long-term view of learning and development often requires a fundamental rethinking of the subject matter under consideration. Historically, decisions about what is worth teaching and learning have been informed not by knowledge about learning and development, but by politics and custom. These decisions are often strongly influenced by the organizational structure and constraints of schooling. The curricular shape of a school discipline is laid down by historical tradition and can be very difficult to reenvision. The way a subject has been previously taught comes to take on canonical status as it is encapsulated in textbooks, standards, tests, and preservice teacher education, and (equally important) in the expectations of parents and the public at large. These historically entrenched views about what science learning or history learning or mathematics learning should be like can be very difficult to change (Dow, 1991), as the current "math wars" amply illustrate. Yet, as we will show, a developmental perspective, coupled with longitudinal research on learning, tends to raise fundamental questions about the status quo vision of school disciplines. Taken seriously, thinking developmentally may change the landscape considerably, both for what should be learned and for how it is learned.

The third and final major section of the chapter illustrates in greater detail how these issues play out, using as an illustrative case a design investigation conducted over 10 years by the authors. Although in principle, any of the examples in this chapter might serve as the case for this analysis, the issues we discuss in this section require exposing the way design research works under the hood, information that is usually known well only to those close to the project in question. Matters usually dismissed as "implementation" or "logistical" issues seldom appear in journals or other public presentations, but in design research they should be accounted for as part of the theory of action, rather than dismissed as side issues. The purpose of this final section is to show how this form of investigation requires researchers to find new ways of addressing research concerns such as representativeness, generalizability, and replication, which cannot always be handled in the same ways as in laboratory investigations (although closer inspection of experimental laboratory studies suggests some clear parallels, especially in new domains of research; see, e.g., Gooding, 1990).

A word on what the chapter will *not* address. There are many fields of research that bear on the issues that are discussed here. They include science education, social studies of science, semiotics, the history and philosophy of science, and cognitive models of learning and development. To avoid taking the chapter too far afield, we keep our central focus trained on classroom studies that take a developmental approach to science learning and scientific reasoning. Research in related fields is introduced only as it bears directly on the chapter's primary focus.

IMAGES OF SCIENCE

Images of the nature of science set the stage for the study of development. They inform what researchers choose to study and suggest appropriate means of study.

We have identified three images that appear to have attracted broad research support: science-as-logic, science-as-theory, and science-as-practice. Here we briefly describe each of these views of science and then further exemplify these positions by contrasting their stance toward the idea of experiment, which is an epistemic form characteristic of and central to the practice of science.

Science-as-Logical Reasoning

Science-as-logic emphasizes the role of domain-general forms of scientific reasoning, including formal logic, heuristics, and strategies, whose scope ranges across fields as diverse as geology and particle physics. This image figures prominently in three early programs of research that have been especially influential in the way researchers conceptualize scientific thinking. These include Inhelder and Piaget's (1958) pioneering work on formal operations; the Bruner, Goodnow, and Austin (1956) studies on concept development; and Wason's (1960, 1968) four-card task studies demonstrating that people tend to avoid evidence that disconfirms their prior theories. The image of scientist-as-reasoner continues to be influential in contemporary research (Case & Griffin, 1990). Learning to think scientifically is conceived as a matter of acquiring strategies for coordinating theory and evidence (D. Kuhn, 1989), mastering counterfactual reasoning (Leslie, 1987), distinguishing patterns of evidence that do and do not support a definitive conclusion (Fay & Klahr, 1996), or understanding the logic of experimental design (Chen & Klahr, 1999; Tschirgi, 1980). These heuristics and skills are considered important targets for research and for education because they are assumed to be widely applicable and to reflect at least some degree of domain generality and transferability (D. Kuhn, Garcia-Mila, Zohar, & Andersen, 1995).

A general feature of studies conducted in this vein is that researchers often attempt to rule out the use of knowledge by relying either on unfamiliar tasks based on knowledge that children are considered unlikely to have, or on tasks that are intrinsically content lean. For example, in a study of problem-solving strategies, D. Kuhn and Phelps (1982) asked children to investigate mixtures of clear, unlabeled chemical solutions in an attempt to find out "for sure" which mixtures, when added to a mixing liquid, would reliably turn pink. The content of this problem was considered unlikely to evoke participants' prior content knowledge in ways that would either help or hinder them in solving the problem, as preadolescent children typically know little about chemical solutions. Moreover, only alphabetical labels on the test tubes identified the chemicals, and all of the chemicals were indistinguishable clear liquids. The labels were changed after every trial, making it impossible for participants to develop cumulative knowledge about the materials over time. Indeed, the authors were not interested in how children think about chemical solutions; they chose this content because they wished to understand the kinds of evidence-generation and evidence-interpretation strategies children would employ in solving problems that involve multivariable causality and, in particular, how those strategies might evolve over repeated trials as children received feedback from observable changes in the physical materials.

A point on which there is no consensus is whether these forms of reasoning should be conceived of as specialized knowledge that is difficult to acquire and that emerges only gradually over development, and in many people never appears at all (D. Kuhn et al., 1995), or alternatively, whether they are appropriately viewed as the application of problem-solving strategies that are common to all kinds of thinking (Klahr, 2000). In either case, the task for developmental researchers is to identify origins, patterns of change, and underlying mechanisms of change in skills and strategies that are presumed to be useful across a wide variety of situations and problems particular to science (and perhaps everyday thinking as well).

Science-as-Theory Change

Science-as-theory change draws from philosophical studies of science and compares individual conceptual change to broader historical trends in science, especially the periodization (i.e., normal and revolutionary science) of science identified by T. S. Kuhn (1962). Among others, Carey (1985b) and Koslowski (1996) have suggested that disciplinary knowledge evolves in ways that typically involve the gradual accretion of new facts (e.g., Kuhn's normal science) and knowledge or, occasionally, the replacement of one idea by another. At critical junctures there may even be wholesale restructuring of the theoretical landscape (e.g., Kuhn's scientific revolutions). In this case, the entire network of concepts and their relationships is reconfigured (Chi, 1992). Not only do new concepts enter the domain; in addition, existing concepts may change their meaning in fundamental ways because the theoretical structure within which they are situated radically changes. Consider, for example, the meaning of the concept *force* or *combustion*. *Force* in Aristotelian theory is not the same concept as *force* in Newtonian theory. Note, however, that we would be unlikely to conclude that scientists who believed in the phlogiston theory or who held Aristotelian notions of force and motion were illogical, in the sense of lacking or violating important canons of reasoning. Instead, we accept that scientists of earlier times reasoned in ways that depended on their knowledge and theories. Under different assumptions about the way the world worked, different kinds of conclusions and inferences would seem quite logical, perhaps even obvious.

If the development of scientific reasoning in individuals is like the development of scientific knowledge over the course of history, the argument goes, it is best conceived not as the mastery of domain-general logic, heuristics, or strategies, but as a process of conceptual or theory change. In fact, some of the research in this tradition is aimed toward demonstrating that children's reasoning per se does not differ in important ways from adults' (e.g., Carey, 1985a; Samarapungavan, 1992).

Carey (1985a), for example, claimed that there is nothing about the power or structure of children's logic that develops, at least beyond the preschool years. In her landmark studies challenging Piaget's (1962) earlier assertions about the "magical" or "animistic" thinking of preadolescent children, Carey (1985b) demonstrated that this apparent animism did not entail failures of children's reasoning, but instead reflected their theories about properties that distinguish living organisms from nonliving objects. Her results suggested that children lack some of the fundamental biological knowledge that adults have. Even more important, the knowledge that

children do have is organized into conceptual systems (i.e., theories) that do not reflect either the overall structure or the categories typically possessed by adults. For example, when asked to provide examples of things that were "not alive," children's responses suggested that they were conflating a number of distinctions that an adult would honor into a general, undifferentiated alive/not alive opposition. As examples of things that are "not alive," children proposed organisms that had been alive but were now dead (a cat run over by a car) or extinct (dinosaurs), were representations (a drawing of an animal rather than a "real" animal) or imaginary. On the basis of responses like these (and a number of other clever experimental tasks), Carey showed that it may be a mistake to assume that when a child judges an example as "alive" or "not alive," he or she is relying on a conceptual system like the one that most adults have in mind. Carey concluded that there is no evidence that children think magically or illogically. Rather, their judgments make perfect sense given their conceptual understanding of the world. Developmental change, under this account, is conceived not as the mastery of thinking processes or a new form of logical or abstract thinking, but as changes over time in one's stock of knowledge about the meaning of terms like "alive," as children collect both first- and secondhand experience with organisms and their properties. These changes in the knowledge system accumulate, and when they reach a critical level the conceptual system restructures to accommodate the inconsistencies.

Indeed, all the relevant logical equipment can be presumed to be intact at least by the time children begin school. (Whether parts of this knowledge are already in place at birth, learned at very early ages, or governed by inborn constraints is a question being actively investigated.) Even participants in content-lean studies import knowledge in an attempt to make sense of the problems and tasks they encounter. Researchers in the science-as-logic tradition have generally acknowledged that it not really possible to rule out the influence of prior knowledge and have instead focused more directly on *how* knowledge and other factors might systematically influence participants' reasoning strategies and heuristics (D. E. Penner & Klahr, 1996; Schauble, 1990, 1996). From the theory change perspective, reasoning strategies and heuristics are tools for theory development. Epistemic commitments of theories are especially important targets for development, including, for example, whether or not a new theory is free of contradiction, accords well with previous theoretical commitments, and accounts for evidence, both actual and potential (Posner, Strike, Hewson, & Gertzog, 1982).

Science-as-Practice

Science-as-practice is an image formulated from studies of science that emphasize observational studies of scientific activity, both in the short term (e.g., studies of activity in a particular laboratory or of a program of study) and historically (e.g., studies of laboratory notebooks, published texts, eyewitness accounts). Science-as-practice suggests that theory development and reasoning are components of a larger ensemble of activity that includes networks of participants and institutions (Latour, 1999); specialized ways of talking and writing (Bazerman, 1988); development of representations that render phenomena accessible, visualizable, and transportable (Gooding, 1989; Latour, 1990); and efforts to manage material contingency, because no theory ever specifies instrumentation and measurement in sufficient detail to prescribe practice. The alignment of instruments, measures, and theories is never entirely principled (e.g., Pickering, 1995). What the other two images of science take as foundational (reasoning and theory) together comprise only one leg of a triangle that also includes material procedures (e.g., making instruments and other contexts of observation, almost always involving machines) and models of how the material procedures function to render nature visible (Pickering, 1989).

The descriptions of science that are produced in this tradition of research suggest that science includes many different forms of practice, ranging from experiment to comparative study. For example, experimental physics tends to favor experiment as a critical form of argument, a tradition initiated several centuries ago (Sibum, 2004). As examples of this, see Shapin and Schaffer's (1985) description of the epistemic controversies aroused by Boyle's then novel experimental approach in the seventeenth century and Bazerman's (1988) description of Newton's role in the genesis of the experimental report. In contrast, even contemporary studies of evolution rely on comparative methods. For example, Van Valkenburgh, Wang, and Damuth (2004) recently tested tenets of natural selection by examining the fossil record of North American carnivores during the past 50 million years. Their argument was comparative in the sense that predictions were made about the effects of individual selection on extinction rates of large carnivores, and these were then compared to the extant fossil record.

Each of the components of practical activity cited in social studies of science appears critical for the overall success of the enterprise. Consider, for example, inscriptions (representations that are written). Latour (1990) suggests that systems of scientific inscription share properties that make them especially well suited for mobilizing cognitive and social resources in the service of scientific argument. His candidates include (a) the literal mobility and immutability of inscriptions, which tend to obliterate barriers of space and time and thus "fix" change so that it can be an object of reflection; (b) the scalability and reproducibility of inscriptions, which guarantees their economy but preserves the configuration of relations among elements of the represented phenomenon; (c) the potential for recombining and superimposing inscriptions, operations that generate structures and patterns that might not otherwise be visible or even conceivable; and (d) the control of reference, because inscriptions "circulate" throughout a program of study, taking the place of phenomena, yet maintaining an index to the original events that inspired their creation (Latour, 1999, p. 72). Lynch (1990) adds that inscriptions not only preserve change, they edit it as well: Inscriptions both reduce *and* enhance information.

Inscriptions serve epistemic commitments. Gooding (1989) examined how patterns made by iron filings in magnetic fields were transformed into displays featuring geometric curves and lines of force. These new technologies of display helped establish a language of description for the new phenomenon of electromagnetism "while also reinforcing the scientific values it embodied" (p. 186). Similarly, Kaiser (2000, pp. 76–77) suggested that the enduring and recurrent use of Feynman diagrams in particle physics was due to the diagrams sharing visual elements with the inscriptions of paths in bubble chambers, a correspondence that appealed to realism: "Feynman diagrams could evoke, in an unspoken way, the scatterings and propagation of real particles, with 'realist' associations for those physicists already awash in a steady stream of bubble chamber photographs."

Science-as-practice emphasizes the complicated and variable nature of science. What develops, then, must include logic and theory (Dunbar, 1993, 1998) but also ways of talking about phenomena and otherwise participating in a community of practice (Gee & Green 1998; Lemke, 1990; Warren & Rosebery, 1996); inventing and appropriating display technologies, sometimes called representational competence (diSessa, 2002, 2004; Goodwin, 1994; Greeno & Hall, 1997; Roth & McGinn, 1998); becoming initiated into the lore of managing contingency within domains, including how to construct variables when Nature does not tell (e.g., Ford, 2004; Lehrer, Carpenter, Schauble, & Putz, 2000); and appreciating the different forms of method employed in different sciences. Because science-as-practice must, by definition, include opportunities to participate in these practices, studies of development that are guided by this image typically track long-term change in environments designed to support participation in scientific practices. As Warren and Rosebery (1996) summarize:

> From this perspective, learning in science cannot be reduced simply to the assimilation of scientific facts, the mastery of scientific process skills, the refinement of a mental model, or the correction of misconceptions. Rather, learning in science is conceptualized as the appropriation of a particular way of making sense of the world, of conceptualizing, evaluating, and representing the world. (p. 104)

Rethinking Images of Science: What Is Experiment?

A comparative analysis of *experiment* may serve to heighten the contrast among these images of science. Science-as-logic regards experiment as a form of reasoning dominated by a singular rationale: control of variables. To experiment is to control, and what develops is an appreciation of this logic. Experiments are valid with respect to the space of possible manipulations of variables. Science-as-theory takes a different tack, treating experiment as a "critical test" of a theory. Critical experiments under gird theory change because they have the potential to produce anomaly and thus initiate conceptual change. Science-as-practice regards experiment as a resolution of an apparent paradox (Latour, 1999). Experimental facts are made—with instruments, material, and ingenuity—and so never can be regarded simply as nature observed (Galison & Assmus, 1989). Theories thus always have a practical side. They rest on foundations of mediated activity (e.g., representations, apparatus, instrument readings, interactions with other participants, design of the experiment). Yet, this practical activity becomes less visible to those who routinely practice it. As initiates are taught to see in particular ways, the products of experiment are treated as ascendant, and the activity whereby they are made becomes transparent, so that experimental facts become unmoored from their original settings (Gooding, 1989, 1990; Shapin & Schaffer, 1985; Sibum, 2004). Thus, from the science-as-practice perspective, experiment is complex and textured.

Implications of Images of Science for Education and Development

As noted, the images of science-as-logic and science-as-theory have dominated the debate about appropriate explanations for developmental change. These two views seek their support in different forms of evidence. Moreover, they tend to be associated with different views of the most appropriate goals for science education. It is interesting that science education has also engaged in its own long-standing debate about the relative importance of scientific knowledge and theories, on the one hand, versus scientific thinking, on the other. In general, school science has tended to emphasize learning what Duschl (1990) calls "final form science," that is, its end products: concepts, facts, and theories. However, school texts that communicate this "rhetoric of conclusions" (Schwab, 1962) often fail to reveal how that knowledge was produced. Teaching facts, concepts, and theories as final form science may leave students in the dark about the way knowledge is generated and may also distort the nature of scientific knowledge, inappropriately conveying that it is unchangeable and uncontested. Partly as a corrective to traditional textbook approaches, educators in the 1960s began to argue that the focus of education should instead be on "science process skills," such as observing, predicting, measuring, and inferring. Indeed, one of the most influential post-*Sputnik* National Science Foundation curricula was titled *Science: A Process Approach* (American Association for the Advancement of Science, 1964). However, it quickly became evident that the learning of domain-general processes could easily become as ritualized and meaningless as the learning of textbook facts. Moreover, the application of these skills seems to be tightly tuned to particular situations, tasks, and content. They are not easily acquired in one realm and then transferred to others, even when their use would be advantageous. Perhaps for these reasons, "process skills" approaches have largely fallen out of favor in science education research (although they still seem appealing to curriculum designers and school faculty; they appear regularly in published commercial curricula and school standards documents).

Science educators agree on the importance of helping students appreciate the epistemology of science, although there is little consensus on how to do so. National science standards, for example, emphasize the importance of providing an opportunity for students to get a taste of doing science at their own level of knowledge and expertise. Indeed, inquiry is a major theme in the National Science Education Standards (Minstrell & van Zee, 2000; National Research Council, 1996). The reference to inquiry (rather than reasoning or process skills) is intended to communicate that scientific knowledge *and* scientific thinking should be inseparable goals of education, always pursued hand in hand (Bransford, Vye, Kinzer, & Risko, 1990). In the context of developing and pursuing scientific investigations that are focused on scientific knowledge, students learn inquiry skills *and* science content. As yet, however, little agreement has been achieved on what these skills might be, the extent to which they are transferable across domains, or how (indeed, whether) their mastery can be assessed (see D. Kuhn, Black, Keselman, & Kaplan, 2000, for a discussion of these matters).

As in the education field's attempt to substitute the process/content dichotomy for an integrated emphasis on inquiry, the field of research has also increasingly acknowledged that science involves *both* characteristic ways of thinking *and* conceptual structures. In research, as in education, there has been growing interest in seeking to understand these as complementary aspects of scientific reasoning. Researchers are investigating how they coevolve and are building and testing models of thinking that coordinate these two aspects of science.

For example, Klahr and Dunbar's (1988) Scientific Discovery in Dual Spaces model describes scientific reasoning as a process of integrated search through two problem spaces: a space of hypotheses and a space of evidence. In this model, moves in each of these problem spaces affect the potential movements in the other, either by constraining potential moves or opening new possibilities. As described in much of the general research on problem solving, a scientific reasoner generates a mental representation of the problem (the "problem space"), and his or her solution of the problem is modeled as a heuristic search through that set of possibilities. In the dual search space model, goals include generating observations that may lead to the formulation of hypotheses, finding evidence that confirms or disconfirms hypotheses that are currently being entertained, or deciding among competing hypotheses. Therefore, the model incorporates hypotheses (which presumably have their origins in beliefs, concepts, or theories), strategies for generating and evaluating evidence, and descriptions of the interactions of search in these spaces in the course of scientific reasoning. In addition to this modeling approach, researchers (Klahr, 2000; D. Kuhn, Amsel, & O'Loughlin, 1988; D. E. Penner & Klahr, 1996; Schauble, 1990, 1996) have pursued empirical studies that systematically examine the effects of prior beliefs on students' strategies and heuristics for generating and evaluating evidence (and conversely, the effects of different strategies on changes in participants' theories).

Note, however, that whether a researcher believes that "what develops" is scientific concepts, scientific reasoning, or both, an assumption common to these perspectives is that the goal is to identify the most important aspect or essence of science, so that researchers can investigate its development and educators will know what to teach. Maybe, however, there is no such kernel. Perhaps what is most important about science is not its essence or core, but its variability. The science-as-practice image suggests that sciences span multiple epistemologies and practices. Moreover, perhaps what is important with respect to development is not characterizing changes that are internal to individuals, but understanding how individuals are initiated into and participate in these variable ways of knowing and doing science. From an educational perspective, the goal in that case would be to consider which forms of practice provide the greatest educational leverage, and then to understand how to assist students in beginning to participate. Primary attention would go not to investigating the developing knowledge or logic of individuals, but to characterizing the role of the systems in which cognition occurs, with special attention given to the array of semiotic and other tools that support and mediate thought.

WHAT IS DEVELOPMENT?

These views about the appropriate focus for research and education are closely associated with perspectives on the nature and mechanisms of development. This, of course, is the "What is development?" issue introduced earlier in the chapter. From its origins as a field and throughout its history, developmental psychology has always preferred explanations based on the internal mental properties of individuals. There seems to be a bias toward seeking some form of biological essence as the ultimate explanation for development. This has been true from the origins of the field in Gesell's maturationist accounts to today's emphasis on identifying innate knowledge and genetically predetermined constraints on learning. It has been difficult in practice to conceptualize a developmental psychology that is not deeply rooted in assumptions about maturation and teleology. Indeed, for some investigators, what defines a phenomenon as *developmental* is that it has a universal character and appears to be governed at least in part by biological predispositions. With some important exceptions, the field of developmental psychology has largely regarded context, culture, history, and education primarily as noise, or at best, as *factors* that affect the course of development. Agreeing on how to legitimately bring these concerns into the purview of developmental study remains a struggle in the field.

As an alternative, one could conceive of development as inseparable from the means that support it, so that an account of "Under what conditions?" is considered an obligatory question that an adequate explanation of development must address. This kind of perspective is useful for scholars and practitioners who are concerned not just with describing or explaining development, but also with catalyzing and supporting it, or in some cases, changing its course in particular ways. Yet in general, mainstream developmental psychology has made little progress with the thorny problem of conceptualizing development and context. Indeed, the increasing attention in the field to younger and younger children could arguably be interpreted, at least in part, as an attempt to sidestep these difficult issues of culture and context.

Research on scientific reasoning that is conducted from a psychological perspective has relied mainly on cross-sectional investigations of individuals at different ages (less frequently, amount of education is used as an independent variable). A second, less frequently pursued methodology has been to track a group of individuals over the short term, conducting dense measurements to document the onset and pattern of change (D. Kuhn, 1989; D. Kuhn et al., 1988; D. Kuhn & Phelps, 1982). However, with one exception (Bullock & Ziegler, 1999), we know of no longitudinal research on scientific rea-

soning from a psychological perspective that extends beyond several weeks in duration. Indeed, cross-sectional studies (Klahr, Fay, & Dunbar, 1993; D. Kuhn et al., 1995) seem to suggest that there is more overlap than separation across age groups in the skills or heuristics typically investigated, and that education seems to be at least as important as whatever else is implicated by looking at individuals of different ages.

Although informed by the psychological research, much of the work featured in the second section of this chapter emphasizes the role of education and other semiotic means that constitute thinking. From this perspective, science entails the deployment of a set of very broad and eclectic psychological functions, marshaled in relationship to a web of complex and varying goals, pursued by a community over a changing history, and supported and shaped by culturally developed tools and semiotics. Under this view, there is no one psychological "essence" of science. Instead, science is regarded as a complex form of human practice. The term *practice* as used here refers not to the external organization of behavior, but to patterns of activity that are initiated and embedded within goals and thoroughly saturated with human meaning and intentions. "What develops" is a capability to participate in these practices of science. Researchers who pursue this perspective do not necessarily deny that scientific thinking entails logic, epistemology, and theory change. However, they argue that what is essential to account for is how these psychological functions are constructed by, contingent on, and expressed within social contexts and mediational means. Moreover, scientific reasoning is not conceived as knowing how to design experiments *plus* understanding patterns in evidence *plus* building a consistent and coherent knowledge base about a domain. Rather, each of these functions is viewed as fundamentally contingent on the others, so studying them as a collection of independent capabilities or *skills* may generate a distorted understanding of the intact enterprise.

This perspective on research tends to turn attention to sources and forms of variability, rather than to a search for universal or general forms of cognition. Variability is conceived as being understandable (and produced) by attending to the mediational features that support and provide meaning for scientific thinking or, from an educational perspective, that can be deployed as design features to instigate and support developmental change. These features may include histories of learning, teaching, and other forms of assistance; cultural expectations of all levels and kinds; tasks and tools; genres of writing and argument; inscriptional and notational systems; and recurrent activity structures. Note that these items are conceptualized neither as internal psychological resources nor as external environmental stimuli; rather, they are understood to be externally instantiated (i.e., they have material expression) but imbued with meaning that is conferred by people.

The perspective of this chapter is not that either the psychological or practice view is "more right" than the other. However, one advantage that the practice view holds for education is that the elements that it takes as primary are potential instruments of change. One cannot directly engineer changes in people's psychological capabilities. Educating involves understanding and deploying tools, tasks, norms of argument, and classroom practices to bring about desired ends (Lehrer & Schauble, 2000c). Understanding how these and other designable features serve to generate and sustain cognition is, therefore, a useful goal for scholars and practitioners concerned with education.

Regardless of one's view on development, there remain unresolved questions concerning the characterization of science that is most appropriate for school science. The next section is devoted to describing current classroom investigations in which researchers work in partnership with teachers and others in school organizational structures to craft conditions that can best support the long-term development of students' participation in the practice of science. Each program emanates from prior developmental research, so we include these antecedents to situate the design studies. Taken collectively, the design investigations emphasize somewhat different views of scientific practice and, therefore, result in educational designs based on different bets about ways of conceiving scientific practice that serve to catalyze development. The way to understand the implication of these bets is to instantiate the designs and conduct longitudinal study on the development of student thinking that results. Debates about the best way to conceptualize scientific reasoning (for educational purposes, at least) are difficult to resolve unless the bets can be cashed in and the outcomes compared. Each approach is very likely to have both strengths and characteristic weaknesses; as in any design enterprise, these need to be evaluated as trade-offs.

CLASSROOM DESIGN STUDIES AND DEVELOPMENT

In this section, we describe current classroom studies in which scholars are working to coordinate two interrelated agendas. First, they seek to change educational practice in ways that foster the development of scientific thinking. As will become evident, each of the projects featured here exemplifies a somewhat different sense of "what develops." Thus, there is variability in what is taken as important early origins or precursors to scientific thinking, as well as in what is supported and studied along the way. Second, as these educational change experiments come into play and evolve over time, researchers study the cognitive and other forms of development that result among participating students. An important related goal is to understand the variety of means by which development is supported (Cobb et al., 2003), reflecting a general commitment to conceiving development as a culturally supported enterprise rather than a naturally occurring phenomenon.

Of course, there have been hundreds of classroom investigations that feature attempts to support students' scientific reasoning and knowledge. This chapter does not attempt to review all of them, or even all those that may be relevant to the development of children's scientific thinking and knowledge. Instead, we focus on a few cases that, collectively, exemplify the landscape of design studies in science, investigations in which scholars are pursuing the study of development by trying to change it. Examples that are featured here were selected for their fit to the following criteria:

- First and most important, these are projects that are developmental in their focus. In some cases, this means that the educational intervention was constructed on a foundation of knowledge from the literature in cognitive development. In others, the project may not be directly motivated by developmental studies, but it is conceptually consistent with current findings about development and makes new contributions to our understanding of development, typically by challenging what is "known" about development. These challenges often take the form of generating forms of thinking and learning that have not been previously documented. As a group, these investigations are concerned both with identifying early origins or precursors of valued forms of thinking, and also with documenting change over time in the target forms of reasoning. In addition to describing the classroom studies on their own terms, for each, we also briefly summarize related research from developmental psychology that shows how the project links to the mainstream concerns of that field.

- In addition to focusing on the development of children's thinking, these projects take a developmental stance toward the domain of *school science*. Each embodies a perspective about how what is taught can contribute to a broader agenda of science literacy. The view of change is long term and looks well beyond the learning of a particular skill or concept. The typical grain size of interest is what can be accomplished over years of instruction, not within a lesson or a unit. All the work described here has given careful thought to what should count as a "big idea" in science education. As we will see, at this point the research agenda for most of this work still lags far behind the conceptualization.

- In each research project presented here, education is taken seriously. That is, the educational agenda is regarded as having intrinsic value. Accordingly, schools are not regarded merely as places to find participants for research, and education is conceived as more than tasks designed to tap some psychological function. The projects are situated in schools that are not unusually privileged with respect to student populations and resources. All of them have had to grapple with the actual conditions of schools, and all have had to address the thorny problem of sustainability.

Our intent is not to catalogue all work that fits these criteria, but to provide examples that illustrate the variety and breadth in the ways that investigators are conceiving of the intersection between science and development.

Not all the scholars whose work is reflected in this section identify themselves as conducting design research, but their research shows many of the commitments that design studies exemplify. Design studies are coordinated efforts to design learning environments and then to study the transitions in teaching and learning that follow. Those studies typically take many methodological forms, from traditional experiments or quasi-experiments to descriptive or ethnographic work.

The distinguishing characteristic of this approach is not its use of any particular method, but a tight and cyclical interaction between two complementary aspects of work: instructional design and research. Working from a base of previous research, analysis of the domain, and theory, researchers plan and craft the design of a learning environment, which may vary with respect to scope. Concurrently, they conduct a careful and systematic program of research on the learning that results as the design coalesces. As the research proceeds, it produces findings that call for revisions to the design. Sometimes these changes are minor, sometimes radical. The changes, in turn, generate new questions for investigation.

An assumption of the design studies approach is that many forms of learning that are important targets of inquiry cannot, in fact, be studied unless the conditions for their generation are present. Thus, they are particularly applicable to the study of forms of development that require sustained education for their emergence. As we mentioned, each design investigation places different emphases on which practices are important to sustain over longer periods of time. Often, these "best bets" have roots in developmental approaches informed by one or more of the three images of science, although in practice, all prolonged studies are hybrids.

Supporting the Development of Scientific Reasoning

Inhelder and Piaget (1958) asserted that only at the onset of formal operations, around the beginning of adolescence, do children become capable of understanding the logic of scientific experimentation. This claim, like many others concerning presumed deficits in children's cognitive capabilities, eventually fell to evidence generated by subsequent research. Microgenetic studies conducted by D. Kuhn and her associates (1988, 1995; Schauble, 1990, 1996) confirmed that only small percentages of preadolescents initially produced valid scientific reasoning strategies or heuristics when attempting to solve multivariable problems without much guidance from adults. However, when given extended opportunities to conduct repeated trials in microgenetic designs (D. Kuhn & Phelps, 1982), most of the children in these studies began to show increasing use of more effective strategies for designing and interpreting experiments (D. Kuhn et al.,

1995; D. Kuhn, Schauble, & Garcia-Mila, 1992; Schauble, 1996). These strategies included investigating all relevant combinations of variables and their levels, controlling extraneous variation, and making inferences that are appropriately based on the available quality and quantity of evidence. Indeed, many of the participants went beyond simply beginning to use the new strategies to mastering and consolidating them. That is, they almost always used the new strategies when it was appropriate to do so; the earlier, flawed strategies were eventually abandoned altogether; and participants even transferred the new strategies to unfamiliar problems that did not share surface features with the original learning context (D. Kuhn et al., 1992).

Indeed, the origins of these heuristics are evident even as early as the preschool years. In a carefully constructed sequence of studies, Sodian, Zaitchik, and Carey (1991) demonstrated that preschoolers could consider two alternative tests of a hypothesis and reliably identify which would actually settle the question. However, their succeeding appeared to depend on a number of simplifying circumstances: that the alternatives did not confirm or challenge strongly held prior beliefs, that the number of choices and variables was kept very restricted, and that children were asked simply to evaluate alternatives rather than to propose an experimental design on their own. Nevertheless, these studies do show that at least in a rudimentary way, children can differentiate their beliefs from evidence that bears on those beliefs.

Promoting Understanding of Experimental Design via Instruction

Building from earlier findings that children can understand the logic of experimental design (Tschirgi, 1980), Chen and Klahr (1999) suggested that the kernel of a science education for children is mastery of the logic of the control of variables. They recommended that children should be taught to ignore or look behind particular content to focus on structural relationships. This is precisely what children were trained to do in Chen and Klahr's educational studies. In one investigation, students learned to evaluate the design of experiments by making judgments about the informativeness of pairs of trials presented by a researcher as a "test" of causes and effects in a multivariable context. Each trial included several potentially causal independent variables (that could be set at different levels) and an outcome variable

(also with several levels). Students understood that the point of the comparisons was to make a decision about whether one of the independent variables was causally related to the outcome.

For example, in one context, students were told that their task was to evaluate an experimental trial's utility for helping to decide which factors determine how far a ball will roll down a ramp. The experimental comparison included two small ramps that could be set at either steep or shallow angles, with starting gates set at different positions on the ramps. The ramps were fitted with a reversible insert that would produce either a rough or a smooth ramp surface. Two different test balls were provided, a golf ball and a rubber squash ball. Children observed pairs of configurations of these materials and were asked whether or not each comparison supported a definitive conclusion.

Among the trials shown to children were various forms of invalid tests. For example, the two-ramp setups might differ in multiple ways, making it impossible to tell whether one of the variables was the causal one. In such a case, a child might observe a golf ball rolled down a steep ramp with a rough surface, and the comparison case would involve a rubber ball rolled down a shallow ramp with a smooth surface. If the two conditions led to a different outcome, it would be impossible to know why, because several variables had been varied simultaneously. The 7- to 10-year-old participants in the study were shown several examples of both confounded comparisons like these and other comparisons where extraneous variation was controlled. In each case, the participant was asked to decide whether the comparison was a "good test" or a "bad test." In a training condition, participants were provided explicit feedback after each trial; the experimenter also explained why the test either was or was not flawed. Chen and Klahr (1999) reported that not only were they able to improve children's abilities to judge the informativeness of experiments and to make inferences based on them; in addition, the older children were able to transfer the strategies they had learned to novel contexts, even after a 7-month delay. Moreover, Klahr and Nigam (2004) demonstrated that children who were taught these strategies were able to use them to evaluate science fair posters a week afterward.

The instruction designed by Chen and Klahr (1999) was tightly focused on the logic of control of variables. Although science-like materials (ramps, springs, and sinking objects) were used, the logic would have been precisely the same if the tasks had borne no relationship whatsoever to science topics. Hence, this body of work is a particularly clear example of science-as-reasoning.

Practices of Investigation as a Route to Developing Reasoning

Like Chen and Klahr (1999), Kathleen Metz (2004) emphasized developing skills and strategies important to the conduct of scientific inquiry. However, in Metz's classroom investigations, the focus on domain-general forms of reasoning was not pursued at the expense of domain-specific conceptual knowledge. Instead, children received repeated opportunities to plan, conduct, and revise related *programs* of research in the service of developing coherent conceptual structures concerning important biological ideas such as behavior and adaptation. In this sense, the practices of children were similar to those of scientists.

For nearly a decade, Metz has been pursuing classroom design research with the ultimate goal of maximizing children's capability to conduct independent inquiry. A main conjecture of her research is that the learning of skills and knowledge is best supported in contexts that maintain the integrity of the original goal-focused enterprise where those skills and knowledge originated. Therefore, research methods and strategies should be introduced to students not as disembodied skills, but as tools for pursuing real questions that children pose in domains where they have opportunities to develop significant content knowledge.

In Metz's work, children are deeply immersed in one discipline, often for a year or longer. Metz (2004) makes the case that students should concentrate intensively in a relatively small number of domains, rather than learning a little bit about a wide variety of topics. After all, one cannot conduct inquiry in a field in which one knows nothing, so a curriculum that emphasizes breadth over depth is not a good one for supporting inquiry. Properly supported, the development of content knowledge and the development of scientific reasoning should bootstrap each other.

Inquiry depends on students being able to generate fruitful questions, acquiring a repertoire of appropriate methods for investigating those questions, and developing a sense of the forms and qualities of evidence (and counterevidence) that can inform the answers. Consistent with this view, Metz's participants study one scientific domain at a time—such as animal behavior, ornithology, botany, or ecology—for an extended period in which they repeatedly encounter the core ideas

of the domain in multiple contexts. Initial investigations are carefully structured and scaffolded; subsequent inquiries are planned and conducted by the children themselves, who are increasingly given independent responsibility for the progress and evaluation of the scientific work.

For example, as an introduction to animal behavior, students in second and fourth/fifth grade began by conducting observations of a rodent confined to a small space in the center of the classroom. The fact that every child was observing the same animal meant that, inevitably, they selected different behaviors to describe, interpreted the behaviors differently, or failed to record them in a common form. These occurrences motivated debates about the need for standard ways to observe and also provoked awareness of the fact that under some conditions (such as loud talking), observation can change the behavior of the organism being observed. Children typically attribute intentions and thoughts to animals, so the observations also produced a forum for discussing the difference between observations and inferences, a distinction that Metz considered fundamental for subsequent work. In small teams, children recorded and displayed their data, and the different data displays generated a reason to talk about how data representations of different design communicate different information.

After these initial observations, students were reorganized into pairs and each pair was given their own organism to study, in this case, one or more crickets. Crickets available for observation varied both between species and within species (gender, age, etc.), raising questions about relationships between these variables and observable animal behaviors (such as chirping, fighting, or eating). Various forms of controls and research methods specific to the domains of study (e.g., time sampling as a technique commonly used in animal behavior) were introduced. To pursue the goal of building a rich knowledge base that could inform inquiry, students supplemented their direct observations with reading material, videotapes, and other media. The research teams independently generated questions about the crickets, and then the whole class compiled their questions and categorized them on a number of dimensions, including whether the questions were amenable to empirical inquiry ("Is this a question that you can collect data on?"). In some cases, students explicitly noted differences between forms of thinking in everyday contexts, as contrasted with their use in science.

For example, students concluded that in science, they might not always achieve consensus and that this was acceptable if they had good justifications for failing to agree. Students learned to recognize and mark sources of uncertainty in their developing knowledge.

Initial investigations with crickets were planned by the whole class working together and then were conducted individually by pairs working as research teams. The teacher assisted in recording and categorizing questions, summarizing observations, and developing a table that displayed classes of questions that might be investigated and methods appropriate for doing so. For subsequent investigations, both the direction and the procedures were increasingly ceded to the students. Finally, using the previously developed list of heuristics for evaluating potential questions and the class-generated list of domain-specific methods for investigating questions, each team planned and conducted its own investigation. The investigations culminated with a poster presentation in which each team presented its question, methods, and findings.

The notion of inquiry exemplified in these sequences contrasts sharply with the typical cookbook laboratory exercises in which students carefully carry out step-by-step procedures, and also with hands-on science activities and kits in which a preordained course of investigation is followed. Students in Metz's classrooms have much more (although not boundless) freedom to select their own question to pursue. This means that it is essential for curriculum designers to identify domains of study that support a wide variety of student questions, all of which, however, must be very likely to lead students directly into confrontation with one or more important scientific ideas. An important topic of Metz's research is to identify domains that have these properties. Metz's approach differs, as well, from those advocated by Chen and Klahr (1999) or D. Kuhn (1989), in which the content and surface features of inquiry tasks are considered secondary and the emphasis is on repeated practice at making logical judgments about problems with varying surface features that preserve a common underlying structure.

Metz (2000) identified five different aspects of children's knowledge that were the primary foci of this instruction: children's conceptual knowledge of the domains under investigation, their understanding of the enterprise of empirical inquiry, their knowledge of domain-specific methodologies, data representation and analysis, and tools. Careful study of the progress of chil-

dren's investigations, coupled with postinvestigation interviews of the children's research teams (Metz, 2004), provided information about children's achievement of these goals. Findings were reported for one class of second graders and one class of mixed fourth/fifth graders, both from a public elementary school in a rural area, who had participated in the first iteration of the animal behavior curriculum.

All 10 of the second-grade research teams and 14 fourth/fifth-grade teams formulated both a researchable question and a method for investigating their question, although one second-grade team initially chose a research method that was not appropriate. Most of the second graders and about half of the fourth graders relied on the class-generated heuristics for identifying a good question. Interestingly, about half of the older teams pursued questions about social behavior, although none of the younger children did. The majority of the younger children conducted studies of the effect of some variable on cricket behavior by comparing the behavior of the crickets under different conditions. In sum, children showed considerable competence at taking charge of their investigations, even coming up with sophisticated proposals for controlling extraneous variation that seem surprising, given the previous literature about children's spontaneous performance on problems that require them to produce or evaluate comparisons that involve controls (Chen & Klahr, 1999; D. Kuhn et al., 1988).

After instruction, each team was individually interviewed about their conceptualization of their question and the method used to investigate it, their findings, and whether they could think of a way to increase their confidence level in the findings. In addition, each team was asked whether they could think of any way to improve the study. In her analysis of these interviews, Metz (2004) paid particular attention to how children conceptualized the sources of uncertainty in their study and the strategies they pursued in trying to resolve the uncertainty. A few of the younger children apparently held the simple idea that the point of inquiry is to produced a desired outcome, so that what was uncertain was how to make the experiment "work," a notion that has shown up repeatedly in previous research with preadolescent children (i.e., Schauble, 1990; Tschirgi, 1980). About 25% of the children focused primarily on the possibilities of uncertainty in their data that were due to imprecision of their instruments or experimenter error. About 15% of the children (approximately equal percentages in both grades) described themselves as uncertain about the generalizability of the trend in their data. The most frequent reasons given for this uncertainty were that the study was conducted within a limited range of experimental conditions or that the variability of the crickets made children uncertain that results achieved with some crickets would apply to others. Nearly 40% of the second graders and 25% of the older children were uncertain that their theory was adequate to account for the trend that they observed in the data. Finally, the most common source of uncertainty was attributed to the trend identified in the data (over 40% of the second graders and 85% of the fourth/fifth graders). In most (but not all) of these cases, children were able to propose at least one strategy to resolve the uncertainty.

In sum, the participants seemed to understand the problematic nature of knowledge in several respects: that uncertainty can enter the data generation process in a variety of ways, that what they know about their research question is mediated by the study they conducted and its inherent flaws and uncertainties, and in general, that the relationship between the world and the scientist's knowledge of it is far from straightforward, but rather complex and interpretation laden. Metz (2004, p. 282) concluded, "At least by the second-grade level, the decontextualization and decomposition of the elementary science curriculum appear to be more a function of curricular traditions than developmental need."

Instruction that is organized around self-directed investigations needs to maintain the right balance between investigation skill and the development of conceptual knowledge. But it is not always a simple matter to find that balance. In practice, teachers must be skillful to negotiate the tension between these two components and must continually work against the tendency for one to fade into the background as the other takes center stage. Metz advised extended study within a coherent domain of knowledge as a way of balancing the focus on methodology with a corresponding emphasis on the development of a rich knowledge base. Because children's knowledge built cumulatively over weeks and months, their repeated opportunities to conduct and interpret investigations not only familiarized them with a repertoire of methodologies, but also provided opportunities to construct expertise in a bounded but complex domain of investigation.

In summary, Metz's approach to supporting development of scientific reasoning has a methodological bent: It places its bets on introducing children to methods commonly employed by scientists, but it does so in con-

texts of prolonged investigation of a rich content domain. It borrows from studies of scientific practice to instantiate aspects of scientific community. Questions and investigations have both a self-directed and a communal nature. What we know less about from these studies is the nature of the conceptions children are developing about the domains under investigation. Clearly, they are developing methodological commitments akin to those of scientists. But do their evolving understandings of crickets serve as gateways to larger conceptual structures in biological sciences? And if so, how? These questions have been more explicitly addressed in research guided by science as theory development.

The Development of Theories

We contrast two programs of research, both of which are centered in theory change but that make different commitments to origins and analysis of what develops. The first, Intentional Conceptual Change, draws from science education and is informed by a view of science as a process of conceptual change. The second, Pathways to Science, as its name suggests, draws from studies of early origins of children's theories about nature and seeks to capitalize on these origins to create developmentally appropriate education.

Intentional Conceptual Change

For many years, Sister Gertrude Hennessey was the sole science teacher for grades 1 though 7 in a small parochial school in Wisconsin. As a result, she had the unusual opportunity to think about the goals and trajectory for students' scientific reasoning across all those grades of schooling. Fortunately, she had both the educational background and the wisdom to capitalize on this opportunity to pursue long-term development (she holds degrees in biology and science education). Hennessey not only planned the course of instruction and taught her students daily; she also kept detailed records and videotapes of her students' learning and conducted regular interviews of individuals, small groups, and intact classes. She pursued a structured approach to science instruction that made students' thinking visible and therefore accessible to her observation. From time to time, she collaborated with university researchers from both developmental psychology and science education to conduct cross-sectional and longitudinal studies of student learning (e.g., Beeth & Hewson, 1999; Smith, Maclin, Houghton, & Hennessey, 2000).

Hennessey (2002) regarded science learning primarily as conceptual change. However, in pursuing this characterization of science, she drew primarily on the field of science education rather than psychology. She was particularly influenced by the work of Posner and his colleagues (1982) and later revisions by Hewson and Hewson (1992), who pursued what they called a conceptual change model (CCM) to account for how students' mental representations of the world might shift from initial, naive notions to the conventionally accepted explanations of science. The CCM described conceptual change as a process by which a concept might be replaced by another, modified, or simply dropped. Critical to the conceptual change model is the assumption that the relative overall *status* of a concept for a particular learner determines whether the concept will be maintained or changed when an alternative is under consideration. Status refers to how the concept is evaluated relative to a consistent set of criteria. How an individual applies those criteria depends on his or her prior knowledge, motivation or stakes in both the new concept and those that it may replace, and ontological and epistemological commitments. Specifically, the evaluative criteria associated with status include the learner's evaluation of the concept's *intelligibility* (how comprehensible is it?), *plausibility* (is it believable?), and *fruitfulness* (how useful is it for getting things done in the world or for motivating new investigations?). A fourth factor, not directly included in status but important nonetheless in whether a concept is maintained or changed, is *conceptual coherence,* whether and how the new concept fits or fails to fit into the preexisting network of related knowledge. Hewson and Hewson used the analogy of a "conceptual ecology" to refer to the balanced interrelationships among beliefs. As in ecological systems in biology, the metaphor of conceptual ecology emphasizes the importance of interdependencies. Changing one concept is very difficult or impossible to do without changing others that are closely related. According to Hewson and Hewson, each concept occupies a niche within its conceptual ecology. Concepts, like organisms, may compete for survival within a niche. However, a concept is unlikely to be discarded or changed unless the individual becomes dissatisfied with it. Therefore, helping children clearly articulate the beliefs that they hold and, in some cases, helping them notice the inconsistencies or insufficiencies of those beliefs are reasonable strategies for a teacher who hopes to help children make conceptual progress toward accepted scientific theories.

Hennessey's instructional approach was to explicitly teach students the evaluative criteria in the Conceptual Change Model, starting with the earliest grades of instruction. Her emphasis was not primarily on learning what each criterion meant in a disembodied way, but on putting the criteria to use in the context of building their own explanations for scientific phenomena and deciding among competing explanations produced by other members of the class.

Hennessey placed a great deal of importance on students' developing metacognition, hence the emphasis on scientific reasoning as *intentional* conceptual change. Becoming aware of one's own theories and explicitly evaluating them against the conceptions proposed by peers was fundamental to her goals for students. Notice, however, that in contrast to a more general emphasis on self-regulation and self-evaluation, Hennessey's classrooms were focused on a more restricted sense of metacognition, one tightly tied to the CCM epistemology of science. Hennessey was adamant that her interest in improving metacognitive understanding was not a general, all-purpose goal for students conceived as transferable across content and disciplines. Rather, student metacognition was pursued in the service of achieving domain-specific conceptual change. Moreover, neither metacognitive development nor conceptual change was regarded primarily as an end in itself, but rather both were considered to be ways of helping students achieve the more fundamental goal of engaging with deep, domain-specific ideas in science.

Given this strong emphasis on epistemology of science, it is not surprising that Hennessey's instruction was frequently based on direct experience with the natural world. Students frequently began a unit of instruction by directly exploring a phenomenon carefully chosen to provoke surprise (again, the emphasis on anomaly in theory change), given students' likely prior beliefs and assumptions. Students worked with the phenomena, typically in a laboratory or field setting, recording questions that came up in the context of their explorations. Then, as in Metz's (2004) work, they planned and carried out investigations to answer their questions. These were more likely to be investigations with physical materials than "research" in books or online. In the course of these investigations, students were encouraged to represent their ideas in a variety of formats (charts, graphs, diagrams) and to compare their ideas with those being developed by other students. The emphasis was on first clarifying one's own ideas and then, after evaluating theories against the evidence and against competing theories posed by others, evaluating and revising those ideas to account for anomalies experienced in the course of ongoing investigations.

In sum, the view of science portrayed in Hennessey's program was that science is a matter of developing and building progressively more adequate theories about the world. Moreover, what develops is not only the scientific theories but, equally important, students' critical standards for defending, adapting, or replacing those theories. Although Hennessey did not discuss development in depth in her published articles, she clearly had ideas about the general course of development of these metacognitive criteria. At each grade, students were expected to build on accomplishments in earlier grades, constructing a progressively more sophisticated capability to reflect on and evaluate their own theories and those of their classmates. Her goals for first graders were modest, focused primarily on helping students become adept at stating their own beliefs and providing reasons for them. By the fourth grade, students were expected to understand and apply all four criteria of intelligibility, plausibility, fruitfulness, and conceptual coherence as they evaluated their evolving beliefs. By sixth grade, students were also monitoring the beliefs of others, especially their peers, and considering the fit of competing explanations to patterns of evidence.

Hennessey's sixth graders, who at that point had received a total of a half-dozen years of instruction under her tutelage, were interviewed with an instrument previously developed by Carey and colleagues (Carey, Evans, Honda, Jay, & Unger, 1989) to ascertain their understanding of the nature of science. In this study, their performance was compared to a demographically similar group of sixth graders who were taught with a more traditional elementary program. The Nature of Science Interview (Carey et al., 1989) was designed to roughly classify students' responses with respect to their conceptual grasp of the epistemology of science. Level 1 ideas, compatible with what Carey and Smith (1993) called a *knowledge unproblematic epistemology,* reflect a belief that knowledge is certain and unproblematically true. It is a relatively simple matter to know what is true; one simply has to look (or be told). Responses classified as Level 2 reflect an understanding that scientists are concerned with explanation and testing, but nonetheless, knowledge is still regarded as true, certain, and discernible. Level 3 responses, in contrast, explicitly note that knowledge is tentative, changeable, and significant only within an interpretive framework.

In previously published research involving Massachusetts public school students (Carey et al., 1989), all seventh graders had provided interview responses that were classified as Level 1. In contrast, 83% of the students in Hennessey's classroom produced responses that were classified at least as Level 2. Smith and her colleagues found four clusters of issues that differentiated Hennessey's students from those in the comparison classroom. First, when asked about the *goals of science,* the Intentional Conceptual Change students said that scientists are involved in understanding and developing ideas. In contrast, the comparison students mentioned simply doing things and gathering information. The two classes also differed on the *type of questions that scientists ask.* Hennessey's students more frequently described questions about explanations and theories, whereas the majority of the comparison students' examples were about procedures (how to do things) or questions that Smith et al. (2000) referred to as "journalistic" (identifying who, what, where, when). When asked about the *nature and purpose of experiments,* Hennessey's students were likely to highlight testing a particular idea or to refer to the role of experiments in developing theories. The comparison students, in contrast, referred to experiments as a way to try things out or to find (unproblematic) answers to questions. Finally, when students were asked *what causes scientists to change their ideas,* many of the Intentional Conceptual Change students responded that scientists change their ideas when they are able to develop a better explanation, or pointed out in other ways that change is a response to complex evidence. In contrast, the dominant answer provided by the traditional students was that scientists decide to either keep or throw out an idea after one simple observation or experiment. Only a third of the comparison students spontaneously noted that changing a scientific idea requires hard work or careful thought.

By and large, Hennessey's students had not yet achieved a sophisticated Level 3 view that included either the logic of hypothesis testing or an acknowledgment of how framework theories entail coherent principles that shape the development of hypotheses. Yet, these findings from the Nature of Science Interviews suggested that most of her students had achieved an understanding of the epistemology of science that is quite unusual for their grade. Indeed, Smith et al. (2000) reported that they found these sixth graders' replies to be similar or superior to responses typically given by 11th graders.

Although Hennessey does not explicitly mention it, there are close conceptual ties between her Intentional

Conceptual Change project and developmental research on children's criteria for evaluating theories. Samarapungavan (1992) investigated first graders', third graders', and fifth graders' criteria for scientific rationality in a study in which children observed a phenomenon and then were asked to select which of two explanations accounted better for their observations. The pairs of explanations were constructed to be identical in surface features, but to contrast on one of four "metaconceptual criteria," as she called them. These criteria, which seem quite similar to the criteria that Hennessey emphasized, included such issues as *range of explanation* (how much of the observational data does the theory account for?), *non-ad hocness* (is the theory simple or does it include a number of added-on assumptions that are not testable?), *consistency with empirical evidence,* and *logical consistency* (internal consistency, lacking mutually contradictory claims). Samarapungavan found that even the youngest children in her sample preferred theories that met these criteria when they were choosing between competing theories that were consistent with their own prior beliefs. Even the first graders preferred the empirically and logically consistent theory to theories that were inconsistent. These children also preferred theories that could account for a broader range of observations. On the other hand, when the theory of broader range contradicted their prior beliefs, they were less likely to favor it. The most difficult criterion was the one Samarapungavan called ad hocness. Only the 11-year-olds reliably rejected theories that were overelaborated with special conditions or auxiliary hypotheses that could not be directly tested.

In her interpretation of these results, Samarapungavan (1992) cautioned that she thought of these criteria as heuristic only, not as definitive of the value of competing explanations. In her view, any of these criteria could legitimately be overridden by a more important concern, that is, whether the content or meaning of the new idea being considered was compatible with existing scientific ideas held with a reasonable amount of confidence (Hennessey's conceptual coherence criterion). Therefore, like Hennessey, Samarapungavan also gave highest priority to the fit between a concept and other related knowledge, or, as Hewson and Hewson (1992) might describe it, how and where a concept fit into the individual's "conceptual ecology."

Samarapungavan (1992) also pointed out the importance of understanding that although children may use these criteria in a simple forced-choice task, this does not mean they have mastered them or even that they were consciously aware of them. Students in her studies merely chose between two options and were never asked, for example, to formulate an explanation on their own. In some cases, students' choices were consistent with one of the criteria, but they did not explicitly mention the criterion in their justification for that preference. Samarapungavan suggested that children hold some of these criteria only implicitly. Therefore, she recommended, it would be helpful to highlight these "metaconceptual dimensions" in science instruction to foster awareness of them and support their systematic use.

We turn now to a more direct kind of connection between developmental research and an educational program. In this case, the educational intervention followed directly from a major trend in developmental research. This is not very surprising, given that one of the program developers is a prominent developmental scholar who conducts research on the origins of children's concepts and theories. Preschool Pathways to Science, which we describe shortly, resulted from a collaboration between developmental researchers and educators.

Early Resources for Scientific Thinking

Shortly after the seminal work of Jean Piaget became widely known in the United States, scholars began to investigate further his findings and conclusions, especially his claims that infants and young children literally do not possess the same forms of logic that adults do. Piaget's theory held that logic must be painstakingly constructed anew by each individual as he or she grapples with the regularities of objects, space, time, and cause that (in Piaget's view) necessarily structure our experience with the world and our evolving conceptual systems. These concepts and more complex forms of intelligence are developed gradually as each person adapts to the structure of the world through his or her actions upon it.

These claims inspired a flurry of interest in identifying more precisely the cognitive resources of infants and young children. Gelman and Baillargeon (1983) summarized the research on the development of Piagetian concepts and concluded that the evidence was not consistent with the idea that there are major, domain-general qualitative shifts in children's reasoning. Rather, Gelman and Baillargeon interpreted this research as suggesting that both the nature and the development of cognitive abilities are domain specific. Moreover, given the robustness and regularity with which some domain-specific concepts emerge, it may well be that their development is governed by mechanisms that are genetically governed. As they remarked, "One lesson of modern research in child psychology is that accounts of how development proceeds can no longer ignore the possibility that at least some of the structures that underlie our systems of knowledge are innate" (p. 220).

The notion that infants may enter the world with well-formed knowledge in some domains—or at least, may be especially prepared for ready learning in them—was influenced and informed by related work in the field of ethology. For any animal, some things are very easy to learn, whereas others are very difficult. For example, as Gallistel, Brown, Carey, Gelman, and Keil (1991) point out, pigeons learn relatively easily to peck a key to obtain food but find it difficult to learn to peck a key to avoid receiving a shock. In contrast, they easily learn to flap their wings to avoid a shock. Like pigeons, humans also seem to be genetically prepared for some forms of learning. A frequently cited example of preferential learning is the relative ease with which most infants learn their native language. Moreover, babies learn language in a remarkably orderly way; both the sequence and timing of the emergence of language components are quite consistent across children and across cultures.

Not only do babies learn certain things with relative ease; they also seem to arrive in the world already possessing forms of knowledge that are relatively complex. In contrast to Piaget, who believed that infants' knowledge of objects developed very slowly over the first months of life, most contemporary developmentalists now believe that babies' conceptions of objects are much like those of adults. Recall that Piaget believed that young infants do not initially integrate information that comes from different sensory modalities, so that the appearance of a bouncing ball, the sound it makes as it bounces, and the way it feels when grasped may not be perceived as related aspects of a single, intact object. Yet, recent research suggests that infants are born prepared to process a world full of three-dimensional objects and that their perception of these objects is amodal (i.e., knowledge that comes in from different sensory modalities is integrated in a common mental representation: Children perceive objects, rather than uncoordinated sights, sounds, and tactile sensations). The child's mental representations of the world are interrelated from the very beginning; they are rich and complex and support all kinds of inferences and predictions about the appearance, motion, and qualities of objects.

Early findings along these lines, coupled with the invention of new technologies for studying cognition in preverbal children, have resulted in an explosion of research on the cognitive capacities of increasingly younger children and infants. Researchers have produced surprising new knowledge about infants' capabilities that was previously unforeseen. For example, even infants in the first year of life seem to know that two objects cannot simultaneously occupy the same place (Baillargeon, 1987). They directly perceive causality in displays in which one object seems to bump into and propel another (Leslie, 1984). They know about the continued existence of an object even when it is hidden from view after being observed (Baillargeon & Graber, 1988). On the other hand, they do not apparently expect unsupported objects to fall (Baillargeon & Hanko-Summers, 1990; Hood, Carey, & Prasada, 2000). At this point, it is not settled whether (and if so, which types of) this infant knowledge is intact at birth, develops as a result of innate predispositions to attend to some things at the expense of others, or emerges as the result of general learning mechanisms, perhaps operating under constraints.

Knowledge about objects and motion supports predictions and expectations, delineates the kinds of events and evidence that will be salient to the perceiver, and provides constraints on the kinds of inferences that are made. Moreover, children's knowledge about objects is not simply a list or collection of ideas; it appears to be organized in a tight network of interrelated concepts that are internally structured. Knowledge about objects also participates in wider knowledge structures, such as the coherent system of ontological classification that children develop (Gopnik & Meltzoff, 1997; Keil, 1992). Because the knowledge of objects (and certain other fundamental domains) appears to be structured in these ways, some researchers have argued that at least certain classes of infant knowledge can be appropriately described as early "theories," which serve the function of organizing both past experience and the generation of new knowledge. The so-called theory theorists emphasize that even babies' mental representations are structured, abstract, and complex. Therefore, although babies' theories may differ in content from those of adult scientists, the theories of both groups nonetheless share important defining properties. Moreover, these theories may be revisable as experience strengthens them or requires their elaboration or adaptation (Gopnik & Meltzoff, 1997). Revisability, of course, is an attribute also characteristic of the theories of adult scientists.

Debate continues about how "theory like" these mental structures are and what forms of early knowledge can be presumed to share these theory-like properties. Frequently mentioned candidates include children's "theories" of physical objects and their interactions, biology and living things, number/quantity, and the nature of human mental life.

Attempts to identify and characterize these "core theories" and to understand their character, their origins, and the mechanisms of their development currently account for considerable research activity in the field of cognitive development. The resulting domain-specific accounts of the ways that children's theories emerge and develop over early years of life have now come to the awareness of science educators, who, for their part, have tended to pay close attention to the influence of naive theories, but only later in the life span. The "misconceptions" literature in science education has been conducted mainly with students at high school or university age. Hundreds of studies have now amply demonstrated that even after succeeding at high levels in school science instruction, students often continue to cling to naive preconceptions about the way the world works. In many cases, these preconceptions are at direct odds with the implications of the science that students have just "mastered."

The growing research base about the origins of young children's theories, considered against this context of older students' failures to deeply understand the scientific theories they have been taught, suggests that it may be valuable to seek and develop potential links between children's unschooled theories of the world and the concepts and theories introduced in school science.

Preschool Pathways to Science

This concern is reflected in Preschool Pathways to Science, a program for prekindergarten children (Gelman & Brenneman, 2004). In this program, instruction is organized around core concepts, such as *biological change,* that are central in children's naive theories and also seem to hold the potential to serve as a firm foundation for acquiring important disciplinary understanding in science. The goal of instruction is the development of conceptual knowledge—not isolated definitions, but systems of concepts that are linked into the kind of rich, interconnected knowledge structures described in the research on core theories. The instruction also includes a focus on communication, including language and other forms of representation, such as writing, drawing, mapping, and charting. Students are encouraged to learn and use precise vocabulary, such as *observe, predict,* and *check,* that makes processes of their inquiry more visible to them and, hence, more open to inspection and self-evaluation.

Children's science work in this program is designed to first capitalize on and then extend children's initial theories about the world. One example described by Gelman and Brenneman (2004) involves a series of investigations about the distinction between what one knows and how one knows, a distinction that the "theory of mind" research identifies as difficult (and not only for young children). The teacher began with a discussion of the five senses, discussing what could be learned about an apple via each of the senses. Students were encouraged to record their observations and eventually to make predictions about things that could not be observed (such as the appearance of the inside of the apple, or the number of seeds). Children checked their predictions by opening the apple and making new observations. As a general principle, learning how to "talk science" (Lemke, 1990) and do science always occurs in the context of learning scientific concepts. Children develop their conceptual knowledge by doing science, and scientific processes and tools are regarded not as disembodied skills, but as a means to learn more about the domain at hand.

The emphasis throughout is on strengthening deep conceptual connections by revisiting the central concepts in a domain via a variety of activities and contexts. Because relevant prior knowledge enhances learning, the topics and concepts in the curriculum deliberately build on domains in which children already have relevant knowledge, such as the core theories about biology and physical properties of objects that have been identified by the theory theorists. Some of the concepts that teachers have developed from these starting points include change (biological, chemical, physical), insides and outsides of objects and organisms, relationships between form and function, and systems and interactions (Gelman & Brenneman, 2004), all topics in which children's early intuitions provide potential starting points for instruction. In each case, the goal is to capitalize on a child's-eye view of a topic, building on these early intuitions by providing additional illustrations, elaborations, and, in some instances, counterexamples that can challenge children's initial mental schemas.

Strengths of this program include that the classroom work is innovative and well connected to a solid research base. As in most of the educational interventions we have described to this point, an important principle is to build deep knowledge within a few content domains, rather than to sample broadly. Children's prior knowledge is to be identified and harnessed, not dismissed or overridden with correct conventional explanations. At the same time, capitalizing on children's intuitive ideas does not mean stopping there. In all cases, the point is to build on these ideas along what Gelman and Brenneman (2004) refer to as a "learning path." Particular emphasis is paid to explicitly marking for children the forms of thinking that are valued and helping underline distinctions between these and everyday kinds of thinking. Specialized vocabulary is cultivated to assist in achieving this goal.

In spite of the many strengths of this program, its long-term outcomes are as yet unknown. Perhaps because of the commitment to tying education tightly to existing research, the developmental trajectory of the program is somewhat restricted, in that it does not extend beyond first grade (although Gelman has been involved in science programs for high school students that share some similarities with this general approach; see, e.g., Gelman, Romo, & Francis, 2002). A critical next step is to first conceptualize and then test empirically the central thesis of the approach: how the extended elaboration of a few central ideas can pay off in the long term with a deeper understanding of scientific ideas that have traditionally been challenging for students to learn. In short, what does the learning pathway look like farther down the road? Conducting conceptual analyses of the links between early theories and later learning can provide first hints, but testing these ideas will require longitudinal study. At this point, little is known about how those relationships are ideally expected to develop or how consistently they can be supported across years of education. Understanding these important questions may require extending the learning research on this program into elementary school, possibly beyond.

Learning to Participate in Scientific Practice

As we mentioned earlier, all long-term investigations of development make commitments to initiating students in forms of practice. In this section, we review programs in which this orientation served as the overriding rationale, although each program clearly also draws from developmental studies conducted with images of theory change or reasoning-skills/heuristics in mind. We contrast a founder program of work, Fostering Communities of Learners (Brown & Campione, 1994, 1996), which explicitly designed instruction to mimic the workings of a scientific community, with later programs that placed primary bets elsewhere, on supporting students' efforts to participate in practices of invention and revision of models of nature.

A Landmark in Developmental Science Education: Fostering Communities of Learners

One of the first attempts to implement and test a long-term developmental view of science education was the Fostering Communities of Learners (FCL) project, directed by Ann L. Brown and Joseph Campione over the course of a decade and a half in the 1980s and 1990s. This project was influential as an educational approach and as a way of conducting developmental research, although the influence on the field of development has been less pervasive than that on education. This work was pioneering in many ways, and all of the long-term projects described in this chapter have been influenced by it, in spite of some differences of opinion about goals and approaches.

In FCL, Brown and Campione (1994, 1996) sought to identify and test "developmental corridors," that is, pathways of the typical development of student knowledge from intuitive ideas to understanding of deep principles in the domains of investigation (like Gelman and Brenneman's, 2004, learning pathways). The shape and direction of these corridors was viewed as being determined by interactions among the capabilities and prior knowledge of students, the forms of teaching and support provided to learners, and the content and structure of the discipline being taught. These pathways were conceived both as conjectured trajectories for instruction (considered as continually revisable, based on emerging results) and as typical patterns of student change. The image of science was one of social community, where theories were developed and subjected to test according to criteria developed within that community. The vision of community was not insular: It included textual accounts and interactions with domain experts, including demonstration lessons. FCL was one of the first developmentally inspired projects in science learning that took seriously the importance of students' learning histories within the content domain of science.

Brown's earlier work in developmental psychology played an important role in the design of FCL. Indeed, as early as 1978, Brown was foreshadowing a key assumption of FCL:

> Our estimates of a child's competencies are sometimes dramatically changed if we consider them in naturally occurring situations. If, therefore, we are in the business of delineating the cognitive competencies of the 4-year-old, we will have a distorted picture if we see the 4-year-old only in a laboratory setting. (Brown & DeLoache, 1978, p. 27)

FCL was entirely consistent with Brown's early emphasis on studying cognitive functioning in the contexts where thinking is naturally put to work. Brown (1992) conceived of school as a place where learning and development could be studied in their interaction. As Vygotsky argued (see Brown & Reeves, 1987), development and learning are related in close and complex ways, a view that contrasts with the typical assumption that development precedes learning and acts as a constraint on it. Children are smarter in contexts where being smart has a function, is expected, and is supported; understanding development relies on opportunities to study it in contexts of that kind. These assumptions led Brown out of the psychological laboratory and into the business of engineering contexts that nurture development and, therefore, produce opportunities to observe and understand it. Although this was by no means the first design study, because of Brown's prominence in developmental psychology, it was the first to become widely known to scholars in that field.

Brown's investigations of memory development in the 1970s were also influential in the direction taken in FCL. Her specific interest in metacognition and self-regulation, a topic where her research was especially influential, foreshadowed the role of metacognition as a pervading theme in FCL. In FCL classrooms, the overriding goal was to progressively turn over to students the responsibility for both the progress and the evaluation of their own learning and to help them construct the tools for managing this responsibility. This goal was pursued in a number of specific ways and was a prominent concern motivating everything from the activity structures in the classroom to the forms of discourse that were favored and supported. Much of the class's learning occurred in small research groups organized and directed by the students themselves. Students, rather than the teacher, were the ones to decide both who contributed to class discussions and the order of participation. Students learned to talk to, convince, and challenge each other rather than the teacher. The teacher, in turn, guided the topic selection and student work in instructionally fruitful directions and worked to build a sense of accountability, both to one's fellow students and to other audiences of a variety of kinds (students were regularly responsible for making presentations, preparing teaching materials for younger children and reports directed to classmates, and communicating with scientists from outside the classroom). Standards for evaluation of classroom work were consensually developed, publicly shared, and, as far as possible, transparent.

A recurring activity structure in the FCL classrooms was reciprocal teaching, a reading comprehension program that Brown had developed in collaboration with Anne Marie Palincsar (Palincsar & Brown, 1984). Reciprocal teaching was another means of placing self-regulation front and center in students' learning, in this case, for understanding information presented in textual form. In reciprocal teaching, students acquired, practiced, and eventually mastered the kinds of comprehension strategies that more expert readers use spontaneously. Students first learned to imitate strategies modeled by the teacher and eventually, with assistance, began to take over key roles themselves. For example, readers might be asked to provide a summary, ask a clarifying question, or make an inference on the basis of the given information. As students became more expert, the teacher progressively ceded responsibility to student group leaders for these kinds of functions; eventually, students read together in small groups and group members negotiated meaning. The studies on reciprocal teaching documented impressive and lasting gains in the reading comprehension of even struggling readers.

FCL teachers relied heavily on reciprocal teaching to carry out the central activity in FCL classrooms, namely, the conduct and sharing of research in cycles that Brown and Campione (1996) referred to as "research-share-perform." The research conducted in these classrooms primarily involved reading, analyzing, and compiling texts of various kinds (written, electronic, or video). Products of the children's research were also typically in the form of text or talk; they might be posters, public presentations, written reports, or teaching materials intended for younger children. The heavy emphasis on reading, analyzing, integrating, and preparing written information was consistent with Brown's earlier work in reading comprehension with reciprocal teaching and also with the general emphasis on metacognition and self-regulation that permeated FCL.

Typically, a research cycle began with the teacher introducing an important disciplinary theme (e.g., biological adaptation). These themes and topics were identified by the project team, which included domain experts, as being fruitful for supporting deep understanding of important disciplinary ideas and productive for focusing the research of student teams. Topics were introduced with an "initiating event," such as a compelling story or a video, which provided a jumping-off point for students' questions and interests. Students would next convene in a whole-class discussion to generate a list of questions that the story, video, or classroom visit raised for them. The teacher categorized and guided questioning with an eye to ensuring that the important themes identified by the project team were represented in the questions that were subsequently investigated. Small teams of students would adopt one of the questions to "research." Commonly, an overarching theme like "food webs and chains" would be divided among the students, so that members of each research group became specialists in a single part of the problem. In the example explained in Brown and Campione (1996), the students studying food webs convened in specialty groups studying photosynthesis, energy exchange, competition, consumers, and decomposition. In another classroom, the same topic was subdivided in a different way, each group studying food webs in a different kind of ecosystem: the rain forest, grasslands, oceans, fresh water bodies, or deserts.

Over the course of these investigations, students were encouraged to develop expertise and knowledge in their own interest areas, to the point where some students became class experts whose knowledge exceeded that of most of the adults. For example, one student might become acknowledged for computer expertise, another for drawing and graphics, and a third for personal expertise in a related subject matter, for instance, a child who had sickle cell disease brought related personal biological knowledge to bear in the classroom investigations. This phenomenon, which Brown and Campione (1996) referred to as "majoring," was explicitly encouraged. In contrast to typical classrooms, where the goal is for all students to know the same things at approximately the same time, teachers in FCL classrooms explicitly encouraged variability, both in what individual students knew and in the distribution of knowledge across groups.

For an extended period (typically weeks or even months), students worked in their research teams to identify and consult a variety of text and electronic resources to assist them in coming to an answer to their question. From time to time, the research teams would

form "jigsaw" groups composed of one "expert" from each of the subtopic specialty teams. Within the jigsaw groups, children taught each other about their own area of expertise and attempted to coordinate their disparate knowledge into a more integrated view of the problem. Often, a culminating "consequential event" (such as a performance, design task—e.g., "Design an animal of the future"—report, or parent visit) was planned to provide the motivation for this integrative work. Occasionally, outside experts (scientists, animal care professionals) would visit the classroom to conduct "benchmark lessons" in which they introduced new disciplinary concepts or modeled thinking from a disciplinary perspective. In "cross-talk" sessions, students convened in whole-class discussions to get preliminary feedback on their progress well before the consequential event, so that they might undertake corrective action or additional investigation, if it was considered warranted. In the class discussions, all assertions that students made were considered open to legitimate challenge from any group member. Students readily learned that they were expected to be able to produce evidence and refer to at least one identifiable source to back up a contested claim. Hence, the norms in the classroom included the idea that sources were to be recruited to support arguments whose purpose was to decide among alternative explanations.

For Brown and Campione (1996) and their colleagues, designing appropriate measures was a central challenge in conducting the research. Developmental researchers have considerable experience with interviews and pre- and posttests of conceptual knowledge, but these are not usually designed to track the development of deep forms of content knowledge that emerge over an extended period of time in ways that vary considerably from student to student. Moreover, in addition to the conceptual structures of science that were the targets of instruction, the FCL program had a broader set of learning goals. For example, researchers constructed ways to track changes in students' ability to read, comprehend, and integrate textual information. They attempted to demonstrate increasing sophistication in classroom performances that are not typically assessed, such as children's scientific reasoning in their groups and whole-class discussions. In this case, they classified the forms of classroom talk that students produced and sought to observe changes in frequency of use and levels of analogies, causal explanations, uses of evidence, argumentation, and predictions.

Beyond pioneering the FCL program and conducting research on students' cognitive development, Brown and

Campione (1996) were also concerned with being able to capture the spirit of the program in a set of design principles that would serve to explain the mechanisms that sustained ongoing implementations and therefore to inform the spread of the program to new sites. This concern for principled explanation may partly have been motivated by Brown's experiences with reciprocal teaching. She noted that a weakness of reciprocal teaching and other strategy training programs is the danger that teachers and students may focus too literally on the processes of learning to the neglect of the underlying goal that motivated them. As Brown and Campione put it, "Without adherence to first principles, surface procedures tend to be adopted, adapted, and ritualized in such a way that they cease to serve the 'thinking' function they were originally designed to foster" (p. 291). In the case of reciprocal teaching, Brown and Campione observed that in its widespread dissemination, teachers sometimes focused too much on surface procedures, such as summarizing or questioning, that were not deployed for the original purpose of helping students learn to read for understanding. Sometimes these strategies were even practiced outside of the context of reading actual texts and were introduced as rituals rather than reflective strategies. It is as if the husk of the intervention had been communicated, but the germ had been left out.

Perhaps as a result of these earlier experiences, Brown and Campione struggled repeatedly through the 1990s to encapsulate and refine the design principles that motivated the FCL intervention in a way that would help the field understand both what FCL actually looked like in practice and how those systems of activity followed from their particular commitments to learning theory. For example, their 1996 chapter delineates 37 principles under six major headings: systems and cycles (a description of the recurrent activity structures utilized in FCL), metacognitive environment, discourse, deep content knowledge, distributed expertise, instruction and assessment, and community features. With some variation and adaptation, many of these features have been preserved in educational interventions that followed FCL.

With respect to science learning specifically, FCL was a sustained classroom project that attempted to identify "big ideas" in science that children might learn cumulatively, and to try to understand how those ideas might be developmentally constructed, given appropriate forms of instructional assistance. In spite of its stature and influence, two questions about FCL remain open. The first concerns the utility of principles as a way to both describe and spread new educational programs. We do not doubt that principles may help readers understand the basis for the particulars of the intervention, but we do question their sufficiency for supporting the replication and adaptation of an intervention in a new site. As yet, little is known about the content and form of knowledge that are necessary and sufficient for catalyzing and sustaining changes in teaching practices. The Schools for Thought experiment, which attempted to capitalize on what was learned through FCL and two other successful classroom-based research projects, did not generate the results and sustainability that participants had hoped (Lamon et al., 1996). Participants in this work, including Brown and Campione, found that their principles were highly meaningful to those who had generated them, but were apparently open to all kinds of interpretations to outsiders who had not shared in the background experiences that motivated the principles in the first place. Principles seemed common sense after the fact, but as a means for prescribing what to do, they did not sufficiently constrain a designer's choices. For example, although one might agree in practice that it is a good idea to encourage shared discourse and common knowledge among students (one of the FCL principles), accepting the principle unfortunately provides no guidance about how to follow it or how one could know if the goal had been satisfactorily achieved.

A second major question about FCL is whether it is a good idea for school science to be so exclusively focused on the reading and integration of textual information. Certainly reading is an important way to build knowledge in science, but arguably, students should also experience direct forms of inquiry with the natural world. Ironically, the domain-general nature of FCL activity structures and goals—something that Brown and Campione probably considered a strength—may also entail a weakness from the perspective of a particular discipline. The activities and goals in the FCL classrooms would probably apply equally well to the learning of history or literature. However, one might legitimately wonder whether learning *about* science is sufficient for coming to appreciate its epistemology. One might legitimately take the position that students should also get some experience *doing* science. Indeed, Palincsar and Magnussun (2001) have subsequently developed an approach that blends textual instruction, which they call "secondhand investigations," with direct or firsthand investigations. In their educational approach, young students read from carefully fabricated journals that explicitly display the thinking of a scientist, who explains in the text how she conceptualized a scientific problem, used graphs and other representational devices to interpret data, or otherwise made her thinking visible so that young children could model it in their own parallel investigations with physical materials.

The Development of Model-Based Reasoning

Philosophers of science have pointed out that the central activity of science is the generation and test of models (Giere, 1988; Hesse, 1974). In fact, Giere argues that all that distinguishes scientific explanation from everyday explanation is that the former is constructed with models that have been developed in the sciences: "Little can be learned . . . about science that could not be learned more directly by examining the nature of scientific models and how they are developed" (p. 105).

Until recently, modeling practices have taken a peripheral place, at best, in school science. Even in model-populated disciplines such as physics, students' modeling activity is typically restricted to applying models developed previously by scientists, perhaps to solve textbook problems or to analyze a situation presented in a laboratory. In school, the word "model" usually denotes a noun, the product of the modeling enterprise, rather than a verb describing the practice of science. Students tend to be interpreters and users of models, but they do not generate and test them. Recently, however, scientists, mathematicians, and educators have been impressed with the potential of new computer tools to put modeling within the reach of school students. Although many investigations of modeling in mathematics and science education are focused relatively tightly on the acquisition of a specific body of disciplinary knowledge, they have also led to a more general interest in the early origins and subsequent development of model-based reasoning—a more general capability and propensity to play what Hestenes (1992) referred to as "the modeling game." In the following section, we describe two classroom-based programs that seek to foster students' capabilities to generate and test models of scientific phenomena, one at the middle school level and the second in elementary grades. The intent of these programs is to help students develop along two tracks simultaneously. First, students develop conceptual understanding of the specific scientific ideas in the domain of study. That is, students come to understand particular models and eventually to acquire a repertoire of models usable across a variety of situations. Over a longer time span, the focus is on their understanding of modeling as a key epistemology of science.

Briefly, by modeling, we refer to the construction and test of representations that serve as analogues to systems in the real world. These representations can be of many forms, including physical models, computer programs, mathematical equations, or propositions. Objects and relations in the model are interpreted as representing theoretically important objects and relations in the represented world. A key hurdle for students is to understand that models are not copies; they are deliberate simplifications. Error is a component of all models, and the precision required of a model depends on the purpose for its current use. The two instructional programs that we describe take different approaches to the forms of models that they regard as central, so we will defer further discussion about the nature of models until the examples are introduced.

Causal Models: Understandings of Consequence. Perhaps the most ubiquitous and general kind of structural relationship that can be captured in a model is the relationship of cause and effect. Causal models are ubiquitous in science, so the value of understanding the kinds of causal models that people can learn and the sources of learning difficulty seems straightforward (White, 1993). An extensive literature on the development of causal reasoning, conducted during the 1980s, suggests that even preschool children are adept at using a variety of cues from the environment to identify the cause of an event from a set of potential candidates. Among these cues are temporal contiguity, spatial contiguity, consistent covariation between the candidate cause and the effect, and mechanism, that is, whether there is a plausible mechanism that would account for A causing B (Leslie, 1984; Shultz, 1982).

Recently, Gopnik and her colleagues (Gopnik & Sobel, 2000; Gopnik, Sobel, Schulz, & Glymour, 2001) conducted a series of investigations with children as young as 2 years in an attempt to identify both *how* young children learn about new causal relations and whether these learning systems are domain specific or applied across different domains of knowledge, such as biological or physical systems. The strategy was to observe online as children went about learning a causal relation that they had not previously encountered or been taught. In one series of studies, children were introduced to the "blicket detector," a machine that lights up and plays music when (and only when) "blickets" are placed on it. Participants were shown several small blocks and told that one or more of them were blickets. Children were asked to identify which of the blocks were the blickets, either by observing patterns of placement and the resulting outcomes and then drawing a conclusion based on those observations or, in some studies, by taking direct action themselves to place blocks on the blicket detector. Across trials within a study and across studies, the patterns of evidence that children observed became increasingly complex, ultimately including multiple causes and probabilistic relationships. In most cases, even the 2-year-olds made correct conclusions about causality by observing patterns of contingency, although these young children did not perform as well as older preschoolers on tasks in which two additive causes were required to set off the blicket detector. Children demonstrated their reasoning in multiple forms, suggesting that they genuinely were reasoning about causes, not simply making judgments of association. These forms included causal conclusions and justifications made on the basis of observation, predictions about novel events on the basis of earlier learning, and direct production of requested outcomes. Moreover, children seemed to use similar kinds of causal learning principles across different content domains of knowledge.

Gopnik and her colleagues (2001) conjectured that data-driven formal learning procedures like these might be used in conjunction with innate, domain-specific causal schemas like those described in the prior section on the "theory theory." She proposed that both kinds of causal reasoning are important and serve complementary and useful roles in children's developing knowledge. The innate theories determine what features the child is likely to attend to and, therefore, what the data-driven procedures will operate on. In turn, the formal causal learning mechanisms provide a means by which initial theories can be modified or extended, as well as a way to learn new information not implicated in a core theory (Gopnik et al., 2001). Both kinds of knowledge are fundamentally important in determining the course of learning.

Research with young children (Bullock, Gelman, & Baillargeon, 1982; Gopnik et al., 2001; Shultz, 1982) emphasizes their competence at reasoning about causally complex situations. However, the developmental literature also tells another story that seems difficult to reconcile with these findings. As often occurs in developmental psychology, findings of early competence stand side by side with studies that emphasize the reasoning flaws and biases shown by adults in situations that are described in similar ways. In this case, the developmental literature seems to conclude that very young children understand causality, whereas adults do not. For example, research conducted by D. Kuhn and her associates (D. Kuhn, 1989; Kuhn et al., 1988, 1992, 1995) demonstrates that adults frequently show characteristic flaws in reasoning about multivariable causal situations. Indeed, they make many of the same errors that children do: generating experiments that are not valid tests, interpreting evidence that is flawed or insufficient, avoiding evidence that challenges their prior theories, and failing to systematically search the space of possibilities, entertain alternative interpretations of data, or rely on evidence rather than mere examples.

Perkins and Grotzer (2000), who direct the Understandings of Consequence project, suggested that the difficulties many students have in learning science concepts stem from differences in the ways that students and scientists think about cause and effect. Nonscientists, they argue, hold a few simplistic causal structures into which all new information gets assimilated. (Similar arguments have been made by Chi, 1992.) Most of the time, these simple causal structures do a perfectly adequate job of supporting our actions and interpretations in the world, and these are the relationships that young children appear to master easily. However, when less familiar forms of cause are involved, as is often the case in science, these structures can be misleading. In contrast to novices, scientists entertain a wide array of causal structures, which vary in complexity. Perkins and Grotzer attempted to identify the features that account for this complexity and to summarize them in a taxonomy that permits estimating the difficulty of any particular causal model with respect to these features.

The taxonomy describes four aspects of causal structures: mechanism, interaction pattern, probability, and agency. Each of these varies across several levels of complexity (and, by implication, difficulty of learning). Perkins and Grotzer (2000) propose that any model or explanation can be identified on the taxonomy with respect to its hypothetical difficulty level by locating it within these four dimensions. For example, a model may vary with respect to sophistication in the level of *mechanism* that it ascribes to the phenomenon being modeled. Very simple models rely on surface generalizations or explanations at the same level of description as the events being explained. At the more sophisticated end of the spectrum, a model may appeal to analogical mapping or underlying mechanisms, including properties, entities, and rules that account for the situation at an underlying level of description. Similarly, simple *interaction patterns* include those that appeal in a straightforward way to one thing acting on another, via pushes, pulls, supports, resistances, and so on. The entities on this level seem similar to the simple schemas that diSessa (1993) referred to as phenomenological primitives, that is, schemas at a midlevel of abstraction that are automatically activated to support interpretations of physical events. According to diSessa, these interpretations seem self-evident and do not require justification; instead, people simply "recognize" an event as belonging to one class or another. At more complex levels, students may entertain mediating causes, interactive causality, feedback loops, or constraint-based systems. The dimension of *probability* specifies whether a particular explanation is deterministic or appeals to chance, chaotic systems, or fundamental uncertainty. The final dimension concerns the perspective taken on *agency:* Does the model assume that a central agent is the causal actor, or are other, more complex possibilities considered, such as additive causes, long causal chains, self-organizing systems, or emergent properties? At this point in the research, the taxonomy should probably be considered hypothetical; the dimensions of complexity were derived via rational analysis rather than empirical test. Moreover, the taxonomy appears to capture only *order* of complexity, not *degree;* there is no claim that difficulty level increases in measurable quantitative steps from the least to the most complex level of each dimension. Also, it is not clear how to cumulate these dimensions to make a judgment about the overall complexity of a model. The best use of the taxonomy at this time seems to be heuristic, and the authors do not comment on whether they consider it to have scale properties.

Along with their analysis of models and model explanations, Perkins and Grotzer (2000) have also developed an analysis of what they call *epistemological moves* toward better models. These are the cognitive behaviors with respect to modeling that they find worthy of encouraging in students. They include seeking a model with no gaps or missing parts, putting the model at risk by actively seeking counterevidence or contrasting cases, detecting flawed evidence, and entertaining reasonable criteria for revising or replacing the model in the face of different forms of counterevidence. These

epistemological moves are similar to the criteria for changing theories that were delineated in the Conceptual Change model, described earlier. Presumably, acquiring and using these epistemological moves increases the likelihood that students will come to understand and, when appropriate, apply the most appropriate causal schema from their repertoire.

Initial research findings suggest that students who participated in activities that emphasized the underlying causal structure of a scientific topic and participated in direct discussions of these causal relationships performed better on measures of conceptual understanding of that topic than did students who worked on similar units that did not directly emphasize causal relationships (Grotzer, 2000; Perkins & Grotzer, 2000). However, the project had ambitions beyond simply boosting conceptual understanding domain by domain. In particular, the goal was that students who learned about causal structures in one topic (e.g., density) would transfer those structures to other topics (e.g., pressure) when it was appropriate to do so, and that importing the new causal structures would provide a firmer base for understanding the new material. Research to this point (Grotzer, 2003) suggests that there is some limited transfer of this kind from one topic to another when the causal structure in both tasks is isomorphic. However, the researchers found no evidence of spontaneous transfer when the causal structures between the two topics were not isomorphic. In other words, so far there is no evidence that students have acquired a general propensity to search among candidates for an appropriate causal model and then try to use it to understand novel cases. Grotzer (2003) observed that situation-specific default concepts like diSessa's (1993) phenomenological primitives seemed to interfere with transfer of the appropriate causal relationships. The investigators are now seeking to enhance the metacognitive aspects of the instruction in an effort to learn whether more explicit reflection on the nature and uses of causal models might help improve the transfer of causal structures between science contexts.

An attractive feature of causal models is that they have both a domain-general aspect, derived from the general structure of the causal relationship that is expressed, and a domain-specific aspect, in that the relationship represents structure in a particular domain or situation (Gopnik et al., 2001). Because of this integrative quality, modeling approaches at least hold the potential of avoiding the process/content or syntax/

substance dichotomies that sometimes plague science education (and psychological accounts of scientific reasoning). The causal modeling approach being developed by Perkins and Grotzer (2000) may be described as a top-down modeling approach. Through rational analysis, the investigators first attempted to exhaustively describe the landscape of kinds of causal models, and content domains for study were apparently selected because they exemplified one or more of these target forms of causal reasoning. It is not clear whether considerations of conceptual development guided the selection of domain topics beyond a commitment to generating opportunities for the acquisition, transfer, or comparison of causal models. Therefore, in this program, development of scientific conceptual knowledge is probably a more important focus within units rather than across domains. Over years of a student's education, the acquisition of a repertoire of causal schemas takes priority as an educational objective over the development of any particular conceptual knowledge base.

Of course, when scientists construct, test, and revise models, they do so in the service of contributing to a base of knowledge within a coherent content domain. The final classroom research program we describe, our own, aims to open the activity of modeling to school students. It integrates Perkins and Grotzer's (2000) emphasis on refining a repertoire of structural analytical tools with the focus on conceptual development within a coherent domain that is favored by investigators like Gelman and Brenneman (2004) and Metz (2004).

Modeling Nature. The kinds of models that scientists construct vary widely, both within and across disciplines. Nevertheless, the rhetoric and practice of science are governed by efforts to invent, revise, and contest models. We (Lehrer & Schauble, 2005) have been investigating the implications of this view of science for the education of students in elementary and middle school grades. Our primary interest was not just on students' understanding of models per se, but, more specifically, on their understanding of modeling. To provide a context where the development of model-based reasoning could be studied, participating teachers worked collaboratively and systematically to build on young children's interests and abilities in representing aspects of the world in all kinds of ways—via language, drawings, physical models, maps and globes, rules that capture regularities and patterns—and to provide effective forms of instructional support, building on chil-

dren's initial modeling attempts to help them achieve a progressively more sophisticated grasp of science. Early emphasis on representational form, especially on purposes and uses, was derived from developmental studies that suggested a rich repertoire of such resources (e.g., Karmiloff-Smith, 1992) and from social studies of science, which indicated their critical role in model building (e.g., Latour, 1999). We were especially interested in those forms of representation that would help children "mathematize" (Kline, 1980) natural phenomena, such as growth or relations between structure and function. By mathematizing, we mean the common scientific practice of quantifying or visualizing phenomena geometrically (or both). Privileging mathematics meant introducing mathematics to elementary children that went beyond arithmetic to include space and geometry, measurement, and data/uncertainty (e.g., Lehrer & Chazan, 1998; Lehrer & Schauble, 2002). The focus of the research that was coordinated with this instructional agenda was on the early emergence and subsequent development of model-based reasoning. A secondary agenda concerned students' conceptual development in target forms of mathematics and science.

The developmental literature illustrates that there are myriad ways in which even preschool children come to regard one thing as representing another. This representational capacity provides roots for the development of a modeling epistemology. For example, long before they arrive at school, children have some appreciation of the representational qualities of pictures, scale models, and video representations (DeLoache, 2004; DeLoache, Pierroutsakos, & Uttal, 2003; Troseth, 2003; Troseth & DeLoache, 1998; Troseth, Pierroutsakos, & DeLoache, 2004). In pretend play, children treat objects as stand-ins for others (a block stands in for a teacup, a banana for a telephone), yet they still understand that the object has not really changed its original identity, character, or function (Leslie, 1987). Later in school, they will capitalize on very similar understandings to use counters for "direct modeling" to solve simple early arithmetic problems that involve grouping and separating.

However important, these early symbolic capacities do not yet capture all the key aspects of a scientific modeling epistemology. Although they certainly know the difference between a model and its referent, children do not usually self-consciously think about the separation of the model and the modeled world. Consequently, they often show a preference for copies over true models, because they tend to resist symbolic depictions that leave out information, even if the information is not important to the current theoretical purposes (Grosslight, Unger, Jay, & Smith, 1991; Lehrer & Schauble, 2000b). For example, children using paper strips to represent the height of plants may insist on the strips being colored green (like the plant stems) and demand that each strip be adorned with a flower (Lehrer & Schauble, 2002). Students are unlikely to spontaneously consider issues of precision and error of a representation or the implications of deviations between the model and the modeled world in light of current goals (although they certainly have intuitions that are helpful as starting points; see Masnick & Klahr, 2003; Petrosino, Lehrer, & Schauble, 2003). Having identified a way to represent one or more aspects of the world, they may be unable to entertain the possibility of alternatives. Indeed, the search for and evaluation of rival models in evaluating alternative hypotheses is a form of argument that does not typically emerge spontaneously (Driver, Leach, Millar, & Scott, 1996; Grosslight et al., 1991).

In addition to these general symbolic capacities, the development of specific representational forms and notations is also a critical part of being able to enter what Hestenes (1992) referred to as the "modeling game." Representational tools such as graphs, tables, computer programs, and mathematical expressions do not simply communicate thought; they also shape it (Olson, 1994), so acquiring a vocabulary of inscriptions and notations and a critical understanding of their design qualities was considered essential. Accordingly, helping students develop their metarepresentational competence (diSessa, Hammer, Sherin, & Kolpakowski, 1991) was a central target of both instruction and the related research.

Particular emphasis was placed on mathematics as a tool that both describes the world and serves as a resource for meaning making (Lehrer, Schauble, Strom, & Pligge, 2001; E. Penner & Lehrer, 2000). Often, science educators delay the mathematization of scientific ideas, believing that students should first develop a qualitative analysis of the science underlying the phenomenon, and that too early attention to mathematical description may encourage an emphasis on computation rather than understanding. This assumes, however, that students have no history of learning mathematics as a sense-making enterprise. Experience and research suggest that this need not be the case. With good instruction even young students can meaningfully consider the epistemic grounds of generalization and even proof (Lampert, 2001; Lehrer et al., 1998; Lehrer & Lesh, 2003).

These epistemic considerations often arise when children investigate the mathematics of shape and form, measurement, and data. Therefore, developing and testing appropriate inroads to these new mathematical ideas was an important part of the program (e.g., Lehrer & Chazan, 1998; Lehrer, Jacobson, Kemeny, & Strom, 1999; Lehrer & Romberg, 1996; Lehrer & Schauble, 2000c, 2005). If they are lacking these mathematical resources, it is unlikely that students' conjectures can be held accountable in any meaningful way to data, which has mathematical qualities that need to be appreciated if their interpretations are to be disciplined. The aim was to develop students' mathematical understanding to the point where it would be sufficient to support description and systematization of the natural world—the heart of modeling.

In the science class, we attempted to orient instruction around a cumulative focus on important core themes, such as growth and diversity, behavior, and structure and function, as described in national science standards (National Research Council, 1996). Themes were selected in part for their centrality to science disciplines, but also for their potential for engaging students in the progressive mathematization of nature (e.g., Kline, 1980). Central concepts such as diversity and structure derive their power from the models that instantiate them, so to fulfill the promise of the "big ideas" outlined in national standards, students must realize these ideals as models. Moreover, models are not simply constructed; equally important, they must be mobilized—that is, put to work—to support socially grounded arguments about the nature of physical reality (Bazerman, 1988; Latour & Woolgar, 1979; Pickering, 1995). Achieving these goals with school students meant identifying forms of modeling that are well aligned with children's development.

We concluded that in children's instruction, it is advisable to begin with models that resemble their target systems (i.e., the phenomena being described or explained) in ways that can be easily detected, because resemblance helps children make and preserve the mappings between models and their referents (Brown, 1990; Lehrer & Schauble, 2000c). For example, when first graders were given a variety of materials from a hardware store and asked to construct a device that "works like your elbow," initial models were guided by a concern for copying perceptually salient features (Grosslight et al., 1991). Most of the children insisted on using round foam balls to simulate the "bumps" in their elbow joints and Popsicle sticks to simulate fingers (D. E. Penner, Giles, Lehrer, & Schauble, 1997). However, this beginning concern with "looks like" lost importance over multiple revisions of the models, which eventually began to focus on "works like": relations among and functions of components in the target system, in this case, ways of constraining the motion of the elbow. Consistent with the emphasis on mathematics in children's modeling activity, third graders went on to mathematically explore relationships between the position of a load and the point of attachment of the tendon in a more complex elbow model (D. E. Penner, Lehrer, & Schauble, 1998).

Modeling is a form of disciplinary argument, one that students learn to participate in over a long and extended period of practice and only with good teaching assistance. Lehrer and Schauble (2005) argued that acquiring disciplinary forms of argument requires emphasizing students' long-term development of central conceptual and epistemic structures, not the acquisition of nuggets of instruction that are delivered within brief periods. Decisions about what is taught should be informed by a long-term view, one that regards learning as a historical activity in which current learning builds from and on learning achieved in earlier weeks, months, and years. Therefore, the research focused on identifying and empirically testing science themes that provide easy entry for young children, while supporting plenty of conceptual challenge for students in the upper grades. Identifying mathematical and scientific models and concepts that could potentially serve as a core and then working with teachers to investigate the potential of these ideas across grades of schooling constituted an important part of the design research agenda.

An example is the theme of growth and change. Students in primary grades represented the growth of flowering bulbs planted under different conditions (in soil or water), using paper strips to depict the heights of plant stems at different points in the growth cycle (Lehrer, Carpenter, et al., 2000). Depiction of height required a transformation in children's thinking from considering the plant as an intact whole to thinking of it as a set of attributes, height being the most salient. Representing and comparing heights required working out standard ways of measuring and a firm understanding of the mathematics of measure, which was developed systematically during this investigation. Indeed, it is worth noting that understanding an attribute and understanding how to measure it are related ideas, regardless of the grade of the "scientist." When children raised the question *how much faster* one plant grew than another, their attention turned from comparing final heights to noting successive differences in the lengths of the strips from day to day. These questions relied on the arithmetic of comparative difference, a form of mathematics within their grasp. They noted that the amaryllis grew faster at the beginning of the life cycle and then slowed, whereas the paperwhite narcissus grew very slowly at the beginning and then "catched up."

In the third grade, students investigated change of Wisconsin Fast Plants™ in a variety of ways (Lehrer, Schauble, Carpenter, & Penner, 2000). (Wisconsin Fast Plants, or *brassica rapta,* complete an entire life cycle in about 40 days, making it feasible to use them in population studies or other classroom investigations that require comparisons of groups of plants that can be readily grown within one school semester.) They developed pressed plant silhouette graphs that recorded changes in the plants over time, coordinate graphs that showed relations between plant height and time, rectangles that represented relationships between plant height and canopy "width," and three-dimensional prisms and cylinders to capture changes in plant volume. These diverse representations raised new questions about the plants. Students wondered whether the growth of roots and shoots were the "same" or "different." They concluded that the rates of growth were different at similar points in the life cycle, but that the general shape of growth (S-shaped logistic curves) was similar. Why, students wondered, might the growth of different plant parts have the same form? When was growth the fastest, and when the slowest, and what features in the plants were changing in ways that might account for this? Teachers played a central role in helping students compare and evaluate their questions, produce and contrast different kinds of representational displays, and generate evidence-based claims. Although it is not possible to include detailed information here about the data on teachers' professional development and changing teaching practices, these were necessary conditions for the student learning that was observed (more information on this aspect of the program is provided in Lehrer & Schauble, 2000c, 2005).

In the fifth grade, students compared populations of plants and reasoned about features of distributions of the plant measurements to decide whether growth factors such as fertilizer and amount of light were affecting variables such as height and reproductive capacity (i.e., number of seeds and seed pods) of the plants (Lehrer & Schauble, 2004). Features of distributions such as typicality and spread were investigated thoroughly, and different representations of these statistics were invented and explored. Sampling experiments based on the students' measurements of plant height at a particular day of growth supported discussions about typical plant height and its variability under different numbers of samples and samples of different sizes. Children learned to read the shape of different distributions as signatures of growth processes. For example, a distribution with a left wall was interpreted as representing the plants early in their life cycle because, as one child explained, "You can't get any shorter than zero mm."

As these examples illustrate, at each grade children's representational repertoires were systematically stretched, making it possible to expand their knowledge about growth and change in new ways. In turn, as their knowledge grew, there was change in children's considerations about what might next be worthy of investigation.

Lehrer and Schauble (2000c, 2003, 2005) reported observing characteristic shifts in understanding of modeling over the span of the elementary school grades, from an early emphasis on literal depictional forms to representations that were progressively more symbolic and mathematically powerful. Diversity in representational and mathematical resources both accompanied and produced conceptual change. As children developed and used new mathematical means for characterizing growth, they understood biological change in increasingly dynamic ways. For example, once students understood the mathematics of ratio and changing ratios, they began to conceive of growth not as simple linear increase, but as a patterned rate of change. These transitions in conception and inscription appeared to support each other, and they opened up new lines of inquiry. Children wondered whether plant growth was like animal growth, and whether the growth of yeast and bacteria on a petri dish would show a pattern like the growth of a single plant. These forms of conceptual development required a context in which teachers systematically supported a restricted set of central ideas, building successively on earlier concepts over grades of schooling.

Learning research was conducted to investigate the development and use of a variety of mathematical and scientific models. One strategy was to conduct detailed studies of student thinking in the context of, or immediately following, particular units of study. The purpose of these investigations was to learn whether and how students developed new models, to identify the variability in student understanding of the mathematical and scientific concepts at hand, and to document how students appropriately applied mathematical concepts learned in

one context to novel situations. For example, in one study, students explored the mathematics of ratio via geometry by investigating the properties of families of similar rectangles (Lehrer & Schauble, 2001). Subsequently, while investigating properties of materials, they spontaneously wondered whether materials might also come in families, a reference to whether there might be constant ratios between volume and weight for objects made of Styrofoam, wood, Teflon, and brass. Pursuing this question led to an extended investigation of the properties of coordinate graphs and linear relationships as models (the plots of weight by volume seemed nearly linear, but many of the points did not lie directly on the line). Lehrer and Schauble conducted numerous classroom investigations of student model-based reasoning in the context of instruction in mathematics (e.g., data modeling, classification, distribution, similarity) and science (e.g., growth, diversity, motion, density). Details of this work are reported in a variety of publications (Horvath & Lehrer, 1998; Lehrer, Carpenter, et al., 2000; Lehrer & Schauble, 2005; Lehrer, Schauble, & Petrosino, 2001; Lehrer, Schauble, Strom, et al., 2001; D. E. Penner et al., 1997, 1998). Most of these investigations were cross-sectional; they either focused on students within a classroom or classrooms at the same grade or drew comparisons of the performance of students in different grades at the same time point.

In addition to these within-grades and between-grades studies, longitudinal investigations were conducted to confirm whether and, if so, how students' understanding of mathematics was growing systematically over years of instruction, because mathematics was the primary tool employed for modeling. Because students were learning forms of mathematics that are not typically taught in elementary grades or measured by current standardized assessments, the project team created a series of standardized measures to assess student achievement, organized into a 3-hour test that could be administered to groups of students. There were two forms for this instrument, one for the primary grades and the other for upper elementary grades. Each form was revised every year, although a core pool of items was administered each year to all students. Several released items from the National Assessment of Educational Progress were included to benchmark student achievement to national performance. The results, reported in detail in Lehrer and Schauble (2005), found gains in student learning that were reliable at each grade from grades 1 through 5 (effect sizes ranged from 0.43 to 0.72). The average gain scores indicated substantial growth in student understanding, and the gains were widespread (i.e., not confined to selected strata of students). Moreover, on the nationally benchmarked items, students in the early grades outperformed those from much higher grades in the national sample.

Of course, there is much yet to be learned. One issue is the relationship between mathematics and science. We generally first introduce students to mathematics, so that they have opportunities to explore and understand mathematical structure before these structures are employed to model nature. We are concerned that if we introduce only the mathematics that students need to model a particular system, then much else about the mathematics will be lost (e.g., its more general, systematic quality). However, this approach clearly contrasts with curricular approaches that emphasize integrating mathematics and science. A related issue is how students view epistemologies within each discipline. For example, in some of our classroom studies, we have noted children drawing clear distinctions between mathematical (e.g., general by definition) and scientific (e.g., general by model) senses of generalization (Lehrer & Schauble, 2000a). How these epistemologies unfold over time is not yet understood.

Summary: Classroom Design Studies

In this section, we reviewed seven extended programs of classroom research in which researchers studied the development of student thinking in contexts that were engineered to support it. Although these are by no means the only developmentally informed investigations of scientific thinking in classrooms, they do represent a range of visions about what scientific literacy should entail. Each vision was either consistent with or directly informed by related research in cognitive development. Many, although not all, of the scholars who conducted this work also articulated an explicit perspective on the relationship between learning and development.

In the chapter's introduction, we claimed that new answers to the questions "What develops?" and "What is development?" were being raised within this niche of classroom-based developmental research. We next briefly summarize what these investigations, taken as a group, suggest about potential answers to these two questions.

With respect to their views of science and science literacy, all of the investigators reviewed in this section acknowledge the complexity and variability of science. The focus on what develops is necessarily much broader than in typical studies of learning and thinking, which appropriately tend instead to focus tightly on particular skills or concepts. This broader focus is necessary, of course, for seeking to characterize and understand development that occurs only over years of education. The wider perspectives taken here may also be useful for considering the implications of more traditional research on scientific thinking with respect to the goals of education. For example, consider Chen and Klahr's (1999) research on the control of variables strategy in juxtaposition to Metz's (2004) broader agenda of helping students conduct self-initiated and self-regulated inquiry. Both studies share a focus on helping children understand the logic and methods of research, yet they do not come to the same conclusion about what should happen in classrooms. Indeed, one of the unresolved issues in science education is this disagreement about whether children should first explicitly be taught strategies and procedures for conducting inquiry and then later learn to apply them, or whether they should learn these strategies and methods in contexts of their use, so that they are situated within a larger, coherent process of inquiry. This question takes on special poignancy when the children are struggling students or come from cultures where they have had less exposure to forms of thinking valued in school. Lee and Fradd (1996) have argued that in these situations, it is important to directly instruct children first on processes and strategies of inquiry, so that they do not come to science instruction with a disadvantage. In contrast, Warren and Rosebery (1996) have emphasized the many points of contact between everyday thinking and scientific thinking, which seem to hold for all children, even those whose first language may not be English and whose first culture may not be Anglo-European. In their view, with sensitive instruction children are quite capable of sophisticated forms of inquiry, and the evidence seems to bear out these claims. It may be, however, that the dispute is more apparent than real. The need to be explicit and clear about the forms of argument and evidence valued in science is widely accepted, and there is plenty of evidence that this need is not restricted to students who are struggling. The reason for contrasting Chen and Klahr's position with Metz's is not to suggest that one conclusion necessarily is associated with psychological research and the other with classroom research. It is to make the more general point that in many cases, taking the wider view that an educational perspective demands, leads to a realignment of what is valued, so that design researchers are not simply involved in bringing together in one site interventions that have individually been more thoroughly studied in psychology laboratories.

Whether one thinks it is more useful for purposes of instruction to highlight science as building knowledge or theories, conducting investigations, or generating and testing models, these are probably best regarded as partially overlapping rather than mutually exclusive views of science and science literacy. They may lead to somewhat different commitments with respect to choices of topics of study or classroom activities. Regardless, theory change, inquiry, and modeling are mutually reinforcing. Therefore, any well-formulated program may focus on all of these goals, even though the relative emphasis or proportions of time spent on each may differ. Similarly, there may be differences in what teachers are oriented toward in professional development, perhaps leading to discernibly different results in teachers' practices and student learning. At this point, we do not know.

There is both a normative (What *should* students be learning?) and empirical (How *does* development typically unfold?) aspect to these guiding perspectives. Taking a longer-term developmental view raises questions about what educators should be trying to achieve in the long term and also about the instructional pathways that can best lead students toward these goals from their current conceptual resources. Ideas about instructional pathways should be conceived as rational analyses that require empirical testing. It is impossible to know in advance how students' cognition is likely to develop given the right kinds of instructional support, partly because we cannot know in advance which kinds of instruction are optimal and partly because our initial views of students' capabilities almost always are distorted by knowing the way they usually perform under typical (or lacking) instructional conditions (Brown & Campione, 1996).

For the most part, the research reviewed in this chapter reflects a preference for students doing science over simply learning final-form science concepts. This preference is due not to a naive belief that knowledge is somehow better if it is reinvented by students, but to a commitment to providing opportunities for students to experience one of civilization's most powerful forms of epistemology. We would probably agree that all students should learn to write to some level of fluency, even though few will eventually become employed as professional authors. Similarly, all students should get a taste of doing science, and those opportunities should not be restricted to those bound for careers in science or technology.

The emphasis on doing science, however, does not imply that nobody cares if students learn any scientific knowledge. Without exception, the emphasis in the programs we have reviewed is on doing science for the purpose of building rich, elaborated bases of knowledge. That is why the programs reviewed in this section value extended study within a bounded content domain over broad sampling of science topics. Focusing deeply in a domain provides a base from which students can develop criteria for evaluating their changing theories about the domain and also provides the foundation of knowledge necessary for inquiry to be both fruitful and meaningful. Not all of these researchers, however, have a clear vision of how science content knowledge is expected to cumulate over a student's education, or even whether having such a vision is considered important. Some investigators (e.g., Metz and Gelman) expect that students will sequentially investigate domains of study in depth, one at a time, but they do not say much about what space of domains needs to be visited by the time a student leaves elementary education. Lehrer and Schauble seek scientific and mathematical themes, such as growth, structure and function, and behavior that can connect inquiry across years of schooling. These themes serve as the criteria for selecting specific topics of study. However, Lehrer and Schauble (2005) argue that it is necessary to empirically test conjectures about the themes that best permit easy entry to younger or less sophisticated students and, at the same time, provide abundant curricular challenge for those who are more knowledgeable. Hennessey and Grotzer and Perkins appear to be focused primarily at a more domain-general level on causal schemas and criteria for conceptual change. Presumably, domain knowledge is selected for its exemplification of the variety of causal schemas that students need to learn about or its potential to highlight criteria for theory change.

To varying degrees, all of these investigators place instructional emphasis on one or another form of metacognition. That said, what is meant by metacognition varies somewhat from program to program, and the actual cognitive processes involved may have little or nothing in common. Brown and Campione generally encouraged students to assume responsibility for their own learning, a goal that Metz also adopted but applied in a more focused way to student planning and conduct of empirical investigations. As we have seen, Hennessey wanted students to understand and apply specific evaluative criteria to their own theories and the theories of classmates. This is a view of metacognition that seems more closely related to the one articulated by Grotzer and Perkins, who expected students to notice and describe the causal structure underlying content domains whose surface features varied. Lehrer and Schauble regarded metacognition somewhat differently, as learning to use varying forms of representation that allow one to literally grasp thought, and as putting these representations to use in the service of arguments about qualities of natural systems.

There was widespread agreement on the importance of data representation and other forms of symbolization. Many of these researchers endorsed the value of capitalizing on the variability in students' invented representations. Repeatedly producing, critiquing, and revising representations helps students appreciate the uses and purposes for inscriptions, what they communicate, and the design trade-offs entailed in their construction. In traditional classrooms, students are taught conventional forms for graphing, making tables, drawing maps, and the like, as context-free tools. They may be given a variety of problems to practice on, but these are regarded merely as contexts to serve the primary goal of learning how to construct and use the inscription in its conventional form. In contrast, a theme common to the programs we reviewed is tying education about forms and uses of representation and inscription to contexts of their use. Other tools as well, from scientific instruments to rulers, are introduced when students have encountered a problem that the tool would be helpful in addressing.

Views on the nature of development emphasize continuity from children's early intuitions and theories to their instruction in conventional theories of science disciplines. In distinction to the misconceptions literature in science education, which tends to draw sharp contrasts between students' conceptions and those of experts, these investigators see early theory building as a resource for rather than a barrier to instruction. Attention to the features of learning contexts that optimize development is considered an essential part of an account of development for these researchers, although the extent to which they focus on cataloguing these features varies somewhat. Brown and Campione, with their 39 principles, are probably most exhaustive in their attempt to specify the features that account for developmental change in a classroom context. Across the six projects, a range of features was proposed that varied from the kinds of tasks presented to students (all of the researchers in this section) to the forms of activity repeatedly engaged, the classroom norms, and the kinds of evidence and argument that characterize classroom discourse.

We have briefly described seven classroom design studies organized around investigation of the development of some aspect of scientific thinking. Each was grounded in a particular vision of what develops in scientific thinking and literacy, and each provides at least initial data about the learning potential of the program. However, at this point in time, none of these projects has secured a base of longitudinal research that is extensive enough or has been sustained for a long enough period to permit clear comparisons about the long-term educational consequences of pursuing one design rather than another. We still know little about what we might expect of a student who participates in one of these programs for an extended period. What capabilities or propensities would this student develop, and what forms of practice would he or she master that graduates from the other programs might not? From a design perspective, the point of having longitudinal comparative data would be not to find out which approach is best, in the simple sense of winning a horse race, but to better understand the characteristic profile of strengths and weaknesses of each, so that choices about educational directions can be informed by their fit to more clearly articulated values. Do some of these programs provide a smoother transition to becoming a generally literate citizen, whereas others provide a better pathway to the professional practice of science? Do some do a better job than others of providing foundational tools that will pay off consistently over the scope of a child's education? What does each approach emphasize, and what does it tend to move to the background?

We now know something about how education starts off under these approaches and a little about how it proceeds, but we know little or nothing about how it ends up many years down the road. In the final section of the chapter, we seek to understand what it takes to build and sustain conditions that permit the acquisition of comparative data of this sort. This question is pursued in the context of discussing the implementation challenges of conducting classroom design research.

IMPLEMENTATION ISSUES IN DESIGN STUDIES: WHY AREN'T WE MAKING FASTER PROGRESS?

Why is it so difficult to conduct the kind of longitudinal, comparative work that can inform educational decisions about science literacy in a systematic, scientific way? There are both conceptual and logistical challenges to developing and refining educational programs that are informed by developmental theory and research, sustaining those programs in ways that preserve and extend their educational integrity, and assessing learning in organizational systems that are both highly changeable and politically sensitive. Rather than discussing these implementation issues in general, we will view them through the lens of our own work. As explained earlier, information about these matters is seldom openly discussed. Therefore, we resort here to our own experience, trusting that it is more common than uncommon.

Challenge 1: Developing and Refining the Design

Although previous and concurrent research can be of help in identifying likely starting points for children's learning, learning research insufficiently constrains educational design. A significant amount of conceptual and empirical work is required to develop and refine an educational design that can foster long-term development. The more extensive the target of educational concern, the more conceptual and empirical work is required to cash in, test, and revise the elements of the educational design. Careful consideration of what is to be done, day by day, does not follow obviously and smoothly from a few key principles or even from hypothetical prospective trajectories of student learning. For instance, deciding that we intend to support the development of model-based reasoning in children, that we will seek to build on early origins of this form of thinking, and that we will systematically provide mathematical resources, representational tools, and appropriate classroom norms still leaves us with the need to make day-to-day decisions about how to accomplish these goals. If the means are wrong, it will not matter if the principles are right.

The instantiation of an educational design routinely requires the revision of initial plans and assumptions. Students have a way of getting stuck on forms of learning that seem relatively straightforward until one tries to help children achieve them, or to the contrary, of readily producing forms of thinking that seemed unlikely on first consideration. At key points during instruction, it is necessary to be able to predict the near landscape of educational possibilities most likely to unfold and to foretell the consequences of following one or another path through this landscape (Lehrer &

Schauble, 2001). Developing this kind of knowledge requires replicating the "same" lesson sequences—while exploring key variants—on multiple occasions and often at different grades. Cross-grade study helps us better understand both what is developing and the likely pathways of development.

For example, we deliberately adopted a developmental focus with the previously described study of data classification (Lehrer & Schauble, 2000b), in which children developed models to predict the age of the artists of a series of self-portraits. This investigation was conducted in grades 1, 4, and 5. The first graders readily classified the portraits by the presumed grade of the artist and identified the features that they felt differentiated the pictures drawn by kindergarteners ("dinosaur" hair, no feet) from those drawn by fifth graders ("lots of detail," all five fingers). However, their classification systems were merely post hoc descriptions applied to decisions they had already made via casual inspection. Tellingly, they did not use their feature lists to make predictions about a set of novel portraits. Therefore, to the first graders, the lists did not really serve as models at all. In contrast, the fourth graders did develop models and apply them to support predictions, but it took many attempts to use the models and rounds of subsequent revision before students came to prefer models that did not include extraneous detail. These fourth graders struggled with the idea that a model that did not include all discernible information about a portrait might be preferable to one that did. Fifth graders not only eliminated features that were not predictive from their models; they even developed quantitative estimates of the predictive power of their features ("A portrait drawn by a fifth grader is twice as likely to have eyelashes as it is to have shoes with shoelaces"; "Two thirds of the time, a fourth-grade portrait will include eyelashes").

To the extent feasible, we replicate instructional sequences to understand more about what is repeatable, what varies, and what routes development typically takes. Our purpose is to achieve a clearer understanding of what constitutes the intervention. That is, what is essential to produce desired outcomes and what is peripheral? What variations in features still produce similar results, and what forms of variation fundamentally change the character of the outcomes? What is the permissible window of variability of each key feature within which we would judge that the intervention maintains its integrity? Failing to understand these issues, we believe, accounts for much of the difficulty experienced in attempting to "scale up" educational interventions—much of the time, what is being "scaled" is only dimly understood. For this reason, we seek to understand the generalization (and generativity) of a pathway of learning by investigating how lesson sequences play out with a variety of different student and teacher populations. We attempt to replicate within and across grades in a participating school, across schools in a district, and across sites. Portions of our work have been replicated in both suburban and urban school districts in the upper Midwest, in Phoenix, Arizona, and currently in Nashville, Tennessee. Yet replicating educational interventions that extend over several years is a very slow process, one that should be pursued before comparative trials are undertaken. At a minimum, they involve considerable challenges in assisting teachers' professional development to a level where the intervention can be reliably produced. Treating a program as if it were transparent to teachers is an invitation to the kinds of lethal mutations discussed earlier.

Challenge 2: Implementing and Sustaining the Program and Its Integrity

So far, we have been discussing the conceptual challenges involved in identifying the defining features of an educational program. There are equally daunting logistical challenges, which require solutions that are every bit as intellectually demanding. These solutions are costly in terms of both researcher time and resources, and our training typically does not equip us to address problems of this kind. First among the implementation challenges is the difficulty of marshaling and maintaining capacity to do this kind of work within our own organizational setting, in this case, the university.

The education of graduate students poses challenges. Rather than introducing students in a gentle way to well-understood and routine procedures, we must help graduate students learn within and make productive contributions to an enterprise that is under continual evolution. One is always updating newcomers of all kinds (staff as well as students) to an ongoing effort that existed before they came and will extend beyond their tenure. Participants at all levels need to continually recalculate the relationships between the part of the project in which their contributions are made and the larger enterprise in which it resides. These features of the research sometimes generate difficulties for the indoctrination and socialization of new students into this form of research.

Classroom design research requires interdisciplinary teams and multiple forms of talent that are unlikely to reside within one individual. We have found it helpful to form collaborations with individuals from other disciplines: in-service teachers and school administrators, of course, but also biologists, mathematicians, and psychometricians. Identifying and coordinating multiple participants and forms of expertise over extended time periods is a goal that does not always align well with the expectations of university promotion and tenure committees, resources and cycles of funding agencies, or colleagues' existing disciplinary allegiances. We have needed to play multiple roles ourselves, including educator, professional development provider, and community politician, in addition to education researcher.

Sometimes these roles involve managing contingencies as they emerge and cannot be identified in principle beforehand. For example, our decade-long program of work in a school district was preceded by a decade of work that one of us conducted in classrooms in that district. This earlier work involved coming to be seen as a member of the school district by teachers, administrators, and parents. It entailed countless conversations "in the cracks" that gradually built trust, so that stakeholders, especially teachers, did not perceive research as something done to them and their children. Some of these events might be viewed as extraordinary, even bizarre, from some perspectives. For example, one parent was concerned that the screen image of the Logo programming language might be a form of idolatry prohibited by her religion. Concerns like this were not anticipated by the researcher but, nonetheless, had to be addressed in ways that preserved the integrity of all concerned. An outcome of this previous work was increased capacity for teacher leadership, so that teachers were prepared to build on the changes they had already begun. This preparation served as an essential foundation to the research we described; without it, it is highly unlikely that we would have been able to achieve significant levels of student learning within a 3-year period. Hence, this history proved relevant to the conduct of the research program, but it also raised the problem of identifying which aspects of history should be judged relevant when reporting current design research.

Schools, of course, are daunting organizations in which to pursue research, especially if they are organized around an educational change agenda. This is particularly the case in today's climate of politicized education. The leadership in most districts is unstable, schools are vulnerable to all sorts of competing political pressures, and their goals and activities are publicly contested. In our work, we have struggled with an array of havoc-producing events, including the resignation of a supportive superintendent, a shift in the school board's political affiliation, the serious illness of a teacher-leader's young child, internal disagreements among the faculty (e.g., over whether to pursue *looping,* in which teachers graduate with their students across one or more grades, or multiage classes). We are confident that other classroom researchers have similar tales to tell. The legitimate agendas of schools often inadvertently put them at cross-purposes to the goals of the research. At one site, we were making good progress at consolidating a cross-grade team of like-minded teachers who had worked for several years together on professional development oriented around the study of student learning. Over the years, the group had achieved strong community affiliation and had amassed impressive technical knowledge about the development of student thinking, achievements that were central to our shared goal of supporting a systematic and consistent approach to mathematics and science education. However, this district was one of the fastest growing in the state. As the district expanded, it became necessary to build a new elementary school. To our dismay and that of the teachers, administrators moved several of the participating teachers to the new school to colonize the reform in this new site. Although the intentions were noble—administrators hoped to see these new forms of teaching spread more widely—the result was the disruption of the cross-grade community and our capability to follow students longitudinally across grades in which the experimental instruction was being implemented. Even when radical changes of this kind are not occurring, the degree of teacher and student mobility that is typical of American schools makes longitudinal research difficult to sustain.

Within the past several years, we have found the politics of education to be especially disruptive to any agenda that includes systematic capacity building. Lack of consensus over the role and form of education leaves teachers highly vulnerable to disagreements about standards, testing, curriculum, grading, student grouping, and almost every other aspect of education. It is not uncommon for the major focus of a district's educational effort to shift suddenly in response to a biannual school board election or the arrival of a new member of the administrative staff. Mandatory testing is now highly consequential for both students and teachers, yet national and state tests lag behind curricular innovation. Hence, research and development aimed at upping the ante for what is taught and learned may not show up on widely accepted measures. Under these circumstances, it is difficult to maintain the sustained focus required to effect educational improvement.

Sometimes logistical and conceptual difficulties become intertwined, for example, the problem of deciding whether the educational program has, in fact, been implemented. All change in schools is uneven, and at any point in time it is far from complete, even if the change has been supported or even mandated by district leadership. Some teachers are early adopters who become essential to the maintenance of the program; others hang on the periphery. Some are enthusiastic about the program but never achieve more than a superficial understanding of it; some resist in active or passive ways. This unevenness of implementation poses problems for the research, especially if the design includes comparison between schools or classrooms that are and are not considered participants. How much and what kinds of participation make a teacher a participant?

In sum, design researchers do not just need to address the conceptual and measurement problems involved in changing and studying the long-term development of learning. In addition, they must cultivate and maintain relationships with the research site, a role that usually includes providing the forms of professional development that support desired forms of teaching and learning. (Professional development that produces generative change in teachers' practice is a difficult and important goal to which an entire base of literature is devoted. See, e.g., Grossman, 1990; Palincsar, Magnussun, Marano, Ford, & Brown, 1998.) Researchers must assist the participating site in managing change, a process that is not always comfortable and that may perturb roles and identities for some individuals. Developing a test bed for extended research is a full-time job in itself. The effort invested in this enterprise means that it is not feasible to step away from site activity to spend a year in uninterrupted analysis of data. One cannot wave goodbye to a school that has come to depend on your support, leaving teachers and students with a promise that you will return when the sabbatical is completed or the book written. Although change may become self-sustaining over time, it is impossible to predict in advance when this will occur, as the organization and constraints of schooling are powerful forces that operate continually to push teaching and learning back into their more conventional forms. As Spillane (2000) and others have demonstrated, educational reforms usually get assimilated into the patterns of knowledge and practice that preexist in a school, with the result that they are often distorted and rendered sterile.

Challenge 3: Assessing Learning

In these classroom investigations, it is necessary to coordinate fine-grained studies of change in individual students (to identify typical strategies and typical forms of change over time) with coarser-grained measures of achievement in groups of students. The finer-grained studies are required to learn more about the development of scientific thinking that is taken by researchers to be the desirable core of scientific literacy, whether the focus is on change in theories, in students' capabilities to conduct self-regulated investigations, or to engage in modeling practices. As suggested earlier, studies of development that span multiple years pose significant measurement problems because at the outset, little solid evidence exists about how thinking develops when it is systematically supported in an educational context. Therefore, it is unclear when one should look for expected benchmark changes. Coarser-grained studies of student achievement must simultaneously address educators' and parents' concerns about performance on assessments that are consequential with respect to progress, graduation, and college, and at the same time must be sensitive to the goals that are specific to the design.

In our work, we found that developing, revising, and retuning the achievement measures constituted a psychometric project of considerable scope. First, there were no measures of long-term development for the forms of thinking we wished to study (e.g., students' representational competence, spatial visualization, data interpretation, statistical reasoning). Therefore, we developed and/or borrowed items based on our own and others' previous research and initial conjectures about likely forms and rates of student learning. In advance, we were not always able to accurately foretell when it would be reasonable to expect particular benchmark changes. As the educational design unfolded, it was frequently necessary to recalibrate the measures, leading to some undesirable shift from year to year in the data we could collect. Other data collection problems followed from student mobility, the bane of longitudinal designs.

Students who studied in collaborating classrooms for 2 contiguous years constituted a reasonably large proportion of our sample, but the proportions of those in project classrooms for 3 years in a row or longer dropped considerably.

There were design issues that followed from the problem of how to identify a fair comparison. The difficulties of accounting for teacher effects and differences in student populations are well established in education research, and these are certainly contributors to the complications of understanding variation in the design, as described earlier. But these difficulties are not just logistical; they are also conceptual. We do not favor control groups that do not control for anything in particular, and moreover, we felt it unlikely that we could persuade teachers in comparison classrooms to spend 3 hours per year testing students on difficult forms of mathematics that they had never studied. Rather than setting up strawperson comparisons of experimental classrooms with those that pursue business as usual, we feel that much more could be learned if the field would pursue a collaborative assessment strategy. Specifically, we hope that in the near future it will be possible to compare the development of student thinking across a few key design studies that vary in interesting ways. The overall strategy would be to develop and use a negotiated common bank of items to assess the learning of students enrolled in different research programs. Because each lead researcher could identify the features theoretically considered central to his or her intervention, the results of such a comparison would be more informative than a typical experimental versus traditional instruction comparison. Presumably, the results would show characteristically different patterns of strengths and weaknesses associated with identifiable instructional approaches. In our opinion, this kind of comparison is a potentially powerful strategy for better understanding the developmental affordances of different designs. We might find, for example, that some approaches produce impressive results in the short term, but others do a far better job over the long haul of producing and sustaining valued outcomes.

Challenge 4: Explaining Contingency

Although design studies offer new opportunities for educational inquiry, they differ from more traditional kinds of study in their purpose, scope, and form of explanation. Like evolutionary biologists and practitioners in some other disciplines (see, e.g., Rudolph & Stewart,

1998), researchers engaged in explaining extended inter-relationships between instruction and learning need to account for phenomena that are contingent and historical. Because classroom learning has this character, an important goal for research is to identify and explain the contingencies that the design accounts for—in other words, the patterns of learning and change that, broadly speaking, can reliably be expected to emerge if the design is instantiated. These contingencies need to be teased out from the broad array of features that are not accounted for in the explanatory structure (Lehrer & Schauble, 2001).

One way that researchers address this problem is to generate a set of conjectures that, collectively, take the form of a learning trajectory or pathway. Collectively, these conjectures form a hypothesized sequence or route, one that describes our best-informed guesses of how students typically progress along the path from less expert to more expert forms of thinking. The sequence is conjectural because design studies are typically employed to investigate the teaching and learning of unexplored or underexplored content. For that reason, one cannot be confident that the trajectory will play out as foreseen. Although less detailed and broader in scope, a learning trajectory is a little like an instructional task analysis in cognitive psychology. Its purpose is to guide the overall direction of instruction in domains in which little research currently exists to inform teaching and learning. Accordingly, a learning trajectory embodies one's best bets (informed by research, general knowledge of children's thinking, and reconceptualization of central ideas in the relevant domain) about how development is likely to occur. Of course, as instruction based on a hypothetical learning trajectory is instantiated, the trajectory needs to be revised in real time, in response to what one is learning in the classroom.

Although this brief description captures the general purposes and processes of design studies, there is some danger to taking the analogy too literally. The metaphors of "developmental corridors" and "learning trajectories" do not foreground contingency and variability, which we have argued are very important to understand. What comes to mind when one thinks of "corridor" is an invariant and circumscribed path from a particular beginning place to a known goal. Thinking of development as a path supports the sense of going from somewhere to somewhere else but does not capture the kind of variability in student thinking and performance that often serves as a fundamental mechanism of change.

For this reason, it may be more accurate to conceive of development as an ecology that emerges in interactions determined (in part) by the learning opportunities and constraints of tasks, semiotic means (e.g., tools, systems of inscription), recurrent activity structures, and the ways teachers or other members of the community recruit, select, and enhance the contributions of participants (see Lehrer, Strom, & Confrey, 2002).

From this perspective, corridors or trajectories are retrospective accounts of particular realizations of this prospective space of interaction. Designing for education must encourage emergence and variability or else risk pruning the potential for development to sanctioned pathways. Faced with such complexity, educators can choose the path for students and use teaching assistance primarily to minimize straying from the predetermined route. Or instead, one can foster and encourage variability in student thinking and then capitalize on the local opportunities that emerge from it. In that case, the design problem is to craft situations and tasks that are most likely to produce forms of variability that are rich with instructional potential. Of course, one needs an overall vision of where instruction is headed, but that vision can be an elastic one, modifiable at all points by an ongoing assessment of what next move best capitalizes on the contingencies that emerge in the classroom. We argue that this approach is best for capitalizing on students' cognitive resources and performances, but it admittedly makes it more difficult to explain conceptual change. If one reconceives of variability not as error or noise but as grist for development (Siegler, 1996), then documenting and accounting for contingency become an essential part of the research enterprise.

For purposes of tractability, we often ignore these contingencies; indeed, much research is designed so that we can safely do so. But explaining learning entails explaining a phenomenon that is fundamentally historical. Students come to classrooms with learning histories, and moreover, teachers seek to build on those histories. If they succeed, those histories coalesce into enduring propensities and capabilities of the kind that we sometimes call "development." Effective learning does not simply cumulate; instead, later learning transforms what we knew earlier on. Understanding development means understanding those histories, not just their shape, but also their causes. Indeed, the internal psychological characteristics of the learner are important mechanisms, but to understand how scientific thinking and scientific literacy take shape, instruction and other forms of assistance must also be accounted for. One cannot understand these forms of development without understanding the means by which they are supported. In that sense, an account of development is an account of its history. As Gopnik and Metlzoff (1997) explain:

> Like Darwinian biology, the view presented here suggests that explanations in cognitive science will often be historical and contingent. If we want to say why we have a conceptual structure of a particular kind, we will typically not be able to reduce that structure to some set of first principles. Rather, we will need to trace the historical route that led from our innate theories to the theory we currently hold. On this view, all of cognitive science would be developmental. (p. 218)

Recognizing contingency is an important first step. Developing sound models of history is an enduring challenge.

REFERENCES

American Association for the Advancement of Science (1964). *Science: A process approach*. Annapolis Junction, MD: Author.

Baillargeon, R. (1987). Young infants' reasoning about the physical and spatial characteristics of a hidden object. *Cognitive Development, 2*(4), 179–200.

Baillargeon, R., & Graber, M. (1988). Evidence of location memory in 8-month-old infants in a nonsearch AB task. *Developmental Psychology, 24*(4), 502–511.

Baillargeon, R., & Hanko-Summers, S. (1990). Is the top object adequately supported by the bottom object? Young infants' understanding of support relations. *Cognitive Development, 5*(1), 29–54.

Bazerman, C. (1988). *Shaping written knowledge: The genre and activity of the experimental article in science*. Madison: University of Wisconsin Press.

Beeth, M. E., & Hewson, P. W. (1999). Learning goals in an exemplary science teacher's practice: Cognitive and social factors in teaching for conceptual change. *Science Education, 83*, 738–760.

Bransford, J. D., Vye, N., Kinzer, C., & Risko, V. (1990). Teaching thinking and content knowledge: Toward an integrated approach. In B. F. Jomes & L. Idol (Eds.), *Symbolizing, communicating, and mathematizing: Perspectives on discourse, tools, and instructional design* (pp. 275–324). Mahwah, NJ: Erlbaum.

Brown, A. L. (1990). Domain-specific principles affect learning and transfer in children. *Cognitive Science, 14*(1), 107–133.

Brown, A. L. (1992). Design experiments: Theoretical and methodological challenges in evaluating complex interventions in classroom settings. *Journal of the Learning Sciences, 2*, 141–178.

Brown, A. L., & Campione, J. C. (1994). Guided discovery in a community of learners. In K. McGilly (Ed.), *Classroom lessons: Integrating cognitive theory and classroom practice* (pp. 229–270). Cambridge, MA: MIT Press.

Brown, A. L., & Campione, J. (1996). Psychological theory and the design of innovative learning environments: On procedures, principles, and systems. In L. Schauble & R. Glaser (Eds.), *Innova-*

tions in learning: New environments for education (pp. 289–326). Hillsdale, NJ: Erlbaum.

Brown, A. L., & DeLoache, J. (1978). Skills, plans, and self-regulation. In R. S. Siegler (Ed.), *Children's thinking: What develops?* (pp. 3–36). Hillsdale, NJ: Erlbaum.

Brown, A. L., & Reeves, R. (1987). Bandwidths of competence: The role of supportive contexts in learning and development. In L. Liben (Ed.), *Development and learning: Conflict or congruence?* (pp. 173–221). Hillsdale, NJ: Erlbaum.

Bruner, J. S., Goodnow, J. J., & Austin, G. A. (1956). *A study of thinking*. New York: Wiley.

Bullock, M., Gelman, R., & Baillargeon, R. (1982). The development of causal reasoning. In W. J. Friedman (Ed.), *The developmental psychology of time* (pp. 209–254). New York: Academic Press.

Bullock, M., & Ziegler, A. (1999). Scientific reasoning: Developmental and individual differences. In F.E. Weinert & W. Schneider (Eds.), *Individual development from 3 to 12: Findings from the Munich longitudinal study* (pp. 38–54). Cambridge, England: Cambridge University Press.

Carey, S. (1985a). Are children fundamentally different kinds of thinkers than adults? In S. Chipman, J. Segal, & R. Glaser (Eds.), *Thinking and learning skills* (Vol. 2, pp. 485–518). Hillsdale, NJ: Erlbaum.

Carey, S. (1985b). *Conceptual change in childhood*. Cambridge, MA: MIT Press.

Carey, S., Evans, R., Honda, M., Jay, E., & Unger, C. (1989). An experiment is when you try it and see if it works: A study of grade 7 students' understanding of the construction of scientific knowledge. *International Journal of Science Education, 11*, 514–529.

Carey, S., & Smith, C. (1993). On understanding the nature of scientific knowledge. *Educational Psychologist, 28*, 235–251.

Case, R., & Griffin, S. (1990). Child cognitive development: The role of central conceptual structures in the development of scientific and social thought. In E. A. Hauert (Ed.), *Developmental psychology: Cognitive, perceptuo-motor, and neurological perspectives* (pp. 193–230). Amsterdam, The Netherlands: Elsevier.

Chen, Z., & Klahr, D. (1999). All other things being equal: Acquisition and transfer of the control of variables strategy. *Child Development, 70*(5), 1098–1120.

Chi, M. T. (1992). Conceptual change within and across ontological categories: Examples from learning and discovery in science. In R. Giere (Ed.), *Cognitive models of science: Minnesota studies in the philosophy of science* (pp. 129–186). Minneapolis: University of Minnesota Press.

Cobb, P., Confrey, J., diSessa, A., Lehrer, R., & Schauble, L. (2003). Design experiments in education. *Educational Researcher, 32*(1), 9–13.

DeLoache, J. S. (2004). Becoming symbol-minded. *Trends in Cognitive Sciences, 8*(2), 66–70.

DeLoache, J. S., Pierroutsakos, S. L., & Uttal, D. H. (2003). The origins of pictorial competence. *Current Directions in Psychological Science, 12*(4), 114–118.

diSessa, A. A. (1993). Toward an epistemology of physics. *Cognition and Instruction, 10*(2/3), 105–225.

diSessa, A. A. (2002). Students' criteria for representational adequacy. In K. Gravemeijer, R. Lehrer, B. van Oers, & L. Verschaffel (Eds.), *Symbolizing, modeling and tool use in mathematics education* (pp. 105–129). Dordrecht, The Netherlands: Kluwer Press.

diSessa, A. A. (2004). Metarepresentation: Native competence and targets for instruction. *Cognition and Instruction, 22*, 293–331.

diSessa, A., Hammer, D., Sherin, B., & Kolpakowski, T. (1991). Inventing graphing: Meta-representational expertise in children. *Journal of Mathematical Behavior, 10,* 117–160.

Dow, P. B. (1991). *Schoolhouse politics: Lessons from the Sputnik era.* Cambridge, MA: Harvard University Press.

Driver, R., Leach, J., Millar, R., & Scott, P. (1996). *Young people's images of science.* Buckingham, England: Open University Press.

Dunbar, K. (1993). Scientific reasoning strategies for concept discovery in a complex domain. *Cognitive Science, 17*(3), 397–434.

Dunbar, K. (1998). How scientists really reason: Scientific reasoning in real-world laboratories. In R. J. Sternberg & J. F. Davidson (Eds.), *The nature of insight* (pp. 265–395). Cambridge, MA: MIT Press.

Duschl, R. A. (1990). *Restructuring science education: The importance of theories and their developments.* New York: Teachers College Press.

Fay, A., & Klahr, D. (1996). Knowing about guessing and guessing about knowing: Preschoolers' understanding of indeterminacy. *Child Development, 67,* 689–716.

Ford, M. J. (2004). *The game, the pieces, and the players: Coherent dimensions of transfer from alternative instructional portrayals of experimentation.* Manuscript submitted for publication.

Galison, P., & Assmus, A. (1989). Artificial clouds, real particles. In D. Gooding, T. Pinch, & S. Schaffer (Eds.), *The uses of experiment: Studies on the natural sciences* (pp. 225–274). Cambridge, England: Cambridge University Press.

Gallistel, C. R., Brown, A. L., Carey, S., Gelman, R., & Keil, F. C. (1991). Lessons from animal learning for the study of cognitive development. In S. Carey & R. Gelman (Eds.), *The epigenesis of mind* (pp. 3–36). Hillsdale, NJ: Erlbaum.

Gee, J. P., & Green, J. (1998). Discourse analysis, learning, and social practice: A methodological study. *Review of Research in Education, 23,* 119–169.

Gelman, R., & Baillargeon, R. (1983). A review of some Piagetian concepts. In J. H. Flavell & E. M. Markman (Eds.), *Cognitive development* (pp. 167–230). New York: Wiley.

Gelman, R., & Brenneman, K. (2004). Science learning pathways for young children. *Early Childhood Research Quarterly, 19*(1), 150–158.

Gelman, R., Romo, L., & Francis, W. S. (2002). Notebooks as windows on learning: The case of a science-into-ESL program. In N. Granott & J. Parziale (Eds.), *Microdevelopment: Transition processes in development and learning* (pp. 269–293). Cambridge, England: Cambridge University Press.

Giere, R. N. (1988). *Explaining science: A cognitive approach.* Chicago: University of Chicago Press.

Gooding, D. (1989). "Magnetic curves" and the magnetic field: Experimentation and representation in the history of a theory. In D. Gooding, T. Pinch, & S. Schaffer (Eds.), *The uses of experiment: Studies on the natural sciences* (pp. 183–223). Cambridge, England: Cambridge University Press.

Gooding, D. (1990). *Experiment and the making of meaning.* Dordrecht, The Netherlands: Kluwer Press.

Goodwin, C. (1994). Professional vision. *American Anthropologist, 96*(3), 606–633.

Gopnik, A., & Meltzoff, A. N. (1997). *Words, thoughts, and theories.* Cambridge, MA: MIT Press.

Gopnik, A., & Sobel, D. M. (2000). Detecting blickets: How young children use information about novel causal powers in categorization and induction. *Child Development, 71*(5), 1205–1222.

Gopnik, A., Sobel, D. M., Schulz, L. E., & Glymour, C. (2001). Causal learning mechanisms in very young children: Two-, three-, and four-year-olds infer causal relations from patterns of variation and covariation. *Developmental Psychology, 37*(5), 620–629.

Greeno, J., & Hall, R. (1997, January). Practicing representation: Learning with and about representational forms. *Phi Delta Kappan,* 361–367.

Grosslight, L., Unger, C., Jay, E., & Smith, C. (1991). Understanding models and their use in science: Conceptions of middle and high school students and experts. *Journal of Research in Science Teaching, 28,* 799–822.

Grossman, P. (1990). *The making of a teacher: Teacher knowledge and teacher education.* New York: Teachers College Press.

Grotzer, T. A. (2000, April). *How conceptual leaps in understanding the nature of causality can limit learning: An example from electrical concepts.* Paper presented at the annual meeting of the American Educational Research Association, New Orleans, LA.

Grotzer, T. A. (2003, March). *Transferring structural knowledge about the nature of causality: An empirical test of three levels of transfer.* Paper presented at the annual meeting of the National Association of Research in Science Teaching, Philadelphia, PA.

Hennessey, M. G. (2002). Metacognitive aspects of students' reflective discourse: Implications for intentional conceptual change teaching and learning. In G. M. Sinatra & P. R. Pintrich (Eds.), *Intentional conceptual change* (pp. 103–132). Mahwah, NJ: Erlbaum.

Hesse, M. B. (1974). *The structure of scientific inference.* Berkeley: University of California Press.

Hestenes, D. (1992). Modeling games in the Newtonian world. *American Journal of Physics, 60*(8), 732–748.

Hewson, P. W., & Hewson, M. G. (1992). The status of students' conceptions. In R. Duit, F. Goldburg, & H. Niedderer (Eds.), *Research in physics learning: Theoretical issues and empirical studies* (pp. 59–73). Kiel, Germany: University of Kiel, Institute for Science Education.

Hood, B., Carey, S., & Prasada, S. (2000). Predicting the outcomes of physical events: Two-year-olds fail to reveal knowledge of solidity and support. *Child Development, 71*(6), 1540–1554.

Horvath, J., & Lehrer, R. (1998). A model-based perspective on the development of children's understanding of chance and uncertainty. In S. P. Lajoie (Ed.), *Reflections on statistics: Learning, teaching, and assessment in grades K to 12* (pp. 121–148). Mahwah, NJ: Erlbaum.

Inhelder, B., & Piaget, J. (1958). *The growth of logical thinking from childhood to adolescence.* New York: Basic Books.

Kaiser, D. (2000). Stick-figure realism: Conventions, reification, and the persistence of Feynman diagrams, 1948–1964. *Representations, 70,* 49–86.

Karmiloff-Smith, A. (1992). *Beyond modularity: A developmental perspective on cognitive science.* Cambridge, MA: MIT Press.

Keil, F. C. (1992). The origins of an autonomous biology. In M. R. Gunnan & M. Maratsos (Eds.), *Minnesota Symposia on Child Psychology: Modularity and constraints on language and cognition* (pp. 103–137). Hillsdale, NJ: Erlbaum.

Klahr, D. (2000). *Exploring science: The cognition and development of discovery processes.* Cambridge, MA: MIT Press.

Klahr, D., & Dunbar, K. (1988). Dual search space during scientific reasoning. *Cognitive Science, 12,* 1–55.

Klahr, D., Fay, A. L., & Dunbar, K. (1993). Heuristics for scientific experimentation: A developmental study. *Cognitive Psychology, 25*(1), 111–146.

Klahr, D., & Nigam, M. (2004). The equivalence of learning paths in early science instruction. *Psychological Science, 15*(10), 661–667.

Kline, M. (1980). *Mathematics: The loss of certainty.* Oxford: Oxford University Press.

Koslowski, B. (1996). *Theory and evidence: The development of scientific reasoning.* Cambridge, MA: MIT Press.

Kuhn, D. (1989). Children and adults as intuitive scientists. *Psychological Review, 96*(4), 674–689.

Kuhn, D., Amsel, E. D., & O'Loughlin, M. (1988). *The development of scientific thinking skills.* New York: Academic Press.

Kuhn, D., Black, J., Keselman, A., & Kaplan, D. (2000). The development of cognitive skills to support inquiry learning. *Cognition and Instruction, 18*(4), 495–523.

Kuhn, D., Garcia-Mila, M., Zohar, A., & Andersen, C. (1995). Strategies of knowledge acquisition. *Monographs of the Society for Research in Child Development, 60*(4, Serial No. 245), 1–128.

Kuhn, D., & Phelps, E. (1982). The development of problem solving strategies. In H. Reese (Ed.), *Advances in child development and behavior* (Vol. 17, pp. 1–44). New York: Academic Press.

Kuhn, D., Schauble, L., & Garcia-Mila, M. (1992). Cross-domain development of scientific reasoning. *Cognition and Instruction, 9*(4), 285–327.

Kuhn, T. S. (1962). *The structure of scientific revolutions.* Chicago: University of Chicago Press.

Lamon, M., Secules, T., Petrosino, A. J., Hackett, R., Bransford, J. D., & Goldman, S. R. (1996). Schools for Thought: Overview of the project and lessons learned from one of the sites. In L. Schauble & R. Glaser (Eds.), *Innovations in learning: New environments for education* (pp. 243–288). Mahwah, NJ: Erlbaum.

Lampert, M. (2001). *Teaching problems and the problems of teaching.* New Haven: Yale University Press.

Latour, B. (1990). Drawing things together. In M. Lynch & S. Woolgar (Eds.), *Representation in scientific practice* (pp. 19–68). Cambridge, MA: MIT Press.

Latour, B. (1999). *Pandora's hope: Essays on the reality of science studies.* London: Cambridge University Press.

Latour, B., & Woolgar, S. (1979). *Laboratory life: The construction of scientific facts.* Princeton, NJ: Princeton University Press.

Lee, O., & Fradd, S. H. (1996). Literacy skills in science learning among linguistically diverse students. *Science Education, 80*(6), 651–671.

Lehrer, R., Carpenter, S., Schauble, L., & Putz, A. (2000). Designing classrooms that support inquiry. In J. Minstrell & E. van Zee (Eds.), *Inquiring into inquiry learning and teaching in science* (pp. 80–99). Washington, DC: American Association for the Advancement of Science.

Lehrer, R., & Chazan, D. (Eds.). (1998). *Designing learning environments for developing understanding of geometry and space.* Mahwah, NJ: Erlbaum.

Lehrer, R., Jacobson, C., Kemeny, V., & Strom, D. (1999). Building on children's intuitions to develop mathematical understanding of space. In E. Fennema & T. A. Romberg (Eds.), *Mathematics classrooms that promote understanding* (pp. 63–87). Mahwah, NJ: Erlbaum.

Lehrer, R., Jacobson, C., Thoyre, G., Kemeny, V., Danneker, D., Horvath, J., et al. (1998). Developing understanding of space and geometry in the primary grades. In R. Lehrer & D. Chazan (Eds.), *Designing learning environments for developing under-standing of geometry and space* (pp. 169–200). Mahwah, NJ: Erlbaum.

Lehrer, R., & Lesh, R. (2003). Mathematical learning. In W. Reynolds & G. Miller (Eds.), *Handbook of psychology: Vol. 7. Educational psychology* (pp. 357–391). Hoboken, NJ: Wiley.

Lehrer, R., & Romberg, T. (1996). Exploring children's data modeling. *Cognition and Instruction, 14*(1), 69–108.

Lehrer, R., & Schauble, L. (2000a). The development of model-based reasoning. *Journal of Applied Developmental Psychology, 21*(1), 39–48.

Lehrer, R., & Schauble, L. (2000b). Inventing data structures for representational purposes: Elementary grade students' classification models. *Mathematical Thinking and Learning, 2*(1/2), 51–74.

Lehrer, R., & Schauble, L. (2000c). Modeling in mathematics and science. In R. Glaser (Ed.), *Advances in instructional psychology: Vol. 5. Educational design and cognitive science* (pp. 101–159). Mahwah, NJ: Erlbaum.

Lehrer, R., & Schauble, L. (2001, April). *Accounting for contingency in design experiments.* Paper presented at the annual meeting of the American Educational Research Association, Seattle, WA.

Lehrer, R., & Schauble, L. (2002). Symbolic communication in mathematics and science: Co-constituting inscription and thought. In E. D. Amsel & J. Byrnes (Eds.), *The development of symbolic communication* (pp. 167–192). Mahwah, NJ: Erlbaum.

Lehrer, R., & Schauble, L. (2003). Origins and evolution of model-based reasoning in mathematics and science. In R. Lesh & H. M. Doerr (Eds.), *Beyond constructivism: A models and modeling perspective on mathematics problem-solving, learning, and teaching* (pp. 59–70). Mahwah, NJ: Erlbaum.

Lehrer, R., & Schauble, L. (2004). Modeling natural variation through distribution. *American Educational Research Journal, 41*(3), 635–679.

Lehrer, R., & Schauble, L. (2005). Developing modeling and argument in the elementary grades. In T. Romberg & T. P. Carpenter (Eds.), *Understanding mathematics and science matters* (pp. 29–53). Mahwah, NJ: Erlbaum.

Lehrer, R., Schauble, L., Carpenter, S., & Penner, D. E. (2000). The inter-related development of inscriptions and conceptual understanding. In P. Cobb, E. Yackel, & K. McClain (Eds.), *Symbolizing and communicating in mathematics classrooms: Perspectives on discourse, tools, and instructional design* (pp. 325–360). Mahwah, NJ: Erlbaum.

Lehrer, R., Schauble, L., & Petrosino, A. J. (2001). Reconsidering the role of experiment in science education. In K. Crowley, C. D. Schunn, & T. Okada (Eds.), *Designing for science: Implications from everyday, classroom, and professional settings* (pp. 251–278). Mahwah, NJ: Erlbaum.

Lehrer, R., Schauble, L., Strom, D., & Pligge, M. (2001). Similarity of form and substance: Modeling material kind. In S. M. Carver & D. Klahr (Eds.), *Cognition and instruction: Twenty-five years of progress* (pp. 39–74). Mahwah, NJ: Erlbaum.

Lehrer, R., Strom, D., & Confrey, J. (2002). Grounding metaphors and inscriptional resonance: Children's emerging understanding of mathematical similarity. *Cognition and Instruction, 20,* 359–398.

Lemke, J. L. (1990). *Talking science: Language, learning and values.* Norwood, NJ: Ablex.

Leslie, A. M. (1984). Spatiotemporal continuity and the perception of causality in infants. *Perception, 13,* 287–305.

Leslie, A. M. (1987). Pretense and representation: The origins of "theory of mind." *Psychological Review, 94*(4), 412–426.

Lynch, M. (1990). The externalized retina: Selection and mathematization in the visual documentation of objects in the life sciences. In M. Lynch & S. Woolgar (Eds.), *Representation in scientific practice* (pp. 153–186). Cambridge, MA: MIT Press.

Masnick, A. M., & Klahr, D. (2003). Error matters: An initial exploration of elementary school children's understanding of experimental error. *Journal of Cognition and Development, 4*(1), 67–98.

Metz, K. E. (1995). Re-assessment of developmental assumptions in children's science instruction. *Review of Educational Research, 65*(2), 93–127.

Metz, K. E. (2000). Young children's inquiry in biology: Building the knowledge bases to empower independent inquiry. In J. Minstrell & E. H. van Zee (Eds.), *Inquiring into inquiry learning and teaching in science* (pp. 371–404). Washington, DC: American Association for the Advancement of Science.

Metz, K. E. (2004). Children's understanding of scientific inquiry: Their conceptualization of uncertainty in investigations of their own design. *Cognition and Instruction, 22*(2), 219–290.

Minstrell, J., & van Zee, E. (Eds.). (2000). *Inquiring into inquiry teaching and learning in science.* Washington, DC: American Association for the Advancement of Science.

National Research Council (1996). *National science education standards.* Washington, DC: National Academy Press.

Olson, D. R. (1994). *The world on paper: The conceptual and cognitive implications of writing and reading.* New York: Cambridge University Press.

Palincsar, A. S., & Brown, A. L. (1984). Reciprocal teaching of comprehension-fostering and monitoring activities. *Cognition and Instruction, 1*(2), 117–175.

Palincsar, A. S., & Magnussun, S. (2001). The interplay of first-hand and second-hand investigations to model and support the development of scientific knowledge and reasoning. In D. Klahr & S. Carver (Eds.), *Cognition and instruction: Twenty-five years of progress* (pp. 151–193). Mahwah, NJ: Erlbaum.

Palincsar, A. S., Magnussun, S. J., Marano, N., Ford, D., & Brown, N. (1998). Designing a community of practice: Principles and practices of the GIsML community. *Teaching and Teacher Education, 14*, 5–19.

Penner, D. E., Giles, N. D., Lehrer, R., & Schauble, L. (1997). Building functional models: Designing an elbow. *Journal of Research in Science Teaching, 34*(2), 125–143.

Penner, D. E., & Klahr, D. (1996). The interaction of domain-specific knowledge and domain-general discovery strategies: A study with sinking objects. *Child Development, 67*, 2709–2727.

Penner, D. E., Lehrer, R., & Schauble, L. (1998). From physical models to biomechanics: A design-based modeling approach. *Journal of the Learning Sciences, 7*(3/4), 429–449.

Penner, E., & Lehrer, R. (2000). The shape of fairness. *Teaching Children Mathematics, 7*(4), 210–214.

Perkins, D. N., & Grotzer, T. A. (2000, April). *Models and moves: Focusing on dimensions of causal complexity to achieve deeper scientific understanding.* Paper presented at the annual conference of the American Educational Research Association, New Orleans, LA.

Petrosino, A. J., Lehrer, R., & Schauble, L. (2003). Structuring error and experimental variation as distribution in the fourth grade. *Mathematical Thinking and Learning, 5*(2/3), 131–156.

Piaget, J. (1962). *Play, dreams and imitation in childhood.* New York: Norton.

Pickering, A. (1989). Living in the material world: On realism and experimental practice. In D. Gooding, T. Pinch, & S. Schaffer (Eds.), *The uses of experiment: Studies on the natural sciences* (pp. 275–297). Cambridge, England: Cambridge University Press.

Pickering, A. (1995). *The mangle of practice: Time, agency, and science.* Chicago: University of Chicago Press.

Posner, G. J., Strike, K. A., Hewson, P. W., & Gertzog, W. A. (1982). Accommodation of a scientific conception: Towards a theory of conceptual change. *Science Education, 66*(2), 211–227.

Roth, W., & McGinn, M. K. (1998). Inscriptions: Toward a theory of representing as social practice. *Review of Educational Research, 68*(1), 35–59.

Rudolph, J. L., & Stewart, J. H. (1998). Evolution and the nature of science: On the historical discord and its implications for education. *Journal of Research in Science Teaching, 35*(10), 1069–1089.

Samarapungavan, A. (1992). Children's judgments in theory-choice tasks: Scientific rationality in childhood. *Cognition, 45*(1), 1–32.

Schauble, L. (1990). Belief revision in children: The role of prior knowledge and strategies for generating evidence. *Journal of Experimental Child Psychology, 49*(1), 31–57.

Schauble, L. (1996). The development of scientific reasoning in knowledge-rich contexts. *Developmental Psychology, 32*(1), 102–119.

Schwab, J. (1962). The teaching of science as enquiry. In J. Schwab & P. Brandwein (Eds.), *The teaching of science* (pp. 1–103). Cambridge, MA: Harvard University Press.

Shapin, S., & Schaffer, S. (1985). *Leviathan and the air pump.* Princeton, NJ: Princeton University Press.

Shavelson, R. J., & Towne, L. (Eds.). (2002). *Scientific research in education.* Washington, DC: National Research Council.

Shultz, T. R. (1982). Casual reasoning in the social and nonsocial realms. *Canadian Journal of Behavioral Science, 14*, 307–322.

Sibum, H. O. (2004). What kind of science is experimental physics? *Science, 306*(5693), 60–61.

Siegler, R. S. (1996). *Emerging minds: The process of change in children's thinking.* New York: Oxford University Press.

Sloane, F., & Gorard, S. (2003). Exploring modeling aspects of design experiments. *Educational Researcher, 32*(1), 29–31.

Smith, C. L., Maclin, D., Houghton, C., & Hennessey, M. G. (2000). Sixth grade students' epistemologies of science: Experiences on epistemological development. *Cognition and Instruction, 18*(3), 349–422.

Sodian, B., Zaitchik, D., & Carey, S. (1991). Young children's differentiation of hypothetical beliefs from evidence. *Child Development, 62*, 753–766.

Spillane, J. (2000). Cognition and policy implementation: District policymakers and the reform of mathematics education. *Cognition and Instruction, 18*, 141–179.

Strauss, S. (1998). Cognitive development and science education: Toward a middle level model. In W. Damon, I. Sigel, & K. A. Renninger (Eds.), *Handbook of child psychology* (Vol. 4, pp. 357–399). New York: Wiley.

Troseth, G. L. (2003). Getting a clear picture: Young children's understanding of a televised image. *Developmental Science, 6*(3), 247–253.

Troseth, G. L., & DeLoache, J. S. (1998). The medium can obscure the message: Young children's understanding of video. *Child Development, 69*, 950–965.

Troseth, G. L., Pierroutsakos, S. L., & DeLoache, J. S. (2004). From the innocent to the intelligent eye: The early development of pictorial competence. In R. Kail (Ed.), *Advances in child development and behavior* (Vol. 32, pp. 1–35). New York: Academic Press.

Tschirgi, J. E. (1980). Sensible reasoning: A hypothesis about hypotheses. *Child Development, 51,* 1–10.

Van Valkenburgh, B., Wang, X., & Damuth, J. (2004). Cope's rule, hypercarnivory, and extinction in North American canids. *Science, 306*(5693), 101–104.

Warren, B., & Rosebery, A. S. (1996). This question is just too, too easy! Students' perspectives on accountability in science. In L. Schauble & R. Glaser (Eds.), *Innovations in learning: New environments for education* (pp. 97–126). Mahwah, NJ: Erlbaum.

Wason, P. C. (1960). On the failure to eliminate hypotheses in a conceptual task. *Quarterly Journal of Experimental Psychology, 12*(4), 129–140.

Wason, P. C. (1968). Reasoning about a rule. *Quarterly Journal of Experimental Psychology, 20,* 273–281.

White, B. Y. (1993). Intermediate causal models: A missing link for successful science education. *Cognition and Instruction, 10*(1), 1–100.

CHAPTER 6

Education for Spatial Thinking

LYNN S. LIBEN

One of the limitations of verbal language—the medium of this *Handbook* and hence of this chapter—is its linear nature. This linearity permits only a single opening paragraph, and the problem is that I would like to write three. Each would be designed to seduce a different audience to read the chapter that follows. The first would be a paragraph aimed at attracting scholars who are interested in cognitive development in general and in the development of spatial thinking and spatial representation in particular. The second would be aimed at attracting developmental scholars who, although not

necessarily interested in spatial thinking per se, have an interest in the interplay between theory and practice and are themselves perhaps in the throes of designing applied research or intervention programs related to some substantive domain. Learning about experiences in linking theory and practice in one domain may be useful for identifying opportunities and challenges in another. Finally, the third would be a paragraph aimed at attracting individuals who have responsibility for children's educational lives, including anyone who has (or will some day have) responsibility for planning, selecting, or implementing educational experiences or who is in a position to teach those who will eventually assume these positions. This is a broad group that includes personnel in both formal education (e.g., teachers, school administrators) and informal education (e.g., museum professionals, youth group leaders),

Much of the research reported here was funded by the National Institute of Education (G-83–0025) and by the National Science Foundation (ESI 01–01758, RED-9554504, REC-0411686), although the opinions expressed are those of the author and not necessarily those of either agency.

those who develop and distribute educational materials (e.g., curriculum writers, textbook publishers, television programmers, software designers), faculty in institutions of higher education (e.g., professors of curriculum and instruction), those who set educational policy (e.g., school board members, political leaders), and those who affect even one or two individual children's experiences directly (e.g., parents).

I have written this chapter for all three audiences. Following this introduction, in the section "Conceptualizing Spatial Thinking," I offer examples of spatial thinking intended to demonstrate its pervasiveness and importance. I then provide more formal definitions of the constructs of space and spatial thinking and illustrate the relevance of spatial thinking for a wide range of disciplines, concepts, tasks, and settings.

To the degree that my examples are convincing, readers may conclude that spatial thinking is, indeed, important and pervasive, but perhaps so much so that education for spatial thinking appears to be unnecessary. I would offer here an analogy to Molière's *Bourgeois Gentleman,* in which Monsieur Jourdain is shocked to discover that he has been speaking prose all his life. The point is that it is easy to take for granted that which one is accustomed to using freely. Prose is indeed pervasive and important, and even preschoolers are adept at using it. Yet, none of these facts leads us to ignore language in our educational curriculum. Instead, our schools provide instruction in all aspects of English—skills needed for comprehension and production of the written word, lessons in the beauty and traditions of great literature, and exercises in designing and delivering spoken arguments. Our informal educational systems are also designed to foster language skills, as in teaching young children the basics of reading through television programs, computer software, or games, or as in public service campaigns encouraging parents to read to their children. At all educational levels, the performance of individual students and institutions is assessed by measuring verbal functioning.

Monsieur Jourdain would probably have been equally shocked if he had stopped to consider how pervasively spatial thinking is used in our mental, physical, and social worlds. However, as with language, the fact that spatial thinking is pervasive should not be taken to imply that it is mastered automatically and effortlessly, nor to obviate the need for spatial education. In the section "Individual and Group Differences in Spatial Thinking

and Spatial Development," I draw from scholarship in developmental psychology to show that masterful levels of spatial thinking are not universally achieved by all individuals and groups, and to review briefly some of the explanations that have been given to account for these differences.

Having established the existence of individual and group differences in spatial thinking, in "The Case for Spatial Interventions: When Differences Are Deficits," I address the question of whether these differences matter for educational goals. After enumerating several reasons why spatial performance does, indeed, matter, I present illustrations from laboratory and classroom contexts to suggest that spatial skills can be facilitated through interventions.

In "The Place of Geography and Map Education in Developing Spatial Thinkers," I consider the means by which one might address the goal of enhancing spatial thinking in the real world of education. I first review reasons for rejecting one possible approach: adding spatial education as a stand-alone curriculum. I then turn to discussing an alternative approach: infusing spatial education within existing school subjects. Ideally, an infusion approach would involve enhancing spatial thinking in a diverse set of school subjects. In this chapter, I focus on a single school subject—geography—as an illustrative case. I argue that geography is an excellent vehicle for spatial education because at its core, the discipline involves explaining spatial patterns and processes. Further, I argue that—within geography—map education is a particularly useful focus for developing spatial thinking. To explain the power of maps as tools for spatial thinking, I provide a mini tutorial on the principles, challenges, functions, and diversity of maps.

There are several motivations for my focus on maps. First, the skills involved in producing, understanding, and using maps are like the spatial skills that have been identified as important for a wide range of observational and representational tasks in many sciences (e.g., distinguishing figure from ground; using distal frames of reference even in the face of proximal, embedding frames of reference; mentally rotating objects or diagrams; determining cross sections). Second, maps are pervasive. They are central tools not only in geography, but also in many other school subjects, occupations, and daily life activities. Third, there is extensive evidence that, without instruction, neither children nor adults exploit the full representational and spatial meaning maps offer.

A fourth and more personal reason is that map education has been at the center of much of my own applied developmental research. Particularly relevant are two ongoing collaborations. The first involves roughly 2 decades of collaborative work with Roger Downs, a geographer. Our projects have included designing and teaching a curriculum unit on geography and mapping for elementary school children (Liben & Downs, 1986), advising Children's Television Workshop on their design of a geography curriculum for *Sesame Street* (Liben & Downs, 1994, 2001), and partnering with the National Geographic Society in a study of boys' and girls' dramatically differential success on the National Geographic Bee (Liben, 2002a). The second collaboration is with Kim Kastens, a marine geologist. Our interactions began when she was funded by the National Science Foundation to develop materials for teaching elementary school children to read and use maps (*Where Are We?* [*WAW?*]; Kastens, 2000) and I was an advisor to the project. Our interactions evolved into a number of collaborative research projects aimed at investigating children's spatial thinking in map use, evaluating the effectiveness of the *WAW?* curriculum, and exploring college students' three-dimensional spatial thinking while learning geological skills in the field (Kastens, Ishikawa, & Liben, 2004; Kastens & Liben, 2004; Liben, Kastens, & Stevenson, 2002).

I draw from these collaborative projects to address various developmental and educational issues related to map understanding. Specifically, in "The Developmental Pathway to Map Understanding," I characterize the developmental course of map understanding, and in "Map Education: Illustrative Materials and Activities," I discuss educational interventions. In the final section of the chapter, "Educating Spatial Thinkers: Conclusions and Questions," I summarize key lessons and highlight remaining questions relevant for each of the three audiences identified in the opening paragraph of this chapter.

CONCEPTUALIZING SPATIAL THINKING

Because space literally surrounds us, and because we so often use spatial metaphors and spatial representations automatically, we often fail to notice or analyze these concepts, or to define terminology explicitly. In this section, I thus highlight the many ways in which spatial thinking enters human life, offer definitions of key terms, and provide a developmental perspective with which to approach spatial thinking.

The Pervasiveness of Spatial Thinking

Our daily lives are filled with space-related action, perception, and representation. When we awaken in the dark, we know where to reach to hit the snooze button; our stored representation of the bedroom allows us to avoid stubbing our toes as we move to the bathroom; we know which cabinet door to open to find our toothpaste or hairbrush; where to look for our clothes; where to find the orange juice. When we read the morning paper, we see aerial photographs of the East Coast during a blackout, a map of a battlefield, a bar graph reporting the results of a recent political poll, a satellite image of a storm system. We drive to work and draw upon a cognitive map of the city to detour around a traffic jam. When we arrive at the office, we examine graphs showing the relative costs, income, and profits for the new digital cameras we have been involved in developing; we examine maps showing the spatial distributions of the factories that manufacture them; we compare the resolutions of the images they create. Our elementary school children wait at the right corner for the school bus; they notice that the driver took a different route to avoid a construction site; once they get to school, they learn to color within the lines and the direction in which to write their letters to form their words; they learn to produce graphs and maps. Our high school children examine the positions of various organs from a frog dissection in biology class and draw and label pictures of each in their lab notebooks; they learn about how hydrogen and oxygen atoms combine by using three-dimensional models in chemistry class. In earth science, they search the Web to find information about the latest earthquakes, clicking the mouse at the right locations on their screen, and negotiating the hierarchically organized and modeled site map; in social studies they use a Geographic Information System (GIS) to explore the links between income level and voting patterns. After school, they get and follow directions to bike to their friend's house; they play a video game when they get there, and then infer the villain's location from a series of discrete elevation views of the castle's rooms. In short, human lives are filled with spatial thinking at home, at work, at school, and at play.

Definitions

Although there would probably be general agreement that the examples just given draw on various aspects of spatial thought, there would probably be far less agreement about how to define or parse the constituent constructs of *space* and *spatial thinking*. That is, unlike the more commonly studied symbolic domain of language, for which there is a well-established taxonomy of components (phonology, syntax, and semantics) and formalization of the domain (grammars), the constructs of space and spatial thinking have no commonly agreed upon set of components or universally shared formalisms, at least as they are studied in human development. As a consequence, answers to the foundational questions *What is space?* and *What is spatial thinking?* are complex and controversial and would require far more pages than the current chapter allows. Thus, the brief answers offered here can provide only the foundations for the topics developed in later sections of this chapter. More fully articulated answers may be found in earlier reviews and collections on space, spatial cognition, and spatial representation (Cassirer, 1950; R. Cohen, 1985; Eliot, 1987; Gattis, 2001; Jammer, 1954; Liben, 1981, 2002b; Liben, Patterson, & Newcombe, 1981; Newcombe & Huttenlocher, 2000; O'Keefe & Nadel, 1978; Olson & Bialystok, 1983; Piaget & Inhelder, 1956).

Space

Space—like many words and ideas we use casually and frequently in daily language—is a surprisingly difficult concept to define. In earlier days, one might have used a dictionary definition or an encyclopedia to demonstrate the range and perhaps even the elusiveness of a concept; today one is more likely to turn to an Internet search. A search with the words "space definition" in *Google*© returns as the first entry a page titled "Definitions of space on the Web" that includes definitions from (and links to) mathematics ("the infinite extension of the three-dimensional field in which all matter exists"), astronomy ("the expanse in which the Solar System, stars, and galaxies exist"), film ("story space, the locale of the totality of the action . . . and plot space, the locales visibly and audibly represented in the scenes"), music ("areas between or below or above the lines of a musical

staff"), time ("the interval between two times . . . [as] in the space of 10 minutes"), typography ("a blank character used to separate successive words in writing or printing"), and kinesthetics ("where the body is moving"), to sample only some.

Embedded within these and other definitions of space is the ancient tension between conceptualizing space as absolute versus relative. In the former, space is defined as a framework that remains unchanged irrespective of whether anything is contained within it, where its contents are located, or from what perspective the space and its contents are viewed. For example, a Cartesian coordinate grid offers such a framework. In the latter, space is conceptualized as an expression of relationships among objects. The space between words, for example, emerges only in relation to characters that come before and after it. In this relative conceptualization of space, the space changes as objects within it change or move. The conception of space as absolute is associated with Plato and Clarke in philosophy and with Newton in physics; the conception of space as relative is associated with Leibniz and Kant in philosophy and with Einstein in physics.

Fortunately, just as physics can progress by modeling light as waves and as particles even though the two models are physically incompatible, developmental science can progress by asking how individuals acquire, refine, use, and consciously reflect on both absolute and relative space. Illustrative of a developmental question within the former is asking how children come to establish and use abstract, homogeneous coordinate systems that, even when empty, provide frameworks for *potential* locations or distances (Piaget, Inhelder, & Szeminska, 1960; Somerville & Bryant, 1985). Illustrative of a developmental question within the latter is asking when and how individuals come to appreciate relational topological spatial concepts such as "above" and "between" (Piaget & Inhelder, 1956; Quinn, 2003).

Also embedded within the illustrative definitions are a number of different views on the metaphysical nature of space. Some definitions imply that space is a physical reality (as in planetary outer space or as in the environment through which individuals move or dance), a cognitive construct (as in a formal spatial model created to represent some spatial or nonspatial content), a metaphorical construction (as in time as space), or an emergent reality (as in the spaces created by drawing lines of a music staff). One parsing of space relevant to these alternatives is that proposed by

O'Keefe and Nadel (1978, pp. 6–7), who distinguished between *psychological* and *physical* space. The former was said to be "any space which is attributed to the mind . . . and which would not exist if minds did not exist," and the latter, "any space attributed to the external world independent of the existence of minds." As behavioral scientists (rather than, say, physicists or geologists), we are presumably interested in the former rather than the latter. And indeed, this is the position taken by O'Keefe and Nadel.

However, to say that our focus is on psychological space in no way denies the relevance of physical space. First, the qualities of the physical world set conditions for human action and cognition, although, as well articulated in embodiment theories (see Liben, 2005, in press; Overton & Müller, 2002), the reverse holds as well. That is, qualities of the human actor (both physical and mental) likewise set conditions for human action and cognition. Second, insofar as important aspects of psychological space are concerned with the physical world, physical space is a critical substantive domain for much of human cognition. For example, much of psychological space is devoted to knowledge about or cognitive representations of the world that allow people to solve inferential problems (see Stevens & Coupe, 1978) or to navigate within it (Allen, 2004; Downs & Stea, 1973, 1977; Garling & Evans, 1991; Golledge, 1999; Kitchin & Blades, 2002). Third, at least some scholars take the position that characteristics of physical space determine (in whole or in part) characteristics of psychological space. For example, Lynch (1960) observed that the Aleuts (who depend on waterways for travel) attend to and label water features of their environment in detail, but differentiate little among landforms. In short, focusing on psychological space does not make physical space irrelevant. Its relevance is, however, mediated through human thought, which is, of course, necessarily the central focus of a chapter entitled "Education for Spatial Thinking." Thus, I turn from definitions of space to definitions of spatial thinking.

Spatial Thinking

Although authors of books and articles concerned with spatial cognition often write very briefly (if at all) about the meaning of the "space" to which the cognition refers, they are usually very deliberate in defining what they mean by spatial cognition or spatial thinking. However, as noted earlier, there is no single definition to which all or even most scholars subscribe. The one I

have chosen to provide here is that offered in the recent report issued by the National Research Council (NRC; 2005) on thinking spatially. I have selected it for several reasons. First, it is one of the broadest definitions of spatial thinking in the literature. Its breadth is probably explained, at least in part, by the fact that the definition was generated by a committee of scientists representing not only the behavioral sciences (psychology, education, human development) but also the physical sciences, for which spatial thinking is central (geology, physics, geology, astronomy, geography). Second, because it is recent, and because NRC reports are consensus reports written by committee, it builds from, and is viewed as compatible with, a range of earlier and alternative conceptualizations and definitions. Finally, because the charge to this particular NRC committee was focused on educational issues (as evident in its title, *Learning to Think Spatially: GIS as a Support System in the K–12 Curriculum*), the definition is well-suited to educational topics that are also the focus of this chapter.

Specifically, the report identifies three components of spatial thinking as follows:

> To think spatially entails knowing about (1) *space,* for example, the relationships among units of measurement (e.g., kilometers versus miles), different ways of calculating distance (e.g., miles, travel time, travel cost), the basis of coordinate systems (e.g., Cartesian versus polar coordinates), the nature of spaces (e.g., number of dimensions [two- versus three-dimensional]); (2) *representation*—for example, the relationships among views (e.g., plans versus elevations of buildings or orthogonal versus perspective maps), the effect of projections (e.g., Mercator versus equal-area map projections), the principles of graphic design (e.g., the roles of legibility, visual contrast, and figure-ground organization in the readability of graphs and maps); and (3) *reasoning*—for example, the different ways of thinking about shortest distances (e.g., as the crow flies versus route distance in a rectangular street grid), the ability to extrapolate and interpolate (e.g., projecting a functional relationship on a graph into the future or estimating the slope of a hillside from a map of contour lines), and making decisions (e.g., given traffic reports on a radio, selecting an alternative detour). (pp. 12–13)

In essence, the first and third components fit fairly readily into the common distinction in cognitive psychology between, respectively, declarative knowledge ("knowing what," as in knowing various systems or models of space) and procedural knowledge ("knowing how," as in knowing how to manipulate or transform spatial information). The second is more closely identified with the spatial domain in particular and highlights the centrality that spatial-graphic representations play in spatial thinking (see Liben, 1999, 2001, 2005; Tversky, 2001).

Spatial Thinking across the Life Span

Developmental psychologists have been interested in the way that understanding spatial concepts, interpreting or creating external spatial representations, and establishing, manipulating, and remembering spatial images evolve over the life course, beginning with infancy (see Kellman & Arterberry, 1998), continuing through childhood (see Liben, 2002b), and extending through adulthood and old age (see Kirasic, Allen, Dobson, & Binder, 1996). Although there can be little debate that spatial behaviors look very different during infancy, childhood, and adulthood, there is relatively little agreement about whether the age-linked differences in observed behaviors signify qualitative differences in the way that space is represented and thought about, or instead signify only quantitative changes in other cognitive skills or structures (e.g., changes in speed of processing; see Kail, 1991).

Undoubtedly, the theoretical position arguing most emphatically for qualitative change in spatial development is that proposed by Piaget and Inhelder in *The Child's Conception of Space,* first published in French as *La Representation de l'Espace chez l'Enfant* in 1948 and appearing in English in 1956 (referenced in this chapter as Piaget & Inhelder, 1956). In this view, children were said to come to construct spatial constructs gradually through their interactions with the physical and social worlds. The notion of the self-regulatory construction of spatial concepts was thus an instantiation in a particular domain—space—of the more general developmental processes described by Piaget (1970). In Piaget's description of this general process, neonates are thought to be biologically endowed with a very small repertoire of behaviors (e.g., the sucking reflex) and a few key processes (assimilation and accommodation) aimed at general states or end points (equilibrium). Environments are understood as important for presenting certain opportunities and challenges that support individuals in exercising and extending their repertoires. In applying these general processes to spatial development, Piaget (1954) argued that infants gradually come to interact

with and understand the spatial world in a physical or sensorimotor sense (e.g., coming to appreciate that objects have a permanent existence even when out of the child's own view; learning to adjust grasping movements in relation to an object's location in space) and later, at the end of the sensorimotor period, in a representational manner (e.g., solving problems about relations between two objects by mental imagery).

Once having developed representational thought, children were said to develop, first, topological spatial concepts and later, in tandem, projective and Euclidean spatial concepts (Piaget & Inhelder, 1956). Topological spatial concepts discussed by Piaget may be described as "rubber sheet" spatial concepts, that is, those that are conserved even as a rubber sheet is stretched. Illustrative are concepts such as *next to, on, on the border of,* and *between,* which are relationships that are conserved even as metric qualities are distorted through stretching. A preschool child who has constructed only topological concepts can, for example, differentiate between open and closed figures (e.g., a circular versus a U-shaped figure) but not between two figures that differ only with respect to metrics (e.g., four-sided figures with equal versus unequal sides or equal versus unequal angles).

Projective spatial concepts are "point of view" spatial concepts, that is, those that are affected by vantage point. Probably the best known measure of the child's understanding of the effect of viewing position on the appearance of an object or group of objects is the classic *three mountains task.* Children are shown a table-top model of three (papier-mâché) mountains and asked to indicate (e.g., by selecting one of several pictures) how the mountains would look to someone seated in a different location (e.g., directly across the table). Of interest is whether children can appreciate that the other person's view is different from their own (i.e., can overcome egocentrism), and if so, whether they can identify the spatial characteristics of that view. For example, questions may address whether a young boy understands that a small mountain that is visible to him (because from his vantage point, it is in front of the large mountain) would be entirely invisible to an adult seated directly across the table, or that a blue mountain that appears to him to be to the left of the yellow mountain would appear to be to the right of the yellow mountain to the adult facing him. Understanding the relevance of point of view is also critical for using principles of projective geometry in drawing (as in Renaissance art, for example; see Hagen, 1986) or in predicting the shape of the shadows cast by light falling on objects as they are rotated toward or away from a screen (Merriwether & Liben, 1997; Piaget & Inhelder, 1956).

Finally, Euclidean concepts are what might be called "abstract spatial system" concepts because they provide the structures by which locations and objects are represented in reference to an abstract, stable, general system. The classic illustration of such a system, and the one that plays a central role in Piaget's own empirical work on space (Piaget & Inhelder, 1956; Piaget et al., 1960), is a Cartesian coordinate system, which establishes a point of origin and a grid of horizontal and vertical axes. Such systems allow for stable measurement and hence conservation of distance and angles. Although mature spatial systems are typically conceptualized as Euclidean, it might be more useful to characterize maturity as the ability to understand and use abstract spatial systems in general (Liben, 2003). First, a more pluralistic approach appears to be more consistent with the notion of hypothetico-deductive reasoning that Piaget ascribed to formal operational thought. Second, a more flexible characterization would offer closer links to a broader range of phenomena that include those better conceptualized with non-Euclidean spatial models. For example, when modeling outer space, the hyperbolic geometry of Lobachevskian space might be more useful; when modeling Earth space, the spherical geometry of Riemannian space might be more useful.

Indeed, Piaget himself revised his own position on spatial development and substituted a sequence of intra-, inter-, and transfigural relations in the place of topological, projective, and Euclidean concepts (Piaget & Garcia, 1989). Others have offered sequences that concern a particular aspect of spatial development rather than spatial development in general. For example, those who have studied infants or toddlers (Acredolo, 1981) observed a developmental shift in which spatial behaviors are based on *egocentric* coding (in which the infant's own bodily experiences provide the referent by which locations in space are organized) to *allocentric* (in which external objects or external frameworks are used to code location). Conceptually, this shift parallels Piaget's description of the developing understanding of vantage point (projective spatial concepts), although it suggests a dramatically earlier developmental shift than proposed in the original Piagetian work.

Another model of spatial development is the sequence proposed by Siegel and White (1975; see also Siegel, Kirasic, & Kail, 1978) with respect to environmental knowledge. They suggested that children first master landmarks, then routes, and finally develop integrated configurational or survey knowledge of the environment. These three stages are similar to the developmental sequence initially suggested by Piaget and Inhelder (1956) insofar as the use of landmarks is akin to the use of topological concepts (e.g., knowing that the school is *next to* the supermarket); the use of routes is akin to the use of projective concepts (e.g., knowing that when traveling from home to school, one turns right at the traffic light, but on the return trip, one turns left at the light); and the use of survey knowledge is akin to the use of Euclidean concepts (e.g., conceptualizing locations of places and pathways by using metric distances and angles).

Although these various alternatives thus differ in the way that the developmental sequences are characterized or in the chronological ages associated with transitions, they retain the fundamental notion of qualitative developmental change that was posited by Piaget. More radical alternatives have also been proposed in which qualitative developmental change is explicitly said to be minimal or even absent entirely. One of the most explicit positions rejecting the notion of qualitative developmental change was proposed by Hagen (1986), whose focus was on the geometries used by various cultures in the drawings and paintings of representational art. As noted earlier, Piaget and Inhelder (1956) saw an individual's ability to use projective geometry in drawing as reflective of having constructed projective spatial concepts. Thus, in the Piagetian view, young children—those who had constructed only topological concepts—should be unable to understand the consequences of viewing position, and thus be unable to create or appreciate graphic representations that employ projective geometry (as in the vanishing points of Renaissance art). In contrast, Hagen argued that it was different cultures—rather than different levels of ontogenetic maturity—that affected the way space was conceptualized and represented. Under this view, the reason that mature individuals in the Western cultures studied by Piaget favor projective geometry in their spatial-graphic representations is that they have been exposed to such representations in their daily lives. Individuals exposed to spatial-graphic representations that use alternative geometries would thus be expected to follow a different representational path.

Consistent with this view, Hagen (1985) offered evidence that those living in cultures that use other geometries in their representational art (e.g., affine geometry in Asian art; orthogonal projections or metric geometry in Northwest Indian art) do not evidence the developmental increases in projective geometry reported for Swiss children.

In contemporary work, Newcombe and Huttenlocher (2000) explicitly offer their own position as falling between the nativist position that attributes high levels of spatial competency to the neonate and the Piagetian position that posits significant qualitative change from infancy through late childhood. In particular, they cite their empirical finding that infants are able to identify specific locations in space as challenging both views. That is, they argue that their data support neither the nativist position that infants under a year are sensitive to metrics, nor the Piagetian proposition that it is not until middle childhood that children evidence metric understanding. Elsewhere, I have suggested that their position is actually more consistent with that of Piaget than they themselves have painted it (Liben, 2003), but irrespective of precisely where on the continuum their theoretical stance may be said to fall, it is evident from the approaches mentioned here as well as from others not discussed here (see R. Cohen, 1985; Kitchin & Blades, 2002; Liben, 2002b) that various theories of spatial development fall along a continuum defined by the degree to which development is presumed to involve qualitative shifts in underlying competence in spatial thinking.

However, despite the presence of scholarly disagreements about whether there are qualitative changes in *competencies* of spatial thinking, there is little disagreement that there are age-linked differences in *performance* on a wide range of spatial tasks. From an educational perspective, then, it may or may not be necessary to intervene to help children establish basic competencies; however, it is surely necessary to intervene to facilitate children's propensity for activating existing spatial competencies and using them effectively. In this light, it is interesting to return to the recent NRC report on *Learning to Think Spatially,* which identifies as its overriding goal fostering "a generation of students (1) who have the habit of mind of thinking spatially, (2) who can practice spatial thinking in an informed way, and (3) who adopt a critical stance to spatial thinking" (2005, pp. 3–4). These goals imply that the challenge is to find ways to facilitate students' application of spatial

thinking rather than to find ways to establish students' facility in spatial thinking in the first place.

INDIVIDUAL AND GROUP DIFFERENCES IN SPATIAL THINKING AND DEVELOPMENT

As illustrated in the preceding discussions, there is a tendency for developmental psychologists to discuss change as if it occurred for children in general. Although some programs of developmental research concentrate on describing age-linked differences at the group level, others are more concerned with identifying and explaining differences among children in developmental rates or end points. In this section, I consider the way that both perspectives are relevant for the study of spatial thinking.

In Theory: The Universality of Spatial Thinking and Spatial Development

The "grand theories" of child development describe age-linked progressions as if they were universal. This is most obviously true of those theories that are unabashedly addressed to universal human development such as Piaget's (1970) or evolutionary psychology (Geary & Bjorklund, 2000), but it is arguably also true even for most theories that are specifically concerned with development in social contexts (Vygotsky, 1978). That is, even as culturally sensitive theorists identify the way specific social traditions and environments vary over time and place, they typically do so in the context of identifying the similar developmental functions that are being served. For example, ecological or contextual theorists may examine the varying ways adults transmit the knowledge and skills of their culture to the next generation. The function is thus viewed as similar across settings, even though the instantiation of that function is said to differ in form (e.g., whether it occurs in situ, as in teaching children to weave via an apprentice, or in a formal educational setting that draws on abstract representations such as words and diagrams; Bruner, 1964; Gauvain, 1993; Rogoff, 1993).

Descriptions of the more focused topic of spatial development likewise tend to imply that developmental mechanisms and outcomes are universal. Given a shared biological heritage that provides humans with certain kinds of sensorimotor capacities (e.g., the ability to see visible but not infrared light; the ability to walk but not fly), and given a shared environmental heritage that surrounds humans with a certain kind of physical world (e.g., a world that has a gravitational field that defines an axis for up and down even if the specifics of the landscape vary), it might be reasonable to anticipate that humans will develop spatially along similar paths and with similar outcomes. Indeed, consistent with this view, the two major monographs on spatial development that have been written during the past 50 years (Newcombe & Huttenlocher, 2000; Piaget & Inhelder, 1956) are completely silent about variability within any given age group or developmental achievement being discussed. This is not meant to imply that these scholars are ignorant of or inattentive to variability. Indeed, much Piagetian and neo-Piagetian work is specifically addressed to identifying mechanisms that promote development in both natural and educational settings (Inhelder, Sinclair, & Bovet, 1974). Similarly, Newcombe (1982), in other aspects of her research, has explicitly studied gender-related variation in spatial behavior. Nevertheless, in these monographs as in much of developmental psychology, the focus is on the development of "the" child, just as in much of cognitive psychology the focus is on characterizing "the" human (most often instantiated by the college student in an English-speaking culture).

As with most generalizations, there are exceptions. In the field of human development in general, probably the most sustained exceptions to characterizing development as if it follows a single trajectory and reaches a single outcome are found in the scholarship in developmental psychology that is labeled "life span." In part, the term is used to underscore the notion that development does not end at adolescence (as might be erroneously inferred from theories such as Piaget's or from the content of many developmental psychology textbooks). Consistent with this thrust of the life span approach, a number of investigators have studied spatial development in the years beyond childhood and adolescence (Willis & Schaie, 1986). But even more important for the question of universality is the observation that researchers associated with the life span approach investigate not only interindividual commonalities or regularities of development, but also interindividual differences (Baltes, Staudinger, & Lindenberger, 1999). In practice, however, few if any investigators immersed in the theo-ries and methods of life span developmental psychology have focused their research on spatial development during the portions of the life course that are of greatest interest to educators (i.e., prekindergarten through grade 12). This lacuna is presumably the result of the assumption that during infancy and childhood, the major sources of influence are biological maturation processes and age-graded socialization experiences that are common across contexts (Baltes, 1987). Thus, life span investigators who are interested in studying the effects of history-graded and nonnormative influences have tended to concentrate their efforts on later rather than earlier portions of the life course. In principle, however, a life span approach might be used to study early spatial development in relation to contextual factors; in fact, it is possible to interpret extant research from other empirical traditions in this light (see Liben, 1991a). It is not only a life span approach, however, that has led to an interest in factors other than chronological age that are associated with different levels of spatial performance, a point developed in the section that follows.

In Reality: The Diversity of Spatial Thinking and Spatial Development

At the same time that most theories of spatial development seem to assume, posit, or imply universality across historical time, individuals, demographic subgroups, and national cultures, there are forces that challenge the characterization of spatial development as a universal. In this section, I consider work leading to the conclusion that spatial development is not, in reality, as universal as our overarching theories might appear to imply. I begin with a discussion of work that stems from the research tradition addressed to individual differences, and then turn to work addressed to group differences.

Individual Differences

As argued earlier, developmental theories tend to focus on the universals of cognitive functioning, even if they vary with respect to whether they posit qualitative age-linked differences or context-linked differences in the details of that functioning. A second tradition in psychology, the psychometric approach, instead focuses on the *differences* among individuals. Psychometricians, or differential psychologists, begin from the premise that individuals differ among themselves on virtually all physical and behavioral human characteristics (e.g., height, weight, muscle mass, memory span, inferential reasoning). Given this starting point, one would anticipate differences among individuals in the domain of spatial thinking as well.

In a review of the psychometric approach to the study of spatial functioning, Eliot (1987) proposed that work in this tradition could be divided into three major phases. The first, which Eliot dated as occupying roughly the first third of the twentieth century, was focused largely on establishing the existence of a specific spatial factor as distinct from general intelligence. The precursors of this first phase lay in the mental testing movement that was driven by practical concerns stemming largely from the social Darwinism and eugenics movements. These movements were concerned with optimizing the quality of the genetic pool of the population or maximizing the way the raw genetic material was used. Thus, for example, early testing efforts were employed to make decisions about matters such as who should be allowed to enter the United States, which young students should be assigned to vocational versus college-bound educational paths, who should be institutionalized, and which applicants should be accepted into the armed forces and for what positions.

Early measures of intellectual functioning typically produced some index of general intelligence, with measures relying on the verbal modality. However, there were conditions under which verbal testing was impossible (e.g., immigrants who did not know English; deaf children), and thus nonlanguage "performance" intelligence tests were developed. Such tests required respondents to solve various kinds of sensorimotor or graphic challenges, for example, completing construction tasks or paper-and-pencil mazes. Whether skills in these domains should appropriately be considered "intelligence" was controversial. Some, some such as Terman (1921, as quoted in Eliot, 1987, p. 43), argued in the negative because "an individual is intelligent in proportion as he is able to carry out abstract thinking." Others, such as Wechsler (1950, as quoted in Eliot, 1987, p. 43), argued in the affirmative, suggesting that there are "several kinds of intelligences, namely abstract (an ability to work with symbols), social (an ability to deal with people) and practical (an ability to manipulate objects)." The latter interpretation took on increasing weight in the psychometric movement as intellectual assessments included a diverse range of tasks, and as analyses of response patterns in samples of those tested

revealed coherent factors, including a spatial factor (Thurstone, 1938).

With the work in phase 1 having provided evidence for a spatial factor as a separate domain of intelligence, the work in phase 2, covering roughly the next quarter-century, was focused on trying to identify component subskills within the broader spatial domain and to understand how they related to one another. Different investigators have identified different factors over the years (e.g., the ability to encode and store spatial patterns), but no single set of factors has been endorsed by all investigators. Indeed, Eliot (1987, p. 55) suggested that various "descriptions of spatial factors were frustrating to other researchers because they appeared at best vague and at worst self-contradictory." Despite this relatively discouraging conclusion that there is no single, universally accepted way to characterize spatial subskills, this work has generated a number of internally coherent alternative models for conceptualizing the structure of spatial ability (see Eliot, 1987, for detailed presentation of these models).

Eliot (1987) distinguished a third phase beginning in the early 1960s, during which the focus turned to identifying the sources of variance affecting performance on spatial tasks. Work since the publication of Eliot's review in 1987 has generally continued along the same lines, although with an increasing emphasis on neuroscience foundations and consequences of spatial thinking (Shelton & Gabrieli, 2004).

In summary, work in the psychometric tradition has identified the spatial domain as a component of intellectual functioning that shows variability among individuals. Before leaving the topic of individual differences, however, it is important to note that one need not be working within the psychometric tradition to focus on differences among people rather than central tendencies. Many developmental investigators have noted that within a given age (even within a demographically homogeneous sample), there are dramatic differences among children in their performance on spatial tasks. Some investigators have studied whether the observed variations in performance are linked to variations in theoretically prerequisite concepts (Liben & Downs, 1993). Others have attempted to identify subgroups of individuals (latent classes) that underlie the observed distributions and thereby generate hypotheses about different strategies that people may be using to solve the tasks at hand (Thomas & Lohaus, 1993; Thomas & Turner, 1991). When the latent groups so identified differ on some salient group membership (e.g., different proportions of males and females that fall into the identified classes; Thomas & Lohaus, 1993), the individual difference approach blends into the group difference approach discussed next.

Group Differences

Variations among individuals at any given moment in time could represent differences among them with respect to the degree to which they are endowed with the quality of interest (here, spatial skills). Alternatively, they could represent differences among individuals with respect to how far along the developmental pathway they have traveled at the point at which they are tested. In either case, once one has documented that there *are* differences among individuals, a key question becomes how to account for those differences. One means of formulating hypotheses about what factors may account for within-group variation is to explore between-group differences. If groups that differ systematically in spatial performance also differ on some biological or experiential factor, that factor becomes a good candidate to examine for its possible relevance to spatial performance. Ideally, in addition to testing whether variations in the identified factor are also systematically related to variations in spatial performance *within* a given group, investigators study whether experimental manipulation of that factor (assuming such manipulation is both possible and ethical) affects spatial performance. Although a finding that the manipulated factor significantly affects some spatial outcome cannot prove that it accounts for differential outcomes in the course of natural development, it shows that it *can* affect outcomes, and thus that it has potential educational utility.

One category of group comparisons that may be informative about spatial outcomes are those that are in some way related to culture, that is, the qualities of the ecology in which individuals develop and live. Any number of cultural variables are potentially relevant. Language is one obvious way cultures vary, and the way that languages mark and use space may affect spatial thinking. For example, different spoken languages differentially privilege absolute versus relative frames of references (Levinson, 2003) and differentially mark spatial features such as whether there is a distinction between something contained within a loose-fitting versus a tightly fitting container (see Choi & Bowerman, 1991). Languages in visual-gestural modes (such as American Sign Language; see Emmorey, Kosslyn, &

Bellugi, 1993) use space explicitly, unlike languages in oral-aural modes (such as spoken English). These different linguistic environments may well effect differences in spatial thinking. Another ecological contrast concerns terrain and navigation through that terrain. Thus, for example, whether one is surrounded by a "carpentered" or "uncarpentered" environment, travels roads that are laid out in a regular grid or a spaghetti-like arrangement, navigates by land or by sea, are factors that may affect one's spatial representational systems (see Berry, 1966, 1971; Cole & Scribner, 1974; Liben, 1981; Norman, 1980). Another cultural variable that may be important concerns the geometric traditions of representational art mentioned earlier. Exposure to different geometries in art may in turn affect the kinds of geometric concepts and mental representations about space that individuals develop (see Hagen, 1986).

A second kind of group comparison that may be informative about spatial outcomes concerns special populations. That is, individuals who are atypical in some way provide "experiments of nature" in which some kind of potentially important experience is absent, reduced, or modified in ways that could not otherwise be manipulated in humans. For example, comparisons of spatial outcomes in blind and sighted children may illuminate the role of vision for spatial thinking (Landau, Spelke, & Gleitman, 1984; Millar, 1994; Morrongiello, Timney, Humphrey, Anderson, & Skory, 1995), investigations of children with Williams syndrome may help to disentangle the role of executive versus attentional processes in completing spatial tasks (Hoffman, Landau, & Pagani, 2003), investigations of children with early brain injury may illuminate neurological bases of spatial development (Stiles, Bates, Thal, Trauner, & Reilly, 2002), and investigations of children with motor impairments such as cerebral palsy or childhood arthritis may reveal the role of autonomous self-exploration (Foreman, Orencas, Nicholas, Morton, & Gell, 1989).

It is a third set of group comparisons that has attracted the most attention in the developmental literature—those related to participant sex. One reason for the popularity of this focus is probably that sex differences had not been predicted a priori. The unexpected nature of the difference has led many to see these differences as an intellectual puzzle to be solved (Vasta & Liben, 1996). A second reason is practical. It is far easier to identify well-matched samples of males and females (e.g., drawn from the same elementary school or university) and to obtain them in adequate numbers than it is to identify adequate and well-matched samples drawn from other potentially interesting comparison groups (e.g., across cultures or special populations). A third reason is that so much is already known about factors that differentiate males and females, factors that thus supply ready-made candidate explanations for differential spatial outcomes.

Studies of children and adults in Western cultures have demonstrated robust sex-related differences on spatial tasks, with the observed advantage for males often falling between what have been labeled by J. Cohen (1977) as medium and large effect sizes (Linn & Petersen, 1985; McGee, 1979; Voyer, Voyer, & Bryden, 1995). Although some of the earliest reports of sex-related differences in spatial skills suggested that they did not emerge until adolescence (Maccoby & Jacklin, 1974), more recent work suggests that at least some differences emerge earlier. For example, Johnson and Meade (1987) reported a male advantage on a range of spatial tasks by 10 years, and S. C. Levine, Huttenlocher, Taylor, and Langrock (1999) reported a substantial male advantage by 4½ years on both spatial translation and rotation tasks.

In what has become a classic paper on sex-related differences in spatial skills, Linn and Petersen (1985) used meta-analyses to identify three components of spatial skills. The first, *spatial perception,* refers to the ability to recognize one's own position (e.g., gravitational upright) in relation to the surrounding environment, even when that environment presents conflicting or embedding cues. The second, *mental rotation,* refers to skill in manipulating, in imagination, figures or objects as they move through two- or three-dimensional space. The third, *spatial visualization,* refers to the use of some combination of verbal or visual strategies to perform multistep spatial tasks. The largest and most robust sex differences have been found in the first two subcomponents. There has been a less consistent pattern of sex differences in the third.

In addition to programs of research that have attempted to identify which categories of spatial skills show sex differences, there have also been programs of research on sex differences on particular tasks. One task that has attracted considerable attention is the water-level task, originally designed by Piaget and Inhelder (1956) to study the child's developing ability to conceptualize space with a Cartesian coordinate system. Specifically, Piaget and Inhelder argued that the ability to represent invariant horizontals and verticals in the physical world (e.g., the horizontal position of water; the vertical position of a plumb line) would depend on the child's having constructed a conceptual grid of horizontals and verticals. To test this notion, they asked children to indicate the position of water and plumb lines under stimulus conditions that provided conflicting (nonparallel or nonorthogonal) alternative frames of reference, as when the water line needed to be drawn in a tilted bottle. The original description of the task and data seemed to imply that children would master this understanding by the age of 9 or 10, and thus investigators were surprised when reports began appearing showing that many adults had serious difficulty on the task and that women were disproportionately evidencing difficulty (Liben, 1978; Rebelsky, 1964; Thomas, Jamison, & Hummel, 1973).

Explaining Individual and Group Differences in Spatial Thinking

The take-home message from the material presented thus far in this section of the chapter is that people vary with respect to performance on spatial tasks. These variations might reflect different rates of progress through developmental spatial achievements, different developmental end points, differential access to nonspatial component skills that are needed for spatial processing (e.g., working memory), or differential success in activating competencies in a given test environment (e.g., as a consequence of test anxiety). In trying to understand the observed differences, investigators have studied a range of factors drawn from both biological and social domains.

Within the domain of biology, a number of mechanisms have been studied to illuminate both individual differences and sex differences (see review in Liben, Susman, et al., 2002). Genetic influences on spatial skills have been one area of focus. From the perspective of individual differences, investigators have reported significant heritability for spatial visualization and spatial orientation abilities in both children and adolescents (Bratko, 1996; Plomin & Vandenberg, 1980). From the perspective of group (sex) differences, investigators have proposed an X-linked recessive gene for good spatial skills as one explanation for males' higher performance (Bock & Kolakowski, 1973; Thomas, 1983; Thomas & Kail, 1991; Vandenberg & Kuse, 1979). Hormonal effects have also been considered as an explanation of both individual and sex differences in spatial skills. For example, investigators have explored links between fluctuating levels of circulating hormones (e.g., as a consequence of pubertal, cyclical, or exogenously administered hormones) and spatial performance with mixed results (see reviews in Kimura, 1999; Liben, Susman, et al., 2002). There is more consistent evidence for effects of prenatal hormones on spatial outcomes. Experimental research with animals has shown direct effects of manipulating prenatal hormones (see Kimura, 1999; Liben, Susman, et al., 2002), and correlational research with humans has linked prenatal exposure to androgens to later spatial abilities. For example, girls with congenital adrenal hyperplasia who are exposed to atypically high levels of prenatal androgen later show elevated spatial skills in comparison to their unaffected sisters (Hampson, Rovet, & Altmann, 1998; Resnick, Berenbaum, Gottesman, & Bouchard, 1986).

Given that biological interventions are unlikely, it is the other major category of explanations, those in the social or environmental domain, that holds more interest for educators. Most of the research linking experience to spatial outcomes has been framed within the study of sex differences. There are plentiful data showing that boys and girls are socialized for different kinds of play, leisure activities, and educational experiences that are thought to be relevant for developing spatial skills (Etaugh, 1983; Serbin & Connor, 1979; Sherman, 1967). Correlational data show significant links between selected kinds of experience and spatial skills both within as well as between sexes (Newcombe, Bandura, & Taylor, 1983; Signorella, Jamison, & Krupa, 1989; Voyer, Nolan, & Voyer, 2000). However, it may be that children who begin with higher spatial skills choose to participate in these kinds of activities, and it may be that children with better initial skills benefit more from similar opportunities (see Casey, 1996; Casey, Brabeck, & Nuttall, 1995).

Only a few studies to date have attempted to examine the role that experiences unrelated to sex typing may play in accounting for differences in spatial outcomes. Illustrative is research showing that the frequency with which parents direct their 5-year-old children's attention to spatial-graphic features of a picture book relates to their children's success on spatial-graphic tasks (Szechter & Liben, 2004). Thus, research to date suggests that certain kinds of experiences do appear to foster spatial development, although considerably more research is needed to separate what effects are linked to experience separately from biological sex or socialized gender. From an educational perspective, what is most interesting is whether the experiences (e.g., different levels of play with spatial toys) that have been linked to higher spatial performance in correlational research can be exploited as educational interventions to enhance spatial skills.

THE CASE FOR SPATIAL INTERVENTION: WHEN DIFFERENCES ARE DEFICITS

In this section, I turn to interventions, first considering whether interventions are justified and then considering whether there is reason to think that interventions can be effective.

Why Might Spatial Performance Matter?

The research reviewed in the preceding section has established that there is a wide range of performance on any given spatial task at any given chronological age. From an educational perspective, the critical question is whether these performance differences matter. Consider, for example, the water-level task. Should anyone be concerned that some children perform poorly on it at an age at which the majority of children perform well? Should anyone be concerned that, on average, the task elicits significantly worse performance in groups of girls or women than in groups of boys or men? Should anyone be concerned that even by adulthood, a sizable portion of the population fails, even though the task was designed for young children and even though the initial Piagetian description of responses to the task implied that it would be universally mastered by middle or late childhood?

There are at least three potential reasons that these kinds of differences in performance might be of concern. The first is when performance on a given task directly affects the educational or occupational opportunities open to the individual student. It is easiest to appreciate the direct impact of test-specific performance by example. Consider elementary children's scores on an intelligence test such as the Stanford-Binet Test of Intelligence that may be used to decide on admission to a gifted program or a magnet school, or consider high school students' scores on national tests such as the

Scholastic Aptitude Test (SAT) that may be used to decide on admission to a selective college or eligibility for a scholarship. Unquestionably, performance on specific tests can play a critical role in opening or closing educational doors to individual students. If the water-level task (or some other spatial test) were used for educational decisions of this kind, performance would indeed matter to the individual student.

Second, performance on a given task, amalgamated at the level of an educational institution, can play a powerful role in how the institution is evaluated, and thus ultimately on how that institution operates. Again, the point is made most dramatically by considering the way teachers, schools, and school districts are being evaluated by their students' performance on national, standardized tests of reading and mathematics. Units whose students are judged to demonstrate inadequate levels of performance may be subject to various kinds of administrative sanctions. If students' performance on spatial tests were added to performance on English and math tests in evaluating institutions, then performance on the specified spatial tasks would be educationally critical.

Third, and conceptually most important, performance on a given spatial task may be educationally important because it reveals something about the child's mastery of cognitive tools that are truly needed for myriad educational challenges in their current and future educational, occupational, and daily lives. Again, by way of analogy, consider the arguments made for concern about students' performance on English tests. Performance on, say, a reading comprehension test is considered important not because it shows that the individual has understood the particular passages used in that test, but because it is taken as indicative of verbal literacy. Educational institutions and society as a whole view verbal literacy as critical for individuals' roles as students (e.g., learning from textbooks), workers (e.g., reading equipment manuals, reading and writing memos), and competent and informed citizens (e.g., reading newspapers to acquire knowledge relevant to political choices). A similar argument holds for tests of quantitative skills and mathematical literacy, which are likewise understood as necessary for school subjects (e.g., chemistry and social studies), occupations (e.g., sales and engineering), and daily life (e.g., adjusting a recipe, calculating how many gallons of paint are needed for one's house). If spatial literacy were judged to be similarly important for educational, occupational, and life tasks, performance on tests that assessed relevant components of that literacy would also be judged to be educationally important.

Does Spatial Performance Matter?

In the preceding section, I argued that under certain conditions, performance on particular assessment tasks would matter educationally. Do any of these conditions hold for spatial assessments?

The first condition concerns whether an individual's performance on particular spatial tasks directly affects the educational or occupational opportunities afforded that individual. In general, performance on spatial tasks is not used as a criterion for selection into academic programs. That is, most admissions or selection committees use performance on verbal and quantitative assessments in their decisions, and typically do not even ask applicants to submit data from explicit spatial assessments. This may well explain why research samples drawn from a given school population (e.g., a highly selective university) typically have a wide distribution of scores on spatial assessments such as the water-level task (Sholl & Liben, 1995). There are, however, some specialized programs in which performance on spatial tasks is explicitly used as part of selection criteria. For example, dental schools require applicants to take the American Dental Association's admission test that includes a Perceptual Ability Test designed to assess visual spatial skills. Many schools of architecture employ institutionally designed tests with spatial skill components. For younger students, it is unusual although not impossible to find selection through spatial testing. One example is the Johns Hopkins University Center for Talented Youth (CTY), which includes performance on a spatial test battery as one route for admission into its special programs. Interestingly, and consistent with the general assertion that spatial testing is not common, the spatial test battery is one that was developed and is administered through CTY. This home-grown approach contrasts markedly to the way CTY handles verbal and mathematical assessments. For these, applicants are simply asked to submit test results from any of a large set of national and state tests (e.g., the SATs, California Achievement Tests, Differential Aptitude Test, Independent School Entrance Examination, Iowa Test of Basic Skills). Thus, to summarize, there is some evidence that performance on spatial tests does open or close doors to some kinds of educational and occupational opportunities, although performance on tests designed to test verbal and mathematical skills or achievement is generally used far more pervasively.

With respect to the second potential reason that scores on spatial measures might be of educational importance, I am aware of no case in which students' spatial performance is used to evaluate the efficacy of educators or educational institutions. In the closing section of this chapter, I return to this issue from the perspective of educational policy.

Finally, as noted in the prior section, the third and most important reason that one might be concerned if an individual performed poorly on a particular spatial task is that this performance indicates inadequacy in a cognitive tool that is needed (or useful) for achieving valuable educational goals. The empirical work on which one can draw to answer this question is somewhat spotty, in large part as a consequence of the relatively sparse use of spatial testing (noted in discussing the first of the three conditions). There are data showing a relationship between performance on spatial tests and success in specialties that are—on their face—highly spatial in nature. As summarized by Shea, Lubinski, and Benbow (2001):

> Proficiency in spatial ability has long been associated with success in cognitively demanding educational tracks and occupations such as engineering, architecture, physics, chemistry, and medical surgery, as well as trades such as artisan, certain industrial positions (e.g., die checker, detailer, and pattern checker), surveyor, draftsman, and cartographer. (p. 604)

This is, of course, the rationale behind using spatial testing for admissions decisions for entry into some of these fields.

What is less well established is the relationship between performance on spatial tests and success in more universal components of education. The most commonly examined link between spatial ability and standard educational curriculum is in mathematics, again with much of this work being driven by an interest in accounting for sex-related differences. For example, in one program of research addressed to the role of spatial abilities in mathematics (Casey, 1996), mental rotation scores predicted to math ability as measured by the mathematics portion of the SAT. Combining these data with those from other research paradigms, Casey suggested that what accounts for the relation is not merely that some mathematical thinking is explicitly spatial (e.g., geometry), but also that effective mental rotation skills may

mark a general predisposition to using spatial strategies to process information. Such strategies may be generally helpful for mathematical reasoning that is not explicitly spatial (e.g., as in using spatial representations to solve algebra problems or transitive reasoning tasks). This interpretation has been supported by findings from research with middle school children as well (see Casey, Nuttall, & Pezaris, 2001), and by various studies examining strategies for solving different kinds of math problems (e.g., Johnson, 1985; Pattison & Grieve, 1984).

The other major educational domain that has been linked to spatial skills is science. The most dramatic links come not from research correlating spatial test performance to science outcomes, but from autobiographical accounts of scientific discoveries. Among the best known is Kekule's (1965) attribution of his discovery of the benzene ring to a dream in which he saw a serpent of atoms seizing its own tail, Einstein's claim that "he rarely thought in words at all" and that his visual and "muscular" images had to be translated "laboriously" into conventional verbal and mathematical terms, and Feynman's use of "Feynman diagrams" rather than lists of equations to work on quantum mechanics (Ferguson, 1992, p. 45). Working at an entirely different size and time scale, Wegener (1915/1966) noticed the "fit" between the coastlines of Africa and South America, leading him to develop the theory that continents were once one encompassing continent (Pangaea).

These descriptions from the history of science suggest that spatial thinking may well be important for dramatic scientific discoveries, but they do not necessarily bear on the question of whether spatial skills facilitate mastery of existing science curriculum among students in general. A number of scholars interested in science education have hypothesized that there should be such a connection (Mathewson, 1999), and investigators have tested this relation empirically in particular disciplines. In chemistry, for example, Bodner and colleagues (Bodner & McMillen, 1986; Carter, LaRussa, & Bodner, 1987) have reported significant correlations between performance on a variety of spatial assessments and success in solving various chemistry problems. Interestingly, however, the associations between variables have been found not only for chemistry problems that are analyzed as being "spatial" but also for chemistry problems that do not, at least on their face, appear to require spatial reasoning. One possible reason for finding an association between higher spatial skills and better performance on chemistry problems in general might be that the spatial assessment taps students' general intellectual levels. It is also possible that students with better spatial skills are more likely to create spatial-graphic representations (diagrams) to stand for nonspatial problems and hence organize the relevant information more effectively (Wu & Shah, 2004). Additional research is needed to test increasingly specific hypotheses about what spatial skill or skills are required for solving particular scientific problems, and then focus directly on these more specific relations.

In the research just described, the strategy has been to identify, analytically, spatial skills that underlie learning science concepts, and then to test for a correlation between that spatial skill and learning. A second research strategy is to provide instruction in the spatial skill so identified, and then study whether there is concomitant improvement in science learning. Finding a positive effect of the intervention would not only provide converging evidence for the hypothesis that the identified spatial skill is relevant to the math or science outcome, but, in addition, would support the utility of using interventions aimed at enhancing spatial skills. In the next section, I turn to work in this tradition.

Can Spatial Thinking Be Improved?

Before promulgating greater attention to spatial education in our educational system and before identifying routes through which it might be offered, it is important to ask whether there is any evidence that spatial skills can be affected by intentional interventions. Two major strands of work are encouraging in this regard. The first is found in the psychological research literature. This work has focused largely on the degree to which abilities are subject to intervention in general, with particular interest in whether it is possible to overcome the well-documented sex-related difference in spatial performance through training. The second is found largely in the professional or disciplinary education literatures, where the work has focused on developing and evaluating curricula designed to improve students' educational success.

Illustrative of work in the psychological tradition is laboratory research showing that performance on traditional spatial tests can be improved with training. For example, Kail and Park (1990) gave children and adults (11- and 20-year-olds) extensive practice and feedback on mental rotation tasks and found that speed of rotation improved significantly. The improvement, however, was confined to the same kinds of stimuli that were used in

training. Similar findings were reported by Sims and Mayer (2002) using the computer game Tetris in which the user must rotate shapes as they fall downward so that they fit neatly into openings as they reach the bottom of the screen. Students who were already skilled with Tetris performed better on a mental rotation task than did non-Tetris-players, but only when the shapes to be rotated were similar to those familiar from Tetris itself. Parallel findings have been reported for training on the water-level task: Participants given experience with feedback on the water-level task improved relative to controls. However, the advantage was found largely on items that were highly similar to those used in training (i.e., same-shaped containers at the same angles). These findings suggest that it may be specific angular relations between the water line and the bottle side that are learned rather than a generalized representation of invariant horizontality (Liben, 1991b). On the other hand, some training studies have shown positive effects of practice from mental rotation games or water-level stimuli to later performance on paper-and-pencil tests with different stimuli (De Lisi & Wolford, 2002; Okagaki & Frensch, 1994; Vasta, Knott, & Gaze, 1996). More generally, Baenninger and Newcombe (1989) summarized spatial training effects by a meta-analysis of training studies that were aimed at examining whether the sex differences in spatial performance are amenable to instruction. From the perspective of gender, what is particularly interesting about their findings is the conclusion that sex differences remained comparable even after training. From the perspective of spatial education, however, what is particularly interesting about their findings is the conclusion that training affected spatial performance significantly and often with considerable generality in both males and females.

Illustrative of work in the professional education tradition is work in engineering. For example, engineering students who performed at relatively low levels on a mental rotation test were given a curriculum to teach 3-D visualization skills prior to entering the required course in engineering graphics (Sorby & Baartmans, 1996, 2000). Participation in this curriculum increased performance on later standardized tests (e.g., the Spatial Relations test of the Differential Aptitude Test), and improved student retention. There have also been various spatial training programs as part of science education. For example, Pallrand and Seeber (1984) provided college students taking a college physics course with practice in drawing outdoor scenes, instruction in geometry and geometric transformations, and other curricula that focused students' attention on how views differ from different positions. Instructional sessions were over an hour long and were given weekly for roughly 2½ months. The intervention was successful: Visual skills and physics grades were higher in the intervention group than in a control group. In chemistry, interventions have also been shown to have a positive effect. For example, giving students training on visualization skills later elicited higher performance on test questions requiring the use of 3-D models (Small & Martin, 1983), and practice on several kinds of visual thinking relevant to chemistry improved students' test performance (Tuckey, Selvaratnam, & Bradley, 1991). Educational interventions of these kinds have not, however, been uniformly successful in improving outcomes or in generalizing to new settings. For example, engineering students whose performance on spatial tasks had improved from software used in an engineering graphics course were no more likely to remain in the program (Devon, Engel, & Turner, 1998). Chemistry students who showed gains from spatial training did not transfer those gains to new settings (Tuckey & Selvaratnam, 1993). The pattern of both positive and negative results establishes that educational interventions *can* be effective, although we are far from knowing precisely the detailed conditions required to make them so.

Should Spatial Performance Be Improved?

A strong case for spatial education may be built from the kinds of evidence described earlier indicating that spatial thinking is important not only for generating scientific discoveries but also for mastering routine educational curricula in math and science. Furthermore, it is likely to become increasingly important as technology offers increasingly sophisticated and complex spatial-graphic displays of voluminous quantities of information relevant to our occupational, educational, and everyday lives. Even apart from facilitating cognitive outcomes, research suggests that enhancing spatial skills may offer motivational benefits. Relevant is work by Casey and her colleagues (Casey, Nuttall, & Pezaris, 1997, 2001), who examined the role that spatial abilities may have in girls' attitudes toward math. Casey et al. (1997) found that 10th-grade girls' (but not boys') attitudes toward math were affected by their scores on a mental rotation task. Given that attitudes have a powerful effect on whether students decide to take more advanced mathe-

matics classes and whether they are motivated to apply themselves to master the material (Jacobs & Eccles, 1992), enhancing spatial skills may have a positive impact even apart from their direct facilitation of mastering mathematical or scientific material.

Taken together, these issues lead to the conclusion that there is great value in incorporating education for spatial thinking into the school curriculum. Indeed, given the wide range of educational, occupational, and daily activities that draw on spatial thinking, it is puzzling that spatial education does not already occupy central stage. One might hypothesize that the omission is simply a reflection of the pervasiveness of spatial thought discussed in the introductory section of this chapter. But it is relevant to recall that Molière's Monsieur Jourdain was shocked to discover he had been speaking prose all his life, not shocked to discover that he had been thinking spatially all his life. Yet, so much of our educational curriculum explicitly focuses on verbal, not spatial, skills. One might hypothesize that the balance is linked to the differential need for verbal versus spatial education in boys versus girls. It is interesting to observe that the educational community provides extensive education and remedial programs in the verbal arena that traditionally presents more problems for boys, but not in the spatial arena that traditionally presents more problems for girls. There are many potential attributions for this difference, ranging from chance, to political beliefs about the differential importance of having the full range of occupational opportunities open to males versus females, to beliefs about the role of biological foundations of verbal versus spatial abilities, to beliefs about their differential susceptibility to environmental input. But regardless of which (if any) of these factors has played a role in creating an educational environment that emphasizes verbal but not spatial education, it is time to begin to redress the balance. In the remainder of this chapter, I turn to one avenue by which spatial thinking might be fostered in the school context.

THE PLACE OF GEOGRAPHY AND MAP EDUCATION IN DEVELOPING SPATIAL THINKERS

Thus far in this chapter, I have argued for the pervasive nature of spatial thinking and its importance for a range of educational goals and have reviewed various kinds of evidence leading to the conclusion that it is risky to leave children entirely to their own devices to develop spatial concepts and to become fluent in developing and applying spatial skills. That is, psychometric studies and research by cognitive and cognitive-developmental psychologists show that not all individuals excel in the declarative, procedural, and representational skills that constitute spatial thinking, nor in the metacognitive skills that allow students to identify and implement potentially useful spatial strategies. At the same time, data from intervention studies show that certain kinds of experiences can be effective in enhancing spatial performance. This does not imply that interventions will necessarily bring all children to the same skill level (any more than instruction in English or in mathematics brings all children to the same level of sophistication in reading, writing, calculating, or mathematical reasoning). But it does imply that it is possible to enhance spatial thinking, and that there is a role for spatial education it in our schools.

Spatial Education in the School Context

Even if one accepts the conceptual arguments about the importance of spatial thinking and the empirical conclusion that spatial thinking can be facilitated through interventions, there remains the practical question of how spatial thinking might be taught in the school environment. There are two potential avenues to implement spatial education.

One approach is to target spatial skills for education much the way verbal and mathematical skills are targeted for education, that is, as domains in their own right that are taught through specific courses and evaluated through specific achievement assessments. This approach may be rejected on two grounds, one conceptual and the other practical. The conceptual argument against it is that we do not currently have the kind of analysis of concepts and skills to support a developmentally sequenced abstract curriculum of this kind (see, e.g., the discussion in the introductory section on definitions concerning formalisms in language versus space). The practical argument against a stand-alone spatial curriculum is compelling. Quite simply, the pressures on instructional time already overwhelm teachers, and adding an entirely new core curriculum would be unworkable.

The second and more realistic approach is to infuse spatial education into disciplinary instruction that is already in the curriculum. Ideally, the infusion process would involve making spatial education explicit in a broad range of school subjects. Courses in science and mathematics provide obvious examples. One might, for example, explicitly contrast two- versus three-dimensional models of chemical molecules, provide practice in linking rotations of concrete models to mental rotations of internally stored images, and perhaps explore what might be understood or communicated differently with alternative models of the same molecule. But even school subjects that are not as obviously spatial in nature can offer relevant opportunities. For example, in discussing literature, spatial representations might be used to model the flow and interconnections among plot lines of the story or among characters.

Even this second approach is subject to practical constraints, however, because teachers, like most of us who have been educated in the United States during the past century, are unlikely to have experienced explicit spatial education themselves. It is thus likely that they would find it difficult to identify opportunities for explicit instruction in spatial thinking and representations. A more realistic approach is to identify one or more existing school subjects that are transparently relevant for studying and facilitating spatial thinking and to use that subject as a vehicle for providing instruction aimed at developing spatial thinking. There are a number of desiderata for selecting a school subject: It should be viewed as an important component of any child's education; it should be taught across a range of grades; and it should be a subject that explicitly places all three aspects of spatial thinking identified earlier (i.e., declarative, procedural, and representational) at its core. I would argue that one school subject that satisfies these desiderata well is geography. In the remainder of this section of the chapter, I develop the argument that geography education is an important and viable route for educating spatial thinkers, and that a core component of geography education—map education—is a particularly valuable vehicle through which to develop spatial thinkers.

Geography and Geography Education

In the period following the founding of the United States as a nation, geography was viewed as an essential part of education. A citizen would have been considered educated only if educated in geography. This point was argued by John Adams in a letter to Abigail Adams in 1776 when he wrote:

> Geography is a Branch of Knowledge, not only very useful, but absolutely necessary, to every Person of public

Character whether in civil or military life. Nay it is equally necessary for Merchants. . . . America is our country, and therefore a minute Knowledge of its Geography, is most important to Us and our Children. (as quoted in Downs, 2004, p. 184)

The centrality of geography as a school discipline has since declined. Indeed, there was a long period in the United States in which geography was not taught systematically in the classroom. Following one such era in the 1980s, the media began carrying articles about shocking levels of geographic ignorance among U.S. citizens. Illustrative was a report that 20% of 12-year-olds in North Dallas misidentified Brazil as the United States on a map of the world, and that only about a third of students tested in a North Carolina college knew that the Seine was in France (*U.S. News & World Report,* March 25, 1985). Stories like these led to the proclamation of Geography Awareness Week by the U.S. Congress and to the establishment of an annual National Geography Bee by the National Geographic Society (see Liben, 2002a). From the perspective of formal education, however, probably the most significant sign of the reemergence of geography as a school discipline was its inclusion in federal legislation that established goals for K–12 educators. Specifically, the third goal of *Goals 2000: Educate America Act* (Public Law 103-227, March 31, 1994) included geography among the list of subjects that students should master.

As was the case for other school subjects named in *Goals 2000,* leaders in the discipline worked together with consultation from other stakeholders to develop national standards. Standards were designed to specify the knowledge and skills that children should acquire in the course of their education in each of the *Goals 2000* disciplines. Assuming that many readers would approach the geography standards with the regrettable assumption that geography is merely the compilation of endless place location and product production facts (e.g., that Paris is the capital of France, or that cheese is a major product of Wisconsin), the writers of *Geography for Life: National Geography Standards 1994* (Geography Education Standards Project, 1994) began their definition of geography by saying what it is *not:* "Geography is not a collection of arcane information." Rejecting the notion of geography as "the rote memorization of isolated facts," the authors went on to define geography as

the study of spatial aspects of human existence . . . an integrative discipline that brings together the physical and human dimensions of the world in the study of people, places, and environments. Its subject matter is Earth's surface and the processes that shape it, the relationships between people and environments, and the connections between people and places. (p. 18)

Myriad examples of what geography is and why it matters may be found in the *National Geography Standards.*

Once one appreciates that geography is more than place locations, it becomes apparent that geographic ignorance is more than a failure to know endless strings of location facts. And just as there is ample evidence that children (and even many adults) are ignorant about location facts, so, too, there is ample indication that many individuals are ignorant about deeper geographic thinking, and make geographically uninformed decisions as a result. Illustrative are the industrial decisions that lead to venting manufacturing pollutants into the air or water without considering possible global effects, building new residential developments without adequate thought to infrastructure demands, and making military or political decisions without knowledge of the terrain or the way the terrain is used by local inhabitants. Recognizing the costs of geographic ignorance has in part motivated more attention to geography education in our public schools (although the commitment contributes to ebb and flow even in contemporary times; Downs, 2005).

In the context of the current chapter, what is particularly important about geography education is that it provides an entrée into spatial thinking: "At its core, geographic thinking is *spatial* thinking. Geography is concerned with the explanation of spatial patterns and processes, and therefore the discipline is by its nature one that requires and fosters spatial thought" (Liben & Downs, 2001, p. 223). Geographic spatial thought takes place not only in abstract ideas and concepts, and is recorded and communicated not only in words and numbers, but also with maps.

Maps and Map Education

In this section, I turn more explicitly to the importance of maps and map education, not only as a support for geographic understanding, but also as an important kind of representation for a variety of other disciplines, intellectual processes, and educational goals. Given my expectation that most readers will be products of an educational era in which geography has held a relatively small role, I also include a brief tutorial on the principles and functions of maps. Only if one appreciates the richness of map forms and functions can one appreciate the role that map education may play in educating spatial thinkers.

Maps as Tools within and beyond Geography. Maps are arguably the single most important tool for geographical thinking and hence for geographic education. Their centrality is made readily apparent by the role they play in the *National Geography Standards* (Geography Education Standards Project, 1994). It is telling that the very first standard explicitly states that students should know "how to use maps and other geographic representations, tools, and technologies to acquire, process, and report information from a spatial perspective" (p. 61). This general standard, like all standards, is then translated into recommendations for the knowledge and skills that children of different ages should master. For example, the standards prescribe: "By the end of the fourth grade, the student knows and understands . . . characteristics and purposes of geographic representations—such as maps, globes, graphs, diagrams, aerial and other photographs, and satellite-produced images" (p. 106). The standards identify the kinds of observable behaviors that may be used to indicate that the child has, in fact, acquired the prescribed knowledge and skills. To continue with the illustration of the first standard, by the end of fourth grade, the student should be able to "interpret aerial photographs or satellite-produced images to locate and identify physical and human features. Examine a variety of maps to identify and describe their basic elements. . . . Design a map that displays information selected by the student" (p. 106). But the role of maps is not limited to the first standard. Of the 18 standards listed in *Geography for Life,* 13 of them refer explicitly to maps or other kinds of representations of spatial distributions. Of the remaining five, maps are strongly implicated in three and implicitly relevant to the other two (Liben & Downs, 2001).

Even in the absence of geography lessons, most people are familiar with maps. In the United States, maps appear at information booths of shopping malls, in newspapers, in travel brochures, in parks, and in cars, to name only a few of the many venues. In light of this pervasiveness, it is perhaps not surprising that both children and adults are highly familiar with some kinds of maps and map functions. For example, when preschool children were asked "Do you know what a map is? What's a map?" (Liben & Yekel, 1996, p. 2786), over half were able to explain maps as archives of location information (e.g., "Where things are" and "Things with different countries"), as navigation tools (e.g., "Something to get around places" and

"Something if you get lost, it helps you to get somewhere . . . maybe home"), or as both (e.g., "Something you see around the world. You can know where to go. If you get lost, you can look at a map and know where to go"). When college students were asked similar questions (Liben & Downs, 2001), responses likewise revealed familiarity with maps, although again, with an almost exclusive focus on archiving and wayfinding functions (rather than on other map functions discussed later). Similarly, both children and adults readily recognize that certain kinds of graphic representations are maps. However, for children, the map category tends to be relatively restricted to a small set of prototypical maps (e.g., state road maps and political maps like those hanging on classroom walls). Adults have a broader category, but even many adults reject graphic representations of place that expert geographers categorize as maps (Downs, Liben, & Daggs, 1988). It is thus important to review the broad range of maps and the functions that they serve.

Map Definitions and Map Principles. Just as the writers of the *National Geography Standards* began their definition of geography by saying what it is not, it is helpful to begin defining *map* by saying what it is not. Maps are not simply miniaturizations of some singular reality: "A map is a generalized, reduced, symbolic spatial representation of reality that has been transformed from the spherical surface of the Earth (or any celestial body) in some dimensionally systematic way" (Liben & Downs, 1989, p. 180). All maps instantiate three general principles (Liben, 2001):

1. The *duality principle:* A map has a dual existence: It *is* something and it *stands* for something.

2. The *spatialization principle:* A map has a spatial essence: It not only represents something, it represents something *in relation to* space.

3. The *purpose principle:* A map has purpose: It is not only *of* something, it is *for* something.

The Duality Principle. The duality principle is one that applies to any concrete, physical, spatial representation (or *spatial product;* see Liben, 1981, 2005). Anything used to stand for something else simultaneously has an existence in its own right as well as an existence as a representation or symbol that stands for its referent, a fact long recognized about representations and symbols (Goodman, 1976; Potter, 1979). The duality principle means that some but not all map qualities carry representational meaning about the referent. As an illustration, consider a road map of Pennsylvania such as one that might be stored in the glove compartment of a car. Many qualities of the map carry representational meaning about the environmental referent for which it stands. The lines stand for roads, the bends in the lines stand for the bends in the roads, and different colored lines represent different categories of roads. The first two qualities of the road symbols—that they are linear symbols and that they bend in certain directions—are motivated by the properties of the referent. That is, both the representation and the referent are linear and bend. The third quality of the road symbols—their color—is arbitrary. The different line colors do not imply different pavement colors; instead, they are used to symbolize different kinds of roads (e.g., toll roads, two-lane roads). The cartographer's choice of colors might be entirely arbitrary, based on convention, motivated by an aesthetic judgment, driven by metaphor, or chosen because they are perceptually easy to discriminate (see Brewer, 1997; Brewer, MacEachren, Pickle, & Herrmann, 1997). Users must refer to a map key to interpret the referential meaning of each colored line.

Not all qualities of the representation, however, carry referential meaning. For example, the fact that the map is a flat piece of paper is not meant to suggest that the state itself is flat, nor are the layers of the folded map meant to represent the geological folds of the mountains of central Pennsylvania; the width of the road lines is not informative about the road width, but is instead selected for legibility. For example, if one were to apply the scale given in the National Geographic Society (1998) *Road Atlas of the United States* to the road symbols, the roads would be calculated to be over five miles wide. In these examples, the flatness, folds, and line width are incidental features of the map. Interpreting the relationship between the referent and the representation, or what have been called the *representational correspondences* between the symbol and map (see Liben & Downs, 1989), is a necessary component of map understanding. In the absence of understanding representational correspondences, map users will draw incomplete or incorrect meanings from representations, a point discussed at greater length later in this chapter.

The Spatialization Principle. Implicit in the examples used to discuss the duality principle have been allusions to spatial qualities of maps. For example, the road symbols were referred to as linear, with the placements and bends in the lines following an analogous path to locations and bends in the road. Linear symbols may be contrasted to "point" symbols, appropriately used for

specific locations (e.g., highway exits), and to "areal" symbols, appropriately used for regions (e.g., areas of national forests). The type of symbol is not determined solely by the type of referent, however; it also reflects the scale of the map. Thus, for example, Chicago would be represented by a point symbol on a small-scale map of the entire world, but would be represented by an areal symbol on a large scale map of Illinois. These spatial qualities of symbols and referents (see Muehrcke & Muehrcke, 1998) thus segue to the spatialization principle, which highlights the central place of space in all maps. The centrality of space is evident in an introductory statement about maps taken from a classic cartography textbook, "All maps have the same basic objective of serving as a means of communicating spatial relationships and forms" (Robinson, Sale, Morrison, & Muehrcke, 1984, p. 4), and in a dictionary definition of maps that begins: "a representation, usually on a flat surface, as of the features of an area of the earth or a portion of the heavens, showing them in their respective forms, sizes, and relationships according to some convention of representation" (Flexner & Hauck, 1997, p. 1173).

The spatial qualities of any given map may be described by reference to the three dimensions of the "cartographic eye" (Downs, 1981) or the "mapmaker's vantage point" (Muehrcke & Muehrcke, 1998), illustrated in Figure 6.1. These include viewing distance,

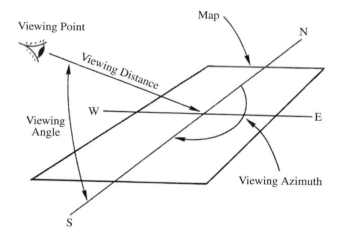

Figure 6.1 The cartographic eye showing the three dimensions of viewing distance, viewing angle, and viewing azimuth. *Source:* From "Maps and Mappings as Metaphors for Spatial Representation" (pp. 143–166), by R. M. Downs, in *Spatial Representation and Behavior across the Life Span: Theory and Application,* L. S. Liben, A. H. Patterson, and N. Newcombe (Eds.), 1981, New York: Academic Press. Reprinted with permission.

viewing angle, and viewing azimuth. Thus, just as there are representational correspondences that refer to which aspects of the referent are depicted on the map and the symbolic forms that are used to depict them, so, too, there are *geometric correspondences* that refer to the way the spatial qualities of the referent are represented by the spatial qualities of the map. Interpreting these geometric correspondences, like interpreting representational correspondences, is critical for map understanding.

The first dimension of the cartographic eye, viewing distance, refers to the distance from which the referent space is depicted. Viewing distance translates into the scale of the map. A map of any given referent space (i.e., the area being depicted) shown on any given representational space (i.e., the size of the particular piece of paper on which it is drawn) fixes the map scale (in cartographic terms, the "representative fraction"). For example, a piece of paper that measures $8\frac{1}{2}'' \times 11''$ might be used to represent all of Chicago, in which case the scale would be roughly $1:12,000$. Alternatively, it might be used to represent a room, in which case the scale would be roughly $1:20$. The second dimension of the cartographic eye, viewing angle, refers to the direction along the vertical dimension from which the referent space is depicted. The most common viewing angle is 90° (straight down), producing what are known as orthogonal, overhead, nadir, or vertical views, resulting in plan view maps like those commonly posted on hotel doors to show the locations of fire escapes. Shallower or oblique views (e.g., of 30° or 45°) depict the referent space from a slanted angle; these are often seen in historical maps of cities and are sometimes used in contemporary times for tourist maps. Oblique maps make landmarks (such as buildings) more recognizable and depict important topography (e.g., the steep hills of San Francisco). Illustrations of plan and oblique maps are shown in Figure 6.2. Finally, the third dimension of the cartographic eye, viewing azimuth, refers to the direction from which the referent space is depicted, conventionally expressed as angular disparity from north. Figure 6.3 shows an oblique map of the same region from two different viewing azimuths.

When small or even medium-size areas are being mapped (e.g., rooms, buildings, neighborhoods, cities), the relationship between referent space and paper space remains constant because over these distances, one can generally disregard the Earth's curvature (at least with maps that use parallel rather than central perspective; see

Figure 6.2   A circular plan map (top) and a square oblique map (bottom) of the Penn State campus.

Muehrcke & Muehrcke, 1998). However, when larger areas are mapped (e.g., states, countries, or continents), the Earth's curvature becomes relevant, and geometric solutions are needed to project the curved surface of the spherical Earth onto the flat surface of the map. The kind of surface on which the three-dimensional sphere is projected before being "unfolded" (e.g., a cone, a cylinder) and the location at which it is centered (e.g., centering the representation on the equator versus the North Pole)

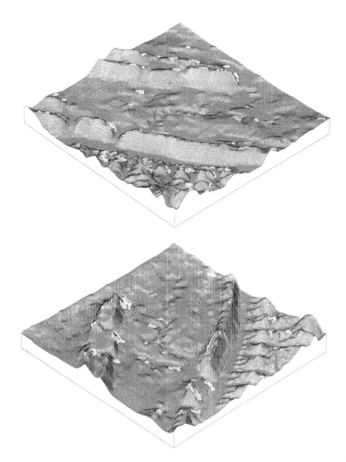

representational and geometric qualities used to represent the chosen content). This diversity of content and form is another way of reinforcing the general point made earlier that maps are not simply some externally determined and singular miniaturization of some fixed reality. The purpose of a map affects the form that a map takes. Thus, for example, a map intended to show major political divisions and perhaps the role of physical geography in those divisions (e.g., the locations of rivers, ports, and mountain ranges that might be used for determining political boundaries) would sensibly be created in a smaller scale (i.e., depict a larger space) than would a map intended to allow someone to plan a car trip across the same areas. The former would omit roads; the latter would show them in detail. Although decisions to omit or include particular kinds of information (e.g., roads) may reflect practical matters (e.g., the room for the symbols given a particular map size), more important, they reflect the cartographer's intentions to highlight certain ideas and relationships.

Consider the two examples of world maps shown in Figure 6.4. The first is the highly familiar Mercator projection; the second is an equal area projection. Both distort spatial features of the real world, as they must,

Figure 6.3 Two oblique perspective representations. In both images, the viewing angle is 30°. The viewing azimuth of the top representation is 315° clockwise from north (0°), and the viewing azimuth of the bottom representation is 45° clockwise from north.

also play powerful roles in determining the appearance of the representation. It is important to appreciate that whenever a three-dimensional space is projected on to a two-dimensional surface, at least one spatial property of the referent space (area, direction, distance, or shape) *must* be distorted. Thus, there is no single "correct" solution to this projection problem. A solution used for a particular map should be driven by the purpose the map serves, thus leading to the third map principle.

The Purpose Principle. As might be inferred from the examples given in the course of discussing the duality and spatialization principles, there are virtually limitless choices with respect to the "what" for any given map (i.e., the referential content that is depicted) as well as with respect to the "how" of any given map (i.e., the

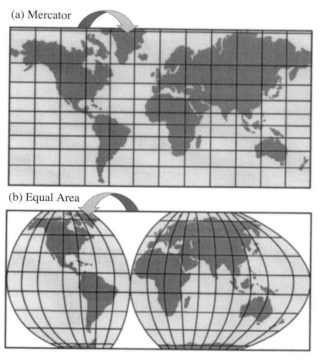

Figure 6.4 World maps in (a) a Mercator projection and (b) an interrupted flat polar quartic equal-area projection. Arrows point to Greenland.

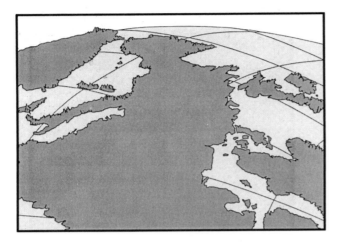

Figure 6.5   An oblique perspective map of Europe as viewed from the east. *Source:* From "Thinking through Maps" (p. 53), by L. S. Liben, in *Spatial Schemas and Abstract Thought*, M. Gattis (Ed.), 2001, Cambridge, MA: MIT Press. Reprinted with permission.

given the need to project the three-dimensional oblate spheroid of Earth onto two-dimensional paper. But the choice of distortions is linked to the purpose of the map. The Mercator projection distorts area but preserves direction; the equal area projection distorts direction but preserves area. The former is no less accurate than the latter, and it serves the purpose for which it was intended, namely, sea navigation. As another example, consider the map of Europe shown in Figure 6.5. It suggests the vulnerability of Western Europe to military action from the east. It thereby offers a vision of "reality" that is different—but no less "accurate"—from the one most of us will have developed from repeated exposure to the more common north-at-the-top, vertical view maps of Europe.

Map Functions.   From the perspective of using map education as a means of the more general goal of spatial education, it is useful to summarize map functions from the perspective of geography, and in the course of doing so, provide a few additional illustrative maps that fall outside the prototypical maps commonly found in cars, psychology journals, and teacher-preparation classes. A useful list of map functions is the following one, taken from a basic cartography text by Muehrcke (1986, p. 14):

1. Record and store information.

2. Serve as computational aids.

3. Serve as aids to mobility.

4. Summarize complex, voluminous data.

5. Help us to explore data (analyze, forecast, spot trends).

6. Help us to visualize what would otherwise be closed to us.

7. Serve as trigger devices to stimulate thought.

As noted earlier, both children and adults tend to be most familiar with archival (1) and wayfinding (3) functions, and, by implication, computational functions (2). It is important to recognize that using maps even for just these first three functions depends on understanding the representational and geometric correspondences discussed earlier. For example, if users do not understand the relationships between referent space and paper (or computer screen) space that hold for different projections, they may make faulty inferences about the referent space or computing distances in that space. There is evidence that just such faulty inferences occur. For example, many adults hold the belief that Greenland is larger than Brazil (Nelson, 1994), presumably a consequence of failing to understand the distortions of area that occur on a Mercator projection but are avoided on an equal-area projection (see Figure 6.4). As another example, President Ford was criticized for stopping in Alaska to give a campaign speech as he traveled (at taxpayer expense) to Japan. However, when the route is shown as a great circle route, the justification for giving the speech as part of an efficient refueling stop becomes evident (see Figure 6.6).

The other map functions (4 through 7) listed by Muehrcke (1986) are rarely represented in children's or adults' responses to questions about map functions, or in psychologists' investigations of map understanding. However, these are key map functions in geography as well as in the many other disciplines for which maps are central tools (e.g., anthropology, ecology, urban planning, military science, agriculture, meteorology, demography, criminal justice, epidemiology, history, geology, astronomy, environmental science, oceanography, and political science). An example is provided by the thematic maps shown in Figure 6.7 (p. 222), which show cancer rates for men and for women, by county, over a 20-year period. Patterns emerge from representations like these that would be virtually impossible to detect in tabular lists of cancer rates. Such patterns raise a host of questions, some of which may be answered by overlaying other data on the same base map. For exam-

(a) Mercator

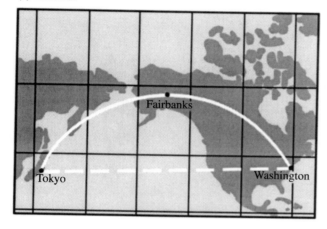

(b) Orthographic

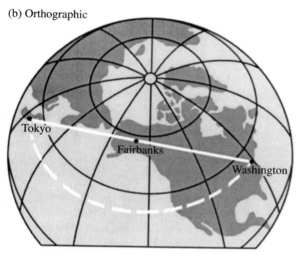

Figure 6.6 Depictions of the route taken by President Ford from Washington, DC, to Tokyo, Japan, with a stop in Fairbanks, Alaska, using a Mercator projection (a) and an orthographic projection (b). Adapted from *Map Use: Reading, Analysis, and Interpretation* (4th ed., p. 10), by P. Muehrcke and J. O. Muehrcke, 1998, Madison, WI: JP Publications. Reprinted with permission from "Thinking through Maps" (p. 72), by L. S. Liben, in *Spatial Schemas and Abstract Thought*, M. Gattis (Ed.), 2001, Cambridge, MA: MIT Press.

ple, are there lifestyles, employment patterns, features of physical geography, sources of water or food supplies that covary with these incidence patterns? What characterizes the living patterns of men versus women residing in the northwest corner of Nevada that may help to pinpoint disease etiology? Maps may also be used to reveal patterns of change or events over time, which, in turn, may suggest mechanisms of change. Plotting the locations of earthquakes over time has been used to generate hypotheses about the existence of tectonic plate bound-

aries; plotting the changing distributions of disease has been used to generate hypotheses about routes of contamination (see MacEachren, 1995).

In short, maps are important not only because they can archive place information per se, but also because they can reveal patterns and help to generate and test hypotheses. They provide excellent models of spatial thinking that can be applied across a wide range of educational and occupational tasks, as well as useful for the real-world tasks encountered in daily living (see Liben, Kastens, et al., 2002).

Summary

The title of this section of the chapter, "The Place of Geography and Map Education in Developing Spatial Thinkers," is meant to carry two meanings. First, it is meant to imply that geography and map education have a place (i.e., a role) in helping to develop (i.e., to create) spatial thinkers. The subject matter of geography, which describes and explains the spatial distribution of phenomena, necessarily involves and promotes spatial thinking. Furthermore, the key tool of geography—the map—is inherently spatial. Maps challenge users to understand a wide range of declarative spatial knowledge (e.g., measurement), spatial representations (e.g., the symbolic meaning of a particular map), and procedural spatial skills (e.g., using mental rotation to compensate for a map that is unaligned with the space it represents). Many other school subjects (e.g., chemistry, history, mathematics) also draw on and challenge students' spatial thinking, and make plentiful use of both concrete and mental spatial representations, but they generally do so only implicitly. Thus, geography education in general, and map education in particular, can have an important place in developing spatial thinkers.

Second, the title it is meant to imply that geography and map education take place in the context of developing spatial thinkers (i.e., children who are themselves developing *as* spatial thinkers). In other words, just as the process of becoming educated in geography and maps enhances spatial thinking in the students who learn these topics, so, too, students come to this material with certain qualities as spatial thinkers. Children's own cognitive qualities influence the way the material can be taught and processed, and, particularly important, these qualities evolve as part of normal cognitive developmental processes more generally. In the next section, I turn to considering how these two meanings are entwined in children's developing understanding of maps.

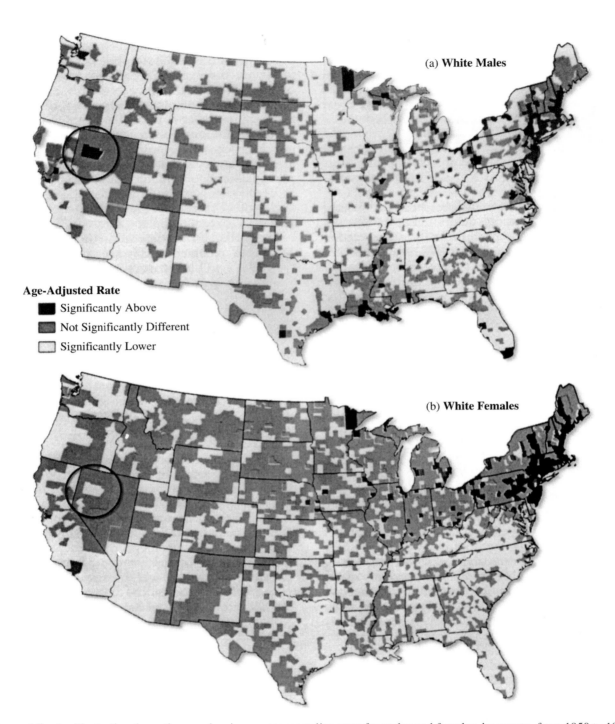

Age-Adjusted Rate

- ■ Significantly Above
- ▨ Not Significantly Different
- □ Significantly Lower

Figure 6.7 An illustrative thematic map showing cancer mortality rates for males and females, by county, from 1950 to 1969. Adapted from *Map Use: Reading, Analysis, and Interpretation* (4th ed., p. 10), by P. Muehrcke and J. O. Muehrcke, 1998, Madison, WI: JP Publications. Reprinted with permission from "Thinking through Maps" (p. 73), by L. S. Liben, in *Spatial Schemas and Abstract Thought,* M. Gattis (Ed.), 2001, Cambridge, MA: MIT Press.

THE DEVELOPMENTAL PATHWAY TO MAP UNDERSTANDING

Thus far, I have defined spatial thinking and provided an argument for its importance, reviewed empirical work showing that individuals and groups vary with respect to their spatial thinking skills when left to develop in their natural ecologies, and provided data demonstrating that spatial performance can be facilitated through educational interventions. In addition, I presented arguments for why geography education in general and map education in particular offer good vehicles for educating spatial thinkers. In recognition that most readers will not have had extensive training in geography or cartography, and with the knowledge that even adults without such training typically have restricted views of maps and map functions, I provided a brief tutorial aimed at expanding readers' appreciation for the diversity in appearance and function of maps. In this section of the chapter, I focus in more detail on what map understanding entails, and highlight findings from our research on children's developing understanding of maps.

Figure 6.8 illustrates one way of organizing the components of map understanding and, hence, map education. There are two critical links in the enterprise, depicted by the arrows shown in the figure. The left arrow links the referent and the map. Map education involves teaching the connections between the referent and the representation, connections that involve representational correspondences (what is mapped) and geometric correspondences (the spatial content), discussed earlier. These two are intimately entwined. For example, a map that depicts the topography of a region has certain

referential content (e.g., information about elevations of land, size and locations of lakes) that is itself spatial (e.g., height above sea level, how much area is covered by the lake). In some sense, the symbols are nonspatial (e.g., different elevations might be shown by different colors, or by hachure lines, or by relief shading, or by contour lines labeled with elevation data; lakes may be shown in blue), but the symbols also have spatial qualities that are driven both by the spatial qualities of the referent space (e.g., the placement of the colors to indicate elevation depends on the way the land is contoured; the area of blue depends in part on how large the lake is) as well as by various cartographic decisions (e.g., the area of colors used for various elevations or the lake also depends on scale and the kind of projection that is used). Students (and the educators teaching them) need to understand these links.

The right arrow links the map user and the map. Two kinds of map user connections are relevant. First, qualities of the user affect the way the map is processed. This statement is an instantiation of the more general constructivist view of knowledge that holds that meaning emerges through interactions shaped by qualities of the stimulus (here, the map) and qualities of the person (here, the child's spatial concepts). When applied to the domain of spatial-graphic representations such as maps, the details of this constructive process may be conceptualized by the embedded model (Liben, 1999), shown in Figure 6.9.

Three aspects of the embedded model are central. First, various perceptual and cognitive processes (such as projective spatial concepts) are used by the child for learning from referents themselves (e.g., acquiring knowledge about the locations of building from moving around a campus), for learning from representations (e.g., extracting meaning from a map or photograph of the campus), and for learning about the strategies used to create representations (e.g., learning about photographic or cartographic techniques). Second, as a result of interacting with each of these three types of stimuli (referents, representations, and representational strategies), the child acquires specific declarative and procedural knowledge (e.g., information about the campus itself; understanding of distance between two landmarks shown on the map; skill in making maps). These interactions may also facilitate more general development (e.g., helping the child to appreciate that vistas look different from different vantage points, thus fostering projective spatial concepts).

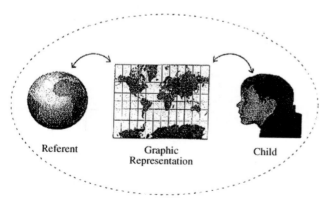

Figure 6.8 Components of map understanding and map education.

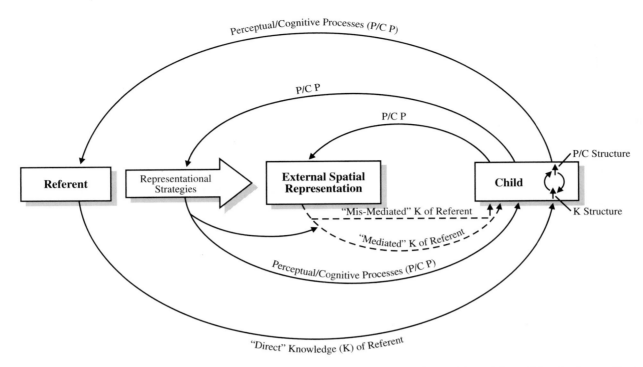

Figure 6.9   The embedded model of understanding external spatial representations. Adapted from "Developing an Understanding of External Spatial Representations" (pp. 297–321), by L. S. Liben, in *Development of Mental Representation: Theories and Applications,* I. E. Sigel (Ed.), 1999, Mahwah, NJ: Erlbaum. Reprinted with permission.

Third, an understanding of representational strategies plays an important role in allowing the child to use representations to construct knowledge of the referent. With an understanding of the representational process (e.g., how a Mercator projection works), the child can use the representation to obtain knowledge about the referent. The child thus obtains "mediated" knowledge of the referent (e.g., learning about the relative land sizes of Greenland and Brazil). Absent an understanding of the relevant representational strategies, however, the child runs the risk of inferring the wrong information, or obtaining what I have referred to (Liben, 1999) as "mis-mediated" knowledge of the referent (e.g., thinking that Greenland is larger than Brazil).

The second relevant connection between the map user and the map is the spatial relationship between the person and the space depicted on the map. This connection is relevant any time the map user is within the depicted space. Figure 6.10 illustrates this situation by showing a person in a room that has, within it, a map of that room. The map shows the location of the person "on the map." This map marks the "self-map relationship" (a relationship that would exist even if the map had not been physically marked). In addition to the self-map relationship, there is also a "self-space relationship." In

Figure 6.10, this relationship is shown by the drawing of the person in the room. In actuality, this is a representation as well. A real person-space relationship is your current position in relation to the room, town, country, state, region, country, continent, planet, solar system, and universe in which you find yourself as you read this chapter. In addition, whenever there is a map of a space (as depicted in Figure 6.10), there is also a "map-space relationship" that relates the map and the space irrespective of any viewer. In the particular case shown in Figure 6.10, the map-space relationship is unaligned;

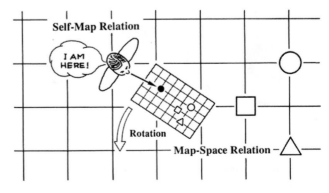

Figure 6.10   The map-space-self relation.

that is, the map and the room are not oriented exactly in the same direction. To bring the map into alignment with the room, the map would need to be rotated as shown by the arrow labeled "rotation."

Different map tasks vary with respect to the degree to which they call on the user's understanding of the relationships among map, space, and person. In many uses of maps, one may work successfully within the map space itself. For example, given a map of the United States, someone might be asked whether Chicago or Atlanta is closer to New York City. This question can be answered correctly without attending to the connection between the mapped cities and the real cities. Other map uses require attention only to the map-space relationship. For example, given a map of a room, one might be asked to align the map with the room. If the map and room are as shown in Figure 6.10, one would need to rotate the map as indicated by the rotation arrow to bring the map into alignment. In neither of these two tasks would it be necessary to figure out one's own location in the room or "on the map." Still other map uses, however, require attention to the self-map relationship. For example, given a map of a campus, one might be asked to walk from one's current location to, say, a building marked with a star on the map. To succeed on this task, it would be necessary to find one's current location and the target building on the map, plan a route on the map, and then relate the mapped space to the real space, updating one's place "on the map" as one executed the route.

In the two subsections that follow, I describe illustrative findings from our research on children's developing understanding of various kinds of map-space-person relationships (Downs & Liben, 1991, 1993; Downs et al., 1988; Liben & Downs, 1986, 1989, 1991, 1994). Some of the data come from stand-alone investigations in which children were interviewed or tested in sessions designed to collect research data. Most of the data, however, were collected in the course of teaching children about maps in their regular classrooms. We served as classroom teachers for a 5-week map curriculum given to 265 children in 11 kindergarten and first- and second-grade classes. In addition, we also conducted individual assessments (e.g., on standardized and Piagetian measures of spatial abilities or concepts) of those children from whom we had received signed parental permission (roughly 75% of the sample). Portions of the curriculum (with associated data collection) were also given in smaller units (ranging from a day or two to a week or two) to children in later elementary school grades and in middle schools.

Classroom lessons thus simultaneously served two purposes. One was to introduce students to a wide range of maps and map functions and to give them experience in interpreting and using maps. The second was to collect data that would enable us to characterize children's developing understanding of maps. These dual goals necessitated some compromises with respect to each. For example, sometimes pedagogical requirements led us to use activities in a fixed sequence even though research design would have dictated counterbalancing orders; sometimes research requirements led us to ask students to work individually even though pedagogical considerations might have led us to ask students to work collaboratively. The findings from this program of research have fed into the design of a number of subsequent educational interventions, ranging from brief consultancies to extended development and evaluation of educational curriculum. Highlights of our research findings are presented in the remainder of the current section. Illustrations of educational interventions from these and other curricula are given in the section that follows.

Developing Representational Map Understanding

As noted earlier, one of the key aspects of map understanding is interpreting the referential content of maps. Fundamental challenges may be inferred from the earlier discussion of the duality principle of maps: the need to (a) distinguish which qualities of the representation are symbolic and which qualities of the representation are incidental, (b) avoid assuming that qualities of the symbol necessarily reflect qualities of the referent, and (c) avoid assuming that qualities of the referent will be evident in qualities of the symbol. In addition, having understood that meaning cannot be determined by inferring qualities of the referent from qualities of the representation, the map user is also challenged by the need to (d) understand how to consult a map key to obtain the necessary information about the assigned meaning of symbolic qualities.

There are two levels of representational meaning that need to be understood (Liben & Downs, 1989). The first level, *holistic,* refers to understanding the referential meaning as a whole, that is, understanding the meaning of the representation at a molar level. At least for familiar map forms, even very young children generally show good holistic understanding of the referential meaning of maps or other place representations. For example, when preschoolers (age 3 to 6 years) were interviewed and asked what a Rand McNally road map of Pennsylvania showed, virtually all children named some kind of place referent. Where they faltered was in identifying the particular place. Illustrative was one child who responded that the map showed "part of Africa" and another who responded particularly expansively that it showed "California, Canada, the West, and the North Coast" (Downs et al., 1988). Given preschoolers' lack of reading skills, it is not surprising that they were unable to identify it as Pennsylvania, but what is more telling was their apparent willingness to make assumptions about what the map might depict. Even holistic understanding, however, depends on the child's familiarity with the map form. A less familiar tourist map of Washington, DC (in which streets were depicted in white on a blue background), that was readily interpreted by adults as showing a city was either entirely uninterpretable to preschool children or was interpreted incorrectly even at the holistic level (e.g., identifying it as, for example, "a cage" or "a space ship").

The second level, *componential,* refers to understanding the referential meaning of individual pieces or components of the map. Even children who are successful in interpreting the meaning of the map as a whole often show dramatic errors in interpreting individual symbols. Results from our interviews of children (Liben & Downs, 2001) showed that preschool children often inferred meaning on the basis of what the symbol looked like even when the interpretation would be impossible given the holistic meaning of the map they had just identified. For example, preschoolers who had just correctly identified the environmental referent of the road map as a place (even if California rather than Pennsylvania), went on to interpret the yellow symbols for populated regions as "eggs" and "firecrackers," apparently because the splotchy yellow areas looked like eggs or firecrackers. Errors of this kind suggest that the child assumes that the symbol stands in an iconic relation to a referent and fails to use the referential context to constrain interpretations of resemblance. Even when children interpreted the referential category correctly, they tended to overextend qualities of the symbol to the referent. Illustrative were children who inferred that a red line used to represent a road meant that the road itself was actually red. Similar assumptions informed children's production of symbols. Illustrative from our classroom studies was the finding that when asked to produce maps of their classrooms, first and second graders almost always generated iconic symbols (Liben

& Downs, 1994). Furthermore, they typically rejected abstract symbols suggested to them, as when children laughed at our suggestion that they might use asterisks to show the file cabinets because "file cabinets don't look like stars" (Liben & Downs, 1989).

More systematic evidence for the powerful effect of children's belief in iconicity is provided by an investigation in which 5- and 6-year-old children watched two videotapes of people placing symbols on a map (Myers & Liben, 2005). One videotape showed a person placing green dots on the map with actions and comments that conveyed a symbolic, functional intent. This person commented that her intent was to "use this," and she explicitly related locations in the room to locations on the map. Before placing each dot, she looked up as if watching someone in the room and made comments about the connection between the room location and the dot location, such as, "Hmm. . . . I see that she hid the next one over there in the room, and that means I should draw a green dot here on my paper." The second videotape showed a person placing red dots on the same map but with actions and comments that conveyed an aesthetic intent. For example, she commented on selecting a red pen because red was her favorite color, mentioned her intent to make it prettier, and explained her plan to hang it on the wall. Furthermore, as she decided where to place the dots, she looked at only the representation itself.

After viewing both videotapes, children were asked about the two characters' intents, and then asked which of the two drawings they would use to help them find hidden fire trucks. Almost all the children, including those who were able to explain the actors' aesthetic and symbolic intentions correctly, incorrectly selected the drawing with the red dots, suggesting that they were seduced by the match between the color of the dots and fire trucks.

These data, along with findings that have been reported elsewhere (Liben & Downs, 1989, 1991, 1994), provide evidence that interpreting the full range of representational meaning of maps continues to challenge children at least through the early elementary school grades. This is true not only for maps that are created primarily to present or record location information (as in the road and room maps used in the work described earlier) but also for maps that are created to spatialize other kinds of information (e.g., thematic maps such as the kind illustrated in Figure 6.7). For example, in an investigation of kindergarten through third-grade children's understanding of thematic maps (Newman & Liben, 1996), children had difficulty interpreting the graphic symbolization of population density in several kinds of maps.

At first glance, it might seem difficult to reconcile the conclusion that the representational meaning of maps is challenging for children of these ages with the well-known finding from scale-model tasks and related symbol tasks (DeLoache, 1987; Troseth, 2003) that children understand the "stand for" relationship by 3 years of age. The latter tasks, however, typically place only very minimal demands on children's understanding of symbols because there is usually a unique symbol for each unique referent. When representation tasks include symbols that are less iconic or include multiple instances of the same symbol, performance is significantly worse (see Blades & Spencer, 1994; Liben & Yekel, 1996). In such cases, children may need to rely on spatial understanding to disambiguate which of two or more identical symbols stands for a particular referent. In the next section, I focus on children's understanding of the spatial meaning of maps more explicitly.

Developing Spatial Map Understanding

The second major set of challenges in map understanding is presented by the spatial qualities of maps shown in the cartographic eye, discussed earlier (see Figure 6.1). As was true in the representational domain, empirical data concerning the spatial domain also show a mixture of understanding and confusion.

Viewing Distance

The first dimension, viewing distance, involves the various scale, proportional, and metric features of maps. Although children are, in general, able to understand the general concept that something small, like a map, can stand for something large, like a room or town, that understanding is somewhat fragile. First, young children are sometimes confused by the disparity between the size of symbols and the size of their referents. In our research with the Pennsylvania road map described earlier, for example, we encountered a number of preschool children who had difficulty interpreting particular symbols because of their size. Illustrative was a child who denied the possibility that the road lines actually showed roads because they were "not fat enough for two cars to go on" (Liben & Downs, 2001). Another child who was shown a plastic relief map of the local area rejected the idea that the raised portions could be mountains, saying that "they're not high enough" to be mountains.

Second, children in both preschool and early elementary school grades have difficulty completing map tasks that require sensitivity to proportional measurement, even allowing for fairly wide margins of error. One illustration from our research comes from a task in which first- and second-grade children were first given a copy of an aerial photograph of Chicago, reproduced in Figure 6.11 (Liben & Downs, 1991). After class discussions about how the photograph was taken and how it might be used to help create a map of the city, each child was asked to use it as the basis for drawing a sketch map of the city. Each child was then given a copy of a black-and-white map of a portion of Chicago. Children were given some time to try to figure out which section of the aerial photograph was depicted in the map, and were then given an acetate sheet to place over the photograph. The acetate contained a rectangle outlining the area shown on the map as well as eight numbered circles marking locations. Children were asked to place numbered stickers on the map to show the locations analogous to those circled on the photograph. Results are also shown in Figure 6.11. Not surprisingly, second-grade children performed better than first-grade children. What is more interesting, though, are the differential levels of success across the locations. Although there are many potential hypotheses about what might account for the pattern of data, one possible explanation concerns the kind of spatial cues available for given items. When children could use a topological or landmark clue (e.g., the bend in the breakwater), they did very well. When, however, they needed to judge location based on proportional distances on the two representations at different scales, they performed more poorly.

Research by other investigators is consistent with the notion that children find it particularly difficult to understand the scale relation between a space and its representation. For example, in a study in which 6- to 12-year-old children were asked to select symbols of the appropriate size to represent buildings on a map, only those in the oldest group chose symbols that were scaled consistently (Towler & Nelson, 1968). In a task that required children to scale up from a map to the referent space (Uttal, 1996), 4- to 6-year-old children first learned where toy symbols belonged on a map of a room. Once locations were learned to criterion, children were asked to place the real toys in the real room in their analogous locations. Consistent with the idea that scale is challenging was the finding that children generally performed well with respect to reproducing the configurations among the toys,

Figure 6.11 Aerial photograph of Chicago (left) on which locations were marked. Maps (right) show percentages of correct responses at each location.

but often performed poorly with respect to scaling the configuration appropriately to the room-size space (e.g., clustering the toys in one corner).

Viewing Angle

The second dimension of the cartographic eye, viewing angle, challenges children's understanding of how changes in vantage point affect the appearance of graphic representations. Again, there are several kinds of data showing that unfamiliar viewing angles make it challenging for children to interpret maps. One line of evidence comes from the spontaneous errors children make in interpreting symbols on plan (overhead) maps. For example, an overhead view of a double sink on a plan map of the preschool classroom was interpreted as a "door" (Liben & Yekel, 1996), an interpretation that makes sense if one assumes that the child thought of the graphic as a straight-ahead view of door panels. Similar findings have been obtained in research using aerial photographs, as, for example, when primary school children identified tennis courts as doors (Spencer, Harrison, & Darvizeh, 1980) and railroad cards lined up in parallel as "bookshelves" (see Liben & Downs, 2001). Another line of evidence that children have

difficulty interpreting representations that depict referents from unfamiliar vantage points comes from their differential performance on maps using different viewing angles. Preschool children were more accurate in placing stickers to show objects' locations on an oblique map of their class that more closely mirrors their own viewing experience than on a plan map that depicts the room in a way that is never experienced directly (Liben & Yekel, 1996).

A third line of evidence comes from production tasks in which children were asked to take an overhead viewing angle in producing maps. Illustrative data come from first- and second-grade children who were asked to draw their school building as it would look to a bird flying overhead and looking straight down. Following the drawing task, children were asked to select the overhead view of their school from among six alternatives. Children's drawings were scored as elevation (eye-level) views, overhead views, mixed elevation and overhead views, or unscorable (because an undifferentiated rectangle could be either a windowless side or a roof of a rectangular building). Figure 6.12 shows two sample responses. One is an elevation view of a generic building

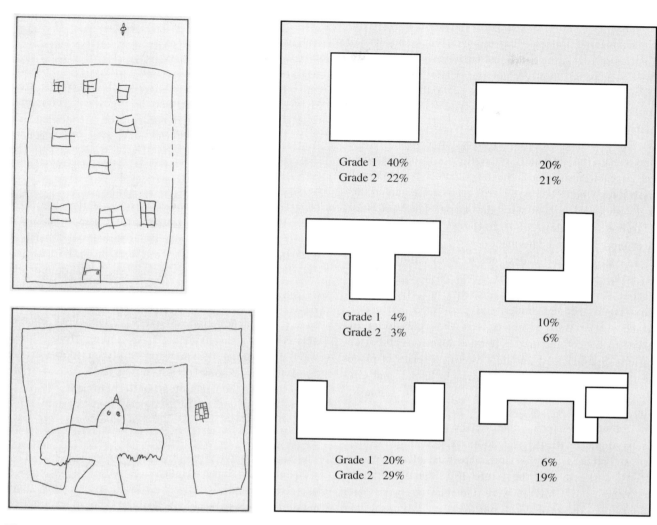

Figure 6.12 Two first-grade children's responses when asked to draw their school as it would look to a bird flying overhead and looking straight down (left) and distributions of choices when asked to select an overhead view of the school (right). Lower right shows the correct response.

that bears no relation to the school other than the fact that both are buildings. The second is a plan view that is remarkably close to accurate except for omitting an enlarged area at the end of one wing of the school. Interestingly, both examples come from students in the same first-grade class, providing a dramatic illustration of the individual differences within chronological age and demographic group discussed in an earlier section of this chapter. Overall, though, second-grade children were systematically better at this task than first-grade children: There was a decrease in the incidence of elevation views from first to second grade (32% to 8%), an increase in plan views (27% to 44%), and little change in either the incidence of mixed view drawings (8% in

each) or unscorable drawings (34% to 40%). Choices given on the selection task are also shown in Figure 6.12. As may be seen from the distributions of selections, as anticipated, children at both grades were better able to select than produce a correct overhead view, and performance improved with age.

Viewing Azimuth

The third dimension, viewing azimuth, refers to the orientation from which the referent space is depicted. One kind of challenge in this domain arises from the need to understand the relationship between the orientation of the map in relation to the space it represents, particularly when the two are unaligned. This situation arises in many wayfinding or navigation tasks in real life, as when someone is using a map to navigate, and because of a series of turns, the relationship between the map and the space is constantly changing. Under such circumstances, the map user must either mentally compensate for the misalignment (e.g., by mentally rotating the map) or physically compensate (by actively turning the map with each change in physical direction so that the map and space are continually brought back into alignment). In some circumstances, the map cannot be physically moved (as when "You Are Here" maps are mounted on a wall out of alignment with the space; see M. Levine, Marchon, & Hanley, 1984); in these circumstances, the user must accommodate mentally.

In one investigation designed to study children's ability to respond to challenges raised by unaligned maps (Liben & Downs, 1993), children from kindergarten, first-grade, second-grade, and combined fifth/sixth-grade classes were given maps of their classroom and asked to use colored arrows to mark locations and orientations. Specifically, an adult went to a series of places in the classroom and pointed straight ahead, and children were asked to place colored arrows on their maps to show where he was standing and in which direction he was pointing. After completing the task once with the maps aligned with the classroom, a second set of maps was distributed, but this time maps were placed on children's desks so that they were 180° out of alignment with the room. Children were told that they were going to be doing the task again, but this time while the map was "turned around." Children were asked to leave the map on their desks as it was placed, and a colored dot was visible to teachers to ensure that the map remained in the intended orientation. As the task progressed, periodic reminders were given, such as "Remember, think carefully. It's hard because your map is turned around."

A summary of children's accuracy in placing and orienting arrows is given, by grade, in Figure 6.13. As shown, children improved with age, reaching high levels of performance when the map was aligned sooner than when it was unaligned. Also shown in Figure 6.13 are composites of all responses in one first-grade classroom to one location under both aligned and unaligned conditions. What the distribution of the arrow responses suggests is that in the unaligned condition, many children were unable to compensate for the 180° rotation of the map, with a cluster of errors in location exactly opposite the correct one. This impression is supported by examining the directions of arrows for each of the six individual

items (details are given in Liben & Downs, 1993). Among kindergarten children, even for the single item that elicited the best performance, the modal response was an arrow with a 180° error. This is precisely the error that would occur if the child failed to compensate for the map's rotation. Although by grade 1, the modal response to the easiest item was correct, the modal error was still 180°. By grade 2, the modal response was correct, with some disproportionate appearance of 180° errors for some items. By grades 5 and 6, virtually the only errors that occurred were errors of precision (i.e., off by only a small number of degrees), with 180° errors virtually absent (only 3% of the responses on a single one of the six items). As on other tasks, and consistent with the picture painted of the striking individual differences in spatial thinking discussed earlier, performance varied dramatically even within each age group. Table 6.1 gives the percentages of children receiving each score in each grade. What is perhaps most remarkable is that some (albeit very few) kindergarten children were performing perfectly or nearly perfectly at the same time that some (again, albeit few) second-grade children were incorrect on all or all but one item.

Similar kinds of tasks have been used to examine the developing ability to solve problems that involve different viewing azimuths. For example, in research with first- and second-grade children (Liben & Downs, 1986), participants were shown oblique-angle aerial photographs of their school and asked to place arrow stickers on a plan map of their school neighborhood to show the direction from which the photographs were taken; then they were

TABLE 6.1   Percentage of Children Receiving Each Score on Classroom Person Location Task, by Alignment Condition and Grade

	Total Number Correct						
	0	1	2	3	4	5	6
Aligned							
Kindergarten	22	11	14	13	22	16	2
Grade 1	4	9	7	15	22	25	18
Grade 2	0	3	3	7	9	36	42
Grade 5/6	0	0	3	3	6	61	27
Unaligned							
Kindergarten	41	29	10	10	6	3	2
Grade 1	9	11	16	18	16	19	12
Grade 2	1	9	15	10	12	39	14
Grade 5/6	0	0	0	3	30	52	15

Source: Adapted from "Understanding Person-Space-Map Relations: Cartographic and Developmental Perspectives," by L. S. Liben and R. M. Downs, 1993, *Developmental Psychology, 29,* p. 739–752.

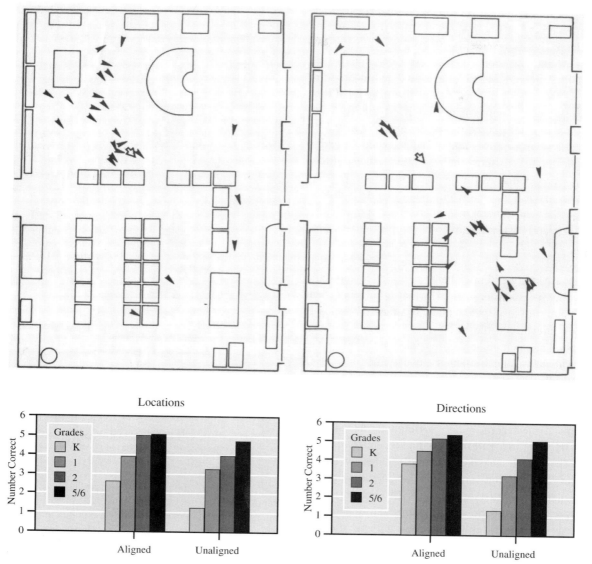

Figure 6.13   Graphs show mean numbers correct, by grade, on the classroom person location and direction task under aligned and unaligned conditions. Maps show composites of all responses to one item in one first-grade class under aligned (left) and unaligned (right) conditions. Open arrows indicates correct responses. Adapted from "Understanding Person-Space-Map Relations: Cartographic and Developmental Perspectives," by L. S. Liben and R. M. Downs, 1993, *Developmental Psychology, 29,* pp. 739–752. Reprinted with permission.

shown oblique perspective drawings (Figure 6.3) and asked to place arrow stickers on a contour map of the same local region to show the vantage point of those drawings. In research with high school students (Liben, Carlson, Szechter, & Marrara, 1999; see Liben, 2001), participants were shown a directional arrow pointing to a place shown on one representation of an environment (a plan map or oblique aerial photograph). They were then asked to place a directional arrow on a second representa-

tion of the same environment (in a different scale and azimuth) so that it would point to the same environmental location from the same general direction. The data from these various tasks converge on the conclusion that understanding and coordinating viewing azimuths across representations is challenging, even at older ages, with striking individual differences evident at all ages tested.

The same general conclusion may be drawn from tasks in which individuals must identify their own orientation on a map or to relate their own position in space to other locations (i.e., the self-map-space relation discussed earlier). Illustrative is research with college students who were tested early in their first semester on campus (see Liben, 2005; Liben, Kastens, et al., 2002). Students were taken to a series of locations. At the first five locations, they were given a campus map (modified slightly from the campus map distributed to visitors and posted at various locations on campus) and asked to place an arrow sticker on the map to show their location and the direction they were facing. At the next five locations, participants were given a map on which one building had been marked and asked to point a spinner arrow to that building (not currently within sight from the participant's location).

Figure 6.14 (top) shows a composite map of the location responses to one item. What is remarkable about the distribution of responses is not only that so many of them are incorrect, but also that so many of them are impossible if one interpreted the referential symbols even at a basic level. For example, in the item used in this example, the participant was positioned at a courtyard-like corner of the building so that there was a wall to the participant's left as well as straight ahead. There were also additional buildings to the right and directly behind. Yet, as evident in the figure, many participants placed their stickers adjacent to a building that had no courtyard-like right angle and that lacked other buildings nearby. Directional data showed the same kind of variability as the location data. To illustrate, Figure 6.14 (bottom) presents data from one of the spinner items. Similar to patterns observed among children, some college students were able to perform almost perfectly on both location and direction tasks, whereas others erred dramatically on every item.

Qualities of the Map User

Implicit in the preceding discussion of research related to individuals' understanding of maps are qualities of the particular map user (depicted by the right arrow of Figure 6.8). One grouping variable that has been used explicitly throughout the discussion is chronological age (or school grade), but from a developmental perspective, age is more appropriately understood as a marker for more differential levels of relevant cognitive development. Some investigators have included direct assessments of the cognitive concepts hypothesized to be relevant to map understanding. Of interest is whether these assess-

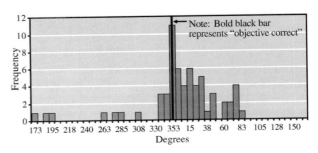

Figure 6.14 Composite of sticker locations by college students asked to show their current location (which was at the intersection of the two arrows) on a campus map (top). Graph shows distribution of pointing directions for a single spinner task item (bottom). Adapted from "Real-World Knowledge through Real-World Maps: A Developmental Guide for Navigating the Educational Terrain," by L. S. Liben, K. A. Kastens, and L. M. Stevenson, 2002, *Developmental Review, 22,* pp. 267–322. Reprinted with permission.

ments predict to map performance better than age per se, perhaps thereby accounting for the wide range of differences in performance observed within given age groups. In our work, for example, we have assessed children's topological, projective, and Euclidean concepts by using classic Piagetian tasks (see Liben & Downs, 1993). We have made the argument that at the group level, there should be relatively early success on map tasks that can be solved by using landmark features because these theoretically call on developmentally early topological understanding. In contrast, there should be relatively later success on tasks that require an understanding of, first, viewing angle or azimuth or, second, scale, because these theoretically call on, respectively, developmentally more advanced projective and Euclidean concepts (Piaget & Inhelder, 1956). The data at the individual level should show that within a given age group, the children who perform particularly well on tasks that draw on understanding viewing angle, azimuth, and scale should be the children who are especially far along in their understanding of spatial concepts.

The empirical data were reasonably consistent with the hypothesized links at the level of groups. For example, better performance was elicited in location tasks on items on or near unique landmarks that provided topological cues than on items in undifferentiated regions of a room, neighborhood, or city that require metric understanding (Liben & Downs, 1993). The data were somewhat, but not strongly, consistent with the hypothesized link at the individual level. That is, there were significant correlations between children's performance on the mapping tasks and the Piagetian spatial tasks, a relationship that held even after scores on a more general test of spatial abilities were statistically removed. However, the correlations were only moderate, and although children who performed very well on the mapping tasks were typically those who performed well on the Piagetian spatial tasks (and the reverse), there were some children whose performance was inconsistent with this pattern. Of course, tasks used to assess spatial concepts are not perfect, and participants may be differentially motivated to apply the concepts that they have to any given mapping task. Thus, additional research is needed to further explore the relationship between performance on general spatial tasks and performance on mapping tasks, and to find ways to study the moment-by-moment processing strategies used in solving mapping tasks.

Summary

The research discussed in this section of the chapter converges on the conclusion that understanding of both representational and geometric correspondences improves with age. However, there is also ample evidence of striking individual differences, with some children performing remarkably well, and some adults performing remarkably poorly. Far more research is needed to identify the factors that are responsible for different levels of performance across ages and individuals. Although we are far from understanding all components of map understanding that are

problematic, and why some components are especially problematic for some individuals, we cannot postpone map education until all these factors are understood. As argued in the earlier section, "*Can* Spatial Thinking Be Improved?" there is already considerable evidence that interventions can have positive effects on spatial thinking.

MAP EDUCATION: ILLUSTRATIVE MATERIALS AND ACTIVITIES

In this section of the chapter, I turn to a discussion of interventions addressed at enhancing students' skill in understanding and using maps.

A Time and Place for Map Education

At a broad level of generalization, the prior section on map understanding leads to the conclusion that, at the group level, children of different ages bring different concepts and knowledge to maps. At very young ages (in the preschool years), children typically have some concept of maps and some understanding of their function, but their concepts and associated skills are limited. They tend to make assumptions about shared qualities of maps and their referents that may interfere with their understanding of both the representational content (e.g., falsely presuming that red lines stand for red roads) and the spatial content (e.g., falsely presuming that lines cannot stand for roads because they are not fat enough for two cars to go on). At somewhat older ages (during the elementary school years), children come to recognize that spatial representations can move from generic to specific (e.g., as in the shift from generic to specific representations of their school; see Figure 6.12), they come to understand the consequences of changing viewing angle (again, see Figure 6.12), and they become increasingly facile at understanding viewing azimuths (as in their ability to handle unaligned maps; see Figure 6.13).

Although at still older ages (late elementary and middle school) children routinely perform well on the kinds of tasks that are challenging to younger children (see Figure 6.13), even adults continue to evidence nontrivial limitations in understanding and using maps. When actually out in a real (rather than laboratory) environment and when actually using a real (rather than a simplified) map, many adults are often confused about their current location and the direction of target locations that are represented on the map but physically beyond view (see

Figure 6.14). Furthermore, it is not only college students participating in research studies who evidence confusion. There are also dramatic examples from the everyday world, such as a logger who was taken to court for cutting down trees on the wrong land and who defended himself by arguing, "The way the map was shown to me didn't help, as it should have been turned the other way" ("Pair Awarded," 1989), and a case in which a Dutch tourist was killed in an incident in which she "and her husband got lost and stopped to ask for directions in a poor, crime-ridden Miami neighborhood.... As her husband got out of their rental car with a map in hand, [one of the men] fired a shot through the car window" (Skipp & Faiola, 1996). It is not only that adults have difficulty using maps for navigation. Students in a professional master's degree program in environmental policy made serious mistakes in interpreting climate forecast maps that depicted the probability of various precipitation data into the future (Ishikawa, Barnston, Kastens, Louchouarn, & Ropelewski, 2005).

At least some confusions evident in adults are likely to stem from incomplete, confusing, or misleading education during early childhood, and thus it is valuable to begin map education during the preschool years. In this context, it is important to point out that the fact that our research shows that preschoolers are confused about some aspects of maps should not be taken to imply that map education is inappropriate during these years. Even a theoretical position such as Piaget's, which posits that preschoolers lack relevant projective and Euclidean concepts, does not imply that instruction should be postponed until the child acquires these concepts (an implication claimed by Blaut, 1997a, 1997b). Rather, it implies the importance of designing developmentally appropriate curricula that take these developmental trajectories into account (see Downs & Liben, 1997; Liben & Downs, 1997, 2001).

The geography and map education experiences in which I have participated have included working on various aspects of museum exhibits, television programs, academic competitions, and curriculum design. Next, I draw from some of these experiences to illustrate ways that developmental theory and educational practice may productively interact.

Locating Maps within a Broader Framework

Before turning to any specific educational intervention designed to enhance children's understanding of maps, it is useful to remember that the overarching focus of this chapter is on spatial thinking. The general argument I have made is that spatial thinking is an important and valuable way of guiding interactions with and thoughts about the world. This includes "the world" not only in the sense of continents and oceans of the planet Earth, as might be studied in geography or geology, but also "the world" in the sense of all its component physical and behavioral systems, as might be studied in fields such as chemistry or economics. In parallel, I have argued that maps are an important tool for spatial thinking, and thus that educating children to understand and use maps is an avenue for educating children to become better spatial thinkers more generally. Thus, it is important to reiterate that the general significance of maps in the context of this chapter lies not their capacity to provide facts about the geographic places that they represent, but in their capacity to model the creation and use of graphic representations for representing and manipulating referents that might otherwise be unseen, unknown, unreal, or untouchable. Thus, one broader framework into which maps must be fit is the framework of spatial thinking.

But there is a second broader framework relevant to maps, and that is how the information that is internal to the map (e.g., the distance and angular relationships among, say, three cities on a map) is related to the broader external world. To operate in space (mentally or physically), it is critical to have a frame of reference. Because there is a magnetic pole and needle technology that permits the identification of magnetic north from any location on Earth, north is a useful external anchor point to which places and maps can be related. North is pervasive (e.g., in language, in graphics, in weather directions, in navigation), and it thus becomes a key concept for maps and education. Especially important, theoretical and empirical work in developmental psychology leads to the expectation that north will be a challenging concept to teach. Given these factors, it is the topic that I focus on in illustrating educational practice. I first describe some of the ways that the concept of north has been covered in others' educational materials, then describe the way we approached teaching the concept of north in our classroom work and, finally, review the instructional approach to north in the *Where Are We?* curriculum (Kastens, 2000), with which I have recently been working.

Characterizing Traditional Curricula

In addressing the concept of north, it is useful to begin by considering the more general issue of how maps and the external world are connected in mapping curricula. In general, curriculum materials tend to focus on maps as worlds in and of themselves, rather than on relationships between what is represented in the map and external reality (Liben, Kastens, et al., 2002). When they do address map-reality relationships, the reality is typically very limited in scope. Thus, for example, mapping curricula often begin by having children create maps of their home or classroom and use these maps to teach the importance of map elements, such as scale and keys. They rarely, however, address the relationship between the mapped space and some larger frame of reference, for example, orienting the classroom map in relation to regional landmarks, to distant physical features (e.g., a mountain range), or to magnetic north. Mapping exercises often ask children to create maps of imaginary lands that are not positioned in relation to any earthly frame of reference. When children are asked to use maps for "navigation," the exercise is typically entirely representational. For example, children may be given a worksheet that shows city blocks, symbolizes and labels buildings such as school, church, and town hall, and asked to draw the route to go from, say, Sally's house to her school. Such tasks can be solved without regard for links between the map and any referential reality.

One means of summarizing traditional mapping materials is by using a classification scheme that was developed to categorize research methods used to study children's emerging understanding of spatial place representations (Liben, 1997a). Two of the methods, *production* and *comprehension methods,* ask children to relate representation and reality: in the former, by taking information from the reality and applying it to (or creating) a representation, in the latter, by taking information from the representation and applying it to the real space. In *representational correspondence methods,* children are asked to relate two or more representations, but the task does not really require the child to link either representation to the reality; the link is between the two representations. In *metarepresentational methods,* children are asked to reflect on the purpose of representations or their components or perhaps talk about a representation-referent link, but only in the abstract. This classification system was used to analyze map materials that were available in the Bank Street Bookstore in New York City over a 2-year period (Kastens & Liben, 2004). All materials that required some student pencil-and-paper product and that were marketed for elementary school ages were included in the analysis. In-

terestingly, and parallel to the way the research literature may be characterized (see Liben, Kastens, et al., 2002), these educational materials showed an overwhelming emphasis on representations per se. Production and comprehension exercises were very rare.

Despite the general paucity of attention to the link between mapped spaces and the larger environmental framework, there has been considerable curricular attention to the concept of north in educational materials. Unfortunately, however, this attention is often misguided. A book entitled *How to Read a Highway Map* (Rhodes, 1970, p. 46), for example, explicitly tells children, "North is always at the top of the map." In a unit entitled "Orienting Ourselves in the Classroom," Rushdoony (1988, Lesson 1.2, p. 6) instructs teachers to place on the chalkboard "a large chart that shows the four cardinal (main) directions." The figure provided shows a large cross with north at the top and with each cardinal direction labeled. Teachers are told to "explain that there are four main directions—north, south, east, and west. Have the class read the words aloud. Then put the manila strips on the walls (one on each wall—north on the wall behind your desk)." It is obviously impossible that every teacher using this curriculum will have a desk in front of a north wall. As another example, in a student workbook (Carratello & Carratello, 1990, p. 8), the page labeled "Do You Know Your Directions?" explains that "directions will make it easier to tell where we are and where we would like to go." The page is illustrated with a picture of a boy from the back, facing the top of the page. Above his head appears "NORTH is at the top," just below his right hand is "EAST is on the right side," at his feet is written "SOUTH is at the bottom," and below his left hand appears "WEST is on the left side."

In summary, many materials designed to teach maps that are used in school do little to link the child and map to an external frame of reference. Further, there are not only errors of omission. As the examples just given show, there are also errors of commission. Curriculum problems like these are among the reasons that children may be challenged in trying to understand the concept of a fixed external referent like magnetic north.

A Developmentally Motivated Approach to Teaching North

Our approach to map education (Liben & Downs, 1986) was an interdisciplinary one that attempted to bring together ideas from both developmental psychology and geography. In the process of teaching various lessons that exposed children to a wide range of map forms and functions, we included some instruction on cardinal directions. We were aware that it was likely that at least some of the children in the first- and second-grade classes we worked with had been exposed to the kinds of misleading information about north described earlier. Given this background, we began by asking students to close their eyes and point to north. As expected, common responses included pointing straight ahead and straight up in the air.

When they opened their eyes, children were surprised to see the variety of responses among their peers. We then discussed the idea of magnetic north, and took out a compass. Based on our knowledge of developmental research on egocentrism and the importance of action in cognition, we invited students to come to the front of the room, one at a time, so that they could see the needle and could point to north (which in this classroom was over children's left shoulder). Although most of the children seemed to be prepared to believe that their original notion that north was straight ahead or straight up was wrong, a few of the children were having difficulty giving up their original beliefs. In one of the second-grade classes, a boy became visibly upset and finally jumped out of his seat, walked over to the wall, and pulled down the wall map to show everyone that indeed he was correct and north was pointing toward the ceiling. Errors like these in each class provided us with the opportunity to discuss the relationship between directions in maps and in the real world. In the course of doing so, we included maps in which north was *not* at the top of the page.

We thought we had been successful in conveying to children the need to use a referent outside their own bodies to find north (e.g., the sun, a compass). We tested our impression during a field trip that occurred a few weeks following the original lesson on north. The students were driven out to a recreational center by bus and gathered inside one of the buildings for some additional map work. Once again, we began by asking children to close their eyes and point to north. We were anticipating that they would either ask for a compass or say that they could not tell. Instead, to our dismay, most of the students simply pointed, quite confidently, over their left shoulders. All we had succeeded in doing was to replace one fixed body-centered belief (that north was straight ahead or straight up) with another (that north was over

the left shoulder). Thus, although we were correct in anticipating children's likely confusions, we were not successful in overcoming them.

Where Are We? Curriculum Attempts to Overcome Misconceptions about North

The final example is drawn from the *Where Are We? (WAW?)* curriculum (Kastens, 2000) targeted for second- through fourth-grade children. Two major premises of this curriculum are, first, that the links between reality and map are at the core of understanding maps, and second, that there are practical difficulties in providing children with extensive reality-map experiences. Thus, a key feature of *WAW?* is computer software designed to provide simulated reality-map experience.

Specifically, and as illustrated by a screen from the *WAW?* software shown in Figure 6.15, the software shows two representations of a park simultaneously. One is a plan map, and the other is an inset of a color video that shows eye-level views recorded on walks through the park. Users control the video that appears in the inset by clicking on one of three arrows. Clicking on the straight arrow starts the video clip to show what would be seen as one continues walking straight ahead on the path. Clicking on the left or right arrows leads to video

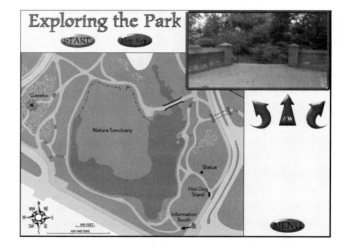

Figure 6.15   Annotated screen from *Where Are We?* in the "Exploring the Park" mode. *Source:* From *Where Are We?* by K. A. Kastens, 2000, Watertown, MA: Tom Snyder Productions. Reprinted with permission from "Real-World Knowledge through Real-World Maps: A Developmental Guide for Navigating the Educational Terrain," by L. S. Liben, K. A. Kastens, and L. M. Stevenson, 2002, *Developmental Review, 22,* pp. 267–322.

clips showing, respectively, what would be seen if one turned to the left or right.

The software operates in four modes. One, "Exploring the Park," orients children to the software, the videotaped scenes, and the map. By clicking on one of the arrows, the user sees the park on the video as if walking or turning and, simultaneously, sees a red dot with a directional arrow marker moving on the map. Because of the scale relation between the walk and representation, a long "walk" in the videotape moves the red dot only a short distance on the map. The explicit display of the red dot and orientation arrow is used consistently only in this introductory mode. In a second mode, "Are We There Yet?" the user is given a starting point and orientation (indicated by the red dot and arrow) and asked to reach a given target location by moving through the space via arrow clicks. In "Lost!" the user is simply dropped at some unknown location in the park and is challenged to discover the location by moving around in the park (via arrow clicks). When users believe they have located themselves on the map, they click on the hypothesized location and receive a message that says either "Sorry, try again," "You're close," or "You got it!" Finally, in "Add to the Map," users again move through the (video) park via arrow clicks and watch for certain objects (e.g., lampposts) that are in the "real" (videotaped) world but not yet on the map. Between clicks, the user drags symbols to the map to show the selected objects' locations. This mode is meant to parallel the field mapping tasks that are common in many occupations and disciplines (e.g., as when an ecologist records distributions of vegetation data on a base map).

A list of the topics of the classroom lessons that compose the *WAW?* curriculum is given in Table 6.2. Of particular interest for the current focus on north is the two-session Lesson 9 (pp. 66–73), entitled "The Compass Rose." Many aspects of the lesson are directly relevant for the kinds of body-centered misunderstandings that have been identified in the research discussed earlier. The three overarching goals for the lesson are to "teach students to use a compass rose in conjunction with a compass," "have students differentiate between North as a region and north as a direction," and "show students when to use north/south/east/west rather than right/left."

It is informative to examine some of the specific recommended activities. Unlike the approach to north often found in traditional curriculum materials described earlier, much of the *WAW?* lesson is specifically aimed at re-

TABLE 6.2   List of Lessons Included in the *Where Are We?* Curriculum

1. *Exploring Maps.* Students examine a variety of paper maps and discuss the uses of maps.
2. *Bird's-Eye View Mapping.* Students draw a simple map of the objects on their desks.
3. *Map Symbols.* Students use the key on the *Where Are We?* poster map to identify objects on the map and to imagine what is seen by someone standing at a particular location.
4. *Introducing the Software.* Students learn how the software works by using "Exploring the Park" mode.
5. *Landmarks.* The lesson introduces the value of landmarks in map reading and navigation through guided use of the "Are We There Yet?" mode.
6. *Keeping Track of Where You've Been.* Students keep track of their route in the "Are We There Yet?" mode and practice returning to their starting point.
7. *Planning a Route.* Students plan a route to a destination and anticipate what they should see along that route. Using the "Exploring the Park" mode, students test their predictions and verify their plan.
8. *Map Scale.* By contrasting the distance traveled in the *Where Are We?* video with the distance the dot advances across the map, students see the difference in size (scale) between the map and the represented landscape. They use the map scale to estimate sizes and distances in the *Where Are We?* scene and on other maps.
9. *The Compass Rose.* Students use a compass rose in the classroom and on the computer map to figure out the direction someone is facing or moving.
10. *Putting New Information on the Map.* Students find some features that are in the video but missing from the map, figure out where these should be located on the map, and add the appropriate symbols. This lesson models the use of maps by geologists, ecologists, architects, town planners, and many others who use maps as tools for organizing spatial information.
11. *Lost!* Using map symbols, landmarks, and compass directions, students make observations about the landscape around them to infer their location on the map. This lesson simulates the situation where walkers or motorists realize they are lost, pull the map out of a backpack or glove compartment, and use visual clues in the surrounding terrain to figure out where they are on the map.
12. *Summing Up: Comparing Maps with the Real World.* Students demonstrate their understanding of the similarities and differences between a map and the real world by completing a table.

Source: Summarized from *Where Are We?* by K. A. Kastens, 2000, Watertown, MA: Tom Snyder Productions.

lating the child's immediate space and representation to an external frame of reference. For example, after discussing the use of a compass or the sun's path to establish where north is, the teacher is asked to have a child put a "large paper compass rose on the floor matching its N with the real north. Place a compass on top of the compass rose to check that the norths are aligned." Signs with cardinal directions are then posted, but unlike the workbook described earlier, north does not automatically get placed at the front of the room, but rather on the north wall as determined by the compass.

As developmental research and theory would imply is important, activities in the lesson are specifically designed to help children differentiate bodily directional referents (e.g., left and right) from external spatial referents (north). This approach is thus in sharp contrast to the traditional curricula described earlier in which activities and materials conflate, rather than distinguish, bodily referents and external referents (e.g., erroneously teaching that the child's right hand identifies east). In *WAW?*, activities involve children following directions to move a figurine around so that the child learns to differentiate regions from directions (e.g., learning that one can be heading, say, northeast even if one is in, say, the southeast region of a state) and to differentiate left/right from cardinal directions. If students are having difficulty making these distinctions with the figurines, teachers are led to use additional exercises that address common misconceptions. These exercises are particularly well grounded in developmental theory insofar as they require children to move through the real space using alternative referential systems. For example, children are asked to divide up into two lines facing each other, and then everyone is asked to turn to the left. The two lines therefore end up facing in opposite directions. Students are then asked to return to their original positions so that the lines again face one another. Students are then instructed to face east. Now all students face in the same direction. Activities such as these are intended to have children come to appreciate the difference between egocentric, body-centered frameworks and external, stable frames of reference.

The second session of the "Compass Rose" lesson involves using the *WAW?* software, which provides continual information about compass heading as one "walks" through the park. The map, however, remains in the same orientation, thus giving children practice in using unaligned maps, something that the research reviewed earlier shows is typically difficult for children of this age. In short, the theoretical foundations of *WAW?* are similar to those that informed the classroom activities used in our integrated research and teaching efforts (Liben & Downs, 1986). The *WAW?* curriculum, however, is far more sustained and is thus likely to be more effective than our own attempt to teach north. However, evidence of such effectiveness must await additional evaluation efforts currently under way (e.g., Kastens & Liben, 2004).

Summary

In this section, I have described and discussed a number of specific classroom materials and activities that are related in some way to helping students to understand the relationship between a representation and a reality. I have focused on frame of reference because keeping track of representations of spaces or objects in space depends on remaining oriented in some way. An examination of the map education materials that are commonly available suggests that many materials and lessons ignore the connection between representations and reality entirely, and at least some of them address the connection in ways that are seriously misleading. As our own unsuccessful attempt to teach the concept of north demonstrates, even being aware of children's likely misconceptions and even grounding a curriculum in developmental and cartographic principles does not ensure success. The *WAW?* curriculum was enriched by what had been learned in earlier work, but whether it will prove to be adequate awaits evaluation data (see Liben, Kastens, et al., 2002). There are, however, already a number of general conclusions that can be drawn, as discussed in the next section of the chapter.

CONCLUSIONS AND QUESTIONS

In this chapter, I began with the argument that spatial thinking plays an important role in a wide range of educational, occupational, and everyday activities. I reviewed data showing that spatial thinking varies markedly between groups (e.g., those defined by age and sex) and within groups (i.e., individual differences), and that these differences are linked to differential success in both general and specialized curricula (e.g., mathematics, engineering). I described research showing that interventions can enhance spatial performance and associated educational outcomes across the curriculum. Given the conclusion that skilled spatial thinking is important but does not develop to high levels automatically and universally, I considered educational routes that might be used to facilitate spatial thinking. For both practical and conceptual reasons, the approach recommended (consistent with the recommendation of the report *Learning to Think Spatially;* NRC, 2005) was to infuse spatial education within courses already taught in our schools. I identified geography as one potential target for infusion because it places spatial reasoning at its disciplinary core and because it routinely includes lessons on maps (which are prototypical exemplars of spatial thinking). As currently configured, however, map lessons are often geared simply to helping children use maps to obtain specific factual information (e.g., to find state capitals, to identify which cities are near which rivers, to find the locations of countries in the news). Map education has the potential to offer much more. The myriad map forms and functions described earlier suggest some of the ways that maps draw on and may thereby facilitate more general spatial and representational skills. I reviewed research showing the developmental emergence of map understanding and sampled from educational curricula designed to teach the concept of north.

In this final section, I revisit my opening paragraph, in which I noted that the material in this chapter is relevant to three audiences. The first is composed of traditional cognitive-developmental psychologists whose primary interests are in basic research on the development of spatial cognition. The second includes applied developmental psychologists who aspire to move their work from the laboratories of the academy to the lives of children in the real world. The third encompasses educators who design or provide educational experiences for children. I highlight some key points relevant to each audience and close by commenting on the need to consider the challenges and opportunities presented by the changing technological environment.

Scholars of the Development of Spatial Cognition

For those readers whose primary interest is in studying the development of spatial cognition, the key lessons from this chapter largely concern the existence and implications of variability. First, the work reviewed here highlights variability among individuals. When one is describing children in the abstract, it is relatively simple to place the primary focus on the commonalities of children within age groups and the distinctions between children across age groups. However, when one takes these abstract descriptions into real classrooms with real children trying to master real lessons, it is the variability rather than the similarity among children that is striking. Data show variability not only with respect to levels of performance, but often also with respect to the cognitive strategies that underlie performance. Differences among individuals with respect to the rates at which they pass through developmental milestones or

with respect to the end points they ultimately reach provide potential windows into developmental processes. That is, detailed observation of natural correlates of different developmental rates and outcomes (e.g., different parental behaviors, different toy play) may illuminate microgenetic changes in spatial development, and, when possible, these correlates may be manipulated experimentally to test their impact on later spatial thinking. Thus, one conclusion from the work described throughout this chapter is that even as there are age progressions in spatial development, there are also individual and group differences in spatial development, differences that imply the need for observational and experimental research that goes beyond descriptions of age-linked differences in spatial thinking.

Second, the work reviewed in this chapter highlights variability in performance across tasks. There is a temptation for developmental psychologists who work primarily within the walls of the academy to assume that the most (or perhaps even the only) important questions about cognitive functioning are those that address the *emergence* of some cognitive skill. From this perspective, for example, it is particularly important to find that young infants encode metric information about objects' locations because these findings appear to discredit the Piagetian proposition that metric concepts do not emerge until middle or late childhood. However, when developmental psychologists look outside the laboratory and turn to the kinds of educational, occupational, and daily tasks discussed in earlier sections of this chapter, they confront fascinating and nontrivial questions concerning the ways cognitive competencies, task demands, and environmental contexts interact to facilitate or impede success. It is arguably as intriguing to study the range of conditions under which an underlying competency can be activated and applied as it is to study the conditions under which an underlying competency emerges in the first place. At a more general level, this conclusion is a reminder of why it is better to avoid conceptualizing developmental phenomena as dichotomies in which children either do or do not have some competency (see Liben, 1997b; Overton, 1998).

Applied Developmental Psychologists

For those readers whose primary interest is in taking theoretical work from developmental psychology and applying it to the world of education, the key lessons from this chapter largely concern challenges of communication and implementation of concepts and the associated need for appropriate assessment. That is, although there are many important connections between what has been learned in cognitive-developmental research and a wide range of educational goals, it is often difficult to bridge the gap between theory and application and to know when one has succeeded in doing so. One striking illustration described earlier was our own failed attempt to teach children the concept of north (Liben & Downs, 2001). Despite our theoretical understanding of children's potential overreliance on body-centered frames of reference, we provided a classroom lesson that led some children to replace their erroneous belief that north was invariably straight ahead with the erroneous belief that north was invariably over their left shoulder.

This illustration carries with it another key lesson: the importance of including assessments to monitor communicative and instructional success. In the previous example, had we not assessed children's understanding of north in an entirely new context during a field trip, we would have been unaware of continued misunderstandings. It is critical that assessments require students to apply their knowledge in new ways and in new contexts rather than to repeat information in exactly the same way and context in which it was initially presented. A classic example of the importance of this caveat in the domain of spatial thinking comes from the work of Vosnaidou and Brewer (1992). They found that elementary school children were extremely proficient in responding to questions about Earth when the questions tapped information as taught. Thus, when asked about the shape of Earth, almost all children were able to answer correctly by responding verbally that Earth is round or spherical and by drawing a round shape. When asked novel questions (e.g., what would happen if one were to keep walking and walking and walking), responses revealed that many children were actually working from faulty mental models (e.g., a pancake rather than spherical model of Earth).

It is particularly important that assessments tap something other than rote learning or near transfer when the lesson is intended to enhance some general understanding or skill. For example, in the context of the overarching goal of educating spatial thinkers, lessons about north are aimed not only at teaching cardinal directions per se, but also at teaching the use of stable distal frames of reference even in the face of changing proximal referents. Thus, assessments of instructional suc-

cess must go beyond testing whether children know that west is to their left and east is to their right under the imposed condition (or incorrect assumption) that they are facing north.

The communicative challenges encountered when bridging theory to practice and the need to monitor understanding applies not only when trying to teach children directly, but also when trying to convey to other professionals the information that they need to design educational materials. One illustration comes from a project mentioned earlier in which we (Liben & Downs, 1994, 2001) consulted with Children's Television Workshop as they planned to introduce geography to *Sesame Street*. Based on our knowledge that young children would be likely to have difficulty understanding representations that depict referents from unfamiliar vantage points, we suggested showing objects or vistas from views other than the prototypical child's-eye view. In particular, we suggested using bird's-eye views (perhaps Big Bird's-eye views) and worm's-eye views. We had intended that our suggestion be translated into video clips of the same objects or vistas viewed from straight ahead (child's-eye views), from above (bird's-eye views), and from below (worm's-eye views).

Our suggestion for bird's-eye views was cleverly implemented. In one clip, for example, the school playground was shown, sequentially, from a child's-eye view of what would be seen while walking onto the playground, then from a tree top, and then from a distant crane. Playground objects (e.g., the basketball hoop) were then shown being transformed into plan-map symbols that were located on a map. The implementation of our suggestion for a worm's-eye view was less successful. We were surprised to find that the worm-related geography video clip showed two worms racing across the United States (by crawling on a small-scale map of the United States) as their progress was narrated (e.g., "They are arriving in Chicago!" "They are crossing the Rockies!"). Not only did this video clip fail to offer children the chance to view the same referent from varying vantage points, but it conflated representational and referential space and symbols. For example, the worms simply moved across the paper without regard to whether they followed roads, crawled over lakes, and so on, and clearly the scale relation between movement on the map and travel through the referent country was grossly misleading. This example serves as a reminder of the importance of continually monitoring understanding of the theoretician's intended message, whether the message is directed to students or to the professionals designing materials to teach them.

Educators

For readers whose primary interest is in educating children, either directly (e.g., teachers or parents) or indirectly (e.g., faculty members in colleges of education or members of school boards), the central messages of this chapter are that spatial thinking is important and pervasive, that many children do not develop strong spatial thinking skills in their natural home and school environments, and, thus, that explicit spatial education is needed. Although the relevant research base is somewhat restricted, those data that are available support the conclusion that educational interventions can be successful in enhancing at least some spatial skills, and that these improvements have positive consequences for at least some broader educational goals. Illustrative are studies cited earlier by Pallrand and Seeber (1984) showing that college students given various kinds of spatial experiences (e.g., drawing outdoor scenes, instruction in geometry) received higher scores on tests of visual skills and higher grades in physics, and by Casey et al. (1997, 2001) showing significant relationships between spatial skills and mathematics motivation and performance.

For an audience of educators, however, there are some extremely important questions that remain unanswered and that must be addressed in future work. One group of questions is pedagogical. First, from an instructional perspective, there remains the practical question of how to implement the recommendation to infuse spatial education into existing school subjects. It will be necessary to catalogue spatial concepts and skills (see NRC, 2005), identify individual courses that are relevant at each grade level, select concepts within those courses that could be infused with spatial education, and design specific materials and activities that can simultaneously facilitate spatial thinking and deliver specific course content.

Undoubtedly, these steps are easier to list than to follow. Again, I draw from our own research to illustrate this point. In one study (Liben & Szechter, 2002), we hypothesized that children's understanding of vantage points might be facilitated by digital photography lessons. Our reasoning was that digital photography would

repeatedly expose children to the representational consequences of changes in viewing position. For the experimental condition, adult research assistants were asked to take individual children (8 to 10 years old) on a campus walk while children took photographs of their own choosing. These adults were asked to guide the child's photographic experience in a way that would emphasize the role of vantage point. However, pilot testing revealed that research assistants found it exceedingly difficult to devise, spontaneously, experiences that would serve this purpose. For the investigation itself, we therefore substituted a method in which photographic requests were scripted (e.g., every child was asked to take a photograph of a lion sculpture so that only one of two paws would be visible in the image). For the current discussion, what is relevant is the observation that adults do not necessarily find it easy to identify opportunities for spatial education.

Another line of evidence leading to the same conclusion comes from a study (Szechter & Liben, 2004) in which parents were given a picture book that was based on a spatially challenging concept (each page progressively zoomed away from the initial scene). When asked to read the book to their preschool child, some parents attempted to explain the spatial premise of the book in multiple and creative ways. Others, however, entirely ignored the spatial challenge of zooming and instead simply labeled individual objects depicted in the book. The examples from both studies suggest that many adults find it difficult to recognize and use potential opportunities to encourage spatial thinking, a difficulty that must be anticipated among classroom teachers as well. Ideally, professional development (e.g., in-service workshops on spatial education) might help to foster these skills, but at a minimum, curriculum development would need to involve collaboration between those who have expertise in teaching the specific course content and those who have expertise in developmental spatial cognition.

Apart from the need to identify concrete opportunities to teach spatial thinking within specific courses, future work must address other general pedagogical questions. One question is whether teachers should make the spatial components of their classes explicit. For example, would it suffice to have children use maps that show the same referent space from many different viewing distances, angles, and azimuths, or would it be necessary for children to learn metacognitive formalisms (e.g., the cartographic eye shown in Figure 6.1) and use these to analyze individual maps? Another question is whether teachers should link spatial instruction across domains. For example, should teachers be facilitating children's use of spatial thinking within the confines of individual courses (e.g., within art, geography, and biology), or should teachers guide children to see common spatial operations and representations across disciplines (e.g., highlighting the use of coordinate axes across disciplines)?

In addition to questions about how to implement the curricular recommendations, there are also questions about how to evaluate the effectiveness of whatever programs are implemented. The core claim of this chapter is that infused spatial education will enhance spatial thinking skills, and that these, in turn, will facilitate success in problem solving in a wide range of school, occupational, and life contexts. Thus, evaluation must address both categories of outcomes. The first, for example, could be assessed by examining children's performance on standardized tests of spatial skills (e.g., solving mental rotation tasks or linking two- and three-dimensional representations); the second could be assessed by testing children's ability to master novel problems in educational, daily, or occupational settings (e.g., interpreting mineral crystal structure in a geology course, assembling furniture from a manufacturer's graphic instructions, or reading an architectural blueprint).

Before leaving the topic of assessment, it is also important to acknowledge that spatial assessment is critical not merely as a means of curriculum evaluation, but also as a marker of, and an influence on, the judged importance of the domain. This statement reflects the common adage "We assess what we value and we value what we assess." In the contemporary educational era defined by the No Child Left Behind [NCLB] legislation (U.S. Department of Education, 2002), it is particularly clear that a decision about what is assessed is a decision about what is taught. As children's performance on English and math assessments has become the criterion by which not only children, but also teachers, schools, and districts are judged, the classroom time devoted to English and math has grown, while the time devoted to other curricula (e.g., social studies, languages, and the arts) has been reduced (e.g., see Goldsmith, 2003). It is possible that the recent addition of science to NCLB assessments may provide an opening for intentional and focused spatial education given that so much of science draws on spatial skills (see NRC, 2005).

It should be obvious that it would take significant human and financial capital to insert specific spatial goals into the implementation of NCLB, to answer the pedagogical and evaluation questions raised in this chapter, and to develop, implement, and sustain spatial education programs themselves. The justification for those resources is equally obvious: We need only join Monsieur Jourdain in contemplating how we operate in our daily lives. Spatial thinking, like verbal and mathematical thinking, is central to our intellectual world, and it deserves to be central to our educational world as well.

Evolving Questions in Evolving Environments

In closing, it is important to note that just as individual children change over time, so, too, the environment that surrounds them changes over time. Changes are particularly rapid in the representational environment. Although societies have long had spatial-graphic representations such as maps and charts (Harvey, 1980; Tversky, 2001), it is only during recent decades that we have had the representational technology to build and rotate images (e.g., computer-assisted design [CAD] software), combine data from multiple geo-referenced databases (e.g., geographic information systems), image internal organs and workings of the human body (e.g., computer-assisted tomography scans), and identify positions within meters on Earth's surface (e.g., global positioning systems), to name only a subset of the burgeoning technology. Indeed, the twenty-first century has been labeled "The Spatial Century" (Gould, 1999).

These changes raise fascinating questions about development and education. In some ways, technologies like these place new spatial demands on users (e.g., an image of a cross section of the brain requires the surgeon to understand where the cross section fits into the patient's head), but in other ways, they may reduce spatial demands (e.g., a car navigation system allows the driver to know whether to turn right or left even without attending to the self-map-space relations shown in Figure 6.10). Thus, just as people have off-loaded spelling functions from their long-term memory to their word processing programs and their multiplication tables to their calculators, it may be that people will off-load mental rotation to their CAD programs and wayfinding to their in-car navigation systems. Much research will be needed to discover which new technologies serve to exercise and hence foster children's spatial skills and which new technologies serve to take over and hence diminish children's spatial skills. What this research is likely to reveal is that, as with most tools, a given technology can be used profitably or badly. The challenge for educators will be to find ways to achieve the former rather than the latter. Although it is impossible to predict precisely where new technologies will lead and the effects they will have on human cognition, it is safe to predict that they will require users who are facile in spatial as well as verbal thinking. The traditions of developmental psychology must be combined with the traditions of education to prepare spatial thinkers who can meet the challenges and opportunities of our evolving world.

REFERENCES

Acredolo, L. P. (1981). Small- and large-scale spatial concepts in infancy and childhood. In L. S. Liben, A. H. Patterson, & N. Newcombe (Eds.), *Spatial representation and behavior across the life span: Theory and application* (pp. 63–81). New York: Academic Press.

Allen, G. L. (Ed.). (2004). *Human spatial memory.* Mahwah, NJ: Erlbaum.

Baenninger, M., & Newcombe, N. (1989). The role of experience in spatial test performance: A meta-analysis. *Sex Roles, 20,* 327–344.

Baltes, P. B. (1987). Theoretical propositions of life-span developmental psychology: On the dynamics between growth and decline. *Developmental Psychology, 23,* 611–626.

Baltes, P. B., Staudinger, U. M., & Lindenberger, U. (1999). Lifespan psychology: Theory and application to intellectual functioning. *Annual Review of Psychology, 50,* 471–507.

Berry, J. W. (1966). Temne and Eskimo perceptual skills. *International Journal of Psychology, 1*(3), 207–229.

Berry, J. W. (1971). Ecological and cultural factors in spatial perceptual development. *Canadian Journal of Behavioral Science, 3*(4), 324–336.

Blades, M., & Spencer, C. (1994). The development of children's ability to use spatial representations. In H. W. Reese (Ed.), *Advances in child development and behavior* (Vol. 25, pp. 157–199). New York: Academic Press.

Blaut, J. M. (1997a). Children can. *Annals of the Association of American Geographers, 87,* 152–158.

Blaut, J. M. (1997b). Piagetian pessimism and the mapping abilities of young children: A rejoinder to Liben and Downs. *Annals of the Association of American Geographers, 87,* 168–177.

Bock, R. D., & Kolakowski, D. (1973). Further evidence of sex-linked major gene influence on human spatial visualizing ability. *American Journal of Human Genetics, 25,* 1–14.

Bodner, G. M., & McMillen, T. L. B. (1986). Cognitive restructuring as an early stage in problem solving. *Journal of Research in Science Teaching, 23,* 727–737.

Bratko, D. (1996). Twin study of verbal and spatial abilities. *Personality and Individual Differences, 21,* 621–624.

Brewer, C. A. (1997). Spectral schemes: Controversial color use on maps. *Cartography and Geographic Information Systems, 24,* 203–220.

Brewer, C. A., MacEachren, A. M., Pickle, L. W., & Herrmann, D. J. (1997). Mapping mortality: Evaluating color schemes for choropleth maps. *Annals of the Association of American Geographers, 87,* 411–438.

Bruner, J. S. (1964). The course of cognitive growth. *American Psychologist, 19,* 1–15.

Carratello, J., & Carratello, P. (1990). *Beginning map skills.* Westminster, CA: Author.

Carter, C. S., LaRussa, M. A., & Bodner, G. M. (1987). A study of two measures of spatial ability as predictors of success in different levels of general chemistry. *Journal of Research in Science Teaching, 24,* 645–657.

Casey, M. B. (1996). Understanding individual differences in spatial ability within females: A nature/nurture interactionist framework. *Developmental Review, 16,* 240–261.

Casey, M. B., Brabeck, M. M., & Nuttall, R. L. (1995). As the twig is bent: The biology and socialization of gender roles in women. *Brain and Cognition, 27,* 237–246.

Casey, M. B., Nuttall, R. L., & Pezaris, E. (1997). Mediators of gender differences in mathematics college entrance test scores: A comparison of spatial skills with internalized beliefs and anxieties. *Developmental Psychology, 33,* 669–680.

Casey, M. B., Nuttall, R. L., & Pezaris, E. (2001). Spatial-mechanical reasoning skills versus mathematics self-confidence as mediators of gender differences on mathematics subtests using cross-national gender-based items. *Journal of Research in Mathematics Education, 32,* 28–57.

Cassirer, E. (1950). *The problem of knowledge.* New Haven, CT: Yale University Press.

Choi, S., & Bowerman, M. (1991). Learning to express motion events in English and Korean: The influence of language-specific lexication patterns. *Cognition, 41,* 83–121.

Cohen, J. (1977). *Statistical power analysis for the behavioral sciences.* San Diego: Academic Press.

Cohen, R. (Ed.). (1985). *The development of spatial cognition.* Hillsdale, NJ: Erlbaum.

Cole, M., & Scribner, S. (1974). *Culture and thought.* New York: Wiley.

De Lisi, R., & Wolford, J. L. (2002). Improving children's mental rotation accuracy with computer game playing. *Journal of Genetic Psychology, 163,* 272–282.

DeLoache, J. S. (1987). Rapid change in the symbolic functioning of very young children. *Science, 238,* 1556–1557.

Devon, R., Engel, R., & Turner, G. (1998). The effects of spatial visualization skill training on gender and retention in engineering. *Journal of Women and Minorities in Science and Engineering, 4,* 371–380.

Downs, R. M. (1981). Maps and mappings as metaphors for spatial representation. In L. S. Liben, A. H. Patterson, & N. Newcombe (Eds.), *Spatial representation and behavior across the life span: Theory and application* (pp. 143–166). New York: Academic Press.

Downs, R. M. (2004). From globes to GIS: The paradoxical role of tools in school geography. In S. D. Brunn, S. I. Cutter, & J. W. Harrington (Eds.), *Geography and technology* (pp. 179–199). Dordrecht, the Netherlands: Kluwer Academic Publishers.

Downs, R. M. (2005, January). *Geography and the "No Child Left Behind" legislation.* Paper presented at the Penn State Geography Coffee Hour, University Park, PA.

Downs, R. M., & Liben, L. S. (1991). The development of expertise in geography: A cognitive-developmental approach to geographic education. *Annals of the Association of American Geographers, 81,* 304–327.

Downs, R. M., & Liben, L. S. (1993). Mediating the environment: Communicating, appropriating, and developing graphic representations of place. In R. H. Wozniak & K. Fischer (Eds.), *Development in context: Acting and thinking in specific environments* (pp. 155–181). Hillsdale, NJ: Erlbaum.

Downs, R. M., & Liben, L. S. (1997). The final summation: The defense rests. *Annals of the Association of American Geographers, 87,* 178–180.

Downs, R. M., Liben, L. S., & Daggs, D. G. (1988). On education and geographers: The role of cognitive developmental theory in geographic education. *Annals of the Association of American Geographers, 78,* 680–700.

Downs, R. M., & Stea, D. (Eds.). (1973). *Image and environment.* Chicago: Aldine.

Downs, R. M., & Stea, D. (1977). *Maps in minds.* New York: Harper & Row.

Eliot, J. (1987). *Models of psychological space: Psychometric, developmental, and experimental approaches.* New York: Springer-Verlag.

Emmorey, K., Kosslyn, S., & Bellugi, U. (1993). Visual imagery and visual-spatial language: Enhanced imagery abilities in deaf and hearing ASL signers. *Cognition, 46,* 139–181.

Etaugh, C. (1983). The influence of environmental factors on sex differences in children's play. In M. B. Liss (Ed.), *Social and cognitive skills: Sex roles and children's play* (pp. 1–19). New York: Academic Press.

Ferguson, E. S. (1992). *Engineering and the mind's eye.* Cambridge, MA: MIT Press.

Flexner, S. B., & Hauck, L. C. (Eds.). (1997). *Random House unabridged dictionary.* New York: Random House.

Foreman, N. P., Orencas, C., Nicholas, E., Morton, P., & Gell, M. (1989). Spatial awareness in 7- to 11-year-old physically handicapped children in mainstream schools. *European Journal of Special Needs Education, 4,* 171–179.

Garling, T., & Evans, G. W. (Ed.). (1991). *Environment, cognition, and action.* New York: Oxford University Press.

Gattis, M. (Ed.). (2001). *Spatial schemas and abstract thought.* Cambridge, MA: MIT Press.

Gauvain, M. (1993). The development of spatial thinking in everyday activity. *Developmental Review, 13,* 92–121.

Geary, D. C., & Bjorklund, D. F. (2000). Evolutionary developmental psychology. *Child Development, 7,* 57–65.

Geography Education Standards Project. (1994). *Geography for life: National geography standards 1994.* Washington, DC: National Geographic Research and Exploration.

Goldsmith, S. S. (2003). The liberal arts and school improvement. *Journal of Education, 184,* 25–36.

Golledge, R. G. (Ed.). (1999). *Wayfinding behavior: Cognitive mapping and other spatial processes.* Baltimore: Johns Hopkins University Press.

Goodman, N. (1976). *Languages of art: An approach to a theory of symbols.* Indianapolis, IN: Hackett.

Gould, P. (1999). *Becoming a geographer.* Syracuse, NY: Syracuse University Press.

Hagen, M. A. (1985). There is no development in art. In H. H. Freeman & M. V. Cox (Eds.), *Visual order* (pp. 59–77). Cambridge, England: Cambridge University Press.

Hagen, M. A. (1986). *Varieties of realism: Geometries of representational art.* New York: Cambridge University Press.

Hampson, E., Rovet, J. F., & Altmann, D. (1998). Spatial reasoning in children with congenital adrenal hyperplasia due to 21-hydroxylase deficiency. *Developmental Neuropsychology, 14,* 299–320.

Harrison, R. E. (1994). *Look at the world: The Fortune atlas for world strategy.* New York: Knopf.

Harvey, P. D. A. (1980). *The history of topographical maps: Symbols, pictures and surveys.* London: Thames & Hudson.

Hoffman, J. E., Landau, B., & Pagani, B. (2003). Spatial breakdown in spatial construction: Evidence from eye fixations in children with Williams syndrome. *Cognitive Psychology, 46,* 260–301.

Inhelder, B., Sinclair, M., & Bovet, M. (1974). *Learning and the development of cognition.* Cambridge, MA: Harvard University Press.

Ishikawa, T., Barnston, A. G., Kastens, K. A., Louchouarn, P., & Ropelewski, C. F. (2005). Climate forecast maps as a communication and decision-support tool: An empirical test with prospective policy makers. *Cartography and Geographic Information Science, 32,* 3–16.

Jacobs, J. E., & Eccles, J. S. (1992). The impact of mothers' gender-role stereotypic beliefs on mothers' and children's ability perceptions. *Journal of Personality and Social Psychology, 63,* 932–944.

Jammer, M. (1954). *Concepts of space.* Cambridge, MA: Harvard University Press.

Johnson, E. S. (1985). Sex differences in problem solving. *Journal of Educational Psychology, 76,* 1359–1371.

Johnson, E. S., & Meade, A. C. (1987). Developmental patterns of spatial ability: An early sex difference. *Child Development, 58,* 725–740.

Kail, R. V. (1991). Developmental change in speed of processing during childhood and adolescence. *Psychological Bulletin, 109,* 490–501.

Kail, R. V., & Park, Y.-S. (1990). Impact of practice on speed of mental rotation. *Journal of Experimental Child Psychology, 49,* 227–244.

Kastens, K. A. (2000). *Where are we?* Watertown, MA: Tom Snyder Productions.

Kastens, K. A., Ishikawa, T., & Liben, L. S. (2004, October). *How do people learn to envision three-dimensional geological structures from field observations?* Poster presented at the Research on Learning and Education PIs meeting, National Science Foundation, Washington, DC.

Kastens, K. A., & Liben, L. S. (2004, May). *Where are we? Understanding and improving how children translate from a map to the represented space and vice versa.* Poster presentation at the Instructional Materials Development PIs meeting, National Science Foundation, Washington, DC.

Kekule, F. A. (1965). Studies on aromatic compounds. *Annals of Chemistry, 137,* 129–196.

Kellman, P. J., & Arterberry, M. E. (1998). *The cradle of knowledge: Development of perception in infancy.* Cambridge, MA: MIT Press.

Kimura, D. (1999). *Sex and cognition.* Cambridge, MA: MIT Press.

Kirasic, K. C., Allen, G. L., Dobson, S. H., & Binder, K. S. (1996). Aging, cognitive resources, and declarative learning. *Psychology of Aging, 11,* 658–670.

Kitchin, R., & Blades, M. (2002). *The cognition of geographic space.* London: Tauris.

Landau, B., Spelke, E., & Gleitman, H. (1984). Spatial knowledge in a young blind child. *Cognition, 16,* 225–260.

Levine, M., Marchon, I., & Hanley, G. (1984). The placement and misplacement of you-are-here maps. *Environment and Behavior, 16,* 139–158.

Levine, S. C., Huttenlocher, J., Taylor, A., & Langrock, A. (1999). Early sex differences in spatial skill. *Developmental Psychology, 35,* 940–949.

Levinson, S. C. (2003). *Space in language and cognition.* Cambridge, England: Cambridge University Press.

Liben, L. S. (1978). Performance on Piagetian spatial tasks as a function of sex, field dependence, and training. *Merrill-Palmer Quarterly, 24,* 97–110.

Liben, L. S. (1981). Spatial representation and behavior: Multiple perspectives. In L. S. Liben, A. H. Patterson, & N. Newcombe (Eds.), *Spatial representation and behavior across the life span: Theory and application* (pp. 3–36). New York: Academic Press.

Liben, L. S. (1991a). Environmental cognition through direct and representational experiences: A life-span perspective. In T. Garling & G. W. Evans (Eds.), *Environment, cognition, and action* (pp. 245–276). New York: Oxford University Press.

Liben, L. S. (1991b). The Piagetian water-level task: Looking beneath the surface. In R. Vasta (Ed.), *Annals of child development* (Vol. 8, pp. 81–143). London: Jessica Kingsley.

Liben, L. S. (1997a). Children's understanding of spatial representations of place: Mapping the methodological landscape. In N. Foreman & R. Gillett (Eds.), *A handbook of spatial research paradigms and methodologies* (pp. 41–83). East Sussex, England: Psychology Press, Taylor & Francis Group.

Liben, L. S. (1997b, Fall). Standing on the shoulders of giants or collapsing on the backs of straw men? *Developmental Psychologist,* 2–14.

Liben, L. S. (1999). Developing an understanding of external spatial representations. In I. E. Sigel (Ed.), *Development of mental representation: Theories and applications* (pp. 297–321). Mahwah, NJ: Erlbaum.

Liben, L. S. (2001). Thinking through maps. In M. Gattis (Ed.), *Spatial schemas and abstract thought* (pp. 44–77). Cambridge, MA: MIT Press.

Liben, L. S. (2002a). The drama of sex differences in academic achievement: And the show goes on. *Issues in Education, 8,* 65–75.

Liben, L. S. (2002b). Spatial development in children: Where are we now? In U. Goswami (Ed.), *Blackwell handbook of childhood cognitive development* (pp. 326–348). Oxford: Blackwell.

Liben, L. S. (2003). Extending space: Exploring the expanding territory of spatial development. *Human Development, 46,* 61–68.

Liben, L. S. (2005). The role of action in understanding and using environmental place representations. In J. Rieser, J. Lockman, & C. Nelson (Eds.), *Minnesota Symposia on Child Development* (pp. 323–361). Mahwah, NJ: Erlbaum.

Liben, L. S. (in press). Representational development and the embodied mind's eye. In W. F. Overton & U. Müller (Eds.), *Body in mind, mind in body: Developmental perspectives on embodiment and consciousness.* Mahwah, NJ: Erlbaum.

Liben, L. S., Carlson, R. A., Szechter, L. E., & Marrara, M. T. (1999, August). *Understanding geographic images.* Paper/poster presented at the 107th annual convention of the American Psychological Association, Boston, MA.

Liben, L. S., & Downs, R. M. (1986). *Children's production and comprehension of maps: Increasing graphic literacy.* Final Report to National Institute of Education (No. G-83-0025).

Liben, L. S., & Downs, R. M. (1989). Understanding maps as symbols: The development of map concepts in children. In H. W. Reese (Ed.), *Advances in child development and behavior* (Vol. 22, pp. 145–201). New York: Academic Press.

Liben, L. S., & Downs, R. M. (1991). The role of graphic representations in understanding the world. In R. M. Downs, L. S. Liben, & D. S. Palermo (Eds.), *Visions of aesthetics, the environment, and development: The legacy of Joachim Wohlwill* (pp. 139–180). Hillsdale, NJ: Erlbaum.

Liben, L. S., & Downs, R. M. (1993). Understanding person-space-map relations: Cartographic and developmental perspectives. *Developmental Psychology, 29,* 739–752.

Liben, L. S., & Downs, R. M. (1994). Fostering geographic literacy from early childhood: The contributions of interdisciplinary research. *Journal of Applied Developmental Psychology, 15,* 549–569.

Liben, L. S., & Downs, R. M. (1997). Canism and can'tianism: A straw child. *Annals of the Association of American Geographers, 87,* 159–167.

Liben, L. S., & Downs, R. M. (2001). Geography for young children: Maps as tools for learning environments. In S. L. Golbeck (Ed.), *Psychological perspectives on early childhood education* (pp. 220–252). Mahwah, NJ: Erlbaum.

Liben, L. S., Kastens, K. A., & Stevenson, L. M. (2002). Real-world knowledge through real-world maps: A developmental guide for navigating the educational terrain. *Developmental Review, 22,* 267–322.

Liben, L. S., Patterson, A. H., & Newcombe, N. (Eds.). (1981). *Spatial representation and behavior across the life span: Theory and application.* New York: Academic Press.

Liben, L. S., Susman, E. J., Finkelstein, J. W., Chinchilli, V. M., Kunselman, S. J., Schwab, J., et al. (2002). The effects of sex steroids on spatial performance: A review and an experimental clinical investigation. *Developmental Psychology, 38,* 236–253.

Liben, L. S., & Szechter, L. S. (2002). A social science of the arts: An emerging organizational initiative and an illustrative investigation of photography. *Qualitative Sociology, 25,* 385–408.

Liben, L. S., & Yekel, C. A. (1996). Preschoolers' understanding of plan and oblique maps: The role of geometric and representational correspondence. *Child Development, 67,* 2780–2796.

Linn, M. C., & Petersen, A. C. (1985). Emergence and characterization of sex differences in spatial ability: A meta-analysis. *Child Development, 56,* 1479–1498.

Lynch, K. (1960). *The image of the city.* Cambridge, MA: MIT Press.

Maccoby, E. E., & Jacklin, C. N. (1974). *The psychology of sex differences.* Stanford: Stanford University Press.

MacEachren, A. M. (1995). *How maps work.* New York: Guilford Press.

Mathewson, J. H. (1999). Visual-spatial thinking: An aspect of science overlooked by educators. *Science Education, 83,* 33–54.

McGee, M. (1979). Human spatial abilities: Psychometric studies and environmental, genetic, hormonal, and neurological influences. *Psychological Bulletin, 86,* 889–918.

Merriwether, A. M., & Liben, L. S. (1997). Adults' failures on Euclidean and projective spatial tasks: Implications for characterizing spatial cognition. *Journal of Adult Development, 4,* 57–69.

Millar, S. (1994). *Understanding and representing space.* Oxford: Clarendon Press.

Morrongiello, B. A., Timney, B., Humphrey, G. K., Anderson, S., & Skory, C. (1995). Spatial knowledge in blind and sighted children. *Journal of Experimental Child Psychology, 59,* 211–233.

Muehrcke, P., & Muehrcke, J. O. (1998). *Map use: Reading, analysis, and interpretation* (4th ed.). Madison, WI: JP Publications.

Muehrcke, P. C. (1986). *Map use* (2nd ed.). Madison, WI: JP Publications.

Myers, L. J., & Liben, L. S. (2005, April). *Can you find it? Children's understanding of symbol-creators' intentions in graphic representations.* Poster presented at the Society for Research in Child Development, Atlanta, GA.

National Geographic Society. (1998). *Road atlas of the United States.* Washington, DC: Author.

National Research Council. (2005). *Learning to think spatially: GIS as a support system in the K–12 curriculum.* Washington, DC: National Academy Press.

Nelson, B. D. (1994, April). *Location and size geographic misperceptions: A survey of junior high through undergraduate college students.* Paper presented at the annual meeting of the Association of American Geographers, San Francisco.

Newcombe, N. (1982). Sex-related differences in spatial ability. In M. Potegal (Ed.), *Spatial abilities: Developmental and physiological foundations* (pp. 223–243). New York: Academic Press.

Newcombe, N., Bandura, M. M., & Taylor, D. G. (1983). Sex differences in spatial ability and spatial activities. *Sex Roles, 9,* 377–386.

Newcombe, N., & Huttenlocher, J. (2000). *Making space.* Cambridge, MA: MIT Press.

Newman, A. K., & Liben, L. S. (1996, August). *Elementary school children's understanding of thematic maps: The concept of areal density.* Paper presented at the American Psychological Association, Toronto, Canada.

Norman, D. K. (1980). A comparison of children's spatial reasoning: Rural Appalachia, suburban, and urban New England. *Child Development, 51,* 288–291.

Okagaki, L., & Frensch, P. A. (1994). Effects of video game playing on measures of spatial performance: Gender effects in late adolescence. *Journal of Applied Developmental Psychology, 15,* 33–58.

O'Keefe, J., & Nadel, L. (1978). *The hippocampus as a cognitive map.* Oxford: Oxford University Press.

Olson, D. R., & Bialystok, E. (1983). *Spatial cognition: The structure and development of mental representations of spatial relations.* Hillsdale, NJ: Erlbaum.

Overton, W. F. (1998). Developmental psychology: Philosophy, concepts, and methodology. In W. Damon (Series Ed.) & R. M. Lerner (Vol. Ed.), *Handbook of child psychology: Vol. 1. Theoretical models of human development* (5th ed., pp. 107–188). New York: Wiley.

Overton, W. F., & Müller, U. (2002, June). *The embodied mind and consciousness.* Introduction to the 32nd annual meetings of the Jean Piaget Society, Philadelphia, PA.

Pair awarded $51,000 for trees felled in error. (1989, March 29). *Los Angeles Times* [Southland Edition: National Desk], p. 14.

Pallrand, G., & Seeber, F. (1984). Spatial ability and achievement in introductory physics. *Journal of Research in Science Teaching, 21*(5), 507–516.

Pattison, P., & Grieve, N. (1984). Do spatial skills contribute to sex differences in different types of mathematical problems? *Journal of Educational Psychology, 76,* 678–689.

Piaget, J. (1954). *The construction of reality in the child.* New York: Ballantine Books.

Piaget, J. (1970). Piaget's theory. In P. Mussen (Ed.), *Carmichael's manual of child psychology* (pp. 703–732). New York: Wiley.

Piaget, J., & Garcia, R. (1989). *Psychogenesis and the history of science.* New York: Columbia University Press.

Piaget, J., & Inhelder, B. (1956). *The child's conception of space.* New York: Norton.

Piaget, J., Inhelder, B., & Szeminska, A. (1960). *The child's conception of geometry.* New York: Basic Books.

Plomin, R., & Vandenberg, S. G. (1980). An analysis of Koch's (1966) primary mental abilities test data for 5- to 7-year-old twins. *Behavior Genetics, 10,* 409–412.

Potter, M. C. (1979). Mundane symbolism: The relations among objects, names, and ideas. In N. R. Smith & M. B. Franklin (Eds.), *Symbolic functioning in childhood* (pp. 41–65). Hillsdale, NJ: Erlbaum.

Quinn, P. C. (2003). Concepts are not just for objects: Categorization of spatial relation information by infants. In D. H. Rakison & L. M. Oakes (Eds.), *Early category and concept development* (pp. 50–76). New York: Oxford University Press.

Rebelsky, F. (1964). Adult perception of the horizontal. *Perceptual and Motor Skills, 19,* 371–374.

Resnick, S. M., Berenbaum, S. A., Gottesman, I. I., & Bouchard, T. J. (1986). Early hormonal influences on cognitive functioning in congenital adrenal hyperplasia. *Developmental Psychology, 22,* 191–198.

Rhodes, D. (1970). *How to read a highway map.* Los Angeles: Elk Grove Press.

Robinson, A. H., Sale, R. D., Morrison, J. L., & Muehrcke, P. C. (1984). *Elements of cartography.* New York: Wiley.

Rogoff, B. (1993). Children's guided participation and participatory appropriation in sociocultural activity. In R. H. Wozniak & K. Fischer (Eds.), *Development in context: Acting and thinking in specific environments* (pp. 121–153). Hillsdale, NJ: Erlbaum.

Rushdoony, H. A. (1988). *Exploring our world with maps.* New York: McGraw-Hill.

Serbin, L. A., & Connor, J. M. (1979). Sex-typing of children's play preferences and patterns of cognitive performance. *Journal of Genetic Psychology, 134,* 315–316.

Shea, D. L., Lubinski, D., & Benbow, C. P. (2001). Importance of assessing spatial ability in intellectually talented young adolescents: A 20-year longitudinal study. *Journal of Educational Psychology, 93,* 604–614.

Shelton, A. L., & Gabrieli, J. D. E. (2004). Neural correlates of individual differences in spatial learning strategies. *Neuropsychology, 18,* 442–449.

Sherman, J. (1967). Problem of sex differences in space perception and aspects of intellectual functioning. *Psychological Review, 74,* 290–299.

Sholl, M. J., & Liben, L. S. (1995). Illusory tilt and Euclidean schemes as factors in performance on the water-level task. *Journal of Experimental Psychology: Learning, Memory, and Cognition, 21,* 1624–1638.

Siegel, A. W., Kirasic, K., & Kail, R. (1978). Stalking the elusive cognitive map: Children's representations of geographic space. In I. Altman & J. Wohlwill (Eds.), *Human behavior and the environment: Advances in theory and research: Vol. 3. Children and the environment* (pp. 223–258). New York: Plenum Press.

Siegel, A. W., & White, S. H. (1975). The development of spatial representations of large-scale environments. In H. W. Reese (Ed.), *Advances in child development and behavior* (Vol. 10, pp. 9–55). New York: Academic Press.

Signorella, M. L., Jamison, W., & Krupa, M. H. (1989). Predicting spatial performance from gender stereotyping in activity preferences and in self-concept. *Developmental Psychology, 25,* 89–95.

Sims, V. K., & Mayer, R. E. (2002). Domain specificity of spatial expertise: The case of video game players. *Applied Cognitive Psychology, 16,* 97–115.

Skipp, C., & Faiola, A. (1996, February 24). Dutch woman slain in Miami armed robbery. *Washington Post* [Final ed.], p. A3.

Small, M. Y., & Martin, M. E. (1983). Research in college science teaching: Spatial visualization training improves performance in organic chemistry. *Journal of College Science Teaching, 13,* 41–43.

Somerville, S. C., & Bryant, P. E. (1985). Young children's use of spatial coordinates. *Child Development, 56,* 604–613.

Sorby, S. A., & Baartmans, B. J. (1996). A course for the development of 3-D spatial visualization skills. *Engineering Design Graphics Journal, 60,* 13–20.

Sorby, S. A., & Baartmans, B. J. (2000). The development and assessment of a course for enhancing the 3-D spatial visualization skills of first year engineering students. *Journal of Engineering Education, 89,* 301–307.

Spencer, C., Harrison, N., & Darvizeh, Z. (1980). The development of iconic mapping ability in young children. *International Journal of Early Childhood, 12,* 57–64.

Stevens, A., & Coupe, P. (1978). Distortion in judged spatial relations. *Cognitive Psychology, 10,* 422–437.

Stiles, J., Bates, E. A., Thal, D., Trauner, D. A., & Reilly, J. (2002). Linguistic and spatial cognitive development in children with pre- and perinatal focal brain injury: A 10-year overview from the San Diego longitudinal project. In M. H. Johnson, Y. Munakata, & R. O. Gilmore (Eds.), *Brain development and cognition: A reader* (2nd ed., pp. 272–291). Malden, MA: Blackwell.

Szechter, L. E., & Liben, L. S. (2004). Parental guidance in preschoolers' understanding of spatial-graphic representations. *Child Development, 75*(3), 869–885.

Thomas, H. (1983). Familial correlational analyses, sex differences, and the X-linked gene hypothesis. *Psychological Bulletin, 93,* 427–440.

Thomas, H., Jamison, W., & Hummel, D. D. (1973). Observation is insufficient for discovering that the surface of still water is invariably horizontal. *Science, 181,* 173–174.

Thomas, H., & Kail, R. (1991). Sex differences in speed of mental rotation and the X-linked genetic hypothesis. *Intelligence, 15,* 17–32.

Thomas, H., & Lohaus, A. (1993). Modeling growth and individual differences in spatial tasks. *Monographs of the Society for Research in Child Development, 58*(9, Serial No. 237).

Thomas, H., & Turner, G. F. W. (1991). Individual differences and development in water-level task performance. *Journal of Experimental Child Psychology, 51,* 171–194.

Thurstone, L. L. (1938). Primary mental abilities. *Psychometric Monographs, 1.*

Towler, J. O., & Nelson, L. D. (1968). The elementary school child's concept of scale. *Journal of Geography, 67,* 24–28.

Troseth, G. L. (2003). Getting a clear picture: Young children's understanding of a televised image. *Developmental Science, 6,* 247–253.

Tuckey, H., & Selvaratnam, M. (1993). Studies involving three-dimensional visualization skills in chemistry: A review. *Studies in Science Education, 21,* 99–121.

Tuckey, H., Selvaratnam, M., & Bradley, J. (1991). Identification and rectification of student difficulties concerning three-dimensional structures, rotation, and reflection. *Journal of Chemical Education, 68,* 460–464.

Tversky, B. (2001). Spatial schemas in depictions. In M. Gattis (Ed.), *Spatial schemas and abstract thought* (pp. 79–112). Cambridge, MA: MIT Press.

U.S. Department of Education, Office of Elementary and Secondary Education. (2002). *No child left behind.* Washington, DC: Author.

Uttal, D. H. (1996). Angles and distances: Children's and adults' reconstructions and scaling of spatial configurations. *Child Development, 67,* 2763–2779.

Vandenberg, S. G., & Kuse, A. R. (1979). Spatial ability: A critical review of the sex-linked major gene hypothesis. In M. A. Wittig & A. C. Petersen (Eds.), *Sex-related differences in cognitive functioning* (pp. 67–95). New York: Academic Press.

Vasta, R., Knott, J., & Gaze, C. (1996). Can spatial training erase the gender differences on the water-level task? *Psychology of Women Quarterly, 20,* 549–567.

Vasta, R., & Liben, L. S. (1996). The water-level task: An intriguing puzzle. *Current Directions in Psychological Science, 5,* 171–177.

Vosniadou, S., & Brewer, W. F. (1992). Mental models of the earth: A study of conceptual change in childhood. *Cognitive Psychology, 24,* 535–585.

Voyer, D., Nolan, C., & Voyer, S. (2000). The relation between experience and spatial performance in men and women. *Sex Roles, 43,* 891–915.

Voyer, D., Voyer, S., & Bryden, M. P. (1995). Magnitude of sex differences in spatial abilities: A meta-analysis and consideration of critical variables. *Psychological Bulletin, 117,* 250–270.

Vygotsky, L. S. (1978). *Mind in society.* Cambridge, MA: Harvard University Press.

Wegener, A. (1966). *The origin of continents and oceans.* Mineola, NY: Dover. (Original work published 1915)

Willis, S. L., & Schaie, K. W. (1986). Training the elderly on the ability factors of spatial orientation and inductive reasoning. *Psychology of Aging, 1,* 239–247.

Wu, H.-K., & Shah, P. (2004). Exploring visuospatial thinking in chemistry learning. *Science Education, 88,* 465–492.

CHAPTER 7

Character Education

DANIEL K. LAPSLEY and DARCIA NARVAEZ

Character education is both popular and controversial. In this chapter, a psychological approach to understanding its central constructs is proposed. We review philosophical conceptions of virtues and conclude that character education cannot be distinguished from rival approaches on the basis of a distinctive ethical theory. We review several educational issues, such as the manner in which the case is made for character education, the implications of broad conceptions of the field, whether character education is best defined by treatments or outcomes, and whether character education is

best pursued with direct or indirect pedagogies, a debate that is placed into historical context. We note that character education requires robust models of character psychology and review several new approaches that show promise. Six general approaches to character education are then considered. Integrative Ethical Education is described as a case study to illustrate theoretical, curricular, and implementation issues. We summarize issues of implementation that are challenges to research and practice. We conclude with several challenges to character education, chief of which is the need to find a distinctive orientation in the context of positive youth development. Problem-free is not fully prepared, but fully prepared is not morally adept.

The moral formation of children is one of the foundational goals of socialization. The ambitions that most parents have for their children naturally include the development of important moral dispositions. Most parents

We express our appreciation to the following colleagues, who read and commented on previous versions of this chapter: Jack Benninga, Jerrell Cassady, Kathryn Fletcher, Lisa Huffman, Jim Leming, Tom Lickona, Kristie Speirs Neumeister, Sharon Paulson, Ben Spiecker, Jan Steutel, Larry Walker, and Marilyn Watson.

want to raise children to become persons of a certain kind, persons who possess traits that are desirable and praiseworthy, whose personalities are imbued with a strong ethical compass. Moreover, other socialization agents and institutions share this goal. The development of moral character is considered a traditional goal of formal education. It is a justification for the work of youth organizations, clubs, and athletic teams. It is the object of homily and religious exhortation. It shows up in presidential speeches. It has preoccupied writers, educators, curriculum experts, and cultural scolds. The number of titles published on character and its role in private and public life has increased dramatically over past decades. So have curricula for teaching the virtues in both schools and homes. Several prominent foundations have thrown their resources behind the cause, and professional meetings dedicated to character education are marked by significant commitment, energy, and fervor. In 2003 a new periodical, the *Journal of Research in Character Education,* was launched to bring focus to scholarly inquiry.

Yet, for all the apparent consensus about the need to raise children of strong moral character, and for all the professional attention devoted to the cause, it is a striking fact that character education occupies contested ground in American society. Indeed, the issues that surround character education are riven with such partisan rivalry that the very terms of reference seem to function like code words that betray certain ideological and political commitments. Whether one is for or against the character education movement is presumably a signal of whether one is a liberal or a conservative, whether one is sympathetic toward traditional or progressive trends in education, whether one thinks the moral life is more a matter of cultivating excellence than submitting to obligation or whether moral evaluation is more about agents than about acts, or whether one prefers the ethics of Aristotle and classical philosophy to that of Kant and the "Enlightenment Project."

This ideological division sometimes surfaces as a technical argument about pedagogy, for example, whether one should endorse direct or indirect methods of instruction. It shows up in how one conceives fundamental questions concerning, for example, the source of our moral values or the epistemological status of our moral claims. It shows up in our understanding of the very goals and purposes of education in liberal democratic polities and in our understanding of what an ethical life consists of: what it means to be a moral agent,

to possess virtue, and to live well the life that is good for one to live. It shows up, too, in the sort of developmental literatures, constructs, and metaphors that one finds compelling.

There is a certain value, of course, in casting large, fundamental, and deeply felt perspectives into such stark relief. It often is useful to draw sharp boundaries around contesting points of view to discern better their strengths and weaknesses. Yet Dewey (1938) warned of the folly of construing educational options in terms of either/or. In so doing, he argued, one runs the danger of advancing one's view only in reaction against the rival, which means that one's vision is controlled unwittingly by that which one struggles against. "There is always the danger in a new movement," he writes, "that in rejecting the aims and methods of that which it would supplant, it may develop its principles negatively rather than positively and constructively" (p. 20), with the result that it fails thereby to address "a comprehensive, constructive survey of actual needs, problems and possibilities" (p. 8).

In this chapter, we review the literature on character education but in a way that avoids, we hope, the dangers of either/or. It is necessary, of course, to sketch the contours of the great debates that have characterized this field. Fortunately, however, there has emerged in recent years a literature that has attempted to bridge the conceptual and ideological divide (e.g., Benninga, 1991a, 1991b; Berkowitz & Oser, 1985; Goodman & Lesnick, 2001; Nucci, 1989; Ryan & Lickona, 1992), or at least to face it squarely. Our search is for the via media that provides, in Dewey's words, the "comprehensive, constructive survey of actual needs, problems and possibilities."

We do not approach our task in complete neutrality. Our own view is that character education would profit from advances in other domains of psychological science (Lapsley & Narvaez, 2005). Indeed, character is a concept with little theoretical meaning in contemporary psychology, although it has been the source of ethical reflection since antiquity. An approach to character education that is deeply "psychologized" would look for insights about moral functioning in contemporary literatures of cognitive and developmental science, in the literatures of motivation, social cognition, and personality. Researchers in these areas rarely draw out the implications of their work for understanding the moral dimensions of personality and its formation. Yet it is our contention that a considered understanding of what is required for effective character education will be forth-coming only when there emerges a robust character psychology that is deeply informed by advances in developmental, cognitive, and personality research. Moreover, effective character education will require deep integration with the educational psychology literatures that constitute the knowledge base for instructional best practice. In short, *character* education must be compatible with our best insights about psychological functioning; character *education* must be compatible with our best insights about teaching and learning (Lapsley & Power, 2005; Narvaez, 2005a).

In the next section, we take up important preliminary issues that establish the context for our review. First, we attempt to understand the various ways character has been conceptualized. Second, we discuss what is at stake with these different conceptualizations for the various theoretical, philosophical, and educational perspectives that have taken up positions on the question of moral character. Third, we attempt to place this discussion in a historical context. As we will see, there is an enduring quality to much of the debate around character education. Fourth, we review recent research on moral personality that could serve as a basis for an integrated psychology of character. Following this discussion, we review promising character education strategies, describe an integrative approach to ethical education, discuss various implementation issues that are common to character education, and outline possible futures for the field.

HOW IS CHARACTER DEFINED?

Character is derived from a Greek word that means "to mark," as on an engraving. One's character is an indelible mark of consistency and predictability. It denotes enduring dispositional tendencies in behavior. It points to something deeply rooted in personality, to its organizing principle that integrates behavior, attitudes, and values. There have been numerous attempts to define character more precisely. It is a "body of active tendencies and interests" that makes one "open, ready, warm to certain aims and callous, cold, blind to others" (Dewey & Tufts, 1910, p. 256). It is made up of a set of dispositions and habits that "patterns our actions in a relatively fixed way" (Nicgorski & Ellrod, 1992, p. 143). It refers to the good traits that are on regular display (Wynne & Ryan,

1997). Character is an individual's "general approach to the dilemmas and responsibilities of social life, a responsiveness to the world that is supported by emotional reactions to the distress of others, the acquisition of prosocial skills, knowledge of social conventions and construction of personal values" (Hay, Castle, Stimson, & Davies, 1995, p. 24). It includes the capacity for self-discipline and empathy (Etzioni, 1993; 1996). It allows ethical agents, as Baumrind (1999, p. 3) put it, "to plan their actions and implement their plans, to examine and choose among options, to eschew certain actions in favor of others, and to structure their lives by adopting congenial habits, attitudes and rules of conduct."

As one can see, defining character is no straightforward matter. Still, one can point to habits, traits, and virtues as three concepts that are foundational to most traditional accounts of moral character. These concepts are interdependent and mutually implicative. Moral character, on this view, is a manifestation of certain personality *traits* called *virtues* that dispose one to *habitual* courses of action. Habits and traits carry a heavy semantic load in the history of psychology that complicates their being used in the context of character education with much conceptual clarity. Virtue is a notion derived from ethics but has very little traction in psychological science unless it is translated into terms such as "habits" and "traits" that are themselves larded with conceptual implications that are controversial.

The Problem with Habits

According to a traditional view, a habit is a disposition to respond to a situation in a certain way. Repeating a behavior or set of procedures over the course of socialization develops this disposition. But not only does right behavior serve to establish habits; they are its consequence as well. Persons of good character behave well without much temptation to do otherwise (W. J. Bennett, 1980), nor is their right behavior a matter of much conscious deliberation: "They are good by force of habit" (Ryan & Lickona, 1992, p. 20). Habits are sometimes used as synonyms for virtues and vices, as in the claim that "character is the composite of our good habits, or virtues, and our bad habits, or vices" (Ryan & Bohlin, 1999, p. 9), and habits also stand in for the dispositional (or "trait") qualities of character.

The appeal for character educators of the role of habits in the moral life has important classical sources. In Book

II of the *Nicomachean Ethics,* Aristotle (350/1985) takes up the nature and definition of virtues. He argues that moral virtue is not a natural part of the human endowment but must come about as a result of habituation. We acquire virtues, on this account, by exercising them. We learn what virtue requires by acting virtuously. No one has the prospect of becoming good unless one practices the good. This would not be unlike the acquisition of skill in the arts or in crafts. Just as individuals become "builders by building and harp players by playing the harp, so also, then, we become just by doing just actions, temperate by doing temperate actions, brave by doing brave actions" (l. 1103b).

According to Steutel and Spiecker (2004; Narvaez & Lapsley, 2005), the Aristotelian notion of habituation is best understood as learning by doing with regular and consistent practice under the guidance and authority of a virtuous tutor. This is not unlike the cultivation of skills through coached practice, although the affinity of skills and virtues is controversial (Peters, 1981; Ryle, 1972). The habits that result from Aristotelian habituation are permanent or settled dispositions to do certain kinds of things on a regular basis but automatically, without reflective choice, deliberation, or planning (Steutel & Spiecker, 2004). In our view, there is a way of understanding Aristotelian habits that is completely compatible with contemporary models of social cognition and cognitive science, including the requirement of automaticity (Lapsley & Narvaez, 2004). For example, Aristotelian habituation can be understood by reference to developing expertise and skill development, notions that underwrite an integrative approach to ethical education that we discuss later (Narvaez, 2005a).

However, retaining the language of habits comes at a cost. When the notion of habits is invoked in the present context, what comes to mind is not classical ethical theory but a certain strand of behavioral learning theory whose core epistemological assumptions have long been challenged. It is linked with an epistemology that locates the developmental dynamic solely in the environment and not with the active child. It is linked with a mechanistic worldview that understands the person to be reactive, passive in his or her own development, and shaped by external contingencies arranged by others. It suggests that learning takes place from the outside *in,* where learning is the acquisition of a repertoire of conditioned responses—habit family hierarchies—that take little notice of the child's own initiative in transforming the learning environment in constructive acts of cognitive mediation.

Hence, an unvarnished behavioral account of habits is belied by contemporary models of developmental science that emphasize the cognitive-constructive activity of the developing child, who is in dynamic interaction with changing ecological contexts across the life course. Consequently, when the notion of habits is invoked to account for moral character, it seems at odds with what is known about developmental processes and constructivist best practice in education (Kohn, 1997). Although invoking habits seems to keep faith with a certain understanding of character in the classical sources, it also has made it more difficult for educators and researchers who reject the behaviorist paradigm to rally around the cause of character education with much enthusiasm (Nucci, 2001). This is unfortunate, in our view, because Aristotelian habits are not coterminous with the habits of behavioral theory. Aristotelian habituation is not coterminous with behavioral laws of learning that use the same term. Aristotelian perspectives contribute much of value to our current understanding of character and its formation, although an understanding adequate for psychological analysis will require translation into contemporary models of developmental and cognitive science.

The Problem with Traits

The language of traits also presents a terminological challenge. The notion that the dispositional features of character are carried by a set of personality traits called *virtues* is both deeply entrenched and controversial. In one sense, there is something completely obvious about trait language, at least in common parlance. Human personality is marked by important continuities. We are disposed to reach certain cognitive interpretations and judgments of events and to experience certain affective and behavioral responses in ways that are predictable and consistent, and these dispositional patterns we designate with the language of traits. We use trait terms to pick out the dispositional tendencies that serve as the basis for charting individual differences. Moreover, our differential valuation of these trait differences provides the basis for moral evaluation of persons. Some displays of individual differences warrant praise and encouragement, and we designate them virtues; others warrant condemnation and admonishment, and we designate those vices.

This view of traits typically comes with two additional assumptions. One is that traits denote stable behavioral patterns that are evident across situations. Another is that traits coalesce as a unity within the person of moral or vicious character. Both assumptions are problematic. The first follows from a traditional understanding that traits-of-character generate dispositional tendencies that are on "regular display." They are adhesive, deeply constitutional aspects of our personality, elements that are engraved "on our essence" (Ryan & Bohlin, 1999, p. 10) that bid us to respond to situations in ways typical of our character. Ryan and Bohlin's example of character is instructive:

> If we have the virtue of honesty, for example, when we find someone's wallet on the pavement, we are characteristically disposed to track down its owner and return it. If we possess the bad habit, or vice, of dishonesty, again our path is clear: we pick it up, look to the right and left, and head for Tower Records or the Gap. (p. 9)

This example illustrates what we take to be the received view: Dispositions are habits; some habits are good and carry the honorific title "virtues," other habits are bad and are designated vices; and habit possession clears the path to predictable and characteristic action. Indeed, a dispositional understanding of traits seems part of our folk theory of human personality and would seem to translate into a straightforward goal for character education: See to it that children come to possess the virtues as demonstrable traits in their personality; see to it that children come to possess good habits.

Yet, to say that moral dispositions coalesce in individuals as traits (or even as "habits") strikes many researchers as a peculiar thing to say. Indeed, in personality research, the nomothetic trait approach has not fared well. This is because the cross-situational generality and consistency of trait behavior has not been demonstrated empirically, nor do trait models have much to say about how dispositions are affected by situational variability. As Mischel (1968, p. 177) put it, "Individuals show far less cross-situational consistency in their behavior than has been assumed by trait-state theories. The more dissimilar the evoking situations, the less likely they are to produce similar or consistent responses from the same individual."

This is remarkably close to conclusions reached by Hartshorne and May (1928–1930) in their classic *Studies in the Nature of Character,* published in three volumes. In one "terse but explosive statement" (Chapman, 1977, p. 59), Hartshorne and May (1929) concluded that the

> consistency with which he is honest or dishonest is a function of the situations in which he is placed so far as (1) these situations have common elements, (2) he has learned to be honest or dishonest in them, and (3) he has become aware of their honest or dishonest implications or consequences. (p. 379)

These studies indicated that the virtue of honesty is not an enduring habit marked indelibly on the essence of a child's character, nor is dishonesty a similarly enduring vice. Children cannot be sorted cleanly into behavioral types on the basis of presumptive traits, habits, or dispositions. In these studies, traits associated with moral character showed scant cross-situational stability and very pronounced situational variability, which is precisely the findings that later personality researchers would report for other traits.

The pessimistic conclusions of Hartshorne and May (1928–1930) have been described variously as a "body blow" (Leming, 1997, p. 34) or "death blow" (Power, Higgins, & Kohlberg, 1989a, p. 127) to the cause of character education. Indeed, they are often cited by partisans of the cognitive developmental tradition as evidence of the poverty of the character approach (e.g., Kohlberg, 1987). Certainly these studies, along with Mischel's (1990, 1999) analysis, seemed to cast doubt on the fundamental assumption of the received view of character traits. Consequently, the ostensible failure of traits in the study of personality made recourse to virtues an unappealing option for many researchers in moral psychology (Lapsley & Narvaez, 2004).

Still, one should not draw the wrong conclusions from evidence that traits show significant situational variability. What is doubted is not the fact that personality shows important dispositional continuity; what is doubted is the implausible view that trait possession invariably trumps the contextual hand that one is dealt. The reality of cross-situational variability is not a failure of the dispositional approach to personality; it is a failure only of the received view of traits. There is, indeed, coherence to personality, but personality coherence cannot be reduced simply to mere stability of behavior across time and setting (Cervone & Shoda, 1999). Instead, coherence is evident in the dynamic, reciprocal interaction among the dispositions, interests, and potentialities of the agent and the changing contexts of learning, development, and socialization. Person variables and contextual variables dynamically interact in complex ways, and both are mutually implicated in behavior. It is here, at the intersection of person and context, where one looks for a coherent behavioral signature (Mischel, 2005; Mischel & Shoda, 1995; Mischel, Shoda, & Mendoza-Denton, 2002; Shoda, Mischel, & Wright, 1994).

The inextricable union of person and context is the lesson both of developmental contextualism (Lerner, 1991) and social cognitive approaches to personality (Cervone & Shoda, 1999; Mischel, 1999), and a robust character psychology will have much in common with these paradigms. Indeed, recent research already vindicates the promise of this perspective. For example, Kochanska's research program shows that the development of conscience and internalization in early childhood requires a goodness-of-fit between styles of parental socialization and children's dispositional temperament (Kochanska, 1993, 1997; Kochanska & Thompson, 1997). In one study, toddlers (age 2 to 3 years) who were temperamentally fearful showed strong evidence of internalization when maternal discipline was mildly coercive, whereas toddlers who were temperamentally fearless profited from mother-child interactions that were mutually cooperative, positive, and responsive (Kochanska, 1995), a pattern that was longitudinally stable 2 years later (Kochanska, 1997). Other studies showed that the quality of the parent-child relationship, as reflected in attachment security, can itself moderate the relationship between parenting strategies and moral internalization (Kochanska, Aksan, Knaack, & Rhines, 2004), and that power assertion can have heterogeneous outcomes for moral behavior and moral cognition (Kochanska, Aksan, & Nichols, 2003). Similarly, Eisenberg and her colleagues showed that a prosocial personality disposition emerges in early childhood and is consistent over time (Eisenberg et al., 2002), although the manifestation of the "altruistic personality" is mediated by individual differences in sympathy (Eisenberg et al., 1999) and the demand characteristics of social contexts (Carlo, Eisenberg, Troyer, Switzer, & Speer, 1991). Finally, Mischel and his colleagues (Shoda, Mischel, & Wright, 1994; Wright & Mischel, 1987) showed that dispositional aggression in children is not, in fact, on regular display across settings but is observed typically when aggressive children are placed in settings of a certain kind, in settings, for example, where demands are placed on their sense of competence. In these exam-

ples, evidence of dispositional coherence requires contextual specification.

A second assumption is that traits hang together to form a unitary consistency within a person. On this view, the various virtues cohere in unified practice. One cannot adequately display courage unless one is also prudent; one cannot be just without temperance; one cannot display any one virtue without all the others. The unity of virtues is a notion that has classical sources, and it is at least implicitly assumed in many discussions about the role of character in public life. Carr (1991, p. 266) points out that the unity-of-virtues perspective is simply the claim that "if a quality of character is a *genuine* virtue it is not *logically* inconsistent with any other real virtue," and that virtues "form a unity because they stand in a certain direct relationship to the *truth* in human affairs." The unity of virtues is a logical possibility; it is an ideal aspiration of the virtuous life.

Still, there are doubts about the adequacy of the unity thesis on both ethical (Carr, 2003; Kent, 1999; MacIntyre, 1981) and psychological grounds. One is not so much concerned with whether the various virtues cohere as a logical possibility, but with whether the unity thesis satisfies a basic criterion of minimal psychological realism that it be a possibility for creatures like us (O. Flanagan, 1991). It is possible after all, given the exigent contingencies of human development, that not all good qualities are equally compatible, or that a good life lived well requires the full range of human excellence. Rather, we become specialists in limited domains of application as a result of the particularities of our developmental experiences, the choices we make, and the environments we select. Our choices canalize the development of dispositions proper to our commitment and to our aspiration, while leaving others unselected, undeveloped, and unobserved in our behavioral repertoire. As a result, certain character blind spots might well be the price one pays for cultivating excellence in other domains of one's life. It may even be the case that our virtues are made possible *just because* other aspects of our character have gone undeveloped.

The Problem with Virtues

The "Character Education Manifesto" (Ryan & Bohlin, 1999, p. 190) asserts that the business of character education "is about developing virtues—good habits and dispositions which lead students to responsible and mature adulthood." We have seen that the appeal to habits and dispositions is not entirely satisfactory given the status of these notions in contemporary psychology. But talk about virtues is also fraught with difficulties. One problem for virtue is the specification of what it entails. How does one "fill out" a particular virtue? How should any virtue be manifested in concrete situations? Aristotle argued famously that virtue lies in the mean between excess and defect. Virtue aims for the intermediate of passions, appetites, and actions: "To feel them at the right times, with reference to the right objects, toward the right people, with the right motive, and in the right ways, is what is both intermediate and best, and that is characteristic of virtue" (1985, l. 1106b). Of course, it is a complication that some actions and passions have no mean, and many states of character have no name: "Now most of these states also have no names, but we must try, as in other cases, to invent names ourselves" (l. 1108a). Kupperman (1999) points out that Aristotle's main point here is not moderation, as many assume, but judgment and flexible response to individual cases. The virtuous person does not follow habits or rules inflexibly but adapts conduct to particular circumstances.

Noddings (2002) noted that the specification of the content of virtue often derives from one's religion or philosophy. Take, for example, Lickona's (1991a, p. 364) view that character education must take a stand on whether it's a good idea for adolescents to masturbate, use condoms, or engage in sexual activity, all behaviors "which [are] clearly wrong for students to do." "The truth is," he writes, "that sexual activity by unmarried teenagers is harmful to them and harmful to society. The morally right value is for young people to avoid such activity" (p. 364). Although this makes the content of virtue quite clear, and quite possibly correct, it does not entirely settle the matter, and one suspects that very different calculations of what is "clearly wrong" and "harmful to society" are possible given a different starting point.

At other times, the moral basis for a specification of virtue is not entirely apparent. One account of the characteristics of a moral teacher suggests, for example, that teacher morality is made evident by small actions, such as "presenting well-planned, enthusiastically taught classes," not being petty, not gossiping, getting homework and test papers returned to students promptly, removing the wad of gum from the water fountain, planning a surprise birthday party for a fellow teacher, or going the extra mile for a struggling student (Wynne & Ryan, 1997, p. 123). Good student character is similarly reflected in small acts: being a member of the math team, tutoring, cleaning up the classroom, joining a sports team, serving as an aide or monitor. One should not minimize praiseworthy behavior or gainsay the value of small kindnesses and good deeds well done, yet the present examples either underspecify the content of moral virtue (insofar as these behaviors could be motivated by a consideration not of virtue but of duty and obligation) or else link it with such commonplaces that virtue is indistinguishable from any behavior that is simply well regarded by others.

Most approaches to character education stress the importance of practical reasoning in the life of virtue (e.g., Lickona, 1991a; Ryan & Bohlin, 1999). Knowing the good, sizing up the situation, gaining insight about how to apply or use moral rules are the work of practical wisdom. Its importance to virtue is evident in Aristotle's (350/1985, l. 1107a) definition of virtue: "It is a state [of character] concerned with choice lying in a mean relative to us, which is defined by reference to reason and in the way in which the person of practical wisdom would determine it." Moreover, Aristotle seems to acknowledge that the proper display of virtue would require keen attention to situational complexity, "to know the facts of the case, to see and understand what is morally relevant and to make decisions that are responsive to the exigencies of the case" (Sherman, 1999, p. 38). Or, as Aristotle put it, "For nothing perceptible is easily defined, and since these circumstances of virtuous and vicious actions are particulars, the judgments about them *depend on perception*" (l. 1109b, emphasis added).

So, if virtues are habits, they must be habits of a certain kind. The kind of habituation proper to virtues is a critical facility; it includes learning how to discern, make distinctions, judge the particulars of the case, and make considered choices (but sometimes automatically). They are dispositions of interpretation (Rorty, 1988) that cognitive psychologists might conceptualize as schemas, prototypes, or scripts whose accessibility and activation make possible the discriminative facility that allows one to act in ways appropriate to the situation (and whose functional readiness could approach automaticity).

The context specificity that attaches to the work of virtues would suggest that one goal of character education would be to help children sort through moral ambiguity by learning when and how to activate what virtue requires given the concrete requirements of a specific context (Noddings, 2002). Of course, what the concrete situation requires of us, say, by way of honesty might well conflict with the demands of compassion, for example. This means that no account of the virtues can be absent the lesson of developmental contextualism, which is that person and context interpenetrate in complex ways and cannot be separated. One must learn, during the course of character development, that the exercise of virtue requires contextual specification; it requires *triage* with respect to the dispositions required for particular settings and an ordering of priorities for their expression given the requirements of the situation. The work of virtues is not unlike the work of any dispositional quality in that the coherence of moral character, its dispositional signature, is to be found at the intersection of person and context (Mischel, 2005).

PHILOSOPHICAL CONSIDERATIONS

Character is fundamentally an ethical concept that struggles for psychological specification. Consequently, the nature of character, both as the moral dimension of personality and as an object of education, invites significant philosophical reflection. In this section we take up two fundamental issues. First, we describe the role that character education plays in responding to concerns about ethical relativism. Second, we examine whether character education can be distinguished from other educational objectives by its commitment to a particular ethical theory associated with Aristotle and the virtue ethics tradition.

Bag of Virtues and Foundations

One suspects that there is deep ambivalence among theorists of character education to consider how virtue works in context for fear that it invites comparison to "situational ethics" and ethical relativism. This is a charge that character education has had to fend off ever since Kohlberg derisively characterized character education as the "bag of virtues" approach. For Kohlberg and the cognitive developmental tradition, the study of moral development was a way to provide the psychological resources by which to defeat ethical relativism. In answer to the ethical relativist who claims that moral perspectives are incommensurable, Kohlberg (1969, p. 352) asserted Piaget's "doctrine of cognitive stages," which provides a developmental criterion for assessing the adequacy of moral judgment. Moral judgments that approach the moral ideal represented by the final stage

of moral reasoning were more adequate on both psychological and ethical grounds (Kohlberg, 1971, 1973). Moreover, justice reasoning at the highest stages made possible a set of operations that could generate consensus about hard case moral quandary. One defeats ethical relativism, then, by motivating justice reasoning to higher stages of development (Lapsley, 2005).

But Kohlberg's project left no room for traits, virtue, or character, for two reasons. First, there was no sensible way to talk about virtues if they are conceptualized as traits-of-character. After all, the Hartshorne and May (1928–1930) studies appeared to show that the psychological reality of traits could not be empirically confirmed (see also Puka, 2004, for trenchant doubts about the reality of virtues) or else could not be relied on to document dispositional consistency in moral behavior. Second, and perhaps more to the point, the language of traits did not provide what was wanted most, which was a way to defeat ethical relativism on psychological grounds. For Kohlberg, any compilation of favored or approved virtues is completely arbitrary. It entails sampling from a "bag of virtues" until a suitable list is produced that has something for everyone. What's more, and worse, given Kohlberg's project, the meaning of virtue trait words is relative to particular communities, for, as Kohlberg and Mayer (1972) put it, one person's integrity is another person's stubbornness; one person's honesty in expressing true feelings is another person's insensitivity to the feelings of others. Not surprisingly, the character education movement uniformly rejects the notion that character education gives comfort to ethical relativism. Indeed, as we will see shortly, the reconstruction of educational history favored by advocates of character education typically pins the blame for "youth disorder" on the ethical relativism promoted by other trends in American culture and education, for which character education is the remedy.

If the problem of settings and context specificity is taken up at all, it takes the form of addressing the question of "whose values" are to be taught in the schools. But this is unproblematic for many character educators because, it is asserted, there are objective values universally agreed on that schools should address with confidence (Lickona, 1991a). For example, one might appeal to natural law theory to "define morality in rational terms agreeable to all" (p. 141). One might distinguish between universal core values that we all do agree on (e.g., respect, responsibility, honesty, justice, caring), possibly because they meet certain canons of objectivity (e.g., Kant's categorical imperative or Kohlberg's "Piagetian" criteria of reversibility) and additional values that are unique to certain communities, such as the Amish, who might endorse, in addition to core values, such things as piety, simplicity, and modesty (Davidson, 2005). Although the list of "common moral values" might differ among communities, there is, nonetheless, a "core" and a "large overlap in the content that emerges" (Ryan & Bohlin, 1999, p. 50).

Still, we think this debate has gone on long enough. The specter of ethical relativism has been a bogey haunting moral psychology and education for decades, but it has been a distraction, and it has distorted the work of both the cognitive developmental and character education paradigms. It has prevented the cognitive developmental tradition from considering the role of personality and selfhood in moral reasoning because these variables could not secure the autonomy of reason or the universality of judgments (Lapsley, 1996; Walker, 2002; Walker & Hennig, 1998). It has distracted character education with worries about moral objectivity and foundations, and with the seeming necessity to show that it is just as sternly antirelativist as the committed stage theorist. However, whether moral claims are universal or incommensurable, whether there is anything like objective moral facts that vouchsafe our moral convictions, are ethical-philosophical or theological issues that psychological research is ill equipped to address with its armamentarium of empirical tools (Blasi, 1990). The attempt to resolve philosophical problems with empirical data has been a big mistake, in our view, and has led to cramped and truncated research programs restricted by perceived philosophical restrictions and boundaries.

Carr (1991) suggested that much of the anxiety about foundations in moral education has got things the wrong way round. In his view, we do not start with principles and then derive practices; rather, the principles are induced from within the practices and experiences of our social life. The principles, in other words, are underwritten by practices, not practices by the principles. Practices are the "product of a fallible human attempt to understand the web of moral association by reference to consideration of . . . what sort of conduct conduce to good and ill, well-being and harm" (p. 4). One can reject the balm of foundationalism and still affirm that workable criteria of right and wrong, of good and evil, of virtue and vice can be discovered "in the rough and tumble of human interpersonal relations and conduct"

(p. 4). Virtues, then, are not foundational axioms or first principles; they are not

> hard and fast principles which may be applied to any conceivable circumstance but general patterns or tendencies of conduct which require reasonable and cautious adjustment to particular and changing circumstances and which may even, in some situations, compete with each other for preference and priority. (p. 5)

And although different communities may well flesh out the meaning of virtues (e.g., courage, caring) in different ways, "it is hard to envisage a human community in which these qualities are not needed, recognized or held to be of any value at all" (p. 6), given the affordances of our shared biological and social nature (see also Nussbaum, 1988).

One appreciates in Carr's (1991) account of virtues and foundations the notion broached earlier, that virtues, and traits generally, do not trump invariably the contextual hand one is dealt; that virtues must be contextually specified and situationally ordered; that virtues are socially implicated dispositions; and that the desired schedule of virtues, their meaning and mode of expression, are deeply embedded in the practices, customs, and expectations of communities—and that none of this should give comfort to the ethical relativist (or else the issue of ethical relativism is a different sort of conversation). This also suggests, as we will see later, that moral education can never be simply about the character of children without also addressing the context of education, that is to say, the culture, climate, structure, and function of classrooms and schools (Berkowitz & Bier, 2005). Persons and contexts are inextricably linked and cannot be separated.

If Carr's (1991) view is correct, that virtues are dispositional templates induced from social practices, whose meaning can be discovered in the "rough and tumble of human interpersonal relations" (p. 4), then one way to approach the problem of whether there are "core values" that overlap is to determine if such templates are evident in the way ordinary people think about character. That is, rather than nominate core values from some alleged objective standpoint, from natural law or the perspective of eternity, one might proceed inductively from the standpoint of individual informants.

There have been recent attempts to address the matter empirically. Lapsley and Lasky (1999) provided evidence that conceptions of good character are organized as a cognitive prototype, and that this prototype has a significant influence on recognition memory and information processing. In this study, the top 10 traits with the highest prototypicality ratings are honest, trustworthy, genuine, loving, dependable, loyal, trusting, friendly, respectful, and caring.

Similarly, Walker (2004; Walker & Pitts, 1998) has pursued naturalistic studies of the prototype structure of a "highly moral person" and has identified clusters or themes that commonly show up in people's understanding of moral maturity. One cluster, for example, is a set of "principled-idealistic" commitments to strongly held values. Another includes themes of "fairness." Other clusters identify dependable-loyal, caring-trustworthy, and confident-agency themes. Subsequent research examined the prototype structure of conceptions of just, brave, and caring persons (Walker & Hennig, 2004). Although these attributes differ somewhat from the prototypical good character, as one might expect with different targets, it would appear that a common core of trait attributes for character and moral personality can be identified empirically.

Character and Virtue Ethics

It is widely assumed that Kohlberg's cognitive developmental approach to moral education represents an instantiation of an ethical theory associated with Kant, whereas character education focuses on a different set of ethical concerns represented by Aristotelian virtue ethics. Indeed, Steutel and Carr (1999; Carr & Steutel, 1999; Steutel, 1997) argued that if character education is to be distinguished from other forms of moral education, such as Kohlberg's, it must be grounded in an explicit commitment to virtue ethics and not to other ethical theories. If character education is in fact committed to virtue ethics, what might that entail?

G. Watson (1990) suggested a useful tripartite division of ethical theory: the ethic of requirement (where the primary moral considerations concern rational judgments of obligation and duty and the moral appraisal of action), the ethic of consequences (various forms of utilitarianism), and the ethic of virtue. An ethics of virtue is distinguished from the others by its claim that the basic moral facts are facts about the quality of character (*arête*); that judgments about agents and their traits have explanatory primacy over judgments about duty, obligation, and utility; and that deontic judgments

about obligation and action appraisal are, in fact, derived from the appraisal of character and ancillary to it. "On an ethics of virtue," he writes, "how it is best or right or proper to conduct oneself is explained in terms of how it is best for a human being to be" (p. 451).

Hence, a virtue ethics has two features: (1) It makes a claim of explanatory primacy for aretaic judgments about character, agents, and what is required for flourishing; and (2) it includes a theory about "how it is best or right or proper to conduct oneself" in light of what is known about human excellence. Surprisingly, neither feature has much resonance in character education. In most accounts of character education, one cultivates virtues mostly to better fulfill one's obligation and duty (the ethics of requirement) or to prevent the rising tide of youth disorder (character utilitarianism, or the ethics of consequences). Although one can conceive of virtues as providing action-guiding prescriptions just as deontological theory does (Hursthouse, 2003), the point of virtues in most accounts of character education is to live up to the prescriptions derived from deontic considerations: to respect persons, fulfill one's duty to the self and to others, and submit to the natural law. When the goal of character education is to help children "know the good," this typically means coming to learn the "cross-cultural composite of moral imperatives and ideals" (Ryan & Bohlin, 1999, p. 7). Rather than emphasize agent appraisal, the animating goal of many character educators is appraisal of actions, for, as Wynne and Hess (1992, p. 31) put it, "Character is conduct," and the best test of a "school's moral efficiency" is "pupils' day-to-day conduct, displayed through deeds and words" (Wynne 1991, p. 145).

It would appear, then, that character education and cognitive developmental moral education cannot be distinguished on the basis of the ethical theory that animates them. Character education, for all its appeal to virtues, seems to embrace the ethics of requirement just as surely as does moral stage theory, rather than an ethics of virtue. The most important moral facts for both paradigms are still facts about obligation, universal principles, and duty. The most important object of evaluation for both paradigms is still action and conduct; it is still deciding the good thing to do rather than the sort of person to become. The fact that character education is so thoroughly deontological and utilitarian with so little in common with virtue ethics is not inherently problematic, although it does attenuate some hope that virtue ethics would open up a new front in moral psychology and education (Campbell & Christopher, 1996; Campbell, Christopher, & Bickhard, 2002; Punzo, 1996).

EDUCATIONAL CONSIDERATIONS

If character education cannot be distinguished from rival approaches in terms of its justifying ethical theory, then perhaps its singularity is to be found elsewhere, say, in terms of its educational practices or in the way that it frames its educational mission. There does seem to be something quite distinctive about the way the case is made for character education, what has been called the *genre of discontent* (Lapsley & Power, 2005) and the *litany of alarm* (Arthur, 2003).

Typically, the first move in making the case for character education is to review a long list of social ills that characterize children and adolescents to document the rising tide of youth disorder. Brooks and Goble (1997, p. 6) point to youth crime, violence, drug addiction, and "other forms of irresponsible behavior." Wynne and Hess (1992; also Wynne & Ryan, 1997) review the statistics for homicide, suicide, out-of-wedlock births, premarital sex, illegal drug use, delinquency and crime rates, and plunging academic achievement test scores. Lickona (1991a) notes the increase in violence and vandalism, stealing, cheating, disrespect, peer cruelty, bigotry, bad language, self-centeredness, and use of illegal substances.

After cataloguing these trends, there is an attempt to understand their source. Lickona's (1991a) account is paradigmatic. Like other writers in this genre, he draws attention to troubling evidence of cultural decline that is attributed to broad changes in American education. In the early days of the republic children were instructed intentionally on matters of character by the exhortation, discipline, and example of teachers, by the models of virtue encountered in the Bible and the McGuffey Reader, and elsewhere in the curriculum. Eventually, however, this "old-fashioned character education" was forced into retreat by a convergence of larger forces that undermined the confidence of schools in taking on their traditional moral educational responsibilities.

The influence of Darwin's theory, for example, led people to wonder if even moral sensibilities could be uprooted from fixed and static foundations and regarded as something changeable and evolutionary. Einstein's theory of relativity encouraged a kind of moral perspectivism that viewed moral claims as relative to a certain

point of view. The Hartshorne and May (1928–1930) studies highlighted the role of situations in moral behavior. And the general rise of logical positivism encouraged the view that the only sensible things to say were those amenable to publicly verifiable empirical demonstrations (as "facts"), whereas everything else ("values") was held to be subjective, personal, and quite literally "non*sense*" (see, e.g., Ayer, 1952).

These four trends, then, according to Lickona (1991a), forced character education into retreat. "When much of society," he writes, "came to think of morality as being in flux [Darwin], relative to the individual [Einstein], situationally variable [Hartshorne and May] and essentially private [logical positivism], public schools retreated from their once central role as moral educator" (p. 8).

This reconstruction of history, and others like it, has been called the "cultural declinist" perspective (Nash, 1997) for perhaps the obvious reason that it sees an empirical relationship between the neglect or abandonment of intentional character education and the rise of disorder and immorality among young people. This way of making the case serves as a preface for three additional issues that we will consider here. The first issue concerns whether the singularity of character education can be identified on the basis of the sort of problems it attempts to address, or the manner in which it attempts to address them, or whether any conceivable intervention targeting problematic behavior would qualify as an instance of character education. Second, is character education identified by a commitment to direct or indirect methods of instruction? We will see that this debate is best understood in the context of much larger histories of teaching practice and of the idea of liberal education. Third, in what sense is the cultural declinist genre itself a recurring movement in educational history, and how can we understand its resurgence over the past 2 decades? An examination of the historiography of character education will show that there are recurring cycles of concern about character education during periods of rapid change, and that character education movements typically fail without well-attested models of self and personality.

Broad Character Education

When the case is made for character education by appealing to troubling social trends or to the epidemiology of adolescent risk behavior, there is an implication that any program that attempts to drive down these trends or ameliorate the incidence of risk behavior might reasonably fall under the broad umbrella of character education. If getting bad grades, cheating, dropping out of school, having sex, bearing children, using drugs, getting into fights, committing status offenses, breaking the law, attempting suicide, showing disrespect, being a bully—if these are the mark of poor moral character, then programs designed to encourage school persistence, prevent teen pregnancy, discourage the use of drugs and alcohol, improve social skills and social problem solving, increase resilience to social-affective problems, and the like might qualify as moral character interventions. There is evidence for such a sweeping view of character education. In her study of the character education practices of 350 Blue Ribbon schools, Murphy (1998) reported a wide range of practices, including self-esteem programs, general guidance counseling, drug education, citizenship, discipline, and conflict management. However, in only 11% of schools was there explicit mention of any program called "character education."

Similarly, Berkowitz and Bier (2004b) identified 12 recommended and 18 promising practices in a review of what works in character education. These practices covered a wide range of purposes, including problem solving, health education, empathy, social skills and social competence training, conflict resolution, peace making, life skills training, developmental assets, and positive youth development. Although Berkowitz and Bier (2004a) concluded that these programs work, they also noted that most of them do not use the term "character" to describe their intentions and objectives. Very few of them were designed with any notion of virtues, character, or morality in mind, and were not described as instances of moral or character education. Nonetheless, the success of these programs is claimed for character education because their methods, outcomes, and justifications are similar to what might be expected of character education programs. "After all," they write, "they are all school based endeavors designed to help foster the positive development of youth" (p. 5).

By these criteria it is difficult to imagine what would *not* count as character education or be excluded from its purview. If character education is all of these things, and if the success of character education is parasitic on the success of any well-designed intervention or prevention program, then the singularity of character education as a distinctive educational objective or pedagogy,

with unique curricular and programmatic features, appears to vanish.

It would seem paradoxical that the manner in which the case has been made for character education actually results in its disappearance as a distinctive educational objective in its own right. If the case is made on the basis of disturbing trends in the epidemiology of adolescent risk behavior, then it bids one to look for the success of character education in the diminution of this behavior. But then character education becomes any program that has a positive outcome with respect to adolescent risk behavior. It becomes a catalogue of psychosocial intervention, promotion, and prevention programs whose objectives are framed by reference to an entirely different set of theoretical literatures that make no reference to morality, virtue, or character. Moreover, there is little reason to appeal to character education, or use the language of moral valuation, to understand the etiology of risk behavior or how best to prevent or ameliorate exposure to risk or promote resilience and adjustment.

The problem with the broad view, then, is that it does not point to anything distinctive about character education. Yet, perhaps the problem of singularity derives from the fact that all good causes in education, from social-emotional learning to positive youth development, risk reduction, psychosocial resilience, academic achievement, and character education, are driven effectively by a common set of school practices. Just as problem behaviors are interrelated and are predicted by a similar profile of risk factors, so, too, are adaptive and prosocial behaviors interrelated and linked to a common set of developmental factors and instructional practices. Indeed, Berkowitz and Bier (2004b) nominate "positive youth development" as the inclusive term to cover all of the program objectives and suggest that these objectives are simply part of "good education" generally. The downside of this maneuver is that character education appears to lose its singular focus. But the loss of conceptual distinctiveness for character education is offset by the gain in instructional clarity for practitioners. The problem for the practitioner is not the problem of knowing which program "works" or of correctly labeling curricular and programmatic activities, but of mastering the instructional best practices that are common to all of them (see Howard, Dryden, & Johnson, 1999, for a similar point with respect to promoting resilience).

Yet, there is a case to be made for character education that has little need for troubling epidemiological trends. The case is made simply by pointing to the fact that moral considerations are immanent to the life of classrooms and schools, that teaching and learning are value-laden activities, and that moral aims are intrinsic to education (Bryk, 1988; Goodlad, 1992; D. T. Hansen, 1993; Strike, 1996). The case is made by reference to the developmental objectives of schools and to the role of schools in inculcating the skills proper to democratic citizenship and to full participation in the life of the community. The immanence of values and the inevitability of moral education is an argument almost always found in the character educator's brief, but mostly for countering the charge of indoctrination rather than for making the case. Yet the immanence-and-inevitability thesis would seem to arm the character educator with all the resources that are needed to defend an intentional and transparent commitment to the moral formation of students. Moreover, the case that is made from this standpoint is a positive one; it makes reference to developmental purposes, to a conception of what it means to flourish, to the skills, dispositions, and excellences that are required to live well and competently, the life that is good for one to live in a democratic society. This is in contradistinction to the traditional argument that builds the case negatively by making character education just another prevention program, viewing character education as a kind of prophylaxis or cultural defense against "youth disorder."

Direct and Indirect Methods

In an early essay, Dewey (1908) defined the terms of this debate. It "may be laid down as fundamental," he asserted, "that the influence of direct moral instruction, even at its very best, is *comparatively* slight in influence, when the whole field of moral growth through education is taken into account" (p. 4, emphasis in original). Rather, it is the "larger field of indirect and vital moral education, the development of character through all the agencies, instrumentalities and materials of school life" (p. 4), that is far more influential. This larger field of indirect education reproduces within the school the typical conditions of social life to be encountered without. "The only way to prepare for social life is to engage in social life" (p. 15).

Moreover, this sort of moral education is possible only when the school itself becomes an "embryonic typical community" (Dewey, 1908, p. 15). Indeed, for Dewey, the school has no moral aim apart from participation in social life. The rules of school life must point to something larger, outside of itself, otherwise education becomes a mere "gymnastics exercise" that trains faculties that make no sense and have no moral significance just because they are disconnected from larger purposes. Absent these purposes, moral education is pathological and formal. It is pathological when it is alert to wrongdoing but fails to cultivate positive service, when it stresses conformity to school routines that are arbitrary and conventional but lack inherent necessity. Moral training is formal when it emphasizes an ad hoc catalogue of habits that are "school duties," not "life duties." To the extent that the work of schools is disconnected from social life, insistence on these moral habits is "more or less unreal because the ideal to which they relate is not itself necessary" (p. 17). The moral habits of interest to Dewey concern an interest in community welfare, in perceiving what is necessary for social order and progress, and in the skills necessary to execute principles of action. All school habits must be related to these "if they are to be animated by the breath of life" (p. 17).

Dewey (1908) was critical of a traditional pedagogy of exhortation, didactic instruction, and drill. Such pedagogy fails to cultivate a social spirit; it emphasize individualistic motives, competition, comparative success, dispiriting social comparison; it encourages passive absorption and emphasizes preparation for life but in the remote future. It reduces moral instruction to simply teaching *about* virtues or in instilling certain attitudes about them. What is required instead is an approach to education that links school subjects to a social interest; that cultivates children's ability to discern, observe, and comprehend social situations; that uses methods that appeal to the "active constructive powers" of intelligence; that organizes the school along the lines of a genuine community and selects curricular materials that gives children a consciousness of the world and what it will demand. Only if schools are prepared to take on these principles can they be said to meet their basic ethical requirements.

Dewey's vision of moral education is sometimes called a "progressive" or "indirect" approach because it eschews traditional pedagogy that relies on didactic instruction and direct transmission of moral content. Instead, indirect approaches emphasize the child's active construction of moral meaning through participation in democratic practices, cooperative groupings, social interaction, and moral discussion (e.g., DeVries & Zan, 1994).

In contrast, the direct approach to instruction is widely associated with traditional character education (Benninga, 1991b; Solomon, Watson, & Battistich, 2001). In a defense, Ryan (1989, p. 15) asserted that "character development is directive and sees the teacher in a more active role than does the cognitive developmental tradition." There is sympathy for what is called the Great Tradition that views the educational encounter as one of transmission from adults to children (Wynne & Ryan, 1997). For traditional character education, morality is ready-made and good character requires submission to its preexisting norms. It is suspicious of indirect or constructivist approaches that seemingly allow adults to abdicate their role as moral teachers in favor of "consensual" democratic practices in schools. Such practices are antitradition because they seem to allow students to engage in "highly relativistic discussions about value laden issues" where alternative views might emerge with respect to such things as obedience or the limits of loyalty to one's country (p. 35). These practices seem to let the kids decide what important values are and naively assumes that children will choose well when given opportunities for self-direction. "Is it wise," writes Wynne (1991, p. 142, emphasis added), "to 'teach' pupils that basic moral principles and conventions generally accepted by responsible adults should be considered de novo, and possibly rejected, by each successive adolescent cohort? *Must each generation try to completely reinvent society?*"

Mimesis and Transformation

The debate over direct and indirect methods of character education has a much longer history and, when properly considered, points to a middle way for practitioners. Jackson (1986) captures much of this history in his useful distinction between mimetic and transformative traditions of education. Both traditions are centuries old and describe a complex worldview about the nature of teaching and learning. These traditions are at the nexus of partisan rivalry not simply because they articulate different perspectives on what constitutes proper teaching, but because they each comprise a different "form of life" (following Wittgenstein, 1968), a fact that raises the stakes considerably.

The mimetic tradition embraces a transmission model of teaching and learning. Knowledge is considered something detachable (it can be preserved), secondhand (it first belongs to someone else before it is transmitted), and reproducible (which facilitates its transmission). As such, knowledge is presented to the learner, rather than discovered by the learner. It can be judged as right or wrong, correct or incorrect. The mimetic teacher is directive, expert in the substantive bodies of knowledge and in methodological competence. The student is a novice, without knowledge of what teachers know, and hence the object of transmission. "In more epigrammatic terms, the slogan for this tradition might be: 'What the teacher knows, that shall the student come to know'" (Jackson, 1986, p. 119).

In contrast, the transformative tradition intends a qualitative change in that which is deeply foundational in a person: in one's character, set of traits, or other enduring aspects of one's psychological makeup. The goal of teachers in this tradition is to:

> bring about changes in their students (and possibly in themselves as well) that make them better persons, not simply more knowledgeable or more skillful, but better in the sense of being closer to what humans are capable of becoming—-more virtuous, fuller participants in the evolving moral order. (Jackson, 1986, p. 127)

And transformative teachers attempt to bring about these changes not through dogmatic presentation of foundational texts, not by means of didactic instruction, but by discussion, argumentation, and demonstration. The transformative teacher, in other words, attempts to influence students by philosophical means. As Jackson put it, "Armed only with the tools of reason the transformative teacher seeks to accomplish what can be attained in no other way" (p. 127).

Oratorical and Philosophical Traditions

The distinction between direct and indirect character education can be framed historically not only by reference to (mimetic and transformative) traditions of teaching, but also by reference to the history of liberal education. According to Kimball (1986), the history of liberal education from the ancients to the present is the struggle between two distinct traditions that he termed "philosophical" and "oratorical." Moreover, the value conflicts between these traditions have resulted in recurring cycles of educational reform as first one then the other tradition becomes ascendant.

The "philosophical" tradition is aligned historically with Socrates, Plato, and Aristotle. It asserts that the pursuit of knowledge and truth is the highest good; that because truth is elusive and because there are many uncertainties, one must cultivate the philosophical dispositions, be open-minded, judge fairly, reason critically. In this tradition, it is freedom of the intellect and diligent inquiry that is the goal and purpose of education.

The "oratorical" tradition is aligned historically with Isocrates and Cicero. It is committed to the public expression of what is known through classic texts and tradition. One becomes a virtuous citizen-orator by becoming acquainted with the wisdom evident in rhetoric and in the classics. If the philosophical tradition saw truth and goodness as something elusive and unsettled, as something not yet realized or achieved, but that can be grasped only by the critical discernment of speculative reason, the oratorical tradition locates truth and goodness in the great texts and past traditions. If the philosophical tradition conceives the search for truth as an act of discovery, it is an act of recovery for the oratorical tradition. If the philosophical tradition intends to equip individuals to face an uncertain future, the oratorical tradition intends to equip individuals with the certain and settled verities of the past.

Featherstone (1986) points out that the great strength of the philosophical tradition is its emphasis on the free exercise of reason in pursuit of the truth, but that its weakness as an educational philosophy is its silence on just what is to be taught. It urges one to seek the truth like a philosopher, but cannot say what truth is with much certainty. It is strong on method, weak on content. This is where the oratorical tradition has an advantage. The educational point of the oratorical tradition is to master the content of traditional texts. In the oratorical tradition, the task of education is to impart the truth, not to help students seek it (Featherstone, 1986). It is strong on content, weak on method.

It would seem, then, that the contemporary debate concerning direct and indirect methods reflects deeper and longer-standing conflicts over the role of mimesis or transformation in teaching, or the relative value of preparing orators or philosophers in education. Yet it also seems clear that the modern expression of direct character education reveals a fundamental confusion about its sources, aims, and traditions. For example, although direct character education intends to transform students' character in the direction of virtue, it attempts to do so with teaching that is mimetic rather than transformative. Moreover, in spite of its frequent invocation of classical sources such as Socrates, Plato, and Aristotle, it is apparent that direct approaches to character education are not, in fact, the heirs of the philosophical tradition but of the oratorical tradition. Indeed, the direct approach is largely mimetic and oratorical, whereas the indirect approach is transformative and philosophical.

Of course, it is not hard to see the middle way in this debate. There are occasions in teaching for both mimesis and transformation. We need both orators and philosophers. The best teachers are experts in pedagogical content knowledge (Shulman, 1987; Wilson, Shulman, & Richert, 1987) and are able therefore to use instructional methods appropriate for teaching specific content. The best approaches to character education flexibly balance the philosophical methods of inquiry, discussion, and discernment with the oratorical respect for text and tradition; both direct and indirect approaches find a place in the curriculum (Benninga, 1991b). Lickona's (1991a, 1991b, 1992, 1997; Lickona & Davidson, 2004) integrated approach to character education is a good example. Although this approach has decided oratorical sympathies and resorts to the genre of discontent to makes its case, there is also significant and welcome appreciation of the constructivist nature of learning and of the necessity for transformative approaches to teaching. Alongside directive advocacy of certain value positions there is use of indirect strategies as well, including cooperative learning, conflict resolution, classroom democratic processes, moral discussion and reflection, and the need to build a sense of moral community within the school.

Historical Lessons

We noted earlier that a "cultural declinist" reading of American history is commonly used to make the case for character education. And that the debate between traditionalists and progressives, between advocates of direct and indirect methods of character education, is just the contemporary manifestation of more fundamental conflicts concerning the nature of teaching (mimesis versus transformative) and of liberal education (oratorical versus philosophical) that have quite long-standing histori-cal roots. But what of the history of character education itself? Chapman's (1977) observation summarizes a common theme. "It is curious to note," he writes, "how the concern for character seems to have been associated with times of rapid social change" (p. 65).

McClellan (1999) notes, for example, in his influen-tial history of moral education, that the nineteenth cen-tury ushered in a revolution in moral education that was motivated by massive social upheaval and the collapse of the old order brought about by urbanization, mobility, and immigration. "Traditional sources of social order—stable hierarchical social structures, patterns of cultural and political deference, webs of extended kinships and tight-knit communities—weakened as images of control and orderly change gave way to visions of movement and opportunity" (p. 15). The response was to urge early in-struction of a common moral code, taught largely through a new genre of children's stories and by the suf-fusion of maxims and moral lessons throughout text-books. Typical themes included the certainty of progress and the perfection of the United States, love of country, duty to parents, the importance of thrift, honesty, and hard work for accumulation of property.

In the early twentieth century, the demands of modernity further sundered the seamless weave of the community into largely disconnected sectors of home, employment, marketplace, church, and recreation, each operating with seemingly different value systems. Schools were now required to prepare students to take up "a variety of roles across the differentiated spheres of a segmented social order" (McClellan, 1999, p. 47). Schools became complex institutions with varied pur-poses, only one of which was moral education.

Among character educators there was a sense that modernity presented important challenges to traditional values that could be mastered only by vigorous teaching of specific virtues and character traits, not just in school but in a variety of clubs and youth organizations that proliferated in the early twentieth century. Codes of con-duct were promulgated, and teachers were expected to use these codes to provide themes for instruction. Much like today, these themes were exhibited in classroom posters and laws of the month. Citizenship and comport-ment grades were commonly taken as signs of character development. Moral education itself was directed largely to the problem of motivation and will rather than to rea-soning. The problem was how to make moral conduct ha-bitual rather than to teach ethical decision making, a no-tion that has a familiar ring a century later.

The progressive alternative, as we have seen, rejected the emphasis on teaching particular virtues as being un-suited to help children meet the demands of a changing social order, and it rejected, too, the direct approaches to instruction as pedagogically ineffective. Instead, it emphasized ethical sensitivity to the demands of chang-ing society, the ability to make moral judgments, and the larger civic and political purposes of moral education as opposed to the traditional emphasis on private virtue and conduct. Hence, rather than focus on traditional texts, the progressive alternative encouraged democratic decision making, critical thinking, and scientific in-quiry as the methods best able to equip students to take up their obligations in modern society. These are the very terms of reference for the current debate concern-ing character education.

Indeed, Cunningham (2005) points to many common themes between the current popularity of character edu-cation and its predecessor movements earlier in the twentieth century. He notes that many modern propo-nents of character education who ardently look back to the Great Tradition, when traditional character educa-tion was allegedly pervasive, widely embraced, and suc-cessfully implemented, might be surprised to learn that the educational "tradition" they seek was not apparent to contemporaries. Widespread anxiety about social dis-integration was as common to the first decades of the twentieth century as to the later decades. Both periods exhibited alarm at the sorry state of moral character among business leaders and politicians, as well as youth. Both periods saw evidence of cultural decline, loss of traditional values, and abandonment of foundational principles. Both periods saw the formation of character education lobbies, pressure groups, and professional so-cieties; both saw state action by legislatures to mandate character education in the schools; both saw the need for experiential or service learning; both saw the promulga-tion of widely divergent lists of urgently needed virtues, debates about direct and indirect methods, and the proper place of coercion and democratic practices in the schools. Moreover, the chasm between educators and re-searchers, between the ardent confidence of character educators in their favored curriculum and the skepticism of researchers about its efficacy, also has a long history (see Leming, 1997). Moreover, Cunningham argues that whereas the "rise" of traditional character education in the twentieth century typically accompanied periods of great social ferment and rapid social change, when there were profound challenges to national identity and widespread anxiety about social cohesion and the unsettling forces of modernity, its "fall" was inevitable without an adequate character psychology to guide curricular development and instructional practice. "Unless psychology can provide a better model of human development," he writes, "character will continue to receive sporadic and faddish treatment and the public's common school will continue to be undermined" (p. 197).

We return, then, to a central claim of this chapter, which is that the conceptual grounding required for any minimally adequate character education must be found in robust models of character psychology (Cunningham, 2005; Lapsley & Power, 2005). Although ideological commitments are notoriously immune to influence, it is our view that consensual frameworks for addressing character education will be forthcoming when controversies are anchored to appropriate psychological literatures. In the next section, we take note of relatively recent approaches to character psychology that provide new ways of conceptualizing the moral dimensions of personality.

NEW APPROACHES TO CHARACTER PSYCHOLOGY

There are at least two new approaches that have emerged for conceptualizing moral character. One approach argues that a moral identity results when the self identifies with moral commitments or a moral point of view. A second approach conceptualizes character in terms of the literatures of cognitive and personality psychology. We briefly consider each approach in turn.

Identity, Exemplars, and the Moral Self

One way to conceptualize character is in terms of moral identity. According to Hart (2005), moral identity includes self-awareness, a sense of self integration and continuity over time, a commitment to plans of action and an attachment to one's moral goals. Moreover, he argues that the contours of moral identity are constrained by stable aspects of personality but also by characteristics of family and neighborhood. Moral identity is a joint product of personal and contextual factors. Indeed, moral identity is influenced by factors beyond the con-

trol of the adolescent, which introduces an element of "moral luck" in the sort of commitments a young person might identify with. Yet there is plasticity in moral identity development. Moral identity is open to revision across the lifecourse, particularly when one is given opportunities to engage in moral action. This possibility underscores the importance of providing youth with opportunities for service learning and community service, a topic we take up later.

Blasi's (1984, 1985, 1995) account of moral identity shares some similarity with Hart's (2005). According to Blasi one has a moral identity to the extent that the self is organized around moral commitments. One has a moral identity when moral notions are central, important, and essential to one's self-understanding. This yields a personality imbued with a deep, affective, and motivational orientation toward morality. Blasi (1984) insists, however, that any account of the moral personality be grounded on the premise that rationality is the core of the moral life. To have a moral identity is to have good moral reasons for the identity-defining commitments that one makes.

Of course, not everyone has a self-concept that is constructed by reference to moral reasons. Some individuals organize self-related information around moral categories, others do not. Some individuals let moral notions penetrate to the core of what and who they are as persons; others have only a glancing acquaintance with moral notions but choose to define the self in other ways, by reference to other values and commitments (Walker, Pitts, Hennig, & Matsuba, 1995). Even those who define the self in moral terms may do so in different ways, emphasizing different sets of moral priorities. In this way, moral identity is a dimension of individual differences; it is foundational to the moral personality (Blasi, 1995). When moral commitments are vital for one's self-understanding, and one commits to live in a way that keeps faith with these identity-defining commitments, one has a moral identity. Indeed, not to act in accordance with one's identity is to put the integrity of the self at risk. Not to act with what is essential, important, and central to one's self-understanding is to risk losing the self, a possibility that introduces a motivational property to the moral personality (Bergman, 2002; Blasi, 1999; Hardy & Carlo, 2005).

Blasi (2005) recently proposed a psychological approach to moral character that trades on these themes. According to this view moral character is best described not by reference to lower-order virtues, such as honesty, generosity, and humility, among numerous others, but by three sets of higher-order virtues that include willpower (as self-control), integrity, and moral desires.

Willpower as self-control is a toolbox of strategic and metacognitive skills that allow one to break down problems, set goals, focus attention, delay gratification, avoid distractions, and resist temptation. These virtues are necessary to deal with obstacles that we encounter invariably in the pursuit of long-range objectives. The cluster of integrity virtues connects our commitments to a sense of self and is responsible for feelings of responsibility and identity. Integrity is felt *as responsibility* when we constrain the self with intentional acts of self-control, effort, and determination in the pursuit of our moral desires; when we make the self conform to the moral law out of a felt sense of necessity and obligation; and when we hold the self accountable for the consequences of actions. Integrity is felt *as identity* when a person constructs the very meaning of the self by reference to moral categories. In this case, living out one's moral commitments does not feel like a choice; living in ways that offend what is central and essential about oneself is unthinkable self-betrayal.

But the virtues of self-control and integrity do not have inherent moral significance. Both are morally neutral unless they are attached to moral desires. Both require a will that desires and tends toward the moral good. The language of moral desires is distinctive of Blasi's (2005) theoretical system, but "moral desires" is an expression he prefers to the closely related notion of moral motivation, and for three reasons. First, the expression connotes an intensity of affect that connects to traditional notions of character as that gives direction to one's life. Second, insofar as moral desires clearly belong to a person, they are preferred over other psychological accounts that treat motivation as an impersonal regulatory system or in terms of cybernetic models of self-control. Third, the notion of desires aligns closely with Frankfurt's (1988) concept of will and his distinction between first- and second-order desires. A person certainly has (first-order) desires, but one can also reflect on them, order them, and have desires about some of them (second-order desires). One has a will when one desires to implement and put into effective action that which is a first-order desire. Here one transforms impulses into something that is reflected on from a greater psychological distance. The will is an intervention on oneself that turns a first-order impulse into something that can be rejected or accepted, and on this foundation

rests the possibility of a moral self if the distancing and appropriating is governed by a consideration of the moral good.

Blasi's approach to moral self-identity is associated with an important line of research on moral exemplars. Colby and Damon (1992) interviewed 23 individuals whose lives demonstrated exceptional moral commitment in such areas as civil rights, civil liberties, poverty, and religious freedom. Although the specific commitments of each exemplar were a unique adaptation to the situational challenges that each faced, one of the most important common characteristics of exemplars was the fact that moral goals were so closely aligned with personal goals. There was an identification of self with moral commitments. Moral goals were central to their self-understanding, to their sense of identity, to such a degree that moral choices were not seen as a burden but simply as a way to advance one's personal objectives. Exemplars also were characterized by a sense of certainty and clarity about what was right and wrong, of their own personal responsibility, and by a sense of optimism about how things would turn out.

A similar theme is evident in the research by Hart and his colleagues (Hart, Atkins, & Ford, 1998; Hart & Fegley, 1995; Hart, Yates, Fegley, & Wilson, 1995), who studied inner-city adolescents who had been nominated by community organizations for their uncommon prosocial commitment. In contrast to matched comparison adolescents, care exemplars more often included moral goals and moral traits in their self-descriptions; and ideal self-representations and parental representations in their actual self-descriptions; articulated a mature self-understanding whereby beliefs generated coherence among elements of the self; and perceived continuity of the self that extended from the remembered past into the projected future. Moral exemplars also have been reported to show advanced moral reasoning, more mature faith and identity development, and an affinity toward agreeableness (Matsuba & Walker, 2004).

In a separate line of research, Aquino and Reed (2002) designed an instrument that measures the degree to which having a moral identity is important to one's self-conception. They assumed, following Blasi (1984, 1985), that moral identity varies in content and in the degree to which moral traits are central to one's self-understanding. They identified nine moral traits (caring, compassionate, fair, friendly, generous, helpful, hardworking, honest, kind) that individuals regard as characteristic of a moral person, which then served as "salience induction stimuli" to activate a person's moral identity when rating the self-importance of these traits on their instrument. Factor analysis revealed two factors: a Symbolization factor (the degree to which the traits are reflected in one's public actions), and an Internalization factor (the degree to which traits are central to one's private self-concept).

Aquino and Reed (2002) showed that both dimensions predict the emergence of a spontaneous moral self-concept and self-reported volunteering, but that internalization showed the stronger relation to actual donating behavior and to moral reasoning. Subsequent research (Reed & Aquino, 2003) showed that individuals with a strong internalized moral identity report a stronger moral obligation to help and share resources with outgroups, to perceive the worthiness of coming to their aid, and to display a preferential option for outgroups in actual donating behavior. Hence, individuals with internalized moral identity are more likely to expand the circle of moral regard to include outgroup members. Moreover, moral identity is thought to mediate the relationship between deviant organizational norms and deviant behavior. If moral identity is highly salient in comparison to other identities within the self-system, then internalized moral identity is likely to inhibit the motivation to respond to deviant norms within the culture of organizations (R. J. Bennett, Aquino, Reed, & Thau, in press). The authors have in mind employee behavior in business organizations, but there is no reason to limit the identity-moderator hypothesis solely to this context.

Research on moral self-identity and on the qualities of individuals who demonstrate exceptional moral commitment is a promising avenue for character psychology, although the implications for character education are not clearly understood. One implication of Blasi's theory is that character education should encourage children and adolescents to develop the proper moral desires and master the virtues of self-control and integrity. But how is this possible? How do children develop self-control and a wholehearted commitment to moral integrity? There are intriguing clues about possible pathways to moral identity from research on the development of conscience in early childhood. For example, Kochanska and her colleagues (Kochanska, 2002; Kochanska et al., 2004; Kochanska, Aksan, & Koenig, 1995) proposed a two-step model of emerging morality that begins with the quality of parent-child attachment. A secure, mutu-ally responsive relationship with caregivers characterized by shared, positive affect orients the child to be receptive to their influence and eager to comply with parental suggestions, standards, and demands. This encourages wholehearted, willing, self-regulated, and "committed" compliance on the part of the child to the norms, values, and expectations of caregivers, which, in turn, motivates moral internalization and the emergence of conscience. The model moves, then, from security of attachment to committed compliance to moral internalization. Moreover, the child's experience of eager, willing, and committed compliance with the parents' socialization agenda is presumed to influence the child's emerging internal representation of the self:

> Children who have a strong history of committed compliance with the parent are likely gradually to come to view themselves as embracing the parent's values and rules. Such a moral self, in turn, comes to serve as the regulator of future moral conduct and, more generally, of early morality. (Kochanska, 2002, p. 340)

Indeed, children are more likely to regulate their conduct in ways that are consistent with their internal working model of the self.

This model of the emergence of conscience in early childhood suggests that the source of wholehearted commitment to moral considerations, and the cultivation of the proper moral desires characteristic of what Blasi requires of a moral personality, lie in the mutual positive affective relationship with socialization agents and the quality of the child's network of interpersonal relationships. The source of self-control, integrity, and moral desires is deeply relational. It is motivated by the sense of moral self-identity that emerges within a history of secure attachment. If true, such a model underscores the importance of school bonding (Catalano, Haggerty, Oesterle, Fleming, & Hawkins, 2004; Libby, 2004; Maddox & Prinz, 2003), caring school communities (Payne, Gottfredson, & Gottfredson, 2003; Solomon, Watson, Battistich, Schaps, & Delucchi, 1992), and attachment to teachers (M. Watson, 2003) as a basis for prosocial and moral development. For example, Payne et al. showed that schools that were organized and experienced as a caring community had higher levels of student bonding to school and greater internalization of common norms and goals, which, in turn, was related to less delinquency. Similarly, the Seattle Social Development Project has documented its theoretical claim that strong bonds of attachment and commitment to school and clear standards of behavior create a press toward behavior consistent with these standards (Hawkins, Catalano, Kosterman, Abbott, & Hill, 1999; Hawkins, Guo, Hill, Battin-Pearson, & Abbott, 2001). Evidence from the Child Development Project showed that elementary school children's sense of community leads them to adhere to the values that are most salient in the classroom (Solomon, Watson, Battistich, Schaps, & Delucchi, 1996). Moreover, perceptions of moral atmosphere in high school promote prosocial and inhibit norms-transgressive behavior (Brugman et al., 2003; Power, Higgins, & Kohlberg, 1989). These findings are quite close to Kochanska's model of early conscience development: Secure attachment promotes committed compliance, which leads to internalization of norms and standards. Hence, there appears to be continuity in the mechanisms of socialization in both families and schools in early and middle childhood and adolescence.

The moral exemplar research holds out another goal for character education, which is to encourage the sort of prosocial commitment observed in care exemplars. This would certainly be a welcome alternative to the more typical understanding of character education as a risk-and-deficits prevention program. How do individuals come to align personal goals with moral ones, or to identify the actual self with ideal representations? One mechanism suggested by Colby and Damon (1995) is social influence. In their view, social influence plays a decisive role in transforming personal goals into important moral commitments. Social influence instigates moral development. It provides a context for reappraisal of one's current capabilities, guidance on how best to extend one's capabilities, and the strategies required to pull it off. "For those who continually immerse themselves in moral concerns and in social networks absorbed by such concerns, goal transformation remains the central architect of progressive change throughout life" (p. 344). Other mechanisms include participation in voluntary organizations (C. Flanagan, 2004; Hart et al., 1998), school attachment (Atkins, Hart, & Donnely, 2004), and service learning opportunities more generally (Waterman, 1997; Youniss, McLellan, Su, & Yates, 1999; Youniss, McLellan, & Yates, 1997; Youniss & Yates, 1997).

These mechanisms may provide not just the means for the transformation of personal into moral goals, but also an opportunity for adolescents to experience other char-acteristics of moral exemplars, such as coming to see moral concerns with greater clarity, developing a greater sense of personal responsibility for the welfare of their communities, and developing a sense of optimism and efficacy that personal effort pays off and makes a difference. We will have more to say about community service and service learning. But if these mechanisms are critical to the formation of moral identity (Hart, 2005), then the challenge for character educators is how best to transform the culture of schools so that they become places where social networks are absorbed by moral concerns, where attachment to school is encouraged, where opportunities abound for broad participation in the sort of voluntary associations that predict prosocial engagement with the community.

Models of Personality Psychology

One strategy for framing models of moral personality is to appeal to the theoretical resources, constructs, and mechanisms of personality psychology. Yet, personality psychology is not a unified domain. According to Cervone (1991), there are two disciplines of personality psychology that are distinguished by how the basic units of personality are conceptualized. One discipline favors trait/dispositional constructs and understands personality structure in terms of between-person variation that is described by "top-down" abstract latent variable taxonomies, such as the Big 5. The second discipline favors cognitive-affective mechanisms, or social cognitive units, and understands personality structure in terms of "bottom-up" within-person processes (Cervone, 2005). Each discipline of personality psychology is reflected in recent attempts to understand the moral personality.

For example Walker and his colleagues examined the personality structure of moral exemplars by reference to the Big 5 trait dimensions. In one study (Walker & Hennig, 2004, Study 2) prototype descriptors of moral exemplars was examined with the interpersonal circumplex and the five-factor model of personality. The prototype of the just person was described as a moderate blend of nurturance and dominance, and aligned with conscientiousness and openness to experience. An earlier study (Walker & Pitts, 1998) reported a relationship between trait dimensions and three kinds of moral exemplars. The brave exemplar was linked with a complex of traits associated with extraversion; the caring exemplar was associated with agreeableness; while the just exemplar was a complex mixture of conscientiousness, emotional stability, and openness to experience. Hart (2005) reports an association between the care exemplar and three of the Big 5 trait dimensions (openness to experience, agreeableness, and conscientiousness), while Matsuba and Walker (2004) showed that the personality structure of young adults who were nominated for their moral exemplarity was characterized by traits associated with agreeableness.

In contrast to trait taxonomic approaches, we have attempted to understand moral personality from the perspective of social cognitive theory, the second discipline of personality psychology (Lapsley & Narvaez, 2004; Narvaez & Lapsley, 2004). Social cognitive theory draws attentions to cognitive-affective mechanisms (scripts, schemas, prototypes, and other cognitive frameworks) that influence social perception but also serve to create and sustain patterns of individual differences. If schemas are readily primed and easily activated ("chronically accessible"), for example, then they direct our attention selectively to certain features of our experience at the expense of others. This selective framing disposes one to choose compatible or schema-relevant life tasks, goals, and settings that are congruent with one's social perceptions. Repeated selection of schema-congruent tasks, goals, and settings serves over time to canalize and sustain dispositional tendencies and to result in highly practiced behavioral routines that provide "a ready, sometimes automatically available plan of action in such life contexts" (Cantor, 1990, p. 738). According to Cantor, this makes one a "virtual expert" in highly practiced regions of social experience demarcated by chronically accessible schemas and allows schemas to function as the cognitive carriers of dispositions.

In our view, the moral personality can be understood similarly in terms of the accessibility of moral schemas for social information processing (Narvaez & Lapsley, 2005). A moral person, a person who has a moral character or identity, is one for whom moral constructs are chronically accessible. These chronically accessible categories provide a dispositional preference or readiness to discern the moral dimensions of experience, as well as underwrite a discriminative facility in selecting situationally appropriate behavior. Recent research has shown, for example, that moral chronicity is a dimension of individual differences that influences spontaneous trait inferences as well as the kind of evaluative moral inferences that are generated when reading stories (Narvaez, Lapsley, Hagele, & Lasky, in press). Moreover, available constructs can be made accessible by situational priming as well as by chronicity, which combine in an additive fashion to influence social perception (Bargh, Bond, Lombardi, & Tota, 1986). This supports the social cognitive view that dispositional coherence is to be found at the intersection of person (chronicity) and context (situational priming), and that stable behavioral signatures are to be found in patterns of situational variability rather than cross-situational consistency (Mischel, 2005; Shoda & Mischel, 2000).

A social cognitive approach to moral character has a number of benefits. It provides an explanation for moral identity. For Blasi (2005), one has a moral identity when moral notions are central, essential, and important to one's self-understanding. We would add that moral notions that are central, essential, and important to self-understanding would also be chronically accessible for appraising the social landscape. The social cognitive approach also accounts for at least one characteristic of moral exemplars. As Colby and Damon (1992) have shown, individuals who display extraordinary moral commitment rarely report engaging in an extensive decision-making process. Rather, they "just knew" what was required of them, automatically as it were, without recourse to elaborate and effortful cognitive exertion. This is also experienced by exemplars as a kind of moral clarity or as a felt conviction that one's judgments are appropriate, justified, and true. Yet, this is precisely the outcome of preconscious activation of chronically accessible constructs: that it induces strong feelings of certainty or conviction with respect to one's social judgments (Bargh, 1989; Narvaez & Lapsley, 2005). Moreover, the automaticity of schema activation contributes to the tacit, implicit qualities often associated with Aristotelian and traditional understanding of the "habits" of moral character. To put it differently, the moral habits of virtue theory are social cognitive schemas whose chronic accessibility favors automatic activation.

One challenge for a social cognitive theory of moral character is to specify the developmental sources of moral chronicity. Indeed, our preference for the social cognitive option reflects a strategic bet that it will more likely lead to integrative developmental models of moral personality than would the taxonomic approach (Narvaez et al, in press). One speculation is that moral personality development is built on the foundation of generalized event representations, behavioral scripts, and episodic memory that characterize early sociopersonality development (Kochanska & Thompson, 1997; Lapsley & Narvaez, 2004; Thompson, 1998). Event representations have been called the "basic building blocks of cognitive development" (Nelson & Gruendel, 1981, p. 131), and it is our contention that they are the foundation as well of emergent moral character. They are working models of how social routines unfold and of what one can expect of social experience. These prototypic knowledge structures are progressively elaborated in the early dialogues with caregivers who help children review, structure, and consolidate memories in script-like fashion (Fivush, Kuebli, & Chubb, 1992). But the key characterological turn of significance for moral psychology is how these early social cognitive units are transformed from episodic into autobiographical memory. Autobiographical memory is also a social construction elaborated by means of dialogue within a web of interlocution. Parental interrogatives ("What happened when you pushed your sister?"; "Why did she cry?"; "What should you do next?") help children organize events into personally relevant autobiographical memories which provide, as part of the self-narrative, action-guiding scripts ("I share with her" and "I say I'm sorry") that become frequently practiced, overlearned, routine, habitual, and automatic. These interrogatives might also include moral character attributions so that the ideal or "ought" self becomes part of the child's autobiographical narrative. In this way, parents help children identify morally relevant features of their experience and encourage the formation of social cognitive schemas that are chronically accessible (Lapsley & Narvaez, 2004). Moreover, as Kochanska's (2002) model suggests, there is every reason to suppose that this developmental process is affected both by variations in the quality of the parent-child relationship and its goodness-of-fit.

One implication of this account, and of Kochanska's (2002) research on the emergence of conscience, is that character education is not something that takes place initially in schools as a formal curriculum, but rather is embedded within the fabric of family life and early socialization experiences. In the next section, we take up school- and community-based programs that are of significance to character education.

APPROACHES TO CHARACTER EDUCATION

In this section, we review promising or prominent school- and community-based approaches to character

education. The range of programs that are claimed for character education is quite diverse, and there are very many of them. Our intention here is not to review the full range of specific programs but to identify general categories of programs that make some claim for character education. Some of the programs that we review might also be considered examples of one or more of the 11 Principles of Effective Character Education (Lickona, Schaps, & Lewis, 2003) adopted by the Character Education Partnership (CEP). We begin our review by a consideration of these principles given their prominence among character educators.

Eleven Principles of Effective Character Education

The Character Education Partnership is a coalition of organizations and individuals dedicated to helping schools develop moral and character education programs. Many school districts embrace approaches to character education that are guided by principles developed by the CEP. The first principle asserts that good character is built on the foundation of core ethical values, such as caring, honesty, fairness, responsibility, and respect. Sometimes core values (alternatively, traits or virtues) are selected by school districts after broad consultation with the community. More often, the core values are those endorsed by national advocacy organizations, such as the six "pillars" of character (trustworthiness, respect, responsibility, fairness, caring, citizenship) articulated by the Aspen Declaration and the Character Counts movement. What is critical is that the values selected for character education be universally valid, promote the common good, affirm human dignity, contribute to the welfare of the individual, deal with issues of right and wrong, and facilitate democratic practices.

Accordingly, programs should teach core values holistically with cognitive, affective, and behavioral components (Principle 2) and in a way that engages school personnel in an intentional, proactive, and comprehensive way (Principle 3). It is particularly important to create caring school communities (Principle 4) and to provide students with opportunities to engage in moral action, such as service learning and community service (Principle 5). Effective character education does not neglect rigorous, challenging academic curricula (Principle 6). It fosters intrinsic motivation to do the right thing by building a climate of trust and respect, by encouraging a sense of autonomy, and by building shared norms through dialogue, class meetings, and democratic decision making (Principle 7). Moreover, the core values that animate student life should engage the school staff as well (Principle 8). For character education to take root it must result in shared educational leadership that makes provision for long-term support of the initiative (Principle 9); it must engage families and community stakeholders (Principle 10); and it must be committed to ongoing assessment and evaluation (Principle 11).

This remarkable set of principles provides a useful guidepost for the design and implementation of intentional, programmatic, and comprehensive character education. It insists that ethical considerations be the transparent rationale for programmatic activities and, on this basis (e.g., Principle 3), would not support efforts to broaden the definition of character education to include all manner of prevention and intervention programs absent an explicit, intentional concern for moral development. It endorses a set of well-attested pedagogical strategies that are considered educational best practice, including cooperative learning, democratic classrooms, and constructivist approaches to teaching and learning. It endorses practices that cultivate autonomy, intrinsic motivation, and community engagement (Beland, 2003c). Indeed, the CEP Principles look like a blueprint for progressive education, and would seem to settle the historical debate concerning direct and indirect approaches to character education in favor of the latter paradigm.

Yet, the Principles are not without their discontents. Principle 1 insists on core values that are foundational, objectively true, universally valid, immanent to human dignity, and crucial to democratic practice, yet its elision of familiar anxieties about the source and selection of favored values gives one pause. This insistence that character education first be grounded on objectively valid core values is, in our view, a misleading and unnecessary distraction. It is misleading because it assumes that practices are derived from principles rather than the other way around (see, e.g., Carr, 1991). It is distracting because it forces educators to defend a transparent and intentional approach to the moral formation of children on grounds other than its immanence and inevitability in the life of schools.

Moreover, the first Principle smuggles a premise into character education; for example, that core values are objectively true, foundational, and universally valid is itself a deeply contentious matter for epistemology and

ethics, and attempts to settle an argument about ethical relativism that it is ill equipped to address except by dogmatic assertion.

But the necessity, inevitability, and desirability of character education does not hinge on the outcome of this argument. Indeed, to suggest that it does is to repeat the mistake on the educational front that the cognitive developmental tradition commits on the psychological front. Just as Kohlberg (1981, 1983) attempted to use stage theory to provide the psychological resources to defeat ethical relativism, so, too, does the first Principle of the Character Education Partnership attempt to take up arms against the bogey of relativism on the educational front.

Although the Principles call for comprehensive infusion of ethical concerns throughout the curriculum and in all facets of school life, and although the *Eleven Principles Sourcebook* (Beland, 2003c) encourages a variety of pedagogical strategies that are compatible with best instructional practice, we observe that not much of contemporary character education gets past the first Principle, or else reduces character education to simply teaching *about* values and the *meaning* of trait words. The broad school reform and commitment to best practice required by the remaining Principles are too often neglected in favor of fussing over the meaning of words denoting core values (leaving aside the problem of how one fills in the meaning of these words). The hard work of character education is not *learning about* core value words, but *learning to* engage the range of developmental and educational experiences countenanced by the remaining Principles.

Although there is value in a first Principle that requires educators to make explicit the moral implications of school practices, it would be far better, in our view, if CEP's first Principle articulated a commitment to a distinctly virtue-centered approach to education that gave primacy to aretaic concerns about agents and flourishing rather than Kantian concerns about universality and objectivity. What is required as a first Principle is not a disguised stance on the epistemological status of "values"—that certain of them are foundational, universal, and objectively valid—but a statement that makes explicit the ethical commitments immanent to educational practices endorsed in the remaining Principles. The goal of character education, in other words, is less about enlisting children in the battle against ethical relativism, and more about equipping them with the moral dispositions and skills required for effective citizenship in a liberal democracy.

A Conceptual Framework

We think there is a better way to make the case for character education that has little to do with taking a stance on the question of ethical foundations. The conceptual framework for character education is adequately anticipated by a commitment to a developmental systems orientation. A developmental systems approach to character education draws attention to embedded and overlapping systems of influence that exist at multiple levels, to the fact that dispositional coherence is a joint product of personal and contextual factors that are in dynamic interaction across the life course. As Masten (2003, p. 172) put it, "Dynamic multisystem models of human learning, development and psychopathology are transforming science, practice and policies concerned with the health, success and well-being of children and the adult citizens of society they will become." A credible character education must resemble dynamic multisystems models of development and be located within contemporary theoretical and empirical frameworks of developmental science if it is going to understand adequately the mechanisms of change, plasticity, prevention, resilience, and the very conditions and possibilities of what it means to flourish—to live well the life that is good for one to live.

Moreover, a developmental systems perspective already underwrites more specific approaches to youth development. For example, Lerner and his colleagues (Lerner, Dowling, & Anderson, 2003; Lerner, Fisher, & Weinberg, 2000) make the case for "thriving" as a basis for understanding the role of adaptive person-context relations in human development. "An integrated moral and civic identity," they write, "and a commitment to society beyond the limits of one's own existence enables thriving youth to be agents both in their own healthy development and in the positive enhancement of other people and of society" (Lerner et al., 2003, p. 172). Indeed, thriving and character education point to the same end, as do other notions derived from developmental contextualism, such as developmental assets, resilience, and positive youth development. Moreover, developmental contextualism provides not only a basis for understanding the dispositional qualities of personality ("character"), but also a vision of what it means to flourish (e.g., thriving and positive development). These developmen-

tal considerations already carry the conceptual load for understanding constructs that are crucial to broad conceptualizations of character education and thus would serve much better as a first principle of character education than the CEP's current emphasis on foundational core values.

Educating for Character

Lickona (1991a, 1991b, 1997, 2004) has developed an integrative approach to character education that is largely congruent with CEP principles. Along with a commitment to core values, he also advocates a variety of strategies that are broadly compatible with instructional best practice for elementary (Lickona, 1992) and high schools (Lickona & Davidson, 2004). A distinction is drawn between two aspects of character: performance character and moral character. Performance character is oriented toward mastery of tasks and includes such qualities as diligence, perseverance, a positive attitude, and a commitment to hard work. Performance character is what is required to develop talents, skills, and competencies. Moral character, in turn, is a relational orientation that is concerned with qualities of integrity, caring, justice, respect, and cooperation. It is an ethical compass that guides the pursuit and expression of performance character. If performance character makes it possible to live a productive life, moral character is required to live an ethical life (Lickona & Davidson, 2004). Effective education should aim to develop both aspects of character.

Lickona and Davidson (2004) recently articulated seven principles of schools that effectively address elements of moral and performance character. These schools:

1. Make the development of character the cornerstone of the school's mission and identity.
2. Cultivate an ethical learning community that includes staff, students, and parents, who share responsibility for advancing the school's character education mission.
3. Encourage the professional staff to form a professional ethical learning community to foster collaboration and mutual support in advancing the ethical dimensions of teaching and student development.
4. Align all school practices, including curriculum, discipline, and extracurricular activities, with the goals of performance excellence and moral excellence.

5. Use evaluation data to monitor progress in the development of strength-of character and to guide decision making with respect to educational practices.

6. Integrate ethical material into the curriculum while encouraging lifelong learning and a career orientation.

7. Treat classroom and schoolwide discipline as opportunities to support the ethical learning community by emphasizing the importance of caring, accountability, shared ownership of rules, and a commitment to restitution.

One salutary feature of this framework is that it urges schools to understand their educative mission in terms of a moral framework. A second salutary feature is that many of its instructional strategies are informed by the research literatures of developmental and educational psychology. It promotes, for example, instructional practices that encourage mastery motivation, metacognitive instruction, and cooperative learning. It sanctions constructivist strategies that embrace the active participation of students in learning. It advocates strategies (e.g., dilemma discussion, just community) more commonly associated with development of a moral education. Indeed, many of the suggested practices that attempt to link home and school, influence school culture, involve community stakeholders, or capitalize on the unique developmental needs of students could be underwritten by a developmental systems orientation.

Caring School Communities

The fourth of the CEP's Principles of Effective Character Education states, "Effective character education creates a caring school community." (Beland, 2003a, p. 1). There is a strong consensus that effective character education must include efforts to promote "communities of caring" in classrooms and schools (Battistich, Solomon, Watson, & Schaps, 1997; Berkowitz & Bier, 2005). A school climate that encourages social and emotional bonding and promotes positive interpersonal experiences is one that provides the minimum necessary grounding for the formation of character (Schaps, Battistich, & Solomon, 1997). Indeed, as Berkowitz (2002, pp. 58–59) put it, "Relationships are critical to character education, so character education must focus on the quality of relationships at school."

Research has shown, for example, that the quality of early teacher-student relationships can have a strong influence on academic and social outcomes that persist through eighth grade (Hamre & Pianta, 2001). Moreover, in schools where there is a strong perception of communal organization there is less student misconduct (Bryk & Driscoll, 1988) and lower rates of drug use and delinquency (Battistich & Hom, 1997). Student attachment or bonding to school also improves school motivation (Goodenow, 1993) and counterindicates delinquency (Welsh, Greene, & Jenkins, 1999) and victimization of teachers and students (Gottfredson & Gottfredson, 1985). In a study of a nationally representative sample of 254 high schools, Payne et al. (2003) found a connection between communal organization and student bonding to school. Schools characterized by communal organization, that is, by mutually supportive relationships among teachers, administrators, and students, a commitment to common goals and norms, and a sense of collaboration, tend to have students who report an attachment to school (an emotional bond to teachers or school and a sense of belonging), a belief in the legitimacy of rules and norms, and a high value placed on schoolwork. Moreover, bonding to school was related, in turn, to lower levels of student misconduct and victimization. Payne et al. suggested that by "improving the relationships among school members, the collaboration and participation of these members and the agreement on common goals and norms, schools could increase students' attachment to school, commitment to education and belief in school rules and norms" (p. 773) and thereby reduce misconduct, delinquency, and victimization.

The work of two research teams, the Social Development Research Group at the University of Washington and the Child Development Project of the Developmental Studies Center (Oakland, CA), has provided particularly impressive evidence on the role of school bonding and caring school communities for a range of outcomes of interest to character educators.

Social Development Research Group

This group launched the Seattle Social Development Project (SSDP) in 1981 in eight Seattle public elementary schools. The project initially provided an intervention to first-grade pupils, but the program expanded by 1985 to include all fifth-grade students in 18 elementary schools, with additional intervention components that targeted parents and teachers as well. The longitudinal assessments of participants continued throughout adolescence and subsequently every 3 years after graduation until age 27. The SSDP was guided by a social development model that assumes that behavior is learned within social environments. One becomes socialized within the norms of a social group to the extent that (a) one perceives opportunities for involvement, (b) becomes actually involved, (c) has the skill for involvement and interaction, and (d) perceives that it is rewarding to do so. When socialization goes well, a social bond of attachment and commitment is formed. This social bond, in turn, orients the child to the norms and expectations of the group to which one is attached and to the values endorsed by the group. "It is hypothesized that the behavior of the individual would be prosocial or antisocial depending on the predominant behaviors, norms and values held by those individuals and institutions to which/whom the individual bonded" (Catalano, Haggerty, et al., 2004, p. 251).

The SSDP included interventions that targeted three primary socialization agents of school-age children: teachers, parents, and peers. Teachers were given training in proactive classroom management, interactive teaching to motivate learners, and cooperative learning. The intervention for children targeted social and emotional skill development, including interpersonal cognitive problem-solving skills and refusal skills. Parent training targeted behavior management, how to give academic support, and skills to reduce risk for drug use.

Research showed that training teachers to use targeted teaching practices was successful in promoting both school bonding and academic achievement (Abbott et al., 1998). Moreover, the SSDP demonstrated long-term positive effects on numerous adolescent health-risk behaviors (e.g., violent delinquency, heavy drinking, sexual intercourse, having multiple sex partners, pregnancy, and school misconduct) and on school bonding (Hawkins, Catalano, Kosterman, Abbott, & Hill, 1999; Hawkins, Guo, Hill, Battin-Pearson, & Abbott, 2001). For example, school bonding at grade 12 and increases in school bonding between grades 7 and 12 was negatively correlated with use of alcohol, cigarettes, marijuana, and other drug use at grade 12. Students bonded to school at grades 5 and 6 were less likely to become minor or major offenders in middle school. Students with a lower sense of school attachment and commitment were twice as likely to join gangs as were students with a stronger sense of school bonding. Moreover, school bonding also had positive academic outcomes. For example, an increase in school bonding between grades 7 and 12 was associated with higher GPA and lower student misconduct at grade 12. Students with greater bonding

to school at grade 8 were less likely to drop out of school by grade 10 (see Catalano, Berglund, Ryan, Lonczak, & Hawkins, 2004, for a review).

Thus, the intensive, multicomponent interventions of the SSDP had clear effects on school bonding and on a range of outcomes of traditional interest to character educators, including substance use, delinquency, gang membership, violence, academic problems, and sexual activity. But is this character education? It depends on whether character education is defined by treatment or by outcomes. The SSPD has generated empirical outcomes that are claimed for character education broadly defined, although the SSPD "treatment" is guided by the theoretical considerations of the social development model and not of virtue, morality, or character. Still, if character education is to be considered a treatment or intervention in its own right, then it must possess the characteristics of successful interventions like the SSDP: It must be guided by explicit theory; it must be comprehensive; it must involve multiple components; and it must be initiated early in development and sustained over time.

Developmental Studies Center

The Developmental Studies Center (DSC) has been particularly influential in documenting the crucial role that children's sense of community plays in promoting a wide range of outcomes commonly associated with character education, including altruistic, cooperative, and helping behavior, concern for others, prosocial conflict resolution, and trust in and respect for teachers (Solomon, Watson, Delucchi, Schaps, & Battistich, 1988; M. Watson, Battistich, & Solomon, 1997). The research agenda of the DSC assumed that children have basic needs for belonging, autonomy, and competence and that their engagement with school depends on whether these needs are adequately met (Battistich et al., 1997). It was assumed further that "when children's needs are met through membership in a school community, they are likely to become affectively bonded with and committed to the school, and therefore inclined to identify with and behave in accordance with its expressed goals and values" (Schaps et al., 1997, p. 127).

In 1982, the DSC initiated the Child Development Project (CDP) in three program schools in suburban San Francisco to examine these core assumptions. It was first implemented by teachers in kindergarten, with one grade level added each year until 1989. Program evaluation followed the cohort annually from kindergarten to sixth grade, with a 2-year follow-up assessment when the program cohort was in eighth grade. The evaluation also included students and teachers from three demographically similar comparison schools.

The programmatic focus of the CDP was designed to enhance prosocial development by creating the condition for a caring school community (Battistich et al., 1997). A sense of community was encouraged through activities such as collaborating on common academic goals; providing and receiving help from others; discussion and reflection on the experiences of self and others as these relate to prosocial values such as fairness, social responsibility, and justice; practicing social competencies; and exercising autonomy by participating in decisions about classroom life and taking responsibility for it. Moreover, the CDP encouraged an approach to classroom management that emphasized induction and developmental discipline (M. Watson, 2003).

Hence, the CDP provided numerous opportunities for children to collaborate with others in the pursuit of common goals, to give and receive help, to discuss and reflect on prosocial values, to develop and practice prosocial skills, and to exercise autonomy through democratic classroom structures.

Research studies of CDP implementations indicate that in comparison to control schools, students make positive gains in targeted areas. In classroom observations, individual interviews, and student questionnaires, program students exhibited more prosocial behavior in the classroom (Solomon et al., 1988), more democratic values and interpersonal understanding (Solomon, Watson, Schaps, Battistich, & Solomon, 1990), and more social problem-solving and conflict resolution skills (Battistich, Solomon, Watson, Solomon, & Schaps, 1989). Students in CDP schools were more likely to view their classrooms as communities, which led them to adhere to whatever norms and values were salient in the classroom. For example, in classrooms that emphasized teacher control and student compliance, student reasoning about prosocial dilemmas was oriented toward heteronomy and reward and punishment. In contrast, in classrooms that emphasized student participation, autonomy, democratic decision making, and interpersonal concerns, student prosocial reasoning emphasized autonomy and other-oriented moral reasoning (Solomon et al., 1992, 1996). When program and control students entered the same intermediate school, former program students were rated higher by teachers at eighth grade in conflict resolution skills, self-esteem, assertion, and popularity (Solomon, Watson, & Battistich, 2002).

The most important variable positively influenced by participation in CDP programs is students' sense of community, which is promoted through structures of the classroom and the school (Watson et al., 1997). For example, teachers who hold class meetings, use cooperative learning strategies, and discuss prosocial values are more likely to foster a sense of community in students. Schools that provide cross-age buddies, homework that links school and family, and schoolwide projects also promote a sense of community. Student sense of community is positively related to self-reported concern for others, conflict resolution skills, altruistic behavior, intrinsic prosocial motivation, trust in and respect for teachers, enjoyment of helping others learn, and positive interpersonal behavior and academic engagement (Battistich, Solomon, Watson, & Schaps, 1996; M. Watson, Battistich, & Solomon, 1997).

Other Approaches

Other approaches have focused similarly on building a sense of community within classrooms and schools. For example, the *Don't Laugh at Me* curriculum attempts to sensitize children to the painful effects of peer ridicule, ostracism, and bullying and to help them transform their classroom and school into "ridicule-free zones" characterized by a climate of respect. A recent efficacy study using a within-school quasi-experimental methodology showed that program participants (fourth and fifth graders) reported significant gains in a psychological sense of school membership, increases in quality of relational experiences and in the desire to stop dissing and ridicule, and declines in bullying, compared to youngsters in the control group (Mucherah, Lapsley, Miels, & Horton, 2004).

Similarly, the Resolving Conflicts Creatively Program (RCCP) attempts to build peaceable schools and classrooms through an emphasis on conflict resolution and positive communication skills (Lantieri & Patti, 1996). The curriculum cultivates a selected set of skills that target conflict resolution, cooperation, caring, appreciating diversity and countering bias, responsible decision making, and appropriate expression of feelings. The curriculum emphasizes the importance of adults coaching these skills as students practice them across a variety of contexts. Students learn to give "I" messages about their feelings, listen actively to others, mediate peer conflict, and become interculturally competent. An evaluation of RCCP performed by the National Center for Children in Poverty at Columbia University (Aber, Brown, & Heinrich, 1999; Aber, Pedersen, Brown, Jones,

& Gershoff, 2003) showed that students from grades 2 through 6 who were involved in an average of 25 lessons per year had a significantly slower growth rate in self-reported hostile attributions, aggressive fantasies, and greater problem-solving strategies than students who received fewer lessons. High-exposure students also showed greater improvement on academic achievement scores in the 2-year study.

Service Learning and Community Service

As we have seen, classroom practices that include democratic cooperation, problem solving, and decision making encourage the cultivation of skills and dispositions that are crucial for citizenship, and hence are an important component of character education. The fifth of the CEP's Principles of Effective Character Education (Beland, 2003c) urges schools to provide students with opportunities for moral action. In some sense, democratic classrooms include important moral lessons concerning fair play, civility, civic friendship, and cooperation. Children learn how to sustain moral conversation in the context of joint decision making. They develop a "deliberative competence" (Guttman, 1987) in solving problems, resolving conflict, establishing shared norms, balancing perspectives, and other skills crucial for effective citizenship (Power et al., 1989a). But the effort to cultivate democratic dispositions and a sense of community within classrooms is being joined by efforts to connect students to the larger community through service learning and community service.

According to Tolman (2003):

> Service learning is rooted in the notion that acts of "doing good" for others—anything from cleaning up neighborhoods, to teaching younger students, to spending time with elderly community members—are the basis for significant learning experiences, for community development and for social change. (p. 6)

Service learning is distinguished from community service by the degree to which it links service activities to clearly defined learning objectives and to an academic curriculum (Pritchard, 2002). Both kinds of activities are now a ubiquitous and pervasive feature of American education. A national survey conducted by the National Center for Educational Statistics estimates that 64% of all public schools, including 87% of public high schools, had students participating in community service activities. About a third of these organized service learning as part of their curriculum, which is typically justified by the desire to strengthen relationships among students, the school, and the community (Skinner & Chapman, 1999).

The desire to strengthen connections among home, school, and community is supported by ecological perspectives on human development. There are adaptational advantages for children whose developmental ecology is characterized by a richly connected mesosytem (Bronfenbrenner, 1979). Indeed, Warter and Grossman (2002) appeal to developmental contextualism to provide a justification for the specific case of service learning and its implementation. Yates and Youniss (1996b; Youniss & Yates, 1997) argue similarly for a developmental perspective on service learning that is strongly influenced by Erikson's (1968) conceptualization of identity. According to this view, service learning opportunities provide an important context for helping adolescents sort out identity issues. For Erikson, identity work requires psychosocial reciprocity between the characteristics, identifications, and ideals of the young person and the affirmation of the community that give these choices significance and meaning. Identity is deeply characteristic of persons, to be sure, but like dispositional coherence of any kind, it plays out in dynamic interaction with community, culture, and context. In this way, identity is compatible with the person-context interactionism that is characteristic of a developmental systems approach.

Research has documented outcomes that are of interest to character education. Service learning experiences and participation in voluntary organizations increase one's sense of social agency, responsibility for the moral and political dimensions of society, and general moral-political awareness (Youniss et al., 1997). Indeed, youth who participate in service experiences often report significant transformation in personal values and orientations, an increased civic-mindedness and sense of social responsibility, along with enhanced learning and better grades (Markus, Howard, & King, 1993; Pancer & Pratt, 1999; Pratt, Hunsberger, Pancer, & Alisat, 2003; Scales, Blyth, Berkas, & Kielsmeier, 2000). They report higher levels of trust and more positive views of others in their communities (Hilles & Kahle, 1985). Similar findings were reported in national evaluations of two federally funded national service learning initiatives (Serve America, Learn and Serve). Melchior and Bailis (2002) report, for example, positive effects of service learning on the civic attitudes of adolescents. In addition, there was a reduction in school absenteeism for program participants and a lower incidence of teenage pregnancy. High school participants showed more school engagement, better math and science achievement, and a lower incidence of course failure. Middle school participants did more homework, got better grades in social studies, and got into serious legal and disciplinary problems less often.

Moreover, service learning and community service may be critical to political socialization and the process of forming a moral-civic identity (C. Flanagan, 2004; Yates & Youniss, 1999a). In one study, Yates and Youniss (1996a) examined the reflective narratives of Black parochial high school juniors who worked at a soup kitchen for the homeless as part of a service learning commitment. Over the course of a year, the researchers noticed that these youth came to invest their service with greater meaning and at a higher level of transcendence. Initially, participants tended to view the homeless in terms of stereotypes; then, at a higher level of transcendence, they started to think about the consequences of homelessness for their own life, or to compare the lot of the homeless to theirs; finally, they were able to reflect on homelessness from the perspective of social justice or in terms of appropriate political action. Over the course of a year, then, serving the homeless in a soup kitchen motivated reflective judgments about weighty matters of justice, responsibility, and political engagement.

In addition to promoting moral-civic identity, there is evidence that participation in service activities and voluntary organizations also increases civic participation in later adulthood (Youniss et al., 1997). Indeed, C. Flanagan (2004, p. 725) argued that membership in community-based organizations, along with extracurricular activities at school, provides a "sense of place" wherein youth "develop an affection for the polity." "Affection for the polity," she writes, "and engagement in community affairs are logical extensions of the sense of connection youth develop from involvement in community-based organizations" (p. 725).

Service learning and community service, then, are significant components of a school's commitment to character education (Hart, 2005). They are justified on the grounds that service significantly transforms moral-civic identity and predicts civic engagement in later adulthood (Youniss & Yates, 1999), both of which are foundational goals of character education. Of course, much depends on how service learning is implemented. It is generally agreed that successful service learning programs include opportunities for significant student reflection as part of the experience. Matching students to projects consistent with their interests and holding them accountable for outcomes but giving them autonomy in selecting goals are also important program elements (Stukas, Clary, & Snyder, 1999; Warter & Grossman, 2002). There is evidence that service learning is particularly effective at high school compared to middle school, and that positive outcomes are most likely to be evident in areas directly related to the service learning experience (Melchior & Bailis, 2002).

Positive Youth Development

We noted earlier that a developmental systems approach (Lerner et al., 2003) might well serve as a conceptual framework for character education, as opposed to the current epistemological preoccupation with core values. A developmental systems orientation is foundational to the positive youth development perspective that has emerged as a counter to a risks-and-deficits model of adolescent development. Although adolescents certainly do face risks and obstacles, there is an emerging consensus that effort to ameliorate risk exposure, overcome deficits, or prevent problems is not sufficient to prepare young people adequately for the competencies that will be required of them for successful adaptation to adulthood. The mantra of positive youth development is "Problem-free is not fully prepared." Children and adolescents must be equipped with the strengths that will allow them to thrive, be resilient, take initiative, and contribute productively to society (Larson, 2000). This will require programmatic efforts to help children develop what Lerner (2001, 2002) calls the "5C's of positive youth development": competence, confidence, character, caring and compassion, and connection to the institutions of civil society.

The work of the Search Institute on the developmental assets is one instantiation of this general approach (Benson, Scales, Leffert, & Roehlkepartain, 1999; Scales & Leffert, 1999). Developmental assets are those features of a developmental system that promote positive outcomes. Forty assets have been identified on the basis of research, 20 of which are external and contextual, and 20 of which are internal and personal. The external assets are grouped into four categories: support (assets 1 to 6), empowerment (assets 7 to 10), boundaries and expectations (assets 11 to 16), and constructive use of time (assets 17 to 20). These refer to the positive developmental experiences that result from the network of relationships that youth have with adults in their family, school, and community. The internal assets are grouped similarly into four categories: commitment to learning (assets 21 to 25), positive values (assets 26 to 31), social competencies (assets 32 to 36), and positive identity (assets 37 to 40). These refer to endogenous skills, dispositions, and interests that emerge over the course of education and development.

In many ways, the developmental assets approach already constitutes a richly articulated conceptual framework for character education that has little need for epistemological wrangling over foundational core values. Virtually all of the internal assets are familiar targets of character education, such as the positive values assets (caring, equality and social justice, integrity, honesty, responsibility), social competency assets (decision making, interpersonal competence, cultural competence, resistance skills, conflict resolution), and identity assets (personal power, self-esteem, sense of purpose, positive view). The external assets are similarly crucial for any comprehensive approach to character education insofar as it targets sources of mesosytem support for positive development (e.g., family support, caring schools and neighborhoods, parental involvement in schooling), ways to empower youth (perceptions of communal support, service learning), the importance of setting appropriate boundaries and expectations (e.g., adult role models, positive peer influence, and high expectations), and constructive use of time (e.g., creative activities, youth programs, participation in a religious community, and time spent at home away from peer influence).

Moreover, all of the CEP Principles of Effective Character Education (Beland, 2003c), save the first Principle, are well in evidence among the 40 developmental assets. Principle 10 is of particular interest. It states, "Effective character education engages families and community members as partners in the character-building effort" (Beland, 2003b). The Search Institute has argued similarly that the success of positive youth development depends on community resolve to construct the building blocks ("assets") of its developmental infrastructure. However, communities vary in the assets that are available to support positive youth development (Benson et al., 1999).

One study assessed the perceived availability of assets in a 1996–1997 survey of more than 99,000 youth in grades 6 through 12 from 213 cities and towns across the United States (Benson, Leffert, Scales, & Blyth, 1998). In this sample, 62% of adolescents experience at most half of the developmental assets associated with positive youth development. The mean number of assets for the aggregate sample was 18, and the least and most affluent communities in the sample differed by only three assets (in favor of the more affluent community), indicating that students typically experience less than half of the developmental assets and that even wealthy communities have work to do on building their developmental infrastructure. Notably, from the perspective of positive youth development and character education, three of the least experienced assets are a caring school, youth being treated as a resource, and community valuing youth (Scales, 1999).

Benson et al. (1998) reported dramatic differences in the percentage of youth with low (0 to 10) and high (31 to 40) assets who engage in risk behavior: Low asset youth are more likely than high asset youth to use alcohol (53% versus 3%); to smoke tobacco (45% versus 1%); to use illicit drugs at least 3 or more times in the past year (45% versus 1%); to have had sexual intercourse at least 3 or more times (42% versus 1%); to report frequent depression or to have made a suicide attempt (40% versus 4%); to report at least 3 incidents of antisocial behavior (52% versus 1%); to engage in at least 3 acts of violence (61% versus 6%); to report school problems (43% versus 2%); to drink and drive (42% versus 4%) and gamble (34% versus 6%). The conclusion is inescapable: Youth who report fewer developmental assets tend to engage in more risk behavior; youth who report more assets engage in fewer risk behaviors (see also Oman et al., 2004). Moreover, youth who are more vulnerable, that is, who have more deficits and risk factors (e.g., experience physical abuse, violence, unsupervised time), profit the most from assets (Scales, 1999).

Benson et al. (Benson, Leffert, Scales, & Blyth, 1998) also report a strong connection between asset levels and thriving factors. High asset youth are more likely than low asset youth to report getting mostly As in school (53% versus 7%); to place a high value on cultural diversity (87% versus 34%); to help friends or neighbors at least 1 hour a week (96% versus 69%); to be a leader in a group or organization in the past year (87% versus 48%); to resist doing dangerous things (43% versus 6%); to delay gratification by saving money rather than spending it right away (72% versus 27%); and to overcome adversity and not give up when things get tough (86% versus 57%). Although not as dramatic in every instance as in the comparison of risk behavior, these data indicate that youth who report the fewest assets also report fewer thriving factors and, conversely, that youth who report more developmental assets also report more thriving indicators.

These data underscore the importance of Principle 10 for effective character education. It requires a fundamental mobilization of the community. There must be an intentional commitment to become an asset-building community, to construct the developmental infrastructure to support the positive development of all youth. The Search Institute suggests some core principles of asset-building communities. There must be broad *collaboration* among all of the socializing systems within a community. The community initiative must be *comprehensive;* it should seek to promote all 40 assets and not just a subset. It should promote the *civic engagement* not just of traditional leaders but of all the residents within the boundaries of a community. It should involve *youth as partners* with adults.

Many adolescents participate in largely community-based youth programs that are guided by a positive youth development orientation. Roth and Brooks-Gunn (2003) surveyed 71 youth-serving organizations to determine the characteristics of programs designed to promote healthy adolescent development. Consistent with the youth development philosophy, 77% of the programs said that their primary goal was to build competencies; 54% also indicated prevention goals. However, prevention goals were strongly in evidence when asked specifically about whether the program was designed as prevention against high risk behaviors, such as substance abuse (76%), school dropout (63%), violence (73%), and gang activity (59%). Interestingly, not one of the youth development programs apparently viewed their competency-building and prevention work in terms of moral or character development.

Another perspective is what adolescents themselves report learning in organized youth activities. In one study (D. M. Hanson, Larson, & Dworkin, 2003), 450 adolescents in a medium-size, ethnically diverse school responded to the Youth Experiences Survey (YES), which asks respondents to report their experiences in several domains (identity, initiative, basic emotional, cognitive, and physical skills, teamwork and social skills, interpersonal relatedness, connections with adults, and negative experiences). Learning in these contexts was compared against "hanging out with friends" and with academic classes. The results showed that organized youth activities were a better context for learning initiative skills (e.g., goal setting, problem solving, effort, time management), exploring identity and reflection, and learning to manage anger, anxiety, and stress than hanging out with friends or taking required classes. Moreover, adolescents reported learning about teamwork, social, and leadership skills in organized youth activities. Interesting learning differences emerged among program activities. For example, the development of identity, prosocial norms, and ties to the community were said to be learned in faith-based, community service, and vocational activities, but participation in sports was associated with mostly gains in personal development (e.g., self-knowledge, physical skills, and emotional regulation) but not teamwork, social skills, prosocial norms, or positive peer interactions. Perhaps the competitive nature of sports works against the development of skills required for interpersonal competence (see Shields & Bredemeier, 2005).

Two reviews have attempted to gauge the effectiveness of youth development programs. Roth, Brooks-Gunn, Murray, and Foster (1998) examined 15 program evaluations that met criteria for methodological rigor. Six programs largely met the goals of the positive youth development framework by focusing on competency and asset building. Six programs were designed as preventions against specific problem behaviors, albeit by strengthening competencies and assets. Three programs were preventions designed to teach skills for avoiding risk behaviors (e.g., assertiveness training, peer resistance, planning for the future) and were the least representative of the ideal youth development program. In general, all 15 programs showed evidence of effectiveness, although a number of general distinctions emerged. For example, programs that are more comprehensive and sustained tend to result in better outcomes. Program effectiveness was also linked to the continuity of caring adult-youth relationships and the extent and quality of youth engagement with program activities.

Catalano, Berglund, et al. (2004) identified 25 programs that addressed one or more positive youth development constructs (e.g., bonding, resilience, socioemotional, cognitive, behavioral or moral competence, self-efficacy, self-determination, spirituality, identity, belief in the future, recognition for positive behavior, prosocial norms, and prosocial involvement) in multiple socialization domains (or many constructs in a single domain), using children from the general or at-risk population (but not in treatment). These studies also met strong methodological criteria. The analysis of program characteristics showed that effective programs addressed a minimum of five positive youth development constructs. Competence, self-efficacy, and prosocial norms were addressed in all 25 programs; opportunities for prosocial involvement, recognition for positive behavior, and bonding were noted in over 75% of the programs; and positive identity, self-determination, belief in the future, resiliency, and spirituality were noted in 50% of the programs. Effective programs also measured both positive and problem outcomes, had a structured curriculum and frequent youth contact for at least 9 months, and took steps to ensure fidelity of implementation.

Social-Emotional Learning

We noted earlier that a developmental systems orientation that focused on positive youth development would constitute a powerful conceptual framework for character education. A similar claim can be made for social-emotional learning (SEL). The Collaborative to Advance Social and Emotional Learning (CASEL) has developed a unifying framework to promote the development of important competencies that both enhance strengths and prevent problem behaviors (Graczyk et al., 2000; Payton et al., 2000; Weissberg & Greenberg, 1998). Its focus on competence and prevention place it well within the positive youth development framework (Catalano, Hawkins, Berglund, Pollard, & Arthur, 2002), although its long-standing concern with school-based implementation makes it particularly attractive for character education (CASEL, 2003; Elias, Zins, Graczyk, & Weissberg, 2003; Elias et al., 1997). Indeed, CASEL insists that effective programming for SEL competencies has an instructional component with well-designed and organized lesson plans that are sequenced in a coherent curriculum that is programmatic over consecutive grades (Payton et al., 2000), as well as broad parent and community involvement in planning, implementation, and evaluation (Weissberg & O'Brien, 2004).

The key SEL competencies identified by CASEL include self-other awareness (awareness and management of feeling, realistic self-assessment of abilities, perspective taking), self-management (self-regulation of emotions, setting goals, persevering in the face of obstacles), responsible decision making (identifying problems, discerning social norms, accurate and critical appraisal of information, evaluation solutions, taking responsibility for decisions), and relationship skills (cooperation, expressive communication, negotiation, refusal, help seeking, and conflict resolution skills). All of these competencies are familiar targets of character education.

A substantial research base links these competencies to effective and adaptive functioning and to prevention of risk behavior. For example, evidence cited earlier for the Child Development Project and the Seattle Social Development Project are claimed as support for school-based SEL objectives (Greenberg et al., 2003; Weissberg & O'Brien, 2004). Similarly, a substantial literature shows that programs that address SEL competencies are effective in preventing problem behaviors (Durlak & Wells, 1997; D. B. Wilson, Gottfredson, & Najaka, 2001), drug use (Tobler et al., 2000), and violence (Greenberg & Kusche, 1998; Greenberg, Kusche, Cook, & Quamma, 1995). SEL is also a strong predictor of academic outcomes (Elias et al., 2003). One study showed, for example, that the best predictor of eighth-grade academic achievement was not third-grade academic achievement but indices of social competence (Caprara, Barbanelli, Pastorelli, Bandura, & Zimbardo, 2000).

One crucial issue that CASEL has taken on concerns program implementation and sustainability. As Elias et al. (2003, p. 308) put it, "Even widely acclaimed evidence-based approaches to classroom organization and instruction that integrate both academics and SEL are dependent for their success on the delivery systems into which they are embedded." We review various implementation issues in a later section.

Character and Higher Education

Character education does not end with high school. Indeed, a developmental systems perspective on moral character would lead us to expect opportunities for dynamic change across the life course. Although there has been comparatively less programmatic emphasis or research on character development in postsecondary institutions, there are notable recent efforts to explore the contributions of the collegiate experience to the moral formation of undergraduates (e.g., Colby, Ehrlich, Beaumont, & Stephens, 2003; Mentkowski & Associates, 2000). One survey, for example, identified an honor roll of 134 colleges and universities to serve as exemplars of character-building institutions (Schwartz & Templeton, 1997; Sweeney, 1997). These institutions emphasized students' moral reasoning skills, community-building experiences, and spiritual growth, while advocating for a drug-free environment. They also conducted critical assessments of their character-building assets and programs.

The emphasis on moral reasoning skills is premised on the expectation that the critical engagement and inquiry that is ideally characteristic of postsecondary education will stimulate moral deliberation to higher stages of complexity. Indeed, one of the best-documented changes that results from the collegiate experience is a significant increase in the quality and complexity of moral reasoning (Pascarella & Terenzini, 1991), demonstrating the effect of college on humanizing "values and attitudes concerning the rights and welfare of others" (Pascarella & Terenzini, 2005, p. 348). College environments that encourage questioning, inquiry, and openness to evidence and argument foster the largest gains in moral reasoning (e.g., Rest & Narvaez, 1991; Rogers, 2002), although this relationship is attenuated in collegiate environments that are narrowly careerist and where critical inquiry is not valued (McNeel, 1994).

There are indeed differences among colleges and universities in the degree to which they make moral and civic education a central institutional commitment. Colby et al. (2003) noted that moral and civic development is not a high priority for most American universities and colleges. "We have been struck again and again," they write, "by the very many lost opportunities for moral and civic growth in curricular and extracurricular programs on most campuses" (p. 277). In their study of 12 universities that do make moral and civic growth an institutional commitment, Colby et al. identify (a) the important dimensions of moral and civic maturity that should be addressed, (b) the sites where these dimensions can be exploited, and (c) the thematic perspectives that a fully rounded commitment to moral and civic education should embrace.

With respect to the dimensions of moral and civic maturity, Colby et al. (2003) nominated three categories: *understanding* (e.g., key ethical and civic concepts, knowledge of democratic principles, expertise in one's field), *motivation* (e.g., hope and compassion, desire to be an engaged citizen, sense of political efficacy, sense of civic responsibility as a part of self-understanding), and *skills* (e.g., communication skills, ability to collaborate, forge consensus, compromise). These dimensions are exploited in the curriculum, in extracurricular activities, and in the general campus culture. The curriculum, for example, presents numerous opportunities to cultivate moral and civic maturity. Moral and civic understanding, motivation, and skills can mutually enhance academic learning (e.g., Markus et al., 1993). A wide range of pedagogical strategies, including service learning, project-based learning, field placements, site-base practicum experiences, and collaborative work, encourages student engagement with the broader community and has significance for moral learning (Brandenberger, 2005). Moral and civic issues can be framed in core courses and in the coursework of one's major and can be the target of faculty development.

Finally, a comprehensive and intentional commitment to moral and civic growth by universities and colleges takes on three themes: community connections, moral and civic virtue, and social justice ("systemic social responsibility"). According to Colby et al. (2003, p. 284), "Moral and civic education is incomplete if it does not somehow take account of all these themes." Feeling a connection to a community cultivates a sense of allegiance and duty, where the benefits and burdens of cooperation, and of citizenship, can be experienced and practiced. Postsecondary institutions are also places where the virtues proper to democratic citizenship can be cultivated. Although these dispositions have been variously conceived, there is a strong consensus that a deliberative character (Guttman, 1987) is minimally required, a character that is able to carry on the public conversation in a way that is tolerant, respectful, and generous. Nash (1997) has noted, too, that democratic dispositions are essentially "conversational virtues" that take on moral significance because they are necessary for living well in a democracy. The democratic citizen must engage in public discourse with toleration, fairness, and respect for different perspectives and for the canons of civility. Civic engagement in a democratic society requires a disposition to listen with generosity, to compromise, to argue on the basis of factual evidence, to abide by outcomes, and to affirm the validity of a democratic process even if it results in outcomes that are contrary to one's own preferences (Knight Higher Education Collaborative, 2000). Moreover, the democratic citizen must have hope and confidence in the value of deliberation and be able to engage in adversarial discussion in a way that does not compromise civic friendship, mutual respect, and sense of common purpose. Hence, an important moral responsibility of higher education is to cultivate "dialogic competence in public moral language" (Strike, 1996, p. 889), and to provide occasions, in the context of scholarly engagement and intellectual inquiry, where these virtues are on frequent display and avidly practiced.

The third theme encourages curricular and extracurricular activities that allow undergraduates to take on "systemic social responsibility": to be active in the democratic process, to take a stand, to take an interest in social policy, and to view the life of the community through the lens of social justice and one's own responsibility as an engaged citizen. Postsecondary institutions vary in how they address these three themes, but what is crucial is that colleges and universities make moral and civic maturity an explicit, intentional, and comprehensive part of their educational mission.

Character and Professional Education

"Professional practice," according to Bebeau (2002, p. 271), "is predominantly a moral enterprise." Indeed, ethical development is a concern for schools across the professional landscape, including business, law, medicine, dentistry, nursing, and education. An increasing number of professional schools are adopting ethics education with greater frequency.

Rest and Narvaez (1994a) point out specific methods that promote moral reasoning development in professional educational programs. First, following Dewey's advocacy of immediate experience and active problem solving, one of the most effective methods is deliberative psychological education, reading academic theory, providing direct experience, and reflection that integrates theory with the direct experience (Sprinthall, 1994). The individual's conceptual frameworks developed from these integrated experiences are not only more sophisticated but are resilient. Studies have documented that the most popular and successful methods of instruction for moral reasoning development involves student discussion about dilemmas and cases in the field (e.g., Hartwell, 1995). Moral dilemma discussion is particularly effective when students are coached to develop the skills necessary for expert moral problem solving, using profession-specific ethical constructs (Bebeau & Thoma, 1999), such as role taking and logical analysis for determining valid and invalid arguments (McNeel, 1994; Penn, 1990). However, even less experiential courses such as film-based courses and writing-intensive courses can have positive effects (e.g., Bebeau, 1994, 2002; Self, Baldwin, & Olivarez, 1993).

The most integrative programs have moved beyond a sole focus on moral reasoning to include other aspects of moral functioning, such as those described by the four component model (Rest, 1983). For example, programs at the University of Minnesota assist nursing and dentistry students in developing the four components: ethical sensitivity, ethical motivation, and ethical implementation as well as ethical judgment (Bebeau, 1994; Duckett, 1994). Recently, Bebeau (2002) has addressed the importance of developing a professional moral identity. She suggests that "the conceptual frameworks of professional identity are not part of an initial self-understanding, and must be revisited frequently during professional education" (p. 286). The study of professional exemplars is a useful method for providing concrete models for professional ethical identity formation (Rule & Bebeau, 2005). Such studies offer glimpses to novices of what a virtuous professional looks like and how to conduct oneself in typical and nontypical situations and provide role models for initiates.

A CASE STUDY: INTEGRATIVE ETHICAL EDUCATION

Integrative Ethical Education (IEE) is a conceptual framework that attempts to incorporate insights of developmental theory and psychological science into character education (Narvaez, 2005a; Narvaez, Bock, & Endicott, 2003). It is integrative in several senses. It attempts to understand character and its development in terms of cognitive science literatures on expertise and the novice-to-expert mechanisms of best practice instruction. It attempts to keep faith with classical sources by linking Greek notions of *eudaemonia* (human flourishing), *arête* (excellence), *phronesis* (practical wisdom), and *techne* (expertise) with developmental and cognitive science. It is compatible with positive youth development in its claim that the goal of integrative ethical education is the development of important competencies that contribute to productive adaptation to the demands of adulthood, but that these competencies are understood as clusters of skills that one may learn or practice to varying degrees of expertise. It assumes that the best context for expertise development is a caring relationship with teacher-mentors wherein skills are learned by means of coached practice and "guided autonomy." In delineating the elemental skills of good character, IEE addresses *character* education by integrating the findings from developmental psychology, prevention science, and positive psychology. In proposing the best approach to instruction, IEE addresses character *education* by integrating contemporary findings from research in learning and cognition.

In this section, we outline some of the key features of IEE. Integrative Ethical Education is predicated on the importance of caring classroom environments, but we focus on just three components of the model: character as expertise development, the cultivation of character as the cultivation of expertise, and the importance of self-regulation for developing and maintaining virtuous character.

Character as Expertise Development

Human learning is increasingly conceptualized as a matter of novices developing greater expertise in domains of study (Ericsson & Smith, 1991; R. Sternberg, 1998). A domain expert differs from a novice by having a large, rich, organized network of concepts or schemas that include declarative, procedural, and conditional knowledge. Unlike novices, experts know what knowledge to access, which procedures to apply, and how to apply them and when. Expertise refers not to mere technical competence but to the multitrack capacities and sensibilities of an exemplar, the refined, deep understanding built from lived experience that is evident in practice and action (Hursthouse, 1999, 2003; Spiecker, 1999).

In the *Republic,* Plato describes virtue as a type of *techne,* or "know-how" that is characteristic of experts (e.g., painters, writers, politicians) in specific domains. Similarly, the virtuous person has ethical know-how, that is, ethical skills honed to a high degree of expertise. Ethical expertise refers not only to behaviors, sensibilities, and orientations but also to feelings, motives, and drives. Ethical expertise is not just what a person does but that which the person *likes* to do (Urmson, 1988). It is a complex of characteristics, skills, and competencies that enable ethical behavior and sustain one in pursuing the life that is good for one to live.

Rest (1983; Narvaez & Rest, 1995) identified four psychologically distinct processes that must occur to enable ethical behavior: ethical sensitivity, ethical judgment, ethical motivation/focus, and ethical action. The four-process model provides a holistic understanding of the ethical exemplar, one who is able to demonstrate keen perception and perspective taking, skilled reasoning, ethical focus, and skills for completing moral action (Bebeau, Rest, & Narvaez, 1999; Narvaez, 2005a; Narvaez, Bock, Endicott, & Lies, 2004). Each process is represented by a set of skills (Narvaez et al., 2004; Narvaez et al., 2003). For example, experts in the skill of ethical sensitivity are able to more quickly and accurately read the moral implications of a situation and determine a suitable response. They are better at generating usable solutions due to a greater understanding of the consequences of possible actions. Experts in ethical judgment are more skilled in solving complex

problems and seeing the syntactic structure of a problem quickly and bring with them many schemas for reasoning about possible courses of action. Their information-processing abilities are both complex and efficient. Experts in the skill of ethical focus are able to sustain moral priorities in light of the commitments of a moral self-identity. Experts in the skills of ethical action engage the self-regulation that is necessary to get the ethical job done.

Pedagogy for Cultivating Character Expertise

The IEE model emphasizes two critical features of successful pedagogy: First, it must be constructivist; second, it must attend simultaneously to cultivating expertise on two fronts: conscious, explicit understandings and intuitive, implicit understanding. Integrative Ethical Education adopts the cognitive-mediational view that learning depends on the cognitive activity of students; that learning occurs when incoming information is actively transformed in light of prior knowledge; and that teachers facilitate learning by engaging students in active cognitive processing about content and facilitating self-monitoring understanding (L. M. Anderson, 1989). It assumes that learners are active constructors of meaning, competencies, and skills and that individuals build conceptual frameworks—declarative, procedural, and conditional—in the process of learning to get along with others. When these skills are practiced extensively in multiple contexts, they take on the qualities of tacit, implicit knowledge and the automaticity characteristic of the "unconscious" mind (Hassin, Uleman, & Bargh, 2005; Hogarth, 2001).

A model of instruction that captures these pedagogical goals is coached apprenticeship. A coached apprenticeship model involves using both direct and indirect instruction, mimesis and transformation, a focus on both content and process, tuning both the deliberate conscious mind and the intuitive mind. In an apprenticeship, the guide provides examples and models of skilled behavior and the theoretical explanation for why things are done one way and not another. At the same time, the apprentice is immersed in well-structured environments that cultivate appropriate intuitions (Hogarth, 2001).

Teaching for ethical expertise requires coached apprenticeship and extensive practice in multiple contexts. Integrative Ethical Education offers instructional guidelines for helping children move along a continuum from novice to expert in each ethical content domain that is studied. To do this, children must experience a type of expert-in-training pedagogy, that fosters appropriate intuitions and deliberative understanding for each skill that they learn. Teachers can set up instruction to help students develop appropriate knowledge by designing lessons according to the following four levels (based on Marshall, 1995). At Level 1 ("Immersion in examples and opportunities"), teachers draw students' attention to the big picture in a subject area and help them learn to recognize basic patterns. At Level 2 ("Attention to facts and skills"), teachers focus students' attention on the details and prototypical examples in the domain to build more elaborate concepts. At Level 3 ("Practice procedures"), the teacher provides opportunities for the students to try out many skills and ideas in a domain to build a procedural understanding of how skills are related and best deployed to solve domain-relevant problems. Finally, at Level 4 ("Integrate knowledge and procedures"), students gradually integrate and apply systematically knowledge across many contexts and situations.

Self-Regulation for Sustainability

The role of self-regulation in character development is of long-standing interest. Aristotle emphasized that virtues are developed with extended practice, effort, and guidance from parents, teachers, and mentors until the child is able to self-maintain virtue (Urmson, 1988). Recent research demonstrates that the most successful learners are those who self-monitor their success and alter strategies when necessary. Thus, self-regulation requires sophisticated metacognition. According to a social cognitive view, self-regulation is a cyclical, ever-changing interaction among personal, behavioral, and environmental factors, involving three phases: forethought, performance or volitional control, and self-reflection (Zimmerman, 2000).

Integrative Ethical Education infuses self-regulation on two levels: the teacher level and the student level. For school reforms to be sustainable, educators must take on a self-regulatory orientation for the implementation of character education. This means taking a systematic intentional approach to building a caring ethical school community, facilitating the development of instructional and ethical skills in all members of the school community, including teachers, administrators, and other staff, as members of a comprehensive learning community.

For students to develop and maintain ethical skills, they must increase their metacognitive understanding,

self-monitoring skills, and self-regulation for ethical and academic development. Individuals can be coached to domain-specific self-efficacy and self-regulation (Zimmerman, Bonner, & Kovach, 2002). In the IEE model, teachers continuously draw student attention to the moral issues immanent in classroom life and learning (Narvaez, 2005b). Students are provided guidance and tools to answer one of the central questions of their lives: Who should I be? As McKinnon (1999, p. 42) points out, individuals must "do the work necessary for constructing a character." The IEE model helps students develop the skills for ethical behavior but requires their active participation in making the decisions that are crucial and relevant for the construction of their own characters. To develop ethical know-how, one must be self-directive; one must take seriously the charge of continually building one's character. Ethical know-how must be trained holistically, as a type of expertise, at first coached, then increasingly self-directed.

An Implementation of IEE: The Community Voices and Character Education Project

The Community Voices and Character Education Project (CVCE) was an early prototype of the Integrative Ethical Education conceptual framework. The CVCE was a federally funded project implemented in the state of Minnesota from 1998 to 2002.* It was a collaborative effort among the Minnesota Department of Education (called at the time the Department of Children, Families, and Learning), the University of Minnesota, and educators across the state. The focus of the CVCE project was to develop and provide a research-based framework for character education at the middle school level with teacher-friendly guidelines for how to incorporate ethical development into standards-driven instruction. Classroom activity guidebooks were created along with other supportive materials, including teacher-designed lesson plans.

Reflecting both an empowerment model and the historical and legislative emphasis in Minnesota on local

*U.S. Department of Education Office of Educational Research and Improvement Grant # R215V980001. Copies of CVCE materials on CD are available from the Minnesota Department of Education or from the Center for Ethical Education, University of Notre Dame, 154 Institute for Educational Initiatives, Notre Dame, IN 46556; e-mail: cee@nd.edu; downloadable from http://cee.nd.edu.

control of curricular decisions, the CVCE project used a "common morality" (Beauchamp & Childress, 1994) approach of presenting research-based principles (top-down) to a local team who adapted them for the local context (bottom-up), formulating a unique intervention. The top-down recommendations included fostering a caring climate conducive to character growth, using a novice-to-expert approach to ethical skill instruction, developing self-regulatory skills in students as they practice ethical skills, and including parents and community members in cultivating character in students. School teams and their leaders were guided in designing a local vision for character education with specific action steps for how to incorporate ethical skill instruction with links to the community. As Elias et al. (2003) pointed out, all program implementations are limited because they must be adapted to local circumstances. "Too often it is assumed," they write, "that evidence-based programs can be 'plugged-in' and then work effectively" (p. 310). Each team developed a unique approach to cultivating character, using schoolwide projects, advisory/homeroom lessons, and/or infusion into academic instruction into some or all subjects. Some teams incorporated existing character interventions (e.g., Lions Quest) into their CVCE intervention. Indeed, the IEE framework provides a comprehensive approach within which existing character education programs can be integrated, extended, and strengthened.

Evaluation of the Community Voices and Character Education Project

In the final year evaluation, only five of eight experimental schools and one control school provided completed pretest-posttest data. The evaluation had several components that correspond to the emphasis of the project (for a more detailed discussion, see C. Anderson, Narvaez, Bock, Endicott, & Lies, 2003; Narvaez, Bock, Endicott, & Lies, 2004).

The primary focus of the project was to design a conceptual framework for character education at the middle school level along with activity books to guide teams of teachers in incorporating character skill development into standards-driven instruction. Both participating and nonparticipating teachers from partner schools thought the framework was valuable. The majority of respondents reported "easy" or "so-so" for the ease of use of the activity books.

We also evaluated the quality of the implementation. Implementation varied across sites in terms of depth and breadth. Differences in local implementation design, leadership, and stability of the leadership and of the core team, as well as demands on teachers, led to differences in depth and quality of implementation and how many students were influenced. In only two of the five schools was there full implementation of the model. In these schools, all teachers were involved in teaching ethical skills during advisory/homeroom, in their academic instruction, and in schoolwide projects. In these two schools, significant effects were found in student pre/posttests. The other schools addressed a wide number of skills in a limited manner by only a subset of teachers. Other approaches have required the full participation of the school for implementation (e.g., the Child Development Project) so that the student experience is consistent across teachers; as a pilot program emphasizing local control, CVCE did not.

The substantive evaluation addressed effects on students and school climate. Four student measures of climate were used: staff tolerance, student tolerance, student self-report of climate perceptions and attachment to school, and student perception of peer ethical behavior. One or more general measures of each of the four ethical processes were also used. For ethical sensitivity, we used the Child Development Project's Concern for Others Scale. For ethical judgment, we used a global moral judgment scale. For ethical focus, we used measures of citizenship, community bonding, and ethical identity. For ethical action, we used a measure of moral assertiveness and prosocial responsibility.

Student survey responses were compared with a matched comparison group ($n = 125$) from another school not involved in the project. Across schools, the findings with the ethical development scales were mixed. Most scales indicated nonsignificant improvements over the comparison group, with one exception. Program students reported more sensitivity to intolerance than did control students. The two schools that fully implemented the program emphasized ethical sensitivity. When contrasted with the comparison group, program students in full-implementation schools reported significant gains on ethical sensitivity. Climate was used as a covariate in a MANOVA with school group as factor (full implementation schools, partial implementation schools, comparison school). For climate, effect sizes were moderate for citizenship and community bonding and small for ethical identity. For school group, effect sizes were small for concern for others, community bonding, and ethical identity. These findings suggest that climate may mediate the majority of effects of ethical skill instruction.

There were three challenges to finding significant differences in pre/post student assessments. First, leadership changes at three schools undermined the test administration in one way or another so that only five sets of usable pre/post data were extant. Second, given the amount of time required for successful interventions to demonstrate an effect, it was deemed a challenge to find significant pre/post differences within 1 year. Third, one of the strengths of the program—local control and local distinctiveness—meant that cross-site comparisons were not possible, insofar as each site's implementation was not strictly comparable with those at other sites. Thus, for a particular implementation, the numbers tested were small.

These features of CVCE are relevant also to the question of replicability. Replicability typically refers to successful implementation in more than one school. This definition assumes that what is being implemented is identical across sites. This is contrary to the approach taken in the CVCE project. Instead, the emphasis was on local control and local adaptation of the conceptual framework. Replicability did not refer to identical implementation but instead to the replicability of the process and the general features of the model. Based on the lesson plans teachers created in virtually every subject area, CVCE evaluators determined that teachers were able to integrate character skills development into standards-driven academic instruction. Based on the teacher-created lesson plans and the local team and local leader reports, educators were generally able to implement the model with minimal supervision.

The key features of the model were largely followed by most schools. Most teams viewed character as a set of ethical skills derived from four processes. According to the lesson plans teachers devised, most sites did use a novice-to-expert approach to teach character skills. Most sites at least attempted to involve the community in planning and implementation in one way or another, although outcomes were mixed. It is not clear how empowered the students felt as the university Human Subjects Committee did not give permission to interview student participants.

Lessons Learned

The IEE model provides a conceptual framework for character cultivation that guides educators in how to think about what character entails and how to nurture it in students. The implementation of IEE in the CVCE project was locally controlled, providing maximum flexibility and allowing for adaptations that met local needs and issues (and that are unforeseeable by a curriculum writer). However, the fact that CVCE did not provide a script for teachers made it necessary for teachers to put in time to modify their lessons to incorporate ethical skill development. With minimal training, teacher teams were able to construct multiple units and lessons. Lessons that a teacher modified himself or herself were lessons that he or she would use again and again. This is an advantage. Nevertheless, sometimes modifying lessons can be a daunting first step in character education, especially for inexperienced teachers. Consequently, a year-long scripted curriculum for homeroom/advisory purposes (currently being piloted) could more easily familiarize teachers with the conceptual framework and scaffold understanding of how to apply the model to classroom activities. Maximum flexibility and local control also made it difficult to measure replicable program effects. A scripted approach will make possible a cleaner estimation of replicable program effects.

ISSUES OF IMPLEMENTATION

Our examination of the IEE case study revealed a number of interesting challenges to successful implementation of a character education intervention. In this section, we summarize some of the enduring implementation issues that have emerged in the various character education literatures and from our own experience.

One enduring problem concerns the fidelity of implementation (Laud & Berkowitz, 1999). In the CVCE project, the quality of implementation was related to disparate outcomes. Schools with a broader (across more classrooms and by more teachers) and deeper (more frequent and focused) implementation were more successful, a finding corroborated by other character development programs (see Solomon et al., 2002). This underscores a point made by Elias et al. (2003) that interventions are rarely delivered as planned, even in trials marked by stringent methodological rigor. And even if the program is implemented and delivered as planned, there are few assurances that it will be received by students as intended. As Elias et al. put it, "If children are inattentive, a classroom is chaotic, or the material is not at the right developmental level, 'delivery' by instructors may not strongly predict children's skill acquisition and use" (pp. 309–310). Thus, in addition to implementation fidelity, one must also attend to factors that limit student exposure to the intervention (Berkowitz & Bier, 2004a).

In their analysis of implementation and sustainability of social-emotional interventions, Elias et al. (2003) note a number of additional obstacles that are highly relevant to character education. For example, implementation fidelity can be threatened by turnover in teachers and program staff. Characteristics of educators and their roles can support or undermine implementation. Not all roles are equally satisfying, level of commitment varies, and tacit knowledge is not communicated to new staff. As the authors put it, "It is not the same thing to create, to deliver, to administer and to continue" an innovative program (p. 314). Working out role differences and supporting new staff is crucial to sustainable programming. Indeed, "success seems to accompany a spirit of continuous improvement and reinvention without excessive divergence from what exists" (p. 314). In addition, although virtually every approach to character education calls for extensive and active collaboration with family and community, the difficulties in forming, effectively utilizing, and sustaining these partnerships are often underestimated.

Elias et al. (2003) summarize a number of factors associated with successful and sustainable program implementation. Such programs (a) have a program coordinator, preferably with appropriate preparation, or a committee, to oversee implementation; (b) involve committed individuals who have a sense of ownership of the program; (c) have continuous formal and informal training; (d) have varied and engaging instructional materials that map onto goals of the school or district; and (e) have buy-in of key educational leaders and the consistent support of critical constituencies. Elias et al. also suggest that a pragmatic, theoretically informed perspective is essential. "Local ecologies," they write, "will not support an infinite variety of possibilities. What has a chance to work is what fits" (p. 314). What is required, in other words, is a goodness-of-fit between program planning, its objectives and goals, and its flexible implementation "in the spirit of continuous improvement."

The reference to the local ecology of schools and to obstacles and opportunities that are endemic to complex organizations draws attention to the culture of schools as an arena for character education. The cultivation of a professional learning community within a school is critical to sustainable school reform efforts (Fullan, 1999, 2000). For example, schools that were successful in raising student achievement and improving school climate had staffs that developed a professional learning community, addressed student work through assessment, and changed their practice to improve results (Newmann & Wehlage, 1995; Pankake & Moller, 2003). Professional learning communities have particular characteristics. They take the time to develop a shared vision and mutually held values that focus on student learning and foster norms for improving practice. Leadership is democratic, shared among teachers and administrators. The entire staff seeks and shares knowledge, skills, and strategies to improve practice. The school structure supports an environment that is collaborative, trusting, positive, and caring. Peers open their classrooms to the feedback and suggestions of others to improve student achievement and promote individual and community growth. We believe that these same practices are critical to sustain a commitment not only to academic achievement but to moral learning as well, and it is welcome to see a commitment to learning communities in a prominent report on high school character education (Lickona & Davidson, 2004).

We suggest that if character education is to be considered an instance of primary prevention then it should possess the features of any well-designed intervention. It should be comprehensive, have multiple components, address multiple assets at different levels of the ecological setting, and be implemented in the early grades and sustained over time. It is now a truism to remark that one-trial or short-term intervention programs have little lasting impact. Moreover, insofar as dispositional coherence is located at the interaction of persons and context, there is little hope for enduring character education that does not attend also to the climate and culture of classrooms and schools. Effective character education requires a pervasive commitment to change the culture of schools as much as to change the behavior of children.

Payton et al. (2000) note a number of specific features of quality social emotional learning programs. These programs (a) articulate a conceptual framework that guides the selection of program and learning objectives; (b) provide professional development instruction to teachers to enable their effective implementation across the regular academic curriculum; and (c) include well-organized and user-friendly lesson plans with clear objectives and learning activities and assessment tools. Moreover, they note that successful programs take steps to improve schoolwide cooperation and school-family and school-community partnerships.

There is a significant literature on the school characteristics that promote academic achievement. Schools with high achievement are orderly and safe; they are respectful and provide students with moral and personal support while expecting them to achieve (Sebring, 1996). Achieving schools have a strong sense of community and high academic standards (strong norms and high expectations for achievement; Bryk, Lee, & Holland, 1993). Interestingly, the characteristics that foster achievement overlap with characteristics that nurture prosocial development. Schools that foster prosocial development have caring climates that nurture a feeling of belonging and competence in students (M. Watson et al., 1997). In other words, there are not two sets of instructional best practice, one for academic achievement and one for character. Both objectives work out of the same playbook. In this sense, effective character education is, indeed, good education. A recent study in Catholic schools using structural equation modeling showed, for example, that climate influenced directly character development. Moreover, character development mediated the effect of climate on academic motivation moreso than climate's direct effect on motivation (Mullen, Turner, & Narvaez, 2005).

This suggests, of course, that effective character education ultimately comes down to what teachers do in their classrooms. The extent to which moral and character education is taught explicitly in teacher preparation programs is not clear. It is well known that teachers who have more expertise in both content and pedagogical content knowledge conduct their classes more effectively than do novice teachers (Berliner, 1994a, 1994b; Shulman, 1987; Sternberg & Horvath, 1995). However, if explicit instructional focus on moral content knowledge and pedagogy is limited or absent during preservice teacher training, then one cannot be optimistic that efforts to expand character education will be met with the requisite levels of teacher expertise.

On the other hand, Carr (1991) argued that if teachers fail in their implementation of moral education it is not because they lack knowledge of curriculum theory or lack pedagogical skills. Indeed, he argues that we do our student teachers in education programs "no great favors by proceeding as though education and learning to teach are matters only of the mastery of certain pedagogical skills, knacks or strategies apt for the successful transmission of value-neutral knowledge or information" (p. 11). Rather, teachers fail because the value questions immanent to teaching are not systematically addressed in their professional formation. Instead, there is "something approaching a conspiracy of silence among teacher educators on this topic" (p. 10). Carr contends that when teacher education programs do not require "sensible reflection upon the moral character of human life and experience, the nature of values and the ethical aspects of the educationalist's role," then the resulting intellectual vacuum leaves teachers vulnerable to faddism; it leaves them ill-prepared to make transparent the immanence and inevitability of fundamental value questions that attend education, teaching, and learning. Sensible reflection might also point to how preservice teachers are taught to frame the moral significance of daily classroom life. Teacher educators might take direction from Jackson, Boostrom, and Hansen (1993), *The Moral Life of Schools,* when thinking about cultivating awareness among preservice teachers of the immanence and inevitability of morality in the classroom. Jackson et al. (1993), for example, pointed out that teachers who maintain ethical classrooms model a strong moral character and expect students to do the same. These teachers point out the moral aspects of subject matter materials and choose materials based on these characteristics. Moreover, in these classrooms moral discussions become part of the classroom flow, occurring spontaneously in and outside of the classroom. In any case, teacher educators need to complete the task of linking best practice with moral character development, a task started by Williams and Schaps (1999).

OPEN QUESTIONS AND FUTURE DIRECTIONS

We have argued that character education requires a defensible psychological understanding of dispositional coherence and of development and a defensible approach to education that conforms to what is known about effective teaching and learning. We proposed a developmental systems perspective as a conceptual framework for character education and reviewed several categories of youth development and prevention programs that show promise as school-based or community-based interventions.

It is an enduring question, however, whether these programs are rightfully considered instances of character education. We made a distinction between character education as a treatment and character education as an outcome. As our review makes clear, there is very little that is distinctive about traditional character education that warrants it be considered an educational treatment in its own right. Indeed, when advocates point to character education programs that work, these are programs motivated by an entirely different theoretical agenda than one of morality, virtue, or character. Programs that work are associated with positive youth development or social-emotional learning. Developmental science, including developmental psychopathology and the science of prevention, already provide powerful frameworks for understanding risk, resilience, adaptation, and thriving that has little need for the language of character. On the other hand, if character is considered not a treatment but a set of outcomes, then, of course, there is nothing untoward about claiming the findings of developmental interventions as its own. In this case, interventions that are motivated by developmental science, by perspectives on youth development and SEL, for example, provide outcomes that are relevant to a certain understanding of character and give insights about how to prepare youth for the travails and opportunities of adulthood.

Yet we do not want to give up on the idea that character education can be a distinctive educational intervention. Although the literatures on youth development and social-emotional learning provide an attractive vision of adaptation, thriving, and positive adjustment, and although it is tempting for character educators to want to claim these literatures as their own, we think that this vision of successful adulthood is incomplete without a specification of the moral dimensions of selfhood, identity, and community. The metaphors of thriving and flourishing and positive development point mostly toward the notion of what it means to live well. But living well is only half of the challenge. We must not only live well, but live well *the life that is good for one to live.* Discerning the life that is good for one to live is a moral question; it has profound moral dimensions that are not exhausted by avoiding risks and acquiring social-affective competencies.

Certainly, the life that is good for one to live requires avoidance of significant risk behavior, and so character education embraces the science of prevention as a prophylaxis against risks and deficits. Certainly, the life that is good for one to live requires the cultivation of competencies that prepare one for the challenges of adulthood, and so character education embraces positive youth development in its several forms, along with its slogan: Problem-free is not fully prepared. Yet fully prepared is not morally adept. In our view, character education should aim minimally for full preparation of

young people for adulthood, but should not be content with full preparation for living well; it should aim, too, at helping students cope with the ethical dimensions of the *good* life lived well.

The challenge for character education, then, is how to maintain a distinctive voice in educational innovations, psychosocial interventions, and youth programming. An approach to positive youth development that is also an instance of character education would be marked, in our view, by an explicit conceptual framework that embraces a developmental systems orientation while articulating a moral vision of what it means to flourish. This moral vision is ideally a virtue ethic that articulates a positive conception of moral agency as a deeply relational and communitarian achievement that expresses the nature of our self-identity through our lived moral desires.

Another challenge is to exploit the resources of psychological science in framing a defensible notion of moral agency, self-identity, and dispositional coherence. We have made a number of suggestions along the way for a "psychologized" approach to moral character. In our view, social cognitive theories of personality and the cognitive science literatures on expertise provide useful frameworks for understanding the moral dimensions of personality, although other literatures may be exploited with profit as well. We reiterate our conviction that an adequate character education will require robust models of character psychology, characterized by deep integration with multiple psychological frameworks.

Moreover, a developmental systems orientation broadens our perspective on character and character education. There is a tendency, for example, to regard character education as something that takes place in schools as a formal curriculum. Yet, as we have seen, the foundations of emergent morality and of conscience are evident quite early in childhood, and the developmental dynamic and pattern of socialization in early family life is most assuredly a kind of character education that will be of interest to researchers for some time to come. What's more, a developmental systems perspective bids us to examine the possibilities of dynamic change in character psychology throughout the life course and within the multiple life worlds of the individual beyond family and schooling in areas such as leisure activities and peer relations. Perhaps a life course perspective on character will require additional constructs, such as wisdom (Staudinger & Pasupathi, 2003; R. J. Sternberg, 1998), purpose (Damon, Menon, & Bronk, 2003), personal goals (Emmons, 2002), spirituality and self-transcendence (Seligman & Csikszentmihalyi, 2000), ecological citizenship (Clayton & Opotow, 2003), and character strengths (Peterson & Seligman, 2004), to capture adequately the complexity of phase-relevant dispositional coherence and human flourishing.

REFERENCES

Abbott, R. D., O'Donnell, J., Hawkins, J. D., Hill, K. G., Kosterman, R., & Catalano, R. F. (1998). Changing teaching practices to promote achievement and bonding to school. *American Journal of Orthopsychiatry, 68,* 542–552.

Aber, J. L., Brown, J. L., & Henrich, C. C. (1999). *Teaching conflict resolution: An effective school-based approach to violence prevention.* New York: National Center for Children in Poverty.

Aber, J. L., Pedersen, S., Brown, J. L., Jones, S. M., & Gershoff, E. T. (2003). *Changing children's trajectories of development: Two-year evidence for the effectiveness of a school-based approach to violence prevention.* New York: National Center for Children in Poverty.

Anderson, C., Narvaez, D., Bock, T., Endicott, L., & Lies, J. (2003). *Minnesota Community Voices and Character Education: Final evaluation report.* Roseville: Minnesota Department of Education.

Anderson, L. M. (1989). Learners and learning. In M. C. Reynolds (Ed.), *Knowledge base for the beginning teacher* (pp. 85–99). Oxford: Pergamon Press.

Aquino, K., & Reed, A., II. (2002). The self-importance of moral identity. *Journal of Personality and Social Psychology, 83,* 1423–1440.

Aristotle. (1985). *Nicomachean ethics* (T. Irwin, Trans.). Indianapolis, IN: Hackett. (Original work written 350)

Arthur, J. (2003). *Education with character: The moral economy of schooling.* London: Routledge Falmer.

Atkins, R., Hart, D., & Donnelly, T. M. (2004). Moral identity development and school attachment. In D. K. Lapsley & D. Narvaez (Eds.), *Moral development, self and identity* (pp. 65–82). Mahwah, NJ: Erlbaum.

Ayer, A. J. (1952). *Language, truth and logic.* New York: Dover.

Bargh, J. A. (1989). Conditional automaticity: Varieties of automatic influence in social perception and cognition. In J. S. Uleman & J. A. Bargh (Eds.), *Unintended thought* (pp. 3–51). New York: Guilford Press.

Bargh, J. A., Bond, R. N., Lombardi, W. J., & Tota, M. E. (1986). The additive nature of chronic and temporal sources of construct accessibility. *Journal of Personality and Social Psychology, 50,* 869–878.

Battistich, V., & Hom, A. (1997). The relationship between students' sense of their school as a community and their involvement in problem behavior. *American Journal of Public Health, 87,* 1997–2001.

Battistich, V., Solomon, D., Watson, M., & Schaps, E. (1996). *Enhancing students' engagement, participation, and democratic values and attitudes.* Ann Arbor, MI: Society for the Psychological Study of Social Issues.

Battistich, V., Solomon, D., Watson, M., & Schaps, E. (1997). Caring school communities. *Educational Psychologist, 32,* 137–151.

Battistich, V., Solomon, D., Watson, M., Solomon, J., & Schaps, E. (1989). Effects of an elementary school program to enhance prosocial behavior on children's social problem-solving skills and strategies. *Journal of Applied Developmental Psychology, 10,* 147–169.

Baumrind, D. (1999). Reflection on character and competence. In A. Colby, J. James, & D. Hart (Eds.), *Competence and character through life* (pp. 1–30). Chicago: University of Chicago Press.

Beauchamp, T. L., & Childress, J. F. (1994). *Principles of biomedical ethics* (4th ed.). New York: Oxford University Press.

Bebeau, M., Rest, J. R., & Narvaez, D. (1999). Beyond the promise: A framework for research in moral education. *Educational Researcher, 28*(4), 18–26.

Bebeau, M. J. (1994). Influencing the moral dimensions of dental practice. In J. Rest & D. Narvaez (Eds.), *Moral development in the professions* (pp. 121–146). Hillsdale, NJ: Erlbaum.

Bebeau, M. J. (2002). The defining issues test and the four component model: Contributions to professional education. *Journal of Moral Education, 31,* 271–295.

Bebeau, M. J., & Thoma, S. J. (1999). Intermediate concepts and the connection to moral education. *Educational Psychology Review, 11*(4), 343–360.

Beland, K. (2003a). Creating a caring school community: Vol. 4. A guide to Principle 4 of the eleven principles of effective character education. In K. Beland (Series Ed.), *Eleven principles sourcebook: How to achieve quality character education in K–12 schools.* Washington, DC: Character Education Partnership.

Beland, K. (2003b). Engaging families and community members: Vol. 10. A guide to Principle 10 of the eleven principles of effective character education. In K. Beland (Series Ed.), *Eleven principles sourcebook: How to achieve quality character education in K–12 schools.* Washington, DC: Character Education Partnership.

Beland, K. (Series Ed.). (2003c). *Eleven principles sourcebook: How to achieve quality character education in K–12 schools.* Washington, DC: Character Education Partnership.

Bennett, R. J., Aquino, K., Reed, A., II., & Thau, S. (in press). Morality, moral self-identity and employee deviance. In S. Fox & P. Spector (Eds.), *Differing perspectives on counter-productive behavior in organizations.* Washington, DC: American Psychological Association.

Bennett, W. J. (1980). The teacher, the curriculum and values education development. In M. L. McBee (Ed.), *New directions for higher education: Rethinking college responsibilities for values* (pp. 27–34). San Francisco: Jossey-Bass.

Benninga, J. (Ed.). (1991a). *Moral, character and civic education in the elementary school.* New York: Teachers College Press.

Benninga, J. (1991b). Synthesis and evaluation in moral and character education. In J. Benninga (Ed.), *Moral, character and civic education in the elementary school* (pp. 265–276). New York: Teachers College Press.

Benson, P. L., Leffert, N., Scales, P. C., & Blyth, D. A. (1998). Beyond the "village" rhetoric: Creating healthy communities for children and adolescents. *Applied Developmental Science, 2,* 138–159.

Benson, P. L., Scales, P. C., Leffert, N., & Roehlkepartain, E. C. (1999). *A fragile foundation: The state of developmental assets among American youth.* Minneapolis, MN: Search Institute.

Bergman, R. (2002). Why be moral? A conceptual model from a developmental psychology. *Human Development, 45,* 104–124.

Berkowitz, M. (2002). The science of character education. In W. Damon (Ed.), *Bringing in a new era in character education* (pp. 43–63). Stanford, CA: Hoover Institution Press.

Berkowitz, M., & Bier, M. (2004a). Research-based character education. *Annals of the American Academy of Political and Social Science, 391,* 72–85.

Berkowitz, M., & Bier, M. (2004b). *What works in character education: A research-driven guide for educators*. Washington, DC: Character Education Partnership.

Berkowitz, M., & Bier, M. (2005). The interpersonal roots of character education. In D. K. Lapsley & F. C. Power (Eds.), *Character psychology and character education*. Notre Dame, IN: University of Notre Dame Press.

Berkowitz, M. W., & Oser, F. (Eds.). (1985). *Moral education: Theory and application*. Hillsdale, NJ: Erlbaum.

Berliner, D. C. (1994a). Expertise: The wonder of exemplary performances. In J. N. Mangieri & C. C. Block (Eds.), *Creating powerful thinking in teachers and students* (pp. 161–186). Forth Worth, TX: Holt, Rinehart and Winston.

Berliner, D. C. (1994b). Teacher expertise. In B. Moon & A. S. Mayes (Eds.), *Teaching and learning in the secondary school*. London: Routledge/Open University.

Blasi, A. (1984). Moral identity: Its role in moral functioning. In W. M. Kurtines & J. J. Gewirtz (Eds.), *Morality, moral behavior and moral development* (pp. 128–139). New York: Wiley.

Blasi, A. (1985). The moral personality: Reflections for social science and education. In M. W. Berkowitz & F. Oser (Eds.), *Moral education: Theory and application* (pp. 433–443). New York: Wiley.

Blasi, A. (1990). How should psychologists define morality? Or the negative side effects of philosophy's influence on psychology. In T. Wren (Ed.), *The moral domain: Essays on the ongoing discussion between philosophy and the social sciences* (pp. 38–70). Cambridge, MA: MIT Press.

Blasi, A. (1995). Moral understanding and the moral personality: The process of moral integration. In W. Kurtines & J. L. Gewirtz (Eds.), *Moral development: An introduction* (pp. 229–253). Boston: Allyn & Bacon.

Blasi, A. (1999). Emotions and moral motivation. *Journal for the Theory of Social Behavior, 29*, 1–19.

Blasi, A. (2005). Moral character: A psychological approach. In D. K. Lapsley & F. C. Power (Eds.), *Character psychology and character education* (pp. 67–100). Notre Dame, IN: University of Notre Dame Press.

Brandenberger, J. (2005). College, character and social responsibility: Moral learning through experience. In D. K. Lapsley & F. C. Power (Eds.), *Character psychology and character education* (pp. 305–334). Notre Dame, IN: University of Notre Dame Press.

Bronfenbrenner, U. (1979). *The ecology of human development*. Cambridge, MA: Harvard University Press.

Brooks, B. D., & Goble, F. G. (1997). *The case for character education: The role of the school in teaching values and virtues*. Northridge, CA: Studio 4 Productions.

Brugman, D., Podolskij, A. J., Heymans, P. G., Boom, J., Karabanova, O., & Idobaeva, O. (2003). Perception of moral atmosphere in school and norm transgressive behavior in adolescents: An intervention study. *International Journal of Behavioral Development, 27*, 289–300.

Bryk, A. S. (1988). Musings on the moral life of schools. *American Journal of Education, 96*(2), 256–290.

Bryk, A. S., & Driscoll, M. (1988). *The school as community: Shaping forces and consequences for students and teachers*. Madison: University of Wisconsin, National Center for Effective Secondary Schools.

Bryk, A. S., Lee, V. E., & Holland, P. B. (1993). *Catholic schools and the common good*. Cambridge, MA: Harvard University Press.

Campbell, R. L., & Christopher, J. C. (1996). Moral development theory: A critique of its Kantian presuppositions. *Developmental Review, 16*, 1–47.

Campbell, R. L., Christopher, J. C., & Bickhard, M. H. (2002). Self and values: An interactionist foundation for moral development. *Theory and Psychology, 12*, 795–823.

Caprara, G. V., Barbanelli, C., Pastorelli, C., Bandura, A., & Zimbardo, P. G. (2000). Prosocial foundations of children's academic achievement. *Psychological Science, 11*, 302–306.

Carlo, G., Eisenberg, N., Troyer, D., Switzer, G., & Speer, A. L. (1991). The altruistic personality: In what contexts is it apparent? *Journal of Personality and Social Psychology, 61*, 450–458.

Carr, D. (1991). *Educating the virtues: An essay on the philosophical psychology of moral development and education*. London: Routledge.

Carr, D. (2003). Character and moral choice in the cultivation of virtue. *Philosophy, 78*, 219–232.

Carr, D., & Steutel, J. (Eds.). (1999). *Virtue ethics and moral education*. London: Routledge.

Catalano, R. F., Berglund, M. L., Ryan, J. A. M., Lonczak, S., & Hawkins, J. D. (2004). Positive youth development in the United States: Research findings on evaluations of positive youth development programs. *Annals of the American Academy of Political and Social Science, 591*, 98–124.

Catalano, R. F., Haggerty, K. P., Oesterle, S., Fleming, C. B., & Hawkins, J. D. (2004). The importance of bonding to school for healthy development: Findings from the Social Development Research Group. *Journal of School Health, 74*(7), 252–261.

Catalano, R. F., Hawkins, J. D., Berglund, M. L., Pollard, J. A., & Arthur, M. W. (2002). Prevention science and positive youth development: Competitive or cooperative frameworks. *Journal of Adolescent Health, 31*, 230–239.

Cervone, D. (1991). The two disciplines of personality psychology. *Psychological Science, 2*, 371–377.

Cervone, D. (2005). Personality architecture: Within-person structures and processes. *Annual Review of Psychology, 56*, 423–452.

Cervone, D., & Shoda, Y. (1999). Social-cognitive theories and the coherence of personality. In D. Cervone & Y. Shoda (Eds.), *The coherence of personality: Social-cognitive bases of consistency, variability and organization* (pp. 3–36). New York: Guilford Press.

Chapman, W. E. (1977). *Roots of character education: An exploration of the American heritage from the decade of the 1920s*. New York: Character Research Press.

Clayton, S., & Opotow, S. (Eds.). (2003). *Identity and the natural environment*. Cambridge, MA: MIT Press.

Colby, A., & Damon, W. (1992). *Some do care: Contemporary lives of moral commitment*. New York: Free Press.

Colby, A., & Damon, W. (1995). The development of extraordinary moral commitment. In M. Killen & D. Hart (Eds.), *Morality in everyday life: Developmental perspectives* (pp. 342–370). Cambridge, England: Cambridge University Press.

Colby, A., Ehrlich, T., Beaumont, E., & Stephens, J. (2003). *Educating citizens: Preparing America's undergraduates for lives of moral and civic responsibility*. San Francisco: Jossey-Bass.

Collaborative for Academic, Social, and Emotional Learning (CASEL). (2003). *Safe and sound: An educational leader's guide to evidence-based social and emotional learning programs*. Chicago: Author.

Cunningham, C. A. (2005). A certain and reasoned art: The rise and fall of character education in America. In D. K. Lapsley & F. C. Power (Ed.), *Character psychology and character education* (pp. 166–200). Notre Dame, IN: University of Notre Dame Press.

Damon, W., Menon, J., & Bronk, C. K. (2003). The development of purpose during adolescence. *Applied Developmental Science, 7,* 119–128.

Davidson, M. (2005). Harness the sun, channel the wind: The promise and pitfalls of character education in the 21st century. In D. K Lapsley & F. C. Power (Eds.), *Character psychology and character education* (pp. 218–244). Notre Dame, IN: University of Notre Dame Press.

DeVries, R., & Zan, B. (1994). *Moral classrooms, moral children: Creating a constructivist atmosphere in early education.* New York: Teachers College Press.

Dewey, J. (1908). *Moral principles in education.* Boston: Houghton Mifflin.

Dewey, J. (1938). *Experience and education.* New York: Macmillan.

Dewey, J., & Tufts, J. H. (1910). *Ethics.* New York: Henry Holt.

Duckett, L. (1994). Ethical education for nursing practice. In J. Rest & D. Narvaez (Eds.), *Moral development in the professions* (pp. 51–69). Mahwah, NJ: Erlbaum.

Durlak, J. A., & Wells, A. M. (1997). Primary prevention mental health programs for children and adolescents: A meta-analytic review. *American Journal of Community Psychology, 25,* 115–152.

Eisenberg, N., Guthrie, D. K., Cumberland, A., Murphy, B. C., Shepard, S. A., Zhou, Q., et al. (2002). Prosocial development in early adulthood: A longitudinal study. *Journal of Personality and Social Psychology, 82,* 993–1006.

Eisenberg, N., Guthrie, D. K., Murphy, B. C., Shepard, S. A., Cumberland, A., & Carlo, G. (1999). Consistency and development of prosocial dispositions: A longitudinal study. *Child Development, 70,* 1360–1372.

Elias, M. J., Zins, J. E., Graczyk, P. A., & Weissberg, R. P. (2003). Implementation, sustainability, and scaling up of social-emotional and academic innovations in public schools. *School Psychology Review, 32,* 303–319.

Elias, M. J., Zins, J. E., Weissberg, R. P., Greenberg, M. T., Haynes, N. M., Kessler, R., et al. (1997). *Promoting social and emotional learning: Guidelines for educators.* Alexandria, VA: Association for Supervision and Curriculum Development.

Emmons, R. A. (2002). Personal goals, life meaning, and virtue: Wellsprings of a positive life. In C. L. Keyes & J. Haidt (Eds.), *Flourishing: Positive psychology and the life well lived* (pp. 105–128). Washington, DC: American Psychological Association.

Ericsson, K. A., & Smith, J. (1991). *Toward a general theory of expertise.* Cambridge, England: Cambridge University Press.

Erikson, E. H. (1968). *Identity: Youth and crisis.* New York: Norton.

Etzioni, A. (1993). *The spirit of community: The reinvention of American society.* New York: Simon & Schuster.

Etzioni, A. (1996). *The new golden rule.* New York: Basic Books.

Featherstone, J. A. (1986). Foreword. In B. A. Kimball. *Orators and philosophers: A history of the idea of liberal education* (pp. ix–xiv). New York: Teachers College Press.

Fivush, R., Kuebli, J., & Chubb, P. A. (1992). The structure of event representations: A developmental analysis. *Child Development, 63,* 188–201.

Flanagan, C. (2004). Volunteerism, leadership, political socialization and civic engagement. In R. Lerner & L. Steinberg (Eds.), *Handbook of adolescent psychology* (2nd ed., pp. 721–746). New York: Wiley.

Flanagan, O. (1991). *The varieties of moral personality: Ethics and psychological realism.* Cambridge, MA: Harvard University Press.

Frankfurt, H. G. (1988). *The importance of what we care about.* New York: Cambridge University Press.

Fullan, M. (1999). *Change forces: The sequel.* London: Falmer Press.

Fullan, M. (2000). The return of large-scale reform. *Journal of Educational Change, 1,* 1–23.

Goodenow, C. (1993). The psychological sense of school membership among adolescents: Scale development and educational correlates. *Psychology in the Schools, 30,* 79–90.

Goodlad, J. (1992). The moral dimensions of schooling and teacher education. *Journal of Moral Education, 21*(2), 87–98.

Goodman, J. F., & Lesnick, H. (2001). *The moral stake in education: Contested premises and practices.* New York: Longman.

Gottfredson, G., & Gottfredson, D. (1985). *Victimization in schools.* New York: Plenum Press.

Graczyk, P. A., Matjasko, J. L., Weissberg, R. P., Greenberg, M. T., Elias, M. J., & Zins, J. E. (2000). The role of the Collaborative to Advance Social and Emotional Learning (CASEL) in supporting the implementation of quality school-based prevention programs. *Journal of Educational and Psychological Consultation, 11,* 3–6.

Greenberg, M. T., & Kusche, C. A. (1998). *Promoting alternative thinking strategies: Blueprint for violence prevention* (Book 10). Boulder: University of Colorado, Institute for the Behavioral Sciences.

Greenberg, M. T., Kusche, C. A., Cook, E. T., & Quamma, J. P. (1995). Promoting emotional competence in school-aged children: The effects of the PATHS curriculum. *Development and Psychopathology, 7,* 117–136.

Greenberg, M. T., Weissberg, R. P., O'Brien, M. U., Zins, J. E., Fredericks, L., Resnick, H., et al. (2003). Enhancing school-based prevention and youth development through coordinated social, emotional and academic learning. *American Psychologist, 58,* 466–474.

Guttman, A. (1987). *Democratic education.* Princeton, NJ: Princeton University Press.

Hamre, B. K., & Pianta, R. C. (2001). Early teacher-child relationships and the trajectory of children's school outcomes through eighth grade. *Child Development, 72,* 625–638.

Hansen, D. T. (1993). From role to person: The moral layeredness of classroom teaching. *American Educational Research Journal, 30,* 651–674.

Hanson, D. M., Larson, R. W., & Dworkin, J. B. (2003). What adolescents learn in organized youth activities: A survey of self reported developmental experiences. *Journal of Research on Adolescence, 13,* 25–55.

Hardy, S., & Carlo, G. (2005). Moral identity theory and research: An update with directions for the future. *Human Development, 48,* 232–256

Hart, D. (2005). The development of moral identity. *Nebraska Symposium on Motivation, 51,* 165–196.

Hart, D., Atkins, R., & Ford, D. (1998). Urban America as a context for the development of moral identity. *Journal of Social Issues, 54,* 513–530.

Hart, D., & Fegley, S. (1995). Prosocial behavior and caring in adolescence: Relations to self-understanding and social judgment. *Child Development, 66,* 1346–1359.

Hart, D., Yates, M., Fegley, S., & Wilson, G. (1995). Moral commitment in inner-city adolescents. In M. Killen & D. Hart (Eds.), *Morality in everyday life: Developmental perspectives* (pp. 317–341). New York: Cambridge University Press.

Hartshorne, H., & May, M. A. (1928). *Studies in the nature of character: Vol. 1. Studies in deceit.* New York: Macmillan.

Hartshorne, H., & May, M. A. (1929). *Studies in the nature of character: Vol. 2. Studies in self-control.* New York: Macmillan.

Hartshorne, H., & May, M. A. (1930). *Studies in the nature of character: Vol. 3. Studies in the organization of character.* New York: Macmillan.

Hartwell, S. (1990). Moral development, ethical conduct and clinical education. *New York Law School Review, 107,* 505–539.

Hassin, R. R., Uleman, J. S., & Bargh, J. A. (Eds.). (2005). *The new unconscious.* New York: Oxford University Press.

Hawkins, D. J., Catalano, R. F., Kosterman, R., Abbott, R., & Hill, K. G. (1999). Preventing adolescent health-risk behavior by strengthening protection during childhood. *Archives of Pediatrics and Adolescent Medicine, 153,* 226–234.

Hawkins, D. J., Guo, J., Hill, G., Battin-Pearson, S., & Abbott, R. D. (2001). Long-term effects of the Seattle Social Development intervention on school bonding trajectories. *Applied Developmental Science, 5,* 225–236.

Hay, D. F., Castle, J., Stimson, C. A., & Davies, L. (1995). The social construction of character in toddlerhood. In M. Killen & D. Hart (Eds.), *Morality in everyday life: Developmental perspectives* (pp. 23–51). Cambridge, England: Cambridge University Press.

Hilles, W. S., & Kahle, L. R. (1985). Social contract and social integration in adolescent development. *Journal of Personality and Social Psychology, 49,* 1114–1121.

Hogarth, R. M. (2001). *Educating intuition.* Chicago: University of Chicago Press.

Howard, S., Dryden, J., & Johnson, B. (1999). Childhood resilience: Review and critique of literature. *Oxford Review of Education, 25*(3), 307–323.

Hursthouse, R. (1999). *On virtue ethics.* Oxford: Oxford University Press.

Hursthouse, R. (2003). Normative virtue ethics. In S. Darwall (Ed.), *Virtue ethics* (pp. 184–202). Oxford: Blackwell.

Jackson; P. W. (1986). *The practice of teaching.* New York: Teachers College Press.

Jackson, P. W., Boostrom, R. E., & Hansen, D. T. (1993). *The moral life of schools.* San Francisco: Jossey-Bass.

Kent, B. (1999). Moral growth and the unity of the virtues. In D. Carr & J. Steutel (Eds.), *Virtue ethics and moral education* (pp. 109–124). London: Routledge.

Kimball, B. A. (1986). *Orators and philosophers: A history of the idea of liberal education.* New York: Teachers College Press.

Knight Higher Education Collaborative. (2000). Disputed territories. *Policy Perspectives, 9*(4), 1–8.

Kochanska, G. (1993). Toward a synthesis of parental socialization and child temperament in early development of conscience. *Child Development, 64,* 325–347.

Kochanska, G. (1995). Children's temperament, mothers' discipline and security of attachment: Multiple pathways to emerging internalization. *Child Development, 66,* 597–615.

Kochanska, G. (1997). Multiple pathways to conscience for children with different temperaments: From toddlerhood to age 5. *Developmental Psychology, 33,* 228–240.

Kochanska, G. (2002). Committed compliance, moral self, and internalization: A mediational model. *Developmental Psychology, 38,* 339–351.

Kochanska, G., Aksan, N., Knaack, A., & Rhines, H. M. (2004). Maternal parenting and children's conscience: Early security as moderator. *Child Development, 75,* 1229–1242.

Kochanska, G., Aksan, N., & Koenig, A. L. (1995). A longitudinal study of the roots of preschoolers' conscience: Committed compliance and emerging internalization. *Child Development, 66*(6), 1752–1769.

Kochanska, G., Aksan, N., & Nichols, K. E. (2003). Maternal power assertion in discipline and moral discourse contexts: Commonalities, differences and implications for children's moral conduct and cognition. *Developmental Psychology, 39,* 949–963.

Kochanska, G., & Thompson, R. (1997). The emergence and development of conscience in toddlerhood and early childhood. In J. E. Grusec & L. Kuczynski (Eds.), *Parenting and children's internalization of values* (pp. 53–77). New York: Wiley.

Kohlberg, L. (1969). Stage and sequence: The cognitive-developmental approach to socialization. In D. Goslin (Ed.), *Handbook of socialization theory and research* (pp. 347–480). Chicago: Rand McNally.

Kohlberg, L. (1971). From is to ought: How to commit the naturalistic fallacy and get away with it in the study of moral development. In T. Mischel (Ed.), *Cognitive development and epistemology* (pp. 151–284). New York: Academic Press.

Kohlberg, L. (1973). The claim to moral adequacy of the highest stage of moral development. *Journal of Philosophy, 70,* 630–646.

Kohlberg, L. (1987). The development of moral judgment and moral action. In L. Kohlberg (Ed.), *Child psychology and childhood education* (pp. 259–328). New York: Longman.

Kohlberg, L., & Mayer, R. (1972). Development as the aim of education. *Harvard Educational Review, 42,* 449–496.

Kohn, A. (1997, February). How not to teach values: A critical look at character education. *Phi Delta Kappan,* 429–439.

Kupperman, J. (1999). Virtues, character, and moral dispositions. In D. Carr & J. Steutel (Eds.), *Virtue ethics and moral education* (pp. 199–209). London: Routledge.

Lantieri, L., & Patti, J. (1996). *Waging peace in our schools.* New York: Beacon Press.

Lapsley, D. K. (1996). *Moral psychology.* Boulder, CO: Westview Press.

Lapsley, D. K. (2005). Moral stage theory. In M. Killen & J. Smetana (Eds.), *Handbook of moral development* (pp. 37–66). Mahwah, NJ: Erlbaum.

Lapsley, D. K., & Lasky, B. (1999). Prototypic moral character. *Identity, 1,* 345–363.

Lapsley, D. K., & Narvaez, D. (2004). A social cognitive approach to the moral personality. In D. K. Lapsley & D. Narvaez (Eds.), *Moral development, self and identity: Essays in honor of Augusto Blasi* (pp. 191–214). Mahwah, NJ: Erlbaum.

Lapsley, D. K., & Narvaez, D. (2005). Moral psychology at the crossroads. In D. K. Lapsley & F. C. Power (Eds.), *Character psychology and character education* (pp. 18–35). Notre Dame, IN: University of Notre Dame Press.

Lapsley, D. K., & Power, F. C. (Eds.). (2005). *Character psychology and character education.* Notre Dame, IN: University of Notre Dame Press.

Larson, R. W. (2000). Toward a psychology of positive youth development. *American Psychologist, 55,* 170–183.

Laud, L., & Berkowitz, M. (1999). Challenges in evaluating character education programs. *Journal of Research in Education, 9,* 66–72.

Leming, J. S. (1997). Research and practice in character education: A historical perspective. In A. Molnar (Ed.), *The construction of children's character: Ninety-sixth yearbook of the National Society for the Study of Education* (pp. 11–44). Chicago: National Society for the Study of Education and the University of Chicago Press.

Lerner, R. M. (1991). Changing organism-context relations as the basic process of development: A developmental contextual perspective. *Developmental Psychology, 27,* 27–32.

Lerner, R. M. (2001). Promoting promotion in the development of prevention science. *Applied Developmental Science, 5,* 254–257.

Lerner, R. M. (2002). *Adolescence: Development, diversity, context and application.* Upper Saddle River, NJ: Prentice-Hall.

Lerner, R. M., Dowling, E. M., & Anderson, P. M. (2003). Positive youth development: Thriving as a basis of personhood and civil society. *Applied Developmental Science, 7,* 172–180.

Lerner, R. M., Fisher, C. B., & Weinberg, R. A. (2000). Toward a science for and of the people: Promoting civil society through the application of developmental science. *Child Development, 71,* 11–20.

Libby, H. P. (2004). Measuring student relationship to school: Attachment, bonding, connectedness and engagement. *Journal of School Health, 74,* 274–283.

Lickona, T. (1991a). *Educating for character: How our schools can teach respect and responsibility.* New York: Bantam.

Lickona, T. (1991b). An integrated approach to character development in elementary schools. In J. Benninga (Ed.), *Moral, character and civic education in the elementary school* (pp. 67–83). New York: Teachers College Press.

Lickona, T. (1992). Character development in the elementary school classroom. In K. Ryan & T. Lickona (Eds.), *Character development in schools and beyond* (2nd ed., pp. 141–162). Washington, DC: Council for Research in Values and Education.

Lickona, T. (1997). Educating for character: A comprehensive approach. In A. Molnar (Ed.), *The construction of children's character* (pp. 45–62). Chicago: University of Chicago Press.

Lickona, T. (2004). *Character matters.* New York: Touchstone.

Lickona, T., & Davidson, M. (2004). *Smart and good high schools: Developing excellence and ethics for success in school, work and beyond.* Cortland, NY: Center for the 4th and 5th Rs (Respect and Responsibility).

Lickona, T., Schaps, E., & Lewis, C. (2003). *The eleven principles of effective character education.* Washington, DC: Character Education Partnership.

MacIntrye, A. (1981). *After virtue.* Notre Dame, IN: University of Notre Dame Press.

Maddox, S. J., & Prinz, R. J. (2003). School bonding in children and adolescents: Conceptualization, assessment and associated variables. *Clinical Child and Family Psychology Review, 6,* 31–49.

Markus, G. B., Howard, J. P. F., & King, D. C. (1993). Integrating community service and classroom instruction enhances learning: Results from an experiment. *Educational Evaluation and Policy Analysis, 15,* 410–419.

Marshall, S. P. (1995). *Schemas in problem solving.* Cambridge, England: Cambridge University Press.

Masten, A. S. (2003). Commentary: Developmental psychopathology as a unifying context for mental health and education models, research and practice in schools. *School Psychology Review, 32,* 169–173.

Matsuba, K., & Walker, L. (2004). Extraordinary moral commitment: Young adults working for social organizations. *Journal of Personality, 72,* 413–436.

McClellan, B. W. (1999). *Moral education in America: Schools and the shaping of character from colonial times to the present.* New York: Teachers College Press.

McKinnon, C. (1999). *Character, virtue theories, and the vices.* Toronto, Canada: Broadview Press.

McNeel, S. (1994). College teaching and student moral development. In J. R. Rest & D. Narvaez (Eds.), *Moral development in the pro-fessions: Psychology and applied ethics* (pp. 27–50). Hillsdale, NJ: Erlbaum.

Melchior, A. L., & Bailis, L. N. (2002). Impact of service-learning on civic attitudes and behaviors of middle and high school youth: Findings from three national evaluations. In A. Furco & S. H. Billig (Eds.), *Service learning: Essence of the pedagogy* (pp. 201–222). Greenwich, CT: Information Age Publishing.

Mentkowski, M., & Associates. (2000). *Learning that lasts: Integrating learning, development, and performance in college and beyond.* San Francisco: Jossey-Bass.

Mischel, W. (1968). *Personality and assessment.* New York: Wiley.

Mischel, W. (1990). Personality dispositions revisited and revised: A view after 3 decades. In L. Pervin (Ed.), *Handbook of personality: Theory and research* (pp. 111–134). New York: Guilford Press.

Mischel, W. (1999). Personality coherence and dispositions in a cognitive-affective personality system (CAP) approach. In D. Cervone & Y. Shoda (Eds.), *The coherence of personality: Social cognitive bases of consistency, variability and organization* (pp. 37–60). New York: Guilford Press.

Mischel, W. (2005). Toward an integrative science of the person. *Annual Review of Psychology, 55,* 55–122.

Mischel, W., & Shoda, Y. (1995). A cognitive-affective system theory of personality: Reconceptualizing situations, dispositions, dynamics and invariance in personality structure. *Psychological Review, 102,* 246–268.

Mischel, W., Shoda, Y., & Mendoza-Denton, R. (2002). Situation-behavior profile as a locus of consistency in personality. *Current Directions in Psychological Science, 11,* 50–55.

Mucherah, W., Lapsley, D. K., Miels, J., & Horton, M. (2004). An intervention to improve socio-moral climate in elementary school classrooms: An evaluation of Don't Laugh at Me. *Journal of Research on Character Education, 2,* 45–58.

Mullen, G., Turner, J., & Narvaez, D. (2005, April). *Student perceptions of climate influence character and motivation.* Paper presented at the annual meeting of the American Education Research Association, Montreal, Canada.

Murphy, M. M. (1998). *Character education in America's Blue Ribbon schools: Best practices for meeting the challenge.* Lancaster, PA: Technomic.

Narvaez, D. (2005a). Integrative ethical education. In M. Killen & J. Smetana (Eds.), *Handbook of moral development* (pp. 703–733). Mahwah, NJ: Erlbaum.

Narvaez, D. (2005b). The neo-Kohlbergian tradition and beyond: Schemas, expertise and character. In C. Pope-Edwards & G. Carlo (Eds.), *Nebraska Symposium Conference papers* (Vol. 51, pp. 119–163). Lincoln: University of Nebraska Press.

Narvaez, D., Bock, T., & Endicott, L. (2003). Who should I become? Citizenship, goodness, human flourishing, and ethical expertise. In W. Veugelers & F. K. Oser (Eds.), *Teaching in moral and democratic education* (pp. 43–63). Bern, Switzerland: Peter Lang.

Narvaez, D., Bock, T., Endicott, L., & Lies, J. (2004). Minnesota's community voices and character education project. *Journal of Research in Character Education, 2,* 89–112.

Narvaez, D., & Lapsley, D. K. (2005). The psychological foundation of moral expertise. In D. K. Lapsley & F. C. Power (Eds.), *Character psychology and character education* (pp. 140–165). Notre Dame, IN: University of Notre Dame Press.

Narvaez, D., Lapsley, D. K., Hagele, S., & Lasky, B. (in press). Moral chronicity and social information processing: Tests of a social cognitive approach to the moral personality. *Journal of Research in Personality.*

Narvaez, D., & Rest, J. (1995). The four components of acting morally. In W. Kurtines & J. Gewirtz (Eds.), *Moral behavior and moral development: An introduction* (pp. 385–400). New York: McGraw-Hill.

Nash, T. (1997). *Answering the virtuecrats: A moral conversation on character education.* New York: Teachers College Press.

Nelson, K., & Gruendel, J. (1981). Generalized event representations: Basic building blocks of cognitive development. In M. Lamb & A. Brown (Eds.), *Advances in developmental psychology* (pp. 131–158). Hillsdale, NJ: Erlbaum.

Newmann, F., & Wehlage, G. (1995). *Successful school restructuring.* Madison: University of Wisconsin, Center on Organization and Restructuring of Schools.

Nicgorski, W., & Ellrod, F. E., III. (1992). Moral character. In G. F. McLean & F. E. Ellrod (Eds.), *Philosophical foundations for moral education and character development: Act and agent* (pp. 142–162). Washington, DC: Council for Research in Values and Philosophy.

Noddings, N. (2002). *Educating moral people.* New York: Teachers College Press.

Nucci, L. P. (Ed.). (1989). *Moral development and character education: A dialogue.* Berkeley, CA: McCutcheon.

Nucci, L. (2001). *Education in the moral domain.* Cambridge, England: Cambridge University Press.

Nussbaum, M. (1988). Non-relative virtues: An Aristotelian approach. *Midwest Studies in Philosophy, 13,* 32–53.

Oman, R. F., Vesely, S., Aspy, C. B., McLeroy, K. R., Rodine, S., & Marshall, L. (2004). The potential protective effect of youth assets on adolescent alcohol and drug use. *American Journal of Public Health, 94,* 1425–1430.

Pancer, S. M., & Pratt, M. W. (1999). Social and family determinants of community service involvement in Canadian youth. In M. Yates & J. Youniss (Eds.), *Community service and civic engagement in youth: International perspectives* (pp. 32–55). Cambridge, England: Cambridge University Press.

Pankake, A. M., & Moller, G. (2003). Overview of professional learning communities. In J. B. Huffman & K. K. Hipp (Eds.), *Reculturing schools as professional learning communities* (pp. 3–14). Lanham, MD: Scarecrow Press.

Pascarella, E. T., & Terenzini, P. (1991). *How college affects students: Findings and insights from 20 years of research.* San Francisco: Jossey-Bass.

Pascarella, E. T., & Terenzini, P. (2005). *How college affects students: Vol. 2. A third decade of research.* San Francisco: Jossey-Bass.

Payne, A. A., Gottfredson, D. C., & Gottfredson, G. D. (2003). Schools as communities: The relationship among communal school organization, student bonding and school disorder. *Criminology, 41*(3), 749–776.

Payton, J. W., Wardlaw, D. M., Graczyk, P. A., Bloodworth, M. R., Tompsett, C. J., & Weissberg, R. P. (2000). Social and emotional learning: A framework for promoting mental health and reducing risk behavior in children and youth. *Journal of School Health, 70,* 179–185.

Penn, W. (1990). Teaching ethics—A direct approach. *Journal of Moral Education, 19*(2), 124–138.

Peters, R. S. (1981). *Moral development and moral education.* London: Allen & Unwin.

Peterson, C., & Seligman, M. (2004). *Character strengths and virtues: A classification and handbook.* Washington, DC: American Psychological Association.

Power, F. C., Higgins, A., & Kohlberg, L. (1989a). The habit of the common life: Building character through democratic community schools. In L. Nucci (Ed.), *Moral development and character education: A dialogue* (pp. 125–143). Berkeley, CA: McCutchan.

Power, F. C., Higgins A., & Kohlberg, L. (1989b). *Lawrence Kohlberg's approach to moral education.* New York: Columbia University Press.

Pratt, M. W., Hunsberger, B., Pancer, M., & Alisat, S. (2003). A longitudinal analysis of personal values socialization: Correlates of moral self-ideal in late adolescence. *Social Development, 12,* 563–585.

Pritchard, I. (2002). Community service and service-learning in America: The state of the art. In A. Furco & S. H. Billig (Eds.), *Service learning: The essence of the pedagogy* (pp. 3–20). Greenwich, CT: Information Age Press.

Puka, B. (2004). Altruism and character. In D. Lapsley & D. Narvaez (Eds.), *Moral development, self and identity: Essays in honor of Augusto Blasi* (pp. 163–190). Mahwah, NJ: Erlbaum.

Punzo, V. A. (1996). After Kohlberg: Virtue ethics and the recovery of the moral self. *Philosophical Psychology, 9,* 7–23.

Reed, A., II., & Aquino, K. (2003). Moral identity and the expanding circle of moral regard towards outgroups. *Journal of Personality and Social Psychology, 84,* 1270–1286.

Rest, J. (1983). Morality. In P. H. Mussen (Series Ed.), J. Flavell & E. Markman (Vol. Eds.), *Handbook of child psychology: Vol. 3. Cognitive development* (4th ed., pp. 556–629). New York: Wiley.

Rest, J., & Narvaez, D. (1991). The college experience and moral development. In W. Kurtines & J. Gewirtz (Eds.), *Handbook of moral behavior and development* (pp. 229–245). Hillsdale, NJ: Erlbaum.

Rest, J., & Narvaez, D. (1994). *Moral development in the professions.* Mahwah, NJ: Erlbaum.

Rogers, G. (2002). Rethinking moral growth in college and beyond. *Journal of Moral Education, 31,* 325–338.

Rorty, A. O. (1988). Virtues and their vicissitudes. *Midwest Studies in Philosophy, 13,* 136–148.

Roth, J., Brooks-Gunn, J., Murray, L., & Foster, W. (1998). Promoting healthy adolescents: Synthesis of youth development program evaluations. *Journal of Research on Adolescence, 8,* 423–459.

Roth, J. L., & Brooks-Gunn, J. (2003). What exactly is a youth development program? Answers from research and practice. *Applied Developmental Science, 7,* 94–111.

Rule, J. T., & Bebeau, M. J. (2005). *Dentists who care: Inspiring stories of professional commitment.* Chicago: Quintessence.

Ryan, K. (1989). In defense of character education. In L. P. Nucci (Ed.), *Moral development and character education: A dialogue* (pp. 3–18). Berkeley, CA: McCutcheon.

Ryan, K., & Bohlin, K. E. (1999). *Building character in schools: Practical ways to bring moral instruction to life.* San Francisco: Jossey-Bass.

Ryan, K., & Lickona, T. (Eds.). (1992). *Character development in schools and beyond.* Washington, DC: Council for Research in Values and Philosophy.

Ryle, G. (1972). Can virtue be taught? In R. F. Dearden, P. H. Hirst, & R. S. Peters (Eds.), *Education and the development of reason* (pp. 434–447). London: Routledge & Kegan Paul.

Scales, P. C. (1999). Reducing risks and building developmental assets: Essential actions for promoting adolescent health. *Journal of School Health, 69,* 113–119.

Scales, P. C., Blyth, D. A., Berkas, T. H., & Kielsmeier, J. C. (2000). The effects of service learning on middle school students' social responsibility and academic success. *Journal of Early Adolescence, 20,* 332–358.

Scales, P. C., & Leffert, N. (1999). *Developmental assets: A synthesis of the scientific research on adolescent development.* Minneapolis, MN: Search Institute.

Schaps, E., Battistich, V., & Solomon, D. (1997). School as a caring community: A key to character education. In A. Molnar (Ed.), *The construction of children's character: Pt. 2. Ninety-sixth yearbook of the National Society for the Study of Education* (pp. 127–139). Chicago: University of Chicago Press.

Schwartz, A. J., & Templeton, J. M., Jr. (1997). The Templeton honor roll. *Educational Record, 78,* 95–99.

Sebring, P. B. (1996). (Ed.). *Charting school reform in Chicago: The students speak.* Chicago: Consortium on Chicago School Research.

Self, D., Baldwin, D. C., Jr., & Olivarez, M. (1993). Teaching medical ethics to first year students by using film discussion to develop their moral reasoning. *Academic Medicine, 68*(5), 383–385.

Seligman, M. E. P., & Csikszentmihalyi, M. (2000). Positive psychology: An introduction. *American Psychologist, 55,* 5–14.

Sherman, N. (1999). Character development and Aristotelian virtue. In D. Carr & J. Steutel (Eds.), *Virtue ethics and moral education* (pp. 35–48). London: Routledge.

Shields, D. L., & Bredemeier, B. L. (2005). Can sports build character? In D. K. Lapsley & F. C. Power (Eds.), *Character psychology and character education* (pp. 121–139). Notre Dame, IN: University of Notre Dame Press.

Shoda, Y., Mischel, W., & Wright, J. (1994). Interindividual stability in the organization and patterning of behavior: Incorporating psychological situations into the idiographic analysis of personality. *Journal of Personality and Social Psychology, 67,* 674–688.

Shulman, L. S. (1987). Knowledge and teaching: Foundations of the new reform. *Harvard Educational Review, 57,* 1–22.

Skinner, D., & Chapman, C. (1999). *Service learning and community service in K–12 public schools* (Publication No. 1999043). Washington, DC: National Center for Educational Statistics.

Solomon, D., Watson, M., & Battistich, V. (2002). Teaching and schooling effects on moral/prosocial development. In V. Richardson (Ed.), *Handbook of research on teaching* (pp. 566–603). Washington, DC: American Educational Research Association.

Solomon, D., Watson, M., Battistich, V., Schaps, E., & Delucchi, K. (1992). Creating a caring community: Educational practices that promote children's prosocial development. In F. K. Oser, A. Dick, & J.-L. Patry (Eds.), *Effective and responsible teaching: The new synthesis* (pp. 383–396). San Francisco: Jossey-Bass.

Solomon, D., Watson, M., Battistich, V., Schaps, E., & Delucchi, K. (1996). Creating classrooms that students experience as communities. *American Journal of Community Psychology, 24,* 719–748.

Solomon, D., Watson, M., Delucchi, K., Schaps, E., & Battistich, V. (1988). Enhancing children's prosocial behavior in the classroom. *American Educational Research Journal, 25,* 527–554.

Solomon, D., Watson, Schaps, E., Battistich, V., & Solomon, J. (1990). Cooperative learning as part of a comprehensive program designed to promote prosocial development. In S. Sharan (Ed.), *Cooperative learning: Theory and research* (pp. 231–260). New York: Praeger.

Spiecker, B. (1999). Habituation and training in early moral upbringing. In D. Carr & J. Steutel (Eds.), *Virtue ethics and moral education* (pp. 210–223). London: Routledge.

Sprinthall, N. (1994). Counseling and social role taking: Promoting moral and ego development. In J. R. Rest & D. Narvaez (Eds.), *Moral development in the professions: Psychology and applied ethics* (pp. 85–100). Hillsdale, NJ: Erlbaum.

Staudinger, U. M., & Pasupathi, M. (2003). Correlates of wisdom-related performance in adolescence and adulthood: Age-graded differences in "paths" toward desirable development. *Journal of Research on Adolescence, 13,* 239–268.

Sternberg, R. (1998, April). Abilities and expertise. *Educational Researcher,* 10–37.

Sternberg, R. J. (1998). A balance theory of wisdom. *Review of General Psychology, 2,* 347–365.

Sternberg, R. J., & Horvath, J. A. (1995). A prototype view of expert teaching. *Educational Researcher, 24,* 9–17.

Steutel, J. (1997). The virtue approach to moral education: Some conceptual clarifications. *Journal of the Philosophy of Education, 31,* 395–407.

Steutel, J., & Carr, D. (1999). Virtue ethics and the virtue approach to moral education. In D. Carr & J. Steutel (Eds.), *Virtue ethics and moral education* (pp. 3–17). London: Routledge.

Steutel, J., & Spiecker, B. (2004). Cultivating sentimental dispositions through Aristotelian habituation. *Journal of the Philosophy of Education, 38*(4), 531–549.

Strike, K. (1996). The moral responsibilities of educators. In J. Sikula, T. Buttery, & E. Grifton (Eds.), *Handbook of research on teacher education* (2nd ed., pp. 869–882). New York: Macmillan.

Stukas, A. A., Clary, G. E., & Snyder, M. (1999). Service learning: Who benefits and why? *Social Policy Report: Society for Research in Child Development, 13,* 1–19.

Sweeney, C. (1997). *Honor roll for character-building colleges: 1997–1998.* Radnor, PA: John Templeton Foundation.

Thompson, R. A. (1998). Early sociopersonality development. In W. Damon (Editor-in-Chief) & N. Eisenberg (Vol. Ed.), *Handbook of child psychology: Vol. 3. Social, emotional and personality development* (pp. 25–104). New York: Wiley.

Tobler, N. S., Roona, M. R., Ochshorn, P., Marshall, D. G., Streke, A. V., & Stackpole, K. M. (2000). School-based adolescent drug prevention programs: 1998 meta-analysis. *Journal of Primary Prevention, 20*(4), 275–335.

Tolman, J. (2003). *Providing opportunities for moral action: A guide to Principle 5 of the eleven principles of effective character education.* Washington, DC: Character Education Partnership.

Urmson, J. O. (1988). *Aristotle's ethics.* Oxford: Blackwell.

Walker, L. J. (2002). Moral exemplarity. In W. Damon (Ed.), *Bringing in a new era in character education* (pp. 65–83). Stanford, CA: Hoover Institution Press.

Walker, L. J. (2004). Gus in the gap: Bridging the judgment-action gap in moral functioning. In D. K. Lapsley & D. Narvaez (Eds.), *Moral development, self and identity* (pp. 1–20). Mahwah, NJ: Erlbaum.

Walker, L. J., & Hennig, K. H. (1998). Moral functioning in the broader context of personality. In S. Hala (Ed.), *The development of social cognition* (pp. 297–327). East Sussex, England: Psychology Press.

Walker, L. J., & Hennig, K. H. (2004). Differing conceptions of moral exemplarity: Just, brave and caring. *Journal of Personality and Social Psychology, 86,* 629–647.

Walker, L. J., & Pitts, R. C. (1998). Naturalistic conceptions of moral maturity. *Developmental Psychology, 34,* 403–419.

Walker, L. J., Pitts, R. C., Hennig, K. H., & Matsuba, M. K. (1995). Reasoning about morality and real-life moral problems. In M. Killen & D. Hart (Eds.), *Morality in everyday life: Developmental perspectives* (pp. 371–408). Cambridge, England: Cambridge University Press.

Warter, E. H., & Grossman, J. M. (2002). An application of developmental contextualism to service learning. In A. Furco & S. H. Billig (Eds.), *Service learning: The essence of pedagogy* (pp. 83–102). Greenwich, CT: Information Age Publishing.

Waterman, A. J. (Ed.). (1997). *Service learning: Applications from the research*. Mahwah, NJ: Erlbaum.

Watson, G. (1990). The primacy of character. In O. J. Flanagan & A. Rorty (Eds.), *Identity, character and morality* (pp. 449–470). Cambridge, MA: MIT Press.

Watson, M. (with L. Ecken). (2003). *Learning to trust: Transforming difficult elementary classrooms through developmental discipline*. San Francisco: Jossey-Bass.

Watson, M., Battistich, V., & Solomon, D. (1997). Enhancing students' social and ethical development in schools: An intervention program and its effects. *International Journal of Educational Research, 27*, 571–586.

Weissberg, R. P., & Greenberg, M. T. (1998). Social and community competence-enhancement and prevention programs. In W. Damon (Editor-in-Chief) & I. E. Sigel & A. K. Renniger (Vol. Eds.), *Handbook of child psychology: Vol. 5. Child psychology in practice* (5th ed., pp. 877–954). New York: Wiley.

Weissberg, R. P., & O'Brien, M. U. (2004). What works in school-based social and emotional learning programs for positive youth development. *Annals of the American Academy of Political and Social Science, 591*, 86–97.

Welsh, W., Greene, J., & Jenkins, P. (Eds.). (1999). School disorder: The influence of individual, institutional and community factors. *Criminology, 37*, 73–115.

Williams, M. M., & Schaps, E. (1999). *Character education: The foundation for teacher education*. Washington, DC: Character Education Partnership.

Wilson, D. B., Gottfredson, D. C., & Najaka, S. S. (2001). School-based prevention of problem behaviors: A meta-analysis. *Journal of Quantitative Psychology, 17*, 171–247.

Wilson, S. M., Shulman, L. S., & Richert, A. E. (1987). "150 different ways" of knowing: Representations of knowledge in teaching. In J. Calderhead (Ed.), *Exploring teachers' thinking* (pp. 104–124). London: Cassell Education Limited.

Wittgenstein, L. (1968). *Philosophical investigations* (3rd ed.). New York: Macmillan.

Wright, J. C., & Mischel, W. (1987). A conditional approach to dispositional constructs: The local predictability of social behavior. *Journal of Personality and Social Psychology, 53*, 1159–1177.

Wynne, E. A. (1991). Character and academics in the elementary school. In J. Benninga (Ed.), *Moral, character and civic education in the elementary school* (pp. 139–155). New York: Teachers College Press.

Wynne, E. A., & Hess, M. (1992). Trends in American youth character development. In K. Ryan & T. Lickona (Eds.), *Character development in schools and beyond* (pp. 29–48). Washington, DC: Council for Research in Values and Philosophy.

Wynne, E. A., & Ryan, K. (1997). *Reclaiming our schools: Teaching character, academics and discipline* (2nd ed.). Upper Saddle River, NJ: Merrill.

Yates, M., & Youniss, J. (1996a). Community service and political-moral identity in adolescence. *Journal of Research on Adolescence, 6*, 271–284.

Yates, M., & Youniss, J. (1996b). A developmental perspective on community service in adolescence. *Social Development, 5*, 85–111.

Yates, M., & Youniss, J. (Eds.). (1999). *Roots of civic identity: International perspectives on community service and activism in youth*. Cambridge, England: Cambridge University Press.

Youniss, J., McLellan, J. A., Su, Y., & Yates, M. (1999). The role of community service in identity development: Normative, unconventional and deviant orientations. *Journal of Adolescent Research, 14*, 248–261.

Youniss, J., McLellan, J. A., & Yates, M. (1997). What we know about engendering civic identity. *American Behavioral Scientist, 40*, 620–631.

Youniss, J., & Yates, M. (1997). *Community service and social responsibility in youth*. Chicago: University of Chicago Press.

Youniss, J., & Yates, M. (1999). Youth service and moral-civic identity: A case for everyday morality. *Educational Psychology Review, 11*(4), 361–376.

Zimmerman, B. J. (2000). Attaining self-regulation: A social-cognitive perspective. In M. Boekaerts, P. R. Pintrich, & M. Zeidner (Eds.), *Handbook of self-regulation* (pp. 13–39). San Diego: Academic Press.

Zimmerman, B. J., Bonner, S., & Kovach, R. (1996). *Developing Self-Regulated Learners: Beyond Achievement to Self-Efficacy*. Washington, DC: American Psychological Association.

CHAPTER 8

Learning Environments

PHYLLIS C. BLUMENFELD, RONALD W. MARX, and CHRISTOPHER J. HARRIS

The term "learning environments" is used in many fields, including education, architecture, and psychology. Although definitions vary, most agree that learning environments encompass the learner, the context, and the content of tasks. The concept of learning environments in education has become more prevalent as theories of learning have evolved (Bransford, Brown, & Cocking, 2000; De Corte, Verschaffel, Entwistle, & van Merriënboer, 2003; Jonassen & Land, 2000; Schauble & Glaser, 1996). Recent theories emphasize that understanding results from active construction by the learner.

One type of learning environment, based on cognitive psychology, focuses on helping students accomplish tasks and engage in specific thinking processes. Information-processing theories explore how learners remember information, relate new information to prior knowledge to build schemas that organize ideas, and develop understanding. The breadth and depth of schemas determine whether the learner is able to apply ideas to new problems. Learning environments of this type often stem from research on differences in expert-novice thinking and often provide tutoring and guidance in the use of strategies and thinking processes typical of experts.

A second type of environment is based on ideas about social contexts and practices, focusing on activities, skills, and discourse used in those contexts. These ideas were discussed by Dewey (1938) and Vygotsky (1978) and more recently by American researchers who have used Vygotsky's theoretical approach. Environments developed along these lines include tasks that are typical of those used in the disciplines, instructional scaffolding by more knowledgeable others, tool use that supports learning, and development of learning communities that engage in practices representative of the subject area under study. A frequent goal of these learning environments is to create intentional or adaptive learners (e.g., Bereiter & Scardamalia, 1989).

The success of learning environments in achieving their goals depends on the experience and knowledge of learners, the knowledge of the teacher, the design of tasks, and the nature of community that is developed. Consider inquiry as an example. Inquiry is a central learning activity for many subject matter-based learning environments. To promote construction of understanding, teachers help students raise questions, decide on information or experiments needed to answer those questions, collect and interpret the information, and draw conclusions. This type of activity differs from those in more traditional instructional approaches. It changes the role of the teacher from information delivery to scaffolder. That is, it requires that teachers scaffold activities so that students understand how to think about them as well as gain the procedural knowledge of how to do them. It requires that teachers help students to collaborate and form a community, to take risks, and to recognize that some questions do not have one right answer.

In this chapter, we describe learning environments that reflect the information processing and social cognitive approaches to learning environments. We begin by presenting selection criteria for the learning environments we discuss. In the first section, we present a unifying scheme to characterize programs, describing several learning environments according to the scheme. The purpose is to illustrate the range of learning environments and the similarities and differences in features they contain and what they emphasize. The second section addresses how learning environments are designed, implemented, and refined. We highlight the interplay of theory and practice in this process. The third section discusses what happens and what needs to be considered as learning environments are scaled. It is often the case that learning environments are developed and revised based on experiences in a few classrooms. When more teachers, children, and settings are involved, issues arise that were not initially problematic. These can affect whether learning environments need to be redesigned and whether they are successful. The fourth section contains a summary and conclusions about what we have learned about designing, implementing, and scaling learning environments and offers suggestions for future work.

SELECTION CRITERIA

Four criteria guide our selection of learning environments for our discussion. We primarily focus on classroom learning environments that are theoretically based. We also include some environments designed for use in afterschool programs. Our search for programs was not exhaustive. Our list includes a range of programs that exemplify the characteristics needed to describe learning environments and advance theoretical development and empirical research. The criteria* are:

1. *Explicit academic learning goals:* Many learning environments are designed to engage students in interesting activities but have vague academic learning goals. We include only those that have specifically identified and assessed subject matter learning goals. These are likely to be the most informative in considering issues of design, implementation and scaling of learning environments. They also are the most likely to meet the other criteria.

2. *Ambitious scope:* By this we mean a learning environment designed to address academic material in either breadth or depth. Many learning environments in education are aligned with national subject matter standards or frameworks recommended by professional organizations. Programs tied to national standards or frameworks are preferred.

3. *Highly specified and developed materials:* Drawing on descriptions of innovations proposed by D. K. Cohen and Ball (1999), we include learning environments that are highly specified and developed. Highly specified programs have clear theoretical backgrounds, design principles based on research and theory, and guidelines for enactment. Highly developed programs have materials for teachers and students to use, such as student workbooks and readers, assessments, teacher manuals, and professional development materials that exemplify desired enactments. Programs can be highly specified but not highly developed, thereby leaving a considerable opportunity for customization to local contexts, but also running the risk of enactments that stray considerably from the theoretical principles. Similarly, materials can be highly developed but have little theoretical specification, such as commonly used textbooks for teachers and students.

4. *Published research:* Reports on the program and its outcomes are necessary for inclusion. Learning environments that do not include reviewed research may

---

* An example of a learning environment that is widespread but would not fit these criteria is the JASON project. This widely disseminated program draws on popular topics and creates packages of material for students and teachers, often including technology. But its design is not explicitly based on a learning theory. Other popular programs are designed to provide simulation experiences, such as a model United Nations, simulating

a meeting of the Organization of American States, or arguing a case in Moot Court. These are what we consider grassroots programs that can serve as useful examples of what to include in learning environments. Often popular and used in many settings, they nevertheless are not designed to link to specific educational standards, have limited scope (even though they consider important topics), are not specifically based on a theory of learning or environment, and, although they provide valuable learning experiences, they vary considerably in the types and rigor of assessment of learning outcomes.

be popular but are not likely to yield theoretical or practical insights necessary to advance knowledge by informing theory, design principles, or practice recommendations.

Table 8.1 lists learning environments that match our selection criteria. This is a purposeful sampling to illustrate the wide range of programs that match. The programs are clustered according to whether they have a disciplinary content focus, knowledge-building emphasis, or an extracurricular learning focus. Each program is accompanied by a brief description and a Web site link. We refer to many of these programs as examples throughout the remaining sections.

FEATURES AND DESCRIPTIONS OF LEARNING ENVIRONMENTS

This section describes selected learning environments based on the four criteria. The programs vary by age of students, subject matter, and goals. Many of the more recently developed learning environments include technology, such as personal computers or Web-based communication tools, either as a primary focus or as an important component. We sample from such programs where there is a strong theory and research base because they are powerful ways to extend learning environments beyond the classroom.

Features of Learning Environments

Table 8.2 (p. 302) presents a framework for examining features of learning environments. We use the features to describe three learning environments that represent both information processing and social cognitive theory. Finally, we present a chart based on the features that characterizes and compares several widely used learning environments. Our point is to illustrate commonality and variety in the design of learning environments. Descriptions of programs in this section contrast environments designed around information-processing approaches and social cognitive approaches to learning.

There are many different ways to describe learning environments. For instance, a tetrahedral model originally developed by Jenkins (1979) and modified by A. L. Brown and colleagues (A. L. Brown, Bransford, Ferrara, & Campione, 1983), presents a framework for examining aspects of learning environments. The Jenkins model, as modified

by A. L. Brown et al., identifies four factors that interact within a learning setting: (1) learning activities, (2) characteristics of the learners, (3) nature of the content to be learned, and (4) the end products or goals of the learning setting. These factors are interdependent: A change in one will influence the impact of others. Another framework, more recently developed by Paavola, Lipponen, and Hakkarainen (2004) examine the models of learning that underlie learning environments. In their approach, they focus on the processes of knowledge creation to explore how learning environments are organized. Quite differently, De Kock, Sleegers, and Voeten (2004) examine learning environments around learning goals, teacher and learner roles, and the roles of learners in relation to one another. They consider these to be basic aspects of learning environments that influence student performance and learning. They suggest that these three aspects of the learning environment can provide a classification scheme for designing and evaluating learning environments in secondary education. A framework proposed in *How People Learn* (Bransford, Brown, & Cocking, 2000) provides a set of four design characteristics that can be used to analyze the quality of learning environments. The framework takes into account the degree to which learning environments are knowledge-centered, learner-centered, assessment-centered, and community-centered.

Our framework attempts to provide greater detail about features of learning environments that are important to consider in design and evaluation. Learning environments can be described by the goals, the types of tasks and instructional materials used to reach the goals, the role of the teacher, and how learning is assessed. Technology also may be a central feature. Learning environments encompass different types or combinations of types of social organization. In the design of learning environments, these features are presumed to be interdependent; they work together to affect outcomes. The goals and instantiations of each feature derive from underlying theoretical ideas about learning.

Goals

The goals of learning environments can be academic, social, metacognitive, and developmental; particular learning environments might encompass all four types or only one or two. Academic goals of recently designed classroom-based learning environments tend to focus on standards-based frameworks following recommendations from professional organizations. The National Research Council (NRC; 1996) and the American Association for the Advancement of Science (1993) have disseminated

TABLE 8.1   Selected Learning Environments

Cluster	Learning Environment	Description	Web Site
Discipline-based programs: Mathematics	Cognitive Tutors (Anderson, Corbett, Koedinger, & Pelletier, 1995; Corbett, Koedinger, & Hadley, 2001)	Intelligent software environment for high school mathematics classrooms	http://www.carnegielearning.com
	Connected Mathematics Project (Lappan, Fey, Fitzgerald, Friel, & Phillips, 2002, 2006)	Problem-centered middle school mathematics program	http://www.mth.msu.edu/cmp
	Jasper (Cognition and Technology Group at Vanderbilt, 1992, 1997)	Video-based mathematics program for middle schools	http://peabody.vanderbilt.edu /projects/funded/jasper /Jasperhome.html
Discipline-based programs: Science	Biology Guided Inquiry Learning Environments (BGuILE; Resier et al., 2001)	Technology-infused inquiry for middle school and high school biology	http://www.letus.org/bguile
	GenScope™/BioLogica™ (Horwitz & Christie, 2000; Hickey, Kindfield, Horwitz, & Christie, 2003)	Computer-based genetics program for middle school and high school	http://www.concord.org /biologica
	Guided Inquiry Supporting Multiple Literacies (GIsML; Magnusson & Palincsar, 1995; Palincsar & Magnusson, 2001)	Guided inquiry science program for elementary students	http://www.soe.umich.edu/gisml
	Kids as Global Scientists/BioKIDS (Huber, Songer, & Lee, 2003; Songer, 1996, in press; Songer, Lee, & Kam, 2002)	Technology-based inquiry science program for upper elementary and middle school students	http://www.biokids.umich.edu
	Learning by Design (LBD; Kolodner, Camp, et al., 2003; Kolodner, Gray, & Fasse, 2003)	Design-based middle school science program	http://www.cc.gatech.edu /edutech/projects/lbdview.html
	Project Based Science (PBS; Marx, Blumenfeld, Krajcik, & Soloway, 1997; Singer, Marx, Krajcik, & Chambers, 2000)	Science inquiry curricula focused on everyday experiences for middle school students	http://www.hi-ce.org
	ThinkerTools (White, 1993; White & Frederiksen, 1998, 2000)	Scientific inquiry and modeling software and curricula for middle school science	http://thinkertools.soe.berkeley .edu
	Web-Based Integrated Science Environment (WISE; Linn, Clark, & Slotta, 2003; Slotta, 2004)	Online science inquiry learning environment for grades 5–12	http://wise.Berkeley.edu
	Geographic Data in Education Initiative/World Watcher (GEODE; Edelson, 2001; Edelson, Gordin, & Pea, 1999)	Inquiry-based environmental science program for middle school and high school	http://www.worldwatcher .northwestern.edu
Discipline-based programs: Literacy	Literacy Innovation that Speech Technology Enables (LISTEN; Mostow & Aist, 2001; Mostow & Beck, in press)	Computerized reading tutor for elementary students	http://www.cs.cmu.edu/~listen

TABLE 8.1   *Continued*

Cluster	Learning Environment	Description	Web Site
Discipline-based programs: Social sciences	Problem-Based Economics (Maxwell & Bellisimo, 2003; Maxwell, Bellisimo, & Mergendoller, 2001)	Problem-based learning for high school economics	http://www.bie.org/index.php
Knowledge-building programs	Computer-Supported Intentional Learning Environments/ Knowledge Forum™ (CSILE; Bereiter & Scardamalia, 2003; Scardamalia, Bereiter, & Lamon, 1994)	Computer-based environment for intentional learning and knowledge building	http://www.knowledgeforum.com
	Fostering Communities of Learners (A. L. Brown & Campione, 1994, 1996, 1998)	Guided inquiry environment supporting a metacognitive culture of learning	
	Schools for Thought (Lamon et al., 1996)	Whole-day guided inquiry program emphasizing learning with understanding for grades 5–8	
Extracurricular programs	Fifth Dimension (Cole, 1995, 1996; K. Brown & Cole, 2000, 2002)	Mixed activity system of education and play for elementary and middle school children	http://129.171.53.1/blantonw /5dClhse/clearingh1.html
	Kids Learning in Computer Klubhouses (KLICK; Zhao, Mishra, & Girod, 2000; Girod, Martineau, & Zhao, 2004)	Afterschool technology-based learning environment for middle school students	http://www.klick.org/kids /klubhouses

science standards; the National Council of Teachers of Mathematics (1989, 1991, 2000) has prepared standards for mathematics teaching. Similarly, history standards have been developed by the National Center for History in the Schools (1996) and the National Council for the Social Studies (1994). Although the standards advocated by professional organizations may be consistent with federal No Child Left Behind legislation, the professional standards are guidelines and are not tied specifically to high-stakes assessment. They might be consistent with standards adopted by states and local education authorities, but they are not mandated by local school districts or states. Academic goals focus on learning particular subject matter content. They also entail learning about disciplinary practices and norms such as what constitutes evidence, how conclusions are drawn, how ideas are communicated, how progress in knowledge is made, and how change in knowledge frameworks occur. For instance, student learning about the nature of science might include how science progresses, the role and design of inquiry, and acceptable methods of interpretations.

Goals can also be social, such as the interpersonal goal of learning to work cooperatively. Motivational goals entail improving attitudes and promoting interest, thereby enhancing students' desire to learn and willingness to exert effort to do so. Communicative goals stem from epistemic frameworks of knowledge in disciplines. They focus on accuracy and use of language as it is practiced in the discipline. Within the discipline of history, examples are students who present information in a historically correct manner, using terms and making arguments and explanations as historians would. These communication capabilities can be part of classroom discourse or embedded in artifacts like reports, models, or visual representations.

A third type of goal addresses the promotion of a disposition for thinking and reasoning: mental habits such as persistence and posing questions that support self-directed or self-regulated learning (Costa & Kallick, 2000). Some habits of mind relate to skills in the discipline; others are more global and considered necessary to become a lifelong intentional learner. They can be

TABLE 8.2 Framework for Examining Features of Learning Environments

Goals	Tasks	Instructional Materials	Social Organization	Teacher	Technology	Assessment
Academic	*Content*	*Theoretical Explicitness*	*Structure*	*Responsibility*	*Tools*	*Types*
Standards	Subject matter knowledge	Design principles	Activity structures:	Topic selection	Web based	Tests
Academic frameworks	Inquiry	*Detail for Enacting*	–Individual	Task design	Communication	Portfolios
Disciplinary content	Problem solving	Premises	–Small groups	Assessment	Learning tools	Performance assessments
Social and Interpersonal	Interdisciplinary	Explicitness of enactment	–Whole class	*Centrality*	Software:	Artifacts
Social	*Sequence*	*Resources*	Roles:	Position in enacting	–Off-the-shelf	*Targets*
Motivational	Degree of specification	Teacher materials	–Teacher	Level of student guidance	–Custom-designed	Content knowledge
Communicative	Skill acquisition	Student materials	–Student	*Competencies*	*Centrality*	Skills
Habits of Mind	Knowledge acquisition		*Communities of Practice*	Subject matter knowledge	Core component	Nature of discipline
Discipline-based	*Authenticity*		Professional practice	Curricular knowledge	Pervasive	
Intentional learners	Real world		Discourse	Knowledge of students	*Function*	
Developmental	Student interest		Knowledge building	Pedagogical expertise	Curricular integration	
Cognitive	Discipline based		*Beyond the Classroom*	Technological expertise	Individual/collaborative	
Social	*Contextualization*		Community participation		Scaffold	
	Frame for engaging in tasks:		Consultation with experts			
	–Discipline-based		Family engagement			
	–Socially based					
	Artifacts					
	Cognitive complexity					
	Purpose:					
	–Represent learning					
	–Drive learning					

metacognitive, such as promoting students' proficiency in the use of learning and self-regulatory strategies. The latter involves planning, monitoring progress, and revising approaches where necessary as well as maintaining concentration. Sometimes habits of mind goals focus on creating adaptive and intentional learners who identify what needs to be learned, are thoughtful and effective in deciding how to accomplish their ends, and use strategies proficiently in the service of their aims (Bereiter & Scardamalia, 1989, 2003).

A fourth type of goal is developmental. Most learning environments are not designed for students of multiple ages. They typically focus on subject matter teaching for one age group, such as late elementary, middle, or high school students. Learning environments attempt to move students forward in terms of their levels of knowledge and in their mirroring of expert thinking, problem solving, and use of discipline-based practice. To do so, they draw on research about learning in the subject areas, student misconceptions, and developmental differences in information processing and use of learning strategies. An example of such an environment is a problem-centered math program for middle school students, Connected Mathematics. This program draws from contemporary research on teaching and learning in this subject area, as well as national mathematics standards (Lappan & Phillips, 1998; Lappan, Fey, Fitzgerald, Friel, & Phillips, 2002).

Developers of learning environments are less explicit in identifying social development as part of design principles. Nevertheless, many designs have features that are compatible with what Eccles and Midgley (1989) describe as classroom-based, age-stage environmental fit. Most feature collaboration with others, meaningful problems, active learning, and varying degrees of student responsibility and choice.

Tasks

Tasks are what students do to learn subject matter content and practices. Tasks include the content, the level of complexity of the material to be learned, and the openness of how the task can be accomplished. Learning environments usually feature tasks that are conceptually and procedurally complex. They require students to use learning strategies to remember and organize material and metacognitive strategies to plan a course of action and evaluate results. They often ask students to solve problems or design artifacts with unprescribed routes to solution and with several or even unlimited answers. For

instance, in the science program Learning by Design (LBD; Kolodner, Camp, et al., 2003), students learn about force and motion by designing and building miniature vehicles and their propulsion systems. The collection of tasks in a learning environment may include only one discipline or combine several subject areas, such as mathematics and science or history and language arts. They may require students to engage in research to answer questions by doing experiments, conducting surveys in their community, or consulting primary or secondary sources through library or Web-based searches.

The sequence of tasks and topics in a learning environment can vary from tightly specified to very open. The former is likely to be part of programs that highlight the acquisition of well-defined and specific academic content or skills. For instance, skill acquisition models are usually sequential and hierarchical, designed to move learners to higher levels of expertise. The American Association for the Advancement of Science (2001) has published specific strand maps of science concepts and process skills for primary through secondary grades that underlie science programs that match their standards. Similarly, intelligent software programs like Carnegie Learning's Geometry Tutor are sequenced so that students learn to solve progressively more difficult problems. On the other hand, the sequence of content, lessons, or experiences may not be as tightly prescribed in some learning environments. Instead, students might explore different topics at different times, such as working on different projects in an online environment for learning, like the Web-based Integrated Science Environment (WISE; Linn, Davis, & Bell, 2004).

Tasks can vary in degree of authenticity. Newmann and Wehlage (1993) define authentic tasks as those that mirror tasks found in the discipline to some extent, require transformation of information, and have meaning beyond the classroom. Tasks may reflect real-world experiences of students, such as their community's air quality, or they may involve topics of potential interest with which students have had no direct experience, such as space travel or dinosaurs. They also may be designed to reflect the work of professionals in a discipline. For example, students might develop historical interpretations of reasons for population migration to northern cities during the first half of the twentieth century, or they might mirror how engineers create designs that solve problems of how to better insulate homes or construct tall buildings.

Content and skills to be learned may be contextualized within a problem or question. For instance, students in LBD are asked to solve design-and-build challenges that involve constructing working devices or models to illustrate science concepts; students in project-based science classrooms are asked to answer such questions as How can good friends make me sick? Similarly, mathematical problem-solving skills are anchored in a videodisc series of more complex adventures of a character named Jasper (Cognition and Technology Group at Vanderbilt, 1997). Tasks also may be designed to reflect disciplinary concepts such as exploring the principles of force and motion or genetics.

Students' artifacts usually are designed to represent their learning. The process of their creation fosters construction of knowledge; for instance, when students create models, they need to decide on what to include, what relationships to illustrate, how to explain reasons for what they have done and what their model shows. In some programs, creation of the artifact is the central feature that drives learning. In LBD, students go through cycles of design as they solve problems; revision of designs should reflect greater understanding of underlying concepts they have studied. Artifacts such as models and designs can be considered open or not predetermined. In contrast, artifacts that demonstrate solution of a math problem can be considered more closed, although there may be various routes to the solution.

Instructional Materials

Materials provided by designers of learning environments range in their level of theoretical explicitness, detail for enactment, and resources provided for teachers and students. Programs chosen for inclusion in this chapter are based on theoretically explicit principles derived from either cognitive or sociocognitive perspectives. These programs are highly specified, but vary in their degree of development. That is, they include a range of examples, materials, and resources for teachers and students to put the ideas into practice.

Most of the programs included are fairly well developed. They usually include professional development in their efforts. The materials provided, however, may vary in how explicitly the principles underlying the program are linked to suggestions for enactment. They also vary in the types of teacher and student material provided to make the program readily usable. Some programs provide curriculum guides with suggestions for enactment and for evaluation along with information about the rationale for the activities and educative materials that help teachers with their own understanding of content

and student learning. Other programs provide suggestions but have many fewer examples of how to enact these suggestions, such as strategies for scaffolding student learning or for building communities of learners. Still others provide reading materials, problems to solve, and suggestions for students to follow when conducting inquiry via information or data gathering. Others also provide software to aid in knowledge construction. When materials are not extensively developed and teachers play a central role in carrying out the learning environment, teachers need to have a greater range and depth of expertise to successfully meet the goals envisioned by designers of the learning environment. This point is discussed more fully in the section on teachers.

Social Organization

A community of practice describes a situation where people are engaged in a collective process of learning that produces common norms, practices, and frameworks for knowledge (Lave & Wenger, 1991; Wenger, 1998). Over time, they develop a common sense of purpose and shared understandings. The communities may have one or several foci. The understandings can involve professional practices such as how problems are framed and solved. The solutions entail processes such as how evidence is collected, what counts as evidence, and how evidence is interpreted or solutions justified. Discourse, how members of a discipline communicate, is another aspect of community that often is emphasized in learning environments. Here students report findings and interpretations in language that mirrors those of the subject area. The discourse emphasizes the difference between everyday language and styles and the more formal ones of the subject matter areas. Language and patterns of social interaction and debate shape meaning making and help students understand how knowledge is built and verified in the discipline (A. L. Brown, Metz, & Campione, 1996; Rogoff, 1995). For instance, in Guided Inquiry supporting Multiple Literacies (GIsML), an approach to science instruction developed by Palincsar and Magnusson (2001; Magnusson & Palincsar, 1995), the learning environment is designed around the notion of community. A tenet of GIsML instruction is that science classrooms are communities that should reflect key elements of the culture of science. In GIsML classrooms, teachers and students engage in a collective process of learning that produces shared understandings of scientific ideas and practices. Science learning involves becoming socialized into the practices of science, such as using the discourse tools of talking, listening, reading, and writing. Language, then, is considered central and necessary for constructing scientific understanding.

Some learning environments are less formal in their focus on disciplinary practice and discourse. They stress intentional learning that is fostered by developing group knowledge about a topic through asking questions, information gathering, debating, critiquing, and synthesizing. For instance, in A. L. Brown and Campione's (1994, 1998) Fostering Communities of Learners, students select a topic of interest, break into cooperative jigsaw groups, and share with peers who have collected other information. Together they synthesize the information and apply the principles derived to solve problems or pursue further questions. Similar interactions are promoted by the Computer-Supported Intentional Learning Environments (CSILE; Scardamalia & Bereiter, 1991). The environment provides a community space that supports collaborative inquiry through information searching and sharing for the purpose of knowledge building. The class explores a common topic and posts information and comments about the information on the multimedia community knowledge space.

Learning environments often are linked to communities that extend beyond the classroom in various ways. Some encourage community participation, such as drawing on "funds of knowledge" (Moll, Amanti, Neff, & Gonzalez, 1992) to bring skills, knowledge, and experiences related to student background to bear on subject matter. Some attempt to bridge in- and out-of-school discourse and ways of knowing (Lee, 2002; Moje, Collazo, Carrillo, & Marx, 2001) by drawing on commonly held beliefs and contrasting these with how experts in the discipline might study and explain a phenomenon. Community engagement is encouraged as students survey communities and present findings to audiences in the community, such as local interest groups and students in other classes or in other schools via Web-based publication. Technology-based learning environments, such as Kids as Global Scientists (Songer, 1996) and WISE, often connect students with graduate students or scientists via telecommunication; students share data, ask questions about findings or interpretations, or get feedback on their artifacts. Students often collaborate with other students across school sites to collect, share, and interpret data.

Teacher

Teacher responsibility in learning environments varies with respect to topic selection, task design, and assess-

ment. Some programs have built-in topics and instructional sequences, whereas in others teachers can choose from a list of designated topics and set their own sequence. Some include a combination of both. For instance, in GIsML, teachers use a heuristic to design their own approach to suggested topics. The heuristic conceptualizes instruction in guided inquiry science as a series of cycles of investigation involving engagement, investigation, and reporting. Teachers play a central role in orchestrating instruction by guiding students through cycles at an appropriate pace and ensuring that students develop scientific knowledge and reasoning. WISE provides a library of inquiry projects for which materials, including lesson plans, have been developed. WISE teachers can use the projects as stand-alone science units or integrate them into their existing curricula.

Few, if any, programs leave task design solely to teachers. Some come with intelligent instructional software that provides specific hierarchical tasks and guides student learning, such as Cognitive Tutors (Aleven & Koedinger, 2002) and the computer-based reading environment Literacy Innovation That Speech Technology Enables (LISTEN; Mostow & Aist, 2001; Mostow & Beck, in press). Other programs, such as Project Based Science (PBS), offer comprehensive materials for teachers that include suggested tasks but assume that teachers will adapt them to local conditions. The key is that the adaptations made by teachers are congruent with the underlying principles on which the learning environments are designed.

All programs include assessments for evaluating student understanding. They differ in how much the teacher is encouraged to use classroom-based assessments to inform instruction. Some programs include pretests and posttests. Several programs also encourage teachers to create their own assessments; for instance, they may provide guidelines for how students might create a multimedia presentation to showcase learning. Many programs also encourage evaluation of artifacts and provide rubrics for doing so. Other programs contain built-in assessments that determine whether students can progress to higher-level activities. For instance, in the after-school program Fifth Dimension (K. Brown & Cole, 2002; Cole, 1995), children must achieve goals specified on task cards before moving to the next level of activities. Most of the activities use educational software and computer games that emphasize problem-solving and literacy skills across a range of content areas, including math, language arts, social studies, science, technology, and fine arts. Task cards accompany each activity and help children get started, specify expected achievements, and provide information for obtaining a credential as an expert in the Fifth Dimension. Similarly, students cannot progress in Cognitive Tutors unless they reach a certain degree of proficiency in solving math problems at their current level.

The role of the teacher varies considerably. In some environments, the teacher's position in enacting the learning environment is central to helping students meet their goals. For instance, instructional efforts by the teacher to scaffold student learning, diagnose difficulties, and assess understanding is an important part of making WISE work. In Connected Mathematics, the teacher works closely with students to help them make sense of the problems under study. In contrast, guiding student understanding is less critical in Cognitive Tutors and LISTEN, where the technology provides a high level of guidance and is the major influence on student learning.

The more teachers have responsibility for topic selection and design, the greater the range of competencies they must have to make learning environments work. Subject matter knowledge refers to the understanding of the key ideas, the connection among ideas, disciplinary practices, and the nature of the discipline. Some environments, such as Cognitive Tutors, are based on a careful analysis of learning so that the teacher does not need to have as deep an understanding of subject matter as in a program like CSILE or Fostering Communities of Learners. In the case of knowledge-building programs like CSILE, teachers must be able to select topics, understand key ideas, and assess understanding based on their own expertise.

Curricular knowledge refers to how to design and sequence tasks. Some programs, such as WISE, are designed to supplement the curriculum so that teachers must decide how to best incorporate Web-based inquiry into their existing curricular structure in a manner that enhances what already exists. Other programs, such as PBS, are designed to replace existing units within a curriculum; a teacher needs to determine what the learning environment affords, the new unit's benefits, and whether it fits well with other aspects of the curriculum to determine whether to make a substitution.

Knowledge of students refers to teachers' ability to draw on student prior knowledge and skills, student experiences, and student motivation as the basis for content representation and diagnosis of student understanding. As in the other areas of competence, the more the teacher

is central to content representation—providing examples, activities, evaluations—the greater the degree of knowledge of students the teacher must have.

Pedagogical expertise refers to knowledge of different types of instructional formats: discussion, small group work, or demonstrations and how to carry them out. In learning environments, the pedagogy also includes how to enact these instructional formats and support student learning in a manner that is warranted, given the premises underlying program design. For instance, in Connected Mathematics, teachers need to be able to support group problem solving; in GIsML, teachers need to actively guide students through an inquiry cycle; in WISE, teachers scaffold students' Web searches; in CSILE, the teacher has to understand and carry out the knowledge-building process according to how it is conceptualized by the Knowledge Forum and create a community of learners while doing so.

Technology expertise, including knowledge of how to use and maintain the technology (troubleshooting) and how to use the technology as a learning tool for students, is critical in some learning environments. Those that use highly structured technology programs where the teacher is not central require somewhat less expertise about using the technology as a learning tool, yet still require the teacher to be a skilled troubleshooter. Other technology-based programs, such as WISE, Kids as Global Scientists, BGuILE, and GEODE, require considerable expertise in helping students exploit the benefits of the technology to support thinking.

Technology

Learning environments utilize a variety of technologies for a range of purposes. Participants in many innovative learning environments are actively involved in information gathering, such as searching on the Internet, information sharing by means of e-mail or instant messaging, and using simulations to generate information for further study, data modeling to aid in information assimilation, and information representation tools like visualization software. For example, students interacting with ThinkerTools software (White, 1993) learn about basic principles of physics through direct interaction with simulations of force and motion phenomena. Online learning environments and workspaces, such as WISE and CSILE, provide custom-designed software tools to support students' knowledge building and knowledge integration. These types of environments are often designed to foster collaboration. CSILE provides a communal database and Web-based communication tools; WISE has interfaces to support collaboration around the technology and via the technology. Other computer-based environments are designed for individual work. Cognitive Tutor software assigns problems to students on an individual basis, monitors students' solution steps, and provides feedback and hints. LISTEN software displays stories on a computer screen and provides individual assistance as children read aloud.

Computer-based environments such as Cognitive Tutors and LISTEN have technology as the core of the learning environment. Although other components may augment the technology in these programs, the technology is the main delivery system for instruction. For instance, in Cognitive Tutors, group problem-solving tasks and discussions are meant to support or reinforce the learning targeted by the instructional software. Whereas some computer-based environments may contain all of the content, others, like CSILE and WISE, help to organize learning by scaffolding individual or group research processes. Still other programs may use a variety of technologies, but these are not the key elements of the environment. In Connected Mathematics, LBD, and Project Based Science, technology tools are intended to leverage learning within the environment. For example, in Project Based Science, technology is utilized to support students as they create artifacts of their learning, such as using handheld computers to create concepts maps.

Assessment

Most learning environments include or recommend several types of assessments to evaluate participants' learning, although some types are more critical than others. Individual and group portfolios, student reports and presentations, and pretests and posttests are characteristic of many programs. In some, the design and evaluation of artifacts is central. In an LBD physical science unit, for instance, students design and build miniature vehicles. As students go through the design process, they move back and forth between cycles of design and redesign as they design, build, and test miniature vehicles that can travel over varied surfaces (Kolodner, Camp, et al., 2003).

Discipline-based programs focus on all or some of the following targets: content knowledge, reasoning skills, and the nature of the discipline. Those that are more general might include content assessments and also dispositions to learning such as intentionality in posing questions and seeking information to answer those questions. Some programs also assess motivation in terms of student interest, feelings of efficacy, and use of learning strategies.

Program Descriptions

We describe three programs to illustrate variations in how designers emphasize and instantiate features. The descriptions include discussion of features that are central to the learning environment depicted; therefore, not all features are included in an individual program description even though they may operate in the program. For instance, many programs include collaboration among students as they discuss ideas or conduct investigations. However, some programs are specifically designed to foster collaboration, such as Knowledge Forum and Kids as Global Scientists. Similarly, some programs include artifact creation as a critical element in evaluating student learning; others rely on more conventional assessments even though students do produce artifacts such as reports.

Project-Based Science

Project-based learning is an approach that has been popular since Dewey. In the 1980s, TERC (www.terc.edu) developed a project curriculum that incorporated new telecommunication technology. It posed questions about environmental topics like air quality and trash decomposition, and students did experiments, collected data, and shared results with their counterparts in other locations.

More recently, the University of Michigan and the Detroit Public Schools have worked collaboratively to design project-based learning environments tied to social constructivist principles. The projects last from 6 to 8 weeks and are an integral part of the middle school science curriculum; project content is selected to meet national science standards proposed by the American Association for the Advancement of Science (1993) and the NRC (1996), as well as district and state science objectives, which are compatible with national standards.

The essential components of project-based science are that it (a) uses a "driving" question that encompasses science content and activities; (b) results in a series of artifacts, or products, that address the question; (c) allows students to engage in authentic investigations; (d) involves collaboration among students and teachers; and (e) supports knowledge construction through use of learning technologies (for more detailed description of the components, see Krajcik & Blumenfeld, in press; Singer, Marx, Krajcik, & Chambers, 2000).

Goals. The standards emphasize the need for students to investigate the everyday world. Engaging in inquiry is presumed to help students learn science content and science processes and to experience the academic framework within which scientists work. Student understanding derives from the need for students to plan investigations, collect and analyze data, keep track of the process, and evaluate their findings in light of the aim of the experiment and their own methods. Critical thinking and problem solving are necessary as students interpret data, consider discrepancies between their predictions and findings as well as discrepancies between their findings and the findings of others, and discuss and debate possible reasons why discrepancies exist. These opportunities also help students to understand the nature of science, such as how questions are generated and investigated, what counts as evidence, how scientists interpret and report results, and how ideas are advanced in science.

Improvement in students' ability to use scientific forms of communication is accomplished by highlighting how scientific language, discourses, and writing genres differ from the technical discourses of other content areas and from everyday discourse. Students have opportunities to explain their ideas about scientific phenomena in oral and written form. The experience of inquiry in the service of studying questions relevant to students' lives is assumed to contribute to students' attitudes toward and valuing of science and to influence their decisions to take more science courses.

Tasks. A driving question serves to organize science content and tasks. Sample questions for projects include "What is the quality of air in my community?" (chemistry); "Can good friends make me sick?" (biology); and "Why do I have to wear a helmet when I ride my bike?" (physics). As students pursue solutions to the driving question, they develop meaningful understanding of key scientific concepts.

Good questions are related to the real world and reflect important aspects of students' daily lives. They are selected to be scientifically worthwhile, to contain rich science content that reflects standards, and to be feasible in that students can design and perform investigations in classrooms to answer the question. Questions

also must be broad enough to generate smaller questions that students can raise and address depending on their interests. Although the projects highlight one area of science, to answer the question students might use concepts from different areas. They also employ math and literacy skills as they compute results, graph data, and write reports.

Projects are sequenced within grade levels. A greater level of scaffolding for science processes and for technology use is provided earlier in the year. For example, initial projects might contain benchmark lessons helping students learn to make explanations by stating a claim, citing supporting evidence, and linking the evidence to a conclusion that supports the claim. Supports are faded as students become more proficient in engaging in inquiry and using learning tools. Projects are also sequenced by grade level. Driving questions for each year of middle school are designed to encompass content that is identified by national, state, and/or local standards for that grade. However, teachers might also use projects regardless of sequence, which might be necessary based on circumstances, school calendars, and individual school policy.

In addition to the real-world nature of the driving question, PBS contextualizes learning in several ways. Students experience phenomena by conducting observations and collecting data in their neighborhoods, such as taking measurements of water quality of a nearby stream or collecting indices of air pollution during a neighborhood walk. These activities draw on students' prior knowledge and experience and serve as anchoring events that are referred to throughout the project. For instance, teachers use a driving question board that includes data collected from these activities; they add information relevant to answering the driving question as the project progresses.

Students produce artifacts, or products, that represent their learning. The artifacts reflect emergent states of knowledge and understanding about solutions to the driving question. The artifacts are cognitively complex and are relatively open. For instance, students create models where they must decide on variables to include, relationships among the variables, and explanations for their choices. Students create concept maps to illustrate relationships among key constructs. They prepare presentations that are attended by community members and other teachers and classes. They write books that address the driving question to share with younger students. Because artifacts are concrete and explicit (e.g., a physical model, report, videotape, or computer program), they can be shared and critiqued. This allows others (students, teachers, parents, and members of the community) to provide feedback and permits learners to reflect on and extend their emergent knowledge and revise their artifacts. The creation and sharing of artifacts makes doing project-based science more like doing real science and mirrors the work of scientists.

Technology. PBS makes extensive use of learning tools (Krajcik, Blumenfeld, Marx, & Soloway, 2000) that are integrated into the curriculum. They are used to support the learning goals of the curriculum, rather than the curriculum's being built to capitalize on the technology's affordances.

Using concepts from learner-centered software design (Quintana et al., 2004; Soloway, Guzdial, & Hay, 1994), each tool has been designed to take into consideration the unique characteristics of novice learners. Such tools have specially designed supports that help students complete inquiry tasks they normally would not be able to complete. For example, Model-It illustrates principles of learner-centered design by representing information in a way that is familiar to learners but also helps to introduce them to more professional or symbolic representations (Jackson, Krajcik, & Soloway, 2000). Students select variables, indicate relationships among them, and then test their models. Similarly, students engage in Web searches using Artemis, a tool designed to help students keep track of what they have found and what is useful. Librarians select Web content to increase the likelihood that middle schoolers will find material relevant to their project and with an eye toward appropriate levels of reading comprehension. To improve access, recent technology includes handheld computers, so that all students can have frequent and immediate access to their own technology tools. These are used in conjunction with desktop computers located in classrooms and computer labs. Software for handhelds allows students to draw representations, share artifacts, store information, and write explanations.

Learning tools expand the range of questions that students can investigate, the types of data and information that can be collected, and the types of data representations that can be displayed to aid interpretation. The tools are used across several curriculum projects and years, so that students become familiar with them and can benefit from repeated use (Krajcik et al., 2000; Wu, Krajcik, & Soloway, 2001). Students can work individu-

ally or collaboratively. When using desktop computers, students usually work collaboratively because of the limited number of machines; handhelds, which are less costly and thereby more plentiful, allow for ubiquitous individual work.

Teacher. The teacher plays a central role in the enactment of PBS. Teachers must have considerable knowledge of the curriculum because they must make adaptations to fit their circumstances in ways that are congruent with underlying principles. Knowledge of the content and of how students learn it is essential because teachers provide crucial benchmark lessons about science content and processes that prepare students for inquiry. Teachers also must be familiar with the technology and be able to capitalize on its potential as a learning tool for students. All of this requires support for student learning; thus, early in the term, teachers do a considerable amount of scaffolding. They model thinking, structure tasks by preparing lists of criteria that students can use to evaluate whether the research questions they choose are valuable and feasible, and distribute charts to help students organize data collection and data analysis. Later, students are expected to be able to carry out procedures or produce artifacts with less help.

Assessment. Assessment of learning in individual projects is based on a combination of student artifacts, project specific pre- and posttest scores, and content interviews with a sample of students. The tests contain both closed and open-ended questions that range from low to high levels of cognitive difficulty. That is, students respond to questions about facts and also to scenarios that ask them to apply their knowledge to a new situation (Marx et al., 2004). Scores on statewide tests are used to determine how students who have participated in PBS curriculum compare with their counterparts who have engaged in other district-supported standard-based science instruction efforts (Geier et al., 2004).

In addition to measures of students' learning, a range of perception and motivation constructs are assessed. Student perceptions of the classroom environment (e.g., real-world nature of the question, opportunities for collaboration, and teachers' press for understanding) and its influence on attitudes toward science and technology and motivation to learn and self-regulation (e.g., use of learning and metacognitive strategies) are explored using a combination of surveys and interviews (Blumenfeld, Soloway, Krajcik, & Marx, 2004).

Instructional Materials. As D. K. Cohen and Ball (1999) recommend, the curricula and materials we designed for PBS are highly specified (the theoretical principles and methods are clearly defined) and developed (materials for teachers and learners are available and usable). The materials, developed collaboratively by science educators, scientists, and classroom teachers, contain extensive information about each lesson in the project along with reading selections, handouts, and worksheets. In addition, educative materials for teachers focus on content and content representation, potential problems with student understanding, and suggestions for management to avoid potential enactment problems (Davis & Krajcik, 2005; Schneider & Krajcik, 2002).

Professional development is tailored to helping teachers enact the curriculum. Instructional technologies support the ongoing development of teachers. Summer institutes and Saturday and late afternoon working sessions make use of data on student learning outcomes, content and pedagogical content concerns, and teacher enactment difficulties (Fishman, Marx, Best, & Tal, 2003). Technology is also used to support teachers and to help them manage their instructional responsibilities. A Web-based teacher support system called Knowledge Networks on the Web (KNOW; www.umich.soe.know.edu) was designed and is used to distribute curriculum materials, illustrate enactment of lessons, share teacher commentary about enactment issues, and display examples of student work. KNOW can be accessed by professional development leaders and by individual teachers who also can query others as they plan enactments.

Web-Based Integrated Science Environment

An example of a virtual community for learning is the Web-based Integrated Science Environment (WISE; http://wise.Berkeley.edu). WISE is an online environment for middle and high school that engages students in collaborative inquiry projects, supported by the use of Web resources (Cuthbert, Clark, & Linn, 2002; Linn, Davis, & Bell, 2004; Linn & Slotta, 2000).

Technology. WISE utilizes Web-based technology and the classroom teacher to enable students to engage in sustained investigations around phenomena as a route to deepening students' scientific understanding. Features include a browser-based interface for students, lesson plans for teachers, and an online library of inquiry projects. The student interface incorporates an inquiry map that guides students in their investigation of a topic. The map provides a level of guidance to enable students to work independently on a project by showing the steps that students need to follow as they work. The software also includes an electronic guidance tool, or an avatar, that provides hints and reminds students of the purpose of the activity. Other custom-designed software tools help students use the Internet to gather and critique evidence, take notes, design approaches, and participate in online discussions with peers and scientists.

Tasks. WISE projects range from several days to several weeks and involve students in investigating scientific phenomena, designing solutions to problems, critiquing scientific ideas, and debating real-world scientific controversies (Linn, Clark, & Slotta, 2003; Slotta, 2004). Typical projects involve students in such diverse activities as investigating the nature and cause of frog deformities, designing a house that is comfortable for desert living, and debating different perspectives on how to control malaria worldwide.

Goals. Academic goals of the program include developing students' conceptual understanding of standards-based science content (NRC, 1996) and promoting scientific, language, and technology literacy skills (Linn & Slotta, 2000). Social and interpersonal goals focus on promoting students' autonomy in learning, helping students to learn from peers, and promoting a positive disposition toward science.

Social Organization. WISE science instruction emphasizes knowledge building within a scientifically oriented classroom community (Linn, Clark, & Slotta, 2003). Students primarily work collaboratively and independently in small groups. Web-based communication tools enable students to connect with peers and scientists to share data, discuss and debate ideas, and report findings. The classroom teacher interacts with groups as they progress through a WISE project, guiding and assisting students when necessary. Students and teacher have a shared purpose of making sense of scientific ideas and practices.

Instructional Materials. The WISE learning environment provides students with an online workspace for working individually or collaboratively through a sequence of activities that constitute an inquiry project. The workspace is a browser-based interface that helps students navigate through activity steps by incorporating prompts, such as pop-up windows for note taking, windows that provide hints, and evidence pages that add ideas about the topic of inquiry. Online investigations are further supported by classroom hands-on activities and explorations. For example, in a project called "Plants in Space," students use the WISE interface and Internet resources to investigate plant life and explore different conditions for growing plants on earth and growing plants in space (Williams & Linn, 2002). They collaboratively create a small hydroponics garden in their classroom and conduct investigations of their plants to analyze factors relevant to plant growth and then use their analyses to consider factors important for plant growth in a space station environment. The project involves students in critiquing Web evidence regarding factors for plant growth, such as soil, water, air, and light; participating in online discussions with peers and scientists; and critiquing additional evidence to determine feasibility of particular plants for growth in a space station environment. Students conduct daily observations on plant growth and development from their own garden as well as local gardens, design and carry out investigations on their plants, and report their recommendations for growing plants in space. The WISE interface provides students with information on plants, as well as additional evidence on conditions on space stations to help raise questions and guide the investigation of ideas about plant growth. WISE software helps students keep track of data, take notes on evidence, and then use evidence to respond to questions and speculate on which plants would be the best option for a space station environment. Student-generated artifacts, such as notes from investigations and presentations, are intended to reinforce literacy skills and showcase learning.

WISE projects are designed to appeal to students' interests and curiosities, relate to real-world scientific topics, and help students develop scientific inquiry skills. Projects are created collaboratively through partnerships with a wide range of participants from science agencies, professional organizations, museums, schools, and universities. For instance, the "Plants in Space" project partnership included scientists, classroom teachers, science education researchers, and technology specialists (Williams & Linn, 2002). WISE partners work together to design a pilot project, observe its implementation in classrooms, and then refine the project based on the classroom trials. These design teams follow design principles that draw from a theory of learning as scaffolded knowledge integration (Linn, Davis, & Eylon, 2004). This perspective suggests that cohesive understanding is best promoted when learners are supported in connecting new ideas and perspectives to their ideas about the scientific phenomenon they are investigating (Linn, Davis, & Eylon, 2004). WISE design teams use the scaffolded knowledge integration perspective to create discipline-focused activities and technology features to support student inquiry in WISE projects. In addition, WISE provides an online authoring environment to enable design teams to create and refine diverse curriculum projects that align with WISE design principles and relevant science standards (Linn, Clark, & Slotta, 2003). WISE partnerships have designed and refined an online library of more than 50 inquiry projects (Shear, Bell, & Linn, 2004).

Teacher. WISE provides the classroom teacher with online support that includes a curriculum library of inquiry projects with accompanying lesson plans, descriptions of learning goals, information on likely student prior conceptions, assessments, and links to national science standards. The teacher workspace provides scaffolds to help teachers plan and run WISE projects. Technology features that support teachers include grading tools, classroom management tools, formative assessment tools, and customization tools that enable teachers to tailor projects. The projects are intended to be flexible and adaptive for teachers so that they can easily incorporate them into existing science programs. This flexibility enables teachers to select a project for use as part of a larger unit of study, or use a project as a stand-alone science unit. The role of the teacher, then, is to select relevant projects from the WISE online library and customize them for local classroom use. The teacher's role also is to facilitate student work through a project. The teacher interacts with small groups of students, assisting them in interpreting Web-gathered information and materials and helping them to link their experiences with scientific concepts (Slotta, 2004).

Assessment. To assess content learning, the teacher has online access to multiple-choice and short-essay subject matter tests. WISE also incorporates opportunities for students to create artifacts and presentations that can serve as assessments of science content and inquiry skills.

Cognitive Tutors

Researchers at the Pittsburgh Advanced Cognitive Tutor Center have developed computer-based learning environments, called Cognitive Tutors, for high school mathematics classrooms (Aleven & Koedinger, 2002; Anderson, Corbett, Koedinger, & Pelletier, 1995; Corbett, Koedinger, & Hadley, 2001). A Cognitive Tutor program integrates classroom instruction with intelligent instructional software that provides students with individual support for math learning. The program is a full curriculum, composed of classroom learning activities, student text materials, and instructional software.

Goals.   The Cognitive Tutor curriculum is aligned with standards for mathematics instruction and curriculum emphasized by the National Council of Teachers of Mathematics (2000). Goals of the program include developing students' math problem-solving abilities and deepening procedural and conceptual knowledge as a means to raise students' mathematics achievement.

Tasks.   Cognitive Tutor software assigns problems to students individually, monitors students' solution steps, and provides feedback and hints. The Geometry Cognitive Tutor, for instance, presents students with geometry problems dealing with such concepts as angles, area, and the Pythagorean theorem (Aleven & Koedinger, 2002). The tutor displays error messages in response to mistakes, provides a geometry glossary and on-demand hints, and keeps track of students' mastery of each skill to be learned. The tutor is part of an integrated full-year geometry curriculum called Cognitive Tutor Geometry. In addition to geometry, Cognitive Tutor software and curricula have been developed for high school algebra and integrated mathematics courses.

Tasks presented by the tutor are problems that connect to real-world situations. For instance, the algebra tutor emphasizes algebraic reasoning through such problems as estimating the cost of a car rental, planning profits for shoveling snow, and organizing to sell ads for a school yearbook (Corbett, McLaughlin, Scarpinatto, & Hadley, 2000). Problems involve multiple math concepts and skills and provide extensive skill practice. The tutor provides a problem-solving space consisting of question sets, worksheets in a window, and feedback

that ensures students reach a successful solution (Corbett et al., 2000).

Instructional Materials.   The design of Cognitive Tutors is based on principles that draw from adaptive character of thought (ACT-R) theory, which proposes that complex cognition arises from an interaction between declarative knowledge of information and procedural knowledge of how to use information to do various cognitive tasks (Anderson, 1993, 1996; Anderson & Schunn, 2000). A fundamental assumption of ACT-R is that procedural knowledge can be learned only by doing. Tutor software is designed, then, to provide skill practice in a variety of problem-solving contexts so that students can acquire and strengthen their procedural knowledge (Anderson, 1993).

Accompanying the software are instructional materials that help orchestrate whole-class instruction and collaborative problem-solving activities that emphasize real-world situations. The materials include a problem-based textbook for students and a teacher's guide that consists of assignments, assessments, teaching suggestions, and classroom management techniques. The purpose of the textbook and classroom activities is to parallel and extend the development of concepts emphasized in the software.

Technology.   The tutor software is specially designed for monitoring individual students' problem solving. Cognitive Tutors are able to monitor students' problem-solving performance and keep track of their mastery of each skill to be learned. To do this, each Cognitive Tutor employs a cognitive model that represents the skills and strategies of students at various levels of competence (Corbett, Koedinger, & Hadley, 2001). The tutor uses the model to analyze an individual student's problem-solving performance. When a student makes an error and cannot produce the correct action, the tutor suggests what action should be taken. The tutors provide tailored practice on math skills until students reach mastery performance levels. Once a student reaches a mastery level of performance in a particular section of a tutor curriculum, the tutor stops presenting new problems. In this way, a student's learning time is spent on strengthening requisite skills for successful problem solving.

Because the tutor is meant to provide suggestions to a student when that student experiences difficulty, the tutor's ability to diagnose student errors and provide useful feedback is crucial. For a tutor to diagnose effectively and give feedback requires that its cognitive model be based on an accurate task analysis. In the design of a tutor, a task analysis is done for each task to develop cognitive models to represent the competencies required to complete each task. The strength of such an analysis is that the cognitive processes engaged in solving a problem are thoroughly mapped. With some degree of certainty, then, the tutor is able to match errors to a family of error types and is thus able to take advantage of prior knowledge and enable careful scaffolding by following students' solution paths through the problem-solving space. For instance, when an error occurs, the tutor initially displays an error message and provides on-demand hints, with multiple levels of hints available for each step of a problem to ensure that the correct path to a solution is followed. Seeing a brief error message, the student is allowed to correct errors without assistance. Multiple hint levels allow the student to succeed with minimum possible assistance. Problems are selected and designed to reflect real-world situations and allow for the practice of specific skills. Multiple representations from the discipline (tables, graphs, symbolic expressions) are built into the software.

Teacher.   The Cognitive Tutor curriculum integrates individual tutor use with classroom instruction and collaborative problem-solving practice. Students spend about 40% of classroom time working individually on problems assigned by the tutor and the remaining time engaged in collaborative problem-solving activities and whole-class instruction (Aleven & Koedinger, 2002). The role of the teacher is to facilitate the problem-solving activities and class discussions and circulate and assist students as they work in the tutor environment. To succeed, the teacher needs to have subject matter knowledge, be familiar with tutor software, and be comfortable in facilitating collaborative problem solving.

Assessment.   Assessment is an integral part of the Cognitive Tutor curriculum. Cognitive Tutor software includes step-by-step assessments of students' mathematical skills and provides a skill report to identify math skills levels and progress for each student. Assessment tools are also provided in the teacher's materials and include pretests and culminating exams, quizzes (answer keys provided), and rubrics for grading class presentations. Teachers are also encouraged to create

and share their own assessments, consisting of quizzes and tests, on an online teacher community.

Comparing Programs

Table 8.3 compares six programs across the features of learning environments. The table characterizes and allows comparison of several widely used learning environments. Our point is to illustrate commonality and variety in the design of learning environments. The entries in Table 8.3 use language that we have drawn from respective descriptions of the programs. In some instances, programs describe similar features, but use different terms.

Summary

The environments described in this section have academic goals, are theoretically based, wide in scope, and have published research on their effectiveness. The descriptions illustrate that while programs have similar features, they differ in how each translates theory into practice. One difference is in which features are central to a particular learning environment. For instance, technology is the core in many programs; in others it is secondary or not present at all. Another difference is that content might be addressed using problem, project or design based units. Content might be linked to students' daily lives or in issues that are derived from those encountered by scientists, mathematicians, or other experts.

Goals usually focus on understanding of the content and processes of a discipline. Development of expertise is an aim shared by most learning environments, and some programs emphasize intentional learning as a goal. Age related developmental goals are mostly absent, although program features match recommendations for instruction based on developmental needs of late elementary and middle school students. Highly sequenced learning environments are usually based on information processing theory, which emphasizes individual construction of knowledge. To guide knowledge development these environments rely on detailed models of expert and novice thinking. Other environments emphasize social aspects of learning and focus on development of learning communities.

The success of any learning environment depends on the teacher, although the programs vary with respect to teachers' roles. In some programs, much of the burden of instruction is shared with technological tools or materials

TABLE 8.3 Program Comparisons

	Goals			
Program	Academic	Social and Interpersonal	Habits of Mind	Developmental
Connected Mathematics (Lappan et al., 2002; Lappan & Phillips, 1998; Reys et al., 2003)	Math knowledge, understanding, and skill; math content and process goals aligned with national standards	Mutually supportive learning	Become independent learners; intellectual methods of the discipline	
CSILE/Knowledge Forum™ (Bereiter & Scardamalia, 2003; Scardamalia, 2004; Scardamalia & Bereiter, 1994; Scardamalia, Bereiter, & Lamon, 1994)	Knowledge-building skills; deep understanding in different academic domains	Interpersonal skills	Habits of mind for lifelong learning; intentional learners	
Fifth Dimension (Cole, 1995; K. Brown & Cole, 2000, 2002; Gallego & Cole, 2000)	Learning through play: Cognitive outcomes include computer literacy, comprehension, and problem-solving skills	Build relationships between children and young adults	Develop autonomy, knowledge, and skills for everyday practices	Extend children's cognitive and social development
GenScope™/BioLogica™ (Horwitz & Christie, 2000; Hickey, Kindfield, Horwitz, & Christie, 1999, 2003; Hickey, Wolfe, & Kindfield, 2000; Horwitz, Neumann, & Schwartz, 1996)	Use basic concepts in genetics to reason and solve problems in the domain		Acquire the habits of mind of professional scientists	
GIsML (Hapgood, Magnusson, & Palincsar, 2004; Magnusson & Palincsar, 1995; Palincsar & Magnusson, 2001; Palincsar, Magnusson, Collins, & Cutter, 2001)	Science content understandings; scientific reasoning	Work in a community of learners	Enculturation into scientific community	
Kids as Global Scientists/BioKIDS (Huber, Songer, & Lee, 2003; Mistler-Jackson & Songer, 2000; Songer, 1996, in press; Songer, Lee, & Kam, 2002)	Conceptual understanding of standards-based science content; longitudinal development of scientific reasoning skills; technology skills	Positive motivational beliefs toward science	Develop understanding of nature of science	

	Tasks				
Program	Content	Sequence	Authenticity	Contextualization	Artifacts
Connected Mathematics	Math problem-solving activities	Sequenced to develop understanding and skills	Real-world, purely mathematical, and whimsical situations	Problem-centered: Math concepts embedded in problems	Represent learning
CSILE/Knowledge Forum™	Knowledge-building workspace to produce and improve ideas	Open sequence: Supports multiple curriculum areas	Tied to interest of classroom community	Self-selected inquiry by students and/or teacher	Contribute to community knowledge
Fifth Dimension	Problem-solving and communication activities	Children move through a maze of activities at own pace	Children select activities and level of challenge	Socially oriented	Illustrate how tasks were accomplished

TABLE 8.3 *Continued*

Program	Tasks				
	Content	Sequence	Authenticity	Contextualization	Artifacts
GenScope™/ BioLogica™	Genetics problem-solving activities	Interactive software presents problems and guides learning	Tied to student interest; domain-focused	Framed by the domain: Tasks focus on genetics	Represent students' mental models
GIsML	Inquiry science investigations	Cycle of investigation guided by teacher	Real-world science; firsthand and secondhand investigations	Knowledge production in a scientific community	Reflect content knowledge and reasoning skills
Kids as Global Scientists/BioKIDS	Inquiry-focused activities	Sequenced to support inquiry readiness and foster science learning	Real-world; discipline-based	Interactive inquiry around science themes	Showcase content and inquiry knowledge acquisition

Program	Instructional Materials		
	Theoretical Explicitness	Detail for Enacting	Resources
Connected Mathematics	Drawn from cognitive sciences research: Students develop understandings from direct experience with mathematics	Complete middle school curriculum; comprehensive guides for enactment	Teachers follow a guidebook; students use unit books
CSILE/Knowledge Forum™	Principles of knowledge building	Online knowledge-building courses, resources, discussions, and tutorials for teachers	Online workspace is used by teacher and students; scaffolds and resources for students in workspace
Fifth Dimension	Design principles derive from cultural-historical activity theory; explicit principles for site design	General implementation guidelines for site design and management; core principles frame program design	Adaptable model: Each site is run by a community and university partnership that develops a unique program based on core principles
GenScope™/ BioLogica™	Model-based teaching and learning framework: Learners need to construct, elaborate, and revise mental models of biological phenomena	Online demonstration of Web-based lab activities illustrates use for teacher and students; activities can supplement or supplant teacher's course	Teacher guide and student worksheets; software provides prompts for students as they engage in investigations
GIsML	Sociocultural theory: Learning arises from individual activity and social interaction in the social and cultural world	Teacher learns tenets of GIsML instruction via professional development; unit activities provided	Teacher's guide for supporting use of student text materials
Kids as Global Scientists/BioKIDS	Constructivist learning theory and learning cycle approach serve as theoretical frame; promoting readiness for inquiry provides explicit guidance in design	Downloadable curriculum to help teachers plan and enact lessons: Includes descriptions of activities, information on using digital resources, annotated student worksheets	Curriculum binder consisting of teacher guide and student worksheets; handheld software; online database for students and teachers

(continued)

315

TABLE 8.3 *Continued*

	Social Organization		
Program	Structure	Communities of Practice	Beyond the Classroom
Connected Mathematics	Multiple arrangements: Individual, pairs, small groups, and whole class	Ways of thinking, reasoning, and communicating in mathematics	Home connections: Newsletters and activities for home
CSILE/Knowledge Forum™	Collaborative knowledge work within a multimedia community space	Knowledge-building practices and discourse	Online network of databases for community participation
Fifth Dimension	Children pair with adult mentors as coparticipants	Social and discourse practices in a playful activity system	Cross-site activities via communication technologies
GenScope™/ BioLogica™	Pairs or individual students engage in activities	Practices of the scientific community; focus on scientific inquiry and reasoning	
GIsML	Students work together with guidance and support from teacher	Cultural elements of the scientific community: Scientific values, conventions, norms, beliefs	
Kids as Global Scientists/BioKIDS	Students work collaboratively with teacher as guide and facilitator	Inquiry knowledge development in a learning community: Science inquiry reasoning, communication	Online discussions and data sharing with peers at other school sites and with experts; students utilize Internet resources

	Teacher		
Program	Responsibility	Centrality	Competencies
Connected Mathematics	Enact curriculum units; assign homework; assess student work	Primary position in enacting; work closely with students to make sense of math	Facilitate problem-centered curriculum; pedagogical expertise
CSILE/Knowledge Forum™	Prepare students for knowledge-building work; set expectations; initiate inquiry	Allow for student-directed inquiry; scaffold students in the process of knowledge building	Understand knowledge-building process; technology expertise
Fifth Dimension	College-age adults partner with children throughout every activity	Role of teacher and learner is flexibly shared by adults and children; adults guide as much as necessary for children to make progress and have fun	Ability to regulate the quality of interaction around the tasks; maintain role as a capable peer
GenScope™ /BioLogica™	Coordinate class and computer activities; assess student progress	Monitor students during computer activities; lead peripheral activities; provide individual assistance to students as needed	Course planning; integrate computer activities with classroom activities; technology expertise
GIsML	Determine the initial inquiry; guide and shape students' interactions with materials, ideas, and classmates	Central role in mediating students' interactions: Guide students through the inquiry cycle	Knowledgeable about science content, nature of science, and scientific practices; support students' knowledge building
Kids as Global Scientists/BioKIDS	Adapt program for classroom use; guide inquiry activities; assess student work	Key facilitator for learning: Guide students through inquiry phases as they investigate and research	Ability to tailor lessons to support students; science content and technology knowledge

	Technology		
Program	Tools	Centrality	Function
Connected Mathematics	Graphing calculators; optional computers and third-party commercial software	Students use calculators regularly; computer software activities are optional	Calculators are integrated into the curriculum as a tool for solving problems
CSILE/Knowledge Forum™	Electronic group workspace: Communal database and Web-based communication tools	Workspace is used for note taking, searching, organizing, and sharing information	Scaffold individual or group research process

TABLE 8.3 *Continued*

Program	Technology		
	Tools	Centrality	Function
Fifth Dimension	Computers and third-party commercial educational software	Computer software and telecommunications activities are pervasive	Computer-mediated activity that interweaves play and learning
GenScope™/ BioLogica™	Computer-based software learning environment consisting of custom-designed tools for exploring genetics	Technology-supported science learning: Structures and guides learning activities	Provide individual students with a sequence of activities and scaffolds for investigation work
GIsML	Technology, such as computers and software, used to leverage learning	Technology used when advantageous to make ideas visible for students	Support the development of conceptual understanding
Kids as Global Scientists/BioKIDS	Web-based databases, handheld technology, and the Internet for interactive inquiry	Technology tools and resources utilized in inquiry activities	Scaffold inquiry process for students: Technology used to gather and organize data, analyze data, communicate with peers and experts, and create reports and presentations

Program	Assessment	
	Types	Targets
Connected Mathematics	Pencil-and-paper quizzes and unit tests; self-assessments; projects	Math concepts and skills; disposition toward mathematics; work habits
CSILE/Knowledge Forum™	Individual and group portfolios of research work; reports, multimedia presentations, and demonstrations	Depth of understanding and ways of thinking in different academic areas
Fifth Dimension	Children complete task cards after each activity; progress is noted in a log	Monitor students' progress through activities
GenScope™/ BioLogica™	Electronic portfolios of students' investigations	Modeling and explanation of processes and mechanisms of genetics
GIsML	Student reports and presentations; written responses in science notebook	Understanding of science concepts; scientific reasoning and explanation
Kids as Global Scientists/BioKIDS	Individual and group generated artifacts and presentations	Science content knowledge and scientific inquiry abilities

on the Internet. In others, teachers have the primary role in instruction so that they have considerable responsibility for making instructional choices such as what questions or topics to pursue, how to represent content, and how to adapt the learning environment materials in a manner that is congruent with basic premises but also tailored to specific circumstances. These types of environments require greater teacher knowledge of content and pedagogy and of the principles that guide the design in order for goals to be achieved.

All programs make use of artifacts as reflections of student understanding. Students synthesize and apply concepts through artifact creation and revision. However, program developers also are under pressure from funding agencies and school systems to demonstrate effects on more conventional and widely understood methods. Most use performance on curriculum specific tests and on high stakes standardized tests as evidence of increased achievement.

The criteria we used narrowed the range of programs included in our descriptions, although even in this limited sample there is considerable variation in how features are designed. Our descriptive framework differentiates specific aspects within each feature and therefore is useful for providing considerable detail about overall program design. Researchers, designers and practitioners can use this detailed information to match their ideas about development of a learning environment with ones that already contain aspects of interest in each feature. Developers then might look across programs to study techniques for instantiating these aspects and making modifications to fit their goals.

DESIGN AND IMPLEMENTATION OF LEARNING ENVIRONMENTS: INTERPLAY OF THEORY AND PRACTICE

In this section, we describe how theory is used to design learning environments, how data are gathered on enactment and student outcomes to shape design revision, and how this cycle helps to inform theory and practice. We begin by examining the role that design principles play in guiding the development process. We then illustrate the process by showing how difficulties in implementation common to many learning environments are addressed via iterative cycles of implementation, evaluation, and revision. Finally, we discuss debates about the merits of design research, which is used extensively in the field of learning environments.

Design Principles

The design and building of learning environments is an iterative process. As illustrated in the previous section, most programs use theory as the basis for design. Developers collect data on enactment and outcomes and revise features that do not work as anticipated. As Ann L. Brown (1992) argued in her groundbreaking paper on design experiments, the idea is that enactment and theory inform each other; consequently, designers generally do not see the innovation as a fixed entity. Through cycles of revision to make features work as intended, they provide valuable information on how theory works in practice and under what circumstances. This information is used to generate design principles for the creation of new learning environments.

Design principles bridge the gap between theory and practice. They are an interpretation of a program's theoretical base and are meant to inform the development of instructional sequences and activities. The initial articulation of design principles is usually tentative, and principles are revisited and strengthened through the iterative design process. They are of central concern to program developers because they provide guidance for the design process by delineating design principles for environments and describing instructional practices that make them work as intended in varying contexts. This more specified level of theoretical analysis is important because the results provide direct guidance for organizing instruction. This is the type of approach Burkhardt and Schoenfeld (2003) argue is necessary for making progress in solving tough educational problems. In this way, the iter-

ative work can lead to stronger connections between theory and classroom practice.

Design principles can take different shape and forms. Some are very general; others are heuristics that inform sequences and activities; and others dictate the prominent features and how they can be instantiated. One example is Edelson's (2001) Learning-for-Use framework, which is drawn from cognitive science principles. The framework is meant to help curriculum designers integrate content and process learning in the design of their own programs. Edelson and colleagues (2001; Edelson, Salierno, Matese, Pitts, & Sherin, 2002) are currently applying this model to the design of technology-supported science learning environments. His framework articulates four principles for design: (1) Learning involves the constructing and modifying of knowledge structures; (2) knowledge construction is a goal-directed process; (3) situations in which knowledge is constructed and used determine its accessibility for future use; and (4) knowledge must be constructed in a usable form before it can be applied. Note that the principles are not detailed enough to spell out every design decision.

In GIsML, a more specific heuristic is used for the design and implementation of guided inquiry (Magnusson & Palincsar, 1995). The heuristic is based on a conceptualization of instruction as a series of cycles involving engagement, investigation, and reporting. This heuristic, derived from a sociocultural perspective, is intended to reflect how scientific knowledge production actually occurs in the professional science community. Because inquiry in the scientific community also involves a combination of firsthand investigation of phenomena and secondhand investigation of the work of others, the heuristic also emphasizes these culturally authentic practices. Similarly, LBD design principles provide guidance for how students can learn science content and practices in the context of design-and-build activities. LBD's cognitive constructivist framework emphasizes the role of routines and procedures in helping learners organize and access their knowledge so that they can apply it and relate it to new situations (Kolodner, Gray, et al., 2003).

Another example is the backward design framework of Wiggins and McTighe (1998), which is aimed at creating effective curricula linked to standards. It begins with learning outcomes based on standards that specify what students should know and be able to do. It includes three stages for design: Identify desired results, determine acceptable evidence, and plan learning experiences and instruction. The design process is based on a broad theory of understanding informed by Dewey (1933), Bloom (1956), Gardner (1991), and others (see Wiggins & McTighe, 1998) and is compatible with a range of instructional approaches.

Design principles are not detailed enough to spell out every design decision; they are midlevel propositions that are not specific enough so that one designer's particular instantiation of the principle can be readily incorporated into a different environment. In fact, many programs derive similar design principles even when their design principles are not explicitly stated. However, it is uncommon for researchers to compare instantiations of the same principle across programs to see which are most effective and under what conditions. Nor is it common for them to compare different ways to instantiate design principles within a program or across programs (Collins, Joseph, & Bielaczyc, 2004). Cobb, Confrey, diSessa, Lehrer, and Schauble (2003) argue that designers can help each other avoid pitfalls by reporting initial designs and doing retrospective analyses to explain how experiences informed final designs. One example is an attempt by Quintana et al. (2004) to create common design principles for technology scaffolds based on a synthesis of other's work in the field. Another is a recent paper by Puntambekar and Hubscher (2005), which reviews and critiques the current state of scaffolding in design. What is needed now is a synthesis across programs that can be part of a framework of design principles. The framework presented in the previous section may prove useful for program designers as they seek to find principles within each area that might inform their own efforts.

Iterative Cycles of Design

We provide examples from our own and others' work on how design and implementation interplay to improve theory. The interplay enables a more well-developed, grounded, and nuanced understanding of constructs, a range of examples of the constructs and their interactions within context, and illustrations of their value for teachers and students. The data collected usually includes some combination of classroom field notes, teacher reports, and video records of instructional interactions, including technology use. In addition, evaluation of learning includes examination of artifacts, student performances, test scores, and interview responses.

We discuss contextualization and design of learning tools as examples of how designs are tested and revised. We also highlight findings about consistent challenges faced by teachers and students that also influence revision and result in more specified design principles.

Contextualization

Theoretically, the principle that learning is situated makes contextualization important for designing learning environments. Contextualization situates student learning by making content concrete and meaningful. It organizes subject matter concepts and skills, helps students draw on prior knowledge, provides a common and continuous reference point for discussion, and motivates learning. Some programs strive for authenticity in how contextualization is achieved. Authenticity, as defined by Newmann and Whelage (1993), involves tasks that are worthwhile and meaningful for learners, supports active constructing of knowledge, and reflects disciplinary practices.

Bransford and his group (Cognition and Technology Group at Vanderbilt, 1997) contextualize through anchoring instruction in a videodisc series called *The Adventures of Jasper Woodbury*. The program materials consist of a series of video-based narrative adventures that pose problems for fifth- through eighth-grade students to solve, such as developing and evaluating a business plan for raising funds for a student-run project. All the information necessary to solve the problem is embedded in the video adventure story. Adventures address such math topics as introductory statistics, geometry, and algebra. The problems are created and sequenced based on a model called the IDEAL problem solver (Bransford & Stein, 1993). The emphasis of *Jasper* is on developing students' mathematical problem-solving, reasoning, and communication skills.

Others, like Learning by Design (LBD), use the design of everyday artifacts to organize instruction around something concrete that students need to build and test. LBD is an approach to science learning that has sixth- through eighth-grade students learn science by engaging in design-and-build challenges (Kolodner, Camp, et al., 2003). The challenges are centered on the design and construction of working devices or models that illustrate science concepts. For example, students learn about force and motion by designing, building, and testing miniature vehicles; they learn about the human respiratory system by designing artificial lungs and building partial working models; and they learn about erosion by designing and constructing a model erosion management system.

Project-based science is organized around a driving question that is related to students' everyday lives. For instance, students explore ideas about force and motion to answer the question "Why should I wear a helmet when I ride my bike?" In addition, anchoring events such as a film about head injuries or demonstrations are used to illustrate big ideas and are referred to throughout the unit as the focus of discussion as students learn more about phenomena under study. Students also experience the phenomena directly whenever feasible, such as doing an "air walk" to examine signs of pollution in their neighborhood.

Contextualization poses problems for instantiating theory into practice. For instance, there were differences in the effectiveness of driving questions that were selected to contextualize PBS units. Students considered some to be more real-world than others. Those that focused on ecology, such as "What is the quality of air in my community?" were perceived as more relevant than questions focused on physical science, such as "How can we build big things?"

We noted problems in instructional practice in use of the driving question and anchoring events. Because teachers are more familiar with stand-alone activities or lessons, they varied in their use of the driving question to organize and synthesize instruction. Some attempted to use student experiences to contextualize concepts but failed to relate that experience clearly to the idea. Instead, to promote participation, they encouraged long discussions of experiences students shared that often diverted from and did little to help students understand how those experiences related to the point. Moreover, some teachers had difficulty helping students experience phenomena because of local circumstances, rules, or resources. For example, visits to a local river were not permitted by some principals, and some schools were not located close to a body of water.

As a result of these experiences, we experimented with different driving questions, altered contextualization activities, created new professional development material, and revised our curriculum materials. For example, we developed driving question boards for the class to post what they learned after completing each main investigation, activity, and artifact to indicate how it contributed to answering the question. We provided

alternatives to experience the phenomena through video of the teacher visiting a river and through the design of virtual field trips presented on CD ROMs. The cycles taught us how to make contextualization more effective, how to help teachers use contextualization, and how to provide alternative possibilities to aid teachers in tailoring for their own students and settings (for more detail, see Krajcik & Blumenfeld, in press).

Our experiences with contextualization are similar to those of other groups. For instance, the designers of *Jasper* needed to tinker with the use of video and stories to make them meaningful to students and to make the mathematical problem involved clear, rather than clouded by too much extraneous detail. Holbrook and Kolodner (2000) found that although design challenges in LBD were intended to provide the context for learning science concepts and practices, teachers would fail to contextualize instruction. Instead, they often attempted to teach the science first and then introduce the design challenge. Design activities were often more like arts-and-crafts activities as students and teachers focused on constructing working models and neglected to make links to the underlying science concepts (Kolodner, Camp, et al., 2003). In the process of redesigning LBD to work better in middle school science classrooms, the designers consulted with teachers to develop a 3-week introductory unit called a launcher unit comprising a series of short design challenges meant to introduce science, design, and collaboration practices (Holbrook & Kolodner, 2000). To accomplish this, the launcher unit emphasizes the norms for doing science and design independent of the science content. Rather than introduce science and design processes at the same time students learn science content, the principle is to establish a classroom culture first, to better prepare students for learning science from design activities during regular LBD units. Launcher units also reduce the complexity of instruction for teachers so that they can transition more easily into new teaching practices required when using design to contextualize learning (Kolodner, Camp, et al., 2003).

Technology

Many recently designed learning environments rely on technology; in fact, the use of technology tools that scaffold learning constitutes one of their hallmarks. Designers usually find that creating software that is usable in classroom situations requires multiple research cycles. For instance, during early implementation efforts, Cognitive Tutors' designers found that the software required computers with greater computational power than was typically found in schools. They also found that the computer interface was confusing to students, and sometimes the tutors gave inappropriate feedback about student problem-solving attempts (Anderson, Boyle, Corbett, & Lewis, 1990). Continuous refinement via cycles of implementation and evaluation allowed designers to respond to challenges. Developers closed the gap between school computers and tutor software, improved the interface and the tutor's cognitive model, and transformed Cognitive Tutors into a complete mathematics curriculum (Corbett et al., 2001; Koedinger & Anderson, 1998).

A related challenge for design is how to make the technology user-friendly. The cost of learning new software and new uses of technology is often high for students and teachers. First-time use of new technology with students can preoccupy teachers with managing the technology and keep teachers from effectively interacting with students to support learning during technology use. To address this problem, WISE designers developed a mentorship model of professional development (Slotta, 2004). Experienced WISE teachers work with novice teachers in workshops in which videos of WISE master teachers are discussed and social supports such as peer networks and close mentor relationships are provided. Also, because many software applications are tailored for a particular learning environment approach, all the features and affordances contained in any one piece of software may not be used easily across programs.

Another challenge is to create programs that are learner-centered so that the degree of scaffolding can be tailored to students' level of expertise (Quintana et al., 2004; Soloway, Guzdial, & Hay, 1994). In addition, designers need to determine what constitutes effective scaffolding to promote student thoughtfulness. For the most part, each learning environment uses software of specially designed scaffolds to support the learning of novices. Customized scaffolding is provided at the macro level in terms of organization and functionality (notebooks, drawing boards) and at the micro level through prompts. Some learning tools promote inquiry, such as those that ask students to make predictions or provide databases and ways to keep track of information gathered; others aid collaboration via mutual visualization, common notebooks, or group databases; some help with interpretation and modeling. How scaffolds are designed tends to be unique to each program, which means

students must learn to respond to different sources of support each time they encounter new software. Greater attention is being paid to the variations in how scaffolding is designed, and there is interest in identifying more common design features to aid students (Puntambekar & Hubscher, 2005; Quintana et al., 2004).

Project Based Science makes use of several software tools. Students use Model-It to easily build, test, and evaluate qualitative, dynamic models. Students can import the functional relationships they developed into DataViz. Students plan their models by recording ideas and creating objects and factors. Next, they build relationship links between the factors using qualitative and quantitative representations. A graphical view of each relationship is also provided. For data visualization, Model-It provides meters and graphs to view factor values. As students test their models they can change the values of factors and immediately see the effects.

The incorporation of learning supports or scaffolding that addresses the differences between learners and professionals is central to learner-centered design. By guiding the selection of goals and processes, scaffolding enables the learner to achieve goals or accomplish processes that would otherwise be too difficult. Reducing complexity is a common design principle for scaffolding. The software incorporates three types of scaffolding (Jackson et al., 2000). Supportive scaffolding guides learners through steps within phases of inquiry; for example, when constructing a model, students are reminded to make a plan of variables to include before building and testing. Reflective scaffolds support learners' metacognitive activities. For instance, they are prompted to test individual relationships or a sequence of relationships before evaluating the entire model. Functionality in the software supports testing and debugging, allowing students to determine which relationships work and which may need revision. Intrinsic scaffolding supports different levels of user expertise; it makes the simplest level of functionality available to the novice learner, but allows learners to access advanced features as their capability grows.

Wallace and colleagues (Wallace, Kupperman, Krajcik, & Soloway, 2000) used observations of how students search for and make use of information on the Internet to learn how to support students in using online resources. They found that many students do not behave as intentional learners who aim to increase or build knowledge as they search. Instead, students interpret the task of seeking information as one of getting a single right answer or numerous good hits. Moreover, students' background knowledge about their question often is limited; as a result, they have trouble generating any keywords other than those used in their questions. Failure to create synonyms may also be due to limited appreciation for the significance of keywords or a lack of understanding about how the technology works.

In addition, Wallace et al. (2000) report that students do not have efficient ways to monitor what they have accomplished; they lose their place if the search continues over a period of time, often repeating what they have done before or not making use of the information they have already gathered. Moreover, they have few strategies for reading or evaluating a considerable amount of material online. Perhaps it is because students are used to looking up brief answers in textbooks or other reference sources such as encyclopedias and dictionaries that they may have neither skills nor inclination to critique what they find.

These findings point to some of the areas in which students need support if they are to conduct effective searches, and suggest that a major challenge to using digital information resources is to provide tools that allow students to embed information seeking in a sustained process. Such tools must support both searching for simple answers where students are looking for factual information, and also complex exploration of information when learners are trying to understand a multifaceted problem.

Based on classroom observations of students, Artemis was created to support students as they access and use digital information over the Internet (Wallace et al., 1998). Artemis allows students to accomplish multiple tasks within a single computer environment. This keeps work from becoming fragmented and allows students to return to where they left off in prior sessions. The workspace allows for recording of searches and includes links to actual documents, helping students sustain the information-seeking process over time. One feature, the question folders, supports students in thinking about and organizing the information they find in terms of their query. They also help students to note what other questions or information they might usefully pursue. Students can store links to items they find interesting in question folders and can create multiple folders that reflect different areas of the search or the refinements of an initial question. The folders allow flexibility in storing links and are available across multiple work sessions so that students can draw on what they have done before. Students can add or delete items or evaluate what they have found to date. Also, past results windows keep a live list of student searches so that they can see how they searched previously and what they have found. This feature is helpful, as observations indicate that students forget which queries they have submitted and consequently repeat the same questions. It also allows students to index what they found and to review their process over time.

There is a broad topics feature that includes a list of topics organized by domain. The topics present a hierarchy of terms that can be browsed or searched as the first step in creating a query. It is intended to help students generate keywords and draw on prior knowledge as well as giving them a view of the structure of the content area they are exploring and providing them with alternative and productive ways to search.

Artemis is connected to the University of Michigan Digital Library, which contains a collection of relevant sites for middle school students (see http://umdl.soe .umich.edu). The objective is to alleviate the frustrating problem students often have of getting numerous irrelevant hits when performing an Internet search. Teachers and students also have the ability to critique, comment on, and recommend sites. Reading others' recommendations and their accompanying rationales and contributing their own critiques can help students learn to evaluate information and sites and also increase motivation.

Design changes similar to those made to the software programs described above can be adapted by other developers as they seek to create learning tools that are theoretically based and that work in classrooms.

Teachers and Students

Most developers of learning environments find that their innovations pose predictable enactment challenges for teachers and students. As some of the examples about contextualization and technology illustrate, quite often, the intended program envisioned by designers differs dramatically from what actually unfolds in classrooms. This is almost always the case in early implementations.

A significant challenge, then, for those designing learning environments is to anticipate difficulties and create innovations that will support teachers and students in engaging in new modes of teaching and learning. Designers need to think through how a learning environment can be enacted and sustained in real-world instructional settings. This process entails making modifications to accommodate to a range of classroom issues. In early implementations of PBS, we found that as teachers tried unfamiliar instructional strategies or new arrangements, the results were often less than ideal; teachers ran out of time and did not relate back to the driving question during lessons, artifacts were left unfinished, and discussions did not facilitate the construction of key ideas (Marx, Blumenfeld, Krajcik, & Soloway, 1997; Singer, Marx, Krajcik, & Chambers, 2000). Time, we learned, is a precious commodity in classrooms; teachers struggle to cover curriculum, address mandated requirements such as testing and test preparation, and incorporate new requirements such as programs on drug awareness or character education. Because time is at a premium, teachers often dropped activities that enabled discussion, reflection, and revision, all of which are essential for knowledge construction. Some teachers proceduralized and simplified artifact development to save time rather than help students to develop, share, and revise their work. Others failed to devote class time for students to compare findings from investigations and consider what varied results meant, an essential component of the inquiry process.

Another difficulty for teachers is the management of groups working on different questions or activities. This challenge is increased when students have difficulty self-regulating and staying on task. The problem is magnified when technology is involved and computer access is limited, so that work time must be organized and coordinated.

Building a community of learners is also problematic. To foster collaboration and create appropriate norms, teachers must help students learn to work together productively, to respect, share, discuss, and critique each other's ideas. This interaction pattern takes time to develop and to carry out. Also, it may not result in "correct" answers, which is troubling to many teachers. When facing challenges of managing complex collaborations, teachers often cut these interactions short and give children the answers.

Teachers also have difficulty scaffolding experiences so that students can take responsibility for learning. They often give students too much independence without adequately modeling thinking processes, structuring the situation, or providing feedback. When students are unsure about what questions to pursue or how to design an investigation to answer questions, teachers simply give students a question and an experiment rather than let them develop and critique their own design as a route to learning about scientific processes. Mergendoller and colleagues (Mergendoller, Markham, Ravitz, & Larmer, in press) discuss in detail what types of scaffolding are necessary across time as problem-based learning curricula unfold. They stress that scaffolding is the key to management and also to student learning.

These problems led our PBS group to change our initial designs so that our materials provided greater support for teachers and students and could be used effectively across different classroom settings. For example, we shortened projects and focused on essential content, simplified artifacts, and provided alternatives to accomplish tasks when small-group work was too demanding (Krajcik & Blumenfeld, in press). We also included educative materials for teachers in the curriculum packages that contained information about management, content, and difficulty students might have with the content. We included ideas for adaptations and the principles underlying designs, so that teachers might adapt them in a manner congruent with the basic principles underlying the goals (Davis & Krajcik, 2005; Schneider, Krajcik, & Blumenfeld, 2005).

We used what we observed as the basis for discussion during professional development. During these sessions, an important part of the process of making revisions was collaboration among school personnel, teachers, and university researchers. Often, researchers identified a problem and teachers would work on strategies or suggest revisions to solve the problem. For example, we worked on ways to introduce inquiry so that students' early experiences were more highly structured and scaffolded and less complex. At other times, teachers complained about activities that did not work or technology design that was confusing. We worked on ways to introduce modeling technology to separate issues of learning to manage the software from learning what models are. We also worked on strategies to help students understand scientific explanations by creating a rubric for students and teachers and scenarios where students contrasted explanations they might make to a parent to explain the meaning results of an investigation from those a scientist might make. We highlighted scientific language, use of evidence, and ways of interpreting data. We also tried to link our professional development to student and teacher learning (Fishman et al., 2003).

Students. Significant design challenges involve promoting student participation, thoughtfulness, and motivation. The learning environments described here represent a considerable departure from the type of classroom experience with which students are familiar. These learning environments require greater participation, more personal responsibility for learning, more self-direction, and more self-regulation (Blumenfeld et al., 1991; Blumenfeld, Kempler, & Krajcik, in press). Constructivist approaches require students to be motivated to ask questions, join in discussion, engage in sustained inquiry, and produce and revise artifacts. Not all students are willing to participate at this level; Scardamalia and Bereiter (1991) report unequal amounts of participation in their Computer-Supported Intentional Learning Environments (CSILE). As students built a class database, less able and less assertive students seemed to be somewhat "sidelined" from the action.

Linn (1992) reports that students were often not respectful of each other (e.g., would refuse to share computer keyboards or information), and groups developed status hierarchies and norms consistent with gender stereotypes in her Computer as Learning Partner environment. She found that quality collaboration was difficult to achieve; less dominant students tended to agree with more dominant ones, and students reported a variety of perspectives rather than try to understand the merits of different points of view and come to common understanding. One reason students might not collaborate productively is because they may not know how to do so. Palincsar, Anderson, and David (1993) addressed this problem by designing a program to help students learn scientific argumentation as a way to enhance the quality of dialogue and improve student learning.

Reports of enactment problems from several of the programs attest to the challenge of eliciting thoughtfulness. Linn (1992) notes that students using the Computer as Learning Partner environment experienced difficulties generalizing from laboratory experiments to their everyday experiences and to new material they had not studied. Students tended to continue to respond to questions with their intuitive ideas rather than with the scientific principles integral to the topic under study. Also, there is evidence that students who collaborate via networks need help engaging in substantive conversations (Linn & Songer, 1988). As described earlier, Wallace et al. (2000) found that although students were on task while doing Web searches, the search frequently did not reflect engagement with the subject matter. Scardamalia and Bereiter (1991) also report that

students have trouble generating questions that allow them to explore a topic in depth. They suggest that students' approaches to learning can be characterized as a "schoolwork module" where, rather than engaging with the material so as to ask significant questions and enhance their knowledge, their aim is to find the right answer and get the work done. As a result, they developed ways to help students evaluate questions and inserted prompts into CSILE, a community knowledge-building software tool, that promoted more thoughtful interaction (Scardamalia & Bereiter, 1991).

Descriptions of middle school students' first experiences with inquiry in PBS reflect what others report (Krajcik et al., 1998). Students tended to select questions for inquiry quickly, without considering their merits. They did not think through what data would be necessary to answer these questions and often were not systematic in data collection. Only when the teacher asked for rationales for how the questions related to the issues under study did the students begin active discussions.

Issues of participation and thoughtfulness are closely linked to motivation. A fundamental goal of new learning environments is for students to take responsibility for and ownership of their own learning by inquiring, discussing, collecting, synthesizing, analyzing, and interpreting information. For these opportunities to be productive, students must invest considerable mental effort and persist in the search for answers to questions and solutions to problems.

However, whether students will be motivated to do so is not certain. On the one hand, there is reason to assume that students will respond positively to constructivist-based learning environments. Instructional factors that affect motivation include challenging work, opportunities for active learning, emphasis on topics that are perceived as valuable and that have personal or real-world relevance, provision of choice and decision making, use of collaboration, incorporating a variety of instructional techniques, and use of technology (Fredricks, Blumenfeld, & Paris, 2004; Guthrie & Wigfield, 2000). Also, Hickey (1997) argues that practices promoted by constructivist-based curricula are likely to minimize the effects of individual differences in motivation, as students participate in and become members of communities of practice. In fact, standards-based programs that incorporate these features promote positive attitudes (Hickey, Moore, & Pellegrino, 2001; Kahle, Meece, & Scantlebury, 2000). Participation in PBS stems the decline in interest in science typically found during the middle school years (Blumenfeld, Soloway, Krajcik, & Marx, 2004). Case studies of sixth graders by Mistler-Jackson and Songer (2000) suggest that their technology-based inquiry program promoted a high level of motivation and satisfaction.

However, findings from several studies demonstrate that student reactions are not uniformly positive. Individual differences influence how students approach tasks in learning environments. Meyer, Turner, and Spencer (1997) found that fifth- and sixth-grade students differed in their motivation, strategy use, and engagement depending on their disposition to seek or to avoid challenge. They suggest that teachers need to create a climate where task focus, not ability focus, is encouraged, where mistakes are viewed as opportunities for learning, where seeking help is seen as adaptive, and where collaboration to solve problems and use others' expertise is the norm.

Veermans and Jarvela (2004) showed individual differences in fourth graders' reactions to the Knowledge Forum (CSILE) learning environment. They found that students who reported higher learning goals demonstrated more self-regulation. These students moved beyond thinking about procedures and focused on the key ideas of the inquiry task. Consequently, the teacher responded by scaffolding the content rather than procedures of inquiry learning. In contrast, students whose goals for learning were lower, who wanted to avoid work or look smart rather than understand the material, faced more challenge in mastering the content.

Renninger and her colleagues (Hidi, Renninger, & Krapp, 2004; Renninger & Hidi, 2002) have shown the importance of interest on individual student motivation. Students are likely to engage more deeply and benefit from activities that they perceive to be personally meaningful. They are likely to be more motivated and more self-regulating when they study content in which they are interested. Motivated students are more likely to organize information and relate it to prior knowledge, promoting deeper understanding of content. Krajcik et al. (1998) and Patrick and Middleton (2002) showed that students' behavior during science projects differed depending on individual interest in the project question and on whether the inquiry tasks afforded enough situational interest to sustain engagement. Situational interest can "catch" students. Opportunities for making choices, working with others, and using technology can

trigger a short-term response that may not "hold" over time. Situational interest may eventually lead to more intrinsic interest in the material being explored. However, if investment in understanding does not occur, then ways to hold situational interest need to be incorporated into learning environments so that students will be more likely to engage with the ideas (Renninger, 2000).

Revisions in features of LBD illustrate responses to problems of teachers and students. Kolodner, Camp, et al. (2003) initially found that their instructional program was not specific enough to work in middle school science classrooms. So LBD designers made a number of changes to support teachers and students. They revised the initial focus on design to a redesign approach that emphasizes the role of iteration in refining and developing understanding (Kolodner, Camp, et al., 2003). They accomplished this by sequencing activities to ensure that students were guided through multiple trials of testing and building. Designers also added core activities, called rituals, in which students and teachers repeatedly engage as they progress through LBD cycles (Kolodner, Gray, et al., 2003). The repetition of core activities is meant to help students become familiar with scientific and design practices. Additional changes by designers included adding a student text, providing optional software to support student design activities, and integrating design worksheets, called diary pages, into the design cycle (Kolodner, Camp, et al., 2003; Putambekar & Kolodner, 2005).

As they went through the iterative design and research process, LBD designers drew from other approaches, such as Fostering Communities of Learners (A. L. Brown & Campione, 1994), to better support collaboration (Kolodner, Camp, et al., 2003). By drawing from design principles of other programs, they were able to make their own approach more complete. Similar problems and alternative solutions have been reported by the Cognition and Technology Group at Vanderbilt (Barron et al., 1998).

Merits of Design Research

Research on learning environments incorporates methodological traditions from several related fields. The work is highly interdisciplinary, with research teams drawn from psychology, computer science, education, and cognitive sciences; often, the teams include disciplinary specialists from mathematics, the sciences, or the social sciences. Over the past decade or two, the new, hybrid field of learning sciences has emerged with which many of the designers and researchers discussed here affiliate. A new journal, the *Journal of the Learning Sciences,* has appeared, and the International Society of the Learning Sciences (www.isls.org) has been organized. Moreover, educational journals (in particular, *Educational Researcher*) have published a lively and spirited debate about the epistemological strengths and weaknesses of research associated with learning environments. This debate has influenced discussions about the broader field of educational research and even the structure and role of colleges of education (Burkhardt & Schoenfeld, 2003). The NRC has published a book presenting the findings of a committee it constituted to contribute to this debate (Shavelson & Towne, 2002). And the newly formed Institute for Educational Sciences in the U.S. Department of Education has contributed through its research standards for funding (www.ed.gov/about /offices/list/ies/index.html) and through the What Works Clearinghouse, a Web-based service (www. whatworks.ed.gov) that evaluates and reports on educational research in support of reform.

The main points of contention in this debate concern a number of fundamental issues. Articles about research on design, which includes learning environments, point to differences with more traditional variable-centered research (see, e.g., the theme issue of *Educational Researcher,* vol. 32, no. 1, 2003, on the role of design in educational research and the special issue of the *Journal of the Learning Sciences,* vol. 13, no. 1, 2004, on design-based research). One point of debate concerns the integrated nature of learning environments. Some (Blumenfeld, Fishman, Krajcik, Marx, & Soloway, 2000) argue that all features (see Table 8.2) are presumed to work together; therefore, when doing research on a learning environment, it may not be possible to unpack contributions of various features. This is a common problem when learning environments are key elements in systemic reform programs (Fishman et al., 2003). By disaggregating the elements, for example, in a factorial experimental design, the value of some variables may be diminished. It might be possible to design large enough experiments for learning environments that have several factors, but the size of such an experiment is likely to be unmanageable.

The problem of losing the essential qualities of learning environments when disaggregating for experimental

studies has contributed, along with other issues, to the concept of design experiments (A. L. Brown, 1992; Collins, 1992) and, more recently, design research (Kelly, 2003). Design research is more akin to engineering, or maybe architecture, than it is to natural science. Simon (1996) distinguishes between natural sciences and sciences of the artificial, or design sciences. The latter include, for example, engineering, computer science, and medicine. When applied to the study of learning, as in research associated with learning environments, design research addresses four challenges (Collins et al., 2004): creating theory that addresses learning in context; studying learning phenomena in real settings rather than in rarified laboratory settings; employing a broader range of learning measures; and linking research findings to formative evaluation. In addressing these issues, Collins et al. point out that design research also has its own challenges: addressing the complexity of real settings and the difficulty of control in such contexts; volumes of data associated with mixed qualitative and quantitative research methods; and comparing findings that emerge from different types of designs.

One of the premises of design experiments is that the intervention is integrated: It works as a whole. The elements are not orthogonal, and changing one element of the system affects all elements. Thus, one cannot decompose the program as if each element were an independent variable in a more conventional experimental design. As a result, usually there is no attempt to separate variables to test their independent and interactive contributions to the instructional program as the basis for making recommendations for practice. In addition, comparison among features across programs is not likely to be attempted because they emphasize different aspects of the theory and are designed for somewhat different purposes. Instead, the research strategy is to modify individual programs based on evaluations and to track whether changes in features affect student learning. The idea is to obtain outcomes that are reliable and replicable for the entire program so that eventually it can be disseminated with minimal support. Therefore, it is unlikely that enough information about the effect of each program's features will be available so that a mix-and-match strategy of selecting and combining effective parts of each based on empirical findings can be used. Also, standardization of features is not likely to occur, because constructivist theory is formulated in a way that does not lead to explicit prescriptions for action. Rather, it encourages adaptation and modification of program features based on design principles as a way to enact the principles derived from theory. It is interesting to note, however, that recently an attempt has been made to integrate various aspects of these efforts in a learning environment called Schools for Thought (Lamon et al., 1996).

Well-done design research can provide findings that are more contextualized, have more detailed descriptions of learning in real settings, and present nuanced and complex examples of the range of outcomes when students engage in learning environments. But there has been considerable criticism of the failure to compare results of learning environments with results of other educational approaches or to use control groups. More recently there have been reviews of effects across problem-based learning environments (e.g., Gjibels, Dochy, Bossche, & Segers, 2005; Hmelo-Silver, 2004).

Among others, Cook and Payne (2002) have called for more use of experimental methods, including randomization of subjects to conditions, for policy-relevant research in education. The recent NRC book edited by Shavelson and Towne (2002) on scientific research in education raises similar points. One of the crucial points of argument concerns the validity of inferences drawn from design research studies. Without randomization and the use of control groups to which learning environments can be compared, there are many threats to internal validity of the research, thereby weakening the power of causal inferences.

Depending on the unit of analysis and length of time that an intervention might take, it is possible to conduct randomized experiments in real settings (see an early example by Clark et al., 1979). But substantial barriers exist. For example, in our work we engage teachers in long-term professional development in order for them to learn how to do inquiry in urban middle school classrooms. For some teachers, it takes a number of years to gain proficiency in the complexities of the curriculum and the instructional model (Geier, 2005). A number of researchers (e.g., Hawley & Valli, 1999) have argued that teacher support systems ought to be used to help teachers master complex instruction. Based on these arguments, we have collaborated with teachers with whom we have worked in Detroit in the creation of such a teacher support system. As a consequence, teachers act like professionals: They talk to each other, share ideas and challenges, and support each other through difficulties. Moreover, they work in the context of a districtwide systemic reform program, so their collaboration is strongly supported by district officials who encourage teachers to share their practices with each other. Because it takes about 3 years for some teachers to master the instruction and even longer to gain expertise, it would be impossible and, in the eyes of district officials, counterproductive to isolate teachers from each other. As a consequence, an experiment in this context would most assuredly result in the blending of practices across treatment groups as teachers share their practices, thus confounding treatments and weakening causal inferences.

Problems also are apparent in the definition and enactment of control groups. For example, if designers are serious about integrating technology and capitalizing on the affordances that new technologies provide, then comparing an instructional unit with the technology to one without it would be tantamount to comparing quite different instructional units. Moreover, there may be no way to create truly comparable control groups that do not have technology if, in fact, the technology provides unique affordances. For example, there may be no way to enable students to conduct simulations of complex systems without using the processing power of computers.

There have also been calls for more mixed-method research designs (Johnson & Onwuegbuzie, 2004) to be employed in evaluating outcomes of educational and social innovations that could be applied to research on learning environments. Indeed, Collins and colleague's (2004) approach to design research employs a range of methods, from ethnography to quantitative assessments of learning. The advantages of mixed-methods studies include the broader range of data that can be used to understand the learning environment as it is actually enacted, the impact the learning environment has on students, and the opportunity to use the strengths of one method to balance the weaknesses of another. The weaknesses include greater cost in time and dollars and the need for a broader range of expertise, thus almost necessitating a team of researchers rather than one. Methodological purists might also object to mixing epistemological systems.

SCALING LEARNING ENVIRONMENTS

Once learning environments have been tested in a small number of settings, the challenge is to test their usability in a wide variety of circumstances. Designs for learning environments stem from research on learning, development, and motivation. Initial implementation combines insights from this work with best practices. As we discussed earlier, initial implementation results in new information about theoretical warrants for design and about teacher practices that make the designs work. Usually in initial development, proof of concept is salient; scaling is not a critical issue.

Scaling of learning environments involves another level of effort and draws on findings from organizational and policy research. This work provides insights into how contexts into which learning environments are scaled impact enactment and success. Thus, designs that work initially may need to be modified to deal with new sites. As a result, design principles for scaling need to be developed as a new round of implementation that includes more sites occurs.

To discuss context issues in scaling, we present ideas about usability reform, problems of scaling of learning environments that use technologies, and research on the role of leadership in scaling. Many of these problems are not unique to scaling of learning environments. Because learning environments include multiple features, they pose special complications; features work together, and change in one feature to accommodate circumstances in different sites may necessitate change in others.

Types of Scaling

One type of scaling involves an increase in the number of users across settings. Work on diffusion of innovations is pertinent here. There are two primary points of view about diffusion. Rogers (2003) and his group view diffusion from the point of view of fixed innovations, examining how organizations take up and use the innovation. Van de Ven and colleagues (Van de Ven, Polley, Garud & Venkataraman, 1999) examine how innovations are modified as they become part of an organization's approach to its work. In this view, innovations that are not sufficiently malleable to be made part of local organizational culture will not succeed. Of course, this raises the problem of how changeable an innovation can be before it ceases to be an innovation. A. L. Brown and Campione (1996) refer to this issue as the problem of lethal mutations.

Scaling involves further tests of theory and practice; as the innovation meets a variety of different circumstances, adaptation is necessary. Warranted adaptations can teach us more about instantiations of features and also about practices that make them work. Features of the learning environments will need to be adapted to deal with the setting and resources of the schools, variations in the capability of teachers, and the background of the students. A standard rule of scale is this: For an innovation to have staying power, enactors must make it their own.

Generally, as programs go to scale they are first taken up by "early adopters." These teachers are risk takers who are enthusiastic about trying new things and about what the new program can offer. In the second phase of scaling, more adaptation likely will be required, and more of the adaptations will be of the "lethal" type. That is, one can expect teachers to change the innovation to match what they are used to or what their circumstances allow. This change is most likely when the learning environment differs from the "grammar of schooling" (Tyack & Cuban, 1995). The grammar of schooling reflects the day-to-day life of classroom instruction, including the formal curriculum and instructional activities, but also the rhythm and flow of interactions within the classroom and across the school. It also encompasses the unacknowledged but highly practiced assumptions and norms that guide roles and routines in school. Innovations such as learning environments that require considerable knowledge and skill and substantial changes in the teacher role are likely to challenge the grammar of schooling and therefore be subject to more pressure to conform. The problem of lethal mutations resulting from adaptation may be lessened when the learning environment is more self-contained, with teachers as managers rather than key figures in implementation.

A second type of scaling involves increasing numbers of users within a system. When scaling within a system, problems of adding numbers remain the same, but additional issues emerge. One big difference between the two types is that in the former, solutions to problems posed by context can be idiosyncratic. Solutions to problems in systemic scaling involve dealing with district and state policy and management. As numbers of users within the system grows, unique solutions become more difficult to create, and more systemwide solutions are needed. For example, when one teacher needs more computers, the principal might buy a few new ones or might borrow some from another department or the technology laboratory. When many teachers in the school or the system have the same problem, such borrowing or moving of resources will not work. Similarly, when one or two teachers need extended class time for students to conduct an investigation, they might trade periods with a colleague. When many teachers need extra time, systemic scaling may require new or flexible scheduling.

The success of systemic scaling will be influenced by the gaps between the demands of the innovation and school culture, capability, and policies. If considerable change in practice is required by a learning environment, teacher study groups can provide opportunities for information exchange about strategies and support for experimentation. However, if the culture does not support risk taking, or policy makes study group meetings and common planning times hard to arrange, then such change is less likely. Similarly, if content emphasized on district and state tests differs significantly from the content and learning goals of the learning environment, administrators and teachers are not likely to support the innovation or work for its success. Gomez and colleagues (Gomez, Fishman, & Pea, 1998) suggest "test bed" research as a way to see if a setting has enough of the requisites to take on the innovation. Research on social welfare and community-based programs suggests that interventions work only when there are enough resources (personal, monetary, social) for participants to take up the innovation. For instance, resource issues come into play with afterschool programs such as Fifth Dimension because each site often has its own funding structure and responsibility for budget and space. Sometimes even a successful program will be short-lived due to resource issues.

Adaptation

In addition to knowledge of how environments influence the success of innovations, adaptations necessitated by scaling to new circumstances also provide valuable information about design, theory, and practice of specific features of learning environments. The need for adaptation or tailoring raises questions of malleability and theoretical warrants. That is, in what ways can critical features of a learning environment be enacted differently, yet still remain true to their theoretical foundation?

Culture and Adaptation. The degree of explicitness in instruction is one example of the tension between adaptability and warrants. Among others, Lee (2002), Moje and colleagues (2001), and Ladson-Billings (1995) discuss the need to be explicit when teaching science to children from different cultures. Explicitness involves making very clear how one communicates, thinks, and proceeds in scientific endeavors

while at the same time addressing the students' cultural ways of explaining phenomena or using evidence. Exploring approaches to explicit instruction that honor children's cultural backgrounds and scaffolds learning that conforms with premises of constructivist learning environments can help to identify when adaptations are "lethal" and contradict warrants.

Adapting learning environments to make them explicit can mean making thought processes very transparent, such as contrasting how scientists talk with how students talk with friends, or contrasting what counts as evidence in science with what counts as evidence in conversations with your mother (Moje et al., 2004). Adaptation may result in more direct instruction. In a learning environment that assumes children should engage in inquiry to learn content, making the scientific processes explicit might short-circuit children's exploration of what are good questions or what are reasonable and feasible designs, as teachers tell students questions to ask or procedures to follow. Teachers are likely to be very explicit in response to their concerns that students will generate wrong answers or misconceptions as they explore phenomena or solve problems. However, helping students construct understanding from their inquiry might require explicit instruction, especially when students are inexperienced or not skilled in keeping track of results, interpreting findings, or drawing conclusions. The defining problem is to strike a balance between adaptations that create more explicit instruction in support of thinking and adaptations that convert inquiry to direct instruction with little opportunity for deep thinking. The former can preserve the intent of learning environments to achieve national science education standards; the latter capitulates to the grammar of schooling.

Social organizational features also will need to be adapted to student cultural backgrounds. Learning environments that entail building discourse communities, in which students debate ideas, critique each others' work, or explore alternative answers to problems, will need to adapt to students whose backgrounds limit questioning of adults, limit argumentation, or foster an orientation to one right answer. Participation structures that vary from those used in the home also will pose problems, especially for younger students (Phillips, 1972). In addition, adaptation will be necessary when the learning environment depends on small-group work and is scaled to places where students come from backgrounds that differ in status. A variety of instantiations of group work have been developed to deal with problems of dominance in groups by nonminority or wealthy students (E. G. Cohen, Lotan, Scarloss, & Arellano, 1999).

Cultural background of students and school setting also affects whether the driving question and anchors make sense and are appealing. Solving this problem stretches our understanding of theory and practice. Are there some contextualizations that work across populations? Are there others that do not? What characterizes them? Moreover, whereas a premise of inquiry is for students to explore questions of interest, once the learning environment is scaled and needs to be developed to suit many different settings and to address specific learning standards, there are constraints on the variation of questions that can be used.

The pressure to create highly developed but adaptable materials illustrates a major tension in scaling. Teachers may not be prepared to change topics in different classes or each year in response to student interest. Teachers and administrators also will be hesitant to consider driving questions that students initiate that do not lend themselves to content that meets national, state, or district standards. Receptivity to student interests is more feasible when projects are supplementary to the curriculum than when they are the main route to convey material mandated by state and local curriculum frameworks. Moreover, even if teachers are motivated and knowledgeable enough to do so, constant changes limit the learning benefits that accrue to teachers from engaging in multiple enactments of the same curriculum material (Geier et al., 2004). One solution we and others have found is to have students raise questions of interest in the context of a driving question around which the unit is developed. Curriculum materials offer advice on types of questions students are likely to raise and how teachers might proceed. This solution keeps key ideas consistent but gives students input.

Technology and Adaptation. Learning environments that use technology also will face tensions of adaptability as they scale. One problem involves interfaces. Learning environments may spread to sites where other technology is in use. If the interfaces differ dramatically from those already in use, teachers and students will have the extra burden of learning something new and possibly a way of operating that differs dramatically from what they know. Utilization of many different applications in the same or different innovations

creates difficulty and sometimes resistance to use that requires redesign of the technology in a way that still supports learning as envisioned in the original design.

Another problem with technology is accessibility. If the learning environment requires frequent use of technology for individual or small-group use, accessibility and number of machines becomes important. Adaptation will be necessary in situations where technology is limited or where access is restricted. The result may be that alternative forms of learning support will be needed or that different ways of getting the benefits of the technology will have to be found. For example, handheld computers are much less expensive than desktop machines, but they lack some of the power and affordances of desktops. In some cases, access might be improved through a handheld program at the expense of power. The designer of a learning environment then has to choose whether the cost of power is worth the benefits of access. For some activities, such as word processing or collecting scientific data in the field, the cost is worth the benefit. For some, such as modeling complex systems, the affordance of the technology might be lost when less powerful devices are used (Fishman, Marx, Blumenfeld, Krajcik, & Soloway, 2004).

Research on Scaling of Learning Environments

One type of research on scaling of learning environments involves examination of how the innovation is adapted, whether these adaptations are warranted, and how well they work. Here researchers examine enactment and student outcomes to compare different instantiations by teachers. Data include observations, student tests, and interviews. As with design work during development phases, the role of iterative cycles of revision based on student outcomes and field-based data collection are discussed.

Another type of research examines how innovations are adapted to make them usable in systems with varying policies, resources, populations, and capabilities (e.g., Lee & Luykx, 2005). Here the focus is on gaps between existing conditions and the requirements of the innovation. This research shows that when the gaps are large, the innovation is extensive, and considerable change is needed for it to work (e.g., altering a substantial part of a curriculum). Researchers examine how policies are adapted and how the system develops capacity to deal with the demands of the innovation (Fishman et al., 2004; McLaughlin, 1990).

A third type of research involves comparison of outcomes of learning environments with other innovations or with control groups, either in fully randomized trials or in quasi-experimental studies. Arguments for such approaches are based on the need to know the added value of new programs and to draw causal inferences. As we discuss in the section on research, there is considerable debate about how experimental designs might or might not work in the context of schools and school districts. For example, there is the problem of selecting and controlling appropriate comparison groups so that they really do control for the full range of parameters that might affect outcomes.

When used in the real world of schools, innovations are not static. Teachers in control groups hear about interesting innovations and often introduce elements into their own classrooms; the result is that their classes are no longer controls. For example, we were interested in how we might help urban students become more successful at making scientific explanations as they learn in PBS curricula that we designed collaboratively with teachers in Detroit Public Schools through the Center for Learning Technologies in Urban Schools (LeTUS; Marx et al., 2004). We designed a three-group, quasi-experimental study to test our instructional approach. The study was designed to contrast non-LeTUS classrooms with LeTUS classrooms using the explanation instruction and LeTUS classrooms not using the explanation instruction. In the larger LeTUS reform effort, some of the teachers who were enacting the explanation instruction also happened to be peer leaders in the professional development program for other LeTUS teachers. Unknown to us, they incorporated the explanation instruction into their professional development activities, thereby changing the nature of one of the comparison groups. The other LeTUS teachers who were not supposed to be enacting the explanation strategies had been exposed to them during professional development. In effect, the teachers were acting professionally; they had reason to think that what they were doing in their classrooms would be useful in other district classrooms, so they made it available to their colleagues.

Critics of randomized experiments also argue that the numerous innovations that exist in most schools also make it impossible to do clean comparisons. For example, outcomes from innovations in the area of science might be influenced by new literacy or math programs that improve student skills and abilities to benefit from the science learning environments. In the high-stakes environment of American public education we are currently experiencing, no school principal who wants to keep his or her job would be willing to leave known achievement problems unaddressed because one of the departments, say, the science department, is engaged in an experiment studying a learning environment. If the principal knows that there is a literacy problem in the school, he or she is going to bring resources to bear on that problem. If the principal is successful and the literacy problem begins to be solved, it is likely that it will affect the students who are in the science department's learning environment study. Most likely, the researchers conducting the learning environment study will not even know about the changes in the school's literacy program. They will proceed with inferences about the value of their program without knowing the threats to validity that the other activities in the school pose.

Professional Development

Scaling also requires professional development to help teachers enact the innovation in a warranted manner and realize the intended goals of learning environments. A significant problem for designers as they scale is the amount of time it takes teachers to become proficient in implementing learning environments. In our experience, initial attempts to change from a didactic model of instruction to a more constructivist approach rendered teachers novices once more. As they tried unfamiliar instructional strategies or new arrangements for which their practical or event knowledge was limited, the results were choppy; teachers ran out of time, left activities unfinished, and did not respond to or return to student suggestions or questions. Also, attempts to deal with one feature inevitably entailed problems with other features. That is, teachers not only had difficulty with individual features of PBS, they had difficulty orchestrating among them (Marx et al., 1997).

At the end of the first year of their work in PBS, each teacher's practices represented a profile of enactment, with some features instantiated in a manner more congruent with the premises underlying the innovation than others. Overall, teacher progress was not linear; they moved back and forth between new and old ideas and practices. Generally, as Shulman (1987) suggests, development was "dialectic." Teachers advanced and retreated as they confronted dilemmas and attempted to meet challenges posed by the new approaches to teaching for understanding. In fact, it took almost 3 years for teachers to grasp the ideas underlying PBS and to become proficient enactors of the innovation.

Obviously, the process of change to promote student construction and understanding is difficult. It is essential that we find ways to assist teachers so that they are willing to try new approaches and persist in their attempts. Supporting teachers as they collaborate, enact, and reflect is time-consuming, labor-intensive, and expensive. Professional development is time-consuming, labor-intensive, and expensive as well. As typically practiced, it requires all participants to be in the same place. Scaling provides challenges in that teachers may be in many different geographical locations and require different types of help. Harnessing the potential of the new technologies is one promising route to make professional development more effective and efficient (Fishman et al., 2004; Hunter, 1992; Lampert & Ball, 1990; Roup, Gal, Drayton, & Pfister, 1992).

Virtual learning environments are now being designed as a vehicle for professional development for teachers. Web-based learning environments are one way to develop communities that help teachers understand premises, develop new knowledge of content and pedagogy, discuss and solve problems, and view video of teaching strategies that aid enactment of the innovation. Interactive technologies make it possible to illustrate new instructional possibilities, to enhance understanding of premises underlying interventions, to demonstrate challenges of enacting the new approaches and strategies for meeting them, and to illustrate a range of practices congruent with the innovation. It also can extend the benefits of face-to-face meetings via telecommunication.

An example of an online community is The Math Forum, a group of individuals who use computers and the Internet to interact and build knowledge about mathematics and mathematics teaching and learning (Renninger & Shumar, 2002; www.mathforum.org). The Math Forum supports a network of relationships around the exchange of resources supporting teachers, students, researchers, parents, and others who have an interest in mathematics and mathematics education. This online community includes Math Forum staff, whose primary role is to provide interactive services that foster discussion, support the creating and sharing of resources, and encourage collaboration on problem posing and problem solving (Renninger & Shumar, 2002). Services include Web-based discussion areas

and ask-an-expert services for teachers and students, interactive projects and math challenges for students in grades 3 through 12, math-related Web resources, an online mathematics library, and an area for teachers to exchange math units and lessons for use across all grade levels, from preschool to college.

The interactive nature of The Math Forum serves as the basis for community building and sustained community participation. Participants interact around the services and resources within an open community that is designed to promote communication between Math Forum staff and participants, as well as among participants. The Math Forum is structured to invite participation and sustain it by providing opportunities for participants to pose questions, receive support tailored to their needs, and contribute to the site. Students, for instance, are invited to work online with a Math Forum "mentor" who provides individual feedback on students' problem-solving efforts. Teachers are invited to participate in online discussions with other educators, pose questions about mathematics and mathematics instruction directly to a Math Forum staff member, and contribute their own ideas to the Forum community. The Math Forum site does not specify what teachers should do; rather, the site makes available services and resources for teachers to explore and make use of for their own professional needs (Renninger & Shumar, 2002).

Another example is Knowledge Networks on the Web (KNOW), developed by Fishman and colleagues (Fishman, 2003). In contrast to The Math Forum, this tool is curriculum-specific; it is designed to support teachers as they enact PBS. It contains clips of teacher enactment of lessons, teacher commentary on what they did and what they might change, and information about content, management, and student learning. In addition, teachers can send questions to others who have recently enacted the same lessons or to senior staff. KNOW is developed so that it can be used as a platform for other learning environments to use with teachers as they scale. That is, developers can customize videotape clips, comments, and information for their own innovation.

CONCLUSIONS

The information in this chapter has implications for design, research, and policy. We discuss how the material reviewed can inform future work in each of these areas.

Design

Three critical issues in design need to be addressed in future work on learning environments. These include the need to specify more clearly the design of features of learning environments, the design of environments for different subject areas and populations, and the creation of usable designs.

Features

Although effective design for all elements of learning environments is challenging, three features illustrate difficulties. First, technology is a central part of many learning environments, yet teachers are not likely to effectively help students use technology as learning tools if the cost of learning how to use the technology is high in terms of time and effort. The technology needs to be easy for teachers and students to use or its benefits will not be realized. In addition, further work is needed on how to design technology to encourage students' deep cognitive engagement. There are enough technology tools in use that it is time to consolidate knowledge and create design principles. Recent efforts on how to build common scaffolds are an example of what is necessary. A recently published special issue of the *Journal of the Learning Sciences* devoted to scaffolding highlights our improved understanding of the effects of scaffolding in complex learning environments (Davis & Miyake, 2004). What we do know is that these principles must address both teacher and student needs.

Addressing infrastructure issues is critical in design for technology. Problems of access, maintenance, and support need to be addressed if technology is to function as envisioned. When sufficient technology is not available in the classroom, when teachers do not have necessary software, or when computers are not configured properly and maintained frequently, instructional time cannot be effectively used. Relying on teachers to carry out these tasks as different classes in different subject areas use computers during the day is not feasible. Attention to these issues is even more important as an innovation scales.

Another design challenge is how to effectively reach beyond classrooms to involve communities. Designers have attempted to create conditions for community involvement, including telecommunications with experts or with other students, working with community groups, and drawing on community knowledge. There are problems to be solved for each of these strategies. We have not yet found ways to optimize the effect of community building to enrich students' learning experiences.

Assessment for designers, assessments for teacher use, and assessments for policymakers need further development. Assessments used by designers to evaluate the effectiveness of learning environments vary considerably from scoring artifacts, using posttests or gain scores, to employing standardized tests that are also of interest to policymakers. Each of these types of assessments varies in how closely it is aligned to goals of the learning environment. The tension between assessing whether learning goals have been met and using policy-oriented assessments such as state or nationally standardized tests that are not aligned with program goals is an old but enduring problem. Moreover, traditional forms of assessment do not usually address other important goals of learning environments such as better understanding of the nature of the disciplines or developing new dispositions toward learning. To complicate matters, assessments that provide information to designers or policymakers are not likely to be very useful to teachers who need to judge learning as it unfolds in the day-to-day enactment of learning environments in their classrooms. Classroom assessments should include a range of artifacts: models, reports, presentations, visual representations, and problem solutions. Designers need to build these into their programs along with scoring rubrics for teachers so that each is aligned tightly with the goals of the learning environment. Moreover, there are continuing challenges in the design of authentic assessments for classroom use that are feasible and economical of time and resources.

Subject Areas and Populations

Another set of issues the field must address is to develop design principles across subject areas and populations of learners. Robust learning environments exist in all subject areas, and others are being tested and refined. There is a continuing need to design new environments that cover a range of important subject matter content and skills. Continuing development will allow the field to address the questions regarding whether design principles are general or vary by discipline. One way to answer these questions is to apply design principles used to create existing environments in one discipline to different subject areas.

We also need to create learning environments that address learners of different ages. A goal should be to establish design principles that take account of developmental needs, interests, and capacities. Developmental literature provides considerable information for designers to make educated guesses about how to tailor environments for different ages. This information needs to be put in practice and tested empirically to determine what specific components of designs are important so that environments work for learners of different ages.

A related point is the need to address issues of diversity and individual differences. For the most part, designers have not been specific about how different types of learners respond to and benefit from their programs and what design principles work. Although there are some general guidelines about the importance of attending to student culture in instruction and in addressing community characteristics, there is little work on variations in design of learning environments that consider adaptations required to meet the needs of diverse groups of learners. In light of the growing diversity in our classrooms, developing and testing design principles to support students from different backgrounds is essential. Similarly, we need to examine how learning environments can be created or adapted for inclusiveness of special needs learners. There is evidence that such environments can help address diversity because they offer a variety of instructional techniques, activities, technology tools, and different ways for students to participate. Some learning environments emphasize different ways for students to demonstrate knowledge through creation of artifacts such as models, designs, visual representations, and oral presentations. This variety allows students to use modalities that draw on their strengths.

Usability

We need to consider how to design learning environments for different contexts to determine how design principles can reflect conditional variation. This variation might include availability of resources such as technology and equipment, scheduling, and the nature of communities that schools serve. Differences might influence how learning is best contextualized, what community knowledge can be drawn on, and what sources of support are available.

There is a need to anticipate predictable challenges of enactment to make learning environments usable. To make learning environments work, designers need to have a deep understanding about the reality of classrooms and schools. All learning environments create common challenges in addition to unique ones associated with context, yet design principles are not always clear about how to adapt as these challenges are confronted. The recent trend toward working closely with groups of teachers during the design and revision phases is a step in the right direction. Collaborations allow incorporation of the craft knowledge of teachers about what skills are necessary for teachers and students and help identify potential difficulties in enactment. Such collaborations enrich designs and make them more feasible for actual classroom use, and they show the need for careful and long-term collaborations to create robust learning environments that have the potential to scale up.

Another issue in designing learning environments is how to build in adaptability. Design groups report that teachers, pressed for time and worried about content coverage, do not always make effective modifications that are warranted. Many teachers are likely to eliminate or truncate opportunities for construction of understanding that are the hallmark of learning environments. Designers might include principles for modification along with examples of enactments that are faithful to the intent of the innovation and that are explicit about why this is the case. Online environments for teachers are an especially useful way to address this problem. A significant tension for designers is how to make designs responsive to the many issues that might arise while at the same time not straying far from basic principles underlying the design of the learning environment. Essentially, designers face a balancing act or trade-off in creating models that are fixed or creating models that are adaptable but specified and developed enough that they can minimize fatal mutations.

Problems of enactment also call for creating learning environments for teachers, not just students. Attention to teacher understanding is critical so that their modifications are congruent with the basic premises of the learning environment. Learning environments vary in the centrality of the teacher's role. As teacher centrality increases, the problem of how to design professional development to build teacher capability becomes more critical. Recent efforts point to some promising approaches, but they have not been compared in terms of the key features that need to be incorporated, nor is there a robust empirical literature on the effectiveness of teacher professional development. As the number of teachers using a learning environment increases, designers also have to consider how to build system capacity so that growing teacher knowledge and skill can be used to help inform others.

Research

A critical question for consideration is this: Has the research and development community working on learning environments matured sufficiently to enable us to make stronger causal inferences about the efficacy of designing learning environments of the type discussed here? We argue that there are enough learning environments at sufficient levels of sophistication and maturity that have been through cycles of design and proven their efficacy that we can start doing more causal studies to evaluate impact as compared with other types of instruction. We are at a point where more comprehensive and systematic research is possible and necessary to compare different designs and to provide evidence allowing the field to make causal attributions of effectiveness. A step in this direction may be to draw from the framework for examining learning environments presented in Table 8.2 as well as the program comparisons presented in Table 8.3.

For such a program of research to have value for developers and policymakers, we also need to identify a range of dependent variables that are consistent with the intent of the designers and that are calibrated against important outcomes such as state and national standards. Some programs stress content knowledge, others skills, others dispositions toward learning, and others the nature of the discipline. Because programs differ in their desired outcomes, learning environments are not easily contrasted, nor are comparison groups easily defined.

Longitudinal research is essential to determine the enduring benefits of participating in learning environments. What learning, social, and economic benefits accrue over time? Are students more likely to show higher achievement, stay in school and earn high school diplomas, and continue selecting courses in subjects where they have participated in such programs? Do the skills and dispositions toward learning transfer to other areas of learning and continue to improve with the degree of participation in learning environments? Moreover, are the benefits associated with participating in learning environments equally distributed across different types of students, or are there interactions between student background characteristics and participation?

With respect to teachers, there is ample evidence that learning environments pose significant instructional challenges (Windschitl, 2002). Although there are several ways professional development is undertaken, there is general agreement that these efforts should focus on enacting the learning environment, rather than improving general teaching skills or attitudes. Teachers need help with content and with the specifics of the pedagogical features of learning environments, such as managing multiple activities, building collaborative communities, using technology as a learning tool, and assessing student understanding.

Little is known about how teachers change over time and the factors that support or inhibit teacher learning and their growing instructional competence. There is some evidence that it takes about 3 years for teachers to learn to use learning environments productively in their instruction. However, studies have not systematically determined whether teachers continue to improve, whether there are individual differences in their learning trajectories, and whether new approaches and instructional skills transfer to teaching for which theoretically designed and developed learning environments are not available.

The learning environments research community needs to create a consensus about the way research on these environments should proceed. Recently published special issues of the *Journal of the Learning Sciences* (Barab, 2004) and *Educational Researcher* (Kelly, 2003) have started to address differences of opinion and build systematic methodological principles that can create a more rigorous approach to design and to determining effectiveness of learning environments.

Finally, most of the research and development we describe here on learning environments is based on an underlying theory of learning. Designers have learned a great deal about how to instantiate theory into practice. They have enriched theory by grounding it conceptually and contextually. They have demonstrated how models of learners, goals, settings, and instruction work together and how each needs to be addressed. It is time to consider the implications of design for learning theory. Design principles developed from this experience are what might be called midlevel theory. That is, they are statements about what needs to be considered in creating a learning environment. We also need critical analyses and reviews of how the findings affirm or disconfirm underlying learning theories.

These environments provide the context for interdisciplinary research. They combine learning, motivation, development, subject matter, and culture and discourse. Combining insights from each field can be used to improve design principles, because each field has explicit assumptions about it's own topics and implicit assumptions about the topics of others. Drawing on the knowledge and strength of each field can help make the design stronger and more explicit. This diverse expertise can be used to improve designs. For instance, learning theorists often assume that creating interest and increasing participation in activities will result in greater cognitive engagement. Motivation researchers find that such situational interests does not necessarily translate into willingness to invest effort in using the types of strategies necessary to construct deep level understanding of content. Similarly, motivation researchers pay less attention to subject matter instruction. When insights from both fields are combined, they are likely to result in better understanding and instantiation of theory into practice.

Policy

Without question, one of the primary goals of designers of learning environments is to have them used by learners. There are certainly questions of theory and research, just described, but ultimately, the goal of this work is to improve learning and other valued educational goals. Schools and other institutions focused on children exist in a social and political matrix in which public and private policies have great impact. To achieve their goals of widespread use of their intellectual efforts, designers and their colleagues must attend to the policy environments for success. To influence policy, designers of learning environments need to attend to issues of scale. They must show that the program can work in many places and retain effectiveness as numbers of participants grow. This requires that adaptability, changeability, sustainability, and achievability are realized in design. These characteristics also require support from policymakers. They are not ensured by good design alone. The importance of issues that arise in scaling will depend on whether the decision maker is at the building, district, or state level.

For adaptability, designers have to consider local conditions. The original design might be highly tailored to circumstances. To scale, designers will need to build in ways to modify aspects of the design to meet a variety of circumstances. As we discussed, these circumstances might differ in the languages and cultures students bring with them to school, different types of individual needs, and different ages. They might include diverse community values, a range of political expressions, and differ-

ent state, district, or building policies. They might include variations in curricular objectives or different high-stakes assessments.

Policymakers can have a huge impact on the quality of enactment of learning environments through a range of actions, from recruitment and retention policies for teachers to resource allocation decisions for infrastructure and operations and sustained professional development that addresses classroom enactment. Policies are key to support adaptability for programs so they can stay true to the basic principles underlying their design. Programs that are based on adaptability to local conditions, including variable classroom situations within a district or school, may be challenged to survive in an increasingly standardized climate where the goal of achieving higher scores on standardized tests dominates. In a very real sense, the learning environment literature that we discuss here constitutes a source of innovation—new ideas in pursuit of values ends—that exists in a fragile ecosystem of, on the one hand, research and development, and on the other, the rough-and-tumble of federal, state, and local policies.

Innovations are not static. It takes time for an innovation to take hold and mature as it is adapted to new circumstances. Consequently, using very early summary evaluations in making decisions to continue the effort can over- or underestimate the impact. To be effective, the enactment of learning environments in schools over time requires a stable staff; recent evidence suggests that the longer teachers enact a learning environment, the greater their contribution to student learning. This kind of stability is very hard to achieve with the enormously high turnover rates in teaching and the loss of a high percentage of teachers early in their careers as they leave for different careers, for personal reasons, or because of inadequate or even hostile working conditions.

For learning environments to be sustainable, designers need to be sure that they align with objectives and disciplinary frameworks of district, state, and national standards. Decision makers need to attend to alignment of policy with the needs of the learning environments they adopt. This alignment needs to occur at multiple levels of administration, from space, time, and resources at the building level to attention to teacher professional development, resource allocation, and objectives at high levels.

The goals of learning environments cannot be achieved without alignment with learning objectives and without alignment of policy and practice that support the innovation. This alignment is what makes possible attaining outcomes such as improved achievement. The alignment should be focused on building dimensions of school capacity, such as teacher capability, knowledge at the building and district level of what is required, and leadership to meet those requirements. Moreover, judging if the goals are achieved depends on choosing assessments that are aligned with curricular goals and with policy needs. Whether the learning environment is deemed successful may differ on whether the criteria used are gain scores on content area tests, raw scores on standardized tests, or pass rates on high-stakes assessments. But policies regarding alignment need to conform with and contribute to the policy environment of high pass rates on high-stakes tests. School leaders working in an era of adequate yearly progress defined by federal legislation ignore high-stakes assessments at their peril. If learning environments that are used in schools do not contribute a response to the very real imperative of federal policy, then administrators are not likely to support their adoption. The ultimate question in schools may be: Does the learning environment contribute to or detract from teachers' ability to increase test performance? For designers, the challenge is to meet these goals while at the same time addressing other important goals.

Conclusion

During the past 10 to 15 years, many exciting learning environments have been designed and implemented in and out of school. These environments represent new approaches to learning. Some are focused on individual learning based on information-processing theory that promotes more expert performance and ways of thinking. Analysis of task requirements and thinking of experts are the basis for these environments. Others stress that learning is situated and social. More knowledgeable individuals, such as teachers, scaffold experiences of learners so that they can accomplish tasks they could not complete on their own. Both approaches use tools to facilitate learning.

As a result of these learning environments, students have been exposed to new ways of learning: solving meaningful problems, working with others, using technology, creating artifacts. They have gained knowledge and skills, appreciation for disciplinary practices, and new dispositions to learning. Designing, enacting, and scaling these types of learning environments is difficult for all involved—researchers, teachers, and students. In

this chapter, we highlight the premises and problems and point to what we have learned and what we still need to know. Most important, we argue that these challenges and ways to address them inform both theory and practice. It is true that enacting these environments is challenging, yet the challenges should not be a deterrent to adoption. The environments described represent ambitious pedagogy and strive for ambitious outcomes. As we think about creating the learner, worker, and citizen of tomorrow, we also need to think about how we envision the next generation of schools. These types of environments offer the promise of creating adaptive learners, effective information users, collaborative workers, and citizens who understand how knowledge is generated in different disciplines. For all the challenges, well-designed learning environments offer considerable promise in attaining these goals.

Note: This work was prepared while the authors were supported by grants from the National Science Foundation (grants ESI-0101780, ESI-0227557, and REC-0106959). All opinions expressed are the responsibility of the authors and do not necessarily reflect the views of the National Science Foundation.

REFERENCES

Aleven, V., & Koedinger, K. R. (2002). An effective metacognitive strategy: Learning by doing and explaining with a computer-based cognitive tutor. *Cognitive Science, 26*(2), 147–179.

American Association for the Advancement of Science. (1993). *Benchmarks for science literacy.* New York: Oxford University Press.

American Association for the Advancement of Science. (2001). *Atlas of science literacy.* Washington, DC: Author.

Anderson, J. R. (1993). *Rules of the mind.* Hillsdale, NJ: Erlbaum.

Anderson, J. R. (1996). ACT: A simple theory of complex cognition. *American Psychologist, 51*(4), 355–365.

Anderson, J. R., Boyle, C. F., Corbett, A., & Lewis, M. W. (1990). Cognitive modeling and intelligent tutoring. *Artificial Intelligence, 42,* 7–49.

Anderson, J. R., Corbett, A. T., Koedinger, K., & Pelletier, R. (1995). Cognitive Tutors: Lessons learned. *Journal of the Learning Sciences, 4,* 167–207.

Anderson, J. R., & Schunn, C. D. (2000). Implications of the ACT-R learning theory: No magic bullets. In R. Glaser (Ed.), *Advances in instructional psychology: Vol. 5. Educational design and cognitive science* (pp. 1–33). Mahwah, NJ: Erlbaum.

Barab, S. (Ed.). (2004). Design-based research: Clarifying the terms [Special issue]. *Journal of the Learning Sciences, 13*(1).

Barron, B. J. S., Schwartz, D. L., Vye, N. J., Moore, A., Petrosino, A., Zech, L., Bransford, J. D., & The Cognition and Technology Group at Vanderbilt. (1998). Doing with understanding: Lessons from research on problem and project-based learning. *Journal of the Learning Sciences, 7*(3/4), 271–311.

Bereiter, C., & Scardamalia, M. (1989). Intentional learning as a goal of instruction. In L. B. Resnick (Ed.), *Knowing, learning, and instruction: Essays in honor of Robert Glaser* (pp. 361–392). Hillsdale, NJ: Erlbaum.

Bereiter, C., & Scardamalia, M. (2003). Learning to work creatively with knowledge. In E. D. Corte, L. Verschaffel, N. Entwistle, & J. V. Merrienboer (Eds.), *Powerful learning environments: Unravelling basic components and dimensions* (pp. 55–68). Oxford: Pergamon Press.

Bloom, B. S. (Ed.), Engelhart, M. D., Furst, E. J., Hill, W. H., & Krathwohl, D. R. (1956). *The taxonomy of educational objectives: Handbook I: Cognitive domain.* New York: David McKay.

Blumenfeld, P. C., Fishman, B. J., Krajcik, J., Marx, R. W., & Soloway, E. (2000). Creating usable innovations in systemic reform: Scaling up technology-embedded project-based science in urban schools. *Educational Psychologist, 35,* 149–164.

Blumenfeld, P. C., Kempler, T., & Krajcik, J. S. (in press). Motivation and engagement in learning environments. In R. K. Sawyer (Ed.), *Cambridge handbook of the learning sciences.* Cambridge, UK: Cambridge University Press.

Blumenfeld, P. C., Soloway, E., Krajcik, J., & Marx, R. W. (2004). Technologies to enable inquiry: The influences on student learning and motivation. Final Report: Spencer Foundation.

Blumenfeld, P. C., Soloway, E., Marx, R. W., Krajcik, J. S., Guzdial, M., & Palincsar, A. (1991). Motivating project-based learning: Sustaining the doing, supporting the learning. *Educational Psychologist, 26,* 369–398.

Bransford, J., Brown, A. L., & Cocking, R. R. (Eds.). (2000). *How people learn: Brain, mind, experience, and school* (Expanded ed.). Washington, DC: National Academy Press.

Bransford, J. D., & Stein, B. S. (1993). *The IDEAL problem solver* (2nd ed.). New York: Freeman.

Brown, A. L. (1992). Design experiments: Theoretical and methodological challenges in creating complex interventions in classroom settings. *Journal of the Learning Sciences, 2,* 141–178.

Brown, A. L., Bransford, J. D., Ferrara, R. A., & Campione, J. C. (1983). Learning, remembering, and understanding. In P. H. Mussen (Ed.), *Handbook of child psychology* (4th ed., Vol. 3, pp. 77–166). New York: Wiley.

Brown, A. L., & Campione, J. C. (1994). Guided discovery in a community of learners. In K. McGilly (Ed.), *Classroom lessons: Integrating cognitive theory and classroom practice* (pp. 229–270). Cambridge, MA: MIT Press.

Brown, A. L., & Campione, J. C. (1996). Psychological theory and the design of innovative learning environments: On procedures, principles, and systems. In L. Schauble & R. Glaser (Eds.), *Innovations in learning: New environments for education* (pp. 289–325). Mahwah, NJ: Erlbaum.

Brown, A. L., & Campione, J. C. (1998). Designing a community of young learners: Theoretical and practical lessons. In N. M. Lambert & B. L. McCombs (Eds.), *How students learn: Reforming schools through learner-centered education* (pp. 153–186). Washington, DC: American Psychological Association.

Brown, A. L., Metz, K. E., & Campione, J. C. (1996). Social interaction and individual understanding in a community of learners: The influence of Piaget and Vygotsky. In A. Tryphon & J. Voneche (Eds.), *Piaget-Vygotsky: The social genesis of thought* (pp. 145–171). East Sussex, UK: Psychology Press.

Brown, K., & Cole, M. (2000). Socially-shared cognition: System design and the organization of collaborative research. In D. H. Jonassen & S. M. Land (Eds.), *Theoretical foundations of learning environments* (pp. 197–214). Mahwah, NJ: Erlbaum.

Brown, K., & Cole, M. (2002). Cultural historical activity theory and the expansion of opportunities for learning after school. In G. Wells & G. Claxton (Eds.), *Learning for life in the twenty-first century: Sociocultural perspectives on the future of education* (pp. 225–238). Oxford: Blackwell.

Burkhardt, H., & Schoenfeld, A. (2003). Improving educational research: Toward a more useful, more influential, and better-funded enterprise. *Educational Researcher, 32*(9), 3–14.

Clark, C. M., Gage, N., Marx, R., Peterson, P., Stayrook, N., & Winne, P. (1979). A factorial experiment on teacher structuring, soliciting, and reacting. *Journal of Educational Psychology, 71*(4), 534–552.

Cobb, P., Confrey, J., diSessa, A., Lehrer, R., & Schauble, L. (2003). Design experiments in educational research. *Educational Researcher, 32*(1), 9–13.

Cognition and Technology Group at Vanderbilt. (1992). The Jasper series as an example of anchored instruction: Theory, program description, and assessment data. *Educational Psychologist, 27,* 291–315.

Cognition and Technology Group at Vanderbilt. (1997). *The Jasper project: Lessons in curriculum, instruction, assessment, and professional development.* Mahwah, NJ: Erlbaum.

Cohen, D. K., & Ball, D. L. (1999). *Instruction, capacity, and improvement* (CPRE Research Report Series, No. RR-43). Philadelphia: University of Pennsylvania, Consortium for Policy Research in Education.

Cohen, E. G., Lotan, R. A., Scarloss, B. A., & Arellano, A. R. (1999). Complex instruction: Equity in cooperative learning classrooms. *Theory into Practice, 38*(2), 80–86.

Cole, M. (1995). Socio-cultural-historical psychology: Some general remarks and a proposal for a new kind of cultural-genetic methodology. In J. Wertsch, D. R. Pablo, & A. Alvarez (Eds.), *Sociocultural studies of mind* (pp. 187–214). New York: Cambridge University Press.

Cole, M. (1996). *Cultural psychology: A once and future discipline.* Cambridge, MA: Harvard University Press.

Collins, A. (1992). Toward a design science of education. In E. Scanlon & T. O'Shea (Eds.), *New directions in educational technology* (pp. 15–22). New York: Springer-Verlag.

Collins, A., Joseph, D., & Bialaczyc, K. (2004). Design research: Theoretical and methodological issues. *Journal of the Learning Sciences, 13*(1), 15–42.

Cook, T. D., & Payne, M. R. (2002). Objecting to the objections to using random assignment in educational research. In F. Mosteller & R. F. Boruch (Eds.), *Evidence matters: Randomized trials in education research* (pp. 150–178). Washington, DC: Brookings Institution.

Corbett, A. T., Koedinger, K. R., & Hadley, W. (2001). Cognitive Tutors: From the research classroom to all classrooms. In P. S. Goodman (Ed.), *Technology enhanced learning: Opportunities for change* (pp. 235–263). Mahwah, NJ: Erlbaum.

Corbett, A. T., McLaughlin, M. S., Scarpinatto, K. C., & Hadley, W. S. (2000). Analyzing and generating mathematical models: An Algebra II Cognitive Tutor design study. In G. Gauthier, C. Frasson, & K. VanLehn (Eds.), *Intelligent tutoring systems: Proceedings of the Fifth International Conference, ITS 2000* (pp. 314–323). New York: Springer.

Costa, A., & Kallick, B. (Eds.). (2000). *Discovering and exploring habits of mind.* Alexandria, VA: Association for Supervision and Curriculum Development.

Cuthbert, A. J., Clark, D. B., & Linn, M. C. (2002). WISE learning communities: Design considerations. In K. A. Renninger & W. Shumar (Eds.), *Building virtual communities: Learning and change in cyberspace* (pp. 215–248). Cambridge, England: Cambridge University Press.

Davis, E. A., & Krajcik, J. S. (2005). Designing educative curriculum materials to promote teacher learning. *Educational Researcher, 34*(3), 3–14.

Davis, E. A., & Miyake, N. (Eds.). (2004). Scaffolding [Special issue]. *Journal of the Learning Sciences, 13*(3).

De Corte, E., Verschaffel, L., Entwistle, N., & van Merriënboer, J. (Eds.). (2003). *Powerful learning environments: Unravelling basic components and dimensions.* Oxford: Pergamon.

De Kock, A., Sleegers, P., & Voeten, M. J. M. (2004). New learning and the classification of learning environments in secondary education. *Review of Educational Research, 74*(2), 141–170.

Dewey, J. (1933). *How we think: A restatement of the relation of reflective thinking to the educative process.* Boston: Henry Holt.

Dewey, J. (1938). *Experience and education.* New York: Collier Macmillan.

Eccles, J. S., & Midgley, C. (1989). Stage-environment fit: Developmentally appropriate classrooms for young adolescents. In C. Ames & R. Ames (Eds.), *Research on motivation in education: Goals and cognitions* (pp. 13–44). New York: Academic Press.

Edelson, D. C. (2001). Learning-for-Use: A framework for the design of technology-supported inquiry activities. *Journal of Research in Science Teaching, 38*(3), 355–385.

Edelson, D. C., Gordin, D. N., & Pea, R. D. (1999). Addressing the challenges of inquiry-based learning through technology and curriculum design. *Journal of the Learning Sciences, 8*(3/4), 391–450.

Edelson, D. C., Salierno, C., Matese, G., Pitts, V., & Sherin, B. (2002, March). *Learning-for-Use in earth science: Kids as climate modelers.* Paper presented at the annual meeting of the National Association for Research in Science Teaching, New Orleans, LA.

Fishman, B. (2003). Linking on-line video and curriculum to leverage community knowledge. In J. Brophy (Ed.), *Advances in research on teaching: Using video in teacher education* (Vol. 10, pp. 201–234). New York: Elsevier.

Fishman, B., Marx, R. W., Best, S., & Tal, R. T. (2003). Linking teacher and student learning to improve professional development in systemic reform. *Teaching and Teacher Education, 19*(6), 643–658.

Fishman, B., Marx, R. W., Blumenfeld, P. C., Krajcik, J. S., & Soloway, E. (2004). Creating a framework for research on systemic technology innovations. *Journal of the Learning Sciences, 13*(1), 43–76.

Fredricks, J. A., Blumenfeld, P. C., & Paris, A. H. (2004). School engagement: Potential of the concept, state of the evidence. *Review of Educational Research, 74*(1), 59–109.

Gallego, M. A., & Cole, M. (2000). Success is not enough: Challenges to sustaining new forms of educational activity. *Computers in Human Behavior, 16,* 271–286.

Gardner, H. (1991). *The unschooled mind: How children think and how schools should teach.* New York: Basic Books.

Geier, R. (2005). *A longitudinal study of individual teachers' impact on urban student achievement in standards-based science curricula.* Unpublished doctoral dissertation. University of Michigan, Ann Arbor.

Geier, R., Blumenfeld, P. C., Marx, R. W., Krajcik, J. S., Fishman, B., & Soloway, E. (2004). Standardized test outcomes of urban students participating in standards and project based science curricula. In Y. Kafai, W. Sandoval, N. Enyedy, A. Nixon, & F. Herrera (Eds.), *Proceedings of the Sixth International Conference of the Learning Sciences* (pp. 310–317). Mahwah, NJ: Erlbaum.

Gijbels, D., Dochy, F., Bossche, P., & Segers, M. (2005). Effects of problem-based learning: A meta-analysis from the angle of assessment. *Review of Educational Research, 75*(1), 27–61.

Girod, M., Martineau, J., & Zhao, Y. (2004). After-school computer clubhouses and at-risk teens. *American Secondary Education, 32*(3), 63–76.

Gomez, L., Fishman, B., & Pea, R. (1998). The CoVis Project: Building a large scale science education testbed. *Interactive Learning Environments, 6*(1/2), 59–92.

Guthrie, J. T., & Wigfield, A. (2000). Engagement and motivation in reading. In M. L. Kamil, & P. B. Mosenthal (Eds.), *Handbook of reading research* (Vol. 3, pp. 403–422). Mahwah, NJ: Erlbaum.

Hapgood, S., Magnusson, S. J., & Palincsar, A. S. (2004). Teacher, text, and experience: A case of young children's scientific inquiry. *Journal of the Learning Sciences, 13*(4), 455–505.

Hawley, W., & Valli, L. (1999). The essentials of effective professional development: A new consensus. In L. Darking-Hammnd & G. Sykes (Eds.), *Teaching as the learning profession: Handbook of policy and practice* (pp. 127–150). San Francisco: Jossey-Bass.

Hickey, D. T. (1997). Motivation and contemporary socio-constructivist instructional perspectives. *Educational Psychologist, 32*(3), 175–193.

Hickey, D. T., Kindfield, A. C. H., Horwitz, P., & Christie, M. A. (1999). Advancing educational theory by enhancing practice in a technology-supported genetics learning environment. *Journal of Education, 181*(2), 25–55.

Hickey, D. T., Kindfield, A. C. H., Horwitz, P., & Christie, M. A. (2003). Integrating curriculum, instruction, assessment, and evaluation in a technology-supported genetics learning environment. *American Educational Research Journal, 40*(2), 495–538.

Hickey, D. T., Moore, A. L., & Pellegrino, J. W. (2001). The motivational and academic consequences of two innovative mathematics environments: Do curricular innovations and reforms make a difference? *American Educational Research Journal, 38,* 611–652.

Hidi, S., Renninger, K. A., & Krapp, A. (2004). Interest, a motivational variable that combines affective and cognitive functioning. In R. Sternberg (Ed.), *Motivation, emotion, and cognition: Perspectives on intellectual development and functioning* (pp. 89–115). Mahwah, NJ: Erlbaum.

Hmelo-Silver, C. (2004). Problem-based learning: What and how do students learn? *Educational Psychology Review, 16*(3), 235–266.

Holbrook, J., & Kolodner, J. L. (2000). Scaffolding the development of an inquiry-based (science) classroom. In B. Fishman & S. O'Connor-Divelbiss (Eds.), *Proceedings of the Fourth International Conference of the Learning Sciences* (pp. 221–227). Mahwah, NJ: Erlbaum.

Horwitz, P., & Christie, M. A. (2000). Computer-based manipulatives for teaching scientific reasoning: An example. In M. J. Jacobson & R. B. Kozma (Eds.), *Innovations in science and mathematics education: Advanced designs for technologies of learning* (pp. 163–191). Mahwah, NJ: Erlbaum.

Horwitz, P., Neumann, E., & Schwartz, J. (1996). Teaching science at multiple space time scales. *Communications of the ACM, 39*(8), 100–103.

Huber, A. E., Songer, N. B., & Lee, S.-Y. (2003, March). *BioKIDS: A curricular approach to teaching biodiversity through inquiry in technology-rich environments.* Paper presented at the annual meeting of the National Association of Research in Science Teaching, Philadelphia, PA.

Hunter, B. (1992). Linking for learning: Computer-and-communications network support for nationwide innovation in education. *Journal of Science Education and Technology, 1,* 23–34.

Jackson, S., Krajcik, J. S., & Soloway, E. (2000). Model-it: A design retrospective. In M. Jacobson & R. Kozma (Eds.), *Advanced designs for the technologies of learning: Innovations in science and mathematics education* (pp. 77–116). Hillsdale, NJ: Erlbaum.

Jenkins, J. J. (1979). Four points to remember: A tetrahedral model of memory experiments. In L. S. Cermak & F. I. M. Craik (Eds.), *Levels of processing in human memory* (pp. 429–446). Hillsdale, NJ: Erlbaum.

Johnson, R. B., & Onwuegbuzie, A. J. (2004). Mixed methods research: A research paradigm whose time has come. *Educational Researcher, 33*(7), 14–26.

Jonassen, D. H., & Land, S. (Eds.). (2000). *Theoretical foundations of learning environments.* Mahwah, NJ: Erlbaum.

Kahle, J. B., Meece, J., & Scantlebury, K. (2000). Urban African-American middle school science students: Does standards-based teaching make a difference? *Journal of Research in Science Teaching, 37*(9), 1019–1041.

Kelly, A. E. (Ed.). (2003). The role of design in educational research [Special issue]. *Educational Researcher, 32*(1).

Koedinger, K. R., & Anderson, J. R. (1998). Illustrating principled design: The early evolution of a cognitive tutor for algebra symbolization. *Interactive Learning Environments, 5,* 161–179.

Kolodner, J. L., Camp, P. J., Crismond, D., Fasse, B. B., Gray, J. T., Holbrook, J., et al. (2003). Problem-based learning meets case-based reasoning in the middle-school science classroom: Putting learning-by-design into practice. *Journal of the Learning Sciences, 12*(4), 495–548.

Kolodner, J. L., Gray, J. T., & Fasse, B. B. (2003). Promoting transfer through case-based reasoning: Rituals and practices in learning by design classrooms. *Cognitive Science Quarterly, 3*(2), 119–170.

Krajcik, J., & Blumenfeld, P. (in press). Project-based science: Promoting active learning. In K. Sawyer (Ed.), *Cambridge handbook of the learning sciences.* Cambridge, UK: Cambridge University Press.

Krajcik, J. S., Blumenfeld, P. C., Marx, R. W., Bass, K. M., Fredricks, J., & Soloway, E. (1998). Inquiry in project-based science classrooms: Initial attempts by middle school students. *Journal of the Learning Sciences, 7*(3/4), 313–350.

Krajcik, J. S., Blumenfeld, P. C., Marx, R. W., & Soloway, E. (2000). Instructional, curricular, and technological supports for inquiry in science classrooms. In J. Minstrell & E. H. V. Zee (Eds.), *Inquiring into inquiry learning and teaching in science* (pp. 283–315). Washington, DC: American Association for the Advancement of Science.

Ladson-Billings, G. (1995). Toward a theory of culturally relevant pedagogy. *American Educational Research Journal, 32*(3), 465–491.

Lamon, M., Secules, T., Petrosino, A. J., Hackett, R., Bransford, J. D., & Goldman, S. R. (1996). Schools for Thought: Overview of the project and lessons learned from one of the sites. In L. Schauble & R. Glaser (Eds.), *Innovations in learning: New environments for education* (pp. 243–288). Mahwah, NJ: Erlbaum.

Lampert, M., & Ball, D. L. (1990). *Using hypermedia technology to support a new pedagogy of teacher education* (Issue paper 90–5). East Lansing, MI: National Center for Research on Teacher Education, Michigan State University.

Lappan, G., Fey, J. T., Fitzgerald, W. M., Friel, S. N., & Phillips, E. D. (2002). *Getting to know connected mathematics: An implementation guide.* Glenview, IL: Prentice Hall.

Lappan, G., Fey, J. T., Fitzgerald, W. M., Friel, S. N., & Phillips, E. D. (2006). *Implementing and teaching connected mathematics 2.* Boston, MA: Prentice Hall.

Lappan, G., & Phillips, E. (1998). Teaching and learning in the Connected Mathematics project. In L. Leutzinger (Ed.), *Mathematics in the middle* (pp. 83–92). Reston, VA: National Council of Teachers of Mathematics.

Lave, J., & Wenger, E. (1991). *Situated learning: Legitimate peripheral participation.* New York: Cambridge University Press.

Lee, O. (2002). Science inquiry for elementary students from diverse backgrounds. In W. Secada (Ed.), *Review of research in education* (Vol. 26, pp. 23–69). Washington, DC: American Educational Research Association.

Lee, O., & Luykx, A. (2005). Dilemmas in scaling up innovations in science instruction with nonmainstream elementary students. *American Educational Research Journal, 42*(5), 411–438.

Linn, M. C. (1992). The computer as learning partner: Can computer tools teach science? In K. Sheingold, L. G. Roberts, & S. M. Malcom (Eds.), *This year in school science 1991: Technology for teaching and learning* (pp. 31–69). Washington, DC: American Association for the Advancement of Science.

Linn, M. C., Clark, D., & Slotta, J. D. (2003). WISE design for knowledge integration. *Science Education, 87*(4), 517–538.

Linn, M. C., Davis, E. A., & Bell, P. (Eds.). (2004). *Internet environments for science education.* Mahwah, NJ: Erlbaum.

Linn, M. C., Davis, E. A., & Eylon, B. S. (2004). The scaffolded knowledge integration framework for instruction. In M. C. Linn, E. A. Davis, & P. Bell (Eds.), *Internet environments for science education* (pp. 47–72). Mahwah, NJ: Erlbaum.

Linn, M. C., & Slotta, J. D. (2000). WISE science. *Educational Leadership, 58*(2), 29–32.

Linn, M. C., & Songer, N. B. (1988, April). *Curriculum reformulation: Incorporating technology into science instruction.* Paper presented at the American Educational Research Association Annual Meeting, New Orleans, LA.

Magnusson, S. J., & Palincsar, A. S. (1995). Learning environments as a site of science education reform. *Theory into Practice, 34,* 43–50.

Marx, R. W., Blumenfeld, P., Krajcik, J., Fishman, B., Soloway, E., Geier, R., et al. (2004). Inquiry-based science in the middle grades: Assessment of learning in urban systemic reform. *Journal of Research in Science Teaching, 41*(10), 1063–1080.

Marx, R. W., Blumenfeld, P., Krajcik, J., & Soloway, E. (1997). Enacting project-based science. *Elementary School Journal, 97*(4), 341–358.

Maxwell, N., & Bellisimo, Y. (2003). *Problem Based Economics Overview.* Novato, CA: Buck Institute for Education.

Maxwell, N., Bellisimo, Y., & Mergendoller, J. (2001). Problem based learning: Modifying the medical model for teaching high school economics. *The Social Studies, 92*(2), 73–78.

McGilly, K. (Ed.). (1994). *Classroom lessons: Integrating cognitive theory and classroom practice.* Cambridge, MA: MIT Press.

McLaughlin, M. W. (1990). The Rand change agent study revisited: Macro perspectives and micro realities. *Educational Researcher, 19,* 11–16.

Mergendoller, J. R., Markham, T., Ravitz, J., & Larmer, J. (in press). Pervasive management of project based learning: Teachers as guides and facilitators. In C. M. Evertson & C. S. Weinstein (Eds.), *Handbook of classroom management: Research, practice, and contemporary issues.* Mahwah, NJ: Erlbaum.

Meyer, D. K., Turner, J. C., & Spencer, C. A. (1997). Challenge in a mathematics classroom: Students' motivation and strategies in project-based learning. *Elementary School Journal, 97*(5), 501–521.

Mistler-Jackson, M., & Songer, N. B. (2000). Student motivation and Internet technology: Are students empowered to learn science? *Journal of Research in Science Teaching, 37*(5), 459–479.

Moje, E., Collazo, T., Carrillo, R., & Marx, R. W. (2001). "Maestro, what is 'quality'?": Language, literacy, and discourse in project-based science. *Journal of Research in Science Teaching, 38,* 469–498.

Moje, E. B., Peek-Brown, D., Sutherland, L. M., Marx, R. W., Blumenfeld, P., & Krajcik, J. (2004). Explaining explanations: Developing scientific literacy in middle-school project-based science reforms. In D. Strickland & D. E. Alvermann (Eds.), *Bridging the gap: Improving literacy learning for preadolescent and adolescent learners in grades 4–12* (pp. 227–251). New York: Carnegie Corporation.

Moll, L. C., Amanti, C., Neff, D., & Gonzalez, N. (1992). Funds of knowledge for teaching: Using a qualitative approach to connect homes and classrooms. *Theory into Practice, 31,* 132–141.

Mostow, J., & Aist, G. (2001). Evaluating tutors that listen: An overview of Project LISTEN. In K. Forbus & P. Feltovich (Eds.), *Smart machines in education* (pp. 169–233). Menlo Park, CA: MIT/AAAI Press.

Mostow, J., & Beck, J. E. (in press). When the rubber meets the road: Lessons from the in-school adventures of an automated reading tutor that listens. In B. L. Schneider (Ed.), *Conceptualizing scale-up: Multidisciplinary perspectives.*

National Center for History in the Schools. (1996). *National standards for history.* Los Angeles: University of California, Los Angeles, National Center for History in the Schools.

National Council for the Social Studies. (1994). *Curriculum standards for social studies: Expectations of excellence.* Silver Spring, MD: Author.

National Council of Teachers of Mathematics. (1989). *Curriculum and evaluation standards for school mathematics.* Reston, VA: Author.

National Council of Teachers of Mathematics. (1991). *Professional standards for teaching mathematics.* Reston, VA: Author.

National Council of Teachers of Mathematics. (2000). *Principles and standards for school mathematics.* Reston, VA: Author.

National Research Council. (1996). *National science education standards.* Washington, DC: National Academy Press.

Newmann, F., & Wehlage, G. (1993). Five standards of authentic instruction. *Educational Leadership, 50,* 8–12.

Paavola, S., Lipponen, L., & Hakkarainen, K. (2004). Models of innovative knowledge communities and three metaphors of learning. *Review of Educational Research, 74*(4), 557–576.

Palincsar, A. S., Anderson, C. W., & David, Y. M. (1993). Pursuing scientific literacy in the middle grades through collaborative problem solving. *Elementary School Journal, 93,* 643–658.

Palincsar, A. S., & Magnusson, S. J. (2001). The interplay of first-hand and second-hand investigations to model and support the development of scientific knowledge and reasoning. In S. Carver & D. Klahr (Eds.), *Cognition and instruction: Twenty-five years of progress* (pp. 151–193). Mahwah, NJ: Erlbaum.

Palincsar, A. S., Magnusson, S. J., Collins, K. M., & Cutter, J. (2001). Making science accessible to all: Results of a design experiment in inclusive classrooms. *Learning Disability Quarterly, 24,* 15–32.

Patrick, H., & Middleton, M. J. (2002). Turning the kaleidoscope: What we see when self-regulated learning is viewed with a qualitative lens. *Educational Psychologist, 37*(1), 27–39.

Phillips, S. U. (1972). Participant structures on communicative competence: Warm Springs children in community and classroom. In C. Cazden, V. John, & D. Hymes (Eds.), *Functions of language in the classroom* (pp. 370–394). New York: Teachers College Press.

Puntambekar, S., & Hubscher, R. (2005). Tools for scaffolding students in a complex learning environment: What have we gained and what have we missed? *Educational Psychologist, 40*(1), 1–12.

Puntambekar, S., & Kolodner, J. L. (2005). Toward implementing distributed scaffolding: Helping students learn science from design. *Journal of Research in Science Teaching, 42*(2), 185–217.

Quintana, C., Reiser, B. J., Davis, E. A., Krajcik, J., Fretz, E., Duncan, R., et al. (2004). A scaffolding design framework for software to support science inquiry. *Journal of the Learning Sciences, 13*(3), 337–386.

Reiser, B., Tabak, I., Sandoval, W. A., Smith, B. K., Steinmuller, F., & Leone, A. J. (2001). BGuILE: Strategic and conceptual scaffolds for scientific inquiry in biology classrooms. In S. M. Carver & D. Klahr (Eds.), *Cognition and instruction: Twenty-five years of progress* (pp. 263–305). Mahwah, NJ: Erlbaum.

Renninger, K. A. (2000). Individual interest and its implications for understanding intrinsic motivation. In C. Sansone & J. M. Harackiewicz (Eds.), *Intrinsic and extrinsic motivation: The search for optimal motivation and performance* (pp. 373–404). New York: Academic Press.

Renninger, K. A., & Hidi, S. (2002). Student interest and achievement: Developmental issues raised by a case study. In S. Hidi (Ed.), *Development of achievement motivation* (pp. 173–195). San Diego: Academic Press.

Renninger, K. A., & Shumar, W. (2002). Community building with and for teachers in The Math Forum. In K. A. Renninger & W. Shumar (Eds.), *Building virtual communities: Learning and change in cyberspace* (pp. 60–95). New York: Cambridge University Press.

Reys, R., Reys, B., Lapan, R., Holliday, G., & Wasman, D. (2003). Assessing the impact of standards-based middle grades mathematics curriculum materials on student achievement. *Journal for Research in Mathematics Education, 34*(1), 74–95.

Rogers, E. M. (2003). *Diffusion of innovations* (5th ed.). New York: Free Press.

Rogoff, B. (1995). Observing sociocultural activity on three planes: Participatory appropriation, guided participation, and apprenticeship. In J. Wertsch, P. Del Rio, & A. Alvarez (Eds.), *Sociocultural studies of mind* (pp. 139–164). Cambridge, England: Cambridge University Press.

Roup, R. R., Gal, S., Drayton, B., & Pfister, M. (Eds.). (1992). *LabNet: Toward a community of practice.* Hillsdale, NJ: Erlbaum.

Scardamalia, M. (2004). CSILE/Knowledge Forum. In A. Kovalchick & K. Dawson (Eds.), *Education and technology: An encyclopedia* (pp. 183–192). Santa Barbara, CA: ABC-CLIO.

Scardamalia, M., & Bereiter, C. (1991). Higher levels of agency for children in knowledge-building: A challenge for the design of new knowledge media. *Journal of the Learning Sciences, 1*(1), 37–68.

Scardamalia, M., & Bereiter, C. (1994). Computer support for knowledge-building communities. *Journal of the Learning Sciences, 3*(3), 265–283.

Scardamalia, M., Bereiter, C., & Lamon, M. (1994). The CSILE project: Trying to bring the classroom into World 3. In K. McGilly (Ed.), *Classroom lessons: Integrating cognitive theory and classroom practice* (pp. 201–228). Cambridge, MA: MIT Press.

Schauble, L., & Glaser, R. (Eds.). (1996). *Innovations in learning: New environments for education.* Mahwah, NJ: Erlbaum.

Schneider, R. M., & Krajcik, J. (2002). Supporting science teacher learning: The role of educative curriculum materials. *Journal of Science Teacher Education, 13*(3), 221–245.

Schneider, R. M., Krajcik, J., & Blumenfeld, P. (2005). Enacting reform-based science materials: The range of teacher enactments in reform classrooms. *Journal of Research in Science Teaching, 42*(3), 283–312.

Shavelson, R. J., & Towne, L. (Eds.). (2002). *Scientific research in education.* Washington, DC: National Academy Press.

Shear, L., Bell, P., & Linn, M. C. (2004). Partnership models: The case of the deformed frogs. In M. C. Linn, E. A. Davis, & P. Bell (Eds.), *Internet environments for science education* (pp. 289–311). Mahwah, NJ: Erlbaum.

Shulman, L. S. (1987). Knowledge and teaching: Foundations of the new reform. *Harvard Educational Review, 57*(1), 1–22.

Simon, H. A. (1996). *The sciences of the artificial.* Cambridge, MA: MIT Press.

Singer, J., Marx, R. W., Krajcik, J., & Chambers, J. C. (2000). Constructing extended inquiry projects: Curriculum materials for science education reform. *Educational Psychologist, 35*(3), 165–178.

Slotta, J. D. (2004). The Web-based Inquiry Science Environment (WISE): Scaffolding knowledge integration in the science classroom. In M. C. Linn, E. A. Davis, & P. Bell (Eds.), *Internet environments for science education* (pp. 203–231). Mahwah, NJ: Erlbaum.

Soloway, E., Guzdial, M., & Hay, K. H. (1994). Learner-centered design: The challenge for HCI in the 21st century. *Interactions, 1*(2), 36–48.

Songer, N. B. (1996). Exploring learning opportunities in coordinated network-enhanced classrooms: A case of kids as global scientists. *Journal of the Learning Sciences, 5*(4), 297–327.

Songer, N. B. (in press). BioKIDS: An animated conversation on the development of curricular activity structures for inquiry science.

In R. K. Sawyer (Ed.), *Cambridge handbook of the learning sciences.* Cambridge, UK: Cambridge University Press.

Songer, N. B., Lee, H. S., & Kam, R. (2002). Technology-rich inquiry science in urban classrooms: What are the barriers to inquiry pedagogy? *Journal of Research in Science Teaching, 39*(2), 128–150.

Tyack, D., & Cuban, L. (1995). *Tinkering toward Utopia: A century of public school reform.* Cambridge, MA: Harvard University Press.

Van de Ven, A. H., Polley, D. E., Garud, R., & Venkataraman, S. (1999). *The innovation journey.* New York: Oxford University Press.

Veermans, M., & Jarvela, S. (2004). Generalized achievement goals and situational coping in inquiry learning. *Instructional Science, 32,* 269–291.

Vygotsky, L. S. (1978). *Mind in society: The development of higher psychological processes.* Cambridge, MA: Harvard University Press.

Wallace, R. M., Kupperman, J., Krajcik, J., & Soloway, E. (2000). Science on the Web: Students online in a sixth-grade classroom. *Journal of the Learning Sciences, 9*(1), 75–104.

Wallace, R. M., Soloway, E., Krajcik, J., Bos, N., Hoffman, J., Hunter, H. E., et al. (1998). Artemis: Learner-centered design of an information seeking environment for K–12 education. In C. M. Karat, A. Lund, J. Coutaz, & J. Karat (Eds.), *Human Factors in Computing Systems* (Computer Human Interaction 1998 Conference Proceedings, pp. 195–202). New York: ACM Press.

Wenger, E. (1998). *Communities of practice: Learning, meaning, and identity.* Cambridge, England: Cambridge University Press.

White, B. Y. (1993). ThinkerTools: Causal models, conceptual change, and science education. *Cognition and Instruction, 10,* 1–100.

White, B. Y., & Frederiksen, J. R. (1998). Inquiry, modeling, and metacognition: Making science accessible to all students. *Cognition and Instruction, 16*(1), 3–118.

White, B. Y., & Frederiksen, J. R. (2000). Metacognitive facilitation: An approach to making scientific inquiry accessible to all. In J. Minstrell & E. V. Zee (Eds.), *Inquiring into inquiry learning and teaching in science* (pp. 331–370). Washington, DC: American Association for the Advancement of Science.

Wiggins, G., & McTighe, J. (1998). *Understanding by design.* Alexandria, VA: Association for Supervision and Curriculum Development.

Williams, M., & Linn, M. C. (2002). WISE inquiry in fifth-grade biology. *Research in Science Education, 32*(4), 415–436.

Windschitl, M. (2002). Framing constructivism in practice as the negotiation of dilemmas: An analysis of the conceptual, pedagogical, cultural, and political challenges facing teachers. *Review of Educational Research, 72*(2), 131–175.

Wu, H.-K., Krajcik, J., & Soloway, E. (2001). Promoting conceptual understanding of chemical representations: Students' use of a visualization tool in the classroom. *Journal of Research in Science Teaching, 38,* 821–842.

Zhao, Y., Mishra, P., & Girod, M. (2000). A clubhouse is a clubhouse is a clubhouse. *Computers in Human Behavior, 16,* 287–300.

Research Advances and Implications for Clinical Applications

CHAPTER 9

Self-Regulation and Effort Investment

MONIQUE BOEKAERTS

Case Example

Thalia was a clever 2-year-old when her baby sister was born. She had a large vocabulary and could express all her thoughts. Her parents praised her verbal skills but chided her stubbornness with respect to toilet training. On the day her baby sister was born, Thalia was sitting in the kitchen waiting for her favorite television program to start when her grandmother said, "You are a big girl now, Thalia, and I would be very happy if you let me help you to get rid of your Pampers. I am sure you agree that walking around in wet Pampers is such a nuisance." Thalia simply said that she was afraid to sit on the toilet. A few minutes later, the phone rang and Grandma told her that she had a baby sister and that they had to leave for the hospital immediately. Thalia threw a temper tantrum; she did not want a baby sister and did not want to go to the hospital; she only wanted to watch her program.

On their way to the hospital, Thalia was silent. She realized that her baby sister would be her big rival from now on, and this premonition was confirmed when they entered the hospital room and all eyes were on Jenny. Thalia tried several times to get her parents' attention, then gave up and silently slipped away. Grandma found her in the bathroom and asked her why she left the room. Thalia replied, "I hate Jenny." She refused to go back to the room and started sobbing: "I do not know what to do about it." Grandma understood; she took her in her arms and said, "Tell you what, you come back with me and ask your daddy to lift you up to have a close look at Jenny. Then you tickle him the way he likes it and tell him you love him very much. How is that?" Thalia still sulked but did as Grandma suggested. Her father cuddled her and said, "You are my big girl, Thalia."

On their way home, Thalia was quiet for a while, then—out of the blue—she announced, "Grandma, I am a big girl now and only babies wear Pampers. Will you teach me to use the bathroom? I know it will be difficult, but I will do my very best. And, Grandma, can you do it real fast?"

At home, Grandma began to lead Thalia through a series of toilet-training activities that, on the surface, might look familiar to anybody who has helped a child use the bathroom. However, there were a number of significant and purposeful differences. Grandma first explained that she had taught a lot of children to use the bathroom and that all these children felt confident that they could do it her way. Next she explained that children might want to use the toilet seat in a different direction than adults do, because they need to have a firm grip on something for support, for example, the toilet paper holder. They went through the successive motions together. "First, you observe what the best sitting direction is and which object you can use for support. Can you tell me what this could be, Thalia? Yes, the toilet paper holder would be a good choice. Then you lower your pants, and when you have a firm grip on the toilet paper holder, you lower your body on the toilet seat. When you're finished, you pull yourself up and use some paper to clean up. Finally, you flush the toilet and pull up your pants." Thalia repeated in her own words what she did while performing the successive actions. Then she went through the successive motions herself while Grandma pretended to clean the bathroom.

Grandma laughed when she heard Thalia say to herself, "Hold your hands firmly on the toilet paper holder for support." She remembered that one of her teachers had stated that Vygotsky was the first to describe how young children use private speech as a way to develop internal control of their thoughts, feelings, and actions. Then she heard Thalia scream and discovered that she was hanging halfway between the wall and the toilet seat. While Grandma was helping the child to find her balance, Thalia said, "Grandma, I tried to tear off some toilet paper but I lost my balance. I still cannot do it alone but I will try again later."

In the next few days, Grandma encouraged the training process by giving appropriate feedback and emotional support. Thalia reflected on her actions and asked several questions, such as, "Grandma, what will happen if there is no toilet paper holder to hang on to? What can I do if the toilet seat is too high to sit on? Can we practice in another bathroom?" By the time her mother and baby sister came home from the hospital, Thalia had become a competent user of the bathroom, who was independent of the adult who had instructed her.

Thalia's case provides a real-world context for this chapter. I selected this true story because I was impressed by the self-regulation strategies that a 2-year-old could use to pursue her own goals. Thalia formed a mental representation of the hospital situation. She observed that her parents were focused on Jenny and that they neglected her. She interpreted her parents' behavior as a signal that they loved Jenny more than her. She wanted to do something to change the situation for the better but felt helpless.

Thalia has a goal and she is aware that she does not have a plan of action to pursue this goal. Hence, Thalia provides us with evidence that she searched her memory for a strategy that she had used in the past that would be appropriate in the present context. Winne and Perry (2000) have referred to this type of knowledge as "conditional knowledge," or if–then chains that link conditions to cognitive operations. This knowledge is necessary to produce new cognitions or behavior products.

Why is self-regulation an important construct, and what might the reader find in this review? In longitudinal classroom studies, my colleagues and I have examined the relative contribution of high school students' work habits and their perception of situational cues on the intensity of reported effort after completing mathematics homework. We found (e.g., Boekaerts, 2002c) that the intensity of effort was predicted by the students' learning style (i.e., the type of learning strategies they preferentially used in a domain), their volition style (i.e., whether they had access to volition strategies that promote taking initiative, persisting, and disengaging from ruminating thoughts), and their appraisal of the actual homework task. Our results showed that, after controlling for work habits, the self-regulation of effort in relation to mathematics homework is uniquely determined by students' perception of the task characteristics and their phenomenological experience. We found that perceived difficulty predicted the investment of effort negatively, and perceived task value predicted it positively. I think that these and similar results have shed light on the whys of students' self-regulation of motivation and effort and that these results are important for the design of new studies and for the promotion of self-regulation in the classroom.

In the first section of this chapter I argue that laypeople and researchers still have a hazy sense of what self-regulation entails. I highlight recent conceptualizations and empirical findings related to the self-regulation of motivation and effort, documenting why we cannot comprehend children's and adolescents' engagement and persistence in the classroom unless we understand how they steer and direct their behavior in the direction of valued goals and away from undesired goals. Accordingly, I propose to look at engagement and disengagement patterns from a self-regulation perspective. I supply examples from recent research, including my own research program, to illustrate how we have translated our theorizing about self-regulation of motivation and effort into research designs and into practice (guided principles for intervention), but also how practice led back into theory. In the final section, I offer some principles for research and practice and also point to some unresolved issues.

SELF-REGULATION IN THE CLASSROOM

Self-regulation is a construct that has been around for quite a while. As early as 1978, Vygotsky argued that young children are capable of regulating their own learning and can be most deliberate, involved, and committed to steering and directing their own actions. In the past 2 decades, educational psychologists have systematically explored the various ways that children and adolescents use self-regulatory strategies as a means to develop internal control of their thoughts and actions during the learning process. Numerous research studies have described the critical and complex relationships that exist between various aspects of self-regulation and achievement. What is self-regulation and which aspects of self-regulation have been studied extensively?

Recent theories of self-regulation locate the sources of individual functioning neither in static personality traits (e.g., hardiness or conscientiousness) nor in environmental constraints and affordances, but in across-episode patterns of self-regulation. Boekaerts, Maes, and Karoly (2005) defined self-regulation as a multilevel, multicomponent process that targets affect, cognitions, and actions, as well as features of the environment for modulation in the service of one's goals. Given this definition, the key self-regulation processes are goal-related and include goal establishment, making an action plan, goal striving, and goal revision (Austin & Vancouver, 1996). In the classroom, the most salient goals that students need to establish, plan, strive for, and revise are *learning and achievement goals*.

A scan of the literature on self-regulation in the classroom reveals that educational psychologists proposed several evolving models of classroom self-regulation (for a review, see Boekaerts & Corno, 2005; Boekaerts, Pintrich, & Zeidner, 2000; Perry, 2002; Schunk & Zimmerman, 1998; Winne, 1995). Each of the models emphasized slightly different aspects of self-regulation, yet all share some basic assumptions. All investigators assume that students who are capable of steering and directing their own learning process are engaged actively and constructively in a process of meaning generation, adapting at the same time their thoughts, feelings, and actions to steer and direct the learning process.

Despite this agreement, most educational psychologists involved in self-regulation research in the classroom have adopted a specific focus on self-regulation; they concentrate on the learning and achievement goals that students pursue in the classroom, thus narrowing the scope of students' ability to self-regulate through a deliberate focus on the cognitive aspects of self-regulation that are necessary and sufficient to steer and direct the learning process. The advantage of such a clear and deliberate focus on the regulation of the *learning* process itself is that these self-regulation models have been firmly grounded in domain-specific theories of competence development.

Detailed information is now available on the regulation strategies that successful students use in different subject matter areas, such as on how children become competent text processors (Pressley, 1995), composition writers (Scardamalia & Bereiter, 1985), and problem solvers in science and mathematics (De Corte, Verschaffel, & Op 't Eynde, 2000). The basic assumption of most self-regulation models that focus on the regulation of the learning process is that students cannot steer and direct their own learning unless the conditions for self-regulation are present. What are these conditions? An answer provided by educational psychologists who primarily focused on the learning process is that students need to have ready access to a large repertoire of cognitive and learning strategies, awareness of these strategies, and knowledge of the contexts in which these strategies will be effective (Hattie, Biggs, & Purdie, 1996). Investigators who took the students' motivation as their focal point of interest give a different answer. These researchers argued that students need to have ready access to a large repertoire of motivation and volition strategies, awareness of these strategies, and knowledge of the contexts in which these strategies will be effective (Boekaerts & Corno, 2005; Paris & Paris, 2001; Wolters & Rosenthal, 2000). In the next two sections, I briefly review studies that documented these complementary viewpoints.

Self-Regulation Is Metacognitively Governed

Winne (1996, p. 327) defined self-regulated learning as a "metacognitively governed behavior wherein learners adaptively regulate their use of cognitive tactics and strategies in tasks." Winne and Hadwin (1998) further argued that self-regulated learning consists of four interdependent and recursive phases: defining the task, goal setting and planning, enacting the plan, and adapting one's approach and strategies when a desired goal or outcome has not been met. Winne's work followed the tradition of Flavell (1979), who had made a clear distinction between cognition and metacognition (cognition about cognition). In the 1970s and 1980s, the work of two developmental psychologists, Flavell (1979) and Brown (1978) was influential as a way of studying the development of students' capabilities over time. Both theorists highlighted the construct of metacognition and defined it as students' knowledge about cognitive processes (e.g., study skills, cognitive and learning strategies) and their self-awareness of a knowledge base in which information is stored about which cognitive strategies are useful and effective to reach specific learning goals. Since then, numerous studies have shown that access to a coherent metacognitive knowledge base as well as the ability to use this knowledge base to reflect on one's learning and regulation processes are essential preconditions for the regulation of learning (P. A. Alexander, 2003; Pressley, 1995; Winne, 1995). The conclusion reached by three independent meta-analyses of learning skill interventions (Haller, Child, &

Walberg, 1988; Hattie et al., 1996; Rosenshine, Meister, & Chapman, 1996) was that promotion of a high degree of metacognitive awareness is a crucial feature of effective learning skill training.

Although not all of the research mentioned in this section has been categorized in the literature under the heading of "metacognition," these scholars all assume that self-awareness of and access to metacognitive knowledge directs learning (e.g., monitoring difficulty level, a feeling of knowing) and forms the basis for task analysis and determining task demands. Hence, self-regulating one's learning is best defined as an executive process that makes use of the available metacognitive knowledge and consists of a combination of metacognitive strategies by which students orient on the task at hand, plan and implement their actions, monitor and evaluate their choice of strategies, and remedy ineffective strategies (De Corte et al., 2000; Pressley, 1995).

Worldwide, children have profited from these insights and their applications. Teachers and school consultants have been informed on how to design intervention programs that target the development of cognitive and metacognitive strategies that form a prerequisite for self-regulated learning in everyday classroom activities. For example, De Corte et al. developed an intervention for the development of cognitive and metacognitive strategies in mathematics for primary school children and showed that students who learned to use these strategies were more competent problem solvers than students receiving traditional instruction. Similar results were reported with different age groups and in relation to different school subjects (for a review, see Boekaerts & Corno, 2005). Furthermore, worked examples of different self-regulation strategies have found their way into textbooks and homework assignments, and new instruction methods have been designed to improve children's cognitive and metacognitive strategies. An excellent example is the highly successful reciprocal teaching program designed by Palincsar and Brown (1984), in which teachers model comprehension and integration strategies, such as analyzing the text, asking questions, giving clarifications, summarizing, paraphrasing, and predicting.

Self-Regulation Is Consequential in Nature and Affectively Charged

Let us now turn to those researchers who provided an alternative answer to the question What are the conditions for self-regulation to occur? Motivation researchers pointed out that many students have the capacity to use their metacognitive knowledge and (meta)cognitive strategies to direct their own learning, but they lack the motivation and volition to apply this knowledge when learning in a new domain.

Classroom life is complex; biological, developmental, contextual, and individual difference constraints interfere with or support students' self-regulation (Pintrich, 2000). There may be many reasons why students do not feel the need to invest time and effort in the selection of those cognitive and learning strategies that are most appropriate in a given learning context. Skill does not automatically create will; accordingly, students' appraisal of the learning conditions and their access to motivation and volitional strategies needs to be brought to the foreground to gain better insight into the self-regulation process as it occurs in real time (e.g., Boekaerts, 1997, 2002a; Corno, 2001; Pintrich, 2000; Randi & Corno, 2000; Rheinberg, Vollmeyer, & Rollett, 2000; Volet, 1997; Wigfield, Eccles, & Rodriguez, 1998; Zimmerman, 2000).

How do students choose the tasks and activities that they engage in? When are they willing to heighten their cognitive and behavioral engagement? Why do students lower effort during goal pursuit? Why do they quit certain learning activities more frequently than others? These and related questions are important to researchers, teachers, and anybody who is involved in student learning. Educational psychology abounds with terms that refer to motivated behavior in the classroom, including (school, intellectual, emotional, behavioral, and cognitive) engagement, effort (management, allocation, regulation), and persistence. Robust bodies of literature address each of these constructs. Reviewing this literature is a substantial task, but it is not my intention to duplicate excellent reviews, such as those by Corno and Mandinach (2004) and Fredricks, Blumenfeld, and Paris (2004). Instead, I want to draw attention to the lack of consensus on definitional components of motivation, interest, and effort regulation. In my opinion, we cannot comprehend children's and adolescents' engagement and disengagement patterns in the classroom unless we understand how they steer and direct their behavior in the direction of valued goals and away from undesired goals, especially when they are faced with obstacles, breakdowns, and setbacks. Boekaerts and Corno (2005) pointed out that, at present, the phenomenology of self-regulation strategies is heterogeneous, involving diverse types of patterns of self-regulation with different purposes, learning trajectories, and suscepti-

bility to intervention. What is needed is a comprehensive theory in which self-regulation is conceptualized as a systems construct and the different purposes that self-regulation serves are clearly defined, operationalized, and integrated.

DIFFERENT PURPOSES OF SELF-REGULATION: TOP-DOWN, BOTTOM-UP, AND VOLITION-DRIVEN SELF-REGULATION

In this section, I explain how the different purposes of self-regulation are conceptualized in my dual processing self-regulation model (see Boekaerts, 1993; Boekaerts & Niemivirta, 2000).

Top-Down or Higher-Order Goal-Driven Self-Regulation

I begin with a short introduction to my dual processing model of self-regulation as it is currently conceived. This model was first introduced in 1992 but was elaborated and extended over the years as theory building in self-regulation progressed and empirical studies shed light on the phenomena described in the model. The dual processing model of self-regulation that I developed together with my colleagues used insights from social psychology (Kuhl, 1985; Leventhal, 1980) to describe two goal priorities that students strive for in the context of the classroom, namely, achieving gains in their resources (e.g., extending their domain-specific knowledge bases, improving cognitive strategy use, increasing competence) and keeping their well-being within reasonable bounds (e.g., feeling safe, secure, happy, satisfied). Students try to achieve a balance between these two goal priorities by straddling the divide between the so-called mastery or growth pathway (e.g., striving for mastery goals; see broken lines in Figure 9.1) and the well-being pathway (e.g., striving for security; see dotted lines in Figure 9.1).

It is assumed that students who are invited to participate in a learning activity use three sources of information to form a mental representation of the task-in-context and to appraise it: (1) current perceptions of the task and the physical, social, and instructional context within which it is embedded; (2) activated domain-specific knowledge and (meta)cognitive strategies related to the task; and (3) motivational beliefs, including domain-specific capacity, interest, and effort beliefs. Task and self-appraisals hold a central position in

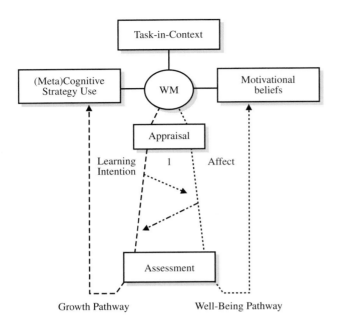

Figure 9.1 Dual processing self-regulation model depicting the different purposes of self-regulation: top-down self-regulation (– – –), bottom-up self-regulation (- - -), and volition-driven self-regulation (– – · – – ·).

the model. It is assumed that students are ready to start activity in the growth pathway when a learning opportunity, and the tasks or activities within it, is congruent with their salient personal goals or when they were successful in bringing the learning task in line with the core guiding principles of their goal system. In the latter case, they have adopted the learning goal, meaning that they have formed a learning intention, and start activity in the growth pathway. Hence, favorable task appraisals lead to self-driven self-regulation, meaning that students steer and direct the flow of energy from the top down. *Top-down self-regulation* implies that students' own values, interests, and higher-order goals, which are located at the apex of their goal hierarchy, drive their goal pursuit. At such a point, students' learning intention is firmly in place and they engage actively in the learning process (they start crossing the Rubicon; see later discussion for an explanation).

Bottom-Up or Cue-Driven Self-Regulation

As Kuhl and Fuhrman (1998) pointed out, good intentions may not be put into use and result in goal accomplishment. Many obstacles might occur en route to the learning goal, and students need access to specific self-regulation strategies to overcome these obstacles. For

example, environmental cues may signal to students that the learning environment is not safe. At such a point, students will start exploring the environment for further cues or quit the situation, rather than devoting attention and energy to the learning task itself. In other words, when children or adolescents detect cues that signal threat to psychological well-being, they will redirect their attention to the threat, thus drawing attention and processing capacity away from the learning task. This shift in focus is visualized in Figure 9.1 by the dotted line, marked 1, that runs from the growth pathway to the well-being pathway. In such instances, students are engaged in self-appraisal rather than task appraisal and bring different questions to bear on the situation, such as: Can any harm or loss of face come to me? Will I look stupid if I do this? or Is this a cool thing to do? My argument is that at some earlier point in time, a linkage has been created between specific environmental cues and the child's safety goals, and that activation of this linkage triggers negative emotions, experienced as turbulence, disturbance, or a discrepancy in the affect system (see also Covington, 2004; Pekrun, Goetz, Titz, & Perry, 2002).

The point being made here is that perception of specific environmental cues (task-in-context) may create a mismatch with the students' current learning intention and trigger cue-driven or *bottom-up forms of self-regulation* with the purpose of preventing threat, harm, or loss. Hence, unfavorable task appraisals prompt students to steer and direct the flow of energy bottom-up; cues in the environment and the anticipated negative consequences they call forth drive the students' goal pursuit. Boekaerts (1999) and Boekaerts and Corno (2005) described the purpose of this form of self-regulation as engaging in activities that maintain or restore the equilibrium in the well-being system. Several researchers have referred to this form of self-regulation as "coping" (Boekaerts, 1993, 1999; Frydenberg, 1999). Three basic forms of coping have been discerned: emotion-focused coping (e.g., crying, shouting, self-blame, denial, distraction, avoidance, delay), problem-focused coping (e.g., search for information, active and instrumental behavior, soliciting social support, mindful problem solving), and reappraisal of the situation (making a new mental representation of the stressor). Stress researchers emphasized that use of the different coping strategies critically depends on the students' appraisal of the situation and their awareness of and access to coping strategies that are effective to restore their well-being in a given context. Note that this definition recognizes the criticality of metacognitive or conditional knowledge for effective coping, even though the term metacognition is totally alien in this field of study. By the same token, educational psychologists have not borrowed any insights from research on coping. Yet, the distinction that coping researchers have made between the different ways that children and adolescents deal with obstacles, setbacks, failures, and breakdowns is highly relevant for the self-regulation processes in the classroom.

Volition-Driven Self-Regulation

Accordingly, Boekaerts and colleagues (Boekaerts, 1993, 1999; Boekaerts & Corno, 2005) blended constructs and research findings from both these fields and proposed that students use two types of self-regulation strategies when environmental cues trigger emotions and a shift to the well-being pathway. At such a point in time, students may use their regulation strategies to explore the extent of the threat, loss, or harm to well-being in order to restore well-being to a reasonable level as fast as possible. However, they may also use their regulation strategies to target obstacles and setbacks for modulation in the service of the *learning* goal. Hence, the dual processing model of self-regulation assumes that students have two alternatives when obstacles arise. They may want to address the noted discrepancy in the well-being system urgently (i.e., emotion-focused coping) and stay on the well-being pathway. Alternatively, they may want to reroute their activities toward growth goals when environmental cues have triggered activity in the well-being pathway. This rerouting is visualized in Figure 9.1 by the path marked 2 that runs from the well-being pathway to the growth pathway.

The former way to target one's cognitions, feelings, and actions is relabeled *bottom-up self-regulation* to contrast it to top-down self-regulation (here a contrast is made between value-driven and interest-driven self-regulation versus cue-driven and emotion-driven self-regulation). The latter way of targeting one's cognitions, feelings, and actions is renamed *volition-driven self-regulation* because it refers to the effort students invest to stay on, or get back on, the growth path despite detected obstacles (here the contrast is between value-driven and interest-driven self-regulation versus volition-driven self-regulation). It might help to conceptualize volitional strategies as the switching track

of a railway system. By turning all lights to red in the affective system, students can continue with the learning activity; they stay on the growth pathway by blocking or attenuating activity in the well-being pathway temporarily.

It is important to realize that students who are on the growth pathway have direct access to motivation strategies that inject value and interest into the task or activity. Next, I provide a brief overview of theories, models, and research findings that underscore this statement.

SELF-REGULATION OF MOTIVATION

Thalia's case illustrates that self-regulation in a natural environment is consequential in nature and affectively charged. Learning experiences that occur in a natural context are often self-initiated or occur spontaneously. Another characteristic of natural environments is that learning is cumulative and socially situated. Thalia's example shows that a specific event (her baby sister is born) and her interpretation of that event *motivates* her to self-regulate her actions to develop a skill that she had considered difficult and redundant till that moment. What explains her motivation to acquire the new skill and her persistence despite setbacks?

One of the basic assumptions of my dual processing self-regulation model is that favorable task appraisals lead to value-driven or interest-driven self-regulation, meaning that the flow of energy fueling the learning process is coming from students' higher-order goals, based on their values, needs, and interests. In other words, learning acquisition is energized and directed from the top down. Several theorists made a clear distinction between goal-directed behavior where the meaning and value comes from the self and goal-directed behavior where individuals pursue goals that are valued by others, either because they cannot avoid these goals or because they are prepared to endorse them. (Kuhl & Fuhrman, 1998 preferred to label this form of regulation "self-control" to contrast it to true forms of self-regulation.) Clearly, many goals that individuals pursue in real-life classroom situations are located in between goals that are truly valued by the self and imposed goals. Nevertheless, the distinction between self-regulation and self-control is crucial because there is emerging evidence that the self-regulatory processes that steer and direct individuals' behavior toward these two different types of goals are distinctive (e.g., Grolnick & Ryan, 1987; Kehr,

Bless, & Rosenstiel, 1999; Kuhl & Fuhrman, 1998; Reeve, 2002; R. M. Ryan & Deci, 2002). I will take up this point again later in the discussion, but first I refer to two major forms of the self-regulation of motivation, namely, experiencing need satisfaction and attaching value to a task or activity.

Top-Down Self-Regulation: Experiencing Need Satisfaction

Deci and Ryan (1985) and R. M. Ryan and Deci (2002) placed the origin of people's motivation in three basic psychological needs: the need for competence, autonomy, and social relatedness. Anticipation of fulfillment of these basic psychological needs forms the basis for intrinsic motivation and autonomous self-regulation. These researchers predicted and found that when the learning conditions support a person's basic psychological needs, he or she will experience need satisfaction and show active and constructive engagement as well as positive emotions. By contrast, when the learning conditions frustrate one of the basic psychological needs, individuals will anticipate negative consequences and experience negative emotions. Thalia feels the need for social relatedness. She wants to relate to her parents and maintain the close bonds that she had with them prior to her sister's arrival. To keep their attention and love, she wants to impress them by showing that she can use the bathroom on her own. Anticipation of their positive reactions has created the need for competence; she wants to master a skill that she had not valued before. She also feels a need for autonomy; she wants to practice the new skill—not because her parents think she should not wet her pants but because she has decided that this skill is important for her.

This example illustrates that very young children can represent an immediate and urgent need mentally. It also shows that it is important that the environment facilitate the fulfillment of a given set of needs. The presence of her grandmother, who can help her focus on her needs by creating a succession of successful learning experiences, sets the scene for the development of effective self-regulation (e.g., "Grandma, what will happen if there is no toilet paper holder to hang on to? Can we practice somewhere else?").

My main point is that optimal conditions for the development of self-regulation can be created when children are given the chance to pursue goals that they themselves find personally relevant and are invited to develop their self-regulation skills by selecting their own tasks and activities, taking initiative, showing active engagement, and making their own decisions. Numerous studies have shown that satisfaction of the three basic psychological needs promotes well-being and positive functioning in individuals of all ages, whereas frustration of those needs creates ill-being (Kasser & Ryan, 1993, 1996; A. M. Ryan, 2000). Hence, information about the fulfillment of children's basic psychological needs will provide a basis for researchers, teachers, and school consultants to learn which aspects of the environment are supportive of children's active engagement and which are antagonistic to engagement and effort.

Fulfillment of Psychological Needs in a Classroom Context

There are a number of reasons why learning activities that foster self-regulation may be harder to realize in a classroom context than in a natural learning environment. Teachers often set learning goals for their students that are specified in the curriculum, and they create several successive learning episodes in which students are invited (read: coerced, coaxed) to show goal-directed behavior. Unfortunately, most teacher-provided learning opportunities do not automatically create a felt need, implying that students are not intrinsically motivated to acquire the new skill and that their behavior will not be guided by autonomous self-regulation.

Ryan and Deci (2002) gave the need for autonomy a primary role in the self-regulation process and described different types of motivation along a continuum of self-regulation. On the left end of the continuum they located controlled behavioral regulation; it occurs when a child feels coerced to attain a goal (e.g., "My parents would feel upset if I did not do my homework"). Autonomous self-regulation is located at the other extreme of the self-regulation continuum; it occurs when individuals choose the goal themselves because they feel a psychological need (e.g., "I want to solve this problem because I want to find out why this strategy did not work"). There is abundant evidence that when individuals feel ownership of their goals—either because they inherently enjoy the activity or because it fits with their values or higher-order goals—they devote more time, show greater concentration, and process information deeper (Grolnick & Ryan, 1987), experience flow (Csikzentmihalyi, 1990), and persist longer (R. M. Ryan

& Connell, 1989). Conversely, when individuals feel co-erced to achieve a goal—either because they believe that external contingencies are the cause of their behavior (external regulation) or because they would feel guilty or anxious if they did not pursue the goal (introjected regulation)—they score lower on these outcomes. Lemos (2002) provided evidence that pressure to comply with goals of others hinders the personalization of goals and leads to overcontrolled, rigid behavior or undercon-trolled behavior governed by one's urges (e.g., aggres-sive behavior).

In line with the theoretical assumptions of Ryan and Deci (2002), researchers and teachers expect that stu-dents' behavior will be guided from the top down by their own learning or mastery goals, yet they forget that most learning tasks that students have to complete in the classroom are not self-chosen and might frustrate the students' need for autonomy. Strong evidence supports the need for autonomy hypothesis in elementary school children. Children who work in classrooms where the teacher supports their need for autonomy (i.e., where teachers offer choices and create opportunities for deci-sion making) work more strategically and persist longer when they meet obstacles (Nolen, 2003; Perry, 1998; J. C. Turner, 1995). However, no such strong effects were found in junior high school (Midgley & Feldlaufer, 1987). Eccles et al. (1993) explained these findings by reference to the large amount of teacher control, as well as the strong emphasis on rules and regulations, in jun-ior high school. Interestingly, Kendall (1992) compared children from a Montessori school, where one of the main features is that students are given the opportunity to pursue their own goals by selecting tasks and activi-ties that they value, with children from a traditional school. The Montessori children showed higher levels of initiative, autonomy, and self-regulation. Hence, it is important to have a closer look at how instructional methods interact with students' need for autonomy.

Nolen's (2003) recent classroom studies illustrated the autonomy hypothesis quite convincingly in ongoing classroom interaction. She studied second and third graders' states of mind in relation to writing and read-ing classes and found that these states of mind were de-pendent on the teacher's skills in setting up these classes. Nolen described how, in some classrooms, the teacher presented writing assignments as opportunities for creative self-expression and a way to share ideas. In those classrooms, children considered writing exercises

as a game. The wording they chose to describe their ac-tivities in class showed that they felt fully volitional in their actions and considered the classroom environment as supporting their autonomy. Examples of such utter-ances were: "You get to write about your own life" and "You get to make up your own stories." These state-ments contrasted to utterances recorded in classrooms where the teacher exerted more control over topics and style of writing assignments and assigned writing exer-cises primarily for evaluation purposes. The students in these classrooms viewed improving their writing skills as something done for school: "We had to copy all the words" and "You are supposed to write about your own ideas." Nolen concluded that the development of interest in reading and writing is influenced by the way students characterize reading and writing activity: as a job to be done for school, or as a way to share ideas and be enter-tained. It is important to note that feeling coerced or controlled does not reside exclusively in the environ-ment. It can also be a state of mind that is triggered when being confronted with a domain by thinking about external rules and constraints that apply in that domain (R. M. Ryan, 1982).

Top-Down Self-Regulation: Attaching Value and Experiencing Interest

In the previous section, the emphasis was on the stu-dents' psychological needs and how need fulfillment fuels top-down self-regulation. In this section, I want to illustrate that the flow of energy might also come from the students' values and interest.

Attaching Positive Value to Tasks and Activities

Hickey and McCaslin (2001) argued that when learning is viewed as intrinsic sense making, engagement in the learning process occurs quite naturally. These theorists argued that engagement in learning is a function of prior experiences, learning, and understanding how the con-text interacts with the learning process. If students do not have a favorable expectation that they will be able to make sense of a learning task and its context, hardly any learning will occur. These assumptions underlie ex-pectancy value theory, which assumes that individuals are motivated to perform tasks and actions that they value and perceive as manageable.

Eccles and her colleagues (Eccles, 1987; Eccles & Wigfield, 2002; Wigfield & Eccles, 1992) developed and tested the expectancy value model in relation to the choices students make in achievement situations. One of the basic assumptions of the model is that all choices come at a cost: If you choose to solve one problem, read one text, or enroll for a particular course, it often means that you eliminate other options. Therefore, the relative *value* that students attach to each alternative and their perceived probability of success on the task are key elements in their decision-making process. Eccles and her colleagues identified four components of task value: intrinsic value (How much will I enjoy doing the task?), utility value (Is this task instrumental for attaining current or future goals?), attainment value (How important is it for me to do well on the task?), and cost (What will I lose or give up by doing the task?).

Eccles and colleagues also studied how students' competence beliefs influence the value they attach to a task or activity, and vice versa. In line with Bandura's (1997) self-efficacy theory, Eccles and Wigfield (2002) reported that changes in students' competence beliefs over a semester predicted changes in their value component, rather than the other way around. Wigfield (1994) pointed out the interesting developmental trend that young children's values and competence beliefs seem to start out relatively independent, but, over time, they might attach more value to achievement tasks that they can complete successfully and less value to activities that they find difficult. In fact, Wigfield et al. (1998) showed that at some point in time, values and competence-related beliefs become positively linked, thus ensuring that the individual maintains a positive sense of self. Accordingly, Eccles and Wigfield assumed that the positive affect that is experienced when one can successfully complete a task becomes attached to these activities and is triggered on later occasions. By the same token, negative affect may become attached to tasks and activities that one cannot perform well.

It is important to note that several of the value constructs that Eccles and her colleagues identified have been studied under different labels. For example, there is an extensive body of research on instrumentality, which is akin to utility value (e.g., Husman & Lens, 1999), and intrinsic value has been studied under different headings, most specifically under the heading of intrinsic motivation and interest (Hidi & Harackiewicz, 2001; Krapp & Lewalter, 2001; Renninger, 1990). Note further that self-efficacy and expectancy beliefs have long been identified as crucial in self-regulation and that the beneficial effect of self-efficacy on student interest and en-

gagement has been well documented at all ages (Bandura, 1997; Pintrich, 2000; Zimmerman, 2000).

Experiencing Interest

Sansone and Harackiewicz (1996) drew attention to the fact that theorists who focused on intrinsic motivation also considered expectancies and goal valuation processes as crucial components of their models, yet assigned specific meaning to these constructs. They also acknowledge that there are two aspects of outcome-derived motivation (expectancy and value) and that these two aspects work multiplicatively (students needs both aspects to regulate their motivation effectively). Sansone and Harackiewicz argued convincingly that it is important to make an explicit distinction between purpose goals and target goals. The former type of goal provides a reason for performing a task or activity (What am I trying to achieve and why?). For example, Thalia wants to learn to use the bathroom in order to impress her parents. The latter type of goal provides more concrete guidelines as to which steps should be taken at a specific point in time. Thalia wants to know what objects she can use for support in order not to lose her balance. In other words, Thalia derives motivation from activated knowledge about the purpose of her activities and she realizes that she needs to have access to concrete scripts (behavioral sequences) to keep her motivation alive.

Sansone and Harackiewicz (1996) proposed that motivation to reach the goal is also derived from the activity itself. In line with the extensive body of literature on interest (Ainley, Hidi, & Berndorff, 2002; Krapp, 2003) they described the positive phenomenological experience of intrinsic interest. Students feel like doing a task or activity when they are cognitively and affectively absorbed in a task and show high task involvement. Sansone and Harackiewicz predicted and found that individuals' phenomenological experience while working toward their goals exerts a greater influence on their willingness to engage actively in the activity than the initial motivation based on purpose and target goals. Applying these insights to Thalia's case means that outcome-derived motivation may be necessary and sufficient to draw Thalia into the toilet-training activity, but process-derived motivation is necessary to maintain performance over time. If Thalia does not have problematic affective experiences during goal pursuit, she will feel good about the training sessions and will be willing to invest time and effort to reach the goal.

The importance of students' phenomenological experiences while working toward the attainment of academic learning goals, particularly their emergent interest, in facilitating and maintaining performance in educational settings has been the object of investigation of interest researchers. For example, Ainley et al. (2002) showed that the nature of a task may have a major impact on students' phenomenological experiences and their engagement in the task. They reported several studies that showed the effect of emergent interest on students' continued engagement. These researchers found that students who were given a choice between two learning activities (e.g., which problem to solve, which topic to read or to write a composition about) activated stored information about the type of learning activity. The level of their reported interest in the topic, triggered by the teacher's brief description of the content of the learning activity, predicted the students' choice of activity and initiated engagement with the activity. Unfortunately, students discontinued the activity when they did not feel good about the task any longer, that is, when the learning experience did not live up to their interest expectation.

Interest researchers have also shown that students do not develop an interest in a study area or course unless they are invited to participate in learning situations that catch and hold their interest. Interest theory (Hidi & Harackiewicz, 2001; Krapp, 2003; Renninger, 1998, 2000) makes a distinction between situational interest and individual interest. The former develops during concrete interactions between the person and the object of (potential) interest, whereas the latter form of interest refers to a relatively stable tendency to engage in interaction with an object of interest. Krapp outlined how an object, topic, or activity that is introduced to a person evolves from an interesting situational event to a longer-lasting individual interest. He describes the growth of an individual interest out of a situational interest as a multistage process and considers attention and curiosity essential prerequisites for a longer-lasting interest to develop. The learner's attention should be caught and held long enough to allow experimentation and exploration; keeping the momentum going after the initial attention given to the object of interest is essential to proceed from situational interest to a stabilized interest stage that produces deep learning. A well-developed interest in a domain of study is reflected in a highly differentiated knowledge domain and many connections to other related domains.

Translating Value and Interest into an Intention to Learn

Researchers and teachers expect students to be interested in a multitude of topics, courses, instructional methods, and learning environments. They realize that when students have developed an individual interest in a domain, this ensures that they show a high readiness to acquire new information and to enlarge their competencies in that domain. However, students do not show longer-lasting interests with all school subjects, and it is essential that teachers support their students' meaning-, value-, and interest-generation processes.

Crossing the Rubicon

Heckhausen and Kuhl (1985) argued that for learning goals to be pursued, students' motivation in a domain has to be transformed into an *intention* to engage actively and constructively in concrete learning activities. These researchers also argued that intentions to act—even those that are self-intentional—might be abandoned later on because individuals do not invest enough effort in maintaining their intentions and protecting them from competing action tendencies. In other words, students may have established a goal and translated it into an intention to act in the goal-setting stage but give up on the goal in the goal-striving stage. The Rubicon model proposed by Heckhausen and Kuhl and later elaborated by Gollwitzer (1990, 1999) describes the link between the goal-setting and goal-striving stages as a path connecting two sides of a river representing commitment. Goal-setting processes precede commitment. These processes refer to the individuals' conscious and preconscious attempts to transform a motivational state into an intention to act. In the goal-setting stage, students make decisions about the targets, focus, expectancies, and type of engagement that they will commit themselves to. They may raise several "what, how, and why" questions before they begin to cross the Rubicon, such as "What is in it for me? How can I make this task more fun? Why is this skill important?" It is evident that it is much easier for students to commit themselves to a learning goal while crossing the Rubicon when (a) they value the activity; (b) they experience a positive experiential state, characterized by joy, excitement, a feeling of competence and interest in the activity; and/or (c) the environmental conditions catch their interest and hold it long enough for the activity or task to be completed.

Motivation Regulation Strategies. Several researchers have described the motivation regulation strategies that students use spontaneously or can learn to use to enhance their motivation in the goal-setting stage. Sansone and colleagues (e.g., Sansone & Smith, 2000) described a variety of avenues by which students may purposely enhance their interest and hold it during the pursuit of relatively uninteresting but important activities. One of these motivation strategies is self-consequating. This motivation strategy refers to students' attempts to anticipate the extrinsic consequences for their engagement or lack of engagement (Purdie & Hattie, 1996). An example of a self-consequating strategy that students use was provided by one of the teachers in our Partnership Program. One of her students said, "I prefer to use paraphrasing a paragraph in my own words as a memory strategy, but you give preference to writing down your own comprehension questions and answering them. I guess you will check whether we are studying your way, so I better start practicing this comprehension question technique." Evidence that students use self-consequating motivation strategies was found in children of different ages and different cultures (see Wolters & Rosenthal, 2000).

A second type of motivation strategy described in the literature is environmental control (Xu, 2004). This motivation strategy refers to students' skill at arranging their surroundings in such a way that it is easier to complete the task without interruption (e.g., switching off the television before starting homework). A third type of motivation regulation strategy is interest or value enhancement (Boekaerts, 2002b; Sansone & Harackiewicz, 1996). This refers to students' ability to make a task more enjoyable or more situationally interesting to complete. For example, students may vary their seating position when doing their homework, facing the door when they do their math homework and facing the map of Great Britain with photographs of the school trip to England while doing their language homework.

Goal-Striving Processes. When students arrive on the other side of the river, their learning intention is firmly in place and a volitional state of mind takes over. Gollwitzer (1999) referred to this state as an implementation mind-set. As the goal-striving process begins, the focus is on the best way to implement the goal, meaning that the necessary learning strategies are set in motion and that students need to have ready access to volitional

strategies to protect their intention from competing action tendencies. I will come back to the volitional strategies that students use in the goal-striving stage in the next part of the chapter.

Summary

The main conclusion that can be drawn on the basis of the reviewed literature on the self-regulation of motivation is that students who act on their felt needs, values, and longer-lasting interests self-regulate their motivation for learning automatically; their self-regulation is *primed* by their higher-order goals. In contrast, students, who do not attach value to an action or are not interested in a topic are not motivated to engage in the learning activity. These students have two main options. Their first option is to deliberately target their own cognitions, feelings, and actions in order to infuse value into the current learning task. I briefly described motivation strategies that students use to infuse value in learning tasks, and I referred to the interest-enhancing strategies that they use during the pursuit of relatively uninteresting but important activities. The second option is that they change the learning situation in such a way that it is brought in line with their own values, interests, and needs. For example, they can ask the teacher whether they are allowed to refocus their composition or their paper on a related issue that they are more interested in. Both these options refer to *nonprimed* decision making and thus may require conscious effort on the part of the student.

Bargh and Gollwitzer (1994) made an explicit distinction between deliberate self-regulation efforts and self-regulation that seems to take place with little thinking or effort on the part of the individual. They showed, for example, that performing a well-learned skill or an inherently interesting activity is initiated and maintained by processes that occur beneath the level of conscious awareness. In the next section, I focus on the role of conscious effort in the learning process, addressing volitional forms of self-regulation.

Self-Regulation of Effort

It is actually strange that we do not have a comprehensive theory of effort regulation that can guide interventions in the classroom, despite the well-established value of the construct for understanding student behavior and the practical applications it might engender. Reasons for the unpopularity of effort research might be traced to only a few factors. There is no evidence that effort is a cognitive construct, a common metric to measure effort is missing, and our models of self-regulated learning are not well equipped to study effort as it reveals itself in real time.

What Is Effort?

A first question that should be raised is What is effort? Is it a cognitive construct, or is it the emergent result of a constellation of properties of the learning task? If the latter is the case, what are the properties from which effort emerges? For example, do students take stock only of the time spent doing a task, or do they also take account of the number of (in)correct responses that they have generated so far? How do students conceptualize an effortless and an effortful accomplishment, and what are their ideas about hard work? To date, these questions remain largely unanswered. In my opinion, researchers have not capitalized on the potential of effort for theory building and practice.

There are several problems with the definitions, operationalizations, and assessment instruments that have been used in relation to this construct. The definitions vary, and it is not at all clear how the different constructs that are used in the literature, such as (emotional, cognitive, and behavioral forms of) engagement, effort investment, effort allocation, persistence, and perseverance, are related to self-regulation. For example, in their review on school engagement, Fredricks et al. (2004) defined effort as an aspect of behavioral engagement. Clearly, effort should be defined in relation to engagement, but its characteristic features should be operationalized in such a way that it adds to the explanatory power of the larger system of self-regulation.

Developmental psychologist Bloom and colleagues (e.g., Bloom & Beckwith, 1989; Bloom & Turner, 2001) argued that, from a developmental perspective, engagement is distinct from effort. They explained that engagement provides the motivation (energy) and directedness for development and effort ensures that this process goes forward. Children who are already engaged in a learning activity may—consciously or unconsciously—increase or decrease their level of engagement by investing more energy or time in the activity. The former decision refers to the *intensity* of effort and the latter to the *duration* of effort (persis-

tence). Bloom and Turner further explained that engagement and effort are two opposing principles that operate with an essential tension between them. In line with Kuhn's (1977) theorizing about theory emergence, these researchers hypothesized that developmental change in a domain is not simply quantitative or cumulative. For example, children do not become more proficient in understanding and expressing verbal messages by adding up words and sentences.

Bloom and Turner (2001) showed that very young children (13 to 24 months) want to talk about the things that interest them. However, toddlers often find that they cannot accommodate new experiences because their language skills are insufficient. At such a point, they use emotional expression to get their message across, such as pointing, shouting, hitting, and crying. These researchers showed that developmental change in language acquisition is the result of *effort* invested in experiencing and working through a succession of tensions between the old (e.g., what the child already can express in one-word sentences and emotional expressions) and the new (using syntax). Bloom's theorizing can also explain Thalia's behavior. She knew that it would be hard to acquire the going-alone-to-the-bathroom skill in a short period of time, but she was prepared to go through a succession of tensions to acquire it. Bloom and Turner's (2001) explanation can also be extended to include learning new skills in formal learning contexts, as I illustrate later in the discussion.

In educational psychology, researchers have adopted a multidimensional view of effort. For example, Weinert, Schrader, and Helmke (1989) have separated qualitative effort from quantitative effort, and Salomon and Perkins (1989) separated mindful effort from mindless effort. Weinert et al. distinguished between time spent (quantitative effort) and the type of cognitive strategies used (qualitative effort) and found that these different types of effort affected mathematics performance differentially in 10- to 12-year-old students. They found that students who had high scores on indices of mathematics ability (measured as either scores on the pretest or their self-concept of mathematics ability at the start of the study) spent high qualitative effort, and this in turn had a positive effect on their math achievement measured 2 years later. In contrast, students who scored low on indices of mathematics ability at the start of the study spent more quantitative effort, and this led to more anxiety, and in turn, to low math achievement. Notably, all students invested effort, but not every type of effort produced learning.

What Assessment Instruments Have Been Used?

A second question concerns the validity of the assessment instruments that are used to measure quantitative and qualitative effort. Researchers have tried to measure effort quantitatively by using various indices of mental effort and processing load. Some researchers measured the number and duration of responses required to solve a problem, others measured students' time on task, and still others used physiological measures to assess ongoing mental activity (for a review, see Eisenberger, 1992). Kahnman (1973) argued that the total energy that can be exerted at any point in time is limited. Accordingly, it was proposed that dual task performance or multitasking increases processing load relative to single task performance. To the extent that these concurrent activities require attention and tap into the same pool of resources, they compete for processing capacity and tend to interfere with one another (Bloom & Turner, 2001; Case, 1992). This explains why low-achieving, less knowledgeable, or less skilled students often experience a *feeling of difficulty* and report having to invest high levels of effort into a task. I come back to this issue later.

How sound are the instruments we use to measure the effort that students invest in the classroom? Most researchers have used self-report instruments. Open-ended self-report measures ask respondents to tell in their own words how much effort they invested in a task, their homework, or exam preparation. Content analyses of the responses allow the researcher to quantify the level of effort reported by students who worked on the same task. An issue that complicates measurement when using narratives is that students may report effort in an unspecified way and there is no way of comparing their reported effort. Consider a teacher's or researcher's problem in interpreting the narrative of two students: Sarah says, "I spent the whole weekend preparing for this exam and I am totally exhausted. I really need a break." Howard says, "I studied real hard during the weekend and did my best to understand all the material." Judging from what these students reported, they each invested considerable time in exam preparation, but do these statements necessarily imply that the quality of the invested effort was high?

Self-report questionnaires of the Likert variety may give the impression that the assessment of effort is less problematic; they consist of a series of items that re-

quire respondents to reflect on the effort expended and then indicate on 4-, 5-, or 7-point Likert scales what level of effort fits their perception of the energy invested in a task or activity (e.g., "I invested *little* effort, *some* effort, *considerable* effort, and *great* effort"). The alternatives provided in most scales seem straightforward and easy to use, and they are rarely questioned psychometrically. Yet, one should ask what the exact meaning of the alternatives is for each respondent. What does "little effort" mean? Is it really less than "some effort"? How wide is the gap between "some effort" and "considerable effort"? Are students aware of the amount of effort they have invested? What metric do they use to communicate to others what the level of invested effort was? Kruger, Wirtz, Van Boven, and Altermatt (2004) found that individuals use an effort heuristic to judge the quality of a performance. Students seem to believe that the more (alleged) time somebody had invested in his or her performance, the better the product is. These researchers also found that the influence of students' perceived effort on their judgment of "quality" was bigger when the ambiguity of the outcome was high.

An issue that further complicates matters is that effort investment is not a linear process; for example, Howard and Sarah might have set themselves a rather general study goal and allocated effort quasi-automatically on Saturday morning, but they may have specified the goal further and revised their level of effort as the weekend progressed. For instance, Sarah's narrative informed us that, initially, she was satisfied with getting a B with reasonable effort. Feedback regarding time needed to work through the material indicated to Sarah that she could easily get an A if she strained herself a little more and did all the provided exercises as well. The favorable time feedback triggered a new aspiration level, prompting Sarah to add some effort that she might not normally have invested. In contrast, Howard started off with an A aspiration, working really hard on Saturday but scaling back on Sunday when he realized that it was next to impossible to cover all the study material and do all the exercises before Monday morning.

My argument is that these students may have started out with a specific idea of how much effort they were going to invest, changing the intensity and duration of their effort depending on certain characteristics of the task or the learning process. In other words, it is difficult to capture the dynamic quality of effort regulation during the goal-striving process. What is needed is a measurement instrument that can register the changing levels of effort over time. To do that we need to establish an idiographic metric (Austin & Vancouver, 1996) that students can use to register and report on their changing effort levels during the different stages of exam preparation, goal pursuit, or a course. Idiographic measures facilitate within-person comparisons across time and subject matter areas but are problematic for comparisons across individuals. Future research on effort should address two dynamic aspects of the self-regulation of effort: how effort is allocated initially, and how it is maintained during the goal-striving stage.

CURRENT KNOWLEDGE ABOUT STUDENTS' EFFORT

In this section, I summarize what is currently known about students' effort beliefs and how these beliefs may influence increases and decreases in effort.

Students' Theory of Effort

Developmental psychologists have examined students' theory of effort. For example, Dweck (2003) deduced from her longitudinal research that to engage actively and constructively in a domain and overcome obstacles, children need to have access to a *coherent* network of beliefs, a meaning system in which they can integrate emerging new ideas and inject them with motivational value. An increasing body of knowledge endorses this view. In the early years of schooling, children seem to draw on isolated pieces of knowledge to interpret learning tasks and activities. Several researchers (e.g., Dweck, 1991, 1998; Nicholls, 1984; Paris, Byrnes, & Alison, 2001) showed that young children have fragmentary ideas about what good work is and what it takes to achieve it. They do not differentiate between ability and effort, believing that everybody who puts in effort will perform well.

Paris et al. (2001) clarified that children's theory of effort develops gradually over the middle childhood years; they unmasked the unrealistic belief that persistence, good work habits, and good conduct are sufficient to succeed in school, independent of ability. By the age of 10, children have developed ideas about their ability, and they begin to understand that ability is an internal quality that can predict their outcomes (Stipek & Daniels, 1990). They have also come to realize that putting in effort cannot compensate for low ability. An interesting finding reported by Dweck and her colleagues

was that, in the early school years, children may realize that they have not done well on a task and certainly performed worse than their peers. However, these unfavorable beliefs neither decreased interest nor elicited avoidance behavior, as they do in older children (Butler, 1992). Dweck (2003) argued that the reason why unfavorable experiences do not systematically affect actions in this age group is that their emerging ideas about ability and effort are not yet integrated into a coherent meaning system and have, as such, not yet gained consistent motivational value.

Dweck and her colleagues (e.g., Cain & Dweck, 1995) were also able to demonstrate that, between the ages of 10 and 12 years, children seem to have access to a theory of intelligence that reflects either an incremental view of intelligence or an entity view. A well-established line of research links the two theories of intelligence to goal orientation; the incremental view of intelligence is consistently linked to task orientation, whereas the entity view is linked to performance orientation (Pintrich, 2003). Blackwell, Dweck, and Trzesniewski (2002) found that at about the transition to middle school (12 to 13 years), children's ideas about ability and effort come together in a network of motivational beliefs around their theory of intelligence and begin to show their impact on the goals they want to achieve and their academic behavior. Based on her longitudinal studies with freshmen in junior high school, Dweck (2003) outlined how children build their motivational meaning system around their theory of intelligence: Children who have built their meaning system around an incremental conception of intelligence focus on improvement and attainment. They view effort as instrumental to improvement and as a sign of involvement and commitment. These children have no problem admitting that they invested effort, even when their performance is (still) poor or when the teacher gives unfavorable feedback on their performance. They interpret errors and setbacks as a signal that more time (duration) and energy (intensity) is needed to increase competence; thus, persisting in the face of hardship, strategizing, and asking for help when necessary comes naturally (J. C. Turner & Meyer, 1999).

Conditional Knowledge Is Necessary for the Self-Regulation of Effort

In one of our own studies (Boekaerts, Otten, & Voeten, 2003), we found that students' activated effort and ability beliefs led them to refrain from seeking control through effort in some domains at the benefit of gaining control in other domains. We asked freshmen in junior high school to indicate how much time they spent preparing for three regular end-of-term exams: history, mathematics, and text processing in their native language. We also examined their attribution processes of the exam results. Students seldom used effort as an explanation for failure in any of the school subjects studied, but they used it as the dominant factor to explain success in history (average preparation time = 120 minutes), in combination with level of difficulty in mathematics (average preparation time = 60 minutes), and not at all in relation to text processing (preparation time = 10 minutes). Based on these results, Boekaerts et al. suggested that students' willingness to invest time and effort in the acquisition of new skills is determined to a large extent by precoded information about subject matter-specific task demands and about their perceived capacity to meet these demands. This knowledge is akin to the metacognitive knowledge that I have discussed previously and is propaedeutic for the self-regulation of effort in a domain.

From the current research on effort and persistence it is gradually becoming clear that the best predictor of students' self-regulation of effort is conditional knowledge. Kuhl and Kraska (1989) showed that the knowledge that elementary school children had about the obstacles they might encounter during goal pursuit and the way to deal with these obstacles effectively predicted the intensity of their effort. In a similar vein, Efklides, Papadaki, Papantoniou, and Kiosseoglou (1999) reported that high school students who lacked metacognitive knowledge to interpret strategy failure in a specific domain could not decide whether or not it was worthwhile to invest further effort. These investigators showed that students who can act on their feelings of difficulty regulate their actions more effectively. In other words, knowing what effort entails in relation to different tasks and when it is needed is conditional to students' self-regulation of effort. Students also need to be aware of the strategies that are effective to increase or decrease effort, and they need knowledge of the contexts in which these strategies will be effective. The tendency to increase effort when needed and to maintain it despite distracters and obstacles refers to students' volitional competence. Volition is one of the most crucial factors of self-regulation; it is the main topic in our next section.

Promoting Volitional Strategies in the Service of Attaining Learning Goals

Many studies have examined how cues in the learning environment interact with students' felt needs to increase or decrease their active engagement (e.g., Connell, 1990; Skinner & Belmont, 1993); some researchers focused explicitly on how instruction strategies and task characteristics promote or inhibit participation and persistence. It is clear that many common educational practices actually reduce students' intrinsic interest in academic learning (Corno & Randi, 1999; McCombs & Pope, 1994). Educational practices that decrease students' sense making, particularly in disadvantaged students, include a focus on evaluations and grading, normative and relative grading, creating competition between students, public announcements of grades, retention, and acceptance of dropping out. Hickey and McCaslin (2001) argued that engagement in learning is enhanced when obstacles to intrinsic sense making are removed and intrinsic sense making is provoked. Over the years, several suggestions have been formulated for teachers to promote intrinsic sense making and persistence in the classroom. Before I look more closely at these suggestions, I try to answer the question What are volitional strategies?

Development of Volitional Competence

Volitional strategies are aspects of self-management; they refer to persistence, perseverance, and buckling down to work. Corno (1994) defined these strategies as students' tendency to maintain focus and effort toward their goals despite potential distractions. When do students need volitional strategies in the classroom? Many students experience difficulty getting started on an assignment or homework task. They may also get distracted while working on an assignment, for example, when they meet with obstacles or are sidetracked by competing goals (e.g., a telephone call, a program that starts on television, or a noise in the street). Corno reported that weaker students experience difficulty in implementing what she called "good work habits" that protect their intentions, particularly when difficult work must be completed. She argued that these students would benefit from instructions in good work habits. She listed several good work habits, including how to set goals and subgoals, how to prioritize goals, how to organize one's work, how to make a time schedule, how to stick to that schedule, how to determine the time needed to do various assignments, and how to monitor time spent.

Are there specific situations in which students need volitional strategies? Boekaerts (2002a) and Corno (2001) formulated a number of hypothetical situations in which students need to control their learning environment. Examples are situations where there is a lot of noise in the classroom or where students would prefer to work on another task or with another person. There are also situations where students show a lot of anxiety, anger, irritation, or frustration that obstructs or interferes with their intention to take actions. Indeed, some learning situations may be tedious and boring, requiring a lot of willpower to stay focused on task. Other learning situations are complex and taxing and students might realize that they will meet many obstacles and will have to invest a great deal of effort to finish the assignment. I come back to the phenomenological experience of felt difficulty later in this section.

There are also a great number of learning situations that pose problems to students' intention to stay on track because competing goals catch their interest or concern. Hijzen, Boekaerts, and Vedder (2004) described social learning situations, where students in the group show various forms of low effort, such as preferring to chat instead of working with their peers, taking advantage of other students' work, skip meetings, and, generally, being unreliable about following up on work arrangements (see also Dowson & McInerney, 2001; Wentzel, 1991a, 1991b).

A question raised by educational psychologists as teachers alike is this: Are volitional strategies trainable? Kuhl and his colleagues (Kuhl, 1985, 2000; Kuhl & Fuhrman, 1998; Kuhl & Kraska, 1989) convinced educational psychologists that they are. In fact, volitional strategies develop from early childhood well into adolescence. What is needed for children to develop these strategies is a growing awareness of their own functioning, including their cognitive, motivational, and affective functioning. Kuhl and Kraska illustrated that socialization practices impact the development of volitional strategies in the home, in the peer group, and at school. Xu (2004) emphasized the importance of parents and teachers supporting and actively coaching children to develop willpower. How can teachers assist students in developing their willpower? Kuhl and his colleagues (see, e.g., Kuhl, 2000) proposed that the best way to train volitional strategies is in an "interactive partnership,"

where pairs of individuals work together and constructively react to each other's attempts at self-regulation, highlighting those aspects of goal pursuit that still pose problems for sustained effort. Several educational psychologists (Boekaerts, 1997, 1999; Boekaerts & Simons, 1995; Corno, 1994, 2001, 2004; Lemos, 2002; Perry, 1998; Xu, 2004; Xu & Corno, 1999) provided guidelines for teachers to enhance students' volitional strategies. A recommendation given to teachers and parents is to model volitional strategies and to discuss their effectiveness with students. In the next section, I take a closer look at the contextual factors that promote the self-regulation of effort.

Contextual Factors Impede or Promote Self-Regulation of Effort

Vygotsky (1978) described how adults can help young children to promote intrinsic sense making by helping them to form and retrieve mental images of an action plan (see my example of Thalia). Zimmerman (1998, 2000) reported the beneficial effects of parents, peers, and teachers who modeled self-regulation skills and encouraged children of all ages to copy their behavior. Zimmerman, Bandura, and Martinez-Pons (1992) described in detail how parents can function as explicit and implicit role models when they want their children to acquire a new competency. There is ample evidence that observational learning has a positive effect on children's and adolescents' learning as well as on their persistence when a task proves to be difficult. Adolescents who observed peer models persist on a difficult task showed increased self-efficacy, persisted longer on similar tasks, and improved their problem-solving skills (Martinez-Pons, 1996; Schunk & Zimmerman, 1998).

Students Need to Pick Up Environmental Cues

Increasingly, researchers advise teachers to interact with their students on the work floor, inviting them to monitor their actions and reflect on their attempts to self-regulate their effort while they work. Boekaerts (2002b) and Boekaerts and Simons (1995) described the monitoring instructions that teachers could give their students to build conditional knowledge about the intensity and duration of effort that is required to complete different types of assignments and about effective ways to see that the effort is maintained when the task becomes boring or difficult. Such monitoring instructions, as well as the recording of the volitional strategies that were undertaken, will make students aware of the situations where volitional strategies are in order and the environmental cues that will tell them whether they have to maintain effort or can discontinue it. Consider the following:

Case Example

Anne Marie is a 16-year-old who wants to become a language teacher. She is well aware that it takes effort to acquire a foreign language at a native speaker level. Her attempts at self-regulation inform her mother that she is willing to invest all the effort it takes to reach her goal. For example, when her mother asked her how much time she still needed to finish her homework, she replied, "I will go on practicing until I can read this French text flawlessly. I will first isolate all the words that I have difficulty with and practice them. Then, I will underline them in the text so that I can see them come up in the corner of my eye while reading."

This example shows that Anne Marie has set herself a purpose and a target goal. These goals allow her to follow the scripts she has specified beforehand, picking up cues in relation to her progress. Oettingen, Honig, and Gollwitzer (2000) and Corno (2004) showed that when such scripts have been put firmly in place before students need to use them in action, they can easily be activated at the time of use, thus acting as conditional knowledge.

Scripts to Deal with Distracters

Corno (1994) emphasized the key role of environmental cues, particularly *distracters,* in triggering the use of volitional strategies. She advised teachers to have their students draw up a list of possible distracters when studying and categorize them as to where and when they occur. She further suggested that teachers make an inventory of how their students deal with these distracters, comparing the volitional strategies they use and asking students to evaluate how well they worked. This procedure allows teachers to discuss the volitional strategies that their students have marked as "effective" and "ineffective" with the whole class and ask the students to explain why they thought these strategies were (in)effective to deal with a particular distracter. For example, Anne Marie told the class that she had dealt successfully with a distracter in the library. She said, "When I realized that I could not find the necessary resource material for my paper in the library because

other students pressured me to hurry up and vacate the computer, I told them that they would have to wait much longer if they kept bothering me. They took the hint and went for coffee." Students might even model effective ways to deal with distracters while role-playing these strategies. As a follow-up on Anne Marie's statement, they could practice effective ways to tell students to stop bullying their peers.

In my own intervention program with students in vocational education, I found that teachers who invite their students regularly to note down effective volitional strategies create a classroom environment where students enjoy discussing their own functioning in the classroom. One of the teachers even asked her students to write their effective volitional strategies on a poster and illustrate them with visual cues. This nicely decorated poster was put up on the wall in the classroom and students enjoyed adding new volitional strategies to the list. At a certain point, the teacher invited her students to consult the poster and pick out one or more volitional strategies that they thought appropriate in the situation they found themselves in. In this way, she coached them to build their conditional knowledge of the type of volitional strategies that are effective in specific contexts, using the information displayed on the poster. After a while, the students called the poster "Tommy" and recommended that their peers spontaneously "Ask Tommy" when one of them expressed doubts as to what to do in a difficult situation.

How Do Contextual Factors Interact with Self-Regulation?

Several intervention programs are currently being set up with students of different ages, and promising results have been reported. I will not describe these ongoing intervention programs. The interested reader is referred to Boekaerts and Corno (2005) and to the special issue on volitional strategies in *a special issue of Teacher College Record* (Corno, 2004). I do make one exception, because I want to draw the reader's attention to a group of researchers who started to use a wide variety of recording techniques to study *in detail* (a) the self-regulation strategies that students of various age groups actually use to achieve their learning goals and (b) how contextual factors interact with students' attempts at self-regulation (e.g., Perry & Vandekamp, 2000; Stipek et al., 1998; J. C. Turner & Meyer, 1999). The recording techniques that this group of researchers used included observations, interviews, stimulated recall, recording students' motivation strategies as they work, self-reports, traces of mental events and processes, and keeping diaries.

Various aspects of the classroom environment seem to contribute to the emergence of self-regulatory skills, such as the types of assignments that the children had to work on, whether or not they had a choice, the type of instructions that were provided, the quality of the student-teacher interactions, and the type of assessment and evaluation procedures that were used. In one of these studies, Perry and her colleagues (Perry, 1998; Perry, Vandekamp, Mercer, & Nordby, 2002) showed that second- and third-grade students engaged constructively in complex writing activities provided their teachers used ongoing assessment, challenging them to make progress without threatening their self-efficacy. All the students who worked with teachers who coached their self-regulation skills demonstrated high self-regulation; they tried to manage all aspects of the writing process independently and flexibly. These students monitored their writing progress in productive ways and self-assessed their performance. Interestingly, when these students met with obstacles, they sought social support from their peers and teachers, and—remarkably—even the low-achieving students in these classrooms showed high self-efficacy for learning and did not avoid challenging tasks.

Second and third graders who had traditional teachers showed different behavior; they avoided challenging tasks and depended on their teachers for feedback and assessment. In fact, these students demonstrated various forms of bottom-up self-regulation, including hiding their work, reducing effort, avoiding different forms of external regulation, and procrastination. What have we learned from this and related studies about effective ways to promote students' volitional strategies? The variety of recording techniques used in these studies allows researchers to pinpoint those instructional techniques that foster intrinsic sense making and top-down self-regulation and contrast them to instructional techniques that promote various forms of bottom-up self-regulation and impede the self-regulation of effort. This information is of high theoretical and practical importance and can be used to design intervention programs to help teachers promote the self-regulation of motivation and effort in their students.

In the previous pages, I have concentrated on the volitional strategies that students need when they en-counter distracters that draw their attention away from the task at hand. I have also discussed some techniques that teachers might use to help their students buckle down to work. There is also another category of situations that calls for the self-regulation of effort, namely, learning situations where students meet with obstacles en route to the goal. These situations are the next focus of attention.

Interpreting the Phenomenological Experience of Felt Difficulty

Why are some students successful in overcoming obstacles and difficulties to ensure the attainment of academic goals and other students are not? Perhaps one of the greatest barriers to students' volitional control is that they do not have easy access to volitional strategies when they encounter obstacles en route to the goal. These students need external regulation and a great deal of scaffolding to finish the task, mainly because they do not know how to deal with the phenomenological experience of "felt difficulty." Experiencing a feeling of difficulty during goal pursuit may imply several things. It may simply mean that students have met with obstacles of some sort that they had not anticipated and that they need to find their way around them. It may also imply that they are aware that they do not have ready access to cognitive and metacognitive strategies to go around the obstacle and that this awareness causes worries, low expectations, and self-doubt (see also Covington, 2004). My argument is that obstacles en route to the goal and the concomitant feeling of difficulty act for some students as a signal that more effort is temporarily needed to self-regulate the learning process (see also Zimmerman, 2000). In others, a feeling of difficulty may elicit negative emotions, thereby forcing students to change their appraisal of the task and of the self in relation to the task.

I have suggested elsewhere (e.g., Boekaerts, 1999) that students who are willing to increase the intensity and duration of effort when they meet with obstacles have a good chance of remaining on the growth pathway. In contrast, students who experience negative emotions when breakdowns or setbacks occur may tend to conclude prematurely that they are unable to reroute activity from the well-being pathway to the growth pathway because their phenomenological experience inhibits them from dealing with the obstacles in an effective way. They want to attend promptly to an immediate and urgent need to restore their well-being by disengaging temporarily or permanently from the task. These students may come back to the task later on, but in a smaller way (e.g., by scaling down). Redefining the effort that is needed to perform a task or activity can be seen in Figure 9.1 by following the dotted line connecting the growth pathway with the well-being pathway (marked 1) in combination with the line (marked 2) that leads the student back to the growth pathway.

Clearly, insight into the cognitions and feelings that students experience when they meet with obstacles, setbacks, breakdowns, and strategy failures is essential to help them self-regulate their effort when they meet with obstacles. Several researchers described what actually happens when individuals experience a feeling of difficulty during goal pursuit (e.g., P. A. Alexander, Graham, & Harris, 1998; Carver & Scheier, 1981, 1998, 2000; Efklides et al., 1999; Winne, 1995). These accounts can roughly be subdivided into affectively charged insights and metacognitively oriented insights. I discuss each in turn.

Experience of Difficulty: Low Confidence and Doubt

Two social psychologists Carver and Scheier (1981) theorized that effort reflects both the presence of a goal and awareness of how one is doing relative to standards. For example, Anne Marie told her mother that she would keep practicing till she could read the text flawlessly. Hence, she set herself a high standard, implying that she had a clear purpose and expectancy as well as a ready script to attain the goal. As argued previously, expectancies have a profound influence on motivation, whatever their source. Individuals generate expectancies about the outcome of their actions as they work, and these expectancies (confidence or doubt) influence the effort they are prepared to invest. Individuals who have experienced obstacles in relation to an activity (domain) in the past may interrupt their efforts periodically to assess in a more thoughtful way than occurs while acting the likelihood of a successful outcome. This assessment presumably depends to a large extent on their prior learning history in relation to the activity, on their knowledge about the reasons why these obstacles occur, and on their anticipation of the additional resources they might need to overcome the problem.

Carver and Scheier (1998) showed that college students invest effort and renew effort investment provided expectancies for a successful outcome are sufficiently favorable. If doubts are strong enough, individuals are inclined to disengage from further effort and even from the goal itself. Disengagement may take the form of overt or covert avoidance behavior. Examples of the former type of avoidance are various forms of giving up, such as quitting the situation, dropping a course, and redirecting one's actions. Illustrations of covert avoidance are daydreaming, wishful thinking, and denying the importance of a goal. Note that these are examples of what I previously labeled emotion-focused coping or bottom-up self-regulation.

Wrosch, Scheier, Carver, and Schultz (2003) maintained that disengagement requires a person to withdraw not only effort but also commitment from unattainable goals. They showed that disengagement can be beneficial to well-being and is most adaptive if the person engages in other meaningful activities. The "scaling back" phenomenon described by Carver and Scheier (1998) and illustrated in Howard's example is a form of partial disengagement. When scaling back, students have in fact given up on the initial goal (e.g., an A grade) while simultaneously substituting it with a more manageable goal. Scaling back is a way to stay in the situation in a meaningful way, even though in a smaller way than originally planned. Students who scale back perceive progress toward an important goal and experience positive affect and confidence, two important ingredients of effortful accomplishment.

An interesting question is this: What makes an individual decide that investing more effort (persistence) is to no avail and that he or she needs to reduce effort, delay, or give up? Several researchers referred to a point in time when an individual considers effort as fruitless and stops trying. They conceptualized this discontinuity between engagement effort and giving up as a perceived shift in difficulty level (e.g., Efklides et al., 1999) or as perceived loss of control (Schwarzer, Jerusalem, & Stiksrud, 1984). Based on insights from their own research, Carver and Scheier (2000) reconceptualized the point of discontinuity as a *region* of discontinuity. This region marks the range of tasks where task demands are close to the individual's limits of performance. In this region, there is a greater variability in observed patterns of engagement effort. Carver and Scheier posited that a person might enter this region from two different directions, leading to different predictions. Individuals who starts out confident but meet many obstacles on their way to the goal will continue to invest effort, even if situational cues imply less and less basis for confidence. By contrast, individuals who enter the region of discontinuity from the low confidence direction but perceive environmental cues indicating otherwise will continue with little effort, even when situational cues imply more and more basis for confidence. Note that Thalia entered the region of discontinuity from the high confidence direction and continued to invest effort even when she met with obstacles (e.g., when she lost her balance).

Experience of Difficulty: Taxing Processing Demands

Winne (1995) provided a metacognitively oriented insight of what happens when students experience a feeling of difficulty. He explained that students who are still novices in a domain make relatively more errors than competent learners, mainly because the newly acquired knowledge has not been proceduralized yet. For example, in mathematics, students may regress to number crunching when they have difficulty detecting the key words in a word problem that inform them what type of algorithm they have to apply. A request often made to these students is that they have to monitor cues that prevent errors from occurring. However, the monitoring processes that are relevant in the new domain may not have automated yet, meaning that the monitoring process heavily taxes the students' limited attentional resources and working memory capacity. Two social psychologists, Kanfer and Ackerman (1989), neatly showed that fewer cognitive resources are needed to run a proceduralized skill than to perform multiple accesses of propositions strung together in a declaratively encoded rule. They explained that once the transformation from declarative knowledge to proceduralized skills has taken place, which occurred in their experiment around the seventh trial, individuals were able to shift their cognitive resources from the learning process per se (i.e., proceduralizing the new skill) to the regulation of the learning process.

These and similar experiments show that the performance of novices will be disrupted by increasing processing demands, simply because novices have a fragmentary, poorly integrated domain of knowledge and do not yet perform many subprocesses on automatic pilot. P. A. Alexander et al. (1998) shed some light on this issue. They described the multiple stages of exper-

tise development in a domain and reported that students from different types and levels of education proceed through three successive stages of skill development: acclimation, competence, and expertise/proficiency. During the acclimation stage, individuals have limited and quite fragmented knowledge of the domain, and they basically use shallow information processing. During the competence stage, students' domain knowledge becomes more coherent, and they start building up knowledge about the obstacles that might occur during task performance and about various ways to deal with obstacles (metacognitive or conditional knowledge). In the proficiency stage, individuals express personal interest in a domain and have access to a rich and principled knowledge base in which a large repertoire of (meta)cognitive strategies is stored as well as metacognitive knowledge about the context in which these strategies are effective. A great deal of information is currently available about how experts in a domain self-regulate the acquisition of new knowledge by selecting, combining, and coordinating cognitive and metacognitive strategies in functions of their reading and writing goals and the perceived contextual cues (e.g., P. A. Alexander, 2003; Pressley, 1995). Zimmerman (1998) listed the volitional strategies that experts in different disciplines (i.e., students, writers, athletes, musicians) use to stay on track. Czikszentmihalyi (1990) described the all-engrossing task engagement of proficient learners. Like experts, proficient learners experience flow, which is characterized by positive affect and a feeling of being lost in time. This timeless experience might explain why expert learners have recollection of an *effortless* performance (i.e., they report low effort despite high-quality deep-level processing).

In contrast to these experts, novices may have recollections of effortful performance despite poor results. Alexander, Graham, and Harris (1998) characterized *effortful* processors as students who perform adequately in the early years of schooling, in part because they are goal-directed and are prepared to expend high levels of strategic effort in the pursuit of understanding or commendable performance, even despite limited topic knowledge and when facing obstacles. These students are aware that they need to invest a lot of effort in their schoolwork and are willing to do so, provided the teacher provides a great deal of scaffolding. Nevertheless, effortful processors seem to have difficulty building a rich and coherent knowledge base in which declarative, procedural, and conditional knowledge about a domain are well integrated. They also lack standards against which to monitor their effort investment. This raises the following question: When and why are students willing to invest effort in their schoolwork?

PROMOTING STUDENTS' WILLINGNESS TO INVEST EFFORT INTO SCHOOL WORK

In the previous three sections, I have reviewed the literature on the self-regulation of motivation, interest, and effort. It should be evident from this review that students' theory of effort, particularly the knowledge they have about the type of distracters and obstacles that may occur during a task or activity and how to deal with distracters and obstacles, is crucial to move the learning and self-regulation process forward. Based on the insights provided in the literature, I have formulated my own working definition of the self-regulation of effort in the classroom. It refers to the extension of mental and physical energy over time toward the achievement of a learning goal based on one's motivation meaning system and one's perception of the demand-capacity ratio. In my way of thinking, self-regulation of effort implies students':

- Awareness that a discrepancy may exist between their current goal state and the desired goal state
- Willingness to work through a series of tensions to reach the desired outcomes
- Willingness to interrupt their action plan when distracters or obstacles occur
- Willingness to reflect on the whys of distraction and strategy failure and on possible ways of dealing with perceived obstacles and with the emotions they trigger
- Willingness to select from their repertoire those strategies that ensure progress in competence development in the present context

This working definition illustrates what is presently known about the self-regulation of effort. It allows researchers and teachers to concentrate on specific aspects of the self-regulation of effort. Next, I provide an example from my own research program to illustrate some issues that were raised in the previous sections. The study that I report on illustrates how difficult it is to measure and interpret effort in the classroom. I want to show how theory about the self-regulation of effort led into practice and how practice led back into theory.

How Taxing Are Processing Demands in the Classroom?

Payne and colleagues (Payne, Bettman, Coupey, & Johnson, 1992) defined effort involved in the decision-making process in terms of the mental operations required to come to an accurate decision, including reading, analyzing, and making comparisons. The effort a decision maker has to invest is considered the "cost," and the accuracy of his or her response is considered the "benefit" of a decision-making process. These researchers argued that individuals adjust their processing mode flexibly to maximize benefits and minimize costs during decision making. Cost-benefit trade-offs account for many findings in the decision-making literature but have also found their way into stress research, work psychology, and educational psychology (e.g., Eisenberger, 1992).

In educational psychology, several researchers attempted to define and operationalize the mental operations and the processing load involved in various learning tasks. For example, Entwistle (1988) sorted text-processing strategies into two main classes: surface-level and deep-level processing. He showed that students who dominantly process information in a text by reading, skipping unfamiliar words, rereading, and memorizing use a shallow processing mode, whereas students who supplement and enrich these processing activities by structuring the information read and critically relating ideas and arguments expressed in the text to their own experiences use a deep processing mode. Entwistle assumed that deep-level processing requires more mental effort than surface-level processing.

In one of our own studies, we borrowed the cost-benefit construct from Payne and his colleagues and the surface-level and deep-level processing distinction from Entwistle and his colleagues. The question that we set ourselves was this: Do students adjust their processing strategies flexibly in order to maximize benefits and minimize costs while learning? I next briefly describe this study and then illustrate that several competing conclusions could be drawn for practice on the basis of the obtained results.

Training in the Use of Deep-Level Processing Strategies

During a 6-month training program, teachers explained to students in vocational school (between 15 and 18 years old) the benefits of deep-level processing strategies for text comprehension and trained them to enrich their processing activities by structuring information read and critically relating ideas and arguments expressed in a text to their own experiences (see Boekaerts & Minnaert, 2003; Rozendaal, Minnaert, & Boekaerts, 2003). Our hypothesis was that after such a training program, motivated students would show an increase in reported deep-level processing strategies and a decrease in surface-level processing strategies. We expected that students low on motivation would go on using surface-level strategies. In addition, we predicted that anxiety (operationalized as performance and test anxiety) increases the use of surface-level processing and decreases deep-level processing. The anxiety hypothesis was confirmed, but motivation was positively associated with both types of processing. We also learned from these data that surface- and deep-level processing are not the opposite ends of a continuum, as assumed in the literature, but two distinct processing modes. Inspection of our data and interviews with students and teachers revealed that some students use both processing modes, others rely on a dominant mode, and still others are low on both processing modes. At that point in the data analysis, we went back to the drawing board and theorized that students cannot select cognitive strategies flexibly unless they have easy access to both processing modes; that is, they have a *choice* of strategy use.

Accordingly, Rozendaal et al. (2003) split up the available data set into four groups: students who dominantly used surface-level processing (SLP; 10%), deep-level processing (DLP; 20%), used both DLP and SLP (50%), and used neither DLP nor SLP (10%). We then estimated the relationships between motivation, anxiety, and the two processing modes for each group separately. We found that motivation and anxiety had a different effect on the processing modes in the respective groups. Motivated students tended to make use of their *preferred* processing mode(s), and anxiety was inversely related to the use of deep-level strategies. Does that mean that anxious students put more confidence in their preferential processing strategies, or rather that they tend to shy away from using the "more demanding" deep-level processing strategies, when they perceive the learning task (environment) as anxiety-provoking? Observations and interviews with students and teachers suggested that anxiety and lack of confidence played a key role in the selection of a processing mode. However, alternative explanations were also given for the phenomenon that students relapsed to surface-level processing

after the training period. Indeed, several theoretical perspectives have something to say on this issue and in the following I formulate some testable hypotheses about students' self-regulation of effort.

Willingness to Pay the Cost for the Anticipated Benefits?

It is important to realize that all students in our study, whether they used deep- or surface-level processing strategies or a combination of both, are self-regulating their effort, using their own theory of effort. To advise the teachers in the program how to coach their students' self-regulation of effort, it is essential to gain insight into the underlying mechanism, especially in the groups that do not use the new strategies consistently. What do modern theorists have to say about the mechanism that underlies the increase and decrease of effort?

Willingness to Work through a Series of Tensions

Developmental psychologist Carol Dweck (2003) shed some light on this issue. She and her colleagues gave children between 3½ and 5 years old the choice of continuing with puzzles that they had already solved before or trying new ones. Thirty-seven percent of the children opted to redo the puzzles they had already successfully completed. The main reason they gave the researchers was that they enjoyed doing these puzzles. By contrast, children who opted for the new puzzles said that they wanted to find out whether they could do a harder one. Interestingly, the children who opted for the new puzzles made significantly fewer negative statements about themselves and their puzzle-solving skills than the children who elected to continue with the puzzles for which they already had the necessary strategies. It is easy to imagine that for these children, familiar activities created less uncertainty and the impression of lower cost.

In line with Bloom and Turner's (2001) model of developmental change in language acquisition, I assume that the children who opted to do the familiar puzzles objected to investing *effort* in experiencing and working through a succession of tensions between the old (e.g., the puzzles they already can solve) and the new. Based on Dweck's and Bloom's findings, I suggest that the driving force for acquiring deep-level processing strategies reflects the essential tension between students' current engagement experiences (i.e., using surface-level processing) and their perception of the effort needed to master and feel comfortable with deep-level processing strategies. This essential tension might have occurred only in those students who were *aware* that the teacher invited them to learn how to accommodate experiences that they could not accommodate yet but considered relevant. In other words, a hypothesis that could be tested in further studies is that students are willing to invest effort in learning to process a text using deep-level processing strategies *only* if they truly believe that they cannot achieve the same result by using already familiar processing strategies (i.e., surface-level processing strategies) and are prepared to work through a succession of tensions to master the new skill and tolerate the anxiety it produces (i.e., pay the cost).

My dual processing self-regulation model specifies the role of negative emotions, such as anxiety, in the self-regulation process. Debilitating thoughts and the concomitant negative affect create an internal context for the task or activity and change the task and self-appraisals. I have explained previously that the infusion of negative affect into task appraisals alters the students' perceptions of the task and triggers bottom-up self-regulation, which may block or attenuate all forms of volitional control to stay on the growth pathway. Kuhl (2000) described the characteristic ways that individuals who tend to experience negative affect when they meet with obstacles dwell on anticipated difficulties. Their processing capacity is overtaxed by questions such as "What if I will not finish reading the text in time?" or "What if there are too many words that I will not understand?" Boekaerts and Corno (2005) argued that students' skill in blocking these ruminations as well as the negative emotions that trigger them (i.e., switch these lights to red) will help students to reroute from the well-being pathway to the growth pathway.

Substituting a "Feeling Unconfident" State with a "Feeling Confident" State

A second explanation for the phenomenon we observed in vocational school relates to what Carver and Scheier (1998) referred to as the phenomenological experience of "feeling confident" about the task. Recall that these investigators found a greater variability in observed patterns of effort in the region of discontinuity, that is, in the range of tasks where task demands are close to the individual's limits of performance. Students who stuck to surface-level processing despite the training they received might have entered this region from the low confidence direction. This would imply that they continue

to use little effort, even when they perceive environmental cues that indicate that the task is not so difficult. The "scaling back" phenomenon described by Carver and Scheier (1998) might also apply here. The students who fell back on surface-level processing may have given up on the initial goal (i.e., process the text using deep-level processing strategies) while simultaneously substituting it with a more manageable goal (i.e., use the more familiar surface-level strategies).

As argued previously, scaling back is a way to stay in the situation in a meaningful way, even though in a smaller way than originally planned. Students who keep using the familiar surface strategies perceive progress toward an important goal and experience positive affect and confidence, two important ingredients of the self-regulation of motivation. Achieving this positive phenomenological state may, in their opinion, be a far greater benefit than the alleged processing benefits the teacher mentioned.

Novices Rely Heavily on Surface-Level Processing to Extend Their Domain Knowledge

A third explanation of the observed phenomenon relates to the students' appraisal that the tasks are too taxing. As illustrated previously, different streams of information are present in the students' working memory. On the one hand, there is information about the qualities and outputs of their *learning process* in progress. For example, students may think, "I do not understand what I am reading. What does this new heading mean?" On the other hand, there is information about various aspects of the *self-regulation of the learning process* in progress, including information about the monitoring processes (e.g., "There are so many new words and I do not know whether we have to look them up or read on and see whether we can grasp the meaning of the text without consulting a dictionary," or "We have to relate what we read to personal experiences. But I do not know anything about this text"). There is also information about the *self-regulation of motivation* in working memory (e.g., "I get the feeling that this text is too complicated for me to read. It is also so boring. I don't feel like continuing. Why am I doing this?").

All these why, where, how, when questions tax students' limited processing capacity while reading the text. They might react to this information overload by simply slipping back to what they normally do when processing a text, namely, reading, rereading, skipping unfamiliar words, rehearsing, and memorizing. P. A. Alexander et al.'s (1998) model of stages of developing expertise predicts that only those students who are in the competence or proficiency stage will use deep-level processing strategies consistently. These researchers showed that students who are still in the acclimation stage rely on surface-level processing strategies rather than deep-level processing strategies to extend their knowledge base and make it more coherent. Most students in our sample who relapsed to SLP might have had limited, fragmentary knowledge about the content of the texts they had to read and of the conditions in which deep-level strategies are superior to surface strategies. This lack of prior knowledge would categorize them as novices in the domain, and such categorization quasi-automatically implies that they make use of SLP rather than DLP (P. A. Alexander et al., 1998). In other words, what we had expected from these students was unwarranted, given their present competence level. I will add yet another explanation for low effort in the classroom that I have not mentioned previously, namely, effort minimalization due to conflicting goals.

Effort Minimalization Due to Conflicting Goals

Corno (2004) explained that students who have worked for a long time under unfavorable classroom conditions are likely to show unproductive work habits. I have previously referred to this phenomenon as low effort due to the perception of suboptimal conditions for learning, and I used Nolen's (2003) recent studies as an illustration of this principle. I believe it is essential to distinguish effort reduction due to suboptimal conditions from low effort due to conflicting goals. I prefer to refer to the latter phenomenon with the term *effort minimalization*.

As mentioned previously, modern students have much more on their mind than doing homework and preparing for quizzes and exams. Teacher-set assignments have to compete for limited resources with other activities, such as sports, dancing, going out with friends, and surfing the Internet. To the extent that preparation time and follow-up activities required for school fit into their overfull agenda, students are willing to invest the required effort in school tasks. Remarkably, Western teachers complain about their students' low effort for their academic studies, and students complain about their teachers' lack of insight into their overall task load. Why these conflicting views? I think that teachers assess benefits and costs

of homework tasks in terms of their instrumentality for future performance in school and beyond. In other words, teachers and researchers have a long-term time perspective, which often contrasts sharply with their students' short-term time perspective.

A study conducted in Leiden (Du Bois-Reymond & Metselaar, 2001) described the phenomenon of the "calculating student." These researchers found that high school students want to get the most out of the system (a certificate) as well as having a "fun" school time with the least effort. If they calculate well, they can have it both ways. They realize that if they miscalculate the resources they have to invest (attention, time, and effort), they have to bear the costs. The peer group and even their parents provide information, help, and support in this important matter. To straddle the divide between surviving in a school system on which they have no influence and enjoying autonomy and emancipation outside school they allocate resources by using modern media (mobile telephone, e-mail, fax, and the Internet) and their social network to share the work load and reduce time spent on homework and preparing for tests and exams. Valuable information about negotiation strategies that work with specific teachers is also exchanged. Du Bois-Reymond and Metselaar (2001) emphasized that modern students are aware of their personal and social assets (e.g., their social status, their parents' influence, their competence and energy, their skills to earn money to pay for their consumer needs), and they negotiate with teachers about how much effort is required for homework and to pass the exams (for further discussion, see Boekaerts, 2003a).

Is the work style described here an example of effort reduction due to suboptimal conditions, and if so, does it rely on the same underlying principles? I do not think it is. I speculate that the effort reduction observed in calculating students is not due to lack of value and interest in the task or to high perceived demand-capacity ratio. Rather, this type of effort regulation depends on societal factors that impact student behavior through peer-group influence (Rydell Altermatt & Pomerantz, 2003). Elliott and Hufton (2002) defended the view that societal changes have a powerful effect on students' perception of work rates and workload. For example, students' conception of hard work may undergo changes when it is common practice in schools that students have a part-time job to pay for their consumer needs (Steinberg & Sanford, 1991).

Summary

What I wanted to illustrate in this section is that different conclusions for practice could be drawn on the basis of our results. Due to a poor conceptualization of the mental load construct in relation to text processing, an inadequate assessment of students' self-regulation of effort, and a total neglect of the different stages of competence development in a domain, we were not able to identify the mechanisms that underlie the relapse to surface-level processing strategies observed in some of our students after the training period. However, we learned that modern theorists have a great deal to say about this phenomenon. We now have a better idea of why students do not make use of newly acquired processing strategies. One reason is that they judge these strategies as "benefits" but are not able to pay the cost for these benefits. Another reason is that they are not willing to pay the extra cost. Our results and the discussions that followed with teachers and fellow researchers helped me to conceptualize where effort is located in the self-regulation system and to formulate new hypotheses.

Where Is Effort Located within the Self-Regulation Process?

I explained previously that in my dual processing model, a distinction is made between two parallel pathways. Activity in the growth pathway is energized by top-down processing, and activity in the well-being pathway by bottom-up processing. At several points in the discussion, I have argued that students who have easy access to volitional strategies and are prepared to use them could stay on the mastery pathway and reroute activity from the well-being pathway to the growth pathway. I would like to suggest at this point that the underlying mechanism responsible for changes in the level of effort coincides with volition-driven self-regulation. More concretely, I have conceptualized volitional strategies as a switching track between the growth pathway and the well-being pathway. Is there evidence that students' conscious or unconscious decisions to increase or decrease effort during the learning process are located in the self-regulation system at the level of volitional strategies?

Student reports confirm that using volitional strategies to stay on the growth pathway or get off the well-being pathway comes at a cost. Students view volition-driven self-regulation to support top-down self-regulation as effortful. Likewise, they report that recovering from emotions and redirecting attention to the learning task is effortful. J. E. Turner and Schallert (2001) illustrated that students who are on the well-being pathway can move into the growth direction if they (re)appraise the goal as instrumental and call upon volitional strategies to prevent unproductive rumination about shame and manage resources in the task. Preliminary evidence also comes from recent studies reported in social psychology by Baumeister and his colleagues. Baumeister (2003) reasoned that using willpower to resist temptation or to control emotional reactions costs energy that needs to be restored. They asked participants to complete a geometrical puzzle that was in fact unsolvable and measured the time participants persisted on the puzzle. However, before starting the puzzle, these participants, who had skipped a meal, were tempted with freshly baked cookies and chocolates. Half the participants were instructed to resist the temptation and instead eat radishes. Interestingly, those who resisted the treats tended to give up faster on the puzzle than either the participants who had not been tempted or those who had been allowed to eat the sweets. It seems that the effort needed to resist temptation interacted with the effort needed to persist on the task. A similar pattern emerged in a second experiment, in which individuals were requested to focus on their emotional responses as they viewed an upsetting video and either had to suppress or amplify them. Baumeister and Eppes (2005) found that participants who had to focus on their emotions and control them tended to give up faster on a successive handgrip-squeezing task than those who did not have to control their emotions. These researchers suggested that the self-regulation strategies that are needed to resist temptation or control emotions interfere with active engagement and persistence on a task (i.e., with the self-regulation of effort) unless the spent energy is restored.

Obviously, these results need to be taken to the classroom. Researchers need to study what types of volitional strategies students use when they are recovering from emotions and find it difficult to redirect their attention to the learning process.

CULTURAL DIFFERENCES IN THE SELF-REGULATION OF MOTIVATION AND EFFORT

In the 1970s and 1980s, investing effort into a task was considered akin to task engagement and was measured as students' time-on-task (e.g., Fischer & Berliner, 1985). Researchers discovered that classrooms differ considerably in the time their students engage in academic learning, and that students who spent more time off-task scored considerably lower on standardized tests than students who were actively engaged in completing exercises. In the 1970s and early 1980s, students in typical classrooms paid attention to what they had to do about 70% of the time. This finding made headline news when the results of cross-cultural research in mathematics (e.g., Stevenson, Lee, & Stigler, 1986) revealed that Asian students show higher school achievement than U.S. students. Comparing the classroom behavior of students in Japan, Taiwan, and the United States and interviewing teachers and parents, Stevenson and colleagues had found that 65% of U.S. fifth graders' school days are devoted to academic activities, compared with 90% for Asian students. Asian teachers seemed to manage their classrooms differently, leading to more time-on-task. Moreover, attitudes of Asian parents and teachers toward learning and effort differed from those of their Western peers; they fostered a learning orientation that reassured students that effort and persistence are necessary and sufficient ingredients of the learning process. A prominent line of investigation in cross-cultural psychology clarified that divergent motivational practices exist between East and West. Markus and Kitayama (1991) and Kitayama and Markus (1999) reviewed the literature, showing that in Western countries, the key words describing students' motivational beliefs are *self-efficacy, self-esteem,* and attribution of success and failure to *ability.* Self-criticism is not encouraged and weaknesses are played down. As I have explained elsewhere (Boekaerts, 1998, 2003b), such a conceptualization of learning and achievement implies that Western students focus on their strengths and are motivated to invest effort only if they view success as being within easy reach. By contrast, Asian students have a fixed social role and want to fulfill that role to perfection. It is their responsibility to adjust to the context of the school and improve their academic and social skills. The key words that describe Asian students' motivational beliefs are attribution to *effort, living up to one's role expectations,* and *self-discipline.*

A number of recent cross-country and cross-cultural studies (R. Alexander, 2000; Elliott & Hufton, 2002; Larson & Verma, 1999) shed some light on cultural and societal influences that affect students' perception of task engagement, effort, and hard work. For example, R.

Alexander reported that student classroom engagement varies across different countries, and that students' understanding of the nature of authority and autonomy influenced their academic engagement to a considerable extent. He noted that students' academic engagement was lower in countries where they were allowed more freedom of action. Beaton et al.'s (1996) study confirmed yet again that Asian students (here: students from Korea and Japan), though ranking among the very best in mathematics and science in international comparative studies, have a relative low self-concept of ability compared with German students, but that they hold a firm belief that effort is necessary and sufficient to achieve in these subject areas.

Elliott and Hufton (2002) also reported consistent cross-cultural differences in effort beliefs. They found that Western students (here: students from the United States and the United Kingdom) put a greater emphasis on the instrumentality of effort for academic success than students in the Russian Federation (St. Petersburg) but seemed to have a different understanding of what "hard work" means. When asked about their work habits, Western students described lifestyles that did not underscore their statement that they worked "hard." Academic standards and achievement, as well as academic demands and work rates, tended to be much higher in St. Petersburg (before the massive changes that occurred in the social, economic, and educational systems of their country) than in the two Western countries. Russian students fully realized that effort (intensity) and persistence (duration) are essential to survive the harsh educational system, and they simply acted accordingly. Interestingly, Elliott and Hufton observed that Russian adolescents' conditions of growing up changed considerably after the massive changes. Their current understanding of freedom and authority is also different from before, and they follow their Western peers in their search for greater material gains. Like their Western peers, adolescents in the Russian Federation are nowadays confronted with multiple goals and many environmental distractions; they have to make many choices and their decision-making seems to impact favorably or unfavorably on their effort investment in school (see also R. Alexander's, 2000, results mentioned previously).

A word of caution is in order here. Many cross-country comparisons are restricted to a rather superficial description of the contrasting personality characteristics that different cultures value and promote during the socialization process. Important aspects of children's and adolescents' everyday functioning are left out of the equation. In my view, students' self-regulation of motivation and effort can be understood only if we use a conceptual framework that casts children's and adolescents' behavior in terms of the self-regulation processes that they activate and generate to steer and direct their behavior.

GUIDELINES FOR FURTHER RESEARCH AND APPLICATIONS

In this section, I summarize what is presently known about students' self-regulation of motivation and effort in a set of principles that may guide further research and practice. I also point to some gaps in our understanding of the self-regulation of motivation and effort.

Principles for Research and Practice

Based on the literature reviewed previously, I have formulated 10 principles that may guide teachers when they coach their students to enhance their self-regulation:

1. *Mastery:* Effort investment leads to mastery.
2. *Compensation:* Effort might compensate for low ability.
3. *Familiarity:* Familiar activities create less uncertainty and cost less effort than unfamiliar or complex activities, which may create a phenomenological state of felt difficulty.
4. *Perceived demand-capacity ratio:* Effort is not needed if perceived capacity exceeds task demands.
5. *Interest:* Meaningfulness and task enjoyment create a phenomenological state that boosts motivation and effort.
6. *Cost-benefit ratio:* Students are prepared to invest effort if the perceived benefits exceed the perceived costs.
7. *Flow:* All-engrossing task engagement does not require conscious effort.
8. *Confidence and doubt:* When task demands are close to one's level of performance, confidence will increase effort and doubt will decrease it.
9. *Accommodation:* When new experiences cannot be accommodated, students need to understand that it is necessary to work through a series of tensions.

10. *Volitional strategies:* Self-regulation of effort requires that students are aware that volitional strategies are needed to achieve the goal, that they have easy access to these strategies, and that they are willing to use them.

These 10 principles are the cumulative results of current research from different research lines. What is the meaning of this information? Are these principles actionable? The good news is that, together, the 10 principles provide teachers and educational practitioners with a heuristic for predicting students' self-regulation of motivation and effort and for creating learning environments that stimulate students to invest effort. Taken together, the 10 principles predict low effort when students want to hide low ability, shy away from going through a series of tensions to accommodate new experiences, opt for activities they are already familiar with, doubt their capacity, are not aware of or do not have easy access to volitional strategies, expect high costs for low benefits, do not value the activity, or perceive the demand-capacity ratio as suboptimal.

Insight into the variables that impact students' self-regulation of motivation and effort is necessary to guide researchers who want to set up intervention programs, teaching consultants who advise teachers in the use of more effective instruction methods, and teachers who actually coach students in the classroom.

The bad news is that the 10 principles are of different breeds and that it is difficult to integrate them into a coherent framework. Some principles represent if-then rules of the type "If the task is such that the perceived benefits exceed the perceived cost, then students will invest effort." These principles describe the antecedents of effort. Other principles represent students' instrumentality beliefs about effort (e.g., effort is instrumental to achieve mastery). These principles describe the outcomes of effort. Principle 10 specifies the underlying mechanism of effort.

In other words, the 10 principles summarize what we currently know about the antecedents and outcomes of effort and about the mechanism itself. Unfortunately, next to nothing is known about whether all students are aware of these principles and endorse them, whether they are linked to specific content domains in a coherent way, or whether they exist in the individual's meaning system as fragmentary ideas about effort investment. Much is still to be learned about gender and cultural differences in students' self-regulation of motivation and effort in different content domains.

Questions with Which the Field Is Still Struggling

At the beginning of this chapter, I observed that the concept of self-regulation is receiving increased attention because it represents a systems approach. A systems approach allows researchers to focus simultaneously on students' attempts to target their cognitions, feelings, and actions in the service of their goals and on their skill to pick up environmental cues to assist their self-regulation process. Studying all these aspects of self-regulation in one comprehensive framework offers several benefits for research, interventions, and classroom practice. A systems approach has the potential to interconnect areas of research and practice that have been studied in isolation. Integrating the results of isolated fields of study not only provides a richer description of the self-regulation processes that students engage in, it also provides an excellent framework for taking stock of our current knowledge and identifying gaps in our understanding.

Despite the large amount of information that is currently available on how students regulate their learning in the classroom, the literature has several gaps. It is in fact strange that we do not have access to a great deal of information on gender differences in self-regulation and that we have little information about the development of self-regulation over time. The evidence that I reviewed in this chapter suggests that the concept of self-regulation, particularly the self-regulation of motivation and effort, merits further exploration. Future research should address questions such as the following: How does the self-regulation of motivation and effort evolve over time? How do children build up their theory of engagement and effort? What types of contexts are beneficial (impede) the development of self-regulation of motivation and effort? How do differences in the self-regulation of motivation and effort affect school success? Answers to these and similar questions are essential to set up intervention programs that help teachers and schools to counteract the well-documented decline in intrinsic motivation after primary school. My conclusion is that the potential contribution of the self-regulation construct has yet to be realized, especially the *development* of self-regulation and the factors that influence this development.

REFERENCES

Ainley, M., Hidi, S., & Berndorff, D. (2002). Interest, learning, and the psychological processes that mediate their relationship. *Journal of Educational Psychology, 94*(3), 545–561.

Alexander, P. A. (2003, August). *Expertise and academic development: A new perspective on a classic theme.* Paper presented at the 10th biennial conference of the European Association for Research on Learning and Instruction, Padua, Italy.

Alexander, P. A., Graham, S., & Harris, K. R. (1998). A perspective on strategy research: Progress and prospect. *Educational Psychology Review, 10*(2), 129–153.

Alexander, R. (2000). *Culture and pedagogy: International comparisons in primary education.* Oxford: Blackwell.

Austin, J. T., & Vancouver, J. B. (1996). Goal constructs in psychology: Structure, process, and content. *Psychological Bulletin, 120*(3), 338–375.

Bandura, A. (1997). *Self-efficacy: The exercise of control.* New York: Freeman.

Bargh, J. A., & Gollwitzer, P. M. (1994). Environmental control of goal-directed action: Automatic and strategic contingencies between situations and behavior. In W. Spaulding (Ed.), *Nebraska Symposium on Motivation: Vol. 41. Integrative views of motivation, cognition, and emotion* (pp. 71–124). Lincoln: University of Nebraska Press.

Baumeister, R. F. (2003). Ego depletion and self-regulation failure: A resource model of self-control. *Alcoholism: Clinical and Experimental Research, 27*(2), 281–284.

Baumeister, R. F., & Eppes, F. (2005). *The cultural animal: Human nature, meaning, and social life.* Oxford: Oxford University Press.

Beaton, A. E., Mullis, I. V., Martin, M. O., Gonzales, E. J., Kelly, D. L., & Smith, T. A. (1996). *Mathematics achievement in the middle school years: IEA's Third International Mathematics and Science Study.* Boston: Center for the Study of Testing.

Blackwell, L. S., Dweck, C. S., & Trzesniewski, K. (2002). *Theories of intelligence and the adolescence transition: A longitudinal study and an intervention.* Manuscript submitted for publication.

Bloom, L., & Beckwith, R. (1989). Talking with feeling: Integrating affective and linguistic expression in early language development. *Cognition and Emotion, 3,* 313–342.

Bloom, L., & Turner, E. (2001). The intentionality model and language acquisition. *Monograph of the Society for Research in Child Development, 66*(4).

Boekaerts, M. (1993). Being concerned with well being and with learning. *Educational Psychologist, 32*(3), 137–151.

Boekaerts, M. (1997). Self-regulated learning: A new concept embraced by researchers, policy makers, educators, teachers, and students. *Learning and Instruction, 7*(2), 11–186.

Boekaerts, M. (1998). Do culturally rooted self-construals affect students' conceptualization of control over learning? *Educational Psychologist, 33*(2/3), 87–108.

Boekaerts, M. (1999). Coping in context: Goal frustration and goal ambivalence in relation to academic and interpersonal goals. In E. Frydenberg (Ed.), *Learning to cope: Developing as a person in complex societies* (pp. 15–197). Oxford: Oxford University Press.

Boekaerts, M. (2002a). Bringing about change in the classroom: Strengths and weaknesses of the self regulated learning approach. *Learning and Instruction, 12*(6), 589–604.

Boekaerts, M. (2002b). Motivation to learn. In H. Walberg (Ed.), *Educational practices series* (pp. 1–27). International Academy of Education-International Bureau of Education (United Nations Educational, Scientific and Cultural Organization). Geneva, Switzerland: World Health Organization.

Boekaerts, M. (2002c). The On-line Motivation Questionnaire: A self-report instrument to assess students' context sensitivity. In P. R. Pintrich & M. L. Maehr (Eds.), *Advances in motivation and achievement: Vol. 12. New directions in measures and methods* (pp. 77–120). New York: JAI Press.

Boekaerts, M. (2003a). Adolescence in Dutch culture: A self-regulation perspective. In F. Pajares & T. Urdan (Eds.), *Adolescence and education: Vol. 3. International perspectives on adolescence* (pp. 101–124). Greenwich, CT: Information Age Publishing.

Boekaerts, M. (2003b). How do students from different cultures motivate themselves for academic learning? In F. Salili & R. Hoosain (Eds.), *Research on multicultural education and international perspectives: Vol. 3. Teaching, learning and motivation in a multicultural context* (pp. 13–31). Greenwich C. T: Information Age Publishing.

Boekaerts, M., & Corno, L. (2005). Self-regulation in the classroom: A perspective on assessment and intervention. *Applied Psychology: An International Review, 54,* 199–231.

Boekaerts, M., Maes, S., & Karoly, P. (2005). Self-regulation across domains of applied psychology: Is there an emerging consensus? *Applied Psychology: An International Review, 54,* 267–299.

Boekaerts, M., & Minnaert, A. (2003). Measuring behavioral change processes during an ongoing innovation project: Scope and limits. In E. De Corte, L. Verschaffel, N. Entwistle, & J. Merrienboer (Eds.), *Powerful learning environments* (pp. 71–87). New York: Pergamon Press.

Boekaerts, M., & Niemivirta, M. (2000). Self-regulated learning: Finding a balance between learning goals and ego-protective goals. In M. Boekaerts, P. R. Pintrich, & M. Zeidner (Eds.), *Handbook of self-regulation* (pp. 417–451). San Diego: Academic Press.

Boekaerts, M., Otten, R., & Voeten, M. (2003). Exam performance: Are students' causal ascriptions school-subject specific? *Anxiety, Stress and Coping, 16*(3), 331–342.

Boekaerts, M., Pintrich, P. R., & Zeidner, M. (2000). Self-regulation: An introductory overview. In M. Boekaerts, P. R. Pintrich, & M. Zeidner (Eds.), *Handbook of self-regulation* (pp. 1–9). San Diego: Academic Press.

Boekaerts, M., & Simons, P. R. J. (1995). *Leren en Instructie: Psychologie van de leerling en het leerproces* [Learning and instruction: The psychology of the student and the learning process] (2nd rev. ed.). Assen, The Netherlands: Royal Van Gorcum.

Brown, A. (1978). Knowing when, where, and how to remember: A problem of metacognition. In R. Glaser (Ed.), *Advances in instructional psychology* (pp. 77–165). Hillsdale, NJ: Erlbaum.

Butler, R. (1992). What young people want to know when: Effects of mastery and ability goals on interest in different kinds of social comparison. *Journal of Personality and Social Psychology, 62,* 934–943.

Cain, K. M., & Dweck, C. S. (1995). The development of children's achievement motivation patterns and conceptions of intelligence. *Merrill-Palmer Quarterly, 41,* 25–52.

Carver, C. S., & Scheier, M. E. (1981). *Attention and self-regulation: A control theory approach to human behavior.* New York: Springer Verlag.

Carver, C. S., & Scheier, M. E. (1998). *On the self-regulation of behavior.* New York: Cambridge University Press.

Carver, C. S., & Scheier, M. E. (2000). On the structure of behavioral self-regulation. In M. Boekaerts, P. Pintrich, & M. Zeidner (Eds.), *Handbook of self-regulation* (pp. 42–85). San Diego: Academic Press.

Case, R. (1992). *The mind's staircase.* Hillsdale, NJ: Erlbaum.

Connell, J. P. (1990). Context, self, and action: A motivational analysis of system processes across the life-span. In D. Cicchetti (Ed.), *The self in transition: Infancy to childhood* (pp. 61–97). Chicago: University of Chicago Press.

Corno, L. (1994). Student volition and education: Outcomes, influences, and practices. In B. J. Zimmerman & D. H. Schunk (Eds.), *Self-regulation of learning and performance* (pp. 229–254). Hillsdale, NJ: Erlbaum.

Corno, L. (2001). Volitional aspects of self-regulated learning. In B. J. Zimmerman & D. Schunk (Eds.), *Self-regulated learning and academic achievement: Theoretical perspectives* (pp. 191–126). Mahwah, NJ: Erlbaum.

Corno, L. (2004). Work habits and work styles: The psychology of volition in education. *Teachers College Record, 106,* 1669–1694.

Corno, L., & Mandinach, E. B. (2004). What we have learned about student engagement in the last 20 years. In D. M. McInerny & S. van Etten (Eds.), *Big theories revisited* (pp. 299–328). Greenwich, CT: Information Age Publishing.

Corno, L., & Randi, J. (1999). A design theory for classroom instruction in self-regulated learning. In C. M. Reigluth (Ed.), *Instructional design theories and models* (pp. 293–318). Mahwah, NJ: Erlbaum.

Covington, M. V. (2004). Self-worth theory: Goes to college. In D. M. McInerny & S. van Etten (Eds.), *Big theories revisited* (pp. 91–114). Greenwich, CT: Information Age Publishing.

Csikszentmihalyi, M. (1990). *Flow: The psychology of optimal experience.* New York: Harper & Row.

Deci, E. L., & Ryan, R. M. (1985). *Intrinsic motivation and self-determination in human behavior.* New York: Plenum Press.

De Corte, E., Verschaffel, L., & Op 't Eynde, P. (2000). Self-regulation: A characteristic and a goal of mathematics education. In P. Pintrich, M. Boekaerts, & M. Zeidner (Eds.), *Self-regulation: Theory, research, and applications* (pp. 687–726). Mahwah, NJ: Erlbaum.

Dowson, M., & McInerney, M. (2001). Psychological parameters of students' social and work avoidance goals: A qualitative investigation. *Journal of Educational Psychology, 93*(1), 35–42.

Du Bois-Reymond, M., & Metselaar, J. (2001). Contemporary youth and risk taking behavior. In I. Sagel-Grande (Ed.), *In the best interest of the child: Conflict resolution for and by children and juveniles* (pp. 49–62). Amsterdam: Rozenberg.

Dweck, C. S. (1991). Self-theories and goals: Their role in motivation, personality, and development. In R. A. Dienstbier (Ed.), *Nebraska Symposium on Motivation, 1990: Vol. 38. Perspectives on motivation* (pp. 199–235). Lincoln: University of Nebraska Press.

Dweck, C. S. (1998). The development of early self-conceptions: Their relevance for motivational processes. In J. Heckhausen & C. S. Dweck (Eds.), *Motivation and self-regulation across the life span* (pp. 257–280). Cambridge, England: Cambridge University Press.

Dweck, C. S. (2003). Ability conceptions, motivation, and development [Monograph]. *British Journal of Educational Psychology, 2,* 13–28.

Eccles, J. S. (1987). Gender roles and women's achievement-related decisions. *Psychology of Women Quarterly, 11,* 135–172.

Eccles, J. S., Midgley, C., Wigfield, A., Buchanan, C. M., Reuman, D., Flanagan, C., et al. (1993). Development during adolescence. *American Psychologist, 48,* 90–101.

Eccles, J. S., & Wigfield, A. (2002). Motivational beliefs, values, and goals. *Annual Review of Psychology, 53,* 109–132.

Efklides, A., Papadaki, M., Papantoniou, G., & Kiosseoglou, G. (1999). Individual differences in school mathematics performance and feelings of difficulty. *European Journal of Psychology of Education, 14*(4), 461–476.

Eisenberger, R. (1992). Learned industriousness. *Psychological Review, 99,* 248–267.

Elliot, J., & Hufton, N. (2002). Achievement motivation in real contexts [Monograph]. *British Journal of Educational Psychology, 2,* 155–172.

Entwistle, N. (1988). Motivational approaches in students' approaches to learning. In R. R. Schmeck (Ed.), *Learning strategies and learning styles* (pp. 21–51). New York: Plenum Press.

Fischer, C. W., & Berliner, D. C. (Eds.). (1985). *Perspectives on instructional time.* New York: Longmans.

Flavell, J. (1979). Metacognition and cognitive monitoring: A new area of cognitive-development inquiry. *American Psychologist, 34,* 906–911.

Fredricks, J. A., Blumenfeld, P. C., & Paris, A. H. (2004). School engagement: Potential of the concept, state of the evidence. *Review of Educational Research, 74*(1), 59–109.

Frydenberg, E. (1999). *Learning to cope: Developing as a person in complex societies.* Oxford: Oxford University Press.

Gollwitzer, P. M. (1990). Action phases and mind-sets. In E. T. Higgins & R. M. Sorrentino (Eds.), *Handbook of motivation and cognition: Vol. 2. Foundations of social behavior* (pp. 53–92). New York: Guilford Press.

Gollwitzer, P. M. (1999). Implementation intentions: Strong effects of simple plans. *American Psychologist, 54,* 493–503.

Grolnick, W., & Ryan, R. M. (1987). Autonomy in children's learning: An experimental and individual difference investigation. *Journal of Personality and Social Psychology, 52,* 890–898.

Haller, E. P., Child, D. A., & Walberg, H. J. (1988). Can comprehension be taught? A quantitative synthesis of "metacognitive" studies. *Educational Researcher, 17*(9), 5–8.

Hattie, J., Biggs, J., & Purdie, N. (1996). Effects of learning skills interventions on student learning: A meta-analysis. *Review of Educational Research, 66,* 99–136.

Heckhausen, H., & Kuhl, J. (1985). From wishes to action: The deadends and short-cuts on the long way to action. In M. Frese & J. Sabini (Eds.), *Goal-directed behavior: The concept of actions in psychology* (pp. 134–160). Hillsdale, NJ: Erlbaum.

Hickey, D. T., & McCaslin, M. (2001). A comparative, sociocultural analysis of context and motivation. In S. Volet & S. Järvelä (Eds.), *Motivation in learning contexts: Theoretical advances and methodological implications* (pp. 33–55). Amsterdam: Elsevier.

Hidi, S., & Harackiewicz, J. M. (2001). Motivating the academically unmotivated: A critical issue for the 21st century. *Review of Educational Research, 70,* 151–179.

Hijzen, D., Boekaerts, M., & Vedder, P. (2004, September/October). *The relationship between students' goal preferences and the quality of cooperative learning.* Paper presented at the sixth WATM conference, Lisbon, Portugal.

Husman, J., & Lens, W. (1999). The role of the future in student motivation. *Educational Psychologist, 34,* 113–125.

Kahnman, D. (1973). *Attention and effort.* Englewood Cliffs, NJ: Prentice-Hall.

Kanfer, R., & Ackerman, P. L. (1989). Motivation and cognitive abilities: An integrative aptitude-treatment approach to skill acquisition [Monograph]. *Journal of Applied Psychology, 4,* 657–690.

Kasser, T., & Ryan, R. M. (1993). A dark side of the American dream: Correlates of financial success as a central life aspiration. *Journal of Personality and Social Psychology, 65,* 410–422.

Kasser, T., & Ryan, R. M. (1996). Further examining the American dream: Well-being correlates of intrinsic and extrinsic goals. *Personality and Social Psychology Bulletin, 22,* 281–288.

Kehr, H. M., Bless, P., & Von Rosenstiel, L. (1999). Self-regulation, self-control and management training transfer. *International Journal of Educational Research, 31,* 487–493.

Kendall, S. (1992). *The development of autonomy in children: An examination of the Montessori educational model.* Unpublished doctoral dissertation, Walden University, Minneapolis, MN.

Kitayama, S., & Markus, H. (1999). Yin and yang of the Japanese self: The cultural psychology of personality coherence. In D. Cervone & Y. Shoda (Eds.), *The coherence of personality* (pp. 242–302). New York: Guilford Press.

Krapp, A. (2003). Interest and human development: An educational-psychological perspective. *British Journal of Educational Psychology, 2,* 57–84.

Krapp, A., & Lewalter, D. (2001). Development of interest and interest-based motivational orientation: A longitudinal study in vocational school and work settings. In S. Volet & S. Järvelä (Eds.), *Motivation in learning contexts: Vol. 11. Theoretical and methodological implications* (pp. 209–232). New York: Pergamon.

Kruger, J., Wirtz, D., Van Boven, L., & Altermatt, T. W. (2004). The effort heuristic. *Journal of Experimental Social Psychology, 40,* 91–98.

Kuhl, J. (1985). Volitional mediators of cognition-behavior consistency: Self-regulatory processes and action versus state orientation. In J. Kuhl & J. Beckman (Eds.), *Action control: From cognition to behavior* (pp. 101–128). New York: Springer Verlag.

Kuhl, J. (2000). A functional design approach to motivation and self-regulation: The dynamics of personality systems and interactions. In M. Boekaerts, P. Pintrich, & M. Zeidner (Eds.), *Handbook of self-regulation* (pp. 111–163). San Diego: Academic Press.

Kuhl, J., & Fuhrman, A. (1998). Decomposing self-regulation and self-control: The volitional components checklist. In J. Heckhausen & C. Dweck (Eds.), *Life span perspectives on motivation and control* (pp. 15–49). Mahwah, NJ: Erlbaum.

Kuhl, J., & Kraska, K. (1989). Self-regulation and metamotivation: Computational mechanisms, development, and assessment. In R. Kanfer, P. I. Acherman, & R. Cudeck (Eds.), *Minnesota Symposia on Individual Differences: Abilities, motivation, and methodology* (pp. 343–368). Hillsdale, NJ: Erlbaum.

Kuhn, T. (1977). *The essential tension.* Chicago: University of Chicago Press.

Larson, R. W., & Verma, S. (1999). How children and adolescents spend time across the world: Work, play, and developmental opportunities. *Psychological Bulletin, 125,* 701–736.

Lemos, M. S. (2002). Social and emotional processes in the classroom setting: A goal approach. *Anxiety, Stress and Coping, 15*(4), 383–400.

Leventhal, H. (1980). Towards a comprehensive theory of emotion. In L. Berkowitz (Ed.), *Advances in experimental social psychology* (Vol. 3, pp. 140–208). New York: Academic Press.

Markus, H., & Kitayama, S. (1991). Culture and the self: Implications for cognition, emotion, and motivation. *Psychological Review, 98,* 224–253.

Martinez-Pons, M. (1996). Test of a model of parental inducement of academic self-regulation. *Journal of Experimental Education, 64,* 213–227.

McCombs, B. L., & Pope, J. E. (1994). *Motivating hard to reach students.* Washington, DC: American Psychological Association.

Midgley, C., & Feldlaufer, H. (1987). Students' and teachers' decision-making fit before and after the transition to junior high school. *Journal of Early Adolescence, 7,* 225–241.

Nicholls, J. G. (1984). Achievement motivation: Conceptions of ability, subjective experience, task choice, and performance. *Psychological Review, 91,* 328–346.

Nolen, S. (2003, August). *The development of motivation to read and write in young children.* Paper presented at the 10th biannual conference of the European Association of Learning and Instruction, Padua, Italy.

Oettingen, G., Honig, G., & Gollwitzer, P. H. (2000). Effective self-regulation of goal attainment. *International Journal of Educational Research, 33,* 705–732.

Palincsar, A. S., & Brown, A. L. (1984). Reciprocal teaching of comprehension-fostering and monitoring activities. *Cognition and Instruction, 1,* 117–175.

Paris, S. G., Byrnes, J. P., & Alison, H. P. (2001). Constructing theories, identified cognitions, and actions of self-regulated learners. In B. J. Zimmerman & D. H. Schunk (Eds.), *Self-regulated learning and academic achievement* (pp. 253–288). Mahwah, NJ: Erlbaum.

Paris, S. G., & Paris, A. H. (2001). Classroom applications of research on self-regulated learning. *Educational Psychologist, 36,* 89–101.

Payne, J. W., Bettman, J. R., Coupey, E., & Johnson, E. J. (1992). A constructive processing view of decision making: Multiple strategies in judgment and choice. *Acta Psychologica, 80,* 107–141.

Pekrun, R., Goetz, T., Titz, W., & Perry, R. P. (2002). Academic emotions in students' self-regulated learning and achievement: A program of quantitative and qualitative research. *Educational Psychologist, 37*(2), 91–105.

Perry, N. E. (1998). Young children's self-regulated learning and contexts that support it. *Journal of Educational Psychology, 90,* 715–729.

Perry, N. E. (2002). Using qualitative methods to enrich understandings of self-regulated learning [Special issue]. *Educational Psychologist, 37.*

Perry, N. E., & Vandekamp, K. O. (2000). Creating classroom contexts that support young children's development of self-regulated learning. *International Journal of Educational Research, 33,* 821–842.

Perry, N. E., Vandekamp, K. O., Mercer, L. K., & Nordby, C. J. (2002). Investigating teacher-student interactions that foster self-regulated learning. *Educational Psychologist, 37*(1), 5–15.

Pintrich, P. R. (2000). The role of goal orientation in self-regulated learning. In M. Boekaerts, P. R. Pintrich, & M. Zeidner (Eds.), *Handbook of self-regulation* (pp. 452–502). San Diego: Academic Press.

Pintrich, P. R. (2003). A motivational science perspective on the role of student motivation in learning and teaching contexts. *Journal of Educational Psychology, 95,* 667–686.

Pressley, M. (1995). More about the development of self-regulation: Complex, long-term, and thoroughly social. *Educational Psychologist, 30*(4), 207–212.

Purdie, N., & Hattie, J. (1996). Cultural differences in the use of strategies for self-regulated learning. *American Educational Research Journal, 33,* 845–871.

Randi, J., & Corno, L. (2000). Teacher innovations in self-regulated learning. In M. Boekaerts, P. R. Pintrich, & M. Zeidner (Eds.), *Handbook of self-regulation* (pp. 651–685). San Diego: Academic Press.

Reeve, J. (2002). Self-determination theory applied to educational settings. In E. L. Deci & R. M. Ryan (Eds.), *Handbook of self-determination research* (pp. 183–203). Rochester, NY: University of Rochester Press.

Renninger, A. (1990). Children's play interests: Representation and activity. In R. Fivush & J. Hudson (Eds.), *Emory Symposia in Cognition, Knowing and Remembering in Young Children.* New York: Cambridge University Press.

Renninger, A. (1998). The roles of individual interest and gender in learning: An overview of research on preschool and elementary school-aged children/students. In L. Hoffmann, A. Krapp, A. K. Renninger, & J. Baumert (Eds.), *Interest and learning: Proceedings of the Seeon conference on interest and gender* (pp. 105–175). Kiel, Germany: University of Kiel, Institute for Science Education.

Renninger, K. A. (2000). How might the development of individual interest contribute to the conceptualization of intrinsic motivation? In C. Sansone & J. M. Harackiewicz (Eds.), *Intrinsic and extrinsic motivation: The search for optimal motivation and performance.* New York: Academic Press.

Rheinberg, F., Vollmeyer, R., & Rollett, W. (2000). Motivation and action in self-regulated learning. In M. Boekaerts, P. R. Pintrich, & M. Zeidner (Eds.), *Handbook of self-regulation* (pp. 503–531). San Diego: Academic Press.

Rosenshine, B., Meister, C., & Chapman, S. (1996). Teaching students to generate questions: A review of the intervention studies. *Review of Educational Research, 66,* 181–221.

Rozendaal, J. S., Minnaert, A., & Boekaerts, M. (2003). Motivation and self-regulated learning in secondary vocational education. *Learning and Individual Differences, 13*(4), 273–289.

Ryan, A. M. (2000). Peer groups as a context for the socialization of adolescents' motivation, engagement, and achievement in school. *Educational Psychologist, 35,* 101–111.

Ryan, R. M. (1982). Control and information in the interpersonal sphere: An extension of cognitive evaluation theory. *Journal of Personality and Social Psychology, 43,* 450–461.

Ryan, R. M., & Connell, J. P. (1989). Perceived locus of causality and internalization: Examining reasons for acting in two domains. *Journal of Personality and Social Psychology, 57,* 749–761.

Ryan, R. M., & Deci, E. L. (2002). An overview of self-determination theory: An organistic-dialectical perspective. In E. L. Deci & R. M. Ryan (Eds.), *Handbook of self-determination research* (pp. 3–34). Rochester, NY: University of Rochester Press.

Rydell Altermatt, E., & Pomerantz, E. M. (2003). The development of competence relations and motivational beliefs. *Journal of Educational Psychology, 95*(1), 111–123.

Salomon, G., & Perkins, D. N. (1989). Rocky roads to transfer: Rethinking mechanisms of a neglected phenomenon. *Educational Psychologist, 24,* 113–142.

Sansone, C., & Harackiewicz, J. M. (1996). "I don't feel like it": The function of interest in self-regulation. In L. L. Martin & A. Tesser (Eds.), *Striving and feeling: Interactions among goals, affect, and self-regulation* (pp. 203–228). Mahwah, NJ: Erlbaum.

Sansone, C., & Smith, J. L. (2000). The "how" of goal pursuit: Interest and self-regulation. *Psychological Inquiry: An International Journal of Peer Commentary and Review, 11*(4), 306–309.

Scardamalia, M., & Bereiter, C. (1985). Fostering the development of self-regulation in children's knowledge processing. In S. F. Chipman, J. W. Segal, & R. Glaser (Eds.), *Thinking and learning skills: Vol. 2. Research and open questions* (pp. 65–80). Hillsdale, NJ: Erlbaum.

Schunk, D., & Zimmerman, B. J. (1998). *Self-regulated learning: From teaching to self-reflective practice.* New York: Guilford Press.

Schwarzer, R., Jerusalem, M., & Stiksrud, A. (1984). The developmental relationship between test anxiety and helplessness. In H. M. Van der Ploeg, R. Schwarzer, & C. D. Spielberger (Eds.), *Advances in test anxiety research* (Vol. 3., pp. 265–399). Lisse, The Netherlands: Swets & Zeitlinger.

Skinner, E. A., & Belmont, M. J. (1993). Motivation in the classroom: Reciprocal effect of teacher behavior and student engagement across the school year. *Journal of Educational Psychology, 85*, 571–581.

Steinberg, L., & Sanford, M. I. (1991). Negative correlates of part-time employment during replication and elaboration. *Developmental Psychology, 27*(2), 304–313.

Stevenson, H. W., Lee, S-Y., & Stigler, J. W. (1986). Mathematics achievement of Chinese, Japanese, and American children. *Science, 231*, 693–699.

Stipek, D., Salmon, J. H., Givvin, K. B., Kazemi, E., Saxe, G., & MacGyvers, V. L. (1998). The value (and convergence) of practices suggested by motivation research and promoted by mathematics education reformers. *Journal for Research in Mathematics Education, 29*, 465–488.

Stipek, D. J., & Daniels, D. (1990). Children's use of dispositional attributions in predicting the performance and behavior of classmates. *Journal of Applied Developmental Psychology, 11*, 13–28.

Turner, J. C. (1995). The influence of classroom contexts on young children's motivation for literacy. *Reading Research Quarterly, 30*, 410–441.

Turner, J. C., & Meyer, D. K. (1999). Integrating classroom context into motivation theory and research: Rationale, methods, and implications. In T. C. Urdan (Ed.), *Advances in motivation and achievement: Vol. 11. The role of context* (pp. 87–122). Greenwich, CT: JAI Press.

Turner, J. E., & Schallert, D. L. (2001). Expectancy-value relationships of shame reactions and shame resiliency. *Journal of Educational Psychology, 93*(2), 320–329.

Volet, S. E. (1997). Cognitive and affective variables in academic learning: The significance of direction and effort in students' goals. *Learning and Instruction, 7*(3), 235–254.

Vygotsky, L. (1978). *Mind in society: The development of higher mental process.* Cambridge, MA: Harvard University Press.

Weinert, F. E., Schrader, F. W., & Helmke, A. (1989). Quality of instruction and achievement outcomes. *International Journal of Educational Psychology, 13*, 895–912.

Wentzel, K. R. (1991a). Social and academic goals at school: Motivation and achievement in context. In M. L. Maehr & P. R. Pintrich (Eds.), *Advances in motivation and achievement: Vol. 7. Goals and self-regulatory processes* (pp. 185–212). Greenwich, CT: JAI Press.

Wentzel, K. R. (1991b). Social competence at school: Relation between social responsibility and academic achievement. *Review of Educational Research, 61*, 1–2.

Wigfield, A. (1994). Expectancy-value theory of achievement motivation: A developmental perspective. *Educational Psychology Review, 6*, 49–78.

Wigfield, A., & Eccles, J. (1992). The development of achievement task values: A theoretical analysis. *Developmental Review, 12*, 265–310.

Wigfield, A., Eccles, J. S., & Rodriguez, D. (1998). The development of children's motivation in school contexts. *Review of Research in Education, 23*, 73–118.

Winne, P. H. (1995). Inherent details in self-regulated learning. *Educational Psychologist, 30*, 173–187.

Winne, P. H. (1996). A metacognitive view of individual differences in self-regulated learning. *Learning and Individual Differences, 8*, 327–353.

Winne, P. H., & Hadwin, A. F. (1998). Studying as self-regulated learning. In D. Hacker, J. Dunlosky, & A. C. Graesser (Eds.), *Metacognition in educational theory and practice* (pp. 277–304). Hillsdale, NJ: Erlbaum.

Winne, P. H., & Perry, N. E. (2000). Measuring self-regulated learning. In M. Boekaerts, P. R. Pintrich, & M. Zeidner (Eds.), *Handbook of self-regulation* (pp. 531–566). San Diego: Academic Press.

Wolters, C. A., & Rosenthal, H. (2000). The relation between students' motivational beliefs and their use of motivational regulation strategies. *International Journal of Educational Research, 33*, 801–820.

Wrosch, C., Scheier, M. F., Carver, C. S., & Schultz, R. (2003). The importance of goal disengagement in adaptive self-regulation: When giving up is beneficial. *Self-and-Identity, 2*(1), 1–20.

Xu, J. (2004). Family help and homework management in urban and rural secondary schools. *Teachers College Record, 106*(9), 1786–1805.

Xu, J., & Corno, L. (1999). Case studies of families doing third-grade homework. *Teachers College Record, 100*, 402–436.

Zimmerman, B. J. (1998). Academic studying and the development of personal skill: A self-regulatory perspective. *Educational Psychologist, 33*, 73–86.

Zimmerman, B. J. (2000). Attaining self-regulation: A social cognitive perspective. In M. Boekaerts, P. R. Pintrich, & M. Zeidner (Eds.), *Handbook of self-regulation* (pp. 13–40). San Diego: Academic Press.

Zimmerman, B. J., Bandura, A., & Martinez-Pons, M. (1992). Self-motivation for academic attainment: The role of self-efficacy beliefs and personal goal setting. *American Educational Research Journal, 29*, 663–676.

CHAPTER 10

Risk and Prevention

ROBERT L. SELMAN and AMY J. DRAY

In the past 30 years, much has been written about the application of research to practice in order to promote the positive social development of children and youth. Many prevention and intervention programs have been designed to ameliorate the effects of risk factors that predict negative life experiences and promote positive contexts and capacities that optimize children's health, social welfare, and academic capabilities. The National Institute of Mental Health's report in 1977 (Klein & Goldstein, 1977), the publication of *14 Ounces of Prevention* in 1988 (Price, Cowen, Lorion, & Ramos-McKay, 1988), the Institute of Medicine report in 1994 (Mrazek & Haggerty, 1994), and the 2003 special issue of *American Psychologist,* "Prevention That Works for

Children and Youth" (Weissberg, Kumpfer, & Seligman, 2003) stand as historical markers of our progress. They document both the research and the debates that evolved over time as we moved as a discipline toward an emphasis on prevention and intervention in children's mental health and socioemotional competence. These documents expertly address the issues of children at risk and detail findings from intervention programs, thereby furthering our understanding of how to best help children and their families.

In contrast, we do not intend to write another review of evidence-based programs that prevent disorder or promote competence and wellness. Any one of the excellent summaries that have been published recently can direct the practitioner, policymaker, or researcher to what is now called prevention science or evidence-based practice in the area of child and youth development (see, e.g., Catalano, Berglund, Ryan, Lonczak, & Hawkins, 2002; Greenberg, Domitrovich, & Bumbarger, 2001; Nation et al., 2003; Wandersman & Florin, 2003).

Instead, this chapter is about the ways social development research in child psychology can be applied in school settings, and how research and theory in turn can be transformed by practice. The first part of the chapter begins by documenting the challenges faced by an urban public school in Boston as it negotiates the tricky terrain of choosing an intervention program designed to promote positive social development and reduce the risks of negative student outcomes such as school failure, conduct disorder, depression, and relational difficulties. In describing this school's story, we focus on the challenges faced by practitioners as they try to translate academic theory and research into daily practices that support social and emotional competence while under enormous pressure to achieve academic standards. Using this case study as a context, we focus on two critical questions: What aspects of social development are the teachers and administrators most interested in and How does research and theory fit into their everyday practice?

We outline and document some prevention/intervention programs that are available to the school and discuss the benefits and drawbacks of each as identified by the school in the process of choosing a program. This first part of the chapter introduces you to an "elementary school in distress," not the usual subject in developmental research or the usual patient in child clinical psychology. This story is about the challenges and problems of implementing research-based practice in an applied setting and the ways research may or may not meet the everyday needs and practices of an urban school.

The second half of the chapter begins by introducing a classroom in the school. Using our own domain of social development as a context, we describe the challenges and problems we faced in theory building and conducting research in an applied school setting. This case illustrates how our work in an applied school setting did not simply draw from previous research but also led to new knowledge. This second analysis not only considers what the academic discipline of social development has to offer to schools, but also shows how doing research embedded in a school contributes to the knowledge base of developmental psychology as a discipline.

Rather than simply evaluating research-based practice, we also discuss the process of what we call "practice-based research."

Finally, the chapter integrates the two cases to illustrate how we have come to a new way of thinking about the relationship among theory, practice, and research from what we believe is more common in academic, and even practical, settings. From the perspective of academics, we suggest that both researchers and practitioners alike overly privilege, if not idealize, the impact of theory and research on practice but do not always appreciate the value of the reverse. Despite the commonly heard rhetoric that practice and research ought to be integrated, we believe there remains a deeply held belief in the academic disciplines that there is a unidirectional, straight-line orientation from evidence generated by the sciences to its application in practice. Knowledge generated from research informs practice and policy: That is the tenet we have been consciously or unconsciously taught—by policymakers who seek to make informed policy decisions, by foundations offering us grants to further our work, by educators looking for ways to teach in their schools, for parents seeking help for their children. As researchers, we are seen as the "experts," and we often buy into this idea ourselves.

In the final section of the chapter, we suggest ways to reexamine this view. Using the two case studies describing the school and the children in the school, we demonstrate how and why we have begun to reevaluate our own definition of applied research. We use the discipline of social development as a base—our own area of so-called expertise—to show how we have attempted to bridge the gap between the researcher's scientific knowledge of child development and the practitioner's everyday experiential and clinical knowledge of children and adolescents.

Both case studies were taken from experiences we had while conducting research and managing prevention programs in Boston public schools over the past several years. The school and its administrators, teachers, school staff, and students are composites of real people and situations we have observed. We hope they will become as real to you as they have been to us.

PREVENTION RESEARCH IN THE LAST DECADES

Since the 1980s, prevention and intervention has become a dominant focus in child psychology. Just as medical

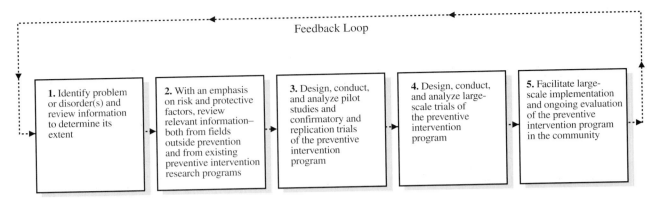

Figure 10.1   Institute of Medicine prevention intervention model.

health professionals are focused on reducing risks for heart disease, prevention and intervention programs are seen as essential for reducing the complex mental health risk factors facing today's children and youth (Mrazek & Haggerty, 1994). Research in developmental and child clinical psychology has been the foundation for many of the programs that have evolved. In these disciplines, a number of factors have been identified that can place children at risk for psychopathology and negative life outcomes. These factors range from biological, cognitive, and neurological problems to relational difficulties within families or with peers to contextual and environmental factors such as poverty and racial injustice (Cicchetti & Toth, 1998; Coie, Lochman, Terry, & Hyman, 1992; Dryfoos, 1990, 1997; Luthar & Zigler, 1992). At the same time, research has also identified assets and protective factors that can ameliorate these risks and promote healthy development, such as positive relationships with adults and peers, a sense of community, and success in school (Benson, Scales, Leffert, & Roehlkepartain, 1999; Catalano et al., 2003; Luthar, Cicchetti, & Becker, 2000; Roberts, Brown, Johnson, & Reinke, 2002; Scales et al., 2001).

In 1994, the Institute of Medicine (IOM) Committee on the Prevention of Mental Disorders established rigorous standards for prevention research. Although advances had been made in diagnosing and treating many mental illnesses, efforts to prevent the occurrence of problems in children and adults lagged behind (Mrazek & Haggerty, 1994). Although many programs had been created to reduce the risk of mental disorders, no clear guidelines existed to direct their development or evaluation. The Preventive Intervention Research Cycle (Figure 10.1) was created as a road map that researchers

should follow to foster psychological health among children and families in a systematic and scientific way. One of its main emphases was on making sure that program outcomes were scientifically evaluated using clinical trials. Too many programs, it seemed, were using research simply as support for their underlying principles and interventions, rather than making the next step toward using outcome research to discover whether the interventions actually worked (Wandersman & Florin, 2003).

Step 1 in the IOM cycle was to identify the problem and review research on its prevalence. Program developers, it was recommended, should inquire into the level of community concern around the problem, review its costs to the wider society, and develop a relationship with the members of the community who are most affected (Mrazek & Haggerty, 1994).

To illustrate how this step could play out in reality, we introduce you to our first case: the teachers, students, and staff at the Gilmore School in Boston, Massachusetts. This case is based on real people and real schools with whom we have worked over the past several years, although names have been changed to protect their privacy. It is, in effect, an introduction to a community of people who may be at risk for any number of negative outcomes, including psychopathology (at the student level) and school failure (a community problem).

Nothing that is worth doing can be achieved in our lifetime; therefore we must be saved by hope.

—Reinhold Niebuhr[1]

[1] Reinhold Niebuhr (1892–1971) was an American theologian and the author of *The Irony of American History* (1952).

CASE STUDY 1: THE SCHOOL HAS A MENTAL HEALTH PROBLEM, CAN IT BE TREATED?

The Gilmore School is located in an urban neighborhood in Boston. The Gilmore has a student enrollment of about 250 students, with 84% identified as Black or African American, about 10% Latino/Hispanic, 3% White, 1.5% Asian, and 2% other/mixed. These racial and ethnic categories reflect the U.S. census and the demographic categories used by the Boston city government and Boston Public School system (Auerbach, 2001).

The 2002/2003 school year was particularly difficult for the school. Like many schools struggling under state and federal mandates, the Gilmore was under state review and labeled an "underperforming school" because it had not made "adequate yearly progress" on the Massachusetts Comprehensive Assessment System (MCAS). Under the No Child Left Behind Act (2002), which links Title 1 funds to academic performance, schools that have not made adequate yearly progress for 5 years are "identified for corrective action" (Boston Public Schools, 2003). The MCAS is the statewide student assessment initiative; since its inception in 1999 the Gilmore students had performed poorly in both English Language Arts and Mathematics. Because of the lack of demonstrated improvement, a team from the Massachusetts Board of Education conducted regular evaluations of school functioning. Their presence contributed to an overall sense of uneasiness and stress felt by the teachers and the students alike.

In addition, the City of Boston had experienced a major budget crisis during the school year, and millions of dollars were cut from the education budget. The budget crisis depleted school resources and further contributed to teacher stress because it resulted in staff layoffs and undercut job security. Therefore, in the 2002/2003 school year, the Gilmore experienced both diminished teacher human resources, due to stress, and low monetary resources, due to budget cuts. The school was undernourished.

To help the students succeed academically, the school needed to focus on literacy. All teachers were trained to link assessment with instruction and used the Reader's and Writer's Workshop models to improve reading and writing skills (Boston Plan for Excellence, 2004). In addition, the school provided a number of other instructional resources: Title I Reading, Reading Recovery (Clay, 1993), a resource room, literacy/math

tutors, transition services for grades 3 and 4, and MCAS skills class for students in grades 2 through 5. For the 2002/2003 school year, the biggest challenges at the Gilmore were raising teacher morale and trying to help students succeed academically and raise their scores on the MCAS. Essentially, the staff from the State Department of Education gave the Gilmore an ultimatum: Grow (in the percentage of students who meet the minimal requirements for academic achievement) or go (be shut down, with the chance that teachers in the school would lose their jobs, for under state guidelines once a school enters this probationary period, the teachers are no longer protected by the union).

Mr. Martinez has been the principal of the Gilmore for the past 4 years. During his tenure, Mr. Martinez worked with Boston business leaders to raise funds for academic programs in school and after school. His approach to social development and mental health issues has been to partner with programs that provide classroom, family, and school climate support. Part of Mr. Martinez's responsibility as principal is to ensure that the projects and interventions serving the school are appropriate to the school's needs. When he came on board, one of the first things he did was to cut back on the number of outside interventions, as he felt the school was suffering from "projectitis." He now believes that the programs in place are strong and relevant ones: A mental health agency provides pull-out counseling to supplement that offered by the school's part-time counselor; a university partnership brings in graduate students to do social skills group work with students through classroom and small-group sessions; a local corporation sends volunteers once a month to read to students and provides considerable financial support; a religious organization from a nearby suburban community offers once-a-week literacy tutoring for targeted students; and Americorps provides similar tutoring services in math.

In addition, Mr. Martinez brought in an afterschool program that now serves over one-third of the student body. Although Mr. Martinez is aware that some of the coordinators of the various organizations feel they are competing for his attention, he believes that each is serving an important role and is loath to pare down the list any further. His challenge, however, is figuring out how to coordinate the programs better, so that the sum ends up equaling more than its combined parts. Whether or not he is successful in this goal, he at least knows that each of the programs is delivering skills development. His number one assessment in considering any new or existing approach involves asking the following question: Are the students gaining skills?

This is a school in seriously poor health, at high risk for expiring within the next 12 to 24 months, and yet if one were to make a casual visit to it today, or examine the evidence as presented so far, one might not be able to diagnose the causes of its problems, let alone be aware of its precarious position. Disciplinary actions are down since several years ago, and the classrooms are bright and cheerful. Furthermore, since the summer, when the staff and principal worked through their vacation with the state examiners to develop a school improvement plan, morale among the faculty has perceptibly improved. Beginning with the start of school in the fall, all those involved with the Gilmore have been trying to follow the school improvement plan.

Also, as we can see, the Gilmore has many friends in the neighborhood: outside social and mental health agencies, volunteers from corporate organizations invested in tutoring and mentoring, and local businesses and corporate foundations of one kind or another who are trying to provide financial resources to help the children in the Gilmore do well in school. These attempts to meet the standards will be tested again in the spring, and that is when we will get another reading on the health and vital signs of the Gilmore School.

Our Involvement in the Gilmore

As a friend of the Gilmore for the past 5 years, we are a partner of the school based in a local university. We are interested in the social development of children and schools from the perspective of research, teaching/training, and education. The Gilmore School has been one of our practicum service and research training sites for the past 5 years. Master's-level students from the Risk and Prevention Program are trained in psychological prevention, both at the individual and the classroom climate level. Doctoral students are trained in research, with an emphasis on human development and cultural psychology.

Like many professionals whose interests in the development of children are expressed from a base in an academic setting, in our case a research-oriented professional graduate school of education, a major reason we are in the Gilmore is that several years ago we received funds from a private foundation to bring some of what we call either "practice-based research" or "research-based practice" into the school as well as to several others in the Boston Public Schools. The focus of our own practice work is on the promotion of children's social development, a need the Gilmore principal and faculty felt their students warranted, but which, given the emphasis the school needed to place on instructional improvements, they felt they could not focus on by themselves. So, when we came with a well-funded service project that made sense to the school, we were generally welcomed in. But our progress at the school has been one of fits and starts as we continue to work toward improving both our delivery of social development programs and our understanding of what the school and the students need.

Our Expertise

We have been involved in psychosocial interventions (treatment, prevention, education/promotion) for over 30 years (Selman, 1980, 2003; Selman, Watts, & Schultz, 1997). Although we have worked in partnership with a wide range of child development professionals, each influenced by one or more disciplines, for the most part our approaches have been based in the discipline of basic and applied developmental psychology, with influences that also can be traced to clinical and educational psychology and child psychiatry (Beardslee, 2002; Beardslee & Gladstone, 2001).

Although over the past 5 years we have had many different relationships with the Gilmore School, for the purposes of this case, we have been cast in the role of "school doctors," that is, as "outside" professionals who are supposed to make a diagnosis of certain aspects of the school's health and write up a prescription. Our role may be unusual for traditional researchers in the field of developmental psychology, but in applied developmental psychology, working in similar school-based projects has become more common (Aber, Brown, & Jones, 2003; Adalbjarnardottir, 1993).

The Symptoms of the Problem

We next share with you the "symptoms," the concerns expressed by the principal as well as teachers and students about what we call school climate: the institutional policies, practices, structures, ethos, internal social, and community dynamics that support or do not support instruction. Each person's story is a composite based on conversations we have had with a variety of individuals about their classes, individual students, and how they perceive their role within the school system. We then share information about four intervention and treatment approaches that are available to schools today.

We have selected these four programs for several reasons. First, they have each been by reviewed for scientific merit by The Collaborative for Academic, Social, and Emotional Learning (CASEL, 2004). CASEL describes its mission thus: "To enhance children's success in school and life by promoting coordinated, evidence-based social, emotional, and academic learning as an essential part of education from preschool though high school." CASEL synthesizes the latest empirical findings and theoretical developments and provides leadership to foster progress in what they call social and emotional learning research and practice.

Second, we selected these four programs because they differ in ways that are reflective of programs that are generally available to schools. For example, some programs direct their intervention toward the prevention of disorders or the reduction of exposure to social and emotional risks; others focus on promoting social strengths and competencies. Some interventions are classroom-based, others work within the whole school, and still others work across districts, enlisting schools, families, and communities. A few of the programs are located in university settings and have their own research units, and others have grown out of applied settings and have recruited outside evaluators to do the type of outcome research that will enable them to claim they are evidence-based.

Each of the four approaches we describe is multidisciplinary, outcome-evaluated, and, to varying degrees, research- and evidence-based. Each program—or intervention, if you will—also has a cost, and we need to consider cost in our intervention planning. This case is designed to illustrate the services, preventions, interventions, and treatments available for an ailing school such as the Gilmore.

From Each Person's Perspective: What Issues of Social Relationship Matter the Most to Teachers, Students, and Administrators?

We have selected six key individuals to be profiled: two students (Robert and Reanna), two teachers (Ms. Li and

Ms. McCarthy), the school adjustment counselor (Ms. Curtis), and the principal (Mr. Martinez).[2]

Robert

Robert sits in one of the three red chairs lined up against the wall to the right of the principal's closed door. He contemplates swinging his feet up onto the adjacent chair to curl up with knees to chest, but thinks again when his eyes meet those of the school secretary, who sits in her office directly across the hall. Some of the kids in the school love Ms. Thompson, bringing her drawings they've done in art class and always calling out her name when passing by in the hall. But nearly all of Robert's interactions with the secretary have been antagonistic. Earlier in the year, when he was sent to her office, his head would always hang low. Only when she demanded that he look at her partway through the reprimand would he force himself to meet her gaze. Now he matches her stare from the moment he appears at the door, and the phrases she barks at him, repetitive and rhetorical, roll right by. He has learned the routine and has chosen the chair closest to the window as his regular favorite.

Today, Robert has been sent to the office for being disruptive in music class. It started when Jamil pushed him from behind as the class entered the music room, crammed together in a line that neither the hallway nor the classroom could fully accommodate. Robert, along with most of his classmates, finds Jamil annoying; he talks too much and has trouble keeping his hands to himself. Robert is able to tolerate Jamil's talking but has no patience for his pushing and shoving. Today, Robert had pushed back a little harder than usual, his level of frustration heightened by the fact that the whole class had been forced to stay in for recess yet again. The Friday before, a group of boys in Robert's fourth-grade class, including Jamil, had gotten into a fight on the playground. As a result, the teacher, Ms. McCarthy, decided that the entire class would be kept in from recess for 2 weeks. Robert and a number of his classmates had complained that this was unfair punishment, but Ms. McCarthy said her mind was made up and no one could unmake it. Students would have to think twice about the consequences of bullying. Robert didn't understand why

[2] We would like to thank Miranda Lutyens, a former EdM student in the Risk and Prevention Program, for her assistance in writing the story of this school.

the teacher called a regular old recess fight "bullying," unless it was because Jamil had been involved and she always defended him. Maybe if Jamil hadn't been one of the boys who got pushed around, Ms. McCarthy wouldn't have punished the entire class. Jamil lost even more points with Robert for being the teacher's pet.

Denial of recess time had particularly harsh repercussions in Robert's world. Apart from the physical frustration of not being able to run around outside, Robert felt his recent playground successes slipping away. A few weeks back, he had started playing football with some of the fifth-grade boys—the fourth and fifth grades share recess time after lunch—and he was just beginning to win their respect. They had even let him play quarterback a couple of times, and a few of the fifth graders would call out his name and shake his hand when passing in the hallway. Then recess had been taken away, and within a few days Robert felt the attention from the older boys fade away. Now, sitting in the red chair, Robert gets angry again, thinking about all the outside time that has passed without him. Grabbing onto the edge of the chair with both hands, he shifts angrily in his seat, but then looks up to see that Ms. Thompson is watching him.

Reanna

Twenty minutes later, Reanna walks into the secretary's office, her backpack over her shoulder and her coat stuffed under her arm. Ms. Thompson smiles at the new arrival, greeting her with a "Hi, Sweetheart!" Reanna grins back and squeezes behind Ms. Thompson's desk to seat herself at a little table by the window. She pulls out a book and begins reading silently to herself. Reanna is one of the few students in the school who actually likes Drop Everything and Read (DEAR) time, which is supposed to comprise the last 15 minutes of every school day. She's not sure her teacher, Ms. Li, likes DEAR, since she rarely has her students engage in the intended practice. Or maybe it's just that her teacher can't manage to get 24 kids to read silently at the end of the day, especially when she's trying to work with individual students on incomplete homework assignments, test preparation, and all the other things the class needs.

Not long after Reanna was chosen as the Thursday bus announcer, she had asked Ms. Li if she could report to the office 15 minutes early to do DEAR on her own. Tired of being made fun of openly for her studious habits and worn down by the whispers and looks directed toward her by other girls in her class, Reanna looks for escape options. She jumps at any opportunity to spend time away from the classroom—deliveries from Ms. Li to the office, visits to the nurse for her asthma shots, working with John, the Americorps student who tutors her in math once a week. Not surprisingly, Ms. Li agreed to Reanna's spending her DEAR time with Ms. Thompson on Thursdays. Reanna senses that Ms. Li understands and is sympathetic to her plight, and she appreciates Ms. Li's efforts in helping her avoid the unfriendly environment of the classroom. She's not sure what else her teacher could do for her, nor is she certain that she'd want her teacher to take any further measures. For now, at least, Thursday afternoons in the office seems her best defense.

Reanna looks forward to Thursday afternoons. She is happy to have the attention from Ms. Thompson and she appreciates the quiet space, far from the afternoon commotion of her classroom upstairs. Most of all, Reanna loves announcing buses. Hearing her voice amplified throughout the halls and seeing the waves of students bustle by on her command, gives Reanna great pleasure. Whatever the girls in her class might be saying about her, it matters much less when she is safely separated from them and when her voice drowns out theirs. She also likes the sense of responsibility that comes with the position. If it weren't for her accurate announcements, students would be stranded and the school would be thrown into chaos. All the adults in the school are constantly talking about "responsibility," and the word seems to be printed or posted on everything she sees throughout the school day, often coupled with "respect." But until being chosen as a bus announcer, Reanna had not found many opportunities in her school to demonstrate responsibility. Even as a fifth grader, she doesn't feel like a leader. Only when her voice guides the younger students and her peers through the exit and out to the bus stop does she feel that she is proving herself as a responsible member of the school.

Unlike the children she directs onto the crowded buses, Reanna has always walked to school. Next year, she will take the bus to the local middle school, which is over a mile from her home. Although she is excited at the prospect of traveling far to school, she is also nervous. Plenty of stories have circulated at school and in her neighborhood about scary things happening on middle school buses. A seventh-grade friend was forced to smoke part of a joint before two eighth graders would let her off at her stop, and Reanna has heard rumors of worse, such as forced sexual acts encouraged by other kids on the bus. She wonders how she will protect herself next year and is glad to know that some of her friends live further from the school than she does. They will be on the bus when she gets on in the morning and when she gets off at the end of the day. Reanna's big hope for middle school is that a larger student body will allow her to have a strong group of friends and avoid the persecution she's lived through this year. Reanna wants nothing more than to keep a low profile.

Ms. Li

As Reanna's voice rings out in her fifth-grade classroom, Ms. Li urges the remaining few students in her room to remember to bring back their signed permission slips for the upcoming field trip. The math instruction professional development workshop scheduled for the afternoon has been cancelled, and although Ms. Li knows she should stay and put up a new display of student work—a recently mandated activity, aimed at demonstrating standards-based achievement—she decides to head home. The day has been no more exhausting than any other, but the week feels as if it should be over. Perhaps today was more challenging, as the resource teacher had been out sick, which meant that the entire class had been with Ms. Li for the full day. She has come to anticipate eagerly the period when she is relieved of six of her more challenged learners, the majority of whom are her most difficult students. When the class is at its full size, Ms. Li has trouble accomplishing anything of substance. And she feels that this is beginning to be reflected in her students' work.

A second-year teacher, Ms. Li came to the profession from the world of management consulting, where she felt professionally challenged but personally unfulfilled. Committed to city life, she saw urban education as a field that would allow for an important give-and-take: She'd be contributing to positive social change, and, in turn, her work would be meaningful and motivating. Although less overwhelmed now than during her rookie year, Ms. Li feels that her master's degree in education left her completely unprepared for the reality of the classroom. The theory learned in her teacher training practices—advocating for a constructivist, child-centered approach—seems unattainable given the circumstances in which she finds herself on a daily basis. She is fond of her students and recognizes a desire to learn in many of them. Moreover, she believes that all her students have potential, both academically and so-

cially. But the behavior of a few consistently disrupts the classroom environment, and other students, worn down by the constant interruptions, quickly lose motivation. As a result, Ms. Li feels incapable of tapping into her students' strengths, let alone helping them realize and appreciate their own potential. Her greatest fear is that she will reach the point of exhaustion or desperation where she resorts to the tactics used by other adults in the school. The constant yelling of her colleague across the hall is distracting. Ms. Li also refuses to employ the tactic used by the third-grade teacher, who keeps his cell phone within reach and pretends to dial home whenever a child misbehaves. Ms. Li prefers to promote positive feelings in her class, rather than fear and mistrust. She sees the bullying that goes on among her students and wants to discourage, not emulate, this behavior. How can she discourage the use of threats among students if she herself employed threats as a behavior management tactic?

Ms. Li is not naive about the stance of her principal and of the school system as a whole: Academics must come first. But as hard as she works to support her students' academic learning, she feels that she can't be successful without devoting some of her focus to social and emotional learning. She holds the philosophical belief—one that she keeps close to her chest—that the teacher's role as promoter of social and ethical awareness is just as important as that of academic instructor. This belief, however, only takes her so far. When she is actually faced with a challenge in the classroom, she feels unequipped to respond in a way that leads to positive results for everyone involved.

Ms. Li is well aware of the teasing and whispering among the girls in her class. Part of the reason she had chosen to teach at the elementary rather than middle school level was to avoid dealing with the challenges of girls' peer relations at that age. Now, as a fifth-grade teacher, she realizes that girls being mean to one another also occurs in elementary school. Ms. Li talked with the school counselor about the problem, and the counselor spent a few lunchtimes with the most egregious offenders, but the results were undetectable. Ms. Li knows it is her responsibility to work on these social issues in the classroom, but she doesn't know how to address them in a way that might have a lasting effect. Instead, she tends to look for opportunities to split up the perpetrator girls, and when that isn't possible, she tries to relieve the victims being trapped among the victimizers. Ms. Li well remembers being teased by mean girls during her own school years. She knows that, despite the phenomenon now having the more official title of "relational aggression," the feelings of girls like Reanna are no different from what she experienced years ago.

Ms. McCarthy

It's the time of day when Ms. McCarthy closes all the windows she has left ajar during the day, an attempt to counteract the building's overactive heating system. It's also the time of day when Ms. McCarthy pays a visit to the vending machine in the faculty room, two doors down, to buy a package of chips. As much as she hates to see her kids eating so much junk food, by the time her classroom empties out she needs a pick-me-up. To put it mildly, her class this year is a nightmare; her kids fight and bully each other, disrespect her and other teachers, steal, and swear. Ms. McCarthy didn't come into the year blindly, either. The third-grade teachers had warned her about this class: As the cohort progressed through each grade level, their behavior had worsened until pervasive poor behavior was the norm. In anticipation of inheriting this notorious group, Ms. McCarthy had voiced her concerns to the school principal, Mr. Martinez, and had even talked about trying to transfer within the system. Days into this year at the school, Ms. McCarthy began expressing her grievances to the principal, claiming that in her 21 years of teaching she had never had such a troublesome class. The veteran teacher also questioned how a group like this could have moved through the school without the students' individual and collective behavior problems being more systematically addressed. No doubt regarding this question as a direct attack, the principal had countered that efforts had been made by the student support services team to deal with the extreme challenges of this specific class. However, like many of her colleagues, Ms. McCarthy sees the student support services as unorganized and ineffective. Most of the services seem to involve Band-Aid approaches to individual students, rather than the macro-level behavior management problems she faces in her classroom.

Over her 2 decades of teaching, Ms. McCarthy has seen a general trend of chronic behavioral dysfunction among the students. She knows that the recent economic downturn may be exacerbating the poverty experienced by many of her students. She is also aware of the cultural shifts playing into the lives of youngsters, from sex and violence in the media to less opportunity for creative play, exercise, and quality time with family. These so-cial realities, however acute and actual they may be, all blur together and fade into the background when it comes to Ms. McCarthy's everyday experience in the classroom. Disruptive behavior is disruptive behavior, whatever the causes. She feels that the rise in behavior problems has been answered by increased numbers of professional development trainings on behavior management, none of which she has found particularly useful.

As a result, Ms. McCarthy has resorted to collective punishment, such as the recent recess ban resulting from a playground fight. At this point, she believes that peer pressure may be the only language her students understand. Maybe being denied time outside will lead to a critical mass of students discouraging others from repeating such behavior. Ms. McCarthy is especially frustrated by students' behavior on the playground and in the hallways. One minute she feels she is making some progress in the classroom, with students speaking to her in respectful ways and asking if anyone has seen a missing item rather than shouting out the blanket accusation of "who stole my_____?!" The next minute, her students are mouthing off to other teachers in the hallway or fighting on the playground. Even when in class they seem to understand what it means to behave acceptably toward others, they are rarely able to turn that thought into action once they are out from under the eyes of Ms. McCarthy.

Ms. Curtis

Picking up the toy trucks and teddy bears strewn about the carpet, Ms. Curtis looks around to make sure she hasn't left anything else in the resource teacher's room. Permitted the use of the sunny, spacious room due to her colleague's absence that day, the school adjustment counselor dreads returning to her tiny closet of an office on the north side of the building. She sits there 3 days a week, doing her best to manage a caseload of students with problems ranging from withdrawn behavior that looks like diagnosable depression to chronic aggression, which is harder to diagnose because in some students it seems reactive to perceived threats and in others it seems to be the way they want to manage their social relationships. Currently, she sees some students individually on a regular basis, pulling them out of class time to engage in 30- to 45-minute counseling sessions. She also runs lunch groups and social skills groups when she can. The majority of her students are boys, and most of them are referred for reasons relating to aggressive behavior.

Ms. Curtis is a trained clinical social worker with a background in working with families. As an African American raised by a single mother, Ms. Curtis believes one of the strengths she brings to her job is being able to culturally understand and connect with the families in the school district. Unfortunately, she has a difficult time making contact with the families. Many parents simply won't show up at the school. One boy's mother has missed four appointments, despite friendly reminder phone calls each time from Ms. Curtis. Unable to work with children without parental consent, Ms. Curtis feels that her hands are tied.

In contrast, she finds herself wanting to throw her arms around those parents who take an active interest in their child's counseling. One mother showed up one morning at the school, unannounced, and asked to speak with the school counselor. Luckily, it had been one of Ms. Curtis's days at the school, and she ended up talking with the mother for over an hour. The mother shared her concerns about her fourth-grade son, Robert, whose father had just been sent to jail for the second time in 5 years. She was seeing increasingly violent tendencies in her son and was concerned that this behavior would begin to crop up in school. In fact, Ms. McCarthy had been talking about this student repeatedly in student support services meetings, and Ms. Curtis was surprised that Ms. McCarthy had not already been in touch with the boy's mother. But rather than share this fact, Ms. Curtis chose to focus their conversation on the mother's own assessment of her son. The mother explained that she worked until six each night, so she only got to spend a couple of hours with the boy. In her place, his grandmother looked after him in the afternoons, and he was allowed to play and do homework at their housing development's community center from the time he returned from school until the center closed at five. He had recently been kicked out of the community center three times in one week for pushing and even hitting other kids, and the mother was concerned that this would become a pattern.

As Ms. Curtis sat and listened, her emotions were mixed. On the one hand, she was disturbed to hear the details of this boy's situation. At the same time, she was thrilled that a parent was taking the time to share these kinds of details with her. Without an understanding of students' home life, Ms. Curtis often feels that she is the blind leading the blind.

Even when Ms. Curtis sees progress in her one-on-one sessions with her students, the reports from the teachers are rarely as encouraging. Behavior contracts and other methods involving rewards for positive behavior seem to have only a limited effect with the more difficult students. As much as she believes that her work with the students has merit, she is well aware that what ultimately counts is how well they are able to adjust to the social and emotional demands of the classroom. Occasionally, Ms. Curtis spends time in her students' classrooms, observing their behaviors and interactions with other students and the teachers. She sees how the environment in many classrooms only exacerbates her students' problems: a constant exchange of put-downs, arbitrary reprimands from teachers, and overlooked acts of bullying. She is not surprised that fights break out frequently, both inside the classroom and on the playground. Realizing that she needs to help her students develop concrete skills in resisting the urge to act out toward others, Ms. Curtis knows that these skills must be reinforced in the classroom. But she doesn't see much hope of it at present.

Mr. Martinez

Robert has long since vacated the red chair outside the principal's door when Mr. Martinez emerges from his office, ducking slightly to reduce his towering size as he passes under the door frame. Accompanying him is the school's literacy coach, who shares her time among four elementary schools in the city. They have been meeting for over 2 hours to discuss their joint concerns regarding English Language Arts (ELA) instruction at the school. Fourth-grade MCAS results were released a week before and were not encouraging: ELA passing scores are down 20% from the previous year. At such a small school—250 students in total—one class's scores count for a lot. Last year's fourth-grade class had difficult behavior issues, and he's even more concerned about this year's fourth graders. He has heard nonstop from Ms. McCarthy regarding her class's chronic behavior problems. His discussions with her, a veteran teacher who has held a leadership position among the faculty ever since he took the principal's position 4 years ago, always come back to one central issue: school support services. Both principal and teacher know that these services should be creating a better school atmosphere. But while Mr. Martinez believes there is overall school improvement, Ms. McCarthy sees little evidence at the classroom level.

Problems relating to classroom and school climate frustrate Mr. Martinez. Under constant pressure to improve instruction and raise test scores, he realizes that these aims are unrealistic when behavior management remains the number one concern (and complaint) of his faculty. Survey results from a recent district-wide study of student support services show that elementary school teachers rate "a caring and supportive school environment" as the most effective means of reducing barriers to learning. Mr. Martinez does not doubt that his teachers would agree with this finding. But, unlike the other "activities" listed in the support services survey, such as breakfast and lunch programs, health education, and community linkages, "a caring and supportive school environment" seems vague and difficult to measure. Although Mr. Martinez wants to make school climate an integral part of the school's overall improvement plan, he believes that the only practical way of achieving this is through attaining more immediate, concrete outcomes, such as improved levels of literacy and increased attendance rates. He is not willing to make school climate its own priority when he can't ensure that the efforts made toward improving climate will result in measurable and lasting academic results. There is too much else at stake. As he returns to his office, having bid the literacy coach good-bye, Mr. Martinez lets his mind spin around these quandaries, but only for a few minutes. There are phone calls to return and reports to write. What's most important right now about the school environment is that the place is quiet and Mr. Martinez will be able to work in peace.

The Approach to Treatment and Prevention

The good news for the Gilmore is that there is a widespread proliferation of programs available to the school. In the 1980s, the American Psychological Association launched a task force to find and evaluate prevention programs. At the time, not many quality programs were discovered, but today there are many research-based prevention programs that work (Weissberg et al., 2003). Most follow the theoretical framework clearly outlined in the IOM report, where prevention was positioned as part of a spectrum of treatment for mental health and disorders that also included treatment and maintenance (Mrazek & Haggerty, 1994). This framework has been adapted successfully by many youth development programs seeking to ameliorate the difficulties experienced by children and families (Dryfoos, 1990, 1997; Weissberg et al., 2003).

In the IOM preventive intervention research cycle, the first step is to identify the problem and/or disor-

der(s) and review the information. For the Gilmore School, the first step of a researcher or practitioner who was interested in providing some kind of "best practice" would be to gain epidemiological information about the disorder. In this instance, as we were the "experts" working with the Gilmore School, we saw the school's problem (or disorder) as being focused on issues of social competence and social skills, that is, getting along with others. A researcher from another discipline, such as sociology or economics, could frame and diagnose the problem differently. From our perspective, based on what we were told by teachers and staff at the Gilmore, the school suffered from a series of relationship illnesses: Teachers struggled with behavior management, students struggled to get along with peers, and administrators tried to address behavior issues while feeling enormous pressure to meet academic standards.

At the student level, Robert lacks impulse control and pushes back physically at Jamil instead of using words to solve his problem. Social exclusion is acute; both Robert and Reanna feel isolated from their peers. Most of their interactions with the other students are unfriendly, and they are socially miserable. In response, Robert fights and Reanna withdraws into books. And, although Reanna's withdrawal may help her academically, in the future she may lack the appropriate social skills to move forward in developing positive friendships. Neither Robert nor Reanna seems to know how to interact with other children their age, and both have difficulties juggling teachers' expectations of behavior.

At the teacher level, none of the teachers at the Gilmore knows for sure how to manage the kids. Ms. Li is kind but ineffective. She feels powerless to stop Reanna from being socially bullied, so she prefers to go home at the end of the day rather than try to come up with inadequate ways to stop the harassment. She remembers this type of "relational aggression" when she was in school, but even as an adult she admits she has no idea how to go about preventing it. In contrast, Ms. McCarthy chooses to punish the children for their physical conflicts—no recess for 2 weeks—instead of teaching conflict resolution and fostering connections between the kids. She relies on peer pressure to change her students' behavior, but these students are not relating to each other in positive ways. As a result, the lessons they learn from each other will be negative ones, such as Robert blaming Jamil for causing the recess ban. Interestingly, we noticed that Ms. Li's response bore a strong resemblance to Reanna's strategy of withdrawing, and Ms. McCarthy's was remarkably similar to Jamil's and Robert's of pushing back.

The school adjustment counselor, Ms. Curtis, recognizes that families need to be involved if the school wants to solve student behavioral issues. But the families in this neighborhood are overstressed: Not enough economic and social supports exist to help them. As a result, they lack the time and energy to come to the school and sometimes don't understand why their participation is so important. Ms. Curtis's role in the school is reduced to seeing individual students one-on-one. Without more administrative support and funding, she lacks the resources to organize schoolwide social competence programs or develop teacher education programs on the topic of behavioral management. Furthermore, her clinical training primarily equipped her to deal with students individually; she is not sure she'd be able to organize a school program even if it was requested. What topics would she focus on? How would she help teachers and students?

From the principal's perspective, the social problems and academic problems of the students are separate. Despite paying lip service to the notion that students cannot function well academically when their social lives and relationships are a mess, Mr. Martinez prefers to focus on the immediate problem he faces: the need to get the school operating at a better level of performance. Ms. McCarthy's complaints are seen as nagging. Ultimately, both Mr. Martinez and Ms. McCarthy blame the current crop of students: "This year is worse than ever."

For better or worse, we have diagnosed a problem in the school on both the community and individual levels. We believe the problems faced by the students and teachers in this school are not unique. In diagnosing these problems, we do not want to come across as pathologizing the individuals involved; all of the teachers and staff in this school face a hard task, and trying to figure out what is best for their students individually and as a whole is daunting. Mr. Martinez is doing the best he can to turn around a failing school. Ms. Li and Ms. McCarthy just want their students to get along and respect their authority. Similarly, the school hierarchy, lack of parental involvement, and a clinical training that emphasized individual rather than systematic problem-solving prevent Ms. Curtis from making progress. Finally, Jamil, Robert, and Reanna are negotiating their social worlds the best they know how.

What can these individuals do differently in their lives? How would they know the best thing to do in a given social situation? What individual, family, school, and systemwide intervention is needed to solve the Gilmore School's distress? It seems to us that although schools have begun to learn how to solve the problem of lack of literacy skills—and they are having a tough enough time trying to do that—they are still at a complete loss as to how to manage social problems. Even if they had the funding to develop a wide-scale approach, how would a school negotiate the wide variety of programs available to them? What criteria would they use to choose?

How Can the Institute of Medicine Model Help the Gilmore School?

The second and third steps of the IOM model recommend that research should lead the way toward developing an intervention. First, by evaluating the existing literature on school climate, social competence, and youth development, the prevention program should choose a theoretical model that will guide the intervention. Next, based on a model and research, the program should design the necessary activities, hire staff, get cooperation from the site, and choose the methodology they will use to do formative and evaluative research. In the fourth and fifth steps, the program should move toward designing large-scale trials of the program and eventually provide a manual outlining the program and delineating core elements and characteristics (Mrazek & Haggerty, 1994).

The benefit of the model is that it focuses on interventions that can be implemented at a scale that will affect not only individuals but also populations beyond individuals. For instance, in this first case, the Gilmore School, our initial point of departure was the desire to improve the mental health and social development of the children in the school through thoughtful services. Over time, however, our concerns mounted as we worked with students and teachers struggling to live in and be supported in a school with a vulnerable social atmosphere. We realized we had to think beyond the individual student at the Gilmore; one-on-one interventions were not stemming the tide of behavioral and social competence issues that permeated every hallway of the school.

The strategy we articulated was to use the IOM framework to seek "mature" outside preventive interventions from a range of options, each with its own theoretical framework and evidence base. In our case, we reviewed the literature on prevention programs (Weissberg et al., 2003) and also examined research that emphasized positive youth development programs. Rather than focus only on the risks children face, these programs seek to develop the positive influences in children's lives that can help promote positive outcomes (Catalano et al., 2002). For the Gilmore School, we needed a program that not only would help ameliorate the mental and social problems of future students of the school but that would also promote positive development among the students who were currently enrolled. In other words, we needed to focus on helping students in the present as well as in the future—combining intervention (a k a "treatment") with prevention.

Some Possible Choices

What are some possible options for the Gilmore School? How should we, as the school's "doctors," the so-called experts, proceed toward making a recommendation of how the school should solve its social and behavioral problems? It is important to keep in mind that many schools are left on their own to make these types of intervention decisions. Some cities have begun school-reform programs that focus on social-emotional competence and decreasing negative attitudes and behaviors (see, e.g., the Reading, Writing, Respect, and Resolution [4Rs] program currently being evaluated in several New York City public schools). But many schools, like the Gilmore, are left to find their way through a confusing landscape of options as best they can. How do they know which programs will work? How much do the various programs cost, and what will they get for their money? These are critical questions from a practice perspective.

Researchers understand that although two programs may rest on the same fundamental research base, their approach and choice of solution may depend on their theoretical orientation, that is, a program that is based on socioemotional learning versus one that views a school as a community. Neither approach is wrong and in fact may share many common attributes, yet for practitioners it can create confusion about which one is best. The realization that even experts may have vastly different points of view about the development of social competence in children, for example, is frustrating and can lead practitioners to doubt the benefit of research.

One option for schools is to turn to CASEL. Under the current direction of Roger P. Weissberg and based in

the Department of Psychology at the University of Illinois, Chicago, CASEL partners with researchers and practitioners in the fields of social and emotional learning, prevention, positive youth development, service learning, character education, and education reform. It does not develop or market educational programs, but rather brings together the work of different researchers across disciplines to promote social and emotional learning. In 2003, it recommended 22 programs across the country that are effective in promoting social and emotional learning and providing staff development (CASEL, 2003).

Even with an array of programs to choose from, and a fairly solid guarantee that the programs are beneficial, schools need to decide which one is best for their particular situation. Should the intervention take place only within classrooms or across schools and communities? Should it work with school staff and students only, or include families? What does it cost? How long does it take to be implemented? Will it focus on conflict resolution, violence and drug prevention, the promotion of social learning, or a combination of different approaches? These are just some of the questions Mr. Martinez needs to have answered. Even though all of the programs CASEL recommends have been outcome-evaluated and are research-based, each has its own particular agenda.

Although there are many programs to choose from, this chapter focuses on four programs in depth. Our intention is not to evaluate the programs, but to illustrate the ways developmental, applied developmental, and clinical psychology research can be (and have been) integrated with other disciplines and translated into practice.

Second Step

Second Step (Committee for Children, 2005) is an elementary school violence prevention curriculum focused on developing three competencies in children: empathy, impulse control/problem solving, and anger management. Studies of Second Step suggest that students of different age groups from kindergarten through sixth grade demonstrated increased positive interactions and empathy, a decline in anxious and depressed behavior, and less disruptive, hostile, and aggressive behavior (Frey, Nolen, Van Schoiack-Edstrom, & Hirschstein, 2001; Grossman et al., 1997; Orpinas, Parcel, McAlister, & Frankowski, 1995).

Second Step's goals for children are to recognize and understand their own feelings, keep anger from escalating into violence, and make positive rather than negative behavior choices. In addition, Second Step aims to help teachers recognize and deal with classroom disruptions and behavior issues. Because Second Step is prepackaged and requires very little teacher preparation time, it seems easy for teachers to follow, and the recommended time commitment is 30 minutes several times a week. Products for purchase in elementary school include puppets for role-playing (e.g., the Slow-Down Snail helps children stop and think before acting or speaking), videos, and photo lesson cards. Teachers use stories as the basis of a lesson (e.g., on the theme of anger management), and visuals are used to depict children's faces in the social situation to display feelings and help young students make the link between the face, the feeling, and the story (Committee for Children, 2005).

In theory, Second Step could be utilized to solve schoolwide as well as individual problems. For instance, to change the Gilmore School's climate from one of punishment to problem solving, teachers could come to agreement around behavior management. Instead of banning recess, teachers could assign "reflection sheets" that prompt students with behavior issues to walk back through the incident and think of a better solution. This could arm the students with the skills needed to proactively address social problems and potentially change future behavior, instead of simply punishing them after the fact. As a reward, students would be given an "I am a Second Step Star" button. Signs listing the problem-solving steps would be posted in the recess area so that paraprofessionals, students, and even lunch mothers would be aware of the format. The signs would also communicate the Second Step values to visiting community members and parents.

Students like Robert would be helped by a change in the language of behavior management (emphasizing student reflection rather than punishment). Teachers and students would partner to reflect on behaviors and plans for the future, opening communication. "Reflections" help students understand why they are being singled out for behavior changes and would prevent them from feeling frustrated that they have no voice in the development of consequences.

At the classroom level, although the program includes some standardized lessons (e.g., anger management), there is also room for teachers to tailor lessons to specific conflict situations. For instance, Ms. Li could create a lesson card for the class to role-play issues of social exclusion to expose the emotions involved and encourage empathy. The curriculum is specific about problem-solving steps that are needed to resolve the conflict productively.

Mr. Martinez and Ms. McCarthy would be pleased with a social problem-solving program that is consistent across the whole school. Progress made in the classroom could be continued at recess, in halls, and at home because other staff and families would be informed of the values and strategies the children were learning. Students of different grades would learn similar strategies and could employ them at recess and after school.

The cost of Second Step is fairly reasonable. Although kits can be purchased for each grade, a comprehensive preschool through grade 5 kit costs around $900 (Committee for Children, 2005).

Social Development Research Group

The Social Development Research Group (SDRG) is affiliated with the School of Social Work at the University of Washington in Seattle. There are several interventions associated with SDRG; one that we consider to be relevant to the Gilmore School is the Raising Healthy Children (RHC) project (SDRG, 2004a). An 8-year intervention funded by the National Institute on Drug Abuse, RHC was designed to promote school success as a protective factor that promotes healthy child and adolescent development and prevents problem behaviors (Catalano et al., 2003). During the 2002/2003 school year, this intervention was running only in the Edmonds School District in Washington, but other districts throughout the country could presumably adapt its principles and publications. RHC, unlike Second Step, is a district-oriented program that works with all elementary, middle, and high schools within the district. It focuses its attention on parents as well as schools to promote positive development. Parents can attend workshops, such as "How to Help Your Child Succeed in School," "Raising Healthy Children," and "Moving into Middle School." During the high school years, parents are even offered home visits that reinforce the training sessions they attended earlier (SDRG, 2004a).

Teachers and school administrators, on the other hand, receive training that helps them keep the school atmosphere focused on learning, not just identification of problem behaviors. Positive social interactions are praised and students are encouraged to remain involved and work in small teams to help each other learn. RHC research suggests that these methods provide an atmosphere in which children feel good about themselves and their ability to learn (Catalano et al., 2003).

Unlike Second Step, however, RHC is less of a packaged curriculum that schools could follow easily. The program would have to be specifically adapted to the Boston Public School district and extended beyond its current existence in a Washington-area school district. The cost of adapting RHC to the district (with the program's permission and supervision) is difficult to calculate, although funding opportunities may be available through the National Institute on Drug Abuse, other federal agencies, or philanthropic organizations. The grant-writing process and application would have to be factored into the cost and more research would be needed.

The benefits for the Gilmore School, however, could be substantial. RHC philosophies seem to be in line with what is needed at the Gilmore. For instance, part of the problem at the school is a lack of positive relationships between students and teachers (e.g., Robert, Jamil, and Ms. McCarthy; Reanna and Ms. Li). There is also a lack of clear, schoolwide standards for behavior and shared decisions about classroom management. Under RHC training, teachers would be able to begin to share strategies for creating a socially appropriate classroom atmosphere that would promote, rather than take away from, the academic learning that is supposed to take place in schools. Also, from Ms. Curtis's point of view, RHC would be beneficial because it does not limit its intervention simply to the school but works to involve parents, recognizing that it is often necessary to get parents on board when designing and implementing school-based interventions. Whether parents would attend or not, however, is hard to say, considering that Ms. Curtis is having a difficult time getting them to attend even parent-teacher conferences.

Although books and other curriculum materials are available for purchase, teachers and administrators would have to spend a substantial amount of time figuring out how the program could be adapted in the district. Although the SDRG programs and research base seems in line with the Gilmore's needs, the practical application of the program would be a district decision, involving the Boston superintendent as well his cluster leaders.

Promoting Alternative Thinking Strategies

The Promoting Alternative Thinking Strategies (PATHS; Greenberg, Kusché, & Mihalic, 1998) program is a K–sixth-grade violence prevention program affiliated with Pennsylvania State University and sold by a commercial publisher, Channing-Bete. Named as one of 10 Blueprints for Violence Prevention by the U.S. Department of Justice and the Center for the Study and Prevention of Violence, PATHS is in place in more than 500 schools throughout the world. Like Second Step, PATHS teaches children nonviolent conflict resolution strategies, to stop and think before acting, and to manage and express their emotions. For teachers, PATHS can be easily integrated into existing classrooms, and the timing and frequency of the lessons can be adapted based on the teacher's needs. The curriculum comes with an instructor's manual as well as a curriculum guide that includes information on how to present the lessons, an overview of the important concepts to get across, and a list of necessary materials. Furthermore, PATHS is fairly cost-effective: A complete program costs around $700 (Greenberg et al., 1998).

For the students, PATHS provides them with ways to evaluate their responses to conflict so that they can learn to prevent future incidences. For the teachers, it recommends that they stop and think about their feelings before responding with yelling or punishment or other negative strategies. Clinical trials have shown decreases in teacher reports of student aggressive behavior and increases in teacher reports of self-control as well as students' emotional vocabularies and cognitive skill test scores (Greenberg et al., 1998; Greenberg, Kusché, Cook, & Quamma, 1995; Greenberg et al., 2003). This would be good news to both Ms. McCarthy and Ms. Li. Furthermore, because the curriculum would be schoolwide, Mr. Martinez could feel confident that all teachers were following the same behavior management strategies.

Developmental Studies Center: Child Development Project

The fourth and final program we discuss is the Developmental Studies Center Child Development Project (CDP, 2003). Rather than focus on student problem behaviors, CDP tries to revamp school climate to create "communities of learners." The Developmental Studies Center provides whole-school training in social and ethical as well as academic development. The CDP's focus is on improving school design to improve students' literacy skills as well as relational connections among students, teachers, and administrative staff. It has created a literacy program that combines decoding with reading comprehension through the use of literacy activities such as guided reading, group reading, and individual instruction (CDP, 2003). In addition, CDP works to train teachers as well as administrators in how to foster a positive school climate. Like the other programs we introduced, CDP has been evaluated for positive outcomes (Battistich, Schaps, Watson, & Solomon, 1996; Solomon, Battistich, Watson, Schaps, & Lewis, 2000).

CDP's focus on literacy as well as social development would appeal to Mr. Martinez, as he is primarily focused on raising students' performance on academic tests. In addition, CDP staff provide development and consulting services to assist in implementation, relieving the Gilmore staff from having to worry about adapting a packaged curriculum to their school. However, to successfully implement CDP, a school must commit over several years to its program and to ongoing professional development. Furthermore, the cost to the school is individually negotiated with the school and the district, depending on the program elements that would be used and the type of support, services, or materials that are required. Mr. Martinez would need to explore whether CDP was cost-effective compared to the other programs. Yet, CDP also provides assistance in identifying grants that could be available for schools and districts and even offers a grant-writing service to help schools apply for them (CDP, 2003).

Implementation

Each of these four programs is research-based. That is, they have not only been empirically evaluated with regard to positive outcomes, but their ideas, models, and implementation rest firmly on solid theoretical and empirical foundations in academic disciplines such as social psychology, developmental psychology, and even cultural anthropology. Yet, although each has been acknowledged as a top program in the United States, the founders, practitioners, and researchers affiliated with each intervention are not equally invested in the management process of implementing the interventions in school systems.

In the process of development, each intervention (and their founders, both practitioners and researchers) had to decide where it wanted to spend its time and energy. Research and practice do not always go hand in hand;

it is extremely difficult to design and implement programs, run training sessions, and sell products while also initiating new practice-inspired research projects, writing grant proposals, and managing data collection and analysis. Once the effectiveness of a program has been proven, its dissemination usually depends on a committed principal investigator who decides to replicate the study with larger samples over time, works with policymakers to ensure a steady stream of funding, and pushes for implementation. In the world of academia, program implementation, even for the most well-regarded research, is not always praised; there is an expectation that researchers must continue to break new ground conducting research and publishing findings (Rotheram-Borus & Duan, 2003).

So each program we presented had (at one time or another) decided what type of "social development" intervention it wished to be. Would it become market-oriented, for example, geared toward meeting the needs of school systems? Or would it contract the business to outside vendors and concentrate on designing and researching future interventions and doing basic research? Among the four programs we have discussed, there is a split down the middle. For instance, Second Step and Developmental Studies Center are business-oriented, market-driven programs. They are not affiliated with any one particular university; Developmental Studies Center conducts its own practice-driven research while contracting with school systems to provide both curriculum materials and professional development. With excellent random assignment outcome evaluations already under its belt (Solomon et al., 2000), Developmental Studies Center has recently turned its attention to doing research that is more formative, focused on identifying the best practices that create a sense of community in schools (Schaps, 2003). Second Step, on the other hand, hires outside researchers to conduct independent evaluations. This research, like that of Developmental Studies Center, is primarily driven by the needs of practice. At this point in their evolution, both programs are geared toward issues of implementation, be it marketing and selling social skills "products" or promoting positive school climates with teacher professional development.

PATHS and SDRG are structured differently. They are affiliated with universities and are less hands-on than Second Step and CDP. The PATHS research base, for instance, is considered one of several middle childhood projects in the Prevention Research Center (PRC) at Pennsylvania State University. Currently, the PRC seems less interested in trying to sell a curriculum or work with school systems to implement it, and more interested in continuing to do both applied and basic research (PRC, 2003).

The ways and means of implementing SDRG are not obvious when you visit the organization's Web site. Like the Prevention Research Center, the Social Development Research Group is located in a university and is a collaboration of researchers sharing common research goals. For these programs, success is not measured by selling a curriculum; instead, like most university-based research programs, they live off grants, doing practice-oriented research on system change and writing publications. The most recent intervention program at SDRG, for instance, is a 5-year study designed to test the effectiveness of the Communities That Care system, an intervention designed to reduce violence, drug abuse, and dropout while fostering healthy development by working at the community level (Hawkins & Catalano, 2003). The outcome research will be funded by several federal agencies (i.e., the National Institute on Drug Abuse and the National Institute on Mental Health) and will involve the participation of treatment and control communities across seven states (SDRG, 2004b).

So, what program did the Gilmore eventually choose? As it turned out, the Massachusetts Department of Public Health awarded $5 million to the Boston Public Schools to implement a district wide violence-prevention program. Senior administrators decided that Second Step was the best fit for the targeted schools in the city. Funds were used to bring in professional development from Second Step and to hire "social skills coaches," akin to literacy coaches, and certain schools, including the Gilmore, were selected to participate. Second Step was implemented in the district until the money ran out a few years later. Currently, neither Second Step nor any other prevention program is in use at the Gilmore. Second Step's principles seem to have disappeared, like many other reform efforts that fail to thrive in urban schools. Although Second Step may still be used in other Boston schools, at the Gilmore we have not seen it in action, nor has it been spoken of by any of the teachers in recent years.

The ending to this story suggests that the implementation process at the Gilmore was less than ideal. Unfortunately, this may be all too common in "disorganized" schools, where there are schoolwide discipline problems, high rates of suspension, low student attendance, and low faculty morale (Gottfredson, Jones, & Gore, 2002). It is disappointing, yet not surprising, that mental health intervention programs are often less successful precisely in the contexts where they are most needed. The implementation of school-based programs can vary widely from school to school and even from classroom to classroom. When the Resolving Conflicts Creatively program was implemented in New York, for example, some teachers taught the program frequently and with fidelity to program goals. Other schools and teachers did not embrace the program as enthusiastically. The dosage and level of buy-in of the program at the classroom level had an effect on the success of the program at the student level (Aber, Brown, Chaudry, Jones, & Samples, 1996; Aber et al., 2003; Brown, Roderick, Lantieri, & Aber, 2004).

Recently, Wandersman and his colleagues (Wandersman & Florin, 2003; Wandersman, Imm, Chinman, & Kaftarian, 2000) have come up with an approach to program implementation, Getting to Outcomes (GTO), that suggests positive outcomes depend on several factors. They have devised a fairly comprehensive list of accountability questions that need to be asked before, during, and after program implementation and they map out the steps from conducting a needs assessment to evaluation program success and sustainability.

It is important, for example, to look at who makes the decisions about implementation. One of the problems at the Gilmore was the extent to which the school bought into the program. It was unclear, for instance, whether Second Step was a program that met the school's needs (as the faculty and staff would describe them), or whether it was something that someone else (in this case, the district) told them they had to do. One question that should be asked, therefore, is What is the best process for working with schools and communities in the decision-making process?

For instance, although the teachers and administrators at the Gilmore clearly needed help, they tended to respond to individual crises as they emerged rather than develop plans to anticipate and solve behavioral problems at a school level. When the district sent Second Step to the school, it is doubtful the faculty saw the program as one with which they needed to partner. Too often, outside programs are viewed either with skepticism (as yet another reform effort with which schools must comply and that will go away eventually) or as a magic bullet that will immediately and easily solve all their problems. The Gilmore may also have realized that not all schools in Boston received Second Step and felt like the poorly performing sibling in the school district family. Assessing a school's readiness to participate in prevention programs seems to be an important preliminary step to implementation that is often overlooked (Brown, Roderick, Lantieri, & Aber, 2004; Wandersman et al., 2000).

A second important issue Wandersman et al. (2000) point out is that all prevention programs need to have diverse streams of funding. By relying entirely on funds from the Massachusetts Department of Public Health, the Boston school district seemed to have set themselves up for disappointment: The program ended when the funding ran out. Sustainability is a term we hear often in the field of mental health, particularly as it applies to prevention and evaluation, and the challenges of sustainability are evident in the failure to keep the program in place at the Gilmore.

Sustainability, however, refers not only to funding, but also to the ability to train teachers and faculty successfully in the program. Ideally, if the school embraced Second Step fully, and if the program was successful, the teachers would not need any additional funding or coaching to continue the program at the school. The program's pedagogy would be embedded in the day-to-day classroom practices of the teacher and reinforced by the overall school climate. The school would then "own" the program and in time maybe even forget that they learned these ideas from Second Step in the first place. Clearly, then, extensive training and skill at the teacher and school level is needed for prevention programs to achieve desired outcomes (Brown et al., 2004; Gottfredson et al., 2002). However, this can be especially challenging in environments where teachers have experienced burnout, are skeptical of new ideas coming from the top, and where typical classrooms are characterized by off-task time and poor student attendance (Gottfredson et al., 2002).

Urban schools face tough issues at the individual, district, and national levels. We hope the Gilmore School's case points to the persistent gap that still exists between research and practice and the challenges we face when we try to bridge this gap. There is a strong need for applied researchers to work in close and ongoing partnership with the sites where they work.

The Tension of Research, Practice, Service, and Training

When we first began working with the Gilmore School, we, too, had our own agenda. On the one hand, we wished to provide a training site—a practicum—for master's-level practice-focused students who wished to gain experience working in schools and with children. On the other hand, we also wished to gain a foothold within the school to further our own research. Basic research in clinical and developmental psychology, after all, needs not only participants but also new ideas. The Gilmore, along with other schools in the Boston system, was an active environment within which we could conduct research.

Like many similar research/practice partnerships, our plan may seem colonialistic. We intended to "take" from the Gilmore—to do research within its walls—and in return we would "give" service provided by our interns under supervision. Both parties agreed to the idea; in fact, the Gilmore administration was happy with the quid pro quo approach. The organizations that provided funding for our project literally and figuratively bought into our plan, as did all the necessary university organizations (e.g., human subjects review) through which any research project has to progress.

Although we intended to work within the Gilmore doing research, truthfully the opportunity to provide a practicum site for master's-level interns was a primary goal. From Mr. Martinez's perspective, the Gilmore would receive both the practical experience of free (or at least, no direct cost) interns and the expert advice of a university partnership. Mr. Martinez's teachers, however, were skeptical of our arrival. They questioned what "services" interns could provide in 1 year—would they be helpful, or would their presence translate into more work for the teachers? The status of a university partnership was not a plus for the teachers; they felt they were under enough scrutiny to improve children's academic performance without interns and/or researchers giving more advice or taking their time.

At the time, it did not occur to us exactly how the Gilmore would contribute to our thinking or be more than a context in which to provide service and conduct research. In the years since we first entered the

Gilmore, however, we have begun to question the stance with which we entered the partnership. We also began to wonder about broader, discipline-wide assumptions regarding the relationship of research to practice. In the fields of child and adolescent psychology (and psychiatry), how can the experience and knowledge of the practitioner, whose primary mission is the healthy development and education of children and adolescents, best be integrated with the expertise of the researcher, whose primary mission is to generate fundamental knowledge about development during childhood and adolescence? Can we serve in both these roles? What part, then, does the applied researcher play?

We realized that certain basic issues, such as knowledge about the development of pathways of individuals from different social backgrounds, or the relationships among thought, language, and action in social relationships, are of interest to both researchers and practitioners alike. However, although both groups share a common interest in improving outcomes for children, very often the communication among these professions—how one can learn from the other—could be improved. As a discipline, we need to connect the researcher's scientific knowledge of childhood and adolescence with the practitioner's everyday experiential and clinical knowledge of children and adolescents. We need the practitioner's role of "consumer" and the researcher's role of "knowledge producer" to shift to one of true "partner," each learning and teaching one another.

To bridge this gap, in our second case we continue to examine how researchers build connections with practitioners and policymakers, using the Gilmore School as our context. However, we shift our focus from the first case, where we put ourselves in the position of the practitioner: specifically, diagnosticians and prescribers of research-based interventions. Now, we take the perspective of practice-based researchers, whose interests are both fundamental and applied. As applied developmental psychologists, we are interested in the degree to which the promotion of self and social awareness as individual competencies in childhood can serve as psychosocial protectors against negative life outcomes such as mental illness and prejudicial attitudes, as well as ways to optimize human development and potential. As fundamental researchers, we are interested in studying psychological and social development in all its complexity. Often, the fundamental researcher receives inspiration from practice to study social processes and problems, while the applied researcher focuses on ways to design and evaluate approaches to solve them. Yet, in both instances, we are interested in the interdisciplinary and interprofessional collaborations that best serve the interests of children growing up.

> Nothing which is true or beautiful or good makes complete sense in any immediate context of history; therefore we must be saved by faith.
>
> —Reinhold Niebuhr (1952)

CASE STUDY 2: PRACTICE-EMBEDDED RESEARCH—MOVING FROM RESEARCH TO PRACTICE TO POLICY AND BACK AGAIN

The second case in this chapter tells the story of our current intellectual journey from research, to practice, to policy and back again to research. By using our own work as examples, we do not intend to aggrandize our initiatives but to demonstrate why we conceptualize the partnership of research and practice in the prevention field differently from the way many researchers, as well as practitioners in this field, tend to think about it. It has often seemed to us as though our expedition—from research to practice to policy—has been like a metaphorical set of travels along a tidal river.

Over the past 30 years, a loosely formed collaborative we call the Group for the Study of Interpersonal Development (GSID) has studied the development of social and ethical awareness in children and their links to social action and conduct, always in conjunction with efforts to promote them. Our earliest efforts focused on the psychological treatment of those youth who already were burdened with severe psychiatric disorders and psychological problems (Selman, 1980; Selman & Schultz, 1990). Subsequently, we adapted these approaches to youth who were identified (targeted) as at risk for these psychological difficulties (Selman et al., 1997). For the past decade we have focused on primary or universal prevention, often working with students in schools (Selman, 2003; Selman & Adalbjarnardottir, 2000; Selman et al., 1992, 1997). Like the four programs profiled in the first part of this chapter, we were researchers embedded in practice, although less driven by the needs of practitioners as oriented toward them.

Our most recent preventative strategy was to integrate the promotion of children's social competence directly into the heart of mainstream education—into the academic literacy practice—as a way to prevent social isolation and miscommunication (Selman, 2003). Up until this point, our model had been used to understand one-on-one social interactions between two individuals, for example, interpersonal development. By moving our ideas into a curriculum, we hoped to scale up our intervention and see if and how it applied to intergroup development, that is, children's understanding of relations within and between groups such as those from different cultures and identity groups.

Our method of delivery was to identify high-quality children's literature, in particular stories that have powerful social themes, and to design research-based teachers' guides for these texts.[3] The books were chosen to appeal to students who come from diverse backgrounds, and the guides focused on exercises to promote students' social understanding and skills. Books were selected and accompanying guides were designed for grades K–6 (Selman, 2003).

In the late 1990s, we began working with Angela Burgos, a fifth-grade teacher at the Gilmore, as she implemented the literacy curriculum that incorporated reading comprehension, vocabulary, and writing skills as well as a heavy dose of social skills training and social awareness promotion. We wanted to know whether our framework was effective, whether it would be supported by evidence, and whether it would have a detectable effect on practice. We were primarily concerned with steps 1 through 3 of the IOM model: We had an idea about the scope (incidence and prevalence) of the problem, we wished to explore it in depth, and we had designed several pilot studies to begin the research process. As part of our partnership with the Gilmore, the school became the context in which we would explore our ideas.

When we entered this partnership and we adapted the developmental framework—a guide for understanding children's social development—to a practice-based method of literacy instruction, this represented to us a modest flow from theory to evidence, then to practice, and then back up the river again to theory. We had made this kind of journey twice before; in fact, the theory

of peer relationships and interpersonal development stemmed from years of going back and forth between practice and research (Selman, 2003).

This time, we started in the knowledge pool at the confluence of developmental, cultural, and social psychology and flowed down toward the delta of practice. Specifically, we were interested in exploring whether our framework of children's social development could help promote students' comprehension of stories they read during language arts classes. Could the lessons students learn from reading literature that deals with social justice, for instance, influence their own lives? Alternatively, does their own understanding of social issues influence their comprehension of these stories? These were the questions that guided our research in the Gilmore School.

As we demonstrated in our first case, when we entered the Gilmore—expecting to apply our model, provide service, collect some data, and return upstream to our laboratory for analysis—we were unprepared for the reality of doing applied research in schools in today's educational climate. For example, we ran into a confluence of political and policy issues, such as the increasing focus on literacy standards, the No Child Left Behind Act, and the economy of the state of Massachusetts and its influence on school budgets. A multitude of political and research agendas were waiting to divert funding and attention away from our interests. The day-to-day decisions faced by the Gilmore School, like many schools across the United States, not only would affect the individual students and teachers within the school, but were representative of the wider concerns facing the educational community and the role of developmental and cultural psychology in contributing to this field.

We did not, however, hold the conviction that we were the experts. We did not naively believe that our research could remain "uncontaminated" by political, economic, and social forces. Although intellectually we understood that contexts such as family, neighborhood, and environment played a role in the development of social competence, we knew we did not fully comprehend the extent to which a school's climate, the concerns of its teachers, and the complexity of a school system could have an impact on the children. We viewed developmental psychology as the domain of the individual, not the school system, but hoped through the application process to learn more about the link between the two.

Nevertheless, in our work at the Gilmore we experienced an identity crisis that was relevant to ourselves as

---

[3] Our partner in this endeavor was Voices of Love and Freedom (VLF), a literacy-based character education program based in Boston under the direction of Patrick Walker. See Selman (2003) for more information on VLF.

well as the larger field of child psychology. Were we basic researchers who happened to work in a school? Or were we applied researchers with a strong theory and research knowledge base? These are simple questions to ask, but not so easy to answer. Although many of us in the field of developmental psychology might be reluctant to admit there is a gap between these two identities, we often run into instances that challenge this assumption. In the field of social development, for example, there are many well-published applied researchers whose research interests center on designing, applying, and evaluating prevention and intervention programs. The work of this group of researchers is highly prized by practitioners because they can easily translate their research into practices that may quickly and directly improve the lives of children. On the other hand, a different group of researchers may do groundbreaking basic research in cognitive science that could someday have implications for improving practice, but they have little expertise in talking with teachers about how to improve students' social competence, little knowledge of social policy, and little experience in working with children. Which type of research is more valuable in today's environment? What type of researcher did we wish to be? Could one be both?

This case is designed to reframe this dichotomy. Instead of choosing sides in the debate, we have struggled to maintain both identities. Doing so has not been without its challenges, as we will point out, but we have found that the rewards of bridging this gap have far outweighed the problems. By keeping a foot in both camps, we have learned to appreciate what both the applied and the basic researcher bring to the field.

From Research to Practice: The Integration of a Theory of Interpersonal and Intergroup Development into a Literacy Curriculum

We worked with Angela Burgo's class for several months in the late 1990s as she implemented the literacy/social skills curriculum. Following the IOM model, we collected data (step 3) in the form of videotaped classroom discussions, teacher interviews, and homework. The following passages come from one of the books we selected to use in this approach. The excerpt is from a novel chosen for fifth grade, *Felita*, by Nicholasa Mohr (1979, pp. 36–37), which tells the experiences of a third-grade Puerto Rican girl and her family living in New York City in the late 1950s:

I stood on the stoop, watching the group of girls I had seen from my window. They had stopped playing rope and were now playing hopscotch. . . . They were having a good time, using bottle caps and keys to toss on the chalked squares. Hopscotch was one game I was really good at.

"Hi! Hey you!" a girl with short brown hair and glasses wearing blue jeans called out. "You wanna play with us?"

The first chapter of the novel introduces the young narrator, Felita, and her friends and family, who live in a neighborhood in Spanish Harlem. Although Felita is reluctant to leave this neighborhood, her parents are intent on moving to a place with better schools and safer streets. In Chapter 2, Felita and her family move to a new neighborhood where few Puerto Rican families live. Once there, Felita faces the awkwardness of making new friends and attending a new school. Understandably, she is nervous. She begins to play hopscotch with some girls on her street in the new neighborhood, but their parents do not welcome this new girl from a strange (Spanish-speaking) family into their community. The children's initial friendliness turns into hostility and aggression once they fall under the influence of their parents, and a painful confrontation takes place.

The other girls all huddled together with the grown-ups. They all spoke in low voices. I waited. Were they coming back to play? They all stared silently at me. . . . Suddenly I felt frightened and all alone. I wanted to get home, upstairs, where I would be safe with Mami. . . . Now the adults and girls were standing in a group beside the stoop steps. As I approached my building, I lowered my eyes and quickened my pace. I figured I would walk around them and get up the steps as fast as I could.
Thelma quickly stepped in front of me, blocking my way. "Why did you move here?"

"Why don't you stay with your own kind?" Mary Beth stood next to Thelma.

As I tried to get by them the other three girls ran up the stoop and formed a line across the building entrance. I turned toward the grown-ups. Some were smiling. Others looked angry.

"She should stay in her own place, right, Mama?"

"Can't you answer? No speak the English no more?" The grown-ups laughed.

". . . so many colors in your family. What are you?"

"Her mother is black and her father is white."

"They ain't white . . . just trying to pass!"

"Niggers."

"Shh, don't say that."

"All right, spicks. God only knows what they are!"

"Let me through!" I screamed.

"Nobody's stopping you." Mary Beth and Thelma stepped aside.

I took a deep breath, tried not to cry, walked up the stoop, and began to push past the other three girls blocking the entrance.

"Watch it!" They pushed back, shoving me down a couple of steps.

"Mami!" I looked up at the window. No one was there. "Let me go by!" I shouted.

I pushed again. I felt a sharp punch in my back and a fist hit the side of my face. Then a wall of arms came crashing down. I began to cry hard.

"Mami . . . Mamita . . ."

"Here now. That's enough!" a man said.

"Let her go," a woman shouted. "She knows now she's not wanted here. Girls, let her through."

As I ran past, someone pulled at my skirt and I heard it rip. I ran up three flights of stairs, crying until I was safe inside my apartment. I made sure the front door was bolted behind me. I ran right into Mami's arms.

The first day *Felita* was introduced, Ms. Burgos encouraged her students to consider, "What is a neighborhood?" The class had a conversation about what it means to be part of a neighborhood and what it would feel like to move to some place new and unfamiliar. They drew pictures of their own neighborhoods, pinned them up on the wall, and learned from Ms. Burgos about the history of Puerto Rican immigration to specific communities in the United States. The children engaged with the book and connected it to their own personal experiences.

A few days later, Ms. Burgos asked her students, "How do you think Felita feels about moving to a neighborhood where there are no Puerto Rican families?" The question, and the discussion that developed, was particularly meaningful to this class of Spanish-speaking bilingual students, most of whom were recent immigrants. During the next 2 weeks, the students participated in learning activities centered on incidents like the one described earlier in Chapter 2, as well as those in Chapter 3, when Felita and her family painfully decided to move back to their old neighborhood because they could no longer endure the discrimination.

From the beginning, Angela Burgos's class was riveted by Felita's story. We discovered that to the fifth graders in the class, *Felita* did not always read like a work of fiction. For these children, whose school is

in a neighborhood that had one of the highest immigration rates in the city, and who were referred to as the "Spanish class" by other fifth graders in the school, Felita's tale was relevant and personally meaningful.

As observers in this classroom in Boston, we saw how powerfully the children engaged in the story, and how the teacher connected the novel to her students' personal lives. We also realized that children seemed to vary in their understanding of the characters' motivation and had different suggestions for dealing with the conflict. Some children supported the family's decision to move back to their old neighborhood. Others felt they should have stayed and fought the discrimination. These observations led to the formulation of several questions: What accounted for the variation we observed? Were some of the students more sophisticated in their understanding of the issues faced by Felita's family? If so, how could we systematize and validate our intuitive observations of developmental differences among the students in the class?

When we first developed a strategy for promoting social competence in the literacy curriculum used by Angela Burgos, we relied on a theoretical model of psychosocial understanding grounded in developmental theory and basic empirical research. The model delineates children's developing awareness of the linkages between the challenges or risks they face (e.g., the risk Felita takes in challenging her persecutors) and the important social relationships in their lives (e.g., Felita's family and the community in the new neighborhood; Adalbjarnardottir, 2002; Levitt & Selman, 1996; Levitt, Selman, & Richmond, 1991; Selman & Adalbjarnardottir, 2000). It analyzes the development and connection of three psychological components of social awareness:

1. The *general level of understanding* individuals have about how social risks influence and are influenced by social relationships (social knowledge).

2. The *repertoire of interpersonal strategies* individuals have available to manage these challenges (social skills).

3. The *awareness individuals have of the personal meaning* these challenges and relationships actually have for themselves: how they understand the actions they take as they relate to the quality of the personal relationships they seek to form and maintain (social relationships and values).

This theoretical model asserts that the greater one's capacity to integrate the social perspectives of oneself and others in the context of dealing with life's social challenges, the better the chances of successfully navigating social relationships (Selman & Schultz, 1990; Selman et al., 1997). Figure 10.2 depicts the connection among the components of the model in visual terms. The broadening of this figure with age suggests that with development, awareness within each of the three components becomes more differentiated. It also suggests that, with development, the components themselves become more integrated with one another, but that there can be regression as well as progression.

Each of the three components of this developmental model—the social understanding, social strategies, and awareness of the personal meaning of relationships and their risks—helped us to define questions in the teacher guides and subsequently analyze the children's responses. For example, we created reading comprehension questions that probed for each of the three theoretical components within the model. One set of reading comprehension/social awareness questions specifically investigated the students' *understanding* of

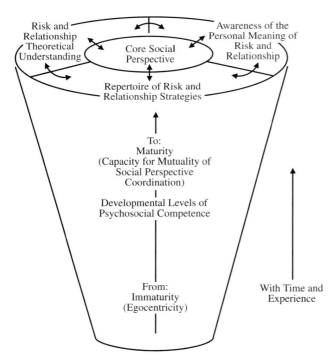

Figure 10.2   A developmental view of risk and social relationships: An analysis of three psychosocial competencies.

the connection between the social relationships and living conditions in Felita's two neighborhoods by asking the students to consider: "How are Felita's new and old neighborhoods alike? How are they different?" A second kind of reading comprehension/social awareness question focused on students' awareness of the *strategies* the family had available to deal with the conflict in which they found themselves, for example: "What is the problem Felita is facing? What can Felita and her family do to deal with the way the people in the new neighborhood treat them?" Finally, a third reading comprehension/social awareness question evaluated how the students interpreted what *personal meaning* the events in the story had for the characters—and for themselves. How did they understand Felita's dilemma when, in conversation with her grandmother, she grappled with her decision to run away from the confrontation in the neighborhood? "Felita says to her abuelita, 'I never said anything to those girls. Never. It was as if they were right, because I just walked away, you know?' What does Felita mean?"

Once we collected the responses from the students, we explored the possibility that the students' ability to understand fictional social experiences was a window into their ability to think about, negotiate, and make meaning of the social risks and relationships in their own lives. We hypothesized that students who displayed more sophisticated social perspective-coordination—the ability to connect multiple viewpoints and think deeply about the actions and motivations of the characters in the book—would also display a richer understanding of the texts they read (Dray, 2005; Selman & Dray, 2003). For example, we observed differences in the way children understood the question about differences between the two neighborhoods (the social understanding question).

Frederico, a boy with limited English proficiency, wrote the following response:

> The kitchen was almost alike. The bilden [building] was desein [designed] like the other bilden. The street of the new neighborhood was clean.

Amalia, a shy girl in the class, wrote:

> They are alike in the neighborhood because both the neighborhoods had a school and some stores. They are different in that in the old neighborhood she got friends and in the new neighborhood she doesn't.

Claudia, a soft-spoken but assertive student, wrote:

> The things that the new and old neighborhood had in common were the stores, schools and building. The difference was the people's attitudes and how they treated other people just because they speak Spanish.

As we attempted to make sense of these responses, they became our data. Because we believed we could identify differences in the ways the children responded to this question, we tackled the question of how to code the responses both developmentally and culturally. For example, with respect to developmentally oriented coding, each of these students' answers was to some degree accurate. As Frederico pointed out, Felita's new neighborhood is cleaner, and it is true that Felita's family originally moved in part because of the better physical qualities of the new neighborhood. But we noted that Frederico was focused on the impersonal qualities that contrasted Felita's old and new communities: the buildings and the streets. He did not refer to the social relationships in the story: Although the family did indeed move to the new neighborhood for the benefit of better living conditions, they moved back because of the negative social conditions (the prejudice and discrimination they experienced). Frederico's response did not (according to our coding scheme) capture the arguably more important definition of a neighborhood.

Now, compare the responses of the two girls, Amalia and Claudia. Amalia wrote, "In the old neighborhood she got friends and in the new neighborhood she doesn't." Her response acknowledged that it is the relationships among the people in each neighborhood that were most important in the story. Unlike Frederico, she was able to express her knowledge of relationships more explicitly, if not more clearly. However, we found it intriguing that Amalia looked at the people in each neighborhood from a self-referential perspective: They were either Felita's friends or they were not her friends. Claudia, on the other hand, suggested that the people in the new neighborhood *had beliefs* and *acted* in ways that prevented Felita from making friends: "The difference was the people's attitudes and how they treated other people." Whereas Amalia implied that someone is either a friend or not (as if by magic), Claudia's response suggested that she understood that the characters' internal beliefs (their attitudes) drove their actions (how they treated people).

She further implied that perhaps these attitudes and actions were influenced by the perception of the group Felita belonged to, a group seen by parents and kids in the new neighborhood as being different and unwelcome. From our theoretical perspective, Claudia's response displayed a more complex understanding of how people become friends and the importance of trust and actions in forming relationships. By enlarging her view to encompass intergroup relationships, she indicated a more sophisticated social awareness.

From Practice Back to Research: The Theory and Promotion of Social Awareness

What do we mean by "social awareness"? Until now, our theory had been successful in investigating social relationships, usually one-on-one interpersonal relationships such as friendships (Selman & Schultz, 1990; Selman et al., 1992, 1997). But, as we realized that some children displayed an interpretation of the text that went beyond a *social* understanding to a *societal* understanding, we reexamined our original ideas. What if the theory of social development that had attempted to explain children's understanding and strategies within friendships could be expanded to help explain their understanding and strategies for solving questions of social justice? This was a shift for us from not just using research to support effective practice, but allowing practice to inspire theory and research.

For example, we found that two other students took their analysis of the neighborhood differences one step further. They pointed out qualities they believed the girls in Felita's new neighborhood lacked. The words they used to describe these qualities were striking to us:

> They are alike because they both are calm neighborhoods. They are both different because the people there (in the new neighborhood) have a hard heart and they make spanish people miserable. (Juan)

> In the old neighborhood they have the hopscotch game. The houses are the same sides. [In the new neighborhood] kids don't respect adults. There is no respect for each other. There are selfish people. (Rosario)

Rosario and Juan, unlike Amalia and Claudia, looked beyond specific actions and attitudes to identify the important internal and enduring feelings of the people in both neighborhoods that contrasted them: respect, selfishness, and "hard hearts." Juan, for instance, demonstrated to us that he perceived correctly that the girls' dislike of Felita originated from their dislike of anyone Spanish. Unlike Amalia, Juan's understanding of the conflict went beyond just seeing the girls as being "friends" or "not friends." He was able to express a level of awareness that included a cultural perspective on the qualities of the neighborhoods. Similarly, Rosario captured an essential meaning of prejudice: that people do not respect each other's differences.

As we examined the responses to *Felita*'s reading comprehension questions, we focused on several developmental research questions: Were the students able to describe how the people in the neighborhoods differed in their attitudes toward Spanish speakers? To what did they attribute these differences? Did they see it simply as a problem of Felita "having friends" or "not having friends," or did they really understand the complexity of prejudice in the story? We began to write our answers down, and in doing so, we began to create a set of rubrics designed to code social awareness (Selman & Dray, 2003).

It is important to step back for a minute to consider the broader implications of these data. In the IOM model we discussed earlier, research and theory feed into practice: The flow goes from the knowledge pool of research to the delta of practice, with practice being the beneficiary of good research. But here our primary prevention program (the literacy infused with social awareness curriculum) was hit midstream with a whirlpool, so to speak. Our original theory of interpersonal development did not easily map onto the intercultural and intergroup responses given by the children. So we did not try to force it to fit; instead, we listened to our data and attempted to make sense of what the students described to us.

From Awareness to Practice: How Children Learn Strategies of Coping with Discrimination

Thus far, we have analyzed how the children comprehended the differences between the two neighborhoods using a developmental analysis. Next, we questioned how they would solve the discrimination the family faced in the new neighborhood. We did not as yet know how their understanding would translate into actions:

How would the students solve the problem Felita and her family actually faced?

Embedded into the curriculum were exercises that allowed the students to practice their social problem solving and interpersonal negotiation skills. One worksheet was called, "ABC: Ask, Brainstorm, and Choose." The students were instructed to "ask" what the problem is, "brainstorm" different ways to solve it, and then "choose" the solution that is best in this particular situation. This type of exercise is fairly common to conflict resolution curricula and is similar to the "stop and think" exercises of Second Step (Committee for Children, 2005).

One kind of fundamental social-cognitive research that underlies this type of exercise conceptualizes the link between social thought and action as a series of information-processing steps, from defining the problem to evaluating the outcome (Coie & Dodge, 1998; Dodge, Pettit, McClaskey, & Brown, 1986). This approach attempts to understand or predict behavior at any particular moment; it is in this sense *proximal*.[4] Our developmental method tends to examine both conduct and the way children make meaning of it over time and is thus more *distal*. These two approaches are not mutually exclusive but instead are complimentary in their methods of explaining behavior in the moment and over time and across children (Selman, Beardslee, Schultz, Krupa, & Podorefsky, 1986).

As part of our data collection, we videotaped the students as they role-played and worked through the exercises. As we expected, the students' responses to Felita's dilemma were illuminating. After about 3 months in Ms. Burgos's class, the students trusted their teacher enough to say what was on their mind—what they really thought as opposed to what they thought she wanted to hear. The class had been instructed to work through the ABC exercise on their own for homework and they would discuss the exercise as a group the following day. That morning, Ms. Burgos called on one student, Luis, to present to the class his homework assignment from the night before. We were on hand with our video recorders to capture the responses and the ensuing discussion.

Luis read the first question on his homework assignment, "What is the problem Felita is facing?" He paused

---

[4] As recounted by K. A. Dodge in 2004 in personal conversation with the first author.

for a moment and then declared, "Felita is facing the problem of living in the new neighborhood and getting insulted by other people." Then Luis read the next question on the sheet, "What advice would you give to Felita to deal with and cope with the difficult situation?" Luis briefly looked up from his homework before replying, "I would advise Felita to ignore everybody and get on with her life."

On the videotape, it is clear this suggestion went over with the rest of the students like a lead balloon. An awkward silence fell over the class as Luis's classmates exchanged knowing smirks and eye rolls. In the class discussion that followed, under Ms. Burgos's careful guidance, we found that most of the students disagreed with Luis's suggestion to ignore the provocation. Instead, most of the students strongly felt Felita's family should do something—anything—in response to the discrimination they experienced.

What strategies did the students choose to handle this conflict? Based on the videotapes and their homework assignments, we identified four thematic groups of responses:

1. *Fight back:* If someone pushes you, push them back (e.g., "call the police," "beat the bullies up for doing that," "ask friends from the old neighborhood to help beat up the bullies"). Most of the boys fell into this category.

2. *Retreat:* Walk away from these situations (e.g., "move back to the old neighborhood," "play with friends in the old neighborhood," "move back to Puerto Rico"). Many of the girls fell into this category.

3. *Ignore:* "Felita should ignore the problem." Only Luis chose this strategy.

4. *Organize:* Rally support to protest the injustice. "Have a celebrating differences day." One girl, Juanita, suggested this option.

Any researcher in social psychology could interpret these children's responses based on his or her own theoretical and interpretive framework. A clinical perspective, for instance, would look to Luis's biographical life experiences to help explain his reaction. We knew, for instance, that in fact Luis had lived in a homeless shelter and had been exposed to life on the streets. Using this type of analysis, Luis's response may be considered adaptive in that he learned that the best strategy to resolve conflicts is avoidance. From a cultural or gender

perspective, it is worth paying attention to how the girls tended to cluster together around the theme of "go back to the old neighborhood," whereas most of the boys preferred the "beat up the bullies" strategy. Cultural psychologists would note, too, that these children are Latino and either are recent immigrants or children of immigrants. That type of analysis would look to the cultural values and preferences rooted in these children's own lives, and their family histories, for explanations of their behavioral strategies. It would also compare Angela's class to other classes.

Using our framework, we began by identifying two main themes in the responses: "forget about it" and "push them back." The "forget about it" category (the left column in Figure 10.3) included a range of options: move back to the old neighborhood, ignore the girls and maybe they will leave you alone, and walk away from the conflict and reflect on it so that you can make a better decision in the future. We called these responses "self-transforming" because they recommended that Felita and her family walk away from the situation (at least at first) by avoiding it, moving back to the old neighborhood, or giving the situation some time and thought.

In contrast, the "push them back" category (the right column in Figure 10.3) included responses in which Felita and her family would take outward action toward the girls and the families in the community.

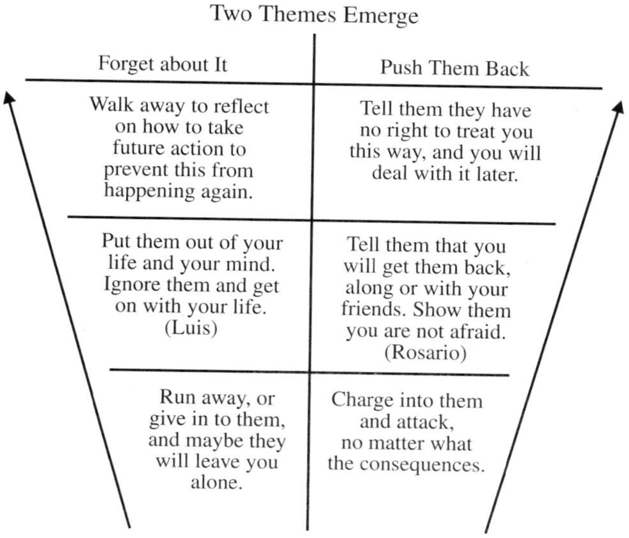

Two Themes Emerge

Forget about It	Push Them Back
Walk away to reflect on how to take future action to prevent this from happening again.	Tell them they have no right to treat you this way, and you will deal with it later.
Put them out of your life and your mind. Ignore them and get on with your life. (Luis)	Tell them that you will get them back, along or with your friends. Show them you are not afraid. (Rosario)
Run away, or give in to them, and maybe they will leave you alone.	Charge into them and attack, no matter what the consequences.

Figure 10.3   Developmental and thematic framework.

These actions ranged from "beat them up immediately" to "get friends from the old neighborhood to beat them up" to "tell them they have no right to treat us this way." Using either words or behavior, this group of responses preferred taking action rather than spending time reflecting on or avoiding the conflict.

However, there is also variation within each thematic group. From our developmental perspective, some responses seemed to be more mature than others. For example, comparing the responses in the "forget about it" column, we felt that reflecting on the problem was more appropriate than ignoring it. Similarly, talking over the problem within the community (a "push them back" option) was preferable to beating them up. Therefore, the widening of the cone in Figure 10.3 reflected by the side arrows illustrates a broadening of perspectives being taken into consideration and a subsequently more developmentally mature social understanding of the problem and strategy.

Why This Type of Analysis Matters

Our interpretation of the students' responses to the reading comprehension questions was intriguing for several reasons. First, it offered a new insight into our preexisting theory: that how children develop an understanding of interpersonal relationships could be broadened to include an awareness of cultural and societal forces. We could identify differences in the children's understanding of Felita's story, and our model of understanding the development of social relationships could classify these differences.

Second, our method of assessing social awareness—through reading comprehension questions in literature—offered a new way to study how children comprehend social situations. In addition to observing behavior and conducting interviews, we could investigate how children make meaning and negotiate social situations through their responses to questions about fictional characters in novels. Combined with the more traditional methods of assessment, this was another tool in the study of the development of social competence, one that integrates well with practice.

Finally, the application of a developmental theory of social awareness (and research that supports it) to the fields of language arts and literacy was important because it suggested the possibility of mutually supporting literacy and social awareness development in children. Of course, the idea that multicultural literature can be used to teach children about their own lives is not new.[5] A variety of programs that teach social skills through literacy have been integrated into schools recently (Developmental Studies Center, 2004; Educators for Social Responsibility [ESR Metro], 1999; Leming, 2000; Narvaez, 2001; Walker, 2000). For many schools, the programs may be a solution to their dilemma of needing to promote literacy, yet not wanting to sideline social skills. If we could come up with a way to assess children's social awareness reliably, then we could work as a discipline toward promoting it. Instead of literature simply being the vehicle through which social relationships are introduced, it could become a mechanism for deepening understanding.

However, these ideas are not without challenges. For instance, we still do not know whether what we captured was a more developed awareness of interpersonal and intergroup relationships, or simply more advanced literacy skills. Literacy researchers, for example, would point to the bilingualism of the students as a factor in their understanding of the novel; perhaps Rosario had better language skills than Frederico and therefore could read and communicate her ideas more fluently in English. In our analysis, we primarily interpreted what we believed the children meant to say. We hypothesized that although many students, including those who were bilingual, would not be sophisticated enough in their writing or reading skills to use the word "prejudice," they knew when they experienced it. However, not everyone would agree with this interpretation. Whether children's social awareness can be disentangled from language and literacy remains to be seen.

Finally, even if we could conduct research that would adequately disentangle the effects of language and literacy skills from the reading comprehension assessments, and if we found ways to validate that in fact we were capturing social skill and understanding, we wondered about the implications of this type of analysis. Would practitioners adopt it as an effective method of teaching

---

[5] See, for example, the Developmental Studies Center's programs, such as Character Development and Academic Competence through Literature; the Yale University School Development Program developed by James Comer; the Collaborative for Academic, Social and Emotional Learning at the University of Chicago, Illinois; and the Reading, Writing, Respect, and Resolution program based out of the Educators for Social Responsibility in New York City.

social skills? How would this method of assessment fit within the more traditional psychological methods of behavior observation, measurement, and interviews? What level of professional and teacher development would be needed to teach the awareness that we considered to be essential? We decided these were important questions to be explored.

From Policy to Practice: Where the Promotion of Social Awareness Fits within Educational Policy in the Field of Literacy

We decided to first tackle the question of language and literacy. Could existing research in reading comprehension explain what we identified in the students' responses—their social awareness? How should we begin to validate our coding? To answer these questions, we needed to do some research in the field of language and literacy—not the usual home of social developmental psychologists.

We discovered that the field is one of the most closely watched and researched domains in education. Faced currently with one of the largest growth spurts in immigration in the history of the United States, the demands of the labor market for jobs requiring a literate workforce, and a widening gap between the wealthy and the very poor, policymakers (and politicians) have responded to these changing social demographics with a focus on academic achievement for all (Bronfenbrenner, McClelland, Wethington, Moen, & Ceci, 1996). The importance of creating a literate nation has become one of, if not the most important goals of education (Hill & Larsen, 2000; MacGinitie & MacGinitie, 1986; Sarroub & Pearson, 1998; Snow, Burns, & Griffin, 1998).

We also discovered that reading comprehension is an important area of research and practice. Although decoding has been acknowledged as a critical step in reading development, researchers and practitioners have come to realize that even the most fluent readers do not necessarily comprehend well (Snow & Sweet, 2003). Good comprehenders not only are skilled decoders but also can navigate different types of texts (Walpole, 1999). When students read fiction, they need to learn how to make inferences about characters' motivations and feelings. They also need to comprehend plot developments that result from characters' actions (Oakhill & Yuill, 1996). Students with good comprehension actively make connections between what they currently read and their background knowledge. They monitor

their own understanding and work to make meaning of the author's ideas (Spires & Donley, 1998; Vacca & Newton, 1995).

Yet, despite knowing what good reading comprehension looks like in action, trying to teach it well or assess it effectively remains a challenge (Snow & Sweet, 2003). Trying to disentangle children's content knowledge (what they actually read about) from their reading skill in assessments is no easy task. In fact, our attempt to figure out how much of what we captured was social awareness versus literacy skill is similar to questions of background knowledge and comprehension confronting literacy assessments.

The Massachusetts Comprehensive Assessment System (MCAS) is one example of how reading comprehension has become an indicator of acquired literacy skills. In the Commonwealth of Massachusetts, as in many states, the recent educational reform movement has focused much of its considerable energy and funding on improving academic achievement by raising literacy standards. MCAS exams are used to identify areas of improvement in individual students, teachers, schools, and districts. Across the state, teachers, principals, and superintendents work hard to prepare students for the yearly MCAS exams. "Teaching to the test" has become an everyday phrase, and teachers not only admit to structuring curriculum and classes according to the MCAS standards, but are in fact expected to do so. The exams are a fact of life in Massachusetts, and a bar all students (including Angela Burgos's) have to jump over to move to the next grade and to graduate. A single test has become a very high-stakes measure indeed, for students, parents, and school professionals.

Outside of Massachusetts, the Stanford Achievement Test (Harcourt Educational Measurement, 1997) is a widely used national measure that evaluates writing and reading comprehension across grade levels. It attempts to assess how well the student understands the story as a whole, connects relationships among ideas, considers why and for whom the story was written, comprehends character's motivations, and understands setting and plot. Assessments such as the MCAS and the Stanford series have broad goals. But often, the objectives of the assessments are distilled into short-answer reading comprehension questions that rarely probe beyond the main idea of a paragraph or passage (Sarroub & Pearson, 1998).

For example, in Figure 10.4 the Stanford Nine (Harcourt Educational Measurement, 1997) tries to determine

---

Reading Selection:
Faster Than the Wind, by Lois Grambling.

Somewhere near you lives a boy like Peter. Peter is in the fourth grade. It takes him a long time to do his work at school, and often he needs help with it…But Peter always does his best. His family taught him that.

Every afternoon when school is over, Peter runs to his house… Peter likes to run. He feels good when he runs, because his legs do what he wants them to do. His arms and feet do too. The wind hits his face and blows his hair. When he runs, Peter feels as if he is flying…

One day, Peter's big brother told Peter that he should try out for the school track team. His brother said the team needed fast and steady runners…All that day, Peter thought about it…The next day, Peter ran over to the track field to try out for the team.

Some things are different for Peter…Peter gets home from school late now, but his family doesn't mind. They're proud of Peter, who may be slow at doing some things, but is faster than the wind when he runs.

Comprehension Question:
Peter's family says that he is faster than the wind. What does that mean? How do you know that?

Coded Responses (with our corrected spelling) from low (bottom) to high (top) levels:
"That means in figurative language it means that he can run very fast. I know that because it would be impossible for a human to run faster than the wind."

"Faster than the wind means he runs very very fast. Because he runs and so if he runs fast his parents use that expression to say he is a fast runner."

"Peter can run very fast. It is a comparison."

"It means that he runs fast because he runs everywhere and he runs on the track team Peter likes to run. Because I read the story and that's what it says Peter runs fast also because he like to run and has good practice at it."

Figure 10.4 An analysis of a short-answer reading comprehension coding rubric from the Stanford Achievement Test 9/e scoring guides. *Source:* From *Stanford Achievement Test Series*, ninth edition, [Technical data report], by Harcourt Educational Measurement, 1997, San Antonio, TX: Author.

if children in the fifth grade can understand the meaning of a "figurative phrase" such as "run faster than the wind." Reading comprehension requires being able to understand literary devices such as figurative phrases; if children cannot utilize these expressions, they will not learn to communicate deeply. We applaud instruction guided toward developing children's capacity to read well, but we cannot help but feel something can be added to the type of assessment represented by the Stanford Nine approach.

One difference in our approach is our theoretical and practical perspective. A social awareness approach focuses on the comprehension of the *understanding, management, and personal meaning* of the powerful challenges inherent in the social and societal relationships in fictional as well as biographical stories. Therefore, our method of assessment needs to be based on narratives where these challenges in social relationships are the primary themes. Traditional measures of reading comprehension contain elements we consider particularly important, such as understanding character motivations, traits, and thoughts (Vacca & Newton, 1995). However, our coding and analysis also tries to capture how deeply the student can see beyond the literal meaning of a text and grasp the personal meaning of the social situations experienced by the characters.

Developmentally speaking, we argue that fifth grade is an important time for learning the kind of social issues raised by texts such as *Felita*. Every day, the students in Angela Burgos's class experience conflicts with each other, with their family, and with students in other classes. It is inevitable that such experiences engage the students' energy and their attention. We cannot ignore this energy; their ideas about relationships will affect their social behavior. Instead of avoiding socially charged themes, as traditional assessments may try to do, we embrace them.

Of course, there are risks to the approach we advocate. For instance, children have to read across different subject areas and need to comprehend texts about science as well as about social relationships (Snow & Sweet, 2003). We don't want to overemphasize our approach and ignore the need for a balanced research agenda in reading comprehension. Our method is not the only way, nor is it all these students need for literacy skills.

A second concern is that we may misdiagnose students using this method of assessment. For example, we could underestimate what they are capable of understanding, or we may mistake differences in cultural beliefs about social issues for variation in social and cognitive development. It is important that we understand and research the ways people from various cultures and backgrounds, with diverse beliefs and values, would infuse Felita's story with different meanings and interpretations.

These risks and prospects suggest a challenge for research and theory. The potential pitfalls and opportunities suggest the need for a next round of research to fill in the picture of what students at different ages and from different backgrounds understand of social issues in stories. We need to return to the area of fundamental research to consider the issues that were raised when we moved into the world of practice.

Reviewing the Map: The Institute of Medicine Principles in Light of the Two Cases

The two cases we have provided, the Gilmore School and Angela Burgos's classroom, are snapshots from the first two phases of our journey from research to practice, and from practice to policy. We return now to our original topics: the role of the Institute of Medicine's Prevention and Intervention Cycle (Mrazek & Haggerty, 1994) and the relationships between practice and research, both fundamental and applied.

In the first case, the school in distress, we illustrated how basic research in psychology (clinical, developmental, social, and/or cultural) can be integrated into programs that may help turn a school around in its approach toward social behavior and school climate. We introduced four programs that are very successful in integrating research with practice. All rest on a foundation of theory and research and all have been outcome-evaluated. By describing the people at the Gilmore to you, we hoped to illustrate how practitioners experience the everyday world of social relationships in school and the challenges they face in trying to sift through research to find the answers to their essential problems.

The second case, the story of Felita and our interpretation of the children's reading comprehension questions, illustrates how even basic research can be, and should be, influenced by contextual issues such as classroom atmosphere and systemic issues such as educational policy. With the current focus on academic standards, social development and character education programs are often sidelined or integrated into content areas such as history or language arts. In our example, reading and social development seem to be a natural fit. But without a structured research plan of how the children's responses and participation in the program can be assessed, we will never know how influential are books about multiculturalism, prejudice, or interpersonal conflicts on the development of children. Nor will we know how to assess the role of teachers. We must have faith that basic research, no matter how modest in relation to the forces of practice, will be of some value. Therefore, our own research agenda has changed direction, becoming more basic as opposed to applied, and

we are currently engaged in designing a new pilot study that may help us disentangle more clearly the role children's literacy skills play in understanding stories of social justice.

In its report on prevention research, the IOM recommended that comprehensive initiatives in this field be guided by five principles (Mrazek & Haggerty, 1994). Consider the two cases we have described in light of each of these characteristics. The first principle is to have clearly specified theory-linked hypotheses to guide both the intervention and the methods of evaluation. Both cases fit this requirement. In the case of the Gilmore School, each intervention program we described had its own underlying research base in the risk and resilience field; all shared an interest in promoting children's social and emotional competence and reducing the risks of conduct disorder, violence, and other social behavioral problems. In the second case, Angela Burgos's class, our working hypothesis was that literacy programs that focus on reading, writing about, and discussing books with powerful social themes and issues will promote better abilities in fundamental academic skills such as reading comprehension and writing. We also believe these programs may improve children's abilities to deal with adversity, risk, and injustice in their lives, such as negotiating conflict, developing self- and social awareness, and expressing their own point of view. In both cases, these theory-driven hypotheses were not just tested once, but require both the continual design and implementation of a range of practices as well as ongoing basic research.

The second IOM principle is that interventions should strive to randomly assign participants to well-defined conditions, where there are clearly specified manuals to guide the intervention and methods to constantly monitor the fidelity of the way the intervention is provided or delivered (Mrazek & Haggerty, 1994). This guideline may work better in models where the target participants are individuals with identifiable disorders or risk factors, although with enough resources evaluation studies at the classroom or school level can be undertaken (Solomon et al., 2000).

The third principle is that potential participants in intervention (or clinical) trials should be fully assessed prior to their (random) assignment to one of the conditions in the study. In addition, once under way, the study should have well-specified measures of expected outcomes that are objectively rated. Here we see an interesting difference in the cases. In their research, the investigators of each program profiled in the first case set up two conditions, participation and nonparticipation, and explored the evaluation literature for the kinds of measures that could objectively (with validity/reliability) measure the effects of each program. The best available measures in the field were imported into the study for use, and the outcomes captured.

In the second case, the pilot work has neither compared results across different conditions (steps 3 and 4) nor gone to the literature for validated measures. Instead, we went in a different direction from that suggested by the evidence in step 3. Rather than move to step 4, we returned to the empirical domain to explore our ideas, construct new hypotheses, and develop measures that could be used in a field where few objective and validated measures previously existed. We then began working on another pilot study to test the measures and our research methods. In other words, the feedback loop to step 1 occurred earlier than the feedback loop outlined in the IOM cycle. Before moving to steps 4 and 5, we needed to spend more time circling between identifying the problem, reviewing literature, and conducting pilot studies.

The final principle of the IOM model is that evaluations should continue beyond the immediate end of the intervention trials (Mrazek & Haggerty, 1994). This is a principle important not only to the model but to all research-based practice that thinks about both individuals (and populations) in developmental terms. At the Gilmore School, for example, we need to know whether cases of conduct disorder diminished over time for those who participated in the school-based prevention program Second Step. In addition, we need to better understand the economic and contextual factors that influenced its implementation. In the literacy classroom, on the other hand, we also must investigate what happened to students who got a good dose of social awareness mixed in with their reading program. In both cases, we want to know if the students were in better shape, academically and socially, than they otherwise might be 3, 5, or 7 years down the line.

Most likely, the IOM model suggests the final principle primarily to find out whether an intervention with any immediately positive effect has some kind of staying power or whether the effects strengthen or weaken over time. These compelling practice-driven questions need to be answered if they are to turn into policies. Nevertheless, this recommendation does not assume

there is some definable end to the intervention/prevention. For instance, the approaches suggested in both cases are really long-term interventions. In the case of the school-based prevention programs, there is evidence that school and individual problems cannot be solved in the short term and that the prevention needs to be ongoing. In the case of the promotion of social awareness, the ideal method of choice is to infuse this approach at every grade level. It is not a circumscribed intervention implemented in a relatively short period of time. In fact, the intervention probably should be adopted for at least 6 years, for example, from kindergarten through fifth grade, with appropriate teacher professional development, for it to be considered implemented with fidelity.

In both cases, longitudinal follow-up studies are essential. All the interventions we presented in both case studies target school-age children, and children are in school from ages 6 to 17. Clearly, there are developmental differences in how children across this age range understand the nature of and make meaning of social interactions in school. We need to study what this process looks like across ages as well as contexts such as school, social class, and cultural background. We also need to know the effect of teacher training and family and contextual interventions. Only with further, long-term, longitudinal research can any of these issues be explored thoroughly.

Nothing we do, however virtuous, can be accomplished alone; therefore we must be saved by love.
—Reinhold Niebuhr (1952)

Enlarging the Map: Connecting the Institute of Medicine Principles to the Public Policy Circle

The cases in this chapter also point to the necessity of integrating public policy into our discussion of the IOM research cycle. Initially, our point of departure was the desire to improve the mental health and social development of youth through thoughtful services. At the Gilmore School, this concern grew from our experience working with children and teachers struggling to live in and be supported in a school with a vulnerable social atmosphere. The strategy we presented was to seek outside preventive interventions from a range of options, each with its own theoretical framework and evidence base. We witnessed how the Gilmore strove to adapt to a new era of educational policy changes that enormously influenced their decision in choosing and implementing a prevention program. In the second case, our goal was to pilot-test a theory and a research-based approach to the promotion of social awareness. Our intervention did not have an empirical outcome seal of approval. Even so, we still found ourselves having to negotiate national policies on literacy assessment and instruction to do research on children's social development. Instead of being cases that simply addressed the relationship between knowledge and practice, in both instances we moved quickly to having to consider issues of policy.

In thinking about the interaction among research, practice, and policy, we have found a framework initially articulated by Julius Richmond, former U.S. surgeon general, to be very useful as a guide to locate the kind of integrative work we both describe and do, the movements we have made, and to plan our next steps. This map not only locates the work of our cases on a larger landscape, but it needs to be considered as a way to view explicitly how this kind of work evolves over time.

Throughout his 60-year career, Richmond, a pediatrician by training, traveled across the worlds of research, practice, and policy in the fields of child development and child health. He has analyzed how members of the child development professions, be they researchers, practitioners, policymakers, politicians, or advocates, can be more effective in influencing public policy. In several articles, Richmond presented a three-factor model to guide child health public policy (Richmond & Kotelchuck, 1983; Richmond & Leaf, 1985; Richmond & Lustman, 1954). To explain it, we will refer to Figure 10.5.

There are three territories, Richmond claims, with which those of us who want to impact public policy in child development must gain some familiarity: (1) the analysis and development of a scientific knowledge base, (2) the analysis and development of a social strategy, and (3) the analysis and development of political will. The three must work together to develop and implement public policy.

For example, a knowledge base provides the scientific foundation on which to make health care policy decisions. Health care policy requires basic research before we can make progress toward the eradication of disease. In addition, however, Richmond and his colleagues suggest that the knowledge base must also in-

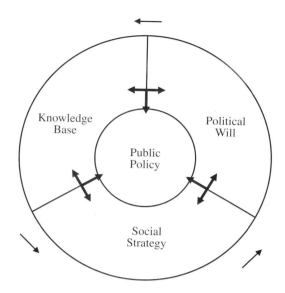

Figure 10.5   Three-factor approach to policy: The Richmond Model.

clude an understanding of the social and economic factors that encompass the health risk, the culture in which the problems exist, and the delivery systems (such as prevention programs) that work to ameliorate the risks. In other words, two kinds of knowledge are necessary: knowledge provided by the basic researcher who does fundamental research on questions related to children's mental health (e.g., the risks they face) and the expertise of the applied researcher who refines and evaluates the context and systems of delivery (i.e., the prevention programs that may work to ameliorate those risks). Without an understanding of both the health risk and the process by which our efforts will make a difference, policies will proceed incrementally in many different directions.

However, basic and applied knowledge are necessary but not sufficient to sway public policy. Knowledge must work hand in hand with social strategy. A social strategy, as defined by Richmond, is a national or international blueprint of how our goals should be accomplished. As a field, child psychology must work across disciplines and domains and bridge gaps between basic and applied research to come to agreement about the steps we should follow to achieve our policy goals. Social strategy is not in itself policy; it is simply the outline and plan of a child health or education policy (Richmond & Kotelchuck, 1983).

Finally, even when we have a strong knowledge base in an area and a blueprint for change, transformations in public policy depend on political will. How committed are we as a society to develop new programs or reinvent old ones? We need to create a process by which constituencies will be created and resources are generated to accomplish our child-care goals.

Developmental psychology as a discipline that contributes to prevention science and practice needs to contribute to the movement among all three domains, as suggested by the bidirectional arrows linking knowledge, strategy, and political will in Figure 10.5. We need to value each domain and acknowledge the contributions each make to the other. Furthermore, when activity in one domain is weak, it needs to have resources invested to strengthen it. No matter where one starts in Figure 10.5, one should not abandon that experience as one moves to a different area. Engagement in all three territories must come together before one can really influence the development and implementation of public policy.

In our case of applied social development, we now know that academic skills alone will not suffice to ensure that children will have successful lives. We realize that supportive schools lead to better academic performance (Goodenow, 1993; Larson & Richards, 1991; Wentzel, 1996; Zins, Weissberg, Wang, & Walberg, 2004), but how does one raise the consciousness among the public or decision makers that high standards in education need to include standards of social understanding and ethical conduct? How can we influence the policies faced by the Gilmore? What are the next steps our field needs to take to deepen our knowledge, map out our social strategy, and invigorate the political will?

These are critical questions our field needs to address. However, as we grappled with them in our own work, we came up with a different question we believe we needed to answer first: In Richmond's model, what role does practice play? Where is the "practice" in the three fields of the model? Is the practitioner simply the person who carries out the work of the knowledge base, or the facilitator in our research studies? Does the practitioner help map social strategy or contribute to political will?

Let us now return to our second case, the students in Angela Burgos's class at the Gilmore School and their responses to reading comprehension questions, to describe the challenges we faced when our knowledge base met the politics and practice of implementation.

The Journey from Practice and Policy Back to Research: Reversing the Direction of the Feedback Loop

While analyzing the data Angela Burgos's students provided, we realized that gaps in our own knowledge base required that we return to the domain of basic research to explore social awareness more deeply. But to do basic research, we had to stay within practice, in Angela Burgos's classroom. We grappled with fundamental ideas about what children understand by continuing to do applied yet basic research—by doing what we call "practice-based" research.

For example, we found that the most challenging question the students faced originated in Chapter 3 of the book. Several weeks after moving back to her old neighborhood, the character of Felita talked with her grandmother about the conflict with the neighborhood girls:

> "Abuelita, I don't want Mami or anybody else to know that I . . . I feel like this."
>
> "Like how, Felita?"
>
> "Bad . . . and like I can't stand up for myself."
>
> "Well, then I promise you, nobody will know but us, yes?" She smiled and hugged me real tight.
>
> "It's about when I lived in that new neighborhood and what happened to me." I told Abuelita the whole story, just like it happened. "Probably Mami told you already, but I don't think she really knows how I feel."
>
> "Now what makes you say that?"
>
> "Abuelita, I never said anything to those girls. Never. It was as if they were right, because I just walked away, you know?" (Mohr, 1979, p. 59)

We were intrigued by this part of the story, where Felita grapples with her own actions and reactions while talking to her grandmother. We wondered, what was the personal meaning of the incident for Felita? Do the students understand why Felita is upset? To explore these ideas, our reading comprehension/social awareness question was this: "Felita says to her Abuelita, 'I never said anything to those girls. Never. It was as if they were right, because I just walked away, you know?' What does Felita mean?"

This question does not just require the students to look back at a passage in the story. Rather, it probes for the levels of awareness children have of the social world around them. In a developmental framework, the responses offered insight into how the students thought about social relationships generally and Felita's situation specifically. How, then, do we interpret the students' responses—their "thoughts"?

Most students fell into one of two groups. Some believed Felita meant she was sorry she had run away from the physical confrontation with the girls, because now they thought she was chicken. Others thought Felita was upset because the girls rejected her for no good reason—she did nothing wrong. However, a small number of students believed that what most upset Felita was how she herself reacted to the neighborhood kids, and how they in turn judged what *they* had done as a function of her reaction. One student, Juanita, wrote, "Felita means when she says, '[it] is as if they were right because I just walked away you know.' She means that they had the reason . . . to beat her up because she walked away and didn't say anything while she was leaving." Although Juanita's sentence is grammatically confusing at first, she catches something most of the other children missed: Juanita realizes that Felita thinks that, because she walked away, she implicitly validated her attackers' view of their discriminatory behavior. The girls believe "they had the right" to act the way they did.

Developmentally speaking, Juanita's comprehension represented to us a deeper level of social awareness as well as a deeper level of reading comprehension, and we believe it is a level that we should strive to promote in all students as they move across the elementary grades. When we talk to educators about this analysis of how students interpret *Felita,* many initially agree with us. However, as soon as we recommend using findings like these to create developmental social awareness benchmarks, patterned after literacy benchmarks, the resolve of these educators quickly evaporates. They say, "Whoa, you can't do that." Why not?

Educators usually object for one of two reasons. One group tends to believe this type of assessment might *underestimate* the student's social awareness, or worse, that it will not recognize that there are alternative, and equally sophisticated, ways to express deeper social awareness. They are concerned that a developmental approach will incorrectly label the level of the student's expressed awareness as some fixed ability of the child. In other words, they mistakenly confuse, and hence fear, the organization of responses to classify the emergence of social awareness as a kind of *absolute* diagnosis of fixed abilities.

On the other hand, other educators have argued that even an accurate assessment of students' social awareness will not tell us how children will act when faced with similar situations. These educators want a clear path of action—a right choice—that students will know needs to be taken. They are concerned especially with giving credit to the student who develops the capacity to express an understanding of the social situation but may not ultimately "do the right thing." In other words, our approach may not emphasize absolute virtues and values. This group mistakenly confuses the ability for *reflection* with an inability to *see* the right course of action.

Frankly, we are not saying that a single method or measure can fully assess the social competencies of any particular student. Nor should we expect to predict how students will themselves behave based on what they say a character should do. The method we used in the *Felita* example accepts the limits of words to express thoughts, and subsequently, of thoughts to predict actions, and we need to acknowledge that the analysis of our observations captures only the depth of awareness that a particular student (or group of students) expresses at a particular time in that single assignment. It does not generalize to students' social development overall. Despite these limitations, however, we believe it is possible to use this approach to develop a method of measuring social and ethical awareness. The *Felita* example demonstrates why such an assessment is essential if we continue to integrate the promotion of social and ethical awareness in elementary school language arts programs.

For instance, reconsider Juanita's interpretation of Felita's comments alongside the other students' interpretations. It is very likely that Felita actually *did not* want to be seen as chicken and *did* want to be friends with the kids in the new neighborhood. However, the other students expressed less depth of awareness about why Felita later struggled with her decision to walk away and why she said to her grandmother, "It was as if they were right." Unlike the other students in her class, Juanita is aware that Felita was less concerned about looking like a chicken or losing friends and more concerned about the interpretation her antagonists would make of her not challenging the girls' opinions of Spanish people.

Accountability and Assessment

We believe the development of research-based standards for measuring students' level of social awareness will enable teachers at all grade levels to better determine how well students have acquired a deeper understanding of social and ethical issues. But the research on assessment will need to move quickly to catch up with policy. For example, as part of a network in the state of Illinois, a consortium on risk and prevention recently helped to define a set of social and emotional learning standards for students in grades K to 12 (Illinois State Board of Education, 2004). The standards focus on three goals for each of five "benchmark" levels: early elementary (grades K to 3), late elementary (grades 4 to 5), middle/junior high (grades 6 to 8), early high school (grades 9 to 10), and late high school (grades 11 to 12). The three broad social and emotional goals are to (1) develop self-awareness and self-management skills for school and life success, (2) use social awareness and interpersonal skills to establish and maintain positive relationships, and (3) demonstrate decision-making skills and responsible behaviors in personal, school, and community contexts.

However, standards are meaningless unless we come up with ways of effectively measuring whether students attained them. This is where we feel practice-based research can make a contribution. If teachers or schools were able to use carefully selected children's literature that reiterated themes from personal identity to social responsibility, they would be able to analyze students' responses to key questions to study how social awareness grows in each student over time.

In addition, if teachers had an empirically validated map that located students' responses to meaning-oriented questions about social awareness on a developmental continuum, they could determine how well the whole class understands the complexity of social issues via a particular book in the literacy program and be able to assist those students who need additional help in developing and understanding their own social awareness. The teachers we have worked with have been fascinated by the prospect of interpreting their students' writing beyond a straight literacy analysis. They well understand that promoting social awareness requires students to understand the meaning these characters make of social events in their lives. They know that students cannot—or will not—always say what they mean, but that practice sharing their thoughts about difficult social issues through writing and discussion is an essential step toward making that connection. Frameworks that organize their students' responses would be very helpful to this practice.

Teachers also know that fostering students' mature social conduct, either in the moment of a critical incident or in relationships over time, is not something that happens as a simple and direct effect of promoting their capacity for social awareness. Both social awareness and social actions fluctuate, and they continue to change depending on conditions in the social atmosphere. But systematic analysis of children's writings on these matters provides one necessary scale for assessing those changes and fluctuations, even if it should not be used as the only indicator.

When students write about what Felita means, the material can be used in multiple ways: as worksheets for teachers to use to evaluate their literacy and social awareness skills, by teachers to assess the classroom culture with respect to intergroup conflict and its resolution, by the district for outcome or program evaluation, and by researchers as data to study basic questions such as the connection or disconnection between social awareness and social conduct or between language and thought. In addition it can be used, in conjunction with teachers and practitioners, to help come to agreement on the topic of what is social development. Practitioners can and should use our research (or at least our research methods) as a basis for coming up with their own knowledge and standards of social developmental growth.

All these initiatives, taken together, constitute what we mean by practice-based research. We did not have to retreat upstream to the usual laboratory location of the basic researcher to create knowledge. Instead, we tried to commit to doing the type of rigorous scientific theory building and research that is necessary to understand children's social competencies while also being sensitive to the needs of the teachers and the complexities of the Gilmore School. Of course, this process is far from easy. It is difficult to relinquish control of our standards of what is developmentally mature or best for the Gilmore School and allow practitioners to engage with us in a dialogue about what is appropriate for their classroom, their school, and their students. But if we had not been willing to listen to what the children told us in their own natural context, and work with Angela Burgos and the other practitioners in the Gilmore School, we would not have been able to gain the inspiration we needed into our own work to move it to the next level of its own development.

Developing Our Knowledge Base: Triangulating Research with Practice

The need to link research to practice is a rhetorical mantra in the field of child psychology that has been repeated often enough to lose much of its meaning. Of course we must link research to practice, we say. We make our regular obeisance to this truth, then go back to doing whatever research (or practice) we were doing before. It may be that the phrase "linking research to practice" is too common and hackneyed to be rescued at this point. Instead, we will argue that there are at least three ways that one could be working at the intersection of research and practice, three possible conversations between researchers and practitioners that could and should take place. They are represented in Figure 10.6, the research-practice triangle.[6]

In this triangle, researchers live at points A (applied) and B (basic), and practitioners live at P (practice). Clearly, however, there is movement along the sides of the triangle from one point to the next. An easy path to understand is between B and A—between the basic researcher doing work in a discipline (e.g., ways to assess and test hypotheses about the social development of children) and the applied researcher. Those who travel along this route apply theory and research to practical matters (e.g., the interpersonal competence of children at risk for depression) or work with applied researchers to design and evaluate interventions. We call this type of work *practice-oriented research.*

A second, fairly easy path to understand is between A and P—the path of the applied researchers who bring their work into the day-to-day life of practice, such as schools, teachers, and hospitals. Often, the type of researcher who bridges this gap lives in two camps, with a primary home in the applied research world and a second home in the practice world. We call this *practice-driven research;* it is akin to our first case, where the Gilmore School was in distress and needed a research-based prevention program. This type of work may also

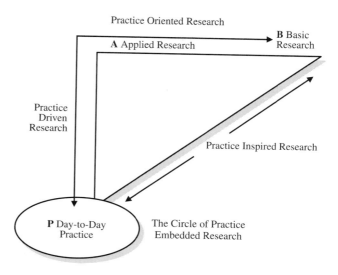

Figure 10.6 The practice-based research triangle.

be called evidence-based practice, when the emphasis is on the P to A direction, for example Second Step's need for evaluation. It is also represented in part by our second case study, when we entered Angela Burgos's classroom with an intervention program and stayed there to do applied research.

The last connection, between P and B, is often the most complicated to grasp and by far the most difficult path to traverse. We think of this link as *practice-inspired research.* It is the partnership that is possible when the basic researcher meaningfully integrates the ideas and concerns of practice and reconceptualizes his or her own research (and theory) based on this new knowledge. In Angela Burgos's classroom, for example, when we realized that our preexisting theory did not account for the complexity of children's thoughts about social issues and certainly did not take into consideration their cognitive language and literacy skills, we returned to the drawing board. We are currently engaged in the process of doing new pilot work that seeks to integrate the knowledge contributed by practitioners, language and literacy researchers, and our own field of social development in an effort to better understand how children make meaning of stories about social justice.

We have taken the risk of introducing these terms—practice-oriented, practice-driven, and practice-inspired research—to replace the old adage "Link theory and research with practice." It is the connections between the points of the triangle in Figure 10.6 that are important. The three research-practice paths have allowed us to think in alternative ways about our own work and the

---

[6] We would like to thank our colleague Catherine Snow for participating in the creation of this triangle and helping us to articulate the practice-research issues we describe in this chapter.

gaps that exist among applied research, basic research, and practice. It is not simply the task of the applied researcher to connect basic research and practice—we must find ways as a field to integrate the knowledge each brings to the domain (in our case, social development) to move forward in developing our knowledge base. Finally, we need to decide as a field how we wish to influence public policy, to create a road map for social change, and to develop the political will necessary to make that change happen.

The circle surrounding the P (practice) in Figure 10.6 also points to the merit of introducing one last term and making the case for its importance. We call this circle the zone of *practice-embedded research*. Practice-embedded research can be either applied or basic, but its fundamental feature is that it is research, as exemplified by our second case of Angela Burgos's classroom, which is located directly in the heart of the practice. Keeping in mind that in our case the social development of the child is nested in context, the social atmosphere of the classroom and school, the triangulation in Figure 10.6 of practice (P), applied research (A), and basic research (B) helped us to see that the zone of practice-embedded research is less well populated by researchers than we would like and yet probably is the area that needs to be the most integrated by researchers if child development practitioners (educators, clinicians, youth workers) are to embrace the evidence-based approaches researchers have convinced policymakers are so important.

Figure 10.6 also clarifies two matters that are obscured in the IOM model and not detailed in the Richmond model. First, although less often traversed, in this triangle there is a direct route between basic research and practice, although the waters around P are not ideal for basic researchers who seek calm and control to do their research. Second, if there was more two-way traffic along this path, it might reduce the amount of time it takes to make the translations that usually follow a path from B to A to P.

In applied research, practice is often the locale where good formative evaluation is conducted in the shifting tide between efficacy and effectiveness trials. We argue that it is also an area well suited to descriptive basic research work, for example, in social development, on what theories children at different ages and from different backgrounds have about racism and prejudice, or what they think the causes and consequences of these social phenomena are, as expressed in the natural and authentic context of the classroom. Although practice-embedded basic research may be a slower process, and it may take longer to publish in conventional research peer-review journals, we believe there is much to be said for basic researchers spending more time embedded in the circle of practice.

CONCLUSION

This chapter used a case study approach to discuss the connections among research and practice, risk and prevention, and social and academic (specifically literacy) development. We have used two complementary cases. One focused on the story of a school at risk and how it reached out to preventive interventions offered by a group of program developers who were informed by innovative applied developmental research. The other case focused on a team of academics and how we found in the Gilmore School not only a place to do applied research but also an inspiration for our own basic research and theory building.

We also presented two intervention/prevention models for the future of the discipline of psychology, specifically social development as it connects to the field of risk and prevention. The first model, the IOM paradigm, is a linear model, or in our metaphor, a downstream-upstream model, in which discipline knowledge flows down along a river from a mountain reservoir and either settles in among the practice or takes the problems and ideas inherent in the practice and returns upstream to do applied research (such as program design or implementation) or more basic research.

In contrast, the Richmond model is a partnership or integrative model. It describes an approach that encourages a commute and conversation across three domains: the knowledge base, the social strategy, and the political will. In Richmond's model, the social strategy component is not synonymous with practice; it represents neither the practice nor the applied research that will achieve desired outcomes. Instead, it represents the wider social processes that need to take place in order for the knowledge base to have an effect in conjunction with political will on policy: the "scaling up" that is necessary to achieve societal and systematic change. Similarly, political will is not specific policies that effect change but rather the momentum that needs to gather within and behind substantive knowledge and research about a problem (i.e., poverty, health care, violence) to make a lasting change in society.

We argue that the latter model is more effective than the former for influencing policy, but also that we need a triangulation of conversation within our own knowledge base between the points of applied and basic research and practice. For one thing, the power and effect of research within a knowledge base on social and societal problems is often much weaker than the researcher in the thick of the research might suspect. It is unlikely, in any field, that any one empirical study in a journal article will have a major impact. As a result, basic researchers must have faith, in Niebuhr's sense of the term: a genuine desire to continue to grow the knowledge base within a particular discipline despite the realization that any individual contribution most likely will be modest, even if and when it attracts temporary attention. We continue to have faith, however, that over time the evidence will build up.

As researchers, both applied and basic, we also continue to hope: to persist within a discipline where progress is measured not in even increments but rather fits and starts. Enduring progressive social policies are rarely implemented in the lifetime of one professional generation; instead, it takes a continuous stream of individuals, each having hope as well as faith that his or her contribution will be beneficial. Even if, as Niebuhr says, "nothing worth doing can be done in one lifetime," the process of engagement with others toward a common cause is mutually transformative, inherently developmental, and worth doing.

Finally, both researchers and practitioners need love: the continued formation and development of ongoing partnerships that work together to promote both applied and basic research and effect change. If nothing else, in the years of doing applied research we have learned that one group can't do it alone. Researchers need practice in the same way that practitioners need research. Ultimately, applied and basic researchers as well as practitioners belong to the same camp in the Richmond model: We all contribute to the knowledge base of our domain, whether by conducting experimental research in laboratories, working with teachers in schools, or providing direct service to children.

We can envision a time when the story of the two cases we presented in this chapter might someday come together—when the basic research on social awareness we do in the Gilmore might actually help the school with its day-to-day problems. But, at this moment in time, we want to use the images these two cases project as a background to end this chapter with some tough questions

our analysis of these cases raised. There are three themes that speak to professional roles for the future. The first illuminates the gap between practice and applied research, the second demonstrates the disconnection between applied and basic research, and the third exemplifies the gaps between basic research back to practice (the biggest gap to bridge).

Although the connection between applied research and practice might in theory be the easiest to traverse, it has its own set of problems. As we pondered the dilemma of the Gilmore School and the prevention and intervention programs designed to ameliorate the school's problems, we questioned how we would go about bridging the gap between practice and applied research in developmental psychology. For instance, do you have to be a practitioner first to develop effective intervention programs?[7] Are the gaps between the two groups more easily bridged by those who have worked in both domains? We believe the answer to this question is no, but more applied developmentalists need to find work commuting between applied research and practice in the same practice context.

There is a precedent for this model in academic medicine. Teaching hospitals are settings for both research and practice. Clinical investigators do research on the problems faced by individuals and also direct the practices that provide services for them. But hospitals (and federal agencies such as the National Institutes of Health) have to offer strong incentives to practitioners to pull them away from practice to clinical research. In our first case of the Gilmore School, if it had been an affiliate of a school of education, then the principal, Mr. Martinez, could have had research objectives as well as practitioner duties. Although this may not be realistic across all elementary schools, perhaps it is not so unrealistic to have a few such principals and schools in place. Advanced training in (applied) developmental psychology would be one good kind of training experience for a clinical investigator (or a school practitioner). Experience in practice would help the applied researcher foresee problems of implementation; experience in research

---

[7] For an accessible story of one psychosocial investigator in the field of prevention, in this case child and adolescent depression, who began in practice as a child psychiatrist, learned risk research in order to study epidemiological risk factors, designed a pilot intervention, conducted a random assignment efficacy study, and moved toward the challenge of effectiveness studies, see Beardslee (2002).

would help the practitioner do a better job of understanding issues of accountability and evaluation.

There are also tensions affiliated with the connection between basic and applied research. In Richmond's model, the knowledge base includes both basic research about the health problem and understanding of the influences of contextual factors and the effectiveness of different preventive measures. Too often, however, when we think of the knowledge base of a domain, we tend to consider only the scientific, cognitive, or biological issues that need to be fully explained before we can begin to think about the surrounding context and/or systems of prevention that will help ameliorate the problem. As represented by the IOM model, for instance, the flow of knowledge seems to indicate that the applied researcher should first learn from the basic researcher, then apply research to practice, and then immediately evaluate it, not necessarily swim back upstream to the area of basic research.

Applied researchers can be frustrated by basic researchers who seem disconnected from real-life needs and concerns; correspondingly, basic researchers may not be concerned with the applications of their work and/or may be unwilling to consider doing research that is too messy or contaminated by practice and applied settings to test fundamental hypotheses. Our questions to bridge this gap are therefore these: How does one keep doing both basic and applied research at the same time, and even in the same place? What kind of value has to be given to applied research in the area of basic research, and what type of basic research, albeit messy and sometimes not very experimental, can and should be published, simply because it contributes novel ideas taken from applications? What kind of bridges can we build across institutions and departments (e.g., from a school of education to the department of psychology or to the interdisciplinary field of human development) to create places where conversations about similar topics are encouraged?

Finally, we are left with the gap between practice and basic research. Too often, practitioners fail to recognize or value the contribution of research that is at first glance far removed from the day-to-day issues they face. For example, they may overvalue the insights provided by their peers and underestimate the knowledge provided by research. Or they are so focused in the moment, on the daily needs of their students, children, or clients, that they are not willing or able to step back to look across a field of research to find out where they should go or what

they should do next. Similarly, basic researchers may be so concerned with the perhaps minute process of conducting their own research that they cannot distance themselves enough to recognize the valuable contributions practitioners can make to their work. Alternatively, they may follow a research agenda of their own, instead of being reconnected to what is actually needed by the field.

Of course, sometimes the nearsightedness of both practitioners and basic researches is exactly what the field requires. We need basic researchers to follow seemingly incomprehensible trains of thought because often this creativity (or simple doggedness) can lead to the next big breakthrough. We also need practitioners to be responsible for the daily needs of our society, not lost in some abstract world of their own. But without some kind of dialogue, or at least recognition of the value of each to the other, our field (on a macro level) will never fully traverse the practice-research triangle. As in the Richmond model, the discipline needs to constantly move among the three points to make progress in expanding our knowledge base. With this type of knowledge development, we will move confidently forward into the realms of social strategy and political will to affect the type of change that will move the fields of risk, prevention, and social development into the future and create sustainable, well-considered policy changes.

REFERENCES

Aber, J. L., Brown, J. L., Chaudry, N., Jones, S. M., & Samples, F. (1996). The evaluation of the Resolving Conflict Creatively program: An overview. *American Journal of Preventive Medicine, 12*(Suppl. 5), 82–90.

Aber, J. L., Brown, J. L., & Jones, S. M. (2003). Developmental trajectories toward violence in middle childhood: Course, demographic differences, and response to school-based intervention. *Developmental Psychology, 39*(2), 324–348.

Adalbjarnardottir, S. (1993). Promoting children's social growth in the schools: An intervention study. *Journal of Applied Developmental Psychology, 14*(4), 461–484.

Adalbjarnardottir, S. (2002). Adolescent psychosocial maturity and alcohol use: Quantitative and qualitative analyses of longitudinal data. *Adolescence, 37*(145), 19–53.

Auerbach, J. (Ed.). (2001). *Report to the mayor: Health of Boston 2001.* Boston: Boston Public Health Commission.

Battistich, V., Schaps, E., Watson, M., & Solomon, D. (1996). Prevention effects of the Child Development Project: Early findings from an ongoing multisite demonstration trial. *Journal of Adolescent Research, 11,* 12–35.

Beardslee, W. R. (2002). *Out of the darkened room.* Boston: Little, Brown.

Beardslee, W. R., & Gladstone, T. R. G. (2001). Prevention of childhood depression: Recent findings and future prospects. *Biological Psychiatry, 49*(12), 1101–1110.

Benson, P. L., Scales, P. C., Leffert, N., & Roehlkepartain, E. (1999). *A fragile foundation: The state of developmental assets among American youth*. Minneapolis, MN: Search Institute.

Boston Plan for Excellence. (2004, November 10). *Effective practice characteristics*. Retrieved November 18, 2004, from http://www .bpe.org.

Boston Public Schools. (2003, February). *No Child Left Behind federal law implementation: No Child Left Behind and school choice*. Retrieved October 18, 2005, from http://boston.k12.ma.us/nclb.

Bronfenbrenner, U., McClelland, P., Wethington, E., & Moen, P. (1996). *The state of Americans: This generation and the next*. New York: Free Press.

Brown, J. L., Roderick, T., Lantieri, L., & Aber, J. L. (2004). The Resolving Conflict Creatively program: A school-based social and emotional learning program. In J. E. Zins, R. P. Weissberg, M. C. Wang, & H. J. Walberg (Eds.), *Building academic success on social and emotional learning: What does the research say?* (pp. 151–169). New York: Teachers College Press.

Catalano, R. F., Berglund, M. L., Ryan, J. A. M., Lonczak, H. S., & Hawkins, J. D. (2002). Positive youth development in the United States: Research findings on evaluations of positive youth development programs. *Prevention and Treatment, 5*(15). Retrieved October 19, 2005, from http://journals.apa.org/prevention/volume5 /pre0050015a.html.

Catalano, R. F., Mazza, J. J., Harachi, T. W., Abbott, R. D., Haggerty, K. P., & Fleming, C. B. (2003). Raising healthy children through enhancing social development in elementary school: Results after 1.5 years. *Journal of School Psychology, 41*(2), 143–164.

Child Development Project. (2003, November 21). *Child Development Project*. Retrieved February 17, 2004, from http://www.devstu .org/cdp/index.html.

Cicchetti, D., & Toth, S. (1998). Perspectives on research and practice in developmental psychopathology. In W. Damon (Editor-in-Chief) & I. Sigel, & K. A. Renninger (Vol. Eds.), *Handbook of child psychology: Vol. 4. Child psychology in practice* (5th ed., pp. 479–583). New York: Wiley.

Clay, M. M. (1993). *Reading Recovery: A guidebook for teachers in training*. Portsmouth, NH: Heinemann.

Coie, J. D., & Dodge, K. A. (1998). Aggression and antisocial behavior. In W. Damon (Editor-in-Chief) & N. Eisenberg (Vol. Ed.), *Handbook of child psychology: Vol. 3. Social, emotional, and personality development* (5th ed., pp. 779–862). New York: Wiley.

Coie, J. D., Lochman, J. E., Terry, R., & Hyman, C. (1992). Predicting early adolescent disorder from childhood aggression and peer rejection. *Journal of Consulting and Clinical Psychology, 60*, 783–792.

Collaborative for Academic, Social, and Emotional Learning. (2004, September 29). *Safe and sound: An education leader's guide to evidence-based social and emotional learning programs*. Retrieved October 19, 2005, from http://www.casel.org/projects_products /safeandsound.php.

Committee for Children. (2005). *Second Step: A violence prevention curriculum*. Retrieved October 19, 2005, from http://www .cfchildren.org.

Developmental Studies Center. (2003, February 21). *Child Development Project: A comprehensive school program*. Retrieved October 19, 2005, from http://www.devstu.org/cdp/index.html.

Dodge, K. A., Pettit, G. S., McClaskey, M. L., & Brown, M. M. (1986). Social competence in children. *Monographs of the Society for Research in Child Development, 51*(2, Serial No. 213). Boston: Blackwell.

Dray, A. J. (2005, April). *The meaning children make of multicultural literature: A study of social awareness and reading comprehension*. Paper presented at the Society for Research in Child Development, Atlanta, GA.

Dryfoos, J. G. (1990). *Adolescents at risk: Prevalence and prevention*. London: Oxford University Press.

Dryfoos, J. G. (1997). The prevalence of problem behaviors: Implications for programs. In R. P. Weissberg, T. P. Gullotta, R. L. Hampton, B. A. Ryan, & G. R. Adams (Eds.), *Healthy children 2010: Enhancing children's wellness* (pp. 17–46). San Francisco: Jossey-Bass.

Educators for Social Responsibility. (1999). *The 4Rs Program (Reading, Writing, Respect and Resolution)*. Retrieved October 19, 2005, from http://www.esrmetro.org/programs_conflict.html#4Rs.

Frey, K. S., Nolen, S. B., Van Schoiack-Edstrom, L., & Hirschstein, M. (2001, June). *Second Step: Effects on social goals and behavior*. Paper presented at the Society for Prevention Research, Washington, DC.

Goodenow, C. (1993). Classroom belonging among early adolescent students: Relationships to motivation and achievement. *Journal of Early Adolescence, 13*(1), 21–43.

Gottfredson, G., Jones, E. M., & Gore, T. W. (2002). Implementation and evaluation of a cognitive-behavioral intervention to prevent problem behavior in a disorganized school. *Prevention Science, 3*(1), 43–56.

Greenberg, M. T., Domitrovich, C., & Bumbarger, B. (2001). The prevention of mental disorders in school-age children: Current state of the field. *Prevention and Treatment, 4*(1). Retrieved October 19, 2005, from http://journals.apa.org/prevention/volume4 /pre0040001a.html.

Greenberg, M. T., Kusché, C. A., Cook, E. T., & Quamma, J. P. (1995). Promoting emotional competence in school-aged deaf children: The effect of the PATHS curriculum. *Development and Psychopathology, 7*, 117–136.

Greenberg, M. T., Kusché, C. A., & Mihalic, S. F. (1998). Blueprints for violence prevention. *Book Ten: Promoting Alternative Thinking Strategies (PATHS)*. Boulder, CO: Center for the Study and Prevention of Violence.

Greenberg, M. T., Weissberg, R. P., O'Brien, M. U., Zins, J. E., Fredericks, L., Resnick, H., et al. (2003). Enhancing school-based prevention and youth development through coordinated social, emotional, and academic learning. *American Psychologist, 58*(6/7), 466–474.

Grossman, D. C., Neckerman, H. J., Koepsell, T. D., Liu, P. Y., Asher, K., Beland, K., et al. (1997). The effectiveness of a violence prevention curriculum among children in elementary school: A randomized controlled trial. *Journal of the American Medical Association, 277*, 1605–1611.

Harcourt Educational Measurement. (1997). *Stanford Achievement Test Series* [Technical data report] (9th ed.). San Antonio, TX: Author.

Hawkins, J. D., & Catalano, R. F. (2003). *Community Youth Development Study*. Retrieved October 19, 2005, from http://depts .washington.edu/sdrg/page3.html.

Hill, C., & Larsen, E. (2000). *Children and reading tests*. Stamford, CT: Ablex Press.

Illinois State Board of Education. (2004). Illinois learning standards. Springfield, IL: Author. Retrieved January 16, 2005, from http://www.isbe.state.il.us/ils.

Klein, D. C., & Goldstein, S. E. (1977). *Primary prevention: An idea whose time has come* (DHEW Publication No. ADM 77-447). Washington, DC: U.S. Government Printing Office.

Larson, R., & Richards, M. (1991). Daily companionship in late childhood and early adolescence. *Child Development, 62,* 284–300.

Leming, J. (2000). Tell me a story: An evaluation of a literature-based character education programme. *Journal of Moral Education, 29*(4), 411–427.

Levitt, M. Z., & Selman, R. L. (1996). The personal meaning of risky behavior: A developmental perspective on friendship and fighting. In K. Fischer & G. Noam (Eds.), *Development and vulnerability* (pp. 201–233). Hillsdale, NJ: Erlbaum.

Levitt, M. Z., Selman, R. L., & Richmond, J. B. (1991). The psychological foundations of early adolescents' high risk behavior: Implications for research and practice. *Journal of Research on Adolescence, 1*(4), 349–378.

Luthar, S., Cicchetti, D., & Becker, B. (2000). The construct of resilience: A critical evaluation and guidelines for future work. *Child Development, 71*(3), 543–562.

Luthar, S., & Zigler, E. (1992). Intelligence and social competence among high-risk adolescents. *Development and Psychopathology, 4,* 287–299.

MacGinitie, W. H., & MacGinitie, R. K. (1986). Teaching students not to read. In S. de Castell, A. Luke, & K. Egan (Eds.), *Literacy, society, and schooling: A reader* (pp. 256–269). Cambridge, UK: Cambridge University Press.

Mohr, N. (1979). *Felita.* New York: Bantam Doubleday Dell.

Mrazek, P., & Haggerty, R. J. (Eds.). (1994). *Reducing risk for mental disorders: Frontiers for prevention intervention research.* Washington, DC: National Academy Press.

Narvaez, D. (2001). Moral text comprehension: Implications for education and research. *Journal of Moral Education, 30*(1), 43–54.

Nation, M., Crusto, C., Wandersman, A., Kumpfer, K. L., Seybolt, D., Morrissey-Kane, E., et al. (2003). What works in prevention. *American Psychologist, 58*(6/7), 449–456.

Niebuhr, R. (1952). *The irony of American history.* New York: Charles Scribner's Sons.

No Child Left Behind. (2002). *No Child Left Behind Act.* Washington, DC: U.S. Department of Education.

Oakhill, J., & Yuill, N. (1996). Higher order factors in comprehension disability: Processes and remediation. In C. Cornoldi & J. Oakhill (Eds.), *Reading comprehension difficulties: Processes and intervention* (pp. 69–92). Hillsdale, NJ: Erlbaum.

Orpinas, P., Parcel, G. S., McAlister, A., & Frankowski, R. (1995). Violence prevention in middle schools: A pilot evaluation. *Journal of Adolescent Health, 17,* 360–371.

Prevention Research Center. (2003). *Prevention Research Center: Five Year Anniversary Report.* University Park, PA: The Pennsylvania State University. Retrieved October 19, 2005, from http://www.prevention.psu.edu/pubs/documents/Five-YearReport.pdf.

Price, R. H., Cowen, E. L., Lorion, R. P., & Ramos-McKay, J. (Eds.). (1988). *14 ounces of prevention: A casebook for practitioners.* Washington, DC: American Psychological Association.

Richmond, J. B., & Kotelchuck, M. (1983). Political influences: Rethinking national health policy. In C. McGuire, R. Foley, A. Gorr, & R. Richards (Eds.), *Handbook of health professions and education* (pp. 386–404). San Francisco, CA: Jossey-Bass.

Richmond, J. B., & Leaf, A. (1985). Public policy and heart disease prevention. *Cardiology Clinics, 3*(2), 315–321.

Richmond, J. B., & Lustman, S. L. (1954). Total health: A conceptual visual aid. *The Journal of Medical Education, 29*(5), 23–30.

Roberts, M. C., Brown, K. J., Johnson, R. J., & Reinke, J. (2002). Positive psychology for children: Development, prevention and promotion. In C. R. Snyder & S. J. Lopez (Eds.), *Handbook of positive psychology* (pp. 663–675). New York: Oxford University Press.

Rotheram-Borus, M. J., & Duan, N. (2003). Next generation of prevention interventions. *Journal of the American Academy of Child and Adolescent Psychiatry, 42*(5), 518–526.

Sarroub, L., & Pearson, P. D. (1998). Two steps forward, three steps back: The stormy history of reading comprehension assessment. *Clearing House, 72,* 97–105.

Scales, P. C., Benson, P. L., Roehlkepartain, E., Hintz, N., Sullivan, T., & Mannes, M. (2001). The role of neighborhood and community in building developmental assets for children and youth: A national study of social norms among American adults. *Journal of Community Psychology, 29*(6), 365–389.

Schaps, E. (2003). Creating a school community. *Educational Leadership, 60*(6), 31–33.

Selman, R. L. (1980). *The growth of interpersonal understanding: Developmental and clinical analyses.* Orlando, FL: Academic Press.

Selman, R. L. (2003). *The promotion of social awareness.* New York: Russell Sage Foundation.

Selman, R. L., & Adalbjarnardottir, S. (2000). A developmental method to analyze the personal meaning adolescents make of risk and relationship: The case of "drinking." *Applied Developmental Science, 4*(1), 47–65.

Selman, R. L., Beardslee, W. R., Schultz, L. H., Krupa, M., & Podorefsky, D. (1986). Assessing adolescent interpersonal negotiation strategies: Toward the integration of structural and functional models. *Developmental Psychology, 22*(4), 450–459.

Selman, R. L., & Dray, A. J. (2003). Bridging the gap: Connecting social awareness with literacy practice. In R. L. Selman (Ed.), *The promotion of social awareness* (pp. 231–250). New York: Russell Sage Foundation.

Selman, R. L., & Schultz, L. H. (1990). *Making a friend in youth: Developmental theory and pair therapy.* Chicago: University of Chicago Press.

Selman, R. L., Schultz, L. H., Nakkula, M., Barr, D., Watts, C. L., & Richmond, J. B. (1992). Friendship and fighting: A developmental approach to the study of risk and prevention of violence. *Development and Psychopathology, 4*(4), 529–558.

Selman, R. L., Watts, C. L., & Schultz, L. H. (Eds.). (1997). *Fostering friendship.* New York: Aldine de Gruyter.

Snow, C., Burns, M. S., & Griffin, P. (Eds.). (1998). *Preventing reading difficulties in young children.* Washington, DC: National Academy Press.

Snow, C., & Sweet, A. P. (2003). *Rethinking reading comprehension.* New York: Guilford Press.

Social Development Research Group. (2004a). *Raising Healthy Children.* Retrieved February 17, 2004, from http://depts.washington.edu/sdrg/index.html.

Social Development Research Group. (2004b). *Community Youth Development Study*. Retrieved October 14, 2005, from http://depts.washington.edu/sdrg/page3.html#CYDS.

Solomon, D., Battistich, V., Watson, M., Schaps, E., & Lewis, C. (2000). A 6-district study of educational change: Direct and mediated effects of the Child Development Project. *Social Psychology of Education, 4,* 3–51.

Spires, H. A., & Donley, J. (1998). Prior knowledge activation: Inducing engagement with informational texts. *Journal of Educational Psychology, 90,* 249–260.

Vacca, R., & Newton, E. (1995). Responding to literary texts. In C. Hadley, P. Antonacci, & M. Rabinowitz (Eds.), *Thinking and literacy: The mind at work* (pp. 283–302). Hillsdale, NJ: Erlbaum.

Walker, P. (2000). *Voices of Love and Freedom: A multicultural ethics, literacy, and prevention program.* Brookline, MA: Voices of Love and Freedom.

Walpole, S. (1999). Changing text, changing thinking: Comprehension demands of new science textbooks. *Reading Teacher, 52*(4), 358–369.

Wandersman, A., & Florin, P. (2003). Community interventions and effective prevention. *American Psychologist, 58*(6/7), 441–448.

Wandersman, A., Imm, P., Chinman, M., & Kaftarian, S. (2000). Getting to outcomes: A results-based approach to accountability. *Evaluation and Program Planning, 23,* 389–395.

Weissberg, R. P., Kumpfer, K. L., & Seligman, M. (Eds.). (2003). Prevention that works for children and youth [Special issue]. *American Psychologist, 58*(6/7), 425–440.

Wentzel, K. (1996). Motivation and achievement in adolescence: A multiple goals perspective. In D. Schunk & J. Meece (Eds.), *Student perceptions in the classroom* (pp. 287–306). Hillsdale, NJ: Erlbaum.

Zins, J. E., Weissberg, R. P., Wang, M. C., & Walberg, H. J. (Eds.). (2004). *Building academic success on social and emotional learning: What does the research say?* New York: Teachers College Press.

CHAPTER 11

A Developmental Approach to Learning Disabilities

VIRGINIA W. BERNINGER

This chapter provides an overview of the various disciplines that have contributed to the conceptualization, diagnosis, and treatment of learning disabilities, with a focus on the field of developmental psychology and representative contributions of this discipline, including a life-span approach. Developmental changes in expression of learning disabilities are illustrated with cases.

The contributions of linguistics and psycholinguistics are also emphasized. The unresolved issues related to defining learning disabilities for purposes of practice

Grants R01 HD25858 and P50 33812 from the National Institute of Child Health and Human Development (NICHD) supported the preparation of this chapter and much of the research reported in it.

and of research are highlighted. Recent approaches to differential diagnosis of specific learning disabilities are discussed, and research on effective prevention and treatment of learning disabilities is reviewed. The chapter ends with current challenges for the field of learning disabilities with respect to research and practice. The unresolved controversies are related to definition and effective service delivery in schools.

I am not being facetious when I characterize my line of research as studying a phenomenon—dyslexia—that schools do not believe exists and that the experts cannot define. Despite these challenges, progress is being made on the research front across the world, but many obstacles remain in translating this scientific knowledge into educational practice, for which cases in this chapter serve as reminders.

LIFE-SPAN APPROACH

Biologically based learning problems may respond to treatment but persist over development in changing forms of behavioral expression. What is initially a problem in *phonological awareness, phonological working memory,* and/or *accurate phonological decoding* (e.g., Liberman, Shankweiler, & Liberman, 1989; Snowling, 1980; Stanovich, 1986; Vellutino & Scanlon, 1987; Wagner, Torgesen, & Rashotte, 1994) may resolve or persist but is likely to become a problem in *automatic word recognition* and/or *reading fluency for text* (Biemiller, 1977–1978; Blachman, 1997; Breznitz, 1987; Kuhn & Stahl, 2003; Levy, Abello, & Lysynchuk, 1997; Perfetti, 1985; Wolf, 2001; Young, Bowers, & Mackinnon, 1996) and *spelling and written expression* (Berninger, Abbott, Thomson, & Raskind, 2001). Despite early intervention, some reading and writing problems persist (Bruck, 1992, 1993; McCray, Vaughn, & Neal, 2001; Pennington, Van Orden, Smith, Green, & Haith, 1990; Shaywitz, Shaywitz, Fletcher, & Escobar, 1990; Singleton, 1999) across development.

Case Illustrating Behavioral Expression in Early Childhood

Susan's dyslexia was first evident to her teachers at the end of second grade. A bright girl with superior oral vocabulary and background knowledge, she once told her second-grade teacher that she thought the other children were missing the nuances in the stories they read and talked about. It was only when the research team asked her to pronounce real words on a list outside story context or pseudowords that can only be decoded based on letter-sound knowledge that the nature of her reading problem was apparent: Her reading was overly dependent on guessing at words in context and on memorizing a few words without understanding how to decode unfamiliar words. These are the hallmark signs of dyslexia early in schooling. Because her school did not recognize these hallmark signs in first grade and provide appropriate instruction, Susan's written language learning came to a standstill in third grade.

Case Illustrating Behavioral Expression in Middle Childhood

Sean had the same problems as Susan in the primary grades but received special education that emphasized phonics and oral reading. He learned to read, but his oral reading was not fluent and his silent reading was slow. In addition, his written work was peppered with misspellings that reflected omissions of sounds, additions of sounds, transposition of sounds, and plausible spellings (but not for the specific word used). He often did not complete written assignments satisfactorily. However, because he could read silently with reasonable comprehension, the school dismissed him from special education services. The school did not understand that the hallmark features of dyslexia during middle childhood are persisting reading rate, spelling, and written expression problems in students who have learned to decode sufficiently well to read silently with adequate comprehension. Without additional explicit instruction in these skills, Sean floundered in the regular program.

Case Illustrating Behavioral Expression in Early Adolescence

Sam, who is in eighth grade, has the hallmark signs of dyslexia in adolescence: impaired executive functions for self-regulation of reading, writing, learning from lectures, and completion of long-term assignments. Many schools provide explicit instruction for dyslexics when they are in the early grades, but not in middle school and high school, when they would benefit from systematic, explicit language arts instruction that prepares them for the reading and writing requirements across the curriculum, study skills, note taking, and test taking. Sam, like many other adolescents with dyslexia, does not receive any explicit instruction related to his learning disability but does receive pull-out services to help him with his assignments in the regular program. However, the school wants to dismiss him from all pull-out services for special help because he passed the state's high-stakes writing test. Both Sam and his parents wanted him to continue to receive special education because he is barely passing most of his written assignments in the regular program. However, according to his school, his learning disability does not have an adverse impact on his performance in the regular program because he receives Ds and that is satisfactory progress. Moreover, because he asks too many questions and does not always raise his hand when answering questions, the school recommended that he be placed in a program for students with behavioral disabilities. They do not think that Sam's verbal IQ in the very superior range, his history of Attention-Deficit/Hyperactivity Disorder (ADHD), or test results using research-supported measures and diagnostic procedures showing that he has dyslexia and dysgraphia are reasons to reconsider dismissing him from special education. His parents are advised by special education officials that if they do not agree, they should hire a lawyer and go to a court hearing.

Sam's own story about his learning problems at different stages of his schooling is reproduced in Figure 11.1. Readers are encouraged to read this story before reading the rest of this chapter in order to understand what it is like to have dyslexia from the perspective of an affected individual during the school years.

Case Illustrating Behavioral Expression in Young Adult Years

Sharon was the first in her family to complete a college education, which she paid for by working many jobs. She did reasonably well but had an enormous struggle learning foreign languages, which has been well documented by researchers (e.g., Ganschow & Sparks, 2000) as the hallmark feature of dyslexia during the college years. Her university graduation was held up because she could not meet the foreign language requirement. She tried three times, twice with one language and once with another language (and even spent a year living in that country to learn the language). She was told by her department that there was no point in being evaluated by the disabled student services on campus because disabilities affect physical skills like walking and using one's hands. She had had a history of reading rate and spelling problems, but the public school she attended refused to evaluate her because she was so bright. Our research team evaluated her in her early adult years (3 years after she should have graduated) and documented that she met research-supported criteria for severe dyslexia. Based on the test results, we obtained permission for her to substitute an alternative course for the foreign language requirement. By the time this volume is published, she should have her undergraduate degree.

At the end of this chapter, these cases are discussed again from the perspective of how their literacy development might have been different had appropriate educational programs been in place. Appropriate educational programs include both diagnostic assessment and differentiated instruction.

SIGNIFICANCE OF LEARNING DISABILITIES FOR CHILD PSYCHOLOGY

Five domains of development have proved reliable and valid in understanding and assessing child development: cognitive and memory, aural receptive and oral expressive, gross and fine motor, attention and executive function for self-regulation, and social-emotional (Berninger, 2001). Children with mental retardation (global developmental disability) fall outside the normal range in each of these domains of development. Children with Pervasive Developmental Disorders (including Autism Spectrum Disorder) fall outside the normal range in two or more of these developmental domains. Some children have primary impairment in one developmental domain (e.g., primary language disorder). Children with mental retardation, Pervasive Developmental Disorder, or primary language disorder will have some difficulty with learning academic subjects and are unlikely to achieve at the population mean. However, there are other children who are generally within the normal range in most areas of development, but who have a specific kind of learning problem, a learning disability. If unidentified and untreated, learning disabilities can significantly impair a child's overall cognitive and social developmental functioning.

One in five children has some kind of learning disability. The most frequently occurring developmental

Figure 11.1   "My Story," told by eighth-grader with dyslexia, dysgraphia, and ADHD (Inattentive subtype).

disorder of childhood is specific learning disability in children whose development is otherwise in the normal range. Sometimes a child's problem may be specific to one academic domain (reading, writing, or math). Sometimes a child's learning problem is in aural/oral language, nonverbal reasoning, or social cognition, which affects school functioning even though none of these is a subject in the school curriculum. Sometimes a child has disabilities in more than one domain. The focus of this chapter is on learning disabilities that affect written language. Learning disabilities that are specific to reading and/or writing are among the most frequently occurring learning disabilities in school-age children and youth and have received the most research attention. Dyslexia, which was used to illustrate the

changing developmental expression of a learning disability across schooling, is only one kind of learning disability.

MULTIDISCIPLINARY STREAMS OF KNOWLEDGE ABOUT LEARNING DISABILITIES

Federal special education law in the United States specifies that multiple disciplines should be involved in the assessment and educational planning of students with learning disabilities. Some other countries (e.g., Canada and England) have comparable laws for identifying and educating children with learning disabilities. Multiple disciplines have also contributed to both research and clinical practice in the field of learning disabilities. These include neurology, experimental cognitive psychology, special education, linguistics, psycholinguistics, speech and child language, clinical and school psychology, and developmental psychology.

Neurology

Neurologists were the first to identify the extreme difficulty some otherwise normal children have in learning to read. One of the most informative introductions to the pioneering contributions of neurologists at the end of the nineteenth and beginning of the twentieth century is "The Historical Roots of Dyslexia" (Shaywitz, 2003, chap. 2). Neurology continued throughout the twentieth century to contribute, primarily through clinical studies (e.g., Orton, 1937). Now in the twenty-first century, this field continues to contribute through the use of in vivo brain imaging (scanning the brains of living children and adults as they perform cognitive and language tasks; for review, see Berninger & Richards, 2002).

Experimental Cognitive Psychology

Beginning early in the twentieth century, psychology contributed to the available literature by developing scientifically defendable paradigms for investigating mental processes involved in reading (e.g., Huey, 1908/1968). By the middle of the twentieth century, the psychology of reading had generated a wealth of knowledge about teaching children to read (e.g., Bond & Tinker, 1967; Gates, 1947; Gray, 1956; Harris, 1961), and this knowledge was transmitted in many (but not all) teacher training programs. Many schools had reading specialists who were well trained in reading (often with 60 to 90 graduate credits) and who were available for assessment, consultation, and small group instruction in local buildings. Decisions about who to test and teach and about how to work with teachers was left to specially trained professionals who were allowed to function in a flexible manner without burdensome regulations and paperwork. Unfortunately, not all schools had access to such professionals. Parents often had to turn to services outside the public school if their child had a specific learning disability in reading or writing.

Special Education

By the early 1960s, a national political movement led by parents was gaining momentum. Parents wanted to understand why schools could not teach children who had normal intelligence to read and write. This movement led to a parent-organized, landmark conference in 1963 in Chicago where Samuel Kirk (Kirk & Kirk, 1971) first proposed the label "learning disabilities." Following that conference, parents of children with learning disabilities partnered with parents of children with mental retardation to mount a national effort in the United States that culminated in the 1975 federal legislation, Public Law 94-142, that guarantees a free and appropriate education for all students with educationally handicapping conditions. Because professionals could not agree about how to define what a learning disability is (inclusionary criteria), the federal law defined it on the basis of what it is not (exclusionary criteria: It is not due to mental retardation, sensory acuity or motor impairment, lack of opportunity to learn, or cultural difference).

To support this new field of special education, the U.S. Department of Education provided funding for training programs for special educators, model demonstration projects, and research on teaching special populations of students with educationally handicapping conditions. (See Torgesen, 2004, for the history of the field of special education; see Johnson & Myklebust, 1967, and Kirk & Kirk, 1971, for a description of early conceptualization and practices in special education.) However, because "appropriate" was not defined on the basis of developmental and educational science, this legislation has often resulted in costly legal proceedings and adversarial relationships between parents and schools, without resulting in better academic achievement of students with learning disabilities. In fact, meta-analyses indicate that special education for students with learning disabilities has not been effective (e.g., Bradley, Danielson, & Hallahan, 2002; Steubing et al., 2002), especially in reading (Vaughn, Moody, & Schumm, 1998).

One reason for the relative ineffectiveness of special education is that special education teachers are not given much preservice training in the psychology of teaching reading; they also are not taught instructional practices that cover all reading and writing skills in the general education curriculum in a grade-appropriate manner from K to 12. Currently, many preservice teacher training programs advocate philosophical approaches (e.g., constructivism, which advises against explicit instruction) that are not consistent with what research in developmental science and educational science during the past 3 decades has shown is effective in teaching students with specific learning disabilities—namely, explicit instruction to bring language processes into conscious awareness. (See Berninger & Winn, in press; and Mayer, 2004, for shortcomings of constructivism in contemporary educational practices.) There is a myth that explicit instruction is skill and drill, but that is not the case (see Berninger, Nagy, et al., 2003, for examples of explicit instruction for developing linguistic awareness in reflective ways that are intellectually engaging).

Moreover, paraprofessionals, most of whom do not have specialized training in teaching reading or as much professional preparation as general educators, are increasingly providing instruction for students with learning disabilities. Many schools hire reading specialists trained outside professional preparation programs and in primarily a single method. There is unlikely to be a single program that meets the needs of all students. Children with specific reading and writing disabilities are more likely to learn to read and write if taught by professionals who are skilled in differentiated instruction; that is, they can construct programs that address all the necessary reading and writing skills at a specific stage of reading or writing development and individualize, if necessary, for specific students in group learning settings (Berninger, 1998).

In short, there are a number of unresolved problems in identification and service delivery for students with specific learning disabilities. It may not be possible to achieve the desired goals by simply legislating them; these goals probably require educating the educators as well as teaching the affected individuals (Berninger, Dunn, Lin, & Shimada, 2004; Berninger & Richards, 2002).

Developmental Psychology

In contrast to special education, which is an applied discipline, developmental psychology is a scientific discipline that contributes relevant basic knowledge to understanding learning disabilities. These contributions, which are discussed later in the chapter, include understanding rule-learning deficits; multiple levels of language; automaticity, fluency, efficiency, and timing deficits; comorbidities, normal variation, gender differences; nature-nurture interactions; life-span approaches;

prevention and treatment validity; and randomized, controlled longitudinal experiments. Many of these contributions draw on earlier and concurrent contributions from linguistics and psycholinguistics.

Linguistics and Psycholinguistics

Linguistics specifies how speech is represented in English orthography in a rule-governed (not purely arbitrary) way and documents the morphophonemic nature of English (e.g., Venezky, 1970, 1999). Although spelling units (typically one or two letters in length) generally represent speech sounds, called phonemes, in a predictable manner (alternations or a set of rule-governed options such as the /k/ and /s/ sound associated with the letter *c*), not all spellings are perfectly predictable. Much of the predictability of American spelling relies on the morphology as well as the phonology of the language; for example, signal preserves the spelling of the stem *sign*. It has also been well established that knowledge of alphabetic principle (one- and two-letter spellings that represent the phonemes) can explain the acquisition of one- and two-syllable words of Anglo-Saxon origin that occur with high frequency in reading materials in the lower elementary grades (for reviews, see Balmuth, 1992; Ehri, Nunes, Stahl, & Willows, 2001; Rayner, Foorman, Perfetti, Pesetsky, & Seidenberg, 2001).

However, knowledge of morphology is critical to the acquisition of the *longer, more complex written words* that occur with high frequency in reading materials from mid-elementary school through high school and college (Carlisle, 2004; Carlisle & Stone, 2004; Carlisle, Stone, & Katz, 2001; Nagy, Anderson, Schommer, Scott, & Stallman, 1989; Nagy, Osborn, Winsor, & O'Flahavan, 1994). From fourth grade on, students encounter in their school texts an increasing number of complex words in terms of sound-letter relations and internal structure (i.e., syllabic or morphemic structure; Carlisle, 2000; Carlisle & Fleming, 2003; Nagy & Anderson, 1984). Students who earlier struggled with mastering alphabetic principle because of difficulties in phonological processing (Liberman et al., 1989) face additional challenges in learning to recognize specific words automatically: (a) creating and linking precise phonological and orthographic representations (Ehri, 1992; Perfetti, 1992), and (b) encountering low-frequency written words frequently enough (White,

Power, & White, 1989). Students who were earlier taught phonics and may have learned letter-sound correspondences in alphabetic principle, word family patterns (e.g., -at in pat, bat), and syllable types (e.g., open and closed, vowel teams, silent e, r-controlled, and -le) may need additional strategies to deal with the complexity of English orthography (Schagal, 1992), especially in content area texts, which may have spellings unique to word origin (Anglo-Saxon, Latinate, or Greek), complex word structures, and unfamiliar, low-frequency words.

Another contribution of linguistics was demonstrating that most language knowledge is implicit (unconscious), but learning to read requires explicit instruction that brings this implicit knowledge to conscious awareness (Mattingly, 1972). Programs of explicit instruction in word decoding that draw on alphabetic principle and morphological structure have been developed by Henry (1988, 1989, 1990, 1993, 2003) and Lovett and colleagues (e.g., Lovett et al., 1994, 2000). Both programs require children to manipulate units of phonology, orthography, and morphology (see Figure 11.2). Both programs combine explicit instruction and strategy instruction and practice, which a meta-analysis showed

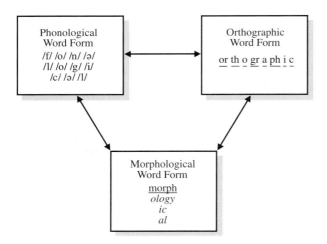

Figure 11.2 Schema of three word forms and their parts that are interrelated in decoding in working memory and creating precise orthographic word forms in long-term memory. *Sources:* From "Processes Underlying Timing and Fluency of Reading: Efficiency, Automaticity, Coordination, and Morphological Awareness" (Extraordinary Brain Series, pp. 383–414) by V. Berninger, R. Abbott, F. Billingsley, and W. Nagy, 2001, in *Dyslexia, Fluency, and the Brain,* M. Wolf (Ed.), Baltimore: York Press; and *Brain Literacy for Educators and Psychologists,* by V. Berninger and T. Richards, 2002, San Diego: Academic Press.

was the most effective approach for improving reading skill (Swanson, 1999).

Henry's (1990, 2003) program focuses on reading and spelling words from different etymological backgrounds: words of Anglo-Saxon, Romance, and Greek origins. For each word origin, students are taught linguistic units in written words (i.e., letter-sound correspondences, syllable types, morphemes). Before receiving such instruction, third, fourth, and fifth graders had letter-sound knowledge but little knowledge of syllable or morpheme patterns; the third and fifth graders who received the morphophonemic training linked to word origin improved significantly more in reading and spelling than those who received only basic phonics (Henry, 1988, 1989, 1993). Lovett (e.g., Lovett et al., 1994, 2000) validated methods to improve the word-reading skills of students with reading disabilities: PHAB/DI (direct instruction in sound analysis, blending skills, and letter-sound correspondences), WIST (four word identification strategies: using analogy, seeking the part of the word you know, attempting variable vowel pronunciations, and peeling off affixes), and Combined PHAB/DI and WIST (Phonological and Strategy Training Program [PHAST]). Clinical studies showed positive gains in reading both trained and untrained (transfer) words (Lovett, 2000).

However, the concept of how knowledge of morphological structure in low-frequency words can help students read content area texts from the fourth grade on is less widely understood. Analysis of the number of distinct words in printed school English showed that students encountered more than 88,000 "distinct" words in texts through ninth grade (Nagy & Anderson, 1984). About half the words in printed texts through ninth grade occur once in a billion words of text or less (e.g., *inflate, extinguish, nettle*), so knowledge of word-formation processes becomes necessary (Nagy & Anderson, 1984). For every word a student learns, there are between one and three related words that should be understandable to the student because of semantic transparency of words—whether the meaning of the base word is apparent in a longer word that contains that base word (e.g., *red* and *redness* have relative semantic transparency, whereas *apply* and *appliance* do not)—that reduces the number of distinct words that need to be learned (Nagy & Anderson, 1984). About 60% of the unfamiliar words encountered by students in the middle school years and beyond are sufficiently semantically transparent that a reader might be able to infer the meaning of the word from context (Nagy et al., 1989). Thus, students with reading and writing disability also need explicit instruction in the word formation processes and inferring word meaning from context.

Triple Word Form Theory

Studies that integrated treatment and brain imaging provided support for the theory depicted in Figure 11.2. Both unique neural signatures for the three word forms (Richards et al., 2005, 2006) and cross-over effects (Richards, Aylward, Raskind, et al., in press) were observed: Individuals who received *morphological treatment* showed significant changes in *phoneme mapping* during brain scans, whereas individuals who received *phonological treatment* showed significant changes in *morpheme mapping* during brain scans. Richards et al. (2002) showed that morphological awareness training improved efficiency (rate) of phonological decoding and led to greater metabolic efficiency in neural processing during phonological judgment while the brain was scanned than did training in only phonological awareness. In addition, structural equation modeling of subphenotypes in the family genetics study showed that a second-order factor modeled on indicators of each word form factor predicts reading and spelling outcomes better than the first-order factors for each word form (Berninger, Abbott, Thomson, Wijsman, & Raskind, in press). The benefits of Wolf et al.'s (2003) RAVO, an intervention that trains rapid automatic retrieval of spoken names (phonology), vocabulary, and orthography, for the reading disabled may be related to the way it integrates phonological, orthographic, and morphological word forms.

Speech and Language Pathology and Child Language

Linguistics is a basic discipline. A professional specialization for applying basic knowledge of child language is speech and language pathology. All public schools at the beginning of the twenty-first century, in large part because of the federal special education laws, now have access to practitioners with professional training in speech and language pathology. Although they primarily work with children who qualify for services under the category of Communication Disorders, many of whom have more severe problems in receptive aural language, speech, or expressive oral language than those with specific learning disabilities, they are typically the professionals in the schools with the most training in language.

Thus, they are a valuable resource for other educational professionals because children with reading and writing disabilities often have associated aural/oral language processing deficits. Developmental studies by speech and language specialists have shown that speech and language problems during the preschool years are associated with a variety of developmental outcomes during the school-age years, including (a) mental retardation, (b) specific aural/oral language impairment, (c) specific reading disabilities, (d) specific writing disabilities, and (e) normal reading function (e.g., Aram, Ekelman, & Nation, 1984; Bishop & Adams, 1990; Catts, Fey, Zhang, & Tomblin, 1999, 2001).

Clinical Psychology and School Psychology

Clinical psychology and school psychology are applied disciplines that have contributed scientific research knowledge about learning disabilities and train the practitioners who serve individuals with specific learning disabilities in the private and public school sectors. They are typically trained in cognitive, academic, social, and emotional assessment that yields relevant information for diagnosing and treating specific learning disabilities. Historically, they have relied on education to translate the assessment results into instructional practice. However, recently, there is growing interest in the treatment validity of linking psychological assessment with research-supported instructional practices (see Berninger, Dunn, & Alper, 2004). Because the federal special education law stipulates that all students with educationally handicapping conditions have the right to evaluation, whether or not they attend public schools, psychologists who work in school settings assess students attending public schools, students referred from private schools, and students who are home-schooled. However, there is a large and growing market for clinical psychologists, especially those with neuropsychological training, because many parents seek independent evaluations outside the public school. This trend is likely to increase because student achievement standards continue to increase in this era of educational accountability and are linked to high school graduation in some states.

Developmental Pediatrics

The child's pediatrician or family physician is the professional who often has the best knowledge of an individual child across development. Levine, who has been a leader in developmental pediatrics, has (a) increased awareness of the normal variation among learners (Levine, 1993, 1998, 2002), (b) demystified learning problems for affected individuals (Levine, 1990), (c) documented that many learning disabled have developmental output failure (writing problems; Levine, Overklaid, & Meltzer, 1981), and (d) emphasized that students who do not complete written work satisfactorily are more likely to have undiagnosed processing problems than to be lazy (Levine, 2003). Most students want to succeed—if only a caring, competent teacher could teach them in a way they can learn (Berninger & Hidi, in press). Because of my earlier clinical and research experience in the Ambulatory Pediatrics Department at Boston's Children's Hospital, headed by Levine, I began a programmatic line of research on normal variation as a reference point for understanding learning disabilities and focused on writing as well as reading.

CONTRIBUTIONS OF DEVELOPMENTAL PSYCHOLOGY

In this section, we highlight a few of the representative contributions of the discipline of developmental psychology to the field of learning disabilities.

Rule-Learning Deficit and Computational Mechanisms

Manis and Morrison (1985) and Manis et al. (1987) questioned whether the problems of the reading disabled in learning alphabetic principle (correspondences between letters and phonemes) reflects a more general underlying difficulty in inducing and applying rules. To test this hypothesis, Manis et al. paired words with visual symbols (arrows, squares, triangles plus dots or asterisks) so that rules were consistent across some situations but not others (as is the case in language, which tends to have predictable but flexible regularities). Their findings supported their hypothesis and are also consistent with recent brain imaging research showing activation in the fusiform gyrus (a brain region associated with pattern recognition and abstracting rules or regularities and pattern) in normal readers (e.g., Booth et al., 2003; Booth, Perfetti, & MacWhinney, 1999) and dyslexics (e.g., Richards et al., 2005). If the reading disabled have difficulty inducing the rule-governed patterns of regularities and/or flexibly adapting these as

necessary across contexts, then they are likely to benefit from explicit instruction that assists them in abstracting those regularities and applying them strategically.

Connectionist models, which simulate computational processes in the brain during written word learning (e.g., Seidenberg & McClelland, 1989), demonstrated that overt, verbally articulated rules are not necessary to learn to read written words, and that one computational mechanism may underlie regular and irregular word reading. Manis and Seidenberg (e.g., Manis, Seidenberg, Doi, McBride-Chang, & Petersen, 1996), who collaborated in longitudinal studies of how children learn rule-governed phonological decoding and irregular word reading, identified subtypes of children with deficits in decoding or irregular word reading, but the subtypes were not completely stable across reading development. Over time, regular and irregular reading may converge because phonological decoding (often assessed by regular word reading) contributes to automatic word recognition (Ehri, 1992; Uhry & Shephard, 1997), which may be assessed with real words that are regular and irregular because exception words are at least partially decodable (Berninger, 1998; Berninger, Vaughan, et al., 2002). The contribution of the connectionist models was showing that procedural knowledge (unconscious computations without overt verbalizations of declarative knowledge of phonics rules) may guide reading development. Our instructional studies apply this principle in teaching connections between letters and sounds explicitly (both out of word context and in word context) but without overtly articulating any rules (e.g., Berninger et al., 1999; Berninger, Abbott, et al., 2000).

The research on the rule-deficit and computational modeling suggests that there is a *continuum of rule-learning in reading,* ranging from (a) highly implicit to (b) moderately implicit to (c) moderately explicit to (d) highly explicit:

1. Computational procedures out of conscious awareness induce connections between spoken and written words that support reading of unknown and familiar words.
2. Through repeated practice in word reading (applying procedural knowledge based on those connections between spoken and written words), *an autonomous lexicon is created* that can be accessed automatically for specific words.
3. Explicit instruction engages children in active manipulations of spoken and written words and their parts and in the process creates conscious linguistic aware-

ness of phonemes, spellings, and morphemes (see Figure 11.2).

4. Explicit instruction in deductive application of the verbalized phonics, morphology, or spelling rules (patterns within and between written and spoken words) creates strategic readers who consciously apply this knowledge to unknown words.

For individuals without the genetic influences associated with learning disabilities (discussed later in the chapter), 1 and 2 alone may be sufficient. For many children, with or without learning disabilities, 3 and 4 may be necessary for learning to read. There are individual differences in how much explicit instruction and what kind of explicit instruction students of the same age and grade level need. One of the greatest challenges in teaching reading is to provide differentiated instruction in the general education program during early and middle childhood so that children receive the appropriate degree of explicit instruction they require for mapping spoken words they already know onto written words they are learning, and recognizing new written words that may not be in their spoken vocabulary. Preservice teachers should be prepared to assess how much explicit instruction individual children require and to provide appropriate instruction along the continuum of explicit rule learning.

Is Phonology the Only Language Deficit?

Phonological skills appear to be impaired across development in reading disability (e.g., Berninger, Abbott, Thomson, et al., 2001, in press; Bruck, 1992, 1993; Pennington & Lefly, 2001; Scarborough, 1984). At the same time, there is evidence that other aspects of language (e.g., vocabulary or syntax) may contribute to reading development and its disorders, and which is the most important may change across development (Scarborough, 1984, 1989, 1990, 1991, 2001; Scarborough, Ehri, Olson, & Fowler, 1998). However, phonological processing is complex and may refer to at least three separable skills: phonological awareness of sound segments in spoken words, phonological working memory (storing and manipulating sound units in temporary working memory), and phonological decoding (translating orthographic units in written words into spoken words; Wagner & Torgesen, 1987).

Each of these phonological processes may be related to multiple levels of aural/oral or written language. For example, aural nonword repetition (see Bishop & Snowling, 2004) may be related to vocabulary (Gathercole & Baddeley, 1989), sentence processing (Willis & Gathercole, 2001), comprehension (Montgomery, 2003; Nation, Clarke, Marshall, & Durand, 2004), and executive functions (Baddeley & Della Sala, 1996). Thus, in the complex brain systems supporting reading (Berninger, 2004a) and writing (Berninger & Winn, in press), there are *systems within systems,* and it can be misleading to attribute any complex skill to a single underlying process. Nevertheless, there are identifiable language skills that can be assessed and taught explicitly for specific reading or writing skills at specific phases in reading and writing development. If professionals are not aware that language is a multilayered, complex system (Berninger & Richards, 2002) and use this knowledge in their assessment and treatment practices, some children will be *assessment casualties,* their problems going undetected, or *curriculum casualties,* children who can learn to read but have not been taught in a developmentally appropriate way. Teaching preservice teachers about the complexities of language may prevent learning disabilities.

Rapid Automatic Naming, Fluency, Efficiency, and Timing

One of the most reliable predictors that a prereading child will have a reading disability is inability to name objects or colors (assuming the child is not color blind; Manis, Seidenberg, & Doi, 1999; Wagner et al., 1994; Wolf, Morris, & Bally, 1986). By first grade and thereafter, the time required for naming multiple rows of continuous letters is one of the most frequent concurrent deficits in individuals with reading disabilities (e.g., Wolf & Bowers, 1999) and writing disabilities (e.g., Berninger, Abbott, Thomson, et al., 2001, in press). Students who have a double deficit in rapid naming of letters and phonological awareness are more impaired than those who are impaired in only one of those skills (Wolf & Bowers, 1999). Number of deficits in phonological, orthographic, and rapid naming skills predicts severity of reading disability (Berninger, Abbott, Thomson, et al., 2001).

Rapid automatic naming (RAN) is a deceptively simple task that reflects complex processing (see Wolf & Bowers, 1999): attention to visual stimuli (colors, pictures, or alphanumeric stimuli), rapid automatic access to familiar phonological codes in long-term memory, and coordinating codes on different time scales (one visual/orthographic code and one oral linguistic code, for lexical or word-level representations) in real time (Breznitz, 2002).

Not all timing problems in reading disability involve rapid retrieval of single lexical items. Some appear to involve fluency (quick, smooth, coordinated processing of serial items), which is influenced by the efficiency of each of the language processes involved (e.g., Perfetti, 1985). A precise timing mechanism for coordinating reading processes may be impaired in reading disability (Wolf, 1999). Treatment that accelerates rate of processing appears to increase efficiency of the multiple processes involved and thus fluency (Breznitz, 1987, 1997a, 1997b).

Dyslexia (a specific kind of reading disability) may cause undue difficulty in *sustaining mental effort over time*. On the first row of the Wolf et al. (1986) RAN tasks (10 items), the child dyslexics do not differ significantly from grade norms, but on the remaining four rows of 10 items each they do (Berninger & Hidi, in press). Dyslexics appear to have an invisible difficulty in sustaining time-sensitive, goal-directed activity carried out in working memory. Many teachers have no empathy for students who cannot complete written assignments in a timely manner. They cannot directly observe this hidden disability in sustained effortful word retrieval, which is apparent on the clinically administered RAN task. In contrast, oral reading dysfluency is a publicly visible disability.

Comorbidities

Reading disability may occur with or without other learning or behavior problems. Some gifted children have disabilities in low-level writing skills that interfere with their high-level composing skills (Yates, Berninger, & Abbott, 1994) or low-level reading skills that interfere with high-level comprehension skills (e.g., untreated child dyslexics in our family genetics study). Many children with behavioral disabilities have undiagnosed and untreated learning disabilities in academic content domains and in aural/oral language (Berninger & Stage, 1996). Reading or writing disabilities may also occur along with developmental psychopathology, including ADHD (especially the Inattentive subtype) and/or Conduct Disorder (see Pennington, 2002, for further discussion of the issue of comorbidity that complicates both research and treatment and for a review of research on this topic).

Normal Variation in Reading and Writing

In contrast to comorbidities based on categorical variables, normal variation is based on quantitative traits modeled as continuous variables. *Normal variation (interindividual and intraindividual differences)* occurred in the processing skills related to reading and writing in a large, representative sample of typically developing primary grade students (Berninger & Hart, 1992). Intermediate grade students in another large, representative sample exhibited *intraindividual variation* in their profiles of word reading and text-level reading skills (Berninger, 1994) and their profiles of word choice, sentence construction, and discourse organization in composing (Whitaker, Berninger, Johnston, & Swanson, 1994). We observed *normal variation in response to the same instruction*. Berninger and Abbott (1992) documented normal variation among individual children in response to the same reading instruction across first grade. Traweek and Berninger (1997) and Abbott, Reed, Abbott, and Berninger (1997) documented normal variation in response to the same instruction during second grade. Among children who do not have ADHD, normal variation in their ability to self-regulate attentional focus and goal-directed attention uniquely predicts their ability to process the orthographic word form (see Figure 11. 2; Thomson et al., 2005).

Taken together, these various studies show that variation among learners is *normal;* the typical classroom will have students exhibiting many individual differences in processes and skills related to literacy learning. Thus, one of the pressing needs in an era of increasing expectations for high levels of academic performance is to prepare teachers to deal effectively with the normal diversity in cognitive processes among the students in their classrooms. This diversity requires a continuum of explicit instruction to create awareness of language processes. Another pressing need is to understand learning disabilities in reference to the normal variation in reading and writing acquisition (Berninger, 1994) and typical reading (e.g., Chall, 1983, 1996) and writing (e.g., Templeton & Baer, 1992; Treiman, 1993).

Gender Differences

Gender differences in reading disabilities appear to be related to referral biases (Shaywitz et al., 1990). However, gender differences do occur in writing. Typically developing boys are more impaired in handwriting automaticity and its related orthographic (not motor) skills (Berninger & Fuller, 1992; Berninger, Fuller, & Whitaker, 1996). Boys with dyslexia are impaired on a wide variety of writing skills (handwriting, spelling, written composition, and related neuropsychological processes in our family genetics phenotyping battery; Berninger, Nielsen, Abbott, Wijsman, & Raskind, 2005; Nielsen, Berninger, & Raskind, 2005).

Nature and Nurture

Although some think of the biological and experiential influences on learning and its disorders as mutually exclusive, independent factors, it is more likely that they are interacting variables. In this section, we consider studies of environmental influences, genetic influences, and then of combined brain imaging and instructional interventions to study nature-nurture interactions in individuals with learning disabilities.

Role of Education and Experience

Although developmental research historically emphasized the biologically constrained maturational processes in development, during the past 15 years there has been a more balanced approach that acknowledges the role of experience. Morrison, Smith, and Dow-Ehrensberger (1995) conducted groundbreaking school cutoff studies showing that children who just made the cutoff and entered kindergarten outperformed, during the current and subsequent years, their age-equivalent peers who just missed the cutoff. Vellutino and Scanlon's (e.g., Vellutino et al., 1996) longitudinal instructional study showed that explicit instruction could eliminate many (but not all) reading problems; these findings, based on direct manipulation of experience, added to those based on indirect measures of experience (self-reported print exposure; Cunningham & Stanovich, 1998) to make the case that instruction and reading experience matter (Morrison et al., 1995). A number of longitudinal treatment studies pointed to the same conclusion: Reading problems could be prevented or the severity of their expression reduced to a large extent with appropriate early intervention, even if children came from low-literacy homes (Foorman, Francis, Fletcher, Schatschneider, & Mehta, 1998; Foorman et al., 1996; Torgesen, Wagner, & Rashotte, 1997; Torgesen et al., 1999). Yet, close scrutiny of data showed that not all children were treatment responders

in early intervention (Torgesen, 2000) or over the course of schooling (Shaywitz et al., 2003). That is, even though most reading problems can be prevented with appropriate instruction, some will not be totally eliminated because there is a genetic (Olson, 2004) and neurological (Hynd, Semrud-Clikeman, Lorys, Novey, & Eliopulos, 1990; Shaywitz et al., 2003) basis for reading disability, which may persist throughout schooling in some form in some individuals.

Genetic Influences in Reading and Writing

Heritability studies with twins (e.g., Byrne et al., 2002; Olson, Datta, Gayan, & DeFries, 1999; Olson, Forsberg, Wise, & Rack, 1994) and family genetics studies (e.g., Chapman et al., 2003, 2004; Raskind, 2001, Raskind et al., 2005) have documented genetic influences on reading disability. Genetic influences on phonological processes and verbal working memory emerge in the preschool years (Byrne et al., 2002). These are the same two areas of functioning that we observed showed the greatest genetic influences during the school-age and adult years (Berninger, Abbott, Thomson et al., 2005; Berninger & O'Donnell, 2004). Considering these genetic influences on processes that affect ease of learning written language, students would probably benefit from learning environments that are optimally designed for their genetically influenced, reading-related processing characteristics (cf. Plomin, 1994) that include anomalies in phonological processing and working memory (Swanson & Siegel, 2001).

Brain Constraints in Infancy versus Plasticity of the Brain during Childhood and Adult Years

Electrophysiological recording in newborns identified event-related potential (ERP) components for speech discrimination of stop consonants in consonant-vowel patterns that predicted language development at age 3 and 5 and reading (including diagnosis of dyslexia) at age 8 (D. Molfese et al., 2002). Newborn ERP recordings were more isolated within brain regions, and adults showed more interactions between brain regions (D. Molfese et al., 2002). Not only brain variables but also social and other environmental variables influenced reading development at the brain and behavioral levels (V. Molfese & Molfese, 2002). Event-related potent-waveforms change as a result of training in infants and adults (D. Molfese et al., 2002).

Plasticity of Brain in Middle Childhood and Adult Years

At least nine studies, using a range of imaging methodologies, including functional magnetic resonance imaging (fMRI), functional magnetic spectroscopic imaging, magnetic source imaging, and electrophysiological recordings of ERPs, now show that the brains of beginning readers (Shaywitz et al., 2004; Simos et al., 2002), developing readers (Aylward et al., 2003; Richards et al., 2000, 2002; Temple et al., 2000, 2003), and adults (Eden et al., 2004; D. Molfese et al., 2002) change in processing related to reading in normal and disabled readers.

The University of Washington brain imaging studies have shown that the brain responds to reading and spelling instruction. The treatment that contained all the instructional components recommended by the National Reading Panel (Berninger, Nagy, et al., 2003) resulted in significant lactate reduction (increased efficiency during neural metabolism) in left frontal regions during phonological judgment (Richards et al., 2002) and increased fMRI Blood Oxygen-Dependent Level (BOLD) activation in frontal and parietal regions (Aylward et al., 2003). In both cases, pretreatment differences between dyslexics and controls disappeared after treatment. Evidence of *treatment-specific brain responding* (e.g., Richards et al., 2005) have also been observed, for example, robust changes during scanning on a spelling task following orthographic treatment but not morphological treatment in dyslexics in grades 4, 5, and 6. Richards et al. (2005) proposed a paradigm for analyzing the results of combined brain imaging and treatment studies that takes into account (a) reliability of responding in controls from time 1 to time 2, (b) significant pretreatment differences between dyslexics and controls in regions that are reliably activated in controls, and (c) significant change following treatment in those regions in the direction of normalization (activating regions that controls had activated or deactivating regions that controls had not activated).

Prevention and Treatment Validity

We conclude this section on contributions of developmental psychology to learning disabilities with an example of a programmatic line of research at the University of Washington that is grounded in theory of reading and writing development and instructional interventions for preventing and treating reading and writing disabilities. Berninger, Stage, Smith, and Hildebrand (2001) pro-

posed a three-tier model to redirect psychologists' attention from diagnosis of chronic failure in reading and writing to early intervention and prevention. The first tier focuses on screening for early intervention, similar to approaches taken to prevent developmental psychopathology and social-emotional problems (see Cicchetti & Toth, Chapter 13, and Selman & Dray, Chapter 10, this *Handbook,* this volume). The second tier focuses on ongoing progress monitoring and supplementary intervention throughout schooling. The third tier focuses on differential diagnosis and specialized treatment for those with persisting, biologically based specific learning disabilities. At each tier, randomized controlled instructional experiments have been conducted, and the assessment measures that were validated in the studies of intraindividual and interindividual differences are used as predictors of response to intervention and/or outcome measures. In contrast to many instructional studies that use convenience samples or school-identified samples, our samples are ascertained on the basis of well-defined subject inclusion criteria for individuals who are at risk or disabled in specific reading or writing skills.

Randomized, Controlled, Longitudinal Experimental Studies

A brief overview of findings is provided that is based on large-scale studies in the schools for tiers 1 and 2 and on smaller-scale studies at the University of Washington Multidisciplinary Center for Learning Disabilities (UWLDC) for tier 3. A summary of instructional design principles implemented in all three tiers follows the research review.

Effective Tier 1 and Tier 2 Reading Instruction

At-risk first graders improved more in word reading when their attention was drawn explicitly to letters in words corresponding to phonemes than to the whole word (all letters and the word name; Berninger et al., 1999). At-risk first graders learned taught words and transfer words better when taught the alphabetic principle in isolation, in word context, and in story context than when only phonological awareness of spoken words was taught (Berninger, Abbott, et al., 2000). Explicit instruction for 20 minutes twice a week for 24 lessons over a 4-month period resulted in half the at-risk readers reaching grade level by the end of the year and maintaining gains at the beginning and end of second grade; the other half reached average levels after a second dose of 24 additional, explicit lessons at the beginning of second grade and maintained the gains at the end of second grade (Berninger, Abbott et al., 2002).

Combined explicit instruction in reading comprehension and decoding led to greater improvement in word decoding than decoding instruction alone for at-risk second-grade readers (Berninger, Vermeulen, et al., 2003). Integrated reading instruction aimed at linguistic awareness, word decoding, automatic word reading, oral reading fluency, and reading comprehension resulted in greater improvement in word decoding and fluency than did the regular, balanced reading program for at-risk second-grade readers (Berninger, Abbott, Vermeulen, & Fulton, in press).

Effective Tier 1 and Tier 2 Writing Instruction

First graders at risk in handwriting improved more in handwriting legibility and automaticity than did children in the contact control group or four alternative handwriting treatments when given a treatment combining (a) studying numbered arrow cues in model letters, and (b) holding the letter forms in memory for increasing duration. All children practiced composing from teacher prompts, but only the treatment combining numbered arrow cues and writing letter forms from memory generalized to both improved handwriting and better compositional fluency (Berninger et al., 1997). At-risk second-grade spellers given instruction in multiple correspondences between units of written words and spoken words did better in dictated spelling and spelling during composition than did the control group given phonological awareness training (Berninger, Vaughan, et al., 1998). Training phonological awareness of six syllable types in English had some added value to training alphabetic principle for spelling polysyllabic words (Berninger, Vaughan, et al., 2000). Explicit instruction in alphabetic principle facilitated learning to spell structure words that were not as phonologically predictable as content words, and explicit instruction in planning, translating, and revising/reviewing led to improved composing (Berninger, Vaughan, et al., 2002).

Effective Tier 3 Treatment in the Multidisciplinary Center for Learning Disabilities

Teaching struggling readers multiple correspondences between units of written and units of spoken words resulted in greater improvement in reading than teaching a single correspondence (Hart, Berninger, & Abbott,

1997). At-risk spellers learned to spell equally well with pencil or keyboard (Berninger, Abbott, et al., 1998). At-risk writers taught integrated handwriting, spelling, and composing skills improved more in each of these skills than the controls at posttest and 6-month follow-up (Berninger, Abbott, Whitaker, Sylvester, & Nolen, 1995). Children taught content reading skills improved more than those in the wait-list control group (Berninger, Abbott, Abbott, Graham, & Richards, 2001). Morphological awareness treatment improved rate of phonological decoding more than phonological awareness treatment did (Berninger, Nagy, et al., 2003), suggesting that dyslexics in upper elementary grades need to learn to coordinate phonological, morphological, and orthographic processes to develop efficient phonological decoding (see Figure 11.2). Morphological awareness training benefited the spelling of pseudowords, and orthographic awareness training benefited the spelling of real words (Berninger & Hidi, in press).

It is never too late to remediate: Upper elementary and middle school students responded positively to instructional interventions that emphasized linguistic awareness and executive functions (Abbott & Berninger, 1999). See Hooper, Swartz, Wakely, deKruif, & Montgomery, 2002, for the importance of executive functions in writing.

Effective Tier 3 Treatment in Schools

Second graders meeting research criteria for dyslexia who used rate criteria in phonological decoding training and progress monitoring improved more in real word reading than those who used accuracy criteria (Berninger, Abbott, Billingsley, Nagy, 2001). For dyslexics in grades 4, 5, and 6, prior attention training did not transfer directly to improved written composition but did lead to greater improvement in written composition, compared to the control group, once written composition instruction was introduced for both groups (Chenault, Thomson, Abbott, & Berninger, in press). Prior attention training also improved oral verbal fluency significantly more in the treatment group that had received reading fluency training.

Instructional Design Principles for Educational Treatment for Biological Problems

All UWLDC treatment research is grounded in a *nature-nurture perspective*. Dr. Raskind, the principal investigator of the Family Genetics Study, emphasizes that the value of genetics research lies in identifying the subphenotypes that have a genetic basis so that instruction is uniquely designed to help dyslexics overcome these genetic influences. For example, based on the aggregation (Raskind, Hsu, Thomson, Berninger, & Wijsman, 2000), segregation (Wijsman et al., 2000), linkage and brain imaging results (Richards, Berninger, et al., submitted) for aural nonword repetition, all our *phonological training starts with spoken words before we introduce the same written words.* Students clap the number of syllables and count with color tokens the number of phonemes in each word to develop precise phonological word forms before they are ever shown the written form of the word.

Also, based on the finding of a unique genetic pathway for rate of phonological decoding (Chapman, Raskind, Thomson, Berninger, & Wijsman, 2003), we use *rate criteria for training alphabetic principle in "Jibberwacky" words* (our modification of Lewis Carroll's Jabberwocky) to teach children to apply alphabetic principle when meaning cues are not available; we use both accuracy and rate criteria in progress monitoring (Berninger, Nagy, et al., 2003). Children with persisting reading problems are typically assessed with pseudowords and often have aversive reactions to them. We use them in instruction in playful ways to reduce the negative affect associated with them. Another instructional design principle is *teaching to all levels of language close in time and to low-level and high-level skills close in time so that the working memory architecture works efficiently* (Berninger & Abbott, 2003).

A final instructional design principle is *externalizing cognition for purposes of overcoming limitations in working memory* and learning *strategies for self-regulation that do not require overt verbalization of rules.* Instructional approaches that externalize cognition render students' ideas visible to themselves and to others so that they can be objectively viewed and manipulated. Once cognition is externalized, students can experiment with their ideas in ways that are difficult to do internally (possibly because of overloading working memory). We *externalize cognition through cue cards that are designed to cue orthographic and phonological awareness of units in the alphabetic principle during teacher-directed instructional activities and for self-regulation during independent reading and writing activities.* (For further information, see the chapter on instructional design principles in Berninger & Abbott, 2003.)

Treatment Validity

A new approach to assessment examines the validity of assessment-intervention links. Results of the UWLDC

programmatic research are relevant to treatment validity and have been presented in a way practitioners can use in practice with time-efficient branching diagnosis, validated instructional based assessment, and multilevel profile assessment (Berninger, Dunn, & Alper, 2004). Berninger and Abbott (2003) have developed lesson plans based on the tier 1, tier 2, and tier 3 interventions.

Social and Cognitive Development

Although learning disabilities involving written language are academic problems, they have important implications for both social and cognitive development. Using the gold-standard treatment research paradigm (evaluate whether a new treatment has added value over and beyond that usual treatment), Weiss, Catron, Harris, and Phung (1999) showed that traditional psychotherapy was no more effective than academic instruction in changing mental health status. This finding implies that fostering academic learning may have positive effects on social and emotional development. Moreover, chronic cognitive learning problems can cause social problems, even though social or emotional problems are not the initial cause of the learning problems. Effective treatment may require both cognitive and social/affective components. Many research-supported approaches for fostering social/affective development in the general education program are now available (e.g., Frey et al., in press; Frey, Nolen, Van Schoiack-Edstrom, & Hirschstein, 2005; Van Schoiack-Edstrom, Frey, & Beland, 2002). Emotional coaching implemented in whole classrooms consistently throughout the school year may enhance learning by improving social relationships in the classroom (Lovitt, 2005). Likewise, interventions designed to improve social relationships between teachers and students are proving fruitful in enhancing school learning (Pianta, 1999; see Vaughn, Sinaguh, & Kim, 2004, for a review of social competence and social skills of students with learning disabilities).

ALTERNATIVE APPROACHES TO DEFINING LEARNING DISABILITIES

In this section controversies regarding how to define learning disabilities for purposes of research and of service delivery in the schools are discussed, along with recent developments that take into account response to early intervention in identifying students with learning disabilities.

Defining Reading Disabilities for Research Purposes

There is a continuing lack of consensus around the world about how to define dyslexia (one kind of specific reading disability; Chapman et al., 2003, 2004; Igo et al., 2005; Raskind et al., 2005), which may confound interpretation of results across research groups. We adopted the definition proposed by the International Dyslexia Association (Lyon, Shaywitz, & Shaywitz, 2003) in the UWLDC Family Genetics Study: unexpectedly low word reading, decoding, spelling, and oral reading fluency of neurobiological origin.

The Verbal Comprehension Factor (based on prorated Verbal IQ without arithmetic or digit span subtests) is used rather than Full-Scale IQ in determining relative criteria for two reasons. First, evidence from studies funded by the National Institutes of Health (NIH) and available at the time this family genetics study began showed that Verbal IQ (VIQ) is a better predictor than Performance IQ of reading disability in referred samples (Greenblatt, Mattis, Trad, 1990) and unreferred samples (Vellutino, Scanlon, & Tanzman, 1991). Second, since then, the publishers of the Wechsler scales recommend using factor scores rather than Full-Scale IQ in identifying students with learning disabilities (e.g., Prifitera, Weiss, & Saklofske, 1998). Also, site visit reviewers in 1995 recommended setting an IQ cutoff at the 25th percentile (standard score of 90 for a scale with a mean of 100 and standard deviation of 15) because it is well documented that prevalence of developmental disorders of genetic origin is significantly higher in children whose IQs fall in the bottom quartile of the population, and these genetic disorders may cause development to fall outside the normal range in specific developmental domains, including cognitive, language, motor, attention/executive, and/or social-emotional function, and could confound a study seeking the genetic mechanisms for a specific learning disorder that affects only written language in children whose development is otherwise normal. In addition, the NIH-funded research of Olson et al. (1999) showed that reading disabilities identified on the basis of relative criteria (low reading relative to IQ) are more

likely to have a genetic basis than those identified only on the basis of low achievement.

The size of VIQ-achievement discrepancy that we required (at least 1 standard deviation) is much less than that required by the special education law in the state where this research was conducted and that is used by other research groups, particularly in England. So that the discrepancy could not be attributed to normal intraindividual variation, we required that the achievement be below the population mean as well as discrepant from IQ on the inclusion measures for reading and spelling. This approach, using simple differences relative to VIQ and low achievement relative to the population mean, has been fruitful in genetic linkage studies that replicated others' work (Chapman et al., 2004) and identified novel chromosome sites for fluency-related subphenotypes for dyslexia (Igo et al., in press; Raskind et al., 2005).

Definitions Related to Providing Services in Schools

Berninger, Hart, Abbott, and Karovsky (1992) adopted a systems approach (of multiple component processes in the reading and writing systems) and applied the Mahalanobis statistic to determine how many students might be at risk for specific kinds of learning disabilities. Mahalanobis D^2 measures the distance a set of scores is from the centroid formed by the means of the joint distribution of the scores, taking the correlations among the measures into account. For two scores, Mahalanobis measures the distance that the value of X is from the mean of X and the distance that the value of Y is from the mean of Y, taking the XY correlation into account. In regression, only the distance of the predicted Y from the actual Y is considered. Results showed that different children were identified depending on whether only low achievement was considered or whether that and discrepancy from VIQ were both considered. We therefore took the position that flexible definitions, based on both absolute (low achievement) and relative (IQ-achievement discrepancy) criteria, were needed to meet the needs of all students in educational settings. In our early intervention, we studied any child whose VIQ appeared to be at least in the low-average range (standard score of 6 on the Wechsler Intelligence Scale for Children, third edition [WISC-III] Vocabulary subtest) and whose word reading and/or decoding accuracy was at least 1 standard deviation below the mean. However, in our family genetics research, we took a different approach based on existing research literature at the time and feedback from the site visitors, as previously explained.

We recognize that there is widespread dissatisfaction with the rigid approach to IQ-achievement discrepancy for qualifying students for special education services (e.g., Bradley et al., 2002; Lyon et al., 2001; Siegel, 1989; Steubing et al., 2002; Vellutino, Scanlon, & Lyon, 2000). Others (e.g., Fletcher et al., 1994) used other data analysis approaches to support the claim that the same children are identified for special education services whether IQ is or is not used. However, those analyses were conducted in a state that uses different criteria for identifying students with learning disabilities for special education and for dyslexia in general education. The results of the Mahalanobis analyses and procedures in place in our state lead to a different conclusion, and we are concerned that all students with learning differences are served appropriately: those with low IQs, those with high IQs, and all those in between (Berninger, 1998).

Thus, the flexibility in the recently revised federal special education law (IQ-achievement discrepancy shall not be the sole criterion for identifying learning disabilities) will allow school professionals in many states to serve students whose learning disabilities express themselves in ways that are difficult to capture in a single diagnostic algorithm and also to focus more on early intervention than in the past. The concept of response to intervention, discussed next, is relevant to the new approach to identifying children needing special help in reading and writing.

Response to Instruction

This emerging approach for defining learning disability—failure to respond to intervention—is relevant in early childhood. Rice (1913) conducted the first large-scale application of the scientific method to evaluate effective educational methods based on student response to instruction. She studied spelling instruction in classrooms throughout the United States and found that children who received 15 minutes of spelling instruction a week achieved significantly higher spelling test scores than those who were drilled for an hour or more a week. This result suggests that explicitness of instruction may be more important than intensity. Chall (1967/1996) showed that primary grade children responded better to

explicit phonics instruction than to the basals in use at that time. Brown and Felton (1990) reported evidence that explicit phonics instruction was associated with better student learning outcomes. Despite this research knowledge regarding the importance of explicit phonics instruction, many teachers in the last 3 decades of the twentieth century favored whole-language methods over explicit reading instruction. Left untreated, early reading problems persist (Juel, 1988). Thus, it was not always clear whether reading disabilities resulted from a biological basis or lack of explicit instruction.

In 1993, NIH sponsored a working conference for researchers in the field of learning disabilities at which these issues were discussed; it resulted in *New Frames of Measurement* (Lyon, 1994). Analyzing change by modeling individual growth (Francis, Fletcher, Stuebing, Davidson, & Thompson, 1991) was a theme in the NIH conference on new frames of measurement. Berninger and Abbott (1994) proposed response to intervention as a research tool to control for effects due to lack of opportunity to learn. We subsequently carried out our proposed research on early intervention in reading and writing outlined in our chapter for the conference. Results were analyzed for individual growth curves, treatment effects, classes of responses (faster and slower responses to instruction), and process measures that predicted individual response to treatment (the earlier discussed tier 1 and tier 2 interventions).

Following that conference, Slavin, Madden, Dolan, and Wasik (1996) showed that the effects of poverty and low literacy could be overcome by changing educational practice at the system level. Vellutino and colleagues (1996) showed that longitudinal early intervention in reading could eliminate most (but not all) reading disabilities. Compton (2000a, 2000b, 2002, 2003a, 2003b) documented that (a) there are individual differences prior to the beginning of instruction, (b) dynamic change occurs in response to instruction for children in general, and (c) processes such as phonological awareness, knowledge of letter-sound correspondence, and rapid automatic naming predict the slopes of individual growth curves.

From its inception (Deno, Marston, & Mirkin, 1982; Fuchs, 1986; Fuchs, Deno, & Mirkin, 1984), curriculum-based measurement (CBM) has been a progress-monitoring, response to intervention model. Unfortunately, with the widespread use of literature-based texts in the whole-language movement, it was often not possible to link the assessment to actual instruction, and CBM made increasing use of standard passages unrelated to those used during classroom instruction. Nevertheless, at a time when prevailing practices were to assess only accuracy and not rate, even though children may have either accuracy and rate reading disabilities or only rate disabilities (Lovett, 1987), CBM provided a useful fluency metric. Another contribution of CBM was that it encouraged teachers to assess student progress on a more regular basis than typically happens in the general education classroom or than is required by federal special education law (every 3 years). A new form of CBM, *instructionally based assessment,* which is more closely yoked to teacher's instructional goals and cognitive processes for adapting instruction, has been introduced (Peverley & Kitzen, 1998; Wong, 2000) and is used in the UWLDC reading and writing lessons (Berninger & Abbott, 2003). One view is that norm-referenced tests are not sensitive to change in response to instruction, but we have not found that to be the case for the explicit instructional treatments we evaluated in randomized, controlled designs. Thus, we use a mix of standardized tests and instructionally based assessments in evaluating response to instruction.

Processes That Mediate Written Language Learning

Some believe that all that needs to be done to prevent reading and writing disabilities is to teach children. Others value the importance of assessment of mediating processes and designing instruction that improves these processes in the context of comprehensive reading and writing instruction. A large body of research points to processes that are concurrent and longitudinal predictors of written language acquisition: *phonological* (e.g., Bishop & Snowling, 2004; Catts et al., 2001; Catts, Fey, Tomblin, & Zhang, 2002; Manis et al., 1999; Mattingly, 1972; Scarborough, 1998; Snowling, 1980; Stanovich, 1986; Torgesen et al., 1997; Vellutino & Scanlon, 1987; Wagner et al., 1994); *letter naming* (Catts et al., 2001), *rapid letter naming* (Compton, 2003a, 2003b; Manis et al., 1999; Meyer, Wood, Hart, & Felton, 1998; Wolf et al., 1986), *rapid switching between letter and number naming* (Wolf, 1986) or *rate* (Wolf, 1999); *orthographic* (e.g., Berninger, Abbott, Thomson, et al., 2001, in press;

Olson, Forsberg, & Wise, 1994; Schlagal, 1992); *morphological* (Carlisle, 2000; Carlisle & Stone, 2004; Carlisle et al., 2001; Nagy & Anderson, 1984; Nagy, Anderson, Shommer, Scott, & Stallman, 1989; Nagy, Berninger, Abbott, Vaughan, & Vermeulen, 2003; Singson, Mahony, & Mann, 2000; White et al., 1989); *syntactic* (e.g., Scarborough, 1990); and *attention* (Berninger et al., 1999; Thomson et al., 2005; Torgesen et al., 1999). Individual differences in *both vocabulary and phonological skills* predict whether children require teacher-directed, explicit instruction to respond optimally to instruction (Connor, Morrison, & Katch, 2004). Just as medical professionals now screen newborns for markers of medical disorders that can be prevented (e.g., mental retardation or other handicaps due to phenylketonuria, thyroid deficiency, RH factor incompatibility), so should educational professionals now screen children during early or middle childhood for marker processes associated with specific reading or writing disabilities and, when necessary, provide supplementary or specialized instruction with frequent progress monitoring (assessment of student response to instruction) and instructional adaptation as needed.

Developmental Expression of Dyslexia Subphenotype(s)

Which of the processes that impair written language learning in early or middle childhood are impaired throughout development? In a dyslexia phenotyping study based on families who were enrolled after a major revision in the test battery, we sought the developmentally stable, impaired processes. Based on relative criteria (for VIQ) and absolute criteria (for population mean), on average, child probands ($n = 122$; affected children who qualified the family) had a mean of 6.0 ($SD = 2.8$) deficits on the nine reading measures used for inclusion and a mean of 4.1 deficits on the six writing measures used for inclusion. Their affected parents had on average a mean of 1.9 ($SD = 1.7$) deficits on the same reading measures and 1.8 ($SD = 1.6$) deficits on the same writing measures.

Table 11.1 summarizes which subphenotypes met both absolute (low achievement at or below 1 SD) and relative (at least 15 standard score points difference between VIQ and measure based on transformation to make scales comparable if necessary) criteria at each developmental level. Six met both criteria at both

Table 11.1   Impaired Phenotypes Based on Absolute and Relative Criteria in Children Only and Children and Adults with Dyslexia

Child and adult	CTOPP nonword repetition, TOWRE pseudoword reading efficiency, Wolf RAN letter naming, UW alphabet letter writing, Wolf RAS letter and number, and Wolf RAS color, letter, and number.
	Note: D-KEF color word inhibition and verbal fluency repetitions met only the relative criteria in both child and adult dyslexics.
Child only	WRMT-R Word Identification and Word Attack, TOWRE sight word efficiency, GORT3 accuracy and rate, UW morphological decoding and accuracy, WRAT 3 and WIAT II spelling, WIAT II written expression, PAL receptive and expressive orthographic coding, CTOPP phoneme reversal, Wolf RAN color, Wolf RAN number, D-KEF color word inhibition.
	Note: Only in child dyslexics did inhibition on the Stroop meet both absolute and relative criteria.
Adult only	None.

Notes: CTOPP = Comprehensive Test of Phonological Processing; D-KEF = Delis Kaplan Executive Functions; PAL = Process Assessment of the Learner; RAN = Rapid Automatic Naming; RAS = Rapid Automatic Switching; TOWRE = Test of Word Reading Efficiency; WIAT II = Wechsler Individual Achievement Test, second edition; WRAT3 = Wide Range Achievement Test, third edition; WRMT-R = Woodcock Reading Mastery Test Revised.

Source: From "Modeling Developmental Phonological Core Deficits within a Working-Memory Architecture in Children and Adults with Developmental Dyslexia," by V. Berninger, R. Abbott, J. Thomson, et al., in *Scientific Studies in Reading,* in press; and "Research-Supported Differential Diagnosis of Specific Learning Disabilities" (pp. 189–233), by V. Berninger and L. O'Donnell, in *WISC-IV Clinical Use and Interpretation: Scientist-Practitioner Perspectives,* A. Prifitera, D. Saklofske, L. Weiss, & E. Rolfhus (Eds.), 2004, San Diego: Academic Press.

developmental levels and are stable hallmark features across development. Many subphenotype measures met both criteria in children but not adults and thus are more likely to show compensation (normalization) over development. No impairments met both criteria only in the adults, but the adults met both the absolute and relative criteria for impaired real word reading efficiency but not for real word reading accuracy (Berninger & O'Donnell, 2004); and real word reading accuracy and rate appear to have different genetic mechanisms based on chromosome linkage (Igo et al., in press).

The stable impaired skills represent the three components of working memory: phonological storage (aural

nonword repetition), phonological loop (rapid letter naming and writing), and executive functions (switching attention and inhibition; e.g., Baddeley, 2002; Baddeley & Della Sala, 1996). The stable phonological deficits (cf. Morris et al., 1998) may explain the word decoding problems, and the set of all three deficits may explain the persistent fluency problems of dyslexics due to inefficient working memory (Berninger, Abbott, Thomson, et al., in press; Berninger & O'Donnell, 2004).

The findings raised new questions we are still investigating. The phonological loop has a role in learning new written words by coordinating linguistic codes (e.g., Baddeley, Gathercole, & Papagano, 1998) and in accessing familiar words rapidly and efficiently in long-term memory. Does the RAN deficit reflect the impaired time-sensitive phonological loop? Did the Vicar of Nibbleswicke, whom Roald Dahl introduced us to, have a recurrence of childhood dyslexia moments with written text in his adult years when he faced his first adult job as a pastor delivering sermons where he transposed the sounds in spoken words (e.g., God and dog; Dahl, 1990)? If inefficiency in the executive functions for phonologically coded working memory is the underlying problem, it may make it more difficult to learn to read (coordinate spoken and written words) in childhood but also to express oneself later in life when working memory is being taxed as in learning a new job and may affect oral expression as well as reading or written expression. More than phonological decoding may be impaired in dyslexia.

Research-Supported Inclusionary Criteria

Resolving issues of definition for research purposes is also important for educational practice if both assessment and instruction are ever to be grounded in scientific research. It is no wonder that educators are confused about what dyslexia is and whether it exists if neither federal legislation nor professionals can define it on the basis of *inclusionary criteria.* Toward the goal of developing inclusionary criteria, we carefully examined cases of children who did and did not have discrepancies between VIQ and reading and spelling achievement. Based on Snow (1994) and Snow, Cancino, Gonzales, and Shriberg (1989), Nagy, who is on the UWLDC research team, proposed that defining words is really a metalinguistic awareness index of a child's ability to use words in a decontextualized manner, distinct from contextualized use of language in conversation (see Berninger, Abbott, Vermeulen, et al., in press). It follows that VIQ, which is highly correlated with expressive vocabulary, may be a general metalinguistic awareness index.

Further group analyses showed that dyslexics appeared to be primarily impaired in phonological and orthographic processing, rapid automatic naming, and executive functions (such as supervisory switching attention and inhibition) but to have intact oral language skills for morphology and syntax, that is, good metalinguistic awareness at those levels of language. However, the language learning disabled (Butler & Silliman, 2002; Wallach & Butler, 1994) children appeared to be impaired in those oral language skills as well as in phonological skills and also to be more impaired in reading comprehension than the dyslexics. Their impaired metalinguistic awareness of morphology and syntax may account for their lower VIQs.

Differential diagnosis for dyslexia versus language learning disability has implications for research and treatment. Dyslexics and language learning disabled individuals are probably included in many studies of reading disability, and results may or may not generalize across studies depending on the relative proportion of these individuals in a particular study. For dyslexics, all that may be needed is explicit instruction in orthographic and phonological awareness and decoding, but for those with language learning disability affecting all aspects of metalinguistic awareness, effective treatment may require explicit instruction in phonological, morphological, and syntactic awareness.

Drawing on Chall's (1983) observation that students first learn to read and then use reading to learn, we have observed that the language learning disabled have *significant problems in using language to learn.* School learning requires using language to understand teachers' instructional language, using language to self-regulate the internal mental processes in learning across the academic curriculum, and using language to self-regulate emotions and behavior. Thus, the language learning disabled need special instruction in using language to learn. The Appendix describes assessment procedures for the differential diagnoses among dyslexia, language learning disability, and dysgraphia (also see Berninger & O'Donnell, 2004). In addition, some individuals have specific comprehension disability without any language disability (e.g., Oakhill & Yull, 1996) or combinations of dyslexia, dysgraphia, and/or language learning disability.

Differential Diagnosis for Teaching versus Labels

Many parents and teachers reject terms such as learning disabilities as labels that stigmatize and do not make a difference in instruction. In contrast, we use the terms *dyslexia, dysgraphia,* and *language learning disability* because they identify both the nature of the problem and the need for specialized instruction in the affected academic skills:

Dyslexia: Impaired word reading and spelling (see Berninger, 2001)

Dysgraphia: Impaired handwriting and/or spelling (forming the letters of the language by hand; see Berninger, 2004b)

Language learning disability: Impairments in both aural/oral and written language (see Berninger & O'Donnell, 2004)

These terms can be used in the general education program, without the legal and paperwork constraints of special education, as well as in special education.

Effective Instruction for Dyslexia and Dysgraphia

Although there is a long-standing clinical research literature on treating dyslexia and specific reading disabilities, studies employing randomized, controlled designs have increased in recent years. Three programmatic lines of research on effective treatment of children with dyslexia include the groundbreaking studies of Wise and Olson at the University of Colorado Learning Disabilities Center with Talking Computers (e.g., Wise, Ring, & Olson, 1999), Lovett and colleagues at Toronto Children's Hospital (e.g., Lovett et al., 1994, 2000), and Torgesen and colleagues (e.g., Torgesen et al., 1999, 2001). More recently, a large randomized controlled study across three sites was conducted by Morris, Wolf, and Lovett (Wolf et al., 2003).

There has been a recent explosion of knowledge in evidence-based, effective reading instruction (e.g., McCardle & Chhabra, 2004; National Reading Panel, 2000; Snow, Burns, & Griffin, 1998); although there is not as much knowledge available for writing instruction, there is some (e.g., Berninger & Richards, 2002, chap. 9; Hooper et al., 1993; Swanson, Harris, & Graham, 2003, chaps. 16, 20, 21). High-stakes tests in many states require writing skills for assessing all domains, not just reading (Jenkins, Johnson, & Hileman, 2004). Also, many of the reviews of research-supported instruction are focused on early reading—and in the general education classroom. There is need for continuing research on instructional interventions that are effective across development and that are validated for specific kinds of learning and development problems, including but not restricted to dyslexia and dysgraphia.

Effective Instruction for Language Learning Disability

Little is known about effective reading or writing treatment for students with reading disabilities and additional oral language disabilities, which increasingly are referred to as language learning disabilities (e.g., Butler & Silliman, 2002; Wallach & Butler, 1994). In our experience, these children show mild to moderate indicators of difficulty in learning aural/oral language during the preschool years; although these oral language problems resolve in terms of production during the school-age years, lingering problems in metalinguistic awareness remain that may affect oral as well as written language. They may also have written expression problems (Fey, Catts, Proctor-Williams, Tomblin, & Zhang, 2004). Effective treatment is needed to help them improve in using decontextualized language to learn (to self-regulate internal learning processes for reading and writing and across the content subjects in the curriculum). They may learn more easily nonverbally (the twenty-first-century curriculum is very verbally oriented), but more research is needed on this issue.

Summary Position on Definitional Issues

We believe the trends toward more flexible criteria for qualifying children for services in the schools and the addition of a response to intervention component are steps in the right direction to prevent severe learning disabilities. Response to intervention will establish dynamic assessment as standard psychological practice (see Grigorenko & Sternberg, 1998; Lidz & Elliott, 2000). At the same time, it is important to retain comprehensive assessment and introduce scientifically supported differential diagnosis that has treatment validity for those who fail to respond to early intervention and have biologically based learning disabilities. Differential diagnosis relies on cognitive tests and associated phenotypic markers of specific learning disabilities.

CONTINUING CHALLENGES

Validity of Special Education Categorical versus Research-Supported Practices

The special education categories for qualifying children for services are not the same as research-supported diagnoses (Berninger, 1998). The shortcomings of the categories for qualifying children for special education services go beyond problems in IQ-achievement discrepancy the way it has been implemented. Often, cluster scores that are composites of more than one subtest are used to qualify students for special education services. This practice is problematic because when subtests are combined; a relative strength on one subtest may mask impairment on another subtest that contributes to the cluster. For example, beginning at-risk readers show *intraindividual differences in the growth curves for real word reading and pseudoword reading* (Berninger, Abbott, et al., 2002). Children who show significant growth in both of these single-word reading skills have the best outcomes; those who show significant growth in only one of these have significantly lower outcomes in reading. Combining these two subtests may miss a significant deficit in either pseudoword reading or real word reading that has important implications for diagnosis and treatment (see Berninger & O'Donnell, 2004).

Likewise, in computing IQ-writing achievement discrepancy, only accuracy measures of writing achievement—cluster scores on the Woodcock-Johnson, third edition (WJ-III) or Wechsler Individual Achievement Test, second edition (WIAT-II) that confound quality of writing samples and writing fluency—are often used. In addition, impaired spelling, handwriting, or compositional fluency are often not recognized as learning disabilities, but 15 years of our National Institute of Child Health and Human Development (NICHD) supported research indicates they are. For example, higher scores on WJ-III Writing Samples (an untimed test that does not require sustained writing and that is scored for content and ideas but not the mechanics of written expression with which students with learning disabilities have difficulty) may mask problems in writing fluency (speed of composing). However, when WJ-III Writing Samples is compared to writing fluency or writing fluency is compared to VIQ, the disparity is evident (significantly lower writing fluency) and typically is confirmed through examination of daily written work.

Thus, children with persisting reading or spelling problems may not qualify for any specialized instruction if they are significantly impaired in (a) accuracy of word decoding (reading pseudowords) but not word reading (real words) or of real word but not pseudoword reading; (b) rate of single word or pseudoword reading or rate of oral reading of passages; (c) spelling; and/or (d) handwriting. It does not matter if it is obvious that the child cannot read classroom materials with accuracy and fluency, spell at a grade-appropriate level in daily written work, and/or has illegible or painfully slow handwriting. There also is no procedure in place to identify or serve students with language learning disability, which may account for more cases of specific learning disability than classic dyslexia or dysgraphia.

The Problem Is Lack of Knowledge, Not Lack of Money

Given the sociopolitical context in which we conduct our research (11 local schools have sued the state superintendent of education, director of special education, and governor because they do not think they have enough money to teach students who qualify for special education), we frequently remind educators that *there is nothing in the special education law that says it is illegal or unethical or unprofessional to help students with learning disabilities in the general education program by implementing research-supported assessment and teaching practices.* Although qualifying students for special education is sometimes an appropriate goal, some parents want appropriate diagnosis and services in general education. Unfortunately, schools are reluctant to accept the research-based definitions of learning disability (many of which have been shown to have a genetic or neurological basis) because they fear the state auditors will penalize them by decreasing their funding if they do not use the current legally mandated procedures even if they are not supported by research and children who have obvious reading or writing problems do not qualify under one of the existing legal definitions. Even though the federal regulations now require that science-based reading instruction be used in schools accepting No Child Left Behind funding, there are no regulations that support use of scientifically supported diagnostic categories for diagnosing or treating reading, writing, or math disabilities.

Although students with tier 3 problems benefit from specialized instruction, it is not cost-effective to provide *all* of their reading, writing, and math instruction in pull-out programs. Therefore, students with these specific learning disabilities in reading, writing, math, or language learning should be given the option of a special section within general education taught by a qualified teacher who provides *explicit, language-based, intellectually engaging instruction*. Although affected individuals can learn to decode and read real words if given appropriate, explicit instruction, the underlying genetic basis for the disorder appears to exert its effects in different ways as affected individuals advance in schooling and the curriculum requirements change. Persisting spelling and written expression problems and silent reading fluency problems are typically observed in older students unless new kinds of instructional interventions are put in place. Unfortunately, many schools offer older students only accommodations rather than continuing explicit instruction aimed at fluent reading, spelling, and written expression and executive functions. Schools might benefit from a return to the flexible model of building-based, well-trained academic learning specialists who provide direct services and also collaborate with teachers to plan and implement differentiated instruction. Such an approach would necessitate more comprehensive teacher training in explicit instruction strategies (e.g., Cunningham, 1990) and domain knowledge relevant to literacy (e.g., Cunningham, Perry, Stanovich, & Stanovich, 2004; McCutchen & Berninger, 1999).

High-Stakes Tests

Based on the experiences of students in our research studies, we wonder whether the high-stakes tests, which are aimed at high-level thinking skills, are adequately assessing low-level decoding, word reading, fluency, handwriting, and spelling skills that can compromise performance on daily school assignments, whether or not students pass the high-stakes tests. (See Figure 11.1, which is a recent writing sample from an eighth grader who passed the high-stakes test in writing.)

Another issue is that high-stakes tests often require writing across all academic domains (reading, math, and writing; Jenkins et al., 2004). Many students who have writing rather than reading problems may perform poorly on these tests because, although they have the domain-specific knowledge, they lack adequate writing skills to express what they know. As one adolescent suicide survivor told me, "I am good at math [and individually administered psychometric tests support this self-perception] and I can explain my math thinking by talking, but I cannot explain my math thinking in writing. I thought my life was over because I can do math but not write about it." Although federal initiatives emphasize the importance of research-supported reading instruction and now annual reading and math assessment, they have not yet included writing in that mandate for scientifically supported instruction and annual assessment. Many students who are failing in course work or achieving far below grade-appropriate levels are mistakenly thought to be not motivated; yet, when they are given tests of writing-related processes validated in research, they are typically shown to have undiagnosed and untreated writing disabilities (Berninger & Hidi, in press). Introducing research-supported writing interventions so that they can become successful in writing often transforms a reluctant writer into an able and willing writer.

Increasingly, students with learning disabilities are brought to our attention because they have not passed the high-stakes test or teachers fear they will not pass it. One of the worst cases we have encountered was the school who refused to listen to parents' concerns that their child was not learning to read during the early grades. Later, a teacher asked the parents to agree to a special education placement for learning disabilities so that the child's scores on the high-stakes test would not bring down her class average. According to the UWLDC assessment results, the child was a nonreader. Had tier 1 research-supported screening and early intervention been in place in this school, this child would probably not have had years of chronic failure and likely would have been a reader and writer. There are many more such stories that constantly remind us that there is still an enormous job yet to be done in educating educators about learning disabilities and effectively teaching students with learning disabilities.

PROFESSIONALS WHO PRACTICE THE THREE Cs: CARE, CONNECT, AND COMMUNICATE

Instructional Research Is Necessary but Not Sufficient

Basic laboratory research may not generalize to real-world settings. Therefore, when applying research results, the effectiveness of the implementation should also be evaluated on the basis of evidence. Achieving desired results in practice may well require both art as well as science. The art involves clinical skills for direct services

and consulting with other professionals (Rosenfield, 1987; Rosenfield & Gravois, 1996). Over the years, we have encountered many dedicated, competent professionals who work hard and effectively to help students with learning disabilities. At the same time, we have encountered many cases in which the students were not being served well and the schools were resistant to outside professional assistance in helping the students with learning disabilities.

Professional Approach

In our professional preparation program for psychologists, I emphasize the three Cs for effective clinical practice: *caring* about the individuals affected with learning disabilities, *connecting* with them and their families, and *communicating* effectively with parents and teachers regarding ways to help children with learning disabilities. This kind of professional practice, reflecting the spirit of federal legislation that guarantees the civil rights of children with educationally handicapping conditions, cannot be legislated. It involves opening one's heart to others (see "Open Hearts," the March 2 reflection in *Native Wisdom for White Minds*, Schaef, 1995). Well-trained professionals, knowledgeable about scientifically supported assessment and instruction, able to open their hearts to care about the plight of children who learn differently because of biological influences (which make it harder but not impossible to learn) are as necessary as laws to optimize academic success during childhood and workplace success during adulthood of individuals with specific learning disabilities. Professionals who practice the three Cs develop collaborative rather than adversarial relationships with parents. Because the parents know that the educators care, there is no need to turn to lawyers who are not professional educators to resolve disputes. This emphasis on caring about others is consistent with progressive pedagogy that underscores the need to meet student strengths and needs (Barth, 2002; Bruner, 1966; Dewey, 1963) through caring (Noddings, 1992).

VISION OF APPROPRIATE EDUCATION FOR STUDENTS WITH LEARNING DISABILITIES

This chapter ends with a vision of what could be so that students like Susan, Sean, Sam, and Sharon do not come to a standstill, flounder, or agonize over why no one can teach them, or waste precious years of their lives because they learn in a different way. This vision does not require more money, but rather more creative and intelligent use of the limited resources available to schools so that they are not needlessly drained by expensive legal proceedings. What follows is implemented fully within general education, with building-level flexibility, and without special education auditors, paperwork, and legal procedures. Special education still exists to provide an appropriate education for students with more severe handicapping conditions, but those with dyslexia, dysgraphia, and language learning disability are appropriately diagnosed and served within the general education program in a manner that provides the specialized instruction they require.

To begin with, schools make greater use of the *language arts block,* during which all teachers at the same grade level or across grade levels teach language arts at the same time. In keeping with the continuum of explicit instruction discussed earlier in the chapter, each school designates at least one class or section at the elementary and middle school level for offering explicit, intellectually engaging reading and writing instruction for those who require, depending on grade level, highly explicit instruction for phonological, orthographic, and morphological awareness (see Figure 11.2, p. 426), alphabetic principle, word families, structure words, decoding, automatic word recognition, oral and silent reading fluency, reading comprehension, handwriting automaticity, spelling, compositional fluency, or genre-specific composing, including report writing, note taking, study skills, and test taking. Not all children require highly explicit instruction, but those with dyslexia, dysgraphia, and language learning disability and others need this option in the general education curriculum. (See Berninger, 1998, and Berninger & Richards, 2002, for the inspiring story of a special education teacher who organized such a language arts block in the general education program and showed that the children with learning disabilities who start out behind can reach the same literacy outcomes as their peers without learning disabilities if provided explicit, intellectually engaging instruction.)

The *role of the school psychologist* changes from giving a battery of tests for the sole purpose of deciding whether children qualify for costly pull-out, special education services, to that of assessment specialist (funded by general education) who serves two important roles in meeting the needs of students with learning disabilities. First, the school psychologist organizes a schoolwide screening and progress monitoring program. The purpose of the tier 1 screening is to identify those students who

are at risk for dyslexia, dysgraphia, language learning disability, or other developmental or learning problems. When children show indications of being at risk, the school psychologist shares this information with the general educator (and parents, to create collaborative rather than adversarial relationships) and uses problem-solving consultation skills (Rosenfield, 1987; Rosenfield & Gravois, 1996) to help the general educator provide differentiated instruction to meet individual students' instructional needs within a group setting. The school psychologist also assists with progress monitoring so that teachers, parents, and the children themselves know if they are making reasonable progress in specific reading and writing skills. Second, when a child is not making adequate progress in response to the initial intervention and possibly tier 2 additional intervention, the school psychologist then conducts tier 3 assessment and administers standardized tests, obtains a developmental history from parents, collects work samples, and observes the child in the classroom to determine if any of the differential diagnoses in the Appendix or others apply. The goal of diagnosis is to (a) understand why a child has struggled, (b) identify an educationally handicapping condition that qualifies the child for both explicit instruction *and* accommodation in the regular program, and (c) plan differentiated instruction for this student within the language arts section that is explicit, intellectually engaging, and appropriate for the diagnosis.

Had this kind of approach been in place, Susan would have been identified in the kindergarten and first-grade screening and given tier 1 supplementary reading and writing instruction in the general education program. By third grade, she would not have been at a standstill, but would probably have been flagged again in fourth grade for reading and writing rate and spelling problems and then again given supplementary instruction for those skills. Likewise, the teachers and psychologists would have realized that just because Sean has learned to decode and read with accuracy does not mean that his dyslexia no longer has implications for his instructional needs. Sean would have continued to receive explicit instruction in silent reading fluency, spelling, and written composition during the upper elementary grades until those skills were well developed. Sam (see Figure 11.1, p. 423) would not be begging for someone to teach him to read and write better. What is unfortunate in his case is that with appropriate intervention at school (supplemented with university assistance), Sam was reading and writing on grade level up through the end of elementary school. He lost relative ground when all explicit instruction in reading and writing was eliminated in middle school, highlighting the *necessity for sustained explicit instruction across schooling for students with dyslexia and dysgraphia (and also language learning disability)*. Finally, Sharon's mother's pleas to have her assessed during the school years would not have been dismissed with the misguided assumption that she cannot possibly have a learning disability because she is bright. Her dyslexia would have been diagnosed and treated and she may even have fared better in learning a second language with specialized instruction; she would have graduated from college at the same time as her peers and found employment commensurate with a college education.

Translating this vision of research into practice requires keeping abreast of the rapidly expanding body of research on learning disabilities. It also requires common sense, caring, and commitment to educating all students, even those who pose more challenges because they do not learn as easily despite being intelligent. There is no teacher-proof curriculum that will bring about this vision. Achieving this vision will require developing more informed and collaborative relationships between educators and state legislators to pass legislation that affirms the professionalism of educators entrusted with bringing about this vision and delegates to them the responsibility of doing so.

APPENDIX WITH HALLMARK FEATURES FOR DIFFERENTIAL DIAGNOSIS

Inclusionary Hallmark Criteria for Dyslexia Constellation

- Verbal IQ (or Verbal Comprehension Factor) at least 90.

- Meets at least one of the following criteria (most will probably meet several):
  - Decoding or real word reading accuracy or rate is below the population mean and at least 1 *SD* (15 standard score points) below VIQ.
  - Oral reading accuracy or rate is below the population mean and at least 1 *SD* (15 standard score points) below VIQ.
  - Spelling is below the population mean and at least 1 *SD* (15 standard score points) below VIQ.

- Does not meet any exclusionary criteria related to other neurodevelopmental disorder, brain injury or disease, or psychiatric disorder, and is not an English-language learner.

Comorbidity Issues

Oral language milestones are normal during the preschool years except in phonology. Rarely do the children who meet this criterion meet the criteria for ADHD specified in the *Diagnostic and Statistical Manual for Mental Disorders (DSM-IV),* but they do show individual variation along a continuum of inattention (based on parental ratings).

Inclusionary Hallmark Criteria for Language Learning Disability Constellation

- Preschool history of some indicator of slower language milestones (first words, first sentences, early intervention in speech or expressive language).

- Performance IQ or Perceptual Organization Factor at least 90 (to reduce probability of confounding developmental neurogenetic disorders); WISC-III or WISC-IV VIQ may be below 90 (or Vocabulary subtest below 8).

- Meets at least one of the following criteria (most will probably meet several):
  - Decoding or real word reading accuracy or rate at least 1 *SD* below the mean.
  - Oral reading accuracy or rate at least 1 *SD* below the mean.
  - Spelling at least 1 *SD* below the mean.
  - Oral or reading vocabulary at least 1 *SD* below the mean.
  - Reading comprehension at least 1 *SD* below the mean.

- Does not meet any exclusionary criteria related to other neurodevelopmental disorder, brain injury or disease, or psychiatric disorder, and is not an English-language learner.

Comorbidity Issues

The following indicators are typical: (a) slower preschool language milestones, (b) preschool motor milestones are possibly slower, (c) some oral language skills (morphological and syntactic awareness and sentence formulation) during the school-age years are outside the normal range, and (d) comorbid diagnosis of ADHD (especially Inattention), although the attention problems may be the result of language-processing problems.

Inclusionary Hallmark Criteria for Dysgraphia Constellation

- No preschool history of slower language milestones (first words, first sentences, early intervention in speech or expressive language) but may have preschool indicators of motor delays or dyspraxias or attentional difficulties.

- VIQ at least 90.

- Meets at least one of the following criteria (most will probably meet several):

  —Does not meet the criteria for dyslexia for word decoding, real word reading, or oral reading of passages.

  —Does meet one or more of the following criteria:

  - Handwriting is below the population mean and either at least 15 standard score points below VIQ or at least 1 *SD* below population mean.
  - Spelling is below the population mean and at least 15 standard score points below VIQ.
  - Does not meet any exclusionary criteria related to other neurodevelopmental disorder, brain injury or disease, or psychiatric disorder, and is not an English-language learner.

Comorbidity Issues

Does not tend to have slower language milestones during the preschool years or oral language skills during the school-age years that are outside the normal range. Some of these children meet *DSM-IV* criteria for ADHD and are more likely to have Hyperactivity symptoms (particularly impulsivity) than the other subtypes but also show signs of Inattention.

Note well: Some children meet the inclusionary criteria for more than one specific learning disability and may have combinations of dyslexia, disgraphia, and/or language learning disability.

REFERENCES

Abbott, S., & Berninger, V. (1999). It's never too late to remediate: A developmental approach to teaching word recognition. *Annals of Dyslexia, 49,* 223–250.

Abbott, S., Reed, L., Abbott, R., & Berninger, V. (1997). Year-long balanced reading/writing tutorial: A design experiment used for dynamic assessment. *Learning Disabilities Quarterly, 20,* 249–263.

Aram, D., Ekelman, B., & Nation, J. (1984). Preschoolers with language disorders: Ten years later. *Journal of Speech and Hearing Research, 27,* 232–244.

Aylward, E., Richards, T., Berninger, V., Nagy, W., Field, K., Grimme, A., et al. (2003). Instructional treatment associated with changes in brain activation in children with dyslexia. *Neurology, 61,* 212–219.

Baddeley, A. (2002). Is working memory still working? *European Psychologist, 7,* 85–97.

Baddeley, A., & Della Sala, S. (1996). Executive and cognitive functions of the prefrontal cortex. *Philosophical Transactions: Biological Sciences, 351*(1346), 1397–1403.

Baddeley, A., Gathercole, S., & Papagno, C. (1998). The phonological loop as a language learning device. *Psychological Review, 105,* 158–173.

Balmuth, M. (1992). *The roots of phonics: A historical introduction.* Baltimore: York Press.

Barth, R. S. (2002). *Learning by heart.* San Francisco: Jossey-Bass.

Berninger, V. (1994). Intraindividual differences in levels of language in comprehension of written sentences. *Learning and Individual Differences, 6,* 433–457.

Berninger, V. (1998). *Guides for reading and writing intervention.* San Antonio, TX: Harcourt Brace.

Berninger, V. (2001). Understanding the lexia in dyslexia. *Annals of Dyslexia, 51,* 23–48.

Berninger, V. (2004a). The reading brain in children and youth: A systems approach. In B. Wong (Ed.), *Learning about learning disabilities* (3rd ed., pp. 197–248). San Diego: Academic Press.

Berninger, V. (2004b). Understanding the graphia in dysgraphia. In D. Dewey & D. Tupper (Eds.), *Developmental motor disorders: A neuropsychological perspective* (pp. 328–350). New York: Guilford Press.

Berninger, V., & Abbott, R. (1992). Unit of analysis and constructive processes of the learner: Key concepts for educational neuropsychology. *Educational Psychologist, 27,* 223–242.

Berninger, V., & Abbott, R. (1994). Redefining learning disabilities: Moving beyond aptitude-achievement discrepancies to failure to respond to validated treatment protocols. In G. R. Lyon (Ed.), *Frames of reference for the assessment of learning disabilities: New views on measurement issues* (pp. 163–202). Baltimore: Paul H. Brookes.

Berninger, V., Abbott, R., Abbott, S., Graham, S., & Richards, T. (2001). Writing and reading: Connections between language by hand and language by eye. *Journal of Learning Disabilities, 35,* 39–56.

Berninger, V., Abbott, R., Billingsley, F., & Nagy, W. (2001). Processes underlying timing and fluency of reading: Efficiency, automaticity, coordination, and morphological awareness. In M. Wolf (Ed.), *Dyslexia, fluency, and the brain* (Extraordinary Brain Series, pp. 383–414). Baltimore: York Press.

Berninger, V., Abbott, R., Brooksher, R., Lemos, Z., Ogier, S., Zook, D., et al. (2000). A connectionist approach to making the predictability of English orthography explicit to at-risk beginning readers: Evidence for alternative, effective strategies. *Developmental Neuropsychology, 17,* 241–271.

Berninger, V., Abbott, R., Rogan, L., Reed, L., Abbott, S., Brooks, A., et al. (1998). Teaching spelling to children with specific learning disabilities: The mind's ear and eye beat the computer or pencil. *Learning Disability Quarterly, 21,* 106–122.

Berninger, V., Abbott, R., Thomson, J., & Raskind, W. (2001). Language phenotype for reading and writing disability: A family approach. *Scientific Studies in Reading, 5,* 59–105.

Berninger, V., Abbott, R., Thomson, J., Wagner, R., Swanson, H. L., Wijsman, E., et al. (in press). Modeling developmental phonological core deficits within a working-memory architecture in children and adults with developmental dyslexia. *Scientific Studies in Reading.*

Berninger, V., Abbott, R., Vermeulen, K., & Fulton, C. (in press). Paths to reading comprehension in at-risk second grade readers. *Journal of Learning Disabilities.*

Berninger, V., Abbott, R., Vermeulen, K., Ogier, S., Brooksher, R., Zook, D., et al. (2002). Comparison of faster and slower responders: Implications for the nature and duration of early reading intervention. *Learning Disability Quarterly, 25,* 59–76.

Berninger, V., Abbott, R., Whitaker, D., Sylvester, L., & Nolen, S. (1995). Integrating low-level skills and high-level skills in treatment protocols for writing disabilities. *Learning Disability Quarterly, 18,* 293–309.

Berninger, V., Abbott, R., Zook, D., Ogier, S., Lemos, Z., & Brooksher, R. (1999). Early intervention for reading disabilities: Teaching the alphabet principle within a connectionist framework. *Journal of Learning Disabilities, 32*(6), 491–503.

Berninger, V., & Abbott, S. (2003). *PAL Research-supported reading and writing lessons.* San Antonio, TX: Psychological Corporation.

Berninger, V., Dunn, A., & Alper, T. (2004). Integrated, multi-level model for branching assessment, instructional assessment, and profile assessment. In A. Prifitera, D. Sakolfske, & L. Weiss (Eds.), *WISC-IV clinical use and interpretation: Scientist-practitioner perspectives* (pp. 151–185). New York: Academic Press.

Berninger, V., Dunn, A., Lin, S., & Shimada, S. (2004). School evolution: Scientist-practitioner educators creating optimal learning environments for ALL students. *Journal of Learning Disabilities, 37,* 500–508.

Berninger, V., & Fuller, F. (1992). Gender differences in orthographic, verbal, and compositional fluency: Implications for diagnosis of writing disabilities in primary grade children. *Journal of School Psychology, 30,* 363–382.

Berninger, V., Fuller, F., & Whitaker, D. (1996). A process approach to writing development across the life span. *Educational Psychology Review, 8,* 193–218.

Berninger, V., & Hart, T. (1992). A developmental neuropsychological perspective for reading and writing acquisition. *Educational Psychologist, 27,* 415–434.

Berninger, V., Hart, T., Abbott, R., & Karovsky, P. (1992). Defining reading and writing disabilities with and without IQ: A flexible, developmental perspective. *Learning Disability Quarterly, 15,* 103–118.

Berninger, V., & Hidi, S. (in press). Mark Twain's writers' workshop: A nature-nurture perspective in motivating students with learning disabilities to compose. In S. Hidi & P. Boscolo (Eds.), *Motivation in writing.* Dordrecht, The Netherlands: Kluwer Academic.

Berninger, V., Nagy, W., Carlisle, J., Thomson, J., Hoffer, D., Abbott, S., et al. (2003). Effective treatment for dyslexics in grades 4 to 6. In B. Foorman (Ed.), *Preventing and remediating reading difficulties: Bringing science to scale* (pp. 382–417). Timonium, MD: York Press.

Berninger, V., Nielsen, K., Abbott, R., Wijsman, E., & Raskind, W. (2005). *Dyslexia: More than a reading disorder.* Manuscript submitted for publication.

Berninger, V., & O'Donnell, L. (2004). Research-supported differential diagnosis of specific learning disabilities. In A. Prifitera, D. Saklofske, L. Weiss, & E. Rolfhus (Eds.), *WISC-IV clinical use and interpretation: Scientist-practitioner perspectives* (pp. 189–233). San Diego: Academic Press.

Berninger, V., & Richards, T. (2002). *Brain literacy for educators and psychologists.* San Diego: Academic Press.

Berninger, V., & Stage, S. (1996). Assessment and intervention for writing in students with writing disabilities and behavioral disabilities. *British Columbia Journal of Special Education, 20*(2), 2–23.

Berninger, V., Stage, S., Smith, D., & Hildebrand, D. (2001). Assessment for reading and writing intervention: A 3-tier model for prevention and intervention. In J. Andrews, H. D. Saklofske, & H. Janzen (Eds.), *Ability, achievement, and behavior assessment: A practical handbook* (pp. 195–223). New York: Academic Press.

Berninger, V., Vaughan, K., Abbott, R., Abbott, S., Brooks, A., Rogan, L., et al. (1997). Treatment of handwriting fluency problems in beginning writing: Transfer from handwriting to composition. *Journal of Educational Psychology, 89,* 652–666.

Berninger, V., Vaughan, K., Abbott, R., Begay, K., Byrd, K., Curtin, G., et al. (2002). Teaching spelling and composition alone and together: Implications for the simple view of writing. *Journal of Educational Psychology, 94,* 291–304.

Berninger, V., Vaughan, K., Abbott, R., Brooks, A., Abbott, S., Reed, E., et al. (1998). Early intervention for spelling problems: Teaching spelling units of varying size within a multiple connections framework. *Journal of Educational Psychology, 90,* 587–605.

Berninger, V., Vaughan, K., Abbott, R., Brooks, A., Begay, K., Curtin, G., et al. (2000). Language-based spelling instruction: Teaching children to make multiple connections between spoken and written words. *Learning Disability Quarterly, 23,* 117–135.

Berninger, V., Vermeulen, K., Abbott, R., McCutchen, D., Cotton, S., Cude, J., et al. (2003). Comparison of three approaches to supplementary reading instruction for low achieving second grade readers. *Language, Speech, and Hearing Services in Schools, 34,* 101–116.

Berninger, V., & Winn, W. (in press). Implications of advancements in brain research and technology for writing development, writing instruction, and educational evolution. In C. MacArthur, S. Graham, & J. Fitzgerald (Eds.), *The writing handbook.* New York: Guilford Press.

Biemiller, A. (1977–1978). Relationship between oral reading rates for letters, words, and simple text in the development of reading achievement. *Reading Research Quarterly, 13,* 223–253.

Bishop, D., & Adams, C. (1990). A prospective study of the relationship between specific language impairment, phonological disorders, and reading retardation. *Journal of Child Psychology and Psychiatry and Allied Disciplines, 31,* 1027–1050.

Bishop, D. V. M., & Snowling, M. J. (2004). Developmental dyslexia and specific language impairment: Same or different? *Psychological Bulletin, 130,* 858–886.

Blachman, B. (1997). *Foundations of reading acquisition and dyslexia: Implications for early intervention* (pp. 163–190). Mahwah, NJ: Erlbaum.

Bond, G., & Tinker, T. (1967). *Reading difficulties: Their diagnosis and correction.* New York: Appleton-Century-Crofts.

Booth, J., Burman, D., Meyer, J., Gitelman, D., Parrish, T., & Mesulam, M. (2003). Relation between brain activation and lexical performance. *Human Brain Mapping, 19,* 155–169.

Booth, J., Perfetti, C., & MacWhinney, B. (1999). Quick, automatic, and general activation of orthographic and phonological representations in young readers, *Developmental Psychology, 35,* 3–19.

Bradley, R., Danielson, L., & Hallahan, D. (2002). *Identification of learning disabilities: Research to practice.* Mahwah, NJ: Erlbaum.

Breznitz, Z. (1987). Increasing first grader's reading accuracy and comprehension by accelerating their reading rates. *Journal of Educational Psychology, 79,* 236–242.

Breznitz, Z. (1997a). The effect of accelerated reading rate on memory for text among dyslexic readers. *Journal of Educational Psychology, 89,* 287–299.

Breznitz, Z. (1997b). Enhancing the reading of dyslexics by reading acceleration and auditory masking. *Journal of Educational Psychology, 89,* 103–113.

Breznitz, Z. (2002). Asynchrony of visual-orthographic and auditory-phonological word recognition processes: An underlying factor in dyslexia. *Journal of Reading and Writing, 15,* 15–42.

Brown, I., & Felton, R. (1990). Effects of instruction on beginning reading skills in children at risk for reading disability. *Reading and Writing: An Interdisciplinary Journal, 2,* 223–241.

Bruck, M. (1992). Persistence of dyslexics' phonological awareness deficits. *Developmental Psychology, 28,* 874–886.

Bruck, M. (1993). Word recognition and component phonological processing skills of adults with childhood histories of dyslexia. *Developmental Review, 13,* 258–268.

Bruner, J. S. (1966). *Toward a theory of instruction.* Cambridge, MA: Harvard University Press.

Butler, K., & Silliman, E. (2002). *Speaking, reading, and writing in children with language learning disabilities.* Mahwah, NJ: Erlbaum.

Byrne, B., Delaland, C., Fielding-Barnsley, R., Quain, P., Samuelsson, S., Høien, T., et al. (2002). Longitudinal twin study of early reading development in three countries: Preliminary results. *Annals of Dyslexia, 52,* 4–73.

Carlisle, J. F. (2000). Awareness of the structure and meaning of morphologically complex words: Impact on reading. *Reading and Writing: An Interdisciplinary Journal, 12,* 169–190.

Carlisle, J. (2004). Morphological processes that influence learning to read. In A. Stone, E. Silliman, B. Ehren, & K. Apel (Eds.), *Handbook of language and literacy: Development and disorders* (pp. 318–339). New York: Guilford Press.

Carlisle, J. F., & Fleming, J. (2003). Lexical processing of morphologically complex words in the elementary years. *Scientific Studies of Reading, 7,* 239–253.

Carlisle, J. F., & Stone, C. A. (2004). The effects of morphological structure on children's reading of derived words. In E. Assink & D. Santa (Eds.), *Reading complex words: Cross-language studies.* Amsterdam: Kluwer Press.

Carlisle, J. F., Stone, C. A., & Katz, L. A. (2001). The effects of phonological transparency in reading derived words. *Annals of Dyslexia, 51,* 249–274.

Catts, H., Fey, M., Tomblin, B., & Zhang, X. (2002). A longitudinal investigation of reading outcomes in children with language impairments. *Journal of Speech, Language, and Hearing Research, 45,* 1142–1157.

Catts, H., Fey, M., Zhang, X., & Tomblin, J. (1999). Language basis of reading and reading disabilities. *Scientific Studies of Reading, 3,* 331–361.

Catts, H., Fey, M., Zhang, X., & Tomblin, J. (2001). Estimating the risk of future reading difficulties in kindergarten children: A research based model and its clinical implications. *Language, Speech, and Hearing Services in Schools, 32,* 38–50.

Chall, J. (1983). *Stages of reading development.* New York: McGraw-Hill.

Chall, J. (1996). *Learning to read: The great debate* (3rd ed.). Fort Worth, TX: Harcourt Brace. (Original work published 1967)

Chapman, N., Igo, R., Thomson, J., Matsushita, M., Brkanac, Z., Hotzman, T., et al. (2004). Linkage analyses of four regions previously implicated in dyslexia: Confirmation of a locus on chromosome 15q. *American Journal of Medical Genetics (Neuropsychiatric Genetic), 131B,* 67–75 and *American Journal of Medical Genetics Supplement, 03174 9999, 1.*

Chapman, N., Raskind, W., Thomson, J., Berninger, V., & Wijsman, E. (2003). Segregation analysis of phenotypic components of learning disabilities: Pt. 2. Phonological decoding. *Neuropsychiatric Genetics, 121B,* 60–70.

Chenault, B., Thomson, J., Abbott, R., & Berninger, V. (in press). Effects of prior attention training on child dyslexic's response to composition instruction. *Developmental Neuropsychology.*

Compton, D. (2000a). Modeling the growth of decoding skills in first-grade children. *Scientific Studies of Reading, 4,* 219–259.

Compton, D. (2000b). Modeling the response of normally achieving and at-risk first grade children to word reading instruction. *Annals of Dyslexia, 50,* 53–84.

Compton, D. (2002). The relationships among phonological processing, orthographic processing, and lexical development in children with reading disabilities. *Journal of Special Education, 35,* 201–210.

Compton, D. (2003a). The influence of item composition on RAN letter performance in first-grade children. *Journal of Special Education, 37,* 81–94.

Compton, D. (2003b). Modeling the relationship between growth in rapid naming speed and growth in decoding skill in first-grade children. *Journal of Educational Psychology, 95,* 225–239.

Connor, C., Morrison, F., & Katch, L. (2004). Beyond the reading wars: Exploring the effect of child-instruction interactions on growth in early reading. *Scientific Studies of Reading, 8,* 305–336.

Cunningham, A. (1990). Explicit versus implicit instruction in phonemic awareness. *Journal of Experimental Child Psychology, 50,* 429–444.

Cunningham, A., Perry, K., Stanovich, K., & Stanovich, P. (2004). Disciplinary knowledge of K–3 teachers and their knowledge of calibration in the domain of early literacy. *Annals of Dyslexia, 54,* 139–167.

Cunningham, A., & Stanovich, K. (1998). Assessing print exposure and orthographic processing skill in children: A quick measure of reading experience. *Journal of Educational Psychology, 82,* 733–740.

Dahl, R. (1990). *The vicar of Nibbleswicke.* New York: Penguin Books.

Deno, S. L., Marston, D., & Mirkin, P. (1982). Valid measurement procedures for continuous evaluation of written expression. *Exceptional Children, 48*(3), 68–71.

Dewey, J. (1963). *Experience and education.* New York: Collier Books.

Eden, G., Jones, K., Cappell, K., Gareau, L., Wood, F., Zeffiro, T., et al. (2004). Neurophysiological recovery and compensation after remediation in adult developmental dyslexia. *Neuron, 44*(3), 411–422.

Ehri, L. (1992). Reconceptualizing the development of sight word reading and its relationship to recoding. In P. Gough, L. Ehri, & R. Treiman (Eds.), *Reading acquisition* (pp. 107–144). Hillsdale, NJ: Erlbaum.

Ehri, L., Nunes, S., Stahl, S., & Willows, D. (2001). Systematic phonics instruction helps students learn to read: Evidence from the National Reading Panel's meta-analysis. *Review of Educational Research, 71,* 393–447.

Fey, M., Catts, H., Proctor-Williams, K., Tomblin, B., & Zhang, X. (2004). Oral and written story composition skills of children with language impairment. *Journal of Speech, Language, and Hearing Research, 47,* 1301–1318.

Fletcher, J., Shaywitz, S., Shankweiler, D., Katz, L., Liberman, I., Stuebing, K., et al. (1994). Cognitive profiles of reading disability: Comparisons of discrepancy and low achievement definitions. *Journal of Educational Psychology, 86,* 6–23.

Foorman, B., Francis, D., Fletcher, J., Schatschneider, C., & Mehta, P. (1998). The role of instruction in learning to read: Preventing reading failure in at-risk children. *Journal of Educational Psychology, 90,* 37–55.

Foorman, B., Francis, D., Winikates, D., Mehta, P., Schatschneider, C., & Fletcher, J. (1996). Early interventions for children with reading disabilities. *Scientific Studies of Reading, 1,* 255–276.

Francis, D., Fletcher, J., Steubing, K., Davidson, K., & Thompson, N. (1991). Analysis of change: Modeling individual growth. *Journal of Consulting and Clinical Psychology, 59,* 27–37.

Frey, K. S., Hirschstein, M. K., Snell, J. L., Edstrom, L. V., MacKenzie, E. P., & Broderick, C. (in press). Reducing playground bullying and supporting beliefs: An experimental trial of the Steps to Respect program. *Developmental Psychology.*

Frey, K. S., Nolen, S. B., Van Schoiak-Edstrom, L., & Hirschstein, M. (2005). Evaluating a school-based social competence program: Linking behavior, goals and beliefs. *Journal of Applied Developmental Psychology, 26,* 171–200.

Fuchs, L. (1986). Monitoring progress among mildly handicapped pupils: Review of current practice and research. *Remedial and Special Education, 7,* 5–12.

Fuchs, L., Deno, S., & Mirkin, P. (1984). The effects of frequent curriculum-based measures and evaluation in pedagogy, student achievement, and student awareness of learning. *American Educational Research Journal, 21,* 449–460.

Ganschow, L., & Sparks, R. L. (2000, April/June). Reflections on foreign language study for students with language learning problems: Research, issues, and challenges. *Dyslexia, 6,* 87–100.

Gates, A. (1947). *The improvement of reading* (3rd ed.). New York: Macmillan.

Gathercole, S. E., & Baddeley, A. D. (1989). Evaluation of the role of phonological STM in the development of vocabulary in children: A longitudinal study. *Journal of Memory and Language, 28,* 200–213.

Gray, W. (1956). *The teaching of reading and writing.* Chicago: Scott, Foresman.

Greenblatt, E., Mattis, S., & Trad, P. (1990). Nature and prevalence of learning disabilities in a child psychiatric population. *Developmental Neuropsychology, 6,* 71–83.

Grigorenko, E., & Sternberg, R. J. (1998). Dynamic testing. *Psychological Bulletin, 124*(1), 75–111.

Harris, A. (1961). *How to increase reading ability* (4th ed.). New York: Longsman.

Hart, T., Berninger, V., & Abbott, R. (1997). Comparison of teaching single or multiple orthographic-phonological connections for word recognition and spelling: Implications for instructional consultation. *School Psychology Review, 26,* 279–297.

Henry, M. (1990). *Words: Integrated decoding and spelling instruction based on word origin and word structure.* Austin, TX: ProEd.

Henry, M. (2003). *Unlocking literacy: Effective decoding and spelling instruction.* Baltimore: Paul H. Brookes.

Henry, M. K. (1988). Beyond phonics: Integrated decoding and spelling instruction based on word origin and structure. *Annals of Dyslexia, 38,* 259–275.

Henry, M. K. (1989). Children's word structure knowledge: Implications for decoding and spelling instruction. *Reading and Writing: An Interdisciplinary Journal, 2,* 135–152.

Henry, M. K. (1993). Morphological structure: Latin and Greek roots and affixes as upper grade code strategies. *Reading and Writing: An Interdisciplinary Journal, 5,* 227–241.

Hooper, S. R., Swartz, C., Montgomery, J., Reed, M., Brown, T., Wasileski, T., et al. (1993). Prevalence of writing problems across three middle school samples. *School Psychology Review, 22,* 608–620.

Hooper, S. R., Swartz, C., Wakely, M., deKruif, R., & Montgomery, J. (2002). Executive functions in elementary school children with and without problems in written expression. *Journal of Learning Disabilities, 35,* 57–68.

Huey, E. B. (1968). *The psychology and pedagogy of reading.* Cambridge, MA: MIT Press. (Original work published 1908)

Hynd, G., Semrud-Clikeman, M., Lorys, A., Novey, E., & Eliopulos, D. (1990). Brain morphology in developmental dyslexia and attention deficit disorder/hyperactivity. *Archives of Neurology, 47,* 919–926.

Igo, R. P., Jr., Chapman, N. H., Berninger, V. W., Matsushita, M., Brkanac, Z., Rothstein, J., et al. (in press). Genomewide scan for real-word reading subphenotypes of dyslexia: Novel chromosome 13 locus and genetic complexity. *American Journal of Medical Genetics/Neuropsychiatric Genetics.*

Jenkins, J., Johnson, E., & Hileman, J. (2004). When reading is also writing: Sources of individual differences on the new reading performance assessments. *Scientific Studies in Reading, 8,* 125–151.

Johnson, D., & Myklebust, H. (1967). *Learning disabilities.* New York: Grune & Stratton.

Juel, C. (1988). Learning to read and write: A longitudinal study of 54 children from first through fourth grades. *Journal of Educational Psychology, 80,* 437–447.

Kirk, S., & Kirk, D. (1971). *Psycholinguistic learning disabilities: Diagnosis and remediation.* Chicago: University of Chicago Press.

Kuhn, M., & Stahl, S. (2003). Fluency: A review of developmental and remedial practices. *Journal of Educational Psychology, 95,* 3–21.

Levine, M., Overklaid, F., & Meltzer, L. (1981). Developmental output failure: A study of low productivity in school-aged children. *Pediatrics, 67,* 18–25.

Levine, M. D. (1990). *Keeping a head in school.* Cambridge, MA: Educators' Publishing Service.

Levine, M. D. (1993). *All kinds of minds*. Cambridge, MA: Educators' Publishing Service.

Levine, M. D. (1998). *Developmental variation and learning disorders* (2nd ed.). Cambridge, MA: Educators' Publishing Service.

Levine, M. D. (2002). *A mind at a time*. New York: Simon & Schuster.

Levine, M. D. (2003). *The myth of laziness*. New York: Simon & Schuster.

Levy, B., Abello, B., & Lysynchuk, L. (1997). Transfer from word training to reading in context: Gains in reading fluency and comprehension. *Learning Disability Quarterly, 20,* 173–188.

Liberman, I. Y., Shankweiler, D., & Liberman, A. M. (1989). The alphabetic principle and learning to read. In D. Shankweiler & I. Y. Liberman (Eds.), *Phonology and reading disability: Solving the reading puzzle* (IARLD Research Monograph Series). Ann Arbor: University of Michigan Press.

Lidz, C. S., & Elliott, J. G. (Eds.). (2000). *Dynamic assessment: Prevailing models and applications*. Amsterdam: JAI/Elsevier Science.

Lovett, M. (1987). A developmental perspective on reading dysfunction: Accuracy and speed criteria of normal and deficient reading skill. *Child Development, 58,* 234–260.

Lovett, M., Borden, S., DeLuca, T., Lacerenza, L., Benson, N., & Brackstone, D. (1994). Training the core deficits of developmental dyslexia: Evidence of transfer of learning after phonologically- and strategy-based reading training programs. *Developmental Psychology, 30,* 805–822.

Lovett, M., Lacerenza, L., Borden, S., Frijters, J., Steinbach, K., & De Palma, M. (2000). Components of effective remediation of developmental reading disabilities: Combining phonological and strategy-based instruction to improve outcomes. *Journal of Educational Psychology, 92,* 263–283.

Lovitt, D. (2005). *Emotional coaching in the classroom*. Unpublished manuscript. Available from dlovitt@u.washington.edu.

Lyon, G. R. (Ed.). (1994). *Frames of reference for the assessment of learning disabilities: New views on measurement issues*. Baltimore: Paul H. Brookes.

Lyon, G. R., Fletcher, J., Shaywitz, S., Shaywitz, B., Torgesen, J., Wood, F., et al. (2001). Rethinking learning disabilities. In C. Finn, J. Rotherham, & C. Hokanson (Eds.), *Rethinking special education for a new century* (pp. 259–287). Washington, DC: Thomas B. Fordham Foundation.

Lyon, G. R., Shaywitz, S., & Shaywitz, B. (2003). A definition of dyslexia. *Annals of Dyslexia, 53,* 1–14.

Manis, F., & Morrison, F. (1985). Reading disability: A deficit in rule learning. In L. Siegel & F. Morrison (Eds.), *Cognitive development in atypical children: Progress in cognitive development research* (pp. 1–26). New York: Springer-Verlag.

Manis, F., Savage, P., Morrison, F., Horn, C., Howell, M., Szeszulski, P., et al. (1987). Paired associate learning in reading-disabled children: Evidence for a rule-learning deficiency. *Journal of Experimental and Child Psychology, 43,* 25–43.

Manis, F., Seidenberg, M., & Doi, L. (1999). See Dick RAN: Rapid naming and the longitudinal prediction of reading subskills in first and second graders. *Scientific Studies of Reading, 3,* 129–157.

Manis, F., Seidenberg, M., Doi, L., McBride-Chang, C., & Petersen, A. (1996). On the basis of two subtypes of developmental dyslexia. *Cognition, 58,* 157–195.

Mattingly, I. G. (1972). Reading, the linguistic process, and linguistic awareness. In J. F. Kavanagh & I. G. Mattingly (Eds.), *Language by ear and by eye: The relationship between speech and reading* (pp. 133–147). Cambridge, MA: MIT Press.

Mayer, R. (2004). Should there be a three-strikes rule against pure discovery learning? *American Psychologist, 59,* 14–19.

McCardle, P., & Chhabra, V. (2004). *The voice of evidence in reading research*. Baltimore: Paul H. Brookes.

McCray, A. D., Vaughn, S., & Neal, L. V. I. (2001). Not all students learn to read by third grade: Middle school students speak out about their reading disabilities. *Journal of Special Education, 35,* 17–30.

McCutchen, D., & Berninger, V. (1999). Those who know, teach well. *Learning Disabilities: Research and Practice, 14*(4), 215–226.

Meyer, M., Wood, F., Hart, L., & Felton, R. (1998). Selective predictive value of rapid automatized naming in poor readers. *Journal of Learning Disabilities, 31,* 106–117.

Molfese, D., Molfese, V., Key, S., Modglin, A., Kelley, S., & Terrell, S. (2002). Reading and cognitive abilities: Longitudinal studies of brain and behavior changes in young children. *Annals of Dyslexia, 52,* 99–120.

Molfese, V., & Molfese, D. (2002). Environmental and social influences on reading skills as indexed by brain and behavioral responses. *Annals of Dyslexia, 52,* 121–137.

Montgomery, J. W. (2003). Working memory and comprehension in children with specific language impairment: What we know so far. *Journal of Communication Disorders, 36,* 221–231.

Morris, R., Stuebing, K., Fletcher, J., Shaywitz, S., Lyon, G. R., Shakweiler, D., et al. (1998). Subtypes of reading disability: Variability around a phonological core. *Journal of Educational Psychology, 90,* 347–373.

Morrison, F., Smith, L., & Dow-Ehrensberger, M. (1995). Education and cognitive development: A natural experiment. *Developmental Psychology, 31,* 789–799.

Nagy, W. E., & Anderson, R. (1984). How many words in printed school English? *Reading Research Quarterly, 19,* 304–330.

Nagy, W. E., Anderson, R. C., Schommer, M., Scott, J., & Stallman, A. (1989). Morphological families and word recognition. *Reading Research Quarterly, 24,* 262–282.

Nagy, W., Berninger, V., Abbott, R., Vaughan, K., & Vermeulen, K. (2003). Relationship of morphology and other language skills to literacy skills in at-risk second graders and at-risk fourth grade writers. *Journal of Educational Psychology, 95,* 730–742.

Nagy, W., Osborn, J., Winsor, P., & O'Flahavan, J. (1994). Structural analysis: Some guidelines for instruction. In F. Lehr & J. Osborn (Eds.), *Reading, language, and literacy* (pp. 45–58). Hillsdale, NJ: Erlbaum.

Nation, K., Clarke, P., Marshall, C. M., & Durand, M. (2004). Hidden language impairments in children: Parallels between poor reading comprehension and specific language impairment? *Journal of Speech, Language, and Hearing Research, 47,* 199–211.

National Reading Panel. (2000, April). *Teaching children to read: An evidence-based assessment of the scientific research literature on reading and its implications for reading instruction* (NIH Publication No. 00-4754). Washington, DC: U.S. Government Printing Office.

Nielsen, K., Berninger, V., & Raskind, W. (2005, June). *Gender differences in writing of dyslexics*. Poster session presented at the International Neuroscience meeting, Dublin, Ireland.

Noddings, N. (1992). *The challenge to care in schools: An alternative approach to education.* New York: Teachers College Press.

Oakhill, J., & Yull, N. (1996). Higher order factors in comprehension disability: Processes and remediation. In C. Cornaldi & J. Oakland (Eds.), *Reading comprehension difficulties: Processes and intervention* (pp. 69–92). Mahwah, NJ: Erlbaum.

Olson, R. (2004). SSSR, environment, and genes. *Scientific Studies in Reading, 8,* 111–124.

Olson, R., Datta, H., Gayan, J., & DeFries, J. (1999). A behavioral-genetic analysis of reading disabilities and component processes. In R. Klein & P. McMullen (Eds.), *Converging methods for understanding reading and dyslexia* (pp. 133–151). Cambridge, MA: MIT Press.

Olson, R., Forsberg, H., & Wise, B. (1994). Genes, environment, and the development of orthographic skills. In V. W. Berninger (Ed.), *The varieties of orthographic knowledge: Vol. 1. Theoretical and developmental issues* (pp. 27–71). Dordrecht, The Netherlands: Kluwer Academic Press.

Olson, R., Forsberg, H., Wise, B., & Rack, J. (1994). Measurement of word recognition, orthographic, and phonological skills. In G. R. Lyon (Ed.), *Frames of reference for the assessment of learning disabilities* (pp. 243–277). Baltimore: Paul H. Brookes.

Orton, S. (1937). *Reading, writing, and speech problems in children.* New York: Norton.

Pennington, B. (2002). *The development of psychopathology: Nature and nurture.* New York: Guilford Press.

Pennington, B., & Lefly, D. (2001). Early reading development in children at family risk for dyslexia. *Child Development, 72,* 816–833.

Pennington, B., Van Orden, G., Smith, S., Green, P., & Haith, M. (1990). Phonological processing skills and deficits in adult dyslexics. *Child Development, 61,* 1753–1778.

Perfetti, C. (1985). *Reading ability.* New York: Oxford University Press.

Perfetti, C. (1992). The representation problem in reading acquisition. In P. Gough, L. Ehri, & R. Treiman (Eds.), *Reading acquisition* (pp. 145–174). Hillsdale, NJ: Erlbaum.

Peverley, S. T., & Kitzen, K. R. (1998). Curriculum-based assessment of reading skills: Considerations and caveats for school psychologists. *Psychology in the Schools, 35,* 29–47.

Pianta, R. (1999). *Enhancing relationships between children and teachers.* Washington, DC: American Psychological Association.

Plomin, R. (1994). *Genetics and experience: The interplay between nature and nurture.* Thousand Oaks, CA: Sage.

Prifitera, A., Weiss, L., & Saklofske, D. (1998). The WISC-III in context. In A. Prifitera, L. Weiss, & D. Saklofske (Eds.), *WISC-III clinical use and interpretation: Scientist-practitioner perspectives* (pp. 1–38). San Diego: Academic Press.

Raskind, W. (2001). Current understanding of the genetic basis of reading and spelling disability. *Learning Disability Quarterly, 24,* 141–157.

Raskind, W., Hsu, L., Thomson, J., Berninger, V., & Wijsman, E. (2000). Family aggregation of dyslexic phenotypes. *Behavior Genetics, 30,* 385–396.

Raskind, W., Igo, R., Chapman, N., Berninger, V., Thomson, J., Matsushita, M., et al. (2005). A genome scan in multigenerational families with dyslexia: Identification of a novel locus on chromosome 2q that contributes to phonological decoding efficiency. *Molecular Psychiatry, 10,* 699–711.

Rayner, K., Foorman, B., Perfetti, C., Pesetsky, D., & Seidenberg, M. (2001). How psychological science informs the teaching of reading. *Psychological Science in the Public Interest, 2,* 31–74.

Rice, J. M. (1913). *Scientific management in education.* New York: Hinds, Noble, & Eldredge.

Richards, T., Aylward, E., Berninger, V., Field, K., Parsons, A., Richards, A., et al. (2006). Individual fMRI activation in orthographic mapping and morpheme mapping after orthographic or morphological spelling treatment in child dyslexics. *Journal of Neurolinguistics, 19,* 56–86.

Richards, T., Aylward, E., Raskind, W., Abbott, R., Field, K., Parsons, A., et al. (in press). Converging evidence for triple word form theory in child dyslexics [Special issue]. *Developmental Neuropsychology.*

Richards, T., Berninger, V., Aylward, E., Richards, A., Thomson, J., Nagy, W., et al. (2002). Reproducibility of proton MR spectroscopic imaging: Comparison of dyslexic and normal reading children and effects of treatment on brain lactate levels during language tasks. *American Journal of Neuroradiology, 23,* 1678–1685.

Richards, T., Berninger, V., Nagy, W., Parsons, A., Field, K., & Richards, A. (2005). Brain activation during language task contrasts in children with and without dyslexia: Inferring mapping processes and assessing response to spelling instruction. *Educational and Child Psychology, 22,* 62–80.

Richards, T., Berninger, V., Winn, W., Stock, S., Wagner, R., Muse, A., & Maravilla, K. (submitted). *fMRI activation in children with dyslexia during pseudoword aural repeat and visual decode.*

Richards, T., Corina, D., Serafini, S., Steury, K., Dager, S., Marro, K., et al. (2000). Effects of phonologically-driven treatment for dyslexia on lactate levels as measured by proton MRSI. *American Journal of Radiology, 21,* 916–922.

Rosenfield, S. (1987). *Instructional consultation.* Hillsdale, NJ: Erlbaum.

Rosenfield, S., & Gravois, T. (1996). *Instructional consultation teams: Collaborating for change.* New York: Guilford Press.

Scarborough, H. (1984). Continuity between childhood dyslexia and adult reading. *British Journal of Psychology, 75,* 329–348.

Scarborough, H. (1989). Prediction of reading disability from familial and individual differences. *Journal of Educational Psychology, 81,* 101–108.

Scarborough, H. (1990). Very early language deficits in dyslexic children. *Child Development, 61,* 1726–1743.

Scarborough, H. (1991). Early syntactic development of dyslexic children. *Annals of Dyslexia, 41,* 207–220.

Scarborough, H. (1998). Predicting the future achievement of second graders with reading disabilities: Contributions of phonemic awareness, verbal memory, rapid naming, and IQ. *Annals of Dyslexia, 48,* 115–136.

Scarborough, H. (2001). Connecting early language and literacy to later reading (dis)abilities: Evidence, theory, and practice. In S. Neuman & D. Dickson (Eds.), *Handbook for research in early literacy* (pp. 97–110). New York: Guilford Press.

Scarborough, H., Ehri, L., Olson, R., & Fowler, A. (1998). The fate of phonemic awareness beyond the elementary school years. *Scientific Studies in Reading, 2,* 115–142.

Schaef, A. (1995). *Native wisdom for White minds: Daily reflections inspired by native peoples of the world.* New York: Ballantine Books.

Schlagal, R. C. (1992). Patterns of orthographic development into the intermediate grades. In S. Templeton & D. Bear (Eds.), *Development of orthographic knowledge and the foundations of literacy: A memorial festschrift for Edmund H. Henderson* (pp. 31–52). Hillsdale, NJ: Erlbaum.

Seidenberg, M., & McClelland, J. (1989). A distributed developmental model of word recognition and naming. *Psychological Review, 96,* 523–568.

Shaywitz, S. (2003). *Overcoming dyslexia.* New York: Alfred A. Knopf.

Shaywitz, S., Fletcher, J., Holahan, J., Shneider, A., Marchione, K., Steubing, K., et al. (2004). Development of left occipitotemporal systems for skilled reading in children after a phonologically-based intervention. *Biological Psychiatry, 55*(9), 926–933.

Shaywitz, S., Shaywitz, B., Fletcher, J., & Escobar, M. (1990). Prevalence of reading disabilities in boys and girls (Results of the Connecticut Longitudinal Study). *Journal of the American Medical Association, 264,* 998–1002.

Shaywitz, S., Shaywitz, B., Fulbright, R., Skudlarski, P., Mencl, W., Constable, R., et al. (2003). Neural systems for compensation and persistence: Young adult outcome of childhood reading disability. *Biological Psychiatry, 54,* 25–33.

Siegel, L. (1989). Why we do not need intelligence scores in the definition and analysis of learning disabilities. *Journal of Learning Disabilities, 22,* 514–518.

Simos, P. G., Fletcher, J. M., Bergman, E., Breier, J. I., Foorman, B. R., Castillo, E. M., et al. (2002). Dyslexia-specific brain activation profile becomes normal following successful remedial training. *Neurology, 58*(8), 1203–1213.

Singleton C. (1999). *Dyslexia in higher education: Policy, provision and practice* (Report of the Working Party on Dyslexia in Higher Education). Hull, England: University of Hull.

Singson, M., Mahony, D., & Mann, V. (2000). The relation between reading ability and morphological skills: Evidence from derivational suffixes. *Reading and Writing: An Interdisciplinary Journal, 12,* 219–252.

Slavin, R., Madden, N., Dolan, L., & Wasik, B. (1996). *Every child every school: Success for all.* Thousand Oaks, CA: Corwin Press.

Snow, C. (1994). What is so hard about learning to read? A pragmatic analysis. In J. Duchan, L. Hewitt, & R. Sonnenmeier (Eds.), *Pragmatics: From theory to practice* (pp. 164–184). Engelwood Cliffs, NJ: Prentice-Hall.

Snow, C., Burns, M., & Griffin, P. (1998). *Preventing reading difficulties in young children.* Washington, DC: National Academic Press.

Snow, C., Cancino, H., Gonzales, P., & Shriberg, E. (1989). Giving formal definitions: An oral language correlate of school literacy. In D. Bloome (Ed.), *Literacy in classrooms* (pp. 233–249). Norwood, NJ: Ablex.

Snowling, M. (1980). The development of grapheme-phoneme correspondence in normal and dyslexic readers. *Journal of Experimental Child Psychology, 29,* 294–305.

Stanovich, K. (1986). Matthew effects in reading: Some consequences of individual differences in the acquisition of literacy. *Reading Research Quarterly, 21,* 360–407.

Steubing, K., Fletcher, J., LaDoux, J., Lyon, G. R., Shaywitz, S., & Shaywitz, B., et al. (2002). Validity of IQ-achievement discrepancy classifications of reading disabilities: A meta-analysis. *American Educational Research Journal, 39,* 469–518.

Swanson, H. L. (1999). *Interventions for students with learning disabilities: A meta-analysis of treatment outcomes.* New York: Guilford Press.

Swanson, H. L., Harris, K., & Graham, S. (2003). *Handbook of learning disabilities.* New York: Guilford Press.

Swanson, H. L., & Siegel, L. (2001). Learning disabilities as a working memory deficit. *Issues in Education, 7,* 1–48.

Temple, E., Poldrack, R. A., Deutsch, G. K., Miller, S., Tallal, P., Merzenich, M. M., et al. (2003). Neural deficits in children with dyslexia ameliorated by behavioral remediation: Evidence from fMRI. *Proceedings of the National Academy of Sciences, 100,* 2860–2865.

Temple, E., Poldrack, R. A., Protopapas, A., Nagarajan, S., Saltz, T., Tallal, P., et al. (2000). Disruption of the neural response to rapid acoustic stimuli in dyslexia: Evidence from functional MRI. *Proceedings of the National Academy of Sciences, USA, 97,* 13907–13912.

Templeton, S., & Bear, D. (Eds.). (1992). *Development of orthographic knowledge and the foundations of literacy: A memorial festschrift for Edmund H. Henderson.* Hillsdale, NJ: Erlbaum.

Thomson, J., Chenault, B., Abbott, R., Raskind, W., Richards, T., Aylward, E., et al. (2005). Converging evidence for attentional influences on the orthographic word form in child dyslexics. *Journal of Neurolinguistics, 18,* 93–126.

Torgesen, J. K. (2000). Individual differences in response to early interventions in reading: The lingering problem of treatment resisters. *Learning Disabilities: Research and Practice, 15,* 55–64.

Torgesen, J. K. (2004). Learning disabilities: An historical and conceptual overview. In B. Wong (Ed.), *Learning about learning disabilities* (3rd ed., pp. 3–40). San Diego: Academic Press.

Torgesen, J. K., Alexander, A., Wagner, R., Rashotte, C., Voeller, K., Conway, T., et al. (2001). Intensive remedial instruction for children with severe reading disabilities: Immediate and long-term outcomes from two instructional approaches. *Journal of Learning Disabilities, 34,* 33–58.

Torgesen, J. K., Wagner, R. K., & Rashotte, C. A. (1997). Prevention and remediation of severe reading disabilities: Keeping the end in mind. *Scientific Studies of Reading, 1,* 217–234.

Torgesen, J. K., Wagner, R., Rashotte, C., Rose, E., Lindamood, P., Conway, T., et al. (1999). Preventing reading failure in young children with phonological processing disabilities: Group and individual responses to instruction. *Journal of Educational Psychology, 91,* 579–593.

Traweek, D., & Berninger, V. (1997). Comparison of beginning literacy programs: Alternative paths to the same learning outcome. *Learning Disability Quarterly, 20,* 160–168.

Treiman, R. (1993). *Beginning to spell: A study of first-grade children.* New York: Oxford University Press.

Uhry, J., & Shephard, M. (1997). Teaching phonological recoding to young children with phonological processing deficits: The effect on sight-vocabulary acquisition. *Learning Disability Quarterly, 20,* 104–125.

Van Schoiack-Edstrom, L., Frey, K. S., & Beland, K. (2002). Changing adolescents' attitudes about relational and physical aggression: An early evaluation of a school-based intervention. *School Psychology Review, 31,* 201–216.

Vaughn, S., Moody, S., & Schumm, J. (1998). Broken promises: Reading instruction in the resource room. *Exceptional Children, 64,* 211–225.

Vaughn, S., Sinaguh, J., & Kim, A. (2004). Social competence/social skills of students with learning disabilities: Interventions and issues. In B. Wong (Ed.), *Learning about learning disabilities* (3rd ed., pp. 341–373). San Diego: Academic Press.

Vellutino, F., & Scanlon, D. (1987). Phonological coding, phonological awareness, and reading ability: Evidence from a longitudinal and experimental study. *Merrill-Palmer Quarterly, 33,* 321–363.

Vellutino, F., Scanlon, D., & Lyon, G. R. (2000). Differentiating between difficult-to-remediate and readily remediated poor readers: More evidence against IQ-achievement discrepancy definitions of reading disability. *Journal of Learning Disabilities, 33,* 223–238.

Vellutino, F., Scanlon, D., Sipay, E., Small, S., Pratt, A., Chen, R., et al. (1996). Cognitive profiles of difficult-to-remediate and readily remediated poor readers: Early intervention as a vehicle for distinguishing between cognitive and experiential deficits as basic causes of specific reading disability. *Journal of Educational Psychology, 88,* 601–638.

Vellutino, F., Scanlon, D., & Tanzman, M. (1991). Bridging the gap between cognitive and neuropsychological conceptualizations of reading disabilities. *Learning and Individual Differences, 3,* 181–203.

Venezky, R. (1970). *The structure of English orthography.* The Hague, The Netherlands: Mouton.

Venezky, R. (1999). *The American way of spelling.* New York: Guilford Press.

Wagner, R., & Torgesen, J. (1987). The nature of phonological processing and its causal role in the acquisition of reading skills. *Psychological Bulletin, 101,* 192–212.

Wagner, R., Torgesen, J., & Rashotte, C. (1994). The development of reading-related phonological processing abilities: New evidence of bi-directional causality from a latent variable longitudinal study. *Developmental Psychology, 30,* 73–87.

Wallach, G., & Butler, K. (1994). *Language learning disabilities in school-age children and adolescents: Some principles and applications.* Needham Heights, MA: Allyn & Bacon.

Weiss, B., Catron, T., Harris, V., & Phung, T. (1999). The effectiveness of traditional child psychotherapy. *Journal of Consulting and Clinical Psychology, 67,* 82–94.

Whitaker, D., Berninger, V., Johnston, J., & Swanson, L. (1994). Intraindividual differences in levels of language in intermediate grade writers: Implications for the translating process. *Learning and Individual Differences, 6,* 107–130.

White, T., Power, M., & White, S. (1989). Morphological analysis: Implications for teaching and understanding vocabulary growth in diverse elementary schools—Decoding and word meaning. *Journal of Educational Psychology, 82,* 281–290.

Wijsman, E., Peterson, D., Leutennegger, A., Thomson, J., Goddard, K., Hsu, L., et al. (2000). Segregation analysis of phenotypic components of learning disabilities: Pt. 1. Nonword memory and digit span. *American Journal of Human Genetics, 67,* 31–646.

Willis, C. S., & Gathercole, S. E. (2001). Phonological short-term memory contributions to sentence processing in young children. *Memory, 9*(4/5/6), 349–363.

Wise, B., Ring, J., & Olson, R. (1999). Training phonological awareness with and without explicit attention to articulation. *Journal of Experimental Child Psychology, 72,* 271–304.

Wolf, M. (1986). Rapid alternating stimulus naming in the developmental dyslexias. *Brain and Language, 27,* 360–379.

Wolf, M. (1999). What time may tell: Towards a new conceptualization of developmental dyslexia. *Annals of Dyslexia, 49,* 3–28.

Wolf, M. (Ed.). (2001). *Dyslexia, fluency, and the brain.* Timonium, MD: York Press.

Wolf, M., & Bowers, P. (1999). The double-deficit hypothesis for the developmental dyslexias. *Journal of Educational Psychology, 91,* 415–438.

Wolf, M., Morris, R., & Bally, H. (1986). Automaticity, retrieval processes and reading: A longitudinal study of average and impaired readers. *Child Development, 57,* 988–1000.

Wolf, M., O'Brien, B., Adams, K., Joffe, T., Jeffrey, J., Lovett, M., et al. (2003). Working for time: Reflections on naming speed, reading fluency, and intervention. In B. Foorman (Ed.), *Preventing and remediating reading difficulties: Bringing science to scale* (pp. 356–379). Baltimore: York Press.

Wong, B. Y. L. (2000). Writing strategies instruction for expository essays for adolescents with and without learning disabilities. *Topics in Language Disorders, 20*(4), 29–44.

Yates, C., Berninger, V., & Abbott, R. (1994). Writing problems in intellectually gifted children. *Journal for the Education of the Gifted, 18,* 131–155.

Young, A., Bowers, P., & Mackinnon, G. (1996). Effects of prosodic modeling and repeated reading on poor readers' fluency and comprehension. *Applied Psycholinguistics, 17,* 59–84.

CHAPTER 12

Mental Retardation

ROBERT M. HODAPP and ELISABETH M. DYKENS

For developmental psychologists, mental retardation is a topic that is both old and new. On one hand, developmental research in mental retardation predates studies of most other applied topics. In the 1940s, Inhelder and Piaget (Inhelder, 1943/1968; Piaget & Inhelder, 1947) examined children with mental retardation to determine whether Piagetian sequences were traversed in universal, invariant order. At about the same time, Werner (1938, 1941) examined children with mental retardation to help develop his orthogenetic principle ("development proceeds from a state of relative globality . . . to a state of differentiation, articulation, and hierarchic integration"; 1957, p. 126). Even earlier, during the 1920s and 1930s, Vygotsky's "defectology"

studies used children with mental retardation to explore the developmental interplay between children and their surrounding cultural environments (Rieber & Carton, 1993; van der Veer & Valsiner, 1991).

Granted, mental retardation would probably not be considered central to the work of Piaget, Werner, or Vygotsky. Each theorist tackled many developmental phenomena; their studies of children with mental retardation generally occurred at the beginning of each theorist's career and were not sustained over time (Hodapp, 1998). Still, to varying extents, Piaget, Werner, and Vygotsky all realized that children with mental retardation could be used to apply, extend, and test out their theories.

Yet, despite these early explorations, in other ways mental retardation is a new topic for developmental psychology. Bluntly stated, many developmentally oriented researchers and practitioners feel that children with mental retardation are somehow less theoretically important or interesting, and that these children simply require instruction that presents less material at a slower pace. Partly reflecting this view, few training programs in developmental psychology or applied developmental psychology offer specializations in mental retardation or developmental disabilities. In journals such as *Child Development* and *Developmental Psychology*—even in the *Journal of Applied Developmental Psychology* and *Applied Developmental Science*—only a few articles feature children with mental retardation and their families. Mental retardation remains less prominent in both child development and applied child development.

To be fair, mental retardation's second-class status is not limited to developmental psychology. Mental retardation is also a part of—but not prominent in—many other disciplines. Mental retardation is the first disorder addressed in the fourth edition of the *Diagnostic and Statistical Manual of Mental Disorders* (American Psychiatric Association, 1994, pp. 39–46), but holds only a minor place in psychiatry, child psychiatry, or clinical psychology (King, State, Shah, Davanzo, & Dykens, 1997; Routh, 2003). Similarly, special education exists but is not prominent in education. One could make similar observations about nursing, social work, genetics and clinical genetics, pediatrics, speech-language pathology, and a host of other disciplines. In each field, mental retardation exists as a subfield, but its place is not prominent.

And yet, this situation may be changing, for two reasons. First, increasing numbers of studies have moved from examining children with mental retardation to examining children with different types of mental retardation (Dykens & Hodapp, 2001). In contrast to prior years, we now have many more studies of children with Down syndrome, fragile X syndrome, Williams syndrome, Prader-Willi syndrome, and other of the 1,000+ genetic mental retardation disorders (Hodapp & Dykens, 2004).

These studies, in turn, are producing many new findings about these disorders. For example, certain genetic syndromes show particular, etiology-related cognitive or linguistic strengths or weaknesses. Others show etiology-related trajectories (or rates) of development in different areas, and still others have much higher rates of particular maladaptive behaviors or co-occurring psychiatric conditions. Although we later detail these intriguing findings, suffice it to note here that different genetic mental retardation disorders show different, etiology-related behaviors.

Developmentally oriented researchers are among those intrigued by such findings. If, for example, individuals with a specific genetic disorder show particular strengths in one area (e.g., language) and weaknesses in another area (e.g., visual-spatial skills), what does this say about the "modularity" of intelligence? How do such profiles develop over time? Which environmental factors enter in, which neurological factors, when, in what ways, to what effect(s)? Just as, in prior decades, Piaget, Werner, and Vygotsky were intrigued by development in children with mental retardation, so are modern-day developmentalists interested in children with different types of mental retardation. Modern-day developmentalists are reaching out to such children to test, extend, and apply what we think we know about how development operates.

In addition to their importance to our theoretical understandings of human development, etiology-related behaviors also have implications for interventions. For this reason, parents, special and general educators, speech-language pathologists, and clinical psychologists and psychiatrists have all become increasingly excited about how etiology-related behavioral profiles might be used for intervention efforts. Consider the idea that children with certain genetic syndromes show etiology-related strengths in one area and weaknesses in another. If so, it may be possible to play to the child's strengths in terms of how or what information is presented. Although the application of research into practice has, until now, rarely been attempted, recent advances provide hope for more targeted, etiology-oriented types of special education services (Hodapp & Fidler, 1999).

A second reason for interest in mental retardation concerns the meaning of "development" to developmentally oriented professionals. Like the larger field of child development, developmentally oriented researchers in mental retardation increasingly examine the environments in which children with mental retardation develop. As they examine these environments, researchers and practitioners realize that environments can have both good and bad effects on children with mental retardation. Indeed, from an earlier perspective on parental and familial pathology, the field has recently noted that a range of child, parent, and family characteristics may help or hinder the functioning of both the child with mental retardation and his or her family.

In a related way, developmentally oriented professionals are realizing just how little we currently know about the larger ecology of children with mental retardation. As in any child's development, the child with mental retardation interacts with many, outside-of-family systems, including the child's school, peers, and other environments. In mental retardation, these outside systems have changed drastically over the past few decades; indeed, one could almost argue that parents and families rearing children with mental retardation in 2005 face an entirely different social service world—with entirely different advantages and challenges—than did parents and families in 1980 or 1970 (Glidden, 2002).

From the perspective of both the child and the ecology, then, mental retardation constitutes an important area of applied developmental psychology. But as a topic that may be less known to many readers, we begin this chapter by briefly defining mental retardation, as well as describing issues of classification within the population itself. We then discuss findings arising from an approach that classifies children with mental retardation by genetic etiology. From such child-centered discussions, we proceed to developmental issues relating to parents, families, and larger ecologies. After discussing several research issues, we end this chapter with examples of preliminary interventions and remaining issues that such interventions entail.

DIAGNOSIS AND CLASSIFICATION

Before summarizing new findings, it is first necessary to define the term mental retardation and to present different ways of classifying these children. As noted in the discussion that follows, controversies arise in both the definition and classification of mental retardation. Such definitional and classificatory controversies are mainly examined as background for later, more expanded discussions of developmental findings and their applications.

Diagnosis

From the early 1960s on, definitions of mental retardation have included three basic factors. First, the person (child or adult) must display impaired intellectual functioning. Second, that person must show concomitant impairments in adaptive behavior. Third, such intellectual and adaptive impairments should begin during the childhood years; thus, cognitive-adaptive impairments involving adult-onset diseases or accidents are not considered to involve mental retardation. These three basic principles are generally referred to as the three-factor definition of mental retardation.

Unfortunately, the specifics of all except the final criterion have been the subject of long-standing, often heated debate. Consider the first criterion, impaired intellectual functioning. In definitions from the 1960s (Heber, 1961), the IQ cutoff was placed at 85; that is, all persons with IQs below 85 were considered to have mental retardation. More recently, most definitional manuals have placed the IQ cutoff 2 standard deviations below the mean of 100 (i.e., IQ 70 or below). Even now, however, some influential systems (e.g., American Association on Mental Retardation [AAMR], 1992) have noted that the IQ cutoff should be placed at IQ 70 or 75 and below, which may have the unintended effect of vastly increasing the number of persons eligible for the diagnosis of mental retardation (e.g., MacMillan, Gresham, & Siperstein, 1993). In addition, all other controversies with intelligence tests apply, including whether IQ tests really measure intelligence and whether one can achieve a "culturally fair" IQ test.

Similarly, controversy also surrounds the second criteria. The idea is simple: Children or adults should be considered to have mental retardation only when, in addition to cognitive-intellectual deficits, these individuals also show impairments in their everyday, adaptive functioning. Directly following from the first tests of adaptive behavior during the 1950s (Doll, 1953), adaptive impairments have constituted an explicit diagnostic criterion in diagnostic-classificatory manuals from the early 1970s on (e.g., Grossman, 1973).

Again, the devil is in the details. What are the "correct" dimensions or factors of adaptive behavior? No one really knows. In one major test of adaptive behavior, the Vineland Adaptive Behavior Scales, Sparrow, Balla, and Cicchetti (1984) identify three domains: communication, daily living skills, and socialization. In the 1992 version of the AAMR's (1992) manual, 10 different domains are proposed: communication, self-care, home living, social skills, community use, self-direction, health and safety, functional academics, leisure, and work. In that same organization's more recent manual, three domains are proposed (conceptual, social, and practical adaptive skills; AAMR, 2002).

Factor analytic studies provide some help, but these findings are also not definitive. In general, studies reveal from two to seven factors of adaptive behavior, with a single primary factor accounting for most of the variance (Harrison, 1987; McGrew & Bruininks, 1989). Most researchers and practitioners therefore agree that mental retardation involves impaired intellectual and adaptive functioning. But problems arise when one specifies the nature of the construct, how it is to be measured, and what cutoff scores will bring about the diagnosis of mental retardation.

For our purposes, mental retardation should be diagnosed when a child or adult has an IQ below 70 and has impairments in adaptive behavior (as tested by the Vineland or other standardized instrument), and when onset occurs during the childhood years. Interested readers should refer to more detailed explanations and discussions (e.g., Switzky & Greenspan, 2003).

Classification: Three Approaches

Most people would agree that children and adults with mental retardation differ one from another. As before, the problem is exactly which classifications are most meaningful for research, intervention, or policy. In general, three approaches characterize attempts to classify individuals with mental retardation.

Degree-of-Impairment Approach

Over the years, most researchers and clinicians have employed a system that classifies persons with mental retardation by their degree of intellectual impairment. This classification system designates persons with mental retardation as mildly, moderately, severely, or profoundly retarded.

Although Table 12.1 describes each level, a few points should be made. First, the degree-of-impairment system has predominated in both research and practice over many years. Granted, names have changed over the years, and different fields use slightly different terms. Still, most professionals are familiar with categorizing mental retardation by the child's degree of impairment.

Second, although adaptive behavior is a part of mental retardation's three-factor definition, most professionals classify individuals by levels of intellectual, not adaptive, impairment. As noted in Table 12.1, individuals at identical IQ levels vary in their adaptive functioning. This variability in adaptive behavior is particularly common for individuals with mild (IQ 55 to 69) and

moderate (IQ 40 to 54) mental retardation; individuals with severe or profound mental retardation usually show closer ties of adaptive and intellectual impairments.

Third, the degree-of-impairment system says nothing about the causes of the person's mental retardation. Individuals with moderate mental retardation might have Down syndrome, Williams syndrome, another genetic disorder, fetal alcohol syndrome (FAS), anoxia at birth, or no clear cause for their mental retardation. The relevant issue pertains to the person's degree of intellectual

TABLE 12.1 Degree-of-Impairment Classification System

Mild mental retardation (IQ 55–70): This group constitutes as many as 90% of all persons with mental retardation (American Psychiatric Association, 1994). These individuals appear similar to typical individuals, and often blend into the nonretarded population in the years before and after formal schooling. As adults, some of these individuals hold jobs, marry, and raise families and are indistinguishable from nonretarded people. More persons with mild mental retardation come from minority and low socioeconomic (SES) backgrounds than would be expected from their numbers in the general population (Hodapp, 1994; Stromme & Magnus, 2000).

Moderate mental retardation (IQ 40–54): The second most prevalent group are those individuals who are more impaired intellectually and adaptively. More of these individuals are diagnosed as having mental retardation during the preschool years. Many individuals with moderate mental retardation show one or more clear organic causes for their mental retardation (e.g., Down syndrome, fragile X syndrome). Although some persons with moderate mental retardation require few supportive services, most continue to require some help throughout life. In one study, 20% of persons with IQs from 40 to 49 lived independently, 60% were considered dependent, and 20% were totally dependent on others (Ross, Begab, Dondis, Giampiccolo, & Meyers, 1985). In a similar way, some of these individuals hold jobs in the outside workforce as unskilled laborers, and others work in supervised workshop programs.

Severe mental retardation (IQ 25–39): This category refers to persons with more severe impairments. The majority of these individuals suffer from one or more organic causes of mental retardation. Many persons with severe mental retardation show concurrent physical or ambulatory problems; others have respiratory, heart, or other co-occurring conditions. Most persons with severe mental retardation require some special assistance throughout their lives. Many live in supervised group homes or small regional facilities, and most work in either workshop or "pre-workshop" settings.

Profound mental retardation (IQ below 25 or 20): In this group are persons with the most severe levels of intellectual and adaptive impairments. These persons generally learn only the rudiments of communicative skills, and intensive training is required to teach basic eating, grooming, toileting, and dressing behaviors. Persons with profound mental retardation require lifelong care and assistance. Most show organic causes for their mental retardation, and many have severe co-occurring conditions that sometimes lead to death during childhood or early adulthood. Some persons with profound mental retardation can perform preworkshop tasks, and most live in supervised group homes or small, specialized facilities.

impairment, not any causes or etiologies of the mental retardation per se.

Finally, controversy exists in that the 1992 edition of the AAMR's diagnostic and classificatory manual proposes to do away with this degree-of-impairment classificatory system. The AAMR asserts that the degree-of-impairment system does not give enough weight to the interplay between the individual and the environmental supports needed by that individual. Therefore, in that 1992 version (and again in the 2002 version), the AAMR instead categorizes individuals by the amount and length of the supportive services that they need. Instead of the mild-moderate-severe-profound distinction, the AAMR 1992 manual classifies individuals by their need for intermittent, limited, extensive, or pervasive environmental supports. Because these support levels somewhat relate (albeit imperfectly) to the person's degree of impairment, we ignore this modification, as do almost all researchers; the system appears in fewer than 2% of recently published behavioral research articles in the main mental retardation journals (Polloway, Smith, Chamberlain, Denning, & Smith, 1999).

Two-Group Approach

A second approach categorizes by the cause of mental retardation. An early form of this process is called the "two-group approach" to mental retardation. Formalized by Edward Zigler (1967, 1969) in the late 1960s, variants of this approach have existed from the early twentieth century (Burack, 1990). By the mid-1960s, researchers had long discussed two groups of persons with mental retardation.

Proponents of the two-group approach hold that the first group consists of persons who show no identifiable cause for their mental retardation. Such individuals are generally more mildly impaired and tend to blend in with other, nonretarded persons. Causes probably range from polygenetic inheritance to environmental deprivation (or overstimulation); different persons may have different polygenic or environmental causes, or there may be an interplay between the two (Hodapp, 1994). This type of mental retardation has been referred to as familial, cultural-familial, or sociocultural-familial; nonorganic, nonspecific, or undifferentiated; and mental retardation due to environmental deprivation. Even this listing highlights the discrepant beliefs about the causes of mental retardation in these individuals.

In contrast to those with cultural-familial mental retardation, other individuals show one or more organic causes for their mental retardation. Such causes include hundreds of separate organic insults. These insults can occur prenatally, perinatally, or postnatally. Prenatal causes include all of the 1,000+ genetic mental retardation disorders, FAS, fetal alcohol exposure (FAE), and rubella, as well as all accidents in utero. Perinatal causes include prematurity, anoxia at birth, and other birth-related complications. Postnatal causes range from sicknesses (meningitis) to head trauma. In addition, those with organic mental retardation are more likely to show greater degrees of intellectual impairments; in most surveys, as IQ levels decrease, increasingly higher percentages of persons show an identifiable organic cause (Stromme & Hagberg, 2000).

Etiological Approach

In many ways, classifying by specific etiology of the child's mental retardation updates the earlier two-group approach. Instead of examining a single organic group, one now begins to examine behavioral development in many different groups (Burack, Hodapp, & Zigler, 1988).

This more detailed etiological approach also reflects recent biomedical advances. In contrast to earlier years, when little was known about mental retardation's causes, more than 1,000 different genetic anomalies have now been linked to mental retardation (King, Hodapp, & Dykens, 2005). For most such disorders, we can go back and forth between the beginning point, the genetic anomaly itself, and the endpoint, the behavior that seems predisposed by having that specific genetic anomaly (as well as the many different medical and physical sequelae). Over the past few decades, we have come to realize that persons with different genetic disorders are prone to different behavioral characteristics. We now turn to genetic disorders' effects on behavior.

BEHAVIORAL PHENOTYPES: EXAMPLES, CONCEPTUAL ISSUES, AND DEVELOPMENTAL IMPLICATIONS

To provide a flavor of how genetic disorders affect behavior—the subfield of "behavioral phenotypes"—we first briefly describe Down syndrome, Prader-Willi syndrome, and Williams syndrome. From there we step back a bit, explaining what we mean by the term behavioral phenotypes and highlighting that definition's most important features.

Down, Prader-Willi, and Williams Syndromes

Although one could choose as examples any of the 1,000+ genetic mental retardation syndromes, we here pick three: Down syndrome, Prader-Willi syndrome, and Williams syndrome. These three disorders are reasonably well-known and feature recent studies that have produced some interesting behavioral findings.

Down Syndrome

Caused in most cases by the occurrence of three (instead of two) chromosome 21s, Down syndrome is the best-known and the most prevalent genetic (i.e., chromosomal) abnormality, occurring once in every 800 to 1,000 live births. First described in 1866 by J. Langdon Down (see Dunn, 1991), Down syndrome has for many years been the focus of genetic and behavioral research.

Children with Down syndrome usually have characteristic physical features, including an epicanthic fold above the eyes (leading to the syndrome's original label, "mongolism"), a protruding tongue, short stature, and, during infancy, hypotonia (weak muscle tone). Down syndrome often occurs together with such medical conditions as heart defects, leukemia, and gut atresia (Leshin, 2002). Although in the past, persons with Down syndrome were often institutionalized and had a short life span, most individuals now live at home and medical treatments for all ages have increased the life span (Cohen, 2002). Down syndrome may be detected during pregnancy through chorionic villus sampling or amniocentesis; such procedures are usually recommended in women above age 35, who bear a substantially higher risk (Pueschel, 1990).

Three behavioral characteristics appear in most individuals with Down syndrome. The first involves a specific set of cognitive-linguistic strengths and weaknesses. In various studies, persons with Down syndrome appear particularly impaired in language. Such impairments, which are more pronounced than overall levels of mental age, occur in linguistic grammar (Chapman & Hesketh, 2000), in expressive (as opposed to receptive) language (Miller, 1999), and in articulation (Kumin, 1994). Conversely, persons with Down syndrome often show relatively higher performance on tasks of visual short-term memory, and the "visual-over-auditory" pattern of short-term memory seems to become more pro-

nounced beginning in the late teen years (Hodapp & Ricci, 2002).

A second behavioral issue involves the rate of development, with children with Down syndrome developing at slower rates as they get older. Most studies show that children with Down syndrome have their highest IQ scores in the earlier years, with gradually decreasing IQ as time goes on. These children continue developing, but at slower and slower rates as they get older (Hodapp, Evans, & Gray, 1999). Such slowings of development may relate to age-related changes or to difficulties these children have in achieving certain cognitive tasks (e.g., language; Hodapp & Zigler, 1995).

A third, possibly related change concerns Alzheimer's disease. It is now known that neuropathological signs of Alzheimer's disease appear to be universal in individuals with Down syndrome by age 35 (Wisniewski, Wisniewski, & Wen, 1985). Geneticists continue to explore the connection of Down syndrome with Alzheimer's and to learn more about pathological segments of chromosome 21 involved in overlapping conditions.

Case Example of a Young Adult Woman with Down Syndrome

Julie, a 21-year-old with Down syndrome, sits in the clinic with her mother. "It's just us," offers mother, "and we have our routines, but I am worried that she doesn't get out enough, like she used to in school." Julie did well in school, her reading and math skills were between the fourth- and sixth-grade levels, and Julie also had very well-developed daily living skills, especially in performing personal grooming and household chores. Julie chimes in, "Overland High School, I graduate," and with increased animation, starts to list the names of her former classmates. Her mother smiles and nods and adds that Julie was well-liked by her high school friends and was greeted warmly by students and teachers alike. Julie was always quick with a smile or an enthusiastic high-five, and much to her delight, received a standing ovation from her classmates at graduation!

But since then, things had not gone as well. The vocational training program that Julie was slated to attend after graduation had a long waiting list, and in the interim, Julie attended a social program three mornings a week. Her mother was concerned that this was not enough for Julie, that the program did not encourage Julie to practice or learn new academic skills, nor to interact with new friends. With her mother working full time, most of Julie's days were spent watching TV alone at home and helping to take care of a neighbor's cat. Julie has lost some of her "sparkle," complained her mother, and she was also becoming a bit more "into herself" and passive, not to mention overweight.

Ultimately, the clinic staff, Julie, and her mother agreed on a plan of action. The social worker would check on the status of the vocational program, and should the wait be excessive, identify alternative training programs that met for at least 5 hours a day. The idea of an advocate was raised, although Julie's mother declined the need for one. Julie offered that she wanted to take care of more cats, and she and her mother agreed to explore the possibility of volunteering at a local animal shelter. Julie and her mother agreed to try to take walks after dinner, and Julie, once an avid swimmer, was encouraged to reenroll in the Special Olympics swimming program.

Julie's story demonstrates several concerns for persons with Down syndrome and other young adults:

- The difficulties families face when services are no longer provided at school
- The need for families to advocate for quality adult services
- The propensity for adults with Down syndrome to become more sedentary and withdrawn
- The need for innovative programs that foster lifelong learning in adults with mental retardation (adapted from Hodapp & Dykens, 2003)

Prader-Willi Syndrome

Prader-Willi syndrome is caused by missing genetic material from the chromosome 15 derived from the father—either a deletion on the paternally derived 15 or two chromosome 15s from the mother (maternal uniparental disomy). Most individuals with Prader-Willi syndrome are short in stature (about 5′ in adulthood) and show extreme hyperphagia (overeating). Such hyperphagia (and resultant obesity) have long been considered the hallmarks of Prader-Willi syndrome, and most cases of early death in the syndrome relate to obesity and its related heart and circulatory problems (Butler et al., 2002; Whittington et al., 2001).

In addition to hyperphagia, many individuals show high levels of many different maladaptive behaviors. Along with hyperphagia, many persons with Prader-Willi syndrome also show temper tantrums and other acting-out

behaviors. Dykens, Leckman, and Cassidy (1996) also showed the very high presence of obsessions and compulsions in this group. In both children and adults with Prader-Willi syndrome, non-food-related obsessions and compulsions occurred at similar levels among nonretarded children and adults who had been clinically diagnosed with obsessive-compulsive disorder.

Intellectually, most children with Prader-Willi syndrome show relative weaknesses on tasks involving consecutive, step-by-step order in problem solving, or sequential processing. In contrast, these children perform well on tasks requiring integration and synthesis of stimuli as a unified whole, or simultaneous processing (Dykens, Hodapp, Walsh, & Nash, 1992). Dykens (2002) has recently found that many individuals with Prader-Willi syndrome demonstrate particularly high-level abilities in jigsaw puzzles. Such high levels in jigsaw puzzles are, on average, even above those shown by typical children of comparable chronological ages. Why such spared areas of functioning occur remains unknown, nor are we currently clear about whether these children's skills in jigsaw puzzles are specific to this single task or instead reflect a more general visual-spatial ability.

Case Example of a Boy with Prader-Willi Syndrome

"We have reached the point where we need to lock." Jake, age 11 years, was busy at the table, working at a puzzle, while his mother brought the clinic team up to date on Jake's diet. Jake was diagnosed with Prader-Willi syndrome shortly after birth and has since demonstrated the classic features of the syndrome: hypotonia in infancy, delayed milestones, and a marked interest in eating and food that began at about age 5. From preschool on, Jake had a "stubborn" streak that evolved into a more pervasive insistence that certain things be "just so," such as his collection of airplane books and book bag. Jake was also now having troubles at school because he insisted on erasing and reworking his letters to the point where he wore holes through the paper and couldn't move on to the next activity.

Further, adds his mother, his food seeking is much worse. Although the clinic staff had previously discussed with the family the possibility of locking the cabinets and refrigerator, the family had not yet felt the need to do so; they could manage Jake's food seeking with a watchful eye from parents and older sister. Now, though, Jake's weight was creeping up, as were instances of food snitching at home and school.

"Now that we are locking," notes Jake's mother, "he asks about food less and less, and it relieves his older sister, who is 15, from being the 'food police.' If he knows that he can't get into it, he is more apt to get involved with other things, like his puzzles." Indeed, Jake, who has just completed a 50-piece puzzle with remarkable speed, looks up with a grin. "This one was easy," he boasts. "I thought you said you had hard puzzles!"

As suggested by this brief case, many youngsters with Prader-Willi syndrome show a host of behavioral concerns, especially hyperphagia and compulsions. For children like Jake, the management of diet and behavior needs to be carefully coordinated between school and home, and later between work and home (or group home). As families struggle to maintain a low-calorie diet, managing their offspring's compulsive behaviors and tantrums are often more stressful for them. As Jake demonstrates, however, many persons with Prader-Willi syndrome have relatively well-developed expressive vocabulary and visual-spatial strengths, especially in solving jigsaw puzzles. In Jake's case, the school teacher and staff used special "puzzle time" at school as an incentive for letting go of his rewriting and erasing and to make easier transitions.

Williams Syndrome

Occurring in about 1 per 20,000 births, Williams syndrome is caused by a microdeletion on one of the chromosome 7s that includes the gene for elastin, a protein that provides strength and elasticity to tissues of the heart, skin, blood vessels, and lungs (Ewart et al., 1993). Children with this syndrome generally show a characteristic, "elfin-like" facial appearance, along with heart and other health problems (Dykens, Hodapp, & Finucane, 2000). As many as 95% of these children suffer from hyperacusis, or a hypersensitivity to sound.

Williams syndrome is best known for its cognitive-linguistic profile. Specifically, children with Williams syndrome appear strikingly good at many linguistic tasks. Indeed, earlier studies even hinted that these children might be able to perform linguistically at or nearly at levels shown by nonretarded age-mates (Bellugi, Marks, Bihrle, & Sabo, 1988). Recent studies dispute this finding, showing that only about 5% of children with Williams syndrome seem spared in language abilities (Bishop, 1999; Mervis, Morris, Bertrand, & Robinson, 1999). Still, language skills are relatively strong

(compared to overall mental age) in children with Williams syndrome.

In contrast, many children with Williams syndrome perform poorly on visual-spatial measures (Udwin & Yule, 1991; Udwin, Yule, & Martin, 1987), including such tasks as putting together a jigsaw puzzle and drawing (Bellugi, Wang, & Jernigan, 1994; Dykens, Rosner, & Ly, 2001). These children seem to have difficulties in "constructive visuo-spatial skills": visuospatial activities requiring one to mentally put together an object's various pieces or parts. In addition, the discrepancies between the higher-level language skills and the lower-level language abilities appear to become increasingly pronounced as children get older (Jarrold, Baddeley, Hewes, & Phillips, 2001).

In contrast to work on cognitive-linguistic profiles, studies have yet to fully examine the personality or psychiatric features of people with Williams syndrome. Early descriptions hinted at a "classic" Williams syndrome personality, described as pleasant, unusually friendly, affectionate, loquacious, engaging, and interpersonally sensitive and charming (e.g., Dilts, Morris, & Leonard, 1990). Such qualities may change over the course of development, with adults being more withdrawn and less overly friendly than children (Gosch & Pankau, 1997).

Recent findings expand these observations. Using the Reiss Personality Profiles (Reiss & Havercamp, 1998), Dykens and Rosner (1999) found that, relative to controls, adolescents and adults with Williams syndrome are more likely to initiate interactions with others (87% of sample), to enjoy social activities (83%), to be kind-spirited (100%) and caring (94%), and to empathize with others' positive feelings (75%) or when others are in pain (87%). At the same time, however, these subjects had difficulties making or keeping friends and were often dangerously indiscriminate in their relating to others.

Recently, attention has also begun to focus on anxieties and fears in this population. Generalized anxiety, worry, and perseverative thinking are commonly seen in Williams syndrome (e.g., Einfeld, Tonge, & Florio, 1997), and people with the syndrome appear to show unusually high levels of fears and phobias. Relative to suitably matched controls, fears in persons with Williams syndrome are more frequent, wide-ranging, and severe and are also associated with impaired social-adaptive adjustment. In one study, Dykens (2003) compared fears in 120 people with Williams syndrome (ages 6 to 48 years) to those with mental retardation of mixed etiologies. Only two fears, getting a shot and going to the dentist, were mentioned by over 50% of the group with mixed causes of mental retardation. In contrast, 50 different fears were mentioned by over 60% of subjects with Williams syndrome. Such fears ran the gamut. Some involved interpersonal issues such as being teased, getting punished, or getting into arguments with others; others involved such physical issues as injections, being in a fire or getting burned, or getting stung by a bee; still others related to these children's hyperacusis or clumsiness (loud noises/sirens, falling from high places, thunderstorms). Though not every person with Williams syndrome shows one or all of these fears, the vast majority seem overly fearful compared to most others with intellectual disabilities.

Case Example of a Teenage Girl with Williams Syndrome

Susie, a highly energetic 14-year-old with Williams syndrome, declared with great enthusiasm, "Why, everyone is my friend!" Indeed, so it seemed to her parents, who were both tickled and worried by their daughter's quest to interact with everyone they met. On the one hand, they loved her sociable nature; on the other, they worried about her poor social judgment and vulnerability as she entered adolescence.

Diagnosed with Williams syndrome at 10 months of age, Susie had come through corrective heart surgery and an infancy marked by fussiness and feeding difficulties. At around age 3, however, Susie "came around," and her language and interest in the world took off. She stared intently at the faces of teachers and therapists, an endearing quality that adults loved. After a period of language delay, she quickly caught up, and on formal testing as a first-grader, Susie's vocabulary skills exceeded her overall cognitive abilities. Although her educational testing also showed that Susie had poorly developed visual-spatial abilities, this had always been less a source of worry for her parents than her increasing anxiety and social disinhibition.

Increasingly, Susie frets and worries about things — what will happen next, or what if the car breaks down or her piano teacher has a heart attack. Her father affectionately calls her his "worrywart." Even so, her anxiety can get out of hand at times, but never to the point that it stops her from getting in the car or taking her piano lesson. Along with her growing anxiety, Susie has a grow-

ing interest in music. She is persistent at the keyboard, yet not necessarily "gifted" in the way that some persons with Williams syndrome seem to be. She simply loves music and often hums tunes to herself as she plunks at the piano, what she herself calls "my creative me in motion." Her father observes that this activity seems to calm her down and helps her to settle for the night. Recently, Susie has asked to try another instrument so that she can play in the school band, or to join the glee club, so that she can sing with others.

Susie thus demonstrates many of the key behavioral features of Williams syndrome:

- Well-developed expressive language
- A strong social orientation coupled with poor social judgment and disinhibition
- A worried, fretful stance
- An interest in music that may or may not reflect remarkable "talent" but that is emotionally compelling and gratifying

Concepts and Issues

Although these descriptions provide a quick sense of etiology-related behavioral characteristics in three syndromes, we have left until now several conceptual issues concerning the nature and study of behavioral phenotypes.

The first issue is one of basic definition. While interest in behavioral phenotypes has increased enormously over the past 2 decades, the very term itself has been debated widely. What is a behavioral phenotype? To us, a behavioral phenotype involves "the heightened probability or likelihood that people with a given syndrome will exhibit certain behavioral and developmental sequelae relative to those without the syndrome" (Dykens, 1995, p. 523). In contrast to other definitions, such a definition focuses on probabilities, the idea that genetic disorders predispose those who have them to a greater chance or likelihood of showing a particular behavior or set of behaviors. Compared to groups with mental retardation in general (arising from any number of other causes), groups with a particular genetic cause will show certain behaviors to a greater extent or in a higher percentage of individuals. Such behaviors might be a particular pattern of cognitive-linguistic strengths and weaknesses, or a particular age at which development slows, or a particular type of maladaptive behavior.

This more probabilistic definition highlights three basic facts, which we discuss next.

Many, but Not All, Individuals Show the Syndrome's "Characteristic" Behaviors

A more probabilistic definition acknowledges the large amount of variance within specific etiologies. Rarely are etiology-related behaviors found in every person with a particular syndrome. Consider the case of Down syndrome. Even compared to their overall mental age, children and adults with Down syndrome generally show deficits in linguistic grammar (Fowler, 1990) and often show receptive language abilities in advance of expressive abilities (Miller, 1999). In addition, approximately 95% of mothers of children with Down syndrome report that others have difficulty understanding their child's articulation of words and phrases (Kumin, 1994).

Yet, despite such commonly observed deficits, not every person with Down syndrome shows particular difficulties with grammar, articulation, or expressive language. Rondal (1995) reported on the case of Françoise, a 32-year-old woman whose IQ is 64. Although Françoise has trisomy 21, she nevertheless utters long and complex sentences. Rondal reports her saying (translated), "And that does not surprise me because dogs are always too warm when they go outside" ("Et ça m'étonne pas parce que les chiens ont toujours trop chaud quand ils vont à la port"; p. 117). Although grammatical, articulatory, and expressive language problems may be common in Down syndrome, not every person with the syndrome shows such behavioral characteristics.

Some Etiology-Related Behaviors Are Unique to a Single Syndrome, Others Are Common to Two or More Syndromes

A more probabilistic definition's second corollary involves the Uniqueness Question (Pennington, O'Connor, & Sudhalter, 1991): To what extent is any etiology-related behavior or pattern of behaviors unique to a single syndrome, as opposed to being shared by a few genetic disorders?

At this point, both unique and partially shared behavioral phenotypes occur, although partially shared phenotypes are probably more common (Hodapp, 1997). Considering unique or totally specific behavioral outcomes first, the following behaviors seem unique to a single syndrome:

- Extreme hyperphagia (Dykens, 1999) in Prader-Willi syndrome
- The "cat cry" (Gersh et al., 1995) in 5p- syndrome (formerly called cri-du-chat—or cry of the cat—syndrome)
- Extreme self-mutilation (L. T. Anderson & Ernst, 1994) in Lesch-Nyhan syndrome
- Stereotypic hand washing or hand wringing (Van Acker, 1991) in Rett syndrome
- Body self-hugging (Finucane, Konar, Haas-Givler, Kurtz, & Scott, 1994) and putting objects into bodily orifices (Greenberg et al., 1996) in Smith-Magenis syndrome

In contrast to what seems likely to remain a fairly short list, many more instances will probably be discovered in which partial specificity is at work. To give but a few examples, a particular advantage in simultaneous (i.e., holistic, Gestalt-like) processing compared to sequential (step-by-step) processing has now been found in children with Prader-Willi syndrome (Dykens et al., 1992) and in boys with fragile X syndrome (Dykens, Hodapp, & Leckman, 1987; Kemper, Hagerman, & Altshul-Stark, 1988). Similarly, compared to groups with intellectual disabilities in general, hyperactivity is more frequently found in children with 5p- syndrome (Dykens & Clarke, 1997) and in boys with fragile X syndrome (Baumgardner, Reiss, Freund, & Abrams, 1995). In both instances, a pattern of strengths and weaknesses or a particular type of maladaptive behavior-psychopathology is found in a few genetic disorders to much greater degrees (or in higher percentages of individuals) than is commonly noted among others with mental retardation.

Finally, partially specific behavioral effects seem more in line with many areas of genetics, child psychiatry, and psychiatry. Across these different disciplines, researchers are now discussing the many pathways, both genetic and environmental, by which one comes to have one or another psychiatric disorder. The clinical geneticist John Opitz (1985, p. 9) put it well when he noted, "The causes are many, but the common developmental pathways are few."

Etiology-Related Behaviors Occur across Many Behavioral Domains

When considering behavioral phenotypes, most researchers probably think of salient maladaptive behaviors. We therefore see a keen interest in hyperphagia, obsessive-compulsive disorder, and tantrums in Prader-

Willi syndrome; autism or autism-like behavior in fragile X and Rett syndromes; and extreme self-mutilation in Lesch-Nyhan syndrome. To many professionals, the term "behavioral phenotypes" connotes the different, etiology-related maladaptive behavior-psychopathology seen in several syndromes.

Without discounting the excitement brought about by the study of etiology-related maladaptive behavior and psychopathology, behavioral phenotypes also involve many other domains of functioning. Thus, etiology-related strengths and weaknesses occur in language, cognition, and social and adaptive behaviors and within specific subdomains. Etiology-related profiles of strengths and weaknesses also exist across these various domains and show distinct patterns of development. One could also examine sequences across various developmental domains to determine whether early language, social, emotional, or cognitive development (or developments within subareas of each; e.g., theory of mind) show the "usual" or normative orderings. Rates of development are also open to etiology-related analyses. In short, we envision the purview of behavioral phenotypes as very large indeed, and sample from this large purview in the next section.

DEVELOPMENTAL IMPLICATIONS

Although one could discuss many different developmental issues, we here examine sequences, cross-domain relations, and how those cross-domain relations might change with increasing chronological age.

Sequences

From Piaget on, developmentalists have been interested in identifying universal, invariant sequences of development. Similarly, from the 1960s on, usual or normative developmental sequences have been linked to children with mental retardation. In Zigler's (1967, 1969) original developmental approach to mental retardation, he described what came to be known as the "similar sequence hypothesis." This hypothesis held that children with mental retardation, like children who are typically developing, will traverse Piagetian, early language, or other universal developmental sequences in the same, invariant order.

But even in Zigler's earliest formulations, the similar-sequence prediction was also tied to the child's type of mental retardation. In contrasting cultural-familial from organic forms of mental retardation, Zigler (1969) held that only children with cultural-familial mental retardation would necessarily show sequences in their development similar to that of nonretarded children. In contrast, he was unclear as to whether normative developmental processes applied to children with organic forms of mental retardation. To quote Zigler:

> If the etiology of the phenotypic intelligence (as measured by an IQ) of two groups differs, *it is far from logical* to assert that the course of development is the same, or that even similar contents in their behaviors are mediated by exactly the same cognitive processes. (p. 533, emphasis added)

To date, however, the findings generally support the similar sequence hypothesis for most children with mental retardation (of either cultural-familial or organic forms). Several reviews indicate that most children, on most developmental tasks, do seem to progress in the usual, invariant order (Hodapp, 1990; Weisz, Yeates, & Zigler, 1982). Possible exceptions involve children with severe seizure disorders, but here difficulties arise in relation to what constitutes a valid test of these children's abilities. Children with mental retardation may also become less systematic or differently sequential when tasks are more social—or occur later in development—as opposed to these children's more usual, invariant sequential development on earlier and less social tasks (Hodapp, 1990).

Until recently, such findings have generally characterized the similar sequence hypothesis. But over the past few years, it has become apparent that not all developments occur in the usual, invariant order in every genetic etiology. Specifically, consider the finding that young, typically developing children usually show pointing before labeling in their earliest communications. Most 10- to 12-month-olds will gesturally point to or show an object in order to get adults to attend (what Bates, Camaioni, & Volterra, 1975, call "proto-declaratives"), achieving the appropriate verbal labels only sometime during their 2nd year of life. But Mervis, Robinson, Rowe, Becerra, and Klein-Tasman (2003) have recently reported that this sequence of pointing before speaking was not found in 9 of 10 children with Williams syndrome. On average, these 9 children with Williams syndrome produced referential object labels ("ball") 6 months before beginning to comprehend or produce referential pointing gestures. As we note later, this finding makes sense given the relatively strong linguistic skills and relatively weak visuospatial skills shown by most children with William syndrome. Still, such findings are interesting and have many theoretical and practical implications.

Cross-Domain Relations

Cross-domain relations in children with mental retardation also feature a long history. In addition to his similar sequence hypothesis, Zigler (1969) also proposed what came to be called the "similar structure hypothesis." This hypothesis implicitly drew on developmental theories of the 1960s that asserted that children's development was "all of a piece," that a child's level of development in one area (e.g., language) was roughly equal to that same child's development in all other areas (e.g., cognitive, social). And again, Zigler explicitly applied this similar structure hypothesis only to children with cultural-familial mental retardation.

This time, the findings seem clearer. The similar structure hypothesis holds up reasonably well for children with cultural-familial mental retardation, although even here children display performance that is below overall mental age levels on some attentional and information-processing tasks (Weiss, Weisz, & Bromfield, 1986). Less clear is why such lower than expected functioning occurs. Some researchers have postulated that children with cultural-familial mental retardation really do have a deficit in their information-processing abilities (Mundy & Kasari, 1990); conversely, any seeming deficit may be due more to the boring, repetitive nature of many information-processing tasks (Weisz, 1990).

In contrast, all would agree that children with organic mental retardation show performance on several cognitive-linguistic tasks that falls below their overall mental age. As noted earlier, the specifics of such deficits vary widely. Summarizing from our earlier discussions, the following characterize the cognitive-linguistic profiles of children with Down syndrome, Prader-Willi syndrome, and Williams syndrome:

- *Down syndrome:* Children with Down syndrome show relative strengths in visual versus auditory short-term memory (Hodapp et al., 1999; Pueschel, Gallagher, Zartler, & Pezzullo, 1986), as well as weaknesses in expressive language and in grammar (Chapman & Hesketh, 2000; Miller, 1999).
- *Prader-Willi syndrome:* In addition to showing abilities in simultaneous, or holistic (Gestalt), processing relative to sequential, step-by-step processing (Dykens et al., 1992), children with Prader-Willi syndrome solve jigsaw puzzles at levels well above both mental age-matched children with mental retardation *and* chronological age-matched, typically developing children (Dykens, 2002).
- *Williams syndrome:* Children with Williams syndrome show extreme weaknesses in many visuospatial tasks, even as they show relative strengths in several areas of language (Bellugi, Mills, Jernigan, Hickok, & Galaburda, 1999; Mervis et al., 1999).

Such findings obviously lead to many new questions. Given that each syndrome has a different pattern of strengths and weaknesses, how does one divide up cognitive functioning? Examining only Down syndrome, one might conclude that intelligence is divided into visual versus auditory short-term memory, or into linguistic versus nonlinguistic functioning. If one were instead to examine the other two syndromes, then simultaneous versus sequential processing (in Prader-Willi syndrome) or linguistic versus visuospatial functioning (Williams syndrome) might seem the preferred way of cutting up the intellectual pie. At this point, no one can say for certain, but findings from genetic syndromes definitely must be included when considering the possible connections and disconnections among diverse areas of human functioning.

A second issue concerns connections among various domains. Particularly in earlier studies, language functioning was thought to be modular in Williams syndrome. Modularity, in Fodor's (1983) sense, refers to an encapsulated system that develops with little or no contact with other of the child's developments (see also Gardner's, 1983, multiple intelligences). But unlike what might be predicted from a modular perspective, Mervis et al. (1999) found strong correlations (from .47 to .64) between various measures of short-term memory and grammatical levels. Although language is relatively strong—and visuospatial skills weak—in Williams syndrome, the language of these children is also not totally modular. In line with typically developing children, language in children with Williams syndrome connects to other areas of these children's cognition.

Cross-Domain Relations over Age

Although etiology-related strengths and weaknesses do not appear fully formed at birth, how such strengths and weaknesses appear has only begun to be examined. During the past few years, several researchers have examined cognitive-linguistic profiles over time in children with several different etiologies of mental retardation. Most such studies have been cross-sectional, although a few recent studies have examined evolving profiles as the child develops.

Across several etiological groups, with increasing chronological age the children's strengths develop more quickly than do their weaknesses. In Down syndrome, the pattern of visual over auditory short-term memory becomes more pronounced during the late teen years (Hodapp & Ricci, 2002), and, among boys with fragile X syndrome, the advantage of simultaneous over sequential processing also becomes more pronounced as these children get older (Hodapp, Dykens, Ort, Zelinsky, & Leckman, 1991). In the sole longitudinal study, Jarrold et al. (2001) examined children with Williams syndrome to determine the development in vocabulary (a relative strength in this syndrome) versus visuospatial skills (a relative weakness). Examining 15 children/adolescents on six occasions over a 4-year period, Jarrold et al. found that vocabulary levels developed much more quickly over time than did visuospatial skills. Figure 12.1 illustrates developmental trajectories by plotting age-equivalent (mental age-like) scores for both vocabulary and visuospatial abilities, averaged over all children and

all testings. Such divergent trajectories allow already existing relative strengths to become gradually stronger and relative weaknesses gradually weaker as these children get older.

Although no good explanations exist as to why strengths become stronger and weaknesses weaker over time, one possibility involves an interplay between the child's etiology-related propensities and subsequent experiences. One measure of experience involves the child's everyday, leisure-time activities, that is, those behaviors that children (or their parents) choose to perform every day. In one study, Rosner, Hodapp, Fidler, Sagun, and Dykens (2004) examined the everyday leisure activities of three groups of children: those with Williams syndrome, those with Prader-Willi syndrome, and those with Down syndrome. Using parent reports of leisure-time behavior from Achenbach's (1991) Child Behavior Checklist, behaviors were grouped into those involving music, reading, visual-motor activities, athletics, pretend play, and focused interests.

Our findings mostly reflect etiology-related strengths and weaknesses. In line with their excellent skills in jigsaw puzzles, a full 50% of children with Prader-Willi syndrome played with jigsaw puzzles, whereas only 9% and 2%, respectively, of persons with Down syndrome and Williams syndrome engaged in this activity. Conversely, in line with their visuospatial weaknesses, children with Williams syndrome did not engage in visuospatial activities. In the overall category of visual-motor activities, only 31% of the sample with Williams syndrome participated in any visual-motor activities, compared to 76% and 60% of persons with Prader-Willi and Down syndromes, respectively. Specific behaviors such as arts-and-crafts activities were listed in 35% of the group with Down syndrome and in 30% of individuals with Prader-Willi syndrome, but in only 7% of those with Williams syndrome. Persons with Williams syndrome (or their parents) seem to be avoiding activities that these children may find difficult to perform.

Our suspicion is that genetic etiologies predispose children to particular cognitive-linguistic profiles, but that these profiles then become more pronounced due to the child's ongoing experiences. For most syndromes, the degree of difference between levels of "strong" versus "weak" areas is probably relatively small during the early years. As children more often perform activities in strong areas and avoid activities in weaker areas, however, increasing discrepancies arise. A snowball effect may thus result from the interplay of the child's

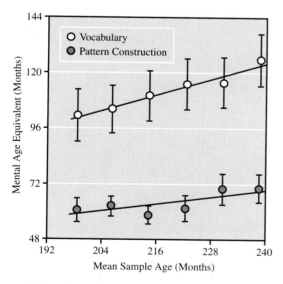

Figure 12.1 Average vocabulary and pattern construction ages at 6 time points (average best fit lines). *Source:* From "A Longitudinal Assessment of Diverging Verbal and Non-Verbal Abilities in the Williams Syndrome Phenotype," by C. Jarrold, A. D. Baddeley, A. K. Hewes, and C. Phillips, 2001, *Cortex, 37,* pp. 423–431.

etiology-related propensities and the child's ongoing transactions with the environment. Such views also seem consonant with the late-appearing gestures (as opposed to verbal labels) in the early communication of children with Williams syndrome (Mervis et al., 2003). For now, how etiology-related profiles evolve is relatively unknown, and much more work is needed.

Summary

Beginning with several tricky definitional and classificatory issues, this section explored the many interesting issues and findings relating to children with mental retardation. The most provocative findings relate not to development in children with mental retardation per se—or even to children with cultural-familial versus organic forms—but instead to children with different genetic syndromes of mental retardation.

As we examine these syndromes in more fine-grained studies, the old, familiar senses of development are giving way to more intricate, nuanced understandings. Although the usual or normative developmental sequences appear for most children with mental retardation in most domains, such is not always the case. With their relative weakness in visuospatial abilities, children with Williams syndrome violate the usual ordering by not engaging in communicative gestures (i.e., pointing and showing) in their earliest communications, behaviors that are simple and early occurring for typically developing children.

In the same way, cross-domain relations become complicated when one considers children with different types of mental retardation. Many children, both typical and with mental retardation, show areas of stronger and weaker development, but here we see specific, etiology-related profiles. As a group, children with Williams syndrome show relative strengths in many linguistic tasks, while they simultaneously demonstrate relative weaknesses in many visual-spatial tasks. Children with Down syndrome show linguistic (particularly grammatical and expressive) weaknesses, as well as etiology-related strengths in visual (as opposed to auditory) short-term memory. In several syndromes, already existing patterns of strengths and weaknesses then become more pronounced, and environmental, genetic, or other factors all seem implicated.

In short, children with Prader-Willi, Down, Williams, and other genetic syndromes are telling us much about how development operates. Partly for this reason, the amount of behavioral research on these disorders has exploded during the past few years (Hodapp & Dykens, 2004), and a wide array of developmental psycholinguists, cognitive developmentalists, and others have been drawn to children with these intriguing syndromes. Just as children who have been adopted, are twins, have experienced maternal deprivation, or are otherwise "natural experiments" all tell us much about typical developmental processes (Rutter, Pickles, Murray, & Eaves, 2001), so, too, do we learn from the behavioral development of children with different genetic forms of mental retardation. We are gradually learning more specifically how atypical development informs typical development (Cicchetti, 1984), an approach first advocated (in more primitive forms) by Piaget, Werner, and Vygotsky.

CONTEXTUALIST VIEWS OF DEVELOPMENT: INTERACTIONS, TRANSACTIONS, ECOLOGIES

In our discussions so far, we have considered development only in its organismic, child-related sense. But as developmentalists have increasingly realized over the past 40 years, development also involves children's larger environments and ecologies. From the late 1960s on, a major strand in developmental psychology has highlighted the child's ongoing interactions and transactions with others. Bell (1968), Sameroff and Chandler (1975), Bronfenbrenner (1979), and others may each focus on slightly different aspects of the child's interactions and transactions with the world, but each highlights ways in which child-environment interactions are important and worthy of study.

Such changes in the intellectual landscape have also influenced developmentally oriented studies of children with mental retardation. Although Zigler's original developmental approach to mental retardation focused mainly on child-related aspects of development, developmentally oriented research from the 1980s on has included parents, families, siblings, and other outside-of-the-child influences. Granted, such studies are newer and less advanced than is similar work in developmental or applied developmental psychology. Still, mother-child interaction, families, and ecologies definitely persist as ongoing, important areas of developmentally oriented mental retardation research (Hodapp & Zigler, 1995).

Before discussing such work, we provide a brief theoretical background. In contrast to more child-centered discussions, we here need to adapt several well-known, contextualist developmental perspectives in light of issues specific to children with mental retardation and their families.

Issues Specific to Mental Retardation

When thinking about the interactions and transactions with various environments over time of children with mental retardation, we need to consider issues of socialization and interaction, parental reactions, history of the mental retardation field itself, and the changing ecology of mental retardation.

Socialization-Interaction

From the late 1960s until today, those interested in parent-child relations have generally adopted one of two perspectives. In the first, or socialization, perspective, parents influence children. Parents directly instruct, model, reward, punish, and encourage or discourage their children at certain times and in certain ways, and children undoubtedly are affected as a result. The most well-known example of socialization probably involves Baumrind's (1973, 1989) studies of the effects of parent socialization styles on children's later adjustment. Parents can also be thought of as indirectly engineering their children's environments by living in certain neighborhoods, choosing certain schools, making friends with certain families, and exposing their children to some, but not other, environments and experiences. In each instance, the direction of causality goes from the parent to the child.

Conversely, others have emphasized the ways children affect parents. Best exemplified by Bell's (1968, 1979) concept of interactionism, this perspective holds that children and parents mutually affect one another. Thus, just as parents socialize children into gradually becoming adults, so, too, do the child's level of functioning, temperament, personality, maladaptive behaviors, and interests all change parental behavior. Other, more "status" characteristics—such as whether the child is a boy or a girl, or considered attractive or unattractive—might also influence parental behaviors.

When dealing with children with mental retardation, both behavioral and status characteristics differ from those of most typically developing children. By definition, children with mental retardation develop at slower rates, and such rates may be differentially slowed in stronger versus weaker areas in certain syndromes. Children with several genetic syndromes are also predisposed to have particular personalities and amounts and types of maladaptive behavior and psychopathology. Most children with Down syndrome do appear to others as sociable and upbeat in personality (Hodapp, Ricci, Ly, & Fidler, 2003; Wishart & Johnston, 1980); children with Prader-Willi syndrome are prone to hyperphagia, obsessions-compulsions, temper tantrums, and other maladaptive behaviors (Dykens & Cassidy, 1999). Etiology-related health problems and physical or facial features might also influence parental behaviors.

We have recently become intrigued by these special twists of Bell's (1968) interactionism (Hodapp, 1997, 1999). Briefly, if children with particular genetic syndromes are predisposed to show one or more etiology-related behaviors, might not others be more likely to react to these children in specific, predictable ways? If so, then genetic disorders have "indirect effects" on others: Genetic disorders predispose children to show particular behaviors (i.e., direct effects), which in turn elicit specific behaviors and reactions from others in their surrounding environments (indirect effects).

Parental Reactions

Unlike parents of typical children, parents of children with mental retardation often experience strong negative reactions on the birth or diagnosis of their child with mental retardation. Earlier studies even talked of how parents thought of themselves as failures for having produced children with mental retardation. At the very least, parental perceptions of their children's development and needs may differ from the usual reactions and perceptions of parents of children with mental retardation (Hodapp, 2002).

Over 40 years ago, Solnit and Stark (1961) exemplified this perspective by hypothesizing that mothers experienced a mourning reaction in response to the birth of a child with mental retardation. Following Freud's (1917/1957) article on "Mourning and Melancholia," these psychoanalytically oriented researchers hypothesized that maternal reactions to the birth of a child with mental retardation were akin to reactions to a death or, more generally, to any experience of loss in which a person feels disappointed, hurt, or slighted. Partly in response to the maternal mourning idea, various stage theories were developed to conceptualize how mothers react emotionally to these children over time. Although differing in specifics, most such models predicted that parents first feel shock or denial, then depression or anger, and finally emotional acceptance. Although such stage theories have been criticized (Blacher, 1984), they do highlight ways in which the emotions and perceptions of parents of children with mental retardation may differ from the emotions and perceptions of parents of typically developing children.

History of the Mental Retardation Field

Apart from Bell, Sameroff, and Bronfenbrenner, mental retardation's small field of behavioral researchers has itself long been interested in the environments of children with mental retardation. Blacher and Baker (2002) have recently compiled 100 years of articles on families of children with mental retardation that have appeared in the *American Journal on Mental Retardation* (and its earlier, differently named forerunner journals). In addition to predating most studies by developmental or applied developmental psychologists on these issues, recent family and ecological research in mental retardation has not been so tightly tied to similar research on typically developing children.

One example illustrates this separate history within the mental retardation field. Until the early 1980s, most studies on families of children with mental retardation were negatively tinged, emphasizing how different family members were negatively affected by raising the child with mental retardation. Over many studies during the 1960s and 1970s, researchers concluded that (compared to parents and families of same-age, typically developing children):

- Mothers of children with mental retardation were more often depressed (W. L. Friedrich & Friedrich, 1981) and preoccupied with their children and had more difficulty handling anger at their children (Cummings, Bayley, & Rie, 1966).
- Fathers experienced "role constriction" (Cummings, 1976) and more depression and neuroticism (Erickson, 1969).
- Couples showed lower levels of marital satisfaction (W. L. Friedrich & Friedrich, 1981).
- Families were considered to be "economically immobile" (Farber, 1970) and "stuck" in earlier stages of family development (Farber, 1959).

Beginning in the early 1980s, this focus on negative effects began to change. Crnic, Friedrich, and Green-

berg (1983) noted that children with mental retardation were better thought of as stressors on the family system. Like illness, moving, loss of a job, or natural disasters, a child with mental retardation could either negatively or positively affect parents and families as a whole. The child with mental retardation did not necessarily negatively impact the family. Although some researchers question the degree to which perspectives have changed over the past 2 decades (Dunst, Humphries, & Trivette, 2002; Helff & Glidden, 1998), most would agree that studies of parents, families, and siblings of children with mental retardation have become less negative. We thus see a historical change in research orientation that is specific to mental retardation family research.

Changing Ecology of Mental Retardation

In addition to shifting research perspectives, major changes have occurred in children's ecologies. Consider even the living status of children with mental retardation. Forty years ago, many more persons, including children, resided in large, often impersonal institutions. In 1967, almost 200,000 Americans lived in institutions, including 91,000 children. By 1997, that number had fallen to 56,161, including fewer than 3,000 children (L. L. Anderson, Lakin, Mangan, & Prouty, 1998; Lakin, Prouty, Braddock, & Anderson, 1997). Children with mental retardation now live in their own family home; adults are living either in their family home or in group homes, apartments, or other community-based settings.

As these children increasingly live in their family home, community-based services have increased many times over. Again, comparisons to the 1960s and early 1970s are instructive. Until the mid-1970s, children with mental retardation were not guaranteed access to public schooling during the school-age years. Access to formal education therefore varied widely, depending mainly on the generosity of the family's particular town or state. Only in 1975, with the passage of the federal Education for All Handicapped Children Act (PL 94-142), were states and towns in the United States required to provide a "free, appropriate public education" to all students, including those with disabilities (Hallahan & Kauffman, 2002).

Over the past 3 decades, other services have also been instituted that cover the preschool and the afterschool years. In addition to school services from age 3 through 21 years, states now provide early intervention services during the 0- to 3-year period. Under federal law PL 99-457, educational and support services have been expanded to the 0- to 3-year-old group, allowing a bridging of services from birth into the school years. A major component of PL 99-457 is its provision of an Individualized Family Service Plan, thereby recognizing that the family, as opposed to the child alone, needs services during these early years (Krauss & Hauser-Cram, 1992). And later, after the school-age years, so-called transitional services help persons with disabilities to make the transition from the school years to lives in which young adults work and live as independently as possible (for helpful programs, services, and agencies, see Morris, 2002). Services for individuals and their families are thus lifelong, and one must consider the interplay between children-parents-families and the service-delivery system from a life-span perspective.

Finally, one must appreciate changes in how all services are being conceptualized. No longer are children, parents, siblings, and families conceptualized as patients who need to be cured; instead, they are seen as persons—or consumers of services—who require long- or short-term support to enable them to cope more effectively. The goal, then, is to provide individualized supports to address the needs of each family. One family may require more information about a range of state-supported services, another respite care (i.e., short-term out-of-family care) so that the family can get a break from the full-time care of the offspring with disabilities. Still other parents may need to be put in touch with parents of children with similar problems, or who have dealt with the same school district, or who can otherwise help in their particular situation. This "support revolution" has changed the nature of services and how such services are understood by families and professionals (Hallahan & Kauffman, 2002).

Children, parents, the mental retardation field, and society at large, then, must all be considered when discussing larger ecological issues for children with mental retardation. We now discuss parent-child interactions, parental perceptions, parent-family reactions, and larger environments.

Parent-Child Interactions

Influenced by interactionism and the work on maternal input language begun in the early 1970s (Snow, 1972), developmentally oriented researchers began to examine interactions between parents and their children with mental retardation. These findings yielded inconsistent results. Sometimes parents of children with mental re-

tardation acted the same as parents of typically developing children, sometimes they differed markedly.

These inconsistent findings, however, were not random. Instead, two dimensions seemed important. The first concerned whether one compared parents of children with mental retardation to typical children who were of the same chronological age or the same level of functioning (such as the child's mental age or language age). When chronological age comparisons were employed, parents of children with mental retardation showed different behaviors. Buium, Rynders, and Turnure (1974) and Marshall, Hegrenes, and Goldstein (1973) both found that mothers of children with Down syndrome provided less complex verbal input and were more controlling in their interactive styles than were mothers of same-age nonretarded children. In both of these early studies, however, children with mental retardation were compared to typically developing children of the same chronological age. With Rondal's (1977) work in the late 1970s, researchers began to appreciate that parental behaviors might best be compared using typically developing groups of the same mental or language age, as opposed to the same chronological age.

But a second dimension was also at play. Specifically, one needed to distinguish the structure versus the style of parental behaviors. Structure, in this sense, includes the grammatical sophistication (the mean length of utterance, or MLU) or the degree of information (type-token ratio) of sentences uttered by the parent to the child. In contrast, style refers to the degree to which the parent teaches the child, leads or follows the child in the interaction, and is generally didactic and intrusive.

Once one makes this second, structure-style distinction, findings have been fairly consistent. Rondal (1977, p. 242) noted that, when children with Down syndrome and nonretarded children were matched on the child's MLU, "None of the comparisons of mothers' speech to normal and to Down Syndrome children led to differences that were significant or close to significant" between the two groups. Additionally, both groups of mothers adjusted their language upward (i.e., longer MLUs, type-token ratios) as the children's language levels increased. Rondal concluded that "the maternal linguistic environment of DS children between MLU 1 and 3 is an appropriate one" (p. 242).

In contrast, mothers of children with mental retardation are different when one focuses on their styles of interaction. Even when children with versus without mental retardation are equated on overall mental or linguistic age, mothers of children with mental retardation are generally more didactic, directive, and intrusive compared to mothers of nonretarded children (Marfo, 1990). Tannock (1988) found that, compared to mothers of nonretarded children, mothers of children with Down syndrome took interactive turns that were longer and more frequent; in addition, these mothers more often "clashed," or spoke at the same time as, their children (see also Vietze, Abernathy, Ashe, & Faulstich, 1978). Mothers of children with Down syndrome also switched the topic of conversation more often, and less often silently responded to the child's utterance. The result was a greater percentage of more asymmetrical conversations, conversations in which mothers controlled the topic, the child's response, and the nature of the back-and-forth conversation.

Why this difference between the structure and the style of parent-child interactions vis-à-vis typically developing children? The most common explanation is that mothers of children with mental retardation inject their parenting concerns into the interactive session. Compared to mothers of typically developing children, more of the mothers of children with mental retardation consider interactions as "teaching sessions," as moments not to be squandered in the nonstop effort to intervene effectively. As one mother said about interacting with her child with Down syndrome, "It's sit him on your knee and talk to him, that's the main object. Play with him, speak to the child, teach him something" (quoted in Jones, 1980, p. 221). Other parents also spoke of their desires to intervene with their children, even in situations in which mothers of nonretarded children feel fine with playing or becoming emotionally close to their offspring (Cardoso-Martins & Mervis, 1984).

Further complicating matters are behavioral characteristics of the children themselves. Here we again note differences relating to children with specific types of mental retardation. Specifically, young children with Down syndrome are often more lethargic and more hypotonic than are infants and young children with mental retardation in general. As a result, young children with Down syndrome may provide fewer and less clear interactive cues, at least in the months directly prior to intentional communication (Hyche, Bakeman, & Adamson, 1992). These infants may be less "readable" to the mother (Goldberg, 1977; Walden, 1996), even as mothers gradually learn to interpret their child's vague or slight communicative behaviors (Sorce & Emde, 1982; Yoder, 1986).

Similarly, one might speculate about the effects on others of the facial appearance of children with Down syndrome. In general, children (and adults) with Down syndrome possess a face that appears more infantile and "babylike," rounder and with smaller facial features. As Zebrowitz (1997) has shown, adults perceive more baby-faced individuals as friendlier, more social, and more compliant. Such attributions also occur when rating the faces of children with Down syndrome compared to typically developing children or to children with another (more adult-looking) genetic mental retardation syndrome (Fidler & Hodapp, 1999). Compared to mothers of children with other forms of mental retardation, mothers of children with Down syndrome give vocalizations that are at a higher register and that show greater pitch variance (i.e., sing-songy; Fidler, 2003). Such vocalizations are congruent with the intonations of "motherese" that have been universally found by Fernald (1989) and others.

Two additional issues deserve mention. First, several studies have now examined variation in maternal behaviors *within* samples with mental retardation (usually with Down syndrome). In the first direct examination of this issue, Crawley and Spiker (1983) rated maternal sensitivity and directiveness of mothers in their interactions with their 2-year-old children with Down syndrome. They found wide individual differences from one mother to another. Some mothers were highly directive, whereas others followed the child's lead; similarly, mothers varied widely in their rated degrees of sensitivity to their children. Because the two dimensions of sensitivity and directiveness were somewhat orthogonal, mothers could be high or low on either sensitivity or directiveness. All four combinations were demonstrated in this study. Just as mothers of nonretarded children vary widely on both directiveness and sensitivity, so, too, do mothers of children with Down syndrome.

A second issue concerns the effects of different maternal behaviors on children's development. In the sole study of this issue, Harris, Kasari, and Sigman (1996) examined the effects of maternal interactive behaviors on the expressive and receptive language behaviors of children with Down syndrome. Examining children when they were 2 and again at 3 years of age, Harris et al. found that the mean length of time in which mothers and children were engaged in joint attention (i.e., focusing on the same object) was correlated to the child's degree of receptive language gain over the 1-year interval. In addition, the child's receptive language gains were also correlated with the amount of time that mothers maintained the child's attention to child-selected toys, and (negatively) to instances of redirecting the child's focus of attention and of engaging in greater numbers of separate joint-attention episodes. Such findings parallel those found for interactions between mothers and typically developing infants, where increased maternal sensitivity (Baumwell, Tamis-LeMonda, & Bornstein, 1997) and more joint-attention episodes (Tomasello & Farrar, 1986) also promote young children's early language abilities. For both typically developing children and children with Down syndrome, then, mothers facilitate children's processing of maternal input language when they attempt to prolong episodes of mother-child joint attention by following their child's lead and responding to the child's interests and behaviors (Paparella & Kasari, 2004). The child's receptive language abilities increase accordingly.

Parent-child interactions are, then, the same in structure and different in style when the child has mental retardation. Although maternal emotions and perceptions may account for style differences, differences may also reside in the children themselves. As we examine children's behaviors and maternal emotions and perceptions, we come to understand what is happening, why, and how such interactions may be most useful for intervention efforts.

Perceptions

Although most would acknowledge that parental perceptions probably differ when raising a child with versus without mental retardation, how such perceptions differ is less well understood, nor do we know how any differences in parental perceptions might relate to differing behaviors or to different child outcomes. It is important, too, to acknowledge just how widespread parental perceptions truly are, ranging all the way from parental emotions to parental attributions of their children's needs and abilities.

Considered in these ways, the finding of differing parental interactive behaviors is most likely due to differences in parental perceptions. More didactic and controlling parental behaviors may indeed reflect parents' perceptions that they need to teach, stimulate, and push their children. Such differences in style seem common among parents of children with mental retardation and with other forms of disability as well (e.g., children with motor impairments, blindness, deafness, autism).

It is also possible to consider parental perceptions in light of the child's cause of mental retardation. Moreover, the very fact that there is a clear, identifiable cause may be helpful to parents. In one study, Goldberg, Marcovitch, MacGregor, and Lojkasek (1986) found that mothers of children with mental retardation from unknown causes suffered greater amounts of stress compared to mothers of children with either Down syndrome or mental retardation caused from specific neurological impairments. Being able to identify a clear cause may itself help parents of children with mental retardation.

Recently, we have begun to explore the idea of using attribution theory to help explain parental behaviors in response to children with different genetic mental retardation syndromes (with their specific, etiology-related strengths and weaknesses). In prior work with typically developing children, Graham (1991) found that, in accordance with attribution theory (Weiner, 1985), teachers showed different patterns of attributions when their students were perceived to have high versus low levels of skills in particular activities. When children were judged to be skilled at a particular task, teachers and parents attributed these children's success to their children's high levels of skill, whereas failure was attributed to the child's not trying (i.e., lack of effort). In contrast, children perceived to have low levels of skill were perceived to succeed at a task only by effort (if children failed, it was due to their low level of ability). Such perceptions then linked to subsequent adult behaviors, such that adults gave greater amounts of help and reward to lower- than to higher-skill children when each succeeded (the idea being that higher-skill children do not need as much help/reward to successfully complete the task).

Given such clear predictions from attribution theory—and such clearly divergent levels of ability in specific etiological groups—Ly and Hodapp (2005) recently examined maternal helping and reinforcement behaviors in children with two genetic syndromes. Recall that, as a group, children with Prader-Willi syndrome perform especially well on jigsaw puzzles (Dykens, 2002); in contrast, children with Willliams syndrome show deficits (beyond their overall mental age) in most tasks of visuospatial functioning (Mervis et al., 1999). Capitalizing on this contrasting strength-weakness across these two syndromes, Ly and Hodapp had mothers and their children with either Prader-Willi or Williams syndromes interact around a novel jigsaw puzzle.

As might be expected from an attributional perspective (Graham, 1991), mothers of children with Williams syndrome gave over twice as many reinforcers (praises, clapping) and helping behaviors to their children as did parents of children with Prader-Willi syndrome. Looking further, such etiology-group differences appeared due both to the child's ability level in puzzles (measured separately from the mother, in another room) and to the child's etiology (Prader-Willi syndrome versus Williams syndrome). Parents respond not only to the child's actual level of ability, but also to ability profiles that generally characterize each of these two syndromes.

Attribution theory has also been used to help explain the perceptions of parents of children with Down syndrome. Ly and Hodapp (2002) gave parents of children with Down syndrome versus parents of children with other, non-Down syndrome forms of mental retardation hypothetical vignettes. These vignettes involved the child's noncompliance to parental commands: one command to clean up his or her room, another to turn down the television set when the mother received a phone call. In addition to rating various reasons for why their child would not comply in these two instances, mothers also were asked to rate their child's personality and maladaptive behaviors.

Again, parents reacted to the child's more sociable, upbeat personality, but also to the child's specific etiological label. Specifically, parents of children with Down syndrome more often attributed the child's noncompliant behaviors to normative concerns ("My child is acting like other children his or her age"). But such connections between child personality and normalizing behaviors were found only within the Down syndrome group. Among parents of children with Down syndrome, those who saw their child as more sociable also more highly rated normalizing as the reason for their child's noncompliance ($r = .43$, $p < .01$). But among parents of children with mixed forms of mental retardation, no such connections existed between child personality and parental ratings of normalizing attributions ($r = .05$, ns).

Although intriguing, these studies merely scratch the surface in our understandings of parental perceptions. We continue to know little about these parents' perceptions, or how such perceptions might relate to the child's etiology, overall abilities, or specific abilities on individual tasks. We know little as well about any changes in attributions, perceptions, and expectations by different adults (mothers, fathers, teachers), in different contexts (schools, homes, communities), and when the child is faced with different tasks (academic, leisure, specific tasks reflecting etiology-related skills). Finally, we have no idea how parents develop these perceptions, how parental perceptions link to behaviors, and how parental perceptions (and subsequent behaviors) link in turn to the child's own behaviors or perceptions.

Parent and Family Reactions

As noted earlier, the conceptualization of parental and familial reactions has changed markedly over the years, as have the nature and philosophy of service delivery. Partly as a result of such changes, changes have also occurred in how studies are performed. In effect, moving from a pathology to a stress-and-coping perspective emphasizes those risks and protective factors that foster better parental and familial coping. From the earlier view that all parents and families of children with mental retardation are prone to depression, conflict, and other negative consequences, we can now better appreciate characteristics—in the children themselves, in parents, and in families—that might predict more successful reactions. We now turn to findings showing different child, parent, and family factors predisposing to better or worse outcomes.

Child Factors

Certain aspects of children seem to be associated with better parent and family functioning, whereas others are not. In most studies, the child's overall degree of impairment (i.e., IQ), level of functioning (mental age), and gender are unassociated with better or worse parent and family reactions. In contrast, the child's degree and amount of maladaptive behavior and psychopathology seem to adversely influence parent and family functioning, whereas the child's sociability and interest in people seem helpful to parents.

The influences of maladaptive behavior can be seen in groups with mixed forms of mental retardation and in children with specific etiologies. Minnes (1988) and Margalit, Shulman, and Stuchiner (1989) have found that more child maladaptive behavior is associated with greater amounts of parental stress. Similarly, higher levels of child maladaptive behavior is associated with higher parental stress levels in children with Prader-Willi syndrome (Hodapp, Dykens, & Masino, 1997) and comparing parents of children with Prader-Willi, Down, and Smith-Magenis syndromes (Fidler, Hodapp, & Dykens, 2000).

From the opposite perspective, parents and families of children with Down syndrome may cope better compared to parents of children with other disability conditions. Such an advantage arises in studies that compare parents of children with Down syndrome to children with autism (Holroyd & MacArthur, 1976; Kasari & Sigman, 1997), with mixed forms of mental retardation (Hodapp et al., 2003), with other disabilities (Hanson & Hanline, 1990), and with emotional problems (but without mental retardation; Thomas & Olsen, 1993). Granted, a few studies do not find this advantage for parents of children with Down syndrome (Cahill & Glidden, 1996). Overall, however, most studies do find that parents of children with Down syndrome experience less parental stress than do parents of children with other disabilities.

Three further issues deserve mention. First, the so-called Down syndrome advantage probably occurs only in comparison to parents of children with other disabilities. In most studies, parents of typically developing children report less stress than do parents of children with Down syndrome (Roach, Orsmond, & Barratt, 1999; Scott, Atkinson, Minton, & Bowman, 1997; although see also Sanders & Morgan, 1997; Wolf, Noh, Fisman, & Speechley, 1989).

Second, certain aspects of parental reactions might show more of a Down syndrome advantage. Across several studies, parents of children with Down syndrome rate their children as more rewarding and as more acceptable than do parents of children with other disabilities. Hoppes and Harris (1990) found that, relative to parents of children with autism, parents of children with Down syndrome regarded their children as more rewarding. Noh, Dumas, Wolf, and Fisman (1989) also found the same pattern when contrasting parents of children with Down syndrome to parents of children with autism or with conduct disorder. Likewise, Hodapp et al. (2003) found that, relative to parents of children with heterogeneous causes of mental retardation, mothers of children with Down syndrome considered their child more acceptable and more rewarding. Some studies even find that parental reinforcement and acceptability are equal in parents of children with Down syndrome versus same-age typically developing children (e.g., Roache et al., 1999). In a few studies, parents of children with Down syndrome even exceed parents of typically developing children on these two specific measures. Thus, Noh et al. conclude that, although parents of children with Down syndrome rated their children as less attractive, socially appropriate, and intelligent, they regarded "their children as happier and as a greater source of positive reinforcement than the parents of normal children" (p. 460).

Third, one must consider the age of the child with Down syndrome. In a large cross-sectional study, Dykens, Shah, Sagun, Beck, and King (2002) noted that adolescents with Down syndrome, in addition to showing lesser amounts of stubbornness and other externalizing problems, may become more "inward" during the adolescent years (see also Meyers & Pueschel, 1991; Tonge & Einfeld, 2003). Using a personality questionnaire, Hodapp et al. (2003) found a similar, subtle withdrawal, and parents of these older teens and young adults reported that their children were less rewarding and acceptable (see also Cunningham, 1996). Though there may be a Down syndrome advantage for parents and families of children with Down syndrome, this advantage may be affected by the inwardness gradually occurring in many adolescents and young adults with this disorder.

Finally, although we view the child with Down syndrome as eliciting reactions from parents and families, we acknowledge that children with Down syndrome may differ in other ways from children with other disabilities. Down syndrome is a common disorder, is diagnosed at birth, is widely known to both professionals and the lay public alike, and has several active parent and advocacy groups. As such, some of the Down syndrome advantage may come about through characteristics that are separate from the child's behavior. The question boils down to whether any Down syndrome advantage arises from behaviors of the children themselves, or from parental or societal characteristics that are associated with Down syndrome. We suspect that child and associated characteristics may both be operating, but more studies are needed.

Parent and Family Factors

In addition to various child factors, one must also realize the importance of parent and family factors on parent and family coping. A first important issue concerns the outlook and general problem-solving style of parents (usually mothers) themselves. Following Folkman, Schaefer, and Lazarus (1979), mothers can be identified as predominantly using either "problem-focused" or "emotion-focused" coping strategies (for a review, see Turnbull et al., 1993). In the first, mothers essentially address their child's mental retardation as a practical, concrete problem to be dealt with. These mothers make plans to address everyday problems, work hard to alleviate those problems, and feel that they have learned from their experiences. In contrast, another group of mothers either totally deny their feelings about their child and the disability, or instead become overly concerned, almost obsessed, with their own feelings of depression and grief.

Across a range of studies, such differences seem intricately involved with the mother's emotional outcomes. Those mothers who are active, problem-focused copers do better. Several studies have now documented that those parents who engage in active, problem-based styles of coping experience less depression than those who either deny their emotional feelings or who engage in what has been called "emotion-based coping" (e.g., Essex, Seltzer, & Krauss, 1999).

A final set of characteristics concerns family demographics. To list briefly, the following have been shown in various studies:

- Families who are more affluent cope better with rearing a child with disabilities than do those making less money (Farber, 1970).
- Two-parent families cope better than one-parent families (Beckman, 1983).
- Women in better marriages cope better than those in troubled marriages (Beckman, 1983; W. N. Friedrich, 1979).

Although none of these findings is surprising, each nevertheless highlights the ways family or couple demographics or dynamics affect the coping of both parents and families.

Schools, Neighborhoods, and Larger Ecologies

In contrast to the work on parent-child interactions, parental perceptions, and parent and family factors, much less research has been done on the larger ecologies of children with mental retardation. Unlike, for example, Bryant's (1985) neighborhood walk with typically developing children to determine these children's support network, few studies examine the neighborhoods or larger ecologies of children with mental retardation. Although schooling has been of interest within the special education field, most studies do not look at schools in what might be considered ecological ways; instead, dominant issues include parental satisfaction with different types of placements for their children, or school-

parent connections, or the effects of the child's specific school placement (fully integrated or mainstreamed only some of the day) on these children's academic and social achievements (Freeman & Alkin, 2000).

Such inattention to ecological matters is surprising given the many societal changes in the lives of children with disabilities and their families. As noted earlier, changes have occurred in where children with mental retardation live, in the increased amount of community-based services, and in the changes from pathological to supportive philosophies underlying those services. Such changes make more complicated the lives of children with mental retardation and their families. Consider the experience of giving birth and raising a child with mental retardation, as seen from the perspective of parents. With only a few exceptions (e.g., parents who adopt children with Down syndrome; Flaherty & Glidden, 2002), most parents are unprepared for the birth of a child with disabilities. If the child has Down syndrome or another easily diagnosed disorder, parents learn at birth about their child's diagnosis. Physicians and other health personnel are also feeling guilty and upset, and stories abound about parents who were told about their child's diagnosis in uncaring, unprofessional ways, or were given wildly pessimistic outcomes about their child's ultimate capabilities and life outcome (Turnbull & Turnbull, 1997). For parents who do not learn of their children's diagnosis at birth, nagging suspicions often persist that somehow their child is not right, even as pediatricians and others often tell them that the child will grow out of it.

Apart from diagnosis itself, these parents are generally unprepared to navigate the entire gamut of existing services. When parents give birth to a child with a disability, they must negotiate the service-delivery system. In every state, parents thus begin dealing with such agencies as the Department of Developmental Disabilities (differently named from state to state), and with that department's various agencies or centers, who actually administer the funds and programs. Later, during the school years, parents work most closely with their child's school district, school administrators, and teachers. After the school years, transition and adult services enter in. These departments and services are generally unknown to most people in the general public.

As these interactions proceed, parents are faced with a wide array of rights and responsibilities. Consider schools, the main service provider from the time the child is 3 to the time he or she is 21 years old (Hallahan

& Kauffman, 2002). Federal laws such as the Individuals with Disabilities Education Act (passed in 1990; amended in 1997 and 2004) now provide as a right a free, appropriate public school education for all children with disabilities. But parents need to be aware of an entire gamut of hearings, appeals, and procedures (Council for Exceptional Children, 1998).

Such hearings and procedures then culminate in the child's actual placement within a specific educational setting. Ideally, all children should be educated in the "least restrictive environment" (LRE), with "least restrictive" generally referring to environments that are most like the typical, general education classroom. Depending on the child's individual needs, LRE allows for full-time integration with nondisabled children, part-time integration with a resource room or specialist, special classes within a public school, and even special classes or special residential schools when necessary to meet the child's educational needs.

In whatever setting education takes place, the child's teachers, administrators, and parents must agree on the various goals, services, and practices that will be put in place to educate the student with disabilities. Such goals and practices are codified in the child's individualized educational plan (IEP; Bateman & Linden, 1998), which has been developed out of the series of legal hearings and appeals mentioned earlier.

Although we often think of disabilities as pertaining mostly to children, children with disabilities eventually grow up to become adults. In this regard, one of the most widespread adaptations has involved transition services. To simplify slightly, transition services focus on skills needed for independent living and working. The goal is that, upon graduation, young adults with disabilities will be able to live either on their own or in a community group home, and to be competitively employed in the community (Rusch & Chadsey, 1998). To live independently, students are taught to shop for clothes and food within a budget, to use the post office, to understand schedules and take public buses or trains, and to visit a doctor or dentist. To be able to be competitively employed by community businesses, students are trained in a variety of vocational skills. Such training addresses more general issues such as being punctual, courteous, and on task, as well as providing actual practice in working in unskilled or semiskilled jobs in the community.

Clearly, the amount and complexity of such information are staggering to most parents, who generally have little knowledge or experience of child development, spe-

cial education, social service systems, law, or other relevant areas. In addition, parents must simultaneously deal with all of the usual transitions that arise when they embark on parenting any child (Bornstein, 2002; Heinicke, 2002). For these reasons, parenting children with mental retardation has often been likened to entering a foreign country, a country in which the language, customs, and expectations are all different from expected.

Fortunately, some guideposts are available to help parents and families in navigating this new, foreign world. In each state, a lead agency has been designated to be in charge of early intervention services, and all states have some version of a Department of Mental Retardation or Department of Developmental Disabilities. In every state, the federal government has set up one (or a few) University Centers for Excellence in Developmental Disabilities (UCEDD; formerly called University Affiliated Programs). These centers provide family resource centers, support groups for parents and siblings, conferences, and advocacy services to deal with schools or regional centers. Local and state educational organizations can also help parents, as can local hospitals and social service agencies.

On the national level, many informational services exist to help parents of children with disabilities. Some organizations, such as the Arc of the United States (originally, the Association for Retarded Citizens), can help parents find resources in their area, and the Council for Exceptional Children can help parents locate educational resources. Others involve parent-professional groups (e.g., National Organization of Rare Disorders) or federally sponsored Web sites (National Institutes of Health). Compared to only a few decades ago, families can access an almost bewildering amount of supportive services, contacts, and educational and medical information. This exponential increase in potential knowledge and support is an important change in the "culture" of disabilities. More knowledge and supportive services are created every day, and parents are both helped and challenged by these vast information and service systems. See Table 12.2 for a listing of helpful resources.

Summary

By definition, children with mental retardation are different from typically developing children, and any studies of parent-child interactions, parental perceptions, families, or even neighborhoods and schools all need to consider these differences. One must acknowledge the

TABLE 12.2 Support and Informational Organizations

National Information Center for Children and Youth with Disabilities
P.O. Box 1492
Washington, DC 20013
(800) 695-0285
www.nichcy.org

Association of Retarded Citizens of the United States (The ARC)
100 Wayne Avenue, Suite 650
Silver Spring, MD 20910
(301) 565-3842
www.thearc.org

American Association on Mental Retardation (AAMR)
1710 Kalorama Road, NW
Washington, DC 20009-2683
(800) 424-3688
www.aamr.org

Council for Exceptional Children (CEC)
1110 North Glebe Road, Suite 300
Arlington, VA 22201-5704
(888) CEC-SPED
www.cec.sped.org

Association of University Centers on Disabilities (AUCD)
8630 Fenton Street, Suite 410
Silver Spring, MD 20910
(301) 588-8252
www.aucd.org

The Association for Persons with Severe Handicaps (TASH)
29 West Susquehanna Avenue, Suite 210
Baltimore, MD 21204
(410) 828-8274
www.tash.org

Clearinghouse of Disability Information (CDI)
Office of Special Education and Rehabilitation Services
Switzer Building, Room 3132
330 C Street, SW
Washington, DC 20202-2524
(202) 334-8241

National Information Center for Children and Youth with
  Disabilities (NICHCY)
P.O. Box 1492
Washington, DC 20013
(800) 695-0285
www.nichcy.org

Resources for Children with Special Needs, Inc.
116 E. 16th Street, 5th floor
New York, NY 10003
(212) 677-4650
www.resourcesnyc.org

CAPP National Parent Resource Center
Federation for Children with Special Needs
95 Berkeley Street, Suite 104
Boston, MA 02116
(617) 482-2915

National Parent Network on Disabilities (NPND)
1727 King Street, Suite 305
Alexandria, VA 22314
(703) 684-6763
www.npnd.org

Sibling Information Network
1775 Ellington Road
South Windsor, CT 07074
(203) 648-1205

National Organization for Rare Disorders (NORD)
55 Kenosia Avenue
P.O. Box 1968
Danbury, CT 06813-1968
(203) 744-0100
(800) 999-6673 (voicemail only)
www.rarediseases.org

Association for Children with Down Syndrome
4 Fern Place
Plainview, NY 11779
(516) 933-4700 X100
www.acds.org

National Down Syndrome Society
666 Broadway
New York, NY 10012
(800) 221-4602
www.ndss.org

National Down Syndrome Congress (NDSC)
1370 Center Drive, Suite 102
Atlanta, GA 30338
http://ndscenter.org

National Fragile X Syndrome Foundation
P.O. Box 190488
San Francisco, CA 94119
(800) 688-8765
www.fragilex.org

Prader-Willi Syndrome Association
5700 Midnight Pass Rd.
Sarasota, FL 34242
(800) 926-4797
www.pwsausa.org

The Williams Syndrome Association
P.O. Box 297
Clawson, MI 48017-0297
(800) 806-1871
www.williams-syndrome.org

many reactions that parents have to rearing a child with mental retardation, the parallel history of parent and family studies in the mental retardation field, and the many historical changes in how society has treated and conceptualized children with mental retardation and their families.

Given these important background issues, we note the ways interactions are the same but different when considering parents and their children with mental retardation. When compared to typically developing children of the same levels of functioning on structural aspects of maternal input language, such interactions seem similar. In contrast, differences emerge in parent-child interactions when children in the typical versus retarded groups are matched on chronological age (not on mental or language age) and when one examines maternal style. Stylistically, mothers of children with mental retardation (versus mothers of typically developing children matched for mental or language age) seem much more didactic and controlling.

Such stylistic differences lead one to consider the perceptions of parents of children with mental retardation. Although a general consensus holds that these parents differ from parents of typically developing children in their strong desires to teach their children, other aspects of parental perceptions seem much less well examined. In addition, only a few studies have yet used attribution theory in relation to children with mental retardation, or to children whose genetic etiologies lead to relatively strong versus weak performances on particular tasks.

So, too, is more work needed on many issues relating to families of children with mental retardation. Family work has changed dramatically in its orientation over the past 30 years, as researchers now adopt perspectives focusing on the child as a stressor on the family system. Conceptualized as a stressor, children with mental retardation might contribute to better, worse, or unchanged family functioning. To date, a few risk and protective factors have been identified using this stress-and-coping perspective, but many areas of family functioning remain open for research.

Finally, the reaction of the wider society has changed markedly in regard to children with mental retardation and their families. Even compared to 20 or 30 years ago, the amount and type of services have increased enormously, as have the ways that professionals and families think about such services. Such changes have mostly been helpful, as children with mental retardation and their families can now benefit from a lifelong array of services. Nevertheless, such services raise new challenges for parents, who must increasingly learn their child's disability, available services, and how and when parents can access such services. We know little about how parents come to know about or use such services, how they overcome barriers to knowledge or access, or what the effects of such services are on children themselves or on family members.

RESEARCH ISSUES

In summarizing findings of the child's and environment's development, we have often mentioned gaps in our understanding. But in addition to gaps related to content knowledge, other gaps also exist concerning how best to perform developmentally oriented behavioral research. Such research issues include but go beyond similar issues in child or applied child development. Four such issues are discussed next.

The Nature of Research Groups

The first unresolved issue in mental retardation research concerns the nature of the group itself. As noted earlier, researchers differ in how they classify persons with mental retardation, with some choosing to examine groups based on level of impairment (mild, moderate, severe, or profound mental retardation), others on mental retardation's two groups (cultural-familial versus organic), still others on the individual's etiology.

Although historically the degree-of-impairment approach has predominated, newer mental retardation behavioral research is more often taking etiology into account. Consider Figure 12.2, a graph of articles published in the *American Journal on Mental Retardation (AJMR)*, the most prominent journal devoted to behavioral studies in the mental retardation field (Hodapp, 2004a). The large majority of behavioral research articles in *AJMR* published during the 1970s and 1980s classified their research subjects by level of impairment; similar conclusions arise when considering other mental retardation journals (Hodapp & Dykens, 1994) and when surveying articles on persons with both mental retardation and emotional-behavioral problems (Dykens, 1996). But as the figure illustrates, such a state of affairs may be changing; at present, almost one-third of behavioral research articles in *AJMR* now separate their groups by etiology.

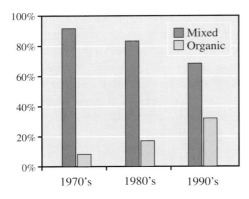

Figure 12.2 Percentage of articles, by type, in the *American Journal on Mental Retardation,* 1975–1980, 1985–1990, and 1995–2000. *Source:* From "Behavioral Phenotypes: Going beyond the Two-Group Approach," by R. M. Hodapp, 2004a, *International Review of Research in Mental Retardation, 29,* pp. 1–30. Reprinted with permission from Elsevier.

This recent rise in etiology-based behavioral articles can be illustrated in other ways as well. Consider the numbers of behavioral research articles on such disorders as Down syndrome, Prader-Willi syndrome, Williams syndrome, and fragile X syndrome. Comparing these numbers during the 1980s (1980 to 1989) versus the 1990s (1990 to 1999), one finds that empirical journal articles on the behavior of individuals with Williams syndrome increased from 10 to 81; on Prader-Willi syndrome, from 24 to 86; on fragile X syndrome, from 60 to 149. Even for Down syndrome, the single genetic syndrome with a long-term, well-established history of behavioral research, the numbers of behavioral studies almost doubled from the 1980s to the 1990s (607 to 1,140; Hodapp & Dykens, 2004). With intriguing findings occurring in many of these syndromes, the numbers of articles should continue rising in the decades to come.

But such steep rises tell only a part of the story. At least 1,000 genetic syndromes are now thought to be associated with mental retardation. Many such syndromes are fairly rare, making it difficult to attain large enough subject groups. Still, not a single study exclusively devoted to behavior or behavioral development exists for the large majority of these syndromes. Although our knowledge of individuals with different etiologies of mental retardation has increased tremendously, we still have a long way to go.

Control-Contrast Groups to Examine Children's Own Behavioral Functioning

Once one settles on the nature of the subject group, the next problem concerns control or comparison groups. To whom, exactly, should one compare one's group with mental retardation? We begin with a historical sense of this issue, then discuss the ways the control-contrast group issue has played out when considering etiology-based behavioral research.

Historical Issues

Over the years, a long-standing controversy has related to two types of comparisons to typically developing children (Hodapp & Zigler, 1995). One group, referred to by the term "defect theorists," has asserted that etiology does not matter, that all children with mental retardation suffer from organic defects. These researchers have generally compared their children with mental retardation to typically developing children of the same chronological age. An entire research tradition has shown that, relative to typically developing children, numerous aspects of cognition and language are deficient in children with mental retardation (e.g., Ellis & Cavalier, 1982).

In contrast, developmentally oriented researchers have generally favored comparisons to typically developing children of the same mental ages. These researchers have considered it a given that children with mental retardation perform worse than chronological age matches on virtually every cognitive task. Instead, they see their job as one of determining whether these children show specific areas of relative strength or weakness. Or, as Cicchetti and Pogge-Hesse (1982, p. 279; emphasis in original) aver, children with mental retardation function below children of the same chronological age in most areas of cognition, but *the important and challenging research questions concern the developmental processes.* Such processes can be determined only by using mental age-matched typically developing controls, thereby showing which areas are more or less affected.

Contrast Groups in Etiology-Based Research

With the rise of etiology-based research, specifying the appropriate control-contrast groups has become more complex. We present six research approaches, organized around three research questions, that have been commonly used in etiology-based behavioral research (Hodapp & Dykens, 2001; see Table 12.3).

Do Children Show an Etiology-Related Profile?
Recall that children with Williams syndrome show relative strengths in language and weaknesses in visuospatial skills; that children with Prader-Willi syndrome show strengths in simultaneous processing (particularly

TABLE 12.3   Strengths and Weaknesses of Some Common Etiology-Based Research Approaches

Control Group	Characteristics	Strengths and Weaknesses
Strategies to Determine Whether a Specific Disorder Has Strengths/Weaknesses		
1. None	Performance "against self"	Shows etiology strength.
2. Typical	Equated on MA Equated on CA	Shows relative strength (versus MA) or intact functioning (versus CA); unclear if profile is unique, partially shared, or similar to all persons with MR.
Strategies to Determine Whether Behavioral Characteristics Differ from Others with Mental Retardation		
3. Mixed MR	Mixed causes of MR	Shows that etiology strength/weakness is not due to MR. Control group changes across studies; mixed ≠ nonspecific.
4. Down syndrome	Down syndrome	Shows behavior not due to any syndrome, but DS has its own behavioral characteristics (may lead to inaccurate conclusions if DS = "all MR").
Strategies to Further Delineate Etiology-Specific Behaviors		
5. Same-but-different MR	Etiology similar in behavior to group	Highlights fine-grained differences in behavior if two or more etiologies have similar behaviors to make contrast meaningful.
6. Special non-MR	Group with special behavior	Shows ways that etiology is similar to or different from (nonretarded) group with special problem or profile.

Source: From "Strengthening Behavioral Research on Genetic Mental Retardation Disorders," by R. M. Hodapp and E. M. Dykens, 2001, *American Journal on Mental Retardation, 106,* pp. 4–15. Reprinted with permission.

in putting together jigsaw puzzles); and that children with Down syndrome show relative weaknesses in linguistic grammar. The word "relative" relates to the child's overall mental age; a relative strength denotes that children of a particular etiology perform significantly above mental age levels, a relative weakness denotes that group performance is below overall mental age levels.

Given this interest in relative strengths and weaknesses, a first, commonly used strategy is to have *no control or contrast group.* To determine whether children with Williams syndrome show strengths in language versus visuospatial processing, Bellugi et al. (1999) compared each child's functioning on a language domain to that same child's performance on another domain. Similarly, we have found simultaneous processing strengths in boys with fragile X syndrome (Dykens, Hodapp, & Leckman, 1987) and in children with Prader-Willi syndrome (Dykens et al., 1992) by comparing each child's performance on domains of Simultaneous Processing versus Sequential Processing on the Kaufman Assessment Battery for Children (Kaufman & Kaufman, 1983). In Down syndrome, higher-level performance has been shown on tasks involving visual (as opposed to auditory) short-term memory (Hodapp et al., 1999; Pueschel et al., 1987). Children thus become their own controls, as their functioning levels in one domain are compared to more general, overall functioning levels.

Although widely used, this self-as-control technique has several limitations. Technically, one can compare the person's performance only on one versus another domain on the same test. Different tests are standardized on different samples, and intelligence test scores tend to increase from decade to decade (the so-called Flynn effect; Flynn, 1999). At the very least, one should stick to different domains of the same test.

Another problem involves the existence of appropriate psychometric instruments. In areas such as IQ, adaptive behavior, and language functioning, many well-normed, standardized tests exist. Such tests easily lend themselves to comparisons between a single subtest and the overall age-equivalent score. But in other areas, few good tests exist. Such is the case for developmentally interesting areas such as emotional development, self-image, theory of mind, and empathy. In areas for which no psychometrically sound measures exist, researchers cannot use children with a specific etiology as their own control.

A second technique also attempts to answer the relative strength or weakness question. Here the researcher compares persons with mental retardation to *typically developing children of the same mental age* (mental age matches). Depending on the question of interest, the comparison might more generally be thought of as comparing the child with mental retardation to typical children of similar functioning levels. To determine areas of adaptive strength or weakness, one might compare children with Down syndrome to typically developing children using the Vineland Adaptive Behavior Scales; to determine whether specific aspects of language are relative strengths (a major issue in current Williams syndrome work), one might match on the child's MLU to examine aspects of pragmatics or semantics. In each case, the researcher compares children with a particular genetic syndrome to typically developing children of identical age-equivalent performance.

Given our knowledge of etiology-based strengths and weaknesses, it is also important to sometimes use chronological age matches. Specifically, when certain etiological groups perform above mental age matches, one has evidence that the group shows a relative strength in that area of behavior. But it is only in comparison to typically developing children of similar chronological ages that one can determine if certain groups are spared in their functioning in a behavioral domain. The best example involves Williams syndrome, long thought to be spared in certain areas of language. To determine whether language in Williams syndrome is indeed spared, a typical, chronological age-matched group is needed. Although sparing now seems unlikely for groups (as opposed to for a few individuals) with Williams syndrome (Karmiloff-Smith et al., 1996; Mervis et al., 1999), the test for spared functioning involves comparing to typically developing age-mates either explicitly (using a typical chronological age-matched group) or implicitly (using standard scores from a standardization sample).

Finally, showing that a particular etiological group has a specific strength or weakness does not, by itself, show that such a profile is unique to one etiological group, is shared with several other etiologies, or is something that occurs in most children with mental retardation. Instead, all (or most) persons with mental retardation may show a particular pattern of cognitive, linguistic, adaptive, or other strengths and weaknesses. If so, then lowered intellectual abilities are the problem, and the profile is not etiology-related. Such conclusions require our second set of specific research techniques, to which we now turn.

Are Such Profiles Seen in Children with Mental Retardation More Generally?   As Table 12.3 shows, this second general research question also features two often-used techniques. In the first, researchers compare persons with a particular mental retardation syndrome to a *mixed or nonspecific group* who are equated on both

mental age and chronological age. If behavioral phenotypes do indeed involve "the heightened probability or likelihood that people with a given syndrome will exhibit certain behavioral and developmental sequelae relative to those without the syndrome" (Dykens, 1995, p. 523), such a mixed or heterogeneous group best approximates "those without the syndrome."

As before, several issues arise. The first concerns the proper mixture of the mixed group, and how to ensure that one's sample does indeed approximate the larger retarded population. Unfortunately, in contrast to our knowledge about many psychiatric disorders, the field of mental retardation has performed few such epidemiological studies. Among all persons with mental retardation, what percentage has Down syndrome? Or Prader-Willi syndrome? At present, we do not have precise answers.

A second technique in this class compares one etiological group against *children with Down syndrome*. Although groups with Down syndrome are often used as a "mentally retarded control group," we consider this strategy to be inappropriate. As a group, persons with Down syndrome show relative weaknesses in grammar (Fowler, 1990) and in expressive language (Miller, 1999); most persons with Down syndrome also show articulation problems (Kumin, 1994). Compared to others with mental retardation, children with Down syndrome more often show "sociable" behaviors such as more looking and smiling at others (Kasari & Freeman, 2001; Kasari, Freeman, Mundy, & Sigman, 1995). So, too, may these children show psychopathology less often and less severely than others with mental retardation (Dykens & Kasari, 1997; Meyers & Pueschel, 1991). Especially in studies involving language, social skills, or maladaptive behavior-psychopathology, using samples with Down syndrome as a control group seems ill advised.

How Do Children in a Specific Etiological Group Compare to Nonretarded Persons with Similar Conditions or Behaviors?   This final approach compares persons who have a genetic syndrome to "specialized" nonretarded persons in an area of specific interest. Here again, the general approach can be seen through the use of two specific research techniques. In the first, persons with a particular syndrome are compared to *nonretarded persons with a diagnosed psychiatric disorder*. Dykens et al. (1996) compared persons with Prader-Willi syndrome to nonretarded outpatients with obsessive-compulsive disorder. With very few exceptions, the two groups were very similar in their mean number and severity of compulsions and in percentages within each group displaying most behaviors (e.g., cleaning, ordering/arranging, repeating rituals).

Such a specialized-group strategy can also be shown in a second technique, this one comparing to *nonretarded persons who show particular cognitive-linguistic profiles*. How, for example, might children with Prader-Willi syndrome—who show simultaneous over sequential processing abilities—compare to nonretarded persons who similarly show such simultaneous advantages? How do children with Prader-Willi syndrome compare to typically developing children who are "good puzzlers"? Are the two groups approaching problems in the same way? In many ways, this final research strategy best approaches Cicchetti and Pogge-Hesse's (1982) call for research that examines developmental processes in children with mental retardation.

The single drawback is that, by using specialized nonretarded groups, one risks designing a "no-difference" study, a study in which the two groups do not show significant differences. For instance, when compared to typical children who are also high on simultaneous processing or on jigsaw puzzle abilities, children with Prader-Willi syndrome may look identical. Though interesting theoretically, no-difference findings are always more problematic statistically.

Comparisons in Studies of Families and Ecologies

In discussing control-contrast groups involving families and other ecologies, different issues arise. In fact, most studies compare families of children with mental retardation to families of typically developing children of the same chronological, not mental, age. The reasoning here involves family life cycles. Carter and McGoldrick (1988) identify six stages of family life, beginning with the young adult's leaving home, then getting married, having young children, then seeing those children through adolescence, launching those children into adult life, and, finally, accepting shifting generational roles, as when children begin to take care of their parents. This type of stage theory also conceptualizes the family as multigenerational, with shifting roles and responsibilities for each member. Each person adopts different roles depending on which family member is the focus, with parents themselves leaving home at earlier ages, becoming grandparents many years later.

Like all theories of adult development, Carter and McGoldrick's (1988) stages might be better conceptualized as general guidelines. Still, these stages do make salient that parents of different-age children have different concerns. Parents worried about their 2-week-old infant's eating, sleeping, and physical development differ greatly from parents concerned about their 16-year-old's new peers and developing sexuality. Such parent-family differences based on the child's chronological age are behind the decision to compare families of children with mental retardation to families of same-age typically developing children (Seltzer & Ryff, 1994). Mental-age comparisons seem most appropriate when considering children with mental retardation, chronological age comparisons when considering their families.

And how should one approach parent-child interactions? As noted earlier, early studies examined parental (mainly maternal) behaviors toward children of the same chronological age as typically developing children. In some studies, it was even strongly hinted that mothers were deficient in their input to their children, as they were speaking at lower levels than were mothers of typically developing children. Beginning with Rondal (1977), groups came to be equated more on age-equivalent scores, and the use of either mental age or language age comparisons has predominated over the past few decades.

As we gain in our knowledge of children with different types of mental retardation, such issues become even trickier. Consider the finding that children with Williams syndrome show relative strengths in language (compared to overall levels of mental age), or that children with Prader-Willi syndrome show excellent performance—even above typical children of identical chronological age—on jigsaw puzzles. What is the appropriate maternal input relative to these tasks?

One suggestion is that children with different genetic mental retardation syndromes might be used as proxies for particular emotional-behavioral problems, personalities, or skill levels on specific tasks (Hodapp, 2004b). In such analyses, one might use children with Down syndrome as a proxy for a sociable, upbeat personality. Conversely, one might use children with Prader-Willi syndrome versus with Williams syndrome as good versus poor jigsaw puzzlers, respectively. Other syndromes might also be used as proxies for one or another etiology-related behavior. One could then ask whether parents or others react similarly or differently to nonretarded children who have similar problems, personalities, or high or low skills on a specific task.

Granted, one must be careful in performing this type of analysis, as a single etiology often predisposes individuals to multiple behavioral characteristics. Children with Prader-Willi syndrome are excellent at putting together jigsaw puzzles, but, in other contexts, such children might be thought of as proxies for children with extreme eating problems and obesity, or children with obsessive-compulsive disorder. Other genetic syndromes can similarly be considered to have more than one behavioral outcome, and reactions or interactive behaviors might also differ based on the interactor or the task.

Using genetic disorders as behavioral proxies extends the many applied developmental studies on so-called natural experiments. In each of these studies, one must essentially disentangle several factors. Consider Rutter's (Rutter, Pickles, Murray, & Eaves, 2001) work on psychiatric risks of such events-situations as maternal deprivation, early institutionalization, being a twin, or being adopted. In each case, the question is not only whether one or another of these situations increases the risks of psychiatric problems, but why.

Direction of Effects, Mediators-Moderators, and Associated Variables

Similar to Bell's (1968) original question many years ago, the direction of effects remains unclear in many studies of mother-child interaction and of family child relations. Does the mother influence the child, or the child the mother?

Under different circumstances, both directions seem to be operating. In a study examining children with mental retardation when children were 3, 7, and 11 years old, Keogh, Garnier, Bernheimer, and Gallimore (2000) found that the more likely direction of effects was from child to parent. In path analyses, the child's higher levels of behavior problems, greater degrees of cognitive impairment, and lower levels of personal-social competence affected parent and family adaptation. In contrast, parental changes and accommodations of the family routine usually did not influence later child behaviors.

From the other direction, parents and families may also influence children. Harris et al. (1996) found that mothers who more often followed the child's lead and prolonged joint attention episodes "produced" young children with Down syndrome whose language developed at a faster rate. Conversely, when mothers more often redirected the child's focus of attention and engaged in greater numbers of separate joint-attention episodes, children showed smaller gains in receptive language skills. Using hierarchical linear modeling to examine changes over the child's first 5 years of life, Hauser-Cram et al. (1999) found that more cohesive families and mothers who more sensitively interacted

with their children "produced" children with Down syndrome who showed greater amounts of development on the adaptive behavior domains of communication, daily living skills, and socialization. Depending on the study, then, children may influence parents or parents may influence children.

In considering these studies, one begins to appreciate just how rare are good, longitudinal studies of children with mental retardation and their parents, families, schools, and other surrounding environments. Even fewer studies examine mediators or moderators of developmental change, and little of what we know about longitudinal effects, mediators, or moderators has been examined in children with different genetic syndromes and their parents, families, or larger environments.

Finally, certain methodological issues pertain only to children with different genetic syndromes and their families. Consider so-called associated variables, those variables that go together with different syndromes but that are separate from the child's behavior per se. The best examples involve Down syndrome. In contrast to other syndromes or to mental retardation in general, Down syndrome is a widely known disorder, occurs more often in births to older mothers, is usually diagnosed at birth, and is fairly common. Parents have access to several well-known, active, and powerful parent groups, as well as books, articles, Web sites, and other informational supports.

One might be tempted to attribute all differences in parents or families of children with versus without Down syndrome to such associated characteristics. Although such differences exist between Down syndrome and other disabilities, they probably do not totally account for the Down syndrome advantage. Moreover, associated characteristics cannot account for changes with age in parent or family stress or perceptions of their children (Hodapp et al., 2003), or the connections between the child's personality and parental attributions (Ly & Hodapp, 2002). We currently know little about formal and informal supports vis-à-vis parents and families of children with different genetic mental retardation syndromes.

Summary

Mental retardation research has gaps that both include and transcend those found in studies of child development and applied child development. In one sense, studies on children with mental retardation mirror gaps found in studies of typically developing children. We need more studies that are longitudinal, that look at moderators and mediators, that worry more about direction of effects, and that use more sophisticated statistical techniques.

Yet in other ways, research issues in mental retardation are specific to this population. Research on few other populations seems to have as much trouble in deciding how research groups should best be divided. Few feature as many as six or seven strategies concerning control or contrast groups. Similarly, few nowadays generally compare to typical children of the same mental age when examining children's functioning, but of the same chronological age when family functioning is the issue. Few fields struggle as mightily with what (if anything) their population's findings tell us about the typical or normative processes of children's development, or of the typical or usual reactions and behaviors of parents and families.

MAKING THE LEAP FROM KNOWLEDGE TO PRACTICE

Like the field of child development itself (Sears, 1975), mental retardation behavioral researchers have historically valued applied work, and basic and applied interests have existed side-by-side in the mental retardation field (Hodapp, 2003). Even the most basic of researchers strive, through their findings, to allow children with mental retardation to develop more optimally, to develop faster in one or another area of functioning, to avoid maladaptive behaviors that make everyday living more difficult. Similarly, those interested in parent-child interaction, families, schools, and neighborhoods desire to improve the developmental ecologies of children with mental retardation.

And yet, although basic and applied interests coexist in the mental retardation field, basic research findings have not always been easily translated into more sophisticated, appropriate interventions. This basic-to-applied gap may simply reflect the fact that, as a field, we know too little. But other issues relate to societal changes, mixing generic and specialized approaches, noncategorical philosophies, and cross-level and interdisciplinary issues. Before describing interventions, then, we first turn to each of these matters.

A Changing Society and a Changing Population

Both philosophically and demographically, American society is changing. Philosophically, over the past few decades Americans have increasingly come to accept the full participation in society of individuals with disabilities. Such societal changes have been embodied in a series of legal and legislative changes that have come to be referred to as the disabilities movement. This movement followed the civil rights and women's movements in demanding full participation of all individuals in school, at work, in the community, and in the law. Major successes include the Education for All Handicapped Children Act, or Public Law 94-142, in 1975, and the Americans with Disabilities Act of 1990, which ensured full access in employment. Each act has codified into law that it is a right—not a privilege—for individuals with disabilities to take their full place in American society.

In addition to such societal changes, changes are also occurring in the American population itself. Not so many years ago, the United States could more or less accurately be considered a country in which the "usual" family was White and middle class, with two parents, one of whom worked outside (usually the father) and the other inside (usually the mother) of the family home. But in recent years, an increasing percentage of the American population has become non-White, most families (including many with young children) have mothers who work outside the family home, and divorced, single, and unmarried parents are all increasingly common. Each issue obviously affects children with mental retardation and their families, although service, research, and policy practices have all yet to catch up.

Consider the impact of another demographic change: the aging of the American population. Demographers note that the American population has gotten increasingly older over the past few decades; the median age of Americans rose from 26.5 years in 1930 to 35.3 years in 2000. In only a few years' time, the leading edge of the Baby Boomers (i.e., those born between 1946 and 1964) will begin retiring. Medicare payments will rise exponentially, health systems will face increased stressors, and few politicians have either the foresight or the courage to address such issues.

A corollary concerns the aging of the population with disabilities. Currently in the United States, 526,000 adults with disabilities are 60 years or older, and that number is expected to triple—to over 1.5 million—by 2030 (National Center for Family Support, 2000). Given that at least 60% of these adults live at home and are now cared for by aging parents, who will care for these adults with disabilities when their parents die or are no longer able to care for them? The adult siblings of adults with disabilities are the assumed future caregivers, but the needs of adult siblings—and all issues relating to life-span development—have so far remained almost totally unexamined in the mental retardation field.

Generic and Specialized Issues

When considering interventions for children with mental retardation and their families, one must think in terms of three separate levels. First, certain programs and services are needed by everyone. All children require caregiving, adequate food and shelter, safe neighborhoods, decent schools, and affordable health care. Such services might be considered common needs of all children and their families.

A second level of services is general to all children with mental retardation and their families. Again, such services and interventions are mostly generic: early intervention programs, special education services, transition, family support, and adult services relating to the adults working and living in the community. Such interventions apply to all children with mental retardation, as well as to children with any disabling condition (deafness, blindness, motor, or emotional problems).

A final set of services and interventions are specific to children with specialized needs. Some children with mental retardation have specialized health care needs, often relating to heart problems or motor impairments. Although estimates vary, approximately ¼ to ⅓ of children with mental retardation also show significant psychiatric impairment (Bouras, 1999; Dykens, 2000; Tonge & Einfeld, 2003).

Many of these health and psychiatric concerns also relate to specific etiological groups. Many children with Down syndrome show heart and respiratory problems,as well as higher prevalence rates of leukemia and (in early mid-adulthood) Alzheimer's disease (Leshin, 2002; Pueschel, 1990). Children with Prader-Willi syndrome are prone to obsessive-compulsive disorder (Dykens et al., 1996), those with Williams syndrome to clinically high levels of anxiety and fears (Dykens, 2003). Etiology-based interventions might address such health, psychiatric, and cognitive-linguistic concerns.

Obviously, each type of intervention is necessary, but the three types of intervention also mutually influence one another. Consider the connections between specialized health or habilitative services and services to help families survive economically. Birenbaum and Cohen (1993) note that families of children with more severe impairments often have associated expenses that, in most cases, these families must pay for themselves. Compared to average health care costs of less than $1,000 per year for all American children, Birenbaum and Cohen's families spent an average of $4,000 a year on health care for their children with severe or profound mental retardation. For about 10% of these families, costs of home or car modifications for their children exceeded $2,000 per year. Such expenses, while unknown to parents of typically developing children, are commonplace to parents of children with mental retardation (particularly those at severe or profound levels). Although Medicaid and state-run cash assistance programs can sometimes offset these costs (Agosta, 1989; Agosta & Melda, 1995), issues of shelter, safety, and well-being are not necessarily separate from intervention discussions within the mental retardation field.

Noncategorical Philosophies

Noncategorical programming refers to the intervention practice of considering together children with many different disabilities (Reynolds, 1990). Most prominent in the field of special education, the idea is that a category, or label, is rarely helpful in the educational process and that different types of children can therefore be educated together. Even if several disabilities do benefit from distinct educational approaches, Forness and Kavale (1994) contend that we could eventually reach the unwieldy situation of many groups requiring their own, specialized classrooms. Such a "Balkanization" of special education services would cause administrative nightmares for schools, teachers, and districts.

Although sympathetic to potential adverse effects of labeling or a Balkanization of special education, we nevertheless feel that certain labels, or genetic diagnoses, may matter. If children show etiology-related profiles of development, personalities, and maladaptive behavior or psychopathology, it seems possible to design interventions that might capitalize on such etiology-based information. To us, the noncategorical philosophy ignores the many etiology-related behavioral findings that have appeared over the past 10 to 15 years. Whether categories are beneficial should be an empirical issue, not one decided on the assertion that labels do not matter.

Cross-Level and Cross-Disciplinary Matters

A final issue relates to cross-level and cross-disciplinary matters. Table 12.4 gives a partial listing of several dis-

TABLE 12.4   Professions Associated with Different Syndromes of Mental Retardation

Profession	Syndrome	Issues
Pediatrics	All	Various pediatric concerns, some specific to particular syndromes.
Genetics	FX, PWS	Number of repeats and methylation status (FX); deletion-disomy (PWS).
Nutrition	PWS, DS	Weight control in PWS and DS; weight reduction in life-threatening cases.
Dentistry	WS, PWS, DS	Dental crowding, caries, saliva, and other issues.
Occupational and Physical Therapy	DS, WS, PWS	Joint stability and flexibility; help in fine- and gross-motor functioning; mobility, balance, movement.
Speech-Language Pathology	DS	Grammar and articulation.
Social Work	All	Mother, father, sibling, and family issues; help in dealing with state social service agencies, thinking and planning about future.
Genetics Counseling	DS, FX, other	Family risk assessment due to parent age, family history, or other.
Child Psychiatry and Clinical Psychology	WS, PWS, FX, Rett	Anxiety (WS), obsessive-compulsive disorder (PWS), autism or autistic-like behaviors (FX, Rett).
Psychopharmacology	PWS, WS	Pharmacological treatments for any maladaptive behavior or psychopathology.
Neurosciences	All	Brain-behavior connections involving brain regions, structures, interconnections, and development.

DS = Down syndrome; FX = Fragile X syndrome; PWS = Prader-Willi syndrome; Rett = Rett syndrome; WS = Williams syndrome.

ciplines interested in children with mental retardation. Although we present professions that deal with children with specific genetic disorders, an equally impressive list of professions and interests could be developed for children with mental retardation in general.

Although impressive in its numbers of disciplines, this list also highlights that mental retardation is not owned by any single discipline. Unlike, say, obsessive-compulsive disorder or depression, which are considered to fall mainly within the purview of mental health professionals, children with mental retardation are not predominantly the concern of child psychiatrists and clinical psychologists. Depending on the specific issues involved, many different professionals help persons with mental retardation. Some might even consider this large list a curse; unlike other disorders, mental retardation has no single professional group that is mostly or totally responsible or interested.

A related issue arises in research. To truly understand children with mental retardation, one needs to be comfortable working in an interdisciplinary fashion. But such collaborations are difficult. Consider even the problem of terminology. To geneticists, each of the following are common terms: cytogenetics and molecular genetics; imprinting; alleles; full versus partial mutation; deletion, disomy, and amplification; and trisomy, translocation, and mosaicism. Many subbranches of developmental psychology have equally strange-seeming terms and interests, and it is difficult to explain enough

of what one does to professionals from different disciplines to achieve some common understandings. But if we are ever to reach sophisticated understandings of behavioral development in many types of mental retardation, it seems essential to navigate such cross-cultural disciplinary divides.

Some Examples of Interventions

In the pages that follow, we provide examples of educational, clinical, and family-based interventions.

Educational Interventions: Reading Instruction for Children with Down Syndrome

Children with Down syndrome show relative weaknesses in grammar, expressive language, and articulation. Conversely, these children show relative strengths in visual (as opposed to auditory) short-term memory.

Using these findings, as well as several decades of intervention work, Buckley and her colleagues (Buckley & Bird, 2002) have long advocated teaching reading to these children. So far, the findings are mixed. On one hand, many children can establish reading vocabularies of numerous sight words, even during the preschool years (Buckley, 1995). Half of all children and adolescents may be able to read more than 50 words, with some reaching much higher levels (Buckley, Bird, & Byrne, 1996; Johansson, 1993).

In addition, reading may constitute an entryway into other areas of language. Laws, Buckley, Bird, MacDonald, and Broadley (1995) compared children with Down syndrome who were readers with those who were not. Over a 4-year span, readers were ahead of nonreaders on tests of receptive vocabulary, receptive grammar, auditory memory, and visual memory. For many measures, an interaction also occurred between receiving reading instruction and developmental changes from time 1 to time 2.

On the other hand, questions persist concerning the degree to which children with Down syndrome have or can acquire reading's component skills. Essentially, literacy intervention capitalizes on the relative strength of visual short-term memory for most children with Down syndrome. But reading is more than a visual skill; higher levels of reading can come about only when one attains various aspects of phonemic awareness. Through their ability to segment, delete, and count phonemes, children become able to identify and manipulate phonemes (Gombert, 2002). In typical children, phonetic decoding is a strong predictor of both first- and third-grade reading skills (McGuinness, 1997); levels of phonological awareness and reading also correlate in children with Down syndrome (Fowler, Doherty, & Boynton, 1995; Laws, 1998).

How good are children with Down syndrome at phonological awareness and, if not so good, can they read in some other way? In three studies, Snowling, Hulme, and Mercer (2002) compared typical children to children with Down syndrome on segmentation, nursery rhyme knowledge, rhyme detection, and phoneme detection. They also examined letter names and sounds, print in the daily environment, single-word reading, and nonword reading. Predictors of reading ability were different for the two groups. Although children with Down syndrome with good phonological skills were better readers than those with poorer skills, their letter-sound knowledge was not a concurrent predictor of reading performance. Children with Down syndrome performed worse than control children on rhyme judgment. Other studies have also documented deficits in specific phonemic awareness tasks by children with Down syndrome (Cardoso-Martins, Michalick, & Pollo, 2002; Gompert, 2002).

Compared to typical children, then, children with Down syndrome may follow a qualitatively different path in their development of reading and phonological skills. Children with Down syndrome identify initial syllable and onset phonemes, but have more difficulty with rhyme ("rhyme deficit"). Letter-sound knowledge does not appear related to reading and/or phonological skills. Children with Down syndrome are therefore reading without the full understanding of all aspects of phonemic awareness. They use grapheme-phoneme strategies to some extent, but are also accessing such other strategies as whole-word recognition.

A related issue concerns whether developing literacy skills might constitute an entryway into language. Although several researchers have suggested that reading is the visual route to improved spoken language, longitudinal research does not support this relationship. In a 5-year longitudinal study of 30 individuals with Down syndrome on language, memory, and reading, Laws and Gunn (2002) found that readers performed better on language and nonverbal ability measures at both assessments. There were no significant interactions, however, between reading progress and progress in memory or language. Similarly, no interaction was found between reading skills (or progress) and developments in expressive language. In contrast to earlier formulations, in Down syndrome the direction of effects seems to be language to reading—language abilities influence reading acquisition—as opposed to reading influencing language acquisition.

Reading instruction for children with Down syndrome thus remains intriguing but in need of further study. We need to know more about how children with Down syndrome read, and whether their reading processes are the same as or different from those used by typically developing children. Given such knowledge, we then need to know which strategies might work best for children with Down syndrome who are beginning to read.

Interventions for Maladaptive Behavior-Psychopathology

As noted earlier, as many as $\frac{1}{4}$ to $\frac{1}{3}$ of children with mental retardation also show associated maladaptive behavior-psychopathology, and several different genetic syndromes seem predisposed to specific types of psychopathology. In response to the need for clinical, pharmacological, and other interventions, several etiology-based clinical services have arisen for children with specific types of mental retardation and their families.

University-Based Behavior Genetics Clinic. One example is the UCLA-Lili Claire Behavior Genetics Clinic at UCLA's Neuropsychiatric Institute. The clinic, which meets one morning per week, was founded in

1996. Its original focus was to serve the mental health and dietary needs of children and young adults with Prader-Willi syndrome. Since that time, the clinic has also served children with Down syndrome, Williams syndrome, and other genetic disorders, as well as these children's family members, teachers, group home workers, and others involved in the child's life.

Although housed in child psychiatry and focused mainly on the management of maladaptive behaviors, the clinic's focus is interdisciplinary. Children and families come for an initial 1- to 2-hour visit with a child psychiatrist, child clinical psychologist, social worker, and special educator. Given the dietary issues in Prader-Willi syndrome, a licensed nutritionist is also often on hand, and consultations are common to (and from) clinical genetics, pediatrics, cardiology, speech-language pathology, and other disciplines. The clinic's medical director has long experience in prescribing drugs to children and adults with mental retardation (and with these syndromes).

In their initial visit and in follow-ups every few months, the children, parents, and others receive numerous, interrelated services. The social worker helps navigate the social service system and brings along information about specific syndromes and parent support groups. The social worker and special educator advocate for the children and their families with the school and with state social service agencies, and the clinical psychologist and child psychiatrist assess child and family needs and strengths. Working together, clinic personnel offer parents with several different disorders practical advice and follow-up, knowledge and contact information about the syndrome, behavioral and pharmacological interventions, and other help as needed.

Behavior Analysis. A second intervention is more strictly behavior-analytic in orientation, successor to an approach that was earlier referred to as "behavior modification." This approach has been extremely helpful to children with mental retardation and their parents in three distinct ways.

First, behavior analysis has been remarkably successful in teaching adaptive skills to children and adolescents with mental retardation, many at the more severe to profound levels. Such behaviors as grooming, toileting, eating, and dressing have all been taught to individuals at the profound and severe levels of mental retardation (Carr et al., 1999). At later ages, techniques such as task analysis and token economies have allowed

many persons with mental retardation to work successfully in supported work environments (Wehman, Sale, & Parent, 1992). Again, such direct, labor-intensive interventions have allowed these individuals to achieve skills and produce in jobs that were previously beyond their reach.

Second, behavioral techniques have been helpful for parents. Parents of very impaired or difficult-to-control children are often at a loss as to how to proceed. Such parents are helped by the behavior analyst's specific behavioral interventions and charting of the environmental precursors of child behavior (and of the consequences of different parent behaviors). Parents have been taught how to model desired behaviors, break down complex tasks into smaller components, and chain together these components (Baker & Brightman, 1997).

Third, behavior analyses have been particularly helpful in eliminating maladaptive behaviors. Although maladaptive behavior-psychopathology is especially prevalent in children with mental retardation, the children's inability to use language to describe their feelings and needs often makes "talk therapies" less effective. In contrast, behavior-analytic techniques generally do not require high levels of communication from the client being treated.

Although many examples could be cited of successful behaviorally oriented treatments, one will suffice. Craig Kennedy has recently begun the Vanderbilt Kennedy Center Behavior Analysis Clinic to intervene with children and young adults who show severe aggressive behaviors. In their model, aggression is considered a form of communication that the aggressive person is giving to the outside world. The clinician must first decipher the exact communicative functions of the individual's aggressive acts, and then institute therapies that might eliminate such aggressive behaviors (Kennedy, 2003).

Two advances distinguish the Vanderbilt Kennedy Center Behavior Analysis Clinic from other interventions with a similar philosophy. First, in a clinical sense, the interventions are provided to the clients, but parents and group home workers are then taught how to continue these interventions in the community. This newly begun clinic is thus combining interventions with parent training. Second, the Vanderbilt group is also interested in the so-called setting conditions of aggressive behaviors. In a series of studies, Kennedy and his colleagues have begun to examine the possibility that such child characteristics as sleep deprivation (Harvey & Kennedy, 2002) or genetic status (having or not having a genetic variant predisposing to aggression; May, Potts, Phillips, Blakely, & Kennedy, 2004) might make aggressive behaviors more likely. In essence, behavior-analytic approaches, which began as predominantly environmental in orientation, have begun to join both environmental and child-related characteristics of children showing aggressive behaviors.

Parent-Family Support Groups

Although many would not consider parent support groups as an intervention per se, these groups have become important, influential organizations for many parents and families of children with mental retardation. In addition, such groups range widely in their targeted population, their orientation, and their desired outcomes for the many parents who participate (see Table 12.2).

Although research on parent support groups is only beginning, preliminary findings are intriguing. In studying groups for parents of children with disabilities, Solomon, Pistrang, and Barker (2001) examined members of the United Kingdom's Contact a Family, a group whose aim was to encourage mutual support among families of children with disabilities. Examining 56 parents of 9-year-old children with a wide variety of disabilities, Solomon et al. discovered that parents (who, on average, had been in the group for 4 years) were very satisfied with their groups, found them helpful, and rated them high on group cohesion and task orientation.

Follow-up focus groups provide more detail about how parents benefited from these groups in three broad areas. First, parents felt that they achieved a sense of control from the information gained from other group members. As one parent noted, "When you have a child with special needs, you don't know the best services, the best care, and so on. You get that information from the group" (Solomon et al., 2001, p. 121). Second, parents felt a strong sense of belonging to a community. The authors thus note, "Parents reported feeling 'less alone,' 'less isolated,' 'not the only one,' 'not different anymore,' as a result of group membership" (Solomon et al., 2001, p. 123).

The third benefit of these parent self-help groups seemed to relate to parents' own emotional growth and development. Solomon et al. (2001) write:

> Parents most commonly said that they felt "far more confident" when dealing with other people than they used to before coming to their group: they were more assertive, "tougher," and felt less intimidated, inhibited, embar-

rassed, awkward, and shy. The group helped them to feel "refocused" and "strengthened." (p. 124)

Other, analogous studies are also instructive. In these studies, parents and caregivers of persons with mental illness, Alzheimer's disease, or alcoholism all describe the benefits and limitations of parent support groups. Findings show that parents and families do benefit from these groups, mainly from receiving information and giving and receiving support. In addition, consumer-led versus professional-led groups focus more on advocacy than on emotional issues (Pickett, Heller, & Cook, 1998), and the two types of group differ greatly in cohesion, leader activities, group structure and task orientation, and fostering independence in group members (Toro, Rappaport, & Seidman, 1987).

Although much more research is needed, parent support groups seem an important ecology of families of children with disabilities. As with other self-help groups, the most effective groups probably involve high-quality relationships, high expectations for personal growth, and a moderate level of structure (Moos, 2003). Although all such groups have both strengths and weaknesses, "relatively cohesive, goal-directed, and well-organized intervention programs and life contexts can help distressed individuals recover and lead essentially normal lives" (p. 6).

CONCLUSION

Combining analyses of children and of their surrounding environments, mixing basic research with applications of that research, the mental retardation field seems almost the quintessential case of applied developmental psychology. From earlier days to today's studies of cognitive and language development, the specific issues may have changed, but the basic approaches have remained remarkably consistent. Such approaches can be summarized through the use of four related themes.

Perspectives and Approaches of Developmental Psychopathology

When most people think of developmental psychopathology, they date its origin to the 1970s and 1980s. In 1974, Thomas Achenbach published his landmark work, *Developmental Psychopathology*. A few years later, Cicchetti (1984) began writing about the larger approach of developmental psychopathology, in 1989 Cicchetti and Nurcombe founded the journal *Development and Psychopathology,* and the nascent field's various handbooks began appearing in the early to mid-1990s (Cicchetti & Cohen, 1995; Lewis & Miller, 1990).

Although such recent inaugural dates may be accurate for developmental psychopathology overall, developmental approaches to children with mental retardation go back much further. Piaget, Werner, and Vygotsky all examined children with mental retardation, and Zigler's (1967) developmental approach to mental retardation dates to the mid- to late 1960s. More important, developmentally oriented researchers conceptualized these children's development as informing us about typical developmental processes. From the earliest days through to today's studies of cognition, language, modularity, and theory of mind, developmentally oriented researchers have adopted Cicchetti's (1984, p. 1) dictum that we "can learn more about the normal functioning of an organism by studying its pathology, more about its pathology by studying its normal condition."

The Changing Sense of Development

Particularly over the past few decades, the very meaning of the word "development" has changed, both for those studying typically developing children and for those studying children with mental retardation. Within the child development field more generally, interests in interactions, transactions, and ecologies were propelled by the researchers most tied to each term: Bell (1968), Sameroff and Chandler (1975), and Bronfenbrenner (1979), respectively. For the smaller field of mental retardation, especially for those interested in developmental issues of these children, the interactional, transactional, and ecological movements in developmental psychology proper have served as a point of reference, a way to extend, apply, and test out our (expanded) notions of development (Hodapp & Zigler, 1995).

As a result, developmental approaches to children with mental retardation now easily include analyses of mother-child interactions, parents, families, friends, schools, and neighborhoods. Just as developmental psychology now concerns itself with all things related to children and children's development, so, too, is a wider view of children's development now intrinsic to the mental retardation field. Although neighborhoods, families,

siblings, and intersystem connections may be less well-studied for children with mental retardation, developmental analyses include each of these issues.

Similar but Different Concerns and Complications

And yet, even as mental retardation's developmental studies simply apply and extend findings from typically developing children, so, too, does this area have its own, idiosyncratic issues and concerns. Consider the very issue of how one defines mental retardation, or how one classifies research groups within the population, or to what extent one should examine children with specific genetic syndromes. Each issue is specific to the mental retardation field.

Similarly, when one considers the wider ecology, mental retardation has its separable concerns. In mental retardation, one must concern oneself with the wider service-delivery systems and (at least implicitly) acknowledge how that system has changed dramatically over the years. Indeed, many studies in the 1950s and 1960s examined children with mental retardation who resided in large public institutions; nowadays, such children almost all live in their family home. Even today, almost every study in such journals as the *American Journal on Mental Retardation, Mental Retardation,* and the *Journal of Intellectual Disability Research* (the three main research journals in the mental retardation field) routinely note the types of classrooms their school-age subjects are attending (specialized, mainstreamed, fully integrated); such information is rarely provided for school-age subjects of articles in journals such as *Child Development* and *Developmental Psychology.*

Such field-specific issues also arise in separate, almost parallel histories and research concerns of particular issues in each field. For instance, the movement from negative to stress-and-coping views of parents and families of children with mental retardation has no counterpart in the larger child development field. Few family studies in child development need concern themselves with the outside formal supports offered to their families, or to the amount, costs, or availability of services the child is receiving outside of school. Similarly, few researchers of typically developing children need to worry about mental age versus chronological age comparison groups, different comparison groups when dealing with children's development versus the functioning of their parents, or how to best classify different children with mental retardation. All are research issues specific to the field of mental retardation.

Simultaneous Concern with Basic and Applied Information

Still, if mental retardation research is "the same but different" relative to the wider child development field, it nevertheless shares with child development its status as a "mixed" discipline. Like researchers in mental retardation, most child development researchers would argue that their work has applied implications and that their ultimate goal is not simply to understand the processes of children's development. Instead, most child development researchers would argue that their goals include using that knowledge to better educate children or to foster children's development. So, too, is the field of mental retardation both basic and applied, simultaneously searching for information about the processes by which these children develop and considering how such basic information can be used to improve the lives of children and their families.

Mental retardation, then, is one among many areas of applied developmental psychology. Whether one is considering gene-brain-behavior relations, or mother-child interactions, or how to use basic research to best educate children, our respective concerns overlap greatly. Such similar basic and applied concerns, such similar uses of many disciplines to examine many domains of functioning, have remained constant over the years. One might argue that, in many ways, we have not advanced much from the days of Piaget, Werner, or Vygotsky. In the spiral-staircase view of development, however, we argue that, although we are in some ways at the same point, our questions and answers have become increasingly specific, increasingly interesting, and increasingly helpful to addressing a greater number of basic and applied issues. May we continue—even increase—our joint efforts as we further understand typical development and development of children with mental retardation, this "old and new" topic within the larger field of child development.

REFERENCES

Achenbach, T. (1974). *Developmental psychopathology.* New York: Ronald Press.

Achenbach, T. M. (1991). *Manual for the Child Behavior Checklist/4–18 and 1991 profile.* Burlington: University of Vermont, Department of Psychiatry.

Agosta, J. (1989). Using cash assistance to support family efforts. In G. H. S. Singer & L. K. Irvin (Eds.), *Support for caregiving families: Enabling positive adaptation to disability* (pp. 189–204). Baltimore: Paul H. Brookes.

Agosta, J., & Melda, K. (1995). Supporting families who provide care at home for children with disabilities. *Exceptional Children, 62,* 271–282.

American Association on Mental Retardation. (1992). *Mental retardation: Definition, classification, and systems of supports* (9th ed.). Washington, DC: Author.

American Association on Mental Retardation. (2002). *Mental retardation: Definition, classification, and systems of supports* (10th ed.). Washington, DC: Author.

American Psychiatric Association. (1994). *Diagnostic and statistical manual of mental disorders* (4th ed.). Washington, DC: Author.

Anderson, L. L., Lakin, K. C., Mangan, T. W., & Prouty, R. W. (1998). State institutions: Thirty years of depopulation and closure. *Mental Retardation, 36,* 431–443.

Anderson, L. T., & Ernst, M. (1994). Self-injury in Lesch-Nyhan disease. *Journal of Autism and Developmental Disorders, 24,* 67–81.

Baker, B. L., & Brightman, A. J. (1997). *Steps to independence: Teaching everyday skills to children with special needs* (3rd ed.). Baltimore: Paul H. Brookes.

Bateman, B. D., & Linden, M. A. (1998). *Better IEPs: How to develop legally correct and educationally useful programs* (3rd ed.). Longmont, CO: Sopris West.

Bates, E., Camaioni, L., & Volterra, V. (1975). The acquisition of performatives prior to speech. *Merrill-Palmer Quarterly, 21,* 205–226.

Baumgardner, T. L., Reiss, A. L., Freund, L. S., & Abrams, M. T. (1995). Specification of the neurobehavioral phenotype in males with fragile X syndrome. *Pediatrics, 95,* 744–752.

Baumrind, D. (1973). The development of instrumental competence through socialization. In A. D. Pick (Ed.), *Minnesota Symposia on Child Psychology* (Vol. 7, pp. 3–46). Minneapolis: University of Minnesota Press.

Baumrind, D. (1989). Rearing competent children. In W. Damon (Ed.), *Child development today and tomorrow* (pp. 349–378). San Francisco: Jossey-Bass.

Baumwell, L., Tamis-LeMonda, C. S., & Bornstein, M. H. (1997). Maternal verbal sensitivity and child language comprehension. *Infant Behavior and Development, 20,* 247–258.

Beckman, P. (1983). Influence of selected child characteristics on stress in families of handicapped children. *American Journal of Mental Deficiency, 88,* 150–156.

Bell, R. Q. (1968). A reinterpretation of direction of effects in studies of socialization. *Psychological Review, 75,* 81–95.

Bell, R. Q. (1979). Parent, child, and reciprocal influences. *American Psychologist, 34,* 821–826.

Bellugi, U., Marks, S., Bihrle, A., & Sabo, H. (1988). Dissociation between language and cognitive functions in Williams syndrome. In D. Bishop & K. Mogford (Eds.), *Language development in exceptional circumstances* (pp. 177–189). London: Churchill Livingson.

Bellugi, U., Mills, D., Jernigan, T., Hickok, G., & Galaburda, A. (1999). Linking cognition, brain structure, and brain function in Williams syndrome. In H. Tager-Flusberg (Ed.), *Neurodevelopmental disorders* (pp. 111–136). Cambridge, MA: MIT Press.

Bellugi, U., Wang, P., & Jernigan, T. (1994). Williams syndrome: An unusual neuropsychological profile. In S. H. Broman & J. Grafman (Eds.), *Atypical cognitive deficits in developmental disorders* (pp. 23–56). Hillsdale, NJ: Erlbaum.

Birenbaum, A., & Cohen, H. J. (1993). On the importance of helping families: Policy implications from a national study. *Mental Retardation, 31,* 67–74.

Bishop, D. V. M. (1999). An innate basis for language? *Science, 286,* 2283–2284.

Blacher, J. (1984). Sequential stages of parental adjustment to the birth of the child with handicaps: Fact or artifact? *Mental Retardation, 22,* 55–68.

Blacher, J., & Baker, B. (Eds.). (2002). *Best of AAMR: Families and mental retardation—A collection of notable AAMR journal articles across the twentieth century.* Washington, DC: American Association on Mental Retardation.

Bornstein, M. (Ed.). (2002). *Handbook of parenting: Vol. 3. Being and becoming a parent* (2nd ed.). Mahwah, NJ: Erlbaum.

Bouras, N. (Ed.). (1999). *Psychiatric and behavioural disorders in developmental disabilities and mental retardation.* Cambridge, England: Cambridge University Press.

Bronfenbrenner, U. (1979). *The ecology of human development.* Cambridge, MA: Harvard University Press.

Bryant, B. K. (1985). The neighborhood walk: Sources of support in middle childhood. *Monographs of the Society for Research on Child Development, 50*(3, Serial No. 122).

Buckley, S. (1995). Teaching children with Down syndrome to read and write. In L. Nadel & D. Rosenthal (Eds.), *Down syndrome: Living and learning in the community* (pp. 158–169). New York: Wiley-Liss.

Buckley, S., & Bird, G. (2002). Cognitive development and education: Perspectives on Down syndrome from a 20-year research programme. In M. Cuskelly, A. Jobling, & S. Buckley (Eds.), *Down syndrome across the life-span* (pp. 66–80). London: Whurr.

Buckley, S., Bird, G., & Byrne, A. (1996). The practical and theoretical significance of teaching literacy skills to children with Down's syndrome. In J. A. Rondal, J. Perera, L. Nadel, & A. Comblain (Eds.), *Down's syndrome: Psychological, psychobiological, and socio-educational perspectives* (pp. 119–128). London: Whurr.

Buium, N., Rynders, J., & Turnure, J. (1974). Early maternal linguistic environment of normal and Down syndrome language learning children. *American Journal of Mental Deficiency, 79,* 52–58.

Burack, J. A. (1990). Differentiating mental retardation: The two-group approach and beyond. In R. M. Hodapp, J. A. Burack, & E. Zigler (Eds.), *Issues in the developmental approach to mental retardation* (pp. 27–48). New York: Cambridge University Press.

Burack, J. A., Hodapp, R. M., & Zigler, E. (1988). Issues in the classification of mental retardation: Differentiating among organic etiologies. *Journal of Child Psychology and Psychiatry, 29,* 765–779.

Butler, J. V., Whittington, J. E., Holland, A. J., Boer, H., Clarke, D., & Webb, T. (2002). Prevalence of, and risk factors for, physical ill health in people with Prader-Willi syndrome: A population-based study. *Developmental Medicine and Child Neurology, 44,* 248–255.

Cahill, B. M., & Glidden, L. M. (1996). Influence of child diagnosis on family and parent functioning: Down syndrome versus other disabilities. *American Journal on Mental Retardation, 101,* 149–160.

Cardoso-Martins, C., & Mervis, C. (1984). Maternal speech to prelinguistic children with Down syndrome. *American Journal of Mental Deficiency, 89,* 451–458.

Cardoso-Martins, C., Michalick, M., & Pollo, T. C. (2002). Is sensitivity to rhyme a developmental precursor to sensitivity to phoneme? Evidence from individuals with Down syndrome. *Reading and Writing: An Interdisciplinary Journal, 15,* 438–454.

Carr, E. G., Horner, R. H., Turnbull, A. P., Marquis, J. G., McLaughlin, D. M., McAtee, M. L., et al. (1999). *Positive behavior support for people with developmental disabilities: A research synthesis* [Monograph]. Washington, DC: American Association on Mental Retardation.

Carter, B., & McGoldrick, M. (1988). *The changing family life cycle: A framework for family therapy* (2nd ed.). New York: Gardner Press.

Chapman, R. S., & Hesketh, L. J. (2000). Behavioral phenotype of individuals with Down syndrome. *Mental Retardation and Developmental Disabilities Research Reviews, 6,* 84–95.

Cicchetti, D. (1984). The emergence of developmental psychopathology. *Child Development, 55,* 1–7.

Cicchetti, D., & Cohen, D. J. (Eds.). (1995). *Manual of developmental psychopathology.* New York: Wiley.

Cicchetti, D., & Pogge-Hesse, P. (1982). Possible contributions of the study of organically retarded persons to developmental theory. In E. Zigler & D. Balla (Eds.), *Mental retardation: The developmental-difference controversy* (pp. 277–318). Hillsdale, NJ: Erlbaum.

Cohen, W. I. (2002). Health care guidelines for individuals with Down syndrome: 1999 revision. In W. I. Cohen, L. Nadel, & M. Madnick (Eds.), *Down syndrome* (pp. 237–245). New York: Wiley-Liss.

Council for Exceptional Children. (1998). *What every special educator must know* (3rd ed.). Reston, VA: Author.

Crawley, S., & Spiker, D. (1983). Mother-child interactions involving 2-year-olds with Down syndrome: A look at individual differences. *Child Development, 54,* 1312–1323.

Crnic, K., Friedrich, W., & Greenberg, M. (1983). Adaptation of families with mentally handicapped children: A model of stress, coping, and family ecology. *American Journal of Mental Deficiency, 88,* 125–138.

Cummings, S. (1976). The impact of the child's deficiency on the father: A study of fathers of mentally retarded and chronically ill children. *American Journal of Orthopsychiatry, 46,* 246–255.

Cummings, S., Bayley, H., & Rie, H. (1966). Effects of the child's deficiency on the mother: A study of mentally retarded, chronically ill, and neurotic children. *American Journal of Orthopsychiatry, 36,* 595–608.

Cunningham, C. C. (1996). Families of children with Down syndrome. *Down Syndrome: Research and Practice, 4*(3), 87–95.

Dilts, C. V., Morris, C. A., & Leonard, C. O. (1990). Hypothesis for development of a behavioral phenotype in Williams syndrome. *American Journal of Medical Genetics, 6*(Suppl. 6), 126–131.

Doll, E. A. (1953). *Measurement of social competence: A manual for the Vineland Social Maturity Scale.* Circle Pines, MN: American Guidance Services.

Dunn, P. M. (1991). Down, Langdon (1828–1896) and mongolism. *Archives of Disease in Childhood, 66,* 827–828.

Dunst, C. J., Humphries, T., & Trivette, C. M. (2002). Characterizations of the competence of parents of young children with disabilities. *International Review of Research in Mental Retardation, 25,* 1–34.

Dykens, E. M. (1995). Measuring behavioral phenotypes: Provocations from the "new genetics." *American Journal on Mental Retardation, 99,* 522–532.

Dykens, E. M. (1996). DNA meets DSM: The growing importance of genetic syndromes in dual diagnosis. *Mental Retardation, 34,* 125–127.

Dykens, E. M. (1999). Prader-Willi syndrome. In H. Tager-Flusberg (Ed.), *Neurodevelopmental disorders* (pp. 137–154). Cambridge, MA: MIT Press.

Dykens, E. M. (2000). Psychopathology in children with intellectual disabilities. *Journal of Child Psychology and Psychiatry, 41,* 407–417.

Dykens, E. M. (2002). Are jigsaw puzzles "spared" in persons with Prader-Willi syndrome? *Journal of Child Psychology and Psychiatry, 43,* 343–352.

Dykens, E. M. (2003). Anxiety, fears, and phobias in Williams syndrome. *Developmental Neuropsychology, 23,* 291–316.

Dykens, E. M., & Cassidy, S. B. (1999). Prader-Willi syndrome. In S. Goldstein & C. R. Reynolds (Eds.), *Handbook of neurodevelopmental and genetic disorders in children* (pp. 525–554). New York: Guilford Press.

Dykens, E. M., & Clarke, D. J. (1997). Correlates of maladaptive behavior in individuals with 5p- (cri du chat) syndrome. *Developmental Medicine and Child Neurology, 39,* 752–756.

Dykens, E. M., & Hodapp, R. M. (2001). Research in mental retardation: Toward an etiologic approach. *Journal of Child Psychology and Psychiatry, 42,* 49–71.

Dykens, E. M., Hodapp, R. M., & Finucane, B. M. (2000). *Genetics and mental retardation syndromes: A new look at behavior and interventions.* Baltimore: Paul H. Brookes.

Dykens, E. M., Hodapp, R. M., & Leckman, J. F. (1987). Strengths and weaknesses in intellectual functioning of males with fragile X syndrome. *American Journal of Mental Deficiency, 92,* 234–236.

Dykens, E. M., Hodapp, R. M., Walsh, K. K., & Nash, L. (1992). Profiles, correlates, and trajectories of intelligence in Prader-Willi syndrome. *Journal of the American Academy of Child and Adolescent Psychiatry, 31,* 1125–1130.

Dykens, E. M., & Kasari, C. (1997). Maladaptive behavior in children with Prader-Willi syndrome, Down syndrome, and nonspecific mental retardation. *American Journal on Mental Retardation, 102,* 228–237.

Dykens, E. M., Leckman, J. F., & Cassidy, S. B. (1996). Obsessions and compulsions in Prader-Willi syndrome. *Journal of Child Psychology and Psychiatry, 37,* 995–1002.

Dykens, E. M., & Rosner, B. A. (1999). Refining behavioral phenotypes: Personality-motivation in Williams and Prader-Willi syndromes. *American Journal on Mental Retardation, 104,* 158–169.

Dykens, E. M., Rosner, B. A., & Ly, T. M. (2001). Drawings by individuals with Williams syndrome: Are people different from shapes? *American Journal on Mental Retardation, 106,* 94–107.

Dykens, E. M., Shah, B., Sagun, J., Beck, T., & King, B. Y. (2002). Maladaptive behaviour in children and adolescents with Down's syndrome. *Journal of Intellectual Disability Research, 46,* 484–492.

Einfeld, S. L., Tonge, B. J., & Florio, T. (1997). Behavioral and emotional disturbance in individuals with Williams syndrome. *American Journal on Mental Retardation, 102,* 45–53.

Ellis, N. R., & Cavalier, A. R. (1982). Research perspectives in mental retardation. In E. Zigler & D. Balla (Eds.), *Mental retardation: The developmental-difference controversy.* Hillsdale, NJ: Erlbaum.

Erickson, M. (1969). MMPI profiles of parents of young retarded children. *American Journal of Mental Deficiency, 73,* 727–732.

Essex, E. L., Seltzer, M. M., & Krauss, M. W. (1999). Differences in coping effectiveness and well-being among aging mothers and fathers of adults with mental retardation. *American Journal on Mental Retardation, 104,* 454–563.

Ewart, A. K., Morris, C. A., Atkinson, D., Jin, W., Sternes, K., Spallone, P., et al. (1993). Hemizygosity at the elastin locus in a developmental disorder, Williams syndrome. *Nature Genetics, 5,* 11–16.

Farber, B. (1959). The effects of the severely retarded child on the family system. *Monographs of the Society for Research in Child Development, 24*(2).

Farber, B. (1970). Notes on sociological knowledge about families with mentally retarded children. In M. Schreiber (Ed.), *Social work and mental retardation* (pp. 118–124). New York: John Day.

Fernald, A. (1989). Intonation and communicative intent in mothers' speech to infants: Is the melody the message? *Child Development, 60,* 1497–1510.

Fidler, D. J. (2003). Parental vocalizations and perceived immaturity in Down syndrome. *American Journal on Mental Retardation, 108,* 425–434.

Fidler, D. J., & Hodapp, R. M. (1999). Craniofacial maturity and perceived personality in children with Down syndrome. *American Journal on Mental Retardation, 104,* 410–421.

Fidler, D. J., Hodapp, R. M., & Dykens, E. M. (2000). Stress in families of young children with Down syndrome, Williams syndrome, and Smith-Magenis syndrome. *Early Education and Development, 11,* 395–406.

Finucane, B. M., Konar, D., Haas-Givler, B., Kurtz, M. D., & Scott, C. I. (1994). The spasmodic upper-body squeeze: A characteristic behavior in Smith-Magenis syndrome. *Developmental Medicine and Child Neurology, 36,* 78–83.

Flaherty, E. M., & Glidden, L. M. (2002). Positive adjustments in parents rearing children with Down syndrome. *Early Education and Development, 11,* 407–422.

Flynn, J. R. (1999). IQ gains over time: Toward finding the causes. In U. Neisser (Ed.), *The rising curve: Long-term gains in IQ and related measures* (pp. 25–66). Washington, DC: American Psychological Association.

Fodor, J. (1983). *Modularity of mind: An essay on faculty psychology.* Cambridge, MA: MIT Press.

Folkman, S., Schaefer, C., & Lazarus, R. S. (1979). Cognitive processes as mediators of stress and coping. In V. Hamilton & D. S. Warburton (Eds.), *Human stress and cognition* (pp. 265–298). New York: Wiley.

Forness, S., & Kavale, K. (1994). The Balkanization of special education: Proliferation of categories for "new" behavioral disorders. *Education and Treatment of Children, 17,* 215–227.

Fowler, A. (1990). The development of language structure in children with Down syndrome. In D. Cicchetti & M. Beeghly (Eds.), *Children with Down syndrome: A developmental approach* (pp. 302–328). Cambridge, England: Cambridge University Press.

Fowler, A. E., Doherty, B. J., & Boynton, L. (1995). The basis of reading skill in young adults with Down syndrome. In L. Nadel & D. Rosenthal (Eds.), *Down syndrome: Living and learning in the community* (pp. 182–196). New York: Wiley-Liss.

Freeman, S. F. N., & Alkin, M. C. (2000). Academic and social attainments of children with mental retardation in general education and special education settings. *Remedial and Special Education, 21,* 3–18.

Freud, S. (1957). Mourning and melancholia. In J. Rickman (Ed.), *A general selection from the works of Sigmund Freud* (pp. 124–140). Garden City, NY: Doubleday. (Original work published 1917)

Friedrich, W. L., & Freidrich, W. N. (1981). Psychosocial assets of parents of handicapped and nonhandicapped children. *American Journal of Mental Deficiency, 85,* 551–553.

Friedrich, W. N. (1979). Predictors of coping behavior of mothers of handicapped children. *Journal of Consulting and Clinical Psychology, 47,* 1140–1141.

Gardner, H. (1983). *Frames of mind.* New York: Basic Books.

Gersh, M., Goodart, S. A., Pasztor, L. M., Harris, D. J., Weiss, L., & Overhauser, J. (1995). Evidence for a distinct region causing a cat-like cry in patients with 5p- deletions. *American Journal of Human Genetics, 56,* 1404–1410.

Glidden, L. M. (2002). Parenting children with developmental disabilities: A ladder of influence. In J. L. Borkowski, S. L. Ramey, & M. Bristol-Powers (Eds.), *Monographs in parenting: Parenting and the child's world—Influences on academic, intellectual, and socioemotional development* (pp. 329–344). Mahwah, NJ: Erlbaum.

Goldberg, S. (1977). Social competence in infancy: A model of parent-infant interaction. *Merrill-Palmer Quarterly, 23,* 163–177.

Goldberg, S., Marcovitch, S., MacGregor, D., & Lojkasek, M. (1986). Family responses to developmentally delayed preschoolers: Etiology and the father's role. *American Journal on Mental Retardation, 90,* 610–617.

Gombert, J. (2002). Children with Down syndrome use phonological knowledge in reading. *Reading and Writing: An Interdisciplinary Journal, 15,* 455–469.

Gosch, A., & Pankau, R. (1997). Personality characteristics and behavior problems in individuals of different ages with Williams syndrome. *Developmental Medicine and Child Neurology, 39,* 527–533.

Graham, S. (1991). A review of attribution theory in achievement contexts. *Educational Psychology Review, 3,* 5–39.

Greenberg, F., Lewis, R. A., Potocki, L., Glaze, D., Parke, J., Killian, J., et al. (1996). Multidisciplinary clinical study of Smith-Magenis syndrome: Deletion 17p11.2. *American Journal of Medical Genetics, 6*(2), 247–254.

Grossman, H. (1973). *Manual on terminology and classification in mental retardation* (Special Publications Series, No. 2). Washington, DC: American Association on Mental Deficiency.

Hallahan, D. P., & Kauffman, J. M. (2002). *Exceptional children: Introduction to special education* (9th ed.). Boston: Allyn & Bacon.

Hanson, M., & Hanline, M. F. (1990). Parenting a child with a disability: A longitudinal study of parental stress and adaptation. *Journal of Early Intervention, 14,* 234–248.

Harris, S., Kasari, C., & Sigman, M. (1996). Joint attention and language gains in children with Down syndrome. *American Journal on Mental Retardation, 100,* 608–619.

Harrison, P. (1987). Research with adaptive behavior scales. *Journal of Special Education, 21,* 37–68.

Harvey, M. T., & Kennedy, C. H. (2002). Polysomnographic phenotypes in developmental disabilities. *International Journal of Developmental Neuorscience, 20,* 443–448.

Hauser-Cram, P., Warfield, M. E., Shonkoff, J. P., Krauss, M. W., Upshur, C. C., & Sayer, A. (1999). Family influences on adaptive development in young children with Down syndrome. *Child Development, 70,* 979–989.

Heber, R. (1961). Modifications in the manual on terminology and classification in mental retardation. *American Journal of Mental Deficiency, 65,* 499–500.

Heinicke, C. M. (2002). The transition to parenting. In M. Bornstein (Ed.), *Handbook of parenting: Vol. 3. Being and becoming a parent* (2nd ed., pp. 363–388). Mahwah, NJ: Erlbaum.

Helff, C. M., & Glidden, L. M. (1998). More positive or less negative? Trends in research on adjustment of families rearing children with developmental disabilities. *Mental Retardation, 36,* 457–464.

Hodapp, R. M. (1990). One road or many? Issues in the similar sequence hypothesis. In R. M. Hodapp, J. A. Burack, & E. Zigler (Eds.), *Issues in the developmental approach to mental retardation* (pp. 49–70). Cambridge, England: Cambridge University Press.

Hodapp, R. M. (1994). Cultural-familial mental retardation. In R. Sternberg (Ed.), *Encyclopedia of intelligence* (pp. 711–717). New York: Macmillan.

Hodapp, R. M. (1997). Direct and indirect behavioral effects of different genetic disorders of mental retardation. *American Journal on Mental Retardation, 102,* 67–79.

Hodapp, R. M. (1998). *Development and disabilities: Intellectual, sensory, and motor impairments.* New York: Cambridge University Press.

Hodapp, R. M. (1999). Indirect effects of genetic mental retardation disorders: Theoretical and methodological issues. *International Review of Research in Mental Retardation, 22,* 27–50.

Hodapp, R. M. (2002). Parenting children with mental retardation. In M. Bornstein (Ed.), *Handbook of parenting: Vol. 1. How children influence parents* (2nd ed., pp. 355–381). Hillsdale, NJ: Erlbaum.

Hodapp, R. M. (2003). A re-emergence of the field of mental retardation: Review of International Review of Research in Mental Retardation (Vols. 24–25). *Contemporary Psychology, 48,* 722–724.

Hodapp, R. M. (2004a). Behavioral phenotypes: Going beyond the two-group approach. *International Review of Research in Mental Retardation, 29,* 1–30.

Hodapp, R. M. (2004b). Studying interactions, reactions, and perceptions: Can genetic disorders serve as behavioral proxies? *Journal of Autism and Developmental Disorders, 34,* 29–34.

Hodapp, R. M., & Dykens, E. M. (1994). The two cultures of behavioral research in mental retardation. *American Journal on Mental Retardation, 97,* 675–687.

Hodapp, R. M., & Dykens, E. M. (2001). Strengthening behavioral research on genetic mental retardation disorders. *American Journal on Mental Retardation, 106,* 4–15.

Hodapp, R. M., & Dykens, E. M. (2004). Studying behavioral phenotypes: Issues, benefits, challenges. In E. Emerson, C. Hatton, T. Parmenter, & T. Thompson (Eds.), *International handbook of applied research in intellectual disabilities* (pp. 203–220). New York: Wiley.

Hodapp, R. M., Dykens, E. M., & Masino, L. L. (1997). Families of children with Prader-Willi syndrome: Stress-support and relations to child characteristics. *Journal of Autism and Developmental Disorders, 27,* 11–24.

Hodapp, R. M., Dykens, E. M., Ort, S. I., Zelinsky, D. G., & Leckman, J. F. (1991). Changing patterns of intellectual strengths and weaknesses in males with fragile X syndrome. *Journal of Autism and Developmental Disorders, 21,* 503–516.

Hodapp, R. M., Evans, D., & Gray, F. L. (1999). What we know about intellectual development in children with Down syndrome. In J. A. Rondal, J. Perera, & L. Nadel (Eds.), *Down's syndrome: A review of current knowledge* (pp. 124–132). London: Whurr.

Hodapp, R. M., & Fidler, D. J. (1999). Special education and genetics: Connections for the twenty-first century. *Journal of Special Education, 33,* 130–137.

Hodapp, R. M., & Ricci, L. A. (2002). Behavioural phenotypes and educational practice: The unrealized connection. In G. O'Brien (Ed.), *Behavioural phenotypes in clinical practice* (pp. 137–151). London: Mac Keith Press.

Hodapp, R. M., Ricci, L. A., Ly, T. M., & Fidler, D. J. (2003). The effects of the child with Down syndrome on maternal stress. *British Journal of Developmental Psychology, 21,* 137–151.

Hodapp, R. M., & Zigler, E. (1995). Past, present, and future issues in the developmental approach to mental retardation and developmental disabilities. In D. Cicchetti & D. J. Cohen (Eds.), *Manual of developmental psychopathology* (pp. 299–331). New York: Wiley.

Holroyd, J., & MacArthur, D. (1976). Mental retardation and stress on parents: A contrast between Down syndrome and childhood autism. *American Journal on Mental Deficiency, 80,* 431–436.

Hoppes, K., & Harris, S. (1990). Perceptions of child attachment and maternal gratification in mothers of children with autism and Down syndrome. *Journal of Child Clinical Psychology, 19,* 365–370.

Hyche, J., Bakeman, R., & Adamson, L. (1992). Understanding communicative cues of infants with Down syndrome: Effects of mothers' experience and infants' age. *Journal of Applied Developmental Psychology, 13,* 1–16.

Inhelder, B. (1968). *The diagnosis of reasoning in the mentally retarded* (W. B. Stephens, Trans.). New York: John Day. (Original work published 1943)

Jarrold, C., Baddeley, A. D., Hewes, A. K., & Phillips, C. (2001). A longitudinal assessment of diverging verbal and non-verbal abilities in the Williams syndrome phenotype. *Cortex, 37,* 423–431.

Johansson, I. (1993). Teaching prereading skills to disabled children. *Journal of Intellectual Disability Research, 37,* 413–417.

Jones, O. (1980). Prelinguistic communication skills in Down syndrome and normal infants. In T. Field, S. Goldberg, D. Stern, & A. Sostek (Eds.), *High-risk infants and children: Adult and peer interaction* (pp. 205–225). New York: Academic Press.

Karmiloff-Smith, A., Grant, J., Berthoud, I., Davies, M., Howlin, P., & Udwin, O. (1996). Language and Williams syndrome: How intact is "intact"? *Child Development, 68,* 246–262.

Kasari, C., & Freeman, S. F. N. (2001). Task-related social behavior in children with Down syndrome. *American Journal on Mental Retardation, 106,* 253–264.

Kasari, C., Freeman, S. F. N., Mundy, P., & Sigman, M. (1995). Attention regulation by children with Down syndrome: Coordinated joint attention and social referencing. *American Journal on Mental Retardation, 100,* 128–136.

Kasari, C., & Sigman, M. (1997). Linking parental perceptions to interactions in young children with autism. *Journal of Autism and Developmental Disorders, 27,* 39–57.

Kaufman, A. S., & Kaufman, N. L. (1983). *Kaufman Assessment Battery for Children.* Circle Pines, MN: American Guidance Service.

Kemper, M. B., Hagerman, R. J., & Altshul-Stark, D. (1988). Cognitive profiles of boys with fragile X syndrome. *American Journal of Medical Genetics, 30,* 191–200.

Kennedy, C. H. (2003, Fall). Understanding and treating problem behaviors. *Discovery, 2,* 1–2.

Keogh, B. K., Garnier, H. E., Bernheimer, L. P., & Gallimore, R. (2000). Models of child-family interactions for children with developmental delays: Child-driven or transactional? *American Journal on Mental Retardation, 105,* 32–46.

King, B. H., Hodapp, R. M., & Dykens, E. M. (2005). Mental retardation. In H. I. Kaplan & B. J. Sadock (Eds.), *Comprehensive textbook of psychiatry* (8th ed., Vol. 2, pp. 3076–3106). Baltimore: Williams & Wilkins.

King, B. H., State, M. W., Shah, B., Davanzo, P., & Dykens, E. M. (1997). Mental retardation: Pt. 1. A review of the past 10 years. *Journal of the American Academy of Child and Adolescent Psychiatry, 36,* 1656–1663.

Krauss, M. W., & Hauser-Cram, P. (1992). Policy and program development for infants and toddlers with disabilities. In L. Rowitz (Ed.), *Mental retardation in the year 2000* (pp. 184–196). New York: Springer-Verlag.

Kumin, L. (1994). Intelligibility of speech in children with Down syndrome in natural settings: Parents' perspectives. *Perceptual and Motor Skills, 78,* 307–313.

Lakin, C., Prouty, B., Braddock, D., & Anderson, L. (1997). State institution populations: Smaller, older, more impaired. *Mental Retardation, 35,* 231–232.

Laws, G. (1998). The use of non-word repetition as a test of phonological memory in children with Down syndrome. *Journal of Child Psychology and Psychiatry, 39,* 1119–1130.

Laws, G., Buckley, S., Bird, G., MacDonald, J., & Broadley, I. (1995). The influence of reading instruction on language and memory development in children with Down syndrome. *Down Syndrome: Research and Practice, 3,* 59–64.

Laws, G., & Gunn, D. (2002). Relationships between reading, phonological skills and language development in individuals with Down syndrome: A 5-year follow-up study. *Reading and Writing: An Interdisciplinary Journal, 15,* 527–548.

Leshin, L. (2002). Pediatric health update on Down syndrome. In W. I. Cohen, L. Nadel, & M. Madnick (Eds.), *Down syndrome* (pp. 187–201). New York: Wiley-Liss.

Lewis, M., & Miller, S. (Eds.). (1990). *Handbook of developmental psychopathology.* New York: Plenum Press.

Ly, T. M., & Hodapp, R. M. (2002). Maternal attribution of child noncompliance in children with mental retardation: Down syndrome versus other etiologies. *Journal of Developmental and Behavioral Pediatrics, 23,* 322–329.

Ly, T. M., & Hodapp, R. M. (2005). Children with Prader-Willi syndrome versus Williams syndrome: Indirect effects on parents during a jigsaw puzzle task. *Journal of Intellectual Disability Research, 49,* 929–939.

MacMillan, D. L., Gresham, F. M., & Siperstein, G. N. (1993). Conceptual and psychometric concerns about the 1992 AAMR definition of mental retardation. *American Journal on Mental Retardation, 98,* 325–335.

Marfo, K. (1990). Maternal directiveness in interactions with mentally handicapped children: An analytical commentary. *Journal of Child Psychology and Psychiatry, 31,* 531–549.

Margalit, M., Shulman, S., & Stuchiner, N. (1989). Behavior disorders and mental retardation: The family system perspective. *Research in Developmental Disabilities, 10,* 315–326.

Marshall, N., Hegrenes, J., & Goldstein, S. (1973). Verbal interactions: Mothers and their retarded children versus mothers and their nonretarded children. *American Journal of Mental Deficiency, 77,* 415–419.

May, M. E., Potts, T., Phillips, J. A., Blakely, R. D., & Kennedy, C. H. (2004). *A functional polymorphism in the monoamine oxidase: A promoter gene predicts aggressive behavior in developmental disabilities.* Manuscript submitted for publication.

McGrew, K., & Bruininks, R. (1989). Factor structure of adaptive behavior. *School Psychology Review, 18,* 64–81.

McGuinness, D. (1997). Decoding strategies as predictors of reading skill: A follow-up study. *Annals of Dyslexia, 47,* 117–150.

Mervis, C. B., Morris, C. A., Bertrand, J., & Robinson, B. F. (1999). Williams syndrome: Findings from an integrated program of research. In H. Tager-Flusberg (Ed.), *Neurodevelopmental disorders* (pp. 65–110). Cambridge, MA: MIT Press.

Mervis, C. B., Robinson, B. F., Rowe, M. L., Becerra, A. M., & Klein-Tasman, B. P. (2003). Language abilities of individuals with Williams syndrome. *International Review of Research in Mental Retardation, 27,* 35–81.

Meyers, B. A., & Pueschel, S. M. (1991). Psychiatric disorders in persons with Down syndrome. *Journal of Nervous and Mental Diseases, 179,* 609–613.

Miller, J. (1999). Profiles of language development in children with Down syndrome. In J. F. Miller, M. Leddy, & L. A. Leavitt (Eds.), *Improving the communication of people with Down syndrome* (pp. 11–39). Baltimore: Paul H. Brookes.

Minnes, P. M. (1988). Family resources and stress associated with having a mentally retarded child. *American Journal on Mental Retardation, 93,* 184–192.

Moos, R. H. (2003). Social contexts: Transcending their power and their fragility. *American Journal of Community Psychology, 31,* 1–13.

Morris, M. (2002). Economic independence and inclusion. In W. I. Cohen, L. Nadel, & M. E. Madnick (Eds.), *Down syndrome: Visions for the twenty-first century* (pp. 17–81). New York: Wiley-Liss.

Mundy, P., & Kasari, C. (1990). The similar structure hypothesis and differential rate of development in mental retardation. In R. M. Hodapp, J. A. Burack, & E. Zigler (Eds.), *Issues in the developmental approach to mental retardation* (pp. 71–92). Cambridge, England: Cambridge University Press.

National Center for Family Support. (2000, Winter). Aging family caregivers: Needs and policy concerns. *Family support policy brief no. 3.* Available from National Center for Family Support@HSRI.

Noh S., Dumas, J. E., Wolf, L. C., & Fisman, S. N. (1989). Delineating sources of stress in parents of exceptional children. *Family Relations, 38,* 456–461.

Opitz, J. M. (1985). Editorial comment: The developmental field concept. *American Journal of Medical Genetics, 21,* 1–11.

Paparella, T., & Kasari, C. (2004). Joint attention research in special needs populations: Translating research to practice. *Infants and Young Children, 17,* 269–280.

Pennington, B., O'Connor, R., & Sudhalter, V. (1991). Toward a neuropsychology of fragile X syndrome. In R. J. Hagerman & A. C. Silverman (Eds.), *Fragile X syndrome: Diagnosis, treatment, and research* (pp. 173–201). Baltimore: Johns Hopkins University Press.

Piaget, J., & Inhelder, B. (1947). Diagnosis of mental operations and theory of intelligence. *American Journal of Mental Deficiency, 51,* 401–406.

Pickett, S. A., Heller, T., & Cook, J. A. (1998). Professional-led versus family-led support groups: Exploring the differences. *Journal of Behavioral and Health Services and Research, 25,* 437–445.

Polloway, E. A., Smith, J. D., Chamberlain, J., Denning, C. B., & Smith, T. E. C. (1999). Levels of deficits or supports in the classification of mental retardation: Implementation practices. *Education and Training in Mental Retardation, 34,* 200–206.

Pueschel, S. R. (1990). Clinical aspects of Down syndrome from infancy to adulthood. *American Journal of Medical Genetics* (Suppl. 7), 52–56.

Pueschel, S. R., Gallagher, P. L., Zartler, A. S., & Pezzullo, J. C. (1986). Cognitive and learning processes in children with Down syndrome. *Research in Developmental Disabilities, 8,* 21–37.

Reiss, S., & Havercamp, S. H. (1998). Toward a comprehensive assessment of functional motivation: Factor structure of the Reiss profiles. *Psychological Assessment, 10,* 97–106.

Reynolds, M. C. (1990). Noncategorical special education. In M. C. Wang, M. C. Reynolds, & H. J. Walberg (Eds.), *Special education: Research and practice* (pp. 57–80). Oxford: Pergamon Press.

Rieber, R. W., & Carton, A. S. (Eds.). (1993). *The fundamentals of defectology: Vol. 2. The collected works of L. S. Vygotsky* (J. Knox & C. B. Stephens, Trans.). New York: Plenum Press.

Roach, M. A., Orsmond, G. I., & Barratt, M. S. (1999). Mothers and fathers of children with Down syndrome: Parental stress and involvement in childcare. *American Journal on Mental Retardation, 104,* 422–436.

Rondal, J. (1977). Maternal speech in normal and Down syndrome children. In P. Mittler (Ed.), *Research to practice in mental retardation: Vol. 3. Education and training* (pp. 239–243). Baltimore: University Park Press.

Rondal, J. (1995). *Exceptional language development in Down syndrome.* New York: Cambridge University Press.

Rosner, B. A., Hodapp, R. M., Fidler, D. J., Sagun, J. N., & Dykens, E. M. (2004). Social competence in persons with Prader-Willi, Williams, and Down syndromes. *Journal of Applied Research in Intellectual Disabilities, 17,* 209–217.

Ross, R. T., Begab, M. J., Dondis, E. H., Giampiccolo, J., & Meyers, C. E. (1985). *Lives of the retarded: A 40-year follow-up study.* Stanford, CA: Stanford University Press.

Routh, D. K. (2003). A retrospective view of doctoral training in psychology and behavior analysis for research on intellectual disability and emotional problems. *Psychology in Mental Retardation and Developmental Disabilities, 28*(1), 2–5.

Rusch, F. R., & Chadsey, J. G. (Eds.). (1998). *Beyond high school: Transition from school to work.* Belmont, CA: Wadsworth.

Rutter, M., Pickles, A., Murray, R., & Eaves, L. (2001). Testing hypotheses on specific environmental causal effects on behavior. *Psychological Bulletin, 127,* 291–324.

Sameroff, A., & Chandler, M. (1975). Reproductive risk and the continuum of caretaker casualty. In F. D. Horowitz, M. Hetherington, S. Scarr-Salapatek, & G. Siegel (Eds.), *Review of child development research* (Vol. 4, pp. 187–244). Chicago: University of Chicago Press.

Sanders, J. L., & Morgan, S. B. (1997). Family stress and adjustment as perceived by parents of children with autism or Down syndrome: Implications for intervention. *Child and Family Behavior Therapy, 19,* 15–32.

Scott, B. S., Atkinson, L., Minton, H. L., & Bowman, T. (1997). Psychological distress of parents of infants with Down syndrome. *American Journal on Mental Retardation, 102,* 161–171.

Sears, R. R. (1975). Your ancients revisited: A history of child development. In E. M. Hetherington (Ed.), *Review of child development research* (Vol. 5, pp. 1–73). Chicago: University of Chicago Press.

Seltzer, M. M., & Ryff, C. (1994). Parenting across the lifespan: The normative and nonnormative cases. *Life-Span Development and Behavior, 12,* 1–40.

Snow, C. E. (1972). Mothers' speech to children learning language. *Child Development, 43,* 549–565.

Snowling, M. J., Hulme, C., & Mercer, R. C. (2002). A deficit in rime awareness in children with Down syndrome. *Reading and Writing: An Interdisciplinary Journal, 15,* 471–495.

Solomon, M., Pistrang, N., & Barker, C. (2001). The benefits of mutual support groups for parents of children with disabilities. *American Journal of Community Psychology, 29,* 113–132.

Solnit, A., & Stark, M. (1961). Mourning and the birth of a defective child. *Psychoanalytic Study of the Child, 16,* 523–537.

Sorce, J. F., & Emde, R. (1982). The meaning of infant emotional expression: Regularities in caregiving responses in normal and Down syndrome infants. *Journal of Child Psychology and Psychiatry, 23,* 145–158.

Sparrow, S. S., Balla, D. A., & Cicchetti, D. V. (1984). *Vineland Adaptive Behavior Scales.* Circle Pines, MN: American Guidance Service.

Stromme, P., & Hagberg, G. (2000). Aetiology in severe and mild mental retardation: A population-based study of Norwegian children. *Developmental Medicine and Child Neurology, 42,* 76–86.

Stromme, P., & Magnus, P. (2000). Correlations between socioeconomic status, IQ and aetiology in mental retardation: A population-based study of Norwegian children. *Social Psychiatry and Psychiatric Epidemiology, 35,* 12–18.

Switzky, H., & Greenspan, S. (Eds.). (2003). *What is mental retardation: Ideas for an evolving disability.* Washington, DC: American Association on Mental Retardation. (Available as an e-book at www.aamr.org)

Tannock, R. (1988). Mothers' directiveness in their interactions with children with and without Down syndrome. *American Journal on Mental Retardation, 93,* 154–165.

Thomas, V., & Olsen, D. H. (1993). Problem families and the circumplex model: Observational assessment using the Clinical Rating Scale (CRS). *Journal of Marital and Family Therapy, 19,* 159–175.

Tomasello, M., & Farrar, M. J. (1986). Joint attention and early language. *Child Development, 57,* 1454–1463.

Tonge, B. J., & Einfeld, S. L. (2003). Psychopathology and intellectual disability: The Australian child to adult longitudinal study. *International Review of Research in Mental Retardation, 26,* 61–91.

Toro, P. A., Rappaport, J., & Seidman, E. (1987). Social climate comparison of mutual help and psychotherapy groups. *Journal of Consulting and Clinical Psychology, 55,* 430–431.

Turnbull, A. P., Patterson, J. M., Behr, S. K., Murphy, D. L., Marquis, J. G., & Blue-Banning, M. J. (Eds.). (1993). *Cognitive coping, families, and disability.* Baltimore: Paul H. Brookes.

Turnbull, A. P., & Turnbull, H. R. (1997). *Families, professionals, and exceptionality: A special partnership* (3rd ed.). Upper Saddle River, NJ: Merrill.

Udwin, O., & Yule, W. (1991). A cognitive and behavioural phenotype in Williams syndrome. *Journal of Clinical and Experimental Neuropsychology, 13,* 232–244.

Udwin, O., Yule, W., & Martin, N. (1987). Cognitive abilities and behavioral characteristics of children with idiopathic infantile hypercalcaemia. *Journal of Child Psychology and Psychiatry, 28,* 297–309.

Van Acker, R. (1991). Rett syndrome: A review of current knowledge. *Journal of Autism and Developmental Disorders, 21,* 381–406.

van der Veer, R., & Valsiner, J. (1991). *Understanding Vygotsky: A quest for synthesis.* Oxford: Blackwell.

Vietze, P., Abernathy, S., Ashe, M., & Faulstich, G. (1978). Contingency interaction between mothers and their developmentally delayed infants. In G. P. Sackett (Ed.), *Observing behavior* (Vol. 1, pp. 115–132). Baltimore: University Park Press.

Walden, T. A. (1996). Social responsivity: Judging signals of young children with and without developmental delays. *Child Development, 67,* 2074–2085.

Wehman, P., Sale, P., & Parent, W. S. (Eds.). (1992). *Supported employment: Strategies for integration of workers with disabilities.* Boston: Andover Medical.

Weiner, B. (1985). An attributional theory of achievement and motivation. *Psychological Review, 92,* 548–573.

Weiss, B., Weisz, J. R., & Bromfield, R. (1986). Performance of retarded and nonretarded persons on information-processing tasks: Further tests of the similar-structure hypothesis. *Psychological Bulletin, 100,* 157–175.

Weisz, J. R. (1990). Cultural-familial mental retardation: A developmental perspective on cognitive performance and "helpless" behavior. In R. M. Hodapp, J. A. Burack, & E. Zigler (Eds.), *Issues in the developmental approach to mental retardation* (pp. 137–168). Cambridge, England: Cambridge University Press.

Weisz, J. R., Yeates, O. W., & Zigler, E. (1982). Piagetian evidence and the developmental-difference controversy. In E. Zigler & D. Balla (Eds.), *Mental retardation: The developmental-difference controversy* (pp. 213–276). Hillsdale, NJ: Erlbaum.

Werner, H. (1938). Approaches to a functional analysis of mentally handicapped problem children. *American Journal of Mental Deficiency, 43,* 105–108.

Werner, H. (1941). Psychological processes investigating deficiencies in learning. *American Journal of Mental Deficiency, 46,* 233–235.

Werner, H. (1957). The concept of development from a comparative and organismic point of view. In D. Harris (Ed.), *The concept of development* (pp. 125–148). Minneapolis: University of Minnesota Press.

Whittington, J. E., Holland, A. J., Webb, T., Butler, J., Clarke, D., & Boer, H. (2001). Population prevalence and estimated birth incidence and mortality rate for people with Prader-Willi syndrome in one U.K. health region. *Journal of Medical Genetics, 38,* 792–798.

Wishart, J. G., & Johnston, F. H. (1990). The effects of experience on attribution of a stereotyped personality to children with Down syndrome. *Journal of Mental Deficiency Research, 34,* 409–420.

Wisniewski, K. E., Wisniewski, H. M., & Wen, G. Y. (1985). Occurrence of Alzheimer's neuropathology and dementia in Down syndrome. *Annals of Neurology, 17,* 278–282.

Wolf, L. C., Noh, S., Fisman, S. N., & Speechley, M. (1989). Psychological effects of parenting stress on parents of autistic children. *Journal of Autism and Developmental Disorders, 19,* 157–166.

Yoder, P. (1986). Clarifying the relation between degree of infant handicap and maternal responsivity to infant communicative cues: Measurement issues. *Infant Mental Health Journal, 7,* 281–293.

Zebrowitz, L. A. (1997). *Reading faces: Window to the soul?* Boulder, CO: Westview Press.

Zigler, E. (1967). Familial mental retardation: A continuing dilemma. *Science, 155,* 292–298.

Zigler, E. (1969). Developmental versus difference theories of retardation and the problem of motivation. *American Journal of Mental Deficiency, 73,* 536–556.

CHAPTER 13

Developmental Psychopathology and Preventive Intervention

DANTE CICCHETTI and SHEREE L. TOTH

In this chapter, we focus on child maltreatment and the offspring of a parent with a Major Depressive Disorder as illustrative exemplars of how theory and research guided by a developmental psychopathology perspective can help to elucidate the etiology, course, and sequelae of these high-risk conditions and to inform the implementation of preventive interventions. We also address decision points and challenges that emerge when developing and implementing the intervention evaluations and when attempting to apply resulting findings to clinical contexts. Our discussion of these topics is guided by an adherence to an organizational perspective on development because we believe that sound theory is critical for organizing research and intervention efforts in the field. To begin our discussion, we provide a brief description of the field of developmental psychopathology as it applies to clinical practice. A more comprehensive description of the discipline, as well as an articulation of its similarities to and divergences from related fields of inquiry, is presented in *Developmental Psychopathol-* *ogy* (Cicchetti & Cohen, 1995a, 1995b, in press-a, in press-b, in press-c).

PRINCIPLES OF DEVELOPMENTAL PSYCHOPATHOLOGY AND IMPLICATIONS FOR CLINICAL PRACTICE

Developmental psychopathology is an integrative scientific discipline that strives to unify, within a life span framework, contributions from multiple fields of inquiry with the goal of understanding the mutual interplay between psychopathology and normative adaptation (Cicchetti, 1984, 1989, 1993; Cicchetti & Toth, 1998b; Rutter, 1986; Rutter & Garmezy, 1983; Rutter & Sroufe, 2000; Sroufe & Rutter, 1984). Prior to the emergence of developmental psychopathology as an integrative perspective with it is own integrity, the efforts of those working in these areas had been separate and distinct. Some of the lack of integration stemmed from long-standing tensions between the philosophical traditions underlying clinical practice and academic training and between experimental versus applied research (see Cahan & White, 1992; Cicchetti, 1984; Cicchetti & Toth, 1991; Santostefano, 1978; Santostefano & Baker, 1972).

Developmental psychopathologists are as interested in individuals at high risk for the development of psychopathology but who do not manifest it over time as they are in individuals who develop an actual disorder (Cicchetti & Garmezy, 1993; Luthar, 2003; Luthar, Cicchetti, & Becker, 2000; Masten, 2001). Relatedly, developmental psychopathologists are committed to discovering pathways to competent adaptation despite exposure to conditions of adversity (Bonnano, 2004; Cicchetti & Toth, 1991; Luthar, 2003). For example, in a longitudinal investigation of the pathways to maladaptation and resilience from childhood to late adolescence, Masten and her colleagues (1999) found that better adolescent intellectual functioning and parenting resources were associated with good outcomes across a variety of competence domains, even in the context of severe, chronic adversity. Resilient adolescents had much in common with their low-adversity competent peers, including average or better IQ, good quality parenting, and higher psychological well-being. Comprehending the factors contributing to positive outcomes despite the presence of significant adversity (i.e., resilience) can help to broaden the understanding of developmental processes that may not be evident in "good enough" normative environments (Cicchetti & Rogosch, 1997; Masten, Best, & Garmezy, 1990). As researchers increasingly conceptualize and design their investigations at the outset with the differential pathway concepts of equifinality and multifinality as a foundation (cf. Cicchetti & Rogosch, 1996; Richters, 1997), we will come progressively closer to achieving the unique goals of the discipline of developmental psychopathology: to explain the development of individual patterns of adaptation and maladaptation (Cairns, Cairns, Xie, Leung, & Heane, 1998; Sroufe & Rutter, 1984).

A central principle of developmental psychopathology is that individuals may move between psychopathological and nonpsychopathological modes of functioning (Zigler & Glick, 1986). Additionally, developmental psychopathologists underscore that, even in the midst of psychopathology, patients may display adaptive coping mechanisms. Only through the consideration of both adaptive and maladaptive processes does it become possible to delimit the presence, nature, and boundaries of the underlying psychopathology.

Furthermore, developmental psychopathology is a perspective that is especially applicable to the investigation of transitional turning points in development across the life span (Rutter, 1990; Schulenberg, Sameroff, & Cicchetti, 2004). Rutter has conjectured that key life turning points may be times when the presence of protective mechanisms could help individuals redirect themselves from a risk trajectory onto a more adaptive developmental pathway (Elder, 1974; Quinton & Rutter, 1988). With respect to the emergence of psychopathology, all periods of life are consequential in that the developmental process may undergo a pernicious turn toward mental disorder at any phase (Cicchetti & Cannon, 1999; Cicchetti & Walker, 2003; Moffitt, 1993; Post, Weiss, & Leverich, 1994; Rutter, 1996; Zigler & Glick, 1986). In contrast to the often dichotomous world of mental disorder/nondisorder depicted in psychiatry, a developmental psychopathology perspective recognizes that normality often fades into abnormality, adaptive and maladaptive may take on differing definitions depending on whether one's time referent is immediate circumstances or long-term development, and processes within the individual can be characterized as having shades or degrees of psychopathology.

Additionally, there has been an intensification of interest in biological and genetic factors (Cicchetti & Cannon, 1999; Cicchetti & Walker, 2001, 2003; Marenco & Weinberger, 2000; Plomin & Rutter, 1998) and in social-contextual factors related to the development of maladaptation and psychopathology (Boyce et al., 1998; Cicchetti & Aber, 1998; Sameroff, 2000). There is increasing recognition of the dynamic interplay of influences over developmental time. Perhaps the most dramatic example of this is the work on experience-dependent brain development (Greenough, Black, & Wallace, 1987). The viewpoint is now widely shared that neurobiological development and experience are mutually influencing (Cicchetti & Tucker, 1994; Eisenberg, 1995; E. R. Kandel, 1998; C. A. Nelson & Bloom, 1997). Brain development exerts an impact on behavior, of course; however, the development of the brain itself is affected by experience (Black, Jones, Nelson, & Greenough, 1998; Cicchetti, 2002a; Francis, Diorio, Liu, & Meaney, 1999; Meaney, 2001; Ray, 2004). Specifically, it has been demonstrated that social processes and psychological experiences can modify gene expression and brain structure, functioning, and organization (Black et al., 1998; E. R. Kandel, 1998). Alterations in gene expression induced by social processes and psychological experiences produce changes in patterns of neuronal and synaptic connections (E. R. Kandel, 1998, 1999; Sanchez, Ladd, & Plotsky, 2001). These changes not only contribute to the biological bases of individuality, but also play a prominent role in initiating and maintaining the behavioral anomalies that are induced by social and psychological experience.

There also has been a veritable explosion in our knowledge of developmental neurobiology, that area of neuroscience that focuses on factors regulating the development of neurons, neuronal circuitry, and complex neuronal organization systems, including the brain. In addition, advances in the field of molecular genetics (see, e.g., Lander & Weinberg, 2000; Lewin, 2004) have contributed to the understanding of neurological disease, allowing scientists for the first time to understand the genetic basis of certain diseases without requiring foreknowledge of the underlying biochemical abnormalities (Ciaranello et al., 1995). These accomplishments have helped to engender renewed excitement for the potential contributing role that the field of molecular genetics can make to comprehending the development of psychopathology (Caspi et al., 2002, 2003; Cowan, Kopnisky, & Hyman, 2002; Plomin & Rutter, 1998).

Likewise, as we have drawn the distinction between factors that initiate pathways and factors that maintain or deflect individuals from pathways, there is a growing recognition of the role of the developing person as a processor of experience (Cicchetti, 2002b; Cicchetti & Tucker, 1994). The environment does not simply act on the child; the child selects, interprets, and exerts an impact on the environment in a dynamic way (Bergman & Magnusson, 1997; Rutter et al., 1997; Wachs & Plomin, 1991).

Furthermore, developmental psychopathologists recognize that the milieu in which an individual develops is likely to profoundly influence the developmental course (Garcia Coll, Akerman, & Cicchetti, 2000; Garcia Coll et al., 1996; Hoagwood & Jensen, 1997; Richters & Cicchetti, 1993). The dynamic interplay of risk and protective processes may have differential impact depending on the cultural norms, practices, values, and beliefs. Cultures may be characterized on a continuum ranging from sociocentric (emphasizing community, family, and interconnectedness) to individualistic (emphasizing individuality, autonomy, and personal achievement; Garcia Coll et al., 2000; Shweder & Bourne, 1991). The

ideal self correspondingly varies with respect to the degree to which the self is defined in terms of relatedness to others versus in terms of autonomy and achievement. As such, cultural groups differ in their socialization goals for desired outcomes for well-functioning members of the culture. Norms for appropriate and inappropriate behavior have different thresholds, and discipline strategies vary in accord with what behaviors are regarded as desirable or unacceptable. Moreover, risk and protective processes and the manner in which they transact may vary depending on priorities of the culture. Consequently, the individual's response to an event, as well as the reactions of other members of the culture, will influence the salience of the event and how it is responded to. Culture also may influence the mode of symptom expression. Cultural values, beliefs, and practices may tend to suppress manifestation of distress in one domain (e.g., socioemotional) while tolerating the expression in another domain (e.g., physical). For example, Serafica (1997) noted a tendency for greater physical manifestations of distress to be tolerated among Asian American families, as compared with less acceptance of psychological expression.

Bridging Research and Practice

Throughout its evolution as an increasingly mature discipline, an ongoing goal of the field of developmental psychopathology has been to become a science that not only bridges fields of study and aids in the discovery of important new truths about the processes underlying adaptation and maladaptation across the life span, but also provides the best means of preventing and ameliorating maladaptive and psychopathological outcomes (Cicchetti, 1990, 1993; Cicchetti & Hinshaw, 2002; Cicchetti & Toth, 1992, 1998b, 1999). Moreover, developmental psychopathologists have sought to reduce the dualisms that exist between behavioral and biological sciences, between basic and applied research, and between empirical research and the clinical study and treatment of childhood and adult high-risk conditions and disorders.

In this vein, developmental psychopathologists believe that efforts to prevent the emergence of psychopathology or to ameliorate its effects also can be informative for understanding processes involved in psychopathological development (Cicchetti & Hinshaw, 2002; Cicchetti & Toth, 1992; Kellam & Rebok, 1992). For example, if the developmental course is altered as a result of the implementation of preventive interventions and the risk for negative outcomes is reduced, then prevention research helps to specify processes that are involved in the emergence of psychopathology or other negative developmental outcomes. As such, prevention research can be conceptualized as true experiments in altering the course of development, thereby providing insight into the etiology and pathogenesis of disordered outcomes (Cicchetti & Hinshaw, 2002; Howe, Reiss, & Yuh, 2002).

Prevention research is based on theoretical models of how risk conditions are related to adverse outcomes, positing processes that link the risk conditions to the negative outcome (Institute of Medicine, 1994; Munoz, Mrazek, & Haggerty, 1996; Reiss & Price, 1996). For example, poverty and single and teenage parenthood constitute risks for adverse family functioning, such as child abuse and neglect, increased negative developmental outcomes, and welfare dependence (Coley & Chase-Lansdale, 1998; McLoyd, 1998). Olds and his colleagues (1997) posited that maternal isolation, lack of parenting skills, and poor understanding of child development were processes mediating or linking the risk conditions to negative outcomes. A pre- and postnatal home visitation program was implemented to reduce these intervening processes, and the long-term effects of the intervention have been studied. The effectiveness of the intervention helps to establish the importance of the specified mediators as processes explaining how the risk factors contribute to negative outcomes (Hinshaw, 2002; Kraemer, Wilson, Fairburn, & Agras, 2002). Kellam and colleagues (Kellam, Rebok, Ialongo, & Mayer, 1994; Kellam, Rebok, Mayer, Ialongo, & Kalonder, 1994), in studying risk for negative outcomes among predominately poor urban children, identified early disruptive classroom behavior as a process contributing to school failure and Conduct Disorder, and poor achievement (specifically, in reading) as a factor contributing to heightened depressive symptomatology. Interventions were implemented to decrease classroom disruptive behavior and to improve reading skills, with the goal of reducing Conduct Disorder and depression symptomatology, respectively. In summary, prevention research not only leads to support or lack of support for theoretical formulations accounting for the development of psychopathology, but also can contribute to the knowledge base of strategies that can be implemented to reduce psychopathology and promote positive adapta-

tion (see, e.g., Conduct Problems Prevention Research Group, 2002a, 2002b, 2002c).

Comparisons of treated individuals to normative groups on diverse aspects of functioning provide a stringent test of treatment efficacy beyond symptom remission, and knowledge of normal variation on various indicators of adaptation is vital for informing such evaluations (Cicchetti & Rogosch, 1999). Knowledge of developmental norms, appreciation of how developmental level may vary within the same age group, sensitivity to the changing meaning that problems have at different developmental levels, attention to the effects of developmental transitions and reorganizations, and understanding of the factors that are essential features to incorporate into the design and implementation of preventive interventions all may serve to enhance the potential for optimal intervention efficacy (Cicchetti & Hinshaw, 2002; Cicchetti & Toth, 1992, 1999; Coie et al., 1993; Institute of Medicine, 1994; Noam, 1992; Shirk, Talmi, & Olds, 2000; Toth & Cicchetti, 1999).

Unfortunately, inquiries regarding developmental theory and findings on basic developmental processes are all too often quite removed from both clinical practice and clinical research (Cicchetti & Toth, 1998b; Kazdin, 1999; Shirk, 1999; Shirk et al., 2000). Despite rhetoric directed to the principle that developmental theory should inform active clinical intervention—and the converse contention that treatment research should inform relevant theory—the gap between these two endeavors is still broad. Indeed, in many ways, those who perform basic developmental research and promote developmental theory appear to constitute a different culture from those who pursue prevention and intervention efforts. At the extremes, clinically oriented investigators and practitioners perceive "basic" academic developmental science as overly concerned with central tendencies and universal, developmental norms, to the exclusion of the rich variability and nonnormative behavior patterns that they confront on a daily basis. Conversely, theorists and academic scientists appear to construe much of the clinical endeavor as atheoretical, practical, and ungrounded in core scientific principles and theories (Cicchetti & Toth, 1998b).

This state of affairs is particularly distressing given the advances that have been made in a host of basic behavioral and biomedical sciences and the urgent clinical needs of large numbers of individuals and families afflicted by mental disorders (U.S. Department of Health and Human Services [DHHS], 1999). Because of the field's still nascent ideas as to the underlying mechanisms of most forms of psychopathology, the need for direct application of basic research advances toward the enhancement of clinical efforts can only be described as essential. Yet, despite the increasing call for "translational" research that can bridge basic and applied efforts, barriers that exist regarding the application of such basic research advances to clinically relevant work are real (Institute of Medicine, 2000). It is essential that so-called basic investigators receive greater exposure to training in clinical realities and that clinical investigators receive updated information about fundamental processes that are relevant to clinical disorders. As Rees (2002) has noted with respect to medicine, basic science (e.g., genetics, biochemistry) and clinical science (e.g., patient-oriented research) are interdependent endeavors. Rees argued that both forms of science are complementary and essential; clinical investigations should not be replaced by basic research, nor should the provision of service be devoid of empirical support.

In addition to their basic scientific endeavors and their growing appreciation of the importance of conducting developmentally informed preventive interventions, from the outset of the field, developmental psychopathologists have been cognizant of the need to translate empirical research into action. From its inception, contributors to the flagship journal of the field, *Development and Psychopathology,* have been urged to consider and address social policy aspects of their research.

The parameters of developmental psychopathology lend themselves to fostering research with implications for society and for policymakers. The very subject matter of the field, which encompasses risk and psychopathology, the elucidation of precipitants of mental illness, the mediating and moderating processes that contribute to or mitigate against the emergence and maintenance of psychopathology, prevention and intervention, and the incorporation of principles of normal development into the conduct of empirical investigations, necessitates thinking clearly about the implications of the work and devising strategies that will remedy the problems being studied. In his discussion of normal child development, Zigler (1998, p. 530) maintains that "those of us who study children must recognize that they are not merely subjects but partners in our research and we owe something to them." To this sentiment we add that all participants in developmental psychopathology research, whether infants, children,

adolescents, adults with serious mental disorders such as Schizophrenia or bipolar illness, or the elderly, deserve to be beneficiaries of newfound knowledge, as well as contributors to initiatives that will promote societal good. We believe that it is essential for the field to move beyond trying to arrive at post hoc explanations of the relevance of research for policy and to design investigations with policy questions at the forefront. This century presents us all with a unique opportunity to translate rhetoric into action and to truly achieve a research-informed policy agenda that will benefit the welfare of all.

An Organizational Perspective: Implications for Investigating the Nature of the Relation between Normality and Psychopathology

Before turning to the specific risk conditions addressed in this chapter, it is important to provide a framework within which research and intervention can be understood. Much research conducted in developmental psychopathology utilizes an organizational perspective on development, a powerful theoretical framework for conceptualizing the intricacies of the life-span perspective on risk and psychopathology, as well as on normal development (Cicchetti & Schneider-Rosen, 1986; Cicchetti & Sroufe, 1978; Sroufe & Rutter, 1984).

The organizational perspective focuses on the quality of integration both within and between the biological and psychological systems of the individual. Moreover, the organizational perspective addresses how development occurs, specifically identifying a progression of qualitative reorganizations within and among the biological, psychological, and social systems that proceed through differentiation and subsequent hierarchical integration (Werner & Kaplan, 1963). In accord with the organizational perspective, development is not viewed as consisting of a series of tasks that need to be accomplished and that subsequently decrease in importance. Rather, development is conceived as comprising a number of age- and stage-relevant tasks. Although the salience of these tasks may wane in relation to newly emerging issues, the tasks remain important to adaptation over time (Cicchetti, 1993). A hierarchical picture of adaptation emerges in which the successful resolution of an early stage-salient issue increases the probability of subsequent successful adjustment (Sroufe & Rutter, 1984). As each new stage-salient issue comes to the fore, opportunities for growth and consolidation, as well as challenges associated with new vulnerabilities, arise. Thus, an ever changing model of development in which newly formed competencies or maladaptations may emerge throughout the life course and transact with the individual's prior developmental organization is proffered (Cicchetti & Tucker, 1994). Although early adaptation probabilistically portends the quality of future functioning, the possibility of developmental divergence and discontinuity is recognized in this dynamic model (i.e., probabilistic epigenesis).

A principle of importance to developmental psychopathologists is that individuals exert an active role in directing the course of their development. Although more distal historical factors and current influences are important to the process of development, individual choice and self-organization have increasingly been viewed as exerting critical influences on development (Cicchetti & Rogosch, 1997; Cicchetti & Tucker, 1994). Across the developmental course, the evolving capacities of individuals and their active choices allow for new aspects of experience, both internal (e.g., genetic/biological) and external, to be coordinated in increasingly complex ways. Moreover, not only because biological factors can influence psychological processes, but also because social and psychological experiences exert actions on the brain by feeding back on it to modify gene expression and brain structure, function, and organization (Cicchetti & Tucker, 1994; Eisenberg, 1995; E. R. Kandel, 1998; C. A. Nelson & Bloom, 1997), developmental plasticity can be brought about by both biological and psychological self-organization (Cicchetti, 2002a; Cicchetti & Tucker, 1994). Thus, for example, the fact that most maltreated children evidence at least some self-righting tendencies in the face of extreme adversity attests to the strong biological and psychological strivings toward resilience that virtually all humans and living organisms possess (Cicchetti & Rogosch, 1997; Curtis & Cicchetti, 2003; Waddington, 1957). In contrast, the absence of such resilient self-strivings in some maltreated children attests to the deleterious and pernicious impact that traumatic experiences can exert on core biological and psychological developmental processes.

Now that we have described the parameters of the field of developmental psychopathology, provided a description of an organizational perspective on development, and addressed the relevance of these concepts for clinical research and practice, we direct our attention to high-risk conditions that have resulted in the development and evaluation of preventive interventions in our

laboratory at Mt. Hope Family Center. We begin this journey of discovery with child maltreatment and then turn our attention to offspring of mothers with Major Depressive Disorder.

CHILD MALTREATMENT

The study of maltreated children affords an opportunity to examine environmental experience that is far beyond the range of what is normatively encountered. Child maltreatment exemplifies a pathogenic relational environment that poses substantial risk for maladaptation across diverse domains of biological and psychological development (Cicchetti, 2002b; Cicchetti & Lynch, 1995; De-Bellis, 2001). Both the proximal environment of the immediate family and the more distal factors associated with the culture and the community, as well as the transactions that occur among these ecological contexts, conspire to undermine normal biological and psychological developmental processes in maltreated children (Cicchetti & Lynch, 1993; Cicchetti & Toth, 2000).

Research on the biological and psychological sequelae of child maltreatment is extremely important for enhancing the quality of clinical, legal, and policymaking decisions for maltreated children (Cicchetti & Toth, 1993; Toth & Cicchetti, 1993, 1998). Decisions concerning such issues as whether to report a child as maltreated, whether to coercively remove a child from the home, how to develop services and interventions to meet the specific psychological and medical needs of maltreated children, and how to evaluate the efficacy of these services and interventions all benefit from a solid and sophisticated database on the biological and psychological sequelae of child maltreatment (Cicchetti & Toth, 1993; Toth & Cicchetti, 1993, 1998). Thus, conducting research that elucidates the developmental processes by which maltreatment exerts its deleterious impact on children, as well as developing theoretically and empirically informed interventions for maltreated children and their families, should be a national priority (Cicchetti & Toth, 1993; National Research Council, 1993).

Moreover, in times of fiscal austerity, human services in general, including social and psychological services for maltreated children and their families, come under the scrutiny of budget-conscious government administrators and legislators. Increasingly, service providers are asked to document the beneficial impact of their service efforts. The inability to provide documentation through scientific research renders the services in question more vulnerable to the budget-cutter's knife. Thus, basic research on the psychological and biological development of maltreated children potentially can contribute to the development of the kind of evaluation research methodology required to justify service dollars to skeptical administrators and legislators and to modify ineffective programs to better serve maltreated children and their families. Clearly, closer collaboration between researchers and decision makers is warranted and in the long-term interests of better research and service on behalf of maltreated children.

Likewise, the investigation of developmental processes in maltreated children may affirm, augment, or challenge extant theories of biological and psychological growth in normally developing children. Child maltreatment may represent the greatest failure of the environment to provide opportunities for normal development. By investigating the effects of severe environmental disturbances, such as child maltreatment, on individual development, it may be possible to examine processes that normally occur so subtly and gradually that they are not readily observed (cf. Cicchetti & Pogge-Hesse, 1982; Cicchetti & Sroufe, 1976). Although maltreatment is a heterogeneous phenomenon (Cicchetti & Barnett, 1991b; Cicchetti & Rizley, 1981), it is unified by an experience of caregiving that does not optimize normal development. Through the examination of atypicalities in the developmental process of maltreated children, our theories of normal development may be enhanced.

According to the most recently published U.S. government statistics (DHHS, 2001), over 2.9 million children were reported as abused or neglected in the United States in 1999, and an estimated 826,000 children were confirmed as having been victims of maltreatment. There is no doubt that child maltreatment is an enormous problem that exerts a toll, not only on its victims, but also on society more broadly (Cicchetti & Rogosch, 1994). In a National Institute of Justice report (Miller, Cohen, & Wiersema, 1996), the direct costs (e.g., medical expenses, lost earnings, public programs for victims) as well as indirect costs (e.g., pain, diminished quality of life) of child abuse and neglect were estimated at $56 billion annually. Furthermore, a 2001 study funded by the Edna McConnell Clark Foundation and conducted by Prevent Child Abuse America estimated that the total cost (i.e., direct and indirect costs combined) of child abuse in the United States is over $94 billion per year. Annual direct costs, estimated at $24,384,347,302, include hospitalization, chronic physi-

cal health problems, mental health care, welfare costs, law enforcement, and court action. Yearly indirect costs (i.e., long-term costs), estimated at $69,692,535,227, include special education, mental and physical health care, delinquency, criminality, and lost productivity to society. The investigative team at Prevent Child Abuse America utilized stringent inclusion criteria for child maltreatment in their study. Specifically, children had to manifest documented harm as a result of child abuse and/or neglect in order to be included in the sample of maltreated children utilized to generate annual and long-term cost estimates of child maltreatment.

Definitional Considerations in Child Maltreatment

To adequately address the needs of maltreated children, an accurate and agreed upon definition of what constitutes maltreatment must be present. According to the developmental psychopathology perspective, a recognition of the developmental and contextual aspects of maltreatment is a requisite for understanding its causes and consequences. A caregiver must be able to adapt to the changing needs of a child. Failure to do so could constitute an act of maltreatment, depending on the developmental level of the child. Thus, whereas close monitoring and physical proximity are expected with a newborn, a similar parenting style with an adolescent would be inappropriate and, taken to extremes, emotionally abusive. The actual consequences of child maltreatment also manifest themselves differently according to a number of factors, including the perpetrator and the child's developmental level. Accordingly, methods of documenting psychological harm will need to vary with the child's age for an accurate assessment of possible sequelae. In addition to child-relevant considerations, alterations in the parent, the family, and the broader extrafamilial environment need to be considered in any definition of maltreatment (see Barnett, Manly, & Cicchetti, 1993).

Because extensive research information is required if it is to be useful in making policy decisions, researchers must be able to communicate their findings and compare their results across laboratories and across samples. Standardizing and unifying definitions of child maltreatment reflect fundamental steps toward improving research and hence the knowledge base about abuse and neglect. Systematized definitions also represent an essential aspect of ensuring consistent and adequate services to children in need. The problems in constructing effective operational definitions include a lack of social consensus about what forms of parenting are unacceptable or dangerous; uncertainty about whether to define maltreatment based on adult behavior, child outcome, or some combination of the two; controversy over whether criteria of harm or endangerment should be included in definitions of maltreatment; and disagreements about whether similar definitions should be used for scientific, legal, and clinical purposes.

The last issue in particular has proved to be a continuing source of disagreement because scientists, lawmakers, and clinicians all use separate definitions of maltreatment to best suit their particular needs. In legal settings, for example, definitions focusing on the demonstrable harm done to the child may be useful in prosecuting cases (Juvenile Justice Standards Project, 1977). However, a number of investigators have argued that for research purposes, definitions of maltreatment that focus on the specific acts that endanger children may be more appropriate (Barnett et al., 1993; Cicchetti & Barnett, 1991b). This allows researchers to concentrate on identifiable behaviors that make up part of the child's caretaking environment rather than the uncertain consequences of those parental actions, such as some form of harm that may or may not be demonstrable. The challenge for researchers, though, is to develop precise operational definitions that minimize relying on professional opinion. This lack of consensus about what constitutes maltreatment makes clear communication and collaboration among the respective fields difficult.

In general, four categories of child maltreatment are usually distinguished from each other:

1. *Physical abuse:* The infliction of bodily injury on a child by other than accidental means.

2. *Sexual abuse:* Sexual contact or attempted sexual contact between a caregiver or other responsible adult and a child for purposes of the caregiver's gratification or financial benefit.

3. *Neglect:* The failure to provide minimum care and the lack of appropriate supervision.

4. *Emotional maltreatment:* Persistent and extreme thwarting of a child's basic emotional needs.

Each of these subtypes of maltreatment represents a clear deviation from the average expectable environment. However, even an issue as seemingly straightfor-

ward as identifying maltreatment subtypes can become unclear. It would be a mistake to think that maltreatment always occurs in discrete subtypes. There is a high degree of comorbidity among maltreatment subtypes, indicating that many maltreated children experience more than one form of maltreatment (Cicchetti & Barnett, 1991b). In many instances, it may be theoretically or clinically necessary to focus on the major subtype of maltreatment in a particular case; however, the actual experience of many children is much more complicated, and this presents significant challenges for both researchers and clinicians. For more detailed operational definitions of subtypes of maltreatment, the reader is referred to Barnett et al. (1993).

Moving toward uniform agreement on what constitutes maltreatment and instituting a standardized means of recording the pertinent information regarding identified maltreatment are essential steps for the future. Despite some important groundbreaking work in this direction, much research remains to be conducted. The challenge is to adopt a consistent method of systematizing maltreatment that is feasible and that satisfies the needs of individuals addressing various related issues.

The Need for a Nosology of Child Maltreatment

A fundamental difficulty inherent in the investigation of child maltreatment is that the range of phenomena covered by the term is enormously varied. We believe there are four primary types of heterogeneity that merit our foremost attention: (1) symptom pattern or type of maltreatment, (2) etiology, (3) developmental sequelae, and (4) response to treatment. The first type acknowledges the fact that a spectrum of different problems is subsumed under the term child maltreatment (Giovannoni & Becerra, 1979). The second recognizes that etiological pathways or causal networks exist, giving rise to the spectrum of different types of maltreatment. The third type of heterogeneity is revealed in the existing data on the consequences of maltreatment on child developmental outcome (Cicchetti & Lynch, 1995). Not surprisingly, there is no specific single pattern exhibited by maltreated children that can be described as the profile of abuse or neglect. Children of different ages, at different developmental stages, from diverse environments, and with differing experiences, who are exposed to vastly different forms of maltreatment, are likely to manifest vulnerabilities and disabilities in a wide variety of age-specific ways. The fourth type of heterogeneity underscores the observation that there is wide variability in response to treatment interventions among families where there has been maltreatment (Daro, 2000; Toth & Cicchetti, 1993; Wolfe, 1987). We believe that the failure to attend to these four sources of heterogeneity, each of which also is interrelated, has contributed to our less than complete understanding of this important problem.

As one solution to alleviating these definitional concerns, in our laboratory we have developed and implemented an operational system for classifying the subtypes, severity, frequency/chronicity, perpetrator(s), and developmental period(s) during which maltreatment occurred (Barnett et al., 1993; Cicchetti & Barnett, 1991b). Our nosological approach, known as the Maltreatment Classification System (MCS), is utilized by raters who code official maltreatment incidents that are reported to Child Protective Services (CPS) units and that are kept as permanent records. Both maltreating and nonmaltreating parents grant permission for us to examine their CPS files.

There are several advantages to utilizing only legally identified protective service cases of abuse and neglect. First, the field of social work has a longer and more extensive history of documenting occurrences of child maltreatment than the psychological or medical professions (B. Nelson, 1984). Second, all maltreatment filings in the state registry are legally substantiated. By having the abuse and neglect reports verified by an outside party and not by individuals conducting the research, investigators avoid the risk of alienating families who otherwise might have participated in the research program. In addition, studies of legally identified occurrences of child maltreatment are more representative of cases in protective services and therefore more directly applicable to this broad segment of the population.

The MCS is presently being used in more than 40 research laboratories across the United States. Because 49 of the 50 states, as well as the District of Columbia, have state registries for logging child abuse and neglect reports, the MCS has been able to be used on state record keeping procedures that vary from those employed in New York State, where the MCS was developed. The MCS has demonstrated excellent reliability and validity in all laboratories that have utilized it (Manly, 2005; Manly, Cicchetti, & Barnett, 1994; Manly, Kim, Rogosch, & Cicchetti, 2001).

The use of protective service families for research has not gone uncriticized. Gelles (1982) argued that researchers' reliance on official reports of maltreatment results in the study of the factors that lead to being "caught" as much as, if not more than, the study of maltreatment per se. We acknowledge this criticism but also believe that coding child protective records is the best currently available approach and it contributes to our understanding of the families that social service agencies, clinicians, and the courts deal with most frequently. In addition, it is likely that the reports that are brought to the attention of CPS are among the most severe instances of maltreatment. This is especially true as limited community resources force only the most severe instances of maltreatment to receive attention and treatment. More broadly, the problem is that protective service records underrepresent the true incidence of child maltreatment (Giovannoni & Becerra, 1979; DHHS, 1988). In addition to the unspecifiable number of maltreated children who go unreported, many incidents of maltreatment are difficult to substantiate and thus go unproven.

To reduce some of these problems, we also administer the Maternal Maltreatment Classification Interview (MMCI; Cicchetti, Toth, & Manly, 2003) to mothers in the families who participate in our research. Both maltreating and nonmaltreating comparison mothers are interviewed with the MMCI. Nonmaltreating comparison families must be matched with maltreating families on a variety of sociodemographic indices to differentiate the effects of maltreatment from the consequences of poverty and its associated risk factors (Elmer, 1977; Trickett, Aber, Carlson, & Cicchetti, 1991). Accordingly, it is highly probable that some percentage of nonmaltreated comparison participants may, in reality, be undetected maltreaters or that, over time, some may receive an indicated CPS report. To address these issues, we check the child abuse registry at 6-month intervals as part of our ongoing cross-sectional and longitudinal research projects. This approach enables us to ascertain whether any participants in our comparison groups have become maltreaters.

Likewise, we reexamine the CPS records of the maltreated children in all of our investigations. Especially in longitudinal studies, additional subtypes of maltreatment incidents may occur, and such chronic, severe, and diverse experiences of malevolent care may exert deleterious effects on biological and psychological developmental processes (Cicchetti & Manly, 2001; Cicchetti & Rogosch, 2001; English, 2003; Manly et al., 2001).

The Effects of Maltreatment on the Developmental Process

We next provide illustrative evidence on how growing up in an environment that deviates from the average expectable conditions affects maltreated children's individual development and functioning. It is in children's ontogenic (i.e., individual) development that the effects of maltreatment, and the environmental failure that maltreatment represents, can be seen. Our research on the biological and psychological consequences of child maltreatment is guided by the organizational perspective described earlier.

In our presentation of the developmental sequelae of child maltreatment, we present only research that helped to inform our preventive interventions for maltreated infants, toddlers, and preschoolers. This entails a focus on infancy through early childhood and on those domains of development that have been addressed in our evaluations of interventions for maltreated children. For a more extensive review of extant research on the sequelae of child maltreatment across the life span and in additional biological, psychological, and socioemotional domains of development, the reader is referred to Cicchetti (2002b), Cicchetti and Toth (2000), Cicchetti and Valentino (in press), DeBellis (2001), and Trickett and McBride-Chang (1995).

Affect Regulation

Affect regulation is defined as the intra- and extraorganismic mechanisms by which emotional arousal is redirected, controlled, modulated, and modified so that an individual can function adaptively in emotionally challenging situations (Cicchetti, Ganiban, & Barnett, 1991). Appropriately developed affect regulation helps the individual to maintain arousal within a manageable range, thereby optimizing performance. Because the infant relies on the caregiver for external scaffolding and support, the quality of care and interactions with the caregiver contributes to *experience-dependent* individual differences in patterns of affect differentiation, expression, and regulation that emerge (Schore, 2003a, 2003b; Sroufe, 1996). Because early affect regulatory processes arise in the context of the caregiver-child relationship, it is not surprising that disruptions in the development of affect regulation occur more commonly in maltreated children than in nonmaltreated comparison youngsters. Thus, in accord with a developmental psychopathology perspective, adequate affect regulation serves as a foundation for the development of secure attachment relationships, an autonomous and coherent self system, and effective relations with peers, whereas early affect-regulatory failures increase the probability that a child will develop future insecure attachment relationships, self system impairments, and peer difficulties (Cicchetti & Lynch, 1995; Cicchetti, Lynch, Shank, & Manly, 1992).

The roots of affect regulation deficits have been noted in maltreated infants. Gaensbauer, Mrazek, and Harmon (1981) observed four patterns of affect differentiation in infants who had been maltreated: developmentally and affectively retarded, depressed, ambivalent and affectively labile, and angry. These investigators believed that the pattern displayed was dependent on an interaction between the caregiving experienced and the infant's biological predisposition. In a case study design, different types of maltreatment were related to the development of various affective patterns (Gaensbauer & Hiatt, 1984). Infants who were physically abused were found to demonstrate high levels of negative affects such as fear, anger, and sadness, and a paucity of positive affect, whereas emotionally neglected infants presented as affectively blunted, evidencing little negative or positive affect.

This early emergence of negative affect in physically abused infants is in contrast to the normal pattern seen in nonmaltreated infants, where fear, anger, and sadness do not appear until approximately 7 to 9 months of age (Sroufe, 1996). It is likely that early malevolent care accelerates the development of negative affect pathways in the brains of maltreated infants. We believe that this may be accomplished by excessive synaptic pruning of the positive affect neurobiological pathways as a result of inadequate or insufficient early positive experiences by abused babies.

In a related investigation, Pollak, Cicchetti, Hornung, and Reed (2000) conducted two experiments on the recognition of emotion among physically abused, physically neglected, and nonmaltreated preschoolers to examine the effects of atypical experience on emotional development. In the first study, children were required to match a facial expression to an array of emotion-recognition vignettes. Neglected children had more difficulty discriminating emotional expressions than did the physically abused and the nonmaltreated comparison youngsters. Signal detection analyses revealed that neglected children used a more liberal bias for selecting sad faces and that physically abused children displayed a response bias for angry facial expressions (see also Pollak & Kistler, 2002; Pollak & Sinha, 2002). For the physically abused child, displays of anger may be the strongest predictor of threat; however, increased sensitivity to anger could result in decreased attention to other emotional cues (Pollak & Tolley-Schell, 2003). In contrast, the physically neglected child may suffer from an extremely impoverished emotional learning environment.

The findings from the second experiment indicated that maltreatment appears to affect children's understanding of particular emotional displays. Neglected children saw greater similarity between happy and sad expressions than did the other groups. This outcome is especially surprising because recognition of happiness usually emerges developmentally early (Sroufe, 1996), suggesting that even relatively simple aspects of emotional recognition are affected through neglectful parenting. Physically abusive environments appear to compromise children's ability to recognize and differentiate some emotions, while concurrently heightening their awareness of other emotions. For example, physically abused children were as able as nonmaltreated preschoolers to perceive dissimilarities between anger and other negative expressions. In comparison, neglected children perceived fewer distinctions between anger and other negative expressions than did either nonmaltreated or physically abused children. Another compelling finding was that, unlike nonmaltreated children, both physically abused and physically neglected children rated expressions of both anger and sadness as very similar to an exemplar of an emotionally neutral face. Pollak et al. (2000) conjectured that maltreated children may have attributed anger or sadness to the neutral face or that maltreated children may interpret happy or neutral faces as masks for more malevolent emotions.

In addition to the early affect expression, regulation, and regulatory anomalies found among maltreated infants, physically abused children also demonstrate later affect regulatory problems in the coping that they employ when confronted with interadult anger. For example, physically abused preschool-age boys who observe simulated anger directed at their mother by an adult female confederate evidence more aggression (e.g., physical and verbal expressions of anger directed toward the female confederate) and more coping designed to minimize their mother's distress (e.g., helping mother, comforting mother) than do nonabused boys (Cummings, Hennessy, Rabideau, & Cicchetti, 1994). It appears that physically abused boys do not habituate to anger as a result of being exposed to familial hostility; rather, they are more aroused and angered by it and more likely to try to stop it. In general, the hypervigilance and arousal

in response to hostility seen among abused children might contribute to the development of their aggressive behavior, especially if conflict in the home is chronic.

Likewise, Maughan and Cicchetti (2002) examined the unique and interactive effects of child maltreatment and interadult violence on preschool children's developing strategies of emotion regulation and socioemotional adjustment, as well as the mediational role of emotion dysregulation in the link between children's pathogenic relational experiences and behavioral outcomes. Person-oriented emotion regulation patterns (EMRPs) were determined based on children's emotional, behavioral, and self-reported responses to simulated interadult anger. Maltreatment history was found to predict children's EMRPs, with approximately 80% of the maltreated preschoolers exhibiting dysregulated emotion patterns (i.e., undercontrolled/ambivalent and overcontrolled/unresponsive types) compared with only 37% of the nonmaltreated comparison youngsters. Undercontrolled/ambivalent EMRPs were associated with maternal reports of child behavior problems, and this type of EMRP was found to mediate the link between maltreatment and children's anxious/depressed symptoms.

In a related study, physically abused and nonabused school-age boys were presented with videotaped vignettes of adults in angry and friendly interactions (Hennessy, Rabideau, Cicchetti, & Cummings, 1994). After viewing these vignettes, abused boys reported experiencing more distress than nonabused boys in response to interadult hostility, especially when the hostility involved unresolved anger between adults. Moreover, physically abused boys described more fear in response to different forms of angry adult behavior. These results support a sensitization model in which repeated exposure to anger and familial violence leads to greater, rather than less, emotional reactivity. Similarly, the distress responses to interadult anger that abused children display may provide an early indication of an increased potential for developing internalizing problems among children exposed to high levels of familial violence (cf. Kaufman, 1991; Toth, Manly, & Cicchetti, 1992).

Additional evidence about the affective coping strategies of maltreated children can be seen in studies of cognitive control functioning. Rieder and Cicchetti (1989) found that maltreated children are more hypervigilant to aggressive stimuli and recall a greater number of distracting aggressive stimuli than do nonmaltreated children. Maltreated children also assimilate aggressive stimuli more readily, even though this impairs their efficiency on tasks. Although hypervigilance and quick assimilation of aggressive stimuli may emerge as adaptive coping responses in a maltreating environment, these strategies become less adaptive when children are faced with nonthreatening situations. Eventually, such a response pattern may adversely affect children's adaptation under normal conditions and impair their ability to negotiate subsequent tasks of development successfully.

In support of this assertion, Shields, Cicchetti, and Ryan (1994) have shown in an observational study that maltreated children are deficient in affective and behavioral regulation, and that this attenuated self-regulation mediates the negative effects of maltreatment on children's social competence with peers. As an organizational perspective would predict, although affective and behavioral self-regulatory processes were interrelated, each appeared to represent a distinct developmental system that differentially and individually affects children's competence.

Corroboration for the prediction, emanating from the organizational perspective, that maltreated children are at increased risk for evidencing a developmental progression from affect-regulatory problems to behavioral dysregulation has been obtained in a number of cross-sectional investigations. Maltreated toddlers have been shown to react to peer distress with poorly regulated and situationally inappropriate affect and behavior, including anger, fear, and aggression, as opposed to the more normatively expected response of empathy and concern (Main & George, 1985; Troy & Sroufe, 1987). Likewise, maltreated preschool and school-age children have been found to exhibit a range of dysregulated behaviors that are frequently characterized by disruptive and aggressive situations (Cicchetti & Manly, 2001; Cicchetti & Toth, 1995).

In an investigation conducted in the context of a research summer day camp, Shields and Cicchetti (1998) examined the interplay among emotion, attention, and aggression in a sample of school-age maltreated and nonmaltreated children. A central focus of this investigation was to examine mechanisms underlying maltreatment's deleterious effects on behavioral and emotional dysregulation.

Shields and Cicchetti (1998) found that maltreated children were more verbally and physically assaultive than were the nonmaltreated comparison children, with physical abuse placing children at heightened risk for aggression. Maltreated children also were more likely than comparison children to exhibit the distractibility, over-

activity, and poor concentration characteristic of children who experience deficits in attention modulation. Physically and sexually abused children also displayed attention disturbances suggestive of subclinical or nonpathological dissociation, including daydreaming, blank stares, and confusion. Deficits in emotion regulation also were evident, in that maltreated children were less likely than comparison children to show adaptive regulation and more likely to display emotional lability/negativity and contextually inappropriate emotion expressions. Such pervasive deficits in maltreated children's regulatory capacities are cause for special concern, as the ability to modulate behavior, attention, and emotion underlie children's adaptive functioning in a number of key domains, including self-development, academic achievement, and interpersonal relationships (Cicchetti, 1989, 1991; Shonk & Cicchetti, 2001).

Shields and Cicchetti (1998) also demonstrated that impaired capacities for attention modulation contribute to emotion dysregulation in maltreated children. Specifically, attention deficits mediated maltreatment's effects on emotional lability/negativity, inappropriate affect, and attenuated emotion regulation. Attention processes that suggest subclinical or nonpathological dissociation also contributed to maltreated children's deficits in emotion regulation. Thus, abuse seems to potentiate disruptions in attention that result in both a relative detachment from and unawareness of one's surroundings, as well as in hyperattunement and hyperreactivity to the social surround (Pollak & Tolley-Schell, 2003; Rieder & Cicchetti, 1989). Together, these deficits appear to compromise maltreated children's ability to regulate behavior and affect in social settings.

In another investigation, Shields and Cicchetti (2001) examined children who were maltreated by their caregivers in order to ascertain whether these children would be more likely to bully others and to be at increased risk for victimization by peers than would nonmaltreated comparison children. An additional focus was to investigate emotion's role in bullying and victimization among maltreated children. Maltreated children were found to be more likely than nonmaltreated children to bully other children. Bullying was especially prevalent among abused children who experienced maltreating acts of commission (physical or sexual abuse). Maltreatment also placed children at risk for victimization by peers. As expected, both bullies and victims evidenced problems with emotion regulation. Furthermore, logistic regression analyses suggested that emotion dysregulation made a unique contribution to differentiating bullies and victims from children who did not evidence bully or victim problems. In addition, maltreatment's effects on children's risk for bullying and victimization were mediated by emotion dysregulation.

In summary, investigations of preschool and school-age maltreated children reveal that emotion regulatory abilities may mediate the link between maltreatment experiences and developmental outcomes. Difficulties with emotion regulation have been shown to adversely affect maltreated children's peer relations and to contribute to the emergence of behavior problems and psychopathology. Moreover, an organizational perspective on development suggests that, in the absence of adaptive self-organization, positive experiences with other adult figures, and/or successful intervention, these difficulties are likely to persist across the life span, resulting in future difficulties in the relationship arena and in overall functioning.

The Development of Attachment Relationships

The capacity for preferential attachment originates during early affect regulation experiences and interactions with the caregiver. These early parent-child experiences provide a context for children's emerging biobehavioral organization (Hofer, 1987; Pipp & Harmon, 1987). Specifically, the preattachment parent-child environment helps to shape children's physiological regulation and biobehavioral patterns of response (Gunnar & Nelson, 1994; Schore, 1994, 2003a; Sroufe, 1996).

More overt manifestations of attachment become salient toward the end of the 1st year of life, when infants derive feelings of security from their caregivers and use them as a base from which to explore the environment (Sroufe, 1996). Parent-child interactions characterized by synchrony and relatedness and by appropriate affective interchange are associated with successful adaptation during this stage of development. The knowledge that a caregiver is reliable and responsive also is critical because the absence of contingent responsiveness on the part of the caregiver can impede infants' ability to develop feelings of security in their primary attachment relationship (Cummings & Davies, 1996; Sroufe & Waters, 1977). Ultimately, the task for the child is to enter into a goal-corrected partnership, where the caregiver and the child share internal states and goals (Bowlby, 1969/1982). Based on the relationship history with their primary caregivers, children form representational models of attachment figures, of themselves, and of themselves in relation to others (Bowlby, 1969/1982; Bretherton, 1985; Crittenden, 1990). Through these mental representational models, children's affects, cognitions, and expectations about future interactions are organized and carried forward into subsequent relationships (Sroufe & Fleeson, 1988).

Although maltreated children do form attachments, the main issue concerns the quality of their attachments and their internal representational models of attachment figures, the self, and the self in relation to others. Studies conducted to date converge in revealing that the attachments maltreated children form with their caregivers are significantly more likely to be insecure than are those of nonmaltreated children (see, e.g., Egeland & Sroufe, 1981; Schneider-Rosen, Braunwald, Carlson, & Cicchetti, 1985). Utilizing the traditional Ainsworth, Blehar, Waters, and Wall (1978) tripartite classification system, approximately 70% of maltreated children have been classified as insecure anxious/avoidant (Type A) or insecure anxious/resistant (Type C). The remaining 30% of children were classified as securely attached (Type B).

Careful observation of a number of videotapes from several laboratories with samples of maltreated infants and young children led to the discovery that the behavior of these children in the Strange Situation (Ainsworth & Wittig, 1969) did not readily conform with the criteria of the Ainsworth et al. (1978) classification system (see, e.g., Egeland & Sroufe, 1981; Main & Solomon, 1990). Unlike infants with the more typical Type A, B, or C patterns of attachment, maltreated infants were often found to lack organized strategies for dealing with separations from and reunions with their caregivers. Main and Solomon (1986, 1990) described this pattern of attachment as disorganized/disoriented (Type D). In addition, these infants displayed bizarre behaviors in the presence of their caregiver, such as interrupted movements and expressions; dazing, freezing, and stilling; and apprehension.

In a related vein, Crittenden (1988) has identified another atypical pattern of attachment in her observations of children who have experienced various forms of maltreatment. Crittenden discovered that a number of maltreated children displayed unusual patterns of moderate to high levels of avoidance of the mother in combination with moderate to high levels of resistance. She labeled this pattern avoidant-resistant (Type A-C). Although theoretical distinctions exist between Main and Solomon's (1986, 1990) and Crittenden's views of disorganization, most investigators have chosen to consider the A-C category as a subtype of the disorganized/disoriented Type D attachment pattern (Cicchetti, Toth, & Lynch, 1995). All researchers consider the A-C and D classifications to represent atypical patterns of attachment.

In a revised attachment classification scheme that includes these atypical patterns, maltreated infants and toddlers demonstrate a preponderance of insecure and atypical attachments (Barnett, Ganiban, & Cicchetti, 1999; Carlson, Cicchetti, Barnett, & Braunwald, 1989; Crittenden, 1988; Lyons-Ruth, Connell, Zoll, & Stahl, 1987). Studies that incorporate atypical attachments into their classification scheme typically reveal rates of attachment insecurity for maltreated youngsters to be as high as 90%. Furthermore, approximately 80% of maltreated infants and toddlers exhibit disorganized attachments, a rate that far exceeds those observed in nonmaltreated infants and toddlers from similar low-socioeconomic status (SES) backgrounds (Barnett et al., 1999; Carlson et al., 1989; Lyons-Ruth, Repacholi, McLeod, & Silva, 1991).

Moreover, maltreated infants and toddlers show substantial stability of insecure attachment, whereas securely attached maltreated youngsters evidence instability of attachment organization (Cicchetti & Barnett, 1991a; Schneider-Rosen et al., 1985). In contrast, for nonmaltreated youngsters, secure attachments are highly stable, whereas insecure attachments are more likely to change (Thompson, 1998). Furthermore, substantial stability of disorganized attachments has been shown across the ages cf 12, 18, and 24 months (Barnett et al., 1999).

The Development of an Autonomous Self System

During the second half of the 2nd year of life, children experience an increased sense of themselves as autonomous. Before this age, processes of emotion regulation are primarily sensorimotor in origin. As a sense of self emerges, an increase in representational capacities arises (Sroufe, 1996). Consequently, children become able to use symbolic capacities such as play and language to convey their needs and feelings. This developmental transition also marks a shift in the burden of self-regulation from the caregiver to the child. However, caregiver availability and responsivity continue to remain necessary to the facilitation of this developmental task. Throughout this period, children are able to rely on representations of caregivers to alleviate their distress during separations. Thus, the representational models of self and other that had their origins in the early caregiving relationship exert a significant impact on the continued development of the self system.

As self-organization is brought forward to the new tasks of development, a number of aspects of maltreated children's self-development are likely to be affected, with possible implications for their subsequent interpersonal relationships. Studies on the development of self-recognition of maltreated children provide some insight into their emerging self-concept. Although there are no deficits in maltreated infants' ability to recognize their rouge-marked selves in a mirror, they are more likely than nonmaltreated infants to display neutral or negative affect on visual self-recognition (Schneider-Rosen & Cicchetti, 1991).

Other impairments in maltreated children's self systems have been noted as well. For example, maltreated children talk less about themselves and about their internal states than do nonmaltreated children (Beeghly & Cicchetti, 1994). Maltreated children with insecure attachments display the most compromised internal state language (Beeghly & Cicchetti, 1994). The ability to talk about internal states and feelings is a development of late toddlerhood that is believed to reflect toddlers' emergent self-other understanding and to be fundamental to the regulation of social interaction (Beeghly & Cicchetti, 1994). Maltreated children's negative feelings about themselves and their inability to talk about their own activities and states may impede their ability to engage in successful social relationships.

In particular, maltreated children appear to be most reluctant to talk about their negative internal states (Beeghly & Cicchetti, 1994). This finding is corroborated by reports that maltreated children may actually inhibit negative affect, especially in the context of their relationship with their caregiver (Crittenden & DiLalla, 1988; Lynch & Cicchetti, 1991). It is possible that some maltreated children adopt a strategy designed to suppress the expression of their own negative feelings to avoid eliciting adverse responses from their caregiver (Cicchetti, 1991). Although this approach may be adaptive in the context of a maltreating relationship, it can become maladaptive and lead to incompetence in other interpersonal contexts. Additionally, the inability of maltreated children to identify and discuss their own distress may play a major role in these children's difficulties in displaying empathy toward their peers (Main & George, 1985; Troy & Sroufe, 1987).

In another investigation of self-development, Alessandri and Lewis (1996) examined the self-conscious emotion expressions of shame and pride in maltreated children. These self-conscious emotions evolve, in part, from the child's burgeoning cognitive abilities between the 2nd and 3rd year of life. Included among the self-conscious emotions are embarrassment, pride, shame, and guilt. In particular, the ability to mentally represent standards for comparison, objective self-awareness and self-evaluation, and the capacity to reflect on and attribute outcomes to personal competence appear to be the prerequisite cognitive capabilities for the development of shame and pride (Kagan, 1981; Lewis & Brooks-Gunn, 1979; Sroufe, 1996).

Alessandri and Lewis (1996) found that maltreated girls displayed more shame and less pride than nonmaltreated girls. On the other hand, maltreated boys exhibited less shame and pride than nonmaltreated boys. Notably, the finding that maltreated girls manifested less pride and more shame in the achievement-like situations used to evoke these self-conscious emotions suggests that these girls are at high risk for developing dysfunctions or disorders of the self and for adapting poorly to school (cf. Cicchetti, 1989). In contrast, maltreated boys displayed a reduction of the self-conscious emotions of shame and pride, developed strategies that attributed their difficulties to characteristics of others, and employed acting-out behaviors to cope with their interpersonal difficulties.

Koenig, Cicchetti, and Rogosch (2000) examined child compliance and noncompliance behavior in maltreated and nonmaltreated comparison preschoolers. These children were observed with their mothers during a toy cleanup situation that followed a semistructured free play. Features of child compliance/noncompliance involve a shift from reliance on external controls to internal mechanisms, thereby reflecting child internalization of the maternal agenda (Kochanska, Aksan, & Koenig, 1995). Two subtypes of maltreated preschoolers were investigated: physically abused and neglected. Compared with nonmaltreated children, abused youngsters were found to exhibit less internalization, whereas neglected youngsters displayed significantly more negative affect. Specifically, abused children were more likely to show situational rather than committed compliance. The strategy of situational compliance involves suppression of negative behaviors and immediate compliance with the maternal directive. Because abused children appear to distort their own perceptions and

emotional responses, these youngsters could develop a "false self," wherein the overt presentation does not accurately reflect internal states. This could impede physically abused children's ability to express their true needs to others, thus contributing to lack of need fulfillment and difficulties in emotion regulation.

In addition, the increased negative affect seen in neglected children could prove to be highly detrimental to these children's moral development because turning anger or negative feelings inward, instead of directing them toward others, is crucial for the development of guilt. Internalized guilt is essential to motivate children to inhibit antisocial and engage in prosocial behaviors. Alternatively, instead of indicating anger, the negative affect seen in neglected children may represent feelings of shame or embarrassment, thereby placing these children at risk for the development of depression. Furthermore, maltreated and nonmaltreated groups differed in the maternal variables that predicted child internalization. A lower level of maternal negative affect was linked to child internalization in maltreated children, whereas a lower level of maternal joy predicted internalization for the nonmaltreated children.

Intervention directed at aiding maltreated children in the identification and expression of their cognitions and emotions, especially with regard to their attachment figures, can decrease disturbances to the self system. Interventions focused on improving mothers' sensitivity and responsiveness to their children's feelings and needs also is crucial.

In a further investigation of self-related development, Cicchetti, Rogosch, Maughan, Toth, and Bruce (2003) examined false belief understanding, an aspect of a theory of mind (TOM), in low-SES maltreated, low-SES nonmaltreated, and middle-SES nonmaltreated 3- to 8-year-old children. The development of false belief understanding, the ability to make inferences about what other persons believe to be the case in a specific situation, is a capacity regarded as a critical component of mature social skills and thought (Perner, 1991; Wellman, 1990). Possessing the knowledge that different individuals can have different thoughts about the same situation is an important achievement that makes it possible to predict what other persons will do across a variety of scenarios. As such, false belief understanding has been conceived as a hallmark of a representational theory of mind (Perner, 1991). Although young children have knowledge about mental states as early as the 2nd year of life, they fail to comprehend representational states necessary to infer the thoughts of others until age 4. This conceptual advance has been described as a shift from a situation-based to a representation-based understanding of behavior (Perner, 1991). Moreover, the acquisition of false belief understanding by age 4 is a well-replicated and remarkably robust experimental finding (Wellman, Cross, & Watson, 2001).

Among children with a verbal mental age of 49 months or greater, maltreatment was related to delays in the development of TOM, beyond the influence of chronological age and SES (Cicchetti, Rogosch, et al., 2003). The occurrence of maltreatment during the toddler period, onset during the toddler period, and physical abuse were features of maltreatment associated with delay in the development of TOM. The centrality of the relation between maltreatment during the toddler period and TOM deficits flows from the importance of self-development for false belief understanding. Internal state language, increased individuation and self-other differentiation, advances in language, conceptual development and symbolic maturity, and the development of self-conscious emotions all occur during early childhood. Maltreated youngsters manifest difficulties in these aspects of self-development, each of which is a precursor of TOM development (Cicchetti, 1991). Thus, harsh caregiving, especially early in a child's life, impairs the development of TOM abilities.

In summary, child maltreatment exerts harmful effects on the development of an autonomous and coherent self system. In the most extreme cases, maltreatment experiences may lead to basic and severe disturbances in self-definition and self-regulation (Fischer & Ayoub, 1994; Westen, 1994), including the development of dissociative disorders.

Representational Models

Representational models (Bowlby, 1969/1982; Bretherton, 1985; Crittenden, 1990) are thought to play an important role in the continuity of development across different domains of functioning. For example, in normative populations, the quality of children's attachment relationships to their primary caregiver has been associated with the complexity of their knowledge of self and others (Beeghly & Cicchetti, 1994; Sroufe, 1996). Among maltreated children, their attachment histories contribute to the victimization observed in these children's relationships with their peers (Main & George, 1985; Shields & Cicchetti, 2001; Troy & Sroufe, 1987).

Additionally, maltreated children's perception of the quality of their relationships with their mother exerts a significant effect on these youngsters' feelings of relatedness to others (i.e., peer groups, best friend, teacher; Lynch & Cicchetti, 1991, 1992; Toth & Cicchetti, 1996).

Initially, the young child develops expectations about the nature of future interpersonal contacts through repeated interactions with the caregiver. These expectations form the basis of representational models of the self, others, and the self in relation to others (Bowlby, 1969/1982). Children's models reflect expectations about the availability and probable actions of others with complementary models of how worthy and competent the self is.

It has been theorized that children are able to form independent representational models of different relationship figures with their complementary models of the self (see, e.g., Lynch & Cicchetti, 1991; Toth & Cicchetti, 1996). Representational models of individual relationships contain information that is specific to those relationships. Expectations about the availability of the other person, how effective the self is likely to be in eliciting desired responses from that person, attitudes and commitment toward the relationship, and the affective tone of the relationship are the kinds of information that may be incorporated into models of specific relationships.

During the course of development, information from these *specific models* may become integrated as part of more *generalized models* of relationships (Crittenden, 1990). These generalized models of self and other allow the individual to forecast how others will act and react and how successful the self is likely to be in the broader social context.

Given their caregiving experiences, maltreated children are highly likely to develop negative expectations of how others will behave and of how successful the self will be in relation to others. In generating these expectations, maltreated children may evaluate information both from models that are specific to a given relationship and from more generalized models of relationships.

Initially, both specific and general representational models remain more or less open to new input and consequent readjustment (Crittenden & Ainsworth, 1989). Open models such as these are akin to Bowlby's (1969/1982) notion of a "working" model. With increasing verbal and cognitive abilities, however, children's representational models may become more closed to experience (Crittenden & Ainsworth, 1989). Conceptual processes and symbolic function replace actual episodes of experience in the formulation and integration of representational models. In the absence of effective intervention, it may not be until adolescence, when children attain formal operations, that a rethinking of previous experiences is likely to occur.

Having representational models that are closed to new interpersonal information may be especially detrimental to children who have experienced insecure attachments and maltreatment. Parents' explanations that their harsh behavior is for their children's own good become organizing principles for children's models of themselves and others. Moreover, some children may begin to employ a form of cognitive screening for relationship-relevant information to avoid the emotional discomfort of an angry relationship (Bowlby, 1980). It has been shown, for example, that abused children tend to split off from consciousness the more negative aspects of their perceptions (Beeghly & Cicchetti, 1994; Stovall & Craig, 1990). As a result, these children's representations of themselves and others may not be open to alternative and potentially positive experiences with others. Instead, they approach their interactions with others with more generalized negative expectations, leading to less competent dealings with others. Repeated experiences of incompetent interactions with others serve to confirm their negative representational models, making it even less likely that they will be open to positive interpersonal experiences in the future.

Research has begun to document differences in maltreated and nonmaltreated children's representational models. Maltreated children differ from nonmaltreated children in their perceptions of self and other on a variety of projective assessments and in the negativity of their view of the relational world, as demonstrated in projective stories (McCrone, Egeland, Kalkoske, & Carlson, 1994; Stovall & Craig, 1990). Additionally, maltreated children tell fewer stories in which adults and peers reciprocate the kind acts of children than do nonmaltreated children; they also relate more stories in which they justify their parents' unkind acts on the basis of their own bad behavior (Dean, Malik, Richards, & Stringer, 1986).

In our laboratory, we have conducted several studies on preschool- and school-age maltreated children's representations of their caregivers, of themselves, and of themselves in relation to others. These investigations typ-

ically have utilized the MacArthur Story Stem Battery (MSSB; Bretherton, Ridgeway, & Cassidy, 1990). The MSSB contains story beginnings that describe a range of emotionally laden interactions among family members. Each story stem involves a combination of family dolls, including a mother, a father, and two same-sex children. The gender and race of the dolls are matched to those of the child. For each narrative, the child is instructed to listen to the beginning of a story told by the experimenter and then to finish it using the characters and simple toy props. Narratives are videotaped and coded according to the MacArthur Narrative Coding Manual (Robinson, Mantz-Simmons, & Macfie, 1991), with a system that involves a presence-absence method of rating content, representation, and child performance. Content areas include, for example, codes for aggression, child injury, oppositionality, and empathy (Robinson et al., 1991). Representations of parents and of self, as well as the child's behavior, also are coded. Among the dependent variables that have been reliably coded across a number of investigations with normal and high-risk children are positive and negative maternal representations, positive and negative self-representations, controllingness, and relationship with the examiner (see, e.g., Emde, Wolf, & Oppenheim, 2003; Oppenheim, Emde, & Warren, 1997).

Toth, Cicchetti, Macfie, and Emde (1997) utilized the MSSB to examine maternal and self-representations in neglected, physically abused, sexually abused, and nonmaltreated preschool children. The narratives of the maltreated youngsters contained more negative maternal representations and more negative self-representations than did the narratives of nonmaltreated children. Maltreated preschoolers also were more controlling with and less responsive to the examiner. In our investigation of the differential impact of maltreatment subtype differences on maternal and self-representations, physically abused children evidenced the most negative maternal representations; moreover, they also had more negative self-representations than did nonmaltreated children. Sexually abused youngsters manifested more positive self-representations than did the neglected children. Despite the differences exhibited in the nature of their maternal and self-representations, physically and sexually abused preschoolers both were found to be more controlling and less responsive to the examiner than were the neglected and nonmaltreated children.

The examination of the different patterns evidenced by physically abused, sexually abused, and neglected children on the self-representation variables suggests interesting interpretations for the representational models of these respective groups. The finding that the sexually abused children had a high level of positive self-representations raises the possibility that these representations are not genuine but are more consistent with the "false self" that has been described in the literature (Calverly, Fischer, & Ayoub, 1994; Crittenden & DiLalla, 1988).

Whereas physically abused children have high levels of negative self-representation, it was the neglected children who had low levels of positive self-representation. Thus, these two groups of maltreated children differ in the positive versus negative valence of their self-views. The fact that neglected children have restricted positive self-representations is consistent with the reality of these children's lives, in which they most likely receive minimal attention to their basic needs. Conversely, physically abused children, although also confronted with parenting dysfunction, may experience periods during which they are responded to, possibly even positively, by their physically abusive parents. Thus, it may well be that physically abused children are more likely to develop some sense of self as positive, whereas neglected children have far fewer opportunities to do so. Additionally, the tendency for neglect to be a more ongoing, chronic condition involving parental acts of omission, whereas physical abuse may involve intermittent acts of commission, also may be influencing the differences evidenced between these groups of children. The fact that physically abused children also seem to accurately perceive the negativity of their caregiving environments, as evidenced by their elevated negative maternal representations, attests to a possible strength that they possess. It may be more realistic to help children move beyond a history of maltreatment if they are in touch with its negativity than if they are prone to deny the realities that confront them.

In view of the differences evidenced among maltreated children, some interesting implications for intervention also can be derived from this investigation. Specifically, for sexually abused children, intervention may need to address the genuineness of their representations of parent and of self, especially if the children are evidencing behavioral difficulties such as might be suggested by their controllingness and lack of responsivity to the examiner. For physically abused children, their high levels of negative representations and the possible generalization of these negative representations to other relationship figures might best be addressed by utilizing a therapeutic relationship to foster a more positive self-representation, which, in turn, could result in greater receptivity to developing positive relationships with others. Finally, the low levels of positive self-representation evidenced by neglected children, in conjunction with their relatively average levels on other variables (e.g., differing neither from nonmaltreated children nor from other maltreated children), suggest that these children are at considerable risk for falling between the cracks of intervention systems that could bolster their sense of self. It is these children who may be most easily ignored, thereby perpetuating the experiences of neglect that have permeated their lives.

In a related investigation, Macfie et al. (1999) examined the narrative representations of preschool-age maltreated and nonmaltreated youngsters. Utilizing the MSSB narratives, Macfie and colleagues found that, compared with nonmaltreated youngsters, maltreated children represented both parents and children as responding less often to relieve distress in child characters. Moreover, it was discovered that maltreated children broke the narrative frame and stepped in more often to relieve distress in the narrative child characters. In addition, the maltreatment subgroups showed different patterns. Both abused children (sexually or physically, or both; most also were neglected) and neglected children (without sexual or physical abuse) depicted parents as responding less often to relieve distress in children than did nonmaltreated children. Furthermore, neglected children portrayed children responding less often to relieve distress in child characters than did the abused or the nonmaltreated children. It also was found that the abused children interjected themselves more often to relieve distress in child characters than did the nonmaltreated children or the neglected children. Moreover, it was the abused children who portrayed more role reversal than did the nonmaltreated children.

If neglected children who have not been sexually or physically abused do not represent parents or other children as likely to respond to children in distress, then these neglected children may grow up relatively passive in the face of others' distress. If, however, abused (particularly physically abused) children portray parents as unlikely to respond to children's distress, yet see children as taking on a role reversal with their parents, then the abused children may develop representational models that associate relationships with the need to give care rather than to receive it (Cicchetti, 1989). Normative development appears to depend on the internalization of responsive parents without children being expected to assume the role of excessive responding to parents' needs. Role reversal may superficially simulate maturity; however, while feeling compelled to understand and care for others, maltreated children may not learn how to meet their own needs. What is adaptive in the maltreating environment may prove to be maladaptive in the wider world (Cicchetti, 1991).

In another investigation of maltreated children's representational models, Shields et al. (2001) discovered that maladaptive representations are related to a continuity in relationship disturbances across the family and peer domains. Specifically, these investigators found that maltreated school-age children's representations, coded from the Rochester Parenting Story Narratives developed in our laboratory, were more negative/constricted and less positive/coherent than those of nonmaltreated children. Furthermore, children's representations of their parents mediated maltreatment's influences on peer rejection.

Shields and colleagues (2001) also identified a mechanism whereby representations appear to exert their influences: by undermining children's emotion regulation on entry to new social groups. Anxiety, arousal, and angry reactivity serve important functions when attachment relationships are disrupted, thereby helping children regulate proximity to caregivers and to mobilize resources in response to danger or threat (Cassidy, 1994; Kobak, 1999; Thompson & Calkins, 1996). However, maladaptive representations can trigger similar emotional reactions in even neutral or friendly peer contexts because representations provide a filter through which information about new social encounters is processed. Maladaptive defense styles, which presumably underlie the lack of coherence in children's representations, would also compromise children's ability to manage their emotional arousal in social contexts. Peers, in turn, may respond to maltreated children's dysregulated emotions and behaviors with avoidance, rejection, and even victimization (Rogosch & Cicchetti, 1994; Shields & Cicchetti, 2001). Thus, maladaptive representations may contribute to the emotion dysregulation that has been documented among maltreated children (Shields & Cicchetti, 1998), setting in motion a complex chain of transactions that reinforce and maintain poor peer relationships and negative representations of social relationships.

How, then, might prevention and intervention interrupt these intergenerational cycles of disturbed relationships? One potentially fruitful arena might be to enhance the accuracy and efficiency of social information processing in maltreated children, with a special focus on how processing patterns influence children's emotional responsiveness in relationships outside of the family (Dodge, Bates, & Pettit, 1990; Dodge, Pettit, & Bates, 1997; Rogosch, Cicchetti, & Aber, 1995). Interventions that enhance maltreated children's coping and problem solving with peers also may increase the likelihood that abused and neglected children will develop and experience more positive peer relationships.

In a longitudinal investigation of the representational models of maltreated children, Macfie, Cicchetti, and Toth (2001) found that maltreated preschoolers evidenced more dissociation in their MSSB story-stem completions than did nonmaltreated children. Further, maltreatment subtype analyses revealed that the sexually abused and the physically abused youngsters displayed more dissociation than the nonmaltreated group; however, the neglected children did not. Thus, it appears that maltreatment that reflects the commission of abuse is more likely to be associated with dissociation than is maltreatment that reflects deficiencies of care.

Additionally, dissociation trajectories during the preschool period differed for maltreated and nonmaltreated children. Maltreated children, especially those who had experienced sexual or physical abuse, exhibited increasingly more dissociation over the course of this 1-year longitudinal investigation, whereas nonmaltreated children showed a decrease in dissociation. Thus, in maltreated children, there was no evidence for the self becoming more coherent during the preschool period (cf. Cicchetti, 1991). However, nonmaltreated children did maintain a more coherent self than did the maltreated children.

Toth, Cicchetti, Macfie, Maughan, and VanMeenan (2000) conducted an additional 1-year longitudinal investigation of the narrative representations of parents and of self, as well as of child behavior during the MSSB assessment, in maltreated and nonmaltreated comparison youngsters. Interestingly, at the first measurement period, when children were approximately 4 years old, the only significant difference obtained was that the maltreated preschoolers evidenced fewer positive representations of parent and of self. However, 1 year later, maltreated and nonmaltreated children were found to exhibit more negative representations of parent and of self as well as more negative behavior with the examiner. Consequently, during the preschool period, a time noted for developmental transformations in the self, the representational models of maltreated children appear to become increasingly more negative.

These findings suggest that it may be critical to intervene with maltreated children early in the preschool period, when their representational models may be more open to being modified by experiences with relationship partners who challenge their negative experiences with caregivers. As we discussed earlier, several investigations have revealed that there is substantial concordance in maltreated children between relationship insecurity with primary caregivers and with noncaregiving figures. The fact that maltreated children are likely to generalize such negative representational models of attachment figures to future relationship partners underscores the need for intervening before relationship models become less open to change. Therefore, the initiation of intervention prior to the consolidation of negative representational models of self and other may be much more effective than would intervention that is begun subsequent to the crystallization of negative representational models.

TRANSLATING MALTREATMENT RESEARCH INTO PRACTICE: THE DEVELOPMENT AND IMPLEMENTATION OF PREVENTIVE INTERVENTIONS

Empirical research has documented that maltreatment in the early years of life poses severe risks for the development and adaptation of young children. Efforts to prevent further maltreatment and its deleterious consequences are thus of critical importance. Guided by an organizational perspective on development, and by empirical research that documents that maltreated children manifest impairments in attachment organization, self-development, and representational models, in our laboratory we have implemented two randomized controlled intervention trials early in the life course of maltreated children, one in infancy and the other during the preschool period, to prevent the compromised developmental attainments that accompany maltreatment and that are precursors to later maladjustment. Due to space constraints, our selective research review focuses on aspects of individual development that are compromised

as a function of child maltreatment. However, it is important to note that maltreatment and its effects involve transactions across multiple levels of an individual's social ecology. Our broader programs of research take these ecological influences into account and, where relevant, they also have guided the development of our preventive interventions. These intervention trials are discussed next.

Preventive Interventions for Maltreated Infants

A number of interventions informed by attachment theory have been developed for high-risk, multiproblem populations (Egeland & Erickson, 1990; Erickson, Korfmacher, & Egeland, 1992; Lieberman, Weston, & Pawl, 1991; Lyons-Ruth, Connell, Grunebaum, & Botein, 1990). With respect to attachment, theoreticians continue to debate whether modifying parents' attachment organization, including their representations of their child, will result in improved parenting or, conversely, whether improving parenting may, independent of attention to parental attachment representations, lead to more secure attachment relationships between parent and child. In a meta-analysis of 12 studies of the effectiveness of preventive or therapeutic interventions in enhancing parental sensitivity or children's attachment security, van IJzendoorn, Juffer, and Duyvesteyn (1995) concluded that interventions were more effective in improving maternal sensitivity than in fostering children's attachment security. Of particular importance, van IJzendoorn et al. also found that the link between parental representational models and infant attachment was stronger than the link between maternal sensitivity and attachment and that the former remained significant after sensitivity was included as a moderator variable. In a more recent meta-analysis of the effectiveness of preventive interventions for enhancing parental sensitivity and infant attachment security, Bakermans-Kranenburg, van IJzendoorn, and Juffer (2003) concluded that the most effective interventions used a moderate number of sessions and a behavioral focus. However, within the meta-analysis, only three randomized studies, all conducted with multiproblem populations, were described as intensive and having numerous sessions. These interventions also were very broad and included a combination of behavioral, representational, and supportive interventions. Therefore, we believed that the effectiveness of specific types of behavioral versus nonbehavioral interventions remained open to further investigation and we provided competing models of intervention, one being more problem-oriented and the other being more focused on maternal representation.

With the common goals of improving attachment insecurity to avert maladaptive development in maltreated infants, we implemented two interventions that differed in their strategies for attaining this goal. The first model, psychoeducational parenting intervention (PPI), is consistent with an ecological perspective; it is based on etiological models of maltreatment that emphasize the role of parental stress and parenting skills deficits in maltreatment and that therefore advocate for the provision of increased social support and parent training to alleviate stress, promote more positive parenting, and decrease child maltreatment. The second model, infant-parent psychotherapy (IPP), is based on research that points to the importance of parent-child attachment in fostering positive child development, improved parent-child interaction, and decreases in child maltreatment. This model involves dyadic mother-infant therapy sessions designed to improve the parent-child attachment relationships by altering the influences of negative maternal representational models on parent-child interaction. We compared the pre- and postintervention functioning of mothers and maltreated infants in both models of intervention with the functioning of mothers and maltreated infants who were receiving services typically available in the community (community standard [CS] group). A fourth, nonmaltreated comparison (NC) group, comprising demographically comparable mothers and their nonmaltreated infants, also were assessed. All maltreated infants and their mothers were randomly assigned to either the PPI, IPP, or the CS group.

Interventions were initiated when infants were approximately 12 months of age and continued for a period of 1 year. Assessments of the quality of attachment, utilizing the Strange Situation, were conducted at baseline (12 months) and at the conclusion of the intervention (24 months) to evaluate the efficacy of the interventions.

The group of mothers and infants who participated in this investigation were demographically comparable with respect to gender, SES, race/ethnicity, and household composition. All babies resided with their biological mother. In addition, the mothers of the maltreated infants were identified as perpetrators of maltreatment. Families were not excluded from study participation because of ethnic or racial considerations, and the racial/ethnic backgrounds of the participants were reflective of the national demographics of victims of child

maltreatment. To be included in the preventive intervention, mothers and infants could not have any significant cognitive or physical limitations that would hamper their ability to understand and/or participate in the research or clinical interventions.

Rather than relying solely on substantiated reports of maltreatment as made by DHHS (i.e., those deemed to be cases of legally designated maltreatment), we made independent determinations of maltreatment on all reports received by DHHS. Although this strategy is a departure from a more legalistic approach to the classification of maltreatment, we considered it to be the best course of action for a number of reasons. Perhaps most important, the past decade has witnessed a decrease in substantiated reports of maltreatment as a concomitant of decreasing financial resources that have been available to address this societal problem. Moreover, this decrease in substantiated reports has been evidenced even in the midst of the increased numbers of reports being made. These trends suggest that authorities are substantiating only the most severe cases of maltreatment, leaving many children vulnerable and without services. This is of significant concern in view of the findings of Manly et al. (1994) that more severe maltreatment is not necessarily related to worse child outcome. Rather than excluding maltreated children due to the false negative approach suggested by current DHHS actions, where children who have been maltreated are not classified as such, we made independent evaluations of the events that were reported to authorities or considered to suggest high risk for maltreatment. To this end, DHHS records were coded using the structured nosological system developed by Barnett et al. (1993).

To facilitate enrollment of maltreated infants and their mothers into our program, DHHS agreed to allow one of their child protective team supervisors to be retained by us and to serve as the liaison between families and our program. We paid a portion of the DHHS person's salary to ensure that his or her allegiance was to the goals of our investigation, not simply to his or her DHHS role. Moreover, due to constraints imposed by confidentiality, only a DHHS staff member had knowledge of families being assessed due to maltreatment concerns. Thus, the initial gatekeeper for approaching families had to be a staff member employed by DHHS. We asked our DHHS liaison to approach all families who met our inclusion criteria and ask if they were willing to be contacted by our project staff; thus, the DHHS liaison did not use any selection biases to determine whom to approach. We also requested the DHHS liaison to record information on all families who refused to be contacted by our staff. Finally, our project staff, not DHHS, was solely responsible for randomization of families to treatment condition. All mothers of maltreated infants who met our enrollment criteria were informed of our investigation and asked whether they were willing to participate.

To avoid any possible perceptions of coercion, the voluntary nature of the program was stressed, and mothers were assured that their refusal to participate would have no adverse effects on their status with DHHS. Rather, the benefits of participation through the potential provision of supplemental services for the mother and her infant were emphasized. By working closely with a DHHS liaison, timely recruitment in conjunction with the maintenance of family confidentiality was assured. A family's name was released to our project's staff only after a consent release form was signed. It is important to clarify that because we also examined the CS group, referral to our project did not necessarily result in assignment to one of our intervention models. Rather, referral indicated a willingness to participate in our research project and the possibility of receiving enhanced services.

All families, maltreating and nonmaltreating alike, were informed that, as mandated reporters, our project staff was obliged to report any suspected cases of child maltreatment to DHHS. Based on our experience conducting research with maltreating and nonmaltreating families from low-SES backgrounds, we have found that families are generally accepting of these reports if they are conducted in an open, sensitive fashion and framed as efforts to get the family the support it needs.

Nonmaltreating families were chosen randomly from the county list of recipients of Temporary Assistance to Needy Families (TANF). Because prior experience has revealed that the majority of maltreating families referred to DHHS are socioeconomically disadvantaged, utilization of TANF lists provided us with access to a demographically similar population. Although all families were asked whether they had ever received protective services, we have learned that families are not always forthcoming with this information. Therefore, during our initial contact, consent was obtained to verify nonmaltreatment status by accessing DHHS central registry data. Additionally, we also administered the MMCI to mothers in the NC group as an independent

verification of nonmaltreating status. If a family refused to consent to this procedure, then they were not enrolled in the investigation. Only those families who had never received child protective or preventive services through DHHS were included in the comparison sample. Throughout the intervention trial, DHHS records were accessed annually for both maltreatment and comparison participants to determine whether any maltreatment reports had been filed; the MMCI also was administered annually.

Challenges to Implementation

To begin, it is important to underscore that, because this intervention evaluation involved a randomized controlled clinical efficacy trial, rigorous inclusion and exclusion criteria were necessary to ensure sufficient homogeneity among participants. Treatment was manualized, and all therapists received extensive training and ongoing supervision. In all of our intervention evaluations, we conducted weekly individual supervision, weekly group presentations, and discussions of videotaped cases. Moreover, checklists were utilized to assess adherence to the parameters of the intervention. This approach is very different from clinical effectiveness trials that are carried out in real-world clinical settings and that provide much less latitude regarding who constitutes a "case." Unfortunately, much of our current evidence regarding the effectiveness of interventions for children has been derived from efficacy trials; studies that have tried to determine the effectiveness of clinic treatments have found much lower success rates that are not substantially different from outcomes for children not receiving treatment (Weisz, Donenberg, Han, & Weiss, 1995; Weisz, Rudolph, Granger, & Sweeney, 1992). This reality underscores the importance not only of establishing efficacy, but also of determining how best to transfer the knowledge gained from efficacy trials into implementation in real-world clinical settings.

In conducting efficacy trials such as this, initial recruitment can be challenging. To begin, it often is difficult for community partners to understand why someone is not eligible for the intervention. Efforts to adhere to strict inclusion/exclusion criteria can come across as off-putting to community service providers. Moreover, explaining randomization procedures to individuals not accustomed to conducting research can be difficult. We have found that it is important to try to convey that, initially, the intervention is conceived in the best possible way to optimize the likelihood of establishing its efficacy. Once this occurs, the intervention can be utilized with more heterogeneous groups of multiproblem clients. Unless the intervention evaluation adheres to scientific standards, efforts to demonstrate its efficacy will not be credible and its ultimate translation into clinic settings will be compromised.

Similarly, potential clients may have difficulty understanding why they cannot receive their treatment of choice. From an ethical practice standpoint, families were told that the treatment that they might be eligible for would "be determined by the flip of a coin," and we sought their agreement to accept this chance outcome. If a potential participant was not willing to accept randomization to treatment condition, then they were ineligible to continue in the research program and were referred to other community providers.

Once they are enrolled, retaining participants in intervention evaluations is especially important. Transportation was provided for all research visits; even so, cancellation and no show rates were approximately 50%. Given the population served, attrition can be a major consideration. Frequent moves, involvement in illegal activities and incarceration, and placement of the child in foster care all may erode the number of participants available for the conduct of a longitudinal investigation. A case example is helpful in illustrating this point.

During a home-based research visit, our research assistants arrived at the residence of a single mother; at the time of the visit, the child enrolled in our project was 24 months of age and the family had been participating in the project for 1 year. The researchers heard a baby crying when they knocked, but repeated loud knocking and calling went unanswered, and the baby continued to wail. Concerned, our staff approached a policeman who was in the vicinity and explained the situation. The dwelling was entered by the police and an infant of 8 months was found alone. The mother returned home shortly with her 2-year-old child to find the police taking her unsupervised infant into custody. She shared that she had left the infant briefly to go to the store. There was a history of neglect in the family, and the infant was subsequently placed in foster care and the mother charged with lack of supervision and incarcerated. The 2-year-old also was placed in care. Our research staff was distraught and felt very bad. We contacted the mother while she was in jail and she conveyed that she understood what had transpired; she acknowledged that

she needed help to care for her children adequately. Although we remained in contact with her, she did not regain custody in time to allow for continued participation in the evaluation.

Unfortunate on many levels, this case description conveys the reality of conducting intervention evaluations with maltreating populations. All staff are trained in the ethics of reporting suspected maltreatment. When possible, we talk with caregivers first and let them know that we are legally and ethically bound to file a report if we suspect child maltreatment.

The fact that the families enrolled in our preventive intervention were primarily members of ethnic and racial minority groups also required knowledge of cultural mores and expectations. Although we tried to recruit a diverse staff, the majority of our research staff were nonminorities. Moreover, as recent college graduates, their backgrounds were such that they had limited experience traversing inner-city environments. We stressed the criticality of nonjudgmental attitudes and sensitivity to the contexts in which the families resided. However, at times, cognition and training gave way to panic. One particularly poignant event was recalled by a mother who had participated in our research over a number of years. She laughingly repeated a story about being interviewed in her home when a car backfired on the street; fearing that gunshots had occurred, one of our young researchers jumped to the floor. We incorporated this vignette into our training sessions to help young staff members understand that their actions are not unnoticed and that they can convey derision by subtle looks or actions, even if unintentionally.

We also exert considerable effort in retaining contact with participants. Newsletters with community events and child activities are sent out regularly. We also send birthday cards and holiday cards and periodically hold raffles for self-care products. Raffle numbers are listed in our periodic newsletters, and we ensure that all participants win at least one of the raffles. It has been enlightening to see how meaningful these gestures are to an impoverished, generally isolated population. We have found that even nonintervention cases benefit from the attention they receive and from feeling part of an important endeavor.

Description of the Interventions

Now that we have provided examples of challenges that arise in the evaluation of preventive interventions with low-income maltreating populations, we turn our attention to the interventions themselves. As previously described, two theoretically informed models of intervention were evaluated in the proposed investigation. Manuals were developed and implemented for each of the two interventions. Because DHHS becomes active via case monitoring, management, or referral when reports of child maltreatment are received, this served as a constant across all conditions. Therefore, all families in which maltreatment had been identified received some services, even if they were not randomized to our theoretically guided intervention conditions.

The provision of intervention to multiproblem populations such as those with whom we intervened requires flexibility and responsivity to the frequent crises and challenges that confront these families. Because DHHS was active with all families, they provided a consistent monitoring function with respect to issues such as adequate food and housing. Although we strove to evaluate the potential efficacy of two theoretically different models of treatment, from an ethical practice standpoint, issues such as domestic violence, inadequate housing, and substance abuse needed to be addressed as they arose. Our models of treatment were focused on the improvement of parenting and the elimination of maltreatment and its sequelae, but we also had to be responsive to myriad related issues that we encountered during our clinical contacts with this population. To this end, therapists in both intervention models not only received extensive training on the respective models of treatment that they were providing, but also on the importance of cultural sensitivity and on how to deal with the extensive needs experienced by these families. In our view, neither treatment model could be effective in the absence of responsivity to the needs of maltreating families. The ability to respond to such needs also increases the portability of the models into clinic settings. Because the interventions were home-based, comfort and skill in navigating inner-city neighborhoods where drug use and violence were normative were necessary.

Community Standard. In the CS condition, DHHS managed cases in accord with their standard approach. Although variability existed, with service provision ranging from no service to referral to existing community clinics, this condition represents the community standard with which the PPI and IPP models were compared. The use of a CS comparison group en-

abled us to determine the effects of standard practices on child and family functioning, as compared with theoretically informed delivery of services. Such an approach is consistent with that of other treatment studies, such as the National Institutes of Health MTA study of children with Attention-Deficit/Hyperactivity Disorder (Arnold et al., 1997). The approaches that DHHS used with families who have been reported for maltreatment and are participating in the proposed investigation were systematically recorded via a standardized services questionnaire.

Psychoeducational Parenting Intervention Model. In addition to services typically made available to maltreating parents (CS), weekly home visitation was provided via the PPI model. This intervention approach has reemerged in recent years as an effective model for preventing damage to vulnerable children (National Commission to Prevent Infant Mortality, 1989; Shirk et al., 2000; U.S. Congress, 1988). In fact, the U.S. Advisory Board on Child Abuse and Neglect (1990) identified home visitation services as the best documented strategy for preventing child maltreatment. Data on the effectiveness of home visitation have emerged (Olds et al., 1997, 1998); yet to be conducted are studies on the effectiveness of home visitation services for families where maltreatment has already occurred, as well as assessments of whether home visitation services can alter the future life course development in infants who have been maltreated.

The PPI model utilized in this investigation was provided by therapists on a weekly basis in 1-hour home-based sessions, with a focus on two primary goals: the provision of parent education regarding infant development and developmentally appropriate parenting skills and the development of adequate maternal self-care skills, including assisting mothers with personal needs, fostering adaptive functioning, and improving social supports.

In accord with the home visitation model of Olds and his colleagues (Olds & Kitzman, 1990), therapists were trained in the provision of an ecologically informed model of influences on mother and child. This model strives to address how factors at different levels of proximity to the mother and child interact to form a system of influences on functioning. Practically, this results in the simultaneous examination of maternal personal resources, social support, and stresses in the home, family, and community that can affect maternal caregiving. We employed as interveners master's-level therapists who were adept at attending to the needs of multiproblem families, were knowledgeable regarding accessing community resources, and had expertise in addressing intrafamilial violence. Weekly 60-minute home visits were conducted over a period of 12 months.

The PPI model was a psychoeducationally based model grounded in the present that strives to educate, improve parenting, decrease maternal stress, and increase life satisfaction. The approach is didactic in nature, providing mothers with specific information, facts, procedures, and practices. Within a core agenda of topics on parenting and improved social skills to be addressed, flexibility and latitude in the amount of time spent on various topics was stressed in order to respond to individual needs of each mother. This flexibility is consistent with that utilized by other home-based interveners working with disadvantaged populations. An initial assessment of client needs within the domains of parenting and maternal self-care was conducted to delineate specific areas most in need of intervention. Thus, although there was a consistent range of issues to be addressed with each mother, the model allows for special emphasis on areas particularly germane to individual mothers.

Infant-Parent Psychotherapy Model. In addition to services typically available for maltreating parents (CS), mother-infant dyads in this intervention received weekly IPP. This intervention approach emanated from the seminal writings of Selma Fraiberg in her classic article, "Ghosts in the Nursery" (Fraiberg, Adelson, & Shapiro, 1975). Building on the work of Fraiberg, Albert Solnit, and Sally Provence, to name a few pioneers in the field, Alicia Lieberman (1991) provided the first evidence-based investigation of infant-parent psychotherapy.

Proponents of IPP believe that parent skills training alone is insufficient to alter the complex matrix of influences that lead to maladaptive mother-infant attachment relationships and future maladaptation. Although in our IPP intervention, developmental guidance was provided as necessary, it is important to stress that such guidance reflected responsivity to issues raised by the mother and did not involve didactic teaching, parent skills training, or modeling. Rather, IPP focused on the relationship between mother and infant and the effect of maternal history on current caregiving.

In accord with the IPP approach, the following goals were addressed:

1. The therapist expanded the mother's empathic responsiveness, sensitivity, and attunement to her infant.
2. The therapist promoted maternal fostering of infant autonomy and positive negotiation of maternal and child goals.
3. Distorted perceptions and reactions to the infant stemming from maternal representational models were altered and more positive representations of the infant were developed.

Each mother-child dyad was seen on a weekly basis by a master's-level therapist who was supervised by a PhD-level clinical psychologist. Sessions were home-based in order to experience mother-child interaction and its challenges in a real-world context. Reaching out to mothers in their homes also conveys respect and sensitivity for their situations. Meetings were 60 minutes in duration. The joint observation of the mother and infant is vital to this approach. As comments about the infant's behavior and the mother's experience of the infant emerge through this naturalistic observation, the therapist becomes able to respond empathically to the mother and expand parental understanding of stage-salient issues as they arise, as well as explore maternal misperceptions of the infant.

Unlike the PPI model, which focused on current behavior, the core of the IPP model resides in the mother's interactional history and its effect on her representation of relationships, most significantly that of her infant. Thus, rather than focusing only on the present, this model of therapy links the maternal past with current maternal perceptions of, and responses to, her infant. Unlike the PPI model, where therapist and mother meet to address parenting issues and caregiver self-care, the IPP approach relies on the mother-infant dyad as the "port of entry" (Stern, 1995) for therapeutic work. Therapeutic insights into the influence of maternal representation on parenting can be gained as maternal representations and distortions are enacted in the context of infant-parent interaction.

A number of aspects of IPP distinguish it as a unique approach to intervention. To begin, the "patient" in IPP is not a person, but a relationship that exists between mother and baby. Because many mothers may not wish to be seen individually in more traditional therapies, the focus on the relationship reduces the stigma and self-blame that might engender resistance to seeking treatment (Stern, 1995). Because much of the action of early mother-child relationships occurs preverbally in interactions, the value of being able to observe interactions is critical to understanding and being able to address relationship disturbances.

In the language of attachment theory, the intervention is designed to provide the mother with a corrective emotional experience in the context of the relationship with the therapist. Maltreating mothers, with their childhood histories of disturbed parent-child relationships and frequent negative experiences of social services helpers, typically expect rejection, abandonment, criticism, and ridicule. Overcoming these negative expectations in the course of establishing a positive therapeutic alliance with the therapist is essential. Often, initial concrete support and service provision create the opportunity for mothers to begin to trust the therapist. The therapist, through empathy, respect, concern, accommodation, and unfailing positive regard, creates a holding environment for the mother and infant in which new experiences of self in relationship to others and to the infant may be internalized. Evolving positive representations of the therapist can then be utilized to contrast with maternal representations of the self in relationship to parents. As the mother is able to reconstruct representations of the self in relationship to others through the therapeutic relationship, she also is able to reconstruct representations of herself in relationship with her infant.

Intervention Outcome

One of our primary intervention outcome measures was that of attachment. The Strange Situation was utilized and subsequently coded by individuals unaware of maltreatment status or treatment condition. Different coders rated baseline and postintervention tapes and interrater reliability was established. At baseline, there were no differences among the three maltreatment groups (IPP, PPI, CS) in the percentage of infants who were securely attached to their mother in the Strange Situation procedure (Ainsworth et al., 1978). This finding attests to the success of our randomization procedure. Notably, 3.6% of the infants in the IPP, and 0% of the babies in PPI and CS groups, had secure attachments at baseline. Thus, consistent with the prior maltreatment literature that included the coding of Type D attachments (Barnett et al., 1999; Carlson et al., 1989), very few maltreated babies had developed secure attachments with their mother.

Although significantly more of the nonmaltreated comparison babies were securely attached than were any of the babies in the maltreatment groups, the 39% rate of security in the nonmaltreated group underscores that this is a very high-risk comparison group. Indeed, their lower than average rate of attachment security (most nonrisk samples manifest security rates between 50% and 60%) is not surprising. Recall that these comparison youngsters were very closely matched to the maltreated infants on a variety of sociodemographic indices.

Additionally, at baseline, the three groups of maltreated infants all displayed extremely high rates of attachment disorganization. In particular, the Type D attachment organizations were 86% for the IPP, 82% for the PPI, and 91% for the CS groups. These high rates of disorganized attachment are consistent with findings in the literature on maltreated infants (Bakermans-Kranenburg et al., 2003; Barnett et al., 1999; Carlson et al., 1989; Lyons-Ruth et al., 1991). In contrast, the rate of disorganized attachment in the NC group was 20%.

The postintervention findings were quite compelling. The maltreated infants in the CS group had a 1.9% security rate, a nonsignificant improvement over their 0% baseline security results. In contrast, infants in each of the two interventions exhibited large increases in attachment security from baseline to postintervention (IPP: 3.6% to 60.7%; PPI: 0% to 54.5%). Finally, the percentage of attachment security in the NC group was 39% at both baseline and postintervention assessments.

Statistical analyses revealed that the IPP and the PPI interventions were equally successful in modifying attachment insecurity. This finding is interesting given the meta-analysis of Bakermans-Kranenburg et al. (2003), where the PPI model would have been predicted to be more effective. The attachment security rates in the IPP and PPI interventions were significantly greater than those found in the CS group. Furthermore, there were no statistically significant differences among the IPP, PPI, and NC groups, even though the intervention groups attained higher percentages of attachment security than did the NC group.

Furthermore, assessments conducted at the conclusion of the intervention revealed that the percentage of Type D attachment had declined from 86% to 32% for the IPP group and 82% to 46% for the PPI group. Conversely, the infants in the CS group continued to exhibit high rates of disorganization (91% to 78%); the percentages of Type D attachment in the NC group at baseline and postintervention were virtually identical (20% and 19%).

An examination of the stability of attachment organization across the four groups of infants provides further corroboration of the efficacy of the two interventions. Specifically, 57.1% of the infants in the IPP intervention and 54.5% of the infants in the PPI intervention changed their attachment organization from insecure to secure. In contrast, only 1.9% of the infants in the CS group evidenced a similar progression from insecure to secure attachment.

Likewise, 57.1% of the babies who received the IPP intervention and 45.5% of the infants who were in the PPI intervention exhibited a change in their attachment classification from Type D disorganized/disoriented to an organized pattern of attachment. Both of the intervention groups evidenced a greater diminution in Type D attachment than either the CS or NC groups.

The results of this randomized preventive intervention trial demonstrate that an intervention informed by attachment theory (IPP) and an intervention that focuses on improving parenting skills, increasing maternal knowledge of child development, and enhancing the coping and social support skills of maltreating mothers (PPI), both were successful in altering the predominantly insecure attachment organizations of maltreated infants. Thus, following Bowlby (1969/1982), the representational models of attachment figures and of the self in relation to others of the maltreated infants in intervention became positive as a function of the provision of the preventive intervention.

Given the success of this intervention, it becomes important to consider why these therapeutic models were effective in altering attachment security when previous investigations did not yield such findings. A number of components of these interventions may have contributed to their success. First, all therapists received extensive training before implementing the interventions, and they were familiar not only with the intervention modality, but also with the theory from which the interventions was derived. All therapists also had considerable prior experience working with low-income maltreating families. Both models were manualized, weekly individual and group supervision was provided, and therapists' adherence to their respective model was monitored for each case throughout the provision of the intervention. Caseloads were maintained at levels considerably lower than is typical of outpatient mental health settings; therapists were therefore able to devote considerable time to engaging mothers and to conceptualizing treatment plans. The positive outcome of this investigation supports the importance of investing in more costly interventions, including allowing therapists sufficient time for training and supervision.

Clearly, as predicted by the organizational perspective, the early insecure, generally disorganized attachments displayed by maltreated infants do not doom these youngsters to have poor-quality relationship expectations and negative self-representations throughout development. The success of the interventions, informed by basic research knowledge on the etiology and developmental sequelae of child maltreatment, suggests that attachment organization is modifiable, even if a high percentage of Type D attachment is initially characteristic of the sample. Following the organizational perspective, it is expected that these maltreated youngsters, now that they are traversing a more positive developmental trajectory, will be more likely to continue on an adaptive pathway and successfully resolve future salient developmental tasks (cf. Sroufe, Carlson, Levy, & Egeland, 1999). The preventive interventions have demonstrated that behavioral plasticity is possible, at least in the early years of life.

Preventive Interventions for Maltreated Preschoolers

The preschool years are an especially important time for symbolic and representational development; it is during this period that representational models of self and of self in relation to others evolving from the attachment relationship become increasingly structured and organized. Although developing children are likely to maintain specific models of individual relationships, these models become increasingly integrated into more generalized models of relationships over time (Crittenden, 1990), thereby affecting children's future relationship expectations. Because maltreated children internalize relational features of their caregiving experiences, they are likely to generalize negative representations of self and the self in relation to others to novel situations and relationship partners (Howes & Segal, 1993; Lynch & Cicchetti, 1991; Toth & Cicchetti, 1996).

As documented in our literature review earlier in this chapter, a considerable body of research has documented the deleterious effects of maltreatment on the representational development of abused and neglected children. The cross-sectional and longitudinal studies reported provide a solid foundation on which to conclude that maltreatment does exert negative effects on representational development, that these effects become more entrenched as development proceeds, and that the representational themes enacted in children's narratives are reflective of their maltreatment experiences and are related to child behavior problems (see Toth et al., 2000). Based on our empirical work, we concluded that it made sound sense to develop and implement interventions designed to modify maladaptive representational development in maltreated preschoolers.

Participant Recruitment

Procedures consistent with those described for the recruitment of maltreated and comparison infants were employed to enlist mothers and their preschool-age children.

Intervention Outcome

At baseline and at postintervention, 11 narrative story-stems, selected from the MSSB (Bretherton et al., 1990) described previously, were individually administered to child participants. The narratives utilized depicted moral dilemmas and emotionally charged events in the context of parent-child and family relationships. Narrative story-stems included vignettes designed to elicit children's perceptions of the parent-child relationship, of self, and of maternal behavior in response to child transgressions, intrafamilial conflicts, and child accidents.

Maternal representations were coded from the children's narratives. These included *positive mother* (the maternal figure is described or portrayed in the narrative as protective, affectionate, providing care, warm, or helpful); *negative mother* (the maternal figure is described or portrayed in the narrative as punitive, harsh, ineffectual, or rejecting); *controlling mother* (the maternal figure is described or portrayed in the narrative as controlling the child's behavior, independent of disciplining actions); *incongruent mother* (the maternal figure is described or portrayed in the narrative as dealing with child-related situations in an opposite or inconsistent manner); and *disciplining mother* (the maternal figure is described or portrayed in the narrative as an authority figure who disciplines the child; inappropriate and harsh forms of punishment were not scored here, but rather were coded as negative mother). A presence/absence method of coding was used to score children's maternal representations.

Self-representation scores were also coded from the children's narratives and were derived from coding any behaviors or references that were made in relation to any child character or when the child participant appeared to be experiencing relevant feelings in response to narrative content. Representational codes of self included *positive self* (a child figure is described or portrayed in the narrative as empathic or helpful, proud, or feeling good about self in any domain); *negative self* (a child figure is described or portrayed in the narrative as aggressive toward self or other, experiencing feelings of shame or self-blame, or feeling bad about self in any domain); and *false self* (a child figure is described or portrayed in the narrative as overly compliant or reports inappropriate positive feelings, for example, in an anger- or fear-producing situation). Consistent with maternal representation coding procedures, a presence/absence method of scoring was used to assess children's self-representations.

In addition to maternal and self-representation codes, a modified version of Bickham and Fiese's (1999) global relationship expectation scale was utilized to capture children's expectations of the mother-child relationship. For the current investigation, the scale was modified to assess children's global expectations of the mother-child relationship as portrayed in the children's 11 narratives. In accord with Bickham and Fiese's coding procedures, children's expectations of the mother-child relationship were determined by the overall degree of predictability and trustworthiness portrayed between mother and child characters across all 11 narrative administrations. Specifically, the following five relationship dimensions were used to aid in coding children's overall expectation of the mother-child relationship; predictable versus unpredictable, disappointing versus fulfilling, supportive or protective versus threatening, warm or close versus cold or distant, and genuine or trustworthy versus artificial or deceptive. Global mother-child relationship expectation ratings were based on a 5-point scale, ranging from very low (participant's narratives describe or portray the mother-child relationship as dissatisfying, unpredictable, and/or dangerous) to very high (participant's narratives describe or portray the mother-child relationship as fulfilling, safe, rewarding, and reliable).

Clinical Relevance of Results

Because a considerable body of prevention and intervention research has emerged based on attachment theory (cf. Lieberman, 1991; Lieberman et al., 1991; Lieberman & Zeanah, 1999), efforts designed to examine the implications of prevention and intervention for developmental theory are especially timely. Congruent with Bowlby's (1969/1982) theory and the organizational perspective on development (Cicchetti & Schneider-Rosen, 1986; Sroufe & Rutter, 1984), maltreated children, who develop insecure attachment relationships with their caregivers, also manifest impairments in self system functioning and in their representational models of attachment figures, the self, and the self in relation to others (Cicchetti, 1991). Thus, an intervention aimed at altering representational models of maltreated children is of vital importance. However, decisions needed to be made regarding the type of intervention that would be most likely to improve attachment security in maltreated children.

Children in the preschooler-parent psychotherapy (PPP) intervention evidenced a greater decline in maladaptive maternal representations over time than did children in the PPI and CS interventions. Moreover, children who took part in the PPP intervention displayed a greater decrease in negative self-representations than did children in the CS, PPI, and NC groups. Additionally, the mother-child relationship expectations of PPP children became more positive over the course of the intervention as compared with children in the PPI and NC groups. These results suggest that a model of intervention informed by attachment theory (PPP) is more effective at improving representations of self and of caregivers than is a didactic model of intervention (PPI) directed at parenting skills. Again, these results are contrary to predictions that would emanate from the meta-analysis of interventions targeting maternal sensitivity and child attachment (Bakermans-Kranenberg et al., 2003). Because the intervention focused on changing representational models utilizing a narrative story-stem measure, outcomes that might be expected to improve more dramatically in the PPI model (e.g., parenting skills, knowledge of child development) could not be addressed. Consistent with the approach described in our discussion of factors contributing to the success of the mother-infant interventions, we believe that the utilization of skilled and well-trained therapists, adherence to manualized treatment models, and monitoring of the fidelity of the provision of the interventions contributed to the efficacious findings. Moreover, given prior research that has found that the type of maternal attachment insecurity that is present may affect maternal responsivity to various intervention strategies (Bakermans-Kranenburg, Juffer, & van IJzendoorn, 1998), it will be important to assess baseline attachment organization of mothers in relation to intervention outcome.

These intervention results point to the potential malleability of these representations of self and of self in relation to others most significantly when an intervention derived from attachment theory (PPP) is provided. Rather than assuming that "sensitive" periods exist during infancy when the attachment relationship becomes less amenable to change, our findings suggest that, at least during the preschool years, the internalized mother-child relationship continues to evolve and remains open to reorganizations.

The fact that maltreated children in the PPP intervention evidenced increases in positive and decreases in negative self-representations is consistent with the findings of Cicchetti and Rogosch (1997) on pathways to resilience in maltreated school-age children. Differential predictors of resilient functioning were found in maltreated versus nonmaltreated children, with the former being more resilient when positive personality and self-system processes were present, and the latter being linked more to relationship variables. The improvements found in the self system processes of children in the PPP intervention are a positive sign that resilient strivings may have been initiated. If so, then the gains evidenced by these youngsters may continue to serve beneficial protective functions in future years. The positive changes in the PPP children's representations of maternal figures also bode well for these children's future receptivity to peers and other potential relationship partners, thereby moving them forward on a more adaptive relationship trajectory.

Next, we direct our attention toward another group of children at risk for maladaptive development and psychopathology: the offspring of depressed mothers.

DEFINITIONAL AND EPIDEMIOLOGICAL CONSIDERATIONS IN DEPRESSION

Point prevalence estimates for Major Depressive Disorder (MDD) in investigations that utilize structured diagnostic interviews yield rates of current Major Depression of less than 1% in samples of children, approximately 6% in samples of adolescents, and 2% to 4% in samples of adults (Kessler, 2002). Additionally, epidemiological surveys utilizing diagnostic interviews report lifetime prevalence rates of MDD that range from as low as 6% to as high as 25% by the end of adolescence and in adulthood (Kessler, Avenenoli, & Merikangas, 2001).

The National Comorbidity Study, the only nationally representative general population data in the United States based on a structured diagnostic interview, discovered that nearly 16% of respondents met diagnostic criteria for a lifetime episode of MDD (Kessler, Davis, & Kender, 1997; Kessler, McGonagle, Zhao, & Nelson, 1994). Furthermore, recurrent episodes of depression are quite common; existing estimates are that more than 80% of persons with a history of MDD experience recurrent episodes. When one also factors in the documented high rates of subsyndromal depression (Kessler, 2002), it is clear that a high percentage of individuals are confronted with the pain, suffering, and other dire consequences that depression and its variants engender.

Over the past several decades, as we have witnessed the managed care revolution in the field of mental health, economists and behavioral scientists alike have begun to substantiate the societal costs of illness (Gold, Hughes, & Swingle, 1996). Consequently, far more attention is being paid to investigating the consequences of mental illness such as MDD than on estimating prevalence and discovering modifiable risk factors, as has traditionally been the case in psychiatric epidemiology (Kessler, 2002).

In this new focus, depression has been shown to exert a major cost on individuals and on society. The World Health Organization's Global Burden of Disease (GBD) study ranked depression as the most burdensome disease in the world (Murray & Lopez, 1996). Among all diseases, the GBD study found that depression was the leading cause of the number of years individuals worldwide lived with disability, and the second leading cause of disease burden in terms of disability adjusted life years (DALYs) in developed regions of the world. Moreover, unipolar depression was documented to be the leading cause of disease burden DALYs among people in the middle years of life. Projecting to the year 2020, the GBD investigators predicted that unipolar depression will become the leading cause of disease burden in females and in developing countries (Murray & Lopez, 1996). The high burden of disease for depression is due to the combination of relatively high prevalence, high impact on quality of life and morbidity, early age of onset, and high likelihood of recurrence and chronicity (Wells, Subkoviak, & Serlin, 2002).

The social and economic effects of depression include stigmatization and discrimination, impairment in functioning, lower educational attainment, lost work productivity, greater marital instability, and increased utilization of health services (Hinshaw & Cicchetti, 2000; Simon, 2003). Depression also imposes a substantial burden on individuals through the pain and suffering it inflicts, not only on individuals, but also on the family.

Given the deleterious consequences that often accompany depressive disorder, it is not surprising that the children of depressed mothers are at increased risk for developing maladaptively. In the next section, we examine the known effects that maternal depression exerts on biological and psychological developmental processes in the early years of life. Subsequently, we illustrate how we have translated this research, much of which was undertaken in our laboratory, into the development and implementation of preventive interventions for young offspring of mothers with MDD.

A Developmental Psychopathology Perspective on Maternal Depression

Depressive conditions may be viewed as forming a spectrum of severity from transient and universally experienced dysphoria, to elevated levels of depressive symptoms that do not meet the diagnostic criteria for disorder, to extended periods of Dysthymic Disorder (i.e., chronic, low-level depression), to episodes of Major Depressive Disorder. Given the prevalence of depressive disorders across extensive periods of development and the various risk factors associated with depression, it is critical to have a firm grasp of the developmental processes that contribute to the emergence and maintenance of depressive disorders.

Because of the complex interplay among psychological (e.g., affective, cognitive, socioemotional, social-cognitive), social (e.g., cultural, community), and biological (e.g., genetic, neurobiological, neurophysiological, neurochemical, neuroendocrine) components, developmentalists have begun to invest great attention in examining the pathways, mechanisms, and sequelae involved in the ontogenesis and perpetuation of mood disorders (Beardslee, Versage, & Gladstone, 1998; Cicchetti & Toth, 1995, 1998a; Goodman & Gotlib, 2002). In this section, we focus on the effects of maternal MDD on two major developmental processes in the early years of life that have been investigated in our laboratory: attachment and the self system. We chose to focus on these topics because research investigations have shown that these issues have played an instrumental role in the generation, development, and implementation of interventions with depressed caregivers and their young children. Given the multiplicity of systems affected by depressive disorders, a developmental psychopathology approach serves to direct attention to the early developmental attainments that may be related to later-appearing patterns of Depressive Disorder. In adaptively functioning children, a coherent organization among diverse developmental systems is expected. In contrast, offspring of depressed mothers are at increased risk for either an incoherent organization among these developmental systems, or an organization of pathological structures, that is, a depressotypic organization (Cicchetti & Toth, 1998a).

The development of Depressive Disorder, as well as the individual's age at onset, is influenced not only by the emergence of salient issues that must be confronted and successfully resolved, but also by timed genetic events that create challenges and provide new opportunities as they figure prominently in every developmental phase. Moreover, two biological systems have received attention in research on the effects of maternal depression on offspring: EEG hemispheric activation asymmetry and stress regulatory dysfunction. At birth, hemispheric interconnections are incomplete and continue to develop. Davidson and Fox (1982) demonstrated that relatively greater left-sided activation was observed when infants were shown a happy video, and greater right-sided activation was observed when a sad video segment was presented. Early individual differences among infants in tendencies to approach versus withdraw from novelty and concomitant emotionality may reflect variations in the relative dominance and reactivity of the left and right hemispheres to stimulation, respectively (Fox & Davidson, 1984). Furthermore, experience may influence the manner in which the hemispheric connections develop. Infants with greater right hemisphere activation may be prone to overstimulation, with greater sensitivity and distraction to environmental change contributing to distress; conversely, infants with greater left activation may appear less distressed by environmental change and may have difficulty shifting and refocusing attention.

Infants as young as 1 month of age whose mothers were depressed have been found to exhibit greater relative right-frontal EEG asymmetry (due to reduced left-frontal activation) than 1-month-old infants of nondepressed mothers (Jones, Field, Fox, Lundy, & Davalos, 1997). These asymmetries were found to persist upon longitudinal follow-up when the babies were 3 months of age. Additionally, Field, Fox, Pickens, and Nawrocki (1995) discovered that depressed mothers and their 3- to 6-month-old infants both displayed right-

frontal EEG asymmetry. Dawson and her colleagues (Dawson, Grofer Klinger, Panagiotides, Hill, & Spieker, 1992; Dawson, Grofer Klinger, Panagiotides, Spieker, & Frey, 1992) examined the EEGs of 14-month-old babies of mothers with elevated depressive symptomatology and of same-age babies of nonsymptomatic mothers during various emotion-eliciting situations. Infants of the symptomatic mothers were found to display reduced left-frontal brain activation during baseline and playful interactions. Securely attached infants of symptomatic mothers evidenced left-frontal EEG hypoactivation, whereas securely attached babies of nonsymptomatic mothers did not. Further, during distress-eliciting maternal separation, the infants of the symptomatic mothers did not display a greater right-frontal activation or the same degree of distress that was observed in the babies of the nonsymptomatic mothers; these group differences were obtained regardless of the attachment status of the infants of the symptomatic mothers. Taken together, the results of the studies on hemispheric activation asymmetries in young offspring of depressed mothers suggest that a genetic diathesis for depression and the quality of caregiving experienced by the infant both exert an impact on neurobiological development.

Relatedly, empirical evidence with rodents and nonhuman primates suggests that disruptions in early caregiving can exert long-term effects on the limbic-hypothalamic-pituitary-adrenal axis, which mediates the stress response (Francis et al., 1996; Gunnar, Morison, Chisholm, & Shchuder, 2001; Plotsky & Meaney, 1993; Sanchez et al., 2001). To determine whether these findings were applicable to humans, Ashman, Dawson, Panagiotides, Yamada, and Wilkinson (2002) collected salivary cortisol samples from young school-age children of depressed and nondepressed mothers. Samples were collected immediately upon arrival to the research laboratory and after a mild laboratory stressor; in addition, samples were collected at home after awakening and before bedtime. Children who were reported to have elevated levels of internalizing symptoms and whose mother had a history of Depressive Disorder displayed elevated laboratory baseline cortisol levels. Children reported as having clinically significant internalizing symptoms also were more likely to evidence an elevated stress response to the mild laboratory stressor. Interestingly, the best predictor of elevations in children's baseline cortisol at age 7 was the presence of maternal depression within the first 2 years of the child's life. These findings suggest that, as has been demonstrated in the animal literature, early caregiving may be related to later dysregulation in neurobiological stress systems (see also Gunnar et al.'s, 2001, work with Romanian orphans). Future longitudinal investigations that integrate biological assessments, such as EEG hemispheric activation asymmetry and stress-reactivity paradigms, with psychological measurements hold great potential for elucidating mechanisms underlying the efficacy of preventive interventions.

The Development of an Attachment Relationship

Mothers who suffer from MDD are likely to struggle with the demands of providing early care for their infants. The features of the disorder, including anhedonia, difficulty regulating negative affect, feelings of worthlessness, helplessness, and hopelessness, sleep disturbances, and decrements in role functioning, conspire to generate an early relational context that may impair parenting and the development of the mother-child relationship and consequent child adaptation (Cicchetti, Rogosch, & Toth, 1998; Goodman & Gotlib, 2002). Moreover, depressive disorders frequently have evolved from difficulties in mothers' own childhood attachment experiences (Bowlby, 1980). Linkages between disturbances in parent-child relations and the emergence of depression have been made by theoreticians operating in the tradition of psychoanalytic and object relations theory (Arieti & Bemporad, 1978; Bowlby, 1980). Additionally, many retrospective studies have found that depressed adults report histories involving inadequate or abusive parental care (Bemporad & Romano, 1992).

Thus, insecurity in childhood attachment relationships of depressed mothers not only may contribute to their depressive disorders, but also may influence the manner in which they are able to relate to their young offspring via the operation of their representational models of attachment relationships. In attempting to understand the effects of maternal depression on the attachment relationship with a child, the issue of psychological unavailability must be considered. From the perspective of attachment theory, physical absence of a caregiver may be much less important than the child's experience of the parent as psychologically unavailable. Moreover, during periods of parental depression, children are likely to be confronted with caregivers who are inconsistent, unpredictable, insensitive, hostile, and/or intrusive (Cummings & Cicchetti, 1990; Egeland &

Sroufe, 1981). Such behavior in depressed caregivers may interfere with the capacity to relate to their child in a way that promotes the development of a secure attachment relationship.

Although children of depressed caregivers are more at risk of experiencing deviations in care as a consequence of their caregivers' struggles with their disorder, these children also may experience a sense of loss, akin to actual loss of a parent (Bowlby, 1980), when caregivers suffer from episodes of Major Depression. Insecure representational models may place these children in a more tenuous position in terms of coping with the experience of psychological loss of the availability of the caregiver as MDD episodes occur. Prolonged anxiety, sustained grieving, and difficulty in resolving the loss may further contribute to aberrations in the organization of cognitive, affective, representational, and biological systems. Subsequent loss experiences, either real or symbolic, may precipitate depressive episodes (Beck, 1967).

The quality of attachment in infants and children of mothers with depressive disorders has been examined in a number of investigations. To date, the results are varied (Martins & Gaffan, 2000). In view of the heterogeneous outcomes evidenced by children with depressed mothers, developmental researchers have been confronted with the challenge of specifying the processes underlying this diversity.

Because children with depressed parents are especially likely to be faced with the parents' psychological unavailability, the role of depression in contributing to insecure attachment relationships has been a fertile area of inquiry. In general, investigations of attachment security in infants, toddlers, and preschoolers with depressed caregivers suggest that offspring of depressed mothers are more likely to evidence increased rates of insecurity (Martins & Gaffan, 2000) than are offspring of nondepressed mothers from comparable SES backgrounds. With respect to the type of insecure attachment experienced, a meta-analytic investigation conducted by Martins and Gaffan concluded that the young offspring of depressed mothers have increased rates of anxious-avoidant (Type A) and disorganized (Type D) attachments. However, findings regarding attachment insecurity vary as a function of sample characteristics (e.g., depressed poverty-stricken mothers versus depressed middle-SES mothers; hospitalized versus community samples of depressed mothers), as well as transient versus more prolonged exposure to maternal depression (Cicchetti et al., 1995). Specifically, chronic maternal depression that occurs during their offspring's infancy and toddlerhood has been demonstrated to be associated with lags in verbal abilities, a lack of school readiness skills, and behavior problems (National Institute of Child Health and Development [NICHD], 1999). Additionally, issues such as the presence or absence of other supportive individuals (e.g., nondisordered fathers), as well as the overall family context in which the depressed mother resides, are likely to exert a major impact on the child's ultimate functioning (Cicchetti et al., 1998; Downey & Coyne, 1990).

The Development of the Self System

Toddlerhood may be a particularly sensitive period for the formation of a depressotypic organization because many of the social, emotional, and cognitive competencies implicated in the development of later Depressive Disorder (e.g., the development of autonomy, the emergence of the affect of shame, and the construction of a representational model of the availability of the self and of the self in relation to others) are at crucial stages of development.

The quality of attachment relationships contributes to the development of representational models of self and other that organize cognition, affect, and behavior, and these models serve to canalize perceptions and experiences as ontogenesis proceeds. Consistent with the propositions of an organizational perspective, the representational models of insecurely attached offspring of depressed mothers are likely to contribute to the development of a depressotypic organization of psychological and biological systems (Cicchetti & Toth, 1998a). Affect regulation and expression are less optimal, and significant others are perceived as unavailable or rejecting, while the self is regarded as unlovable. These attachment-related aspects of a depressotypic organization may contribute to a proneness to self-processes that have been linked to depression (e.g., low self-esteem, helplessness, hopelessness, negative attributional biases).

In a study conducted by Rogosch, Cicchetti, and Toth (2004), expressed emotion was examined in families of toddlers whose mothers had experienced MDD occurring since the child's birth and contrasted with expressed emotion in demographically comparable families with no history of parental mental disorder. Mothers provided 5-minute speech samples on their child, their spouse, and themselves and completed measures of toddler behavior

problems. Expressed emotion scores of criticism and emotional overinvolvement were determined for mothers for each of the individuals noted. Depressed mothers expressed significantly higher criticism in regard to self, spouse, and toddler than did nondepressed mothers. No depression group differences were found for emotional overinvolvement. Thus, higher levels of criticism across relationships mark the emotional climate in the families of the depressed group. Moreover, mothers with MDD reported significantly higher levels of child behavior problems than did mothers in the nondepressed group. However, high expressed emotion levels of maternal criticism did not serve as a mediator of the relation between depression group status and higher maternal report of child behavior problems.

The greater criticism of depressed mothers in regard to their toddlers is consistent with previous research demonstrating that depressed mothers express more criticism toward their school-age and adolescent children (Brennan, Hammen, Katz, & Le Broque, 2003; Schwartz, Yerushalmy, & Wilson, 1993). The findings of Rogosch et al. (2004) demonstrate that the negativity and criticism expressed are likely to emerge earlier in development than suggested by prior work. Furthermore, toddlers also are more likely to be exposed to criticism communicated between their parents, resulting in a family emotional climate rife with negativity across relationships.

Even when the young child is not the object of maternal criticism, the toddler in the families of mothers with MDD is nevertheless likely to be subjected to family system processes operating in response to criticism in other relationships. Children in families with depressed mothers are more likely to be exposed to reciprocal criticism between their parents, and such a conflicted marital relationship poses risks for these children's socioemotional development (Cummings & Davies, 1999; Rogosch et al., 2004). The highly negative and critical relational environment of families with a depressed mother likely influences emerging self-representations of the toddler and may inculcate a negative self-structure that may form the foundation for a depressotypic developmental organization (Cicchetti & Toth, 1998a).

A number of empirical studies attest to the difficulties in self-development and corresponding affective functioning in toddlers of depressed mothers. Maternal attribution patterns have been shown to affect the types of self-attributions that young children make. For example, Radke-Yarrow, Belmont, Nottelmann, and Bottomly

(1990) found that mothers with mood disorders conveyed significantly more negative affect in their attributions, particularly in regard to negative attributions about child emotions. Moreover, among the mood disordered mothers and their toddlers, there was a higher correspondence in the affective tone of attributions and statements about the self. This finding suggests a heightened vulnerability among these children for negative self-attributions, with negative implications for an increased risk for the development of later depression.

The development of self-knowledge during early toddlerhood has been examined most extensively through studies of visual self-recognition (M. Lewis & Brooks-Gunn, 1979). These investigations have relied on the presence of mark-directed behavior involving touching the nose while inspecting oneself in a mirror after a spot of rouge has been applied as the criterion for self-recognition. This capacity to recognize oneself visually emerges during the 2nd year of life and is considered to be one of the early precursors in the ontogenetic sequence of self-awareness. Cognitive, social, and experiential factors have been examined as they relate to individual differences in the development of visual self-recognition. Consistent with Kagan's (1981) conclusion, based on cross-cultural research, that self-awareness is a maturational attainment, findings to date coalesce to demonstrate that self-recognition is primarily a cognitive maturational phenomenon. This assertion has been further substantiated through investigation of atypical populations (cf. Mans, Cicchetti, & Sroufe, 1978; Schneider-Rosen & Cicchetti, 1991).

Research conducted with normative samples has revealed that visual self-recognition is predominantly accompanied by positive affective displays. Despite the fact that the attainment of visual self-recognition does not differ in high-risk populations, empirical investigations have revealed a high percentage of neutral or negative affect accompanying self-recognition in these youngsters (Schneider-Rosen & Cicchetti, 1991; Spiker & Ricks, 1984).

Because the offspring of mothers with MDD are exposed to a nonnormative, affectively extreme rearing environment, Cicchetti, Rogosch, Toth, and Spagnola (1997) examined visual self-recognition in the toddlers of depressed and nondepressed mothers. These investigators discovered that the achievement of visual recognition was not related to differences in level of cognitive development, timing of rouge application, affective expression, or maternal depression. However, toddlers who

exhibited self-recognition and who had mothers with MDD were more likely than toddlers of nondepressed mothers to display nonpositive affect and to shift affect from positive to nonpositive in the rouge condition.

Within the group of toddlers of mothers with MDD, toddlers who did not evidence self-recognition and who shifted affect from positive to nonpositive had lower attachment Q-Sort (Waters, 1995) security ratings and had mothers with less positive affect characteristics. These findings are consistent with the predictions of the organizational perspective on development (Cicchetti & Schneider-Rosen, 1986), which posits relations between attachment security and self-development. Furthermore, self-recognition and affective instability from the nonrouge to the rouge condition were related to differences in cognitive developmental level among toddlers of depressed mothers. Whether the differing patterns of affect-cognition relations discovered in the toddlers of depressed mothers in this investigation will influence the development, quality, or stability of emerging self-cognitions is an important empirical question that is currently being investigated in our laboratory. Such work will enable an examination of how affective components of the self (e.g., self-esteem) that are relevant to the development of depressive disorders relate to growing cognitive and representational components of the self (e.g., self-understanding, self-cognitions, self-schemata; see Cicchetti & Toth, 1995).

Cole, Barratt, and Zahn-Waxler (1992) observed a group of toddlers during two mishaps: a doll breaking and juice spilling. In general, toddlers exhibited two reactions to these mishaps: concerned reparation, and tension and frustration. Consistent with Kagan's (1981) notions that self-awareness, the appreciation of standards, and a moral sense emerge during this period, most toddlers tried to repair the mishap. The presence of depressed and anxious symptomatology in mothers was associated with a suppression of frustration and tension in their toddlers. It may be that the toddlers' exposure to mothers with depressed and anxious symptomatology served to inhibit the development of more normal affective expression, thereby contributing to a sense of lack of efficacy in interfacing with the environment.

Cicchetti, Maughan, Rogosch, and Toth (in press) investigated false belief understanding, an important aspect of a representational theory of mind and an aspect of self-other differentiation that is typically acquired during the preschool period (Wellman et al., 2001). Early maternal depression was found to have a significant effect on children's false belief understanding at age 5, with fewer children of depressed mothers passing the false belief criteria than youngsters with nondepressed caregivers. Interestingly, mothers who experienced depression during the first 2 years of their child's life and during the year prior to the false belief assessments had children who performed most poorly on the TOM tasks. These findings suggest that the experience of both early and recent maternal depression exerted a more detrimental effect on the development of TOM in preschool offspring.

Our review of research on the effects of maternal depression on offspring underscores the deleterious effects that this major mental disorder may exert on the developing child. It also highlights the importance of intervening not just directly with the depressed mother, but also with offspring exposed to maternal depression. Therefore, we next discuss a program of intervention that has incorporated results derived from studies of attachment and self in offspring of depressed mothers.

Preventive Interventions for Toddlers of Depressed Mothers

Based on our knowledge of the effects of maternal depression on the functioning of their young offspring, we sought to examine the efficacy of a preventive intervention to promote mother-child attachment security and positive child adaptation. The intervention was predicated on the importance of addressing the interplay among maternal representational models of their attachment experience in childhood, the mother's representations of her child, and the quality of the developing attachment relationship between mother and child.

Although a number of attachment-informed interventions have been developed (Bakermans-Kranenburg et al., 2003; van IJzendoorn et al., 1995), they typically have involved the provision of treatment to multiproblem populations (see, e.g., Egeland & Erickson, 1990; Erickson et al., 1992; Lieberman et al., 1991; Lyons-Ruth et al., 1990). Consequently, an array of services has been provided to meet the extensive needs of the families being served. This diversity in service outcomes has made it difficult to evaluate outcomes that may be attributed to changes in representational models versus results that may be due to other factors, such as a reduction of environmental stressors. Therefore, the application of attachment-informed interventions to populations with more circumscribed problems, such as mothers experi-

encing MDD without co-occurring risk factors, can be informative through more effectively isolating the specific factors that influence outcome.

To date, two interventions have been conducted that have sought to modify attachment security in the young offspring of depressed mothers. Gelfand, Teti, Seiner, and Jameson (1996) found that a home-based intervention designed to improve maternal self-efficacy was not effective in improving attachment security in offspring. Similarly, Cooper and Murray (1997) evaluated four types of intervention for mothers with postpartum depression. Mothers were assigned randomly to either routine primary care, nondirective counseling, cognitive-behavioral therapy, or attachment theory-guided dynamic psychotherapy. With the exception of the primary care condition, all treatment groups evidenced fewer relationship difficulties with their children postintervention. However, improvements in attachment security did not occur. Thus, preventive interventions have yet to demonstrate the ability of attachment-informed therapies to foster attachment security in diverse groups of high-risk populations, including the offspring of depressed mothers.

An Attachment Theory-Informed Preventive Intervention for Toddlers with Depressed Mothers

In view of the potential challenges to the development of secure attachment relationships that confront children with depressed caregivers, the continued provision and evaluation of preventive interventions for this population are extremely important. Although it is not uncommon for depressed women to receive therapeutic interventions for their depression that involve pharmacological treatments, individual therapy, or both, it is much less likely that such interventions recognize the woman as a mother and, consequently, address the relationship that is forming between mother and child. Unfortunately, disregard for this evolving relationship may result in greater risk for the emergence of an insecure attachment relationship and associated developmental difficulties for the child. Inattention to mother-child relationship issues in depressed mothers, in turn, may serve to perpetuate maternal depression, as the caregiver may be confronted with current and future child behavior problems and the associated guilt resulting from the fear that her depression has interfered with effective parenting.

In our laboratory, we conducted a controlled randomized preventive intervention trial with mothers with

MDD and their toddler offspring. Participants in this preventive intervention were recruited for a longitudinal study designed to evaluate the efficacy of a preventive intervention (toddler-parent psychotherapy [TPP]) for toddlers of depressed mothers and to examine the effects of maternal depression on child development, including child attachment. The sample included 168 mothers and their toddlers. At the time of enrollment, the average age of the toddlers was 20.4 months. Of the toddlers, 102 had mothers with a history of MDD that minimally involved a major depressive episode occurring at some time since the toddler had been born. The remaining 66 children had mothers with no current or prior history of major psychiatric disorder. The mean maternal age of the sample was 31.6 years.

To minimize the co-occurring risk factors that often accompany parental depression (Downey & Coyne, 1990), we decided not to recruit families from low-SES backgrounds. Initially, we wanted to conduct this intervention with low-SES mothers and their young offspring; however, because no study had succeeded in demonstrating that an attachment-informed intervention could successfully alter attachment security and child functioning in the offspring of depressed mothers, we concluded that it was first necessary to ascertain whether such an intervention could be effective with depressed mothers from the middle-SES population. Accordingly, parents were required to have at least a high school education and families could not be reliant on public assistance. A community sample of mothers with a history of Depressive Disorder was recruited through referrals from mental health professionals and through notices placed in newspapers, community publications, and medical offices and on community bulletin boards. In addition to having a child of approximately 20 months of age, mothers in the depressed groups had to meet diagnostic criteria for MDD occurring at some period since the birth of their toddler. The depressed mothers also had to be willing to accept random assignment to either the intervention or the nonintervention group following completion of baseline assessments. Among depressed mothers, 92.8% had been depressed during the postpartum period. Only 12.4% had been depressed exclusively in the postpartum period since the toddler was born. Forty-six depressed mothers were randomly assigned to receive the TPP intervention. The length of the intervention period averaged 57 weeks, and the mean number of intervention sessions conducted was 45.

Recruitment of control group mothers without a history of psychiatric disorder was achieved by contacting families living in the vicinity of the families of depressed mothers. Names of potential families with a toddler of the targeted age were obtained from birth records. In addition to the same demographic characteristics required for families with depressed mothers, the control group mothers were screened for the presence or history of major psychiatric disorder using the Diagnostic Interview Schedule III-R (Robins et al., 1985); only mothers without a current or past history of major psychiatric disorder were retained. Thus, this control group constitutes a "super normal" comparison group, given what is known from epidemiological studies about the prevalence of mental disorders in the general population.

We based our decision to recruit depressed mothers when their offspring were approximately 20 months of age on research as well as clinical considerations. Because several studies have found shifts from secure to insecure attachment between 12 and 18 months of age in offspring of depressed mothers, it appears that the toddler period confronts the mother-child dyad with challenges that are not met effectively. The chronicity of maternal depression may impede the toddler from being able to rely on the mother as a secure base. During toddlerhood, depressed mothers may become especially overwhelmed by the demands associated with parenting an active, inquisitive, and increasingly independent child who strives for initial individuation from the mother (Cicchetti & Toth, 1995). As these strivings for autonomy reach ascendance, a depressed mother may feel rejected by her child's increased interest in aspects of the world not related to the dyadic relationship. This tendency might be especially likely to occur in women who themselves had histories of rejection and who therefore are sensitized to perceiving rejection even in generally benign circumstances. To prevent the coalescence of insecure attachment and to help mothers accurately interpret the changes associated with toddlerhood, we felt that the provision of a preventive intervention during this developmental period was especially important.

Participants in the depressed intervention (DI), depressed control (DC), and nondepressed control (NC) groups were comparable on a range of basic demographic characteristics. Mothers were predominantly Caucasian (92.4%), and minority representation did not differ across groups. Maternal education also was comparable across groups. Overall, 53.8% of the mothers were college graduates or had received advanced degrees. Family SES based on Hollingshead's (1975) four-factor index also was consistent across groups: 73.4% were ranked in the two highest socioeconomic group status levels (IV and V).

Baseline assessments took place when toddlers were approximately 20 months of age and depressed mothers were randomly assigned to the intervention group (DI) or the nontreatment control (DC) group. Postintervention assessments occurred subsequent to the child turning 3 years old, when the DI group had completed the course of intervention. Extensive analyses of baseline measurements were conducted and differences between the DI and DC groups, in contrast to the normative group of non-depressed mothers (NC), were examined. Consistently, across diverse measurements, including stress, social support, parenting hassles, marital harmony and satisfaction, and levels of conflict, the two groups of depressed mothers were found to be indistinguishable, verifying the effectiveness of the randomization procedures. In all cases, the two groups of depressed mothers were found to have less adaptive functioning (Cicchetti et al., 1998); moreover, each of the features on which the depressed mothers differed from the mothers in the control group are detrimental to facilitating optimal child development and secure attachment relationships. Although not all mothers in the depressed groups were experiencing a depressive episode at the initiation of the preventive intervention, it was apparent that vulnerabilities in the two groups were substantial and continued beyond the confines of depressive episodes. These findings underscore the adverse emotional climate in which the toddler offspring of depressed mothers are immersed.

TPP is consistent with the IPP intervention described earlier in the chapter, with therapeutic adjustments made for the child's developmental level (Lieberman, 1992). Modifications in the treatment model also were made based on the socioeconomic status of participants. For example, rather than providing the intervention in homes, as was the case with low-income maltreating mothers, TPP was provided in the office setting. We found that our middle-income participants were not comfortable having someone provide services in their home, as they viewed it as somewhat intrusive. They also were much more accustomed to professional settings. Thus, although we initially considered providing the treatment in the homes as has been done in other seminal studies of this model of intervention (cf. Lieberman et al., 1991), it quickly became apparent that this would

be counterproductive. This realization is an important one, as it underscores the importance of tailoring an intervention to the needs of the population being served rather than rigidly adhering to a model developed with another population.

Challenges to Implementation. Although initially we expected the implementation of a preventive intervention with middle-income families in which fewer co-occurring risks were present to be much easier than our experiences in providing and evaluating services to low-income multiproblem families, we quickly learned that a different set of challenges was present. Our description of the modification to the provision of TPP provides one example of how a new population required a different approach. A number of other issues also emerged, many of them directly related to the diagnosis of depression.

First, we needed to ascertain how best to communicate with women regarding their depression. Although some women clearly self-identified as depressed, others had never actively sought treatment for depression. Thus, challenges posed by enrolling a sample that was recruited from the community and that was not necessarily comfortable with the utilization of diagnostic nomenclature needed to be addressed. Although we decided not to focus on the clinical diagnosis, we did describe symptoms and discussed how the symptoms were consistent with the presence of depression. The fact that the symptom pattern could affect parenting also was discussed. Sharing information that we were "preventing" something also proved to be a very delicate issue. We found that many of the mothers who were depressed feared that they had somehow "damaged" their offspring. Thus, even though we carefully described our randomization procedures, when contacted regarding participation in intervention, many women became alarmed. After completing baseline visits and being invited to participate in the intervention based on random assignment, one mother anxiously responded, "I knew there was something wrong with my son because I took antidepressants when I was pregnant. I know you're calling me because he looks really bad." We consistently needed to emphasize that not all children exposed to maternal depression had problems and that participation in the preventive intervention might just maintain an already positive developmental trajectory.

Actual recruitment of the population of depressed women also posed challenges. Initially, we planned to enlist participants from providers who were treating the maternal depression. Because we were focusing on the mother-child relationship and not on maternal depression per se, this approach seemingly posed no interference with any treatment being provided to the mother for her depression and also ensured that all women would be receiving necessary treatment for their depressive disorders. Surprisingly, we found that despite extensive outreach efforts, community providers of services to depressed women were reluctant to refer possible participants. In fact, we received a much more positive response from non-mental health providers. In retrospect, we realized that despite protestations to the contrary, many providers feared that they would lose their clients if they referred them to our program. Therefore, we modified our recruitment strategy to reach out directly to mothers.

The reputation of Mt. Hope Family Center as a facility serving low-income populations also posed obstacles. We needed to establish a separate name for the intervention program, relying on our university affiliation, which we minimized in our work with low-income participants, for whom that affiliation was typically off-putting. We also obtained a separate phone line, utilized a different entrance, and provided more upscale décor in efforts to decrease perceptions of stigmatization that our participants might feel attending a clinic-like setting known for treating child abuse and neglect. Our location in an urban community also resulted in some resistance, with suburban mothers fearing for their safety when venturing into the city. Procedures needed to be developed to increase comfort with traveling to our facility. Research staff would meet mothers in the parking lot and offer to pick them up if they were uncomfortable with the drive.

Because mothers were struggling with depression, concerted outreach needed to occur to ensure that they had the energy to meet the demands of participation in the research. We provided a single point of contact for mothers so that they could develop a relationship with a member of our staff. The designated "mom experimenter" was a constant who guided participants through all aspects of the longitudinal research program. Unfortunately, staff turnover is unavoidable over the course of a longitudinal project; when staff attrition occurred, we made great efforts to have the departing staff member introduce the new contact person.

Interestingly, the remission of MDD also posed a challenge to the conduct of the longitudinal investigation. We found that well mothers sometimes wanted to distance themselves from the period during which they had been clinically depressed. Remaining involved with a research program that had recruited them because of their mental illness reminded them of a difficult period in their lives. Moreover, as offspring became older, we found that some mothers were reluctant to discuss their history of depression with their children for fear of stigmatizing either themselves or their children. Efforts to help these women understand that both research and clinical case studies (e.g., Beardslee, 2000; Hinshaw, 2002) suggest that honest disclosure and the provision of information about past and current mental illness is helpful for children met with mixed results. Although some mothers expressed a willingness to continue involvement in the project as a function of this information, others adamantly insisted that they did not want their or their child's life in any way linked with the history of depression. The latter scenario was most typical in families where significant life changes, such as divorce and remarriage, had occurred. The fear of stigmatization was very real, and its presence speaks to the need for increased efforts to battle the societal stigmatization of mental illness.

Finally, our project staff struggled with how best to share the results of the project when mothers requested information. Because we were working with bright women who utilized library and Internet resources, they were interested in reading publications that emanated from their involvement. However, we were concerned that depressed mothers who had not participated in the intervention would be alarmed about the effects of their depression on their child, given our positive findings for intervention. Therefore, we prepared synopses of our results, always emphasizing that conclusions were based on group data and did not apply to individuals.

Intervention Efficacy. Given the centrality of attachment organization to early personality development and competent adaptation, a critical question involved whether the toddlers of a middle-class group of depressed mothers would evidence heightened rates of attachment insecurity at baseline. At baseline and at postintervention completion at 36 months, attachment was assessed via the attachment Q-set (AQS; Waters, 1995), a measure that has been found to provide a valid assessment of attachment. Mothers were given detailed instructions and training on how to complete the AQS prior to the baseline assessment and were asked to observe their child for 2 weeks before completing the

AQS. In accordance with the findings of others, toddlers with depressed mothers evidenced higher rates of insecurity than toddlers of nondepressed mothers. Subsequently, the effectiveness of the attachment theory-based intervention for fostering attachment security of toddlers with depressed mothers was examined (Cicchetti, Toth, & Rogosch, 1999).

Although, at baseline, the toddlers in the DI and DC groups evidenced equivalent rates of insecure attachment and both groups had higher rates of insecure attachment than the NC group, at follow-up the DC group continued to have higher rates of insecure attachment than the NC group. In contrast, the DI group at postintervention follow-up was not significantly different from the NC group in terms of the rate of insecure attachment. For toddlers who had taken part in the intervention, there was greater maintenance of secure attachment organization among those who were initially secure, as well as a greater shift from insecure to secure attachment groupings. These findings demonstrate the efficacy of TPP in promoting secure attachment organization among young offspring of depressed mothers and are among the first in the literature to demonstrate the effectiveness of a preventive intervention for altering attachment organization.

Maternal sorts of the AQS have been shown to relate to Strange Situation attachment classifications, as well as in theoretically expected ways to maternal internal working models and child security (Eiden, Teti, & Corns, 1995; Vaughn & Waters, 1990). It is unlikely that the maternal reports were biased because the Q-set method, unlike face-valid, self-report measures, requires the respondent to make forced-choice decisions across items, thereby reducing potential for biased responding. Moreover, mothers were not informed as to what constitutes secure attachment and they were unaware of our experimental hypotheses. In addition, mothers were neither trained in attachment theory nor knowledgeable about the security criterion ratings for the AQS. Consequently, it is improbable that demand characteristics affected maternal ratings of attachment security. In this regard, the nondidactic nature of the intervention provided becomes important. Unlike interventions that strive to teach sensitive responding or utilize modeling, the TPP intervention never provided such techniques.

In addition to AQS assessments, attachment security also was examined in the Strange Situation; this paradigm was utilized at baseline and postintervention to further elucidate the impact of TPP on attachment organization (Toth, Cicchetti, & Rogosch, in press). At baseline, toddlers in the DI and DC groups were significantly more likely to be insecurely attached to their mother than were toddlers in the NC group. Specifically, 13% of the toddlers in the DI and 20% of the toddlers in the DC group exhibited insecure attachment. Although their insecurity rates were not significantly different from each other, the security rate of 55% in the NC group differed significantly from both depression groups. Consistent with the extant literature, the toddlers in the DC group also had significantly greater rates of disorganized (Type D) attachment than the toddlers in the NC group. There also was a trend for toddlers in the DI group to manifest higher rates of Type D attachment than was the case for youngsters in the NC group. Specifically, the rates of disorganized attachment were 45%, 37%, and 20% for the DC, DI, and NC groups, respectively.

At postintervention, statistically significant differences were obtained in security of attachment between the DI (67%) and the DC (17%) groups. Furthermore, the DC group had significantly less attachment security than the NC group (48%). Of particular importance, despite the large differences in security that existed between the DI and NC groups at baseline, upon completion of the intervention, toddlers in these two groups showed no differences in attachment security. Whereas, at baseline, there were no statistically significant differences between the DI and NC groups in attachment disorganization, at postintervention there was less Type D attachment in the DI than in the DC group and a greater rate of Type D attachment in the DC than in the NC group. The percentages of Type D attachment at postintervention were 11%, 41%, and 21% in the DI, DC, and NC groups, respectively.

An examination of change in attachment security from baseline to postintervention revealed striking findings. The toddlers in the DI group displayed a greater percentage of change in attachment from baseline to postintervention than did either of the nonintervention groups. Specifically, toddlers in the DI group were more likely to change from attachment insecurity to attachment security. In addition, the toddlers in the DC group were more likely to change from attachment security to insecurity than were toddlers in the NC group.

Clinical Implications of Attachment Results. The results of the TPP intervention for toddlers of mothers with MDD provide compelling support for the potential malleability of attachment insecurity. The TPP intervention was effective at modifying attachment insecurity and in maintaining existing security in the toddler offspring of depressed mothers. Conversely, offspring of depressed mothers not receiving the TPP intervention were less likely than intervention offspring to maintain secure attachments at the postintervention assessment. These findings emphasize the importance of providing preventive interventions to offspring of depressed mothers so as to minimize the likelihood that insecurity will emerge over time. That is, even if offspring of mothers with MDD are securely attached early in life, the parenting milieu and the emotional climate of the home that accompany maternal depression, even once an active episode has remitted, may militate against the continuance of their secure attachment.

In view of the findings on the effectiveness of TPP, it is important to try to ascertain why this is one of the first interventions found to effectively improve security of attachment in young children. One possibility lies in the characteristics of the sample. Even though these mothers were struggling with MDD, they had fewer stressors than typical in populations frequently participating in preventive interventions. For example, the majority of women were married, had a postsecondary education, and were not members of the lower socioeconomic strata. Therefore, they may have been better able to utilize an insight-oriented mode of therapy than women confronted with a multitude of daily living challenges.

Additionally, the selection of a sample with fewer risk factors than that present in multiproblem populations allowed therapists to provide a "pure" form of therapy without needing to depart from the intervention protocol to address crisis situations. Because TPP sessions revealed that many of the depressed mothers in this investigation themselves had histories of negative caregiving and accompanying unresolved issues from childhood, the ability to maintain a focus on the dynamic roots of intergenerational patterns and to explore the current impact of past history on caregiving is considered to be of paramount importance in the success of this intervention. We speculate that as mothers became freed from the ghosts from their pasts, their representational models became more positive and they were increasingly able to focus on the present, including their relationship with their child. Moreover, as this occurred, we believe that mothers were better able to derive pleasure from their offspring and that, consequently, caregivers were invested in fostering and maintaining positive interactions. As mothers became more grounded in the present, we believe that they were more sensitive to their children and better able to

respond to the cues of their offspring. It remains an open, and critical, question as to whether this intervention would be equally effective with a more high-risk population of depressed women (e.g., depressed and impoverished mothers).

After the intervention, youngsters in the DI, DC, and NC groups were followed up 1 year later to determine whether the youngsters in the DI group would continue their positive trajectory and manifest more positive representations of their mother than youngsters in the DC group. At the age of 4, youngsters were individually administered a story-stem completion task by examiners unaware of group diagnosis, intervention status, and child attachment organization (Toth, Maughan, Manly, Spagnola, & Cicchetti, 2002). Consistent with the predictions of an organizational perspective, it was found that the children in the DI group were significantly more likely than those in the DC group to display positive expectations of their relationship with their mother.

The percentage of children with positive representational models of their caregivers was equivalent in the DI and NC groups; moreover, the DI and NC groups both exhibited more positive representations of their mother than did the youngsters in the DC group. Furthermore, the positive relationship between attachment security and positive self-representations demonstrates that the positive effects of the intervention were maintained 1 year after the conclusion of TPP.

The Efficacy of Toddler-Parent Psychotherapy for Fostering Cognitive Development in Offspring of Depressed Mothers. Offspring of depressed mothers are frequently confronted with a caregiver who has cognitive difficulties, including negative self-cognitions, concentration and memory impairments, and delayed information-processing abilities (American Psychiatric Association, 1994). Not surprisingly, a number of investigations have examined the impact that maternal depression has on young children's cognitive development. Although some evidence has emphasized the significance of maternal depression during the postpartum period and found that cognitive impairments remit over time, other investigations have found continued cognitive difficulties into the preschool years (Cicchetti, Rogosch, & Toth, 2000).

The role of preventive interventions in remediating the detrimental effects of maternal depression on cognitive development has been examined. Neither Cooper and Murray (1997) nor Gelfand et al. (1996) found any intervention effects on the cognitive functioning of offspring of depressed mothers; in contrast, Lyons-Ruth et al. (1990) found significant treatment effects for a home-visiting intervention among offspring of depressed mothers. Eighteen-month-old toddlers of depressed mothers who had not taken part in the preventive intervention obtained Mental Development Index (MDI) scores on the Bayley Scales of Infant Development that were 10 points lower than those toddlers whose mother participated in the intervention.

In our intervention for toddler offspring of mothers with MDD, we also examined the impact of TPP on the course of cognitive development in toddlers from middle-SES backgrounds whose mothers had experienced MDD prior to the child's age of 18 months. During the toddler period, the emergence of self-awareness and the development of symbolic representation are central issues (Cicchetti & Schneider-Rosen, 1986). Through facilitating communication and expressiveness between mother and child and optimizing the emotional quality of the mother-child relationships, the TPP intervention enhanced children's resolution of the competent developmental tasks of infancy and toddlerhood. Competent development during toddlerhood results in a positive emerging self in which children are more autonomous, free to explore and engage their environment, and more likely to have greater facility in the expression of their internal experience (Cicchetti & Toth, 1995).

At baseline, the DI, DC, and NC groups did not differ on the Bayley MDI. At the postintervention follow-up, a decline in IQ was found in the DC group, whereas the DI and NC groups continued to be equivalent, with higher Wechsler Preschool and primary Scale of Intelligence-Revised (WPPSI-R, 1989) Full-Scale and Verbal IQs than in the DC group. The worst outcome was found among the DC children whose mother had experienced subsequent depressive episodes. In contrast, among children of depressed mothers in the DI groups, no differences in cognitive development were observed for those children of mothers in the intervention who did or did not have subsequent depressive episodes between baseline and age 3. Thus, TPP contributed to children's making normative cognitive advances, even when mothers continued to struggle with recurrent depression. Conversely, children in the DC group were more delayed when their mother experienced recurrent depressive episodes. Specifically, among children whose mother had subsequent depressive episodes, there was nearly a

15-point difference in Verbal IQ favoring children in the intervention group (Cicchetti et al., 2000).

Taken in tandem, the efficacy of the TPP intervention in fostering attachment security, positive representational models, and normative cognitive development, even in the presence of ongoing maternal depression, underscores the criticality of providing prevention interventions for children of depressed mothers. The fact that more difficulties emerged over time among the offspring of mothers with subsequent depressive episodes further highlights the need for intervening preventively in the lives of these children. Without intervention, it is highly likely that the young offspring of mothers with MDD in the DI group, as appears to be the case with the youngsters in the DC group, would develop a depressotypic organization that forebodes later maladaptation and possible depressive illness. It is important to note that the provision of TPP did not result in a reduction of maternal depression. Although not a surprising outcome, given the effects of recurrent depressive episodes on child development, further attention needs to be directed toward effectively treating MDD in mothers.

CONCLUSION AND FUTURE PERSPECTIVE

A central objective of this chapter has been to illustrate the essential role that a developmental psychopathology perspective can play in bridging the worlds of basic research and clinical practice. We invoked a number of the principles of developmental psychopathology to guide the research conducted in our laboratory on maltreated children and the offspring of mothers with MDD. We chose to focus on the research we carried out with infants, toddlers, and preschoolers from these high-risk conditions as exemplars of how research findings could be utilized to conduct and implement preventive interventions. Guided by an organizational perspective on development that informed the discoveries of our basic research, we demonstrated the efficacy of several randomized clinical trials with maltreated infants, toddlers, and preschoolers, as well as with the infant and toddler offspring of mothers with MDD.

The experimental nature of randomized clinical trials provides an unprecedented opportunity to make causal inferences in the field. Independent variables manipulated in prevention trials may be several steps removed from underlying etiologic factors because such trials are primarily concerned with alleviating suffering and promoting competence. Nonetheless, careful research design and assiduous measurement of ancillary process variables through which intervention effects may occur can shed light on the theory-driven mechanisms underlying healthy and pathological outcomes (Cicchetti & Hinshaw, 2002; Kraemer, Stice, Kazdin, Offord, & Kupfer, 2001).

Recent initiatives at the National Institute of Mental Health, wherein funding decisions are tied to the real-world applications of research findings and to research capable of reducing the burden of mental illness, certainly will increasingly encourage investigators to devise and conduct investigations that break down the dualisms that exist between basic research and clinical intervention. In a report of the National Advisory Mental Health Council (2000, p. v) entitled *Translating Behavioral Science into Action,* the workgroup concluded that "too few researchers are attempting to bridge across basic, clinical, and services research, and not enough are working with colleagues in related allied disciplines to move research advances out of the laboratory and into clinical care, service delivery, and policy making." In this report, "translational research is defined as research designed to address how basic behavioral processes inform the diagnosis, prevention, treatment, and delivery of services for mental illness and, conversely, how knowledge of mental illness increases our understanding of basic behavioral processes" (p. iii). This formulation of translational research is in direct accord with principles of developmental psychopathology—namely, the reciprocal interplay between basic and applied research and between normal and atypical development (Cicchetti & Toth, 1998b).

In recent years, developmental psychopathologists have advocated a multiple-levels-of-analysis approach to the investigation of maladaptation and psychopathology (Chicchetti & Blender, 2004; Cicchetti & Dawson, 2002). Thus, the examination of multiple systems, domains, and levels of the ecology on the same individuals is thought to eventuate in a more complete depiction of individual patterns of adaptation and maladaptation. We believe it is essential that this multiple-levels-of-analysis approach be adopted by scientists who are conducting randomized controlled clinical preventive intervention trials. For example, the inclusion of molecular genetic methods (e.g., sequencing DNA and utilizing functional polymorphisms to examine gene × environment interactions), neuroimaging techniques (e.g., to investigate brain structure and function, pre- and postintervention), and stress-reactivity paradigms (e.g., to ascertain whether neurobiological stress systems are modifiable as a result of treatment), in conjunction with psychological outcomes, will enhance the understanding of the impact of interventions on brain-behavior relations (see, e.g., Caspi et al., 2002, 2003; Cicchetti & Posner, 2005; Fishbein, 2000; Goldapple et al., 2004). Similarly, the incorporation of biological measures into the research armamentaria of researchers investigating pathways to competence in the presence of significant adversity, as well as the translation of this integrative research into resilience-promoting interventions that assess biological, psychological, and ecological variables, will contribute to greatly reducing the schisms that exist between research and practice (Cicchetti, 2003; Curtis & Cicchetti, 2003; Luthar & Cicchetti, 2000).

Given the substantial monetary investment in supporting both basic research with relevance to the understanding and treatment of mental illness and in randomized prevention and treatment trials, it is of paramount importance that the knowledge gained from such endeavors be transported into real-world contexts. Researchers must be advocates, not only for the scientific dissemination of knowledge, but also for reaching policymakers and clinicians who may lack the understanding or resources needed to provide interventions that have been found to be efficacious. It would be naive to suggest that impediments to implementing evidence-supported treatments in nonresearch settings do not exist. However, although efforts to traverse the path from the university laboratory to the clinical world may cause apprehension, avoidance, and resistance, such a journey must not be eschewed. Rather, as a field we need to embrace the diversity among us, equally welcoming potentially elucidating contributions from basic researchers and frontline professionals. Such collaborative endeavors and active efforts to improve the conduct and utilization of research and the scientific base of practice will benefit researchers, practitioners, policymakers, and, most important, children and families in need of support and treatment.

REFERENCES

Ainsworth, M. D. S., Blehar, M. C., Waters, E., & Wall, S. (1978). *Patterns of attachment: A psychological study of the Strange Situation.* Hillsdale, NJ: Erlbaum.

Ainsworth, M. D. S., & Wittig, B. A. (1969). Attachment and the exploratory behavior of 1-year-olds in a Strange Situation. In B. M. Foss (Ed.), *Determinants of infant behavior* (Vol. 4, pp. 113–136). London: Methuen.

Alessandri, S. M., & Lewis, M. (1996). Differences in pride and shame in maltreated and non-maltreated preschoolers. *Child Development, 67,* 1857–1869.

American Psychiatric Association. (1994). *Diagnostic and statistical manual of mental disorders* (4th ed.). Washington, DC: Author.

Arieti, S., & Bemporad, J. (1978). *Severe and mild depression.* New York: Basic Books.

Arnold, L. E., Abikoff, H. B., Cantwell, D. P., Conners, C. K., Elliot, G. R., Greenhill, L. L., et al. (1997). NIMH collaborative multi-model treatment study of children with ADHD (MTA): Design, methodology, and protocol evolution. *Journal of Attention Disorders, 2,* 141–158.

Ashman, S. B., Dawson, G., Panagiotides, H., Yamada, E., & Wilkinson, C. W. (2002). Stress hormone levels of children of depressed mothers. *Development and Psychopathology, 14,* 333–350.

Bakermans-Kranenburg, M. J., Juffer, F., & van IJzendoorn, M. H. (1998). Interventions with video feedback and attachment discussions: Does type of maternal insecurity make a difference? *Infant Mental Health Journal, 19,* 202–219.

Bakermans-Kranenburg, M. J., van IJzendoorn, M. H., & Juffer, F. (2003). Less is more: Meta-analysis of sensitivity and attachment interventions in early childhood. *Psychological Bulletin, 129,* 195–215.

Barnett, D., Ganiban, J., & Cicchetti, D. (1999). Maltreatment, negative expressivity, and the development of Type D attachments from 12- to 24-months of age. *Society for Research in Child Development Monograph, 64,* 97–118.

Barnett, D., Manly, J. T., & Cicchetti, D. (1993). Defining child maltreatment: The interface between policy and research. In D. Cicchetti & S. L. Toth (Eds.), *Child abuse, child development, and social policy* (pp. 7–73). Norwood, NJ: Ablex.

Beardslee, W. R. (2000). Prevention of mental disorders and the study of developmental psychopathology: A natural alliance. In J. L. Rapoport (Ed.), *Childhood onset of "adult" psychopathology: Clinical and research advances* (pp. 333–355). Washington, DC: American Psychological Association.

Beardslee, W. R., Versage, E. M., & Gladstone, T. R. G. (1998). Children of affectively ill parents: A review of the past 10 years. *Journal of the American Academy of Child and Adolescent Psychiatry, 37,* 1134–1141.

Beck, A. T. (1967). *Depression: Clinical, experimental, and theoretical aspects.* New York: Harper & Row.

Beeghly, M., & Cicchetti, D. (1994). Child maltreatment, attachment, and the self system: Emergence of an internal state lexicon in toddlers at high social risk. *Development and Psychopathology, 6,* 5–30.

Bemporad, J. R., & Romano, S. J. (1992). Childhood maltreatment and adult depression: A review of research. In D. Cicchetti & S. L. Toth (Eds.), *Rochester Symposium on Developmental Psychopathology: Vol. 4. Developmental perspectives on depression* (pp. 351–376). Rochester, NY: University of Rochester Press.

Bergman, L. R., & Magnusson, D. (1997). A person-oriented approach in research on developmental psychopathology. *Development and Psychopathology, 9,* 291–319.

Bickham, N., & Fiese, B. (1999). *Child narrative coding system.* Syracuse, NY: Syracuse University Press.

Black, J., Jones, T. A., Nelson, C. A., & Greenough, W. T. (1998). Neuronal plasticity and the developing brain. In N. E. Alessi, J. T. Coyle, S. I. Harrison, & S. Eth (Eds.), *Handbook of child and adolescent psychiatry* (pp. 31–53). New York: Wiley.

Bonanno, G. A. (2004). Loss, trauma, and human resilience: Have we underestimated the human capacity to thrive after extremely aversive events? *American Psychologist, 59,* 20–28.

Bowlby, J. (1982). *Attachment and loss* (Vol. 1). New York: Basic Books. (Original work published 1969)

Bowlby, J. (1980). *Attachment and loss: Vol. 3. Loss, sadness, and depression.* New York: Basic Books.

Boyce, W. T., Frank, E., Jensen, P. S., Kessler, R. C., Nelson, C. A., Steinberg, L., et al. (1998). Social context in developmental psychopathology: Recommendations for future research from the MacArthur Network on Psychopathology and Development. *Development and Psychopathology, 10,* 143–164.

Brennan, P. A., Hammen, C., Katz, A. R., & Le Broque, R. M. (2003). Maternal depression, paternal psychopathology, and adolescent diagnostic outcomes. *Journal of Consulting and Clinical Psychology, 70,* 1075–1085.

Bretherton, I. (1985). Attachment theory: Retrospect and prospect. *Monographs for the Society for Research in Child Development, 50,* 3–35.

Bretherton, I., Ridgeway, D., & Cassidy, J. (1990). Assessing internal working models of the attachment relationship: An attachment story completion task for 3-year-olds. In M. Greenberg, D. Cicchetti, & E. M. Cummings (Eds.), *Attachment in the preschool years* (pp. 273–308). Chicago: University of Chicago Press.

Cahan, E., & White, S. (1992). Proposals for a second psychology. *American Psychologist, 47,* 224–235.

Cairns, R. B., Cairns, B., Xie, H., Leung, M. C., & Heane, S. (1998). Paths across generations: Academic competence and aggressive behaviors in young mothers and their children. *Developmental Psychology, 34,* 1162–1174.

Calverley, R. M., Fischer, K. W., & Ayoub, C. (1994). Complex affective splitting in sexually abused adolescent girls. *Development and Psychopathology, 6,* 195–213.

Carlson, V., Cicchetti, D., Barnett, D., & Braunwald, K. (1989). Disorganized/disoriented attachment relationships in maltreated infants. *Developmental Psychology, 25,* 525–531.

Caspi, A., McClay, J., Moffitt, T., Mill, J., Martin, J., Craig, I. W., et al. (2002). Role of genotype in the cycle of violence in maltreated children. *Science, 297,* 851–854.

Caspi, A., Sugden, K., Moffitt, T. E., Taylor, A., Craig, I. W., Harrington, H. L., et al. (2003). Influence of life stress on depression: Moderation by a polymorphism in the 5-HTT gene. *Science, 301,* 386–389.

Cassidy, J. (1994). Emotion regulation: Influences of attachment relationships. *Monographs of the Society for Research in Child Development, 59,* 228–283.

Ciaranello, R., Aimi, J., Dean, R. S., Morilak, D., Porteus, M. H., & Cicchetti, D. (1995). Fundamentals of molecular neurobiology. In D. Cicchetti & D. J. Cohen (Eds.), *Developmental psychopathology: Vol. 1. Theory and method* (pp. 109–160). New York: Wiley.

Cicchetti, D. (1984). The emergence of developmental psychopathology. *Child Development, 55,* 1–7.

Cicchetti, D. (1989). How research on child maltreatment has informed the study of child development: Perspectives from developmental psychopathology. In D. Cicchetti & V. Carlson (Eds.), *Child maltreatment: Theory and research on the causes and consequences of child abuse and neglect* (pp. 377–431). New York: Cambridge University Press.

Cicchetti, D. (1990). A historical perspective on the discipline of developmental psychopathology. In J. Rolf, A. Masten, D. Cicchetti,

K. Nuechterlein, & S. Weintraub (Eds.), *Risk and protective factors in the development of psychopathology* (pp. 2–28). New York: Cambridge University Press.

Cicchetti, D. (1991). Fractures in the crystal: Developmental psychopathology and the emergence of the self. *Developmental Review, 11,* 271–287.

Cicchetti, D. (1993). Developmental psychopathology: Reactions, reflections, projections. *Developmental Review, 13,* 471–502.

Cicchetti, D. (2002a). How a child builds a brain: Insights from normality and psychopathology. In W. W. Hartup & R. A. Weinberg (Eds.), *Minnesota Symposia on Child Psychology: Vol. 32. Child psychology in retrospect and prospect* (pp. 23–71). Mawah, NJ: Erlbaum.

Cicchetti, D. (2002b). The impact of social experience on neurobiological systems: Illustration from a constructivist view of child maltreatment. *Cognitive Development, 17,* 1407–1428.

Cicchetti, D. (2003). Neuroendocrine functioning in maltreated children. In D. Cicchetti & E. F. Walker (Eds.), *Neurodevelopmental mechanisms in psychopathology* (pp. 345–365). New York: Cambridge University Press.

Cicchetti, D., & Aber, J. L. (1998). Contextualism and developmental psychopathology. *Development and Psychopathology, 10,* 137–141.

Cicchetti, D., & Barnett, D. (1991a). Attachment organization in pre-school-aged maltreated children. *Development and Psychopathology, 3,* 397–411.

Cicchetti, D., & Barnett, D. (1991b). Toward the development of a scientific nosology of child maltreatment. In W. Grove & D. Cicchetti (Eds.), *Thinking clearly about psychology: Vol. 2. Essays in honor of Paul E. Meehl—Personality and psychopathology* (pp. 346–377). Minneapolis: University of Minnesota Press.

Cicchetti, D., Beeghly, M., Carlson, V., & Toth, S. L. (1990). The emergence of the self in atypical populations. In D. Cicchetti & M. Beeghly (Eds.), *The self in transition: Infancy to childhood* (pp. 309–344). Chicago: University of Chicago Press.

Cicchetti, D., & Blender, J. A. (2004). A multiple-levels-of-analysis approach to the study of developmental processes in maltreated children. *Proceedings of the National Academy of Sciences, 101,* 17325–17326.

Cicchetti, D., & Cannon, T. D. (1999). Neurodevelopmental processes in the ontogenesis of psychopathology. *Development and Psychopathology, 11*(3), 375–393.

Cicchetti, D., & Cohen, D. J. (Eds.). (1995a). *Developmental psychopathology: Vol. 1. Theory and method.* New York: Wiley.

Cicchetti, D., & Cohen, D. J. (Eds.). (1995b). *Developmental psychopathology: Vol. 2. Risk, disorder, and adaptation.* Hoboken, NJ: Wiley.

Cicchetti, D., & Cohen, D. J. (Eds.). (in press-a). *Developmental psychopathology: Vol. 1. Theory and method* (2nd ed.). Hoboken, NJ: Wiley.

Cicchetti, D., & Cohen, D. J. (Eds.). (in press-b). *Developmental psychopathology: Vol. 2. Developmental neuroscience* (2nd ed.). Hoboken, NJ: Wiley.

Cicchetti, D., & Cohen, D. J. (Eds.). (in press-c). *Developmental psychopathology: Vol. 3. Risk, disorder, and adaptation* (2nd ed.). Hoboken, NJ: Wiley.

Cicchetti, D., & Dawson, G. (Eds.). (2002). Multiple levels of analysis [Special issue]. *Development and Psychopathology, 14*(3), 417–666.

Cicchetti, D., Ganiban, J., & Barnett, D. (1991). Contributions from the study of high risk populations to understanding the development of emotion regulation. In J. Garber & K. A. Dodge (Eds.), *The development of emotion regulation and dysregulation* (pp. 15–48). New York: Cambridge University Press.

Cicchetti, D., & Garmezy, N. (1993). Prospects and promises in the study of resilience. *Development and Psychopathology, 5,* 497–502.

Cicchetti, D., & Hinshaw, S. P. (Eds.). (2002). Prevention and intervention science: Contributions to developmental theory [Special issue]. *Development and Psychopathology, 14*(4), 667–981.

Cicchetti, D., & Lynch, M. (1993). Toward an ecological/transactional model of community violence and child maltreatment: Consequences for children's development. *Psychiatry, 56,* 96–118.

Cicchetti, D., & Lynch, M. (1995). Failures in the expectable environment and their impact on individual development: The case of child maltreatment. In D. Cicchetti & D. J. Cohen (Eds.), *Developmental psychopathology: Vol. 2. Risk, disorder, and adaptation* (pp. 32–71). New York: Wiley.

Cicchetti, D., Lynch, M., Shonk, S. M., & Manly, J. T. (1992). An organizational perspective on peer relations in maltreated children. In R. D. Parke & G. W. Ladd (Eds.), *Family-peer relationships: Modes of linkage* (pp. 345–383). Hillsdale, NJ: Erlbaum.

Cicchetti, D., & Manly, J. T. (Eds.). (2001). Operationalizing child maltreatment: Developmental processes and outcomes [Special issue]. *Development and Psychopathology, 13*(4), 755–1048.

Cicchetti, D., Maughan, A., Rogosch, F. A., & Toth, S. L. (in press). Predictors of false belief understanding in preschool offspring of mothers with Major Depressive Disorder. *Development and Psychopathology.*

Cicchetti, D., & Pogge-Hesse, P. (1982). Possible contributions of the study of organically retarded persons to developmental theory. In E. Zigler & D. Balla (Eds.), *Mental retardation: The developmental difference controversy* (pp. 277–318). Hillsdale, NJ: Erlbaum.

Cicchetti, D., & Posner, M. I. (Eds.) (2005). Integrating cognitive and affective neuroscience and developmental psychopathology [Special issue]. *Development and Psychopathology, 17*(3), 569–891.

Cicchetti, D., & Rizley, R. (1981). Developmental perspectives on the etiology, intergenerational transmission, and sequelae of child maltreatment. *New Directions for Child Development, 11,* 32–59.

Cicchetti, D., & Rogosch, F. A. (1994). The toll of child maltreatment on the developing child: Insights from developmental psychopathology. *Child and Adolescent Psychiatric Clinics of North America, 3,* 759–776.

Cicchetti, D., & Rogosch, F. A. (1996). Equifinality and multifinality in developmental psychopathology. *Development and Psychopathology, 8,* 597–600.

Cicchetti, D., & Rogosch, F. A. (1997). The role of self-organization in the promotion of resilience in maltreated children. *Development and Psychopathology, 9,* 799–817.

Cicchetti, D., & Rogosch, F. A. (1999). Conceptual and methodological issues in developmental psychopathology research. In P. C. Kendall, J. N. Butcher, & G. N. Holmbeck (Eds.), *Handbook of research methods in clinical psychology* (pp. 433–465). New York: Wiley.

Cicchetti, D., & Rogosch, F. A. (2001). Diverse patterns of neuroendocrine activity in maltreated children. *Development and Psychopathology, 13,* 677–694.

Cicchetti, D., Rogosch, F. A., Maughan, A., Toth, S. L., & Bruce, J. (2003). False belief understanding in maltreated children. *Development and Psychopathology, 15,* 1067–1091.

Cicchetti, D., Rogosch, F. A., & Toth, S. L. (1998). Maternal depressive disorder and contextual risk: Contributions to the development of attachment insecurity and behavior problems in toddlerhood. *Development and Psychopathology, 10,* 283–300.

Cicchetti, D., Rogosch, F. A., & Toth, S. L. (2000). The efficacy of toddler-parent psychotherapy for fostering cognitive development in offspring of depressed mothers. *Journal of Abnormal Child Psychology, 28,* 135–148.

Cicchetti, D., Rogosch, F. A., Toth, S. L., & Spagnola, M. (1997). Affect, cognition, and the emergence of self-knowledge in the toddler offspring of depressed mothers. *Journal of Experimental Child Psychology, 67,* 338–362.

Cicchetti, D., & Schneider-Rosen, K. (1986). An organizational approach to childhood depression. In M. Rutter, C. Izard, & P. Read (Eds.), *Depression in young people: Clinical and developmental perspectives* (pp. 71–134). New York: Guilford Press.

Cicchetti, D., & Sroufe, L. A. (1976). The relationship between affective and cognitive development in Down syndrome infants. *Child Development, 47,* 920–929.

Cicchetti, D., & Sroufe, L. A. (1978). An organizational view of affect: Illustration from the study of Down syndrome infants. In M. Lewis & L. Rosenblum (Eds.), *The development of affect* (pp. 309–350). New York: Plenum Press.

Cicchetti, D., & Toth, S. L. (1991). The making of a developmental psychopathologist. In J. Cantor, C. Spiker, & L. Lipsitt (Eds.), *Child behavior and development: Training for diversity* (pp. 34–72). Norwood, NJ: Ablex.

Cicchetti, D., & Toth, S. L. (1992). The role of developmental theory in prevention and intervention. *Development and Psychopathology, 4,* 489–493.

Cicchetti, D., & Toth, S. L. (1993). Child abuse research and social policy: The neglected nexus. In D. Cicchetti & S. L. Toth (Eds.), *Child abuse, child development, and social policy* (pp. 301–330). Norwood, NJ: Ablex.

Cicchetti, D., & Toth, S. L. (1995). A developmental psychopathology perspective on child abuse and neglect. *Journal of the American Academy of Child and Adolescent Psychiatry, 34,* 541–565.

Cicchetti, D., & Toth, S. L. (1998a). The development of depression in children and adolescents. *American Psychologist, 53,* 221–241.

Cicchetti, D., & Toth, S. L. (1998b). Perspectives on research and practice in developmental psychopathology. In W. Damon (Ed.), *Handbook of child psychology* (5th ed., Vol. 4, pp. 479–583). New York: Wiley.

Cicchetti, D., & Toth, S. L. (Eds.). (1999). *Rochester Symposium on Developmental Psychopathology: Vol. 9. Developmental approaches to prevention and intervention.* Rochester, NY: University of Rochester Press.

Cicchetti, D., & Toth, S. L. (2000). Developmental processes in maltreated children. In D. Hansen (Ed.), *Nebraska Symposium on Motivation* (Vol. 46, pp. 85–160). Lincoln: University of Nebraska Press.

Cicchetti, D., Toth, S. L., & Lynch, M. (1995). Bowlby's dream comes full circle: The application of attachment theory to risk and psychopathology. *Advances in Clinical Child Psychology, 17,* 1–75.

Cicchetti, D., Toth, S. L., & Manly, J. T. (2003). *Maternal maltreatment interview.* Unpublished manuscript.

Cicchetti, D., Toth, S. L., & Rogosch, F. A. (1999). The efficacy of toddler-parent psychotherapy to increase attachment security in offspring of depressed mothers. *Attachment and Human Development, 1,* 34–66.

Cicchetti, D., Toth, S. L., & Rogosch, F. A. (2005). *The efficacy of interventions for maltreated infants in fostering secure attachment.* Manuscript in preparation.

Cicchetti, D., & Tucker, D. (1994). Development and self-regulatory structures of the mind. *Development and Psychopathology, 6,* 533–549.

Cicchetti, D., & Valentino, K. (in press). An ecological transactional perspective on child maltreatment: Failure of the average expectable environment and its influence upon child development. In D. Cicchetti & D. J. Cohen (Eds.), *Developmental psychopathology: Vol. 3. Risk, disorder, and adaptation* (2nd ed.). Hoboken, NJ: Wiley.

Cicchetti, D., & Walker, E. F. (Eds.). (2001). Stress and development: Biological and psychological consequences [Special issue]. *Development and Psychopathology, 13*(3), 413–753.

Cicchetti, D., & Walker, E. F. (Eds.). (2003). *Neurodevelopmental mechanisms in psychopathology.* New York: Cambridge University Press.

Coie, J. D., Watt, N. F., West, S. G., Hawkins, D., Asarnow, J. R., Markman, H. J., et al. (1993). The science of prevention: A conceptual framework and some directions for a national research program. *American Psychologist, 48,* 1013–1022.

Cole, P., Barratt, K., & Zahn-Waxler, C. (1992). Emotion displays in 2-year-olds during mishaps. *Child Development, 63,* 314–324.

Coley, R. L., & Chase-Lansdale, P. L. (1998). Adolescent pregnancy and parenthood: Recent evidence and future directions. *American Psychologist, 53,* 152–166.

Conduct Problems Prevention Research Group. (2002a). An end of third-grade evaluation of the impact of the Fast Track prevention trial with children at high risk for adolescent conduct problems. *Journal of Abnormal Child Psychology, 30,* 19–35.

Conduct Problems Prevention Research Group. (2002b). The implementation of the Fast Track program: An example of a large-scale prevention science efficacy trial. *Journal of Abnormal Psychology, 30,* 1–17.

Conduct Problems Prevention Research Group. (2002c). Using the Fast Track randomized prevention trial to test the early-starter model of the development of serious conduct problems. *Development and Psychopathology, 14,* 925–943.

Cooper, P., & Murray, L. (1997). The impact of psychological treatment of postpartum depression on maternal mood and infant development. In L. Murray & P. Cooper (Eds.), *Postpartum depression and child development* (pp. 201–220). New York: Guilford Press.

Cowan, W. M., Kopnisky, K. L., & Hyman, S. E. (2002). The human genome project and its impact on psychiatry. *Annual Review of Neuroscience, 25,* 1–50.

Crittenden, P. M. (1988). Relationships at risk. In J. Belsky & T. Nezworski (Eds.), *Clinical implications of attachment theory* (pp. 136–174). Hillsdale, NJ: Erlbaum.

Crittenden, P. M. (1990). Internal representational models of attachment relationships. *Infant Mental Health Journal, 11,* 259–277.

Crittenden, P. M., & Ainsworth, M. D. S. (1989). Child maltreatment and attachment theory. In D. Cicchetti & V. Carlson (Eds.), *Child maltreatment: Theory and research on the causes and consequences of child abuse and neglect* (pp. 432–463). New York: Cambridge University Press.

Crittenden, P. M., & DiLalla, D. (1988). Compulsive compliance: The development of an inhibitory coping strategy in infancy. *Journal of Abnormal Child Psychology, 16,* 585–599.

Cummings, E. M., & Cicchetti, D. (1990). Toward a transactional model of relations between attachment and depression. In M. T. Greenberg, D. Cicchetti, & E. M. Cummings (Eds.), *Attachment in the preschool years* (pp. 339–372). Chicago: University of Chicago Press.

Cummings, E. M., & Davies, P. T. (1996). Emotional security as a regulatory process in normal development and the development of psychopathology. *Development and Psychopathology, 8,* 123–139.

Cummings, E. M., & Davies, P. T. (1999). Depressed parents and family functioning: Interpersonal effects and children's functioning and development. In T. Joiner & J. C. Coyne (Eds.), *The interactional nature of depression: Advances in interpersonal approaches* (pp. 299–327). Notre Dame, IN: University of Notre Dame Press.

Cummings, E. M., Hennessy, K., Rabideau, G., & Cicchetti, D. (1994). Responses of physically abused boys to interadult anger involving their mothers. *Development and Psychopathology, 6,* 31–42.

Curtis, W. J., & Cicchetti, D. (2003). Moving research on resilience into the twenty-first century: Theoretical and methodological considerations in examining the biological contributors to resilience. *Development and Psychopathology, 15,* 773–810.

Daro, D. A. (2000). Child abuse prevention: New directions and challenges. In D. J. Hansen (Ed.), *Nebraska Symposium on Motivation: Vol. 46. Motivation and child maltreatment* (pp. 161–219). Chicago: University of Chicago Press.

Davidson, R. J., & Fox, N. A. (1982). Asymmetrical brain activity discriminates between positive versus affective stimuli in human infants. *Science, 218,* 1235–1237.

Dawson, G., Grofer Klinger, L., Panagiotides, H., Hill, D., & Spieker, S. (1992). Frontal lobe activity and affective behavior of infants of mothers with depressive symptoms. *Child Development, 63,* 725–737.

Dawson, G., Grofer Klinger, L., Panagiotides, H., Spieker, S., & Frey, K. (1992). Infants of mothers with depressive symptoms: Electroencephalographic and behavioral findings related to attachment status. *Development and Psychopathology, 4,* 67–80.

Dean, A., Malik, M., Richards, W., & Stringer, S. (1986). Effects of parental maltreatment on children's conceptions of interpersonal relationships. *Developmental Psychology, 22,* 617–626.

DeBellis, M. D. (2001). Developmental traumatology: The psychobiological development of maltreated children and its implications for reserach, treatment, and policy. *Development and Psychopathology, 13,* 539–564.

Dodge, K. A., Bates, J. E., & Pettit, G. S. (1990). Mechanisms in the cycle of violence. *Science, 250,* 1678–1683.

Dodge, K. A., Pettit, G. S., & Bates, J. E. (1997). How the experience of early physical abuse leads children to become chronically aggressive. In D. Cicchetti & S. L. Toth (Eds.), *Rochester Symposium on Developmental Psychopathology: Vol. 8. Trauma—Perspectives on theory, research, and intervention* (pp. 263–288). Rochester, NY: University of Rochester Press.

Downey, G., & Coyne, J. C. (1990). Children of depressed parents: An integrative review. *Psychological Bulletin, 108,* 50–76.

Egeland, B., & Erickson, M. F. (1990). Rising above the past: Strategies for helping new mothers break the cycle of abuse and neglect. *Zero to Three, 11,* 29–35.

Egeland, B., & Sroufe, L. A. (1981). Developmental sequelae of maltreatment in infancy. *New Directions for Child Development, 11,* 77–92.

Eiden, R. D., Teti, D., & Corns, K. (1995). Maternal working models of attachment, marital adjustment, and the parent-child relationship. *Child Development, 66,* 1504–1518.

Eisenberg, L. (1995). The social construction of the human brain. *American Journal of Psychiatry, 152,* 1563–1575.

Elder, G. H. (1974). *Children of the great depression.* Chicago: University of Chicago Press.

Elmer, E. (1977). *Fragile families, troubled children.* Pittsburgh, PA: University of Pittsburgh Press.

Emde, R. N., Wolf, D. P., & Oppenheim, D. (Eds.). (2003). *Revealing the inner worlds of young children.* Oxford: Oxford University Press.

English, D. J. (2003). The importance of understanding a child's maltreatment experience cross-sectionally and longitudinally. *Child Abuse and Neglect, 27,* 877–882.

Erickson, M. F., Korfmacher, J., & Egeland, B. (1992). Attachments past and present: Implications for therapeutic intervention with mother-infant dyads. *Development and Psychopathology, 4,* 495–507.

Field, T. M., Fox, N., Pickens, J., & Nawrocki, T. (1995). Relative right frontal EEG activation in 3- to 6-month old infants of "depressed" mothers. *Developmental Psychology, 31,* 358–363.

Fischer, K. W., & Ayoub, C. (1994). Affective splitting and dissociation in normal and maltreated children: Developmental pathways for self in relationships. In D. Cicchetti & S. L. Toth (Eds.), *Rochester Symposium on Developmental Psychopathology: Vol. 5. Disorders and dysfunction of the self* (pp. 149–222). Rochester, NY: University of Rochester Press.

Fishbein, D. (2000). The importance of neurobiological research to the prevention of psychopathology. *Prevention Science, 1,* 89–106.

Fox, N. A., & Davidson, R. J. (1984). Hemispheric substrates of affect. In N. A. Fox & R. J. Davidson (Eds.), *The psychobiology of affective development* (pp. 353–381). Hillsdale, NJ: Erlbaum.

Fraiberg, S., Adelson, E., & Shapiro, V. (1975). Ghosts in the nursery: A psychoanalytic approach to impaired infant-mother relationships. *Journal of the American Academy of Child Psychiatry, 14,* 387–421.

Francis, D., Diorio, J., LaPlante, P., Weaver, S., Seckl, J. R., & Meaney, M. J. (1996). The role of early environmental events in regulating neuroendocrine development: Moms, pups, stress, and glucocorticoid receptors. In C. F. Ferris & T. Grisso (Eds.), *Annals of the New York Academy of Sciences: Vol. 794. Understanding aggressive behavior in children* (pp. 136–152). New York: New York Academy of Sciences.

Francis, D., Di Orio, J., Liu, D., & Meaney, M. J. (1999). Nongenomic transmission across generations of maternal behavior and stress responses in the rat. *Science, 286,* 1155–1158.

Gaensbauer, T., & Hiatt, S. (1984). Facial communication of emotion in early infancy. In N. A. Fox & R. J. Davidson (Eds.), *The psychobiology of affective development* (pp. 207–230). Hillsdale, NJ: Erlbaum.

Gaensbauer, T., Mrazek, D., & Harmon, R. (1981). Emotional expression in abused and/or neglected infants. In N. Frude (Ed.), *Psy-

chological approaches to child abuse (pp. 120–135). Totowa, NJ: Rowman & Littlefield.

Garcia Coll, C., Akerman, A., & Cicchetti, D. (2000). Cultural influences on developmental processes and outcomes: Implications for the study of development and psychopathology. *Development and Psychopathology, 12,* 333–356.

Garcia Coll, C., Crnic, K., Lamberty, G., Wasik, B., Jenkins, R., Garcia, H., et al. (1996). An integrative model for the study of developmental competencies in minority children. *Child Development, 67,* 1891–1914.

Gelfand, D. M., Teti, D. M., Seiner, S. A., & Jameson, P. B. (1996). Helping mothers fight depression: Evaluation of a home-based intervention program for depressed mothers and their infants. *Journal of Clinical Child Psychology, 25,* 406–422.

Gelles, R. J. (1982). Toward better research on child abuse and neglect: A response to Besharov. *Child Abuse and Neglect, 6,* 495–496.

Giovannoni, J., & Becerra, R. M. (1979). *Defining child abuse.* New York: Free Press.

Gold, S. N., Hughes, D. M., & Swingle, J. M. (1996). Characteristics of childhood sexual abuse among female survivors in therapy. *Child Abuse and Neglect, 20,* 323–335.

Goldapple, K., Segal, Z., Garson, C., Lau, M., Bieling, P., Kennedy, S., et al. (2004). Modulation of cortical-limbic pathways in major depression. *Archives of General Psychiatry, 61,* 34–41.

Goodman, S., & Gotlib, I. H. (Eds.). (2002). *Children of depressed parents: Mechanisms of risk and implications for treatment.* Washington, DC: American Psychological Association.

Greenough, W., Black, J., & Wallace, C. (1987). Experience and brain development. *Child Development, 58,* 539–559.

Gunnar, M., & Nelson, C. A. (1994). Event-related potentials in year-old infants: Relations with emotionality and cortisol. *Child Development, 65,* 80–94.

Gunnar, M. R., Morison, S. J., Chisholm, K., & Shchuder, M. (2001). Salivary cortisol levels in children adopted from Romanian orphanages. *Development and Psychopathology, 13,* 611–628.

Hennessy, K. D., Rabideau, G. J., Cicchetti, D., & Cummings, E. M. (1994). Responses of physically abused and nonabused children to different forms of interadult anger. *Child Development, 65,* 815–828.

Hinshaw, S. P. (2002). Prevention/intervention trials and developmental theory: Commentary on the Fast Track Special Section. *Journal of Abnormal Child Psychology, 30,* 53–59.

Hinshaw, S. P., & Cicchetti, D. (2000). Stigma and mental disorder: Conceptions of illness, public attitudes, personal disclosure, and social policy. *Development and Psychopathology, 12,* 555–598.

Hoagwood, K., & Jensen, P. S. (1997). Developmental psychopathology and the notion of culture: Introduction to the special section on "The fusion of cultural horizons: Cultural influences on the assessment of psychopathology in children and adolescents." *Applied Developmental Science, 1,* 108–112.

Hofer, M. A. (1987). Early social relationships: A psychobiologist's view. *Child Development, 58,* 633–647.

Hollingshead, A. (1975). *Four-factor index of social status.* Unpublished manuscript, Yale University.

Howe, G. W., Reiss, D., & Yuh, J. (2002). Can prevention trials test theories of etiology? *Development and Psychopathology, 14,* 673–694.

Howes, C., & Segal, J. (1993). Children's relationships with alternative caregivers: The special case of maltreated children removed from their homes. *Journal of Applied Developmental Psychology, 14,* 71–81.

Institute of Medicine. (1994). *Research on children and adolescents with mental, behavioral, and developmental disorders.* Washington, DC: National Academy Press.

Institute of Medicine. (2000). *Bridging disciplines in the brain, behavioral, and clinical sciences.* Washington, DC: National Academy Press.

Jones, N. A., Field, T., Fox, N. A., Lundy, B., & Davalos, M. (1997). EEG activation in 1-month-old infants of depressed mothers. *Development and Psychopathology, 9,* 491–505.

Juvenile Justice Standards Project. (1977). *Standards relating to child abuse and neglect.* Cambridge, MA: Ballinger.

Kagan, J. (1981). *The second year: The emergence of self-awareness.* Cambridge, MA: Harvard University Press.

Kandel, E. R. (1998). A new intellectual framework for psychiatry. *American Journal of Psychiatry, 155,* 469–475.

Kandel, E. R. (1999). Biology and the future of psychoanalysis: A new intellectual framework for psychiatry revisited. *American Journal of Psychiatry, 156,* 505–524.

Kaufman, J. (1991). Depressive disorders in maltreated children. *Journal of the American Academy of Child and Adolescent Psychiatry, 30,* 257–265.

Kazdin, A. E. (1999). Current (lack of) theory in child and adolescent therapy research. *Journal of Clinical Child Psychology, 28,* 533–543.

Kellam, S. G., & Rebok, G. W. (1992). Building developmental and etiological theory through epidemiologically based preventive intervention trials. In J. McCord & R. E. Tremblay (Eds.), *Preventing antisocial behavior: Interventions from birth through adolescence* (pp. 162–195). New York: Guilford Press.

Kellam, S. G., Rebok, G. W., Ialongo, N., & Mayer, L. S. (1994). The course and malleability of aggressive behavior from early first grade into middle school: Results of a developmental epidemiologically-based preventive trial. *Journal of Child Psychology and Psychiatry, 35.* 259–281.

Kellam, S. G., Rebok, G. W., Mayer, L. S., Ialongo, N., & Kalonder, C. R. (1994). Depressive symptoms over first grade and their responsiveness to a preventive trial aimed at improving achievement. *Development and Psychopathology, 6,* 463–489.

Kessler, R. C. (2002). Epidemiology of depression. In I. H. Gotlib & C. L. Hammen (Eds.), *Handbook of depression* (pp. 23–42). New York: Guilford Press.

Kessler, R. C., Avenenoli, S., & Merikangas, K. R. (2001). Mood disorders in children and adolescents: An epidemiologic perspective. *Biological Psychiatry, 49,* 1002–1014.

Kessler, R. C., Davis, C. G., & Kender, K. S. (1997). Childhood adversity and adult psychiatric disorder in the United States National Comorbidity Study. *Psychological Medicine, 27,* 1079–1089.

Kessler, R. C., McGonagle, K. A., Zhao, S., & Nelson, C. B. (1994). Lifetime and 12-month prevalence of DSM-III-R psychiatric disorders in the United States: Results from the National Comorbidity Study. *Archives of General Psychiatry, 51,* 8–19.

Kobak, R. (1999). The emotional dynamics of disruptions in attachment relationships: Implications for theory, research, and clinical intervention. In J. Cassidy & P. R. Shaver (Eds.), *Handbook of attachment: Theory, research, and clinical applications* (pp. 21–43). New York: Guilford Press.

Kochanska, G., Aksan, N., & Koenig, A. L. (1995). A longitudinal study of the roots of preschoolers' conscience: Committed compliance and emerging internalization. *Child Development, 66,* 1752–1769.

Koenig, A. L., Cicchetti, D., & Rogosch, F. A. (2000). Child compliance/noncompliance and maternal contributors to internalization in maltreating and nonmaltreating dyads. *Child Development, 71,* 1018–1032.

Kraemer, H. C., Stice, E., Kazdin, A., Offord, D., & Kupfer, D. (2001). How do risk factors work together? Mediators, moderators, and independent, overlapping, and proxy risk factors. *American Journal of Psychiatry, 158,* 848–856.

Kraemer, H. C., Wilson, G. T., Fairburn, C. G., & Agras, W. S. (2002). Mediators and moderators of treatment effects in randomized clinical trials. *Archives of General Psychiatry, 59,* 877–884.

Lander, E. S., & Weinberg, R. A. (2000). Genomics: Journey to the center of biology. *Science, 287,* 1777–1782.

Lewin, B. (2004). *Genes VIII.* Upper Saddle River, NJ: Pearson Education, Inc., Pearson Prentice-Hall.

Lewis, D. O. (1992). From abuse to violence: Psychological consequences of maltreatment. *Journal of the American Academy of Child and Adolescent Psychiatry, 31,* 282–391.

Lewis, M., & Brooks-Gunn, J. (1979). *Social cognition and the acquisition of self.* New York: Plenum Press.

Lieberman, A. F. (1991). Attachment theory and infant-parent psychotherapy: Some conceptual, clinical, and research considerations. In D. Cicchetti & S. L. Toth (Eds.), *Rochester Symposium on Developmental Psychopathology: Vol. 3. Models and integrations* (pp. 261–287). Rochester, NY: University of Rochester Press.

Lieberman, A. F. (1992). Infant-parent psychotherapy with toddlers. *Development and Psychopathology, 4,* 559–574.

Lieberman, A. F., Weston, D., & Pawl, J. H. (1991). Preventive intervention and outcome with anxiously attached dyads. *Child Development, 62,* 199–209.

Lieberman, A. F., & Zeanah, C. H. (1999). Contributions of attachment theory to infant-parent psychotherapy and other interventions with infants and young children. In J. Cassidy & P. R. Shaver (Eds.), *Handbook of attachment* (pp. 555–574). New York: Guilford Press.

Luthar, S. S. (Ed.). (2003). *Resilience and vulnerability: Adaptation in the context of childhood adversities.* New York: Cambridge University Press.

Luthar, S. S., & Cicchetti, D. (2000). The construct of resilience: Implications for intervention and social policy. *Development and Psychopathology, 12,* 857–885.

Luthar, S. S., Cicchetti, D., & Becker, B. (2000). The construct of resilience: A critical evaluation and guidelines for future work. *Child Development, 71,* 543–562.

Lynch, M., & Cicchetti, D. (1991). Patterns of relatedness in maltreated and nonmaltreated children: Connections among multiple representational models. *Development and Psychopathology, 3,* 207–226.

Lynch, M., & Cicchetti, D. (1992). Maltreated children's reports of relatedness to their teachers. *New Directions for Child Development, 57,* 81–107.

Lyons-Ruth, K., Connell, D., Grunebaum, H., & Botein, S. (1990). Infants at social risk: Maternal depression and family support services as mediators of infant development and security of attachment. *Child Development, 61,* 85–98.

Lyons-Ruth, K., Connell, D., Zoll, D., & Stahl, J. (1987). Infants at social risk: Relationships among infant maltreatment, maternal behavior, and infant attachment behavior. *Developmental Psychology, 23,* 223–232.

Lyons-Ruth, K., Repacholi, B., McLeod, S., & Silva, E. (1991). Disorganized attachment behavior in infancy: Short-term stability, maternal and infant correlates, and risk-related subtypes. *Development and Psychopathology, 3,* 377–396.

Macfie, J., Cicchetti, D., & Toth, S. L. (2001). Dissociation in maltreated versus nonmaltreated preschool-aged children. *Child Abuse and Neglect, 25,* 1253–1267.

Macfie, J., Toth, S. L., Rogosch, F. A., Robinson, J., Emde, R. N., & Cicchetti, D. (1999). Effect of maltreatment on preschoolers' narrative representations of responses to relieve distress and of role reversal. *Developmental Psychology, 35,* 460–465.

Main, M., & George, C. (1985). Response of abused and disadvantaged toddlers to distress in agemates: A study in the day care setting. *Developmental Psychology, 21,* 407–412.

Main, M., & Solomon, J. (1986). Discovery of a disorganized/disoriented attachment pattern. In T. B. Brazelton & M. W. Yogman (Eds.), *Affective development in infancy* (pp. 95–124). Norwood, NJ: Ablex.

Main, M., & Solomon, J. (1990). Procedures for identifying infants as disorganized/disoriented during the Ainsworth Strange Situation. In M. Greenberg, D. Cicchetti, & E. M. Cummings (Eds.), *Attachment in the preschool years* (pp. 121–160). Chicago: University of Chicago Press.

Manly, J. T. (2005). Advances in research definitions of child maltreatment. *Child Abuse and Neglect, 29*(5), 425–439.

Manly, J. T., Cicchetti, D., & Barnett, D. (1994). The impact of subtype, frequency, chronicity, and severity of child maltreatment on social competence and behavior problems. *Development and Psychopathology, 6,* 121–143.

Manly, J. T., Kim, J. E., Rogosch, F. A., & Cicchetti, D. (2001). Dimensions of child maltreatment and children's adjustment: Contributions of developmental timing and subtype. *Development and Psychopathology, 13,* 759–782.

Mans, L., Cicchetti, D., & Sroufe, L. A. (1978). Mirror reactions of Down syndrome infants and toddlers: Cognitive underpinnings of self-recognition. *Child Abuse and Neglect, 49,* 1247–1250.

Marenco, S., & Weinberger, D. R. (2000). The neurodevelopmental hypothesis of schizophrenia: Following a trail of evidence from cradle to grave. *Development and Psychopathology, 12,* 501–528.

Martins, C., & Gaffan, E. A. (2000). Effects of early maternal depression on patterns of infant-mother attachment: A meta-analytic investigation. *Journal of Child Psychology and Psychiatry, 41,* 737–746.

Masten, A. S. (2001). Ordinary magic: Resilience processes in development. *American Psychologist, 56,* 227–238.

Masten, A. S., Best, K., & Garmezy, N. (1990). Resilience and development: Contributions from the study of children who overcome adversity. *Development and Psychopathology, 2,* 425–444.

Masten, A. S., Hubbard, J. J., Gest, S. D., Tellegen, A., Garmezy, N., & Ramirez, M. (1999). Competence in the context of adversity: Pathways to resilience and maladaptation from childhood to late adolescence. *Development and Psychopathology, 11,* 143–169.

Maughan, A., & Cicchetti, D. (2002). The impact of child maltreatment and interadult violence on children's emotion regulation abilities. *Child Development, 73,* 1525–1542.

McCrone, E., Egeland, B., Kalkoske, M., & Carlson, E. A. (1994). Relations between early maltreatment and mental representations of relationships assessed with projective storytelling in middle childhood. *Development and Psychopathology, 6,* 99–120.

McLoyd, V. C. (1998). Socioeconomic disadvantage and child development. *American Psychologist, 53,* 185–204.

Meaney, M. J. (2001). Maternal care, gene expression, and the transmission of individual differences in stress reactivity across generations. *Annual Review of Neuroscience, 24,* 1161–1192.

Miller, T. R., Cohen, M. A., & Wiersema, B. (1996). *Victim costs and consequences: A new look.* Washington, DC: National Institute of Justice.

Moffitt, T. E. (1993). Adolescence-limited and life-course-persistent anti-social behavior: A developmental taxonomy. *Psychological Review, 100,* 674–701.

Munoz, R. F., Mrazek, P. J., & Haggerty, R. J. (1996). Institute of Medicine report on prevention of mental disorders. *American Psychologist, 51,* 1116–1122.

Murray, C. J. L., & Lopez, A. D. (Eds.). (1996). *The global burden of disease and injury* (Vol. 1). Cambridge, MA: Harvard School of Public Health.

National Advisory Mental Health Council. (2000). *Translating behavioral science into action: Report of the National Advisory Mental Health Counsel's behavioral science workgroup* (No. 00-4699). Bethesda, MD: National Institute of Mental Health.

National Commission to Prevent Infant Mortality. (1989). *Home visiting: Opening doors for America's pregnant women and children.* Washington, DC: National Commission to Prevent Infant Mortality.

National Institute of Child Health and Development, Early Child Care Research Network. (1999). Chronicity of maternal depressive symptoms, maternal sensitivity, and child functioning at 36 months. *Developmental Psychology, 35,* 1297–1310.

National Research Council. (1993). *Understanding child abuse and neglect.* Washington, DC: National Academy of Sciences.

Nelson, B. (1984). *Making an issue of child abuse.* Chicago: University of Chicago Press.

Nelson, C. A., & Bloom, F. E. (1997). Child development and neuroscience. *Child Development, 68,* 970–987.

Noam, G. (1992). Development as the aim of clinical intervention. *Development and Psychopathology, 4,* 679–696.

Olds, D., Eckenrode, J., Henderson, C., Kitzman, H., Powers, J., Cole, R., et al. (1997). Long-term effects of home visitation on maternal life course and child abuse and neglect: Fifteen-year follow-up of a randomized trial. *Journal of the American Medical Association, 278,* 637–643.

Olds, D., Henderson, C., Kitzman, H., Eckenrode, J., Cole, R., & Tatelbaum, R. (1998). The promise of home visitation: Results of two randomized trials. *Journal of Community Psychology, 26,* 5–21.

Olds, D. L., & Kitzman, H. (1990). Can home visitation improve the health of women and children at environmental risk? *Pediatrics, 86,* 108–116.

Oppenheim, D., Emde, R. N., & Warren, S. (1997). Children's narrative representations of mothers: Their development and associations with child and mother adaptation. *Child Development, 68,* 127–138.

Perner, J. (1991). *Understanding the representational mind.* Cambridge, MA: MIT Press.

Pipp, S., & Harmon, R. J. (1987). Attachment as regulation: A commentary. *Child Development, 58,* 648–652.

Plomin, R., & Rutter, M. (1998). Child development, molecular genetics, and what to do with genes once they are found. *Child Development, 69,* 1223–1242.

Plotsky, P. M., & Meaney, M. J. (1993). Early, postnatal experience alters hypothalamic corticotropin-releasing factor (CRF) mRNA, median eminence CRF content and stress-induced release in adult rats. *Molecular Brain Research, 18,* 195–200.

Pollak, S. D., Cicchetti, D., Hornung, K., & Reed, A. (2000). Recognizing emotion in faces: Developmental effects of child abuse and neglect. *Developmental Psychology, 36,* 679–688.

Pollak, S. D., & Kistler, D. (2002). Early experience alters categorical representations for facial expressions of emotion. *Proceedings of the National Academy of Sciences, USA, 99,* 9072–9076.

Pollak, S. D., & Sinha, P. (2002). Effects of early experience on children's recognition of facial displays of emotion. *Developmental Psychology, 38,* 784–791.

Pollak, S. D., & Tolley-Schell, S. A. (2003). Selective attention to facial emotion in physically abused children. *Journal of Abnormal Psychology, 112,* 323–338.

Post, R., Weiss, S. R. B., & Leverich, G. S. (1994). Recurrent affective disorder: Roots in developmental neurobiology and illness progression based on changes in gene expression. *Development and Psychopathology, 6,* 781–814.

Prevent Child Abuse America. (2001). *Total estimated cost of child abuse and neglect in the United States.* Available from www.preventchildabuse.org/research_ctr/cost_analysis.pdf.

Quinton, D., & Rutter, M. (1988). *Parenting and breakdown: The making and breaking of intergenerational links.* Aldershot, England: Avebury.

Radke-Yarrow, M., Belmont, B., Nottelmann, E., & Bottomly, L. (1990). Young children's self-conceptions: Origins in the natural discourse of depressed and normal mothers and their children. In D. Cicchetti & M. Beeghly (Eds.), *The self in transition* (pp. 345–361). Chicago: University of Chicago Press.

Ray, O. (2004). How the mind hurts and heals the body. *American Psychologist, 59*(1), 29–40.

Rees, S. (2002). Functional assay systems for drug discovery at G-protein coupled receptors and ion channels. *Receptors Channels, 8*(5/6), 257–259.

Reiss, D., & Price, R. H. (1996). National research agenda for prevention research: National Institute of Mental Health report. *American Psychologist, 51,* 1109–1115.

Richters, J. E. (1997). The Hubble hypothesis and the developmentalist's dilemma. *Development and Psychopathology, 9,* 193–229.

Richters, J. E., & Cicchetti, D. (1993). Mark Twain meets DSM-III-R: Conduct disorder, development, and the concept of harmful dysfunction. *Development and Psychopathology, 5,* 5–29.

Rieder, C., & Cicchetti, D. (1989). Organizational perspective on cognitive control functioning and cognitive-affective balance in maltreated children. *Developmental Psychology, 25,* 382–393.

Robins, L., Helzer, J., Orvaschel, H., Anthony, J., Blazer, D. G., Burnam, A., et al. (1985). Diagnostic Interview Schedule. In W. Eaton & L. Kessler (Eds.), *Epidemiologic field methods in psychiatry* (pp. 143–170). New York: Academic Press.

Robinson, J., Mantz-Simmons, L., & Macfie, J. (1991). *The narrative coding manual.* Unpublished manuscript.

Rogosch, F. A., & Cicchetti, D. (1994). Illustrating the interface of family and peer relations through the study of child maltreatment. *Social Development, 3,* 291–308.

Rogosch, F. A., Cicchetti, D., & Aber, J. L. (1995). The role of child maltreatment in early deviations in cognitive and affective processing abilities and later peer relationship problems. *Development and Psychopathology, 7,* 591–609.

Rogosch, F. A., Cicchetti, D., & Toth, S. L. (2004). Expressed emotion in multiple subsystems of the families of toddlers with depressed mothers. *Development and Psychopathology, 16,* 689–710.

Rutter, M. (1986). Child psychiatry: The interface between clinical and developmental research. *Psychological Medicine, 16,* 151–160.

Rutter, M. (1990). Psychosocial resilience and protective mechanisms. In J. Rolf, A. S. Masten, D. Cicchetti, K. Nuechterlein, & S. Weintraub (Eds.), *Risk and protective factors in the development of psychopathology* (pp. 181–214). New York: Cambridge University Press.

Rutter, M. (1996). Developmental psychopathology: Concepts and prospects. In M. F. Lenzenweger & J. J. Haugaard (Eds.), *Frontiers of developmental psychopathology* (pp. 209–237). New York: Oxford University Press.

Rutter, M., Dunn, J., Plomin, R., Simonoff, E., Pickles, A., Maughan, B., et al. (1997). Integrating nature and nurture: Implications of person-environment correlations and interactions for developmental psychopathology. *Development and Psychopathology, 9,* 335–364.

Rutter, M., & Garmezy, N. (1983). Developmental psychopathology. In E. M. Hetherington (Ed.), *Handbook of child psychology* (4th ed., Vol. 4, pp. 774–911). New York: Wiley.

Rutter, M., & Sroufe, L. A. (2000). Developmental psychopathology: Concepts and challenges. *Development and Psychopathology, 12,* 265–296.

Sameroff, A. J. (2000). Developmental systems and psychopathology. *Development and Psychopathology, 12,* 297–312.

Sanchez, M. M., Ladd, C. O., & Plotsky, P. M. (2001). Early adverse experience as a developmental risk factor for later psychopathology: Evidence from rodent and primate models. *Development and Psychopathology, 13,* 419–450.

Santostefano, S. (1978). *A bio-developmental approach to clinical child psychology.* New York: Wiley.

Santostefano, S., & Baker, H. (1972). The contribution of developmental psychology. In B. Wolman (Ed.), *Manual of child psychopathology* (pp. 1113–1153). New York: McGraw-Hill.

Schneider-Rosen, K., Braunwald, K., Carlson, V., & Cicchetti, D. (1985). Current perspectives in attachment theory: Illustrations from the study of maltreated infants. *Monographs of the Society for Research in Child Development, 50,* 194–210.

Schneider-Rosen, K., & Cicchetti, D. (1991). Early self-knowledge and emotional development: Visual self-recognition and affective reactions to mirror self-image in maltreated and nonmaltreated toddlers. *Developmental Psychology, 27,* 481–488.

Schore, A. N. (1994). *Affect regulation and the origin of the self: The neurobiology of emotional development.* Hillsdale, NJ: Erlbaum.

Schore, A. N. (2003a). *Affect regulation and disorders of the self.* New York: Norton.

Schore, A. N. (2003b). *Affect regulation and the repair of the self.* New York: Norton.

Schulenberg, J., Sameroff, A., & Cicchetti, D. (Eds.). (2004). The transition from adolescence to adulthood [Special issue]. *Development and Psychopathology, 16*(4).

Schwartz, J. L., Yerushalmy, M., & Wilson, B. (Eds.). (1993). *The geometric supposer: Vol. 6. What is it a case of?* Hillsdale, NJ: Erlbaum.

Serafica, F. C. (1997). Psychopathology and resilience in Asian American children and adolescents. *Applied Developmental Science, 1,* 145–155.

Shields, A., & Cicchetti, D. (1998). Reactive aggression among maltreated children: The contributions of attention and emotion dysregulation. *Journal of Clinical Child Psychology, 27,* 381–395.

Shields, A., & Cicchetti, D. (2001). Parental maltreatment and emotion dysregulation as risk factors for bullying and victimization in middle childhood. *Journal of Clinical Child Psychology, 30,* 349–363.

Shields, A., Cicchetti, D., & Ryan, R. M. (1994). The development of emotional and behavioral self regulation and social competence among maltreated school-age children. *Development and Psychopathology, 6,* 57–75.

Shields, A., Ryan, R. M., & Cicchetti, D. (2001). Narrative representations of caregivers and emotion dysregulation as predictors of maltreated children's rejection by peers. *Developmental Psychology, 37,* 321–337.

Shirk, S. R. (1999). Integrated child psychotherapy: Treatment ingredients in search of a recipe. In S. W. Russ & T. H. Ollendick (Eds.), *Handbook of psychotherapies with children and families: Issues in clinical child psychology* (pp. 369–384). Dordrecht, The Netherlands: Kluwer Academic.

Shirk, S. R., Talmi, A., & Olds, D. (2000). A developmental psychopathology perspective on child and adolescent treatment policy. *Development and Psychopathology, 12,* 835–855.

Shonk, S. M., & Cicchetti, D. (2001). Maltreatment, competency deficits, and risk for academic and behavioral maladjustment. *Developmental Psychology, 37,* 3–14.

Shweder, R. A., & Bourne, E. J. (1991). Does the concept of the person vary cross-culturally? In R. A. Shweder & R. A. LeVine (Eds.), *Culture theory: Essays on mind, self and emotion* (pp. 158–199). Cambridge: Cambridge University Press.

Simon, G. E. (2003). Social and economic burden of mood disorders. *Biological Psychiatry, 54*(3), 208–215.

Spiker, D., & Ricks, M. (1984). Visual self-recognition in autistic children: Developmental relationships. *Child Development, 55*(1), 214–225.

Sroufe, L. A. (1996). *Emotional development: The organization of emotional life in the early years.* New York: Cambridge University Press.

Sroufe, L. A., Carlson, E. A., Levy, A. K., & Egeland, B. (1999). Implications of attachment theory for developmental psychopathology. *Development and Psychopathology, 11,* 1–13.

Sroufe, L. A., & Fleeson, J. (1988). The coherence of family relationships. In R. A. Hinde & J. Stevenson-Hinde (Eds.), *Relationships within families: Mutual influences* (pp. 27–47). Oxford: Oxford University Press.

Sroufe, L. A., & Rutter, M. (1984). The domain of developmental psychopathology. *Child Development, 55,* 17–29.

Sroufe, L. A., & Waters, E. (1977). Attachment as an organizational construct. *Child Development, 48,* 1184–1199.

Stern, D. N. (1995). *The motherhood constellation: A unified view of parent-infant psychotherapy.* New York: Basic Books.

Stovall, G., & Craig, R. J. (1990). Mental representations of physically and sexually abused latency-aged females. *Child Abuse and Neglect, 14,* 233–242.

Thompson, R. (1998). Early sociopersonality development. In W. Damon & N. Eisenberg (Eds.), *Handbook of child psychology* (5th ed., Vol. 3, pp. 25–104). New York: Wiley.

Thompson, R. A., & Calkins, S. D. (1996). The double-edged sword: Emotional regulation for children at risk. *Development and Psychopathology, 8,* 163–182.

Toth, S. L., & Cicchetti, D. (1993). Child maltreatment: Where do we go from here in our treatment of victims? In D. Cicchetti & S. L. Toth (Eds.), *Child abuse, child development, and social policy* (pp. 399–438). Norwood, NJ: Ablex.

Toth, S. L., & Cicchetti, D. (1996). Patterns of relatedness and depressive symptomatology in maltreated children. *Journal of Consulting and Clinical Psychology, 64,* 32–41.

Toth, S. L., & Cicchetti, D. (1998). Remembering, forgetting, and the effects of trauma on memory: A developmental psychopathology perspective. *Development and Psychopathology, 10,* 589–605.

Toth, S. L., & Cicchetti, D. (1999). Developmental psychopathology and child psychotherapy. In S. Russ & T. Ollendick (Eds.), *Handbook of psychotherapies with children and families* (pp. 15–44). New York: Plenum Press.

Toth, S. L., Cicchetti, D., Macfie, J., & Emde, R. N. (1997). Representations of self and other in the narratives of neglected, physically abused, and sexually abused preschoolers. *Development and Psychopathology, 9,* 781–796.

Toth, S. L., Cicchetti, D., Macfie, J., Maughan, A., & VanMeenan, K. (2000). Narrative representations of caregivers and self in maltreated preschoolers. *Attachment and Human Development, 2,* 271–305.

Toth, S. L., Manly, J. T., & Cicchetti, D. (1992). Child maltreatment and vulnerability to depression. *Development and Psychopathology, 4,* 97–112.

Toth, S. L., Maughan, A., Manly, J. T., Spagnola, M., & Cicchetti, D. (2002). The relative efficacy of two interventions in altering maltreated preschool children's representational models: Implications for attachment theory. *Development and Psychopathology, 14,* 777–808.

Trickett, P. K., Aber, J. L., Carlson, V., & Cicchetti, D. (1991). The relationship of socioeconomic status to the etiology and developmental sequelae of physical child abuse. *Developmental Psychology, 27,* 148–158.

Trickett, P. K., & McBride-Chang, C. (1995). The developmental impact of different types of child abuse and neglect. *Developmental Review, 15,* 311–337.

Troy, M., & Sroufe, L. A. (1987). Victimization among preschoolers: The role of attachment relationship history. *Journal of the American Academy of Child and Adolescent Psychiatry, 26,* 166–172.

United States Advisory Board on Child Abuse and Neglect. (1990). *Child abuse and neglect: Critical first steps in response to a national emergency.* Washington, DC: U.S. Department of health and Human Services.

United States Congress. (1988). *Healthy children: Investing in the future.* Washington, DC: U.S. Government printing Office.

U.S. Department of Health and Human Services. (1988). *Executive summary: Study of national incidence and prevalence of child abuse and neglect.* Washington, DC: Author.

U.S. Department of Health and Human Services. (1999). *Mental health: A report of the surgeon general.* Rockville, MD: Author.

U.S. Department of Health and Human Services. (2001). *Child maltreatment.* Washington, DC: U.S. Government Printing Office.

van IJzendoorn, M. H., Juffer, F., & Duyvesteyn, M. G. C. (1995). Breaking the intergenerational cycle of insecure attachment: A review of the effects of attachment-based interventions on maternal sensitivity and infant security. *Journal of Child Psychology and Psychiatry, 36,* 225–248.

van IJzendoorn, M. H., Tavecchio, L. W. C., Stams, G. J. J. M., Verhoeven, M. J. E., & Reiling, E. J. (1998). Attunement between parents and professional caregivers: A comparison of child-rearing attitudes in different child-care settings. *Journal of Marriage and the Family, 60,* 771–781.

Vaughn, B. E., & Waters, E. (1990). Attachment behavior at home and in the laboratory: Q-Sort observations and Strange Situation classifications of 1-year-olds. *Child Development, 61,* 1965–1973.

Wachs, T. D., & Plomin, R. (Eds.). (1991). *Conceptualization and measurement of organism-environment interaction.* W. Lafayette, IN: Purdue University Press.

Waddington, C. H. (1957). *The strategy of genes.* London: Allen & Unwin.

Waters, E. (1995). Appendix A: The Attachment Q-set (version 3.0). *Monographs of the Society for Research in Child Development, 60,* 234–246.

Wechsler, D. (1989). *Manual for the Wechsler Preschool and Primary Scale of Intelligence-Revised (WPPSI-R).* San Antonio, TX: Psychological Corporation.

Weisz, J. R., Donenberg, G. R., Han, S. S., & Weiss, B. (1995). Bridging the gap between laboratory and clinic in child and adolescent psychiatry. *Journal of Consulting and Clinical Psychology, 63,* 688–701.

Weisz, J. R., Rudolph, K. D., Granger, D. A., & Sweeney, L. (1992). Cognition, competence, and coping in child and adolescent depression: Research findings, developmental concerns, therapeutic implications. *Development and Psychopathology, 4,* 627–653.

Wellman, H. M. (1990). *The child's theory of mind.* Cambridge, MA: MIT Press.

Wellman, H. M., Cross, D., & Watson, J. (2001). Meta-analysis of theory-of-mind development: The truth about false beliefs. *Child Development, 72,* 655–684.

Wells, C. S., Subkoviak, M. J., & Serlin, R. C. (2002). The effect of item parameter drift on examinee ability estimates. *Applied Psychological Measurement, 26*(1), 77–87.

Werner, H., & Kaplan, B. (1963). *Symbol formation.* New York: Wiley.

Westen, D. (1994). The impact of sexual abuse on self structure. In D. Cicchetti & S. L. Toth (Eds.), *Rochester Symposium on Developmental Psychopathology* (Vol. 5, pp. 223–250). Rochester, NY: University of Rochester Press.

Wolfe, D. A. (1987). *Child abuse: Implications for child development and psychopathology.* Newbury Park, CA: Sage.

Zigler, E. (1998). A place of value for applied and policy studies. *Child Development, 69,* 532–542.

Zigler, E., & Glick, M. (1986). *A developmental approach to adult psychopathology.* New York: Wiley.

CHAPTER 14

Families and Early Childhood Interventions

DOUGLAS R. POWELL

Ensuring the well-being of at-risk children through supportive assistance to their families is a powerful idea that has driven a substantial amount of early intervention research and program development activity. Since the early 1970s, a diverse set of interventions has been developed to help families promote positive child outcomes. Programs vary in the substantive focus of assistance to families, from parenting and child-rearing responsibilities, to family connections with community services, to job skills. Intervention methods may include home visiting, group sessions at a program center, and/or case management, sometimes provided in a concurrent or sequential arrangement with a center-based early childhood program. Staff who work directly with families may be professionals or paraprofessionals.

In spite of varied program efforts, the expectation that intervention with families will enable children to succeed in life has yet to be fully realized. Some interventions have produced short- and long-term positive effects; many other interventions have yielded weak effects, sometimes on a small number of outcomes, or no effects.

Reasons for the overall mixed picture of results have received limited attention in the scholarly literature. Reviews of early intervention research have tended to juxtapose direct work with the child versus the family in an attempt to identify the most beneficial approach. The problem with this analysis strategy is that it ignores issues of quality in intervention design, implementation, and evaluation. Discerning what seems to work and not work in approaches to families in early interventions requires respectful attention to variations in intervention design. Considerations of quality also necessitate a careful look at common problems in intervention re-

I am grateful to Carolyn Pape Cowan, Philip A. Cowan, and Joan E. Grusec for thoughtful reviews of an earlier draft of this chapter; to Karen E. Diamond, K. Ann Renninger, and Irving E. Sigel for helping me shape the chapter's focus; and to James S. Bates for gathering material and reviewing successive drafts.

search: simplistic or poorly conceptualized program models, mismatches between program approach and population circumstances, inadequate implementation of a program model, and faulty research designs, including inappropriate and/or insensitive measures.

An increasingly common conclusion of analyses of the early intervention literature is that researchers need to look more carefully into the "black box" of programs to determine the process by which interventions contribute, or fall short of contributing, to improvements in children's well-being (e.g., Brooks-Gunn, Berlin, & Fuligni, 2000; Gomby, Culross, & Behrman, 1999; National Research Council and Institute of Medicine, 2000). Accordingly, a closer examination of research on the role of families in early interventions holds promise of identifying factors and patterns that warrant attention in program design decisions and in future intervention research.

CHAPTER PURPOSE AND ORGANIZATION

The purpose of this chapter is to identify potentially critical characteristics of effective approaches to families in interventions aimed at enhancing the well-being of at-risk children from birth to 5 years of age. To this end, the chapter examines variations in the design of interventions with regard to programmatic elements of support to families (e.g., staffing, intensity) and different combinations of program content and participant roles. It also describes conceptual and empirical influences on program design and identifies needed directions in research aimed at discerning what works in the relation of families to early childhood interventions.

A premise of the chapter is that a major decision in the design and delivery of early childhood interventions is how much and what type of programmatic room to make for families. The issue is not a dichotomous matter of whether early interventions should include provisions for families. Even early interventions that seek to compensate for deficiencies in family functioning by providing a year-round, full-day educational program for young children include modest voluntary options for connecting with families. The current sociopolitical climate—particularly values underlying parental rights and respect for family cultures and traditions—ensures that, at a minimum, interventions will give rhetorical if not nominal attention to families.

Consistent with purposes of this volume, an assumption of the chapter is that readers have an interest in the

application of research to pressing societal problems. Most of the chapter is organized by program variables, and attention is given to issues in translating research to practice and in conducting intervention research.

After defining key terms and the literature included in this chapter, I describe in general terms how conceptualizations of families and empirical knowledge from developmental and intervention researches have shaped the development of family interventions. A goal of this section is to provide an orientation to substantive bases of intervention approaches to families. At the same time, the section acknowledges the limitations of the extant research literature and provides a case description of the process of applying conceptualizations of families and research knowledge to the development of practice guidelines for a federally sponsored family intervention program.

The chapter then moves to a major section on elements of program support to families with young children. The section is organized around seven areas requiring decisions in the design and implementation of family interventions. The variables examined here include leading candidates for indicators of quality in interventions with families. If the field eventually is successful in a search for what works in early intervention, the list of attributes of effective interventions with families likely will include some of the factors described here. This section partly addresses the chapter's secondary interest in the translation of research to practice. It is organized by program variables and draws on developmental and intervention research literatures in an attempt to demonstrate the benefits of using findings from both types of investigations.

The section on elements of program support to families is followed by an examination of five basic designs of family interventions in early childhood. The designs are defined by the program participant status of parents (i.e., adjunct, supplementary, primary) and by the scope of program goals and content focused on family functioning (i.e., child- versus broad-focused). These two dimensions represent dominant perspectives on how best to achieve better outcomes for children at risk. Illustrative interventions are described in each of the five basic program designs, with attention to program content and methods, effects, and whether and how parent or family factors contribute to child outcomes.

The chapter's concluding section identifies needed directions in family intervention program development and research. Themes of this section emphasize intervention responsiveness to family circumstances and use of rigorous research methods in an incremental manner to determine effective intervention elements.

DEFINITIONAL AND LITERATURE PARAMETERS

Early intervention refers to *a broad array of activities designed to enhance a young child's development* (Ramey & Ramey, 1998, p. 110). These activities typically are provided through programs of early education and care, services aimed at promoting positive parenting and/or family functioning, and individualized developmental or therapeutic services. Individual programs provide activities in one or more of these areas through center- and/or home-based delivery systems.

There are two main literatures on early intervention, defined by population group: children considered to be at risk of developmental delay or academic difficulty, generally due to family economic or educational status, and children with identified disabilities or developmental delays. Programs serving the at-risk group tend to emphasize the prevention of negative outcomes, whereas interventions serving children with identified disabilities or delays typically are viewed as remediation or treatment programs (Ramey & Ramey, 1998).

Although the two literatures on early intervention are seldom combined, in practice the program and population boundaries are blurred. For example, early intervention for young children with identified disabilities and developmental delays supported by the federal Individuals with Disabilities Education Act may, at state discretion, provide supports to children judged to be at risk (e.g., multiproblem family). Head Start, conceived as a program for children at risk due to poverty, requires that a minimum of 10% of children have identified disabilities but does not impose a low-income requirement as a program eligibility criterion for children with disabilities. Families with children receiving early intervention services do not fall neatly into two groups. One recent study of state early intervention services for children with identified disabilities and developmental delays found that families of children with developmental delay had a median annual gross income just above the poverty level (Diamond & Kontos, 2004).

This chapter focuses primarily on early intervention for children deemed to be at risk of developmental delay or academic difficulty. The risk indicators here generally include family socioeconomic status, adolescent parenthood, and premature and low birthweight status. In a modest step toward bridging the two early intervention literatures, the chapter also draws on research on early intervention for children with identified disabilities or developmental delays. Certainly there are issues unique to poverty and to disabilities that deserve careful attention in designing and understanding early intervention, and caution is needed with generalizations. At the same time, consideration of commonalities and differences in findings across the two literatures provides a stronger empirical base for contemplating advances in intervention design and delivery.

Because the parent-child dyad is of special interest to work with families in early intervention, the chapter gives specific attention to *parenting*. I use an adaptation of Bornstein's (2000) definition of parenting, particularly *direct effects on children of experiences that parents provide, including parents' beliefs and behaviors, and indirect effects which take place through parents' relationships with each other, the daily routines and objects (e.g., books) available in the home environment, and their connections to extrafamilial support systems.*

Due to space limitations, the chapter is based on early intervention research conducted in the United States. The international literature offers a rich comparative perspective on early childhood intervention (Boocock & Larner, 1998), including research on several family interventions similar to programs examined in the United States (e.g., Westheimer, 2003) and follow-up studies of intervention effects such as a recent set of longitudinal investigations sponsored by the Bernard van Leer Foundation (www.bernardvanleer.org).

INFLUENCES ON THE ROLE OF FAMILIES IN EARLY CHILDHOOD INTERVENTIONS

Approaches to families in early childhood interventions in the United States have been shaped by conceptualizations of families and the findings of research on interventions and on children's development in diverse family contexts. Each of these domains of influence is described here. To illustrate the contribution of these influences to intervention work with families, the section ends with a case description of the process through which a content framework was developed for the parenting education component of the federal Even Start Family Literacy Program.

Conceptualizations of Families

The form, substance, and process of approaches to family interventions may be traced to powerful ideas about family contributions to children's development, the contexts of family functioning, and family resourcefulness. Origins of these ideas include theory and research as well as sociopolitical developments, particularly growing population diversity in the United States, the Civil Rights movement, and the War on Poverty. Influential constructs are the object of critical commentary and periodic refinement, and, as noted in the following discussion, each of the prevalent perspectives on families is in transition as intervention programs yield information on the experiences of putting ideas into practice, scholars question the empirical base of prevailing assumptions, and social policies such as welfare reform shape family life.

Families as Developmental Contexts

Central to the early intervention field is the idea that families are a significant context of early development. For decades the notion that "families matter" has been bolstered by theories and scientific evidence pointing to the lasting impact of families on children's development and by research on the formative quality of the early years.

Results of research linking family variables to child outcomes do not necessarily lead to rationales for interventions aimed at changing and supporting families. Some scholars have concluded from the family effects literature that early intervention should compensate for, and seek to reduce, family deficiencies by placing the child in a high-quality early childhood program for most of the child's waking hours, preferably as early in life as possible. In extrapolations based on results of a longitudinal study of family language interactions and children's intellectual outcomes, for example, Hart and Risley (1995) estimated that children in families receiving welfare would need 41 hours per week of language-rich, out-of-home experiences per week from birth to equal the language experiences of children in average working-class families.

In contrast, other researchers have inferred from the family effects literature that a potentially more power-

ful and efficient way to improve child outcomes is to support family capacity to promote the healthy development of children. Early childhood interventions that include complementary or exclusive work with families are assumed to produce more powerful effects through enduring changes in parenting and other family processes than interventions that give minimal or no substantive attention to parents and other family members. An influential report by Bronfenbrenner (1974, p. 300) on effects of early intervention bolstered this argument with the conclusion that "without family involvement, intervention is likely to be unsuccessful, and what few effects are achieved are likely to disappear once the intervention is discontinued." This conclusion was based largely on findings of several intervention studies (e.g., Radin, 1972) indicating that parent participation in the intervention helped to sustain IQ gains after the program ended. Hence, the report reinforced the expectation of continuing support for improved child outcomes through enduring changes in families.

The merits of child- and family-oriented programs have long been debated in the early intervention literature (e.g., Zigler & Berman, 1983) and today remain an active area of empirical investigation (e.g., Barnett, Young, & Schweinhart, 1998; Reynolds, Ou, & Topitzes, 2004). At the core of this main feature of intervention design are theoretical differences in whether the primary locus of forces regulating developmental change is internal or external to the child or a product of interaction between internal and external forces (P. A. Cowan, Powell, & Cowan, 1998). Although treatments of this topic often dichotomize the issue as child-versus parent-focused intervention, in reality programs differ in the amount and type of attention given to parents. All theories of child development have assumed that laypersons need expert guidance in the rearing of young children (Kessen, 1979), and parent education has been viewed as a part of early childhood programs since the establishment of nursery schools in the United States in the early 1900s (D. R. Powell & Diamond, 1995). A major distinction across programs, then, is the extent to which intervention with the family is considered integral to achieving sustained positive effects on the child.

The magnitude of family effects on children—overstated at times in research, policy, and early intervention arenas—has been challenged vigorously since the mid-1990s (Rowe, 1994), notably in Harris's (1995,

1998) argument that parents have little or no influence on their children's outcomes. Her position has received considerable academic attention (e.g., Collins, Maccoby, Steinberg, Hetherington, & Bornstein, 2000; Okagaki & Luster, 2005), and it remains to be seen whether a "parents don't matter" perspective ultimately will influence early intervention approaches to families. For the short term, criticisms of the family effects literature have increased research interest in family interventions because interventions with parents are the best means available to social scientists for testing the magnitude of family effects on children (P. A. Cowan & Cowan, 2002), including Harris's (2002) argument that changes in child behavior via intervention in the home environment will not transfer to changes in a child's behavior at school or in other settings that do not involve the parent.

Families in Context

Since the mid-1970s, the early intervention field has been influenced by the idea that families are embedded in an interconnected system of formal and informal resources at neighborhood and community levels that vary dramatically in the provision of supports for individual and family well-being. Interveners often communicate the essence of the developmental literature on contextualism by citing the African proverb "It takes a whole village to raise a child." The prominence of this idea has been advanced in part by societal interest in the consequences of a rapidly changing social landscape characterized by increases in single-parent households, mothers working outside the home, and the racial, ethnic, and linguistic diversity of families.

A major contribution of ecological perspectives to the early intervention field is increased awareness of population differences. A priori assumptions cannot be made that characteristics identified in one or several groups exist or function in the same way in another group (Lerner, 1998), and interventions found to be effective or ineffective with one population or context may have a different pattern of results with a different population or context. The notion that a particular program model or strategy can work with any family or parent has been replaced by questions about appropriate ways to achieve program responsiveness to family circumstances (D. R. Powell, 2005).

Theory and research on the ecology of human development also has expanded the content boundaries of intervention interest in family functioning. The popularity of the "whole village" statement represents a broadening, and sometimes abandonment, of program models that assume the primary task with families is to provide information on child development and parenting. In addition to or in lieu of parenting education, interventions increasingly seek to strengthen a family's connections with its larger environment as a means of improving family support of positive child outcomes. One of four goals of the federal Early Head Start Program, for example, is community development, including improvements in child care quality, community collaboration, and the integration of supportive services to families (Love et al., 2002). Programs also may attempt to facilitate use of social support provided through informal sources such as family, friends, and neighbors (Dunst, 2000).

Many interventions targeted at low-income families take special interest in parents' economic self-sufficiency skills as a pathway to improved family functioning and child outcomes. To this end, programs provide services aimed at strengthening parents' employment-related skills as well as child development services that may include early childhood programs, parenting education, and preventive health care. Interventions adhering to this approach, commonly called two-generation programs (Smith & Zaslow, 1995), are congruent with welfare reform policies that require labor force participation and with changes in norms regarding women's roles in society.

Family interventions have encountered challenges in translating broad constructs about family contexts to the level of program design and implementation. A critical and unresolved matter is determining specific variables that can be efficiently and effectively targeted in myriad interrelated and powerful influences on the daily functioning of families living in poverty and other high-risk conditions. In recognition of the absence of a magic bullet, program designers have embraced the concept of comprehensive services to families but struggled with the availability, integration, and quality of existing services provided by different agencies operating under different categorical funding streams and assumptions about how best to support families (e.g., St. Pierre, Layzer, & Barnes, 1998). There is a risk of minimal or diffused focus on the child in social support interventions (Dunst, 2000) and limited clarity on how to substantively combine child- and family-oriented services (Mahoney et al., 1999). The field also has had to grapple with some naive expectations of the rapidity and ease by which education and employment-related services for parents contribute to improved child outcomes (e.g., teach parents to read so they can read to their children).

Families as Resourceful

A third idea with growing influence on early intervention is that family strengths should be marshaled toward the optimal development of children and parents. The strengths-based concept is supported by scholarly work on the flow of social support in natural helping systems (Cohen, Underwood, & Gottlieb, 2000), the benefits of building on strengths in efforts to promote individual and family well-being (Trivette, Dunst, & Deal, 1997), and growing interest in the promotion of positive development in contrast to the customary focus on the treatment and prevention of negative outcomes (Lerner, Fisher, & Weinberg, 2000; Pollard & Rosenberg, 2003).

The "build on family strengths" idea is in part a backlash against early intervention assumptions and practices that emphasize family deficits. The early 1960s origins of intervention programs for children from low-income families were based on a view of limitations in family child-rearing practices, particularly in the area of language use with children, as the primary cause of low-income children's school failures. A high level of optimism about the plasticity of human development during this era led to the expectation that early education programs could provide children with school readiness experiences missing in their home, thereby moving children to a more productive developmental trajectory in life. According to this view, readiness for school resides in the child, and inadequate mothering is an indirect cause of school failure. Early interventions built on these premises were deemed to be blatant forms of institutional racism (Baratz & Baratz, 1970), and policies and practices that imposed middle-class European American values and practices on other populations were harshly criticized (Laosa, 1983).

These criticisms plus the press of the Civil Rights movement and the War on Poverty led to an erosion of support for the deficit perspective beginning in the late 1960s. Significant in this paradigm change was seminal research such as Labov's (1970) work on African American dialect and Heath's (1983) study of language use in low-income communities and the success of teachers in building on cultural differences among children. There was prompt abandonment of the term "deficits" in the scholarly literature and an emphasis on "differences" in depictions of family and community language systems (Vernon-Feagans, 1996) and in descriptions of child-rearing practices (Yando, Seitz, & Zigler, 1979).

Legislative actions in the 1960s and 1970s supported the principle that families have resources to contribute to intervention programs. The call for "maximum feasible participation" of families in programs supported by the Economic Opportunity Act of 1964 functioned as an impetus for Head Start's eventual decisions on how to work with families (e.g., 51% of local policy council members are parents), and federal legislation included provisions for parental rights in decisions about a child's educational placement and treatment plan. This occurred in the context of larger concerns about rapidly increasing professional involvement in functions and decisions historically handled by the family (Lasch, 1977), ethical concerns about professional manipulation of parents in intervention programs (Hess, 1980; Sigel, 1983), and whether the scientific base of child development was sufficiently rigorous and definitive to warrant professional edicts about how to rear young children (Cochran & Woolever, 1983), particularly in racial and ethnic minority families.

Current professional standards for early intervention reflect a view of families as resourceful contributors to program decisions and actions. The emphasis is on partnerships that promote family capacities and ensure shared decision making with program staff rather than view parents as helpmates in implementing program-determined agendas (D. R. Powell, 2001). Early intervention work with families is to focus on promotion (versus treatment), individuals exercising existing capabilities and developing new competencies (versus professionals solving problems for people), defining practice from a broad range of community resources (versus mostly or exclusively professional services), and programs as agents of families, responsive to family desires and concerns (versus professionals as experts who determine clients' needs; Dunst & Trivette, 1997).

Evidence suggests there is a gap between principles and practice in the implementation of standards regarding program relationships with families. Studies point to limited attention to family outcomes and supports in individualized family service plans (e.g., McWilliam et al., 1998), for example. The emphasis on family resourcefulness has triggered clarifications of the roles of professionals in early interventions (Buysse & Wesley, 1993) and reconsiderations of professional preparation for working with families (McBride & Brotherson, 1997; D. R. Powell, 2000) as programs seek ways to carry out a strengths-based approach. This situation in the early intervention field reflects conditions in a broader movement toward the promotion of child well-being wherein there is an upsurge of interest in policies and programs that promote positive outcomes, but considerable conceptual, methodological, and empirical work is needed (Moore & Keyes, 2003).

Empirical Knowledge

Prominent ideas about families provide intervention designers and staff with a common point of reference for work with families and an accessible language for communicating with policymakers and the lay public about intervention goals and practices. By themselves, however, big ideas generally offer insufficient guidance for fine-tuning the design and implementation of an intervention. Sound bite representations of basic constructs (e.g., "families matter") may foster simplistic program assumptions and actions (e.g., "when the family is okay, the child is okay"). To add essential details, program designers and staff have long turned to professional knowledge or clinical judgment derived from accumulated experiences with a population and intervention modality (Shonkoff, 2000). To a lesser extent, they also have turned to empirical research as a source of information on family intervention design and implementation. The use of education and social science to inform practice is a complex and poorly understood topic (Shonkoff, 2000; Sigel, 1998), and family interventions in early childhood are no exception to a general pattern of limited or missing connections between research and design and implementation of education and human services.

Expansion of the early intervention field has occurred along several paths with regard to the role of empirical knowledge. One is the classical research and program development strategy wherein an intervention model is tested in a single or multiple sites and replicated in additional sites only after outcome data offer promise of positive effects. Another path is implementation of a program on a large-scale basis without the benefit of results from rigorous study of smaller-scale programs to guide staged or incremental expansion of the model (Yoshikawa, Rosman, & Hsueh, 2002).

With a few striking exceptions, our knowledge of causal relations regarding the role of families in early interventions is too limited to support widespread expansion and replication of most program models. Although the use of random assignment is growing in intervention research, investigations designed to identify what works in early interventions—that is, studies with the greatest potential to inform program design and implementation decisions—generally have not used experimental designs. For instance, within-group comparisons are commonly used to determine whether intervention effects vary by population characteristics, sometimes in a post hoc search for *any* intervention effects (D. R. Powell, 2005). Moreover, randomized trials in intervention research commonly examine the effectiveness of a treatment variable that is actually a composite of many variables (e.g., curriculum, intensity, staffing), usually organized in a complex manner. In D. T. Campbell's (1986) proposed renaming of *internal validity* with *local molar causal validity,* the word *molar* represented this multivariate quality of interventions. Results of experimental study of an intervention that, in essence, is an intervention package leave to speculation the identification of important elements of an intervention. Thus, interveners who adopt some but not all of an intervention run the risk of omitting a key attribute of the program package (Shadish, Cook, & Campbell, 2002).

Our understanding of family contributions to children's development is also limited. Most of what is known about child-family context relations is derived from correlational studies. Because children cannot be randomly assigned to different environmental conditions, researchers have depended, sometimes brilliantly (e.g., effects of the Great Depression; Elder, 1974), on naturally occurring variations to examine links between child and environment. Self-selection is among the serious problems of this approach.

Further, growing interest in the role of context in child development and early intervention has accentuated issues in generalizing the results of developmental and intervention research. Three factors underlie this problem. One is the shallow level of empirical science on the diverse populations increasingly served by programs. Context and diversity have been addressed in theoretical work to a greater extent than in research, and existing research on group differences is often limited by insufficient attention to individual differences within groups and by overlaps among race, ethnicity, culture, and socioeconomic status (Garcia Coll & Magnuson, 2000). A second factor is that, as noted earlier, evidence pointing to population-specific links between child-rearing patterns and child outcomes raises questions about the need for population-specific intervention content. A small but impressive set of early intervention models have had the opportunity to address external validity questions through consecutive randomized trials with different populations and contexts (Kitzman et al., 2000; Olds, Henderson, Chamberlin, & Tatelbaum, 1986; Olds et al., 2002) or implementation with a sufficient number of ethnically diverse families to permit analyses by population group (Reid, Webster-Stratton, & Beauchaine, 2001). A third factor is disagreements both in developmental and intervention research literatures regarding the extent to which universal knowledge is possible. Relativistic arguments that all developmental processes are culturally dependent (e.g., Shweder, 1993) or that interventions cannot be objectively defined (e.g., Olson, 2003) essentially imply that each intervention needs to invent itself.

An obvious consequence of this state of developmental and intervention research is that empirical science cannot be used to significantly help interventions act on some currently prominent ideas on how to work with families. One example is the growing interest in fathers. Research on father-child relationships across different contexts has matured in the past 2 decades (Lamb, 2003), but intervention research has not kept pace with increases in the range of programs and program components targeted at fathers (Mincy & Pouncy, 2002). Another example is the emphasis on family systems. References to families and to family systems dominate descriptions of early intervention understandings of children's developmental contexts, but family systems research is an emerging topic in the developmental sciences. The empirical literature on family effects is primarily about parenting and parent-child interactions and relationships (Parke & Buriel, 1998). Not surprisingly, most "family-oriented" program practices are a variant of parenting education generally aimed at mothers. A less obvious consequence of research limitations is that ethical problems arise when interveners fill data voids with information or advice to families that transcends the limits of empirical science or overstate the effectiveness of an intervention to participants and policymakers (P. A. Cowan et al., 1998).

Future generations of intervention programs may have the benefit of more and better information on causal relations in child-family interactions and intervention processes. Currently, there is strong emphasis on internal validity in experimental research. Influential reports recommend greater use of rigorous intervention studies to improve child outcomes (e.g., National Research Council, 2002; National Research Council and Institute of Medicine, 2000), for example, and the federal government is shaping the dissemination of findings from research on replicable interventions within a "best practices" framework (e.g., the What Works Clearinghouse established by the Institute of Education Science).

More and better research data on context and diversity eventually may provide an empirical basis for determining what type of population-specific content is needed in interventions with particular populations. In time, a more robust database also may help shift the focus of existing debates about the utility of generalizations. A major task in generating a culturally sensitive approach to the study of child development is to strike a balance between cultural relativism and absolute universalism (Parke, 2004). In the absence of adequate research knowledge, a strategy of forming relationships with families that enable their idiosyncratic strengths to shape the intervention process is far superior to the risks of attempting to translate a limited database into intervention content (Brinker, 1992).

A certain level of local reinvention in the development of an intervention may be a necessary step as interveners actively learn the boundaries and details of their collective and individual work. Generalizations are broadband by definition and typically in need of fine-tuning in applications to particular contexts. Local data can play a complementary role here. For example, Neuman and her colleagues (Neuman, Hagedorn, Celano, & Daly, 1995) gathered data on African American adolescent mothers' beliefs about children's literacy development and used their findings, which emphasized within-group differences, to individualize the presentation of program content. As a complement to locally generated data and to the relatively small samples common to developmental research, national survey data on families and young children offer a potentially useful source of information to developers and implementers of intervention programs. One recent national survey, for example, found that nearly 80% of parents reported that grandparents lived within an hour's drive from their home, and 70% reported having many friends and relatives they can count on. These data appear to refute the typical portrayal of young families disconnected from family and friends due to geographic mobility (Halfon & McLearn, 2002).

A Case Illustration

In 1998, I was invited by the federal administrator responsible for the Even Start Family Literacy Program in the U.S. Department of Education to develop guidance to local programs regarding the content and method of the parenting education component of the Even Start Program. The assignment was carried out in collaboration with Diane D'Angelo, a seasoned early childhood practitioner and senior staff member at the RMC Research Corporation, and resulted in a U.S. Department of Education publication (D. R. Powell & D'Angelo, 2000; see also D. R. Powell, 2004) widely distributed to Even Start Programs as well as numerous presentations at national and regional Even Start meetings. In essence, the assignment was an experiment in translating dominant conceptualizations of families and research on family literacy environments into concrete suggestions for programs on how to promote parenting that fosters early literacy development.

The Even Start Program was created as a demonstration program in 1988 through congressional action that called for the integration of early childhood, adult education, and parenting education into a program aimed at improving the literacy skills of all family members. Goals are to help parents become full partners in the education of their children, to assist children in reaching their full potential as learners, and to provide literacy training for their parents. Core services include early childhood education from birth to 8 years of age, adult education services that develop basic educational and literacy skills, parenting education, and joint parent-child activities focused on early literacy development. There is emphasis on programmatic integration of these core services, and families are expected to participate in all core services. To be eligible for program participation, a family must have an adult who is eligible for adult basic education and a child less than 8 years of age (St. Pierre & Swartz, 1995). The program was implemented in 76 sites in 1989, and by 1999 to 2000 had grown to more than 800 local projects.

Since the inception of Even Start, the parenting component has been a challenging aspect of the program for several reasons. One is that parenting education was defined in general terms in the legislation establishing Even Start, and programs have used a variety of commercial and locally developed curricula that generally focus on ages and stages of child development, often with little focused attention to early literacy development. Second, many Even Start Programs appeared to be staffing the parenting education component with individuals who had limited preparation for the role. In most

communities in the United States, the availability of qualified personnel to provide parenting education is severely restricted because there are few baccalaureate degree programs and certification programs in parenting education. In general, the field of parenting education is less well developed than the fields of adult education and early childhood education. There are no commonly accepted standards for parenting education; in contrast, there are highly regarded benchmarks of appropriate practice in early childhood education and in adult education. Third, across a range of programs, there have been reports of resistance from some parents to participate in parenting education (e.g., it is seen by some as a distraction from work toward the general equivalency diploma). An early national evaluation of Even Start indicated that the parenting education component was not one of the main appeals for participation. Although the anticipated results of the guidance on how the Even Start Program might improve its work with parents—a federal publication and series of conference presentations—could not be expected to significantly change this situation, the development of a conceptual framework on the role of parents in fostering children's literacy was viewed as an essential foundation for improving the Even Start parenting education component.

The guidance to programs was developed through a review of research literatures on family contributions to young children's early literacy development and early school success and on methods of parenting education; extensive consultation with family literacy program practitioners; visits to 12 local Even Start Programs for the purpose of observing promising practices in parenting education that might serve as illustrations to other programs; and feedback on early drafts of the guidance document provided by local Even Start Program staff, state coordinators of Even Start Programs, researchers familiar with the Even Start Program, and U.S. Department of Education officials.

Our first direct exposure to the challenges of finding common ground involving research-based guidance on family practices regarding early literacy and the diversity of prevailing approaches to parenting education in Even Start occurred in early consultations with practitioners about a goal statement for the parenting education component. We proposed a goal statement focused on children's literacy outcomes, in view of the larger literacy goals of the Even Start Family Literacy Program. This was well received by some practitioners but deemed to be too narrow by others who viewed the parenting education component as appropriately addressing a wide range of content, including self-esteem, the "empowerment" of parents, and coping with the difficult contexts of poverty. The compromise was a goal statement fully focused on children's literacy outcomes and content that embraces a range of topics coupled with suggestions that programs "begin where parents are" by initially engaging parents around content that seems most appropriate to their current circumstance (e.g., moved to a safer neighborhood) and eventually moving toward sustained focus on family practices that directly support children's literacy development. The goal statement is as follows: "The overall goal of parenting education in Even Start Family Literacy Programs is to strengthen parents' support of their young children's literacy development and early school success" (D. R. Powell & D'Angelo, 2000, p. 5). The content is organized into five domains:

1. Engage in language-rich parent-child interactions.
2. Provide supports for literacy in the family.
3. Hold appropriate expectations of child's learning and development.
4. Actively embrace the parenting role.
5. Form and maintain connections with community and other resources.

This compromise position initially was of concern to practitioners who wanted a report focused on a small set of specific family practices. Some Even Start Programs, for instance, promote the primary message "Read to your child," and their representatives to the consultation process wanted the guidance document to focus exclusively on this message. Our description of studies indicating that shared book reading accounted for about 8% of the variance in children's early reading abilities (e.g., Scarborough & Dobrich, 1994) often was met with disbelief. Further, our argument that research suggests there is not a silver bullet for school readiness, that many studies use composite measures of family literacy environment that make it impossible to identify specific practices or environmental conditions, and that other practices, including *how* to read with young children, should be emphasized in a guidance document typically was met with the response that program staff and parents may become confused with information on

too many family correlates of early literacy development. For these programs, content in the domain of "form and maintain connections with community and other resources" appeared to be viewed as social work, not parenting education. Further, our document did not communicate key practices through acronyms or key words found in some other research-based recommendations for parenting practices (e.g., Borkowski, Ramey, & Stile, 2002).

The literature review work also encountered the persistent issues of causality and generalizability noted in the prior section of this chapter. Our numerous consultations with practitioners made clear that prospecive users of the program guidance work desired clear language about effects of family environments and parenting practices on children's literacy outcomes. Practitioners noted, for instance, the extensive trade book literature on "10 steps to a brighter child" and indicated that, to ensure use of the guidance document, we would need to offer assurances that specific family conditions "produce" early school success, as commonly found in mass circulation periodicals and books. Our final report attempted to accommodate this situation through text that reflected the correlational nature of existing studies but a one-page summary chart that used a sentence-completion format beginning with the stem, "Parents strengthen their children's literacy development and school-related competence when they . . ." (D. R. Powell & D'Angelo, 2000, p. 6). Although confined to one page, the chart entailed more sentence-completion bullets (17 in the five aforementioned domains) than some practitioners preferred, as noted earlier.

The generalizability issues we encountered in our work stemmed primarily from the limited amount of research on low-income and ethnic minority populations—the Even Start target population—regarding family factors associated with children's literacy outcomes. Most of the research on family literacy environments focuses on parents (typically mothers), not family variables, in middle-class European American populations. Although research on parenting seems compatible with the goal of developing guidance for a parenting education component, it would be far preferable to speak to family factors in a program that seeks to serve the entire family.

Responses to these issues in the field of family literacy programs illustrate possible implications for the content of work with families in early interventions. By design, family literacy programs typically serve families with adult members who have limited levels of education and income and often are English-language learners relatively new to the United States.

The fact that the extant research literature on family contributions to children's literacy development generally does not represent populations that family interventions typically serve has generated a range of responses in the family literacy program field (D. R. Powell, Okagaki, & Bojczyk, 2004). At one end of a continuum are rationales for sharing with lower-income, ethnic minority families what we know from research on how primarily middle-class European American families successfully support children's early reading success. At the approximate midpoint are programs that seek to learn about and accommodate the interests and preferences of culturally diverse parents, while promoting practices known to foster children's literacy development in middle-class European American families. At the other end are programs organized exclusively around and within the sociocultural contexts of participants. The family support field has many historical and contemporary examples of programs that assume "the most valid and useful knowledge about the rearing of children is lodged among the people . . . rather than in the heads of college professors, trained professionals, or the books written by so-called experts" (Cochran & Woolever, 1983, p. 229). Clearly, this is a field with strikingly different perspectives on family resourcefulness.

In our consultations for development of the Even Start guide, practitioners who saw value in sharing results of existing research saw no difficulty with our plan to develop a conceptual framework based on the extant literature. For those adhering to a sociocultural perspective on family literacy, however, there was a high level of concern about a guide based heavily on research involving middle-class populations. There was specific criticism of the design and results of the aforementioned Hart and Risley (1995) study, which appeared to command a high level of receptive attention in the Department of Education at the time of our work. Some practitioners took issue with the Hart and Risley comparisons of professional, working-class, and welfare families, arguing that the language environments of low-income families had distinctive qualities not appreciated by mainstream society and that schools and other institutions needed to accommodate diverse family culture rather than expect families to change their interaction styles to accommodate schools. This is a familiar argument, of course, yet the final draft of the guide endorsed a perspective that all parties involved in the schooling enterprise, including schools and families, share joint responsibility for children's learning. Further, the guidance document's emphasis on responsiveness to cultural diversity addressed specific program practices that, based on our visits to program sites, might facilitate fuller participation of adults from diverse families in program services. For instance, we found that in many programs, the preschool component's curriculum emphasis on "follow the child's lead" in teaching practices was also carried out in the parent-child interaction time component of the program. Yet, our observations suggested that in programs strongly adhering to this approach, some parents (e.g., Latinas) appeared to view the concept as a foreign idea, apparently preferring that adults, not children, take the lead in directing the learning interaction. In contrast, programs subscribing to a more adult-led approach seemed to have a higher level of parent participation during the parent-child literacy interaction time. Our report's suggestion that programs remain flexible and responsive in their approaches to the adult-child interaction time, because not all parent populations appear to see value in the "follow the child's lead" philosophy, was controversial among practitioners expressing support for a child-centered curriculum and opposition to adult-directed learning experiences.

In many ways, development of the guidance document was a goodness-of-fit journey that entailed negotiated understandings of how programs make use of the strengths and limitations of existing research and work with what families bring to program settings. The consultation process and site visits introduced us to numerous program assumptions, often unspoken yet fully evident in program services, and our greatest challenges occurred when our understanding of the extant research literature conflicted with prevailing program ideas and practices. Because research is far from definitive in this arena, we found it appropriate and useful to organize and communicate research results through a focus on general principles and illustrative practices rather than prescriptions for practice. Perhaps the most important contribution of the guidance document is clarity on outcome (children's literacy development).

ELEMENTS OF PROGRAMMATIC SUPPORT TO FAMILIES

The design and implementation of family interventions require decisions in the following seven areas: content, participants, delivery format, intensity, staffing, targeting and recruiting families, and host agency supports for program implementation. Each of these areas may be viewed as a program lever for supporting family contributions to children's growth and development.

In this section, research on families and child development and on early intervention work with families is reviewed selectively in each of the seven program design and implementation areas to highlight options in determining the substance and form of program connections with families. The focus of many early childhood intervention studies was broadened in the mid-1980s to include questions about "what works" and "what works for whom," in addition to customary attention to program effects (Guralnick, 1997; Korfmacher, 2001; D. R. Powell, 2005). The current yield of searches for what works in early interventions is promising but insufficiently robust to offer a list of indicators of quality in intervention work with families. Accordingly, the treatment of the seven program design and implementation areas does not offer a summary of best practices.

The family and child development studies noted briefly and selectively emphasize research trends worthy of consideration in intervention design decisions. It is well beyond the scope of this chapter to summarize the family and child development research literature relevant to the specific populations and developmental domains that particular interventions address.

Distinctions between basic and applied research are increasingly blurred, if not artificial, and intervention research has considerable potential to contribute to our understanding of person-context relations in child development (P. A. Cowan & Cowan, 2002; Lerner, 1998). An intent of organizing this section by key attributes of interventions versus by type of research literatures is to demonstrate the utility of building on coordinated use of developmental and intervention researches to formulate decisions about program design and implementation aimed at improving children's well-being.

Content

A common answer to the question of what information to share with families is to use an early childhood classroom curriculum as the content base of work with families. For programs where children participate in an early childhood classroom, a presumed advantage of this strategy is curriculum continuity: Classroom activities and experiences are extended to and reinforced in the home.

A potential limitation of this arrangement is that the program does not engage a family on its own terms. That is, content may not build on unique contributions of families to children's development, including parents' goals for their children. Research on educational outcomes has long recognized the distinctive influences of families and schools on children's educational attainment (e.g., Coleman et al., 1966), and qualitative differences between parenting and teaching have been set forth theoretically (Katz, 1980). In this vein, a premise of some interventions is that learning at home is often incidental to other ongoing activities (Neuman, 1999) and that suggestions for new parent and child behaviors need to be woven into daily family routines. For interventions seeking to develop or tailor content around family research literature, the four domains of knowledge described next offer implications for program content decisions.

Early Development in Context

A starting point for decisions about the content of work with families in early intervention programs is research on family processes associated with children's development. This literature offers a broad domain of possible content for early intervention work with families, but historically interventions have narrowed their interest in families to parenting. A result is program messages about the importance of parent responsiveness, monitoring, mentoring, and modeling (Borkowski et al., 2002). Parenting is only one dimension of family processes, and, although it is an appropriate way for interveners to think about and connect with families, intervention attention to parenting may be more appropriately situated in the dynamic network of factors that affect children's development.

Research on structural dimensions of families (e.g., one-parent households) and child development has been of interest to interventions in terms of understanding how variables such as household composition might moderate program effects (e.g., Cole, Kitzman, Olds, & Sidora, 1998), but in general, family configuration has been viewed as an ethically inappropriate target of change in early interventions. Currently, this stance is being challenged by prominent initiatives and calls for the promotion of marriage (e.g., Waite & Gallagher, 2000) in federal policies and in social programs such as Head Start.

Research on racial, ethnic, and cultural contexts of family processes and child development is crucial to decisions about the content of early intervention work with families because family child-rearing beliefs and practices are embedded in these contexts (McLoyd, 1998) and because families served by early intervention increasingly represent backgrounds other than European American, although intervention staff often are European American. There is a growing literature on the child-rearing practices and concerns of different population groups, including African American, Latino, Native American, and Asian American (e.g., Parke & Buriel, 1998) and some evidence to suggest that links between parenting practices and child outcomes differ by population group. For example, mothers' reported use of harsh physical discipline has been found to be associated with a higher frequency of children's externalizing behavior problems in school for European American children but not for African American children (Deater-Deckard, Dodge, Bates, & Pettit, 1996), and ethnic group differences have been found in the relation of parents' expectations and beliefs to children's school achievement (Okagaki & Frensch, 1998).

Economic resources and parent education level are similarly influential contextual variables that often are confounded with race and ethnicity. Studies of socioeconomic status (SES) and child development outcomes are especially helpful to decisions about intervention design when results shed light on causal mechanisms by which SES influences family processes and children's outcomes (Duncan, Brooks-Gunn, Yeung, & Smith, 1998; Lerner, 2003) and when attention is given to within-group differences such as cumulative effects of stress when living in poverty (e.g., Evans, 2004; McLoyd, 1998).

At a minimum, research on population group differences in family processes and child development can be used in a due diligence effort to inform intervention staff *in general terms* about the population it seeks to serve. This is a first and critical step toward developing the cross-cultural competence of interveners (Hanson, 1992; Yutrzenka, 1995). Essential understandings here include traditional child-rearing values and practices as well as collective historical experiences such as the Native American boarding school movement (Harjo, 1993). Research on acculturation and assimilation experiences, including bicultural adaptation, is especially useful to interventions such as family literacy programs serving populations that are new to the United States and/or to mainstream systems. In addition to generating a population profile, research findings suggestive of population-

specific links between child-rearing practices and child outcomes imply a need for population-specific content in interventions with families. There has been movement in this direction in the parenting education field for African American and Latino families, but methodological limitations of existing evaluations limit our understanding of the effectiveness of these efforts (Cheng Gorman & Balter, 1997).

Family child-rearing processes are also influenced by person variables such as maternal depression (e.g., Embry & Dawson, 2002) and child temperament (e.g., Kochanska, 1997). Research on effects of a child disability on families suggests that there is increased risk of divorce and financial pressures, and indirect negative consequences for siblings (e.g., Hogan & Msall, 2002). Studies of the role of person variables in family processes, particularly bidirectional influences, can be used to inform intervention content that helps family members appropriately respond to the person characteristics of concern. Interventions that formulate goals and content around parent variables such as depression need to decide whether changes in the targeted variable provide a direct pathway to improved child outcomes *or* desired changes in the targeted parent variable are the first of several steps toward improved child outcomes (e.g., first improve relationship skills, then increase child-rearing knowledge and skills; Booth, Mitchell, Barnard, & Spieker, 1989).

Relationships as Developmental Contexts

One clear trend in child development research is the focus on interpersonal relationships as developmental contexts. Bowlby's (1969) attachment theory offers a substantive foundation of this orientation, and corresponding research now transcends the social-emotional domain generally pursued in attachment studies. For example, in a study of mother-child joint book reading, Bus and van IJzendoorn (1988) found that securely attached dyads paid more attention to reading instruction and engaged in more proto-reading, there was less need to discipline, and children were less distracted than in anxiously attached dyads. A relationships perspective on early development and learning suggests that the content of interventions with families should be framed within dyadic and other family relationships. Guidance on how to read with young children, for example, should account for the interpersonal context in which the reading takes place.

Early intervention work with families typically deals with the mother-child dyad, often independent of a family system that likely includes many other subsystems, including father-child, child-sibling, marital/partner, sibling-parent, and extended kith and kin systems. Theoretical models of linkages among family subsystems (e.g., Luster & Okagaki, 1993; Parke & Buriel, 1998) and of a family systems approach to parenting interventions (C. P. Cowan et al., 1985; P. A. Cowan et al., 1998) have been developed. However, other than research on the direct and indirect relationships of the marital/partner subsystem quality to child outcomes (e.g., Cummings, Goeke-Morey, & Graham, 2002), studies to date neither specify the pathways through which different family subsystems exert their influence (Parke & Buriel, 1998) nor clarify the relative weight of parent-child relationships versus other family relationships in relation to child outcomes (Parke & O'Neil, 1997). Thus, currently there is a limited empirical basis for early interventions to generate specific content that recognizes the embeddedness of the child and parent-child relationships within a system of family influences.

Individual and Family Support Systems

Another program content decision stemming from ecological perspectives on child and family development is how early interventions address social supports for family members, including a parent's life course goals such as additional schooling or employment. Generally, intervention actions aimed at improving family support systems are viewed as requisite to improved individual or family functioning so that focused work eventually can be pursued with child development content.

Intervention attention to individual and family support systems can require considerable staff time and energy (e.g., enrolling a parent in an adult education program most likely will require arrangements for transportation and child care) and is a major undertaking with families living in high-stress circumstances. Home visitors often report that a family's pressing life circumstances take precedence over a program's child development content; for example, "If a mother isn't making it financially, and she's just had a fight with her boyfriend, and he's just split, there ain't no way I can just say to her, 'okay, let's you and I go play a game with the child'" (Mindick, 1986, p. 83).

Interventions run the risk of having no impact on child outcomes if pressing family matters dominate program

work with families. An early example of this point is the Child and Family Resource Program, a family-oriented early intervention that gave minimal attention to parenting and child development content with parents in part because family crises occupied the joint agenda of intervener and family. The intervention improved some aspects of adult functioning but had no effects on child outcomes (Travers, Irwin, & Nauta, 1981; Travers, Nauta, & Irwin, 1982). There appears to be no intervention research evidence to support the idea that improvements in the provision of social supports is a direct pathway to improved child outcomes. A meta-analysis of 88 preventive interventions focused on enhancing parental sensitivity and infant attachment found that interventions with a clear-cut behavioral focus on parental sensitivity were more effective than interventions with a broader content focus that included attention to social support and parents' mental representations as well as parental sensitivity (Bakermans-Kranenburg, van IJzendoorn, & Juffer, 2003).

A major content decision in this domain is the specific focus of attempts to improve supports for individual and family functioning. One option is a mediator role, such as case management aimed at strengthening links with informal and formal resources. The intervener's work here entails referral to needed services and, in some cases, active involvement in ensuring that services are accessed (e.g., driving a family member to a clinic appointment) and are responsive to a family's circumstance (e.g., finding an agency staff person who speaks the family's language). A concurrent or alternative option is to train parents in skills related to effective development and use of support resources (e.g., problem-solving skills; Wasik, Bryant, Lyons, Sparling, & Ramey, 1997).

Family Members' Views of Their Situation

Because early intervention programs generally focus on proximal processes involving the child and family, and not distal contexts, research that increases our understanding of how families make sense of, navigate, and help shape their ecological niches can be especially useful. Studies that link family child-rearing practices to prevailing understandings and beliefs within different types of families may be particularly useful in helping interveners anticipate how to approach the introduction of a program or given topic to families. Parents and other primary caregivers are not blank slates. They filter, edit, and process program information in relation to existing constructs, goals, pressing issues (Goodnow, 2000; D. R. Powell, 1988), and perhaps the views of one or more influential others who may not be visibly involved in the intervention.

The ways family members act on their perceptions of the larger environment are one route by which context influences child rearing. Interventions that focus on content independent of family members' ideas about the world they and their children live in may "take us only along part of the road" toward improved child outcomes (Goodnow, 2000, p. 441). For example, research on strategies used by families to buffer their children from violence in a high-risk African American neighborhood illustrates how mothers' danger management efforts (e.g., monitoring, cautionary warnings, in-home learning, resource brokering) serve as intervening processes that mediate effects of community conditions on family functioning and outcomes (Jarrett & Jefferson, 2003, 2004).

Participants

There is a limited but growing body of research to inform program decisions about what members of a family or household should be encouraged to participate in a family intervention. An early experimental study on this topic regarding adult family members, conducted with well-educated European Americans to determine the effectiveness of newborn interventions, employed the Brazelton Neonatal Behavioral Assessment Scale as a tool for influencing parental behavior. The study found short-term positive effects on mothers and fathers who jointly participated in the intervention (versus mother participating without the baby's father) and who were highly engaged in the intervention (Belsky, 1986). With higher-risk populations, household composition (i.e., whether a new mother lives alone or with her partner or the baby's grandmother; Cole et al., 1998) and mothers' perceived quality of her partner's support (i.e., communicate clearly, express affection, low levels of hostility; Heinicke et al., 1998) have been found to moderate intervention outcomes. A meta-analysis of interventions aimed at improving either parental sensitivity or infant attachment or both found that interventions involving fathers were more effective than interventions focusing on mothers only, but the analysis included a small number of interventions targeting fathers (Bakermans-Kranenburg et al., 2003). More generally, it appears that effects of

planned variation in the joint participation of parent and significant other(s) in an intervention have not been examined in higher-risk populations.

The growing research literature on fathers and child development, coupled with societal concern about the limits or absence of father contributions to child rearing and other family functions, has accelerated intervention attention to fathers, as noted earlier. Many families involved in family interventions differ from the modal family type that developmentalists have examined in father-child relationship studies (Marsiglio, Amato, Day, & Lamb, 2000). Interveners face challenges of determining which fathers to involve in a program when more than one man plays a fathering role in a child's life (e.g., nonresident biological father, a resident stepfather, a grandfather or other male relative; Roggman, Fitzgerald, Bradley, & Raikes, 2002). Program staff also need to recognize the benefits and problems of adapting methods that work with mothers in approaches to fathers (Roggman et al., 2002), a nuance perhaps connected to the finding that mature programs are more likely than newer programs to involve fathers (Raikes, Summers, & Roggman, 2005). The gatekeeping role of women in nonresident fathers' and stepfathers' relationships with their children also needs attention in program designs and actions (Raikes et al., 2005).

A major implication and challenge of viewing relationships as developmental contexts is to establish productive connections with the important relationship systems in a family. The customary practice is for intervention staff to develop separate relationships with each member of a family dyad or triad. Certainly the intervener's relationship with the parent or primary caregiver, typically the priority relationship in interventions, is valuable in its own right and a point of access to the family. But what may be more important is how the intervener manages his or her relationship to the parent-child relationship (Emde & Robinson, 2000) and to the partner relationship (C. P. Cowan, Cowan, & Heming, 2005).

Format

Discussion groups and home visits have rich histories of use in early childhood interventions that reflect different assumptions about how best to facilitate growth and change in families, specifically the peer learning and support presumed to exist in discussion groups and the tailoring to family circumstances afforded in home visits (Bryant & Wasik, 2004). An early quasi-experimental study found that long-term peer discussion groups produced stronger effects on maternal child-rearing attitudes than home visits (Slaughter, 1983), and a meta-analysis of 665 studies of 260 family support programs, 98% of which offered parenting education, found that parent groups produced stronger effects on child outcomes than home visiting (Layzer, Goodson, Bernstein, & Price, 2001). The average effect sizes for parent groups as the primary method of delivering education were .54 when targeted to children at biological risk and .27 when used with nontargeted populations, compared to average effect sizes for home visiting of .36 when targeted to children at biological risk and .09 when used with nontargeted populations. Perhaps program effectiveness increases when the unique strengths of home- and group-based methods are maximized sequentially or concurrently. A 17-site study of the Early Head Start Program found that a combination of center-based and home-based methods yielded a stronger pattern of effects on children's language and social-emotional development and on parents' behavior and participation in self-sufficiency activities (i.e., job training) than center-based or home-based strategies alone (Love et al., 2002).

High expectations of positive results of home visiting were prominently reduced in 1999 when a widely distributed David and Lucile Packard Foundation publication on results of evaluations of six nationally visible home visiting models recommended that policymakers and practitioners maintain modest expectations of home visiting and consider including home visiting as one of a range of services offered to families with young children (Gomby et al., 1999).

Decisions about the use of groups and/or home visits need to recognize that these are delivery systems, not programs, and existing studies of groups and home visits do not control for other important program features (e.g., content, pedagogical approach, frequency, child presence) that program designers need to consider in concert with program delivery methods.

Intensity

A prevailing assumption in the early childhood intervention field is that more is better, and lackluster findings of early intervention work with families are often attributed to insufficient levels of program intensity. Intensity has four dimensions: the frequency of contact with a fam-

ily; the length or duration of an intervention; the point at which an intervention begins working with a family, generally defined by child age (timing); and the extent to which participants are actively engaged in a program.

Frequency

Experimental research on the relation of frequency of intervention contact with families to child outcomes is exceptionally limited (for a review, see D. R. Powell, 2005). Within-group analyses of dose-response relationships in early childhood interventions involving parents typically find that higher levels of participation are associated with stronger program effects (e.g., Ramey et al., 1992). The chief problem of dose-response correlational analyses is the lack of control for population characteristics. Research by C. Powell and Grantham-McGregor (1989) in Jamaica apparently is the only published investigation that systematically varied levels of program frequency. However, this two-study contribution is limited because random assignment to different frequencies of home visiting (twice a month, once a month, control condition) was by neighborhood area (not family) in Study 1. In Study 2, families in a different sample were randomly assigned to either weekly home visits or a control condition. Results of separate analyses for Study 1 and Study 2 indicate that bimonthly visits had a small influence on children's developmental functioning and that there were significant developmental improvements in children in families receiving weekly home visits compared to children in the control group.

Duration

Research on the length of intervention work with families generally has the same population confounds as within-group analyses of the frequency of contact. An additional methodological problem in studies of intervention duration is the high rate of participant attrition. Among the families randomly assigned to the intervention group in one three-site study of a parent-oriented home visiting program, for example, 22% never began any visits and 35% received some visits but dropped out by the year 2 assessment. Attrition was so high in two of the three study sites that the evaluation of the planned 3-year program was discontinued at the end of the second year (Wagner, Spiker, & Linn, 2002). The Bakermans-Kranenburg et al. (2003) meta-analysis found that interventions with fewer than five sessions were as effective (effect size = .42) as interventions with 5 to 16 sessions (effect size = .38), but interventions with more than 16 sessions were less effective (effect size = .21) than interventions with a smaller number of sessions. Follow-up outcome data were not considered in this analysis.

Studies indicating that positive effects of preschool interventions on IQ fade over time (Barnett, 1995; Consortium for Longitudinal Studies, 1983) have led to interest in follow-up interventions in elementary school. Effects of a home-school intervention were examined in a randomized study of the Abecedarian Project, an early intervention program beginning in infancy (Ramey, Dorval, & Baker-Ward, 1983; the infancy/preschool phase of the Abecedarian Project is described in the section on Approaches to Families in Early Interventions). Participants in the infancy/preschool intervention were randomly assigned to a K–2 educational support program at kindergarten entry. This yielded three intervention groups: preschool and K–2 educational support intervention, early intervention only, and K–2 educational support intervention only; a control group was also added. The K–2 educational support intervention consisted of a home-school resource teacher for each child and the child's family. The teachers prepared an individualized set of home activities to supplement the school's basic curriculum in reading and math; they helped families secure such community services as decent housing or adult literacy classes, and they were advocates for the child and family within the school and community.

The K–2 educational support intervention by itself was not as effective as the preschool condition or the preschool plus K–2 educational support condition in increasing school performance, although it did increase parental involvement in their child's education. Follow-up research when children were 15 years old found that the preschool-only condition had a positive effect on grade retention, and both the preschool-only condition and the preschool plus K–2 educational support condition, but not the K–2 educational support-only condition, had positive effects on reading and math performance (Ramey, Ramey, Lanzi, & Cotton, 2002). Intervention effects on reading performance were particularly strong. The effect sizes for the preschool plus K–2 educational support condition and the preschool-only condition were .87 and .53, respectively, but was under .15 for the K–2 educational support-only condition and the control condition (Ramey et al., 2000). Interestingly, between 36% and 48% of children in the intervention conditions involving the K–2 educational support also were placed in special education, perhaps because the home-school resource teachers were special educators

who sought out special education services they believed would be helpful to a child (Ramey et al., 2002).

A follow-up assessment when study participants were 21 years of age found that the school-age intervention helped to maintain preschool benefits for reading, but the effects of the school-age component were weaker than those of the preschool program (Campbell, Ramey, Pungello, Sparling, & Johnson, 2002).

A study of the Abecedarian children's experiences in elementary school found that children had difficulty meeting teachers' expectations of a "middle-class way with words" and that teachers had difficulty responding to the distinctive nature of the Abecedarian children's incorrect answers to questions (Vernon-Feagans, 1996, p. 210). There is anecdotal evidence that public ridicule of individual performance and marginalized status contributed to a loss of interest in school (e.g., an older boy in the Abecedarian community told one of the Abecedarian kindergarteners, "See, Melvin, you stop likin to go to school when you get there"; Vernon-Feagans, 1996, p. 205). Abecedarian children were assigned to low-ability groups even when child ability data such as IQ scores (e.g., 130) indicated that a higher placement would be appropriate. Vernon-Feagans identified the Abecedarian children's low-income African American status as a factor in how school personnel viewed and accommodated nonmainstream children and argues for reforms that would enable schools to be ready for all children.

Timing

A companion to the "more is better" assumption in the early intervention field is the "earlier is better" perspective, driven largely by a view of the earliest years of life as a critical developmental period. Although this premise has been disputed in recent years (e.g., Bruer, 1999), there is scant intervention research to guide decisions about the timing of work with families. In the Bakermans-Kranenburg et al. (2003) meta-analysis of interventions focused on parental sensitivity and infant attachment security, interventions starting 6 months after birth or later were somewhat more effective (effect size = .44) than interventions starting prenatally or within the first 6 months of life (effect size = .28).

Level and Type of Engagement

Intervention methods vary in the extent to which they encourage an active level of participant engagement. For example, presumably, an intervention that includes guided discussion with a program participant about his or her observed behavior is more intense than a didactic presentation of information that entails no tailoring of content to a participant or involvement of a participant in discussion of the content.

Research suggests that participants' active engagement of program content is predictive of outcomes. Liaw, Meisels, and Brooks-Gunn (1995) found that parent and child active experience in an intervention (i.e., parent's interest in the intervention activities during the home visit and child's mastery of tasks taught at the child development center) were stronger predictors of child IQ and quality of home environment scores at age 3 years than program exposure (i.e., number of contacts in home and child development center) and rate of participation (i.e., number of activities presented per visit to parent in the home or per day to the child at the center). A higher level of active experience on the part of both child and parent was more strongly associated with child IQ and home environment quality than a high level of active experience on the part of the child only or the parent only. In another intervention study, the rate at which a curriculum emphasizing adult-child interactions was implemented in home visits and in the child development center added significantly to the prediction of children's IQ scores at 3 years of age (Sparling et al., 1991). An implication of these findings is that interventions may need to give attention to staff practices (e.g., individualization of content) that are likely to support active engagement of an intervention.

Intervention staff often model desired parenting practices, although little is known about the effectiveness of this pedagogical strategy. One qualitative study of a home visiting program found that parents were not always aware that the home visitor was modeling appropriate practices for the parent (Hebbeler & Gerlach-Downie, 2002). Videotaped demonstrations of appropriate practices, found to be effective in parent training for families with conduct-problem children (Webster-Stratton, 1990; Webster-Stratton, Kolpacoff, & Hollinsworth, 1988), are a promising tool. Videotapes of recommended joint book reading practices were found to be more effective than live demonstrations of recommended practices, perhaps because mothers featured in the videotapes were more similar to the demographic characteristics of the intervention participants than the staff person conducting the live demonstration (Arnold, Lonigan, Whitehurst, & Epstein, 1994).

Constructive feedback to individuals based on observations of their parenting behaviors is another interven-

tion method for which there is limited evidence on effectiveness. Coaching adolescent mothers to use labeling, scaffolding, and contingent responsivity in literacy-focused social interactions with their preschool-age children is an illustration of this intervention method (Neuman & Gallagher, 1994). Some interventions videotape parent-child interaction for use in a guided discussion with the parent about parent and child behaviors. A meta-analysis of interventions focused on parental sensitivity and infant attachment security found that interventions with video feedback were more effective (effect size = .44) than interventions without this method (effect size = .31; Bakermans-Kranenburg et al., 2003).

There is some evidence to suggest that the quality of relationship between intervener and family is predictive of intervention outcomes. In an intervention involving nurses as home visitors, a positive relation between nurses' empathy (i.e., trust, understanding, acceptance) toward their client-mothers and the mothers' empathy toward their child was found for mothers with higher levels of psychological resources (e.g., emotional well-being; Korfmacher, Kitzman, & Olds, 1998). In a different intervention also involving nurses as home visitors, therapeutic relationships with mothers that included demonstrations of ways to handle family relationships and problems were found to be effective with mothers with limited social skills (Booth et al., 1989). A review of early family intervention studies in which the relationship between the family and the intervener was viewed as central to intervention outcomes points to positive intervention effects on maternal functioning and quality of family and community support (Heinicke & Ponce, 1999). Many of the interventions included in the Heinecke and Ponce review were represented in the Bakermans-Kranenburg et al. (2003) meta-analysis, which found that randomized interventions were effective in changing insensitive parenting (effect size = .33) and, to a lesser extent, infant attachment insecurity (effect size = .20). With few exceptions (e.g., Arnold et al., 1994), experimental designs have not been employed in research on different methods of working with parents or families.

Staffing

Paraprofessionals have been employed most commonly as staff responsible for direct work with families in early childhood interventions. They are generally selected on the basis of their existing ties to local residents and their ability to establish a strong interpersonal relationship with program participants. Paraprofessionals are expected to provide a high level of personal credibility that aids in recruiting and retaining hard-to-reach families, facilitates parent acceptance of the program, and enhances their effectiveness as a role model for parents (D. R. Powell, 1993). Evaluations of some home-based (Wagner & Clayton, 1999) and group-based (Miller, 1988) interventions staffed by paraprofessionals have produced weak or no positive effects, but the studies do not make clear whether results were a function of the maturity of the program model or the abilities of paraprofessionals.

A randomized trial of a home visiting program model with first-time, low-income mothers in Denver addressed the question of whether paraprofessionals can produce positive results in a well-developed program found to be effective when delivered by professionals (Olds et al., 2002). Results indicated that, when trained in the Nurse-Family Partnership model (previously known as the Nurse Home Visiting Program), paraprofessionals produced small effects that rarely achieved statistical or clinical significance. Nurses produced significant effects on a wide range of maternal and child outcomes. For most outcomes on which either paraprofessionals or nurses produced significant effects, the paraprofessionals typically had effects that were about half the size of those produced by nurses.

Olds and his colleagues (2002) speculate that, from a family's perspective, nurses may have higher levels of legitimacy than paraprofessionals to address concerns about pregnancy complications, labor and delivery, and the care of newborns, and thus may have more power to engage parents and support adaptive behavior change. In their study, nurses spent more time focused on personal health and parenting issues, and paraprofessionals devoted more time to topics related to environmental health and safety. Mothers' ratings of the helping relationship did not differ between nurses and paraprofessionals (Korfmacher, O'Brien, Hiatt, & Olds, 1999). Generalization of the Olds et al. findings is limited to programs serving first-time, low-income mothers with a program model focused on health issues. The study leaves open the question of whether there would be different outcomes if paraprofessionals were trained and supported in a program model uniquely suited to their backgrounds and abilities (Korfmacher, 2001).

Reports from other home visiting interventions indicate that lay home visitors may have special difficulty systematically addressing parenting behaviors, finding it easier to provide material support such as transportation to a clinic appointment, and may avoid discussing sensitive issues faced by families (e.g., adolescent pregnancy) that are also a part of the paraprofessional's life history (Musick & Stott, 2000). Also, a cost-benefit analysis indicates that the amount of training and professional supervision of paraprofessionals has a tendency to erase any economic benefit of employing paraprofessionals (Harkavy & Bond, 1992). This indirectly raises questions about how the quality of supervision of intervention staff contributes to overall program quality and effects.

Targeting and Recruiting Families

There is long-standing concern that the families most likely to benefit from an intervention program may be the least likely to participate. Problems of and strategies for recruiting hard-to-reach families are persistent topics in the field. Most reports identify personal contact as superior to flyers and other impersonal methods of contacting prospective participants. Few intervention studies have addressed the question of who accepts and who declines the invitation to participate (McCurdy & Daro, 2001). A multisite study of Hawaii's Healthy Start Program, a home visiting intervention that serves families identified through screening at birth as highly stressed and/or at risk for child abuse, found that of 897 families offered the possibility of program enrollment, 82% agreed to enroll. Initial willingness to participate was associated with the method of assessment (i.e., odds of accepting the program were twice as great for mothers assessed in person than by telephone), infant biologic risk (i.e., low birthweight, premature), overall score on a measure of family stress, and maternal age and education (i.e., adolescent mothers who had not finished high school were 2.5 times more likely to enroll than adult mothers with a high school education; Duggan et al., 2000).

Agreeing to participate is not to be confused with actually participating. In a multisite study of the Parents as Teachers program, for example, one in five families who initially agreed to enrollment did not subsequently participate in a home visit (Wagner, Spiker, Linn, Gerlach-Downie, & Hernandez, 2003). As noted earlier, attrition rates are typically high in interventions serving at-risk populations. In the model home visiting programs included in the Packard Foundation publication, 20% to 67% of families enrolled in the programs departed before the programs were scheduled to end (Gomby et al.,

1999), a pattern found in childhood intervention research spanning several decades. Whether there is differential attrition is largely unanswered.

Population characteristics have been found to predict level of program participation. Families in the Hawaii Healthy Start Program were more likely to have had at least 12 home visits in the 1st year if the father was violent, substance abusing, and at extremely high risk; if the mother did not use violence unilaterally as a means of dealing with conflict with her partner; and if the mother was not at extremely high risk (Duggan et al., 2000; Duggan et al., 1999). In contrast, a study of the Oregon Healthy Start Program found that mothers were significantly less likely to actively engage in home visits when living in a county that displayed poor community health (i.e., high infant death rate, low birthweight rate) or when isolated from immediate family and friendship networks (McGuigan, Katzev, & Pratt, 2003). A study of psychological characteristics of parents as predictors of patterns of participation in an Early Head Start Program found that mothers who entered the program with a lower sense of mastery, more difficult attitudes toward relationships, and more stressful life events were likely to be classified as superficially engaged in the program (i.e., high frequency of attendance but low engagement in terms of perceived levels of interest and attentiveness; Robinson et al., 2002).

With regard to program outcomes, results of a number of investigations suggest that higher-risk mothers and their children benefit more from early childhood interventions than lower-risk populations. The risk indicators examined in various studies include education level (Brooks-Gunn, Gross, Kraemer, Spiker, & Shapiro, 1997), mother's sense of control over her life (Olds et al., 1986), psychological resources (Olds, Henderson, et al., 1998), social skills (Booth et al., 1989), depression (Lyons-Ruth, Connell, Grunebaum, & Botein, 1990), and mental health risks (Baydar, Reid, & Webster-Stratton, 2003).

Studies indicating that early interventions with families are more effective with higher-risk than with lower-risk populations raise questions about the merits of targeting specific populations. Research on this topic is limited, although programs have pursued various strategies. One option is to use screening data to target higher-risk samples for a program (e.g., Duggan et al., 2000) or, within a universal program, to determine the level of needed services (Daro & Harding, 1999). The reliability and validity of screening tools is critical to these types of practices. Some argue speculatively that

when programs are offered to all parents (e.g., Head Start participants) in a nonstigmatizing manner, higher-risk parents in fact participate and that the inclusion of lower-risk parents in heterogeneous groups enhances program effects on higher-risk parents by providing positive parenting models (Baydar et al., 2003). Another option in a universal intervention is to enhance program supports for higher-risk families. For example, Robinson et al. (2002) studied parents' psychological characteristics of predictors of participation in Early Head Start, conducted as a collaboration between researchers and program staff. Findings led staff to strengthen attention to mental health factors in in-service staff trainings and to supplement the information gathering at the enrollment point with brief assessments of psychological characteristics of mothers that would provide anticipatory guidance to home visitors (e.g., use patience and persistence with a woman with many life stressors and a low sense of mastery who might express few signals of seeking a relationship but in fact may be in need of support).

Supports for Program Implementation

Developers of early interventions have long suggested that program delivery systems, including the host agency and community supports for the program, affect the quality of program implementation (e.g., Weikart, Bond, & McNeil, 1978). There is now a fledgling body of research on program implementation that holds promise of eventually offering guidance on conditions associated with successful implementation of an intervention. This information is particularly needed to inform decisions about taking model programs to scale.

Organizational cultures and capacities appear to shape the ways a host agency carries out an early intervention. A study of the implementation of the Early Head Start Program found that agency experiences in providing services to families and to infants and toddlers prior to becoming an Early Head Start Program were linked to the ease with which Early Head Start components were fully implemented. For example, staff in some agencies with experience in providing parent and family support programs initially resisted the Early Head Start focus on child development services (Kisker, Paulsell, Love, & Raikes, 2002). In a three-site study of the Hawaii Healthy Start Program, Duggan and her colleagues (1999, 2000) found significant differences across agencies in program implementation. The agency with the lowest family retention rate viewed the entire family more than the target child as its primary client, and home visitors were likely to honor family wishes about program participation and focus on more receptive families. The two agencies with higher family retention rates reportedly expected that many at-risk families would be reluctant to participate in home visiting and regarded outreach to an isolated family, for instance, as more important than honoring a family's inclination to be left alone. Home visitors in these two agencies persisted in contacting families by telephone and in person, whereas staff in the agency with low retention rates were advised to send a letter to a reluctant family offering a final chance to participate.

APPROACHES TO FAMILIES IN EARLY INTERVENTION: FIVE BASIC PROGRAM DESIGNS

A premise of this chapter is that considerations of the merits of family interventions require a finer-grained examination of intervention components and processes than is generally provided in the literature. This section describes five basic program designs, defined by the parent's role (adjunct, supplementary, primary) and by whether intervention goals and content aimed at adult family members emphasize child rearing or a broader set of family functions that include child rearing as well as domains such as economic self-sufficiency and use of educational, human, and health services. Key distinctions across the five intervention designs are depicted in Table 14.1.

Participant role and program goals and content, essentially the *who* and *what* dimensions of intervention design, capture conceptual differences in program assumptions about how best to achieve better outcomes for children at risk. The approaches represent contrasting theories of change (Weiss, 1995) regarding pathways of influence or causal linkages within interventions.

In early interventions where the parent is in an adjunct or supplementary role in a program serving children directly, the hypothesized mechanism by which an intervention influences child well-being typically emphasizes strengthening the child's knowledge or skills, such as cognitive ability. This initial boost in ability is expected to expand into further abilities and corresponding outcomes, sometimes called a Matthew effect (e.g., Stanovich, 1986). With regard to the family in this arrangement, the child may be viewed as a mediator of change in parents' behaviors or cognitions (e.g., asking for storybooks to be read at home as at preschool). The

TABLE 14.1 Approaches to Families in Early Childhood Interventions: Five Basic Program Designs

Program Design	Targeted Participant		Targeted Family Function	
	Child	Parent	Child Rearing	Other[a]
Parent is adjunct to child program (e.g., Abecedarian Project)	X			
Parent is supplementary to child program (e.g., Perry Preschool Project)	X	X	X	
Parent is primary participant: child-focused content (e.g., Parents as Teachers)		X	X	
Parent is primary participant: broad-focused content (e.g., Nurse-Family Partnership)		X	X	X
Parent and child are primary participants (e.g., Even Start Family Literacy)	X	X	X	X

[a]For example, family use of educational, human, and health services; parent job skills; parent problem-solving skills.

intervention also may supplement its direct work with the child by regularly conducting home visits or group meetings; these are hypothesized to add value to the child program by providing families with skills and encouragement to reinforce the child's gains during and after child participation in the program.

In interventions where the parent is the sole primary participant, the prevailing hypothesis is that direct, regular work with the parent(s) will lead to changes in parent behaviors, including parent-child interaction, which in turn will improve child outcomes that are sustained over time due to ongoing family support. The content of intervention with the parent may focus primarily on the child-rearing role or a broader set of family functions.

Hypothesized pathways are more complex in interventions where both parent and child are primary participants. The substance of direct work with the parent(s) may be a hypothesized link to both child and parent outcomes. Intervention aimed at improving a parent's problem-solving skills, for instance, may assume that improved problem-solving skills will enable parents to more effectively cope with daily situations and enhance overall parental well-being, which may directly and perhaps indirectly increase the likelihood of positive parent-child relationships (Wasik, Bryant, Lyons, et al., 1997). The timing of intersections among pathways of influence is an important consideration because the focus of direct work with the parent(s) often is a prerequisite to positive influence on the child (e.g., teaching a parent to read so the parent can in turn help the child learn to read).

Although multiple paths of intervention effects are inherent in interventions that cast both parent and child as primary participants, note that more than one hypothesized mediator of intervention effects may be embraced in child-oriented and parent-oriented program designs. With few exceptions (e.g., Reynolds et al., 2004), most intervention research has examined one model of casual linkages, generally focused on child ability.

The discussion follows the order of intervention designs listed in Table 14.1, beginning with interventions in which the parent is adjunct or supplementary to a child program and ending with the most complicated of intervention designs, where both parent and child are primary participants and a range of family functions is addressed. Some preliminary hypotheses about program design are offered at the end of the section.

The interventions described in this section were selected for purposes of illustrating different combinations of program content and status of parent participants. The section does not offer an inclusive or exhaustive review of family interventions and thus does not provide conclusions about intervention effectiveness or design. Most, but not all, of these interventions were developed in the field of early childhood intervention. They were targeted at lower-income families and evaluated with an experimental or strong quasi-experimental research design, often in more than one research site.

Parent as Adjunct to Child Program

It is rare to find an early childhood intervention that does not include some programmatic attention to families because, as noted in this chapter's introduction, early childhood education has a tradition of viewing parents as partners in supporting a young child's development. There is considerable variation in how programs act on the partnership idea, however (D. R. Powell, 2001). Of interest here are early interventions that approach work with families as adjunct to the primary mission of working with the child. These child-focused programs typically provide occasional opportunities for parents to be involved in the program and encourage but do not require

parent participation. Program provisions for parent participation generally follow recommendations of the National Association for the Education of Young Children (NAEYC) for establishing reciprocal relationships with families, including frequent, two-way communication with children's parents; parent participation in decisions about their children's care and education; teacher respect for parents' child-rearing preferences and concerns; family involvement in assessing and planning for individual children; and program assistance in linking families to a range of community services (Bredekamp & Copple, 1997).

Program Approaches

The preschool phase of the Abecedarian Project, begun in 1972 at the Frank Porter Graham Child Development Center at the University of North Carolina, illustrates the ways supportive services may be offered to families in a child-centered intervention. The home-school educational support phase of the Abecedarian Project beginning in kindergarten was described previously. The project was designed to determine whether an educationally focused full-day child care program beginning in infancy could prevent nonorganically caused mild mental retardation in children from high-risk families (Ramey et al., 1983). Families were selected on the basis of scores on an index of factors indicative of risk for school failure. The families were mostly low-income and African American. They were matched on high-risk scores and maternal IQ, and then pair members were randomly assigned to either the intervention group or the control group. Four cohorts of approximately 28 children were selected for the study over a 5-year period (Ramey et al., 1983), resulting in an enrolled sample of 111 children (57 experimental, 54 control).

The center-based educational program for children was year-round (50 weeks), 5 days a week for up to 8 hours a day. Children began attending the center as young as 6 weeks of age; 98% of the children had begun by age 3 months. The program focused on skills that would enhance children's abilities to succeed in the public schools. Primary emphasis was on cognitive and language development. The program used the Learningames curriculum for infants and toddlers, comprising more than 300 items in language, motor, social, and cognitive areas (Sparling & Lewis, 1979). Experiences were tailored to the developmental status of individual children, and teachers maintained a developmental chart for each child to help provide an appropriate match between child functioning and curriculum items. The curriculum beginning at age 3 years emphasized active child functioning and independence with systematic exposure to science, math, and music (Ramey et al., 1983).

Program provisions for establishing and maintaining relationships with parents included many of the practices now recommended by NAEYC. There were regular parent-teacher conferences focused on the child's growth and development and scheduled group discussions on a range of topics related to family and child development. Vans transported children between home and the center, and, although "there was no formal parent involvement or home visiting component to the intervention," many of the center staff had strong ties to the African American community and families served by the program (Vernon-Feagans, 1996, p. 80). Project social workers also were available to provide direct and indirect assistance with housing, social services, and counseling on personal and family matters (Ramey & Ramey, 1992; Ramey et al., 2002). The social work services, also available to families in the control group (Ramey et al., 2002), were provided upon request (Ramey et al., 1983, p. 87). Published reports that provide the most information regarding Abecedarian effects on parents do not indicate the extent to which experimental and control group parents made use of these services, or how frequently experimental group parents participated in meetings and communications with teachers at the center (Ramey et al., 1983; Ramey & Ramey, 1992; Ramey et al., 2002).

Effects

Outcome data indicate that the Abecedarian intervention prevented intellectual decline during the preschool period (Ramey & Campbell, 1984). A subgroup analysis of 13 children of retarded mothers found that intervention effects were greatest for children of mothers with IQ below 70 (Martin, Ramey, & Ramey, 1990).

No differences between experimental and control group mothers were found in child-rearing attitudes when infants were 6 and 18 months of age, and in mothers' locus of control when infants were 3 months old (Ramey et al., 1983). When children were 20 months of age, analyses of videotaped mother-child interaction in a laboratory indicated that experimental group infants were communicating with their mothers at a significantly higher level than control group infants. Experimental group infants were equivalent to infants in a middle-class comparison sample (nonrandomized) in "requesting" behaviors (O'Connell & Farran, 1980 cited in Ramey et al., 1983). At 36 months of age, infants in the experimental

group were four times as likely to attempt to modify their mother's behavior (e.g., ask mother to watch their activity, read them a book) than control group infants, and mutual play activities involving mother and child lasted twice as long for mother-child dyads in the experimental group (Farran & Haskins, 1977 cited in Ramey et al., 1983). It appears, then, that children in the Abecedarian child development center presented different demand characteristics when interacting with their mother and thus may have affected the quality of mother-child interaction by their ability to bring out the best in caregivers (Ramey et al., 2002). There were no differences between experimental and control group families in the quality of the home environment at 54 months (Ramey et al., 1983).

A pattern of positive intervention effects on reading and math performance was found when children were assessed at 8 and 12 years of age (F. A. Campbell & Ramey, 1994, 1995). As reported earlier in this chapter, follow-up research when children were 15 years of age found that the preschool intervention had a positive effect on grade retention (Ramey et al., 2002). Also at the 15-year follow-up, 12% of children in the preschool-only group compared to 48% in the control group had been placed in special education during the 10 years they attended school (Ramey et al., 2000).

At 21 years of age, participants in the preschool intervention earned significantly higher scores on intellectual and academic measures, attained significantly more years of total education, were more likely to attend a 4-year college, and showed a reduction in teenage pregnancy compared to participants in the control group (Campbell et al., 2002). Preschool cognitive gains accounted for a substantial portion of intervention differences in the development of reading and math skills from age 3 to 21 years (Campbell, Pungello, Miller-Johnson, Burchinal, & Ramey, 2001).

Follow-up results suggest that the early childhood program enabled mothers to continue their education. Experimental group mothers had significantly higher education levels (11.9 years) than control group mothers (10.3 years) when their children were 54 months of age despite the fact that the levels of education were comparable (10.30 for experimental and 10.12 for control) at the time of their child's birth (Ramey, 1980). Also, more control group mothers were unemployed or engaged in unskilled employment than experimental mothers, and experimental group mothers held more semiskilled or skilled jobs than control group mothers (Ramey et al., 1983). Adolescent parents seemed to benefit the most. At the time of kindergarten entry, 46% of teenage mothers in the intervention group had graduated from high school and obtained postsecondary training compared to 13% in the control group (F. A. Campbell, Breitmayer, & Ramey, 1986). This pattern continued at follow-up. When children were 15 years of age, 80% of teenage mothers whose children had participated in the preschool intervention compared to 28% of comparable control mothers had attained a postsecondary education. Rates of employment were highest (92%) for teenage mothers in the experimental group and lowest (66%) for teenage mothers in the control group (Ramey et al., 2000).

Parent as Supplementary to Child Program

Early interventions that view parents as supplementary participants require or expect regular involvement in program provisions for parents. This level of frequency is in contrast to occasional opportunities for parent participation characterized by the adjunct role. Regular, supplemental work with parents is expected to add value to intervention effects achieved through direct work with the child. Child-rearing issues typically are the focus of work with parents, although, in keeping with NAEYC standards (Bredekamp & Copple, 1997), it is common for programs to also facilitate access to health, education, and social services when needed, generally through referrals. In this type of program design, a distinction across interventions is whether the content of work with parents primarily addresses a single child-rearing domain (e.g., cognitive development) or multiple child-rearing domains. Each of these two content approaches is discussed next, beginning with interventions that address multiple child-rearing domains in work with parents.

Multiple Child-Rearing Domains

The Perry Preschool Project, launched in 1962 in Ypsilanti, Michigan, is arguably the best-known investigation of the effects of early childhood education on low-income children. The experimental study has gained visibility in policy and early childhood practitioner circles for its follow-up findings regarding real-world variables (e.g., income, criminal behavior, home ownership) at age 27 years (Schweinhart, Barnes, Weikart, Barnett, & Epstein, 1993) and 40 years (Schweinhart et al., 2005) and for its cost-benefit analyses (e.g., Barnett, 1996).

Less well-known is the targeted focus on parents in the Perry Preschool Project: Mothers received weekly home visits lasting about 90 minutes from their child's preschool teacher aimed at involving mothers in providing educational support at home and extending school activities on an individual basis. For each home visit, teachers offered materials (e.g., puppets, clay, art materials) that were conducive to involving the mother and were tailored to areas where a child might need extra work. Informal discussions with the mother about child-rearing practices and the child's preparation for school were viewed as an important part of each home visit. There also were periodic group meetings with content planned in collaboration with parents (mostly mothers) and focused on child-rearing practices (Weikart, Rogers, Adcock, & McClelland, 1971).

The Chicago Child-Parent Center Program represents a second illustration of an early childhood program design in which parents are important supplementary participants. This large-scale program provides educational services to economically disadvantaged children and their parents from preschool to early elementary school, ages 3 through 9 years. It was established in 1967 through funding from the federal Elementary and Secondary Education Act of 1965 (Title 1). The half-day preschool and half-day or full-day kindergarten classrooms emphasize language arts and math through relatively structured experiences offered in a range of settings (e.g., large group, small group, individualized activities).

The parent involvement program in the Chicago Child-Parent Centers is more intensive than what was offered in the Perry Preschool Project. Parent involvement in the Chicago program is expected to promote children's school readiness and school adjustment via enhanced parent-child interactions, parent and child participation in school, and social support among parents. During preschool and kindergarten years, parents were required to participate at least one-half day per week, although average participation rates were lower. Parent participation was expected but not required in the primary grades. A parent room, located adjacent to the children's preschool and kindergarten classrooms and staffed by a full-time parent resource teacher, was a core part of the intervention's work with parents. Parent room activities include participation in parent reading groups, craft projects, and workshops on child development. Other avenues for parent involvement included classroom volunteering, home visits, participation in high school coursework, and parent-teacher conferences and other school meetings.

A full-time staff person responsible for outreach services to families, including referral to health and social service agencies, is located at each center. The outreach worker meets with each family at the beginning of the year and additional visits occur as needed (Reynolds, 2000). Compared to nonparticipants, participants in the Perry Preschool Project experimental group at age 27 years had significantly higher monthly earnings, rates of home ownership, and level of schooling completed, and significantly lower percentages receiving social services at some time in the previous 10 years and fewer arrests (Schweinhart et al., 1993). At age 40 years, adults who had participated in the preschool program had higher earnings, were more likely to hold a job, had committed fewer crimes, and were more likely to have graduated from high school than adults who did not participate in a preschool program (Schweinhart et al., in press).

Long-term effects of the Chicago Child-Parent Centers were examined with a quasi-experimental design involving 1,539 children who participated in the intervention in 1983 to 1989: an intervention group that received the services from ages 3 through 9 years, as described earlier, and a comparison group of children who participated in alternative full-day kindergartens. Results indicated that children who participated in the preschool intervention for 1 or 2 years had a higher rate of high school completion, more years of completed education, and lower rates of school dropout by age 20 years, and lower rates of juvenile arrest, violent arrests, grade retention, and special education placement by age 18 years. The largest gains in educational attainment occurred for boys in the intervention (Reynolds, Temple, Robertson, & Mann, 2001).

Did these interventions have an influence on parents? To what extent did parents mediate intervention effects on children? Follow-up data in the Perry Preschool Project when children were in fourth grade suggested that the experimental mothers had more developmentally supportive child-rearing attitudes but not behaviors than control mothers (Weikart et al., 1978). At age 15 years, more experimental group mothers than control group mothers were satisfied with their child's school performance, and experimental group mothers had higher educational aspirations for their child than control group mothers (Schweinhart & Weikart, 1980). Data were not collected from parents in follow-up studies when study participants were 19, 27, and 40 years of age. In the Chicago Child-Parent Program, parent data were collected when children were 10 to 12 years of age. Parents of program children were more likely than parents of children in the comparison group to have higher educational expectations for their children, higher rates of satisfaction with their children's education, and higher levels of involvement in school activities (Reynolds, 2000).

Perry Preschool Study researchers have consistently emphasized children's intellectual performance in causal models of how preschool participation influences subsequent outcomes, including adult functioning (Barnett et al., 1998; Schweinhart et al., 1993, in press). In models designed to explain preschool program effects at 27 years (Barnett et al., 1998; Schweinhart et al., 1993) and 40 years (Schweinhart et al., in press), preschool experience directly improves early childhood intellectual performance, the gateway to all subsequent intervention effects. Family variables are not included in the models except in relation to entry-level socioeconomic status predictors of intellectual performance. Analyses conducted when children were in fourth grade indicated that the home environment was a more powerful predictor of achievement and school success in the control group than in the experimental group, prompting the investigators to suggest that the intervention reduced the effects of the home environment on the acquisition of academic skills (Weikart et al., 1978).

The limited attention to intervention effects on parents in the Perry Preschool analyses leaves open important questions about the contribution of parents to children's outcomes (Zigler & Seitz, 1993). In a secondary analysis of the Perry Preschool data that combined experimental and control groups, there was a mixed pattern of links between family variables and children's subsequent achievement. For example, maternal involvement in kindergarten was predictive of children's competence and adjustment in kindergarten. However, for male youth during adolescence, there was a negative relationship between how often parents contacted teachers on their own and level of education attained by the child, perhaps because contact with the school was due to concern about student performance. Mothers who were identified by their child as role models at the 27-year follow-up were significantly more involved in their child's school at kindergarten than mothers who were not selected by their children as role models. Children's cognitive competence and academic motivation in kindergarten were more strongly predictive of subsequent achievement and educational attainment (Luster & McAdoo, 1996).

Reynolds et al. (2004) analyzed different mechanisms or pathways through which the Chicago Child-Parent Centers had long-term effects on educational attainment by age 20 and juvenile delinquency by age 18. They found that the primary mediators of effects for both outcomes were literacy skills in kindergarten and avoidance of grade retention (cognitive advantage), parent involvement in elementary school (when children were between 8 and 12 years of age) and avoidance of child maltreatment (family support), and attendance in high-quality elementary schools and lower number of school moves (school support). The model accounted for 58% of preschool links with school completion and 79% of preschool links with juvenile arrest.

Single Child-Rearing Domain

Research on two interventions related to different aspects of child functioning illustrates the benefits of focused attention to a specific domain of child development through educational work with parents and enhanced teacher practices in existing preschool classrooms. The studies also offer indirect evidence regarding the merits of intervention with parents alone versus intervention with parents in combination with curriculum enhancements in a center-based early childhood program.

The first study deals with preventive interventions focused on child conduct problems. In a study involving Head Start Programs, Webster-Stratton (1998) found that a short-term training program offered to all parents (regardless of whether their child had behavior problems) contributed to significant improvements in parenting interactions with children, reductions in children's negative behaviors, and increases in prosocial behaviors for children of parents who participated in the training program compared to children of comparison group parents. There were no significant intervention effects on children's negative behaviors at school, however.

Webster-Stratton and her colleagues (Webster-Stratton, Reid, & Hammond, 2001) hypothesized that an intervention involving parent training combined with in-depth parallel training for teachers in classroom management skills would result in reduced conduct problems and greater social competence at both school and home. In a study involving 14 Head Start centers (36 classes) that were randomly assigned to either an experimental condition or a control condition, a 12-week parent training program offered to all parents and delivered through weekly parent group meetings was combined with 6 monthly 1-day workshops (i.e., 36 hours of training) for teachers in classrooms in the intervention condition. Parent training topics included playing with your child, using praise and encouragement to bring out the best in your child, effective limit setting, and handling misbehavior. Parents viewed videotapes of modeled parenting skills and engaged in a focused group discussion after viewing each 2-minute vignette. The teacher training workshop topics included strengthening student social skills, using incentives to motivate students with behavior problems, and handling misbehavior using effective limit setting, ignoring, time-out, and other strategies. Teachers watched and discussed videotapes of other classroom teachers.

Following the 12-session weekly parent program, experimental mothers had significantly lower negative parenting and significantly higher positive parenting scores than control mothers. Experimental children showed significantly fewer conduct problems at school than control children, and children of mothers who attended six or more intervention sessions showed significantly fewer conduct problems at home than children in the control group. At the end of training, experimental teachers exhibited significantly better classroom management skills than control teachers. Experimental effects were maintained 1 year later for parents who attended more than six parent group trainings (Webster-Stratton et al., 2001).

A comparison of the Webster-Stratton (1998) and Webster-Stratton et al. (2001) findings indirectly suggests that if behavior is to be changed in a particular setting (i.e., home, school), intervention focused on the targeted behavior is needed within the setting of interest. Intervention with parents contributed to changes in children's behaviors at home but not in the Head Start classrooms, whereas intervention both with teachers and parents led to changes in children's behaviors both at home and at school.

Children's early reading abilities are the focus of the second example of an intervention involving concurrent training of parents and teachers. The intervention is the dialogic reading program developed by Whitehurst and colleagues (Whitehurst, Arnold, et al., 1994; Whitehurst, Epstein, et al., 1994; Whitehurst et al., 1988). This program promotes the child's active participation in adult-child shared book reading by shifting the adult's typical role of storyteller to the role of active listener, asking questions, adding information, and prompting the child to increase the sophistication of descriptions of material in the picture book.

In a study of the effects of dialogic reading with low-income children, Whitehurst, Arnold, et al. (1994) randomly assigned children attending publicly subsidized child care centers to one of two intervention conditions or a control condition. In one intervention condition, children were read to by their parents at home and by their child care teachers in small groups of no more than five children. In the second intervention condition, children were read to by their child care teachers in the small group format. A videotape training method (Arnold et al., 1994) was used to train teachers and parents in dialogic reading. Children in both intervention groups experienced significant increases in oral language skills compared to children in the control group at the end of the 6-week intervention, and these gains were maintained on a 6-month follow-up assessment. Children who were read to by both teachers and parents had larger gains than children who were read to by teachers only (Whitehurst, Arnold, et al., 1994).

In a subsequent investigation, Lonigan and Whitehurst (1998) extended the design of the Whitehurst, Arnold, et al. (1994) study by adding a third intervention group where only parents read to their children using the dialogic reading approach. The intent of the Lonigan and Whitehurst experiment was to determine the relative effectiveness of parents versus teachers in implementing dialogic reading. Four child care centers serving mainly families eligible for subsidized child care participated in the study; children were randomly assigned to one of the four study conditions, and teachers and parents in the respective intervention conditions participated in videotape training in dialogic reading methods as carried out in the Whitehurst, Arnold, et al. study. Results of the Lonigan and Whitehurst investigation indicated that at the end of the 6-week intervention, each of the intervention conditions had a significant effect on oral language skills; effects were largest in the two intervention conditions involving home reading. The investigators speculate that a one-on-one reading context provided by parents may be more conducive to a child's active participation in shared reading than the group format most commonly used in classrooms.

Parent as Primary Participant

As noted in the introduction to this chapter, the idea that families are central to achieving meaningful change in children's outcomes has led many designers of early intervention programs to view work with parents in adjunct or supplementary roles in child-focused interventions to be an insufficient influence on families. A better program design, some argue, is to support families through intensive intervention with the parent. Two types of parent-focused interventions are considered next, one with a content emphasis on family child-rearing environments and one with a content emphasis on a broader range of family functions.

Child-Focused Content

Early childhood intervention via parenting education and support has been an active part of the early intervention field since the 1960s. Early efforts in this area include the Florida Parent Education Infant and Toddler Program (Gordon, Guinagh, & Jester, 1977), the Mother-Child Home Program (Levenstein, 1977, 1988), and the Early Training Project (Klaus & Gray, 1968). Later interventions targeted adolescent mothers (e.g., Field, Widmayer, Greenberg, & Stoller, 1982; Osofsky, Culp, & Ware, 1988) and parents of children with disabilities (e.g., Brassell & Dunst, 1978). There also is a rich tradition of family interventions that seek to change antisocial behavior in children through behavioral parent training (e.g., Serketich & Dumas, 1996).

Program Approaches. The Parents as Teachers (PAT) Program is one prominent model representative of this tradition. It was founded in 1981 as the New Parents as Teachers Program by Mildred Winter (Vartuli & Winter, 1989), with program content originally based on Burton White's (White & Watts, 1973) research on early childhood development. PAT is a core element of Edward Zigler's (Zigler, Finn-Stevenson, & Hall, 2002) School of the 21st Century model. A major program component is home visits conducted with the parent (usually the mother) to share age-appropriate activities and child development information aimed at strengthening the quality of mother-child interaction and the home learning environment. There also are periodic group meetings of parents, developmental screenings, and referrals to community services. School readiness is a major program goal.

Effects. The PAT Program has been subjected to a series of randomized trials with low-income populations. A three-site study conducted in geographically dispersed urban areas with a total sample of 665 children and their families found few statistically significant effects on parenting and child development at the end of 2 years in the program (child's 2nd birthday). There were only three statistically significant differences among 28 measures of parent outcomes: a higher frequency of telling stories, saying nursery rhymes, and singing with the child among very low-income intervention group parents compared to very low-income control group parents, and a higher frequency of parents' happiness in caring for their child and acceptance of their child's behavior among the more moderate-income intervention families compared to their control group counterparts. There were no statistically significant effects on child outcomes (Wagner et al., 2002).

In separate randomized trials of the PAT Program with primarily Latino parents in northern California and with adolescent parents in southern California, there were small and inconsistent positive effects on parent knowledge, attitudes, and behavior, and no gains in child development or health when experimental and control groups were compared overall. Subgroup analyses in the northern California site indicated that children in primarily Spanish-speaking Latino families benefited more than either non-Latino or English-speaking Latino families; there were significant child gains in cognitive, communication, social, and self-help development but not a corresponding consistent pattern of positive intervention effects on mothers. Also, subgroup analyses in the southern California site indicated that families receiving both PAT services and comprehensive case management services designed to help mothers improve their life course benefited most (Wagner & Clayton, 1999). Attrition was high and the frequency of home visits was well below the intended monthly contact in each of the PAT studies.

A qualitative study focused on why the PAT Program was not more effective in the two California randomized trials found that home visitors emphasized their social support role and generally did not discuss parenting behaviors that appeared to be in need of change or improvement, even though program goals emphasized both confidence building and focus on parenting behaviors. Mothers viewed the time the home visitor spent interacting with their child as a direct intervention (a "vitamin") that would enhance the child's development, whereas the home visitors saw the same interaction as modeling for the parent (Hebbeler & Gerlach-Downie, 2002).

Implementation issues aside, it is useful to ponder whether a different method (groups) and content (social development) are critical variables here. Recall from the previous section that Webster-Stratton's (1998) group-based intervention with parents regarding children's Conduct Disorder yielded positive effects on parents and children's behaviors at home.

Broad-Focused Content

Since the 1970s, reviewers of the early intervention research literature have argued that parenting education programs aimed at low-income families are likely to yield few or no positive outcomes because they are not equipped to address parents' primary concerns, namely, major sources of stress faced by parents living in poverty (e.g., Chilman, 1973; St. Pierre & Layzer, 1998). Results of the PAT Program in southern California suggest that there are benefits in providing parents with concrete assistance with personal and family life issues combined with support for improvements in parenting knowledge and skills. In an intervention condition that combined the PAT Program with case management for adolescent mothers, experimental group participants were more accepting of their children's behavior, children experienced significant gains of 1 or 2 months in cognitive development, and there were significantly fewer opened cases of child abuse or neglect compared to control group participants. There were no intervention effects on a range of other outcome variables, however (Wagner & Clayton, 1999). Described next are approaches and results of other parent-oriented interventions that have attempted to support parent and family functioning as an avenue to improved child outcomes.

Program Approaches. A case management approach to family support via home visiting was examined in the Comprehensive Child Development Project (CCDP), a 21-site randomized experiment that began in 1989. The project's name is misleading, as the initiative did not provide services directly to children other than developmental screening (Goodson, Layzer, St. Pierre, Bernstein, & Lopez, 2000; see also Gilliam, Ripple, Zigler, & Leiter, 2000). The project was mandated by federal law to serve infants and young children from low-income families who, "because of environmental, health, or other factors, need intensive and comprehensive supportive services to enhance their development" (Goodson et al., 2000, p. 10).

The CCDP was an ambitious intervention designed to work with two or more generations of a family and to involve all family members on a broad range of issues (St. Pierre, Layzer, Goodson, & Bernstein, 1997).

The model of hypothesized CCDP effects speaks to the complexity of the program. The model included five domains of short-term parent/family effects (physical health, mental health, parenting, steps to economic self-sufficiency, employment and income), two domains of short-term child effects (physical health, developmental), plus long-term child effects in four areas (improved school success, reduced special education placement, reduced retention in grade, reduced teen pregnancy) and long-term parent effects on economic self-sufficiency (St. Pierre et al., 1997). Improved parenting knowledge and skills and economic self-sufficiency were the two main hypothesized indirect pathways to improved child well-being, and participation in high-quality programs of early education and care was the primary hypothesized direct pathway to better child outcomes (Goodson et al., 2000).

The CCDP provided case management, parenting education for the mother or primary caregiver, arrangements for developmentally appropriate early childhood education experiences for all children, and developmental screening. Case management was central to the CCDP because without case managers, the CCDP families would have been no different from other low-income families in their community who had access to existing services (Goodson et al., 2000; St. Pierre et al., 1997). Family case managers developed service plans with families based on an assessment of needs (e.g., housing, domestic violence) and identification of goals and necessary actions, and helped families carry out their plans, including referral to health and mental health services and specialists. Referrals also were made to education-related services such as adult literacy education and job training and placement. Emphasis in the case management work was on coordination of services for a family; case managers referred families to services (i.e., provided mother with contact information for a program) and also engaged in brokering of services (i.e., worked with a non-CCDP program on behalf of a CCDP family and followed up to ensure that the family received needed services; St. Pierre et al., 1997). Case managers, usually paraprofessionals, were families' main point of contact with the program, although other CCDP specialists (e.g., health and mental health coordinators, staff responsible for male involvement in the program) interacted with families on an as-needed basis.

When children were between birth and 3 years of age, most early childhood education was delivered through home visits by early childhood specialists. The focus was on educating parents about child development and

parenting skills. Parenting education also was provided through group sessions and printed materials. For older children, program staff linked families to Head Start or high-quality child care. Families were expected to participate for 5 years, beginning during the mother's pregnancy or during the target child's 1st year.

The Nurse-Family Partnership (NFP; previously known as the Nurse Home Visiting Program) also illustrates an intervention approach focused on parents and their contexts. The program seeks to improve (a) the outcomes of pregnancy, (b) quality of caregiving (and related child health and developmental outcomes), and (c) maternal life course development. Nurse home visitors provide information on child development, particularly how to promote sensitive and responsive caregiving (e.g., understanding and responding to infant nonverbal cues, crying behavior, colic). They also attempt to enhance parents' informal social support networks and use of community services, including health and human services that can reduce situational stressors encountered by low-income families. First-time mothers are recruited for the intervention during pregnancy and encouraged to remain in the program through their child's 2nd birthday. Pregnancy and the early years of a child's life are targeted because it is a time when parents are learning the parental role (Olds, Kitzman, Cole, & Robinson, 1997).

The program views the relationship between the nurse home visitor and the mother and other family members beginning during pregnancy as a therapeutic alliance that provides a model to mothers of care and support. An assumption is that this alliance challenges negative views a mother may have of herself as undeserving of attention and care. The intervention also seeks to promote self-efficacy by helping participants set small achievable goals for behavioral change that, if accomplished, would strengthen confidence in dealing with similar situations in the future. The program gives particular attention to women's progressive mastery of their roles as parents and as adults "responsible for their own health and economic self-sufficiency" (Olds, Kitzman, et al., 1997, p. 12).

Effects. Evaluation of the 21 sites of the CCDP, involving a sample of 4,410 families for 5 years, found no statistically significant intervention effects on child outcomes (cognitive, social-emotional, health) or parent outcomes (parenting, family economic self-sufficiency, maternal life course) compared to a control group. Accordingly, there was no empirical support for the two hypothesized indirect pathways (parenting behavior and family economic status) to improved child well-being. Results do not support the hypothesized direct pathway of participation in high-quality programs of early education and care to improved child outcomes. Significantly more CCDP children than control children were enrolled in center-based programs, and program children spent more hours than control children in center-based programs, but overall, the amount of exposure was modest (an average of 2 to 3 hours a day) and data are not available on whether the center-based programs enrolling CCDP children were of higher quality than programs enrolling control group children (Goodson et al., 2000; St. Pierre et al., 1997).

The NFP has been tested in three successive randomized trials. The original trial with predominantly European Americans conducted between 1978 and 1980 in semirural Elmira, New York, found that the intervention reduced rates of child abuse and neglect, maternal welfare dependence, closely spaced successive pregnancies, and maternal criminal behavior related to use of alcohol and other drugs (Olds, Eckenrode, et al., 1997; Olds et al., 1986). Positive intervention effects were concentrated on poor, unmarried adolescents, a subgroup at greatest risk of inappropriate caregiving. Intervention mothers in this high-risk subgroup were significantly less likely to punish and restrict their children, and provided their children with a larger number of appropriate play materials as measured by the Home Observation for Measurement of the Environment (HOME; Caldwell & Bradley, 1984) scale than their counterparts in the comparison group when children were 22 months of age. There were trends when children were 12 and 24 months of age for intervention children to have higher developmental quotients than babies of counterparts in the comparison condition (Olds et al., 1986). A 15-year follow-up of adolescents born to low-income women who received the nurse home visits during pregnancy and postnatally and who were unmarried found fewer instances of running away, fewer arrests, fewer convictions and violations of probation, fewer lifetime sex partners, and fewer days having consumed alcohol in the prior 6 months than youth in the comparison group. Parents who participated in the intervention reported that their children had fewer behavioral problems related to use of alcohol and other drugs, but there were no program effects on other behavioral problems (Olds, Henderson, et al., 1998).

In a subsequent randomized trial conducted with primarily African American women in Memphis, Ten-

nessee, in the early 1990s, nurse-visited mothers held fewer child-rearing beliefs associated with child abuse and neglect, including belief in physical punishment and unrealistic expectations for infants, and had higher quality home environments as measured by the HOME inventory than comparison group mothers when their children were 24 months of age. There was no intervention effect on maternal teaching behavior, child's use of well-child care, immunization status, the child's mental development, or parent report of child behavior problems. Children born to mothers with limited psychological resources were observed to be more responsive to their mother and to communicate their needs more clearly than children of low-resource mothers in the comparison group. At 24 months, nurse-visited mothers reported having fewer second pregnancies and higher levels of perceived mastery than mothers in the comparison group (Kitzman, Cole, Yoos, & Olds, 1997). A 3-year follow-up of the Memphis trial found that intervention mothers had fewer subsequent pregnancies and fewer months of welfare and food stamp use, but the results were smaller in magnitude than those achieved in the Elmira trial (Kitzman et al., 2000).

In the most recent trial, conducted in Denver, Colorado, in the mid-1990s, nurse-visited infants at 6 months of age were less likely to exhibit emotional vulnerability in response to fear stimuli. At 21 months, nurse-visited children born to women with low psychological resources were less likely to exhibit language delays, and at 24 months they exhibited superior mental development compared to counterpart children in the comparison group. There were no intervention effects on women's educational achievement or use of welfare or children's behavior problems (Olds et al., 2002).

Child and Parent as Primary Participants

One of the typical responses to findings of modest or no effects of parent-focused interventions is the argument that early childhood intervention is more effective when it entails direct, intensive work with both parent and child than with the parent alone.

Research-based interventions that work directly with the child and the parent and provide supports for a range of family functions span nearly 4 decades. Initial efforts, launched in the late 1960s and in 1970, include Head Start's Parent-Child Center Program (Lazar et al., 1970), the Parent-Child Development Center (Andrews et al., 1982), the Yale Child Welfare Project (Provence, Naylor, & Patterson, 1977), and the Syracuse Family

Development Research Program (Lally, Mangione, & Honig, 1988). These early interventions, like their contemporary counterparts, differ on theoretical and programmatic dimensions (e.g., whether direct services to parent and to child are offered concurrently or sequentially), but they share a clear goal of improving a range of parent outcomes, including maternal depression, sense of mastery, problem-solving and life management skills, and abilities related to economic self-sufficiency.

Research on the initial wave of interventions in this area yielded positive, albeit modest, program effects on parents and children and provided a basis for further development and testing of program models. For example, a three-site, experimental study of the Parent-Child Development Center (PCDC) Program found that children achieved superior Stanford-Binet scores at the time of program graduation (36 months of age), and program mothers scored significantly higher than control group mothers on dimensions of positive maternal behavior. The PCDC children maintained their IQ gains 1 year after leaving the program (Andrews et al., 1982) but not beyond (Bridgeman, Blumenthal, & Andrews, 1981). A 10-year follow-up study of the Yale Child Welfare Project, which provided families with pediatric care, social work, child care, and psychological services in an individualized manner by a four-person team of professionals, found positive program effects on intervention children's school attendance and boys' use of special school services, but no program effects on children's IQ scores. Program mothers were more likely to be self-supporting, have more formal education, and have smaller family size than mothers who had not been in the program (Seitz, Rosenbaum, & Apfel, 1985). A later follow-up study found positive program effects on intervention children's siblings' school attendance and performance (Seitz & Apfel, 1994). Reduced rates of juvenile delinquency, better school performance, and more positive child and parental attitudes toward self and the environment (i.e., problem-solving orientation) were found for intervention girls but not boys in junior high school in a 10-year follow-up study of the Syracuse Family Development Research Program (Lally et al., 1988). The positive effects of these interventions provided a basis for further development and testing of other program models.

Interventions that seek to improve parent and family functioning differ in the amount of emphasis on the parent's employment skills. The early set of interventions in this area tended to provide referrals to programs providing adult literacy and job training on an as-needed or as-requested basis. Partly in response to welfare reform, more recent child and family interventions include training directly related to economic self-sufficiency as an integral part of service provisions. Illustrations of these contrasting approaches and their effects are described next.

Program Approaches

The Infant Health and Development Program (IHDP) was an eight-site randomized study of a 3-year intervention with low birthweight, premature infants that included three components: home visits through age 3 years, weekly in the 1st year and biweekly in the 2nd and 3rd years; child participation in child development centers beginning at age 1 year through age 3 years for a full day, 50 weeks a year; and parent group meetings every other month during the 2nd and 3rd years. IHDP was launched in 1985.

The home visits promoted knowledge and skill development in child health and development, using the Partners for Learning curriculum for age-appropriate games and activities that foster cognitive, language, and social development (Sparling & Lewis, 1995), and in problem-solving skills, using the Parent Problem Solving Program designed to help parents learn effective ways of coping with stress related to parenting and other life events (Wasik, Bryant, Lyons, et al., 1997). Activities from the Partners for Learning curriculum also were used in the child development center (Ramey, Sparling, Bryant, & Wasik, 1997). Home visitor selection and training included major attention to basic clinical skills (i.e., observing, listening, questioning, probing, prompting, supporting) that would enable visitors to develop an empathic, trusting relationship with parents and other family members (Wasik, Bryant, Lyons, et al., 1997).

The problem-solving curriculum was based on the assumption that daily situations encountered by parents are often complex and demanding, and that problem-solving skills can enhance overall parental well-being and increase the likelihood of positive parent-child relationships. The curriculum views problem solving as a cognitive-behavioral process that includes both thinking and action components. Seven steps are emphasized: problem definition, goal selection, generation of solutions, consideration of consequences, decision making, implementation, and evaluation. Home visitors gave explicit attention to each of these steps in guided discussions with parents and used a booklet and three visual aids as reminders of key words in the problem-solving process: a "Stop" card that includes the words Stop, Think, Act, and Check; and a "Think" card that includes key questions corresponding to the problem-solving steps (What is the problem? What do I want? What can I do? What will happen if? What is my decision? Wasik, Bryant, Lyons, et al., 1997).

The Even Start Family Literacy Program is illustrative of the trend to include job-related training in two-generation interventions. It was described earlier in this chapter in the case illustration.

Effects

In the IHDP study, 985 infants were randomly assigned to either intervention (home visitors, child development center, parent group meetings) or follow-up conditions in each of the eight research sites through a computer-driven process that gave consideration to such key factors as birthweight, gender, maternal education, maternal race, and primary language in the home. Both intervention group and follow-up group infants received medical, developmental, and social assessments, with referral to pediatric care and other services as needed. At 3 years of age, the end of the intervention, intervention children had significantly higher intelligence test scores and receptive vocabulary test scores and lower scores on a parental measure of reported behavior problems than children in the follow-up group. Benefits were more pronounced among heavier low-birthweight than in lighter low-birthweight infants (IHDP, 1990). Child outcomes were positively associated with frequency of family participation in the intervention (Ramey et al., 1992). When children were 5 years of age, there were no significant overall differences in IQ score, receptive vocabulary, or reported behavior problems, but heavier low-birthweight children in the intervention had higher IQ scores, verbal IQ scores, and receptive vocabulary scores than their counterparts in the follow-up group (Brooks-Gunn et al., 1994). At 8 years of age, there were modest intervention effects on cognitive and academic skills of heavier low-birthweight children (McCarton et al., 1997).

There were no intervention effects on the home environment, as measured by the HOME inventory, at 12 months, but at 36 months the home environments of intervention families were higher than follow-up families in total HOME scores, suggesting that the impact of the intervention may be cumulative. At 36 months, there were intervention effects on the learning stimulation, modeling, variety of experience, and acceptance subscales, aspects of the home environment emphasized in the Partners for Learning curriculum (Bradley et al.,

1994). The intervention effect on children's IQ scores at 3 years of age was much greater for children from lower-quality homes, as measured by the HOME inventory. As noted earlier, there were no overall intervention effects on child IQ at 5 and 8 years of age (control group children caught up with treatment group children at age 8 years), and the IQ difference between children from higher- and lower-quality home environments, as measured when children were 3 years of age, declined with child age (Bradley, Burchinal, & Casey, 2001).

Analysis of videotaped mother-child interaction at the child's 30-month clinic visit found small positive effects of the intervention on maternal interactive behavior but not on a rating summarizing maternal affective behavior. A rating of dyadic quality of the mother-child interactions showed that intervention mothers and their children were more synchronous, exhibiting greater cooperation and harmony, than follow-up mother-child dyads, and intervention children were rated as significantly more persistent and goal-directed and more attentive, involved, and enthusiastic while working on a challenging problem-solving task in the presence of the child's mother (Spiker, Ferguson, & Brooks-Gunn, 1993).

Intervention mothers scored higher than follow-up group mothers on a self-report measure of problem-solving skills, but there were no differences between intervention and follow-up group mothers on a measure of coping with health and daily living at 36 months (Wasik, Bryant, Sparling, & Ramey, 1997) and on measures of knowledge or concepts of child development at 12, 24, or 36 months (Benasich, Brooks-Gunn, Spiker, & Black, 1997).

The IHDP intervention reduced maternal distress (depression and anxiety) when children were 1 and 3 years of age, especially for women with less than high school education, but maternal distress did not moderate or mediate intervention effects on child outcomes. IHDP effects on maternal distress at 1 year were likely a result of the home visits because child development center and parent group meetings were not offered during the 1st year. Life events moderated the influence of the intervention on children's test scores; the intervention was more effective for children whose mother had fewer life events (Klebanov, Brooks-Gunn, & McCormick, 2001).

Even Start has been evaluated in three national evaluations beginning in 1989. The third and most recent evaluation, conducted from 1997/1998 through 2000/2001, included an experimental design study to test program effectiveness in 18 sites involving about 460 families who were randomly assigned to either Even Start or a control group (St. Pierre et al., 2003). Results indicated that Even Start Program children and parents did not gain more than control group children and parents, about one-third of whom received early childhood education or adult education through non-Even Start services. Even Start families participated in a small amount of program services relative to their apparent needs and program goals. There was some evaluation evidence to suggest that Even Start early childhood classrooms, though of good quality overall, gave insufficient attention to language acquisition and reasoning skills.

Preliminary Hypotheses about Program Design

Although it is impossible to move toward conclusions about the design of family interventions from a review of programs selected for illustrative purposes only, the patterns of findings across these different approaches to families point to some preliminary hypotheses about central features of program design.

It appears unlikely that the child serves as a mediator of early childhood program effects on family interactions when parents are assigned an adjunct role in an intensive early childhood program. Because interventions targeted to parents living in high-risk circumstances are complicated and difficult enterprises, there is great appeal in the notion that direct work with the child can trigger changes in patterns of interaction within a family, thereby reducing the need to work with parents to achieve positive change in parent-child interactions. Years ago, Lazar (1983) proposed a pattern of "stimulation stimulating," wherein a child comes home from preschool with skills and interests that place new demands on family interactions (i.e., child requests to be read to) and prompt parents to praise the child's accomplishments and to raise their achievement expectations and encouragement of the child to do well in school. Although the Abecedarian findings suggest that experimental group children presented different demand characteristics when interacting with their mother, there is no subsequent evidence to suggest that these behaviors led to changes in family interactions. This is not surprising theoretically. Family systems theory indicates that homeostatic features of families maintain the stability of their patterns of interaction (Minuchin, 1985, 2002).

More generally, it seems that placement of parents in an adjunct role in an intensive early childhood program

is unlikely to impact parents' child-rearing competence. This is an important hypothesis to investigate because the provisions for program connections with parents in the Abecedarian project mirror the widely used NAEYC guidelines for appropriate practice in early childhood programs.

Increasing the frequency of focused program exchanges with parents—represented in the program design where parents assume a supplementary role in an early childhood program—may increase the likelihood of program impact on parenting competence and child outcomes if the content is focused on a single child-rearing domain that is also a curriculum enhancement in the early childhood program. Results of the dialogic reading program (Whitehurst, Arnold, et al., 1994) and the child conduct program (Webster-Stratton et al., 2001) demonstrate the promise of a dual home-and-school focus on well-defined content.

Programs that embrace a broad area of content have greater opportunity than more narrowly focused programs to employ the social work principle "Begin where clients are." The flexibility and, one hopes, the resourcefulness to focus on a range of issues do not necessarily ensure that the program worker will eventually engage parents in child-related topics once other matters have been addressed. The ability to weave child and parent content into a conversation dominated by a parent's legitimate concerns about other pressing personal or family circumstances requires keen clinical skills that may be more readily possessed by professionals than paraprofessionals. A relationship with one staff person also may help parents focus on parent and child issues. For example, in the CCDP, the separation of child development and parenting information (provided by a bachelor's-level staff person in most sites) from case management work (carried out by a paraprofessional) may have seemed artificial to parents and may have suppressed in-depth discussion of child and parenting concerns in the context of other family matters. One striking difference between the CCDP and the NFP is the focus on the nurse-mother-family relationships, parent development, and connections with informal social support networks in NFP and on referral to and brokering with formal services in CCDP. In view of NFP effects on child and parent outcomes, particularly for parents at greatest risk, a relationship-based approach to intervention in the context of informal and formal systems of family support may be central to promoting child and parent well-being.

Program assistance with parents' job-related skills is unlikely to have immediate positive effects on parenting and child outcomes. Parental workplace experiences may increase the value parents place on their child's education, and characteristics of parents' jobs (e.g., autonomy, problem solving) have been found to be significant predictors of child outcomes, such as reduced child behavior problems (Cooksey, Menaghan, & Jekielek, 1997) and early reading ability (Parcel & Menaghan, 1994). Yet, the path to major change in education and employment is slow and uncertain for educationally disadvantaged parents living in poverty (Wilson, Ellwood, & Brooks-Gunn, 1995), and low-pay, low-complexity work for mothers attempting to leave welfare may result in negative child outcomes (Menaghan & Parcel, 1995). Thus, it seems unrealistic to expect that associations found between parenting practices and child outcomes in substantively more complex employment will be realized in a timely manner for low-income young children typically targeted for early intervention.

NEEDED DIRECTIONS IN APPROACHES TO FAMILIES IN EARLY CHILDHOOD INTERVENTIONS

Needed directions in research and program development are set forth below. In both areas, emphasis is given to focusing on the components and processes of interventions with families.

Research

Since the 1960s, the early intervention field has been driven by research on program models that span a range of assumptions about how to improve the outcomes of children at risk. Current funding streams, policies, and practices have been greatly influenced by the design and evaluation results of prominent models. At the same time, the early intervention field is composed mostly of state- and locally developed efforts that may be inspired by but seldom are full replications or adoptions of existing models (Ramey & Ramey, 1998). Moreover, there is a history of model interventions being watered down in the process of taking programs to scale as policymakers trade quantity for quality in stretching program resources (Schorr & Schorr, 1988). One proposed solution to this problem is for developers of model programs to emphasize essential elements of the model (Olds, O'Brien, Racine, Glazner, & Kitzman, 1998). A persua-

sive case for specific model components is difficult to make when research on program models examines an intervention package rather than individual program elements, as noted earlier in this chapter. Too, adaptation to local circumstances is expected practice in the development of new programs or adoption of an existing program model (Yoshikawa et al., 2002). Research on potentially critical elements of intervention programs, then, holds promise of providing guidance to program implementers, particularly when a set of studies can be used to formulate indicators of program quality in work with families.

Rigorous research methods, particularly experimental designs, are essential to searches for critical elements of effective interventions. Within-group comparison analyses are the dominant design of existing research on potentially critical elements of early interventions. An example is the dosage-response relationship. The chief problem with correlational methods is that causality cannot be established. Strong positive correlations between indices of program participation and program outcomes are difficult to interpret, for example, because preintervention population differences may be related to participant-outcome relationships. Needed, then, are experimental studies that systematically vary a program element. Especially informative are between-group comparison studies that entail an enhancement or adaptation of a particular program, found to be effective in prior investigations, to determine whether there are more effective program designs. Movement in this direction requires resources as well as maturity in research-based development of intervention models that currently is limited to a relatively small set of early childhood interventions. Examples include planned variation in the use of videotapes versus in-person staff to demonstrate effective joint book reading strategies with preschool children (Arnold et al., 1994) and in the use of professional nurses versus paraprofessionals to deliver a home visiting program (Olds et al., 2002). Also illustrative of this approach is a federally funded Even Start study, known as the Classroom Literacy Interventions and Outcomes study, initiated in 2003 to assess the relative effectiveness of different family literacy curricula in promoting language and literacy outcomes for children and their parents (St. Pierre, Ricciuti, & Tao, 2004).

In addition to stronger research designs, the investigation of family interventions needs sophisticated measurement approaches and sufficient resources for data collection with a population that often is difficult to track and engage. The customary sample attrition rates alone present multiple challenges for data collection and analyses (McCall & Green, 2004) and interpretation of results (Wagner et al., 2002). Observational methods need to be central to the measurement of program outcomes (particularly among adults) and program processes. Existing studies suggest that the conceptualization and measurement of program processes need to move beyond frequency of program contact with participants (D. R. Powell et al., 2004). Further, the status of program implementation research needs to be elevated through use of rigorous methods to assess treatment fidelity and through contributions to our understanding of links between program variables and participant outcomes.

Especially needed are theoretically driven research designs for examining the mediator and moderator roles of family factors in early intervention processes. Much of the existing research has a post hoc, exploratory quality and, though investigators are to be commended for maximizing the yield of studies originally intended to examine child outcomes with minimal attention to process variables, the results are typically elusive. The early intervention field would benefit from greater use of an incremental, research-based approach to program development. Gradual improvements in the design of a program model based in part on results of repeated experimental study have not been the norm of program development in early intervention (Yoshikawa et al., 2002), yet the more effective interventions have followed this pattern. For example, the content and methods of the NFP were revised after each of three consecutive randomized trials that, as noted earlier, also produced important data on how well the model worked with different populations and in semirural and urban settings. Specifically, the intervention's parent-infant curricula were broadened to promote sensitive and responsive caregiving through refinements and expansions that incorporated activities from other interventions (Olds, Kitzman, et al., 1997). This incremental approach to program development is in contrast with the early intervention field's modal pattern of taking programs to scale without a well-researched model program to provide a solid base of guidance for program design and implementation decisions. Head Start is a classic example of the rapid launching of a program (Zigler & Muenchow, 1992). The quick program rollout pattern has continued with, for example, the 23-site Comprehensive Child Development Program, based partly on the Beethoven Project in Chicago, which had a

history of program implementation problems, and with the Even Start Family Literacy Program, initially implemented in 76 sites and based loosely on a program model (the Parent and Child Education Program in Kentucky; Heberle, 1992) that has not been subjected to a credible experimental study.

A potential limitation of an incremental approach to program development is that the societal context initially giving shape to a program model may shift while the program is in development, rendering the program model incompatible with contemporary circumstances. An example is the Parent-Child Development Center Program. The PCDC research and program development plan was experimental, rigorous, and long term with replications, but some of the intervention's basic assumptions about the target population (e.g., stay-at-home mothers available for frequent, daytime participation at a program center) proved to be problematic while the program was undergoing a randomized outcome study and contributed to premature termination of the larger project. The program was conceived prior to serious national economic troubles, including inflation, and the growth of the women's movement in the 1970s. The PCDC emphasized motherhood and child-rearing skills, but program participants increasingly were interested in other roles, including potential wage earner, and not solely interested in their role as an agent for enhancing their child's development. Many program participants entered or reentered the labor force for personal as well as financial reasons (Andrews et al., 1982).

Program Development

A challenge facing any social intervention is responsiveness to the daily realities of the target population. Interventions aimed at families living in poverty and high-risk conditions have long struggled with this task (e.g., Chilman, 1973). Today, most parents living in poverty are engaged in school, job training, or employment. In the broader population, families with young children increasingly face difficult decisions about use of time for family and work, with employment patterns suggesting, for example, that employed mothers of preschoolers in dual-earner families work about 9 more hours a week than they would prefer and fathers' work hours increasing as the number of children rises (Jacobs & Gerson, 2004). Parent employment is negatively correlated with level of parent participation in Head Start (e.g., Castro, Bryant, Peisner-Feinberg, & Skinner, 2004), and growing numbers of parents are unavailable for participation in time-intensive intervention programs crafted in an earlier era.

The limited availability of many parents for program participation provides a pragmatic basis for dismissing the idea of working with parents and primary caregivers. However, early interventions that programmatically disconnect children from their families reduce the potential of enhancing children's well-being by ignoring a major context of early development. Nonfamilial child care does not reduce the influence of parents on children's behavior and development (e.g., National Institute of Child Health and Human Development Early Child Care Research Network, 1998), and family factors continue to be among the predictors of young children's outcomes when children participate in intensive classroom-based early interventions (Burchinal, Campbell, Bryant, Wasik, & Ramey, 1997).

Contemporary family conditions heighten interest in family program designs that work with parents in conjunction with an early childhood program. A common configuration is for parents to assume an adjunct role in relation to their child's center-based program. A potentially significant limitation of the adjunct role is that it does not appear to lead to improvements in parents' child-rearing competence, as noted in the previous section.

Of greater promise is the program design characterized by a supplementary role for parents, particularly when well-defined program content is shared with parents in a concentrated time period and also emphasized in the early childhood curriculum. The examples in the previous section were curriculum enhancements of existing preschool programs that involved both parent and teacher in focused training aimed at improving children's early reading skills (Whitehurst, Arnold, et al., 1994) and behavior conduct (Webster-Stratton et al., 2001). Efficiency is one of many appeals of these approaches. Work with parents was frequent but within a relatively brief time frame and presumably focused on content of keen interest to parents. Because some studies of early childhood programs have found weak or no effects of an add-on educational component for parents (e.g., Boyce, White, & Kerr, 1993), an important future direction is to identify characteristics of effective approaches. Also needed is follow-up research on the sustainability of short-term effects achieved by these content-specific approaches as well as on the extent to which parents (and teachers) continue to engage in practices promoted by the intervention.

Family interventions aimed at helping parents improve their educational and vocational aspirations while also providing an early childhood program—the "parent and child as primary participants" design described in the previous section—appear on the surface to be responsive to the needs of many low-income families, but considerable program development work is needed to refine the potential of this approach. It is not clear that the current organization of most two-generation programs address in sufficient detail the range of problems experienced by program participants living in poverty. Individual program components may be of insufficient intensity (St. Pierre et al., 1998). One task is to achieve balanced, high-quality attention to both parent and child in two-generation interventions. Anecdotal information from the Even Start Program suggests there is a tendency for some programs to focus on one set of outcomes at the exclusion of others, for example, viewing the preschool component as a custodial arrangement staffed by minimally trained individuals and aimed at freeing parents for participation in parenting or job training classes. The mission of the sponsoring agency (i.e., early childhood or adult education) and the outcomes by which programs are assessed (i.e., children's school readiness or adult GED completion rates) may contribute to imbalances. A related task is to provide quality services in each of the components. For example, most adult education programs are replications of poor high school settings in which most Even Start participants initially failed (St. Pierre et al., 1998).

Important program development work needs to be carried out with program content. The previous section on intervention design suggests that program goals and content are linked to participant outcomes. Intervention programs have a valuable role to play in testing hypotheses offered in developmental literatures (see section on "Elements of Programmatic Support to Families"). Father contributions to family functioning are an example of an area in pressing need of further development. Systematic refinement and assessment of program goals and content require some boundaries. The family functions that interventions seek to support or change—that is, the goals and content of a program—represent many different variables that expand in number and diversity as interventions broaden their reach. The substantive offerings of an intervention also need to be thoughtfully calibrated with target population interests and circumstances. For example, Farran (2000) has speculated that the problem-solving skills curriculum used with parents in the Infant Health and Development Project may have been more frustrating than helpful to parents attempting to cope with poverty-related problems that often are fairly intractable (e.g., inadequate housing, poor health, lack of transportation, little money).

Intervention methods also need thoughtful program development attention. For example, Gomby and colleagues (1999, p. 17) have suggested that home visiting program attrition rates may reflect family views of "a most unusual approach to service delivery. There are very few occasions in America in which a nonfamily member regularly visits the home to persuade someone to change his or her behavior." As suggested in previous sections of this chapter, interventions have a long way to go in applying family systems theory to practices with participants (i.e., working with relationship systems, not individuals per se) and in examining the effects of different pedagogical approaches, particularly strategies that encourage active participant engagement.

The long-neglected area of program implementation needs to be a high priority of program designers. The extant literature contains potent hints of some serious problems in carrying out program plans. Because staffing arrangements appear to be a linchpin in intervention programs, the early intervention field would benefit from future work that refines and transcends the paraprofessional versus professional debate to examine specific skills and background characteristics of effective intervention staff as well as approaches to staff supervision.

Family interventions operate at the intersection of profound sociopolitical changes affecting families, growing societal concern about children's outcomes, a limited base of pertinent empirical science, and often unrealistic expectations of what programs can accomplish. It is difficult to overstate the complexities of research and practice in this terrain. It is equally difficult to overemphasize the opportunities to contribute to an understanding of how the hopes and actions of families can be marshaled on behalf of their children's futures.

REFERENCES

Andrews, S. R., Blumenthal, J. B., Johnson, D. L., Kahn, A. J., Ferguson, C. J., Lasater, R. M., et al. (1982). The skills of mothering: A study of parent child development centers. *Monographs of the Society for Research in Child Development, 47*(6, Serial No. 198).

Arnold, D. H., Lonigan, C. J., Whitehurst, G. J., & Epstein, J. N. (1994). Accelerating language development through picture book reading: Replication and extension to a videotape training format. *Journal of Educational Psychology, 86*, 235–243.

Bakermans-Kranenburg, M. J., van IJzendoorn, M. H., & Juffer, F. (2003). Less is more: Meta-analysis of sensitivity and attachment interventions in early childhood. *Psychological Bulletin, 129*, 195–215.

Baratz, S. S., & Baratz, J. C. (1970). Early childhood intervention: The social science base of institutional racism. *Harvard Educational Review, 40*, 29–50.

Barnett, W. S. (1995). Long-term effects of early childhood programs on cognitive and school outcomes. *Future of Children, 5*, 25–50.

Barnett, W. S. (1996). Lives in the balance: Age-27 benefit-cost analysis of the High/Scope Perry Preschool Program. *Monographs of the High/Scope Educational Research Foundation, 11*.

Barnett, W. S., Young, J. W., & Schweinhart, L. J. (1998). How preschool education influences long-term cognitive development and school success: A causal model. In W. S. Barnett & S. S. Boocock (Eds.), *Early care and education for children in poverty: Promises, programs, and long-term results* (pp. 167–184). Albany: State University of New York Press.

Baydar, N., Reid, M. J., & Webster-Stratton, C. (2003). The role of mental health factors and program engagement in the effectiveness of a preventive parenting program for Head Start mothers. *Child Development, 74*, 1433–1453.

Belsky, J. (1986). A tale of two variances: Between and within. *Child Development, 57*, 1301–1305.

Benasich, A. A., Brooks-Gunn, J., Spiker, D., & Black, G. W. (1997). Maternal attitudes and knowledge about child development. In R. T. Gross, D. Spiker, & C. W. Haynes (Eds.), *Helping low birth weight, premature babies: Infant health and development program* (pp. 290–303). Stanford, CA: Stanford University Press.

Boocock, S. S., & Larner, M. (1998). Long-term outcomes in other nations. In W. S. Barnett & S. S. Boocock (Eds.), *Early care and education for children in poverty* (pp. 45–76). Albany: State University of New York Press.

Booth, C. L., Mitchell, S. K., Barnard, K. E., & Spiker, S. J. (1989). Development of maternal social skills in multiproblem families: Effects on the mother-child relationship. *Developmental Psychology, 25*, 403–412.

Borkowski, J. G., Ramey, S. L., & Stile, C. (2002). Parenting research: Translations to parenting practices. In J. G. Borkowski, S. L. Ramey, & M. Bristol-Power (Eds.), *Parenting and the child's world: Influences on academic, intellectual, and social-emotional development* (pp. 365–386). Mahwah, NJ: Erlbaum.

Bornstein, M. H. (2000). *Handbook of parenting* (2nd ed.). Mahwah, NJ: Erlbaum.

Bowlby, J. (1969). *Attachment and loss: Vol. 1. Attachment.* New York: Basic Books.

Boyce, G. C., White, K. R., & Kerr, B. (1993). The effectiveness of adding a parent involvement component to an existing center-based program for children with disabilities and their families. *Early Education and Development, 4*, 327–345.

Bradley, R. H., Burchinal, M. R., & Casey, P. H. (2001). Early intervention: The moderating role of the home environment. *Applied Developmental Science, 5*, 2–8.

Bradley, R. H., Whiteside, L., Mundfrom, D. J., Casey, P. H., Caldwell, B. M., & Barrett, K. (1994). Impact of the Infant Health and Development Program (IHDP) on the home environment of infants born prematurely and with low birthweight. *Journal of Educational Psychology, 86*, 531–544.

Brassell, W. R., & Dunst, C. J. (1978). Fostering the object construct: Large-scale intervention with handicapped infants. *American Journal Mental Deficiency, 82*, 505–510.

Bredekamp, S., & Copple, C. (1997). *Developmentally appropriate practice in early childhood programs* (Rev. ed.). Washington, DC: National Association for the Education of Young Children.

Bridgeman, B., Blumenthal, J., & Andrews, S. (1981). *Parent-Child Development Center: Final evaluation report* (Submitted to the

U.S. Department of Health and Human Services). Princeton, NJ: Educational Testing Service.

Brinker, R. P. (1992). Family involvement in early intervention: Accepting the unchangeable, changing the changeable, and knowing the difference. *Topics in Early Childhood Special Education, 12,* 306–333.

Bronfenbrenner, U. (1974). *Is early intervention effective? Vol. 2. A report on longitudinal evaluations of preschool programs.* Washington, DC: Department of Health, Education and Welfare, Office of Child Development.

Brooks-Gunn, J., Berlin, L. J., & Fuligni, A. S. (2000). Early childhood intervention programs: What about the family? In J. P. Shonkoff & S. J. Meisels (Eds.), *Handbook of early childhood intervention* (2nd ed., pp. 549–588). New York: Cambridge University Press.

Brooks-Gunn, J., Gross, R. T., Kraemer, H. C., Spiker, D., & Shapiro, S. (1997). Enhancing the cognitive outcomes of LBW, premature infants: For whom is the intervention most effective? In R. T. Gross, D. Spiker, & C. W. Haynes (Eds.), *Helping low birth weight, premature babies: Infant Health and Development Program* (pp. 181–189). Stanford, CA: Stanford University Press.

Brooks-Gunn, J., McCarton, C. M., Casey, P. H., McCormick, M. C., Bauer, C. R., Bernbaum, J. C., et al. (1994). Early intervention in low-birth-weight premature infants: Results through age 5 years from the Infant Health and Development Program. *Journal of the American Medical Association, 272,* 1257–1262.

Bruer, J. T. (1999). *The myth of the first 3 years.* New York: Free Press.

Bryant, D., & Wasik, B. H. (2004). Home visiting and family literacy programs. In B. H. Wasik (Ed.), *Handbook of family literacy* (pp. 329–346). Mahwah, NJ: Erlbaum.

Burchinal, M. R., Campbell, F. A., Bryant, D. M., Wasik, B. H., & Ramey, C. T. (1997). Early intervention and mediating processes in cognitive performance of children of low-income African American families. *Child Development, 68,* 935–954.

Bus, A. C., & van IJzendoorn, M. H. (1988). Mother-child interactions, attachment, and emergent literacy: A cross-cultural study. *Child Development, 59,* 1262–1272.

Buysse, V., & Wesley, P. W. (1993). The identity crisis in early childhood special education: A call for professional role clarification. *Topics in Early Childhood Special Education, 13,* 418–429.

Caldwell, B. M., & Bradley, R. H. (1984). *Home Observation for Measurement of the Environment.* Fayetteville: University of Arkansas Press.

Campbell, D. T. (1986). Relabeling internal and external validity for applied social scientists. In W. M. K. Trochim (Ed.), *Advances in quasi-experimental design and analysis* (pp. 67–77). San Francisco: Jossey-Bass.

Campbell, F. A., Breitmayer, B. J., & Ramey, C. T. (1986). Disadvantaged teenage mothers and their children: Consequences of educational day care. *Family Relations, 35,* 63–68.

Campbell, F. A., Pungello, E. P., Miller-Johnson, S., Burchinal, M., & Ramey, C. T. (2001). The development of cognitive and academic abilities: Growth curves from an early childhood educational experiment. *Developmental Psychology, 37,* 231–242.

Campbell, F. A., & Ramey, C. T. (1994). Effects of early intervention on intellectual and academic achievement: A follow-up study of children from low-income families. *Child Development, 65,* 684–698.

Campbell, F. A., & Ramey, C. T. (1995). Cognitive and school outcomes for high risk African American students at middle adolescence: Positive effects of early intervention. *American Educational Research Journal, 32,* 743–772.

Campbell, F. A., Ramey, C. T., Pungello, E., Sparling, J., & Miller-Johnson, S. (2002). Early childhood education: Young adult outcomes from the Abecedarian Project. *Applied Developmental Science, 6,* 42–57.

Castro, D. C., Bryant, D. M., Peisner-Feinberg, E. S., & Skinner, M. L. (2004). Parent involvement in Head Start programs: The role of parent, teacher and classroom characteristics. *Early Childhood Research Quarterly, 19,* 413–430.

Cheng Gorman, J., & Balter, L. (1997). Culturally sensitive parent education: A critical review of quantitative research. *Review of Educational Research, 67,* 339–369.

Chilman, C. S. (1973). Programs for disadvantaged parents. In B. M. Caldwell & H. N. Ricciuti (Eds.), *Review of child development research* (Vol. 3, pp. 403–465). Chicago: University of Chicago Press.

Cochran, M., & Woolever, F. (1983). Beyond the deficit model: The empowerment of parents with information and informal supports. In I. E. Sigel & L. M. Laosa (Eds.), *Changing families* (pp. 225–245). New York: Plenum Press.

Cohen, S., Underwood, L. G., & Gottlieb, B. H. (2000). *Social support measurement and intervention: A guide for health and social scientists.* New York: Oxford University Press.

Cole, R., Kitzman, H., Olds, D., & Sidora, K. (1998). Family context as a moderator of program effects in prenatal and early childhood home visitation. *Journal of Community Psychology, 26,* 37–48.

Coleman, J. S., Campbell, E. Q., Hobson, C. J., McPartland, J., Mood, A. M., Weinfeld, F. D., et al. (1966). *Equality of educational opportunity.* Washington, DC: U.S. Government Printing Office.

Collins, W. A., Maccoby, E. E., Steinberg, L., Hetherington, E. M., & Bornstein, M. H. (2000). Contemporary research on parenting: The case for nature *and* nurture. *American Psychologist, 55,* 218–232.

Consortium for Longitudinal Studies. (1983). *As the twig is bent . . . Lasting effects of preschool programs.* Hillsdale, NJ: Erlbaum.

Cooksey, E. C., Menaghan, E. G., & Jekielek, S. M. (1997). Life course effects of work and family circumstances on children. *Social Forces, 76,* 637–667.

Cowan, C. P., Cowan, P. A., & Heming, G. (2005). Two variations of a preventive intervention for couples: Effects on parents and children during the transition to school. In P. A. Cowan, C. P. Cowan, J. C. Ablow, V. K. Johnson, & J. R. Measelle (Eds.), *The family context of parenting in children's adaptation to school* (pp. 277–312). Mahwah, NJ: Erlbaum.

Cowan, C. P., Cowan, P. A., Heming, G., Garrett, E., Coysh, W. S., Curtis-Boles, H., et al. (1985). Transitions to parenthood: His, hers, and theirs. *Journal of Family Issues, 6,* 451–481.

Cowan, P. A., & Cowan, C. P. (2002). What an intervention design reveals about how parents affect their children's academic achievement and behavior problems. In J. G. Borkowski, S. L. Ramey, & M. Bristol-Power (Eds.), *Parenting and the child's world: Influences on academic, intellectual, and social-emotional development* (pp. 75–97). Mahwah, NJ: Erlbaum.

Cowan, P. A., Powell, D. R., & Cowan, C. P. (1998). Parenting interventions, family interventions: A family systems perspective. In W. Damon (Editor-in-Chief) & I. E. Sigel & K. A. Renninger (Vol. Eds.), *Handbook of child psychology: Vol. 4. Child psychology in practice* (5th ed., pp. 1113–1132). New York: Wiley.

Cummings, E. M., Goeke-Morey, M. C., & Graham, M. A. (2002). Interpersonal relations as a dimension of parenting. In J. G. Borkowski, S. L. Ramey, & M. Bristol-Power (Eds.), *Parenting and the child's world: Influences on academic, intellectual, and social-emotional development* (pp. 251–263). Mahwah, NJ: Erlbaum.

Daro, D. A., & Harding, K. A. (1999). Healthy Families America: Using research to enhance practice. *Future of Children, 9,* 152–176.

Deater-Deckard, K., Dodge, K. A., Bates, J. E., & Pettit, G. S. (1996). Physical discipline among African American and European American mothers: Links to children's externalizing behaviors. *Developmental Psychology, 32,* 1065–1072.

Diamond, K. E., & Kontos, S. (2004). Relationships between children's developmental needs, families' resources and families' accommodations: Infants and toddlers with Down syndrome, cerebral palsy, and developmental delay. *Journal of Early Intervention, 26,* 253–265.

Duggan, A., McFarlane, E., Windham, A., Rohde, C. A., Salkever, D. S., Fuddy, L., et al. (1999). Evaluation of Hawaii's Healthy Start program. *Future of Children, 9,* 66–90.

Duggan, A., Windham, A., McFarlane, E., Fuddy, L., Rohde, C., Buchbinder, S., et al. (2000). Hawaii's Healthy Start program of home visiting for at-risk families: Evaluation of family identification, family engagement, and service delivery. *Pediatrics, 105,* 250–259.

Duncan, G., Brooks-Gunn, J., Yeung, J., & Smith, J. (1998). How much does childhood poverty affect the life changes of children? *American Sociological Review, 63,* 406–423.

Dunst, C. J. (2000). Revisiting "rethinking early intervention." *Topics in Early Childhood Special Education, 20,* 95–104.

Dunst, C. J., & Trivette, C. M. (1997). Early intervention with young at-risk children and their families. In R. Ammerman & M. Hersen (Eds.), *Handbook of prevention and treatment with children and adolescents: Intervention in the real world* (pp. 157–180). New York: Wiley.

Elder, G. H. (1974). *Children of the Great Depression.* Chicago: University of Chicago Press.

Embry, L., & Dawson, G. (2002). Disruptions in parenting behavior related to maternal depression: Influences on children's behavioral and psychobiological development. In J. G. Borkowski, S. L. Ramey, & M. Bristol-Power (Eds.), *Parenting and the child's world: Influences on academic, intellectual, and social-emotional development* (pp. 203–229). Mahwah, NJ: Erlbaum.

Emde, R. N., & Robinson, J. (2000). Guiding principles for a theory of early intervention: A developmental-psychoanalytic perspective. In J. P. Shonkoff & S. J. Meisels (Eds.), *Handbook of early childhood intervention* (2nd ed., pp. 160–178). New York: Cambridge University Press.

Evans, G. W. (2004). The environment of childhood poverty. *American Psychologist, 59,* 77–92.

Farran, D. (2000). Another decade of intervention for children who are low income or disabled: What do we know now? In J. P. Shonkoff & S. J. Meisels (Eds.), *Handbook of early childhood intervention* (2nd ed., pp. 510–548). New York: Cambridge University Press.

Farran, D. C., & Haskin, R. (1977, March). *Reciprocal control in social interactions of mothers and 3-year-old children.* Paper presented at the biennial meeting of the Society for Research in Child Development, New Orleans, LA.

Field, T., Widmayer, S., Greenberg, R., & Stoller, S. (1982). Effects of parent training on teenage mothers and their infants. *Pediatrics, 69,* 703–707.

García Coll, C., & Magnuson, K. (2000). Cultural differences as sources of developmental vulnerabilities and resources. In J. P. Shonkoff & S. J. Meisels (Eds.), *Handbook of early childhood intervention* (2nd ed., pp. 94–114). New York: Cambridge University Press.

Gilliam, W. S., Ripple, C. H., Zigler, E. F., & Leiter, V. (2000). Evaluating child and family demonstration initiatives: Lessons from the Comprehensive Child Development Program. *Early Childhood Research Quarterly, 15,* 41–59.

Gomby, D. S., Culross, P. L., & Behrman, R. E. (1999). Home visiting: Recent program evaluations—Analysis and recommendations. *Future of Children, 9,* 4–26.

Goodnow, J. J. (2000). Parents' knowledge and expectations: Using what we know. In M. H. Bornstein (Ed.), *Handbook of parenting: Vol. 3. Being and becoming a parent* (2nd ed., pp. 439–460). Mahwah, NJ: Erlbaum.

Goodson, B. D., Layzer, J. I., St. Pierre, R. G., Bernstein, L. S., & Lopez, M. (2000). Effectiveness of a comprehensive, 5-year family support program for low-income children and their families: Findings from the Comprehensive Child Development Program. *Early Childhood Research Quarterly, 15,* 5–39.

Gordon, I. J., Guinagh, B., & Jester, R. E. (1977). Florida parent education infant and toddler programs. In M. C. Day & R. K. Parker (Eds.), *The preschool in action: Exploring early childhood programs* (2nd ed., pp. 95–127). Boston: Allyn & Bacon.

Guralnick, M. J. (1997). Second-generation research in the field of early intervention. In M. J. Gurlanick (Ed.), *The effectiveness of early intervention* (pp. 3–20). Baltimore: Paul H. Brookes.

Halfon, N., & McLearn, K. T. (2002). Families with children under 3: What we know and implications for results and policy. In N. Halfon, K. T. McLearn, & M. A. Schuster (Eds.), *Child rearing in America: Challenges facing parents with young children* (pp. 367–412). New York: Cambridge University Press.

Hanson, M. (1992). Ethnic, cultural, and language diversity in intervention settings. In E. W. Lynch & M. J. Hanson (Eds.), *Developing cross-cultural competence* (pp. 3–18). Baltimore: Paul H. Brookes.

Harjo, S. S. (1993). The American Indian experience. In H. P. McAdoo (Ed.), *Family ethnicity* (pp. 19–207). Newbury Park, CA: Sage.

Harkavy, O., & Bond, J. T. (1992). Program operations: Time allocation and cost analysis. In M. Larner, R. Halpern, & O. Harkavy (Eds.), *Fair start for children: Lessons learned from seven demonstration projects* (pp. 198–217). New Haven, CT: Yale University Press.

Harris, J. R. (1995). Where is the child's environment? A group socialization theory of development. *Psychological Review, 102,* 458–489.

Harris, J. R. (1998). *The nurture assumption.* New York: Free Press.

Harris, J. R. (2002). Beyond the nurture assumption: Testing hypotheses about the child's environment. In J. G. Borkowski, S. L. Ramey, & M. Bristol-Power (Eds.), *Parenting and the child's world: Influences on academic, intellectual, and social-emotional development* (pp. 3–20). Mahwah, NJ: Erlbaum.

Hart, B., & Risley, T. R. (1995). *Meaningful differences in the everyday experiences of young American children.* Baltimore: Paul H. Brookes.

Heath, S. B. (1983). *Ways with words.* Cambridge, England: Cambridge University Press.

Hebbeler, K. M., & Gerlach-Downie, S. G. (2002). Inside the black box of home visiting: A qualitative analysis of why intended outcomes were not achieved. *Early Childhood Research Quarterly, 17,* 28–51.

Heberle, J. (1992). PACE: Parent and Child Education in Kentucky. In T. B. Sticht, M. J. Beeler, & B. A. McDonald (Eds.), *The intergenerational transfer of cognitive skills: Vol. 1. Programs, policy and research issues* (pp. 1261–1348). Norwood, NJ: Ablex.

Heinicke, C. M., Goorsky, M., Moscov, S., Dudley, K., Gordon, J., & Guthrie, D. (1998). Partner support as a mediator of intervention outcome. *American Journal of Orthopsychiatry, 68*, 534–541.

Heinecke, C. M., & Ponce, V. A. (1999). Relationship-based early family intervention. In D. Cicchetti & S. L. Toth (Ed.), *Developmental approaches to prevention and intervention* (pp. 153–193). Rochester, NY: University of Rochester Press.

Hess, R. D. (1980). Experts and amateurs: Some unintended consequences of parent education. In M. D. Fantini & R. Cardenes (Eds.), *Parenting in a multicultural society* (pp. 141–159). New York: Longman.

Hogan, D. P., & Msall, M. E. (2002). Family structure and resources and the parenting of children with disabilities and functional limitations. In J. G. Borkowski, S. L. Ramey, & M. Bristol-Power (Eds.), *Parenting and the child's world: Influences on academic, intellectual, and social-emotional development* (pp. 311–327). Mahwah, NJ: Erlbaum.

Infant Health and Development Program. (1990). Enhancing the outcomes of low-birth-weight, premature infants: A multisite, randomized trial. *Journal of the American Medical Association, 263*, 3035–3042.

Jacobs, J. A., & Gerson, K. (2004). *The time divide: Work, family, and gender inequality.* Cambridge, MA: Harvard University Press.

Jarrett, R. L., & Jefferson, S. M. (2003). "A good mother got too tight for her kids": Maternal management strategies in a high-risk, African-American neighborhood. *Journal of Children and Poverty, 9*, 21–39.

Jarrett, R. L., & Jefferson, S. M. (2004). Women's danger management strategies in an inner-city housing project. *Family Relations, 53*, 138–147.

Katz, L. G. (1980). Mothering and teaching: Some significant distinctions. In L. G. Katz (Ed.), *Current topics in early childhood education* (Vol. 3, pp. 47–63). Norwood, NJ: Ablex.

Kessen, W. (1979). American children and other cultural inventions. *American Psychologist, 34*, 815–820.

Kisker, E. E., Paulsell, D., Love, J. M., & Raikes, H. (2002). *Pathways to quality and full implement in Early Head Start programs.* Princeton, NJ: Mathematica Policy Research.

Kitzman, H., Olds, D. L., Sidora, K., Henderson, C. R., Hanks, C., Cole, R., et al. (2000). Enduring effects of nurse home visitation on maternal life course: A 3-year follow-up of a randomized trial. *Journal of the American Medical Association, 283*, 1983–1989.

Kitzman, H. J., Cole, R., Yoos, H. L., & Olds, D. (1997). Challenges experienced by home visitors: A qualitative study of program implementation. *Journal of Community Psychology, 25*, 95–109.

Klaus, R. A., & Gray, S. W. (1968). Early training project for disadvantaged children: A report after 5 years. *Monographs of the Society for Research in Child Development, 33*(4, Serial No. 120).

Klebanov, P. K., Brooks-Gunn, J., & McCormick, M. C. (2001). Maternal coping strategies and emotional distress: Results of an early intervention program for low birth weight young children. *Developmental Psychology, 37*, 654–667.

Kochanska, G. (1997). Multiple pathways to conscience for children with different temperaments: From toddlerhood to age 5. *Developmental Psychology, 33*, 228–240.

Korfmacher, J. (2001). Early childhood intervention: Now what? In H. E. Fitzgerald, K. H. Karraker, & T. Luster (Eds.), *Infant development: Ecological perspectives* (pp. 275–294). New York: Routledge Falmer.

Korfmacher, J., Kitzman, H., & Olds, D. (1998). Intervention processes as predictors of outcomes in a preventive home-visitation program. *Journal of Community Psychology, 26*, 49–64.

Korfmacher, J., O'Brien, R., Hiatt, S., & Olds, D. (1999). Differences in program implementation between nurses and paraprofessionals providing home visits during pregnancy and infancy: A randomized trial. *American Journal of Public Health, 89*, 1847–1851.

Labov, W. (1970). The logic of nonstandard English. In F. Williams (Ed.), *Language and poverty: Perspectives on a theme* (pp. 153–189). Chicago: Markham.

Lally, J. R., Mangione, P. L., & Honig, A. S. (1988). Syracuse University Family Development Research Program: Long-range impact of an early intervention with low-income children and their families. In D. R. Powell (Ed.), *Parent education as early childhood intervention* (pp. 79–104). Norwood, NJ: Ablex.

Lamb, M. E. (2003). *Role of the father in child development* (4th ed.). New York: Wiley.

Laosa, L. (1983). Parent education, cultural pluralism and public policy: The uncertain connection. In R. Haskins & D. Adams (Eds.), *Parent education and public policy* (pp. 331–345). Norwood, NJ: Ablex.

Lasch, C. (1977). *Haven in a heartless world: The family besieged.* New York: Basic Books.

Layzer, J. I., Goodson, B. D., Bernstein, L., & Price, C. (2001). *National evaluation of family support programs: Vol. A. Final report—The meta-analysis.* Cambridge, MA: Abt Associates.

Lazar, I. (1983). Discussion and implications of the findings. In Consortium for Longitudinal Studies (Ed.), *As the twig is bent . . . Lasting effects of preschool programs* (pp. 461–466). Hillsdale, NJ: Erlbaum.

Lazar, I., Anchel, G., Beckman, L., Gethard, E., Lazar, J., & Sale, J. (1970). *A national survey of the Parent-Child Center Program* (Prepared for Department of Health, Education, and Welfare, Office of Child Development, Project Head Start). Washington, DC: Kirchner Associates.

Lerner, R. M. (1998). Theories of human development: Contemporary perspectives. In W. Damon (Editor-in-Chief) & R. M. Lerner (Vol. Ed.), *Handbook of child psychology: Vol. 1. Theoretical models of human development* (5th ed., pp. 1–24). New York: Wiley.

Lerner, R. M. (2003). What are SES effects effects of? A developmental systems perspective. In M. H. Bornstein & R. H. Bradley (Eds.), *Socioeconomic status, parenting, and child development* (pp. 231–255). Mahwah, NJ: Erlbaum.

Lerner, R. M., Fisher, C. B., & Weinberg, R. A. (2000). Toward a science for and of the people: Promoting civil society through the application of developmental science. *Child Development, 71*, 11–20.

Levenstein, P. (1977). Mother-child home program. In M. C. Day & R. K. Parker (Eds.), *The preschool in action: Exploring early childhood programs* (2nd ed., pp. 27–49). Boston: Allyn & Bacon.

Levenstein, P. (1988). *Messages from the home: Mother-child home program and the prevention of school disadvantage.* Columbus: Ohio State University Press.

Liaw, F., Meisels, S. J., & Brooks-Gunn, J. (1995). Effects of experience of early intervention on low birth weight, premature children: Infant health and development program. *Early Childhood Research Quarterly, 10,* 405–431.

Lonigan, C. J., & Whitehurst, G. J. (1998). Relative efficacy of parent and teacher involvement in a shared-reading intervention for preschool children from low-income backgrounds. *Early Childhood Research Quarterly, 13,* 263–290.

Love, J. M., Kisker, E. E., Ross, C. M., Schochet, P. Z., Brooks-Gunn, J., Paulsell, D., et al. (2002). *Making a difference in the lives of infants and toddlers and their families: Impacts of early Head Start: Vol. 1. Final technical report.* Princeton, NJ: Mathematica Policy Research.

Luster, T., & McAdoo, H. (1996). Family and child influences on educational attainment: A secondary analysis of the High/Scope Perry Preschool data. *Developmental Psychology, 32,* 26–39.

Luster, T., & Okagaki, L. (1993). Multiple influences in parenting: Ecological and life-course perspectives. In T. Luster & L. Okagaki (Eds.), *Parenting: An ecological perspective* (pp. 227–250). Hillsdale, NJ: Erlbaum.

Lyons-Ruth, K., Connell, D. B., Grunebaum, H. U., & Botein, S. (1990). Infants at social risk: Maternal depression and family support services as mediators of infant development and security of attachment. *Child Development, 61,* 85–98.

Mahoney, G., Kaiser, A., Girolametto, L., MacDonald, J., Robinson, C., Safford, P., et al. (1999). Parent education in early intervention: A call for a renewed focus. *Topics in Early Childhood Special Education, 19,* 131–140.

Marsiglio, W., Amato, P., Day, R. D., & Lamb, M. E. (2000). Scholarship on fatherhood in the 1990s and beyond. *Journal of Marriage and the Family, 62,* 1173–1191.

Martin, S. L., Ramey, C. T., & Ramey, S. (1990). The prevention of intellectual impairment in children of impoverished families: Findings of a randomized trial of educational day care. *American Journal of Public Health, 80,* 844–847.

McBride, S. L., & Brotherson, M. J. (1997). Guiding practitioners toward valuing and implementing family-centered practices. In P. J. Winton, J. A. McCollum, & C. Catlett (Eds.), *Reforming personnel preparation in early intervention: Issues, models, and practical strategies* (pp. 253–276). Baltimore: Paul H. Brookes.

McCall, R. B., & Green, B. L. (2004). Beyond the methodological gold standards of behavioral research: Considerations for practice and policy. *Society for Research in Child Developmental Social Policy Report, 18,* 3–19.

McCarton, C. M., Brooks-Gunn, J., Wallace, I. F., Bauer, C. R., Bennett, F. C., Bernbaum, J. C., et al. (1997). Results at age 8 years of early intervention for low-birth-weight premature infants: Infant health and development program. *Journal of the American Medical Association, 277,* 126–132.

McCurdy, K., & Daro, D. (2001). Parent involvement in family support programs: An integrated theory. *Family Relations, 50,* 113–121.

McGuigan, W. M., Katzev, A. R., & Pratt, C. C. (2003). Multi-level determinants of mothers' engagement in home visitation services. *Family Relations, 52,* 271–278.

McLoyd, V. C. (1998). Socioeconomic disadvantage and child development. *American Psychologist, 53,* 185–204.

McWilliam, R. A., Ferguson, A., Harbin, G., Porter, P., Munn, D., & Vandiviere, P. (1998). The family-centeredness of individualized family service plans. *Topics in Early Childhood Special Education, 18,* 69–82.

Menaghan, E. G., & Parcel, T. L. (1995). Social sources of change in children's home environment: Effects of parental occupational experiences and family conditions. *Journal of Marriage and the Family, 57,* 69–84.

Miller, S. H. (1988). Child Welfare League of America's adolescent parents projects. In H. B. Weiss & F. H. Jacobs (Eds.), *Evaluating family programs* (pp. 371–388). New York: Aldine de Gruyter.

Mincy, R. B., & Pouncy, H. W. (2002). Responsible fatherhood field: Evolution and goals. In C. S. Tamis-LeMonda & N. Cabrera (Eds.), *Handbook of father involvement: Multidisciplinary perspectives* (pp. 555–597). Mahwah, NJ: Erlbaum.

Mindick, B. (1986). *Social engineering in family matters.* New York: Praeger.

Minuchin, P. (1985). Families and individual development: Provocations from the field of family therapy. *Child Development, 56,* 289–302.

Minuchin, P. (2002). Looking toward the horizon: Present and future in the study of family systems. In J. P. McHale & W. S. Grolnick (Eds.), *Retrospect and prospect in the psychological study of families* (pp. 259–278). Mahwah, NJ: Erlbaum.

Moore, K. A., & Keyes, C. L. M. (2003). A brief history of the study of well-being in children and adults. In M. H. Bornstein, L. Davidson, C. L. M. Keyes, & K. A. Moore (Eds.), *Well-being: Positive development across the life course* (pp. 1–11). Mahwah, NJ: Erlbaum.

Musick, J., & Stott, F. (2000). Paraprofessionals revisited and reconsidered. In J. P. Shonkoff & S. J. Meisels (Eds.), *Handbook of early childhood intervention* (2nd ed., pp. 439–453). New York: Cambridge University Press.

National Institute of Child Health and Human Development Early Child Care Research Network. (1998). Relations between family predictors and child outcomes: Are they weaker for children in child care? *Developmental Psychology, 34,* 1119–1128.

National Research Council. (2002). *Scientific research in education* (Committee on Scientific Principles for Education Research, R. J. Shavelson & L. Towne, Eds.). Washington, DC: National Academy Press.

National Research Council and Institute of Medicine. (2000). *From neurons to neighborhoods: Science of early childhood development* (Committee on Integrating the Science of Early Childhood Development, J. P. Shonkoff, & D. A. Phillips, Eds.). Washington, DC: National Academy Press, Board on Children, Youth, and Families, Commission on Behavioral and Social Sciences and Education.

Neuman, S. B. (1999). Creating continuity in early literacy: Linking home and school with a culturally responsive approach. In L. B. Gambrell, L. M. Morrow, S. B. Neuman, & M. Pressley (Eds.), *Best practices in literacy instruction* (pp. 258–270). New York: Guilford Press.

Neuman, S. B., & Gallagher, P. (1994). Joining together in literacy learning: Teenage mothers and children. *Reading Research Quarterly, 29,* 383–401.

Neuman, S. B., Hagedorn, T., Celano, D., & Daly, P. (1995). Toward a collaborative approach to parent involvement in early education: A study of teenage mothers in an African-American community. *American Educational Research Journal, 32,* 801–827.

O'Connell, J., & Farran, D. C. (1980, April). *The effects of daycare intervention on the use of intentional communicative behaviors in socioeconomically depressed infants.* Paper presented at the sixth biennial Southeastern Conference on Human Development, Alexandria, VA.

Okagaki, L., & Frensch, P. A. (1998). Parenting and children's school achievement: A multiethnic perspective. *American Educational Research Journal, 35,* 123–144.

Okagaki, L., & Luster, T. (2005). Research on parental socialization of child outcomes: Current controversies and future directions. In T. Luster & L. Okagaki (Eds.), *Parenting: An ecological perspective* (2nd ed., pp. 377–401). Mahwah, NJ: Erlbaum.

Olds, D., Eckenrode, J., Henderson, C. R., Jr., Kitzman, H., Powers, J., Cole, R., et al. (1997). Long-term effects of home visitation on maternal life course and child abuse and neglect: 15-year follow-up of a randomized trial. *Journal of the American Medical Association, 278,* 637–643.

Olds, D., Kitzman, H., Cole, R., & Robinson, J. (1997). Theoretical foundations of a program of home visitation for pregnant women and parents of young children. *Journal of Community Psychology, 25,* 9–25.

Olds, D., O'Brien, R. A., Racine, D., Glazner, J., & Kitzman, H. (1998). Increasing the policy and program relevance of results from randomized trials of home visitation. *Journal of Community Psychology, 26,* 85–100.

Olds, D. L., Henderson, C. C., Jr., Kitzman, H., Eckenrode, J., Cole, R., & Tatelbaum, R. (1998). The promise of home visitation: Results of two randomized trials. *Journal of Community Psychology, 26,* 5–21.

Olds, D. L., Henderson, C. R., Chamberlin, R., & Tatelbaum, R. (1986). Preventing child abuse and neglect: A randomized trial of nurse home visitation. *Pediatrics, 78,* 65–78.

Olds, D. L., Robinson, J., O'Brien, R., Luckey, D. W., Pettitt, L. M., Henderson, C. T., et al. (2002). Home visiting by paraprofessionals and by nurses: A randomized, controlled trial. *Pediatrics, 110,* 486–496.

Olson, D. R. (2003). *Psychological theory and educational reform: How school remakes mind and society.* Cambridge, England: Cambridge University Press.

Osofsky, J. D., Culp, A. M., & Ware, L. M. (1988). Intervention challenges with adolescent mothers and their infants. *Psychiatry, 51,* 236–241.

Parcel, T. L., & Menaghan, E. G. (1994). Early parental work, family social capital, and early childhood outcomes. *American Journal of Sociology, 99,* 972–1009.

Parke, R. D. (2004). Society for Research in Child Development at 70: Progress and promise. *Child Development, 75,* 1–24.

Parke, R. D., & Buriel, R. (1998). Socialization in the family: Ethnic and ecological perspectives. In W. Damon (Editor-in-Chief) & N. Eisenberg (Vol. Ed.), *Handbook of child psychology: Vol. 3. Social, emotional, and personality development* (5th ed., pp. 463–452). New York: Wiley.

Parke, R. D., & O'Neil, R. (1997). The influence of significant others on learning about relationships. In S. Duck (Ed.), *Handbook of personal relationships* (2nd ed., pp. 29–59). New York: Wiley.

Pollard, E. L., & Rosenberg, M. L. (2003). A strength-based approach to child well-being: Let's begin with the end in mind. In M. H. Bornstein, L. Davidson, C. L. M. Keyes, & K. A. Moore (Eds.), *Well-being: Positive development across the life course* (pp. 13–21). Mahwah, NJ: Erlbaum.

Powell, C., & Grantham-McGregor, S. (1989). Home visiting of varying frequency and child development. *Pediatrics, 84,* 157–164.

Powell, D. R. (1988). Support groups for low-income mothers: Design considerations and patterns of participation. In B. Gottlieb (Ed.), *Marshaling social support: Formats, processes, and effects* (pp. 111–134). Beverly Hills, CA: Sage.

Powell, D. R. (1993). Inside home visiting programs. *Future of Children, 3,* 23–38.

Powell, D. R. (2000). Preparing early childhood professionals to work with families. In D. Horm-Wingerd, M. Hyson, & N. Karp (Eds.), *New teachers for a new century: The future of early childhood professional preparation* (pp. 59–87). Washington, DC: U.S. Department of Education.

Powell, D. R. (2001). Visions and realities of achieving partnership: Parent-school relationships at the turn of the century. In A. Goncu & E. L. Klein (Eds.), *Children in play, story, and school* (pp. 333–357). New York: Guilford Press.

Powell, D. R. (2004). Parenting education in family literacy programs. In B. H. Wasik (Ed.), *Handbook of family literacy* (pp. 157–173). Mahwah, NJ: Erlbaum.

Powell, D. R. (2005). Searches for what works in parenting interventions. In T. Luster & L. Okagaki (Eds.), *Parenting: An ecological perspective* (2nd ed., pp. 343–373). Mahwah, NJ: Erlbaum.

Powell, D. R., & D'Angelo, D. (2000). *Guide to improving parenting education in Even Start family literacy programs.* Washington, DC: U.S. Department of Education.

Powell, D. R., & Diamond, K. E. (1995). Approaches to parent-teacher relationships in U.S. early childhood programs during the twentieth century. *Journal of Education, 177,* 71–94.

Powell, D. R., Okagaki, L., & Bojczyk, K. (2004). Evaluating parent participation and outcomes in family literacy programs: Cultural diversity considerations. In B. H. Wasik (Ed.), *Handbook of family literacy* (pp. 551–566). Mahwah, NJ: Erlbaum.

Provence, S., Naylor, A., & Patterson, J. (1977). *The challenge of daycare.* New Haven, CT: Yale University Press.

Radin, N. (1972). Three degrees of maternal involvement in a preschool program: Impact on mothers and children. *Child Development, 43,* 1355–1364.

Raikes, H. H., Summers, J. A., & Roggman, L. A. (2005). Father involvement in Early Head Start programs. *Fathering, 3,* 29–58.

Ramey, C. T. (1980). Social consequences of ecological intervention that began in infancy. In S. Harel (Ed.), *The at-risk infant* (pp. 440–443). Amsterdam: Excerpta Medica.

Ramey, C. T., Bryant, D. M., Wasik, B. H., Sparling, J. J., Fendt, K. H., & LaVange, L. M. (1992). Infant Health and Development Program for low birth weight, premature infants: Program elements, family participation, and child intelligence. *Pediatrics, 3,* 454–465.

Ramey, C. T., & Campbell, F. A. (1984). Preventive education for high-risk children: Cognitive consequences of the Carolina Abecedarian Project. *American Journal of Mental Deficiency, 88,* 454–465.

Ramey, C. T., Campbell, F. A., Burchinal, M., Skimmer, M. L., Gardner, D. M., & Ramey, S. L. (2000). Persistent effects of early childhood education on high-risk children and their mothers. *Applied Developmental Science, 4,* 2–14.

Ramey, C. T., Dorval, B., & Baker-Ward, L. (1983). Group day care and socially disadvantaged families: Effects on the child and the family. In S. Kilmer (Ed.), *Advances in early education and day care* (Vol. 3, pp. 69–106). Greenwich, CT: JAI Press.

Ramey, C. T., & Ramey, S. L. (1992). Effective early intervention. *Mental Retardation, 30,* 337–345.

Ramey, C. T., & Ramey, S. L. (1998). Early intervention and early experience. *American Psychologist, 53,* 109–120.

Ramey, C. T., Ramey, S. L., Lanzi, R. G., & Cotton, J. N. (2002). Early educational interventions for high-risk children: How center-based treatment can augment and improve parenting effectiveness. In J. G. Borkowski, S. L. Ramey, & M. Bristol-Power (Eds.), *Parenting and the child's world: Influences on academic, intellectual, and social-emotional development* (pp. 125–140). Mahwah, NJ: Erlbaum.

Ramey, C. T., Sparling, J. J., Bryant, D. M., & Wasik, B. H. (1997). The intervention model. In R. T. Gross, D. Spiker, & C. W. Haynes (Eds.), *Helping low birth weight, premature babies: Infant Health and Development Program* (pp. 17–26). Stanford, CA: Stanford University Press.

Reid, M. J., Webster-Stratton, C., & Beauchaine, T. P. (2001). Parent training in Head Start: A comparison of program response among African American, Asian American, Caucasian, and Hispanic mothers. *Prevention Science, 2,* 209–227.

Reynolds, A. J. (2000). *Success in early intervention: Chicago Child-Parent Centers.* Lincoln: University of Nebraska Press.

Reynolds, A. J., Ou, S., & Topitzes, J. W. (2004). Paths of effects of early childhood intervention on educational attainment and delinquency: A confirmatory analysis of the Chicago Child-Parent Centers. *Child Development, 75,* 1299–1328.

Reynolds, A. J., Temple, J. A., Robertson, D. L., & Mann, E. A. (2001). Long-term effects of an early childhood intervention on educational achievement and juvenile arrest: A 15-year follow-up of low-income children in public schools. *Journal of the American Medical Association, 285,* 2339–2346.

Robinson, J. L., Korfmacher, J., Green, S., Song, N., Soden, R., & Emde, R. (2002). Predicting program use and acceptance by parents enrolled in Early Head Start. *NHSA Dialog, 5,* 311–324.

Roggman, L. A., Fitzgerald, H. E., Bradley, R. H., & Raikes, H. (2002). Methodological, measurement, and design issues in studying fathers: An interdisciplinary perspective. In C. S. Tamis-LeMonda & N. Cabrera (Eds.), *Handbook of father involvement: Multidisciplinary perspectives* (pp. 1–30). Mahwah, NJ: Erlbaum.

Rowe, D. C. (1994). *Limits of family influence.* New York: Guilford Press.

Scarborough, H. S., & Dobrich, W. (1994). On the efficacy of reading to preschoolers. *Developmental Review, 14,* 245–302.

Schorr, L., & Schorr, D. (1988). *Within our reach.* New York: Anchor Press/Doubleday.

Schweinhart, L. J., Barnes, H. V., Weikart, D. P., Barnett, W. S., & Epstein, A. S. (1993). Significant benefits—High/Scope Perry Preschool study through age 27. *Monographs of the High/Scope Educational Research Foundation, 10.*

Schweinhart, L. J., Montie, J., Xiang, Z., Barnett, W. S., Belfield, C. R., & Nores, M. (2005). Lifetime effects—High/Scope Perry Preschool study through age 40. *Monographs of the High/Scope Educational Research Foundation, 14.*

Schweinhart, L. J., & Weikart, D. P. (1980). Young children grow up: Effects of the Perry Preschool Program on youths through age 15. *Monographs of the High/Scope Educational Research Foundation, 7.*

Seitz, V., & Apfel, N. H. (1994). Parent-focused intervention: Diffusion among siblings. *Child Development, 65,* 677–683.

Seitz, V., Rosenbaum, L. K., & Apfel, N. H. (1985). Effects of family support intervention: A 10-year follow-up. *Child Development, 56,* 376–391.

Serketich, W. J., & Dumas, J. E. (1996). Effectiveness of behavioral parent training to modify antisocial behavior in children: A meta-analysis. *Behavior Therapy, 27,* 171–186.

Shadish, W. R., Cook, T. D., & Campbell, D. T. (2002). *Experimental and quasi-experimental designs for generalized causal inference.* New York: Houghton Mifflin.

Shonkoff, J. P. (2000). Science, policy, and practice: Three cultures in search of a shared mission. *Child Development, 71,* 181–187.

Shweder, R. A. (1993). Cultural psychology: Who needs it? *Annual Review of Psychology, 44,* 497–523.

Sigel, I. E. (1983). Ethics of intervention. In I. E. Sigel & L. M. Laosa (Eds.), *Changing families* (pp. 1–21). New York: Plenum Press.

Sigel, I. E. (1998). Practice and research: A problem developing communication and cooperation. In W. Damon (Editor-in-Chief) & I. E. Sigel & K. A. Renninger (Vol. Eds.), *Handbook of child psychology: Vol. 4. Child psychology in practice* (5th ed., pp. 1113–1132). New York: Wiley.

Slaughter, D. T. (1983). Early intervention and its effects on maternal and child development. *Monographs of the Society for Research in Child Development, 48*(4, Serial No. 202).

Smith, S., & Zaslow, M. (1995). Rationale and policy context for two-generation interventions. In S. Smith (Ed.), *Two generation programs for families in poverty: A new intervention strategy* (pp. 1–35). Norwood, NJ: Ablex.

Sparling, J., & Lewis, I. (1979). *Learningames for the first 3 years: A guide to parent-child play.* New York: Walker & Co.

Sparling, J., & Lewis, I. (1995). *Partners for learning: Birth to 36 months.* Lewisville, NC: Kaplan Press.

Sparling, J., Lewis, I., Ramey, C. T., Wasik, B. H., Bryant, D. M., & LaVange, L. M. (1991). Partners: A curriculum to help premature, low birthweight infants get off to a good start. *Topics in Early Childhood Special Education, 11,* 36–55.

Spiker, D., Ferguson, J., & Brooks-Gunn, J. (1993). Enhancing maternal interactive behavior and child social competence in low birth weight, premature infants. *Child Development, 64,* 754–768.

Stanovich, K. E. (1986). Matthew effects in reading: Some consequences of individual differences in the acquisition of literacy. *Reading Research Quarterly, 21,* 360–407.

St. Pierre, R. G., & Layzer, J. I. (1998). Improving the life chances of children in poverty: Assumptions and what we have learned. *Social Policy Report, 12*(4), 1–25.

St. Pierre, R. G., Layzer, J. I., & Barnes, H. V. (1998). Regenerating two-generation programs. In W. S. Barnett & S. S. Boocock (Eds.), *Early care and education for children in poverty* (pp. 99–121). Albany: State University of New York Press.

St. Pierre, R. G., Layzer, J. I., Goodson, B. D., & Bernstein, L. S. (1997). *National impact evaluation of the Comprehensive Child Development Program: Final report.* Cambridge, MA: Abt Associates.

St. Pierre, R. G., Ricciuti, A. E., & Tao, F. (2004). Continuous improvement in family literacy programs. In B. H. Wasik (Ed.), *Handbook of family literacy* (pp. 587–599). Mahwah, NJ: Erlbaum.

St. Pierre, R. G., Ricciuti, A., Tao, F., Creps, C., Swartz, J., Lee, W., et al. (2003). *Third national Even Start evaluation: Program impacts and implications for improvement.* Washington, DC: U.S. Department of Education, Office of the Under Secretary, Planning and Evaluation Service.

St. Pierre, R. G., & Swartz, J. P. (1995). Even Start family literacy program. In I. Sigel (Series Ed.) & S. Smith (Vol. Ed.), *Two generation programs for families in poverty: A new intervention strategy: Vol. 9. Advances in applied developmental psychology* (pp. 37–66). Norwood, NJ: Ablex.

Travers, J., Irwin, N., & Nauta, M. (1981). *Culture of a social program: An ethnographic study of the Child and Family Resource Program* (Report prepared for the Administration of Children, Youth and Families). Cambridge, MA: Abt Associates.

Travers, J., Nauta, M., & Irwin, N. (1982). *Effects of a social program: Final report of the Child and Family Resource Program's infant-toddler component.* Cambridge, MA: Abt Associates.

Trivette, C. M., Dunst, C. J., & Deal, A. G. (1997). Resource-based approach to early intervention. In S. K. Thurman, J. R. Cornwell, & S. R. Gottwald (Eds.), *Contexts of early intervention: Systems and settings* (pp. 73–92). Baltimore: Paul H. Brookes.

Vartuli, S., & Winter, M. (1989). Parents as first teachers. In M. Fine (Ed.), *Second handbook on parent education* (pp. 99–117). New York: Academic Press.

Vernon-Feagans, L. (1996). *Children's talk in communities and classrooms.* Cambridge, MA: Blackwell.

Wagner, M., Spiker, D., & Linn, M. I. (2002). Effectiveness of the Parents as Teachers program with low-income parents and children. *Topics in Early Childhood Special Education, 22,* 67–81.

Wagner, M., Spiker, D., Linn, M. I., Gerlach-Downie, S., & Hernandez, F. (2003). Dimensions of parental engagement in home visiting programs: Exploratory study. *Topics in Early Childhood Special Education, 23,* 171–187.

Wagner, M. M., & Clayton, S. L. (1999). Parents as Teachers program: Results from two demonstrations. *Future of Children, 9,* 91–115.

Waite, L. J., & Gallagher, M. (2000). *Case for marriage: Why married people are happier, healthier, and better off financially.* New York: Doubleday.

Wasik, B. H., Bryant, D. M., Lyons, C., Sparling, J. J., & Ramey, C. T. (1997). Home visiting. In R. T. Gross, D. Spiker, & C. W. Haynes (Eds.), *Helping low birth weight, premature babies: Infant Health and Development Program* (pp. 27–41). Stanford, CA: Stanford University Press.

Wasik, B. H., Bryant, D. M., Sparling, J. J., & Ramey, C. T. (1997). Maternal problem solving. In R. T. Gross, D. Spiker, & C. W. Haynes (Eds.), *Helping low birth weight, premature babies: Infant Health and Development Program* (pp. 276–289). Stanford, CA: Stanford University Press.

Webster-Stratton, C. (1990). Enhancing the effectiveness of self-administered videotape parent training for families with conduct-problem children. *Journal of Abnormal Child Psychology, 18,* 479–492.

Webster-Stratton, C. (1998). Preventing conduct problems in Head Start children: Strengthening parent competencies. *Journal of Consulting and Clinical Psychology, 66,* 715–730.

Webster-Stratton, C., Kolpacoff, M., & Hollinsworth, T. (1988). Self-administered videotape therapy for families with conduct-problem children: Comparison with two cost-effective treatments and a control group. *Journal of Consulting and Clinical Psychology, 56,* 558–566.

Webster-Stratton, C., Reid, M. J., & Hammond, M. (2001). Preventing conduct problems, promoting social competence: A parent and teacher training partnership in Head Start. *Journal of Clinical Child Psychology, 30,* 283–302.

Weikart, D. P., Bond, J. T., & McNeil, J. T. (1978). Ypsilanti Perry Preschool project: Preschool years and longitudinal results through fourth grade. *Monographs of the High/Scope Educational Research Foundation, 3.*

Weikart, D. P., Rogers, L., Adcock, C., & McClelland, D. (1971). *Cognitively oriented curriculum: A framework for preschool teachers.* Urbana: Educational Resources Information Center Clearinghouse on Early Childhood Education, University of Illinois.

Weiss, C. H. (1995). Nothing as practical as a good theory: Exploring theory-based evaluation for comprehensive community initiatives for children and families. In J. P. Connell, A. C. Kubisch, L. B. Schorr, & C. H. Weiss (Eds.), *New approaches to evaluating community initiatives: Concepts, methods, and contexts* (pp. 65–92). Washington, DC: Aspen Institute.

Westheimer, M. (Ed.). (2003). *Parents making a difference: International research on the Home Instruction for Parents of Preschool Youngsters (HIPPY) program.* Jerusalem: Hebrew University Magnes Press.

White, B. L., & Watts, J. C. (1973). *Experience and environment: Major influences on the development of the young child* (Vols. 1–2). Englewood Cliffs, NJ: Prentice-Hall.

Whitehurst, G. J., Arnold, D. S., Epstein, J. N., Angell, A. L., Smith, M., & Fischel, J. E. (1994). A picture book reading intervention in day care and home for children from low-income families. *Developmental Psychology, 30,* 679–689.

Whitehurst, G. J., Epstein, J. N., Angell, A. C., Payne, A. C., Crone, D. A., & Fischel, J. E. (1994). Outcomes of an emergent literacy intervention in Head Start. *Journal of Educational Psychology, 86,* 542–555.

Whitehurst, G. J., Falco, F., Lonigan, C. J., Fischel, J. E., DeBaryshe, B. D., Valdez-Menchaca, M. C., et al. (1988). Accelerating language development through picture-book reading. *Developmental Psychology, 24,* 552–558.

Wilson, J. B., Ellwood, D. T., & Brooks-Gunn, J. (1995). Welfare-to-work through the eyes of children. In P. L. Chase-Lansdale & J. Brooks-Gunn (Eds.), *Escape from poverty: What makes a difference for children?* (pp. 63–86). New York: Cambridge University Press.

Yando, R., Seitz, V., & Zigler, E. (1979). *Intellectual and personality characteristics of children: Social-class and ethnic group differences.* Hillsdale, NJ: Erlbaum.

Yoshikawa, H., Rosman, E. A., & Hsueh, J. (2002). Resolving paradoxical criteria for the expansion and replication of early childhood care and education programs. *Early Childhood Research Quarterly, 17,* 3–27.

Yutrzenka, B. (1995). Making a case for training in ethnic and cultural diversity in increasing treatment efficacy. *Journal of Consulting and Clinical Psychology, 63,* 197–206.

Zigler, E., & Berman, W. (1983). Discerning the future of early childhood intervention. *American Psychologist, 8,* 894–906.

Zigler, E., & Muenchow, S. (1992). *Head Start: The inside story of America's most successful educational experiment.* New York: Basic Books.

Zigler, E., & Seitz, V. (1993). Invited comments on significant benefits. In L. J. Schweinhart, H. V. Barnes, & D. P. Weikart. *Significant benefits: The High/Scope Perry Preschool Study through age 27* (pp. 247–249). Ypsilanti, MI: High/Scope Press.

Zigler, E. F., Finn-Stevenson, M., & Hall, N. W. (2002). *The first 3 years and beyond.* New Haven, CT: Yale University Press.

CHAPTER 15

School-Based Social and Emotional Learning Programs

JEFFREY S. KRESS and MAURICE J. ELIAS

From the late 1990s schools have been inundated with well-intentioned prevention and promotion programs that address such diverse issues as bullying, HIV/AIDS, alcohol, careers, character, civics, conflict resolution, delinquency, dropout, family life, health, morals, multiculturalism, pregnancy, service learning, truancy, and violence.

At the same time, the year 2002 marked the passage of the No Child Left Behind (NCLB) legislation, which placed a strong emphasis on test scores as the most important and tangible outcome of educational achievement. School funding was tied to progress in test performance, and educators quickly found themselves faced with a dilemma. The needs that had generated the proliferation of prevention-related programs had not abated. However, their accountability structure changed in ways that seemed incompatible with the continuation of those programs.

Signs of this dilemma were evident over a decade ago (Elias, 1995, pp.12–13):

> The continuing undercurrent of emphasis on basic academic skills is probably driven more by economic and workplace forces—both domestic and international—than by a genuine concern with the well-being of our nation's

children and youth. For if the latter were the case, compelling statements about the inextricable bond linking personal, social, affective, and cognitive development would be more in the forefront. Arguments have been made that "Placing an overlay of strong academic demands on the current educational climate is likely to result in few increases in learning and instead exacerbate current stress-related problems and lead to further alienation among our student population." (Elias, 1989, pp. 393–394)

What was previously described as an undercurrent has now become a riptide, and the stress-related sequelae of trying to meet the academic and psychological demands of students in the schools are drowning both students and teachers alike. Efforts to redress these problems by returning attention to the bond across developmental areas have not been absent during this time, but they have undergone both conceptual and practical reformulations. Concomitantly, our understanding of what is required to implement these efforts—most specifically, what is being demanded of those who are expert consultants to implement interventions in schools—has become more sophisticated.

How have schools attempted to respond to growing demands to implement effective educational approaches that promote academic success, enhance health, and prevent problem behaviors? Unfortunately, many child advocates, educational policymakers, and researchers, despite their good intentions, have proposed fragmented initiatives to address problems without an adequate understanding of the mission, priorities, and culture of schools (Sarason, 1996).

For a number of reasons, these uncoordinated efforts often fail to live up to their potential. Typically, they are introduced as a series of short-term, fragmented program initiatives. They are not sufficiently linked to the central mission of schools or to the issues for which teachers and other school personnel are held accountable, which is primarily academic performance. Rarely is there adequate staff development and support for program implementation. Programs that are insufficiently coordinated, monitored, evaluated, and improved over time have reduced impact on student behavior.

Even before the crisis precipitated by the NCLB legislation, concern for the disappointing performance of many prevention and health promotion efforts spurred a 1994 meeting hosted by the Fetzer Institute. Attendees included school-based prevention researchers, educators, and child advocates who were involved in diverse educational efforts to enhance children's positive development, including social competence promotion, emotional intelligence, drug education, violence prevention, sex education, health promotion, character education, service learning, civic education, school reform, and school-family-community partnerships. The Fetzer group first introduced the term *social and emotional learning* (SEL) as a conceptual framework to address both the needs of young people and the fragmentation that typically characterizes the response of schools to those needs (Elias et al., 1997). They believed that, unlike the many "categorical" prevention programs that targeted specific problems, SEL programming could address underlying causes of problem behavior while supporting academic achievement. A new organization, the Collaborative for Academic, Social, and Emotional Learning (CASEL), also emerged from this meeting with the goal of establishing high-quality, evidence-based SEL as an essential part of preschool through high school education (see www.CASEL.org).

Social and emotional learning skills have had several competing conceptualizations, including those of Bar-On (Bar-On & Parker, 2000), Mayer and Salovey (1993), Goleman (1995), and CASEL (Elias, 2003). Of these, CASEL's has been most focused on children and

has served as the guide for virtually all school-based SEL interventions. Hence, we will concern ourselves with CASEL's view of SEL skills. (See Ciarrochi, Forgas, & Mayer, 2001, for an overview of theoretical perspectives.)

The skills of social-emotional learning are presented in Table 15.1. CASEL (2003) posits five interrelated skill areas: self-awareness, social awareness, self-management and organization, responsible problem solving, and relationship management. Within each area, there are specific competencies supported by research and practice as essential for effective social-emotional functioning. The list does not purport to be comprehensive; rather, it is drawn from research and practice and is intended to guide intervention. Further, the conceptualization of the skills is that they are important at all developmental levels; what changes is the level of cognitive-emotional complexity with which they are applied, as well as the situations in which they will be used. Hence, Table 15.1 provides a framework for looking at the skills from the perspective of childhood and beyond. (See Elias et al., 1997, for versions appropriate to other stages of child development.)

The fact that SEL has been part of the popular literature is significant. People reading about it from all walks of life, from various professions, as psychologists, educators, members of the business community, and parents, can share this term (Goleman, 1995). Similarly, SEL and emotional intelligence found their way into psychology, education, business, and other professional journals and in over 30 languages. This has created a base of interest and involvement that far eclipsed prior work in social competence promotion, even though the long history of research and conceptualization in that area clearly provided the foundation from which SEL and emotional intelligence could spring (Consortium on the School-Based Promotion of Social Competence, 1994).

However, SEL also had "value added" as a concept. First, it placed a strong emphasis on such dimensions as emotion and spirituality (Kessler, 2000). Second, it was based in advances in brain research (Brandt, 2003). Third, SEL became tied to factors that were being studied in education and related fields as mediators of academic performance, that is, the emotional state of children, their cognitive capacity to learn, and their style of learning. Just as the education field seemed to be focusing on "back to basics" in terms of both skills and learning approaches, the SEL field was uncovering

TABLE 15.1   Social-Emotional Learning Skills

Self-Awareness

Recognizing and naming one's emotions

Understanding the reasons and circumstances for feeling as one does

Recognizing and naming others' emotions

Recognizing strengths in, and mobilizing positive feelings about, self, school, family, and support networks

Knowing one's needs and values

Perceiving oneself accurately

Believing in personal efficacy

Having a sense of spirituality

Social Awareness

Appreciating diversity

Showing respect to others

Listening carefully and accurately

Increasing empathy and sensitivity to others' feelings

Understanding others' perspectives, points of view, and feelings

Self-Management and Organization

Verbalizing and coping with anxiety, anger, and depression

Controlling impulses, aggression, and self-destructive, antisocial behavior

Managing personal and interpersonal stress

Focusing on tasks at hand

Setting short- and long-term goals

Planning thoughtfully and thoroughly

Modifying performance in light of feedback

Mobilizing positive motivation

Activating hope and optimism

Working toward optimal performance states

Responsible Decision Making

Analyzing situations perceptively and identifying problems clearly

Exercising social decision-making and problem-solving skills

Responding constructively and in a problem-solving manner to interpersonal obstacles

Engaging in self-evaluation and reflection

Conducting oneself with personal, moral, and ethical responsibility

Relationship Management

Managing emotions in relationships, harmonizing diverse feelings and viewpoints

Showing sensitivity to social-emotional cues

Expressing emotions effectively

Communicating clearly

Engaging others in social situations

Building relationships

Working cooperatively

Exercising assertiveness, leadership, and persuasion

Managing conflict, negotiation, refusal

Providing, seeking help

reasons why genuine learning required attention to other factors (Zins, Weissberg, Wang, & Walberg, 2004).

Yet another trend was operating in the late 1990s and early 2000s that is relevant to understanding SEL, its emergence, and why action research in that field has generated such unique insights. Both in the therapeutic field and in education, there was a push for evidence-based interventions. Those who were funding services (managed care companies and federal and state government for the former; federal, state, and local government for the latter) were concerned about accountability. Were children receiving services that were cost-effective? Could they be delivered in prescriptive ways, to ensure fidelity and maximize efficiency? Thus came the push for manualized therapeutic interventions and scripted school reform plans and related interventions. And with these circumscribed interventions came the need for accountability and the gold standard of research: randomized clinical trials.

Randomized clinical trials work best for discrete, time-limited, low-complexity interventions (Elias, 1997). This led to an ascendance of the short-term, focused "program" as the unit of intervention and study, along with the illusion/deception that programs were simple to implement in a controlled, replicable, and consistent manner. Outcomes research focused on the efficacy of such programs as implemented in "model" sites. For example, the American Psychological Association's *14 Ounces of Prevention* (Price, Cowen, Lorion, & Ramos-McKay, 1988) and the 1997 publication *Primary Prevention Works* (Albee & Gullotta, 1997) contain program descriptions and outcome data for SEL programs that address a range of populations across the life span. In the chapter in the latter volume on the Social Decision Making/Social Problem Solving program, which is the focus of this chapter, data were reviewed showing the efficacy of the program in terms of (a) improving teachers' abilities in facilitating students' social decision making and problem solving and (b) improving the social decision-making and problem-solving skills of students. Positive outcomes such as these further boosted interest in the field.

As the field matured, it became evident that there were significant issues to consider in terms not only of the structure of a program, but also of the process by which a program is implemented in a setting. Gager and Elias (1997) showed clearly that so-called model programs were variable in their success, and that their outcomes were related most strongly to implementation considerations. That is, a model program could be carried out successfully and unsuccessfully in almost equal measure. (It should be noted that an essentially asymmetric relationship is suggested by the research, in that sound program design is a necessary but not sufficient condition for positive outcomes, whereas poor program design is highly unlikely to lead to positive outcomes, regardless of implementation.) This was not a reflection on the programs, but showed that the implementation process could no longer be neglected from a research, intervention, or conceptualization point of view. Social-emotional factors in the environment of the program, including its ecological context, had a strong influence on the effectiveness and impact of the program.

THE COMPLEX, LONGITUDINAL NATURE OF SCHOOL-BASED SOCIAL-EMOTIONAL LEARNING INTERVENTIONS

> It is beneficial to provide a developmentally appropriate combination of formal, curriculum-based instruction with ongoing informal and infused opportunities to develop social and emotional skills from preschool through high school. (Elias et al., 1997, p. 33)

It has become widely accepted among researchers and those deeply involved with the SEL field that learning social and emotional skills is similar to learning other academic skills. That is, the effect of initial learning is enhanced over time to address the increasingly complex situations children face regarding academics, social relationships, citizenship, and health. This outcome is best accomplished through effective classroom instruction; student engagement in positive activities in and out of the classroom; and broad student, parent, and community involvement in program planning, implementation, and evaluation (CASEL, 2003; Weissberg & Greenberg, 1998). Ideally, planned, ongoing, systematic, and coordinated SEL instruction should begin in preschool and continue through high school.

Social and emotional learning programs also take many forms, but several generalities can be drawn about them. To begin with, a definition of SEL is provided by CASEL (2003, p. 8):

> Social and emotional learning (SEL) is the process of developing fundamental social and emotional competencies in children. SEL programming is based on the understanding that (1) the best learning emerges from supportive and

challenging relationships, and (2) many different kinds of factors are caused by the same risk factors.

The specifics of how these relationships are formed and how the risk factors are addressed will vary from program to program. Recent years have seen the proliferation of SEL-enhancing programs and efforts. In an effort to help educators navigate among and decide between various programs and to effectively incorporate these into their practice, reviews of effectiveness research (e.g., CASEL, 2003) have been conducted and guidelines established for what constitutes effective programming (e.g., Elias et al., 1997). For example, Elias et al. delineate the scope of SEL programmatic efforts in the first of their 39 "Guidelines for Educators":

> Educators at all levels need explicit plans to help students become knowledgeable, responsible, and caring. Efforts are needed to build and reinforce skills in four major domains of SEL:
>
> 1. Life skills and social competencies.
> 2. Health promotion and problem prevention skills.
> 3. Coping skills and social support for transitions and crises.
> 4. Positive, contributory service. (pp. 21–22)

Successful programmatic approaches include a combination of direct instruction in social and emotional skills as well as opportunities to practice these skills in a variety of situations. Direct instruction involves introducing students to the basic components of complex social and emotional skills. Students practice the use of these skills, and receive guided feedback from the teacher. Teachers may establish prompts for use as cues by students to put the behaviors to use. A basic example can be drawn from the Social Decision Making/Social Problem Solving Program (SDM/SPS; Elias & Bruene-Butler, 2005a, 2005b, 2005c) that is discussed in depth later in this chapter. This curriculum includes instruction in communication skills. In this unit, students learn the prompt "Listening Position," which includes the following behavioral components: (a) Sit or stand straight, (b) face the speaker, (c) look at the speaker. These three components are modeled by the teacher and practiced by the students as the teacher provides feedback on their efforts. The teacher may use a practice activity, such as asking the students to use Listening Position during a game that involves paying auditory attention (e.g., "Clap your hands when you hear me say a certain word"). Again, the teacher provides feedback.

In addition to this type of direct instruction, SEL skills are best taught when infused throughout the school day and in all aspects of a student's experience. To continue with the earlier example, teachers can find opportunities for students to role-play listening skills as part of a discussion about literature or history. A science teacher may reinforce listening skills as part of a lesson on the five senses. A principal, in calling an assembly to order, may use the same "Listening Position" prompt that students learned in their classrooms. Finally, efforts can be made to engage parents in the process by orienting them to the skills and prompts and helping them understand how best to coach their children.

As suggested by these examples, a comprehensively implemented approach to SEL transcends work by individual teachers in individual classes. In addition to the type of curriculum-based work described earlier, J. Cohen (1999, p. 13) points out that SEL can be addressed in less formal, "noncurriculum-based" ways in which educators "discover ways of being further attuned to SEL and how best to incorporate it into all they do at school," thereby "integrating a set of principles and practices with work that is taking place in the classroom." Further, Cohen points out that there are SEL initiatives targeting students at risk. Further, Cohen discusses a dimension of SEL specifically focusing on the educators themselves and the SEL competencies and experiences of those working in the school. Building on Cohen's rubric, we suggest two further related areas in which SEL can be manifested in a school. First, we can think about *systemic SEL,* or SEL initiatives that transcend the classroom and have to do with school policies (such as discipline) and governance (e.g., how students can have meaningful input into the functioning of the school community). Second, we see the importance of *administrative SEL,* or the ability of the administrator to draw on the principles of SEL in his or her interactions with staff and students and in bringing new programs or initiatives to the school.

Numerous successful, multiyear, multicomponent, school-based interventions promote positive academic, social, emotional, and health behavior. Examples include the following:

- Creating coordinated, caring communities of learners and enhancement of school and classroom climate through a combination of class meetings, peer leadership, family involvement, and whole-school community building activities (Battistich, Schaps, Watson, & Solomon, 1996; Solomon, Battistich, Watson, Schaps, & Lewis, 2000). This takes place by having an entire

school staff come together to discuss the potential program and agree that they support the values and procedures that are encompassed by the program and are prepared to implement it over time.

- Strengthening teacher instructional practices and increasing family involvement (Hawkins, Catalano, Kosterman, Abbott, & Hill, 1999). Teachers are taught how to create opportunities for children to bond with one another and participate in and support the creation of school norms; parents are similarly engaged in supporting school norms and in learning skills of nonviolent conflict resolution and anger management with their children.

- Establishing smaller units within schools and building trust among school staff, families, and students, thereby increasing student access, guidance, and support from school staff and other students (Felner et al., 1997). Specifically, students entering middle and high school do so in their own wings of buildings and share classes mostly with students in their own grade to increase camaraderie and mutual support; advisories also provide all students with regular problem-solving opportunities.

- Developing effective classroom-based SEL instructional programs that extend into all facets of the school environments, as well as family and/or community, to enhance students' social-emotional competence and health (Conduct Problems Prevention Research Group, 1999; Elias, Gara, Schuyler, Branden-Muller, & Sayette, 1991; Errecart et al., 1991; Greenberg & Kusché, 1998; Perry, 1999; Shure & Spivack, 1988). The skills imparted in such programs are reinforced by being explicitly used in physical education classes, in hallways, on the school bus, as part of service learning experiences, and for family problem solving. Invoking the skills outside the curriculum and instructional context serves to reinforce and generalize the use of those skills.

Despite the availability of evidence-based programs of varying degrees of complexity, many schools still do not use them (Ennett et al., 2003; Gottfredson & Gottfredson, 2001; Hallfors & Godette, 2002). For example, Ennett et al. surveyed educators from a national sample of public and private schools and found that only 14% use interactive teaching strategies and effective content in delivering substance use prevention programming. Hallfors and Godette's survey results from 81 Safe and Drug-Free School district coordinators across 11 states indicated that 59% had selected a research-based curriculum for implementation, but only 19% reported that their schools were implementing these programs with fidelity. This issue is of equal if not greater importance than generating new and more accurate curricula; the level of practice would be enhanced greatly if even current knowledge was implemented to a greater degree.

The history and trajectory of development of the field of SEL provides insights into what we believe is one of the deep, structural issues maintaining the gap between knowledge and practice. Since the emergence of the SEL field, there has been a reconceptualization of what is needed to be an effective action researcher and practitioner. The field first moved from an emphasis on short-term, discrete programs, to a realization that multicomponent, multilevel, multiyear interventions, linked to the goals and fabric of the organizations for which they are intended, are essential for successful, enduring outcomes (Weissberg & Elias, 1993). Accompanying this view is an evolving understanding of the skills needed to implement such efforts effectively (Elias, 1997). Social and emotional learning, character education, service learning, prevention, and related school-based programs and activities are highly operator-dependent. That is, their success is not linked to some automated technology, but rather to actions carried out by human beings interacting with multiple others across situations over time. Even when such interactions are scripted, there is great potential variation, and the moment-to-moment decisions made by the human operators of an intervention, in ecological relationship to all those around them, greatly influence the ultimate outcomes.

For schools to successfully bring in comprehensive approaches to SEL in enduring and effective ways, they will need consultants who can negotiate a complex, interactive, ecological-developmental process. The remainder of the chapter focuses on a pragmatic-theoretical guide for consultants and researchers working to implement SEL in a variety of contexts.

DEVELOPMENTAL ARENAS IN SOCIAL-EMOTIONAL LEARNING PROGRAM IMPLEMENTATION

As our contribution to the greater likelihood that interactive, ecological-developmental processes will be well-handled, we want to elucidate the developmental nexus within which effective SEL takes place. The centerpiece of our ecological considerations is the consultant and the path that he or she takes to being able to master, or at least address, the evolving complexity of interventions. An additional level of analysis is a set of developmental processes in the host settings that must ultimately be in alignment if SEL is to take root in a school and be a positive influence on children.

Developmental Arena 1: Program Implementation

Finding trends in the changing trajectories of individuals is a difficult endeavor due to the large number of variables that may influence the pathways. Examining the change trajectory of an organization, itself made up of multiple individuals undergoing their own processes of change within the ecology of the setting, yields a literature "that is diverse and often unwieldy" (Commins & Elias, 1991, p. 207). Efforts to summarize the process of program implementation within an organization are necessarily summative generalizations of the efforts of multiple individuals within the organization. A temporal cross section of the setting at a given point in time may reveal individuals whose level of implementation does not correspond to the overall level of implementation within the organization. New teachers come on board and need to be brought up to speed. Veteran teachers differ in terms of their own motivation to implement the program. Individual differences in creativity or drive for innovation will impact the degree to which one adheres to or makes changes to the program being implemented.

However, even with the multitude of factors impacting the process (many of which are discussed later in this chapter), there are trends that emerge as implementation of a new program unfolds in a setting. Novick, Kress, and Elias (2002), basing their work on Hord et al. (1987), summarize these trends by looking at the general levels of use of interventions by individuals within a setting (Table 15.2).

The earliest stage, though technically one of nonuse, is important in forming the foundation of future implementation efforts. All implementation efforts have a "prehistory" (Sarason, 1972) of past experiences with innovation in a setting, of beliefs, values, and experiences held by individuals within a setting, and of the culture of the school

TABLE 15.2   Levels of Use and Concern

Level of Use	Staff Members at This Level	Level of Concern	Staff Members at This Level	Adult Learners at This Level Need
Nonuse	Have little or no knowledge, no involvement, and no actions to help them become involved.	Awareness	May be concerned about the consequences of SEL deficits, but not about SEL programming or implementation.	To gain an understanding of the program rationale, the contextual supports/incentive supports for implementation, and skills needed for implementation.
Orientation	Are acquiring information about SEL and its value orientation and what it will require to carry out the innovation.	Informational	Would like to know more about SEL and how to promote it.	Introductory information about specific program goals, requirements, and time lines.
Preparation	Are preparing to use a new SEL idea or process.	Personal	Are considering using (or not using) SEL and are grappling with the impact that this decision will have on their work and on themselves.	Concrete information on what the innovation will look like, what materials they will use, and how to prepare themselves to take the first steps in getting started.
Mechanical use	Focus on short-term, day-to-day use, mastering the specific tasks and techniques they must carry out.	Management	Are concerned about their ability to handle the logistics of the program implementation.	Support and troubleshooting for implementation (e.g., observing other teachers, additional consultation/supervision, e-mail contact with experts, peer-group meetings to share and learn).
Routine	Have established use of the innovation; regular patterns of implementation predominate and few changes are made in ongoing use.	Consequences (I)	Wonder about the impact that their efforts are having on their students.	Praise and recognition for what they are doing; assistance in making implementation easier or better and assessing outcomes.
Refinement	Fine-tune SEL efforts based on feedback from consumers/clients and from their own experience.	Consequences (II)	Consider how to maximize program effectiveness and improve delivery.	Support and reinforcement for innovation while maintaining the core aspects of the plan.
Integration	Begin to step back and look at the big picture of the SEL work they are doing; they focus on how to combine their own efforts with those of colleagues.	Collaboration	Recognize that impact can be maximized by coordinating efforts with others and continuity over time.	Support for naturally occurring interactions and collaborations; planned contexts in which cooperation can occur.
Renewal	Reevaluate practice in light of factors such as changes in population, student needs, staffing patterns, freshness/relevance of materials.	Refocusing	Begin to supplement and enhance the intervention based on their own experience.	Opportunities for staff to share and discuss desirable, coordinated changes in the school's SEL efforts.

Source: Based on *Taking Charge of Change,* by S. M. Hord, W. L. Rutherford, L. Huling-Austin, and G. E. Hall, 1987, Alexandria, VA: Association for Supervision and Curriculum Development; and *Building Learning Communities with Character: How to Integrate Academic, Social and Emotional Learning,* by B. Novick, J. S. Kress, and M. J. Elias, 2002, Alexandria, VA: Association for Supervision and Curriculum Development.

in terms of such areas as staff collaboration and morale.[1] Does the school have a history of revolving-door innovations that might impact how seriously staff regard yet another new program? Do staff tend to work together proactively to address concerns in the school, or does individual griping predominate? The answers to such questions will impact the trajectory of any programmatic efforts in a setting.

Early use stages are introductions or initiations of a new program into a setting, corresponding to the orientation, preparation, and mechanical use levels in Table 15.2. The goals and rationale of a program are introduced, and implementers are oriented to why such a program is important to the life of the school. Initiation progresses to include planning to take, and then actually embarking on, the first steps in implementing the pro-

---

[1] The prehistory also involves the process by which the innovation was brought to the setting. Who initiated the effort: was it top-down from the principal, grassroots from the teachers, or some combination of the two? What program options were explored? These factors are important, but because they precede the onset of programming, they will not be a focus of this chapter.

gram. For SEL programming, introduction and initiation is a time when implementers consider the importance of SEL skills, the difficulties with deficits in such skills, and basic tenets of best practices for promoting SEL skills. Further, they are learning the nuts and bolts of implementing the specific program being brought to the school (e.g., Are there lessons to learn? Materials to use?) and planning how to incorporate new activities into existing class structures (e.g., When will the lessons be delivered?).

Once a degree of implementation mastery is achieved through repeated mechanical use, initiation gives way to regularity of programming efforts within a school. Such a routine level of use involves fairly consistent patterns of programming with few changes being made. As implementers gain increased fluency with the program and begin to notice subtleties such as differential impact on various students (e.g., based on gender, developmental level, special needs classification) and their own implementation style (e.g., comfort or lack thereof with various programmatic aspects), they may attempt to refine their efforts in light of their experiences and observations.

As staff members become regular users, the program moves toward institutionalization within a setting. The program becomes part of the standard operating procedure of a setting. A visitor would be unable to distinguish the institutionalized program from any other long-standing initiative. Many of the functions once performed by an outside consultant are now owned by the institution (Kress, Cimring, & Elias, 1997). New roles might be created to maintain the program, and the values and goals of the program may be reflected in the rituals and ceremonies of the school.

The institutionalization phase, like the routine use phase before it, is not static. Just as routine use is marked by refinement, institutionalization is marked by integration and renewal. The former term refers to the growing realization by implementers that their individual efforts will be enhanced to the extent to which they support one another and their efforts are carried through over time. The focus of programmatic efforts shifts from isolated classrooms to coordination among faculty members at and across grade levels and/or disciplines. As the overall quality and consistency of implementation continues to progress, implementers will be interested in renewing their efforts in light of contextually based changes. Student populations change, staff turnover occurs, new mandates are mandated, and new materials materialize. Programmatic response to such

changes can be seen in a Piagetian light: Changes may be "assimilated" into existing program structures, or the program "accommodates" to new realities.

A curriculum-based and problem-solving oriented program such as Interpersonal Cognitive Problem Solving (ICPS) (Shure & Spivack, 1988), Open Circle (Seigle, 2001), and SDM/SPS (Elias & Bruene-Butler, 2005a, 2005b, 2005c) is typically introduced in a half-day awareness workshop that shows staff the framework of the program, the key skills, and the problem-solving steps that are embodied in their lessons. Preparation involves another level of training, for at least an entire day, in which specific curriculum materials are presented to staff. What follows next is mechanical use, whereby teachers typically follow the curriculum lessons pretty much as presented in the curriculum but are not overly concerned if they miss an occasional lesson. There is not much flexibility and little spontaneous use of the curriculum in noninstructional time. Use is considered routine once there is an understanding of the importance of regular use if the program is to have an impact on students. Refinement is the next logical level; this is where problem-solving procedures might be modified to make them more clearly remembered or applied by particular students, or whole-class activities are recast into small groups (or vice versa) in an attempt to have a greater impact on students who do not seem to be grasping the skills based on standard presentation. Integration occurs when problem-solving skills are applied not only to social situations, but to academics, such as literature and social studies, and to the discipline system in the form of problem-solving worksheets to help students think through rule infractions and plan better ways to handle troubling situations when they occur in the future. Finally, after perhaps 2 to 3 years, these programs can be at the renewal level of use as the need to modify procedures and supplement materials is evaluated in light of the impact of the curriculum. For example, procedures from the Responsive Classroom program (www.responsiveclassroom.org) that focus on morning meetings, establishing rules, and building a positive sense of community often provide a valuable adjunct to Open Circle and SDM/SPS; self-control techniques from Second Step (www.cfc.org) have been used to bolster readiness skills for problem solving in ICPS. These modifications then go through their own levels of use process, albeit usually at a much quicker pace than shown by the original curriculum.

These trends can be considered developmental in that earlier stages of implementation are seen as enabling later stages to occur. As in individual developmental theories, not all stages are achieved at the same speed (nor by all the implementers in any given setting at the same time), nor will any given setting (or its individual implementers) make their way fully to the "last" stage. Finally, there is a cyclical nature to the process, as modifications that are made during later phases might need to be initiated in a process similar to introducing a new program.

Developmental Arena 2: The Program Implementers

The stage-wise progress of implementing programmatic change on a systemic level has parallels in terms of learning, behavioral change, and innovation adaptation on the part of the implementers of any SEL program. This progression can be framed in terms of Prochaska and DiClemente's (1984) transtheoretical model of behavior change (cf. Edwards, Jumper-Thuman, Plested, Oetting, & Swanson, 2000). In their model, individual readiness is described as an underlying factor in moving through stages of change, beginning with limited awareness of the problem and lack of motivation to change, and progressing through increases in both. With regard to SEL programming, various adult learning needs may emerge as implementers move from initial exposure to the intervention to preliminary inroads in its use to eventual regular usage.

Novick et al. (2002) have discussed a progression of levels of concern, or adult learner-implementer needs, based on Hord, Rutherford, Huling-Austin, and Hall (1987), that emerge as implementers move through the process of implementing an SEL program. As summarized in Table 15.2, these concerns and needs correspond to the levels of use discussed previously. In summary, these levels begin at a limited awareness of the issue of SEL and low motivation to implement SEL programming. As staff become more aware of the importance of SEL, and their own role in addressing SEL skills, basic "how to" issues come to the fore. Once implementers have achieved a degree of mastery of the basics of implementation, needs begin to focus on improving, supporting, and innovating practice.

These levels of concern point out the interplay between the progress of program implementation and implementers' needs to have certain concerns addressed. A consultant must be aware of the particular concerns at any given time and be ready to help see that they are addressed. At some levels, for example, at the informa-

tion level, learners' needs may be filled by a direct intervention on the part of the consultant (in this case, providing more information). Other levels, for example, collaboration, may require a more systemic approach to create the kind of learning communities that would meet some implementers' concerns.

Factors Impacting Initiation into the Implementation Process

Embedded in this discussion is an understanding that the developmental needs of the adult learner-implementers are sensitive to social and emotional factors. At the early levels of concern, for example, beliefs and attitudes will be important in the progression toward initial steps of implementation. Specifically, the beliefs and attitudes held by the implementers regarding the origins of social and emotional skills and the best way to build such skills will impact the degree of motivation to implement any SEL program. Incompatibility between the consultant's and implementers' framing of a target problem can result in the latter group rejecting the program being promoted by the former (Everhart & Wandersman, 2000). Teachers who believe that social and emotional skills are part of a student's immutable genetic makeup will be unlikely to show support for a program based on a social learning model of social and emotional skill development.

Perceptions regarding the importance of deficits in SEL skills and one's responsibility for addressing them may have an impact on implementation, as well. For example, in a study of an antibullying program, degree of implementation was predicted by perceptions held by teachers regarding the extent of bullying behaviors in their school and teachers' assessment of the importance of their role in stemming the problem (Kallestad & Olweus, 2003). Thorsen-Spano (1996) found that elementary school teachers with a favorable attitude toward conflict resolution report a higher level of implementation of a conflict resolution program in their class than do those who report a less favorable attitude. Teachers who do not see SEL skills as a problem (and therefore, "If it ain't broke, don't fix it"), or who see them as a concern but not their concern ("SEL is for the parents/school psychologist/and so on to deal with, not me") will be unlikely to embrace an SEL program. A consultant must work to gauge the attitudes and feelings of the implementers both around the social-emotional climate of the school and about the implementation as it unfolds (Novick et al., 2002).

Factors Impacting Movement toward Regular Use

Implementers must possess a sense of their own ability to successfully carry out an SEL program. That is, a teacher might believe in the premise of the SEL program but have concerns about how he or she will handle factors such as classroom management during program sessions or finding time to implement an additional initiative (e.g., Ghaith & Yaghi, 1997). Such concerns can derail the efforts of the implementer to progress toward regular program use. Although teachers will enter the implementation process with a level of implementation self-efficacy, this factor will also be sensitive to iatrogenic effects. The relative success or failure of initial implementation efforts will have an impact on willingness to regularize programming. As such, Elias et al. (1997) have stressed the importance of "small wins" early on in creating positive momentum.

Growth in skill development will be enhanced by the extent to which individual efforts are given an opportunity to intersect with the efforts of others who are also involved in the process, thereby creating a community of learner-implementers. Such efforts "can enhance relationships, facilitate contextually relevant modifications, and foster understanding of the role of school culture in program implementation" (Nastasi, 2002, p. 222).

Factors Important during Institutionalization

Finally, in considering the development of the implementers qua implementers, it is important to keep in mind parallel developmental processes. Program implementation may be related to an educator's experience level. For example, following a staff development program on cooperative learning, experience was negatively correlated with reported attitudes toward implementation (Ghaith & Yaghi, 1997). Also, as discussed by Everhart and Wandersman (2000), adults in an Eriksonian "generativity" stage may find it more exciting to modify the existing program or to try something new than to maintain implementation as is. Staff turnover ensures that any ongoing implementation cohort includes both those experienced with as well as new to any intervention. As such, a consultant must be careful not to generalize regarding the implementation-developmental level of any group of consultees. Newly hired teachers likely being at a less advanced level of concern (after all, they may enter the school with little or no familiarity with the SEL program being used). Further, teachers new to a set-

ting have these concerns play out in a social and emotional context different from that of the cohort with whom the innovation was introduced (Elias, Zins, Greenberg, Graczyk, & Weissberg, 2003). When first introduced to a program, implementers often have a cohort of colearners who are facing the same excitement, anxieties, and so on related to the program, and can support one another through the process. A new teacher, already needing to gain entry to a new workplace, may be the only one, or one of an isolated few, going through these initial awkward baby steps.

Developmental Arena 3: The Social-Emotional Learning Intervention

Another factor that operates in interplay with others in developmental progression is the nature of the intervention. At its inception, an intervention should be limited, tangible, and scripted. This allows it to incorporate complexity but not require full understanding on the part of implementers to carry it out. As long as its principles and procedures are clearly laid out in training and follow-up materials in ways that allow emulation, the implementer will be able to get a feel for what it is like to carry it out. As in the sensorimotor period of infancy, learning occurs without being accompanied by full understanding. Also, the intervention is not experienced as a flow or systematic sequence, but as a set of discrete events. Yet, operational knowledge sufficient to manage in the world in a rudimentary way is present.

From Discrete Intervention to Establishing a Flow

Feedback during this initial period of use is followed by the intervention being carried out for a full year or cycle (e.g., some interventions are designed for a set period of weeks or months, others go for a full academic year). It is at this point that the flow of an intervention is established and those implementing it can make realistic and comprehensive preparations for carrying it out. Among these plans are how to connect the intervention to other programs and services in the school and other experiences that the child has either in preparation or follow-up to the intervention. For example, in SDM/SPS, a first year of teaching students problem-solving skills led to a decision to provide them with readiness skills in 1 to 2 prior years, and then application opportunities to allow integration of problem-solving skills into academic subject areas in subsequent years.

Integration in the Culture and Climate of Classrooms and Schools

These expansions also go through the process of development, as noted earlier. In addition, within the classroom, an SEL intervention becomes integrated with classroom management—it becomes the umbrella under which related efforts are organized. At this point, the integration might not be clearly visible as such; it has become part of the culture and climate of the class. In Heinz Werner's (1957) terminology, the process of differentiation and integration takes a decisive turn toward the latter.

Yet, the process is not over. Interventions that operate only at the classroom level are still limited in their impact on the student body. The next part of the development of an intervention involves its principles being extracted and applied into building-wide SEL/SPS efforts. This includes such important areas as the overall school climate and the discipline and positive recognition systems used. Among the components one is likely to see that denote this process are administrator training and the training of bus drivers and lunch aides in intervention-linked techniques. Other indicators are an SDM/SPS Lab, Keep Calm Force (a schoolwide, peer-led self-control and problem-solving program), bulletin boards denoting application of intervention principles to everyday interactions and situations and academic content areas, positive recognition systems, and emphases on positive citizenship in and out of the school. In other words, the intervention tends to expand and become more comprehensive.

A Spiraling Process of 3 to 5 Years

At the same time, it becomes a bit harder to bring new people on board into this process because of turnover, changes in the target populations, and changes in the development of the adult learners. Sarason (1996) and others (e.g., Elias, 1997) suggest that it takes 3 to 5 years to proceed from the inception of a pilot intervention to its spreading systematically within an entire school building. To understand this process most accurately, it is best to think of it as a developmental trajectory that is less linear and perhaps more like a spiral in nature.

Developmental Arena 4: The Consultant

There are two aspects of the development of consultants that are of particular relevance. First, consultants gain experience over time, and thus develop expertise and so-

phistication. However, there is a second aspect of development. Over time, consultants are called on to handle more and more advanced stages of the intervention process. Schools call on consultants at different stages in the process of bringing in programs. The stages are:

1. Awareness
2. Training to begin
3. Ongoing consultation/support
4. Leadership team/administrator training
5. Program evaluation (including implementation monitoring, consumer feedback)
6. Intervention development and expansion
7. Contextual integration

Each stage brings its own nuances and requires consultants to have certain knowledge, skills, and perspectives. What happens almost inevitably, especially to effective consultants, is that they are called on to shepherd an SEL program through its various stages in a particular school or district over time. Ready or not, the consultant will have to develop the understandings and skills needed to deal with what is in essence a transformational process. Complexities abound, however, in that consultants might be working at different stages of programs at the same time in different settings, and sometimes they are called in to work at different stages, rather than following the developmental progression of stages during a single consultation.

1. Awareness

At this stage, consultants have the task of introducing an SEL program to potential adopters. This is best understood as marketing the intervention. Typically, the consultant has a limited time period, from 45 minutes to 3 hours, to introduce the intervention to a group that can be homogeneous (from one grade level), heterogeneous (from all elementary grades, or even K–12), to a mix (from the same school, but all different grade levels). The recipients may well be informed about the intervention, but it is more likely that they will not be, other than knowing the title or topic of the presentation and perhaps a synopsis. Rare indeed is the situation in which staff members will read an article in advance of an awareness training. Thus, the mind-set of the consultant must be one of reducing complexity, eschewing comprehensiveness, and maximizing entertainment/engagement as part of the workshop/presentation experience.

2. Training to Begin

If an awareness session goes well, the consultant may be called on to conduct a training with staff to get them started with the intervention. Several pragmatic factors influence the specific nature of the training, such as when during the school year it takes place (e.g., fall, early in the calendar year, May/June, summer, just prior to the start of school), the length of time (2 hours, a full day), the number and nature of staff people attending, and the extent to which the training is voluntary or mandatory (no, it is not incongruous to refer to degrees of mandatory, or even voluntary, attendance). Because the agenda of the consultant is to encourage trainees to begin and persist, whereas the main focus of the trainees is simply to begin in a sound, comfortable, effective way, another concern is the plan and resource allocation to follow up the training. One need not be a veteran consultant to recognize the inherent difficulties of conducting trainings in May/June or early or midsummer. Again, the consultant must balance how much to present the full year-long context of the program versus focusing on a segment but going into it in sufficient depth to allow trainees to begin to implement with confidence. Even in a full-day training, unless the groups are highly homogeneous and well prepared, it is difficult for consultants to give trainees a good feel for how the intervention looks and feels over the course of a school year and also have time to impart the skills and practice needed so that initial implementation goes well. A further consideration is the definition of "begin." How far along in the program should the consultant focus the initial training? In preparing staff from a single grade level from 10 elementary schools in an urban district for a 2-hour workshop, one consultant decided to focus on the generic structure of the lessons and then the first two lessons (out of 22 planned for the school year). Given how long it took staff from 10 buildings to arrive at a single location, functional instructional time was closer to 75 minutes. (Note that the decision about whether to start on time but then have perhaps 50% of the trainees come in while the training is in progress, versus waiting, is a vexing one that beginning consultants often do not anticipate.) Even in a generally positive and receptive climate, completing the two-session focus was a challenge under these circumstances.

It is useful to point out some developmental considerations here. The consultant is being asked to coordinate cognition, emotion, and behavior between the groups of trainees and the tasks for which they are being prepared.

The ability of the consultant to do this effectively increases with experience, reflection, and supervision. Some issues, such as how to address late arrivals, can be thought through in advance with the proper guidance; so can the issue of how to deal with absentees.

Werner's (1957) principle of differentiation and integration is relevant here as well. To do an awareness training, the amount of differentiation the consultant deals with is minimal. Deciding on what to emphasize, the consultant then must think of how to integrate these disparate elements so that he or she can have an integrated approach and the trainees can perceive their experience in an integrative, rather than scattered or disconnected, way. During a training to begin (as would occur at initial stages of implementation), the consultant has more to differentiate, but still not the full context of a year-long program. Integration usually needs to take place around the concept of "What do I do on Monday, and then the next Monday?" assuming that the cognitions, emotions, and behavior of trainees must be coordinated around these primary concerns.

3. Ongoing Consultation/Support

If there is an agreement to continue working with the consultant after the initial training, the consultant's attention must turn to how to support staff in implementing the program. Various studies converge to suggest that this is a pivotal point in the process for both psychological and pragmatic reasons (Diebolt, Miller, Gensheimer, Mondschein, & Ohmart, 2000; Gager & Elias, 1997; Greenberg & Kusché, 1988). The latter is self-evident. People want to be successful and comfortable taking on new tasks and would like to have questions answered before and after the initial session and receive feedback or support in preparation for the next one. The former has to do with the question of the school administration's commitment to the program teachers are being asked to carry out. Teachers want to know that they are not being asked to invest their time in a fad, or in a 1-year, short-lived, tangential intervention. No amount of verbal assurance is a substitute for tangible support. The consultant, then, needs skills in providing supportive consultation and feedback (a skill set that is more interactive and differentiated than doing a frontal group training) and needs to have the ability and perspective to negotiate a system or framework for that consultation to take place. Often, external consultants are constrained in being able to have the time and flexibility to observe and meet with teachers over the course of a school year. Therefore, some procedure for developing local expertise must be developed. (Note that experienced consultants will often want to create initial agreements that include not only the awareness and initial trainings, but also the work that the consultant will do to help develop and sustain a system of ongoing consultation, support, and training.) This brings the consultant into the arena of administrative consultation and requires an understanding of district goals and policies, procedures and practices for staff development, staff schedules, and supervisory practices and methods of compensation.

4. Leadership Team/Administrator Training

It is one thing to have the administration agree to allow some staff members to serve in supervisory/coaching roles, and another for the administration to take ownership of the direction and operation of the program. Setting up an SEL or program-based leadership team is another pivotal task for consultants. To do this effectively requires consultants to understand well the roles of school administrators, social workers, guidance counselors, school psychologists, health educators, and character education and substance abuse and violence/bullying prevention coordinators. Should there be student-family support staff or any position with responsibility as a liaison to parents and the community, that person's input is also important because one of the purviews of the leadership team is funding. Consultants must know these roles because roles that might be assigned must be congruent with existing duties and patterns of availability. Designing and implementing a training for this group requires that the consultant find a way to concisely convey the key elements of the program, its pedagogy, and the expected implementation time line and structure. In addition, attendees should be exposed to basic principles of supportive, constructive supervisory feedback to teachers. And there is yet another level of concern: The leadership team will assume responsibility for program planning and evaluation, and so training in this process and the tasks involved must be provided. As before, the consultant must deal with logistical constraints (such as number and length of sessions and expectations about attendance and absence) and the attitude of staff toward the program and its implementation (Gager & Elias, 1997).

What begins to happen at this stage is that consultants are being asked to switch cognitive, emotional, and behavior gears in an increasingly disparate context. It is one thing to work with multiple schools or districts within the same or adjacent stages; that provides great variation and challenge for the consultant to keep straight. But it is another to shift back and forth between the awareness level, which eschews detail, and the ongoing consultation and support levels, which require it. Many consultants flounder as they experience difficulty inadvertently increasing the complexity of their awareness or initial trainings or, less often, oversimplifying their ongoing consultation and related work in the name of getting easy acceptance. Commins and Elias (1991) showed that such simplification is associated with reduced program longevity in schools, whereas presenting programs at an appropriate and realistic (but not excessive) level of complexity is associated with longer program endurance.

5. and 6. Program Evaluation (Including Implementation Monitoring, Consumer Feedback) and Intervention Development and Expansion

Whereas some level of accountability is a constant concern at every stage of consultancy (including the process by which the consultant monitors and evaluates his or her own efforts), systematic program evaluation efforts usually emerge once a leadership team, social development committee, or similar structure is established (Elias et al., 1997). Program evaluation is deceptively complicated, and consultants who are not trained in this area will find themselves needing to build their expertise or bring on consultative assistance. The first challenge is to find ways of monitoring what is actually happening with the program: who is carrying out lessons, with what frequency, and with what degree of fidelity. Without knowing how the program is implemented, it is impossible to make any inferences about the relationship of the program to any observed outcomes. Consumer feedback is also important, because a program that teachers and other school professionals do not like to implement and that students do not enjoy receiving is unlikely to be carried out in an effective and enduring way. This is not to say that consumer satisfaction is a primary criterion, but it is a necessary, though not sufficient, condition for long-term program success.

Intervention development is the process of refining a program based on feedback. Where something is not working for a subgroup of students, modifications must be made. This is not a simple process. Staff members need to be involved for maximum buy-in, and those modifying the program must know its key elements and make changes that do not change the character of the program (especially if it is an evidence-based program). However, programs tend not to be static, and the most recent view about program effectiveness is that programs must be multiyear in nature. True skill gain in children is cumulative in nature, and so programs must be carried out over multiple years (Weissberg & Greenberg, 1998). If a given program has been created to operate over multiple grade levels, then at least the materials and structure are available for the consultant to work with. Sometimes, however, a program exists only through grade 3, or grade 5, and a school wants to expand it to the next grade level. This will require a new skill set for consultants and will take them into collaborative relationships with teachers and perhaps program developers. Thus, the consultant must develop new skills related to curriculum/program content and be prepared to serve not purely as a consultant but as a collaborator in program development and expansion efforts.

7. Contextual Integration

Another recent insight about SEL programs is that they need to be integrated into the structure, climate, and organization of the classroom if they are to succeed (CASEL, 2003). And if programs are to have an impact on the school, they also must be integrated into the overall structure and climate of the school. Social and emotional learning must become salient outside the classroom and influence what happens in the hallways, lunchrooms, bus rides, discipline procedures, and how everyone in the school interacts with one another. Further, students benefit most when SEL is continuous across schools.

None of this should be surprising because the points are the same for academic skill acquisition. If reading were to be limited to classroom lessons, not continued at all grade levels, not carried out from school to school, and, particularly important, not done with any consistent approach across settings, children would be quite impaired in their literacy development. If children do not receive SEL across grade levels in a coherent and high-quality manner, they may be at risk with regard to developing the skills they need to maximally carry out their responsibilities as adults. Consultants develop from being focused on the delivery of a particular program in one classroom to providing the array of supports necessary to ensure that children develop substantial SEL skills. An extended example of such development is provided in the accompanying vignette.

Developmental Arena 5: The Child

The development of social and emotional competencies has been extensively researched. The scope of the topic

and the various subcomponents of many of these competencies contribute to the amount of research done. For example, emotional skills can be broken down into subunits, including identification of emotions in oneself and others, the regulation of emotion, and the communication—both verbal and nonverbal—of emotions. It is not our intention to review this literature in its entirety. Rather, we trace the trends in the social and emotional expectations that can be held for students as they develop and that can become curricular foci for school-based intervention of the type described in this chapter.

A helpful rubric for organizing this complex literature is provided by Elias et al. (1997), who trace trends in social and emotional development through different age groups (early elementary, elementary/intermediate, middle school, high school) within various developmental contexts (personal, peer/social, family, and school- and community-related). This clustering of age groups not only simplifies understanding of the developmental trends, but also underscores the nondeterministic nature of a child's specific age. Although trends exist, great variability can be expected within any group of same-age children. As readers encounter this review, they might find themselves thinking, "This doesn't describe the 8-, or 10-, or 12-year-olds I know!" This response is anticipated by the authors and is a by-product of the variability within ages mentioned earlier. The approach we take here is one of reviewing what students at this age generally *can* do, especially with proper support from adults, rather than what might be seen in any given interaction or social situation. We take such an approach because the focus of this chapter is on how developmental issues can inform school-based programming. Such programming strives to help students achieve the types of competencies we describe here as reasonable expectations.

Early Elementary

In terms of the personal arena, early elementary students are generally developing the ability to express and manage basic emotions (such as fear, anger, excitement), can differentiate between negative and positive emotions, and can use increasingly complex language to express emotion. They are increasingly able to tolerate frustration and delay gratification and to manage turn taking, although these skills will be demonstrated inconsistently. "Although the preschooler begins to use language to facilitate self-control and begins to engage in cognitive planning in the service of frustration tolerance, the ability to effectively and automatically use these processes transpires primarily during the

One Consultant's Developmental Journey

One of the authors (MJE) worked with an urban school district over a 7-year period, allowing for a journey through all seven of the stages of consultant activity. This example is instructive because it also involves SDM/SPS. However, in the focal school district, an urban, high-risk setting in central New Jersey with poor test score performance, SDM/SPS had to be modified to be sensitive to the predominantly African American population and also the strong literacy needs of the students. Thus, at the 2-hour awareness workshop, attended by teachers from grades 2 and 3 across 10 elementary schools, an attempt was made to introduce SEL, introduce a specific curriculum program, Talking with TJ (Dilworth, Mokrue, & Elias, 2002), show its appropriateness with regard to culture and literacy, and provide teachers with a practice opportunity that would allow them to carry out an initial lesson. There was no additional opportunity to provide training to begin. Teachers were expected to begin, and I, along with an African American graduate student assistant, provided follow-up to teachers in all 10 schools. We did this by meeting with them during available slots between 2:35 and 3:05.

In the course of providing ongoing consultation and support, we became aware of how few teachers had a good feel for the program and recognized that this would have to be accomplished without formal training. We recruited Rutgers undergraduates, trained them in the curriculum, and sent them into many classrooms so that they could provide direct feedback and assistance to teachers and help to convey their feel of the program. This helped make our ongoing consultation efforts more useful. However, we also recognized the limitations of this approach over the long term. Thus, I turned my attention to working with the superintendent of schools and a special assistant assigned to provide administrative support to the SEL effort to develop a leadership team and support structure. My consultation involved a level different from working with and supporting teachers, which was continued by graduate and undergraduate students who had familiarity with the program but not with working with administrators. The key need was to provide channels of communication from the teachers to the Rutgers Social-Emotional Learning Lab team that was supporting the program, and also local building-based leadership in bringing SEL across grade levels and into the school climate beyond its presence in curriculum lessons. Opportunities to address the administrative cabinet were used to help principals understand the theory and pedagogy behind the program and to appreciate the specific actions they needed to take to support teachers in their work (e.g., ask them to submit lesson plans showing when they would implement the program, assist them in finding the time and context if they were having difficulty, and provide feedback based on the lesson plans and direct observation when possible). Administrators also selected "TJ captains" in each building; these were teachers who had the role of speaking with other teachers carrying out the program and raising concerns proactively with members of the Rutgers team. So the consultation task shifted from working with all teachers to working primarily with the TJ captains and occasionally working with teachers who needed special help.

Another consultation task was working with the building-based SEL coordinators. This involved helping them to see ways to extend SEL to schoolwide efforts, such as positive recognition of students and creating school citizenship and service activities, bulletin boards, plays focused on SEL themes, and literacy activities such as the Principal's Book of the Month. They also needed help communicating about SEL within their buildings, across buildings, and to parents.

There were other nuances of consultation not mentioned; for example, another diverse area was evaluation. Here, the primary consultee was the school superintendent. He wanted ways to monitor the implementation of the program and its outcome. Consultation required knowledge of formative and summative evaluation procedures, as well as how to convey them in a practical manner and deal with the logistics of carrying out this assessment in an environment already saturated by standardized tests. Consumer satisfaction surveys were put into place and completed by teachers and students. Teachers also completed an assessment related to levels of use. Teachers rated students' behavior on a standardized teacher rating scale, which was shortened and modified for use with urban, low-income minority populations (at the request of teachers), and students completed measures of SEL skills, self-concept, social support, and school violence and victimization. Clearly, this requires a very different kind of activity by a consultant than any previous stage.

As data from the program indicated positive receptivity and successful outcomes (Dilworth et al., 2002), there was a desire on the part of the school district to develop and expand the intervention. The development included adding a character education component, the Laws of Life essay, to the skills-based Talking with TJ curriculum. The expansion was creating a curriculum for grades 4–5 and then K–1. These changes required work by the consultant to integrate Laws of Life and Talking with TJ into the literacy curriculum. At the same time, the building-based SEL coordinators increased their efforts to better connect the program with other elements of the school day to increase the impact on school climate. For this to take place, the consultant needed to coordinate more with school principals and to grasp the big picture of how SEL could unfold within the culture of each of the schools. Managing this diversity across 10 schools is challenging, as is the need to continue the consultative cycle as each new component to the curriculum was added on.

Other skills that were required over the course of the 7 years included writing school board policy around SEL, dealing with high staff turnover, and following up the program into the two middle schools and high school. In each case, new areas of expertise were required, and sources of support and information had to be tapped for the consultant to effectively meet these needs.

elementary school years" (Greenberg & Snell, 1997, p. 106). However, they still often employ behavioral, rather than cognitive, strategies to deal with stressors (Brenner & Salovey, 1997). Students at this level are beginning to be able to consider the feelings and intentions of others in a reflective, role-taking capacity, even showing early signs of differentiating the feelings of different people in different contexts. They are becoming able to generate alternative possibilities for action in interpersonal situations.

Students at this age are learning basic skills that will remain vital to peer functioning. They are developing competencies in areas such as listening, sharing, cooperating, negotiating, and compromising. These students understand similarities and differences between self and others. They are able to demonstrate empathy toward their peers and become distressed at the suffering of others, and often respond by helping a child in need. They are also learning about themselves, can express themselves through artistic and dramatic representations, can express their likes and dislikes, and are learning about their own strengths. The ICPS, Second Step, and Responsive Classroom Programs are especially strong at this age level.

Middle Elementary

Students at a middle elementary level are moving ahead in many of those competencies initially begun earlier. Their repertoire of labels for emotions is expanding, and they can generally be expected to exercise more control over their anger. They can calm themselves down when upset and verbalize how they are feeling and describe what happened. They can learn strategies to cope with strong emotional situations. They are developing more positive ways to express their feelings. When they do lose their temper or become upset, they can generally calm themselves down, increasingly tending to use cognitive as opposed to behavioral strategies to deal with stressors, and they are forgiving regarding the situation. From this age into the next cohort, students are developing repertoires of coping skills and learning to match different strategies to different types of situations (Brenner & Salovey, 1997).

Students at this grade level are making advances in sociocognitive skills as well. They are increasingly able to set goals and to continue to work toward these even in the face of obstacles. Abilities to anticipate outcomes and consequences of actions are improving. Students at this level are becoming increasingly self-aware, particu-

larly regarding their own strengths and weaknesses and those of others. They are learning not to be derailed by failures. Skills in perspective taking continue to grow.

Social interactions at this level are more complex, with cooperative planning and joint problem solving taking place. They are grappling with a set of social skills such as making new friends and entering new and expanded peer groups. They are accepting of diversity and difference. They call on improved skills in being able to manage a reciprocal conversation and judge and anticipate the thoughts, feelings, and actions of others. They can modify their interactions—verbal and nonverbal—to suit different audiences (e.g., peers, teachers). With the increased peer interactions come an increased awareness of peer norms and sensitivity to pressures for conformity. Also, students at this age are developing skills in assertiveness, boundary setting, and dealing with rejection. In school, students at this age are increasingly able to work on teams and to see projects through to completion and experience pride in a job well done. The skills emphasis of Providing Alternative Thinking Strategies (PATHS; Greenberg & Kusché, 1998), SDM/SPS, and Open Circle are especially well matched to this age level.

Middle School and Beyond

As we turn our attention to middle school, we find students who are entering adolescence, with its attendant social and behavioral changes. In terms of social and emotional development, there are several trends that can be traced. Students at this stage are increasingly self-aware and, often, self-critical. Their sociocognitive skills are making great strides. They are able to understand multiple sides of arguments and disagreements. They are sensitive to perceived social norms and often judge their own abilities and self-worth by others' reactions to them. They can identify their own self-talk and acknowledge its importance. Although they are increasingly able to articulate goals, both long and short term, it is often difficult for them to modify actions to come into line with achieving these goals. As with those that precede it, there is often a great disparity at this age level between what one *can* do under structured conditions and what one *will* do in actual situations.

Peer interactions are undertaken with a great sensitivity to popular trends, but at the same time with increasing introspective thoughtfulness and ability to distinguish between good and bad friends. Belonging becomes an important issue to students at this age, and friends strive to develop ways to deal with conflict and solve problems while maintaining friendships. Throughout adolescence, students are gaining skills in peer leadership.

As students progress into high school, perhaps the most important theme is that of increasing integration among the various developing social and emotional skills under the broad umbrella of developing a stable sense of identity and set of long-range goals.

> During adolescence emotions noticeably become the basis of identity and ideals. What adolescents care about is usually what they feel strongly about—not only feel intensely but also feel variably. . . . Adolescents become aware of feeling everything, and this transforms their values and their understanding. (Haviland-Jones, Gebelt, and Stapely, 1997, p. 244–245)

Adolescents become more interested in questions of personal meaning, transcendence, and goals for personal accomplishment. One's own decisions and behaviors, including those regarding friendships and peer relations, school functioning, balancing independence and interdependence within one's family, all become crucial pieces in an ongoing process of self-definition.

Effective programs at the secondary level include Lions-Quest, and especially their Skills for Action service learning program (www.lions-quest.org), the Giraffe Heroes Program (www.giraffe.org; Graham, 1999), Facing History and Ourselves (www.facing.org), and the Resolving Conflict Creatively Program (www.esrnational.org; DeJong, 1994).

Special Populations

This section began with a caveat that variability is the norm in the development of social and emotional skills. However, consultants must be aware that students with clinical diagnoses or special educational classifications will often show particular patterns of deficit in the development of such skills. In fact, social and emotional skills deficits are in many cases pathognomonic of clinical diagnosis and a part of the defining feature of educational classifications. For example, interpersonal interactions marked by hostility, bullying, and cruelty are among the diagnostic criteria of Conduct Disorder (American Psychiatric Association, 2000). Anxiety and depressive disorders clearly have affective symptomatology as primary features.

Further, as we have discussed elsewhere, "Children with mild disabilities tend not to be accepted by their peers, and they display shortcomings in the way they interact with parents and peers" (Elias, Blum, Gager, Hunter, & Kress, 1998, p. 220). Children classified as learning disabled face an array of social and emotional challenges. For example, as reviewed by LaGreca (1981), these students have more negative peer relations than their nondisabled peers, receive more negative responses from their peers, and are less adept at initiating help-giving behaviors. The specific nature of a child's learning disability may impact the social and emotional manifestations: "For example, students with more severe cognitive impairments may lack age-appropriate social understanding of complex interactions. Language impaired students may have appropriate understanding of social situations but may have difficulty communicating effectively to others" (Elias & Tobias, 1996, p. 124). As reviewed by Elias et al. (1997, p. 65), children with a variety of classifications, including learning disabled, language disordered, with mild mental delays, neurologically disordered, and with hearing loss, "often have related difficulties in the areas of social and communicative competence. They are more likely to show difficulties in effectively reading social cues from others and managing frustration and other high intensity emotions."

Students classified as emotionally disturbed could be differentiated from their nonclassified peers on the basis of deficits in interpersonal problem solving (Elias, Gara, Rothbaum, Reese, & Ubriaco, 1987). For emotionally disturbed (ED) populations, the distinction between skill deficits (i.e., mastery of social skills) and performance deficits (i.e., lack of motivators to use skills that are possessed) becomes particularly salient. In addition, many ED students have incorporated previous negative outcomes in social situations into a set of expectations for continued difficulty and a negative self-image based on such expectations (Elias & Tobias, 1996). Students with a variety of classifications (including LD and ED) show deficits in nonverbal aspects of emotional interactions (see Kress & Elias, 1993, for a review).

Trends in the use of social and emotional skills have been studied in various clinical child populations. For example, depressed children and early adolescents were found to be less likely than nondepressed peers to use cognitive strategies for coping with negative mood states and more likely to use negative behaviors to cope in such situations (Brenner & Salovey, 1997). Research suggests that children with conduct and aggression problems may misread ambiguous nonverbal cues and make hostile attributions for the behaviors of others (Dodge,

1980). Surprisingly, few programs have been developed for special populations. Project OZ and the SDM/SPS program (Elias & Bruene-Butler, 2005a, 2005b, 2005c) are among those that have shown effectiveness in these contexts. Work done by the authors with the SDM/SPS program with a special needs population is highlighted in the discussion later in this chapter.

In conclusion, a consultant's attention to the area of children's development of social and emotional competence must be informed by both possibility and reality. As discussed in this section, there are trends in what can be expected from most students as they move through the school years. However, there is considerable variability in any group and some more systematic deficits found when dealing with clinical or classified subpopulations. As programs are targeted to student needs, efforts must build on strengths of, and address needs in, individual students to move them ahead in their social and emotional functioning. If this process is seen as a social and emotional skill analogue to the Vygotskian (1978) idea of the zone of proximal development, then the consultant is left with the question of how an individual's environment (in this case, primarily but not limited to the school environment) can facilitate skill development and use.

INTEGRATION: THE GRADIENT OF DEVELOPMENTAL RELEVANCE

The previous sections outlined several arenas that exhibit developmental change over the course of implementation. Although these arenas are reviewed individually and separately, it is our strong belief, grounded in our experience as consultants, that these arenas can be better understood as intersecting and existing in dynamic relationship. At any given point in the life of a programmatic effort, a cross-sectional freeze-frame can be taken of each of these arenas, but once the scene is allowed to progress, changes in one arena will bring changes in others. The dynamic nature of these interactions often makes it difficult to state where an evolution of these arenas begins, which is the cause and which is the effect.

As a matter of practice, the beginning of a consultation/intervention program defines the starting point along all of the dimensions, though the starting point is not necessarily at the beginning of the dimension. As an example, in the 2nd year of an intervention, the original group of students typically will be in the next grade

level. The faculty who implemented in the 1st year will now have a year of experience under their belts and will face a new group of students. However, new faculty will not be at that same point. Thus, the experience of the faculty, their need for consultation, and the experience of the students (as well as the impact of the program) will be different. If we look ahead to the following year, teachers in the next grade will find students coming in with greater variability than they experienced after the 1st year of the intervention. This is something for which they need to be prepared and for which consultation will have to take place. The situation is further complicated if the intervention is followed up in the next grade level. To what extent will the consultant be prepared to deal with these issues? They will require considerable flexibility, as well as deep knowledge of the intervention to allow for changes to be made that optimize what particular teachers can do. These new needs and the new perception of needs may necessitate a change in the original programmatic focus. To support this, a consultant may need to plan for increased training and support for a program that had been running with less oversight.

The picture is beyond one of intersecting lines, and more of interdependent forces. That is, although it is the case that any temporal cross section will reveal various points in each of the developmental trajectories, paths of any one arena will influence all the others. The scenario depends on where one starts the story, but in reality the arenas exist in dynamic interrelationship. As the program moves along, staff concerns will change, the needs of the students will change (based on natural factors and on the impact of the program), and the staff's perceptions of the students and their actions and needs might change. To make appropriate consultative decisions, a consultant must be able to judge options against where each arena is in its development. We use the term "gradient of developmental relevance" to refer to the conditions created by the interacting developmental needs of the various arenas. New information, decisions, procedures, and so on can be evaluated against the gradient of developmental relevance to assess where they fit within this ever-evolving system.

An apt analogy might be to the leader of an improvisational jazz band.[2] Each developmental arena can be seen as a band member, playing a particular improvised

_____
[2] We are honored to continue Jim Kelly's line of jazz analogies applied to community psychology concepts!

line of music. Just as a bandleader might go in with a certain set of parameters in mind—a particular tempo or key—the consultant may be guided by research on effective practice (e.g., Elias et al., 1997). The consultant (who, in most cases, embodies all of the band members and has to serve as the conductor) has to work in a dynamic way, without a script, often by feel, to keep the instrumentation moving forward in a harmonious way. There is a framework for guiding the leader's decisions, but there is not note-for-note scripting. It remains up to the consultant to make it all come together. A consultant with an understanding of trends in each of the developmental spheres has the same advantage as a leader of a well-rehearsed (rather than a newly formed) jazz group. Although each member works on his or her own, the leader has come to know about the style and tendencies of each and can anticipate possible next moves (though there is always room for surprise). Likewise, knowing developmental trends allows the consultant to apply additional structure to decision making, while still remaining flexible enough to handle what is essentially a constantly shifting set of contextual realities.

DEVELOPMENTAL SNAPSHOTS

Our developmental snapshots are pulled from work at The Children's Institute (TCI), a private, nonprofit, out-of-district school for students ranging in age from 3 to 16. The school was founded in 1963 and is divided into preschool, elementary, and middle school levels. The school receives out-of-district placements from a broad area throughout northern and central New Jersey, with over 40 different districts represented. As such, the school population is quite diverse in terms of both socioeconomic status and ethnicity, although male students constitute a majority (90%) of the enrollment. Students are referred to TCI with one of three classifications: preschool handicapped, emotionally disturbed, and autistic.

Students at TCI receive instruction in all academic areas and, in addition, receive therapeutic services. These services are provided by two specialty areas. Crisis workers provide a frontline intervention for students exhibiting an acute behavior that can no longer be accommodated in the classroom. The model, at least early on in the chronology of the program, was for crisis workers to be called in an emergency and to remove the indicated student from the classroom until the crisis de-

escalated. The second line of therapeutic intervention was provided by social workers. In contrast to crisis workers, social workers saw children on an ongoing, scheduled basis. The social workers are the object of our first snapshot, and more will be said about them in the next section.

Although a school focusing on students with emotional disorders can be seen as addressing social and emotional needs on an ongoing basis, formal implementation of SEL programming began in 1989, with the implementation of the SDM/SPS program. SDM/SPS was created in 1979 through collaborative efforts among psychologists and educators from Rutgers University, the University of Medicine and Dentistry of New Jersey, and school districts in New Jersey. Over the years, curriculum guides have been developed for the elementary and middle school grades (Elias & Bruene-Butler, 2005a, 2205b, 2005c; Elias & Tobias, 1996). Books written specifically for parents helps carry-over of school-based programming (Elias, Tobias, & Friedlander, 2000, 2002). The program is implemented in the classroom by teachers (or other staff) who are trained to deliver the program. The program has undergone extensive research (Bruene-Butler, Hampson, Elias, Clabby, & Schuyler, 1997) and has received commendation from the National Education Goals Panel, the U.S. Department of Education's Expert Panel on Safe and Drug Free Schools, the Character Education Partnership, and the Collaborative for Academic, Social, and Emotional Learning (CASEL, 2003).

The general structure of the program is shown in Table 15.3. SDM/SPS can be broken down into three phases: readiness, instruction, and application. The readiness skills cover the fundamental components of self-control and social awareness/group participation. This part of the curriculum got its name from the idea that these skills are essential building blocks, or needed tools, for proper decision making. Lacking self-control and social awareness, we are unlikely to engage in productive problem solving and are subject to "emotional hijacking" (Goleman, 1995), which derails rational thought during high-threat situations. Table 15.3 shows the skills covered in the readiness phase. A major focus of the readiness phase has to do with setting the stage for effective conflict management and fostering self-discipline and socially responsible behavior even in the face of situations that might tax such positive outcomes. To begin to address these issues, teachers introduce an interconnected set of skills in conflict resolution and

TABLE 15.3 Basic Structure of the Social Decision Making Approach

Readiness Skills

A. Self-control skills:
 1. Listening carefully and accurately.
 2. Following directions.
 3. Calming oneself when upset or under stress.
 4. Approaching and talking to others in a socially appropriate manner.
B. Social awareness and group participation skills:
 1. Recognizing and eliciting trust, help, and praise from others.
 2. Understanding others' perspectives.
 3. Choosing friends wisely.
 4. Participating appropriately in groups.
 5. Giving and receiving help and criticism.

Skills for Decision Making and Problem Solving

 1. Finding feelings for yourself and others.
 2. Identifying issues or problems.
 3. Generating goals to guide your decision.
 4. Thinking of alternative solutions.
 5. Envisioning possible consequences.
 6. Selecting the best solution.
 7. Planning and making a final check for obstacles.
 8. Noticing what happened and using the information for future decision making and problem solving.

anger management. In introducing this set of skills, a teacher may lead a discussion of the importance of being able to stay calm in stressful situations (e.g., by asking the students to share experiences where they had difficulty calming down and the consequences of that). The teacher may have students discuss situations when it is particularly difficult for them to stay calm ("trigger situations"), and internal "feelings fingerprints" that signal stress. "Keeping calm" is broken down into component skills, which are demonstrated and practiced, with feedback given to the students as they practice. The teacher often has students role-play use of skills as they are introduced. Particularly important, the phrase "Keep Calm" is established as a prompt and cue for the desired behavior. This behavioral shorthand can be used by the teacher and other staff members throughout the school to call for the skill when needed. Students may be prompted to "Keep Calm" during difficult times such as transitions or before exams. Teachers can model use of Keep Calm during situations where they might be feeling particularly stressed. As students become adept at using Keep Calm, the teacher can ask students to share situations in which they used Keep Calm in class or at recess. Aides and other staff can prompt students to use the skill as needed.

In the instructional phase of the curriculum, students are introduced to eight skills of decision making, as summarized in Table 15.3. The acronym FIG TESPN can be used as a mnemonic to assist students in remembering the process. Notably, the first step focuses on feelings. Emotions are seen as important guides through the problem-solving process. The eight decision-making skills are taught directly and through the use of a guided facilitative questioning technique to help students move through the process.

Comprehensive programming involves infusion of SEL skills into all aspects of the educational experience. Application activities provide opportunities to practice new skills in academic and social situations. Once introduced, SDM/SPS skills can be applied to content areas. A teacher may use the terminology of problem solving to analyze a situation in a story (What was the character feeling? What was the problem?) or to make a decision about how a student will present material from a research project. Students can be prompted to use SDM/SPS skills in real-life situations such as recess and lunch, and then this experience can be processed with them.

Implementation of SDM/SPS at TCI began with a pilot group of six teachers and assistants and all of the social workers, crisis workers, speech teachers, and specialists (e.g., physical education). Consultation for the program was provided by graduate students (including JSK) familiar with the program and working under the supervision of one of the program's creators (MJE). From the beginning, the vision of the school leadership called for SEL programming that is "integrated within all aspects of the special educational setting throughout the entire school day" (M. Cohen, Ettinger, & O'Donnell, 2003, p. 127). As such, as the programming progressed efforts were made to train all school personnel and to orient any new staff to the SDM/SPS program. Throughout, consultation was provided by graduate students and their faculty supervisor at Rutgers University.

These descriptive snapshots are drawn from several sources. Aside from the reflections of the authors, who were each involved in a variety of consultative roles at TCI, data are drawn from several written documents. The primary source of documentation is a dissertation written by the school director (Ettinger, 1995) that documents the systemwide changes and initiatives that occurred during the period from approximately 1993 to 1995. Because SEL has such a central role in the school, the documentation of this period provides rich descriptions of the work done in this area. Also, the consultation team was able to publish two journal articles based on their experiences (Kress et al., 1997; Robinson & Elias, 1993), and these provide an additional perspective on efforts at TCI. Finally, school leaders published a chapter describing their efforts (M. Cohen et al., 2003).

Developmental Snapshot 1: Resistant Clinical Constituents

Our first snapshot concerns a difficulty encountered in achieving the outcome of schoolwide implementation. As indicated in a previous section (cf. Novick et al., 2002), successful implementation of any SDM/SPS program depends on mutual acceptance of program goals, methods, and responsibilities on the part of those called on to implement the program. Looking at the developmental trajectory of the TCI implementers, it was clear that not all constituents achieved this, at least not within the same time frame. Within approximately 3 years of initial implementation, use among classroom teachers could be described as moving toward stabilization of programming. Supports were set up for new teacher-implementers, meetings were initiated in which implementers were able to share accomplishments and discuss obstacles, and a committee was formed to address SPS/SDM programming (Robinson & Elias, 1993). However, at the same time, it was noted that the school social workers were not actively participating in implementation efforts.

The participation of social workers emerged as a concern as early as 1993, when results from interviews conducted by the school principal led him to set social worker-teacher collaboration as a goal for enhancing SEL efforts. Further, the nonparticipation of the social workers was a source of dissatisfaction by the classroom teachers, who felt that their own efforts were not extending beyond the classroom.

The roots of the differential readiness of social workers (as opposed to classroom teachers) to implement the program can be speculated on. One cause might have to do with the educational background and subsequent theoretical perspective of the social workers. According to the school principal, "Clinical staff members had extensive training and education in psychodynamic interventions and understanding children's psychopathologies. However, they had minimal course work in education of the emotionally disturbed child" (Ettinger, 1995, p. 15), and in particular, very little with regard to the type of cognitive-behavioral approach that underlies the SDM/SPS program.

The reaction of the social workers to SDM/SPS implementation is best summarized from a segment from the administrator's dissertation tracing program implementation during the period at approximately the 4th year of implementation:

> The social workers' graduate studies had prepared them to work in a traditional mental health setting using a psycho-dynamic approach emphasizing insight therapy with pullout mental health services. They were committed to treating children in a private confidential manner in settings separate and apart from the students' daily routines in school, the classroom, and in the community. They perceived their role with staff members as that of the professional consultant, providing recommendations and advisement. . . . Due to the clinical paradigm the social workers were clinging to, they were resistant and threatened by the psycho-educational model this staff development project promoted. Social workers had expressed concerns that implementing the behavior management program, participating in leading SPS sessions, and conducting social skills training would result in their losing their identities as therapists. (Ettinger, 1995, pp. 36–37)

It is possible to look at this snapshot through the lens of the developmental arenas described previously. The increased emphasis on the role of the social workers, and the concern at their resistance to assuming this role, can be seen as emerging from the developmental needs of the students in the setting. The students at TCI, by virtue of the presenting classification for their referral to the school, exhibit pronounced deficits in social competence, particularly in the areas of self-control. Efforts to remediate these deficits are complicated by the fact that many of these students exhibit learning problems that confound skill development. TCI students are involved with multiple educational and psychotherapeutic personnel throughout every school day.

Combined, these factors point out the need for intensive, coordinated efforts to address SEL outcomes in these students. For one constituency to fail to support this effort raises the concern that efforts will not be enough to overcome the challenges faced by the students. To address this, the intervention model itself began to develop as well. Individual teacher implementation efforts were augmented by ever-widening spheres of schoolwide implementation. In addition to featuring specific expectations placed on the social workers, the period of this snapshot was also characterized by increases in the number and variety of specialists and other school personnel trained. Along with this came increased efforts at developing communication structures so that all implementers would target a similar set of skills with particular students.

This snapshot illustrates the potential for different cohorts of school-based personnel to be at varying developmental stages of both their usage and their concern with regard to an intervention. The concerns expressed by classroom teachers regarding the lack of carry-over by the social workers can generally be thought of as representative of those who have had experience working with an intervention and are looking for ways to maximize impact, particularly by finding others to support their efforts. From a development of implementation standpoint, the teachers were implementing and refining (Table 15.2). However, their efforts to move ahead to the next level of implementation, that of integrating their efforts with those of others, had been complicated by the social workers' resistance. In terms of the teachers' development as adult learners, a similar situation existed. Teachers were interested in the consequences of their work and in improving their efforts. However, movement to collaboration, a common next stage, was hindered.

The nature of the SEL intervention was itself in developmental flux, with increased attention being given to applying specific behavioral techniques to a focused effort on the readiness skills of self-control and social awareness. At this point in the implementation, the Rutgers-based SDM/SPS consultant was also working at several developmental levels. Part of the consultant's focus was on helping to provide training and consultative support, both basic and advanced; the development of institutional ownership (Kress et al., 1997) was a major goal as well. Major SDM/SPS implementation and leadership functions rested in the hands of a multidisciplinary team comprising school leadership and representatives from various school constituencies (teachers, assistants, clinical staff, specialists). The consultant was a member of this team, but did not assume a leadership role.

To summarize, this snapshot of resistance on the part of one constituency occurs within a gradient of developmental relevance understood as the convergence of developmental trajectories of the implementation process, the intervention itself, the needs and concerns of the implementers, the role of the consultant, and the needs of the program recipients. As student needs became clearer regarding collaborative efforts focused on social competence promotion, teachers became frustrated by perceived impediments to the effectiveness of their efforts. The consultant was playing a supportive, rather than a leadership, role. Understanding this gradient not only helps in terms of problem definition—understanding the greater context in which the social workers' resistance took place—but also helps in conceptualizing the way that solutions were implemented.

School leadership, functioning at a point of increasing ownership of the SDM/SPS program, worked to redefine the job description of the social workers "to place more emphasis on social workers serving as case managers who coordinated in and out-of-school services and to include their role in sps [sic], social skill training, and parent education" (Ettinger, 1995, pp. 135–136). Social workers were expected to co-lead SDM/SPS social skills groups along with the classroom teachers and to provide carry-over for skill building in their individual clinical work. Recognizing that the social workers were at a different developmental point in both implementation and concern about the intervention, specific efforts were made to provide training with regard to their role in the skill-building endeavor. Leadership made efforts to make its expectations clear, even going so far as to remove a social worker from a case due to unwillingness to "support the [behaviorally based] plan due to [the social worker's] psychoanalytic orientation" (p. 169). Other structural components were put in place to provide opportunities to reinforce social worker efforts, as well as to increase accountability. For example, social workers and teachers were asked to present at staff meetings the joint social skill lessons they developed and implemented.

To increase the degree to which such training was consistent with the values and expectations of the social workers, the social workers were provided with literature and data regarding the efficacy of social skills interventions. In addition, further training and ongoing consultation were provided by a practicing clinician, who, although coming from a theoretical orientation different from the social workers', could more specifically address the clinical issues they confront. This clinician worked with social workers both on clinical case issues and on their work with social skills groups in the classroom, providing both professional modeling and links among their work. The addition of another consultant also had the benefit of allowing the Rutgers-based SDM/SPS consultant to maintain the focus on transferring ownership and leadership to school personnel. Close supervision and observation of a large cohort of the school might have sent an unintended message about the consultant's interests in the school leadership being empowered to guide implementation.

These efforts appear to have had an impact on the role of the social workers in the school. Several years after the more intensive work with the social workers, M. Cohen et al. (2003, p. 137) updated the role of the school clinical staff: "The clinician combines a cognitive-behavioral approach, classical behavioral principles (TCI's Token Economy), and psychodynamic techniques to promote social competence through social-emotional skills training and social problem solving." However, this should not give the impression that the process was simple and linear. Social workers did not always report satisfaction with their new roles, and sometimes it took changes in staff before appropriate implementation occurred.

Snapshot 2: Integrating Interventions

The second snapshot plays out over the same period of time as the previous one. Feedback from various sources suggested that efforts to promote the desired SEL outcomes in the TCI population would be enhanced by "the use of a social skills curriculum that provides direct instruction and opportunities for practice, rehearsal, and application" (Ettinger, 1995, p. 7). The importance of a structured behavioral approach for emotionally and behaviorally disordered children and adolescents was stressed by program consultants and bolstered by the school executive's reading of research literature related to specific social skills deficits in these populations. The decision was made to integrate another social skills curriculum, Skillstreaming (Goldstein, Sprafkin, Gershaw, & Klein, 1980), into the school's SEL work.

It is notable that this desire for a structured behavioral curricular approach emerged from a setting that was in the midst of implementing a program that was based on a similar array of cognitive-behavioral principles. The "direct instruction . . . practice, rehearsal, and application" mentioned earlier are all elements of recommended practice in the SDM/SPS program. As mentioned previously, a major component of the SDM/SPS curriculum involves building readiness skills in the areas of self-control and social awareness. For example, a lesson on listening skills introduces a set of behaviors associated with "Listening Position" (sit or stand up straight, look at the source of the sound, etc.) and practice activities. Teachers are instructed to give feedback to student efforts and to prompt and rein-

force proper use of "Listening Position" throughout the school day.

It is worth exploring briefly the specific concerns about the behavioral skill content of the SDM/SPS and the perceived benefits of bringing in the Skillstreaming program. In comparing the approaches of the two programs, the school director emphasized the differences rather than the similarities: "Social skills training is behavior specific in comparison to SPS, emphasis is on teaching prosocial skills rather than cognitive strategies" (Ettinger, 1995, p. 57). Clearly, there is an element of perception involved here. As shown by the example of "Listening Position" in the SDM/SPS curriculum, there is a behavioral skills focus to the SDM/SPS program. Further, the Skillstreaming curriculum does contain a section on "Planning Skills," similar to the problem-solving skills of SDM/SPS.

However, perceptions notwithstanding, there are some significant differences between the two approaches. The (behavioral skills-based) readiness section of the SDM/SPS curriculum contains 16 skill areas (e.g., "Learning to listen carefully and accurately," "Giving criticism"). The Skillstreaming program contains 42 distinct behavioral skill areas, plus 8 more in the more cognitively oriented "Planning Skills" section. These 42 skill areas are broken down into a small number (generally 4 to 6) of performance steps. It is likely that this approach was seen as more consistent with the educational approach generally taken with students at TCI. Further, the discrete skill-based approach of Skillstreaming generally lends itself to a more structured approach to teaching the skills.

It is important to note that the approach taken at TCI was not one of replacing one curriculum with another. Rather, the two curricular approaches were integrated into a unique SEL approach. The work of integrating the curricula was guided by the school's interdisciplinary Social Problem Solving Committee, which, as curricular integration progressed, was renamed the Social Development Committee. This new name reflected the growing role of the committee in guiding SEL efforts, expanding beyond the implementation of a specific program. The committee's guiding vision was summarized by the school director: "The SPS curriculum would be followed, which provided the structure, developmental guidelines, and strategies for social skills instruction. The social Skillstreaming curriculum provided more detailed, specific skills to be integrated into the SPS curriculum and additional instructional strategies" (Ettinger, 1995, p. 98). As such, the committee kept the sequence and developmental structure of SDM/SPS while adding a more fine-grained breakdown of skills and extra behavioral rehearsal and practice that characterizes the Skillstreaming approach.

Curricular integration was supported by the consulting psychologist, who understood how to make the approaches work in a complementary way. A constructivist approach was used to bring the teachers along in their understanding of how the new structure might work. A half-day staff training workshop was held on the topic, and teachers developed and presented a lesson illustrating the integration. The implementation model called for classroom teachers and social workers to collaborate in developing and delivering SPS/Skillstreaming lessons. The Social Development Committee would collate the lessons into a unique site-based curriculum guide and spent 3 days during the summer break formalizing and organizing lessons into a "Social Development Curriculum Guide." The guide, and training in using it, was presented to all staff when they returned for the following school year. Sharing of new social development lessons became a regular part of staff meetings.

This initial combination of SPS and Skillstreaming can be seen as the beginning of a cycle of curricular integration and adaptation that resulted in what has been referred to as the TCI Model (M. Cohen et al., 2003). The model is summarized as follows:

> TCI uses a cognitive-behavioral approach with all students. . . . This involves a step-by-step process to teach students what they need to do to develop socially appropriate replacement behaviors. On a regular basis, students also participate in "practice and rehearsal" of skills specific to the needs of the individual child. It is through this technique that students learn to replace inappropriate actions with appropriate ones with a specific situation. This method is based on the extensive works of Dr. Maurice Elias (Elias & Tobias, 1996), Dr. Arnold Goldstein's Skillstreaming curriculum (McGinnis & Goldstein, 1984), and Dr. Frank Gresham's Social Skills Intervention Guide (Elliott & Gresham, 1992). These woks focus on the social and emotional learning of all children: using the cycle of design, implementation, and feedback for more than a decade, TCI staff members revised—and continue to revise today—the works to reflect the unique needs of our students. We then added lessons promoting self-esteem and other social-emotional skills. This evolved into TCI's Social Development Curriculum.

The TCI model incorporates the common vocabulary found in Elias and Clabby's (1989) approach. . . . The use

of this shared language created far greater continuity in care for the students than had previously been in evidence. (M. Cohen et al., 2003, pp. 128–129)

The SDM/SPS provides the structure and language into which a number of other curricular pieces are integrated. The result is a unique product that speaks directly to the needs of the site in which it was created. As with any snapshot taken of a setting, the integration of Skillstreaming and SDM/SPS represents a convergence of the developmental arenas described previously. Perhaps the main motivator was concern for the developmental trajectory of the students and an increasing understanding of how best to address these concerns. Specific behavioral skill deficits, frequently found in populations such as TCI's, seemed to indicate that a more focused skill-building approach was warranted.

As summarized in the previous snapshot, implementation at this point was inconsistent among the various school constituents. Classroom teachers were regularly implementing SDM/SPS lessons, but the clinical staff was generally resistant to refocusing their primarily psychodynamic approach. Teachers were ready to refine their work based on their experiences and the results of initial implementation, which gave rise to a desire for a behavioral skills-based focus. The consultant, as noted previously, was working with a goal of transferring major program SEL ownership to the setting, rather than outside support personnel. Finally, it is evident that this snapshot marks a major developmental change in the intervention itself, moving from the use of a specific program to the creation of an integrative new approach.

The gradient created by this convergence of developmental arenas can help in the understanding of how these events unfolded. In particular, this snapshot is notable for what *did not* happen. In the face of newly understood programmatic needs, school leadership refused to take the commonly trod path of revolving-door programming. That is, the SDM/SPS program was not replaced by Skillstreaming, and a new cycle of implementation was not begun. The decision of the school's director and the Social Development Committee to adapt rather than adopt may be attributable to the already existing level of comfort and competence with the SDM/SPS program on the part of the frontline implementers. Further, school personnel had long-lasting positive relationships with consultants from the SDM/SPS program. This relationship had evolved to the point where the SDM/SPS consultant, rather than supervising or overseeing implementation, was involved as a member of the Social Development Committee, attending meetings and voicing opinions on a par with all other members of this group. This might have helped the consultant, and the program he represented, to move with the committee, rather than setting up an either/or situation between SDM/SPS and Skillstreaming. Finally, school SEL leadership had an appreciation of the unique nature of their student population and recognized the opportunity to do something new in a way that would contribute to the field. For example, from the early stages of SEL curricular integration, the Social Development Committee and school leadership developed a proposal to present their approach at a statewide conference.

CONCLUSIONS

Although we acknowledge the centrality of the five developmental arenas reviewed here, there may be other developmentally linked areas of change that can impact implementation efforts. For example, factors involved in the school leadership might be of relevance. Is the principal new to the setting, or a veteran? What is the principal's history of working with (or failing to work with) various constituents in the school? How much does leadership know about and care about the intervention in question? A second additional area is the life span of the setting itself. How long has the setting been in existence? What other interventions, in SEL and beyond, are currently being implemented, or have been implemented in the past? A school still recovering from a difficult or controversy-filled implementation process of, say, a new block-scheduling approach may present unique challenges to efforts to again initiate something new.

For interventions to succeed, a convergence of a large number of what are essentially developmental influences must take place. Consultants, as well as school leaders, who attempt to implement innovations can hardly keep all of the possible areas clearly in mind and coordinate the affect, cognition, and behavior necessary to do so. Yet, some interventions, like SDM/SPS in TCI, succeed. We hypothesize that for this to happen, a critical mass of those involved in the implementation process must have a generalized, developmental understanding that pervades their work. It may take the form of a generalized expectancy (Rotter, 1954), a superordinate schema, or some other higher-order transactional orga-

nizing structure. This is a matter for future research. What is clear, however, is that our understanding of the implementation process (and consultation process) can be enhanced by adding the perspective of a gradient of developmental relevance and applying it to the context of interventions, as a complement to a developmental perspective on the student recipients and their match to developmental content of the intervention itself.

REFERENCES

Albee, G., & Gullotta, T. G. (Eds.). (1997). *Primary prevention works: Vol. 6. Issues in children's and families' lives.* Thousand Oaks, CA: Sage.

American Psychiatric Association. (2000). *Diagnostic and statistical manual of mental disorders* (4th ed., text rev.). Washington, DC: Author.

Bar-On, R., & Parker, J. (Eds.). (2000). *Handbook of emotional intelligence.* San Francisco: Jossey-Bass.

Battistich, V., Schaps, E., Watson, M., & Solomon, D. (1996). Prevention effects of the child development project: Early findings from an ongoing multi-site demonstration trial. *Journal of Adolescent Research, 11,* 12–25.

Brandt, R. S. (2003). How new knowledge about the brain applies to social and emotional learning. In M. J. Elias, H. Arnold, & C. S. Hussey (Eds.), *EQ + IQ = Best practices for caring and successful schools* (pp. 57–70). Thousand Oaks, CA: Corwin.

Brenner, E. M., & Salovey, P. (1997). Emotional regulation during childhood: Developmental, interpersonal, and individual considerations. In P. Salovey & D. J. Sluyter (Eds.), *Emotional development and emotional intelligence: Educational implications* (pp. 168–192). New York: Basic Books.

Bruene-Butler, L., Hampson, J., Elias, M. J., Clabby, J. F., & Schuyler, T. (1997). Improving social awareness-social problem solving project. In G. Albee & T. G. Gullotta (Eds.), *Primary prevention works: Vol. 6. Issues in children's and families' lives* (pp. 239–267). Thousand Oaks, CA: Sage.

Ciarrochi, J., Forgas, J., & Mayer, J. (2001). *Emotional intelligence in everyday life.* Philadelphia: Taylor & Francis.

Cohen, J. (Ed.). (1999). *Educating minds and hearts: Social and emotional learning and the passage into adolescence.* New York: Teachers College Press.

Cohen, M., Ettinger, B., & O'Donnell, T. (2003). Children's Institute model for building the social-emotional skills of students in special education: A school-wide approach. In M. J. Elias, H. Arnold, & C. S. Hussey (Eds.), *EQ + IQ = Best practices for caring and successful schools* (pp. 124–141). Thousand Oaks, CA: Corwin.

Collaborative for Academic, Social, and Emotional Learning. (2003, March). *Safe and sound: An educational leader's guide to evidence-based social and emotional learning programs.* Retrieved October 1, 2002, from http://www.casel.org.

Commins, W. W., & Elias, M. J. (1991). Institutionalization of mental health programs in organizational contexts: Case of elementary schools. *Journal of Community Psychology, 19,* 207–220.

Conduct Problems Prevention Research Group. (1999). Initial impact of the Fast Track prevention trial for conduct problems: Pt. 2.

Classroom effects. *Journal of Consulting and Clinical Psychology, 67,* 648–657.

Consortium on the School-Based Promotion of Social Competence. (1994). The school-based promotion of social competence: Theory, research, practice, and policy. In R. J. Haggerty, L. R. Sherrod, N. Garmezy, & M. Rutter (Eds.), *Stress, risk, and resilience in children and adolescents: Processes, mechanisms, and interventions* (pp. 268–316). New York: Cambridge University Press.

DeJong, W. (1994). *Building the peace: The Resolving Conflict Creatively Program.* Washington, DC: U.S. Department of Justice, National Institute of Justice.

Diebolt, C., Miller, G., Gensheimer, L., Mondschein, E., & Ohmart, H. (2000). Building an intervention: A theoretical and practical infrastructure for planning, implementing, and evaluating a metropolitan-wide school-to-career initiative. *Journal of Educational and Psychological Consultation, 11*(1), 147–172.

Dilworth, J. E., Mokrue, K., & Elias, M. J. (2002). Efficacy of a video-based teamwork-building series with urban elementary school students: A pilot investigation. *Journal of School Psychology, 40*(4), 329–346.

Dodge, K. A. (1980). Social cognition and children's aggressive behavior. *Child Development, 51,* 162–170.

Edwards, R. W., Jumper-Thuman, P., Plested, B. A., Oetting, E. R., & Swanson, L. (2000). Community readiness: Research to practice. *Journal of Community Psychology, 28,* 291–307.

Elias, M. J. (1989). Schools as a source of stress to children: An analysis of causal and ameliorative factors. *Journal of School Psychology, 27,* 393–407.

Elias, M. J. (1995). Prevention as health and social competence promotion. *Journal of Primary Prevention, 16,* 5–24.

Elias, M. J. (1997). Reinterpreting dissemination of prevention programs as widespread implementation with effectiveness and fidelity. In R. P. Weissberg (Ed.), *Healthy children 2010: Strategies to enhance social, emotional, and physical wellness* (pp. 253–289). Newbury Park, CA: Sage.

Elias, M. J. (2003). *Academic and social-emotional learning* (Educational Practices Booklet No. 11). Geneva, Switzerland: International Academy of Education and the International Bureau of Education (UNESCO).

Elias, M. J., Blum, L., Gager, P., Hunter, L., & Kress, J. S. (1998). Group interventions for students with mild disorders: Evidence and procedures for classroom inclusion approaches. In K. C. Stoiber & T. R. Kratochwill (Eds.), *Handbook of group interventions for children and adolescents* (pp. 220–235). New York: Guilford Press.

Elias, M. J., & Bruene-Butler, L. (2005a). *Social Decision Making/Social Problem Solving: A curriculum for academic, social, and emotional learning, grades 2–3.* Champaign, IL: Research Press.

Elias, M. J., & Bruene-Butler, L. (2005b). *Social Decision Making/Social Problem Solving: A curriculum for academic, social, and emotional learning, grades 4–5.* Champaign, IL: Research Press.

Elias, M. J., & Bruene-Butler, L. (2005c). *Social Decision Making/Social Problem Solving for middle school students: Skills and activities for academic, social, and emotional success.* Champaign, IL: Research Press.

Elias, M. J., & Clabby, J. F. (1989). *Social decision making skills: A curriculum for the elementary grades.* Rockville, MD: Aspen.

Elias, M. J., Gara, M., Rothbaum, P. A., Reese, A. M., & Ubriaco, M. (1987). A multivariate analysis of factors differentiating behaviorally and emotionally dysfunctional children from other groups in school. *Journal of Clinical Child Psychology, 16,* 409–417.

Elias, M. J., Gara, M. A., Schuyler, T. F., Branden-Muller, L. R., & Sayette, M. A. (1991). Promotion of social competence: Longitudinal study of a preventive school-based program. *American Journal of Orthopsychiatry, 61,* 409–417.

Elias, M. J., & Tobias, S. E. (1996). *Social problem solving: Interventions in the schools.* New York: Guilford Press.

Elias, M. J., Tobias, S. E., & Friedlander, B. S. (2000). *Emotionally intelligent parenting: How to raise a self-disciplined, responsible, socially skilled child.* New York: Three Rivers Press.

Elias, M. J., Tobias, S. E., & Friedlander, B. S. (2002). *Raising emotionally intelligent teenagers: Guiding the way to compassionate, committed, courageous adults.* New York: Random House/Three Rivers Press.

Elias, M. J., Zins, J. E., Greenberg, M. T., Graczyk, P. A., & Weissberg, R. P. (2003). Implementation, sustainability, and scaling up of social-emotional and academic innovations in public schools. *School Psychology Review, 32,* 303–319.

Elias, M. J., Zins, J. E., Weissberg, R. P., Frey, K. S., Greenberg, M. T., Haynes, N. M., et al. (1997). *Promoting social and emotional learning: Guidelines for educators.* Alexandria, VA: Association for Supervision and Curriculum Development.

Elliot, S., & Gresham, F. (1992). *Social skills intervention guide.* Circle Pines, MN: American Guidance Service.

Ennett, S. T., Ringwalt, C. L., Thorne, J., Rohrbach, L. A., Vincus, A., Simons-Rudolph, A., et al. (2003). A comparison of current practice in school-based substance use prevention programs with meta-analysis findings. *Prevention Science, 4,* 1–14.

Errecart, M. T., Walberg, H. J., Ross, J. G., Gold, R. S., Fiedler, J. L., & Kolbe, L. J. (1991). Effectiveness of teenage health teaching modules. *Journal of School Health, 61,* 26–30.

Ettinger, B. A. (1995). *A comprehensive staff development project in an elementary and middle school program for emotionally disturbed students.* Unpublished doctoral dissertation, Nova Southeastern University, FL.

Everhart, K., & Wandersman, A. (2000). Applying comprehensive quality programming and empowerment evaluation to reduce implementation barriers. *Journal of Educational and Psychological Consultation, 11,* 177–191.

Felner, R. D., Jackson, A. W., Kasak, D., Mulhall, P., Brand, S., & Flowers, N. (1997). Impact of school reform for the middle years: Longitudinal study of a network engaged in turning points-based comprehensive school transformation. *Phi Delta Kappan, 78,* 528–532, 541–550.

Gager, P. J., & Elias, M. J. (1997). Implementing prevention programs in high-risk environments: Application of the resiliency paradigm. *American Journal of Orthopsychiatry, 67,* 363–373.

Ghaith, G., & Yaghi, H. (1997). Relationships among experience, teacher efficacy, and attitudes toward the implementation of instructional innovation. *Teaching and Teacher Education, 13,* 451–458.

Goldstein, A. P., Sprafkin, R. P., Gershaw, N. J., & Klein, P. (1980). *Skillstreaming the adolescent: A structured learning approach to teaching prosocial skills.* Champaign, IL: Research Press.

Goleman, D. (1995). *Emotional intelligence.* New York: Bantam Books.

Gottfredson, G. D., & Gottfredson, D. C. (2001). What schools do to prevent problem behavior and promote safe environments. *Journal of Educational and Psychological Consultation, 12,* 313–344.

Graham, J. (1999). *It's up to us: The Giraffe Heroes Program for teens.* Langley, WA: The Giraffe Project.

Greenberg, M. T., & Kusché, C. A. (1998). *Blueprints for violence prevention: Vol. 10. PATHS project* (D. S. Elliott, Series Ed.).

Boulder: Institute of Behavioral Science, Regents of the University of Colorado.

Greenberg, M. T., & Snell, J. L. (1997). Brain development and emotional development: Role of teaching in organizing the frontal lobe. In P. Salovey & D. J. Sluyter (Eds.), *Emotional development and emotional intelligence: Educational implications* (pp. 93–119). New York: Basic Books.

Hallfors, D., & Godette, D. (2002). Will the "Principles of Effectiveness" improve prevention practice? Early findings from a diffusion study. *Health Education Review, 17,* 461–470.

Haviland-Jones, J., Gebelt, J. L., & Stapely, J. C. (1997). Questions of development in emotion. In P. Salovey & D. J. Sluyter (Eds.), *Emotional development and emotional intelligence: Educational implications* (pp. 233–253). New York: Basic Books.

Hawkins, J. D., Catalano, R. F., Kosterman, R., Abbott, R., & Hill, K. G. (1999). Preventing adolescent health-risk behaviors by strengthening protection during childhood. *Archives of Pediatric Adolescent Medicine, 153,* 226–234.

Hord, S. M., Rutherford, W. L., Huling-Austin, L., & Hall, G. E. (1987). *Taking charge of change.* Alexandria, VA: Association for Supervision and Curriculum Development.

Kallestad, J. H., & Olweus, D. (2003). Predicting teachers' and schools' implementation of the Olweus Bullying Prevention Program: A multilevel study. *Prevention and Treatment, 6*(Article 21). Available from http://journals.apa.org/prevention/volume6/pre0060021a.html.

Kessler, R. (2000). *Soul of education: Helping students find connection, compassion, and character at school.* Alexandria, VA: Association for Supervision and Curriculum Development.

Kress, J. S., Cimring, B. R., & Elias, M. J. (1997). Community psychology consultation and the transition to institutional ownership and operation of intervention. *Journal of Educational and Psychological Consultation, 8,* 231–253.

Kress, J. S., & Elias, M. J. (1993). Substance abuse prevention in special education: Review and recommendations. *Journal of Special Education, 27,* 35–51.

LaGreca, A. M. (1981). Social behavior and social perception in learning-disabled children: A review with implications for social skills training. *Journal of Pediatric Psychology, 6,* 395–416.

Mayer, J., & Salovey, P. (1993). Intelligence of emotional intelligence. *Intelligence, 17*(4), 433–442.

McGinnis, E., & Goldstein, A. P. (1984). *Skillstreaming the elementary school child: A guide for teaching prosocial skills.* Champaign, IL: Research Press.

Nastasi, B. K. (2002). Realities of large-scale change efforts. *Journal of Educational and Psychological Consultation, 13,* 219–226.

Novick, B., Kress, J. S., & Elias, M. J. (2002). *Building learning communities with character: How to integrate academic, social and emotional learning.* Alexandria, VA: Association for Supervision and Curriculum Development.

Perry, C. L. (1999). *Creating health behavior change: How to develop community-wide programs for youth.* Thousand Oaks, CA: Sage.

Price, R., Cowen, E. L., Lorion, R., & Ramos-McKay, J. (Eds.). (1988). *14 ounces of prevention: A casebook for practitioners.* Washington, DC: American Psychological Association.

Prochaska, J. O., & DiClemente, C. C. (1984). *Transtheoretical approach: Crossing traditional boundaries of therapy.* Homewood, IL: Dow Jones Irwin.

Robinson, B. A., & Elias, M. J. (1993). Stabilizing classroom-based interventions: Guidelines for special services providers and consultants. *Special Services in the Schools, 8,* 159–178.

Rotter, J. B. (1954). *Social learning and clinical psychology.* Englewood Cliffs, NJ: Prentice-Hall.

Sarason, S. B. (1972). *Creation of settings and the future societies.* San Francisco: Jossey-Bass.

Sarason, S. B. (1996). *Revisiting "The culture of the school and the problem of change."* New York: Teachers College Press.

Seigle, P. (2001). Reach Out to Schools: A social competency program. In J. Cohen (Ed.), *Caring classrooms/intelligent schools: The social and emotional education of young children* (pp. 108–121). New York: Teachers College Press.

Shure, M. B., & Spivack, G. (1988). Interpersonal cognitive problem solving. In R. Price, E. L. Cowen, R. Lorion, & J. Ramos-McKay (Eds.), *14 ounces of prevention: A casebook for practitioners* (pp. 69–82). Washington, DC: American Psychological Association.

Solomon, D., Battistich, V., Watson, M., Schaps, E., & Lewis, C. (2000). A six-district study of educational change: Direct and mediated effects of the Child Development Project. *Social Psychology of Education, 4,* 3–51.

Thorsen-Spano, L. (1996). A school conflict resolution program: Relationships among teacher attitude, program implementation, and job satisfaction. *School Counselor, 44,* 19–27.

Vygotsky, L. S. (1978). *Mind in society: Development of higher mental processes.* Cambridge, MA: Harvard University Press.

Weissberg, R., & Greenberg, M. T. (1998). Community and school prevention. In W. Damon (Editor-in-Chief) & I. Sigel & A. Renninger (Vol. Eds.), *Handbook of child psychology: Vol. 4. Child psychology in practice* (5th ed., pp. 877–954). New York: Wiley.

Weissberg, R. P., & Elias, M. J. (1993). Enhancing young people's social competence and health behavior: An important challenge for educators, scientists, policy makers, and funders. *Applied and Preventive Psychology, 3,* 179–190.

Werner, H. (1957). *Comparative psychology of mental development (Rev. ed.).* New York: International Universities Press.

Zins, J. E., Weissberg, R. P., Wang, M. C., & Walberg, H. J. (Eds.). (2004). *Building school success through social and emotional learning.* New York: Teachers College Press.

CHAPTER 16

Children and War Trauma

AVIGDOR KLINGMAN

This chapter addresses children's war-triggered stress responses and the related mental health intervention options. Unlike most disasters, war does not comprise a short, single, violent event but rather a large-scale, protracted, complex, constantly changing, novel, and often unpredictable emergency that encompasses life-threatening exposure, targets an entire society, and creates shared mental suffering. War is a case of extreme societal violence that unsettles entire populations at the personal, familial, and broader social levels (e.g., community, ethnic group, state, or national), while damaging physical property and infrastructures. As a result, civilians' total life experience is disrupted, sometimes even replaced by a state of surreal existence; the victims' pain and suffering often seem devoid of rational explanation, a condition that contradicts the human need for a predictable environment and equilibrium (Kahana, Kahana, Harel, & Rosner, 1998; Williams-Gray, 1999). Wars may take various forms of deliberate, intentionally inflicted violent activities that especially target civilian populations. One such form of contemporary war uses long-range high-technology weapons with biological and chemical warhead capability to "surgically" remove a civilian target, devastating civilians and their environments. Such were the missile attacks by Iraq against populated cities of Israel during the 1991 Gulf War. An-

other instance constitutes ethnic strife, as evinced particularly in the former Soviet republics, as well as in conflicts in the developing world and in the civil wars in the former Yugoslavia (in which harming women and children was often a war strategy). Ethnic fighting frequently results in forced evacuations or flight to refugee camps in neighboring countries. A third example is the "new" form of war targeting innocent civilians, represented by the recent large-scale terrorist attacks of September 11, 2001, on the United States and the massive attacks by suicide bombers during the second Palestinian uprising in Israel, and lately in Iraq. The threat of political terrorism as an act of war has recently succeeded in overturning the enduring sense of national security enjoyed by even the most politically stable, peaceful, and affluent democracies of the world.

As is inevitable in war, many children experience high levels of war-related stress. In this cumulative condition, children who are exposed to the stressors of war and/or political violence/terrorism exhibit *complex biopsychobehavioral disruptions*. These may involve significant alternations in cognitive, emotional, moral, behavioral, and psychosocial functioning. This condition incorporates cultural dynamics and an existential response to sociopolitical upheaval (Parson, 1996). To date, a substantial body of literature has accumulated on the psychological consequences of war for adults, but less is known about the longer-term effects of war on children (Cairns & Dawes, 1996; Dybdahl, 2001; Dyregrov, Gupta, Gjestad, & Mukanoheli, 2000). Literature on psychological interventions with children in the midst of war is almost nonexistent, and so the literature on the effects of therapeutic interventions with children following war remains relatively scarce. Despite the desirability and value of empirical research data in the area of children's responses to and recovery from war, conducting well-designed research is problematic because of the scope, complexity, and uniqueness of war and the various operational pressures involved. Often, neither field conditions nor funds are available for conducting a well-controlled, detailed study during or immediately after war (Klingman & Cohen, 2004; Klingman, Sagi, & Raviv, 1993). In part, the available empirical findings conflict due to methodological diversity and flawed evidence collection (e.g., absence of proper controls, nonrandom selection of participants, use of dissimilar tools). In most cases, reported field experiences and projects and their in-house evaluation provide the best information on the subject of intervention in wartime or in war-affected regions.

This chapter therefore draws on theory and research but also leans heavily on reported field experiences, which are examined in light of theory and research findings. Furthermore, most empirical studies concerning psychological intervention in war have focused intently on Posttraumatic Stress Disorder (PTSD) or the risk for PTSD and on treatment of PTSD-related symptoms. However, this chapter aims to reach beyond a classificatory psychopathological approach to also focus on the overall quality of the child's needs for the adaptation process (American Academy of Child and Adolescent Psychiatry, 1998); the need to intervene with children's war stress reactions, not only with disorders; and the role of positive coping, resiliency, and trauma-induced growth in the recovery process. Many of the intervention cases discussed in this chapter illustrate a preventive response to a wide variety of children's war-related stress reactions and propose the adoption of a wider developmental psychopathology perspective in clinical intervention for PTSD-related symptomatology. Because intense war experiences are shared by children and the significant others in their lives, the multisystemic intervention approach seems especially relevant as the method of choice for war situations. Accordingly, this chapter contextualizes, examines, and treats the impact of war on

children at three levels (Ager, 1996; Klingman & Cohen, 2004): the direct personal, the family-mediated, and the broader social-mediated levels.

The purpose of this chapter is thus threefold. One aim is to present the unique war-related issues faced by children and their implications for intervention. The second is to present war-related multimodal psychological interventions with children in the context of a preventive, multisystemic, generic, society-focused (e.g., school-based, school-linked, and community-initiated) approach that emphasizes positive psychology. The third aim is to review specific war-related therapeutic interventions for individuals and small groups, focusing on those for which PTSD-related symptomatology is considered a useful reference point and which are complementary to and congruent with the two preceding aims.

THE WAR CONTEXT AND IMPACT ON CHILDREN

This section of the chapter presents the major factors constituting the magnitude and breadth of war's psychological effects on children. Interventionists' awareness of the prevalence and especially the combination of these factors will enable the identification of populations, groups, and individuals with special needs and with a high likelihood of developing disorders.

Children in war zones grow up in an atmosphere of *constant fear for life and limb.* In UNICEF's 1996 *State of the World's Children* report, it was estimated that wars in the preceding decade killed 2 million children and left another 4 to 5 million children disabled. Additional life-threatening conditions may result from difficulties in access to transportation, adequate food, medications, and immunizations (which may sometimes be intentionally denied). *Loss of significant others* constitutes another major threat, whose impact varies across the child's development. The greatest threat to an infant is likely to be loss of or separation from the primary caregiver(s) or serious injury to the functioning caregiver(s); adolescents have the potential to experience greater losses of friends and acquaintances outside the family (Wright, Masten, & Hubbard, 1997). In certain types of wars, children may also witness *repeated violent acts against their significant others* (e.g., torture, sexual violence, public display of executed persons). War may also involve large-scale extensive *violations of children's basic rights:* Children may be forced to separate from their parents, be confined in concentration camps, and denied access to education or health services; in some wars, they are even raped or prostituted. In various conflict zones, children are exploited for ideological propaganda or enlisted into civil strife activities. The availability of very lightweight weapons enables younger children to become directly involved; in certain cases, they are recruited forcibly or coaxed into military service (child combatants); others are driven into war and war-related activities by poverty, alienation, discrimination, and/or the desire for revenge (see Silva, Hobbs, & Hanks, 2001). Exposure to the sustained stress of war and violence, combined with dwindling hopes for the future, may result in *desensitization to dangers,* whereby children begin taking further life risks in an effort to establish a sense of control (Garbarino, Dubrow, & Kostelny, 1991). Some children and youth engage in self-engineered patterns of reexposure to traumatic sensory repetition, seeking out situations of affective intensity, excitement, and danger such as child-soldier "status" (Parson, 2000). Children who live surrounded by land mines and dormant (cluster) bombs may become desensitized to them or attracted to their colors, or may think it is brave to be seen handling explosives; this may continue for some time after the war is over (Klingman, 2002c).

During war, *basic infrastructures* such as the economy, public health, medicine, education, social welfare, and psychological services may become overloaded, drastically restricted, seriously impaired, or incapacitated for lengthy periods, or may even collapse. Depending on the severity of the damage, a very long period may be required to reestablish infrastructures even after the war is over. This situation holds direct as well as indirect implications for children, specifically through closure of schools, restrictions on social/recreational activities, and unavailability (at least temporarily) of psychological and welfare services. Prolonged destruction at a societal level may cause adolescents (struggling to define themselves in a changed world) to question the value of schooling or work in a war-torn country or in a nation whose economy has been decimated (Wright et al., 1997).

Another major problem typifying many war-ravaged regions is forced evacuation and the resulting large number of *refugee or displaced children,* sometimes called the "forgotten victims of war." An estimated 12 million children became homeless due to armed con-

flicts between 1988 and 1998 (Southall & Abbasi, 1998). The refugee process advances through three phases: preflight, flight, and resettlement (Gonsalves, 1992). Before evacuation or flight begins, many children may be overwhelmed by war atrocities or undergo a lengthy process of traumatization typically experienced as a psychic trauma. The relocation or flight is in itself socially, culturally, and psychologically complex and can impede the normal process of child development, particularly if children are alone in their migration. In attempting to resettle, children may experience the distress of refugee camp life: malnutrition, which increases the incidence of childhood illnesses (Goldson, 1993); exposure to pervasive discrimination and bias due to their cultural background, skin color, racial origin, or religion; and children's often fundamental ignorance of the host culture (Parson, 2000; Reichman, 1993; van der Veer, 1992). They may have to conceal the actions they took while fleeing and may be suspicious of all authority figures (including psychologists), at least until they are certain about their future legal status. Moreover, refugee parents may instruct their children never to disclose anything to outsiders, which may hinder the process of helping children come to terms with their experiences (van der Veer, 1992; Yule, 2002).

The impact of *mass terror attacks* constitutes a war situation that deserves specific attention, particularly when such attacks become a chronic condition without discrete beginning and end points. A terrorist attack occurs without warning and selects symbolic targets that will not only weaken symbols of power but will also convey the idea that no one is safe (see Gidron, 2002; Klingman & Cohen, 2004). Civilians do not know how to prepare for or respond effectively to such an unfamiliar event and predominantly feel that neither they nor the authorities (police, army, government) can prevent such attacks. People find it hard, if not impossible, to make sense of or find meaning in such deliberate and indiscriminate malicious, violent, inhuman acts.

The specific threat of unconventional *chemical, biological, or radiological weapons* in international as well as domestic terrorism necessitates consideration of specific, direct health effects, and also the resulting primary and secondary psychological effects. Presumably, children will suffer more extreme effects from the release of chemical or biological weapons than will adults. For example, children's higher number of respirations per minute may result in exposure to a relatively greater dosage of aerosolized agents such as sarin and anthrax. Children who witness the weapons' effect also risk developing psychological injuries from the experience. Moreover, the invisibility of biological and chemical agents may lead to false-alarm reactions that may result in mass episodes of sociogenic illness and associated anxiety (see discussion on such effects on children in Klingman & Cohen, 2004). Also, children may become confined indoors or to sealed (gas-proofed) rooms for most of the day due to the threat of unconventional warhead missile attacks. They may experience relative isolation, protracted boredom, and a lack of sustaining structure, as among Israeli children during the 1991 Gulf War (Solomon, 1995).

The previous outline mainly explored the magnitude and duration of war as they affect children. In the next two subsections, first the psychological risk mechanisms involved are detailed, and then the resilient responses. These constitute a complex range of factors present before, during, and after war.

War-Related Psychological Responses and Intervention Challenges

All mass disasters present problems that challenge the coping resources of victims and community services alike; the nature and consequences of war, however, present numerous unique challenges. The psychological effects of war involve contextual, personal, and recovery-environment factors and encompass a wide spectrum of emotional, cognitive, and behavioral outcomes. The practitioner's awareness of the prevalence and combination of these factors will facilitate the identification of populations, groups, and individuals who have a relatively high likelihood of developing distress, adjustment difficulties, and (consequently) disorders. Such awareness will also serve for planning relevant (especially preventive) interventions.

Warfare affects the *child's mental map*, or cognitive and emotional schemata, as life becomes inconsistent with prewar norms. Children of war are exposed to a continuous series of adverse experiences that are potentially traumatic in that they involve multisensory experiences of sights, sounds, and smells that a child may be incapable of comprehending or assimilating within the existing cognitive-emotional schema (Ager, 1996). Warfare forces children to process information that may challenge core beliefs and assumptions that people are

trustworthy, that the world is a meaningful, predictable, and secure environment, and that the self is worthy (Janoff-Bulman, 1992). In general, "maps" that previously guided the child through the world suddenly prove inaccurate, and life becomes unpredictable and untrustworthy. Fearing that the traumatic experiences may return, children may develop catastrophic beliefs. When no opportunities exist to engage in a search for meaning, children and especially adolescents are left with perceived unsolvable contradictions that may lead to greater distress. They may experience an inability to predict or project a meaningful future for themselves. Children may lose trust in others, especially if they witness violent acts by people or groups with whom they maintained a friendly, or at least a stable, prewar relationship (e.g., in Croatia; Williams-Gray, 1999). They may also face contradictions between the values and behaviors inculcated in them in the past (prewar) and those underlying apparently successful adaptations in the violent present. Those clinging to the past may be less prepared for the stresses of war, whereas children who discard prewar sensibilities for a self well-adjusted to the present war (especially child combatants assimilating the virtues of destruction of the enemy) may experience great difficulties with the advent of a peaceful future (Ager, 1996).

The complex childhood environment in war imposes unique demands with regard to children's developmental tasks, such as learning to live with constant fear, struggling with identity formation and moral reasoning, creating intimate relationships, and planning for the future. These may result in *interference with normative developmental tasks,* or with the smooth transition to the next developmental stage, such as emotional regulation in toddler years, controlling aggressive behavior in middle childhood, and forming intimate bonds in adolescence. War is likely to have wide-ranging influences on developmental tasks connected with the formation of successful peer relationships and adaptation to school. Furthermore, children are at risk of *losing previously acquired developmental skills* or regressing to a less mature behavioral mode. Serious risk also exists for growing up too fast and losing childhood too early, for example by being forced to resolve serious moral and emotional conflicts before full maturation (Punamaeki, 2002). Legitimate concerns about child safety in an unpredictable war environment may result in caretakers' overprotection and discouragement of increased independence; conversely, parents attempting to cope with the war's hardships and stresses may expect their children to mature more quickly, thereby easing the demands on their parenting.

A prolonged period of warfare may cause *disruptions in the child's experience of social relationships*. These may stem, for instance, from curfews or restrictions on out-of-home movement, forced evacuation resulting in separation of family members and/or loss of parent(s), peers, or adult significant other(s), and the closure of schools. War-zone children may have problems in gauging interpersonal distance, experiencing attachments that are too close or too distant or vacillating between detachment and enmeshment (Parson, 2000).

Children in war may find themselves with *fewer social outlets and supportive resources* to deal with their adverse experiences. This occurs because war inevitably impinges (directly or indirectly) on both the child's natural (i.e., peer, family, and significant others) and formal (i.e., community psychological and social welfare services) support systems. War may also have indirect consequences, for example, when long-lasting economic damage affects parents' ability to take care of their children. Moreover, parents face the double challenge of processing their own subjective traumatic experience and managing their own individual reactions, while concurrently relating to the children's needs and often also those of other family members (e.g., elderly relatives). In addition, increased functional demands occur in the family, such as those related to a spouse's absence due to deployment or hospitalization or the adjustment difficulties of a homecoming war veteran. The numerous types of family stress may result in parenting change: a more authoritarian parenting style, less supervision of children, or less positive emotional interaction. Moreover, when a parent directly experiences a traumatic event, preoccupation with his or her own symptomatology may reach the point where it is impossible for that parent to appropriately monitor and effectively respond to the young child's needs. Furthermore, in wartime, children and parents often experience traumatization by the same event or different events, but the effects of each victim's symptomatology exacerbate the other's (Scheeringa & Zeanah, 2001). Psychological unavailability of the attachment figure as a secure base may lead to long-term psychological impairment (Cicchetti, Toth, & Lynch, 1997). Parental support is an important factor in explaining both children's resilience and in-

crease in problems (Dybdahl, 2001). Interventionists should strongly consider psychosocial interventions for parents with respect to parenting during wartime (for a detailed discussion, see Klingman & Cohen, 2004).

War necessitates the *adaptation of existing coping strategies and techniques as well as the development of new coping modes*. Effective coping with a prolonged traumatic situation requires the ability to shift and manipulate mental experiences, seek help, rely on soothing and consoling memories, construct new metaphors, and create comprehensive narratives to replace fragmented horrific pictures (Punamaeki, 2002). The child's adaptive coping strategies and techniques may differ across war-induced situations, and at different points in the course of the war new situation-specific needs may become central to the choice of strategy. For example, a problem-focused coping style may not be practical for a child in certain circumstances or points in time. Using a problem-focused strategy may serve as a reminder of the uncontrollability of the situation, whereas emotion-focused coping, or even high defensiveness (e.g., denial, avoidance), might offer the child time to assimilate the trauma more readily. Some data indicate that children who persisted in directly engaging in problem solving and other activities to change an unchangeable situation may have coped less effectively than those relying on emotion-focused coping (Klingman et al., 1993). A wide repertoire of coping modes and their situation-sensitive, flexible, and adequate employment are likely conducive to an enhanced recovery process. Coping modes' effectiveness must be considered in terms of personality differences and goodness-of-fit with the challenges that war situations pose for children. Thus, professionals and parents should not strip children of their personal ways of responding to trauma but rather should expose and guide them toward the utilization or even creation of a new and broader repertoire of strategies (Klingman & Cohen, 2004; Punamaeki, 2002; Rutter, 2000).

War conditions may involve the *intensification of pre-existing anxieties*. For example, Ronen (1996a, 1996b) detailed the case history of ten 9- to 11-year-old Israeli children who were referred for treatment a few weeks after the 1991 Gulf War. Unlike the other members of their families, these children's war-related anxious behaviors did not decrease after the war. They all evidenced anxiety reactions, sleep disorders, and features of separation anxiety as an outcome of the war. An accurate review of each child's past history revealed previous anxieties beginning in early childhood. The war may have affected their prewar anxieties in several ways (Ronen, 1996b): by legitimizing expressions of fear, thereby increasing children's preoccupation with their own fears; by parents' ceasing to insist (as they had before, in peacetime) that their children invest as much in overcoming their fears, thereby reinforcing and maintaining new fears; by legitimizing avoidant behavior, in contrast to peacetime, when the children had been forced to expose themselves in one way or another to anxiety-provoking situations (e.g., remaining in their own beds); and by normalizing and thus reinforcing new wartime life patterns in which the children experienced staying at home and sleeping together with the family in the sealed room. This togetherness actually "released" these children from the need to cope with their anxiety and conditioned them to the new situation of staying at home with their family. Also, wartime may arouse the negative effects of earlier trauma, thus sensitizing an individual to subsequent stress and trauma and creating vulnerability for PTSD (Cicchetti et al., 1997).

The combination of trauma and grief often seen in war may lead to *traumatic grief or bereavement,* which involves a complex overlay of symptoms that arise from the difficulty inherent in moving on with grief work due to one's preoccupation with the trauma. Without first working through the traumatic experience and/or the traumatic nature of a significant other's death, this difficulty may impede the normal work of grief and resolution (Klingman & Cohen, 2004; Malkinson, Rubin, & Witztum, 2000).

Evacuation may involve children's *separation from family.* Several studies have indicated that children separated from their family during war proved more distressed by the separation than by exposure to bombings or by witnessing destruction, injury, or death (Klingman, 2002a, 2002b). Those who experienced constant bombing did not seem adversely affected, provided they remained with their mother or mother substitute and continued their familiar routines.

Discrete war-related effects may develop in children with regard to the *deployment of their loved ones.* (Note that this can have an effect on children even if the conflict is raging in a distant country.) Children must face the possibility that a parent could be wounded or killed in action. Additional stressors may occur as a result of up-to-the-minute information and vivid, often live, combat scenes transferred by way of conventional and satellite-transmitted television, commercial radio, com-

puter modem, fax machine, and the Internet (Figley, 1993a, 1993b). Misinformation and rumors spread easily via these means and cause harm. Reactions of children who are separated from a deployed parent range from sadness, jealousy of children whose parents are not deployed, and increased levels of unruly behavior and anger, to fears, separation anxiety, hostility toward the other parent, and guilt (Costello, Phelps, & Wilczenski, 1994). Some may experience depressive symptoms or (especially among younger children) exhibit acute acting-out behavior. A father's long absence may promote maternal overprotection, indirectly contributing to sex-role development difficulties (e.g., effeminacy, softness) and affecting later father-child bonding. Children may be burdened with extra tasks because of the parent's absence, which requires them to forgo age-appropriate activities and adopt adult-like responsibilities. As mostly fathers are deployed, mothers play the key role in determining whether or not children cope well when faced with their father's prolonged absence (Hunter, 1988).

The *parent's return and reunion* also deserves attention. A parent's prolonged absence may deeply affect children, who may respond with a mixture of relief and anger (which their parents may not understand) at both the prolonged absence and the reunion/reintegration (Figley, 1993a; Hobfoll et al., 1991). The reunion may cause considerable ambivalence, with relief and exhilaration. In addition to the psychosocial residue of combat, the returning parents face changes in society and in the family and may have to deal with new family conflicts related to their prolonged absence as well as the old ones, if they existed. The family may enter power struggles engendered by anxieties over parental role changes and shifts in parent-child loyalties.

Exposure to their *parents' posttraumatic stress* may also affect children. The relationship between parents' war experience and subsequent stress disorder and their children's problems is considered a secondary traumatization. Intense involvement of a child in the emotional life of such a parent may cause high levels of anxiety, guilt, and conscious and unconscious preoccupation with specific events that were traumatic for the parent. These children should receive help to disentangle their experiences from those being relived by their parents (Rosenheck & Nathan, 1985).

Silence and denial about previous traumatic experiences may be common in families exposed to war-produced violence; the basis for this is mutual protection of parents and children. An intergenerational communication pattern referred to as the "conspiracy of silence" has been found in families of survivors (Danieli, 1998). This silence between the survivors and their children regarding the parents' traumatic experience emanated not only from the parents' need to forget (e.g., "We should forget the past and look ahead"), but also from their belief that withholding information about the horrors of the war was crucial to their children's normal development (e.g., "Opening up old wounds can only cause more suffering or harm to my child"). Their children, in turn, became sensitive to their parents' need to keep silent (Bar-On, 1995, 1996). As a result, both generations often mutually supported a "double wall" of silence. Studies of families of the Holocaust survivors (Auerhahn & Laub, 1998; Felsen, 1998), Japanese American internment camps (Nagata, 1998), Dutch war sailors and resistance veterans (Op den Velde, 1998), and Vietnam veterans (Ancharoff, Munroe, & Fisher, 1998), taken together, suggest that the quality of parents' (verbal and nonverbal) communication about traumatic experiences may have major consequences for the inner and interpersonal life of their children (Wiseman & Barber, 2004; Wiseman et al., 2002).

Children often attempt to shield their parents from knowing how much the children's own trauma has affected them. Such protectiveness (or even denial) may be considered an adaptive strategy that supports the capacity of both parents and children to cope and survive in dangerous wartime situations, and it also serves the function of preserving the child's internal representations of his or her parents as a secure base. Yet, it may become an obstacle if, as a result, the child is later (especially when the war is over) left with insufficient parental support and must deal alone with the effects of war trauma; clinicians need to take these family dynamics into consideration (Almqvist & Broberg, 1997; Wiseman & Barber, 2004).

War-relevant coping mechanisms may interfere with postwar adjustment. A wartime environment may render children's dissociative mechanisms, for instance, to be not only normal but even necessary as an important functional defensive maneuver (i.e., a survival strategy) in adapting to danger, violent scenes, and evil. Such defense mechanisms spare the child victim the self-experiences of abject passivity, helplessness, unworthiness, and vulnerability to harm. In prolonged trauma-inducing war events, children may develop impulse-driven, aggressive self-defense responses that can interfere with problem solving and lead to overag-

gressiveness toward peers and parents, difficulty in modulating impulses, problems with social attachment and attention, lack of participation in preparing for the future, and the loss of trust, hope, a sense of agency, and meaningful attachments (Witty, 2002). Also, children in war-affected zones may adopt a revenge-oriented ideology as a simplistic coping mechanism; they may become intolerant and/or suspicious of peers from a different (racial, ethnic, or religious) background or political ideology, or to peers who show nonconforming behavior. In this sense, the role of society or the community in providing a solution to moral conflicts should not be overlooked. When the war is over, such conflicts may affect children's adjustment; some, for example, will not (at least immediately) connect with regular school study projects or a peace dialogue. Moreover, the experience of wartime/political conflict and violence has shown links with aggressive and even delinquent behavior (e.g., Shoham, 1994) due to lowered levels of child supervision, an increase in thrill seeking resulting from excitement attached to the notion of war, social modeling, and the normalization of violence, as well as anxiety and loss of control experienced by children during war and protracted war-like situations (Cairns, 1996; Muldoon, 2000). Postwar psychological intervention should thus examine the need to focus on making these fixations movable again.

The observed *incidence of PTSD* symptomatology in children as a result of exposure to war or war-like events is highly variable. For instance, rates ranged from 6% who met all three symptom criteria (e.g., Dawes, Tredoux, & Feinstein, 1989; Klingman, 2001) to 32% in Cambodian children some 10 years after they witnessed the execution of family members (Clarke, Sack, & Goff, 1993). This variability in prevalence rates may be related to the number, the type, and the intensity of war traumas experienced. Based on a study of Lebanese children, Macksoud and Aber (1996) concluded that in situations of chronic armed conflict, where there is no respite from the traumas of war, children are at risk of developing "continuous" PTSD. Nevertheless, PTSD should not be the only criterion for launching an intervention; the long-term effect of traumatic experiences emerged, for example, in the case of Israeli adolescents taken hostage during a school outing. Most survivors who were investigated reported some forms of trauma-related symptoms even 17 years after their face-to-face encounter with the terrorists (Desivilya, Gal, & Ayalon, 1996a, 1996b). Experts agree that up to one-third of the young people in a community may develop PTSD. However, to date, neither well-designed qualitative data nor quantitative longitudinal data exist to allow conclusions to be drawn on the duration and recurrence of traumatic exposure in children and adolescents following war or on their war-related mental health risks.

Resilience and Coping

These unique effects of war on children are related to various negative impacts. Yet some children *cope reasonably well* despite exposure to the extremely stressful circumstances. Others *cope better when they are offered a sensitive recovery environment,* that is, when their physical safety is ensured and social infrastructures are created (or reestablished) to meet their basic physical and emotional needs.

Successful coping with regard to war also entails an attempt to make the adverse situation more tolerable or to minimize the distress via distancing, denial, and habituation strategies used by children to manage the negative affect generated by a traumatic encounter (Muldoon & Cairns, 1999). Habituation may provide one explanation for findings showing that children exhibit a high level of adaptation to war and warlike situations (Klingman et al., 1993; Muldoon & Cairns, 1999).

It is also important to acknowledge that children actively and creatively engage in their situation and adopt constructive approaches to the management of risk, and in some cases contribute to family maintenance, protection, and survival. For example, children often bear responsibilities within the family for incapacitated adults or younger siblings.

Much of children's resiliency may be attributed to certain personality factors that are known to play a part in responding to and coping with danger. Temperamental dimensions such as the threshold for pain and pleasure, valence and intensity of fear, sadness, and anger, emotional arousal and regulation, and novelty-seeking behavior seem to be especially salient in the course of posttraumatic distress.

The role of parents in enhancing their children's resilience must be highlighted. Family members' responses and behaviors may influence young children's coping behaviors. Attachment-related working models explain how children interpret and evaluate danger and how they adjust to stressful situations (Punamaeki, 2002). There is evidence that young children's experiences within the family, particularly with their primary caregivers, are central to subsequent coping and adaptation (Muldoon & Cairns, 1999). Plausibly, parents serve as a coping model for their children; children model family members' behaviors (e.g., their "calmness") and are influenced by their balanced or "positive" interpretations and outlook (e.g., optimism). The parents' actual behavior in wartime and/or its aftermath probably also significantly communicates to children concerning safety and optimism, which contribute to their resilience. Moreover, war conditions may create an opportunity for both families and children (especially adolescents) to become involved in taking care of or helping others, at the individual level or by joining in some kind of shared proactive, prosocial community activity. In this way, they engage in self-fulfilling activities and experience a sense of mastery and worth.

Furthermore, *response to war can be mediated through the initiation of preventive inoculation programs,* such as stress-inoculation programs. The extended warning or anticipatory period that usually precedes war indicates the need for anticipatory coping strategy interventions (Caplan, 1964), which are usually school-based in the case of children (Klingman & Cohen, 2004). Such intervention constitutes preplanned efforts to manage—reduce, minimize, master, or tolerate—an impending stressful transaction. Although this anticipatory period is extremely stressful and may require crisis intervention assistance in itself, professionals and educators can initiate anticipatory guidance programs to help children, parents, teachers, schools, and the relevant community/state agencies to better prepare, however partially, in real time for the impending war emergencies. Such an anticipatory intervention conducted in Israel prior to the 1991 Gulf War focused on children's familiarity with gas masks and other protective measures against chemical fallout as well as the related anxieties. This intervention was reported effective (Klingman, 2002a, 2002c; Klingman & Cohen, 2004).

The study of children in war and in war-torn zones has led to understanding that *the successful conclusion of difficult experiences can strengthen people* and better prepare them for new difficult experiences that are to come. Children may not only learn to cope better: For some, their struggle with the war ordeal may even positively change them in the long run. In planning interventions, professionals should not underestimate the positive resources of adaptive coping, resiliency, and growth.

Communality and a sense of community are notable recovery factors in wartime. Individuals undergoing the hardships of war pull together, join ranks, and experience a greater sense of community. Individuals thus resolve the suffering that arises in a social context shaped by the meanings and understandings applied to it (Summerfield, 1999). Social networks such as family members, close friends, relatives, and familiar clergy can greatly help people create a sense of safety and meaning under these circumstances.

Also associated with a sense of community and war are strong feelings of *patriotism and ideological commitment.* Some research findings (Punamaeki, 1996) indicate that ideology may contribute to adolescents' successful coping. Strong ideological commitment to a political struggle and active engagement can be protective and increase resilience, on the condition that the children's exposure to hardship is not overwhelming. Furthermore, children's, especially adolescents', attempts to make sense of the conflict (e.g., the cause of the war) may affect their mental health. It is also plausible that the political meaning they give to their mental suffering may lead them to interpret their symptoms as nonproblematic.

In this regard, local as well as national *leadership* such as clergy, local community leaders, and teachers play an important role in communal trauma recovery. By definition, wars affect entire communities, and there is much that community and state leaders can do (e.g., people/children often look to them as meaning makers), especially enhancing social morale. Although basically strong, leaders may become overburdened (if not overwhelmed) by the pressing needs of others in their community, so psychologists need to reach out to these individuals and give them the message that leaders must attend to their own needs as well (Hobfoll et al., 1991).

Considering the roles that communality, ideological commitment, and leadership play in times of war and recovery, it can be argued, as in Israel during the 1991 Gulf War, that the nonwar traditional therapeutic approach, with its focus on pathology and its emphasis on personal (as opposed to societal) recovery and well-being and its professed neutrality of values, may be inappropriate, even damaging, in times of war (Solomon, 1995). Interventionists must consider the collective capacity of survivor populations to mourn, endure, and rebuild, as well as individuals' capacity to cope and engage in self-healing, that is, to manage their suffering,

adapt, recover, and in some cases even grow (Klingman & Cohen, 2004; Summerfield, 1999). The therapist's role is thus not to first focus on or look for "proofs" of pathological response but to consider the natural human ability to self-recover, change, develop, and grow from adversity. The best immediate intervention may have a social focus (Farwell & Cole, 2001–2002; Wessely, 2003), centering on the empowerment of the recovery environments (i.e., social healing) as well as of personal resources (e.g., resiliency, strengths, benefit finding, and growth), which should take precedence. This approach has implications for both the natural recovery process and direct psychological interventions with war-affected children.

Children of war, then, undergo a variety of experiences, necessitating an array of carefully planned intervention programs (in variable war settings) to meet their diverse needs. Large-scale interventions should be the method of choice, and such interventions must be community-based, multifaceted, and generic in nature. To implement this, clinical psychology and community psychology should collaborate and complement one another, focusing on the benefits of a multisystemic approach to trauma due to its greater psychological impact, professional richness, and cost effectiveness.

COMMUNITY AS A CONTEXT OF HEALING: THE SHIFT FROM CLINIC- TO COMMUNITY-BASED INTERVENTIONS

Much of the current emphasis in the war-related trauma intervention literature lies on targeting and reducing PTSD. However, PTSD is not the only psychological consequence of war for youth. Also in war, and often in immediate postwar circumstances, any individual-focused intervention is impractical because both therapists and clients are preoccupied with safety and survival issues. In addition, although victims of war indeed experience acute symptoms and become distressed, these are not necessarily dysfunctional or indicative of a clinical disorder. Most children experiencing difficulties during war eventually adjust, given the availability of certain personal factors, coping patterns, and recovery-environment factors. Even for those whose basic ability to function is blocked, so that clinical labels may indeed be appropriate and helpful, it is possible that PTSD is substantially overdiagnosed. In certain cases, this clinical concept has perhaps been stretched beyond any value by confusing psychiatric disorder with acute but, under the circumstances, "normal" distress (Wessely, 2003). More important, clinical treatment of the individual may not be required because the distress reactions relate to a social situation affecting a whole population. Cultural factors play an important role in individual or group expression of stress reactions, vulnerability to developing PTSD, and treatment responsiveness. Regarding the latter, certain cultures may evidence strong resistance by parents and children alike to mental health professionals or even to the entire concept of mental health intervention. Conversely, cultural routines, traditions, and rituals embedded in a particular culture may better aid distressed and traumatized persons who belong to that culture by defining helpful societal, culture-dependent pathways to recovery.

Accordingly, an expanded view of psychopathology and posttraumatic adaptation (Klingman & Cohen, 2004) advocates the consideration of children's current and potential ability to adapt to the new situation, to invest in age-appropriate activities, and to self-recover. This more general emphasis on the implications of the war considers not only aspects of the acute traumatic experience, but also a range of psychological and socioenvironmental risk and protective factors related to the pretrauma, peritrauma, and posttrauma ecologies.

Multiple factors do influence children's response to war. Some involve aspects of the environment, which may be more distal or more proximal to the individual child, and others lie within the individual child. Cicchetti and colleagues (1997) suggested an ecological transactional perspective for relating to intervention with war-affected children. The model's several co-occurring levels in depicting the child's war-affected environment is useful for understanding how the multiple risk and resilience factors described in the earlier sections can influence children's responses to war. In referring to the *macrosystem,* which includes the beliefs and values of a people/culture, these authors asserted that ideological commitment may be one important protective factor. For example, children with a strong ideological commitment who were exposed to war-related hardships did not show an increase in symptoms of anxiety, insecurity, and depression, whereas those who revealed weak ideological commitment showed a nonlinear increase in symptoms (Punamaeki, 1996). In referring to aspects of the community in which families and individuals live, namely, the *exosystem,* Cicchetti et al. noted that fragmentation of community resources may place children at increased risk for psychological distress at times of war. Such are disrupted peer networks, which may result in the absence of one important source of social support for the children, and interrupted schooling, which might result in alienating an important base of continuity for many children. These authors then referred to the *microsystem,* namely, the immediate setting in which the child exists: the family's level of adaptation in general, the parents' in particular, and how they cope specifically with the stress of war. Parents' level of adaptation can become one critical factor in determining how the individual child responds to the trauma of war. As for the *ontogenic* developmental level, namely, factors within the individual connected to his or her own development and adaptation, Cicchetti et al. pinpointed the role played by the child's affect regulation, attachment patterns, self-management, peer relations, and other extrafamilial relationships (e.g., school participation) in the child's adaptation process. This ecological model provides the rationale for an *ecologically informed,* multisystemic intervention.

Multisystemic intervention refers to the active mutual interdependence of an individual child's self system (e.g., self-esteem, ego identity, affect regulation, temperament) and its sustaining environment: the immediate nuclear family, the extended family, the community (structures, organizations, and services), and the society at large, including policies at the city, county, state, and federal levels of government, especially those underlying national and international psychological trauma intervention programs (Klingman & Cohen, 2004; Parson, 1996; Summerfield, 1999). Thus, intervention planners can direct their efforts at three levels. One is the child's direct experience of the violent war event, or series of events, or their results. The second level relates to the link between family functioning and children's adaptation; it includes difficulties in family members' functioning (e.g., due to loss of home and/or economic resources), their psychological availability for support, and the meanings given by them to the violent acts. The third, societal level concerns the war's impact on fundamental routines, on community resources, and on the mediating capacity of the broader social mechanisms. For children, as described earlier, the societal level of war may involve closure of schools, restrictions on social and recreational activities, and temporary unavailability of psychological and welfare services.

Conducted within the natural ecology of the youth and family (e.g., home, school, and community), coordinated interventions that are enacted simultaneously in more than one system exert a much stronger impact on recovery than does the cumulative impact of separate interventions. They target key factors within and between the multiple systems in which the child is embedded. The prime objective is to reactivate/mobilize the resourcefulness of children, their parents, other caregivers (e.g., teachers), and the community (including the sociopolitical community as a significant context). Such an approach does not view the impact of war as simply impinging on children who are passive recipients of environmental factors; rather, children's responses will vary as a function of their personal resources, the availability and quality of their support system, and their efforts at processing the war-related effects. Strong emphasis is placed on *preventive* strategies and techniques, adapted to massive use.

The multisystemic intervention may require a mental health professional to assume several roles: as *a consultant* to the community, as *a coordinator* of organizational interventions focused on mental health, and often as *a supervisor* to ensure that triage and risk screening are well coordinated and conducted in line with the generic approach. These roles may necessitate a temporary departure from the intervention mode usually practiced. Given the reality of war, the psychologist as a consultant must often take a proactive-directive approach, such as adopting a unilateral (rather than shared), coercive-directive consultation approach (Gutkin, 1999), often relying on his or her own judgment when recommending steps to be taken or when choosing among intervention strategy options.

Psychological intervention must thus be community-based and informed politically, socially, and culturally. This means initiating large-scale preventive measures, relating to the common responses, and first and foremost working for an adaptive resolution of the crises of the war and the postwar period. In other words, intervention should adopt a generic approach.

A primary tenet of *the generic approach* is that certain recognized patterns of response and recovery exist for all (or most) people in crisis, such as process components of grief and bereavement. A specific generic intervention plan should be designed to be effective for all members of the affected population, or a given group, rather than for the particular attributes of one individual, and should aim at an adaptive resolution of the trauma. In addition, such a

plan should emphasize positive psychology with a minimum of clinical therapeutic interference. The generic approach maintains that an individual-focused approach—underscoring the child's unique, diverse intrapsychic and interpersonal processes, needs, and difficulties—can always be initiated later for individuals who fail to respond to generic measures, thus complementing the initial generic intervention. One noted advantage of the generic approach is its feasibility: This mode of intervention can be learned and implemented by paraprofessionals and non-mental health professionals. In practice, generic intervention focuses on supporting children as they attempt to regain control by providing opportunities for ventilation, offering age-appropriate information, and training children in simple techniques of stress/symptom reduction (e.g., relaxation exercises), preferably in the child's natural setting of home, school, or community. Also, caregivers receive assistance in setting limited recovery goals relevant to any situation and in tailoring proactive, meaningful, age-related, solution-focused activities for the children, as much as possible within the specific circumstances.

The following are optimal generic intervention principles:

Immediacy ensures that measures are taken as soon as possible to prevent hiatuses that would deepen the sense of disruption.

Proximity maintains children in a familiar setting with their regular caretakers and prefers intervening in the natural setting.

Simplicity advocates avoidance of sophisticated intervention methods, establishment of limited and clear goals, and employment of situation-specific, easy-to-implement recovery activities such as ventilation, relaxation, and support.

Expectancy establishes confidence in personal as well as communal ability to recover.

Sense of community enhances feelings of belongingness.

Purposeful action espouses being active to serve as a powerful counterresponse to a sense of helplessness.

Finally, the *continuity principle* (Klingman & Cohen, 2004; Omer & Alon, 1994) is the unifying generic guiding principle. To counteract the extreme disruptions in everyday personal and community life triggered by war (or any large-scale disaster), this principle holds that the optimal intervention measures constitute preserving and restoring disrupted continuities at the individual, familial, and organizational/community levels of a personal (historical), functional, and interpersonal nature. Cognitive and emotional working-through restores *personal continuity* by exploring what has happened, ascribing meaning to it, reframing the present situation, and setting modest, situation-specific, personal goals/tasks for the near future. Situation-relevant external action reestablishes *functional continuity* by starting to act, even if on a very elementary level, and gradually broadening the scope and complexity of functioning. Activating (or reinstituting) mutual support and reestablishing trust in others aids in restoring *interpersonal continuity*. Normally, progress in any one of these continuities facilitates progress in others by a ripple effect. The generic approach serves best in cases of massive intervention for survivors of war and political strife.

Organizational continuity and continuity of care can both be added to the continuity principle. *Organizational continuity* entails the restoration of the connections between children and their natural community, in which they can resume their prewar roles. Regarding children's needs, the restoration and reorganization of school is the most important and highest priority (Klingman & Cohen, 2004). Identifying, reactivating, and empowering prewar societal institutions and especially nonstigmatizing, school-based services may significantly enhance a sense of control and expectation of a return to normalcy. This favors the reverberation of the process of recovery even further throughout all the circles of vulnerability.

Continuity of care ideally relates to the restoration of prewar social welfare and mental health community services. From a mental health frame of reference, continuity of care also refers to the proactive provision of a range of accessible multimodal preventive interventions. Specifically, mental health professionals must systematically and continually assess the development of and the reduction in reactions and symptoms in all war-affected children at different points in time, thus also enabling possible identification of delayed PTSD symptoms. Professionals must ensure that the interventions applied are provided as long as necessary and that new ones are offered as needed based on periodical assessments. Schools offer the optimal setting for implementation of continuity of care. In schools, all children can be systematically observed and assessed at different points in time as well as participate directly and indirectly in preventive and other nonstigmatizing recovery programs and activities.

Selected war-related interventions illustrate the implementation of organizational procedures and measures, the generic multisystemic approach, and the unifying continuity principle as employed in war and war-related situations. These are discussed next.

Prewar Generic Anticipatory Interventions

As noted earlier, in many cases, psychoeducational interventions can address war or some aspects of it even before it begins. This anticipatory period enables some preparatory interventions to target organizations (e.g., schools) and the media, thus reaching children and their parents and teachers. The preparations in Israel for attack by unconventional weapons prior to the two Gulf Wars (1991 and 2003) illustrate one aspect of such preparatory intervention with children. *Preparedness intervention* at this period aimed to ensure that children became familiar with and competent at using gas masks and other protective measures, especially for chemical fallout. The preparatory intervention, conducted in schools, involved dissemination of carefully composed, age-appropriate information, followed by gradual exposure and desensitization (a combination of in vivo and participant modeling). Group (separate classes and whole-school) simulations helped students gain a sense of control and envisage themselves withstanding the threat of (unconventional) warfare effectively, should it erupt (Klingman, 2002a, 2002c; Klingman & Cohen, 2004). Psychologists helped in planning a gradual exposure to the aversive aspects of some preparation components (e.g., staying for a long time in a sealed room with the gas mask on, getting acquainted with the large-size syringe, and training in self-injection).

During this anticipatory period, *the mass media* became a central source of information, giving meaning to events and calming fears. Israeli child psychologists appeared as interviewees on psychological educational programs on television and radio that provided parental guidance on various psychological problems. The psychological principles that guided these programs were adapted to the emergency situation. Popular children's television programs were adapted as well. For example, the Israeli version of the well-known *Sesame Street* program* used the familiar characters and puppets that ap-

---

* *Rechov Sumsum*, the Israeli *Sesame Street* produced by T. Steklov, is a well-known program geared toward young viewers, based on the U.S. program, but produced in Israel by local professionals in conjunction with colleagues in the United States.

peared regularly on the program to transmit to child viewers psychological messages aimed at helping them cope with their fears and anxieties (for an extensive discussion and recommendations, see Raviv, 1993). Such programs can be expanded (whenever conditions allow) during the war. Although these measures were specific to Israel in response to the 1991 Gulf War, these and other media interventions can undoubtedly be employed in prewar, wartime, and the immediate postwar periods in other parts of the world.

Another intervention in the anticipatory period before the outbreak of war may concern notification that a parent will be participating in the war, preparation for parental departure, and the expectation of a marked change in the family system due to this absence. It is possible to reduce the impact of separation for children, focusing on factors that most influence their adjustment to parental absence. The most critical factor is explicit, supportive communication that gives the child a rationale and clear understanding of the parents' deployment in the war (Figley, 1993a, 1993b). Attention should be directed, too, to the deployment of other family members (older sibling, uncle, etc.).

The provision of a support group for parents during the anticipatory period (e.g., via schools and community centers) should also be considered. Such support groups enable parents to be more emotionally available to their children, as well as to improve their potential continuity in providing appropriate support for the children (Cicchetti, Toth, & Lynch, 1993). Support groups that address parenting issues relevant to children's fears due to an impending war may lessen the likelihood of insecure attachments (especially in infants and toddlers) at later stages. Children indeed benefit from interventions with parents (Klingman & Cohen, 2004), but during the prewar anticipatory stage, interventions can target children directly in their schools or involve children in small-group formats, especially around art activities in afterschool programs, to include some developmentally appropriate stress inoculation techniques (Meichenbaum & Cameron, 1983).

War and Postwar Community-Based Generic Interventions

Not all wars are alike. Sometimes intervention with children during a war is next to impossible. In other wars, conditions allow for psychologists' involvement (however limited), most often as consultants to parents,

teachers, and those handling emergency reorganization in a community.

Organizational Measures Based on a Generic Frame of Reference: The Case of Evacuation from an Attacked Zone

As an example of implementing the generic approach in wartime, we may examine the case of emergency temporary hotel accommodations provided for Israelis whose homes were badly damaged in the missile strikes by Iraq during the 1991 Gulf War. As the war progressed, many hotels in the Tel Aviv metropolitan area were gradually turned into absorption centers and provisional accommodation facilities. Families were led by the authorities from the rubble of their homes to register at an on-the-scene municipal command post through which they were directed to a designated hotel. The evacuated families would arrive at the hotels in a state of shock, and many expressed a variety of fears induced by the missile attacks, such as fear of remaining alone, fear of impending strikes, and fear of being "chased by the missiles" to this location outside the targeted communities. Some were afraid to part even temporarily from other family members. The victims were anxious and on edge, some still dazed and numb. Families were placed in very small rooms in the overcrowded hotels, therefore also experiencing a lack of privacy. Entire families lingered in the lobby or walked about the hallways, often restless or irritable. Some of the older children who had assumed parental roles and some of the mothers who were trying to "remain strong" for their family "broke down." In addition, the evacuees had to confront the complex bureaucracy that was mobilized to help them. The hotel grounds became flooded with both local municipality assistance personnel and well-meaning volunteers. The entire experience of the evacuees left them feeling helpless and out of control (for an extended discussion, see Solomon, 1995).

As head of the emergency mental health team of the Ministry of Education at the time, I was invited to fulfill the role of consultant to the various (mental health as well as non-mental health) officials in charge. Adopting the preventive/organizational and generic frames of reference, I suggested that priority be given first to concrete relief and organizational (logistical and practical) measures, which would then be followed by generic mental health measures. The logistical/practical measures included supplying basic needs (e.g., beverages to avoid dehydration) and actively engaging the families in their own process of settling down. This required, first, the restoration of evacuees' personal continuity, namely, helping them regain their personal identity (e.g., reframing the present situation, setting modest personal goals, and involvement in simple situation-specific tasks). A basic organizational measure was the officials' restoration of a sense of order, as much as possible under the circumstances, via two means: encouraging informational, instructive communication of a soothing, placating nature by the personnel in charge (i.e., a calming effect) and establishing a situation-specific, relatively structured logistical environment (i.e., an organizing effect). Personnel's soothing communication was achieved by a benevolent yet firm (but not authoritarian) stance. Recall that clarity, structure, and local leadership's confidence building constitute generic measures for intervention in mass trauma.

Referring to the practical logistics, I asked, for example, that large, clearly printed, color signs be placed in the main lobby. These signs included a simplified, clear map of the hotel grounds and facilities, indicating registration points, and a short text about basic procedures to follow. Other signs in different colors directed families who had already registered to their assigned floor and room. Lists of instructions about how to proceed further were posted on each floor. The rationale was the need to convey to parents and children a sense of surrounding order and control and to enable these evacuees to resume at least some of their personal functioning by beginning to follow directions, taking control over making preparations to ease registration, and so on. These simple logistical measures aimed to start the process of transforming evacuees' self-concept from victim to survivor, replacing the experience of helplessness with an acknowledgment of their own resources, however limited under these conditions, in coping with the trauma.

In another organizational measure with corollary mental health objectives, a large, clearly written timetable for the day was posted in the main lobby, referring to organized children's activities and play groups. This timetable further conveyed to the children and their parents that they were expected to gradually resume at least some of their predisaster activities and functioning. These opportunities for children to join in developmentally appropriate, familiar, normative (pretrauma) popular social and peer activities also encouraged functional and personal continuities. Group activities were both fun and relaxing as well as purposeful and useful (e.g., decorating, helping younger children). Thus, the activity itself, with its experience of control and mastery, helped youngsters regain some sense of self-efficacy. Concurrently, a sense of belonging to a group or community and a sense of solidarity emerged. These experiences could also serve as an antidote to possible difficulties ahead. Some of the group activities enabled children to act out (e.g., in puppetry) their worries and express their feelings and fears. Group leaders were recruited from volunteer adult (especially unmarried) evacuees who were experienced in leading children's activities; whenever possible, older adolescent evacuee volunteers were assigned to co-lead younger children's play groups; children identified as talented musicians were asked to entertain. The group leaders were asked to focus on very simple activities, in line with the guiding principle of simplicity.

On the following day, we called volunteer teachers who were familiar to many of the children because they taught in schools and kindergartens in the evacuated areas. These teachers had had prior contact with the mental health themes because they had previously incorporated mental health perspectives into their regular prewar teaching and had engaged in preventive interventions for their classes during the anticipatory period preceding the war. We asked these teachers to now serve as tutors in the hotels for noncompulsory, 1- to 2-hour daily school-related study sessions in small groups or individually. Beyond their teaching expertise and familiarity with the evacuees' background, these teachers also served as attachment figures, mental health promoters, and "clinical mediators." Having prior experience in mental health prevention programs, these teachers required minimal introduction to their new (nonjudgmental) tutoring role and very little help with communicating accepting, empathic, and caring concern, or with conveying reassurance and structure to the children. They also needed little ongoing support from the mental health team in the implementation process. Whenever it was appropriate and feasible, we encouraged parents to join in and become actively involved in sports, drawing, or painting activities. The parents' presence and involvement aimed to enhance their sense of resuming the parenting role.

Parents became a major focus of preventive intervention, inasmuch as this organized evacuation program had intentionally avoided separating children from their family, in line with the view that family was the "first circle" of security for the children. Thus, we guided the parents in establishing a volunteer parents committee to meet daily to discuss parents' and children's pressing concerns and to become proactively involved in planning, organizing, and following up on measures and activities in response to these needs. The most pressing need voiced by the parents concerned guidance on parenting in the present circumstances. In response, we offered parents small-group guidance (rather than counseling) sessions led by mental health professionals. The guidance meetings adopted a structured, solution-focused approach (de Shazer, 1985) in the form of solution-focused guidance (Klingman, 2002b, and see later in this chapter). Only very brief personal ventilation was allowed (as well as some airing of parents' logistical concerns), and then the discussion moved right on to focus on parenting. Early on, these group discussions often touched on individual parents' unhelpful tendencies, such as overprotection, denial, and avoidance; later, parents were led to discover mutual concerns and engage in finding solutions based on their mutual resources as a group. The group facilitators focused on parents sharing their successful means of coping with the situation, and especially how they tapped their inner strengths and familial and social resources, to foster parental empowerment. (See Klingman & Cohen, 2004, for other forms of parents' small-group work relating to trauma designed to attend to different parental needs in other war-related circumstances.)

Our intervention also focused on intensively supporting the mental health professionals involved with the evacuees over the period during which the war continued. By that time, professionals from several mental health disciplines were involved in the hotel-based intervention: psychiatrists, psychologists, social workers, and school counselors. Briefing and debriefing group meetings for the mental health staff were established, to be held twice a day. The morning session consisted of a very short briefing lasting about 20 minutes, which reviewed the upcoming day's schedule, specific assignments, clarification of policies, and so on. The late afternoon sessions comprised a short-term intervention that combined ventilation on the one hand (i.e., sharing and supportive listening via briefing and limited debriefing) and a solution-focused approach on the other hand, which directed attention to both the professional and personal needs of the staff. These mental health professionals found it extremely difficult to dissociate themselves from the war ordeal because they were exposed to the same conditions as the children and their parents and because child victims in particular evoke protective nurturing feelings. The professionals needed to come to terms with and regulate their own war-inflicted reactions before attempting to help others, especially children. The staff also required psychological refueling during their extensive involvement in the trauma work. Considering these circumstances, the daily afternoon meetings provided a short (1-hour), relatively simple, support and empowerment, "helping the helpers" program. Such an intervention with school counselors in different (war-related) situations is discussed later in this chapter; a discussion on its effectiveness and details of the intervention development and protocol is presented elsewhere (Klingman, 2002c).

School-Based Intervention Following a Terrorist Attack Incident

In line with the unifying continuity principle, large-scale interventions should be delivered whenever possible via the school system. The school is the children's natural community system, where they spend much (if not most) of their waking hours, can socialize with peers, and can learn to benefit from adult (teachers') support. Schools may provide a relatively secure and predictable environment by means of a new routine reestablished as soon as possible after the outbreak of war. Substantial improvement in child functioning and adjustment can be rendered by prioritizing the reestablishment of educational and recreational opportunities as soon as possible for the postwar recovery process. Regardless of the inadequacy of the school's physical plant or the inexperience of its teachers at the time, the school remains the major community institution where most if not all children can be reached by mental health professionals through consultation (Klingman & Cohen, 2004; Yule, 2002).

An example of war-related, trauma-focused, school-based intervention utilizing *cognitive-behavior therapy principles with school children in a group* concerns the case of Israeli schoolchildren after a massive terrorist shooting attack on and around their neighborhood beachfront (Klingman & Ben Eli, 1981). The application of expressive and creative processes aimed to forge some sense of mastery and to help make frightening communication more tolerable. To help children examine what had happened more objectively, the psychologist asked them to create a model of the shooting site using clay, Play-Doh, and scrap materials. The psychologist then introduced various age-appropriate relaxation exercises and guided imagery to simulate how they would behave should such a situation occur again, exploring realistic precautions to be taken. Next, the teacher made active efforts to help the children implement their imagined preparations, to decrease their sense of vulnerability and helplessness. The transformation of children's ideas into practical, situation-specific action aimed to address the children's repeated, even somewhat compulsive fears concerning the possibility of more attacks in the very near future (which indeed was a very real concern). The children were thus encouraged to plan specifically how each of them would behave, to look for possible hiding places, and to devise escape routes. Next, in an in vivo desensitization procedure, they were encouraged to visit (in groups and with the teacher) the place on the beach where the incident started. Since the night of the attack, when the terrorists had arrived by boat and landed on that neighborhood beach, the children had not dared approach the place, which was normally very popular with the town's children.

Expressive Activity in Large-Scale Interventions

Many, if not all, large-scale war-related interventions with children reported in the literature involve playing, drawing, and other symbolic activities. Strikingly, for example, almost all supportive interventions in the former Yugoslavia offered art and crafts to war-affected children (Kalmanowitz & Lloyd, 1999). Therapists regard symbolic and imagery processes as effective means to enhance coping under war conditions. However, structured art therapy in itself does not necessarily reduce the symptoms of distress, as attested by a large study of 600 primary school children in Bosnia (Bunjevac & Kuterovac, 1994). Nevertheless, as a means for assisting children to cope with war trauma, art, puppetry, and drama often predominate interventions and are particularly useful with latency-age youngsters affected by the crisis of war. They can act out their worries and express their fears and feelings in ways that are developmentally in tune with their ego development (Williams-Gray, 1999).

Play has been widely acknowledged as an extremely powerful modality for treating children's problems (Chazan, 2002). Given a choice, younger children prefer to interact in a playful way. Play usually supersedes verbalization in the preschool years. Although some play materials may be spurned by latency-age boys who consider them "girls' toys," these same boys may willingly engage in play with animal puppets, for instance. Playing can serve as a safe refuge when anxiety mounts and the child needs to retreat from verbalized connections to his or her "own world." In play, children process their traumatic experience by symbolizing it and modifying its consequences; symbolic activities allow children to divide their excessive and painful experiences into small quantities, work through them, and assimilate them into their existing schemas.

Puppets can serve as an appropriate release for aggression and tension, while allowing the children to control and master a situation (Webb, 1999). In a case of peer group intervention with refugee children adjusting to their new life in the United States (St. Thomas & Johnson, 2001), puppetry served as an important action medium. All these children had experienced one or more traumas induced by the death of a relative or a close friend, were forcibly uprooted from their homeland, and faced immediate issues of survival and adjustment to their new life in an unfamiliar country. At one point in the peer group, a dragon puppet was chosen as an all-powerful character that was merciless toward all other animals. One by one, all the other animal puppets tried to stop the dragon's psychic and verbal abusive onslaught, but to no avail. Each character was jumped on physically and verbally, dismissed, or frightened away. The group facilitator then asked the participants to create a personal puppet that represented power in the natural or imaginative world. Superheroes and superheroines emerged as the youngsters drew and decorated their power symbols, utilizing the puppets to express personal needs. Asking other puppets for help, children exhibited themes of caring, friendship, support, and concern. Altogether, the children talked (through their puppets) about how abused and mistreated they felt as war victims and shared their current fears. Some talked about their hardship adjusting as refugees to the new strange environment.

By late latency or middle childhood, children's verbal communication skills increase; they become significantly more reality-oriented, thus necessitating less reliance on symbolic play. More verbalization, reality-oriented games, and large-muscle play are used. *Board games*, for example, may become useful. In a war zone in Israel, a board game was found especially effective in helping schoolchildren achieve a sense of intellectual control, and it significantly reduced their state of anxiety following a massive terrorist attack in a border town (Klingman & Cohen, 2004; Ophir, 1980). The students actively participated in creating and structuring a customized board game that included moving security and terrorist forces around the board. They thus learned the best positions for placing security forces in and around the town, considered the different security measures taken, assessed the probability of terrorists reaching (the game's) neighborhood, school, class, and homes, and discussed possible steps in case of another attack. This enabled students to positively focus some of their energy on planning, taking action, devising solutions, and gaining a sense of control.

Although well-controlled empirical research has not yet established the specific therapeutic effect of art and play activities, or of their components, reports of large-scale interventions in war-torn zones indicate that they are widely used with children and adolescents, especially in the recovery process. *Art and play activities* include singing, storytelling, dancing, learning to play musical instruments, game playing, and creative-expressive art activities by means of masks and puppets, movement, socio- and psychodrama, creating photo journals, and building simple playing devices out of scrap or accessible natural materials. In the former Yugoslavia, play, drawing, and drama were used with children not only to encapsulate past experiences but also to develop adaptive constructions of the world for their future life (Ager, 1996; Kostarova-Unkovska, 1993).

Undoubtedly, the use of art and play intervention offers an effective way to engage many children in purposeful, active self-healing when there are not enough mental health professionals to reach out to so many children and adolescents (as is the case in wartime and in war-torn regions). This intervention can be primarily handled by local staff in the educational and community settings, and may well involve local artists, too, with only one mental health professional (or very few) present as a consultant. This intervention mode also appears extensively in war-torn regions because traditional therapy is an intervention unfamiliar to children, and most of them are more comfortable exploring psychological issues through familiar play and the expressive arts. In essence, any intervention involving play and the arts is therapeutic in that it provides a supportive, structured, and supervised environment for self-exploration and the processing of emotions and thoughts in a variety of ways. The arts as an expressive medium aptly engage affective, cognitive, and perceptual capacities and allow children to use their own pace in the push and pull between the senses and cognition, between catharsis and control, and between free and structured activity. Beyond providing an avenue for children and adolescents to indirectly express their feelings and thoughts about their war experiences, art and play activities unmistakably involve generic recovery processes that overlap with established trauma-related interventions. Such are gradual exposure, desensitization, cognitive restructuring, re-

framing, and distraction. Via repetition of actions, thoughts, and emotions, the children experience and thus may gain increased tolerance and a sense of mastery. The processes involved also provide a psychological space that enables children to self-examine issues related to identity, relationships, and hope and to identify strengths and assets in the self for engaging in self-healing. When utilized as a doing-and-sharing process, the art and play activities also promote feelings of common bonds and thus enhance the discovery of safety within a group of peers. Children who find it difficult to engage in art activities can be activated in other ways in art projects, such as physically arranging for and creating exhibition space for the artwork of others.

Large-scope play and art activities are especially advantageous in a multicultural setting because they serve as a common language that is basic to all children, overcoming diversity in culture, language, and ethnic background. In addition to the work conducted directly with children, training workshops should target local mental health-related professionals and semiprofessionals, artists, educational staff, and selected volunteers to become qualified to participate in these projects. These training workshops aim to activate local persons and enable them to partake fully in the project, thus ensuring that the direct work with children continues after the mental health professionals leave.

A detailed illustration of this is a project targeting school-age children who suffered traumatic experiences during the war in Kosovo, where schoolteachers underwent training as "mental health promoters" to conduct a comprehensive intervention independently (Simo-Algado, Mehta, Kronenberg, Cockburn, & Kirsh, 2002). This project was based on a community-centered approach (i.e., focusing on the inner potential possessed by communities), a transcultural approach (i.e., reflecting the values and traditions of the culture), and a holistic approach (i.e., incorporating the physical, social, psychological, and spiritual dimensions). Each structured session began with Kosovarian poems and songs (integrating cultural aspects), continued with an indoor or outdoor game, and then moved to an activity such as painting with a free theme. Play included fun activities that, based on play theory (Morrison, Metzger, & Pratt, 1996), were considered therapeutic. Initial discussions focused on helping children identify different feelings. The children gave their artwork a title or a theme and described what they had created, why they chose it, and what they had felt while creating their product. Puppet play helped teach children to realize the importance of discussing emotions. Play activities aimed to provide support, promote insight, and facilitate ventilation of feelings, positive experiences, and success in activities. Most of all, play served as a powerful tool for "the children's return from a land of war to a land of children" (Simo-Algado et al., 2002, p. 205). Children's drawings, performances, and free play evolved from darker themes to more positive thoughts. The fun activities were also reported to be the best moments to observe the children's nonverbal behavior, which allowed teachers to identify children in need of individual attention.

In certain war situations, it may be possible to engage children in art activity while the war is still on, as in Israel during the 1991 Gulf War. Decorating gas mask boxes (which children had to carry with them at all times) became a popular activity with children and adolescents of all ages. Besides the advantage of furnishing creative activity (as previously discussed), the decorations helped disguise the frightening contents, including an atropine injection against nerve gas and powder for burns. Thus, this activity rendered the boxes less threatening and more personal. Also during the war, schools remained closed but Israeli museums remained open and offered unique art projects. Museum paintings were removed from the gallery walls and stored in underground shelters to prevent damage during the massive missile attacks. Large sheets of paper were hung on the empty wall space, and schoolchildren were invited to paint murals and pictures of their perceptions and views of the war. One such project involving children who were evacuated from their destroyed homes served primarily a therapeutic purpose. It consisted of four stages. First, the room was covered with visual images from newspapers. The children were asked to draw their personal stories in comic-strip style with a fine black pen. Pen and ink were used in the second stage and water colors in the third stage. The final result appeared on a large piece of white painted plywood. Many creations depicted destroyed houses and missiles. Interestingly, some of the missiles were drawn to appear floppy instead of straight, perhaps indicating the children's desire to neutralize them. The wish to diminish the power of the missiles also manifested itself in the size of the houses, which towered over the missiles (Shilo-Cohen, 1993).

Nature-assisted projects constitute another way to help children cope in wartime as well in the postwar recovery period. In the former Yugoslavia, children were organized into garden clubs that engaged in planting and finding ways to protect their plants from damage during enemy attacks (Berk, 1998). The therapeutic value in such programs lies in providing children of war with life-renewing energy by promoting active coping, creativity, caring, and a future-oriented outlook.

Nature-assisted support programs are yet another innovative intervention when employed for enhancing children's recovery. Such an intervention can be a nature-oriented program in itself or just one activity within a wider spectrum of activities. Pardess (2002) conducted such an intervention with Israeli children who experienced traumatic loss as a result of ongoing terrorist attacks. Some children had lost several close family members in one attack. This nature-oriented intervention program incorporated verbal and nonverbal techniques such as movement therapy, storytelling, creative art projects, and pet therapy. Its focus was on a multisensory nature hike combined with discussion group sessions led by an expert botanist and supervised by a mental health professional. The hike centered on the process of regeneration and rebuilding following a forest fire or other natural disaster. This activity evoked strong responses among the children and facilitated a discussion about survival. It was followed by an art session entitled "Telling the Story of the Hurt Tree." The children drew and told the story of the recovering tree, thus acknowledging their own loss and considering a personal narrative that may be shared with others (Klingman & Cohen, 2004).

In another *combined action and art activities* program (St. Thomas & Johnson, 2001), refugee children took a nature hike to a large waterfall. They were encouraged to observe the natural world and to gather any natural objects that reminded them of their own strength or ability. These authors also reported that an outing coupled with drawing, journal writing, fishing, guided imagery, playing games, and dramatic play opened the door for personal stories and grief.

Enhancement of Coping and Resiliency in Generic Terms

Many difficulties associated with war loom large and complicated for children. From a generic frame of reference, one of the most effective coping strategies in managing the stress of war involves *breaking down major problems into more manageable subcomponents* (Hobfoll et al., 1991). This may enable more effective coping and the experience of more positive outcomes. Even very small gains lead to a greater sense of mastery and control over the environment. This, in turn, helps individuals to feel and become more effective (Bandura, 1982; Meichenbaum, 1985) and move away from their victim role. Interventionists should thus assist children in disentangling the jumbled aspects of their situation. From the generic frame of reference, this involves setting up small, accomplishable tasks and goals, where the child is rewarded for small successes.

Also, children should receive encouragement to engage in helping behaviors. By taking part in finding solutions for their own family, their peers, and their community, children and adolescents can develop an enhanced sense of mastery and control over their lives and cope more effectively with stressful war events (Hobfoll et al., 1991). For example, during the anticipatory training to use gas masks and other protective equipment against unconventional weapons immediately prior to the 1991 Gulf War, trainers conveyed to the Israeli children the expectation that they should help train younger siblings and older persons in the household and should also help them don the masks properly in real time. This anticipatory guidance intervention was school-based and included all students nationwide. Many schoolchildren were reported to have been very helpful in these roles during the war. Indeed, by becoming involved in problem solving and a part of the solution to others' problems, children can move out of their victim role and enter a mastery role (Klingman & Cohen, 2004).

Experience with war-related generic interventions for children, parents, and teachers attests to the benefit inherent in a broad-spectrum group intervention, especially in the *multimodal coping and resiliency intervention* approach implemented in Israel and in the former Yugoslavia (Klingman & Cohen, 2004; Krkeljic & Pavlicic, 1998; Lahad, Shacham, & Niv, 2000). This approach borrowed from Lazarus's (1997) multimodal psychotherapy, which focused on seven core modalities summed up as the acronym BASIC ID (behavior, affect, sensation, imagery, cognition, interpersonal, and drugs). One such model's modification in terms of generic coping enhancement and resiliency (Lahad et al., 2000) proposed an organization around six BASIC Ph modalities (beliefs, affect, social, imagination, cognition, and physiology). Klingman and Cohen (2004) suggested intervention with parents around eleven integrative components, BASICS PhD B-ORN (beliefs, affects, sensations, imagination, cognitive abilities, social or interpersonal, physiology, drive, behavior-organization, reflective ability, and narrative

systems). The first eight of these parent coping resources (BASICS PhD) may be activated at the beginning, whereas the last three (behavior-organization, reflective, and narrative) require some time to activate.

Smith et al. (1999) developed a more structured and trauma-focused program for large-scale intervention that includes a manual for "Teaching Recovery Techniques." This psychosocial-educational program's five main sessions concentrate on helping children deal with the troubling symptoms of intrusion, arousal, and avoidance. The group facilitator takes children through various warm-up exercises and helps them adopt a problem-solving and group-sharing approach to the difficulty. With regard to intrusion, children learn distraction techniques and dual-attention techniques (similar to some eye movement desensitization and reprocessing [EMDR] techniques). To reduce arousal, children learn to identify their reactions and then to relax at will. With respect to avoidance, children practice imaginal exposure followed by self-reinforcement. Above all, children are encouraged to look to the future rather than to the past. A single session with parents to explain the intervention and give them suggestions on helping their children constitutes an essential element in this package (Yule, 2002). As with the BASIC Ph, this program design permits delivery by persons who possess a minimum of mental health intervention experience, but who receive training and supervision by someone with more mental health expertise. In general, these and similar interventions derive from established theoretical orientations and sound clinical experience; reports on their effectiveness indicate that they are suitable and useful. However, their specific effectiveness still awaits systematic evaluation.

Written generic crisis intervention guides, manuals, or kits for schools also appear helpful. They can serve as a blueprint for the school while organizing in preparation for war, as well as for teachers during war and in the postwar recovery process. Yule and Gold (1993) developed a booklet to help schools in the United Kingdom prepare for responding to crises. The booklet addresses such topics as reactions to major stress in young people, who is likely to be affected, and what the school can do in terms of short- and medium-term action and longer-term planning. This booklet, mailed to every school in the United Kingdom, received very positive feedback on its usefulness (Yule, 2002). Similarly, I developed a guidebook (Klingman, 1991) and an emergency kit (Klingman, 1997) to address Israeli school-based crisis intervention in mass trauma, as well as offering teacher-led classroom activities and tools. The structure and contents are described elsewhere (Klingman & Cohen, 2004, pp. 105–106). The guidebook stated that the activities presented are examples and that teachers are expected to come up with their own; schools should also examine what is best for their individual setting in the specific crisis situation at hand. The Israeli Ministry of Education distributed the guidebook and the kit to all school psychology services and to every school in Israel. The kit was extensively used in schools located in war zones (especially in the occupied territories), which provided highly positive feedback on the materials' helpfulness. In examining the guidebook's usefulness about a year after its distribution, I sent a questionnaire to a sample of 280 school counselors in war-affected areas. From the 227 questionnaires returned, 98% of the counselors reported that the guidebook had been used in their schools, 72% reported that they independently added tools and content from other sources, and 47% reported "creating" (at least two) new tools based on the guidebook's suggestions and tool samples and using them with or instead of the tools offered in the guide. Such guides, manuals, and kits, based on sound clinical experience and the generic approach, do indeed appear useful, whether used as is or employed as a stimulus to select or create school-specific tools. One of their advantages is their package format that can be implemented by paraprofessionals and adults with a minimal level of mental health background and experience. Their cost-effectiveness in reaching a vast child population affected by war should also be noted. Despite these guidebooks' reported usefulness, future systematic evaluation must examine their specific effectiveness.

The School as a Focal Point for Generic Intervention

Many *generic measures can be successfully carried out by schoolteachers* (Klingman & Cohen, 2004). The schoolteacher is placed in a number of significant roles in times of mass trauma, beyond his or her traditional role as an expert in instruction (see Wolmer, Laor, & Yazgan, 2003). The teacher in wartime and its aftermath may actually serve as a "clinical mediator." Although teachers may initially be reluctant to assume such a role, our repeated experience in war-torn zones attests that with appropriate and relatively brief training, teachers can successfully employ active listening and can act as role models who encourage, inspire, and facilitate con-

structive coping with the children. Teachers are valuable in helping children apply coping skills to their everyday life and to new concerns and conflicts as they arise. The teacher also has numerous opportunities to closely observe and follow up students in their natural setting. Practical considerations (e.g., limited resources, shortage of mental health professionals, cost-effectiveness, and the reluctance of victims to seek professional help) and conceptual considerations (e.g., nonstigmatizing approach, "normalization" of stress, empowerment, positive psychology) mandate that intervention efforts should involve as many children as possible by working with them in groups in their natural setting. Local teachers are the most familiar with local traditions and are able to integrate or add them to any generic intervention program. My experience has shown that when schools follow the generic approach and the unifying continuity principle, they become a sort of *therapeutic milieu* and a valuable *focal point for mass (multisystemic) intervention*. The cooperative efforts of the school organization, homeroom teachers, parents, and community (especially welfare and mental health) agencies can proactively create a "protective shield," accentuating empowerment, resiliency, strengths, growth, and a positive outlook in coping with the war's adverse events.

Helping the Helpers

Naturally, most efforts must be invested in the plight of the directly war-affected children. However, a lesson learned from recent wars revealed the vast importance of helping mental health interventionists when they are helping others, especially children. Compassion fatigue (Figley, 1995) poses a major risk for vicarious or secondary traumatization among interventionists in war-torn regions. In many war zones, mental health providers have shared the war experience or the same traumatizing circumstances as the treated population (e.g., a "near miss"). Some professionals may have been exposed to morbid experiences themselves; others may continue to be worried about the recovery of their own children and other family members; and for others, seeing and hearing about the adversities (especially those the children went through) takes its psychological toll. Interventionists often feel overwhelmed by the scope of the recovery task ahead. They may not have immediate relevant answers to many of their clients' needs. Shortage of professionals often results in overwork; the combination of work overload, high commitment, and emotional exhaustion leads to quick burnout. Although the adoption of the generic approach and principles and the unifying continuity principle serve well as a partial solution to this problem, for many professionals this approach entails a shift in professional orientation as well as roles, especially for those who were not previously involved in intervening in mass trauma. Thus, "helping the helper" interventions must become an integral part of any mass war-related intervention with children.

In this regard, *group psychological debriefing* may furnish a suitable tool. Debriefing originally evolved to assist emergency personnel in adjusting to their emotional reactions to events encountered in the course of rescue work (Mitchell & Everly, 1997). Psychological debriefing usually underscores ventilation of feelings, experiential reviewing, and emotional sharing in small groups. Commonly employed helping-the-helper interventions in many war-related specific circumstances in Israel include supportive listening and debriefing-focused methods, especially those focusing on catharsis and attempting to direct participants' attention to internal affects and thought processes through insight-oriented methods. Gal (1998) reported an extensive program for mental health professionals in the former Yugoslavia that involved training in various trauma-relief issues, along with debriefing sessions that dealt with the helpers' stresses and burnout.

However, experience shows that what is needed in wartime and in the immediate postwar circumstances often goes beyond emotional intervention. Professionals also need longer-term *practical support* for handling the enormous tasks at hand. To empower interventionists to cope more effectively with their role-related issues and professional dilemmas, they often need to arrive at practical solutions. This support addresses situation-specific instrumental and personal coping resources as well as effective strategies and techniques for mass intervention. For example, a war-related helping-the-helpers program with school counselors utilized solution-focused methods following a structured brief version of process debriefing (Klingman, 2002b). This intervention was based on a structured group process and directive-active group leadership roles, assigning great responsibility to the group leader(s) to proactively establish a climate favorable for short-term group processes. The debriefing part of the intervention consisted of an introductory lecture; limited in vitro exposure, involving precise labeling for feelings and thoughts to allow limited ventilation of feelings but also to indicate the role of cognitive processing of the affective responses; sharing personal coping, in-

cluding past and present strategies and skills; discussing role-related problems, including clarifying role definitions; and a focus on the positive lessons learned.

The *solution-focused orientation* of this intervention aimed to move quickly onward to focusing on participants' resilience and shifting their attention outward and toward other people and external practical tasks. Purposeful questioning and other techniques helped professionals gain a more realistic sense of what was feasible in the given adverse situation. Dealing with situation-specific practical goals and participants' expectations proved very helpful for setting more modest and manageable goals and expectations for themselves and their clientele. The intervention included discussion of alternative solutions suggested by the participants. This promoted active engagement and a mood of expectation regarding desirable outcomes, and, not least important, it enabled participants to see that no immediate dramatic actions on their part were required, whereas some small steps could be taken effectively. Overall, this solution-focused guidance, rather than a counseling or therapeutic approach, emphasized a gradual but relatively swift shift from "problem talk" to "solution talk," concentrating on strengths and inner resources. A solution-focused approach derives flexibly from several models of social and individual psychology and borrows various techniques from other therapeutic approaches, yet retains its own theoretical integrity.

Another reported intervention adopting the narrative approach (and in part matching the solution-focused approach) was employed extensively with Israeli school psychologists and counselors in areas affected by frequent massive terror attacks (e.g., Shalif & Leibler, 2002). This intervention addressed coping abilities, exceptions to the negative influences of the terror attacks, and meaning giving. It focused on "reauthoring" the talk about the traumatic events, exploring different possible meanings of the traumatic events, and adopting the most validating and empowering ones. Specifically (and in line with some of the solution-focused guidance approach), it included externalizing conversations to create a "reflective distance," mapping the effects of the problem (i.e., discovering areas and spaces where the problem/difficulty has less influence and where greater opportunities of counteracting these influences exist), and finding the exceptions and unique outcomes (i.e., areas in which the problem or difficulty did not take over, against all odds: experiences that instead strengthened or "organized" the person, the community, and society). This specific intervention demonstrated to the participants how attention to language and the power of ideology, religion, and community support could play a central role in deconstructing the negative meaning of "trauma" and in supporting the potential for growth.

INDICATED INDIVIDUAL AND SMALL-GROUP SYMPTOM-FOCUSED INTERVENTIONS FOR POSTTRAUMATIC STRESS DISORDER

Above all, the scope of war's effects on children, and the difficulties involved in reaching out to so many war-affected children, necessitate the adoption of large-scale, generic, community-focused, and preferably school-based intervention. As described earlier, conceptually, the war-affected children, their parents, and their natural community and culture do possess mechanisms for natural recovery. Therefore, an emphasis on community-focused preventive intervention in trauma work is preferable to an emphasis on the reduction of symptoms. Thus, this chapter has heretofore called for an alternative flexible, continuous, health-oriented, generic approach, which addresses various needs at different phases of coping with traumatic war experiences. However, there are exceptions. Some children's symptoms do not remit, but even worsen to fit a clinical diagnosis of PTSD or other trauma-related disorders such as anxiety or depressive disorders. Some children experience the intensification of preexisting problems or evidence delayed posttraumatic responses. For others, extensive war-specific fears may put them in immediate danger, affecting their safety. Children whose problems persist despite the generic intervention efforts will benefit from indicated interventions, which focus less on the generic approach and more on the unique needs and problems of individuals, through individual or small-group counseling or therapy.

War-related symptoms in children may develop around specific war-related fears; such fears, which are based on reality, may become generalized or elicit more fears. Although children are rarely treated in the midst of a war, and almost no reports appear in the literature on individual child treatment at the impact stage of a war, such cases can often be successfully treated with short-term intervention for specific fears.

For example, a *fear-focused intervention* during the impact stage of the 1991 Gulf War targeted a 5-year-old Israeli boy who refused to put on his gas mask during air raids (Klingman, 1992). Here, a short-term, family-mediated, cognitive-behavioral intervention was the method of choice. At intake, the parents' interview centered first on ventilation of their anxiety due to the urgency of the situation: the very high probability of chemical or bacteriological missile warheads and their concern for their son's safety. This was followed by an analysis of the child's behavior (noncompliance, angry tantrums), discussion of the relevance of behavioral principles for compliance, and development of a contract agreement. The parents received step-by-step instructions in recording their child's behavior for the baseline and control phases and in using at-home story reading bibliotherapy, play, and cognitive-behavioral prompts on the target behaviors. They received a specifically designed story and coloring booklet for their child. This booklet depicts a family preparing for and actively coping with the ordeal of the war (e.g., missiles, chemical warfare, confinement in a sealed room, problems with gas masks, anxieties). The story centers on a child's teddy bear, who is very "confused" and "afraid," and for whom a gas mask is made. The boy in the story deals with his teddy bear's noncompliance and anxiety. The story also focuses on looking beyond the ordeal, such as the funny and positive aspects in the present situation (e.g., "My parents look so funny in this mask"; the family's intense experience of togetherness) and a positive future/optimism (e.g., going back to kindergarten when the war is over, and the reunion scene in the kindergarten). The parents received instruction on how to respond to their child's noncompliance by agreeing about the difficulty but not implying that there was any choice about it, by responding with "That's just the way things are," for example. They were told how to praise him with "you" compliments (e.g., "You must be proud of yourself") rather than with "I" compliments (e.g., "I am proud of you") to encourage his self-esteem and confidence. Story sharing, coloring, and playing created psychological space and a relaxed atmosphere.

The results of this intervention, based on a single-case research design (Klingman, 1992), supported the application of the combined procedure. This intervention represents the successful use of a relatively short parent-implemented, home-managed, crisis intervention in the midst of a war, utilizing a combination of contact desensitization and cognitive-behavioral prompts via behavioral guidance to parents, the use of a bibliotherapy-based psychoeducational play method with the child, conveying to the child an expectation of recovery and behavior change, and reinforcing the desired behavior change. The need for professional contact with the child was replaced by training the parents both to assess and to intervene. The professional served as a change agent providing psychological support, training, and some corrective feedback in the course of a 3-day time span. This example demonstrates that in certain cases, when war conditions allow, reactions that center on war-related fears can be treated in the midst of a war using a short-term, problem-focused, or solution-focused intervention. A major component of such interventions concerns conveying the clear message to children that they can overcome the specific difficulty and do what must be done (which may involve suggesting specific alternatives to the child). In addition to the practical advantage in having the parent(s) as the clinical mediators in real time during an ongoing war emergency, most important was the parents' involvement in the treatment. Parents' involvement helps prevent them from projecting their own concerns and anxieties onto the child around his or her difficulty. For example, in war situations, parents may especially tend to shield the child rather than prompt and reinforce independence or self-care behaviors. Such behavior might unintentionally preserve or even enhance the child's sense of helplessness, and in some cases encourage secondary gains that can become predominant in the child's behavioral repertoire.

Interventionists have successfully utilized *play therapy* with children who have been traumatized (Bevin, 1999; Gil, 1991; James, 1989; Pynoos & Eth, 1985; Terr, 1983). Bevin reported on rather extensive use of reconstructive play in a therapy for a 9-year-old Nicaraguan boy a few months after arriving in the United States, representing the typical experience of many children from war-torn countries who enter the United States. The boy, who survived the traumatic experience of illegally crossing a border and watching his mother being raped, received a diagnosis of suffering from symptoms consistent with PTSD. The main treatment goals were to increase his speech production and social interaction and to improve his mood, while decreasing his panic-like reactions, passivity, and tendency to worry excessively. He was treated individually for 1 hour twice a week at school, and the therapist visited his home one evening a week to allow his parents to participate in family sessions as cosurvivors of the trauma. After several initial sessions that included talking, storytelling, drawing, and playing guessing games, more directive

play therapy sessions began. Every session started with a period of relaxation. Through manipulation of dolls, the boy could subconsciously identify his own maladaptive coping techniques and thus be helped to conceptualize the aftereffects of his trauma at some level and to recognize his posttraumatic behaviors and feelings. It was impossible (as it is in many cases) to identify one factor that was critical in the management of this case. Whereas the play reenactment evidently helped turn passivity into activity and provided an outlet for his frustration and anger, overall the therapist attributed the positive outcomes to a combination of the treatment approach and the methods used. In this case, the nine-session directive play therapy was integrated into a longer-term intervention. Also, the involvement of the parents in therapy, their willingness to work with their child, their high level of cooperation with the therapist, and their ability to face their own (trauma-related) difficulties and anger were of primary importance to their child's recovery. The introduction of toy replicas representing aspects of the traumatic event and the therapist's active though sensitive encouragement of the child to process a set of sights and emotions can expedite the child's resolution of difficult aspects of the traumatic experience (Nader, 2002).

In contrast to directive play therapy, some therapists (e.g., Ryan & Needham, 2001) support a nondirective approach to play therapy with traumatized children. They argue that nondirective models avoid direct confrontation with the trauma itself and thus minimize the risk of strong negative reactions in children with PTSD.

Several forms of therapy for posttraumatic response and for PTSD *conform to the continuity principle.* Apparently, at least in war situations, psychotherapists intuitively choose to work with this principle in mind regardless of their formal, preferred, habitual therapeutic approach (Alon & Levine Bar-Yoseph, 1994). Alon and Levine Bar-Yoseph reported an intervention with children that followed the unifying continuity principle. This 10-session case study dealt with an Israeli family whose apartment block had been targeted in a terrorist attack, resulting in several deaths and injuries. All family members narrowly escaped but could not find one another during the event. Although at first they responded well, a financial crisis unrelated to the trauma brought about full-fledged PTSD in all of them. The two sons, ages 6 and 9, were treated at home, and the parents were asked to serve as cotherapists and coaches for the children between sessions, thus fostering vicarious learning as well as the resumption of habitual roles.

First, a debriefing session asked each member to recount his or her actions during and after the assault. A combined picture, depicted in diagrams and broadened as a result of the therapist's questions to include thoughts and emotions, revealed everyone's resourcefulness and delighted all, especially the proud parents. Then, freedom of movement at home was reestablished by conjointly making a hierarchy of fear of the various apartment rooms, from most horrible and therefore not to be tackled before the following week's session, to the most bearable. The children were trained to move from the "panicking room" to their parents' safe room while singing a "Song of Fear," a humorously lamenting, wailing song improvised by the therapist. In the following weeks, family members learned self-relaxation. Next, they underwent desensitization to the place in the house where they had encountered the terrorists; this involved playing ball near the site in such a way that the children would spontaneously run after it when it dropped. Reestablishing and reinforcing family routine and cohesion was achieved by starting each session with a joint family-and-therapist lunch under the pretext that the therapist came from a distant city and needed some refreshment. Discussions with the parents about children, about trauma and its implications, and about the parents' image in the children's eyes all served as an indirect suggestive intervention for the parents. A 2-year follow-up showed satisfactory adjustment.

In sum, the following points deserve note: This intervention taught children self-hypnosis for relaxation and better sleep and provided desensitization to places in the house where they had met the terrorists; the continuity principle was applied throughout the intervention; indirect discussions about the children, about trauma, and about its implications all served as indirect suggestive therapy for the parents; and by asking the parents to serve as cotherapists and coaches for the children between sessions, the therapist fostered not only vicarious learning but also the resumption of habitual roles.

To date, little evidence has shown that drug treatments have a central role in the treatment of children; therefore, cognitive-behavioral treatments have constituted the main interventions aiming to help child survivors make sense of what they experienced, promote emotional processing, and master their feelings of anxiety and helplessness. The problem for the therapist lies in finding the optimal means to help children reexperi-

ence the traumatic event and the emotions it engenders in such a way that the distress can be mastered rather than magnified (Yule, 2002). One means, exposure under supportive circumstances, has been reported as helping children deal well with both intrusive thoughts and behavioral avoidance.

Single-case studies with children's war-related posttrauma symptomatology reported the general efficacy of *in vitro flooding*. This method was employed in treating Lebanese children individually some time after the traumatic incident (Saigh, 1987a, 1987b, 2000). In one case (Saigh, 1986), a 14-year-old male who was abducted and held by militia for 48 hours was referred for evaluation by his school principal 6 months after the abduction. The complaints involved symptoms that were not evident before the trauma: anxiety-evoking recollections of the trauma, abduction-related avoidance behaviors, depression, temper outbursts, and difficulties concentrating and recalling information. Saigh chose in vitro flooding based on the suggestion that it involves fewer treatment sessions than systematic desensitization and that earlier attempts to treat cases of PTSD through systematic sensitization were unsuccessful. The treatment identified four anxiety-evoking scenes involving the chronological sequence of events of the traumatic abduction, and then stimulus-response imagery cues were presented across scenes. A single-case design analysis revealed that this treatment had a positive influence on the client's affective, behavioral, and cognitive outcome measures. The treatment procedure involved therapist-directed relaxation exercises. Other cases reported by Saigh (1987a, 1987b) revealed positive changes using in vitro flooding to treat a 6-year-old boy 25 months after being exposed to a bomb blast, two 11-year-old girls (one who witnessed two pedestrians die during a shelling incident and the other who witnessed the shooting to death of a man by a sniper), and a 12-year-old boy whose home had been partially destroyed during a shelling incident. The overall results suggest that the in vitro flooding package had a palliative influence on the children's affective, behavioral, and cognitive parameters, and these improvements occurred after 8 to 15 treatment sessions.

Criticism of in vitro flooding with children has focused on the risks elicited by the exposure component. Persistent talking about traumatic events to children who are embarrassed or highly resistant may in fact worsen symptoms. Exposure may be counterproductive when excessively gruesome details that evoke strong emotions leave children in a heightened state of arousal, thus sensitizing them rather than helping to habituate anxiety. Younger children in particular may be unable to imagine certain traumatic material, tolerate exposure, or follow relaxation procedures. Avoidant children may resist carrying out instructions to confront the avoided thoughts and images. However, dealing with traumatic issues indirectly through the use of art (e.g., drama, play) may be helpful in such cases. Asking children to draw their experience often assists recall of both the event and the associated emotions, thus employing drawings not as projective techniques but as ways of facilitating talk about the experience. Also, treatment with children is not usually limited to exposure per se: Participants generally receive a multifaceted treatment package that includes parent-child education regarding PTSD, education regarding the flooding process, relaxation training, prolonged imaginal exposure, and debriefing (American Academy of Child and Adolescent Psychiatry, 1998; Klingman & Cohen, 2004; Saigh, 2000; Saigh, Yule, & Inamdar, 1996).

Ronen (1996b) reported a war-related short-term, group-based intervention based on *self-guided, self-control exposure therapy* to treat 8- to 11-year-old Israeli children 4 to 6 weeks following the end of the 1991 Gulf War. All children exhibited anxiety reactions as an outcome of the war and features of preexisting separation anxiety disorders that continued or intensified throughout the war. The children and their parents attended one individualized intake session, two parent-child group intervention sessions, and one follow-up group session. The parents' active participation involved them and the child in constructing graphs together that plotted the improvement in the child's anxiety levels (before, during, and after each exposure assignment), reinforcement procedures for the child's achievements of reality-based predictions, and completion of exposure assignments. A tendency emerged for children's decreased anxiety levels and increased calmness during exposure compared with other days, and the parents learned to compliment the child for small steps toward success every day, compared with the day before. As part of the exposure assignments, the children themselves were placed in charge of selecting the individual kinds of exposure tasks, degree of exposure, and length of exposure. Self-control methods for exposure were the use of imagination, self-reinforcement, commands to the brain, and self-compliments. Preliminary findings indicated that self-guided self-control exposure therapy conserves the

therapist's resources and facilitates rapid improvement in both postwar fears and prewar-initiated separation anxiety. Nonetheless, this intervention's success depended much on the parents' full cooperation.

With regard to PTSD in children, the treatment of children of war is often based on PTSD diagnostic criteria as presented in the *Diagnostic and Statistical Manual of Mental Disorders IV* (*DSM-IV;* American Psychiatric Association, 1994). The *DSM-IV* guidelines, however, tend to be "adult-o-centric" (Yule, 2001) and should be viewed as a work in progress with regard to children. For example, children do not usually experience the unexpected flashbacks that characterize adults' PTSD. Based on research findings, some researchers (e.g., Scheeringa & Zeanah, 2001; Terr, 1985) have suggested accommodations and changes in the use of PTSD criteria for children, especially under the age of 6 years. The suggested *child-specific trauma-related symptoms* that differ from those of adults include repetitive play (possibly a behavioral equivalent of the more cognitive intrusive thoughts and imagery of adults), regression (e.g., to babyish games, baby talk, bedwetting), and a sense of a foreshortened future as a predominant symptom in adolescents. Children, more than adults, may express their distress somatically and demonstrate self-blame. Other child-specific symptoms include restriction of social play, social withdrawal, restricted range of affect, loss of acquired developmental skills, new aggression, new separation anxiety, and new unrelated fears (Klingman & Cohen, 2004; L. Miller, 2003; Scheeringa & Zeanah, 2001).

An *expanded view of posttrauma adaptation and psychopathology* focuses more on the developmental implications and the successful progression of developmental processes of children under the influences of war trauma. It considers a range of psychological and socioenvironmental risk and protective factors related to the pretrauma, peritrauma, and posttrauma ecologies. Such a view targets those factors that cause continuous stress and the natural recovery processes rather than merely using the classificatory psychopathological approach and thus treating only the individual's symptoms (Klingmam & Cohen, 2004; Layne et al., 2001; Saltzman, Pynoos, Layne, Steinberg, & Aisenberg, 2001; Saltzman, Steinberg, Layne, Aisenberg, & Pynoos, 2002; Shalev, 2002).

Along these lines, Ronen (2002) discussed in some detail the difficulties in assessing traumatic reactions in children and suggested guidelines for the assessment and treatment of traumatized children from a cognitive-constructivist frame of reference. She suggested that assessment should derive from PTSD criteria, the context of normal childhood behavior problems, and developmental considerations. Cognitive-constructivist treatment focuses on the child's developmentally linked powers of personal monitoring and meaning making, and on the child's awareness of the processes involved and their functions. Children learn to understand and accept traumatic events as part of life and to give these events new meaning, which can generate better coping and potential growth and maturation (Ronen, 1996a, 2002).

Close to this approach, several *psychosocial group programs* for the treatment of youth exposed to trauma and traumatic loss have been established and studied in recent years. These interventions usually targeted postdisaster stress symptoms (e.g., Chemtob, Nakashima, & Hamada, 2002; March, Amaya-Jackson, Murray, & Schulte, 1998; Saltzman et al., 2002). Although these programs have not yet been specifically developed in the context of war-related events, their structure and techniques lend themselves readily to such use. March et al.'s program emerged as safe, effective, and durable in alleviating PTSD symptoms (as well as depression and anxiety) among 10- to 15-year-olds who evinced a primary, full PTSD diagnosis and who had each individually suffered a single traumatic incident. The intervention consisted of a school-based, group-administered, 8-week, cognitive-behavioral intervention protocol. The design derived from a theoretical model integrating the social and biological foundations of PTSD with social learning theory, conditioning theory, and cognitive information processing. It included anxiety reduction using relaxation training, skills for coping with disturbing affects and physiological sensations, anger control, and positive self-talk.

Another program, the UCLA Trauma Psychiatry Program, was implemented in postwar Bosnia (Layne et al., 2001). This 16- to 20-week intervention comprised trauma- and grief-focused group psychotherapy. Its main foci were the traumatic experience, trauma and loss reminders, secondary adversities, grief, and developmental impact. Unique to this program was its focus on identifying adolescents' missed developmental opportunities and their current difficulties in functioning, and in initiating more desirable developmental progression and prosocial adjustment. Whereas March et al.'s (1998) program did not include the parents, the UCLA program included family therapy. Both these programs seem optimally suitable for the treatment of adolescents.

By contrast, Chemtob and his colleagues (2002) developed a four-session, individual or group integrative psychosocial intervention for postdisaster trauma symptoms in elementary schoolchildren. This program included a standard box of play and art materials and incorporated experiential activities designed to elicit reflections relevant to each session. The interventionists reported the program's effectiveness in reducing disaster-related symptoms in children 2 years after a hurricane disaster. Interestingly, although the group and individual treatments did not differ in efficacy, fewer children dropped out of the group treatment.

Considering that political violence may also affect children indirectly through its impact on their mother's health and well-being (K. Miller, 1996), the best and sometimes the only way to reach out to traumatized children during wartime conditions may be to *help parents in groups* to overcome their anxieties. Thus, parents can develop better situation-specific functioning in the family environment conducive to the recovery of their children. At the same time, this treatment mode addresses the practical limitations of treating massive groups in need with the shortage of mental health professionals available. For example, preschool children who had lost their Iranian soldier father were found to be best helped through supporting their mother to overcome her grief and help her provide a well-functioning home environment (Kalantari, Yule, & Gardner, 1993).

Dybdahl (2001) developed a manualized psychosocial support intervention program consisting of semistructured group discussion meetings designed to help war-exposed mothers with their own psychological problems as well as those of their children, and to facilitate improved mother-child interactions. All participants were victims of the war in Bosnia and Herzegovina, through both war activities and having to flee their home to seek refuge in another part of the region. The psychoeducational approach included provision of information about trauma and trauma reactions in adults and children, as well as suggestions on how to meet common posttraumatic needs and problems. Emphasis was placed on strengthening the participants' own coping, but the group did not receive traditional therapy. The groups reinforced basic communication and interaction skills that already existed. Mothers shared their experiences about the topics discussed, their feelings, and their coping strategies, and also discussed suggestions raised by the group leader. Although the effects of this intervention program on children's symptom reduction and increase in positive characteristics were modest, they coincided with the results envisaged for this type of program. Furthermore, the effects of the intervention were notable relative to the program's simplicity, low expense, and duration (weekly group meetings for 5 months).

As most of the reviewed cases demonstrate, treatment of children during wartime and in war-torn zones should focus particularly on active parent involvement. Furthermore, in many cases, parents are called on to participate actively as cotherapists or even to assume the role of interventionist (clinical mediator), with the professional therapist as a consultant. Such cases involve short but extensive situation- and child-focused parent training.

A review of the available controlled treatment outcome studies for PTSD in children in general does not establish the clear advantage of one treatment over another. Existing data substantiate the need for comprehensive, broad-spectrum, multimodal, and multidimensional treatments of children suffering from PTSD and other trauma-related disorders (American Academy of Child and Adolescent Psychiatry, 1998; Woodcock, 2000). Indeed, several empirically sound studies revealed that cognitive-behavioral therapeutic components proved most effective in treating war-traumatized children. However, results in all these reported cases were obtained through the application of a multicomponent treatment package (i.e., including education, relaxation, and self-monitoring), thus precluding the attribution of success to one sole component (e.g., in vitro flooding) within the overall package (Saigh, 2000). Also, except for one case (Klingman, 1992), the children and their parents were not in any immediate danger due to a state of war at the time of treatment, nor were the activities involved in treatment (e.g., behavioral walks) dangerous.

OPEN QUESTIONS AND CONCLUDING REMARKS

The literature review at the beginning of this chapter surveyed the impact of war on children and their psychological responses to it. Clearly, many of the reviewed topics underwent careful observation but lack sound systematic research data. As one illustration of this gap, the psychological aspects of young people's physical recovery processes have not been directly addressed in the literature, nor are developmentally focused controlled studies available, despite the large number of young

people injured during war. Clinicians emphasize that adolescents, in particular, may be traumatized by their wounds because, for them, the smallest bodily imperfection is of enormous significance (Bronfman, Campis, & Koocher, 1998; Green & Kocijan-Hercigonja, 1998). Plausibly, even minor wounds may pose considerable risk for posttraumatic difficulties and perhaps disorders in children and adolescents. In addition to processing traumatic war experiences and perhaps the loss of significant others, these children possibly have to deal with loss of personal control, injured self-image, dependency, stigma, isolation, anger, intense emotionality, and fears of death or of the future. Moreover, the injured parts of the body may act as a constant reminder of the trauma, further interfering with the processing and resolution of traumatic experiences. Also, as in the case of the combination of trauma and bereavement (see Klingman & Cohen, 2004, for details on this high-risk combination), unsuccessful attempts at processing the traumatic injury may easily complicate the psychological recovery from injury. Despite some clinical testimony and the clinical speculation concerning these issues, at this point in time we must rely mostly on limited clinical observations of nonwar cases, such as the detailed clinical issues for acutely injured and medically traumatized children described by Bronfman et al. (1998). Research is needed in this area, considering that wounded children must be helped with their difficulties in psychological processing of the war-related injurious event. This problem holds true, of course, for many, indeed most, of the other topics presented in the beginning of this chapter.

Obviously, developmental differences in posttraumatic symptom expression require thorough future study, especially with respect to younger children. Some of the *DSM-IV*'s PTSD items (American Psychiatric Association, 1994) require verbal descriptions of experiences and internal states, which are beyond the capacity of infants, toddlers, and even some older children. Indeed, an expanded checklist of behaviorally based, developmentally sensitive symptoms is now available (e.g., Scheeringa & Zeanah, 2001); however, much more remains to be done to facilitate better diagnosis of war trauma in younger children.

PTSD should not be the only phenomenon to concern interventionists. Posttraumatic stress reactions, rather than disorder symptoms, persist in children and adolescents, although their intensity somewhat diminishes over time. Yet, wartime events continue to influence children, potentially affecting their development of personality, moral values, and outlook on life. The psychological impact of war is not over when the fighting ceases (Dyregrov, Gjestad, & Raundalen, 2000; Dyregrov, Gupta, et al., 2000). More research would do well to address obstacles hindering developmental progression and transitions. Researchers working in the attachment theory paradigm (e.g., Wright et al., 1997) should focus and further highlight the long-term effects of war on children's development. Child assessment must consider children's progress in the ability to relate to war and war events without excessive avoidance and distress, as well as advances in children's resumption of "ordinary" life and ability to invest in and enjoy age-appropriate activities (Klingman & Cohen, 2004).

Considering the growing capacity of the mass media (e.g., Internet, television, third-generation cellular phones) to reach out to populations at war concerning mental health, the psychologist's role in the public domain deserves reconsideration. I have stressed here and elsewhere (e.g., Klingman, 2002a, 2002c; Klingman & Cohen, 2004) that resources like the media, the Internet, and the telephone have proved useful as large-scale alternative support systems to reach a population during war, especially because they may be accessible to children and families who are housebound or limited in their ability to travel due to wartime circumstances. In this regard, prior to and during a war or war-related disaster, child psychologists are called on to counsel the public over radio, television, and the Internet, especially with regard to children's reactions and coping. On the one hand, this intervention meets the public's (especially parents') needs for information. On the other hand, the flood of psychological advice and especially the focus on fear, stress, trauma, anxiety, and PTSD-related symptoms may convey the message that the population cannot cope with difficulties on their own. Moreover, psychologists may concentrate excessively on anxiety and disorder-related symptoms, often overemphasizing the value of expression of the anxiety as a major means of coping with the ordeal. The emphasis on anxiety ventilation, more particularly the advice given to parents that they encourage their children to cry and voice their fears and anxieties, may in certain cases be problematic, or even counterproductive, when professional supervision is not readily available, if at all, which is typical in times of war. In their messages, psychologists often overlook the varied human response to stress, including the benefits in such mechanisms as partial denial, repression, avoidance, and isolation, which

are considered counterproductive signs of problems in the clinical setting but may well be functional for different people under different circumstances. In general, messages that are appropriate when addressed to patients in the privacy of the therapeutic setting may be inappropriate and even damaging to the nonpathological population reached through the media (Solomon, 1995). These criticisms are true especially for psychologists who have no experience with, or any background in, mass trauma intervention.

Another, perhaps more fundamental, criticism is that in times of war the task of the psychologist is also to encourage people to trust the local or national leadership, to use modes of overcoming fears, and to use active means of coping not only with their anxieties but with the external threat. Practical advice such as staying alert, keeping informed, and taking measures to promote personal and familial safety can be viewed as important wartime messages for psychologists (as consultants) to incorporate in their traditionally (clinically focused) mental health orientation.

Nor should mental health professionals ignore that the struggle with wartime hardships often leads to positive gains. Some children go beyond mere resiliency. In constructively confronting the traumatic experience, youngsters may also experience greater self-confidence, adopt new coping skills, and develop greater appreciation of life. This phenomenon of trauma-induced growth (Calhoun & Tedeschi, 1999) coincides with the positive psychology approach (Seligman, 2002). In my experience (for further discussion, see Klingman & Cohen, 2004), these and related issues must be discussed with psychologists who are to be involved with the media; an emphasis in the media on potentially strengthened relationships with others, increased closeness and intimacy, altruistic activities, and an augmented experience of oneself as capable and self-reliant should be upheld.

It is also imperative that programs aimed specifically at children, which operate through indirect means, be distinguished from programs geared to parents and teachers, who possess a greater capacity to make use of direct guidance and advice provided by psychologists and to apply them in helping children (Raviv, 1993). When times and circumstances allow, it may be wise to develop a special curriculum for training psychologists in counseling techniques and interventions through the media during war in general and with regard to specific war conditions; these psychologists must be trained for their appearance in the electronic media.

The possible overinvolvement of mental health professionals in the various media should be noted as well. One of the fiercest objections to this overrepresentation in Israel during the 1991 Gulf War was that this was a time for people who could offer moral support, not psychologists. The psychologists undoubtedly meant well, but they were criticized for weakening rather than strengthening the nation during that war. The question, though, should not be whether psychologists should be involved in the various media during war, but how often, to what extent, delivering which messages, and whether they have the proper training in mass disaster intervention. The public activities of well-meaning mental health professionals should be constantly checked and rechecked against their natural wish to help by relaying their prewar professional knowledge that may be inappropriate, or perhaps personal motivations such as the need to alleviate their own anxiety or the desire for self-promotion. (For an extensive discussion of these and related issues as observed in Israel during the 1991 Gulf War, see Solomon, 1995.) Systematic analysis of the amount and types of psychological messages transmitted to the public in war through the media is lacking. It is important to carefully address and further study the foregoing issues. Technology is progressing and the various media are available in ever larger parts of the world, so wars are likely to be accompanied by increasing intervention by mental health professionals through the media.

The role of intervention for recovery from war-related ills does not end with the cessation of hostile activities or with the signing of a formal peace treaty. In times of war, collective narratives play a major societal role, subsuming and determining attitudes, stereotypes, prejudices, and actions that emanate from them (Bar-Tal, Raviv, & Freund, 1994). When the war is over, *reconciliation* (the "art of making peace") between the warring groups entails adjusting their attitudes to one another. Volkan (1990) described the central role of projection mechanisms as a process of inner splitting that takes place in individuals and groups during intergroup conflict. The "good" splits from the "bad," and the rejected elements (e.g., meanness, hatred) are denied as parts of the self and ascribed to the "other" person, group, or nation. When steps toward peacemaking or reconciliation begin to be taken, these psychological mechanisms need to be addressed through psychoeducational programs targeting peace, reconciliation, and coexistence. Salomon (2004) suggested that such psychoeducational programs focus on reversing the de-

legitimization of the collective narrative, leading to the acceptance of the "other's" collective narrative as legitimate and thus addressing perceptions of and tolerance for collectives.

Peace education in most regions of intractable conflict entails elements of conflict resolution, multiculturalism, antiracism, cross-cultural training, and the cultivation of a general peace-oriented outlook. Such education efforts face a number of severe challenges, such as conflicting collective narratives, shared histories, and beliefs; grave inequalities; excessive emotionality; and unsupportive social climates (Bar-Tal, 2004; Salomon, 2004b). The underlying psychological principles and strategies and the educational methods of school-based conflict resolution for peer mediation (especially in multicultural school contexts; e.g., Johnson & Johnson, 1996) show some practical commonalities with the practice of peace education in regions of active political conflict and tension. However, these principles, strategies, and methods in themselves do not suit, or suffice in, regions that experience active political conflict, which necessitates a focus on a narrative-based view of coexistence education. At this point in time, despite the urgent need and the relatively large number of peace education projects operating all over the world, very little research or program evaluation accompanies such activities (Nevo & Brem, 2002). Hardly any information is available concerning their ultimate effectiveness. Although researchers are currently making a noted effort in this area, thus far, only scarce and unsatisfactory guidelines have emerged for psychological practice and peace educators seeking efficient data-based methods to establish reconciliation. This poses a new challenge for social and clinical psychologists as well as for educationalists.

Although much of the foregoing discussion (especially the case studies and conclusions) may be viewed as largely a product of research and experience from the industrialized or developed world (some specific to Israel), my observation of wars elsewhere indicates that the generic principles for large-scale, ecology-based support systems can undoubtedly be employed in international emergency situations in general. In contrast to the Western mental health approaches that focus on the individual, non-Western collectivist cultures focus on the family and the traditional group and therefore need culture-sensitive, community-based generic intervention. Variables such as sense of community, needs and preference for certain types of help, motivation, honor, and pride about getting help (especially psychological aid), political systems, leadership patterns, and political leaders' involvement are but a few of the variables affected by cultural differences. I assume that while following the generic approach and the unifying continuity principle, psychologists in other parts of the world and in different war contexts will engage in creatively translating the knowledge base and experiences presented and discussed in this chapter into their own culture-based war-focused or trauma-focused interventions. This actually holds generally true now, as we live in increasingly multicultural societies the world over.

In sum, from the literature, especially concerning PTSD, it is indeed evident that wars seriously challenge the coping systems of those affected and constitute a considerable and sometimes serious mental health risk to children. It is now generally acknowledged that a high proportion of war-exposed children develop mental health problems. Although mental health professionals have no control over the contextual features of war, we do have much to offer in creating a positive, culturally sensitive recovery environment. First and foremost, professionals should recognize that many war-affected children in need of psychological help can be helped *indirectly* by investment first in the reconstruction of their community institutions (schools, churches, recreational centers, community centers, and afterschool care). Next, consultation should be provided to primary caregivers such as the parents and teachers (the natural support system) and to the persons who operate and supervise these institutions, regarding the children's mental health needs. Psychologists, being experts in traditional clinical interventions, may overlook the other interventions at the community level that may be applied.

Another important message to be gleaned from this chapter is that more emphasis than currently exists should be placed on empowerment, positive coping, morale building, strengths, resilience, and growth. Professional observations, personal accounts, and some of the reviewed literature contend that individuals possess an impressive ability for creatively utilizing inner and outer resources in war and its aftermath to regain mastery over traumatic experiences. The study of war and war-torn zones has led to the understanding that more often than is usually considered, exposure to increased stress also builds up protective mechanisms, and that children in particularly difficult situations can and do learn to cope better (Aptekar & Stoecklin, 1997; Klingman & Cohen, 2004). A further shift is needed

from the purely medical-clinical model, which focuses on individual treatments of those children identified as suffering from a disorder as an outcome of war, to multiple emphases on the recovery environment of all involved children, on preventive efforts within the children's natural environments, and on the use of generic principles.

There is a pressing need to now invest in developing, testing, and evaluating large-scale generic interventions. With the recent rise in wars and war-like events all over the world, including world terrorism, nationalism, violent political conflicts, and civil wars associated with tribalism, a vast number of children are affected. Hence, our best investment would be in (a) tailoring culture-specific versions for the implementation of the generic principles and (b) developing measures to assess the effectiveness of various components of generic interventions across different cultures and war contexts. Of course, this should not come at the expense of continuing to expand our knowledge of specific manifestations of PTSD in children across and within the various cultures, or of conducting better controlled longitudinal studies of children's PTSD and other war-related disorders.

Interventionists must acknowledge that, however good their intentions, knowledge, funding, and interventional designs, no intervention will erase the painful memories and the traumas of war. However, an investment in the generic, multifaceted, multimodal, and multisystemic approach seems a most promising avenue for alleviating the effects of war and displacement on children, helping them develop positive social and emotional skills, and facilitating their capacity to live fulfilling lives despite their painful memories. Such an investment may eventually enable children to adjust to the new postwar normality and to restore their lives as near to normal as possible, with the focus on ensuring the successful progression of developmental processes.

REFERENCES

Ager, A. (1996). Children, war, and psychological intervention. In S. C. Car & J. F. Schumaker (Eds.), *Psychology and the developing world* (pp. 162–172). Westport, CT: Praeger.

Almqvist, K., & Broberg, A. G. (1997). Silence and survival: Working with strategies of denial in families of traumatized pre-school children. *Journal of Child Psychotherapy, 23,* 417–435.

Alon, N., & Levine Bar-Yoseph, T. (1994). An approach to the treatment of post-traumatic stress disorder (PTSD). In P. Clarkson & M. Pokorny (Eds.), *The handbook of psychotherapy* (pp. 451–469). New York: Routledge.

American Academy of Child and Adolescent Psychiatry. (1998). Practice parameters for the assessment and the treatment of children and adolescents with posttraumatic stress disorder. *Journal of the Academy of Child and Adolescent Psychiatry, 37*(10), 4–26.

American Psychiatric Association. (1994). *Diagnostic and statistical manual of mental disorders* (4th ed.). Washington, DC: Author.

Ancharoff, M. R., Munroe, J. F., & Fisher, L. (1998). The legacy of combat trauma: Clinical implications of intergenerational transmission. In Y. Danieli (Ed.), *International handbook of multigenerational legacies of trauma* (pp. 257–279). New York: Plenum Press.

Aptekar, L., & Stoecklin, D. (1997). Children in particularly difficult circumstances. In J. W. Berry, P. R. Dasen, & T. S. Saraswathi (Eds.), *Handbook of cross-cultural psychology* (Vol. 2, 2nd ed., pp. 377–412). Boston: Allyn and Bacon.

Auerhahn, N. C., & Laub, D. (1998). Intergenerational memory of the Holocaust. In Y. Danieli (Ed.), *International handbook of multigenerational legacies of trauma* (pp. 21–41). New York: Plenum Press.

Bandura, A. (1982). Self-efficacy mechanism in human agency. *American Psychologist, 37*, 122–147.

Bar-On, D. (1995). *Fear and hope: Three generations of five Israeli families of Holocaust survivors*. Cambridge, MA: Harvard University Press.

Bar-On, D. (1996). Attempting to overcome the intergenerational transmission of trauma: Dialogue between descendents of victims and of perpetrators. In R. Apfel & B. Simon (Eds.), *Minefields of their hearts: The mental health of children in war and communal violence* (pp. 165–188). New Haven, CT: Yale University Press.

Bar-Tal, D. (2004). Nature, rationale, and effectiveness of education for coexistence. *Journal of Social Issues, 60*, 253–271.

Bar-Tal, D., Raviv, A., & Freund, T. (1994). An anatomy of political beliefs: A study of their centrality, confidence, contents, and epistemic authority. *Journal of Applied Social Psychology, 24*, 849–872.

Berk, J. H. (1998). Trauma and resilience during war: A look at the children and humanitarian aid workers of Bosnia. *Psychoanalytic Review, 85*, 639–658.

Bevin, T. (1999). Multiple traumas of refugees: Near drowning and witnessing of maternal rape—Case of Sergio, age 9, and follow-up at age 16. In N. B. Webb (Ed.), *Play therapy with children in crisis: Individual, group, and family treatment* (pp. 164–182). New York: Guilford Press.

Bronfman, E. T., Campis, L. B., & Koocher, G. P. (1998). Helping children to cope: Clinical issues for acutely injured and medically traumatized children. *Professional Psychology: Research and Practice, 29*, 574–581.

Bunjevac, T., & Kuterovac, G. (1994). *Report on the results of psychological evaluation of the art therapy program in schools in Herzegovina*. Zagreb, Yugoslavia: UNICEF.

Cairns, E. (1996). *Children and political violence*. Malden, MA: Blackwell.

Cairns, E., & Dawes, A. (1996). Children: Ethnic and political violence—A commentary. *Child Development, 67*, 129–139.

Calhoun, L. G., & Tedeschi, R. G. (1999). *Facilitating posttraumatic growth*. Mahwah, NJ: Erlbaum.

Caplan, G. (1964). *Principles of preventive psychiatry*. Oxford: Basic Books.

Chazan, S. E. (2002). *Profiles of play: Assessing and observing structure and process in play therapy*. London: Jessica Kingsley.

Chemtob, C. M., Nakashima, J. P., & Hamada, R. S. (2002). Psychosocial intervention for postdisaster trauma symptoms in elementary school children: A controlled community field study. *Journal of the American Academy of Child and Adolescent Psychiatry, 41*, 1341.

Cicchetti, D., Toth, S. L., & Lynch, M. (1993). The developmental sequelae of child maltreatment: Implications for war-related trauma. In L. A. Leavitt & N. A. Fox (Eds.), *The psychological effects of war and violence on children* (pp. 41–71). Hillsdale, NJ: Erlbaum.

Cicchetti, D., Toth, S. L., & Lynch, M. (1997). Child maltreatment as an illustration of the effects of war on development. In D. Cicchetti & S. L. Toth (Eds.), *Developmental perspectives on trauma: Theory, research, and intervention* (pp. 227–262). Rochester, NY: University of Rochester Press.

Clarke, G., Sack, W. H., & Goff, B. (1993). Three forms of stress in Cambodian adolescent refugees. *Journal of Abnormal Child Psychology, 21*, 65–77.

Costello, M., Phelps, L., & Wilczenski, F. (1994). Children and military conflict: Current issues and treatment implications. *School Counselor, 41*, 220–225.

Danieli, Y. (Ed.). (1998). *International handbook of multigenerational legacies of trauma*. New York: Plenum Press.

Dawes, A., Tredoux, C., & Feinstein, A. (1989). Political violence in South Africa: Some effects on children of the violent destruction of their community. *International Journal of Mental Health, 18*, 16–43.

de Shazer, S. (1985). *Keys to solutions in brief therapy*. New York: Norton.

Desivilya, H. S., Gal, R., & Ayalon, O. (1996a). Extent of victimization, traumatic stress symptoms, and adjustment of terrorist assault survivors: A long-term follow-up. *Journal of Traumatic Stress, 9*, 881–889.

Desivilya, H. S., Gal, R., & Ayalon, O. (1996b). Long-term effects of trauma in adolescence: Comparison between survivors of a terrorist attack and control counterparts. *Anxiety, Stress, and Coping: An International Journal, 9*, 135–150.

Dybdahl, R. (2001). Children and mothers in war: An outcome study of a psychosocial intervention program. *Child Development, 72*, 1214–1230.

Dyregrov, A., Gjestad, R., & Raundalen, M. (2000). Children exposed to warfare: A longitudinal study. *Journal of Traumatic Stress, 15*, 59–68.

Dyregrov, A., Gupta, L., Gjestad, R., & Mukanoheli, E. (2000). Trauma exposure and psychological reactions to genocide among Rwandan children. *Journal of Traumatic Stress, 13*, 3–21.

Farwell, N., & Cole, J. B. (2001–2002). Community as a context of healing: Psychological recovery of children affected by war and political violence. *International Journal of Mental Health, 30*, 19–41.

Felsen, I. (1998). Transgenerational transmission of effects of the Holocaust. In Y. Danieli (Ed.), *International handbook of multigenerational legacies of trauma* (pp. 43–69). New York: Plenum Press.

Figley, C. R. (1993a). Coping with stressors on the home front. *Journal of Social Issues, 49*, 51–71.

Figley, C. R. (1993b). War-related stress and family-centered intervention: American children and the Gulf War. In L. A. Leavitt & N. A. Fox (Eds.), *The psychological effects of war and violence on children* (pp. 339–356). Hillsdale, NJ: Erlbaum.

Figley, C. R. (Ed.). (1995). *Compassion fatigue: Coping with secondary traumatic stress disorder in those who treat the traumatized*. Philadelphia: Bunner.

Gal, R. (1998). Colleagues in distress: "Helping the helpers." *International Review of Psychiatry, 10*, 234–238.

Garbarino, J., Kostelny, K., & Dubrow, N. (1991). What children can tell us about living in danger. *American Psychologist, 46,* 376–383.

Gidron, Y. (2002). Posttraumatic stress disorder after terrorist attacks: A review. *Journal of Nervous and Mental Disease, 190,* 118–121.

Gil, E. (1991). *The healing power of play: Working with abused children.* New York: Guilford Press.

Goldson, E. (1993). War is not good for children. In L. A. Leavitt & N. A. Fox (Eds.), *The psychological effects of war and violence on children* (pp. 3–22). Hillsdale, NJ: Erlbaum.

Gonsalves, C. J. (1992). Psychological stages of the refugee process: A model for therapeutic interventions. *Professional Psychology: Research and Practice, 23,* 382–389.

Green, A. H., & Kocijan-Hercigonja, D. (1998). Stress and coping in children traumatized by war. *Journal of the American Academy of Psychoanalysis, 26,* 585–597.

Gutkin, T. B. (1999). Collaborative versus directive/prescriptive/expert school-based consultation: Reviewing and resolving a false dichotomy. *Journal of School Psychology, 37,* 161–190.

Hobfoll, S. E., Spielberger, C. D., Breznitz, S., Figley, C., Folkman, S., Leppen-Green, B., et al. (1991). War related stress: Addressing the stress of war and other traumatic events. *American Psychologist, 46,* 848–855.

Hunter, E. J. (1988). Long-term effects of parental wartime captivity on children: Children of POW and MIA servicemen. *Journal of Contemporary Psychotherapy, 18,* 312–328.

James, B. (1989). *Treating traumatized children: New insights and creative innovations.* Lexington, MA: Lexington Books.

Janoff-Bulman, R. (1992). *Shattered assumptions: Towards a new psychology of trauma.* New York: Free Press.

Johnson, D. W., & Johnson, R. T. (1996). Conflict resolution and peer mediation programs in elementary and secondary schools: A review of the research. *Review of Educational Research, 66,* 459–506.

Kahana, E., Kahana, B., Harel, Z., & Rosner, T. (1998). Coping with extreme stress. In J. P. Wilson & B. Kahana (Eds.), *Human adaptation to extreme stress from the Holocaust to Vietnam* (pp. 55–70). New York: Plenum Press.

Kalantari, M., Yule, W., & Gardner, F. (1993). Protective factors and behavioral adjustment in preschool children of Iranian martyrs. *Journal of Child and Family Studies, 2,* 97–108.

Kalmanowitz, D., & Lloyd, B. (1999). Fragments of art at work: Art therapy in the former Yugoslavia. *Arts in Psychotherapy, 26,* 15–25.

Klingman, A. (1991). *Hitarvut psichologit-chinuchit be'et ason* [Psychological-educational intervention in disaster]. Jerusalem: Psychological and Counseling Services, Israel Ministry of Education.

Klingman, A. (1992). Stress reactions of Israeli youth during the Gulf War: A quantitative study. *Professional Psychology: Research and Practice, 23,* 521–527.

Klingman, A. (1997). *Hitmodedut beit sifrit be'et ason* [School coping in disaster]. Jerusalem: Psychological and Counseling Services, Israel Ministry of Education.

Klingman, A. (2001). Stress responses and adaptation of Israeli school-age children evacuated from homes during massive missile attacks. *Anxiety, Stress, and Coping, 14,* 149–172.

Klingman, A. (2002a). Children under stress of war. In A. La Greca, W. A. Silverman, E. M. Vernberg, & M. C. Roberts (Eds.), *Help-ing children cope with disaster and terrorism* (pp. 359–380). Washington, DC: American Psychological Association.

Klingman, A. (2002b). From supportive-listening to a solution-focused intervention for counsellors dealing with a political trauma. *British Journal of Guidance and Counselling, 30,* 247–259.

Klingman, A. (2002c). School and war. In S. E. Brock, P. J. Lazarus, & S. R. Jimerson (Eds.), *Best practices in school crisis prevention and intervention* (pp. 577–598). Bethesda, MD: National Association of School Psychologists.

Klingman, A., & Ben Eli, Z. (1981). A school community in disaster: Primary and secondary prevention in situational crisis. *Professional Psychology, 12,* 523–533.

Klingman, A., & Cohen, E. (2004). *School-based multisystemic intervention for mass trauma.* New York: Kluwer Academic/Plenum Press.

Klingman, A., Sagi, A., & Raviv, A. (1993). The effects of war on Israeli children. In L.A. Leavitt & N.A. Fox (Eds.), *Psychological effects of war and violence on children* (pp. 75–92). Hillsdale, NJ: Erlbaum.

Kostarova-Unkovska, L. (Ed.). (1993). *Children hurt by war.* Skopje: General Consulate of the Republic of Macedonia.

Krkeljic, L., & Pavlicic, N. (1998). School project in Montenegro. In O. Ayalon, M. Lahad, & A. Cohen (Eds.), *Community stress prevention* (Vol. 3, pp. 51–61). Jerusalem: Psychological and Counseling Services, Israel Ministry of Education.

Lahad, S., Shacham, Y., & Niv, S. (2000). Coping and community resources in children facing disaster. In A. Y. Shalev & R. Yehuda (Eds.), *International handbook of human response to trauma* (pp. 389–395). Dordrecht, Netherlands: Kluwer Academic.

Layne, C. M., Pynoos, R. S., Saltzman, W. R., Arslanagic, B., Black, M., Savjak, N., et al. (2001). Trauma/grief-focused group psychotherapy school-based postwar intervention with traumatized Bosnian adolescents. *Group Dynamics, 5,* 277–290.

Lazarus, A. A. (1997). *Brief but comprehensive psychotherapy: The multimodal way.* New York: Springer.

Macksoud, M. S., & Aber, J. L. (1996). The war experiences and psychological development of children in Lebanon. *Child Development, 67,* 70–88.

Malkinson, R., Rubin, S. S., & Witztum, E. (Eds.). (2000). *Traumatic and nontraumatic loss and bereavement: Clinical theory and practices.* Madison, CT: Psychological Press.

March, J. S., Amaya-Jackson, L., Murray, M. C., & Schulte, A. (1998). Cognitive-behavioral psychotherapy for children and adolescents with posttraumatic stress disorder after a single-incident stressor. *Journal of the American Academy of Child and Adolescent Psychiatry, 37,* 585–593.

Meichenbaum, D. (1985). *Stress inoculation training.* New York: Pergamon.

Meichenbaum, D., & Cameron, R. (1983). Stress inoculation training: Toward a general paradigm for training coping skills. In D. Meichenbaum & M. E. Jaremko (Eds.), *Stress reduction and prevention* (pp. 115–154). New York: Plenum Press.

Miller, K. (1996). The effects of state terrorism and exile on the indigenous Guatemalan refugee children: A mental health assessment and an analysis of children's narratives. *Child Development, 67,* 89–106.

Miller, L. (2003). Family therapy of terror trauma: Psychological syndromes and treatment strategies. *American Journal of Family Therapy, 31,* 257–280.

Mitchell, J. T., & Everly, G. S. (1997). *Critical incident stress debriefing: An operational manual for the prevention of traumatic stress among emergency services and disaster workers* (2nd ed.). Ellicott City, MD: Chevron.

Morrison, C. D., Metzger, P. A., & Pratt, P. N. (1996). Play. In J. Cash-Smith, A. S. Allen, & P. N. Pratt (Eds.), *Occupational therapy for children* (3rd ed., pp. 504–523). St Louis, MO: Mosby.

Muldoon, O., & Cairns, E. (1999). Children, young people, and war: Learning to cope. In E. Frydenberg (Ed.), *Learning to cope: Developing as a person in complex societies* (pp. 322–337). Oxford: Oxford University Press.

Muldoon, O. T. (2000). Children's experience and adjustment to political conflict in Northern Ireland. *Peace and Conflict, 6,* 157–176.

Nader, K. O. (2002). Treating children after violence in schools and communities. In N. B. Webb (Ed.), *Helping bereaved children: A handbook for practitioners* (2nd ed., pp. 214–244). New York: Guilford Press.

Nagata, D. K. (1998). Intergenerational effects of the Japanese American internment. In Y. Danieli (Ed.), *International handbook of multigenerational legacies of trauma* (pp. 125–141). New York: Plenum Press.

Nevo, B., & Brem, I. (2002). Peace education programs and the evaluation of their effectiveness. In G. Salomon & B. Nevo (Eds.), *Peace education: The concept, principles, and practices around the world* (pp. 271–282). Mahwah, NJ: Erlbaum.

Omer, H., & Alon, N. (1994). The continuity principle: A unified approach to disaster and trauma. *American Journal of Community Psychology, 22,* 273–287.

Op den Velde, W. (1998). Children of Dutch war sailors and civilian veterans. In Y. Danieli (Ed.), *International handbook of multigenerational legacies of trauma* (pp. 147–163). New York: Plenum Press.

Ophir, M. (1980). Mischak hadmaia keshitat tipul becharadah matzavit [Simulation game as an intervention to reduce state anxiety]. In A. Raviv, A. Klingman, & M. Horowitz (Eds.), *Yeladim bematzavey lachatz vemashber* [Children in stress and crisis situations] (pp. 274–279). Tel Aviv: Otzar Hamoreh.

Pardess, E. R. (2002). *Support program for bereaved families in the aftermath of tragedy.* Tel Aviv: Israel Crisis Management Center/SELAH.

Parson, E. R. (1996). "It takes a village to heal a child": Necessary spectrum of expertise and benevolence by therapists, nongovernmental organizations, and the United Nations in managing war-zone stress in children traumatized by political violence. *Journal of Contemporary Psychotherapy, 26,* 251–286.

Parson, E. R. (2000). Understanding children with war-zone traumatic stress exposed to the world's violent environments. *Journal of Contemporary Psychotherapy, 30,* 325–340.

Punamaeki, R. L. (1996). Can ideological commitment protect children's psychosocial well-being in situations of political violence? *Child Development, 67,* 55–69.

Punamaeki, R. L. (2002). Developmental and personality aspects of war and military violence. *Traumatology, 8,* 45–63.

Pynoos, R. S., & Eth, S. (1985). Witnessing acts of personal violence. In S. Eth & R. S. Pynoos (Eds.), *Post-traumatic stress disorder in children* (pp. 19–43).Washington, DC: American Psychiatric Press.

Raviv, A. (1993). The use of hotline and media interventions in Israel during the Gulf War. In L. A. Leavitt & N. A. Fox (Eds.), *The psychological effects of war and violence on children* (pp. 319–337). Hillsdale, NJ: Erlbaum.

Reichman, N. (1993). Annotation: Children in situations of political violence. *Journal of Child Psychology and Psychiatry, 34,* 1286–1302.

Ronen, T. (1996a). Constructivist therapy with traumatized children. *Journal of Constructivist Psychology, 9,* 139–156.

Ronen, T. (1996b). Self-control exposure therapy for children's anxieties: A preliminary report. *Child and Family Behavior Therapy, 18,* 1–17.

Ronen, T. (2002). Difficulties in assessing traumatic reactions in children. *Journal of Loss and Trauma, 7,* 87–106.

Rosenheck, R., & Nathan, P. (1985). Secondary traumatization in children of Vietnam veterans. *Hospital and Community Psychiatry, 36,* 538–539.

Rutter, M. (2000). Resilience reconsidered: Conceptual considerations, empirical findings, and policy implications. In J. Shonkoff & S. Meisels (Eds.), *Handbook of early childhood intervention* (2nd ed., pp. 651–682). New York: Cambridge University Press.

Ryan, V., & Needham, C. (2001). Non-directive play with children experiencing psychic trauma. *Clinical Child Psychology and Psychiatry, 6,* 437–453.

Saigh, P. A. (1986). In vitro flooding in the treatment of a 6-year-old boy's posttraumatic stress disorder. *Behavior Research and Therapy, 24,* 685–688.

Saigh, P. A. (1987a). In vitro flooding of an adolescent's posttraumatic stress disorder. *School Psychology Review, 16,* 203–211.

Saigh, P. A. (1987b). In vitro flooding of childhood posttraumatic stress disorder: A systematic replication. *Professional School Psychology, 2,* 135–146.

Saigh, P. A. (2000). The cognitive-behavioral treatment of PTSD in children and adolescents. In S. E. Brock, P. J. Lazarus, & S. R. Jimerson (Eds.), *Best practices in school crisis prevention and intervention* (pp. 639–652). Bethesda, MD: National Association of School Psychologists.

Saigh, P. A., Yule, W., & Inamdar, S. C. (1996). Imaginal flooding of traumatized children and adolescents. *Journal of School Psychology, 34,* 163–183.

Salomon, G. (2004a). A narrative-based view of coexistence education. *Journal of Social Issues, 60,* 273–287.

Salomon, G. (2004b). Does peace education make a difference in the context of an intractable conflict? *Peace and Conflict: Journal of Peace Psychology, 10,* 257–274.

Saltzman, W. R., Pynoos, R. S., Layne, C. M., Steinberg, A. M., & Aisenberg, E. (2001). School-based trauma/grief focused group psychotherapy program for youth exposed to community violence. *Group Dynamics, 5,* 291–303.

Saltzman, W. R., Steinberg, A. M., Layne, R. S., Aisenberg, E., & Pynoos, R. S. (2002). A developmental approach to school-based treatment of adolescents exposed to trauma and traumatic loss. *Journal of Child and Adolescent Group Therapy, 11,* 43–56.

Scheeringa, M. S., & Zeanah, C. H. (2001). A relational perspective on PTSD in early childhood. *Journal of Traumatic Stress, 14,* 799–815.

Seligman, M. E. P. (2002). Positive psychology, positive prevention, and positive therapy. In C. R. Snyder & S. J. Lopez (Eds.), *Handbook of positive psychology* (pp. 3–9). London: Oxford University Press.

Shalev, A. Y. (2002). Acute stress reactions in adults. *Biological Psychiatry, 51,* 532–543.

Shalif, Y., & Leibler, M. (2002). Working with people experiencing terrorist attacks in Israel: A narrative perspective. *Journal of Systemic Therapies, 21,* 60–70.

Shilo-Cohen, N. (1993). Israeli children paint war. In L. A. Leavitt & N. A. Fox (Eds.), *The psychological effects of war and violence on children* (pp. 93–107). Hillsdale, NJ: Erlbaum.

Shoham, E. (1994). Family characteristics of delinquent youth in time of war. *International Journal of Offender Therapy and Comparative Criminology, 38,* 247–258.

Silva, H., Hobbs, C., & Hanks, H. (2001). Conscription of children in armed conflict: A form of child abuse—A study of 19 former child soldiers. *Child Abuse Review, 10,* 299.

Simo-Algado, S., Mehta, N., Kronenberg, F., Cockburn, L., & Kirsh, B. (2002). Occupational therapy intervention with children survivors of war. *Canadian Journal of Occupational Therapy, 69,* 205–217.

Smith, P., Dyregrov, A., Yule, W., Gupta, L., Perrin, S., & Gjestad, R. (1999). *Children and disaster: Teaching recovery techniques.* Bergen, Norway: Foundation for Children and War.

Solomon, Z. (1995). *Coping with war-induced stress: The Gulf War and the Israeli response.* New York: Plenum Press.

Southall, D., & Abbasi, K. (1998). Protecting children from armed conflict. *British Medical Journal, 316,* 1549–1550.

St. Thomas, B., & Johnson, P. G. (2001). Child as healer. *Migration World Magazine, 29,* 33–46.

Summerfield, D. (1999). A critique of seven assumptions behind psychological trauma programmes in war-affected areas. *Social Science and Medicine, 48,* 1449–1462.

Terr, L. C. (1983). *Play therapy.* New York: Wiley Interscience.

Terr, L. C. (1985). Children traumatized in small groups. In S. Eth & R. S. Pynoos (Eds.), *Posttraumatic stress disorder in children* (pp. 47–70). Washington, DC: American Psychiatric Press.

UNICEF. (1996). *The state of the world's children.* Oxford: Oxford University Press.

van der Veer, G. (1992). *Counselling and therapy with refugees: Psychological problems of victims of war, torture and repression.* Chichester, England: Wiley.

Volkan, V. (1990). Psychoanalytic aspects of ethnic conflicts. In J. V. Moontville (Ed.), *Conflict and peacemaking in multiethnic societies* (pp. 81–92). Washington, DC: Lexington.

Webb, N. B. (1999). Play therapy crisis intervention with children. In N. B. Webb (Ed.), *Play therapy with children in crisis* (2nd ed., pp. 39–46). New York: Guilford Press.

Wessely, S. (2003). War and the mind: Psychopathology or suffering? *Palestine-Israel Journal, 10,* 6–16.

Williams-Gray, B. (1999). International consultation and intervention on behalf of children affected by war. In N. B. Webb (Ed.), *Play therapy with children in crisis: Individual, group, and family treatment* (2nd ed., pp. 448–467). New York: Guilford Press.

Wiseman, H., & Barber, J. P. (2004). The core conflictual relationship theme approach to relational narratives: Interpersonal themes in the context of intergenerational communication of trauma. In A. Lieblich, D. P. McAdams, & R. Josseson (Eds.), *Healing plots: The narrative basis of psychotherapy* (pp. 151–170). Washington, DC: American Psychological Association.

Wiseman, H., Barber, J. P., Raz, A., Yam, I., Foltz, C., & Levine-Snir, S. (2002). Parental communication of Holocaust experiences and interpersonal patterns in offspring of Holocaust survivors. *International Journal of Behavioral Development, 26,* 371–381.

Witty, C. J. (2002). The therapeutic potential of narrative therapy in conflict transformation. *Journal of Systemic Therapies, 21,* 48–59.

Wolmer, L., Laor, N., & Yazgan, Y. (2003). School reactivation programs after disaster: Could teachers serve as clinical mediators? *Child and Adolescent Psychiatric Clinics of North America, 12*(2), 363–381.

Woodcock, J. (2000). Refugee children and their families: Theoretical and clinical perspectives. In K. N. Dwivedi (Ed.), *Posttraumatic stress disorder in children and adolescents* (pp. 213–239). London: Whurr.

Wright, M. O., Masten, A. S., & Hubbard, J. J. (1997). Long-term effects of massive trauma: Developmental and psychobiological perspectives. In D. Cicchetti & S. L. Toth (Eds.), *Developmental perspectives on trauma: Theory, research, and intervention* (pp. 181–225). Rochester, NY: University of Rochester Press.

Yule, W. (2001). Post-traumatic stress disorder in children and adolescents. *International Review of Psychiatry, 13,* 194–200.

Yule, W. (2002). Alleviating the effects of war and displacement on children. *Traumatology, 8*(3), 25–43.

Yule, W., & Gold, A. (1993). *Wise before the event: Coping with crises in schools.* London: Calouste Gulbenkian Foundation.

Research Advances and Implications for Social Policy and Social Action

CHAPTER 17

Cultural Pathways through Human Development

PATRICIA M. GREENFIELD, LALITA K. SUZUKI, and CARRIE ROTHSTEIN-FISCH

CULTURAL PATHWAYS TO INDEPENDENCE AND INTERDEPENDENCE

Our foundational theme is that many children in the United States (and other immigrant-receiving countries) are raised in home cultures that place a higher relative value on interdependence as a goal of development than does the dominant surrounding culture, where independence is more highly valued. This situation derives from differences between the dominant cultural orientation of society at large and the cultural value system of families' ancestral cultures, often Latin American, Asian, African, Native American, or Native Hawaiian (Greenfield & Cocking, 1994). A cultural orientation of independence yields one pathway through universal developmental issues; a cultural orientation of interdependence yields a different one (Greenfield, Keller, Fuligni, & Maynard, 2003). In North America, Australia, Canada, and many parts of Europe, these diverging pathways can cause children and families with a more interdependent home culture to be caught in a conflicting cross-current of socializing influences. Because of the large number of immigrant and Native families in the United States, such conflict constitutes a significant social problem.

This chapter is an extensive revision of a chapter in this *Handbook*'s fifth edition, "Culture and Human Development: Implications for Parenting, Education, Pediatrics, and Mental Health," by Greenfield and Suzuki (1998). The sections titled "Three Approaches to Culture and Human Development" and "Criticisms of Independence/Individualism and Interdependence/Collectivism as Basic Cultural Paradigms" were adapted from "Cultural Pathways through Universal Development" by Greenfield, Keller, et al. (2003). For the first edition of this chapter, the authors would like to express special appreciation to Helen Davis for insightful comments on early drafts, for editing, and for help with manuscript preparation. We also thank Ashley Maynard for reading and commenting on the first draft. And we remember with appreciation the very constructive review of the late Rodney R. Cocking. For the revised chapter, we thank the FPR-UCLA Center for Culture, Brain, and Development for providing a stimulating atmosphere in which to discuss and learn about the issues of culture and human development. We also thank HopeLab for their support of the revision. This revision was completed while the first author was a Fellow at the Center for Advanced Study in the Behavioral Sciences, Stanford, California.

PLAN OF THE CHAPTER

We first review research from around the world demonstrating these two developmental pathways, each with its distinctive socialization goals and practices. We organize this review into four sections according to age periods and agents of socialization: early socialization at home, later socialization at home, socialization by peers, and socialization by the school. After reviewing the relevant research in each section, we discuss implications for practice. At the end of each section, we also present an intervention designed to alleviate conflicting socialization pressures between home and the outside community and the cross-cultural misunderstandings that arise from them.

THREE THEORETICAL APPROACHES TO CULTURE AND HUMAN DEVELOPMENT

Our conception of cultural pathways draws on three major types of theory: the *ecocultural, sociohistorical,* and *values* perspectives. Philosophically, the ecocultural approach emphasizes the causal influence of material conditions in the environment. The values approach, in contrast, emphasizes the causal influence of ideals or meanings inside the psyche. The sociohistorical approach emphasizes the causal influence of social factors: the interactional processes and symbolic tools used in cultural learning; these processes and tools develop over historical time. We begin with the values approach, the most central to our model of cultural pathways through human development.

The Cultural Values Approach

On the side of social development, the distinction between independent and interdependent pathways of development originates in cross-cultural comparative research identifying altruism and egoism as outcomes of different socialization practices under different environmental conditions (J. W. M. Whiting & B. B. Whiting, 1973/1994). On the side of cognitive development, the distinction between a collectivistic and an individualistic worldview originates in Greenfield's (1966) research in Senegal in which she found an assumption of greater unity between self and world, both social and physical, in the indigenous Wolof culture. This contrasted with greater metacognitive self-awareness—a cognitive separation of self and world—as a result of the Western institution of formal schooling (Greenfield & Bruner, 1966).

Out of these historical beginnings has grown a conception of alternative pathways of development. In an independent developmental pathway, social obligations are individually negotiated; opportunities to select social relationships (personal choice) and to act freely in those relationships (individual rights) are maximized (Raeff, Greenfield, & Quiroz, 2000). In an interdependent developmental pathway, in contrast, social obligations and responsibilities are given greater priority, and individual choice is much less important. An independent pathway prioritizes individuation as a developmental goal; an interdependent pathway, by contrast, prioritizes conforming to established social norms as a developmental goal (Kitayama, Markus, & Lieberman, 1995; Nsamenang & Lamb, 1994; Weisner, 2000).

Culturally relevant developmental goals are represented in the form of implicit ethnotheories of development, that is, systems of beliefs and ideas concerning the nature of the ideal child and the socialization practices necessary to achieve this ideal (Goodnow, 1988; Harkness & Super, 1996; McGillicuddy-DeLisi & Sigel, 1995). These ethnotheories are shared (and negotiated) among members of cultural communities. Values concerning preferred developmental goals can be expressed explicitly, as in parental ethnotheories, or implicitly, as in cultural practices, particularly discourse practices (Keller, Voelker, & Yovsi, 2002; Ochs & Schieffelin, 1984; Sigel, McGillicuddy-DeLisi, & Goodnow, 1992). The growing emphasis on indigenous conceptualizations of parenting goals (Chao, 1994; Gutierrez & Sameroff, 1990; Yovsi & Keller, 2003) has unraveled independence and interdependence as core dimensions, applicable to all developmental domains.

Participants from non-Western cultural communities, such as Chinese (Chao, 1994), Japanese (Rothbaum, Weisz, Pott, Miyake, & Morelli, 2000), Indians (Keller, Voelker, et al., 2002; Saraswathi, 1999), West Africans (Ogunnaike & Houser, 2002, for Nigeria; Nsamenang, 1992, and Yovsi, 2001, for Cameroon), and Puerto Ricans (Harwood, Schoelmerich, Ventura-Cook, Schulze, & Wilson, 1996), subscribe to the cultural ideal of interdependence: Their ethnotheories stress closeness, decency (social responsibility, honesty) and proper demeanor (politeness, respect for elders, loyalty to family) for various developmental domains (Harwood, 1992).

Participants from Western industrialized cultural communities, such as Germans (Keller, Zach, & Abels, 2002), European Americans (Harwood et al., 1996), and Dutch (Harkness, Super, & van Tijen, 2000), subscribe to the cultural ideal of independence: Their ethnotheories stress self-maximization and independence (creativity, curiosity, assertiveness, self-esteem). These particular parental goals and practices socialize children to operate effectively in an individualistic society such as the United States. "So basic is the concept of individualism to American society," it has been said, "that every major issue which faces us as a nation invariably poses itself in these terms" (Gross & Osterman, 1971, p. xi). Socialization practices that function to actualize the ethnotheoretical framework within cultural communities begin at birth or even before.

The Ecocultural Approach

The ecocultural approach, pioneered by anthropologists Beatrice Whiting and John Whiting (1975; see also D'Andrade, 1994), sees the child's behavioral development and the acquisition of culture as resulting from the interaction between human biological potentialities and environmental conditions. In short, the ecocultural approach emphasizes development as an adaptation to different environmental conditions and constraints (Berry, 1976; LeVine, 1977; Munroe & Munroe, 1994; Super & Harkness, 1986; Weisner, 1984; B. B. Whiting & Edwards, 1988; B. B. Whiting & J. W. M. Whiting, 1975).

From the ecocultural perspective, particular economic and environmental conditions create different social structures that favor different developmental pathways (cf. Berry, 1994). The pathways therefore arise as adaptations to these physical and economic conditions. Thus, the interdependent pathway appears to be an adaptive response to small face-to-face communities and a subsistence economy; these communities value tradition and therefore change slowly. The independent pathway, in contrast, appears to be an adaptive response to large, anonymous communities and a commercial economy (Greenfield, 2000, 2004; Greenfield, Maynard, & Childs, 2003; Keller, Zach, et al., 2002); these communities value innovation and therefore change more rapidly. In slow-changing, subsistence-based ecologies, ethnotheories are transmitted vertically from generation to generation, maximizing historical continuity. In complex and fast-changing societies, on the other hand, parental ideas are negotiated horizontally within generations, relying on public discourse (media) and experts (e.g., pediatricians), with substantial differences among generations (Hewlett & Lamb, 2002; Keller, Miranda, & Gauda, 1984).

Correlatively, high socioeconomic status (SES) and formal education are associated with a more individualistic orientation (Keller, Zach, et al., 2002; Palacios & Moreno, 1996; Tapia Uribe, LeVine, & LeVine, 1994). Nonetheless, these cultural orientations persist across various socioeconomic and educational backgrounds (Harwood et al., 1996; Keller, Zach, et al., 2002).

The Sociohistorical Approach

The sociohistorical approach emphasizes processes of social construction, particularly cultural apprenticeship, cultural practices and artifacts, and the historical dimension of these processes (Cole, 1996; Lave & Wenger, 1991; Rogoff, 1990; Saxe, 1991; Scribner, 1985; Scribner & Cole, 1973, 1981; Vygotsky, 1962; Wertsch, 1985; Zukow, 1989). Social construction is seen as a set of situation-specific activities.

The sociohistorical perspective is crucial to the model of cultural pathways through human development. According to this model, each pathway results from a value orientation that generates the social construction (often called co-construction to reflect the active involvement of the child) of socializing practices and behaviors in particular situations. These social construction processes include apprenticeship from cultural "experts" in the adult generation, as well as peer interaction (Greenfield & Lave, 1982; Maynard, 2002). The interactional routines and artifacts that are utilized in cultural learning have a key role in socializing a child to proceed on a developmental pathway (Greenfield, 2000; Mistry & Rogoff, 1994; Rogoff, 1990; Saxe, 1991). Construction processes become particularly salient in bicultural people, where one or the other value system can become prominent in a particular situation (Garcia Coll, Meyer, & Brillon, 1995).

CRITICISMS OF INDEPENDENCE/INDIVIDUALISM AND INTERDEPENDENCE/COLLECTIVISM AS CULTURAL PARADIGMS OF HUMAN DEVELOPMENT

One common criticism of this approach is that it is too simplistic and reductionistic; the dichotomous binary quality of independence/individualism and interdependence/collectivism is seen as problematical (Killen & Wainryb, 2000; Rogoff, 2003). However, we do not see these concepts as dichotomous. They are not all or none, but rather exist to different degrees in different individuals in different cultures at different times in different domains (Greenfield, Maynard, & Childs, 2003; Morelli, Rogoff, Oppenheim, & Goldsmith, 1992; Raeff et al., 2000). They also vary with geography, SES, and formal education (Hofstede, 2001; Tapia Uribe et al., 1994). In addition, they are seen as developing through dynamic processes of socialization, which are themselves an important object of study (Greenfield, Maynard, et al., 2003).

The notion of independent and interdependent concerns coexisting in the same culture is put forth as another criticism of the framework (Killen & Wainryb, 2000). In response, we register our agreement, but note that individual enterprise (independence) and social relationships (interdependence) each have distinctive modes of expression in the two cultural frameworks. For example, freely chosen relationships are valued in the independent framework, whereas implicit social obligations are a more valued relationship premise in the interdependent framework (Raeff et al., 2000).

As a closely related response to this same criticism, a given behavior may be valued in both types of culture, but its relative priority may be different. For example, sharing with siblings is valued by parents in mainstream U.S. culture, but sharing is considered a matter of personal choice. Among Mexican immigrants to Los Angeles, by contrast, sharing has a much higher priority; it is simply expected (Raeff et al., 2000). Prioritizing one value over another may involve setting boundary conditions for the exercise of the preferred value (Wainryb, 1995). Boundary conditions may also reflect intergroup contact and cultural change processes. For example, the collectivistic Druze community studied by Wainryb is surrounded by the greater individualism of mainstream Israeli culture. Under these circumstances, the development in Druze children of boundaries on the rightful exercise of authority and the obligation to obey may, among other things, reflect contact with the surrounding national culture.

The existence of individual differences in the same culture is also seen as a criticism of the independence/interdependence framework. For example, Wainryb and Turiel (1994) found more orientation toward autonomy among males than females in collectivistic Druze culture. However, this criticism treats cultural characteristics as independent (*sic!*) traits and fails to take into account the systemic nature of cultures. In response to their example, we see female respect for male authority, a relational feature of collectivistic cultures, as the root of such differential autonomy.

Sometimes the between-culture variability among collectivistic or individualistic cultures is taken as a criticism of the paradigm (Harkness et al., 2000). Qualitative and quantitative variability has been found in both systems (Harkness et al., 2000; Hofstede, 1991). The two value systems are merely ideal paradigms that get instantiated in a multiplicity of concrete and historically differentiated cultural contexts.

CULTURAL PATHWAYS: CONFLICT, INVISIBILITY, AND IMPLICATIONS FOR PRACTITIONERS

When home culture and societal culture differ for any particular family, interesting and, at times, vexing situations arise. Children may be faced with conflicting messages from home and from the outside world (particularly from school) as to the proper values, attitudes, and behaviors they should follow. Parents are also in the position of having to reassess their cultural framework in a new setting where many of their own values may be in direct conflict with those of society at large. Choices will need to be made as to which values in what contexts should be used in raising their children.

The difficulty of such choices is all the greater because cultures are "invisible" (Philips, 1972). That is, they are interpretive lenses that are taken for granted by the wearers. Like the air we breathe, under ordinary conditions, these value frameworks do not rise to conscious awareness. This lack of awareness exacerbates the potential for both personal conflict and interpersonal misunderstanding in multicultural environments. People tend to experience the other pathway's response to a particular situation as "wrong" rather than as simply reflecting a different cultural orientation.

Because they have the task of assessing the behaviors of parents and children who come from diverse cultural backgrounds, counselors, social workers, educators, and health care professionals who work with families must be aware of these intercultural dynamics. Behaviors that may appear strange and perhaps dysfunctional in one cultural context could in fact be seen as normal in others. The professional community that comes into contact with families of differing backgrounds has the challenge of understanding the values and child developmental goals behind cultural differences. Otherwise, they cannot hope to correctly diagnose the source of any problems that arise.

Perhaps even more important, an understanding of diverse cultural values and associated rearing practices reveals the strengths of socialization and child care practices used in diverse cultural groups. Equally important is the awareness of the losses that come from giving up one's ancestral culture in the process of assimilating to the dominant cultural surround.

This is the background for considering cultural pathways in infancy, children's relations with parents, peer relations, and school-home relations. We begin with infancy.

INFANT CARE, SOCIALIZATION, AND DEVELOPMENT

Culture inundates us with information on what is "appropriate" infant rearing. A great degree of variation exists even within middle-class American methods of infant rearing; when we look cross-culturally, we see an even greater variance in child-rearing practices and goals.

What Are Parents' Goals for Their Infants?

In general, parents' goals for their infants include some combination of the following: infant survival and health, the acquisition of economic capabilities, and the attainment of culturally appropriate values (LeVine, 1988). Culturally defined parental goals are crucial in parental behavior toward infants and in the child's eventual socialization process. Normative parental goals both reflect and affect the structure and functioning of society as a whole.

In the United States, parents have many different goals for their children, but one of the most basic and general is the desire to have their babies grow up to be independent and individuated adults. For example, guiding children to learn to make their own decisions and establish their separate, individual existence was found to be one of the most important parental goals mentioned by mothers of infants in Boston (Richman, Miller, & Johnson Solomon, 1988). In infancy, others' contingent responses to babies' autonomous signals support the development of their independent agency (Keller, 2002).

In contrast, parents in Japan showed a different trend in parental goals. Rather than focusing on independence, in Japan, mothers were more likely to perceive themselves as being "one" with their infants. For example, Kawakami (1987, p. 5, quoted in Morelli et al., 1992) claimed, "An American mother-infant relationship consists of two individuals . . . on the other hand a Japanese mother-infant relationship consists of only one individual; that is, mother and infant are not divided." Furthermore, an immediate or even anticipatory reaction to infants' distress signals minimizes the self-other distinction in Japan (Rothbaum et al., 2000), as in Cameroon (Yovsi & Keller, 2000), India (Saraswathi & Pai, 1997), and Mexico (Brazelton, Robey, & Collier, 1969).

This value of extreme closeness between mother and infant is another indication of the interdependent goals of traditional Japanese parenting and is manifested in patterns of interaction, such as in *amae* behavior (variously translated as "dependence" or "interdependence"), that children express toward their mothers (Kim & Choi, 1994; Lebra, 1994). Just as the United States is an example of a society in which individualism is both valued and institutionalized, Japan has been a society in which collectivism—an emphasis on strong, cohesive in-groups (Hofstede, 1991)—has been both valued and institutionalized. However, this may be changing, as we note later in the section on culture change.

How Are Sleeping and Feeding Arrangements Affected by Parental Goals?

One readily observable dimension of cultural difference in the first 2 years of life is the organization of infant sleeping arrangements. In this section we argue that the cultural structuring of parental goals can play a part in determining infant sleeping arrangements.

Where Do Infants Sleep Worldwide?

In the United States and Germany, most infants sleep alone in a separate crib, most often in a separate room from their parents (Keller, Voelker, & Yovsi, 2002; Morelli et al., 1992). However, in many cultures around the world (particularly in Africa, Asia, and Latin America), cosleeping is the predominant sleeping arrangement (Konner & Worthman, 1980). In fact, in a survey taken of sleeping practices around the world, it was found that mothers in approximately two-thirds of cultures surveyed slept with their infant in their bed, and this portion was much higher if mothers sleeping with

their baby in the same room were included (Barry & Paxson, 1971; Burton & Whiting, 1961).

Examples of cosleeping cultures include Japan, where children traditionally have slept with their parents until 5 or 6 years of age (Caudill & Plath, 1966). This cosleeping is often referred to as *kawa,* or "river," in which the parents form the symbolic riverbanks for the children sleeping in their own futons between them (Brazelton, 1990). People from many other cultures share similar cosleeping arrangements with their children.

Although the dominant culture in the United States adheres to separate sleeping practices, many minority and immigrant groups still hold onto cosleeping practices from their ancestral cultures. Many people in the United States have immigrated from countries in which infant-mother cosleeping is customary. For example, Schachter, Fuchs, Bijur, and Stone (1989) found that 20% of Hispanic families in Harlem slept with their children at least 3 times a week. This was in contrast to the 6% of European American families that did so. Lozoff, Wolf, and Davis (1984) found a similar pattern, with more African American than European American infants and toddlers regularly cosleeping with their parent or parents. Although African Americans have been in the United States for many generations, it may be that their original incorporation by slavery provided separation from the broader society and therefore less assimilation to its norms.

What Preferences and Constraints Do Sleeping Arrangements Reflect in the Dominant U.S. Culture?

In the dominant culture of the United States, there is a distinct pressure on parents to push their infants to sleep alone (Brazelton, 1990). In fact, middle-class families who practice cosleeping realize they are going against cultural norms (Hanks & Rebelsky, 1977). According to Morelli et al. (1992), since the early 1900s, American folk wisdom has considered early nighttime separation to be crucial for healthy infant development.

A stress on independence training is an important factor connected to separate sleeping among middle-class parents in the United States (Munroe, Munroe, & Whiting, 1981). Parents have goals of training infants to be independent and self-reliant from the first few months of life, before an undesirable habit of cosleeping may be established that can be difficult to break (Morelli et al., 1992).

Another side of the coin may be parents' need for independence. Adults from the dominant U.S. culture constitute the developmental end point of independence training. A dependent infant threatens parents' own autonomy; therefore, an important motive for separate sleeping arrangements in infancy must be the parents' need to maintain their own independence. Research on the interrelations between parents' goals for themselves and their children is very much needed.

Loss of privacy associated with parental intimacy is another reason for the disapproval of cosleeping (Shweder, Jensen, & Goldstein, 1995). The privileging of marital ties is typical of cultures that stress autonomy or independence as a developmental goal. In contrast, the privileging of intergenerational ties, such as that between mother and child, is typical of cultures that stress interdependence as a developmental goal (Lebra, 1994; Shweder et al., 1995).

Survival as a reason for separate sleeping arrangements has also been cited by parents in the United States. This includes reducing risks such as smothering or catching a contagious illness (Ball, Hooker, & Kelly, 2000; Bundesen, 1944; Holt, 1957; Morelli et al., 1992). Other reasons include psychoanalytic Oedipal issues and fear of incestuous sexual abuse (Brazelton, 1990; Shweder et al., 1995). These rationales have led many middle-class European American women (and others who are part of the dominant U.S. culture) to adhere to sleeping separately from their infants.

Pediatricians, and even the federal government, reinforce this practice. Lozoff et al. (1984) cite sources from pediatric advice books (e.g., Spock, 1976) to government publications that advise parents not to take their children into their bed for any reason. When parents read such advice, however, the authors are viewed as "well respected professionals" (Smaldino, 1995), rather than bearers of folk wisdom or carriers of culture-specific ethnotheories of development.

What Preferences and Constraints Does Cosleeping Reflect?

In many cultures, cosleeping is considered a desirable practice. In fact, separate infant sleeping arrangements are often met with shock. For example, Brahmins in India believe that it is wrong to let young children sleep alone in a separate room in case the child awakens in the middle of the night. They believe that it is the parents' obligation to protect their children from fear and distress at night (Shweder, Mahapatra, & Miller, 1990). Maya Indians and Japanese also express shock and pity when first learning of the American practice of having

infants sleep apart from parents (Brazelton, 1990; Morelli et al., 1992). On learning that American infants sleep in a separate room from their parents, one shocked Maya mother remarked, "But there's someone else with them there, isn't there?" (Morelli et al., 1992, p. 608).

It has been suggested that resource constraints such as lack of space may also be a factor in cosleeping (Brazelton, 1990; Shweder et al., 1995). For example, in many cultures, homes have fewer beds or fewer rooms allotted for sleeping purposes than is common in the United States. Resource constraints, however, may play a relatively small role. For example, the shock and sadness that Maya mothers express when learning of the North American practice of separate sleeping arrangements is an indication that cosleeping is not merely a practical concern. Rather, it constitutes a commitment to a special kind of relationship with the infant (Morelli et al., 1992). Indeed, in large parts of Africa, Asia, and South America infants sleep with their mother because separation of the infant from the mother is beyond imagination (Morelli et al., 1992; Shweder et al., 1998; Yovsi, 2001).

Indeed, in their study of cultural variability in the United States, Lozoff et al. (1984) found that there was no significant relationship between space constraints (number of sleeping rooms available, household size, or the ratio of household size to sleeping rooms) and sleeping arrangements during infancy and toddlerhood. Instead of resource constraints, there seem to be reasons related to cultural values and goals that affect even the seemingly simplest of practices, such as infant sleeping arrangements.

However, other kinds of ecological factors can play a role in moderating the enactment of a culturally specified developmental goal such as independence. For example, in Lozoff et al.'s (1984) study, there was evidence that European American babies were accepted in their parents' bed under constraining conditions, such as when there was familial stress (such as a move or marital tension) or infant illness, or when the baby was old enough to get out of bed by himself or herself and walk into the parents' bedroom or bed.

The Relationship of Sleep to Feeding, Holding, Carrying, and Nursing

Parents in Asia, Africa, and indigenous America put their babies to sleep by nursing and holding (e.g.,

Brazelton et al., 1969; Hewlett, Lamb, Shannon, Leyendecker, & Schölmerich, 1998; LeVine et al., 1994; Miyake, Chen, & Campos, 1985; Morelli et al., 1992; Super & Harkness, 1982). This practice is part of a pattern of almost continual holding, carrying, and nursing (e.g., Brazelton et al., 1969; Miyake et al., 1985; Super & Harkness, 1982).

In cultural communities that value interdependence, the early relational matrix is founded in the ethnotheory of a continuously close mother-child relationship entailing close body contact during the day (holding and carrying) and at night (cosleeping). One Cameroonian Nso mother said in an ethnographic interview that a baby needs to be bonded to the mother's body (Keller, Voelker, & Yovsi, 2002).

From a neurological perspective, Restak's (1979, p. 122) research shows that "physical holding and carrying of the infant turns out to be the most important factor responsible for the infant's normal mental and social development." Hence, we must strongly consider the possibility, suggested by Konner (1982), that sleep problems are a major cultural problem in infant care in the United States precisely because professional advice and the culturally dominant practice are fighting the biology of the human infant that has evolved over hundreds of thousands of years.

What Can We Learn from a Cross-Cultural Perspective on Infant Care Practices? Implications for Parents, Pediatricians, and Other Practitioners

Cultural views and goals may make it difficult for people to realize and incorporate different modes of behavior. Indeed, there can be unintended consequences of changing one piece of a complex, interrelated cultural system. Nonetheless, there are cases in which much can be gained by observing and understanding the practices of other cultures.

Sleep Problems

Many have claimed that in North America, sleep disturbance is one of the most common concerns among parents of young infants today (Brazelton, 1990; Dawes, 1989; Nugent, 1994). In fact, children in the United States who slept alone were more engaged in complex bedtime routines and had longer-standing and stronger attachments to sleep aids and security objects than did

cosleepers (Hayes, Roberts, & Stowe, 1996). Yet sleep problems are less common or even nonexistent in a number of other cultures. For example, Nugent reports that "sleep problems or night waking are less commonly reported as clinical concerns in Japanese settings" (p. 6). Similarly, Super and Harkness (1982) noted that sleep problems were nonexistent among the Kipsigis in Kenya.

Cross-Cultural Exchange

It is clear that there is much to be learned from infant-rearing techniques practiced in different cultures. In terms of the superordinate goal of infant survival, cosleeping may play a part in fostering the development of optimal sleeping patterns in infants (McKenna et al., 1993). This may be because cosleeping permits the sleeping infant to take tactile and rhythmic cues from his or her parent, and these cues help regulate an immature breathing system. This interactive process, in turn, may decrease the risk of sudden infant death syndrome (SIDS; McKenna, 1986). Indeed, in many countries worldwide, cosleeping is associated with low rates of SIDS (McKenna & Mosko, 1994).

The Cultural Relativity of Risk

Perhaps Japanese parents, who traditionally put their babies to sleep by nursing and holding, would agree with the U.S. experts that this practice encourages dependence. However, the Japanese interpretation of dependence would be quite different. Certainly, the Japanese would be in profound disagreement with the "experts'" negative evaluation of dependence as a "risk" factor that could "impair" a child's development. In this way, the notion of developmental risk is clearly culture-bound (Nugent, 1994).

Issues for Pediatricians and Parents to Consider

Thus, many issues surround infant care practices such as sleeping arrangements. Of import are the child's physical well-being (e.g., reducing the risk of SIDS), emotional well-being (e.g., nighttime comforting), parental sleep patterns (e.g., parental privacy, nighttime feeding issues), practical constraints (e.g., housing situation), adult needs (e.g., for autonomy), and cultural goals (e.g., independence versus interdependence). These are issues to consider for parents and pediatricians alike.

Pediatricians have traditionally concluded that infant-parent cosleeping is a risk factor for healthy development. However, have they considered infant sleeping arrangements from all of the relevant angles: physiological, psychological, and cultural? As Nugent (1994) points out, cross-cultural studies demonstrate that the notion of risk is a cultural construction. Pediatricians must be cautious before imposing their own cultural construction on members of various ethnic or social groups with whom they do not share a common culture or common ecocultural niche for infant development.

Differences, Not Deficits

Clearly, there are many ethnic and immigrant groups in the United States (and other industrialized nations) for whom ancestral heritage of infant care practices are apparent. Being aware and accepting of these cultural differences is, in itself, important and beneficial. Because multicultural societies such as the United States contain a variety of ethnic groups and family contexts with a variety of sleeping practices, parents deviating from the dominant norm should not be made to feel they are doing something harmful to their child.

For example, understanding that sleeping alone and cosleeping are two different cultural modes, each with its own set of risks and benefits, will lead to pride in rather than shame for diverse cultural heritages. For members of the dominant majority, such understanding leads to respect for rather than denigration of "nonstandard" practices such as cosleeping. Similarly, understanding the reasons behind alternative practices can also help immigrants understand the cultural norms in their new cultural surround. The dissemination of information on such practices among pediatricians and parents can help in developing this kind of mutual respect.

How Are Attachment Behaviors Affected by Parental Goals?

While the role of cultural goals is readily observed in infant sleeping practices, cross-cultural differences in parental goals are also manifest in attachment behaviors. Harwood, Miller, and Lucca Irizarry (1995) begin their book, *Culture and Attachment,* with Bowlby's (1969) classic definition of "attachment as 'the bond that ties' the child to his or her primary caretaker" (p. 4) and attachment behaviors as "those behaviors that allow the infant to seek and maintain proximity to his primary attachment figure" (p. 4). Nonetheless, the classic attach-

ment assessment procedure, the Strange Situation presented by Ainsworth and Wittig in 1969, uses reactions to brief separations rather than opportunities for proximity maintenance as the foundation for measuring infant attachment.

Infant Responses to the Strange Situation

In the Strange Situation paradigm, *securely* attached children are differentiated from *insecurely* attached children in a laboratory test involving leaving an infant alone with various combinations of mother, stranger, both, or neither. From observations of infant behavior in these situations, infants can be assigned into the categories of avoidant attachment (Group A), secure attachment (Group B), and resistant attachment (Group C). The Group B behavior pattern in the Strange Situation has long been seen as an indicator of such things as healthy mother-infant interaction and emotional growth (Ainsworth, Blehar, Waters, & Wall, 1978).

The role of the mother, particularly maternal sensitivity, is also seen as important in infant attachment. For example, it has been proposed that mothers of future Group A babies express anger and rejection of their babies, mothers of Group C babies are insensitive and inept, and mothers of Group B babies are more affectionate and effective in soothing their babies (Ainsworth, 1979; Campos, Barrett, Lamb, Goldsmith, & Stenberg, 1983; Main & Weston, 1982).

These generalizations, however, do not take into consideration the cultural reasons an infant may behave in a particular way and how a mother might interpret that behavior. Because mothers are the carriers of culture to the next generation, especially during their child's infancy, it is important to consider cultural reasons for the mother's behavior. Some have argued that attachment behaviors in different countries are so different that indigenous theories of attachment are needed to fully describe attachment in different cultures (Rothbaum, Weisz, Pott, Miyake, & Morelli, 2000, 2001); others conclude that attachment is a valuable framework for examining general questions about mothering, biology, and culture in development (Chao, 2001b; Posada & Jacobs, 2001). Whatever the case may be, it is clear that mother-infant attachment is an important phenomenon to consider in studies of culture and development.

In Japan, compared to the United States, more C or resistant babies have been identified from the Strange Situation assessment. In contrast, A or avoidant babies are common in the United States, but rare or absent in Japan (Miyake et al., 1985; Takahashi, 1990; van Ijzendoorn & Kroonenberg, 1988). Why this difference in the way cultures deviate from the "norm"? Cultural differences in parental goals may be the reason. Traditional Japanese mothers, with parental goals such as having the parent and child "become one" (Kawakami, 1987), rarely leave their babies in the care of strangers such as babysitters. Thus, the various separations that take place in the Strange Situation paradigm cause extreme and unusual stress to the infants (Miyake et al., 1985; Takahashi, 1990).

Supporting this hypothesis, a study of working Japanese mothers found the same distribution of attachment patterns as in the United States (Durrett, Otaki, & Richards, 1984); there were avoidant as well as resistant and secure attachments. Clearly, such babies would have had experience with temporary separations from their mother. Confirming this point, studies in the United States by Lamb and colleagues (Lamb & Sternberg, 1990; Roopnarine & Lamb, 1978, 1980) show that unaccustomed separations from the mother, as when a baby begins day care, can raise anxiety about separation that is revealed in Strange Situation behavior, but that habituation to temporary separations removes the behavioral manifestations of this anxiety.

As Takahashi (1990) proposed, the separation history of the child affects responses to the Strange Situation; this separation history is conditioned both by cross-cultural variability in value orientations and by ecological factors within a culture, such as day care. The higher proportion of resistant babies found in Japan could therefore be due to different modal patterns of separation that take place in the daily interactions of Japanese and U.S. mother-child dyads.

In another study, German babies were found to be more likely to be categorized as Group A, or avoidant, and less likely to be labeled as Group C, or resistant, when compared to children in both Japan and the United States (Grossmann, Grossmann, Spangler, Suess, & Unzner, 1985; van IJzendoorn & Kroonenberg, 1988). Like the Japanese and U.S. patterns, this pattern can also be attributed to culture-specific parental goals for their children. In Germany, for example, parents desire their children to be nonclingy and independent (Grossmann et al., 1985). Therefore, the greater proportion of A infants in Germany may be a culturally desired outcome of German parental goals and strategies (Campos et al., 1983).

The United States falls between Japan and Germany in the frequency of both avoidant, independent (Group A) and dependent, resistant (Group C) babies (van Ijzendoorn & Kroonenberg, 1988). If we think of the independence value as having originated in Germany and other parts of northern Europe, this pattern makes sense. The value would have attenuated in its travels to the United States, where it came into contact with people from all over the world, including indigenous Americans, most of whom valued interdependence in their ancestral cultures (Greenfield & Cocking, 1994).

In line with this explanation, Grossman et al. (1985) observe that in Germany,

> as soon as infants become mobile, most mothers feel that they should now be weaned from close bodily contact. To carry a baby who can move on its own or to respond to its every cry by picking it up would be considered as spoiling. (p. 253)

LeVine (1994) notes that German infants not only sleep alone, they are also left alone in the morning for an hour after waking up. In addition, mothers leave babies alone to shop, and German babies are left alone in the evening after 1 year of age. These methods of fostering independence seems more extreme than those used by mothers in the United States. Hence, it is logical for the United States to be between Germany and Japan in both avoidant, independent A babies and resistant, dependent C babies.

However, within the United States, it has been suggested that day care is also associated with more avoidant attachments (Belsky, 1989). This is an ecological factor that could push the value of independence farther than would otherwise be the case. Clarke-Stewart (1989) has suggested that, "although children who are accustomed to brief separations by virtue of repeated day care experiences may behave 'avoidantly,' their behavior might actually reflect a developmentally precocious pattern of independence and confidence rather than insecurity" (quoted by Lamb & Sternberg, 1990, p. 360).

Implications of Cross-Cultural Differences in Attachment for Practice

What, in a multicultural society, is the adaptive significance of minority interpretations of attachment that differ from those of the majority? This is an important question for practice that has not been explored in research. Are minority infants at risk for later maladaptation to the majority culture because their mothers have a different interpretation of the attachment relationship? Psychologists and practitioners concerned with issues of attachment should keep this issue in mind; in understanding attachment for clinical purposes, it may be necessary to go beyond attachment behaviors to understand the culture-specific meaning of those behaviors for the mother-child dyad.

Implications for Measuring Attachment across Cultures and across Subcultures

The stress level engendered by the Strange Situation in Japan raises the question of whether the measuring instrument itself is too culture-specific for cross-cultural research. Indeed, it was originally developed as a culture-specific instrument for the dominant culture of the United States (Clarke-Stewart, Goossens, & Allhusen, 2001). Because it is based on reactions to separation from mother and reactions to strangers, is it a valid measure of attachment in cultures characterized by almost continuous mother-infant contact and the absence of contact with strangers?

On the other side of the coin, the Strange Situation is based on the assumption that brief separations from the mother will provoke mild to moderate stress. Clarke-Stewart, Goossens, and Allhusen (2001) therefore note that the Strange Situation may not be valid for cultural settings (such as day care) in which an infant becomes accustomed to frequent brief separations from the mother and, therefore, is not stressed at all. Clarke-Stewart and her colleagues, in response to these problems with the cross-cultural (and cross-subcultural) use of the Strange Situation, have developed a new attachment measure, the California Attachment Procedure, that does not involve separation from mother and is therefore not affected by experience (or the lack thereof) with brief separations from mother. In line with Bowlby's (1969) evolution-based notion of attachment, their measure operationalizes attachment as the use of a close relationship for a safe haven when danger is sensed. Moderate stressors (such as a loud noise) are presented to the baby in the presence of the mother, and the baby's use of the mother (the safe haven) to cope with fearful reactions to these stressors is then noted. Because it is not affected by specific experience with maternal separation, a measure based on this type of universalistic definition of attachment is much more likely to have cross-cultural validity than the Strange Situation.

How Are Communication Behaviors Affected by Parental Goals?

In this section, we provide evidence that parental goals for child development are also realized through parents' communication strategies with their infants. In some cultures, these strategies are more geared to fostering technological intelligence; in others, they are more geared to fostering social intelligence.

The Content of Communication

Fernald and Morikawa (1993) observed American and Japanese mother-infant dyads playing with toys. The differences found in conversational topics was striking: American mothers tended to focus on calling attention to the object names of the toys. An example given of a typical American interaction is, "That's a car. See the car? You like it? It's got wheels" (p. 653). In contrast, Japanese mothers were less interested in object labeling; instead, they focused more of their attention on verbalizing polite social exchanges. An example of such an interaction is translated as "Here! It's a vroom vroom. I give it to you. Now give it to me. Give me. Yes! Thank you" (p. 653).

Japanese mothers were also more likely to engage in routines that arouse empathy with the object, encouraging positive feelings toward the toy by saying things like "Here! It's a doggy. Give it love. Love love love while patting the toy" (Fernald & Morikawa, 1993, p. 653). In sharp contrast, many U.S. mothers explained that their goals in the interaction were to attract their child's attention and to teach him or her new words. Here, a distinct value is placed on cognitive development. In contrast, Japanese mothers explained that their goals were to talk gently and to use sounds that the infant could easily imitate. The Japanese concern for explicit teaching of cultural norms for politeness in speech was also expressed (Clancy, 1986; Fernald & Morikawa, 1993).

These differences are an operational demonstration of different parental goals. Mundy-Castle (1974) conceptualizes the European-based (Western) way of socializing children as geared to the goal of technological intelligence (intelligence that is related to manipulation of the physical world), and the African way as geared to the goal of social intelligence (intelligence related to the knowledge of others). Clearly, the Japanese mother quoted earlier is also emphasizing the development of social intelligence.

The role of adult-infant communication in actualizing the parental goal of social intelligence is seen in the following interpretation of Bakeman, Adamson, Konner, and Barr's (1990) research among the !Kung, African hunter-gatherers in Botswana. In this culture of intimate social bonds and minimal property, objects are valued as things to be shared, not as personal possessions (Berk, 1993, p. 30).

In !Kung society, no toys are made for infants. Instead, natural objects, such as twigs, grass, stones, and nutshells, are always available, along with cooking implements. However, adults do not encourage babies to play with these objects. In fact, adults are unlikely to interact with infants while they are exploring objects independently. But when a baby offers an object to another person, adults become highly responsive, encouraging and vocalizing much more than at other times. Thus, the !Kung cultural emphasis on the interpersonal rather than physical aspects of existence is reflected in how adults use objects in their interactions with the very youngest members of their community (Berk, 1993, p. 30).

Similar to the !Kung's emphasis on social rather than technological intelligence, the communication of West Africans in Africa and West African immigrants in Paris focuses on integrating the infant into a social group (Rabain, 1979; Rabain-Jamin, 1994; Zempleni-Rabain, 1973). African mothers manifest this emphasis by using verbalizations that relate their infant to a third party, either real (e.g., telling the baby to share some food with brothers or sisters) or imaginary (e.g., "Grandma told you," said by the mother of a family that has immigrated to France, leaving the grandmother in Africa). They also respond more frequently to child-initiated social activity than French mothers do.

European mothers (e.g., French, German, Greek), in contrast, focus on the child-centered mother-child dyad (e.g., face-to-face communication) and on their infants' technological competence (e.g., object manipulation; Keller et al., 2003; Rabain, 1979; Rabain-Jamin, 1994; Zempleni-Rabain, 1973). For example, in comparison with the African mothers, French mothers manifest this focus by more frequent reference to the child's speech (e.g., "What are you saying to your mommy?"; "Is that all you've got to say?"), by less frequently relating the child to a third party, and by responding more frequently to child-initiated object manipulation (Rabain, 1979; Rabain-Jamin, 1994; Zempleni-Rabain, 1973).

One conclusion is that there may be a connection between an independent orientation and technological intelligence. An early orientation to the nonsocial world of things and objects stresses independence from social relationships, for example, in Germany (Keller, Zach, & Abels, 2002) and in France (Rabain-Jamin & Sabeau-Jouannet, 1997). An absence of emphasis on social relationships seems correlated with the presence of an emphasis on the physical world. Although our earlier discussion of sleeping arrangements focused on whether an infant was alone or with a parent, there is another aspect of this difference: When infants are left alone in a crib or playpen, they are usually given toys (e.g., mobiles, rattles) to amuse themselves with. Because toys provide early cognitive socialization for technological intelligence, there is a connection between the socialization of independence and the socialization of technological intelligence. The child left alone with toys is both learning to be alone and learning to interact with the physical world of objects. In contrast, people are more important than the object world in the development of an interdependent orientation or social intelligence.

The Process of Communication

Dyadic communication is the norm in an individualistic value system. However, multiparty communication is the norm in a collectivistic framework (Quiroz, Greenfield, & Altchech, 1999). This leads to differences in the deployment of attention by caregivers and their toddlers in the process of communication. In a Maya community in Guatemala, where interdependence is an important developmental goal, mothers and their toddlers often kept two simultaneous and continuous lines of attention and communication going when there were two competing sources of attentional demand (e.g., an older sib makes a bid to play with a toddler, who is already interacting with his or her mother). In Salt Lake City, Utah, an individualistic setting, mothers and toddlers more often carried on one dyadic interaction at a time when there were two competing bids for attention (e.g., both a toddler and an older sibling want the mother's attention; Chavajay & Rogoff, 2002). In other words, the process of communication between parent and toddler, itself a socializing force in development, reflected the two respective models of human development.

Cultural Coherence and Individual Differences

The different customs and practices of infant care are not random. They are motivated by underlying cultural

TABLE 17.1   Contrasting Cultural Models of Infant Development and Socialization

Developmental Goals	Independence	Interdependence
Valued intelligence	Technological	Social
Socialization practices	Infant sleeps alone; more use of devices (baby seats, strollers, cribs, playpens) that allow separation of awake infant; objects to explore and amuse	Parent-child cosleeping, more holding and carrying, objects to mediate social relationships
Attachment behaviors	More avoidant behavior in response to the Strange Situation	More resistant behavior in response to the Strange Situation

models with overarching socialization goals that provide continuity from one developmental domain to another. How infants are viewed, the developmental goals of the parents for the child, and parental behavior toward the child are all inextricably intertwined with the cultural background of the parents and the child. The coherence, on a cultural level, of developmental goals, socialization practices, child outcomes, and adult interpretations is illustrated in Table 17.1, which serves as a kind of summary of this section.

Philosophical Differences in Child Rearing between Individualistic and Collectivistic Cultures

The two models presented in Table 17.1 must be taken as two idealized systems of cultural norms. Within each ideal type, different societies and cultures will exemplify different varieties of both individualism and collectivism (Kim & Choi, 1994).

Because individual differences are central to U.S. culture and to psychology as a discipline, it is important to point out that, within every culture, there will always be important individual variation around each cultural norm. In other words, cultural typologies do not eradicate or minimize individual differences; they simply point to the norms around which individual differences range. Nonetheless, we must also point out that the scientific and popular concern with individual differences reflects a cultural orientation in which individuation is a primary emphasis (Greenfield, 2004).

Culture Contact and Culture Change

In addition, there will be conflict and compromise between the two idealized models presented in Table 17.1 in situations of culture contact or culture change. Culture contact is particularly important in multicultural societies (e.g., Raeff et al., 2000). Culture change is particularly important in societies undergoing processes of technological or commercial development (Greenfield, 2004; Greenfield, Maynare, & Childs, 2003).

Japan and China, for example, have been undergoing processes of rapid culture change over the past generation. For example, a recent study in Taiwan and the United States did not find more collectivistic child-rearing values in Taiwan (Wang & Tamis-LeMonda, 2003).

Earlier we mentioned that a study of working Japanese mothers found the same distribution of attachment patterns in that subgroup as in the United States (Durrett et al., 1984); we have interpreted this finding as reflecting the greater independence of babies who experience regular brief separations from their mother. But in the period since that study was published in 1984, a much greater proportion of Japanese mothers have gone to work outside the home. We would therefore expect that overall patterns of attachment in the Japanese population as a whole would have become more like the pattern in the United States. We would also expect the cultural ideology about attachment to shift accordingly, adapting to new conditions. Indeed, the most recent studies in Japan that we could find showed no differences between Japanese and U.S. mothers in their preferences about interactions, physical proximity, and contact with their infant (Posada & Jacobs, 2001).

It is also known that the ecologies of wealth (e.g., Georgas, van de Vijver, & Berry, 2004), formal education (e.g., Tapia Uribe et al., 1994), and urban environments (e.g., Fuligni & Zhang, 2004) favor more individualistic adaptations. Germany is a country that has become wealthier, more urban, and more highly educated over the past generation. The first historical study of these issues, by Keller and Lamm (in press), has found that infant care practices in Germany have also moved toward greater socialization for independence of infants. Present-day mothers and fathers of 3-month-old infants display significantly more face-to-face contact and object play and significantly less body contact and body stimulation during free play interactions than parents in similar life conditions 25 years earlier.

Cultural Frameworks and Ethnocentrism

It is an all too natural response to criticize the attitudes and practices generated by a cultural model different from one's own, with no understanding of the model behind the overt behaviors. LeVine et al. (1994) provide a wonderful example of ethnocentric criticism in their comparative look at the Gusii in Kenya and the middle class in the United States:

> The Gusii would be shocked at the slow or casual responsiveness of American mothers to the crying of young infants. . . . This signals incompetent caregiving from their perspective. They would be similarly appalled by the practice of putting babies to sleep in separate beds or rooms, where they cannot be closely monitored at night, rather than with the mother. (pp. 255–256)

According to LeVine et al., the Gusii would think American toddlers unruly and disobedient as well, largely due to the excessive praise they receive and the maternal solicitations of their preferences.

Likewise, LeVine et al. (1994) believe that Americans would also find problems with the way the Gusii choose to raise their infants. For example, leaving an infant under the supervision of a 5- or 6-year-old child, a common practice among the Gusii, would be viewed as neglect in the United States.

However, a 5- or 6-year-old Gusii infant caregiver probably has much more know-how about taking care of babies than a typical U.S. child of the same age would have. Sib caregivers observe and practice caregiving under the watchful eye of the mother in many parts of the world (Ochs & Schieffelin, 1984). They develop sophisticated skills that aid them in carrying out this responsibility (Rabain-Jamin, Maynard, & Greenfield, 2003).

LeVine et al. (1994) also believe that:

> [Americans] would be appalled that Gusii mothers often do not look at their babies when breastfeeding them . . . and that praise is more or less prohibited in the Gusii script of maternal response. . . . They would see the Gusii mothers as unacceptably authoritarian and punitive with children. (pp. 255–256)

In this way, infant care practices that are viewed as moral and pragmatic in one cultural context can be viewed as "misguided, ineffective, and even immoral" (p. 256) in others.

In a multicultural society, ethnocentric criticism has disastrous practical and social consequences. Instead, it is necessary to understand how each model has made sense in its historical context. This means that assessments of pathology or deviance by parents, pediatricians, teachers, and clinicians must always be based on an understanding of the cultural meaning that particular behaviors have for the participants in a social system.

For example, Schroen (1995) explores how a lack of cultural understanding can lead to misinterpretations by social workers. She documents how negative judgments by social workers of cultural practices they do not understand, using criteria from their own culture, can lead to tragedy. For instance, social workers can misinterpret sibling care (a practice in many cultures worldwide) as child neglect, leading to children being taken away from loving parents who may have been following a different cultural model of competent parenting and child development.

One can imagine other situations in which cultural practices may be misinterpreted as forms of neglect or abuse. For example, cosleeping or cobathing practices (acceptable in many cultures, such as in Japan) may be misinterpreted as sexual in nature. Social workers, like other clinicians, must therefore be trained to recognize differences between cultural variations in practice and truly abusive situations.

Teachers and day care workers must also be made aware of these differences in infant rearing practices. For example, the crying (or lack thereof) of children when they are dropped off at school in the morning may be partially attributable to cultural differences in the strangeness of separation. Through a better understanding of these differences, infant care professionals can become more understanding and helpful to the child's transition between home and day care.

Costs and Benefits of Different Cultural Models

Each cultural model has its own set of benefits and costs (LeVine et al., 1994). These can still be seen throughout the life span. For example, the mother-child bond remains strong throughout life in Japan, but the husband-wife tie is of a less romantic and close nature than in the United States (Lebra, 1994).

The costs and benefits of each cultural model are perceptible by the participants and a culturally sensitive outside observer. For example, although European American mothers generally subscribe to the benefits of autonomy as a developmental goal, its cost to them can be seen as the "empty nest syndrome." In this culture, adult children are often gone physically, as well as emotionally.

Different patterns of costs and benefits provide opportunities for useful cross-cultural exchange. From the perspective of both insider and outsider, each cultural model has its strengths and weaknesses, its costs and benefits, and its pathological extremes. For this reason, cross-cultural exchange of values and practices can sometimes serve as a corrective force to counteract the weaknesses, costs, and pathologies of any given cultural system. For example, McKenna and Mosko's (1994) experimental research documents the potential physiological benefits of cosleeping for infants in a society (the United States) with a relatively high rate of SIDS. This practice, which many of the study's participants have brought with them from Mexico and Central America, have direct relevance to pediatric advice on sleeping arrangements.

However, recommendations for cross-cultural exchange of infant care practices must by tempered by the finding of Weisner, Bausano, and Kornfein (1983) that there are strong ecological and cultural constraints on cross-cultural exchange in this domain. An example of such a constraint is the fact that parent-infant cosleeping, while decreasing the risk of SIDS, also decreases husband-wife intimacy, so valued in the United States. Consequently, ecologically valid research on the benefits and costs of adapting infant care practices from a variety of cultures is needed. Cultures are not isolated practices, but coherent wholes. So cross-cultural borrowing must be done with caution: A change in one element may have unwanted repercussions in other domains or at later developmental points. Nonetheless, parents, pediatricians, clinicians, and day care workers are often not fully aware of the range of options available to them in terms of infant caregiving practices.

Culture Conflict

When infants and toddlers from a more collectivistic home culture enter their first mainstream educational institution, the day care center, they often find an institution where individualistic values are simply taken for granted. Janet Gonzalez-Mena (2001) reports the following conflict scene:

"I just can't do what you want," says the caregiver. "I don't have time with all these other children to care for. Besides," she adds hesitantly, "I don't believe in toilet training a 1-year-old."

"But she's already trained!" the mother says emphatically. "All you have to do is put her on the potty."

"She's not trained—you're trained." The caregiver's voice is still calm and steady, but a red flush is beginning to creep up her neck toward her face.

"You just don't understand!" The mother picks up her daughter and diaper bag and sweeps out the door.

"No, *you're* the one who doesn't understand," mutters the caregiver, busying herself with a pile of dirty dishes precariously stacked on the counter. (pp. 34–35)

Gonzalez-Mena (2001) analyzes this conflict as a conflict between the cultural scripts of independence and interdependence:

If the caregiver defines toilet training as teaching or encouraging the child independently to take care of his or her own toileting needs and her goal is to accomplish this as quickly and painlessly as possible, she'll regard 12 months as too early to start. Children of 12 months need adult help. However, if toilet training is regarded as a reduction of diapers and the method is to form a partnership with the child to do just that, you'll start as soon as you can read the children's signals and "catch them in time." In the first case, the focus is on independence; in the second, it is on interdependence or mutual dependence. (p. 34)

INTERVENING TO REDUCE CROSS-CULTURAL VALUE CONFLICT AND MISUNDERSTANDING

The intervention we present here, as in the rest of the chapter, is from a series of Bridging Cultures projects (e.g., Trumbull, Rothstein-Fisch, & Greenfield, 1999). These are interventions designed to reduce the confusion and conflict, both internal and external, that come from the incompatibilities between collectivistic and individualistic developmental norms in a multicultural society. The intervention we describe here was designed to handle conflicts like the toilet training conflict just presented. Janet Gonzalez-Mena was part of the intervention team; her ethnographic observations, such as the one just presented, were the research base for the intervention itself.

According to the National Association for the Education of Young Children (2005) responding to cultural differences is an important part of developmentally appropriate care. However, as we have seen, appropriateness is determined by cultural beliefs and values. The "Guidelines for Developmentally Appropriate Practice" (Bredekamp & Copple, 1997, p. 12) acknowledge that "every culture structures and interprets children's behavior and development" but conclude that "children are capable of learning to function in more than one cultural context simultaneously." Thus, the default assumption is that, although cultures may vary, infants can be expected to negotiate eating and sleeping arrangements different from what they experience at home. Caregivers might mistake this to mean that because babies can adapt, family routines at home (and implicitly the values and beliefs that underlie them) are not really an issue for them to take on. This is an alternative viewpoint to the one on which we have based our Bridging Cultures intervention.

The following scenario is based on a composite of experiences and observations. It provides another example of how culturally based developmental goals of independence and interdependence can lead to cross-cultural misunderstanding and conflict concerning standards of early care. Most important for present purposes, we describe how this kind of ethnographic knowledge can be used in an intervention to produce more culturally sensitive caregiving attitudes and practices. This particular incident is drawn from the *Bridging Cultures in Early Care and Education Module* (Zepeda, Gonzalez-Mena, Rothstein-Fisch, & Trumbull, in press). The Bridging Cultures project was developed to make caregivers more aware of the individualistic assumptions of professional practice and the more collectivistic assumptions of immigrant and other families from nonmainstream cultures.

> The home visitor sits in a small living room near a mother holding a baby. The visitor knows that the baby has some physical challenges and is at risk for developmental delays. While the mother talks to the visitor about some issues going on in her life, the visitor is wiggling a toy in front of the baby. The mother turns the baby around and holds him close so he can't see or reach the toy. When she hears a noise in the other room, she gets up to check on her older children. The home visitor holds out her arms to take the baby. The mother hands him to her.
>
> The home visitor sits on the floor and holds the baby so he can easily reach any one of several toys she has arranged on a blanket. When the mother returns, the home visitor has the baby lying on the blanket, and she is bent over talking to the baby, who is clutching a soft ball and waving it in the air. "Oh you like that ball! It's soft," she says. The mother picks the baby up off the blanket, and the ball falls from his hand. She ignores the ball and takes him back to her chair. As she sits down, the baby reaches for an empty plastic glass on the table beside the chair. The mother puts it out of his reach. She goes back to cuddling

the baby in her arms. The home visitor looks discouraged, and the mother looks puzzled at the expression on the other woman's face. (Zepeda et al., in press)

In this scenario, the mother remains in close physical contact with her baby and communicates nonverbally with him by holding. She also puts him in a relationship of physical closeness with the visitor. She is communicating the importance of social relationships. In contrast, the home visitor lays the baby down on his back and engages him with verbal labeling around the topic of the toy; she also encourages his manipulation of the toy. The visitor creates a physical separation with the baby and communicates about an object, while encouraging the baby's agency in relation to the physical world. When the mother reenters the room, she is surprised to see the baby on the floor, perhaps perceived as distancing, and picks him up immediately, with no apparent regard for the ball. Yet it was the baby's interaction with the object that seemed most important to the home visitor.

This incident provides a further example of cross-cultural value conflict between accepted standards of infant care in the dominant culture and accepted standards of infant care in immigrant cultures. The conflict is potent and fundamental because the home visitor is probably thinking about the baby's need to interact with objects in order to achieve physical and cognitive goals, whereas the mother may be more concerned about social interactions.

This incident is used as part of the Bridging Cultures curriculum. Participants in the training discuss what they perceive as the goals of the mother and the home visitor. The discussion is intended to lead them to acknowledge the importance of both social relationships (developing social intelligence) and knowledge of objects (developing technological intelligence) and the potential for discussion between the mother and the visitor about their goals. However, if the underlying reasons for the differing developmental goals are not made apparent, each adult may simply disapprove of the other's behavior, thus undermining an important partnership between parents and caregivers. Through cross-cultural exchange, both styles of communication could be used to socialize children for both technological and social intelligence.

The early childhood Bridging Cultures workshops are based on an extensive body of ethnographic research (e.g., Gonzalez-Mena, 2001). However, the workshops themselves are new, and very little research on their effects has yet been carried out. One promising indication is that, after a 90-minute workshop, 93% of the participants (*N* = 51) indicated they would change the way they worked with children as a result of their new understanding (Rothstein-Fisch, 2004). When practitioners are open to learning about different cultural values and behavioral options, a new appreciation, and perhaps even successful implementation, of a broader range of practices may be attained.

PARENT-CHILD RELATIONS

Parent-child relations are an important aspect of both child development and child socialization; parents embody and represent the broader cultural context as children learn to become members of their culture. Parents and children become a sort of family microculture with specific norms, customs, and values that reflect a variety of cultural and ethnic norms. In this section, we examine cross-cultural variation in parents' behavior and attitudes toward their children and children's behavior and attitudes toward their parents. The latter is an understudied perspective.

Children's Behavior toward Parents

Consider the following scenario:

> A week ago, you went shopping with your mother, and at the register, she realized that she was short $10. You lent her the money, and after a week, she gives no indication of remembering the loan. What would you do? Why?

In responses to scenarios like this, Suzuki and Greenfield (2002) found an interesting effect. Asian American students, particularly those closer to Asian culture in their acculturative levels and activity preferences, were significantly more likely than European American students to sacrifice certain personal goals for their parents. This finding seems to reflect the collectivistic emphasis on filial piety and respect for parents found in the Confucian worldview of East Asia.

The Confucian value of filial piety deeply influences the desired behavior of children toward their parents. According to Tseng (1973, p. 199), "[Confucius] viewed the parent-child relationship as the foundation from which interpersonal love and trust would grow, and thus interpreted filial piety as the virtue for every person to

follow." Some of the tenets of filial piety are obeying and honoring one's parents, providing for the material and mental well-being of one's aged parents, performing the ceremonial duties of ancestral worship, taking care to avoid harm to one's body, ensuring the continuity of the family line, and in general conducting oneself so as to bring honor and not disgrace to the family name (Ho, 1994, p. 287).

This multidimensional concept of filial piety is believed to be a virtue that everyone must practice, as "the love and affection of a child for his parents, particularly the mother, is the prototype of goodness in interpersonal relationships" (Tseng, 1973, p. 195). From a very young age, children are introduced to these concepts and ideals, and by the time they are teenagers, the extent of filial piety felt among Asians is such that it is not uncommon for Chinese teenagers to hand over entire paychecks to their parents for family use (B. L. Sung, 1985). More recently, researchers have differentiated between different forms of filial piety. For example, filial piety traits can be categorized as authoritarian (suppressing one's wishes and complying with parents' wishes), or reciprocal (emotionally attending to parents out of gratitude), with the former decreasing and the latter increasing in relevance in Chinese society (Yeh & Bedford, 2003).

In the United States, Asian American adolescents also have stronger values and feelings of expectation about assisting, respecting, and supporting their families than do European Americans (Fuligni, Tseng, & Lam, 1999). Greater feelings of family obligation are felt by Latino teens as well (Fuligni et al., 1999). These feelings are strengthened even more during young adulthood (Fuligni & Pedersen, 2002). Suzuki (2000) found that Asian Americans from fifth grade through college, as well as parents of fifth and sixth graders, spoke more favorably about the various components of filial piety—respect, obedience, and eventual care of parents—than did comparable European-American groups.

This pattern is consonant with the fact that traditional European American values are affected by different cultural influences and reflect the importance of individual goals and personal property prominent in the dominant North American worldview. Implicit in this view is a certain personal distance between parent and child; this is consonant with a view of human development that emphasizes the achievement of autonomy by late adolescence. It is also consonant with the predominantly Protestant religious background of the United

States, which stresses each individual's relationship with God rather than family ties and obligations.

In sum, contrasting responses to the scenario manifest and highlight differing models of children's relationships with their parents, models that have deep cultural roots. Given that assimilation to U.S. culture reduced self-sacrifice in Asian Americans in Suzuki and Greenfield's (2002) study, we would expect an even stronger pattern of difference when comparing Asians in Asia with European Americans in the United States.

Many Asian countries (e.g., Japan, China, and Korea) have similar emphases on children's lifelong duties toward their parents (J. S. Choi, 1970; Osako & Liu, 1986; K.-T. Sung, 1990). Some parallel differences emerged when Miller and Bersoff (1995, p. 274) gave subjects in India and the United States the following scenario: "Because of his job, a married son had to live in a city that was a four hour drive from his parents' home. The son made a point of keeping in touch with his parents by either visiting, calling or writing them on a regular basis." The authors note that a typical subject in the United States evaluated "the son's behavior as satisfying in that it enabled him to enhance his relationship with his parents, while still retaining a sense of individual autonomy" (p. 275). A typical Indian subject, in contrast, "focused on the satisfaction associated with fulfilling the obligations of care toward one's parents and of knowing that their welfare needs are being met" (p. 275).

The contrast is, in both scenarios, between a response that values children's obligations to their parents versus one that emphasizes children's autonomy and personal choices concerning their relationship to their parents. In both cases, the dominant cultural response in the United States is for autonomy and choice. Relative to that response, less acculturated Asian Americans emphasized self-sacrifice for parents, while Indians in India emphasized children's obligations to their parents as a positive value.

Parents' Behavior toward Children

In this section, we discuss the other side of the coin, parents' behavior toward their children. Our point is to show that the same two cultural pathways guide parents' behavior toward their children, as they guide children's behavior toward their parents. We will make this point with respect to parental style (discipline), communication, teaching, and patterns of reinforcement. We extrapolate the cultural structuring of parent-

ing through the life span, pointing once again to cultural coherence. Throughout, we explore the impact of cultural dynamics—historical change in demographics or cross-cultural value conflict—on the cultural structuring of parenting behavior.

Styles of Parenting

Baumrind (1967, 1971) offered a now classical formulation of three dstyles: authoritarian, authoritative, and permissive. Each one defines a core relationship between parents and children; the children that have been studied range from preschool (Baumrind, 1967) to high school age (Dornbusch, Ritter, Leiderman, Roberts, & Fraleigh, 1987). The *authoritative* parent is controlling, demanding, warm, rational, and receptive to the child's communication. The *authoritarian* parent is detached and controlling without exhibiting warmth. The *permissive* parent is noncontrolling, nondemanding, and relatively warm (Baumrind, 1983).

How does parenting style relate to European American parents' goals for their children? Although not generally acknowledged in the developmental literature, Baumrind's typology is closely tied to the normative goals for child development in North America. Authoritative parenting is considered to be the most adaptive style because it is associated with children who are "self-reliant, self-controlled, explorative, and content" (Baumrind, 1983, p. 121). These are the qualities of the independent individual so valued in the cultural model of individualism in countries such as the United States. In the United States, authoritative parenting and relationship closeness are also associated with better school performance among European Americans (Leung, Lau, & Lam, 1998). Interestingly, this is not the case for first-generation Chinese Americans (Chao, 2001a). Thus, authoritative parenting may not be the best model for all cultural contexts.

Cross-Cultural Variability in Styles of Parenting. Authoritative parenting is not the norm in every group. Different ethnic groups within the United States and many Eastern and developing countries have been found to utilize an authoritarian parenting style to a greater degree than do middle-class European American parents in the United States. Authoritarian parenting is more common, for example, in East Asia (Ho, 1994; Kim & Choi, 1994), Africa (Nsamenang & Lamb, 1994; LeVine et al., 1994), and Mexico (Delgado-Gaitan, 1994), as well as in ethnic groups derived from these ancestral cultures: Asian Americans (Chao, 1994, 2000, 2001a; Leung et al., 1998), African Americans (Baumrind, 1972), Mexican Americans (Cardona, Nicholson, & Fox, 2000; Delgado-Gaitan, 1994; Reese, Balzano, Gallimore, & Goldenberg, 1995), and Egyptian Canadians (Rudy & Grusec, 2001). (Baumrind's third style, permissive parenting, has not been found to be normative in any identifiable cultural group.)

How does cross-cultural variability in parenting style relate to child behavior and parental goals? Most important in considering cross-cultural variation in parenting styles is the fact that different parental goals can give different meanings and a different emotional context to the same behaviors. Notably, the social and emotional accompaniments of classical authoritarian parenting behavior such as the usage of imperatives may be quite different where the culture has an interdependence-oriented developmental script (Greenfield, 1994). Chao (1994), for example, points out the inadequacy of the notion of authoritarian parenting to describe the Chinese ethnotheory of child socialization. She invokes indigenous Chinese child-rearing ideologies reflected in the concepts of *chiao shun* (training children in the appropriate or expected behaviors) and *guan* (to govern).

For the European American mothers in this study, the word "training" often evoked associations such as "militaristic," "regimented," or "strict" that were interpreted as being very negative aspects of authoritarian parenting. However, although authoritarian parenting was associated with negative effects and images in the United States, the Chinese versions of authoritarianism, chaio shun and guan, were perceived in a more positive light from within the culture, emphasizing harmonious relations and parental concern (Chao, 1994). Chinese chiao shun and guan were seen not as punitive or emotionally unsupportive, but rather as associated with rigorous and responsible teaching, high involvement, and physical closeness (Chao, 1994). In fact, in China (and in India), authoritarian parenting styles are associated with maternal valuing of filial piety and academic achievement (Leung et al., 1998; Rao, McHale, & Pearson, 2003).

Another interesting finding indicative of qualitatively different cultural patterning was that, although Chinese American parents were higher on authoritarian parenting than European American parents, they did not differ on the measure of authoritative parenting. In other words, Chinese parents more often subscribed to authoritarian items (sample authoritarian item: "I do not allow my child to question my decisions"); however,

there was no difference between the groups in subscribing to authoritative items (sample authoritative item: "I talk it over and reason with my child when he misbehaves"). In this group, authoritarianism and aspects of authoritativeness such as affection and rational guidance (illustrated in the example) were complementary, not contradictory.

This finding was mirrored by another study of Chinese American parents, which found that they were more directive than but equally as warm as European American parents in their child-rearing behaviors (Jose, Huntsinger, Huntsinger, & Liaw, 2000). A similar result was found in a study of Egyptian Canadians and Anglo-Canadians; Egyptian Canadian parents scored higher on authoritarian parenting, but they did not differ from Anglo-Canadian parents in overall levels of warmth (Rudy & Grusec, 2001).

Besides Chinese Americans, there are other groups in the United States for whom authoritarian parenting is not always associated with the negative child development outcomes (such as discontent, withdrawal, distrust, and lack of instrumental competence) it has for European American children. For example, Baumrind (1972) found that, in lower middle-class African American families, authoritarian parenting was more frequent and seemed to produce different effects on child development than in European American families. Rather than negative outcomes, authoritarian parenting by African Americans was associated with self-assertive, independent behavior in preschool girls. (Baumrind did not have enough information to carry out the same kind of analysis with African American preschool boys.)

This difference in the frequency and effects of authoritarian parenting may be related to different ecological demands of the African American environment. The fact that African Americans have traditionally been on the bottom of society's power and economic hierarchy may have led them to develop obedience in their children through authoritarian directives. Authoritarian parenting can be essential when children live in potentially hazardous conditions where safety is assured only if parental instructions are followed immediately.

A second possibility is that the relative social isolation of African American communities because of slavery, segregation, and discrimination led to more long-term retention of African culture than was the case for voluntary (in Ogbu's, 1994, sense) immigrants. Indeed, according to Sudarkasa (1988, cited in Harrison, Wilson, Pine, Chan, & Buriel, 1990, p. 354),

"Research has documented the persistence of some African cultural patterns among contemporary African American families." One relevant pattern would be the emphasis on obedience and respect as most important in African child development (LeVine et al., 1994; Nsamenang & Lamb, 1994). On the side of socialization, this pattern is achieved by strictness (Nsamenang & Lamb, 1994) and the use of parental commands as a communication strategy (LeVine et al., 1994). Such a socialization pattern would fit into the rubric of Baumrind's authoritarian parenting.

Similarly, poor immigrant Latino families bring from Mexico and Central America the developmental goal of respect and the socialization mode of authoritarian parenting to achieve parental respect (Reese et al., 1995; Valdes, 1997).

Parent-Child Communication

Another important aspect of parent-child relations is the styles that parents employ in communicating with their children. Although parents everywhere utilize an array of styles, the emphasis is quite different from culture to culture. Here, we take up several dimensions of this variability, relating each style to parental goals (Sigel, 1985; Sigel et al., 1992) and cultural models of human development.

Nonverbal Communication or Verbalization? The Cultural Role of Empathy, Observation, and Participation. Azuma (1994) notes that Japanese mothers (and nursery school teachers) rely more on empathy and nonverbal communication, whereas mothers in the United States rely more on verbal communication with their children. He sees a connection between the physical closeness of the Japanese mother-child pair (discussed in the infancy section of this chapter) and the development of empathy as a mode of communication.

Azuma (1994) points out that verbalization is necessary when there is greater physical and psychological distance between parent and child. The development of empathy paves the way for learning by osmosis, in which the mother does not need to teach directly; she simply prepares a learning environment and makes suggestions. In turn, the child's empathy for the mother motivates learning. This tradition survives in the families of third-generation Japanese American immigrants (Schneider, Hieshima, Lee, & Plank, 1994).

Closely related to empathy and learning by osmosis are the use of observation and participation as forms of

parent-child communication and socialization. Whereas verbal instruction is particularly important in school-based learning, observation and coparticipation of learner and teacher are central to the apprentice-style learning that is common in many cultures (Rogoff, 1990, 2003; Rogoff, Paradise, Arauz, Correa-Chavez, & Angelillo, 2003). Often, master and apprentice are parent and child, as in Childs and Greenfield's (1980; Greenfield, 2004; Greenfield, Maynard, et al., 2003) study of informal learning of weaving in a Maya community of highland Chiapas, Mexico.

Both learning by observation and coparticipation with a parent imply a kind of closeness and empathy between parent and child. For example, in Zinacantec weaving apprenticeship in Chiapas, Mexico, the teacher would sometimes sit behind the learner, positioned so that the two bodies, the learner's and the teacher's, were functioning as one at the loom (Maynard, Greenfield, & Childs, 1999; Greenfield, 2004). Verbal communication and instruction, in contrast, imply using words to bridge the distance through explicitness, thus reducing the need for empathetic communication.

A discourse study by S. H. Choi (1992) reveals a similar pattern of differences between Korean and Canadian mothers interacting with their young children. Comparing middle-class mothers in Korea and Canada, Choi found that Korean mothers and their children manifest a communicative pattern that is relationally attuned to one another in a "fused" state, "where the mothers freely enter their children's reality and speak for them, merging themselves with the children'" (Kagitçibasi, 1996, p. 69). Canadian mothers, in contrast, "withdraw themselves from the children's reality, so that the child's reality can remain autonomous" (S. H. Choi, 1992, pp. 119–120).

Effects of Social Change. With an ecological transition from agriculture and subsistence to money and commerce, apprenticeship learning becomes more independent and less under the control of parents. Greenfield and colleagues (Greenfield, 2004; Greenfield, Maynard, et al., 2003) demonstrated this when they studied weaving apprenticeship in a Maya community across two generations. In response to participation in commercial activities, they found a historical shift from reliance on observation of adult models and careful guidance by adult experts (usually the mother) in the generation studied in 1970 to more involvement of the peers in the apprenticeship process, lessened reliance on observation of others weaving, a reduction in teacher guidance, and more learner independence and initiative in the generation studied in the early 1990s.

Development of Comprehension versus Self-Expression.

Authoritarian parenting brings with it an associated style of parent-to-child communication: frequent use of directives and imperatives, with encouragement of obedience and respect (Greenfield, Brazelton, & Childs, 1989; Harkness, 1988; Kagitçibasi, 1996). This style is used where the primary goal of child communication development is comprehension rather than speaking (e.g., Harkness & Super, 1982). An important aspect of the imperative style is the fact that it elicits action rather than verbalization from the child. This style is found in cultures in Africa (Harkness & Super, 1982) and Mexico (Tapia Uribe et al., 1994) and in Latino populations in the United States (Delgado-Gaitan, 1994).

The comprehension skill developed by an imperative style is particularly functional in agrarian societies in which the obedient learning of chores and household skills is a very important socializing experience (e.g., Childs & Greenfield, 1980), with the ultimate goal of developing obedient, respectful, and socially responsible children (Harkness & Super, 1982; Kagitçibasi, 1996; LeVine et al., 1994). This style of interaction is also useful for apprenticeship learning of manual skills, but it is not so functional for school, where verbal expression is much more important than nonverbal action.

On the other hand, more democratic parenting brings with it a communication style in which self-expression and autonomy are encouraged in the child. This parenting style often features a high rate of questions from the parent, particularly "test questions," in which the answer is already known to the parent (Duranti & Ochs, 1986), as well as parent-child negotiation (cf. Delgado-Gaitan, 1994). Child-initiated questions are also encouraged and accepted. This style is intrinsic to the process of formal education in which the teacher, paradigmatically, asks questions to which he or she already knows the answer and tests children on their verbal expression. An important aspect of the interrogative style is the fact that it elicits verbalization from the child. Such verbal expression is an important part of becoming a formally educated person and is particularly functional and common in commercial and technological societies where academic achievement, autonomy, and creativity are important child development goals. This style is the cultural norm in North America and northern Europe.

Teaching and Learning: The Role of Reinforcement.

In societies that put an emphasis on commands in parental communication, there also tends to be little praise used in parent-child communication (e.g., Chen et al., 2000; Childs & Greenfield, 1980). Where schooling comes into play, praise and positive reinforcement take on importance. Duranti and Ochs (1986, p. 229) make the following observation of Samoan children who go to school:

> In their primary socialization [home], they learn not to expect praises and compliments for carrying out directed tasks. Children are expected to carry out these tasks for their elders and family. In their secondary socialization [school], they learn to expect recognition and positive assessments, given successful accomplishment of a task. In their primary socialization, Samoan children learn to consider tasks as co-operatively accomplished, as social products. In their secondary socialization, they learn to consider tasks as an individual's work and accomplishment.

Thus, there is a connection between more individualistic child development goals and the use of praise and other positive reinforcers.

Correlatively, there is a connection between a tighter primary in-group and the absence of praise and compliments. Where role-appropriate behavior is expected rather than chosen, positive reinforcement does not make sense. Miller (1995) has described how people do not say "thank you" in India; once you are part of the group, you are completely accepted and expected to fulfill your social roles and obligations. B. B. Whiting and Whiting (1975) noted the lesser need for positive reinforcement where the intrinsic worth of the work is evident, as it is in household tasks and chores.

Teaching and Learning: The Nature of Collaborative Problem Solving.

Chavajay and Rogoff (2002) identified two modes of collaborative problem solving between a mother and three related children between 6 and 12 years old (at least two being her own) in a Maya community in Guatemala. One of these modes was shared multiparty engagement, where all four parties simultaneously focused on a single aspect of the task (in this case, a construction task). The other mode was division of labor, in which participants worked on separate aspects of the task. The researchers found that, with increasing maternal schooling, there was a shift from shared engagement in a single aspect of the task to division of labor. In other words, the indigenous mode, consistent with the community's traditional interdependent orientation (Morelli et al., 1992), involved more interdependent interaction, whereas division of labor, fostered by formal schooling, an influence foreign to Maya culture and an individualizer (Tapia Uribe et al., 1994; Trumbull et al., 1999), involved greater independence of the various members of the cooperating family group.

Cultural Models of Parent-Child Relations: Developmental Goals over the Life Span

There are basically two different cultural models describing parent-child relations over the life span. Without considering both models, we cannot adequately encompass cross-cultural variability in child development, parental behavior, and parent-child relations.

In one model, children are viewed as starting life as dependent on their parents and as achieving increasing independence as they grow older (Greenfield, 1994). In the other model, children are viewed as starting life as asocial creatures and as achieving a concept and practice of social responsibility and interdependence as they grow older (e.g., Ochs & Schieffelin, 1984). Under this model, infants are often indulged, whereas older children are socialized to comprehend, follow, and internalize directives from elders, particularly parents. The developmental outcome of the first model is the independent, individuated self; the developmental outcome of the second model is the interdependent and socially responsible self (Markus & Kitayama, 1991; Raeff et al., 2000).

In the interdependent model found in Japan, the mother-child relationship lasts a lifetime and is seen as the model for all human relationships throughout life (Lebra, 1994). The importance of continued respect up the generational ladder is seen in other cultures that subscribe to this model, such as in Mexico, among Mex-

ican Americans (Delgado-Gaitan, 1994), and in Korea (Kim, 1996).

In contrast, the independent model of family relations is distinguished by the "separateness of the generations and both emotional and material investments channeled toward the child, rather than to the older generation" (Kagitçibasi, 1996, p. 84). As Lebra (1994) points out, in this model, characteristic of the United States, the paradigmatic model of parent-child relations is the rebellious adolescent son who is breaking away from his family of origin.

Cultural Coherence

Again, we find evidence of cultural coherence. This coherence has developmental continuity as well. The two cultural models of infant development and socialization (Table 17.1) continue to be expressed in the parent-child relations of children (Table 17.2).

Ecological Factors and Social Change

The interdependence model is particularly adaptive in poor rural/agrarian societies, where it utilizes a "functionally extended family" to carry out subsistence tasks, including child care (Kagitçibasi, 1996). Due to the high poverty level and agricultural lifestyle, such shared work is highly adaptive for survival (Kagitçibasi, 1996). Indeed, in contemporary China, rural adolescents have a greater sense of family obligation than do urban adolescents (Fuligni & Zhang, 2004).

The interdependence between generations, with the younger ultimately responsible for the security of the older, is particularly adaptive in societies lacking old-age pensions and social security systems (Kagitçibasi, 1996). Conversely, the independence model of family relations is particularly adaptive in industrial, technologi-

TABLE 17.2 Contrasting Cultural Models of Parent-Child Relations

Developmental Goals	Independence	Interdependence
Developmental trajectory	From dependent to independent self	Fom asocial to socially responsible self
Communication	Verbal emphasis Atonomous self-expression by child Fequent parental questions to child Fequent praise Child negotiation	Nonverbal emphasis (empathy, observation, participation) Child comprehension, mother speaks for child Fequent parental directives to child Infrequent praise Frequent parental directives
Collaborative problem solving	Division of labor	Shared multiparty engagement
Parents helping children	A matter of personal choice except under extreme need	A moral obligation under all circumstances

cal societies, where the unit of economic employment is the individual, not the family. Furthermore, independence and self-reliance are valued in a sociocultural-economic context where intergenerational material dependencies are minimal, and children's loyalty to their elderly parents is not required to support parents in their old age (Kagitçibasi, 1996). With increasing affluence and education, the interdependence model tends to wane as the independence model waxes (Kagitçibasi, 1996).

But the world as a whole is becoming more affluent and formally educated; these are global trends. A cross-cultural Value of Children survey conducted in 1975 and repeated again a generation later indicated a worldwide decline in parents regarding children for their old-age security value and a worldwide increase in parents focusing on their children's development and achievement for its own sake (Kagitçibasi, & Ataca, 2005; Trommsdorff & Nauck, 2005).

IMPLICATIONS FOR PRACTICE: WHAT CAN WE LEARN FROM A CROSS-CULTURAL PERSPECTIVE ON PARENTING STYLES?

In this section, we will draw out implications of the previous section for the practice of developmental researchers, parents, educators, social workers, and clinicians in a multicultural society.

For Researchers: You Can't Take It with You

There is an important methodological lesson here: It is not valid to take the same measuring instrument from one culture to another, with the goal of making a direct cross-cultural comparison. The same behavior may have a different meaning and therefore a different outcome in different cultures (Greenfield, 1997). This is clearly true when looking at the different styles of parental interaction and discipline used by different cultural groups. For example, taking a measure of authoritarian parenting developed in the United States and using it to study parenting styles in China would provide an inaccurate and incomplete perspective on parenting practices there. It is therefore important to explore different methods of research that utilize the ideas and opinions of people native to the society under study.

One way to do this is to encourage the indigenous psychologies approach when studying culture. Kim and

Berry (1993, p. 2) define this approach as "the scientific study of human behavior (or the mind) that is native, that is not transported from other regions, and that is designed for its people." In other words, instead of taking concepts, methods, and measures from one culture and forcing it into the framework of another, it may be more appropriate and more fruitful to work from within the culture to form concepts, methods, and measures that are designed specifically for that environment. If this is done, indigenous concepts (e.g., chiao shun and guan) can be discovered and investigated from a more culturally salient perspective.

For Parents, Educators, Social Workers, and Other Clinicians

Multicultural understanding has direct implications for clinical work with families. Consider the following case (Carolyn McCarty, personal communication, June 1996): A child in an African American family is punished when a younger sibling, under her care, falls off the bed. The older child feels the punishment is unfair and complains of having too much responsibility in the family. The family seeks family therapy for these issues. In this case, armed with unconscious cultural assumptions about the developmental goal and value of independence, the first reaction of the therapist is to blame the parents for "parentifying" the older child; in this framework, parentification is considered pathological. Parentification of a child compromises the autonomy and opportunities for self-actualization that are implicit developmental goals in psychotherapy, itself an outgrowth of an individualistic framework.

However, after some training concerning the two cultural models described earlier, the clinician understood another possibility: that the parents could be developing familial responsibility in the older child by having her take care of the younger child. In accordance with this value system, the older child's punishment makes sense; it helps socialize the child to carry out the familial responsibility associated with child care. Having understood this perspective, the clinician is in a position to explore the issue of culture conflict. Is this situation, in fact, simply a conflict between an older child who has internalized the individualistic notion of fairness and responsibility for self and parents who hold dear the value of familial responsibility? If so, the clinician can now mediate between the two cultures represented by the two generations within the family.

Another implication of the preceding is that professionals (e.g., social workers, counselors, clinical psychologists, pediatricians, and educators) who advise parents on discipline and other parenting practices need to bear in mind that any advice must be relative to a particular set of developmental goals. Often, they may not realize that a particular set of child development goals is implicit in a particular piece of advice on an issue such as discipline. Insofar as members of many ethnic groups in a multicultural society will not share the socially dominant developmental model of the clinician or teacher, practitioners may need to think twice about whether it is appropriate either to ignore or change the parents' developmental goals for their children.

The Problem of Differential Acculturation of Parents and Children

Because parents often acculturate more slowly than children to a host culture (Kim & Choi, 1994), there is a great potential for parent-child conflict when families immigrate from a collectivistic to an individualistic society. Parents may expect respect, but their children have been taught to argue and negotiate (Delgado-Gaitan, 1994). Parents may see strictness as a sign of caring; adolescents may see it as robbing them of autonomy and self-direction (Rohner & Pettengill, 1985). Acculturation differences between parents and adolescents can be related to family conflict; in one study of Indian Americans, adolescents reported less frequent and less intense conflicts within the family if there was no acculturation difference between themselves and their parents (Farver, Narang, & Bhadha, 2002).

Sometimes immigrant parents bring their children, particularly teenagers, to mental health clinics for problem behaviors, such as rebelliousness, that are considered normal for adolescents in the dominant U.S. society (V. Chavira, personal communication, June 1996). When this happens, a clinician may easily assume the perspective of the dominant culture and simply take the side of the child. However, this approach denigrates the parents without understanding the value perspective that has generated their attitudes and behavior. It should be much more helpful if the clinician could accurately diagnose the parent-child problem as a problem of cross-cultural value conflict and differential acculturation. In this way, the perspectives of both parent and child are validated and understood, and a way is opened for compromise and mutual understanding.

BRIDGING CULTURES IN PARENT WORKSHOPS

Parents can also feel alienated from their children as a result of differential acculturation, specifically, the school's success with its individualistic socialization (Raeff et al., 2000). A Bridging Cultures parent workshop process was developed to address this problem. In a true experiment with random assignment, The Bridging Cultures team compared two kinds of six-session parent education workshops with immigrant Latino parents in a large urban elementary school (Esau, Greenfield, Daley, & Tynes, 2004). Parents of children in grades 1 through 4 were randomly assigned to either the district-based "standard" workshop group concentrating on techniques to improve student achievement and school policies or a second kind of workshop group called Bridging Cultures. The Bridging Cultures workshops were designed to make explicit the differences between individualistic culture (the culture of the school) and collectivistic culture (the culture of many immigrant Latinos, as in Table 17.2). We hoped that this process would help Latino immigrants gain a better understanding of their children and the socialization process they were undergoing at school.

After analyzing the group process in the course of the videotaped workshops, we found that we had made an impact in this arena. The parents discovered ways to improve their relationships with their children. They noted an increased awareness of how cultural differences influence their children's development, including the knowledge that the culture of the United States would play a large role in their children's lives. The parents retained the collectivistic values of sharing and helping, while also coming to accept independence, the importance of self-expression in school, respect for children's decisions and choices, and the value of praise and affection. One mother said (translated from Spanish), "When in school they receive merits, then too [I should] tell them, 'Oh my delight, I am so proud of you!'" (Chang, 2003, p. 24).

Parents' own child-rearing methods were validated in the workshops, as they reflected on how they themselves were raised, as well as how they were helping to foster their children's development and learning. They were also encouraged to speak to their children about the different expectations at home and school. Longitudinal research is needed to see whether this kind of cross-cultural understanding can prevent the alienation between parents and children that often occurs as the schools, representing the dominant culture, become a stronger socializing force than the family, especially as children move into secondary education (Trumbull, Rothstein-Fisch, & Hernandez, 2003).

PEER RELATIONS

Peer relations are the child's first opportunity to take the cultural values and practices learned at home and go forth into a wider world of people who may or may not share these values and practices. This section starts with an overview of different cultural elements that can come into play during peer interaction. We will make inferences from cross-cultural variability in peer behavior in culturally homogenous peer groups to potential intergroup conflict when interacting peers belong to *different* cultural groups. We analyze cultural differences and intergroup peer conflict in a number of different behavioral areas: self-presentation, helping behaviors, competition/cooperation, and conflict resolution.

In several cases, we use adult social-psychological literature to establish developmental end points for peer behavior in different cultures and developmental literature (where available) to see how peer relations develop toward these cultural endpoints. In other words, a cross-cultural perspective on adult behavior is important because adults provide the goals used for child socialization. As a consequence, child behavior grows toward the developmental end points expressed in adult behavior.

Self-Presentation

In many individualistic societies, it is established that people like to perceive themselves as the origin of good effects but not of bad effects (Greenwald, 1980), and the confident attribution of successes to personal ability is commonly practiced (e.g., Mullen & Riordan, 1988). Consequently, self-esteem is a highly desirable quality in these societies. For example, it was found that in the United States, people who scored highest on self-esteem tests (by saying nice things about themselves) also tended to say nice things about themselves when explaining their successes and failures (R. Levine & Uleman, 1979). It appears that self-esteem is somehow correlated with a positive representation of the self.

In collectivistic societies, this tendency to present oneself in a positive light is not as highly valued (Markus & Kitayama, 1991). Research has shown that Americans tend to self-enhancement, whereas Japanese tend to self-deprecation (Heine, Kitayama, & Lehman, 2001; Heine & Lehman, 1997; Kitayama, Markus, Matsumoto, & Norasakkunkit, 1995, 1997). The effect of self-deprecation among Japanese participants was robust, and carried through to their evaluations of their universities and even family members (Heine & Lehman, 1997). The effect of culture in molding self-presentation, and therefore peer relations, is indeed far-reaching.

This cultural difference in peer relations begins in childhood. In a study conducted on the opinions of second, third, and fifth graders in Japan, students were asked to evaluate a hypothetical peer who was either modest and self-restrained or self-enhancing in commenting on his or her athletic performance (Markus & Kitayama, 1991; Yoshida, Kojo, & Kaku, 1982). Yoshida et al. found that, at all ages, the personality of the person giving the modest comment was perceived much more positively than that of the person giving the self-enhancing comment. A developmental trend was also found: Second graders believed the self-enhancing comment of the hypothetical peer to be true, whereas fifth graders did not. In other words, whereas second graders believed that the self-enhancing peer was truly superb in athletics, fifth graders believed that the modest peer was more competent. Therefore, although the cultural value of restraint and modesty was understood as early as second grade, this value expanded with age to incorporate positive attributes of ability and competence (Markus & Kitayama, 1991). Indeed, behaviors such as the verbal devaluation of oneself and even of one's family members is a norm in many East Asian cultures (Toupin, 1980). Not surprisingly, self-effacing values are also stronger in Asian American than European American youth (Akimoto & Sanbonmatsu, 1999).

Implications for Intergroup Peer Relations

Both modes of self-presentation conform perfectly to their respective cultural goals, but one can see how people from one culture can misinterpret and even decry the preferred self-presentation styles of other cultures. The Asian American tendency to present oneself in a self-effacing manner can be evaluated unfavorably by others (Akimoto & Sanbonmatsu, 1999). In college interview situations, for example, Asian American students can be viewed as uninteresting applicants because of their modesty and desire to fit in rather than stand out. On the other side, self-enhancing tendencies of European American youth can be seen as undesirable self-aggrandizement (Suzuki, Davis, & Greenfield, in press).

Helping Behavior

The desirability of helping others appears to be universal. However, people's perceptions of helping behaviors and when they are appropriate can vary drastically from culture to culture. Some societies view helping as a personal choice; others view this as a moral obligation. For example, children in the United States feel that it is a matter of personal choice, not moral responsibility, to help a friend in moderate or minor need, whereas it is a matter of moral responsibility to help a friend in extreme need or to uphold justice (Miller, Bersoff, & Harwood, 1990). Caring and interpersonal responsiveness are seen as a matter of personal choice based on various factors, such as how much one likes the person needing help (Higgins, Power, & Kohlberg, 1984; Miller & Bersoff, 1992, 1998; Nunner-Winkler, 1984). This value of personal choice is highlighted in individualistic societies, such as the United States, where Miller and colleagues found this pattern of results from second grade to college age.

In societies that value group harmony and cooperation, however, helping behaviors can be perceived at a different level of urgency and obligation. This is particularly true in India, where helping is seen not as a personal choice, but as a moral necessity (Miller, 1994; Miller & Bersoff, 1992; Miller et al., 1990). Virtually all Indians from second grade to college age felt that it was legitimate to punish a person who failed to help a friend, even in minor need. Whether or not the helper liked the person in need had no impact on Indian participants' perceptions of moral responsibility to help others (Miller & Bersoff, 1998).

In another study, Miller (1995) found that most U.S. college students would not inconvenience themselves to help their best friend if he or she had not helped them or others in the past. Although Indian college students agreed with U.S. college students that not helping in the past was undesirable behavior, this history would not deter them from helping their best friend.

Choosing not to help others may be met with harsh disapproval in cultures that value the preservation of group interests. In Cameroon, for example, asserting individual rights and interests over those of the community would cause the Cameroonian to be acting "at the expense of his or her peace of mind and at great risk of losing the psychological comfort of a feeling of belonging" (Nsamenang, 1987, p. 279). Such a person would be considered deviant under traditional African thinking (Nsamenang, 1987). In the United States, Latinos viewed helping others as more obligatory and personally desirable than did European Americans (Janoff-Bulman & Leggatt, 2002; Raeff et al., 2000). Given these differences, one can imagine how an Indian, Nigerian, or Latino child may be confused and even shocked when a child from another culture may choose not to help a group member in a time of need.

Ecological Factors

J. W. M. Whiting and Whiting (1973/1994, p. 279) put forth the hypothesis that complex societies must suppress altruistic or helping behavior to friends (as well as to family) to maintain the economic order, "a system of open and achievable occupational statuses." Complex technological society requires the egoistic behaviors of self-development; the essence of obtaining a position in the economic system is individual merit, not social or family connections. Based partly on their cross-cultural child observation data in nontechnological small-scale cultures, Whiting and Whiting view the United States, a complex technological society, as occupying an extreme position on the egoistic side of the egoism/altruism dimension.

Play: Cooperation and Competition

Peer games can bring up important cross-cultural differences in the tendency to emphasize cooperation versus competition and in the ways rewards are allocated. These differences can then create difficulties in peer relations in a culturally diverse society.

In Western societies, both cooperation and competition are valued, and children often learn to interact with one another utilizing both concepts. However, children in the United States, for example, are often placed in situations where competition is more likely to be utilized and even encouraged. In the United States, this tendency to be competitive with one another increases with age (Kagan & Madsen, 1972). This developmental trend was clearly depicted in a study by Madsen (1971) that utilized an interpersonal game in which children could either cooperate with one another (and be more likely to receive a prize) or compete with one another (and be less likely to receive a prize). The result showed a striking effect. In the United States, it was found that younger children (4 to 5 years) were more successful than older children (7 to 8, 10 to 11) in restraining their motivation to compete in order to receive a prize. In older children, the motivation to compete was so strong that it overcame the tendency to act out of mutual self-interest, even when they had the intellectual capacity to act otherwise (Madsen, 1971). In contrast, Mexican children from a small agricultural community behaved cooperatively at the older ages. Small population size may be important because of its role in leading to within-group cohesion.

It is important to note, however, that in-group cooperation is often associated with out-group competition. This was the case for highly cooperative kibbutz children from Israel (Shapira & Madsen, 1969). Israeli kibbutzim are small, collectivistic, agricultural communities with strong in-group ties. Using a game to examine cooperation and competition in peer relations, Shapira and Madsen found that kibbutz children's tendency to cooperate in a game overshadowed their competitive tendencies under different reward conditions. In contrast, Israeli city children would cooperate when there was a group reward, but as soon as rewards were distributed on an individual basis, competition took over.

In kibbutzim, children are prepared from an early age to cooperate and work as a group, and competition is not seen as a socially desirable norm (Shapira & Madsen, 1969). At the time this study was done, kibbutz teachers reported that anticompetitive attitudes are so strong that children sometimes felt ashamed for being consistently at the top of their class (Shapira & Madsen, 1969). Under such cultural norms, it is of no surprise that children in kibbutz communities are much more likely to cooperate than compete with one another in gaming situations. A high level of within-group cooperation was associated with a desire to do better than other groups who had played the game before.

Insofar as an emphasis on cooperation is part of a collectivistic value orientation, it may be that greater differentiation of relations with in-group and out-group members may characterize collectivistic cultures, in comparison with individualistic ones (Triandis, Bontempo, Villareal, Asai, & Lucca, 1988). In a study comparing Japanese and American students in conflict situations against differing opponents, researchers found that the Japanese participants showed a greater behavioral difference between their interactions with in-group members and their interactions with out-group members.

Thus, it is too simplistic to say that children from collectivistic cultures are, on average, more cooperative than children from individualistic cultures. Instead, children from more collectivistic cultures are more cooperative with in-groups and more competitive with out-groups. Also, the cross-cultural mean differences are far from absolute. For example, children from more individualistic environments will cooperate when competition is dysfunctional and there are very strong cues for cooperating, for example, group reward (Shapira & Madsen, 1969).

Ecological Factors and Social Change

As with helping behavior, cooperative behavior appears to be more functional and encouraged in small, simple, nontechnological groups with low levels of formal education, and less functional in large, complex, technological groups with high levels of formal education (Graves & Graves, 1978). Therefore, when members of a small, simple, nontechnological group come into contact with members of a large, complex, technological group, competitiveness in peer relations increases, as Madsen and Lancy (1981) found in New Guinea.

The effects of urbanization are confirmed by studies comparing two ecologies in one country. In one such study, Madsen (1967) found that urban Mexican children were much more competitive and less cooperative than rural children from a small, agricultural community in Mexico. This pattern of findings points to the conclusion that the greater cooperation of Mexican immigrants to the United States may be, to a great extent, a function of their rural, agricultural background.

However, urbanization may play its role in reducing cooperation and increasing competition by loosening the strength of in-group ties in an ethnically diverse milieu. This was the conclusion of Madsen and Lancy (1981), who, in a study of 10 sites in New Guinea, found that, when primary group identification could be separated from rural residence, it was by far the most important factor in children's choice between a cooperative and a competitive strategy in a peer game situation. Children who came from ethnic groups that had retained their tribal coherence were more cooperative, even when exposed to urban centers, than were rural children whose groups had less stability and whose traditional way of life had largely disappeared.

Implications for Intergroup Peer Relations

With this in mind, it is apparent that children (as well as adults) with differing cultural backgrounds can easily have differing ideas concerning cooperation and competition. Without proper awareness of such differentiation in viewpoints, one can imagine the possible confusion and misunderstanding that might occur when one child's assumptions about cooperation, competition, and reward allocation fundamentally differs from that of a playmate. This difference can indeed be yet another source of cross-cultural conflict that can occur among children, particularly following immigration from a collectivistic milieu to an individualistic one.

Conflict Resolution

Conflicts among children are inevitable within any culture. It is clear from the earlier descriptions that the potential for conflict (especially culturally based conflict) is even greater between children of differing backgrounds. However, it is ironic to note that acceptable and preferred measures of conflict resolution also differ from culture to culture.

Cultural Bases of Conflict Resolution

In the United States, success, freedom, and justice are "central strands" of culture (Bellah, Madsen, Sullivan, Swindler, & Tipton, 1985). These values are considered individual rights and are treasured concepts, written into the Constitution and worthy of fighting wars for. Under the precepts of these rights and the resulting economic system of capitalism, competition among people is seen as healthy, necessary, and even desirable. Thus, resolution of conflict may be competitive and confrontational, based on the concept that the individual, rather than the collective, has rights that should be actively pursued.

In other societies, however, behavioral ideals lead to different types of desired behavior. For example, Chinese people were found to prefer nonconfrontational approaches to conflict resolution more than Westerners did (Leung, 1988). In fact, there appears to be a strong inverse relationship between the presence of Chinese values and the degree of competitiveness used in handling conflicts (Chiu & Kosinski, 1994), suggesting a strong tie between cultural values and conflict behavior. In general, Toupin (1980) suggests that East Asian cultures share certain norms, including that of deference to others, absence of verbal aggression, and avoidance of confrontation.

Conflict resolution in West Africa also emphasizes the importance of group harmony. According to Nsamenang (1987, p. 279), West Africans emphasize reconciliation as a means of handling disputes and domestic conflicts in order to "reinforce the spirit of communal life." The preservation of group harmony during conflict resolution is once again crucial in this cultural context. Similarly, college students in Mexico were more likely than students in the United States to prefer conflict resolution styles that emphasize accommodation, collaboration, and concern for the outcome of others (Gabrielidis, Stephan, Ybarra, Pearson, & Villareal, 1997).

Indeed, both the means as well as the goals of conflict resolution vary according to the aspired values and ideals of each culture. We would expect these cultural modes of adult conflict resolution to furnish the developmental goals for the socialization of conflict resolution in children.

Children's Methods of Conflict Resolution Reflect Their Cultural Foundations

In every society, cultural ideals are manifest in the conflict resolution tactics that are encouraged by the adults. According to B. Whiting and Edwards (1988, p. 189), "The manner in which socializers handle children's disputes is one of the ways in which the former transmit their values concerning the legitimate power ascribed to gender and age." That is, through adult intervention, cultural and societal ideals and values are transmitted to the children.

Take, for example, the case of the United States. In American preschools, a child is generally encouraged to use words to "defend oneself from accusations and to seek redress when one feels wronged" (Tobin, Wu, & Davidson, 1989, p. 167). American parents also encourage children to use words to "negotiate disputes or label their emotions" (B. Whiting & Edwards, 1988) when having conflicts with their peers. In a culture that highly values equality, individual rights, and justice, expressing one's personal point of view is very important. By doing so, the hope is that justice can emerge out of learning about each child's individual perspective. Note that the emphasis on verbal dispute resolution reflects the emphasis of European American parents on verbalization.

Individualized attention given to misbehaving children, heralded as an appropriate and effective means of child management in this particular cultural context, would appear strange in others. In the United States, it is quite common and even desirable for teachers, parents, and children to use negotiation, lobbying, voting, pleading, litigation, encouraging, arbitration, and a variety of other means to resolve conflicts in a "just" or "fair" manner (Tobin et al., 1989). However, such individualized attention given to misbehaving children may not be approved of in more collectivistic cultures.

In the same observational field study, Tobin et al. (1989) observed preschool activities in Japan. Here, teachers were described as being "careful not to isolate a disruptive child from the group by singling him out for punishment or censure or excluding him from a group activity" (p. 43). In a society where group interactions and collectivism are highly valued, such a punishment for misbehavior would be seen as extreme. Given this cultural framework, the Japanese teachers would choose instead to take a more unintrusive approach to conflict resolution. When Hiroki, a misbehaving child, causes a stir among his classmates, the Japanese teacher's response is not to single him out but rather to instruct other children to take care of the problem themselves. This technique is in stark contrast to the American tactic of immediate adult intervention and arbitration.

The philosophy behind this mode of conflict resolution is closely linked to cultural beliefs. In Japan, group interactions are highly salient, and teachers therefore believe that "children learn best to control their behavior when the impetus to change comes spontaneously through interactions with their peers rather than from above" (Lewis, 1984, quoted in Tobin et al., 1989, p. 28). In an interview, the Japanese teacher said that she believed that other classmates' disapproval would have a greater effect on misbehaving children, perhaps more so than would any form of adult intervention. Here we see peer pressure as an effective means of conflict control.

In the United States, in contrast, peer pressure is usually seen not as a means of controlling behavior in a positive way, but as a negative form of conformity and lack of personal freedom. In this context, having children work things out on their own without intervention and assessment by others would be unusual indeed.

Cultural differences in children's conflict resolution have been found between other countries as well. For example, preschoolers in Andalusia, Spain, are more likely to resolve conflicts by reaching an agreement or compromise, whereas Dutch children are more likely to give priority to their individual objectives even at the risk of disrupting the activity (Sanchez Medina, Lozano, &

Goudena, 2001). Perhaps the Andalusian tendency to be more harmonious during conflict is related to the Spanish/Latin American notion of *simpatia,* or "pro-active socioemotional orientation and concern with the social well-being of others" (R. V. Levine, Norenzayan, & Philbrick, 2001, p. 546).

Implications for Intergroup Peer Relations

Conflict is unavoidable in any cultural context. However, the modes of dealing with conflict can differ greatly. Conflict resolution is difficult enough in a homogeneous society where children ascribe to the same cultural scripts and norms. When children from differing backgrounds attempt to reconcile their differences, their task is even further exacerbated by an incongruity between the children's conflict resolution styles. Thus, events such as minor playground altercations can lead to greater schisms in children's perceptions of people from other backgrounds and beliefs.

Implications for Practice

In this section, we deal with the implications of culturally heterogeneous peer groups for educators, counselors, and other clinical practitioners.

Education

Teachers are in the position of interacting with large groups of children of differing backgrounds where cultural differences in interactive style are constantly exposed. When interethnic misunderstandings occur, Quiroz (personal communication, January 1996) observed that the injured party often attributes the behavior of the other group to prejudice and discrimination. This might be especially true when the injured party belongs to a minority ethnicity. An understanding of the cultural reasons for peer behavior has the power to decrease attributions of prejudice and discrimination, thus contributing to improved intergroup peer relations.

How teachers resolve conflicts is often determined by the dominant culture. For example, in their book *Conflict Resolution in the Schools,* Girard and Koch (1996, p. 138) emphasize that teachers should develop their students' negotiation skills so that students can "educate one another about their needs and interests." Another strategy recommended is for teachers to teach students to use "I" messages, such as "I feel _____ when _____ because _____, and I need _____"

(p. 138). These kinds of conflict skills may be appropriate for students from individualistic cultures, where the emphasis is on getting one's own needs met. This is a different style of conflict resolution from consensus building, which is built on "an integrative solution . . . a synthesis and blending of solutions" (p. 137). Consensus building, where points are discussed until the group decides on a common decision, reflects a much more collectivistic orientation (Suina & Smolkin, 1994).

Counselors and Other Clinicians

Child counselors and clinicians should likewise be informed and educated on the effects of culture on child behavior and peer interaction. In this way, they can be better prepared to recognize and accommodate culture in their counseling sessions and diagnoses when children from multicultural environments present with difficulties in peer relations.

School counselors are in a strategic position to help students, teachers, and parents understand culture. In one study, middle school counselors were given a three-session Bridging Cultures training similar to that described earlier. The counselors were able to find many examples of the collectivistic home culture among their largely Latino student population. One counselor noted:

> Just today, a female student shared many of her problems that her family has. Problems include poverty, lack of adult supervision and nurturance. She suspects that her mother may be a prostitute. Due to her collectivistic belief she spends all day thinking about ways to possibly solve or improve her home situation for herself and her brothers. That leaves her with no time, energy or motivation to study. (quoted in Geary, 2001, p. 66)

Summary

Differences in peer relations in the areas of self-presentation, helping behavior, play, and conflict resolution organize themselves around what has become a familiar dimension: an idealized cultural model of independent or interdependent functioning. When interacting peers come from home cultures that have different models concerning this dimension, the potential for problematic peer relations arises.

An important source of perceived prejudice and discrimination is failure to understand the cultural values that generate the behavior of others. One can see how differences in cultural value systems have the potential to cause deep misunderstanding and conflict between children from different cultural backgrounds. Interaction between children is never completely conflict-free, but when children play with other children who share their cultural values, peer interaction can often be smoother, based on similar assumptions of what constitutes fair play, proper methods of conflict resolution, and ideal interactive behaviors.

In a multicultural society such as the United States, children from various cultural backgrounds are given the opportunity to interact with one another. However, interaction alone does not breed awareness of other value systems. There is a tendency for each interactant to see the other's behavior through the implicit lens of his or her own value system. It is therefore important for educators and clinicians to be aware of the potential differences between children to help each child to better understand that children may have different perspectives on proper peer interaction, and that these differences can be acknowledged, respected, and even appreciated.

STUDYING AND INTERVENING IN CROSS-CULTURAL PEER RELATIONS: THE CASE OF MULTIETHNIC HIGH SCHOOL SPORTS TEAMS

In a study of cross-cultural conflict among girls volleyball team members in Los Angeles, players' journals, in combination with ethnographic observation at practices and games, unearthed many instances of peer conflict in which one party assumed an individualistic perspective while the other assumed a collectivistic one (Greenfield, Davis, Suzuki, & Boutakidis, 2002). For example, in a "water bottle incident," a Latina girl drank from a water bottle of a European-American girl, and the latter became quite angry (Kernan & Greenfield, 2005). Journal entries relating to this type of conflict indicated that the girl who drinks from the bottle of another assumes the interdependent value of sharing, whereas the owner of the water bottle assumes the value of personal property, bolstered by a desire not to spread germs (an appeal to the physical world). In a later observation of another team composed entirely of Hispanics and Native Americans in Santa Fe, New Mexico, Greenfield (unpublished field note, 2000) observed that a water bottle was passed around the whole team during a team huddle. Here, in a more homogeneous group in which everyone comes from a collectivistic culture (either New Mexico Hispanic or Pueblo Indian), a subsequent interview indicated that sharing water by the whole team was simply taken for granted. However, given the heterogeneous nature of high school sports teams in Los Angeles, an intervention research project was designed.

The goal of the intervention was to promote greater cross-cultural harmony: If teens could learn about the cultural values of both individualism and collectivism, would it increase their tolerance and understanding of each other? The intervention tried to affect peer-group relations in two multiethnic high school girls varsity basketball teams. The two teams were selected because each one represented a mix of ethnicities: European American, Asian American, Latino American, African American, Native American, and mixed ethnicity. The first analysis examined teams over two seasons. During the first season, baseline data concerning the sources of conflict were obtained (Engle & Greenfield, 2005).

During the second season, three workshops were presented to each team to promote tolerance and understanding of cultural value differences within the framework of independence (individualism) and interdependence (collectivism). The workshops included discussions in large and small groups about individualism and collectivism. The girls also developed skits about conflicts in sports from the perspective of both value systems, with the goal of making implicit values explicit and communicating the notion that each value orientation has its own strengths and weaknesses (Engle & Greenfield, 2005). Pre- and postworkshop questionnaires each included eight action scenarios; four were sports team situations and the other four were home and school situations. Each scenario presented a social dilemma that could be resolved in either a more collectivistic or a more individualistic manner. In addition to choosing their own (collectivistic or individualistic) resolution for the dilemma, respondents were asked if they could imagine someone making the other choice and why. This was meant as a measure of understanding the other cultural perspective. We hypothesized that our intervention would increase this type of cross-cultural understanding. However, we did not find the hoped-for effect.

Instead, we found that the values of individualism and collectivism were situational. The sports team scenarios prompted significantly more collectivistic value choices than did home and school scenarios. In the context of sports-based scenarios, the girls did respond to questions indicating that they would work together for the good of the team, demonstrating the development of a superordinate group identity that is important for adolescents.

Equally important was the development over time of a team culture. Questionnaire responses were more collectivistic at the end than at the beginning of the season; playing as a team increased collectivism (Engle & Greenfield, 2005).

In sum, the effective intervention was not the workshops, but the experience of playing on a team. Even here, the effect was not what we expected—a greater understanding of another cultural value system—but rather a push toward a collectivistic perspective. The authors conclude that a dynamic model of cultural values systems exists, adapting to contexts over time.

The second analysis examined how young women begin to think of themselves as a team: negotiating problems and creating shared team values (Kernan & Greenfield, 2005). Besides questionnaires, players kept journals throughout the season. The journals supported the questionnaire results: Whatever the starting value orientation expressed in their journals, almost all of the players became more collectivistic during the basketball season. However, there were differences in the rationale depending on value starting point. Over the course of the season, players starting with both value orientations increasingly valued "showing up" for practices and games, but for different reasons. Showing up was valued by the more individualistic team members because of an agreement or contract to do so. In a sense, this perspective emphasizes a task orientation and an explicit contract, features of a more individualistic orientation. This perspective is in contrast to a more collectivistic approach centering on implicit social obligation as a reason to show up. The personal journals supported the questionnaires in showing that cultural values are not static: Family culture interacts with ecological circumstances to create specific cultural practices in specific contexts. However, they also demonstrated that the value starting point, the result of prior socialization, has an impact as well.

In short, the experience of playing together over time made the group more of a team. This recognition of a superordinate peer group—the team—has great potential for bringing peers from different ethnicities and different cultures together for a common goal (Allport, 1958; Gaertner, Dovidio, Nier, Wsard, & Banker, 1999).

This is an example of a failed intervention. However, the integration of qualitative and quantitative methodology enabled the researchers to understand other important interpersonal dynamics. At the same time, on a theoretical level, much was learned about the power of the situation to shape a value orientation. This process of shaping values through specific experience indicates the adaptive quality and, by extension, the adaptive origin of cultural value systems.

HOME-SCHOOL RELATIONS

Cultural models of human development and socialization are embodied in infant care practices and parent-child relations (both discussed earlier). These practices and relations then influence the cultural models and behaviors that children bring into their peer relations (previous section). One important institution in which peer relations are forged is the school. Schooling involves more than just peer relations, however. It also involves relations between children and teachers and between parents and teachers. These relationships are the focus of the present section.

By the age of 4 or 5 years, most children venture from their home to enter a brand new environment: school. In a culturally homogeneous situation, this shift between home culture and the culture of the school is a relatively smooth transition, based on shared goals and assumptions (Raeff et al., 2000). In a multicultural situation, the problems are different. Cultural diversity, while being colorful and joyous, can also lead to potential misunderstandings and value conflicts between school personnel and parents. Some of these misunderstandings occur in the context of peer relations at school; here the analysis of the previous section is relevant. Still others occur between parents and teachers or between children and teachers. Such culture-based misunderstandings are the central issue of this section.

In the cross-cultural peer conflicts we analyzed in the preceding section, contrasting cultural values were considered to be on an equal footing. However, in school, this is actually not the case. The power belongs to the dominant culture that is part and parcel of formal education in the United States or any other country.

Bringing a Collectivistic Model of Development to School: The Potential for Home-School Conflict

Raeff et al. (2000) studied conceptions of relationships and areas of cross-cultural value conflict among European American and Latino children, their parents, and their teachers. The study was conducted in two different elementary schools in the Los Angeles area: School 1 served a primarily European American population, and School 2 served a primarily immigrant Latino population. Eight open-ended hypothetical scenarios were constructed based on reported experiences of immigrant families. Four scenarios depicted home-based dilemmas and four were school-based (these scenarios were also used in the sports study discussed in the preceding section). The scenarios were presented to all participants on an individual basis. For example: "It is the end of the school day, and the class is cleaning up. Denise isn't feeling well, and she asks Jasmine to help her with her job for the day, which is cleaning the blackboard. Jasmine isn't sure she will have time to do both jobs. What do you think the teacher should do?" (p. 66).

The results indicate that the overwhelming majority of the responses fell into two categories:

1. Find a third person who will volunteer and will not endanger the helper's own task completion; this was considered an individualistic mode of response.
2. Simply help the sick child with her job; this was considered a collectivistic mode of response.

The teachers (multiethnic in both schools) overwhelmingly made the individualistic choice. European American parents and their children were in tune with the teachers' individualistic model of development. However, the overwhelming majority of immigrant Latino parents made the collectivistic choice: Jasmine should help no matter what. This response was shown to be part of a more general model of development: Across four diverse scenarios, Latino immigrant parents overwhelmingly constructed responses that reflected an underlying collectivistic model of development. As would be expected from this choice, Latino immigrant parents were significantly more collectivistic than their children's teachers; this pattern indicated that the children were being subjected to two different socialization influences, a more collectivistic one at home and a more individualistic one at school.

From the point of view of home-school relations, the Latino parents seemed out of tune with the school's value system, and the teachers were equally out of tune with the Latino parents' value system. This is in sharp contrast to the picture of home-school value harmony that exists for European American families (Raeff, Greenfield, & Quiroz, 2000).

Children Caught between Home Culture and School Culture

As a consequence of value harmony between their parents and their teachers, European American children are receiving consistent socialization messages at home and at school. The children of Latino immigrants are not. The results reflect these dynamics: Whereas there are no significant differences in the responses of European American children and their parents, there are significant differences between Latino children and their immigrant parents (Raeff et al., 2000).

Indeed, the Latino children are, overall, significantly more individualistic than their parents and significantly more collectivistic than their teachers (Raeff et al., 2000). That is, they are different from both their major socializing agents. Little is known about whether such children have successfully integrated two cultures or are caught in the middle. Although this research was done with a particular population, it is potentially applicable to the children of other collectivistic minorities in the United States.

Schools often reflect aspects of individualism that highlight independence as a goal of development. For example, classroom interactions and activities emphasize individual achievement, children's autonomous choice and initiative, and the development of logicorational rather than social skills (Delgado-Gaitan, 1993, 1994; Reese et al., 1995).

Academic activities are also intrinsically individualistic insofar as evaluations are generally made on the basis of independent work accomplished by individual students (J. W. M. Whiting & B. B. Whiting, 1975/1994) rather than on the basis of group endeavors. This focus on individual achievement and evaluation is a predominant theme in academic settings; indeed, individual achievement and evaluation are the foundation on which most schools are built (Farr & Trumbull, 1997; Trumbull, 2000).

These aspects of school culture often come into direct conflict with the collectivistic orientation toward education favored not only by Latinos, but by many minority and immigrant cultures that emphasize values such as cherishing interpersonal relationships, respecting elders and native traditions, responsibility for others, and cooperation (Blake, 1993, 1994; Delgado-Gaitan, 1993,

1994; Ho, 1994; Kim & Choi, 1994; Suina & Smolkin, 1994). This perspective is antithetical to the school's emphasis on individual achievement.

Individual Achievement from a Collectivistic Perspective

Encouraging children's individual achievements can be seen in some cultures (e.g., Nigeria) as devaluing cooperation (Oloko, 1993, 1994) or group harmony. Research on conferences between immigrant Latino parents and their children's elementary school teachers revealed incidents when the teacher's praise of an individual child's outstanding achievement made a parent feel distinctly uncomfortable (Greenfield, Quiroz, & Raeff, 2000).

These parents seemed to feel most comfortable with a child's school achievement if the academic skill in question could be applied to helping other family members. For example, in one parent-teacher conference, a Latino mother (with a first-grade education) created common ground with the teacher when she responded to a question about her daughter's home reading by telling the teacher that her daughter had been reading to a younger family member.

Written Knowledge from a Collectivistic Perspective

The reliance on textbooks used in many school settings may also be cause for conflict. In some cultures, knowledge is seen as something that is gleaned not from impersonal texts, but from the wisdom and knowledge of relevant others. In the Pueblo Indian worldview, parents and grandparents are seen as the repositories of knowledge, and this fact provides a social connection between the older and younger generations. In cultures such as these, when objects rather than people become the authorities of knowledge, the introduction of resources such as encyclopedias, reference books, and the like is seen to undermine "the very fiber of the connectedness" (Suina, 1991, p. 153) between people. Given this perspective, the school's emphasis on learning through written material may appear to be an impersonal and even undesirable way of acquiring knowledge.

Valdés (1996) in an ethnographic study of 10 immigrant families from Mexico, found that a mother's communication with her son's elementary school teacher "confirmed the school's lack of interest and caring." In this case, the mother had concerns that her son Saul was eating fish at school, a problem because he was allergic to fish and became sick after eating it, causing him to miss school. She instructed Saul's older brother, 8-year-old Juan, to tell his teacher about this problem. Either the older child failed to deliver the message or the "teacher did not consider it to be her role to pass on the information to the appropriate school personnel" (p. 156). As a result, Saul continued to eat fish and miss school. Valdés concludes that if the mother "had sent a note instead of a message, it might have been that she would have received some response from the teacher or another individual" (p. 156). However, the mother had no way of knowing the greater value of written communication in this instance and assumed that the school had little interest in her child's health.

As this example demonstrates, the problems of home-school communication transcend translation issues. The system of an older child being a knowledgeable, trusted, and responsible care provider of a younger sibling is consistent with the values of collectivistic families. In contrast, the teacher may have believed the older sibling's remarks were unsubstantiated by a formal note and thus discounted entirely. If it were true that the older sibling did not communicate his mother's message to the teacher, then it is possible he had already shifted from his home cultural values to those of the school.

Object Knowledge from a Collectivistic Perspective

Children whose cultural background has emphasized social relations and social knowledge may not understand the privileged position of decontextualized object knowledge in the culture of the school. The following is an example of culture conflict that can occur between teachers and children:

> In a Los Angeles prekindergarten class mostly comprised of Hispanic children, the teacher was showing the class a real chicken egg that would be hatching soon. She was explaining the physical properties of the egg, and she asked the children to describe eggs by thinking about the times they had cooked and eaten eggs. One of the children tried three times to talk about how she cooked eggs with her grandmother, but the teacher disregarded these comments in favor of a child who explained how eggs are white and yellow when they are cracked. (Greenfield, Raeff, & Quiroz, 1996, p. 44)

From the Latino point of view, the first child's answer was typical of the associations encouraged in her invisible home culture of interdependence. That is, objects are most meaningful when they mediate social interactions. The child therefore acted on this value of interpersonal relations in answering the teacher's question. The teacher, however, did not recognize this effort and considered the social descriptions of the time the child had eaten eggs as irrelevant; only physical descriptions of these occasions were valued (Greenfield et al., 1996). The teacher did not even see the invisible culture that generated a description of cooking eggs with one's grandmother; the teacher devalued the child's contribution and, implicitly, the value orientation it reflected. Because she did not understand the collectivistic value orientation, she was also unaware that her question was ambiguous in the following way: Children who shared her value orientation would assume that she was interested in the physical properties of the eggs, even though she did not make this point explicit; those children who did not share the teacher's value orientation would make different assumptions.

Assertiveness from a Collectivistic Perspective

In many collectivistic cultures, the value placed on respecting authority may go as far as to undermine the more individualistic styles of learning that require children to articulate and even argue their views with teachers and other elders on a relatively egalitarian basis (Delgado-Gaitan, 1993, 1994; Valdez, 1997). Consider the following cultural ideal for child communicative behavior for many people of Mexican background. According to Delgado-Gaitan (1994, p. 64): "Children are expected to politely greet their elders; they are not supposed to argue with them. In the company of adults, children are to be good listeners and participate in a conversation only when solicited. To raise questions is to be rebellious."

Valdés (1996) found respect to be so central to the families in her ethnographic study that she titled her book *Con respeto*. "*Respeto* for the mother's role was very much in evidence. . . . When a directive was given, it was followed promptly. If a younger child did not do so, an older sibling soon made certain that the youngster did what he had been told" (p. 120).

A similar view of questioning is found in Japan (Muto, Kubo, & Oshima-Takane, 1980). Given this cultural ideal in child communication, one can imagine the scenario in a U.S. school in which a teacher might falsely interpret a Mexican American child's culturally defined polite compliance or a Japanese child's absence of questioning as a lack of motivation or intellectual curiosity.

As we saw in the section on parent-child relations, many children from different ethnic groups are raised with the notion of respecting and accepting the opinions of elders without question, and this value may be carried with the children to the school setting. The school's emphasis on rational argumentation can be seen to undermine respect for elders. However, when children with respect for authority are not vocal and adept at logicorational modes of argumentation, they can be subjected to criticism by teachers, who focus on fostering individual assertiveness and opinions.

For example, in a study of fall conferences between immigrant Latino parents and their children's elementary school teachers, we showed that the teacher criticized every single child for not sufficiently expressing his or her views in class (Greenfield, Quiroz, & Raeff, 2000). The teacher was unaware that such behavior would be contrary to the Latino parents' goals for their own children's development.

Implications for Educational Practice

In many collectivistic societies, schools have found ways of integrating indigenous cultural values into the school system. In Japanese and Chinese classrooms, for example, classroom practices that focus the attention of teaching on the class as a whole rather than promoting attention to individual students are common and widely accepted (Stigler & Perry, 1988). This technique might be useful in U.S. classrooms that are homogeneous in the sense of containing only children who come from collectivistic backgrounds. Classrooms for immigrants would be one such example.

Implications for Counseling and Clinical Practice

Conflicts between children's experiences at home versus school could cause some degree of distress to children who are too young to realize that their feeling "different" may be due to culture. Cultural differences can be manifested in a variety of areas (religious restrictions, differences in social interaction, differing customs, foods, and beliefs, unusual parenting styles, etc.), and at an age when children want to fit in with their schoolmates, there is a potential for anxiety when home-school conflict occurs. Counselors and therapists who come into contact with school-age children should be aware of cultural conflicts and their potential to af-

fect children's emotional and psychological well-being. Furthermore, they should be properly trained to deal with these issues.

Summary

By and large, the educational implications of cross-cultural research revolve around a single major theme: the need to recognize that patterns and norms of development and education previously thought to be universal are often specific to European American culture and the culture of the schools. More specifically, immigrant and Native American families often come from collectivistic cultures but must put their children into the highly individualistic institution of the school. On the other hand, members of the dominant culture find relative harmony between their individualistic value framework and that of the school.

The major educational implication of cross-cultural value conflict is for teachers first to acquire an awareness and understanding of the individualistic and collectivistic frameworks and then to encourage mutual understanding and accommodation between the two value frameworks in both children and their parents. This was the foundation of our Bridging Cultures teacher-training intervention, to which we next turn.

EXAMPLE OF A HOME-SCHOOL INTERVENTION: BRIDGING CULTURES FOR TEACHERS

As part of a longitudinal action research project called Bridging Cultures, seven bilingual elementary school teachers serving homogeneous immigrant Latino populations were introduced to the concepts of individualism and collectivism (Rothstein-Fisch, Greenfield, & Trumbull, 1999; Trumbull, Diaz-Meza, Hasan, & Rothstein-Fisch, 2000; Trumbull et al., 1999; Trumbull, Rothstein-Fisch, Greenfield, & Quiroz, 2001). Teachers were selected because they had an interest in multicultural education and they represented all grades from kindergarten through grade 5 in the greater Los Angeles area. Four teachers identified themselves as Latino and three as European American. Teachers attended three workshops designed to acquaint them with the cultural value systems of individualism and collectivism. The teachers completed pre- and postassessments to determine if their problem-solving strategies of home- and school-based dilemmas (see Raeff et al., 2000) changed as a result of the training. The teachers shifted from a decidedly strong individualistic orientation (independent of ethnicity) to a culturally open perspective that included a mix of individualistic and collectivistic responses (Rothstein-Fisch Trumbull, Quiroz, & Greenfield, 1997).

After the initial training, the teachers met bimonthly along with the researchers to discuss what kinds of changes they were making to their classrooms. They were introduced to ethnographic research methods and were encouraged to become both observers and change agents in their own classrooms. It is important to keep in mind that these changes were always teacher-generated and the researchers were not prescriptive about what changes to make. In addition to these meetings, over a period of 5 years, several classroom observations were made of each teacher and in-depth interviews occurred several times over the course of the project.

Changes in Classroom Management and Assessment

As a result of the training, teachers began using new classroom management strategies (Rothstein-Fisch, Trumbull, & Greenfield, in press). Building on their sense of shared responsibility for the group (akin to that of siblings discussed earlier), the students began to control each other's behavior, and very few incidents of poor discipline were ever observed in the classrooms. The teachers allowed students to share resources rather than insisting on personal property (Rothstein-Fisch, Trumbull, Daley, Mercado, & Perez, 2003).

But sharing can be problematic when testing occurs; in a test, helping is called cheating (J. W. M. Whiting & B. B. Whiting, 1994/1973). Therefore, Bridging Cultures teachers created ways to incorporate the cultural tendency for Latino children from immigrant families to want to help and share in the service of test preparation, without compromising individual test taking. In one classroom, children worked together to answer practice test questions, while learning that they would have to take the test individually; in another, they took the test individually but debriefed it in a group. In a third-grade class that was struggling with timed math facts, the teacher brought out a popular motivating device: a star chart to indicate the level of facts mastered by individual students. However, these students were not motivated by individual rewards. They saw the chart as representative

of the whole group, and they decided that the goal was to fill in a whole block of stars. Their idea was to have math buddies to help one another succeed. When it was time for the individual test and a child was successful at the next level of math facts, he or she would ring a bell. This signaled the class to stop and clap for the student who had, through his or her individual achievement, added to the collective class chart (Rothstein-Fisch, Trumbull, Isaac, Daley, & Perez, 2003).

Cross-Cultural Exchange: Parents and Teachers

Drawing from the Bridging Cultures project data, another area of dramatic teacher change centered on teachers' relationship with parents (Trumbull, Rothstein-Fisch, & Hernandez, 2003). These changes revolved around three interrelated themes. First, the teachers increased their psychological proximity to families because of their ability to take parents' perspectives. They also increased their contact through use of a personal and informal style, while still maintaining appropriate roles. Second, the teachers designed new classroom practices that demonstrated their understanding of parents' cultural values; they initiated group parent conferences, successfully increased the number of parent volunteers, and changed their schedules to accommodate family needs. Finally, they explored new roles. As mentioned earlier, they became ethnographers in their own classrooms, allowing them an openness to understanding families; they became more effective advocates for students and families; they explained school culture to parents more explicitly; and they supported parents in taking on new roles at school.

Parents in the Bridging Cultures parent training, described at the end of the section on parent-child relations, also learned to increase harmony with the school. They came to understand teacher behavior better and increased their contact with their children's teachers. The parents in the standard workshops did not increase their contact with their children's teachers.

The standard workshop sessions also resulted in benefits, but these revolved around help with homework and knowledge of school policies. Within the framework of school policies, parents learned about the importance of communicating with school personnel. An example of these two approaches can be seen from the third workshop, when a parent felt disrespected by a teacher. The Bridging Cultures parents viewed the situation through the lens of cultural differences, resulting in diminished frustration. On the other hand, the standard workshop participants suggested becoming outspoken advocates, talking with the superintendent, writing letters, and even threatening removing the children from the school.

> The cultural approach introduces integration and mutual understanding of cultural values into conflict situations, without forcing one side to confront to the other. The "standard" approach assumes that everyone holds similar values for child development and that parents should adopt the schools' methods. In resolving a conflict, the cultural approach completely reconstructs a road of understanding that allows for real reconciliation rather than patching over rough spots. (Chang, 2003, p. 40)

CONCLUSION

Every generalization obscures some things while illuminating others. Cultural variability is no exception. It calls attention to normative cultural patterns at the expense of individual differences. However, individual differences always occur around a culturally defined norm, which also serves as the starting point for historical change. Without knowledge of the norm, individual differences become uninterpretable. In addition, individuation and consequent magnification of individual differences is itself a characteristic of individualistic cultures (Greenfield, 2004). In any case, the primary goal of this chapter has been to contribute to a deeper understanding of culturally variable norms around which individual differences can range. A second goal was to contribute to an understanding of the dynamics of intercultural conflict as these affect development and socialization. A third goal has been to present and evaluate practices and interventions that can alleviate such conflict. Research relevant to the second and third goals is in its infancy. Its social importance provides a motive for much further investigation.

The analysis of cultural variability calls attention to cultures at one point in time, thereby obscuring historical change. We have therefore also tried to show that culture is not static; rather, it is constantly reinventing itself through the addition of new ethnic groups to multicultural societies, through changes in educational practices, through widening effects of the mass media, and through transformations in economy and technology. These sociohistorical changes produce constantly evolving cultural modes of socialization and human development (Greenfield, 2004; Greenfield, Maynard, et al., 2003; Keller & Lamm, 2005). The dynamics of cultural change and its impact on socialization and development is an area that has been seriously understudied up to now. As cultural change accelerates, it is ripe for research attack.

Cultural History and Multiculturalism

In a diverse society such as the Unites States, cross-cultural conflict is unavoidable, manifesting itself in interpersonal misunderstandings and altercations. Individuals in every culture must find their own compromise between functioning as an individual and as a member of a group, between independence and interdependence. Some cultures stress one, some the other. Interpersonal differences in this tendency are present in every culture; every culture also has an ideal model of which is more important. Differences in these models and emphases generate cross-cultural differences in many domains of child development. In this chapter, we define domains mainly in terms of socializing influences and social development. They can also be defined in terms of developmental issues, including cognitive development (Greenfield, 2005; Greenfield, Keller, et al., 2003).

Throughout this chapter, cultural models have connected what would otherwise appear to be unrelated cross-cultural differences and, more important, provided an explanation for these differences. The diverse ethnicities that compose the United States and other multicultural societies have their ancestral roots in cultures that have different positions in the cultural complexes of individualism and collectivism. Prior research (Greenfield & Cocking, 1994) has shown that these constructs also generate a historical understanding of the nature of cultural diversity in child development and socialization in diverse societies like the United States.

Although it is clear that such cross-cultural conflicts do exist, it is not enough to simply acknowledge their existence. By educating parents, children, teachers, clinicians, and health care professionals to recognize and deal with cross-cultural difference and conflict, through targeted interventions, children's social, psychological, and educational needs can be better served. It is hoped that in this increasingly multicultural society, children will learn to prepare for and to appreciate the cultural differences that they will inevitably encounter between themselves and others. Future research will tell us whether and how this has been accomplished.

One of our main messages for the application of a cultural perspective on human development is the opportunity for cross-cultural exchange in socialization strategies. Cultural differences are a resource for pediatricians, educators, and mental health professionals who work with parents and children. At the same time, there is an important secondary effect of such cross-cultural exchange: No ethnic group feels that they are parenting the "wrong" way; parents from all ethnocultural backgrounds can receive the message that they have something to contribute to the raising of children in a multicultural society. At the same time, the message can go out to members of the dominant culture that, in a changing world, they have much to learn from other cultural modes of socialization and human development. This intercultural learning process is also a ripe domain for future research.

REFERENCES

Ainsworth, M. D. S. (1979). Infant-mother attachment. *Clinical Psychologist, 38*(2), 27–29.

Ainsworth, M. D. S., Blehar, M. C., Waters, E., & Wall, S. (1978). *Patterns of attachment.* Hillsdale, NJ: Erlbaum.

Ainsworth, M. D. S., & Wittig, B. A. (1969). Attachment and the exploratory behavior of 1-year-olds in a strange situation. In B. M. Foss (Ed.), *Determinants of infant behavior* (Vol. 4, pp. 113–136). London: Methuen.

Akimoto, S. A., & Sanbonmatsu, D. M. (1999). Differences in self-effacing behavior between European and Japanese Americans: Effect on competence evaluations. *Journal of Cross-Cultural Psychology, 30*(2), 159–177.

Allport, G. (1958). *The nature of prejudice* (Abridged version). New York: Doubleday Anchor.

Azuma, H. (1994). Two modes of cognitive socialization in Japan and the United States. In P. M. Greenfield & R. R. Cocking (Eds.), *Cross-cultural roots of minority child development* (pp. 275–284). Hillsdale, NJ: Erlbaum.

Bakeman, R., Adamson, L. B., Konner, M., & Barr, R. G. (1990). !Kung infancy: The social context of object exploration. *Child Development, 61,* 794–809.

Ball, H. L., Hooker, E., & Kelly, P. J. (2000). Parent-infant co-sleeping: Fathers' roles and perspectives. *Infant and Child Development, 9,* 67–74.

Barry, H., III, & Paxson, L. M. (1971). Infancy and early childhood: Cross-cultural codes. *Ethology, 10,* 466–508.

Baumrind, D. (1967). Child care practices antedating three patterns of preschool behavior. *Genetic Psychology Monographs, 75,* 43–88.

Baumrind, D. (1971). Current patterns of parental authority. *Developmental Psychology Monographs, 4*(1, Pt. 2).

Baumrind, D. (1972). An exploratory study of socialization effects on Black children: Some Black-White comparisons. *Child Development, 43,* 261–267.

Baumrind, D. (1983). Socialization and instrumental competence in young children. In W. Damon (Ed.), *Social and personality development: Essays on the growth of the child* (pp. 121–138). New York: Norton.

Bellah, R. N., Madsen, R., Sullivan, W. M., Swindler, A., & Tipton, S. M. (1985). *Habits of the heart.* Berkeley: University of California Press.

Belsky, J. (1989). Infant-parent attachment and daycare. In defense of the Strange Situation. In J. Lande, S. Scarr, & N. Gunzenhauser (Eds.), *Caring for children: Challenge to America* (pp. 23–48). Hillsdale, NJ: Erlbaum.

Berk, L. (1993). *Infants, children, and adolescents.* Needham Heights, MA: Allyn & Bacon.

Berry, J. W. (1976). *Human ecology and cognitive style: Comparative studies in cultural and psychological adaptation.* New York: Sage.

Berry, J. W. (1994). Ecology of individualism and collectivism. In U. Kim, H. C. Triandis, Ç. Kagitçibasi, S.-C. Choi, & G. Yoon (Eds.), *Individualism and collectivism: Theory, method, and applications* (pp. 77–84). Thousand Oaks, CA: Sage.

Blake, I. K. (1993). Learning language in context: The social-emotional orientation of African-American mother-child communication. *International Journal of Behavioral Development, 16,* 443–464.

Blake, I. K. (1994). Language development and socialization in young African-American children. In P. M. G. Greenfield & R. R. Cocking (Eds.), *Cross-cultural roots of minority child development* (pp. 167–196). Hillsdale, NJ: Erlbaum.

Bowlby, J. (1969). *Attachment and loss: Vol. 1. Attachment.* New York: Basic Books.

Brazelton, T., Robey, J., & Collier, G. (1969). Infant development in the Zinacanteco Indians of southern Mexico. *Pediatrics, 44,* 274–283.

Brazelton, T. B. (1990). Commentary: Parent-infant co-sleeping revisited. *Ab Initio, 2*(1), 1–7.

Bredekamp, S., & Copple, C. (Eds.). (1997). *Developmentally appropriate practice in early childhood programs* (Rev. ed.). Washington, DC: National Association for the Education of Young Children.

Bundesen, H. (1944). *The baby manual.* New York: Simon & Schuster.

Burton, R. V., & Whiting, J. W. M. (1961). The absent father and cross-sex identity. *Merrill-Palmer Quarterly, 7,* 85–95.

Campos, J. J., Barrett, K. C., Lamb, M. E., Goldsmith, H. H., & Stenberg, C. (1983). Socioemotional development. In P. H. Mussen (Series Ed.) & M. M. Haith & J. J. Campos (Vol. Eds.), *Handbook of child psychology: Vol. 2. Infancy and developmental psychobiology* (pp. 783–915). New York: Wiley.

Cardona, P. G., Nicholson, B. C., & Fox, R. A. (2000). Parenting among Hispanic and Anglo-American mothers with young children. *Journal of Social Psychology, 140*(3), 357–365.

Caudill, W., & Plath, D. (1966). Who sleeps by whom? Parent-child involvement in urban Japanese families. *Psychiatry, 29,* 344–366.

Chang, P. (2003). *Bridging cultures parent workshop: Developing cross-cultural harmony in minority school communities.* Unpublished honors thesis, UCLA Department of Psychology.

Chao, R. (1994). Beyond parental control and authoritarian parenting style: Understanding Chinese parenting through the cultural notion of training. *Child Development, 65,* 1111–1119.

Chao, R. (2000). The parenting of immigrant Chinese and European American mothers: Relations between parenting styles, socialization goals, and parental practices. *Journal of Applied Developmental Psychology, 21,* 233–248.

Chao, R. (2001a). Extending research on the consequences of parenting style for Chinese Americans and European Americans. *Child Development, 72*(6), 1832–1843.

Chao, R. (2001b). Integrating culture and attachment. *American Psychologist, 56*(10), 822–823.

Chavajay, P., & Rogoff, B. (2002). Schooling and traditional collaborative social organization of problem solving by Mayan mothers and children. *Developmental Psychology, 38,* 55–66.

Chen, X., Liu, M., Li, B., Cen, G., Chen, H., & Wang, L. (2000). Maternal authoritative and authoritarian attitudes and mother-child interactions and relationships in urban China. *International Journal of Behavioral Development, 24*(1), 119–126.

Childs, C. P., & Greenfield, P. M. (1980). Informal modes of learning and teaching: The case of Zinacanteco weaving. In N. Warren (Ed.), *Studies in cross-cultural psychology* (Vol. 2, pp. 269–316). London: Academic Press.

Chiu, R. K., & Kosinski, F. A. (1994). Is Chinese conflict-handling behavior influenced by Chinese values? *Social Behavior and Personality, 22*(1), 81–90.

Choi, J. S. (1970). Comparative study on the traditional families in Korea, Japan, and China. In R. H. Hill & R. Koenig (Eds.), *Families in East and West* (pp. 202–210). Paris: Mouton.

Choi, S. H. (1992). Communicative socialization processes: Korea and Canada. In S. Iwawaki, Y. Kashima, & K. Leung (Eds.), *Innovations in cross-cultural psychology* (pp. 103–121). Lisse, The Netherlands: Swets & Zeitlinger.

Clancy, P. M. (1986). The acquisition of communicative style in Japanese. In B. B. Schieffelin & E. Ochs (Eds.), *Language socialization across cultures* (pp. 213–250). Cambridge, England: Cambridge University Press.

Clarke-Stewart, K. A. (1989). Infant day care: Maligned or malignant? *American Psychologist, 44,* 266–273.

Clarke-Stewart, K. A., Goossens, F. A., & Allhusen, V. D. (2001). Measuring infant attachment: Is the Strange Situation enough? *Social Development, 10,* 143–169.

Cole, M. (1996). *Cultural psychology: A once and future discipline.* Cambridge, MA: Harvard University Press.

D'Andrade, R. (1994). Introduction: John Whiting and anthropology. In E. H. Chasdi (Ed.), *Culture and human development: The selected papers of John Whiting* (pp. 1–13). Cambridge, England: Cambridge University Press.

Dawes, D. (1989). *Through the night: Helping parents and sleepless infants.* London: Free Association Books.

Delgado-Gaitan, C. (1993). Socializing young children in Mexican American families: An intergenerational perspective. *International Journal of Behavioral Development, 16,* 409–427.

Delgado-Gaitan, C. (1994). Socializing young children in Mexican-American families: An intergenerational perspective. In P. M. Greenfield & R. R. Cocking (Eds.), *Cross-cultural roots of minority child development* (pp. 55–86). Hillsdale, NJ: Erlbaum.

Dornbusch, S. M., Ritter, P. L., Leiderman, P. H., Roberts, D. F., & Fraleigh, M. J. (1987). The relation of parenting style to adolescent school performance. *Child Development, 58,* 1244–1257.

Duranti, A., & Ochs, E. (1986). Literacy instruction in a Samoan village. In B. B. Schieffelin & P. Gilmore (Eds.), *Acquisition of literacy: Ethnographic perspectives* (pp. 213–232). Norwood, NJ: Ablex.

Durett, M. E., Otaki, M., & Richards, P. (1984). Attachment and mothers' perception of support from the father. *Journal of the International Society for the Study of Behavioral Development, 7,* 167–176.

Engle, L., & Greenfield, P. M. (2005). *Culture and intergroup relations: Effects of team experience and targeted intervention on cultural values and intercultural understanding.* Manuscript in preparation.

Esau, P. C., Greenfield, P. M., & Daley, C. (2004, May). *Bridging cultures parent workshops: Developing cross-cultural harmony in minority school communities.* University of California Linguistic Minority Research Institute Conference, University of California, Santa Barbara.

Farr, B. P., & Trumbull, E. (1997). *Assessment alternatives for diverse classrooms.* Norwood, MA: Christopher-Gordon.

Farver, J. M., Narang, S., & Bhadha, B. R. (2002). East meets West: Ethnic identity, acculturation, and conflict in East Indian families. *Journal of Family Psychology, 16*(3), 338–350.

Fernald, A., & Morikawa, H. (1993). Common themes and cultural variation in Japanese and American mothers' speech to infants. *Child Development, 64,* 637–656.

Fuligni, A. J., & Pedersen, S. (2002). Family obligation and the transition to young adulthood. *Developmental Psychology, 38*(5), 856–868.

Fuligni, A. J., Tseng, V., & Lam, M. (1999). Attitudes toward family obligations among American adolescents with Asian, Latin American, and European backgrounds. *Child Development, 70*(4), 1030–1044.

Fuligni, A. J., & Zhang, W. (2004). Attitudes toward family obligation among adolescents in contemporary urban and rural China. *Child Development, 75,* 180–192.

Gabrielidis, C., Stephan, W. G., Ybarra, O., Pearson, V. M., & Lucila, V. (1997). Preferred styles of conflict resolution: Mexico and the United States. *Journal of Cross-Cultural Psychology, 28*(6), 661–677.

Gaertner, S. L., Dovidio, J. L., Nier, J. A., Ward, C. M., & Banker, B. S. (1999). Across cultural divides: The value of a superordinate identity. In D. A. Prentice & D. T. Miller (Eds.), *Cultural divides: Understanding and overcoming group conflict* (pp. 173–212). New York: Russell Sage Foundation.

Garcia Coll, C. T., Meyer, E., & Brillon, L. (1995). Ethnic and minority parenting. In M. H. Bornstein (Ed.), *Handbook of parenting: Vol. 2. Biology and ecology of parenting* (pp. 189–209). Hillsdale, NJ: Erlbaum.

Geary, J. P. (2001). *The Bridging Cultures project: A case study with middle school counselors.* Unpublished master's thesis, California State University, Northridge.

Georgas, J., van de Vijver, F. J. R., & Berry, J. W. (2004). The ecocultural framework, ecosocial indices, and psychological variables in cross-cultural research. *Journal of Cross-Cultural Psychology, 35,* 74–96.

Girard, K., & Koch, S. J. (1996). *Conflict resolution in the schools: A manual for educators.* San Francisco: Jossey-Bass.

Gonzalez-Mena, J. (2001). *Multicultural issues in child care* (3rd ed.). Mountain View, CA: Mayfield.

Goodnow, J. J. (1988). Parents' ideas, actions, and feelings: Models and methods from developmental and social psychology. *Child Development, 59*(2), 286–320.

Graves, N. B., & Graves, T. D. (1978, August). *Learning cooperation in a cooperative society: Implications for the classroom.* Paper presented at the annual meeting of the American Psychological Association, Toronto, Ontario, Canada.

Greenfield, P. M. (1966). On culture and conservation. In J. S. Bruner, R. R. Olver, & P. M. Greenfield (Eds.), *Studies in cognitive growth* (pp. 225–256). New York: Wiley.

Greenfield, P. M. (1994). Independence and interdependence as developmental scripts: Implications for theory, research, and practice. In P. M. Greenfield & R. R. Cocking (Eds.), *Cross cultural roots of minority child development* (pp. 1–37). Hillsdale, NJ: Erlbaum.

Greenfield, P. M. (1997). You can't take it with you: Why ability assessments don't cross cultures. *American Psychologist, 52,* 1115–1124.

Greenfield, P. M. (2000). Culture and universals: Integrating social and cognitive development. In L. P. Nucci, G. B. Saxe, & E. Turiel (Eds.), *Culture, thought, and development* (pp. 231–277). Mahwah, NJ: Erlbaum.

Greenfield, P. M. (2004). *Weaving generations together: Evolving creativity in the Zinacantec Maya.* Santa Fe, NM: SAR Press.

Greenfield, P. M. (2005). Paradigms of cultural thought. In K. J. Holyoak & R. G. Morrison (Eds.), *Cambridge handbook of thinking and reasoning* (pp. 663–682). Cambridge, England: Cambridge University Press.

Greenfield, P. M., Brazelton, T. B., & Childs, C. (1989). From birth to maturity in Zinacantan: Ontogenesis in cultural context. In V. Bricker & G. Gossen (Eds.), *Ethnographic encounters in southern Mesoamerica: Celebratory essays in honor of Evon Z. Vogt* (pp. 177–216). Albany: Institute of Mesoamerica, State University of New York.

Greenfield, P. M., & Bruner, J. S. (1966). Culture and cognitive growth. *International Journal of Psychology, 1,* 89–107.

Greenfield, P. M., & Cocking, R. R. (Eds.). (1994). *Cross-cultural roots of minority child development.* Hillsdale, NJ: Erlbaum.

Greenfield, P. M., Davis, H., Suzuki, L., & Boutakidis, I. (2002). Understanding intercultural relations on multiethnic high school sports teams. In M. Gatz, M. A. Messner, & S. Ball-Rokeach (Eds.), *Paradoxes of youth and sport* (pp. 141–157). Albany: State University of New York Press.

Greenfield, P. M., Keller, H., Fuligni, A., & Maynard, A. (2003). Cultural pathways through universal development. *Annual Review of Psychology, 54,* 461–490.

Greenfield, P. M., & Lave, J. (1982). Cognitive aspects of informal education. In D. Wagner & H. Stevenson (Eds.), *Cultural perspectives on child development* (pp. 181–207). San Francisco: Freeman.

Greenfield, P. M., Maynard, A. E., & Childs, C. P. (2003). Historical change, cultural learning, and cognitive representation in Zinacantec Maya children. *Cognitive Development, 18,* 455–487.

Greenfield, P. M., Quiroz, B., & Raeff, C. (2000). Cross-cultural conflict and harmony in the social construction of the child. In S. Harkness, C. Raeff, & C. M. Super (Eds.), *New directions in child development: Vol. 87. Variability in the social construction of the child* (pp. 93–108). San Francisco: Jossey-Bass.

Greenfield, P. M., Raeff, C., & Quiroz, B. (1996). Cultural values in learning and education. In B. Williams (Ed.), *Closing the achievement gap* (pp. 37–55). Alexandria, VA: Association for Curriculum Supervision.

Greenfield, P. M., & Suzuki, L. K. (1998). Culture and human development: Implications for parenting, education, pediatrics, and mental health. In W. Damon (Editor-in-Chief) & I. E. Sigel & K. A. Renninger (Vol. Eds.), *Handbook of child psychology: Vol. 4. Child psychology in practice* (5th ed., pp. 1059–1109). New York: Wiley.

Greenwald, A. G. (1980). The totalitarian ego: Fabrication and revision of personal history. *American Psychologist, 37*(7), 603–618.

Gross, R., & Osterman, P. (Eds.). (1971). *Individualism: Man in modern society.* New York: Dell.

Grossmann, K., Grossmann, K. E., Spangler, G., Suess, G., & Unzner, L. (1985). Maternal sensitivity and newborns' orientation responses as related to quality of attachment in northern Germany. In I. Bretherton & E. Waters (Eds.), *Growing points of attachment theory and research: Monographs of the Society for Research in Child Development, 50*(1/2, Serial No. 209).

Gutierrez J., & Sameroff, A. J. (1990). Determinants of complexity in Mexican-American and Anglo-American mothers' conceptions of child development. *Child Development, 61*(2), 384–394.

Hanks, C., & Rebelsky, F. (1977). Mommy and the midnight visitor: A study of occasional co-sleeping. *Psychiatry, 40,* 277–280.

Harkness, S. (1988). The cultural construction of semantic contingency in mother-child speech. *Language Sciences, 10*(1), 53–67.

Harkness, S., & Super, C. M. (1982). Why African children are so hard to test. In L. L. Adler (Ed.), *Cross-cultural research at issue* (pp. 145–152). New York: Academic Press.

Harkness, S., & Super, C. (1996). *Parents' cultural belief systems: Their origins, expressions and consequences.* New York: Guilford Press.

Harkness, S., Super, C., & van Tijen, N. (2000). Individualism and the "Western mind" reconsidered: Parents' ethnotheories of the child. In S. Harkness, C. Raeff, & C. M. Super (Eds.), *New directions in child development: Vol. 87. Variability in the social construction of the child* (pp. 23–39). San Francisco: Jossey-Bass.

Harrison, A. O., Wilson, M. N., Pine, C. J., Chan, S. Q., & Buriel, R. (1990). Family ecologies of ethnic minority children. *Child Development, 61*(2), 347–362.

Harwood, R., Miller, J., & Lucca Irizarry, N. (1995). *Culture and attachment: Perceptions of the child in context.* New York: Guilford Press.

Harwood, R. L. (1992). The influence of culturally derived values on Anglo and Puerto Rican mothers' perceptions of attachment behavior. *Child Development, 63*(4), 822–839.

Harwood, R. L., Schoelmerich, A., Ventura-Cook, E., Schulze, P. A., & Wilson, S. P. (1996). Culture and class influences on Anglo and Puerto Rican mothers' beliefs regarding long-term socialization goals and child behavior. *Child Development, 67*(5), 2446–2461.

Hayes, M. J., Roberts, S. M., & Stowe, R. (1996). Early childhood co-sleeping: Parent-child and parent-infant nighttime interactions. *Infant Mental Health Journal, 17*(4), 348–357.

Heine, S. J., Kitayama, S., & Lehman, D. R. (2001). Cultural differences in self-evaluation: Japanese readily accept negative self-relevant information. *Journal of Cross-Cultural Psychology, 32,* 434–443.

Heine, S. J., & Lehman, D. R. (1997). The cultural construction of self-enhancement: An examination of group-serving bias. *Journal of Personality and Social Psychology, 72*(6), 1268–1283.

Hewlett, B. S., & Lamb, M. E. (2002). Integrating evolution, culture and developmental psychology: Explaining caregiver-infant proximity and responsiveness in central Africa and the USA. In H. Keller, Y. Portinga, & A. Scholmerich (Eds.), *Between culture and biology: Perspectives on ontogenetic development* (pp. 241–269). New York: Cambridge University Press.

Hewlett, B. S., Lamb, M. E., Shannon, D., Leyendecker, B., & Schölmerich, A. (1998). Culture and early infancy among central African foragers and farmers. *Developmental Psychology, 34*(4), 653–661.

Higgins, A., Power, C., & Kohlberg, L. (1984). The relationship of moral atmosphere to judgments of responsibility. In W. M. Kurtiness & J. L. Gewirtz (Eds.), *Morality, moral behavior, and moral development* (pp. 74–106). New York: Wiley.

Ho, D. Y. F. (1994). Cognitive socialization in Confucian heritage cultures. In P. M. Greenfield & R. R. Cocking (Eds.), *Cross-cultural roots of minority child development* (pp. 285–313). Hillsdale, NJ: Erlbaum.

Hofstede, G. (1991). *Software of the mind.* New York: McGraw-Hill.

Hofstede, G. (2001). *Culture's consequences: Comparing values, behaviors, institutions, and organizations across nations* (2nd ed.). Thousand Oaks, CA: Sage.

Holt, E. (1957). *How children fail.* New York: Dell.

Janoff-Bulman, R., & Leggatt, H. K. (2002). Culture and social obligation: When "shoulds" are perceived as "wants." *Journal of Research in Personality, 36*(3), 260–270.

Jose, P. E., Huntsinger, C. S., Huntsinger, P. R., & Liaw, F.-R. (2000). Parental values and practices relevant to young children's social development in Taiwan and the United States. *Journal of Cross-Cultural Psychology, 31*(6), 677–702.

Kagan, S., & Madsen, M. C. (1972). Rivalry in Anglo-American and Mexican children of two ages. *Journal of Personality and Social Psychology, 24*(2), 214–220.

Kagitçibasi, Ç. (1996). *Family and human development across cultures: A view from the other side.* Mahwah, NJ: Erlbaum.

Kagitçibasi, Ç., & Ataca, B. (2005). Value of children, family, and self: A 3-decade portrait from Turkey. *Applied Psychology: An International Review, 543,* 317–337.

Kawakami, K. (1987, July). *Comparison of mother-infant relationships in Japanese and American families.* Paper presented at the meeting of the International Society for the Study of Behavioral Development, Tokyo, Japan.

Keller, H. (2002). The role of development for understanding the biological basis of cultural learning. In H. Keller, Y. H. Poortinga, & A. Schoelmerich (Eds.), *Between culture and biology* (pp. 213–240). Cambridge: Cambridge University Press.

Keller, H., & Lamm, B. (in press). Parenting as the expression of sociohistorical time: The case of German individualism. *International Journal of Behavioral Development.*

Keller, H., Miranda, D., & Gauda, G. (1984). The naive theory of the infant and some maternal attitudes: A two-country study. *Journal of Cross-Cultural Psychology, 15,* 165–179.

Keller, H., Papaligoura, Z., Kuensemueller, P., Voelker, S., Papaeliou, C., Lohaus, A., et al. (2003). Concepts of mother-infant interaction in Greece and Germany. *Journal of Cross-Cultural Psychology, 34*(6), 677–689.

Keller, H., Voelker, S., & Yovsi, R. D. (in press). Conceptions of good parenting in Cameroonian Nso and northern Germans. *Social Development.*

Keller, H., Zach, U., & Abels, M. (2002). The German family: Families in Germany. In J. Roopnarine (Ed.), *Families across cultures* (pp. 24–258). Boston: Ally & Bacon.

Kernan, C. L., & Greenfield, P. M. (2005). *Becoming a team: Individualism, collectivism, and group socialization in Los Angeles girls' basketball.* Unpublished manuscript.

Killen, M., & Wainryb, C. (2000). Independence and interdependence in diverse cultural contexts. In S. Harkness, C. Raeff, & C. M. Super (Eds.), *New directions in child development: Vol. 87. Variability in the social construction of the child* (pp. 5–21). San Francisco: Jossey-Bass.

Kim, U. (1996). Seminar presented to the Deptartment of Psychology, University of California, Los Angeles.

Kim, U., & Berry, J. W. (1993). Indigenous psychologies: Research and experience in cultural context. *Cross-Cultural Research and Methodologies Series, 17.* Newbury Park, CA: Sage.

Kim, U., & Choi, S. H. (1994). Individualism, collectivism, and child development. In P. M. Greenfield & R. R. Cocking (Eds.), *Cross-cultural roots of minority child development* (pp. 227–258). Hillsdale, NJ: Erlbaum.

Kitayama, S., Markus, H. R., & Lieberman, C. (1995). The collective construction of self esteem: Implications for culture, self, and emotion. In J. Russell, J. Wellenkamp, T. Manstead, & J. M. F. Dols (Eds.), *Everyday conceptions of emotions* (pp. 523–550). Dordrecht, The Netherlands: Kluwer Academic.

Kitayama, S., Markus, H. R., Matsumoto, H., & Norasakkunkit, V. (1997). Individual and collective processes in the construction of the self: Self-enhancement in the United States and self-criticism in Japan. *Journal of Personality and Social Psychology, 72*(6), 1245–1267.

Konner, M. (1982). *The tangled wing: Biological constraints on the human spirit.* New York: Holt, Rinehart and Winston.

Konner, M. J., & Worthman, C. (1980). Nursing frequency, gonadal function and birth-spacing among !Kung hunters and gatherers. *Science, 207,* 788–791.

Lamb, M., & Sternberg, K. J. (1990). Do we really know how daycare affects children? *Journal of Applied Developmental Psychology, 11,* 351–379.

Lave, J., & Wenger, E. (1991). *Situated learning: Legitimate peripheral participation.* New York: Cambridge University Press.

Lebra, T. (1994). Mother and child in Japanese socialization: A Japan-U.S. comparison. In P. M. Greenfield & R. R. Cocking (Eds.), *Cross-cultural roots of minority child development* (pp. 259–274). Hillsdale, NJ: Erlbaum.

Leung, K. (1988). Some determinants of conflict avoidance. *Journal of Cross-Cultural Psychology, 19,* 125–136.

Leung, K., Lau, S., & Lam, W. L. (1998). Parenting styles and academic achievement: A cross-cultural study. *Merrill-Palmer Quarterly, 44,* 157–172.

Levine, R., & Uleman, J. S. (1979). Perceived locus of control, chronic self-esteem, and attributions to success and failure. *Journal of Personality and Social Psychology, 5,* 69–72.

LeVine, R. A. (1977). Child rearing as cultural adaptation. In P. H. Leiderman, S. R. Tulkin, & A. Rosenfeld (Eds.), *Culture and infancy: Variations in the human experience* (pp. 15–27). New York: Academic Press.

LeVine, R. A. (1988). Human and parental care: Universal goals, cultural strategies, individual behavior. In R. A. Levine, P. M. Miller, & M. M. West (Eds.), *Parental behavior in diverse societies: New directions for child development, 40* (pp. 3–12). San Francisco: Jossey-Bass.

LeVine, R. A. (1994, July). *Culture and infant-mother attachment.* Paper presented at the International Society for the Study of Behavioral Development, Amsterdam.

LeVine, R. A., Dixon, S., LeVine, S., Richman, A., Leiderman, P., Keefer, C., et al. (1994). *Child care and culture: Lessons from Africa.* Cambridge, England: Cambridge University Press.

Levine, R. V., Norenzayan, A., & Philbrick, K. (2001). Cross-cultural differences in helping strangers. *Journal of Cross-Cultural Psychology, 32*(5), 543–560.

Lewis, C. (1984). Cooperation and control in Japanese nursery schools. *Comparative Education Review, 28,* 69–84.

Lozoff, B., Wolf, A., & Davis, N. (1984). Cosleeping in urban families with young children in the United States. *Pediatrics, 74*(2), 171–182.

Madsen, M. C. (1967). Cooperative and competitive motivation of children in three Mexican subcultures. *Psychological Reports, 20,* 1307–1320.

Madsen, M. C. (1971). Developmental and cross-cultural differences in the cooperative and competitive behavior of young children. *Journal of Cross-Cultural Psychology, 2*(4), 365–371.

Madsen, M. C., & Lancy, D. F. (1981). Cooperative and competitive behavior: Experiments related to ethnic identity and urbanization in Papua New Guinea. *Journal of Cross-Cultural Psychology, 12*(4), 389–408.

Main, M., & Weston, D. (1982). Avoidance of the attachment figure in infancy: Descriptions and interpretations. In J. Stevenson-Hinde & C. Murray Parkes (Eds.), *The place of attachment in human infancy* (pp. 31–59). New York: Basic Books.

Markus, H., & Kitayama, S. (1991). Culture and the self: Implications for cognition, emotion, and motivation. *Psychological Review, 98*(2), 224–253.

Maynard, A., Greenfield, P. M., & Childs, C. P. (1999). Culture, history, biology, and body: How Zinacantec Maya learn to weave. *Ethos, 27,* 379–402.

Maynard, A. E. (2002). Cultural teaching: The development of teaching skills in Zinacantec Maya sibling interactions. *Child Development, 73*(3), 969–982.

McGillicuddy-DeLisi, A. V., & Sigel, I. E. (1995). Parental beliefs. In M. H. Bornstein (Ed.), *Handbook of parenting: Vol. 3. Status and social conditions of parenting* (pp. 333–358). Hillsdale, NJ: Erlbaum.

McKenna, J. J. (1986). An anthropological perspective on the sudden infant death syndrome (SIDS): The role of parental breathing cues and speech breathing adaptations. *Medical Anthropology, 10*(1), 9–92.

McKenna, J. J., & Mosko, S. S. (1994). Sleep and arousal, synchrony and independence, among mothers and infants sleeping apart and together (same bed): An experiment in evolutionary medicine. *Acta Paediatric Supplement, 397,* 94–102.

McKenna, J. J., Thoman, E. B., Anders, T. F., Sadeh, A., Schectman, V. L., & Glotzbach, S. F. (1993). Infant-parent co-sleeping in an evolutionary perspective: Implication for understanding infant sleep development in the sudden infant death syndrome. *Sleep, 16*(3), 263–282.

Miller, J. G. (1994). Cultural diversity in the morality of caring: Individually oriented versus duty-based interpersonal moral codes. *Cross-Cultural Research, 28*(1), 3–39.

Miller, J. G. (1995, April). Discussion. In C. Raeff (Chair), *Individualism and collectivism as cultural contexts for developing different modes of independence and interdependence.* Symposium conducted at the meeting of the Society for Research in Child Development, Indianapolis, IN.

Miller, J. G., & Bersoff, D. M. (1992). Culture and moral judgment: How are conflicts between justice and interpersonal responsibilities resolved? *Journal of Personality and Social Psychology, 62*(4), 541–554.

Miller, J. G., & Bersoff, D. M. (1998). The role of liking in perceptions of the moral responsibility to help: A cultural perspective. *Journal of Experimental Social Psychology, 34*(5), 443–469.

Miller, J. G., Bersoff, D. M., & Harwood, R. L. (1990). Perceptions of social responsibilities in India and in the United States: Moral imperatives or personal decisions? *Journal of Personality and Social Psychology, 58*(1), 33–47.

Mistry, J., & Rogoff, B. (1994). Remembering in cultural context. In W. J. Lonner & R. S. Malpass (Eds.), *Psychology and culture* (pp. 139–144). Boston: Allyn & Bacon.

Miyake, K., Chen, S., & Campos, J. J. (1985). Infant temperament, mother's mode of interaction, and attachment in Japan: An interim report. In I. Bretherton & E. Waters (Eds.), *Growing points in attachment theory and research: Monographs of Cross-Cultural Human Development, 50*(1/2, Serial No. 209).

Morelli, G. A., Rogoff, B., Oppenheim, D., & Goldsmith, D. (1992). Cultural variation in infants' sleeping arrangements: Questions of independence. *Developmental Psychology, 28*(4), 604–613.

Mullen, B., & Riordan, C. A. (1988). Self-serving attribution in naturalistic settings: A meta-analytic review. *Journal of Applied Social Psychology, 18,* 3–22.

Mundy-Castle, A. C. (1974). Social and technological intelligence in Western and non-Western cultures. *Universitas, 4,* 46–52.

Munroe, R. L., & Munroe, R. H. (1994). *Cross-cultural human development.* Prospect Heights, IL: Waveland Press.

Munroe, R. L., Munroe, R. H., & Whiting, J. W. M. (1981). Male sex-role resolutions. In R. H. Munroe, R. L Munroe, & B. B. Whiting (Eds.), *Handbook of cross-cultural human development* (pp. 611–632). New York: Garland.

Muto, T., Kubo, Y., & Oshima-Takane, Y. (1980). Why don't Japanese ask questions? *Japanese Psychological Review (Shinrigaku Hyouron), 23,* 71–88.

National Association for the Education of Young Children. (2005). *Where we stand: Many languages, many cultures—Respecting and responding to diversity.* Retrieved October 31, 2005, from http://www.naeyc.org/about/positions/pdf/diversity .pdf#xml=http://naeychq.naeyc.org/texis/search/pdfhi.txt?query=multicultural&pr=naeyc&prox=sentence&rorder=750&rprox=500&rdfreq=1000&rwfreq=1000&rlead=1000&sufs=2&order=r&cq=&id=42ea28367.

Nsamenang, A. B. (1987). A West African perspective. In M. E. Lamb (Ed.), *The father's role: Cross-cultural perspectives* (pp. 273–293). Hillsdale, NJ: Erlbaum.

Nsamenang, A. B. (1992). *Human development in cultural context: A Third World perspective.* Newbury Park, CA: Sage.

Nsamenang, A. B., & Lamb, M. E. (1994). Socialization of Nso children in the Bamenda grassfields of northwest Cameroon. In P. M. Greenfield & R. R. Cocking (Eds.), *Cross-cultural roots of minority child development* (pp. 133–146). Hillsdale, NJ: Erlbaum.

Nugent, J. K. (1994). Cross-cultural studies of child development: Implications for clinicians. *Zero to Three, 15*(2), 1, 3–8.

Nunner-Winkler, G. (1984). Two moralities? A critical discussion of an ethic of care and responsibility versus an ethic of rights and justice. In W. M. Kurtiness & J. L. Gewirtz (Eds.), *Morality, moral behavior, and moral development* (pp. 348–361). New York: Wiley.

Ochs, E., & Schieffelin, B. B. (1984). Language acquisition and socialization: Three developmental stories and their implications. In R. Shweder & R. LeVine (Eds.), *Culture theory: Essays on mind, self, and emotion* (pp. 276–320). Cambridge, England: Cambridge University Press.

Ogbu, J. U. (1994). From cultural differences to differences in cultural frame of reference. In P. M. Greenfield & R. R. Cocking (Eds.), *Cross-cultural roots of minority child development* (pp. 365–391). Hillsdale, NJ: Erlbaum.

Ogunnaike, O. A., & Houser, R. F. (2002). Yoruba toddlers' engagement in errands and cognitive performance on the Yoruba Mental

Subscales. *International Journal of Behavioral Development, 26*(2), 145–153.

Oloko, B. A. (1993). Children's street work in urban Nigeria: Dilemma of modernizing tradition. *Journal of Behavioral Development, 16,* 465–482.

Oloko, B. A. (1994). Children's street work in urban Nigeria: Dilemma of modernizing tradition. In P. M. Greenfield & R. R. Cocking (Eds.), *Cross-cultural roots of minority and child development* (pp. 197–224). Hillsdale, NJ: Erlbaum.

Osako, M. M., & Liu, W. T. (1986). Intergenerational relations and the aged among Japanese Americans. *Research on Aging, 8*(1), 128–155.

Palacios, J., & Moreno, M. C. (1996). Parents' and adolescents' ideas on children: Origins and transmission of intracultural diversity. In S. Harkness & C. M. Super (Eds.), *Parents' cultural belief systems: Their origins, expressions and consequences* (pp. 215–253). New York: Guilford Press.

Philips, S. U. (1972). Participant structures and communicative competence: Warm Springs children in community and classroom. In C. B. Cazden, V. P. John, & D. Hymes (Eds.), *Functions of language in the classroom* (pp. 370–394). New York: Teachers College Press.

Posada, G., & Jacobs, A. (2001). Child-mother attachment relationships and culture. *American Psychologist, 56*(10), 821–822.

Quiroz, B., Greenfield, P. M., & Altchech, M. (1999). Bridging cultures with a parent-teacher conference. *Educational Leadership, 56*(7), 68–70.

Rabain, J. (1979). *L'enfant du lignage.* Paris: Payot.

Rabain-Jamin, J. (1994). Language and socialization of the child in African families living in France. In P. M. Greenfield & R. R. Cocking (Eds.), *Cross-cultural roots of minority child development* (pp. 147–166). Hillsdale, NJ: Erlbaum.

Rabain-Jamin, J., Maynard, A. E., & Greenfield, P. M. (2003). Implications of sibling caregiving for sibling relations and teaching interactions in two cultures. *Ethos, 31,* 204–231.

Rabain-Jamin, J., & Sabeau-Jouannet, E. (1997). Maternal speech to 4-month-old infants in two cultures: Wolof and French. *International Journal of Behavioral Development, 20,* 425–451.

Raeff, C., Greenfield, P. M., & Quiroz, B. (2000). Conceptualizing interpersonal relationships in the cultural contexts of individualism and collectivism. In S. Harkness, C. Raeff, & C. M. Super (Eds.), *New directions in child development: Vol. 87. Variability in the social construction of the child* (pp. 59–74). San Francisco: Jossey-Bass.

Rao, N., McHale, J. P., & Pearson, E. (2003). Links between socialization goals and child-rearing practices in Chinese and Indian mothers. *Infant and Child Development, 12,* 475–492.

Reese, L., Balzano, S., Gallimore, R., & Goldenberg, C. (1995). The concept of educación: Latino family values and American schooling. *International Journal of Educational Research, 23*(1), 57–81.

Restak, R. (1979). *The brain.* New York: Doubleday.

Richman, A. L., Miller, P. M., & Johnson Solomon, M. (1988). The socialization of infants in suburban Boston. In R. A. LeVine, P. M. Miller, & M. West (Eds.), *Parental behavior in diverse societies* (pp. 65–74). San Francisco: Jossey-Bass.

Rogoff, B. (1990). *Apprenticeship in thinking: Cognitive development in social context.* Oxford, England: Oxford University Press.

Rogoff, B. (2003). *The cultural nature of human development.* New York: Oxford University Press.

Rogoff, B., Paradise, R., Arauz, R., Correa-Chavez, M., & Angelillo, C. (2003). Firsthand learning through intent participation. *Annual Review of Psychology, 54,* 175.

Rohner, R. P., & Pettengill, S. M. (1985). Perceived parental acceptance-rejection and parental control among Korean adolescents [Special issue]. *Child Development, 56,* 524–528.

Roopnarine, J. L., & Lamb, M. E. (1978). The effects of daycare on attachment and exploratory behavior in a Strange Situation. *Merrill-Palmer Quarterly, 24,* 85–95.

Roopnarine, J. L., & Lamb, M. E. (1980). Peer and parent-child interaction before and after enrollment in nursery school. *Journal of Applied Developmental Psychology, 1,* 77–81.

Rothbaum, F., Weisz, J., Pott, M., Miyake, K., & Morelli, G. (2000). Attachment and culture: Security in the United States and Japan. *American Psychologist, 55*(10), 1093–1104.

Rothbaum, F., Weisz, J., Pott, M., Miyake, K., & Morelli, G. (2001). Deeper into attachment and culture. *American Psychologist, 56*(10), 827–829.

Rothstein-Fisch, C. (2004, February). *Bridging cultures in early care and education.* Workshop presented at the annual Birth to Three Institute, Baltimore.

Rothstein-Fisch, C., Greenfield, P. M., & Trumbull, E. (1999). Bridging Cultures with classroom strategies. *Educational Leadership, 56*(7), 64–67.

Rothstein-Fisch, C., Trumbull, E., Daley, C., Mercado, G., & Perez, A. I. (2003, April). *Classroom management reconsidered: Building on students' cultural strengths.* Paper presented at the American Educational Research Association, Chicago.

Rothstein-Fisch, C., Trumbull, E., & Greenfield, P. M. (in press). *Reconceptualizing classroom management: Building on students' cultural strengths.* Washington, DC: Association for Supervision and Curriculum Development.

Rothstein-Fisch, C., Trumbull, E., Isaac, A., Daley, C., & Perez, A. I. (2003). When "helping someone else" is the right answer: Bridging cultures in assessment. *Journal of Latinos and Education, 2,* 123–140.

Rothstein-Fisch, C., Trumbull, E., Quiroz, B., & Greenfield, P. M. (1997, June). *Bridging cultures in the schools.* Poster session presented at the Jean Piaget Society Conference, Santa Monica, CA.

Rudy, D., & Grusec, J. E. (2001). Correlates of authoritarian parenting in individualist and collectivist cultures and implications for understanding the transmission of values. *Journal of Cross-Cultural Psychology, 32*(2), 202–212.

Sanchez Medina, J. A., Lozano, V. M., & Goudena, P. P. (2001). Conflict management in pre-schoolers: A cross-cultural perspective. *International Journal of Early Years Education, 9*(2), 153–160.

Saraswathi, T. S. (1999). *Culture, socialization, and human development: Theory, research, and applications in the Indian setting.* Thousand Oaks, CA: Sage.

Saraswathi, T. S., & Pai, S. (1997). Socialization in the Indian context. In H. S. R. Kao (Ed.), *Asian perspectives on psychology* (pp. 74–92). Thousand Oaks, CA: Sage.

Saxe, G. B. (1991). *Culture and cognitive development.* Hillsdale, NJ: Erlbaum.

Schachter, F. F., Fuchs, M. L., Bijur, P. E., & Stone, R. (1989). Cosleeping and sleep problems in Hispanic-American urban young children. *Pediatrics, 84,* 522–530.

Schneider, B., Hieshima, J. A., Lee, S., & Plank, S. (1994). Continuities and discontinuities in the cognitive socialization of

Asian-oriented children: The case of Japanese Americans. In P. M. Greenfield & R. R. Cocking (Eds.), *Cross-cultural roots of minority child development* (pp. 323–350). Hillsdale, NJ: Erlbaum.

Schroen, C. (1995, May). *Is it child abuse? Toward a multi-cultural field guide for social workers.* Paper presented at the UCLA Undergraduate Psychology Conference, Los Angeles.

Scribner, S. (1985). Vygotsky's uses of history. In J. Wertsch (Ed.), *Culture, communication, and cognition: Vygotskian perspectives* (pp. 119–145). New York: Cambridge University Press.

Scribner, S., & Cole, M. (1973). Cognitive consequences of formal and informal education. *Science, 182,* 553–559.

Scribner, S., & Cole, M. (1981). *The psychology of literacy.* Cambridge, MA: Harvard University Press.

Shapira, A., & Madsen, M. C. (1969). Cooperative and competitive behavior of kibbutz and urban children in Israel. *Child Development, 40*(2), 609–617.

Shweder, R., Jensen, L., & Goldstein, W. (1995). Who sleeps by whom revisited: A method for extracting the moral goods implicit in practice. In J. Goodnow, P. Miller, & F. Kessel (Eds.), *New directions for child development: Vol. 67. Cultural practices as contexts for development* (pp. 21–39). San Francisco: Jossey-Bass.

Shweder, R. A., Goodnow, J., Hatano, G., LeVine, R. A., Markus, H., & Miller, P. (1998). The cultural psychology of development: One mind, many mentalities. In W. Damom (Editor-in-Chief) & R. M. Lerner (Vol. Ed.), *Handbook of child psychology: Vol. 1. Theoretical models of human development* (5th ed., pp. 865–937). New York: Wiley.

Shweder, R. A., Mahapatra, M., & Miller, J. G. (1990). Culture and moral development. In J. W. Stigler, R. A. Shweder, & G. Herdt (Eds.), *Cultural psychology: Essays of comparative human development* (pp. 130–203). Cambridge, England: Cambridge University Press.

Sigel, I. E. (Ed.). (1985). *Parental belief systems: The psychological consequences for children.* Hillsdale, NJ: Erlbaum.

Sigel, I. E., McGillicuddy-DeLisi, A. V., & Goodnow, J. J. (Eds.). (1992). *Parental belief systems: The psychological consequences for children* (2nd ed.). Hillsdale, NJ: Erlbaum.

Smaldino, C. (1995). Tossing and turning over "crying it out." *Mothering, 74,* 32–37.

Spock, B. (1976). *Baby and child care.* New York: Pocket Books.

Stigler, J. W., & Perry, M. (1988). Mathematics learning in Japanese, Chinese, and American classrooms. In G. B. Saxe & M. Gearhart (Eds.), *Children's mathematics: Vol. 41. New directions of child development* (pp. 27–54). San Francisco: Jossey-Bass.

Suina, J. H. (1991, June/July). Discussion. In P. M. Greenfield & R. R. Cocking (Eds.), *Continuities and discontinuities in the cognitive socialization of minority children.* Proceedings of a workshop, Department of Health and Human Services, Public Health Service, Alcohol, Drug Abuse, and Mental Health Administration, Washington, DC.

Suina, J. H., & Smolkin, L. B. (1994). From natal culture to school culture to dominant society culture: Supporting transitions for Pueblo Indian students. In P. M. Greenfield & R. R. Cocking (Eds.), *Cross-cultural roots of minority child development* (pp. 115–130). Hillsdale, NJ: Erlbaum.

Sung, B. L. (1985). Bicultural conflicts in Chinese immigrant children. *Journal of Comparative Family Studies, 16,* 255–269.

Sung, K.-T. (1990). A new look at filial piety: Ideals and practices of family-centered parent care in Korea. *Gerontologist, 30*(5), 610–617.

Super, C., & Harkness, S. (1982). The infant's niche in rural Kenya and metropolitan America. In L. L. Adler (Ed.), *Cross-cultural research at issue* (pp. 47–55). New York: Academic Press.

Super, C., & Harkness, S. (1986). The developmental niche: A conceptualization at the interface of child and culture. *International Journal of Behavioral Development, 9*(4), 545–569.

Suzuki, L. K. (2000). *The development and socialization of filial piety: A comparison of Asian Americans and Euro-Americans.* Unpublished doctoral dissertation, University of California, Los Angeles.

Suzuki, L. K., Davis, H. M., & Greenfield, P. M. (in press). Self-enhancement and self-effacement in reaction to praise and criticism: The case of multi-ethnic youth. In C. Mattingly & N. Lutkehaus (Eds.), *Psychology meets anthropology: Jerome Bruner and his inspiration.* New York: Palgrave Macmillan.

Suzuki, L. K., & Greenfield, P. M. (2002). The construction of everyday sacrifice in Asian Americans and European Americans: The roles of ethnicity and acculturation. *Cross Cultural Research, 36*(3), 200–228.

Takahashi, K. (1990). Are the key assumptions of the "Strange Situation" procedure universal? A view from Japanese research. *Human Development, 33,* 23–30.

Tapia Uribe, F., LeVine, R. A., & LeVine, S. E. (1994). Maternal behavior in a Mexican community: The changing environments of children. In P. M. Greenfield & R. R. Cocking (Eds.), *Cross-cultural roots of minority child development* (pp. 41–54). Hillsdale, NJ: Erlbaum.

Tobin, J., Wu, D., & Davidson, D. (1989). *Preschool in three cultures: Japan, China, and the United States.* New Haven, CT: Yale University Press.

Toupin, E. A. (1980). Counseling Asians: Psychotherapy in context of racism and Asian American history. *American Journal of Orthopsychiatry, 50,* 76–86.

Triandis, H. C., Bontempo, R., Villareal, M., Asai, M., & Lucca, M. (1988). Individualism and collectivism: Cross-cultural perspectives on self in-group relationships. *Journal of Personality and Social Psychology, 54,* 323–338.

Trommsdorff, G., & Nauck, B. (Eds.). (2005). Factors influencing value of children and intergenerational relations in times of social change: Analyses from psychological and socio-cultural perspectives. *Applied Psychology: An International Review, 543*(3), 317–337.

Trumbull, E. (2000). Avoiding bias in grading systems. In E. Trumbull & B. Farr (Eds.), *Grading and reporting student progress in an age of standards* (pp. 105–127). Norwood, MA: Christopher-Gordon.

Trumbull, E., Diaz-Meza, R., Hasan, A., & Rothstein-Fisch, C. (2000). *The Bridging Cultures 5 year report (1996–2000).* San Francisco: WestEd.

Trumbull, E., Rothstein-Fisch, C., & Greenfield, P. M. (1999). *Bridging Cultures in our schools: New approaches that work* (Knowledge Brief). San Francisco: WestEd.

Trumbull, E., Rothstein-Fisch, C., Greenfield, P. M., & Quiroz, B. (2001). *Bridging Cultures between home and school: A guide for teachers.* Mahwah, NJ: Erlbaum.

Trumbull, E., Rothstein-Fisch, C., & Hernandez, E. (2003). Parent involvement in schooling: According to whose values? *School Community Journal, 13,* 45–72.

Tseng, W. S. (1973). The concept of personality in Confucian thought. *Psychiatry, 36,* 191–202.

Valdés, G. (1997). *Con respeto: Bridging the distances between culturally diverse families and schools—An ethnographic portrait.* New York: Teachers College Press.

van IJzendoorn, M. H., & Kroonenberg, P. (1988). Cross-cultural patterns of attachment: A meta-analysis of the Strange Situation. *Child Development, 59,* 147–156.

Vygotsky, L. S. (1962). *Thought and language.* Cambridge, MA: MIT Press.

Wainryb, C. (1995). Reasoning about social conflicts in different cultures: Druze and Jewish children in Israel. *Child Development, 66*(2), 390–401.

Wainryb, C., & Turiel, E. (1994). Dominance, subordination, and concepts of personal entitlements in cultural contexts. *Child Development, 65*(6), 1701–1722.

Wang, S., & Tamis-LeMonda, C. S. (2003). Do child-rearing values in Taiwan and the United States reflect cultural values of collectivism and individualism? *Journal of Cross-Cultural Psychology, 34,* 661–677.

Weisner, T. S. (1984). Ecocultural niches of middle childhood: A cross-cultural perspective. In W. A. Collins (Ed.) *Development during middle childhood: The years from 6 to 12* (pp. 335–369). Washington, DC: National Academy of Science Press.

Weisner, T. S. (2000). Culture, childhood, and progress in sub-Saharan Africa. In L. E. Harrison & S. P. Huntington (Eds.), *Culture matters* (pp. 141–157). New York: Basic Books.

Weisner, T., Bausano, M., & Kornfein, M. (1983). Putting family ideals into practice: Pronaturalism in conventional and nonconventional California families. *Ethos, 11*(4), 278–304.

Wertsch, J. V. (1985). *Vygotsky and the social formation of mind.* Cambridge, MA: Harvard University Press.

Whiting, B., & Edwards, C. (1988). *Children of different worlds: The formation of social behavior.* Cambridge, MA: Harvard University Press.

Whiting, B. B., & Whiting, J. W. M. (1975). *Children of six cultures.* Cambridge, MA: Harvard University Press.

Whiting, J. W. M., & Whiting, B. B. (1994). Altruistic and egoistic behavior in six cultures. In E. H. Chasdi (Ed.), *Culture and human development: The selected papers of John Whiting* (pp. 267–281). New York: Cambridge University Press. (Original work published 1973)

Yeh, K.-H., & Bedford, O. (2003). A test of the dual filial piety model. *Asian Journal of Social Psychology, 6,* 215–228.

Yoshida, T., Kojo, K., & Kaku, H. (1982). A study on the development of self-presentation in children. *Japanese Journal of Educational Psychology, 30,* 30–37.

Yovsi, R. D. (2001). *Ethnotheories about breastfeeding and mother-infant interaction: The case of sedentary Nso farmers and nomadic Fulani pastorals with their infants 3 to 6 months of age in Mbvein subdivision of the northwest province of Cameroon, Africa.* Unpublished doctoral dissertation, University of Oanabrueck, Germany.

Yovsi, R. D., & Keller, H. (2003). Breastfeeding: An adaptive process. *Ethos, 31,* 147–171.

Zempleni-Rabain, J. (1973). Food and the strategy involved in learning fraternal exchange among Wolof children. In P. Alexandre (Ed.), *French perspectives in African studies* (pp. 221–233). London: Oxford University Press.

Zepeda, M., Gonzalez-Mena, J., Rothstein-Fisch, C., & Trumbull, E. (in press). *Bridging cultures in early care and education module.* Mahwah, NJ: Erlbaum.

Zukow, P. G. (1989). *Sibling interactions across cultures: Theoretical and methodological issues.* New York: Springer-Verlag.

CHAPTER 18

Childhood Poverty, Policy, and Practice

VONNIE C. MCLOYD, NIKKI L. AIKENS, and LINDA M. BURTON

Although fundamentally accepting of wide disparities in economic well-being as an inherent consequence of capitalism, Americans are not inured to economic poverty and its attendant problems. The United States has a long history, dating back to colonial times, of policies, reforms, and interventions ostensibly intended to reduce the incidence and/or ameliorate the human costs of poverty (Demos, 1986; Schlossman, 1976). Most antipoverty efforts have focused on children directly or indirectly through their parents, based on the notion that poverty results from an intergenerational cycle that can best be broken during the victim's childhood (de Lone, 1979). Because of the prevailing ideology among Americans that low motivation, poor choices, and a variety of individual defects are at the core of poverty (Bobo, 2001; Haller, Hollinger, & Raubal, 1990), these efforts primarily have focused on changing poor individuals' putative behavior and characteristics, rather than altering structural conditions that create poverty and its social ills.

This long-standing pattern notwithstanding, the past 15 years marked a period of policy changes in the United States that increased returns from low-wage work, though they did little to remove structural barriers that disproportionately relegated certain groups to low-wage work in the first place (Greenberg et al., 2002). Most notable is the expansion of the Earned Income Tax Credit (EITC), a provision designed to offset the burden of the Social Security payroll tax, supplement low-wage earnings, and promote work as a viable alternative to welfare (Bos et al., 1999). The EITC helps more families escape poverty than any other government program. In 2002, 4.8 million people, including 2.7 million children, were lifted out of poverty as a result of the additional income provided by the federal EITC. It has also achieved some measure of success in inducing more single mothers to work (Llobrera & Zahradnik, 2004). Nonetheless, these policy changes have left a significant number of even full-time workers in poverty (U.S. Census Bureau, 2003). In 2002, of 4.9 million poor families with children in which the parents were not elderly or disabled, 66% were families in which at least one parent was working (Llobrera & Zahradnik, 2004). African American and Hispanic individuals, including children, are more likely than their non-Hispanic White counterparts to be poor despite living in full-time working families (Iceland, 1998).

The sharp rise in childhood poverty during the early 1980s and persistently high rates of childhood poverty through the late 1990s generated intense scholarly interest in poor children and families, manifested most strikingly by the publication of numerous edited volumes and special issues of journals devoted to the topic. The issues around which this scholarship coalesced included the effectiveness of various antipoverty programs (Barnett, 1995; Olds & Kitzman, 1993; St. Pierre, Layzer, & Barnes, 1995), the processes that mediate and temper the adverse effects of poverty and economic stress on children's development (e.g., Duncan & Brooks-Gunn, 1997; Huston, Garcia Coll, & McLoyd, 1994; Korbin, 1992), the consequences of the dynamics and context of poverty for children's development (Duncan & Brooks-Gunn, 1997), and the application of research on poor children and families to welfare policy and practice (Danziger & Danziger, 1995). Scholarly interest in these issues remains high (Arnold & Doctoroff, 2003; Bradley & Corwyn, 2002). New to the landscape in recent years is a generation of studies assessing the effects of welfare reform and different welfare and employment policies on child well-being (e.g., Chase-Lansdale et al., 2003; Gennetian et al., 2002, 2004; Gennetian & Miller, 2002; Morris, Bloom, Kemple, & Hendra, 2003; Morris, Huston, Duncan, Crosby, & Bos, 2001). The impetus for these studies was the Personal Responsibility and Work Opportunity Reconciliation Act of 1996, popularly known as PRWORA, and federal waivers granted to states to implement and test welfare reform policies in anticipation of this federal legislation.

The major goal of this chapter is to illuminate the dynamic relation between programs and policies that target poor children and families, on the one hand, and theoretical and empirical work in the field of child development, on the other. The United States is the focal geographic context within which these issues are discussed, but cross-national data are presented to highlight characteristics distinctive to the United States that shape its antipoverty policies and practices and ultimately affect the economic well-being of its children. Although the centerpiece of this chapter is a discussion of how theoretical and empirical work in the field of child development has influenced policies and programs for poor children, it is important that we underscore two points at the outset to put this discussion in proper perspective.

First, it is our belief that when developmental theory and research have played a role in the formulation of poverty-focused policies and programs, most often it has been a supporting rather than leading role. Political and social forces, not developmental theory and research, typically are the prime movers and wellsprings of social policies and programs directed toward poor children and families. Research often is not a prerequisite and is virtually never a sufficient basis for the formulation and maintenance of such policies and programs. Examples abound of policies directed toward poor families that persisted in the face of strong research evidence that they were not having their desired effect (e.g., Learnfare; Quinn & Magill, 1994). Conversely, in a number of instances, experimental social policies (e.g., negative income tax experiments of the 1960s and early 1970s) shown by research to have salutary effects on poor children's well-being were rejected for universal implementation (Neubeck & Roach, 1981; Salkind & Haskins, 1982). Often underlying such divergences between policy decisions and research are ideological and social forces, especially prevailing public sentiments about how the poor should be treated.

In other instances, the enactment of federal policies with the potential to affect massive numbers of poor children has borne remarkably little imprint from child development research and theory. Cases in point are PRWORA and the Family Support Act of 1988, which sought to increase economic self-sufficiency among recipients of Aid to Families with Dependent Children (AFDC) by mandating participation in educational and employment training programs and strengthening enforcement of existing child support provisions. Both laws, like the welfare debate from which they emerged, lacked a clear, consistent focus on children's developmental needs and well-being (Chase-Lansdale & Vinovskis, 1995; Greenberg et al., 2002). Most theories posit structural factors to explain the underutilization of social science research in policymaking (e.g., the political nature of the policymaking process, the paucity of centralized institutions for integrating research-based knowledge and governmental structures). A more optimistic theory points to communication gaps and limited understanding between social scientists and policymakers, who function in communities that differ in goals, information needs, values, reward systems, and languages. Fortunately, recent years have witnessed growing knowledge and sophistication about effective ways to bridge this gap (Bogenschneider, Olson, Linney, & Mills, 2000).

Delineation of how theoretical and empirical work has sanctioned policies and practices directed toward poor children and families also must be tempered with an appreciation of the often subtle but decided shadows that social and political forces cast on scholarly work itself. The manner in which issues are formulated and, hence, the nature of knowledge generated in the discipline of child development is influenced by sociohistorical context (Riegel, 1972; Wertsch & Youniss, 1987). Scholars in the field of child development, as in any discipline, bring with them predispositions stemming from laws, customs, economic factors, political beliefs, and the prevailing Zeitgeist, among other things, that necessarily shape the nature of and conclusions drawn from their research (Youniss, 1990). Their recommendations about courses of action toward children and interventions in the lives of families follow not just from data, but from the interests they bring to their studies. For these reasons, woven into our review of scholarly work that undergirds policies and programs directed toward poor families and children is a discussion of how social and political forces have shaped both of these entities. It represents our attempt to take seriously Youniss's challenge that "an ethically mature development psychology would not deny its debt to social and cultural forces but seek to know them better for itself and the persons it serves" (p. 287).

The chapter is divided into four major sections. We begin with a brief discussion of the official measure of income poverty and its relation to other indicators of economic well-being, such as socioeconomic status. In the second section, we turn our attention to core substantive issues, namely, linkages among theory, research, and programs that seek to reduce poverty and/or its negative effects. Our analysis is limited primarily to three categories of programs that provide an array of educational and social services to poor infants, preschoolers, and/or their parents, specifically early childhood education programs (primarily Head Start and Early Start), parent education and training programs, and pro-

grams that focus on both parent and child and the broader ecology of family life (e.g., two-generation programs). The organizing framework for our discussion is three assumptions on which these categories of programs are premised: (1) that early experience is a critical determinant of the course of development, (2) that parents and the home environment exert primary influence on children's development, and (3) that the broader ecological context of family life impacts parental behavior and, in turn, children's functioning. We review the theoretical and empirical work that prompted and/or sustained these assumptions and provided the intellectual foundation for these antipoverty programs, along with findings from evaluation studies designed to demonstrate the efficacy of these programs. We also consider these programs and their underlying assumptions in light of more recent poverty-focused research. Given the vastness of relevant bodies of research, our review is necessarily selective.

In the third section, we review nonexperimental studies assessing the relation of child functioning to maternal receipt of and transitions off public welfare (AFDC and PRWORA) and studies that used a random assignment design to test the effects of different welfare and employment policies on parental employment, income, family processes, and child well-being. The chapter concludes with a discussion of the implications of extant research for policy and practice. The ideological bases and limitations of existing antipoverty programs are considered in light of social-structural and macroeconomic forces, and suggestions to guide the practices of those working with poor children and families are offered.

CATEGORIES AND DEFINITIONS OF ECONOMIC DEPRIVATION

This chapter encompasses research on multiple categories of economic deprivation, including income poverty, low socioeconomic status, and economic loss. In this section, we discuss how these constructs differ and the potential importance of these differences for children's development and for policy formulation.

Income Poverty

Sound definitions and corresponding measures of poverty are important for a range of "scientific" and political reasons. They allow comparisons of economic well-being across different groups and across time, identification of individuals, families, and social groups whose most basic needs remain unmet, and assessments of the effects of poverty, policies, and programs on these individuals, families, and social groups (Ruggles, 1990). Most developmental, socialization, intervention, and policy studies relevant to this chapter are concerned with absolute poverty, rather than relative poverty or subjective poverty (see Hagenaars & de Vos, 1988, for a discussion of various definitions of economic poverty).

The most common measure of absolute poverty in these studies is defined by cash income, using the official federal poverty index as a marker. Developed in 1965 by Mollie Orshansky, an economist employed by the Social Security Administration, the federal poverty standard was officially adopted by the government in 1969 during its "War on Poverty" (Haveman, 1987). Cash income was defined as the pretax, posttransfer annual cash income of a family, excluding capital gains or losses. This value was compared with a threshold based on the estimated cost of food multiplied by 3, adjusted to account for economies of scale for larger families and the differing food needs of children under age 18 and adults under and over 65. The estimated cost of food was based on the minimum income a family needed to purchase food delineated in the U.S. Department of Agriculture's (USDA) "thrifty" diet. The food multiplier of 3 was based on a household budget study conducted in 1955 indicating that food typically absorbed about a third of the posttax income of families over a wide range of incomes.

Today, there are well over 100 different poverty thresholds, adjusted annually by the consumer price index so that the purchasing power they represent does not change over time. Hence, they remain close to those calculated with the "thrifty" food plan (Citro & Michael, 1995; Haveman, 1987). Because this index is an absolute dollar amount, not a percent of the median income or a percentile, it is theoretically possible for everyone to be above the poverty threshold.

The official poverty index has several defects and limitations, recognition of which has prompted various corrective efforts in public policy arenas (see McLoyd & Ceballo, 1998, for a discussion). These problems notwithstanding, the official poverty index, or some derivative of it, is widely used in both child-focused research and policy. For example, it has become standard practice among developmental researchers to use

an income-to-needs ratio (calculated as household income/official poverty threshold for household) as an indicator of the degree of poverty or affluence characterizing a household (e.g., Brooks-Gunn, Klebanov, & Liaw, 1995; Gutman, McLoyd, & Toyokawa, 2005; Mistry, Biesanz, Taylor, Burchinal, & Cox, 2004). This ratio tells us how far below or above an individual or family falls relative to the poverty threshold. An income-to-need ratio of 1.0 indicates that a household's income is equal to the poverty threshold, and smaller or larger ratios represent more or less severe poverty (or greater affluence), respectively. Used in this manner, the poverty line becomes a unit of measurement rather than a threshold of need (Hauser & Carr, 1995). An income-to-need ratio has the advantage of being a more sensitive indicator that bears a stronger relation to children's development than does a simple poor/nonpoor dichotomy (Duncan & Brooks-Gunn, 1997). Others define poverty in terms of eligibility for federal or state subsidies to the poor (e.g., reduced-cost or free lunch) or family income cutoffs corresponding to those used to determine eligibility for subsidies.

Low Socioeconomic Status

Another large category of studies pertinent to this chapter focuses on low socioeconomic status (SES) as an indicator of economic deprivation. The term "socioeconomic status" typically is used to signify an individual's, family's, or group's ranking on a hierarchy according to its access to or control over some combination of valued commodities such as wealth, power, and social status (Mueller & Parcel, 1981). Although some dispute exists among social scientists about how SES should be defined or measured, there is considerable agreement that important components of SES include the occupation of the father and/or mother, family income, education, prestige, power, and a certain style of life.

Poverty is not isomorphic with low SES. Unlike SES, poverty is based on an absolute standard or threshold and does not signify relative position. Its marker, cash income, is only one of several components or dimensions of SES and is clearly related to but distinct from occupational status, educational level, prestige, and power. In addition, poverty status is considerably more volatile than SES. During adulthood, income relative to need is more likely to shift markedly from one year to another than SES indicators such as educational attainment and occupational status. Duncan's (1984) examination of adjacent-year pairs of data from the national, longitudinal Panel Study of Income Dynamics for the period 1969 to 1978 indicated that one-third to one-half of those who were poor in one year were not poor in the next year. One of the important distinctions that emerged from this work is persistent versus transitory poverty (Duncan & Brooks-Gunn, 1997).

These distinctions between poverty and low SES are conceptually important and are viewed as crucial for public-policy discussions (Duncan, Yeung, Brooks-Gunn, & Smith, 1998). Some research has indicated, for example, that poverty and income status have effects on children's development independent of parental education (Duncan & Brooks-Gunn, 1997), although it is not yet known how changes in poverty and income status act synergistically with more stable indicators of SES to influence development (Huston, McLoyd, & Garcia Coll, 1994). Policy analysts regard the SES-income distinction as critical partly on the presumption that it is generally easier to design and implement programs that alter family income (e.g., increasing welfare benefits, tax credits, and minimum wage) than programs that modify family characteristics that mark social class (Duncan et al., 1998).

Also important to bear in mind is that neither poverty as measured by official criteria nor low SES can be assumed to be identical to, or even particularly good proxies for, material hardship. Mayer and Jencks (1988) found, for example, that income-to-needs ratios explained less than a quarter of the variance in householders' reports of material hardship (e.g., spending less for food than the "thrifty" food budget published by the U.S. Department of Agriculture; unmet medical and dental needs; housing problems). This is because poverty and low SES rarely come alone. They often represent a conglomerate of conditions and events that amount to a pervasive rather than a bounded stressor. Scarcity of material resources and services frequently is conjoined to a plethora of undesirable events (e.g., eviction, physical illness, criminal assault) and ongoing conditions (e.g., inadequate housing, poor health care, dangerous neighborhoods, poor diets, environmental toxins) that operate concurrently and often precipitate additional crises (Belle, 1984; Evans, 2004). In short, in the context of limited financial resources, stressors are highly contagious (Makosky, 1982). Traditional measures of poverty and SES, then, may underestimate the direct and indirect effects of material hardship and contextual risks on children's development (Ackerman, Brown, & Izard, 2004; Mayer & Jencks, 1988).

Economic Loss

Whereas poverty and low SES are typically conceptualized as ongoing conditions inextricably linked to employment-related factors such as unemployment, underemployment, low wages, and unstable work, another set of studies relevant to our concern here focuses on various events as precipitants of economic deprivation. This research assesses the impact on parents and children of job loss, job demotion, income loss, and economic pressure as experienced by working- and middle-class individuals who characteristically are employed (e.g., Conger, Ge, Elder, Lorenz, & Simons, 1994; Flanagan & Eccles, 1993; McLoyd, 1989, 1990). Although they tend to be overrepresented among poor families, these experiences of economic loss or decline do not necessarily push families into poverty. We review this work to the extent that it helps fill gaps in the poverty literature and, in general, furthers our understanding of the processes by which economic deprivation might influence children's development.

Throughout this chapter, we attempt to maintain distinctions among various categories of economic deprivation, especially poverty and low SES, on the one hand, and economic loss on the other. In our discussion of specific findings, the term is used that most closely approximates the indicator of economic deprivation employed by the researchers. In psychological research published prior to the mid-1980s, the terms "low SES" and "poor" tended to be used interchangeably. Recent research is distinguished by more precise definitions of poverty (e.g., income-to-needs ratios), attention to the multiple dimensions of poverty (e.g., chronicity and contexts of poverty, such as neighborhoods and schools), and a diminution of the tendency to treat poverty as a condition identical to low SES. These conceptual and empirical advances are traceable in large measure to Duncan's (1984) research underscoring the volatility and dynamics of poverty and W. J. Wilson's (1987) seminal analysis of historical changes in the spatial concentration of poverty in inner-city neighborhoods wrought by structural changes in the economy.

The preeminence in research and policy studies of "objective" states of economic deprivation operationalized in terms of the official poverty index, low SES, and economic loss should not obscure the fact that some of the impact on individuals of economic deprivation and ameliorative policies and practices undoubtedly is subjective. How parents and children perceive and feel about their economic circumstances is driven partly by subjective evaluation of their circumstances in comparison to some reference group. In contexts distinguished by extraordinary affluence and conspicuous consumption, such as the United States, this comparison process can accentuate "feeling poor" among individuals who are poor in an objective sense and can engender "feeling poor" among those who are not (Garbarino, 1992). This subjective state can have direct effects on psychological functioning and mediate as well as moderate the influence of "objective" states of poverty and other forms of economic deprivation (Conger et al., 1994; Garbarino, 1992; McLoyd, Jayaratne, Ceballo, & Borquez, 1994).

BASIC ASSUMPTIONS OF ANTIPOVERTY POLICIES AND PROGRAMS: LINKAGES TO CHILD DEVELOPMENT THEORY AND RESEARCH

Programs that aim to reduce the prevalence of poverty and/or ameliorate the negative effects of poverty on children have informed and been influenced by developmental research, and both have been shaped by common political and social forces. Although a mainstay of these programs is their principal focus on infants and preschoolers, the research that undergirds the programs, and the programs themselves, have grown more complex and sophisticated over time. A historical overview of these programs reveals progressive shifts toward more comprehensive models whose precursors include changing conceptual frameworks and research foci within the field of child development and evidence from evaluation studies of the limitations of previous programs based on more simplistic models.

In this section of the chapter, we consider three major premises that are the bedrock of major antipoverty policies and programs in the United States: (1) that early experience is a critical determinant of the course of development, setting the child on a trajectory toward successful or problematic adaptation; (2) that parents and the home environment exert primary influence on children's development; and (3) that the broader ecological context of family life impacts parental behavior and,

in turn, children's functioning. Our primary goal is to illuminate the theoretical and empirical work that gave rise to and/or affirmed these and other guiding assumptions and, hence, helped shaped the nature of antipoverty policies and their implementation. Also reviewed are intervention studies that test the efficacy of programs designed to reduce poverty and/or its negative effects. Historical continuities and discontinuities in the nature of policies and programs for the poor are highlighted, with special attention given to antecedents of discontinuities.

Two qualities of research on poor children are reflected in this review. First, basic and intervention research focused on poor children and families are genealogically and conceptually intertwined. Second, issues of race, ethnicity, culture, and racism are prominently and intricately woven throughout the history of research on poor children, because race and poverty are decidedly confounded as a consequence of America's racial caste system. This confound, however, is not sufficient as an explanation for the fact that the overwhelming majority of basic and intervention studies of poor children focus on African Americans. A few recent studies of the psychological effects, mediators, and moderators of childhood poverty have focused on non-Hispanic White children (e.g., Costello, Compton, Keeler, & Angold, 2003; Evans & English, 2002), but on the whole, these children are scarcely represented in the annals of child development research, despite constituting the plurality of America's poor children. We speculate about the precursors of this bias and make note of the limitations it poses for the formulation and implementation of national antipoverty policies. More extensive historical accounts of child development research and its relation to practice and social policies directed toward poor children and families can be found elsewhere (Condry, 1983; G. Fein, 1980; Laosa, 1984; Schlossman, 1976; Washington & Bailey, 1995; Weissbourd, 1987; Zigler & Muenchow, 1992).

Early Experience as a Critical Determinant of the Course of Development

The notion that experiences during childhood influence poor children's ability to meet the expectations of broader, mainstream society and to acquire skills necessary for successful adulthood was implicit in many early policies and practices directed toward the poor. British colonists, transporting across the Atlantic the attitudes common in England about poverty and its prevention, sought to prevent the development of a pauper class in Boston with the passage of laws mandating parents to provide children with a basic education and marketable skills. Children whose parents did not fulfill these responsibilities, most of whom were indigent, were indentured as servants. The church complemented interventions of the state during the colonial period with efforts to compel parents to rear their children according to religious doctrines and to provide religious instruction to poor children as an antidote to the "temptations of poverty" (Schlossman, 1976).

During the mid- to late nineteenth century, the confluence of industrialization, urbanization, and high rates of immigration sowed urban ghettoes populated by the poor and culturally different. Most newcomers of this period were individuals from southern and eastern Europe whose customs, language, and, to a lesser extent, child-rearing practices were unlike those of earlier immigrants from England and western Europe. Plagued by disease, crime, delinquency, and a host of social problems linked to economic exploitation, these urban ghettoes were perceived as a threat to the stability of American culture. Large numbers of poor, immigrant women entered the workforce with the new wave of immigration preceding World War I, necessitating out-of-home care of their children. Mainstream, more affluent sectors of the society responded with the introduction into these urban ghettoes of three distinct types of interventions: settlement houses, religious missions, and kindergartens. Each was envisioned, in part, as a vehicle of poverty reduction and assimilation of lower-class individuals into mainstream middle-class values, attitudes, and behavior (Braun & Edwards, 1972; Shonkoff & Meisels, 1990). Each had elements of a personal helping strategy that was paradigmatic during the second half of the nineteenth century, namely, "friendly visiting," in which well-to-do women associated with private relief agencies and charity organizations made home visits to poor families "to provide a mixture of support, scrutiny, and advice" (Halpern, 1988, p. 285).

Settlement houses were established during the late nineteenth century in urban neighborhoods, deemed an "experimental effort" by their most prominent exponent, Jane Addams. Young, college-educated professionals staffed and lived in the houses " 'not to uplift the masses, but to be neighbors to the poor and restore communications between various parts of society' " (Addams, cited in Weissbourd, 1987, p. 44). They " 'settled and developed services in the neighborhood' " (Weissman, cited in Halpern, 1988, p. 286) and aimed to strengthen neighborhood and family life by advocating for and empowering the poor, decreasing ethnic, racial, and cultural conflicts, and increasing understanding among individuals from diverse backgrounds (Weissbourd, 1987). Rather than duplicate the services of other family agencies, settlement houses gave priority to linking people with existing services and helping them to utilize them. Settlement workers conducted parent education for immigrant families isolated from traditional sources of child-rearing advice and provided practical assistance with child care, housing, and legal problems. Under the auspices of the settlement movement, nurses also made home visits to care for the sick and to give advice about domestic matters such as child care, diet, and hygiene (Halpern, 1988). Their work and the role of the new social work profession in championing the needs of poor children achieved national attention in the first White House Conference on Children in 1909 (G. Fein, 1980). Many elements of the community work of settlement workers foreshadowed the strategies and goals of today's parent/family support movement, discussed later in the chapter (Halpern, 1988).

Because missions of Protestant crusaders were largely unsuccessful in modifying the behavior of poor urban adults, attention shifted to young children as instruments of social reform. Subsequent religious missions into poor neighborhoods were intended to "improve the living conditions of families through the lessons the children received in cleanliness, morality, and industriousness" (Ross, 1979, p. 24). The focus on young children continued with the establishment of kindergartens in urban ghettoes supported by religious and philanthropic organizations (Braun & Edwards, 1972; Ross, 1979). Espousing the pedagogical philosophy of Froebel, who established the first formal kindergarten classes during the early 1800s in Germany, these kindergartens were grounded in traditional religious values and a belief in the importance of learning through supervised play. However, because of the nature of the social and economic conditions that spawned them, urban kindergartens in the United States sought to satisfy educational and social welfare functions simultaneously. Professional personnel spent mornings as teachers of young children and afternoons as social welfare workers, helping unemployed parents find work, securing health care for children and families, and assisting families in acquiring other needed services. As Braun and Edwards point out, referring to the social welfare functions performed by these employees, "This was the most important contribution of the pioneer kindergartners, as at this period the kindergarten was frequently the only social agency offering a helping hand in the rapidly-increasing slums" (p. 75). This ecologically oriented approach combining educational services to preschoolers and support services to their parents lost ground in the following decades, regaining currency in the late 1970s as interventionists turned their attention to improving the social context of parenthood and children's development (Bronfenbrenner, 1975).

Kindergartens for poor children gave way to nursery schools for middle-class children in the 1930s, which, in turn, served as models for early childhood education programs established in the 1960s to fight poverty. Participation of middle-class families in institutional forms of child care once reserved exclusively for the poor was the result of a confluence of factors operating in the 1930s, including the growing prominence of child development "experts," angst among middle-class parents about their ability to provide a child-rearing environment adequate for positive child development, economic hardship during the Great Depression, pressure on middle-class women to find employment, and the formation of WPA day nurseries (G. Fein, 1980).

Environmentalism as a Cornerstone of Contemporary Antipoverty Programs: The Role of Basic Research

Not until the 1960s was reduction of poverty and its adverse effects formally articulated as federal policy. Initiated by President Lyndon Johnson as a "War on Poverty," this policy and its attendant programs for a "Great Society" were born of a complex configuration of social and political forces operating at the time, including rapid economic growth and the resulting affluence and optimism of Americans, heightened awareness of the high prevalence of poverty in the United States, the struggle for racial equality waged by the civil rights movement, and the emergence of political leaders (i.e., President Johnson, Sargent Shriver) who had notable personal and professional experiences with poor children (Condry, 1983; Laosa, 1984). Educationally oriented early childhood intervention was one of the major categories of antipoverty programs that emerged during this period. Emphasis on "compensatory education" was galvanized by several influential analyses calling attention to widespread school failure among poor children even in the early years and to the correlation between poverty and low levels of education in the adult population (G. Fein, 1980).

Abundant evidence had accrued prior to the 1960s that lower-class children and children from certain ethnic minority groups performed less well than middle-class White children on indicators of academic achievement and cognitive functioning (e.g., Dreger & Miller, 1960; Shuey, 1958). Performance on IQ tests was elevated to major significance partly because of its significant correlation with school achievement (Deutsch, 1973). Inspired by small-scale, demonstration programs crafted by individual researchers in the early 1960s to study their effects on poor preschool children, for example, S. Gray, Ramsey, and Klaus's Early Training Project, initiated in 1962 (S. Gray, Ramsey, & Klaus, 1983), Head Start was established in 1965 as the first national, publicly funded preschool intervention program (Zigler & Valentine, 1979). Early childhood intervention was premised on a strong environmentalist perspective that called for reducing poverty by equipping poor children with academically relevant cognitive skills during the early years of life, which, in turn, was expected to prevent school failure and, ultimately, low employability, poverty, and economic deprivation. In effect, inadequate cognitive skills were seen as a proximal cause and, therefore, the locus for the prevention of poverty.

This marked a major shift toward environmental, rather than genetic, factors as the prevailing explanation for social class and race differences in academic and cognitive performance and the related notion that intelligence is not fixed (Laosa, 1984). In addition, the optimal time for remediation of these presumed cognitive deficits was thought to be the preschool years. Although attempts at social reforms had historically focused on young children partly because they were perceived to be more malleable than adults, the 1960s marked the transformation of this notion into a "scientific" tenet that undergirded antipoverty policies and programs. It is well-known that these core assumptions on which Head Start was based derived principally from two authoritative books, Hunt's (1961) *Intelligence and Experience* and B. S. Bloom's (1964) *Stability and Change in Human Characteristics* (Zigler & Valentine, 1979).

The notion that early childhood is the critical period for the development of skills required for academic success came under attack in later years as it became clear that early intervention did not inoculate children against continuing economic disadvantage. Critics argued that because development is continuous, a series of dovetailed programs appropriate for each major stage of development would have more beneficial effects on poor children's development than intervention limited to the preschool years (Zigler & Berman, 1983). Nonetheless, bolstered by research showing positive effects of early education intervention, belief in the singularly potent influence of early experience held sway. Testament to this is the establishment of Early Head Start in 1994 for poor children ages 1 to 3 and the fact that current intervention programs for the poor overwhelmingly focus on infants and preschoolers and/or their parents (Administration for Children and Families [ACF], 2004a). Recent research indicating that early childhood is a period of elevated vulnerability to the impact of poverty (Duncan & Brooks-Gunn, 1997) and growing evidence about the significance of early experience in brain development (Shore, 1997) make the case stronger than ever for enhancing poor children's learning experiences during early childhood (C. T. Ramey & Ramey, 1998).

Cultural Deprivation as a Corollary Premise. The establishment of preschool intervention was also premised on the assumption that the early experiences of poor children are inadequate as a foundation for academic success and upward economic mobility. Recognition of the etiological significance of environment in children's development stimulated a proliferation of studies documenting SES differences in an ever-widening range of cognitive and social variables presumably related to later academic functioning (e.g., Coleman et al., 1966; Deutsch, 1973; Hess & Shipman, 1965). Collectively, these efforts served to build a case for preschool intervention by claiming that poor children were suffering deficiencies that forecast academic failure and, hence, needed remediation (Laosa, 1984). Implicitly contrasting *cultural* with *genetic* to underscore the environment as a determinant of behavior seen as inferior and undesirable (Condry, 1983), poor children were labeled "culturally deprived" and disparities in their behavior as compared to middle-class children were termed "cultural deficits" (e.g., Bernstein, 1961; Hess & Shipman, 1965).

This terminology is a derivative of the "culture of poverty" concept elaborated by Oscar Lewis (1966). Lewis attributed to poor people living in the ghettoes of Latin America many of the psychological characteristics and behaviors that were later conceived as precursors of school failure. Researchers and scholars concerned with the psychological impact of environmental disadvantage during the 1960s borrowed generously from Lewis's writings, applying his culture of poverty notion most consistently and forcefully to inner-city African Americans, although the majority of America's poor were White and lived in rural areas (Condry, 1983). Attempting to explain this peculiarity, J. Patterson (1981, p. 120) noted, referring to poor, inner-city African Americans, "Their comparative visibility, their geographic concentration, and their color made cultural interpretations of poverty more plausible than they might otherwise have been."

Preschool intervention programs established during the 1960s and 1970s, including Head Start and its educational forebearers (e.g., S. Gray & Klaus, 1965), bore the stamp of the cultural deficiency model and drew sustenance from empirical studies conducted under this banner (Laosa, 1984; Zigler & Berman, 1983). Intervention programs of this period varied greatly in terms of their guiding assumptions, curricula, and structure. This diversity aside, common to these programs was the assumption that poor children were suffering deficits that needed remediation by professionals during the preschool years (Laosa, 1984).

Cultural Difference as an Alternative Perspective. By the early to mid-1970s, the concept of cultural deprivation and its companion studies and programs were under scathing attack. They were criticized as perniciously ethnocentric on the grounds that they exalted White middle-class norms as the standard of health, ignored the vast range of intellectual and social competencies possessed by poor children, and blamed poverty on individual characteristics while ignoring social structural contributors to economic deprivation (e.g., Baratz & Baratz, 1970; Cole & Bruner, 1971; Ginsburg, 1972; Sroufe, 1970; Tulkin, 1972). The most vehement and prodigious criticisms were reserved for the notion that poor, African American children are impoverished in their means of verbal expression and that nonstandard vernacular impedes complex abstract thought (Labov, 1970).

This academic discourse, in concert with forces in preschool intervention programs (e.g., parent involvement), played a role in attenuating the pejorative view of the poor that prevailed in preschool intervention programs and shifting priorities to building on the strengths and cultural experiences that poor children brought to the programs (Zigler, 1985). As we discuss later, criticism of the deficit model eventually tempered the focus on personal behavior as a target of blame. It helped forge a more ecological approach to early childhood intervention, distinguished by a focus on improving the context of child rearing and child development by reducing stressors and increasing social supports (D. Powell, 1988). Nonetheless, the extent to which Head Start and other preschool intervention programs have fully divested themselves of practices rooted in notions of cultural inferiority is still a matter of some debate.

Resilience of Early Intervention as an Antipoverty Policy: The Significance of Evaluation Research

Providing experiences during early life that are presumed to be intellectually stimulating and enriching remains a major cornerstone of antipoverty policies and programs directed toward poor children, although considerable diversity exists in the implementation of this goal (e.g., provision of services directly to parent versus child; home visitation versus center-based education). Head Start is the largest and most enduring exemplar of this antipoverty strategy. It stands as the model for other public, large-scale, non-Head Start preschool education programs established under the auspices of Title I (Chapter I) of the Elementary and Secondary Education Act (Reynolds, 1994, 1995). A multifaceted program that has served more than 22 million children and their families since 1965, Head Start offers a wide range of services that include early childhood education, health screening and referral, mental health services, nutrition education, family support services, and opportunities for parent involvement (ACF, 2004b, 2005b). Head Start programs must adhere to national performance standards but are permitted to adapt components, including the preschool education curriculum, to local needs and resources. Consequently, considerable variation exists among Head Start programs (Zigler & Styfco, 2003).

Currently, Head Start's basic educational component is a center-based preschool program serving children ages 3 to 5. In 2003, the majority (53%) of these children were 4 years old, followed by a large proportion (34%) of 3-year-olds (ACF, 2004b). Head Start serves about 70% of all eligible 4-year-olds but only about 40% of all eligible 3-year-olds (Haskins & Sawhill, 2003). Head Start preschools have an adult:child ratio that

ranges from 1:8 to 1:10 and are gradually shifting away from half-day sessions (U.S. General Accounting Office, 2003), given increased demand due to parents' work schedules. In fact, as of 2003, 54% of Head Start children were served in full-day programs for at least 6 hours daily (Hart & Schumacher, 2004). Most of these programs, however, operate on a 9-month schedule and are not open on weekends. Less than a third of Head Start children (28%) are served for more than 1 year, with most receiving only 1 year or no post-preschool services (Schumacher & Rakpraja, 2003).

In fiscal year 2003, there were 1,670 Head Start grantees (19,200 centers and over 47,000 classrooms) serving more than 909,600 children and their families. Of these children, 31.5% were African American, 28% were Anglo, 31% were Latino, 3% were Native American, and 3% were Asian and Pacific Islander (ACF, 2004b). Federal guidelines require that at least 90% of children enrolled in Head Start programs come from families with incomes at or below the official poverty line and that at least 10% of enrollment consist of children with disabilities. In 2003, nearly three-quarters of families had incomes less than 100% of the federal poverty line, and 21% received Temporary Assistance for Needy Families benefits. Most participating families were single-parent families (56%), and 13% of children had disabilities (Hart & Schumacher, 2004). Head Start receives 80% of its funding from the federal government, with the remaining 20% coming from other sources, usually local, in the form of funds or services (Zigler & Styfco, 2003). Federal expenditures for Head Start have increased by 33% since 1994 and now stand at $4.66 billion, although a considerable portion of this budget is devoted to evaluation efforts (Reynolds, Wang, & Walberg, 2003).

Evaluations of Head Start's Efficacy.   Major landmarks in the evaluation of Head Start include the Westinghouse evaluation (Westinghouse Learning Corporation, 1969), a highly controversial undertaking, followed by the Head Start Evaluation, Synthesis, and Utilization Project, commonly known as the "Synthesis Project" (McKey et al., 1985), the Educational Testing Service (ETS) Head Start Longitudinal Study (Lee, Brooks-Gunn, Schnur, & Liaw, 1990; Schnur, Brooks-Gunn, & Shipman, 1992), and, most recently, the National Head Start Impact Study (ACF, 2005a) mandated by Congress in 1998, when it reauthorized the Head Start program.

Nonexperimental Evaluations. The history of Head Start evaluation is a troubled and contentious one, owing in large measure to the high economic and political stakes attached to the evaluation findings, juxtaposed with the serious methodological problems that have plagued these evaluations (see McLoyd, 1998, for a more detailed discussion of Head Start evaluations). Excluding the National Head Start Impact Study (ACF, 2005a) initiated in 2001, Head Start evaluations have been legitimately criticized for undue focus on cognitive indicators to the neglect of other outcomes that Head Start was designed to improve, nonrepresentativeness of samples, lack of attention to the quality and type of Head Start program in the research design, and lack of systematic attention to moderating and mediating processes.

But the factor that has engendered most consternation is potential selection bias stemming from the nonexperimental research designs of these evaluations. Random assignment is the preferred method of evaluation of program effects because it increases confidence that estimated effects are due to program differences rather than to preexisting differences between comparison groups. Until the National Head Start Impact Study (ACF, 2005a), lack of random assignment to treatment and control groups was a major methodological weakness of all evaluations of large-scale preschool programs, including Head Start (Barnett, 1995). Enrollment in basic Head Start programs has never been under experimental control for political reasons, including the fact that the program was instituted on a national, full-scale level rather than as an experimental pilot program. As a consequence, it theoretically was and continues to be open to all poor children (Condry & Lazar, 1982).

With random assignment precluded as an option, researchers conducting evaluation studies of Head Start and other large-scale preschool programs have typically attempted to match treatment and control group children on various familial and demographic characteristics. Strategies include drawing controls from the same neighborhood or elementary school classes attended by enrollees of the program, selecting children from waiting lists comprising those who are eligible but not enrolled in the program, and/or using statistical techniques to control for initial differences. Although preferable to having no comparison group, matching of groups is problematic because it is virtually impossible to rule out the possibility that differences observed between groups of children simply reflect differences that were present prior to the intervention, rather than differ-

ences resulting from the intervention (Barnett, 1995). Indeed, the ETS Head Start Longitudinal Study compellingly demonstrated selection bias in Head Start enrollment, vindicating critics who believed that failure to control for preintervention differences between Head Start and comparison groups posed a significant threat to the validity of several evaluations of Head Start (Schnur et al., 1992).

The ETS study began with the collection of data from children in the spring prior to their possible entry into Head Start, permitting an assessment of preexisting differences between children who enrolled in Head Start and children who were eligible (i.e., poor), but either did not enroll in Head Start or enrolled in a non-Head Start preschool. Preintervention data indicated that children who subsequently enrolled in Head Start were more disadvantaged than their impoverished counterparts. Children destined for Head Start programs, compared to poor children who attended a non-Head Start preschool or attended no preschool, had mothers with fewer years of schooling, were more likely to live in families in which the father was absent, and lived in more crowded homes, even after controlling for race. Mothers of Head Start attendees had lower expectations for their children's achievement, compared to mothers of children who ultimately attended other preschools. Furthermore, prospective Head Start attendees performed less well on measures of cognitive functioning (administered before entry to preschool) than children who ultimately attended other preschool programs, but were similar to children who attended no preschool after controlling for race, site, and family characteristics.

These findings were consonant with long-standing anecdotal evidence that local Head Start staff, faced with an inability to offer Head Start to all eligible children because of limited funds, tend to select the most disadvantaged children for participation in the program (Haskins, 1989). The findings urge strong caution against ignoring the heterogeneity of the poverty population and suggest that "reports of postintervention differences in evaluations of programs like Head Start that lack initial status information, or that use matching techniques, almost certainly have underestimated the efficacy of the preschool intervention experience" (Schnur et al., 1992, p. 416).

Nonexperimental evaluation studies (using both between-group treatment/no treatment designs, and pre-post intragroup longitudinal designs) tend to find positive effects of Head Start on school readiness, reading and mathematics achievement, and social behavior (controlling for background demographic factors). But even with these gains, Head Start children still score below national norms, below children who did not attend Head Start, and below more economically advantaged children. These gains, though educationally meaningful (e.g., effect sizes of approximately .25 or greater, a convention established on the basis of evidence that differences of this size accompany discernible improvement in classroom performance; Cohen & Cohen, 1983), usually fade during the early grade school years (Lee, Brooks-Gunn, & Schnur, 1988; McKey et al., 1985). However, more fine-grained analyses indicate that fade-out did not occur in a number of samples (Barnett, 1995; Zigler & Styfco, 2003). There is also evidence that African American children are more likely than White children to experience significant gains from attending Head Start and that preschool experience, whether Head Start or non-Head Start, boosts their cognitive and analytic functioning, although not to the level of nonpoor children or to parity with national norms (Lee et al., 1988, 1990; McKey et al., 1985).

In 1997, Head Start launched the Family and Child Experiences Survey (FACES), a study of a national random sample of Head Start programs designed to answer questions about child outcomes and program quality. There is no non-Head Start comparison group in FACES, but the use of assessment measures with national norms permits comparisons between the skills of children in the sample and children of the same ages in the norming samples (Zill, Resnick, Kim, O'Donnell, & Sorongon, 2003). Findings from the year 2000 cohort of FACES (2,800 3- and 4-year-old children and their families in 43 different Head Start programs across the United States) mirror those from studies comparing Head Start children to non-Head Start children recruited for the investigation. On average, children entered Head Start with literacy and math skills substantially below national averages. The gap narrowed during the Head Start year, especially with respect to vocabulary knowledge and early writing skills, but despite these gains, Head Start children still fell below national averages when they exited the program. Children who entered Head Start with lower levels of knowledge and skill showed larger gains. Teacher reports indicate that children also showed growth in social skills and declines in hyperactive behavior during the Head Start year (Zill et al., 2003). This study also highlights parental characteristics (e.g., depression) and behavior (engagement in literacy activities at home, involvement in child's schooling) in relation to children's cognitive and socioemotional functioning, providing clues about factors that may moderate and mediate Head Start effects.

An Experimental Test of Efficacy: National Head Start Impact Study. In 1998, led largely by the U.S. General Accounting Office's concerns about the lack of a rigorous evaluation of Head Start's effectiveness, Congress mandated a national analysis by the Department of Health and Human Services (DHHS) of the impact of Head Start on the families and children the program serves. The evaluation was guided by two principle questions: "What difference does Head Start make to key outcomes of development and learning for low-income children?" and "Under what conditions does Head Start work best and for which children?" (ACF, 2005a).

Aspects of the study design and framework were developed under the direction of an Advisory Committee on Head Start Research and Evaluation chartered by the DHHS secretary. The study design addresses several problems that compromised prior evaluations of Head Start (ACF, 2005a). First, the study used an experimental design with randomized comparison groups (children were randomly assigned to either a group receiving Head Start services or to a control group not receiving program services). Second, sites were selected to maximize representativeness in terms of the range of Head Start characteristics nationwide (i.e., region of the country, race/ethnicity/language, depth of poverty, program length, program options). Sites in heavily saturated Head Start communities, as well as those not complying with Head Start standards or that were new, were excluded from the framework. A multistage sample selection process was completed to select participating Head Start grantee/delegate agencies and children and to maximize similarity in the probability of selection for each (see ACF, 2005a, for specific details of this process). The study was designed to generalize findings to the national program, but the sample overrepresented larger programs and Hispanic/Spanish-speaking children as compared to the national Head Start population (ACF, 2005a). Children (and their parents) will be followed longitudinally through the spring of the first grade year (i.e., 2006; ACF, 2005a).

The evaluation was initiated after refining the full-scale study design through a pilot study. Beginning in fall 2002, data were collected on 2,559 first-time enrolled 3-year-olds and 2,108 newly entering 4-year-olds from 84 nationally representative grantee/delegate agencies and 383 Head Start centers across the United States. Head Start was found to have small to moderate positive effects on several indicators of child functioning after 1 year of participation in the program, with more positive impacts found among 3-year-olds than 4-year-olds. For both age groups, Head Start positively impacted children's pre-reading and pre-writing skills (based on direct assessments), and their literacy skills (parent report), but had no effect on children's oral comprehension, phonological awareness, or early mathematics skills. Positive impacts on 3-year-olds' vocabulary knowledge were also found. Within the socio-emotional domain, Head Start had no effect on children's social skills, approaches to learning, or social competencies, but it lowered the incidence of parent-reported problem behaviors and hyperactive behavior among 3-year-olds. Finally, among both age groups, Head Start had positive effects on children's access to health care (parent-reported), though positive effects on children's health status (parent-reported) were found only for 3-year-olds. Although the impacts were small to moderate they are nonetheless encouraging when put in context. Families that applied to Head Start but were not accepted were more likely than other low-income families to seek center-based care for their children, highlighting the importance a random-assignment design. Center-based arrangements were the principal form of child care for control families, which means that the Head Start group is being compared to a control group with center-based child care experiences, rather than a "no services" group (ACF, 2005a).

Evaluations of the Efficacy of Model Programs. To the extent that research played a role in the survival of Head Start and other large-scale, publicly funded non-Head Start preschool education programs during the late 1970s and 1980s, major credit goes to research evaluations of small-scale model programs rather than to efficacy studies of Head Start that existed during this period. This is because many of the evaluations of small-scale model intervention programs had methodological advantages that made the evidence they yielded more persuasive, among them random assignment, long follow-ups, and relatively low attrition rates (Barnett, 1995; Consortium for Longitudinal Studies, 1983; Haskins, 1989; Zigler & Styfco, 1994b). In the face of growing threats to downsize and eliminate Head Start due to changing government priorities and the disappointing findings of previous evaluations, the Consortium for Longitudinal Studies was formed in 1975. The Consortium consisted of 11 independent researchers

(and their collaborators) who had initiated model preschool intervention programs for poor children between 1962 and 1972; its expressed purpose was to provide a more definitive answer to the question of whether early education programs were effective in preventing school failure among poor children (Condry, 1983).

As a group, model programs in the Consortium, as well as those not represented in the Consortium (e.g., Carolina Abecedarian Project) were very diverse, varying in terms of curriculum, ages and number of children served, length, and years of operation, among other dimensions. For example, age of entry into these programs ranged from the prenatal and early infancy period to approximately 4 years, with most programs enrolling children between ages 3 and 4. A few were home-based, but the vast majority were center-based with frequent to occasional home visits. Program length during the preschool period varied from about 2 years to 5 years. The curriculum was also highly diversified and based on a range of child development and pedagogical models (e.g., Bank Street, Montessorian, Piagetian, Bereiter-Englemann), but most were primarily cognitive in orientation. The majority of model programs operated during the 1960s and had run their course by the early 1970s (Barnett, 1995; Consortium for Longitudinal Studies, 1983).

The methodological advantages of evaluation studies of model programs noted earlier rendered them more rigorous and sound as tests of the effects of early education intervention. Nonetheless, because model programs typically have lower child-staff ratios, smaller group size, and more highly trained staff than large-scale, public programs such as Head Start, scholars cautioned against assuming that the documented effects of model programs would be produced by ordinary, large-scale preschool programs (Haskins, 1989). Additionally, given the greater comparative demands placed on Head Start programs, as well as growing changes in the Head Start population (e.g., diverse language backgrounds; increased growth in immigrant children; parents who are more likely to be younger, single, and unemployed; new demands experienced due to welfare reform), it is unclear whether comparisons between Head Start and model programs is fair or reasonable (Zigler & Styfco, 2004a).

At the same time, however, studies of large-scale and model programs are best seen as complementary, with both providing unique and important information needed to guide policy formulation and service delivery. Studies of model programs are often weak on generalizability but strong on internal validity, documenting the effects that can accrue from early childhood education programs implemented under relatively ideal circumstances (Haskins, 1989; Schweinhart, Barnes, & Weikart, 1993). Studies of large-scale programs, on the other hand, are often strong on generalizability in that they provide a close approximation of what effects can be expected to be produced by ordinary, universally available preschool programs. However, they tend to be weak on internal validity (e.g., control of selection bias, uniformity of treatment implementation and test administration, confounding of preschool with other program variations experienced by children after the preschool years).

Consortium for Longitudinal Studies: Pooled Analyses.
The 11 research groups composing the Consortium for Longitudinal Studies developed a common protocol for the collection of follow-up data from children in their original treatment and control groups (94% of the original samples were African American children), relocated their samples, collected common data, and submitted the data to an independent group for joint analyses. The studies of programs in the Consortium essentially represented independent tests of the hypothesis that early education has positive effects on poor children's development, the value of which is that chance findings tend to cancel each other out. Common findings across projects increase confidence that effects are reliable (Condry, 1983).

Results from the 11 projects were pooled, in accordance with an elaborate, stringent plan of analysis to identify robust effects (Royce, Darlington, & Murray, 1983; see McLoyd, 1998, for further details about this plan of analysis). The pattern of results from the pooled analyses indicated that (a) children in the programs, compared to those in the control groups, had higher levels of mathematics and reading achievements in the early grades, but these differences disappeared in the later grades, and (b) program participants had lower rates of grade retention and/or placement in special education and were more likely to complete high school than were controls. Data from individual projects suggested that positive effects on school progress were mediated through increased IQ scores at age 6 and through several noncognitive variables such as children's self-esteem, classroom behaviors, and attitudes toward teachers, and mothers' parenting skills, expectations for

their children, self-confidence, and ability to work effectively with teachers and other professionals. However, too few projects measured these hypothetical intervening variables to permit rigorous tests of mediation across studies. Analyses appeared to rule out some competing interpretations of noncognitive pathways, among them, that teachers in public schools may have been more reluctant to place children in special education classes who were known to have attended preschool. If this process operated, they argued, the difference between program and control groups should have been greatest after grade 1 or 2 and to decline thereafter. To the contrary, the difference between the two groups increased as children progressed through the grades and, indeed, did not become statistically significant until grade 7.

The Consortium's success in stoking policymakers' enthusiasm for early childhood intervention and ensuring continued and incremental funding of Head Start has been attributed to three factors: (1) positive and robust findings that concerned specific outcomes the interventions were intended to influence and whose importance and validity were easily understood (e.g., placement in special education classes, grade retention, high school graduation, rather than IQ); (2) cost-benefit analyses of one of the Consortium member studies, the Perry Preschool Project, demonstrating a significant return on the original investment of public dollars (Weber, Foster, & Weikart, 1978); and (3) rapid, broad dissemination of the findings to policymakers. The Consortium's findings were disseminated in policy circles as early as 1977 but did not appear in academic publications until the 1980s (Consortium for Longitudinal Studies, 1983; Darlington, Royce, Snipper, Murray, & Lazar, 1980). Further buttressing Head Start's favored status was additional evidence of long-term positive effects of non-Consortium model programs (e.g., Carolina Abecedarian Project) released after the Consortium's major reports. In the following sections, we highlight program features and findings from two highly prominent model programs whose long-term effects are especially impressive.

Perry Preschool Project. Conducted in Ypsilanti, Michigan, between 1962 and 1967, the Perry Preschool Project (Berrueta-Clement, Schweinhart, Barnett, Epstein, & Weikart, 1984; Schweinhart et al., 1993) is perhaps the most prominent of the model projects and was part of the Consortium. Children who participated in the program have been followed through ages 39 to 41, the longest follow-up of any early childhood education program. Overall attrition rates for the study are quite low, with only 5% of cases missing across waves (Schweinhart, 2003).

Researchers identified potential participants from a census of the families of students attending the Perry Elementary School in Ypsilanti, referrals by neighborhood groups, and door-to-door canvassing. The sample consisted of 123 low SES families (58 randomly assigned to the treatment group and 65 to the control group) whose children had IQ scores between 70 and 85 but who showed no evidence of organic handicap. All of the families were African American and about half were mother-headed and receiving welfare. Forty percent of parents were unemployed and only 21% of mothers and 11% of fathers had completed high school.

Children entered the program at ages 3 and 4. Those in the treatment group attended 2.5 hour center-based classes five mornings a week from October to May, most (78%) for a period of 2 years. Teacher-child ratio was 1:5–6. The curriculum was guided by Piagetian theory and emphasized children as active learners. Interactions with children were built around a set of active learning key experiences (e.g., creative representation, language, social relations, movement). Teachers made a weekly home visit during the afternoon (with both mother and child present) lasting 90 minutes to involve the mother in the educational process, to enable the mother to provide her child with educational support, and to implement aspects of the center's curriculum in the child's home. Supportive social services such as assistance with housing and nutritional services were not provided.

Evidence from the 14-, 19-, and 27-year-old followups indicated benefits for children's educational performance, with program children having higher literacy and school achievement scores at ages 19 and 14, respectively, and higher educational attainment at age 27 than control children (71% versus 54% completed high school). The strongest effects were found in the areas of economic well-being and crime prevention. At age 27, compared to their control counterparts, (a) program adults had higher earnings (7% versus 29%, respectively, earning more than $2,000 monthly); (b) program males had better-paying jobs (6% versus 42% earning $2,000 or more monthly); (c) program females had higher employment rates (55% versus 80%); (d) program adults had received less public welfare as adults,

as indicated by public welfare records and self-reports, although the magnitude of these reductions depended on gender and the time period in question; (e) program participants averaged 2.3 fewer arrests for criminal activity; (f) program males had been married twice as long; and (g) program females were more likely to be married and to have fewer out-of-wedlock births. Effects on economic well-being are less clear in data collected at ages 39 to 41. That is, it is not certain whether these effects lasted into midlife. However, effects on violent crime reduction and time spent in prison were maintained (Schweinhart, 2003, 2004). Cost-benefit analyses of the program indicate significant public benefits per participant (e.g., at the age-27 follow-up, $7.16 benefits for every $1 invested). In short, the intervention was an extremely sound economic investment (Barnett & Escobar, 1987; Schweinhart, 2003).

Carolina Abecedarian Project. This project is the most recent vintage of early education model programs and, unlike the Perry Preschool Project, was not part of the Consortium. This center-based program operated between 1972 and 1985 in Chapel Hill, North Carolina (Campbell & Ramey, 1994, 1995; Campbell, Ramey, Pungello, Sparling, & Miller-Johnson, 2002). The program recruited poor families nominated by social welfare departments and prenatal clinics, most of which were African American (98%) and headed by an unmarried mother (mean age = 20 years, with a range from 13 to 44 years; mean IQ = 85) who had not graduated from high school at the time of the child's birth. Fifty-five families were randomly assigned to the experimental group and 54 to the control group.

Children entered the program at 4 months of age, on average, and remained until they entered public kindergarten at age 5. The center operated 8 hours a day, 5 days per week, 50 weeks per year. The caregiver-to-infant ratio was 1:3. Caregiver to child ratios gradually increased to 1:6 as children moved from the nursery into toddler and preschool groupings. The curriculum for infants emphasized cognitive, language, perceptual-motor development, and social and self-help skills. In the later preschool years, emphasis was placed on language development (pragmatic features rather than syntax) and preliteracy skills. Parents served on the center's advisory board and were offered a series of voluntary classes covering such topics as family nutrition, legal matters, behavior management, and toy making. Supportive social services were available to families to help solve problems related to housing, food, and transportation.

Cognitive and academic benefits of the Abecedarian program were stronger than those of most other early childhood programs, a fact attributed to the high intensity of the program (full-day, year-round beginning in early infancy) and its long duration (5 years; Campbell et al., 2002). The most recent follow-up (104 of the original 111 individuals) assessed effects on 21-year-olds (Campbell et al., 2002). Findings indicated a long-lasting effect on cognitive outcomes. Program children had significantly higher cognitive test scores from the toddler years to age 21. In addition, their reading and math achievement scores were significantly higher from the primary grades through early adulthood. Compared to control children, program children completed more years of education (14% versus 35%, respectively, attending or graduated from a 4-year college at age 21), had higher employment rates in young adulthood (50% versus 65% employed), and delayed parenthood longer (17.7 versus 19.1 years of age at birth of first child). Twenty-six percent of those in the program group had children as teenagers, compared to 45% in the control group (Campbell et al., 2002). Few studies of model programs have found effects on adolescent parenthood, although there is fairly strong evidence that preschool intervention increases the likelihood that adolescent mothers will complete high school, mediated partly by reducing the likelihood of grade retention and placement in special education (Schweinhart et al., 1993). Unlike findings from the Perry Preschool Project, there were no significant effects on crime prevention in early adulthood, but significant reductions in drug use and smoking were found (Campbell et al., 2002; Schweinhart, 2003). A recent cost-benefit analysis of the Abecedarian program by researchers at the National Institute of Early Education Research indicates significant returns on taxpayer investments ($4 benefits for every $1 invested; Masse & Barnett, 2002).

Although we have highlighted findings from model programs, it is noteworthy that long-term effects have also been found for the Chicago Child-Parent Center (CPC) program, a large-scale, public, center-based preschool and school-based intervention for low-income children in Chicago, although the evaluation did not use a random assignment design. A 15-year follow-up indicated that children who participated in the pre-

school intervention had a higher rate of high school completion and lower rates of juvenile arrest, violent arrests, and school dropout, relative to children in the comparison group who participated in alternative early childhood programs (full-day kindergarten). In addition, both preschool and school-age participation were significantly associated with lower rates of grade retention and special education services. These findings are among the strongest evidence to date that large-scale education interventions similar to Head Start and administered through public schools can promote children's long-term success (Reynolds, Temple, Robertson, & Mann, 2001).

Early Head Start. Some of the model programs with the largest or most enduring positive effects began educational intervention earlier in development (i.e., during the first 2 years of life) and continued at least until children entered kindergarten (Campbell & Ramey, 1994; Consortium for Longitudinal Studies, 1983; C. T. Ramey & Ramey, 1998). These findings helped pave the way for the establishment in 1994 of Early Head Start, an intervention for low-income infants and toddlers up to age 3 and their families. The most recent, large-scale, and publicly funded early childhood education program, Early Head Start seeks to enhance children's development and health with a palette of coordinated services, including child care, child development services delivered via home visits, parenting education, health care and referrals, and family support. Depending on community needs, programs provide services via three approaches: center-based, home-based, or a mixed approach. Currently, the program operates in 700 communities and serves more than 60,000 low-income children. It has increasingly received a greater share of the Head Start budget, with its budget for 2003 standing at $654 million (ACF, 2004a).

When it established Early Head Start in 1994 as part of the Head Start reauthorization legislation, Congress mandated an early evaluation of the new program across sites. The national evaluation, known as the National Early Head Start Research and Evaluation Project, was guided by two overarching goals: to understand the extent to which the Early Head Start intervention was effective for low-income children and families and to understand the specific programs and services that were effective for families and children with different demographic characteristics and served by programs with diverse characteristics. In short, the evaluation moves beyond the simple question of "What works?" and instead focuses on "What works for whom and under what conditions?"

Beginning in 1995, the evaluation project was carried out in 17 sites selected to represent the Early Head Start programs funded during the first two cycles of the program. Sites were spread across the country, in both urban and rural areas, and initially the research programs were equally divided among center-based, home-based, and mixed approach settings. However, over the course of the evaluation term, the proportion of program approaches changed. A total of 3,001 families across the 17 sites were randomly assigned to participate in Early Head Start ($n = 1,513$) or the control group ($n = 1,488$), yielding groups equivalent on a number of demographic characteristics. Children and families were followed from the time they entered the program until the child was age 3, with assessments done at ages 14, 24, and 36 months.

Findings revealed a number of positive impacts of the program, even though a substantial number of families did not participate for the full eligibility period or at recommended levels. At 36 months, program children, compared to control children, scored higher on standardized measures of cognitive and language development, engaged their parents more, and were less aggressive, less negative toward their parents, and more attentive to objects during play (ACF, 2002). Effects also extended to parental behavior. Compared to control parents, Early Head Start parents provided more stimulating home environments and more support for language and learning. In addition to being more emotionally supportive of the child (observed), they were more likely to read to the children daily and less likely to use physical punishment (self-report). The program also had positive effects on parents' self-sufficiency and on father-child interactions. Program impacts were larger for African American families than White families, families that enrolled during pregnancy, families with a moderate number of risk factors, mixed-approach programs, and programs that achieved full implementation earlier (ACF, 2002). Data collection for a follow-up of children (and families) at entry to kindergarten was recently completed, though at the time of this writing, findings were not available.

Assessing Head Start Policy and Models in Light of Evaluation Findings

It is clear that Head Start is not so potent as to boost enrollees' school readiness and academic competence to the level of nonpoor children, or to parity with national norms. However, findings from the National Head Start Impact Study (ACF, 2005a) bolster confidence that Head Start enhances children's early literacy skills and certain domains of socioemotional functioning and lend support to the claim that the magnitude of Head Start's impact as assessed in nonexperimental studies has been underestimated due to selection bias. This argues in favor of continuing federal support for Head Start, but the argument for seeking ways to improve Head Start's efficacy is equally strong. Head Start quality has been observed to be consistently good over time, as indicated by child-adult ratio, teacher-child interactions, and classroom activities and materials (Zill et al., 2003). Nonetheless, the findings from the FACES 2000 (Zill et al., 2003) assessment of children's functioning when they exited Head Start are clearly regarded among some government officials as disappointing and grounds for substantive changes within Head Start (U.S. Department of Health and Human Services, 2003).

Head Start's basic model has remained largely intact, and until recently, this adherence seemed justified because numerous researchers had looked for, but not found, strong, consistent evidence that program, child, or family characteristics moderate to any significant degree the long-term impact of model or large-scale preschool interventions (McKey et al., 1985; Royce et al., 1983). However, findings from FACES 2000 (Zill et al., 2003) invite reconsideration of this conclusion, and along with findings from evaluations of small-scale model programs, suggest ways that Head Start might be modified to achieve larger impacts on children's competence. This study found that several program and classroom characteristics within Head Start were associated with greater gains in children's cognitive and socioemotional functioning, including use of an integrated curriculum (programs using the High/Scope curriculum versus programs using other curricula), provision of full-day classes, higher educational credentials of teachers (i.e., bachelor or associate degrees), and higher teacher salaries. It is of considerable interest whether these findings will be replicated in the National Head Start Impact Study.

Two large-scale federal initiatives are under way to assess the effectiveness of different early childhood curricula and early childhood interventions and programs in preparing children for school (U.S. Department of Education's Preschool Curriculum Evaluation Research Program; Interagency Early Childhood Research Initiative). Additional experimental studies focusing partly on curriculum issues are being conducted by the Head Start Quality Research Consortium, in keeping with Head Start's tradition of implementing demonstration projects both within and outside its basic core program to ascertain more effective ways of serving poor children and families (U.S. Department of Health and Human Services, 2003; Zigler & Styfco, 1994a). These collective efforts, along with lessons learned from state-level experimentation with new strategies for coordinating early childhood programs and enhancing children's school readiness, are expected to strengthen Head Start and result in stronger and more seamless early childhood systems in the United States (U.S. Department of Health and Human Services, 2003).

The shift in Head Start preschools away from half-day sessions to full-day programs (U.S. General Accounting Office, 2003) is consistent with the aforementioned finding from the FACES study (Zill et al., 2003) and with the pattern found in model programs of larger and more enduring effects on children's cognitive and academic functioning when programs are more intensive (Campbell et al., 2002; C. T. Ramey & Ramey, 1998). This shift has the additional advantage of being more practical for poor women who are working or participating in job programs. The numbers of such women have increased markedly in response to welfare reform (Greenberg et al., 2002). Undoubtedly, many of these mothers were forced to place their children in informal, unregulated child care of much lower quality than that provided in Head Start centers because Head Start preschools offered only half-day sessions or had no slots available. As of 2003, 54% of Head Start children were served in full-day programs for at least 6 hours daily, but most centers operate on a 9-month school year, with most open 5 days or fewer per week (Hart & Schumacher, 2004).

Research findings also buttress Head Start's prevailing practice of providing 1 rather than 2 years of Head Start for most children who participate in the program. Taken together, longitudinal studies of model programs and large-scale public programs such as the Chicago Child-Parent Centers provide little evidence that a 2nd year of preschool intervention confers enduring, educationally meaningful academic advantages beyond a single year (Consortium for Longitudinal Studies, 1983; Reynolds, 1995; Sprigle & Schaefer, 1985). A 2nd year may reinforce the school readiness skills that children have learned during the 1st year, but its unique contribution to the acquisition of academic skills is modest at best and decidedly less than that of the 1st year (Reynolds, 1995). Research findings provide a much stronger case for providing 1 year of publicly funded preschool intervention for all poor children (30% of 4-year-olds and 70% of 3-year-olds eligible for Head Start are currently not served by Head Start), in lieu of 2 years for a smaller number of poor children. Findings from the National Head Start Impact Study (ACF, 2005a) will allow a more rigorous consideration of all of the issues mentioned here.

Effectiveness of Follow-Through Services into Elementary School: Findings in Search of Policy. Paradoxically, although 2 years of preschool may not be markedly more advantageous than 1 year in increasing poor children's cognitive functioning and school achievement, comparisons of treatment effects between and within studies suggest that programs of even longer duration may be optimal (Fuerst & Fuerst, 1993; Madden, Slavin, Karweit, Dolan, & Wasik, 1993; Reynolds, 1995). Consequently, some have advocated for a continuation of Head Start intervention services into the primary grades as a strategy to prevent fade-out (Reynolds, 2003). It was precisely this rationale that led to the creation of Head Start/Follow Through in 1967. Despite original intentions, Follow Through never became a national program, and initial emphasis on comprehensive services was supplanted with a primary focus on innovative curricula. In the early 1990s, it operated in only 40 schools, and few evaluations of its effectiveness exist (Zigler & Muenchow, 1992). However, the Follow Through concept was revamped in 1991 with the National Head Start/Public School Early Childhood Demonstration Transition Project. This project followed Head Start graduates in 31 programs from kindergarten through third grade. Children and parents were introduced to the new school environment and provided comprehensive services and support. Parental involvement was heavily emphasized.

Although evaluations of the Transition Project are incomplete, preliminary findings provide some evidence that the program enhanced children's school transition (S. L. Ramey, Ramey, & Lanzi, 2004; Reynolds, 2003). Also encouraging is the fact that although children initially performed below national norms, by the end of the second and third grades, they performed at essentially the national average in reading and math. Additionally, results of similar transitional programs, most notably the Chicago Child-Parent Centers, lend support to the value of such extended interventions (Reynolds, 2003; Zigler & Styfco, 2003).

No specific plans currently exist for expansion of follow-through services to the larger Head Start population. Direct delivery of educational services to the child and significant changes in the child's learning environment, especially in the school context, appear to be prerequisites for effective follow-on interventions (Barnett, 1995). Follow-on services for children that are parent-mediated (e.g., programs that focus on increasing parent involvement in the child's schooling through home curriculum activities for the parent) and based primarily in the home setting have not been found effective (C. T. Ramey & Ramey, 1998; see McLoyd, 1998, for a more detailed discussion of this issue).

Individual Differences in Program Benefits. There continues to be keen interest in determining whether certain child and family characteristics moderate program effects, in part, because understanding this issue would be the basis for better targeting of early interventions. According to C. T. Ramey and his colleagues (C. T. Ramey, Ramey, & Lanzi, 1998), individual differences in how much children benefit from participation in diverse early interventions tend to be related to aspects of children's initial risk condition. Extrapolating from this generalization, within-group differences in poor children's level of disadvantage or risk for dysfunctional development are likely linked to the individual differences in the benefits they accrue from participating in early education interventions. C. T. Ramey et al. used data from former Head Start children at entry to kindergarten to explore the usefulness of cluster analyses to distinguish among poor families. The analyses identified six major family types on the basis of correlation coefficients among 13 widely used indicators of family characteristics (e.g., maternal education, mother's employment and AFDC status, presence of parenting assistance in the home, maternal age at time of child's entry to kinder-

garten). These clusters or family types were systematically related to children's receptive language, special education placement, and social competence. Identification of risk levels or typologies among poor children prior to entry to Head Start, using this or other procedures, lays the foundation for addressing the question regarding what intervention works best for whom.

To date, questions about what child and family characteristics moderate program effects have not been fully explored in the National Head Start Impact Study (ACF, 2005a), but an initial examination of sources of variation in program impacts indicated that Head Start effects on cognitive competence were larger for children whose primary language was English (as compared to Spanish), for African American and Hispanic children (as compared to non-Hispanic White children), and for children whose primary caregiver had lower levels of depressive symptoms at baseline. Other evaluations of the effects of preschool interventions on poor children point to both child sex and race/ethnicity as moderators of program effects. We discuss these findings below.

Attenuated Gains among African American Boys? A conspicuous number of higher-quality studies (of model programs and large-scale, public programs) serving African American children report stronger intervention and follow-on effects on girls' school competence, school progress, and socioemotional functioning than boys', although program findings by sex interactions have not necessarily been statistically significant. Boys often benefited substantially less from programs than did girls, despite bringing equivalent and, in some instances, superior intellectual abilities to the program. These studies also suggest that sex is a more probable moderator of long-term rather than immediate effects, with gender differences becoming progressively larger over time in some instances (Consortium for Longitudinal Studies, 1983; Fuerst & Fuerst, 1993; Schweinhart et al., 1993).

Researchers have offered several explanations for these differences, but ascertaining which ones are most credible is difficult because longitudinal studies have not tracked the school, family, and broader social experiences of boys and girls in relation to the preschool experience. Explanations centering on post-preschool factors appear more plausible than those centering on the programs themselves because gender differences in immediate effects typically are not found. A combination of gender and racial stereotypes may condition teachers and school staff to more readily ignore or to respond less positively to improvement in school competence among African American boys. Attention may be directed toward boys' conduct at the expense of their academic competence (Jackson, 1999; Schweinhart et al., 1993).

Perhaps poor African American boys, compared to their female counterparts, confront more barriers to academic achievement and/or barriers that are more impervious to preschool intervention. Gender-related barriers may include an indifferent, if not hostile, school climate, peer pressure against school achievement, belief that academic competence is not masculine, low expectations of achievement among parents and teachers, and early school failure (Graham, Taylor, & Hudley, 1998; Jackson, 1999; Kunjufu, 1986; Osborne, 1997). These analyses suggest that African American boys may need follow-through services uniquely tailored to the challenges that confront them in elementary school.

The conditions and underlying processes that encourage divergence between boys and girls in their long-term response to preschool education are intriguing issues. Given the increasingly bleak status of a substantial segment of the African American male population (Gibbs, 1988), few issues are more deserving of systematic study.

Race as a Moderating Variable?   The ETS study of Head Start's efficacy (Lee et al., 1988), as well as more recent evidence from the Early Head Start evaluation (ACF, 2002) and the National Head Start Impact Study (ACF, 2005a) raise the possibility that programs have larger positive impacts on African American children than White children, apparently because of differences in risk exposure and related differences in cognitive performance at the point of preintervention. In the ETS study, children who started out lowest gained the most. African American children were relatively more disadvantaged demographically than White children in the preintervention year and scored significantly lower on all four measures of cognitive functioning (Lee et al., 1988).

In terms of comparative risk, it also bears repeating that African American children are more likely than White children to experience poverty that is both persistent and extreme (income below one-half of the poverty threshold), factors that predict lower levels of cognitive functioning (Duncan & Brooks-Gunn, 1997). In addition, the differential impact of poverty by childhood stage reported by Duncan and his colleagues (i.e., poverty during first 5 years is more detrimental to educational attainment than poverty during middle child-

hood and adolescence) is especially pronounced among African American children (Duncan et al., 1998). Hence, African American children may experience greater benefits from Head Start than White children because they are more vulnerable to the elevated effects of poverty during early childhood as compared to subsequent developmental periods. Other intervention studies of poor children and families have found the greatest relative gains among those at highest risk (C. T. Ramey & Ramey, 1998), although Halpern (2000), in his review of a broad range of early childhood intervention programs for low-income children and families, concluded that research is equivocal and ultimately inconclusive as to whether relatively higher- or lower-risk populations benefit more from participation in early childhood intervention.

In contrast to the ETS findings, Currie and Thomas's (1995) analysis of data from the National Longitudinal Study of Youth (NLSY) child sample revealed no race differences in initial gains from Head Start. However, significant race disparities were found in the rate at which gains dissipated, with White children retaining the benefits of Head Start on the Peabody Picture Vocabulary Test (PPVT) much longer than African American children. By age 10, African American children had lost any gains on the PPVT derived from Head Start, whereas 10-year-old White Head Start enrollees retained a gain of 5 percentile points. Currie and Thomas also found race differences in the impact of Head Start on grade retention. Whereas Head Start reduced the probability of grade retention among White children by 47% compared to their siblings who did not attend preschool, it was unrelated to grade retention among African American children. At least part of the race difference in rate of dissipation may reflect differences in the quality of schools that African American and White children attended once they left Head Start. Curiously, no evidence of a similar race effect in the dissipation of positive effects was found among children who attended non-Head Start preschools. Currie and Thomas's findings conflict not only with the race differences found in other prominent studies of the effects of Head Start and Early Head Start (ACF, 2002, 2005a; Lee et al., 1988), but also with reports of long-term positive effects of other large-scale preschool intervention programs on African American children's cognitive functioning and school progress (e.g., Reynolds, 1994).

What explains these discrepancies is unclear, but it is notable that unlike most studies of preschool effects, Currie and Thomas (1995) used siblings (rather than nonsiblings) of Head Start enrollees who had not attended Head Start as a comparison group (as a strategy to control for family background effects). Another important consideration may be their questionable creation of a "White" comparison group of Head Start children. They combined White non-Latino and Latino children into a single White group and estimated fixed-effects models using this grouping (Barnett, 2004). A reanalysis of the fixed-effects models by Barnett and Camilli (2000) indicated that there was no justification for treating the White non-Latino and Latino children as a single population given their differences in test scores and program participation rates. Additionally, their reanalysis indicated identical short- and long-term effects for White non-Latino and African American children, as well as a fade-out for both groups.

Effects of Preschool Intervention on Whites and Other Ethnic Groups? The discussion about race as a moderator of preschool effects points up a related gap in the research literature, namely, inadequate study of the impact of preschool education on White children and children from other ethnic groups. Studies of preschool effects reveal a preoccupation with African American children (Barnett, 1995). African American children are greatly overrepresented in the population of poor children, but the fact remains that poor White children vastly outnumber poor African American children in an absolute sense. Over the course of Head Start's existence, African American children have constituted from about one-third to two-fifths of its enrollment and Latino children from about one-fifth to one-third (Hart & Schumacher, 2004; National Center for Education Statistics, 1995). Historically, a large percentage of the early growth of Head Start centers occurred in poor, African American communities. Taking account of their rates of enrollment, however, African American children are overrepresented in studies of Head Start effects, whereas White and Latino children are underrepresented.

Model programs provide virtually no insight into the effects of preschool interventions on children from ethnically diverse populations, because with the exception of a few studies of preschool programs that targeted Latino children (Andrews et al., 1982; Johnson & Breckenridge, 1982), they have focused almost exclusively on African American children (see McLoyd, 1998, for a discussion of considerations that led to the racial makeup of model programs). Whatever its underlying cause, this bias has had at least two unfortunate consequences. First, we know little about the utility of Head Start and

preschool education generally for poor White children. The most rigorous evaluations of Head Start (ACF, 2002, 2005a; Lee et al., 1988) raise cautions against generalizing findings based on African American children to White children. Second, it feeds the stereotype of African Americans as invariably poor and economically dependent, while furthering the tendency to render poor White children and families invisible in the field of child development research. Given the changing demographics of the current Head Start population (Zigler & Styfco, 2004a), an understanding of the experiences of all children and families served by the program is essential.

Parents and the Home Environment as Determinants of Development

A second major assumption that undergirds antipoverty programs is that parents and the home environment they afford exert major influence on the course of children's development. During the 1960s, rapid growth in research evidence lending support to this assumption, along with other forces, propelled interest in parent education as a form and a major component of early childhood intervention (Clarke-Stewart & Apfel, 1978; D. Powell, 1988). Parent education programs and, to a lesser extent, opportunities for parent involvement in early education interventions were conceived as strategies to alter poor children's outcomes indirectly by increasing parents' knowledge of the principles of child development and, ultimately, modifying parental behavior.

Parent education as an indirect strategy to influence children's development has a long history in America, dating back to the early 1800s (for historical reviews, see G. Fein, 1980; Halpern, 1988; Schlossman, 1976). Parent education programs proliferated during the 1950s, but their clientele was almost exclusively middle class (Brim, 1959). Parent education rose to prominence again during the late 1960s and 1970s, but in ways that distinguished it from its predecessors. First, it was now a strategy that targeted principally poor families, on the grounds that enhancing parents' child-rearing skills would, in turn, improve children's ability to effect a successful transition from home to school, to benefit from schooling, and to maximize cognitive gains accrued from preschool education (Chilman, 1973; Clarke-Stewart & Apfel, 1978; D. Powell, 1988). Characterized by a focus on mothers of infants and preschoolers as primary recipients of services, parent education programs marked an evolving direction in early childhood intervention from an almost exclusive focus on children to one that gave major consideration to the roles of parents, the home environment, and parent-child interaction in poor children's development. This trend was strengthened by rising rates of single-parent households, unmarried teenage mothers, divorce, unemployment, and economic instability and increased public awareness of child abuse and neglect, all of which evoked concern that the child-nurturing capacities of American families were in decline (D. Powell, 1988).

Research-Based Antecedents

The reincarnation of parent education during the late 1960s was also different from its predecessors in that it had much deeper foundations in empirical child development research (Clarke-Stewart & Apfel, 1978). Proponents cited popular ideas such as "parents are a child's first and most important teacher" (Clarke-Stewart & Apfel, 1978, p. 48) and "every child needs—and has a right to have—trained parents" (Bell, 1975, p. 272), but they relied heavily on a diverse set of research findings from child development research to support their cause. First, the disappointing findings from early evaluations of the effects of Head Start were interpreted by some advocates as evidence that prevention of cognitive deficits required intervention even before preschool and, relatedly, that the source of cognitive deficits resided somewhere in the home (Clarke-Stewart & Apfel, 1978). Second, a major boost for parent training programs came from Bronfenbrenner's (1975) synthesis of findings from early education interventions, wherein he concluded that early education interventions produce greater and more enduring benefits in children the more involved their parents are. Although Bronfenbrenner's conclusion spoke more directly to the enhanced efficacy of family-centered interventions involving parents and their children, it was viewed as support for the narrower concept of parent education as well. What was more, data indicated that the positive effects of interventions involving parents diffused to younger siblings (e.g., S. Gray & Klaus, 1970), making such programs highly cost-effective.

Third, proponents pointed to a panoply of interview and laboratory studies demonstrating the relation of children's cognitive functioning to countless indicators of mothers' knowledge of child development, child-rearing attitudes, and child-rearing practices (e.g., level of maternal stimulation of child, such as playing, talking, and elaborating the child's activities; provision of appropriate play materials; abstractness of the mother's speech; promptness of the mother's responsiveness to the infant's distress signals; use of consistent, firm discipline accompanied by frequent approval). Also contributing to the credibility of parent training was evidence that parents' behavior could be modified by brief interventions (see Clarke-Stewart & Apfel, 1978, for a review of these studies).

A fourth and critical set of studies on which advocates of parent education relied focused on social class differences in children's home and family environment (Clarke-Stewart & Apfel, 1978). One line of work documented SES differences in child-rearing practices (e.g., teaching strategies, maternal speech patterns, influence techniques). On the basis of parent-child correlational data or developmental theory, this research inferred that these differences accounted for social class variation in children's cognitive and academic functioning (e.g., Bee, Egeren, Streissguth, Nyman, & Leckie, 1969; Bernstein, 1961; Deutsch, 1973; Hess & Shipman, 1965; Kamii & Radin, 1967). In a related line of work, poverty, low levels of maternal education, and other indicators of low social status were identified as predictors of both lower cognitive/academic functioning in children and lower levels of various indicators of maternal behavior associated with children's cognitive and academic functioning (e.g., verbal and cognitive stimulation in home environment, emotional support of child, positive reinforcement). Children with higher levels of cognitive and academic competence tended to have mothers who were more accepting, affectionate, and egalitarian, less commanding, threatening, and punishing, and more consistent and rewarding in their interactions, and these were the very dimensions of child rearing that distinguished lower-class from middle-class mothers (Bradley & Caldwell, 1976; Clarke-Stewart & Apfel, 1978; Deutsch, 1973).

In general, the view of lower-class patterns of child rearing painted by 1960s-era research generally was one of wholesale inadequacy (e.g., Bee et al., 1969; Hess & Shipman, 1965; Kamii & Radin, 1967). The culture of poverty notion that held sway during the 1960s and 1970s led inexorably to interpretations of SES differences that disparaged lower-class patterns of child rearing (Bernstein, 1961; Lewis, 1966). These differences were conceptualized as antecedents of retarded cognitive, linguistic, and socioemotional development and, in turn, as a major pathway by which poverty is perpetuated from one generation to the next. A natural extension of these arguments was the assertion that poor parents needed training for their child-rearing role more than parents from more affluent backgrounds (Baratz & Baratz, 1970; Laosa, 1984).

The foundation on which 1970s-era parent education for poor mothers rested was not nearly as sound as proponents made it out to be. First, much of the research on parental effects on children's development was based on White, middle-class families and, hence, of uncertain generalizability to poor families. Second, serious methodological biases against poor parents (e.g., assessments in university laboratories; use of measures normed for middle-class individuals) and race-SES confounds limited interpretations of many of the research findings and their applicability to policy. Third, as an intervention that targeted participants principally on the basis of SES, especially during the early stages of the movement, parent education ignored the considerable heterogeneity that existed among lower-class parents. Typically, modal behavior of parents, like children's, is the same at different SES levels, and heterogeneity within social class typically is greater than variation between social classes. Hence, SES is, at best, an extremely crude proxy of presumed differences in parental behavior and home environment (Clarke-Stewart & Apfel, 1978).

As the parent education movement gained momentum, a number of programs began to target specific groups at high risk for parenting difficulties, such as pregnant adolescents, adolescent mothers, and women identified as drug users or potential child abusers (e.g., Field, Widmayer, Stringer, & Ignatoff, 1980). In the main, though, the eligibility criterion for most programs was simply low SES. Heightened appreciation in subsequent years of the heterogeneity within groups of poor individuals prompted studies of parenting practices, home environment, and extrafamilial factors as sources of psychological resilience and academic competence, rather than problematic development, in poor minority children (e.g., Baldwin, Baldwin, & Cole, 1990; Gutman & McLoyd, 2000).

Recent research on parenting and home environmental factors as determinants of cognitive functioning in poor children diverges from 1960s-era research in that it tends to (a) emphasize social structural rather than cultural deficiencies as causal factors in poverty, (b) focus on income poverty rather than social class, and (c) directly assess provision of stimulating experiences in the home as a mediator of the relation between family income and children's development. Another striking difference is that contemporary researchers tend to interpret links between family income and home environment within an investment model (i.e., the notion that income is associated with children's development because it enables families to invest in the human capital of their children by purchasing materials, experiences, and services that benefit the child's development and well-being), rather than within a cultural deficit model (e.g., Linver, Brooks-Gunn, & Kohen, 2002). In short, they assume a direct link between income and home-based stimulation rather than an indirect one mediated through parenting knowledge and attitudes.

Recent research demonstrates that the provision of cognitively stimulating experiences in the home (e.g., presence of cognitively stimulating toys, reading to child, helping children learn numbers, alphabet) is a strong mediator of the relation between family income and young children's cognitive functioning (Duncan, Brooks-Gunn, & Klebanov, 1994; Klebanov, Brooks-Gunn, McCarton, & McCormick, 1998; Linver et al., 2002), although it appears to play a smaller role in mediating the effects of *across-time, within-family income changes* than mediating the effects of average income (Dearing, McCartney, & Taylor, 2001). Other variables, such as maternal sensitivity, appear to play a much weaker role in mediating the link between family income and children's cognitive functioning (Mistry et al., 2004). Further, these studies have yielded strong, consistent evidence that the relationship between family income and quality of home environment is nonlinear, such that the home environments of children in low-income households are particularly sensitive to income and income changes. Data indicate that the quality of children's home environment, like IQ scores, decreases as families' income-to-need ratios decline and as duration of poverty increases, and further, that improvements in family income have the strongest effects on the quality of children's home environment if children were born poor (versus not born poor) or spent more time in poverty (Dubow & Ippolito, 1994; Garrett, Ng'andu & Ferron, 1994).

In response to concerns that the reported income-home environment link and the home environment-child functioning link are spurious (i.e., that they reflect unmeasured individual differences or omitted variables related to income, income changes, home environment, and child outcome), researchers have used longitudinal fixed effects models to control for stable omitted differences between individuals (e.g., mother and child cognitive abilities) by comparing individuals to themselves over time, which holds these characteristics constant. Studies using this more rigorous test have also found nonlinear relationships. This work indicates that household income is positively related to children's cognitive functioning and the level of cognitive stimulation in children's home environment and, more important, that over-time improvements and reductions in family income (a) have much stronger impacts on the home environments of low-income children than those of middle-income children (Votruba-Drzal, 2003) and (b) bear a strong relationship to young children's cognitive functioning in the expected direction if they are poor, but are of little consequence if the child is not poor (Dearing et al., 2001).

Taken together, recent research makes a stronger case for family income supplements than for parent education as a strategy to promote poor children's cognitive functioning (a) because of the investment model that guides these investigations; (b) because studies have shown that the link between income and home learning environment remains robust after applying various statistical techniques to control for maternal, household, and child characteristics (Votruba-Drzal, 2003); and (c) because investigators have not tested differences in parenting knowledge and attitudes either as a mediator of the income-home environment link or as a direct contributor to income-related disparities in children's cognitive functioning. However, there are data from poor families indicating that maternal knowledge of child development indirectly influences poor children's cognitive test scores through maternal supportiveness (Wacharasin, Barnard, & Spieker, 2003).

Evaluations of the Efficacy of Parent Education Programs

In this chapter, we use the terms "parent education" and "parent training" interchangeably, while acknowledging that differences exist in their meanings. Parent education tends to be regarded as the more general term, whereas parent training is thought of as one category of parent education, distinguished by a process that includes a component devoted to teaching specific skills (Dembo, Sweitzer, & Lauritzen, 1985). Although parent education programs vary in their goals, a large proportion of them generally seek to increase parents' knowledge of child development, enhance the child's home learning environment, and ultimately improve children's cognitive functioning and school success. Another large

category of parent education programs is designed to improve parent-child communication, help parents use effective discipline methods, and foster children's social competence.

The past 2 decades brought a stunning panoply of parent education programs and evaluations of their efficacy (C. Smith, Perou, & Lesesne, 2002). The overwhelming diversity among parent education programs makes it hazardous to compare effects across programs and sites. Parallel with the proliferation of programs has been a growing tendency to embed parent education within broader family support programs or as a component of comprehensive intervention programs for low-income families (Brooks-Gunn, Berlin, & Fuligni, 2000; C. Smith et al., 2002). In terms of assessment, the thorny problem this creates is sorting out the unique effects of parent education per se from other program components such as parent support and social services, because these multifaceted programs invariably are not structured to set apart the impact of the parent education component. Some of the largest and best-evaluated interventions are of this nature, such as the Parent and Child Development Centers and the Comprehensive Child Development Program (Morley, Dornbusch, & Seer, 1993; D. Powell, 1982; St. Pierre & Layzer, 1999). On the other hand, some scholars argue that efforts to dissect multifaceted programs into their constituents are misdirected because it is the sum of the parts and the synergistic processes operating among program components that often account for their success (Olds & Kitzman, 1990).

Another challenge for those interested in the effects of parenting education on low-income parents and children generally derives from the correlation that poverty and low income bear to numerous other demographic and family characteristics that are increasingly the criteria for inclusion in parent education programs. For example, a growing number of programs target teen mothers, parents with limited English proficiency, and parents with limited formal education. These programs may serve parents from socioeconomically diverse backgrounds, and in evaluations of their efficacy, SES/poverty status may be controlled rather than examined as a potential moderator of program effects (e.g., Baker, Piotrkowski, Brooks-Gunn, 1999). More precise targeting of parent education programs on the basis of demographic or family criteria other than poverty that place children at risk for poor cognitive, school, or behavioral outcomes may, in the long run, prove cost-effective. However, compared to programs that specifically target poor or low-income parents, these programs may have comparatively high attrition rates because they incorporate fewer or less effective incentives to curb dropout and low attendance rates or are implemented in ways incompatible with the life circumstances of low-income participants (Gomby, Culross, & Behrman, 1999). Poor and low-income parents are more likely to drop out of or have low levels of involvement in parent training programs, compared to their more advantaged counterparts (e.g., Baker et al., 1999; F. Frankel & Simmons, 1992), a finding that may suggest the need for incentives that are more responsive to the resource needs of poor and low-income parents (e.g., transportation, child care; R. B. Wolfe & Hirsch, 2003).

Most parent education programs that were initiated during the 1970s and that focused primarily on low-income parents emphasized enhancing children's cognitive performance (Clarke-Stewart & Apfel, 1978; Morley et al., 1993; Olds & Kitzman, 1993). Recent years have brought a broader focus that includes fostering social competence and preventing conduct problems in low-income children, partly in response to growing recognition of the role of social skills in early academic success (e.g., Webster-Stratton, 1998). Diverse strategies have been employed to achieve these goals, as reflected in the vast array of dimensions on which parent education and training programs differ. These dimensions include focus (parent-child dyad versus parent alone), method of instruction (one-to-one versus group discussion, toy demonstration and modeling), setting (home- versus center-based), frequency of contact, duration of the program, existence of a predetermined curriculum, and staff credentials (e.g., professional versus paraprofessionals). Content may include information about various milestones in child development, physical and emotional development, and parenting techniques. In programs seeking to enhance cognitive functioning, children generally range in age from young infants to 5-year-olds, though more emphasis is given to the first 3 years of life. Those concerned with children's social competence tend to involve parents of children representing a broader age range. A large number of programs with an evaluation component have focused on African American mothers (e.g., Morley et al., 1993; Olds & Kitzman, 1993; D. Powell, 1982).

The vast majority of parent education and training programs do not include an evaluation component. Among those that do, a variety of methodological problems exist that make it difficult to assess their effects and to determine what aspects or kinds of programs are most effective. Parenting programs (or programs with parent education components) evaluated in rigorous randomized trials were rare in the 1970s and 1980s and remain so (Clarke-Stewart & Apfel, 1978; Dembo et al., 1985; Gomby et al., 1999). Moreover, the advantages of a true random control group is likely lost in some studies because control and experimental groups live in close proximity and the curriculum may be diffused from program mothers and children to control mothers and children. Other common threats to the validity of evaluations of these programs include repeated testing of children with the same instrument, use of nonstandardized and culturally biased measures and measures with unknown psychometric properties, and subject attrition. Few evaluations have included long-term follow-ups or gone beyond demonstrating the overall effectiveness of the program to systematically investigate either processes through which change is effected or factors that moderate overall effectiveness (Clarke-Stewart & Apfel, 1978; Gomby et al., 1999).

Effects on Children. Despite these myriad methodological limitations, existing research supports the general conclusion that well-administered parent education programs can produce immediate effects on low-income children's cognitive functioning (for detailed reviews of these studies, see Clarke-Stewart & Apfel, 1978; Halpern, 1990b; Morley et al., 1993). When cognitive gains have been found among program children, compared to control children, they have been modest and are usually maintained for 1 or 2 years and then gradually fade. In a meta-analysis of the effects of 13 programs that offered parent education either alone or in combination with other intervention services to mothers/parents of children under 3 years of age, Morley et al. found an overall positive effect on children's intellectual functioning that tended to persist for a year or so. Analysis of the effects of parent education alone, unmixed with other interventions, yielded similar findings. In general, though, interventions that rely solely on parent-mediated routes to increase children's cognitive competencies (e.g., parent education that involves only the parent) produce less positive and enduring effects than interventions that provide direct learning experiences to children (C. Ramey, Ramey, Gaines, & Blair, 1995; Wasik, Ramey, Bryant, & Sparling, 1990).

Parenting programs also have been found to enhance low-income children's social competence, though reliance on parent reports is a major limitation in most studies (e.g., Myers et al., 1992). In one of the most rigorously evaluated parenting programs of this genre that used a random assignment design, Head Start children whose mother participated in an 8- to 9-week parenting program (weekly parent group meetings of 8 to 16 parents for 2 hours, once a week) were found to exhibit significantly fewer conduct problems, less noncompliance, less negative affect, and more positive affect (as assessed by home observations and teacher report) than Head Start control children. Most of these improvements were maintained 1 year later (Webster-Stratton, 1998).

Considerably less consensus exists about the degree to which the effectiveness of parent education programs on children's development is moderated by program characteristics such as duration, intensity, location, format, focal child's age at the inception of the intervention, and curriculum content. It is difficult to assess the independent contribution of these program characteristics because they tend to be confounded within and across programs. Several studies have found no difference in the effects of programs lasting 1 versus 2 years, or 2 versus 3 years, but when differences are found, they tend to favor longer programs, the latter tending to produce more enduring rather than larger gains (Clarke-Stewart & Apfel, 1978; Morley et al., 1993). There is suggestive evidence that a more intense program schedule may result in increased benefits, but most studies have confounded intensity with other potentially critical variables. In one of the higher-quality studies of this issue, C. Powell and Grantham-McGregor (1989) varied the frequency with which community health aides provided psychosocial stimulation to infants and toddlers and demonstrated these techniques to their mothers during a 2-year period. At the end of the 1st and the 2nd years, children who were visited biweekly had higher intellectual functioning than those who were visited monthly or not at all. The pattern of scores indicated that the 1st year of biweekly home visiting increased intellectual functioning, whereas the 2nd year served to maintain this benefit or reinforce the skills that children had learned during the 1st year, a pattern reminiscent of that found in studies of the effects of 2 versus 1 year of center-based intervention (e.g., Reynolds, 1995).

Data do not point to any optimal age during the first 5 years of the child's life for initiating parent education.

Studies that systematically vary by about a year the age of the child at the inception of parent education tend to find no significant age-related difference in immediate effects. Beginning at a younger age may be better in the long run (Clarke-Stewart & Apfel, 1978), though there may be no significant advantage to beginning prior to the child's 12th month of life (Morley et al., 1993). Discrepancies in findings regarding the relative effectiveness of different formats (e.g., home-based versus group/center-based), along with cultural insensitivity of programs for ethnic minorities, acknowledgment of individual differences among parents, and evidence that exact replication of model programs was not possible because of the need to adapt programs to local circumstances have led to a shift in the parent education field to matching program content and methods to the needs and characteristics of parents (D. Powell, 1988).

Effects on Maternal Behavior and Attitudes.   A number of parent training programs have been found to positively affect low-income mothers' parenting behavior and attitudes. Effects include use of more complex speech, greater provision of stimulating activities in the home environment, less authoritarian child-rearing attitudes, greater discipline competence, greater use of praise and less harsh critical behavior, greater involvement in the child's education, and increased confidence and perceived efficacy in the role of parent (Clarke-Stewart & Apfel, 1978; Duggan et al., 1999; Morley et al., 1993; Webster-Stratton, 1998; R. B. Wolfe & Hirsch, 2003). Too few long-term studies have been conducted to know whether these maternal effects persist well beyond the end of the programs. Overall, though, parent education programs have stronger immediate effects on mothers' attitudes and behavior and on the quality of the home environment than on children's cognitive functioning (Clarke-Stewart & Apfel, 1978; Morley et al., 1993). An even finer-grained distinction may be warranted, in that some interventions with parent education components have been more effective in modifying parental attitudes and self-reports of behavior than observed home environment or mother-child interaction (Duggan et al., 1999). Because evaluation studies have not assessed the relationship between changes in maternal and child behavior over time, it remains unclear whether gains in children's cognitive and social functioning are indeed caused by increased parental knowledge and changes in parental behavior and attitudes (Clarke-Stewart & Apfel, 1978; Shonkoff & Phillips, 2000).

Parent Participation/Involvement in Early Childhood Interventions

During the mid- to late 1970s, emphasis on parent education in a narrow sense began to give way to the broader concepts of parent participation and involvement, whereby professionals, in effect, were to do things "with rather than to parents in early intervention programs" (D. Powell, 1988, p. 11). This realignment of parent-professional relations, seen by some as more rhetorical than substantive, was the product of several forces, including (a) provisions for parent participation in federal legislation establishing programs for the poor, such as the Economic Opportunity Act of 1964, which called for "maximum feasible participation" for individuals served by Community Action Programs (CAP), the umbrella entity under which Head Start was implemented; (b) the civil rights movement, which sought institutional change and empowerment of the poor partly by pressing for poor people's involvement in decisions that affected them; (c) criticisms of the deficit model; and (d) growing concern about professional meddling in private family matters (Halpern, 1988; D. Powell, 1988).

Although not without strong resistance from those who perceived Head Start parents as deficient in educational and parenting skills and as a primary source of their children's "cultural deficits," parent involvement (and parenting education) ultimately was incorporated as a central component of the Head Start model (Zigler & Muenchow, 1992). By the early 1970s, provisions for parent participation and decision making in Head Start had been clearly enunciated and spanned a wide array of possibilities (e.g., participation in the classroom as paid employees, volunteers, or observers; educational activities for parents which they helped to develop; leading and serving on committees that make decisions about budgetary matters, curriculum development, health services, program goals, and implementation of program services; G. Fein, 1980; Parker, Piotrkowski, Horn, & Greene, 1995). Parent involvement continues to be a salient feature of Head Start. Head Start parents are significantly more involved in school-based activities (e.g., volunteering in child's classroom, going on class trips with child) and conference with teachers and school administrators more frequently than parents whose children attend comprehensive day care centers (Fantuzzo, Tighe, & Childs, 2000), although the two groups do not differ in behaviors that actively promote a learning environment at home for the child.

Parent Participation/Involvement as an Enhancer of Preschool Effects

The legitimacy of parent participation/involvement in preschool interventions increased exponentially following Bronfenbrenner's (1975) conclusion, noted previously, that increased parent involvement enhanced the efficacy of early childhood interventions. Advocates pointed to two potential pathways by which this effect is produced. First, it was asserted that helping parents understand and manage their children's developmental needs helps consolidate and maintain the benefits of early education, given parents' uniquely salient and enduring presence in the child's life. Second, involving parents in the planning, implementation, and assessment of programs was thought to enhance programs' sensitivity to the needs of children and, hence, boost positive effects (White, Taylor, & Moss, 1992).

In subsequent reviews of research bearing on parental participation/involvement as a moderator of the effects of early childhood intervention, researchers have noted limitations in Bronfenbrenner's (1975) analysis (e.g., the sample of programs was small, ages and frequency of home visits were confounded) and concluded that existing research provides no compelling evidence of an enhancing effect of parental participation/involvement (Clarke-Stewart & Apfel, 1978; White et al., 1992). Clarke-Stewart and Apfel identified a number of studies reporting evidence of stronger effects in mother-child programs than programs that focused only on the child. However, they found equally strong evidence that children's cognitive gains were not dependent on their mother's level of participation/involvement in the program. Moreover, they cited studies in which child-focused programs were more effective than mother-child programs in producing gains in children's test competence and school skills. Clarke-Stewart and Apfel's conclusion of an overall null effect, based on a traditional review of the literature, foreshadowed similar findings from a meta-analysis published several years later (White et al., 1992).

Taken together, extant investigations yield no consistent evidence that parent participation/involvement enhances the immediate or long-term effects of early intervention on children's development. This may be due to a lack of consensus about the definition of parent participation/involvement. Parent participation/involvement has evolved into a broad and highly diffuse concept whose operationalizations encompass highly disparate activities, including teaching parents specific skills to assist them in becoming more effective socializers of their children, exchanging information between parents and professionals, participation of parents in the planning and implementation of programs, assisting parents in accessing community resources, and providing emotional and social support to family members (White et al., 1992). Failure to find an enhancing effect of parent participation/involvement also may be due to insufficient attention to a range of parent behaviors across different settings and populations, inadequate implementation of parent participation/involvement components of intervention programs, and poorly designed research (Reynolds, 1992; White et al., 1992).

The most obvious limitation to drawing firm conclusions about the impact of parental participation/involvement, however, is the remarkably sparse number of studies that have been designed expressly to investigate this issue. A strong, venerable presumption exists that parental involvement in child-directed educational efforts, however defined and measured, is desirable (G. Fein, 1980; Reynolds, 1992). Low priority may be given to conducting empirical tests of this assumption because it is so prevalent and held with such certitude. Even if parent participation/involvement does not enhance children's gains from early intervention, this in no way negates its potential importance as a means to achieve other laudable goals (e.g., enhancing poor parents' political power and sense of efficacy).

Although apparently not a robust moderator of effects, parent involvement has been found to mediate preschool effects. In his longitudinal study of children enrolled in a large-scale preschool intervention program similar to Head Start, Reynolds (1991) found that parental involvement mediated the effect of preschool intervention on reading and mathematics achievement during the first 2 years of primary school and the effect of children's achievement motivation during kindergarten on academic achievement in first grade.

Ecological Influences on Parenting and Child Development

Intervention strategies that aim to prevent and ameliorate the negative effects of poverty on children's development traditionally have concentrated on providing direct educational experiences to children and modify-

ing the parenting practices and home environment to which poor children are subject, without major regard for contextual, extrafamilial factors impinging on parents and their children. This perspective and its implicit disavowal of the need to change contextual factors and social systems has always had its critics, though they typically have been a minority voice (Chilman, 1973). During the late 1960s and early 1970s, a handful of demonstration models evinced some degree of departure from this traditional approach (Andrews et al., 1982). In addition to parent education and educational experiences for preschoolers, they offered social services to the entire family and attempted to remediate extrafamilial obstacles to optimal parent and child functioning (Halpern, 1988).

It was not until the 1980s, however, that an ecological perspective achieved notable currency in early childhood intervention. At the heart of this shift was increased appreciation of stress, social support, and broader contextual factors as determinants of parenting behavior, on the one hand, and as conditioners of parents' and children's ability to profit from an intervention program, on the other (Bronfenbrenner, 1975; Chilman, 1973; Halpern, 1984). An overarching goal is improvement of the social and economic context of parenting and children's development. Ecologically sensitive intervention is a highly diverse genre, but a few common denominators distinguish programs in this category. They tend to be expansive in focus (i.e., family-focused rather than child- or parent-focused) and offer a broad complement of services. Emphasis is given to prevention rather than treatment as a cost-effective approach to human service delivery. In addition, these programs claim espousal of a nondeficit orientation dedicated to building on families' strengths rather than simply remediating their weaknesses, though questions exist about whether this is a substantive change or a public relations maneuver (D. Powell, 1988).

A multiplicity of strategies are employed to increase supports and reduce stressors at multiple levels of proximity to the parent, child, and entire family (e.g., psychological, sociological, economic, home, neighborhood, workplace). These include direct provision of emotional support to parents and other family members, facilitation of peer support and social networks, assistance of family members in gaining access to and using educational, health, and social services in the community, reinforcement of links between families and both formal and informal sources of support, and mediation between the family and more distal bureaucracies to help families obtain needed services. Considerable variation exists across programs, however, in the degree of emphasis given to each of these services (Halpern, 1990b; Kagan, Powell, Weissbourd, & Zigler, 1987).

As a form and component of early childhood intervention, parent education also broadened its focus to include ecological factors. By the early 1980s, many parent education programs sought to improve parent functioning via provision of social support to parents, not just dissemination of information about child rearing and the principles of child development. D. Powell (1988) identified two variants of the family/parent support approach that emerged during this period. In the first, the assumption is that parents lack confidence in their child-rearing beliefs and practices. Rather than attempting to modify parental behavior and attitudes in accord with some ideal notion of what a parent should do with children, these programs provide validation and affirmation of the parent's existing child-rearing beliefs and behaviors on the assumption that this alone is sufficient to enhance parental behavior and attitudes. Such programs attempt to replicate some elements of informal support systems traditionally available through networks of friends and family. In the second variant, programs provide social support as a means to increase parents' receptivity to expert information and advice, on the grounds that high levels of stressors and low support inhibit parents' ability to attend to the curriculum content of parent education programs.

The trend toward more ecological approaches to poverty-focused early childhood intervention is part of a broader "family support" movement that surged during the 1980s. Family support programs share the characteristics, emphasis, and perspectives of ecologically sensitive early childhood intervention programs but are distinctive in one major regard. They are committed to universal (rather than means-tested) access to family support services on the grounds that economic and social changes have created widespread support needs that transcend social class and economic boundaries (e.g., increases in costs of living that necessitate two paychecks to maintain a middle-class standard of living; increased geographic mobility that has reduced the availability of extended family members for provision of myriad kinds of support; increase in divorce and single-parent families). Head Start, especially its demonstration models, laid the foundation for the principles underlying the family support movement (Kagan et al., 1987).

The late 1970s and 1980s also brought a broadening of the developmental outcomes considered in both basic and intervention research. With the burgeoning of intervention programs during the late 1960s and early 1970s, several scholars questioned the preoccupation with cognitive enrichment. They asserted that socioemotional factors (e.g., impulsivity, noncompliance) contributed as much to school failure as the lack of academic skills and, hence, that studied attention should be extended to socioemotional functioning and the overall development of poor children and their parents (Chilman, 1973; Zigler & Berman, 1983). Interest in the impact of early interventions on children's socioemotional functioning exploded during the 1980s, strengthened by rising rates of crime, violence, and antisocial behavior among youth; the growing availability of longitudinal data on preschool intervention effects during late adolescence and early adulthood, when antisocial behavior tends to peak (e.g., Berrueta-Clement et al., 1984; Johnson, 1988); and advances in the measurement of socioemotional functioning. Gains in cognitive functioning continue to be regarded as critical indicators of the efficacy of early childhood interventions, but they no longer eclipse a focus on socioemotional outcomes.

In the following section, we discuss conceptual and empirical work that triggered and sustained the evolution toward more ecologically oriented approaches in early childhood intervention for poor children and families. We then turn to an appraisal of different categories of interventions whose content reflects some of the hallmarks of this approach.

Precursors of an Ecological Approach to Early Childhood Intervention

A confluence of factors have been credited for the evolving direction of early childhood intervention toward a more ecological approach (Bronfenbrenner, 1987; Halpern, 1990a; D. Powell, 1988), among them: (a) prominent model programs developed in the late 1960s that exemplified and documented positive effects of ecologically oriented intervention (Andrews et al., 1982; Seitz, Rosenbaum, & Apfel, 1985); (b) Bronfenbrenner's (1975) assertion that ecological intervention and parenting support are essential to effecting positive change in the course of poor children's development and his subsequent elaboration of an ecological model of human development (Bronfenbrenner, 1979); (c) empirical evidence that family processes, including parenting behavior, and children's development can be undermined by stressful events and conditions, including those that occur in extrafamilial settings; (d) empirical evidence that the availability and provision of social support from immediate family members, and persons outside the immediate family such as kin, friends, and neighbors, can enhance psychological functioning and parenting behavior under ordinary and stressful conditions; and (e) persistent criticisms of the deficit model and evidence of its negative effects. We discuss each of these factors, although this is not to suggest that individual interventionists are cognizant necessarily of how these factors have shaped their efforts. Indeed, although the work reviewed here provides strong underpinnings for the policies and practices governing ecologically oriented intervention, its contributions to some of the basic concepts underlying these programs and to some of the programs themselves often have gone unrecognized (Bronfenbrenner, 1987).

Early, Prominent Demonstration Models. Research findings on SES differences in parenting practices and the relations between parenting practices and child development, discussed previously, were widely disseminated among policymakers during the mid-1960s by a cadre of pediatricians, developmental psychologists, and other social scientists. These dissemination efforts, along with the disappointing findings of the Westinghouse evaluation, prompted the Office of Economic Opportunity, and later the Office of Child Development and its successor, the Administration for Children, Youth, and Families, to launch several experimental demonstration projects focused on early parenting in poor families (Halpern, 1988). They included the Parent and Child Centers (PCCs), followed by the Parent and Child Development Centers (PCDCs), and later, the Child and Family Resource Programs (CFRPs). Carefully conceived, implemented, and evaluated to enhance the probability of replication if they proved effective (all were randomized trials), these programs are rightly credited as forerunners of the current family/parent support movement and the source of some of the best evidence about the conditions of effective parent education and support (Halpern, 1988; Zigler & Freedman, 1987).

The PCCs, established in 1967 as the first Head Start experimental programs designed to serve very young children (infants to 3-year-olds) and their families, were multipurpose family centers (about 33 were

established) that provided parent education, health, and social services. Whereas center-based Head Start was seen as remedial, the PCCs reached poor children during the earliest years of life and, hence, were regarded as preventive. This initiative was envisioned as a nationwide program, but its expansion was prevented by shifting political forces and bureaucratic reorganization (Halpern, 1988).

In 1970, three PCCs (located in Birmingham, Houston, and New Orleans) were selected to become experimental Parent and Child Development Centers. Their general purpose was to define the goals of parent-infant intervention, develop different approaches to meet these goals, and establish appropriate evaluation strategies. The centers adopted different methods of program delivery (i.e., in Birmingham, a step system of increasing maternal responsibility for program work, culminating in staff positions; in New Orleans, involvement of paraprofessionals from the community; in Houston, a year of home visits, followed by a year of center programs for both mother and child), but all served families with children from birth to 3 and were developed and implemented within a common framework that emphasized the role of parents in children's development. Core components in all the centers were (a) a comprehensive curriculum for mothers consisting of information on child development and child-rearing practices, home management, nutrition and health, mothers' personal development, and government and community resources (e.g., community colleges) and how to use them; (b) a simultaneous program for the children of these women (ranging in age from 2 to 12 months at the time of entry into the program); and (c) extensive supportive services for participating families, including transportation, some meals, family health and social services, peer support groups, and a small, daily stipend. The programs varied in the amount of weekly participation expected and ended when the child was 36 months of age (Andrews et al., 1982).

Evaluations of short-term effects showed that program children scored higher than control children on the Stanford-Binet, although this difference reached statistical significance in only two of the three sites. In general, immediate effects of the PCDC intervention were stronger for mothers than their children. At graduation, program mothers in all three PCDCs showed more positive maternal behavior than controls in videotaped interactions with their children (e.g., giving child praise and emotional support, being affectionate and accepting, encouraging child's verbal communications, participating actively in child's activities, greater use of language to inform rather than restrict and control child; Andrews et al., 1982). In a follow-up of children in the Houston PCDC when they were in grades 2 through 5, 5 to 8 years after program completion, positive effects were found for children's academic and socioemotional functioning. Compared to the control group, program children scored significantly better on standardized achievement tests and were reliably more considerate of others, less hostile, restless, impulsive, and obstinate, and less likely to be involved in fights (Johnson, 1988). However, a subsequent comprehensive follow-up of all three PCDC samples found no residual program effects on a number of child and family variables (Halpern, 1990b). Efforts to replicate the centers on a broad scale were abandoned, despite evidence of their short-term efficacy, because of budgetary pressures and concerns about their costliness and generalizability (G. Fein, 1980; Halpern, 1988).

The Child and Family Resource Program, initiated in 1973 and funded through 1983, had as its core a 2-year program of bimonthly to monthly home visits for families with infants from birth to 3. Its distinguishing features were (a) an emphasis on parent support and education (e.g., information on prevention and identification of child abuse, domestic management, use of community services), including helping parents resolve serious family problems (e.g., poor health, substandard housing, alcoholism); (b) stress on developmental continuity by providing services before birth and continuing them into elementary school; (c) coordination of comprehensive social services provided directly and via referrals; and (d) an attempt to individualize services through needs assessment and goal setting with each family. Referrals for adult education, literacy, and job training were made by case managers as needed, but this was not a strong component of the program. Each of the 11 local programs was linked to Head Start centers, where 3- to 5-year-olds in the program attended preschool. Once children began elementary school, staff personnel maintained contact with parents to maximize their involvement in their child's academic progress (St. Pierre et al., 1995; Zigler & Freedman, 1987).

Effects of the program on children were much weaker than those produced by the PCDCs, probably because children received fewer direct services and only uneven attention was given to parent-child interaction. The CFRP had no significant effect on children's Bayley scores or on several other measures of development,

health, and behavior. However, the program had significant, positive effects on parenting behavior, feelings of efficacy, and perceived ability to control events. Rate of maternal employment and training, but not household income, also favored program mothers, though this difference was modest (St. Pierre et al., 1995).

Bronfenbrenner's Analyses.   In his analysis of the effectiveness of early intervention, Bronfenbrenner (1975) selected for special attention the famous Skeels (1966) experiment and the extremely invasive and controversial Milwaukee Project (Garber, 1988) to illustrate the potential of ecological interventions to promote cognitive functioning. He noted:

> [The] "enabling act" took the form in both instances, of a major transformation of the environment for the child and the persons principally responsible for his care and development. . . . The essence of the strategy [of ecological intervention] is a primary focus neither on the child nor his parent nor even the dyad or the family as a system. Rather, the aim is to effect changes in the context in which the family lives; these changes in turn enable the mother, the parents, and the family as a whole to exercise the functioning necessary for the child's development. . . . The need for ecological intervention arises when the . . . prerequisites [for the family to perform its child-rearing functions] are not met by the environment in which the child and his family live. This is precisely the situation which obtains for many, if not most, disadvantaged families. Under these circumstances no direct form of intervention aimed at enhancing the child's development or his parents' childrearing skills is likely to have much impact. Conversely, once the environmental prerequisites are met, the direct forms of intervention may no longer seem as necessary. (pp. 584–585)

Bronfenbrenner noted further that ecological intervention is rarely carried out because it "almost invariably requires institutional change" (p. 586).

He continued his theme concerning the importance of the family's ecology on children's development in a subsequent analysis focusing on basic research. Drawing on a theoretically convergent body of research, Bronfenbrenner (1979) argued compellingly that children's development is influenced not only by the family system, but by systems well removed from the family's control, among them, parents' workplace, neighborhoods, schools, available health and day care services, and macroeconomic forces that result in stressors such as parental unemployment and job and income loss. He exhorted researchers to take seriously the potency of the family's ecology by undertaking multilayered, contextual, and more process-oriented analyses of family relations and children's development. Two scholarly contributions were pivotal in sustaining interest in ecological influences, namely Ogbu's (1981) cultural-ecological model, underscoring the potency of extrafamilial forces on the socialization and development of poor African American children, and W. J. Wilson's (1987) historical analyses of changes in the economic character of inner-city neighborhoods and his speculations about the implications of these changes for social norms and children's development (e.g., Brooks-Gunn, Duncan, Klebanov, & Sealand, 1993).

Research on Relations among Stressors, Parenting, and Adult Psychological Functioning. A rich body of research produced during the 1970s and 1980s provided compelling support for the contention that undesirable events and conditions compromised adults' mental health and hence, their parenting behavior and that social support lessened these compromising effects. In the following sections, we highlight some of the most prominent research documenting these relations.

Adverse Events/Conditions as Determinants of Parenting. A considerable amount of research documenting the effects of undesirable life events and chronic conditions on both adult psychological functioning and parenting focused on economic stressors, prompted in part by the economic downturns of the late 1970s and early 1980s (McLoyd, 1989). The most influential work published during this period concerned economic hardship as experienced during the Great Depression of the 1930s. In that research, Elder and his colleagues (Elder, 1974; Elder, Liker, & Cross, 1984) found that fathers who lost jobs and sustained heavy financial loss became irritable, tense, and explosive, which in turn increased their tendency to be punitive and arbitrary in the discipline of their children. These fathering behaviors were predictive of temper tantrums, irritability, and negativity in young children, especially boys, and of moodiness and hypersensitivity, feelings of inadequacy, and lowered aspirations in adolescent girls.

Elder et al.'s (1984) basic causal pathway linking economic loss and economic hardship more generally to the child through the parent's behavior has been replicated in several studies of ethnically diverse contemporary families (Conger et al., 1993; Gutman et al., in press; Lempers, Clark-Lempers, & Simon, 1989). In

Lemper et al.'s study of White working- and middle-class families, for example, economic loss led to higher rates of adolescent delinquency and drug use by increasing inconsistent and punitive discipline by parents.

Further corroboration of the link between economic loss and parenting comes from studies of child abusers and investigations of the relationship between the status of an economy (e.g., unemployment rate, inflation rate) and rates of child abuse. These investigations are consistent in showing that child abuse occurs more frequently during periods of undesirable economic change and in families experiencing economic decline (i.e., job and income loss) than in families with stable resources (Parke & Collmer, 1975). Negative life events and daily hassles more generally were also found to predict lower-quality parenting (e.g., less responsive, more restrictive, and punitive parenting; for example, Gersten, Langner, Eisenberg, & Simcha-Fagan, 1977; G. Patterson, 1988). Adverse events/conditions were also linked to the quality of the home learning environment. Reminiscent of the inverse relationship found between children's IQ and number of risk factors (Sameroff, Seifer, Barocas, Zax, & Greenspan, 1987), Brooks-Gunn et al. (1995), for example, found that as the number of risk factors experienced by the parents increased (e.g., incidence of stressful life events, parental unemployment), the less stimulating the preschooler's home environment.

Psychological Distress as a Mediator of the Adversity-Parenting Link. Several studies conducted during the late 1970s and 1980s yielded direct as well as indirect evidence that psychological distress mediates the link between negative life events/conditions and harsh, inconsistent parenting. This mediational process was clearly demonstrated in work on economic hardship precipitated by parental job and income loss (Conger et al., 1993; Elder, 1974; Lempers et al., 1989) and was thought to operate more generally across a range of stressors. Two types of evidence are relevant to this proposition: research linking adverse events/conditions to adult psychological functioning and investigations documenting an association between parents' psychological functioning and parenting behavior.

A plethora of studies reported strong positive relationships between negative life events/conditions and psychological distress in adults, as indicated by depression, anxiety, hostility, somatic complaints, eating and sleeping problems, and low self-regard (e.g., Kessler & Neighbors, 1986; Liem & Liem, 1978). Parenthetically, several studies conducted during this period found a strong link between negative life events/conditions and psychological distress (including school adjustment problems) in children (e.g., Sandler & Block, 1979; Sterling, Cowen, Weissberg, Lotyczewski, & Boike, 1985). Complementing these studies of adults was evidence linking fluctuations in unemployment rates to aggregate-level indices of psychological distress (e.g., admissions to psychiatric hospitals; Horwitz, 1984). Research demonstrated cogently that these are true effects and not simply selective factors that lead to job loss or unemployment (e.g., Kessler, House, & Turner, 1987).

Turning to the second line of research, enormous amounts of data were generated during the 1980s about how parents' affective states condition the quality of parent-child interaction. These data, most from mothers of infants and preschoolers, directly tied negative psychological states in the parent (e.g., depressive symptoms, as well as clinical depression) to greater parental punitiveness, inconsistency, and unresponsiveness, less reliance on reasoning and loss of privileges in disciplining the child, more negative perceptions of the child, and greater use of conflict-resolution strategies that require little effort, such as dropping initial demands when the child is resistant or enforcing obedience unilaterally rather than negotiating with the child (Downey & Coyne, 1990; McLoyd, 1990). The relationship between psychological distress and parenting is robust, for it has been found to exist in samples of poor individuals where the range of scores is generally more restricted (Crockenberg, 1987; Zelkowitz, 1982).

Parallels between Correlates of Poverty and Correlates of Adverse Events/Conditions. By the mid-1980s, the inverse relationship between SES (and poverty) and various forms of psychological distress was well established. In addition, enough data existed to conclude that the poor's increased exposure to negative life events and chronic conditions was a major cause underlying this relationship (Liem & Liem, 1978). Researchers documented that poor and low SES individuals were more likely than economically advantaged counterparts to be confronted with an unremitting succession of negative life events (e.g., eviction, physical illness, criminal assault, catastrophes resulting from substandard housing) in the context of chronically stressful life conditions outside personal control, such as inadequate housing and dangerous neighborhoods. It was also clear from research that psychological impairment was more severe when negative conditions and events were not under the

control of the individual, a condition more common for the poor (Liem & Liem, 1978). Ongoing stressful conditions associated with poverty and low SES, such as inadequate housing and shortfalls of money, were found to be more debilitating than acute crises and negative events (e.g., Makosky, 1982). In some studies, after chronic stressors were controlled, the effects of life events on psychological distress were diminished to borderline significance (e.g., Gersten et al., 1977; Pearlin, Lieberman, Menaghan, & Mullan, 1981).

If poverty and low SES are markers for a conglomerate of negative life events and chronic stressors and are predictive of higher levels of psychological distress, they should predict child-rearing behaviors and attitudes similar to those linked to specific negative life events, undesirable conditions, and psychological distress as discussed earlier. Abundant evidence accumulated over 3 decades confirms this expectation. These studies found that mothers who are poor or from low SES backgrounds, compared to their economically advantaged counterparts, are more likely to use power-assertive techniques in disciplinary encounters and are generally less supportive of their children. They value obedience more, are less likely to use reasoning, and are more likely to use physical punishment as a means of disciplining and controlling the child. Lower-class parents also are more likely to issue commands without explanation, less likely to consult the child about his or her wishes, and less likely to reward the child verbally for desirable behavior. In addition, poverty has been associated with diminished expression of affection and lesser responsiveness to the socioemotional needs explicitly expressed by the child (Gecas, 1979; Hess, 1970).

Parallels between poverty and low SES, on the one hand, and specific negative life events, undesirable conditions, and psychological distress, on the other, also were found for child abuse. Poverty, like job and income loss, is a significant predictor of child abuse (e.g., Garbarino, 1976). Indeed, it is the single most prevalent characteristic of abusing parents, although it is indisputable that only a small proportion of poor parents are even alleged to abuse their children (Pelton, 1989). Several kinds of data generated during the late 1970s and 1980s contradicted the claim that the relationship between poverty and abuse is spurious because of greater public scrutiny of the poor and resulting bias in detection and reporting. First, although greater public awareness and new reporting laws resulted in a significant increase in official reporting in recent years, the socioeconomic pattern of these reports has not changed (Pelton, 1989). Second, child abuse is related to degrees of poverty even within the lower class, which admittedly is more open to public scrutiny; abusing parents tend to be the poorest of the poor (Wolock & Horowitz, 1979). Third, the most severe injuries occur in the poorest families, even among the reported cases (Pelton, 1989).

In sum, research conducted during the 1970s and 1980s yielded a trove of evidence that poor and low SES individuals are more likely than their economically advantaged counterparts to experience negative life events, undesirable chronic conditions, and psychological distress and that these factors are conducive to less nurturant and more punitive parenting. In addition, the findings of several studies lend support to the hypothesis that child-rearing practices associated with poverty and low SES are partly a function of higher levels of psychological distress brought on by elevated exposure to negative life events and undesirable chronic conditions (McLoyd, 1990). These data, with their clear implications for practice, commanded the attention of the early childhood intervention field. They suggested that in some cases, stressors and their attendant psychological distress can override knowledge of the principles of child development as a determinant of parenting and that removal or amelioration of acute and chronic stressors can be highly effective as a strategy to improve parenting, and presumably child functioning. The multidimensionality of poverty and the conglomeration of acute and chronic stressors experienced by the poor accented the poor's need for a broad range of concrete services. These factors also suggested that service delivery should be integrative in approach (e.g., collaboration among individual service providers and clients in developing intervention and evaluation plans; close proximity of service delivery sites) so that it is not yet another source of stress.

Research on Social Support as a Contributor to Positive Psychological and Maternal Functioning.

Empirical research on social support as a determinant of adults' psychological well-being, family functioning, and parenting behavior, as well as ecological models of the determinants of parenting (Belsky, 1984) and family coping patterns (Barbarin, 1983), were powerful stimulants of interventionists' interest in the social context of parenting. Several of the interpersonal-level strategies chosen to promote poor children's development indirectly through the parent (e.g., peer support, strengthening self-help networks, reinforcing links between families and sources of support) are rooted in this vast literature. They also have been informed by qualitative research that developed methods for professionals to identify and recruit natural helpers in social networks, to collaborate in the matching of needs and resources in neighborhoods, and to link with formal agencies as needed (Watson & Collins, 1982).

The first set of findings from empirical research that proved to be highly significant to the field of early childhood intervention concerned the role of social support as a buffer against the negative effects of stress. Inspired by Caplan's (1974) thesis that social support is a protection against pathology, several studies were published during the late 1970s and thereafter indicating that social support buffered psychological distress among individuals under stress, including unemployed adults (e.g., Kessler et al., 1987) and mothers on welfare (e.g., Zur-Szpiro & Longfellow, 1982). A second set of studies documented naturally occurring patterns of informal help seeking (e.g., Cowen, 1982) and poor African Americans' heavy reliance on kinship ties and social networks for primary support and mutual aid (Barbarin, 1983; Stack, 1974).

A third set of studies based on low-income as well as economically advantaged families demonstrated the salutary effects of various forms of social support on parents' behavior toward their children (main effect, rather than a buffering effect). Emotional support (i.e., companionship, expressions of affection, availability of a confidant) and parenting support (e.g., assistance with child care), for example, were linked to improved mental health in mothers, increases in maternal sensitivity and nurturance, and decreases in coercive discipline (Crnic & Greenberg, 1987; Zur-Szpiro & Longfellow, 1982). Parenting support was also linked to increases in the mother's ability to give effective directions to the child and her effectiveness in getting the child to conform to rules (Weinraub & Wolf, 1983).

Indirect evidence of the salutary effects of social support emerged from the research literature on child abuse as well. Studies reported that parents who abused their children, compared to nonabusing parents, were more isolated from formal and informal support networks, less likely to have a relative living nearby, and usually had lived in their neighborhood for a shorter period (Gelles, 1980). This research suggested that in addition to indirectly preventing child maltreatment by enhancing parents' psychological functioning, members of parents' social networks directly inhibit child abuse by purposive intervention. Network embeddedness increases detection of child abuse, and a strong sense of obligation fosters direct intervention in the interest of the child (E. P. Martin & Martin, 1978). Sometime later, studies documented that children accrued benefits from naturally occurring social support systems (e.g., Cowen, Wyman, Work, & Parker, 1990). For example, researchers found that availability of child care support to the primary caregiver distinguished stress-resilient from stress-affected children (Cowen et al., 1990). Increased parenting or emotional support, and more nurturant parenting behavior as a result, may explain why emotional adjustment in poor African American children living in mother/grandmother families is almost as high as that of children living in mother/father families, and significantly higher than that of children living alone with the mother (Kellam, Ensminger, & Turner, 1977). In general, though, the bulk of the evidence suggests that parents' social networks have more indirect than direct effects on the child through their effects on the mother (M. Wilson, 1989).

Although the research literature provided incontrovertible evidence that social support enhances psychological and maternal functioning, it also sounded a number of cautionary notes that merit careful attention from those formulating and implementing programs that rely on the creation and strengthening of social support systems for families under stress. First, the protective effects of social support vary by context and circumstance. Support relationships exert a more positive influence on emotional and parental functioning when psychological distress is relatively low (Crockenberg, 1987), during times of major life transitions (Crnic & Greenberg, 1987), and when the source of stress is an event rather than a chronic condition such as persistent poverty or economic hardship (Dressler, 1985). Second, support from individuals who are also major sources of distress reduces the effectiveness of the support (Belle, 1982; Crockenberg, 1987). Likewise, embeddedness in an extended family network, though generally providing economic and psychological benefits, is not without its psychological and material costs. These costs include feeling burdened by obligations to the extended family, feeling exploited by those who want more than they need or deserve, disagreement concerning the need for and/or use of aid, and disapproval by extended family members of potential marital partners and child-rearing practices and decisions (Stack, 1974). Hence, although parent/

family support was greeted with enthusiasm and high hopes as a balm for the problems of the poor, the research literature sounded some sobering notes that called for, at the very least, guarded optimism.

Persistent Criticisms and Negative Effects of the Deficit Model. Criticism of the deficit model on which early childhood intervention was premised continued relentlessly through the 1970s and 1980s, although the nature and practice implications of these criticisms varied (Bronfenbrenner, 1987; Halpern, 1988; Laosa, 1989; Washington, 1985). To the extent that early childhood intervention in general has been torn away from its deficit-based moorings—an issue of some debate still—the variant that was most potent in forging this change argued that "failures" in the social environment, not personal deficiencies, were responsible for the problems of the poor. Its effect was to direct attention to the social ecology of poor families, rather than the individual, as the primary target for transformation (D. Powell, 1988).

This perspective, combined with the notion of empowerment of poor parents, is the essence of the compensatory model of helping articulated by Brickman and his colleagues (1982). The core tenet of this model is that people are not blamed for their problems but are held responsible for solving the problems by compelling an unwilling social environment to yield needed resources. People are seen and see themselves as having to compensate, via effort, ingenuity, and collaboration with others, among other strategies, for the hardships and obstacles imposed on them. Likewise, people who help others under the assumptions of this model see themselves as compensating by providing assistance and opportunities that the recipients deserve, but somehow do not have. However, the responsibility for using the help and determining whether the help is successful is seen to lie with the recipients. This ideological perspective is embodied in Jesse Jackson's repeated assertion to urban, economically distressed African Americans, "'You are not responsible for being down, but you are responsible for getting up'" and "'Both tears and sweat are wet and salty, but they render a different result. Tears will get you sympathy, but sweat will get you change'" (quoted in Brickman et al., 1982, p. 372).

An evolving orientation toward transformation of the environment, rather than the individual, was also a product of growing awareness of the ill effects of the deficit or person-blame model. In contrast to the beneficial effects of emotional support from family and friends, several investigations found use of community/neighborhood services to have no enhancing effect on the psychological well-being and parenting behavior of adolescent mothers (e.g., Colletta & Lee, 1983; Crockenberg, 1987). In fact, in one study, adolescent mothers were more dissatisfied with professionals than any other group of helpers. Health professionals were often seen as unsympathetic, impatient, disapproving, uninformative, and offering parenting advice that contradicted that of family members or other professionals. In essence, they provided these mothers little, if any, emotional, informational, or instrumental support and, hence, had no salutary effect on their mental health or parenting (Crockenberg, 1987).

Evidence that attribution biases moderated the impact of economic hardship on adults' psychological functioning also served notice of the dysfunctionality of person-blame attributions. For example, researchers found that men who held themselves responsible for their loss of income or a job (e.g., Buss & Redburn, 1983; Cohn, 1978) and poor African American women who blamed themselves for being on welfare (Goodban, 1985) had more psychological and physical health problems than those who did not blame themselves for their economic difficulties. Extrapolating from these findings, professional helpers who covertly and overtly heap blame on poor parents for their difficult circumstances essentially compromise their avowed mission, because such attributions, reflected in behaviors and attitudes, render them less effective in ameliorating psychological and parenting problems.

Evaluations of Ecologically Oriented Interventions

The research just discussed helped illuminate the ecology of poor families and the multidimensionality of family poverty. As such, it increased understanding of the pathways by which poverty influences children's development and expanded the focal targets of change to include concrete conditions, social circumstances, and other features of the ecology. It also nurtured an appreciation of the heterogeneity of the poverty population and, hence, a tendency toward developing programs for distinct subgroups within the poverty population. In Schorr's (1989) qualitative evaluation of a broad cross-section of programs for poor children and families, whose services spanned the gamut from health, social services, and family support to education, programs judged to be most effective in increasing positive outcomes for poor children were all predicated on an ecological model. Specifically, they typically offered a broad spectrum of coherent, easy-to-use services (rec-

ognizing that social and emotional support and help with concrete problems such as food and housing are often prerequisites to a family's ability to make use of other interventions such as parenting education); provided help to parents as adults so they could make good use of services for their children; and allowed staff members to exercise discretion, redefine their roles, and cross traditional professional and bureaucratic boundaries to respond to clients' needs. Given these characteristics, Schorr's conclusion that many highly successful interventions are "unstandardized and idiosyncratic" (p. 268) is not surprising.

In the sections that follow, we focus attention on the effects of two categories of ecologically oriented interventions that proliferated during the 1980s and 1990s: home visitation programs and two-generation programs. They are but a small sampling of a variety of ecologically oriented programs for poor children and families, but are of special interest because of their comparatively strong research designs and because several have been subject to intensive evaluation.

Home Visitation Programs. As noted previously, home visitation programs date back at least to the second half of the nineteenth century, when well-to-do women associated with private relief agencies and charity organizations made home visits to poor families "to provide a mixture of support, scrutiny, and advice" (Halpern, 1988, p. 285). This helping strategy was revitalized during the late 1970s and 1980s, when several home visitation programs were erected to promote positive functioning in poor mothers and children and prevent several problems associated with poverty. In 1989, the federal government responded to the growing popularity of these programs by authorizing funding of home visitation for pregnant women and infants, by which time a number of state governments had begun supporting maternal and child home visitation programs with Medicaid dollars (Olds & Kitzman, 1990). Home visitation programs are of particular interest because they permit within- and across-study comparisons of the relative effectiveness of programs that are more or less ecological in their approach.

Effects on Maternal Teaching and Children's Cognitive Development. Several studies exist of randomized trials with poor families that aimed to promote cognitively stimulating mother-child interaction and, in turn, children's cognitive development either through parent education alone (e.g., Scarr & McCartney,

1988) or a combination of parent education and social support (Barnard, Magyary, Sumner, & Booth, 1988; Olds, Henderson, Chamberlin, & Tatelbaum, 1986a). Both types of interventions have produced positive effects on maternal parenting and teaching behaviors and on children's cognitive functioning. In general, though, programs that address the broader ecology of the family by providing parent education as well as social support (e.g., help locating needed community resources; establishing a therapeutic alliance between mother and nurse home visitor) produce stronger and more enduring effects on mothers' parenting and teaching behavior and children's cognitive functioning than programs that provide parent education only, or parent education combined with minimal social support (e.g., referrals without establishment of a therapeutic alliance; Olds & Kitzman, 1993; Schorr, 1989). Note that in this schema, provision of parenting education is the distinguishing feature of the ecological approach, with social support provided in both categories of programs. Across-program comparisons also suggest that home visitation programs that target poor families at particularly high risk of parenting problems (e.g., unmarried adolescent mothers living alone with child; drug-addicted mothers) are generally more effective than those focusing on heterogeneous groups of poor children and families (for a more detailed review of efficacy studies of these programs, see Olds & Kitzman, 1990, 1993).

Sweet and Applebaum's (2004) recent meta-analysis of the efficacy of 60 home visiting programs for families with young children points to the advantages to children of programs that target specific populations. Although their analysis is not constrained to the poverty population, 55% of the programs represented in their meta-analysis targeted low-income families. Sweet and Applebaum found that programs that targeted specific populations (e.g., families with a low birthweight child, families with low income, and teenage mothers) had stronger effects on children's cognitive functioning than programs in which families were universally enrolled. Effects on children's cognition outcomes were also larger when families were visited by professionals (as compared to families visited by nonprofessionals), were visited more frequently, and had more hours of visits. However, findings for child outcomes did not necessarily mirror findings for parenting behavior. For example, programs that targeted specific populations had stronger effects on children's

cognitive functioning than programs in which families were universally enrolled, but for parenting behavior, the effect was reversed. That is, effect sizes for parenting behavior were significantly larger when families were universally enrolled than when families were targeted in some way. Moreover, programs that targeted low-income families were less successful in enhancing parenting behavior than programs not targeting low-income families.

Sweet and Applebaum's (2004) meta-analysis also reaffirms the challenge of fostering maternal and child functioning in the same program. Programs in which maternal life enhancement was a primary goal produced larger effects on parenting behavior (i.e., programs in which maternal social support and maternal self-help were primary objectives) but smaller effects on children's cognitive functioning (i.e., programs in which maternal self-sufficiency and maternal self-help were primary objectives) than programs in which these goals were not primary. This finding echoes earlier syntheses of extant research suggesting that interventions that rely solely on parent-mediated routes to increase children's cognitive competencies produce less positive and enduring effects than interventions that provide direct learning experiences to children (C. Ramey et al., 1995; Wasik et al., 1990).

Effects on Child Maltreatment.   The public institution charged with protecting the welfare of dependent, neglected, and abused children is the public child welfare system. In response to criticism that child welfare agencies devote insufficient effort to placement prevention and provide care of questionable quality to children who have been removed from their own home, the Adoption Assistance and Child Welfare Act was passed in 1980. It mandated that a certain portion of funding of child welfare agencies must be allocated to services intended to reduce the need for placement of children in foster care, reunify families, and find adoptive families for those children who cannot return home. Family-centered, home-based service programs are among the options available to meet these requirements. These programs focus on the family system, not just the mother, and its social and physical context as the target for change. They typically provide counseling and concrete services such as homemakers and day care. Unfortunately, very few well-designed studies exist of the effectiveness of this approach versus more traditional approaches in preventing child placement. Existing evaluations tend to be seriously flawed (e.g., lack of comparison or control groups, inadequate descriptions of service activities; H. Frankel, 1988).

One of the higher-quality studies of the effectiveness of different approaches to prevention of child abuse and placement used a design reminiscent of the one employed by Olds et al. (1986a) in their study of intervention effects on preterm delivery and low birthweight. D. A. Wolfe, Edwards, Manion, and Koverola (1988) assessed the relative effects of support services alone versus parent education combined with support services on the parenting behavior of mothers who were under supervision from a child protective service agency because public health nurses suspected that a child living in the home was at high risk of maltreatment. In addition to receiving standard agency services (e.g., informal discussion of topics related to health and family, social activities, periodic home visits from caseworkers), mothers in the parent education intervention received didactic instruction and exposure to modeling and rehearsal procedures to increase positive child management skills (e.g., rewarding compliance, using more praise and less criticism, giving concise demands). Results indicated that, in comparison to mothers who received only standard agency services, mothers in the parent education intervention had more positive attitudes and feelings about parenting and reported less depressive symptomatology, though the two groups did not differ on their child-rearing methods as assessed by home observation. One year following treatment, caseworkers rated mothers in the parent intervention group as managing their children significantly better and at lower risk for maltreating the child than mothers in the comparison group.

These findings are in general accord with those from a randomized trial of nurse home visitation of primiparas mothers who were either teenagers, unmarried, or of low SES (Olds, Henderson, Chamberlin, & Tatelbaum, 1986b). One group received home visits once every 2 weeks during pregnancy. For a second group, home visits continued with decreasing frequency until the child was 2 years of age. During these visits, nurses provided mothers with information about infants' development and socioemotional and cognitive needs (e.g., crying behavior and its meaning; infant's need for progressively more complex motor, social, and intellectual experiences), encouraged involvement of relatives and friends in child care and support of the mother, and connected families with community health and human ser-

vice agencies. Among poor, unmarried teenage mothers, those who were visited by a nurse had fewer instances of verified child abuse and neglect during the first 2 years of the child's life, reported less conflict with and scolding of their 6-month-old infants, and were observed in their home to restrict and punish their children (10- and 22-month-olds) less frequently and to provide more appropriate play materials, compared to those who received either no services or only free transportation to medical offices for prenatal and well-child care. In addition, during the 2nd year of life, regardless of the family's risk status, babies of nurse-visited women were seen in the emergency room less frequently and were seen by physicians less frequently for accidents and poisoning. However, differences in rates of maltreatment did not persist during the 2-year period after the program ended.

Notwithstanding the short-term positive findings from these two studies, randomized trials of programs designed to prevent child maltreatment generally do not demonstrate overall decreases in maltreatment, as evidenced by state child protective services records (Olds & Kitzman, 1990, 1993). Some have found differences that are suggestive of a reduction in maltreatment, such as lower rates of severe diaper rash (Hardy & Streett, 1989) or decreased use of medical services associated with child abuse and neglect (e.g., hospitalizations for serious injury; J. Gray, Cutler, Dean, & Kempe, 1979; Hardy & Streett, 1989). In their detailed review of these randomized trials, Olds and Kitzman (1993) detected no clear pattern in findings as a function of program characteristics (e.g., comprehensiveness, intensity), but noted that two of the programs that produced positive effects in a subsample of women or on at least some variables associated with abuse and neglect employed especially well-trained home visitors who remained through the course of the study. Sweet and Applebaum's (2004) meta-analysis yields additional insights about this general issue. They found that programs were more effective in preventing or reducing the incidence of child abuse if prevention of child abuse was a primary objective of the program, if the home visitors were paraprofessionals rather than professionals, and if low-income families as well as families at risk of child abuse or neglect were targeted. Surprisingly, programs that had maternal social support as a primary goal were less effective in lowering the potential for child abuse than programs not listing this as a primary goal.

Effects on Preterm Delivery and Low Birthweight.
During the 1980s, rapid growth occurred in home visiting programs to prevent preterm delivery and low birthweight and to improve the health and development of preterm or low birthweight infants and their parents. Most of these programs focused on poor, unmarried adolescents and young adult women, and many combined health education, parent education, and various forms of instrumental and emotional support (e.g., Olds et al., 1986a).

The immediate precipitant of these programs was a burgeoning body of research suggesting that poverty adversely affects children's cognitive development partly by impairing their physical health status at birth and restricting their ability to overcome perinatal complications. Numerous studies had found that poor children were overrepresented in premature samples due partly to substandard or total lack of prenatal care and inadequate nutrition. Evidence also existed that poor children were more likely to be exposed prenatally to illegal drugs as well as to legal drugs such as nicotine and alcohol and that such exposure increased perinatal complications such as prematurity, low birthweight, small head circumference, and severe respiratory problems. These complications were found to be risk factors for delayed cognitive development, especially in poor children. In particular, research indicated that poor children were less able than affluent children to overcome the problems created by perinatal complications, apparently because they grow up in circumstances marked by fewer social, educational, and material resources (Escalona, 1984; Werner & Smith, 1977).

Olds and Kitzman (1990) contrasted the effects of four home visiting prenatal programs (all randomized trials) on birthweight and length of gestation, three of which adopted a narrow "social support" model, in contrast to an "ecological" approach followed in the fourth program. The three programs exemplifying a social support model assumed that high rates of preterm delivery and low birthweight among poor women are caused by high rates of psychosocial stress in the absence of social support. To test this assumption, home visitors in the three programs provided various kinds of social support (e.g., serving as a confidant; providing concrete assistance such as help with transportation and child care; facilitating women's use of community services; helping women with their relationships with family members and friends; involving family members and friends in child care and support of the mother), but actively avoided teaching about health-related behaviors or provided such information only on request. In contrast, a fourth program followed a broader "ecological" model, integrating social support with education about health-related behaviors such as smoking, alcohol consumption, nonprescription drug use, and managing the complications of pregnancy. Note that in this across-study comparison, health education, rather than social support, is the distinguishing feature of the approach labeled ecological, as provision of social support to improve the broader context of women's pregnancy is a common denominator of the programs.

Only the ecological program had a discernible positive effect on birthweight and length of gestation, and the effect was concentrated among women who smoked or who were very young (less than 17 years) at the time of program entry (Olds et al., 1986a). This pattern of findings suggests that programs are more likely to be effective if they are more comprehensive in their approach and target women with specific risks for preterm delivery or low birthweight (e.g., smoking, alcohol, illicit drug use). However, more corroborating evidence is needed given that the subsample in which effects were identified in the Olds et al. study was quite small and that no similar effects were found in a subsequent evaluation of a prenatal home visiting program that also combined social support with education (Villar et al., 1992). Moreover, Olds et al.'s prenatal home visitation program had no enduring effects on maternal and child functioning (e.g., cognitive performance), despite nurses' attempts to establish a close working relationship with families and their success in improving women's health-related behaviors, the psychosocial conditions of pregnancy, and the health status of babies born to smokers and young adolescents.

Overall, home visiting prenatal programs of varying levels of comprehensiveness generally have not produced significant reductions in preterm delivery or low birthweight or reliable improvement in utilization of routine prenatal services. Even if successful in improving pregnancy outcomes, prenatal home visitation does not appear sufficient to promote long-term maternal and child functioning (Olds & Kitzman, 1993). This pattern of negative findings may be due to insufficient intensity or poor program implementation, but is more likely attributable to failure of most of these programs to concentrate directly on elimination of known behavioral antecedents of poor pregnancy outcomes (e.g., smoking; for a fuller discussion of these issues and a detailed review of the effects of prenatal home visiting programs, see Olds & Kitzman, 1990, 1993).

Two-Generation Programs. The most recent genre of antipoverty programs, labeled "two-generation" programs, is distinguished by a combination of services for children and a more omnibus parent component that provides parenting education and social support, but gives greater emphasis than most of its predecessors to adult education, literacy training, and other job skills training intended to help parents become economically sufficient. Ancillary services such as transportation, meals, and child care are typically provided so that parents can participate in these activities. The child-focused component of these programs usually includes educational day care or preschool education, although the intensity of child-focused services of this category of programs varies tremendously (S. Smith, 1995).

Two-generation programs, most of which began in the early 1990s, owe their emergence partly to growing recognition that early childhood education programs and other unigeneration programs are not sufficiently broad to address the multidimensional aspects of family poverty (St. Pierre et al., 1995). Among the specific arguments that have laid the groundwork for more omnibus programs are that (a) parenting programs may improve parenting skills, but children cannot wait to accrue the benefits of such programs because some critical aspects of their development occur on their own timetable; (b) early childhood education programs can confer enhanced cognitive and socioemotional skills, but high-quality parenting can increase the prospects that these skills will translate into school success; and (c) neither child-focused nor parent-focused programs alone provide interventions sufficiently expansive to address the multiplicity of problems and needs that poor families face (e.g., unemployment, limited literacy, and job skills) and to significantly improve the economic status of poor families (Larner, Halpern, & Harkavy, 1992; St. Pierre et al., 1995). These arguments, taken together, have been sufficiently cogent to forge this new category of interventions into the ranks of an already complex array of programs designed to serve poor children and families (S. Smith, 1995; St. Pierre et al., 1995).

Several two-generation programs were part of Head Start, among them the Comprehensive Child Development Program (CCDP) and the Head Start Family Service Centers (FSCs; S. Smith & Zaslow, 1995). One of the earliest of these programs, the Child and Family Resource Program, described previously, operated from 1973 to 1983 as a Head Start demonstration project. These programs are in keeping with Head Start's longstanding tradition of implementing demonstration projects both within and outside its basic core program to ascertain more effective ways of serving poor children and families (Zigler & Styfco, 1994a). Well-known two-generation program models that are not part of Head Start include Even Start Family Literacy Program (St. Pierre & Swartz, 1995), Avance Parent-Child Education Program (Walker, Rodriguez, Johnson, & Cortez, 1995), and New Chance (Bos, Polit, & Quint, 1997).

A description of CCDP is presented here to exemplify the approach that characterizes most two-generation programs. Initiated in 1990, CCDP was a national demonstration program that aimed to enhance parents' progress toward economic self-sufficiency by increasing the scope, duration, and intensity of services, while maintaining the services to children provided by Head Start's basic program. It operated in both rural and urban areas and provided integrated, comprehensive, and continuous support services to more than 4,440 low-income families with a newborn child for up to 5 years. On average, families were enrolled in CCDP for 3.3 years. Parents and other adult members of the family received prenatal care, parenting education, health care, adult education, job training, and other supports as needed, such as treatment for mental health problems and substance abuse. Adult literacy education, employment counseling, and job training and placement were typically provided through linkages and referrals to community colleges and other local educational institutions. Job linkages were also made with employers and agencies. CCDP was not conceived as a home visiting program, but the program used home visits as the primary means of delivering early child education and case management (St. Pierre et al., 1999). CCDP provided relatively low-intensive services to children from birth through age 3, using biweekly home visits that usually lasted about 30 minutes. These home visits focused on educating parents in infant and child development and parenting skills, rather than working directly with children. A parent who was present for every session, then, received a maximum of

13 hours of parenting education in a year. By 4 or 5 years of age, at least half of the children in CCDP had enrolled in center-based early childhood education (Head Start); the remainder continued to receive early childhood education by means of parenting education (St. Pierre et al., 1999).

In addition to a stronger focus on adult services, several features of CCDP were intended to improve on Head Start's capacity to deliver two-generation services. These included (a) broader eligibility requirements (e.g., a family could remain in the program even if its income rose above the poverty threshold at any time during the program's 5-year period); (b) provision of services to all members of a participating family, broadly defined to include any children of the primary caregiver under age 18 in the household and any family member residing in the household having major responsibility for the care of the focal child; (c) provision of services to a parent of the focal child who resided outside the household; and (d) expanded and stronger provisions for ensuring that families could gain access to needed services. The impact evaluation was conducted in 21 of the original 24 CCDP project sites (Parker et al., 1995; St. Pierre et al., 1999).

All six of the two-generation programs cited here have been evaluated via randomized trials (St. Pierre et al., 1995; St. Pierre, Layzer, & Barnes, 1996). In general, the findings of these evaluations have been disappointing.

Effects on Children. Efficacy studies indicate that two-generation programs have only small or no effects on children's cognitive development, verbal skills, and school readiness. For example, 5 years after the program began, CCDP had no meaningful impact on children's cognitive or socioemotional functioning or physical health, or on birth outcomes for children born subsequent to the focus children. It also had no important differential effects on various subgroups of participants (e.g., children of teenage mothers versus older mothers; children of mothers who entered CCDP with high school diplomas versus children of mothers who entered without high school diplomas; St. Pierre et al., 1999). Neither Avance nor CFRP had an effect on Bayley scores. Even Start produced a significant gain in children's school readiness skills 9 months after entry to the program, but this difference dissipated once children in the control group began school (St. Pierre et al., 1996). At follow-up, no effects were found for cognitive functioning, social skills, school progress (e.g., percentage of children in special education), or parent reports of child literacy (Ricciuti, St. Pierre, Lee, Parsad, & Rimdzius, 2004). Similarly, at the 3.5-year follow-up, New Chance had no effect on children's cognitive functioning or school readiness and, in fact, increased children's behavioral problems and reduced positive behavior, as reported by the mothers. Negative impacts on children's socioemotional functioning were concentrated among women who were at high risk of clinical depression at random assignment (Bos et al., 1997).

Effects on Mothers. Two-generation programs have stronger effects on parents than on children, although even when effects are found, they are quite modest. Several have produced positive short-term effects on parenting attitudes and behavior. For example, at the end of the 1st year of participation in the Avance program, program mothers compared to control group mothers had a stronger belief in their ability to determine the nature of their children's educational experiences, provided their children a more educationally stimulating home environment, and interacted in a more positive and stimulating manner with their children during videotaped play sessions (e.g., affect, vocalization, contingent praise, initiation of social interaction with child, time spent teaching child; Walker et al., 1995). Other significant changes in parents' attitudes and behavior resulting from participation in these programs include less authoritarian child-rearing attitudes, more emotional support and nurturance of the child (CCDP, CFRP, New Chance), higher expectations for the child's success, increased time spent with the child (CCDP), and increased presence of reading materials in the home (Even Start; St. Pierre et al., 1995, 1996). However, most of these effects did not persist. For example, 5 years after it began, CCDP had no statistically significant impact on mothers' parenting attitudes and beliefs, the quality of parent-child interaction, or the child's home learning environment (St. Pierre et al., 1999). Even Start had no effects on parent reports of parent-child reading, literacy resources in the home, or parent participation in the child's school (Ricciuti et al., 2004). Likewise, at the 3.5-year follow-up, New Chance had no effects on children's home learning environment or mothers' use of harsh discipline, although positive effects in the home environment persisted among mothers who were not at risk of clinical depression at baseline

(Bos et al., 1997). Evaluations generally find relatively high levels of depressive symptomatology in both program and control group mothers, but no evidence that programs are effective in reducing depressive symptoms or increasing mothers' self-esteem or use of social supports (Bos et al., 1997; St. Pierre et al., 1995, 1999; Walker et al., 1995).

Of particular significance to any assessment of two-generation programs is whether programs affect parents' educational attainment, employment status, household income, and use of welfare benefits. Effects appear modest at best and tend to be restricted to educational attainment. Evaluations of Even Start, New Chance, and Avance indicated that program mothers, compared to control group mothers, were significantly more likely to attain a GED certificate, but this educational advancement was not accompanied by positive effects on standardized tests of adult literacy (Bos et al., 1997; Ricciuti et al., 2004; St. Pierre et al., 1995, 1996). New Chance had no effects on women's fertility, fertility-related behavior, contraceptive use, or physical health status (Bos et al., 1997). None of the studies that measured annual household income (or average hourly wage among those employed) found positive effects (Even Start, New Chance, CCDP, CFRP, FSC), and only CFRP increased rates of employment. In general, two-generation programs did not affect use of federal benefits such as AFDC and food stamps, or actually increased participants' use of such benefits by heightening awareness of their availability or by rendering more families eligible for them by virtue of increased participation in educational classes (e.g., CCDP, CFRP, New Chance; Bos et al., 1997; St. Pierre et al., 1995, 1996; Swartz et al., 1995).

The primary reasons for the disappointing pattern of findings from two-generation studies are thought to be insufficient intensity of services to both mothers and children and/or incorrect assumptions about the most appropriate intervention strategies (e.g., assumption that what poor families need most is a case manager to help guide and negotiate as they navigate services in the community; assumption that changing parent behavior is an effective means to promote children's development), rather than poor implementation (Bos et al., 1997; St. Pierre et al., 1999). It is also possible that these studies did not follow mothers long enough to capture longer-term impacts on maternal employment, a factor that may explain why a more favorable picture of employ-

ment effects emerged from evaluations of pre-1990 interventions that provided a combination of services to children and their parents (Benasich, Brooks-Gunn, & Clewell, 1992).

WELFARE AND EMPLOYMENT TRANSITIONS, WELFARE REFORM POLICY, AND THE WELL-BEING OF POOR CHILDREN

Evelia, a Puerto Rican single mother of four, lived in a low-income neighborhood in Milwaukee, Wisconsin and had an income at or below 150% of the poverty line. In the spring of 1998, Evelia worked the second shift (3–11 P.M.) as a casual employee of the U.S. postal service. During that time she either kept her 3-year-old daughter at home with her three older children (the oldest was 13 at that time) or with nearby relatives while she worked in the evening, checking in on them time-to-time by telephone. She did have some concerns leaving her youngest with her other children and she did occasionally consider looking for a child care center or in-home care provider at night for her daughter to ensure adult supervision. But she never looked for one. Evelia did not believe her children would be safe in a formal care center and she also believed that it would be difficult to find a center that would be open as late as she needed it to be.

Things changed in January 1999 when Evelia started working the day shift (7 A.M.–4 P.M.). Evelia's nearby family members were either unreliable or unavailable during the day at the time. Without available family support, she had no alternative but to place her daughter in a day care center. She called the local agency in charge of dispensing Wisconsin Shares for her area to find out what she needed to have in order to receive subsidized care. She was informed that she simply needed to come into the office and fill out a form. However, when Evelia arrived at the office she discovered that she needed a number of additional pieces of information regarding her employment, income, and so on, before she could sign up for the program. Evelia would end up spending an entire day, losing an entire day's wages, running around so that she could enroll her daughter in the subsidy program. She enrolled her daughter in a day care center, but Evelia continued to feel ambivalent. She worried that her daughter might get sick or get lice from other children. Sometimes she felt that her daughter might be healthier in the care of trusted relatives. After a few months of this arrangement, however, Evelia was thrilled with her child's experiences in the day care center. Evelia believed her daughter had really learned a great deal in the day care center in just a short amount of time—lessons she could never have provided at home. Evelia even remarked that her daughter would be the smartest of all her children as a result of having been placed in a formal care setting. (Lowe & Weisner, 2004, p. 144)

Questions about how best to reduce child poverty and enhance the well-being of poor children were not central in congressional debates that culminated in the 1996 federal welfare reform law (PRWORA). Rather, these debates centered on promoting devolution from the federal to the state level, reducing government spending, promoting parental responsibility, requiring work and imposing time limits on welfare receipt, and strategies for reducing out-of-wedlock births (Greenberg et al., 2002). The law that emerged from these debates voided the long-standing principle of federal entitlement to assistance for poor children and adults alike (i.e., AFDC). More specifically, PRWORA (a) replaced AFDC and several related programs with state block grants known as Temporary Assistance for Needy Families (TANF); (b) mandated that recipients of public assistance be working within 2 years of the time they start to receive assistance; (c) lowered to 12 months the age-of-child criterion for exempting parents' work requirements (in prior provisions, mothers of children under 3 years old were exempt from mandatory work-related activities); (d) imposed a 5-year lifetime limit on assistance in the form of cash aid, work slots, and noncash aid such as vouchers to poor children and families, regardless of whether parents can find employment; and (e) required states to have a certain proportion of their welfare caseloads meet work requirements (Greenberg et al., 2002). The law granted states numerous options and discretionary powers, for example, the option to require work of parents with children under 12 months of age, to impose caps so that payments do not increase if recipients have additional children, and to require recipients of public assistance to be working sooner than 2 years from the time they start to receive assistance (Morris et al., 2001; Zaslow, McGroder, & Moore, 2000).

PRWORA's core goals are to reduce long-term welfare dependency, increase employment-based self-support, encourage marriage, and discourage out-of-wedlock childbearing, not directly enhance the well-being of poor children. Nonetheless, advocates of welfare reform foresaw many benefits redounding to children indirectly through increased parental employment (i.e., role models of disciplined work behavior,

more structured daily routines, increases in parents' self-esteem and sense of control) and higher family income—presumed consequences of welfare reform. Opponents, however, predicted a host of detrimental consequences for child well-being, among them, increases in the rate and depth of childhood poverty because of loss of welfare benefits without compensating increases in earnings, placements in low-quality child care, increases in unsupervised time, and decreases in responsive parenting brought on by excessive demands and attendant emotional distress (Chase-Lansdale et al., 2003; Morris et al., 2001). Evelia's case provides a glimpse of the complicated set of factors that may influence how children fare under welfare reform, including the mother's employment circumstances (e.g., work schedule), type and quality of child care, changes and instability in these factors, and the compatibility of employment circumstances and child care arrangements with the mother's values and preferences.

Although sweeping in its changes, PRWORA was the denouement of a more gradual process begun during the 1960s to push welfare recipients to higher levels of employment-based self-support (Morris et al., 2001). Congress passed a law in 1967 requiring AFDC recipients with no preschool children to register for activities, but states did not make serious efforts to enforce work requirements until the early 1980s. The Family Support Act of 1988 sought to increase economic self-sufficiency among recipients of AFDC by mandating participation in educational and employment training programs and strengthening enforcement of existing child support provisions. States' efforts to promote employment and reduce welfare gained full momentum during the mid- to late 1980s, and by the early 1990s, a large number of states had been granted waivers of AFDC rules to experiment with changes in welfare provisions (Morris et al., 2001). States' receipt of waivers from the federal government to experiment with changes in welfare provisions was conditional on use of a random assignment design and evaluation of the program (Gennetian & Morris, 2003). States mixed and matched several kinds of welfare and employment policies, and the resulting diversity of programs provided an opportunity to assess the comparative effects of different program features on child well-being. Because these experimental programs anticipated key elements of the federal law, they offer important lessons about the potential effects on children of welfare reform policies legislated after PRWORA (Morris et al., 2003). In the following, we discuss the findings from some of the evaluations that the Manpower Demonstration Research Corporation (MDRC) conducted under these waivers. It is too soon to know if and how the findings from these programs will influence welfare policies.

Experimental Tests of Welfare and Employment Policies: Two Synthesis Projects

The core dependent variables in the evaluations of these programs were parents' economic outcomes, but some states expanded the focus to include child well-being on the grounds that programs might affect children indirectly as a consequence of their potential to alter important aspects of children's lives. In some sense, this decision harkened back to the historical roots of welfare programs, which were to protect the well-being of children growing up in poor, especially single-parent households (Zaslow et al., 2000). At the time these programs were designed (early to mid-1990s), extant research provided only a limited basis for making predictions about how and through what pathways these programs might affect children. Hence, rather than test specific predictions, most studies with a child-focused component set out to explore in a general sense whether the programs had positive, negative, or no effects on children or whether the program affected only children in certain subgroups (Zaslow et al., 2000). However, some studies (e.g., those testing effects of income supplements) were guided by a well-articulated conceptual framework, accompanied by hypotheses about effects as well as mediators of those effects (e.g., Bos et al., 1999).

Two recent syntheses of the findings of these experiments have significantly advanced our understanding of the potential implications of different welfare policies for children's well-being. These projects are products of the Next Generation Project, a collaboration among researchers at MDRC and several universities devoted to an examination of the effects of welfare, antipoverty, and employment policies on children and families. In this section, we discuss the findings from these two synthesis projects, as well as findings published subsequent to the completion of the synthesis projects about the effects of certain programs that were included in the synthesis. To illustrate some of the processes through which various welfare and employment policies influenced family life and child well-being, we present selected case studies from ethnographies that

were carried out in conjunction with some of these individual projects (e.g., New Hope).

Preschoolers and Elementary School-Age Children

In the first syntheses, Morris et al. (2001) examined the findings from five large-scale studies that together assessed the effects on preschoolers and elementary school-age children of 11 different employment-based welfare and antipoverty programs aimed primarily at single-parent families. They classified these programs on the basis of three features: earnings supplements, mandatory employment services, and time limits on welfare receipt. Four of the programs—Minnesota Family Investment Program (MFIP), the Self-Sufficiency Project (SSP), the New Hope Program, and Florida's Family Transition Program (FTP)—offered *earnings supplements* to compensate for some of the shortcomings of the labor market and to make work more financially rewarding, either by providing working families cash benefits or by increasing the earnings disregard, that is, the amount of earnings that were not counted as income in calculating the amount of a family's welfare benefit (Bos et al., 1999; Gennetian & Morris, 2003; Huston et al., 2001, in press; Morris et al., 2003; Morris & Michalopoulos, 2003). Earnings disregards allowed welfare recipient to keep more of their welfare dollars as their earnings increased, whereas under AFDC, welfare recipients experienced sharp reductions in welfare dollars as their earnings rose. For example, in MFIP, working families continued to receive supplemental benefits until their income reached approximately 140% of the poverty level (Gennetian & Morris, 2003).

These programs differed in a number of respects, however. Some made earnings supplements contingent on full-time employment (at least 30 hours/week; SSP, New Hope, Full MFIP), whereas others provided earnings supplements for any amount of work (MFIP Incentives Only). MFIP Incentives Only was created as a contrast to Full MFIP to help disentangle the effects of MFIP's two components: financial incentives and mandatory employment and training services. Single-parent families in MFIP Incentives Only received MFIP benefits and earnings disregards for part-time as well as full-time work but were not subject to mandatory employment and training services. Some programs provided supplements within the welfare system by raising the earnings disregard, whereas others did so outside of the welfare system (SSP, New Hope). Some programs included additional components, but provision of supplements was the sole feature that the four programs in this category shared. In the New Hope Program, for example, parents who worked full time were eligible for wage supplements sufficient to raise family income above the poverty threshold as well as subsidies for child care and health insurance. In addition, project representatives provided advice and services to participants, and community service jobs were available to people who could not find employment in the unsubsidized labor market (Bos et al., 1999).

Six of the programs provided *mandatory employment services* (e.g., education, training, or immediate job search) in which parents were required to participate in order to receive cash welfare benefits (Atlanta Job Search First, Atlanta Education First, Grand Rapids Job Search First, Grand Rapids Education First, Riverside Job Search First, Riverside Education First, all of which were part of the National Evaluation of Welfare-to-Work Strategies). These programs were generally successful in increasing employment rates but did not provide earnings supplements or institute time limits on family's eligibility for welfare benefits. Each of the three sites (Atlanta, Grand Rapids, Riverside) operated both a program emphasizing job search as a first activity (labor force attachment approach) and a program emphasizing basic education as a first activity (human capital development approach). In the former program, participants usually attended a "job club" that lasted 1 to 3 weeks, and those who were unsuccessful in their job search were then enrolled in short-term adult basic education, vocational training, or work experience. Education First programs initially placed participants in education and training programs to increase knowledge and skills before they attempted to transition into employment. They are founded on the view that welfare recipients should raise their skill levels before searching for work so they can obtain jobs with higher wages and more fringe benefits (D. Bloom & Michalopoulos, 2001; Zaslow et al., 2000).

One of the programs (FTP) put *time limits* on families' eligibility for welfare benefits. Receipt of cash assistance was limited to 24 or 36 months (depending on parents' level of disadvantage) in any 60-month period. Time limits were combined with mandatory employment services and a small earnings supplement in the form of an enhanced earnings disregard (Morris et al., 2003).

In all of these studies, parents were randomly assigned to either a program group, which had access to the new services and benefits and was subject to the new rules, or a control group, which received welfare benefits and were subject to rules governing welfare receipt that existed in the locale where the study was conducted. In most instances, control group members were eligible for cash assistance through AFDC. Children were assessed 2 to 4 years after random assignment and ranged in age from approximately 5 to 12 years at the time of assessment. For the synthesis of child effects, Morris et al. (2001) focused on a subset of measures that were similar across studies; fortunately, these measures represented a wide range of outcomes for children that might be affected by welfare policies. Too few of the studies of these experimental programs assess children under age 3 for conclusions to be drawn about this age group.

Pattern of Effects. Morris et al.'s (2001) synthesis identified a clear-cut pattern of effects. Programs that included earnings supplements increased both parental employment and income. Moreover, these programs had modest, positive effects on a range of behaviors, with effect sizes averaging about .15. All of these programs had positive effects on children's school achievement, and some also reduced behavior problems, increased positive social behavior, and/or improved children's overall health. For example, at 24 months post-random assignment, the New Hope Program had strong positive effects on boys' academic achievement, classroom behavior skills, positive social behavior (e.g., compliance, social competence, sensitivity), and problem behaviors, as reported by teachers (who were given no information about children's participation in New Hope or other interventions), and on boys' own expectations for advanced education and occupational aspirations (though there were not corresponding program effects for girls; Huston et al., 2001).

Subsequent to Morris et al.'s (2001) synthesis, findings regarding the longer-term impact of New Hope became available. A follow-up conducted 60 months after random assignment, when the children were 6 to 16 years old, indicated that New Hope's effects on boys' school achievement, motivation, and social behavior persisted. In comparison to impacts measured 2 years after program onset, effects on school achievement were robust, but effects on social behavior were reduced (Huston et al., in press). The effects of New Hope on child outcomes are particularly persuasive because they appeared on measures obtained from multiple sources.

Measures obtained from parents, who were the most likely to be affected by their knowledge of the New Hope treatment and the evaluation design, showed fewer treatment differences than did measures completed by teachers and children.

The one program included in Morris et al.'s (2001) synthesis that combined mandatory employment services and earning supplements (Full MFIP) increased full-time employment among parents but tended to have no impact on children's outcomes beyond those positive effects (i.e., higher academic performance, higher engagement in school, increases in positive interactions with peers, fewer behavioral problems) found when the program was implemented with earnings supplements alone (i.e., MFIP Incentives Only). It is notable, however, that adding mandatory employment services to MFIP (as compared to MFIP Incentives Only) significantly reduced children's positive behavior, especially their social competence and autonomy (Gennetian & Miller, 2002; Gennetian & Morris, 2003). Overall, programs with mandatory employment services successfully increased parental employment rates and reduced welfare receipt, but generally left family income unchanged because participants lost welfare benefits as their earnings increased. These programs had few effects on children, and the effects found were mixed in direction. The pattern of effects among these programs appeared to be more closely linked to particular sites than to program characteristics (Morris et al., 2001; Zaslow et al., 2000).

The program with time limits produced an increase in parental employment and a modest increase in income but had no consistent pattern of effect on child outcomes. Because this program was combined with mandatory employment services and a small earnings supplement, it is impossible to sort out the impact of time limits (Morris et al., 2001). A recent study of the impact of Connecticut's Job First program found that generous earnings disregards can both increase family income and improve children's outcomes, even when such disregards are combined with a short time limit (i.e., a cumulative total of 21 months of cash assistance receipt). Parents in the program group, compared to those in the control group, reported that their children had fewer internalizing and externalizing problem behaviors and more positive behaviors with peers, although there were no effects on parents' reports of children's performance and engagement in school or on

teacher reports of children's achievement and behavior in school (Gennetian & Morris, 2003).

Mediating Processes. All of the earnings supplement programs had in common one result, an increase in employment and income, but no one mechanism appeared to be responsible for the beneficial effects of these programs on children. Within the corpus of relevant studies, none of the outcomes considered to be possible mediators of effects (i.e., family relations, child care, parental well-being, parenting practices) was affected across all programs (Morris et al., 2001). Full MFIP and MFIP Incentives Only increased marriage among long-term welfare recipients, but SSP and New Hope had no effects on marriage rates (Bos et al., 1999; Gennetian & Miller, 2002; Morris & Michalopoulos, 2000).

Some programs increased the use of formal and stable child care and children's participation in afterschool activities (New Hope, SSP, Full MFIP), though others did not (MFIP Incentives Only; Gennetian & Miller, 2002; Huston et al., 2001; Morris et al., 2001; Morris & Michalopoulos, 2003). For example, at 24 months postrandom assignment, children ages 3 to 12 in the New Hope Program had spent almost twice as many months in center-based care (for preschool and school-age children) and more than twice as many months in school-based extended day care than had control group children. Moreover, among the 9- to 12-year-olds, program group children spent more time in adult-supervised, organized afterschool activities (e.g., lessons, sports, clubs, youth groups) than did control children (Huston et al., 2001). Although evaluations of welfare and employment programs do not provide information on the quality of child care children received, there is some evidence that center-based care, on average, is more likely than home-based care to enhance cognitive, academic, and social skills (Lamb, 1997). Likewise, extended day care for elementary school children has been linked to higher school achievement; this appears to be due partly to tutoring and help with homework received by children in this setting (Pierce, Hamm, & Vandell, 1999; Posner & Vandell, 1999). The case of Evelia, presented at the beginning of this section, provides an example of how center day care may foster children's academic readiness, even when such a child care arrangement was selected as a last resort and is at odds with the mother's original preference. Lynnette's case, presented next, illustrates how an adult-supervised, afterschool program can benefit children's school performance and make it easier for parents to maintain full-time employment. Although a control group parent in the New Hope study, Lynnette's situation could apply to many program group families as well.

> Lynnette, an African American woman, lives with Mark, her fiancé, and her fiancé's younger brother. Lynnette worries about who is caring for her 6-year-old son, Mark, while she is at work. She specifically focused on supplemental or after-school care as having helped her maintain full-time employment. Lynnette took college courses for 1 year and then dropped out. Her employment history has been sporadic and varied—she has worked at Kinko's and Burger King and as a nanny-babysitter. Recently, she was hired full time by the trucking firm for which she had been temping. She works in the accounting department. As a single mother returning to work after the birth of her son, she had no choice but to leave him in the care of someone else. Before Mark entered school, she relied on a network of close friends and family to care for him while she worked. She said that she never considered putting him in a child care program since, from her perspective, "it doesn't matter what you call it, it's still 'stranger care.'" Similarly, now that her son is in first grade she does not think that organizations that provide after-school programs are safe for children. "Boys and girls, that all there is—no supervision." However, last year, when Mark was in kindergarten his school instituted an after-school program, run by teachers whom Lynnette knew, in the school library. Consequently, Lynnette was comfortable leaving her son in what she considered a familiar and well-supervised program. The program focused on school skills as well as play activities. Her only complaint about the program was they did not offer the children a snack. Lynnette was disappointed that the program was terminated for lack of funding after a few months. Lynnette said that while Mark was attending the after-school program he mastered the alphabet and then learned to read, which put him ahead of most students in his class. Even a year later Mark says that he is doing well in school. As he had put it, "I am better than everyone else." His mother explained that he has scored higher on the school district reading tests than any other student in his class. (Bos et al., 1999, p. 201)

Parents' psychological functioning, child-rearing practices, and children's home environment were thought to be key pathways through which earnings supplement programs would impact children, but programs had few effects on these factors (Gennetian & Miller, 2002; Huston et al., 2001; Morris et al., 2001). Some programs improved parents' psychological functioning (e.g., fewer symptoms of depression, less parental stress, greater sense of agency; Gennetian & Miller, 2002; Huston et al., 2001), but others did not, and SSP actually increased depressive symptomatology in parents (Morris & Michalopoulos, 2003).

There are some patterns across these studies, though, suggesting that when mothers are able to choose the number of hours they work, financial incentives may improve children's behavior partly by enhancing their psychological functioning and parenting behavior (Chase-Lansdale & Pittman, 2002). Many of the mothers in MFIP Incentives Only took up the option to work part time rather than full time (D. Bloom & Michalopoulos, 2001). MFIP Incentives Only reduced mothers' depressive symptomatology and harsh parenting (though only the former effect was statistically significant), patterns not found in Full MFIP (which required at least 30 hours of employment per week). Furthermore, MFIP Incentives Only had more uniformly positive impacts on children than did the Full MFIP program (recall that Full MFIP had negative impacts on children's positive behavior, whereas MFIP Incentives Only did not). MFIP's incentives were primarily responsible for the program's beneficial effects on children (Gennetian & Morris, 2002, 2003).

Similarly, New Hope reduced hours of employment among parents in the program group, and this seemed to benefit mothers' psychological functioning, though not child well-being. New Hope required participants to work at least 30 hours per week, but this meant that program participants who were already working full time at random assignment could reduce their work hours. Indeed, this is precisely what many participants did. New Hope reduced hours worked by those employed full time at random assignment, mostly by reducing overtime and employment at second jobs (Bos et al., 1999). Two years after random assignment, New Hope had significantly increased self-reported parental warmth and parent-reported monitoring of the focal child's activities, but only among parents who were employed full time at random assignment. For the most part, the impact of New Hope on child functioning did not depend on parents' employment status at random assignment. Nonetheless, the pattern of findings from these two studies seem to warrant more examination of the conditions under which parenting behavior operates as a mediator of positive effects of earning supplement programs on child functioning.

Moderators of Effects.   There is some suggestion that children in higher-risk families may benefit more from some programs than children in lower-risk families, and conversely, that children in lower-risk families may experience more negative effects than children in higher-risk families. Morris et al.'s (2001) synthesis indicated that the positive effects of earnings supplements on parental employment and family income were stronger for long-term welfare recipients than short-term welfare recipients. Moreover, programs with earnings supplements had more pronounced effects on children of long-term welfare recipients, compared to children of parents with a shorter welfare history, boosting the functioning of the former children to a level near that of the control group children in families that had received welfare for less than 2 years. Essentially, programs with earnings supplements increased children's well-being and reduced problematic functioning to the level of the highest-functioning children in these low-income samples.

Conversely, analyses completed subsequent to the synthesis and focusing on two specific programs (FTP and MFIP) indicate that these programs had more negative effects on children from families with more economic and human capital (e.g., shorter duration of welfare receipt risk prior to program entry, higher educational attainment of parent) than children from more socioeconomically deprived families (e.g., lower school performance, increased likelihood of being suspended from school; Gennetian & Miller, 2002; Morris et al., 2001). In MFIP, for example, children of long-term welfare recipients experienced benefits of the program, whereas those in families that had recently applied to welfare were negatively affected by their parents' participation in the program (compared to the control children; Gennetian & Miller, 2002). Morris et al. speculate that this moderating effect may indicate that the child care that low-income parents were able to purchase failed to compensate for the loss of parental attention experienced by children from families with more economic and human capital.

Morris et al. (2001) found no clear pattern of gender differences across programs with earnings supplements. Some of the earnings supplement programs had positive effects (i.e., increased positive behavior, decreased behavior problems) primarily on boys (e.g., New Hope), whereas others had positive effects primarily for girls (e.g., MFIP). However, there is some suggestion from analyses completed subsequent to the synthesis that African American and Latino children may have benefited more than White children from welfare policies

that enhanced parents' human capital—a suggestion that echoes findings from prominent evaluations of Head Start and Early Head Start (ACF, 2002; ACF, 2005a; Lee et al., 1988). Analyzing data from four programs across two sites in the National Evaluation of Welfare to Work Strategies, Yoshikawa et al. (2003) found that programs emphasizing adult basic education prior to employment (human capital development approach) substantially increased math achievement among 8- to 10-year-old African American and Latino children, but had negative effects on their White counterparts. A similar though less robust pattern was found for reading achievement and in programs emphasizing immediate employment (labor force attachment approach). African American mothers' stronger value (compared to White mothers') for going to work over staying at home and Latino mothers' greater involvement in and valuation of educational activities (compared to White mothers') accounted for ethnic differences in the impact on children's math achievement, suggesting that families from different ethnic groups may experience welfare policies differently and in ways associated with initial differences in values and preferences.

It is also notable that New Hope significantly increased earnings among African American and Hispanic participants but had a negative (but not significant) impact on the earnings of White participants. These ethnic differences in earnings impact were unrelated to full-time employment status at random assignment, and additional analyses failed to produce a clear explanation for the differences. They did not translate into ethnic differences in the effects of New Hope on child functioning, but this may be due to small sample sizes. The assessment of earnings impact was based on a much larger sample (which included adults with and without children) than the one available for assessing child effects. The New Hope child sample included only 93 White children (12.5% of total), compared to 409 African American (55%) and 217 Hispanic (29%) children (Huston et al., 2001).

Adolescent Children

Whereas Morris et al.'s (2001) synthesis concerned effects of welfare and employment policies on preschool and elementary school-age children, Gennetian et al. (2002, 2004) conducted a companion synthesis focusing on adolescents. Using meta-analytic techniques, they integrated survey data collected from parents about their adolescent children in eight studies of 16 different welfare and employment programs, all of which used a random assignment design. Adolescents were roughly 10 to 16 years old at random assignment and 12 to 18 years old when the follow-up survey data on which the synthesis is based were collected. The length of the follow-up period varied, ranging from 24 months to 60 months after random assignment. Gennetian et al.'s synthesis is based on the five experimental studies examined in Morris et al.'s synthesis (the former focusing only on 12- to 18-year-olds and the latter focusing on 10- to 12-year-olds), plus three additional experimental studies (Los Angeles Jobs First Greater Avenues for Independence, Welfare Restructuring Project, Jobs First Evaluation). Like those included in Morris et al.'s analysis, the programs in Gennetian et al.'s synthesis represented various combinations of earning supplements, mandatory employment activities, and time limits on welfare receipt. Of the 16 programs tested in the eight experimental studies, 12 required parents to work or to participate in work-related activities in order to receive welfare; 8 offered earnings supplements to parents who worked (6 allowed parents to continue receiving welfare benefits along with the earning supplements); 2 put time limits on the length of time that families could receive welfare.

Pattern of Effects. The pattern of findings that emerged from Gennetian et al.'s (2004) synthesis is in sharp contrast to that found in Morris et al.'s (2001) synthesis. Specifically, parents in the programs generally reported *worse* school performance, a *higher* rate of grade retention, and *more* use of special education services among their adolescent children than did control group parents. Effects were especially pronounced for adolescents with younger siblings. Of the nine programs examined in the seven studies that measured adolescents' school performance, six lowered performance; for grade repetition, nine of the 15 impacts were unfavorable; and for receipt of special services for an emotional, physical, or mental condition, the impacts were unfavorable in 8 of 12 comparisons. The largest negative impact was on maternal reports of school performance (.10 of a standard deviation). Overall, the sizes of the average effects were small, and many of the programs did not produce statistically significant effects. No consistent effects were found for the three policies. That is, negative effects could not be traced to any one welfare

or employment policy. For example, negative effects were found for both programs that required parents to work or to participate in work activities and programs in which parents' work participation was voluntary. On average, the programs had no effect on school dropout rates, suspension rates, or the proportion of adolescents who completed school or had children.

Mediating Effects. Gennetian et al. (2002, 2004) undertook a series of analyses to examine what might account for the negative effects on school outcomes across the different employment-based welfare and antipoverty programs. Their findings are only suggestive because several studies lacked data needed to assess mediating processes. Gennetian et al. (2002) found some evidence that negative impacts were the result of changes in adolescents' home and out-of-home environments, such as increased pressure to work long hours outside the home, greater domestic responsibilities (e.g., sibling care), and less supervision by adults. For example, SSP, the only project that provided information about adolescent employment, increased the likelihood that adolescents were employed more than 20 hours per week. This increase in adolescent employment may have been responsible for the elevated rates of delinquent behavior found in the SSP program group, in keeping with prior research linking adolescent employment to delinquent behavior (Steinberg & Dornbusch, 1991).

Gennetian et al. (2002) also found that programs that increased maternal employment and that had negative effects on adolescents' school functioning were the same programs that increased adolescents' home responsibilities. When single mothers move into employment, adolescent children may assume greater domestic responsibilities, and this may, in some circumstances, hinder academic achievement and school progress among adolescents already struggling with schoolwork. Gennetian et al. reasoned that if additional home responsibilities are a pathway by which the programs adversely affected adolescents' academic achievement and school progress, negative effects should be especially pronounced among adolescents with younger siblings, on the assumption that expanded domestic responsibilities probably included sibling care. Indeed, they found this to be the case. Whereas control group adolescents who had younger siblings at random assignment functioned similarly to control group adolescents who had no younger siblings at study entry, the detrimental effects of the programs were larger and more consistently negative across outcomes for adolescents who had younger siblings at study entry than those who did not.

The case of Tina illustrates how a mother's entry to employment and her work schedule can adversely affect a child's academic performance by requiring that the child take on responsibilities (i.e., child care) that conflict with school. It is based on ethnographic data collected under the auspices of the Urban Change project to provide insight into how adolescent children were being affected by their mother's adjustment to mandatory work requirements, incentives, and time limits introduced by welfare reform in 1996 (Gennetian et al., 2002).

> Tina is a 35-year-old African American mother of six who has transitioned from welfare to work. Because of Tina's work schedule, the three oldest of her children who were still living at home had to take care of her two youngest children. This added responsibility cut into her older children's free time and appeared to hurt the school performance of Tamara, her eldest daughter. Tamara was responsible for waiting with the younger children for the van that took them to their daycare center. Because the van typically came late, Tamara was usually 20 to 30 minutes late for school. As her mother put it: "She's late every day for her school, every day. And what the school says to me is . . . they gotta do what they, what's their policy. She's gotta stay after school, do her detention . . . or she'll lose her credit out of her, out of that morning class 'cause she didn't get there on time. So she feels sad and I feel bad because I gotta be at work at 7. She can't be at school by 7—she can't. We all can't be at the same place at the same time." Tina suffered tremendous guilt for imposing on her older children a responsibility that she felt was properly her own. (Gennetian et al., 2002, p. 14)

Age of Child as a Moderator of Effects across and within Studies

Whereas Morris et al. (2001) found a pattern of positive effects on preschool and elementary school-age children across programs with earnings supplements, Gennetian et al.'s (2002) analyses indicated that not only did these programs fail to improve adolescents' functioning, but, like programs with mandatory employment services and time limits, they tended to have negative effects on adolescents' school achievement and school progress. This age-related difference in the pattern of effects found in the two syntheses projects parallels age effects found in two studies (SSP and FTP) whose samples included preschoolers, children in middle childhood, and adolescents.

SSP offered a generous earnings supplement for up to 3 years to single parents who left welfare for full-time work (at least 30 hours per week), and its effects varied as a function of age of the child. For very young children (ages 3 to 5 years at 36 months after random assignment), SSP had no effect on children's outcomes. For children in middle childhood (ages 6 to 11 at 36 months after random assignment), SSP increased children's cognitive functioning (as indicated in test performance and parents' reports) and health outcomes, but had no effects on their socioemotional functioning. However, among adolescents ages 12 to 18 at 36 months after random assignment, SSP increased use of tobacco, alcohol, and drugs as well as minor delinquent behavior (e.g., staying out late or all night) and reduced average school performance (as reported by mothers). It had no effect on major delinquent behavior (e.g., stealing, carrying weapons, involvement with police), achievement test performance, or self-reported school achievement among adolescents (Morris & Michalopoulos, 2003). In the second study, the negative effects of FTP on children whose parents were least likely to be long-term dependent were most pronounced among adolescent children (i.e., arrests, convictions, involvement with police), that is, those who were ages 11 to 13 at baseline and 15 to 17 at the 4-year follow-up.

Factors that explain why some adolescents fared less well than others under these new welfare and employment policies may also account for why adolescents, on average, fared less well than preschool and elementary school-age children. These programs tended to change adolescents' ecologies in ways that were largely incompatible with their developmental needs, whereas the reverse seemed true for preschoolers and elementary school-age children. As discussed previously, among adolescents, these policies tended to increase intensive adolescent employment, decrease adult supervision, and increase domestic responsibilities—all factors that have the potential to impose time pressures that interfere with adolescents' engagement in school and homework. In contrast, for preschool and school-age children, many of these programs led to increases in the amount of time they spent in formal child care and organized afterschool activities, both of which have been linked to enhanced cognitive, academic, and social functioning (Lamb, 1997; Pierce et al., 1999; Posner & Vandell, 1999).

Differential Patterns of Involvement

Substantial variation exists in the extent to which individuals take up or use benefits offered by work-based antipoverty and welfare reform demonstrations, driven partly by individuals' personal circumstances, resources, and preferences. Understanding factors that predict involvement in these programs is essential to efforts that aim to modify programs to better fit the needs of the service population. Using ethnographic methods, Gibson and Weisner (2002) found that four categories of personal and family circumstances were associated with take up of the services offered by the New Hope program: (a) lack of information or misinformation about the program, (b) multiple personal problems and disruptive events that prohibited systematic or sustained involvement in the program, (c) circumstances in which the gains of participating were perceived to be greater than the costs, and (d) use of services only if they contributed to a daily routine that parents were already working to achieve.

Yoshikawa, Altman, and Hsueh (2001) addressed the issue of take-up using a quantitative approach. Although the program on which their findings are based was not included in the synthesis projects discussed earlier, the findings are briefly summarized because they help fill a critical gap in our understanding of this issue and because they have important implications for the implementation of welfare reforms. These researchers identified subgroups of participants in the New Chance welfare reform demonstration on the basis of different patterns of employment, child care use, job training, and education and assessed whether subgroup membership predicted young children's cognitive and mental health functioning. New Chance was a 16-site voluntary program for 16- to 22-year-old current and former teen mothers on AFDC who had dropped out of high school. The program consisted of 6 months of GED classes and other educational activities, parenting and life skills classes, provision of free center-based child care, individual case management, and job training, work internships, or college for an additional year. Children, ages 0 to 3 at the onset of the program, were assessed at 42 months following random assignment.

Center care co-occurred with a variety of education and job training activities and with attendance at personal development classes to a greater degree than other forms of child care (e.g., grandparent care, nonrelative care). That is, the provision (at most of the New Chance sites) of on-site child care appeared to facilitate involvement in program activities that were most likely to lead to employment and long-term exits from welfare. Fifty percent of the sample were characterized by low involvement in all program activities and made little use of relative care, nonrelative care, or center-based care. At the 42-month follow-up, these individuals were more likely than expected to be on welfare and less likely than expected to be employed. Ethnicity predicted membership in the low involvement group, with those in the low involvement group more likely to be White than Black or Latino—a finding that runs counter to societal stereotypes. Surprisingly, child demographic factors, maternal depression, and socioeconomic characteristics such as prior employment and educational attainment did not predict level of involvement.

Accounting for the effects of selection, children whose parents were in the low involvement group scored lower on a measure of cognitive school readiness than did children whose parents were in other cluster profiles. Yoshikawa et al. (2001) speculated that low levels of center-based child care experienced by the former children may have denied them opportunities to advance their cognitive functioning. In addition, parents' low levels of involvement in program activities that enhance self-sufficiency and personal development may have denied children the indirect positive influences that such activities might have. Children of mothers in a cluster profile characterized by human capital development (higher-than-average levels of involvement in education, job training, personal development classes, and center-based child care use) had higher levels of cognitive school readiness than children in cluster profiles characterized by either high levels of center-based child care use and job training or high levels of center-based child care use and education. The cumulative effects of education and job training likely increased parents' human capital, which, in turn, may have increased children's educational resources. These advantages appear to have amplified the positive and direct effects of center-based child care on children's cognitive functioning.

Summary

Findings from any single program with an income supplement require tenuous statements about the effects of income because benefits and services within a program were offered as a package, making it impossible to identify the separate effects of different components of the program. However, consideration of findings across multiple programs offering income supplements with a mixture of other program services increases confidence in the causal effects of income supplements, as this was the common feature across these varied programs. Morris et al.'s (2001) synthesis indicates that mandatory employment services increased employment but left income unchanged, and generally had little effect on the well-being of preschool and elementary school-age children. In contrast, increases in employment accompanied by income gains benefited children in this age group. These findings together suggest that income—not employment per se—drove the positive effects on children, a conclusion supported by a comparison of the results for Full MFIP and MFIP Incentives Only (D. Bloom & Michalopoulos, 2001). Income may have improved child well-being by providing a range of cognitive and social resources (e.g., books and other learning materials; participation in organized activities during nonschool hours; stable, higher-quality child care). Parent's psychological functioning, proximal child rearing practices, and children's home environment were not key pathways of influence. There is some suggestion that African American and Latino children may benefit more than White children from programs designed to enhance parents' human capital (emphasizing adult basic education prior to employment), and that the benefits of programs with earnings supplements are greater for children in higher-risk families than those in lower-risk families.

Apparently, in the case of adolescents, the benefits of increased income were insufficient to offset the negative effects of increased unsupervised time, greater domestic responsibilities, and increased adolescent employment occasioned by mother's entry into work and employment training activities. The negative effects of these programs on adolescent outcomes signal the need to seriously reconsider the costs versus benefits of requiring single-parent welfare recipients, especially those with adolescent children, to be involved in work and work-related activities 40 hours per week instead of the current 30 hours per week (Thompson, 2003). We return to this issue briefly in a later section of the chapter.

Among mothers with infant and preschool children, provision of on-site child care appears to enhance mothers' involvement in program activities that are likely to lead to employment and exits from welfare. High levels of maternal involvement in multiple domains of human capital development (e.g., education, job training, personal development classes), combined with high use of center-based child care, appear to boost children's cognitive school readiness.

Estimating the Causal Influence of Income

The differential effect on child well-being of employment-based antipoverty programs with and without earnings supplements brings into focus the question of whether income plays a causal role in child well-being.

There are ongoing debates about whether low income is the critical variable affecting developmental outcomes among poor children, as opposed to attributes such as low ability and low education levels of parents, genetic predispositions, poor mental health, welfare receipt, single-mother family structure, and large family size (Corcoran, 2001; Duncan & Brooks-Gunn, 1997; Huston, McLoyd, & Garcia Coll, 1997; Mayer, 1997; Rowe & Rodgers, 1997). Notwithstanding the potential for genetic-environment confounding in studies conducted within biologically related families, collectively, investigations using a variety of methods provide strong evidence that income poverty and related experiences influence children's cognitive, academic, and socioemotional functioning through environmental processes that go well beyond genetically transmitted attributes (Huston et al., 1997). Included in this corpus of studies are (a) longitudinal studies with statistical controls for genetically based shared variance (e.g., analyses of effects of poverty on children's IQ that control for maternal IQ, maternal education, or both; e.g., Duncan & Brooks-Gunn, 1997); (b) studies that control for enduring family characteristics (and hence, any stable genetically based family attributes) by using children as their own controls or by comparing siblings (e.g., Currie & Thomas, 1995); (c) studies of the effects of naturally occurring income changes (e.g., Garrett et al., 1994); and (d) experimental manipulations of income (Salkind & Haskins, 1982).

Recent findings published by Costello and her colleagues (2003) further bolster the claim that income plays a causal role in child well-being. These investigators were confronted with a natural experiment when, midway through an 8-year longitudinal study of 1,420 rural children ages 9 to 13 years at intake, the opening of a gambling casino on a reservation of the Eastern Band of Cherokee Indians substantially increased income levels in an entire community. Under the terms of the agreement with casino operators, every man, woman, and child on the reservation receives a percentage of the profits, paid every 6 months. Children's earnings are paid into a trust fund until the age of 18 years. The payment has increased each year, reaching approximately $6,000 in 2001. The income supplement moved 14% of study families out of poverty; 53% remained poor, and 32% were never poor (incomes of non-Indian families were not affected). Before the casino opened, children whose family was to move out of poverty had the same number of behavioral psychiatric symptoms (Conduct Disorder, Oppositional Defiant Disorder) as those who were to remain poor, and both groups had significantly more symptoms than did children whose families were never poor, consistent with other research. However, after the casino opened, behavioral symptoms of ex-poor children fell to the levels of never-poor children, and significantly below the levels of persistently poor children. The measure of behavioral symptoms was based on child and parent responses to the Child and Adolescent Psychiatric Assessment, which was used to generate diagnoses following the *Diagnostic and Statistical Manual of Mental Disorders,* fourth edition (American Psychiatric Association, 1994). Analysis indicated that the beneficial effect of moving out of poverty was mediated by an increase in parental supervision resulting from fewer time demands on the index parent and, overall, fewer time constraints in the family.

Nonexperimental Studies of Mothers' Transitions off Welfare and Increased Work Involvement in Relation to Child Well-Being

Random assignment design allows more definitive causal inferences about the effects of different policy options on family life and child well-being than is possible from nonexperimental work. Nonetheless, as with the experimental studies of model preschool education programs (Haskins, 1989), there are questions about the external validity of experimental studies of welfare and employment policies. Most of the experiments were begun prior to the 1996 welfare reform legislation, most of the programs did not have time limits, and the earning supplements and child care subsidies of these programs were more generous than many current state welfare provisions (Chase-Lansdale et al., 2003). In the sections that follow, we turn to nonexperimental studies examining the association between mother's welfare and employment transitions and child well-being. Relevant studies have been conducted both prior to and after the passage of PRWORA. Taken together, these studies may

provide a closer approximation of what effects can be expected to result from welfare reform, but they are limited in their inability to definitively address issues of causality resulting from potential unmeasured characteristics of the mother that may be correlated with welfare and employment transitions and changes in children's well-being. Our review of these studies is followed by a discussion of some of the factors that are likely to influence how children respond to mothers' transitions off welfare and into employment.

Effects on Child Functioning of Receiving and Transitioning off Aid to Families with Dependent Children

Some data suggest that longer duration of welfare receipt is associated with better school performance among African American adolescent girls and higher levels of educational attainment among African American youth (Coley & Chase-Lansdale, 2000; Peters & Mullis, 1997), but the bulk of research generally shows little or no association between receipt of AFDC and child well-being after adjusting for poverty and low income (e.g., Kalil & Eccles, 1998; Zaslow, McGroder, Cave, & Mariner, 1999; Zill, Moore, Smith, Stief, & Coiro, 1995). In the Philadelphia Family Management Study, adolescents' endorsement of mainstream values toward social behavior, level of academic performance, and participation in delinquent behaviors, risky behaviors, or substance use were all unrelated to whether or not their family had received income from AFDC in the previous 12 months, although adolescents in families with a longer history of welfare receipt (number of years on welfare since the adolescent's birth) had slightly lower levels of academic performance (Kalil & Eccles, 1998). In other research, longer duration of welfare receipt predicted lower school readiness but was unrelated to positive social behaviors, internalizing behavior problems, physical health, school delinquency problems, and adolescent work orientation (Coley & Chase-Lansdale, 2000; Zaslow et al., 1999). The lack of sound data on lifetime poverty status and monthly spells of welfare receipt typical of these studies compromises estimates of welfare effects, given the substantial fluidity in welfare and poverty status among low-income families (Bane & Ellwood, 1986; Kalil & Eccles, 1998).

Hofferth and her colleagues (Hofferth, Smith, McLoyd, & Finkelstein, 2000) hypothesized that the transition from welfare to "self-sufficiency"—pre-PRWORA—would be associated with elevated levels of externalizing and internalizing behavior problems in children because their mother would be experiencing the strain and anxiety of supporting the family without AFDC. They further predicted that this increase in behavior problems would be short term and would reverse itself over the longer term. Data from the Panel Study of Income Dynamics Child Development Supplement, a nationally representative sample of children under age 13, were consistent with these predictions. Children of single mothers who had been off welfare for 1 year or less were both more aggressive and more withdrawn than children whose mother had never received AFDC, controlling for background characteristics of the child (e.g., age, gender, race) and the mother (e.g., education, income-needs ratio). Maternal depression, family conflict, and living with a household member with drinking problems mediated some of this association. Children whose mother was currently on welfare and children whose mother had been off AFDC for 1 to 3 years did not differ in level of behavior problems from children whose mother had received no welfare in the past 3 years. Children's cognitive functioning was not consistently related to the transition off welfare.

In one of the few longitudinal studies of welfare transitions focusing on very young children, J. R. Smith and her colleagues (J. R. Smith, Brooks-Gunn, Kohen, & McCarton, 2001) found a negative association between children's cognitive test scores at age 3 and different welfare transition patterns (compared to children who never received AFDC) during the child's first 3 years of life, but most of this association was explained by preexisting maternal and family characteristics and family income, rather than by AFDC status per se. One of the most robust findings was the interactive effects of poverty status and transition off welfare. Children's cognitive test scores were negatively related to leaving AFDC by age 3 (compared to children who never received AFDC), but this effect was much stronger for families who left AFDC but remained in poverty, compared with those who left poverty when they left AFDC. These associations held even after controlling for a host of preexisting child and family characteristics, home learning environments, and parenting behaviors.

Effects on Child Functioning of Mothers' Transitions after the 1996 Welfare Reform Legislation

Research on the effects of PRWORA on child well-being needs to be viewed within the context of post-PRWORA

macroeconomic trends and aggregate-level analyses of the consequences of PRWORA for the material well-being of low-income families. Gauging the impact of welfare reform on families and children is not simply a matter of documenting the relationship of transitions into and out of TANF and employment to child and family well-being, but also assessing how policy differences under TANF versus AFDC are related to resources available to the poor overall, regardless of their welfare and employment transitions. We discuss these issues prior to summarizing what is known about the effects of welfare reform on child well-being.

Macroeconomic Trends. Since the passage of PRWORA in August 1996 and the replacement of AFDC with TANF, welfare caseloads have been cut in half, falling from 4.4 million families to 2.2 million in September 2000 (Greenberg et al., 2002). Child poverty rates also fell during this period, from 22% in 1994 to 16.2% in 2000, the lowest percentage in 20 years (Proctor & Dalaker, 2003). Implementation of TANF coincided with a strong economy that allowed low-income single mothers to enter jobs that had been added to the economy mostly in retail trade and services. It also co-occurred with policy changes that benefited workers in low-wage jobs, including an increase in the minimum wage, expansion of the Earned Income Tax Credit, and increases in child care spending and public health care coverage (Chapman & Bernstein, 2003; Greenberg et al., 2002).

As the U.S. economy took a downturn in 2001, a number of the positive post-PRWORA trends have leveled off or reversed. A sharp decrease occurred in the number of jobs in the sectors that had previously employed low-income single mothers, precipitating higher unemployment rates in this group. In 2002, the average unemployment rate of low-income single mothers was 12.3%, an increase from 9.8% in 2000 (Chapman & Bernstein, 2003). Consistent with this change is evidence from the National Survey of America's Families that the proportion of recent welfare leavers who were working and not receiving TANF was lower in 2002 than it was in 1999—42.2% versus 49.9% (Loprest, 2003a)—and that food stamp receipt among welfare leavers increased from 28% in 1999 to 35% in 2002 (Loprest, 2003b). The number of children living with an unemployed parent dropped from 4.3 million to almost 3 million between 1995 and 2000, but by 2001, this number again stood at 4 million (S. K. Martin & Lindsey,

2003). Moreover, child poverty rates have increased since 2000, and the percentage of children living in deep poverty (those below one-half of the poverty threshold) is rising toward pre-1996 levels (S. K. Martin & Lindsey, 2003; Proctor & Dalaker, 2003).

Changes in Family Material Resources. Studies of aggregate-level changes in the economic resources of low-income families wrought by welfare reform present a mixed picture. Researchers who base their assessment solely on cash income conclude that poverty has declined as a result of welfare reform, whereas those who base their assessment on total family income, including noncash benefits, conclude that a significant segment of families are worse off as a result of welfare reform. Accumulating data suggest that, indeed, those at the bottom of the income distribution have experienced a substantial decline in income since the implementation of TANF, principally because of a sharp drop in receipt of various welfare-related benefits (Greenberg et al., 2002; Zedlewski, 2002). Studies consistently report that about 40% of families leaving welfare are not working and that their transition off welfare was the result of sanctions or noncompliance with program requirements. Adults in these families tend to have very low levels of education, little or no work history, and multiple barriers to employment. These families represent a large percentage of those who experienced a drop in income following welfare reform (Greenberg et al., 2002).

The other 60% of families that leave welfare are working, but in jobs that are typically low paying with no employer-provided benefits. Moreover, a surprisingly large percentage (over 50% in some studies) of these families lack food stamp benefits, Medicaid coverage, and child care subsidies even when eligible—the result being that they face multiple material hardships, including unmet health needs, food insufficiency, and inadequate housing (Greenberg et al., 2002; S. K. Martin & Lindsey, 2003; Zedlewski, 2002). Low participation rates in programs intended to support working poor families have been attributed to ineffective administrative systems in state and local welfare offices, caseworkers' lack of understanding of complex eligibility rules, administrative complexities, and stigma associated with these programs (Zedlewski, 2002). Such findings underscore the important point that gauging the impact of welfare reform on families and children is not simply a matter of documenting the relationship of transitions into and out of TANF and employment to child and fam-

ily well-being, but also assessing how policy differences under TANF versus AFDC are related to resources available to the poor overall, regardless of their welfare and employment transitions.

One of the reasons for the high percentage of poor families who are currently eligible for but not receiving Medicaid coverage is that welfare reform uncoupled eligibility requirements for TANF and Medicaid (Burton et al., 2002). Before TANF, individuals receiving AFDC were automatically eligible for Medicaid. Now, individuals must qualify for TANF and Medicaid separately. This policy change, one of several intended to increase returns from low-wage work and to push welfare recipients to higher levels of employment-based self-support (Morris et al., 2001), made families at higher incomes eligible for Medicaid without regard to TANF or TANF time limits. Paradoxically, studies show a decline in families receiving Medicaid once off TANF rolls, although it is not clear how much of this is due to families being no longer eligible or being unaware of continuing eligibility. Families that are not eligible for enrollment in TANF, or who leave TANF, may not be aware or informed that they may still qualify for Medicaid. In 1997, shortly after passage of PRWORA, Congress passed the States Children's Health Insurance Program, allowing billions to enable states to insure children from working families with incomes too high to qualify for Medicaid but too low to afford private health insurance (Burton et al., 2002).

In Burton et al.'s (2002) ethnography, a complex story about family health insurance unfolded. Families clustered in three health insurance categories: (1) fully insured, (2) partially insured (some family members were covered by health insurance and some were not), and (3) uninsured. In 40% of the families, all household members (primary caregivers and children) were covered by Medicaid, private insurance, or some combination of the two. The variable insurance coverage across and within families was attributed to numerous factors, among them, (a) primary caregivers' confusion about their eligibility for TANF and Medicaid benefits (some did not know whether they or their children were insured even though they were receiving TANF); (b) primary caregivers (e.g., grandparent) who did not have legal custody of the children they cared for and, as such, could not acquire insurance for them; and (c) institutional and informational barriers that primary caregivers encountered in acquiring Medicaid for themselves and their children once they were sanctioned or transitioned off TANF. As one mother said, "Once my caseworker told me I was cut off I figured that was it. I thought that means that I can't get food stamps or medical assistance. Is that right?" (p. 28). Another significant barrier was job schedule and transportation difficulties faced by working poor parents in getting to the appropriate offices to apply for Medicaid or other types of health insurance for their children.

Lowe and Weisner's (2004) ethnographic data from individuals randomly assigned to the New Hope control group provide compelling examples of administrative complexities tied to child care subsidies and the toll they take on families. To use and maintain access to child care subsidies from the state Wisconsin Shares program, for example, families had to complete paper work, meet with agency personnel to find out about child care availability, and travel back and forth between home, work, and the state offices to submit proof of employment or levels of income each month or pay period. Often, these procedures had to be repeated when family economic and child care needs shifted. Evelia's encounter with administrative missteps, briefly noted in the case presented at the beginning of this section, entailed inconvenience, but for some individuals, the barriers to access and the resulting material and psychological costs were especially high. Consider the case of Keisha (Burton et al., 2002, p. 29):

> During the five hours per day Keisha spends on the bus getting back and forth to work, and her 8-hour shift, she can never get to the appropriate office before it closes to apply for Medicaid for herself and her three children. She won't take time off from work to go into the office during regular business hours for fear of losing her job. She prays every day that she and her children don't get too sick.

Danziger, Corcoran, Danziger, and Heflin's (2000) study of post-PRWORA welfare-to-work transitions in a community-based sample of women underscores the mixture of advantages and challenges that accompany the transition from welfare to work. Employment among women who were current or previous recipients of cash assistance reduced, but certainly did not eliminate, economic vulnerability and material hardships. Women currently or previously on welfare who accumulated the most labor market experience over a 20- to 23-month period post-PRWORA had higher levels of financial and subjective well-being. They garnered higher monthly earnings and income net of work-related transportation and child care expenses and experienced fewer material

hardships (e.g., food insufficiency, no phone, utilities cut-off, eviction). In addition, they were less likely to report engaging in other activities to make ends meet, such as pawning possessions, receiving food, clothing, or shelter from a charity, and engaging in illegal behavior. However, regardless of level of work involvement, a substantial proportion of women reported major economic difficulties and high levels of subjective financial strain. For example, among the women who worked every month during the nearly 2-year period, about one-third received cash welfare, two-thirds received food stamps, and one-fifth reported two or more experiences of material hardship.

Child Outcomes. We have very limited knowledge about how children's well-being is related to mothers' transitions off welfare and into employment since the implementation of the 1996 welfare reform law. Data are too sparse and too few welfare recipients have experienced some of the most draconian provisions of the law (e.g., time limits) to draw conclusions yet. That said, extant research suggests that at least in the short run, transitions off welfare into employment bear no negative relation to child well-being and, in some instances, is associated with improved child functioning (Chase-Lansdale et al., 2003; Dunifon, Kalil, & Danziger, 2003). The best known of these research efforts is the Three-City Study of Welfare, Children and Families, a longitudinal study of a sample of 2,404 families from low-income neighborhoods in Boston, Chicago, and San Antonio, with a focus on preschoolers (ages 2 to 4) and children in early adolescence (ages 10 to 14; Chase-Lansdale et al., 2003). Families participated in home interviews in 1999 and again in 2001, on average 16 months after the first interview. Extensive measures of child well-being were collected, including direct measures of children's quantitative and reading skills, adolescent self-reports of psychological distress and delinquent behavior, and maternal reports of children's emotional and behavior problems.

The researchers found that transitions into and out of welfare and employment—whether for 1 or more hours or for 40 hours per week—were not associated with negative outcomes among preschoolers. For adolescents, the predominant pattern was also one of few associations. However, when associations were found, they tended to indicate positive, though small, effects of transitions into employment. In particular, adolescents whose mother transitioned into employment, irrespective of the number of hours of employment, reported better mental health (i.e., lower levels of anxiety and psychological distress). The findings pointed to both increases in income and mother's time with the child as mediating influences. Information from a time diary of the day before the interview was used to estimate hours that mothers spent apart from their children while working and hours that mothers spent apart from their children while not working. For preschoolers, increased family income as a result of mother's entry into employment appeared to be offset by significant decreases in the amount of time they spent with their mother, leading to no net effect of welfare and employment transitions. A trade-off between money and time was not apparent in the case of adolescents. Family income increased when mothers of adolescents entered employment, but these mothers appeared to have compensated for time away from their adolescent children by cutting down on time apart when they were not on the job.

On the whole, Chase-Lansdale et al.'s (2003) findings for preschoolers, but not for adolescents, appear consistent with the random assignment studies reviewed earlier in the chapter showing a pattern of no effects on preschoolers and elementary school-age children of programs with mandatory employment services and time limits, and a pattern of positive effects of earnings supplement programs. Chase-Lansdale et al. have offered a number of explanations for why their findings for adolescents are at odds with those from experimental studies. The Three-City sample includes both mothers on welfare facing work requirements as well as unemployed mothers not on welfare who voluntarily joined the labor force, whereas in the experimental studies, the treatment groups were subject to mandatory work requirements. There is also the possibility that direct assessments of children's reading and math skills (collected in the Three-City Study) may be more valid and reliable than teacher and parent reports of school progress. In addition, adolescents in the Three-City Study, on average, were younger (ages 11.5 to 15.5) than those in the experimental studies (ages 12 to 18) at the time of measurement. Negative effects may emerge in the former study as these teens move into late adolescence (Chase-Lansdale et al., 2003).

In terms of its relevance for the debate about welfare reform policy from the child's perspective, this study and its findings need to be viewed in light of several additional considerations. First, some have questioned how much this study speaks directly to the effects of welfare reform policy on child well-being because the study does not differentiate between women who made welfare and employment transitions because of welfare reform and those who made transitions for other reasons (e.g., greater employment opportunities resulting from a strong economy; Kaestner, 2003). In raising this issue, Kaestner pointed to research indicating that since the implementation of the welfare reform law, only about one-third of the women who transitioned from welfare to work did so in response to public policy changes, arguing that when the causes of such transitions are different, the effect of the transitions may also be quite different. Second, the investigators of the Three-City Study have cautioned against viewing these findings as the final word on the effects of welfare reform on children because (a) findings to date are based on data collected prior to the weakening of the economy in 2001, (b) relatively few welfare families had reached their time limits at the time the data were collected, and (c) findings to date reflect short-term associations between child well-being and mothers' work and welfare transitions that might change in the long term (Cherlin, 2004).

The same cautions hold for Dunifon et al.'s (2003) longitudinal study of how transitions from welfare to work during the period from early 1997 to late 1999 are related to parenting behavior and children's behavior problems (based on maternal report) in a sample of 575 single mothers (all were welfare recipients at Wave 1) and their children ages 2 to 10 (at Wave 1). Relying on life history calendars that measured maternal employment status in each month and administrative records of TANF cash benefits in each month over the study period, at each of three waves, they classified women as being in one of five mutually exclusive categories based on their work/welfare status during at least 7 of the past 12 months: wage-reliant, welfare-reliant, combiners (women who both worked and received welfare payments simultaneously), no work/no welfare, and transitioners (women not in any of the four other categories; these women were transitioning between multiple categories over the study period). Only one of the work/welfare categories was related to child behavior problems. Moving from welfare-reliance to combining welfare and work (combiners) was associated with a decrease in internalizing and externalizing behavior problems. They found no evidence that changes in parenting behavior (e.g., harsh parenting, positive parenting), household income, or perceived financial strain mediated this relation.

Potential Moderating Influences.   As suggested earlier, how economically poor children fare in the context of welfare reform and how they respond when their mothers enter employment is likely to depend on a host of maternal, family-level, and extrafamilial factors, including mothers' human and social capital, values concerning employment, commitment to full-time parenting, proclivity toward depression, and coping skills, as well as child care and school quality, the home environment, the depth and persistence of poverty (especially for young children) that results from time limits as well as other elements of welfare reform, and local economic conditions (Chase-Lansdale et al., 2003; Coley & Chase-Lansdale, 2000; Duncan & Brooks-Gunn, 2000; D. J. Fein & Lee, 2003; Kalil, Schweingruber, & Seefeldt, 2001). Extant research provides a very sound basis for expecting that the nature and quality of the mother's job, maternal work intensity, and child care experiences, in particular, will exert strong moderating influences. Taken together, these factors make it doubtful that robust average effects of mothers' transitions of welfare will emerge (Chase-Lansdale et al., 2003).

Job Quality and the Working Poor.   As previously noted, about 60% of parents who leave welfare are working, but in jobs that are typically low paying with no employer-provided health insurance or pension benefits (i.e., the classic definition of a "bad" job; Greenberg et al., 2002; Kalleberg, Reskin, & Hudson, 2000). Many employees, but especially those with low levels of education, are becoming increasingly less likely to find job security, regular wages and hours, and the benefits that have been associated with regular full-time employment (Kalleberg et al., 2000). The increase in short-term jobs with irregular hours affects the regularity and dependability of paid work available to these individuals (Lambert, Waxman, & Haley-Lock, 2002). Many of these jobs require changes in numbers of hours and shifts worked (Ehrenreich, 2001; Newman, 2001). Rotating shifts and daily or weekly assignment of different hours leave parents unable to plan ahead for their transportation, child care, and other needs (Henly & Lyons, 2000).

Many of the jobs with the highest growth rate in recent years have disproportionately high rates of nonstandard schedules (night, evening, and variable shifts), are in female-dominated occupations, and include some of the most common jobs held by women with low levels of education (e.g., cashier, janitor, maid, waiter, nursing aide, orderly; Silvestri, 1995). Increasing numbers of working poor mothers will hold these jobs to satisfy the work effort mandated by welfare reform. Never-married mothers are more likely than married or divorced mothers to work nonstandard schedules because they have lower levels of education and lack alternative employment opportunities. Remarkably, their employment schedules, unlike those of married mothers, are unrelated to caregiving demands (e.g., having a child under the age of 5, number of children under age 14; Beers, 2000; Presser & Cox, 1997).

There is a significant body of research, much of it conducted prior to the passage of PRWORA, that provides clues about how job characteristics might influence children's home environments and adaptation to their mother's transitions from welfare to work. Research with low-income families with some history of welfare receipt indicates that girls whose mother worked had fewer behavioral problems and higher mathematics achievement scores, but only if the mother earned relatively high wages. Outcomes for girls whose mother earned very low wages were similar to those for girls with a nonworking mother (Moore & Driscoll, 1997). Higher hourly earnings also have been linked to fewer behavioral problems in children of mothers who are disproportionately from low SES backgrounds (Rogers, Parcel, & Menaghan, 1991). Especially low wages may impose severe restrictions on parents' ability to provide children adequate nutrition, health care, and material stimulation (Duncan et al., 1994). They also may diminish the quality of parent-child interaction and reduce parental monitoring of children's health by increasing psychological distress in parents (McLoyd, 1990).

Other work indicates that the quality of children's home environment worsens when single mothers enter low-wage jobs with low complexity (i.e., routine, repetitive, heavily supervised activities with little opportunity for autonomy and initiative), but not when they enter jobs with higher wages and complexity. Low-complexity jobs tend to present minimal cognitive demands to those who hold them. This job characteristic is thought to indirectly and negatively affect the learning, academic, and language stimulation children receive in their home environment (e.g., books, toys that teach academic and language skills, quality of verbal explanation to child) by constricting parents' cognitive functioning and, in turn, lessening the value they hold for cognitive achievement in their children (Parcel & Menaghan, 1997).

In addition to posing unique child care demands for single mothers, nonstandard work schedules (night, evening, and variable shifts), as compared to standard daytime work schedules, may undermine worker health, quality of family life, and child well-being. Although extant data on these issues do not focus on the working poor, they have considerable relevance for this population because individuals with low levels of education are disproportionately represented in jobs with nonstandard work schedules. Nonstandard work schedules have been linked to poor-quality and insufficient sleep, problems with appetite, digestion, and elimination, increased risk of cardiovascular disease, and risky health behaviors (e.g., smoking, high levels of alcohol consumption, use of hypnotics; for example, Barak et al., 1995, 1996; Simon, 1990). Because workers on afternoon and rotating shifts have less regular eating times, they may substitute snacks for main meals, a practice that over time can result in weight gain, weight loss, and/or nutritional deficiency. These health problems and health-related behaviors are thought to result because nonstandard shifts upset diurnal and circadian rhythms that control sleep and wakefulness, body temperature, the cardiopulmonary system, cortisol and growth hormone secretion, metabolic activity, and digestive and eliminative processes (Simon, 1990). Shift workers also are more susceptible to mental health problems, a link thought to be the result of greater social isolation, less access to community services, and more difficulty participating regularly in recreational and social groups in their neighborhood and community, and more sleep disturbances, compared to those who work standard hours (e.g., Muhammad & Vishwanath, 1997).

Given their links to physical and mental health problems, it is not surprising that nonstandard work schedules have been linked also to family problems (e.g., divorce, marital conflict; Presser, 2000; White & Keith, 1990) and compromised child well-being. Nonstandard work schedules are associated with lower school achievement and less positive psychological functioning among children (Barton, Aldridge, & Smith, 1998; Heymann, 2000). Data from the National Longitudinal Study of Youth indicates that the more hours a parent worked evenings or nights, the lower his or her child's math and reading achievement scores and the more likely the child was to have repeated a grade and to have

been suspended from school, even after taking into account family income, parental education, marital status, the child's gender, and the total number of hours the parent worked (Heymann, 2000). Daughters (but not sons) whose father works non-day shifts report more dysphoria, lower self-esteem, and less perceived academic competence, compared to daughters whose father works day shifts (Barton et al., 1998). A standard daytime work schedule affords more parent-child contact than a nonstandard work schedule because it is generally more synchronous with children's daily school schedule. Consequently, parents who work these hours may find it easier to monitor the child's behavior, to set and enforce limits/rules, and to engage in shared activities with the child (Heymann, 2000). Given these differences, it seems likely that nonstandard work schedules undermine children's well-being partly by reducing parent-child interaction, parental involvement in the child's schooling, and parental supervision of children's time use and activities.

Work Intensity. Number of hours of maternal employment is also linked to child well-being, though this work has not focused exclusively on low-income families. Net of maternal background factors and other work characteristics (e.g., hourly wage), children whose mother works part time (20 to 34 hours/week) have greater verbal skills than children whose mother works full-time, who, in turn, have better verbal skills than those whose mother routinely works overtime. Parental work that routinely exceeds 40 hours/week may hinder, rather than facilitate, children's cognitive, social, and physical well-being by diminishing parent mental health, parental availability and involvement, and children's social capital. The combination of overtime hours and having a job low in complexity has been found to exacerbate children's behavior problems (Parcel & Menaghan, 1994).

Extrapolating from extant findings, it is reasonable to hypothesize that children in working poor families, on average, are likely to fare better if their parents work part time, do not routinely work overtime, and hold jobs that afford higher wages, more occupational complexity, and a standard daytime work schedule. The Bush administration's proposal for reauthorization of welfare reform calls for single-parent welfare recipients to be involved in work and work-related activities 40 hours per week instead of the current 30 hours per week (Thompson, 2003). This proposal, if enacted, may well undermine mothers' ability to meet their children's health and developmental needs. Meeting these needs often requires that parents are available to take children to well-child or illness-related medical appointments during regular business hours, to care for sick children, to manage chronic disease exacerbations such as asthma (both chronic diseases and exacerbations are more prevalent among poor children than nonpoor children; Fernandez, Foss, Mouton, & South-Paul, 1998; Halfon & Newachek, 1993), and to have children evaluated for cognitive and behavior problems—caregiving that is especially difficult when a single parent is working full time in a job with little flexibility (Heymann & Earle, 1999). High work intensity in combination with certain nonstandard work schedules is of particular concern as a threat to adolescent well-being because of its potential to markedly undermine parents' ability to monitor and supervise the child's behavior (Gennetian et al., 2002).

Child Care. A full discussion of child care issues in relation to welfare reform is beyond the scope of this chapter. These issues have been considered at length by others (Fuller, Kagan, Caspary, & Gauthier, 2002; Lowe & Weisner, 2004; Lowe, Weisner, Geis, & Huston, 2005). However, several points bear brief mention here. Fuller et al.'s review of studies suggests that age of child, trust and flexibility, costs, and accessibility are prominent considerations in parents' decisions about child care. When mothers' participation in welfare-to-work programs begins, they typically rely on informal child care arrangements, but as they move off welfare and into stable jobs, they are more likely to choose center day care or a family child care home (Fuller et al., 2002). Consistent with the child care preferences of Evelia, whose case was presented earlier, low-income mothers tend to trust kin and friends as caregivers more than center-based caregivers, partly because they share child-rearing values and practices and because caregiver kin and friends tend to be more flexible (Fuller et al., 2002). However, many low-income parents prefer center care when it is available and affordable (Quint, Polit, Bos, & Cave, 1994).

The impact of mothers' employment transitions on children is likely to be influenced by the quality of care children receive in their mother's absence. The impact of child care on children's social and cognitive development depends partly on its quality, which is typically defined by structural features (e.g., low ratios of children to adults, trained caregivers) and process features (e.g., responsiveness of caregiving; Lamb, 1997). Research indicates that when quality is equivalent, formal center-based care is associated with more advanced

cognitive and language development than is home-based child care, and this seems partly due to the educational materials and activities that centers typically provide (Lamb, 1997; NICHD Early Child Care Research Network, 2000). On average, poor children have less access to and are less likely to be enrolled in high-quality child care programs than their more advantaged peers (Fuller et al., 2002). However, when they are enrolled in high-quality center care, they accrue more benefits from such care than their advantaged counterparts (Loeb, Fuller, Kagan, & Carrol, 2004).

Loeb et al. (2004) recently documented the longitudinal effects of type (center care versus family child care home versus individual kith and kin), quality, and stability of child care among low-income children of working poor mothers. Consistent with the experiences of Evelia's daughter recounted earlier, Loeb et al. found strong positive effects of center-based care. Among children who were between 12 and 42 months when their mother entered welfare-to-work programs, those in center-based child care programs had higher levels of performance on several indicators of cognitive functioning than children who remained with individual kith and kin providers (controlling for income and numerous maternal and child background factors). Quality of care (based on half-day observations of centers and home-based care settings) as well as stability of care were associated with higher school readiness and cognitive functioning, but even taking these factors into account, center care predicted more positive cognitive outcomes. Effects of type of child care on children's social competence were less consistent. Children in family child care homes exhibited more behavioral problems than those in other types of care settings, but the only significant effect was for aggression. Children in family child care homes were more aggressive than children cared for by kith and kin.

PROGRAMS FOR POOR CHILDREN AND FAMILIES: POLICY AND PRACTICE CONSIDERATIONS

In this final section of the chapter, we consider the ideological bases and limitations of early childhood education as an antipoverty strategy in light of social-structural and macroeconomic forces, and offer suggestions to guide the practices of those working with poor children and families.

Early Childhood Education in Context

The extent of childhood poverty and the strategies used to reduce its prevalence and its effects are not preordained, but rather reflect society-level choices and, hence, values. Understanding the ideology that undergirds these choices is important partly because forging different or a richer palette of choices is conditional on changes in ideology. Appreciation of the sociostructural, macroeconomic, and historical contexts within which early childhood education is situated is an antidote to unreasonable expectations about the benefits that these interventions can bestow on poor children. We turn to these issues next.

Ideological Context

Americans are far more supportive of government action to ensure educational opportunity than other types of social welfare (e.g., universal minimal income and health insurance), and this disparity in preference is much more pronounced among Americans than among citizens in other Western industrialized countries (Haller et al., 1990). It is not surprising, then, that early childhood education, either alone or in combination with other services, has long been the predominant government-sponsored strategy used in the United States to fight poverty and its negative effects. As a large-scale, publicly funded strategy, it dates back more than 150 years, to the establishment of free and universal public education for White American children and the assurance by its proponent, Horace Mann, that this reform would virtually eradicate poverty. It is a natural outgrowth of America's tendency to focus on children as instruments of reform (de Lone, 1979).

Head Start's broad-based support derives from several sources, including strong support from Head Start parents and staff, public campaigns by advocacy groups such as the Children's Defense Fund, positive media attention, and empirical evidence of early childhood education's effects on children's school readiness and academic achievement (Zigler & Styfco, 1994a). Not to be underestimated as a source of its popularity, though, is Head Start's compatibility with Americans' preference for indirect rather than direct approaches (e.g., universal minimal income) to poverty reduction (Haskins, 1989; Zigler, 1985). It is politically palatable because of its avowed promotion of equality of opportunity rather than equality of condition.

That is, early childhood interventions touted as antipoverty programs essentially hold out the promise of ending poverty in the next generation, while preserving social harmony and buttressing the Protestant work ethic and beliefs about equal opportunity and unlimited economic and social mobility (de Lone, 1979). Because the ideal of equality of opportunity stands in sharp contrast to the reality of gross economic inequality in the United States, "the mission of childhood in this country has been defined to a considerable extent by the promise of equal opportunity" (p. 34). This promise exerts a powerful grip on the American psyche, for what poor parent dares not hold fast to the dream of rearing offspring who "make it," who do better economically than their parents? Reality, however, is more sobering. The escape hatch is not a large one and, indeed, may be growing smaller if research on intergenerational income mobility (Solon, 1992) and the changing prevalence of chronic poverty (Rodgers & Rodgers, 1993) is any indication. Using intergenerational data from the Panel Study of Income Dynamics, Solon found father-son and mother-son correlations of about .40 or higher in long-run earnings, hourly wages, and family income. Based on this estimate, a son whose father is in the bottom 5% of earners has only a 1 in 20 chance of making it into the top 20% of families, a 1 in 4 chance of rising above the median income of American families, and a 2 in 5 chance of staying poor or near poor. The parent-son correlations for earnings and family income reported by Solon are higher than those typically reported in past studies (most report correlations of .20 or less, and most present data on fathers but not mothers). Correlations for ethnic minorities are likely to be even higher due to racial and ethnic barriers. Solon argues compellingly that previous studies systematically underestimated the correlation between father and son income status (and hence overestimated intergenerational income mobility) as a result of flawed and limited data (e.g., single-year measures of earnings) and unrepresentative, homogeneous samples.

The United States espouses a liberal ideology that minimizes class distinctions and proclaims equal opportunity, yet it has intergenerational mobility rates roughly comparable to those in European countries where class distinctions are exaggerated (de Lone, 1979). This contradiction exists because Americans are less likely to interpret intergenerational mobility as tied to family background and more likely to view it as evidence of the openness of their society than are individuals in, for example, Great Britain, West Germany, Austria, or Italy (T. Smith, 1990). Liberal ideology has tempered class consciousness in the United States, but so have ethnicity, religion, and especially race as sources of identity. America's heightened racial and ethnic consciousness is inextricably tied to the lingering effects of its systematic subordination of castelike ethnic and racial minorities, including its enslavement and legal segregation of African Americans, conquest and forced displacement of American Indians and Hispanics, and the economic exploitation of Asian immigrants (Ogbu, 1978).

Sociostructural and Macroeconomic Contexts

Many of the causes of poverty and the difficult life conditions confronting poor families in the United States are largely impervious to child- and family-level interventions (e.g., historic and contemporary racism in the labor market, lending institutions, housing; poor-quality schools; low wages paid by traditionally "female" jobs; unavailability of affordable, high-quality child care). Smeeding and his colleagues (Smeeding, Rainwater, & Burtless, 2001), for example, found that America's exceptionally high rate of child poverty, compared to the rates in other Western industrialized countries, is partly due to a comparatively high incidence of low-paid employment. A substantial proportion of variance in cross-national poverty rates was accounted for by cross-national variation in the prevalence of low-paid employment, defined as the proportion of a nation's full-time workers who earn less than 65% of national median earnings on full-time jobs. In the 1990s, of 14 industrialized countries, the United States had the highest proportion of such workers. The prominence of these sociostructural factors as contributors to poverty do not augur well for the success of antipoverty policies whose core strategy involves educating or ministering to the acute needs of poor youngsters in the absence of job creation and the presence of massive numbers of jobs that do not pay their parents a living wage. As Halpern (1988, 1990a) contends, it is a case of using secondary strategies to deal with primary problems.

Rather than effect structural changes to remedy poverty and its social ills, U.S. policymakers have overly relied on a variety of social services and programs that call for ameliorating poverty and its attendant problems largely by changing individuals, not structures. The evolving ecological approach in early childhood intervention with its emphasis on altering social contexts in ways that enhance family life and children's development surely represents an advance over more unidimensional, person-centered approaches, but it has not and indeed cannot alone produce significant structural or institutional change in American society. The social and economic conditions that produce developmental risks are as prevalent as ever today, despite an ever increasing proliferation of ecologically sensitive home-based and center-based programs and expansion of our national early childhood education program for poor children and families. This overreliance on services and programs, many of which were designed to be a last resort rather than the principal resource base for developing children (Garbarino, 1992), reflects either genuine opacity about the limits of what such programs and services can realistically accomplish, or "an unwillingness to acknowledge that many of our most serious problems are a result of chosen social and economic arrangements and a reluctance to use the political process to alter arrangements even when it is acknowledged that they are harmful" (Halpern, 1991, p. 344). Moreover, because the reforms and programs invariably fall markedly short of their promise, insufficient acknowledgment of what they can accomplish bodes well for the cyclical and predictable resurrection of genetic hypotheses proclaiming the intrinsic inferiority of those individuals whom reformers sought to help (de Lone, 1979; see also Herrnstein & Murray, 1994).

As a genre, early childhood education is no more likely to significantly reduce poverty in the United States than did universal public education, for it does not directly increase material resources or fundamentally alter most of the environmental conditions that produce problematic developmental outcomes and intergenerational poverty. At best, it only blunts the powerful force of poverty and renders modest improvements in children's environmental circumstances and developmental outcomes. As is clearly documented in research studies reviewed in this chapter, although Head Start and other preschool education programs significantly increase poor children's school readiness, they leave wide gaps between poor children's school competence and that of more economically advantaged children and have only weak, if any, impacts on participants' postschool labor market participation (Royce et al., 1983). Moreover, the positive effects on preschoolers of these interventions, especially large-scale, educational programs, are not sustained because of the tangle of environmental risk factors and their multiplicative adverse effects that is the lot of too many poor children in the United States (Rutter, 1979).

This problem is well illuminated in a study by Lee and Loeb (1995) that sought to clarify why the cognitive gains produced by children's participation in Head Start and model programs fade or disappear completely within 2 to 3 years after the intervention. This study, based on a sample of more than 15,000 eighth graders enrolled in 975 middle schools (based on a sample drawn from the National Education Longitudinal Study of 1988), points to poor-quality schooling subsequent to preschool intervention as a potential culprit. Compared to students who attended other preschools, former Head Start enrollees were in middle schools distinguished by considerably less academic rigor as reported by students, parents, and principals, lower overall quality, lower average student performance on mathematics, science, reading, and social studies achievement tests, and lower SES (i.e., average SES of children attending the school). The middle schools of former Head Start enrollees also were perceived to be less safe than those attended by non-Head Start counterparts. These differences were evident after controlling for family income-to-need ratio, parents' education, and children's race and ethnicity. Similar, but less pronounced, differences were also found in school quality favoring students who did not attend preschool, as compared to students who formerly attended Head Start. Additional insight could be brought to bear on this issue by tracking changes in children's academic performance from the preschool years through elementary and secondary school in relation to the quality of schooling.

The challenge of producing positive effects potent enough to be of some long-term or even immediate significance in parents' and children's lives, in spite of a multiplicity of ongoing and unremitting environmental stressors, is no less daunting for service programs that are billed, not as instruments of poverty reduction, but as strategies that prevent or ameliorate poverty's negative effects on family life and children's development. As we have seen, randomized trials of home visitation programs, even those that are more comprehensive in nature, have had little overall success in preventing child maltreatment, preterm delivery, and low birthweight. They have proven more effective in promoting positive child-rearing practices and producing gains in children's cognitive functioning, though it is not known whether these effects translate into better long-term outcomes for children (Olds & Kitzman, 1990, 1993).

Recognizing the negative consequences of overoptimism, some of the most ardent supporters of these programs have conceded and even emphasized the limitations of what early childhood intervention programs and two-generation programs can accomplish (Washington, 1985; Zigler & Styfco, 1994a). Zigler and Styfco, for example, lamented that "neither Head Start nor any preschool program can inoculate children against the ravages of poverty. Early intervention simply cannot overpower the effects of poor living conditions, inadequate nutrition and health care, negative role models, and substandard schools" (p. 129). To argue that early childhood education programs or various other forms of social and educational services are insufficient to reduce poverty to a significant degree is not to suggest that they be eliminated. Rather, in the spirit of Zigler and Styfco's admonition, it is a call to acknowledge that child- and family-level interventions and service programs can "counter some of the injuries of inequality, but . . . cannot destroy inequality itself" (de Lone, 1979, p. 68) and, in so doing, relieve these programs of a responsibility they cannot discharge: producing greater equality. Moreover, program effects on employment status and wages are likely to be highly dependent on circumstances, such as the local economy, that are beyond the control of these programs (Swartz et al., 1995). Ultimately, significant progress toward reducing the high incidence of childhood poverty in the United States is likely to require the creation of government-supported work programs that mix work and benefits (e.g., the New Hope Program; Bos et al., 1999) and the provision of more generous earnings supplements under the Earned Income Tax Credit (Smeeding et al., 2001, W. J. Wilson, 1996), strategies that are more in keeping with American values than the social insurance policies operating in many European countries (Smeeding & Torrey, 1988).

Historical Context

Recent trends in childhood poverty raise questions about whether early childhood intervention and service delivery based on models developed during the 1960s and 1970s are even less effective today than in previous times. Since the mid-1970s, poverty has become more geographically concentrated and its environmental stressors more pervasive and life-threatening (e.g., homelessness, street violence, illegal drugs; Shinn & Gillespie, 1994; W. J. Wilson, 1996). It also appears to have become more chronic and less transitory, though the data on this are less conclusive (Duncan & Rodgers, 1991; Rodgers & Rodgers, 1993). Conversely, jobs, public and private services (e.g., parks, community centers, child care), and informal social supports have become less accessible to the poor (W. J. Wilson, 1996; Zigler, 1994).

These changes in the persistence, context, and environmental correlates of poverty signal more acute needs among the poor. Although Head Start apparently has always served the poorest of the poor (Schnur et al., 1992), the deprivation experienced by that group may well increase over the years as more experience the draconian elements of welfare reform (i.e., time limits). If the disadvantages resulting from poverty have increased, the injurious effects of poverty may have intensified as well, necessitating modifications in extant programs. This inference is supported by evidence that persistent poverty is more deleterious to children's development and home environments than is transitory poverty, and research indicating that neighborhood poverty has adverse effects on children's functioning independent of family-level poverty (Brooks-Gunn et al., 1995; Duncan et al., 1994). Consequently, programs based on models of intervention, prevention, and service delivery developed prior to the mid-1970s may be less effective in buffering the effects of today's poverty (Zigler, 1994). Achieving remediation effects equivalent to those produced by interventions implemented in earlier times may require interventions that are more intensive, comprehensive, and integrative. To some extent, the flexibility accorded Head Start programs, whereby they are permitted to adapt components to local needs and resources, mitigates the latter concern. However, this flexibility does not result in incremental funding if the needs of those to be served increase.

At the very least, the family support services component of Head Start should be intensified and such a component added to early childhood education programs lacking it. Better integration of services also is needed (Illback, 1994; Ramey, 1999). These recommendations are justified on the basis of the changing nature of poverty and strong evidence of the adverse and cumulative effects on children's cognitive functioning and home learning environment of risk factors such as low social support and stressful life events (Brooks-Gunn et al., 1995; Sameroff et al., 1987). The relationship of these risk factors within the family ecology to children's cognitive functioning is consistently stronger in poor families than affluent families, suggesting that need for these support services may be especially acute and their

provision particularly beneficial to children whose parents are poor (Bee et al., 1982).

The potential for devolution, or shifting Head Start from federal to state control—raises yet another historical consideration. If proponents of devolution prevail—and there are strong reasons for concern about the wisdom of such a change in policy—it will be critical to determine how devolution impacts Head Start implementation, quality, access, and efficacy (Ripple, Gilliam, Chanana, & Zigler, 1999; Zigler & Styfco, 2004b).

Working with Poor Children and Families

The effectiveness of programs intended to enhance poor children's intellectual and educational achievement is not only a function of whether the services provided by the programs are sufficiently intensive, comprehensive, content-appropriate, and flexible to meet families' needs. It would be a serious error to ignore the potency of the affective dimension of programs. It is this dimension on which we concentrate here.

Schorr (1989) found that staffs of successful programs were not only technically skilled, but were committed to and respectful of the families they served, making it possible for them to establish caring and trusting relationships with service recipients. According families wide latitude to decide what services to utilize and how they wanted to participate and taking account of the families' particular goals for their children were among the ways respect and trust were established and maintained.

The established link between attribution biases and psychological well-being suggests that blaming the poor for their plight will exacerbate their psychological problems, heighten mistrust and apprehension, and undercut the professional's role as facilitator and helper (Belle, 1984; Crockenberg, 1987). Hence, programmatic efforts to ameliorate or prevent negative outcomes in parental functioning, parental psychological well-being, and children's functioning should be unambivalently supportive rather than punitive in nature. Although the family support movement and ecological approaches to intervention essentially endorse this position, effectively actualizing this principle requires recognition of the formidable cognitive challenges it poses to prevailing sentiments.

Americans harbor a profound ambivalence toward and suspicion of poor people, partly because the value and myth of independence and self-sufficiency are so deeply etched in American society as to be virtually sacrosanct. A sense of morality, ethics, and magnanimity moves us to help them, but our steadfast ideological commitment to individual culpability as a primary explanation of poverty compels us to punish them (Halpern, 1991; Pelton, 1989). Racism, cultural ethnocentrism, and ignorance of nonmainstream cultural traditions intensify these negative attitudes when the poor in question are ethnic minorities. The typical middle-class service provider or teacher has never experienced the stressors that children and families living in concentrated poverty routinely confront. This lack of common history and experience, combined with the negative view of the poor that prevails in American society, means that persons who work with poor children and families in intervention and prevention programs must confront and work arduously and self-consciously to minimize ambivalence about the character and worth of poor people and to bridge the class- and culture-linked chasms between them and the poor. Otherwise, their effectiveness will be undermined. Visits to clients' neighborhoods and homes, when undertaken as a genuine educational experience, can help interventionists appreciate clients' ongoing struggles to survive and raise their children in the midst of daunting environmental realities (Belle, 1984). Educators and service providers also need to grapple with ethical issues that often arise in intervention programs for poor children and parents (e.g., procedures that restrict the autonomy of participants who are highly vulnerable and in greatest need; activities that usurp the parental role and conflict with the child's family heritage and values; McAdoo, 1990).

Knowing and demonstrating sensitivity to the cultural characteristics and class-linked expressions of the families to be served cannot be overemphasized (Slaughter, 1988), although it is equally important to recognize the existence of individual differences within groups of poor and ethnic minority families. Without this competence, status cues assume exaggerated importance in unfamiliar interpersonal situations, often operating to the detriment of lower-class individuals and hindering the establishment of a trusting and mutually respectful relationship. For example, as early as kindergarten, status cues appear to contribute to negative biases about the intellectual capacity of poor children, which in turn can impede their educational and economic mobility through various classroom dynamics (Rist, 1970). In a well-designed study of first-grade teachers and students in a socially

heterogeneous, urban public school system, Alexander, Entwisle, and Thompson (1987) found that first-grade teachers' own social origins tempered their reactions to the status attributes (i.e., race and SES) of their students and that these reactions had significant implications for children's achievement. High-SES teachers (i.e., those who grew up in middle-class homes), compared to low-SES teachers (i.e., those who grew up in lower-class homes), held more negative attitudes about the maturity and social competence of poor, African American first graders and held lower performance expectations for them than for their White peers. African American students in classrooms taught by high-SES teachers began first grade with test scores very similar to their White counterparts, but by year's end they had fallen markedly behind. Race differences in grades were especially pronounced. In classrooms taught by low-SES teachers, however, pupil race was unrelated to teachers' affective orientations and judgments, and no race differences in grades or test performance were found. Alexander et al. speculate that high-SES teachers may be less committed to African American students and think less well of their abilities partly because they are less familiar with poor and minority individuals and their surroundings and culture. This can lead them to misconstrue certain cues (e.g., style of dress, deportment, language usage) as fundamental failings in the child.

It is also the case that negative stereotypes can have untoward effects on the behavior of individuals who are the objects of stereotypy. A case in point is the stereotype of African Americans as intellectually inferior to Whites. In a series of laboratory experiments, Steele and Aronson (1995) found that, controlling for verbal and quantitative scores on the Scholastic Aptitude Test, African American college students at a prestigious private university underperformed in relation to Whites when tests (items taken from the Graduate Record Examination study guides) were presented as diagnostic of intellectual ability, but matched the performance of Whites when the same tests were described as laboratory problem-solving tasks. Even asking students to indicate their race on an information sheet immediately prior to taking the test was sufficient to depress African Americans' performance compared to Whites; when students were not asked to indicate their race, there were no race differences in performance. If these effects are generalizable to the classroom, we would predict that African Americans would perform less well than Whites of equal ability on tests construed as measures of intellectual ability.

Members of stigmatized groups typically buffer their self-esteem from the prejudice of others through a variety of social and psychological mechanisms. In their extensive literature review, Crocker and Major (1989) presented compelling, convergent evidence of the use of three of these self-protective mechanisms: (a) attributing negative feedback to prejudice against members of the stigmatized group, (b) selectively comparing their outcomes with those of members of their own group, and (c) selectively devaluing those attributes on which their group typically fares poorly and valuing those attributes on which their group excels. Although these self-protective mechanisms have positive consequences for self-esteem, each of them may undermine motivation to improve one's individual performance in areas where one's group is disadvantaged. Ultimately, the performance level of stigmatized groups may lag behind that of nonstigmatized groups even when individual capabilities do not warrant these differences. In the domain of school achievement, these processes can lead to academic helplessness and low levels of motivation among poor children and children stigmatized because of their racial and ethnic minority status. Paradoxically, to the degree that they operate, these self-protective strategies advance a trajectory of underachievement set in motion by teachers' prejudiced attitudes and behavior and other stigmatizing experiences in the broader environment. A number of scholars have provided compelling evidence of these dynamics among African American and poor students (Brantlinger, 1991). Treatment of individuals belonging to stigmatized groups in a caring and respectful manner minimizes the need for them to invoke self-protective strategies.

Relatively high rates of immigration among minorities are contributing to the growth in the proportion of racial and ethnic minorities in the American population. Because of the socioeconomic and demographic characteristics of recent immigrants (Portes & Zhou, 1993), the ethnic diversity of the poverty population will increase, which, in turn, may well intensify the challenges of designing and implementing antipoverty programs for poor children and families that are culturally sensitive (e.g., have awareness and respect for socialization values and practices; Williams, 1987). Educational interventions and family support programs that serve African Americans and Latinos have provided valuable lessons about some of the essentials for accomplishing this goal (e.g., Larner et al., 1992; Slaughter, 1988; Walker et al., 1995). However, because newcomers often experience stressors uncommon to or less pronounced among long-time residents (e.g., language barriers, dislocations and separations from support networks, dual struggle to preserve identity and to acculturate, changes in SES status; Rogler, 1994), adaptations in the program content and service delivery may be required to achieve optimal cultural sensitivity and maximum effectiveness in programs serving immigrant parents and their children.

REFERENCES

Ackerman, B. P., Brown, E. D., & Izard, C. E. (2004). The relations between contextual risk, earned income, and the school adjustment of children from economically disadvantaged families. *Developmental Psychology, 40*(2), 204–216.

Administration for Children and Families. (2002). *Making a difference in the lives of infants and toddlers and their families: Vol. 1. Impacts of Early Head Start: Final technical report.* Washington, DC: U.S. Department of Health and Human Services. Retrieved from http://www.acf.hhs.gov/programs/opre/ehs/ehs_resrch/reports/impacts_vol1/impacts_vol1.pdf.

Administration for Children and Families. (2004a). *Early Head Start information folder.* Washington, DC: U.S. Department of Health and Human Services. Retrieved from http://www.headstartinfo.org/infocenter/ehs_tkit3.htm.

Administration for Children and Families. (2004b). *Head Start program fact sheet.* Washington, DC: U.S. Department of Health and Human Services. Retrieved from http://www2.acf.dhhs.gov/programs/hsb/research/2004.htm.

Administration for Children and Families. (2005a, May). *Head Start impact study: First year findings.* Washington, DC: U.S. Department of Health and Human Services. Retrieved from http://www.acf.hhs.gov/programs/opre/hs/impact_study/reports/first_yr_execsum/first_yr_execsum.pdf.

Administration for Children and Families. (2005b). *Head Start programs and services.* Washington, DC: U.S. Department of Health and Human Services. Retrieved from http://www2.acf.dhhs.gov/programs/hsb/programs/index.htm.

Alexander, K., Entwisle, D., & Thompson, M. (1987). School performance, status relations, and the structure of sentiment: Bringing the teacher back in. *American Sociological Review, 52,* 665–682.

American Psychiatric Association. (1994). *Diagnostic and statistical manual of mental disorders* (4th ed.). Washington, DC: Author.

Andrews, S. R., Blumenthal, J. B., Johnson, D. L., Kahn, A. J., Ferguson, C. J., Lasater, T. M., et al. (1982). The skills of mothering: A study of a parent child development center. *Monographs of the Society for Research in Child Development, 47*(6, Serial No. 198).

Arnold, D. H., & Doctoroff, G. (2003). The early education of socioeconomically disadvantaged children. *Annual Review of Psychology, 54,* 517–545.

Baker, A., Piotrkowski, C. S., & Brooks-Gunn, J. (1999). The Home Instruction Program for Preschool Youngsters (HIPPY). *Future of Children, 9*(1), 116–133.

Baldwin, A. L., Baldwin, C., & Cole, E. (1990). Stress-resistant families and stress-resistant children. In J. Rolf, A. S. Masten, D. Cicchetti, K. H. Nuechterlein, & S. Weintraub (Eds.), *Risk and protective factors in the development of psychopathology* (pp. 257–280). Cambridge, England: Cambridge University Press.

Bane, M. J., & Ellwood, D. (1986). Slipping into and out of poverty: The dynamics of spells. *Journal of Human Resources, 21,* 1–23.

Barak, Y., Achiron, A., Kimhi, R., Lampi, Y., Ring, A., Elizur, A., et al. (1996, November/December). Health risks among shift workers: A survey of female nurses. *Health Care for Women International, 17,* 527–534.

Barak, Y., Achiron, A., Lampi, Y., Gilad, R., Ring, A., Elizur, A., et al. (1995). Sleep disturbances among female nurses: Comparing shift to day work. *Chronobiology International, 12,* 345–350.

Baratz, S., & Baratz, J. (1970). Early childhood intervention: The social science base of institutional racism. *Harvard Educational Review, 40,* 29–50.

Barbarin, O. (1983). Coping with ecological transitions by Black families: A psychosocial model. *Journal of Community Psychology, 11,* 308–322.

Barnard, K. E., Magyary, D., Sumner, G., & Booth, C. (1988). Prevention of parenting alterations for women with low social support. *Psychiatry, 51,* 248–253.

Barnett, W. S. (1995). Long-term effects of early childhood programs on cognitive and school outcomes. *Future of Children, 5*(3), 25–50.

Barnett, W. S. (2004). Does Head Start have lasting cognitive effects? In E. Zigler & S. J. Styfco (Eds.), *Head Start debates* (pp. 221–249). Baltimore: Paul H. Brookes.

Barnett, W. S., & Camilli, G. (2000). Compensatory preschool education, cognitive development, and "race." In J. Fish (Ed.), *Race and intelligence: Separating science from myth* (pp. 369–406). Mahwah, NJ: Erlbaum.

Barnett, W. S., & Escobar, C. M. (1987). The economics of early intervention: A review. *Review of Educational Research, 57,* 387–414.

Barton, J., Aldridge, J., & Smith, P. (1998). The emotional impact of shift work on the children of shift workers. *Scandinavian Journal of Work, Environment and Health, 24,* 146–150.

Bee, H., Barnard, K., Eyres, S., Gray, C., Hammond, M., Spietz, A., et al. (1982). Prediction of IQ and language skill from perinatal status, child performance, family characteristics, and mother-infant interaction. *Child Development, 53,* 1134–1156.

Bee, H., Egeren, L., Streissguth, P., Nyman, B., & Leckie, M. (1969). Social class differences in maternal teaching strategies and speech patterns. *Developmental Psychology, 1,* 726–734.

Beers, T. (2000). Flexible schedules and shift work: Replacing the '9-to-5' workday? *Monthly Labor Review, 123,* 33–40.

Bell, T. H. (1975). The child's right to have a trained parent. *Elementary School Guidance and Counseling, 9,* 271–276.

Belle, D. (1982). Social ties and social support. In D. Belle (Ed.), *Lives in stress: Women and depression* (pp. 133–144). Beverly Hills, CA: Sage.

Belle, D. (1984). Inequality and mental health: Low income and minority women. In L. Walker (Ed.), *Women and mental health policy* (pp. 135–150). Beverly Hills, CA: Sage.

Belsky, J. (1984). The determinants of parenting: A process model. *Child Development, 55,* 83–96.

Benasich, A., Brooks-Gunn, J., & Clewell, B. (1992). How do mothers benefit from early intervention programs? *Journal of Applied Developmental Psychology, 13,* 311–362.

Bernstein, B. (1961). Social class and linguistic development: A theory of social learning. In A. Halsey, J. Floud, & C. Anderson (Eds.), *Education, economy, and society* (pp. 288–314). New York: Free Press.

Berrueta-Clement, J., Schweinhart, L., Barnett, W. S., Epstein, A., & Weikart, D. (1984). Changed lives: The effects of the Perry Preschool Program on youths through age 19. *Monographs of the High/Scope Educational Research Foundation, 8.* Ypsilanti, MI: High/ScopePress.

Bloom, B. S. (1964). *Stability and change in human characteristics.* New York: Wiley.

Bloom, D., & Michalopoulos, C. (2001). *How welfare and work policies affect employment and income: A synthesis of research.* New York: Manpower Demonstration Research Corporation.

Bobo, L. (2001). Racial attitudes and relations at the close of the twentieth century. In N. Smelser, W. J. Wilson, & F. Mitchell (Eds.), *America becoming: Vol. 1. Racial trends and their consequences* (pp. 264–301). Washington, DC: National Academy Press.

Bogenschneider, K., Olson, J., Linney, K., & Mills, J. (2000). Connecting research and policymaking: Implications for theory and practice from the Family Impact Seminars. *Family Relations, 49,* 327–339.

Bos, J. M., Huston, A. C., Granger, R. C., Duncan, G. J., Brock, T. W., & McLoyd, V. C. (1999). *New hope for people with low incomes: Two-year results of a program to reduce poverty and reform welfare.* New York: Manpower Demonstration Research Corporation.

Bos, J. M., Polit, D., & Quint, J. (1997). *New chance: Final report on a comprehensive program for young mothers in poverty and their children.* New York: Manpower Demonstration Research Corporation.

Bradley, R., & Corwyn, R. (2002). Socioeconomic status and child development. *Annual Review of Psychology, 53,* 371–399.

Bradley, R. H., & Caldwell, B. M. (1976). The relations of infants' home environments to mental test performance at 54 months: A follow-up study. *Child Development, 47,* 1172–1174.

Brantlinger, E. (1991). Social class distinctions in adolescents' reports of problems and punishment in school. *Behavioral Disorders, 17,* 36–46.

Braun, S., & Edwards, E. (1972). *History and theory of early childhood education.* Belmont, CA: Wadsworth.

Brickman, P., Rabinowitz, V., Karuza, J., Coates, D., Cohn, E., & Kidder, L. (1982). Models of helping and coping. *American Psychologist, 37,* 368–384.

Brim, O. (1959). *Education for child rearing.* New York: Russell Sage Foundation.

Bronfenbrenner, U. (1975). Is early intervention effective? In M. Guttentag & E. Struening (Eds.), *Handbook of evaluation research* (Vol. 2, pp. 519–603). Beverly Hills, CA: Sage.

Bronfenbrenner, U. (1979). *The ecology of human development.* Cambridge, MA: Harvard University Press.

Bronfenbrenner, U. (1987). Foreword. Family support: The quiet revolution. In S. Kagan, D. Powell, B. Weissbourd, & E. Zigler (Eds.), *America's family support programs* (pp. xi–xvii). New Haven, CT: Yale University Press.

Brooks-Gunn, J., Berlin, L. J., & Fuligni, A. (2000). Early childhood intervention programs: What about the family? In J. Shonkoff & S. Meisels (Eds.), *Handbook of early childhood intervention* (2nd ed., pp. 549–588). New York: Cambridge University Press.

Brooks-Gunn, J., Duncan, G., Kelbanov, P., & Sealand, N. (1993). Do neighborhoods influence child and adolescent development? *American Journal of Sociology, 99,* 353–395.

Brooks-Gunn, J., Klebanov, P., & Liaw, F. (1995). The learning, physical, and emotional environment of the home in the context of poverty: The infant health and development program. *Children and Youth Services Review, 17,* 231–250.

Burton, L. M., Tubbs, C., Odoms, A., Oh, H., Mello, Z., & Cherlin, A. (2002). *Welfare reform, poverty, and health: Low income families' health status and health insurance experiences* (Report to Kaiser Commission on Medicaid and the Uninsured). Menlo Park, CA: Henry J. Kaiser Family Foundation.

Buss, T., & Redburn, F. S. (1983). *Mass unemployment: Plant closings and community mental health.* Beverly Hills, CA: Sage.

Campbell, F. A., & Ramey, C. T. (1994). Effects of early intervention on intellectual and academic achievement: A follow-up study of children from low-income families. *Child Development, 65,* 684–698.

Campbell, F. A., & Ramey, C. T. (1995). Cognitive and school outcomes for high-risk African-American students at middle adolescence: Positive effects of early intervention. *American Educational Research Journal, 32,* 743–772.

Campbell, F. A., Ramey, C. T., Pungello, E., Sparling, J., & Miller-Johnson, S. (2002). Early childhood education: Young adult outcomes from the Abecedarian Project. *Applied Developmental Science, 6*(1), 42–57.

Caplan, G. (1974). *Support systems and community mental health.* New York: Behavioral Publications.

Chapman, J., & Bernstein, J. (2003, April 11). *Falling through the safety net: Low-income single mothers in the jobless recovery* (Issue Brief #191). Washington, DC: Economic Policy Institute. Retrieved from http://www.epinet.org/Issuebriefs/ib191/ib191.pdf.

Chase-Lansdale, P. L., Moffitt, R. A., Lohman, B. J., Cherlin, A. J., Coley, R. L., Pittman, L. D., et al. (2003). Mothers' transitions from welfare to work and the well being of preschoolers and adolescents. *Science, 299,* 1548–1552.

Chase-Lansdale, P. L., & Pittman, L. D. (2002). Welfare reform and parenting: Reasonable expectations. *Future of Children, 12*(1), 167–185.

Chase-Lansdale, P. L., & Vinovskis, M. (1995). Whose responsibility? An historical analysis of the changing roles of mothers, fathers, and society. In P. L. Chase-Lansdale & J. Brooks-Gunn (Eds.), *Escape from poverty: What makes a difference for children?* (pp. 11–37). New York: Cambridge University Press.

Cherlin, A. (2004). *Welfare reform and children's well-being* (Poverty Research Insights, Newsletter of the National Policy Center, pp. 7–9). Ann Arbor: University of Michigan, Gerald R. Ford School of Public Policy.

Chilman, C. S. (1973). Programs for disadvantaged parents: Some major trends and related research. In B. M. Caldwell & H. N. Ricciuti (Eds.), *Review of child development research* (Vol. 3, pp. 403–465). Chicago: University of Chicago Press.

Citro, C. F., & Michael, R. T. (Eds.). (1995). *Measuring poverty: A new approach.* Washington, DC: National Academy Press.

Clarke-Stewart, K. A., & Apfel, N. (1978). Evaluating parental effects on child development. In L. S. Shulman (Ed.), *Review of research in education* (Vol. 6, pp. 47–119). Itasca, IL: Peacock.

Cohen, J., & Cohen, P. (1983). *Applied multiple regression/correlation analysis for the behavioral sciences.* Hillsdale, NJ: Erlbaum.

Cohn, R. (1978). The effect of employment status change on self-attitudes. *Social Psychology, 41,* 81–93.

Cole, M., & Bruner, J. (1971). Cultural differences and inferences about psychological processes. *American Psychologist, 26,* 867–876.

Coleman, J. S., Campbell, E., Hobson, C., McPartland, J., Mood, A., Weinfeld, F., et al. (1966). *Equality of educational opportunity.* Washington, DC: U.S. Government Printing Office.

Coley, R. L., & Chase-Lansdale, P. L. (2000). Welfare receipt, financial strain, and African-American adolescent functioning. *Social Service Review,* 381–404.

Colletta, N., & Lee, D. (1983). The impact of support for Black adolescent mothers. *Journal of Family Issues, 4,* 127–143.

Condry, S. (1983). History and background of preschool intervention programs and the Consortium for Longitudinal Studies. In Consortium for Longitudinal Studies (Ed.), *As the twig is bent: Lasting effects of preschool programs* (pp. 1–31). Hillsdale, NJ: Erlbaum.

Condry, S., & Lazar, I. (1982). American values and social policy for children. *Annals of the American Academy of Political and Social Science, 461,* 21–31.

Conger, R., Ge, X., Elder, G., Lorenz, F., & Simons, R. (1994). Economic stress, coercive family process and developmental problems of adolescents. *Child Development, 65,* 541–561.

Conger, R. D., Conger, K., Elder, G., Lorenz, F., Simons, R., & Whitbeck, L. (1993). Family economic stress and adjustment of early adolescent girls. *Developmental Psychology, 29,* 206–219.

Consortium for Longitudinal Studies (Ed.). (1983). *As the twig is bent: Lasting effects of preschool programs.* Hillsdale, NJ: Erlbaum.

Corcoran, M. (2001). Mobility, persistence, and the consequences of poverty for children: Child and adult outcomes. In S. Danziger & R. Haveman (Eds.), *Understanding poverty* (pp. 127–161). New York: Russell Sage Foundation.

Costello, E. J., Compton, S., Keeler, G., & Angold, A. (2003). Relationships between poverty and psychopathology: A natural experiment. *Journal of the American Medical Association, 290*(15), 2023–2029.

Cowen, E. L. (1982). Help is where you find it: Four informal helping groups. *American Psychologist, 37,* 385–395.

Cowen, E. L., Wyman, P. A., Work, W. C., & Parker, G. R. (1990). The Rochester Child Resilience Project: Overview and summary of first year findings. *Development and Psychopathology, 2,* 193–212.

Crnic, K., & Greenberg, M. (1987). Maternal stress, social support, and coping: Influences on early mother-child relationship. In C. Boukydis (Ed.), *Research on support for parents and infants in the postnatal period* (pp. 25–40). Norwood, NJ: Ablex.

Crockenberg, S. (1987). Support for adolescent mothers during the postnatal period: Theory and research. In C. Boukydis (Ed.), *Research on support for parents and infants in the postnatal period* (pp. 3–24). Norwood, NJ: Ablex.

Crocker, J., & Major, B. (1989). Social stigma and self-esteem: The self-protective properties of stigma. *Psychological Review, 96,* 608–630.

Currie, J., & Thomas, D. (1995). Does Head Start make a difference? *American Economic Review, 85,* 341–364.

Danziger, S., Corcoran, M., Danziger, S., & Heflin, C. M. (2000). Work, income, and material hardship after welfare reform. *Journal of Consumer Affairs, 34,* 6–30.

Danziger, S., & Danziger, S. (Eds.). (1995). Child poverty, public policies and welfare reform [Special issue]. *Children and Youth Services Review, 17*(1/2).

Darlington, R., Royce, J., Snipper, A., Murray, H., & Lazar, I. (1980). Preschool programs and later school competence of children from low-income families. *Science, 208,* 202–204.

Dearing, E., McCartney, K., & Taylor, B. A. (2001). Change in family income to needs matters more for children with less. *Child Development, 72*(6), 1779–1793.

de Lone, R. (1979). *Small futures: Children, inequality, and the limits of liberal reform.* New York: Harcourt, Brace, Jovanovich.

Dembo, M., Sweitzer, M., & Lauritzen, P. (1985). An evaluation of group parent education: Behavioral, PET, and Adlerian programs. *Review of Educational Research, 55,* 155–200.

Demos, J. (1986). *Past, present, and personal.* New York: Oxford University Press.

Deutsch, C. (1973). Social class and child development. In B. Caldwell & H. Ricciuti (Eds.), *Review of child development research* (Vol. 3, pp. 233–282). Chicago: University of Chicago Press.

Downey, G., & Coyne, J. (1990). Children of depressed parents: An integrative review. *Psychological Bulletin, 108,* 50–76.

Dreger, R., & Miller, K. (1960). Comparative psychological studies of Negroes and Whites in the United States. *Psychological Bulletin, 57,* 361–402.

Dressler, W. (1985). Extended family relationships, social support, and mental health in a southern Black community. *Journal of Health and Social Behavior, 26,* 39–48.

Dubow, E., & Ippolito, M. F. (1994). Effects of poverty and quality of the home environment on changes in the academic and behavioral adjustment of elementary school-age children. *Journal of Clinical Child Psychology, 23,* 401–412.

Duggan, A. K., McFarlane, E. C., Windham, A. M., Rohde, C. A., Salkever, D. S., Fuddy, L., et al. (1999). Evaluation of Hawaii's Healthy Start Program. *Future of Children, 9*(1), 66–90.

Duncan, G. (1984). *Years of poverty, years of plenty.* Ann Arbor: University of Michigan Institute for Social Research.

Duncan, G., & Brooks-Gunn, J. (Eds.). (1997). *Consequences of growing up poor.* New York: Russell Sage Foundation.

Duncan, G., & Brooks-Gunn, J. (2000). Family poverty, welfare reform, and child development. *Child Development, 71,* 188–196.

Duncan, G., Brooks-Gunn, J., & Klebanov, P. (1994). Economic deprivation and early childhood development. *Child Development, 65,* 296–318.

Duncan, G., & Rodgers, W. (1991). Has children's poverty become more persistent? *American Sociological Review, 56,* 538–550.

Duncan, G., Yeung, W. J., Brooks-Gunn, J., & Smith, J. R. (1998). How much does childhood poverty affect the life chances of children? *American Sociological Review, 63,* 406–423.

Dunifon, R., Kalil, A., & Danziger, S. K. (2003). Maternal work behavior under welfare reform: How does the transition from welfare to work affect child development? *Children and Youth Services Review, 25,* 55–82.

Ehrenreich, B. (2001). *Nickel and dimed: On (not) getting by in America.* New York: Metropolitan Books.

Elder, G. (1974). *Children of the Great Depression.* Chicago: University of Chicago Press.

Elder, G., Liker, J., & Cross, C. (1984). Parent-child behavior in the Great Depression: Life course and intergenerational influences. In P. Baltes & O. Brim (Eds.), *Life-span development and behavior* (Vol. 6, pp. 109–158). Orlando, FL: Academic Press.

Escalona, S. K. (1984). Social and other environmental influences on the cognitive and personality development of low birthweight infants. *American Journal of Mental Deficiency, 88,* 508–512.

Evans, G. (2004). The environment of childhood poverty. *American Psychologist, 59*(2), 77–92.

Evans, G., & English, K. (2002). The environment of poverty: Multiple stressor exposure, psychophysiological stress, and socioemotional adjustment. *Child Development, 73*(4), 1238–1248.

Fantuzzo, J., Tighe, E., & Childs, S. (2000). Family involvement questionnaire: A multivariate assessment of family participation in early childhood education. *Journal of Educational Psychology, 92*(2), 367–376.

Fein, D. J., & Lee, W. S. (2003). The impacts of welfare reform on child maltreatment in Delaware. *Children and Youth Services Review, 25,* 83–111.

Fein, G. (1980). The informed parent. In S. Kilmer (Ed.), *Advances in early education and day care* (Vol. 1, pp. 155–185). Greenwich, CT: JAI Press.

Fernandez, E., Foss, F., Mouton, C., & South-Paul, J. (1998). Introduction to the dedicated issue on minority health. *Family Medicine, 30,* 158–159.

Field, T., Widmayer, S., Stringer, S., & Ignatoff, E. (1980). Teenage, lower-class, Black mothers and their preterm infants: An intervention and developmental follow-up. *Child Development, 51,* 426–436.

Flanagan, C., & Eccles, J. (1993). Changes in parents' work status and adolescents' adjustment at school. *Child Development, 64,* 246–257.

Frankel, F., & Simmons, J. (1992). Parent behavioral training: Why and when some parents drop out. *Journal of Clinical Child Psychology, 21,* 322–330.

Frankel, H. (1988). Family centered, home-based services in child protection: A review of the research. *Social Service Review, 62,* 137–157.

Fuerst, J., & Fuerst, D. (1993). Chicago experience within an early childhood program: The special case of the Child Parent Center Program. *Urban Education, 28,* 69–96.

Fuller, B., Kagan, S., Caspary, G., & Gauthier, C. (2002). Welfare reform and child care options for low-income families. *Future of Children, 12*(1), 97–121.

Garbarino, J. (1976). A preliminary study of some ecological correlates of child abuse: The impact of socioeconomic stress on mothers. *Child Development, 47,* 178–185.

Garbarino, J. (1992). The meaning of poverty in the world of children. *American Behavioral Scientist, 35,* 220–237.

Garber, H. L. (1988). *The Milwaukee Project: Prevention of mental retardation in children at risk.* Washington, DC: American Association of Mental Retardation.

Garrett, P., Ng'andu, N., & Ferron, J. (1994). Poverty experiences of young children and the quality of their home environments. *Child Development, 65,* 331–345.

Gecas, V. (1979). The influence of social class on socialization. In W. Burr, R. Hill, F. Nye, & I. Reiss (Eds.), *Contemporary theories about the family: Vol. 1. Research-based theories* (pp. 365–404). New York: Free Press.

Gelles, R. (1980). Violence in the family: A review of research in the seventies. *Journal of Marriage and the Family, 42,* 143–155.

Gennetian, L. A., Duncan, G. J., Knox, V. W., Vargas, W. G., Clark-Kauffman, E., & London, A. S. (2002). *How welfare and work policies for parents affect adolescents: A synthesis of research.* New York: Manpower Demonstration Research Corporation.

Gennetian, L. A., Duncan, G. J., Knox, V. W., Vargas, W. G., Clark-Kauffman, E., & London, A. S. (2004). How welfare policies affect adolescents' school outcomes: A synthesis of evidence from experimental studies. *Journal of Research on Adolescence, 14*(4), 399–423.

Gennetian, L. A., & Miller, C. (2002). Children and welfare reform: A view from an experimental welfare program in Minnesota. *Child Development, 73*(2), 601–620.

Gennetian, L. A., & Morris, P. A. (2003). The effects of time limits and make work pay strategies on the well being of children: Experimental evidence from two welfare reform programs. *Children and Youth Services Review, 25,* 17–54.

Gersten, J., Langner, T., Eisenberg, J., & Simcha-Fagan, O. (1977). An evaluation of the etiological role of stressful life-change events in psychological disorders. *Journal of Health and Social Behavior, 18,* 228–244.

Gibbs, J. (1988). Young Black males in America: Endangered, embittered, and embattled. In J. Gibbs (Eds.), *Young, Black, and male in America: An endangered species* (pp. 1–36). New York: Auburn House.

Gibson, C. M., & Weisner, T. S. (2002). Rational and ecocultural circumstances of program take up among low income working parents. *Human Organization, 61*(2), 154–166.

Ginsburg, H. (1972). *The myth of the deprived child: Poor children's intellect and education.* Englewood Cliffs, NJ: Prentice-Hall.

Gomby, D. S., Culross, P. L., & Behrman, R. E. (1999). Home visiting: Recent program evaluations. Analysis and recommendations. *Future of Children, 9*(1), 4–26.

Goodban, N. (1985). The psychological impact of being on welfare. *Social Service Review, 59,* 403–422.

Graham, S., Taylor, A., & Hudley, C. (1998). Exploring achievement values among ethnic minority early adolescents. *Journal of Educational Psychology, 90,* 606–620.

Gray, J., Cutler, C., Dean, J., & Kempe, C. (1979). Prediction and prevention of child abuse and neglect. *Journal of Social Issues, 35,* 127–139.

Gray, S., & Klaus, R. (1965). An experimental preschool program for culturally deprived children. *Child Development, 36,* 887–898.

Gray, S., & Klaus, R. (1970). The Early Training Project: A seventh-year report. *Child Development, 41,* 909–924.

Gray, S., Ramsey, B., & Klaus, R. (1983). The Early Training Project: 1962–1980. In Consortium for Longitudinal Studies (Ed.), *As the twig is bent: Lasting effects of preschool programs* (pp. 33–69). Hillsdale, NJ: Erlbaum.

Greenberg, M. H., Levin-Epstein, J., Hutson, R. Q., Ooms, T. J., Schumacher, R., Turetsky, V., et al. (2002). The 1996 welfare law: Key elements and reauthorization issues affecting children. *Future of Children, 12*(1), 27–57.

Gutman, L., McLoyd, V. C., & Toyokawa, T. (2005). Financial strain, neighborhood stress, parenting behaviors, and adolescent functioning of urban African American boys and girls. *Journal of Research on Adolescence, 15,* 425–449.

Gutman, L. M., & McLoyd, V. C. (2000). Parents' management of their children's education within the home, at school, and in the community: An examination of high-risk African American families. *Urban Review, 32,* 1–24.

Hagenaars, A., & de Vos, K. (1988). The definition and measurement of poverty. *Journal of Human Resources, 23,* 211–221.

Halfon, N., & Newachek, P. W. (1993). Childhood asthma and poverty: Differential impacts and utilization of health services. *Pediatrics, 91,* 56–61.

Haller, M., Hollinger, F., & Raubal, O. (1990). Leviathan or welfare state? Attitudes toward the role of government in six advanced Western nations. In J. Becker, J. Davis, P. Ester, & P. Mohler (Eds.), *Attitudes to inequality and the role of government* (pp. 33–62). Rijswijk, the Netherlands: Social and Cultural Planning Office.

Halpern, R. (1984). Lack of effects for home-based early intervention? Some possible explanations. *American Journal of Orthopsychiatry, 54,* 33–42.

Halpern, R. (1988). Parent support and education for low-income families: Historical and current perspectives. *Children and Youth Services Review, 10,* 283–303.

Halpern, R. (1990a). Community-based early intervention. In S. Meisels & J. Shonkoff (Eds.), *Handbook of early childhood intervention* (pp. 469–498). New York: Cambridge University Press.

Halpern, R. (1990b). Parent support and education programs. *Children and Youth Services Review, 12,* 285–308.

Halpern, R. (1991). Supportive services for families in poverty: Dilemmas of reform. *Social Service Review, 65,* 343–364.

Halpern, R. (2000). Early intervention for low-income children and families. In J. Shonkoff & S. Meisels (Eds.), *Handbook of early childhood intervention* (2nd ed., pp. 361–386). New York: Cambridge University Press.

Hardy, J. B., & Streett, R. (1989). Family support and parenting education in the home: An effective extension of clinic-based preventive health care services for poor children. *Journal of Pediatrics, 115/116,* 927–931.

Hart, K., & Schumacher, R. (2004). *Moving forward: Head Start children, families, and programs in 2003* (Center for Law and Social Policy Brief No. 5). Washington, DC: Center for Law and Social Policy.

Haskins, R. (1989). Beyond metaphor: The efficacy of early childhood education. *American Psychologist, 44,* 274–282.

Haskins, R., & Sawhill, I. (2003). *The Future of Head Start* (Welfare Reform and Beyond, Brookings Institution Policy Brief No. 27). Washington, DC: Brookings Institution.

Hauser, R., & Carr, D. (1995). *Measuring poverty and socioeconomic status in studies of health and well-being* (Center for Demographic and Ecology Working Paper No. 94-24). Madison: University of Wisconsin.

Haveman, R. H. (1987). *Poverty policy and poverty research.* Madison: University of Wisconsin Press.

Henly, J., & Lyons, S. (2000). The negotiations of child care and employment demands among low-income parents. *Journal of Social Issues, 56,* 683–705.

Herrnstein, R., & Murray, C. (1994). *The bell curve: Intelligence and class structure in American life.* New York: Free Press.

Hess, R. (1970). Social class and ethnic influences upon socialization. In P. Mussen (Ed.), *Carmichael's manual of child psychology* (pp. 457–557). New York: Wiley.

Hess, R., & Shipman, V. (1965). Early experience and the socialization of cognitive modes in children. *Child Development, 36,* 869–886.

Heymann, J. S. (2000). *The widening gap: Why America's working families are in jeopardy and what can be done about it.* New York: Basic Books.

Heymann, J. S., & Earle, A. (1999). The impact of welfare reform on parents' ability to care for their children's health. *American Journal of Public Health, 89*(4), 502–505.

Hofferth, S. L., Smith, J., McLoyd, V. C., & Finkelstein, J. (2000). Achievement and behavior among children of welfare recipients, welfare leavers, and low-income single mothers. *Journal of Social Issues, 56*(4), 747–774.

Horwitz, A. (1984). The economy and social pathology. *Annual Review of Sociology, 10,* 95–119.

Hunt, J. M. (1961). *Intelligence and experience.* New York: Ronald Press.

Huston, A., Garcia Coll, C., & McLoyd, V. C. (Eds.). (1994). Children and poverty [Special issue]. *Child Development, 65*(2).

Huston, A., McLoyd, V. C., & Garcia Coll, C. (1994). Children and poverty: Issues in contemporary research. *Child Development, 65,* 275–282.

Huston, A., McLoyd, V. C., & Garcia Coll, C. (1997). Poverty and behavior: The case for multiple methods and levels of analysis. *Developmental Review, 17,* 376–393.

Huston, A. C., Duncan, G. J., Granger, R., Bos, J., McLoyd, V. C., Mistry, R., et al. (2001). Work-based antipoverty programs for parents can enhance the school performance and social behavior of children. *Child Development, 72*(1), 318–336.

Huston, A. C., Duncan, G. J., McLoyd, V. C., Crosby, D. A., Ripke, M., Weisner, T. S., et al. (in press). Impacts on children of a policy to promote employment and reduce poverty for low-income parents: New Hope after 5 years. *Developmental Psychology.*

Iceland, J. (1998). *Poverty among working families: Findings from experimental poverty measures* (Current Population Reports). Washington, DC: U.S. Census Bureau.

Illback, R. (1994). Poverty and the crisis in children's services: The need for services integration. *Journal of Clinical Child Psychology, 23,* 413–424.

Jackson, J. F. (1999). Underachievement of African American males in the elementary school years: Neglected factors and action imperatives. In R. Jones (Ed.), *African American children, youth, and parenting* (pp. 83–113). Hampton, VA: Cobb & Henry.

Johnson, D. L. (1988). Primary prevention of behavior problems in young children: The Houston Parent-Child Development Center. In R. Price, E. Cowen, R. Lorion, & J. Ramos-McKay (Eds.), *14 ounces of prevention: A casebook for practitioners* (pp. 44–52). Washington, DC: American Psychological Association.

Johnson, D. L., & Breckenridge, J. N. (1982). The Houston Parent-Child Development Center and the primary prevention of behavior problems in young children. *American Journal of Community Psychology, 10,* 305–316.

Kaestner, R. (2003). Welfare reform and child well-being [Letter to the editor]. *Science, 301,* 1325.

Kagan, S., Powell, D., Weissbourd, B., & Zigler, E. (Eds.). (1987). *America's family support programs.* New Haven, CT: Yale University Press.

Kalil, A., & Eccles, J. S. (1998). Does welfare affect family processes and adolescent adjustment? *Child Development, 69*(6), 1597–1613.

Kalil, A., Schweingruber, H., & Seefeldt, K. (2001). Correlates of employment among welfare recipients: Do psychological characteristics matter? *American Journal of Community Psychology, 29,* 701–723.

Kalleberg, A., Reskin, B., & Hudson, K. (2000). Bad jobs in America: Standard and nonstandard employment relations and job quality in the United States. *American Sociological Review, 65*(2), 256–278.

Kamii, C., & Radin, N. (1967). Class differences in the socialization practices of Negro mothers. *Journal of Marriage and the Family, 29,* 302–310.

Kellam, S., Ensminger, M. E., & Turner, R. (1977). Family structure and the mental health of children. *Archives of General Psychiatry, 34,* 1012–1022.

Kessler, R., House, J., & Turner, J. (1987). Unemployment and health in a community sample. *Journal of Health and Social Behavior, 28,* 51–59.

Kessler, R., & Neighbors, H. (1986). A new perspective on the relationships among race, social class, and psychological distress. *Journal of Health and Social Behavior, 27,* 107–115.

Klebanov, P. K., Brooks-Gunn, J., McCarton, C., & McCormick, M. C. (1998). The contribution of neighborhood and family income to developmental test scores over the first 3 years of life. *Child Development, 69*(5), 1420–1436.

Korbin, J. (Ed.). (1992). Child poverty in the United States [Special issue]. *American Behavioral Scientist, 35*(3).

Kunjufu, J. (1986). *Countering the conspiracy to destroy Black boys* (Vol. 2). Chicago: African American Images.

Labov, W. (1970). The logic of non-standard English. In F. Williams (Ed.), *Language and poverty* (pp. 164–174). Chicago: Markham.

Lamb, M. E. (1997). Nonparental child care: Context, quality, correlates, and consequences. In W. Damon (Editor-in-Chief) & I. Sigel & K. A. Renninger (Vol. Eds.), *Handbook of child psychology: Vol. 4. Child psychology in practice* (5th ed., pp. 73–134). New York: Wiley.

Lambert, S., Waxman, E., & Haley-Lock, A. (2002). *Against the odds: A study of instability in lower-skilled jobs* (Working paper, Project on the Public Economy of Work). Chicago: University of Chicago Press.

Laosa, L. M. (1984). Social policies toward children of diverse ethnic, racial, and language groups in the United States. In H. W. Stevenson & A. Siegel (Eds.), *Child development research and social policy* (pp. 1–109). Chicago: University of Chicago Press.

Laosa, L. M. (1989). Social competence in childhood: Toward a developmental, socioculturally relativistic paradigm. *Journal of Applied Developmental Psychology, 10,* 447–468.

Larner, M., Halpern, R., & Harkavy, O. (Eds.). (1992). *Fair start for children: Lessons learned from seven demonstration projects.* New Haven, CT: Yale University Press.

Lee, V., Brooks-Gunn, J., & Schnur, E. (1988). Does Head Start work? A 1-year follow-up comparison of disadvantaged children attending Head Start, no preschool, and other preschool programs. *Developmental Psychology, 24,* 210–222.

Lee, V., Brooks-Gunn, J., Schnur, E., & Liaw, F. (1990). Are Head Start effects sustained? A longitudinal follow-up comparison of disadvantaged children attending Head Start, no preschool, and other preschool programs. *Child Development, 61,* 495–507.

Lee, V., & Loeb, S. (1995). Where do Head Start attendees end up? One reason why preschool effects fade out. *Educational Evaluation and Policy Analysis, 17,* 62–82.

Lempers, J., Clark-Lempers, D., & Simons, R. (1989). Economic hardship, parenting, and distress in adolescence. *Child Development, 60,* 25–49.

Lewis, O. (1966). The culture of poverty. *Scientific American, 215,* 19–25.

Liem, R., & Liem, J. (1978). Social class and mental illness reconsidered: The role of economic stress and social support. *Journal of Health and Social Behavior, 19,* 139–156.

Linver, M. R., Brooks-Gunn, J., & Kohen, D. E. (2002). Family process as pathways from income to young children's development. *Developmental Psychology, 38*(5), 719–734.

Llobrera, J., & Zahradnik, B. (2004). *A hand up: How state earned income tax credits help working families escape poverty in 2004.* Washington, DC: Center for Budget and Policy Priorities.

Loeb, S., Fuller, B., Kagan, S., & Carrol, B. (2004). Child care in poor communities: Early learning effects of type, quality, and stability. *Child Development, 75,* 47–65.

Loprest, P. (2003a). Fewer welfare leavers employed in weak economy. In K. Finegold (Ed.), *Snapshots of America's families, 5.*

Washington, DC: Urban Institute. Retrieved from http://www
.urban.org/UploadedPDF/310837_snapshots3_no5.pdf.

Loprest, P. (2003b). Use of government benefits increases among families leaving welfare. In K. Finegold (Ed.), *Snapshots of America's
families, 6,* Washington, DC: Urban Institute. Retrieved from
http://www.urban.org/UploadedPDF/310838_snapshots3_no6.pdf.

Lowe, E., & Weisner, T. S. (2004). "You have to push it—Who's
gonna raise your kids?" Situating child care and child care subsidy use in the daily routines of lower income families. *Children
and Youth Services Review, 26,* 143–171.

Lowe, E. D., Weisner, T., Geis, S., & Huston, A. (2005). Child care
instability and the effort to sustain a working daily routine:
Evidence from the New Hope ethnographic study of low-
income families. In C. R. Cooper, C. Garcia-Coll, W. T. Bartko,
H. M. Davis, & C. M. Chatman (Eds.), *Developmental pathways
through middle childhood: Rethinking diversity and contexts as
resources* (pp. 121–144). Mahwah, NJ: Erlbaum.

Madden, N., Slavin, R., Karweit, N., Dolan, L., & Wasik, B. (1993).
Success for all: Longitudinal effects of a restructuring program
for inner-city elementary schools. *American Educational Research
Journal, 30,* 123–148.

Makosky, V. P. (1982). Sources of stress: Events or conditions. In D.
Belle (Ed.), *Lives in stress: Women and depression* (pp. 35–53).
Beverly Hills, CA: Sage.

Martin, E. P., & Martin, J. M. (1978). *The Black extended family.*
Chicago: University of Chicago Press.

Martin, S. K., & Lindsey, D. (2003). The impact of welfare reform
on children: An introduction. *Children and Youth Services Review,
25,* 1–15.

Masse, L. N., & Barnett, W. S. (2002). *A benefit cost analysis of
the Abecedarian early childhood intervention.* Retrieved November 15, 2004, from http://nieer.org/resources/research/
AbecedarianStudy.pdf.

Mayer, S., & Jencks, C. (1988). Poverty and the distribution of material hardship. *Journal of Human Resources, 24,* 88–113.

Mayer, S. E. (1997). *What money can't buy: Family income and children's life chances.* Cambridge, MA: Harvard University Press.

McAdoo, H. P. (1990). The ethics of research and intervention with
ethnic minority parents and their children. In I. Sigel (Series Ed.)
& C. Fisher & W. Tryon (Vol. Eds.), *Advances in applied developmental psychology: Vol. 4. Ethics in applied developmental psychology—Emerging issues in an emerging field* (pp. 273–283).
Norwood, NJ: Ablex.

McKey, R., Condelli, L., Ganson, H., Barrett, B., McConkey, C., &
Plantz, M. (1985). *The impact of Head Start on children, families,
and communities.* Final Report of the Head Start Evaluation,
Synthesis and Utilization Project (DHHS Publication No. OHDS
90-31193). Washington, DC: U.S. Department of Health and
Human Services.

McLoyd, V. C. (1989). Socialization and development in a changing
economy: The effects of paternal job and income loss on children.
American Psychologist, 44, 293–302.

McLoyd, V. C. (1990). The impact of economic hardship on Black
families and children: Psychological distress, parenting, and socioemotional development. *Child Development, 61,* 311–346.

McLoyd, V. C. (1998). Children in poverty: Development, public
policy, and practice. In W. Damon (Editor-in-Chief) & I. Sigel
& K. A. Renninger (Vol. Eds.), *Handbook of child psychology:
Vol. 4. Child psychology in practice* (5th ed., pp. 135–208). New
York: Wiley.

McLoyd, V. C., & Ceballo, R. (1998). Conceptualizing and assessing
economic context: Issues in the study of race and child development. In V. C. McLoyd & L. Steinberg (Eds.), *Studying minority
adolescents: Conceptual, methodological, and theoretical issues*
(pp. 251–278). Mahwah, NJ: Erlbaum.

McLoyd, V. C., Jayaratne, T., Ceballo, R., & Borquez, J. (1994). Unemployment and work interruption among African American single mothers: Effects on parenting and adolescent socioemotional
functioning. *Child Development, 65,* 562–589.

Mistry, R. S., Biesanz, J. C., Taylor, L. C., Burchinal, M., & Cox,
M. J. (2004). Family income and its relation to preschool children's adjustment for families in the NICHD study of early child
care. *Developmental Psychology, 40(5),* 727–745.

Moore, K. A., & Driscoll, A. K. (1997). Low-wage maternal employment and outcomes for children: A study. *Future of Children,
7 (1),* 122–127.

Morley, J., Dornbusch, S., & Seer, N. (1993). *A meta-analysis of education for parenting of children under 3 years of age.* Unpublished
manuscript, Stanford University, CA.

Morris, P., Bloom, D., Kemple, J., & Hendra, R. (2003). The effects
of a time-limited welfare program on children: The moderating
role of parents' risk of welfare dependency. *Child Development,
74(3),* 851–874.

Morris, P., & Michalopoulos, C. (2000). *The Self-Sufficiency Project
at 36 months: Effects on children of a program that increased employment and income.* Ottawa, Canada: Social Research and
Demonstration Corporation.

Morris, P., & Michalopoulos, C. (2003). Findings from the Self-
Sufficiency Project: Effects on children and adolescents of a
program that increased employment and income. *Applied Developmental Psychology, 24,* 201–239.

Morris, P. A., Huston, A. C., Duncan, G. J., Crosby, D. A., & Bos,
J. M. (2001). *How welfare and work policies affect children: A syn-
thesis of research.* New York: Manpower Demonstration Research
Corporation.

Mueller, C., & Parcel, T. (1981). Measures of socioeconomic status:
Alternatives and recommendations. *Child Development, 52,*
13–30.

Muhammad, J., & Vishwanath, V. (1997). Shiftwork, burnout, and
well-being: A study of Canadian nurses. *International Journal of
Stress Management, 4,* 197–204.

Myers, H. F., Alvy, K. T., Arrington, A., Richardson, M. A.,
Marigna, M., Huff, R., et al. (1992). The impact of a parent train-
ing program on inner-city African-American families. *Journal of
Community Psychology, 20,* 132–147.

National Center for Education Statistics. (1995). *Digest of education
statistics: 1995.* Washington, DC: U.S. Department of Education.

Neubeck, K., & Roach, J. (1981). Income maintenance experiments,
politics, and the perpetuation of poverty. *Social Problems, 28,*
308–319.

Newman, K. S. (2001). Hard times on 125th street: Harlem's poor
confront welfare reform. *American Anthropologist, 103,* 762–778.

NICHD Early Child Care Research Network. (2000). The relation of
child care to cognitive and language development. *Child Development, 71,* 960–980.

Ogbu, J. (1978). *Minority education and caste: The American system
in cross-cultural perspective.* New York: Academic Press.

Ogbu, J. (1981). Origins of human competence: A cultural-ecological
perspective. *Child Development, 52,* 413–429.

Olds, D., & Kitzman, H. (1990). Can home visitation improve the health of women and children at environmental risk? *Pediatrics, 86,* 108–116.

Olds, D., & Kitzman, H. (1993). Review of research on home visiting for pregnant women and parents of young children. *Future of Children, 3 (3),* 53–92.

Olds, D. L., Henderson, C., Chamberlin, R., & Tatelbaum, R. (1986a). Improving the delivery of prenatal care and outcomes of pregnancy: A randomized trial of nurse home visitation. *Pediatrics, 77,* 16–28.

Olds, D. L., Henderson, C., Chamberlin, R., & Tatelbaum, R. (1986b). Preventing child abuse and neglect: A randomized trial of nurse home visitation. *Pediatrics, 78,* 65–78.

Osborne, J. W. (1997). Race and academic disidentification. *Journal of Educational Psychology, 89,* 728–735.

Parcel, T. L., & Menaghan, E. G. (1994). Early parental work, family social capital, and early childhood outcomes. *American Journal of Sociology, 99,* 972–1009.

Parcel, T. L., & Menaghan, E. G. (1997). Effects of low-wage employment on family well-being. *Future of Children: Welfare to Work, 7 (1),* 116–121.

Parke, R., & Collmer, C. (1975). Child abuse: An interdisciplinary review. In E. M. Hetherington (Ed.), *Review of child development research* (Vol. 5, pp. 509–590). Chicago: University of Chicago Press.

Parker, F., Piotrkowski, C., Horn, W., & Greene, S. (1995). The challenge for Head Start: Realizing its vision as a two-generation program. In I. Sigel (Series Ed.) & S. Smith (Vol. Ed.), *Advances in applied developmental psychology: Vol. 9. Two generation programs for families in poverty—A new intervention strategy* (pp. 135–159). Norwood, NJ: Ablex.

Patterson, G. (1988). Stress: A change agent for family process. In N. Garmezy & M. Rutter (Eds.), *Stress, coping and development in children* (pp. 235–264). Baltimore: Johns Hopkins University Press.

Patterson, J. (1981). *America's struggle against poverty 1900–1980.* Cambridge, MA: Harvard University Press.

Pearlin, L., Lieberman, M., Menaghan, E., & Mullan, S. (1981). The stress process. *Journal of Health and Social Behavior, 22,* 337–356.

Pelton, L. H. (1989). *For reasons of poverty: A critical analysis of the public child welfare system in the United System.* New York: Praeger.

Pierce, K. M., Hamm, J. V., & Vandell, D. L. (1999). Experiences in after-school programs and children's adjustment in first-grade classrooms. *Child Development, 70,* 756–767.

Portes, A., & Zhou, M. (1993). The new second generation: Segmented assimilation and its variants. *Annals of the American Academy of Political and Social Science, 530,* 74–96.

Posner, J. K., & Vandell, D. L. (1999). After-school activities and the development of low-income urban children: A longitudinal study. *Developmental Psychology, 35,* 868–879.

Powell, C., & Grantham-McGregor, S. (1989). Home visiting of varying frequency and child development. *Pediatrics, 84,* 157–164.

Powell, D. (1982). From child to parent: Changing conceptions of early childhood intervention. *Annals of the American Academy of Political and Social Science, 461,* 135–144.

Powell, D. (1988). Emerging directions in parent-child early intervention. In I. Sigel (Series Ed.) & D. Powell (Vol. Ed.), *Advances in applied developmental psychology: Vol. 3. Parent education as early childhood intervention—Emerging directions in theory, research, and practice* (pp. 1–22). Norwood, NJ: Ablex.

Presser, H. (2000). Nonstandard work schedules and marital instability. *Journal of Marriage and the Family, 62,* 93–110.

Presser, H., & Cox, A. G. (1997, April). The work schedules of low-educated American women and welfare reform. *Monthly Labor Review, 120,* 25–34.

Proctor, B., & Dalaker, J. (2003). *Poverty in the United States: 2002* (U.S. Census Bureau Current Population Reports, P60–222). Washington, DC: U.S. Government Printing Office.

Quinn, L., & Magill, R. (1994). Politics versus research in social policy. *Social Service Review, 68,* 503–520.

Quint, J. C., Polit, D. F., Bos, J. M., & Cave, G. (1994). *New chance: Interim findings on a comprehensive program for disadvantaged young mothers and their children.* New York: Manpower Demonstration Research Corporation.

Ramey, C., Ramey, S., Gaines, K., & Blair, C. (1995). Two-generation early intervention programs: A child development perspective. In I. Sigel (Series Ed.) & S. Smith (Vol. Ed.), *Advances in applied developmental psychology: Vol. 9. Two generation programs for families in poverty—A new intervention strategy* (pp. 199–228). Norwood, NJ: Ablex.

Ramey, C. T., & Ramey, S. L. (1998). Early intervention and early experience. *American Psychologist, 53*(2), 109–120.

Ramey, C. T., Ramey, S. L., & Lanzi, R. (1998). Differentiating development risk levels for families in poverty: Creating a family typology. In M. Lewis & C. Feiring (Eds.), *Families, risk, and competence* (pp. 187–205). Mahwah, NJ: Erlbaum.

Ramey, S. L. (1999). Head Start and preschool education: Toward continued improvement. *American Psychologist, 54,* 344–346.

Ramey, S. L., Ramey, C. T., & Lanzi, R. G. (2004). The transition to school: Building on preschool foundations and preparing for lifelong learning. In E. Zigler & S. J. Styfco (Eds.), *Head Start debates* (pp. 379–413). Baltimore: Paul H. Brookes.

Reynolds, A. (1991). Early schooling of children at risk. *American Educational Research Journal, 28,* 392–422.

Reynolds, A. (1992). Comparing measures of parental involvement and their effects on academic achievement. *Early Childhood Research Quarterly, 7,* 441–462.

Reynolds, A. (1994). Effects of a preschool plus follow-on intervention for children at risk. *Developmental Psychology, 30,* 787–804.

Reynolds, A. (1995). One year of preschool intervention or two: Does it matter? *Early Childhood Research Quarterly, 10,* 1–31.

Reynolds, A., Temple, J., Robertson, D., & Mann, E. (2001). Long-term effects of an early childhood intervention on educational achievement and juvenile arrest: A 15-year follow-up of low-income children in public schools. *Journal of the American Medical Association, 285*(18), 2339–2346.

Reynolds, A. J. (2003). The added value of continuing early intervention. In A. J. Reynolds, M. C. Wang, & H. J. Walberg (Eds.), *Early childhood programs for a new century* (pp. 163–196). Washington, DC: Child Welfare League of America Press.

Reynolds, A. J., Wang, M. C., & Walberg, H. J. (Eds.). (2003). *Early childhood programs for a new century.* Washington, DC: Child Welfare League of America Press.

Ricciuti, A. E., St. Pierre, R., Lee, W., Parsad, A., & Rimdzius, T. (2004). *Third national Even Start evaluation: Follow-up findings from the experimental design study.* Washington, DC: U.S. Department of Education, National Center for Education Evaluation and Regional Assistance.

Riegel, K. (1972). Influence of economic and political ideologies on the development of developmental psychology. *Psychological Bulletin, 78,* 129–141.

Ripple, C. H., Gilliam, W., Chanana, N., & Zigler, E. (1999). Will 50 cooks spoil the broth? The debate over entrusting Head Start to the states. *American Psychologist, 54,* 327–343.

Rist, R. (1970). Student social class and teacher expectations: The self-fulfilling prophecy in ghetto education. *Harvard Education Review, 40,* 411–451.

Rodgers, J., & Rodgers, J. L. (1993). Chronic poverty in the United States. *Journal of Human Resources, 28,* 25–54.

Rogers, S. J., Parcel, T. L., & Menaghan, E. G. (1991). The effects of maternal working conditions and mastery on child behavior problems: Studying the intergenerational transmission of social control. *Journal of Health and Social Behavior, 32,* 145–164.

Rogler, L. H. (1994). International migrations: A framework for directing research. *American Psychologist, 49,* 701–708.

Ross, C. J. (1979). Early skirmishes with poverty: The historical roots of Head Start. In E. Zigler & J. Valentine (Eds.), *Project Head Start: A legacy of the war on poverty* (pp. 21–42). New York: Free Press.

Rowe, D. C., & Rodgers, J. L. (1997). Poverty and behavior: Are environmental measures nature and nurture? *Developmental Review, 17,* 358–375.

Royce, J., Darlington, R., & Murray, H. (1983). Pooled analyses: Findings across studies. In Consortium for Longitudinal Studies (Ed.), *As the twig is bent: Lasting effects of preschool programs* (pp. 411–459). Hillsdale, NJ: Erlbaum.

Ruggles, P. (1990). *Drawing the line: Alternative poverty measures and their implications for public policy.* Washington, DC: Urban Institute Press.

Rutter, M. (1979). Protective factors in children's responses to stress and disadvantage. In M. Kent & J. Rolf (Eds.), *Primary prevention of psychopathology* (pp. 49–74). Hanover, NH: University Press of New England.

Salkind, N., & Haskins, R. (1982). Negative income tax: The impact on children from low-income families. *Journal of Family Issues, 3,* 165–180.

Sameroff, A., Seifer, R., Barocas, R., Zax, M., & Greenspan, S. (1987). Intelligence quotient scores of 4-year-old children: Social-environmental risk factors. *Pediatrics, 79,* 343–350.

Sandler, I. N., & Block, M. (1979). Life stress and maladaptation of children. *American Journal of Community Psychology, 7,* 425–440.

Scarr, S., & McCartney, K. (1988). Far from home: An experimental evaluation of the Mother-Child Home Program in Bermuda. *Child Development, 59,* 636–647.

Schlossman, S. L. (1976). Before Home Start: Notes toward a history of parent education in America, 1897–1929. *Harvard Educational Review, 46,* 436–467.

Schnur, E., Brooks-Gunn, J., & Shipman, V. (1992). Who attends programs serving poor children? The case of Head Start attendees and nonattendees. *Journal of Applied Developmental Psychology, 13,* 405–421.

Schorr, L. (1989). *Within our reach: Breaking the cycle of disadvantage.* New York: Doubleday.

Schumacher, R., & Rakpraja, T. (2003). *A snapshot of Head Start children, families, teachers, and programs: 1997 and 2001* (Center for Law and Social Policy Brief No. 1). Washington, DC: Center for Law and Social Policy.

Schweinhart, L. J. (2003, April). *Benefits, costs, and explanation of the High/Scope Perry Preschool Program.* Paper presented at the biennial meeting of the Society for Research in Child Development, Tampa, FL.

Schweinhart, L. J. (2004). *The High/Scope Perry Preschool Study through age 40.* Ypsilanti, MI: High Scope Educational Research Foundation. Retrieved November 8, 2004, from http://www.highscope.org/Research/PerryProject/PerryAge40SumWeb.pdf.

Schweinhart, L. J., Barnes, H., & Weikart, D. (1993). Significant benefits: The High/Scope Perry Preschool study through age 27. *Monographs of the High/Scope Educational Research Foundation, 10.* Ypsilanti, MI: High/Scope Press.

Seitz, V., Rosenbaum, L., & Apfel, N. (1985). Effects of family support intervention: A 10-year follow-up. *Child Development, 56,* 376–391.

Shinn, M., & Gillespie, C. (1994). The roles of housing and poverty in the origins of homelessness. *American Behavioral Scientist, 37,* 505–521.

Shonkoff, J., & Meisels, S. (1990). Early childhood intervention: The evolution of a concept. In S. Meisels & J. Shonkoff (Eds.), *Handbook of early childhood intervention* (pp. 3–31). New York: Cambridge University Press.

Shonkoff, J., & Phillips, D. (Eds.). (2000). *From neurons to neighborhoods: The science of early childhood development.* Washington, DC: National Academy Press.

Shore, R. (1997). *Rethinking the brain: New insights into early development.* New York: Families and Work Institute.

Shuey, A. (1958). *The testing of Negro intelligence.* Lynchberg, VA: J. P. Bell.

Silvestri, G. (1995). Occupational employment to 2005. *Monthly Labor Review, 118,* 60–87.

Simon, B. L. (1990). Impact of shift work on individuals and families [Special issue: Work and family]. *Families in Society, 71,* 342–348.

Skeels, H. (1966). Adult status of children from contrasting early life experiences. *Monographs of the Society for Research in Child Development, 31*(Serial No. 105).

Slaughter, D. (1988). Programs for racially and ethnically diverse American families: Some critical issues. In H. Weiss & F. Jacobs (Eds.), *Evaluating family programs* (pp. 461–476). New York: Aldine de Gruyter.

Smeeding, T. M., Rainwater, L., & Burtless, G. (2001). U.S. poverty in a cross-national context. In S. Danziger & R. Haveman (Eds.), *Understanding poverty* (pp. 162–189). New York: Russell Sage Foundation.

Smeeding, T. M., & Torrey, B. B. (1988, November 11). Poor children in rich countries. *Science, 242,* 873.

Smith, C., Perou, R., & Lesesne, C. (2002). Parent education. In M. Bornstein (Ed.), *Handbook on parenting: Vol. 4. Social conditions and applied parenting* (pp. 389–410). Mahwah, NJ: Erlbaum.

Smith, J. R., Brooks-Gunn, J., Kohen, D., & McCarton, C. (2001). Transitions on and off AFDC: Implications for parenting and children's cognitive development. *Child Development, 72*(5), 1512–1533.

Smith, S. (Ed.). (1995). *Two generation programs for families in poverty: A new intervention strategy.* Norwood, NJ: Ablex.

Smith, S., & Zaslow, M. (1995). Rationale and policy context for two-generation interventions. In I. Sigel (Series Ed.) & S. Smith (Vol. Ed.), *Advances in applied developmental psychology: Vol. 9. Two generation programs for families in poverty—A new intervention strategy* (pp. 1–35). Norwood, NJ: Ablex.

Smith, T. (1990). Social inequality in cross-national perspective. In D. Alwin, J. Becker, J. Davis, P. Ester, & P. Mohler (Eds.), *Attitudes to inequality and the role of government* (pp. 21–31). Rijswijk, The Netherlands: Social and Cultural Planning Office.

Solon, G. (1992). Intergenerational income mobility in the United States. *American Economic Review, 82,* 393–408.

Sprigle, J., & Schaefer, L. (1985). Longitudinal evaluation of the effects of two compensatory preschool programs on fourth- through sixth-grade students. *Developmental Psychology, 21,* 702–708.

Sroufe, L. A. (1970). A methodological and philosophical critique of intervention-oriented research. *Developmental Psychology, 2,* 140–145.

Stack, C. (1974). *All our kin: Strategies for survival in a Black community.* New York: Harper & Row.

Steele, C., & Aronson, J. (1995). Stereotype threat and the intellectual test performance of African Americans. *Journal of Personality and Social Psychology, 69,* 797–811.

Steinberg, L., & Dornbusch, S. (1991). Negative correlates of part-time employment during adolescence: Replication and elaboration. *Developmental Psychology, 27,* 304–313.

Sterling, S., Cowen, E. L., Weissberg, R. P., Lotyczewski, B. S., & Boike, M. (1985). Recent stressful life events and young children's school adjustment. *American Journal of Community Psychology, 13,* 87–98.

St. Pierre, R., Layzer, J., & Barnes, H. (1995). Two-generation programs: Design, cost, and short-term effectiveness. *Future of Children, 5 (3),* 76–93.

St. Pierre, R., Layzer, J., & Barnes, H. (1996). *Regenerating two-generation programs.* Cambridge, MA: Abt Associates.

St. Pierre, R., & Swartz, J. (1995). The Even Start Family Literacy Program. In I. Sigel (Series Ed.) & S. Smith (Vol. Ed.), *Advances in applied developmental psychology: Vol. 9. Two generation programs for families in poverty—A new intervention strategy* (pp. 37–66). Norwood, NJ: Ablex.

St. Pierre, R. G., & Layzer, J. I. (1999). Using home visits for multiple purposes: The Comprehensive Child Development Program. *Future of Children, 9*(1), 134–151.

Swartz, J., Smith, C., Bernstein, L., Gardine, J., Levin, M., & Stewart, G. (1995). *Evaluation of the Head Start Family Service Center Demonstration Projects* (Second Interim Report: Wave III Projects). Cambridge, MA: Abt Associates.

Sweet, M. A., & Appelbaum, M. L. (2004). Is home visiting an effective strategy? A meta-analytic review of home visiting programs for families with young children. *Child Development, 75,* 1435–1456.

Thompson, T. G. (2003). *Welfare reform: Building on success* (Testimony before the United States Senate Committee on Finance). Retrieved from http://www.os.hhs.gov/asl/testify/t030312.html.

Tulkin, S. R. (1972). An analysis of the concept of cultural deprivation. *Developmental Psychology, 6,* 326–339.

U.S. Census Bureau. (2003). *Statistical abstract of the United States: 2003.* Washington, DC: Author.

U.S. Department of Health and Human Services. (2003). *Strengthening Head Start: What the evidence shows.* Washington, DC: Author.

U.S. General Accounting Office. (2003). *Head Start: Better data and processes needed to monitor underenrollment* (GAO-04-17). Washington, DC: Author.

Villar, J., Farnot, U., Barros, F., Victoria, C., Langer, A., & Belizan, J. (1992). A randomized trial of psychosocial support during high-risk pregnancies. *New England Journal of Medicine, 327,* 1266–1271.

Votruba-Drzal, E. (2003). Income changes and cognitive stimulation in young children's home learning environments. *Journal of Marriage and Family, 65,* 341–355.

Wacharasin, C., Barnard, K., & Spieker, S. (2003). Factors affecting toddler cognitive development in low-income families. *Infants and Young Children, 16*(2), 175–181.

Walker, T., Rodriguez, G., Johnson, D., & Cortez, C. (1995). Advance Parent-Child Education Program. In I. Sigel (Series Ed.) & S. Smith (Vol. Ed.), *Advances in applied developmental psychology: Vol. 9. Two generation programs for families in poverty—A new intervention strategy* (pp. 67–90). Norwood, NJ: Ablex.

Washington, V. (1985). Head Start: How appropriate for minority families in the 1980s? *American Journal of Orthopsychiatry, 55,* 577–590.

Washington, V., & Bailey, U. J. (1995). *Project Head Start: Models and strategies for the twenty-first century.* New York: Garland.

Wasik, B., Ramey, C., Bryant, D., & Sparling, J. (1990). A longitudinal study of two early intervention strategies: Project CARE. *Child Development, 61,* 1682–1696.

Watson, E., & Collins, A. (1982). Natural helping networks in alleviating family stress. *Annals of the American Academy of Political and Social Science, 461,* 102–112.

Weber, C. U., Foster, P., & Weikart, D. (1978). An economic analysis of the Ypsilanti Perry Preschool Project. *Monographs of the High/Scope Educational Research Foundation, 5.* Ypsilanti, MI: High/Scope Press.

Webster-Stratton, C. (1998). Preventing conduct problems in Head Start children: Strengthening parenting competencies. *Journal of Consulting and Clinical Psychology, 66*(5), 715–730.

Weinraub, M., & Wolf, B. (1983). Effects of stress and social supports on mother-child interactions in single- and two-parent families. *Child Development, 54,* 1297–1311.

Weissbourd, B. (1987). A brief history of family support programs. In S. Kagan, D. Powell, B. Weissbourd, & E. Zigler (Eds.), *America's family support programs* (pp. 38–56). New Haven, CT: Yale University Press.

Werner, E., & Smith, R. (1977). *Kauai's children come of age.* Honolulu: University Press of Hawaii.

Wertsch, J., & Youniss, J. (1987). Contextualizing the investigator: The case of developmental psychology. *Human Development, 30,* 18–31.

Westinghouse Learning Corporation. (1969, June). *The impact of Head Start: An evaluation of the effects of Head Start on children's cognitive and affective development* (Ohio University report to the Office of Economic Opportunity). Washington, DC: Clearinghouse for Federal Scientific and Technical Information.

White, K. R., Taylor, M., & Moss, V. (1992). Does research support claims about the benefits of involving parents in early intervention programs? *Review of Educational Research, 62,* 91–125.

White, L., & Keith, B. (1990). The effect of shift work on the quality and stability of marital relations. *Journal of Marriage and the Family, 52,* 453–462.

Williams, K. (1987). Cultural diversity in family support: Black families. In S. Kagan, D. Powell, B. Weissbourd, & E. Zigler (Eds.),

America's family support programs (pp. 295–307). New Haven, CT: Yale University Press.

Wilson, M. (1989). Child development in the context of the Black extended family. *American Psychologist, 44,* 380–383.

Wilson, W. J. (1987). *The truly disadvantaged: The inner city, the underclass, and public policy.* Chicago: University of Chicago Press.

Wilson, W. J. (1996). *When work disappears: The world of the new urban poor.* New York: Knopf.

Wolfe, D. A., Edwards, B., Manion, I., & Koverola, C. (1988). Early intervention for parents at risk of child abuse and neglect: A preliminary investigation. *Journal of Consulting and Clinical Psychology, 56,* 40–47.

Wolfe, R. B., & Hirsch, B. J. (2003). Outcomes of parent education programs based on reevaluation counseling. *Journal of Child and Family Studies, 12*(1), 61–76.

Wolock, I., & Horowitz, B. (1979). Child maltreatment and material deprivation among AFDC recipient families. *Social Service Review, 53,* 175–162.

Yoshikawa, H., Altman, E. A., & Hsueh, J. (2001). Variation in teenage mothers' experiences of child care and other components of welfare reform: Selection processes and developmental consequences. *Child Development, 72*(1), 299–317.

Yoshikawa, H., Gassman-Pines, A., Morris, P., Gennetian, L., Godfrey, E. B., & Roy, A. L. (2003, June). *Racial/ethnic differences in 5 year impacts of welfare policies on middle-childhood standardized achievement.* Paper presented at a Conference on Building Pathways to Success: Research, Policy and practice on Development in Middle Childhood, MacArthur Foundation Research Network on Successful Pathways through Middle Childhood, Washington, DC.

Youniss, J. (1990). Cultural forces leading to scientific developmental psychology. In I. Sigel (Series Ed.) & C. Fisher & W. Tryon (Vol. Eds.), *Advances in applied developmental psychology: Vol. 4. Ethics in applied developmental psychology—Emerging issues in an emerging field* (pp. 285–300). Norwood, NJ: Ablex.

Zaslow, M. J., McGroder, S. M., Cave, G., & Mariner, C. (1999). Maternal employment and measures of children's health and development among families with some history of welfare receipt. *Research in the Sociology of Work, 7,* 233–259.

Zaslow, M. J., McGroder, S. M., & Moore, K. A. (2000). *The national evaluation of welfare to work strategies: Impacts on young children and their families 2 years after enrollment* (Findings from the child outcomes study summary report). Retrieved from http://www.aspe.hhs.gov/hsp/NEWWS /child-outcomes/summary.htm.

Zedlewski, S. (2002). Family economic resources in the post-reform era. *Future of Children, 12*(1), 121–145.

Zelkowitz, P. (1982). Parenting philosophies and practices. In D. Belle (Ed.), *Lives in stress: Women and depression* (pp. 154–162). Beverly Hills, CA: Sage.

Zigler, E. (1985). Assessing Head Start at 20: An invited commentary. *American Journal of Orthopsychiatry, 55,* 603–609.

Zigler, E. (1994). Reshaping early childhood intervention to be a more effective weapon against poverty. *American Journal of Community Psychology, 22,* 37–47.

Zigler, E., & Berman, W. (1983). Discerning the future of early childhood intervention. *American Psychologist, 33,* 894–906.

Zigler, E., & Freedman, J. (1987). Head Start: A pioneer of family support. In S. Kagan, D. Powell, B. Weissbourd, & E. Zigler (Eds.), *America's family support programs* (pp. 57–76). New Haven, CT: Yale University Press.

Zigler, E., & Muenchow, S. (1992). *Head Start: The inside story of America's most successful educational experiment.* New York: Basic Books.

Zigler, E., & Styfco, S. (1994a). Head Start: Criticisms in a constructive context. *American Psychologist, 49,* 127–132.

Zigler, E., & Styfco, S. (1994b). Is the Perry Preschool better than Head Start? Yes and no. *Early Childhood Research Quarterly, 9,* 269–287.

Zigler, E., & Styfco, S. J. (2003). The federal commitment to preschool education: Lessons from and for Head Start. In A. J. Reynolds, M. C. Wang, & H. J. Walberg (Eds.), *Early childhood programs for a new century* (pp. 3–33). Washington, DC: Child Welfare League of America Press.

Zigler, E., & Styfco, S. J. (Eds.). (2004a). *The Head Start debates.* Baltimore: Paul H. Brookes.

Zigler, E., & Styfco, S. J. (2004b). Moving Head Start to the States: One experiment too many. *Applied Developmental Science, 8,* 51–55.

Zigler, E., & Valentine, J. (Eds.). (1979). *Project Head Start: A legacy of the war on poverty.* New York: Free Press.

Zill, N., Moore, K., Smith, E. W., Stief, T., & Coiro, M. (1995). The life circumstances and development of children in welfare families: A profile based on national survey data. In L. Chase-Lansdale & J. Brooks-Gunn (Eds.), *Escape from poverty: What makes a difference for children?* (pp. 38–59). New York: Cambridge University Press.

Zill, N., Resnick, G., Kim, K., O'Donnell, K., & Sorongon, A. (2003). *Head Start FACES 2000: A whole-child perspective on program performance* (Report prepared for the Administration for Children and Families). Washington, DC: U.S. Department of Health and Human Services. Retrieved from http://www.acf.hhs.gov/programs/opre/hs/faces/reports/ executive_summary/exec_summary.pdf.

Zur-Szpiro, S., & Longfellow, C. (1982). Fathers' support to mothers and children. In D. Belle (Ed.), *Lives in stress: Women and depression* (pp. 145–153). Beverly Hills, CA: Sage.

CHAPTER 19

The Child and the Law

MAGGIE BRUCK, STEPHEN J. CECI, and GABRIELLE F. PRINCIPE

Since the 1980s, research in the field of children and the law is one of the fastest growing areas in all of developmental psychology mainly because it calls on the expertise of researchers in such a variety of areas. Yet, despite the diversity of topics, all share the common goal of studying behaviors and processes that impact the legal status of children both in and out of the courtroom. Although the research is oriented toward applied issues, it is grounded in developmental theory and in some cases has produced innovative developmental paradigms, theories, and frameworks.

The wide set of topics included in research on children and the law reflects their importance to current societal problems. For example, there is a growing literature on the effects of family constellations and parenting on children's adjustment, such as the effects of gay or lesbian parenting (Golmbok et al., 2003; Patterson, 1997), effects of divorce and custody arrangements (Amato, 2000; Bauserman, 2002; Emery, Laumann-Billings, Waldron, Sbarra, & Dillon, 2001; Gindes, 1998; Kelly & Lamb, 2003), and adoption and foster parenting (Goodman, Emery, & Haugaard, 1998; Haugaard & Hazan, 2002). Another recent avenue of study involves the child in the juvenile justice system when the

child is the perpetrator. In part, this interest is due to rising crime in this age group and to the fact that a number of jurisdictions have become more conservative in dealing with this group of children in the forensic area. Some of these studies, which mainly focus on older children, examine the extent to which they understand the legal proceedings and their legal rights (Grisso & Schwartz, 2000; Grisso et al., 2003; Salekin, 2002; Steinberg & Cauffman, 1996; Steinberg & Scott, 2003).

The greatest amount of work in the field of children and the law has focused on issues related to the maltreatment of children. In 2002, an estimated 896,000 children in the United States were determined to be victims of child abuse. Although the annual rate of victimization per 1,000 children in the U.S. population has dropped from 13.4 in 1990 to 12.3 in 2002, these figures greatly underestimate the extent of the problem because they are based on cases reported to agencies only. A general theme of the research in this area is the prevalence, correlates, consequences of, and treatments for maltreatment (Kendall-Tacket, Williams, & Finkelhor, 1993).

Issues of maltreatment have also been responsible for perhaps the most significant area of study in children and the law: factors related to children's ability to provide accurate testimony about experienced events. For several reasons, these studies have mainly focused on young children (ages 3 to 7) and have been framed to address issues concerned with sexual abuse. First, there has been a growing awareness and concern about the incidence of child sexual abuse in our society. In the United States, where national archives are kept for each type of maltreatment, the numbers are telling: For the 49 states reporting in the National Center on Child Abuse and Neglect's (NCCAN) 1998 national data system, there were 103,600 cases of *substantiated* sexual abuse (1.5 per 1,000 children), nearly 38% of which involved children age 7 and younger. In 2002, the rate dropped to 1.2 per 1,000 children (Child Maltreatment, 2004).

Second, prior to the 1980s, children were rarely admitted as witnesses in the legal arena (see Ceci & Bruck, 1995). This pattern changed as a result of society's reaction to the dramatic increases in child abuse[1] and as a result of the ineffective prosecution of child abuse cases. During the 1980s, all but a few jurisdictions in the United States dropped their corroboration requirement for children in sexual abuse cases, a crime that by its nature lacks corroboration. Many states began to allow children to testify regardless of the nature of the crime, permitting the jury to determine how much weight to give to the child's testimony. In Canada, with the adoption of Bill C-15, the court could now convict on the basis of a child's unsworn testimony. In England, children over 3 years of age were admitted as witnesses in the courtroom and could provide unsworn corroborated testimony in sexual abuse cases.

Third, in addition to those children who enter the forensic arena for issues related to sexual abuse, there are many others who come into contact each year with the juvenile and criminal justice systems for other reasons (witnesses to domestic violence, hearings for persons in need of supervision, neglect/permanency hearings, and custodial disputes). The numbers of young children involved in the various parts of the justice system become frighteningly large. In all of these situations, children may be asked to provide sworn or unsworn statements, be deposed, and sometimes be required to testify in court proceedings. Thus, young children represent a large and growing legal constituency,

one that possesses a special set of constraints involving basic developmental competencies, involving cognitive, social, and emotional domains, that may constrain their effective participation.

Fourth, beginning in the 1980s, there were a number of highly visible cases that came to court in which young children claimed that their caretakers had abused them. The claims often included a commingling of plausible allegations with fantastic reports of ritualistic abuse, pornography, human and animal sacrifice, multiple perpetrators, and multiple victims (e.g., *California v. Raymond Buckey et al.*, 1990; *Commonwealth of Massachusetts v. Cheryl Amirault LeFave*, 1998; *Lillie and Reed v. Newcastle City Council & Ors*, 2002; *New Jersey v. Michaels*, 1994; *North Carolina v. Robert Fulton Kelly Jr.*, 1995; *State v. Fijnje*, 1995). The defendants in a number of these cases were convicted.

When these types of cases first came to trial, the major issue before the jury was whether or not to believe the children. Prosecutors argued that children do not lie about sexual abuse, that the child witnesses' reports were authentic, and that their bizarre and chilling accounts of events, which were well beyond the realm of most preschoolers' knowledge and experience, substantiated the fact that the children had actually participated in them. Furthermore, they argued that patterns of delayed disclosures and denials and recantations were typical, if not diagnostic, of sexual abuse in children.

The defense argued that the children's reports were the product of repeated suggestive interviews by parents, law enforcement officials, social workers, and therapists. Although the defense was able to point out some of the potentially suggestive interview techniques that were used in eliciting allegations with the children, in the absence of any direct scientific evidence to support the view that such techniques could actually lead children to make incorrect disclosures of a sexual nature and in light of the common belief of that time that children do not lie about sexual abuse, many of these cases eventuated in convictions (for details of the early cases, see Ceci & Bruck, 1995; Nathan & Snedeker, 1995).

The issues raised by these cases were taken up by social scientists and resulted in the most heavily researched topic in children and the law. There are several major areas of study. The first concerns the accuracy of children's autobiographical memory: how well they remembered their past and how well they recalled traumatic events and how they disclosed the traumatic event of child abuse. A second related area

---

[1] Consider the rarity of perceived incest just 35 years ago: "Incestuous sexual relations are indulged in by less than one in every million people in English-speaking countries" (Verville, 1968, p. 372).

concerns the degree to which children will make false reports of nonexperienced events as a consequence of suggestive interviews. A third area concerns the credibility of children's statements using both a juror decision-making paradigm (e.g., McCauley & Parker, 2001; Nightingale, 1993; Quas, Bottoms, Haegerich, & Nysse-Carris, 2002) and, as described later in the chapter, more objective measures of credibility, A fourth area concerns modifications that could be made in and outside of the courtroom to increase the accuracy and the safeguarding of children's testimony. This area has resulted in the development of scientifically validated interviews, the examination of the positive impacts of various courtroom modifications (closed-circuit TV), and the pros and cons of electronically recording interviews with young children.

CASE EXAMPLE AND PRESENTATION OF RELEVANT SCIENTIFIC EVIDENCE

In this section of this chapter, we review the literature on the four major areas of research spurred by the day care cases, with a particular focus on accuracy and suggestibility of autobiographical memory. We do this by drawing on one of the actual cases, *Lillie and Reed v. Newcastle City Council & Ors,*[2] 2002 to illustrate the application of developmental psychology in informing the court about some of the key issues of study in children and the law. Because neither this nor any other case can cover all key issues in this field, we discuss other issues in the second section of this chapter.

Case Facts

Chris Lillie and Dawn Reed were two British day care workers who were accused of sexually abusing 27 children at a day care facility in Newcastle, a city in the northeast of England. The defendants were first declared innocent at their criminal trial in 1994. However, in 1998, a special review committee set up by the town accused them anew of abuse. In 2002, Reed and Lillie then sued the review committee, the town counsel, and the local newspaper for libel. The judge in that case found them innocent of all charges and awarded them monetary damages.

---

[2] For a detailed account of this case, see http://www.richard-webster.net/cleared.html.

The initial allegation was reported to the police by Mrs. Roberts in April 1993. She claimed that her 2-year-old son, Tim, had indicated that Chris Lillie had touched him in the genital area. However, when interviewed by the police and social services a few days later, Tim denied that Lillie had hurt him; physical examination also failed to show any positive evidence of abuse. Nonetheless, the investigation continued, and Chris Lillie was suspended from his duties at the day care. Mrs. Roberts continued to supply the police with additional details that Tim was abused in a house with black doors and Lillie's coworker, Dawn Reed, was involved.

Several weeks after Mrs. Roberts's report, social services met with the parents of the day care children and announced that one of the workers had been suspended because of an allegation of sexual abuse. Dawn Reed was officially suspended from the school soon after that meeting.

Social services contacted families to determine whether the children had made any allegations or whether parents were concerned. At times, they provided parents with advice on how to question their otherwise silent children. Approximately 25 children were interviewed at least once by the police and social services. A number of the children were interviewed two and even three times to elicit allegations of abuse. In June 1993, after 4-year-old Mandy Brown claimed that she had been vaginally penetrated with a crayon at least 9 months previously, Lillie and Reed were arrested. They were successfully granted bail, but just as they were leaving their cells, they were rearrested on the basis of the statement of a 5-year-old child who had not attended the day care for over 1 year. At the end of her third interview, this child alleged that she, too, had been abused. All interviews in this case were videotaped.

On the basis of a disciplinary hearing held by social services in February 1994, Lillie and Reed were dismissed from their positions at the day care, and in July 1994, their criminal trial commenced. There were 11 counts involving 11 children (the index child, Tim, was not a witness). It was a very short trial because the judge dismissed the entire case on the grounds that the evidence was too weak to present to a jury. Lillie and Reed were legally free. However, due to the outrage of the parents and based on the city council's belief that that the pair were guilty, an independent review team was set up to determine what, if anything, went wrong in the investigation. The review team's mandate was to examine how the allegations of abuse arose and to investigate specific complaints made by parents. They were not asked to judge the guilt or innocence of Lillie or Reed. After 4 years of investigation, in 1998 the review team issued its report, titled *Abuse in the Early Years* (Barker, Jones, Saradjian, & Wardell, 1998) and concluded, "From the evidence we have seen it is clear that Chris Lillie and Dawn Reed had conspired as a pair to abuse children and it is also clear that other people outside the nursery were involved" (p. 264). Lillie and Reed became the objects of public hatred, in part incited by the headlines in the local newspaper. They went into hiding. Eventually, due to the efforts of two journalists, they brought suit against the city council, the local evening newspaper (the newspaper made an out-of-court settlement), and the review team itself.

There were two prongs to their case. The first was for the original plaintiffs to show that Lillie and Reed were indeed guilty of child abuse. The second was to show that the plaintiffs acted in bad faith and were indeed guilty of malice and libel toward Chris Lillie and Dawn Reed. After a 6-month trial, the judge ruled in favor of the complainants, awarding them the maximum penalty of £200,000 each. The review team was found guilty of libel; the city council was not found guilty on the grounds of "qualified privilege."

One of the authors of this chapter (MB) served as an expert witness for the complainants. This involved writing a brief that was submitted to the court before the trial and that was to serve as the basis for her cross-examination during the trial. Major parts of the chapter that follow are excerpts from this document that have been updated in terms of the scientific foundation that was presented in 2002.

We selected this case because it contains a variety of ideas that have been examined in research in children and the law. In addition, it shares the following set of characteristics with other cases involving allegations of sexual abuse in institutional settings, usually day cares, that spurred the initial research interest in this area.

First, the children in these cases were all preschoolers attending day care programs; most were 3 or 4 years olds. Second, the first child to make an allegation (the index child) did not initially make spontaneous statements but was questioned by an adult who was suspicious that something had happened to the child. When first questioned, the index child denied harm or wrong-

doing; however, with repeated questioning, allegations began to emerge. Third, on the basis of the index child's uncorroborated allegations, parents of children in the day care were informed that a child had been abused or that abuse was suspected. Parents were instructed to look for symptoms of abuse (bedwetting, crying, nightmares) and to question their children about specific events. Fourth, as was the case with the index child, children at first told their interviewers that nothing had happened; however, after repeated questioning by parents, police, social workers, and/or therapists, some of these children also reported abuse. Sometimes it took months of questioning for them to provide an acceptable report. Fifth, there were a number of contaminating factors that could account for the common allegations of the children: In each case, the same small group of professionals interviewed all of the children, provided therapy for them, and evaluated them for sexual abuse. In addition, parents and children interacted with each other and spoke about the newest claims or rumors. Sixth, although, for the most part, there was no reliable medical evidence of sexual abuse, most parents reported changes in their children's behavior around the time of the alleged abuse, such as nightmares, bedwetting, baby-talking, resistance to going to the bathroom alone, refusal to attend day care, and much more. Finally, the children's reports became more elaborated with time; for example, after naming a specific perpetrator, children began to make disclosures about other workers at the day care, and sometimes they made disclosures about other people in the town. Over a period of time, the children's allegations became quite disturbing and bizarre; they alleged that they were taken out in boats or thrown into pools of sharks or taken to unknown places where they were tied up in chains or hung upside down from trees or ceiling hooks.

The most unifying characteristic of all these cases was the methods or strategies used by interviewers to elicit the children's allegations of abuse. These included, but were not limited to, the following ingredients:

- The child was given little opportunity to say in his or her own words what, if anything, had happened.

- Interviewers quickly resorted to the use of questions that required monosyllabic responses.

- Interviewers' statements and questions contained sexual content and details about the case that may not have been part of children's initial knowledge.

- Questions were repeated within and across interviews.
- Interviews continued or were repeated until the child provided information consistent with sexual abuse.
- Interviewers used bribes or threats of punishment ("I will give you a treat if you tell me" or "We can't go home until you tell what happened").
- Interviewers used selective reinforcement in response to children's statements (rewarding the child for abuse-consistent statements but ignoring or making negative comments in response to denials of abuse or related activities).
- Interviewers made "atmospheric" statements that conveyed the theme that something bad had happened (e.g., telling the children not to be afraid, that they are being brave, that they are going to be protected, or that they are helpers in an investigation).
- Interviewers invoked statements of other people ("Your mom told me that . . ." or "All your friends have talked about this, now it's your turn").
- Interviewers induced negative stereotypes of the suspected perpetrator (e.g., telling the child that the suspect does bad things, that he is in jail).
- Props, such as dolls, toys, sandbox enactments, and drawings, were used to elicit statements about touching.

Bringing Developmental Psychology to the Courtroom

The ultimate goal of presenting to the court the scientific literature on memory and memory distortions is to provide a scientific basis for evaluating the reliability of the witnesses' statements. In this context, reliability refers to the *trustworthiness* of the evidence, not to the honesty or credibility of a witness. Statements or reports can be unreliable due to normal processes of forgetting, of distortion, and of reconstruction. Statements can also be rendered unreliable if they are elicited in certain
suggestive contexts. Thus, the expert's testimony focuses on the factors that enhance or degrade the quality of children's and adults' reports. This was the primary focus of the expert testimony presented to the court in *Lillie-Reed*. Although an assessment of the credibility (believability) of the children's statements and a determination of whether the child witnesses were abused by the defendants are issues within the province of the

jury, not the expert witness, the provision of information on the reliability of the evidence to jurors or to judges is crucial to allow them to draw conclusions about the credibility of the children's allegations and, in this case, about the guilt of Lillie and Reed.

The scientific literature has little to say about the *competence* of a witness. There are several reasons for this. First, there appears to be little if any relationship between children's truthfulness in their recall of experienced events and their performance on competence-type interviews that are often used in the courtroom (e.g., London & Nunez, 2002; Talwar, Kang, Bala, & Lindsay, 2004). Second, because the competence standard is quite undemanding (witnesses are deemed competent if they are sufficiently intelligent to observe, recollect, and recount an event and have a moral sense of obligation to speak the truth), most witnesses are deemed competent by the judge. Thus, the expert's analysis is not that the children were incompetent but that the methods used to gather information from them rendered their statements, and thus the inherent quality of the evidence, unreliable.

The Nature and Time Course of Children's Disclosures of Sexual Abuse

In this section, we first summarize the evolution and landmarks of children's allegations of sexual abuse in Lillie and Reed. Next we summarize the scientific literature on how children disclose abuse and the interpretation of the pattern of disclosure in the target case.

Case Facts

In the present case, none of the children[3] spontaneously told of sexual abuse (with the possible exception of Rosie's statement to her mother that Lillie had touched her privates; this statement was made in September 1992, months before the investigation began; the mother did not know what she was talking about). According to the parents, when they first asked their children if they had been abused, five of the children denied wrongdoing. The electronically preserved recordings of the first official forensic interviews,

---

[3] Examples provided in this chapter focus on the index child and the six child witnesses who were to appear in the 1994 criminal trial.

which occurred days to months after the parents' first questioning, show that none of the children provided consistent allegations that Lillie or Reed had sexually abused them. Consequently, five of the children were interviewed a second time, during which three gave some kind of statement consistent with sexual abuse. One child was interviewed a third time, and only after a very long session, with three interviewers, did she finally provide a few abuse-consistent statements.

Scientific Evidence

It is of primary importance to examine the evolution of the children's reports of sexual abuse. The pattern that occurred in the present case has raised the most concerns: The child is initially silent; she does not make any unsolicited or spontaneous statements about abusive acts. Rather, the allegations emerge once an adult suspects that something has occurred and starts to question the child. At first, the child denies the event happened, but with repeated questioning, interviewing, or therapy, the child may eventually make a disclosure. Sometimes, after the disclosure is made, the child may recant, only to later restate the original allegation after further questioning. The most popular embodiment of this idea is Summit's (1983) description of the *child sexual abuse accommodation syndrome* (CSAAS).

Because the CSAAS model was based not on empirical data but on clinical intuitions, we recently reviewed the literature to determine its empirical support (London, Bruck, Ceci, & Shuman, 2005). We identified 10 studies in which adults with histories of childhood abuse were asked to recall their disclosures in childhood. Across studies, an average of only 33% of the adults remembered disclosing the abuse in a timely fashion. In some studies, approximately 30% of adults reported that they had never told anyone before the current interview about their childhood abuse (Finkelhor, Hotaling, Lewis, & Smith, 1990; Smith et al., 2000). These data support the CSAAS model in that sexually abused children are silent about their victimization and delay disclosure for long periods of time.

Although informative on the issue of delay of reporting, these data are silent with regard to the phenomena of denial and recantation, because the participants were never asked, "As a child, did anyone ever ask you or question you about abuse?" We simply have no way of knowing whether these individuals denied having been abused and then perhaps subsequently recanted their re-

luctant disclosures. Another set of studies provides some data relevant to this point. We identified 17 studies that examined rates of denial and recantation by sexually abused children who *were* asked directly about abuse when they were assessed or treated at clinics. The rates of denial at assessment interviews were highly variable (4% to 76%), as were the rates of recantation (4% to 27%). We found that the methodological adequacy of each study (the representativeness of the sampling procedures and the degree to which sexual abuse was validated) was directly related to the rates of denial and recantation: The weakest studies produced the highest rates of denial and recantation. For the 6 methodologically superior studies, the average rate of denial was only 14% and the average rate of recantation was 7%. Thus, although the retrospective studies of adults show that children often do not disclose their abuse, the studies of sexually abused children's responses in a formal interview indicate that if they are directly asked, they do not deny, but rather disclose that they were abused.

In part, the myth about children's patterns of disclosure has persisted because documentation of the first stage of the CSAAS model (children are silent and delay disclosures) has been interpreted as evidence for the full model, according to which denial and recantation are common. Also, as shown by our recent review and analysis, the most commonly cited studies in the literature are those that support the model—but sadly, these are the methodologically weakest of the studies.

Interviewers of children suspected of abuse who are not aware of the scientific evidence, but rather follow the clinical lore that sexually abused children are afraid to talk, deny abuse, and then recant abuse, may not accept the child's initial statements that nothing occurred and continue to interview until allegations emerge. For example, in the present case, a mother questioned her 3-year-old child, Ned, about abuse in the spring of 1993. He said that nothing had happened to him. As a result, she had no concerns, until August 16, when a social worker explained that in some cases it took children a long time to disclose abuse. By August 18, after additional questioning, there was now enough concern to have Ned interviewed by the investigators.

To summarize, the most consistent finding in the scientific literature is that although a significant proportion of sexually abused children will never report their abuse (spontaneously), when questioned about it by authorities, most will disclose and few will recant. If the children in *Lillie-Reed* had been sexually abused, then based on the scientific literature, one might predict (conservatively) that at least some of them, when directly asked, would have readily admitted that abuse occurred. And only a small proportion would recant allegations once they were made.

Because the patterns of disclosure of the children in *Lillie-Reed* were so discrepant from those reported in the methodologically strongest scientific studies, it raises the hypothesis that children's eventual disclosures were the product of suggestive influences that can sometimes eventuate in false allegations of sexual abuse. This hypothesis requires an analysis of the record to document how the children were questioned and an analysis of the scientific literature to determine the effects of such questioning techniques on the accuracy of children's statements. The next section undertakes such an analysis.

Research on the Effects of Suggestion on Children's Reports

Until the end of the 1980s, most developmental studies of suggestibility focused on children's answers to leading questions or children's incorporation of misleading suggestions into their reports. This focus on leading questions and misinformation did not, however, capture the essential features of the problematic interviews that occurred in a number of legal cases mentioned at the outset of this chapter. Because of the discrepancy between the structure and content of interviews in scientific studies and those occurring in actual cases, at the beginning of the 1990s, the scientific model of suggestibility was greatly expanded into a model of *interviewer bias*.

Interviewer Bias

According to our model of the architecture of suggestive interviews (Ceci & Bruck, 1995) interviewer bias is the defining feature of many suggestive interviews. Interviewer bias characterizes those interviewers who hold a priori beliefs about the occurrence of certain events and, as a result of such beliefs, mold the interview to elicit statements from the interviewee that are consistent with these prior beliefs. One of the hallmarks of interviewer bias is the single-minded attempt to gather only confirmatory evidence and to avoid all avenues that may produce negative or inconsistent evidence. The biased interviewer does not ask questions

about the allegations that might provide alternative explanations that are inconsistent with his or her primary or only hypothesis. When provided with inconsistent or bizarre evidence, biased interviewers either ignore it or else interpret it within the framework of their initial hypothesis. This belief is transmitted to the child via a range of suggestive interviewing techniques that are associated with the elicitation of false reports. Consequently, the child may come to inaccurately report the belief of the interviewer rather than the child's own experience. Finally, it is important to note that a biased interviewer may be a police officer, a therapist, or even a parent.

Interviewer bias has been the focus of much study by developmental forensic psychologists. The following two studies provide a flavor of the methodologies and results of some of these studies.

Chester the Janitor. Thompson, Clarke-Stewart, and Lepore (1997) conducted a study in which children viewed a staged event that could be construed as either abusive or innocent. Some children interacted with a confederate named Chester as he cleaned some dolls and other toys in a playroom. Other children interacted with Chester as he handled the dolls roughly and in a mildly abusive manner. The children were then questioned about this event. The interviewer was (a) *accusatory* (suggesting that the janitor had been inappropriately playing with the toys instead of working), (b) *exculpatory* (suggesting that the janitor was just cleaning the toys and not playing), or (c) *neutral* and nonsuggestive. In the first two types of interviews, the questions changed from mildly to strongly suggestive as the interview progressed. Following the first interview, all children were asked to tell in their own words what they had witnessed and then were asked questions about the event. Immediately after the interview and 2 weeks later, the children were asked by their parents to recount what the janitor had done.

When questioned by a neutral interviewer, or by an interviewer whose interpretation was consistent with the activity viewed by the child, children's accounts were both factually correct and consistent with the janitor's script. However, when the interviewer was biased in a direction that contradicted the activity viewed by the child, those children's stories quickly conformed to the suggestions or beliefs of the interviewer. In addition, children's answers to interpretive questions (e.g., "Was he doing his job or just being bad?") were in agreement with the interviewer's point of view, as opposed to what actually happened. When asked neutral questions by their parents, the children's answers remained consistent with the interviewers' biases.

Surprise Party.   Bruck, Ceci, Melnyk, and Finkelberg (1999) showed how interviewer bias can quickly develop in natural interviewing situations, and how it not only taints the responses of child interviewees but also the reports of the adult interviewers. In this study, a special event was staged for 90 preschool children in their school. In groups of three and with the guidance of research assistant A, the children surprised research assistant B with a birthday party, played games, ate food, and watched magic tricks. Another 30 children did not attend the birthday party; in groups of two, they simply colored a picture with research assistants A and B. These children were told that it was assistant A's birthday.

Interviewers (who were recruited from university graduate degree programs in social work or counseling and who had training and experience in interviewing children) were asked to question four children about what had happened when special visitors came to the school. The interviewers were not told about the events but were simply told to find out from each child what had happened. The first three children that each interviewer questioned attended the birthday party and the fourth child attended the coloring event.

Bruck, Ceci, Melnyk, et al. (1999) found that the children who attended the coloring event and were interviewed last produced twice as many errors as the children who attended the birthday party; 60% of the children who only colored made false claims that involved a birthday party. This result suggests that the interviewers had built up a bias that all the children had attended a birthday party. By the time they interviewed the fourth child, they structured their interviews to elicit claims consistent with this hypothesis. Thus, if interviewers have the belief that all the children they are interviewing have experienced a certain event, it is probable that many of the children will come to make such claims even though they were nonparticipants (or nonvictims). Another important finding was that even when the fourth child denied attending a birthday party, 84% of their interviewers later reported that all the children they interviewed had attended a birthday party. These data suggest that regardless of what children actually say, biased interviewers inaccurately report the

child's claims, making them consistent with their own hypotheses.

These two studies and others like them provide evidence that interviewers' beliefs about an event can influence their judgments as well as their style of questioning. This, in turn, can affect the accuracy of children's testimony. The data highlight the dangers of having only one hypothesis about the event in question—especially when this hypothesis is incorrect.

Interview Bias in Lillie-Reed

Although some children in the present case did utter words or statements that were consistent with the hypothesis that they were touched by Chris Lillie or Dawn Reed, they also made other allegations about other teachers or adults that seem to have been ignored.

One child told the investigative interviewer that Chris Lillie had hurt her bum with a crayon at Lillie's house. When questioned further, she stated in three different parts of the interview that her father was also present:

Interviewer: Was anybody else there?
Child: No. Daddy was . . .
Interviewer: And who did you say was there at Chris's house?
Child: Nobody.
Interviewer: I thought you said somebody called dad was there?
Child: [inaudible]
Interviewer: Was it your dad from home?
Child: Yes.
Interviewer: What did he look like?
Child: He looked at me and he said I see you later. That's what he said. . . .
Interviewer: Do you know when you said that you'd been to Chris's house?
Child: I know my daddy was there.
Interviewer: Your daddy was there?
Child: My daddy [inaudible] was and my mummy wasn't.*

Like other children, this child also named other people who were present or involved in the alleged abuse,

---

Interviews with children in all cases in this chapter were presented in court and are in the official record. Segments of these interviews that are quoted in the present paper are marked with an asterisk and were reported by Bruck in her testimony before the court.

such as Helen, Tommy, Lynn, and the man with the sack at the library. A classmate claimed that Diane and other teachers had driven the children to Lillie and Reed's flat and that Diane had given her a bath. The police did question each of the day care workers, who, like Lillie and Reed, denied any knowledge of the reported activities. But for some reason, whereas the denials of others were accepted, Lillie and Reed were not believed. The multitude of names provided by the children led some to assume that there was an organized group of pedophiles abusing all the children. However, this ring of pedophiles also included adults explicitly mentioned by the children such as their fathers, their doctors, their parents' friends, and their teachers. The investigators seem to have ignored this discrepant evidence.

During the videotaped interviews, at least four children made exculpatory statements about Dawn Reed (and some also did about Chris Lillie), but these were ignored. For example:

> **Interviewer:** What about Dawn because you had some things to tell me about Dawn as well, didn't you, eh?
> **Child:** No.
> **Interviewer:** You said there were some silly things about Dawn, eh?
> **Child:** No, that was ages ago when I come here. . . .
> **Child:** But don't say nothing to Dawn cos she wasn't silly. . . . She just went into jail for nothing. Say Dawn can come out today. Say that. Don't let Chris out!*

When this interviewer presented the evidence of abuse to the disciplinary panel that subsequently dismissed Lillie and Reed, she edited out what *she* thought was irrelevant; she omitted to tell them of this child's denials in two different interviews.

Investigators argued that the children remained silent or denied abuse because they were too frightened to tell of their actual abuse. Nowhere is there evidence that they considered the possibility that the children remained silent because there was nothing to tell. Rather, children were interviewed until they simply could stand it no longer (e.g., Rachel ended up moaning in her mother's lap; Mary whimpered; Nora begged her mother to stop and when she did not, Nora simply left the room). The interviewers interpreted these behaviors as further signs of resistance, reflected in their

continuing to question the children. For example, the two social workers who were present during Rachel's interview interpreted her behavior as follows:

> **Social Worker 1:** Towards the end of the interview, she appeared to become restless. I had visited her at home and not seen her display this sort of behaviour before. Although the interview had been fairly long I do not think she was tired, but rather pretending to be tired in order to avoid answering our questions. I recall that when we went out of the room she was running around and playful.
> **Social Worker 2:** I recall that after the video interview was over, she walked along the street holding on to Social Worker's hand with great relief that she was out of the video room. My impression was that she had been quite frightened.*

These interviewers did not consider the hypothesis that the contents and structure of the interview were aversive to the child rather than any trauma-induced secrecy resulting from past abuse.

Behavioral symptoms pre- and postdisclosure were viewed as primary or additional evidence of sexual abuse. There did not seem to be any recognition that as parents became more convinced that their children were abused, they changed their reports on the frequency, severity, and onset of the symptoms. There was no consideration that the children's symptoms could reflect normal developmental patterns, that they could reflect problems in the household (divorce, leaving of partners, merging of new households, violence, etc.), nor was there any realization that the symptoms may have emerged or become exacerbated because of the manner in which the children were interviewed or treated.

The focus on behavioral symptoms in this case was based on the assumption that there is a common constellation of symptoms that are diagnostic of sexual abuse. However, there are no behavioral symptoms that are diagnostic of sexual abuse. Many of the problems cited by the parents (anxiety, enuresis, fears, night terrors, and even sexual behaviors) either are common in children of this age or can be associated with other types of childhood behavioral disorders (see Kendall-Tackett et al., 1993). Also, a majority of sexually abused children are asymptomatic. Thus, the fact that so many of these children had problems indicates that perhaps other causes should have been examined but they were not.

Suggestive Interviewing Techniques Used by
Biased Interviewers

Interviewer bias influences the entire architecture of interviews and is revealed through a number of different component features, some of which were listed in the first section of this chapter (e.g., repeated questions, selective reinforcement, peer pressure). As will be described in the next sections, the results of the scientific literature indicate that the use of these suggestive techniques, especially in the hands of biased interviewers and especially when used in combination, can bring children to make claims about events that they have never experienced.

Open-Ended versus Specific Questions

To confirm their suspicions, biased interviewers may not ask children open-ended questions, such as "What happened?" but instead quickly resort to a barrage of very specific questions, which require the child to provide one-word answers (yes or no). Sometimes the questions are very leading (e.g., asking the child "Where did your teacher touch you?" is very leading if the child never previously mentioned touching by the teacher), and often the questions are repeated until the child provides a desired response.

Although the strategy of using specific questions, leading questions, and repeating questions ensures that the child will provide information, it is also problematic because children's answers to these types of questions are often inaccurate. For example, Peterson and Bell (1996) interviewed children after they had been treated in an emergency room for a traumatic injury. They were first asked free recall questions ("Tell me what happened"). Then, to obtain additional information, the children were asked more specific questions (e.g., "Where did you hurt yourself?" or "Did you hurt your knee?"). Peterson and Bell found that children were most likely to accurately provide important details in free recall. Across all age groups, errors increased when children were asked more specific questions. The percentage of errors elicited by free recall and specific questions was 9% and 45%, respectively.

Specific questions include yes/no questions ("Did the lady have a dog?") and forced-choice questions ("Was it the man or the woman?"). One reason using these questions is risky is that children rarely reply "I don't know" even when explicitly told that this is an option (Peterson & Grant, 2001) and even when the question is nonsensical and thus incomprehensible (Hughes & Grieve, 1980; Waterman, Blades, & Spencer, 2000). One of the reasons that children so willingly provide answers to specific yes/no or forced-choice questions even though they may not know the answer or understand the question is that young children are cooperative conversational partners, and they perceive their adult interviewer as truthful and not deceptive. To comply with a respected adult, children sometimes attempt to make their answers consistent with what they see as the intent of the questioner rather than consistent with their knowledge of the event (see Ceci & Bruck, 1993, for a review). Because of this compliant, cooperative characteristic, and because of young children's poor performance on specific questions, it is particularly important in interviews to avoid these types of questions until after the child has first provided evidence in response to open-ended questions.

As illustrated throughout this chapter, interviewers in *Lillie-Reed* rarely asked open-ended questions and mostly asked specific questions that can be answered with little effort in one or two words. In the following example, the prosecution's best witness is interviewed by the police and social services for the third time in a period of 3 weeks. She had told her mother in the car prior to the interview that it was all a stupid joke. In the first half of the interview, when bombarded with specific questions by the two interviewers (Helen and Vanessa), she mainly replied that she did not know or did not remember. When she did provide answers to questions, these were so disjointed that it seemed the child had given up and decided to answer each question as it came with no attention to the content or the sequence of previous questions or answers.

Interviewer: Did he have anything on underneath his pants?
Child: Yes, underpants.
Interviewer: Did he take those down?
Child: Yes.
Interviewer: And did you see any bits of his body?
Child: Yes.
Interviewer: And what did that look like?
Child: It was big.
Interviewer: Can you remember which way it was pointing, pointing up or pointing down.
Child: Pointing up, I mean down it was up then down, up then down.
Interviewer: So it was going up and down all the time.

Interviewer: Was it doing that on its own?

Child: Yes.

Interviewer: What colour was it?

Child: Pink.

Interviewer: It was pink; it was going up all the time, and then what?

Child: That was all, those were the only two things that, that I had to tell to do.*

When examining transcript examples, such as this one, it is instructive to focus simply on the child's words to estimate how much the child actually said and how much the interviewers said. As shown in this excerpt, this child said very little besides "Yes," "It was big," and "Pink" before stating that she had fulfilled her promise to tell about two things.

The low frequency of open-ended questions and the high frequency of specific questions are not specific to this one case, but appear to characterize forensic interviews with children in general. For example, analyses of 42 child protective services interviews with children ages 2 to 13 years in one state revealed that 89% of the questions about the suspected abuse were specific (Warren, Woodall, Hunt, & Perry, 1996).

Interviewers often state that they do not frequently use open-ended questions because of cognitive, emotional, and motivational barriers that inhibit children's spontaneous disclosure of abuse and because children must be encouraged to disclose by being asked specific questions over a period of time. Even though there are known risks of using leading or specific questions, perhaps these are necessary to elicit reports or details from sexually abused children who feel frightened, ashamed, or guilty.

This claim has recently been challenged by Lamb and colleagues (2003), who constructed a structured interview protocol and then trained interviewers in its use. The protocol requires trained interviewers to encourage suspected child abuse victims to provide detailed life event narratives through the guidance of open-ended questions (e.g., "Tell me what happened"; "You said there was a man; tell me about the man"). The use of specific questions is allowed only after exhaustive free recall. Suggestive questions are highly discouraged. In a recent study, Lamb et al. examined the interviews of police officers trained on the protocol with 4- to 8-year-old children who had made allegations of sexual abuse. Lamb et al. found that 83% of all allegations and disclo-

sures were elicited through free recall questions (78% for preschoolers), and 66% of all children identified the suspect through open-ended questions (60% for preschoolers). These data dispel the belief that interviewers need to bombard children with suggestive techniques to elicit details of trauma; rather, children can provide detailed information through open-ended prompts, and if a child denies abuse when asked directly, there is no scientifically compelling evidence that the child must be "in denial." As argued in the previous section, abused children usually disclose the abuse when directly asked.

Repeating Interviews and Repeating Questions

In formal investigations, children are often interviewed on many different occasions. There are numerous concerns about the influence of these repeated interviews on children's reports, especially when conducted by biased interviewers. As shown next, the results of several studies indicate that repeated questioning and interviewing in suggestive interviews increase the number of false allegations.

For example, preschool children were interviewed on five different occasions about two true events and two false events (Bruck, Ceci, & Hembrooke, 2002). The two true events involved the child helping a visitor in the school who had tripped and hurt her ankle, and a recent incident where the child was punished by the teacher or the parent. The two false events involved helping a woman find her monkey and witnessing a man steal food from the day care. In the first interview, children were simply asked if each event had ever happened. If they said yes, they were asked to describe the event. During the next three interviews, the children were suggestively interviewed (e.g., they were asked repeated leading questions, they were praised for responses, they were asked to try to think about what might have happened, they were told that their friends had already told and now it was their turn). In the fifth interview, a new interviewer questioned each child about each event in a nonsuggestive manner. Across the five interviews, all children consistently and accurately assented to the true event about helping a woman who fell in the day care. However, children were at first reluctant to talk about the true punishment event; many of the children denied that the punishment had occurred. With repeated suggestive interviews, increasing numbers of children agreed that the punishment had occurred. Similar patterns of disclosure occurred for the two false events; that is, children initially correctly denied the false events, but with repeated suggestive interviews, they began to assent to these events. By the third interview, most children had assented to all true and false events. This pattern continued to the end of the study.

One of the rationales for reinterviewing children is that it provides them additional opportunities to report important information that was forgotten or simply not reported in earlier interviews. Thus, it is assumed that when children provide new details in subsequent interviews, these new reports are accurate memories that were not remembered in previous interviews. Another rationale is to allow children to rehearse so that their memories will not fade over time. However, the results of recent studies dispute this claim. One set of studies consistently shows that reports that emerge in a child's first interview with a neutral interviewer are the most accurate. When children are later interviewed about the same event and report new details not mentioned in a previous interview, the newer details are less accurate than those repeated from the first interview (Peterson, Moores, & White, 2001; Pipe, Gee, Wilson, & Egerton, 1999; Salmon & Pipe, 2000). In some studies, the inaccuracy rates of new, inserted details in neutrally conducted interviews rise to a level of 50% (Peterson et al., 2001; Salmon & Pipe, 2000). Similar results are obtained when children are suggestively questioned about an actual event (Bruck et al., 2002; Scullin, Kanaya, & Ceci, 2002). Thus, insertion of new but inaccurate details can be a natural memory phenomenon; it can be due to prior suggestions that become incorporated into later reports; but it can also be due to the demand characteristics of the interview. When interviewers urge children to tell them anything (that is consistent with the bias of the interviewer), these requests for additional information will sometimes result in false reports that are supplied by the children to comply with their perception of the interviewer's wishes.

Although these studies show the detrimental effects of repeated interviews, there is an important qualification to this conclusion: There are a number of studies in which children who are provided with misinformation across multiple interviews are no more likely to incorporate this information into a later report than children who receive only one suggestive interview. The major factor appears to be the timing of the suggestive interviews: If the first suggestive interview occurs soon after an event and the second interview occurs close to the final interview, then misinformation effects are maximized (Melnyk & Bruck, 2004). There are several points to bear in mind, however; as shown in some of the studies in this chapter, one suggestive interview can destroy the reliability of a child's report; also, it may take several suggestive interviews to move the child from making simple assents to providing some elaboration to the false allegations (see Bruck et al., 2002, in which repeated suggestive interviews were associated with more elaborated narratives of false events).

Just as there are risks associated with repeated interviews, there are also risks associated with repeating questions within the same interview. Biased interviewers sometimes repeatedly ask the same question until the child provides a response that is consistent with their hypothesis. Poole and White (1991) found that asking the same question within an interview, especially a yes/no question, often results in young children changing their original answer (see Cassel, Roebers, & Bjorklund, 1996, for similar effects when children are asked repeated leading questions). Furthermore, when children are asked the same question on numerous occasions, they sound increasingly confident about their statements even if these are false.

It also appears that when interviews contain a preponderance of (mis)leading questions, children will initially resist the suggested response, but with repeated misleading questions (that differ in content), their resistance dissipates. Garven, Wood, Shaw, and Malpass (1998) found that preschoolers provided increasingly inaccurate responses to misleading statements and questions as a suggestive interview proceeded. In this study, children were suggestively interviewed for 5 to 10 minutes about a stranger who came to read their class a story. As a result of the suggestive devices used by Garven and her colleagues, children falsely claimed that the visitor said a bad word, that he threw a crayon, that he broke a toy, that he stole a pen, that he tore a book, and that he bumped the teacher. Of particular importance, the children came to make more false claims as the interview progressed; that is, within a short, 5- to 10-minute interview, children made more false claims in the second half than in the first half of the interview. It seems that it is not simply repeating questions but repeating questions about a specific theme (e.g., the visitor doing bad things) that may compromise the reliability of children's reports.

Forced Confabulation Effects

As will be seen from some of the examples of *Lillie-Reed*, not only were the young child witnesses asked repeated questions within the same interview and across interviews, but this questioning often continued until the children provided answers amid protests that they did not know the answer (i.e., they were forced to give an answer). This practice raises the following question: If the children were forced to knowingly provide an inaccurate answer to a question, would they not correct themselves when given the next opportunity (e.g., in the next interview, or in the same interview)? In other words, if a child first denied abuse until he or she was coaxed to provide abuse-related information and then later produced an abuse-consistent disclosure, doesn't this mean that the child's second statement is unreliable?

Two studies conducted by Zaragoza and colleagues (Ackil & Zaragoza, 1998; Zaragoza, Payment, Kichler, Stines, & Drivdahl, 2001) show that when children are forced to provide an incorrect answer (confabulation), they will not only continue to provide the same incorrect answer but will actually come to believe in the validity of the wrong answer. For example, in the latest study (Zaragoza et al., 2001), children came to a laboratory and played computer games; during this time, a handyman came into the room and fixed some broken things. Immediately after, the child was asked a number of questions about the event and was told to provide an answer no matter what. Children were asked questions about things that really happened and they were asked misleading questions about things that did not happen. For example, children were asked how the handyman had broken the videotape (he had not even touched the videotape). Although most children claimed that he had not broken the videotape, they were told to provide an answer anyway. Sometimes it took several rounds of coaching to get the children to provide an answer. For example:

Interviewer: There's a videotape on top of the VCR that is broken. How did he break it?
Child: I have no clue.
Interviewer: Can you tell me how you think he might have broken it?
Child: I have no clue.
Interviewer: Just make something up then.
Child: I can't think of anything.
Interviewer: Well, what might, what, what might someone do to break a videotape?

Child: Drop it.
Interviewer: That's right! He did drop it.*

Two weeks later, these children were brought back to the laboratory and informed that the original experimenter had made some mistakes and had asked them questions about things that had never happened. The children were asked to report only those things that they actually saw. In this second interview, children at all ages (6 to 10 years) reported that the confabulated false items had actually occurred (they saw it). For example, 60% of the 6-year-old children now reported in the second interview that they saw the handyman break the videotape.

This is an important study because it shows that no matter how resistant to misleading questions a child may be in an earlier interview, with sufficient pressure not only will he or she come to report this false information in a later interview, but he or she will report that it actually happened. Using a milder version of the forced confabulation interview, similarly dramatic suggestibility effects have been reported (Bruck, London, Landa & Goodman, in press; Finnila, Mahlberga, Santtilaa, Sandnabbaa, & Niemib, 2003).

In summary, if children's allegations are elicited by specific leading questions that have been repeated within the same interview or across interviews, there is a high risk that the children's statements will be unreliable. Conversely, children's answers to open-ended questions asked prior to any suggestive interviewing have a high probability of being accurate.

Following are examples of repeated questions and repeated interviews from *Lillie-Reed:*

Interviewer: Did you have anything to tell me about the nursery?
Child: Not actually.
Interviewer: Not actually or I've got that wrong. Can you tell me what it is?
Child: Can't. Don't know what it is.
Interviewer: You don't know what it is. Okay. Is there anything you want to tell me about anything that happened at nursery?
Child: Don't know.
Interviewer: Did anybody do anything at the nursery that they shouldn't have done?
Child: What's this? [about something she has in her hand]
Interviewer: Did anyone do anything at the nursery that they shouldn't have done?

Child: No.

[Child's mother enters the room]

Interviewer: Did Chris do anything to you? Can't you tell me, 'cause I can't hear very well. Can you just tell me?

Mom: Will you tell me?

Child: I can't.

Interviewer: Why can't you tell, 'cause it's alright here, you know? To tell Mummy and me. Hmm? And you won't have to tell anyone again, will you? You just tell us now. Hmm?

Mom: Did something happen that you didn't like?

Child: No! Yeah!

Mom: What?

Child: Chris, Chris hit me and Jill.*

When interviewed for a second time in December 1993, this child's denials of abuse became allegations of abuse after repeated specific questions and perhaps as a result of the repeated interview:

Interviewer: What about Dawn because you had some things to tell me about Dawn as well, didn't you, eh?

Child: No.

Interviewer: You said there were some silly things about Dawn, eh?

Child: No, that was ages ago when I come here.

Interviewer: But you said that you got touched by Dawn and can you—I just need to know where she touched you? It's all right.

Child: On my fairy. [Children used the term fairy to refer to their vagina.]*

The next example shows how suggestive techniques used in one interview may show their influence only in a later interview.

Mom: Right, can you remember when you were sitting in the house? Can you remember when you had a sore fairy? You tell Helen [the interviewer], right, what you said to me when you said a sore fairy. Has anybody ever touched your fairy in the nursery? [child shakes her head "no"] That's not what you told me.

Mom: Remember when you had a sore fairy?

Child: No/What?

Interviewer: Did you have a sore fairy when you went to nursery school?

Mom: Didn't you? You used to have a sore fairy. Did you?

Child: No.

Mom: You did. You told me you did, didn't you? Its ok you know, we're not going to get a smacked bum or anything. . . . You're a good girl. 'Cause you know when you told us you had a sore fairy and I asked you has anybody ever touched your fairy at nursery and you said yes, didn't you? Didn't you?

Child: No.

Mom: [laughing] You did. Stop telling fibs. . . .

Mom: Listen, can you remember when we were talking in the house and you said you had a sore fairy? Come here a minute, two minutes while I just ask you this. Can you remember when we were talking in the house and you said you had a sore fairy? Can you remember? Hmm? [child shrugs no] You can. Tell the truth. Be a big girl like you were, 'cause you're not going to get wrong, you know for a fact you're not. And didn't I say to you has anybody ever touched your fairy at nursery?

Child: No. . . .

Mom: Tell Auntie who touched your fairy.

Child: I don't think so.

Mom: You don't think so? . . .

Mom: Well, can you remember? Can you remember who, who touched your fairy? Can you remember?

Auntie: Are you going to tell us your secret? I'll tell you my secret if you tell me yours.*

In interview 2, when first asked about touching, this child now gave the following answer:

Interviewer: So, what did you want to tell me about this person called Chris?

Child: Touched me.

Interviewer: Can you show me where? If that was you, where did he touch you?

Child: On my fairy.*

Although this analysis focuses mainly on the children's statements in the videotaped interviews, it is important to note that the children were questioned before these official interviews were recorded. The record shows that children had several to many sessions with parents, friends of parents, relatives, and professionals. For example, although one child, Mandy, first told her parents about abuse in May 1993, her parents had questioned her a few times before. It was not until June 28, however, that the parents gave permission for their daughter to be interviewed by the officials; the major reason was that Mandy had made more disclosures when they were questioning her.

Another mother first suspected that her child may have been abused in May 1993. Her child was interviewed at the police station in June 1993 but made no allegations consistent with sexual abuse. Then she was questioned many times between June and December. On December 1, 1993, when she was interviewed for the second time at the police station, she made a few allegations consistent with abuse. Given the denial of wrongdoing in the June interview, followed by an enormous amount of repeated interviewing during the next few months, the few allegations that emerged in the December 1 interview are not "fresh" utterances but may have been contaminated by multiple retellings and questionings.

Atmospherics or Emotional Tone of the Interview

Interviewers can use verbal and nonverbal cues to communicate their bias. These cues can set the emotional tone of the interview. Research shows that children are quick to notice the emotional tones in an interview and to act accordingly. For example, in some studies when an accusatory tone is set by the examiner (e.g., "It isn't good to let people kiss you in the bathtub" or "Don't be afraid to tell"), children are likely to fabricate reports of past events even in cases when they have no memory of any event occurring. In some cases, these fabrications are sexual in nature.

In one such study, children played with an unfamiliar research assistant for 5 minutes while seated across a table from him. Four years later, researchers asked these same children to recall the original experience (Goodman, Batterman-Faunce, Schaaf, & Kenney, 2002). The researchers created "an atmosphere of accusation," telling the children that they were to be questioned about an important event and saying things like, "Are you afraid to tell? You'll feel better once you've told." Although few children had any memory of the original event from 4 years earlier, 5 out of the 15 children incorrectly agreed with the interviewer's suggestive question that they had been hugged or kissed by the confederate, 2 of the 15 agreed that they had their picture taken in the bathroom, and one child agreed that he or she had been given a bath. In other words, children may give inaccurate responses to misleading questions about events for which they have no

memory when the interviewer creates an emotional tone of accusation.

Rewards and punishments shape the emotional tone of an interview and provide another means for interviewers to express bias. The use of rewards and punishments in interviews with children can be beneficial by motivating children to tell the truth. On the other hand, there may also be negative consequences; children may learn that if they produce stories that are consistent with interviewers' beliefs, their interviewers will reward them.

A study conducted by Garven, Wood, and Malpass (2000) illustrates how the use of rewards and punishments in an interview can quickly shape the child's behavior and have long-lasting consequences. Children between the ages of 5 and 7 attended a special story time led by a visitor called Paco. During this 20-minute visit, Paco read the children a story, handed out treats, and placed a sticker on the child's back. One week after the visit, the children were asked mundane questions ("Did Paco break a toy?") and fantastic questions ("Did Paco take you somewhere in a helicopter?"). There were two interviewing conditions. In the neutral-no reinforcement condition, children were simply asked a list of 16 questions and provided no feedback after each question. In the reinforcement condition, children were asked the same 16 questions, but they were provided with feedback after each question, as illustrated by the following example:

Interviewer: Did Paco take you somewhere on a helicopter?
Child: No. [Note this is an accurate denial]
Interviewer: You're not doing good. Did Paco take you to a farm?
Child: Yes. [Note this is an incorrect assent]
Interviewer: Great. You're doing excellent now. [The next question is asked.]*

The reinforcement had large negative effects on the accuracy of children's responses. Children in the reinforcement condition inaccurately assented to 35% of misleading mundane questions and to 52% of the misleading fantastic questions. The comparable rates for the nonreinforcement group were 13% and 15%. In a second interview, a week later, all children were asked the same questions without any reinforcement. The same high error rates continued for the reinforcement children. When children were challenged and asked in the second interview, "Did you see that or just hear about that?" children in the reinforcement group stated that they had personally observed 25% of the misleading mundane events and 30% of the misleading fantastic events. Children in the nonreinforcement group made these claims only 4% of the time.

These findings show how quickly reinforcing statements can shape children to provide inaccurate responses no matter how bizarre the question. Furthermore, the inaccurate responses persist on second questioning, with a number of children claiming that they actually observed the suggested but false event. Of course, as shown in some of the excerpts, rewards and punishments can take a more explicit form, such as promising children a treat if they tell the right answer or threatening the children if they provide an undesirable answer.

Examples from the Lillie-Reed Case

The following excerpts are statements by a child's mother and by her aunt, who were both allowed to help investigators interview the child. There statements were made to induce this young child to make abuse-consistent disclosures.

Aunt: You promised to tell me your secret if I got all the Barbie toys for you and you didn't tell us. Didn't you not?

Aunt: Yes. All right, I'll get them, but are you going to tell me your secret, then? Because you said you would.

Mom: If you can remember who it is, or who it was, we'll get you some clothes for the Barbie.

Aunt: Do you want us to take you to Fenwicks and buy you some clothes for your Barbie?

Aunt: You tell me what you told your mummy last week, right? Are you listening? And I'll let you come sleep at my house a night.

Mom: After you tell AUNT what happened, right and then we'll go downtown and buy your Barbie some new clothes, eh? If you're a good girl, if you tell Auntie Joan.

Aunt: Do you want to tell me about the nursery, eh, and then we'll go to Fenwicks for a McDonald's burger.*

In addition to positive and negative reinforcement, rewards, and bribes, the children were repeatedly told not to be frightened, not to be afraid, and that they were

brave. For example, the word "frighten" was used 9 times in the following excerpt, which also shows the potentially damaging effect of this strategy that was repeated by the investigator, the mother, and the mother's friend.

Interviewer: I was wondering if maybe Grace was frightened.

Interviewer: Do you think she's frightened to tell me?

Friend: I think so and I think I know what she's frightened of.

Interviewer: Grace, have we got this bit right? Grace?

Mom: Listen, Grace, are you frightened?

Interviewer: What of?

Grace: Chris.

Interviewer: What for? You're safe. . . .

Interviewer: We're all there to look after you and there's nothing for you to be frightened of.

Friend: So that nobody can harm her, can they not, Grace. . . .

Friend: What did he do when he was naughty, Grace?

Interviewer: I think Grace's still a little bit frightened but she doesn't have to be.

Mom: What did Chris tell you to be frightened of, Grace? Why were you frightened?

Grace: Monsters.*

Stereotype Induction

Suggestions do not always take the form of explicit (mis)leading questions, such as "Your Dad was mad, right?" One suggestive interviewing technique involves the induction of negative stereotypes by telling a child that the suspect "does bad things."

As a study by Lepore and Sesco (1994) shows, some children will incorporate this negative information into their reports.

In this study, children played games with a man called Dale. Dale played with some of the toys in a researcher's laboratory room and he asked the child to help him take off his sweater. Later, an interviewer asked the child to tell her everything that happened with Dale. For half the children, the interviewer maintained a neutral stance whenever they recalled an action. For the remaining children, the interviewer reinterpreted each of the child's responses in an incriminating way by stating, "He wasn't supposed to do or say that. That was bad. What else did he do?" Thus, in this condition, the bias that Dale had misbehaved was induced. At the conclusion of these incriminating procedures, the children heard three misleading statements about things that had not happened: "Didn't he take off some of your clothes, too?" "Other kids have told me that he kissed them, didn't he do that to you?" and "He touched you and he wasn't supposed to do that, was he?" All children were then asked a series of direct questions, requiring yes or no answers, about what had happened with Dale.

Children in the incriminating condition gave many more inaccurate responses to the direct yes/no questions than children in the neutral condition. Interestingly, one-third of the children in the incriminating condition embellished their responses to these questions, and the embellished responses were always in the direction of the incriminating suggestions. The question that elicited the most frequent embellishments was "Did Dale ever touch other kids at the school?" Embellishments to this question included information about who Dale touched (e.g., "He touched Jason, he touched Tori, and he touched Molly"), where he touched them (e.g., "He touched them on their legs"), how he touched them (e.g., "And some he kissed . . . on the lips"), and how he took their clothes off ("Yes, my shoes and my socks and my pants. But not my shirt"). When they were reinterviewed 1 week later, children in the incriminating condition continued to answer the yes/no questions inaccurately and they continued to embellish their answers.

In *Lillie-Reed,* the children were repeatedly told that Chris Lillie and other people had done "silly" things and they were constantly asked to talk about the silly things.

> **Interviewer:** Why. Because I've heard some stories about silly people at the nursery school doing silly things. So I said to your mummy has Mary told you anything about these silly things at nursery and she said "Oh, yes, shall I bring her to talk to you?" I said "Oh, please. I don't know what all these silly things are." Do you? Did you tell your mummy about them though?*

Interviewers told the children that Lillie was in jail and asked if he had hit or hurt them.

> **Mom:** Remember when mum and you were talking this morning and I asked you if Chris had ever hurt you [The child is lying on her mother's lap and moaning], and I said that the policeman took him away now and he can't ever hurt you again and nothing bad's going to happen to you because you

can tell now? Can you remember what you said to me when I asked if Chris had ever hurt you?*

The children were also asked about "naughty" things that happened or to tell about the naughty things that Chris Lillie and Dawn Reed had done. During one child's first interview, the investigators used the word "naughty" approximately 53 times. The following was the child's response after "naughty" had been mentioned 15 times:

> **Interviewer:** Well, I don't want him to be naughty. You've told us he's been naughty and I don't want him to be.
> **Child:** Why?
> **Interviewer:** 'Cause I don't think he should be, but I need—
> **Child:** He's been nice before and now he's being naughty.*

In the next exchange, "naughty" had been mentioned another 9 times:

> **Interviewer:** So it was something to do with Charlie. Is it something to do with some part of Charlie's body?
> **Child:** No.
> **Interviewer:** Is it something naughty? Is it something nice?
> **Child:** Uh-huh.
> **Interviewer:** I'm still a bit stuck, 'cause it's hard guessing that.
> **Child:** I know something naughty.
> **Interviewer:** It was something naughty, right. That's the bit I cannot think. So it was something naughty and mummy's forgotten and now you're the only one who knows.
> **Child:** I don't know.*

And finally, after approximately 29 more repetitions of the word "naughty," when questioned by the mother's friend, the child produced the major allegation of the interview:

> **Interviewer:** He's naughty, though, isn't he? Why do we say he's naughty? 'Cause what did he do again?
> **Child:** 'Cause he's naughty.
> **Interviewer:** 'Cause what did he do, though, to make him naughty?
> **Child:** He smacked me bum.*

Many of the children's first allegations involved hitting. Vanessa Lyon, one of the main interviewers, also noted this trend and declared that children often begin to disclose abuse by describing the least abusive incident, which allows them to gauge the reactions of people they tell. But in examples such as the present one, the children did not have to gauge the reactions of the adult, who willingly accepted any statement of wrongdoing that involved Chris Lillie or Dawn Reed. Thus, another interpretation of this pattern is that it was the repetitious words and concepts like "naughty" that, when paired with questions about Chris Lillie, prompted Grace to come up with the naughtiest answer that she could think of: Chris smacked her bottom. In this case, as in others, allegations of sexual abuse emerged later, as interviewers provided the children with sexual information that, prior to the interviews, was unfamiliar to these children.

Peer Pressure

The effect of telling children that their friends have "already told" is a much less investigated area in the field of forensic developmental psychology. Certainly, the common wisdom is that a child will go along with a peer group. But will a child provide an inaccurate response just so he or she can be one of the crowd? The most recent and most relevant studies in the literature suggest that the answer is yes (Principe & Ceci, 2002; Principe, Kanaya, Ceci, & Singh, in press).

Preschoolers in groups ranging in age from 6 to 8 took part in a contrived "dig" with a fictitious archaeologist named Dr. Diggs (Principe & Ceci, 2002). Dr. Diggs led the children through an event in which they used plastic hammers to dig pretend artifacts (e.g., dinosaur bones, gold coins). Dr. Diggs also showed the children two special artifacts: a map to a buried treasure and a rock with a secret message. The children were warned not to touch these because they could be ruined. All children in the study participated in or viewed these core events. However, one-third of the children also saw Dr. Diggs ruin the two special artifacts (heretofore referred to as the target activities) and show upset about their loss. A second third of the children were the classmates of those in the first group but did not witness the extra target activities. The remaining children were not the classmates of those who witnessed the target activities, nor did they witness the target activities themselves; they thus served to provide a baseline against which to assess the effects of peer contact. Following

the dig, the children were interviewed in either a neutral or a suggestive manner on three occasions. The suggestive interviews for children who did not view Dr. Diggs ruining the special artifacts provided children with this information. Children in the neutral interview were not given information about the two target events. In a later interview, children were asked questions about the dig. Children who had not reported the two absent special activities were prompted to tell more by the interviewer's telling them that their friends had already told.

Children who were classmates of those who saw Dr. Diggs ruining the two artifacts were more likely to claim that they had viewed the target activities (i.e., they incorporated the misinformation from the previous interview) than children who did not view the special activities and were in another classroom. These data suggest that there was contamination from classroom interactions; children who had not experienced the target events learned of them from their classmates and thus were more likely to assent to false events. Finally, telling children that their friends had told increased their false assent rate.

Principe et al. (in press) conducted another study in which they found that children who overheard a child talking were as likely to falsely claim to have seen the event in question (a rabbit that escaped from a magician) as were peers who actually saw it escape. Moreover, in this study, the effect of suggestive questioning did not notably increase their false reports; they were as likely to report falsely if they overheard peers talking about the rabbit, regardless of whether interviewers employed suggestive questions.

In *Lillie-Reed*, Children were told that their friends had come and talked about "silly things":

> **Interviewer:** You know your friends that you played with at nursery school? I've been talking to them . . . They were telling me about some silly things that happened at the nursery. Do you know about them things? . . .
> **Child:** Don't know that.
> **Interviewer:** Shall I help you a bit? They were telling me about their teachers, when they were in your class.*

After the accusations of abuse, teachers in the day care kept "disclosure logs" to record children's statements about abuse. Some of the examples show how children talked among themselves about abusive subjects in what seemed to be a very playful atmosphere.

Child 1 They had real snakes, they went SSS, they were toys in the cage outside.

Child 2: I saw the snakes and cage, but I ran up the steps, the snakes are called Mandy the same as me. [Note this is the first time Mandy mentions snakes.] . . .

Child 2: And do you know what? Chris and Dawn kicked me.

Child 3: Why did they kick you?

Child 2: 'Cause they thought I was a pirate lady.

Child 1: And they slapped me 'cause they thought I was a doggy. [Both Child 1 and Child 2 laugh and begin to jump on a piece of equipment.]*

It appears that the first allegations of Child 2 and Child 3 may have emerged from these sessions.

Nonverbal Props

Because of the limited language skills of young children, many interviewers use nonverbal props to help children provide details of their past. These props have been particularly used in interviews of sexually abused children as a way to question children about how and where they were touched. Although the use of props seems intuitively useful, the scientific literature indicates that at times, these devices will increase inaccuracy in children's reports. One of the reasons for this is because the prop is being used as a symbol and young children are not symbol-minded. According to Deloache (DeLoache & Smith, 1999), who has conducted the pioneering work in this field, for the child to become symbol-minded, the child must come to understand that symbolic objects have a dual nature: They represent the object itself (e.g., a doll) as well as a specific referent (e.g., the doll represents the child). Until 4 years of age, children do not have this appreciation. One result is that they end up "playing" with the symbol. In this respect, the symbol is a suggestive influence. Some examples of research on the influence of props on children are now presented.

Anatomically detailed and undetailed dolls are frequently used by professionals when interviewing young children about suspected sexual abuse. The major rationale for the use of anatomical dolls is that they allow children to manipulate objects reminiscent of a critical event, thereby cuing recall and overcoming language and memory problems as well as motivational problems of embarrassment and shyness. However, research conducted in the past decade has raised concerns about the suggestiveness of the dolls and their influence on the accuracy of children's reports. There are several important findings of this research. First, there is no consistent evidence to suggest that there are characteristic patterns of doll play for abused children. Many studies show that the play patterns thought to be characteristic of abused children, such as playing with the dolls in a suggestive or explicit sexual manner or showing reticence or avoidance when presented with the dolls, also occur in samples of nonabused children. Second, more recent studies indicate that use of the dolls does not improve accuracy of young children's reports, and in some cases they decrease accuracy. For instance, we found that 3-year-old children (Bruck, Ceci, Francoeur, & Renick, 1995) and 4-year-old children (Bruck, Ceci, & Francoeur, 2000) who had just completed a medical examination at their pediatrician's office made a number of errors when asked direct questions about where the pediatrician had touched them and that these errors increased when children were asked these same questions in conjunction with dolls. Specifically, children inaccurately showed that the doctor had touched their genitalia or buttocks when this did not happen. These inaccurate answers reflect the novelty of the dolls, which prompted the children to explore the genitalia, often in very creative ways; the inaccurate answers also reflect the implicit demands of the interview, which were to show and talk about touching.

There is also a single case study that suggests that repeated exposure to the dolls may lead young children to fabricate highly elaborate accounts of sexual abuse. After a third exposure in a period of a week to an anatomically correct doll, a nonabused 3-year-old told her father that her pediatrician had strangled her with a rope, inserted a stick into her vagina, and hammered an ear scope into her anus (see Bruck, Ceci, Francoeur, & Renick, 1995).

Researchers have examined the effects of giving children real objects (e.g., a stethoscope) or a toy object (e.g., a teddy bear to represent the child, or a toy car to represent a real car) to report their past experiences. In a recent review of the experimental studies examining the use of props in interviews, Salmon (2001) concluded that although real props increase the amount of information that children report about an event, they also increase the number of errors. Further, she concluded that free access to a large number of real props is associated with a relatively large number of errors in children's reports about touching, particularly for younger children. For example, Pipe et al. (1999, experiment 2) reported that repeated interviewing with real props introduced a disproportionate amount of new inaccurate information into children's reports after a 1-year delay. Steward and Steward (1996) found that when children had the opportunity to manipulate real props, the situation turned from one of reporting what actually happened to playing. Similar findings have been found for toys or for small-scale props (i.e., giving the child a toy piece of furniture and asking him to show how he was sitting).

Asking the Child to Draw

In her review, Salmon (2001) concluded that asking children to draw a picture about a specific event in combination with nonleading verbal prompts can enhance the verbal reports of children over the age of 4 years, but it is less effective for younger children. She also concluded, however, that after a long delay, not only will drawing elicit less information than not drawing (i.e., just asking), but it also introduces additional errors into children's accounts. A recent study found that when drawing is accompanied by misleading questions, it is associated with very high error rates in children's subsequent reports (Bruck, Melnyk, & Ceci, 2000).

A striking aspect of the interviews in *Lillie-Reed* was the number of toys available to the children during investigative interviews. On the one hand, these seemed to have put the children at ease and allowed them to enjoy some of the experience. However, generally, their presence was distracting and resulted in the children spending more time playing with the toys than focusing on the interview. As a result, there are times when it is not clear if the child was actually playing or directly responding to the interviewer's question.

Children were shown dolls and sometimes asked to draw or point to body parts to elicit allegations of abuse. The problem with this strategy is that it signals to the child that the focus of concern is the touching of certain areas of the body. Children may provide abuse-consistent responses because they think this is what the adults want to hear. Also, the use of these props makes it easier for adults to ask leading questions about touching ("Show me where he touched you. What do we call this part? Did he touch you here?").

On July 12, Kristen reported in an investigative interview with that Chris Lillie had hurt her bottom with a crayon, that he had tickled her with a crayon, and that he had put a crayon in her "fairy." The context of this last disclosure is as follows. First, Kristen asked to play with a doll and the interviewer encouraged her to undress the doll and name the body parts. When directly asked, the child denied twice that anything bad happened to her at the day care. The interviewer then pointed to the doll and asked:

Interviewer: Has anybody ever hurt those bits on your body?
Child: No. Chris.
Interviewer: How did Chris hurt those bits?
Child: He's hurt mine bum and it's sore now.
Interviewer: So you know you're pointing to that bit between your legs and you said Chris had hurt you. How did he do it?
Child: He'd do it this hard. [As she says this, Kristen, who is sitting on a child's tiny wooden chair, lifts her skirt and points or presses a finger or fingers between her legs—what looks like the vagina area.]
Interviewer: And what was he using to do it with?
Child: He was . . . [there is a brief pause while she looks at the table of toys in front of which she is sitting and then stretches her hand out to a plastic bucket of crayons that she was earlier using to draw] using a crayon.*

Thus, Kristen's disclosure that Chris Lillie had inserted a crayon in her vagina was actually a demonstration with props that were laid out on the table in front of her. Perhaps she named the prop to provide an answer to a question that she had no answer for. In research settings, it is common for children to name surrounding props when asked questions to which they do not know the answer. For example, in the monkey-thief study (Bruck et al., 2002), when children were asked what the thief had stolen, a number of children named objects that were in the interviewing room (e.g., video camera, clock, books). When children in this study were asked to describe the thief, they would often look at the experimenter and describe the very clothes she was wearing. (Interestingly, there were children in the *Lillie-Reed* case who, when asked what they were wearing when they were abused, replied, "These clothes that I am wearing now.")

Kristen's claim that she had a crayon inserted in her fairy is reminiscent of the children in the Bruck, Ceci, Francoeur, and Renick (1995); Bruck et al. (2000) studies; when these children were asked how the doctor touched them, they used available props to make false demonstrations or statements that these had been inserted into their buttocks or genitals. Thus, it is possible that Kristen's initial response reflected her use of an available object to fill in the answer to a question with no knowable answer. It was a response that, once elicited, she repeated and elaborated. On July 20, the medical examiner noted that "Kristen told her" that Chris Lillie had put a crayon in her vulva and made her bleed in her knickers. On the basis of her statements, Lillie was arrested and put in prison on July 24.

Combining Suggestive Techniques

For ease of exposition, we have attempted to discretely categorize a number of suggestive interviewing techniques. As can be seen from so many of the excerpts, these elements rarely occur in a vacuum; each interview was filled with a variety of suggestive interviewing techniques. The scientific literature demonstrates that as interviews become more suggestive, the number of false allegations increases (e.g., Bruck et al., 2002; Leichtman & Ceci, 1995; Scullin et al., 2002). One reason for this is that as the number of techniques increases, the bias of the interviewer becomes clearer.

Generally, the interviews in the *Lillie-Reed* case are so filled with suggestive interviewing techniques that they are best described as chaotic. Children were given toys, they were asked to draw, or the interviewer would draw. Never was there any attempt to identify whether the children were playing or actually describing their alleged abuse. In addition to the props, toys, and drawings, when one interviewer could not deal with the situation, another one was called in, and sometimes parents or friends of parents were asked to join in or take over the interview. Sometimes one of these interviewers would leave (on the promise that the child would tell when the interviewer left), only to reappear later in the interview. Children were promised trips to restaurants if they would tell. Children were told to be brave, or they were told that they were safe because the bad people were in jail. Children were asked leading questions or provided with direct information about touching, about abuse, about Lillie, about Reed, and about trips to Lillie's apartment. And all of this information was repeated within and across interviews, with the goal that the children would come to make statements consistent with the prevailing belief that they had been abused by Lillie and Reed.

The Effects of Suggestion on the Credibility of Children's Reports

It is one thing to demonstrate that children can be induced to make errors and include false perceptual details in their reports, but it is another matter to show that such faulty reports are convincing to an observer, especially a highly trained one. In a series of studies, Ceci and colleagues (Ceci, Loftus, Leichtman, & Bruck, 1994; Ceci, Huffman, Smith, & Loftus, 1994; Leichtman & Ceci, 1995) showed videotapes to experts of children's reports that emerged as a consequence of repeated suggestive interviews. In some cases, the experts also saw videotapes of children who resisted suggestions and denied that anything had happened. These experts were asked to decide which of the events reported by the children actually transpired and then to rate the overall credibility of each child. Experts who conduct research on the reliability of children's reports, who provide therapy to children suspected of having been abused, and who carry out law enforcement interviews with children generally failed to detect which of the children's claims were accurate and which were not, despite being confident in their judgments.

Some professionals state that they can detect suggestion because the children simply parrot the words of their investigators. However, evidence from the past decade provides no support for this assertion. First, children's false reports are not simply repetitions or monosyllabic responses to leading questions. Under some conditions, their answers go well beyond the suggestion and incorporate additional details and emotions. For example, in the Bruck et al. (2002) study, children's false reports contained the prior suggestion that they had seen a thief take food from their day care; but the reports also contained nonsuggested details such as chasing, hitting, and shooting the thief (also see Bruck, Ceci, Francoeur, & Barr, 1995; Ceci, Huffman, et al., 1994).

Finally, linguistic markers do not consistently differentiate true from false narratives that emerge from repeated suggestive interviews. In the Bruck et al. (2002) study, where children were repeatedly and suggestively interviewed about true and false events, the children's narratives of the false events actually contained more embellishments (including descriptive and emotional terms) and details than their narratives of the true events.

Also the false narratives had more spontaneous statements than the true narratives. Although for the most part, the details in false stories were realistic, as suggestive interviews continued, children inserted bizarre details into their stories, a point that we now consider.

In *Lillie-Reed,* some of the children's disclosures became bizarre or fantastic with repeated interviewing, For example, after one suggestive investigative interview, one of the children, Ned, reported that he had been penetrated with a knife (there was no physical evidence); that Dawn Reed had put needles into his bottom; that Chris Lillie had urinated in his face; that Lillie and Reed had swapped bodies, putting each other's head on and different hair and clothes. Ned also spoke of monsters in an elevator. He said that Reed picked him up and put him in a cupboard with no handles or windows but that he turned into a gladiator and killed everyone.

Three hypotheses have been offered to account for the occurrence of such bizarre details. The first is that they are false and are the result of suggestive interviews (Bruck et al., 2002). Second, although reports of fantastic or bizarre events may themselves be false, their presence is claimed by some to be symptomatic of trauma, and as such may be markers for narratives that are otherwise true. According to this latter hypothesis, as a consequence of their abuse, children may misperceive actions or events or use fantasy to deal with their anxieties and to empower themselves to regain control over their victimization (see Everson, 1997, for a full account of explanations). Finally, children may make bizarre allegations because their abusers maliciously suggest false events to the children so that they will not be believed at all. For these reasons, reports of abuse should not be discounted as false if they contain fantastic or bizarre details because fantastic details occur with some frequency in the reports of children who were actually abused (Dalenberg, Hyland, & Cuevas, 2002).

Some of the professionals involved in *Lillie-Reed* expressed belief in the children's bizarre allegations, as reflected by the following statement of the chief medical examiner:

> The bizarre nature of the abuse, almost certainly involving instrumentation, drugs and pornography, at a time when the children's cognitive abilities were so immature, means that triggers are not easily recognized. For example, a soda siphon sound in one room caused hysteric panic to a child in another.

The review team argued that although the content of each and every statement made by the children may be incorrect, nonetheless the substance of the disclosures is correct. Thus, statements that the children had been penetrated with scissors or that they had been taken to specific locations by Lillie and Reed or that Lillie and Reed had swallowed bleach are said to contain important kernels of truth. The argument is that either because the children did not have the vocabulary or because they were misinformed about specifics, there are errors in their statements.

Although some of these arguments seem plausible, there is strong scientific evidence to support only the first hypothesis: that evolving bizarre disclosures reflect suggestive interviewing techniques. The argument is not that interviewers suggested these bizarre details to the children, but that it became clear to the children that the more details they could produce, the more they pleased their interviewers, even if they produced very fantastic and bizarre details.

To summarize, when children have undergone suggestive interviewing or are exposed to some of the components of suggestive interviews, they can appear highly credible when they are inaccurate, even to well-trained professionals. Accordingly, once children have been exposed to the suggestive influences discussed here, it is impossible to support a claim that the reports obtained from them are reliable. Demeanor, affect, spontaneity, and other traditional criteria used to determine credibility are rendered irrelevant to the determination of the accuracy of the postsuggestion report.

Adults' Memories for Conversations with Children

As we have demonstrated, information on the exact wording of each question asked of children during interviews, as well as the number of times questions are repeated and the tone of questioning, is necessary to determine whether strategies recognized as capable of affecting the reliability and accuracy of children's reports were used by interviewers. In Lillie-Reed the lack of such information for the parents', the physicians', and other professionals' reports makes it impossible to make such a determination. Therefore, videotaped interviews of the children must be relied on to examine the instances when children made or denied allegations of abuse.

It is a well-documented fact in the psycholinguistic literature that when asked to recall conversations, most adults may recall the gist (the major ideas, the core content), but they cannot recall the exact words used, nor the sequence of interactions between speakers. This latter linguistic information rapidly fades from memory, minutes after the interactions have occurred (for a review, see Rayner & Pollatsek, 1989). Bruck, Ceci, and Francoeur (1999) videotaped mothers interviewing their 4-year-old children about a play activity that had taken place in the laboratory. Three days later, mothers were asked to recall this conversation. The mothers could not remember much of the actual content of the interview, omitting many details that had been discussed, but much of what they did recall was accurate. Of particular importance, the mothers were especially inaccurate about several aspects of their conversation: They could not remember who said what (e.g., they could not remember if they had suggested that an activity had occurred or if the child had spontaneously mentioned the activity). Mothers also could not remember the types of questions they had asked their children (e.g., if they had used an open-ended question or a series of leading questions to obtain a piece of information). For example, although some mothers in this study remembered that they learned that a strange man came into the room when the child was playing, they could not remember if the child spontaneously gave them this information, or if it was obtained through a sequence of repeated leading questions that the child assented to with monosyllabic utterances. To summarize, although mothers could accurately remember parts of the general content of the conversation, they could not remember how or if they questioned their child.

A similar study was conducted with mental health trainees. This study (the birthday party study; Bruck, Ceci, Melnyk, et al., 1999) was described earlier in the section on interviewer bias. Mental health trainees interviewed four children about an event. They were encouraged to make notes after each of the interviews. A few weeks later, their memories for two of the conversations were tested. The mental health trainees showed the same pattern as the mothers. Even though they were allowed to consult their notes, they could not remember who first mentioned certain pieces of information; also, they could not remember if the child's statements were spontaneous or the result of leading questions. In addition, these trainees mixed up which of the four children said what. That is, they often attributed the actual report of Child A to Child B.

Warren and Woodall (1999) obtained results similar to those reported for mothers and mental health trainees. These researchers studied experienced investigators who created summaries immediately after their interview with a child. When asked what types of questions they had used to elicit information from the children, most of these experienced interviewers answered that they had asked primarily open-ended questions, few stated that they had asked specific questions, and only one reported asking any leading questions. Their estimates were highly inaccurate, as most (over 80%) of the questions asked by these interviewers were specific or leading.[4] Returning to the Bruck, Ceci, Melnyk, et al. (1999) birthday party study, as reported earlier, the interviewers also made factual errors about the content of the children's statements. That is, the interviewers reported that the fourth child had attended a birthday party when it was clear in a number of cases that the child had made no such statement. A recent study conducted by Lamb and colleagues (Lamb, Orbach, Sternberg, Hershkowitz, & Horowitz, 2000) indicates that the findings that are obtained in the laboratory with mothers, mental health trainees, and skilled interviewers generalize to investigators who interview children suspected of sexual abuse. Verbatim contemporaneous accounts of 20 investigative interviews of 20 4- to 14-year-old alleged sexual abuse victims were compared with audiotaped recordings of these interviews. More than 50% of the interviewers' utterances and 25% of the incident-relevant details provided by the children were not reported in the "verbatim" notes. The structure of the interviews was also represented inaccurately in these accounts. Fewer than half (44%) of the details provided by the children were attributed to the correct eliciting utterance type. Investigators systematically misattributed details to more open rather than more focused prompts. In view of the quantity of errors in the Lamb et al. study, where notes were made at the time of the interview, one can begin to appreciate the large number of errors that can occur when adults attempt to recall conversations that occurred days or months previously.

These data provide an empirical basis for the importance of obtaining electronic copies of interviews with children. They suggest that summaries of interviews

---

[4] A number of parents stated that they did not ask leading questions or put words into their children's mouths. The scientific literature shows how difficult it is to evaluate just how we conduct conversations. Our memories are probably molded by how we would like to see ourselves rather than how we are.

based on interviewers' notes and memories may be inaccurate for a number of reasons. Usually, notes contain only pieces of information that the investigator thinks are important at the moment. If the investigator has a bias that the child was sexually abused, this could color his or her interpretations of what the child said or did, and it is this interpretation that appears in the summary rather than a factual account of what transpired. If a number of children are interviewed and the reports are not immediately written, the investigator may confuse which child said what. Finally, summaries of interviews based on interviewers' notes are exactly that—summaries. They do not contain a detailed accounting of how many times the same question was asked or how many times the child denied before finally assenting. No one without stenographic training can possibly record each and every time a question was asked that was not answered. Thus, the literature on adults' inability to accurately recall what children told them, when paired with the literature on forgetting, memory distortions, and biases, highlights the real problem of relying on parents' and investigators' reports of children's behaviors and statements that occurred in the past and that were not recorded at the time of their occurrence.

Examples from Lillie-Reed

All the children in the *Lillie-Reed* case made their initial disclosures to their parent(s), who were the first to question them about abuse. The parents recollected these conversations days, weeks, and months after they allegedly occurred. Some of these descriptions contain contextual statements, such as "I asked . . ." and "He said . . .," but, as the literature clearly shows, the potential for error is extremely high in these recollections, and as a result, the investigators of this case cannot determine the following: (a) whether the child's statement was spontaneous or prompted by dozens of questions (as was the case in the videotaped interviews); (b) how many questions the parent asked and how many different times the parent questioned the child to get any response; (c) whether the parent reported what he or she had said or what the child had said; (d) whether the parent accurately recalled the content of the child's statement; and (e) how much of the original interaction the parent omitted either because it was forgotten or because it was considered nonessential material at the time of recall. Because it is impossible to recapture this information, the most reliable evidence (and maybe the only reliable evidence) of the children's disclosures, and the

amount of prompting required to make these disclosures, is that obtained from the videotaped evidence.

This first example shows changes in one parent's memory of her child's pretend phone call in April 1993:[5]

> May 13 1993 Social Worker Report: Around Easter 1993, her mother left Rachel with some friends while she went shopping. On her return, her friend said that Rachel had said, "My Dad did something with his willie." Her friend had replied "no, no." Rachel did not say anymore when she was questioned further.
>
> August 17 1993 (Mother's statement to the police). On one occasion when Rachel was with a neighbor of mine, she was playing with a toy telephone and pretending to ring her Dad. She said something like someone's willie had been on her hand. When I tried to ask her further about this, she totally clammed up and rushed to another neighbor for reassurance saying, "I'm not naughty, I'm not naughty, am I?" We reassured her that she wasn't.
>
> March 1994 (Signed Statement). On one occasion, I left Rachel to be cared for by two friends. I went out shopping. Jeanie had reported to me when I returned that Rachel had been playing on a toy phone pretending to ring her Daddy. She said that someone's willie was on her hand. When she realized that Jeanie was listening she put the phone down and said, "I am not naughty am I." The next day I tried to talk to Rachel about it but she wasn't able to explain to me what she had said.

This example shows that the content of Rachel's utterance had changed from "My Dad did something with his willie" to "she told her dad that someone's willie was in her hand." With time, the statement became more consistent with the idea that someone besides her father had done something. This example also shows that although the words "no" or "naughty" continued to be mentioned, the specification of the speaker changed. Initially, it was the mother's friend, then it was Rachel in response to her mother's questioning, and finally it was Rachel's response to the adult's listening in on her pretend conversation.

In another example, according to the notes of a social worker who was present at the child's police interview, the child said that Chris Lillie and Dawn Reed were married. However, this statement was not made by this child in the interview.

Throughout their report, *Abuse in the Early Years* (Barker et al., 1998, pp. 210–214), the review team

---

[5] This interchange is a central theme in statements by Rachel's mother, probably because she interpreted it as Rachel's attempt to tell about the abuse.

provided examples of children's statements such as the following:

> Boys and girls describe being sexually assaulted and witnessing other children being sexually assaulted by Chris Lillie and to a lesser extent by Dawn Reed. These assaults were said to have taken place in the toilets, in a cupboard, and in the play house at the nursery. For example, one boy said that Chris Lillie had held his penis and rubbed it until it hurt. . . . Another child describes Chris Lillie weeing on his hair. . . . Several children told of a house with a black door in a named road. Children also talked of being taken in lifts to flats. . . . One child described Chris Lillie's willie pointing to the ceiling . . . one child described how Chris Lillie had put his tiddler in her fairy while she was sitting on the edge of a settee in his house . . . several children described being given an injection which we deduce from their descriptions contained some form of analgesic. . . . Children variously stated that they have been shouted at, sworn at, smacked, hit. . . . Children described how they were threatened, they said that a boy and a girl had been stabbed because they told their mum. . . . Other threats that the children were able to talk about were of monsters and a dog that would hurt you or scratch your fairy.

If indeed these statements were spontaneous, were not preceded by any forms of suggestion, and were the direct words of the children (rather than parents' summaries of conversations or the review team's summary of interactions in an interview), then the children's words would provide important evidence to support the hypothesis of abuse. However, a review of the case facts show that these purported statements of the children were often parents' reports of their child's statements; in other cases, these represent a combination of monosyllabic responses provided to a stream of leading questions or at the end of a very suggestive interview.

To produce their report, the review team interviewed more than 40 sets of parents/carers of children and more than 112 other witnesses. If the interviewing began in October 1995, these adults were recalling events, ideas, and impressions from 3 to 4 years earlier. Examination of the statements of parents at this last inquiry show how much their testimony changed from their first reports of their children's statements. Clearly, the review team relied on unreliable evidence from witnesses who deeply believed that their children had been abused.

The review team concluded that there was no evidence of suggestion in the interviews with the children.

They wrote: "The Review Team saw the evidential videos made by the children. These would not support the view that the questions were in any way leading" (Barker et al., 1998, p. 221). Their impression of the three interviews conducted with one of the child witnesses was this:

> Over three video interviews, she detailed abuse of herself and other children by Chris Lillie, to a lesser extent Dawn Reed, and she also mentioned other nursery staff's names. Her testimony in these videos, which we have seen, is extremely powerful and provided persuasive evidence of her abuse in the nursery and elsewhere. (p. 148)

Based on the analyses of the videotape by the plaintiffs' experts (including the first author of this chapter), it is difficult to understand how the review team came to such a conclusion; these interviews were highly suggestive. The judge agreed with this assessment.

Impact and Criticism of Scientific Studies Cited in Lillie-Reed

The child and law research conducted by developmental psychologists has had a large impact on many aspects of the legal arena. First, as a result of this new scientific evidence, many of the guilty verdicts of the 1980s and early 1990s have been or are being overturned. On appeal, the defendants presented relevant and appropriate scientific evidence to show how suggestibility and memory distortion could produce inaccurate statements of abuse in young children (e.g., *New Jersey v. Michaels*, 1994; *People v. Scott Kniffen, Brenda Kniffen, Alvin McCuan, and Deborah McCuan,* 1996; *Snowden v. Singletary,* 1998; *State of Washington v. Carol M.D. & Mark A.D.,* 1999; *State of Washington v. Manuel Hidalgo Rodriguez,* 1999). It is now rare to find similar cases cropping up in the legal setting, at least in North America. Second, as a result of this scientific literature, there is an awareness of the importance of developing scientifically validated protocols to be followed when interviewing children (e.g., Davies & Westcott, 1999; Lamb et al., 2003). Third, there is a growing awareness of the importance of videotaping the first and all subsequent investigative interviews with children in order to evaluate the degree to which children's initial statements were spontaneous and the degree to which they were elicited by various suggestive interviewing techniques.

Although this work is scientifically based, it is not without its critics (e.g., Lyon, 1999; Meyers, 1995). These critics claim that this area of science has created a backlash that has undermined the credibility of children, that focuses on the weaknesses rather than the strengths of their memory, and that denies the reality of child abuse. They also argue that because scientists have based their studies and analyses on a handful of trials (preschool multivictim, multiabuser cases) that represent the worst-case scenario in terms of interviewing young children, the scientific analyses are overgeneralized to nonproblematic interviews of children involving sexual abuse.

However, this literature should not be viewed as an attack on the credibility or the competence of children, but rather on adults' mishandling of young children and their reports. Although it is true that the suggestibility literature focuses on the ways adults can distort children's memories, it does not deny the strengths of children's memories when these are not tainted by exogenous forces. For example, in cases when children make spontaneous disclosures to parents about past abuse and then report the same event to the police, it is inappropriate to call on the suggestibility literature to demonstrate that children's reports can be tainted by interviewing methods. Clearly, that would be an inappropriate extension of this literature. Similarly, it is just as illogical to dwell on literature that shows how well children can recall their past when asked neutral questions, when the case at hand reveals a multitude of suggestive techniques. Nothing about the strengths of children's memories can inform such cases other than to stress the point that their initial disclosures prior to suggestive interviewing may have been accurate.

The claim that research on suggestibility denies the reality of sexual abuse is a straw man. Researchers who conduct research in this field uniformly agree that most claims that children make of sexual abuse are probably accurate. The scientific findings merely indicate that there are clearly defined situations in which some children's claims should be carefully examined. Just because there are some false allegations does not mean that all allegations are false.

Finally, the argument that the scientific literature rests on issues raised by the very worst of cases is also to some degree a red herring. Cases such as *Lillie-Reed* are of interest to social scientists not simply because of their dramatic components, but also because their complexity provides a vast number of examples and details

that are relevant to many types of cases that end up in the legal arena. Although *Lillie-Reed* may be among those "worst-cases scenarios," it nonetheless shares important structures or components with other cases that commonly come to court.

Further, a specific case does not render the literature on children's suggestibility and autobiographical memory valid or not valid. It is the extent to which the literature is relevant to each individual case. The literature on children's suggestibility is applicable to any type of case in which child witnesses make statements only after suggestive interviewing practices; it does not matter if the case is a day care case or if it involves allegations of abuse by a parent, boyfriend, or stranger.

Summary

If a child's indicting statements are made in the absence of any previous suggestive interviewing and in the absence of any motivation on the part of the child or adults to make incriminating statements, then the risk that the statement is inaccurate is quite low. If, however, the child initially denies any wrongdoing when first asked about a criminal action but later, as a result of suggestive interviewing practices, does make allegations, the statements may be unreliable.

Errors that result from suggestive techniques involve not only peripheral details, but also central events that involve children's own bodies. In laboratory studies, children's false reports can be tinged with sexual connotations. Young children have made false claims about "silly events" that involved body contact (e.g., "Did the nurse lick your knee? Did she blow in your ear?"), and these false claims persisted in repeated interviewing over a 3-month period (Ornstein, Gordon, & Larus, 1992). Young children falsely reported that a man put something "yuckie" in their mouth (Poole & Lindsay, 1995, 2001), and falsely alleged that their pediatrician had inserted a finger or a stick into their genitals (Bruck, Ceci, Francoeur, & Renick, 1995), or that some man touched their friends, kissed their friends on the lips, and removed some of the children's clothes (Lepore & Sesco, 1994). A significant number of preschool children falsely reported that someone touched their private parts, kissed them, and hugged them (Bruck et al., 2000; Goodman, Bottoms, Schwartz-Kenney, & Rudy, 1991; Goodman, Rudy, Bottoms, & Aman, 1990). In addition, when suggestively interviewed, some children will make false allegations about nonsexual events that could have serious legal consequences were they to occur. For example, preschoolers claimed to have seen a thief in their day care (Bruck, Ceci, & Hembrooke, 1997).

The mix of suggestive interviewing techniques in conjunction with the degree of interviewer bias can account for variations in suggestibility estimates across studies. If a (biased) interviewer uses more than one suggestive technique, there is a greater chance for taint than if he or she uses just one technique.

At times, suggestive interviewing techniques result in false beliefs. Children who incorporate the suggestions of their interviewers come to truly believe that they were victims.

Suggestive interviewing affects the perceived credibility of children's statements. The major reason for this lack of accurate discrimination between true and false reports is perhaps due to the fact that suggestive techniques breathe authenticity into the resulting false reports. When false reports emerge as a result of suggestive interviews, these are not simple repetitions or monosyllabic responses to leading questions. Under some conditions, these suggested reports become spontaneous and elaborate, going beyond the suggestions provided by their interviewers. There are no valid scientific tests to determine which aspects of a report or which reports are accurate accounts of the past. There is no scientific "Pinocchio test" that indicates that the child's metaphorical nose is growing longer when his or her statement is inaccurate.

Final Judgment of Lillie-Reed

In a 446-page judgment that reviews in detail all aspects of the case, Judge Eady found the review team guilty of malice on the grounds of a biased and inaccurate investigation that was based on opinion rather than scientifically based findings. As for Lillie and Reed, Judge Eady wrote:

> The allegations made against them were of the utmost gravity and received sustained and widespread coverage. I decided, therefore, that each Claimant was entitled to what is now generally recognised to be the maximum amount for compensatory damages in libel proceedings. I award each of them £200,000. . . . What matters primarily is that they are entitled to be vindicated and recognised as innocent citizens who should, in my judgment, be free to exist for what remains of their lives untouched by the stigma of child abuse. (Approved Judgement *Lillie and Reed v. Newcastle City Council & Ors,* 2002, p. 443)

AUTOBIOGRAPHICAL MEMORY, DEVELOPMENTAL DIFFERENCES, AND MECHANISMS OF SUGGESTIBILITY

In this section, we cover some topics that, although important in the field of children and the law, were not germane to the discussion of *Lilly-Reed.*

Children's Memory for Traumatic Events

The discussion of *Lillie-Reed* focused on the suggestive influences that can compromise reliable reporting because, as noted earlier, children in this case did not provide any abuse-related narratives before this type of suggestive questioning occurred. Although it might be argued that children are incapable of reporting traumatic events without this type of support, the literature clearly does not support this view. Rather, as detailed in this section, a large number of studies show that children are capable of providing accurate, detailed, and useful information about actual events, some of which are traumatic. It is important to note that the studies in this section are characterized by the neutral tone of the interviewer, the limited use of misleading questions (for the most part, if suggestions are used, they are limited to a single occasion), and the absence of any motive for the child to make a false report. When such conditions are present, much, but not all, of what children report can be quite accurate. Unfortunately, these conditions were not present in the interviews of the children in *Lillie-Reed.*

Does Memory for Trauma Differ from Memory in General?

A widespread notion is that memory for traumatic events operates differently from memory for everyday experiences. The origin of this belief can be traced to the psychiatry of the late nineteenth century. From interviews with his patients, Pierre Janet (1889) concluded that traumatic experiences disrupt normal memory and become "dissociated" or split off from conscious awareness as the result of a psychological defense that works to block the recall of painful events. Like Janet, Sigmund Freud (1896/1953) asserted that traumatic memories are subject to "repression" and can seep into consciousness indirectly by way of symptoms of psychological disorders. Freud's claim that memory for trauma operates differently from memory for nontraumatic events has pervaded the clinical literature. Paradoxically, two competing theories have emerged in modern clinical thought. Consistent with Freud's original beliefs, some have asserted that traumatic experiences are too overwhelming for children to endure and are pushed underground and remain difficult to access (e.g., van der Kolk & Fisler, 1995). Others have argued that traumatic experiences are so shocking that they are indelibly fixed in memory and preserved over time in a pristine form (e.g., Koss, Figueredo, Bell, Tharan, & Tromp, 1996).

Two Types of Traumatic Memory?

One widely cited solution for these disparate effects of trauma has been proposed by Terr (1991, 1994). Terr distinguishes between two types of trauma: Type I involves a single, shocking event, such as an attempted murder or a natural disaster, and Type II deals with repeated, chronic traumatic experiences, such as multiple incidents of sexual abuse. According to Terr, Type I traumas create detailed and precise memories, whereas Type II traumas lead to fragmented or even nonexistent memories. After many traumatic events, children learn to cope with the fear or pain by dissociating, or separating themselves from the experience as it is occurring, thereby causing impoverished encoding and limited or no memory.

Evidence for this distinction comes from clinical case reports. Most notably, Terr (1988, 1991) contrasted a group of 5- to 14-year-old children who were kidnapped from their school bus and buried in a truck trailer, with 20 children who were abused repeatedly before 5 years of age. Terr reported that all of the kidnapped children recalled the event in vivid detail after a 5-year delay, whereas the repeatedly traumatized children exhibited poor or no verbal recall because they had learned to repress their memories.

Although seemingly sensible, a careful examination of Terr's (1988, 1991) comparison reveals numerous problems. First, the Type I and Type II children differed in age; the older (Type I) children should have better memory than the younger (Type II) children for any experience, not just traumatic experiences. Second, only four of the Type II children endured repeated sexual abuse, and three of them were under the age of 2 years when they were abused. Based on the empirical literature (reviewed later), however, all events, not just traumatic events, experienced before 2 years of age are inaccessible to verbal recall. Third, Terr's argument that repeated trauma leads to alterations in memory implies that well-organized memories for such occurrences should never be available for retrieval because

these were never completely registered in memory in the first place.

Empirical Studies of Memory for Stressful Events

Given claims in the clinical literature regarding the special nature of traumatic memories, how well have empirical studies squared with these claims? As a whole, the empirical literature on children's recall of distressful events is inconsistent with beliefs that memory for trauma operates differently from memory in general. Rather, existing evidence suggests that memory for traumatic events behaves very much like memory for everyday experiences.

Recall of Traumatic Events Is Generally Accurate. First, numerous investigations have demonstrated that, like everyday experiences, traumatic experiences can be recalled quite well, even by children as young as 3 years of age. Studies of children's memory for natural disasters, such as Hurricane Andrew (Bahrick, Parker, Fivush, & Levitt, 1998; Shaw, Applegate, & Schorr, 1996) and the explosion of the space shuttle *Challenger* (Warren & Swartwood, 1992), present evidence of detailed and generally accurate memories over long delays. Likewise, examinations of children's recall of highly distressful medical procedures, such as emergency room visits for trauma (Howe, Courage, & Peterson, 1995; Peterson & Whalen, 2001), bone marrow transplants (Stuber, Nader, Yasuda, Pynoos, & Cohen, 1991), lumbar punctures (Chen, Zeltzer, Craske, & Katz, 2000), and chemotherapy treatments (Howard, Osborne, & Baker-Ward, 1997), show that children retain enduring and largely faithful memories for these experiences.

To illustrate, research by Ornstein and his colleagues on children's retention of a voiding cystourethrogram (VCUG)—a painful and stressful radiological procedure involving urinary catheterization—has demonstrated that 3- to 7-year-olds can provide highly accurate accounts of this event over a 6-week delay (Merritt, Ornstein, & Spicker, 1994). Related work has shown generally accurate memory for this procedure for children over delays of 5.5 years (Pipe et al., 1997).

Investigators who employ the VCUG paradigm to study the effects of trauma on memory argue that the VCUG is a forensically relevant event because in some ways it is similar to situations of sexual abuse. Children, some of whom are restrained, are handled by adults while the genital area is uncovered. The event is quite painful, as it involves passing a catheter into the urinary bladder and filling the bladder to capacity with contrast fluid. Also, the child is asked to urinate on the examining table—a potentially embarrassing activity, especially for young children who have been toilet-trained recently.

Despite the high levels of anxiety experienced by most of the children who undergo this examination, however, some have questioned the relevance of the VCUG to situations involving sexual abuse because it is a socially sanctioned procedure. However, this criticism may be irrelevant to situations in which an abusive adult provides the young victim a misleading framework characterizing their interactions as conventional, such as describing the abuse as a secret game or a special relationship. Further, to the extent that children lack an understanding of the diagnostic value of the VCUG, some may conceive of this procedure as a betrayal by trusted caregivers rather than a medically necessary examination.

Memories for Trauma Are Subject to Forgetting. Like ordinary memories, memories for trauma become less accessible as the delay interval increases. Usually, with the passage of time, peripheral or inconsequential details are lost most readily and the gist or central details persist (Goodman, Hirschman, Hepps, & Rudy, 1991; Peters, 1997; Peterson & Bell, 1996). To illustrate, Peterson and Whalen (2001) showed that although children maintained generally accurate memory over a 5-year period for an accident (e.g., lacerations, bone fractures, burns, and dog bites) and medical attention in a hospital emergency room, some aspects of the experience, particularly the details of the treatment, were lost during the delay. Moreover, the general components of the injury were retained better than smaller details.

Memories for Trauma Are Susceptible to Constructive Distortions from External Events. Trauma memories, like memories for more mundane events, are vulnerable to constructive distortions or confusions from other, similar experiences. That is, existing memories of trauma can be altered during the course of the interval between the experience and the report of it, when information from intervening experiences becomes incorporated into the original memory. For example, Principe, Ornstein, Baker-Ward, and Gordon (2000) provided evidence that television programs can produce later fabrications of medical procedures that were nonexperienced but seen on television.

Howe et al. (1995) have shown that, as the delay between a trauma and later interviews increases, children become increasingly likely to erroneously incorporate information from intervening, like traumatic events into their accounts of the original occurrence. For example, one child who was asked to recall the details of an emergency room treatment for an eye injury that had taken place 6 months prior mistakenly reported that the doctor had fixed his tooth and put medicine in his mouth—activities consistent with another hospital room visit that had occurred in the preceding month. Of particular importance, although nonexperienced details imported from intervening experiences generally do not hinder the accuracy of children's reports, an interviewer who is not privy to the details of the original event likely would not be able to differentiate the children's reports in terms of actually experienced events versus intervening events—an important point given that forensic interviewers rarely know exactly what happened.

Memories for Trauma Are Vulnerable to Constructive Distortions from Internal Factors. Memories for distressful events may change over time as the result of internal thoughts, such as expectations, feelings, preferences, and goals. To illustrate, Pynoos, Steinberg, and Aronson (1997) reported that some children who witnessed brutal domestic violence erroneously recalled intervening to help the abused parent. Likewise, consider an investigation by Ornstein and his colleagues (1998) in which 4- and 6-year-old children's memory was assessed for a mock physical examination that included some highly expected medical features (e.g., measuring weight) while omitting others, and incorporated several atypical, unexpected features (e.g., collecting a sputum sample). After a 12-week delay, but not during an immediate interview, the children exhibited a relatively high frequency of spontaneous intrusions of typical, but not atypical, medical features that had not been included in their checkups. In fact, 42% of the 4-year-olds and 72% of the 6-year-olds made at least one such intrusion at the 12-week assessment, whereas essentially none of the children reported in their spontaneous recall any of the atypical procedures that had not taken place during their examinations.

Taken together, empirical studies demonstrate convincingly that memories for traumatic experiences act like memories in general. Children's trauma memories are not repressed or hidden from consciousness; rather, the core of the event tends to be well remembered over time. Although trauma memories are enduring, they are not indelibly preserved in storage in their original form.

Rather, their details tend to fade from memory with time. Nor are traumas immune to constructive distortions; intervening events and internal ruminations can alter memory. Thus, it seems that traumatic memories are not of a unique nature, nor do they require special principles to explain their operation.

There is one qualification to these general conclusions, and this involves the long-term memories of very young, often nonverbal children who are later asked to recount an event. In other words, can children or adults accurately recall events that occurred during the first 2 years of life? This is a very complicated issue about which much has been written, but it can be summarized with a few major points.

First, it is clear that throughout infancy, nonverbal memories for certain types of sequenced events develop such that some infants as young as 13 months at the time of original exposure to a simple event are able to nonverbally reenact three-step sequences following delays as long as 12 months (Bauer, Wenner, Dropik, & Wewerka, 2000). Although these investigations provide ample evidence that infants are capable of retaining information about the past, exactly what aspects of their experiences they can remember is unclear. In the infancy work, retention is inferred on the basis of changes in behavior, such as kicking more vigorously or reproducing a set of actions. Behavioral responses, however, are not equivalent to demonstrations of autobiographical memory. Autobiographical memory involves a process in which stored information is made consciously available and remembered as an actual experience, that is, occurring at a particular time, in a particular place, and under particular circumstances.

Nonetheless, these findings of infant retention may be relevant to discussions of children's testimony if early memories first expressible only through behavior later become verbally expressible once children have acquired the ability to talk about past experiences. A number of investigations, however, have provided compelling evidence that children cannot gain verbal access to memories stored without the benefit of language. In a study of children's recall of traumatic injuries that occurred between 13 and 34 months of age, Peterson and Rideout (1998) found that 2-year-olds who were unable to provide a narrative account of the injury immediately after it took place produced fragmentary and moderately inaccurate accounts of this event during subsequent interviews. Similarly, when 3-year-old children were asked to recall a novel event that they had experi-

enced 1 year earlier, they used only words that were part of their vocabulary when the event was experienced (Simcock & Hayne, 2002). These provocative findings suggest that children cannot translate memories into language if the words were not available when the memories were formed. This work indicates, then, that it is difficult, if not impossible, for children or adults to provide verbal testimony about events that occurred before the onset of productive language.

Are Traumatic Events More or Less Memorable Than Everyday Events?

Although it is clear that traumatic memories are subject to the same mechanisms as normal memories, the question remains whether traumatic events are more or less memorable than more mundane events. It is somewhat difficult to answer this question because few studies have directly compared memory for traumatic experiences with memory for nontraumatic experiences within the same children. Nonetheless, what evidence exists suggests that traumatic events often have certain features that make them more or less memorable than most experiences. As such, it is important to understand when and how distress might translate into more or less detailed, accurate, or enduring memories. Factors such as the distinctiveness of an experience, children's understanding of the experience, and their level of distress during the experience can affect the processes involved in encoding, storage, and recall, and consequently affect the memorability of traumatic occurrences.

The Distinctiveness of the Experience. One factor that might affect the memorability of trauma concerns the distinctiveness or uniqueness of the event against the background of the particular child's past experiences (Howe, 1998). Studies of event memory demonstrate that unique events, whether negative or positive in tone, tend to be better remembered than familiar or routine events (Fivush & Schwarzmueller, 1998; Hudson, Fivush, & Kuebli, 1992). For example, by 3 years of age, children are able to retain generally accurate and detailed memories over extended delays for novel events such as airplane rides and visits to Disney World and special museums (see Fivush, 1993, for a review). However, children have great difficulty recalling single episodes of familiar or repeated events, such as what happened one time that they went to McDonald's or what happened on a specific day at preschool (Fivush, 1984; Hudson & Nelson, 1983; Myles-Worsley, Cromer,

& Dodd, 1986). These patterns indicate that single distinctive experiences are more memorable than single episodes of familiar events.

Extending this logic to traumatic events, trauma may be better remembered than other events to the extent that it deviates from the typical experiences of children, rather than merely as a function of the distress that it brings about (Howe, 1998). A fire at a preschool that prompts an emergency response by the fire department might be recalled better than last Monday's snack or trip to the park, not necessarily because of the distress evoked by the situation, but because it stands out from the usual. Like the fire, a visit by the SPCA or a trip to the planetarium might be well remembered because such events are inconsistent with children's expectations of what usually happens at school.

In support of this account is work by Ornstein (1995) examining memory for the VCUG that shows that children's reports of this distressful medical procedure are more complete and more accurate than their accounts of a routine pediatric checkup. One explanation for this finding is that the VCUG is better remembered because it is a single distinctive experience made up of unfamiliar activities, such as a catheterization, a fluoroscopic filming, and urinating on the examining table. In contrast, the well-child checkup is a repeated, familiar event made up of recognizable actions, many of which are often part of young children's pretend play.

Further supporting the notion that the uniqueness of trauma enhances memorability is work by Stein (1996), who found that children's accounts of emotional experiences, both positive and negative, tend to focus on those aspects that are novel or different from what is expected. Stein argues that it is the violation of the typical, not direction of the emotion evoked by the event, that facilitates memory, as distinctive events can elicit positive as well as negative emotions. Consistent with this contention is an investigation by Fivush, Hazzard, Sales, Sarfati, and Brown (2003) that revealed that children living in violent, inner-city neighborhoods recalled positive events in more descriptive detail than negative events. Fivush and her colleagues attribute the heightened recall of positive events to a violation of expectation; for children living in conditions of chronic violence, positive experiences may be distinctive and therefore more completely remembered than negative events. In contrast, a single traumatic event may not stand in stark contrast to their daily lives and would not be expected to persist in memory.

As noted by Howe (1998), this argument is in line with studies showing that as the novelty of stressful situations dissipates, so does their memorability. Consider, for example, individuals in emergency response teams who acclimate to experiences that may seem upsetting to most. This example illustrates that previously distinctive experiences may lose their uniqueness, and hence their memorability, with additional experience. In the next section, we review evidence that directly examines the effects of repeated experience on memorability.

Effects of Repeated Experience on Event Memorability. Despite the lack of evidence supporting Terr's (1994) distinction between Type I and Type II trauma, the experimental literature on children's memory makes it clear that memories of repeated experiences are quite different from memories of single events. However, the reasons for these differences are not the ones proposed by Terr.

Repeated experience with an event can have both beneficial and baleful effects on children's memory, depending on the nature of the event details being recalled. After multiple occurrences of an event, details that generally are experienced the same way during each occurrence are strengthened in memory. Consequently, with repeated experience, children's reports become increasingly general or script-like, focusing on what usually happens (Pezdek & Roe, 1995; Powell & Thomson, 1996). However, with regard to children's recall of details that vary across occurrences (e.g., remembering what clothing was worn by a person the last time the event was experienced, when the items of clothing differed each time), repeated experience has detrimental effects on children's ability to remember a particular occurrence. Specifically, the number of correct details reported about a particular episode of a repeated event is lower than when recalling a one-time event, as details of specific occurrences are omitted or confused among episodes (Hudson, 1990). Although children's general reports of repeated events are largely accurate, in the sense that they describe the gist of what usually happens, they lack detail and may not be veridical with any one instance of the event.

The problems associated with children's recall of the variable details of an occurrence of a repeated event are accentuated under certain conditions. The more frequently events are experienced, the longer the time delay between the event and the interview; the greater the similarity between the events, the more difficult it is for children to keep track of which details were included in a particular occurrence (Lindsay, Johnson, & Kwon, 1991). Further, the accuracy of children's recall of an occurrence of a repeated event is shaped by the manner in which memory is tested. When children are asked to freely report what happened in an occurrence of a repeated event, they provide few specific features that discriminate one occurrence from others in the series. In contrast, when questions are asked that focus the child on specific aspects of the event that were likely to have varied, confusion between the occurrences is more evident (Powell & Thomson, 1997).

Unlike Terr's (1994) speculation that multiple experiences lead to poorer memory, it simply may be that the details of individual episodes are not recalled as well when they have happened on numerous occasions than when they have happened only once. But, as discussed earlier, although the details of repeated events fade as the memory becomes increasingly general and abstract, the gist tends to be well maintained and largely accurate.

The only study to examine children's memory for repeated trauma was done by Howard et al. (1997). Children who were in remission from cancer were asked to recall the details of chemotherapy treatment that had lasted for an average of 21 months and had ended over 2.5 years earlier. The children's reports of their treatment were quite extensive and highly accurate. Further, no parent agreed with the statement "My child cannot recall the treatment because he/she has actively blocked it out." Thus, Terr's (1994) contention that repeated, or Type II, trauma is unavailable to conscious recall is not supported by empirical evidence.

Existing knowledge. A central determinant of what is selected for attention and placed in memory is existing knowledge. Knowledge influences how children monitor the world, interpret events, and encode incoming information (Bjorklund, 1985; Chi & Ceci, 1987; Ornstein & Naus, 1985). One implication of the literature is that in situations where a child does not understand what is happening, he or she will have little basis for later remembering what was experienced. For example, when child abuse victims are young enough to have almost no sexual knowledge, they likely will have trouble interpreting and remembering what took place. Although children as young as 2 or 3 years will understand that "something is wrong" if they experience the physical pain associated with anal or vaginal penetration, when they experience milder forms of abuse, such as

genital touching, they may not be aware of the inappropriateness of genital fondling versus everyday hygiene and, as a result, construct a very different memory for the encounter than do older children who have learned the impropriety of this behavior.

This argument is most relevant to young sexual abuse victims because most abuse with this age group does not involve vaginal or anal penetration. It most often includes exhibitionism, fondling, photography, and oral fellatio. To the extent that children do not interpret these activities as sexual or inappropriate, they may not be perceived as any more distressful than ordinary forms of affection, cleaning, or diapering, and would not be expected to be any more memorable. The important point here is that what is considered traumatic by adult standards might not be construed as such by a young child.

Stress. A number of investigators have proposed that individual differences in children's behavioral reactions to stress can impact their encoding and retention of a traumatic experience (Howe, 2000; Ornstein, Manning, & Pelphrey, 1999). If one child responds to anxiety by closing her eyes and covering her ears, she is preventing encoding of visual and auditory stimuli associated with the event. However, if another child deals with his feelings of fear by asking questions about what is being experienced, he may likely generate a well-organized and enduring memory for the event.

Despite the intuitive appeal of this prediction, measures of stress have faired poorly in how well they predict children's memory for a traumatic event. Some authors argue that stress experienced as an event is taking place strengthens children's abilities to focus and thus facilitates the encoding of information (Fivush, 1998; Goodman, Hirschman, et al., 1991; Shrimpton, Oates, & Hayes, 1998), whereas others have found that elevated levels of stress impede memory (Howard et al., 1997; Merritt et al., 1994; Peters, 1997). Still others have shown mixed or no significant effects of stress on memory (Bruck, Ceci, Francoeur, & Barr, 1995; Goodman & Quas, 1997; Howe et al., 1995; Peterson & Bell, 1996).

To some extent, these discrepancies may be due to the various indices of stress that have been used. Measures used range from self or parental behavioral ratings of stress (ratings of stress as adduced by a parent or objective observer) to physiological (heart rate, blood pressure) and neuroendocrine indicators (salivary cortisol). Not only are few of these measures associated with one another, but few of these measures show a consistent relationship with recall. For example, in an investigation of children's memory for a VCUG, Merritt and her colleagues (1994) observed a negative association between stress and memory with behavioral ratings of stress but not with salivary cortisol.

As discussed by Ornstein and his colleagues (1999), an adequate understanding of the effects of stress on memory may involve using moment-by-moment indicators of arousal as an event is occurring rather than summary measures (be they behavioral, physiological, or neuroendocrine) that essentially result in an estimate of the average level of anxiety experienced during the event. This is important because the amount of stress experienced may vary considerably as the event unfolds, with some moments accompanied by high levels of arousal and other moments experienced with nonchalance.

On the basis of this brief review, it is apparent that special mechanisms are not needed to account for memory for traumatic experiences. Whether the event is a single occurrence or repeated on multiple occasions, traumatic experiences are remembered as least as well as if not better than more mundane experiences. Traumatic memories, however, like ordinary memories, can be fallible, incomplete, and malleable. What a child remembers about a traumatic event is based on constructive processes that result from the complex interactions of a wide range of cognitive and social variables that affect the encoding of the original event, the storage of information memory, and the retrieval of material from storage.

Developmental Differences in Suggestibility and Autobiographical Recall

In the review of the literature that was pertinent to the *Lillie-Reed* case, we focused on studies of preschoolers (because this was the age group under consideration) without discussing developmental differences. Although the research findings demonstrate that preschool children are especially susceptible to the deleterious influence of suggestive interviewing techniques (Ceci & Bruck, 1993; Ceci & Friedman, 2000), their greater vulnerability is a matter of degree only; even much older children and adults will succumb to suggestions and pressures (Bruck & Ceci, 2004). For example, Finnila et al. (2003) staged an event (a version of the Paco visit we described earlier) for 4- to 5-year-olds and 7- to 8-year-olds. One week later, half the children were given a low-pressure interview that contained some misleading questions with abuse themes (e.g., "He

took your clothes off, didn't he?"). The other children received a high-pressure interview; they were told that their friends had answered the leading questions affirmatively, they were praised for assenting to the misleading questions, and when they did not assent, the question was repeated. In both conditions, there were no significant age differences in the percentage of misleading questions answered affirmatively, although a significant number (68%) were assented to in the high-pressure condition (see also Bruck et al., in press; Zaragoza et al., 2001). It has also been found that under some conditions, older children are more suggestible than younger children (e.g., Finnila et al., 2003; Zaragoza et al., 2001).

Many of the suggestive techniques used in the child studies also produce tainted reports or false memories in adults (e.g., see Loftus, 2003). An illuminating piece of evidence for this assertion is the work of Kassin and Kiechel (1996). They have shown that college students will often erroneously claim they broke a computer after being told that they did by an experimenter. Moreover, they will internalize this belief, tell others they accidentally broke the computer, and sign a statement to this effect, agreeing to donate 8 hours of service to the experimenter in reparation for the alleged breakage.

Thus, although suggestibility is highest among preschool children, this type of memory distortion occurs at all ages.

In terms of autobiographical recall, preschoolers are also least able to provide details of actually experienced events (e.g., Baker-Ward, Gordon, Ornstein, Larus, & Clubb, 1993; Cassel et al., 1996; Ceci & Bruck, 1995; Lamb et al., 2003; Quas et al., 1999). When asked open-ended questions, preschool-age children can recall relevant and accurate information, but they often are less responsive and provide fewer spontaneous memory reports than older children and adults (Bahrick et al., 1998; Goodman, Hirschman, et al., 1991; McCauley & Fisher, 1995; Ornstein et al., 1992; Peterson, 1999; Saywitz, 1987).

Mechanisms Underlying Children's Suggestibility

The search for mechanisms underlying children's suggestibility is an enterprise that attempts to integrate developmental differences in basic cognitive skills and social behaviors with developmental differences in suggestibility. The general strategy is to link the reduction in suggestibility with the development of social and cognitive skills. Methodologically, hypotheses that emerge from this exercise are tested in correlational studies whereby the levels of children's suggestibility are correlated with their performance on a range of tasks that assess the predicted mechanisms (see Bruck & Melnyk, 2004, for a review).

Some of the attempts to pinpoint the mechanisms underlying children's suggestibility examine the relative importance of social versus cognitive factors that underlie suggestibility effects. On the one hand, it is argued that the child (or adult) adopts suggestions in order to defer to or comply with the agenda of the questioner. In other words, for social reasons, the children repeat suggestions that they know to be inaccurate. At the other extreme, there is the view that suggestibility effects reflect cognitive weaknesses. For example, the child may incorporate a suggestion because he or she forgets the original event or is confused as to whether he or she saw the original event or the suggestion. Of course, both factors may underlie suggestibility effects; for example, social factors may first influence assents to misinformation or misleading questions, but with time, the assents may lead to cognitive impairments involving memory changes (see Ceci & Bruck, 1995). Or, because of children's less developed cognitive skills, they may be more willing to defer to the perceived agenda of their adult interviewer. In the following paragraphs, we attempt to provide a bird's-eye view of the various hypotheses that have been put forward to account for age-related reductions in children's suggestibility. As will become evident, some of the proposed cognitive mechanisms also account for age-related changes in children's autobiographical memory.

The focus on children's memory is of central interest because it is commonly found that children with poor memory of an event are more suggestible about that event (e.g., Marche, 1999; Marche & Howe, 1995; Pezdek & Roe, 1995). This has led to the following observations and proposals. As children grow older, their memories become more efficient because of the acquisition of strategies, knowledge, and self-insights about their memory (so-called metamemory). Preschool-age children have limited skill at using encoding, storage, and retrieval strategies (Brainerd, 1985; Brainerd & Ornstein, 1991; Loftus & Davies, 1984). They often fail to encode new events efficiently due to their selective focus on salient or central features (Bower & Sivers, 1998), their lack of knowledge about the events

(Ricci & Beal, 1998), and their tendency to rely more on verbatim than gist memory (Brainerd & Reyna, 1990; Foley & Johnson, 1985). Young children have weaker memory traces and show steeper forgetting curves (Baker-Ward et al., 1993; Brainerd, Reyna, Howe, & Kingman, 1990). They are also inferior to school-age children in terms of the strength of stored representations, because use of storage strategies, such as rehearsal and organization of stimuli, is uncommon among preschool children. They exhibit production deficits when it comes to retrieval strategies (e.g., use of category information) needed to search and facilitate their memories (Cox, Ornstein, Naus, Maxfield, & Zimler, 1989; Schneider & Bjorklund, 1998). All of these deficits conspire to render them dependent on external cues, such as an interviewer's prompts or questions, to retrieve information stored in long-term memory (Priestley, Roberts, & Pipe, 1999).

Young children's limited knowledge constrains their ability to incorporate and organize new information (Chi & Ceci, 1987; Johnson & Foley, 1984; Lindberg, 1980; Ornstein, 1990; Schneider & Bjorklund, 1998). Because of a lack of knowledge, they do not introspect into the inner workings of their memories to monitor when they need to engage in more mental work to consolidate a memory. Because young children fail to engage in strategies and insights, their memories are sometimes weaker and more susceptible to alteration by insinuations and false suggestions.

In addition, preschoolers lack skill at distinguishing between two or more sources of input into their memories (Gopnik & Graf, 1988; Wimmer, Hogerfe, & Perner, 1988), thus confusing things they heard with things they saw, and vice versa (Johnson & Foley, 1984; Lindsay et al., 1991). They also are more likely than older groups to exhibit a confusion between reality and fantasy that can lead at times to the belief that something was directly experienced when, in reality, it was merely dreamed about or imagined (Foley & Johnson, 1985; Foley, Santini, & Sopasakis, 1989; Lindsay & Johnson, 1987). This is called "source confusion," and young children are more likely to exhibit it, such as when they misattribute an interviewer's suggestions to actual experiences (Ackil & Zaragoza, 1995).

Another limitation of preschoolers that may be related to suggestibility concerns so-called scripted knowledge. Scripts are temporally organized expectations regarding typical and habitual routines of an event (Ceci & Bruck, 1993). It has been reported that young children are more susceptible than older children to the negative effect of scripted knowledge (Farrar & Goodman, 1992; Hudson, 1990; Hudson & Nelson, 1986; Powell & Thomson, 1996). For example, young children might report erroneously that a certain event occurred as it usually happens in their script, even though the event was not witnessed at that instance. In other words, young children have trouble recalling novel details of a single event that are inconsistent with their generalized script of the event (Farrar & Goodman, 1992). This tendency to overly rely on the scripted knowledge might lead them to be more vulnerable to overgeneralizing their scripts.

For the cognitively unarmed child, an interrogation by experts is no contest: Children can be made to say things that are incriminating, even if they are false. In the summer of 1999, the city of Chicago witnessed a grisly murder and sexual assault of an 11-year-old girl named Ryan Harris. In the aftermath of discovering Ryan's body, two boys, ages 7 and 8, confessed to murdering her. The boys made their confessions without counsel present during a lengthy interrogation. Later, a 27-year-old ex-convict's semen was found on the dead girl's body, and he now stands indicted for her murder. Why would those two boys falsely admit to things they didn't do? One possible answer lies in their eagerness to please adult authority figures by complying with the boys' beliefs about what the police wanted them to say. Children might respond with a very compliant attitude during an interrogation, especially if they are highly praised and given attention that is rare in their everyday life. The boys in the Chicago case sat around a table with two uniformed officers; they held hands around the table and pledged to be on the "same team." The officers bought the boys food and explained that they could go home as soon as they helped the rest of the team clear up Ryan Harris's murder. After several hours of interrogation without the presence of an attorney or family member, each boy ended up admitting to a series of behaviors that they almost certainly could not have enacted, including raping the dead girl.

Without foreseeing the ramifications of their statements, children learn that noncompliance is met with negative reaction by adults, and so they avoid challenging adults' suggestions in their daily experiences and in the courtroom situations as well (Saywitz & Moan-Hardie, 1994). Children's eagerness to please adults is easily exploitable by interrogators as well as defendants seeking their help.

The socioemotional pressure to comply in forensic interviews may result from children's limited perspective-taking skill (Flavell, 1992). They lack the knowledge of the interviewer's motivation, the purpose of questioning, and the forensic relevance of their responses. They sometimes acquiesce to suggestive questions to avoid humiliation, assuming that their lack of knowledge may be viewed unfavorably.

Despite this long list of possible mechanisms, there are very few data to support any of these hypotheses (see Bruck & Melnyk, 2004). One of the implications of this is that at present, we cannot accurately predict the types of children who might be most suggestible.

FUTURE DIRECTIONS

Since the end of the 1980s, developmental psychology has made enormous progress in providing a scientific basis for the studies in children in the law. In this chapter, we have shown the extent of this progress in understanding aspects of children's testimony before they come into the courtroom and once they are there. Although there may be new areas of interest in the coming decade, spurred by current basic research or by current societal problems, the existing research calls for important modifications and changes in the current system.

First, the most significant implication of the research on adults' memories of interviews with children is that interviewers should be mandated to electronically preserve all (and especially the very first) of their interviews with children. If courts are interested in historical accuracy, there is simply no substitute for a tape that can be played to verify the accuracy of the interviewer's recall and the details of the discussion that took place between the interviewer and child. Although there may be times when it is not feasible to electronically record interviews (specifically, when parents question their children at home or in the car), it is nevertheless important for jurors and judges to know how to interpret hearsay testimony and to consider the potential for different types of errors, even though the testimony may be compelling and be offered in good faith.

Despite the dramatically consistent scientific findings that interviewers have poor recall of both the content and the structure of their interviews with children, only a handful of states mandate electronic recordings.

Agencies or jurisdictions defend the absence of this procedure on a number of grounds, including the claim that videotaping would provide the defense with evidence to be used against the child victim, or that agencies do not have the facilities to carry out these procedures, or that the child had already been interviewed prior to the first investigative interview. These are not viable reasons. First, if there is evidence of suggestive interviewing, then this exculpatory evidence must be turned over to the defense. If the interviews are well carried out, however, electronic copies will be useful to the prosecution. In this electronic age, the cost and ease of obtaining videotaped or audiotaped statements from children is negligible. It should be part of every professional's training to know how to obtain the best quality records possible. Finally, although it is true that children are sometimes (suggestively) interviewed by parents or other caretakers prior to their first investigative interview, this does not preclude the necessity of videotaping the first official and subsequent sessions. For example, in *Lillie-Reed,* before the first investigative interview, all parents had reported that their children had disclosed abuse (and their reports also revealed suggestive interviewing techniques); however, careful inspection of the first videotaped interviews with the children by the police showed that the children did not disclose what the parents had reported. With suggestions from the police, the children eventually did disclose. Without the videotape, the nature of the children's police disclosures would have been lost. What would have remained was the parents' reports of disclosures and the police reports of disclosures.

When a crime has been committed and evidence is being collected from the crime scene (the weapon, blood samples), the investigators are not permitted to simply inspect these pieces of evidence, make notes about their appearance, and then throw the evidence away. This would not be allowed into a court of law because the investigators' reports would be unreliable. For the very same reasons, children's reports of victimization should be handled in the same careful way required for physical evidence at crime scenes. The only means to achieve this goal is through electronic recording.

Second, there is a clear need for further work on the development of empirically validated interview schedules for interviewing children. The developmental research has proved the basic foundation for the general structure and constraints of such protocols. Michael

Lamb and his colleagues from National Institute of Child Health and Development have taken the lead in this field. They have developed one such protocol (for details of the protocol, see Orbach et al., 2000; Sternberg, Lamb, Orbach, Esplin, & Mitchell, 2001) that emphasizes the use of open-ended questions to obtain detailed reports from children; specific and leading questions should be used only when necessary and only at the end of the interview. This interview schedule was specifically developed for children suspected of being sexually abused; however, with a few modifications, it is also applicable for interviewing children about a variety of topics.

Although this team of researchers has made enormous contributions to the field, there need to be further studies that examine modifications to protocols (e.g., having different protocols for different age groups). In addition, it is important that these protocols be tested in the laboratory as well as in the field (i.e., interviewing children suspected of abuse). The latter methodology provides information about feasibility, whether it is possible to train interviewers to follow the protocol, whether children can follow the instructions, as well as the amount and quality of information that children provide. However, these studies do not provide information on the reliability or the accuracy of children's reports. This is because interviewers simply do not know the details about the event that the children are reporting. To address issues of accuracy and reliability, the accuracy of children's reports must be verified; this can be achieved through laboratory studies in which children are asked to recall events about which the researcher has full knowledge.

Third, even though there is some progress in the construction of standardized interviewing protocols, this must be accompanied by the development of programs to teach interviewers how to use these protocols. This is not an easy task; training is intensive, often lasting days and sometimes weeks. In part, this is because interviewers in training must give up previous automatic strategies, many of which they may not be aware of using. Anecdotal reports suggest that even after intensive training, interviewers will not faithfully follow the protocols unless there are intermittent reeducation sessions. The cost and time required to retrain a large workforce in this area will be great. However, as a start, one would hope that all professional training programs (undergraduate, graduate, and certificate) would redesign their curriculum to ensure that their graduates will be properly trained to interview children.

REFERENCES

Ackil, J. K., & Zaragoza, M. S. (1995). Developmental differences in eyewitness suggestibility and memory for source. *Journal of Experimental Child Psychology, 60,* 57–83.

Ackil, J. K., & Zaragoza, M. (1998). The memorial consequences of forced confabulation: Age differences in susceptibility to false memories. *Developmental Psychology, 34,* 1358–1372.

Amato, P. R. (2000). The consequences of divorce for adults and children. *Journal of Marriage and the Family, 62,* 1269–1287.

Bahrick, L., Parker, J. F., Fivush, R., & Levitt, M. (1998). The effects of stress on young children's memory for a natural disaster. *Journal of Experimental Psychology: Applied, 4,* 308–331.

Baker-Ward, L., Gordon, B. N., Ornstein, P. A., Larus, D. M., & Clubb, P. A. (1993). Young children's long-term retention of a pediatric examination. *Child Development, 64,* 1519–1533.

Barker, R., Jones, J., Saradjian, J., & Wardell, R. (1998). *Abuse in the early years.* (Report of the independent complaints review team on Shieldfield Day Nursery and related matters). Newcaste upon Tyne, England.

Bauer, P. J., Wenner, J. A., Dropik, P. L., & Wewerka, S. S. (2000). Parameters of remembering and forgetting in the transition from infancy to early childhood. *Monographs of the Society for Research in Child Development, 65*(4, Serial No. 263).

Bauserman, R. (2002). Child adjustment in joint-custody versus sole-custody arrangements: A meta-analytic review. *Journal of Family Psychology, 16,* 91–102.

Bjorklund, D. F. (1985). The role of conceptual knowledge in the development of organization in children's memory. In C. J. Brainerd & M. Pressley (Eds.), *Basic processes in memory development* (pp. 103–142). New York: Springer-Verlag.

Bower, G. H., & Sivers, H. (1998). Cognitive impact of traumatic events. *Development and Psychopathology, 10,* 625–653.

Brainerd, C. J. (1985). Three-state models of memory development: A review of advances in statistical methodology. *Journal of Experimental Child Psychology, 40,* 375–394.

Brainerd, C. J., & Ornstein, P. A. (1991). Children's memory for witnessed events: The developmental backdrop. In J. Doris (Ed.), *The suggestibility of children's recollections* (pp. 10–20). Washington, DC: American Psychological Association.

Brainerd, C. J., & Reyna, V. F. (1990). Gist is the grist: Fuzzy trace theory and the new intuitionism. *Developmental Review, 10,* 3–47.

Brainerd, C. J., Reyna, V. F., Howe, M. L., & Kingman, J. (1990). The development of forgetting and reminiscence. *Monographs of the Society for Research in Child Development* (No. 55).

Bruck, M., & Ceci, S. J. (2004). Forensic developmental psychology: Unveiling four common misconceptions. *Current Directions in Psychological Science, 13*(6), 229–232.

Bruck, M., Ceci, S. J., & Francoeur, E. (1999). The accuracy of mothers' memories of conversations with their preschool children. *Journal of Experimental Psychology: Applied, 5,* 1–18.

Bruck, M., Ceci, S. J., & Francoeur, E. (2000). A comparison of 3- and 4-year-old children's use of anatomically detailed dolls to report genital touching in a medical examination. *Journal of Experimental Psychology: Applied, 6,* 74–83.

Bruck, M., Ceci, S. J., Francoeur, E., & Barr, R. (1995). "I hardly cried when I got my shot!": Influencing children's reports about a visit to their pediatrician. *Child Development, 66,* 193–208.

Bruck, M., Ceci, S. J., Francoeur, E., & Renick, A. (1995). Anatomically detailed dolls do not facilitate preschoolers' reports of a pediatric examination involving genital touch. *Journal of Experimental Psychology: Applied, 1,* 95–109.

Bruck, M., Ceci, S. J., & Hembrooke, H. (1997). Children's false reports of pleasant and unpleasant events. In D. Read & D. S. Lindsay (Eds.), *Recollections of trauma: Scientific research and clinical practice* (pp. 199–219). New York: Plenum Press.

Bruck, M., Ceci, S. J., & Hembrooke, H. (2002). Nature of true and false narratives. *Developmental Review, 22,* 520–554.

Bruck, M., Ceci, S. J., Melnyk, L., & Finkelberg, D. (1999, April). *The effect of interviewer bias on the accuracy of children's reports and interviewer's reports.* Paper presented at the biennial meeting of the Society for Child Development, Albuquerque, NM.

Bruck, M., London, K. Landos, R., Goodman, J. (in press). Autobiographical memory and suggestibility in children with autistic spectrum disorder. *Developmental Psychopathology.*

Bruck, M., & Melnyk, L. (2004). Individual differences in children's suggestibility: A review and synthesis. *Applied Cognitive Psychology, 18,* 947–996.

Bruck, M., Melnyk, L., & Ceci, S. J. (2000). Draw it again Sam: The effect of drawing on children's suggestibility and source monitoring ability. *Journal of Experimental Child Psychology, 77,* 169–196.

California v. Raymond Buckey et al., Los Angeles County Sup. Ct. A750900 (1990).

Cassel, W., Roebers, C., & Bjorklund, D. (1996). Developmental patterns of eyewitness responses to repeated and increasingly suggestive questions. *Journal of Experimental Child Psychology, 61,* 116–133.

Ceci, S. J., & Bruck, M. (1993). The suggestibility of children's recollections: An historical review and synthesis. *Psychological Bulletin, 113,* 403–439.

Ceci, S. J., & Bruck, M. (1995). *Jeopardy in the courtroom: A scientific analysis of children's testimony.* Washington, DC: APA Books.

Ceci, S. J., & Friedman, R. D. (2000). The suggestibility of children: Scientific research and legal implications. *Cornell Law Review, 86,* 34–108.

Ceci, S. J., Huffman, M. L., Smith, E., & Loftus, E. F. (1994). Repeatedly thinking about a non-event. *Consciousness and Cognition, 2,* 388–407.

Ceci, S. J., Loftus, E. F., Leichtman, M., & Bruck, M. (1994). The possible role of source misattributions in the creation of false beliefs among preschoolers. *International Journal of Clinical and Experimental Hypnosis, 42,* 304–320.

Chen, E., Zeltzer, L. K., Craske, M. G., & Katz, E. R. (2000). Children's memories for painful cancer treatment procedures: Implications for distress. *Child Development, 71,* 933–947.

Chi, M. T. H., & Ceci, S. J. (1987). Content knowledge: Its representation and restructuring in memory development [Special issue]. In H. W. Reese & L. Lipsett (Eds.), *Advances in Child Development and Behavior, 20,* 91–146.

Child Maltreatment 2002. (2004). Reports from the States to the National Child Abuse and Neglect Data Systems—National statistics on child abuse and neglect.

Commonwealth v. Amirault, 424 Mass. 618 (1997) 3, 52n., 91, 92, 98.

Cox, B. C., Ornstein, P. A., Naus, M. J., Maxfield, D., & Zimler, J. (1989). Children's concurrent use of rehearsal and organizational strategies. *Developmental Psychology, 25,* 619–627.

Dalenberg, C. J., Hyland, K. Z., & Cuevas, C. A. (2002). Sources for fantastic elements in allegations of abuse by adults and children. In M. L. Eisen (Ed.), *Memory and suggestibility in the forensic interview* (pp. 185–204). Mahwah, NJ: Erlbaum.

Davies, G. M., & Westcott, H. (1999). *The child witness and the memorandum of good practice: A research review.* London: The Home Office.

DeLoache, J. S., & Smith, C. M. (1999). Early symbolic representation. In I. Siegal (Ed.), *Theoretical perspectives in the concept of representation* (pp. 61–86). Hillsdale, NJ: Erlbaum.

Emery, R. E., Laumann-Billings, L., Waldron, M. C., Sbarra, D. A., & Dillon, P. (2001). Child custody mediation and litigation: Custody, contact, and coparenting 12 years after initial dispute resolution. *Journal of Consulting and Clinical Psychology, 69,* 323–332.

Everson, M. (1997). Understanding bizarre, improbable, and fantastic elements in children's accounts of abuse. *Child Maltreatment, 2,* 134–149.

Farrar, M. J., & Goodman, G. S. (1992). Developmental changes in event memory. *Child Development, 63,* 173–187.

Finkelhor, D., Hotaling, G., Lewis, I. A., & Smith C. (1990). Sexual abuse in a national survey of adult men and women: Prevalence, characteristics and risk factors. *Child Abuse and Neglect, 14,* 19–28.

Finnila, K., Mahlberga, N., Santtilaa, P., Sandnabbaa, K., & Niemib, P. (2003). Validity of a test of children's suggestibility for predicting responses to two interview situations differing in their degree of suggestiveness. *Journal of Experimental Child Psychology, 85,* 32–49.

Fivush, R. (1984). Learning about school: The development of kindergartners' school scripts. *Child Development, 55,* 1697–1709.

Fivush, R. (1993). Developmental perspectives on autobiographical recall. In G. S. Goodman & B. Bottoms (Eds.), *Child victims and child witnesses: Understanding and improving testimony* (pp. 1–24). New York: Guilford Press.

Fivush, R. (1998). Children's recollections of traumatic and nontraumatic events. *Development and Psychopathology, 10,* 699–716.

Fivush, R., Hazzard, A., Sales, J. M., Sarfati, D., & Brown, T. (2003). Creating coherence out of chaos? Children's narratives of emotionally positive and negative events. *Applied Cognitive Psychology, 17,* 1–19.

Fivush, R., & Schwarzmueller, A. (1998). Children remember childhood: Implications for childhood amnesia. *Applied Cognitive Psychology, 12,* 455–473.

Flavell, J. H. (1992). Perspectives on perspective taking. In H. Beilin & P. Pufall (Eds.), *Piaget's theory: Prospects and possibilities* (pp. 107–139). Hillsdale, NJ: Erlbaum.

Foley, M. A., & Johnson, M. K. (1985). Confusions between memories for performed and imagined actions: A developmental comparison. *Child Development, 56,* 1145–1155.

Foley, M. A., Santini, C., & Sopasakis, M. (1989). Discriminating between memories: Evidence for children's spontaneous elaborations. *Journal of Experimental Child Psychology, 48,* 146–169.

Freud, S. (1953). Fragment of an analysis of a case of hysteria. In J. Strachey (Ed. & Trans.), *The standard edition of the complete psychological works of Sigmund Freud* (Vol. 7, pp. 3–122). London: Hogarth Press. (Original work published 1896)

Garven, S., Wood, J. M., & Malpass, R. S. (2000). Allegations of wrongdoing: The effects of reinforcement on children's mundane and fantastic claims. *Journal of Applied Psychology, 85,* 38–49.

Garven, S., Wood, J. M., Shaw, J. S., & Malpass, R. (1998). More than suggestion: Consequences of the interviewing techniques from the McMartin Preschool case. *Journal of Applied Psychology, 83,* 347–359.

Gindes, M. (1998). The psychological effects of relocation for children of divorce. *Journal of the American Academy of Matrimonial Lawyers, 15*(1), 119–148.

Golombok, S., Perry, B., Burston, A., Golding, J., Murray, C., Mooney-Somers, J., et al. (2003). Children with lesbian parents: A community study. *Developmental Psychology, 39,* 20–33.

Goodman, G., Batterman-Faunce, J., Schaaf, J., & Kenney, R. (2002). Nearly 4 years after an event: Children's eye witness memory and adult's perceptions of children's accuracy. *Child Abuse and Neglect, 26,* 849–884.

Goodman, G. S., Bottoms, B. L., Schwartz-Kenney, B., & Rudy, L. (1991). Children's testimony about a stressful event: Improving children's reports. *Journal of Narrative and Life History, 1,* 69–99.

Goodman, G. S., Emery, R., & Haugaard, J. J. (1998). Developmental psychology and law: Divorce, child maltreatment, foster care, and adoption. In W. Damon (Editor-in-Chief) & I. E. Sigel & A. Renninger (Vol. Eds.), *Handbook of child psychology: Vol. 4. Child psychology in practice* (5th ed., pp. 775–874). New York: Wiley.

Goodman, G. S., Hirschman, J. E., Hepps, D., & Rudy, L. (1991). Children's memory for stressful events. *Merrill-Palmer Quarterly, 37,* 109–157.

Goodman, G. S., & Quas, J. A. (1997). Trauma and memory: Individual differences in children's recounting of a stressful experience. In N. Stein, P. A. Ornstein, C. J. B. Tversky, & C. J. Brainerd (Eds.), *Memory for everyday and emotional events* (pp. 267–294). Mahwah, NJ: Erlbaum.

Goodman, G. S., Rudy, L., Bottoms, B., & Aman, C. (1990). Children's concerns and memory: Issues of ecological validity in the study of children's eyewitness testimony. In R. Fivush & J. Hudson (Eds.), *Knowing and remembering in young children* (pp. 249–284). New York: Cambridge University Press.

Gopnik, A., & Graf, P. (1988). Knowing how you know: Young children's ability to identify and remember the sources of their beliefs. *Child Development, 59,* 1366–1371.

Grisso, T., & Schwartz, R. (Eds.). (2000). *Youth on trial: A developmental perspective on juvenile justice.* Chicago: University of Chicago Press.

Grisso, T., Steinberg, L., Woolard, J., Cauffman, E., Scott, E., Graham, S., et al. (2003). Juveniles' competence to stand trial: A comparison of adolescents' and adults' capacities as trial defendants. *Law and Human Behavior, 27,* 333–363.

Haugaard, J., & Hazan, C. (2002). Foster parenting. In M. H. Bornstein (Ed.), *Handbook of parenting: Vol. 1. Children and parenting* (2nd ed., pp. 313–327). Mahwah, NJ: Erlbaum.

Howard, A. N., Osborne, H. L., & Baker-Ward, L. (1997, April). *Childhood cancer survivors' memory for their treatment after long delays.* Paper presented at the meetings of the Society for Research in Child Development, Washington, DC.

Howe, M. L. (1998). Individual differences in factors that modulate storage and retrieval of traumatic memories. *Development and Psychopathology, 10,* 681–698.

Howe, M. L. (2000). *The fate of early memories: Developmental science and the retention of childhood experiences.* Washington, DC: American Psychological Association.

Howe, M. L., Courage, M. L., & Peterson, C. (1995). Intrusions in preschoolers' recall of traumatic childhood events. *Psychonomic Bulletin and Review, 2,* 130–134.

Hudson, J. (1990). Constructive processes in children's event memories. *Developmental Psychology, 26,* 180–187.

Hudson, J., & Nelson, K. (1986). Repeated encounters of a similar kind: Effects of familiarity on children's autobiographic memory. *Cognitive Development, 1,* 253–271.

Hudson, J. A., Fivush, R., & Kuebli, J. (1992). Scripts and episodes: The development of event memory. *Applied Cognitive Psychology, 6,* 483–505.

Hudson, J. A., & Nelson, K. (1983). Effects of script structure on children's story recall. *Developmental Psychology, 19,* 625–635.

Hughes, M., & Grieve, R. (1980). On asking children bizarre questions. *First Language, 1,* 149–160.

Janet, P. (1889). *L'Automatisme psychologique.* Paris: Alcan.

Johnson, M. K., & Foley, M. A. (1984). Differentiating fact from fantasy: The reliability of children's memory. *Journal of Social Issues, 40,* 33–50.

Kassin, S. M., & Kiechel, K. L. (1996). The social psychology of false confessions: Compliance, internalization, and confabulation. *Psychological Science, 7,* 125–128.

Kelly, J. B., & Lamb, M. E. (2003). Developmental issues in relocation cases involving young children: When, whether, and how? *Journal of Family Psychology, 17,* 193–205.

Kendall-Tackett, K. A., Williams, L. M., & Finkelhor, D. (1993). Impact of sexual abuse on children: A review and synthesis of recent empirical studies. *Psychological Bulletin, 113*(1), 164–180.

Koss, M. P., Figueredo, A. J., Bell, I., Tharan, M., & Tromp, S. (1996). Traumatic memory characteristics: A cross-validated mediational model of response to rape among employed women. *Journal of Abnormal Psychology, 105,* 421–432.

Lamb, M., Orbach, Y., Sternberg, K., Hershkowitz, I., & Horowitz, D. (2000). Accuracy of investigators' verbatim notes of their forensic interviews with alleged child abuse victims. *Law and Human Behavior, 24,* 699–708.

Lamb, M. E., Sternberg, K. J., Orbach, Y., Esplin, P. W., Stewart, H., & Mitchell, S. (2003). Age differences in young children's responses to open-ended invitations in the course of forensic interviews. *Journal of Consulting and Clinical Psychology, 71*(5), 926–934.

Leichtman, M. D., & Ceci, S. J. (1995). The effects of stereotypes and suggestions on preschoolers' reports. *Developmental Psychology, 31*(4), 568–578.

Lepore, S. J., & Sesco, B. (1994). Distorting children's reports and interpretations of events through suggestion. *Applied Psychology, 79*(1), 108–120.

Lillie and Reed v. Newcastle City Council & Ors EWHC 1600 (QB) (2002).

Lindberg, M. A. (1980). Is knowledge base development a necessary and sufficient condition for memory development? *Journal of Experimental Child Psychology, 30,* 401–410.

Lindsay, S., & Johnson, M. K. (1987). Reality monitoring and suggestibility. In S. J. Ceci, M. P. Toglia, & D. F. Ross (Eds.), *Children's eyewitness memory* (pp. 92–121). New York: Springer Verlag.

Lindsay, S., Johnson, M. K., & Kwon, P. (1991). Developmental changes in memory source monitoring. *Journal of Experimental Child Psychology, 52,* 297–318.

Loftus, E. F. (2003). Make believe memories. *American Psychologist, 58*(11), 867–873.

Loftus, E. F., & Davies, G. (1984). Distortions in the memory of children. *Journal of Social Issues, 40,* 51–67.

London, K., Bruck, M., Ceci, S. J., & Shuman, D. (2005). Children's disclosure of sexual abuse: What does the research tell us about the ways that children tell? *Psychology, Public Policy, and the Law, 11,* 194–226.

London, K., & Nunez, N. (2002). Examining the efficacy of truth-lie discussions in predicting and increasing the veracity of children's reports. *Journal of Experimental Child Psychology, 83,* 131–147.

Lyon, T. D. (1999). The new wave in children's suggestibility research: Critique. *Cornell Law Review, 86,* 1–84.

Marche, T. (1999). Memory strength affects reporting of misinformation. *Journal of Experimental Child Psychology, 73,* 45–71.

Marche, T. A., & Howe, M. L. (1995). Preschoolers report misinformation despite accurate memory. *Developmental Psychology, 31*(4), 554–567.

McCauley, M. R., & Fisher, R. P. (1995). Facilitating children's eyewitness recall with the revised Cognitive Interview. *Journal of Applied Psychology, 80,* 510–516.

McCauley, M. R., & Parker, J. F. (2001). When will a child be believed? The impact of the victim's age and jurors' gender on children's credibility and verdict in a sexual-abuse case. *Child Abuse and Neglect, 25,* 523–539.

Melnyk, L., & Bruck, M. (2004). Timing moderates the effects of repeated suggestive interviewing on children's eyewitness memory. *Applied Cognitive Psychology, 18,* 613–631.

Merritt, K. A., Ornstein, P. A., & Spicker, B. (1994). Children's memory for a salient medical procedure: Implications for testimony. *Pediatrics, 94,* 17–23.

Meyers, J. E. (1995). Expert testimony regarding child sexual abuse. *Child Abuse and Neglect, 17,* 175–185.

Myles-Worsley, M., Cromer, C. C., & Dodd, D. H. (1986). Children's preschool script reconstruction: Reliance on general knowledge as memory fades. *Developmental Psychology, 22,* 22–30.

Nathan, D., & Snedeker, M. (1995). *Satan's silence: Ritual abuse and the making of a modern American witch hunt.* New York: Basic Books.

National Center on Child Abuse and Neglect. (1998). *Child Maltreatment 1996: Reports From the States for the National Child Abuse and Neglect Data System.* Washington, DC: U.S. Department of Health and Human Services.

New Jersey v. Michaels, 625 A.2d 579 *aff'd* 642 A.2d 1372 (1994).

Nightingale, N. N. (1993). Juror reactions to child victim witnesses: Factors affecting trial outcome. *Law and Human Behavior, 17,* 679–694.

North Carolina v. Robert Fulton Kelly Jr., 456 S. E.2d 861 (1995).

Orbach, Y., Hershkowitz, I., Lamb, M., Sternberg, K., Esplin, P., & Horowitz, D. (2000). Assessing the value of structured protocols for forensic interviews of alleged child abuse victims. *Child Abuse and Neglect, 24,* 733–752.

Ornstein, P., Gordon, B. N., & Larus, D. (1992). Children's memory for a personally experienced event: Implications for testimony. *Applied Cognitive Psychology, 6,* 49–60.

Ornstein, P. A. (1990). Knowledge and strategies: A discussion. In W. Schneider & F. Weinert (Eds.), *Interactions among aptitudes, strategies, and knowledge in cognitive performance* (pp. 147–156). New York: Springer-Verlag.

Ornstein, P. A. (1995). Children's long-term retention of salient personal experiences. *Journal of Traumatic Stress, 8,* 581–606.

Ornstein, P. A., Manning, E. L., & Pelphrey, K. A. (1999). Children's memory for pain. *Developmental and Behavioral Pediatrics, 20,* 262–277.

Ornstein, P. A., Merritt, K. A., Baker-Ward, L., Furtado, E., Gordon, B. N., & Principe, G. (1998). Children's knowledge, expectation, and long-term retention. *Applied Cognitive Psychology, 12,* 387–405.

Ornstein, P. A., & Naus, M. J. (1985). Effects of the knowledge base on children's memory strategies. In H. W. Reese (Ed.), *Advances in child development and behavior* (Vol. 19, pp. 113–148). Orlando, FL: Academic Press.

Ornstein, P. A., Naus, M. J., Maxfield, D., & Zimler, J. (1989). Children's concurrent use of rehearsal and organizations strategies. *Developmental Psychology, 25,* 619–627.

Patterson, C. J. (1997). Children of lesbian and gay parents. In T. Ollendick & R. Prinz (Eds.), *Advances in clinical child psychology* (Vol. 19, pp. 235–282). New York: Plenum Press.

People v. Scott Kniffen, Brenda Kniffen, Alvin McCuan and Deborah McCuan, Kern County (Calif.) Sup. Ct. 24208 (1996).

Peters, D. P. (1997). Stress, arousal, and children's eyewitness memory. In N. L. Stein, P. A. Ornstein, B. Tversky, & C. Brainerd (Eds.), *Memory for everyday and emotional events* (pp. 351–370). Mahwah, NJ: Erlbaum.

Peterson, C. (1999). Children's memory for medical emergencies: 2 years later. *Developmental Psychology, 35,* 1493–1506.

Peterson, C., & Bell, M. (1996). Children's memory for traumatic injury. *Child Development, 67,* 3045–3070.

Peterson, C., & Grant, M. (2001). Forced-choice: Are forensic interviewers asking the right questions? *Canadian Journal of Behavioural Science, 33*(2), 118–127.

Peterson, C., Moores, L., & White, G. (2001). Recounting the same events again and again: Children's consistency across multiple interviews. *Applied Cognitive Psychology, 15*(4), 353–371.

Peterson, C., & Rideout, R. (1998). Memory for medical emergencies experienced by 1- and 2-year-olds. *Developmental Psychology, 34,* 1059–1072.

Peterson, C., & Whalen, N. (2001). Five years later: Children's memory for medical emergencies. *Applied Cognitive Psychology, 15,* 7–24.

Pezdek, K., & Roe, C. (1995). The effect of memory trace strength on suggestibility. *Journal of Experimental Child Psychology, 60,* 116–128.

Pipe, M. E., Gee, S., Wilson, J. G., & Egerton, J. M. (1999). Children's recall 1 or 2 years after an event. *Developmental Psychology, 35,* 781–789.

Pipe, M. E., Goodman, G. S., Quas, J., Bidrose, S., Ablin, D., & Craw, S. (1997). Remembering early experiences during childhood: Are traumatic events special. In J. D. Read & D. S. Lindsay (Eds.), *Recollections of trauma: Scientific evidence and clinical practice* (pp. 417–423). New York: Plenum Press.

Poole, D., & White, L. (1991). Effects of question repetition on the eyewitness testimony of children and adults. *Developmental Psychology, 27*(6), 975–986.

Poole, D. A., & Lindsay, D. S. (1995). Interviewing preschoolers: Effects of nonsuggestive techniques, parental coaching and leading questions on reports of nonexperienced events. *Journal of Experimental Child Psychology, 60,* 129–154.

Poole, D. A., & Lindsay, D. S. (2001). Children's eyewitness reports after exposure to misinformation from parents. *Journal of Experimental Psychology: Applied, 7,* 27–50.

Powell, M., & Thomson, D. (1997). Contrasting memory for temporal-source and memory for content in children's discrimination of repeated events. *Applied Cognitive Psychology, 11,* 339–360.

Powell, M. B., & Thomson, D. M. (1996). Children's recall of an occurrence of a repeated event: Effects of age, retention interval, and question type. *Child Development, 67,* 1988–2004.

Priestley, G., Roberts, S., & Pipe, M. E. (1999). Returning to the scene: Reminders and context reinstatement enhance children's recall. *Developmental Psychology, 35,* 1006–1041.

Principe, G. F., & Ceci, S. J. (2002). "I saw it with my own ears": The effects of peer conversations on preschoolers' reports of non-experienced events. *Journal of Experimental Child Psychology, 83*(1), 1–25.

Principe, G. F., Kanaya, T., Ceci, S. J., & Singh, M. (in press). Believing is seeing: How rumors can engender false memories in preschoolers. *Psychological Science.*

Principe, G. F., Ornstein, P. A., Baker-Ward, L., & Gordon, B. N. (2000). The effects of intervening experiences on children's memory for a physical examination. *Applied Cognitive Psychology, 14,* 59–80.

Pynoos, R. S., Steinberg, A. M., & Aronson, L. (1997). Traumatic experiences: The early organization of memory in school-age children and adolescents. In P. S. Applebaum, L. A. Uyehara, & M. R. Elin (Eds.), *Trauma and memory: Clinical and legal controversies* (pp. 272–289). New York: Oxford University Press.

Quas, J. A., Bottoms, B. L., Haegerich, T. M., & Nysse-Carris, K. L. (2002). Effects of victim, defendant, and juror gender on decisions in child sexual assault cases. *Journal of Applied Social Psychology, 24,* 702–732.

Quas, J. A., Goodman, G. S., Bidrose, S., Pipe, M. E., Craw, S., & Ablin, D. S. (1999). Emotion and memory: Children's long-term remembering, forgetting, and suggestibility. *Journal of Experimental Child Psychology, 72,* 235–270.

Rayner, K., & Pollatsek, A. (1989). *The psychology of reading.* Upper Saddle River, NJ: Prentice-Hall.

Ricci, C., & Beal, C. (1998). Effect of questioning techniques and interview setting on young children's eyewitness memory. *Expert Evidence, 6,* 127–144.

Salekin, R. T. (2002). Juvenile transfer to adult court: How can developmental and child psychology inform policy decision making. In B. L. Bottoms, M. B. Kovera, & B. D. McAuliff (Eds.), *Children, social science, and the law* (pp. 203–232). New York: Cambridge University Press.

Salmon, K. (2001). Remembering and reporting by children: The influence of cues and props. *Clinical Psychology Review, 21*(2), 267–300.

Salmon, K., & Pipe, M. E. (2000). Recalling an event one year later: The impact of props, drawing and a prior interview. *Applied Cognitive Psychology, 14,* 99–120.

Saywitz, K. J. (1987). Children's testimony: Age-related patterns of memory errors. In S. J. Ceci, M. P. Toglia, & D. F. Ross (Eds.), *Children's eyewitness memory* (pp. 36–52). New York: Springer Verlag.

Saywitz, K. J., & Moan-Hardie, S. (1994). Reducing the potential for distortion of childhood memories. *Consciousness and Cognition, 3,* 408–425.

Schneider, W., & Bjorklund, D. F. (1998). Memory. In W. Damon (Editor-in-Chief) & D. Kuhn & R. S. Siegler (Vol. Eds.), *Handbook of child psychology: Vol. 2. Cognition, perception, and language* (pp. 467–521). New York: Wiley.

Scullin, M., Kanaya, T., & Ceci, S. J. (2002). Measurement of individual differences in children's suggestibility across situations. *Journal of Experimental Psychology: Applied, 8,* 233–241.

Shaw, J. A., Applegate, B., & Schorr, C. (1996). Twenty-one-month follow-up of school-age children exposed to Hurricane Andrew. *Journal of the American Academy of Child and Adolescent Psychiatry, 35,* 359–364.

Shrimpton, S., Oates, K., & Hayes, S. (1998). Children's memory of events: Effects of stress, age, time delay and location of interview. *Applied Cognitive Psychology, 12,* 133–143.

Simcock, G., & Hayne, H. (2002). Children fail to translate their preverbal memories into language. *Psychological Science, 13,* 225–231.

Smith, D. W., Letourneau, E. J., Saunders, B. E., Kilpatrick, D. G., Resnick, H. S., & Best, C. L. (2000). Delay in disclosure of childhood rape: Results from a national survey. *Child Abuse and Neglect, 24*(2), 273–287.

Snowden v. Singletary, 135 F.3d 732 (11th Cir. 1998).

State v. Fijnje, 84-19728 (11th Cir. 1995).

State of Washington v. Carol, M. D., & Mark, A. D., 983 P.2d 1165 (Wash. Ct. App. 1999).

State of Washington v. Manuel Hidalgo Rodriguez, 17600-2-III (Wa. Ct. App. 1999).

Stein, N. L. (1996). Children's memory for emotional events: Implications for testimony. In K. Pezdek & W. P. Banks (Eds.), *The recovered/false memory debate* (pp. 169–194). San Diego, CA: Academic Press.

Steinberg, L., & Cauffman, E. (1996). Maturity of judgment in adolescence: Psychosocial factors in adolescent decision-making. *Law and Human Behavior, 20*(3), 249–272.

Steinberg, L., & Scott, E. (2003). Less guilty by reason of adolescence: Developmental immaturity, diminished responsibility, and the juvenile death penalty. *American Psychologist, 58,* 1009–1018.

Sternberg, K. J., Lamb, M. E., Orbach, Y., Esplin, P., & Mitchell, S. (2001). Use of a structured investigative protocol enhances young children's responses to free-recall prompts in the course of forensic interviews. *Journal of Applied Psychology, 86,* 997–1005.

Steward, M. S., & Steward, D. S. (with Farquahar, L., Myers, J. E. B., Reinart, M., Welker, J., Joye, N., Driskll, J., & Morgan, J.). (1996). Interviewing young children about body touch and handling. *Monographs of the Society for Research in Child Development, 61*(4/5, Serial No. 248).

Stuber, M. L., Nader, K., Yasuda, P., Pynoos, R. S., & Cohen, S. (1991). Stress response after pediatric bone marrow transplantation: Preliminary results of a prospective longitudinal study.

Journal of the American Academy of Child and Adolescent Psychiatry, 30, 952–957.

Summit, R. C. (1983). The child sexual abuse accommodation syndrome. *Child Abuse and Neglect, 7,* 177–193.

Talwar, V., Kang, L., Bala, N., & Lindsay, R. C. L. (2004). Children's lie-telling to conceal a parent's transgression: Legal implications. *Law and Human Behavior, 28,* 411–435.

Terr, L. (1988). What happens to early memories of trauma? A study of 20 children under age 5 at the time of documented traumatic events. *Journal of the American Academy of Child and Adolescent Psychiatry, 27,* 96–104.

Terr, L. (1991). Childhood traumas: An outline and overview. *American Journal of Psychiatry, 148,* 10–20.

Terr, L. (1994). *Unchained memories: True stories of traumatic memories, lost and found.* New York: Basic Books.

Thompson, W. C., Clarke-Stewart, K. A., & Lepore, S. (1997). What did the janitor do? Suggestive interviewing and the accuracy of children's accounts. *Law and Human Behavior, 21*(4), 405–426.

van der Kolk, B. A., & Fisler, R. E. (1995). Dissociation and the fragmentary nature of traumatic memories: Overview and exploratory study. *Journal of Traumatic Stress, 8,* 505–525.

Verville, E. (1968). *Behavior problems of children.* Philadelphia: Saunders.

Warren, A. R., & Swartwood, J. N. (1992). Developmental issues in flashbulb memory research: Children recall the Challenger event. In E. Winograd & U. Neisser (Eds.), *Affect and accuracy in recall: Studies of "flashbulb" memories* (pp. 95–120). Cambridge, MA: Cambridge University Press.

Warren, A. R., & Woodall, C. E. (1999). The reliability of hearsay testimony: How well do interviewers recall their interviews with children? *Psychology, Public Policy and Law, 5,* 355–371.

Warren, A. R., Woodall, C. E., Hunt, J. S., & Perry, N. W. (1996). "It sounds good in theory, but . . .": Do investigative interviewers follow guidelines based on memory research? *Child Maltreatment, 1,* 231–245.

Waterman, A. H., Blades, M., & Spencer, C. (2000). Do children try to answer nonsensical questions? *British Journal of Developmental Psychology, 18*(2), 211–225.

Wimmer, H., Hogerfe, G. J., & Perner, J. (1988). Children's understanding of informational access as a source of knowledge. *Child Development, 59,* 386–396.

Zaragoza, M., Payment, K., Kichler, J., Stines, L., & Drivdahl, S. (2001, April). *Forced confabulation and false memory in child witnesses.* Paper presented at the 2001 biennial meeting of the Society for Research in Child Development, Minneapolis, MN.

CHAPTER 20

Media and Popular Culture

GEORGE COMSTOCK and ERICA SCHARRER

The second half of the twentieth century has seen what some have called a "revolutionary change" in the role of media in the lives of American children and teenagers (Roberts & Foehr, 2004). The change began with the introduction of television in the late 1940s. This was a new kind of medium—in the home and more convenient and attractive than anything that had preceded it. By the end of the 1950s, almost 9 out of 10 households would have a set. However, it was during the last 2 decades that the most rapid proliferation of media in the lives of young people occurred in the United States. What have changed are the circumstances of growing up. Symbolic models and vicarious experience play a much greater role (Bandura, 1986). Entertainment is starkly predominant in the media use of the young, and much of this entertainment is violent. This scenario raises questions about the consequences of media use for scholastic performance and of entertainment for interpersonal behavior. Media are usually—but not exclusively—supported by advertising, and advertising for cereals, candies, fast foods, toys, and apparel are directed at the young, including those in the early years of childhood. This raises issues of deception, manipulation, and, in the case of

some food products, health. Finally, these media of the twentieth century have stripped from parents their ability to control the symbols and information reaching children—a task that was straightforward in the early 1940s, when there were only newspapers, magazines, radio, and the Saturday matinee (and, in some homes, a phonograph) that could intrude. In fact, in the new environment, a substantial amount of media use occurs out of the sight and hearing of parents in the privacy of the bedrooms of children and teenagers.

Our treatment of the influence of media and popular culture in the lives of the young has three emphases. We cover a wide range of media, but much of our attention goes to television because it is by far the medium with which the young spend the most time—at least until the late teenage years, when music takes up almost as much time. We draw largely on academic research in child development, social psychology, sociology, and communication. The television and advertising industries, as well as manufacturers, engage regularly in research to market products and television programs to the young, but most of this work is not publicly available and not too much would have much application to theory or practice outside of successful marketing. Finally, we identify the pertinence and applications of research on policymaking and in parenting.

Practice has been well-informed by research. One testament is the 39 chapters of the recent *Handbook of Children and the Media* edited by Dorothy G. Singer and Jerome L. Singer (2001). Another is the approximately 900 references in G. Comstock's (1991) *Television and the American Child*. However, the path to application is usually through theory or judicious interpretation of accumulated evidence. It is the rare instance when research directly affects practice, such as the monitoring by Children's Television Workshop of children's attentiveness on a scene-by-scene basis during production to ensure the attention necessary for the intended educational impact of *Sesame Street* (Lesser, 1974).

We cover five topics: the allocation of time and attention to televisual media, scholastic performance, television advertising, violent entertainment, and two issues of current concern and interest—the development of codes warning parents about (and possibly luring young viewers with the promise of forbidden fruit) the violent, adult, or sexual content of media, and the role of new electronic media in the delivery of popular culture. Thus, we begin with the two fundamental requirements for media influence, time and attention, and conclude by examining the implications for time and attention of developing technology.

ALLOCATION OF TIME AND ATTENTION

Our first topic falls outside the usual parameters of child development but is essential not only to our theme—the influences of popular culture—but to the modern lives of American children and teenagers. It is the allocation of time and attention to the media. We draw on our own work: our analysis of the data on use of television and other film-related media (Comstock & Scharrer, 2001) and our analyses of the data on the content and themes of televisual entertainment media (Scharrer & Comstock, 2003).

Use of Television and Other Film-Related Media

There are five questions that are paramount in regard to the use of television and other film-related media by children and teenagers. How much do they view? What makes television viewing different from other media consumption? What are the preferences of young people? Why do children and teenagers view? What changes in viewing occur as children grow up?

Time

Attention to the screen of an operating television set has been recorded as occurring as early as 6 months of age (Hollenbeck & Slaby, 1979). However, viewing on a regular basis usually begins between the ages of 2.5 and 3, with an average of about 1.5 hours per day (Huston et al., 1983). Viewing quickly rises to about 2.75 hours between the ages of 3 and 6 (Huston, Wright, Rice, Kerkman, & St. Peters, 1990), before declining about a half hour between the ages of 5.5 and 7, when the demands of initial school attendance reduce time available for viewing (Figure 20.1). Viewing then increases again until age 12.

The high school years see a sizable decline in viewing because of the greater freedom to be away from home and the greater competition from other activities, such as athletics, dating, and pursuits incompatible with viewing television. Viewing time remains lower for those who go on to college and, later, graduate school. When the years of education have ended, viewing time returns to about the same level as in the elementary school years, before increasing substantially for those in their mid-50s and older.

Based on a number of sources, including Roberts and Foehr (2004) and Robinson and Godbey (1997), we estimate the average amount of viewing for those age 2 to 11 to be 3 hours and 7 minutes a day, or 21 hours and 49 minutes a week. Our estimate for teenagers age 12 to 17 is 2 hours and 28 minutes a day, or 17 hours and 16 minutes a week. These estimates include three levels of viewing: *primary,* when viewing is reported as the sole or foremost activity; *secondary,* when viewing is said to be secondary to some other activity; and *tertiary,* when television is said to be subordinate to other activities but a set is operating (Comstock & Scharrer, 2001).

These averages mask a great deal of variability among individuals. Major factors that affect amount of viewing include *household characteristics:* socioeconomic status (inversely associated with television use), norms about viewing (which may promote or discourage television use), and availability of television sets, other media, and alternative leisure options (which will affect the ability to choose programs for oneself and the comparative attractiveness of the medium); *child attributes,*

(a)

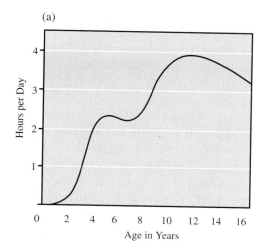

(b)

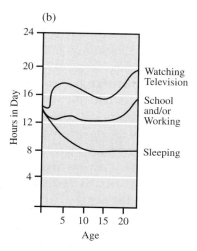

Figure 20.1   Television viewing, school or work, and sleep by age. *Source:* (a) Adapted from *Television and Human Behavior,* by G. Comstock, S. Chaffee, N. Katzman, M. McCombs, and D. Roberts, 1978, New York: Columbia University Press. Copyright by Columbia University Press. Reprinted with permission; (b) *The Psychology of Television,* by J. Condry, 1989, Hillsdale, NJ: Erlbaum. Copyright by Lawrence Erlbaum. Reprinted with permission.

such as age (as we have seen), mental ability (inversely associated with amount of viewing), and comprehension (a prerequisite for enjoying a televised narrative); *situational influences,* such as the presence and behavior of others (who might choose to turn a set on or direct attention to the screen by looking at it themselves), clock and calendar effects, such as hour of day, day of week, and season (the daily cycle of children's viewing rises when school lets out, is greatest during the week on Friday nights when there is no school the next day, and increases during the summer with more leisure time); and

states of mind (viewing often is engaged in to escape anger and stress).

What's Special

The ubiquity of media in the environment of young people sets the present era apart. The household of the 1950s typically had a single television set and sometimes one device that could play recorded music as well as one or more radios. Today's young person grows up surrounded by media and the options for diversion, learning, and play that they provide. Roberts and Foehr (2004) provide up-to-date data from a nationally representative sample of more than 3,000 children and teenagers between the ages of 2 and 18. They found that the typical home contained three television sets, three tape players, three radios, two videocassette recorders (VCRs), two compact disc (CD) players, one video game console, and one computer. When they inquired about direct and private access in the young person's bedroom, they found media in similarly impressive array. Among those age 2 to 7, 43% had radios, 38% had CD players, 32% had television sets, 16% had VCRs, 13% had video game consoles, and 6% had computers. Among those older (8 to 18), the figures were much larger: 88% for CD players, 86% for radios, 65% for television sets, 45% for video game consoles, 36% for VCRs, and 21% for computers. The result, undoubtedly surprising to some, has not been a diminishing of the time spent with television but an expansion of the total time spent with media, which Roberts and Foehr estimate as 3 hours and 38 minutes for those 2 to 7 and 6 hours and 17 minutes for those 8 to18, with total exposure about 20% greater because of multiple use of more than one medium at a time. The greater the time available and the opportunity to be in the vicinity of an operable television set, the greater the amount of viewing that will be registered for an audience segment (thus, children's viewing increases in summer, and teenagers view less than those in elementary school).

Addressing the paucity of research regarding the role of media in the lives of very young children, the Kaiser Family Foundation sponsored a recent study entitled "Zero to Six: Electronic Media in the Lives of Infants, Toddlers, and Preschoolers" (Rideout, Vandewater, & Wartella, 2003). Random-digit dialing was used to secure survey data from a nationally representative sample of more than 1,000 parents of children ranging in age from 6 months to 6 years. Like their older counterparts, these youngsters live in media-rich homes; 50% contain three or more TVs, 73% have a computer, and 49% a video game player. Media are not only present but accessed regularly by very young children. We concentrate our discussion on those 2 years old and younger, as this group is absent from the data reported earlier.

In a "typical" day, parents of these very young children report that 59% watch television, 42% view a videotape or DVD, 5% use a computer, and 3% play video games. Television's supremacy among media forms is apparent, again, in the first years of life. The average amount of time children 2 and under spend watching television per day is 2 hours and 5 minutes. About one in every four children 2 or younger has a television in their own bedroom.

Preferences

Program preferences develop surprisingly early. More than 3 decades ago, Lyle and Hoffman (1972b), in a pioneering study, asked a Los Angeles-area sample of 160 3-, 4-, and 5-year-olds to name a favorite program. About four-fifths of the 3-year-olds did so, and by age 5 almost everyone named a favorite.

Major predictors are gender and age. Both preschool boys and girls like animal characters such as appear on *Sesame Street*. Gender exerts an influence early, with 3 times as many boys as girls (17% versus 5%) naming a violent cartoon and twice as many girls as boys (39% versus 19%) naming a family cartoon (*The Flintstones*) among those 3 to 5 years old. Age makes a big difference. Lyle and Hoffman (1972a) again present pertinent data obtained from about 1,600 Los Angeles-area 1st-, 6th-, and 10th-grade students. Among the first graders, about one-fourth named a cartoon and about half a situation comedy. By the sixth grade, only 1 in 20 named a cartoon; situation comedies remained the most popular, but other general audience formats were gaining. By the 10th grade, drama, action adventure, soap operas, situation comedies, and talk, variety, and music (a category partly replaced now by MTV) were the most popular. *Sesame Street* provides an excellent example of the tyranny of age. Almost 33% of the 3-year-olds in the Lyle and Hoffman (1972b) data named it as a favorite; by age 5, that figure had declined to 12%, and 6- and 7-year-olds have almost wholly deserted the program as something for younger kids (Huston et al., 1990).

Why They View

The three major gratifications driving the use of television by children and teenagers as well as adults are (1)

diversion and escape from stress; (2) social comparison; and (3) keeping aware of what is transpiring in the world (Comstock & Scharrer, 1999). The first derives from the fact that those under stress, lonely, anxious, in negative mood states, or in conflict with others rank higher in their amount of viewing or other measures of attention to television (D. R. Anderson, Collins, Schmitt, & Jacobvitz, 1996; Canary & Spitzberg, 1993; Kubey & Csikszentmihalyi, 1990; Maccoby, 1954; R. Potts & Sanchez, 1994) as well as from the motives that people cite when asked why they view (Albarran & Umphrey, 1993; Bower, 1985). The second was advanced by Harwood (1997) and is consistent with the tendency of viewers to pay greater visual attention to screen personages like themselves, whether the characteristic is race (Comstock, 1991b), age (Harwood, 1997), or gender (Maccoby & Wilson, 1957; Maccoby, Wilson, & Burton, 1958; Sprafkin & Liebert, 1978). The third is based on the great frequency with which people cite learning something as a reason for viewing, though not referring specifically to the news or educational programming (Albarran & Umphrey, 1993; Bower, 1985), and we construe this motive to keep up with things as encompassing what is on television in the way of entertainment, sports, and news and the manner in which television covers events, as well as the events that make up the content of the news.

These motives find expression in two types of attention to the medium: ritualistic viewing and instrumental viewing. What separates the two is the degree to which the specific content of a program can be said to be responsible for viewing (Comstock & Scharrer, 1999; A. M. Rubin, 1983, 1984). The medium has primacy in ritualistic viewing, with the decision to watch television preceding the search for a satisfactory program. Instrumental viewing describes the more careful use of the medium to attend to particular programs. Most viewing is ritualistic, and most viewers are ritualistic most of the time in their attention to the medium. This holds true for children and teenagers as well as adults. The great attentiveness to favorite programs among younger children is certainly an example of instrumental viewing (but would account for no more than a fifth of their total television use). By age 10, they, like adults, have begun to see favorite programs less often (because their scheduling conflicts with other activities) but to spend more time with the medium (Comstock & Scharrer, 1999, 2001; Eron, Huesmann, Brice, & Mermelstein, 1983) and, at the same time, to begin to give less eye attention to the screen (D. R. Anderson, Lorch, Field, Collins, & Nathan, 1986). Young people, like adults, are now usually *monitoring* rather than viewing television, paying enough attention to audio and visual cues to follow the narrative (whatever it might be) while giving less than full attention to the screen.

Developmental Changes

Viewing begins before the age of 3 and reaches a peak at about age 12. These 9 years begin with exposure to imagery that has very limited meaning to the young child, to monitoring television in the manner of an adult (although the inclusion of some of television's darker and morally complex offerings, such as *Law and Order, CSI: Crime Scene Investigation,* and *The Sopranos,* will usually wait until the middle or late teens).

Early instrumental use of educational programs such as *Sesame Street* often will have been the product of parental guidance and will lead to less viewing and greater instrumental use of the medium as a teenager (Rosengren & Windahl, 1989). In contrast, in households where print media are scarce and norms favor the constant use of television, children will view more than average, will largely confine their use of other media to audio or screen media, and will continue to do so as teenagers and adults (Comstock & Scharrer, 1999, 2001; Roberts & Foehr, 2004). Again, household characteristics play a large role in how much and in what ways television is consumed.

Attention to the screen represents involvement. Up to about 6 years of age, greater attention is confined to cartoons (Bechtel, Achelpohl, & Akers, 1972). Attention to television in general then increases up to about age 10, as more programs for general audiences become of interest (D. R. Anderson et al., 1986; Wolf, 1987); attention to the screen then declines, as the young have reached an adult orientation toward the medium. The increasing attention coincides with the shift, between the ages of 7 and 9, from Piaget's preoperational to his concrete operational stage. In the latter stage, children make greater use of verbal elements than appearances and action in interpreting television and become more open to subtleties of plot and character (Kelly & Spear, 1991; Van Evra, 2004). They now also need to give less rapt attention to the screen to follow a narrative, as exemplified by the decline in eye contact.

Most scholars agree that children's attention to the screen is also a function of the comprehensibility of the program (D. R. Anderson, Pugzles Lorch, Field, &

Sanders, 1981; Campbell, Wright, & Huston, 1987), with comprehensibility explained, in part, by the age and cognitive-developmental level of the child (Calvert, Huston, Watkins, & Wright, 1982; Huston et al., 1990). These principles were demonstrated recently in data drawn by Valkenburg and Vroone (2004) via a home observation study with 50 6- to 58-month-olds. Examining attention paid to television segments that varied in content complexity, these researchers found that the youngest children (6 to 18 months) attended more to the least complex program (*Teletubbies*), whereas the oldest children attended more to the most complex program (*Lion King II*). Of particular importance, the two programs were similar in audio and visual features. Thus, a child dedicates attention to something perceived as within his or her cognitive grasp.

Content and Themes of Televisual Media

We begin our treatment of content and themes in the programming that children and teenagers watch with three fundamental parameters that establish the context for all else. We then turn to two forms of behavior depicted that have been the subject of controversy or concern because they present questionable guidance: violence and sexual intimacy. These portrayals and depictions attain importance given the potential for children and teenagers to take television as representative of the world or as a guide for emulation (Bandura, 1986; Comstock & Scharrer, 1999; DeFleur & DeFleur, 1967).

Entertainment Predominates

A large majority of the television viewed by those age 8 to 13 and a substantial proportion of that viewed by 2- to 7-year-olds is entertainment (Roberts & Foehr, 2004). Younger children particularly enjoy cartoons, and these have dominated the blocks of time set aside for children's programming on weekend mornings and after school for decades (Comstock, 1991a; Comstock & Scharrer, 2001), for animation signals to a child that the content is designed for a young viewer. However, children are also present in large numbers for general audience programming, which they will come to prefer. Because television earns most of its revenues from advertising, with some, for cable, coming from subscriber fees, popularity is the paramount goal (with audience demographics that will attract advertisers, such as children on Saturday mornings and young adults in general).

The most effective way to achieve popularity is with undemanding entertainment (Barwise & Ehrenberg, 1988). Thus, this type of programming is preeminent in all parts of the day every day of the week except weekend afternoons, when sports (another undemanding genre) predominate. Entertainment consequently is what children and teenagers mostly view.

Children's Programming: Popular but Limited Role

In a nationally representative sample of more than 3,000 young people in the late 1990s, about 85% of 2- to 7-year-olds, about 50% of 8- to 13-year-olds, and 16% of 14- to 18-year-olds said they watched entertainment created for young viewers the previous day (Roberts & Foehr, 2004). In recent years, children's programs on the three original networks (ABC, CBS, and NBC) have numbered in the high 50s, a decline from a high of 67 in 1979 to 1980 (Pecora, 1998). On cable, two channels, The Disney Channel (funded mostly by subscriber fees) and Nickelodeon (funded by both fees and advertising), use the same formula (Pecora, 1998): morning for preschoolers (who reach a peak of more than 20% at this time in their daily viewing cycle), an afterschool block for those older (who will reach a peak of 40% by 5 P.M. in this phase of their daily cycle), and entertainment for the family in prime time (when all audience segments peak in their daily viewing). The Disney Channel mostly programs its own characters, such as *Little Mermaid, Pooh Corner,* and *Mickey Mouse Club*; Nickelodeon features entertainment popular with older children, such as *Rugrats,* and educational preschool programs such as *Blues Clues, Bob the Builder,* and *Franklin.* However, the combination of children in the audience for general audience programming, the changing tastes of young people as they grow older, and the number and placement in the schedule of programs specifically designed for young people assign them a limited role despite their popularity among younger viewers.

Educational Programming: A Small Role

Educational programs have only a small role in the overall viewing of young people partly because of the small number of such programs in television schedules. The Public Broadcasting System (PBS) has offered the celebrated *Sesame Street* and *Mister Rogers' Neighborhood. Sesame Street* is of particular interest because regular viewing is associated with a number of favorable outcomes, such as the learning of letters and numbers, language learning, school readiness, and better grades years later, although many of these (other than the learning of letters and numbers) may reflect the superior parenting practices of those who also encourage their young children to watch *Sesame Street* rather than effects of viewing the program (Comstock & Scharrer, 1999; Cook et al., 1975; Fisch & Truglio, 2001; Huston et al., 1990; Rice, Huston, Truglio, & Wright, 1990; Wright & Huston, 1995; Zill, Davies, & Daly, 1994). Broadcast television abounds, of course, with advertising and merchandise tie-ins, but other channels are becoming more commercialized. Nickelodeon began without commercials, but after 4 years turned to advertising. Decreases in federal funding have led PBS to product tie-ins for such shows as *Barney and Friends* and *Lamb Chop's Play-Along;* backpacks, books, clothing, lunch boxes, and videotapes carry PBS characters for a price, and the corporate sponsorship announcements between programs resemble the advertising on commercial television. Thus, the experience of even educational fare has a substantial context of commercials and marketing.

In the Children's Television Act of 1990, Congress required commercial stations to offer educational programming as a condition for license renewal. The criterion eventually was set at 3 hours per week (or six half-hour shows), and programs were required by the Federal Communications Commission (FCC) to have as a "significant purpose" cultural or educational benefit. Presumably, the latter phrase will end the initial response of broadcasters to the 1990 legislation of simply labeling a program already on the air as educational on the grounds that admirable behavior was sometimes portrayed (Kunkel, 1998; Kunkel & Canepa, 1994; Kunkel & Goette, 1997), making ostensible educators of *Yogi Bear* and *G. I. Joe.* Whether this definition will enlarge the scope of educational programming remains to be seen; some broadcasters are a hardy lot in pursuing profits and schedule educational programming at hours when children are unlikely to be in the audience because they can sell the time when children would be present to advertisers at a higher price with other offerings (Hamilton, 1998).

Violence

There has been a great deal of violence on television since its introduction in the late 1940s (Head, 1954; Smythe, 1954). This violence is often committed by attractive characters who are typically White males, and usually occurs without inflicting great apparent harm or agony (Comstock & Scharrer, 1999). Flashy weapons are often used. These elements make it very attractive to emulate. The most violent television is children's programming because of the action-adventure cartoons (and this has been true for at least 3 decades), premium movie channels, cable channels that specialize in violence such as TNT, and theater movies shown on broadcast television (Hamilton, 1998; National Television Violence Study, 1998a, 1998b). Violence is best thought of as a staple that oscillates and sometimes migrates (from broadcast to cable channels) but does not change dramatically in frequency and is not at all likely to disappear, despite disapproving presidents and members of Congress.

Sexual Intimacy

There is plenty of sexual content on television reaching young people in the way of talk, allusions, and assignations, but comparatively little in the way of physical sexual contact other than kissing and a modest frequency of implied or depicted intercourse during the day and evening hours of viewing. The preschool educational programs and cartoons favored by young children obviously do not contain sexual references. However, the situation comedies, soap operas, and prime time programs popular with older children and adolescents do. For example, Kunkel, Cope, and Colvin (1996) examined 128 programs during what was once called the "family hour" (the first hour of prime time, beginning at 8 P.M. EST) and found that 61% contained some variety of sexual behavior (from kisses to the depiction of intercourse), 12% implied or depicted intercourse, and 59% contained talk about sex. Cope (1998) examined 95 episodes of programs favored by 12- to 17-year-olds: 67% included talk about sex, 62% depicted various sexual behavior, and 13% implied or depicted intercourse. The same pattern occurs in the comprehensive examination by Kunkel, Cope-Farrar, Biely, Farinola, and Donnerstein (2001) of 900 programs appearing between 7 A.M. and 11 P.M. on 11 channels (the four major broadcast networks, a WB affiliate, four cable channels, PBS, and HBO): Sexual messages occurred at a rate of 4.1 per hour and 66% of the programs contained sexual messages. Unfortunately, most of these depictions were devoid of any emphasis on or reference to the risks and responsibilities of sexual intimacy. Such references oc-

curred at the miserly rate of 6% (Kunkel et al., 1996) to 9% (Cope, 1998).

Applications

The great diversity of media use that occurs among young people is neatly captured by the statistical manipulations of Roberts and Foehr (2004). They performed a cluster analysis on their nationally representative sample of more than 2,000 8- to 18- year-olds and uncovered six groupings that could be aligned on the two dimensions of access to media (from low to high) and use of media (again, from low to high). The result is a very elegant typology because each group represents about one-sixth of the population (Figure 20.2):

1. *Enthusiast:* Highest use of media overall. High home and bedroom access. Uses all media more than others: print, television, computers, movies, video games. Home environment favorable to media.

2. *Vidkid:* Second-highest use of media, but focuses primarily on screen media, and especially television. Bedroom access medium, home access low, but media-favorable home environment.

3. *Interactor:* Moderate media use. Bedroom access low, home access medium to high. Focuses more than average on computer use and print media. Home environment on average neither favorable nor strict toward media.

4. *Restricted:* Low to moderate use of media. Home access high, bedroom access medium, but environment very strict about media use.

5. *Indifferent:* Comparatively low use of media. Bedroom and home access high. Home environment favorable to media.

6. *Media lite:* Lowest use of media overall. Bedroom and home access low. Environment very strict about media use.

Several factors are at work here. Access to multiple television sets and computers, especially access in the young person's bedroom, makes a significant difference. The home environment (whether there are rules restricting television use) makes a big difference. This was measured by three questions about television (how often the set is on, whether there is viewing during meals, and

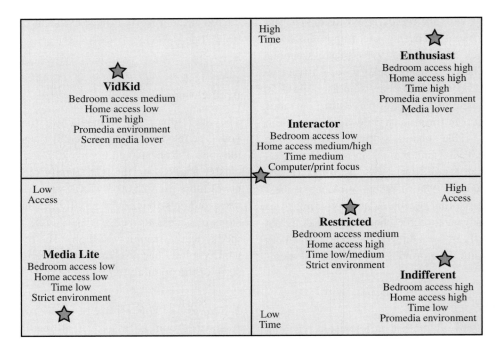

Figure 20.2   Typology of media use, 8- to 18-year-olds. *Source:* From *Kids and Media in America,* by D. F. Roberts and U. G. Foehr, 2004, New York: Cambridge University Press. Reprinted with permission.

whether there are rules about viewing), which turn out to be correlated with a variety of measures of media use as well as with greater television use. Personal interests then enter, with one group (Interactor) emphasizing computer use and print media more than average and another (Indifferent), despite easy access, ignoring media to a large degree, in favor, presumably, of other activities that are engaged in outside the home.

The survey by Roberts and Foehr (2004) leads to four important conclusions:

1. Television remains preeminent among the media in use by young people and has not been diminished by the Internet or computer use, which is mostly employed outside of school work for e-mail with friends.

2. This dominance of television, which is the most used of all the media by each of the six groups, means that it is the somewhat lower-than-average use of television or greater-than-average use of other media that distinguish those who are not among the two high media use groups and not the desertion of the medium.

3. Use of one medium by a young person is correlated with use of other media, so that at the present time, media do not crowd each other out but share a stage that is larger or smaller depending on the favorableness of individual and household toward media.

4. Media are very prominent in the lives of young people by three measures: the variety and number of media available in the home, the variety and number of media to which the young person has direct and private access in his or her bedroom, and the amount of time and attention allocated to media.

PERFORMANCE IN SCHOOL

Since the introduction of television in the late 1940s, evidence has accumulated on the influence of television on the scholastic performance of children and teenagers. Schramm, Lyle, and Parker (1961), in their large-scale examination of the effects of the introduction of television on young persons in the United States, concluded that outcomes related to knowledge and schooling were mixed. Children higher than average in mental ability who watched a great deal seemed to be somewhat impeded; children below average in mental ability who did the same seemed to be helped; and, for most—those average in mental ability—viewing made no difference. The implication that what counted was the quality of the experience for which television substituted would find support in later studies. Similarly bright children who viewed very selectively might be helped; this, too, has found support in later studies. However, on vocabulary tests, first graders in communities with television scored about a year ahead of those in communities without television, although by the sixth grade this advantage had vanished. Future research would fail to confirm optimism over the effects of television on vocabulary.

The data are now rich on a large number of questions about television and school-related performance, and there are some definitive answers. Still, certain aspects of this early pattern have remained in place. Amount of viewing has been identified as a critical variable, but there also is evidence that the content viewed makes a big difference, and this applies to several different types of content with diverse implications. There has been a continued interest in specialized areas where television might make a positive contribution, as exemplified by the early findings on vocabulary.

We divide the literature into two broad areas. The first covers a range of quite specific hypotheses about the relationships between viewing and school-related performance. The second covers the evidence on the relationships between viewing and achievement on standardized tests and the interpretation of that evidence.

Specific Hypotheses

We begin with two hypotheses proposing positive contributions by television. We then turn to four hypotheses offering mixed expectations.

Favorable Outcomes

Television viewing increases vocabulary. Television viewing increases visual skills. These are the two well-tested hypotheses that have proposed positive contributions by television to scholastic achievement.

Vocabulary. On the basis of the findings by Schramm et al. (1961), Williams (1986) and colleagues hypothesized in their three-community quasi-experiment (Cook & Campbell, 1979) that the vocabularies of young persons in Notel (the community to which television was being introduced) would increase compared to earlier cohorts or those in Unitel (with one Canadian channel) or Multitel (with American as well as Canadian channels). At no grade level and on none of three standardized tests—the Stanford-Binet vocabulary subtest, the vocabulary subscale of the Wechsler Intelligence Scale for Children, and the Peabody Picture Vocabulary Test—was there any evidence of a change in vocabulary.

Our interpretation is twofold. First, television may have increased vocabularies when it was introduced, but viewing itself no longer mattered because any contributions traceable to the medium had now become disseminated through the interaction of young people with peers, teachers, and parents. Second, much of what young people might take away from television in vocabulary would pertain to entertainment, sports, news, and commercials and would elude those standardized measures of vocabulary. The exception would be educational television, for which research has supported lexical gains (Naigles & Mayeux, 2001).

Visual Skills. Gavriel Salomon (1979) proposed that the visual imagery and forms of television depictions (such as pan shots, close-ups, cut-aways, and montages) increase skills of recalling, interpreting, and comprehending visual stimuli. An analogy would be exercise, which builds muscles and strength.

The research is quite clear. There are no measurable effects among preschool children (Hofman & Flook, 1980; Salomon, 1979) except for video instruction in serial ordering by height or size (Henderson & Rankin, 1986). Older children improve after seeing video examples in their ability to link portions of a complex painting with the whole and to understand perspective (Rovet, 1983; Salomon, 1979). Visual tasks such as ordering pictures logically and discerning an embedded figure were slightly improved by watching an entertaining educational program, *Sesame Street* (Salomon, 1979). All demonstrated effects were confined to educational videos, with the greatest effects occurring when the pedagogy was most focused. Our conclusion is that ordinary viewing at most would have only minor effects very early in children's lives because of the limited variety of the forms and devices used on the screen and their organization as entertainment (or news and sports) rather than focused video instruction.

Mixed Outcomes

Fantasy play, daydreaming, creativity, and mental ability are four topics where a variety of possible relationships with television viewing have been examined.

Fantasy Play and Daydreaming. Fantasy play occurs when young children pretend to take on a role apart from their actual selves and is generally confined to those between the ages of 3 and 7 (Fein, 1981; D. G. Singer & Singer, 1990). Daydreaming, in contrast, is lifelong, doesn't involve physical activity, and, unlike play, is not always voluntary. Both are developmentally important because they permit young people to experiment with different roles and encourage inventiveness (Valkenburg & van der Voort, 1994).

Several hypotheses have been offered:

- Viewing decreases play and daydreaming by substituting for them.
- Viewing increases play and daydreaming by supplying stimulating ideas.
- Viewing shapes play and daydreaming by providing examples and subject matter.
- Viewing decreases play by some mechanism other than displacement (such as mental exhaustion, arousal, or anxiety and fear).
- Unpleasant thoughts and daydreams increase viewing because it serves as an escape from them.

The evidence on fantasy play is extensive and includes surveys of everyday experiences (Lyle & Hoffman, 1972a, 1972b; J. L. Singer & Singer, 1976, 1981; J. L. Singer, Singer, & Rapaczynski, 1984), quasi-experiments (Gadberry, 1980; Maccoby, 1951; Murray & Kippax, 1978; Schramm et al., 1961), and laboratory-type experiments (D. R. Anderson, Levin, & Lorch, 1977; Friedrich-Cofer, Huston-Stein, McBride Kipnis, Susman, & Clewett, 1979; Noble, 1970, 1973; W. J. Potts, Huston, & Wright, 1986; Silvern & Williamson, 1987; Tower, Singer, Singer, & Biggs, 1979). We find no convincing evidence that television decreases or increases play, except for an increase for educational programs designed to enhance imaginative activity. There is ample evidence that television shapes play. French and Penna (1991), for example, found that adults who had grown up in communities with television recalled more superhero play than those who grew up in communities without television. The viewing of violent programs clearly decreases fantasy play, but the causal mechanism is unclear (Huston-Stein, Fox, Greer, Watkins, & Whitaker, 1981; Noble, 1970, 1973; J. L. Singer & Singer, 1976).

The literature is less extensive for daydreaming. There is a full range of methods and subjects, and respondents largely were 7 years of age and up because, unlike play, daydreaming cannot be observed and information must be elicited by interview or questionnaire, methods that are not feasible with those younger (Feshbach & Singer, 1971; Fraczek, 1986; Hart, 1972; Hues-

mann & Eron, 1986; McIlwraith, Jacobvitz, Kubey, & Alexander, 1991; McIlwraith & Josephson, 1985; McIlwraith & Schallow, 1982–1983; Schallow & McIlwraith, 1986–1987; Sheehan, 1987; Valkenburg & van der Voort, 1995; Valkenberg, Voojis, van der Voort, & Wiegman, 1992; Viemero & Paajanen, 1992). We find no evidence that viewing in general decreases or increases daydreaming (neither does exposure to any mass medium, including books, movies, and compact discs). However, the hypothesis that viewing shapes daydreaming receives some support. Consistently, there are correspondences between what has been viewed and the content of daydreams. Pleasant fantasies are correlated with general drama and comedies and to a somewhat lesser degree with music videos and entertainment. Thoughts about how things work are correlated with science fiction. "Positive-intense" daydreams (in the language of Valkenburg and van der Voort) are correlated with nonviolent children's programs. "Aggressive-heroic" daydreams are positively correlated with violent drama and negatively correlated with nonviolent programs. Although these correlations may be partially explained by the viewing choices of those in these varied states of mind, it is likely that, at least in part, they represent the influence of what has been viewed. This is because they persist when other variables are statistically taken into account that would be correlates of interests, such as gender and age (thus reducing the likelihood of artifactuality), and because Valkenburg and van der Voort were able to trace the daydreams of about 780 third- and fifth-grade children to differences in the television programs viewed in an earlier period.

The most pronounced correspondences were for heroic-aggressive daydreaming and violent drama. For example, Viemero and Paajanen (1992) found that the mental replaying of violent scenes and fantasies about behaving aggressively was predicted by viewing greater numbers of violent programs in a large sample of 8- and 10-year-old Finnish boys and girls.

Finally, fantasies of failure and guilt predict purposeful use of television to counter negative moods and more frequent switching of channels (but not greater viewing, which would be governed by the time available). Thus, the proposition that television serves as an escape receives some support.

Creativity.   The hypothesis that has been advanced most often is that viewing would decrease creativity because of the medium's concreteness and set pace (as compared, say, with reading), which might squash rumination and inventiveness, and the conventionality of its portrayals (Comstock & Scharrer, 1999; Valkenburg, 1991). Evidence comes from three sources: experiments testing the effects of viewing television on the retelling or construction of stories (Greenfield & Beagle-Roos, 1988; Greenfield, Farrar, & Beagle-Roos, 1986; Kerns, 1981; Meline, 1976; Runco & Pedzek, 1984; Stern, 1973; Valkenburg & Beentjies, 1997; Vibbert & Meringoff, 1981; Watkins, 1988), correlational studies comparing measures of creativity for those higher or lower in television use (Childs, 1979; Peterson, Peterson, & Carroll, 1987; J. L. Singer et al., 1984; Williams, 1986; D. M. Zuckerman, Singer, & Singer, 1980), and the three-community British Columbia quasi-experiment (Williams, 1986).

The experiments convincingly demonstrate that exposure to television in the short run diminishes the creative inventiveness of retold or newly constructed stories compared to being read to by an adult. However, this is evidence of a transient state and the greater or lesser immediate facilitation of creativity, and not an alteration in a trait (the children scoring higher or lower would have done the opposite had they been assigned to the other treatment condition). We find no convincing evidence of positive or negative correlations between amount of everyday television use and the ability to generate new ideas (as exemplified by the Alternate Uses test), to think about things in different ways (as exemplified by the Pattern Meanings test), or to elaborate on a theme (as measured by storytelling). However, there is some evidence (Watkins, 1988) that young people who view a lot of television tend to draw on its plots and characters when storytelling, and their stories are more complex but decorated with the conventions of television programs.

Mental Ability. Schramm et al. (1961, p. 79) designated mental ability as "one of the great building blocks (along with personal relationships and social norms, and of course, age and sex) that go into the structure of a child's television viewing patterns." The model they offered remains essentially valid today.

Very early, very bright children viewed large amounts of television, just as they engaged in many activities with enthusiasm. Between the ages of 10 and 13, viewing by most young people declined; this was the now familiar adolescent downward slope. Print use increased. Today, it would be print and computer use. This shift began earlier

and was much more pronounced among brighter children. The authors conclude:

> Both the high and low groups, in mental ability, are settling into adult patterns. The high group will use television less, and more selectively, and will turn to other media for much of its serious information needs. The low group will use television more, and printed media less. (Schramm et al., 1961, pp. 46–47)

More recent data confirm that amount of viewing after the early years of childhood is inversely associated with mental ability (Gortmaker, Salter, Walker, & Dietz, 1990; Morgan & Gross, 1982; Williams, 1986). This occurs independently of the inverse association between viewing and family socioeconomic status (although socioeconomic status is a strong positive predictor of mental ability). Schramm et al. (1961) also were correct to identify these early patterns as lifelong. Heavy use of television in early childhood is associated with heavy use when older, and there is evidence that early preferences for particular types of content are likely to still be in place years later (Huston et al., 1990; Kotler, Wright, & Huston, 2001; Tangney & Feshbach, 1988; Wright & Huston, 1995).

Viewing and Achievement

There is no question that amount of television viewing and performance on standardized tests are inversely associated. Our preference is to draw on the 1980 California Assessment Program (CAP) data because it was a census of enormous size rather than a sampling (282,000 in the sixth-grade and 227,000 in the 12th grade on the day of data collection). The same pattern appeared for both the sixth and 12th grades, although the negative slope of the curves was more pronounced in the 12th grade (probably because anything taking a toll on scholastic performance would have a greater effect where the demands on performance are greater, which would be at the higher grade). As can be seen in the sixth grade data (Figure 20.3), the slope of the curves is negative for reading, writing, and mathematics and for all four social strata. However, the slope of the curve becomes steeper as socioeconomic status increases, and the data of Gaddy (1986) provides the explanation. He divided households into those high, medium, and low in regard to educational resources: newspapers, books, magazines, and in the present day, we would include

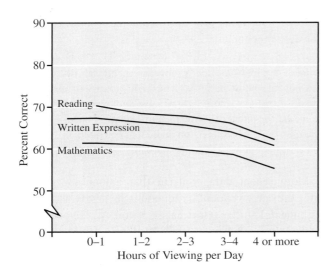

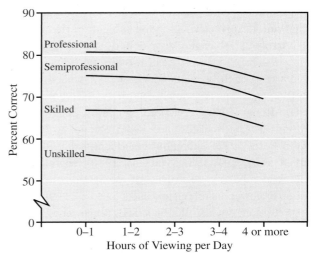

Viewing and Achievement by Socioeconomic Status—Reading

Number of Students by Socioeconomic Status
Hours of Television Viewed per Day

Occupation of Head of Household	0–1	1–2	2–3	3–4	4 or more	Non-response	Total	Percent
Professional	15,731	11,176	7,022	3,787	4,976	337	43,029	15
Semiprofessional	15,634	12,927	9,449	5,812	9,631	495	53,948	19
Skilled	23,713	21,283	16,966	11,301	21,795	1,189	96,247	34
Unskilled	10,408	9,391	7,591	5,211	11,451	769	44,821	16
Nonresponse	11,505	9,866	7,266	4,627	9,481	1,173	43,918	16
Total	76,991	64,643	48,294	30,738	57,339	3,963	281,968	100
Percent	27	23	17	11	20	2		

Figure 20.3   Television viewing, achievement, and socioeconomic status: sixth grade. *Source:* Adapted from *Survey of Sixth Grade School Achievement and Television Viewing Habits,* by California Assessment Program, 1982, Sacramento: California State Department of Education. Reprinted with permission.

computers and Internet access. His negative coefficients between viewing and performance in school were consistently larger in the high-resource households. The implication, again, as in the conclusions of Schramm et al. (1961), is that the role of viewing depends on the quality of experience for which it substitutes. Thus, the curves are steeper where resources that would have some usefulness for in-school performance are present.

These 1980 CAP data do not stand alone. The same pattern appears in two CAP follow-ups (1982, 1986), in the sample of 28,000 seniors from the data collected by the National Center for Educational Statistics (Keith, Reimers, Fehrmann, Pottebaum, & Aubey, 1986), in the sample of 70,000 in three grades collected for the National Assessment of Educational Progress (B. Anderson, Mead, & Sullivan, 1986), and in Neuman's (1988)

pooled data from eight statewide evaluations (California, Connecticut, Maine, Illinois, Michigan, Pennsylvania, Rhode Island, and Texas). We are on firm and confident ground in the conclusion that viewing and achievement are inversely associated. In the earlier grades, here and there are occasional signs of a slight curvilinearity (Fetler, 1984; Neuman, 1988, 1991), but none at all in the later grades, and nowhere does it constitute more than a small portion of a curve that is almost totally negative in slope. The exception may arise among immigrants or ethnic minorities, in which higher levels of television exposure in conjunction with parental communication have been found to positively predict children's educational aspirations (Tan, Fujioka, Bautista, Maldonado, Tan, & Wright, 2000). Tan and colleagues explain that in this context, television viewing may help to acquaint children with the dominant American culture, knowledge of which is instrumental in American schools.

Our interpretation is that the inverse associations represent both the selective media use of young persons less likely to do well in school and some influence of television on scholastic achievement. We would divide the variance about equally, with slightly more allocated to the former than to the latter. We constructed a mock path analysis synthesizing the outcomes of many studies (Figure 20.4).

There have been two analyses of data (Gaddy, 1986; Gortmaker et al., 1990) that seemingly cast doubt on these conclusions, in which a decidedly negative association between amount of viewing and achievement appears to vanish when other variables are controlled. Yet, in both cases, the dependent variable is so truncated in the potential for an association with viewing that none could be expected. In Gaddy's case, it is the use of a change in grades over the last 2 years of high school and an earlier measure of viewing. In the case of Gortmaker

and colleagues, it is the use of measures of intelligence and achievement that are so high in test-retest reliability that they represent traits rather than a changeable state of scholastic achievement.

Selective Media Use

Socioeconomic status and mental ability are both inversely associated with viewing and positively associated with scholastic performance (notice the rankings by socioeconomic status in Figure 20.3). This leads to the expectation that those who view greater amounts of television will perform less well in school. Stressful circumstances and lack of mental and physical well-being predict greater use of television, and these same factors predict lower achievement in school. These patterns have persisted for more than 5 decades, and their present-day validity is attested to by the recent large-scale national survey of Roberts and Foehr (2004), where television viewing on the part of young people was inversely associated with academic achievement and positively associated with psychological and social discontent.

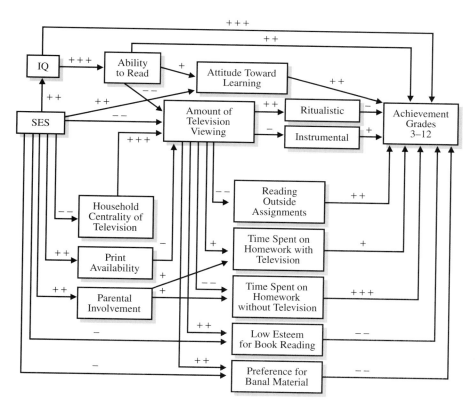

Figure 20.4 Path model: viewing, household and individual variables, and scholastic performance. *Source:* Adapted from *Television: What's On, Who's Watching, and What It Means,* by G. Comstock & E. Scharrer, 1999. San Diego, CA: Academic Press. Reprinted with permission.

Television's Contribution

We conclude that there are three processes by which viewing affects scholastic performance: interference, displacement, and the nurturing of self-defeating tastes and preferences.

Interference. The undertaking of homework, assigned reading, or reading for pleasure while monitoring television programming may somewhat debase these experiences. Several experiments document that homework-like cognitive processing tasks are performed with lower quality or at longer times to completion when there is an operating television set in the background, and this seems to be particularly so for television that presents an interesting narrative (Armstrong, 1993; Armstrong, Bojarsky, & Mares, 1991; Armstrong & Greenburg, 1990; Pool, van der Voort, Beentjes, & Koolstra, 2000). Fetler (1984), in a large CAP follow-up, found a small negative association between homework regularly done in front of an operating television set and scholastic achievement: about one-fourth that for amount of viewing (negative) and one-seventh that for amount of homework (positive). In a Dutch sample of more than 1,000 second and fourth graders, Koolstra and van der Voort (1996) found that greater viewing resulted in lower mental effort when reading, after statistically controlling for mental ability (which could have offered an alternative explanation for both greater viewing and lower effort). The tendency for viewing and reading to become positively correlated as young people grow older (CAP, 1980; Morgan, 1980) is thus actually somewhat ominous, because it implies less concentration and less demanding reading material. Finally, the sample of more than 28,000 seniors examined by Keith et al. (1986) suggests that for those who view for average amounts of time, there is no serious conflict between the blocks of time that could be allocated to homework and television viewing. This is because only modest amounts of homework typically were assigned. Nevertheless, time spent on homework was a predictor of scholastic performance, and parental interest and involvement was a predictor of greater time spent on homework (which may merely indicate that those with discipline and motive do better in school, with time spent on homework an outcome rather than a cause).

The more wide-sweeping and damning allegation that television viewing interferes not just at the moment that homework is being done but in a more insidious and long-term manner by generally reducing children's ability to concentrate and focus their attention has received less research support. One of the few studies to bring data to bear on this frequent complaint was published recently in *Pediatrics* and uses the National Longitudinal Survey of Youth to examine hyperactivity and television viewing (Christakis, Zimmerman, DiGiuseppe, & McCarty, 2004). Hyperactivity was measured using a subscale of the Behavioral Problems Index (covering such indicators as difficulty concentrating, impulsivity, obsessiveness, confusion, and restlessness) among 7-year-olds in the data, and estimates of their television exposure when they were toddlers (1 and 3 years of age) were obtained from the reports of their mothers. Employing numerous covariates (including, but not limited to, demographic characteristics, number of parents and siblings in the home, measures of cognitive stimulation such as reading and playing, and parental emotional support such as communication with parents), number of hours of television viewing at ages 1 and 3 was a significant predictor of attention problems at age 7. However, the lack of additional research to join this investigation, as well as limitations to the present study pointed out by both its authors (Christakis et al., 2004) and others in letters to the editor of *Pediatrics* (Bertholf & Goodison, 2004; Obel et al., 2004)—including the classification of those 1.2 standard deviations above the mean and higher as having attentional difficulties, failure to account for television content viewed, and the possibility of reverse causation—suggest that advancing this claim with conviction is premature.

Displacement. The displacement hypothesis in its more general version proposes that television may consume time and attention that could be better spent on acquiring the three basic skills of reading, writing, and mathematics, although the most attention has been given to the displacement of time that should have been spent acquiring the rudimentary skills of reading between the second and third grades (Chall, 1983; Comstock & Scharrer, 1999; Williams, 1986). Reading achievement is inversely associated with amount of time spent viewing (the downward sloping curve in the CAP data is a good example). Both reading and viewing are sedentary, so they compete for the same blocks of time (Heyns, 1976; Medrich, Roizen, Rubin, & Buckley, 1982), and television would be an enticing alternative to the effort required during the 2 years when reading is not for pleasure (as it will become in the fourth grade) but the tiresome learning of a skill. The 4 or more hours spent with television by 20% of young people (we use the CAP data as an estimate) would place these children at high risk. Similarly, the same argument would apply to writing and mathematics. In our view, the displacement hypothesis should be expanded to a more general proposition (Comstock & Scharrer, 1999, p. 259).

Television viewing is inversely related to achievement when it displaces intellectually and experientially richer stimuli. Viewing is positively related to achievement when the stimuli it supplies are intellectually and experientially richer than the available alternatives.

We view displacement as having two distinct aspects. The first is the usurpation of time that should be spent acquiring the three basic skills, and will have lifelong consequences for most. The second is the consumption of time at any age that might be spent on activities that are scholastically more productive, from reading to visiting a museum (or, for that matter, going to a movie that has aesthetic claims beyond the daily fare of television).

Tastes and Preferences. Television often has been described as a teacher, but unhappily, primarily of the ways of entertainment, news, sports, and commercials. The evidence now goes quite a bit beyond this. Koolstra and van der Voort (1996) collected data over a 2-year period between the second and fourth grades from a Dutch sample of more than 1,000 boys and girls. They found that greater amounts of television viewing in the earlier grade predicted greater reading of comic books and attitudinal dispositions flagrantly and decidedly hostile to the reading of books as dull and boring in the later grade. In a similar 3-year undertaking in the United States that ended with the students in high school, Morgan (1980, p. 164) found that greater amounts of viewing earlier predicted a greater liking for television-like content, "stories about love and families, teenage stories, and true stories about stars." These two sets of data make a strong claim on behalf of a causal disruption of the use of print (and by extension, we argue, other demanding media, such as computers and the Internet) because the findings survive statistical controls for numerous other variables, including mental ability (crucial in this case because mental ability predicts greater viewing and lower reading ability and thus would be the prime candidate as an alternative explanation). Our conclusion is that television socializes young people in regard to tastes and preferences in ways that are self-defeating in regard to scholastic achievement.

Our model (Figure 20.4) assigns large roles to socioeconomic status, mental ability, and the household norms about television use. We see greater amounts of television use as having a negative effect on achievement by reducing reading outside of assignments, by lowering the quality of homework done in the company of an operating television set (while acknowledging that homework with television is better than none at all), and by the socialization of tastes and preferences that disdain books that are perceived as challenging and favor the banal. We see television viewing that is selective—that is, instrumental viewing—as having positive consequences for achievement.

TELEVISION ADVERTISING

Television advertising directed at children and teenagers is an excellent example of an area in which empirical research was called on to help settle a policy issue. It has the requisite properties to be representative in many ways of what often transpires in the attempt to translate science into action. These include a series of questions on which there are disparate opinions, contentious debate, and scant evidence (or even, in many cases, the criteria by which to evaluate evidence); a government agency committed to the possibility of regulatory action; advocacy groups calling for reform confronting an industry defending the status quo; the clear enhancement of knowledge by social research about the responses of children and teenagers to commercials; a disconnect between the interest of the agency in formulating policy based on research and its ability, in the existing political context, to do so; and, finally, the emergence of some real reforms despite the absence of new regulatory initiatives. This sequence—debate and contention, the collecting of data, the political obfuscation of the application of research, and some salutary changes—is quite typical of the oblique but important role of social and behavioral science in the arena of practice.

Background

Television, introduced in the United States in the late 1940s, enjoyed its first 2 decades (during which households with television increased from essentially zero to 96%) with almost no attention given by parents, the public, or regulatory agencies to television advertising directed at children. Children, of course, have always been a central element in various strategies for marketing television. Very early, programming for children was considered to be an effective means of encouraging parents to purchase sets; similar strategies are operating today, with cable systems and premium channels offering programming with special appeal to parents and children. Children also were thought to be particularly influential in what the family watched before their bedtime (by 1960, only 12% of households had more than one set; by the end of the decade, this figure had increased, almost robustly, only to about 33%), and in the 1960s, ABC used situation comedies with characters designed to be appealing to teenagers to compete successfully with CBS and NBC. Les Brown in his 1977 *New York Times Encyclopedia of Television* (still quite useful for the programs, controversies, and personalities that marked the medium's first 3 decades) tells the story:

> Although children helped to build circulation for stations, and good will for the new television medium, they were not initially perceived as a major marketing group for products. Television was considered too high-priced for child-oriented products in the 50s and early 60s when the single or dual sponsorship of programs was the rule. But a number of factors converged around 1965 to make children's programs a major profit center of networks: first, the proliferation of multiset households, which broke up family viewing and loosened the child's control over the program his or her parents would watch; second, the drift to participation advertising as opposed to full sponsorships, which encouraged more advertisers to use the medium; and third, the discovery that a relatively "pure" audience of children could be corralled on Saturday mornings (and to a lesser extent on Sundays) where air time was cheaper, advertising quotas were wide open and children could be reached by the devices used years before by comic books.
>
> By the late 60s television programming aimed at children was confined, with few exceptions, to Saturday mornings in the form of animated cartoons. Moreover, the animation studios developed a form of limited animation for the undiscriminating youngsters, involving fewer movements per second, which was cheaper than standard animation. Recognizing that children enjoy the familiar, the networks played each episode of a series six times over 2 years, substantially reducing costs. And while prime time programs, under the Television Code, permitted 9.5 commercial minutes per hour, Saturday morning children's shows carried as many as 16 commercial minutes per hour. Citizens groups did not become aroused, however, until the networks began to deal excessively—in their competitive zeal—with monsters, grotesque super-

heroes and gratuitous violence to win the attention of youngsters. Advertisers, by then, were making the most of the gullibility of children by pitching sugar-coated cereals, candy-coated vitamins and expensive toys. (pp. 82–83)

> Commercials directed specifically at children . . . became a highly controversial aspect of television, raising questions of the morality of subjecting children to sophisticated advertising techniques. In the 70s consumer groups began protesting the differing commercial standards for children and adults, as well as other allegedly abusive practices, among them promoting nutritionally inadequate foods, using program hosts as salesmen, tempting purchases by offering premiums, and advertising expensive toys in a deceptive manner. (pp. 81–82)

The best known of the advocacy groups was Action for Children's Television, led by the indefatigable Peggy Charren and headquartered in a suburb of Boston. ACT, now disbanded (but hardly yet forgotten), asserted that advertising to children distorted and lowered the quality of programming aimed at them by making audience attractiveness to advertisers rather than child development the foundation on which programs were designed; these commercially attractive shows undeniably would seek large audiences varying in age rather than the smaller audiences that programs tailored to the narrower interests and needs of specific age groups would attract. ACT also argued that young children could not understand the self-interest behind commercials, making them by definition deceptive. Press coverage, complaints to broadcasters, and petitions to the FCC and the Federal Trade Commission (FTC) created an atmosphere favorable to some conciliatory response by broadcasters and advertisers fearful of government regulation or public hostility.

One of the effects of this activity was the nurturing of a considerable amount of research on television advertising directed at children and teenagers. Another, eventually, was a series of hearings by the FTC in conjunction with the FCC on the possibility of rule making.

Three Topics

It is no accident that the voluminous citations of research articles bear dates almost wholly subsequent to the public emergence of the controversy. This is an instance in which research on questions of child development sought to answer questions of public policy and industry practice. Although many issues were pursued, most of the research addressed three broad topics (Comstock, 1991a):

1. Recognizing and understanding commercials
2. Degree of persuasion achieved by commercials
3. Exchanges between parents and offspring

In effect, the issues were deception, influence, and the disruption of parental authority or, at least, comfort.

Recognition and understanding present a clear picture. Several studies document that very young children, as young as 3 years of age, usually can recognize that a commercial is different from or at least not a seamless part of the accompanying program (Butter, Popovich, Stackhouse, & Garner, 1981; Levin, Petros, & Petrella, 1982; P. Zuckerman & Gianinno, 1981), although it is probably not until about age 5 that most children can make this distinction without some confusion, such as correctly applying the term "commercial" but thinking of the commercial as a part of the program (Kunkel, 2001). Performance is similar on another measure of recognition in these same studies: matching characters from commercials with the products they advertise. For example, P. Zuckerman and Gianinno showed 64 4-, 7-, and 10-year-olds photos of animated characters from either commercials or programs. Most at all ages could identify those associated with products and match the characters with the products they represented. However, understanding is a very different matter.

Under the age of 8, a majority do not fully understand the motivated purpose of a commercial as a self-interested vehicle intended to benefit the advertiser by gaining the compliance, eventually if not immediately, of a consumer. Blosser and Roberts (1985) present the definitive evidence. They showed 90 children varying in age from preschool to fourth grade five different kinds of televised messages: commercials aimed at children and at adults, news, educational programming, and public service announcements. The researchers then applied three measures of understanding: comprehending the content, labeling the message correctly, and articulating accurately the message's purpose and character. When the criterion for commercials was the recognition that they presented items that could be purchased, more than half under the age of 7 "understood" what a commercial was. When the criterion was articulating self-interested persuasive intent, it was not until age 8 that a majority could be said to understand commercials. News was correctly described earliest across all mea-

sures; this makes the important point that it is not a matter of exposure, which would be greater for commercials, but the cognitive concept of self-interested persuasion that is the problem.

The brilliant experiment by Gentner (1975) provides insight into why this is the case. She inventively asked children varying in age from 3.5 to 8.5 to dramatize a series of verbs using two puppets from *Sesame Street*: have, give, take, sell, buy, and spend. "Give" and "take" were largely understood by even the youngest, but these same youngest did not comprehend "buy" and "sell." Comprehension of "buy" and "sell" of course increased with age, and for those between 7.5 and 8.5 reached 95% for "buy" and 65% for "sell." Gentner's interpretation, with which we concur, is that selling is too complicated, with its many steps culminating in an exchange of goods, for early comprehension, whereas buying is something children typically see their parents engage in often (and often enjoy the benefits of), and giving and taking are experienced quite early, in both cases with toys and food.

The evidence on persuasiveness is equally clear. Commercials are quite effective in directing children's choices of products within a category but less effective in switching preferences from one genre to another. Product choices have been shown to be influenced by endorsements by liked or respected figures quite apart from any other aspect of a commercial (Ross et al., 1984). The heavy toy and game advertising leading up to Christmas by the end of the shopping season was found to shift choices toward the advertised products, in effect eroding defenses against persuasion (decreasing critical attitudes toward advertising) and preferences for other items among 290 first-, third-, and fifth-grade children (Rossiter & Robertson, 1974). A dissertation (R. S. Rubin, 1972) even queried 72 first-, third-, and sixth-grade children about their recall for products and premiums and found that at all ages the premium was better recalled than the product name and vied quite successfully with the product in being perceived as what the viewer was supposed to want. Later, Shimp, Dyer, and Divita (1976) would report a modest but positive correlation between brand choice and liking for a premium, and Atkin (1975a, 1975b, 1978) reported that a large majority (about three-fourths) of a sample of mothers of children from preschool to fifth grade said that premiums had been specifically mentioned by their children in asking for cereals. One out of 10 children's product requests recorded surreptitiously in supermarket aisles included specific mention of a premium.

Food selections have repeatedly been demonstrated to be influenced by exposure to commercials at all ages (Galst & White, 1976; Goldberg, Gorn, & Gibson, 1978; Gorn & Goldberg, 1982; Meringoff, 1980; Stoneman & Brody, 1981; Story & French, 2004). Between half and two-thirds of commercials directed at children are for food-related products (Kotz & Story, 1994; Taras & Gage, 1995). An effect on selection holds primarily for selections within a genre, exemplified by the selection of one brand or option rather than another. For example, Gorn and Goldberg found among 288 children ranging in age from 5 to 8, exposure over a 2-week period to commercials for orange juice or candy could shift choices away from Kool-aid or fruit, but Galst (1980) found among 3- to 6-year-olds that commercials for nutritional foods did not shift choices unless followed by advice from a live adult. Thus, children can be persuaded to change the means by which they satisfy a preference but not the preference.

The data on parent-child interaction are not quite so clear. There are two reasons. The data focus on three topics: children's requests for products, parental yielding, and intemperate responses from the child when yielding does not occur. These do not lend themselves to straightforward measurement, as do recognizing or understanding commercials and the shift of product choices toward an advertised item, and we are largely left with proportions of children or parents saying requests, yielding, or displays of temper occur often, sometimes, or seldom, so that precise estimates are not available. Furthermore, for none of these three measures is there a recognized criterion or threshold that signals trouble or pathology other than that most would agree that repeated tantrums by the same child probably deserves some attention. Yet, these very concerns are at the heart of any interest in parent-child interaction in regard to television commercials—that they disrupt the orderly process of parenting and make it less effective (by widening children's options while limiting those of parents) or tranquil (by contributing to the dissatisfaction of children and disputes between parents and children).

However, the data do permit some conclusions. Children certainly do regularly ask for products as a consequence of seeing them advertised on television. Atkin (1975b) reported that among 440 children ranging from preschool to fifth grade, those who were classified as heavy viewers said they asked for products "a lot," whereas the figure for light viewers was about half the frequency of requests. Isler, Popper, and Ward (1987) found that one-sixth of the purchase requests of children between 3 and 11 were attributed to television advertising by a sample of 260 mothers, although the requests declined decidedly as children grew older. Yielding also is highly frequent. Parental reports of yielding to cereal requests ranged from 87% to 62% in different samples (Atkin, 1975b; Ward & Wackman, 1972; W. D. Wells & LoScuito, 1966) and decline as the purchase from the genre becomes less obligatory or of less direct interest to the child. For example, Ward and Wackman found that yielding declined steadily as a function of those two variables: from cereal (87%), snack foods (63%), games and toys (54%), candy (42%), toothpaste (39%), shampoo (16%), to a mere 7% for dog food. This descending order represents children's interest in the product and the recognition by parents of the legitimacy of that interest. Both would increase with greater efforts to market products to children, so we would expect toothpastes and shampoos to rank higher today, with their packaging emblazoned with television characters popular with children. We think the best data on yielding are those of Atkin's (1978) supermarket aisle study of 516 sets of parents and children ages 3 to 12 because they trace the process from purchase initiatives by both children and parents (Figure 20.5). The child initiated interactions two-thirds of the time, and more than two-thirds of these were classified as demands. About two-thirds of the time a parent yielded to a demand or request; the figure for rejecting was less than half that.

Disputes between parents and children and the anger of children at the refusal of a request are plagued by the same problems of measurement and interpretation. Nevertheless, we can say that such occurrences are not rare. For example, Atkin (1975a, 1975b) found in one sample of children that one out of five said they became angry "a lot" when toy requests were denied, and one out of six said they argued "a lot" in response to such denials. In his observational study of parents and children in supermarket aisles, Atkin recorded that two-thirds of denials (occurring at a rate of 18%) evoked anger, and one-half induced disappointment.

Enter the National Science Foundation and the Federal Trade Commission

In the late 1970s, the National Science Foundation (NSF) took the extraordinary step of commissioning a review of this burgeoning literature to serve as the evidentiary foundation for possible rule making by the FCC

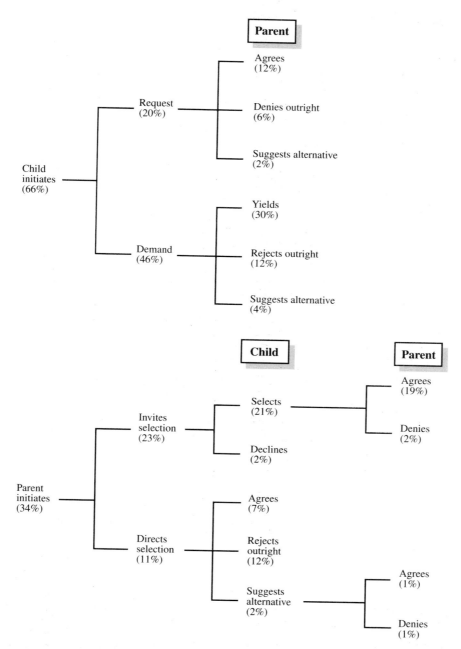

Figure 20.5   Parent-child supermarket aisle interaction over breakfast cereal. *Source:* Adapted from "Observations of Parent-Child Interaction in Supermarket Decisionmaking," by C. K. Atkin, 1978, *Journal of Marketing, 42,* pp. 41–45. Reprinted with permission.

and the FTC. This was a brave attempt to resolve the conjunction of new issues and new science. This painstaking effort, under the direction of Richard P. Adler, stands as a landmark in the literature on television advertising and children and eventually was published commercially in 1980 as *The Effect of Television Advertising on Children* (Adler et al., 1980), although an earlier version first appeared from the U.S. Government

Printing Office in 1977. Its major conclusions matched those we have reported:

- Children at a very early age can recognize that a commercial is different from the program accompanying it, but it is not until much later that they can articulate—and, in our view, be said to understand—the nature of commercials.

- The techniques employed by commercials are very successful in persuading children to desire advertised products, and this is particularly so for foods.
- Purchase requests are common, yielding is typical, and dissatisfied children and parent-child disputes are not rare.

In response to the report, in 1978 the FTC proposed to ban or limit advertising to children. This raised some interesting questions. Would children's entertainment disappear from the air if it were not supported by advertising? Would the FCC be willing to require such programming without supportive advertising, in effect placing a "children's tax" on broadcasters (as ACT advocated)? If limits rather than a ban were imposed, what would be the parameters (in the sense of what would qualify as a consumer product or slice of the broadcast schedule for targeting)? Extensive hearings followed, but economic power and political influence eliminated the need to address these issues. Kunkel (2001, pp. 387–388) tells the story succinctly:

> The painstaking level of detail the FTC pursued in marshaling its supporting evidence contrasted sharply with a serious miscalculation about the extent of the political opposition to its proposal (Kunkel & Watkins, 1987). The broadcasting and advertising industries were joined by many of America's largest corporate conglomerates in opposing the ban. These businesses owned subsidiaries producing toys, sugared cereals, and numerous other types of child-oriented merchandise. Fearing adverse impacts on their profits, these industries initiated campaigns to influence the public to oppose the ban. A key element of their strategy was the claim of First Amendment protection for the right to provide "information" about products to America's budding consumers.
>
> The FTC's formal rule-making process for implementing the proposed ban moved forward. Open hearings were held. Elaborate briefs assessing the research evidence regarding children's comprehension of advertising were submitted by all sides. On this front, the forces seeking regulation fared reasonably well. Although some inevitable qualifications were lodged, a consensus emerged among researchers that young children were indeed uniquely vulnerable to television's commercial claims and appeals.
>
> At the same time, however, a much different outcome was occurring on other fronts of the political battle. Using their influence with elected officials, the FTC's corporate opponents succeeded in derailing the agency's proposal, employing an innovative strategy. Responding to corporate pressure, Congress rescinded the agency's authority to re-

strict advertising deemed unfair by enacting legislation ironically titled the FTC Improvements Act of 1980. Besides removing this aspect of the FTC's jurisdiction, the act specifically prohibited any further action to adopt the proposed children's advertising rules. The agency soon issued a final ruling on the case formally implementing the congressional mandate (FTC, 1981), and since then there has been no further effort to resurrect this initiative.

Reforms and Subsequent Research

The consequences of these events—public displeasure, the rise of advocacy groups, new research in child development, the NSF review, the FTC rule-making hearings—were a series of significant reforms (Comstock, 1991a). The discrepancy between amount of nonprogram material on children's and primetime television was eliminated (and more recently was set by the Children's Television Act of 1990 at no more per hour than 10.5 minutes on weekends and 12 minutes on weekdays). Advertising of vitamins branded and packaged to appeal to children as if they were breakfast cereals was ended. Restraints were placed on the use of television storyline characters in advertising (although only half-heartedly; so-called host-selling was barred accompanying the program in which the character appeared but permitted in commercials accompanying other programs; hosts only had to take a hike). Industry codes were strengthened. "Bumpers" or separators before and after commercials were adopted to aid identification, although research indicates these have been largely ineffective (Comstock, 1991a; Kunkel, 2001).

Subsequent research has turned away from these issues of possible harm toward a topic that also was pursued earlier: the cognitive processing of commercials, and in particular, the characteristics of commercials that lead to a favorable response from a child (Greer, Potts, Wright, & Huston, 1982; John, 1999; Macklin, 1988; Wartella & Ettema, 1974; Wartella & Hunter, 1983). John neatly summarizes the cognitive changes that take place in young people as they mature (Table 20.1), using a Piagetian schema (we have substituted adjacent years for the overlapping ones in the original but have retained the somewhat earlier transition to a more advanced stage because we agree that advertising, while certainly involving many subtleties in its messages, does not impose as severe demands on formal reasoning as occurs in many other topics where cognitive stages predict—and constrain—success at a task). Examples include the shift from approval to skepticism without much in the

TABLE 20.1 Responses to Advertising by Cognitive Stage

Topic	Perceptual Stage, 3–7 Years	Analytical Stage, 8–11 Years	Reflective Stage, 12–16 Years
Advertising knowledge	Can distinguish ads from programs based on perceptual features Believe ads are truthful, funny, and interesting Positive attitudes toward ads	Can distinguish ads from programs based on persuasive intent Believe ads lie and contain bias and deception—but do not use these "cognitive defenses" Negative attitudes toward ads	Understand persuasive intent of ads as well as specific ad tactics and appeals Believe ads lie and know how to spot specific instances of bias or deception in ads Skeptical attitudes toward ads
Transaction knowledge: Product and brand knowledge	Can recognize brand names and beginning to associate them with product categories Perceptual cues used to identify product categories Beginning to understand symbolic aspects of consumption based on perceptual features Egocentric view of retail stores as a source of desired items	Increasing brand awareness, especially for child-relevant product categories Underlying or functional cues used to define product categories Increased understanding of symbolic aspects of consumption Understand retail stores are owned to sell goods and make a profit	Substantial brand awareness for adult-oriented as well as child-relevant product categories Underlying or functional cues used to define product categories Sophisticated understanding of consumption symbolism for product categories and brand names Understanding and enthusiasm for retail stores
Shopping knowledge and skills	Understand sequence of events in the basic shopping script Value of products and prices based on perceptual features	Shopping scripts more complex, abstract, and with contingencies Prices based on theories of value	Complex and contingent shopping scripts Prices based on abstract reasoning, such as input variations and buyer preferences
Decision-making skills and abilities: Information search	Limited awareness of information sources Focus on perceptual attributes Emerging ability to adapt to cost-benefit trade-offs	Increased awareness of personal and mass media sources Gather information on functional as well as perceptual attributes Able to adapt to cost-benefit trade-offs	Contingent use of different information sources depending on product or situation Gather information on functional, perceptual, and social aspects Able to adapt to cost-benefit trade-offs
Product evaluation	Use of perceptually salient attribute information Use of single attributes	Focus on important attribute information—functional and perceptual attributes Use two or more attributes	Focus on important attribute information—functional, perceptual, and social aspects Use multiple attributes
Decision strategies	Limited repertoire of strategies Emerging ability to adapt strategies to tasks—usually need cues to adapt	Increased repertoire of strategies, especially noncompensatory ones Capable of adapting strategies to tasks	Full repertoire of strategies Capable of adapting strategies to tasks in adult-like manner
Purchase influence and negotiation strategies	Use direct requests and emotional appeals Limited ability to adapt strategy to person or situation	Expanded repertoire of strategies, with bargaining and persuasion emerging Developing abilities to adapt strategy to persons and situations	Full repertoire of strategies, with bargaining and persuasion as favorites Capable of adapting strategies based on perceived effectiveness for persons or situations
Consumption motives and values: Materialism	Value of possessions based on surface features, such as "having more" of something	Emerging understanding of value based on social meaning and significance	Fully developed understanding of value based on social meaning, significance, and scarcity

Source: Adapted from "Consumer Socialization of Children: A Retrospective Look at Twenty-Five Years of Research," by D. R. John, 1999, *Journal of Consumer Research, 26*, pp. 183–213. Reprinted with permission.

way of effective defenses against appeals (top), the adoption of a stance of sophisticated (if hooked) consumption (middle), and the eventual awareness of the symbolic role of products and brands (bottom).

Children certainly are exposed to a large quantity of commercials (Comstock & Scharrer, 1999). The average child ages 2 to 11 sees almost 40,000 commercials a year. Discounting for no interest in many product categories, we estimate these children would see at least 12,500 commercials for products in which they might take an interest, with about 90% appearing outside of children's programming. Cereals and candies top the list for children's programming, followed by toys and fast foods; in general audience programming, these are joined by soft drinks, shoes, and clothing. Toys are the crown princes of pre-Christmas advertising, accounting for at least half of the commercials in children's programming. Teenagers 12 to 17 watch less television but would find more products of interest (comparable figures are 27,000 commercials with an estimated 16,000 of possible interest). Thus, advertising likely will remain a fertile area for research, although at a slower pace than during the heated 1970s.

VIOLENT ENTERTAINMENT

Entertainment is the type of television content most often attended to by children and teenagers. Unambiguously, the topic that has received the most attention in child development research in regard to entertainment (with the exception, of course, of the continuing and repeated measurement of audience demographics to satisfy the informational needs of those who buy and sell time slots for commercials, which unavoidably produces data of some interest in regard to child development but is motivated by and designed to serve the needs of marketing) is violent entertainment and its effects on aggressive and antisocial behavior.

Although the investigation of the influence of audiovisual entertainment media on antisocial behavior traces to the Payne Fund movie studies of the early 1930s (Charters, 1933), the contemporary inquiry into this issue dates from the early 1960s. We have constructed a timeline displaying significant events in the empirical examination of the possible influence of violent television and film entertainment on aggressive and antisocial behavior (Figure 20.6). In 1963, two pioneering experiments were published in the *Journal of Abnormal and Social Psychology*. In one, Bandura, Ross, and Ross (1963a) demonstrated that nursery school children would imitate the aggressive antics of those observed on a television screen, including a young adult female clothed in a cat costume intended as a faux representation of a character that might appear in children's entertainment. In the other, Berkowitz and Rawlings (1963) demonstrated that college students would increase their aggressiveness after exposure to an example of justified aggression observed on a television screen. These two investigations began an experimental literature now numbering more than 100 exploring the various factors on which an effect of violent television or film portrayals on behavior are contingent. For example, Bandura, Ross, and Ross (1963b) quickly enlarged the range of variables in their studies of nursery school children to include positive reinforcement or punishment of the portrayed behavior, with positive reinforcement on screen increasing the likelihood of imitation. Berkowitz and colleagues later found in their studies of college students that cues in a portrayal matching real-life circumstances (Berkowitz & Geen, 1966, 1967) and portrayals that depict malevolent motives for aggression (Berkowitz & Alioto, 1973; Geen & Stonner, 1972) enhanced the likelihood of aggressive behavior.

Enter the Surgeon General

By the end of the decade, there was enough evidence from experiments and other research methods to lead the National Commission on the Causes and Prevention of Violence (1969) to conclude that there was a causal link between exposure to violent portrayals in television entertainment and aggressive and antisocial behavior. This commission had been established by President Lyndon Johnson as a result of the assassinations of John and Robert Kennedy and Martin Luther King and widespread urban rioting in Black neighborhoods. Its judgment about the media was not considered particularly credible or important; however, the compilation of commissioned papers on media effects (Baker & Ball, 1969) in academic circles was considered something of a landmark (and a valuable reference) for many years. Senator John Pastore of Rhode Island then extended the concern with the media to an investigation focused exclusively on television. The result was the 1972 federal report *Television and Growing Up: The Impact of Televised Violence* by the Surgeon General's Scientific Advisory Committee on Television and Social Behavior, accompanied by

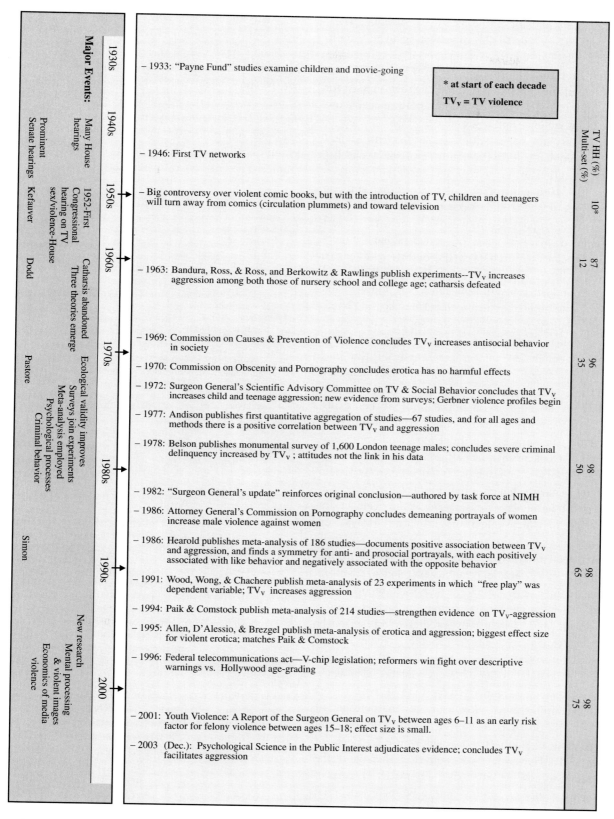

Figure 20.6 TV violence through the ages.

five volumes (Comstock, Rubinstein, & Murray, 1972a, 1972b, 1972c, 1972d, 1972e) representing $1 million in new research. This enterprise substantially enlarged the research literature. More significant, the surgeon general's committee concluded in its report that, at least for some children, there was a causal link between exposure to television violence and aggressive behavior.

Ten years later, the National Institute of Mental Health assembled a special committee of social and behavioral scientists expert in regard to research on television on the 10th anniversary of the original surgeon general's report. This undertaking, known as the "surgeon general's update," produced a committee report accompanied by a volume of commissioned papers covering recent research (Pearl, Bouthilet, & Lazar, 1982a, 1982b). The focus was largely on children and teenagers, and the range of topics in regard to television was now quite broad: cognition and affect, social beliefs and social behavior, and family and social relations, as well as violent portrayals and aggression. This select committee concluded that the research of the past decade had strengthened and reinforced the evidence on which the original surgeon general's committee drew in concluding that there was a causal link between exposure to television violence and aggressive behavior.

In 2001, the surgeon general's report on youth violence (U.S. Department of Health and Human Services, 2001) again raised the issue of effects on aggressive and antisocial behavior, but in a more pronounced way. Accompanied by a judicious evaluation of the evidence for some effect of violent television and film portrayals on behavior (the conclusion is that the evidence supports such an effect, and there is speculation that newer media, with interactivity, greater graphicness, and availability on demand, may have stronger effects), the report incorporates television violence as among the factors empirically documented as causally predictive of seriously harmful antisocial behavior. Specifically, it identifies exposure to television violence as one of 20 early risk factors for the committing of felony violence. The early period of exposure encompassed ages 6 to 11, with the seriously harmful criminal violence occurring between 15 and 18 (p. 58, Box 4.1). The effect size of $r = .13$ would be classified as small (by the widely used criteria of Cohen, 1988). However, so too were three-fourths of the factors said to pose an early risk (Figure 20.7), none of which on the surface would seem to be inconsequential for the welfare or constructive social functioning of a child or teenager.

This is an important conclusion in the debate over the effects of television and film violence, for it both escalates the degree of social harm and heightens the standards of evidence. The effect is now felony violence, and not the more vague and quite encompassing aggressive or antisocial behavior. It also has particular credibility because the authors insisted on data either from meta-analyses quantitatively aggregating the results of a group of studies or data from at least two independent studies. The ignoring of this indictment by the press and

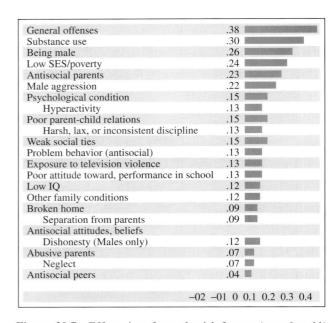

Figure 20.7 Effect sizes for early risk factors (ages 6 to 11) for serious violence at ages 15 to 18. *Source:* From "A Review of Predictors of Youth Violence" (pp. 106–146), by J. D. Hawkins, T. L. Herrenkohl, D. P. Farrington, D. Brewer, R. F. Catalano, and T. W. Harachi, in *Serious and Violent Juvenile Offenders: Risk Factors and Successful Interventions,* R. Loeber and D. P. Farrington (Eds.), 1998, Thousand Oaks, CA: Sage. Reprinted with permission; "Predictors of Violent and Serious Delinquency in Adolescence and Early Adulthood: A Synthesis of Longitudinal Research" (pp. 86–105), by M. W. Lipsey and J. H. Derzon, in *Serious and Violent Juvenile Offenders: Risk Factors and Successful Interventions,* R. Loeber and D. P. Farrington (Eds.), 1998, Thousand Oaks, CA: Sage. Reprinted with permission; "The Effects of Television Violence on Antisocial Behavior: A Meta-Analysis," by H. Paik and G. Comstock, 1994, *Communication Research, 21*(4), pp. 516–546. Reprinted with permission; pooling of outcomes from two or more longitudinal studies of general population samples. Specific factors listed when data permits; *Youth Violence: A Report of the Surgeon General* (p. 60, Table 4.1), by U.S. Department of Health and Human Services, 2001, Rockville, MD: Author. Reprinted with permission.

the public almost certainly has less to do with the substance of the charge or the quality of the evidence than the issuing of the report at the beginning of the inaugural week of George W. Bush (see Figure 20.8).

Aggregating the Evidence

At the time of the original surgeon general's inquiry, about 50 experiments had been published with nursery school children or college students as subjects, with most recording increased aggressiveness as a consequence of exposure to a violent television portrayal. However, these outcomes are problematic for generalizing to everyday viewing; in the jargon of social science methodology, they are weak in external validity (Cook & Campbell, 1979) because of the contrived conditions of the experience, with viewing brief and attenuated rather than continuous, as it would be in ordinary circumstances, and zero likelihood of retaliation from the victim. Today, with the contributions of the research undertaken for the surgeon general's 1972 inquiry and the extensive subsequent research, there are more than twice as many experiments (thereby increasing the credibility, what Cook and Campbell call internal validity, of this body of studies), and many that incorporate elements of everyday viewing (increasing their external validity), as well as evidence from a variety of methods, such as the survey (which does not suffer from the weak external validity of the experiment). Thus, it is possible now to answer the question of whether exposure to violent television portrayals increases aggressive and antisocial behavior with much greater confidence than in the past (in effect, we can test the validity of earlier inferences by asking whether more recent research, more varied in approach and sometimes employing different methods, strengthens or weakens the evidentiary trail).

Happily, we can effectively describe the evidence through a series of seven quantitative aggregations of study outcomes, with most using the techniques of meta-analysis (which, using the standard deviation as a criterion, leads to an effect size, or statistical coefficient, representing the difference across studies between those experiencing or not experiencing a stimulus, or what in an experiment would be the treatment versus the control conditions; Hunt, 1997). These aggregations are more reliable and valid than a single study because the outcomes rest on a much larger number of subjects or respondents and they do not suffer much from the singular weaknesses of a particular study.

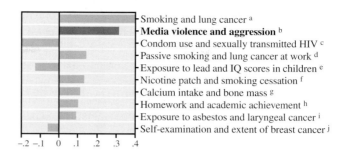

Figure 20.8 Effect size for media violence and aggression compared with effect sizes for other domains. Note: A correlation coefficient can range from −1 (a perfect negative linear relation) to +1 (a perfect positive linear relation), with 0 indicating no linear relation. The effect of smoking tobacco on lung cancer was estimated by pooling the data from Figures 1 and 3 in Wynder and Graham's (1950) classic article. The remaining effects were estimated from meta-analyses. *Sources:* (a) Adapted from "Tobacco Smoking as a Possible Etiological Factor in Bronchiogenic Carcinoma," by E. L. Wynder and E. A. Graham, 1950, *Journal of the American Medical Association, 143,* pp. 329–336. Reprinted with permission; (b) "The Effects of Television Violence on Antisocial Behavior: A Meta-Analysis," by H. Paik and G. Comstock, 1994, *Communication Research, 21*(4), pp. 516–546. Reprinted with permission; (c) "A Meta-Analysis of Condom Effectiveness in Reducing Sexually Transmitted HIV," by S. C. Weller, 1993, *Social Science and Medicine, 36,* pp. 1635–1644. Reprinted with permission; (d) "Lung Cancer from Passive Smoking at Work," by A. J. Wells, 1998, *American Journal of Public Health, 88,* pp. 1025–1029. Reprinted with permission; (e) "Low-Level Lead Exposure and the IQ of Children," by H. L. Needleman and C. A. Gatsonis, 1990, *Journal of the American Medical Association, 263,* pp. 673–678. Reprinted with permission; (f) "The Effectiveness of the Nicotine Patch for Smoking Cessation," by M. C. Fiore, S. S. Smith, D. E. Jorenby, and T. B. Baker, 1994, *Journal of the American Medical Association, 271,* pp. 1940–1947. Reprinted with permission; (g) "A Meta-Analysis of the Effect of Calcium Intake on Bone Mass in Young and Middle Aged Females and Males," by D. C. Welten, H. C. G. Kemper, G. B. Post, and W. A. van Staveren, 1995, *Journal of Nutrition, 125,* pp. 2802–2813. Reprinted with permission; (h) *Homework,* by H. Cooper, 1989, New York: Longman. Reprinted with permission; (i) "Epidemiological Evidence Indicates Asbestos Causes Laryngeal Cancer," by A. H. Smith, M. A. Handley, and R. Wood, 1990, *Journal of Occupational Medicine, 32,* pp. 49–507. Reprinted with permission; (j) "Self Examination of the Breast: Is It Beneficial? Meta-Analysis of Studies Investigating Breast Self Examination and Extent of Disease in Patients with Breast Cancer," by D. Hill, V. White, D. Jolley, and K. Mapperson, 1988, *British Medical Journal, 297,* pp. 271–275. Reprinted with permission; (k) "Media Violence and the American Public: Scientific Facts versus Media Misinformation," by B. J. Bushman and C. A. Anderson, 2001, *American Psychologist, 56*(6/7), pp. 477–489. Reprinted with permission.

In a pioneering aggregation of results (and the one instance in which the techniques of meta-analysis were not employed), Andison (1977) scored the outcomes of 67 experiments and surveys as to direction and magnitude. Hearold (1986) examined 168 studies to estimate effect sizes between exposure to either antisocial or prosocial portrayals and both antisocial and prosocial outcomes. Wood, Wong, and Chachere (1991) focused on 23 experiments with children and teenagers as subjects in which the dependent variable was "unconstrained interpersonal aggression" such as would occur in everyday play. In contrast, M. Allen, D'Alessio, and Brezgel (1995) focused on 33 experiments in which the treatment was exposure to sexually explicit portrayals, including those that combine violence with erotica. Hogben (1998) avoided experiments altogether and confined himself to 56 coefficients from studies where the independent variable was everyday viewing. Bushman and Anderson (2001) calculated effect sizes at 5-year intervals over 25 years for both experimental and nonexperimental designs. Paik and Comstock (1994) updated Hearold's examination of the link between television violence and aggression by including 82 new studies for a total of 217.

This is a challenging body of data because meta-analysis, though increasing reliability and validity, does not absolve the analyst from the anxiety-ridden task of interpretation. It is still necessary to assign meaning to the data: what to make of positive correlations in survey designs where causal inference is ambiguous, whether experimental findings can be generalized to other settings, and how large an association should be to qualify as socially important.

In our view, these aggregations, qualified and amplified by information from individual studies that escapes the broader net of the aggregations, lead to several important conclusions:

1. Because the aggregations *all* produce positive and (when put to this criterion) statistically significant effect sizes between exposure to the portrayals under scrutiny and the dependent variables of aggressive or antisocial behavior, they make it irrefutably clear that there is a positive association between exposure and behavior.

2. This positive association occurs for both experimental and nonexperimental designs (most of which are surveys). These parallel outcomes would produce a strong case for causation should one condition be met: that the positive coefficients in the nonexperimental designs cannot be wholly explained by the influence of something, a so-called third variable, other than exposure to violent portrayals. In fact, this is precisely what occurs. When the studies in the meta-analyses are examined individually, the positive correlations persist when every other measured variable is taken into account (Comstock, 2004; Comstock & Scharrer, 2003). Thus, the case for causation rests on the demonstration of causality in the experiments, which unambiguously permit such an inference, and the documentation of a positive association not otherwise wholly explainable in everyday circumstances. In effect, the surveys, drawing on data representing viewing and behavior outside of the laboratory, confirm the generalizability of the experimental outcomes. This interpretation is strongly reinforced by the failure of the "reverse hypothesis" to provide an explanation. This is the hypothesis that the positive correlations between exposure to violent portrayals and aggression are attributable to the preference on the part of aggressive youths for violent entertainment. There is some evidence that such a phenomenon occurs (Huesmann, 1986, 1998; Slater, Henry, Swaim, & Anderson, 2003), but not on a scale sufficient to absolve television of complicity in television violence-aggression causation. For example, in examining a series of correlations between earlier aggression and later viewing and later viewing and earlier aggression, Kang (1990) found twice as many statistically significant viewing-to-behavior as behavior-to-viewing coefficients, and Belson (1978), in his survey of about 1,600 London male teenagers, reported only a minute link between prior aggression and violence viewing but a link of substantial magnitude between prior viewing violence and aggression. Thus, data are highly supportive (by what they don't provide: an alternative explanation that eliminates the possibility of violence viewing playing a causal role) of violent portrayals in television and film entertainment contributing to aggressive and antisocial behavior.

3. Effects are surprisingly similar for males and females. The early experiments of Bandura (1965; Bandura et al., 1963a, 1963b) with nursery school children so clearly recorded greater aggressiveness by males that this has become almost axiomatic in the child development literature. However, the Paik and Comstock (1994) meta-analysis makes it equally clear that this is an untenable position. As more findings accumulated, outcomes for males and females became more similar and are almost identical in the nonexperimental designs that best represent everyday viewing and behavior.

4. There is definite evidence of a longitudinal influence, with earlier violence viewing contributing to later aggressive or antisocial behavior. One prominent example, of course, is the conclusion of the 2001 surgeon general's report on youth violence that violence viewing between the ages of 6 and 11 heightens the risk of serious violence between the ages of 15 and 18 (U. S. Department of Health and Human Services, 2001). However, there are many examples in the literature in which earlier viewing affects later behavior. These include Eron and colleagues (Eron & Huesmann, 1987; Huesmann, Eron, Lefkowitz, & Walder, 1984), who report positive correlations between violence viewing and aggression not only at 10-year but also at 20- and 30-year intervals; Cook and colleagues (Cook, Kendzierski, & Thomas, 1983) and Kang (1990), who both reported coefficients of increasing size with extended time spans in the 3.5-year panel study of Milavsky and colleagues (Milavsky, Kessler, Stipp, & Rubens, 1982) and with different segments of the panel population; and the very recent analyses by Johnson and colleagues (Johnson, Cohen, Smailes, Kasen, & Brook, 2002) and Huesmann and colleagues (Huesmann, Moise-Titus, Podolski, & Eron, 2003), with the former finding young adult aggression predicted by adolescent television viewing, and the latter finding violence viewing between the ages of 6 and 10 predicting aggression 15 years later, both with samples of several hundred and after numerous potentially contaminating variables had been statistically controlled.

5. When the nonexperimental studies are examined individually, it becomes clear that the recorded effects do not represent outcomes that most people would consider particularly tolerable. The most common dependent variable has been interpersonal aggression, and although this may escape the attention of the law, the hitting, fighting, stealing, and name-calling encompassed would hardly be found pleasant by anyone. In other cases, the dependent measure has been delinquency against property, teachers, or the use of physical violence in an encounter (Cook et al., 1983; Thornton & Voigt, 1984). In fact, one investigator found a convincing causal link between violence viewing and the committing of crimes: using a knife or gun in a fight, rape, or torturing a victim with a lit cigarette (Belson, 1978).

6. The size of effects is not trivial by social standards. Bushman and Anderson (2001) and Bushman and Huesmann (2001) compiled a catalogue of effect sizes for other variables and outcomes, and the overall effect size ($r = .31$) recorded by Paik and Comstock (1994) is among the largest (Figure 20.2). Of course, effect sizes in Paik and Comstock and in other meta-analyses vary for each specific pairing of an independent variable and an outcome, and range (by Cohen's criteria) from small to large. However, even small effect sizes can have social consequences if the behavior in question is of importance because, as Rosenthal and colleagues (Rosenthal, 1986; Rosenthal, Rosnow, & Rubin, 2000) have persuasively argued, a small effect size masks a sizable number of people being shifted above or below the mean by the treatment.

7. The link between exposure to television or film portrayals and behavior applies to a wide variety of circumstances: prosocial behavior (defined to encompass altruism, acceptance of others, and engaging in social interaction, the three most frequent in a much longer list, as would have been seen on *Mister Rogers' Neighborhood, Big Blue Marble,* and, more recently, *Blue's Clues*), which declines after exposure to violent portrayals and increases after exposure to prosocial portrayals (Hearold, 1986); when the experimentally measured behavior is naturally occurring spontaneous aggression on the playground or similar settings (Wood et al., 1991); and when the measure of viewing occurred in everyday circumstances rather than the contrived environment of an experiment (Andison, 1977; Bushman & Anderson, 2001; Hearold, 1986; Hogben, 1998; Paik & Comstock, 1994). This favors the view that the exposure-behavior link is robust across circumstances.

8. There is a stunning symmetry between outcomes for violent and prosocial portrayals (Hearold, 1986). Effect sizes are positive for violent portrayals and aggressive behavior but negative for violent portrayals and prosocial behaviors, and positive for prosocial portrayals and prosocial behavior and negative for prosocial portrayals and aggressive behavior.

The inferences in regard to violent media receive strong endorsement from the recent review in Psychological Science in the Public Interest (Anderson et al., 2003), the American Psychological Society journal whose mission is to adjudicate the empirical evidence on issues of significant public concern. The authors conclude that (a) exposure to violent television or film entertainment facilitates aggressive and antisocial behavior, that (b) this facilitation extends to seriously harmful behavior, and that (c) there is a developmental pattern in which earlier viewing nurtures one or more traits that will be expressed in aggressive and antisocial behavior in a later time period.

Other Violence-Related Hypotheses

Three other hypotheses have seen considerable attention in regard to television and film violence. These include the expectation that media portrayals may induce, as well as temporarily invoke, anxieties and fears (Cantor, 2001), the possibility that media portrayals may desensitize audience members to future displays of violence (Drabman & Thomas, 1974), and the proposition that television cultivates beliefs and impressions that are in accord with the emphases of its programming (Gerbner, Gross, Morgan, Signorielli, & Shanahan, 2002).

Fear

Cantor (1998a, 2001) and her colleagues (Cantor, 1994a, 1994b; Cantor & Hoffner, 1990; Cantor & Nathanson, 1996; Cantor & Reilly, 1982) have explored the relationships between the anxieties and fears of children and teenagers in relation to television and films. Almost half have been frightened at one time and will recall this many years later. Young children are particularly disturbed by visual manifestations of danger, including monsters and transformations such as *The Incredible Hulk* used to undergo. Older children are less frightened by the impossible than by the possible if improbable: kidnappings, abuse, threats to pets. Cataclysmic events such as wars and natural upheavals such as hurricanes and earthquakes are not of much significance to young children (until experienced), although they are quite frightening to older children who are better prepared to imagine the harm and destruction and threat to life that such an event might bring. A highly dramatic portrayal may be particularly powerful; the movie *Jaws* left many young people and particularly teenagers, who would be more apt to venture into deeper waters, avoiding the beach, an effect that would be expected today when reports of shark attacks are prominent in the media (although their effect would certainly be diminished without graphic video).

Desensitization

The evidence is quite convincing that media portrayals of violence may lessen the subsequent responsiveness of children and teenagers to violent stimuli. Drabman and Thomas (1974) and Thomas, Horton, Lippencott, and Drabman (1977) found that third- and fourth-grade children who viewed a violent film were slower to respond to a signal that children they had been assigned to watch over had become engaged in a physical melee. Cline, Croft, and Courrier (1973) found that children between the ages of 5 and 12 who had a history of viewing violent television were emotionally less aroused by new violent television scenes. Donnerstein, Linz, and Penrod (1987) and Linz, Donnerstein, and Adams (1989) report that continuous exposure to violent erotica reduces the readiness of college students to label similar new stimuli as violent or pornographic, and increases the likelihood that they will perceive the female victim of a rape as somehow responsible. It would be far too much to conclude that this desensitization extends to bloody violence witnessed in real life, for all of the studies we have described used television or film to convey the new stimuli that evoked a lessened response (the children in the experiments by Drabman and colleagues were responding to video coverage of their wards' play area). However, media portrayals inevitably figure prominently in the reactions of children and teenagers, as well as adults, to the larger world. Media are the principal means by which children and teenagers, as well as adults, learn of distant events. What media depict impinges on viewers' interpretation of what is transpiring in the world and critically affects the picture that people have of reality. These events often include human suffering, distress, and death. The media also have long been used by nations to justify the retribution imposed on an enemy; this is the process of dehumanization (Bandura, 1986), by which the suffering of others is made more tolerable by the media. The implication is that desensitization to media portrayals may encourage a callous indifference to suffering and a curtailment of empathy (this is, of course, speculation because such outcomes in regard to the news have not been investigated for either young people or adults).

Cultivation

Gerbner and colleagues (Gerbner, Gross, Morgan, & Signorielli, 1980; Gerbner et al., 2002; R. P. Hawkins & Pingree, 1990) have proposed what has become known as "cultivation theory." This formulation takes its name from the notion that television cultivates beliefs and perceptions, with the emphasis on the subtlety and generally small scale of the influence rather than the larger impact connoted by its synonym, effects. Two initial assumptions were that television is homogeneous enough in its presentations—as exemplified by such perennials as ubiquitous violence, preeminence in news, sports, and entertainment of the White male, and a focus on the middle and upper-middle classes—that amount of viewing is a reasonable index of exposure to the emphases of the medium, and that the cultivation effect will be a function of amount viewed.

The first proposition offered by cultivation theory is that those who view more will be more likely to perceive the world as resembling what has been portrayed on television. Morgan (1989) catalogues a large number of such correlations; for example, heavier viewers perceive the world as racially and occupationally more like the demographics of television casts. The two propositions that have been offered in regard to violent entertainment is that heavier viewers will perceive the world as a mean and dangerous place, and that they are more likely to be fearful of falling victim to an attack. The first finds considerable support; after controlling for a large number of other variables, including those that are correlates of both amount of viewing and such pessimistic views (lower socioeconomic status, senior citizen status, or being female) that might artifactually create correlations between viewing and perceptions, the viewing-pessimism correlations hold up stoutly (Hughes, 1980). The second has fared less well (Hughes, 1980; Tyler, 1980, 1984); television viewing in general, as contrasted with the viewing of terrifying or frightening portrayals, is unrelated to fearfulness when the influence of other variables is statistically controlled. The analysis by Hughes presents critical evidence in what is essentially a match-up of mean world and fearfulness responses. In a nationally representative sample of about 2,000 (and thereby particularly credible), he found that after controlling for crucial variables such as age, sex, and race (because they are positively correlated with both amount of viewing and mean world and fearfulness responses), three out of four mean world items were positively associated with amount of viewing to a statistically significant degree; the one item representing fearfulness, after controlling for those same items, reversed in direction, with scores increasing as amount of viewing decreased—exactly the opposite of what cultivation theory would predict.

Thus, the two initial assumptions have held up well enough for data collected under their rubric to support the theory, but on closer examination they do not accurately convey the whole story. There is enough variation in the makeup of television programs for those who watch a particular genre a great deal to display stronger effects for the emphases of that particular genre, and as

a consequence measuring exposure to particular types of programming produces larger correlations between program emphases and beliefs than occur for viewing in general and the overall emphases of programming (R. P. Hawkins & Pingree, 1980, 1982). Ironically, these both follow logically from the initial assumptions, because effects, if present, surely should increase with more specific measures of program emphases and more precise measures of exposure to those emphases.

The data supporting the cultivation perspective mostly has represented adults, but the few instances where children or teenagers have been examined show the same pattern (R. P. Hawkins & Pingree, 1982; R. P. Hawkins, Pingree, & Adler, 1987; Pingree & Hawkins, 1981). In addition, children and teenagers are particularly likely to rely on the media when firsthand knowledge is absent (DeFleur & DeFleur, 1967), and so it is a reasonable speculation that they would be particularly affected by portrayals that take them away from their own world, which would account for a good amount—although certainly not all—of their television exposure.

Theory, the V-Chip, and the Surgeon General

Child development as a field has profited from research on the influence of violent portrayals on aggressive and antisocial behavior. The data identify a developmental pattern in which viewing violence during the elementary school years nurtures a trait of aggressiveness that will persist well into and perhaps throughout adulthood, and large amounts of violence viewing during the teenage years will promote enhanced aggressiveness (but not necessarily a lasting trait) whatever the history of prior viewing (Anderson et al., 2003; Comstock & Scharrer, 1999; Huesmann, 1986). The two theories that guided so much of the research—Bandura's (1986) social cognition and Berkowitz's (1984, 1990) neo-associationism—have certainly benefited by the support from myriad findings, and we have all benefited by being able to apply these explanations of behavior with greater confidence. Social cognition, of course, holds that what children and teenagers see—in the media as well as the real world—is a source for the acquisition (and subsequent performance) of behavior; neo-associationism emphasizes the influence on behavior of the thoughts, semantically linked in the brain, triggered by what is observed. Both predict that media portrayals under some circumstances will influence behavior. Although social cognition emphasizes the learning of behavior and neo-associationism emphasize the performance of learned behavior, the two are essentially identical in the hypotheses they would offer in a given circumstance. Both concur that the context of a portrayal makes a critical difference. Likelihood of an effect is enhanced when a portrayal includes various elements that attribute what Comstock and Scharrer (1999) have termed efficacy, normativeness, or pertinence to a way of behaving, or when there is particular susceptibility to influence on the part of a viewer. These terms refer to the presentation of behavior as likely to be rewarded, successful, or helpful in attaining a goal; as accepted or socially approved; as particularly connected to a viewer through the overlap of the portrayal with viewer attributes or circumstances (such as age, gender, race, potential victim, or some aspect of the setting); and (in regard to susceptibility) in the case of aggression and antisocial behavior, anger, frustration, or provocation. Changes in attitudes, norms, and values attributable to the media, proposed by some as a major factor (Eron & Huesmann, 1987), are not a necessary condition. This is made clear by Belson's (1978) documentation in his monumental survey of about 1,600 male London teenagers that a positive correlation between violence viewing and aggression was not mediated by attitudes, norms, or values; this is a strong finding, because attitudes, norms, and values were operationalized in four distinct, highly reliable scales, and in none of these instances did violence viewing predict dispositions favorable to aggression. Efficacy, normativeness, and pertinence, then, well-documented in the experiments derived from social cognition and neo-associationism, may function, in addition to the possibility of changes in dispositions, through enhancing accessibility by giving ways of behaving greater prominence and preference in the behavioral repertoires of young viewers. The data in turn establish the media as important contributors to the behavior of young people.

This role extends beyond aggressive and antisocial behavior to prosocial behavior, as the symmetry in one meta-analysis (Hearold, 1986) makes clear. Individual studies, as well as portions of the meta-analyses, identify four factors that will vary considerably from situation to situation as critical, with three representing attributes of portrayals and one an attribute of the viewer (Comstock & Scharrer, 1999): *efficacy* (the portrayal of successful goal attainment), *normativeness* (the portrayal of behavior as socially approved), *pertinence*

(the portrayal of a link with the viewer, such as age, setting, or adversary), and *susceptibility* (circumstances that render the viewer vulnerable, such as frustration or anger in the case of aggressive behavior).

The meta-analyses now appear regularly in the literature on media and aggression and thereby establish a superior framework in regard to the reliability and validity of evidence, and thus interpretation (Anderson et al., 2003; Comstock, 2004). They have joined the currency of academic exchange. They have also seen more specific applications. Bushman and Anderson (2001) used the Paik and Comstock (1994) meta-analysis to evaluate how the effect size ranked among socially consequential effect sizes (about as large as they come), and used their own meta-analysis, broken into 5-year segments, to show that whereas the findings have become stronger with time, news coverage has become weaker in regard to a media violence-behavior link. The latter may be a consequence of the preoccupation of the news media with the episodic, for in the specific, dramatic instance, news outlets have been quick to indict the media for responsibility, as exemplified by the death of Princess Diana, the Jenny Jones talk show murder, and the shootings at Columbine High School (Scharrer, Weidman, & Bissell, 2003).

There is much also that must be attributed to the varied research on the effects of violent portrayals as a whole, although the research on portrayals and aggressive and antisocial behavior unambiguously has been at the forefront. The gist of all the research, from the viewpoint of the welfare of the child or teenager, has been that violent portrayals, however enjoyable or, in specific instances, true to life and even inspiring, can be problematic for young viewers, with sometimes undesirable consequences. It is difficult to believe that without the context established by this research, an eminence suitably lustrous with disinterested scientific authority, the warning labels that now grace many programs and particularly cable movies would be appearing on our television screens. The industry has every reason to detest and avoid labels, because they narrow the audience, arouse parental concerns, and frighten advertisers with the very noxious (to the industry) result that commercials sell for less on programs with warning labels (Hamilton, 1998). Not surprising, given the economic consequences of labeling, the industry has leaned toward underlabeling (J. C. Allen, 2001; Kunkel et al., 1998), leaving some programs unlabeled or with less restrictive ratings than the content would seem to call for. Nevertheless, the entire enterprise can be regarded as a potential service to parents (Gentile, Humphrey, & Walsh, 2004), and apparently programs labeled with warnings do draw smaller child audiences (Hamilton, 1998).

EMERGING ISSUES

Children and adolescents continue to spend much of their time—outside of school and absent other obligations—watching television, listening to music, logging on to the Internet, and playing video games. Television, for decades discussed by social scientists as a medium that newly captured our attention, is now often relegated, along with radio, newspapers, and magazines, to the status of "traditional media," in contrast with the newest wave of novel media forms that are computer- and video game console-based. However, despite the semantic shift and the increasing prevalence of new media in the lives of young people, television continues to dominate overall media use and largely commands the way leisure time is spent (Comstock & Scharrer, 1999).

With the growth of new interactive media and the staying power of traditional media have come new concerns about the amount of time young people spend in front of screens as well as about the content to which they are exposed. Neither concern is new in substance. What is new is the cumulative hours spent by young people with media and the recent implementation of ratings and codes to label the media content—in effect, to give warning—delivered through traditional forms (in the case of television) and new forms (in the case of video and computer games). We begin with the codes and ratings, which are now largely (if imperfectly and confusedly) in place. We then turn to the new delivery systems that are becoming increasingly important in the allocation by the young of time and attention to media and popular culture.

Ratings and Codes

Violence is the topic that has garnered the most research and public attention and triggered the most heated and long-standing debates about media. Yet, little to no substantive reform was achieved in past instances in which Congress took up the issue, despite increasing confidence in the causal link between media violence and aggression, desensitization, and fear (C. A. Cooper, 1996). The V-chip and accompanying program labels implemented by the Telecommunications Act of 1996 stand in

stark contrast to the long history of a high degree of attention to the issue of media violence with low levels of responsive changes in the entertainment industry.

In the early to mid-1990s, U.S. Representative Edward Markey began to press for the creation of a policy that would address the issue of media violence, focusing on bringing V-chip technology that had been introduced in Canada to the United States (Price, 1998). This computer chip, contained in television sets, can be programmed to read the rating or codes that are assigned to a television program to flag the presence of potentially objectionable content and allow the user to block the display of the program on the television screen. A parent uses a code or personal identification number to program the V-chip via remote control to block out all programs that carry the label or labels the parent has identified as a concern. The label information of the program is encoded in the television signal using a technology that is similar to that developed for closed captioning (Eastin, 2001; Price, 1998).

Dale Kunkel and Brian Wilcox (2001, p. 592) describe the political process through which the V-chip legislation surfaced:

> In a political context shaped by strong scientific consensus about the harms of violent portrayals, and perhaps even stronger public opinion against media violence, United States Representative Edward Markey began to gain support for his V-chip legislative proposal. . . . When President Clinton endorsed the V-chip in his 1996 State of the Union Address, it was only a matter of weeks until Congress adopted Markey's legislative proposal, adding it as an amendment to the omnibus Telecommunications Act of 1996. Under the law, the television industry was given 1 year to devise its own system of categorizing programs for violence and other sensitive material (including sex and offensive language) and to then submit this system to the FCC for its approval. If the television industry failed to act, or if its system was not deemed "acceptable," then the FCC would have been required to appoint an advisory committee to design a model V-chip rating system. Oddly enough, the industry would not have been bound to actually employ the system designed by the FCC or, for that matter, any system at all. The only firm requirement in the law was that all television sets sold in the United States must be equipped with a V-chip device that would facilitate program-blocking capabilities.

Thus, the two-pronged system—program ratings/codes and the V-chip that can read them—was implemented in a manner that was technically voluntary on the part of the industry but in reality was couched in fairly threatening terms. The opposition of members of the television industry on First Amendment grounds was circumnavigated by their freedom to devise the codes themselves and by the fact that parents could choose whether to use the chip (Eastin, 2001; McDowell & Maitland, 1998). Industry leaders also objected on economic grounds, concerned that the labels would decrease audiences and thereby ward off advertisers (Price, 1998).

Research supports the view that child audiences, but not adults or teens, will be smaller when programs carry warning labels. Hamilton (1998) analyzed the impact of "viewer discretion warnings" on the audience composition for movies airing on the broadcast networks from 1987 to 1993. He found that such warnings "resulted in a decrease in children's ratings of approximately 14%," translating into approximately "220,000 fewer children in the audience" (pp. 76–77).

Facing the possibility of direct FCC involvement, an industry group comprising members of the National Association of Broadcasters, the National Cable Television Association, and the Motion Picture Association of America (MPAA) joined forces to create codes that would be used to label television programs for potentially sensitive content.

Despite the evidence from a national survey of parents that they would prefer codes that communicated information about the actual content of programs (rather than the ages for which they were deemed appropriate) and the support for such content-based (rather than age-based) codes of many social scientists (Cantor, 1998b; Gruenwald, 1997), the industry group unveiled its newly conceived codes that used the MPAA model of assigning age-based ratings only. The ratings included TV-Y (for youth), TV-Y7 (for youth age 7 and older), TV-G (for general audiences), TV-PG ("parental guidance suggested," as used by the MPAA), TV-14 (recommended for those 14 and older, "parents strongly cautioned"), and TV-MA (for mature audiences only; Eastin, 2001). News and sports were exempted from labeling, and the decision was made to label each individual episode of a television series, a task given to the program producers or the syndicated programmers (Eastin, 2001).

The lack of content descriptors in the codes initially generated by the industry group sparked a new round of controversy. In addition to reflecting public interest groups' demands for more informative labels, the ensuing debate was also influenced by the National Televi-

sion Violence Study, a multifaceted, multimillion-dollar research project funded by the cable industry (Kunkel & Wilcox, 2001; S. Smith et al., 1998; Wilson et al., 1997, 1998). One portion of the National Television Violence Study investigated the potential for program labels to actually increase the appeal of a program among young audiences rather than to lead them away (Cantor & Harrison, 1997; Cantor, Harrison, & Nathanson, 1997), a phenomenon that has been referred to as a "boomerang" or "forbidden fruit" effect (Bushman & Stack, 1996; Christenson, 1992). The data from the experiment indicated that age-based labels increased children's interest in television programs, primarily among boys, whereas content-based labels did not. This evidence, impugning the effectiveness of age-based labels, had a prominent role in the critique of the industry's original program coding scheme. After press attention to the fresh controversy and another congressional hearing, the industry agreed fairly quickly to add codes that would signify particular categories of content were present (Kunkel & Wilcox, 2001). Furthermore, the composition of the committee designing the labels was expanded to represent such nonindustry organizations as the American Medical Association, the Center for Media Education, and the Parent Teacher Association (Greenberg, 2001).

The result is the presently used system, in place since October 1997, which employs both the age-based labels and content codes: V for violence, S for sex, L for adult language, D for suggestive dialogue, and FV for fantasy violence (usually used for children's cartoons, and used only in conjunction with the TV-Y7 rating; Eastin, 2001). The combination of the age- and content-based labels introduces the possibility of multiple meanings assigned to the content codes based on the age-related context. A V in a TV-PG program, for instance, signifies "moderate violence," whereas the same V in association with a TV-14 program means "intense violence" and with a TV-MA program means "graphic violence" (Eastin, 2001).

The labels appear in the opening 15 seconds of television programs in the form of a black-and-white box that appears in the corner of the screen. Parents and caregivers can use the label information itself to make decisions about viewing in the household or, if they have a television set that contains the V-chip, can program the chip to block out programs that feature any combination of labels that the parent chooses. In other words, a parent of a young child can block any program labeled with a V for violence, for instance, or any program with a label that exceeds TV-Y7. The parent sets the parameters for acceptable programs and can reset them at any time.

Effectiveness

The V-chip and television program labels are positive developments because they give parents and caregivers information about program content and age-appropriateness that may be useful, as well as provide the means to restrict children's access to such content using the chip. The policy is the only tangible and potentially long-lasting reform to come out of more than 30 years of consistent social scientific support for negative effects of media violence (Kunkel & Wilcox, 2001). In practice and at present, however, the effectiveness of the V-chip and program labels is constrained by many obstacles.

Some criticisms of the V-chip and labels have focused on the potential conflict of interest involved when industry professionals themselves rate their programs, the difficulty parents may encounter in actually programming the chip, and the short amount of time that the labels air that makes them easy to miss. In addition to these concerns, research has identified two major areas in which severe limitations to the effectiveness of the V-chip and labels have surfaced: (1) whether and how accurately and consistently television producers label programs using both age- and content-based ratings and (2) a lack of attention, awareness, and understanding of the system among parents.

To investigate whether television producers were labeling their programs with age- and content-based ratings faithfully and accurately, Greenberg, Eastin, and Mastro (2001) examined a 2-month sample of *TV Guide* listings for the four major broadcast networks and four cable channels at three different times of the day. *TV Guide* and other program listing sources were supposed to have made ratings information available to parents to allow them to plan viewing decisions before programs aired. The *TV Guide*s examined in the study were from 1998, 5 months after the content-based ratings had been devised. Greenberg and colleagues found that of the 4,001 programs eligible for ratings, only 2,911 actually carried a rating. (NBC programs were exempt from the analysis because the network had decided not to submit content codes, with no discernible consequences as of this writing.) Thus, 27% had no rating (either age- or content-based) available at all. Of those programs that had a rating, only 25% carried a content-based label. Although the data certainly reveal a high degree of noncompliance, the researchers observe that the over-

whelming lack of content-based information is partly attributable to the presence of TV-G and TV-Y programs in the sample that, by definition, are not supposed to contain objectionable content. Greenberg and colleagues note that the ostensible victory that public interest groups and social scientists gained in the fight to add content information to labels "resulted in content information being part of the ratings for only one in four shows" (p. 35). The study found that TV-G (32%) and TV-PG (24%) were the most common age-based, and D (for dialogue, 38%) and V (for violence, 33%) the most common content-based codes in the *TV Guide*s. Yet, when the researchers compared the *TV Guide* listed ratings to the ratings that actually aired with the television programs, they determined that "the overall match in ratings between on-air information and *TV Guide* is abysmally low" (p. 50).

Kunkel and colleagues (Kunkel, Farinola, et al., 2001) compared the labels appended to programs with data from content analyses of the treatment of violence and sex. Using a composite week that consisted of 1,147 programs eligible for ratings that aired from early morning to late at night on 10 channels, they chose only those programs that contained violent acts that would cause serious harm. Coders then assigned points for number of acts of violence, sanitization of harm or pain, and graphicness. In the highest-scoring programs in the sample using this procedure (those deemed "high risk" by the researchers), 65% were not labeled with a V for violence and 27% were labeled as appropriate for audience members 14 and older (TV-14). When only children's programs designated as high risk were assessed, only 28% were labeled TV-Y7/FV (indicating fantasy violence, the strictest label available for children's shows). The same pattern was found with sexual content, with a failure to label "high risk sexual portrayals" with an S 80% of the time. The conclusion of the researchers is unambiguous: "Parents cannot rely on the V-chip ratings, as presently applied, to effectively identify and block the most problematic material that poses a risk of harm to their children" (p. 68).

Finally, there is persuasive evidence that young people and parents alike have difficulty ascertaining the meaning of some of the labels used to identify television programs, and children and adolescents pay little attention to the ratings. In 1997, Greenberg, Rampoldi-Hnilo, and Hofschire (2001) surveyed 462 4th, 8th, and 10th graders in Michigan and found that their attention to the television program ratings was low, especially among the older respondents. Only 52% of respondents were aware that the ratings labeled programs for sexual content, compared to 70% for language and 72% for violence. Fewer than half of the respondents knew that cartoons were labeled (47%). Just over half (52%) could correctly identify the meaning of the label TV-Y, whereas the other age-based labels were understood by at least two-thirds of the respondents. The majority of the young people reported that they used the ratings either "not much" or "not much at all." Acknowledgment of the use of the ratings to actually seek out a show with sensitive content was more common among the younger respondents and those with more parental mediation of viewing, demonstrating some evidence of the "forbidden fruit" effect.

Greenberg and Rampoldi-Hnilo (2001) conducted a follow-up study a year later to determine knowledge, attitudes, and use of the newer content-based labels among another sample of 510 4th, 8th, and 10th graders. Attention to and use of the labels continued to be modest, and knowledge of the content-based labels was lower for all age groups than knowledge of the age-based labels. Only 25% of the respondents could identify either D as the label used for "adults talking about topics that should not be heard by children" or FV as the label that "means the TV show has cartoons with violence in them" (p. 126). Over half (56%) could match up the letter L with the labeling of language, and nearly three-fourths (73%) could do the same for S and sex, with these results possibly somewhat inflated as measures of comprehension by the match between the first letters.

In a 1998 survey of 1,358 parents of children ages 2 to 17, Foehr, Rideout, and Miller (2001) found that 18% were unaware of the television ratings system and only 55% reported ever having used it. Comprehension among parents of the meaning of the codes was moderate to low. Only 34% could correctly identify the meaning of TV-Y, 41% TV-Y7 or TV-MA, 55% V, 44% S, 40% L, 7% FV, and 2% D. Comprehension was slightly to significantly higher for the aged-based codes that are similar to the recognizable MPAA ratings (TV-G, TV-PG, TV-14). One year later, a follow-up survey (Kaiser Family Foundation, 1999) found little change, and most data pointed toward reduced rather than increased understanding. Yet, these same two surveys make it clear that parents approve of the idea of ratings (by about a 9:1 ratio) even if only about half use them, and they prefer, as earlier survey research had indicated, content-based to age-based ratings. Therefore, even among the

group that would presumably be most interested in the labeling system—parents of children and teens—awareness, comprehension, and use have been low.

New Delivery Systems

Two new media delivery systems whose rising presence in the lives of young people is difficult to ignore are the Internet and interactive games (either computer- or video game console-based). The best data on the use of both by children and adolescents in the United States is the 1999 Kaiser Foundation survey on which Roberts and Foehr (2004) report. They used two different samples, 2- to 7-year-olds and 8- to 18-year-olds, asking the parents of the younger group to respond but allowing the children and teenagers in the older group to report on their own behavior. To maximize validity and lessen the bias of recall and interpretation of "typical" use that often constrains these measures, time use questions were framed around media use the previous day and were measured by specific blocks or "dayparts." Both samples were nationally representative: The younger group, reached at home, included 1,090 children, and the older group, reached in school, consisted of 2,014 older children and teenagers.

The patterns drawn by the Roberts and Foehr (2004) data assign a staggeringly large role to media in the lives of children and adolescents in the United States (Table 20.2). The new, interactive forms of media—distinguished by technology in which changes in the child's physical behavior (clicking a mouse, hitting a button) dictate alterations in the content to which they are exposed—are increasingly available and escalating in use. Yet, time spent with television dominates overall media use by far.

Almost 70% of households with children under the age of 18 owned a computer, and 45% had Internet access at home. It is apparent that Internet access has grown since the Roberts and Foehr (2004) data were collected. The 2000 Census reported that 53% of households with school-age children had Internet access (Newburger, 2001). The National Center for Education Statistics found that in 2001, 65% of children ages 5 to 17 could access computers in the home, whereas 81% accessed them in school (DeBell & Chapman, 2003).

Among all of the young people in the Roberts and Foehr (2004) sample, the amount of time spent with computers varied from an average of 6 minutes per day for 2- to 7-year-olds to 31 minutes for 11- to 14-year-

TABLE 20.2   Media Availability in the Homes of Young People

Media	2- to 7-year-olds				8- to 18-year-olds			
	Average	1+	2+	3+	Average	1+	2+	3+
TV	2.5	100%	81%	45%	3.1	100%	93%	70%
VCR	1.6	96	47	12	2.0	99	64	26
Radio	2.6	99	78	48	3.4	98	91	73
CD player	1.4	83	36	14	2.6	95	74	48
Tape player	1.8	91	53	26	2.9	98	85	62
Computer	0.8	63	16	3	1.1	74	25	8
Video game console	0.8	53	18	5	1.7	82	49	24
Cable TV		73				74		
Premium channels		40				45		
Internet connection		40				47		

Source: Adapted from *Kids and Media in America,* by D. F. Roberts and U. G. Foehr, 2004, Cambridge, England: Cambridge University Press. Reprinted with permission.

olds and 26 minutes for 15- to 18-year-olds. Among only those with in-home access to computers, the figures were much higher, with 2- to 7-year-olds spending 23 minutes, 8- to 10-year-olds 50 minutes, 11- to 14-year-olds 58 minutes, and 15- to 18-year-olds 47 minutes per day. Generally, boys in these homes spent more time with the computer than girls (an average of 58 compared to 46 minutes), and the gender gap is particularly marked in the older age groups. Among the younger age groups (those 8 to 10 and 11 to 14) who use computers, the largest allocation of time is spent playing computer games, whereas among the 15- to 18-year-olds, playing computer games and visiting Web sites tied for computer time allotment. E-mail and instant messaging, both forms of engaging with others through computer use, also constitute popular practice and enjoyed a substantial proportion of the computer-dedicated time use of young people (Lenhart, Rainie, & Lewis, 2001; Roberts & Foehr, 2004; Roper Starch Worldwide Inc., 1999).

The Roberts and Foehr (2004) data also point to a significant role for video games in the lives of young people. Indeed, the amount of time devoted to console-based games is similar to that devoted to computers. Just over half (53%) of the 2- to 7-year-olds and over three-quarters (82%) of the 8- to 18-year-olds in the sample had a video game console (e.g., Nintendo, Sega Genesis, Xbox) in the home. Children 2 to 7 years old played for an average of 8 minutes per day (2 minutes more than they used the computer), and 8- to 18-year-olds played for an average of 26 minutes (1 minute more than the computer). The data collected by Roberts and Foehr document that the gender differences that were apparent but hardly extreme in computer use appear in more staggering form in video game use. Boys outnumber girls as

video game users in every age group, but never more so than at ages 11 to 14, when 61% of boys and 24% of girls reported playing. Boys also spent significantly more time with video games than girls did and listed action/combat, sports/competition, and simulation/strategic games as preferences more often than girls (Table 20.3).

Access to television has reached a saturation level, where it is about equal across socioeconomic and racial and ethnic differences. Access to computers and the Internet is not at all equal across these groupings. The Roberts and Foehr (2004) data from 1999 showed that among the 2- to 7-year-olds, 71% of White children had computers in the household compared to 45% of Black or African American and 40% of Latino children. Half of White children had Internet access at home, compared to 19% of both Black/African American and Latino children. The differences in access appeared in the older age group as well, although they were somewhat less pronounced. Home computer access in the De-Bell and Chapman (2003) data collected 2 years later was highest for White and Asian families (77% and 76%, respectively), followed by American Indian (54%), and Black/African American and Latino families (each at 41%). Having a computer in the home also increased linearly with household income, from a low access figure of 31% in homes with incomes of less than $20,000 to a high of 89% for incomes of $75,000 or more (DeBell & Chapman, 2003). Thus, the diffusion of these newer technologies to young people in the United States is not universal and is contingent on a multitude of factors, whereas television access and use is omnipresent.

Data reported by Livingstone (2002) and gathered through the General Household Survey of 1,287 households in the United Kingdom and by Livingstone and

TABLE 20.3   Media Exposure by Gender and Age (8 to 18)

	8–18 Years		8–10 Years		11–14 Years		15–18 Years	
	Female	Male	Female	Male	Female	Male	Female	Male
Average exposure time (hr:min):								
Television	2:55[a]	3:15[b]	3:24	3:15	3:13[a]	3:47[b]	2:12[a]	2:34[b]
Videos of TV	0:13	0:15	0:19	0:22	0:13	0:15	0:09	0:11
Commercial videos	0:27	0:28	0:23	0:28	0:28	0:30	0:28	0:27
Movies (in theaters)	0:16	0:19	0:25	0:27	0:17	0:22	0:09	0:09
Video games	0:11[a]	0:39[b]	0:20[a]	0:40[b]	0:09[a]	0:43[b]	0:07[a]	0:34[b]
Print media	0:46[a]	0:41[b]	1:00	0:49	0:44	0:39	0:38	0:36
Radio	0:55[a]	0:38[b]	0:30[a]	0:19[b]	0:55[a]	0:38[b]	1:13[a]	0:55[b]
CDs and tapes	1:14[a]	0:51[b]	0:42[a]	0:22[b]	1:16[a]	0:40[b]	1:36	1:32
Computer	0:24[a]	0:30[b]	0:23	0:23	0:26[a]	0:36[b]	0:22[a]	0:30[b]
Total media exposure	7:21	7:37	7:25	7:03	7:41	8:09	6:53	7:29
Proportion of total media time devoted to:								
Television	38[a]	41[b]	46	45	40[a]	46[b]	30	32
Other screen media	11	12	14	16	10	11	10	10
Video games	2[a]	9[b]	4[a]	9[b]	2[a]	9[b]	2[a]	8[b]
Reading	12[a]	11[b]	16	14	12[a]	9[b]	10	9
Audio media	31[a]	21[b]	15[a]	10[b]	30[a]	18[b]	43[a]	36[b]
Computer	6[a]	7[b]	5	6	5[a]	7[b]	6	6

Source: Adapted from *Kids and Media in America,* by D. F. Roberts and U. G. Foehr, 2004, Cambridge, England: Cambridge University Press. Reprinted with permission.

Note: Figures sharing a superscript within a row do not differ at the *p* = .05 level of significance.

Bovill (1999) collected in a multination survey of Western Europe and Israel indicate that high levels of media access and use are not confined to the United States but are typical of the developed world. In the United Kingdom, 61% of 15- to 17-year-olds and 72% of 12- to 14-year-olds have the ability to use console-based video games in the home, again varying by gender (56% of girls, 78% of boys). The UK data also found that 44% of all boys and 40% of all girls ages 6 to 16 owned a Gameboy, a handheld video game-playing system. Video games are slightly less pervasive in other European locations, lower than UK estimates by about 15 to 20 percentage points for Germany, Spain, France, Switzerland, and Denmark (Livingstone & Bovill, 1999).

Livingstone (2002) also reports on the diffusion of computers and the Internet to British homes, finding in the 1997 data that 53% of homes with young people had a personal computer, yet only 7% had Internet access. These figures are comparable with some other countries in Europe (e.g., Germany and Spain), whereas other locations have higher Internet diffusion rates (e.g., Sweden at 31% and Finland at 26%; Livingstone & Bovill, 1999). However, Livingstone also cites a more recent British poll (Wigley & Clarke, 2000) that estimated 70% of UK homes with children have a personal computer and 36% have Internet access. These latter, more up-to-date diffusion rates for computers and the Internet are very similar to those in the United States and lead us to suspect that as time progresses, computer-related diffusion rates in most Western countries will be much the same.

The bedrooms of children and teens in the United Kingdom, as in the United States, are often replete with personal media. Livingstone (2002) reports that 66% of the young people in the sample had a television, books, and a radio or stereo, 33% a video game console, and 12% a computer in their own room. The distribution of media in bedrooms of children and teens in the United Kingdom is related to their age (older kids have more access) and gender (boys have more access). Other European countries (with the exception of Denmark, which more closely resembles the United States and the United Kingdom on this measure) have significantly fewer young people with access to media in their bedroom (Livingstone & Bovill, 1999). In France, for instance, 28% of children had a television in their bedroom, 25% a video game console, and 3% a computer with a CD-ROM (Livingstone & Bovill, 1999).

Consequences

One of the central concerns about the consequences of high levels of media use is the potential for displacement of time that might otherwise be spent by young people with something more physically active, educationally rewarding, or socially constructive (Comstock & Scharrer, 1999). The concern about the sedentary nature of time spent with screen media has reached a new intensity in light of recent links between television viewing hours and obesity in adults (Hu, Li, Colditz, Willett, & Manson, 2003; Jakes et al., 2003) and children (R. E. Anderson, Crespo, Bartlett, Cheskin, & Pratt, 1998; Berkey, Rockett, Gillman, & Colditz, 2003; Crespo et al., 2001; W. Dietz & Gortmaker, 1985; Gortmaker et al., 1996; Lowry, Wechsler, Galuska, Fulton, & Kann, 2002; Proctor et al., 2003). The Rideout et al. (2003) data representing very young children found that heavy television viewers (watching 2 or more hours per day) spent less time playing outdoors than lighter viewers. Rideout and colleagues also report that among the 4- to 6-year-olds in their national sample, heavy television viewers spent significantly less time reading than other children. This is consistent with past research pointing to television's role in the reduction of time spent reading among young children (Comstock & Scharrer, 1999; Heyns, 1976; Medrich et al., 1982). As we have pointed out, displacement of time by television viewing that might be spent on more educationally rewarding activities has consequences for scholastic performance. Video games exacerbate this problem because the games most preferred by young people would be unlikely to fulfill an educational function (Roberts & Foehr, 2004). In contrast, considerable proportions of the time that children and teenagers spend with computers and the Internet pertain to schoolwork and/or information acquisition, in addition to the more pervasive entertainment (via games) and communication (via e-mail, chatting, and instant messaging) functions (Roberts & Foehr, 2004).

Other consequences of media use by young people and adolescents stem from exposure to particular types of content. The new, interactive media do little to allay or replace such concerns. The vast, unregulated dominion that is the Internet has been criticized for allowing young computer users to easily access pornographic material, perhaps even unwittingly (Mitchell, Finkelhor, & Wolak, 2003). Studies of video game content have found that portrayals parallel—and sometimes even exceed— the narrow depictions of gender and sexualized female characters (Beasley & Collins Standley, 2002; T. Dietz, 1998; Scharrer, 2004; Ward Gailey, 1993) and the prevalent role for violence (T. Dietz, 1998; Scharrer, 2004; S. L. Smith, Lachlan, & Tamborini, 2003; Thompson & Haninger, 2001) found in television.

The accounts by Montgomery (2001) and Tarpley (2001) specifically focus on these perils. Montgomery points out that the Internet offers new and potentially lucrative means to market to young children and teenagers. In addition to the home shopping model, which is plain enough in its intent and purpose, the Internet makes possible the construction of Web sites built around characters and activities appealing to young people, with the goal not of selling today but of building favorable brand images for purchases in the distant tomorrow: of autos, watches, clothing, cosmetics. Thus, the Internet opens the way to a degree of manipulation far beyond that achieved by directing advertising to children too young to comprehend its vested self-interest. Tarpley, on the other hand, points to the unregulated and extraordinary breadth of user access as posing both threats and opportunities. Chat rooms offer access to information and exchanges involving sex, violence, and racial and political hatred, as well as information—such as building a bomb in the basement—that cannot be said to denote or connote pleasant or constructive outcomes. At the same time, the Internet offers the opportunity to pursue educational offerings, such as specialized tutoring and unusual subjects, and the possibility of socializing and participating in group endeavors that by its comparative anonymity may give respite to the shy or otherwise somewhat disenfranchised while also offering possibilities, ranging into the lurid, for young users to disguise their age, gender, race, and opinions.

The very nature of interactive media has led to new anxieties about their potential to exacerbate media effects. Video and computer games inspire a high degree of involvement in the action, trigger more intense identification with characters, and feature a reward structure in which new levels or components of the game are offered to those who perform well, among other differences that may make them more "hazardous" than television (Gentile & Anderson, 2003). As Calvert (1999, p. 36) explains:

> The child is the aggressor in the new technologies, the player of the video or the virtual game. These games certainly amplify personal involvement, because the child identifies more with the character that wins or loses. The child who plays the game directly experiences success or failure when his or her own behaviors lead to those outcomes.

Although no comparative studies pit television violence influence against video game violence influence, recent research has indicated that concern about the latter may be warranted. An increasing number of studies (C. A. Anderson & Dill, 2000; Calvert & Tan, 1994; Gentile, Lynch, Linder, & Walsh, 2004; Kirsch, 1998; Silvern & Williamson, 1987) as well as two meta-analyses (C. A. Anderson & Bushman, 2001; Sherry, 2001) have documented a link between playing violent games and aggression.

In general, the contemporary child or teenager in the United States and, for the most part, around the world has a veritable cornucopia of media at his or her disposal each day and turns very frequently to screen media—video games, computers, and television—for entertainment, information, and communication. The pervasive role of media in the lives of young people has sparked parental concerns that stem from the sheer amount of time spent as well as from consternation about the content to which they are exposed, with violence consistently among the most frequently voiced worries. Although the V-chip and television program labels represent a historical moment for media and public policy and allow parents the means to exercise some control over the content to which their children are exposed, considerable hurdles currently exist that severely constrain their effective use. Parental negotiation of the media-saturated world of youngsters remains a difficult task.

CONCLUSION

The social and behavioral science research on the roles of media and popular culture in the lives of children and teenagers has provided information that has increased knowledge, helped to build theory, and has had implications—if not always fulfilled—for policymaking and parenting. Previously, media and popular culture had occasionally drawn the attention of those concerned with the welfare of the young, as exemplified by the 13-volume Payne Fund studies of the movies in the 1930s (Charters, 1933) and the campaign by New York psychiatrist Frederic Wertham (1954) in the 1950s against comic books as a school for violence and crime in such books as *Seduction of the Innocent*. But it was the introduction of television that initiated the modern scrutiny by scientific methods of young people's use of media and popular culture. The two landmarks were the large-scale examinations of the effects of the introduction of the medium, involving thousands of young people and hundreds of parents and teachers, in the United States

by Schramm et al. (1961) and in Great Britain by Himmelweit, Oppenheim, and Vince (1958). Soon, papers, journal articles, and eventually books by those in child development, social psychology, sociology, and communication began to appear. Although any given study can become the subject of debate over the legitimacy of its data collection, the appropriateness of the interpretations by the author(s), and the generalizability of the findings to other populations or other circumstances, we believe the proper response is to seek out patterns from the total accumulation of studies as we have done here. In approaching the literature from this perspective, we agree with the recent conclusion of Roberts and Foehr (2004, p. 6) that the past half-century represents a research "tradition that has demonstrated clearly that media messages can influence children's and adolescents' beliefs, attitudes, and behavior across a wide range of topic areas."

Our major conclusions, which emphasize television and other screen media because of their very large place in the media budgets of most young persons, begin with the recognition that a wide array of media are used regularly by most young people, many younger children and most of those older have access to these media in the privacy of their bedroom, and substantial amounts of media time are spent alone, without the company of peers or the presence of parents. The amount of time allocated to media among those who are their greatest fans is extraordinary, but even among those who use media comparatively sparsely access and use are substantial. Most of what is offered and most of what is consumed is entertainment, so the experience is enjoyable and rewarding, but content of cultural and educational value is dwarfed by entertainment (this is particularly visible in the television schedule).

We conclude, despite the consistently inverse associations between amount of viewing and scholastic achievement, that only the minority who spend many hours per day viewing are at risk for the displacement of skill acquisition by television and interference with the quality of homework, intellectual tasks, and reading that would diminish scholastic performance. However, we are not so conservative regarding the evidence that television facilitates tastes and preferences that favor plots, topics, and themes similar to those found on television and in comic books, and a contemptuous disdain for books as dull and boring. This cultivation of tastes and preferences, while certainly enhanced by greater viewing (because the evidence in its behalf is correlational), in our judgment would probably affect a much greater proportion because so many view substantial amounts— enough for these effects to occur—in terms of the kind of dispositions with which we are here concerned.

We conclude that children under the age of 8 are deceived by television advertising because at this early stage of cognitive development they cannot usually understand the self-interested motive of the advertiser ("to sell," a necessary component, is beyond the grasp of most). This, and the evidence on persuasion and nutrition along with the climate of manipulation, was thought by the FTC to be enough for regulatory action, but political opposition foreclosed this option.

We conclude, based on seven meta-analyses and our interpretation of several significant individual studies, that violent entertainment facilitates aggressive and antisocial behavior and that this effect extends beyond incivility to behavior that is seriously harmful. Experiments document that young persons of all ages engage in greater aggressive behavior after exposure to violent portrayals. Surveys attest that young people who view greater amounts of violent entertainment engage more frequently in aggressive and antisocial behavior, and nowhere do the data indicate that this is attributable wholly to any other variable than the influence of television, including any preference of those who are particularly aggressive for violent entertainment. In our interpretation, the generalizability of the experiments is confirmed by the surveys; the two jointly make a case that is much stronger than either taken alone.

We conclude that the codes labeling programs for adult, sexual, and violent content are helpful to concerned parents, although the codes are not widely understood. We observed that the television industry has incentives to avoid such labels because they draw controversy and reduce what can be charged for advertising time, so there should be no surprise that more than the occasional program that merits a label goes unlabeled or that a label sometimes seems insufficient for the content.

Finally, we conclude that despite technological developments of great importance, at the present time the traditional media, especially television, account for the large majority of media use by children and teenagers. It remains the major medium of the young even among those who use the media the least. Nevertheless, the VCR and DVD, increasingly available in the unsupervised bedrooms of the young, increase the viewing of theater movies, and these movies sometimes will be rated for audiences that are older than those who now will be able to view them. These two devices, along with interactivity, make available content that often is more involving emotionally and cognitively than most television programming. They also make it possible to focus on a narrow range of content. Technological developments promote private consumption, access, involvement, and exclusivity in regard to content. As a result, the recent surgeon general's report on youth violence (U. S. Department of Health and Human Services, 2001) speculates that technology will enhance media influence on the young (and perhaps beyond effects on aggressive and antisocial behavior). The most recent data available (Roberts & Foehr, 2004) indicate that young people were not yet using computers very much outside of school, but those who did used them more than twice as much as the per capita figure. This pattern identifies a medium that currently is enthusiast-based compared to the universal appeal of television. We expect per capita use to increase with greater access. Technology, as would be expected, is an area for continuing attention to the changes that it may bring to media use. However, it would be our expectation that screen-based media, such as television, VCR, and DVD use, and theater movies in toto will remain paramount because other electronic media will not supplant them in supplying undemanding but enjoyable and occasionally absorbing entertainment, sports, and news.

REFERENCES

Adler, R. P., Lesser, G. S., Meringoff, L. K., Robertson, T. S., Rossiter, J. R., & Ward, S. (1980). *The effect of television advertising on children: Review and recommendations.* Lexington, MA: Lexington Books.

Albarran, A. B., & Umphrey, D. (1993). An examination of television motivations and program preferences by Hispanics, Blacks, and Whites. *Journal of Broadcasting and Electronic Media, 37*(1), 95–103.

Allen, J. C. (2001). The economic structure of the commercial electronic children's media industries. In D. G. Singer & J. L. Singer (Eds.), *Handbook of children and the media* (pp. 477–493). Thousand Oaks, CA: Sage.

Allen, M., D'Alessio, D., & Brezgel, K. (1995). A meta-analysis summarizing the effects of pornography: Pt. 2. Aggression after exposure. *Human Communication Research, 22*(2), 258–283.

Anderson, B., Mead, N., & Sullivan, S. (1986). *Television: What do national assessment tests tell us?* Princeton, NJ: Educational Testing Service.

Anderson, C. A., Berkowitz, L., Donnerstein, E., Huesmann, L. R., Johnson, J. D., Linz, D., et al. (2003). The influence of media violence on youth. *Psychological Science in the Public Interest, 4*(3), 81–110.

Anderson, C. A., & Bushman, B. J. (2001). Effects of violent video games on aggressive behavior, aggressive cognition, aggressive affect, physiological arousal, and prosocial behavior: A meta-analytic review of the scientific literature. *Psychological Science, 12,* 353–359.

Anderson, C. A., & Dill, K. E. (2000). Video games and aggressive thoughts, feelings, and behavior in the laboratory and in life. *Journal of Personality and Social Psychology, 78,* 772–290.

Anderson, D. R., Collins, P. A., Schmitt, K. L., & Jacobvitz, R. S. (1996). Stressful life events and television viewing. *Communication Research, 23*(3), 243–260.

Anderson, D. R., Levin, S., & Lorch, E. (1977). The effects of TV program pacing on the behavior of preschool children. *AV Communication Review, 25*(2), 159–166.

Anderson, D. R., Lorch, E. P., Field, D. E., Collins, P. A., & Nathan, J. G. (1986). Television viewing at home: Age trends in visual attention and time with TV. *Child Development, 57,* 1024–1033.

Anderson, D. R., Pugzles Lorch, E. P., Field, D. E., & Sanders, J. (1981). The effects of TV program comprehensibility on preschool children's visual attention to television. *Child Development, 52,* 151–157.

Anderson, R. E., Crespo, C. J., Bartlett, S. J., Cheskin, L. J., & Pratt, M. (1998). Relationship of physical activity and television watchdog with body weight and level of fatness among children. *Journal of the American Medical Association, 279*(12), 938–942.

Andison, F. S. (1977). TV violence and viewer aggression: A cumulation of study results. *Public Opinion Quarterly, 41*(3), 314–331.

Armstrong, G. B. (1993). Cognitive interference from background television: Structural effects on verbal and spatial processing. *Communication Studies, 44,* 56–70.

Armstrong, G. B., Bojarsky, G. A., & Mares, M. (1991). Background television and reading performance. *Communication Monographs, 58,* 235–253.

Armstrong, G. B., & Greenberg, B. S. (1990). Background television as an inhibitor of cognitive processing. *Human Communication Research, 16*(3), 355–386.

Atkin, C. K. (1975a). *Effects of television advertising on children: Parent-child communication in supermarket breakfast selection* (Report No. 7). East Lansing: Department of Communication, Michigan State University.

Atkin, C. K. (1975b). *Effects of television advertising on children: Survey of children's and mothers' responses to television commercials* (Report No. 8). East Lansing: Department of Communication, Michigan State University.

Atkin, C. K. (1978). Observations of parent-child interaction in supermarket decisionmaking. *Journal of Marketing, 42,* 41–45.

Baker, R. K., & Ball, S. J. (Eds.). (1969). *Violence and the media: A staff report to the National Commission on the Causes and Prevention of Violence.* Washington, DC: U.S. Government Printing Office.

Bandura, A. (1965). Influence of model's reinforcement contingencies on the acquisition of imitative responses. *Journal of Personality and Social Psychology, 1*(6), 589–595.

Bandura, A. (1986). *Social foundations of thought and action: A social cognitive theory.* Englewood Cliffs, NJ: Prentice-Hall.

Bandura, A., Ross, D., & Ross, S. A. (1963a). Imitation of film-mediated aggressive models. *Journal of Abnormal and Social Psychology, 66*(1), 3–11.

Bandura, A., Ross, D., & Ross, S. A. (1963b). Vicarious reinforcement and imitative learning. *Journal of Abnormal and Social Psychology, 67*(6), 601–607.

Barwise, T. P., & Ehrenberg, A. S. C. (1988). *Television and its audience.* Newbury Park, CA: Sage.

Beasley, B., & Collins Standley, T. (2002). Shirts versus skins: Clothing as indicator of gender role stereotyping in video games. *Mass Communication and Society, 5*(3), 279–293.

Bechtel, R. B., Achelpohl, C., & Akers, R. (1972). Correlates between observed behavior and questionnaire responses on television viewing. In E. A. Rubinstein, G. A. Comstock, & J. P. Murray (Eds.), *Television and social behavior: Vol. 4. Television in day-to-day life—Patterns of use* (pp. 274–344). Washington, DC: U.S. Government Printing Office.

Belson, W. A. (1978). *Television violence and the adolescent boy.* Westmead, England: Saxon House, Teakfield.

Berkey, C. S., Rockett, H. R. H., Gillman, M. W., & Colditz, G. A. (2003). One-year changes in activity and in inactivity among 10- to 15-year-old boys and girls: Relationship to change in body mass index. *Pediatrics, 111*(4), 836–844.

Berkowitz, L. (1984). Some effects of thoughts on anti- and prosocial influences of media events: A cognitive-neoassociationistic analysis. *Psychological Bulletin, 95*(3), 410–427.

Berkowitz, L. (1990). On the formation and regulation of anger and aggression: *American Psychologist, 45*(4), 494–503.

Berkowitz, L., & Alioto, J. T. (1973). The meaning of an observed event as a determinant of aggressive consequences. *Journal of Personality and Social Psychology, 28*(2), 206–217.

Berkowitz, L., & Geen, R. G. (1966). Film violence and the cue properties of available targets. *Journal of Personality and Social Psychology, 3*(5), 525–530.

Berkowitz, L., & Geen, R. G. (1967). Stimulus qualities of the target of aggression: A further study. *Journal of Personality and Social Psychology, 5*(3), 364–368.

Berkowitz, L., & Rawlings, E. (1963). Effects of film violence on inhibitions against subsequent aggression. *Journal of Abnormal and Social Psychology, 66*(3), 405–412.

Bertholf, R. L., & Goodison, S. (2004). Television viewing and attention deficits in children [Letter to the editor]. *Pediatrics, 114*(2), 511–513.

Blosser, B. J., & Roberts, D. F. (1985). Age differences in children's perceptions of message intent: Responses to TV news, commercials, educational spots, and public service announcements. *Communication Research, 12*(4), 455–484.

Bower, R. (1985). *The changing television audience in America.* New York: Columbia University Press.

Brown, L. (1977). *New York Times encyclopedia of television.* New York: Times Books.

Bushman, B. J., & Anderson, C. A. (2001). Media violence and the American public: Scientific facts versus media misinformation. *American Psychologist, 56*(6/7), 477–489.

Bushman, B. J., & Huesmann, L. R. (2001). Effects of televised violence on aggression. In D. G. Singer & J. L. Singer (Eds.), *Handbook of children and the media* (pp. 223–254). Thousand Oaks, CA: Sage.

Bushman, B. J., & Stack, A. D. (1996). Forbidden fruit versus tainted fruit: Effects of warning labels on attraction to television violence. *Journal of Experimental Psychology: Applied, 2,* 207–226.

Butter, E. J., Popovich, P. M., Stackhouse, R. H., & Garner, R. K. (1981). Discrimination of television programs and commercials by preschool children. *Journal of Advertising Research, 21*(2), 53–56.

California Assessment Program. (1980). *Student achievement in California schools: 1979–1980 annual report.* Sacramento: California State Department of Education.

California Assessment Program. (1982). *Survey of sixth grade school achievement and television viewing habits.* Sacramento: California State Department of Education.

California Assessment Program. (1986). *Annual report, 1985–1986.* Sacramento: California State Department of Education.

Calvert, S. (1999). *Children's journeys through the information age.* Boston: McGraw-Hill.

Calvert, S., Huston, A. C., Watkins, B. A., & Wright, J. C. (1982). The relationship between selective attention to television forms and children's comprehension of content. *Child Development, 53,* 601–610.

Calvert, S., & Tan, S. L. (1994). Impact of virtual reality on young adults' physiological arousal and aggressive thoughts: Interaction versus observation. *Journal of Applied Developmental Psychology, 15,* 125–139.

Campbell, T. A., Wright, J. C., & Huston, A. C. (1987). Form cues and content difficulty as determinants of children's cognitive processing of televised educational messages. *Journal of Experimental Child Psychology, 43,* 311–327.

Canary, D. J., & Spitzberg, B. H. (1993). Loneliness and media gratification. *Communication Research, 20*(6), 800–821.

Cantor, J. (1994a). Confronting children's fright responses to mass media. In D. Zillmann, J. Bryant, & A. C. Huston (Eds.), *Media, children, and the family: Social scientific, psychodynamic, and clinical perspectives* (pp. 139–150). Hillsdale, NJ: Erlbaum.

Cantor, J. (1994b). Fright reactions to mass media. In J. Bryant & D. Zillmann (Eds.), *Media effects: Advances in theory and research* (pp. 213–246). Hillsdale, NJ: Erlbaum.

Cantor, J. (1998a). *"Mommy, I'm scared": How TV and movies frighten children and what we can do to protect them.* San Diego: Harcourt Brace.

Cantor, J. (1998b). Ratings for program content: The role of research findings [Special issue]. *Annals of the American Academy of Political and Social Science, 557,* 54–69.

Cantor, J. (2001). The media and children's fears, anxieties, and perceptions of danger. In D. G. Singer & J. L. Singer (Eds.), *Handbook of children and the media* (pp. 207–221). Thousand Oaks, CA: Sage.

Cantor, J., & Harrison, K. (1997). Ratings and advisories for television programming. In Center for Communication and Social Policy, University of California, Santa Barbara (Ed.), *National Television Violence Study* (Vol. 1, pp. 361–388). Thousand Oaks, CA: Sage.

Cantor, J., Harrison, K., & Nathanson, A. (1997). Ratings and advisories for television programming. In Center for Communication and Social Policy, University of California, Santa Barbara (Ed.), *National Television Violence Study* (Vol. 2, pp. 267–322). Thousand Oaks, CA: Sage.

Cantor, J., & Hoffner, C. (1990). Children's fear reactions to a televised film as a function of perceived immediacy of depicted threat. *Journal of Broadcasting and Electronic Media, 34,* 421–442.

Cantor, J., & Nathanson, A. (1996). Children's fright reactions to television news. *Journal of Communication, 46*(4), 139–152.

Cantor, J., & Reilly, S. (1982). Adolescents' fright reactions to television and films. *Journal of Communication, 32*(1), 87–99.

Chall, J. S. (1983). *Stages of reading development.* New York: McGraw-Hill.

Charters, W. W. (1933). *Motion pictures and youth: A summary.* New York: Macmillan.

Childs, J. H. (1979). *Television viewing, achievement, IQ, and creativity.* Unpublished doctoral dissertation, Brigham Young University, Provo, UT.

Christakis, D. A., Zimmerman, F. J., DiGiuseppe, D. L., & McCarty, C. A. (2004). Early television exposure and subsequent attention problems in children. *Pediatrics, 113*(4), 708–714.

Christenson, P. (1992). The effect of parental advisory labels on adolescent music preferences. *Journal of Communication, 42*(1), 106–113.

Cline, V. B., Croft, R. G., & Courrier, S. (1973). Desensitization of children to television violence. *Journal of Personality and Social Psychology, 27*(3), 360–365.

Cohen, J. (1988). *Statistical power analysis for the behavioral sciences* (2nd ed.). Hillsdale, NJ: Erlbaum.

Comstock, G. (1991a). *Television and the American child.* San Diego: Academic Press.

Comstock, G. (1991b). *Television in America* (2nd ed.). Newbury Park, CA: Sage.

Comstock, G. (2004). Paths from television violence to aggression: Reinterpreting the evidence. In L. J. Shrum (Ed.), *Blurring the lines: The psychology of entertainment media* (pp. 193–211). Mahwah, NJ: Erlbaum.

Comstock, G., Chaffee, S., Katzman, N., McCombs, M., & Roberts, D. (1978). *Television and human behavior.* New York: Columbia University Press.

Comstock, G., & Scharrer, E. (1999). *Television: What's on, who's watching, and what it means.* San Diego: Academic Press.

Comstock, G., & Scharrer, E. (2001). The use of television and other film-related media. In D. G. Singer & J. L. Singer (Eds.), *Handbook of children and the media* (pp. 47–72). Thousand Oaks, CA: Sage.

Comstock, G., & Scharrer, E. (2003). Meta-analyzing the controversy over television violence and aggression. In D. A. Gentile (Ed.), *Media violence and children* (pp. 205–226). Westport, CT: Praeger.

Comstock, G. A., Rubinstein, E. A., & Murray, J. P. (Eds.). (1972a). *Television and adolescent aggressiveness* (Vol. 3). Washington, DC: U.S. Government Printing Office.

Comstock, G. A., Rubinstein, E. A., & Murray, J. P. (Eds.). (1972b). *Television and social behavior: Vol. 1. Media content and control.* Washington, DC: U.S. Government Printing Office.

Comstock, G. A., Rubinstein, E. A., & Murray, J. P. (Eds.). (1972c). *Television and social learning* (Vol. 2). Washington, DC: U.S. Government Printing Office.

Comstock, G. A., Rubinstein, E. A., & Murray, J. P. (Eds.). (1972d). *Television in day-to-day life: Vol. 4. Patterns of use.* Washington, DC: U.S. Government Printing Office.

Comstock, G. A., Rubinstein, E. A., & Murray, J. P. (Eds.). (1972e). *Television's effects: Vol. 5. Further explorations.* Washington, DC: U.S. Government Printing Office.

Condry, J. (1989). *The psychology of television.* Hillsdale, NJ: Erlbaum.

Cook, T. D., Appleton, H., Conner, R. F., Shaffer, A., Tamkin, G., & Weber, S. J. (1975). *"Sesame Street" revisited.* New York: Russell Sage.

Cook, T. D., & Campbell, D. T. (1979). *Quasi-experimentation: Design and analysis issues for field settings.* Chicago: Houghton Mifflin.

Cook, T. D., Kendzierski, D. A., & Thomas, S. A. (1983). The implicit assumptions of television research: An analysis of the 1982 NIMH report on television and behavior. *Public Opinion Quarterly, 47*(2), 161–201.

Cooper, C. A. (1996). *Violence on television: Congressional inquiry, public criticism, and industry response.* Lanham, MD: University Press of America.

Cooper, H. (1989). *Homework.* New York: Longman.

Cope, K. M. (1998). *Sexually-related talk and behavior in the shows most frequently viewed by adolescents.* Unpublished master's thesis, University of California, Santa Barbara.

Crespo, C., Smit, E., Troiano, R., Bartlett, S., Macera, C., & Anderson, R. (2001). Television watching, energy intake, and obesity in U.S. children. *Archives of Pediatrics and Adolescent Medicine, 155,* 360–365.

DeBell, M., & Chapman, C. (2003). *Computer and Internet use by children and adolescents in 2001* (National Center for Education Statistics). Washington, DC: U.S. Department of Education.

DeFleur, M. L., & DeFleur, L. B. (1967). The relative contribution of television as a learning source for children's occupational knowledge. *American Sociological Review, 32,* 777–789.

Dietz, T. (1998). An examination of violence and gender role depictions in video games: Implications for gender socialization and aggressive behavior. *Sex Roles, 38,* 425–441.

Dietz, W., & Gortmaker, S. (1985). Do we fatten our children at the TV set? Obesity and television viewing in children and adolescents. *Pediatrics, 75,* 807–812.

Donnerstein, E., Linz, D., & Penrod, S. (1987). *The question of pornography: Research findings and policy implications.* New York: Free Press.

Drabman, R. S., & Thomas, M. H. (1974). Does media violence increase children's tolerance of real-life aggression? *Developmental Psychology, 10*(3), 418–421.

Eastin, M. S. (2001). The onset of the age-based and content-based ratings system: History, pressure groups, Congress, and the FCC. In B. S. Greenberg (Ed.), *The alphabet soup of television program ratings* (pp. 1–18). Cresskill, NJ: Hampton Press.

Eron, L. D., & Huesmann, L. R. (1987). Television as a source of maltreatment of children. *School Psychology Review, 16*(2), 195–202.

Eron, L. D., Huesmann, L. R., Brice, P., & Mermelstein, R. (1983). Age trends in the development of aggression, sex typing, and related television habits. *Developmental Psychology, 19*(1), 71–77.

Federal Trade Commission. (1978). *FTC staff report on television advertising to children.* Washington, DC: Author.

Federal Trade Commission. (1981). *In the matter of children's advertising: FTC final staff report and recommendation.* Washington, DC: Author.

Fein, G. G. (1981). Pretend play in childhood: An integrative review. *Child Development, 52,* 1095–1118.

Feshbach, S., & Singer, R. D. (1971). *Television and aggression: An experimental field study.* San Francisco: Jossey-Bass.

Fetler, M. (1984). Television viewing and school achievement. *Journal of Communication, 34*(2), 104–118.

Fiore, M. C., Smith, S. S., Jorenby, D. E., & Baker, T. B. (1994). The effectiveness of the nicotine patch for smoking cessation. *Journal of the American Medical Association, 271,* 1940–1947.

Fisch, S. M., & Truglio, R. T. (2001). *"G" is for growing: Thirty years of research on children and Sesame Street.* Mahwah, NJ: Erlbaum.

Foehr, U. G., Rideout, V., & Miller, C. (2001). Parents and the TV ratings system: A national study. In B. S. Greenberg (Ed.), *The alphabet soup of television program ratings* (pp. 195–216). Cresskill, NJ: Hampton Press.

Fraczek, A. (1986). Socio-cultural environment, television viewing, and the development of aggression among children in Poland. In L. R. Huesmann & L. D. Eron (Eds.), *Television and the aggressive child: A cross-national comparison* (pp. 119–159). Hillsdale, NJ: Erlbaum.

French, J., & Penna, S. (1991). Children's hero play of the twentieth century: Changes resulting from television's influence. *Child Study Journal, 21*(2), 79–94.

Friedrich-Cofer, L. K., Huston-Stein, A., McBride Kipnis, D., Susman, E. J., & Clewett, A. S. (1979). Environmental enhancement of prosocial television content: Effects on interpersonal behavior, imaginative play, and self-regulation in a natural setting. *Developmental Psychology, 15*(4), 637–646.

Gadberry, S. (1980). Effects of restricting first graders' TV viewing on leisure time use, IQ change, and cognitive style. *Journal of Applied Developmental Psychology, 1*(1), 161–176.

Gaddy, G. D. (1986). Television's impact on high school achievement. *Public Opinion Quarterly, 50*(3), 340–359.

Galst, J. P. (1980). Television food commercials and pronutritional public service announcements as determinants of young children's snack choices. *Child Development, 51,* 935–938.

Galst, J. P., & White, M. A. (1976). The unhealthy persuader: The reinforcing value of television and children's purchase attempts at the supermarket. *Child Development, 47*(4), 1089–1096.

Geen, R. G., & Stonner, D. (1972). Context effects in observed violence. *Journal of Personality and Social Psychology, 25*(2), 145–150.

Gentile, D. A., & Anderson, C. A. (2003). Violent video games: The newest media violence hazard. In D. A. Gentile (Ed.), *Media violence and children: A complete guide for parents and professionals* (pp. 131–152). Westport, CT: Praeger.

Gentile, D. A., Humphrey, J., & Walsh, D. A. (2004). *Media ratings for movies, music, video games, and television: A review of the research and recommendations for improvements.* Manuscript under review.

Gentile, D. A., Lynch, P. J., Linder, J. R., & Walsh, D. A. (2004). The effects of violent video game habits on adolescent hostility, aggressive behaviors, and school performance. *Journal of Adolescence, 27,* 5–22.

Gentner, D. (1975). Evidence for the psychological reality of semantic components: The verbs of possession. In D. Norman & D. Rumelhart (Eds.), *Explorations in cognition* (pp. 211–246). San Francisco: Freeman.

Gerbner, G., Gross, L., Morgan, M., & Signorielli, N. (1980). The "mainstreaming" of America. *Journal of Communication, 30*(3), 10–29.

Gerbner, G., Gross, L., Morgan, M., Signorielli, N., & Shanahan, J. (2002). Growing up with television: Cultivation process. In J. Bryant & D. Zillmann (Eds.), *Media effects: Advances in theory and research* (2nd ed., pp. 43–67). Mahwah, NJ: Erlbaum.

Goldberg, M. E., Gorn, G. J., & Gibson, W. (1978). TV messages for snacks and breakfast foods: Do they influence children's preferences? *Journal of Consumer Research, 5*(2), 73–81.

Gorn, G. J., & Goldberg, M. E. (1982). Behavioral evidence of the effects of televised food messages on children. *Journal of Consumer Research, 9,* 200–205.

Gortmaker, S., Must, A., Sobol, A., Peterson, K., Colditz, S., & Dietz, W. (1996). Television viewing as a cause of increasing obesity among children in the United States. *Archives of Pediatric and Adolescent Medicine, 150,* 356–362.

Gortmaker, S. L., Salter, C. A., Walker, D. K., & Dietz, W. H. (1990). The impact of television viewing on mental aptitude and achievement: A longitudinal study. *Public Opinion Quarterly, 54*(4), 594–604.

Greenberg, B. S. (2001). Preface. In B. S. Greenberg (Ed.), *The alphabet soup of television program ratings* (pp. ix–xiii). Cresskill, NJ: Hampton Press.

Greenberg, B. S., Eastin, M. S., & Mastro, D. (2001). Comparing the on-air ratings with the published ratings: Who to believe. In B. S. Greenberg (Ed.), *The alphabet soup of television program ratings* (pp. 39–50). Cresskill, NJ: Hampton Press.

Greenberg, B. S., & Rampoldi-Hnilo, L. (2001). Young people's responses to the content-based ratings. In B. S. Greenberg (Ed.), *The alphabet soup of television program ratings* (pp. 117–138). Cresskill, NJ: Hampton Press.

Greenberg, B. S., Rampoldi-Hnilo, L., & Hofschire, L. (2001). Young people's responses to the age-based ratings. In B. S. Greenberg (Ed.), *The alphabet soup of television program ratings* (pp. 83–116). Cresskill, NJ: Hampton Press.

Greenfield, P., & Beagles-Roos, J. (1988). Television versus radio: The cognitive impact on different socio-economic and ethnic groups. *Journal of Communication, 38*(2), 71–92.

Greenfield, P., Farrar, D., & Beagles-Roos, J. (1986). Is the medium the message? An experimental comparison of the effects of radio and television on imagination. *Journal of Applied Developmental Psychology, 7*(3), 201–218.

Greer, D., Potts, R., Wright, J., & Huston, A. (1982). The effects of television commercial form and commercial placement on children's social behavior and attention. *Child Development, 53,* 611–619.

Gruenwald, J. (1997). Critics say TV rating system doesn't tell the whole story. *Congressional Quarterly, 55,* 424–425.

Hamilton, J. T. (1998). *Channeling violence: The economic market for violent television programming.* Princeton, NJ: Princeton University Press.

Hart, L. R. (1972). *Immediate effects of exposure to filmed cartoon aggression on boys.* Unpublished doctoral dissertation, Emory University, Atlanta, GA.

Harwood, J. (1997). Viewing age: Lifespan identity and television viewing choices. *Journal of Broadcasting and Electronic Media, 41*(2), 203–213.

Hawkins, J. D., Herrenkohl, T. L., Farrington, D. P., Brewer, D., Catalano, R. F., & Harachi, T. W. (1998). A review of predictors of youth violence. In R. Loeber & D. P. Farrington (Eds.), *Serious and violent juvenile offenders: Risk factors and successful interventions* (pp. 106–146). Thousand Oaks, CA: Sage.

Hawkins, R. P., & Pingree, S. (1980). Some processes in the cultivation effect. *Communication Research, 7,* 193–226.

Hawkins, R. P., & Pingree, S. (1982). Television's influence on social reality. In D. Pearl, L. Bouthilet, & J. Lazar (Eds.), *Television and behavior—Ten years of scientific progress and implications for the 1980s: Vol. 2. Technical reviews* (pp. 224–247). Rockville, MD: National Institute of Mental Health.

Hawkins, R. P., & Pingree, S. (1990). Divergent psychological processes in constructing social reality from mass media content. In N. Signorielli & M. Morgan (Eds.), *Cultivation analysis: New directions in media effects research* (pp. 35–50). Newbury Park, CA: Sage.

Hawkins, R. P., Pingree, S., & Adler, I. (1987). Searching for cognitive processes in the cultivation effect: Adult and adolescent samples in the United States and Australia. *Human Communication Research, 13*(4), 553–577.

Head, S. W. (1954). Content analysis of television drama programs. *Quarterly Journal of Film, Radio and Television, 9*(2), 175–194.

Hearold, S. (1986). A synthesis of 1,043 effects of television on social behavior. In G. Comstock (Ed.), *Public communication and behavior* (Vol.1, pp. 65–133). New York: Academic Press.

Henderson, R. W., & Rankin, R. J. (1986). Preschoolers' viewing of instructional television. *Journal of Educational Psychology, 78*(1), 44–51.

Heyns, B. (1976). *Television: Exposure and the effects on schooling.* Washington, DC: National Institute of Education.

Hill, D., White, V., Jolley, D., & Mapperson, K. (1988). Self examination of the breast: Is it beneficial? Meta-analysis of studies investigating breast self examination and extent of disease in patients with breast cancer. *British Medical Journal, 297,* 271–275.

Himmelweit, H. T., Oppenheim, A. N., & Vince, P. (1958). *Television and the child.* London: Oxford University Press.

Hofman, R. J., & Flook, M. A. (1980). An experimental investigation of the role of television in facilitating shape recognition. *Journal of Genetic Psychology, 136,* 305–306.

Hogben, M. (1998). Factors moderating the effect of television aggression on viewer behavior. *Communication Research, 25,* 220–247.

Hollenbeck, A., & Slaby, R. (1979). Infant visual and vocal responses to television. *Child Development, 50,* 41–45.

Hu, F. B., Li, T. Y., Colditz, G. A., Willett, W. C., & Manson, J. E. (2003). Television watching and other sedentary behaviors in relation to risk of obesity and Type 2 diabetes mellitus in women. *Journal of the American Medical Association, 289*(14), 1785–1792.

Huesmann, L. R. (1986). Psychological processes promoting the relation between exposure to media violence and aggressive behavior by the viewer. *Journal of Social Issues, 42*(3), 125–140.

Huesmann, L. R. (1998). The role of social information processing and cognitive schemas in the acquisition and maintenance of habitual aggressive behavior. In R. G. Geen & E. Donnerstein (Eds.), *Human aggression: Theories, research, and implications for policy* (pp. 73–109). New York: Academic Press.

Huesmann, L. R., & Eron, L. D. (Eds.). (1986). *Television and the aggressive child: A cross-national comparison.* Hillsdale, NJ: Erlbaum.

Huesmann, L. R., Eron, L. D., Lefkowitz, M. M., & Walder, L. O. (1984). The stability of aggression over time and generations. *Developmental Psychology, 20*(6), 1120–1134.

Huesmann, L. R., Moise-Titus, J., Podolski, C. L., & Eron, L. D. (2003). Longitudinal relations between children's exposure to TV violence and their aggressive and violent behavior in young adulthood: 1977–1992. *Developmental Psychology, 39*(2), 201–222.

Hughes, M. (1980). The fruits of cultivation analysis: A reexamination of the effects of television watching on fear of victimization, alienation, and the approval of violence. *Public Opinion Quarterly, 44*(3), 287–302.

Hunt, M. (1997). *How science takes stock.* New York: Russell Sage.

Huston, A., Wright, J. C., Rice, M. L., Kerkman, D., Siegle, J., & Bremer, M. (1983, April). *Family environment and television use by preschool children.* Paper presented at the biennial meeting of the Society for Research in Child Development, Detroit, MI.

Huston, A., Wright, J. C., Rice, M. L., Kerkman, D., & St. Peters, M. (1990). Development of television viewing patterns in early childhood: A longitudinal investigation. *Developmental Psychology, 26*(3), 409–420.

Huston-Stein, A., Fox, S., Greer, D., Watkins, B. A., & Whitaker, J. (1981). The effects of action and violence on children's social behavior. *Journal of Genetic Psychology, 138,* 183–191.

Isler, L., Popper, E. T., & Ward, S. (1987). Children's purchase requests and parental responses: Results from a diary study. *Journal of Advertising Research, 27*(5), 28–39.

Jakes, R. W., Day, N., Khaw, K. T., Luben, R., Oakes, S., Welch, A., et al. (2003). Television viewing and low participation in vigorous recreation are independently associated with obesity and markers of cardiovascular disease risk: EPIC-Norfolk population-based study. *European Journal of Clinical Nutrition, 57*(9), 1089–1097.

John, D. R. (1999). Consumer socialization of children: A retrospective look at 25 years of research. *Journal of Consumer Research, 26,* 183–213.

Johnson, J. G., Cohen, P., Smailes, E. M., Kasen, S., & Brook J. S. (2002). Television viewing and aggressive behavior during adolescence and adulthood. *Science, 295,* 2468–2471.

Kaiser Family Foundation. (1999, May 10). *Parents and the V-chip: A Kaiser Family Foundation survey.* Retrieved 10/25/2005 from http://www.kff.org/entmedia/1477-index.cfm.

Kang, N. (1990). *A critique and secondary analysis of the NBC study on television and aggression.* Unpublished doctoral dissertation, Syracuse University, Syracuse, NY.

Keith, T. Z., Reimers, T. M., Fehrmann, P. G., Pottebaum, S. M., & Aubey, L. W. (1986). Parental involvement, homework, and TV time: Direct and indirect effects on high school achievement. *Journal of Educational Psychology, 78*(5), 373–380.

Kelly, A. E., & Spear, P. S. (1991). Intraprogram synopses for children's comprehension of television content. *Journal of Experimental Child Psychology, 52,* 87–98.

Kerns, T. Y. (1981). Television: A bisensory bombardment that stifles children's creativity. *Phi Delta Kappan, 62,* 456–457.

Kirsch, S. J. (1998). Seeing the world through *Mortal Kombat*-colored glasses: Violent video games and the development of a short-term hostile attribution bias. *Childhood, 5,* 177–184.

Koolstra, C. M., & van der Voort, T. H. A. (1996). Longitudinal effects of television on children's leisure-time reading: A test of three explanatory models. *Human Communication Research, 23*(1), 4–35.

Kotler, J. A., Wright, J. C., & Huston, A. C. (2001). Television use in families with children. In J. Bryant & J. A. Bryant (Eds.), *Television and the American family* (2nd ed., pp. 33–48). Mahwah, NJ: Erlbaum.

Kotz, K., & Story, M. (1994). Food advertisements during children's Saturday morning television programming: Are they consistent with dietary recommendations? *Journal of the American Dietary Association, 94,* 1296–1300.

Kubey, R. W., & Csikszentmihalyi, M. (1990). *Television and the quality of life: How viewing shapes everyday experience.* Hillsdale, NJ: Erlbaum.

Kunkel, D. (1998). Policy battles over defining children's educational television. *Annals of the American Academy of Political and Social Science, 557,* 39–54.

Kunkel, D. (2001). Children and television advertising. In D. Singer & J. Singer (Eds.), *Handbook of children and the media* (pp. 375–393). Thousand Oaks, CA: Sage.

Kunkel, D., & Canepa, J. (1994). Broadcasters' license renewal claims regarding children's educational programming. *Journal of Broadcasting and Electronic Media, 38,* 397–416.

Kunkel, D., Cope, K. M., & Colvin, C. (1996). *Sexual messages on family hour television: Content and context.* Menlo Park, CA: Kaiser Family Foundation.

Kunkel, D., Cope-Farrar, K. M., Biely, E., Farinola, W. J. M., & Donnerstein, E. (2001, May). *Sex on TV: Comparing content trends from 1997–1998 to 1999–2000.* Paper presented at the annual meeting of the International Communication Association, Washington, DC.

Kunkel, D., Farinola, W. J. M., Cope, K. M., Donnerstein, E., Biely, E., & Zwarun, L. (1998). *Rating the TV ratings: One year out.* Menlo Park, CA: Kaiser Family Foundation.

Kunkel, D., Farinola, W. J. M., Cope, K. M., Donnerstein, E., Biely, E., Zwarun, L., et al. (2001). Assessing the validity of V-chip rating judgments: The labeling of high-risk programs. In B. S. Greenberg (Ed.), *The alphabet soup of television program ratings* (pp. 51–68). Cresskill, NJ: Hampton Press.

Kunkel, D., & Goette, U. (1997). Broadcasters' response to the Children's Television Act. *Communication Law and Policy, 2,* 289–308.

Kunkel, D., & Watkins, B. (1987). Evolution of children's television regulatory policy. *Journal of Broadcasting and Electronic Media, 31,* 367–389.

Kunkel, D., & Wilcox, B. (2001). Children and media policy. In D. G. Singer & J. L. Singer (Eds.), *Handbook of children and the media* (pp. 589–604). Thousand Oaks, CA: Sage.

Lenhart, A., Rainie, L., & Lewis, O. (2001, June). *Teenage life online: The rise of the instant message generation and the Internet's impact on friendships and family relationships.* Washington, DC: Pew Foundation.

Lesser, G. S. (1974). *Children and television: Lessons from "Sesame Street."* New York: Random House.

Levin, S. R., Petros, T. V., & Petrella, F. W. (1982). Preschoolers' awareness of television advertising. *Child Development, 53*(4), 933–937.

Linz, D., Donnerstein, E., & Adams, S. M. (1989). Physiological desensitization and judgments about female victims of violence. *Human Communication Research, 15*(4), 509–522.

Lipsey, M. W., & Derzon, J. H. (1998). Predictors of violent and serious delinquency in adolescence and early adulthood: A synthesis of longitudinal research. In R. Loeber & D. P. Farrington (Eds.), *Serious and violent juvenile offenders: Risk factors and successful interventions* (pp. 86–105). Thousand Oaks, CA: Sage.

Livingstone, S. (2002). *Young people and new media: Childhood and the changing media environment.* London: Sage.

Livingstone, S., & Bovill, M. (1999). *Young people, new media: Final report of the project "Children, young people and the changing media environment"* (An LSE report). London: London School of Economics and Political Science.

Lowry, R., Wechsler, H., Galuska, D., Fulton, J., & Kann, L. (2002). Television viewing and its association with overweight, sedentary lifestyle, and insufficient consumption of fruits and vegetables among U.S. high school students: Differences in race, ethnicity, and gender. *Journal of School Health, 72*(10), 413–421.

Lyle, J., & Hoffman, H. R. (1972a). Children's use of television and other media. In E. A. Rubinstein, G. A. Comstock, & J. P. Murray (Eds.), *Television and social behavior: Vol. 4. Television in day-to-day life—Patterns of use* (pp. 129–256). Washington, DC: U.S. Government Printing Office.

Lyle, J., & Hoffman, H. R. (1972b). Explorations in patterns of television viewing by preschool-age children. In E. A. Rubinstein, G. A. Comstock, & J. P. Murray (Eds.), *Television and social behavior: Vol. 4. Television in day-to-day life—Patterns of use* (pp. 257–273). Washington, DC: U.S. Government Printing Office.

Maccoby, E. E. (1951). Television: Its impact on school children. *Public Opinion Quarterly, 15*(3), 421–444.

Maccoby, E. E. (1954). Why do children watch television? *Public Opinion Quarterly, 18*(3), 239–244.

Maccoby, E. E., & Wilson, W. C. (1957). Identification and observational learning from films. *Journal of Abnormal and Social Psychology, 55,* 76–87.

Maccoby, E. E., Wilson, W. C., & Burton, R. V. (1958). Differential movie-viewing behavior of male and female viewers. *Journal of Personality, 26,* 259–267.

Macklin, M. C. (1988). The relationship between music in advertising and children's responses: An experimental investigation.

In S. Hecker & D. Stewart (Eds.), *Nonverbal communication in advertising* (pp. 225–243). Lexington, MA: Lexington Books/D. C. Heath.

McDowell, S. D., & Maitland, C. (1998). The V-chip in Canada and the United States: Themes and variations in design and employment. *Journal of Broadcasting and Electronic Media, 42*(4), 401–422.

McIlwraith, R. D., Jacobvitz, R. S., Kubey, R., & Alexander, A. (1991). Television addiction: Theories and data behind the ubiquitous metaphor. *American Behavioral Scientist, 35*(2), 104–121.

McIlwraith, R. D., & Josephson, W. L. (1985). Movies, books, music, and adult fantasy life. *Journal of Communication, 35*(2), 167–179.

McIlwraith, R. D., & Schallow, J. (1982–1983). Television viewing and styles of children's fantasy. *Imagination, Cognition and Personality, 2*(4), 323–331.

Medrich, E. A., Roizen, J., Rubin, V., & Buckley, S. (1982). *The serious business of growing up: A study of children's lives outside of school.* Los Angeles: University of California Press.

Meline, C. W. (1976). Does the medium matter? *Journal of Communication, 26*(3), 81–89.

Meringoff, L. K. (1980). The effects of children's television food advertising. In R. P. Adler, G. S. Lesser, L. K. Meringoff, T. S. Robertson, J. R. Rossiter, & S. Ward (Eds.), *The effects of television advertising on children: Review and recommendations* (pp. 123–152). Lexington, MA: Lexington Books.

Milavsky, J. R., Kessler, R., Stipp, H. H., & Rubens, W. S. (1982). *Television and aggression: A panel study.* New York: Academic Press.

Mitchell, K. J., Finkelhor, D., & Wolak, J. (2003). The exposure of youth to unwanted sexual material on the Internet: A national survey of risk, impact, and prevention. *Youth and Society, 34*(3), 330–359.

Montgomery, K. C. (2001). Digital kids: The new on-line children's consumer culture. In D. G. Singer & J. L. Singer (Eds.), *Handbook of children and the media* (pp. 635–650). Thousand Oaks, CA: Sage.

Morgan, M. (1980). Television viewing and reading: Does more equal better? *Journal of Communication, 30*(1), 159–165.

Morgan, M. (1989). Cultivation analysis. In E. Barnouw (Ed.), *International encyclopedia of communication* (Vol. 3, pp. 430–433). New York: Oxford University Press.

Morgan, M., & Gross, L. (1982). Television and educational achievement and aspiration. In D. Pearl, L. Bouthilet, & J. Lazar (Eds.), *Television and behavior: Vol. 2. Ten years of scientific progress and implications for the eighties—Technical reviews* (pp. 78–90). Washington, DC: U.S. Government Printing Office.

Murray, J. P., & Kippax, S. (1978). Children's social behavior in three towns with differing television experience. *Journal of Communication, 28*(4), 19–29.

Naigles, L. R., & Mayeux, L. (2001). Television as incidental language teacher. In D. G. Singer & J. L. Singer (Eds.), *Handbook of children and the media* (pp. 135–152). Thousand Oaks, CA: Sage.

National Commission on the Causes and Prevention of Violence. (1969). *Final report.* Washington, DC: U.S. Government Printing Office.

National Television Violence Study (Vol. 1). (1997). Thousand Oaks, CA: Sage.

National Television Violence Study (Vol. 2). (1998a). Thousand Oaks, CA: Sage.

National Television Violence Study (Vol. 3). (1998b). Thousand Oaks, CA: Sage.

Needleman, H. L., & Gatsonis, C. A. (1990). Low-level lead exposure and the IQ of children. *Journal of the American Medical Association, 263,* 673–678.

Neuman, S. B. (1988). The displacement effect: Assessing the relation between television viewing and reading performance. *Reading Research Quarterly, 23*(4), 414–440.

Neuman, S. B. (1991). *Literacy in the television age.* Norwood, NJ: Ablex.

Newburger, E. C. (2001, September). *Home computers and Internet use in the United States: August 2000* (P23–207). Washington, DC: U.S. Census Bureau.

Noble, G. (1970). Film-mediated aggressive and creative play. *British Journal of Social and Clinical Psychology, 9*(1), 1–7.

Noble, G. (1973). Effects of different forms of filmed aggression on children's constructive and destructive play. *Journal of Personality and Social Psychology, 26*(1), 54–59.

Obel, C., Henriksen, T. B., Dalsgaard, S., Linnet, K. M., Skajaa, E., Thomsen, P. H., et al. (2004). Does children's watching of television cause attention problems? Retesting the hypothesis in a Danish cohort [Letter to the editor]. *Pediatrics, 114*(5), 1372–1375.

Paik, H., & Comstock, G. (1994). The effects of television violence on antisocial behavior: A meta-analysis. *Communication Research, 21*(4), 516–546.

Pearl, D., Bouthilet, L., & Lazar, J. (Eds.). (1982a). *Television and behavior: Vol. 1. Ten years of scientific progress and implications for the eighties—Summary report.* Washington, DC: U.S. Government Printing Office.

Pearl, D., Bouthilet, L., & Lazar, J. (Eds.). (1982b). *Television and behavior: Vol. 2. Ten years of scientific progress and implications for the eighties—Technical reviews.* Washington, DC: U.S. Government Printing Office.

Pecora, N. O. (1998). *The business of children's entertainment.* New York: Guilford Press.

Peterson, C. C., Peterson, J. L., & Carroll, J. (1987). Television viewing and imaginative problem solving during preadolescence. *Journal of Genetic Psychology, 147*(1), 61–67.

Pingree, S., & Hawkins, R. P. (1981). United States programs on Australian television: The cultivation effect. *Journal of Communication, 31*(1), 24–35.

Pool, M. M., van der Voort, T. H. A., Beentjes, J. W. J., & Koolstra, C. M. (2000). Background television as an inhibitor of performance on easy and difficult homework assignments. *Communication Research, 27*(3), 293–326.

Potts, R., & Sanchez, D. (1994). Television viewing and depression: No news is good news. *Journal of Broadcasting and Electronic Media, 38*(1), 79–90.

Potts, W. J., Huston, A. C., & Wright, J. C. (1986). The effects of television form and violent content on boys' attention and social behavior. *Journal of Experimental Child Psychology, 41*(1), 1–17.

Price, M. E. (Ed.). (1998). *The V-chip debate: Content filtering from television to the Internet.* Mahwah, NJ: Erlbaum.

Proctor, M., Moore, L., Gao, D., Cupples, L., Bradlee, M., Hood, M., et al. (2003). Television viewing and change in body fat from preschool to early adolescence: Framingham Children's Study. *International Journal of Obesity, 27,* 827–833.

Rice, M. L., Huston, A. C., Truglio, R., & Wright, J. C. (1990). Words from "Sesame Street": Learning vocabulary while viewing. *Developmental Psychology, 26*(3), 421–428.

Rideout, V. J., Vandewater, E. A., & Wartella, E. A. (2003, October 28). *Zero to six: Electronic media in the lives of infants, toddlers and preschoolers* (A Kaiser Family Foundation Report). Menlo Park, CA: The Henry J. Kaiser Family Foundation. Retrieved October 30, 2003, from http://www.kff.org/entmedia/3378.cfm.

Roberts, D. F., & Foehr, U. G. (2004). *Kids and media in America.* New York: Cambridge University Press.

Robinson, J. P., & Godbey, G. (1997). *Time for life: The surprising ways Americans use their time.* University Park: Pennsylvania State University Press.

Roper Starch Worldwide Inc. (1999). *America Online/Roper Starch Youth Cyberstudy 1999.* New York: Author.

Rosengren, K. E., & Windahl, S. (1989). *Media matter: TV use in childhood and adolescence.* Norwood, NJ: Ablex.

Rosenthal, R. (1986). Media violence, antisocial behavior, and the social consequences of small effects. *Journal of Social Issues, 42*(3), 141–154.

Rosenthal, R., Rosnow, R. L., & Rubin, D. B. (2000). *Contrasts and effect sizes in behavioral research: A correlational approach.* New York: Cambridge University Press.

Ross, R. P., Campbell, T., Wright, J. C., Huston, A. C., Rice, M. L., & Turk, P. (1984). When celebrities talk, children listen: An experimental analysis of children's responses to TV ads with celebrity endorsement. *Journal of Applied Developmental Psychology, 5*(4), 185–202.

Rossiter, J. R., & Robertson, T. S. (1974). Children's TV commercials: Testing the defenses. *Journal of Communication, 24*(4), 137–144.

Rovet, J. (1983). The education of spatial transformations. In D. R. Olson & E. Bialystok (Eds.), *Spatial cognition: The structures and development of mental representations of spatial relations* (pp. 164–181). Hillsdale, NJ: Erlbaum.

Rubin, A. M. (1983). Television uses and gratifications: The interaction of viewing patterns and motivations. *Journal of Broadcasting, 27*(1), 37–51.

Rubin, A. M. (1984). Ritualized and instrumental television viewing. *Journal of Communication, 34*(3), 67–77.

Rubin, R. S. (1972). *An exploratory investigation of children's responses to commercial content of television advertising in relation to their stages of cognitive development.* Unpublished doctoral dissertation, University of Massachusetts, Amherst.

Runco, M., & Pezdek, K. (1984). The effect of television and radio on children's creativity. *Human Communication Research, 11*(1), 109–120.

Salomon, G. (1979). *Interaction of media, cognition and learning.* San Francisco: Jossey-Bass.

Schallow, J. R., & McIlwraith, R. D. (1986–1987). Is television viewing really bad for your imagination? Content and process of TV viewing and imaginal styles. *Imagination, Cognition and Personality, 6*(1), 25–42.

Scharrer, E. (2004). Virtual violence: Gender and aggression in video game advertisements. *Mass Communication and Society, 7*(4), 393–412.

Scharrer, E., & Comstock, G. (2003). Entertainment televisual media: Content patterns and themes. In E. Palmer & B. Young (Eds.), *Faces of televisual media* (pp. 161–194). Mahwah, NJ: Erlbaum.

Scharrer, E., Weidman, L. M., & Bissell, K. L. (2003). Pointing the finger of blame: News media coverage of popular-culture culpability. *Journalism and Communication Monographs, 5*(2), 49–98.

Schramm, W., Lyle, J., & Parker, E. B. (1961). *Television in the lives of our children.* Stanford, CA: Stanford University Press.

Sheehan, P. W. (1987). Coping with exposure to aggression: The path from research to practice. *Australian Psychologist, 22*(3), 291–311.

Sherry, J. L. (2001). The effects of violent video games on aggression: A meta-analysis. *Human Communication Research, 27*(3), 409–431.

Shimp, T., Dyer, R., & Divita, S. (1976). An experimental test of the harmful effects of premium-oriented commercials on children. *Journal of Consumer Research, 3*, 1–11.

Silvern, S. B., & Williamson, P. A. (1987). The effects of video game play on young children's aggression, fantasy, and prosocial behavior. *Journal of Applied Developmental Psychology, 8*(4), 453–462.

Singer, D. G., & Singer, J. L. (1990). *The house of make-believe.* Cambridge, MA: Harvard University Press.

Singer, D. G., & Singer, J. L. (Eds.). (2001). *Handbook of children and the media.* Thousand Oaks, CA: Sage.

Singer, J. L., & Singer, D. G. (1976). Can TV stimulate imaginative play? *Journal of Communication, 26*, 74–80.

Singer, J. L., & Singer, D. G. (1981). *Television, imagination, and aggression: A study of preschoolers.* Hillsdale, NJ: Erlbaum.

Singer, J. L., Singer, D. G., & Rapaczynski, W. S. (1984). Family patterns and television viewing as predictors of children's beliefs and aggression. *Journal of Communication, 34*(2), 73–89.

Slater, M. D., Henry, K. L., Swaim, R., & Anderson, L. (2003). Violent media content and aggression: A downward-spiral model. *Communication Research, 30*(6), 713–736.

Smith, A. H., Handley, M. A., & Wood, R. (1990). Epidemiological evidence indicates asbestos causes laryngeal cancer. *Journal of Occupational Medicine, 32*, 449–507.

Smith, S., Wilson, B., Kunkel, D., Linz, D., Potter, W. J., Colvin, C., et al. (1998). *National Television Violence Study: Vol. 3. Violence in television programming overall.* Thousand Oaks, CA: Sage.

Smith, S. L., Lachlan, K., & Tamborini, R. (2003). Popular video games: Quantifying the presentation of violence and its context. *Journal of Broadcasting and Electronic Media, 47*(1), 58–76.

Smythe, D. W. (1954). Reality as presented by television. *Public Opinion Quarterly, 18*(2), 143–156.

Sprafkin, J. N., & Liebert, R. M. (1978). Sex-typing and children's preferences. In G. Tuchman, A. K. Daniels, & J. Benet (Eds.), *Hearth and home: Images of women in the mass media* (pp. 288–339). New York: Oxford University Press.

Stern, S. L. (1973). *Television and creativity: The effect of viewing certain categories of commercial television broadcasting on the divergent thinking abilities of intellectually gifted elementary students.* Unpublished doctoral dissertation, University of Southern California, Los Angeles.

Stoneman, Z., & Brody, G. H. (1981). Peers as mediators of television food advertisements aimed at children. *Developmental Psychology, 17*(6), 853–858.

Story, M., & French, S. (2004). Food advertising and marketing directed at children and adolescents in the U.S. *International Journal of Behavioral Nutrition and Physical Activity, 1*, 3. Retrieved January 13, 2005, from http://www.ijbnpa.org/content/1/1/3.

Surgeon General's Scientific Advisory Committee on Television and Social Behavior. (1972). *Television and growing up: The impact of televised violence* (Report to the surgeon general, U.S. Public Health Service). Washington, DC: U.S. Government Printing Office.

Tan, A., Fujioka, Y., Bautista, D., Maldonado, R., Tan, G., & Wright, L. (2000). Influence of television use and parental communication on educational aspirations of Hispanic children. *Howard Journal of Communications, 11*, 107–125.

Tangney, J. P., & Feshbach, S. (1988). Children's television viewing frequency: Individual differences and demographic correlates. *Personality and Social Psychology Bulletin, 14*, 145–158.

Taras, H. L., & Gage, M. (1995). Advertised foods on children's television. *Archives of Pediatric Adolescent Medicine, 149*, 649–652.

Tarpley, T. (2001). Children, the Internet, and other new technologies. In D. G. Singer & J. L. Singer (Eds.), *Handbook of children and the media* (pp. 547–556). Thousand Oaks, CA: Sage.

Thomas, M. H., Horton, R. W., Lippencott, E. C., & Drabman, R. S. (1977). Desensitization to portrayals of real-life aggression as a function of exposure to television violence. *Journal of Personality and Social Psychology, 35,* 450–458.

Thompson, K. M., & Haninger, K. (2001). Violence in E-rated video games. *Journal of the American Medical Association, 286*(5), 591–598.

Thornton, W., & Voigt, L. (1984). Television and delinquency. *Youth and Society, 15*(4), 445–468.

Tower, R., Singer, D., Singer, J., & Biggs, A. (1979). Differential effects of television programming on preschoolers' cognition, imagination and social play. *American Journal of Orthopsychiatry, 49*(2), 265–281.

Tyler, T. R. (1980). The impact of directly and indirectly experienced events: The origin of crime-related judgments and behaviors. *Journal of Personality and Social Psychology, 39*(1), 13–28.

Tyler, T. R. (1984). Assessing the risk of crime victimization: The integration of personal victimization experience and socially-transmitted information. *Journal of Social Issues, 40*(1), 27–38.

U.S. Department of Health and Human Services. (2001). *Youth violence: A report of the surgeon general.* Rockville, MD: U.S. Department of Health and Human Services; Centers for Disease Control and Prevention, National Center for Injury Prevention and Control; Substance Abuse and Mental Health Services Administration, Center for Mental Health Services; and National Institutes of Health, National Institute of Mental Health.

Valkenburg, P. M. (2001). Television and the child's developing imagination. In D. G. Singer, & J. L. Singer (Eds.), *Handbook of children and the media* (pp. 121–134). Thousand Oaks, CA: Sage.

Valkenburg, P. M., & Beentjies, J. W. J. (1997). Children's creative imagination in response to radio and television stories. *Journal of Communication, 47*(2), 21–38.

Valkenburg, P. M., & van der Voort, T. H. A. (1994). Influence of TV on daydreaming and creative imagination: A review of research. *Psychological Bulletin, 116*(2), 316–339.

Valkenburg, P. M., & van der Voort, T. H. A. (1995). The influence of television on children's daydreaming styles: A one-year panel study. *Communication Research, 22*(3), 267–287.

Valkenburg, P. M., Voojis, M. W., van der Voort, T. H. A., & Wiegman, O. (1992). The influence of television on children's fantasy styles: A secondary analysis. *Imagination, Cognition and Personality, 12,* 55–67.

Valkenburg, P. M., & Vroone, M. (2004). Developmental changes in infants' and toddlers' attention to television entertainment. *Communication Research, 31*(1), 288–311.

Van Evra, J. (2004). *Television and child development* (3rd ed.). Mahwah, NJ: Erlbaum.

Vibbert, M. M., & Meringoff, L. K. (1981). *Children's production and application of story imagery: A cross-medium investigation.* Cambridge, MA: Harvard University Press.

Viemero, V., & Paajanen, S. (1992). The role of fantasies and dreams in the TV viewing: Aggression relationship. *Aggressive Behavior, 18*(2), 109–116.

Ward, S., & Wackman, D. B. (1972). Children's purchase influence attempts and parental yielding. *Journal of Marketing Research, 9,* 316–319.

Ward Gailey, C. (1993). Mediated messages: Gender, class, and cosmos in in-home video games. *Journal of Popular Culture, 27*(1), 81–97.

Wartella, E., & Ettema, J. (1974). A cognitive developmental study of children's attention to television commercials. *Communication Research, 1,* 69–88.

Wartella, E., & Hunter, L. (1983). Children and the formats of television advertising. In M. Meyer (Ed.), *Children and the formal features of television* (pp. 144–165). Munich, Germany: K. G. Saur.

Watkins, B. (1988). Children's representations of television and real-life stories. *Communication Research, 15*(2), 159–184.

Weller, S. C. (1993). A meta-analysis of condom effectiveness in reducing sexually transmitted HIV. *Social Science and Medicine, 36,* 1635–1644.

Wells, A. J. (1998). Lung cancer from passive smoking at work. *American Journal of Public Health, 88,* 1025–1029.

Wells, W. D., & LoScuito, L. A. (1966). Direct observation of purchasing behavior. *Journal of Marketing Research, 3,* 227–233.

Welten, D. C., Kemper, H. C. G., Post, G. B., & van Staveren, W. A. (1995). A meta-analysis of the effect of calcium intake on bone mass in young and middle aged females and males. *Journal of Nutrition, 125,* 2802–2813.

Wertham, F. (1954). *Seduction of the innocent.* New York: Rinehart.

Wigley, K., & Clarke, B. (2000). *Kids.net Wave 4.* London: National Opinion Poll Family.

Williams, T. M. (Ed.). (1986). *The impact of television: A natural experiment in three communities.* New York: Praeger.

Wilson, B., Kunkel, D., Linz, D., Potter, W. J., Donnerstein, E., Smith, S., et al. (1997). Violence in television programming overall. In Center for Communication and Social Policy, University of California, Santa Barbara (Ed.), *National Television Violence Study* (Vol. 1, pp. 3–268). Thousand Oaks, CA: Sage.

Wilson, B., Kunkel, D., Linz, D., Potter, W. J., Donnerstein, E., Smith, S., et al. (1998). Violence in television programming overall. In Center for Communication and Social Policy, University of California, Santa Barbara (Ed.), *National Television Violence Study* (Vol. 2, pp. 3–204). Thousand Oaks, CA: Sage.

Wolf, M. A. (1987). How children negotiate television. In T. R. Lindlof (Ed.), *Natural audiences: Qualitative research of media uses and effects* (pp. 58–94). Norwood, NJ: Ablex.

Wood, W., Wong, F., & Chachere, J. (1991). Effects of media violence on viewers' aggression in unconstrained social interaction. *Psychological Bulletin, 109*(3), 371–383.

Wright, J. D., & Huston, A. C. (1995). *Effects of educational TV viewing of lower income preschoolers on academic skills, school readiness, and school adjustment 1 to 3 years later* [Technical report]. Lawrence: University of Kansas.

Wynder, E. L., & Graham, E. A. (1950). Tobacco smoking as a possible etiological factor in bronchiogenic carcinoma. *Journal of the American Medical Association, 143,* 329–336.

Zill, N., Davies, E., & Daly, M. (1994). *Viewing of Sesame Street by preschool children in the United States and its relationship to school readiness* (Report prepared for Children's Television Workshop). Rockville, MD: Westat, Inc.

Zuckerman, D. M., Singer, D. G., & Singer, J. L. (1980). Television viewing, children's reading, and related classroom behavior. *Journal of Communication, 30*(1), 166–174.

Zuckerman, P., & Gianinno, L. (1981). Measuring children's responses to television advertising. In J. Esserman (Ed.), *Television advertising and children: Issues, research and findings* (pp. 83–93). New York: Child Research Service.

CHAPTER 21

Children's Health and Education

CRAIG T. RAMEY, SHARON LANDESMAN RAMEY, and ROBIN G. LANZI

Children's health and education can be facilitated by systematic supports that span traditional and innovative health care, health promotion, and disease prevention and that apply scientific principles about how young children learn and develop. Conversely, children's development can be impaired by disease and injury, nonoptimal lifestyle, the presence of multiple risk factors, and the failure to receive high-quality experiences to promote cognitive, social-emotional, and physical well-being.

During the past half-century, a new field has emerged—prevention developmental science (e.g., Bryant, Windle, & West, 1997; Coie et al., 1993)—that systematically integrates theories and methods from the broad fields of public health, psychology, medicine, sociology, and education to improve developmental outcomes for children at risk for a wide variety of poor outcomes in health and education. Exciting integrative advances in developmental neuroscience have conjoined with prevention science to fuel design and implementation of studies about the fundamental interconnectedness of children's health and education (e.g., C. T. Ramey & Ramey, 2004a; Teti, 2004). Indeed, many of the health disparities and inequities in children's educational attainment are likely the result of this complex interplay between health and education (e.g., Livingston, 2004).

David Satcher, 16th surgeon general of the United States and now director of the National Center for Primary Health Care at Morehouse School of Medicine, has used what is termed a health disparities lens to bring into focus the huge toll taken on the well-being of many individuals from historically marginalized and minority groups, especially children of color and children with disabilities. Satcher (2004, p. xxxi) summarized:

Although major progress has been made in reducing morbidity and mortality, as well as increasing the life expectancy among vulnerable and at-risk populations, such as African Americans, the ethnic divide continues to widen. As a matter of fact, in some cases it has even gotten worse! Because we are essentially dealing with the inherent complexities of human behavior on the micro or individual level, which are inextricably tied to ongoing factors and conditions at the macro or societal level, the reasons for the lack of more substantial improvements over the ensuring years are complex. . . . To suffice, however, it can be reasoned that increased vulnerability to adverse health among [targeted subgroups] is differentially mediated by various environmental factors and conditions. All of these factors and conditions serve to influence individuals' personal choices concerning health lifestyle choices; availability, accessibility, and acceptability of services; and, ultimately, impact negatively on their physiologic functioning, hence the current health disparities dilemma. At the risk of oversimplifying a complex situation, what is desperately needed at the macro level is health-care reform to guide the nation's policies and research agenda.

We concur that such health care reform is imperative, and argue further that the need for educational reform is equally compelling. Satcher's (2004) observations about vulnerability apply soundly to educational inequities as well as to health.

For more than 3 decades, we and many other developmental scientists have constructed broad conceptual frameworks that build on biological systems theory (e.g., Bertalanffy, 1975; Miller, 1978) and social ecology and Gestalt theory (e.g., Binder, 1972; Bronfenbrenner, 1977, 1979; Lewin, 1936, 1951; Stokols, 1992, 1996) and extended it to delineate social transactions (cf. Lewis, 1984; C. T. Ramey & Ramey, 1998a; Sameroff, 1983) that shape the course of individual development. These conceptual frameworks incorporate fundamental assumptions about the interconnectedness of the individual and the environment, biology and behavior, and the dynamic nature of changes over time. Similarly, developmental science has acknowledged that "dividing the child" into separate functional strands of development—such as perceptual, motor, cognitive, social, emotional, and physical growth—is largely arbitrary, based on historical disciplinary fields in which different aspects of human functioning were studied and treated. Today, the evidence compellingly supports the strong interdependencies among multiple domains (outcomes) of development; that is, a child's development is more aptly depicted as intertwined, overlapping, and codetermined by influences within and outside the child.

The historical disciplinary isolation in both academia and clinical and educational practices that serve children (e.g., education, pediatrics, psychiatry, social work, psychology, rehabilitation, nutrition, physical education) contributes to the lack of a common language and an acknowledged awkwardness in finding words to capture this more integrated transdisciplinary and biosocial perspective. Many developmental and biological scientists have demonstrated the inadequacy of simplistic nature-versus-nurture formulations of development (e.g., Borkowski, Ramey, & Bristol-Powers, 2002; Moser, Ramey, & Leonard, 1990; Shonkoff & Phillips, 2000); comparably, others have highlighted the flaws of trying to measure independent contributions of the environment to the individual, and vice versa (e.g., Landesman-Dwyer & Butterfield, 1983; Lewis, 1984; S. L. Ramey, 2002). We, too, struggle to overcome the dominance of the older ways of thinking. This is reflected in the fact that we still emphasize that health includes mental health, that cognition also refers to social and emotional cognition, and that social competence is more than behavioral interactions but includes mental representations and problem solving in the social realm. Indisputably, brain and behavior are interdependent, perhaps fundamentally inseparable; but current measurement strategies and analytic frameworks constrain how we formulate the role of children's experiences in their biological and psychosocial behavioral development, and how health impinges on education and vice versa.

In this chapter, we describe the broad conceptual framework with which we have been working, known as applied biosocial contextual development (ABCD), that considers health and education as key outcomes influenced by individual, family, and environmental contexts and processes, incorporating biological and behavioral factors. We then present an example of a multidisciplinary, longitudinal, large-scale, randomized trial that embraced this conceptual framework to inform study conceptualization, design, measurement, and analytic strategy. We selectively highlight both health and educational outcomes from these studies. Next, we identify five principles of effective early childhood interventions, supported by results from a wide array of randomized controlled trials (RCTs) of early childhood health and education interventions. We conclude that there is great potential to apply theoretical, technological, and practical advances in innovative ways to improve children's well-being, to reduce health disparities, and to ensure educational adequacy for all children (S. L. Ramey & Ramey, 2000). We outline key features of community collaborative and participatory research and recommend that universities, scientific organizations, advocacy groups, philanthropy, government agencies, and professional practices seek new alliances that transcend the historical and political boundaries that contributed to unduly complex, inefficient, and often ineffective systems for the delivery of health and education supports and for vigorous scientific inquiry.

THE CONNECTION BETWEEN HEALTH AND EDUCATION

Higher levels of educational attainment have long been associated with better health status among adults, and poor health among children is widely recognized as an impediment to full participation in formal education (cf. Waldfogel & Danziger, 2001). That both educational attainment and health status are closely linked to socioeconomic status, residential conditions, and the presence of major disabilities also is irrefutable. What has not been explored carefully—particularly via prospective, longitudinal scientific inquiry with ethnically and economically diverse populations—are the ways health and education mutually and dynamically influence the course of a child's life, and how educational and health factors in turn influence subsequent generations.

DEFINING BASIC TERMS: HEALTH, EDUCATION, AND DEVELOPMENT

To help promote a common language for the field of young children's health and education, we provide explicit definitions of basic terms. We endorse the World Health Organization's (World Health Organization, 2005) definition of "health" as *the state of complete physical, mental and social well-being and not merely the absence of disease or infirmity.*" The WHO definition was once considered revolutionary, with its emphasis on health as multifaceted, its endorsement of the centrality of mental and social well-being, and its position that

health was fundamentally synonymous with complete, optimal human functioning.

We regret that the term "education" is frequently used in a quite narrow way to refer only to the formal system of external supports to instruct children academically, often reducing education to a variable measured as "years of education," or "most advanced degree earned." Alternatively, we advocate a broader definition of education intended to reflect an individual's actual attainment and application of knowledge and skills. The Random House Dictionary of the English Language, second edition, Webster's unabridged (1987, p. 621), defines education as "the active process of imparting or acquiring general knowledge, developing the powers of reasoning and judgment, and generally of preparing oneself or others intellectually for mature life." Education, thus defined, encompasses many life experiences outside of formal schooling and didactic instruction. Undeniably, one of the major childhood tasks is to do well in school and to participate in the formal system of education; yet increasingly, social and life skills are recognized by educators and parents as vital to a child's learning. In this chapter, we use the term education to represent *the child's own acquisition of intellectual competencies, including practical, creative, and logical-deductive thinking.* As such, education is a measurable, multifaceted child outcome, just as health is.

We use the term "development" to capture *an ongoing set of biological, psychological, and social processes that result in measurable change(s) at the individual level that reflect increasing differentiation and hierarchical integration of functions.* Development is often described in everyday terms such as increased competencies, greater maturity, and more refined and adaptable skills, which in turn help a child prepare for a large number of diverse and often unexpected encounters and life challenges. Development progresses in ways that alter both internal functioning and external behavior. Internal functioning includes sensory and motor perceptions, feelings, thinking, remembering, and metacognitive strategies that help a child to govern his or her plans, reasoning, and actions; external behavior spans basic actions to complex performance in everyday situations and in formal evaluations or tests of skill, knowledge, and problem solving. Development can include incremental, steady changes as well as major transformations and the emergence of new classes of behaviors at different times and stages of life. Ultimately, development is purposive, such that development contributes to the individual's increased adaptability and effectiveness of thoughts and behavior, including social transactions, which in turn promote the individual's ability to understand the world and successfully contribute in an ethically principled and constructive manner to his or her society and its future.

Collectively, these terms characterize important universal goals for children: that children *develop* in ways that promote their *health* and their *education* and that children's *health* and *education* directly contribute to and are part of their *development*.

APPLIED BIOSOCIAL CONTEXTUAL DEVELOPMENT: A CONCEPTUAL FRAMEWORK FOR UNDERSTANDING, DESIGNING, AND TESTING INTERVENTIONS TO IMPROVE CHILDREN'S HEALTH AND EDUCATION

Figure 21.1 presents the conceptual framework with which we work, named applied biosocial contextual development (C. T. Ramey, MacPhee, & Yeates, 1982; C. T. Ramey & Ramey, 1998a; S. L. Ramey & Ramey, 1992). ABCD incorporates both health and education as explicit outcomes, through pathways that represent multiple levels and sources of influence on a child's development. ABCD is well-suited for designing, implementing, and evaluating early interventions and preventive programs to improve children's health and education outcomes, because ABCD addresses the whole child in the child's natural multiple settings and environments.

In the left column of Figure 21.1, the box labeled Child is centered within the Family, because young children are dependent on the care of others (note: As a convention, we capitalize words that denote major components in the figure). The term Family means those caring for the child, regardless of whether they reside together, and recognizing that roles and legal relationships may fluctuate over time. Family identifies those people who assume the ethical, practical, and legal responsibility for a child. Next, the child and family are surrounded by eight boxes indicating major domains of functioning and influence. The status of the child and family in each domain is hypothesized to be interre-

lated. A holistic picture of a child and family is a central feature of ABCD, such that study of one aspect of development, such as a child's health status or a child's reading achievement, is likely to be advanced through more comprehensive study of what is happening in multiple domains of the child's and the family's life. Though this is cumbersome for research and for those who implement interventions to improve child outcomes, the failure to recognize this reality often becomes a serious obstacle to realizing desired comprehensive outcomes. The eight domains are Survival Resources to meet the child's and family's basic needs; Health and Nutrition; Safety and Security; Appraisal of Self; Motivation and Values related to child and family functioning; Social Support; Communication Skills; and Basic Academic, Social, and Work Skills.

Figure 21.1 shows multiple influences on the eight functional domains, deriving from (a) the Community Context, with its specific Community Resources; and (b) Biology and Prior Experiences. The Community Context can be measured from the closely proximal to more distal relationships in the young child's life, and includes Community Resources, such as Social and Child Care Supports, Supports for Learning, Physical Supports, Health Services, and School Systems. For young children, these community resources often directly influence their health and education status, with resources impinging on family supports for the child (e.g., job training and literacy, parenting programs, substance abuse and mental health treatments for family members) and sometimes directly affecting the child (e.g., exposure to toxic substances, risk while in child care, supports from school readiness programs). Of equal theoretical importance are influences subsumed in the lower box labeled Biology and Prior Experiences. These include Intergenerational Influences, Individual Biology, and the cumulative experiences of a child and the child's family members. We admit that trying to display a dynamic, ever-changing systems theory in a two-dimensional, static, black-and-white format that fits onto one page is a nearly insurmountable challenge, and we judge our pictorial representation to be limited in adequately reflecting the complex pathways and feedback loops that are so eloquently identified by David Satcher (2004; see earlier quote). A video representation illustrating how distinctive, time-distributed inputs and processes would be a more suitable format for capturing the ABCD framework. For now, the words and

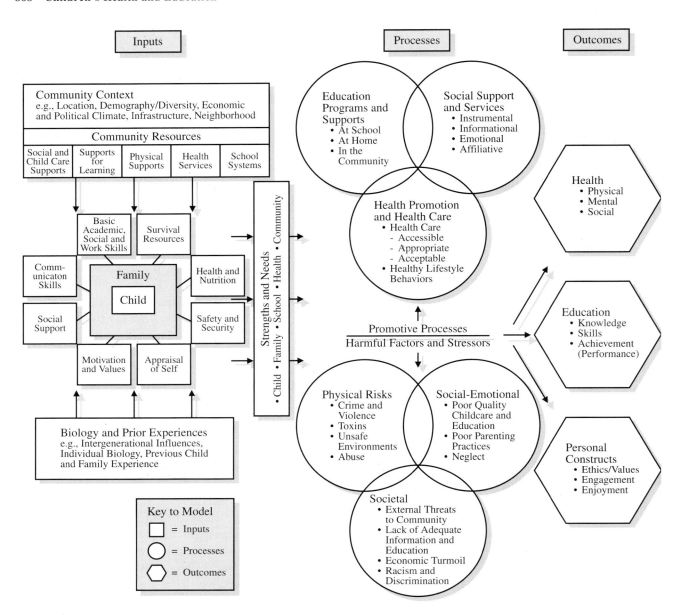

Figure 21.1 Applied biosocial contextual development (ABCD): a conceptual framework for health and education interventions.

the reader's own comprehension of the extensive developmental science findings of the past century will have to suffice.

As a systems theory, a fundamental premise of ABCD is that changes in the child and the family serve to alter both biology and experiences, as well as to possibly alter community context and community resources, particularly when children and families change in ways that affect the availability, the appropriateness, and/or the acceptability of prior community resources.

Together, the child's functioning in all of the major domains serves to undergird what are defined as outcomes, that is, the formal assessment at a specified time or a sequential portrayal of a child's status at multiple time points (i.e., developmental trajectory). We acknowledge that there is considerable ambiguity and circularity in separating an outcome from a child's functioning. In fact, we think these are one and the same, in many cases, because the very processes inextricably linked to a child's development are what become part of the measurement of an identified outcome. For example, a child's experiences in the realm of language and how a child functions in terms of everyday communication and academic aspects of language and literacy are actually simultaneously developmental processes and developmental outcomes. In the realm of health, for instance, how a child's body handles the metabolism of carbohydrates is part of what defines an outcome related to hyperglycemia (e.g., risk for or presence of diabetes). Typically, the term "outcome" is one of convenience for clinical, administrative, and research purposes, as a check on the child's status at a moment in time. Sometimes, an outcome is represented in terms of a more global and personally meaningful or valued outcome, such as "doing well in school," which is a composite or multifaceted outcome with many indicators rather than a single measure. Rarely are outcomes amenable to measurement in absolute terms, even when the outcome is a biomedical marker. For example, over the past several decades, the clinical definitions used to diagnose diabetes, childhood obesity, and childhood autism have changed considerably (they are relative definitions, not absolutes). Similarly, intellectual and education outcomes rely primarily on nationally normed standardized tests, which means that approximately half of all children will always be classified as "below national average," even if all children realized considerable gains in absolute levels of academic achievement. Accordingly, when selecting outcomes, scientists and practitioners benefit from seeking a consensus about what are positive, valued, and adaptive health and education outcomes for young children. Outcomes can never be value-free, although the measurements can become increasingly well specified, standardized, and scored in ways that allow valid comparisons of changes over time, cohorts, and contexts.

This values and relativistic perspective is part of the reason the name of our conceptual model includes the term "contextual." Applied biosocial contextual development is basically an inductive framework to promote incorporating new findings and greater specificity and directionality to its components, and eventually to inform interventions that are designed to be maximally effective and efficient in yielding desired (valued) child health and education outcomes.

In the realm of outcomes (depicted as octagons on the far right of Figure 21.1), we display the well-recognized areas of Health and Education, as well as a third out-

come to encompass dimensions of a child's life that do not easily fit within health and education. We hearken back to the pioneering work of George Kelly (1955), who advanced the concept of "personal constructs." Kelly's innovative contribution was to bring a phenomenological (personal, experiential) perspective to bear on the major issues in psychology. How an individual understands his or her world, and the personal value assigned to experiences, is an undeniable filter, one that perhaps has been overlooked for too long in the field of developmental science. Similarly, Vygotsky (1978) advanced the theory that consciousness was an end product of socialization, and explicitly identified a cognitive-cultural component that served a central role in creating the child's individual reality. Rarely are these dimensions included in the study of young children's health and education. By explicitly including this personal constructs dimension, ABCD advances the idea that children may respond differently (i.e., in an idiographic way) to the same environments—even environments considered "good" or "bad" for most children—and that the reasons for differential responding transcend variables such as age, gender, ethnicity, skill level, and presence/absence of major health conditions. Also, we provide examples of meaningful dimensions of life such as Ethics/Values, Engagement, Enjoyment, and Perceived Social Support because they capture highly valued aspects of life that are not included in conventional outcome measures of health and education.

The processes hypothesized to influence outcomes (depicted in circles in the center of Figure 21.1) are represented in terms of two major types: Promotive Processes and Harmful Factors and Stressors. Depending on the focus of a study and an intervention, greater or lesser specificity about the particular types of processes is needed. Children's outcomes, in general, are hypothesized to be supported by Educational Programs and Supports at School, Home, and in the Community; by Social Support and Services that provide Instrumental, Informational, Emotional, and Affiliative support (e.g., Reid, Ramey, & Burchinal, 1990); and by Health Promotion and Health Care, including Healthy Lifestyle Behaviors. Even when children receive promotive supports, their development can be threatened by Harmful Factors and Stressors. These represent actual risks the child experiences directly, not merely the community or family context that may increase or decrease the probability that risks will occur. Harm can occur in many domains, including the child's physical, social and emotional, and personal constructs development. In general, harmful factors and stressors have exerted a strong effect on children's outcomes, although there has been high interest in children who appear resilient, invulnerable, or successful in overcoming these risk factors (e.g., Garmezy, 1983; Grotberg, 2003; Rutter, 2000; Werner, Bierman, & French, 1971).

OVERVIEW OF APPLICATION OF THE MODEL TO EARLY INTERVENTION RESEARCH

The ABCD conceptual framework has been used for several multidisciplinary RCTs of prevention and intervention programs in early childhood. These include the Abecedarian Project and Project CARE (e.g., Campbell, Pungello, Burchinal, & Ramey, 2001; Campbell, Ramey, Pungello, Sparling, & Miller-Johnson, 2002; C. T. Ramey, Bryant, Campbell, Sparling, & Wasik, 1988; C. T. Ramey & Ramey, 1998b; Wasik, Ramey, Bryant, & Sparling, 1990), which sought to prevent intellectual disabilities and to improve school achievement among extremely low resource families; the eight-site RCT called the Infant Health and Development Program (IHDP), which adapted the Abecedarian Project and CARE early intervention program for use in the first 3 years of life with premature, low-birthweight infants (e.g., IHDP, 1990; C. T. Ramey et al., 1992); and the National Head Start-Public School Transition Demonstration Project conducted in 31 sites to test the effectiveness of 4 continuous years of comprehensive health and education supports (cf. S. L. Ramey, Ramey, & Phillips, 1997; S. L. Ramey et al., 2001; the latter study is described in detail later in the chapter). All of these studies were grounded in theory and prior research findings and adopted an explicit and broad integrative, multidisciplinary conceptual framework, derived from ABCD, (a) to inform the design of the intervention or prevention strategy; (b) to select the measurement approach to document inputs, processes, and outcomes; (c) to guide the data analyses that considered multiple and intersecting influences on the major health and education outcomes; and (d) to refine and further specify the nature and magnitude of influences on child developmental trajectories in specified developmental domains.

In writing this chapter, we would like to acknowledge that it has not been "standard science" to endeavor to conduct a rigorous study of both health and education for young children within a single longitudinal study. Although almost all longitudinal research in developmental psychology includes some marker-level variables in health and education, research historically has been more focused, studying, for example, children's mental illnesses (usually a particular form of mental illness), children's cognitive and academic development, children's social skills and behavioral problems, or children's medical illnesses or injuries. These studies have led to a rich scientific literature in these discrete but remarkably unlinked fields. The scientific journals have multiplied and become, in most cases, narrower and more topic-specific, with only a few integrative and transdisciplinary in their focus. This reflects, in large part, the traditional organization of universities into departments and schools, as well as the scientific review process that favors proposals that are more narrowly focused. For an argument in favor of major university reform to support multidisciplinary and transdisciplinary scientific inquiry and practice related to children's health and education, see S. L. Ramey and Ramey (1997b) and C. T. Ramey and Ramey (1997b).

There is strong evidence that the National Institutes of Health (NIH) has embraced the need for new, innovative, and integrative approaches—with corresponding implications for university organization and operations—in the evolving NIH road map (described on the NIH Web site), as well as the reorganized National Science Foundation, the National Academy of Sciences in the U.S. Department of Education (e.g., see the outstanding summary of early childhood research by Shonkoff & Phillips, 2000), and the Institute of Education Sciences, newly created by the U.S. Congress.

We judge the greatest challenges that derive from ABCD to be the discovery of ways to support the preparation of scientists, practitioners, and policy shapers to work collaboratively and to understand this integrative worldview of how children develop. An urgent priority is to align intervention, prevention, and promotion activities in productive and open ways with research, practice, evaluation, and policies to achieve maximal benefit for children, their families, their communities, and society at large (S. L. Ramey & Ramey, 2000). An exceptionally promising line of scientific inquiry directly addresses the dynamic relationship of a child's education to his or her health and the ways healthier children may be more likely to benefit from opportunities to advance their education. In turn, intergenerational effects of increased health and increased education may convey particular benefits to the next generation, mediated through interdependent biological and social mechanisms.

THE NATIONAL HEAD START-PUBLIC SCHOOL EARLY CHILDHOOD TRANSITION DEMONSTRATION PROJECT: A 31-SITE RANDOMIZED TRIAL TO PROVIDE COMPREHENSIVE HEAD START-LIKE SUPPORTS TO CHILDREN AND FAMILIES FROM KINDERGARTEN THROUGH THIRD GRADE

In this section, we provide an overview of a longitudinal and experimental study that adopted a prevention science approach to the design and measurement of systematic, multipronged health and education interventions to decrease risk and to increase both the educational competence and the health and well-being of young vulnerable children. We selected this study because it represents a well-supported, multiyear effort to transform the field of early childhood inquiry by engaging individuals from multiple disciplines; working closely with practitioners, scientists, and policymakers from the start and throughout the project; establishing internal and external oversight mechanisms to promote scientific rigor and integrity; and creating public use data sets that are amenable to productive secondary data analyses to advance the field. Within the confines and intent of this chapter, we do not strive to provide a compendium of all the findings from this research project. Rather, we selectively describe the project's purposes, delineate the key components of the intervention program and its corresponding data collection strategies, and report some of the findings to date that have implications for practice, policy, and future large-scale studies of health and education.

Study Purpose and History

In 1991, the U.S. Congress passed legislation titled the Head Start Transition Project Act, authorizing funding to test the value of extending comprehensive and contin-

uous Head Start-like service and supports to children for the first 4 years of elementary school. Local sites competed for funding to do the following: (a) develop promising strategies in which Head Start programs, parents, local education agencies (LEA), and other community agencies joined together to plan and implement a coordinated, continuous program of comprehensive services for low-income children and their families beginning in Head Start and continuing through third grade; (b) to develop ways to support the active involvement of parents in their education of their children; and (c) to conduct rigorous research at the local and national levels, using a randomized design to assign children and schools to the transition demonstration condition or the comparison group. The 31 funded sites were dispersed across 30 states and one Indian nation. More than 8,700 former Head Start children were enrolled and nearly 3,000 additional classmates. A distinctive feature of this intervention was that it was provided for the entire classroom, rather than just singling out former Head Start children.

Application of the Conceptual Framework to the Design and Evaluation of the Intervention

Figure 21.2 shows how ABCD was used to help frame the conceptualization of the interventions and to represent, in a general way, how the health and education components of the intervention were hypothesized to improve child health and education outcomes. As shown on the lower left side of the figure, the Planning Stage (a 1-year period) for the Transition Demonstration Program involved local adaptation of a national Program Model that mandated certain components to achieve the "comprehensive Head Start-like" feature of the program. The model established a Governing Board (with at least 51% of membership from parents of children to be served); local decision making regarding Program Implementation (the logistics of who would be hired, how local partnerships would be formed and operate, and specific plans to change Community Resources designed to improve outcomes); and Program Costs (an essential area for ensuring that intervention programs can be adequately implemented and replicated across sites).

The Planning Stage also involved creating and nurturing a National Consortium of the 31 sites, with each site having a three-way partnership of Head Start, the public schools, and an evaluation team typically at a university or research firm. At the national level, the consortium

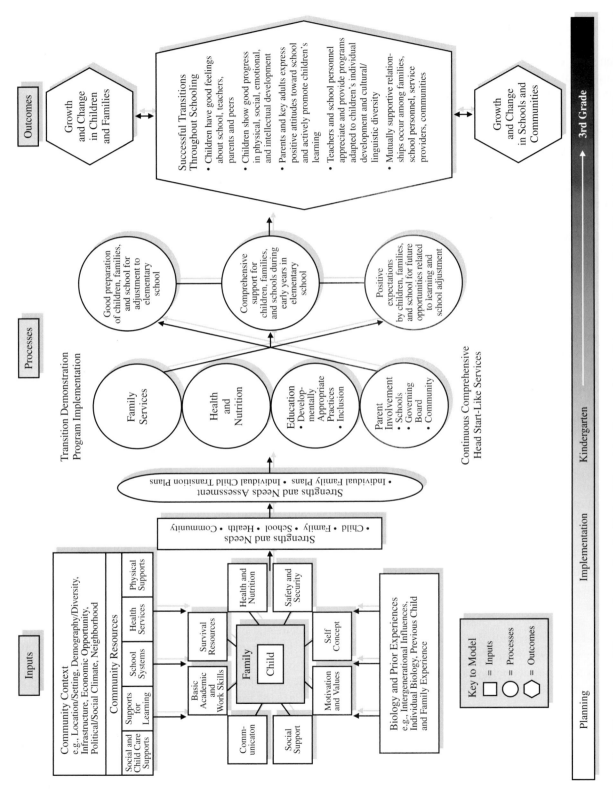

Figure 21.2 The conceptual framework used for the National Transition Demonstration Program. *Source:* From "Evaluating Educational Programs: Strategies to Understand and Enhance Educational Effectiveness" (pp. 274–292), by S. L. Ramey and C. T. Ramey, in *Continuing Issues in Early Childhood Education*, 2nd ed., C. Seefeldt and A. Galper (Eds.), 1997b, Englewood Cliffs, NJ: Prentice-Hall. Reprinted with permission.

872

addressed the eight functional domains (represented by eight boxes surrounding the child and family), endorsing their importance for the intervention and the research, and further specifying how these domains would be assessed at the beginning of the study (baseline) and throughout the course of the study (4 years).

As Figure 21.2 displays in the Implementation Phase (identified along the x-axis at the bottom of the figure), each site was to conduct an individualized Strengths and Needs Assessment for all participating children and families. This assessment was referred to as an Individualized Transition Plan that addressed the strengths and needs of the child and the family. This assessment was designed to maximize early identification of any special supports and services for a successful transition to school. As shown to the right of the oval on assessment, the major components of the Transition Demonstration Program are identified in four major areas: Family Services, Health and Nutrition, Education, and Parent Involvement. Collectively, these four areas constitute the comprehensive Head Start-like services. The time period for implementation was from the planning for kindergarten entry (ideally, in the year children were served by traditional Head Start) through each of the next 4 years in public school, with systematic efforts to ensure continuity of planning and supports from grade to grade.

For evaluation, the ABCD conceptualization was used to identify what would be measured, starting with descriptions of each local site in terms of the Community Context and Community Supports; comprehensive assessment of the child and family's health and education, including multiple measures designed to tap the constructs in each of the eight functional domains; and ongoing and annual documentation of program implementation, combining program participation data from the local site with external multidisciplinary site visits during which additional data were collected and the local site program documentation was verified. In Figure 21.2, the Transition Demonstration Program services are shown to contribute to three general areas (processes). That is, the intervention program was hypothesized to change children's health and education outcomes through three primary pathways. The first was creating "good preparation of children, families, and schools for the child's adjustment to elementary school." The Individualized Transition Plan and the process of creating local partnerships around the topic of positive school transitions were central features altering the

community- and family-specific context for school readiness. The second pathway was "comprehensive support for children, families, and schools during the early years in elementary school." This was hypothesized to result from the many in-school supports and community-based activities for children and parents, increased professional development activities for educators, and multiple parent involvement programs to facilitate children's academic progress. Third, "positive expectations by children, families, and schools for future opportunities related to learning and school adjustment" was included as a specific pathway. Measures of this were obtained by in-depth open-ended and structured interviews with families, teachers, principals, and children themselves.

This project recognized that in many communities, the poor performance of children in the past set the stage for low expectations and concomitant dismal predictions of outcomes for children from low-income families. An explicit component of the intervention was to change these expectations for academic and life success, that is, to create an expectation that the historical health disparities and educational inequities could be significantly reduced or eliminated. Collectively, the processes of increasing preparation for school success, providing supports for health and education during the early elementary school years, and increasing expectations for positive outcomes among a large stakeholder group surrounding the child are the general pathways—each of which was measured by multiple indicators throughout the study—conceptualized as producing positive outcomes.

Finally, Figure 21.2 indicates the outcomes (the octagons in the far right column) specified for the Transition Demonstration Project. These agreed-upon outcomes, building on an earlier shared vision and local community partnerships and input to the national evaluation, transcend the typical academic indicators of test scores only, and reflect the fact that outcomes for a large, intensive intervention or community reform effort should correspond to ways that the stakeholders actually think about children and their well-being. Specifically, we note that some subjective measures are identified as legitimate outcomes, such as "Children have good feelings about school, teachers, parents, and peers" (what most people call "liking school" and "positive school attitudes"), as well as their parents and teachers having positive attitudes and being actively engaged in their children's learning. Although outcomes such as having "mutually supportive relationships among families, school personnel, service providers, and communities" can be challenging for researchers to measure, these are important valid outcomes to target. Of course, children's health and educational status are also measured, but these did not constitute the sole indicators of effectiveness for this National Transition Demonstration Program.

By using the ABCD conceptual framework, the progress of the project and the extent to which goals were realized could be studied in a prospective way, assessing year-by-year changes at the level of the child, the family, the school, the health and social service delivery system, and the community as a whole. More important, the steps from Planning through Implementation could be tracked, so that if intended outcomes did not occur, the supportive processes could be carefully reviewed to consider likely explanations for differential benefits across and within the 31 sites.

Measurement of Inputs, Processes, and Outcomes

The ABCD framework facilitated the identification of constructs to be measured. Table 21.1 presents an overview of the measures selected and links these to the ABCD model. (For further details and references about methodology, see S. L. Ramey et al., 2001.) Note: this data set is now in the public domain, with supportive data dictionaries and summary variables available.

Selected Findings from the National Transition Demonstration Study about Children's Health and Education

In this chapter, we chose findings about three topics often overlooked in conventional studies of children's health and education: children's perceptions about their school experiences, the developmental trajectory of academically gifted former Head Start children, and the ways families protect children from injuries.

Children's Feelings about School

Children's feelings about school, as revealed during a Vygotskian-style dialogue, permitted children as young as 5 years of age to tell the child assessors how they felt about things happening in school. The areas rated by children included how well they got along with their teacher and peers; how important they and their parents (separate queries) thought it was to do well in

school; how much they liked school; how well they thought they were doing in academic areas; and how good their teacher was at teaching them new things. The dialogue "What I Think of School" (Reid et al., 1990) has good psychometric properties and is sensitive to individual differences. For example, S. L. Ramey, Lanzi, Phillips, and Ramey (1998) reported that by the spring of kindergarten, about 7% of former Head Start children were having multiple negative perceptions of school. Especially impressive was the finding that children's negative early perceptions were highly predictive of subsequent academic progress in reading and math, as measured by standardized assessments and teacher ratings, and that children's feelings about school contributed significant information above and beyond the measures of their kindergarten-level language, reading, math, and social skills. Children's impressions of school fit within the outcome labeled Personal Constructs in the ABCD conceptual model (Figure 21.1). We interpreted this finding to support the recommendation that children's experiences warrant inclusion in almost all investigations of children's school adjustment and their mental and physical well-being. Also, this finding exemplifies a practically useful result well suited for sharing with educators and program staff. That is, in a collaborative style of program research and evaluation, information such as this can help inform subsequent changes in the intervention—perhaps to encourage the programs, teachers, and parents to consider children's feelings as important early warning signs that are likely to precede awareness by the adults that things are not going well.

High-Achieving Low-Income Children

Another interesting set of findings from this multisite, multidisciplinary longitudinal study concerns identifying a subgroup of children with exceptionally positive development. Analysis sought to understand the supportive and protective factors in their lives (Robinson, Lanzi, Weinberg, Ramey, & Ramey, 2002; Robinson, Weinberg, Redden, Ramey, & Ramey, 1998). All too often, studies grounded in a commitment to eliminate the health and educational disparities concentrate disproportionately on the negative outcomes, or the reduction in negative outcomes. In the process, the presence of highly accomplished children and families is overlooked, and negative stereotypes are reinforced. Analyses such as these are important for both practical and theoretical reasons. In the Transition Demonstration Project, for example, the children who scored in the upper 3% of this former Head

TABLE 21.1 Data Collection Schedule for National Transition Development Project

Procedure	Functional Domain(s) Addressed	F^K	S^K	S^1	S^2	S^3
Peabody Picture Vocabulary Test	Communication	X	X	X	X	X
Woodcock-Johnson: Reading Achievement	Academic Skills	X	X	X	X	X
Math Achievement		X	X	X	X	X
What I Think of School	Motivation and values, related to school and self-concept		X	X	X	X
Writing Sample	Academic skills and communication				X	X
Information from Family						
Getting to Know Your Family	Motivation, expectations, values, and social support	X				
Family Background Interview (updated annually)	Survival resources, health, security, basic skills, and community context/resources	X	X	X	X	X
Family Resource Scale	Survival resources, security, and social support	X				X
Family Routines Questionnaire	Family context	X				X
Primary Caregiver Health: Depression Screen	Health and security	X			X	X
Social Skills Rating System: Social Skills	Basic skills	X	X	X	X	X
Problem Behavior					X	X
Your Child's Health and Safety	Social and health services in the community context and survival resources	X				X
Parenting Dimensions Inventory	Parent-child transactions and mediating processes		X	X		X
School Climate Survey	School context		X	X	X	X
Neighborhood Scales	School context		X	X		X
Your Child's Adjustment to School	Self-concept, motivation/expectations/values (related to school), social support, and basic skills		X	X	X	X
Family Involvement in Children's Learning	Demonstration program context and school program context				X	X
Information from Teachers						
Child Health Questionnaire for Teachers	Health		X	X	X	X
School Climate Survey	School context		X	X	X	X
Social Skills Rating System: Social Skills	Basic skills		X	X	X	X
Problem Behavior			X	X	X	X
Academic Competence			X	X	X	X
School Survey of Early Childhood Programs (Part C: 1–9)	School context		X	X	X	X

(continued)

TABLE 21.1 *Continued*

Procedure	Functional Domain(s) Addressed	Data Collection Period				
		F[K]	S[K]	S[1]	S[2]	S[3]
Information from Principals						
School Climate Survey	School context		X	X	X	X
School Survey of Early Childhood Programs (Part A: 1–6; Part B: 1–5)	School context		X	X	X	X
Information from Existing Records						
School Archival Records Search	Basic skills and school program context		X	X	X	X
Information from Classroom Observation						
Assessment Profile for Early Childhood Programs	Classroom context		X	X	X	X
ADAPT (to measure use of developmentally appropriate practices in the classroom)	Classroom context		X	X	X	X

Start sample on individually administered standardized tests of vocabulary, reading, and math came from all ethnic groups and many sites; these children also were highly accomplished by national norms, not just project norms. In addition to their academic achievements, these children were thriving socially and emotionally as well, according to both teacher and parent ratings (although, interestingly, parents did not rate their children as more cooperative). The social ecological factors contributing to the positive outcomes for these children included some predictable, and some unexpected, factors. For instance, parents reported significantly fewer stressors in their lives, but they did not report significantly more family strengths. Residential stability, somewhat higher father involvement, fewer single-parent households, and higher rates of parent high school graduation were predictably associated with higher-achieving children. Unexpectedly, however, rates of maternal depression did not differ for the highest-achieving versus remaining children (25% versus 23%), and parental Nurturance and Consistency (factor scores from the Parenting Dimensions Inventory; Slater & Power, 1987) were comparable for these groups. What was important were the dimensions of parent Responsiveness and Nonrestrictiveness, such that children whose parents endorsed less restrictive parenting practices and were more responsive to individual child needs had children with higher academic achievement. Further, teachers rated parents of the highest-achieving former Head Start students as more strongly encouraging of their children to succeed in school, despite the fact that the

parents did not so describe themselves. Parents of the highest-achieving children did not report discussing school with their children, being in touch with the teacher, or participating in planned parent activities at school more than other parents, but they did report volunteering more often at their child's school.

Findings such as these bring into focus the importance of differentiating subgroups or clusters of children and families within a larger at-risk population. Indeed, in this study, we identified and verified six major family types, based on the strengths and needs assessments, living in poverty (e.g., C. T. Ramey, Ramey, & Lanzi, 1998). This type of differentiation permits study of the likelihood of differential courses of development and the importance of different processes to support children having more or less positive outcomes.

Unintentional Child Injuries

Schwebel, Brezausek, Ramey, and Ramey (2004) explored children's unintentional injury risk, the leading cause of deaths among children 1 to 18 years (National Safety Council, 2001). At the time we conducted these analyses, available data supported the view that children's impulsive, hyperactive behavior patterns served to increase risk of injury and that poor parenting might also independently increase injury risk in the same samples. Remarkably, no analyses had considered whether active, positive parenting (supportive processes) could reduce injury among children at risk because of difficult behavior patterns. Using a logistic regression approach that considered child, parenting, and contextual factors and their possible interactions, this data set affirmed that children's hyperactivity was a strong predictor of injuries (odds ratio = 28.4). The ABCD conceptualization, however, contributed to the important additional finding that parents' report of the adequacy of their temporal resources—that is, time available to parents for desired activities, including time to be with their children—was a significant protective factor for this increased-risk group of children. Thus, the family environment and parental behavior emerged as key promotive processes. (For further findings about the National Transition Demonstration Project, see S. L. Ramey, Ramey, & Lanzi, 2004.)

Collectively, these findings provide a window on ways to study developmental pathways to alternative health and education outcomes and to consider how aspects of the child's context, initial status of the child and family, and supportive as well as harmful processes can alter the course of development and children's outcomes.

PRINCIPLES OF EFFECTIVE INTERVENTION SUPPORTED BY LONGITUDINAL RESEARCH ON CHILDREN'S HEALTH AND EDUCATION

For many decades, the single most pressing question in early childhood education was simply "Do early education and health interventions work?" There was robust skepticism that early educational interventions could alter the cumulative negative toll that poverty and other risk circumstances take on the development of young children. But by the mid-1980s, a professional consensus was reached (cf. Guralnick & Bennett, 1987) that early educational interventions can—under certain conditions—produce meaningful benefits, as reflected in the academic achievement and social progress of young children. Just as important, when early interventions fail to produce intended benefits, the likely reasons are important to understand for practice and theory. Given the cross-study consistencies in findings, we summarize findings about early educational interventions in terms of five major scientific principles (C. T. Ramey & Ramey, 1998a; S. L. Ramey & Ramey, 1992). We postulate that these principles are likely to hold true for health interventions, although there is scant scientific support from randomized controlled trials designed to improve the physical health of at-risk children or to prevent prevalent childhood disorders such as asthma, obesity, depression, and chronic dental disease. We have endeavored to incorporate health examples, however, as much as possible, including several dramatic public health interventions that have altered the Community Context and Community Supports directly. These five major principles are (1) the dosage principle, (2) the timing principle, (3) the direct receipt of services principle, (4) the differential benefits principle, and (5) the continuity of supports principle.

The Principle of Dosage

Programs that provide higher amounts of intervention (i.e., full dosage) produce greater benefits in health and education outcomes. This principle of dosage or intervention intensity has considerable scientific support, derived from cross-study comparisons of magnitude of benefits from multipronged and educational interventions that varied in their dosage, as well as some experimental studies that directly tested different dosage levels within the same study, and from post hoc analyses that analyzed rates of participation using sophisticated analytical techniques. Dosage is indexed in different ways, for different types of interventions; we caution that for medical interventions, the intensity principle refers to administering the full dosage, recognizing that overdosage could be dangerous.

For educational interventions in the first 8 years of life, dosage can be indexed by variables such as number of hours per day, days per week, and weeks per year that children receive the educational intervention. An ideal measure—which has never been calculated, to our knowledge, in educational interventions—would be the actual amount of instructional and learning time children have when they attend, multiplied by the child's attendance. Theoretically, the reason that more intensive programs produce significantly larger positive effects than do less intensive programs is straightforward: Children are engaged in more learning, which in turn supports their continued growth and development in the domains in which the learning occurs. For health, the greater the amount of time spent in health promotion activities and the greater the compliance with recommended health care treatments (representing a complex interplay of availability, accessibility, and acceptability of appropriate services), the healthier the child should be.

Many early interventions do not significantly improve children's intellectual or academic performance (see S. L. Ramey & Ramey, 2000, for discussion of some reasons why these likely fail). A key characteristic of many of these unsuccessful interventions is that they were not very intensive. For instance, none of the 16 randomized trials of early interventions for young children with disabilities or delays evaluated by the Utah State Early Intervention Research Institute (White, 1991) provided full-day 5-day/week programs, and none of these programs produced any measurable benefits for children in terms of their competencies. Similarly, Scarr and McCartney (1988) provided intervention only once per week to economically impoverished families in Bermuda in an effort to replicate the findings of Levenstein's (1970) Verbal Interaction Project. They also failed to detect any positive cognitive effects.

In marked contrast, two RCTs conducted in North Carolina using the same educational curriculum, the Abecedarian Project and Project CARE, produced multiple significant benefits to participants in this high-dosage educational intervention. The Abecedarian Project and Project CARE both provided educational supports to children within a full-day, 5 days a week, 50 weeks per year program for 5 consecutive years, using a structured and individualized curriculum delivered in a high-quality, university-based child development center that was continuously monitored and supported for quality of curriculum implementation (C. T. Ramey & Ramey, 2004a, 2004b, 2004c). To our knowledge, these two programs are among the most intensive (high dosage) that have been subjected to rigorous experimental study, and the principle of dosage may account for a large portion of the increased magnitude of benefit detected at ages 8, 12, 15, and 21 years. We particularly note the benefits for language and literacy, as demonstrated in significant gains at every age on every language measure and all reading assessments (C. T. Ramey et al., 2000; C. T. Ramey & Ramey, 2004c). Other educationally important outcomes include markedly lower rates of placement in special education, reduced from 48% in the comparison group to 12% in the educational intervention group (close to the national average of 11%), and reduced rates of grade repetition, from 56% in the control group to 30% in the educational group.

The Milwaukee Project was an RCT that produced large, immediate benefits in intelligence and language (Garber, 1988) and provided a high-dosage, daily early educational intervention from birth through the transition to school, with a university child development program offered daily (see review by S. L. Ramey & Ramey,

2000). However, long-term benefits were not sustained to the same degree as in the North Carolina projects, perhaps because of the influence of the principle of continuity of supports and the differences in the enrollment criteria across these projects (i.e., the North Carolina projects enrolled on a combination of family risk variables; the Milwaukee Project enrolled only children born to mothers with mental retardation).

Two studies provide experimental evidence that program intensity matters: An early intervention home visit program (Grantham-McGregor, Powell, & Fletcher, 1989) that systematically tested different levels of intensity discovered significant cognitive benefits at a dosage level of three visits per week, whereas fewer visits per week did not produce any significant gains, and the Brookline Early Education Project (Hauser-Cram, Pierson, Walker, & Tivnan, 1991) reported that only the most intensive services were sufficient to benefit children from less well-educated families, whereas the lowest and intermediate intensities had no measurable consequences.

The eight-site Infant Health and Development Program RCT systematically investigated program intensity effects at the level of the individual child's participation. Originally, C. T. Ramey et al. (1992) reported that the intensity of educational intervention each child and family received related significantly to cognitive outcomes at age 3. Dosage was a sum of three program components: total days the child attended the child development center between 12 and 36 months; number of home visits from birth to age 3; and number of monthly educational meetings the parents attended. This "participation index" demonstrated a strong, linear relationship to the child's intellectual and behavioral development at 36 months, even after controlling for variables that might have influenced individual rates of participation (such as maternal education, maternal verbal competence, family income, child health status, and ethnicity). When considering the efficacy of this 3-year, multipronged educational intervention to prevent mental retardation (IQ less than 70 points) at age 3, the results showed that children in the highest participation group had nearly a nine-fold reduction in the percentage of low-birthweight children who were mentally retarded (under 2%), compared with control children who received only high-quality pediatric follow-up services (about 18%). Later, Blair, Ramey, and Hardin (1995) demonstrated that year-by-year participation rates produced significant and independent effects on the course of the child's measured cognitive competence at 12, 24, and 36 months of age.

Hill, Brooks-Gunn, and Waldfogel (2003) extended these intensity analyses to answer the question "Do longer-term effects, at ages 5 and 8, relate to participation rates?" When the children were 3, 5, and 8 years of age, multiple assessments of language and cognition were completed, with the 8-year battery including the full Wechsler Intelligence Scale for Children (WISC; Verbal, Performance, and Full-Scale IQ scores), the Woodcock-Johnson Reading and Math assessments, and the Peabody Picture Vocabulary Test-Revised (PPVT-R). On 12 major outcome measures across 3 age periods, all measures showed higher performance for children in two higher-participation groups (attending more than 350 days and attending more than 400 days in the child development center) relative to the randomly assigned follow-up group, which received pediatric and social services, but not the educational component of this multipronged early intervention. The first set of analyses confirmed that children who participated at higher rates differed significantly from the comparison group, with site-specific differences in which variables (e.g., maternal ethnicity, maternal education, maternal use of drugs, and prenatal care) correlated with amounts of participation. Accordingly, this team applied a sophisticated set of data-analytic techniques that are well-known in medical RCTs, involving an adaptation of a propensity score matching procedure coupled with logistic regression to reduce the influence of the natural selection bias when evaluating treatment effects. The results yielded compelling support for the dosage principle, demonstrating differences between matched high-dosage and control children, and between higher- and lower-dosage children within the treatment group. The magnitude of these differences is impressive at all 3 ages analyzed, and extends to the reading and math scores at age 8, with sustained benefits of the early educational intervention corresponding to gains of 6.1 to 11.1 points higher (depending on the definition used for high dosage) on the Woodcock-Johnson, as well as sustained (although slightly reduced) benefits at ages 5 and 8 for PPVT (4.1 to 6.6 points at age 8) and WISC IQ scores (6.5 to 8.4 points at age 8).

The Principle of Timing

Generally, when interventions begin earlier and continue longer, they produce larger and longer-lasting benefits to the participants than do those that begin much later and do not last as long. The age when children enter early educational interventions ranges from birth through 8 years of age. Typically, children from economically disadvantaged families become eligible for early educational interventions (e.g., Head Start, public school pre-K for at-risk children) in their home communities beginning at 4 years of age, and sometimes at 3 years of age. Many of the well-cited early educational interventions, however, began when children were young infants, such as the Abecedarian Project (C. T. Ramey, Bryant, Campbell, Sparling, & Wasik, 1988; C. T. Ramey, Yeates, & Short, 1984), the Brookline Early Education Project (Hauser-Kram et al., 1991), the Milwaukee Project (Garber, 1988), Project CARE (Wasik et al., 1990), and the Infant Health and Development Program (1990). Two noteworthy exceptions, however, are the Perry Preschool Project, conducted in Ypsilanti, Michigan (Schweinhart & Weikart, 1983), and the Early Training Project (Gray, Ramsey, & Klaus, 1982), which began when children were 3 years of age. An important difference in these two interventions that began later in life and did produce significant benefits is that the children were documented to be significantly delayed in their cognitive development at age 3, whereas the other studies that enrolled children earlier sought to prevent intellectual decline linked to early and continued impoverished language and learning environments.

The principle of timing has always been one of high interest and is associated with vigorous debate. Concerning neurobiology and education outcomes, the stunning technology advances to document brain growth and development, coupled with research on early brain development (primarily experimental animal research) and how experiences shape brain activities lend support, in a general way, to the principle that earlier and more sustained educational interventions are especially promising to maximize benefits to children. Even the carefully controlled animal experiments on early experience, which support the general principle of timing, do not refute the possibility that educational interventions begun at later ages can produce measurable gains (S. L. Ramey & Sackett, 2000). One of the most consistently cited areas that lend support to the principle of timing comes from the observational research of Kuhl, Tsao, and Liuh (2003) concerning acquisition of speech and language perception, demonstrating that an infant's exposure (naturally) to his or her first language results in the loss of a generalized discrimination ability that existed at earlier ages. This reflects development (see earlier definition) in which there is increasing selective differentiation and hierarchical integration, that is hypothesized to facilitate (and to reflect) more efficient, higher-order functioning. When young infants are not exposed to certain sensory-perceptual experiences very early in life, they seem to lose their initial capacity (such as the universal ability of young babies to recognize phonemes in all languages, later narrowing to recognize primarily phonemes in their native language).

Just as we cautioned earlier regarding possible negative effects of overdosage, we recognize that certain types of interventions may be infeasible, ineffective, or even iatrogenic (producing unintended negative consequences) if provided too early. There are some historical examples of this, often given in textbooks, such as a study that trained babies to walk earlier than usual by practicing the walking reflex daily, and efforts to teach complex motor skills to nursery school children. Both studies found short-term changes, but these seeming benefits were washed out when the age-typical display of these motor skills occurred for the control (untreated) children.

The Abecedarian Project involved a two-phase educational intervention, with 50% of the children who received 5 consecutive years of early educational intervention and 50% in the control group (receiving nutritional, pediatric, and social services only) who were randomly selected to participate in an elementary school Home-School Resource Program for 3 consecutive years. This partially tested the issue of timing, offering extra educational supports during the school year (provided by individualized assistance to children and their families with schoolwork and school-family communication) and a summer educational camp that sought to increase children's learning opportunities from kindergarten through entry into third grade. The results demonstrate two clear sets of findings. First, the elementary school support program (i.e., the later onset of intervention) did yield measurable benefits to participants, as indexed by higher scores on standardized assessments of reading and math achievement at age 8. However, there were not comparable gains on general tests of intelligence or language, compared to children who received the preschool early education intervention. Second, the magnitude of benefits, even for the reading and math achievement scores, was smaller than for children who received the earlier-onset education intervention (see C. T. Ramey et al., 2000). This study is not germane, however, in helping to resolve the vital

question about differential timing benefits during the preschool years. Further, this study tested a reasonably well-designed and replicable public school enhancement program, but did not seek to directly control the overall classroom curriculum and instruction and thus is not a simple and pure test of timing effects alone.

In summary, the principle of timing has modest support from human studies, but further research is needed for conclusive evidence about its importance for different aspects of language, literacy, and other academic competencies. For health interventions, examples among deaf children such as timing of cochlear implants and age of teaching infants sign language confirm the greater malleability or recoverability of the brain when such corrective procedures are implemented. In general, early detection and treatment are so widely accepted as positive in health care that they rarely are studied systematically. There are no compelling data, at this time, to support the notion of an absolute critical period, such that educational intervention or health supports provided after a certain age cannot be beneficial at all; rather, this is a principle of *relative* timing effects.

The Principle of Direct Receipt of Services

This principle affirms that early educational and health interventions that directly alter children's daily health and education produce larger positive and longer-lasting results than do those interventions that rely primarily on indirect or pass-through routes to change competencies.

Early education and health interventions have been presented in many different forms, including those that are based in child development centers with trained teaching and health staff, those that are home-based and seek to change parents' health behavior and provide environmental enrichments (books, learning games, educational videos), and those that combine center- and home-based components. These different types of early educational and health interventions may be divided into two major categories: those that rely primarily on direct provision of academic and health instruction to children and those that seek indirect means of enhancing child learning, such as seeking to change the parents' behavior and, through that mechanism, to alter the child's health and education.

The empirical findings regarding the differential effects of these two quite different strategies are clear: The indirect interventions that seek to change intermediary factors are not as powerful in changing children's language, reading, intellectual, or health performance (Lewis, 1984; Madden, Levenstein, & Levenstein, 1976; C. T. Ramey, Ramey, Gaines, & Blair, 1995; Scarr & McCartney, 1988; Wasik et al., 1990). This generalization holds true for economically disadvantaged children, seriously biologically disadvantaged children, and high-risk children with both environmental and individual risk conditions.

C. T. Ramey, Bryant, Sparling, and Wasik (1985) conducted the first systematic and experimental study with direct provision of instruction versus intermediary forms of early educational intervention. In an RCT, high-risk children were randomly assigned just after birth to receive one of three interventions: (1) the daily, highly intense child development center program, identical to that provided to children in the Abecedarian Project, coupled with the home visiting program; (2) a home visiting (intermediary) program that lasted for 5 years, used the same educational curriculum as the center-based intervention, and sought to have parents deliver the intervention; and (3) a comparison group that received enhanced nutritional, pediatric, and social services only (both intervention groups also received these health and social support services). An important achievement in this study, the longest-lasting home visiting program we know of, is that participants in all three groups remained highly engaged in the program and the assessments. The home visiting was planned to be weekly during the first 2 years of life and then every other week for the next 3 years. Further, the home visitors received ongoing supervision and continuing support throughout the 5 years and used a structured but adaptable curriculum, and both the home visitors and the families reported that they perceived the home visiting program to very positive. Despite the enthusiasm for the effort to change parents, who in turn could transmit increased learning opportunities to their children, the outcome data demonstrated no measurable gains for the children in the home visiting program compared to the control children, and both of these groups fared significantly worse than the group that received the daily, year-round center-based educational curriculum plus home visiting. Post hoc analyses indicated that magnitude of benefits associated with the children who received direct language and academic instruction (in the center) plus the 5 years of home visiting was almost identical to that reported for the Abecedarian Project participants, who did not receive the same intensive home visiting educational component. On a promising

note, from another home visiting program, Powell and Grantham-McGregor (1989) indicated that three home visits per week—but not less—produced significant child improvement through the intermediary or indirect intervention approach.

Just recently, Olds et al. (2004) reported positive but modest education and health benefits from a nurse home visiting program detected 2 years after the program ended but not during the program. These results were particularly noteworthy in the areas of receptive language and intelligence. These high-risk children were also more likely to have been enrolled in formal out-of-home care, so it is not clear whether a direct or indirect route of influences or a combination best accounts for the results.

There clearly is popular appeal to the idea that increasing the skills and knowledge of young children's first teachers—their parents—will be beneficial, because parents are children's natural support system and, typically, care deeply about their children's well-being. Also, most programs hope that changing parents and improving the home environment will have spillover effects to the next children born into these families and will help to increase the local community's competence in providing the right types of education and health experiences, at the right times, for many other young children. Increasingly, many of these parent-focused educational and health interventions consider that some parents themselves lacked good educational and health opportunities when they were growing up, and some parents lacked positive parenting models in their own lives. Accordingly, the curricula used for the parenting and home visiting programs often address the parent's own developmental needs and crucial aspects of culture and local community, along with "how to parent" issues.

What are the likely reasons that center-based programs with more traditional types of language enrichment, health care, and teacher-provided instruction relating to academic skills yield positive results in terms of academic achievement and cognition, whereas the indirect or intermediary programs do not? We hypothesize that at least four factors may be contributing to this pattern of results. One is that most home visiting programs are not equal in intensity or dosage to the center-based programs. Another is that the natural language and academic skills of some parents in at-risk families may not be equal to those of teachers or caregivers in the center-based programs, even when parents are encouraged to provide more language and academic learning experiences to their preschool children. Thus, the children in the two groups would not receive similar levels of exposure to a rich language environment on an everyday basis (cf. Hart & Risley, 1995; Huttenlocher, 1990). A third reason is that parents who respond positively to the home visiting still may not spend enough time with their children for the children to have the full benefit of their parents' increased skills. For many parents, their children may be in the care of others for extended periods during the day or night, and these other caregivers may not be meeting the needs of these at-risk children (National Institute of Child Health and Human Development [NICHD] Consortium for the Study of Early Child Care, 2005). Fourth and finally, the rate at which participating parents acquire and then implement their enhanced parenting and instructional skills may not be rapid enough to achieve the intended benefits for their children. This harkens back to the principles of both dosage and timing. We note that home visiting programs may serve other valuable purposes, such as preventing child neglect and abuse and increasing children's health and safety, as demonstrated in research projects such as those by Olds and colleagues (2004).

For reasons we do not fully understand, the early childhood community has become polarized around issues that concern direct or explicit teaching of certain skills to young children. It appears common knowledge that babies are born without knowing any specific words or ideas, and that skills related to reading, writing, and math require direct exposure; that is, their advancement cannot occur without some introduction, scaffolding, modeling or demonstration, and practice and feedback. We believe that some practitioners in early childhood programs mistakenly tried to enact kindergarten- or first-grade-level instruction for much younger children, and adopted ineffective methods of repetitive drill, restricted young children's spontaneous play and exploration, and tried to force very young children to attend and behave in ways that were counterproductive. Accordingly, the anti-instruction movement could be viewed as a backlash to such inappropriate applications of early educational interventions. An alternative explanation is that some of the competent caregivers for young children, particularly low-income and minority children, in the United States have low levels of formal education and lack formal teaching credentials. There may be a fear that all of these individuals will be excluded from the future of child care and early education and judged to be incompetent simply because they cannot articulate precisely how they instruct children and help to prepare them for school. Although there are many published studies documenting a general relationship between an adult's level of education, language skills, and intelligence and the adult's skills in promoting children's cognitive and language development (cf. NICHD Consortium for the Study of Early Child Care, 2005), there are many notable exceptions to the generalization. From our own professional experience, we have observed highly competent teachers of young children who come from all types of educational backgrounds and all types of linguistic and cultural backgrounds. Advanced degrees in early childhood education are not a guarantee of high-quality instruction occurring on a responsive and regular basis; neither does the lack of a college degree prohibit an adult from providing high-quality language and academic learning opportunities.

Currently, the Institute of Educational Sciences is coordinating an effort to evaluate RCTs that test the benefits of different published preschool curricula, mostly for 4-year-olds. This effort is designed to yield much needed information about "what works" in pre-K settings. There are, however, already recognized limits that have surfaced in this new research endeavor, such as differences across sites regarding the dosage of the intervention (hours per day, weeks per year), the degree of risk in the children participating, the quality of and control over curriculum implementation, and the levels of participation from the children and families. What is admirable about this research initiative is that both educational science and curriculum development are being advanced, and the practical importance of this type of scientific inquiry has become paramount by creating a national network of projects concerned with children's language and literacy outcomes. Content analysis of existing early educational interventions that have already produced large and lasting benefits through RCTs would be a worthwhile endeavor, as well as efforts to measure the actual classroom instruction at levels that correspond to the particular types of learning and language experiences hypothesized to be the most essential for young children's learning (e.g., C. T. Ramey & Ramey, 1999; S. L. Ramey & Ramey, 1998).

The Principle of Differential Benefits

This principle asserts that some children show greater benefits from participation in early educational and health interventions than do other children. These individual differences appear to relate to aspects of the children's initial risk condition and the degree to which the program meets the child's needs or services to prevent the harmful consequences of those risk conditions over time (e.g., by providing sufficient amounts of direct positive learning experiences that otherwise would not have been present).

A fundamental assumption in the fields of education and social ecology is that of person × environment (read as "person by environment") or person × treatment effects. This assumption is that different individuals respond differently to the same program, and correspondingly, different programs may be needed to produce the same outcome for different participants. These ideas have long prevailed in the clinical and educational literature, but only recently have they been explored systematically in the early intervention field.

In providing broad-based early intervention for premature, low-birthweight infants, the Infant Health and Development Program (1990) reported that children at greater presumed biological risk, as indexed by their lower birthweight (less than 2,000 gm), at age 3 years did not initially benefit as much from the program as did children at lesser presumed risk (with birthweight between 2,000 and 2,499 gm), even though both groups showed significant gains. In a longer-term follow-up of these children at 5 and 8 years of age, Hill et al. (2003) reported large and significant risk × intervention effects, such that the heavier low-birthweight children showed IQ point benefits of about 14 points, and lighter babies had effects of about 8 points, compared to their appropriate-birthweight matched controls who did not receive the educational component of the intervention.

Another study focused on early educational intervention for children with disabilities and considered two influences simultaneously: the degree of the child's impairment and the form of educational intervention provided. Cole, Dale, Mills, and Jenkins (1991) found an aptitude × treatment effect in a randomized design comparing Feuerstein's "mediated learning" techniques and more traditional direct instruction. Contrary to conventional wisdom, students who performed relatively better (as measured on the pretest battery of cognitive, language, and motor tests) gained more from direct instruction, whereas students who performed worse showed greater benefits from the mediated learning treatment.

From the Abecedarian Project, Martin, Ramey, and Ramey (1990) discovered that the children who showed the greatest relative gains (i.e., compared to controls)

were those whose mothers were the most intellectually limited (i.e., maternal IQ scores below 70; in fact, all experimental children whose mother was mentally retarded performed at least 20 points higher and averaged 32 points higher than did their own mother; Landesman & Ramey, 1989). These dramatic findings are comparable to the large benefits reported in the Milwaukee Project, which enrolled only economically disadvantaged mothers with IQs below 75 (Garber, 1988).

Some of the programs that have failed to detect any significant overall benefits may have enrolled a highly heterogeneous group of children, some of whom were at very low or no risk for poor educational outcomes. This could serve to lessen the power to detect real intervention effects if, in fact, only the high-risk children showed benefits. As an example, analyses conducted on children participating in the Infant Health and Development Program showed significantly different levels of benefit based on the educational level of the children's mother. As Figure 21.3 shows, the degree of benefits, as indexed by children's IQ scores on the Stanford-Binet at age 3, displayed a highly orderly relationship to mother's education. The gains were the greatest (comparing treated and control children) for those children whose mother had less than a high school education, followed by those whose mother earned a high school

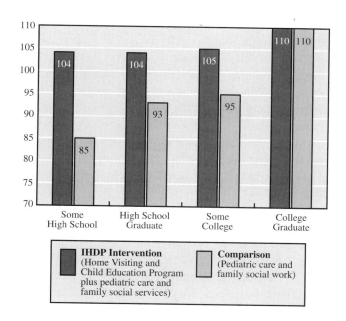

Figure 21.3 Differential effects of the Infant Health and Development Program on age 3 IQ outcomes (Stanford-Binet) as a function of maternal educational status.

degree or GED, and then those whose mother had some college education. Interestingly, there were neither any benefits nor any harm related to participating in this educational intervention for children whose mother had earned a 4-year college degree or higher (see S. L. Ramey & Ramey, 2000). These findings of differential benefits are consistent with an interpretation that these educational interventions supplement children's experiences at home in ways that are essential for the development of average (or above-average) intelligence; accordingly, for children whose cognitive and linguistic development is strongly supported by their family and other natural environments, additional educational interventions are not needed to prevent subaverage performance. We also note that in this study, the control children, like those in all of the RCTs we have reviewed, were never prevented from participating in other programs, and many of the college-educated parents in the Infant Health and Development Program sought, on their own, additional help and information to support the early development of their premature and low-birthweight infants.

The Principle of Continuity of Supports

This principle states that over time, the initial positive effects of early interventions will diminish if there are inadequate later supports to maintain children's positive outcomes. This has been demonstrated mostly in the educational realm, but logically is just as important for children's health. The reason postintervention programs continue to matter is that children continue to learn at high rates, with educational and health progress that depends not only on a child's entry-level skills or health status but his or her continued acquisition of the cognitive, language, and academic skills—complemented by appropriate physical, social, and emotional skills—to have a positive transition to school (S. L. Ramey, Ramey, & Lanzi, 2004).

For many early intervention programs for at-risk children, long-lasting and substantial effects on school achievement, grade retention, and special education placement have been repeated. In some, but not all, studies (e.g., Garber, 1988), the long-term effects of early educational intervention on IQ scores lessen over time. Two important issues are relevant. First, it is not sufficient for disadvantaged children merely to maintain the advantages from effective early educational interventions. Rather, children must continue to develop at normative rates in multiple domains if they are to succeed

in school settings. Second, no currently influential developmental theory is premised on the assumption that positive early learning experiences are sufficient *by themselves* to ensure that children will perform well throughout their lives. A poor school environment, suboptimal health, a seriously disrupted home environment, and many other conditions influence the behavior of children at all ages. Thus, longitudinal inquiry about the long-term effects of early intervention must take into consideration children's subsequent environments and experiences (i.e., after early intervention ceases).

As described earlier, only one RCT early intervention study, the Abecedarian Project, has extended early intervention into the elementary school years to evaluate the importance of additional systematic supports during the transition to school. As Figure 21.4 shows, at 8 years of age, children who had received continuous educational intervention for the first 8 years performed the best of any group in reading and mathematics, followed next by those who received early intervention for 5 years, followed by those who received the elementary school treatment only (Horacek, Ramey, Campbell, Hoffman, & Fletcher, 1987). Longitudinal analysis of IQ scores revealed effects only for the early intervention groups; that is, the supplemental program from kindergarten through age 8 did not result in higher IQ scores (C. T. Ramey & Campbell, 1994). Later, at age 12, children who had received the early intervention continued to show benefits in terms of both academic achievement and IQ scores and a reduction of nearly 50% in the rate of repetition of at least one grade in the elementary school years. Overall, however, the group of children who performed best across all measures were those who had *both* the preschool and school-age educational interventions.

Currie and Thomas (1995) have conducted important analyses of the long-term educational progress of former Head Start children and demonstrated that those who go to average or above-average schools continue to keep up with their age or grade peers, whereas those in the very lowest performing schools show a decline (relative to their school entry level). Tragically, 50 years after *Brown v. Board of Education,* it remains true that African American low-income children disproportionately attend very poor quality schools, at rates far higher than for other ethnic groups even when family income is below the poverty line.

Recently, Barnett (2004) has written an excellent and integrative review that confronts the "myth of fade-out." Although it is true that IQ scores per se show dimin-

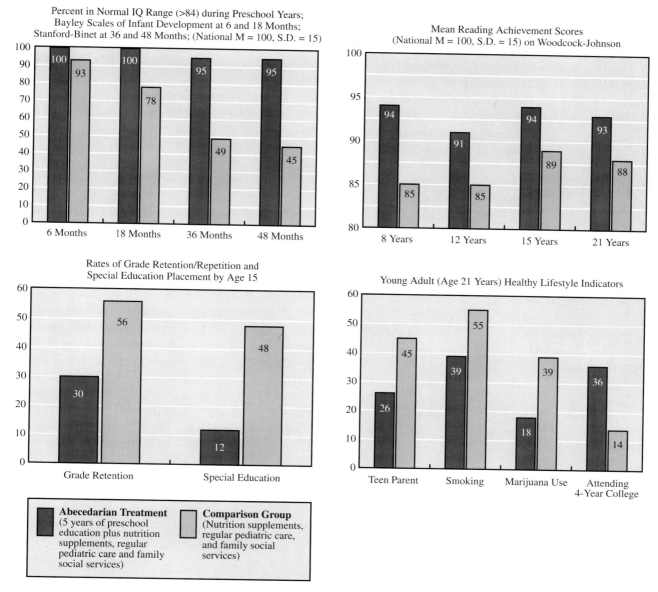

Figure 21.4 The Abecedarian Project: selected health and education outcomes from infancy through young adulthood.

ished group difference over time, achievements in reading, language, math, and overall school adjustment as indexed by grade retention and special education placement show long-lasting benefits. When these sustained effects do not appear, one of the contributing factors—in addition to the principles already detailed in this chapter—may well be the quality and intensity of the educational programs that follow the early educational intervention. The opportunity to conduct more rigorous post hoc analyses about the schools that children attended across the well-conducted RCTs that have longitudinal data would be valuable, as well as more de-

scription about the natural variation in the alignment and educational supports for children transitioning from early educational interventions into public school programs (Kagan, 1994).

KEY FEATURES OF COLLABORATIVE AND COMMUNITY PARTICIPATORY RESEARCH

Traditionally, scientific inquiry about child development has been guided primarily by scientists with interests in advancing scientific theory and practical understanding of what influences the course of human development. Some research has been fueled by advocacy concerns, such as increased research into Autism, mental retardation, AIDS, and learning and reading disabilities. Rarely, however, is research conducted in a way that adequately includes the perspectives of those whose lives are the primary topic of the research. Further, clinicians, educators, and community members often have extensive in-depth knowledge of topics germane to longitudinal research on children and families, yet these individuals seldom participate as full partners in the design and conduct of longitudinal research. Increasingly, scientists recognize the tremendous potential value of conducting research in a way that actively engages and respects a much broader range of expertise, from multiple disciplines, practices, and community experiences. The challenge is how to efficiently and effectively create new types of partnerships in which multiple groups of "experts" can be combined to yield a more complete understanding of important influences on children's health and education.

We have established and used guidelines for conducting collaborative research to evaluate the effects of interventions in education and health settings (S. L. Ramey & Ramey, 1997b). Figure 21.5 summarizes critical activities in planning and conducting responsive, useful research on education and health interventions. Briefly, these include early engagement of key individuals and groups as participants to create a shared vision and framework to guide decision making and the identification of key questions and plans for gathering and analyzing data. Vital to the success of collaborative and community participatory research is the generation of timely interim reports that provide practical information about the progress of program implementation and early evidence about program impact and children's development. Active maintenance of these partnerships is equally important to ensure continuity in the conduct of longitudinal intervention research and to understand other changes occurring over time in the community and families' lives that may affect measured health and education outcomes. These research partnerships facilitate accurate identification of changes in the community and family context that may independently and interactively affect child health and education. These partnerships not only serve to foster scientific integrity in terms of the appropriate measurement of relevant multiple influences, but also set the stage for informed interpretation, dissemination, and application of the results of such re-

search. In addition, the partnerships themselves can serve as an ongoing means of timely exchange of relevant information, including opportunities for scientists to provide practitioners and families with valuable findings from previous research that could be practically applied in the community (see Figure 21.5).

We would be remiss if we did not state there are serious challenges associated with conducting such complex, ambitious, and action-oriented research. These include the importance of identifying the appropriate individuals who will be engaged in the partnership, recognizing that the members in the partnership will change over time (for many reasons), finding ways the partnership can offer tangible benefits and appropriate recognition to all participants throughout the partnership, anticipating and proposing how to resolve likely problems and disagreements, and creating stronger supports within most universities for this type of research. Ideally, clearly written agreements (e.g., memoranda of understanding) signed by key participants and community and university leaders, widespread public media about the partnership, and ongoing documented meetings to exchange information in ways that are open and honest serve as important mechanisms for maintaining project integrity, acceptability, and productivity.

As an example, when we created a long-term research partnership between a geographic community and a major research university, we developed and endorsed a set of guiding operating principles (for more details, see C. T. Ramey & Ramey, 1997a, 1997b). These were (a) a pledge that there will be joint university and community development of all programs; (b) a commitment to research that benefits both the community and the university; (c) a commitment to programs that make a difference in people's everyday lives; (d) a pledge from partners to maintain the partnership for an extended period (e.g., a decade); (e) a belief that over time both the community and the university will become better places as a direct result of the quality of partnership; and (f) a commitment to conducting the partnership in a way that could serve as a model for others (e.g., to expand the benefits and to facilitate productive university-community partnerships).

Universities and Public Policy

Universities have been the largest incubator for model research programs to enhance young children's education and to test health interventions. Unfortunately,

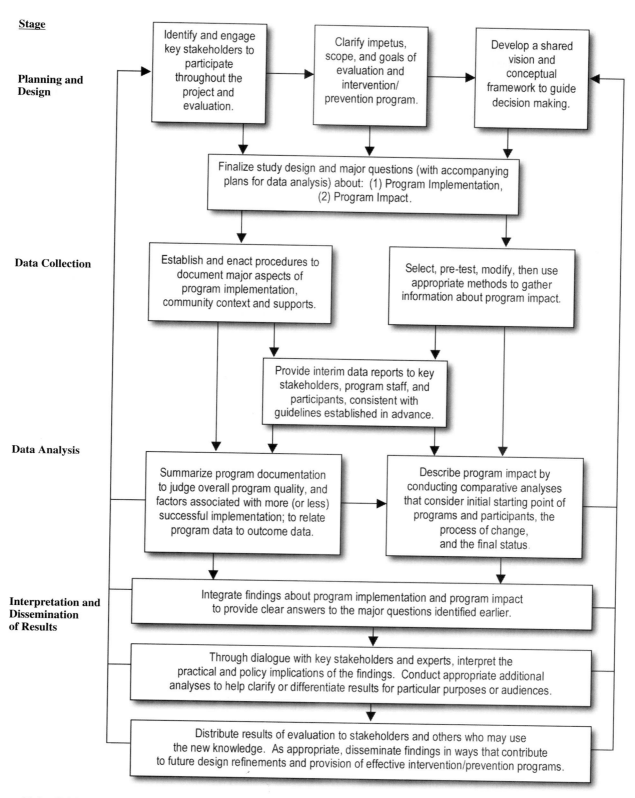

Stage

Planning and Design

Identify and engage key stakeholders to participate throughout the project and evaluation.

Clarify impetus, scope, and goals of evaluation and intervention/ prevention program.

Develop a shared vision and conceptual framework to guide decision making.

Finalize study design and major questions (with accompanying plans for data analysis) about: (1) Program Implementation, (2) Program Impact.

Data Collection

Establish and enact procedures to document major aspects of program implementation, community context and supports.

Select, pre-test, modify, then use appropriate methods to gather information about program impact.

Provide interim data reports to key stakeholders, program staff, and participants, consistent with guidelines established in advance.

Data Analysis

Summarize program documentation to judge overall program quality, and factors associated with more (or less) successful implementation; to relate program data to outcome data.

Describe program impact by conducting comparative analyses that consider initial starting point of programs and participants, the process of change, and the final status.

Interpretation and Dissemination of Results

Integrate findings about program implementation and program impact to provide clear answers to the major questions identified earlier.

Through dialogue with key stakeholders and experts, interpret the practical and policy implications of the findings. Conduct appropriate additional analyses to help clarify or differentiate results for particular purposes or audiences.

Distribute results of evaluation to stakeholders and others who may use the new knowledge. As appropriate, disseminate findings in ways that contribute to future design refinements and provision of effective intervention/prevention programs.

Figure 21.5   Critical activities in planning and conducting responsive, useful health and education evaluations. Adapted from "The Role of Universities in Child Development" (pp. 13–44), by S. L. Ramey and C. T. Ramey, in *Children and Youth: Interdisciplinary Perspectives,* H. J. Walberg, O. Reyes, and R. P. Weissberg (Eds.), 1997b, Thousand Oaks, CA: Sage. Reprinted with permission.

many of the model programs shown to yield positive benefits have not been adopted and implemented in community settings to realize comparable benefits on a large scale. We think this indicates an inherent limitation in the old-style research that has been primarily conducted within one or two major disciplines, led by university scientists, funded by federal agencies without requiring early and sustained engagement of key community stakeholders, and not designed to take into account public policies and practical issues that will determine whether new programs can readily be implemented in the community.

To a remarkable degree, the historical structure of universities also has guided the structure of the research funding and the ways communities are organized to provide supports for children and families (C. T. Ramey & Ramey, 1997b). Specifically, the historical disciplinary training that grants degrees in areas such as social work, psychology, pediatrics, pediatric dentistry, pediatric rehabilitation, early childhood education, special education, educational psychology, child and family nursing, child psychiatry, public health, and urban planning (and many others) contributed to the creation of parallel types of service organizations and community-based practices that have hindered the provision of well-coordinated, efficient, and comprehensive supports for children and families. This dispersion has created a remarkable fragmentation and duplication of services in a time of limited resources and high need. Similarly, within universities, a highly compartmentalized knowledge base about children and families has evolved, with no obvious way to create a unified understanding of child development and effective means of enhancing the development of the most at-risk children.

Potential benefits of reorganization within universities and communities, consistent with the scientific evidence about how children learn and how their health is promoted, are great. Just as the university-led research and demonstration projects are inherently limited, so, too, are many well-intentioned community-based programs that have not realized their intended benefits, even when they have sought to be comprehensive and coordinated. The community initiatives often do not include rigorous research from the beginning, just as many university-led efforts have not adequately included community input and partners. We think this further supports the need for major policy and organizational changes in both universities and communities—changes that will not be easy or welcomed by all. Genuine reorganization would likely mean the end of some disciplines and practices as we know them today and the creation of new combined or coordinated fields and practices designed to better meet the needs of children and families in ways that are more holistic, informed by scientific findings, and responsive to communities and consumers.

This type of research also places universities in a new position, one in which they are actively supporting relationships to improve well-being in the community, while at the same time generating new knowledge. Accordingly, universities may need to consider how to strategically invest in infrastructure support for this type of research (i.e., on a par with planning for new technology and laboratory supports), how to recognize and reward faculty and staff for productively sustaining these research-service partnerships, and how to operate in more flexible and accommodating ways to promote these partnerships (e.g., creating easy-to-handle subcontracts, joint hiring or supervising of staff, reducing indirect cost rates for certain activities, flexibility in paying for community consultation, offering access to university courses and services to community partners). Finally, universities need to anticipate that the emerging results from longitudinal research may sometimes be controversial and politically charged. Ideally, the partnership agreements will have anticipated a full range of results, and active partnerships will accept responsibility for agreed-upon ways to share and act on the findings. Scientific and academic freedom cannot be compromised; neither should the needs of the community and research participants be ignored in how the findings are interpreted and disseminated. These complicated and thorny issues need to be openly discussed and considered in an ongoing fashion, consistent with the overall goal of promoting children's health and education.

SUMMARY

Both early childhood education programs and community-based prevention and health promotion interventions need to incorporate a transdisciplinary approach that builds on recent scientific findings and reflects advances in integrating the historically separate fields of health and education. This relatively new and innovative approach can be characterized as a systematic endeavor to individualize and integrate the supports provided to treat and educate "the whole child." Health is defined consistent with the

WHO definition as including an individual's psychosocial well-being, not merely the absence of disease or disability. Similarly, education is defined as more than just intellectual ability and performance on standardized measures of academic achievement; that is, a child's progress in the educational arena includes social-emotional skills, the ability to adapt to change, and a wide array of cognitive and problem-solving skills that support lifelong learning and competence.

There are many well-intentioned federal, state, and local multicomponent initiatives under way, including the well-known Head Start, Early Head Start, early intervention programs for children with developmental disabilities and risk conditions, subsidized child care quality enhancement efforts, and school readiness and transition-to-school programs. This chapter presented as an example the Head Start-Public School Early Childhood Transition Demonstration Project, a multisite, congressionally mandated intervention to help promote the educational attainment and health of former Head Start children and their classmates, based on an ideology of two-generation, community-based family support.

Children's health and education are widely recognized as vital for their success as contributing members of society, yet relatively few studies have endeavored to understand how health and education mutually influence each other and combine to determine the course of a child's development. Applied biosocial contextual development is a general conceptual framework that is strongly supported by research findings and has proven useful in designing and studying interventions to improve children's health and education. ABCD identifies multiple and co-occurring types of influences on development from a systems theory perspective. Children's development is dimensionalized in terms of biological and social processes that can be more or less supported or hindered by environmental conditions, and thus contribute to three major classes of interrelated outcomes: children's health status and health promotion behaviors (health); children's behavioral, intellectual, and social development, and their educational progress (education); and children's own internal representations of themselves, their environments, and their experiences (personal constructs).

Many carefully planned interventions have yielded scientific findings about what constitutes effective childhood interventions. We reviewed and summarized these findings by delineating five major principles of ef-

fective early intervention. The scientific principles supported by research are the following:

1. The principle of dosage, in which more intensive or higher-dose interventions yield larger and longer-lasting effects, whereas less intensive interventions often yield limited or no demonstrable benefits.

2. The principle of timing, supporting the conclusion that interventions that are well-timed to take advantage of children's neuroplasticity in multiple domains, by beginning fairly early in life and continuing through periods of rapid growth and learning, produce more positive outcomes.

3. The principle of direct receipt of supports, indicating that, to date, programs that seek to change children only by changing their parents and community providers have not produced evidence of significant benefits to children themselves, whereas programs that provide services directly to children (often accompanied by family and community supports) can alter the developmental trajectories of individual children.

4. The principle of differential benefits, which predicts that planned interventions are likely to have greater or lesser impact on children, depending on a combination of factors, such as the initial type and magnitude of a child's risks and needs and the extent to which these are specifically addressed in the intervention. For example, children whose mother has limited resources to meet her young children's cognitive and language learning needs have benefited significantly more from early educational interventions than have children whose mother initially had much greater amounts of educational, economic, and health resources.

5. The principle of continuity of supports, which affirms the importance of children receiving the right types and amounts of environmental supports for health and education throughout their development. That is, there is no evidence that early intervention programs alone can produce large and sustainable benefits in the absence of children receiving reasonably good supports from schools, families, and communities after the planned intervention.

Much remains to be learned about the ways these five major principles interact across different ages and stages of development and within and across diverse cultural and regional settings. The future of scientific inquiry about children's health and education research will depend largely on the degree to which studies are more carefully designed, implemented, documented, and summarized in ways that can be compared and combined within a practically useful knowledge framework.

To conduct such complex research, especially involving large-scale and sustainable prevention and intervention programs, a new style of collaborative research that engages the community and broader expertise from professionals, scientists, and citizens is vitally needed. Engaging individuals and groups in the early stages of planning and implementation has great promise for producing results that are more valid, more sensitive, and more acceptable and useful to families, practitioners, and communities. Conducting such research necessitates an in-depth understanding of the complex and changing ways that policy, economics, politics, and practice operate in the fields of education and health. The goal of such research is undeniably both basic and applied, and potentially may yield insights to move into an era where the large disparities and inequities in health and education for low-income, historically marginalized groups of children are drastically reduced and eventually eliminated.

REFERENCES

Barnett, W. S. (2004). Does Head Start have lasting cognitive effects? The myth of fade out. In E. Zigler & S. J. Styfco (Eds.), *Head Start debates* (pp. 221–249). Baltimore: Paul H. Brookes.

Bertalanffy, L. V. (1975). *Perspectives on general system theory.* New York: George Braziller.

Binder, A. (1972). A new context for psychology: Social ecology. *American Psychologist, 27,* 903–908.

Blair, C., Ramey, C. T., & Hardin, M. (1995). Early intervention for low birth weight premature infants: Participation and intellectual development. *American Journal on Mental Retardation, 99,* 542–554.

Borkowski, J. G., Ramey, S. L., & Bristol-Powers, M. (Eds.). (2002). *Parenting and the child's world: Influences on academic, intellectual, and social-emotional development.* Hillsdale, NJ: Erlbaum.

Bronfenbrenner, U. (1977). Toward an experimental ecology of human development. *American Psychologist, 32,* 513–530.

Bronfenbrenner, U. (1979). *The ecology of human development.* Cambridge, MA: Harvard University Press.

Bryant, K., Windle, M., & West, S. G. (1997). *The science of prevention: Methodological advances from alcohol and substance abuse research.* Washington, DC: American Psychological Association.

Campbell, F. A., Pungello, E., Burchinal, M., & Ramey, C. T. (2001). The development of cognitive and academic abilities: Growth curves from an early childhood educational experiment. *Developmental Psychology, 37,* 231–242.

Campbell, F. A., Ramey, C. T., Pungello, E., Sparling, J., & Miller-Johnson, S. (2002). Early childhood education: Young adult outcomes from the Abecedarian Project. *Applied Developmental Science, 6,* 42–57.

Coie, J., Watt, N., West, S., Haskins, D., Asarnow, J., Markman, H., et al. (1993). The science of prevention: A conceptual framework and some directions for a national research program. *American Psychologist, 48,* 1013–1022.

Cole, K. N., Dale, P. S., Mills, P. E., & Jenkins, J. R. (1991). Effects of preschool integration for children with disabilities. *Exceptional Children, 58,* 36–45.

Currie, J., & Thomas, D. (1995). Does Head Start make a difference? *American Economic Review, 83,* 241–364.

Garber, H. L. (1988). *Milwaukee Project: Preventing mental retardation in children at risk.* Washington, DC: American Association on Mental Retardation.

Garmezy, N. (1983). Stressors of childhood. In N. Garmezy & M. Rutter (Eds.), *Stress, coping and development in children* (pp. 43–84). New York: McGraw-Hill.

Grantham-McGregor, S., Powell, C., & Fletcher, P. (1989). Stunting, severe malnutrition and mental development in young children. *European Journal of Clinical Nutrition, 43,* 403–409.

Gray, S. W., Ramsey, B. K., & Klaus, R. A. (1982). *From 3 to 20: The early training project.* Baltimore: University Park Press.

Grotberg, E. H. (2003). *Resilience for today.* Westport, CT: Praeger.

Guralnick, M. J., & Bennett, F. C. (Eds.). (1987). *The effectiveness of early intervention for at-risk and handicapped children.* San Diego: Academic Press.

Hart, B., & Risley, T. R. (1995). *Meaningful differences in the everyday experience of young American children.* Baltimore: Paul H. Brookes.

Hauser-Cram, P., Pierson, D. E., Walker, D. K., & Tivnan, T. (1991). *Early education in the public schools.* San Francisco: Jossey-Bass.

Hill, J. L., Brooks-Gunn, J., & Waldfogel, J. (2003). Sustained effects of high participation in an early intervention for low-birth-weight premature infants. *Developmental Psychology, 39,* 730–744.

Horacek, H. J., Ramey, C. T., Campbell, F. A., Hoffman, K. P., & Fletcher, R. H. (1987). Predicting school failure and assessing early interventions with high-risk children. *Journal of the American Academy of Child Psychiatry, 26,* 758–763.

Huttenlocher, P. R. (1990). Morphometric study of human cerebral cortex development. *Neuropsychologia, 28*(6), 517–527.

Infant Health and Development Program. (1990). Enhancing the outcomes of low birth weight, premature infants: A multisite randomized trial. *Journal of the American Medical Association, 263,* 3035–3042.

Kagan, S. L. (1994). Defining and achieving quality in family support. In B. Weissbourd & S. L. Kagan (Eds.), *Putting families first: America's family support movement and the challenge of change* (pp. 375–400). San Francisco: Jossey-Bass.

Kelly, G. A. (1955). *The psychology of personal constructs.* Oxford: Norton.

Kuhl, P. K., Tsao, F. M., & Liu, H. M. (2003). Foreign-language experience in infancy: Effects of short-term exposure and social interaction on phonetic learning. *Proceedings of the National Academy of Science, 100*(15), 9096–9101.

Landesman, S., & Ramey, C. T. (1989). Developmental psychology and mental retardation: Integrating scientific principles with treatment practices. *American Psychologist, 44,* 409–415.

Landesman-Dwyer, S., & Butterfield, E. C. (1983). Mental retardation: Developmental issues in cognitive and social adaptation. In

M. Lewis (Ed.), Origins of intelligence: Infancy and early childhood (2nd ed., pp. 479–519). New York: Plenum Press.

Levenstein, P. (1970). Cognitive growth in preschoolers through verbal interaction with mothers. American Journal of Diseases of Children, 136, 303–309.

Lewin, K. (1936). Principles of topological psychology. New York: McGraw-Hill.

Lewin, K. (1951). Field theory in social science: Selected theoretical papers. New York: Harper & Row.

Lewis, M. (1984). Beyond the dyad. New York: Plenum Press.

Livingston, I. L. (Ed.). (2004). Praeger handbook of Black American health: Policies and issues behind disparities in health (Vols. 1–2). Westport, CT: Praeger.

Madden, J., Levenstein, P., & Levenstein, S. (1976). Longitudinal IQ outcomes of the mother-child home program. Child Development, 76, 1015–1025.

Martin, S. L., Ramey, C. T., & Ramey, S. L. (1990). The prevention of intellectual impairment in children of impoverished families: Findings of a randomized trial of educational day care. American Journal of Public Health, 80, 844–847.

Miller, J. G. (1978). Living systems. New York: McGraw-Hill.

Moser, H. W., Ramey, C. T., & Leonard, C. O. (1990). Mental retardation. In A. E. H. Emery & D. L. Rimoin (Eds.), The principles and practice of medical genetics (Vol. 2, pp. 495–511). New York: Churchill Livingstone.

National Institute of Child Health and Human Development Early Child Care Research Network. (2005). Child care and child development: Results from the NICHD Study of Early Child Care and Youth Development. New York: Plenum Press.

National Safety Council. (2001). Injury facts: 2001 edition. Chicago: Author.

Olds, D. L., Kitzman, H., Cole, R., Robinson, J., Sidora, K., Luckey, D. W., et al. (2004). Effects of nurse home-visiting on maternal life course and child development: Age 6 follow-up results of a randomized trial. Pediatrics, 114, 1550–1559.

Ramey, C. T., Bryant, D. M., Campbell, F. A., Sparling, J. J., & Wasik, B. H. (1988). Early intervention for high-risk children: The Carolina Early Intervention Program. In H. R. Price, E. L. Cowen, R. P. Lorion, & J. Ramos-McKay (Eds.), Fourteen ounces of prevention (pp. 32–43). Washington, DC: American Psychological Association.

Ramey, C. T., Bryant, D. M., Sparling, J. J., & Wasik, B. H. (1985). Project CARE: A comparison of two early intervention strategies to prevent retarded development. Topics in Early Childhood Special Education, 5, 12–25.

Ramey, C. T., Bryant, D. M., Wasik, B. H., Sparling, J. J., Fendt, K. H., & LaVange, L. M. (1992). Infant Health and Development Program for low birth weight, premature infants: Program elements, family participation, and child intelligence. Pediatrics, 89, 454–465.

Ramey, C. T., Campbell, F. A., Burchinal, M., Skinner, M. L., Gardner, D. M., & Ramey, S. L. (2000). Persistent effects of early childhood education on high-risk children and their mothers. Applied Developmental Science, 4, 2–14.

Ramey, C. T., MacPhee, D., & Yeates, K. O. (1982). Preventing developmental retardation: A general systems model. In J. M. Joffee & L. A. Bond (Eds.), Facilitating infant and early childhood development (pp. 343–401). Hanover, NH: University Press of New England.

Ramey, C. T., & Ramey, S. L. (1997a). Evaluating educational programs: Strategies to understand and enhance educational effectiveness. In C. Seefeldt & A. Galper (Eds.), Continuing issues in early childhood education (2nd ed., pp. 274–292). Englewood Cliffs, NJ: Prentice-Hall.

Ramey, C. T., & Ramey, S. L. (1997b). The development of universities and children: Commissioned paper for the Harvard University Project on Schooling and Children. Cambridge, MA: Harvard University Press.

Ramey, C. T., & Ramey, S. L. (1998a). Early intervention and early experience. American Psychologist, 53, 109–120.

Ramey, C. T., & Ramey, S. L. (1998b). Prevention of intellectual disabilities: Early interventions to improve cognitive development. Preventive Medicine, 27, 224–232.

Ramey, C. T., & Ramey, S. L. (1999). Beginning school for children at risk. In R. C. Pianta & M. J. Cox (Eds.), The transition to kindergarten (pp. 217–251). Baltimore: Paul H. Brookes.

Ramey, C. T., & Ramey, S. L. (2004a). Early childhood education: The journey from efficacy research to effective practice. In D. Teti (Ed.), Handbook of research methods in developmental science (pp. 233–248). Malden, MA: Blackwell.

Ramey, C. T., & Ramey, S. L. (2004b). Early educational interventions and intelligence: Implications for Head Start. In E. Zigler & S. Styfco (Eds.), Head Start debates (pp. 3–17). Baltimore: Paul H. Brookes.

Ramey, C. T., & Ramey, S. L. (2004c). Early learning and school readiness: Can early intervention make a difference? Merrill-Palmer Quarterly, 50, 471–491.

Ramey, C. T., Ramey, S. L., Gaines, R., & Blair, C. (1995). Two-generation early intervention programs: A child development perspective. In I. Sigel (Series Ed.) & S. Smith (Vol. Ed.), Two-generation programs for families in poverty—A new intervention strategy: Vol. 9. Advances in applied developmental psychology (pp. 199–228). Norwood, NJ: Ablex.

Ramey, C. T., Ramey, S. L., & Lanzi, R. G. (1998). Differentiating developmental risk levels for families in poverty: Creating a family typology. In M. Lewis & C. Feiring (Eds.), Families, risk, and competence (pp. 187–205). Hillsdale, NJ: Erlbaum.

Ramey, C. T., Yeates, K. O., & Short, E. J. (1984). The plasticity of intellectual development: Insights from preventive intervention. Child Development, 55, 1913–1925.

Ramey, S. L. (2002). The science and art of parenting. In J. G. Borkowski, S. L. Ramey, & M. Bristol-Power (Eds.), Parenting and the child's world: Influences on academic, intellectual, and social-emotional development (pp. 47–71). Hillsdale, NJ: Erlbaum.

Ramey, S. L., Lanzi, R., Phillips, M., & Ramey, C. T. (1998). Perspectives of former Head Start children and their parents on school and the transition to school. Elementary School Journal, 98, 311–328.

Ramey, S. L., & Ramey, C. T. (1992). Early educational intervention with disadvantaged children: To what effect? Applied and Preventive Psychology, 1, 131–140.

Ramey, S. L., & Ramey, C. T. (1997a). Evaluating educational programs: Strategies to understand and enhance educational effectiveness. In C. Seefeldt & A. Galper (Eds.), Continuing issues in early childhood education (2nd ed., pp. 274–292). Englewood Cliffs, NJ: Prentice-Hall.

Ramey, S. L., & Ramey, C. T. (1997b). The role of universities in child development. In H. J. Walberg, O. Reyes, & R. P. Weissberg

(Eds.), *Children and youth: Interdisciplinary perspectives* (pp. 13–44). Thousand Oaks, CA: Sage.

Ramey, S. L., & Ramey, C. T. (1998). The transition to school: Opportunities and challenges for children, families, educators, and communities. *Elementary School Journal, 98,* 293–296.

Ramey, S. L., & Ramey, C. T. (2000). Early childhood experiences and developmental competence. In J. Waldfogel & S. Danziger (Eds.), *Securing the future: Investing in children from birth to college* (pp. 122–150). New York: Russell Sage Foundation.

Ramey, S. L., Ramey, C. T., & Lanzi, R. G. (2004). The transition to school: Building on preschool foundations and preparing for lifelong learning. In E. Zigler & S. J. Styfco (Eds.), *Head Start debates* (pp. 397–413). Baltimore: Paul H. Brookes.

Ramey, S. L., Ramey, C. T., & Phillips, M. M. (1997). *Head Start children's entry into public school* (Research Report 1997–2002). Washington, DC: U.S. Department of Health and Human Services, Administration for Children and Families.

Ramey, S. L., Ramey, C. T., Phillips, M. M., Lanzi, R. G., Brezausek, C., Katholi, C. R., et al. (2001). *Head Start children's entry into public schools: A report on the National Head Start/Public School Early Childhood Transition Demonstration Study* (Contract No. 105-95-1935). Washington, DC: U.S. Department of Health and Human Services, Administration on Children, Youth, and Families.

Ramey, S. L., & Sackett, G. P. (2000). The early caregiving environment: Expanding views on non-parental care and cumulative life experiences. In A. Sameroff, M. Lewis, & S. Miller (Eds.), *Handbook of developmental psychopathology* (2nd ed., pp. 365–380). New York: Plenum Press.

Random House Webster's unabridged dictionary (2nd ed.) (1997). Random House.

Reid, M., Ramey, S. L., & Burchinal, M. (1990). Dialogues with children about their families. In I. Bretherton & M. Watson (Eds.), *Children's perspectives on their families: New directions for child development* (pp. 5–28). San Francisco: Jossey-Bass.

Robinson, N. M., Lanzi, R. G., Weinberg, R. A., Ramey, S. L., & Ramey, C. T. (2002). Family factors associated with high academic competence in former Head Start children at third grade. *Gifted Child Quarterly, 46,* 281–294.

Robinson, N. M., Weinberg, R. A., Redden, D., Ramey, S. L., & Ramey, C. T. (1998). Family factors associated with high academic competence among former Head Start children. *Gifted Child Quarterly, 42,* 148–156.

Rutter, M. (2000). Resilience reconsidered: Conceptual considerations, empirical findings, and policy implications. In S. J. Meisels & J. P. Shonkoff (Eds.), *Handbook of early childhood intervention* (2nd ed., pp. 651–682). New York: Cambridge University Press.

Sameroff, A. J. (1983). Developmental systems: Contexts and evolution. In P. H. Mussen (Ed.), *Handbook of child psychology* (Vol. 1, pp. 237–394). New York: Wiley.

Satcher, D. (2004). Foreword to Praeger handbook of Black American health. In I. L. Livingston (Ed.), *Praeger handbook of Black American health: Policies and issues behind disparities in health* (pp. xxxi–xxxiv). Westport, CT: Praeger.

Scarr, S., & McCartney, K. (1988). Far from home: An experimental evaluation of the mother-child home program in Bermuda. *Child Development, 59,* 531–543.

Schwebel, D. C., Brezausek, C. M., Ramey, S. L., & Ramey, C. (2004). Interactions between child behavior patterns and parenting: Implications for children's unintentional injury risk. *Journal of Pediatric Psychology, 29,* 93–104.

Schweinhart, L. J., & Weikart, D. P. (1983). The effects of the Perry Preschool Program on youths through age 15. In Consortium for Longitudinal Studies (Ed.), *As the twig is bent: Lasting effects of preschool programs* (pp. 71–101). Hillsdale, NJ: Erlbaum.

Shonkoff, J. P., & Phillips, D. A. (2000). *From neurons to neighborhoods: The science of early childhood development.* Washington, DC: National Academy Press.

Slater, M. A., & Power, T. G. (1987). Multidimensional assessment of parenting in single-parent families. In J. P. Vincent (Ed.), *Advances in family intervention, assessment and theory* (pp. 197–228). Greenwich, CT: JAI Press.

Stokols, D. (1992). Establishing and maintaining healthy environments: Toward a social ecology of health promotion. *American Psychologist, 47,* 6–22.

Stokols, D. (1996). Translating social ecological theory into guidelines for community health promotion. *American Journal of Health Promotion, 10,* 282–298.

Teti, D. (Ed.). (2004). *Handbook of research methods in developmental science.* Malden, MA: Blackwell.

Vygotsky, L. S. (1978). *Mind in society: The development of higher psychological processes* (M. Cole, V. John-Steiner, S. Scribner, & E. Souberman, Eds. & Trans.). Cambridge, MA: Harvard University Press.

Waldfogel, J., & Danziger, S. (Eds.). (2001). *Securing the future: Investing in children from birth to college.* New York: Sage.

Wasik, B. H., Ramey, C. T., Bryant, D. M., & Sparling, J. J. (1990). A longitudinal study of two early intervention strategies: Project CARE. *Child Development, 61,* 1682–1696.

Werner, E. E., Bierman, J. M., & French, F. E. (1971). *The children of Kauai: A longitudinal study from the prenatal to age ten.* Honolulu: University Press of Hawaii.

White, K. R. (1991). *Longitudinal studies of the effects of alternative types of early intervention for children with disabilities* (Annual report for project period October 1, 1990–September 30, 1991). Logan: Utah State University, Early Intervention Research Institute.

World Health Organization. (2005). Retrieved September 15, 2005, from http://www.who.int/en.

CHAPTER 22

Parenting Science and Practice

MARC H. BORNSTEIN

States Parties agree that the education of the child shall be
directed to:

(a) The development of the child's personality, talents and
    mental and physical abilities to their fullest potential. . . .
(c) The development of respect for the child's parents.
    Article 29

CONVENTION ON THE RIGHTS OF THE CHILD
(UNITED NATIONS CHILDREN'S FUND, 1990)

Each day approximately three-quarters of a million
adults around the world experience the joys and rewards
as well as the challenges and heartaches of becoming a
new parent (Population Reference Bureau, 2000).
As individuals, each of us has had the experience of
being parented, and many of us relive the experience
when we parent our own children. Yet, parenting remains a somewhat mystifying subject about which few

people agree, but about which almost everyone has
opinions. That said, a surprising amount of solid science
is recently accumulating about parenting. Figure 22.1
shows the increasing popularity of parenting studies
today. As a testament to the demands for information

This chapter summarizes selected aspects of my research, and
portions of the text have appeared in previous scientific publications cited in the references. Preparation of this report was supported by the Intramural Research Program of the NIH, NICHD.
I thank H. Bornstein, K. Crnic, M. Heslington, S. Latif, J.
Sawyer, C. S. Tamis-LeMonda, and C. Varron for comments and
assistance; L. Davidson, M. A. Fenley, L. Gulish, E. L. Pollard,
M. F. Rogers, M. Rosenberg, D. C. Smith, and S. Toal of the Center for Child Well-being, and R. Bradley, K. Crnic, E. Galinsky,
M. Juzang, W. Juzang, J. Kagan, S. Lee, R. M. Lerner, V. Murry,
L. Steinberg, and R. Wooden of the Parenting Network.

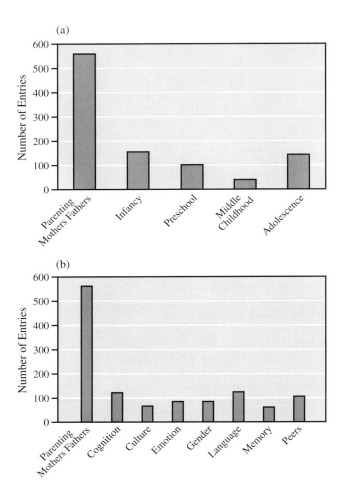

Figure 22.1 (a) Number of entries at the 2005 meeting of the Society for Research in Child Development for parenting, mothers, and fathers versus four phases of childhood. (b) Number of entries for parenting, mothers, and fathers versus the seven next most popular subject areas.

about parenting and to bring order to existing information, this is the first formal chapter on *parenting* per se to appear in the *Handbook of Child Psychology*.

Parenting is a job whose primary object of attention and action is the child—human children do not and cannot grow up as solitary individuals—but parenting is also a status in the life course with consequences for parents themselves. Parents are concerned about the everyday well-being of their children as well as their children's long-term development, and parents are concerned about themselves as parents and want to know how best to cope with the unrelenting demands of parenting. Parenting is a 24/7 job.

Parents are fundamentally invested in their children: their survival, their socialization, and their education.

Evolutionary psychology distinguishes between bringing a new individual into the world and caring for an existing individual, childbearing versus child caring (Bjorklund, Yunger, & Pellegrini, 2002). Whereas species lower in the phylogenetic hierarchy are principally childbearers, mammals such as human beings tend to be devoted child carers perhaps because young human children are totally dependent on parents. Childhood is also the time when we forge our first social bonds, first learn how to express and read basic human emotions, and first make sense of the physical world. In childhood, individual personalities and social styles also first develop. It is parents who lead children through all these dramatic firsts.

Thinking about parent-child relationships highlights parents as agents of child socialization; to a considerable degree, however, parenting is a two-way street. Almost nothing stirs the emotions or rivets the attention of adults more than the birth of a child. Furthermore, by their very coming into existence, children alter the sleeping, eating, and working habits of their parents; they change who parents are and how parents define themselves. In point of fact, parent and child activities are characterized by intricate patterns of synchronous interactions and sensitive mutual understandings (Bornstein, 1989a, 2002b; Kaye, 1982; Stern, 1985; Trevarthen & Aitken, 2001). Infants cry to be fed and changed, and when they wake, they tell parents they are ready to play and to learn. Sometimes, parents' initiatives are proactive; often, however, they are reactive. Parents and their children interact with one another over time to co-construct parenthood as well as childhood.

Historically, theorists of many stripes looked to parents as those thought to influence children the most, although in modern societies, childhood socialization is acknowledged to involve a variety of individuals and to take place in a variety of contexts: families, peer groups, day care centers, school classrooms. Bronfenbrenner (Bronfenbrenner & Morris, 1998) described an apt ecological perspective on parent-child relationships and children's development that has stimulated developmental scientists to think about parents, children, and families from a systemic point of view. This chapter on parenting adheres to that developmental contextual perspective.

Parents are charged with the larger and continuing task to enculturate children, that is, to prepare them for the physical, economic, and psychosocial situations that are characteristic of the environment in which they must survive and, it is hoped, thrive (Benedict, 1938; Bornstein, 1991; LeVine, 2003). Parents have the moment-to-moment job of disambiguating novel, complex, and rapidly changing, uncertain information that arises from children. Yet, despite this flux they are expected to parent consistently, appropriately, and effectively. Parents everywhere appear highly motivated to carry out these assignments. Adults already know (or think they know) something about parenting by the time they first become parents (Zero-to-Three, 1997). Indeed, human beings appear to possess an amount of intuitive knowledge about parenting (Papoušek & Papoušek, 2002), and some characteristics of parenting may be wired into our biological makeup (Fleming & Liu, 2002). For example, parents almost everywhere speak to their infants even though they know that babies cannot understand language per se, and parents even speak to babies in a special speech register. However, human beings also acquire knowledge of what it means to parent by living in a culture: Generational, social, and media images of parenting, children, and family life—handed down or ready made—play significant roles in helping people formulate their parenting cognitions and guide their parenting practices (Holden & Buck, 2002; Sigel & McGillicuddy-De Lisi, 2002). For these reasons, parents from different cultures differ in their opinions about the significance of specific competencies for their children's successful adjustment, they differ in the ages they expect children to reach different milestones or acquire various competencies, and so forth (Goodnow, 2002; Harkness & Super, 1996). Direct experiences with children and self-constructed aspects of parenting are other important factors in developing parenting attitudes and actions.

For their part, children seem primed to profit from parental care. Early childhood in particular has long been thought to be a period in the life cycle when humans are especially plastic, a time when they are open to influences they will carry with them long after they have left their family of origin. The characteristics thought to be especially vulnerable to influence in the first years of children's lives range from the language they speak and the foods they prefer to the politics they follow and religious beliefs they profess.

Parenting is not an activity we normally think of as being especially scientific. Most people just seem to parent, without giving it much thought. Like most things, however, better parenting requires knowledge. Happily, there *is* a science of parenting with much systematic research behind it. The contemporary parenting literature contains thousands of empirical studies. This chapter is based on the emerging science of parenting. One important consequence of the increasingly sophisticated view of the origins and conduct of parenting is the conclusion that parenting can be influenced and modified through education and culture, and thus what we learn about parenting can have far-reaching practical implications.

Scientific analysis of parenting has also helped to shed light on how and why parental practices influence child outcomes. Studies of parenting often rely on correlational designs, but also use experimental manipulations and other techniques that make it possible to examine parenting variables as potential causal mechanisms for specified child outcomes. What forces affect when and how children change? What conditions determine differences among children in their rates of development or their ultimate achievements? These questions constitute the heart of much of parenting science. Of course, children's genetic makeup affects their characteristics and also influences the way they are treated by their parents. However, children's inherited dispositions and their parents' child-rearing choices are closely interwoven and function jointly. There is unassailable evidence that parents can and do influence children.

Parents have many roles to play in child development: to nurture and protect children, to guide children in understanding and expressing proper feelings and emotions, to educate children in behaviors that are acceptable for the stage of childhood they occupy as well as to prepare children for adaptation to a wider range of life roles and contexts they will encounter as they grow (Bornstein, 1989a, 2002a; Badley & Caldwell, 1995). All cultures prescribe certain beliefs and behaviors in their members and proscribe others, and children in the culture must learn both (Maccoby, 2000). For parents, some prescriptions and proscriptions are essentially universal, such as the requirement that patents nurture and protect their offspring. Others, such as what kinds of emotions can be expressed in public, vary from culture to culture. All cultures socialize children in such a way that each new generation acquires relevant prescribed beliefs and behaviors. In the tripartite organization of culture/parent/child, parents bridge cultural practices and ideals to children's everyday life and learning. It is sometimes said that only two kinds of information are transmitted across generations: genes and culture. Parents are "final common pathway" of both. Undergirding all these considerations is the fundamental fact that parenting is requisite to the survival and success of the human race.

PARENTING FOR PARENTS

Parenting is most certainly a functional activity, but parenting is pleasures, privileges, and profits as well as frustrations, fears, and failures. Sociobiological theories of human evolution assert that all individuals are compelled to see their childbearing and child rearing succeed on the argument that it is in that way that they ensure the continuation of their genes (Dawkins, 1976). However, there is much more to parenting than biological continuity. Parenting has its intrinsic rewards. According to a nationwide survey conducted by the National Center for Children, Toddlers, and Families, more than 90% of parents say that when they had their first child, they not only felt "in love" with their baby, but were personally happier than ever before in their lives (Zero-to-Three, 1997). Parents can find interest and derive considerable and continuing pleasure in their relationships and activities with their children.

Parenthood can also enhance one's psychological development, self-confidence, and sense of well-being. Parenting translates into a constellation of new trusts and opens a vista on the "larger picture" of life. Of course, parenthood also gives adults ample opportunity to confront new challenges and to test and display their competencies (Crittenden, 2004). Markus, Cross, and Wurf (1990) reported that feelings of competence as a parent constituted a highly common aspect of the self desired by adults. Furthermore, from infancy, children recognize and show that they prefer the sights, sounds, and smells of their caregivers, and over the course of just the 1st year of life children develop deep and lifelong attachments to sensitive and responsive parents. In essence, then, parents receive a great deal in kind for their hard work and commitment: They are often recipients of unconditional love, and they even pretend to immortality.

Adults are motivated by strong self-interest to parent. Becoming or being a parent means assuming new and vital responsibilities for oneself as well as for others. To parent well, however, parents' own needs must be met. When women are inadequately nourished, for example, their health and social development may be compromised, and their ability to bear and rear healthy children is threatened. Malnourished women fall ill more often, and they have smaller babies. Where birth rates are high and child mortality is also high, women's bodies are stressed and their children are trapped in a cycle of poor health and nutrition.

Mostly, however, parenting is defined by its functional role in the human life cycle. A functionalist approach to parenting asserts that it is desirable to promote traits in children that will lead to their becoming adults who function well within the requirements of the social groups among which they live. The conception of parenting as a set of functions expands the focus of discussion beyond biological parents; other related and nonrelated caregivers may also be centrally engaged in parenting (Leon, 2002). In this functional sense, too, parenting cannot be separated from child development. This chapter focuses on parenting and parents to the degree possible, but does not eschew significant others in the lives of children or children's development.

Becoming a parent is a transforming experience (C. P. Cowan & Cowan, 1992; Heinicke, 2002). New parents experience change in aspects of their personality (i.e., self-efficacy expectations, personal control, anxiety, and depression). Generally during the transition to parenthood, gender roles become more traditional, with women becoming the primary caregiver, and marital satisfaction also normatively declines.

Freud reputedly counted bringing up children as one of the three "impossible professions," the other two being governing nations and psychoanalysis. Some parents are more fully committed than others to the parenting role (Greenberger & Goldberg, 1989; Pulkkinen, 1982). In the end, degree of commitment may rival in importance and for effect the style with which commitment to parent is expressed.

HISTORY AND THEORY OF PARENTING IN BRIEF OVERVIEW

How did parenting studies begin, and how did they arrive at the state we find them in today? A glance backward and a short excursion into parenting theory also helps to show the way we are headed.

A Glance Backward at How Parenting Study Got to be the Way It Is

Child-rearing responsibilities have been viewed as fundamental to societal well-being throughout time, and so every society has paid considerable attention to parenting (French, 2002). Written speculation and sermonizing on parenting date back at least to ancient Egypt, the Code of Hammurabi, and the pre-Socratic philosophers. In the *Laws,* Plato (*ca.* 355 B.C.) theorized about the significance of parenting. Over the centuries since, the writings of clergy and philosophers—as well as popular wisdom—have been replete with theories, convictions, and aphorisms concerning what kinds of child training best ensure social order. Historians, anthropologists, and sociologists of family life have documented evolving patterns of primary child care (Colón with Colón, 1999). However, the formal study of parenting had its beginnings in attempts by philosopher, educator, and scientist parents to do systematically what parents around the world do naturally everyday: observe their children. Such reflections on child rearing first took form as diary descriptions of children in their natural settings written by their own parents, referred to as "baby biographies" (Darwin, 1877; Hall, 1891; Preyer, 1882; Rousseau, 1762; Taine, 1877; Tiedemann, 1787; see Jaeger, 1985; Prochner & Doyon, 1997; Wallace, Franklin, & Keegan, 1994), and they still regularly appear (Brazelton, 1969; Church, 1966; Greene, 1984; Mendelson, 1993; Stern, 1990). These systematic observations of parenting had many salutary effects, heightening awareness in parents and provoking formal studies of how to guide child development. It was only in the twentieth century, however, that parenting became the focus of scientific study.

On account of high rates of child mortality, parents in early times may have cared for but resisted emotional investment in the very young (Dye & Smith, 1986), an orientation that appears to persist where especially dire circumstances reign (Scheper-Hughes, 1989). One historian theorized that parents have generally improved in their orientation to and treatment of children because parents have, through successive generations, improved in their ability to identify and empathize with the special qualities of early childhood (deMause, 1975). Today, advice on parenting children can be found in professional compendia that provide comprehensive medical treatises of prenatal and perinatal development, such as *Effective Care in Pregnancy and Childbirth* (Chalmers, Enkin, & Keirse, 1989); in classic how-to books, such as *Dr. Spock's Baby and Child Care* (Spock & Needlman, 2004) and *Your Baby and Child* (Leach, 1997); in research-grounded academic compilations, such as the *Handbook of Parenting* (Bornstein, 2002a) and *The 10 Basic Principles of Good Parenting* (Steinberg, 2004); as well as in numerous popular periodicals that overflow magazine racks in supermarkets, airports, and pharmacies.

Parenting Theory in Perspective

Historically, many theories in philosophy and psychology focused on parenting. This recapitulation closely follows Maccoby (1992) who observed that at first two overarching theories presumed to encompass most of what was significant about the socialization of children, psychoanalysis and behavior theory, but these all-encompassing perspectives on parenting yielded over time to narrower views specific to domains or ages. Early research also consisted largely of a search for direct connections between parental practices and child outcomes, whereas current work focuses on processes that may mediate the ways parental practices affect a child. Parents were once seen primarily as trainers or transmitters of culture and children as empty vessels who were gradually filled up with the necessary social repertoires; today complex models of socialization involve bidirectional and transactional processes.

Sigmund Freud (1949), founder of *psychoanalytic theory,* asserted the principal role of parenting in child development. Freud hypothesized that the parent's personality determined the nature of parenting, the parent-child relationship, and the child's development as children "internalize" models of their parents and "introject" their values. Another consistent theme among psychoanalytic theorists was that, if parents' emotional needs had not been met during the course of their own development, then their own neuroses would be reflected in their parenting (Holden & Buck, 2002). Anna Freud (1955/1970) described mothers who rejected their children, sometimes due to psychosis but more often because of their own neurotic conflicts. Likewise, Winnicott (1948/1975) and Spitz (1965/1970) saw the roots of aggressive, impulsive, immature, self-centered, and self-critical parenting of abusive parents in the parents' own upbringing. Psychoanalytic theorizing was applied to studies of the role of personality in family life, but the psychoanalytic movement failed to foster much systematic empirical research (Cohler & Paul, 2002). Recent advances redress this imbalance.

Early empirical studies of parenting from a *behavior theory* perspective consisted of straightforward demonstrations that specific behaviors in babies (smiles or vocalizations) could be instrumentally conditioned or extinguished (Rheingold, Gewirtz, & Ross,

1959). From Watson (1924/1970) to Skinner (1976), attempts were made to relate learning theories to socialization. Children's aggression, dependency, sex typing, and identification with parents were often foci of behavioral study. N. E. Miller and Dollard (1941) reformulated hypotheses derived from psychoanalytic theory into simple testable propositions stated in behavior-theoretical terms. Their efforts to predict more complex outcomes such as children's personality attributes from parental socialization methods proved unsuccessful. Sears, Maccoby, and Levin (1957), for example, found few connections between parental child-rearing practices (as reported by parents in interviews) and independent assessments of children's personality characteristics.

Many theories of child psychology place strong emphasis on parents. According to *scaffolding theory,* for example, cognitive and social development occur mainly in interactive contexts with trusted, more competent partners (Rogoff, 1990) who do not reward, punish, or correct children so much as provide a structure for learning that increases the likelihood of children's succeeding in their own attempts to learn. Parents who move their children forward in development arrange circumstances so that the demands of a situation fall beyond the child's "zone of actual development" to within the child's "zone of proximal development." According to Vygotsky (1978), the parent, being more advanced than the child, raises the child's level of competence through reciprocal interactions. This view implies that enduring parental influences stem mainly from the nature of the relationships parents co-construct and continually reconstruct with their children.

Other prominent theories emphasize the active role of the child in parent-child interaction. In one view, children acquire new behaviors without ever performing them overtly and without ever being rewarded, but merely by observing them being performed by nurturant and powerful parents (Bandura, 1962, 1965). A central tenet of this *social learning theory* posits that the primary method by which children learn about the world is through observing the actions of their caregivers. In this way, children gradually internalize the behaviors and values of key figures in their lives (Maccoby, 1959). What children imitate in others, what they remember, and how they process what is remembered all depend on their level of development. Piaget's (1952) *interactionist theorizing,* for example, strongly suggested that children

use parental input rather than parental input into learning determining what children learn.

Bowlby (1969) infused ethological theory into socialization. He contended that parent and child develop reciprocal behaviors particularly through attachment (Ainsworth & Bell, 1969). *Attachment theory* postulates the formation of an internal working model or representation of the attachment relationship, a schema that affects the nature of new relationships formed later in life (Main, Kaplan, & Cassidy, 1985). What is internalized from a child's attachment experience is the quality of the relationship with a parent rather than the personality characteristics of the parent (Sroufe & Fleeson, 1986). A sensitive and responsive parenting style provides a secure base from which children develop cooperation, self-regulation, and social initiative (Putallaz & Heflin, 1990; van IJzendoorn, 1995), internalize social values (Grusec & Goodnow, 1994), and explore the world and engage socially with others (Ainsworth, Blehar, Waters, & Wall, 1978; Sroufe, 1988).

Finally, in the view of *family systems theory,* what transpires between a parent and a child is governed not only by the characteristics of each individual but also by patterns of transaction between them and others (Bornstein & Sawyer, 2005; Broderick, 1993; Cox & Paley, 2003). Parent and child develop in a family system that functions as an organized whole, composed of interdependent elements or subsystems that include individuals as well as relationships among individuals. Each element or subsystem within the family both affects and is affected by other elements; a change in any one aspect of the system can lead to changes in others. How responsive a mother or father may be at any given moment is determined not only by that parent's characteristic warmth and the child's characteristic responsiveness, but also by the patterns they have created jointly and therefore come to expect in their relationship. Moreover, a full family systems approach examines parenting in the context of all relationships within the family and between the family and its many larger social contexts (such as culture). For example, Deal, Hagan, Bass, Hetherington, and Clingempeel (1999) observed that parents behaved one way when the whole family was together and another when each interacted one-on-one with their young child. Like other living systems, families continually strive to attain a dynamic balance amid the experiences of growth and maturation on the one hand, and the need for consistency on the other. In the family systems view, emphasis falls on relationships and interactions as well as contexts that reach beyond the parent and child to encompass the full diversity of the dyad's social embeddedness. "Models that limit examination of the effects of interaction patterns to only the father-child and the mother-child dyads and the direct effects of one individual on another are inadequate for understanding the impact of social interaction patterns in families" (Parke, 2002, p. 41). In family systems theory, interconnected subsystems are also organized in a hierarchical structure; the asymmetrical nature of the parent-child relationship is necessary for child development.

This multidomain family systems model is built on a set of central assumptions. One is that the whole is greater than the sum of its parts. This means that the structure or organization of relationships in the family affects the quality of the relationship between any two family members. For example, each parent's relationships with his or her parents affect their joint ability to work together to parent their child. A major life transition for one family member is likely to affect other family members. Influences within the family system and between the family and other social systems in the culture are transactional. Furthermore, family members are always in the process of development, so that the family system is always in the process of change.

Key questions that must be addressed in parenting theory concern the specification of mechanisms by which parent cognitions and practices produce change in children (Patterson & Fisher, 2002). By the same token, theorists must explain how the child impacts the parent. Successful parenting theories will also have two common characteristics: They will be based on constructs that are readily operationalized, and they will specify effective means of assessment.

Many theoretical accounts for how socialization takes place have been proposed. For most theories, it is primarily through parental control and teaching that the adult culture is passed down to each new generation of children. Parents are the primary agents who set the agenda for what children learn and who administer the rewards and punishments that strengthen desired characteristics and weaken undesired ones in children. More recent theoretical formulations recognize the role of the child in interaction with the parent. Central assumptions of all socialization theories are that, even though socialization and resocialization can occur at any point in the life cycle, childhood is a particularly plastic period

when enduring social skills, personality attributes, and values are inculcated, and that parent-child interactions robustly influence children in other circumstances and at later times.

Looking Ahead to Where Parenting Theory and Research are Going

We know some, but not nearly enough, about parenting. The challenge for the future of the discipline is to acknowledge that up to now we have focused too narrowly on households of predominantly Anglo-Saxon background (Tomlinson & Swartz, 2003), even though such families are in the minority worldwide. Contemporary study fails to adequately represent the cultural diversity and complexity of contemporary parenting. A pervading critique of developmental science is that research in the field has tended to describe the constructs, structures, functions, and processes of child rearing and child development that accord with ideals mostly or exclusively appropriate to middle-class, industrialized and developed, Western societies (Bornstein, 2002c). This unhappy situation cries for change. In the meanwhile, what follows must be seen and understood in light of the extant literature.

PARENTS

The majority of children throughout the world grow up in family systems where there is more than one significant parenting figure guiding more than one child's socialization at a time (McHale et al., 2002). Biological and adoptive mothers and fathers are children's acknowledged principal caregivers. However, parents are not the only agents who contribute to the upbringing and socialization of children. Brothers and sisters (Zukow-Goldring, 2002) and members of the extended family (P. K. Smith & Drew, 2002) all have roles to play. Outside the family, peers (J. R. Harris, 1995, 1998; Hartup, 1992), for example, also have an undeniable impact. Moreover, in different cultures (now and historically) children have been tended by nonparental, nonfamilial care providers—day care workers and metaplot, nurses and slaves—whether in family day care at home, day care facilities, or fields (Clarke-Stewart & Allhusen, 2002). In short, many individuals, other than mother and father, "socially" parent children (Leon, 2002). This chapter is circumscribed to parents, although the choices parents make to share caregiving with nonparents are briefly mentioned.

Mothers

Almost all mammalian species are matrilocal (Wilson, 1975). Trivers (1972, 1974) acknowledged the reality that in land-dwelling mammals after copulation, the female is left in physical possession of the embryo. Even if she lays the fertilized egg almost immediately, the male still has time to abscond, leaving the female with the decision of whether to leave the young to certain death or stay and rear it. On this account, maternal care is more common than paternal care among mammals who are devoted "caregivers" (Bjorklund et al., 2002). Even among species where males show considerable parental altruism, they commonly do less work than females and vanish more quickly (Wilson, 1975). Among human beings, fathers may withdraw from their children when they are unhappily married; mothers typically never do (Kerig, Cowan, & Cowan, 1993). Mothers and fathers do not necessarily share the same parental "investment strategies."

Human cultures distribute the tasks of child care in different ways. Even if fathers' social and legal claims on and responsibilities for children were preeminent historically (French, 2002), most people agree that mothers normally play a more central role in children's development (Barnard & Solchany, 2002; Zero-to-Three, 1997). Cross-cultural surveys and meta-analyses alike attest to the primacy of (biological or adoptive) mothers in child rearing (Holden & Miller, 1999; Leiderman, Tulkin, & Rosenfeld, 1977). The maternal role is better articulated and defined than is the paternal role, and mothers generally have more opportunities to acquire and practice skills that are central to child rearing than do fathers. Normally, mothering helps to interpret and condition fathering, and mothers often serve as gatekeepers to children's fathers and other caregivers (Allen & Hawkins, 1999). DeLuccie (1994) reported that fathers are more involved with their children when mothers assess them to be more competent at caring for children and when mothers are more satisfied with their care of children. Parke (2002) observed that many paternal influences on child development tend to be indirectly mediated through the father's impact on the mother.

For these reasons, theorists, researchers, and clinicians have historically concerned themselves preponderantly with mothering, rather than parenting. Mothers and mothering are investigated much more often and comprehensively than fathers and fathering. There is thus a more extensive body of information about mothers and children than about fathers, siblings, other relatives, or nonfamilial caregivers and children. Western industrialized nations have witnessed increases in the amount of time fathers spend with children; in reality, however, fathers still typically assume little responsibility for child care and rearing, and fathers are primarily helpers to mothers (Cabrera, Tamis-LeMonda, Bradley, Hofferth, & Lamb, 2000). On average, mothers spend between 65% and 80% more time than fathers do in direct one-to-one interaction with their young children (Parke, 2002), and such ratios hold in many different lands (Belsky, Gilstrap, & Rovine, 1984; Collins & Russell, 1991; Greenbaum & Landau, 1982; Jackson, 1987; Kotelchuck, 1976; Montemayor, 1982; Pedersen & Robson, 1969; A. Russell, 1983; G. Russell & Russell, 1987; Szalai, 1972). In both traditional American families (Belsky, Garduque, & Hrncir, 1984) and traditional versus father primary-caregiver Swedish families (Lamb, Frodi, Frodi, & Hwang, 1982), parental gender exerts a greater influence on the quality of parent-child interaction than parental role in the family or employment status.

Fathers

If motherhood goes along with apple pie, the status of fathers is curiously more debatable. Some contemporary observers point to the continuing and widespread abrogation of responsibility by fathers (Blankenhorn, 1995; Popenoe, 1996), whereas others praise fathers' increasing involvement with their children (Lamb, 2000; Parke, 2002; Yeung, Sandberg, Davis-Kern, & Hofferth, 2001). One finds many fewer nonresident moms than dads (King, 1994; Seltzer, 1991). But fathers are neither inept nor uninterested in their children, of course. Fathers engage children in all of the parenting practices that mothers do and hold the same diversity of cognitions. When feeding children, for example, fathers, like mothers, respond to children's cues, either with social bids or by adjusting the pace of the feeding (Parke, 2002). Both father and mother touch and look more closely at a child after the child has vocalized, and both equally increase their rates of speech following a child's vocalizing. Although fathers are capable of performing sensitively, they still yield principal responsibility for child tending to their wives

(Coltrane, 1996). A. Russell (1983) found that most Australian fathers believed in a "maternal instinct" in regard to child care and that fathers who endorsed that belief participated less in child care. But some have argued that fathers are occupied with many more internal family concerns, such as planning, monitoring, and worrying about finances (Palkovitz, 2002). Fathers also contribute uniquely to their children's development; Isley, O'Neil, and Parke (1996) reported that, when maternal affect was accounted for, fathers' affect and control predicted children's social adaptation. Indeed, father presence is critical: Having a resident versus a nonresident father during their first 3 years of life means fewer behavior problems and a better developmental course at ages 4 to 6 in both European American and Latin American children (Crockett, Eggebeen, & Hawkins, 1993).

Coparenting and the Division of Parenting Labor

In point of fact, mothers and fathers appear to interact with and care for children in complementary ways; that is, they tend to divide the labor of caregiving and engage children by emphasizing different types of interactions. When mother-child and father-child play were contrasted developmentally (Power, 1985), both mothers and fathers were found to follow interactional rules of sharing attentional focus on a toy; however, mothers tended to follow the child's focus of interest, whereas fathers tended to establish the attentional focus themselves. Mothers' language but not fathers', and fathers' physical play but not mothers', predict the popularity of boys (MacDonald & Parke, 1984; Parke et al., 1989). Mothers' and fathers' perceptions of their parental efficacy vary in complementary ways as well. Perozynski and Kramer (1999) reported that mothers of young children were more confident than fathers in their ability to use strategies that involve reasoning or talking to the child. In contrast, fathers were more confident than mothers in their use of directives or the threat of force.

Marital relationships affect the quality of mother-child and father-child relationships and child outcomes (Gable, Crnic, & Belsky, 1994; Tamis-LeMonda & Cabrera, 2002), just as how parents work together as a coparenting team can have far-reaching consequences for children (Fincham, 1998). Coparenting *broadly* refers to ways that parents (or parental figures) relate to each other in the role of parent (McHale et al., 2002). Coparenting comprises multiple interrelated components: agreement or disagreement on child-rearing issues; support or undermining of the parental role; and the joint management of family interactions (Feinberg, 2003). This literature closely articulates with the family systems perspective that marital and parent-child relationships are interdependent (Grych, 2002), as each is to the child's development (Cox, Paley, & Harter, 2001; Cummings & Davies, 1994). Mutual emotional support and validation, modeling and sharing parenting skills, buffering marital conflict or dissatisfaction from spilling over into relationships with children constitute some of the ways coparenting functions to nurture child development. The direct-effects model of coparenting postulates that exposure to interparental conflict, for example, influences children's behavior. Erel and Burman (1995) documented changes in children's physiology, cognitions, and emotions in response to marital conflict. Marital discord not only affects children's psychological health and functioning (Cummings, Iannotti, & Zahn-Waxler, 1985; Grych & Fincham, 1990), such as child internalizing and externalizing behaviors and disorders (P. A. Cowan, Cowan, Schultz, & Heming, 1994; Fincham, Grych, & Osborne, 1994), but also their peer relationships (Kerig, 1995; Ladd & Pettit, 2002). The indirect-effects model posits that the impact of marital relationships on children is mediated by the nature and structure of the parent-parent relationship per se (Cummings & Watson-O'Reilly, 1997; Grych & Fincham, 2001), for example, how each parent regulates the other's interactions with the child (gatekeeping). Marital status makes it easy or difficult for a parent to provide social support and opens or limits adults' physical and emotional availability to children.

More specific hypotheses have also been advanced to the effect that emotional security (Davies & Cummings, 1994) and emotion (dys)regulation patterns (Crockenberg & Langrock, 2001) explain the links between parents' interactions as a couple and children's relationships with peers. For example, Cummings (Cummings & Davies, 1995; Cummings & Wilson, 1999) found that destructive marital conflict threatens the child's sense of safety and emotional security in the family.

Other Caregivers

In many underdeveloped societies, siblings or other family members regularly care for children (Zukow-Goldring, 2002), and large numbers of young children today in developed societies normatively participate in nonparental care, enter that care early, stay for longer periods of time, and change types of care often (Clarke-Stewart & Allhusen, 2002; Lamb, 1998). Based on data from the National Longitudinal Study of Youth, Fuller-Thompson, Minkler, and Driver (1997) reported that 11% of grandparents were the primary caregivers of their grandchildren (Chase-Lansdale, Brooks-Gunn, & Zamsky, 1994). Using data from the National Study of Families and Households, Baydar and Brooks-Gunn (1998) reported that approximately 12% of grandmothers resided with a grandchild, and approximately 43% provided child care on a regular basis. An estimated 12.9 million American children under age 6 are enrolled in some kind of nonparental child care on a regular basis (U.S. Bureau of the Census, 1997). Moreover, the National Institute of Child Health and Human Development Early Child Care Research Network (1997) found that the vast majority of children (81%) in a U.S. national study experienced regular nonmaternal child care during their first 12 months of life, with most starting prior to 4 months of age and enrolled for nearly 30 hours per week. Fewer than 20% of children spent their entire 1st year at home with no supplemental care. As a consequence of contemporary social and cultural changes, most notably dual parent employment, the demand for high-quality community-based child care services has burgeoned, and nonparental caregivers have assumed increasing responsibility for meeting children's developmental needs and essentially for preparing children for a future in society (A. E. Gottfried, Gottfried, & Bathurst, 2002). As more families have two parental wage earners earlier in the family life cycle, and more children are cared for by nonparental caregivers earlier in their lives, a looming issue for parents (as well as child care educators, researchers, and policymakers) is the long-term cumulative impact of nonparental child care on parents and children alike.

Summary

Mothers and fathers share central parenting responsibilities for child rearing, although siblings, grandparents, and various nonparental figures also fill salient roles in child care. Often, child caregivers behave in a complementary fashion to one another, dividing the full labor of child rearing by emphasizing mutually reinforcing responsibilities and activities. Still unclear, however, are the long-term cumulative implications of diverse patterns of parenting.

DETERMINANTS OF PARENTING

A critical step on the path to fully understanding parenting is to evaluate forces that shape it. The origins of individual variation in maternal and paternal caregiving, whether of cognitions or practices, are extremely complex. Evolution and history; biology and ethology; family configuration; formal and informal support networks; social, educational, legal, medical, and governmental institutions; socioeconomic class, designed and natural ecology, and culture—as well as children themselves—each contributes to constructing the parent. Nonetheless, certain groups of factors seem to be of paramount importance: (a) intrapersonal and intrapsychic characteristics of parents, (b) actual or perceived characteristics of children, and (c) contextual characteristics. This text follows an ecological orientation from proximal to distal to describe and evaluate the multiple antecedents of parenting (Belsky, 1984; Bronfenbrenner & Morris, 1998). Each of these domains is thought to influence parenting directly and, indirectly through parenting, child development.

Characteristics of Parents Affect Parenting

Forces within the parent shape parenting. Even if most parents face the formidable challenges of parenthood with a degree of psychological naiveté, parents do not meet the test totally unprepared. Both biology and culture equip parents to interpret and respond to the tasks of parenting as well as to childhood and its vicissitudes.

Biological Forces That Shape Parenting

Because securing the survival of offspring is an important element underlying evolutionary selection, it is likely that specific brain mechanisms developed to subserve these operations. Animal studies show that the mammalian forebrain plays an important part in the expression of reproductive behavior, one that is different in female and male animals and is reflected in functional and morphologic sex differences in neural forebrain circuitry (Simerly, 2002). The pivotal role of the forebrain in parenting in mammals is further supported by its involvement in the regulation of specific behaviors during nursing and maternal care of offspring (Champagne, Diorio, Sharma, & Meaney, 2001; Corter & Fleming, 2002; Sheehan & Numan, 2002). Imaging studies reveal that mothers show neural activation in limbic forebrain structures in response to infant crying compared with neutral sounds (Lorberbaum et al., 1999) and bilateral activation of the orbitofrontal cortex while viewing pictures of their own versus unfamiliar infants (Nitschke et al., 2004). Such experience-dependent neuroplastic effects in the human brain are likely to subserve the biological requirements of child care. This can be a critical element in bonding and in securing offspring survival and well-being, thus fostering the reproductive fitness of subsequent generations.

The expression of parental behaviors also depends on hormonal factors that are at least homologous in females and males (Corter & Fleming, 2002; Reburn & Wynne-Edwards, 1999). For example, increases in prolactin levels have been implicated in the expression of parenting behaviors in female as well as male mammals (Dixson & George, 1982), and, whereas estradiol plays a role in regulating maternal behaviors in female animals, the conversion of testosterone into estradiol is believed to be involved in regulating paternal behavior in male animals (Trainor & Marler, 2001, 2002). Human fathers show different peripheral steroid hormone levels compared with childless men (Storey, Walsh, Quinton, & Wynne-Edwards, 2000).

H. Papoušek and Papoušek (2002) developed the notion that some parenting practices are biologically wired in human beings. Intuitive parenting involves responses that are developmentally suited to the age and abilities of the child and that often have the goal of enhancing child adaptation and development. Parents regularly enact intuitive parenting programs in an unconscious fashion; such programs do not require the time and effort typical of conscious decision making, and, being more rapid and efficient, they utilize less attentional reserve. An example of such intuitive parenting is the use of child-directed speech (M. Papoušek, Papoušek, & Bornstein, 1985). Special characteristics of child-directed speech include prosodic features (higher pitch, greater range of frequencies, more varied and exaggerated intonation); simplicity features (shorter utterances, slower tempo, longer pauses between phrases, fewer embedded clauses, fewer auxiliaries); redundancy features (more repetition over shorter amounts of time, more immediate repetition); lexical features (special forms like "mama"); and content features (restriction of topics to the child's world). Cross-cultural study attests that child-directed speech is (essentially) universal (Jacobson, Boersma, Fields, & Olson, 1983; Snow, 1977; but see Ratner & Pye, 1984). Indeed, parents find it difficult to resist or modify such intuitive behaviors, even when asked to do so (Trevarthen, 1979). Additional sup-

port for the premise that some interactions with children are intuitive comes from observations that nonparents (males *and* females) who have little prior experience with children modify their speech as parents do when a young child is present and even when asked to imagine speaking to one (Jacobson et al., 1983). When communicating with their children, even deaf mothers modify their sign language the way hearing mothers use child-directed speech (Erting, Prezioso, & Hynes, 1994). Many parenting cognitions and practices are likewise unconscious, habitual, and possibly thoughtless (see Goodnow, 1997; Kuczynski, 1984).

Personality and Parenting

The idea that personality has a significant part to play in parenting is commonsensical: "One cannot take the 'person' out of the parent" (Vondra, Sysko, & Belsky, 2005, p. 2). This idea has been acknowledged formally at least since Sigmund Freud (1949; see Cohler & Paul, 2002), and a more contemporary view derived from personality psychology is that some features of parenting might reflect general and stable personality characteristics (Kochanska, Clark, & Goldman, 1997). Bronfenbrenner and Morris (1998) contended that personality factors constitute person "force characteristics" most likely to influence children's development because personality not only affects parenting directly but also shapes other social contextual factors and forces that influence parenting, including spouse selection, marital relationships, occupational experiences, and friendships and social supports (Belsky, 1984).

Empirical investigators have long connected various forms of psychopathology with impaired parenting (Downey & Coyne, 1990; Rutter & Quinton, 1984). Belsky, Crinic, and Woodworth (1995), for example, reported that neuroticism is a robust predictor of negativity/rejection toward children, and Kochanska et al. (1997) found that mothers high in the personality characteristics of negative emotionality and disagreeableness were rated by observers as being more rejecting of their children (see also L. A. Clark, Kochanska, & Ready, 2000). Whether fleeting, as in response to economic circumstances or even the birth of the baby (Zahn-Waxler, Duggal, & Gruber, 2002), or enduring, depression affects parenting adversely. Depressed mothers fail to experience—and convey to their children—much happiness with life. Such feelings diminish responsiveness or discoordinate interactions (Tronick & Gianino, 1986), and so depressed parenting is thought to have short- as well as long-term consequences for children (Lyons-Ruth, Zoll, Connell, &

Grunebaum, 1986). Field, Healy, Goldstein, and Guthertz (1990) observed that in face-to-face interactions, children of depressed mothers show less positive and more negative facial affect, vocalize less, protest more, and seem to make less effort to change or improve their lot than do children of nondepressed mothers.

Relative to the amount of attention that has been devoted to studying associations between psychological disorders and parenting, the study of "normal" personality and parenting has been neglected (Belsky & Barends, 2002; Vondra et al., 2005). Parenting reflects transient feelings as well as enduring personality traits (Belsky & Barends, 2002). Features of personality favorable to good parenting might include empathic awareness, predictability, nonintrusiveness, and emotional availability (Martin, 1989). Perceived self-efficacy is also likely to affect parenting positively because parents who feel competent are reinforced and thus motivated to engage in further interactions with their children, which in turn provides them with additional opportunities to read their children's signals fully, interpret them correctly, and respond appropriately. The more rewarding the interaction, the more motivated are parents to seek quality interaction again (Teti & Candelaria, 2002).

Within the normal range, personality characteristics such as self-centeredness and adaptability might be especially pertinent to parenting. For example, adult adaptability would be vital in the first few months, when children's activities appear unpredictable and their cues undifferentiated, and children themselves generally less readable. Self-centered parents may be less likely to put children's needs before their own (Dix, 1991). Women who are more preoccupied with themselves, as measured by physical and sexual concerns, show less effective parenting patterns in the postpartum year (Grossman, Eichler, & Winikoff, 1980). Self-absorbed, these mothers may not show sensitivity to their children's needs (C. P. Cowan & Cowan, 1992), a situation that also seems prevalent among teen mothers (Osofsky, Hann, & Peebles, 1993).

Family of Origin and Parenting

Through intergenerational transmission, via interlocked genetic and experiential pathways, purposefully or unintentionally, one generation influences the parenting beliefs and behaviors of the next (van IJzendoorn, 1992). Fraiberg and her colleagues (Fraiberg, Adelson, & Shapiro, 2003) referred to these influences as "ghosts in the nursery." So a parent's experiences with his or her own parents may have continuing effects on his or her own parenting (Caspi & Elder, 1988; P. K. Smith & Drew, 2002). Mothers who report having had secure and realistic perceptions of their attachments to their own mother, for example, are themselves more likely to have securely attached children (Cummings & Cummings, 2002; Main & Goldwyn, 1984). Ruoppila (1991) found significant correlations between grandparental and parental child rearing in a Finnish sample. Vermulst, de Brock, and van Zutphen (1991) examined parental functioning across generations in a Dutch sample of grandmother-mother dyads. Approximately one-third of the variation in mothers' parental functioning could be explained in terms of earlier parental functioning of the grandmother. The use of physically aggressive and punitive techniques in the grandparent-parent generation predicts similar behavior in the parent-grandchild generation and antisocial behavior in grandchildren (Farrington, 1993; Murphy-Cowan & Stringer, 1999). Marital violence in the family of origin tends to repeat in the successive generation (Stith et al., 2000). When parents abuse their children, the children are at risk of repeating the pattern as adults with their own children (Cicchetti, Toth, & Maughan, 2000; Newcomb & Locke, 2001; Pears & Capaldi, 2001). Sociological studies and meta-analyses find that adult children whose parents divorced are more likely to end their own marriages in divorce (Amato, 1996; Chase-Lansdale, Cherlin, & Kiernan, 1995). Maritally dissatisfied couples are more likely to have had unhappily married parents (Amato & Booth, 2001; Schneewind & Ruppert, 1998).

The Adult Attachment Interview (AAI; George, Kaplan, & Main, 1985) assesses an adult's model of his or her own relationship with his or her parents. A strong predictive link has emerged between the child's attachment with the mother and the mother's own AAI classification (P. K. Smith & Drew, 2002). Van IJzendoorn (1995) reviewed AAI studies that included 854 parent-child dyads and found 75% concordance between the parent's autonomous/nonautonomous classification on the AAI and a child's secure/insecure classification in the Strange Situation. The different components of the person are not equally telling, however. Barends and Belsky (2000) compared the predictive power of three personality traits (Neuroticism, Extraversion, Agreeableness) with that of mothers' working models of attachment, as measured by the AAI: Personality traits predicted mothering observed under naturalistic conditions in the home better than whether a mother's internal working model of attachment was autonomous, dismissive, or preoccupied.

Age and Stage of Life in Parenting

The contemporary demographics of parturition indicate that the rate of teenage motherhood, though epidemic (421,626 babies in the United States in 2003; Hamilton, Martin, & Sutton, 2004), has been decreasing slightly, as has the birth rate for women in their early 20s. At the same time, increasing numbers of older adult women are delaying conception, extending the age range for pregnancy and birth (Hamilton et al., 2004). These demographic changes might be ascribable to several factors. Among teens, the fear of AIDS and the impact of AIDS-prevention education, the introduction and increased use of new forms of birth control, welfare reform, compulsory education, the rise of a more religious and conservative generation, an economic climate with more opportunities for women, and an array of youth sex education programs that stress both abstinence and contraception may have contributed to the decline (McKay & Carrns, 2004). Similarly, multiple factors operate at the other end of the age continuum. The aging of the baby boom generation translates into greater absolute numbers of women in their late 30s and 40s than in previous decades (Ventura, Martin, Curtin, & Mathews, 1997). Moreover, delayed marriage, the pursuit of advanced education, careerism, and high rates of divorce all can contribute to the decision to postpone childbearing. In addition, advances in birth control have made it possible to delay becoming pregnant, and advances in assisted reproductive technologies (*in vitro* fertilization) have made it possible for older women to become pregnant (Golombok, 2002).

These demographic trends, in turn, raise questions about effects that may obtain between age or stage of life and parenting. The psychosocial impacts of early childbirth are fairly well established. Adolescent mothers experience more pregnancy and delivery problems and have less healthy babies than do adult mothers (Coley & Chase-Lansdale, 1998). Very young mothers are also known to express less desirable child-rearing attitudes and to hold less realistic expectations about child development than older mothers (J. Hardy, Astone, Brooks-Gunn, Shapiro, & Miller, 1998; Moore & Brooks-Gunn, 2002). In general, parenthood at very young ages is associated with less favorable maternal actions toward children (Barratt & Roach, 1995; Coley &

Chase-Lansdale, 1998; Moore & Brooks-Gunn, 2002; Pomerleau, Scuccimarri, & Malcuit, 2003).

The effects of aging on parenting are not so clear-cut. A 35-year-old woman has a 1 in 400 chance of conceiving a child with Down syndrome, and this likelihood increases to 1 in 110 by age 40, and to approximately 1 in 35 by the age of 45 (National Down Syndrome Society, 2000). However, older mothers are more likely to adhere to good diets and gain weight appropriately during pregnancy and to begin prenatal care in the first trimester of pregnancy, and are less likely to smoke during pregnancy. Age is often conceived of as a marker for maturity, perspective, and patience; older adult mothers tend to possess more experience and information and may feel more psychologically ready to assume responsibilities of child rearing. When Garrett, Ferron, Ng'andu, Bryant, and Harbin (1994) created a structural model of the determinants of children's motor and social development, for example, mothers' readiness to be a parent was found to be determined by competency and maturity as measured by her age at childbirth.

Whether and how age relates to parenting cognitions or practices appears to depend on specifics of the assessment. On the one hand, mothers of all ages possess implicit beliefs (Holden & Buck, 2002) and engage in child-directed speech (H. Papoušek & Bornstein, 1992). On the other hand, the more mature, experienced, and well-to-do mothers are, the more appropriate and optimal their parenting cognitions and practices are likely to be. However, on the third hand, it was once standard to believe that optimal childbearing takes place between about 20 and about 30 years of age (Rindfuss & Bumpass, 1978). Rossi (1980) proposed a "timing-of-events" model that suggests that socially off-time childbearing results in decreased social reinforcement and leads to the expectation of curvilinear relations between age and parenting. Thus, having a child when very young or very old might represent "off-time" versus "on-time" variations in the progression through this key phase in the life cycle (Helson, Mitchell, & Moane, 1984; Lowenthal, Thurner, & Chiriboga, 1976; Neugarten, 1968).

Of course, age is a "social address" (Wohlwill, 1973), and more proximal intrapersonal factors may play a more central role in parenting. At present, however, there is no comprehensive theory of women's adult development (Roberts & Newton, 1987). For this reason, age usually stands as a reasonable proxy. We can nonetheless point to some critical developmental phenomena that would help to mark adult caregiving.

Executive functions, for example, coordinate cognitive and metacognitive processes through monitoring and controlling the use of knowledge and strategies (Butterfield, Albertson, & Johnston, 1995). Normally, executive functions include self-regulation, sequencing, flexibility, response and inhibition, planning, and organization of behavior (Denckla & Reiss, 1997; Eslinger, 1996). The orderly approach to problems, maintenance of problem solving sets for future goals, control processes for organizing behavior over time, flexibility and effectiveness of verbal self-regulation, skillful use of strategy, and behaviors that alter the likelihood of later events and behaviors are all executive functions and describe well the requirements of parenting.

Grattan and Eslinger (1992) suggested that cognitive flexibility and perspective-taking ability are cognitive prerequisites to empathic understanding; impulse control, temporal integration, and synthesis of multiple pieces of information are cognitive prerequisites to identity formation; symbolic thinking, weighing alternative possibilities, and considering consequences among alternatives are cognitive prerequisites to moral maturity. Thus, executive functions exert powerful influences on social behavior, and immaturity or impairment of executive function can lead to demanding and self-centered behavior, lack of social tact and restraint, impulsive speech and actions, disinhibition, apathy and indifference, and lack of empathy, all of which are hallmarks of dysregulated parenting.

Pennington, Bennetto, McAleer, and Roberts (1996) further detailed the neuropsychological underpinnings of executive function. The prefrontal cortex and its extended networks are thought to mediate executive functions, and they show the most prolonged course of postnatal development of any region of the human brain, with changes in synaptic density detectable even into the teenage years (Huttenlocher, 1990). Giedd et al. (1999) also showed that increases in white matter continue through adolescence into early adulthood, particularly in frontal brain regions. Notably, individuals with localized injury to the prefrontal lobe display poor parenting (Eslinger, Grattan, Damasio, & Damasio, 1992). Consider patient DT, who

> proved unable to anticipate and meet her child's needs, such as planning meals, changing clothing, and providing nurturance and comfort. . . . Her performance has . . . been erratic, impulsive, and marked by poor follow through on required tasks, failure to learn from mistakes,

> and very negative reactions to criticism. . . . [She has] very limited capacity for empathic understanding, inadequate identity development, difficulties in vocational adjustment, and a concrete level of moral reasoning. (Grattan & Eslinger, 1992, p. 185)

DT shows how a profound and devastating lack of executive functions undermines parenting in an individual who otherwise possesses normal motor and sensory functions and a broadly normal range of intellectual performance, perceptual abilities, language, and memory.

Characteristics of Children Affect Parenting

Subtle as well as not so subtle characteristics of children also influence parenting (Hodapp & Ly, 2005; Karraker & Coleman, 2005). Some "child effects" are universal and common to all children; others are unique to a particular child or situation. Children actively select, modify, and create their own environments, including their parenting (Bell, 1968, 1970; Scarr & Kidd, 1983). An experimental study by Anderson, Lytton, and Romney (1986) paired conduct-disordered boys with mothers of conduct-disordered boys and with mothers of normal boys. Conduct-disordered boys elicited negative parenting practices from both sets of mothers. Clearly, in this experimental setting (which controls for genetic effects), characteristics of the child contributed to the type of parenting displayed. A reciprocal effect or transactional model, which asserts that parenting not only affects child behavior but that child behavior also affects parenting, contemporaneously prevails in parenting theory and research.

Some physical features of children likely affect parents everywhere, perhaps in similar ways. By the conclusion of the first trimester, fetuses are felt to move in utero ("quickening"), and soon after (with support) fetuses may survive outside the womb ("viability"). These are significant markers in the life of the child *and* in the lives and psyches of the child's parents. Similarly, after birth, common child characteristics likely influence parenting. The newborn has a large head dominated by a disproportionately large forehead, widely spaced sizable eyes, a small snub nose, an exaggeratedly round face, and a small chin. The ethologist Lorenz (1935/1970) argued that these physiognomic features of "babyishness" provoke adults to express nurturant reactions—even across different species (Alley, 1981, 1983). And from the moment of birth, babies exercise many effective signals that influence parenting: Crying motivates adults to approach and soothe, for example, and smiling encourages adults to stay near (Ainsworth et al., 1978).

Other structural characteristics of children affect parenting and the quality of parent-child interaction; child health status, gender, and developmental age are three significant factors. Preterm children, for example, often have difficulty regulating engagements with parents, as evidenced in increased gaze aversion, decreased play, and lower levels of joint attention, and, reciprocally, their mothers are more active and directive (Goldberg & Di-Vitto, 2002). Although there is evidence that parenting girls and boys is surprisingly similar in many ways (Leaper, 2002; Lytton & Romney, 1991), child gender organizes parents' descriptions, impressions, and expectations of children from the start of life (Condry & Condry, 1976; J. Z. Rubin, Provenzano, & Luria, 1974): Newborn nurseries provide color-coded blankets, accessories, and so forth; baby showers are carefully adorned with regard to sex; and children are fastidiously dressed in sex-typed clothing (Shakin, Shakin, & Sternglanz, 1985). Mondschein, Adolph, and Tamis-LeMonda (2000) found that mothers of 11-month-old males overestimated how well their babies would crawl down a sloped pathway, whereas mothers of 11-month-old females underestimated how well their babies would do, but subsequent tests of crawling ability on the sloped path revealed no sex differences in infant crawling. Finally, stage of child development per se exerts pervasive control over parental behavior. Cross-cultural study shows that mothers of younger children use more affect-laden speech, but that, as children achieve more sophisticated levels of motor exploration and cognitive comprehension, mothers increasingly orient, comment, and prepare children for the world outside the dyad by increasing amounts of information in their speech (Bornstein et al., 1992). Similarly, children's achieving the ability to stand upright and walk alters the nature and quality of parenting (Biringen, Emde, Campos, & Appelbaum, 1995). With each child advance, parenting changes in some corresponding ways.

Idiosyncratic characteristics of individual children are no less stimulating to parents. Goldberg (1977) taxonomized three salient child characteristics that affect parents: responsiveness, readability, and predictability. Responsiveness refers to the extent and quality of child reactivity to stimulation. Readability refers to the definitiveness of child behavioral signals. Predictability refers to the degree to which child behaviors can be anticipated reliably. Each child possesses his or her unique profile of these characteristics that will influence parents. For example, an "easily read" child produces unambiguous cues that allow parents to recognize the child's state of arousal quickly, interpret signals promptly, and thus respond contingently. Having a temperamentally easy child or perceiving a child as temperamentally easy (relatively happy, predictable, soothable, and sociable) enhances a mother's feelings of competence (Deutch, Ruble, Fleming, Brooks-Gunn, & Stangor, 1988).

Childhood is also change, and every child changes at his or her own rate. Understanding, anticipating, and responding to dynamic change in the context of individual variation challenge parents. Parents need to know about and be vigilant to all the complications and subtleties of child development. Child development involves parallel and rapid growth in biological, psychological, and social spheres, and normal development may be nonlinear in nature, stalling sometimes, or even regressing temporarily (Bever, 1982; C. C. Harris, 1983; Strauss & Stavey, 1982).

Every child is an original. Parenting a child is thus akin to trying to judge a moving target, the ever changing child developing in fits and starts at his or her own pace. Interest in the origins and expression of child-to-child variability occupies a central position in parental thinking about child development. The ages at which individual children might achieve a given developmental milestone typically vary enormously (some children say their first word at 9 months, others at 29 months), just as children of a given age vary dramatically among themselves on nearly every index of development (at 1 year, some toddlers comprehend 10 words, others 75). Of course, when and how their children talk or achieve puberty exercises strong psychological and behavioral impacts on parents.

A major problem faced by parents is that, at base, they are constantly trying to divine what is inside their child's head: what children want, what they know, how they feel, what they will do next vis-à-vis the things and people around them. Thus, parents seem constantly in search of patterns, often inferring them on the basis of single transient events.

Contextual Characteristics Affect Parenting

In addition to biology, personality, and children, social and societal factors condition and channel beliefs and behaviors of parents. Family structure, social support networks, socioeconomic class, and culture, for example, encourage or discourage diverse patterns of parenting principles and practices. It is also important to recognize that child-rearing cognitions and practices evolve and change (Bronfenbrenner, 1958; French, 2002), and the attitudes and actions of parents at any one time may differ from those characteristic of parents of different generations.

Family Structure and Parenting

Parenting is influenced by family configuration, among other social situational factors. One of the more dramatic changes in family dynamics is the one that takes place when a second baby is born (Mendelson, 1993; Stewart, 1991); consequently, the social and physical ecologies of first- and later-borns differ (Dunn & Plomin, 1990). Parents treat their second-born children in many ways differently than they treat their first-born children (Sulloway, 1996). Mothers engage, respond, stimulate, talk, and express positive affection more to their firstborns than to later-borns, even when first- and later-borns show no differences in their behavior, indicating that these maternal behaviors do not reflect child effects (Belsky, Gilstrap, & Rovine, 1984). However, mothers are also prone to rate their firstborns as more difficult (J. E. Bates, 1987), which may derive from the fact that firstborns actually are more difficult children, or alternatively, because first-time mothers are less at ease with their children and thus tend to perceive them as more demanding. Reciprocally, multiparas report higher self-efficacy than primiparas (Fish & Stifter, 1993).

The same parents may treat their children in different ways for a multitude of reasons. Dunn (1995), Plomin (1994), and their colleagues (Hetherington, Reiss, & Plomin, 1994) have drawn attention to the importance of understanding variation in parent-child relationship quality within families. Parents may treat children in the same family differently because children differ in age, cognitive level, personality characteristics, sex, or other personal experiences. Combined with variation in genetic makeup, within-family variation in parental treatment is a potent factor in accounting for why children in the same family differ from one another (Dunn & Plomin, 1990; Hetherington et al., 1994).

Social Network and Parenting

Having a baby is a major transition in a person's life, marked by dramatic changes in information seeking, self-definition, and role responsibility (Belsky, 1984; C. P. Cowan & Cowan, 1992). Integration or isolation from potential support networks mitigates or exacerbates parenting (Cochran & Niego, 2002). Social support refers to the psychological and tangible resources available to individuals through their relationships with family, friends, neighbors, work associates, and others (Cutrona & Suhr, 1990; Cutrona & Troutman, 1986; Jennings, Stagg, & Connors, 1991). Crockenberg (1988) taxonomized social support as emotional, instrumental, or informational. Both informal support systems (the extended family) and formal ones (schools, child care, parent education programs, and professionals) influence parenting (Cochran & Niego, 2002; Cotterell, 1986; Crockenberg, 1988; Jennings et al., 1991). Lee and Colletta (1983) studied support-parenting relations in adolescent parents with young children. Mothers who were satisfied with their support reported that they were more affectionate with their children, whereas mothers who were dissatisfied with their support reported more hostility, indifference, and rejection of their children. More child care support is associated with higher-quality face-to-face interactions between mothers and babies (Levine, Garcia Coll, & Oh, 1985). Levitt, Weber, and Clark (1986) confirmed the importance of support from the spouse for mothers' well-being in intact families and extended the impact of that support to differences in the infant-mother relationship. Emotional and child care support from the spouse, but not from other family members, are associated with greater life satisfaction and more positive maternal affect. In fact, intimate support from husbands appears to have the most general positive consequences for maternal competence (Crnic, Greenberg, Ragozin, Robinson, & Basham, 1983). Mothers' social support moderates the effects of daily hassles of parenting (Crnic & Greenberg, 1990): Socially supported mothers are less harried and less overwhelmed, have fewer competing demands on their time, and as a consequence are more available to their children.

A generalized benefit of social support could occur because large social networks provide mothers with regular positive experiences and a set of stable, socially rewarded roles in the community. This kind of support could be related to overall well-being because it provides for positive affect, a sense of predictability and stability in one's life situation, and recognition of self-worth. Members of support networks teach and encourage parents to use more developmentally appropriate caregiving (Bronfenbrenner & Crouter, 1983;

Tolson & Wilson, 1990). A critical question in this literature is whether it is the objective amount of support available to a parent that is important, or parents' perceptions of that support. Hashima and Amato (1994) found in a nationally representative sample that mothers' perceived social support was negatively associated with punitive and other negative parenting behaviors. Another question in this literature relates to the nature and source of support. To establish social support networks for information about child rearing, middle-class American parents typically consult professionals, books, and magazines, as well as relatives and friends (Clarke-Stewart, 1998; Young, 1991). Mothers in other social classes and cultures vary from this mode of data collection, however.

Socioeconomic Status and Parenting

Socioeconomic status (SES) is influential in parenting (Bornstein & Bradley, 2003). Mothers in different SES groups behave similarly in certain ways; however, SES also orders the home environment and other practices of parents toward children (Bornstein, Hahn, Suwalsky, & Haynes, 2003; Hoff, Laursen, & Tardif, 2002). SES-related variation in parenting has diverse effects, as in the likelihood that parents serve their children spinach and read books on child care (Hoff et al., 2002). Large numbers of new mothers in the United States have not finished high school, are not married, or are only teenagers themselves when their babies are born.

Parental education is a key factor in SES (Bornstein et al., 2003). Lower-SES mothers refer to books or other written materials less readily as sources of information about child rearing and child development, whereas middle-SES mothers report that reading material is their primary source of information (Furstenberg, Brooks-Gunn, & Chase-Lansdale, 1989; Hofferth, 1987; Young, 1991), and they seek out and absorb expert advice about child development (Lightfoot & Valsiner, 1992). Parents with more education possess more formal knowledge about child development norms and theories and about child-rearing practices (Conrad, Gross, Fogg, & Ruchala, 1992; MacPhee, 1981; Palacios & Moreno, 1996; Parks & Smeriglio, 1986). Not surprisingly, parent education links to many child health and psychosocial outcomes (E. Chen, Matthews, & Boyce, 2002; J. R. Smith, Brooks-Gunn, & Klebanov, 1997). When Duncan and Brooks-Gunn (1997) statistically controlled for household income and other demographic characteristics, they still found that higher levels of maternal education were associated with better cognitive and educational outcomes in children.

Conversely, low SES and poor education are risk factors in parenting and children's development on many accounts. Low SES adversely affects mothers' psychological functioning and is associated with harsh or inconsistent disciplinary practices (McLoyd, 1998; Simons, Whitbeck, Conger, & Wu, 1991). Low- compared to middle-SES parents typically provide children fewer opportunities for variety in daily stimulation, less appropriate play materials, and less total stimulation (A. W. Gottfried, 1984). Significantly, middle-class mothers converse with their children more, and in systematically more sophisticated ways, than do working-class mothers (Hart & Risley, 1995; Hoff, 2003). These social class differences in maternal speech to children are pervasive: In Israel, for example, upper-class mothers talk, label, and ask "what" questions more often than do lower-middle-class mothers (Ninio, 1980). Higher-SES mothers' encouragement in language undoubtedly facilitates self-expression in children; higher-SES children produce more sounds and later more words than do lower-SES children (Hart & Risley, 1995; M. Papoušek et al., 1985). Parents in higher socioeconomic strata also change more flexibly and more rapidly in response to changes in developmental theory than do parents in lower socioeconomic strata (Bronfenbrenner, 1958). Lower-SES parents believe they have less control over the outcome of their children's development than do higher-SES parents (Elder, Eccles, Ardelt, & Lord, 1995; Luster, Rhoades, & Hass, 1989). Kohn (1963, 1969, 1979) hypothesized that social class differences in fathers' goals and expectations for their children, for example, were related to differences in the requirements and expectations fathers needed to succeed in their jobs.

Overall, financial and social stresses adversely affect the general well-being and health of parents and demand attention and emotional energy from them (Magnuson & Duncan, 2002). In McLoyd's (1998) analysis, great stresses on impoverished parents stemming from the day-to-day struggle to find the resources to pay for food and rent, and the stresses of trying to cope with living in crowded housing and deteriorated, dangerous neighborhoods undermine parenting skills and contribute to disorganizing family life. These circumstances, in turn, may reduce parents' attentiveness, patience, and tolerance toward children (Crnic & Low, 2002). McLoyd found that the deterioration of parenting is responsible for many of the adjustment difficulties of children growing up in impoverished families (see Conger, Ge, Elder, Lorenz, & Simons, 1994). The effects of parental poverty appear to depend on the age and sex of the child, however (Elder, 1974), and parenting in the upper class is not immune from disadvantage either (Luthar, 2003).

Culture and Parenting

Like social class, culture pervasively influences how parents view parenting and how they parent (Bornstein, 1991, 2002c; Harkness & Super, 1996, 2002; LeVine, 2003). Cultural variation in beliefs and behaviors is always impressive, whether observed among different ethnic groups in one society or among groups in different parts of the world. In some cultures, children are reared in extended families in which care is provided by many relatives; in others, mothers and babies are isolated from almost all social contexts. In some groups, fathers are treated as irrelevant social objects; in others, fathers assume complex responsibilities for children. Baumrind's (1967, 1978, 1989) work defined a typology of middle-class European American approaches to parenting children as mixes of control and responsiveness and linked the approach to child outcomes. Other socioeconomic, ethnic, or cultural groups in the United States have different approaches to parenting and value different outcomes (Steinberg, Dornbusch, & Brown, 1992; Steinberg, Mounts, Lamborn, & Dornbusch, 1991). The majority of research in parenting refers to Western psychological traditions and has not situated parenting by specific ethnic groups or within specific cultural traditions. Parenting clearly varies in meaningful ways across ethnicity and culture, however.

Culture influences parenting and child development from very early in life in terms of when and how parents care for children, the extent to which parents permit children freedom to explore, how nurturant or restrictive parents are, which behaviors parents emphasize, and so forth (Benedict, 1938; Whiting, 1981). For example, Japan and the United States maintain reasonably similar levels of modernity and living standards and both are child-centered societies, but the two differ dramatically in terms of history, beliefs, and child-rearing goals (Azuma, 1986; Bornstein, 1989b; Caudill, 1973). Japanese mothers expect early mastery of emotional maturity, self-control, and social courtesy in their offspring, whereas American mothers expect early mastery of verbal competence and self-actualization in theirs. American mothers promote autonomy and organize social interactions with their children so as to foster phys-

ical and verbal assertiveness and independence, and they promote children's interest in the external environment. Japanese mothers organize social interactions so as to consolidate and strengthen closeness and dependency within the mother-child dyad, and they tend to indulge children (Befu, 1986; Doi, 1973; Kojima, 1986).

Culturally defined beliefs are so powerful that parents sometimes act on them as much as or more than on what their senses tell them about their own children. Parents in Samoa, for example, reportedly think of young children as having an angry and willful character, and, independent of what children might actually say, parents consensually report that their children's first word is *tae,* Samoan for "shit" (Ochs, 1988). Likewise, an investigation of expected developmental timetables in new mothers from Australia and Lebanon showed that culture shapes mothers' expectations of children much more than other factors, such as experiences observing their own children, comparing them to other children, and receiving advice from friends and experts (Goodnow, Cashmore, Cotton, & Knight, 1984).

Although social science sometimes succumbs to the mistaken tendency to lump ethnicity and culture, research shows that each is heterogeneous, and across cultures and across subgroups within the same society, different parenting cognitions, different parenting practices, and (not unexpectedly) different patterns of child outcomes prevail (Ogbu, 1993; Stevenson & Lee, 1990).

Ethnic and cultural differences notwithstanding, parents also show striking commonalities in interacting with their children. All must nurture and promote the physical growth of children if their children are to survive (Bornstein, 2002b; LeVine, 2003). Some similarities may reflect biological bases of caregiving, the historical convergence of parenting styles, or the increasing prevalence of a single child-rearing pattern through migration or dissemination via mass media. In the end, different peoples presumably wish to promote some similar general competencies in their young as well as some culture-specific ones. Even where ultimate goals may be similar, however, cultures may differ in proximal ways to achieve them (Bornstein, 1995).

Methodological Note

The literature concerning endogenous and exogenous sources of influence on parenting is rich (R. M. Lerner, Rothbaum, Boulos, & Castellino, 2002). Typically, however, antecedents to parenting have been studied in isolation, and few investigations evaluate multiple influences simultaneously. Thus, the overlap of different antecedents vis-à-vis the unique contribution that any one may make to parenting remains essentially unexplored. For example, parent age may exert important effects on parenting and on children because people who have children at an early age are more likely to have preexisting problems that in turn affect their parenting and their children. Younger parents are likely to have less education (Baldwin & Cain, 1981; Elster, McAnarney, & Lamb, 1983; Luster & Dubow, 1990) and to come from poorer families (Haveman, Wolfe, & Wilson, 1997). With this is mind, family systems theorists have emphasized the importance of considering the possible independence *and* interdependence of organismic, environmental, and experiential determinants of parenting (see Belsky, 1984; Bornstein, 2002b; Bornstein & Sawyer, 2005; Bronfenbrenner & Morris, 1998; R. M. Lerner et al., 2002; Minuchin, 1985).

Summary

To understand variations in parenting, information about multiple domains is required (P. A. Cowan, Powell, & Cowan, 1998), including biological and psychological characteristics of each individual in the family, the quality of relationships in parents' families of origin, the quality of the relationship between parents, their division of roles, communication patterns, and co-parenting, the quality of relationships between parents and each child, and relationships between nuclear family members and key individuals or institutions outside the family (friends, peers, work, child care, school, ethnicity, culture). Parenting stands at the confluence of many complex tributaries of influence; some arise within the individual, whereas others have external sources in the child, in the society, and in the culture.

PARENTING EFFECTS AND THEIR MULTICAUSAL CONTEXT

"As the twig is bent, so grows the tree." "The apple does not fall far from the tree." These sayings reflect the belief (some would say assumption) that parental ideas and actions, and the environments parents create, give rise to differences in children. (The agrarian metaphor for parenting is especially pervasive, stretching as it does from "kindergarten" to "culture.") Much of the early lit-

erature on "parenting effects" built up as a natural consequence of this way of thinking, and much of it used parent-child correlations as its evidentiary base. However true it may be that parents influence children, we recognize that correlation does not prove causation, that the arrow of influence may run in the opposite direction (*viz.,* that children influence parents), and that children's characteristics could be a product of some third familial or extrafamilial factor. There follows next brief comment on parenting effects constructed on correlational designs and thereafter an extended discussion of more powerful and robust approaches to parenting effects. This section concludes with a review of complementary information from behavior genetics and group socialization theory.

Correlational Designs

By some reckoning, parenting is believed to account for 20% to 50% of the variance in child outcomes (Conger & Elder, 1994; Kochanska & Thompson, 1997; Reiss, Neiderhiser, Hetherington, & Plomin, 1999). For example, Patterson and Forgatch (1995) found substantial correlations between parents' disciplinary and monitoring practices and children's negative, coercive behavior both at home and in out-of-home contexts. Chilcoat and Anthony (1996) showed a significant increase in risk of drug sampling for every unit of decrease in parental monitoring after partialling age, sex, and ethnic status.

Most studies of parents and children are correlational in design, the resultant associations have usually been modest, and early advocates sometimes overstated their implications. In actuality, the sizes of zero-order correlations between parent cognitions or practices and child characteristics vary considerably depending on what parent and child variables are considered, the way they are measured, the length of time between predictive and outcome measurements, which analyses are used to investigate the questions, which kinds of children or families living in which circumstances are studied, and whether background variables are statistically controlled. For example, direct behavioral observations yield large effect sizes for environmental associations with social development, whereas parental reports yield small effect sizes. It is not reasonable to expect generalizations about the nature and effects of specific parent-child interactions to span all the ages/stages and domains of child development. Parents foster the development of specific talents (e.g., by providing sports practices) and can influence some activities (e.g., religious beliefs), but may have less influence on others. Research that includes a broader array of parenting attributes and focuses on parenting processes tends to show more robust findings.

Gene-Environment Interactions

Contemporary parenting research has moved beyond a focus on main effects of parenting toward understanding more complex interactions between individuals and their environments. Interactions emerge when a given environment has different effects on an organism depending on the organism's traits. Tienari, Wynne, Moring, Lahti, and Naarala (1994) contrasted children with a schizophrenic biological parent with adopted children who did not carry this risk factor to illustrate how a predisposition can either manifest itself or not, depending on whether certain triggering environmental conditions are present. Adoptees who had a schizophrenic biological parent were more likely to develop a range of psychiatric disorders (including schizophrenia) than adoptees not at risk, but only if they were adopted into dysfunctional families. Bohman (1996) studied adopted children whose biological parents did or did not have a history of criminality. Among adoptees who carried a risk factor from their biological parents, those who had been adopted into dysfunctional homes were much more likely to become criminals than those whose adoptive parents provided stable and supportive environments.

An implicit assumption in parenting studies is that the effects of equivalent parenting are similar for all children. However, studies that pool parenting effects across children with different temperaments might obscure parental effects. There is no reason to expect that a given parenting cognition or practice exerts the same effect on every child. A given parental cognition or practice might have different effects on children with different temperaments. For example, Kochanska (1995, 1997) found that maternal responsiveness and the formation of a close emotional bond with the child fostered the development of conscience in bold, assertive children, whereas maternal gentle child-rearing techniques that de-emphasized power assertion were more effective with shy, temperamentally fearful children.

Experiments

Experimental manipulations help to advance beyond parent-child correlations and interactions to reveal causality. The strongest statement that could be made about parenting effects would be based on experimental treatments or interventions in which parents are assigned randomly to treatment/intervention versus control groups, with resulting changes in the behaviors of both the parents and their otherwise untreated children in the experimental groups. Such experiments show (a) that the intervention alters parenting in the experimental group, (b) that there are no changes in the comparison group, and (c) that change in the mediating mechanisms in the parent effects change in the child.

Animal Studies

When young rhesus monkeys with different reactivity patterns are cross-fostered to mothers that are either reactive or nonreactive, their adult behavior differs from that shown by the biological offspring of reactive and nonreactive mothers (Suomi, 1997). Genetically reactive young animals that are raised by nonreactive mothers for the first 6 months of their lives and then placed in large social groups made up of peers and nonrelated older adults develop normally and rise to the top of their dominance hierarchy. These cross-fostered animals are also adept at avoiding stressful situations and at recruiting social support that enables them to cope with stress. By contrast, reactive animals that are raised by reactive mothers are socially incompetent when placed in the larger living group at 6 months of age and are particularly vulnerable to stress.

Natural Experiments with Human Beings

Studies of children with genetic backgrounds that differ from those of their nurturing families provide a means of simultaneously evaluating the impacts of heredity and experience on child development (H. Z. Ho, 1987; Plomin, 1990; Plomin & DeFries, 1985). In (ideal) natural experiments of adoption, one child shares genes but not environment with biological parents, and another child shares environment but not genes with adoptive parents. In France, children were located who had been given up in infancy by their low-SES parents and adopted by upper-middle-SES parents. These children all had biological siblings or half-siblings who remained with their biological mother and were reared by her in impoverished circumstances. No selective factors differentiated the two groups. When tested in middle childhood, the adopted children's IQs averaged significantly higher than those of their natural siblings, and children who remained with their biological mother were more likely to exhibit failures in school performance (Duyme, Dumaret, & Stanislaw, 1999; Schiff, Duyme, Dumaret, & Tomkiewicz, 1982). Similarly, the Colorado Adoption Project included assessments of rates of communicative development in groups of children either born or adopted into intact families. The language competencies of children correlated with their biological mother's verbal intelligence even though they had not seen their mother since birth. However, adoptive mothers' parenting activities, especially imitating their children's vocalizations and vocalizing contingently to their children's vocalizations, also predicted child language competencies (Hardy-Brown, 1983; Hardy-Brown & Plomin, 1985; Hardy-Brown, Plomin, & DeFries, 1981). These results point to roles for *both* genetics and parenting in child development.

Parenting Interventions

Forgatch (1991) advocated the interpretation of intervention trials as experimental manipulations that test theoretical models of parenting. In interventions to improve the behavioral-training skills of parents of noncompliant children, Forehand and colleagues (Forehand & King, 1977; Forehand, Wells, & Griest, 1980) demonstrated both improvements in parental behavior and behavioral changes in children, as well as increased parental perceptions of improved child behavior and decreased parental depression. Similarly, Belsky, Goode, and Most (1980) found that interventions to increase mothers' didactic interactions with their young children during play resulted in significantly higher exploratory play among children compared to a no-treatment control group. Van den Boom (1989, 1994) demonstrated that an intervention to train lower-class mothers to respond sensitively to their children modified both their negative responses to child irritability and reduced the extent of avoidant attachment in distress-prone children. Dishion, Patterson, and Kavanagh (1992) showed that the reduction of parent-to-child coercive behavior, brought about by a parent-training intervention with a randomly assigned experimental group, produced declining levels of antisocial behavior in aggressive children. P. A. Cowan, Cowan, Ablow, Johnson, and Measelle (2005) observed that parents' participation in classes on effective parenting just prior to their children's kindergarten entry resulted in better school adjustment and higher academic achievement for children in kindergarten and first grade, compared to the children of parents who attended a comparable series of discussion groups without the effective-parenting emphasis. The relative advantage for the children of intervention-group parents persisted through age 10, a period of 6 years.

Studies that randomly assign families to treatment or control groups and that intervene with the parents but do not simultaneously treat the children are rare, but several have shown that, when treatment is able to change parental behavior toward children in specified ways, the behavior of children changes correspondingly. Such experimental studies document that changes in parenting predict changes in children's school adjustment (Forgatch & DeGarmo, 1999), aggressive behavior (Patterson, Dishion, & Chamberlain, 1993), behavior management (Webster-Stratton, 1990), and attachment (P. A. Cowan et al., 1998; Heinicke, Rineman, Ponce, & Guthrie, 2001).

With these sources of data in mind, it is surprising that some critics contend that there is still little compelling evidence that parents influence the psychological functioning of children or adolescents but, rather, that heredity and peers do so. It is illogical and nonscientific to assert the preeminence of one cause over another when each in its own way contributes to an effect. The enterprise is really to understand how these several forces work in concert to shape the developing individual. The following discussion cumulates over the hard-won knowledge of several critiques (see Collins, Maccoby, Steinberg, Hetherington, & Bornstein, 2000; R. M. Lerner et al., 2002; Maccoby, 2000; Vandell, 2000).

The arguments for genetic and social influences on child development complement our understanding of parenting and the effects of parenting.

Behavior Genetics

Behavior genetics seeks to understand biological sources of variation in human characteristics. By studying individuals of varying genetic relatedness (identical and fraternal twins, biological and adopted siblings who live or do not live in the same households), behavioral geneticists attempt to estimate the amount of variation (the heritability; h^2) in characteristics explained by genetic factors. They assume that sources of variation in a characteristic can be separated into independent genetic (G) and environmental (E) components that together (with error variance) add to 100% of the variance in a characteristic. (Note: E is often not directly measured, but estimated as the residual variance not accounted for by G; Caspi, Taylor, Moffitt, & Plomin, 2000.) However, G and E do not play a zero-sum game (Block, 1995; Feldman & Lewontin, 1975; Gottlieb, 1995; Rose, 1995; Turkheimer, 1998).

Furthermore, some behavioral genetic research contends that (a) genetic endowment accounts for child characteristics better than socialization; (b) children with different genetic predispositions elicit different reactions from their parents; and (c) nonshared environments (conceptualized as experiences in and out of the family that result in differences among individuals) play a greater part in child development than shared factors (such as parenting). However, a full consideration of this literature reveals limits on its claims.

1. Heritability can be high at the same time environmental forces are at work. Some environmental factors affect a group or population without altering the rank order of individuals within the group. The prevailing ecological perspective on human development "stresses the interactive and synergistic, rather than additive and competitive, nature of the links between the family and other influences" (Collins et al., 2000, p. 227). Everything that human beings are or do is a joint function of both their genes and their life experiences (Elman et al., 1996).

2. Correlations between child characteristics and parenting reflect genetic linkages between parent and child characteristics but also bidirectional interactive processes. Behavior genetics assigns both child and parent parts of parent-child covariances to the genetic component in the G + E = 100% equation. It may be that the child's part in parent-child covariance (i.e., evocative effects) is genetic, but assigning the parent contribution to genetics is questionable (Maccoby, 2000). Behavior genetics ignores parent-child reciprocal influences. In a developing and unfolding relationship such as the one between a parent and a child, the child influences the parent and the parent influences the child. Parenting is influenced by child characteristics, but parents contribute to child characteristics as well.

3. Behavior genetic designs show parenting effects. Horn (1983) reported that the mean IQ of adopted children was the same as the mean IQ of their adoptive parents, and significantly higher than the mean IQ of their biological parents. This effect presumably follows from how adoptive parents caregive. O'Connor, Deater-Deckard, Fulker, Rutter, and Plomin (1998) identified two groups of adoptees: one at genetic risk for antisocial behavior (i.e., a history of antisocial behavior in the biological mother)

and the other not at risk. At several points during the adoptees' childhood, they assessed both the children's characteristics and the adoptive parents' child-rearing methods. Children carrying a genetic risk for antisocial behavior were more likely to receive negative socialization inputs from their adoptive parents, but parental negative behavior made an independent contribution to children's externalizing, over and above the children's genetic predispositions. Neiss and Rowe (2000) found that parents' education was significantly (if modestly) associated with adopted adolescents' verbal IQ.

4. Behavior genetics assumes that parenting is a shared experience for siblings, and because shared environment effects have sometimes proven to be small, parenting effects must be small. However, parents do not behave toward all their children in the same way, parenting is not perceived by all children in the same way, and parenting does not affect all children in the same way. Twin data support the hypothesis that family environments make a substantial contribution to the child's development (Plomin, 1994; Reiss, 1997). Nonshared environmental effects refer to the influence of events specific to an individual's life, such as illness or particular friends, which are not shared by other family members. Behavioral geneticists have offered two suggestions to account for individual variation among siblings. The first is within-family environmental differences (Dunn & Plomin, 1990; Hoffman, 1991), and the second is differential experience outside the home (J. R. Harris, 1995, 1998; Rowe, 1994). To the extent that siblings perceive differential parental treatment, they experience different environments, which increases the likelihood that they also develop differently in important aspects of intellect and personality compounding genetic dispositions. Genes contribute to making siblings alike, but (as we all recognize) siblings are normally very different from one another, and it is widely held that siblings' different experiences (their nonshared environments) in growing up contribute to making them distinctive individuals (Dunn & Plomin, 1990; Plomin & Daniels, 1987). Even within the same family and home setting, parents (and other factors) help to create distinctive and effective environments for their different children (Stoolmiller, 1999; Turkheimer & Waldron, 2000).

5. Heritability estimates are themselves often indeterminate and variable:

- The genetic contribution might be greater for some human attributes (intellect) than for others (religion).
  - Estimates of the size of the genetic contribution vary depending on the source of information for measuring a trait. Cadoret, Leve, and Devor (1997) reported a range of heritability coefficients for aggressive behavior from .00 for observational studies to .70 for parent-report measures. In a meta-analysis of 24 twin and adoption studies, Miles and Carey (1997) reported substantially greater h^2 values based on parent reports than for those based on adolescent self-reports.
  - Genes function differently in different environments.
  - Meta-analyses show that heredity rarely accounts for as much as 50% of the variation among individuals in a particular population (McCartney, Harris, & Bernieri, 1990).
  - Estimates derived from twin studies might overestimate the genetic contribution because identical twins have more similar environments than do with same-sex fraternal twins.

6. The child outcomes that are the focus of most heritability studies are intelligence and personality, but contemporary parenting studies are concerned with a much broader range of questions. The case for parental influence may be great, for example, for aspects of children's learned behavior. Children's fruit and vegetable consumption is shaped not just by children's taste preferences, but also by their mother's nutritional knowledge, her attitudes about the health benefits of eating more produce, and by her own consumption of fruit and vegetables (Galloway, Fiorito, Lee, & Birch, 2005).

7. Parents' concerns are not only the "final product" of their parenting. They live with their children and are involved in quotidian processes of parenting and cope with a constantly changing set of child-rearing challenges. The upbringing of children is also highly emotional for both parents and children (Pomerantz, Wang, & Ng, 2005). These concerns of parenting are not addressed by behavioral genetics or other approaches to parenting that look only at child outcomes.

8. In behavior genetic twin and adoption studies, degree of biological relatedness between individuals, not specific markers of genetically linked characteristics in the two individuals, is often the primary focus, and variations in environments are infrequently assessed.

Group Socialization Theory

Many researchers have observed that peers exert a strong environmental influence on individual psychological functioning in children.

Lewin (1947) theorized that we change when we participate in peer group interaction, and J. R. Harris (1995, 1998) used this view as a platform from which to assert that experience outside the home, and especially within the peer group, constitutes the major environmental source of influence on development in children. According to J. R. Harris (1995, p. 463), group socialization affects children's behavior, language, cognitions, emotions, and self-esteem, whereas dyadic relationships with parents, teachers, and mentors have minimal effects on these psychological characteristics or functioning in adulthood. However, several counterarguments to this radical proposition mitigate its claims:

1. Parents and peers actually exert joint influences on the developing child (Brown, Mounts, Lamborn, & Steinberg, 1993; Cairns & Cairns, 1994; Dishion, Patterson, Stoolmiller, & Skinner, 1991; Fuligni & Eccles, 1993; Mounts & Steinberg, 1995).

2. The proclivity in individuals to select like-minded peers (Berndt, 1999; Berndt, Hawkins, & Jiao, 1999) might account for observed similarities between children and their friends across a wide array of variables, including school achievement (Epstein, 1983), aggression (Cairns, Cairns, Neckerman, Gest, & Gariepy, 1988), internalized distress (Hogue & Steinberg, 1995), and drug use (Kandel, 1978). Children are not randomly assigned to peer groups; rather, parents and parent-child relationships influence which peers children select.

3. Group socialization may apply to some everyday behaviors and transient attitudes but not to enduring personality traits or values (Brown, 1990).

4. Children vary in their susceptibility to peer influence, and parenting might be a major source of their differential susceptibility. Of course, infants and very young children are hardly exposed to meaningful peer influence.

Social relationship theory posits that multiple relationships are important to children because they meet different developmental needs (Howes, Hamilton, & Phillipsen, 1998; Ladd, Kochenderfer, & Coleman, 1997; MacKinnon-Lewis, Starnes, Volling, & Johnson, 1997; Vandell & Wilson, 1987; Vondra, Shaw, Swearingen, Cohen, & Owens, 1999; Wentzel, 1998). Parents may serve as a source of love, affection, security, protection, advice, and limit setting. Siblings may offer opportunities related to social understanding, conflict management, and differential status. Peer friendships provide mutual commitment, support, and trust. Teachers and nonparental caregivers of young children often act similarly to parents, whereas teachers of older children may be influential for their expertise and access to opportunity. In the end, J. R. Harris (1995) conceded:

> It is important to note that [group socialization theory] does not imply that children can get along without parents. Children are emotionally attached to their parents (and vice versa), are dependent on them for protection and care, and learn skills within the home that may prove useful outside of it; these facts are not questioned. (p. 461)

In short, many individuals in children's lives influence their development, parents prominently included.

Summary

Even parenting's most strident critics acknowledge that parents serve important functions in children's lives: "Parents are the most important part of the child's environment and can determine, to a large extent, how the child turns out" (J. R. Harris, 1998, p. 15). Of course, biological mothers and fathers contribute directly to the nature and development of their children by passing on heritable characteristics (Plomin, 1999). At the same time, all prominent theories of development put experience in the world as either the principal source of individual growth or as a major contributing component (R. M. Lerner, Theokas, & Bobek, 2005; Wachs, 2000). Thus, evidence for heritability effects and peer influences neither negates nor diminishes equally compelling evidence for effects of parenting.

Parenting research today is guided by a developmental contextual perspective. The size of reported parenting effects reflects the fact that parenting is part of a complex developmental system that includes children's own capacities and proclivities, children's and parents' multiple social relationships (with siblings, friends, peers, teachers, and neighbors), and multiple developmental contexts (homes, schools, neighborhoods, so-cioeconomic class, and culture). Within complex developmental systems like the parent-child, it is unlikely that any single factor will account for even substantial amounts of variation. Parenting effects are conditional and not absolute (i.e., true for all children under all conditions). Finally, given the variance related to the number of independent variables, more complex theories that incorporate larger numbers of variables can be expected to account for effects better than simpler theories with fewer variables. Multiple sources of shared and nonshared environmental influences affect the child's life.

PARENTING COGNITIONS AND PRACTICES

What defines parenting? What about parenting affects children? Parenting is instantiated in cognitions and practices. Parenting is also multidimensional, modular, and specific (see Bornstein, 1989a, 2002b), supporting empirical focus on multiple specific cognitions and practices (De Wolff & van IJzendoorn, 1997; MacDonald, 1992; Tamis-LeMonda, Chen, & Bornstein, 1998). Furthermore, the child-rearing cognitions and practices of one's own group may seem natural but may actually be rather unusual when compared with those of other groups.

Parenting Cognitions

When their children are only 1 month of age, 99% of mothers believe that their babies can express interest, 95% joy, 84% anger, 75% surprise, 58% fear, and 34% sadness (Johnson, Emde, Pannabecker, Stenberg, & Davis, 1982). These judgments may reflect children's expressive capacities, or contextual cues, or mothers' subjective inferences. In response to specific questions, mothers describe children's vocal and facial expressions, along with their gestures and arm movements, as the bases of their judgments (H. Papoušek & Papoušek, 2002). Because mothers commonly respond differently to different emotional messages they perceive in their children, they have frequent opportunities to have their inferences fine-tuned or corrected depending on how their children respond in turn. There is therefore good reason to invest confidence in maternal cognitions.

Parenting cognitions include their goals, attitudes, expectations, perceptions, attributions, and actual knowledge of child rearing and child development (Goodnow, 2002; Holden & Buck, 2002; Sigel & McGillicuddy-De Lisi, 2002). Parenting cognitions are generally believed to serve many functions. They affect parents' sense of self, mediate the effectiveness of parenting, and help to organize parenting (Darling & Steinberg, 1993; Dix & Grusec, 1985; Goodnow & Collins, 1990; Harkness & Super, 1996; S. G. Miller, 1988; Murphy, 1992; K. H. Rubin & Mills, 1992; Sigel & McGillicuddy-De Lisi, 2002). Cognitions form a framework from which parents perceive and interpret their children's behaviors. In addition, many theorists reason that because parents' cognitions generate and shape their practices, they in turn shape children's development (Conrad et al., 1992; Darling & Steinberg, 1993; Goodnow, 2002; Holden & Buck, 2002; Hunt & Paraskevopoulos, 1980; Wachs & Camli, 1991). Unfortunately, fewer than a handful of studies have examined the three-term relation among parenting cognitions, parenting practices, and child development completely, although those that have tend to support expected pathways (McGillicuddy-De Lisi, 1982; Seefeldt, Denton, Galper, & Younoszai, 1999). Benasich and Brooks-Gunn (1996), for example, using the prospective longitudinal study data set of a low-birthweight preterm cohort from the multisite Infant Health and Development Program, found that maternal knowledge of child development and child rearing conditioned the quality and structure of the home environment mothers provided, which in turn affected child cognitive and behavioral outcomes.

How parents see themselves vis-à-vis children generally can lead to their expressing one or another kind of affect, thinking, or behavior in child rearing. According to the Zero-to-Three (1997) survey, for example, 90% of new parents in the United States have confidence in their abilities and think of themselves generally as good parents. Mothers who feel efficacious and competent in their role as parents tend to be more responsive, more empathic, and less punitive and have more appropriate developmental expectations (East & Felice, 1996; Parks & Smeriglio, 1986; Schellenbach, Whitman, & Borkowski, 1992). How parents construe childhood in general functions in the same way: Parents who believe that they can or cannot affect children's characteristics modify their parenting accordingly. Zero-to-Three also found that one in four parents in America thinks that a baby is born with a certain level of intelligence that cannot be increased or decreased by how parents interact

with the baby. Mothers who feel effective vis-à-vis their children are motivated to engage in further interactions, which in turn provide them with additional opportunities to understand and interact positively and appropriately with their children (Teti, O'Connell, & Reiner, 1996). Last, how parents see their own children has its specific consequences. Mothers who regard their child as being difficult, for example, are less likely to pay attention or respond to their child's overtures. Their inattentiveness and nonresponsiveness can then foster temperamental difficulties and cognitive shortcomings (Putnam, Sanson, & Rothbart, 2002). In this way, parents' cognitions foster further temperamental problems because they can lead parents to treat children more negatively.

Although it is arguably the case that all parents seek some of the same accomplishments and achievements for their children, notably social adjustment, educational achievement, and economic security, they may do so in substantially different ways. Considerable attention in the parenting literature has focused on variation in parents' cognitions with SES, ethnicity, and culture (see Bornstein & Bradley, 2003; Harwood, Handwerker, Schoelmerich, & Leyendecker, 2001; Kohn, 1963, 1969, 1979; Schulze, Harwood, Schoelmerich, & Leyendecker, 2002). "Beliefs are like possessions" (Abelson, 1986, p. 223), and parents cling to theirs beliefs about parenting and children equally dearly.

A Taxonomy of Parenting Cognitions

Parents' *goals* for their own parenting and for their children arise, in part, out of society's expectations of its adult members (LeVine, 2003). For example, many Western societies encourage independence, self-reliance, and individual achievement among their children, whereas many Asian and Latin cultures encourage interdependence, cooperation, and collaboration (Triandis, 1995). These general values are associated with differences in the socialization goals of parents (Harwood, 1992; Ogbu, 1981). According to D. Y. F. Ho (1994), for example, Confucian ethics emphasize obligation to others rather than individual rights and provide a foundation for parent-child relationships through the notion of filial piety. Among such filial precepts are obeying, honoring, and providing for the material and mental well-being of one's parents, performing the ceremonial duties of ancestral worship, taking care to avoid harm to one's body, ensuring the continuity of the family line, and in general conducting oneself so as to bring honor and not disgrace to the family name. These underlying values are reflected in parents' goals for what it means to be a good parent and what constitutes a good or virtuous child.

Attitudes are a component of social cognition that refer to a tendency, internal state, or explicit evaluation of some object (Eagly, 1992). Some children are relatively relaxed when confronted with an unfamiliar situation and show little indication of distress. Other children react to novel objects and situations with anxiety and try to remain close to their mother. They do not readily explore novel objects or easily interact with unfamiliar people. These actions indicate behavioral inhibition. X. Chen et al. (1998) found cultural differences in mothers' attitudes toward such behavioral inhibition in children. Chinese mothers, who traditionally value mutual interdependence, view behavioral inhibition in toddlers as a positive trait. Behavior inhibition was positively associated with maternal acceptance of the child and maternal belief in encouraging children's achievement. In contrast, for Canadian parents of European origin, who traditionally hold a more individualistic orientation, behavioral inhibition is negatively associated with maternal acceptance and encouragement of children's achievement. Among Chinese families, children who displayed higher levels of behavioral inhibition had a mother who was less likely to believe that physical punishment is the best way to discipline the child and who was less likely to feel angry toward the child. However, maternal punishment orientation was positively correlated with behavioral inhibition in Canadian families; mothers whose children displayed higher levels of behavioral inhibition were more likely to believe that physical punishment was the best discipline strategy. In short, behavioral inhibition in children was associated with positive attitudes in Chinese mothers and negative attitudes in Canadian mothers.

Expectations about developmental norms and milestones—when a child is expected to achieve a particular developmental skill—affect parents' appraisals of their child's development and of child development per se. Adult caregivers—parents, teachers, or others—normally harbor ideas about when children should be capable of certain achievements (Becker & Hall, 1989), and these ideas can themselves affect development. For example, Hopkins and Westra (1989, 1990) surveyed English, Jamaican, and Indian mothers living in the same city and found that Jamaican mothers expected their children to sit and to walk earlier, whereas Indian moth-

ers expected their children to crawl later. In each case, children's actual attainment of developmental milestones accorded with their mother's expectations. Higher-SES mothers generally give earlier age estimates for children's attainment of developmental milestones than lower-SES mothers (Mansbach & Greenbaum, 1999; von der Lippe, 1999). When Filipino mothers of preschool-age children were asked to estimate the age at which their child would acquire a variety of cognitive, psychosocial, and perceptual-motor skills (Williams, Williams, Lopez, & Tayko, 2000), mothers with higher educational attainment had earlier expectations for children's cognitive and psychosocial development (e.g., emotional maturity, independence).

Especially salient *self-perceptions* of parenting have to do with parents' feelings of competence in the role of caregiver, satisfaction gained from caregiving relationships, investment in caregiving, and ability to balance caregiving with other social roles. These distinctive self-perceptions function in child rearing and child development in unique ways. Most is known about parenting competence (Bornstein, Hendricks, et al., 2003; Teti & Candelaria, 2002). Functionally, perceptions of competence in parenting are associated with parents' use of effective child-rearing strategies (Johnston & Mash, 1989; Teti & Gelfand, 1991). Self-efficacy theory posits that adults who evaluate themselves as competent, who know what they can do, and who understand the likely effects of their actions will, as parents, more likely act as constructive partners in their children's development (Bandura, 1986, 1989; Coleman & Karraker, 1998; Conrad et al., 1992; King & Elder, 1998). Feelings of competence relate to behavioral choice and help to determine how much time, effort, and energy to expend in parenting. Eccles and Harold (1996) reported that parents' confidence in their ability to influence their children's academic performance and school achievement was associated with parents' school involvement and predicted parents' helping with children's academic interests (see, too, Hoover-Dempsey & Sandler, 1997).

Investment in, involvement with, and commitment to children is integral to child rearing; indeed, Baumrind and Thompson (2002, p. 3) defined ethical parenting "above all [as] requiring of parents enduring investment and commitment throughout their children's long period of dependency." High-investment parents believe that they can meet their children's needs better than other adults; they hold higher maturity expectations, are more responsive, and view their children more positively

(Greenberger & Goldberg, 1989). In turn, parental involvement relates to developmental outcomes in children (Bogenschneider, 1997; E. V. Clark, 1983; Eccles & Harold, 1996). Parental investment in children's lives and parental responsibility for children's care ensure that children receive the preventive medical attention, physical activity, and proper nutrition they require (Cox & Harter, 2003).

How individuals balance their roles in life, such as parent, spouse, and employee, reflects on their effectiveness in those diverse roles (Perry-Jenkins, Repetti, & Crouter, 2000). People who maintain greater balance score lower on measures of role strain and depression and higher on measures of self-esteem and other indicators of well-being (Marks & MacDermid, 1996). J. V. Lerner and Galambos (1985, 1986) found that mothers' role balance had more of an impact on child development than did mothers' work status per se. Mothers who are unhappy with their roles are more rejecting of their children (Stuckey, McGhee, & Bell, 1982; Yarrow, Scott, DeLeeuw, & Heinig, 1962). Thus, research supports a positive association between the balance struck by employed mothers and their parenting behaviors (Harrell & Ridley, 1975; Stuckey et al., 1982).

In certain circumstances, parents will tend to believe their children are behaving intentionally in one or another way, when the child's behavior may in fact be developmentally typical (K. H. Rubin & Mills, 1992). Thus, parents' *attributions* about their children (often vis-à-vis developmental norms) help to shape parents' caregiving practices, which in turn affect children's lives. Numerous studies have documented that Asian American parents as compared to European American parents attribute the effort the child directs toward school work as most important contributor to the child's academic success (Hess, Chang, & McDevitt, 1987; Okagaki & Sternberg, 1993; Stevenson & Lee, 1990). Cultural variation also characterizes parents' attributions about successful parenting. For example, mothers from Argentina, Belgium, Italy, Israel, Japan, and the United States were asked if being able to successfully comfort their child when the child cries was due to their parenting ability (e.g., "I am good at this."), effort (e.g., "I have tried hard."), mood (e.g., "I am in a good mood."), task difficulty (e.g., "This is easy to do."), or a child characteristic (e.g., "My child makes this easy to do."). Among the culturally differentiated patterns of findings that emerged, Japanese mothers were less likely than mothers from all other nations to attribute success to

their own ability and more likely to indicate that, when they were successful, it was because of the child's behavior (Bornstein et al., 1992).

Parenting *knowledge* encompasses understanding how to care for children, how children develop, and the diverse roles parents play in children's lives. Studies of parents' knowledge of child rearing and child development investigate what kinds of knowledge parents have, how accurate their knowledge is, how parents of different social statuses, ethnicities, or cultures vary in their knowledge, where parents acquire their knowledge, and what factors are related to differences in knowledge. The general state of knowledge that parents possess constitutes a frame of reference from which they interpret their children's behaviors, and knowledge about children's development affects parents' everyday decisions about their children's care and upbringing (Conrad, Gross, Fogg, & Ruchala, 1992; Holden & Buck, 2002; S. G. Miller, 1988; Murphy, 1992). Knowledgeable parents have more realistic expectations and are more likely to behave in developmentally appropriate ways with their children (Grusec & Goodnow, 1994), whereas parents who harbor unrealistic developmental expectations that are not informed by accurate knowledge experience greater stress as a result of mismatches between expectations and actual child behaviors (Teti & Gelfand, 1991).

Parents' knowledge of children's health and safety is measured in terms of awareness of health care, the identification and treatment of illnesses, and accident prevention. These cognitions guide parents' decisions about how to maintain child health and when to seek care if children manifest symptoms (Hickson & Clayton, 2002; Melamed, 2002). For example, sudden infant death syndrome (SIDS) is the leading cause of reported neonatal deaths in the United States (C. A. Miller, 1993), and sleeping prone or on too soft bedding that may cover the child's mouth and nose increases the likelihood of asphyxiation (Scheers, Rutherford, & Kemp, 2003). Yet approximately 20% of infants ages 1 to 3 months are still placed on their stomachs during sleep (Gibson, Dembofsky, Rubin, & Greenspan, 2000).

Parenting knowledge includes understanding the various approaches appropriate to fulfilling the physical and biological and socioemotional and cognitive needs of children as they develop (Goodnow & Collins, 1990). Proper parenting practices follow knowledge of principles related to early experience, bidirectionality of social influences, atypical development, individual differences, instrumental beliefs, management of the child through tuition or modeling, and the responsibilities of being a parent.

Extant research points to definite individual variation in parenting knowledge (Young, 1991; Zero-to-Three, 1997). Parenting researchers have also identified multiple antecedents of parenting knowledge (Belsky, Youngblade, & Pensky, 1989; Cochran, 1993; Goodnow & Collins 1990; MacPhee, 1981). Clarke-Stewart (1998), for example, reported that books and magazine articles were a popular source of advice about general child development, and their most frequent users were first-time and middle-class parents (Deutsch et al., 1988). Friends and relatives constitute a major base of information for younger parents with little child-rearing experience (Belsky et al., 1989). Pediatricians are a resource for all social classes and ages of parent, but they appear to be turned to most often for advice about current or specific problems (Hickson & Clayton, 2002). Mothers' own knowledge tends to relate to their formal, objective experience—exposure to books and manuals, pediatricians, and courses about child rearing—whereas previous informal or subjective experience with children (through babysitting or professional services alone) has been found to correlate not at all or negatively with parenting knowledge (Frankel & Roer-Bornstein, 1982; MacPhee, 1981).

Of course, differences in parents' cognitions may reflect differences in children's prior performance (Entwisle & Hayduk, 1988; Seginer, 1983). A hierarchical regression in which the previous year's grades and parents' perceptions of their child's ability were used to partial out differences in actual and perceived school performance still resulted in group differences in parents' expectations for their child's school attainment. This finding supports the hypothesis that differences in parental cognitions are not simply a response to children's prior achievements, but reflect differences in broader cultural values.

Parenting Practices

In the 1983 *Handbook*, Maccoby and Martin reasoned that parenting style could be assessed along two separate broad dimensions, responsiveness (child-centeredness and warmth) and demandingness (control), which they combined to produce four parenting types: authoritative, authoritarian, permissive, and disengaged. Baumrind's

(1967, 1978, 1991) categories of parenting involve just such an emphasis on style and content. She hypothesized that these practices contribute differentially to child identity formation and cognitive and moral development. Her findings show that some parenting practices facilitate growth (social competency), whereas others do not. An authoritative style combines high levels of warmth with moderate to high levels of control. In middle-class European American children, it is associated with achievement of social competence and overall better adaptation. Authoritarian parenting, by contrast, contains high levels of control but little warmth or responsiveness to children's needs, and it is generally associated with poorer developmental outcomes. In different social classes or ethnic groups, however, different outcome patterns appear to obtain. For example, adolescents from European American and Latin American authoritative homes perform well academically, and better than those coming from nonauthoritative households. However, school performance is similar for authoritatively and for nonauthoritatively reared Asian Americans and African Americans (Dornbusch, Ritter, Leiderman, Roberts, & Fraleigh, 1987).

A small number of domains of parenting practices has been identified as a common core of parental care (Bornstein, 1989a, 2002b; LeVine, 1988; for other componential systems, see Bradley & Caldwell, 1995). They have also been studied for their variation, stability, continuity, and covariation, as well as for their influences on child development.

A Taxonomy of Parenting Practices

In infrahuman primates, the majority of maternal behaviors consist of biologically requisite feeding, grooming, protection, and the like (Bard, 2002; Rheingold, 1963). Some related acts focus on examining offspring and assessing and monitoring their behavioral and physical state. Perhaps these mothers also encourage motor development with physical exercise. Other residual activities among higher primate parents include playing with offspring.

The contents of human parent-child interactions are more dynamic, varied, and discretionary. Moreover, like cognitions, parenting practices tend to be multidimensional, modular, and specific. Several categories of human parental caregiving can be identified: They are nurturant, physical, social, didactic, verbal, and material. Together, these modes are perhaps universal among human beings in different societies, even if their instantiation or emphases (in terms of frequency or duration) vary across groups. These categories capture the most prominent of human parents' activities with children. For their part, human children are reared in, influenced by, and adapt to a social and physical ecology commonly characterized by this parenting taxonomy and its elements.

When parents *nurture,* they meet the biological, physical, and health requirements of their offspring. From a biological evolutionary stance, survival and reproduction are the ultimate criteria of adaptation. After reproduction, survival is achieved through protection of the child and provision of nourishment, but also through processes that involve sharing information and maintaining social order (Wilson, 1975). Child mortality is a perennial parenting concern, and parents are centrally responsible for promoting children's wellness and preventing their illness from the moment of conception, or even earlier. Parents in virtually all higher species nurture their young, providing sustenance, protection, supervision, grooming, and the like. Parents shield children from risks and stressors. Nurturance is a prerequisite for children's survival and well-being; seeing a child's survival to reproductive age enhances parents' probability of passing on their genes (Bjorklund et al., 2002).

Parents promote children's *physical development,* that is their gross and fine motor skills. Parents foster their children's physical growth in many direct and indirect ways. Parents physically move and manipulate babies to reach or step, and they set goals and place rewards for children to achieve. In turn, child growth and maturation affect the ways parents treat a child. How parents organize the physical environment and interact with and speak to children who vary in their physical abilities differ substantially (Campos et al., 2000; Campos, Kermoian, Witherington, & Chen, 1997). Parents talk to the walking as opposed to the crawling toddler differently, just as they interact with the pubertal adolescent differently from the prepubertal.

Parenting in the *social* domain includes the variety of visual, verbal, affective, and physical behaviors parents deploy in engaging children in loving interpersonal exchanges. Through positive feedback, openness and negotiation, listening, and emotional closeness, parents make their children feel valued, accepted, and approved of. Social caregiving includes all the ways parents help and direct children to regulate their own affect and emotions

and influence the communicative styles and interpersonal repertoires that children use to form meaningful and sustained relationships with others. Early in life, dyadic organization is a foundation for an intricate system of communication and interpersonal interaction. Later in childhood, parents mediate and monitor their children's social relationships with others, such as peers (Ladd & Pettit, 2002; K. H. Rubin, Bukowski, & Parker, 1998; Stattin & Kerr, 2000).

Parenting also consists of a variety of *didactic* strategies used to stimulate children to engage and understand the wider natural and designed environments. Didactics organize the young child's attention to properties, objects, or events in the surroundings; introduce, mediate, and interpret the external world; describe and demonstrate; as well as provoke or provide children with opportunities to observe, to imitate, and to learn. Education is a vital and fundamental human parenting function.

Language in parenting is fundamental to child development and to the parent-child bond in itself. The motivation to acquire language is social and is born in interaction, usually with parents (Bloom, 1998). Language also cross-cuts the foregoing domains, as speech to children supports and enriches all domains of child development (Hoff, 2003).

Finally, caregiving includes those ways in which parents *materially* provision and organize the child's world, especially the home and local environments (Wachs, 2000). Parents influence their children not only by what they do but also by the role they play in structuring the physical and social surround. Adults are responsible for the number, variety, and composition of inanimate objects (toys, books, tools) available to the child, the level of ambient stimulation, the situations and locales children find themselves in, the limits on their physical freedom, and the overall physical dimensions of children's experiences. The amount of time children spend interacting with their inanimate surroundings rivals or exceeds the time children spend in direct social interaction with parents or others.

Together, these categories encompass virtually all of parents' important activities with their children. Although these modes of caregiving are conceptually and operationally distinct, in practice parent-child interaction is dynamic, intricate, and multidimensional, and parents regularly engage in combinations of them. Taken as a totality, this constellation of parenting practices constitutes a varied and demanding set of caregiving tasks, and adults differ considerably in terms of how they recognize, esteem, and engage in components of the caregiving repertoire, as well as in how successful they are in executing different components. Traditionally, the mechanisms asserted to convey intergenerational transmission of beliefs and behaviors amongst human families include socialization, teaching, and scaffolding, conditioning and reinforcement, and modeling. Elements of the parenting taxonomy via these means constitute direct parenting experience effects on children's development.

Certain characteristics of this parenting taxonomy merit brief comment:

1. From an evolutionary adaptive view, nurturant and physical parenting seem compulsory; by contrast, social, didactic, language, and material elements appear more discretionary.

2. Nurturant, physical, social, didactic, and verbal parenting are active forms of interaction; physical and material parenting may be active or passive.

3. No one category of parenting is the most prominent all the time, although any one may best characterize a given parent-child interaction at a given time.

4. There is initially asymmetry in parent and child contributions to parenting. As childhood progresses, children play more active and anticipatory roles in their upbringing, whereas initial responsibility for nurturing, promoting physical growth, sociability, teaching, language, and material provisions in child development appear to lie more unambiguously with parents.

Some Prominent Principles of Parenting Cognitions and Practices

For parent-provided experiences to play a meaningful role in child development, they need to meet some psychometric criteria and the mechanism of their action should be explained.

Psychometric Characteristics of Parenting Cognitions and Practices

Four significant psychometric characteristics help to further define and distinguish parenting cognitions and practices. The first has to do with *variation* among parents. Adults vary among themselves in terms of how tenaciously they cling to various parenting cognitions and how often and long they engage in various parenting practices, even when they come from socioeconomically homogeneous groups and from the same culture. For example, the amounts of language which parents address to children varies enormously: Some mothers talk to their infants during as little as 3% and some during as much as 97% of a naturalistic home observation, even when the mothers are sampled from a relatively homogeneous population in terms of education and SES (Bornstein & Ruddy, 1984). As a consequence, the range in amount of language that washes over babies is virtually as large as it can be. This is not to say that there are not also systematic group differences by SES or culture; there are.

The second psychometric feature of parenting has to do with developmental stability and the third with continuity. *Stability* is consistency in the relative ranks of individuals in a group over time, and *continuity* is consistency in the mean level of group performance over time; the two are independent developmental constructs (Bornstein, Brown, & Slater, 1996; McCall, 1981). Summarizing over a variety of samples, time intervals, and types of home assessments, A. W. Gottfried (1984) concluded that parent-provided experiences tend to be stable. Holden and Miller (1999) analyzed the short-term reliability of attitude questionnaires and behavioral observations of parents (mothers) in 11 studies and arrived at a median correlation of .59. The fact that parenting is stable (in some degree) implies that cognitions and practices assessed at one point can be assumed to reflect past as well as future parenting. It also means that indices of parenting can be related systematically to concurrent or future parent and child behavior or performance. Mothers' behavior toward their first- and second-borns when each child was 1 and then 2 years of age shows similar stability (Dunn, Plomin, & Daniels, 1986; Dunn, Plomin, & Nettles, 1985).

Individual parents do not vary in themselves much from day to day. Over longer periods, of course, parenting changes, and it certainly does in response to children's development. The ratio of adult-directed speech to child-directed speech increases across just the first postpartum year (Bornstein & Tamis-LeMonda, 1990); more generally, there is a reduction in time devoted to parenting activities (Fleming, Ruble, Flett, & Van Wagner, 1990), especially caregiving (Holden & Miller, 1999), as children grow and develop. Parents also adjust their behaviors relative to both child age and child capacity or performance (Bellinger, 1980): Sensitive parents tailor their parenting to match their children's developmental progress (Adamson & Bakeman, 1984; Carew, 1980), for example, by providing more didactic experiences as children age (Bornstein & Tamis-LeMonda, 1990; Bornstein et al., 1992; Klein, 1988). They do so as well to children's changing capacities. The mean length of mothers' utterances tends to match the mean length of those of their 12- to 32-month-olds (McLaughlin, White, McDevitt, & Raskin, 1983).

The fourth characteristic of parenting assesses *covariation* among parenting domains. Despite the wide range of activities parents naturally engage in with children, classical authorities, including notably psychoanalysts, personality theorists, ethologists, and attachment theorists, historically and theoretically conceptualized maternal behavior as traitlike and more or less unitary, often denoted as "good," "good enough," "sensitive," "warm," or "adequate" (Ainsworth et al., 1978; Brody, 1956; Brody & Axelrad, 1978; Hunt, 1979; MacPhee, Ramey, & Yeates, 1984; Mahler, Pine, & Bergman, 1975; Rothbaum, 1986; Schaefer, 1959; Symonds, 1939; Wachs & Gruen, 1982; Winnicott, 1957). This view is that parents package the variety of their beliefs and behaviors together into a monolithic set and show the selfsame beliefs or behaviors across domains of interaction, time, and context. Operationally, that is, a parent who engages the child in more emotional and interpersonal exchanges is also the parent who engages the child in more teaching and learning experiences and does so across situations. This trait conceptualization projects parenting as more or less fixed in recurrent patterns, so that the particular pattern embodied by a parent represents the essence of that parent's child rearing.

However, trait approaches have led to erroneous conclusions about the nature of parenting. For example, Thomas and Chess (1977) observed that trait formulations assume an all-or-nothing character and are credited with exclusive significance in determining the child's development; they argued (pp. 78–79) that it is insufficient and inaccurate to characterize a parent in an overall, diffuse way as rejecting, overprotective, insecure, and so on. Rather, a parent's behavior may vary relative to the situation. Moreover, the trait approach to parenting does not invite more differentiated developmental questions or allow for bidirectionality, the fact that different child characteristics may affect or interact with particular factors of parenting. Yet, the child effects position recognizes the manifest behavioral adjustments parents make to children's age and gender, behavior and appearance, temperament and activity. Child-rearing practices reflect the interaction of child, parent, and context. Thus, parent cognition or practice is a joint product of multiple parent and child characteristics based on a history of shared interactions and transformations over time.

Parents naturally engage their children in a range of diverse activities, and parents do not only or necessarily behave in uniform ways. Research has shown that, rather than employing one broad style, parents are adaptable (Smetana, 1994). They change their approach to children of different ages and temperaments and in response to situational constraints such as time available or whether they are in public or in private. In a similar way, Mischel and Shoda (1995) delineated a unified view of personality in which there is consistency across contexts as well as situational specificity (see Fleeson, 2004).

Different domains of parenting are conceptually and operationally distinct, but in practice parents regularly engage in combinations of domains. Positions alternative to the trait conceptualization are that frequently performed activities are not necessarily or rigidly linked psychologically, and that individuals vary in the constellation and pattern of their activities so as to call into question any monistic organization of parenting. The different domains of parenting children constitute coherent but distinctive constructs (Bornstein, 1989a, 2002b). In shorter words, parenting is multidimensional, modular, and specific, and individual parents may possess particular cognitions and emphasize particular practices with their children.

Direct and Indirect Effects of Parenting Cognitions and Practices

Empirical research attests to the short- and long-term influences of parent cognitions and practices on child development. Maternal attentiveness and mood during feeding in the first months predict 3-year child language (Bee et al., 1982). Mothers' affectionately touching, rocking, holding, and smiling at their 6-month-olds predict cognitive competencies at 2 years (Olson, Bates, & Bayles, 1984). Mothers who speak more, prompt more, and respond more during the 1st year have 6-month-olds to 4-year-olds who score higher in standardized evaluations of language and cognition (Bornstein, 1985; Bornstein, Tamis-LeMonda, & Haynes, 1999; Nicely, Tamis-LeMonda, & Bornstein, 1999). Even features of the parent-outfitted physical environment appear to influence child development directly (Wachs & Chan, 1986): New toys and changing room decorations influence child language acquisition in and of themselves, and independent of proximal parenting.

Indirect effects are more subtle and perhaps less noticeable than direct effects, but no less meaningful. One primary type of indirect effect is marital support and communication. Effective coparenting bodes well for child development (McHale et al., 2002), and mothers who report supportive relationships with "secondary parents" (grandparents and the like) are more competent and sensitively responsive to their children than are women lacking such relationships (Grych, 2002). In the extreme, conflict between spouses may reduce the availability of an important source of support in child rearing, namely, one's partner. Short of that, parents embroiled in marital conflict may miss the sometimes subtle signals children use to communicate their needs. Children in these homes may learn that their caregivers are unreliable sources of information or assistance in stressful situations. For example, even 1-year-old children are less likely to look to their maritally dissatisfied father for information or clarification in the face of stress or ambiguity than are like-age children of maritally satisfied fathers (Parke, 2002).

Specificity, Transaction, and Interdependence in Parenting Cognitions and Practices

Parents' cognitions and practices each can influence children via different paths. A common assumption in parenting is that the overall level of parental involvement or stimulation affects the child's overall level of development (see Maccoby & Martin, 1983). An example of this simple model suggests that the development of language in children is determined (at least to some degree) by the amount of language children hear (Hart & Risley, 1995). Indeed, mothers' single-word utterances are just those that appear earliest in their children's vocabularies (Chapman, 1981), and specific characteristics of maternal speech appear to play a part in children's specific styles of speech (E. Bates, Bretherton, & Snyder, 1988).

Increasing evidence suggests, however, that more sophisticated and differentiated mechanisms need to be brought to bear to explain parenting effects (Collins et al., 2000). First, specific (rather than general) parental cognitions and practices appear to relate concurrently and predictively to specific (rather than general) aspects of child competence or performance (Bornstein, 1989b, 2002b; Bradley, Caldwell, & Rock, 1988; Hunt, 1979; Wachs, 2000). It is not the case that overall level of parental stimulation directly affects children's overall level of functioning and compensates for selective deficiencies: Simply providing an adequate

financial base, a big house, or the like does not guarantee, or even speak to, children's development of healthy eating habits, an empathic personality, verbal competence, or other valued capacities. The *specificity principle* states that specific cognitions and practices in specific parents at specific times exert specific effects in child development in specific children in specific ways (Bornstein, 1989a, 2002b).

The specificity principle helps to explain numerous observations and discrepancies in the parenting literature. For example, "Parents who are highly effective at one stage in the child's life [are] not necessarily as effective at another. . . . Similar practices do not necessarily produce the same effects at successive stages in [a] child's life" (Baumrind, 1989, p. 189). Mothers' responses to their children's communicative overtures are central to children's early acquisition of language, but exert less influence on the growth of motor abilities (Tamis-LeMonda & Bornstein, 1994).

The specificity principle is apparently counterintuitive because, according to the Zero-to-Three (1997) national survey, 87% of parents simplistically think that the more stimulation a baby receives, the better off the baby is. In fact, parents need to carefully match the amount and kinds of stimulation they offer to a specific child's specific level of development, specific interests, temperament, and mood at the moment. The specificity principle accords with a situational contextual view of parenting. It is not that there do not exist consistent parenting styles, but parenting is best conceptualized as multidimensional, modular, and specific, reflecting the interactional context. Parenting undergoes frequent adjustments and represents the product of multiple transactional processes. This is person-situation interaction brought to parenting (Dix, 1992; Grusec & Goodnow, 1994; Luster & Okagaki, 2005).

One implication of this position for parenting is that estimates of the strength of parental effects are likely specific to particular parenting cognitions or practices in specific circumstances for specific children at specific points in time. To detect regular relations between antecedents in parenting, experience, and environment on the one hand and outcomes in child characteristics and values on the other, we need to seek and to find precisely the right combinations of independent and dependent variables.

Consider timing as one key term of the specificity formulation. Ethological and attachment theories of parenting posit a special role for early experience in child development. Early parenting influences the child at a particular time point in a particular way, and the consequence for the child endures, independent of later parenting and of any other contribution of the child. This early experience model is consonant with a sensitive period interpretation of parenting effects (Bornstein, 1989c), and data derived from ethology, attachment, psychoanalysis, behaviorism, and neuropsychology support this model with regard to some child outcomes. Wakschlag and Hans (1999), for example, found maternal responsiveness in infancy was related to a decreased risk of behavioral problems in middle childhood after controlling for concurrent parenting.

Early childhood may be a period of plasticity and adaptability to transient conditions, but early effects may not persist or they may be altered or supplanted by subsequent conditions that are more consequential. On this argument, some theorists have questioned the importance of early experience (Kagan, 1998; Lewis, 1997). Alternatively, they argue, parents exert unique influences over their children at points in development that override the effects of earlier experiences and independent of whatever individual differences children carry forward. Empirical support for contemporary experience models typically consists of recovery of functioning from early deprivation and failures of early interventions to show sustained effects (Clarke & Clarke, 1976; Lewis, 1997; Rutter and English and Romanian Adoptees Study Team, 1998).

Third, a cumulative/additive/stable environment model, which combines the first two views, contends that, with repeated and successful experiences, children develop important associations as they assimilate information from one learning experience and apply it to information gained in the next (Rovee-Collier, 1995). That is, a parent-provided experience at any one time does not necessarily affect the child, but meaningful longitudinal relations are structured by similar parenting interactions continually repeating and aggregating through time (Bornstein & Tamis-LeMonda, 1990; Coates & Lewis, 1984; Landry, Smith, Swank, Assel, & Vellet, 2001; Olson et al., 1984). Although longitudinal data provide evidence for unique early, unique contemporary, and cumulative experiential effects between parents and children, for the most part children are reared in stable environments (Holden & Miller, 1999), so that cumulative experiences are very likely.

Furthermore, concurrent and predictive correspondences begin to define the mutual influences that parent and child continuously exert on one another. The *transactional principle* in development acknowledges that the characteristics of an individual shape his or her experiences and, reciprocally, that experiences shape the characteristics of the individual through time (Sameroff, 1983). Bell (1968; Bell & Harper, 1977) was among the first to emphasize the key role that bidirectional effects play in the socialization process. Biological endowment and experience mutually influence development from birth onward, and each life force affects the other as development proceeds to unfold through the life span (R. M. Lerner et al., 2002; Overton, 1998). By virtue of their unique characteristics and propensities—state of arousal, perceptual awareness, cognitive status, emotional expressiveness, and individuality of temperament and personality—children actively contribute, through their interactions with their parents, to producing their own development. Children influence which experiences they will be exposed to, and they interpret and appraise those experiences, and so (in some degree) determine how those experiences will affect them (Scarr & McCartney, 1983). Child and parent bring distinctive characteristics to, and each is believed to change as a result of, every interaction; both parent and child then enter the next round of interaction as changed individuals. For example, child temperament and maternal sensitivity operate in tandem to affect one another and eventually the attachment status of babies (Cassidy, 1994; Seifer, Schiller, Sameroff, Resnick, & Riordan, 1996).

In addition, parents and children are embedded in complex social systems marked by strong forms of *interdependence* associated with responsibilities and functions of family members through time. Interdependence means that to understand the responsibilities and functions of any one family member necessitates recognizing the complementary responsibilities and functions of other family members (Bornstein & Sawyer, 2005). When one member of the family changes in some way, all members of the family are potentially affected. Beyond the nucleus family system, all families are also embedded in, influence, and are themselves affected by larger social systems. These include both formal and informal support systems, extended families, community ties with friends and neighbors, work sites, social, educational, and medical institutions, and the culture at large.

To fathom the nature of parenthood and parent-child relationships within families, therefore, requires a *multivariate* and *dynamic* stance. Only by taking multiple circumstances into consideration simultaneously can we appreciate individual-, dyadic-, and family-level aspects within the family and the embeddedness of the family within its many relevant extrafamilial systems. The multiple pathways and dynamics of parenting and child development present really quite messy facts of life, and it makes everyone's job harder: Researchers are challenged to develop new paradigms and methodologies to accommodate this chaos; similarly, the use of this perspective in the development and implementation of parenting interventions as well as policy is made problematic. Yet, it is only out of this complexity and chaos that we can possibly understand more about the reality of families and children and parenting.

Cognition-Practice Relations in Parenting

Are parents' cognitions about their own practices accurate and valid? Intuitively, parents' child-rearing beliefs might be expected to relate to their child-rearing behaviors. Indeed, parents' cognitions are hypothesized by many to direct parents' child-rearing practices (Darling & Steinberg, 1993; Sigel & McGillicuddy-De Lisi, 2002). Nonetheless, the relation between beliefs and behaviors is historically an unsettled area in social psychology (Festinger, 1964; Green, 1954; LaPiere, 1934), and relations between parental beliefs and behaviors specifically are equally problematic (Okagaki & Bingham, 2005; Goodnow & Collins, 1990; Holden, 2002; S. G. Miller, 1988; Sigel & McGillicuddy-De Lisi, 2002). Coordinate relations between parents' beliefs and behaviors have often proven elusive (S. G. Miller, 1988), with many researchers reporting no relations between mothers' professed parenting attitudes and their activities with their children (Cote & Bornstein, 2000; McGillicuddy-De Lisi, 1992). In many cases, those parenting beliefs and behaviors that have been studied have been general and have not been conceptually corresponding, and so there has been little reason to expect covariation. Other studies have reported correlations between parents' beliefs and behaviors that are relatively weak or positive but nonsignificant (Coleman & Karraker, 2003; Mantzicopoulos, 1997; Sigel & McGillicuddy-De Lisi, 2002).

When more circumscribed and corresponding domains are studied, some maternal beliefs relate to some self-reported or observed maternal child-rearing behaviors (Kinlaw, Kurtz-Costes, & Goldman-Fraser, 2001; Stevens, 1984). Thus, the strength of the association between parents' cognitions and practices appears to depend, at least in part, on the closeness of the conceptual match between the contents of the beliefs and the types of behaviors that are measured (DeBaryshe, 1995), for example, between mothers' authoritative attitudes and discipline strategies (Kochanska, Kuczynski, & Radke-Yarrow, 1989), beliefs about child-rearing practices and actual caregiving behaviors (Wachs & Camli, 1991), and beliefs about parenting effectiveness and caregiving competence (Teti & Gelfand, 1991). The degree to which mothers believe that children's development can be facilitated by their social environment is positively correlated with the amount and type of language that mothers use during mother-child interactions (Donahue, Pearl, & Herzog, 1997). Harwood, Miller, and Irizarry (1995) found that European American mothers underscore the importance of values such as independence, assertiveness, and creativity when asked to describe their ideal child, whereas Latina mothers underscore the importance of obedience and respect for theirs. In line with these expressed values, U.S. mothers foster independence in their children; for example, in naturalistic mother-child interactions during feeding, U.S. mothers encourage their children to feed themselves at 8 months of age. In contrast, Latina mothers hold their children close on their lap during mealtimes and take control of feeding them meals from start to finish.

Of course, associations between parents' cognitions and practices could, also in part, be a methodological artifact of shared source variance: Much of the research that has reported significant correlations between parents' cognitions and practices has utilized parents' self-reports to measure both, inflating relations between the variables being studied (S. G. Miller, 1988).

Summary

Biological parents endow a significant and pervasive genetic makeup to their children, with its beneficial or other consequences for children's proclivities and abilities. Beyond parents' genes, prominent theories of human development put experience in the world as either the principal source of individual growth or as a major contributing component. It falls to parents (and other caregivers) to shape most, if not all, of young children's experiences, and parents directly influence child development both by the beliefs they hold and by the behaviors they exhibit. Parenting cognitions include, for example, perceptions about, attitudes toward, and knowledge of all aspects of parenting and childhood. Out of the dynamic range and complexity of individual activities that constitute parenting, major domains of parent-child interaction have been distinguished. These domains are conceptually separable but fundamentally integral, and each is developmentally significant.

Caregiving behaviors and styles constitute direct experience effects of parenting. Indirect effects are more subtle and less noticeable than direct effects, but perhaps no less meaningful. Parents indirectly influence their children by virtue of their influence on each other, for example, by marital support and communication and the multiple contexts in which they live. Whether direct or indirect, parental influences on children operate on several noteworthy principles. The specificity principle states that specific experiences specific parents provide specific children at specific times exert effects over specific aspects of child growth in specific ways. The transaction principle asserts that the experiences parents offer their children shape the characteristics of the child through time, just as, reciprocally, the characteristics of the child shape his or her experiences. Thus, children influence which experiences they will be exposed to, as well as how they interpret those experiences, and therefore ultimately how those experiences affect them.

PREVENTION AND INTERVENTION IN PARENTING

Infanticide was practiced historically, and although it is rare today, it is not unknown (Hrdy, 1999). Short of that, children are common victims of abuse and neglect, babies are born drug addicted, and many youngsters are never immunized. It is a sad fact of everyday life that parenting children does not always go as planned. Almost two in five parents (37% in the Zero-to-Three, 1997, survey) say that one of the chief reasons they need to improve as parents is that they do not spend as much quality time with their children as they would like. Modern parents typically complain that they have too many balls in the air already: working, errands, multiple commitments. This is not to trivialize the daunting problems that parents face: In the 1940s and 1950s, chewing gum and talking out of turn were the classroom problems listed by teachers as most prominent; today drug abuse and violence—witnessed in its most extreme form in the school shootings at Pearl, Peducah, Edinbiro, Jonesboro, and Columbine High Schools—top their list. A significant proportion of parents need assistance to find more effective strategies to create more satisfying relationships with children, but

only a fraction of parents who need such services receive them (Saxe, Cross, & Silverman, 1988). When parents suffer from individual, marital, and parenting problems, children are more likely to have academic and behavior problems and difficulty relating to their peers.

Strong secular and historical trends operating in modern society—industrialization, urbanization, poverty, increasing population growth and density, and especially widespread dual parental employment—constitute centrifugal forces on parenting. Society at large is also witnessing the emergence of striking permutations in parenthood and the constellation of the family structure, notably in the rise of single-parent households, divorced and blended families, and teenage and 50s first-time parents. In short, the family generally, and parenthood specifically, are today in an agitated state of question, flux, and redefinition. Because these societywide changes exert many unfortunately debilitative influences on parenthood, on interactions between parents and children, and consequently on children and their development, organizations at all levels of society increasingly feel the need to intercede in child rearing and to right some of society's ills through parenting preventions and interventions. For these and other reasons, contemporary parenting has witnessed an explosive growth in information and support programs. This trend also leads away from a focus on parents as the proximal protectors, providers, and proponents of their own progeny. In reality, however, parents are children's primary advocates and their frontline defense. Parents are the corps available in the greatest numbers to lobby and labor for children. Few ethical or sentient parents want to abrogate their child-rearing responsibilities. Insofar as parents can be enlisted and empowered to provide children with experiences and environments that optimize children's development, society can obviate after-the-fact remediation.

Prevention and Intervention

Little wonder that a one-time U.S. commissioner of education opined that every child has a right to a trained parent. Preventions are concerned with identifying risk and protective factors that ultimately lead to empirically based interventions (Coie, Watt, West, & Hawkins, 1993; Mrazek & Haggerty, 1994). Contemporary parenting prevention and intervention programs are normally guided by several assumptions. Parents are usually the most consistent and caring people in the lives of their children. If parents are provided with knowledge, skills, and supports, they can respond more positively and effectively to their children. Parents' own emotional and physical needs must be met if they are to rear children optimally.

Certain tools can help to address these parenting requirements successfully. First, parents benefit from knowledge of how children develop. Therefore, the normative patterns and stages of children's physical, verbal, cognitive, emotional, and social development, as well as their nutritional and health needs, should be part of the knowledge base for parenthood. Second, parents need to know how to observe children. Informed child watching helps to clarify a child's level of development in relation to what parents want children to learn and to accomplish. Observing also allows parents to spot potential trouble early and may help them respond to a child's daily frustrations more skillfully. Third, parents need all manner of skills for managing their children's behaviors. Knowledge of alternative methods of discipline and problem avoidance are basic. Parents need to understand the tremendous impact they have on their children's lives through the simplest things they do: their attention, expressed pleasure, listening, and interest. Fourth are supports for development. Knowing how to take advantage of settings, routines, and activities to create learning and problem-solving opportunities enhances parenthood and childhood. Finally, parents need to be patient, flexible, and goal-oriented—to call on their personal sources of support—and they must command an ability to extract pleasure from their encounters with children.

Positive prevention and intervention programs for parents are guided by beliefs in the consummate role of families in rearing their own children and the importance of family participation in defining its priorities and identifying appropriate prevention and intervention strategies. The responsibility for determining the child's best interests rests first and foremost with parents. Therefore, the doctrine of parental rights remains a fundamental premise of parent education efforts.

Contemporary parents from families all along the continuum from low risk to serious distress can and do seek assistance to become more effective parents. Preventions and interventions designed to help parents come in a variety of venues (psychotherapy, classes, print and broadcast media), settings (homes, schools, health clinics, houses of worship), and formats (individual, family, groups). Child-focused programs are based on theories that emphasize biological and psychological change mechanisms within the child; parent-focused programs relate primarily to changing parents' cognitions and practices; transactional programs combine child- and parent-focused perspectives to improve the quality of parent-child relationships (P. A. Cowan et al., 1998).

Experimental designs yield the best causal evidence on what works in a prevention or intervention. Early reviewers of parenting programs arrived at the unhappy conclusion that research results were often confusing and failed to demonstrate support for program effectiveness (Dembo, Switzer, & Lauritzen, 1985; Levant, 1988; Powell, 1998). To overcome design and measurement flaws in existing studies, prevention and intervention studies require large samples, inclusion of fathers as well as mothers, recruitment of no-treatment or alternative treatment controls and comparisons, random assignment to conditions, and multimeasure, multimethod assessments that include parent self-reports, parents' reports about children, and independent observations of parents' and children's behavior. Researchers also need to be mindful of the specificity principle and its implications. Researchers rarely find problem-free organizational settings to host programs, consistently uniform program implementation, or consensus among staff on a program's theory of change (Cook & Payne, 2002). With sufficient sample sizes, however, such variability in implementation can be systematically examined as part of outcome research. Many parenting preventions and interventions aimed at at-risk populations have failed to produce anticipated or desired effects on parents or children (St. Pierre & Layzer, 1999), leading to a closer examination of process. For example, small effects from randomized trials of six prominent home visiting programs led one group of analysts to call for research "crafted to primarily help programs improve quality and implementation: for example, to explore which families are most likely to engage in and to benefit from the services . . . and to determine the threshold levels of intensity and duration of services" (Gomby, Culross, & Behrman, 1999, p. 22).

Interest in what works for parenting reflects the general desire to ensure that resources are well spent and, more specifically, coincide with governmental efforts to use findings from scientifically based research (Powell, 2005). For example, the U.S. Department of Education's Institute of Education Sciences established a What Works Clearinghouse (WWC) to provide educators, policymakers, and the public with high-quality reviews of scientific evidence of the effectiveness of replicable educational interventions, including programs, practices, products, and policies.

Program research has generally focused on three categories of variables in searches for what works in parenting: program features, population characteristics, and program participation (Powell, 2005). Program features have been considered in relation to outcomes and have also been studied as a context of program participation. There are structural characteristics such as the mode of delivery (group, home-based); the onset, duration, and frequency of program services; and whether the parenting program is part of a larger effort that includes other services (early childhood education). A related characteristic is program staffing. For example, in a review of 15 randomized trials of home visiting programs aimed at promoting the cognitive and verbal development of young children in low-SES families, Olds and Kitzman (1993) found that only six produced significant overall program benefits for children. Five of the six successful programs employed professionals or highly trained staff: nurses, teachers, or psychology graduate students. In total, compared with randomized controls, 71% of the interventions that employed professionals, but only 29% of the programs staffed by paraprofessionals, produced significant positive outcomes for children. However, employing professional staff did not guarantee program success, nor were intervention failures attributable solely to the lack of professional training. Goals and content represent other critical sets of program features. Last, parenting programs differ in the pedagogical or clinical strategies they employ to support change in parents.

Contemporary studies also use randomized trials and repeated measures of family processes and child outcomes over long-term follow-up intervals (Forgatch & DeGarmo, 1999; Kellam, Rebok, Ialongo, & Mayer, 1994; Reid, Eddy, Fetrow, & Stoolmiller, 1999). With improved design features, positive effects of programs often prove stronger over time, sometimes more than a year or two after the conclusion of the program (C. P. Cowan et al., 1985; Markman, Renick, Floyd, & Stanley, 1993; Olds, Henderson, Kitzman, & Cole, 1995). A program may stimulate initial disequilibria of organized systems, which may result in replacing disorganization with reorganization at a new structural level only with some delay. Also, treatment groups might remain intact

or at the same level or they may show positive gains, whereas control groups decline. Even small effects of parenting have the potential to become large effects over time (Abelson, 1985). Because parenting has been shown to be stable (Holden & Miller, 1999), specific parental influences, consistently experienced, could accumulate to produce larger meaningful outcomes in childhood.

Case History of a Parenting Intervention

The Center for Child Well-being (CCW; 2004), a branch of the Task Force for Child Survival in Atlanta, Georgia, recognizes that the healthy development of children is not simply a result of eliminating health problems that occur in childhood, but requires proactive nurturing of strengths and positive behaviors, skills, characteristics, and values that promote physical growth and health, cognitive development, and social and emotional well-being. The CCW undertakes projects that engage diverse groups of parents, policymakers, scientists, practitioners, and advocates in synthesizing their knowledge and experience in child health and development. To meet these goals, the CCW has created five networks: Parenting, Early Child Care and Education, Health and Safety, Early Child Development, and Community Support. Each network consists of approximately one dozen geographically dispersed core members who represent a wide range of disciplines, professions, sectors of society, perspectives, ethnicities, and cultural viewpoints.

The Parenting Network and Its Work

The Parenting Network (PN) was recruited by the CCW to apply science and experience to strengthen parenting skills by creating and disseminating practical products that would make a difference for parents. Topics of interest to the PN included parenting stress (time management, setting priorities, work/family issues, social support networks, and parenting skill development); effective parental relationships with caregivers, pediatricians, teachers, and bosses/supervisors; regulating environmental influences on children (media and peers); parental education (recognizing and promoting strengths in children and coping with weaknesses); and nontraditional parenting (single parents, divorced parents, foster parents, and grandparents). The PN has generated a number of products: books, pamphlets, book lists, Web postings, and the like (e.g., Bornstein, Davidson, Keyes, Moore, & Center for Child Well-Being, 2003).

For one project, the PN reviewed the scientific literature concerned with supporting parents, conducted an online survey of parents and parenting professionals, and evaluated more than 1,000 parenting products (in terms of consumer cost, publication, ease of acquisition, endorsement by official organizations, the organizations responsible for product development, and intended audiences). It observed that very few products were developed for parents of low SES or for minority parents. Rather, approximately 75% of available parenting products were primarily geared to general audiences; the majority were literature-based materials, but more than 100 videos were developed for parents or for use in parenting classes. Of those, only a handful were developed for low-SES parents and only a dozen for minority parents, at an average cost per video of over $100. Evident throughout the PN's initial review was the thread of awareness that they were to create a product that would serve as a medium—through which knowledge would pass—and that their challenge was to create a vehicle that would effectively deliver their work into the hands of parents who would benefit from this conveyance.

The PN decided to pursue the issue of stress-related parenting, including stress related to normal child development, selection and supervision of child care, balancing work and family, child temperament, discipline and daily hassles, illness or disability, stress associated with intrafamilial conflict, coping with stress, cultivating social support, and building parenting strengths to counteract stress. Parenting is inherently stressful. Decreasing parental stress promises to improve the parent-child relationship as well as the well-being of both parties. Economic stress, for example, has a negative impact on parents, erodes parenting skills, and also undermines children's development (Conger et al., 1994). Connections exist between parental stress and child abuse (Holden, Willis, & Foltz, 1989), harsh parenting styles (Emery & Tuer, 1993), and decreased sensitivity to child cues and more negative feelings toward children (Crnic et al., 1983).

Parental stress that occurs in everyday interactions with children also relates to normal child development. Lack of knowledge about child development often leads to inappropriate expectations, which in turn lead to negative interactions between parents and children. This logic became a central theme of a planned intervention project. If parents better understood normative developmental issues, then they would have more realistic expectations for their children's behavior. The presence of unrealistic expectations, based on a lack of understanding of normal child development, for example, leads to frustrated interactions and increased daily stressors. Increasing parents' knowledge of their children's development would then decrease stress, which would directly benefit both parents and children. Zero-to-Three (1997) conducted a survey of 3,000 adults regarding what parents know about child development. Specific areas of misinformation included expectations of young children at different ages and stages, and spoiling and spanking. A report from the Commonwealth Fund, "Child Development and Medicaid: Attitudes of Mothers with Young Children Enrolled in Medicaid," indicated that mothers want simple and easily accessible materials about their child's development and about easing pressures of child rearing (Kannel & Perry, 2001).

The PN conducted two focus groups at Head Start programs. Taking an emic approach, the PN endeavored to learn about the intended audience: what topics interested this audience, by which channels this audience preferred to receive messages, which product formats might most appeal to it, and what barriers prevented it from accessing and using existing information about child development.

One message the PN heard repeatedly was that parents wanted to participate in groups where they could talk to other parents and learn more about how to improve their parenting skills. On this basis, the PN decided to develop a parenting intervention for young African American parents in low-SES circumstances. The PN determined that starting at a local level would increase the likelihood of success.

The culmination of planning led the PN to propose that the CCW develop a "Community Kit" to help these parents reduce parent-related stresses and improve their parenting skills. The proposed kit would be used in a group setting to foster a support network for parents and would include videos and complementary multimedia materials for facilitators and participants. The information included in the kit would address general categories: child development specific to age/stages, stage-specific parenting, and coping with stresses specific to those stages.

The final proposal was the result of a dynamic exchange between parents and parenting experts. The PN had sought and received input directly from parents representative of the ultimate target audience to discover what those parents felt they most needed, how that information would best be received, and how the information to be contained in the Community Kit could reflect the members' own child development, experiences, and parenting expertise.

Partnerships

The CCW also initiated partnerships with organizations that agreed to field-test, fine-tune, and implement the Community Kit. Expert interviews and focus groups were used to obtain information from African American cultural authorities and behavior change theorists, service providers, and parents. In particular, four critical pieces of information about content and delivery of messages were sought and obtained:

1. *Message style:* How messages about child development and child rearing, stress and coping, should best be formulated to meet with the highest level of recognition and understanding?
2. *Messenger:* Who should present those messages?
3. *Barriers:* What impediments stand between recognition and understanding of such messages and behavior change related to child development and child rearing, stress and coping?
4. *Success:* What are the best ways to overcome barriers to recognition and understanding of target messages?

Findings indicated that low-SES African American parents were most concerned with stresses related to finding time for self, finances, balancing work and family, and ensuring quality child care. Parents reported that they needed to learn more about their child's development and talked about issues such as discipline, attachment, and establishing a routine as being important. Parents also preferred parenting classes held in a support group setting, and wanted to see videos with real-life parents, with whom they could identify, instead of celebrities or white-coated child development experts. Parents stressed the importance of authenticity and avoiding a judgmental tone. Many parent education programs have been criticized for attempting to impose middle-SES values on all types of families and failing to acknowledge the strengths and values of minorities. Furthermore, many parenting education materials undermine parents' feelings of efficacy (C. Smith, Perou, & Lesesne, 2002).

These parents' focus groups provided the framework for the design of the main CCW parenting intervention.

Based on comments from parents, several features of the intervention were considered vital to its success:

1. *Support:* Group formation should be used to increase support networks that also constitute a product of the project.
2. *Appropriateness:* The intervention should be primarily focused on low-education/low-income African American mothers and fathers, but can be modified to fit various languages, racial and ethnic norms, and generations.
3. *Incentives:* The work focused heavily on addressing both barriers and incentives to participation.
4. *Reinforcement:* In addition to messages discussed and reinforced in the group setting, participants would be provided with materials to take home to reinforce messages at the time when they need the information to achieve behavior change.

Parenting in the Real World

On the basis of findings from the background research and focus groups, the PN developed a targeted intervention for parents of children from birth through 3 years of age called Parenting in the Real World: Kids Don't Come with Instructions (a name generated by focus group participants). Parenting in the Real World (PRW) is a system of parenting classes for low-income African Americans that addresses the most critical aspects of parenting young children, as identified by the PN and in focus groups of actual parents. The main goals of PRW are to help parents reduce their parenting stress and improve their parenting knowledge and skills. PRW consists of seven 90-minute sessions, including an introductory session, five topic sessions, and a graduation. Topics covered are knowledge of child development; discipline; attachment; juggling work, school, and family; and taking care of self. The PRW tool kit was developed for group facilitators, such as Early Head Start family support coordinators, and consists of a video, facilitator's guide, a parent handbook, marketing material, and message reinforcement materials, such as pens and key chains imprinted with key concepts.

Each PRW session begins with a short video clip designed to trigger discussion among the participants. Parenting stresses and coping techniques are identified and discussed. Sessions also contain exercises designed to build parents' skills and improve their understanding of child development. These exercises include a judicious mix of role-play, quizzes, and peer education. At the end of each session, parents are given take-home materials and asked to identify one area to work on during the following week. Parents are asked to report on their activities at the next session. One important goal of each session is to have parents build on their strengths to improve their parenting skills and increase their feelings of competence. The intervention was also designed to foster connections among participants.

Assessment

Three groups of parents participated in an initial assessment of PRW: (1) Parents whose children were enrolled in Early Head Start and who took part in the PRW intervention served as the treatment group; (2) parents whose children were enrolled in Early Head Start, but who did not participate in the PRW intervention, served as the first control group; and (3) parents whose children were not enrolled in Early Head Start served as the second control group. (Sample sizes were small due to limited funding for the evaluation phase of the project.) All parents were African American, and most were mothers. On average, parents were about 30 years of age, had two children, and almost half had never been married. Over a quarter of parents had a high school diploma or less education, about half had completed either partial college or specialized training, and another quarter had completed a 4-year college degree. Reported annual income ranged from under $10,000/year to between $40,001 and $50,000/year. The parents in the three groups did not significantly differ in age, education, or income levels.

To test the feasibility of the kit, parents and facilitators in the PRW program completed ongoing evaluations of each of the seven sessions. Almost all parents reported that the number of sessions was appropriate and that the length of the sessions (90 minutes) was appropriate. Parents' evaluations of program content and structure were very positive. Upon graduation, parents were asked a variety of questions, including whether the program helped to improve their parenting skills and their confidence about their parenting skills, and if they would recommend the program.

Parent perceptions of the program's effects were overwhelmingly positive. Parents agreed that the information presented across the seven sessions was understandable and interesting and that the video segments were informative and entertaining. The topics covered in the program were deemed relevant to parenting. They reported a good balance among lecture, discussion, and activities, and that the facilitator did a good job of teaching the sessions. Parents reported having learned new parenting skills or strategies across the seven sessions. Similarly, they reported that the sessions had reduced their parenting stress. Overall, parents agreed that the PRW program helped to improve their parenting, made them feel more confident about their parenting, and reduced their parenting stress. The treatment group also reported less depression than the control groups at posttest, controlling for pretest levels of depression. All parents reported that they would recommend the program to a friend.

Facilitators were asked similar questions about the comprehensibility of the material; balance among lecture, discussion, and activities; and video segments. They were also asked whether the facilitator's guide was easy to use, helpful, clear, and thorough; whether parents were interested in the topics; and whether it was easy to get parents to participate. Like the parents, the facilitators reported that the information presented across the seven sessions was understandable to the parents and maintained parents' interest, and they found it easy to get parents to participate. They agreed that the video segments were informative and entertaining and that they achieved a good balance among lecture, discussion, and activities. Facilitators found the teaching guide easy to use and thorough.

The final stage of the evaluation process included focus groups for parents who participated in the classes, conducted within 2 weeks after the sessions were completed and facilitated by an independent consultant. These exit focus groups gave participants the opportunity to talk about their experiences in the classes and how the classes impacted their parenting beliefs and behaviors. Parents had the opportunity to offer suggestions about the sessions and provide feedback to be used to revise the contents of the PRW kit. Facilitators also participated in a focus group. They were asked about the sessions and whether or not they felt that the structure and content were likely to improve parenting and child development. Issues such as attendance, time of sessions, incentives, and facilitator characteristics were also discussed.

Transcriptions from these focus groups were analyzed for themes. For parent focus groups:

1. The group discussions and the support group setting were deemed very helpful. Interacting with other parents and being able to come to the session and talk helped to relieve parenting stress.

2. Parents agreed that the sessions had the appropriate amount of information and found the information to be understandable and relevant to their lives.

3. Participants reported learning new information and using new skills that helped to reduce their stress: establishing a routine, yelling at their children less, reassessing their beliefs about child development, becoming more patient with their children, and learning that all children are different.

4. Parents enjoyed the take-home items and found them to be useful reminders of the main messages.

5. Parents formed support networks with one another. Some exchanged phone numbers and helped one another with babysitting.

6. All parents would recommend the PRW course to their friends.

For facilitator focus groups:

1. Each facilitator found the PRW kit easy to use. They liked the organization of the topics as well as the content in each section.

2. The facilitators felt that the participants could relate to the parents in the video.

3. Facilitators found the content to be understandable and relevant (although they wanted to see more time spent covering discipline).

4. Facilitators suggested that homework assignments be made more user-friendly and simpler.

5. Facilitators agreed that they would continue to use the PRW kit for their parent education classes.

Ongoing Efforts

Based on feedback from both parents and facilitators, the PRW kit was revised. Obtaining real-world feedback throughout each stage of development and refinement was essential to making the CCW parenting intervention both accessible and relevant to the target population. Further dissemination and continued evaluation of the PRW kit are aimed at improving parental involvement, and at the same time arming Early Head Start centers with a valuable tool for parent education. The topics covered in PRW are issues that all parents face, and par-

ents who took part in PRW classes reported that the support group atmosphere was extremely helpful, the topics especially relevant, and the information contained in the classes effective in reducing their stress and affording them strengths and strategies to be more available and consistent with their children. Furthermore, participation in the PRW classes ameliorated depression in parents, and many parents reported that they changed their parenting behaviors, which increased their feelings of competence and improved their relationships with their children.

CONCLUSIONS

Parents intend much in their interactions with their children: They promote their children's mental development through the structures they create and the meanings they place on those structures, and they foster their children's emotional regulation, development of self, and social sensitivities and participation in meaningful relationships and experiences outside of the family through the models they portray and the values they display. The complex of parent cognitions and practices with children is divisible into domains, and parents tend to show consistency over time in certain of those domains. Some aspects of parenting are frequent or significant from the get-go and wane thereafter; others wax over the course of childhood. Parenting, along with other forces, exerts powerful influences on children's psychological development. Although not all parenting is critical for later development, and single events are rarely formative, parenting certainly has long-lasting effects. Little and big consistencies of parenting aggregate over childhood to co-construct the person. The interactive and intersubjective aspects of parent and child have telling consequences for development. Researchers and theoreticians today do not ask *whether* parenting affects child development, but *which* parent cognitions and practices affect *which* aspects of development *when* and *how,* and they are interested also to learn the *ways* in which individual children are so affected, as well as the ways individual children affect their own development.

Children bring unique social styles and an active, physical, social, and mental life to everyday interactions with adults that shape their caregiving experiences. Children alter the environment as they interact with it, and they interpret their experiences and environment in idiosyncratic ways. In addition, biology, personality, and contexts all play important roles in determining the nature and function of parenting. A full understanding of what it means to parent children depends on the several ecologies in which parenting takes place. Family composition, social class, and cultural variation all exert salient influences on the ways parents rear their children and what they expect of children as they grow.

Of course, human development is too subtle, dynamic, and intricate to maintain that parenting alone determines the course and outcome of ontogeny; stature in maturity is shaped by the actions and vicissitudes of individuals themselves across the life span. Parenthood does not fix the route or the terminus of the child's development. Parent and child convey distinctive characteristics to every interaction, and both are changed as a result. In short, parent and child actively construct one another through time.

Parents have central roles to play in children's physical survival, social growth, emotional maturation, and cognitive development. A better understanding of the nature of the human being is afforded by examining parents' cognitions, practices, and their consequences—the unique and specific influences of parents. As children achieve autonomy, parenthood ultimately means having facilitated a child's self-confidence, capacity for intimacy, achievement motivation, pleasure in play and work, friendships with peers, and continuing academic success and fulfillment. Within-family parenting experiences exercise a major impact over growth in each of these spheres of development. In parenting, we sometimes don't know what to do, but we can find out; we sometimes do know what to do, but still don't get into the trenches and do it.

So, parenting is a peculiar kind of life's work, marked by challenging demands, changing and ambiguous criteria, and all too frequent evaluations. Principles such as specificity, interdependence, and transaction, and indirect and direct effects, do not make it easy. Successful parenting entails both affective components—in terms of commitment, empathy, and positive regard for children, for example—as well as cognitive components—the how, what, and why of caring for children. Moreover, the path to achieving satisfaction and success in parenting is not linear or incremental, but tends to meander. Different tasks are more or less salient and challenging at different periods in the course of child rearing. It is obvious that parenthood is central to childhood, to child development, and to society's long-term investment in children. Parents are fundamentally committed to the survival, socialization, and education of young children. But parenthood is also a critical component of adulthood. So we are motivated to know about the meaning and importance of parenthood as much for itself as out of the desire to improve the lives of children and society. Parenting is a process that formally begins before pregnancy and continues through the balance of the life span. Practically speaking, *once a parent, always a parent.*

REFERENCES

Abelson, R. P. (1985). A variance explanation paradox: When a little is a lot. *Psychological Bulletin, 97,* 129–133.

Abelson, R. P. (1986). Beliefs are like possessions. *Journal for the Theory of Social Behaviour, 16,* 223–250.

Adamson, L. B., & Bakeman, R. (1984). Mothers' communicative acts: Changes during infancy. *Infant Behavior and Development, 7,* 467–478.

Ainsworth, M. D. S., & Bell, S. M. (1969). Some contemporary patterns of mother-infant interaction in the feeding situation. In A. Ambrose (Ed.), *Stimulation in early infancy* (pp. 133–170). New York: Academic Press.

Ainsworth, M. D. S., Blehar, M. C., Waters, E., & Wall, S. (1978). *Patterns of attachment: A psychological study of the Strange Situation.* Hillsdale, NJ: Erlbaum.

Allen, J. M., & Hawkins, A. J. (1999). Maternal gatekeeping: Mothers' beliefs and behaviors that inhibit greater father involvement in family work. *Journal of Marriage and the Family, 61,* 199–212.

Alley, T. R. (1981). Head shape and the perception of cuteness. *Developmental Psychology, 17,* 650–654.

Alley, T. R. (1983). Infantile head shape as an elicitor of adult protection. *Merrill-Palmer Quarterly, 29,* 411–427.

Amato, P. R. (1996). Explaining the intergenerational transmission of divorce. *Journal of Marriage and the Family, 58,* 628–640.

Amato, P. R., & Booth, A. (2001). The legacy of parents' marital discord: Consequences for children's marital quality. *Journal of Personality and Social Psychology, 81,* 627–638.

Anderson, K. E., Lytton, H., & Romney, D. M. (1986). Mothers' interactions with normal and conduct-disordered boys: Who affects whom? *Developmental Psychology, 22,* 604–609.

Azuma, H. (1986). Why study child development in Japan? In H. W. Stevenson, H. Azuma, & K. Hakuta (Eds.), *Child development and education in Japan* (pp. 3–12). New York: Freeman.

Baldwin, W., & Cain, V. S. (1981). The children of teenage parents. In F. F. Furstenberg Jr., R. Lincoln, & J. Menken (Eds.), *Teenage sexuality, pregnancy, and childbearing* (pp. 265–279). Philadelphia: University of Pennsylvania Press.

Bandura, A. (1962). Social learning through imitation. In M. R. Jones (Ed.), *Nebraska Symposium on Motivation* (pp. 211–274). Lincoln: University of Nebraska Press.

Bandura, A. (1965). Influence of models' reinforcement contingencies on the acquisition of imitative responses. *Journal of Personality and Social Psychology, 1,* 589–595.

Bandura, A. (1986). *Social foundations of thought and action: A social cognitive theory.* Englewood Cliffs, NJ: Prentice-Hall.

Bandura, A. (1989). Human agency in social cognitive theory. *American Psychologist, 44,* 1175–1184.

Bard, K. A. (2002). Primate parenting. In M. H. Bornstein (Ed.), *Handbook of parenting: Vol. 2. Biology and ecology of parenting* (2nd ed., pp. 99–140). Mahwah, NJ: Erlbaum.

Barends, N., & Belsky, J. (2000). *Adult attachment and parent personality as determinants of mothering in the second and third years.* Unpublished manuscript, Penn State University, University Park, PA.

Barnard, K. E., & Solchany, J. E. (2002). Mothering. In M. H. Bornstein (Ed.), *Handbook of parenting: Vol. 3. Status and social conditions of parenting* (2nd ed., pp. 3–25). Mahwah, NJ: Erlbaum.

Barratt, M. S., & Roach, M. A. (1995). Early interactive processes: Parenting by adolescent and adult single mothers. *Infant Behavior and Development, 18,* 97–109.

Bates, E., Bretherton, I., & Snyder, L. (1988). *From first words to grammar.* New York: Cambridge University Press.

Bates, J. E. (1987). Temperament in infancy. In J. D. Osofsky (Ed.), *Handbook of infant development* (2nd ed., pp. 1101–1149). New York: Wiley.

Baumrind, D. (1967). Child-care practices anteceding three patterns of preschool behavior. *Genetic Psychology Monographs, 75,* 43–88.

Baumrind, D. (1978). Reciprocal rights and responsibilities in parent-child relations. *Journal of Social Issues, 34,* 179–196.

Baumrind, D. (1989). Rearing competent children. In W. Damon (Ed.), *Child development today and tomorrow* (pp. 349–378). San Francisco: Jossey-Bass.

Baumrind, D. (1991). Effective parenting during the early adolescent transition. In P. A. Cowan & E. M. Hetherington (Eds.), *Family transitions: Advances in family research series* (pp. 111–163). Hillsdale, NJ: Erlbaum.

Baumrind, D., & Thompson, R. A. (2002). The ethics of parenting. In M. H. Bornstein (Ed.), *Handbook of parenting: Vol. 5. Practical parenting* (2nd ed., pp. 3–34). Mahwah, NJ: Erlbaum.

Baydar, N., & Brooks-Gunn, J. (1998). Profiles of grandmothers who help care for their grandchildren in the United States. *Family Relations, 47,* 385–393.

Becker, J. A., & Hall, M. S. (1989). Adult beliefs about pragmatic development. *Journal of Applied Developmental Psychology, 10,* 1–17.

Bee, H. L., Barnard, K. E., Eyres, S. J., Gray, C. A., Hammond, M. A., Spietz, A. L., et al. (1982). Prediction of IQ and language skill from perinatal status, child performance, family characteristics, and mother-infant interaction. *Child Development, 53,* 1134–1156.

Befu, H. (1986). The social and cultural background of child development in Japan and the United States. In H. W. Stevenson, H. Azuma, & K. Hakuta (Eds.), *Child development and education in Japan* (pp. 13–27). New York: Freeman.

Bell, R. Q. (1968). A reinterpretation of the direction of effects in studies of socialization. *Psychological Review, 75,* 81–95.

Bell, R. Q. (1970). Sleep cycles and skin potential in newborns studied with a simplified observation and recording system. *Psychophysiology, 6,* 778–786.

Bell, R. Q., & Harper, L. (1977). *Child effects on adults.* Hillsdale, NJ: Erlbaum.

Bellinger, D. (1980). Consistency in the pattern of change in mothers' speech: Some discriminant analyses. *Journal of Child Language, 7,* 469–487.

Belsky, J. (1984). The determinants of parenting: A process model. *Child Development, 55,* 83–96.

Belsky, J., & Barends, N. (2002). Personality and parenting. In M. H. Bornstein (Ed.), *Handbook of parenting: Vol. 3. Status and social ecology of parenting* (2nd ed., pp. 415–438). Mahwah, NJ: Erlbaum.

Belsky, J., Crnic, K., & Woodworth, S. (1995). Personality and parenting: Exploring the mediating role of transient mood and daily hassles. *Journal of Personality, 63,* 905–929.

Belsky, J., Garduque, L., & Hrncir, E. (1984). Assessing performance, competence, and executive capacity in infant play: Relations to home environment and security of attachment. *Developmental Psychology, 20,* 406–417.

Belsky, J., Gilstrap, B., & Rovine, M. (1984). The Pennsylvania Infant and Family Development Project: Pt. 1. Stability and change in mother-infant and father-infant interaction in a family setting at one, three, and nine months. *Child Development, 55,* 692–705.

Belsky, J., Goode, M. K., & Most, R. K. (1980). Maternal stimulation and infant exploratory competence: Cross-sectional, correlational, and experimental analyses. *Child Development, 51,* 1168–1178.

Belsky, J., Youngblade, L., & Pensky, E. (1989). Childrearing history, marital quality, and maternal affect: Intergenerational transmission in a low-risk sample. *Development and Psychopathology, 1,* 291–304.

Benasich, A. A., & Brooks-Gunn, J. (1996). Maternal attitudes and knowledge of child-rearing: Associations with family and child outcomes. *Child Development, 67,* 1186–1205.

Benedict, R. (1938). Continuities and discontinuities in cultural conditioning. *Psychiatry: Journal for the Study of Interpersonal Processes, 2,* 161–167.

Berndt, T. J. (1999). Friends' influence on children's adjustment to school. In W. A. Collins & B. Laursen (Eds.), *Minnesota Symposia on Child Psychology: Vol. 30. Relationships as developmental contexts* (pp. 85–107). Mahwah, NJ: Erlbaum.

Berndt, T. J., Hawkins, J. A., & Jiao, Z. (1999). Influences of friends and friendship on adjustment to junior high school. *Merrill-Palmer Quarterly, 45,* 13–41.

Bever, T. G. (Ed.). (1982). *Regressions in mental development.* Hillsdale, NJ: Erlbaum.

Biringen, Z., Emde, R. N., Campos, J. J., & Appelbaum, M. I. (1995). Affective reorganization in the infant, the mother, and the dyad: The role of upright locomotion and its timing. *Child Development, 66,* 499–514.

Bjorklund, D. F., Yunger, J. L., & Pellegrini, A. D. (2002). The evolution of parenting and evolutionary approaches to childrearing. In M. H. Bornstein (Ed.), *Handbook of parenting: Vol. 2. Biology and ecology of parenting* (2nd ed., pp. 3–30). Mahwah, NJ: Erlbaum.

Blankenhorn, D. (1995). *Fatherless America: Confronting our most urgent social problem.* New York: Basic Books.

Block, N. (1995). How heritability misleads about race. *Cognition, 56,* 99–128.

Bloom, L. (1998). Language acquisition in its developmental context. In W. Damon (Editor-in-Chief) & D. Kuhn & R. S. Siegler (Vol. Eds.), *Handbook of child psychology: Vol. 2. Cognition, perception, and language* (5th ed., pp. 309–370). New York: Wiley.

Bogenschneider, K. (1997). Parental involvement in adolescent schooling: A proximal process with transcontextual validity. *Journal of Marriage and the Family, 59,* 718–733.

Bohman, M. (1996). Predispositions to criminality: Swedish adoption studies in retrospect. In G. R. Bock & J. A. Goode (Eds.),

Ciba Foundation Symposium: Vol. 194. Genetics of criminal and anti-social behavior (pp. 99–114). New York: Wiley.

Bornstein, M. H. (1985). How infant and mother jointly contribute to developing cognitive competence in the child. *Proceedings of the National Academy of Sciences, USA, 82,* 7470–7473.

Bornstein, M. H. (1989a). Between caretakers and their young: Two modes of interaction and their consequences for cognitive growth. In M. H. Bornstein & J. S. Bruner (Eds.), *Interaction in human development* (pp. 197–214). Hillsdale, NJ: Erlbaum.

Bornstein, M. H. (1989b). Cross-cultural developmental comparisons: The case of Japanese-American infant and mother activities and interactions—What we know, what we need to know, and why we need to know. *Developmental Review, 9,* 171–204.

Bornstein, M. H. (1989c). Sensitive periods in development: Structural characteristics and causal interpretations. *Psychological Bulletin, 105,* 179–197.

Bornstein, M. H. (Ed.). (1991). *Cultural approaches to parenting.* Hillsdale, NJ: Erlbaum.

Bornstein, M. H. (1995). Form and function: Implications for studies of culture and human development. *Culture and Psychology, 1,* 123–137.

Bornstein, M. H. (Ed.). (2002a). *Handbook of parenting* (2nd ed., Vols. 1–5). Mahwah, NJ: Erlbaum.

Bornstein, M. H. (2002b). Parenting infants. In M. H. Bornstein (Ed.), *Handbook of parenting: Vol. 1. Children and parenting* (2nd ed., pp. 3–43). Mahwah, NJ: Erlbaum.

Bornstein, M. H. (2002c). Toward a multiculture, multiage, multimethod science. *Human Development, 45,* 257–263.

Bornstein, M. H., & Bradley, R. H. (Eds.). (2003). *Socioeconomic status, parenting, and child development.* Mahwah, NJ: Erlbaum.

Bornstein, M. H., Brown, E. M., & Slater, A. M. (1996). Patterns of stability and continuity in attention across early infancy. *Journal of Reproductive and Infant Psychology, 14,* 195–206.

Bornstein, M. H., Davidson, L., Keyes, C. M., Moore, K., & Center for Child Well-Being (Eds.). (2003). *Well-being: Positive development across the life course.* Mahwah, NJ: Erlbaum.

Bornstein, M. H., Hahn, C.-S., Suwalsky, J. T. D., & Haynes, O. M. (2003). Socioeconomic status, parenting, and child development: The Hollingshead Four-Factor Index of Social Status and the Socioeconomic Index of Occupations. In M. H. Bornstein & R. H. Bradley (Eds.), *Socioeconomic status, parenting, and child development* (pp. 29–82). Mahwah, NJ: Erlbaum.

Bornstein, M. H., Hendricks, C., Hahn, C.-S., Haynes, O. M., Painter, K. M., & Tamis-LeMonda, C. S. (2003). Contributors to self-perceived competence, satisfaction, investment, and role balance in maternal parenting: A multivariate ecological analysis. *Parenting: Science and Practice, 3,* 285–326.

Bornstein, M. H., & Ruddy, M. G. (1984). Infant attention and maternal stimulation: Prediction of cognitive and linguistic development in singletons and twins. In H. Bouma & D. G. Bouwhuis (Eds.), *Attention and performance X: Control of language processes* (pp. 433–445). London: Erlbaum.

Bornstein, M. H., & Sawyer, J. (2005). Family systems. In K. McCartney & D. Phillips (Eds.), *Blackwell handbook of early childhood development* (pp. 381–398). Malden, MA: Blackwell.

Bornstein, M. H., Tal, J., Rahn, C., Galperin, C. Z., Pecheux, M. G., Lamour, M., et al. (1992). Functional analysis of the contents of maternal speech to infants of 5 and 13 months in four cultures: Argentina, France, Japan, and the United States. *Developmental Psychology, 28,* 593–603.

Bornstein, M. H., & Tamis-LeMonda, C. S. (1990). Activities and interactions of mothers and their firstborn infants in the first six months of life: Covariation, stability, continuity, correspondence, and prediction. *Child Development, 61,* 1206–1217.

Bornstein, M. H., Tamis-LeMonda, C. S., & Haynes, O. M. (1999). First words in the second year: Continuity, stability, and models of concurrent and predictive correspondence in vocabulary and verbal responsiveness across age and context. *Infant Behavior and Development, 22,* 65–85.

Bowlby, J. (1969). *Attachment and loss: Vol. 1. Attachment* (2nd ed.). New York: Basic Books.

Bradley, R. H., & Caldwell, B. M. (1995). The acts and conditions of the caregiving environment. *Developmental Review, 15,* 92–96.

Bradley, R. H., Caldwell, B. M., & Rock, S. L. (1988). Home environment and school performance: A 10-year follow-up and examination of three models of environmental action. *Child Development, 59,* 852–867.

Brazelton, T. B. (1969). *Infants and mothers: Differences in development.* New York: Delacorte Press.

Broderick, C. B. (1993). *Understanding family process: Basics of family systems theory.* Thousand Oaks, CA: Sage.

Brody, S. (1956). *Patterns of mothering: Maternal influence during infancy.* Oxford: International Universities Press.

Brody, S., & Axelrad, S. (1978). *Mothers, fathers, and children.* New York: International Universities Press.

Bronfenbrenner, U. (1958). *Socialization and social class through time and space.* New York: Holt.

Bronfenbrenner, U., & Crouter, A. C. (1983). The evolution of environmental models in developmental research. In P. H. Mussen (Series Ed.) & W. Kessen (Vol. Ed.), *Handbook of child psychology: Vol. 1. History, theory, and methods* (4th ed., pp. 357–414). New York: Wiley.

Bronfenbrenner, U., & Morris, P. A. (1998). The ecology of developmental processes. In W. Damon (Editor-in-Chief) & R. M. Lerner (Vol. Ed.), *Handbook of child psychology: Vol. 1. Theoretical models of human development* (5th ed., pp. 993–1028). New York: Wiley.

Brown, B. (1990). Peer groups and peer cultures. In S. Feldman & G. Elliott (Eds.), *At the threshold: The developing adolescent* (pp. 171–196). Cambridge, MA: Harvard University Press.

Brown, B., Mounts, N., Lamborn, S. D., & Steinberg, L. (1993). Parenting practices and peer group affiliation in adolescence. *Child Development, 64,* 467–482.

Butterfield, E. C., Albertson, L. R., & Johnston, J. C. (1995). On making cognitive theory more general and developmentally pertinent. In F. E. Weinert & W. Schneider (Eds.), *Memory performance and competencies: Issues in growth and development* (pp. 181–205). Hillsdale, NJ: Erlbaum.

Cabrera, N. J., Tamis-LeMonda, C. S., Bradley, R. H., Hofferth, S., & Lamb, M. E. (2000). Fatherhood in the twenty-first century. *Child Development, 71,* 127–136.

Cadoret, R. J., Leve, L. D., & Devor, E. (1997). Genetics of aggressive and violent behavior. *Psychiatric Clinics of North America, 20,* 301–322.

Cairns, R. B., & Cairns, B. D. (1994). *Lifelines and risks: Pathways of youth in our time.* New York: Cambridge University Press.

Cairns, R. B., Cairns, B. D., Neckerman, H., Gest, S., & Gariepy, J. L. (1988). Social networks and aggressive behavior: Peer support or peer rejection? *Developmental Psychology, 24,* 815–823.

Campos, J. J., Anderson, D. I., Barbu-Roth, M. A., Hubbard, E. M., Hertenstein, M. J., & Witherington, D. (2000). Travel broadens the mind. *Infancy, 1,* 149–219.

Campos, J. J., Kermoian, R., Witherington, D., Chen, H., & Dong, Q. (1997). Activity, attention, and developmental transitions in infancy. In P. J. Lang & R. F. Simons (Eds.), *Attention and orienting: Sensory and motivational processes* (pp. 393–415). Mahwah, NJ: Erlbaum.

Carew, J. V. (1980). Experience and the development of intelligence in young children at home and in day care. *Monographs of the Society for Research in Child Development, 45*(6–7, Serial No. 187).

Caspi, A., & Elder, G. H., Jr. (1988). Emergent family patterns: The intergenerational construction of problem behaviour and relationships. In R. A. Hinde & J. Stevenson-Hinde (Eds.), *Relationships within families: Mutual influences* (pp. 218–240). Oxford: Clarendon Press.

Caspi, A., Taylor, A., Moffitt, T. E., & Plomin, R. (2000). Neighborhood deprivation affects children's mental health. *Psychological Science, 11,* 338–342.

Cassidy, J. (1994). Emotion regulation: Influences of attachment relationships. *Monographs of the Society for Research in Child Development, 59,* 228–283.

Caudill, W. A. (1973). The influence of social structure and culture on human behavior in modern Japan. *Journal of Nervous and Mental Disease, 157,* 240–257.

Center for Child Well-Being. (2004). *An interim report on the parenting program: Parenting in the real world.* Unpublished manuscript, Center for Child Well-Being, Atlanta, GA.

Chalmers, I., Enkin, M., & Keirse, M. J. N. C. (Eds.). (1989). *Effective care in pregnancy and childbirth.* New York: Oxford University Press.

Champagne, F., Diorio, J., Sharma, S., & Meaney, M. J. (2001). Naturally occurring variations in maternal behavior in the rat are associated with differences in estrogen-inducible central oxytocin receptors. *Proceedings of the National Academy of Sciences of the USA, 98,* 12736–12741.

Chapman, R. S. (1981). Mother-child interaction in the second year of life: Its role in language development. In R. Schiefelbusch & D. Bricker (Eds.), *Early language: Acquisition and intervention* (pp. 201–250). Baltimore: University Park Press.

Chase-Lansdale, P. L., Brooks-Gunn, J., & Zamsky, E. S. (1994). Young African-American multigenerational families in poverty: Quality of mothering and grandmothering. *Child Development, 65,* 373–393.

Chase-Lansdale, P. L., Cherlin, A. J., & Kiernan, K. E. (1995). The long-term effects of parental divorce on the mental health of young adults: A developmental perspective. *Child Development, 66,* 1614–1634.

Chen, E., Matthews, K. A., & Boyce, W. T. (2002). Socioeconomic differences in children's health: How and why do these relationships change with age? *Psychological Bulletin, 128,* 295–329.

Chen, X., Hastings, P. D., Rubin, K. H., Chen, H., Cen, G., & Stewart, S. L. (1998). Child-rearing attitudes and behavioral inhibition in Chinese and Canadian toddlers: A cross-cultural study. *Developmental Psychology, 34,* 677–686.

Chilcoat, H. D., & Anthony, J. C. (1996). Impact of parent monitoring on initiation of drug use through late childhood. *Journal of the American Academy of Child and Adolescent Psychiatry, 35,* 91–100.

Church, J. (1966). *Three babies: Biographies of cognitive development.* New York: Random House.

Cicchetti, D., Toth, S. L., & Maughan, A. (2000). An ecological-transactional model of child maltreatment. In A. J. Sameroff, M. Lewis, & S. M. Miller (Eds.), *Handbook of developmental psychopathology* (2nd ed., pp. 689–722). New York: Kluwer Academic/Plenum Press.

Clark, E. V. (1983). Meanings and concepts. In P. H. Mussen (Series Ed.) & J. H. Flavell & E. M. Markman (Vol. Eds.), *Handbook of child psychology: Vol. 3. Cognitive development* (4th ed., pp. 787–840). New York: Wiley.

Clark, L. A., Kochanska, G., & Ready, R. (2000). Mothers' personality and its interaction with child temperament as predictors of parenting behavior. *Journal of Personality and Social Psychology, 79,* 274–285.

Clarke, A. M., & Clarke, A. D. B. (Eds.). (1976). *Early experience: Myth and evidence.* New York: Free Press.

Clarke-Stewart, K. A. (1998). Historical shifts and underlying themes in ideas about rearing young children in the United States: Where have we been? Where are we going? *Early Development and Parenting, 7,* 101–117.

Clarke-Stewart, K. A., & Allhusen, V. D. (2002). Nonparental caregiving. In M. H. Bornstein (Ed.), *Handbook of parenting: Vol. 3. Status and social conditions of parenting* (2nd ed., pp. 215–252). Mahwah, NJ: Erlbaum.

Coates, D. L., & Lewis, M. (1984). Early mother-infant interaction and infant cognitive status as predictors of school performance and cognitive behavior in 6-year-olds. *Child Development, 55,* 1219–1230.

Cochran, M. (1993). Parenting and personal social networks. In T. Luster & L. Okagaki (Eds.), *Parenting: An ecological perspective* (pp. 149–178). Hillsdale, NJ: Erlbaum.

Cochran, M., & Niego, S. (2002). Parenting and social networks. In M. H. Bornstein (Ed.), *Handbook of parenting: Vol. 4. Applied parenting* (2nd ed., pp. 123–148). Mahwah, NJ: Erlbaum.

Cohler, B. J., & Paul, S. (2002). Psychoanalysis and parenthood. In M. H. Bornstein (Ed.), *Handbook of parenting: Vol. 3. Status and social conditions of parenting* (2nd ed., pp. 563–599). Mahwah, NJ: Erlbaum.

Coie, J. D., Watt, N. F., West, S. G., & Hawkins, J. D., Asarnaw, J. R., Markman, H. J., Ramey, S. L., Shure, M. B., & Long, B. (1993). The science of prevention: A conceptual framework and some directions for a national research program. *American Psychologist, 48,* 1013–1022.

Coleman, P. K., & Karraker, K. H. (1998). Self-efficacy and parenting quality: Findings and future applications. *Developmental Review, 18,* 47–85.

Coleman, P. K., & Karraker, K. H. (2003). Maternal self-efficacy beliefs, competence in parenting, and toddlers' behavior and developmental status. *Infant Mental Health Journal, 24,* 126–148.

Coley, R. L., & Chase-Lansdale, P. L. (1998). Adolescent pregnancy and parenthood: Recent evidence and future directions. *American Psychologist, 53,* 152–166.

Collins, W. A., Maccoby, E. E., Steinberg, L., Hetherington, E. M., & Bornstein, M. H. (2000). Contemporary research on parenting: The case for nature and nurture. *American Psychologist, 55,* 218–232.

Collins, W. A., & Russell, G. (1991). Mother-child and father-child relationships in middle childhood and adolescence: A developmental analysis. *Developmental Review, 11,* 99–136.

Colón, A. J. (with Colón, P. A.). (1999). *Nurturing children: A history of pediatrics.* Westport, CT: Greenwood Press.

Coltrane, S. (1996). *Family man: Fatherhood, housework, and gender equity*. New York: Oxford University Press.

Condry, J., & Condry, S. (1976). Sex differences: A study of the eye of the beholder. *Child Development, 47*, 812–819.

Conger, R. D., & Elder, G. H., Jr. (Eds.). (1994). *Families in troubled times: Adapting to change in rural America*. Hawthorne, NY: Aldine.

Conger, R. D., Ge, X., Elder, G. H., Jr., Lorenz, F. O., & Simons, R. L. (1994). Economic stress, coercive family process, and developmental problems of adolescents. *Child Development, 65*, 541–561.

Conrad, B., Gross, D., Fogg, L., & Ruchala, P. (1992). Maternal confidence, knowledge, and quality of mother-toddler interactions: A preliminary study. *Infant Mental Health Journal, 13*, 353–362.

Cook, T. D., & Payne, M. R. (2002). Objecting to the objections to using random assignment in educational research. In F. Mosteller & R. F. Boruch (Eds.), *Evidence matters: Randomized trials in education research* (pp. 150–178). Washington, DC: Brookings Institution.

Corter, C. M., & Fleming, A. S. (2002). Psychobiology of maternal behavior in human beings. In M. H. Bornstein (Ed.), *Handbook of parenting: Vol. 2. Biology and ecology of parenting* (2nd ed., pp. 141–181). Mahwah, NJ: Erlbaum.

Cote, L. R., & Bornstein, M. H. (2000). Social and didactic parenting behaviors and beliefs among Japanese American and South American mothers of infants. *Infancy, 1*, 363–374.

Cotterell, J. L. (1986). Work and community influences on the quality of child rearing. *Child Development, 57*, 362–374.

Cowan, C. P., & Cowan, P. A. (1992). *When partners become parents*. New York: Basic Books.

Cowan, C. P., Cowan, P. A., Heming, G., Garrett, E., Coysh, W. S., Curtis-Boles, H., et al. (1985). Transitions to parenthood: His, hers, and theirs. *Journal of Family Issues, 6*, 451–481.

Cowan, P. A., Cowan, C. P., Ablow, J., Johnson, V. K., & Measelle, J. (2005). *The family context of parenting in children's adaptation to elementary school*. Mahwah, NJ: Erlbaum.

Cowan, P. A., Cowan, C. P., Schulz, M. S., & Heming, G. (1994). Prebirth to preschool family factors in children's adaptation to kindergarten. In R. D. Parke & S. G. Kellam (Eds.), *Exploring family relationships with other social contexts* (pp. 75–114). Hillsdale, NJ: Erlbaum.

Cowan, P. A., Powell, D., & Cowan, C. P. (1998). Parenting interventions: A family systems perspective. In W. Damon (Editor-in-Chief) & I. E. Sigel & K. A. Renninger (Vol. Eds.), *Handbook of child psychology: Vol. 4. Child psychology in practice* (5th ed., pp. 3–72). New York: Wiley.

Cox, M. J., & Harter, K. S. M. (2003). Parent-child relationships. In M. H. Bornstein, L. Davidson, C. L. M. Keyes, & K. A. Moore (Eds.), *Well-being: Positive development across the life course* (pp. 191–204). Mahwah, NJ: Erlbaum.

Cox, M. J., & Paley, B. (2003). Understanding families as systems. *Current Directions in Psychological Science, 12*, 193–196.

Cox, M. J., Paley, B., & Harter, K. (2001). Interparental conflict and parent-child relationships. In J. H. Grych & F. D. Fincham (Eds.), *Interparental conflict and child development: Theory, research, and applications* (pp. 249–272). New York: Cambridge University Press.

Crittenden, A. (Ed.). (2004). *If you've raised kids, you can manage anything: Leadership begins at home*. New York: Gotham Books.

Crnic, K., & Low, C. (2002). Everyday stresses and parenting. In M. H. Bornstein (Ed.), *Handbook of parenting: Vol. 5. Practical parenting* (2nd ed., pp. 243–267). Mahwah, NJ: Erlbaum.

Crnic, K. A., & Greenberg, M. T. (1990). Minor parenting stresses with young children. *Child Development, 61*, 1628–1637.

Crnic, K. A., Greenberg, M. T., Ragozin, A. S., Robinson, N. M., & Basham, R. (1983). Effects of stress and social support on mothers and premature and full-term infants. *Child Development, 54*, 209–217.

Crockenberg, S. B. (1988). Social support and parenting. In W. Fitzgerald, B. Lester, & M. Yogman (Eds.), *Research on support for parents and infants in the postnatal period* (pp. 67–92). New York: Ablex.

Crockenberg, S. B., & Langrock, A. (2001). The role of specific emotions in children's responses to interparental conflict: A test of the model. *Journal of Family Psychology, 15*, 163–182.

Crockett, L. J., Eggebeen, D. J., & Hawkins, A. J. (1993). Father's presence and young children's behavioral and cognitive adjustment. *Journal of Family Issues, 14*, 355–377.

Cummings, E. M., & Cummings, J. S. (2002). Parenting and attachment. In M. H. Bornstein (Ed.), *Handbook of parenting: Vol. 5. Practical parenting* (2nd ed., pp. 35–58). Mahwah, NJ: Erlbaum.

Cummings, E. M., & Davies, P. T. (1994). *Children and marital conflict: The impact of family dispute and resolution*. New York: Guilford Press.

Cummings, E. M., & Davies, P. T. (1995). The impact of parents on their children: An emotional security perspective. In R. Vasta (Ed.), *Annals of child development: Vol. 10. A research annual* (pp. 167–208). Philadelphia: Jessica Kingsley.

Cummings, E. M., Iannotti, R. J., & Zahn-Waxler, C. (1985). Influence of conflict between adults on the emotions and aggression of young children. *Developmental Psychology, 21*, 495–507.

Cummings, E. M., & Watson-O'Reilly, A. (1997). Fathers in family context: Effects of marital quality on child adjustment. In M. E. Lamb (Ed.), *The role of the father in child development* (3rd ed., pp. 49–65). New York: Wiley.

Cummings, E. M., & Wilson, A. (1999). Contexts of marital conflict and children's emotional security: Exploring the distinction between constructive and destructive conflicts from the children's perspective. In M. J. Cox & J. Brooks-Gunn (Eds.), *Conflict and cohesion in families: Causes and consequences—Advances in family research series* (pp. 105–129). Mahwah, NJ: Erlbaum.

Cutrona, C. E., & Suhr, J. A. (1990). The transition to parenthood and the importance of social support. In S. Fisher & C. L. Cooper (Eds.), *On the move: Psychology of change and transition* (pp. 111–125). New York: Wiley.

Cutrona, C. E., & Troutman, B. R. (1986). Social support, infant temperament, and parenting self-efficacy: A mediating model of postpartum depression. *Child Development, 57*, 1507–1518.

Darling, N., & Steinberg, L. (1993). Parenting style as context: An integrative model. *Psychological Bulletin, 113*, 487–496.

Darwin, C. R. (1877). A biographical sketch of an infant. *Mind, 2*, 286–294.

Davies, P. T., & Cummings, M. E. (1994). Marital conflict and child adjustment: An emotional security hypothesis. *Psychological Bulletin, 116*, 387–411.

Dawkins, R. (1976). Hierarchical organization: A candidate principle for ethology. In P. P. Bates & R. A. Hinde (Eds.), *Growing points in ethology*. Oxford: Cambridge University Press.

Deal, J. E., Hagan, M. S., Bass, B., Hetherington, E. M., & Clingempeel, G. (1999). Marital interaction in dyadic and triadic contexts: Continuities and discontinuities. *Family Process, 38,* 105–115.

DeBaryshe, B. D. (1995). Maternal belief systems: Linchpin in the home reading process. *Journal of Applied Developmental Psychology, 16,* 1–20.

DeLuccie, M. F. (1994). Mothers as gatekeepers: A model of maternal mediators of father involvement. *Journal of Genetic Psychology, 156,* 115–131.

deMause, L. (Ed.). (1975). *The new psychohistory.* New York: Psychohistory Press.

Dembo, M. H., Switzer, M., & Lauritzen, P. (1985). An evaluation of group parent education: Behavioral, PET, & Adlerian programs. *Review of Educational Research, 55,* 155–200.

Denckla, M. B., & Reiss, A. L. (1997). Prefrontal-subcortical circuits in developmental disorders. In N. A. Krasnegor, G. R. Lyon, & P. S. Goldman-Rakic (Eds.), *Development of the prefrontal cortex: Evolution, neurobiology, and behavior* (pp. 283–294). Baltimore: Paul H. Brookes.

Deutsch, F. M., Ruble, D. N., Fleming, A., Brooks-Gunn, J., & Stangor, C. (1988). Information-seeking and maternal self-definition during the transition to motherhood. *Journal of Personality and Social Psychology, 55,* 420–431.

De Wolff, M., & van IJzendoorn, M. H. (1997). Sensitivity and attachment: A meta-analysis on parental antecedents of infant attachment. *Child Development, 68,* 571–591.

Dishion, T., Patterson, G., Stoolmiller, M., & Skinner, M. (1991). Family, school, and behavioral antecedents to early adolescent involvement with antisocial peers. *Developmental Psychology, 27,* 172–180.

Dishion, T. J., Patterson, G. R., & Kavanagh, K. A. (1992). An experimental test of the coercion model: Linking theory, measurement, and intervention. In J. McCord & R. E. Tremblay (Eds.), *Preventing antisocial behavior: Interventions from birth through adolescence* (pp. 253–282). New York: Guilford Press.

Dix, T. (1991). The affective organization of parenting: Adaptive and maladaptive processes. *Psychological Bulletin, 110,* 3–25.

Dix, T. (1992). Parenting on behalf of the child: Empathic goals in the regulation of responsive parenting. In I. E. Sigel & A. V. McGillicuddy-De Lisi (Eds.), *Parental belief systems: The psychological consequences for children* (2nd ed., pp. 319–346). Hillsdale, NJ: Erlbaum.

Dix, T., & Grusec, J. E. (1985). Parent attribution processes in the socialization of children. In I. Sigel (Ed.), *Parental belief systems: The psychological consequence for children* (pp. 201–233). Hillsdale, NJ: Erlbaum.

Dixson, A. F., & George, L. (1982). Prolactin and parental behaviour in a male New World primate. *Nature, 299,* 551–553.

Doi, T. (1973). *The anatomy of dependence* (J. Bester, Trans.). Tokyo: Kodansha International.

Donahue, M. L., Pearl, R., & Herzog, A. (1997). Mothers' referential communication with preschoolers: Effects of children's syntax and mothers' beliefs. *Journal of Applied Developmental Psychology, 18,* 133–147.

Dornbusch, S. M., Ritter, P. L., Leiderman, P. H., Roberts, D. F., & Fraleigh, M. J. (1987). The relation of parenting style to adolescent school performance. *Child Development, 58,* 1244–1257.

Downey, G., & Coyne, J. C. (1990). Children of depressed parents: An integrative review. *Psychological Bulletin, 10,* 50–76.

Duncan, G. J., & Brooks-Gunn, J. (1997). *Consequences of growing up poor.* New York: Russell Sage Foundation.

Dunn, J. (1995). Stepfamilies and children's adjustment. *Archives of Disease in Childhood, 73,* 487–489.

Dunn, J., & Plomin, R. (1990). *Separate lives: Why siblings are so different.* New York: Basic Books.

Dunn, J. F., Plomin, R., & Daniels D. (1986). Consistency and change in mothers' behavior toward young siblings. *Child Development, 57,* 348–356.

Dunn, J. F., Plomin, R., & Nettles, M. (1985). Consistency of mothers' behavior toward infant siblings. *Developmental Psychology, 21,* 1188–1195.

Duyme, M., Dumaret, A. C., & Stanislaw, T. (1999). How can we boost IQs of "dull" children? A late adoption study. *Proceedings of the National Academy of Sciences, 96,* 8790–8794.

Dye, N. S., & Smith, D. B. (1986). Mother love and infant death, 1750–1920. *Journal of American History, 73,* 329–353.

Eagly, A. H. (1992). Uneven progress: Social psychology and the study of attitudes. *Journal of Personality and Social Psychology, 63,* 693–710.

East, P. L., & Felice, M. E. (1996). *Adolescent pregnancy and parenting: Findings from a racially diverse sample.* Mahwah, NJ: Erlbaum.

Eccles, J. S., & Harold, R. D. (1996). Family involvement in children's and adolescents' schooling. In A. Booth & J. F. Dunn (Eds.), *Family-school links: How do they affect educational outcomes?* (pp. 3–34). Hillsdale, NJ: Erlbaum.

Elder, G. H. (1974). *Children of the Great Depression.* Chicago: University of Chicago Press.

Elder, G. H., Eccles, J. S., Ardelt, M., & Lord, S. (1995). Inner-city parents under economic pressure: Perspective on the strategies of parenting. *Journal of Marriage and the Family, 57,* 771–784.

Elman, J. L., Bates, E. A., Johnson, M. H., Karmiloff-Smith, A., Parisi, D., & Plunkett, K. (1996). *Rethinking innateness: A connectionist perspective on development.* Cambridge, MA: MIT Press.

Elster, A. B., McAnarney, E. R., & Lamb, M. E. (1983). Parental behavior of adolescent mothers. *Pediatrics, 71,* 494–503.

Emery, R. E., & Tuer, M. (1993). Parenting and the marital relationship. In T. Luster & L. Okagaki (Eds.), *Parenting: An ecological perspective* (pp. 121–148). Hillsdale, NJ: Erlbaum.

Entwisle, D. R., & Hayduk, L. A. (1988). Lasting effects of elementary school. *Sociology of Education, 61,* 147–159.

Epstein, J. L. (1983). The influence of friends on achievement and affective outcomes. In J. L. Epstein & N. Karweit (Eds.), *Friends in school* (pp. 177–200). New York: Academic Press.

Erel, O., & Burman, B. (1995). Interrelatedness of marital relations and parent-child relations: A meta-analytic review. *Psychological Bulletin, 118,* 108–132.

Erting, C. J., Prezioso, C., & Hynes, M. O. (1994). The interfactional context of deaf mother-infant communication. In V. Volterra & C. J. Erting (Eds.), *From gesture to language in hearing and deaf children* (pp. 97–106). Washington, DC: Gallaudet University Press.

Eslinger, P. J. (1996). Conceptualizing, describing, and measuring components of executive function: A summary. In G. R. Lyon &

N. A. Krasnegor (Eds.), *Attention, memory, and executive function* (pp. 367–395). Baltimore: Paul H. Brookes.

Eslinger, P. J., Grattan, L. M., Damasio, H., & Damasio, A. R. (1992). Developmental consequences of childhood frontal lobe damage. *Archives of Neurology, 49,* 764–769.

Feinberg, M. E. (2003). The internal structure and ecological context of coparenting: A framework for research and intervention. *Parenting: Science & Practice, 3,* 95–131.

Feldman, M. W., & Lewontin, R. C. (1975). The heritability hangup. *Science, 190,* 1163–1168.

Festinger, L. (1964). *Conflict, decision, and dissonance.* Oxford: Stanford University Press.

Field, T., Healy, B., Goldstein, S., & Guthertz, M. (1990). Behavior state matching and synchrony in mother-infant interactions of nondepressed versus depressed dyads. *Developmental Psychology, 31,* 358–363.

Fincham, F. D. (1998). Child development and marital relations. *Child Development, 69,* 543–574.

Fincham, F. D., Grych, J. H., & Osborne, L. N. (1994). Does marital conflict cause child maladjustment? Directions and challenges for longitudinal research. *Journal of Family Psychology, 8,* 128–140.

Fish, M., & Stifter, C. A. (1993). Mother parity as a main and moderating influence on early mother-infant interaction. *Journal of Applied Developmental Psychology, 14,* 557–572.

Fleeson, W. (2004). Moving personality beyond the person-situation debate: The challenge and the opportunity of within-person variability. *Current Directions in Psychological Science, 13,* 83–87.

Fleming, A. S., & Liu, M. (2002). Psychobiology of maternal behavior in its early determinants in nonhuman mammals. In M. H. Bornstein (Ed.), *Handbook of parenting: Vol. 2. Biology and ecology of parenting* (2nd ed., pp. 61–97). Mahwah, NJ: Erlbaum.

Fleming, A. S., Ruble, D. N., Flett, G. L., & Van Wagner, V. (1990). Adjustment in first-time mothers: Changes in mood and mood content during the early postpartum months. *Developmental Psychology, 26,* 137–143.

Forehand, R., & King, H. E. (1977). Noncompliant children: Effects of parent training on behavior and attitude change. *Behavior Modification, 1,* 93–108.

Forehand, R., Wells, K. C., & Griest, D. L. (1980). An examination of the social validity of a parent training program. *Behavior Therapy, 11,* 488–502.

Forgatch, M. S. (1991). The clinical science vortex: A developing theory of antisocial behavior. In D. J. Pepler & K. H. Rubin (Eds.), *The development and treatment of childhood aggression* (pp. 291–315). Hillsdale, NJ: Erlbaum.

Forgatch, M. S., & DeGarmo, D. S. (1999). Parenting through change: An effective prevention program for single mothers. *Journal of Consulting and Clinical Psychology, 67,* 711–724.

Fraiberg, S., Adelson, E., & Shapiro, V. (2003). Ghosts in the nursery: A psychoanalytic approach to the problems of impaired infant-mother relationships. In J. Raphael-Leff (Ed.), *Parent-infant psychodynamics: Wild things, mirrors and ghosts* (pp. 87–117). London: Whurr.

Frankel, D. G., & Roer-Bornstein, D. (1982). Traditional and modern contributions to changing infant-rearing ideologies of two ethnic communities. *Monographs of the Society for Research in Child Development, 4,* 1–51.

French, V. (2002). History of parenting: The ancient Mediterranean world. In M. H. Bornstein (Ed.), *Handbook of parenting: Vol. 2. Biology and ecology of parenting* (2nd ed., pp. 345–376). Mahwah, NJ: Erlbaum.

Freud, A. (1970). The concept of the rejecting mother. In E. J. Anthony & T. Benedek (Eds.), *Parenthood: Its psychology and psychopathology* (pp. 376–386). Boston: Little, Brown. (Original work published 1955)

Freud, S. (1949). *An outline of psycho-analysis.* New York: Norton.

Fuligni, A. J., & Eccles, J. S. (1993). Perceived parent-child relationships and early adolescents' orientation toward peers. *Developmental Psychology, 29,* 622–632.

Fuller-Thomson, E., Minkler, M., & Driver, D. (1997). A profile of grandparents raising grandchildren in the United States. *Gerontologist, 37,* 406–411.

Furstenberg, F. F., Jr., Brooks-Gunn, J., & Chase-Lansdale, P. L. (1989). Adolescent fertility and public policy. *American Psychologist, 44,* 313–320.

Gable, S., Crnic, K., & Belsky, J. (1994). Coparenting within the family system: Influences on children's development. *Family Relations: Interdisciplinary Journal of Applied Family Studies, 43,* 380–386.

Galloway, A. T., Fiorito, L., Lee, Y., & Birch, L. L. (2005). Parental pressure, dietary patterns, and weight status among girls who are "picky eaters." *Journal of the American Dietetic Association, 105,* 541–548.

Garrett, P., Ferron, J., Ng'andu, N., Bryant, D., & Harbin, G. (1994). A structural model for the developmental status of young children. *Journal of Marriage and the Family, 56,* 147–163.

George, C., Kaplan, N., & Main, M. (1985). *Adult Attachment Interview.* Unpublished manuscript, University of California, Berkeley.

Gibson, E., Dembofsky, C. A., Rubin, S., & Greenspan, J. S. (2000). Infant sleep position practices 2 years into the "back to sleep" campaign. *Clinical Pediatrics, 39,* 285–289.

Giedd, J. N., Blumenthal, J., Jeffries, N. O., Castellanos, F. X., Liu, H., Zijdenbos, A., et al. (1999). Brain development during childhood and adolescence: A longitudinal MRI study. *Nature Neuroscience, 2,* 861–863.

Goldberg, S. (1977). Infant development and mother-infant interaction in urban Zambia. In P. H. Leiderman, S. R. Tulkin, & A. Rosenfeld (Eds.), *Culture and infancy: Variations in the human experience* (pp. 211–243). New York: Academic Press.

Goldberg, S., & DiVitto, B. (2002). Parenting children born preterm. In M. H. Bornstein (Ed.), *Handbook of parenting: Vol. 1. Children and parenting* (2nd ed., pp. 329–354). Mahwah, NJ: Erlbaum.

Golombok, S. (2002). Parenting and contemporary reproductive technologies. In M. H. Bornstein (Ed.), *Handbook of parenting: Vol. 3. Status and social conditions of parenting* (2nd ed., pp. 339–360). Mahwah, NJ: Erlbaum.

Gomby, D. S., Culross, P. L., & Behrman, R. E. (1999). Home visiting: Recent program evaluations—Analysis and recommendations. *Future of Children, 9,* 4–26.

Goodnow, J. J. (1997). Parenting and the transmission and internalization of values: From social-cultural perspectives to within-family analyses. In J. E. Grusec & L. Kuczynski (Eds.), *Parenting and children's internalization of values: A handbook of contemporary theory* (pp. 333–361). New York: Wiley.

Goodnow, J. J. (2002). Parents' knowledge and expectations: Using what we know. In M. H. Bornstein (Ed.), *Handbook of parenting: Vol. 3. Status and social conditions of parenting* (2nd ed., pp. 439–460). Mahwah, NJ: Erlbaum.

Goodnow, J. J., Cashmore, R., Cotton, S., & Knight, R. (1984). Mothers' developmental timetables in two cultural groups. *International Journal of Psychology, 19,* 193–205.

Goodnow, J. J., & Collins, W. A. (1990). *Development according to parents: The nature, sources, and consequences of parents' ideas.* Hillsdale, NJ: Erlbaum.

Gottfried, A. E., Gottfried, A. W., & Bathurst, K. (2002). Maternal and dual-earner employment status and parenting. In M. H. Bornstein (Ed.), *Handbook of parenting: Vol. 2. Biology and ecology of parenting* (2nd ed., pp. 207–229). Mahwah, NJ: Erlbaum.

Gottfried, A. W. (1984). Home environment and early cognitive development: Implications for intervention. In A. W. Gottfried (Ed.), *Home environment and early cognitive development* (pp. 329–342). New York: Academic Press.

Gottlieb, G. (1995). Some conceptual deficiencies in "developmental" behavior genetics. *Human Development, 38,* 131–141.

Grattan, L. M., & Eslinger, P. J. (1992). Long-term psychological consequences of childhood frontal lobe lesion in patient D. T. *Brain and Cognition, 20,* 185–195.

Green, R. (1954). Employment counseling for the hard of hearing. *Volta Review, 56,* 209–212.

Greenbaum, C. W., & Landau, R. (1982). The infant's exposure to talk by familiar people: Mothers, fathers and siblings in different environments. In M. Lewis & L. Rosenblum (Eds.), *The social network of the developing infant* (pp. 229–247). New York: Plenum Press.

Greenberger, E., & Goldberg, W. A. (1989). Work, parenting, and the socialization of children. *Developmental Psychology, 25,* 22–35.

Greene, B. (1984). *Good morning, merry sunshine: A father's journal of his child's first year.* New York: Athenaeum.

Grossman, F. K., Eichler, L. W., & Winikoff, S. A. (1980). *Pregnancy, birth and parenthood.* San Francisco: Jossey-Bass.

Grusec, J. E., & Goodnow, J. J. (1994). Impact of parental discipline methods on the child's internalization of values: A reconceptualization of current points of view. *Developmental Psychology, 30,* 4–19.

Grych, J. H. (2002). Marital relationships and parenting. In M. H. Bornstein (Ed.), *Handbook of parenting: Vol. 4. Applied parenting* (2nd ed., pp. 203–225). Mahwah, NJ: Erlbaum.

Grych, J. H., & Fincham, F. D. (1990). Marital conflict and children's adjustment: A cognitive-contextual framework. *Psychological Bulletin, 108,* 267–290.

Grych, J. H., & Fincham, F. D. (Eds.). (2001). *Interparental conflict and child development: Theory, research, and applications.* New York: Cambridge University Press.

Hall, G. S. (1891). Notes on the study of infants. *Pedagogical Seminary, 1,* 127–138.

Hamilton, B. E., Martin, J. A., & Sutton, P. D. (2004). *Births: Preliminary data for 2003* (National Statistics Reports, Vol. 53, No. 9). Hyattsville, MD: National Center for Health Statistics.

Hardy, J., Astone, N. M., Brooks-Gunn, J., Shapiro, S., & Miller, T. (1998). Like mother, like child: Intergenerational patterns of age at first birth and associations with childhood and adolescent characteristics and adult outcome in the second generation. *Developmental Psychology, 34,* 1220–1232.

Hardy-Brown, K. (1983). Universals in individual differences: Disentangling two approaches to the study of language acquisition. *Developmental Psychology, 19,* 610–624.

Hardy-Brown, K., & Plomin, R. (1985). Infant communicative development: Evidence from adoptive and biological families for genetic and environmental influences on rate differences. *Developmental Psychology, 21,* 378–385.

Hardy-Brown, K., Plomin, R., & DeFries, J. C. (1981). Genetic and environmental influences on rate of communicative development in the first year of life. *Developmental Psychology, 17,* 704–717.

Harkness, S., & Super, C. M. (1996). *Parents' cultural belief systems: Their origins, expressions, and consequences.* New York: Guilford Press.

Harkness, S., & Super, C. M. (2002). Culture and parenting. In M. H. Bornstein (Ed.), *Handbook of parenting: Vol. 2. Biology and ecology of parenting* (2nd ed., pp. 253–280). Mahwah, NJ: Erlbaum.

Harrell, J. E., & Ridley, C. A. (1975). Substitute child care, maternal employment and the quality of mother-child interaction. *Journal of Marriage and the Family, 37,* 556–564.

Harris, C. C. (1983). *The family and industrial society.* London: Allen & Unwin.

Harris, J. R. (1995). Where is the child's environment? A group socialization theory of development. *Psychological Review, 102,* 458–489.

Harris, J. R. (1998). *The nurture assumption.* New York: Free Press.

Harrison, A. O., Wilson, M. N., Pine, C. J., Chan, S. Q., & Buriel, R. (1990). Family ecologies of ethnic minority children. *Child Development, 61,* 347–362.

Hart, B., & Risley, T. R. (1995). *Meaningful differences in the everyday experience of young American children.* Baltimore: Paul H. Brookes.

Hartup, W. W. (1992). Peer relations in early and middle childhood. In V. B. Van Hasselt & M. Hersen (Eds.), *Handbook of social development: A lifespan perspective—Perspectives in developmental psychology* (pp. 257–281). New York: Plenum Press.

Harwood, R. L. (1992). The influence of culturally derived values on Anglo and Puerto Rican mothers' perceptions of attachment behavior. *Child Development, 63,* 822–839.

Harwood, R. L., Handwerker, W. P., Schoelmerich, A., & Leyendecker, B. (2001). Ethnic category labels, parental beliefs, and the contextualized individual: An exploration of the individualism/sociocentrism debate. *Parenting: Science and Practice, 1,* 217–236.

Harwood, R. L., Miller, J. G., & Irizarry, N. L. (1995). *Culture and attachment: Perceptions of the child in context.* New York: Guilford Press.

Hashima, P. Y., & Amato, P. R. (1994). Poverty, social support, and parental behavior. *Child Development, 65,* 394–403.

Haveman, R., Wolfe, B., & Wilson, K. (1997). Childhood poverty and adolescent schooling and fertility outcomes: Reduced-form structural estimates. In G. Duncan & J. Brooks-Gunn (Eds.), *Consequences of growing up poor* (pp. 419–460). New York: Sage.

Heinicke, C. M. (2002). The transition to parenting. In M. H. Bornstein (Ed.), *Handbook of parenting: Vol. 3. Status and social conditions of parenting* (2nd ed., pp. 363–388). Mahwah, NJ: Erlbaum.

Heinicke, C. M., Rineman, N. R., Ponce, V. A., & Guthrie, D. (2001). Relation-based intervention with at-risk mothers: Outcome in the second year of life. *Infant Mental Health Journal, 22,* 431–462.

Helson, R., Mitchell, V., & Moane, G. (1984). Personality patterns of adherence and nonadherence to the social clock. *Journal of Personality and Social Psychology, 46,* 1078–1096.

Hess, R. D., Chang, C. M., & McDevitt, T. M. (1987). Cultural variations in family beliefs about children's performance in mathematics: Comparisons among People's Republic of China, Chinese-American, and Caucasian-American families. *Journal of Educational Psychology, 79,* 179–188.

Hetherington, E. M., Reiss, D., & Plomin, R. (Eds.). (1994). *Separate social worlds of siblings.* Hillsdale, NJ: Erlbaum.

Hickson, G. B., & Clayton, E. W. (2002). Parents and their children's doctors. In M. H. Bornstein (Ed.), *Handbook of parenting* (Vol. 5, pp. 439–462). Mahwah, NJ: Erlbaum.

Ho, D. Y. F. (1994). Cognitive socialization in Confucian heritage cultures. In P. M. Greenfield & R. R. Cocking (Eds.), *Cross-cultural roots of minority child development* (pp. 285–313). Hillsdale, NJ: Erlbaum.

Ho, H. Z. (1987). Interaction of early caregiving environment and infant developmental status in predicting subsequent cognitive performance. *British Journal of Developmental Psychology, 5,* 183–191.

Hodapp, R. M., & Ly, T. M. (2005). Parenting children with developmental disabilities. In T. Luster & L. Okagaki (Eds.), *Parenting: An ecological perspective* (2nd ed., pp. 177–201). Mahwah, NJ: Erlbaum.

Hoff, E. (2003). Causes and consequences of SES-related differences in parent-to-child speech. In M. H. Bornstein & R. H. Bradley (Eds.), *Socioeconomic status, parenting, and child development* (pp. 147–160). Mahwah, NJ: Erlbaum.

Hoff, E., Laursen, B., & Tardif, T. (2002). Socioeconomic status and parenting. In M. H. Bornstein (Ed.), *Handbook of parenting: Vol. 2. Biology and ecology of parenting* (2nd ed., pp. 231–252). Mahwah, NJ: Erlbaum.

Hofferth, S. L. (1987). The children of teen childbearers. In S. L. Hofferth & C. D. Hayes (Eds.), *Risking the future: Adolescent sexuality, pregnancy and childbearing* (pp. 174–206). Washington, DC: National Academy Press.

Hoffman, L. W. (1991). The influence of the family environment on personality: Accounting for sibling differences. *Psychological Bulletin, 110,* 187–203.

Hogue, A., & Steinberg, L. (1995). Homophily of internalized distress in adolescent peer groups. *Developmental Psychology, 31,* 897–906.

Holden, G. W. (2002). Perspectives on the effects of corporal punishment: Comment on Gershoff. *Psychological Bulletin, 128,* 590–595.

Holden, G. W., & Buck, M. J. (2002). Parental attitudes toward child-rearing. In M. H. Bornstein (Ed.), *Handbook of parenting: Vol. 3. Status and social conditions of parenting* (2nd ed., pp. 537–562). Mahwah, NJ: Erlbaum.

Holden, G. W., & Miller, P. C. (1999). Enduring and different: A meta-analysis of the similarity in parents' child rearing. *Psychological Bulletin, 125,* 223–254.

Holden, G. W., Willis, D. J., & Foltz, L. (1989). Child abuse potential and parenting stress: Relationships in maltreating parents. *Psychological Assessment, 1,* 64–67.

Hoover-Dempsey, K. V., & Sandler, H. M. (1997). Why do parents become involved in their children's education? *Review of Educational Research, 67,* 3–42.

Hopkins, B., & Westra, T. (1989). Maternal expectations of their infants' development: Some cultural differences. *Developmental Medicine and Child Neurology, 31,* 384–390.

Hopkins, B., & Westra, T. (1990). Motor development, maternal expectation, and the role of handling. *Infant Behavior and Development, 13,* 117–122.

Horn, J. (1983). The Texas Adoption Project: Adopted children and their intellectual resemblance to biological and adoptive parents. *Child Development, 54,* 268–275.

Howes, C., Hamilton, C. E., & Phillipsen, L. C. (1998). Stability and continuity of child-caregiver and child-peer relationships. *Child Development, 69,* 418–426.

Hrdy, S. B. (1999). *Mother nature: A history of mothers, infants, and natural selection.* New York: Pantheon.

Hunt, J. M., & Paraskevopoulos, J. (1980). Children's psychological development as a function of the inaccuracy of their mothers' knowledge of their abilities. *Journal of Genetic Psychology, 136,* 285–298.

Hunt, J., McV. (1979). Psychological development: Early experience. *Annual Review of Psychology, 30,* 103–143.

Huttenlocher, P. R. (1990). Morphometric study of human cerebral cortex development. *Neuropsychologia, 28,* 517–527.

Isley, S., O'Neil, R., & Parke, R. D. (1996). The relation of parental effect and control behavior to children's classroom acceptance: A concurrent and predictive analysis. *Early Education and Development, 7,* 7–23.

Jackson, S. (1987). *Education of children in care* (Papers in Applied Social Studies No. 1). Bristol, England: University of Bristol.

Jacobson, J. L., Boersma, D. C., Fields, R. B., & Olson, K. L. (1983). Paralinguistic features of adult speech to infants and small children. *Child Development, 54,* 436–442.

Jaeger, S. (1985). The origin of the diary method in developmental psychology. In G. Eckhardt, W. G. Bringmann, & L. Sprung (Eds.), *Contributions to a history of developmental psychology* (pp. 63–74). Berlin, Germany: Mouton.

Jennings, K., Stagg, V., & Connors, R. (1991). Social networks and mothers' interactions with their preschool children. *Child Development, 62,* 966–978.

Johnson, W., Emde, R. N., Pannabecker, B., Stenberg, C., & Davis, M. (1982). Maternal perception of infant emotion from birth through 18 months. *Infant Behavior and Development, 5,* 313–322.

Johnston, C., & Mash, E. (1989). A measure of parenting satisfaction and efficacy. *Journal of Clinical Child Psychology, 18,* 167–175.

Kagan, J. (1998). *Three seductive ideas.* Cambridge, MA: Harvard University Press.

Kandel, D. (1978). Homophily, selection, and socialization in adolescent friendships. *American Journal of Sociology, 84,* 427–436.

Kannel, S., & Perry, M. J. (2001). *Child development and Medicaid: Attitudes of mothers with young children enrolled in Medicaid.* New York: Commonwealth Fund.

Karraker, K. H., & Coleman, P. K. (2005). The effects of child characteristics on parenting. In T. Luster & L. Okagaki (Eds.), *Parenting: An ecological perspective* (2nd ed., pp. 147–176). Mahwah, NJ: Erlbaum.

Kaye, K. (1982). *The mental and social life of babies.* Brighton, England: Harvester Press.

Kellam, S. G., Rebok, G. W., Ialongo, N., & Mayer, L. S. (1994). The course and malleability of aggressive behavior from early first grade into middle school: Results of a developmental epidemiologically-based preventive trial. *Journal of Child Psychology and Psychiatry and Allied Disciplines, 35,* 259–281.

Kerig, P. K. (1995). Triangles in the family circle: Effects of family structure on marriage, parenting, and child adjustment. *Journal of Family Psychology, 9,* 28–43.

Kerig, P. K., Cowan, P. A., & Cowan, C. P. (1993). Marital quality and gender differences in parent-child interaction. *Developmental Psychology, 29,* 931–939.

King, V. (1994). Nonresident father involvement and child well-being: Can dads make a difference? *Journal of Family Issues, 15,* 78–96.

King, V., & Elder, G. H., Jr. (1998). Perceived self-efficacy and grandparenting. *Journals of Gerontology Series B: Psychological Sciences and Social Sciences, 53B,* S249–S257.

Kinlaw, R., Kurtz-Costes, B., & Goldman-Fraser, J. (2001). Mothers' achievement beliefs and behaviors and their children's school readiness: A cultural comparison. *Journal of Applied Developmental Psychology, 22,* 493–506.

Klein, P. (1988). Stability and change in interaction of Israeli mothers and infants. *Infant Behavior and Development, 11,* 55–70.

Kochanska, G. (1995). Children's temperament, mothers' discipline, and security of attachment: Multiple pathways to emerging internalization. *Child Development, 66,* 597–615.

Kochanska, G. (1997). Multiple pathways to conscience for children with different temperaments: From toddlerhood to age five. *Developmental Psychology, 33,* 228–240.

Kochanska, G., Clark, L., & Goldman, M. (1997). Implications of mothers' personality for parenting and their young children's developmental outcomes. *Journal of Personality, 65,* 389–420.

Kochanska, G., Kuczynski, L., & Radke-Yarrow, M. (1989). Correspondence between mothers' self-reported and observed child-rearing practices. *Child Development, 60,* 56–63.

Kochanska, G., & Thompson, R. A. (1997). The emergence and development of conscience in toddlerhood and early childhood. In J. E. Grusec & L. Kuczunski (Eds.), *Parenting and children's internalization of values* (pp. 53–77). New York: Wiley.

Kohn, M. L. (1963). Social class and parent-child relationships: An interpretation. *American Journal of Sociology, 68,* 471–480.

Kohn, M. L. (1969). *Class and conformity: A study in values.* Oxford: Dorsey.

Kohn, M. L. (1979). The effects of social class on parental values and practices. In D. Reiss & H. Hoffman (Eds.), *American family: Dying or developing?* (pp. 45–68). New York: Plenum Press.

Kojima, H. (1986). Child rearing concepts as a belief-value system of the society and the individual. In H. W. Stevenson, H. Azuma, & K. Hakuta (Eds.), *Child development and education in Japan* (pp. 39–54). New York: Freeman.

Kotelchuck, M. (1976). The infants' relationship to the father: Experimental evidence. In M. E. Lamb (Ed.), *The role of the father in child development* (pp. 329–344). New York: Wiley.

Kuczynski, L. (1984). Socialization goals and mother-child interaction: Strategies for long-term and short-term compliance. *Developmental Psychology, 20,* 1061–1073.

Ladd, G. W., Kochenderfer, B. J., & Coleman, C. C. (1997). Classroom peer acceptance, friendship, and victimization: Distinct relational systems that contribute uniquely to children's school adjustment? *Child Development, 68,* 1181–1197.

Ladd, G. W., & Pettit, G. D. (2002). Parents and children's peer relationships. In M. H. Bornstein (Ed.), *Handbook of parenting: Vol. 5. Practical parenting* (2nd ed., pp. 269–309). Mahwah, NJ: Erlbaum.

Lamb, M. E. (1998). Nonparental child care: Context, quality, correlates, and consequences. In W. Damon (Editor-in-Chief) & I. E. Sigel & K. A. Renninger (Vol. Eds.), *Handbook of child psychology: Vol. 4. Child psychology in practice* (5th ed., pp. 73–133). New York: Wiley.

Lamb, M. E. (2000). The history of research on father involvement: An overview. *Marriage and Family Review, 29,* 23–42.

Lamb, M. E., Frodi, A. M., Frodi, M., & Hwang, C.-P. (1982). Characteristics of maternal and paternal behavior in traditional and nontraditional Swedish families. *International Journal of Behavioral Development, 5,* 131–141.

Landry, S. H., Smith, K. E., Swank, P. R., Assel, M. A., & Vellet, S. (2001). Does early responsive parenting have a special importance for children's development or is consistency across early childhood necessary? *Developmental Psychology, 37,* 387–403.

LaPiere, R. T. (1934). Attitudes versus actions. *Social Forces, 13,* 230–237.

Leach, P. (1997). *Your baby and child: From birth to age five.* New York: Knopf.

Leaper, C. (2002). Parenting girls and boys. In M. H. Bornstein (Ed.), *Handbook of parenting: Vol. 1. Children and parenting* (2nd ed., pp. 189–225). Mahwah, NJ: Erlbaum.

Lee, D., & Colletta, N. (1983, April). *Family support for adolescent mothers: The positive and negative impact.* Paper presented at the biennial meetings of the Society for Research in Child Development, Detroit, MI.

Leiderman, P. H., Tulkin, S. R., & Rosenfeld, A. (Eds.). (1977). *Culture and infancy: Variations in the human experience.* New York: Academic Press.

Leon, I. G. (2002). Adoption losses: Naturally occurring or socially constructed? *Child Development, 73,* 652–663.

Lerner, J. V., & Galambos, N. L. (1985). Maternal role satisfaction, mother-child interaction, and child temperament: A process model. *Developmental Psychology, 21,* 1157–1164.

Lerner, J. V., & Galambos, N. L. (1986). Temperament and maternal employment. *New Directions for Child Development, 31,* 75–88.

Lerner, R. M., Rothbaum, F., Boulos, S., & Castellino, D. R. (2002). Developmental systems perspective on parenting. In M. H. Bornstein (Ed.), *Handbook of parenting: Vol. 2. Biology and ecology of parenting* (2nd ed., pp. 285–309). Mahwah, NJ: Erlbaum.

Lerner, R. M., Theokas, C., & Bobek, D. L. (2005). Concepts and theories of human development: Contemporary dimensions. In M. H. Bornstein & M. E. Lamb (Eds.), *Developmental science: An advanced textbook* (pp. 3–44). Mahwah, NJ: Erlbaum.

Levant, R. F. (1988). Education for fatherhood. In P. Bronstein & C. P. Cowan (Eds.), *Fatherhood today: Men's changing role in the family* (pp. 253–275). Oxford: Wiley.

Levine, L., Garcia Coll, C. T., & Oh, W. (1985). Determinants of mother-infant interaction in adolescent mothers. *Pediatrics, 75,* 23–29.

LeVine, R. A. (1988). Human parental care: Universal goals, cultural strategies, individual behavior. In R. A. LeVine & P. M. Miller (Eds.), *Parental behavior in diverse societies: New directions for child development* (Jossey-Bass Social and Behavioral Sciences Series No. 40, pp. 3–12). San Francisco: Jossey-Bass.

LeVine, R. A. (2003). *Childhood socialization.* Hong Kong: University of Hong Kong Press.

Levitt, M. J., Weber, R. A., & Clark, M. C. (1986). Social network relationships as sources of maternal support and well-being. *Developmental Psychology, 22,* 310–316.

Lewin, K. (1947). Group decision and social change. In T. Newcomb & E. Hartley (Eds.), *Readings in social psychology* (pp. 330–344). New York: Holt, Rinehart and Winston.

Lewis M. (1997). *Altering fate: Why the past does not predict the future.* New York: Guilford Press.

Lightfoot, C., & Valsiner, J. (1992). Parental beliefs about developmental processes. *Human Development, 25,* 192–200.

Lorberbaum, J. P., Newman, J. D., Dubno, J. R., Horwitz, A. R., Nahas, Z., Teneback, C. C., et al. (1999). Feasibility of using fMRI to study mothers responding to infant cries. *Depression and Anxiety, 10,* 99–104.

Lorenz, K. (1970). *Studies in animal and human behavior* (R. Martin, Trans.). London: Methuen. (Original work published 1935)

Lowenthal, M. F., Thurner, M., & Chiriboga, D. (1976). *Four stages of life*. San Francisco: Jossey-Bass.

Luster, T., & Dubow, E. (1990). Home environment and maternal intelligence as predictors of verbal intelligence: A comparison of preschool and school-age children. *Merrill-Palmer Quarterly, 38*, 151–175.

Luster, T., & Okagaki, L. (Eds.). (2005). *Parenting: An ecological perspective* (2nd ed.). Hillsdale, NJ: Erlbaum.

Luster, T., Rhoades, K., & Haas, B. (1989). The relation between parental values and parenting behavior: A test of the Kohn hypothesis. *Journal of Marriage and the Family, 51*, 139–147.

Luthar, S. S. (2003). The culture of affluence: Psychological costs of material wealth. *Child Development, 74*, 1581–1593.

Lyons-Ruth, K., Zoll, D., Connell, D., & Grunebaum, H. U. (1986). The depressed mother and her 1-year-old infant: Environment, interaction, attachment, and infant development. *New Directions for Child Development, 34*, 61–82.

Lytton, H., & Romney, D. M. (1991). Parents' differential socialization of boys and girls: A meta-analysis. *Psychological Bulletin, 109*, 267–296.

Maccoby, E. E. (1959). Role-taking in childhood and its consequences for social learning. *Child Development, 30*, 239–252.

Maccoby, E. E. (1992). The role of parents in the socialization of children: An historical overview. *Developmental Psychology, 28*, 1006–1017.

Maccoby, E. E. (2000). Parenting and its effects on children: On reading and misreading behavior genetics. *Annual Review of Psychology, 51*, 1–27.

Maccoby, E. E., & Martin, J. A. (1983). Socialization in the context of the family: Parent-child interaction. In P. H. Mussen (Series Ed.) & E. M. Hetherington (Vol. Ed.), *Handbook of child psychology: Vol. 4. Socialization, personality, and social development* (4th ed., pp. 1–101). New York: Wiley.

MacDonald, K. (1992). Warmth as a developmental construct: An evolutionary analysis. *Child Development, 63*, 753–773.

MacDonald, K., & Parke, R. D. (1984). Bridging the gap: Parent-child play interaction and peer interactive competence. *Child Development, 55*, 1265–1277.

MacKinnon-Lewis, C., Starnes, R., Volling, B., & Johnson, S. (1997). Perceptions of parenting as predictors of boys' sibling and peer relations. *Developmental Psychology, 33*, 1024–1031.

MacPhee, D. (1981). *Manual for the knowledge of infant development inventory*. Unpublished manuscript, University of North Carolina, Chapel Hill.

MacPhee, D., Ramey, C. T., & Yeates, K. O. (1984). Home environment and early cognitive development: Implications for intervention. In A. W. Gottfried (Ed.), *Home environment and early cognitive development* (pp. 343–369). New York: Academic Press.

Magnuson, K. A., & Duncan, G. J. (2002). Parents in poverty. In M. H. Bornstein (Ed.), *Handbook of parenting: Vol. 4. Applied parenting* (2nd ed., pp. 95–121). Mahwah, NJ: Erlbaum.

Mahler, M., Pine, A., & Bergman, F. (1975). *The psychological birth of the human infant*. New York: Basic Books.

Main, M., & Goldwyn, R. (1984). Predicting rejection of her infant from mother's representation of her own experiences: Implications for the abused-abusing intergenerational cycle. *Child Abuse and Neglect, 8*, 203–217.

Main, M., Kaplan, N., & Cassidy, J. (1985). Security in infancy, childhood, and adulthood: A move to the level of representation. *Monographs of the Society for Research in Child Development, 50*, 66–104.

Mansbach, I. K., & Greenbaum, C. W. (1999). Developmental maturity expectations of Israeli fathers and mothers: Effects of education, ethnic origin, and religiosity. *International Journal of Behavioral Development, 23*, 771–797.

Mantzicopoulos, P. Y. (1997). The relationship of family variables to Head Start children's preacademic competence. *Early Education and Development, 8*, 357–375.

Markman, H. J., Renick, M. J., Floyd, F. J., & Stanley, S. M. (1993). Preventing marital distress through communication and conflict management training: A 4- and 5-year follow-up. *Journal of Consulting and Clinical Psychology, 61*, 70–77.

Marks, S. R., & MacDermid, S. M. (1996). Multiple roles and the self: A theory of role balance. *Journal of Marriage and the Family, 58*, 417–432.

Markus, H., Cross, S., & Wurf, E. (1990). The role of the self-system in competence. In R. J. Sternberg & J. Kolligian Jr. (Eds.), *Competence considered* (pp. 205–225). New Haven, CT: Yale University Press.

Martin, J. A. (1989). Personal and interpersonal components of responsiveness. In M. H. Bornstein (Ed.), *Maternal responsiveness: Characteristics and consequences—New directions for child development* (pp. 5–14). San Francisco: Jossey-Bass.

McCall, R. B. (1981). Nature-nurture and the two realms of development: A proposed integration with respect to mental development. *Child Development, 52*, 1–12.

McCartney, K., Harris, M. J., & Bernieri, F. (1990). Growing up and growing apart: A developmental meta-analysis of twin studies. *Psychological Bulletin, 107*, 226–237.

McGillicuddy-DeLisi, A. V. (1982). Parental beliefs about developmental processes. *Human Development, 25*, 192–200.

McGillicuddy-DeLisi, A. V. (1992). Parents' beliefs and children's personal-social development. In I. Sigel & A. V. McGillicuddy-DeLisi (Eds.), *Parental belief systems: The psychological consequences for children* (2nd ed., pp. 115–142). Hillsdale, NJ: Erlbaum.

McHale, J., Khazan, I., Erera, P., Rotman, T., DeCourcey, W., & McConnell, M. (2002). Co-parenting in diverse family systems. In M. H. Bornstein (Ed.), *Handbook of parenting: Vol. 3. Status and social conditions of parenting* (2nd ed., pp. 75–107). Mahwah, NJ: Erlbaum.

McKay, B., & Carrns, A. (2004, November 17). As teen births drop, experts are asking why. *Wall Street Journal*. B1.

McLaughlin, B., White, D., McDevitt, T., & Raskin, R. (1983). Mothers' and fathers' speech to their young children: Similar or different? *Journal of Child Language, 10*, 245–252.

McLoyd, V. C. (1998). Children in poverty: Development, public policy, and practice. In W. Damon (Editor-in-Chief) & I. E. Sigel & K. A. Renninger (Vol. Eds.), *Handbook of child psychology: Vol. 4. Child psychology in practice* (5th ed., pp. 135–208). New York: Wiley.

Melamed, B. G. (2002). Parenting the ill child. In M. H. Bornstein (Ed.), *Handbook of parenting* (Vol. 5, pp. 329–348). Mahwah, NJ: Erlbaum.

Mendelson, M. J. (1993). *Becoming a brother: A child learns about life, family, and self*. Cambridge, MA: MIT Press.

Miles, D., & Carey, G. (1997). Genetic and environmental architecture of human aggression. *Journal of Personality and Social Psychology, 72*, 207–217.

Miller, C. A. (1993). Maternal and infant care: Comparisons between Western Europe and the United States. *International Journal of Health Services, 23,* 655–664.

Miller, N. E., & Dollard, J. (1941). *Social learning and imitation.* New Haven, CT: Yale University Press.

Miller, S. G. (1988). Parents' beliefs about children's cognitive development. *Child Development, 59,* 259–285.

Minuchin, P. (1985). Families and individual development: Provocations from the field of family therapy. *Child Development, 56,* 289–302.

Mischel, W., & Shoda, Y. (1995). A cognitive-affective system theory of personality: Reconceptualizing situations, dispositions, dynamics, and invariance in personality structure. *Psychological Review, 102,* 246–268.

Mondschein, E. R., Adolph, K. E., & Tamis-LeMonda, C. S. (2000). Gender bias in mothers' expectations about infant crawling. *Journal of Experimental Child Psychology, 77,* 304–316.

Montemayor, R. (1982). The relationship between parent-adolescent conflict and the amount of time adolescents spend alone and with parents and peers. *Child Development, 53,* 1512–1519.

Moore, M. R., & Brooks-Gunn, J. (2002). Adolescent parenthood. In M. H. Bornstein (Ed.), *Handbook of parenting: Vol. 3. Status and social conditions of parenting* (2nd ed., pp. 173–214). Mahwah, NJ: Erlbaum.

Mounts, N. S., & Steinberg, L. (1995). An ecological analysis of peer influence on adolescent grade point average and drug use. *Developmental Psychology, 31,* 915–922.

Mrazek, P. J., & Haggerty, R. J. (1994). *Reducing risks for mental disorders: Frontiers for preventive intervention research.* Washington, DC: National Academy Press.

Murphy, D. A. (1992). Constructing the child: Relations between parents' beliefs and child outcomes. *Developmental Review, 12,* 199–232.

Murphy-Cowan, T., & Stringer, M. (1999). Physical punishment and the parenting cycle: A survey of Northern Irish parents. *Journal of Community and Applied Social Psychology, 9,* 61–71.

National Down Syndrome Society. (2000). *About Down syndrome.* Available from http://www.ndss.org/aboutds.html.

National Institute of Child Health and Human Development Early Child Care Research Network. (1997). Child care in the first year of life. *Merrill-Palmer Quarterly, 43,* 340–360.

Neiss, M., & Rowe, D. C. (2000). Parental education and child's verbal IQ in adoptive and biological families in the National Longitudinal Study of Adolescent Health. *Behavior Genetics, 30,* 487–495.

Neugarten, B. L. (1968). Adult personality: Toward a psychology of the life cycle. In B. L. Neugarten (Ed.), *Middle age and aging: A reader in social psychology* (pp. 137–147). Chicago: University of Chicago Press.

Newcomb, M. D., & Locke, T. F. (2001). Intergenerational cycle of maltreatment: A popular concept obscured by methodological limitations. *Child Abuse and Neglect, 25,* 1219–1240.

Nicely, P., Tamis-LeMonda, C. S., & Bornstein, M. H. (1999). Mothers' attuned responses to infant affect expressivity promote earlier achievement of language milestones. *Infant Behavior and Development, 22,* 557–568.

Ninio, A. (1980). Picture-book reading in mother-infant dyads belonging to two subgroups in Israel. *Child Development, 51,* 587–590.

Nitschke, J. B., Nelson, E. E., Rusch, B. D., Fox, A. S., Oakes, T. R., & Davidson, R. J. (2004). Orbitofrontal cortex tracks positive mood in mothers viewing pictures of their newborn infants. *Neuroimage, 21,* 583–592.

Ochs, E. (1988). *Culture and language development: Language acquisition and language socialization in a Samoan village.* Cambridge, England: Cambridge University Press.

O'Connor, T. G., Deater-Deckard, K., Fulker, D., Rutter, M., & Plomin, R. (1998). Genotype-environment correlations in late childhood and early adolescence: Antisocial behavioral problems and coercive parenting. *Developmental Psychology, 34,* 970–981.

Ogbu, J. U. (1981). Origins of human competence: A cultural-ecological perspective. *Child Development, 52,* 413–429.

Ogbu, J. U. (1993). Differences in cultural frame of reference. *International Journal of Behavioral Development, 16,* 483–506.

Okagaki, L., & Bingham, G. E. (2005). Parents' social cognitions and their parenting behaviors. In T. Luster & L. Okagaki (Eds.), *Parenting: An ecological perspective* (2nd ed., pp. 3–33). Mahwah, NJ: Erlbaum.

Okagaki, L., & Sternberg, R. J. (1993). Parental beliefs and children's school performance. *Child Development, 64,* 36–56.

Olds, D. L., Henderson, C. R., Jr., Kitzman, H., & Cole, R. (1995). Effects of prenatal and infancy nurse home visitation on surveillance of child maltreatment. *Pediatrics, 95,* 365–372.

Olds, D. L., & Kitzman, H. (1993). Review of research on home visiting for pregnant women and parents of young children. *Future of Children, 3,* 53–92.

Olson, S. L., Bates, J. E., & Bayles, K. (1984). Mother-infant interaction and the development of individual differences in children's cognitive competence. *Developmental Psychology, 20,* 166–179.

Osofsky, J. D., Hann, D. M., & Peebles, C. (1993). Adolescent parenthood: Risks and opportunities for mothers and infants. In C. H. Zeanah Jr. (Ed.), *Handbook of infant mental health* (pp. 106–119). New York: Guilford Press.

Overton, W. F. (1998). Developmental psychology: Philosophy, concepts, and methodology. In W. Damon (Editor-in-Chief) & R. M. Lerner (Vol. Ed.), *Handbook of child psychology: Vol. 1. Theoretical models of human development* (5th ed., pp. 107–188). New York: Wiley.

Palacios, J., & Moreno, M. C. (1996). Parents' and adolescents' ideas on children: Origins and transmission of intracultural diversity. In S. Harkness & C. M. Super (Eds.), *Parents' cultural belief systems: Their origins, expressions, and consequences* (pp. 215–253). New York: Guilford Press.

Palkovitz, R. (2002). *Involved fathering and men's adult development: Provisional balances.* Mahwah, NJ: Erlbaum.

Papoušek, H., & Bornstein, M. H. (1992). Didactic interactions: Intuitive parental support of vocal and verbal development in human infants. In H. Papousek, U. Jurgens, & M. Papousek (Eds.), *Nonverbal vocal communication: Comparative and developmental approaches—Studies in emotion and social interaction* (pp. 209–229). New York: Cambridge University Press.

Papoušek, H., & Papoušek, M. (2002). Intuitive parenting. In M. H. Bornstein (Ed.), *Handbook of parenting: Vol. 2. Biology and ecology of parenting* (2nd ed., pp. 183–203). Mahwah, NJ: Erlbaum.

Papoušek, M., Papoušek, H., & Bornstein, M. H. (1985). The naturalistic vocal environment of young infants: On the significance of homogeneity and variability in parental speech. In T. M. Field & N. Fox (Eds.), *Social perception in infants* (pp. 269–297). Norwood, NJ: Ablex.

Parke, R. D. (2002). Fathers and families. In M. H. Bornstein (Ed.), *Handbook of parenting: Vol. 3. Status and social conditions of parenting* (2nd ed., pp. 27–73). Mahwah, NJ: Erlbaum.

Parke, R. D., MacDonald, K. B., Burks, V. M., Carson, J., Bhavnagri, N. P., & Barth, J. M. (1989). Family and peer systems: In search of the linkages. In K. Kreppner & R. M. Lerner (Eds.), *Family systems and life-span development* (pp. 65–92). Hillsdale, NJ: Erlbaum.

Parks, P. L., & Smeriglio, V. L. (1986). Relationships among parenting knowledge, quality of stimulation in the home and infant development. *Family Relations: Journal of Applied Family and Child Studies, 35*, 411–416.

Patterson, G. R., Dishion, T. J., & Chamberlain, P. (1993). Outcomes and methodological issues relating to treatment of antisocial children. In T. R. Giles (Ed.), *Handbook of effective psychotherapy: Plenum behavior therapy series* (pp. 43–88). New York: Plenum Press.

Patterson, G. R., & Fisher, P. A. (2002). Recent developments in our understanding of parenting: Bi-directional effects, causal models, and the search for parsimony. In M. H. Bornstein (Ed.), *Handbook of parenting: Vol. 5. Practical parenting* (2nd ed., pp. 59–88). Mahwah, NJ: Erlbaum.

Patterson, G. R., & Forgatch, M. S. (1995). Predicting future clinical adjustment from treatment outcome and process variables. *Psychological Assessment, 7*, 275–285.

Pears, K. C., & Capaldi, D. M. (2001). Intergenerational transmission of abuse: A two-generational prospective study of an at-risk sample. *Child Abuse and Neglect, 25*, 1439–1461.

Pedersen, F. A., & Robson, K. S. (1969). Father participation in infancy. *American Journal of Orthopsychiatry, 39*, 466–472.

Pennington, B. F., Bennetto, L., McAleer, O., & Roberts, R. J., Jr. (1996). Executive functions and working memory: Theoretical and measurement issues. In R. Lyon & N. A. Krasnegor (Eds.), *Attention, memory, and executive function* (pp. 327–348). Baltimore: Paul H. Brookes.

Perozynski, L., & Kramer, L. (1999). Parental beliefs about managing sibling conflict. *Developmental Psychology, 35*, 489–499.

Perry-Jenkins, M., Repetti, R. L., & Crouter, A. C. (2000). Work and family in the 1990s. *Journal of Marriage and the Family, 62*, 981–998.

Piaget, J. (1952). *The origins of intelligence in children* (2nd ed.). New York: International Universities Press. (Original work published 1936)

Plomin, R. (1990). The role of inheritance in behavior. *Science, 248*, 183–188.

Plomin, R. (1994). *Genetics and experience: The interplay between nature and nurture.* Thousand Oaks, CA: Sage.

Plomin, R. (1999). Behavioral genetics. In M. Bennett (Ed.), *Developmental psychology: Achievements and prospects* (pp. 231–252). Philadelphia: Psychology Press.

Plomin, R., & Daniels, D. (1987). Why are children in the same family so different from each other? *Behavioral and Brain Sciences, 10*, 1–16.

Plomin, R., & DeFries, J. C. (1985). A parent-offspring adoption study of cognitive abilities in early childhood. *Intelligence, 9*, 341–356.

Pomerantz, E. M., Wang, Q., & Ng, F. F.-Y. (2005). Mothers' affect in the homework context: The importance of staying positive. *Developmental Psychology, 41*, 414–427.

Pomerleau, A., Scuccimarri, C., & Malcuit, G. (2003). Mother-infant behavioral interactions in teenage and adult mothers during the first 6 months postpartum: Relations with infant development. *Infant Mental Health Journal, 24*, 495–509.

Popenoe, D. (1996). *Life without father: Compelling new evidence that fatherhood and marriage are indispensable for the good of children and society.* New York: Martin Kessler Books.

Population reference bureau. (2000). Retrieved from http://www.prb.org. Washington, DC: Author.

Powell, D. R. (Ed.). (1998). *Parent education as early childhood intervention: Emerging directions in theory, research and practice.* Westport, CT: Ablex.

Powell, D. R. (2005). Searches for what works in parent interventions. In T. Luster & L. Okagaki (Eds.), *Parenting: An ecological perspective* (2nd ed., pp. 343–373). Mahwah, NJ: Erlbaum.

Power, T. G. (1985). Mother- and father-infant play: A developmental analysis. *Child Development, 56*, 1514–1524.

Preyer, W. (1882). *Die Seele des Kindes* [The mind of the child]. Leipzig, Germany: Grieben.

Prochner, L., & Doyon, P. (1997). Researchers and their subjects in the history of child study: William Blatz and the Dionne quintuplets. *Canadian Psychology, 38*, 103–110.

Pulkkinen, M. O. (1982). Pregnancy maintenance after early luteectomy by 17-hydroxyprogesterone-capronate. *Acta Obstetrica et Gynecologica Scandinavica, 61*, 347–349.

Putnam, S. P., Sanson, A. V., & Rothbart, M. K. (2002). Child temperament and parenting. In M. H. Bornstein (Ed.), *Handbook of parenting: Vol. 1. Children and parenting* (2nd ed., pp. 255–277). Mahwah, NJ: Erlbaum.

Puttallaz, M., & Heflin, A. H. (1990). Parent-child interaction. In S. R. Asher & J. D. Coie (Eds.), *Peer rejection in childhood: Cambridge studies in social and emotional development* (pp. 189–216). New York: Cambridge University Press.

Ratner, N. B., & Pye, C. (1984). Higher pitch in BT is not universal: Acoustic evidence from Quiche Mayan. *Journal of Child Language, 11*, 512–522.

Reburn, C. J., & Wynne-Edwards, K. E. (1999). Hormonal changes in males of a naturally biparental and a uniparental mammal. *Hormones and Behavior, 35*, 163–176.

Reid, J. B., Eddy, J. M., Fetrow, R. A., & Stoolmiller, M. (1999). Description and immediate impacts of a preventive intervention for conduct problems. *American Journal of Community Psychology, 27*, 483–517.

Reiss, D. (1997). Mechanisms linking genetic and social influences in adolescent development: Beginning a collaborative search. *Current Directions in Psychological Science, 6*, 100–106.

Reiss, D., Neiderhiser, J., Hetherington, E. M., & Plomin, R. (1999). *Relationship code: Deciphering genetic and social patterns in adolescent development.* Cambridge, MA: Harvard University Press.

Rheingold, H. L. (Ed.). (1963). *Maternal behavior in mammals.* Oxford: Wiley.

Rheingold, H. L., Gewirtz, J., & Ross, H. (1959). Social conditioning of vocalizations in the infant. *Journal of Comparative and Physiological Psychology, 52*, 68–73.

Rindfuss, R. R., & Bumpass, L. L. (1978). Age and the sociology of fertility: How old is too old? In K. E. Taeuber, L. L. Bumpass, & J. A. Sweet (Eds.), *Social demography* (pp. 43–56). New York: Academic Press.

Roberts, P., & Newton, P. M. (1987). Levinsonian studies of women's adult development. *Psychology and Aging, 2*, 154–163.

Rogoff, B. (1990). *Apprenticeship in thinking: Cognitive development in social context.* New York: Oxford University Press.

Rohner, R. P., & Pettengill, S. M. (1985). Perceived parental acceptance-rejection and parental control among Korean adolescents. *Child Development, 56*, 524–528.

Rose, R. (1995). Genes and human behavior. *Annual Review of Psychology, 46,* 625–654.

Rossi, A. S. (1980). Life-span theories and women's lives. *Signs: Journal of Women in Culture and Society, 6,* 4–32.

Rothbaum, F. (1986). Patterns of maternal acceptance. *Genetic, Social, and General Psychology Monographs, 112,* 435–458.

Rousseau, J. J. (1762). *Emile.* New York: Barron's Educational Series.

Rovee-Collier, C. (1995). Time windows in cognitive development. *Developmental Psychology, 31,* 147–169.

Rowe, D. C. (1994). *The limits of family influence: Genes, experience, and behavior.* New York: Guilford Press.

Rubin, K. H., Bukowski, W., & Parker, J. G. (1998). Peer interactions, relationships, and groups. In W. Damon (Editor-in-Chief) & N. Eisenberg (Volume Ed.), *Handbook of child psychology: Vol. 3. Social, emotional, and personality development* (5th ed., pp. 619–700). New York: Wiley.

Rubin, K. H., & Mills, R. S. L. (1992). Parents' thoughts about children's socially adaptive and maladaptive behaviors: Stability, change, and individual differences. In I. Sigel, J. Goodnow, & A. McGillicuddy-De Lisi (Eds.), *Parental belief systems* (pp. 41–68). Hillsdale, NJ: Erlbaum.

Rubin, J. Z., Provenzano, F., & Luria, Z. (1974). The eye of the beholder: Parents' view on sex of newborns. *American Journal of Orthopsychiatry, 44,* 512–519.

Ruoppila, I. (1991). The significance of grandparents for the formation of family relations. In P. K. Smith (Ed.), *The psychology of grandparenthood: An interactional perspective* (pp. 123–139). London: Routledge.

Russell, A. (1983). Stability of mother-infant interaction from 6 to 12 months. *Infant Behavior and Development, 6,* 27–37.

Russell, G., & Russell, A. (1987). Mother-child and father-child relationships in middle childhood. *Child Development, 58,* 1573–1585.

Rutter, M., & English and Romanian Adoptees Study Team. (1998). Developmental catch-up, and deficit, following adoption after severe global early privation. *Journal of Child Psychology and Psychiatry and Allied Disciplines, 39,* 465–476.

Rutter, M., & Quinton, D. (1984). Long-term follow-up of women institutionalized in childhood: Factors promoting good functioning in adult life. *British Journal of Developmental Psychology, 2,* 191–204.

Sameroff, A. J. (1983). Developmental systems: Contexts and evolution. In P. H. Mussen (Series Ed.) & W. Kessen (Vol. Ed.), *Handbook of child psychology: Vol. 1. History, theory, and methods* (4th ed., pp. 237–294). New York: Wiley.

Saxe, L., Cross, T., & Silverman, N. (1988). Children's mental health: The gap between what we know and what we do. *American Psychologist, 43,* 800–807.

Scarr, S., & Kidd, K. K. (1983). Developmental behavior genetics. In P. H. Mussen (Series Ed.) & M. M. Haith & J. J. Campos (Vol. Eds.), *Handbook of child psychology: Vol. 2. Infancy and developmental psychobiology* (4th ed., pp. 345–433). New York: Wiley.

Scarr, S., & McCartney, K. (1983). How people make their own environments: A theory of genotype-environment effects. *Child Development, 54,* 424–435.

Schaefer, E. S. (1959). A circumplex model for maternal behavior. *Journal of Abnormal and Social Psychology, 59,* 226–235.

Scheers, N. J., Rutherford, G. W., & Kemp, J. S. (2003). Where should infants sleep? A comparison of risk for suffocation of infants sleeping in cribs, adult beds, and other sleeping locations. *Pediatrics, 112,* 883–889.

Schellenbach, C. J., Whitman, T. L., & Borkowski, J. G. (1992). Toward an integrative model of adolescent parenting. *Human Development, 35,* 81–99.

Scheper-Hughes, N. (1989, October). Human strategy: Death without weeping. *Natural History Magazine.* pp. 8–16.

Schiff, M., Duyme, M., Dumaret, A., & Tomkiewicz, S. (1982). How much could we boost scholastic achievement and IQ scores? A direct answer from a French adoption study. *Cognition, 12,* 165–196.

Schneewind, K. A., & Ruppert, S. (1998). *Personality and family development: An intergenerational comparison.* Mahwah, NJ: Erlbaum.

Schulze, P. A., Harwood, R. L., & Schoelmerich, A. (2001). Feeding practices and expectations among middle-class Anglo and Puerto Rican mothers of 12-month-old infants. *Journal of Cross-Cultural Psychology, 32,* 397–406.

Schulze, P. A., Harwood, R. L., Schoelmerich, A., & Leyendecker, B. (2002). The cultural structuring of parenting and universal developmental tasks. *Parenting: Science and Practice, 2,* 151–178.

Sears, R. R., Maccoby, E. E., & Levin, H. (1957). *Patterns of child rearing.* Oxford: Row, Peterson.

Seefeldt, C., Denton, K., Galper, A., & Younoszai, T. (1999). The relation between Head Start parents' participation in a transition demonstration, education, efficacy and their children's academic abilities. *Early Childhood Research Quarterly, 14,* 99–109.

Seginer, R. (1983). Parents' educational expectations and children's academic achievements: A literature review. *Merrill-Palmer Quarterly, 29,* 1–23.

Seifer, R., Schiller, M., Sameroff, A. J., Resnick, S., & Riordan, K. (1996). Attachment, maternal sensitivity, and infant temperament during the first year of life. *Developmental Psychology, 32,* 12–25.

Seltzer, J. (1991). Relationships between fathers and children who live apart: The father's role after separation. *Journal of Marriage and the Family, 53,* 79–101.

Shakin, M., Shakin, D., & Sternglanz, S. H. (1985). Infant clothing: Sex labeling for strangers. *Sex Roles, 12,* 955–964.

Sheehan, T., & Numan, M. (2002). Estrogen, progesterone, and pregnancy termination alter neural activity in brain regions that control maternal behavior in rats. *Neuroendocrinology, 75,* 12–23.

Sigel, I. E., & McGillicuddy-De Lisi, A. V. (2002). Parental beliefs and cognitions: The dynamic belief systems model. In M. H. Bornstein (Ed.), *Handbook of parenting: Vol. 3. Status and social conditions of parenting* (2nd ed., pp. 485–508). Mahwah, NJ: Erlbaum.

Simerly, R. B. (2002). Wired for reproduction: Organization and development of sexually dimorphic circuits in the mammalian forebrain. *Annual Review of Neuroscience, 25,* 507–536.

Simons, R. L., Whitbeck, L. B., Conger, R. D., & Wu, C. (1991). Intergenerational transmission of harsh parenting. *Developmental Psychology, 27,* 159–171.

Skinner, B. F. (1976). *Walden two.* Englewood Cliffs, NJ: Prentice-Hall.

Smetana, J. G. (Ed.). (1994). *Beliefs about parenting: Origins and developmental implications.* San Francisco: Jossey-Bass.

Smith, C., Perou, R., & Lesesne, C. (2002). Parent education. In M. H. Bornstein (Ed.), *Handbook of parenting: Vol. 4. Applied parenting* (2nd ed., pp. 389–410). Mahwah, NJ: Erlbaum.

Smith, J. R., Brooks-Gunn, J., & Klebanov, P. K. (1997). Consequences of living in poverty for young children's cognitive and verbal ability and early school achievement. In G. Duncan & J. Brooks-Gunn (Eds.), *The consequences of growing up poor* (pp. 133–189). New York: Russell Sage Foundation.

Smith, P. K., & Drew, L. M. (2002). Grandparenthood. In M. H. Bornstein (Ed.), *Handbook of parenting: Vol. 3. Status and social conditions of parenting* (2nd ed., pp. 141–172). Mahwah, NJ: Erlbaum.

Snow, C. E. (1977). Mothers' speech research: From input to interactions. In C. E. Snow & C. A. Ferguson (Eds.), *Talking to children: Language input and acquisition* (pp. 31–49). London, England: Cambridge University Press.

Spitz, R. A. (1970). *The first year of life.* New York: International Universities Press. (Original work published 1965)

Spock, B., & Needlman, R. (2004). *Dr. Spock's baby and child care* (8th ed.). New York: Simon & Schuster.

Sroufe, L. A. (1988). The role of infant-caregiver attachment in development. In J. Belsky & T. Nezworski (Eds.), *Clinical implications of attachment: Child psychology* (pp. 18–38). Hillsdale, NJ: Erlbaum.

Sroufe, L. A., & Fleeson, J. (1986). Attachment and the construction of relationships. In W. Hartup & Z. Rubin (Eds.), *Relationships and development* (pp. 51–71). Hillsdale, NJ: Erlbaum.

Stattin, H., & Kerr, M. (2000). Parental monitoring: A reinterpretation. *Child Development, 71,* 1072–1085.

Steinberg, L. (2004). *The 10 basic principles of good parenting.* New York: Simon & Schuster.

Steinberg, L., Dornbusch, S. M., & Brown, B. (1992). Ethnic differences in adolescent achievement: An ecological perspective. *American Psychologist, 47,* 723–729.

Steinberg, L., Mounts, N. S., Lamborn, S. D., & Dornbusch, S. M. (1991). Authoritative parenting and adolescent adjustment across varied ecological niches. *Journal of Research on Adolescence, 1,* 19–36.

Stern, D. (1985). *The interpersonal world of the infant.* New York: Basic Books.

Stern, D. (1990). *Diary of a child.* New York: Basic Books.

Stevens, J. H. (1984). Child development knowledge and parenting skills. *Family Relations, 33,* 237–244.

Stevenson, H. W., & Lee, S. Y. (1990). Contexts of achievement: A study of American, Chinese, and Japanese children. *Monographs of the Society for Research in Child Development, 55,* 1–123.

Stewart, R. B., Jr. (1991). *The second child: Family transition and adjustment.* Newbury Park, CA: Sage.

Stith, S. M., Rosen, K. H., Middleton, K. A., Busch, A. L., Lundeberg, K., & Carlton, R. P. (2000). The intergenerational transmission of spouse abuse: A meta-analysis. *Journal of Marriage & the Family, 62,* 640–654.

Stoolmiller, M. (1999). Implications of the restricted range of family environments for estimates of heritability and nonshared environment in behavior genetic adoption studies. *Psychological Bulletin, 125,* 392–409.

Storey, A. E., Walsh, C. J., Quinton, R. L., & Wynne-Edwards, K. E. (2000). Hormonal correlates of paternal responsiveness in new and expectant fathers. *Evolution and Human Behavior, 1,* 79–95.

St. Pierre, R. G., & Layzer, J. I. (1999). Using home visits for multiple purposes: The comprehensive child development program. *Future of Children, 9,* 134–151.

Strauss, S., & Stavey, R. (1982). U-shaped behavioral growth: Implications for theories of development. In W. W. Hartup (Ed.), *Review of child development research* (Vol. 6, pp. 547–599). Chicago: University of Chicago Press.

Stuckey, F., McGhee, P. E., & Bell, N. J. (1982). Parent-child interaction: The influence of maternal employment. *Developmental Psychology, 18,* 635–644.

Sulloway, F. J. (1996). *Born to rebel: Birth order, family dynamics, and creative lives.* New York: Vintage.

Suomi, S. J. (1997). Long-term effects of different early rearing experiences on social, emotional and physiological development in non-human primates. In M. S. Kesheven & R. M. Murra (Eds.), *Neurodevelopmental models of adult psychopathology* (pp. 104–116). Cambridge, England: Cambridge University Press.

Symonds, P. M. (1939). *The psychology of parent-child relationships.* Oxford: Appleton-Century.

Szalai, A. (1972). *The use of time.* The Hague, The Netherlands: Mouton.

Taine, H. (1877). On the acquisition of language by children. *Mind, 2,* 252–259.

Tamis-LeMonda, C. S., & Bornstein, M. H. (1994). Specificity in mother-toddler language-play relations across the second year. *Developmental Psychology, 30,* 283–292.

Tamis-LeMonda, C. S., & Cabrera, N. (Eds.). (2002). *Handbook of father involvement: Multidisciplinary perspectives.* Mahwah, NJ: Erlbaum.

Tamis-LeMonda, C. S., Chen, L. A., & Bornstein, M. H. (1998). Mothers' knowledge about children's play and language development: Short-term stability and interrelations. *Developmental Psychology, 34,* 115–124.

Teti, D. M., & Candelaria, M. (2002). Parenting competence. In M. H. Bornstein (Ed.), *Handbook of parenting: Vol. 4. Applied parenting* (2nd ed., pp. 149–180). Mahwah, NJ: Erlbaum.

Teti, D. M., & Gelfand, D. M. (1991). Behavioral competence among mothers of infants in the first year: The mediational role of maternal self-efficacy. *Child Development, 62,* 918–929.

Teti, D. M., O'Connell, M. A., & Reiner, C. D. (1996). Parenting sensitivity, parental depression and child health: The mediational role of parental self-efficacy. *Early Development and Parenting, 5,* 237–250.

Thomas, A., & Chess, S. (1977). *Temperament and development.* New York: Brunner/Mazel.

Tiedemann, D. (1787). Beobachtungen aaber die entwicklung der seetenfaahrigkeiten bei kindern [Tiedemann's observations on the development of the mental faculties of children]. *Hessischen Beitraage zur Gelehrsamkeit und Kunst, 2/3,* 313–315, 486–488.

Tienari, P., Wynne, L. C., Moring, J., Lahti, I., & Naarala, M. (1994). The Finnish adoptive family study of schizophrenia: Implications for family research. *British Journal of Psychiatry, 23,* 2026.

Tolson, T. F., & Wilson, M. N. (1990). The impact of two- and three-generational Black family structure on perceived family climate. *Child Development, 61,* 416–428.

Tomlinson, M., & Swartz, L. (2003). Imbalances in the knowledge about infancy: The divide between rich and poor countries. *Infant Mental Health Journal, 24,* 547–556.

Trainor, B. C., & Marler, C. A. (2001). Testosterone, paternal behavior, and aggression in the monogamous California mouse (Peromyscus californicus). *Hormones and Behavior, 40,* 32–42.

Trainor, B. C., & Marler, C. A. (2002). Testosterone promotes paternal behaviour in a monogamous mammal via conversion to oestrogen. *Proceedings of the Royal Society of London. Series B: Biological Sciences, 269,* 823–829.

Trevarthen, C. (1979). Communication and cooperation in early infancy: A description of primary intersubjectivity. In M. Bullowa (Ed.), *Before speech: The beginning of interpersonal communication* (pp. 321–347). New York, NY: Cambridge University Press.

Trevarthen, C., & Aitken, K. J. (2001). Infant intersubjectivity: Research, theory, and clinical applications. *Journal of Child Psychology and Psychiatry and Allied Disciplines, 42,* 3–48.

Triandis, H. C. (1995). *Individualism and collectivism*. Boulder, CO: Westview Press.

Trivers, R. L. (1972). Parental investment and sexual selection. In B. Campbell (Ed.), *Sexual selection and the descent of man 1871–1971* (pp. 136–179). Chicago: Aldine.

Trivers, R. L. (1974). Parent-offspring conflict. *American Zoologist, 14*, 249–264.

Tronick, E. Z., & Gianino, A. F. (1986). The transmission of maternal disturbance to the infant. *New Directions for Child Development, 34*, 5–11.

Turkheimer, E. (1998). Heritability and biological explanation. *Psychological Review, 105*, 1–10.

Turkheimer, E., & Waldron, M. (2000). Nonshared environment: A theoretical, methodological, and quantitative review. *Psychological Bulletin, 126*, 78–108.

United Nations Children's Fund. (1990). *Convention on the rights of the child*. New York: Author.

U.S. Bureau of the Census. (1997). *Who's minding our preschoolers? Current population reports, Series P-70–62*. Washington, DC: U.S. Government Printing Office.

Vandell, D. L. (2000). Parents, peer groups, and other socializing influences. *Developmental Psychology, 36*, 699–710.

Vandell, D. L., & Wilson, K. S. (1987). Infant's interactions with mother, sibling, and peer: Contrasts and relations between interaction systems. *Child Development, 58*, 176–186.

Van den Boom, D. C. (1989). Neonatal irritability and the development of attachment. In G. A. Kohnstamm & J. E. Bates (Eds.), *Temperament in childhood* (pp. 299–318). Oxford: Wiley.

Van den Boom, D. C. (1994). The influence of temperament and mothering on attachment and exploration: An experimental manipulation of sensitive responsiveness among lower-class mothers with irritable infants. *Child Development, 65*, 1457–1477.

van IJzendoorn, M. H. (1992). Intergenerational transmission of parenting: A review of studies in nonclinical populations. *Developmental Review, 12*, 76–99.

van IJzendoorn, M. H. (1995). Adult attachment representations, parental responsiveness, and infant attachment: A meta-analysis on the predictive validity of the adult attachment interview. *Psychological Bulletin, 117*, 387–403.

Ventura, S. J., Martin, J. A., Curtin, S. C., & Mathews, T. J. (1997). Report of final natality statistics, 1995. *Monthly Vital Statistics Report, 45*(11, Suppl. 2/4), 73.

Vermulst, A. A., de Brock, A. J. L. L., & van Zutphen, R. A. H. (1991). Transmission of parenting across generations. In P. K. Smith (Ed.), *The psychology of grandparenthood: An interactional perspective* (pp. 100–122). London: Routledge.

von der Lippe, A. L. (1999). The impact of maternal schooling and occupation on child-rearing attitudes and behaviours in low income neighbourhoods in Cairo, Egypt. *International Journal of Behavioral Development, 23*, 703–729.

Vondra, J., Sysko, H. B., & Belsky, J. (2005). Developmental origins of parenting: Personality and relationship factors. In T. Luster & L. Okagaki (Eds.), *Parenting: An ecological perspective* (2nd ed., pp. 35–71). Mahwah, NJ: Erlbaum.

Vondra, J. I., Shaw, D. S., Swearingen, L., Cohen, M., & Owens, E. B. (1999). Early relationship quality from home to school: A longitudinal study. *Early Education and Development, 10*, 163–190.

Vygotsky, L. (1978). *Mind in society*. Cambridge, MA: Harvard University Press.

Wachs, T. D. (2000). *Necessary but not sufficient: The respective roles of single and multiple influences on individual development*. Washington, DC: American Psychological Association.

Wachs, T. D., & Camli, O. (1991). Do ecological or individual characteristics mediate the influence of the physical environment upon maternal behavior? *Journal of Environmental Psychology, 11*, 249–264.

Wachs, T. D., & Chan, A. (1986). Specificity of environmental action, as seen in environmental correlates of infants' communication performance. *Child Development, 57*, 1464–1474.

Wachs, T. D., & Gruen, G. (1982). *Early experience and human development*. New York: Plenum Press.

Wakschlag, L. S., & Hans, S. L. (1999). Relation of maternal responsiveness during infancy to the development of behavior problems in high-risk youths. *Developmental Psychology, 35*, 569–579.

Wallace, D. B., Franklin, M. B., & Keegan, R. T. (1994). The observing eye: A century of baby diaries. *Human Development, 37*, 1–29.

Watson, J. B. (1970). *Behaviorism*. New York: Norton. (Original work published 1924)

Webster-Stratton, C. (1990). Enhancing the effectiveness of self-administered videotape parent training for families with conduct-problem children. *Journal of Abnormal Child Psychology, 18*, 479–492.

Wentzel, K. R. (1998). Parents' aspirations for children's educational attainments: Relations to parental beliefs and social address variables. *Merrill-Palmer Quarterly, 44*, 20–37.

Whiting, J. W. (1981). Environmental constraints on infant care practices. In R. H. Munroe, R. L. Munroe, & B. B. Whiting (Eds.), *Handbook of cross-cultural human development* (pp. 155–179). New York: Garland STPM Press.

Williams, P. D., Williams, A. R., Lopez, M., & Tayko, N. P. (2000). Mothers' developmental expectations for young children in the Philippines. *International Journal of Nursing Studies, 37*, 291–301.

Wilson, E. O. (1975). *Sociobiology: The new synthesis*. Cambridge, MA: Harvard University Press.

Winnicott, D. W. (1957). *The child and his family: First relationships*. Oxford: Petite Bibliotheque Payot.

Winnicott, D. W. (1975). *Through pediatrics to psycho-analysis: Collected papers*. Philadelphia: Brunner/Mazel. (Original work published 1948)

Wohlwill, J. F. (1973). *The study of behavioral development*. Oxford: Academic Press.

Yarrow, M. R., Scott, P., Deleeuw, L., & Heinig, C. (1962). Child-rearing in families of working and nonworking mothers. *Sociometry, 25*, 122–140.

Yeung, W. J., Sandberg, J. F., Davis-Kean, P. E., & Hofferth, S. L. (2001). Children's time with fathers in intact families. *Journal of Marriage and the Family, 63*, 136–154.

Young, K. T. (1991). What parents and experts think about infants. In F. S. Kessel, M. H. Bornstein, & A. J. Sameroff (Eds.), *Contemporary constructions of the child* (pp. 79–90). Hillsdale, NJ: Erlbaum.

Zahn-Waxler, C., Duggal, S., & Gruber, R. (2002). Parental psychopathology. In M. H. Bornstein (Ed.), *Handbook of parenting: Vol. 4. Applied parenting* (2nd ed., pp. 295–327). Mahwah, NJ: Erlbaum.

Zero-to-Three. (1997). *Key findings for a nationwide survey among parents of 0- to 3-year-olds*. Washington, DC: Peter D. Hart Research Associates.

Zukow-Goldring, P. (2002). Sibling caregiving. In M. H. Bornstein (Ed.), *Handbook of parenting: Vol. 3. Status and social conditions of parenting* (2nd ed., pp. 253–286). Mahwah, NJ: Erlbaum.

CHAPTER 23

Nonparental Child Care: Context, Concepts, Correlates, and Consequences

MICHAEL E. LAMB and LIESELOTTE AHNERT

INTRODUCTION

What type and how much care do young children receive from adults other than their parents? What effects do such care arrangements have on their development? Although the latter question has been the focus of heated ideological debate for more than 30 years, the issues are actually more complicated than the shrill polemics suggest, and interpretation of the burgeoning literature is often difficult. In addition, researchers have learned in recent years to be wary of facile generalization across cultures or circumstances when studying such issues. It is naive to ask whether nonparental child care is good or bad for children or whether center care is better for chil-

dren than home-based child care. Instead, researchers must examine children's development in the context of the rich array of people, experiences, and settings to which children are exposed, recognizing that the effects are likely to differ from child to child, from one phase of life to the next, and from setting to setting.

Most of the published research on the effects of child care has been conducted in the United States, where ideologically driven passions have been most intense, but we have tried in this chapter to report and evaluate relevant research conducted in other countries as well. Such studies help place in context and perspective the results of research conducted in the United States and should foster caution about the universality, generalizability, and interpretability of the research literature. Unfortunately, social scientists tend to have a very myopic view of human history, often treating popular or widespread practices as basic species-typical givens

The authors gratefully acknowledge the many constructive comments and suggestions offered by Jay Belsky.

without analyzing their origins and history. Because formal schooling has been mandatory in most developed countries for several generations, for example, the potential effects of schooling on child-parent relationships are largely ignored, and concerns are raised about the potential effects of nonparental care on younger children. By contrast, the fact that formal education (or productive labor away from family members) is a much more recent and culturally restricted innovation than nonparental child care is seldom recognized. The transition to school is viewed as normal and normative; enrollment in child care, by contrast, has been widely questioned, popularly and professionally. Hrdy (1999, 2002, 2005) has argued persuasively, however, that humans evolved as cooperative breeders and thus that human child rearing has always been characterized by extensive involvement by multiple relatives and conspecifics.

Of course, preoccupation with the potentially harmful effects of nonparental care in early childhood is not accidental; it reflects the belief, partially attributable to psychoanalysis and its incorporation into popular North American belief systems, that early experiences have disproportionately powerful influences on child development. Fortunately, commitment to the early experience hypothesis is not as profound today as it was as little as 4 decades ago, when psychologists implied that major early experiences had long-lasting effects that were nearly impossible to overcome. Many researchers and theorists have since come to believe that all developmental periods are critical and that development is best viewed as a continuing process in which successive experiences modify, modulate, amplify, or ameliorate the effects of earlier experiences on remarkably plastic individuals (J. S. Kagan, 1980; Lerner, 1984; Lewis, 1998). This life span view of development undeniably complicates efforts to study longer-term effects on child development—particularly the effects of less salient and significant events—but appears to represent better the determinants and course of human development.

Over the past decade, researchers have also come to recognize the diversity and complexity of child care arrangements and their effects on children. Children grow up in a heterogeneous array of cultural and family circumstances, and many also experience multiple types of nonparental care. The diversity of family circumstances, the disparate array of nonparental care arrangements that exist, and the complex effects of en-

dogenous differences among children all ensure that nonparental child care per se is unlikely to have clear, unambiguous, and universal effects, either positive or negative, when other important factors are taken into account (Lamb & Sternberg, 1990). Instead, researchers must focus on the nature, extent, quality, and age at onset of care, as well as the way these factors together affect children with different characteristics, from different family backgrounds, and with different educational, developmental, and individual needs. In this endeavor, contemporary researchers will need to focus increasingly on the crucial intersection between home and out-of-home care settings and their complementary impact on children.

In the first substantive section of this chapter, we attempt to place contemporary patterns of child care in their broader sociocultural and historical context. Nonparental care is a universal practice with a long history, not a dangerous innovation representing a major deviation from species-typical and species-appropriate patterns of child care (Hrdy, 2005; Lamb & Sternberg, 1992). Specific patterns of child care vary cross-culturally, of course, with different nations emphasizing different goals and mechanisms. These differences are revealing to the extent that they underscore the need to view any research on the "effects" of "child care" in the context of the goals, values, and practices of particular cultures at specific points in time.

We next sketch changing patterns of child care in the United States and other industrialized countries. Over the past 3 decades, nonparental care has become a normative experience for preschoolers in the industrialized countries, although there are broad inter- and intracultural differences in the types of care received and in the ages at which most children begin receiving such care.

The effects of day care on child development then become central. In the past 15 years, most researchers have emphasized the need to evaluate the quality of care when assessing effects on children, and the parameters of this debate, as well as the popular indices of quality, are introduced in the third section. The increasing belief that the quality of care plays a crucial role in determining how children are affected by nonparental care has fostered efforts to understand *how* care providers behave and how they should be trained to provide growth-promoting care for children (Bredekamp, 1987a, 1987b).

Unfortunately, "high-quality" alternative care is difficult to define, measure, and promote comprehensively, even though some simple and concrete measures—including adult-child ratios, levels of care provider training and experience, staff stability and pay, and the adequacy of the physical facilities—can be used to assess structural aspects of the quality of care. These dimensions are most likely to be emphasized by state standards, which set the minimal acceptable standards on a state-by-state rather than federal basis (Phillips & Zigler, 1987). Structural characteristics affect the likelihood of high-quality care, but they do not guarantee it: Centers that are characterized by good adult-child ratios and are staffed by well-trained providers may still provide care of poor quality. Extensive training, education, and experience, like generous adult-child ratios, have to be translated into sensitive patterns of interaction, displays of appropriate emotion, and the intuitive understanding of children that make the experiences richly rewarding for them. The ease with which and the extent to which structural factors are translated into quality clearly vary depending on the culture, the context, and the alternative opportunities available to children, care providers, and parents. Furthermore, even the benefits of high-quality care may be compromised when the demands of the parents' work roles result in excessively long periods of nonparental care. It is thus impossible to write a recipe for high-quality care that is universally applicable. High-quality care needs to be defined with respect to the characteristics and needs of children and families in specific societies and subcultures rather than in terms of universal dimensions.

Debates about the effects of child care on children's development, which are the focus of the fourth section, have varied over time in response to a multitude of social, economic, and scientific factors. Initially, research efforts were focused on 3- and 4-year-old children in an attempt to address the implicit question "Is out-of-home care bad for young children?" Anxieties about the effects of nonmaternal care on child-mother attachment predominated, with professionals warning that damaged attachments would in turn lead to maladaptation in other aspects of development. Only in discussions regarding the benefits of compensatory education for impoverished children were these concerns submerged, presumably because the risks were viewed as less serious than the potential gains. By the early 1980s, however, the results of several studies, most conducted in high-quality day care centers, had fostered a widespread consensus that, contrary to the dire predictions of attachment theo-

rists, nonparental care begun in the 3rd year of life or later need not have adverse effects on psychosocial development (Belsky & Steinberg, 1978; Belsky, Steinberg, & Walker, 1982; Clarke-Stewart & Fein, 1983). This conclusion had to be qualified, however, because most of the studies involved atypically good programs, ignored home-based child care and in-home sitter arrangements, and paid no attention to group differences in parental values or attitudes prior to enrollment in nonparental care.

These limitations notwithstanding, public concerns about child care changed in the 1980s, by which time out-of-home care had become a normative and manifestly nonharmful experience for preschoolers. Instead, concern was focused on the many infants and toddlers who began receiving nonparental care before they had time to establish and consolidate attachments to their parents. Intensive and contentious research has since established that infant day care does not typically harm infant-mother attachment, but uncertainty persists concerning the interpretation, universality, and implications of the established effects. Focus on infant-mother attachment has also fostered research concerned with the effects of infant child care of varying quality on other important aspects of development, such as compliance with adults, peer relationships, behavior problems, and cognitive/intellectual development.

Unfortunately, recent preoccupation with the way the quality of care mediates the effects of nonparental child care on young children has led researchers to overstate the demonstrated importance of quality of care. Just as quality clearly makes a difference, so, too, is it clear that the effects of quality are considerably less profound than expected. Whether this reflects difficulties measuring quality or the reality that human development is shaped by so many factors that any one factor seldom has a large and dramatic effect is not clear, but both policymakers and researchers need to address this point much more forthrightly than they have in the past.

Public and professional concerns about the effects of nonparental care have been focused on infants, toddlers, and preschool-age children, but human children remain dependent on adults through adolescence and into early adulthood. The effects of the educational system and school personnel are discussed elsewhere in this *Handbook*, but the effects of before- and afterschool care on elementary, middle, and high school students have attracted some attention recently as well. As with younger children, increases in the rates and extent of maternal employment have forced many parents to arrange supervision and care for their children by others. The diverse effects of self-care and various forms of afterschool care are summarized in the fifth section. The chapter ends with an integrative summary and conclusion.

CHILD CARE IN CULTURAL CONTEXT

Recent media hyperbole notwithstanding, arrangements regarding nonparental child care do not represent a new set of problems for the world's parents. In fact, decisions and arrangements about children's care and supervision are among the oldest problems faced by human society. The fact that they were not discussed frequently in the past may reflect the failure of the men with political and intellectual power to discuss a "women's issue" as well as the fact that maternal care at home has been the dominant mode of early child care in the groups and eras most familiar to contemporary social and political scientists.

Unfortunately, the long history of attempts to make child care arrangements has not reduced the complexity of the issues faced by parents and policymakers today, although it has ensured that a diverse array of solutions have been tried. In this section, we sketch some of the arrangements that have developed in various parts of the world. Our goal is to provide a framework for analyzing these individual solutions and for making cautious and informed comparisons among them. In the first subsection, we place child care in the context of species-typical behavior patterns and needs. We then discuss the various purposes that nonparental child care can be designed to serve in industrial societies. In the third subsection, we describe the ideological dimensions along which countries can be arrayed and the resulting dangers of superficial generalization from one country to another. Finally, we summarize implications for policymakers, researchers, and practitioners, which we revisit later in the chapter after examining the empirical literature.

Human Evolution and Ecology

Our species is one for whom decisions about child care arrangements and the division of time and energy among child care, provisioning, and other survival-relevant ac-

tivities have always been necessary (Lancaster, Rossi, Altmann, & Sherrod, 1987). Humans are born at a much earlier stage of development than are the young of any other mammalian species, and a larger proportion of development takes place outside of the womb in humans than in any other mammal (Altmann, 1987). The period of dependency, and thus the process of socialization, is extremely prolonged among humans, with offspring dependent on conspecifics into adulthood, whereas the young of most mammals become nutritionally independent at the time of weaning. As a result, parental investment in each child is extremely high, and recent scholarship makes clear that other conspecifics typically make invaluable contributions as well (Hrdy, 2002, 2005). Humans have long been forced to develop complex and extended alliances and arrangements with others to ensure the survival of both themselves and their offspring; studies in many contemporary cultures underscore the survival value of these contributions (Hewlett & Lamb, 2005; Hrdy, 2002, 2005). Many theorists believe that pair-bonding represents one adaptation to the basic needs of human parents to cooperate in the provisioning, defense, and rearing of their offspring (Lancaster & Lancaster, 1987). In many environments, multifamily units developed to maximize individual survival in circumstances where, for example, hunting or gathering required cooperative strategies.

Studies of modern hunter-gatherers provide insight into the social organizations that might have developed in circumstances such as these (contributors to Hewlett & Lamb's, 2005, anthology describe child care practices in several foraging societies). In many such societies, within-family divisions of responsibility between men and women are paralleled by cooperative hunting strategies among men and cooperative gathering strategies among women. Depending on the task, the season, the children's ages, the availability of alternatives, and the women's condition, children accompany one or other parent at work or are left under the supervision of alloparents, often older children or adults.

Prior to weaning, mothers assume the heaviest portion of child care responsibilities in most societies, although alloparents are active long before weaning in many cultures where weaning is delayed and nursing coexists alongside other forms of feeding (Fouts, Hewlett, & Lamb, 2005; Fouts, Lamb, & Hewlett, 2004). Although the strategies of provisioning, protection, and child care are different in industrialized countries and in those societies where pastoral or agricultural traditions have replaced nomadic hunting and gathering, similar choices must always be made. Exclusive maternal care throughout the period of dependency was never an option in what Bowlby (1969) called "the environment of evolutionary adaptedness" and was seldom an option in any phase of human society even through early childhood; it emerged as a possibility for a small elite segment of society during one small recent portion of human history. Infants in 40% of the cultures sampled by Weisner and Gallimore (1977) were cared for more than half the time by people other than their mother, for example, and rates are surely higher where toddlers, preschoolers, and young children are concerned. It is thus testimony to the power of recent mythology and ignorance of the dominant human condition throughout history that exclusive maternal care came to be labeled as the "traditional" or "natural" form of human child care, with all deviations from this portrayed as unnatural and potentially dangerous. Braverman (1989) decries this "myth of motherhood," and Silverstein (1991) has bemoaned the way the historically recent "essentializing" of maternal care has shaped the popular and scholarly approach to conceptualizing and studying various forms of nonmaternal care. Nonmaternal child care is portrayed as deviant, even though it is universal and normative. Only the need for parents in industrialized countries to leave their children in the care of paid care providers, rather than neighbors or kin, is novel, and the possible implications of this situation have received little attention from researchers or theorists (see Daly & Wilson, 1995).

Economic Influences on Child Care Practices

In contemporary industrial societies, the availability of nonparental child care is determined by economic circumstances, local social demography, history, and cultural ideology. Of these, economic factors often play the major role in determining whether and what types of nonparental care arrangements are available. To complicate matters, however, economic, demographic, ideological, and historical factors often exert inconsistent and contrasting pressures. In North America, for example, employed parents began to seek help caring for their infants and young children before such practices were popularly endorsed. Economic circumstances thus forced families to make nonmaternal care arrangements, of which many family members and neighbors disapproved.

The central prominence of economic forces can be illustrated with many examples. In agricultural societies, for example, infants are typically left in the care of siblings, relatives, or neighbors while their mothers work in the fields (e.g., Fouts, 2002; Hewlett, Lamb, Shannon, Leyendecker, & Schölmerich, 1998; Leiderman & Leiderman, 1974; Nerlove, 1974; Weisner & Gallimore, 1977). Economic factors are also important in more developed countries. Mason and Duberstein (1992) have shown that the availability and affordability of child care influences maternal employment in the United States. Similarly, Sweden's family policy was developed because rapid industrialization produced a national labor shortage. To increase the number of women who were employed and to increase the willingness of young families to bear and rear future workers, it was necessary to develop a comprehensive system in which women were paid well, in which early child care could be accomplished without professional or financial sacrifices, and in which the assured availability of parental leave and high-quality nonparental child care facilities motivated parents to have and rear children (Broberg & Hwang, 1991; Gunnarsson, 1993; Haas, 1992; Hwang & Broberg, 1992; Lamb & Levine, 1983).

The communist countries of Eastern Europe likewise made child care facilities widely available to facilitate the increased participation of women in the paid labor force (Ahnert & Lamb, 2001; Kamerman & Kahn, 1978, 1981). Similarly, the U.S. and Canadian governments became involved in the financial support and supervision of nonmaternal child care facilities during the Second World War to encourage women to work in war-time industries while male potential workers were away at war (Griswold, 1993; Tuttle, 1993).

Meanwhile, in what is now Israel, small agricultural settlements called kibbutzim were established in the early part of the twentieth century by Jewish socialists from Eastern Europe (Infield, 1944). The malaria-infested swamplands and rocky desert soils posed severe problems for the idealistic and inexperienced farmers, and the need for female labor made it expedient to have one person, usually a woman, take care of several children rather than have mothers individually care for their own children. To maximize productivity and minimize the amount of housing needed, the original kibbutznikim (inhabitants of the kibbutz) also decided that children should live in collective dormitories, visiting their parents only for several hours every day (Neubauer, 1965). Over the ensuing decades, the emergence of the communal child care system has been attributed to ideological commitment (gender equality), and the role played by economic necessity has been downplayed.

The tendency to develop post hoc ideological explanations for popular behavior patterns tends to obscure the central role of economic circumstances in the development of nonparental care arrangements. Lamb, Sternberg, Hwang, and Broberg (1992) could identify no country in which the introduction of nonmaternal child care policies was not driven primarily by economic forces, although subgroups (e.g., the British upper class) occasionally sought child care assistance (e.g., nannies) for other reasons.

Other Goals and Purposes of Nonparental Child Care

Nonparental child care serves a variety of additional purposes, the most prominent of which include fostering equal employment opportunities, acculturation and ideological indoctrination, the encouragement of economic self-sufficiency, and the enrichment of children's lives.

Fostering Female Employment

As mentioned earlier, child care policies in many countries have been designed at least in part to promote female employment and to equalize the potential employment opportunities of men and women (Cochran, 1993; Lamb, Sternberg, Hwang, et al., 1992). The formerly communist countries of Asia and Eastern Europe, for example, made this a central feature of their family policies (Ahnert & Lamb, 2001; Foteeva, 1993; Kamerman & Kahn, 1978, 1981; Korczak, 1993; Nemenyi, 1993; Zhengao, 1993). Unfortunately, equality of opportunity has never been achieved anywhere despite the costly and extensive investment in child care facilities, and women do not enjoy equitable pay, whether or not their professions are integrated.

Influencing Demographic Patterns

The limited availability of high-quality child care also appears to have affected fertility rates in European countries such as Germany, with an especially dramatic effect on well-educated women (Ahnert et al., 2005; Kreyenfeld, 2004). Concerns about these demographic trends have led the government of reunified Germany not only to strengthen the child care system in the east that it had initially attempted to dismantle but also to

improve the underdeveloped child care infrastructure in the west (Ahnert & Lamb, 2001).

Acculturation and Indoctrination

Child care facilities have frequently been used to facilitate acculturation or ideological indoctrination. In northern Italy, for example, the number of children in preschools nearly doubled in the 1960s because the educational philosopher Ciari believed that preschools could be used to provide cultural foundations for children from different backgrounds (Corsaro & Emiliani, 1992). In Israel, meanwhile, the speed with which successive waves of Jewish immigrants have risen to positions of economic and political power can be attributed in the main to the participation of immigrant children in preschool programs where they learn Hebrew and the norms of Israeli culture (M. K. Rosenthal, 1992). The children in turn socialize and teach their parents. In the People's Republic of China, child care was made available in the early 1950s ostensibly to help children learn the importance of hard work and individual sacrifice (Lee, 1992). Universal day care also permitted parents to participate in reeducation programs, sponsored by the new communist government as part of its plan for the reconstruction of China. Finally, Shwalb and his colleagues (Shwalb, Shwalb, Sukemune, & Tatsumoto, 1992) point out that preschool education was made widely available to 4- and 5-year-old Japanese children in 1941 in part because the government wanted to use kindergarten as a means of fostering nationalism.

Encouragement of Economic Self-Sufficiency

Child care facilities have also been provided to encourage women to seek job training or paid employment and thus to cease being the beneficiaries of welfare; in the United States, pursuit of this goal led politicians to completely reshape the welfare system in the mid-1990s (National Academy of Science, 2003). Ironically, this goal was promoted with greatest vigor by conservative politicians who opposed governmental involvement in child care and emphasized the importance of maternal care and the "traditional family" while instituting policies that required parents to become economically self-sufficient and promoted this by subsidizing nonparental child care (Knitzer, 2001).

Enrichment of Children's Lives

The impetus to develop and invest in intervention or enrichment programs grew in the late 1950s and early

1960s, following the determination by experts that poor children experienced understimulation, overstimulation, or inappropriate stimulation, which in turn led them to perform poorly in school and on achievement tests (Clarke-Stewart, 1977; Fein & Clarke-Stewart, 1973; Hess, 1970). The development in the United States of the Head Start program in 1965 exemplified such a motivation to enrich the lives of children from the poorest and most disadvantaged families (Zigler & Valentine, 1979). Likewise, despite its strong opposition to nonmaternal care, the Catholic Church in Italy came to view preschools as a medium for socializing children from impoverished homes whose parents were considered incapable of effective socialization (Corsaro & Emiliani, 1992; New, 1993). Only later was preschool deemed acceptable for children in better socioeconomic circumstances. Until very recently, similarly, child care was widely viewed in Great Britain as a service for children at risk because their parents could not cope (Melhuish & Moss, 1992) and government funding was largely channeled to centers serving disadvantaged, troubled, and disabled children. In Canada, meanwhile, it took the recommendations of a government task force in the mid-1980s to recast day care as a service of potential value to all Canadian families, rather than as a service for disadvantaged and immigrant children (Goelman, 1992; Pence, 1993).

Exemplary programs like Head Start notwithstanding, a desire to enrich the lives of children did not motivate the initial development of nonparental care facilities in most countries. Parents and their government representatives may hope for care of adequate quality, but there is ample evidence that parents often accept care of lower quality because they simply have no choice (National Academy of Science, 1990, 2003). Where parents, groups, and societies have seriously considered the needs and best interests of children, these have often been secondary considerations. Many politicians and social commentators argue further that few societies, whether industrialized or nonindustrialized, have addressed children's needs satisfactorily.

Dimensions of Cross-Cultural Variation

Cultures clearly differ with respect to the goals—other than supervising children while their parents are employed—that nonparental child care is expected to serve. In addition, there are four major philosophical

or ideological dimensions along which contemporary societies can be compared. The first is one that has already been broached: the ideology concerning *equality between men and women* and how the availability of nonmaternal care programs increases female labor participation and allows women to advance themselves economically and professionally.

Consider international variations in the extent to which the provision of child care is viewed as a *public responsibility* rather than a *private or individual concern*. The United States probably represents the extreme among the industrial societies holding that decisions about child care should be left to individual families, that the cost and quality of care should be set by competition between the unregulated forces of supply and demand, and that governmental intrusions of all kinds should be resisted on the grounds that they would simply reduce efficiency (Blau, 2000; B. Cohen, 1993; Lamb, Sternberg, Hwang, et al., 1992; Spedding, 1993). Since 1997, the United Kingdom has moved from a position alongside the United States to one in which the role of the state is ensuring access to high-quality child care has been embraced and major investments have been made in building up the child care infrastructure. At the other extreme stand the democratic socialist countries of Scandinavia and the formerly communist countries of Eastern Europe, in which society as a whole is believed to share responsibility for the care and welfare of all children (Ahnert & Lamb, 2001; Hwang & Broberg, 1992; Kamerman & Kahn, 1978, 1981; Stoltenberg, 1994). The child care systems that evolved in each country necessarily reflected that society's position regarding public and private responsibilities. Contributors to Lamb, Sternberg, Hwang, et al.'s volume suggested that the best quality nonparental care was provided or regulated by governmental agencies in the context of comprehensive family policies. By contrast, countries or regions that have failed to develop comprehensive family policies tend to provide care of much poorer average quality.

Third, societies vary with respect to whether child care is viewed as a *social welfare program* or an *early education program*. Because all industrialized countries and most developing countries regularly assign responsibility for children older than 5 or 6 years to educational authorities, many countries have expanded the availability of care settings for young children by emphasizing the educational value of preschool care. Higher percentages of preschoolers are in nonparental care settings when societies attribute educational rather than custodial goals to them (Olmsted, 1992). Because public education is a widely accepted concept, it has also proven relatively easy to direct public finances to the support of preschool nonparental care when such facilities are represented as the early stages of a universal educational process, as they are in France, Belgium, Italy, Iceland, New Zealand, and Spain (see next section). By contrast, when nonparental care is viewed as a custodial babysitting service addressing the goals of social welfare, it has proven harder to obtain public support and harder yet to make quality of care a relevant dimension. Thus, the presumed character of nonparental care has major and far-reaching implications for the quality, type, and public support for nonparental care services. In Italy, the United Kingdom, France, and the Netherlands, for example, the portrayal of day care or nursery schools as an educational service rather than a welfare service altered perceptions of its value by middle- and upper-class families and thus legitimized its utilization (Clerkx & van IJzendoorn, 1992; Corsaro & Emiliani, 1992; Lamb, Sternberg, Hwang, et al., 1992; Melhuish & Moss, 1992). Analogously, whereas day nurseries and kindergartens both emerged in St. Louis at the start of the twentieth century, the latter came to be seen as part of the educational process and flourished, whereas day nurseries experienced the struggle for support that continues to this day. Cahan (1989), too, has chronicled the emergence of separate child care and early childhood education pathways in the nineteenth and twentieth centuries.

The last, infrequently considered, factor concerns *basic conceptions of childhood and developmental process.* Many inhabitants of the Western industrialized countries are steeped in the Freudian and post-Freudian belief that early experiences are crucially important. Endogenous tendencies may directly affect development, too, of course and, perhaps more important, interact with and alter the impact of diverse experiences on developmental processes and outcomes. Variations in the conceptualization of developmental processes have major implications for child care practices and the seriousness of concerns about the quality of care.

Students of comparative child care practices and policies need to consider these four dimensions (ideologies concerning male and female roles, perceptions of private and public responsibilities, educational and custodial goals, and conceptions of developmental

processes) when evaluating the policies and systems of diverse countries because international differences on these dimensions make it difficult and often inappropriate to generalize from one country to another and to use any country's social policies as models for adoption by others. Only when we fully understand the social structures and the ideologies that led to the development of a particular child care system are social scientists likely to learn from the experiences of other societies.

In addition, differences in parental and national goals lead to differences in the implementation of programs and in the effects of child care, and the evaluation of those outcomes differs from society to society. In some of the Western industrial countries, for example, assertiveness is viewed as a desirable goal, whereas others view it as one manifestation of undesirable aggression. Everywhere debate persists over the relative values of individualism and cooperation: Is compliance an index of passive acquiescence or of being well socialized? As long as disagreements persist concerning these values, it becomes impossible, for example, to state objectively that any given pattern of child care has positive or negative effects on behavioral adjustment.

Few countries have actually developed integrated child care systems that address all the functions of child care equally well. Even the best-developed and most carefully integrated systems must deal with the contradictory impulses created by pursuit of these different goals, and in most countries a patchwork array of solutions has emerged over time, with different and often contradictory policies designed to address each of these needs. At its best, pursuit of the highest possible quality of care forces ideologically liberal governments into a dilemma. Better quality care almost invariably involves more adults taking care of fewer children, and this becomes expensive. In fact, it is cheaper to provide infant care at home than to provide out-of-home care of good quality. As a result, successive Swedish governments gradually extended the duration of paid parental leave permitting parents to stay at home with their children — a generous resolution that may strengthen parent-child relationships at the expense of other worthy goals for both parents and children. Does high-quality nonparental care provide some unique and valuable formative experiences of which children in exclusive parental care will be deprived? What happens to the goals of gender equality and salary equity when families almost invariably conclude that mothers rather than fathers should withdraw from paid work to care for their children? What values are conveyed by the assignment of child care to members of an immigrant lower class (Wrigley, 1995)? How can one satisfy the competing agendas that child care policies must address?

Summary

Clearly, individuals and societies have developed a large number of solutions to age-old needs for child care. The variety and diversity of these solutions illustrate the ways historical, economic, ideological, and demographic realities shape the context in which individuals, families, and societies operate and constrain the solutions or policies they can develop. Employed parents need to obtain care for their children, and this chapter is concerned largely with the circumstances in which they make these decisions as well as with their effects on child development.

The development of child care policies has become increasingly important to governments around the world. As a result, new policies, plans, and practices are being developed worldwide. But despite the development of family policies and child care facilities, the demand for child care far outstrips the available supply in almost every country. This in turn maintains the pressure on governments, private agencies, and parents to make arrangements that are not optimal.

Interestingly, discussions of the needs for child care have, with few exceptions, portrayed child care as a women's issue, even though decisions about how and where children will be raised should concern both mothers and fathers. Swedish sociologists and policymakers recognized more than 4 decades ago (e.g., Dahlström, 1962) that major changes in maternal employment and paternal child care were unlikely unless they were preceded by changes in the underlying expectations about the appropriate roles and responsibilities of men and women and without changes in the opportunities available to men and women within the home as well as in the world of paid employment. Reformers hoped that group care settings might instill greater concern for the community and a commitment to less sexist values, but the near exclusive reliance on female care providers makes it unlikely that child care gives children a less sexist view of adult responsibility, whether or not their mother is employed.

Decades of research have made clear that one cannot make blanket statements about the superiority of any particular form of child care (Lamb, 1986; Lamb & Sternberg, 1990). In each case, the development of most children is affected by the quality of care received both at home and in out-of-home care facilities and by the extent to which the care is sensitively adjusted to children's developmental and individual needs. The implication is that societies need to provide an array of options that allow parents to choose child care arrangements that are most appropriate given their children's ages and individual styles, their economic and social circumstances, and the values and attitudes they hold.

Furthermore, nonparental child care must be viewed in the context of the whole ecology of socialization, because child care patterns are manifestations of the wider social structure. Development is a complex, multifaceted process, and thus we are only likely to understand it if we look, not simply at patterns of nonparental care, but at these patterns of care in the context of other experiences, ideologies, and practices. Nonparental child care arrangements do not exist in social vacuums and are likely to have relatively small, discrete, and direct effects on development, though they may be important parts of the web of influences and experiences that shape children's development. Because development is such a multifaceted and complicated process, it is essential to understand the role played by each of those experiences in shaping the course of human development. With that in mind, we next consider evidence concerning the extent to which children in the major industrial countries experience nonparental care in the first few years of their lives.

CHANGING PATTERNS OF CARE IN THE UNITED STATES AND EUROPE: PARENTING AND ALLOPARENTING

In this section, we review statistics concerning changing patterns of early child care in developed countries over the past few decades. As we show, these decades have been marked by the availability of increasingly detailed social statistics as well as by dramatic secular changes in marital, fertility, and employment practices that have had powerful and tangible effects on patterns of child care. Broadly similar changes and trends have been evident in most of the developed countries, although meaningful and significant international differences are evident as well. Changes in the utilization of nonparental child care of course affect the extent to which children in these countries may be affected by non-parental child care experiences.

Patterns of Shared Care

Most is known about pattern of child care in North America and Western Europe. As a result, we begin our analysis by considering statistics concerning patterns of child care in the United States.

The United States

In the United States, child care was once viewed as a service valued primarily by single mothers and disadvantaged Black families, whereas middle-class families supplemented maternal care by sending their children to part-day nursery schools and child development centers (Phillips, 1989). The proportions of employed Black and White mothers of preschoolers were the same by 1995, however, with a larger proportion of White than Black mothers in the workforce when they had school-age children. By the mid-1990s, similarly, 48% of single mothers whose youngest child was 3 or under and 52% of those with children age 5 and under were employed, compared with 57% and 59% of married mothers, respectively (Casper & Bianchi, 2002; H. Hayghe, personal communication, October 17, 1995). By 2001, however, these groups had diverged again: 64% of single mothers with children of 3 and under and 67% of those with children age 5 or under were employed, compared with 56% and 58% of married mothers, respectively (Casper & Bianchi, 2002). Overall, most of the 22 million under-5s in the United States had an employed father and 12.2 million had an employed mother by 2000 (U.S. Bureau of the Census, 2003). Employed mothers averaged 36 hours of paid work per week in 2001, mean-

ing that the majority of employed parents had full-time paid responsibilities (Casper & Bianchi, 2002). Perhaps most important, the majority of new mothers now return to paid work before their child's 1st birthday, whereas mothers formerly remained out of the workforce for considerably longer (U.S. Bureau of Labor Statistics, 2000).

Because the majority of the parents who live with their children are now employed, formal nonparental care arrangements are experienced by almost all children, although the industrial countries differ with respect to when these arrangements tend to be initiated, with the United States distinguished as the country where nonparental home-based day care, care by relatives, in-home babysitters, nursery schools, and child care centers for anywhere between 5 and 55 hours per week is initiated earliest.

The Census Bureau's annual reports, entitled *Who's Minding the Kids?* which use survey of income and program participation (SIPP) data, provide the most extensive and up-to-date information about child care patterns drawn from nationally representative samples of the U.S. population. Information about child care has been collected as a supplement to the SIPP since 1984, and the most recently published census data on child care were collected between April 1999 and July 1999 in the 10th interview with the 1996 SIPP panel. Initially, the SIPP collected child care information only when the mothers were employed, but the data gathered in the spring of 1999, released in January 2003, are informative regarding care arrangements for all children. The 1999 National Survey of American Families also provided valuable information regarding the child care arrangements made by employed parents (Sonenstein, Gates, Schmidt, & Bolshun, 2002).

As indicated earlier, and as shown in Table 23.1, the majority of children in the United States were receiving

TABLE 23.1   Child Care Arrangements for 0- to 5-Year-Olds in the United States (1999 SIPP), Expressed in Percentages

Age of Child	Parents	Grandparents	Other Relatives[a]	Child Care Centers[b]	Family Day Care	Own Home	No Regular Arrangement	Multiple
<1 year	23.9	24.6	8.9	20.8	13.4	3.4	35.1	16.3
1–2 years	21.9	23.8	11.1	30.1	13.9	5.9	32.9	18.5
3–4 years	19.6	21.2	13.4	71.7	13.9	4.1	31.1	21.0

[a] Including sibling care.
[b] Including Head Start, day care centers, nursery schools, and preschools.
Note: Percentages in a row may sum to more than 100 because children may have multiple care arrangements.
Source: From *Who's Minding the Kids?* by U.S. Bureau of the Census, 2003, Washington, DC: U.S. Government Printing Office. Reprinted with permission.

care regularly from persons other than their parents in 1999. The number for whom the parents were the primary designated care providers fell modestly from nearly a quarter of children under 1 to around a fifth of those over 3 years of age. Home-based nonparental care arrangements were used for about one-seventh of the children, regardless of age, and the number attending some kind of center increased from just over 20% for 1-year-olds to a remarkable 72% of 3- to 4-year-olds.

Table 23.2, which summarizes information only concerning the children whose mother was employed (and thus excludes children who lived alone with their father and those whose mother was unemployed or was a full-time student) makes clear that many of the children received care from centers on a part-time basis, although the proportion of children for whom it was the primary form of care doubled between the ages of 1 and 4 years. Notwithstanding this increase, it is noteworthy that the majority of infants and toddlers were cared for primarily by relatives, and another 20% received care from an individual nonrelative. Evidently, formal or institutional forms of care are not widely utilized by American parents with children age 4 and under. The tendency to seek care providers related to the child was most marked in Native American (73%), Asian and Pacific Islander (64%), and Black (61%) families, and less common in White (54%) and Hispanic (53%) families (see also National Institute of Child Health and Human Development [NICHD] Early Child Care Research Network, 2004). In every group, however, the majority of children received care regularly from relatives. Of course, many children have more than one child care arrangement, and Table 23.2 documents only the most important for each child.

As one might expect, child care arrangements vary depending on the mother's employment status and work schedule (U.S. Bureau of the Census, 2003), and changes in maternal employment are the best predictor of changes in child care arrangements (Han, 2004), which are extremely frequent (NICHD Early Child Care Research Network, 2004). Mothers working full time in 1999 were more likely than those employed part time to use child care centers or schools (86% versus 25%) or home-based child care (24% versus 15%), although both of these differences were less marked than they had been in 1991 (U.S. Bureau of the Census, 2003). As in 1991, however, fathers were more likely to be the regular nonmaternal care providers when mothers were employed part time (38%) rather than full time (25%; U.S. Bureau of the Census, 2003), with both figures representing increases from 1991. Fathers were also more likely to be the regular nonmaternal care providers when mothers worked a nonday shift (39%) rather than a day shift, and these percentages would undoubtedly be higher if the sample was limited to children living with both of their parents; not surprisingly, fathers are less involved in care when separated from or never married to the mothers.

When mothers are not employed, families make less use of nonparental care, although it is clear from Table 23.1 that the vast majority of 3- to 4-year-olds are enrolled in some kind of center-based care, with minimal differences between families with nonemployed and employed mothers (U.S. Bureau of the Census, 1993, 2003). As would be expected, however, children of nonemployed mothers spent much less time in care than peers whose mothers were employed: According to the 1993 Census Bureau report, about 80% of children with

TABLE 23.2   Primary Child Care Arrangements for U.S. Children Age 4 and Younger Whose Mother Was Employed (Spring 1999 SIPP), Expressed in Percentages

Age of Child	Parents	Grandparents	Other Relatives[a]	Child Care Centers[b] or School	Family Day Care[c]	No Regular Arrangement
<1 year	27.7	24.1	8.3	16.0	19.7	5.8
1–2 years	24.0	22.9	7.7	20.7	24.0	4.4
3–4 years	18.9	19.6	9.1	34.1	18.9	4.9

[a] Includes sibling care.

[b] Includes Head Start, day care centers, nursery schools, preschools, and schools.

[c] Includes other nonrelatives, some of whom may care for the child at home.

Note: Percentages in a row may sum to more than 100 because children may have multiple care arrangements.

Source: From *Who's Minding the Kids?* by U.S. Bureau of the Census, 2003, Washington, DC: U.S. Government Printing Office. Reprinted with permission.

nonemployed mothers spent less than 20 hours a week in child care, whereas 55% of the children with employed mothers spent 35 or more hours a week at child care facilities. A decade later, 63% of 3- to 5-year-olds with employed mothers were in center-based programs, compared with 67% of those with nonemployed mothers (NCES Early Child Care Research Network, 2002). Participation in educationally oriented center programs continued declining among 3- to 5-year-olds through 2001 (Child Trends, 2003).

Examination of Table 23.3 reveals that, between 1977 and 1999, primary care arrangements made by employed mothers in the United States changed remarkably little in the intervening quarter-century, despite dramatic increases in the number of employed mothers with young children and concomitant increases in the proportion of young children who were thus receiving nonparental as opposed to exclusive parental care. Between 20% and 25% of contemporary families rely on parental care, and as the proportions of women who can care for their children while working have declined (from 11% to 3%), the population of children cared for by their fathers while mothers work has increased from 14% to 19%. Care by grandparents has increased by about 25%, whereas care by other relatives has remained stable at around 8%. The popularity of child care centers and nursery schools initially increased but has declined since the mid-1990s, perhaps in response to well-publicized but exaggerated concerns about the adverse effects of center care, especially on infants and toddlers (see later discussion). By contrast, the utilization of informal and formal home-based child care arrangements has increased, although it

is unclear how much of this increase may reflect changes in the way information was solicited since 1995.

Whatever the reason for the dramatic apparent increase in 1995, reliance on home-based child care has steadily declined by about 33% since that time. In-home care by nannies and babysitters was never very common, and its importance has declined over the last quarter-century.

Other Industrial Countries

As suggested in the previous section, the nonparental care picture looks quite different in most other industrial countries than it does in the United States (Tietze & Cryer, 1999). Principally, this is because most industrial countries other than the United States offer various incentives to allow or encourage new parents, particularly new mothers, to remain at home to care for their infants throughout the 1st year of life. Parental leave has only recently (1993) been mandated in the United States, but even though half the private sector workers and all public sector workers are now entitled to 12 weeks of job-protected leave, few can afford to remain out of work long because the mandatory leave is unpaid (Asher & Lenhoff, 2001). In other industrial countries, by contrast, new mothers (and, in some countries, new fathers) are entitled to extended periods of paid leave. In countries of the Organization for Economic Cooperation and Development (OECD), for example, the average paid leave is 10 months (the minimum outside the United States is 6 months), with pay levels ranging from a basic daily stipend to as much as 90% of the parent's regular salary (Kamerman,

TABLE 23.3   Historical Changes in Primary Child Care Arrangements for U.S. Children under 5 Years of Age with an Employed Mother (Percentages)

	1977	1985	1988	1990	1991	1993	1995	1997	1999
Mother	11	8.1	7.6	6.4	8.7	6.2	5.4	3.3	3.1
Father	14	15.7	15.1	16.5	20.0	15.9	16.6	19.0	18.5
Grandparents	N/A	15.9	13.9	14.3	15.8	17.0	15.9	18.4	20.8
Other relatives	N/A	8.2	7.2	8.8	7.7	9.0	5.5	7.4	8.0
Day care/school	13	23.1	25.8	27.5	23.1	29.9	25.1	21.6	22.1
In child's home	7	5.9	5.3	5.0	5.4	5.0	4.9	4.0	3.3
Family day care	22	22.3	23.6	20.1	17.9	16.6	46.0[a]	36.3	33.8
Other[b]	N/A	0.8	1.6	1.3	1.6	1.1	2.9	8.1	7.3

[a] In 1995, the Census Bureau first distinguished between all forms of care in the providers' home, family day care, and other forms of care by nonrelatives. Changes in the questions used may account for the dramatic increase in the number of children in various forms of "family day care."

[b] Includes self-care, no regular arrangement, and other arrangements.

Source: From *Who's Minding the Kids?* by U.S. Bureau of the Census, 2003, Washington, DC: U.S. Government Printing Office. Reprinted with permission.

2000; Waldfogel, 2001). Whereas the statistics reported earlier show that the majority of infants in the United States begin nonmaternal care during the 1st year of life, therefore, enrollment can be delayed until the 2nd and even 3rd year of life in other industrial countries. Because maternal or parental care is thus nearly universal in the 1st year, good statistics documenting the enrollment of European children in nonparental child care facilities in the first 2 to 3 years of life are not widely available. The statistics shown in panel a of Figure 23.1 refer only to enrollment in publicly subsidized settings (Waldfogel, 2001), and these figures vastly understate the number of children in private facilities, particularly in countries like the United States, where publicly subsidized facilities are scarce. The figures for the other listed countries are probably more representative and

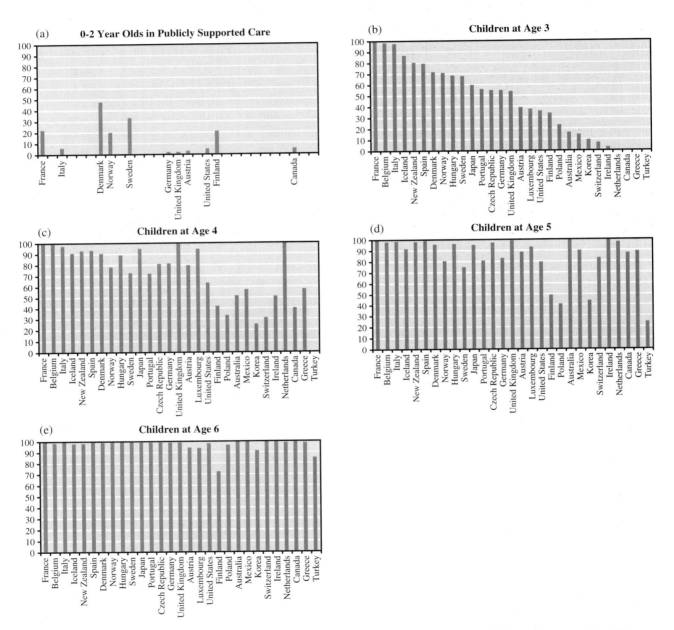

Figure 23.1   (a) 0- to 2-year-olds in publicly supported care, (b) Children at age 3, (c) Children at age 4, (d) Children at age 5, (e) Children at age 6.

underscore how few infants and toddlers in these countries are enrolled in formal child care facilities.

The panel b of Figure 23.1 shows dramatic cross-national variations in the number of 3-year-old children enrolled in educationally oriented programs (OECD, 2002). Notice that, by the age of 3, almost all children in Belgium, France, and Italy are already enrolled in such programs (which are formally affiliated with the public education systems), as are two thirds or more of the children in Denmark, Hungary, Iceland, New Zealand, Norway, Spain, and Sweden. (The comparable figure for the United States is 37%.) By the age of 4 (Figure 23.1, panel c), two-thirds or more of the children in Austria, the Czech Republic, Germany, Japan, Luxembourg, The Netherlands, Portugal, the Slovak Republic, and the United Kingdom are enrolled as well, along with 65% of the children in the United States. Children in the remaining countries become enrolled as either 5- or 6-year-olds (see panels d and e). Thus, whereas nonparental child care is much more common in the United States than elsewhere in the first years of life, educational programs in several Western countries embrace most children much earlier than they do in the United States. The programs themselves are also viewed and funded as part of the educational system in these countries, thereby fostering care of more homogeneous quality that is more easily regulated, administered, and publicly funded (Tietze & Cryer, 1999).

Parental Decisions about Nonparental Care

A variety of factors, including role conflicts, anxieties about daily separations, and fears that children may have difficulty adapting to settings with unfamiliar or undesirable characteristics, and fears that children might develop closer relationships to care providers than parents, influence parents' child care decisions (e.g., Fein, Gariboldi, & Boni, 1993; Hock, McBride, & Gnezda, 1989; Stifter, Coulehan, & Fish, 1993). Furthermore, perhaps because many parents in the United States prefer within-family care when they return to paid work early in their children's lives (Sonenstein & Wolf, 1991), more than half the children with employed parents are initially cared for by their mother, father, or other relatives, mostly grandparents (see Tables 23.1 and 23.2). Such families are characterized either by concerns about the effects of nonparental care on their infants or have limited resources that constrain their access to more costly nonparental care arrangements (NICHD Early Child Care Research Network, 1997c). Not surprisingly, American families with annual incomes exceeding $54,000 in 2003 were more apt to use center care than those whose incomes were either less than $18,000 or between $18,000 and $36,000 per annum (28%, 19%, and 18%, respectively; U.S. Bureau of the Census, 2003).

Reliance on care by fathers is more common when parents have less traditional child-rearing beliefs, marital intimacy is greater, and fathers want to be involved in care (NICHD Early Child Care Research Network, 2000b), whereas the avoidance of paternal care is associated with elevated emotional problems (Vandell, Hyde, Plant, & Essex, 1997). Father care is also higher when mothers work nonstandard hours and is highest when both parents have nonstandard work schedules (Han, 2004). Care by grandparents is more likely in families of color, when grandparents live in the household, and when mothers are very young, work nonstandard hours, or have extended workdays (NICHD Early Child Care Research Network, 2004; Vandell, McCartney, Owen, Booth, & Clarke-Stewart, 2003). Unfortunately, care by grandparents also tends to be quite unstable.

The heterogeneity of family circumstances in the United States leads many parents to rely on more than one child care arrangement during the first years of life (see Table 23.1) and probably explains why children in the United States experience such frequent changes in child care arrangements (NICHD Early Child Care Research Network, 2004). Interestingly, the extensiveness of maternal employment does not predict the type or number of child care arrangements, even though the availability of nonparental child care facilitates the simultaneous pursuit of both child-rearing and career goals (NICHD Early Child Care Research Network, 1997c).

Some professionals have been especially skeptical about the ability of young parents to pursue these two goals simultaneously, but associations between maternal age and either the types or extent of child care usage have seldom been studied. Older German mothers seemed better able to limit the time that their children spent in center-based care than younger mothers with similar working schedules, however (Ahnert, Rickert, & Lamb, 2000).

Since the late 1980s, parents in the United States have been increasingly willing to utilize center-based rather than home-based care by nonrelatives (Haber &

Kafka, 1992; Kisker & Silverberg, 1991). Perhaps this trend reflects increased understanding of children's needs for intellectual and social stimulation and of the possible disadvantages associated with more informal care arrangements, as well as improvements in the available quality of center care (e.g., Johansen, Leibowitz, & Waite, 1996; NICHD Early Child Care Network, 1997a). Over the past decade, these associations between parental education and child care preferences have increasingly been moderated by child age, however: Regardless of their educational backgrounds, parents of infants and toddlers (as opposed to parents of preschoolers) emphasize health and well-being and thus seek environments likely to minimize stress rather than those that maximize educational opportunities (e.g., Britner & Phillips, 1995; Cryer & Burchinal, 1997).

Furthermore, because many families, especially in Europe, have two or fewer children, parents may fear that exclusive family care may deprive children of enriching and diverse social experiences, especially with other children (Sturzbecher, 1998). In this context, parental decisions about child care may reflect the parents' willingness to offer their children opportunities to develop additional close relationships outside the family, with some mothers feeling particularly threatened when their children develop close relationships with others.

Relationships between Parents and Other Care Providers

Within-family and out-of-home care environments obviously differ in many important ways. To what extent do parents and care providers understand the differences between their roles and these environments? Parents and child care professionals value the same care characteristics, but, perhaps because they have difficulty monitoring it, parents tend to be poorly informed about the quality of care that their children receive. Nevertheless, parents who provide solicitous, stimulating care clearly tend to select child care arrangements with these characteristics (Bolger & Scarr, 1995). Relief at finding much needed child care and anxiety about the possible risks associated with nonparental care may also prevent some parents from evaluating their children's placements accurately and lead them to deny obvious problems. This may explain why parents of all education and income levels tend to overestimate the quality of their children's programs and relationships with their care

providers, reporting that these are satisfactory even when trained observers recognize that the quality of care is poor (e.g., Brown Miller, 1990; Clarke-Stewart, Gruber, & Fitzgerald, 1994; Cryer & Burchinal, 1997). Not surprisingly, parents also tend to report that they have positive relationships with care providers even when the partnerships may not be as good as they claim.

For their part, care providers seldom see parents as partners, perhaps perceiving themselves as professionals who have greater expertise regarding child care. In addition, they may be somewhat judgmental about parents, attributing children's perceived difficulties to inadequacies on the part of the parents, for example (Kontos & Dunn, 1989; Shpancer, 1998). Care providers also believe that parents need opportunities to develop their caregiving skills (Elicker, Noppe, Noppe, & Fortner-Wood, 1997).

Even when parents and care providers are mutually appreciative and respectful, they often have divergent views of one another's confidence and collaboration. Instead of developing the types of friendships that care providers would prefer, for example, parents often decline to share information about their families or to use care providers as sources of information and guidance (Elicker et al., 1997; Kontos & Dunn, 1989). As a result, parent-care provider conversations tend to be brief, infrequent, and nonsubstantive. The two partners also tend to be most available at different times: Whereas care providers are more accessible at drop-off times in the mornings, parents are more accessible during pick-up times in the afternoons (Endsley & Minish, 1991).

The notion that parent-care provider partnerships are formatively important is intuitively appealing, but empirical data have accumulated slowly. For example, Owen, Ware, and Barfoot (2000) reported that more communication between mothers and care providers (based on mothers' and care providers' reports) was significantly associated with more sensitive and supportive interactions between care providers and children. Van IJzendoorn, Tavecchio, Stams, Verhoeven, and Reiling (1998) reported that better communication was associated with indices of child well-being. In addition, Kontos and Dunn (1989) found that care providers tended to have the lowest regard for the parenting abilities of parents who communicated less; the children of these parents were also less advanced developmentally. This underscores the difficulties that may arise when the relationships between parents and care providers are not adequately bridged and the need for professional care providers to foster improved relationships with parents. Ghazvini and Readdick (1994) reported a positive correlation between the quality of center care and the frequency of parent-care provider communication.

Summary

Nonparental care during the preschool years has become normative in the United States and other industrialized countries. Children outside the United States often begin nonparental care as toddlers because more generous parental leave policies allow them to be cared for by their parents in infancy, whereas the majority of children in the United States begin nonparental care as infants, typically some time before their 1st birthday. American mothers often attempt to arrange for early care to be provided within the family by fathers, grandparents, or other relatives when exclusive maternal care is not possible, although care provided by relatives tends to be unstable and changing care arrangements are very common. Children who begin nonparental care before their 1st birthday and experience three or more different nonparental care arrangements may be at special risk because the instability of infant care predicts behavioral maladjustment (see later discussion). From a policy perspective, it is thus important to determine why so many young children have unstable patterns of care and why the child care available in the United States is of such uneven quality.

Parents have limited insight into their children's child care experiences even when they monitor their children's responses closely, so it is misleading to assume that market forces will regulate the available quality of child care. Instead, quality of care tends to be best when it is evaluated and regulated by professionals, as in most European countries.

QUALITY OF CARE

Just as researchers have come to appreciate the diverse array of care arrangements that children experience and the possible importance of wide variations in their preenrollment characteristics and backgrounds, so, too, have they come to acknowledge vast differences in the quality of care that children experience both in and outside their homes. This realization led researchers to develop measures that have, in turn, advanced efforts to understand how quality of care affects children's development.

Process Measures of Quality

Researchers have developed both process and structural measures of quality. Process measures are observational measures of the settings and interactions between care providers and children, although some emphasize the experiences of individual children, whereas the majority assess the experiences of groups of children. The best known of these are standardized measures developed by Thelma Harms and Richard Clifford. The latest versions of the Infant/Toddler Environment Rating Scale (ITERS; Harms, Cryer, & Clifford, 2003) and the Early Childhood Environment Rating Scale (ECERS; Harms, Clifford, & Cryer, 1998) contain 39 and 43 items, respectively, on which the quality of care is rated by trained observers; from these ratings, scores on seven highly intercorrelated scales can be computed (see Table 23.4). Scores can also be reduced to two factors, Appropriate Caregiving and Developmentally Appropriate Activities, although scores on these two dimensions of the original measures tended to be highly intercorrelated as well (Phillips, Voran, Kisker, Howes, & Whitebook, 1994). The Family Day Care Rating Scale (FDCRS; Harms & Clifford, 1989) was developed to provide a six-factor assessment of the quality of home-based care using 32 items; a revision of this scale is currently in preparation. The FDCRS has been used much less than the ITERS and ECERS, not least because home-based care has been studied less extensively than center-based care. Harms, Jacobs, and White (1996) also developed a companion measure to use when evaluating the quality of afterschool programs.

Measures other than the ECERS, ITERS, and FDCRS have been used in major studies as well. Abbott-Shim and Sibley (1987, 1992) developed the Assessment Profile for Early Childhood Programs with over 150 items designed, like the measures developed by Harms and Clifford, to assess the entire setting. A briefer (26-item) Classroom Practices Inventory (CPI) was developed by Hyson, Hirsh-Pasek, and Rescorla (1990) to tap those aspects of quality subsumed under the National Association for the Education of Young Children's "Guidelines for Developmentally Appropriate Practices" (Bredekamp, 1987b). The CPI has not yet been

TABLE 23.4   Items on Some Popular Process Measures of Quality

ECERS[a]	Global Rating Scale[b]	APECP[c]
Space and Furnishings	Positive Relationship	Safety and Health
1. Indoor space	1. Speaks warmly to children	1. Classroom safe
2. Furniture for routine care, play, and learning	2. Listens when children speak	2. Supplies and materials safe
3. Furnishings for relaxation and comfort	3. Seems to enjoy children	3. Teacher prepared for emergencies
4. Room arrangement for play	4. Explains rule violations	4. Personal hygiene encouraged
5. Space for privacy	5. Encourages new experiences	5. Teacher responsible for basic health care
6. Child-related display	6. Seems enthusiastic	Learning Environment
7. Space for gross motor play	7. Attentive to individuals	6. Physical layout encourages independence
8. Gross motor equipment	8. Talks at appropriate level	7. Classroom respects individuality
Personal Care Routines	9. Encourages prosocial behavior	8. Outdoor materials support varied opportunities
9. Greeting/departing	10. Adopts children's level	9. Teacher active outdoors
10. Meals/snacks	Punitiveness	Scheduling
11. Nap/rest	11. Seems critical of children	10. Scheduling occurs
12. Toileting/diapering	12. Values obedience	11. Varied activities on written schedule
13. Health practices	13. Speaks with irritation	12. Teacher-organized reasoning skills
14. Safety practices	14. Threatens	13. Varied classroom activities
Language/Reasoning	15. Punishes without explanation	Curriculum
15. Books and pictures	16. Finds fault	14. Materials support varied experiences
16. Encouraging children to communicate	17. Prohibits many activities	15. Materials encourage cultural awareness
17. Using language to develop	18. Unnecessarily harsh	16. Alternative techniques used
18. Informal use of language	Permissiveness	17. Children active in learning
Activities	19. Doesn't control	18. Individualization
19. Fine motor	20. Doesn't reprimand misbehavior	Interacting
20. Art	21. Firm when necessary	19. Teacher initiates positive interactions
21. Music/movement	22. Expects self-control	20. Teacher is responsive
22. Blocks	Detachment	21. Teacher manages children positively
23. Sand/water	23. Seems distant/detached	22. Food served in positive atmosphere
24. Dramatic play	24. Spends time in other activities	23. Children happy and involved
25. Nature/science	25. Uninterested in children's activities	Individualizing
26. Math/number	26. Not close supervision	24. Systematic child assessment
27. Use of TV, video, computers		25. Assessments used in planning activities
28. Promoting acceptance of diversity Interaction		26. Teacher identifies special needs
29. Supervision of gross motor activities		27. Teacher cooperative with adults
30. General supervision		28. Provisions made for special needs
31. Discipline		29. Conferences planned regularly
32. Staff-child interactions		30. Parental activity encouraged
33. Interactions among children		
Program Structure		
34. Schedule		
35. Free play		
36. Group time		
37. Provisions for children with disabilities		
Parents and Staff		
38. Provisions for parents		
39. Provisions for personal needs of staff		
40. Provisions for professional needs of staff		
41. Staff interactions and cooperation		
42. Supervision and evaluation of staff		
43. Opportunities for professional growth		

[a] Early Childhood Environment Rating Scale-Revised (Harms, Clifford, & Cryer, 1998). All items are rated on a 7-point scale, anchored by definitions of Inadequate (1), Minimal (3), Good (5), and Excellent (7). Similar items, adjusted for age and context, appear on the Infant/Toddler Environment Rating Scale–Revised (Harms, Cryer, & Clifford, 2003). *Sources:* From *The Early Childhood Environment Rating Scale,* revised edition, by T. Harms, R. M. Clifford, and D. Cryer, 1998, New York: Teachers College Press. Reprinted with permission; and *Infant/Toddler Environment Rating Scale,* revised edition, by T. Harms, D. Cryer, and R. M. Clifford, 2003, New York: Teachers College Press. Reprinted with permission.

[b] All rated on 4-point scale, with item scores combined into 4 factor scores. *Source:* From "Caregivers in Day Care Centers: Does Training Matter?" by J. Arnett, 1989, *Journal of Applied Developmental Psychology, 10,* pp. 541–552. Reprinted with permission.

[c] Assessment Profile for Early Childhood Programs (Abbott-Shim & Sibley, 1987). Each of the 30 topics listed here subsumes several specific items (150 in all), each rated as "present" or "absent" on the basis of observations or reports. *Source:* From *Assessment Profile for Childhood Programs,* by M. Abbott-Shim and A. Sibley, 1987, Atlanta, GA: Quality Assistance. Reprinted with permission.

widely used, although L. Dunn (1993) reported that higher ECERS scores were associated with more developmentally appropriate practices, as assessed using the CPI. In addition, Arnett (1989) developed an observational measure of teacher sensitivity that has been used in several large-scale studies and can be used to assess the experiences of individual children. Items on the most widely used of these process measures are listed in Table 23.4.

Many recent reports concerned with the effects of nonparental child care have used data obtained in the NICHD Study of Early Child Care (1996), for which a new process measure of the quality of child care, the Observational Record of the Caregiving Environment (ORCE), was developed to permit comparable assessments of both home- and center-based care. The ORCE lists 18 specific types of interactions between the target child and the caregiver or other children (see Table 23.5) and is distinguished from other popular measures of quality because it emphasizes the experiences of individual children rather than those of the group as a whole. The observer observes each child for three 10-minute periods, during each of which the observer alternately observes and records descriptions of the child's experiences. In addition to recording these specific ex-

periences, the observers also take qualitative notes at the end of each 10-minute session and in a special 14-minute session after the three 10-minute sessions; these notes are used to make qualitative ratings of the care providers' behavior on the eight dimensions or scales displayed in Table 23.6. To maximize the reliability of the measures obtained in the NICHD Study of Early Child Care, furthermore, the observations described here (each comprising 44 minutes of observation, with both specific behavioral and qualitative ratings obtained) were repeated within 2 weeks. For purposes of analysis, scores on conceptually related items (e.g., those concerned with language simulation) can be combined or used individually to assess specific aspects of the quality, or the scores can be used to provide a more comprehensive assessment.

In the United States, scores on the various process measures are highly correlated with one another. This makes it possible to use composite measures of quality containing fewer items than the complete measures do (Scarr, Eisenberg, & Deater-Deckard, 1994). All of the standardized process measures have proven to be less useful as indices of the quality of care in Western Europe, however, perhaps because the quality of care available there is less variable and of higher average

TABLE 23.5 Behaviors Recorded on the Observational Record of the Caregiving Environment (Infant Version)[a]

Behavior	Definition
Share positive affect	Caregiver and infant laugh, smile, coo
Positive physical contact	Caregiver holds infant, touches warmly
Responds to vocalization	Caregiver responds verbally to infant's nondistressed vocalization
Asks questions	Caregiver directs a question to infant
Other talk	Caregiver makes declarative statement to infant
Stimulates cognitive development	Caregiver encourages a skill like rolling over or focuses infant's attention on something in the environment
Stimulates social development[b]	Caregiver plays social game with infant, moves infant so he or she can see, touch another infant
Reads	Caregiver reads aloud to infant
Facilitates behavior	Caregiver provides help, entertainment for the infant
Responds to negative affect	Caregiver responds when the infant fusses, cries (as proportion of infant fussing, crying)
Restricts infant's activities	Caregiver restricts infant's activity physically or verbally
Restricts in physical container	Infant is in a highchair, playpen, crib, etc.
Speaks negatively to infant	Caregiver speaks to infant in negative tone
Uses negative physical actions[c]	Caregiver slaps, yanks, pushes infant
Physical care	Caregiver provides physical care to the infant: feeding, bathing, diapering
Other activity	Caregiver involved in any activity with infant except physical care
Infant solitary	Infant playing or exploring alone
Infant watching or unoccupied	Infant is not involved in any activity

[a] Separate versions, with age-appropriate definitions, were available for each phase.
[b] This behavior was not recorded reliably.
[c] This behavior did not occur often enough for the frequency counts to be meaningful.

TABLE 23.6 Dimensions Rated on the Qualitative Portion of the Observational Record of the Caregiving Environment[a]

Dimension	Definition
Sensitivity/responsiveness to nondistressed communication	Caregiver responds to the infant's social gestures and is attuned to the infant's needs and moods
Detachment-disengagement	Caregiver is emotionally uninvolved, disengaged, and unaware of infant's needs
Intrusiveness	Caregiver is highly controlling and adult-centered in interactions with the infant
Stimulation of cognitive development	Caregiver engages in activities that can facilitate the infant's learning, such as talking to the infant or demonstrating a toy
Positive regard	Caregiver expresses positive feelings in interaction with the infant
Negative regard	Caregiver expresses negative feelings in interaction with the infant
Flat affect	Caregiver expresses no emotion or animation
Sensitivity/responsiveness to infant distress	Caregiver responds to the infant's distress signals consistently, promptly, and appropriately

[a] Definitions provided here apply to infants; separate versions, with age-appropriate definitions, were prepared for each phase of the NICHD Early Child Care Study.

quality (e.g., Beller, Stahnke, Butz, Stahl, & Wessels, 1996; Tietze, Cryer, Bairrao, Palacios, & Wetzel, 1996). Recognizing the need for more systematic and comprehensive measures that could be used internationally, Pierrehumbert and his colleagues (Pierrehumbert, Ramstein, Krucher, et al., 1996) in Switzerland developed measures of quality that could be used in Switzerland, Sweden, and other countries characterized by high-quality child care. Subsequent research by Pierrehumbert, Ramstein, Karmaniola, Miljkovitch, and Halfon (2002) established the validity of this measure by way of correlates with outcomes that should be (and were) affected by the quality of care. Another measure, the Child Care Facility Schedule, was developed for use in countries outside the United States where quality is highly variable (Dragonas, Tsiantis, & Lambidi, 1995). Its predictive and construct validity have yet to be established, however. Neither Pierrehumbert's nor Drogonas's measures have been used widely enough to determine whether they might have broader utility.

Structural Measures of Quality

Instead of process variables, many researchers assess quality using structural indices: measures of teacher training and experience, group size, teacher-child ratios, crowding, staff turnover, and the like (e.g., Barnas & Cummings, 1994; Howes & Olenick, 1986). Most of these factors can be, and often are, regulated, although such factors as stability and continuity obviously cannot be regulated. Conceptually, structural and process measures differ to the extent that factors indexed by the structural measures potentiate high-quality interaction and care but do not guarantee it, whereas process measures try to quantify the actual care received by children.

Group size and staff-child ratios are popular structural measures. The Panel on Child Care Policy of the U.S. National Research Council (1991) recommended group sizes of 6 to 8 for infants, 6 to 12 for 1- to 2-year-olds, 14 to 20 for 3-year-olds, and 16 to 20 for 4- and 5-year-olds, as well as staff-child ratios of 4 to 1 for infants and 1-year-olds, between 4 and 6 to 1 for 2-year-olds, between 5 and 10 to 1 for 3-year-olds, and between 7 and 10 to 1 for 4- and 5-year-olds. These standards were not very demanding, especially where infants were concerned, and ratios of 2 or at most 3 infants per adult are now considered more appropriate (American Academy of Pediatrics, American Public Health Association, & National Resource Center for Health and Safety in Child Care, 2002; American Public Health Association & American Academy of Pediatrics, 1992a, 1992b). Standards vary dramatically internationally and among states in the United States, not surprisingly, with only about half of the states even requiring that licensed care providers be trained (Morgan et al., 1993; Phillips, Lande, & Goldberg, 1990). Licensed care providers are also more likely to offer stimulating environments and nutritious food than unlicensed providers (Fosburg et al., 1980; Stallings, 1980).

Howes (1983) suggested more than 2 decades ago that the adult-child ratio and the extent of teacher training were the best structural indices of quality in centers, whereas group size, the degree of safety, and the appropriateness of care provider behavior best measured the quality of home-based care. Care providers' salaries have also proved to be valuable, if indirect, measures of the quality of care in a number of studies in the United States (Phillips, Howes, & Whitebook, 1992; Phillips, Mekos, Scarr, McCartney, & Abbott-Shim, 2001; Phillipsen, Burchinal, Howes, & Cryer, 1997; Scarr et al., 1994). Howes also introduced an important distinction between the conventional structural measures of quality (group size, adult-child ratio, care provider training) and more comprehensive and empirically derived measures, such as number of care providers present at any given time, staff turnover, number of settings experienced by each child, care provider sensitivity and involvement, and the provision of developmentally appropriate activities. Unfortunately, site- or care provider-specific measures of quality fail to take account of the substantial frequency of moves by children from one setting to another (NICHD Early Child Care Research Network, 1995a). These transitions may adversely affect children even when all facilities provide high-quality care.

Relations between Structural and Process Measures of Quality

Because the many structural measures of quality are all believed to reflect conditions conducive to high-quality interactions and experiences, one might expect at least modest relationships among them; this is usually, but not always, the case. Scarr et al. (1994) found that scores on various structural measures of quality were poorly correlated with one another and were not correlated with scores on the process measures of quality. In their large multisite study, only teachers' wages predicted the quality of care they provided, as indexed on process measures. Petrogiannis (1995), too, reported no significant associations among the observed quality of care provider-child interaction, ITERS scores, and structural indices of quality in his study of Greek child care centers.

Other researchers, including those participating in the multisite NICHD Study of Early Child Care, have reported clearer and stronger associations between scores on structural and process measures of quality:

The better the salaries, benefits, and level of training received by care providers, the better the quality of care they provide and the less they are likely to quit their jobs (Berk, 1985; Kontos & Stremmel, 1988; Phillips, Howes, & Whitebook, 1991; Ruopp, Travers, Glantz, & Coelan, 1979). The researchers in the NICHD Child Care Research Network (1995b, 2000a, 2002a) reported that the observed quality of care provider-child interaction was higher when group sizes were smaller, child-adult ratios were lower, and care providers were better trained. Howes, Phillips, and Whitebook (1992) reported that classrooms with appropriate teacher-child ratios were more likely than those with higher ratios to provide care of better quality and to promote secure child-teacher attachments.

In four large multisite studies (one of them multinational in scope and one conducted in the United Kingdom), the quality of child care—assessed using process measures of quality—was correlated with structural measures of quality, including higher staff-child ratios, better staff training and education, and higher teacher wages (*Cost, Quality, and Child Outcomes in Child Care Centers,* 1995; Cryer, Tietze, Burchinal, et al., 1999; Phillips et al., 2001; Sylva, Melhuish, Sammons, Siraj-Blatchford, & Taggert, 2004). In the two large U.S. studies, average levels of quality within the states sampled were related to the stringency of state standards: States with more demanding licensing standards had fewer centers providing care of poor quality, thereby underscoring the benefits of demanding and well-enforced standards (Vandell & Wolfe, 2000). In an interesting natural experiment, Howes, Smith, and Galinsky (1995) reported that the introduction of stricter standards of training and provider-child ratios statewide led to improvements in the quality of child-care provider interaction and higher scores on the ECERS scale. Similarly, the NICHD Early Child Care Research Network (1999b) reported that children in classrooms that met more of the recommended guidelines regarding ratio, group size, teacher training, and teacher education were less likely to have behavior problems and more likely to have better school readiness and language comprehension scores. Except in North Carolina, where licensing regulations are quite lax and for-profit centers provided care of significantly lower quality, the *Cost, Quality, and Child Outcomes in Child Care Centers* (1995) study revealed no difference in the quality of care provided by for-profit and not-for-profit centers, in part because nonprofit church-based centers often provided care of such poor quality. Nonprofit centers did have higher staff-child ratios, better educated, trained, and more experienced staff, and lower rates of staff turnover, however.

Similar findings were obtained in studies focused on family day care homes (Clarke-Stewart, Vandell, Burchinal, O'Brien, & McCartney, 2002). Galinsky, Howes, Kontos, and Shinn (1994) and Galinsky, Howes, and Kontos (1995) reported that home-based child care providers who received training were more likely to behave warmly, attentively, and responsively. Trained providers also received higher scores on Harms and Clifford's (1989) FDCRS, perhaps because the training enhanced their self-esteem and professionalism (Dombro, 1995; Dombro & Modigliani, 1995). In an independent sample of home-based child care providers, training was in fact the most powerful predictor of the observed quality of care as indexed on the FDCRS (Fischer & Eheart, 1991). Bollin (1993) reported that home-based care providers were most likely to continue providing care when they had held previous child care jobs and were not trying to combine paid child care work with care of their own young children. Quality of care provider-child interaction has also been linked to group size in home-based care (Kontos, 1994; Stith & Davis, 1984) and care provider-child ratios in both center and home-based care (Howes, 1983; Howes & Rubenstein, 1985). In Israel, however, M. K. Rosenthal (1991a) found little association between the quality of care provider-child interaction and the quality of the education that caregivers provided.

Overall, there is substantial evidence that scores on diverse structural and process indices of quality are intercorrelated, with Scarr et al.'s (1994) findings representing the exception rather than the rule. The convergence reported by most researchers validates the notion that structure affects function and underscores the substantial consensus regarding the components and nature of high- (or low-) quality care, despite the rather heterogeneous range of items considered as indices of quality. This consensus should also increase the amount of attention paid to reports that the average quality of care in the United States is barely adequate or mediocre (*Cost, Quality, and Child Outcomes in Child Care Centers*, 1995; Galinsky et al., 1994; Kontos, Howes, Shinn, & Galinsky, 1994; NICHD Early Child Care Research Network, 1995d, 2000a; Whitebook, Howes, & Phillips, 1989) and prompt efforts to narrow the gap between parents' and researchers' evaluations of quality (Clarke-Stewart et al., 1994; Galinsky, 1992; Mason & Duberstein, 1992; Phillips, 1992).

The mean quality of care, as indexed by provider training and education level, improved during the 1980s in the United States, but average group size and turnover rates increased over this period (Hofferth, 1992). According to the NICHD Early Child Care Research Network (2000a, p. 116), "Positive caregiving was . . . very uncharacteristic" for 8% of children in the United States ages 1 to 3 years, "somewhat uncharacteristic" for 53%, "somewhat characteristic" for 30%, and "highly characteristic" for only 9%. This conclusion is especially alarming because the centers and care providers providing care of higher quality are likely to be overrepresented and those providing poorer quality care underrepresented in such studies, thanks to variations in their willingness to participate in research. Haskins (1992) and Clarke-Stewart (1992) have questioned the assumption that "adequate" day care quality represents a case for concern, however, and the results of the NICHD Early Child Care Research Network (1995d) suggested that three-quarters of the infants studied had sensitive care providers.

Correlates of the Quality of Care

In the early 1980s, several researchers noted a disturbing tendency in both Canada and the United States for quality of care and social class to be confounded. Children from economically and socially disadvantaged backgrounds appeared to receive nonparental care of poorer quality than those from more advantaged backgrounds. This led researchers to fear that disadvantaged children were doubly handicapped, suffering the adverse effects of poor-quality care both at home and in their out-of-home care settings (Anderson, Nagle, Roberts, & Smith, 1981; Clarke-Stewart et al., 1994; Goelman, 1988; Goelman & Pence, 1987a, 1987b; Howes & Stewart, 1987; Kontos & Fiene, 1987). Although the NICHD Early Child Care Research Network (1995c) reported that children receiving better out-of-home care had superior home environments as well, most recent research has revealed a curvilinear rather than linear relationship between social class and the quality of out-of-home care (Phillips et al., 1994; Voran & Whitebook, 1991; Waite, Leibowitz, & Witsberger, 1991; Whitebook et al., 1989; Zaslow, 1991). Centers serving children from advantaged backgrounds indeed seem to provide care of the highest quality (see also Holloway & Reichhart-Erickson, 1989; Kontos, 1991), but the worst care tends to be provided by centers predominantly serving children from middle-income families rather than the poorest families. Centers serving children from low-income families do not differ from those serving advantaged families on most measures of quality, although the teachers in centers serving poorer children tend to be less sensitive and harsher, perhaps because the children behave more poorly. According to the survey by Phillips and her colleagues, quality varies across an especially wide range in centers serving disadvantaged families. Community-based centers had smaller groups and better teacher-child ratios, although their teachers had obtained less education and were more poorly trained. Interestingly, children from middle-income families are especially likely to attend for-profit centers, where quality is often significantly poorer (Coelen, Glantz, & Calore, 1979; S. L. Kagan, 1991; Phillips et al., 1992). In the NICHD Early Child Care Research Network (1995b) study, however, the quality of observed care provider behavior was not predicted by family income level, although it was predicted by the quality of home care (NICHD Early Child Care Research Network, 1995c).

Family social status, parental income, and parental education are not the only factors correlated with indices of the quality of care children receive. Bolger and Scarr (1995) reported that authoritarian attitudes toward child rearing were also associated with lower-quality care, and that, at least in the middle-class sample they studied, variation in the state standards for child care quality did not attenuate the powerful association between family background and child care quality. Phillips, McCartney, and Scarr (1987) reported that parents who valued social skills tended to choose centers with higher quality than those who valued conformity. Children may also end up in centers of lower quality if their parents are too preoccupied with other problems to evaluate their child care options thoroughly (Howes & Olenick, 1986).

Much of the literature reviewed next confirms that quality of care is indeed an important consideration: Children perform better on many dimensions when they have received care of higher quality. Such findings raise obvious questions: How good is good enough? Is there a linear relationship between quality of care and children's adjustment? Is there a threshold beyond which improvements in quality no longer have demonstrable effects? The results of the Goteborg Child Care Study provided an early answer to these questions (Broberg, Hwang, Lamb, & Ketterlinus, 1989; Hwang, Broberg, & Lamb, 1991; Lamb, Hwang, Bookstein, et al., 1988; Lamb, Hwang, Broberg, & Bookstein, 1988). In Sweden, nonparental care is government-subsidized and strictly regulated to ensure high quality (Broberg & Hwang, 1991; Hwang & Broberg, 1992). Despite limited variations in the quality of care across settings, however, quality of out-of-home care was one of the most important and consistent correlates of children's personality maturity, social skills, and compliance with maternal requests in the early assessments conducted as part of the Goteborg Child Care Study.

The results of the much larger and more comprehensive NICHD Early Child Care Study (2002a, 2003b) likewise revealed that the effects of quality were continuous across the wide range encountered in this study. Interestingly, however, careful analyses revealed no dose-response relations, meaning that the beneficial efforts of high-quality care and the adverse effects of poor-quality care were similar regardless of the amount of time spent in care. Similar findings were reported by Sylva et al. (2004) in the Effective Provision of Preschool Education (EPPE) Study.

Scarr and her colleagues (Scarr, 1992, 1998; Scarr, McCartney, Abbott-Shim, & Eisenberg, 1995) have not only reported poor intercorrelation among measures of quality, but were among the first to offer the more skeptical opinion that the quality of out-of-home care is much less significant than many advocates believe. Their research suggested that socioeconomic and family background variables were much more influential sources of variance than the quality of care, which explained statistically significant but small portions of the variance in behavioral adjustment. Measures of the quality of care also had small (but reliable) effects in the NICHD study: The NICHD Early Child Care Research Network and Duncan (2003) estimated that a 1 standard deviation increase in the quality of care between 36 and 54 months was associated with an increase of between .50 and 1.50 points on standardized cognitive test scores. Further research involving diverse samples and measures is obviously necessary to evaluate the merits of this argument, which has substantial implications for both parents and public authorities. Quality matters, it seems, but not as much as researchers and policymakers hoped (Lamb, 2000). In addition, the type, quality, and extent of out-of-home care must be viewed in broader context: Child care does not replace home care and does not render family processes and family background irrelevant.

Summary

The results of both small- and large-scale studies over the past 2 decades have revealed substantial agreement among experts regarding the components of high-quality care, even though parents' assessments of quality and their appraisals of satisfaction seem to be determined very differently from experts' assessments. Researchers have distinguished between process indices of quality, which quantify development-promoting care provider behavior, and structural indices, which identify conditions in which such behavior should be more likely. Empirical evidence confirms that the many objective indices of high-quality care are highly intercorrelated, and that observable aspects of appropriate care provider behavior are more likely to be evident when the structural indices suggest auspicious circumstances for such high-quality care. Research reviewed later in this chapter also supports the assumption that high-quality care promotes adaptive development in a variety of developmental domains, although the effects of quality are much smaller than most researchers or policymakers typically acknowledge.

Unfortunately, the most popular indices of quality have proven less useful when employed in Western and Northern European countries. Their failure has been attributed to measurement insensitivity when levels of quality are very high, but cultural differences in the definition of quality may restrict the validity of these measures as well. Exploration and specification of these cultural differences would be extremely informative, not only to students of nonparental care but also to those who study cultural practices and beliefs. In addition, as noted earlier, repeated reports that the quality of care is correlated with various outcome measures often lead researchers to ignore the small size of the associations, especially in predictive analyses. At least in part, these disappointing findings can be attributed to the rather general way that quality is typically measured. In the next decade, researchers might profitably focus their efforts on attempts to identify more precisely the particular aspects of quality that promote or impede development in specific domains, and for children with particular characteristics, thereby moving beyond global indices of quality and sharpening our understanding of quality and its effects (see Kontos, Burchinal, Howes, Wisseh, & Galinsky, 2002, for an example of such research).

CORRELATES AND CONSEQUENCES

With the exception of theorists such as Piaget (e.g., 1965) and Harris (1998), who have described how regular interactions with peers promote social and moral development, early childhood educators who have endorsed enrichment programs for children from impoverished backgrounds, and sociobiologists (e.g., Daly & Wilson, 1995) warning that biologically unrelated care providers are less motivated than relatives to meet children's needs, most contemporary theories of socialization focus almost exclusively on the ways parents (especially mothers) influence their children's development, largely ignoring the possible effects of nonparental care providers and extrafamilial environments. Only attachment theorists have conceptually analyzed the developmental consequences of nonparental care in any depth, proposing that care by a single care provider is needed to promote healthy social and emotional development (Bowlby, 1951, 1958, 1969–1973). Warnings that child-parent separations might damage child-parent relationships and thereby cause social maladjustment and pathological emotional development have in turn prompted researchers to examine the ways children cope with and are affected by nonparental care. For the most part, however, research on the effects of nonparental care has been surprisingly atheoretical rather than conceptually driven.

In this section, we review research designed to illuminate the effects of nonparental child care on children's development and adjustment. We begin with an analysis of the processes whereby children adjust to novel care providers and contexts, with emphasis on emotional reactions and factors associated with individual variations in the magnitude of children's responses. We then examine the effects of these transitions on the quality of child-parent interaction before turning to the issue that has been most contentious: the effects of child care on the security of infant-parent (especially child-mother) attachment relationships.

The initiation of nonparental care of course involves opportunities as well as stresses. In particular, children in care settings are able to form and be affected by meaningful relationships with other adults (care providers) as well as other children (peers). In fact, most children do establish such relationships, which range in quality and thus have the potential to affect children's development in positive as well as less desirable ways, as we show in our analysis of these developing relationships. Children in care settings are at increased risk of developing behavior problems, as we then show, noting that the magnitude and reliability of this effect appears to be a consequence of the time of enrollment and the quality of care, including the quality of the relationships with care providers. Effects on cognitive and linguistic development, in both community and special intervention programs, are discussed in the final subsection.

Processes of Adaptation to Nonparental Care

In this section, we discuss research on children's initial reactions to the start of out-of-home care, focusing first on separation responses and then on processes of familiarization with the new setting.

Separation Responses

Bowlby (1969, 1973) initially described children's reactions to extended maternal separations by reference to successive phases of protest, despair, and detachment similar to the observable stages of bereavement in adults. Passage through these phases was believed to proceed at a pace that varied depending on the length of the separations. Bowlby's theory was informed by observations of children in orphanages and residential homes during and after the Second World War, but comparable data were obtained by professionals working in East European child care centers during the 1970s. These educators and pediatricians reported sleeping and eating disorders, infectious diseases, and declines in levels of play and communication after enrollment (Schmidt-Kolmer, Tonkowa-Jampolskaja, & Atanassowa, 1979). Bowlby's colleagues, Robertson and Robertson (1972, 1975), reported that a variety of factors modified children's emotional and physical reactions to extended separations, but little systematic research on factors affecting children's responses to repeated separations was conducted until much more recently (cf. Field, 1991b).

Most research on the transition from home to child care has been conducted in Europe, perhaps because national policies there encourage extended periods of subsidized parental care during the first years of life to ensure that most children enter nonparental care settings after child-parent relationships have already been established (Lamb, Sternberg, Hwang, et al., 1992). In Italy, Fein and her colleagues (Fein, 1995; Fein et al., 1993) observed that infants (ages ranged from 4.5 to 19.5 months) enrolled full time in high-quality centers continued to show despair-like behavior (negative affect, immobilization, and self-comforting) 6 months after enrollment. In Germany, Rauh and her colleagues (Rauh, Ziegenhain, Müller, & Wijnroks, 2000) found that infants who were enrolled in child care between 12 and 18 months of age (late entry) were more irritable and negative than those enrolled before 12 months (early entry), both at home and in child care centers. As children grow older, however, emotional reactions to child care entry become less intense, so that, for example, kindergartners regulate their emotions better and cope better with the first stressful days in child care than infants and toddlers do (Field et al., 1984).

Reactions to maternal separation may vary depending on the quality of the child-mother relationship prior to enrollment. According to attachment theorists, mothers who provide children with emotional security help children develop self-regulatory abilities that facilitate adaptation to separations (Ainsworth, 1979). Consistent with this view, infants from secure dyads appear less stressed (i.e., they have lower cortisol levels 30 minutes after the last separation) than infants from insecure dyads when observed in a setting (the Strange Situation) that involves brief mother-child separations (Spangler & Grossmann, 1993; Spangler & Schieche, 1998).

By comparison with the separations studied in the laboratory, however, nonparental child care involves longer, repeated separations which may violate children's expectations about their mother's return. The intensity of the stress involved may explain why cortisol levels were similarly elevated in securely and insecurely attached toddlers when the daily mother-child separations associated with child care began (Ahnert, Gunnar, Lamb, & Barthel, 2004). These findings suggest that enrollment in child care places a special stress on children who are too young to cope effectively with violations of expectations about the parents' availability, even when they have established attachments to their parents. M. K. Rosenthal (1994) found that Israeli toddlers in family day care were most distressed when they had younger and more stressed mothers, when their coenrollees tended to be older than they, and when their care providers had age-inappropriate expectations.

Processes of Familiarization

Quite often, care providers can do little to modulate children's responses to stress. Fein et al. (1993) reported, for example, that the levels of negative affect 6 months after enrollment in child care were predicted by measures of immobility and reduced levels of positive affect at entry but not by variations in the care providers' behaviors, even though the care providers comforted, maintained proximity to, and initiated interactions with unhappy children more than with other children during the transitional period.

To help children adjust, many European child care centers have implemented adaptation programs in which mothers are allowed to accompany their children during the transitional period of enrollment. As expected by the proponents of such programs, Rauh and her colleagues (2000) reported that abrupt transitions to child care prolonged negative emotions and made adaptation more difficult, especially when children were enrolled as toddlers rather than infants. When mothers familiarized their children to child care in a more leisurely manner and accompanied their children in the center, by contrast, adjustment was easier. Similarly, Ahnert, Gunnar, et al. (2004) found that child-mother attachments remained secure or shifted from insecure to secure when mothers accompanied their children to child care for a longer period. In addition, securely attached toddlers had markedly lower cortisol levels than insecurely attached infants while the mothers accompanied them, suggesting that secure infant-mother relationships reduced the perceived stressfulness of the novel child care environment.

Effects on Child-Parent Relationships

In this section, we turn attention from the children's initial emotional responses to the effects of child care on the relationship between children and their parents.

Changes in Parenting

Perhaps in defensive response to widespread concerns about the riskiness of nonparental care, many researchers noted that employed and unemployed mothers behaved similarly with their children (Bornstein,

Maital, & Tal, 1997; Easterbrooks & Goldberg, 1985; Rubenstein & Howes, 1979; Rubenstein, Pedersen, & Yarrow, 1977; Stith & Davis, 1984), or they emphasized that employed mothers paid more attention, vocalized more, and expressed more positive emotions to their children than stay-at-home mothers did (Caruso, 1996; Schubert, Bradley-Johnson, & Nuttal, 1980; Schwartz, 1983). Such inconsistencies were at least partially attributable to situational variability (Crockenberg, & Litman, 1991; Zaslow, Pedersen, Suwalsky, & Rabinovich, 1989), underscoring the importance of assessing children in a variety of social situations. In addition, surprisingly few researchers studied the experiences of the same children at home and in child care centers; indeed, many researchers have implicitly failed to recognize that children in child care facilities are not only exposed daily to an additional set of experiences at child care, but also have experiences at home that differ from those experienced by peers who do not receive regular nonparental care.

Ahnert, Rickert, et al. (2000) detailed the weekday experiences of German toddlers who either attended or did not attend child care facilities. The children's social experiences differed depending on where they were observed, and the children in the two groups also had different experiences at home with their parents. At home, parents interacted more intensely with the child care children, as if attempting to make up for the time they were apart; during comparable portions of the day, they attended to, communicated with, and stimulated their children more than parents of home-only children. Similarly, Booth, Clarke-Stewart, Vandell, McCartney, and Owen (2002) reported that mothers of children in child care spent more time interacting with their children, even on weekends, than did mothers of home-only children. Burchinal, Bryant, Lee, and Ramey (1992) likewise found that mothers of children in child care were more involved with their 6- to 12-month-olds than were mothers of home-only children.

However, maternal sensitivity and levels of positive child engagement decline when children—especially infants and toddlers—spend many hours in child care facilities (NICHD Early Child Care Research Network, 2003a). This means that the quality of mother-child relationships also declines in such circumstances, especially when the child care is of poor quality (NICHD Early Child Care Research Network, 1999a; Sagi, Koren-Karie, Gini, Ziv, & Joels, 2002). For example, Ahnert, Rickert, et al. (2000) found that mothers of children in child care tended to respond hesitantly to their children's distress signals in the evenings, even when the children indicated by intensified levels of whining that they wanted their mother's attention. Similar patterns of interaction were described by Nelson and Garduque (1991), who found that 2- to 4-year-olds behaved more negatively when interacting with their parents than with their care providers. Rubenstein and Howes (1979) likewise showed that more negative affect was displayed at home than in care settings. To foster secure child-parent relationships and promote children's emotional equilibrium, families thus need to titrate and adjust the children's experiences at home, especially when poor child care experiences further tax the children's relationship skills (Ahnert & Lamb, 2003; Lamb, 2005). Specifically, parents need to be especially attentive to children and their needs, responding sensitively to fusses and cries when they are together, thereby providing the emotion-regulating support that children typically do not obtain from care providers in group settings.

Measuring Child-Parent Relationships

Although changes in parental behavior typically accompany enrollment in child care, adverse effects on child-parent relationships are not inevitable, especially when parents and children have established harmonious relationships. Fears about adverse effects of early and extended nonparental child care have long been prominent, however.

Many of the early studies involved the Strange Situation procedure, which was designed to measure the quality of child-parent attachment by observing children's reactions to reunion with their parents following two 3-minute separations in an unfamiliar context (Ainsworth, Blehar, Waters, & Wall, 1978) and has become popular in part because it is one of few measures providing valid insight into children's early socioemotional development. Following the brief separations involved in the Strange Situation, most infants greet the returning parent warmly, either by approaching, asking to be picked up, or smiling and vocalizing. Children who behave in this fashion are deemed securely attached (Ainsworth et al., 1978). Other children are deemed insecure because they behave avoidantly (ignoring the adults' bids, failing to greet, and perhaps even withdrawing) or resistantly (ambivalently mingling bids for contact with angry rejection of contact offered to them).

In a widely cited early study, Blehar (1974) compared 2- and 3-year-old children receiving full-time child care with children of similar ages cared for exclusively at home. When the children were observed in the Strange Situation, many of those in child care appeared insecurely attached to their mother. Because Blehar's findings seemed to confirm widespread fears that child care had negative effects on child-parent relationships, several investigators attempted—unsuccessfully—to replicate her findings (e.g., Portnoy & Simmons, 1978; Ragozin, 1980).

Is it appropriate to use the Strange Situation when evaluating children whose daily experiences of separation might have affected their tolerance for brief separations like those involved in the Strange Situation? Clarke-Stewart (1989) and Thompson (1988) in fact suggested that children enrolled in child care might appear insecure even when they were securely attached to their parents. In addition, Clarke-Stewart and her colleagues (1994) reported that child care children appeared more independent than home-only children when observed in unfamiliar test situations with their mother. Because independence from mother was correlated with several measures of social competence with unfamiliar adults, Clarke-Stewart et al. worried that the children's independence might be misinterpreted as insecurity, but later assessments (at 15 months) of 1,153 infants participating in a longitudinal study revealed that infants with extensive child care experiences were neither less distressed nor more independent in the Strange Situation than peers without nonparental care experiences (NICHD Early Child Care Research Network, 1997b). The validity of the Strange Situation remains an issue when children as old as those studied by Blehar are concerned, however, because the procedure was initially developed and validated for use with toddlers under 20 months of age (Ainsworth et al., 1978).

Variation in Child-Parent Relationships

Beginning in 1986, a series of reports in both the popular media and the professional literature again fanned fears that early initiated nonparental care might adversely affect child-parent attachment and related aspects of psychosocial development (e.g., Belsky, 1986). This conclusion was largely supported by studies in which the Strange Situation was used to assess socioemotional adjustment. Reviewing the results of four such studies, Belsky (1988) reported that the proportion of insecure (especially insecure/avoidant) attachments was higher (41%) among children receiving out-of-home care than among home-only children (26%). He thus concluded that extensive nonmaternal care in the 1st year of life made insecure child-mother attachments more likely.

Noting that Belsky's (1986; see also Belsky & Rovine, 1988) review was selective (he had deliberately focused only on children from more advantaged and stable backgrounds), Clarke-Stewart (1989) combined data from all known studies in which the Strange Situation had been used, regardless of socioeconomic status. In this rather heterogeneous sample, 36% of the infants in full-time care were classified as insecure compared with 29% of the infants whose mothers were employed part-time or were not employed. Acknowledging an "elevated risk" of insecure attachment among infants in child care, Clarke-Stewart emphasized the needs (a) to explore a variety of factors other than emotional insecurity that might explain these differences in child behavior and (b) to use a wider range of measures when evaluating adjustment to child care. Shortly thereafter, Lamb, Sternberg, and Prodromidis (1992) obtained raw data from several investigators, recoded the data, and reexamined the effects of child care on the security of infant-mother attachment. Access to raw data allowed Lamb et al. to assess the effects of such factors as extent of care and age of enrollment more fully than had hitherto been possible. Their reanalysis showed that children who began receiving nonmaternal care between 7 and 12 months were more likely to be insecurely attached (37%) than were those cared for exclusively by their mother (29%). Subsequent meta-analyses by Erel, Oberman, and Yirmiya (2000) of data obtained in 59 studies revealed no significant effect of child care on the security of child-mother attachment, however, and suggested that earlier enrollment was preferable. Interestingly, adverse effects were more commonly found in earlier studies, whereas positive effects or no differences were more common in later studies.

When children in the large NICHD Study of Early Child Care (1997b) were observed in the Strange Situation at 15 months, there were no differences in the proportion of secure attachments depending on whether or not these infants had experienced nonmaternal care. In the NICHD study, furthermore, the effects of child care on attachment at both 15 and 36 months were moderated by the mother's involvement and sensitive parenting. Greater maternal sensitivity was associated with increases in the probability that children would be classified as securely attached to their mother, and maternal sensitivity moderated estimated effects of the amount, quality, and instability of child care. Children whose mothers were less sensitive were more likely to be insecurely attached to them, especially when the children

spent long hours in care and the child care was of poor quality (NICHD Early Child Care Research Network, 1997b, 2001b). Such findings indicated that parenting continues to shape the quality of child-parent relationships even when children experience child care, and that sensitive parenting moderates the effects of child care on attachment security. In addition, the results of the NICHD study identified amount of early child care as a risk factor that made children more susceptible to the adverse effects of insensitive parenting, probably because these parents were unable to provide their children with the types of soothing, emotion-regulating attention in the evenings that allowed the children to return to child care the next day in states of emotional equilibrium (Ahnert & Lamb, 2003; Lamb, 2005). In Israel, however, the link between maternal sensitivity and attachment security is not evident when children attend poor-quality child care centers (Aviezer, Sagi-Schwartz, & Koren-Karie, 2003). Insecure infant-mother attachments appear more common when Israeli children attend centers providing care of poor quality (Sagi et al., 2002).

As indicated earlier, the observation of Strange Situation behavior at best provides a very narrow assessment of the effects of child care on child-parent relationships. Associations between Strange Situation behavior and measures of later performance tend to be impressive only when there is stability over time with respect to family circumstances and caretaking arrangements (Ahnert, 2004; Belsky & Fearon, 2002; Goldsmith & Alansky, 1987; Lamb, Thompson, Gardner, & Charnov, 1985). Thus, the hypothesized links between nonparental care, insecure/avoidant attachment, and subsequent behavior problems need to be evaluated more thoroughly. There is as yet no evidence that avoidant infants who have experienced nonparental care in fact behave any differently in future years than similar infants who behave securely in the Strange Situation (Grossmann, Grossmann, & Waters, in press; Lamb et al., 1985). In addition, it is obviously important to view out-of-home care in the context of other social and familial variables that affect child-parent relationships.

Because sensitive parenting continues to shape the quality of child-parent relationships when children attend child care facilities, it is important to note that sensitivity is itself conditioned by parental motivation and attitudes (see Bell & Richard, 2000). Harrison and Ungerer (2002), for example, reported that Australian mothers who returned to the workforce because they wanted to do so described many benefits for themselves, their families, and their children, expressed less separation anxiety, and were less likely to have insecurely attached children than unemployed mothers were. Likewise, Stifter et al. (1993) found that mothers who returned to work early and reported more separation anxiety were more likely to behave intrusively and to have insecurely attached infants. Scher and Mayseless (2000) reported an association between the number of hours spent at work, separation anxiety, and insecure patterns of attachment. There is also some evidence that variables such as birth order (Barglow, Vaughn, & Molitor, 1987), temperament (Belsky, 1988; Melhuish, 1987), level of familial stress, differences in maternal personality (Belsky & Rovine, 1988), maternal role satisfaction (Hock, 1980), cultural differences in parenting values (Burchinal, Ramey, Reid, & Jaccard, 1995), and the availability of social support (Crockenberg, 1981) may mediate the effects of child care experiences on infant-mother attachment. As a result, it is important to identify, measure, and take these factors into account when interpreting the effects of child care on the quality of child-parent relationships, and to recognize that family factors remain the best predictors of children's development, even when they attend child care facilities (Lamb, 1998; NICHD Early Child Care Research Network, 1998b).

Relationships with Care Providers

Whatever happens to child-parent relationships when children begin attending out-of-home care facilities, enrollment also offers opportunities to form relationships with other adults. We consider the development of this relationship, next.

Concepts and Measures

Enrollment in child care allows children to form significant relationships with providers but does not lead care providers to displace mothers as primary attachment figures. After observing infants interacting with their mother and care providers in the laboratory, for example, early researchers reported that children overwhelmingly preferred to interact with and be near their mother and were often upset when left alone with care providers. Positive responses to care providers were more common in the presence of strangers, however (Cummings, 1980; Farran & Ramey, 1977; Fox, 1977).

In child care settings, children show a preference for stable over unstable care providers when their parents are absent. They also show more positive emotions and

explore more in the presence of regular care providers and those who have provided their care longer. For example, toddlers consistently seek comfort from stable and familiar care providers when distressed, interact with them preferentially when not distressed, and are more rapidly soothed by them than by unstable providers (Anderson et al., 1981; Barnas & Cummings, 1994; Rubenstein & Howes, 1979). Such differences may reflect in part some characteristics or skills of the providers because stable providers were often the head teachers and were highly involved with children. Barnas and Cummings thus speculated that the children had been able to form secure attachments to those care providers who had been reliable sources of care.

In more recent studies, many researchers have used Ainsworth et al.'s (1978) Strange Situation (SS) or Waters's (1995) Attachment Q-set (AQS) to examine the quality or security of the relationships between children and their care providers. Although scores on the two measures are highly correlated (Sagi et al., 1995), they capture different aspects of child-adult relationships. Specifically, the SS emphasizes the adequacy of adult responses to children's separation distress and children's feeling about the comfort and protection they receive, especially when distressed (Ainsworth et al., 1978; Lamb et al., 1985), whereas the AQS explores adult-child interactions in a variety of everyday situations, capturing child behaviors that include security, comfort, and attention seeking (Booth, Kelly, Spieker, & Zuckerman, 2003; Waters, 1995). In a recent meta-analysis, Ahnert, Pinquart, and Lamb (in press) found that the SS and AQS revealed equivalent proportions of secure (as opposed to insecure) child-care provider attachments, although secure relationships to care providers were less common than secure relationships to mothers or fathers. The security of children's attachments to their mother, father, and care providers were minimally but significantly intercorrelated, suggesting that children construct intertwined internal working models of significant relationships with adults. For the most part, however, the characteristics of interaction with particular individuals shape the quality of specific relationships. The security of child-care provider attachment is not simply determined by the security of child-parent attachment, as many attachment theorists once hypothesized.

Correlates and Antecedents

As with parents, the security of infant-care provider attachment is associated with the sensitivity, involvement, and quality of the care provided by care providers, although considerable disagreement exists about the ways the qualities underlying secure child-care provider attachments should be conceptualized and assessed. Some researchers argue that, as with mother-child dyads, the security of child-care provider attachments depends on the sensitivity of the care providers' behavior with individual children. Consistent with this view, Galinsky et al. (1995) reported that infants behaved as though they were more securely attached to their providers in home-based settings after the care providers' participated in a training program designed to enhance their sensitivity.

Highly trained care providers can appear even more sensitive than mothers in one-on-one free-play situations (Goossens & van IJzendoorn, 1990), but dyadic sensitivity necessarily decreases in group settings because care providers have to divide their attention among multiple children (Goossens & Melhuish, 1996). This may explain why some researchers have found no significant associations between the security of child-care provider attachment and measures of the care providers' sensitivity in child care settings (e.g., Howes & Smith, 1995). Children in specific groups also tend to develop relationships with their shared care providers that are of similar quality (Sagi et al., 1985, 1995), and the security of child-care provider attachment remains the same even when care providers change (Howes, Galinsky, & Kontos, 1998). These findings suggest that the security of child-care provider attachments is shaped primarily by group-directed rather than individual-focused behavior, with relationships between care providers and children reflecting group dynamics rather than the dynamics of individual dyads (Ahnert & Lamb, 2000; Ahnert, Lamb, & Seltenheim, 2000).

Because some researchers have assessed the promptness and adequacy of care providers' responses to individual children, whereas others have used group-focused measures of responsiveness, Ahnert et al. (in press) were able to examine the differential impact of the two types of responsiveness on emerging child-care provider relationships. Meta-analyses revealed that children's relationships with care providers, especially in centers, were predominantly shaped by behavior toward the group as a whole. Only in small groups was the security of relationships with care providers predicted by measures of dyadic responsiveness similar to those that predict the security of children's attachments to their parents (De Wolff & van IJzendoorn, 1997).

Factors such as group size and adult-child ratio appear to moderate the associations between care providers' behavior and the security of child-care provider relationships. In group settings, sensitive care providers clearly need to monitor children's emotional needs, and in small groups (or those with high adult-child ratios) they may be able to respond to almost every social bid. They cannot do so in large groups, however, and characteristics others than group size may thus become important. For example, gender (which is normally seen as an individual characteristic) becomes a powerful group-structuring feature when many children are grouped together (Leaper, 1994, 2002; Maccoby, 1998). In such contexts, gender not only divides groups but changes the context and dynamics of the subgroups as well. Boys are more likely to be accepted if they are ranked high in dominance (e.g., Sebanc, Pierce, Cheatam, & Gunnar, 2003), whereas emotional patterns—such as happy-positive and angry-negative patterns—affect girls' popularity (Denham & Holt, 1993; Denham et al., 2001).

If care providers' activities in centers are primarily group-oriented, then group dynamics and interactions may be affected by group characteristics of this sort, as well as by the fact that care providers tend to be females whose professional attitudes might reflect (female) emphases on safety and relaxation more than (male) emphases on excitement and exploration. The meta-analyses conducted by Ahnert et al. (2005) in fact revealed that girls tended to develop secure relationships with care providers more often than boys did; similar gender-based differences are evident in other measures of the quality of child-care provider interactions (e.g., Leaper, 2002). Such findings suggest that care providers tend to provide care that fits their own gender-stereotyped attitudes and that, as a result, boys may have more difficulty forming close relationships with (female) teachers, establishing connections to the (female) world of education, and thus benefiting from later education. Antecedents of individual differences in care provider sensitivity have received little attention from researchers, although Hamre and Pianta (2004) found that care providers (especially in home-based settings) were less sensitive and more withdrawn when they were depressed.

Children's backgrounds, characteristics, and child care histories also affect the security of their attachments to care providers. For example, children with better-educated and more affluent families are more socially responsive and may thus establish new social relationships more easily than less advantaged children (e.g., Belsky, Woodworth, & Crnic, 1996; Crockenberg & Litman, 1991), although this appears to be true only when the children are in home-based care arrangements (Elicker, Fortner-Wood, & Noppe, 1999); socioeconomic background appears to be less influential when children attend child care centers. Perhaps this is because care providers in center contexts are forced to focus on group integration rather than on the children's family backgrounds. Howes and Smith (1995) reported that secure child-care provider relationships were more common when children were younger, but other researchers have not found similar correlations between age and the security of child-care provider attachment (e.g., Cassibba, van IJzendoorn, & D'Odorico, 2000). Reasoning that this might be because age is often confounded with child care history, Ahnert et al. (in press) predicted and found that older children were less likely to form secure attachments to their care providers only when their child care histories had been discontinuous. This underscores the importance of stable care experiences, which allow child-care provider relationships time to develop and deepen.

Predictive Value

Relationships with care providers merit attention because they significantly affect children's development. The security of both infant-mother and infant-care provider attachment are correlated with the level of competence evident when children play with adults as well as the degree of engagement in play with peers (Howes & Hamilton, 1993; Howes, Matheson, & Hamilton, 1994). More impressive, Israeli infants who behaved securely with care providers in the Strange Situation were less ego-controlled and more empathic, dominant, purposive, achievement-oriented, and independent 4 years later than those whose relationships were insecure-resistant (Oppenheim, Sagi, & Lamb, 1988). School children's perceptions of their relationships with teachers are also predicted by the quality of their first attachment to care providers, underscoring the long-lasting impact of these early relationships (Howes, Hamilton, & Philipsen, 1998).

Relationships with Peers

Just as enrollment in child care provides opportunities to form relationships with adult care providers, so does it increase opportunities for relationships with peers and other children.

Developmental Functions of Peer Relationships

The opportunity to interact with peers in child care settings may be especially valuable for children from small families who do not have siblings and thus would not otherwise interact with developmentally matched partners who, unlike adults and children, have similar levels of social understanding and behavior. Peer interactions permit communications from which children gain insight into other children's daily lives, share experiences, and learn from one another. These exchanges most often occur during pretend play (e.g., McCune, 1995), when children as young as 2 years can relate to the fictive play scenarios of their partners, agreeing on themes, roles, and rules and adjusting them as necessary in the course of play. Pretend play is more successful when peers or siblings rather than adults (even mothers) are involved (Brown, Donelan-McCall & Dunn, 1996). Peer interactions also provide a protected environment in which children can deal with emotions and explore intimate themes. For example, when children elaborate being-afraid-of-the dark themes with their peers, the peers' emotional supportiveness determines whether the peers are trusted and whether the interactions continue (Hughes & Dunn, 1997).

Mutual interests characterize early friendships and distinguish them from other peer relationships. When Werebe and Baudonniere (1991) observed two young friends interacting in a laboratory playroom with another peer, for example, interactions between the friends were more specific, complex, and extended than interactions with the other child, even though the children interacted in a friendly manner with the unfamiliar peer. Peer interactions also provide opportunities to test social exchange strategies, explore social bids and dialogue structures, develop rules, and deal with compromises. Peer conflicts are especially important because they promote children's awareness of discrepancies between their intentions and those of their peers. Whereas conflicts with adults lead children to merely accept the adults' more competent solutions, conflicts among peers are more challenging developmentally because they force children to compromise if they want interactions to continue (Hartup & Moore, 1990). Peer interactions also play an important role in the formation of social identity, particularly with respect to gender. Peer groups tend to be structured by gender, and this may foster the imitation of same-sex behaviors as well as gender identification (Maccoby, 1998).

Developmental Course of Peer Relations

Peers are not only attractive to growing children but also become sources of social, emotional, and cognitive stimulation and support, particularly when stable and enduring relationships develop. Patterns of reciprocal interaction are evident in child care facilities even among toddlers (e.g., Brownell & Carriger, 1990; Finkelstein, Dent, Gallacher, & Ramey, 1978; Rubenstein & Howes, 1976; Vandell & Wilson, 1987), although these early interactions typically involve simple rituals because infants and toddlers have difficulty coordinating their actions with peers. The everyday encounters with peers made possible by enrollment in child care may facilitate the acquisition of social skills, however.

As soon as children acquire the ability to reference and transform actions in ways that other children understand, they begin to imitate one another. Thereafter, imaginative play allows preschoolers to share meanings and learn from each other (e.g., Hartup & Moore, 1990; McCune, 1995; Mueller, 1989). Regular interactions with the same peers permit children to develop friendships characterized by specific patterns of interaction (Kenny & La Voie, 1984). Describing the early development of friendships among 2-year-olds over a 10-month period, Whaley and Rubenstein (1994) noted striking elements of intimacy (the dyad's tendency to separate itself from other peers), similarity (the tendency to imitate the other's behavior and to create routines based on them), loyalty (the tendency to defend one another against other peers), and support (the tendency to sooth each other when they were distressed). Based on such observations of children in child care facilities, Howes (1996) reported that the first friendships appear after age 2, mainly involve one or two same-sex peers, and are stable over periods of 1 to 2 years.

It seems likely that sensitive care providers might help young children to cope with and learn from unsuccessful interactions with peers, but little relevant research has been conducted. Interestingly, Lollis (1990) found no differences in the quality of early peer interactions when adults either intervened by offering cautious support (minimal intervention group) or by getting actively involved (interactive intervention group). When the adults left, however, peers in the interactive intervention group were able to maintain high levels of play longer. Rubin, Hastings, Chen, Stewart, and McNi-

chol (1998) found that controlling and intrusive adult behaviors were associated with aggressive interactions among peers.

Preconditions for Peer Relationships in Child Care

The development of relationships with peers is affected not only by specific developmental attainments, especially in the social-cognitive and social-emotional realms, but also by socialization practices within the family (e.g., NICHD Early Child Care Research Network, 2001a). Child-parent relationships are believed to have the greatest impact on peer relationships, such that children who experience warm parenting styles and harmonious families tend to be well adjusted socially, unaggressive, and popular (e.g., Ladd & Le Sieur, 1995). Moreover, maternal sensitivity predicts peer competence in a variety of settings, including child care facilities (NICHD Early Child Care Research Network, 2001a). Attachment theorists have further predicted that children who have secure relationships with their parents should be sociable and socially competent (e.g., Elicker, Englund, & Sroufe, 1992; Sroufe, 2000), but the empirical evidence is contradictory (e.g., NICHD Early Child Care Research Network, 1998a), suggesting that parent-child relationships are not the only family factors affecting the peer system. For example, children also benefit from relationships with siblings, from whom they learn (among other things) how to deal with disrupted interactions (J. Dunn, Creps, & Brown, 1996). Children with siblings may also have more appropriate expectations of peers and thus be better prepared to interact with peers in child care settings than children who have no siblings (Hoff-Ginsberg & Krueger, 1991; Perner, Ruffman, & Leekam, 1994).

Many of the skills that children use when interacting with parents are not directly transferable to interactions with peers (e.g., Mueller, 1989; Vandell & Wilson, 1987). It is thus important to understand the unique features of peer culture that shape group dynamics in child care settings. Clearly, to form enduring relationships with peers, children must not only understand their peers' intentions and feelings but also orient their own intentions and feelings accordingly (e.g., Brown et al., 1996). Observing preschoolers in child care, Denham and her colleagues (Denham & Holt, 1993; Denham et al., 2001) described contrasting patterns of emotional communication—happy-positive and angry-negative—that reliably differentiated groups of children. These patterns were so pervasive that they even differentiated subgroups and affected the children's popularity. The ability to regulate emotions and adjust behavior to changing demands and circumstances also affects the quality of peer relationships (Fabes et al., 1999; Raver, Blackburn, Bancroft, & Torp, 1999; Thompson, 1993; Walden, Lemerise, & Smith, 1999).

Prosocial and Agonistic Interactions with Peers in Child Care

Empathetic and prosocial behaviors first appear between 12 and 18 months of age, when infants recognize their individuality, become aware of their feelings, and begin to realize that others have feelings as well (Eisenberg, Shea, Carlo, & Knight, 1991). In group care settings, 2-year-olds no longer respond contagiously to their peers' emotions, crying and wanting to be soothed when their peers cry. Instead, toddlers observe their peers' negative emotions carefully and attempt to respond appropriately (e.g., Bischof-Koehler, 1991). Their responses are typically prosocial (soothing, helping, giving or sharing) and gender-differentiated: Girls respond prosocially to peers more often than boys do.

The development of prosocial behaviors in group settings has been the focus of little systematic research, however. Hay and her colleagues (Hay, 1994; Hay, Castle, Davies, Demetriou, & Stimson, 1999) have shown that children adjust behaviorally to the demands of particular situations and persons and thus come to respond empathically in more clearly defined circumstances as they grow older. Other researchers have described increases in prosocial behaviors as a result of successful socialization (Eisenberg & Fabes, 1998; Zahn-Waxler, Radke-Yarrow, Wagner, & Chapman, 1992), yet others have reported no associations between child age and prosocial behavior (e.g., Farver & Branstetter, 1994), even though toddlers understand the concept of empathy and base friendships on it.

Peer relationships are frequently characterized by conflicts. In the early years (1 to 4 years), conflicts often emerge when children simultaneously want the same toys (e.g., Caplan, Vespo, Pedersen, & Hay, 1991; Hay, Castle, & Davies, 2000; O'Brien, Roy, Jacobs, Macaluso, & Peyton, 1999). Caplan et al. have shown that the frequency of possession conflicts does not vary depending on the number of toys available. Indeed, conflict occurred even when identical alternative toys were available! Hay and her colleagues further distinguished between reactive (child snatches the desired toy from a peer) possession conflicts, which involve defense of the child's possessions and thus appear normal, as opposed to proactive (child attacks the peer in anticipation of the latter's desire for a toy) possession conflicts that reflect either misunderstanding of peers' intentions or social dominance strategies, and in both cases presage later aggressiveness (Calkins, Gill, & Williford, 1999).

Students of peer interaction in child care settings seldom encounter the types of intimidating or hurtful aggressiveness described by Coie and Dodge (1998) in school-age peer groups. Among preschoolers, however, researchers have identified temperaments that reflect poor inhibitory control and negative emotional expressions (such as anger) that could lead to "high approach-low avoidance" (Fox, 1994) behavior patterns. Such children appear actively involved in interactions with peers, although their social skills are inadequate. When they need to cope with conflicts and frustrations, for example, these children cannot fall back on positive interaction strategies and thus often fail to maintain constructive interactions with their peers (Rubin et al., 1998; Shaw, Keenan, & Vondra, 1994). Although such children may have difficulty being accepted by other children, they do appear to develop friendships.

The Impact of Child Care on Peer Relationships

Because many parents choose child care arrangements in the belief that peer interactions play an important role in social development, especially by fostering the development of empathy and the acquisition of social skills, it was surprising when some early reports suggested that infant child care was associated with increased aggressiveness toward peers (see review by Clarke-Stewart, 1988). However, most of these studies involved unrepresentative high-risk samples and did not control for family variables, or were conducted in facilities providing care of low quality (e.g., Haskins, 1985; Vandell & Corasaniti, 1990b). Other researchers reported no increases in aggression and assertiveness on the part of children who had experienced infant child care (e.g., Hegland & Rix, 1990).

Family experiences and children's personalities indeed affect levels of agonistic interactions with peers in child care settings. For example, Klimes-Dougan and Kistner (1990) reported that infants from disadvantaged families responded to signals of distress from their peers with anxiety, anger, and physical attacks, even when the peers had previously interacted with them prosocially. Watamura, Donzella, Alwin, and Gunnar (2003) found that shy and fearful children had special difficulty interacting with more socially competent children. This made child care settings more stressful for them and could thus lead to social isolation and, perhaps, internalizing behavior problems if care providers did not intervene successfully.

According to Farver and Branstetter (1994), prosocial behaviors with peers are associated with positive expectations of peers' behaviors, friendship formation, and easy temperaments, suggesting that care providers may need to focus special attention on children with difficult behavioral dispositions or adverse family backgrounds. Unsatisfactory relationships with peers may develop when care providers fail to provide adequate and appropriate supervision. For example, Howes and Hamilton (1993) found significant correlations between peer aggression and staff turnover in a longitudinal study of children ages 1 to 4 years, and Kienbaum (2001) described positive associations between warm care provider behaviors and prosocial behaviors among kindergartners. In a longitudinal study, Howes, Hamilton, and Matheson (1994) followed 48 children who entered full-time child care (either center- or home-based) in the 1st year of life (the average age at enrollment was 5 months). The first data collection took place 1 year after enrollment and subsequent data gathering occurred every 6 months thereafter. The more secure the child-care provider relationship, the more complex and gregarious and the less aggressive was the play observed with peers at age 4, whereas dependence on care providers was associated with social withdrawal and hostile aggressive behaviors. These predictive associations parallel other reports that preschoolers who have secure relations with their teachers and care providers are more socially competent with peers (e.g., Howes, 1997; Mitchell-Copeland, Denham, & DeMulder, 1997; Oppenheim et al., 1988; Pianta & Nimetz, 1991). In addition, gendered cultures develop in the preschool years, influencing children's relationships with (overwhelmingly female) care providers in different ways (see "Relationships with Care Providers"). Care providers should thus be aware of these processes and strive to build secure relationships with both girls and boys in their care.

The quality of interactions with peers is also affected by group characteristics. Unstable and large groups may leave peers to negotiate conflicts in isolation, whereas stable small groups delineate domains of conflict clearly and allow care providers to intervene promptly and effectively. J. J. Campbell, Lamb, and Hwang (2000) showed that such group characteristics significantly affected the quality of early peer interactions. Stimulating programs also help to minimize peer conflict at every age. For example, M. K. Rosenthal (1994) reported that children in home-based care developed more positive relationships with their peers when care providers organized group activities on a regular basis. In selected centers providing care of excellent quality, Rubenstein and Howes (1979) noted that conflicts with peers were infrequent, whereas home-reared counterparts and peers in other centers experienced conflict more frequently. These results underscore the benefits of regular positive encounters with peers in stable small groups and may explain why children appear more sociable and popular when they have been exposed to regular child care of high quality from infancy (Andersson, 1992; Field, 1991a; Howes, 1990).

The effects of many child care characteristics remain unclear or unknown, however. For example, whereas many American researchers advocate small groups, large groups with low adult-child ratios are preferred in some countries, because small groups are believed to impede positive group dynamics (Boocock, 1995). Other researchers have asked whether same-age or mixed-age groups best support peer interactions (e.g., Goldman, 1981; Rothstein-Fisch & Howes, 1988). Howes and her colleagues reported peer interactions of higher quality in mixed-age groups in which older children can serve as models for younger children (Howes & Farver, 1987), whereas children in same-age groups experienced more reciprocal interactions (Howes & Rubenstein, 1981). Nevertheless, when Bailey, Burchinal, and McWilliam (1993) compared the development of social competence in 2- to 4-year-olds from same-age and mixed-age groups longitudinally, they found no differences. Gender and cultures in preschool may promote different pathways for boys and girls, however. If peer acceptance is correlated with age in mixed-age groups (Lemerise, 1997), for example, and, as reported earlier, peer acceptance of boys but not of girls is correlated with dominance ranking (Sebanc et al., 2003), then younger boys might do better in same-age groups, whereas girls would function equally well in same- and mixed-age groups.

Clearly, we do not understand group dynamics in child care very well and have inadequately conceptualized the ways care providers can shape children's peer relationships while effectively supervising groups of young children. In addition to continued research on care providers' behaviors and child-care provider attachments, research is needed on group dynamics and the "connectedness" of individuals in child care centers (Maccoby & Lewis, 2003).

Behavior Problems, Compliance, and Personal Maturity

Independent of the social relationships potentiated by child care, many researchers have examined the effect on children behavioral tendencies and adjustment.

Compliance with Parents and Care Providers

Researchers such as Belsky (1988, 1989) have portrayed insecure infant-mother attachments as a likely consequence of early and extensive nonmaternal care and have argued that as a result, noncompliance is likely to follow enrollment in child care (Ainsworth et al., 1978; Arend, Gove, & Sroufe, 1979; Londerville & Main, 1981). Consistent with this hypothesis, the results of several early studies suggested that nonmaternal child care was associated with noncompliance, both at home and in child care centers (Belsky & Eggebeen, 1991; Belsky, Woodworth, & Crnic, 1996; Crockenberg & Litman, 1991; Finkelstein, 1982; Rubenstein, Howes, & Boyle, 1981; Schwarz, Strickland, & Krolick, 1974; Thornburg, Pearl, Crompton, & Ispa, 1990; Vandell & Corasaniti, 1990a, 1990b).

In a study of 18-, 24-, 30-, and 36-month-olds assessed at home, in their child care centers, and in a standardized laboratory situation, however, Howes and Olenick (1986) reported that compliance with adult requests at home and in the laboratory did not vary depending on the quality of out-of-home care or even on whether the children had any regular out-of-home care experiences, although children without child care experiences were least likely to regulate their own behavior and emotions in the laboratory. In the laboratory, children from high-quality centers were more compliant and less resistant than children in low-quality centers. In exploratory regression analyses, the quality of center care was the most powerful predictor of compliance, but unfortunately, the different measures of compliance were not stable over situations, making it inappropriate to speak of compliance and noncompliance as traits. Simi-

lar findings were obtained in the Goteborg Child Care Study, in which compliance with mother's requests were assessed in home observations when the children were 28 and 40 months of age (Ketterlinus, Bookstein, Sampson, & Lamb, 1989; Sternberg et al., 1991). No reliable dimension of compliance was evident at 28 months, but individual differences in noncompliance at 40 months were predicted by the quality of both home and alternative care and by the amount of nonparental care received before age 2. Compliance was highly correlated with the degree of parent-child harmony, suggesting that compliance is best viewed as an aspect of cooperation with the parents rather than as a characteristic of the individual child. Subsequently, Prodromidis, Lamb, Sternberg, Hwang, and Broberg (1995) supplemented the observational measures of mother-child compliance with ratings made by teachers and parents through 80 months of age. Once again, no consistent or reliable dimension was evident at 28 months; indices of compliance with teachers and mothers loaded on the same factor but were not stable over time and were uncorrelated with any aspects of the children's child care histories. Noncompliant children received care of poorer quality at home and were more likely to have controlling parents regardless of their child care experiences.

Like Prodromidis et al. (1995) and Sternberg et al. (1991), Clarke-Stewart et al. (1994) reported that different indices of compliance did not form a single coherent dimension. In this study, middle-class 2- to 4-year-old children in child care, especially those in center care, were more compliant with unfamiliar experimenters than those in the exclusive care of their parents, especially when the children experienced intermediate amounts of high-quality care on a regular basis (10 to 30 hours per week). Observed levels of compliance with parents at home were also higher for children in child care, whereas measures of family characteristics and parental behavior had a greater impact on compliance than child care variables did. Similar results were obtained in the large multisite study undertaken by the NICHD Early Child Care Research Network (1998a, p. 1164): "Although 2-year-olds who spent more time in nonmaternal care were reported by their mothers to be less cooperative and by their caregivers to exhibit more behavior problems . . . by the time the children were 3 years of age, no significant effects of amount of child care experience could be detected." Measure of the quality of care had very little impact on measures of the children's behavior in this study, whereas measures of the quality of home care and child-mother relationships were more strongly related to measures of the children's behavior. DeSchipper, Tavecchio, van IJzendoorn, and Linting (2003) reported that Dutch infants and toddlers were more noncompliant with care providers the more their child care schedules varied from day to day, although these effects were not statistically significant. Feldman and Klein (2003) reported that Israeli toddlers were similarly compliant with mothers, fathers, and care providers, that warm adult control was the most reliable correlate of child compliance, and that maternal sensitivity predicted compliance with care providers.

Taken together, these reports reveal a tendency for early enrollment in child care to be associated with noncompliance and less harmonious child-mother interactions at home. However, several contradictory findings and evidence that noncompliance does not constitute a coherent cross-situational trait imply that the association is context-specific and poorly understood. This signals the need for further efforts to understand the origins, reliability, and implications of these potentially important associations.

Behavior Problems

Research on the effects of child care on behavior problems other than compliance has also yielded results that at first glance appear inconsistent. On the one hand, Balleyguier (1988) reported that French infants in day care cried more, threw more tantrums, and were more oppositional at home during the 2nd year of life than were those who remained in the exclusive care of their parents. Similarly, in a large retrospective study, Bates et al. (1994) assessed associations between the extent of nonmaternal care in the 1st, 2nd to 4th, and 5th year of life and scores on multiple teacher- and mother-reported indices of adjustment after controlling for family background, gender, and other possible correlates. The extent of care in the most recent period was most influential, with children who were currently in child care appearing to be most poorly adjusted. In addition, infant care predicted less positive adjustment in kindergarten even after the effects of later care histories were taken into account. Interestingly, however, greater child care exposure was associated with teacher reports of fewer internalizing symptoms (e.g., somatic complaints, anxiety, depression). And in the multisite EPPE Project, enrollment in group care prior to the age of 2 was associated with increased behavior problems when these British

children were 3 and 5 years of age (Sylva et al., 2004). Analyzing data from the National Longitudinal Study of Youth (NLSY), furthermore, Baydar and Brooks-Gunn (1991) reported that White 4-year-olds who began receiving nonmaternal care in the 1st year were believed by their mother to have more behavior problems than those who began receiving nonmaternal care later, or not at all. By contrast, using the same data set but different statistical controls, Ketterlinus, Henderson, and Lamb (1992) reported that children who started child care in the 1st or 2nd year of life and were in day care for at least 2 years did not have more reported behavior problems than children who experienced no day care. Ephemeral effects of nonparental care on behavioral problems were also suggested by Borge and Melhuish (1995), who followed all the children in a rural Norwegian community from their 4th birthday through third grade. Behavior problems were no more common at either 4 or 8 years of age among those who had received nonmaternal care in their first 3 years. Children who experienced more center care between ages 4 and 7 had significantly fewer behavior problems at ages 7 and 10 years in the views of both mothers and teachers, even though there was little association between the behavior problems reported by mothers and teachers. Teachers, but not parents, reported that children who experienced more day care before 4 years of age behaved more poorly at age 10.

In a retrospective study of 6- to 12-year-olds in middle-class families, Burchinal et al. (1995) reported that infant day care had no effect on maternal reports of children's externalizing and internalizing behavior problems, although children with preschool experiences had higher levels of externalizing problems than did children with no preschool experiences, and preschool experiences predicted more positive ratings of social behavior in African American but not White children. High-quality child care, initiated at 12 months of age for preterm low-birthweight infants participating in an intensive intervention study, was even associated with a decline in the incidence of behavior problems reported by mothers when their children were 26 to 36 months old (Brooks-Gunn, Klebanov, Liaw, & Spiker, 1993; Infant Health and Development Program, 1990). And in annual assessments from kindergarten through sixth grade, children from impoverished families who entered child care in infancy did not have more externalizing behavior problems than children who did not receive infant day care (Egeland & Hiester, 1995).

Pierrehumbert (1994; Pierrehumbert & Milhaud, 1994) reported that Swiss children who behaved insecurely with their mother in the Strange Situation at 21 months were rated more aggressive by their mother at 5 years of age unless they had experienced more than average amounts of nonmaternal care in the first 5 years, in which case their levels of aggression were not elevated. In a later study of 89 Swiss families with 3-year-olds, however, Pierrehumbert et al. (2002) reported no association between behavior problems and either the amount or type of nonparental care experienced, although the care providers' values and attitudes were associated in the expected directions with measures of the children's behavior problems. Furthermore, Scarr et al. (1995) reported that length of time in center care had no effect and the observed quality of care had minimal effects on children's behavioral adjustment and manageability as reported by both parents and teachers. Family background (social class, parental stress, ethnicity) accounted for substantial portions of the variance in this large multisite study of infants, toddlers, and preschoolers, however. In addition, Jewsuwan, Luster, and Kostelnik (1993) reported that 3- and 4-year-old children who were rated by their parents as anxious had more difficulty adjusting to preschool, whereas children rated by their parents as sociable had a more positive reaction, especially to their peers. Similarly, DeSchipper, Tavecchio, Van IJzendoorn, and van Zeijl (2004) found that children who had easy temperaments adapted to parallel child care arrangements more readily and had fewer behavior problems than those with difficult temperaments. These results underscore the importance of considering individual differences among children when examining the effects of child care.

Against this confusing background, a recent report from the NICHD Early Child Care Research Network (2003a) attracted considerable attention because of the clear indication that the amount of nonmaternal care in the first 4.5 years of life predicted the level of externalizing behavior problems (including assertiveness, disobedience, and aggression) displayed at home or in kindergarten. The elevated risk of behavior problems on the part of children with extensive child care histories was evident in reports by mothers, care providers, and teachers, and the effects remained significant even when the effects of maternal sensitivity, family background, and the type, quality, and stability of child care were taken into account (see also NICHD Early Child Care Research Network, 1998a, 2002a).

Interestingly, much less attention has been paid to an article published in the same journal (Love et al., 2003) indicating that similar associations were not evident in three other large multisite studies. Love et al. attributed the differences to the fact that the NICHD researchers studied centers that tended to provide care of mediocre quality, whereas the centers he and his coauthors studied provided care of higher quality. Quality of care also proved to be important in another multisite study, this involving children from low-income families in three cities. Votruba-Drzal, Coley, and Chase-Lansdale (2004) reported that 2- to 4-year-old children had fewer externalizing and internalizing behavior problems the higher the quality of out-of-home care experienced, and for these children, increases in the amount of time spent in nonparental care facilities had a salutary effect, rather than the adverse effect reported by the NICHD Early Child Care Research Network (2003a). Boys, in particular, benefited from care of higher quality. In a similar multisite study of 4-year-olds, Loeb, Fuller, Kagan, and Carrol (2004) found that children in family day care settings had more behavior problems than children in other types of care, especially those who were cared for by individual relatives. In the NICHD Early Child Care Study (2004), however, high-quality child care did not appear to moderate the adverse effects of family risk factors, except that 3-year-olds from minority and single-parent families who received low-quality nonparental care were rated as less prosocial by their mother. Overall, the results of the NICHD Early Child Care Study confirmed that family background and relationship factors had a greater impact on the children's adjustment than either the extent or quality of nonparental child care, although the extent of care had a significant, negative, effect.

In sum, whether or not it is mediated through the quality of attachments to care providers, the quality of nonparental child care appears to modulate the effects of nonparental child care on many aspects of child behavior and adjustment, although family experiences appear to have the most important impact on child behavior. Thus, children who have experienced nonparental care from infancy tend to be more aggressive, more assertive, and less compliant with adults than peers who have not had these experiences, but the associations are weaker, if not nonexistent, when the quality of care is better. Effects on noncompliance with adults are not as clear, however, both because compliance and noncompliance have been studied less extensively and because noncompliance appears to be situation- and relationship-specific rather than trait-like. Unfortunately, many of the studies focused on behavior problems have not assessed quality of care systematically, and the actual behavior problems at issue are a heterogeneous melange, including poor relationships with peers, aggression, and noncompliance.

Personal Maturity

The personal maturity of children in day care has not often been studied, although there is some evidence that nonparental care of high quality fosters personality development. In the Goteborg Child Care Study, mothers described the children's personalities at 28 and 40 months of age using Block and Block's (1980) California Child Q-set (CCQ). Their ratings were used to generate scores for the children's ego resilience, ego control, and field independence (Broberg et al., 1989; Lamb, Hwang, Bookstein, et al., 1988; Lamb, Hwang, Broberg, & Brookstein, 1988). Perceived personality maturity was quite stable over time and was best predicted by observational measures of the quality of care received at home and in the alternative care settings. The children viewed as most mature by mothers were those who had received care of higher quality from nonparental care providers as well as from their parents. There were no differences between children in the home-based care, family care, and center care groups on any of the personality measures at either age.

Most (87%) of the children in this study were reassessed immediately prior to enrollment in first grade (80 months of age) and toward the end of second grade (101 months of age). Once again, personal maturity was assessed using the CCQ, but a different pattern of results was now evident. Children who had been enrolled since toddlerhood in home-based child care settings appeared less mature than those in the other groups (Wessels, Lamb, Hwang, & Broberg, 1997). Over time, in addition, ego undercontrol decreased less, whereas ego resilience and field independence increased less in the children who had received home-based care than in those who had remained at home with their parents or attended child care centers.

No other researchers have explored type of care effects, and most have examined contemporaneous associations rather than longitudinal relations. Hestenes, Kontos, and Bryan (1993) showed that 3- to 5-year-olds expressed more positive affect when their child care arrangements were of higher quality. The appropriate-

ness of the adults' behavior, along with the extent to which they manifested high levels of engagement, was especially significant. Positive self-perceptions were also correlated with high-quality care, even after controlling for differences in social class, ethnicity, and family background, in a large-scale study of infants, toddlers, and preschoolers in child care centers (*Cost, Quality, and Child Outcomes in Child Care Centers*, 1995). Reynolds (1994) reported that preschool and elementary school intervention were associated with improved teacher ratings on various indices of mature adjustment to school in the fifth grade. And, as discussed earlier (see section on "Relationships with Care Providers"), children who had secure relationships with their care providers were more ego-resilient and more appropriately ego-controlled than those who had insecure relationships (Howes, Matheson, et al., 1994).

In sum, although the number of studies is quite small, the available evidence suggests that center care of high quality has positive effects on personal maturity, whereas children receiving care of lower quality tend to be less mature. Further exploration in large samples is called for, however, particularly in light of Wessels et al.'s (1997) findings that the effects of quality diminish over time.

Cognitive and Linguistic Competence

Many researchers have studied the effects of child care arrangements or children's cognitive and linguistic competence. Only over time have the findings revealed a clear pattern.

Early Findings

At first glance, research over the past 15 years on the effects of nonmaternal care on cognitive and linguistic competence appears to have yielded quite contradictory and inconsistent results. These apparent inconsistencies underscore the fact that the effects of child care must be viewed in the context of a complex constellation of phenomena, including family and parent characteristics as well as characteristics of the child care arrangements. When all of these factors are taken into account, a much clearer picture of child care and its impact emerges. In this subsection, we first review research on the effects of standard or community child care arrangements before turning to studies focused on child care programs specifically designed to enhance the development of children whose circumstances place them at risk of later academic failure.

Some early researchers reported that child care had negative effects on cognitive development. In a retrospective study of third graders, for example, Vandell and Corasaniti (1990a, 1990b) reported that extensive care beginning in infancy was associated with poorer scores on standardized measures of cognitive development, and in a smaller study of Swiss infants, nonmaternal infant child care was associated with lower cognitive test performance at age 2 (Pierrehumbert, Ramstein, & Karmaniola, 1995). Using data from the NLSY ($N = 1,181$), Brooks-Gunn and her colleagues (e.g., Baydar & Brooks-Gunn, 1991; Brooks-Gunn, Han, & Waldfogel, 2002) reported that maternal employment during the 1st year of life was associated with poorer cognitive abilities in 3- and 4-year-olds, and Desai, Chase-Lansdale, and Michael (1989) reported poorer verbal abilities on the part of boys in the sample. The children received varying types of early nonmaternal care (often by relatives), and few of the children were enrolled in center-based care during the 1st year of life.

Other early researchers reported neither positive nor negative effects. Thornburg et al. (1990), for example, found that early child care (full or part time, initiated before or after infancy) did not affect the cognitive achievement scores of a large group of Missouri kindergartners. Likewise, Ackerman-Ross and Khanna (1989) reported no differences in receptive language, expressive language, and IQ between middle-class 3-year-olds who either remained home or received child care beginning in infancy. Burchinal et al. (1995) found only weak positive associations between preschool or center-based child care and either cognitive or linguistic performance scores Wechsler Intelligence Scales for Children-Revised and Problem Picture Vocabulary Test (WISC-R and PPVT scores) at 6 to 12 years of age in a sample of middle-class children.

By contrast, Clarke-Stewart (1987; Clarke-Stewart et al., 1994) reported that middle-class 2- to 4-year-old children in centers scored better on many measures of cognitive development than children who remained in the exclusive care of their parents, had in-home sitters, or were in home-based care, and that the effects were greater in centers of higher quality (see later discussion). Another prospective longitudinal study of children from educationally advantaged backgrounds revealed that boys, but not girls, who attended a 1-year preschool program performed better on a battery of

achievement measures administered in second and third grade (Larsen & Robinson, 1989). In Sweden, Broberg, Hwang, Lamb, and Bookstein (1990) assessed verbal intelligence when the children participating in the Goteborg Child Care Study were nearing the end of second grade (average age 101 months). The children's performance on standardized measures of cognitive ability was predicted by the number of months the children had spent in center-based care before 3.5 years of age. By contrast, children in home-based care performed more poorly than those in the center-based care and home-only comparison groups. In a retrospective study, Andersson (1989, 1992) similarly found that Swedish children who entered child care in infancy scored significantly better on standardized measures of cognitive ability and teacher ratings of academic achievement at both 8 and 13 years of age, even after controlling for differences in their family backgrounds. These results were largely consistent with those of studies from Norway (Hartmann, 1991), New Zealand (A. B. Smith, Inder, & Ratcliff, 1993), and Britain (Wadsworth, 1986).

Differential rates of illness may account for some of the inconsistencies evident in this literature. For example, Feagans, Kipp, and Blood (1994) showed that, when children in child care had chronic ear infections, they were much less likely to pay attention during book-reading sessions than children without ear infections. These children were also rated more distractible and inattentive by their mother. Unfortunately, researchers have paid little attention to the role that illness may play in mediating the effects of child care. Children in group care settings are obviously more susceptible to illness and infection than children who are exposed to fewer sources of possible infection, and this might work to children's disadvantage, especially in the first 2 years of life, when the immune system is still immature.

Reflecting the inconsistencies summarized here, a meta-analysis of 59 studies conducted by Erel et al. (2000) revealed no reliable differences in cognitive competence between children with and without histories of nonparental child care. If one focuses on studies conducted in Europe, where the quality of child care tends to be higher, positive effects on children's cognitive and linguistic outcomes have been reported more consistently, however (Boocock, 1995; Scarr, 1998). For example, Sylva et al. (2004) found that preschool experiences, especially in high-quality settings, enhanced the academic and cognitive performance of children in the large multisite EPPE study, with benefits evident during the preschool years as well as when the children were 5 and 7 years old. As we note later, effects generally appear to differ depending on the backgrounds of the children involved as well, with children from disadvantaged backgrounds more likely to benefit then those from more advantaged backgrounds unless the care is of very high quality, in which case all children may benefit.

Children from Low-Income Families

As discussed in the section on enrichment programs, many researchers in the United States have shown that children from low-income families benefit from participation in programs, such as Head Start and Early Head Start, designed to enhance the school readiness and academic performance of children from disadvantaged family backgrounds (Spieker, Nelson, Petras, Jolley, & Barnard, 2003). However, these effects are often attenuated over time when not supplemented by continued enrichment.

Child care arrangements can mitigate the adverse effects of unstimulating or confusing family environments on cognitive and linguistic development even when special intervention programs are not involved. In a study focused on low-income mothers and their second graders, for example, Vandell and Ramanan (1992) reported that maternal employment in the first 3 years was associated with superior academic performance, especially when the mother remained employed for the remainder of the preschool years. Similarly, center care of the quality typically available in poor communities in the United States had positive effects on development over the first 3 to 4 years of life for children from low-income families (Loeb et al., 2004). Some preschool enrichment programs are not stimulating enough to enhance the competencies of children from advantaged backgrounds, however. For example, Caughy, DiPietro, and Strobino (1994) reported that enrollment in child care before age 1 was associated with better reading recognition scores for 5- and 6-year-old children from impoverished backgrounds but poorer scores for children from more advantaged backgrounds. Center-based care begun in the first 3 years was also associated with higher math performance scores in children from impoverished backgrounds and lower math scores for children from more stimulating homes. Children from more disadvantaged backgrounds also benefited more from preschool experiences than did peers from more advantaged backgrounds in the large EPPE study conducted in Great Britain (Sylva et al., 2004). Likewise, African American but not White children benefited from preschool in

a study of middle-class 6- to 12-year-olds conducted by Burchinal et al. (1995).

Overall, it seems that children from low-income families benefit when they attend stimulating child care centers. By contrast, recent evaluations of both Sure Start in the UK and Early Head Start in the USA found that early intervention had negative effects on children from the most disadvantaged backgrounds (Belsky et al., 2005; Early Head Start Research and Evaluation Project, 2002a). Children from more advantaged backgrounds do not consistently profit from child care in this way, presumably because they enjoy rich stimulating environments at home. Indeed, early and extensive child care can even have negative effects, especially on language development, when the benefits attributable to growing up in advantaged families are attenuated by child care (Burchinal, Peisner-Feinberg, Bryant, & Clifford, 2000). Children from all family backgrounds appear to benefit when child care is of high quality, however. Positive family factors (such as greater family income, more sensitive mothering, and less authoritarian child-rearing attitudes) are associated with indices of more positive child functioning and continue to affect children positively even when they spend much time in child care settings (NICHD Early Child Care Research Network, 1998b, 2001c). Indeed, family factors are more reliable predictors of children's cognitive competencies than the quality or type of nonparental child care (NICHD Early Child Care Research Network, 2002a).

Quality and Types of Child Care

Higher-quality care is positively associated with better cognitive and language development, whereas lower-quality care is associated with poorer outcomes. Such findings have been obtained in the Bermuda Study (McCartney, 1984; Phillips, McCartney, & Scarr, 1987), the Chicago Study (Clarke-Stewart, 1987), the Child Care and Family Study (Kontos et al., 1994), the Cost, Quality, and Child Outcomes Study (Peisner-Feinberg & Burchinal, 1997), the Goteborg Child Care Study (Broberg et al., 1990; Broberg, Wessels, Lamb, & Hwang, 1997), the NICHD Study of Early Child Care (NICHD Early Child Care Research Network, 1994, 1999b, 2003b, in press), the EPPE Study (Melhuish, Sylvia et al., 2001; Sammons et al., 2002, 2003; Sylva et al., 2004), and in a large multisite study in Northern Ireland (Melhuish, Quinn et al., 2001; Melhuish et al., 2002a, 2002b), as well as in several smaller studies (Field, 1991a; Hartmann, 1995). Similar results have been reported internationally regardless of how quality is measured or of the specific types of educational programs implemented (Boocock, 1995; Tietze & Cryer, 1999). The effects diminish over time, however, presumably because the beneficial effects of high-quality care are undercut by increasing exposure to less stimulating environments, both at home and at school.

With regard to the characteristics of cognitively stimulating environments, high-quality cognitive and linguistic stimulation is more likely when positive adult-child relationships (Meins, 1997; van IJzendoorn, Dijkstra, & Bus, 1995; Williams & Sternberg, 2002) and egalitarian peer interactions (see "Relationships with Peers") prevail. Not surprisingly, therefore, the NICHD Early Child Care Research Network's (2002a) structural equation model revealed that both care provider training and adult-child ratios affected cognitive competence via their impact on the quality of care (i.e., care providers' sensitivity to nondistress, detachment, stimulation of cognitive development, and intrusiveness; classroom characteristics of chaos, overcontrol, and emotional climate; see also Burchinal et al., 2000; Peisner-Feinberg et al., 2001). Likewise, home-based care providers who were better educated (more recent and higher levels of training) provided richer learning environments as well as warmer and more 9sensitive care. The associations were amplified when settings had groups of the recommended sizes (Clarke-Stewart et al., 2002).

We might expect that any effects of the type of care would vary depending on the differential opportunities for child-care provider relationships in center-based and home-based setting (see "Relationships with Care Providers"). Unfortunately, variations in the quality of care received and the fact that some children experience a variety of care settings either sequentially or simultaneously complicates research on these topics, but the results of the NICHD Early Child Care Research Network study (2000c) provide some insight into the relative merits of home-based and center-based care of equivalent quality. As in other studies (Broberg et al., 1997; Burchinal et al., 1995; Caughy et al., 1994; Clarke-Stewart et al., 1994; NICHD Early Child Care Research Network, 2002b, 2003b), center-based care appears to have some advantage over home-based care with respect to cognitive and language development, perhaps because children in centers are typically exposed to a richer language environment and have more opportunities to encounter developmentally stimulating events than children in less formal settings. Children in center-based care are also more likely than those in home-based care

to have peers who engage them in discussions and arguments that promote the effective use of language.

Researchers have also asked whether experiences in child care during specific developmental periods have distinctive effects. In the NICHD study (NICHD Early Child Care Research Network, 2000c) as well as in studies of maternal employment (Baydar & Brooks-Gunn, 1991; Brooks-Gunn et al., 2002), sensitive care and individual language stimulation during the first 2 years had a greater effect on subsequent cognitive and linguistic functioning than high-quality parenting in later years (Siegel, 1999). In addition, children whose mothers were not employed full time and children in home-based child care had better cognitive and language skills at age 3 than those who experienced other types of high-quality care. Perhaps as a result, the positive effects of home-based nonparental care on cognitive and linguistic development are evident at 24 and 36 but not 54 months, by which time peer (as opposed to adult) stimulation starts to become more important (NICHD Early Child Care Research Network, 2000c).

Enrichment Programs

The effects of child care on diverse aspects of development, but especially cognitive skills and academic performance, have also been elucidated by studying the effects of especially designed enrichment programs, particularly in the United States.

History of Head Start Programs

Numerous attempts have been made to evaluate the long- and short-term effects of compensatory enrichment programs for children from disadvantaged backgrounds. The amount of attention paid to this topic reflects in large part the tremendously optimistic fanfare that accompanied the rapid nationwide expansion of these programs in the mid-1960s as part of President Johnson's twin crusades, the Great Society and the War on Poverty (Steiner, 1976; Zigler & Muenchow, 1992; Zigler & Valentine, 1979). In this context, the establishment of Head Start in 1965 took and retains center stage in U.S. efforts to enhance the welfare of its children. Because of its tremendous costs and broad constituency, furthermore, the debates have been prolonged, although systematic efforts to study the effects of Head Start have been surprisingly inadequate.

In the late 1950s, social scientists began to marshal evidence suggesting that human abilities were more pliable than previously recognized (e.g., Bloom, 1964; Hunt, 1961). In response to this, a small number of model preschool programs were developed and evaluated. The results obtained documented the value of compensatory education, although most researchers sought primarily to contrast the relative efficacy of different curricula and pedagogical approaches rather than the utility of compensatory preschool education per se (e.g., Bereiter & Engelmann, 1966; Caldwell & Richmond, 1968; Copple, Sigel, & Saunders, 1984; Gray & Klaus, 1965; Stanley, 1973). Before this programmatic research had advanced enough to permit the evaluation and fine-tuning of intensive model interventions, political pressures and the availability of funds led to the premature launching of Head Start on a nationwide scale. Originally intended as a summer-long pilot program for children from impoverished backgrounds, Head Start quickly became a year-round program attended by preschoolers in the year or two before they entered the school system. A half-million children were enrolled by the summer of 1965, and by 1998, some 800,000 children attended Head Start programs, mostly for a few hours per day, while some of the mothers attended parent education and skill development classes, often in the same building (Administration for Children & Families, 1999).

Head Start programs have always varied greatly, in large part because federal administrators have explicitly deferred to the grassroots clientele whose loyalty has allowed the program to prosper for 4 decades. Most programs emphasize the direct delivery of services to children, and this is viewed as most effective (S. L. Ramey & Ramey, 1992; Roberts, Casto, Wasik, & Ramey, 1991; Wasik, Ramey, Bryant, & Sparling, 1990). Similarly, parent participation is widely viewed as an important adjunct to successful early intervention programs, but its extent varies greatly from program to program (Comer, 1980; C. Powell & Grantham-McGregor, 1989; D. R. Powell, 1982; Seitz, 1990), and potentially valuable home-visiting components are provided by only a small number of Head Start programs (Roberts & Wasik, 1990, 1994).

Originally intended as a broadly focused compensatory and enrichment program, Head Start's political proponents quickly came to depict it as a program designed (in large part) to enhance children's school performance. Evaluations shortly after enrollment could not, of course, track either behavior or achievement at school, and so the fateful decision was made to measure

IQ, a construct with which psychologists and educators had extensive experience and that they were able to measure quickly and reliably (J. S. Kagan et al., 1969). Unfortunately, this decision and the initial results helped foster unrealistic and simplistic views of the problems posed by poverty, and of their susceptibility to intervention (Sigel, 1990).

Despite evidence that short-term increases in IQ could be attributed to enhanced motivation rather than intelligence (Zigler & Butterfield, 1968), initial reports pleased Head Start's political and academic progenitors: The IQ scores of children in Head Start programs increased over the time they were enrolled, and the IQ scores of children attending Head Start programs were significantly higher than those of comparable children who did not attend the programs. The euphoria quickly faded following publication of the Westinghouse Report in 1969 (Cicirelli, 1969), however. The results of this large multisite evaluation confirmed that children who had attended Head Start programs indeed had higher IQs, although these advantages quickly faded after the children left the programs and entered the regular public school system. The methodological sophistication of the Westinghouse Report was widely criticized at the time (D. T. Campbell & Erlebacher, 1970; Datta, 1976; Lazar, 1981; M. Smith & Bissell, 1970), but similar findings were reported by other researchers (e.g., McKey et al., 1985). Together, these reports fueled (a) criticisms that compensatory education was a wrong-headed failure that should be abandoned (Jensen, 1969; Spitz, 1986); (b) efforts to underscore that the major—nonintellectual—goals of Head Start (such as improved medical, mental health, and dental care) had not been evaluated (D. J. Cohen, Solnit, & Wohlford, 1979; Hale, Seitz, Zigler, 1990; National Head Start Association, 1990; North, 1979; Zigler, Piotrkowski, & Collins, 1994); (c) arguments that practitioners needed to build on the acknowledged short-term contributions of Head Start by complementing them with continuing enrichment following enrollment in public school (Doernberger & Zigler, 1993; S. L. Ramey & Ramey, 1992); (d) recommendations that interventions would be more effective if children were enrolled at much younger ages (S. L. Ramey & Ramey, 1992); and (e) awareness that poverty had multiple facets and impacts, such that amelioration of its effects would require complex, multifaceted, multidisciplinary, and extensive interventions (Sigel, 1990). The emergence in the 1990s of Early Head Start for children under 3 years of age represents one be-lated response to some of these issues, as did the earlier introduction of Parent Child Centers.

Later Evaluations of Preschool Intervention Programs

The Consortium for Longitudinal Studies (1978, 1983; Darlington, Royce, Snipper, Murray, & Lazar, 1980; Lazar, Darlington, Murray, Royce, & Snipper, 1982) followed participants in 11 early intervention studies using a uniform set of measures. Their analyses confirmed that effects on IQ quickly faded following graduation from the programs, although the researchers were able to identify impressive group differences in other aspects of school performance, including retentions in grade and premature school leaving (see also Barnett, 1995; Karoly et al., 1998). Few of these longitudinal studies involve Head Start graduates, in part because assignment to Head Start and comparison groups is not random and in part because there is so much diversity among Head Start programs that consistent effects should perhaps not be expected. Notwithstanding such methodological shortcomings, other reports suggest better school performance on the part of Head Start graduates. For example, Hebbeler (1985), McKey et al. (1985), and Copple, Cline, and Smith (1987) reported that Head Start graduates were more likely than children from comparable backgrounds who did not attend Head Start to be promoted, perform adequately at school, and have adequate nutrition and health care. Because the quality of Head Start programs is so variable, it is possible that the effects of Head Start would appear greater and more enduring if focus was placed on the good programs and their graduates (Gamble & Zigler, 1989). Consistent with this hypothesis, Bryant, Burchinal, Lau, and Sparling (1994) reported that the quality of Head Start classrooms, assessed using Harms and Clifford's (1980) ECERS scales, was correlated with scores on standardized measures of achievement, school readiness, and intelligence at the end of the Head Start year, regardless of the quality of home care. Most of the classrooms were rated "adequate" in quality; none were deemed "developmentally appropriate." Such findings, of course, underscored the need for improvements in the overall quality of Head Start (see also Gamble & Zigler, 1989).

Currie and her colleagues (Currie, 2001; Currie & Thomas, 1995, 1999, 2000; Garces, Thomas, & Currie, 2002) have examined the long-term effects of Head Start not by following graduates and nongraduates over time, but by selecting subjects retrospectively from large, nonexperimental, longitudinal studies such as the National Longitudinal Survey (NLS) and the Panel Study of Income Dynamics (PSID). In their first study, Currie and Thomas (1995) selected children in the NLS who had attended Head Start programs and compared them with siblings who had not been in Head Start, reasoning that the sibling comparisons would control for family background effects. Their analyses revealed the expected increases in test scores associated with Head Start attendance. Currie and Thomas were the first researchers able to compare outcomes for individuals from different racial backgrounds, and they found that the gains associated with Head Start attendance persisted into adolescence for the White children, who continued to experience less in-grade retention, whereas they faded out in the early elementary grades for African American children, probably because the African American children studied attended poorer-quality elementary schools—poorer even than the schools attended by African American children on average (Currie & Thomas, 2000). Similar findings regarding the greater benefits of early intervention for children at greatest risk have been reported by other researchers (Brooks-Gunn, 2003).

In a later study, Whites and African Americans born between 1965 and 1977 were interviewed in the 1995 wave of the PSID, when they ranged between 18 and 29 years of age. After controlling for background variables, Garces et al. (2002) found that Whites who attended Head Start were 20% more likely to complete high school and 28% more likely to attend college than siblings who did not, whereas Head Start attendance had no comparable effect on African Americans. On the other hand, African Americans who attended Head Start were 12% less likely to report being booked or charged with a criminal offense than siblings who did not attend Head Start, and in this case there was no comparable difference among Whites. Using an innovative analytic technique, general growth mixture modeling, Kreisman (2003) likewise showed that different groups of children who attended Head Start had different developmental trajectories, but she was unable to explore the characteristics (e.g., racial background) of children in the different groups.

Of the early intervention programs that have managed to follow their graduates over extended periods of time, most attention has been paid to the Perry Preschool Program in Ypsilanti, Michigan, which began in 1962 (Barnett, 1985, 1993a, 1993b; Berrueta-Clement, Schweinhart, Barnett, Epstein, & Weikart, 1984). One hundred and twenty-eight African American children from low-income families were randomly assigned to control and intervention groups. Beginning when they were 3 to 4 years old, children in the intervention group received 2.5 hours of class instruction per day throughout a 30-week school year, 13 of them for 1 year and 45 of them for 2 years. In addition, mothers and children were visited at home weekly for about 90 minutes. The children and their official records were reevaluated annually through 11 years of age as well as at 14, 15, 19, and 28 years of age using a battery of measures primarily focused on achievement, ability, and school performance (Schweinhart, Barnes, & Weikart, 1993). These data revealed that children in the program had higher achievement scores at ages 9 and 14, were more likely to graduate from high school, were more likely to be employed and not to have been arrested by age 19, earned more, were less likely to have a history of frequent arrests by age 28, and were less likely to go on welfare than those in the comparison group.

Much of the popular attention paid to this program reflects the decision to estimate in dollar terms the costs and benefits of enrollment in the preschool program (Barnett, 1993a, 1993b). The most widely publicized figures suggest that an average investment of $12,356 per child who participated in the program resulted in benefits through age 28 of $70,876. These benefits reflected the additional costs of completed education and higher wages and the lower costs of incarceration and welfare. Benefits are projected to continue as well, presumably justifying an initial investment that was substantially greater than the average cost of typical preschool programs or Head Start programs.

The results of the Perry Preschool Project underscore the potential value of an extended preschool intervention of high quality, but do not reflect the likely effects of large established programs like Head Start, which serve a somewhat different clientele over a briefer period of time with much less rigorous control over quality (Zigler & Styfco, 1994). Greater attention to quality might improve the average effectiveness of early intervention programs like Head Start. Likewise, extension of the programs by enrolling children at younger ages, providing full-day services, and/or continuing to provide enriching services after school enrollment typically enhance the effects of preschool on the intellectual performance of children from impoverished backgrounds (see also Clark & Kirk, 2000; Cryan, Sheehan, Wiechel, & Bandy-Hedden, 1992; Elicker & Mathur, 1997; Fusaro, 1997; Gullo, 2000;

Sheehan, Cryan, Wiechel, & Bandy, 1991; Vecchiotti, 2003), although the large EPPE study showed no differences between the effects of full-day and part-day programs in the United Kingdom (Sylva et al., 2004).

European Intervention Programs

In most European countries, preschool programs (often akin to American kindergarten) are mandatory in the year or years before school officially begins; as a result, the effects of preschool programs on school preparedness have not been studied extensively. Nevertheless, considerable public debate about the structure, components, and goals of these preschool programs is now taking place throughout Europe. Some educators want emphasis placed on cognitive competencies rather than socialization and exploration, and the debate has only become more intense in response to evidence of major cross-cultural variation in the basic reading and mathematics competencies of eighth graders in the 39 industrialized countries studied (OECD, 2002). This has raised questions not only about the quality of the different school systems but also about how preschool programs should prepare children for school. Sure Start programs in the UK have modest but positive effects on most children and mothers, although effects on the most disadvantaged children were negative (Belsky et al., 2005).

Earlier Intervention

C. T. Ramey and his colleagues (C. T. Ramey, 1992; C. T. Ramey & Smith, 1977) have continued to study a small cohort of children who entered the Abecedarian intervention project in North Carolina as infants in the late 1960s. All of the children came from impoverished African American backgrounds. When they were 3 months old, half of the children were enrolled in a full-time, full-year, center-based intervention program designed to prepare them for school, and this program continued until kindergarten. Upon enrollment in kindergarten, half of the children in each group began an intervention program that continued through the first 3 years of elementary school.

In every assessment between 6 and 54 months, a greater proportion of the children in the intervention group had an IQ in the normal range (Martin, Ramey, & Ramey, 1990), and at the time of entry into kindergarten, the children in the experimental group had IQ scores 8.5 points higher than those of children in the comparison group, although the difference narrowed to 5 IQ points by second grade (C. T. Ramey & Campbell,

1984, 1987, 1991, 1992). At the beginning of kindergarten, the children in the enrichment group also performed better on measures of narrative skills than children in the control group, but these differences were no longer evident by the spring (Feagans & Farran, 1994), and other children in their classrooms performed better on measures of paraphrasing than did children from either the enrichment or comparison groups. Children in the intervention group also performed better on tests of conservation at ages 5, 6, and 7; their school performance and academic achievement were better; they were less likely to repeat grades; and they were less likely to have special education needs when they received the preschool intervention as well (F. A. Campbell et al., 1995; F. A. Campbell & Ramey, 1990; Hovacek, Ramey, Campbell, Hoffman, & Fletcher, 1987). Later assessments showed that children in the intervention group completed more years of school than those who did not (F. A. Campbell, Pungello, Miller-Johnson, Burchinal, & Ramey, 2001; F. A. Campbell, Ramey, Pungello, Sparkling, & Miller-Johnson, 2002). Somewhat surprisingly, the elementary school enrichment component had little impact (F. A. Campbell & Ramey, 1994, 1995).

Wasik et al. (1990) later showed that the Abecedarian intervention was even more influential when it was supplemented by a home-based family education program, which became Project CARE. At every assessment through 54 months of age, children receiving both center- and family-focused intervention in Project CARE performed better than those receiving only center-based intervention. According to C. T. Ramey, Ramey, Hardin, and Blair (1995), however, intensive home visits by themselves had no effect on the children's performance or on their families, even though home visiting has proven effective in other studies (Seitz, 1990).

Burchinal, Lee, and Ramey (1989) compared the developmental trajectories of Black children from impoverished backgrounds who (a) entered the intensive intervention programs at 2 to 3 months of age, (b) were enrolled in community child care at an average of 20 months, or (c) had minimal or no child care experiences. Semiannual assessments between 6 and 54 months using the Bayley Mental Development Index (MDI), the Stanford-Binet, and the McCarthy scales revealed that the children in the intervention group consistently performed the best, followed by those in community care settings, followed by those who had minimal child care experiences. This suggests that community child care can have beneficial effects on the cognitive performance of children from impoverished unstimulating homes, although the lack of random assignment to the two nonexperimental comparison groups compromises the assessment of causality. The same is true of the New York City Infant Day Care Study (Golden et al., 1978), in which disadvantaged children whose parents chose to enroll them in day care centers had higher IQ scores at 18 and 36 months than children whose parents chose to keep them primarily at home.

Sparling et al. (1991) later developed an intensive intervention program modeled after the Abecedarian program for a large-scale randomized control study of low-birthweight premature babies, the Infant Health and Development Program (1990). Mothers and infants in this study were randomly assigned to either program (intervention) or control groups. The program involved weekly home visits for 3 years after hospital discharge, high-quality educationally oriented day care from 12 to 36 months of age, and parent group meetings on a bimonthly basis. Enrollment in this program led to significant improvements in the IQs of infants at age 36 months (Brooks-Gunn et al., 1993; C. T. Ramey et al., 1995). The effects on the heavier babies was greater than on the lighter babies, but was statistically significant in either case at the time of the 3-year follow-up (C. T. Ramey et al., 1995), although by 5 years of age, significant effects were evident only among those who were heavier at birth (Brooks-Gunn et al., 1994). Intervention had substantially more powerful effects on the infants of mothers with the lowest education, and had no effect on the infants of mothers who were college graduates (C. T. Ramey et al., 1995). Subsequent analyses showed that the magnitude of the effects on IQ varied depending on the extent to which the families participated and took advantage of the services offered to them (Blair, Ramey, & Hardin, 1995; C. T. Ramey et al., 1992). This is consistent with other evidence suggesting that more intensive programs have a greater impact on child development than less intensive programs do (S. L. Ramey & Ramey, 1992). Furthermore, the results of the Infant Health and Development Program, the Abecedarian Program, and Project CARE all underscore the importance of providing care and stimulation directly to children in out-of-home contexts.

Responding to calls that intervention for children at psychosocial risk should begin as early as possible, the U.S. Administration for Children, Youth, and Families (ACYF) developed Early Head Start in 1994 and funded the first 143 programs in 1995. By 2002, 664 programs nationwide were serving 55,000 children. As with Head Start, programs vary widely depending on local needs and resources, with some programs providing home-based, some center-based, and some both home- and center-based services to infants, toddlers, and their parents from pregnancy through the 3rd year of life (Early Head Start Research and Evaluation Project, 2002b). To assess the implementation and effectiveness of Early Head Start, ACYF also commissioned a random assignment study of families who were and were not offered services through local programs. The Early Head Start Research and Evaluation Project (2001, 2002a) found that Early Head Start services had a significant impact on the supportiveness and positiveness of the mothers' and fathers' behavior as well as on the cognitive performance, language development, and social-emotional behavior of the children at ages 2 and 3. Effects tended to be stronger when families were enrolled in programs that had implemented a wider range of services, especially when they provided both home- and center-based services. African American children tended to benefit the most and White children the least, and children from the most disadvantaged programs were adversely affected. Although children receiving Early Head Start services performed much better than peers in the control groups, it is noteworthy that they continued to score far below national norms, whereas children in the more intensive and extensive Abecedarian Project performed at around national norms.

Supplementary Enrichment for Graduates of Preschool Programs

Unfortunately, public school enrichment programs (such as Program Follow Through) designed to attenuate the IQ decline that typically occurs when children leave enrichment programs (Doernberger & Zigler, 1993; Kennedy, 1993) have never been well funded, and thus implementation has been limited despite a small but persuasive body of evidence showing that programs of this sort can indeed be beneficial. Abelson, Zigler, and DeBlasi (1974) and Seitz, Apfel, Rosenbaum, and Zigler (1983) showed that one cohort of children who went from Head Start to Follow Through programs in New Haven, Connecticut, maintained higher scores on measures of IQ, school achievement, and social-emotional development than children who attended traditional school programs through grade 9. A comparable demonstration program involving comprehensive preschool and

school-age intervention, complemented by parental involvement during the preschool and early elementary years, was conducted in Chicago, although, as in New Haven, children were not assigned randomly to the two groups. Fuerst and Fuerst (1993) and Reynolds (1992a, 1992b, 1994, 1998, 2000; Reynolds, Temple, Robertson, & Mann, 2001; Temple, Reynolds, & Miedel, 2000) reported that, after controlling for family background, graduates had better reading and mathematics achievement scores, were significantly less likely to be retained in grade, were less likely to be referred for special education, were less likely to engage in criminal activities, and were more likely to graduate from high school than children who received traditional schooling. Reynolds (1994) further found that participation in the elementary school component of the program had beneficial effects independent of the preschool component. Interestingly, there was very little difference between the effects of 1- and 2-year enrollment periods, suggesting that it might be more effective to expand the number of children served rather than to extend the length of time each was enrolled (Reynolds, 1995). Taylor and Machida (1994) reported that parental participation in school activities was associated with learning skills and more strongly associated with classroom behavior after several months in Head Start. Maintenance of parental involvement also played an important role in ensuring the long-term continuity of effects on the children's performance in the Chicago Child-Parent Centers (CPC; Reynolds, 1992b), although site-level factors, such as location, curriculum, parental participation rates, family stability, and the proportion of children who came from low-income families, had much less impact on the children's outcomes than preschool participation (Clements, Reynolds, & Hickey, 2004).

Summary

The onset of nonparental child care stresses children, especially those who enter child care after becoming attached to their mother. Secure child-mother relationships do not appear to help children cope with these stresses as much as attachment theorists originally believed, and thus familiarization programs and supportive child-care provider relationships are needed to help children adjust to the onset of child care.

Parental sensitivity remains a key determinant of children's adjustment even after the onset of child care, and the life changes that accompany the onset of maternal employment and child care often affect the quality of parental behavior. Families need to find ways to compensate for the time they spend apart and to respond sensitively to children's needs to minimize or avoid adverse effects on attachment security. Supportive and secure child-care provider relationships can also play an important role in promoting children's well-being. Care providers are not mother substitutes, however. Whereas dyadic interactions are central to parent-child relationships, the quality of care providers' behavior in relation to groups of children is crucial. Both child-care provider interactions and group dynamics define the climate that powerfully affects children's adjustment, for good and for ill.

For children without siblings, child care may provide unique opportunities for socialization with and by peers on a regular basis. However, the development and significance of relationships with peers are affected not solely by enrollment in child care but also by social-cognitive and social-emotional characteristics that are significantly shaped by socialization in the family. In addition, child care practices can foster good and hinder poor interaction skills, which in turn affect later behavioral adjustment and personality maturation. Extensive experience of mediocre or poor-quality care is associated with increased behavior problems.

Longitudinal studies are disappointingly rare, but all show that the positive cognitive effects of high-quality intervention are attenuated over time unless maintained by continuing care or education of high quality. Of course, success at school demands cognitive and linguistic competencies that are affected by experiences both at home and in child care facilities. High-quality child care can thus counteract the adverse effects of poorer experiences with parents. High-quality child care is not as helpful for children from more advantaged backgrounds, however. Instead, care of poorer quality has effects that vary depending on its quality relative to the quality of care and stimulation that children would receive at home. As a result, the performance of some children from supportive and stimulating families may be affected adversely by out-of-home care experiences.

Unfortunately, few attempts have been made to evaluate the relative effectiveness of different curricula or pedagogical approaches, so we cannot identify which features of successful programs are particularly valuable for which children. Likewise, the literature permits us to offer only the most general conclusions about the beneficial effects of high-quality care rather than empirically supported conclusions about the value of particular programs and approaches. Research on particular programs and approaches will be particularly helpful in the face of growing evidence that the effects of quality are considerably less powerful than expected. It is also surprising that such little evidence exists concerning the effects of Head Start, particularly considering the enormous cumulative and annual public costs of the program.

AFTERSCHOOL CARE

The need for nonparental care does not end when children enter the elementary education system at around 6 years of age (enrollment ages vary across cultures and communities), particularly as parental employment rates continue to rise in association with children's ages, and have always been higher for parents with school-age rather than preschool-age children or infants (see "Changing Patterns of Care in the United States and Europe: Parenting and Alloparenting"). In the United States, an estimated 78% of the mothers with school-age children were employed outside the home by 1997, compared with 40% in 1970 and 75% in 1995 (H. Hayghe, personal communication, October 17, 1995; Hofferth & Phillips, 1987; U.S. Bureau of Labor Statistics, 1987, 1998). The typical school day extends for only 6 hours, and in many European countries, some children go home for lunch at the end of or in the middle of the school day. These practices were institutionalized at a time when mothers were expected to be working in and around the home, able to care for their children when they were not in school. Obviously, these conditions no longer exist in most industrialized countries. Instead of returning from (or going to) school from a home supervised by their mother, many children attend formal afterschool programs, are supervised informally by neighbors, relatives, or babysitters, or are left unsupervised. By 1999, 49% of the 6- to 11-year-olds in the United States whose primary caregivers were employed received some kind of regular afterschool care, including care by relatives (25%), before- and afterschool programs (15%), or home-based child care (7%: Sonenstein et al., 2002). Before- and afterschool nonmaternal care arrangements are more common when mothers are single or work longer hours (NICHD Early Child Care Research Network, 2004), and two somewhat unconnected bodies of literature have emerged, one concerned with the characteristics of children who are unsupervised, and one with the effects of formal afterschool programs. These literatures are reviewed separately here.

Self-Care

According to the 1999 National Survey of America's Families (NSAF), 3.3 million school-age children (15% of the 6- to 12-year-olds in the United States) stay at home, unsupervised by an adult, on a regular basis (Vandivere, Tout, Zaslow, Calkins, & Capizzano, 2003). Closer analysis of the NSAF data shows that self-care becomes more common as children grow older: 7% of 6- to 9-year-olds but 26% of 9- to 12-year-olds and 47% of 14-year-olds were left regularly to care for themselves in 1999 (K. Smith, 2002; Vandivere et al., 2003), and the average amounts of time spent unsupervised also increase as children grow older (Vandivere et al., 2003). Contrary to popular belief, unsupervised children are not more likely to be found in impoverished, minority communities. In fact, Vandivere et al. reported that low-income and less-educated parents were less likely to leave their children unsupervised after school than were parents with higher incomes or higher levels of education. Similarly, Vandell and Ramanan (1991), using data from the NLSY, reported that children were more likely to be supervised after school when family income and social support levels were lower. Self-care is also more common when mothers work full time or parents are divorced/separated (K. Smith & Casper, 1999; Steinberg, 1986; Vandivere et al., 2003). Hispanic children are much less likely than non-Hispanic children to be left unsupervised (Vandivere et al., 2003).

Since the 1970s, great concern has been expressed about the safety and welfare of unsupervised young children (Bronfenbrenner, 1976; Genser & Baden, 1980), whose circumstances fit the legal definition of child neglect in most states. Perhaps because this legal characterization makes parents unwilling to admit the care status of their children, there has been much less research on the psychosocial and behavioral adjustment of young children than on the status of children in middle school, with surprisingly little attention paid to their differing developmental needs. Whereas a case can be made that eighth graders benefit from learning to be responsible and independent during periods of unsupervised self-care, for example, the same argument should not be made with respect to first graders living in urban communities.

Much of the concern about "latchkey" children was prompted by Woods (1972), who studied African American fifth graders in the inner city and found that the latchkey girls scored more poorly on measures of cognitive/academic, social, and personality adjustment than did peers in the care of adults. In particular, unsupervised girls had poorer achievement test scores and poorer relationships with their peers at school. On the basis of open-ended interviews with children in self-care arrangements, furthermore, Long and Long (1983, 1994) concluded that latchkey children were at risk for a wide variety of social, academic, and emotional problems. Richardson et al. (1989) later reported that eighth graders in the Los Angeles and San Diego metropolitan areas were more likely to abuse illicit substances when they spent more time in self-care. Similarly, adolescents who were regularly unsupervised after school were more likely to smoke cigarettes, consume alcohol, and use drugs (Mott, Crowe, Richardson, & Flay, 1999; Mulhall, Stone, & Stone, 1996). Vandell and Posner (1999) reported that third graders who cared for themselves regularly had more behavior problems in both third and fifth grade, whereas self-care by fifth graders was not associated with behavior problems. Pettit, Laird, Bates, and Dodge (1997) reported that sixth graders were less socially competent and performed more poorly in academic contexts when they had spent more time in self-care as first and third graders. These associations remained even after controlling for differences in earlier child adjustment and family social class. As in Vandell and Posner's study, the amount of self-care in fifth grade was not associated with problematic behavior in sixth grade. Colwell, Pettit, Meece, Bates, and Dodge (2001) also reported that self-care beginning in the first grade was associated with behavior problems in the sixth grade. Socioeconomic status affects these associations; children in less-advantaged families are more likely to be characterized by significant correlations between self-care and either behavior problems or poorer academic performance (Marshall et al., 1997; Vandell & Posner, 1999).

By contrast, Galambos and Garbarino (1983) reported no differences in achievement, classroom orientation, adjustment to school, and fearfulness on the part of fifth and seventh graders who were either adult-supervised or cared for themselves after school in a rural community; neither did Rodman, Pratto, and Nelson (1985), who studied fourth and seventh graders matched on age, gender, family composition, and socioeconomic status. There were no differences in locus of control, behavioral adjustment, and self-esteem. Similarly, Vandell and Corasaniti (1988) reported that White suburban middle-class third graders in self-care after school did not differ from children in the care of their mother on any dimensions. In fact, the latchkey children appeared to function better at school and in the peer group than peers who went to formal afterschool programs. The mother's marital status did not moderate any of these differences or nondifferences.

Vandell and Ramanan (1991) later studied third to fifth graders whose mother was a participant in the NLSY; the children were thus disproportionately likely to be born to adolescent, poor, minority parents, but only 28 of the 390 children were unsupervised after school, which limits the strength of the conclusions that can be drawn from the study. There were no differences between latchkey and mother- or other-care children in the total number of behavior problems, although those who were unsupervised after school were rated as more headstrong and hyperactive than those in other- (but not mother-) care after school. Children in other-care after school had fewer behavior problems and higher PPVT scores than children cared for by their mother after school. All of these differences disappeared following statistical controls for family income and emotional support, however, presumably because mother-care was the arrangement most likely to be chosen by the poorer, less emotionally supported families. Likewise, analyses of nationally representative data gathered in the 1999 NSAF showed no differences in behavior problems in 6- to 12-year-olds depending on whether or not they regularly cared for themselves (Vandivere et al., 2003).

As Steinberg (1986, 1988) pointed out, researchers need to distinguish among several groups of children who are all unsupervised by their parents after school: some stay home alone; some go to a friend's house, where they may be but typically are not supervised by the friend's parent; some "hang out" in the mall or some other public place. These differences may be associated with important differences in the psychosocial status of the children concerned, argued Steinberg, particularly if they lead to differences in exposure to antisocial peer pressure. As predicted, suburban fifth, sixth, eighth, and ninth graders appeared more susceptible to antisocial peer pressure (as indexed by the children's responses to hypothetical vignettes on a measure developed by Berndt, 1979) when they tended to hang out in public places, and those who went to a friend's house were more susceptible than those who stayed home alone (Steinberg, 1986). Children who stayed

home alone did not in fact differ from those who were under adult supervision. Steinberg also reported group differences in the children's reports of their parents, with the parents of boys in self-care being more permissive than those of boys in adult care of some sort, and the permissiveness of girls' parents being correlated with the degree to which they were unsupervised (adult care, self-care at home, at friend's house, hanging out). Parental permissiveness was itself associated with the susceptibility to peer pressure, whereas authoritative parental practices (Baumrind, 1968) were associated with greater resistance to peer pressure.

Comparable results were obtained by Galambos and Maggs (1991) in a longitudinal study of sixth graders living with both of their parents in suburban Canadian communities. Children who were not at home after school were more involved with peers, and unsupervised girls were more likely to have deviant peers, poor self-images, and be at risk of problem behavior, although the risks were reduced by less permissive and more accepting parental behavior. As earlier reported by Steinberg (1986) and Rodman et al. (1985), children who stayed at home unsupervised did not differ from those who were under adult supervision.

Formal Afterschool Programs

Just as self-care may have varied effects depending on the children's characteristics and circumstances, afterschool care likely has diverse effects on children's adjustment, but unfortunately these issues have not been well explored. School-age child care (SACC) programs serving several million children in the United States operate in diverse locations, and the types and quality of care vary widely. In one study of 30 SACC programs, R. Rosenthal and Vandell (1996) reported that children and parents evaluated the programs more positively when they were smaller, staff-child ratios were lower, the staff was more emotionally supportive, the variety of possible activities was greater, and negative staff-children interactions were less common. Pierce, Hamm, and Vandell (1999) similarly found that lower child-adult ratios were associated with more positive staff-child interactions and more time spent in constructive activities. These variations in quality are obviously important: High-quality programs are associated with more positive academic and social outcomes, whereas programs have negative or ambiguous effects when the quality is poorer (Vandell & Pierce, 1999, 2001; Vandell, Shuman, & Posner, 1999).

Focusing on 6-year-olds in a variety of programs, Pierce et al. (1999) found that children, especially boys, in programs characterized by positive interactions with the staff had fewer behavior problems, better academic grades, and better social skills than children in settings characterized by negative staff-child and peer relationships even after controlling for family background characteristics. Subsequent assessment of these children and programs revealed that the majority of programs provided care of mediocre or barely adequate quality (Vandell & Pierce, 2001) and that the higher the quality of afterschool care received by those children through fourth grade, the better their academic performance and the less they reported feeling lonely. In addition, girls, but not boys, had better work habits and social skills when they had attended higher-quality programs. Better peer relations in the SACC programs were associated with less depression.

In an earlier study of third graders in Milwaukee in which single-parent, African American, low-income families were oversampled, Posner and Vandell (1994) sought to describe the components and effects of formal afterschool programs. Formal care was more likely when mothers were better educated and family incomes were lower; Whites were more likely to leave their children unsupervised, and African Americans were more likely to count on informal afterschool care arrangements. After controlling statistically for these factors, Posner and Vandell found that children attending formal afterschool programs received better grades for mathematics, reading, and conduct than did peers in the mother-care and other-care groups. The former also had better work habits and better peer relations than those in the other-care group. These results are perhaps attributable to the fact that, in comparison with the other children, children in the formal settings spent more time in academic and enrichment activities with both adults and peers, but less time watching television or playing with siblings. Unlike Vandell and Ramanan (1991), Posner and Vandell found that children in the other-care group performed more poorly than those in mother-care with respect to reading grades, work habits, and behavior problems, perhaps because these arrangements seemed quite inconsistent and variable from day to day. The more time these children spent in unstructured outdoor activities, the poorer their grades, work habits, and emotional adjustment. When reassessed as fourth and fifth graders, children who were performing better and were better behaved as third graders engaged in more constructive afterschool activities as fifth graders (Posner & Vandell, 1999). In addition, African American children who engaged in more nonsport activities over the study years were better adjusted in fifth grade. White children had poorer grades and more behavior problems when they spent more time in unstructured activities. Finally, in the multisite NICHD Study of Early Child Care (2004), kindergartners and first graders had higher standardized test scores when they participated in extracurricular activities after school, but all other types of before- or afterschool arrangements were unrelated to measures of the children's functioning after controlling for background factors.

Summary

Overall, the data suggest that the lack of direct supervision in afterschool hours has effects on children that vary depending on their age, what they are doing, and the extent to which they are monitored by their parents. Direct adult supervision appears to remain an important determinant of children's adjustment at least through midadolescence, although researchers have paid inadequate attention to developmental differences and have failed to study the psychosocial adjustment of the youngest children left unsupervised. Self-care is associated with poorer outcomes among 8- to 9-year-olds (American third graders) but is not consistently associated with poor outcomes among older preadolescents. Among adolescents, there are few consistent effects when children are at home alone and are (loosely) monitored by their parents, but those who are not monitored and especially those who hang out with peers unsupervised are most likely to get into trouble, have behavior problems, and perform poorly at school. It is not clear whether the widespread availability of cell or mobile phones may affect the level of supervision or give parents a false sense of security regarding their children's whereabouts and activities.

In light of demographic data suggesting that some kindergartners are left alone regularly, it is noteworthy that the research literature has focused on children in third grade or higher, with most studies concerned with young adolescents. From the fifth grade, children who are regularly at home after school behave and perform similarly whether or not an adult is present, but the distance from adult supervision explains differences in the outcomes of unsupervised children who do not go home after school. Parental disciplinary practices appear to modulate these differences in predictable ways. Unfortunately, all of these findings are compromised by the absence of longitudinal data and the strong possibility that differences among children (in their preferences to be and do things with their peers, for example) may precede rather than be consequences of the differing types of supervision.

Third and fourth graders seem to do better academically and behaviorally when they are in formal after-school programs, although this may not be true of children from more affluent families. Participation in formal programs by such children appears to promote more constructive uses of time as the children mature, though there has yet to be much research on children older than 10 or 11 years. Interestingly, however, recreational programs for disadvantaged teenagers and teenagers considered at risk for antisocial behavior have tended not to have the expected positive effects on adolescents (McCord, 1990).

CONCLUSION

After nearly 3 decades of intensive research on nonparental child care, considerable progress has been made, although we still have much to learn about the mechanisms by which out-of-home care affects children's development. In large part, our continuing ignorance about developmental processes reflects the extent to which researchers were preoccupied too long with the wrong questions—first asking "Is day care bad for children?" instead of "How does child care affect children's development?"—and later remained focused on the effects of child care and the effects of child care quality instead of recognizing that child care has myriad incarnations and must always be viewed in the context of children's intrinsic characteristics, developmental trajectories, and other experiences. We should not be surprised that children's experiences away from home are formatively significant, although simplistic assessments of these experiences and limited opportunities for truly experimental research have impeded progress. In addition, there is vast (and often poorly specified) variability within and among studies with respect to the actual care arrangements studied, the amount and quality of care received, the age at which it began, the number and type of changes in the patterns of care, and the ways outcomes were assessed. Even when the same outcomes are assessed, variations in the ages of assessment and enrollment, means of quantification, and the composition and selection of comparison groups often preclude anything more than tentative conclusions about specific care arrangements.

Clumsy investigative strategies notwithstanding, we can actually answer a few of the simpler questions with some confidence. We now know, for example, that child care experiences *need not* have harmful effects on children's development and on their family relationships, although they *can* do so. Most children's relationships with their parents do not differ systematically depending on whether or not they receive regular nonparental care. Most children in out-of-home facilities remain attached to their parents and still prefer their parents over teachers and care providers. Meaningful relationships are often established with peers and care providers, however, and these can affect children's later social behavior and personality maturity. In addition, exposure to peers may offer some children (e.g., those who are singletons or have shy temperament) opportunities they could not experience at home, thereby launching them on different developmental trajectories.

Early exposure to nonparental care of poorer quality also fosters excessive assertiveness, aggression, and behavior problems in some children for reasons that are not yet well understood. Insecure parent-child attachments do not modulate these effects, as once believed, because nonparental care experiences are not reliably associated with insecure infant-mother attachment, but poor relationships with care providers do appear to mediate the effects of nonparental care on children's aggressiveness. Children in higher-quality facilities who enjoy good relationships with stable providers are not more aggressive than peers who have experienced care only from their parents.

The onset of regular nonparental care for infants and toddlers has complex psychobiological and behavioral effects on their functioning both at home and in child care centers. As a result, maladaptive behavior on the part of children who spend many hours in child care may reflect not the direct effects of nonparental care, but the inability of parents to buffer the enhanced levels of stress occasioned by the time spent in child care. Successful adaptation demands careful equilibration of the contrasting limitations and benefits of the two environments, with parental care characterized by stress reduction and emotional regulation, whereas care providers emphasize cognitive stimulation and behavioral regulation. Home remains the center of children's lives even when children spend considerable amounts of time in child care, and thus parents who fail to recognize and respond to their children's need for emotion regulation when they are reunited after long hours in stress-inducing child care arrangements are at least partly responsible for the dysregulation that becomes manifest in misbehavior.

Assertions that nonparental care does not consistently or inevitably have either positive or adverse effects on children's development must be further qualified on a number of grounds. Some of the most important stem from the fact that, with few exceptions, quasi-experimental studies have not been possible. Because the children and families studied are not assigned randomly to nonparental and exclusive parental care groups, preexisting group differences—particularly those that led to the enrollment of some but not other children in nonparental care settings in the first place—may continue to explain at least some of the between-group variance discerned. Statistical controls for some of the known group differences and potentially influential factors (such as social class) reduce but do not completely eliminate the problem, limited as they are to imperfect measures of factors that are operationalized as linear and independent sources of influence. Still, it is comforting to note that researchers are continuing to refine their understanding of these factors.

In addition, although researchers have more recently done a much better job of sampling the range of settings experienced by most children, settings providing care of the poorest quality are disproportionately excluded from studies. The most intensive studies still tend to overrepresent middle-class White North Americans in placements of better-than-average quality, whereas the larger multisite studies and surveys include more diverse and ethnically representative groups. For a variety of reasons, the large multisite studies (but not the NICHD study) are least likely to include microanalytic components, however, so sampling limitations are an especially important consideration when behavioral observations are at issue.

Over time, researchers' focus has clearly shifted from between-group to within-group (correlational) strategies. Most researchers embracing such strategies have attempted to assess the predictive importance of the quality of care, and there is a clear consensus that the quality of care, broadly defined and measured, modulates the effects of nonparental child care on child development. Interestingly, improvements in quality appear to have significant positive effects even at the highest end of the range sampled, suggesting that there is no threshold beyond which quality of care no longer matters. The magnitude of the effect is considerably smaller than expected, however, although the fact that researchers must estimate the importance of quality in the context of complex correlational models that also include a range of other potential influences makes it doubtful that we will ever really know how important quality is in an absolute sense. The recent and widespread focus on the quality of care has also led researchers to neglect many of the other factors that affect children's development. Developmentalists now know that all aspects of behavioral development are multiply and redundantly determined; as a result, the absolute magnitude of each individual influence is likely to be quite small when all important factors are taken into account simultaneously. It would thus be a mistake to conclude, for example, that quality of care is not really important because its coefficients are small; by this logic, almost any factor could be deemed insignificant. A realistic appreciation of how complex developmental processes really are should instead foster a shift from the simplistic search for magic bullets to the patient but tedious evaluation of complex models of development. By the same token, however, researchers have a responsibility not to misrepresent either the costs or the benefits of variations in the quality of care, particularly in the face of political pressures to do so. For similar reasons, it is important to determine why early intervention programs with generally positive effects sometimes affect the most disadvantaged children negatively.

Nonparental care of superior quality is clearly beneficial to children and preferable to care of poor quality; parents and regulators need to evaluate the relative costs and benefits of incremental improvements in quality, however. Researchers, meanwhile, need to shift their attention to more detailed considerations of quality so as to define, more clearly than has been possible with the current generation of measures, what characteristics of care providers and out-of-home care settings have the greatest impact on specific aspects of development. Nonparental care needs to be designed to serve the needs of children and, in particular, to recognize that children of different ages and backgrounds have different needs and experience stress for different reasons. Thus, the global indices of quality that have served a first generation of researchers and regulators so well must now yield center stage to a generation of more refined measures and concepts that allow practitioners to determine whether and how specific practices have unique effects on children's learning and development.

Type of care may also have varying effects depending on the age at which children enter nonparental care settings, with the planned curricula of child care centers become increasingly advantageous as children get older. It also appears likely that different children will be affected differently by various child care experiences, although we remain ignorant about most of the factors that modulate these differential effects. Child temperament, parental attitudes and values, preenrollment differences in sociability, curiosity, and cognitive functioning, gender, and birth order may all be influential, but reliable evidence is scanty.

In all, we have learned a great deal about the effects of out-of-home care and, in so doing, we have learned that these effects are a good deal more complex than was once thought. The challenge for the next decade is to determine how different experiences inside and outside the home are associated with specific outcomes for children in defined contexts and cultures.

REFERENCES

Abbott-Shim, M., & Sibley, A. (1987). *Assessment profile for childhood programs*. Atlanta, GA: Quality Assist, Inc.

Abbott-Shim, M., & Sibley, A. (1992). *Research version of the assessment profile for childhood programs*. Atlanta, GA: Quality Assist, Inc.

Abelson, W. D., Zigler, E. F., & DeBlasi, C. L. (1974). Effects of a 4-year follow through program on economically disadvantaged children. *Journal of Educational Psychology, 66*, 756–771.

Ackermann-Ross, S., & Khanna, P. (1989). The relationship of high quality day care to middle-class 3-year-olds' language performance. *Early Childhood Research Quarterly, 4*, 97–116.

Administration for Children and Families. (1999). *Head Start 1998 fact sheet*. Washington, DC: U.S. Department of Health and Human Services.

Ahnert, L. (2005). Parenting and alloparenting: The impact on attachment in humans. In S. Carter, L. Ahnert, K. E. Grossmann, S. B. Hardy, M. E. Lamb, & S. W. Porges (Eds.), *Attachment and bonding: A new synthesis* (Dahlem Workshop Report 92). Cambridge, MA: MIT Press.

Ahnert, L., Gunnar, M., Lamb, M. E., & Barthel, M. (2004). Transition to child care: Associations of infant-mother attachment, infant negative emotion and cortisol elevations. *Child Development, 75*, 639–650.

Ahnert, L., & Lamb, M. E. (2000). Infant-careprovider attachments in contrasting German child care settings: Pt. 2. Individual-oriented care after German reunification. *Infant Behavior and Development, 23*, 211–222.

Ahnert, L., & Lamb, M. E. (2001). The East German child care system: Associations with caretaking and caretaking beliefs, children's early attachment and adjustment. *American Behavioral Scientist, 44*, 1843–1863.

Ahnert, L., & Lamb, M. E. (2003). Shared care: Establishing a balance between home and child care. *Child Development, 74*, 1044–1049.

Ahnert, L., Lamb, M. E., & Seltenheim, K. (2000). Infant-careprovider attachments in contrasting German child care settings: Pt. 1. Group-oriented care before German reunification. *Infant Behavior and Development, 23*, 197–209.

Ahnert, L., Pinquart, M., & Lamb, M. E. (in press). Security of children's relationships with non-parental care providers: A meta-analysis. *Child Development*.

Ahnert, L., Rickert, H., & Lamb, M. E. (2000). Shared caregiving: Comparisons between home and child care settings. *Developmental Psychology, 36*, 339–351.

Ainsworth, M. D. S. (1979). Infant-mother attachment. *American Psychologist, 34*, 932–937.

Ainsworth, M. D. S., Blehar, M. C., Waters, E., & Wall, S. (1978). *Patterns of attachment: A psychological study of the Strange Situation*. Hillsdale, NJ: Erlbaum.

Altmann, J. (1987). Life span aspects of reproduction and parental care in anthropoid primates. In J. B. Lancaster, J. Altmann, A. S. Rossi, & L. R. Sherrod (Eds.), *Parenting across the life span: Biosocial perspectives* (pp. 15–29). Hawthorne, NY: Aldine de Gruyter.

American Academy of Pediatrics, American Public Health Association, & National Resource Center for Health and Safety in Child Care. (2002). *Caring for our children: The national health and safety performance standards for out-of-home child care* (2nd ed.). Elk Grove Village, IL: American Academy of Pediatrics.

American Public Health Association & American Academy of Pediatrics. (1992a). *Caring for our children: National health and safety performance standards—Standards for out-of-home child care programs*. Ann-Arbor, MI: Authors.

American Public Health Association & American Academy of Pediatrics. (1992b). *National health and safety performance standards: Guidelines for out-of-home child care programs*. Arlington, VA: National Center for Education in Maternal and Child Health.

Anderson, C. W., Nagle, R. J., Roberts, W. A., & Smith, J. W. (1981). Attachment to substitute caregivers as a function of center quality and caregiver involvement. *Child Development, 52*, 53–61.

Andersson, B. E. (1989). Effects of public day care: A longitudinal study. *Child Development, 60*, 857–866.

Andersson, B. E. (1992). Effects of day care on cognitive and socioemotional competence of 13-year-old Swedish schoolchildren. *Child Development, 63*, 20–36.

Arend, Z., Gove, F., & Sroufe, L. A. (1979). Continuity in early adaptation from attachment security in infancy to resiliency and curiosity at age five. *Child Development, 50*, 950–959.

Arnett, J. (1989). Caregivers in day care centers: Does training matter? *Journal of Applied Developmental Psychology, 10*, 541–552.

Asher, L. J., & Lenhoff, D. R. (2001). Family and medical leave: Making time for family is everyone's business. *Future of Children, 11*, 112–121.

Aviezer, O., Sagi-Schwartz, A., & Koren-Karie, N. (2003). Ecological constraints on the formation of infant-mother attachment relations: When maternal sensitivity becomes ineffective. *Infant Behavior and Development, 26*, 285–299.

Bailey, D. B., Burchinal, M. R., & McWilliam, R. A. (1993). Relationship between age of peers and early child development: A longitudinal study. *Child Development, 64*, 848–862.

Balleyguier, G. (1988). What is the best mode of day care for young children? A French study. *Early Child Development and Care, 33,* 41–65.

Barglow, P., Vaughn, B. E., & Molitor, N. (1987). Effects of maternal absence due to employment on the quality of infant-mother attachment in a low-risk sample. *Child Development, 58,* 945–954.

Barnas, M. V., & Cummings, E. M. (1994). Caregiver stability and toddlers' attachment-related behavior towards caregivers in day care. *Infant Behavior Development, 17,* 141–147.

Barnett, W. S. (1985). Benefit-cost analysis of the Perry Preschool Programs and its policy implications. *Educational Evaluation and Policy Analysis, 7,* 333–342.

Barnett, W. S. (1993a). Benefit-cost analysis. In L. J. Schweinhart, H. V. Barnes, & D. P. Weikart (Eds.), *Significant benefits: The High/Scope Perry Preschool Study through age 27* (pp. 142–173). Ypsilanti, MI: High/Scope Press.

Barnett, W. S. (1993b). Benefit-cost analysis of preschool education: Finding from a 25-year follow-up. *American Journal of Orthopsychiatry, 63,* 500–508.

Barnett, W. S. (1995). Long-term effects of early childhood programs on cognitive and school outcomes. *Future of Children, 5,* 25–50.

Bates, J. E., Marvinney, D., Kelly, T., Dodge, K. A., Bennett, D. S., & Pettit, G. S. (1994). Child-care history and kindergarten adjustment. *Developmental Psychology, 30,* 690–700.

Baumrind, D. (1968). Authoritarian versus authoritative parental control. *Adolescence, 3,* 255–272.

Baydar, N., & Brooks-Gunn, J. (1991). Effects of maternal employment and child-care arrangements on preschoolers' cognitive and behavioral outcomes: Evidence from the children of the National Longitudinal Survey of Youth. *Developmental Psychology, 27,* 932–945.

Bell, D. C., & Richard, A. J. (2000). Caregiving: The forgotten element in attachment. *Psychological Inquiry, 11,* 69–83.

Beller, E. K., Stahnke, M., Butz, P., Stahl, W., & Wessels, H. (1996). Two measures of quality of group care for infants and toddlers. *European Journal of Psychology of Education, 11,* 151–167.

Belsky, J. (1986). Infant day care: A cause for concern? *Zero to Three, 7,* 1–7.

Belsky, J. (1988). The "effects" of infant day care reconsidered. *Early Childhood Research Quarterly, 3,* 235–272.

Belsky, J. (1989). Infant-parent attachment and day care: In defense of the Strange Situation. In J. Lande, S. Scarr, & N. Gunzenhauser (Eds.), *Caring for children: Challenge to America* (pp. 23–48). Hillsdale, NJ: Erlbaum.

Belsky, J., & Eggebeen, D. (1991). Early and extensive maternal employment and young children's socioemotional development: Children of the National Longitudinal Survey of Youth. *Journal of Marriage and the Family, 53,* 1083–1098.

Belsky, J., & Fearon, R. M. P. (2002). Early attachment security, subsequent maternal sensitivity, and later child development: Does continuity in development depend upon continuity of caregiving? *Attachment and Human Development, 3,* 361–387.

Belsky, J., Melhuish, E., Barnes, J., Leyland, A. H., Romaniuk, H., and the NESS Research Team (2005). Effects of Sure Start local programmes on children and families: Early findings. Unpublished report, Birkbeck College, London.

Belsky, J., & Rovine, M. J. (1988). Nonmaternal care in the first year of life and the security of infant-parent attachment. *Child Development, 59,* 157–167.

Belsky, J., & Steinberg, L. D. (1978). The effects of daycare: A critical review. *Child Development, 49,* 929–949.

Belsky, J., Steinberg, L. D., & Walker, A. (1982). The ecology of daycare. In M. E. Lamb (Ed.), *Nontraditional families: Parenting and child development* (pp. 71–116). Hillsdale, NJ: Erlbaum.

Belsky, J., Woodworth, S., & Crnic, K. (1996). Trouble in the second year: Three questions about family interaction. *Child Development, 67,* 556–578.

Bereiter, C., & Engelmann, S. (1966). *Teaching disadvantaged children in the preschool.* Englewood Cliffs, NJ: Prentice-Hall.

Berk, L. E. (1985). Relationship of caregiver education to child-oriented attitudes, job satisfaction, and behavior toward children. *Child Care Quarterly, 14,* 103–129.

Berndt, T. (1979). Developmental changes in conformity to peers and parents. *Developmental Psychology, 15,* 608–616.

Berrueta-Clement, J. R., Schweinhart, L. J., Barnett, W. S., Epstein, A. S., & Weikart, D. P. (1984). *Changed lives: The effects of the Perry Preschool Program on youths through age 19.* Ypsilanti, MI: High/Scope Press.

Bischof-Koehler, D. (1991). The development of empathy in infants. In M. E. Lamb & H. Keller (Eds.), *Infant development: Perspectives from German-speaking countries* (pp. 245–273). Hillsdale, NJ: Erlbaum.

Blair, C., Ramey, C. T., & Hardin, J. M. (1995). Early intervention for low birthweight, premature infants: Participation and intellectual development. *American Journal on Mental Retardation, 99,* 542–554.

Blau, D. M. (2000). The production of quality in child-care centers: Another look. *Applied Developmental Science, 4,* 136–148.

Blehar, M. C. (1974). Anxious attachment and defensive reactions associated with day care. *Child Development, 45,* 683–692.

Block, J. H., & Block, J. (1980). The role of ego-control and ego-resiliency in the organization of behavior. In W. A. Collins (Ed.), *Minnesota Symposia on Child Psychology* (Vol. 13, pp. 39–101). Hillsdale, NJ: Erlbaum.

Bloom, B. S. (1964). *Stability and change in human characteristics.* New York: Wiley.

Bolger, K. E., & Scarr, S. (1995). *Not so far from home: How family characteristics predict child care quality.* Unpublished manuscript, University of Virginia, Charlottesville.

Bollin, G. G. (1993). An investigation of job stability and job satisfaction among family day care providers. *Early Childhood Research Quarterly, 8,* 207–220.

Boocock, S. S. (1995). Early childhood programs in other nations: Goals and outcomes. *Future of Children, 5,* 94–114.

Booth, C. L., Clarke-Stewart, K. A., Vandell, D. L., McCartney, K., & Owen, M. T. (2002). Child-care usage and mother-infant "quality time." *Journal of Marriage and Family, 64,* 16–26.

Booth, C. L., Kelly, J. F., Spieker, S. J., & Zuckerman, T. G. (2003). Toddler's attachment security to child-care providers: The Safe and Secure Scale. *Early Education and Development, 14,* 83–100.

Borge, A. I. H., & Melhuish, E. C. (1995). A longitudinal study of childhood behavior problems, maternal employment and day care in a rural Norwegian community. *International Journal of Behavioral Development, 18,* 23–42.

Bornstein, M. H., Maital, S. L., & Tal, J. (1997). Contexts of collaboration in caregiving: Infant interactions with Israeli kibbutz mothers and caregivers. *Early Child Development and Care, 135,* 145–171.

Bowlby, J. (1951). Maternal care and mental health. *Bulletin of the World Health Organization, 3*, 355–533.

Bowlby, J. (1958). The nature of the child's tie to his mother. *International Journal of Psychoanalysis, 39*, 350–373.

Bowlby, J. (1969). *Attachment and loss: Vol. 1. Attachment.* New York: Basic Books.

Bowlby, J. (1973). *Attachment and loss: Vol. 2. Separation.* New York: Basic Books.

Braverman, L. B. (1989). Beyond the myth of motherhood. In M. McGoldrick, C. M. Anderson, & F. Walsh (Eds.), *Women and families* (pp. 227–243). New York: Free Press.

Bredekamp, S. (Ed.). (1987a). *Accreditation criteria and procedures of the National Academy of Early Childhood Programs.* Washington, DC: National Association for the Education of Young Children.

Bredekamp, S. (1987b). *Developmentally appropriate practice in early childhood programs serving children from birth through age 8.* Washington, DC: National Association for the Education of Young Children.

Britner, P. A., & Phillips, D. A. (1995). Predictors of parent and provider satisfaction with child day care dimensions: A comparison of center-based and family child day care. *Child Welfare, 74*, 1135–1168.

Broberg, A. G., & Hwang, C. P. (1991). The Swedish childcare system. In E. C. Melhuish & P. Moss (Eds.), *Day care and the young child: International perspectives* (pp. 75–101). London: Routledge.

Broberg, A. G., Hwang, C. P., Lamb, M. E., & Bookstein, F. L. (1990). Factors related to verbal abilities in Swedish preschoolers. *British Journal of Developmental Psychology, 8*, 335–349.

Broberg, A. G., Hwang, C. P., Lamb, M. E., & Ketterlinus, R. D. (1989). Child care effects on socioemotional and intellectual competence in Swedish preschoolers. In J. S. Lande, S. Scarr, & N. Gunzenhauser (Eds.), *Caring for children: Challenge to America* (pp. 49–75). Hillsdale, NJ: Erlbaum.

Broberg, A. G., Wessels, H., Lamb, M. E., & Hwang, C. P. (1997). Effects of day care on the development of cognitive abilities in 8-year-olds: A longitudinal study. *Developmental Psychology, 33*, 62–69.

Bronfenbrenner, U. (1976). Who cares for America's children? In V. C. Vaughn & T. B. Brazelton (Eds.), *The family: Can it be saved?* (pp. 3–32). Cambridge, MA: Harvard University Press.

Brooks-Gunn, J. (2003). Do you believe in magic? What we can expect from early childhood intervention programs. *Social Policy Reports, 17*(1), 3–14.

Brooks-Gunn, J., Han, W.-J., & Waldfogel, J. (2002). Maternal employment and child cognitive outcomes in the first 3 years of life: The NICHD study of early child care. *Child Development, 73*, 1052–1072.

Brooks-Gunn, J., Klebanov, P. K., Liaw, F., & Spiker, D. (1993). Enhancing the development of low-birthweight, premature infants: Changes in cognition and behavior over the first 3 years. *Child Development, 64*, 736–753.

Brooks-Gunn, J., McCarton, G. M., Casey, P. H., McCormick, M. C., Bauer, C. R., Bernbaum, J. G., et al. (1994). Early intervention in low-birthweight premature infants: Results through age 5 years from the Infant Health and Development Program. *Journal of the American Medical Association, 272*, 1257–1262.

Brown, J. R., Donelan-McCall, N., & Dunn, J. (1996). Why talk about mental states? The significance of children's conversations with friends, siblings, and mothers. *Child Development, 67*, 836–849.

Brownell, C. A., & Carriger, M. S. (1990). Changes in cooperation and self-other differentiation during the second year. *Child Development, 61*, 1164–1174.

Brown Miller, A. (1990). *The day care dilemma: Critical concerns for American families.* New York: Plenum Press.

Bryant, D. M., Burchinal, M., Lau, L. B., & Sparling, J. J. (1994). Family and classroom correlates of Head Start children's developmental outcomes. *Early Childhood Research Quarterly, 9*, 289–309.

Burchinal, M. R., Bryant, D. M., Lee, M. W., & Ramey, C. T. (1992). Early day care, infant-mother attachment, and maternal responsiveness in the infant's first year. *Early Childhood Research Quarterly, 7*, 383–396.

Burchinal, M. R., Lee, M., & Ramey, C. T. (1989). Type of day care and preschool intellectual development in disadvantaged children. *Child Development, 60*, 182–187.

Burchinal, M. R., Peisner-Feinberg, E., Bryant, D. M., & Clifford, R. (2000). Children's social and cognitive development and childcare quality: Testing for differential associations related to poverty, gender, or ethnicity. *Applied Developmental Science, 4*, 149–165.

Burchinal, M. R., Ramey, S. L., Reid, M. K., & Jaccard, J. (1995). Early child care experiences and their association with family and child characteristics during middle childhood. *Early Childhood Research Quarterly, 10*, 33–61.

Cahan, E. D. (1989). *Past caring: A history of United States preschool care and education for the poor, 1820–1965.* New York: National Center for Children in Poverty.

Caldwell, B. M., & Richmond, J. (1968). The Children's Center in Syracuse. In C. P. Chandler, R. S. Lourie, & A. P. Peters (Eds.), *Early child care* (pp. 326–358). New York: Atherton Press.

Calkins, S. D., Gill, K., & Williford, A. (1999). Externalizing problems in 2-year-olds: Implications for patterns of social behavior and peers' responses to aggression. *Early Education and Development, 10*, 267–288.

Campbell, D. T., & Erlebacher, A. (1970). How regression artifacts in quasi-experimental evaluations can mistakenly make compensatory education look harmful. In J. Hellmuth (Ed.), *Compensatory education: Vol. 3. A national debate* (pp. 185–210). New York: Brunner/Mazel.

Campbell, F. A., Burchinal, M., Wasik, B. H., Bryant, D. M., Sparling, J. J., & Ramey, C. T. (1995). *Early intervention and long term predictors of school concerns in African American children from low-income families.* Unpublished manuscript, University of North Carolina, Chapel Hill.

Campbell, F. A., Pungello, E. P., Miller-Johnson, S., Burchinal, M., & Ramey, C. T. (2001). The development of cognitive and academic abilities: Growth curves from an early childhood educational experiment. *Developmental Psychology, 37*, 231–242.

Campbell, F. A., & Ramey, C. T. (1990). The relationship between Piagetian cognitive development, mental test performance, and academic achievement in high-risk students with and without early educational experience. *Intelligence, 14*, 293–308.

Campbell, F. A., & Ramey, C. T. (1994). Effects of early intervention on intellectual and academic achievement: A follow-up study of children from low-income families. *Child Development, 65*, 684–698.

Campbell, F. A., & Ramey, C. T. (1995). Cognitive and school outcomes for high-risk African American students at middle-adolescence: Positive effects of early intervention. *American Educational Research Journal, 32*, 743–772.

Campbell, F. A., Ramey, C. T., Pungello, E. P., Sparling, J., & Miller-Johnson, S. (2002). Early childhood education: Young adult outcomes from the Abecedarian Project. *Applied Developmental Science, 6,* 42–57.

Campbell, J. J., Lamb, M. E., & Hwang, C. P. (2000). Early child-care experiences and children's social competence between 1.5 and 15 years of age. *Applied Developmental Science, 4,* 166–175.

Caplan, M., Vespo, J., Pedersen, J., & Hay, D. F. (1991). Conflict and its resolution in small groups of 1- and 2-year-olds. *Child Development, 62,* 1513–1524.

Caruso, D. A. (1996). Maternal employment status, mother-infant interaction, and infant development in day care and non-day care groups. *Child and Youth Care Quarterly, 25,* 125–134.

Casper, L. M., & Bianchi, S. M. (2002). *Continuity and change in the American family.* Thousand Oaks, CA: Russell Sage Foundation.

Cassibba, R., van IJzendoorn, M. H., & D'Odorico, L. (2000). Attachment and play in child care centers: Reliability and validity of the Attachment Q-sort for mothers and professional caregivers in Italy. *International Journal of Behavioral Development, 24,* 241–255.

Caughy, M. O. B., DiPietro, J. A., & Strobino, D. M. (1994). Day care participation as a protective factor in the cognitive development of low-income children. *Child Development, 65,* 457–471.

Child Trends. (2003). *Early childhood program enrollment.* Washington, DC: Author.

Cicirelli, V. G. (1969). *The impact of Head Start: An evaluation of the effects of Head Start on children's cognitive and effective development.* Washington, DC: Westinghouse Learning Corporation.

Clark, P., & Kirk, E. (2000). All-day kindergarten. *Childhood Education, 76,* 228–231.

Clarke-Stewart, K. A. (1977). *Child care in the family: A review of research and some propositions for policy.* New York: Academic Press.

Clarke-Stewart, K. A. (1987). Predicting child development from child care forms and features: The Chicago Study. In D. Phillips (Ed.), *Quality in child care: What does research tell us?* (pp. 21–42). Washington, DC: National Association for the Education of Young Children.

Clarke-Stewart, K. A. (1988). The "effects" of infant day care reconsidered: Risks for parents, children, and researchers. *Early Childhood Research Quarterly, 3,* 293–318.

Clarke-Stewart, K. A. (1989). Infant day care: Maligned or malignant? *American Psychologist, 44,* 266–273.

Clarke-Stewart, K. A. (1992). Consequences of child care for children's development. In A. Booth (Ed.), *Child care in the 1990s: Trends and consequences* (pp. 63–83). Hillsdale, NJ: Erlbaum.

Clarke-Stewart, K. A., & Fein, G. C. (1983). Early childhood programs. In P. H. Mussen (Series Ed.) & M. M. Haith & J. J. Campos (Vol. Eds.), *Handbook of child psychology: Vol. 2. Infancy and developmental psychobiology* (4th ed., pp. 917–999). New York: Wiley.

Clarke-Stewart, K. A., Gruber, C. P., & Fitzgerald, L. M. (1994). *Children at home and in day care.* Hillsdale, NJ: Erlbaum.

Clarke-Stewart, K. A., Vandell, D. L., Burchinal, M., O'Brien, M., & McCartney, K. (2002). Do regulable features of child-care homes affect children's development? *Early Childhood Research Quarterly, 17,* 52–86.

Clements, M. A., Reynolds, A. J., & Hickey, E. (2004). Site-level predictors of children's school and social competence in the Chicago Child-Parent Centers. *Early Childhood Research Quarterly, 19,* 273–296.

Clerkx, L. E., & van IJzendoorn, M. H. (1992). Child care in a Dutch context: On the history, current status, and evaluation of nonmaternal child care in the Netherlands. In M. E. Lamb, K. J. Sternberg, C.-P. Hwang, & A. G. Broberg (Eds.), *Child care in context: Cross-cultural perspectives* (pp. 55–79). Hillsdale, NJ: Erlbaum.

Cochran, M. (Ed.). (1993). *International handbook of child care policies and programs.* Westport, CT: Greenwood Press.

Coelen, C., Glantz, F., & Calore, D. (1979). *Day care centers in the United States: A national profile, 1976–1977.* Cambridge, MA: ABT Associates.

Cohen, B. (1993). The United Kingdom. In M. Cochbran (Ed.), *International handbook of child care policies and programs* (pp. 515–534). Westport, CT: Greenwood Press.

Cohen, D. J., Solnit, A. J., & Wohlford, P. (1979). Mental health services in Head Start. In E. Zigler & J. Valentine (Eds.), *Project Head Start: A legacy of the War on Poverty* (pp. 259–282). New York: Free Press.

Coie, J. D., & Dodge, K. A. (1998). Aggression and antisocial behavior. In W. Damon (Editor-in-Chief) & N. Eisenberg (Vol. Ed.), *Handbook of child psychology: Vol. 5. Social, emotional, and personality development* (5th ed., pp. 779–862). New York: Wiley.

Colwell, M. J., Pettit, G. S., Meece, D., Bates, J. E., & Dodge, K. A. (2001). Cumulative risk and continuity in nonparental care from infancy to early adolescence. *Merrill-Palmer Quarterly, 47,* 207–234.

Comer, J. P. (1980). *School power.* New York: Free Press.

Consortium for Longitudinal Studies. (1978). *Lasting effects after preschool* (Final report to the Administration on Children, Youth, and Families). Washington, DC: U.S. Government Printing Office.

Consortium for Longitudinal Studies. (1983). *As the twig is bent: Lasting effects of preschool programs.* Hillsdale, NJ: Erlbaum.

Copple, G., Cline, M., & Smith, A. (1987). *Paths to the future: Long-term effects of Head Start in the Philadelphia school district.* Washington, DC: U.S. Department of Health and Human Services.

Copple, G., Sigel, I. E., & Saunders, R. (1984). *Educating the young thinker: Classroom strategies for cognitive growth.* Hillsdale, NJ: Erlbaum.

Corsaro, W. A., & Emiliani, F. (1992). Child care, early education, and children's peer culture in Italy. In M. E. Lamb, K. J. Sternberg, C. P. Hwang, & A. G. Broberg (Eds.), *Child care in context: Cross-cultural perspectives* (pp. 81–115). Hillsdale, NJ: Erlbaum.

Cost, Quality, and Child Outcome in Child Care Centers. (1995). Denver: University of Colorado at Denver, Economics Department.

Crockenberg, S., & Litman, C. (1991). Effects of maternal employment on maternal and 2-year-old child behavior. *Child Development, 62,* 930–953.

Crockenberg, S. B. (1981). Infant irritability, mother responsiveness and social support influences on the security of infant-mother attachment. *Child Development, 52,* 857–865.

Cryan, J., Sheehan, R., Wiechel, J., & Bandy-Hedden, I. (1992). Success outcomes of full-school-day kindergarten: More positive behavior and increased achievement in the years after. *Early Childhood Research Quality, 7,* 187–203.

Cryer, D., & Burchinal, M. (1997). Parents as child care consumers. *Early Childhood Research Quarterly, 12,* 35–58.

Cryer, D., Tietze, W., Burchinal, M., Leal, T., & Palacios, J. (1999). Predicting process quality from structural quality in preschool programs: A cross-country comparison. *Early Childhood Research Quarterly, 14,* 339–361.

Cummings, E. (1980). Caregiver stability and daycare. *Developmental Psychology, 16,* 31–37.

Currie, J. (2001). Early childhood education programs. *Journal of Economic Perspectives, 15,* 213–238.

Currie, J., & Thomas, D. (1995). Does Head Start make a difference? *American Economic Review, 85,* 341–384.

Currie, J., & Thomas, D. (1999). Does Head Start help Hispanic children? *Journal of Public Economics, 74,* 235–262.

Currie, J., & Thomas, D. (2000). School quality and the long-term effects of Head Start. *Journal of Human Resources, 35,* 755–774.

Dahlström, E. (Ed.). (1962). *Kvinnors liv och arbete* [Women's lives and work]. Stockholm: Studieförbundet Näringsliv och Samhälle.

Daly, M., & Wilson, M. I. (1995). Discriminative potential solicitude and the relevance of evolutionary models to the analysis of motivational systems. In M. Gazzaniga (Ed.), *The cognitive neurosciences* (pp. 1269–1286). Cambridge, MA: MIT Press.

Darlington, R. B., Royce, J. M., Snipper, A. S., Murray, H. W., & Lazar, I. (1980). Preschool programs and the later school competence of children from low-income families. *Science, 208,* 202–204.

Datta, L. (1976). The impact of the Westinghouse/Ohio evaluation on the development of Project Head Start. In C. C. Abt (Ed.), *The evaluation of social programs* (pp. 129–181). Beverly Hills, CA: Sage.

Denham, S. A., & Holt, R. W. (1993). Preschoolers' likeability as cause or consequence of their social behavior. *Developmental Psychology, 29,* 271–275.

Denham, S. A., Mason, T., Caverly, S., Schmidt, M., Hackney, R., Caswell, C., et al. (2001). Preschoolers at play: Co-socialisers of emotional and social competence. *International Journal of Behavioral Development, 25,* 290–301.

Desai, S., Chase-Lansdale, P. L., & Michael, R. T. (1989). Mother or market? Effects of maternal employment on the intellectual ability of 4-year-old children. *Demography, 26,* 545–561.

DeSchipper, J. C., Tavecchio, L. W. C., van IJzendoorn, M. H., & Linting, M. (2003). The relation of flexible child care to quality of center day care and children's socio-emotional functioning: A survey and observational study. *Infant Behavior and Development, 26,* 300–325.

DeSchipper, J. C., Tavecchio, L. W. C., van IJzendoorn, M. H., & van Zeijl, J. (2004). Goodness-of-fit in center day care: Relation of temperament, stability, and quality of care with the child's adjustment. *Early Childhood Research Quarterly, 19,* 257–272.

De Wolff, M., & van IJzendoorn, M. H. (1997). Sensitivity and attachment: A meta-analysis on parental antecedents of infant attachment. *Child Development, 68,* 571–591.

Doernberger, C., & Zigler, E. F. (1993). Project Follow Through: Intent and reality. In E. F. Zigler & S. J. Styfco (Eds.), *Head Start and beyond: A national plan for extended childhood intervention* (pp. 43–72). New Haven, CT: Yale University Press.

Dombro, A. L. (1995). *Child care aware: A guide to promoting professional development in family child care.* New York: Families and Work Institute.

Dombro, A. L., & Modigliani, K. (1995). *Family child care providers speak about training, trainees, accreditation, and professionalism: Findings from a survey of family-to-family graduates.* New York: Families and Work Institute.

Dragonas, T., Tsiantis, J., & Lambidi, A. (1995). Assessing quality day care: The child care facility schedule. *International Journal of Behavioral Development, 18,* 557–568.

Dunn, J., Creps, C., & Brown, J. (1996). Children's family relationships between two and five: Developmental changes and individual differences. *Social Development, 5,* 230–250.

Dunn, L. (1993). Proximal and distal features of day care quality and children's development. *Early Childhood Research Quarterly, 8,* 167–192.

Early Head Start Research and Evaluation Project. (2001). *Building their futures.* Washington, DC: Administration on Children, Youth, and Families.

Early Head Start Research and Evaluation Project. (2002a). *Making a difference in the lives of infants and toddlers and their families: The impacts of Early Head Start.* Washington, DC: Administration on Children, Youth, and Families.

Early Head Start Research and Evaluation Project. (2002b). *Pathways to quality and full implementation in Early Head Start programs.* Washington, DC: Administration on Children, Youth, and Families.

Easterbrooks, M. A., & Goldberg, W. A. (1985). Effects of early maternal employment on toddlers, mothers, and fathers. *Developmental Psychology, 21,* 774–783.

Egeland, B., & Hiester, M. (1995). The long-term consequences of infant daycare and mother-infant attachment. *Child Development, 66,* 474–485.

Eisenberg, N., & Fabes, R. A. (1998). Prosocial development. In W. Damon (Editor-in-Chief) & N. Eisenberg (Vol. Ed.), *Handbook of child psychology: Vol. 5. Social, emotional, and personality development* (5th ed., pp. 701–778). New York: Wiley.

Eisenberg, N., Shea, C. L., Carlo, G., & Knight, G. (1991). Empathy-related responding and cognition: A "chicken and the egg" dilemma. In W. Kurtines & G. Gerwitz (Eds.), *Handbook of moral behavior and development: Vol. 2. Research* (pp. 63–88). Hillsdale, NJ: Erlbaum.

Elicker, J., Englund, M., & Sroufe, L. A. (1992). Predicting peer competence and peer relationships in childhood from early parent-child relationships. In R. D. Parke & G. W. Ladd (Eds.), *Family-peer relationships: Modes of linkage* (pp. 77–106). Hillsdale, NJ: Erlbaum.

Elicker, J., Fortner-Wood, C., & Noppe, I. (1999). The context of infant attachment in family child care. *Journal of Applied Developmental Psychology, 20,* 319–336.

Elicker, J., & Mathur, S. (1997). What do they do all day? Comprehensive evaluation of a full-school-day kindergarten. *Early Childhood Research Quarterly, 12,* 459–480.

Elicker, J., Noppe, I. C., Noppe, L. D., & Fortner-Wood, C. (1997). The Parent-Caregiver Relationship Scale: Rounding out the relationship system in infant child care. *Early Education and Development, 8,* 83–100.

Endsley, R. C., & Minish, P. A. (1991). Parent-staff communication in day care centers during morning and afternoon transitions. *Early Childhood Research Quarterly, 6,* 119–135.

Erel, O., Oberman, Y., & Yirmiya, N. (2000). Maternal versus nonmaternal care and seven domains of children's development. *Psychological Bulletin, 126,* 727–747.

Fabes, R. A., Eisenberg, N., Jones, S., Smith, M., Guthrie, I., Poulin, R., et al. (1999). Regulation, emotionality, and preschoolers' socially competent peer interactions. *Child Development, 70,* 432–442.

Farran, D. C., & Ramey, C. T. (1977). Infant day care and attachment behaviors toward mothers and teachers. *Child Development, 48,* 1112–1116.

Farver, J., & Branstetter, W. (1994). Preschoolers' prosocial responses to their peers' distress. *Developmental Psychology, 30,* 334–341.

Feagans, L. V., & Farran, D. C. (1994). The effects of day care intervention in the preschool years on the narrative skills of poverty children in kindergarten. *International Journal of Behavioral Development, 17,* 503–523.

Feagans, L. V., Kipp, E., & Blood, I. (1994). The effect of otitis media on the attention skills of day-care-setting toddlers. *Developmental Psychology, 30,* 701–708.

Fein, G. G. (1995). Infants in group care: Patterns of despair and detachment. *Early Childhood Research Quarterly, 10,* 261–275.

Fein, G. G., & Clarke-Stewart, K. A. (1973). *Day care in context.* New York: Wiley.

Fein, G. G., Gariboldi, A., & Boni, R. (1993). The adjustment of infants and toddlers to group care: The first 6 months. *Early Childhood Research Quarterly, 8,* 1–14.

Feldman, R., & Klein, P. S. (2003). Toddlers' self-regulated compliance to mothers, caregivers, and fathers: Implications for theories of socialization. *Developmental Psychology, 39,* 680–692.

Field, T. (1991a). Quality infant day-care and grade school behavior and performance. *Child Development, 62,* 863–870.

Field, T. M. (1991b). Young children's adaptations to repeated separations from their mothers. *Child Development, 62,* 539–547.

Field, T. M., Gerwitz, J. L., Cohen, D., Garcia, R., Greenberg, R., & Collins, K. (1984). Leavetakings and reunions of infants, toddlers, preschoolers and their parents. *Child Development, 55,* 628–635.

Finkelstein, N. (1982). Aggression: Is it stimulated by day care? *Young Children, 37,* 3–9.

Finkelstein, N. W., Dent, C., Gallacher, K., & Ramey, C. T. (1978). Social behavior of infants and toddlers in a day-care environment. *Developmental Psychology, 14,* 257–262.

Fischer, J. L., & Eheart, B. K. (1991). Family day care: A theoretical basis for improving quality. *Early Childhood Research Quarterly, 6,* 549–563.

Fosburg, S., Hawkins, P. D., Singer, J. D., Goodson, B. D., Smith, J. M., & Brush, L. R. (1980). *National day care home study.* Cambridge, MA: ABT Associates.

Foteeva, Y. V. (1993). The commonwealth of independent states. In M. Cochran (Ed.), *International handbook of child care policies and programs* (pp. 125–142). Westport, CT: Greenwood Press.

Fouts, H. H., Hewlett, B. S., & Lamb, M. E. (2005). Parent-offspring conflicts among the Bofi farmers and foragers of Central Africa. *Current Anthropology, 46,* 29–50.

Fouts, H. N. (2002). *The social and emotional contexts of weaning among the Bofi farmers and foragers of Central Africa.* Unpublished doctoral dissertation, Washington State University, Pullman.

Fouts, H. N., Lamb, M. E., & Hewlett, B. S. (2004). Infant crying in hunter-gatherer cultures. *Behavioral and Brain Sciences, 27,* 462–463.

Fox, N. (1977). Attachment of kibbutz infants to mother and metapelet. *Child Development, 48,* 1228–1239.

Fox, N. A. (1994). Dynamic cerebral processes underlying emotion regulation. *Monographs of the Society for Research in Child Development, 59*(2/3).

Fuerst, J. S., & Fuerst, D. (1993). Chicago experience with an early education program: The special case of the Child Parent Center program. *Urban Education, 28,* 69–96.

Fusaro, J. (1997). The effects of full-school-day kindergarten on student achievement: A meta-analysis. *Child Study Journal, 27,* 269–277.

Galambos, N. L., & Garbarino, J. (1983, July/August). Identifying the missing links in the study of latchkey children. *Children Today,* 2–4, 40–41.

Galambos, N. L., & Maggs, J. L. (1991). Out-of-school care of young adolescents and self-reported behavior. *Developmental Psychology, 27,* 644–655.

Galinsky, E. (1992). The impact of child care on parents. In A. Booth (Ed.), *Child care in the 1990s: Trends and consequences* (pp. 159–172). Hillsdale, NJ: Erlbaum.

Galinsky, E., Howes, C., & Kontos, S. (1995). *The family child care training study.* New York: Families and Work Institute.

Galinsky, E., Howes, G., Kontos, S., & Shinn, M. (1994). *The study of children in family child care and relative care.* New York: Families and Work Institute.

Gamble, T., & Zigler, E. F. (1989). The Head Start Synthesis Project: A critique. *Journal of Applied Developmental Psychology, 10,* 267–274.

Garces, E., Thomas, D., & Currie, J. (2002). Longer-term effects of Head Start. *American Economic Review, 92,* 999–1012.

Genser, A., & Baden, C. (Eds.). (1980). *School-aged child care: Programs and issues.* Urbana: ERIC Clearinghouse, University of Illinois.

Ghazvini, A. S., & Readdick, C. A. (1994). Parent-caregiver communication and quality of care in diverse child care settings. *Early Childhood Research Quarterly, 9,* 207–222.

Goelman, H. (1988). A study of the relationship between structure and process variables in home and day care settings on children's language development. In A. R. Pence (Ed.), *Ecological research with children and families: From concepts to methodology* (pp. 16–34). New York: Teachers College Press.

Goelman, H. (1992). Day care in Canada. In M. E. Lamb, K. J. Sternberg, C.-P. Hwang, & A. G. Broberg (Eds.), *Child care in context: Cross-cultural perspectives* (pp. 223–263). Hillsdale, NJ: Erlbaum.

Goelman, H., & Pence, A. R. (1987a). Effects of child care, family, and individual characteristics on children's language development: The Victorian day care research project. In D. A. Phillips (Ed.), *Quality in child care: What does research tell us?* (pp. 89–104). Washington, DC: National Association for the Education of Young Children.

Goelman, H., & Pence, A. R. (1987b). The relationships between family structure and child development in three types of day care. In S. Kontos & D. L. Peters (Eds.), *Advances in applied developmental psychology* (Vol. 2, pp. 129–146). Norwood, NJ: Ablex.

Golden, M., Rosenbluth, L., Grossi, M., Policare, H., Freeman, H., & Brownlee, E. (1978). *New York City infant day care study.* New York: Medical and Health Resource Association of New York City.

Goldman, J. A. (1981). Social participation of preschool children in same- versus mixed-age groups. *Child Development, 52,* 644–650.

Goldsmith, H. H., & Alansky, J. A. (1987). Maternal and infant temperamental predictors of attachment: A meta-analytic review. *Journal of Consulting and Clinical Psychology, 55,* 805–816.

Goossens, F. A., & Melhuish, E. C. (1996). On the ecological validity of measuring the sensitivity of professional caregivers: The laboratory versus the nursery. *European Journal of Psychology of Education, 11,* 169–176.

Goossens, F. A., & van IJzendoorn, M. H. (1990). Quality of infants' attachments to professional caregivers: Relation to infant-parent attachment and day-care characteristics. *Child Development, 61,* 832–837.

Gray, S. W., & Klaus, R. A. (1965). An experimental preschool program for culturally deprived children. *Child Development, 36,* 889–898.

Griswold, R. (1993). *Fatherhood in America: A history.* New York: Basic Books.

Grossmann, K. E., Grossmann, K., & Waters, E. (Eds.). (in press). *The power and dynamics of longitudinal attachment research*. New York: Guilford Press.

Gullo, D. (2000). The long-term educational effects of half-day versus full-school day kindergarten. *Early Child Development and Care, 160,* 17–24.

Gunnarsson, L. (1993). Sweden. In M. Cochran (Ed.), *International handbook of child care policies and programs* (pp. 491–514). Westport, CT: Greenwood Press.

Haas, L. (1992). *Equal parenthood and social policy: A study of parental leave in Sweden.* Albany: State University of New York Press.

Haber, S., & Kafka, H. (1992). The other mommy: Professional women's solutions and compromises. *Psychotherapy in Private Practice, 11,* 27–39.

Hale, B. A., Seitz, V., & Zigler, E. F. (1990). Health services and Head Start: A forgotten formula. *Journal of Applied Developmental Psychology, 11,* 447–458.

Hamre, B., & Pianta, R. (2004). Self-reported depression in non-familial caregivers: Relevance and association with caregiver behavior in child care settings. *Early Childhood Research Quarterly, 19,* 297–318.

Han, W.-J. (2004). Nonstandard work schedules and child care decisions: Evidence from the NICHD Study of Early Child Care. *Early Childhood Research Quarterly, 19,* 231–256.

Harms, T., & Clifford, R. M. (1980). *The Early Childhood Environment Rating Scale.* New York: Teachers College Press.

Harms, T., & Clifford, R. M. (1989). *The Family Day Care Rating Scale.* New York: Teachers College Press.

Harms, T., Clifford, R. M., & Cryer, D. (1998). *The Early Childhood Environment Rating Scale* (Rev. ed.). New York: Teachers College Press.

Harms, T., Clifford, R. M., & Cryer, D. (2002). *Escala De Calificacion Del Ambiente De La Infancia Temprana* (Edicion revisada) [Early Childhood Environment Rating Scale (Rev. ed.)]. New York: Teachers College Press.

Harms, T., Cryer, D., & Clifford, R. M. (2003). *Infant/Toddler Environment Rating Scale* (Rev. ed.). New York: Teachers College Press.

Harms, T., Jacobs, E., & White, D. (1996). *School-Age Care Environment Rating Scale.* New York: Teachers College Press.

Harris, J. R. (1998). *The nurture assumption.* New York: Simon & Schuster.

Harrison, L., & Ungerer, J. A. (2002). Maternal employment and infant-mother attachment security at 12 months postpartum. *Developmental Psychology, 38,* 758–773.

Hartmann, E. (1991). Effects of day care and maternal teaching on child educability. *Scandinavian Journal of Psychology, 32,* 325–335.

Hartmann, E. (1995). *Long-term effects of day care and maternal teaching on educational competence, independence and autonomy in young adulthood.* Unpublished manuscript, University of Oslo, Norway.

Hartup, W. W., & Moore, S. G. (1990). Early peer relations: Developmental significance and prognostic implications. *Early Childhood Research Quarterly, 5,* 1–17.

Haskins, R. (1985). Public school aggression among children with varying day-care experience. *Child Development, 56,* 689–703.

Haskins, R. (1989). Beyond metaphor: The efficacy of early childhood education. *American Psychologist, 44,* 274–282.

Haskins, R. (1992). Is anything more important than day-care quality? In A. Booth (Ed.), *Child care in the 1990s: Trends and consequences* (pp. 101–116). Hillsdale, NJ: Erlbaum.

Hay, D. F. (1994). Prosocial development. *Journal of Child Psychology and Psychiatry, 35,* 29–71.

Hay, D. F., Castle, J., & Davies, L. (2000). Toddlers' use of force against familiar peers: A precursor of serious aggression? *Child Development, 71,* 457–467.

Hay, D. F., Castle, J., Davies, L., Demetriou, H., & Stimson, C. A. (1999). Prosocial action in very early childhood. *Journal of Child Psychology and Psychiatry, 40,* 905–916.

Hebbeler, K. (1985). An old and a new question on the effects of early education for children from low income families. *Educational Evaluation and Policy Analysis, 7,* 207–216.

Hegland, S. M., & Rix, M. K. (1990). Aggression and assertiveness in kindergarten children differing in day care experiences. *Early Childhood Research Quarterly, 5,* 105–116.

Hess, R. D. (1970). Social class and ethnic influences upon socialization. In P. H. Mussen (Ed.), *Carmichael's manual of child psychology* (Vol. 2, 3rd ed., pp. 457–557). New York: Wiley.

Hestenes, L. L., Kontos, S., & Bryan, Y. (1993). Children's emotional expression in child care centers varying in quality. *Early Childhood Research Quarterly, 8,* 295–307.

Hewlett, B. S., & Lamb, M. E. (Eds.). (2005). *Hunter-gatherer childhoods.* New Brunswick, NJ: Transaction/Aldine.

Hewlett, B. S., Lamb, M. E., Shannon, D., Leyendecker, B., & Schölmerich, A. (1998). Culture and early infancy among Central African foragers and farmers. *Developmental Psychology, 34,* 653–661.

Hock, E. (1980). Working and nonworking mothers and their infants: A comparative study of maternal caregiving characteristics and infants' social behavior. *Merrill-Palmer Quarterly, 46,* 79–101.

Hock, E., McBride, S., & Gnezda, M. T. (1989). Maternal separation anxiety: Mother-infant separation from the maternal perspective. *Child Development, 60,* 793–802.

Hofferth, S. L. (1992). The demand for and supply of child care in the 1990s. In A. Booth (Ed.), *Child care in the 1990s: Trends and consequences* (pp. 3–26). Hillsdale, NJ: Erlbaum.

Hofferth, S. L., & Phillips, D. A. (1987). Child care in the United States, 1970 to 1995. *Journal of Marriage and the Family, 49,* 559–571.

Hoff-Ginsberg, E., & Krueger, W. M. (1991). Older siblings as conversational partners. *Merrill-Palmer Quarterly, 37,* 465–481.

Holloway, S. D., & Reichhart-Erickson, M. (1989). Child care quality, family structure, and maternal expectation: Relationship to preschool children's peer relations. *Journal of Applied Developmental Psychology, 10,* 281–298.

Hovacek, H. J., Ramey, C. T., Campbell, F. A., Hoffman, K. P., & Fletcher, R. H. (1987). Predicting school failure and assessing early intervention with high risk children. *Journal of the American Academy of Child and Adolescent Psychiatry, 26,* 758–763.

Howes, C. (1983). Caregiver's behavior in center and family day care. *Journal of Applied Developmental Psychology, 4,* 99–107.

Howes, C. (1990). Can the age of entry into child care and the quality of child care predict adjustment in kindergarten? *Developmental Psychology, 26,* 292–303.

Howes, C. (1996). The earliest friendships. In W. M. Bukowski & A. F. Newcomb (Eds.), *The company they keep: Friendship in childhood and adolescence* (pp. 66–86). New York: Cambridge University Press.

Howes, C. (1997). Teacher-sensitivity, children's attachment and play with peers. *Early Education and Development, 8,* 41–49.

Howes, C., & Farver, J. (1987). Social pretend play in 2-year-olds: Effects of age of partner. *Early Childhood Research Quarterly, 2,* 305–314.

Howes, C., Galinsky, E., & Kontos, S. (1998). Child care caregiver sensitivity and attachment. *Social Development, 7,* 25–36.

Howes, C., & Hamilton, C. E. (1993). The changing experience of child care: Changes in teachers and in teacher-child relationships and children's social competence with peers. *Early Childhood Research Quarterly, 8*, 15–32.

Howes, C., Hamilton, C. E., & Matheson, C. C. (1994). Children's relationships with peers: Differential associations with aspects of the teacher-child relationship. *Child Development, 65*, 253–263.

Howes, C., Hamilton, C. E., & Philipsen, L. C. (1998). Stability and continuity of child-caregiver and child-peer relationships. *Child Development, 69*, 418–426.

Howes, C., Matheson, C. C., & Hamilton, C. (1994). Maternal, teacher, and child care history correlates of children's relationship with peers. *Child Development, 65*, 264–273.

Howes, C., & Olenick, M. (1986). Family and child care influences on toddler compliance. *Child Development, 57*, 202–216.

Howes, C., Phillips, D. A., & Whitebook, M. (1992). Thresholds of quality: Implications for the social development of children in center-based child care. *Child Development, 63*, 447–460.

Howes, C., & Rubenstein, J. L. (1981). Toddler peer behavior in two types of day care. *Infant Behavior and Development, 4*, 387–393.

Howes, C., & Rubenstein, J. L. (1985). Determinants of toddler's experience in day care: Age of entry and quality of setting. *Child Care Quarterly, 14*, 140–151.

Howes, C., Smith, E., & Galinsky, E. (1995). *Florida Child Care Quality Improvement Study.* New York: Families and Work Institute.

Howes, C., & Smith, E. W. (1995). Children and their child care caregivers: Profiles of relationships. *Social Development, 4*, 44–61.

Howes, C., & Stewart, P. (1987). Child's play with adults, toys, and peers: An examination of family and child care influences. *Developmental Psychology, 23*, 423–430.

Hrdy, S. B. (1999). *Mother nature: A history of mothers, infants, and natural selection.* New York: Pantheon Books.

Hrdy, S. B. (2002). On why it takes a village: Cooperative breeders, infant needs and the future. In G. Peterson (Ed.), *The past, present, and future of the human family* (pp. 86–110). Salt Lake City: University of Utah Press.

Hrdy, S. B. (2005). Comes the child before man: How cooperative breeding and prolonged post-weaning dependence shaped human potentials. In B. S. Hewlett & M. E. Lamb (Eds.), *Hunter-gatherer childhoods* (pp. 65–91). New Brunswick, NJ: Tranaction/Aldine.

Hughes, C., & Dunn, J. (1997). "Pretend you didn't know": Preschoolers' talk about mental states in pretend play. *Cognitive Development, 12*, 381–403.

Hunt, J., McV. (1961). *Intelligence and experience.* New York: Ronald Press.

Hwang, C. P., Broberg, A., & Lamb, M. E. (1991). Swedish childcare research. In E. C. Melhuish & P. Moss (Eds.), *Day care for young children* (pp. 75–101). London: Routledge.

Hwang, C. P., & Broberg, A. G. (1992). The historical and social context of child care in Sweden. In M. E. Lamb, K. J. Sternberg, C. P. Hwang, & A. G. Broberg (Eds.), *Child care in context: Cross-cultural perspectives* (pp. 27–54). Hillsdale, NJ: Erlbaum.

Hyson, M. C., Hirsh-Pasek, K., & Rescorla, L. (1990). Classroom Practices Inventory: An observation instrument based on NAEYC's guidelines for developmentally appropriate practices for 4- and 5-year-old children. *Early Childhood Research Quarterly, 5*, 475–494.

Infant Health and Development Program. (1990). Enhancing the outcomes of low-birthweight, premature infants: A multisite, randomized trial. *Journal of the American Medical Association, 263*, 3035–3042.

Infield, H. F. (1944). *Cooperative living in Palestine.* New York: Dryden.

Jensen, A. R. (1969). How much can we boost IQ and scholastic achievement? *Harvard Educational Review, 39*, 1–123.

Jewsuwan, R., Luster, T., & Kostelnik, M. (1993). The relation between parents' perceptions of temperament and children's adjustment to preschool. *Early Childhood Research Quarterly, 8*, 33–51.

Johansen, A. S., Leibowitz, A., & Waite, L. J. (1996). The importance of child-care characteristics to choice of care. *Journal of Marriage and the Family, 58*, 759–772.

Kagan, J. S. (1980). *Infancy.* Cambridge, MA: Harvard University Press.

Kagan, J. S., Hunt, J. M., Crow, J. F., Bereiter, G., Elkand, D., Cronbach, L. J., et al. (1969). How much can we boost IQ and scholastic achievement? A discussion. *Harvard Educational Review, 39*, 273–356.

Kagan, S. L. (1991). Examining profit and non-profit child care in an odyssey of quality and auspices. *Journal of Social Issues, 47*, 87–104.

Kamerman, S. B. (2000). From maternity to parental leave policies: Women's health, employment, and child and family well-being. *Journal of the American Women's Medical Association, 55*, 96–99.

Kamerman, S. B., & Kahn, A. J. (Eds.). (1978). *Family policy: Government and families in fourteen countries.* New York: Columbia University Press.

Kamerman, S. B., & Kahn, A. J. (1981). *Child care, family benefits, and working parents.* New York: Columbia University Press.

Karoly, L. A., Greenwood, P. W., Everingham, S. S., Haube, J., Kilburn, M. R., Rydell, P. C., et al. (1998). *Investing in our children: What we know and don't know about the worths and benefits of early childhood interventions.* Santa Monica, CA: RAND Corporation.

Kennedy, E. M. (1993). Head Start transition project: Head Start goes to elementary school. In E. F. Zigler & S. J. Styfco (Eds.), *Head Start and beyond: A national plan for extended childhood intervention* (pp. 97–109). New Haven, CT: Yale University Press.

Kenny, D. A., & La Voie, L. (1984). Social relation model. In L. Berkowitz (Ed.), *Advances in experimental social psychology* (pp. 141–182). Orlando, FL: Academic Press.

Ketterlinus, R. D., Bookstein, F. L., Sampson, P. D., & Lamb, M. E. (1989). Partial least squares analysis in developmental psychopathology. *Development and Psychopathology, 1*, 351–371.

Ketterlinus, R. D., Henderson, S. H., & Lamb, M. E. (1992). Les effets du type de garde de l'emploi maternel et de l'estime de soi sur le comportement des enfants [The effect of type of child care and maternal employment on children's behavioral adjustment and self-esteem]. In B. Pierrehumbert (Ed.), *L'accueil du jeune enfant: Politiques et recherches dans les différents pays* [Child care in infancy: Policy and research issues in different countries] (pp. 150–163). Paris: ESF Editeur.

Kienbaum, J. (2001). The socialization of compassionate behavior by child care teachers. *Early Education and Development, 12,* 139–153.

Kisker, E. E., & Silverberg, M. (1991). Child care utilization by disadvantaged teenage mothers. *Journal of Social Issues, 47,* 159–178.

Klimes-Dougan, B., & Kistner, J. (1990). Physically abused preschoolers' responses to peers' distress. *Developmental Psychology, 26,* 599–602.

Knitzer, J. (2001). Federal and state efforts to improve care for infants and toddlers. *Future of Children, 11,* 79–97.

Kontos, S. (1991). Child care quality, family background, and children's development. *Early Childhood Research Quarterly, 6,* 249–262.

Kontos, S. (1994). The ecology of family day care. *Early Childhood Research Quarterly, 9,* 87–110.

Kontos, S., Burchinal, M., Howes, C., Wisseh, S., & Galinsky, E. (2002). An ecobehavioral approach to examining the contextual effects of early childhood classrooms. *Early Childhood Research Quarterly, 17,* 239–258.

Kontos, S., & Dunn, L. (1989). Attitudes of caregivers, maternal experiences with daycare, and children's development. *Journal of Applied Developmental Psychology, 10,* 37–51.

Kontos, S., & Fiene, R. (1987). Child care quality, compliance with regulations, and children's development: The Pennsylvania study. In D. A. Phillips (Ed.), *Quality in child care: What does research tell us?* (pp. 57–80). Washington, DC: National Association for the Education of Young Children.

Kontos, S., Howes, C., Shinn, M., & Galinsky, E. (1994). *Quality in family child care and relative care.* New York: Teachers College Press.

Kontos, S., & Stremmel, A. J. (1988). Caregivers' perceptions of working conditions in a child care environment. *Early Childhood Research Quarterly, 3,* 77–90.

Korczak, E. (1993). Poland. In M. Cochran (Ed.), *International handbook of child care policies and programs* (pp. 453–467). Westport, CT: Greenwood Press.

Kreisman, M. B. (2003). Evaluating academic outcomes of Head Start: An application of general growth mixture modeling. *Early Childhood Research Quarterly, 18,* 238–254.

Kreyenfeld, M. (2004). Fertility decisions in the FRG and GDR: An analysis with data from the German fertility and family survey. *Demographic Research, 3,* 275–318.

Kreyenfeld, M., Spiess, C. K., & Wagner, G. G. (2001). *Finanzierrungs-und organisationsmodelle institutioneller kinderbetreuung* [Fiscal and organizational models for child care]. Berlin, Germany: Luchterhand.

Ladd, G. W., & Le Sieur, K. D. (1995). Parents and child's relationships. In M. H. Bornstein (Ed.), *Handbook of parenting* (Vol. 4, pp. 377–409). Mahwah, NJ: Erlbaum.

Lamb, M. E. (1986). The changing roles of fathers. In M. E. Lamb (Ed.), *The father's role: Applied perspectives* (pp. 3–27). New York: Wiley.

Lamb, M. E. (1998). Nonparental child care: Context, quality, correlates, and consequences. In W. Damon (Editor-in-Chief), & I. E. Sigel, & K. A. Renninger (Vol. Eds.), *Handbook of child psychology: Vol. 4. Child psychology in practice* (5th ed., pp. 73–133). New York: Wiley.

Lamb, M. E. (2000). The effects of quality of care on child development. *Applied Developmental Science, 4,* 112–115.

Lamb, M. E. (2005). Développement socio-émotionnel et scolarisation précoce: Recherches expérimentale [Socioemotional development and early education: Experimental research]. In J.-J. Ducret (Ed.), *Constructivisme et education (II): Scolariser la petite enfance?* [Constructivism and education: Pt. 2. Infant education?]. Genève, Switzerland: Service de la recherche en éducation.

Lamb, M. E., Hwang, C. P., Bookstein, F. L., Broberg, A., Hult, G., & Frodi, M. (1988). Determinants of social competence in Swedish preschoolers. *Developmental Psychology, 24,* 58–70.

Lamb, M. E., Hwang, C. P., Broberg, A., & Bookstein, F. L. (1988). The effects of out-of-home care on the development of social competence in Sweden: A longitudinal study. *Early Childhood Research Quarterly, 3,* 379–402.

Lamb, M. E., & Levine, J. A. (1983). The Swedish parental insurance policy: An experiment in social engineering. In M. E. Lamb (Ed.), *Fatherhood and family policy* (pp. 39–51). Hillsdale, NJ: Erlbaum.

Lamb, M. E., & Sternberg, K. J. (1990). Do we really know how day care affects children? *Journal of Applied Developmental Psychology, 11,* 351–379.

Lamb, M. E., & Sternberg, K. J. (1992). Sociocultural perspectives on nonparental child care. In M. E. Lamb, K. J. Sternberg, A. Broberg, & C. P. Hwang (Eds.), *Child care in context: Cross-cultural perspectives* (pp. 1–23). Hillsdale, NJ: Erlbaum.

Lamb, M. E., Sternberg, K. J., Hwang, C. P., & Broberg, A. G. (Eds.). (1992). *Child care in context: Cross-cultural perspectives.* Hillsdale, NJ: Erlbaum.

Lamb, M. E., Sternberg, K. J., & Prodromidis, M. (1992). Nonmaternal care and the security of infant-mother attachment: A reanalysis of the data. *Infant Behavior and Development, 15,* 71–83.

Lamb, M. E., Thompson, R. A., Gardner, W. P., & Charnov, E. L. (1985). *Infant-mother attachment: The origins and developmental significance of individual differences in Strange Situation behavior.* Hillsdale, NJ: Erlbaum.

Lancaster, J. B., & Lancaster, C. S. (1987). The watershed: Change in parental investment and family formation strategies in the course of human evolution. In J. S. Lancaster, J. Altmann, A. Rossi, & L. R. Sherrod (Eds.), *Parenting across the life span: Biosocial perspectives* (pp. 187–205). Hawthorne, NY: Aldine de Gruyter.

Lancaster, J. B., Rossi, A., Altmann, J., & Sherrod, L. R. (Eds.). (1987). *Parenting across the life span: Biosocial perspectives.* Hawthorne, NY: Aldine de Gruyter.

Larsen, J. M., & Robinson, C. C. (1989). Later effects of preschool on low-risk children. *Early Childhood Research Quarterly, 4,* 133–144.

Lazar, I. (1981). Early intervention is effective. *Educational Leadership, 38,* 303–305.

Lazar, I., Darlington, R., Murray, H., Royce, J., & Snipper, A. (1982). Lasting effects of early education: A report from the Consortium for Longitudinal Studies. *Monographs of the Society for Research in Child Development, 47*(Serial No. 195).

Leaper, C. (1994). Exploring the correlates and consequences of gender segregation: Social relationships in childhood, adolescence and adulthood. In C. Leaper (Ed.), *New directions for child development: The development of gender relationships* (pp. 67–86). San Francisco: Jossey-Bass.

Leaper, C. (2002). Parenting girls and boys. In M. H. Bornstein (Ed.), *Handbook of parenting: Vol. 2. Children and parenting* (2nd ed., pp. 189–225). Mahwah, NJ: Erlbaum.

Lee, L. C. (1992). Day care in the People's Republic of China. In M. E. Lamb, K. J. Sternberg, C. P. Hwang, & A. G. Broberg (Eds.), *Child care in context: Cross-cultural perspectives* (pp. 355–392). Hillsdale, NJ: Erlbaum.

Leiderman, P. H., & Leiderman, G. F. (1974). Affective and cognitive consequences of polymatric infant care in the East African highlands. In *Minnesota Symposia on Child Psychology* (Vol. 8, pp. 81–110). Minneapolis: University of Minnesota Press.

Lemerise, E. A. (1997). Patterns of peer acceptance, social status, and social reputation in mixed-age preschool and primary classrooms. *Merill-Palmer Quarterly, 43,* 199–218.

Lerner, R. M. (1984). *On the nature of human plasticity.* New York: Cambridge University Press.

Lewis, M. (1998). *Altering fate: Why the past does not predict the future.* New York: Guilford Press.

Loeb, S., Fuller, B., Kagan, S. L., & Carrol, B. (2004). Child care in poor communities: Early learning effects of type, quality, and stability. *Child Development, 1,* 47–65.

Lollis, S. P. (1990). Effects of maternal behavior on toddler behavior during separation. *Child Development, 61,* 99–103.

Londerville, S., & Main, M. (1981). Security of attachment, compliance, and maternal training methods in the second year. *Developmental Psychology, 17,* 281–299.

Long, T. J., & Long, L. (1983). *The handbook of latchkey children and their parents.* New York: Arbor House.

Long, T. J., & Long, L. (1984). Latchkey children. In L. Katz (Ed.), *Current topics in early childhood education* (Vol. 5, pp. 141–164). Norwood, NJ: Ablex.

Love, J. M., Harrison, L., Sagi-Schwartz, A., van IJzendoorn, M. A., Ross, C., Ungerer, J., et al. (2003). Child-care quality matters: How conclusions may vary with context. *Child Development, 74,* 1021–1033.

Maccoby, E. E. (1998). *The two sexes: Growing up apart, coming together.* Cambridge, MA: Harvard University Press.

Maccoby, E. E., & Lewis, C. C. (2003). Less day care or different day care? *Child Development, 74,* 1069–1075.

Marshall, N. L., Garcia Coll, C., Marx, F., McCartney, K., Keefe, N., & Ruh, J. (1997). After-school time and children's behavioral adjustment. *Merill-Palmer Quarterly, 43,* 497–514.

Martin, S. L., Ramey, C. T., & Ramey, S. (1990). The prevention of intellectual impairment in children of impoverished families: Findings of a randomized trial of educational day care. *American Journal of Public Health, 80,* 844–847.

Mason, K. O., & Duberstein, L. (1992). Consequences of child care for parents' well-being. In A. Booth (Ed.), *Child care in the 1990s: Trends and consequences* (pp. 127–159). Hillsdale, NJ: Erlbaum.

McCartney, K. (1984). Effect of quality of day care environment on children's language development. *Developmental Psychology, 20,* 244–260.

McCord, J. (1990). Problem behaviors. In S. S. Feldman & G. R. Elliott (Eds.), *At the threshold: The developing adolescent* (pp. 414–430). Cambridge, MA: Harvard University Press.

McCune, L. (1995). A normative study of representational play in the transition to language. *Developmental Psychology, 31,* 198–206.

McKey, R. H., Condelli, L., Ganson, H., Barrett, B. J., McConkey, C., & Plantz, M. C. (1985). *The impact of Head Start on children, family, and communities: Final report of the Head Start Evaluation, Synthesis, and Utilization Project.* Washington, DC: U.S. Government Printing Office.

Meins, E. (1997). Security of attachment and maternal tutoring strategies: Interaction within the zone of proximal development. *British Journal of Developmental Psychology, 15,* 129–144.

Melhuish, E. C. (1987). Socio-emotional behavior at 18 months as a function of daycare experience, gender, and temperament. *Infant Mental Health Journal, 8,* 364–373.

Melhuish, E. C., & Moss, P. (1992). Day care in the United Kingdom in historical perspective. In M. E. Lamb, K. J. Sternberg, C. P. Hwang, & A. G. Broberg (Eds.), *Child care in context: Cross-cultural perspectives* (pp. 157–183). Hillsdale, NJ: Erlbaum.

Melhuish, E. C., Quinn, L., Sylva, K., Sammons, P., Siraj-Blatchford, I., Taggart, B., et al. (2001). *Cognitive and social/behavioural de-velopment at 3 to 4 years in relation to family background.* Belfast, Northern Ireland: Stranmillis University Press.

Melhuish, E. C., Quinn, L., Sylva, K., Sammons, P., Siraj-Blatchford, I., Taggart, B., et al. (2002a). *Pre-school experience and cognitive development at the start of primary school.* Belfast, Northern Ireland: Stranmillis University Press.

Melhuish, E. C., Quinn, L., Sylva, K., Sammons, P., Siraj-Blatchford, I., Taggart, B., et al. (2002b). *Pre-school experience and social/behavioral development at the start of primary school.* Belfast, Northern Ireland: Stranmillis University Press.

Melhuish, E. C., Sylva, K., Sammons, P., Siraj-Blatchford, I., & Taggart, B. (2001). *Effective provision of pre-school education project: Technical paper 7. Social/behavioral and cognitive development at 3 to 4 years in relation to family background.* London: Institute of Education.

Mitchell-Copeland, J., Denham, S. A., & DeMulder, E. K. (1997). Q-sort assessment of child-teacher attachment relationships and social competence in the preschool. *Early Education and Development, 8,* 27–39.

Morgan, G., Azer, S. L., Costley, J. B., Genser, A., Goodman, I. F., Lombardi, J., et al. (1993). *Making a career of it: The state of the states report on career development in early care and education.* Boston: Wheelock College.

Mott, J. A., Crowe, P. A., Richardson, J., & Flay, B. (1999). After-school supervision and adolescent cigarette smoking: Contributions of the setting and intensity of after-school self-care. *Journal of Behavioral Medicine, 22,* 35–58.

Mueller, E. (1989). Toddlers' peer relations: Shared meaning and semantics. In W. Damon (Ed.), *Child development today and tomorrow* (pp. 313–331). San Francisco: Jossey-Bass.

Mulhall, P. F., Stone, D., & Stone, B. (1996). Home alone: Is it a risk factor for middle school youth and drug use? *Journal of Drug Education, 26,* 39–48.

National Academy of Science. (1990). *Who cares for America's children?* Washington, DC: Author.

National Academy of Science. (2003). *Working families and growing kids.* Washington, DC: Author.

National Center for Educational Statistics. (2002). *The condition of education 2002* (NCES 2002-025). Washington, DC: U.S. Government Printing Office.

National Head Start Association. (1990). *Head Start: The nation's pride, a nation's challenge* (Report of the Silver Ribbon Panel). Alexandria, VA: Author.

National Institute of Child Health and Human Development Early Child Care Research Network. (1994). Child care and child development: The NICHD study of early child care. In S. L. Friedman & H. C. Haywood (Eds.), *Developmental follow-up: Concepts, domains, and methods* (pp. 377–396). New York: Academic Press.

National Institute of Child Health and Human Development Early Child Care Research Network. (1995a, April). *The dynamics of child care experiences during the first year of life.* Poster presented to the biennial meeting of the Society for Research in Child Development, Indianapolis, IN.

National Institute of Child Health and Human Development Early Child Care Research Network. (1995b, April). *Family economic status, structure, and maternal employment as predictors of child care quantity and quality.* Poster presented to the biennial meeting of the Society for Research in Child Development, Indianapolis, IN.

National Institute of Child Health and Human Development Early Child Care Research Network. (1995c, April). *Future directions: Testing models of developmental outcome.* Poster presented to the biennial meeting of the Society for Research in Child Development, Indianapolis, IN.

National Institute of Child Health and Human Development Early Child Care Research Network. (1995d, April). *Measuring child care quality in the first year.* Poster presented to the biennial meeting of the Society for Research in Child Development, Indianapolis, IN.

National Institute of Child Health and Human Development Early Child Care Research Network. (1996). Characteristics of infant child care: Factors contributing to positive caregiving. *Early Childhood Research Quarterly, 11,* 269–306.

National Institute of Child Health and Human Development Early Child Care Research Network. (1997a). Child care in the first year of life. *Merrill-Palmer Quarterly, 43,* 340–360.

National Institute of Child Health and Human Development Early Child Care Research Network. (1997b). The effects of infant child care on infant-mother attachment security: Results of the NICHD study of early child care. *Child Development, 68,* 860–879.

National Institute of Child Health and Human Development Early Child Care Research Network. (1997c). Familial factors associated with the characteristics of nonmaternal care for infants. *Journal of Marriage and Family, 59,* 389–408.

National Institute of Child Health and Human Development Early Child Care Research Network. (1998a). Early child care and self-control, compliance, and problem behavior at 24 and 36 months. *Child Development, 69,* 1145–1170.

National Institute of Child Health and Human Development Early Child Care Research Network. (1998b). Relations between family predictors and child outcomes: Are they weaker for children in child care? *Developmental Psychology, 34,* 1119–1128.

National Institute of Child Health and Human Development Early Child Care Research Network. (1999a). Child care and mother-child interaction in the first 3 years of life. *Developmental Psychology, 35,* 1399–1413.

National Institute of Child Health and Human Development Early Child Care Research Network. (1999b). Child outcomes when child care center classes meet recommended standards for quality. *American Journal of Public Health, 89,* 1072–1077.

National Institute of Child Health and Human Development Early Child Care Research Network. (1999c). Chronicity of maternal depressive symptoms, maternal sensitivity and child functioning at 36 months: Results from the NICHD Study of Early Child Care. *Developmental Psychology, 35,* 1297–1310.

National Institute of Child Health and Human Development Early Child Care Research Network. (2000a). Characteristics and quality of child care for toddlers and preschoolers. *Applied Developmental Science, 4,* 116–125.

National Institute of Child Health and Human Development Early Child Care Research Network. (2000b). Factors associated with fathers' caregiving activities and sensitivity with young children. *Journal of Family Psychology, 14,* 200–219.

National Institute of Child Health and Human Development Early Child Care Research Network. (2000c). The relation of child care to cognitive and language development. *Child Development, 71,* 960–980.

National Institute of Child Health and Human Development Early Child Care Research Network. (2001a). Child care and children's peer interaction at 24 and 36 months: The NICHD study of early child care. *Child Development, 72,* 1478–1500.

National Institute of Child Health and Human Development Early Child Care Research Network. (2001b). Child-care and family predictors of preschool attachment and stability from infancy. *Developmental Psychology, 37,* 847–862.

National Institute of Child Health and Human Development Early Child Care Research Network. (2001c). Nonmaternal care and family factors in early development: An overview of the NICHD study of early child care. *Applied Developmental Psychology, 22,* 457–492.

National Institute of Child Health and Human Development Early Child Care Research Network. (2002a). Child care structure-process-outcomes: Direct and indirect effects of child care quality on young children's development. *Psychological Science, 13,* 199–206.

National Institute of Child Health and Human Development Early Child Care Research Network. (2002b). Early child care and children's development prior to school entry: Results from the NICHD study of early child care. *American Educational Research Journal, 39,* 133–164.

National Institute of Child Health and Human Development Early Child Care Research Network. (2003a). Does amount of time spent in child care predict socioemotional adjustment during the transition to kindergarten? *Child Development, 74,* 976–1005.

National Institute of Child Health and Human Development Early Child Care Research Network. (2003b). Does quality of child care affect child outcomes at age $4\frac{1}{2}$? *Developmental Psychology, 39,* 451–469.

National Institute of Child Health and Human Development Early Child Care Research Network. (2003c). Early child care and mother-child interaction from 36 months through first grade. *Infant Behavior and Development, 26,* 234–370.

National Institute of Child Health and Human Development Early Child Care Research Network. (2004). Are child development outcomes related to before and after school care arrangements? Results from the NICHD Study of Early Child Care. *Child Development, 75,* 280–295.

National Institute of Child Health and Human Development Early Child Care Research Network (in press). Type of care and children's development at 54 months. *Early Childhood Research Quarterly.*

National Institute of Child Health and Human Development Early Child Care Research Network, & Duncan, G. J. (2003). Modeling the impacts of child care quality on children's preschool cognitive development. *Child Development, 74,* 1454–1475.

National Research Council. (1991). *Caring for America's children.* Washington, DC: National Academy Press.

Nelson, F., & Garduque, L. (1991). The experience and perception of continuity between home and day care from the perspectives of child, mother, and caregiver. *Early Child Development and Care, 68,* 99–111.

Nemenyi, M. (1993). Hungary. In M. Cochran (Ed.), *International handbook of child care policies and programs* (pp. 231–245). Westport, CT: Greenwood Press.

Nerlove, S. B. (1974). Women's workload and infant feeding practices: A relationship with demographic implications. *Ethnology, 13,* 207–214.

Neubauer, P. B. (Ed.). (1965). *Children in collectives: Childrearing aims and practices in the kibbutz.* Springfield, IL: Thomas.

New, R. (1993). Italy. In M. Cochran (Ed.), *International handbook of child care policies and programs* (pp. 291–311). Westport, CT: Greenwood Press.

North, A. F., Jr. (1979). Health services in Head Start. In E. Zigler & J. Valentine (Eds.), *Project Head Start* (pp. 231–258). New York: Free Press.

O'Brien, M., Roy, C., Jacobs, A., Macaluso, M., & Peyton, V. (1999). Conflict in the dyadic play of 3-year-old children. *Early Education and Development, 10,* 289–313.

Olmsted, P. P. (1992). A cross-national perspective on the demand for and supply of early childhood services. In A. Booth (Ed.), *Child care in the 1990s: Trends and consequences* (pp. 26–33). Hillsdale, NJ: Erlbaum.

Oppenheim, D., Sagi, A., & Lamb, M. E. (1988). Infant-adult attachments on the kibbutz and their relation to socioemotional development 4 years later. *Developmental Psychology, 24,* 427–433.

Organization for Economic Cooperation and Development. (2002). *Learning for tomorrow's world: First results from Pisa 2003* [OECD e-book]. Available from http://pisa.oecd.org.

Owen, M. T., Ware, A. M., & Barfoot, B. (2000). Caregiver-mother partnership behavior and the quality of caregiver-child and mother-child interactions. *Early Childhood Research Quarterly, 15,* 413–428.

Peisner-Feinberg, E., & Burchinal, M. (1997). Relations between preschool children's child care experience and concurrent development: The Cost, Quality, and Outcomes Study. *Merrill-Palmer Quarterly, 43,* 451–477.

Peisner-Feinberg, E. S., Burchinal, M. R., Clifford, R., Culkin, M. L., Howes, C., Kagan, S. L., et al. (2001). The relations of preschool child-care quality to children's cognitive and social developmental trajectories through second grade. *Child Development, 72,* 1534–1553.

Pence, A. R. (1993). Canada. In M. Cochran (Ed.), *International handbook of child care policies and programs* (pp. 57–81). Westport, CT: Greenwood Press.

Perner, J., Ruffman, T., & Leekam, S. R. (1994). Theory of mind is contagious: You catch it from your sibs. *Child Development, 65,* 1228–1238.

Petrogiannis, K. G. (1995). *Psychological development at 18 months of age as a function of child care experience in Greece.* Unpublished doctoral dissertation, University of Wales, Cardiff.

Pettit, G. S., Laird, R. D., Bates, J. E., & Dodge, K. A. (1997). Patterns of after-school care in middle childhood: Risk factors and developmental outcomes. *Merrill-Palmer Quarterly, 43,* 515–538.

Phillips, D. (1989). Future directions and need for child care in the United States. In J. S. Lande, S. Scarr, & N. Gunzenhauser (Eds.), *Caring for children: Challenge to America* (pp. 257–274). Hillsdale, NJ: Erlbaum.

Phillips, D., Lande, J., & Goldberg, M. (1990). The state of child care regulations: A comparative analysis. *Early Childhood Research Quarterly, 5,* 151–179.

Phillips, D., Mekos, D., Scarr, S., McCartney, R., & Abbott-Shim, M. (2001). Within and beyond the classroom door: Assessing quality in child care centers. *Early Childhood Research Quarterly, 15,* 475–496.

Phillips, D. A. (1992). Child care and parental well-being: Bringing quality of care into the picture. In A. Booth (Ed.), *Child care in the 1990s: Trends and consequences* (pp. 172–180). Hillsdale, NJ: Erlbaum.

Phillips, D. A., Howes, C., & Whitebook, M. (1991). Child care as an adult work environment. *Journal of Social Issues, 47,* 49–70.

Phillips, D. A., Howes, C., & Whitebook, M. (1992). The social policy context of child care: Effects on quality. *American Journal of Community Psychology, 20,* 25–51.

Phillips, D. A., McCartney, K., & Scarr, S. (1987). Child care quality and children's social development. *Developmental Psychology, 23,* 537–543.

Phillips, D. A., Voran, M., Kisker, E., Howes, C., & Whitebook, M. (1994). Child care for children in poverty: Opportunity or inequity? *Child Development, 65,* 472–492.

Phillips, D. A., & Zigler, E. F. (1987). The checkered history of federal child care regulation. In E. Z. Rothkopf (Ed.), *Review of research in education* (Vol. 14, pp. 3–41). Washington, DC: American Educational Research Association.

Phillipsen, L. C., Burchinal, M. P., Howes, C., & Cryer, D. (1997). The prediction of process quality from structural features of child care. *Early Childhood Research Quarterly, 12,* 281–303.

Piaget, J. (1965). *The moral judgment of the child.* New York: Free Press.

Pianta, R., & Nimetz, S. L. (1991). Relationships between children and teachers: Associations with classroom and home behavior. *Journal of Applied Developmental Psychology, 12,* 379–393.

Pierce, K. M., Hamm, J. V., & Vandell, D. L. (1999). Experiences in after school programs and children's adjustment in first grade classrooms. *Child Development, 70,* 756–767.

Pierrehumbert, B. (1994, September). *Socio-emotional continuity through the preschool years and child care experience.* Paper presented to the British Psychological Society, Developmental Section conference, Portsmouth, England.

Pierrehumbert, B., & Milhaud, K. (1994, June). *Socio-emotional continuity through the preschool years and child care experience.* Paper presented to the International Conference on Infant Studies, Paris, France.

Pierrehumbert, B., Ramstein, T., & Karmaniola, A. (1995). Bèbès á partager [Babies to share]. In M. Robin, I. Casati, & D. Candilis-Huisman (Eds.), *La construction des liens familiaux pendant la première enfance [The construction of family ties in infancy]* (pp. 107–128). Paris: Presses Universitaires de France.

Pierrehumbert, B., Ramstein, T., Karmaniola, A., & Halfon, O. (1996). Child care in the preschool years, behavior problems, and cognitive development. *European Journal of Educational Research, 11,* 201–214.

Pierrehumbert, B., Ramstein, T., Karmaniola, A., Miljkovitch, R., & Halfon, O. (2002). Quality of child care in the preschool years: A comparison of the influence of home care and day care characteristics on child outcome. *International Journal of Behavioral Development, 26,* 385–396.

Pierrehumbert, B., Ramstein, T., Krucher, R., El-Najjar, S., Lamb, M. E., & Halfon, O. (1996). L'evaluation du lieu de vie du jeune enfant. *Bulletin do Psychologie, 49,* 565–584.

Portnoy, F. C., & Simmons, C. H. (1978). Day care and attachment. *Child Development, 49,* 239–242.

Posner, J. K., & Vandell, D. L. (1994). Low-income children's after-school care: Are there beneficial effects of after-school programs? *Child Development, 63,* 440–456.

Posner, J. K., & Vandell, D. L. (1999). After-school activities and the development of low income urban children: A longitudinal study. *Developmental Psychology, 35,* 868–879.

Powell, C., & Grantham-McGregor, S. (1989). Home visiting of varying frequency and child development. *Pediatrics, 84,* 157–164.

Powell, D. R. (1982). From child to parent: Changing conceptions of early childhood intervention. *Annals of the American Academy of Political and Social Science, 481,* 135–144.

Prodromidis, M., Lamb, M. E., Sternberg, K. J., Hwang, C. P., & Broberg, A. G. (1995). Aggression and noncompliance among Swedish children in center-based care, family day care, and home care. *International Journal of Behavioral Development, 18,* 43–62.

Ragozin, A. (1980). Attachment behavior of day-care children: Naturalistic and laboratory observations. *Child Development, 51,* 409–415.

Ramey, C. T. (1992). High-risk children and IQ: Altering intergenerational patterns. *Intelligence, 16,* 239–256.

Ramey, C. T., Bryant, D. M., Wasik, B. H., Sparling, J. J., Fendt, K. H., & LaVange, L. M. (1992). Infant health and development program for low-birthweight, premature infants: Program elements, family participation, and child intelligence. *Pediatrics, 89,* 454–465.

Ramey, C. T., & Campbell, F. A. (1984). Preventive education for high-risk children: Cognitive consequences of the Carolina Abecedarian Project. *American Journal of Mental Deficiency, 88,* 515–523.

Ramey, C. T., & Campbell, F. A. (1987). The Carolina Abecedarian Project: An educational experiment concerning human malleability. In S. S. Gallagher & C. T. Ramey (Eds.), *The malleability of children* (pp. 127–139). Baltimore: Paul H. Brookes.

Ramey, C. T., & Campbell, F. A. (1992). Poverty, early childhood education, and academic competence: The Abecedarian experiment. In A. C. Huston (Ed.), *Children in poverty: Child development and public policy* (pp. 190–221). New York: Cambridge University Press.

Ramey, C. T., Ramey, S. L., Hardin, M., & Blair, C. (1995, May). *Family types and developmental risk: Functional differentiations among poverty families.* Paper presented to the fifth annual conference of the Center for Human Development and Developmental Disabilities, New Brunswick, NJ.

Ramey, C. T., & Smith, B. (1977). Assessing the intellectual consequences of early intervention with high risk infants. *American Journal of Mental Deficiency, 81,* 318–324.

Ramey, S. L., & Ramey, C. T. (1992). Early educational intervention with disadvantaged children: To what effect? *Applied and Preventive Psychology, 1,* 131–140.

Rauh, H., Ziegenhain, U., Müller, B., & Wijnroks, L. (2000). Stability and change in infant-mother attachment in the second year of life: Relations to parenting quality and varying degrees of day-care experience. In P. M. Crittenden & A. H. Claussen (Eds.), *The organization of attachment relationships: Maturation, culture, and context* (pp. 251–276). New York: Cambridge University Press.

Raver, C. C., Blackburn, E. K., Bancroft, M., & Torp, N. (1999). Relations between effective emotional self-regulation, attentional control, and low-income preschoolers' social competence with peers. *Early Education and Development, 10,* 333–350.

Reynolds, A. J. (1992a). *Effects of a multi-year child-parent center intervention program on children at risk.* Unpublished manuscript.

Reynolds, A. J. (1992b). Mediated effects of preschool intervention. *Early Education and Development, 3,* 139–164.

Reynolds, A. J. (1994). Effects of a preschool plus follow-on intervention for children at risk. *Developmental Psychology, 30,* 787–804.

Reynolds, A. J. (1995). One year of preschool intervention or two: Does it matter? *Early Childhood Research Quarterly, 10,* 1–31.

Reynolds, A. J. (1998). Extended early childhood intervention and school achievement: Age thirteen findings from the Chicago longitudinal study. *Child Development, 69,* 231–246.

Reynolds, A. J. (2000). *Success in early intervention: The Chicago Child-Parent Centers.* Lincoln: University of Nebraska Press.

Reynolds, A. J., Temple, J. A., Robertson, D. L., & Mann, E. A. (2001). Long-term effects of an early childhood intervention or educational achievement and juvenile arrest: A 15-year follow-up of low-income children in public school. *Journal of the American Medical Association, 285,* 2339–2346.

Richardson, J. L., Dwyer, K., McGuigan, K., Hansen, W. B., Dent, C., Johnson, C. A., et al. (1989). Substance use among 8th-grade students who take care of themselves after school. *Pediatrics, 84,* 556–566.

Roberts, R. N., Casto, G., Wasik, B., & Ramey, C. T. (1991). Family support in the home: Programs, policy, and social change. *American Psychologist, 46,* 131–137.

Roberts, R. N., & Wasik, B. H. (1990). Home visiting programs for families with children from birth to three: Results of a national survey. *Journal of Early Intervention, 14,* 274–284.

Roberts, R. N., & Wasik, B. H. (1994). Home visiting options within Head Start: Current positive and future directions. *Early Childhood Research Quarterly, 9,* 311–325.

Robertson, J., & Robertson, J. (1972). Quality of substitute care as an influence on separation responses. *Journal of Psychosomatic Research, 16,* 261–265.

Robertson, J., & Robertson, J. (1975). Reaktionen kleiner Kinder auf kurzfristige Trennung von der Mutter im Lichte neuer Beobachtungen [Children's responses to maternal separation in light of recent research]. *Psyche, 29,* 626–664.

Rodman, H., Pratto, D., & Nelson, R. (1985). Child care arrangements and children's functioning: A comparison of self-care and adult-care children. *Developmental Psychology, 21,* 413–418.

Rosenthal, M. K. (1991). Behaviors and beliefs of caregivers in family day care: The effects of background and work environment. *Early Childhood Research Quarterly, 6,* 263–283.

Rosenthal, M. K. (1992). Nonparental child care in Israel: A cultural and historical perspective. In M. E. Lamb, K. J. Sternberg, C. P. Hwang, & A. G. Broberg (Eds.), *Child care in context: Cross-cultural perspectives* (pp. 305–330). Hillsdale, NJ: Erlbaum.

Rosenthal, M. K. (1994). *An ecological approach to the study of child care: Family care in Israel.* Hillsdale, NJ: Erlbaum.

Rosenthal, R., & Vandell, D. L. (1996). Quality of care at school-aged child-care programs: Regulatable features, observed experiences, child perspectives, and parent perspectives. *Child Development, 67,* 2434–2445.

Rothstein-Fisch, C., & Howes, C. (1988). Toddler peer interaction in mixed-age groups. *Journal of Applied Developmental Psychology, 9,* 211–218.

Rubenstein, J., & Howes, C. (1976). The effects of peers on toddlers interaction with mother and toys. *Child Development, 47,* 597–605.

Rubenstein, J. L., & Howes, C. (1979). Caregiving and infant behavior in day care and in homes. *Developmental Psychology, 15,* 1–24.

Rubenstein, J. L., Howes, C., & Boyle, P. (1981). A 2-year follow-up of infants in community-based day care. *Journal of Child Psychology and Psychiatry, 8,* 1–11.

Rubenstein, J. L., Pedersen, F. A., & Yarrow, L. J. (1977). What happens when mother is away: A comparison of mothers and substitute caregivers. *Developmental Psychology, 13,* 529–530.

Rubin, K. H., Hastings, P., Chen, X., Stewart, S., & McNichol, K. (1998). Intrapersonal and maternal correlates of aggression, conflict, and externalizing problems in toddlers. *Child Development, 69,* 1614–1629.

Ruopp, R., Travers, J., Glantz, F., & Coelen, G. (1979). *Children at the center.* Cambridge, MA: ABT Associates.

Sagi, A., Koren-Karie, N., Gini, M., Ziv, Y., & Joels, T. (2002). Shedding further light on the effects of various types and quality of early child care on infant-mother attachment relationship: The Haifa study of early child care. *Child Development, 73,* 1166–1186.

Sagi, A., Lamb, M. E., Lewkowicz, K. S., Shoham, R., Dvir, R., & Estes, D. (1985). Security of infant-mother, -father, and -metapelet attachments among kibbutz-reared Israeli children. *Monographs of the Society for Research in Child Development, 50,* 257–275.

Sagi, A., van IJzendoorn, M. H., Aviezer, O., Donnell, F., Koren-Karie, N., Joels, T., et al. (1995). Attachments in a multiple-caregiver and multiple-infant environment: The case of the Israeli kibbutzim. *Monographs of the Society for Research in Child Development, 60,* 71–91.

Sammons, P., Smeas, R., Taggat, B., Sylva, K., Melhuish, E. C., Siraj-Blatchford, I., et al. (2003). *Effective provision of pre-school education project: Technical paper 86. Measuring the impact on children's social behavioral development over the pre-school years.* London: Institute of Education.

Sammons, P., Sylva, K., Melhuish, E. C., Siraj-Blatchford, I., Taggat, B., & Elliot, K. (2002). *Effective provision of pre-school education project: Technical paper 8a. Measuring the impact on children's cognitive development over the preschool years.* London: Institute of Education.

Scarr, S. (1992). Keep our eyes on the prize: Family and child care policy in the United States, as it should be. In A. Booth (Ed.), *Child care in the 1990s: Trends and consequences* (pp. 215–223). Hillsdale, NJ: Erlbaum.

Scarr, S. (1998). American child care today. *American Psychologist, 53,* 95–108.

Scarr, S., Eisenberg, M., & Deater-Deckard, R. (1994). Measurement of quality in child care centers. *Early Childhood Research Quarterly, 9,* 131–151.

Scarr, S., McCartney, K., Abbott-Shim, M., & Eisenberg, M. (1995). *Small effects of large quality differences among child care centers on infants', toddlers', and preschool children's social adjustment.* Unpublished manuscript, Department of Psychology, University of Virginia, Charlottesville.

Scher, A., & Mayseless, O. (2000). Mothers of anxious/ambivalent infants: Maternal characteristics and child-care context. *Child Development, 71,* 1629–1639.

Schmidt-Kolmer, E., Tonkowa-Jampolskaja, R., & Atanassowa, A. (1979). *Die soziale Adaptation der Kinder bei der Aufnahme in Einrichtungen der Vorschulerziehung* [Children's social adaptation at entry to child care centers]. Berlin, Germany: Volk und Gesundheit.

Schubert, J. B., Bradley-Johnson, S., & Nuttal, J. (1980). Mother-infant communication and maternal employment. *Child Development, 51,* 246–249.

Schwartz, P. (1983). Length of day-care attendance and attachment behavior in 18-month-old infants. *Child Development, 54,* 1073–1078.

Schwarz, J. C., Strickland, R., & Krolick, G. (1974). Infant day care: Behavioral effects at preschool age. *Developmental Psychology, 10,* 502–506.

Schweinhart, L. J., Barnes, H. V., &, Weikart, D. P. (Eds.). (1993). *Significant benefits: The High/Scope Perry Preschool Study through age 27.* Ypsilanti, MI: High/Scope Press.

Sebanc, A. M., Pierce, S. L., Cheatam, C. L., & Gunnar, M. R. (2003). Gendered social worlds in preschool: Dominance, peer acceptance and assertive social skills in boys' and girls' peer groups. *Social Development, 12,* 91–106.

Seitz, V. (1990). Intervention programs for impoverished children: A comparison of educational and family support models. *Annals of Child Development, 7,* 78–103.

Seitz, V., Apfel, N. H., Rosenbaum, L., & Zigler, E. F. (1983). Long-term effects of project Head Start. In Consortium for Longitudinal Studies (Eds.), *As the twig is bent: Lasting effects of preschool programs* (pp. 299–332). Hillsdale, NJ: Erlbaum.

Shaw, D. S., Keenan, K., & Vondra, J. I. (1994). Developmental precursors of externalizing behavior: Ages 1 to 3. *Developmental Psychology, 30,* 355–364.

Sheehan, R., Cryan, J., Wiechel, J., & Bandy, I. (1991). Factors contributing to success in elementary schools: Research findings for early childhood educators. *Journal of Research in Childhood Education, 6,* 66–75.

Shpancer, N. (1998). Caregiver-parent relationships in daycare: A review and re-examination of the data and their implications. *Early Education and Development, 9,* 239–259.

Shwalb, D. W., Shwalb, B. J., Sukemune, S., & Tatsumoto, S. (1992). Japanese nonmaternal child care: Past, present, and future. In M. E. Lamb, K. J. Sternberg, C. P. Hwang, & A. G. Broberg (Eds.), *Child care in context: Cross-cultural perspectives* (pp. 331–353). Hillsdale, NJ: Erlbaum.

Siegel, D. J. (1999). *The developing mind: Toward a neurobiology of interpersonal experience.* New York: Guilford Press.

Sigel, I. E. (1990). Psychoeducational intervention: Future directions. *Merrill-Palmer Quarterly, 36,* 159–172.

Silverstein, L. B. (1991). Transforming the debate about child care and maternal employment. *American Psychologist, 46,* 1025–1032.

Smith, A. B., Inder, P. M., & Ratcliff, B. (1993). Relationships between early childhood center experience and social behavior at school. *New Zealand Journal of Educational Studies, 28,* 13–28.

Smith, K. (2002). *Who's minding the kids? Child care arrangements: Fall 1995* (Current Population Reports, pp. 70–86). Washington, DC: U.S. Bureau of the Census.

Smith, K., & Casper, L. (1999, March). *Home alone: Reason parents leave their children unsupervised.* Paper presented to the Population Association of America Convention, New York.

Smith, M., & Bissell, J. S. (1970). Report analysis: The impact of Head Start. *Harvard Educational Review, 40,* 51–104.

Sonenstein, F. L., Gates, G. J., Schmidt, S., & Bolshun, N. (2002). *Primary child care arrangements of employed parents: Findings from the 1999 National Survey of America's Families.* Washington, DC: Urban Institute.

Sonenstein, F. L., & Wolf, D. A. (1991). Satisfaction with child care: Perspectives of welfare mothers. *Journal of Social Issues, 47,* 15–31.

Spangler, G., & Grossmann, K. E. (1993). Biobehavioral organization in securely and insecurely attached infants. *Child Development, 64,* 1439–1450.

Spangler, G., & Schieche, M. (1998). Emotional and adrenocortical responses of infants to the Strange Situation: The differential function of emotional expression. *International Journal of Behavioral Development, 22,* 681–706.

Sparling, J., Lewis, I., Ramey, C. T., Wasik, B. H., Bryant, D. M., & La Vange, L. M. (1991). Partners: A curriculum to help premature, low birthweight infants get off to a good start. *Topics in Early Childhood Special Education, 11,* 36–55.

Spedding, P. (1993). United States of America. In M. Cochran (Ed.), *International handbook of child care policies and programs* (pp. 535–557). Westport, CT: Greenwood Press.

Spieker, S. J., Nelson, D. C., Petras, A., Jolley, S. N., & Barnard, K. E. (2003). Joint influence of child care and infant attachment security for cognitive and language outcomes of low-income toddlers. *Infant Behavior and Development, 26,* 326–344.

Spitz, H. H. (1986). *The raising of intelligence: A selected history of attempts to raise retarded intelligence.* Hillsdale, NJ: Erlbaum.

Sroufe, L. A. (2000). Early relationship and the development of children. *Infant Mental Health Journal, 21,* 67–74.

Stallings, J. A. (1980). An observational study of family day care. In J. C. Colbert (Ed.), *Home day care: A perspective.* Chicago: Roosevelt University.

Stanley, J. C. (Ed.). (1973). *Compensatory education for children, ages 2 to 8: Recent studies of educational intervention.* Baltimore: Johns Hopkins University Press.

Steinberg, L. (1986). Latchkey children and susceptibility to peer pressure: An ecological analysis. *Developmental Psychology, 22,* 433–439.

Steinberg, L. (1988). Simple solutions to a complex problem: A response to Rodman, Pratto, and Nelson. *Developmental Psychology, 24,* 295–296.

Steiner, G. Y. (1976). *The children's cause.* Washington, DC: Brookings Institution.

Sternberg, K. J., Lamb, M. E., Hwang, C. P., Broberg, A., Ketterlinus, R. D., & Bookstein, F. L. (1991). Does out-of-home care affect compliance in preschoolers? *International Journal of Behavioral Development, 14,* 45–65.

Stifter, C., Coulehan, C. M., & Fish, M. (1993). Linking employment to attachment: The mediating effects of maternal separation anxiety and interactive behavior. *Child Development, 64,* 1451–1460.

Stith, S. M., & Davis, A. J. (1984). Employed mothers and family day-care substitute caregivers: A comparative analysis of infant care. *Child Development, 55,* 1340–1348.

Stoltenberg, J. (1994). Day care centers: Quality and provision. In A. E. Borge, E. Hartmann, & S. Strom (Eds.), *Day care centers: Quality and provision* (pp. 7–11). Oslo, Norway: National Institute of Public Health.

Sturzbecher, D. (Ed.). (1998). *Kindertagesbetreuung in Deutschland: Bilanzen und Perspecktiven* [Child care in Germany: Results and perspective]. Freiberg, Germany: Lambertus.

Sylva, K., Melhuish, E., Sammons, P., Siraj-Blatchford, I., & Taggart, B. (2004). *Effective pre-school education.* London: Institute of Education, University of London.

Taylor, A. R., & Machida, S. (1994). The contribution of parent and peer support to Head Start children's early school adjustment. *Early Childhood Research Quarterly, 9,* 387–405.

Temple, J. A., Reynolds, A. J., & Miedel, W. T. (2000). Can early intervention prevent high school dropout? Evidence from the Chicago Child-Parent Centers. *Urban Education, 35,* 31–56.

Thompson, R. A. (1988). The effects of infant day care through the prism of attachment theory: A critical appraisal. *Early Childhood Research Quarterly, 3,* 273–282.

Thompson, R. A. (1993). Socioemotional development: Enduring issues and new challenges. *Developmental Review, 13,* 372–402.

Thornburg, K. R., Pearl, P., Crompton, D., & Ispa, J. M. (1990). Development of kindergarten children based on child care arrangements. *Early Childhood Research Quarterly, 5,* 27–42.

Tietze, W., & Cryer, D. (1999). Current trends in European early child care and education. *Annals of the American Academy, 563,* 175–193.

Tietze, W., Cryer, D., Bairrao, J., Palacios, J., & Wetzel, G. (1996). Comparisons of observed process quality in early child care and education in five countries. *Early Childhood Research Quarterly, 11,* 447–475.

Tuttle, W. M., Jr. (1993). *"Daddy's gone to war": The Second World War in the lives of America's children.* New York: Oxford University Press.

U.S. Bureau of Labor Statistics. (1987). *Statistical abstract of the United States* (107th ed.). Washington, DC: U.S. Department of Commerce.

U.S. Bureau of Labor Statistics. (1998). *Handbook of labor statistics.* Washington, DC: U.S. Government Printing Office.

U.S. Bureau of Labor Statistics. (2000). *Handbook of labor statistics.* Washington, DC: U.S. Government Printing Office.

U.S. Bureau of the Census. (1993). *Statistical abstract of the United States, 1993.* Washington, DC: U.S. Government Printing Office.

U.S. Bureau of the Census. (2003). *Who's minding the kids?* Washington, DC: U.S. Government Printing Office.

Vandell, D. L., & Corasaniti, M. A. (1988). The relation between third graders' after-school care and social, academic, and emotional functioning. *Child Development, 59,* 868–875.

Vandell, D. L., & Corasaniti, M. A. (1990a). Child care and the family: Complex contributors to child development. *New Directions for Child Development, 49,* 23–37.

Vandell, D. L., & Corasaniti, M. A. (1990b). Variations in early child care: Do they predict subsequent social, emotional, and cognitive differences? *Early Childhood Research Quarterly, 5,* 555–572.

Vandell, D. L., Hyde, J. S., Plant, E. A., & Essex, M. J. (1997). Fathers and "others" as infant-care providers: Predictors of parents' emotional well-being and marital satisfaction. *Merrill-Palmer Quarterly, 43,* 361–385.

Vandell, D. L., McCartney, K., Owen, M. T., Booth, C. L., & Clarke-Stewart, K. A. (2003). Variations in child care by grandparents during the first 3 years. *Journal of Marriage and Family, 65,* 375–381.

Vandell, D. L., & Pierce, K. M. (1999, April). *Can after-school programs benefit children who live in high crime neighborhoods?* Poster presented at the Society for Research in Child Development Convention, Albuquerque, NM.

Vandell, D. L., & Pierce, K. M. (2001, April). *Experiences in after school programs and children's well-being.* Paper presented at the Society for Research in Child Development Convention, Minneapolis, MN.

Vandell, D. L., & Posner, J. K. (1999). Conceptualization and measurement of children's after-school environments. In S. L. Friedman & T. D. Wachs (Eds.), *Assessment of the environment across the lifespan* (pp. 167–196). Washington, DC: American Psychological Association.

Vandell, D. L., & Ramanan, J. (1991). Children of the National Longitudinal Survey of Youth: Choices in after-school care and child development. *Developmental Psychology, 27,* 637–643.

Vandell, D. L., & Ramanan, J. (1992). Effects of early and recent maternal employment on children from low-income families. *Child Development, 63,* 938–949.

Vandell, D. L., Shuman, L., & Posner, J. K. (1999). Children's after school programs: Promoting resiliency or vulnerability. In H. McCubbin (Ed.), *Resiliency in families and children at risk: Interdisciplinary perspectives*. Thousand Oaks, CA: Sage.

Vandell, D. L., & Wilson, K. S. (1987). Infants' interactions with mother, sibling, and peer: Contrasts and relations between interaction systems. *Child Development, 58,* 176–187.

Vandell, D. L., & Wolfe, B. (2000). *Child care quality: Does it matter and does it need to be improved?* (IRP Special Report No. 78). Madison: University of Wisconsin, Institute for Research on Poverty.

Vandivere, S., Tout, K., Zaslow, M., Calkins, J., & Capizzano, J. (2003). *Unsupervised time: Family and child factors associated with self care.* Washington, DC: Child Trends.

van IJzendoorn, M. H., Dijkstra, J., & Bus, A. (1995). Attachment, intelligence, and language: A meta-analysis. *Social Development, 4,* 115–128.

van IJzendoorn, M. H., Tavecchio, L. W. C., Stams, G. J., Verhoeven, M., & Reiling, E. (1998). Attunement between parents and professional caregivers: A comparison of childrearing attitudes in different child-care settings. *Journal of Marriage and the Family, 60,* 771–781.

Vecchiotti, S. (2003). Kindergarten: An overlooked educational policy priority. *Social Policy Report, 17*(2), 3–19.

Voran, M. J., & Whitebook, M. (1991, April). *Inequity begins early: The relationship between day care quality and family social class.* Paper presented at the meeting of the Society for Research in Child Development, Seattle, WA.

Votruba-Drzal, E., Coley, R. L., & Chase-Lansdale, P. L. (2004). Child care and low-income children's development: Direct and moderated effects. *Child Development, 75,* 296–312.

Wadsworth, M. E. J. (1986). Effects of parenting style and preschool experience on children's verbal attainment: Results of a British longitudinal study. *Early Childhood Research Quarterly, 5,* 55–72.

Waite, L. J., Leibowitz, A., & Witsberger, C. (1991). What parents pay for: Child care characteristics, quality, and costs. *Journal of Social Issues, 47,* 33–48.

Walden, T., Lemerise, E., & Smith, M. C. (1999). Friendship and popularity in preschool classrooms. *Early Education and Development, 10,* 351–371.

Waldfogel, J. (2001). International policies toward parental leave and child care. *Future of Children, 11,* 99–111.

Wasik, B. H., Ramey, C. T., Bryant, D. M., & Sparling, J. J. (1990). A longitudinal study of two early intervention strategies: Project CARE. *Child Development, 61,* 1682–1696.

Watamura, S., Donzella, B., Alwin, J., & Gunnar, M. (2003). Morning to afternoon increases in cortisol concentrations for infants and toddlers at child care: Age differences and behavioral correlates. *Child Development, 74,* 1006–1020.

Waters, E. (1995). The Attachment Q-set (version 3.0). *Monographs of the Society for Research in Child Development, 60,* 71–91.

Weisner, T. S., & Gallimore, R. (1977). My brother's keeper: Child and sibling caretaking. *Current Anthropology, 18,* 971–975.

Werebe, M. G., & Baudonniere, P. M. (1991). Social pretend play among friends and familiar preschoolers. *International Journal of Behavioral Development, 14,* 411–428.

Wessels, H., Lamb, M. E., Hwang, C. P., & Broberg, A. G. (1997). Personality development between 1 and 8 years of age in Swedish children with varying child care experiences. *International Journal of Behavioral Development, 21,* 771–794.

Whaley, K. L., & Rubenstein, T. S. (1994). How toddlers "do" friendship: A descriptive analysis of naturally occurring friendships in a group child care setting. *Journal of Social and Personal Relationships, 11,* 383–400.

Whitebook, M., Howes, C., & Phillips, D. A. (1989). *Who cares? Child care teachers and the quality of care in America.* Oakland, CA: Child Care Employee Project.

Willer, B., Hofferth, S., Kisker, E., Divine-Hawkins, P., Farquhar, E., & Glantz, F. (1991). *The demand and supply of child care in 1990: Joint findings from the National Child Care Survey 1990 and a Profile of Child Care Settings.* Washington, DC: National Association for the Education of Young Children.

Williams, W. M., & Sternberg, R. (2002). How parents can maximize children's cognitive abilities. In M. H. Bornstein (Ed.), *Handbook of parenting* (Vol. 5, pp. 169–194). Mahwah, NJ: Erlbaum.

Woods, M. B. (1972). The unsupervised child of the working mother. *Developmental Psychology, 6,* 14–25.

Wrigley, J. (1995). *Other people's children.* New York: Basic Books.

Zahn-Waxler, C., Radke-Yarrow, M., Wagner, E., & Chapman, M. (1992). Development of concern for others. *Developmental Psychology, 28,* 126–136.

Zaslow, M. J. (1991). Variation in child care quality and its implications for children. *Journal of Social Issues, 47,* 125–138.

Zaslow, M. J., Pedersen, F. A., Suwalsky, J. T., & Rabinovich, B. A. (1989). Maternal employment and parent infant interaction at 1-year. *Early Childhood Research Quarterly, 4,* 459–478.

Zhengao, W. (1993). China. In M. Cochran (Ed.), *International handbook of child care policies and programs* (pp. 83–106). Westport, CT: Greenwood Press.

Zigler, E. F., & Butterfield, E. C. (1968). Motivational aspects of changes in IQ test performance of culturally deprived nursery school children. *Child Development, 39,* 1–14.

Zigler, E. F., & Muenchow, S. (1992). *Head Start: The inside story of America's most successful educational experiment.* New York: Basic Books.

Zigler, E. F., Piotrkowski, C., & Collins, R. (1994). Health services in Head Start. *Annual Review of Public Health, 15,* 511–534.

Zigler, E. F., & Styfco, S. J. (1994). Is the Perry Preschool better than Head Start? Yes and no. *Early Childhood Research Quarterly, 9,* 241–242.

Zigler, E. F., & Valentine, J. (1979). *Project Head Start.* New York: Free Press.

CHAPTER 24

Research to Practice Redefined

IRVING E. SIGEL

Do research findings in child development influence relevant practice and is practice influential in planning research? I contend that at least for child development or child psychology the answer is often "no," although this situation has changed dramatically in recent years. Research as the term is used in child psychology refers to results gathered in scientifically based studies. Practice is the use of research findings in service settings. Despite change, research findings are likely to be underused in practical settings like school classrooms, child guidance clinics, or policy settings. In fact, there is an oft-held view that research studies are not "user friendly" from the perspective of the classroom teacher, the clinician, or the policymaker. The underuse of research in practice stems from diversity in researchers' and practitioners' conceptual frameworks, problems that are addressed, and worldviews, or Root Metaphors (Pepper, 1942).

The field of human development embraces a variety of conceptual frameworks. In the last few decades, this diversity has included those who are trained and conduct research as Piagetians, neo-Piagetians, Vygotskyans, Wernerians, Freudians, and Behaviorists. There are also, of course, the mini-theorists, who espouse their own philosophies or "schools," who have devel-

oped groups of followers. Some have even labeled themselves as specialists in particular areas of development, such as cognitive science, neural development, behavior modification, and social cognition with a social psychological twist. There are also investigators who are problem-centered in their focus (e.g., the children's concept of mind, language development, or development of self), who build on a range of theoretical perspectives. Disagreements arise within these groups because of differences of interpretation. The theoretical perspective and/or problem-centered focus of research that is undertaken provides the basis of a group or an organization that shares a common language—a language with its own working definitions of concepts. Similar types of variations can be observed in practice settings, also. Some practitioners apply theory to practice, and others make up their own theories of practice.

Not only is there diversity in the assumptions and theoretical and/or conceptual foci of study, but researchers and practitioners also diverge in their professional functions. Child psychology researchers have tended to perceive of themselves as engaged in basic theory-driven research in contrast to applied researchers who work with more concrete concerns. The basic researcher, as scientist, is trained to seek scientific generalization with experimental research, and may have little interest in developing technologies or practical suggestions (Polanyi, 1958).

On the other hand, there is a growing interest in blending science with application. There are researchers who

Thanks to K. Ann Renninger for helpful and constructive suggestions that have helped make this chapter more focused and to the point. Thanks also to Vanessa Gorman and Marsha Satterthwaite for editorial suggestions.

as science practitioners apply their research to what they see as relevant and appropriate real life situations. Other researchers conduct research in real-life contexts, adjusting or weighting variables in order to make comparisons and assess change. Yet, another group of researchers are practitioners who use research to inform their work with children in child guidance clinics, hospitals, schools, and juvenile courts. These researchers are clinicians who share responsibility for helping children (and often their families) cope with the worlds in which they live. These researchers can also be consumers who use the products of research when they become accessible and are appropriate for the work in which they are engaged.

Thus, although the researchers of child development undertake work based on the "research literature," there is no reason to believe that all studies work within the same view of what is a science of child psychology, and this has an impact on the way in which research impacts practice. Debates on this issue abound, not only as to the definition, but also as to the appropriateness of the model of science currently in use. This was clearly reflected in articles by Bevan and Kessel (1994):

> psychology's methods and methodology must be far less rigid and our discipline's view of what is scientifically acceptable must be far more pragmatic than has been the case for many decades. (Bevan & Kessel, 1994, p. 507)

They argued that psychology needs to be sensitive to human experience. Their position contrasted with that of Kimble (1994) who wrote:

> If psychology is to be a science, it must play by the scientific rules, of which the most important is that it must be about observables. It must be a science of stimuli and responses, because the only public facts available are the things that organisms do (responses) and the situations in which they do them (stimuli). (p. 510)

The difference between these two views of science is profound. They suggest that the field is fractured and that the information available to the practitioner who is not trained in the field needs to be considered. How does research look to the practitioner? What does the practitioner need?

HOW DOES RESEARCH LOOK TO THE PRACTITIONER?

The field of child psychology with its diversity of interests and theoretical orientations has created a mixed and blurry image for itself. A substantial amount of scientific laboratory research has been conducted and developmental methods are increasingly being used to approach problems in practice—a recognition that developmental approaches have much to offer in terms of mitigating social and individual dysfunction and much to contribute to the health and well-being of society. Whether child psychology is a basic or an applied science is no longer a useful question. Research is increasingly focused on real-life problems. A more important issue has become whether the application of scientific methods to real-life problems can serve practice and realistically be science.

Does the scientific study of complex social problems preclude careful science? Does the use of rigid scientific procedures narrow the problems for study and lead to the study of trivial questions? An effort to delineate some of the sources of the problem, including a discussion of the expected impact of scientific research findings on social change and social transformations is likely to increase understanding of the utility and application of research to practice. In spite of the claims made by psychologists as to their actual and potential contributions to the social welfare (Wiggins, 1994), there are those who are dismayed by psychology's failure to address important human questions (e.g., Bevan & Kessel, 1994). There are also child developmental psychologists who argued that setting up a special field of applied developmental psychology might result in an eschewing of basic research (Morrison, Lord, & Keating, 1984).

The effort to apply science to practice is complicated. It is influenced by issues of time, context, and agenda. It is also influenced by how research is understood: its purposes and practices, and its complexities. Criticisms of researchers by practitioners are based in part on promises made and promises unfulfilled. The promise that research can be of social value needs to be tempered by its consumer's awareness that there is an inevitable time lag between the time a project has begun and its acceptance and use in the field. The medical research on poliomyelitis and diphtheria are good examples from the past. Research on AIDS, cancer, and many other diseases reveals the same time lag—the time between the onset of research and its completion is highly unpredictable. A further complication is that there are so many factors in the life of a child that are reasonable sources of influence that it is difficult to evaluate the role and influence of each. While, disseminating current knowledge base can be slow and difficult, it is also the case that service providers and policymakers have their own agendas. These agendas have to be recognized, understood, and reconciled by both parties.

The researcher may view practitioners as being concrete, atheoretical, and pragmatic. The practitioner may view the researcher as engaged in using rigid and meaningless approaches to study trivial questions, driven by sometimes esoteric and unworldly theory. Research reports can be couched in probability terms that are useless for the day-to-day work of some practitioners. Practitioners sometimes accuse scientists of engaging with a fanatic and uncritical devotion to science. Therefore, why should a busy practitioner waste time reading such meaningless material? Not to be outdone by this type of criticism, the researcher is often disdainful of the practitioner's lack of understanding of science and the significance of data, even if it has been derived from careful methodology.

Interestingly, because of diversity of conceptual frameworks and roles, there is no definitive center that gives the field of child psychology a coherent view of childhood.

> Images [of childhood] are basic assumptions or conceptions about children and the factors that influence their ontogeny. Images thus include beliefs regarding the existence of innate tendencies or dispositions, the susceptibility to external influences, the limits of human modifiability, the special importance of early experience, and the role of the individual. (Hwang, Lamb, & Sigel, 1996, p. 3)

The diversity of how childhood is described is a complication for researchers and practitioners alike—there is a sense in which both researchers and practitioners have a shared agenda to understand childhood, but the difference of lens affects the usefulness of the research. In a review of two major journals, for example, different images of childhood were found to stem from different perceptions of variables important to study (Sigel & Kim, 1996). We compared the topics studied, the methods used, and the samples described over 5 years. Of importance for this discussion is the finding that there were only rarely suggestions about "how" to use information from this research in the articles.

ON THE PROXIMAL AND DISTAL RELEVANCE OF RESEARCH, OR WHAT THE PRACTITIONER NEEDS

Child psychology includes a wide-range of problems of study; it contains many voices and languages. It draws on different methods, and yet each has its claims to science. I suggest that we reconsider Pepper's *Root*

Metaphor (1942), as a frame for understanding these differences. According to Pepper, the root metaphor a person selects (consciously or not) is his or her worldview.

In terms of researchers and practitioners, and the application of research to practice, the degree to which parties share the same, or approximately the same, root metaphor, the greater their mutual understanding and consequent communication. For example, if the researcher and the practitioner have a contextual perspective, they should communicate more effectively than when one views the world from a mechanistic root metaphor and the other a contextualist. It does not matter with which root metaphor a person works. If the researcher and the practitioner do not share the same metaphor, their communication will be compromised. For example, beliefs may not change despite evidence to the contrary (Sigel & McGillicuddy-De Lisi, 2002). Recognizing difference is of particular value in reaching consensus. Dialogue is enriched when there is an acknowledged awareness of operating belief systems that are derivatives of the root metaphors. A person's root metaphor can only be influenced by what he or she knows and understands.

Findings from research can only be used if the practitioner understands how to use them in the course of practice. I call this the *proximity index,* defined as the distance between the readiness for findings to be used and the understanding of the meaning and the comprehensibility of the research report. For example, if a teacher reads about the virtues of an inquiry discovery approach, but has always taught with a didactic approach, he or she needs to assess the implications of shifting pedagogical approaches without mastering procedures. If the approach is not mastered, or, as in the case of a research approach, the underlying assumptions are not understood, then any research results are likely to be compatible with the objectives of education, but incompatible with the goals of the instructor. If on the other hand, there is compatibility between the research and the atmosphere in the class, the new findings may aid the teacher in elaborating the approaches in the classroom. In terms of a proximity index, this could be labeled a Level 1 application. Each subsequent score on this type of hypothetical index requires additional judgments. At Level 2, the practitioners judge the findings of the study to be closer in terms of specific techniques used, but they may be uncertain about the level of their comparability. This requires that the practitioner assumes the role of evaluator or interpreter of the research. As one approaches Level 5 in this continuum, the research may increasingly feel removed from classroom practice. The idea of weighting degrees of comparability involves consideration of how similar the children in the study were to those in his or her classroom, whether what was accomplished is a goal for his or her classroom, and whether the demonstrated effect seems applicable. In effect, the practitioner needs to reflect on a number of extrapolations, before deciding to apply it to his or her own practice (Morgan, Gliner, & Harmon, 2003).

Moreover, applicability does not need to be action-based. The practitioner can use the research to rethink the way he or she does his or her work, and to reflect about other areas to explore. For example, if one focused on the effects of culture, then there is reason to expect that the instructor will change his or her understanding of some of the events in his her classroom or clinic. By definition, even if different terms are used, this focus also includes consideration of reliability and validity. The question is no longer one of basic or applied science. Rather, the question becomes one of the practical use of any scientifically acquired knowledge: what function research serves, what the products of such efforts are, and how and when research can be used.

Several years ago, I participated in an intervention program in a middle-class elementary school system. The program was derived from Piagetian theory. One of the stipulations in their type of curriculum required the teachers to ask questions, to engage in dialogue, and to get the children to interact with each other, and with the teacher. The study was undertaken to observe teachers' question-asking techniques and follow-through, how they engaged the group, and whether or not they allowed the children to discover and share ideas. Observers went into the classroom with permission of the teacher, set up a rigorous observation schedule, and observed teachers' verbalizations every six seconds during a 30-minute extended play period. The results showed that the teachers asked many questions, but the questions were didactic and directive, such as: What is the name of this? What is the color of that? There was very little, if any, follow through. Instead, considerable attention was paid to the precise way in which the children spoke their answers. After the program was evaluated it was found that the children were no different in responsiveness and verbalization from children enrolled in traditional programs in that same school system, and that the teachers' questions never created a dialogue or a discussion. When these re-

sults were reported to the school committee, there was an immediate objection to the fact that the observers were new, unknown to the teachers, segmented in their approach, and so on. Rather than discussing the implications of the findings, the committee rejected them out of hand because they were not what were expected.

Resolution of this conflict took intense discussion and explanation. The committee eventually accepted the observation of the researcher as valid once audiotapes of the classroom were shared. It was not the quality of science that resolved the issue but the development of interpersonal trust and willingness of everyone to reexamine the research process. Clarifying the goals for the research together with the opportunity to think about these goals with data led the school committee and the leaders to alter their intervention efforts over time.

In order to enhance the proximity of research for the practitioner, a number of issues need to be addressed: (a) Who poses the research question? (b) How are data collected and analyzed? (c) How are data disseminated? The conflicts between general findings and any specifications for application and the practical problems that are involved in integrating research findings into practice need to be explored.

Who Poses the Research Questions and How Is Research Conducted?

The posing of the research question is one of the most difficult intellectual challenges. The structuring of the research question is part of the scientist's way of working. Each participant in any collaborative effort will frame the question of interest from his or her own frame of reference. The scientist will put it into the genre of science with the precision necessary for subsequently setting up a study whereas a practitioner may phrase the question within an action based practical framework that is consistent with his or her setting. The process of identifying *the* research question is difficult and will require considerable discussion.

The typical situation is one in which the researcher and the practitioner come from different settings, however, the researcher and the practitioner can be the same person (e.g., Blechman, 1990, where the therapist is also the researcher) and/or of the same root metaphor.

In the situation where the practitioner wishes to study a particular question (e.g., evaluation of a curriculum or a mode of psychotherapy) and to do so requires a working relationship with a researcher, their partnership requires equal status so that the study meets the interests of both parties. As Scholnick (2002) points out, partnerships can support change, and yield products that differ qualitatively from what any one person can accomplish independently. The effectiveness of the partnership will depend on how the relationship is structured, the personalities of the principals, clarification of theoretical views, and shared goals.

Most so-called partnerships are not truly equal when one researcher takes charge because of his or her expertise. I hope that this asymmetry is accepted and justified, but it is also the case that researchers may treat the practitioners insensitively and arrogantly. This type of interaction is most frequent when the practitioner is coerced by the administration, job situation, and so on to participate in an experimental research project. For research to inform practice, it needs to be undertaken on the basis of an authentic question.

How Are Data Collected and Analyzed?

Studies usually focus on a limited number of variables. They can be limited by the size of the population and also the research question. Thus, the probability is great that practitioners may think that constricted experimental environments decontextualize children. From this perspective, the child essentially becomes a partitioned object of study as defined by the variables of interest to the investigator. For example, most studies that investigate children's conservation of quantity or number rarely ask whether these children were studying these subjects in school. Is it not possible that the child's academic experience confounds the findings? The child in the experiment is treated as a participant unrelated to any other source of influence, and randomization of children is considered to address potential sources of error. In fact, phenomena are studied by partitioning not only the child, but also the problem. It is as though studies of cognition or motivation are insulated from other psychological systems. Yet, it is the case that the whole child is the person responding to whatever is being asked of him or her. This is a particular concern for the practitioner, especially as he or she thinks about applying research to practice.

Moreover, data obtained are often aggregated so that group variability is reported, not how particular individuals vary. Yet, the practitioner needs to know how a particular child might function given the use of those particular findings, or how a particular strategy will af-

fect a particular child. If this is the case, what are the limits as to how the teacher, therapist, or clinician can work with this child in a particular setting? The researcher is testing hypotheses to seek support for a theory and can as a result generalize about how a particular phenomena functions. The practitioner, on the other hand, is typically more interested in individual differences in a particular classroom, with a particular child or group of children, at a particular point in time.

The researcher works from a nomothetic model, eschewing idiographic or impassive analyses. The reason for this is probably due to his or her interest in generalizability. Unfortunately, the distal quality of the nomothetic model limits its contribution to practice. From a practitioner's perspective, idiographic reports are more meaningful because they present an integrated view of the person, more akin to profile analyses or case histories. Coupled with ideographic methods, nomothetic approaches assume power to inform both theory and practice.

How Are Data Disseminated?

Research results are usually presented in quantitative terms; the assumption is that the number tells an objective story whose meaning every reader shares. However, the fact is that the numbers are derived from the investigator's perspective. He or she chooses the methods by which to collect the data and the means of quantification. Since every quantitative method has its limits and biases, the reported numbers are subject to interpretation. The decision as to how to evaluate the numbers goes back to the initial organization and classification of the data, in addition to the data themselves.

How and when research information is disseminated depends on the target audience and the person who is disseminating the information. The audiences targeted to receive reports of research are typically the scientific community (including students in training to become researchers and practitioners), practitioners, and the lay public. Usually this task involves different discourses. More to the point are the traditional, and hence conventional, methods of reporting research.

Typically, research findings are written and published in books and journals that are primarily accessible to the researcher. Its accessibility is only limited by its comprehensibility and that depends on the familiarization with the particular discourse of the author. For scientists, the discourse is familiar. For the practitioners, especially those unfamiliar with the scientific jargon and style of writing, the research findings and their interpretation are elusive and hence neither accessible nor useful. While the researchers should be intimately acquainted with the setting to which they claim their research applies, so too the practitioner should assume some responsibility for becoming informed about how to read and interpret this material in order to form a rational basis for evaluating the quality and the appropriateness of what he or she finds. Research reviews, if carefully structured to clarify concepts and ground examples in practice may be useful to practitioners; the lay public may need still another form of communication.

On a more informal level, disseminating research findings can be done in the course of researchers consulting with service providers. How this is done will depend on the relationship of the researcher to the service partners. Often practitioners would like information that they can use immediately. However, carrying out any research project takes time. The gap between discovery and implementation is not only due to the length of time required to do the research, but also to the commitment of scientists and practitioners to their own construction of knowledge: what counts as a research question, what is expected as findings, and how well the research process, including its limits and possibilities, is understood and explained.

CONCLUSIONS

The field of child psychology is in ferment. In the past, we accepted this since we believed the field to be a young science—it just needed to grow and mature. Scientific knowledge was, we believed, cumulative and linear in its development. After 100 years, we can no longer claim youth. Fermentation reflects effervescence, a bubbling change that alters the character of substance. To carry on the analogy, the process is not linear and, in addition, it is in the current vernacular "chaotic," becoming transformed into a new whole. In a sense, those of us in child psychology are sharing the same crisis that our idealized physics colleagues are facing—the new scientific revolution, *the science of chaos* (Gleick, 1987). Does that not sound like an oxymoron? We have been encouraged to think in terms of stability, equilibrium, and homeostasis. Our science is grounded in the precepts of prediction. To predict means to be able to control, to define, to be precise,

and to identify the ingredients of the whole. Yet, in order to work in and with practice requires moving away from linear models and comfort with complexity and change.

What kinds of mechanisms can be devised so that empirical research can be brought to the fore to provide answers to questions dealing with *how* and *why* children develop as they do? What are the mechanisms that aid in keeping the trajectory of development optimal? What contributions can be made to prevent dysfunctional development? What are the requirements to optimal development? Should not developmental research offer useful and meaningful explanations for the course of development and where needed provide approaches for the prevention and amelioration of conditions that may hinder the optimization of the developmental trajectory?

Efforts to apply research to practice require acknowledging the inherent tensions of trying to validate theory and research in practical settings. They require stretching and/or adapting the root metaphors in which we have been trained so that collaborations between researchers and practitioners are the basis of research and of any application of research to practice.

REFERENCES

Bevan, W., & Kessel, F. (1994). Plain truths and home cooking: Thoughts on the making and remaking of psychology. *American Psychologist, 49,* 505–509.

Blechman, E. (1990). A new look at emotions and the family: A model of effective family communication. In E. A. Blechman (Ed.), *Emotions and the family: For better or for worse* (pp.lnbl201–224). Hillsdale, NJ: Erlbaum.

Gleick, J. (1987). *Chaos: Making a new science.* New York: Penguin Books.

Hoffman, M. L., & Hoffman, L. W. (Eds.). (1964). *Review of child development research* (Vol. 1). New York: Russell Sage Foundation.

Hwang, C. P., Lamb, M. E., & Sigel, I. E. (Eds.). (1996). *Images of childhood.* Mahwah, NJ: Erlbaum.

Kimble, G. A. (1994). A frame of reference for psychology. *American Psychologist, 49,* 510–519.

Morgan, G. A., Gliner, J. A., & Harmon, R. J. (2003). Selection and use of inferential statistics. *Journal of the American Academy of Child and Adolescent Psychiatry, 42*(10), 1253–1257.

Morrison, F. J., Lord, C., & Keating, D. P. (Eds.). (1984). *Applied developmental psychology* (Vol. 1). Orlando, FL: Academic Press.

Pepper, S. C. (1970). *World hypotheses: A study in evidence.* Berkeley: University of California Press. (Original work published 1942)

Polanyi, M. (1958). *Personal knowledge: Toward a post-critical philosophy.* Chicago: University of Chicago Press.

Scholnick, E. K. (2002). Forming a partnership. In E. Amsel & J. P. Byrnes (Eds.), *Language, literacy, and cognitive development* (pp. 3–23). Mahwah, NJ: Erlbaum.

Sigel, I. E., & Kim, M.-I. (1996). The images of children in developmental psychology. In C. P. Hwang, M. E. Lamb, & I. E. Sigel (Eds.), *Images of childhood* (pp. 47–62). Mahwah, NJ: Erlbaum.

Sigel, I. E., & McGillicuddy-De Lisi, A. V. (2002). Parent beliefs are cognitions. In M. H. Bornstein (Ed.), *Handbook of Parenting* (2nd ed., pp. 484–508). Mahwah, NJ: Erlbaum.

Wiggins, J. G. (1994). Would you want your child to be a psychologist? *American Psychologist, 49,* 485–492.

Author Index

Subject Index